Smith and Roberson's
BUSINESS LAW
Uniform Commercial Code
Fifth Edition

Smith and Roberson's
BUSINESS LAW
Uniform Commercial Code
Fifth Edition

Len Young Smith
Chairman of the Department of Business Law
Northwestern University (Retired)
Member of the Illinois Bar

G. Gale Roberson
Professorial Lecturer in Business Law
Northwestern University (Retired)
Member of the Illinois Bar

Richard A. Mann
Associate Professor of Business Law
The University of North Carolina at Chapel Hill
Member of the North Carolina Bar

Barry S. Roberts
Associate Professor of Business Law
The University of North Carolina at Chapel Hill
Member of the North Carolina and Pennsylvania Bars

WEST PUBLISHING COMPANY
St. Paul   New York   Los Angeles   San Francisco

A study guide has been developed to assist you in mastering concepts presented in this text. Prepared by Dennis R. Hower and Peter T. Kahn of the University of Minnesota, this practical student study guide includes chapter overviews, key terms, and exercises that match key terms to definitions. Your comprehension can be tested with multiple choice, true/false, and short essay problems. Answers are provided for all exercises and are keyed to the text material. The study guide is available from your local bookstore under the title *Study Guide to Accompany Smith and Roberson's Business Law, Fifth Edition*. If you cannot locate it in the bookstore, ask your bookstore manager to order it for you.

COPYRIGHT © 1962, 1966, 1971, 1977 By WEST PUBLISHING CO.

COPYRIGHT © 1982 By WEST PUBLISHING CO.
50 West Kellogg Boulevard
P.O. Box 3526
St. Paul, Minnesota 55165

Library of Congress Cataloging in Publication Data

Smith, Len Young, 1901–
    Smith and Roberson's Business Law.

Includes index.
    I. Commercial law—United States.
    I. Roberson, G. Gale (George Gale), 1903–
    II. Title.
    III. Mann, Richard A., joint author.
    IV. Roberts, Barry S., joint author.
KF888.S554   1982   346.73′07′02632   81–16352
ISBN 0–314–63286–7   347.306702632   AACR2

Preface

The format of the Fifth Edition is the same as that of the prior four editions, in that each chapter contains narrative text, cases consisting of selected court decisions, and problems. Five new chapters have been added, namely, Legal Process, Chapter 2; Torts, Chapters 4 and 5; Securities Regulation, Chapter 42; and Consumer Protection, Chapter 43.

The Edition is considered necessary in view of the changes and developments in the law since the publication of the Fourth Edition in April, 1977. These developments include two significant Federal Statutes, the Bankruptcy Reform Act of 1978, and the Economic Recovery Tax Act of 1981, as well as recent cases interpreting and applying various sections of the Uniform Commercial Code.

The Fifth Edition contains a total of 237 cases, in which the court opinions are edited to show the essential facts of the case, the issue or issues involved, the decision of the court, and the reason for its decision. A total of 67 of these cases were decided in the period of 1976 to 1981. Each of the 237 cases is headed by a brief notation stating the nature of the subject matter of the case. This will indicate to the student the importance of the case and the reason for its inclusion in the particular chapter. The readability of the text material in the Fifth Edition has been improved by including in each chapter numerous sub-headings in bold face type which indicate briefly the subject matter of the discussion that follows.

Business Law is an important required course, or courses, for undergraduates in Schools of Commerce in Universities and Colleges, and in Schools of Business Administration. It is also required for students of Accounting. Classroom use and study of this book should provide for the student the following benefits and skills:

(1) Perception and appreciation of the scope, extent, and importance of the law.

(2) Basic knowledge of the fundamental concepts, principles, and rules of law that apply to business transactions.

(3) Acquisition of knowledge of the function and methods of operation of courts and governmental administrative agencies.

(4) Ability to recognize the possibility of the potential legal problem or problems which may arise in a doubtful or complicated situation, and the necessity of consulting a lawyer and obtaining competent professional legal advice.

(5) Development of analytical skills and reasoning power through the thoughtful study of a subject of which reason is its life.

(6) A deep feeling of gratitude and pride resulting from a knowledge of legal principles and precepts which are enforced by the Federal courts and by the courts of the 50 States.

In the preparation of the Fifth Edition, we wish to acknowledge with gratitude the continuous, unremitting, and valuable assistance and cooperation of Richard A. Mann and Barry S. Roberts, both of whom are

Associate Professors of Legal Studies in the School of Business Administration, University of North Carolina, Chapel Hill, N.C. They did the major share of the legal research required, prepared the original drafts of the five new chapters previously mentioned herein, as well as the preliminary redrafts of all of the other chapters in the book, and all of the problems at the end of the chapters.

We also express our gratitude for the revisions and helpful comments by the following Professors: David Webster, College of Business, University of South Florida, Tampa; Joe W. Fowler, College of Business Administration, Oklahoma State University, Stillwater; Wells J. Wright, College of Business Administration, University of Minnesota, Minneapolis; Donald Cantwell, Department of Finance and Real Estate, University of Texas, Arlington; Telford F. Hollman, School of Business, University of Northern Iowa, Cedar Falls; Charles H. Walker, School of Business Administration, University of Mississippi, University; Duane R. Lambert, Department of Accounting, School of Business and Economics, California State University, Hayward.

We are also grateful to Maurice P. Wolk, of the Illinois Bar, Chicago, for his excellent assistance in connection with the text discussion of the Tax Reform Act of 1976, and the Economic Recovery Tax Act of 1981, in Chapters 44 and 51. We also thank Josephine B. Roberson for her careful reading and corrections of galley proofs.

We extend our thanks and appreciation to Cheryl Ingold, Sheri Farrell, and Mary Crump for typing the manuscript of the Fifth Edition, and to Joanne Erwick Roberts and Karlene Fogelin Knebel for their support. In addition, we are thankful for the helpful assistance of Robert J. Barten, Sherry H. Romig, and Judith S. Fifer of West Publishing Company in connection with the preparation of the Fifth Edition.

Len Young Smith
G. Gale Roberson

Wilmette, Illinois
January 8, 1982

Summary of Contents

Table of Contents

ix

Table of Statutes

Table of Cases

Cases in roman are those cited in text.

References are to pages.

xxix

The Legal System

Chapter

1

INTRODUCTION TO LAW

The importance of law needs no brief or argument. The laws of the United States affect and influence the lives of every American citizen, and the laws of each state affect and influence the life of each of its citizens and residents. The rights possessed and the duties owing by every individual to others, and the safety and security of every individual and his property depend upon the law.

Individual men and women, in accordance with the rational side of their nature, admire and respect law and order, truth, honesty, honorable conduct, fair dealing, and consideration of the reasonable interests of others. However, their ever-present animalistic nature is a strong influence favoring their individual self-interests and desire for personal gain at the expense of others, and sometimes in a manner harmful to others.

Blackstone, the English jurist, firmly believed that "a competent knowledge of the laws of one's country is the proper accomplishment of every gentleman and scholar, and is almost an essential part of a liberal education." He bemoaned the fact that whereas in Cicero's time young boys learned the principles of Roman law by heart and in Continental countries no education was complete without considerable study of the laws of one's native land, yet Englishmen were then largely ignorant of the great common law. Likewise, Americans, while often knowledgeable in many areas, are generally uninformed with respect to the legal system which profoundly affects their everyday lives.

The legal system interacts with and influences the political, economic, and social systems of every civilized society. When a society functions peacefully, efficiently and prosperously, its legal system is a primary cause. When a society appears to break down, it may be the result of the abuse, corruption, or malfunction of its legal system, as every civilized society is founded upon law and none has ever survived without law or without an efficient legal system. Hence, the beginning of all progress and improvement in any society must be based upon an understanding of the purpose and necessity of law, a knowledge of some of its fundamental principles, and a comprehension of the legal systems whereby the law is formulated and made effective. The law is pervasive. It permits, forbids, and regulates or moderates practically every known human activity, and affects all persons either directly or indirectly. Without law, there is no guarantee of liberty and freedom of the individual.

Judge Learned Hand, in *The Spirit of Liberty*, stated: "Without it [law] we cannot live; only with it can we insure the future which by right is ours. The best of man's hopes are enmeshed in its success; when it fails it must fail; the measure in which it can reconcile our passions, our wills, our conflicts, is the measure of our opportunity to find ourselves."

In his 1981 *Report on the Education of Lawyers,* Rev. Raymond Baumhart, S. J. stated: "A value oriented Law School should provide students not only with legal expertise, but also with a knowledge of ethics which sustains the desire to be just."

When Margaret Fuller (1810–1850), a talented intellectual, announced publicly, "I accept the universe" (and George Bernard Shaw responded, "E Gad, she'd better"), she undoubtedly included in such a sweeping statement the laws of life and of governments. The law is universal, although different according to time and place.

NATURE OF LAW

The law is not a pure science based upon immutable and universal truths but rather a continuous striving to attain a workable set of rules to adjust the individual and group rights of a society within the fixed framework of its political premises and amidst the constant changing and progression of its sociology and technology. When it is understood that the law is formed by a creative admixture of inductive, deductive and intuitive techniques, the ultimate question remains: What should the law be?

Numerous philosophers and jurists (legal scholars) have attempted to answer this question.

Definition of Law

The American jurists, Holmes and Cardozo, defined law in a functional sense as prophecies or predictions of the way that a court will probably decide specific legal questions. This definition may represent the point of view of many but does not provide a comprehensive understanding of law. Blackstone defined law as "a rule of civil conduct prescribed by the supreme power in a state, commanding what is right, and prohibiting what is wrong."

Similarly, Austin, a nineteenth-century English jurist, defined law as a general command of a state or sovereign to those who are subject to its authority by laying down a course of action which is sanctioned because sanction is implied in command and enforced by judicial or administrative tribunals. However, a concept of law as merely the command of the sovereign or ruling power is not entirely satisfactory because it is not all embracing as it fails to include pre-existing precepts which have not been formalized into a command but nonetheless are "found" by courts to have always existed as part of the common law and are "made" into an announced rule of law whereby a legal duty is found to exist and is enforced.

A definition of the law for our purposes must also relate to the basis of the American political legal system and its premises of freedom, equality and cooperation, and encompass the body of rules which this country has adopted in order to function effectively in a constitutional manner. Furthermore, any system of rules must have the support and respect of those whom it governs. To this end, the system must be capable of adapting to ever-changing social, industrial and political conditions. Judge Jerome Frank, in his classic work,

"Law and the Modern Mind," observes that the fluidity of the law is what makes it most meaningful, yet elusive of definition:

The law always has been, is now, and will ever continue to be, largely vague and variable. And how could this well be otherwise? The law deals with human relations in their most complicated aspects. The whole confused, shifting helter-skelter of life parades before it—more confused than ever, in our kaleidoscopic age.

Even in a relatively static society, men have never been able to construct a comprehensive, eternized, set of rules anticipating all possible legal disputes and formulating in advance the rules which would apply to them. Even in such a social order no one can foresee all the future permutations and combinations of events; situations are bound to occur which were never contemplated when the original rules were made. How much less is such a frozen legal system possible in modern times. New instruments of production, new modes of travel and of dwelling, new credit and ownership devices, new concentrations of capital, new social customs, habits, aims and ideals—all these factors of innovation make vain the hope that definitive legal rules can be drafted that will forever after solve all legal problems. When human relationships are transforming daily, legal relationships cannot be expressed in enduring form. The constant development of unprecedented problems requires a legal system capable of fluidity and pliancy. Our society would be strait-jacketed were not the courts, with the able assistance of the lawyers, constantly overhauling the law and adapting it to the realities of ever-changing social, industrial, and political conditions; although changes cannot be made lightly, yet rules of law must be more or less impermanent, experimental and therefore not nicely calculable. *Much of the uncertainty of law is not an unfortunate accident: it is of immense social value.*

Roscoe Pound, a distinguished American jurist and legal scholar, in an address to the American Bar Association in 1933, stated that law may mean any of three things:

The term "law" has more than one meaning. As we use it commonly, it may mean any of three things, or sometimes all three.

First, we may mean the legal order, that is, the régime of ordering human activities and relations through systematic application of the force of politically organized society, or through social pressure in such a society backed by such force. We use the term "law" in this sense when we speak of "respect for law" or for the "end of law." Indeed, historical jurists have been wont to go further and use "law" to mean the whole régime of social control of which the legal order is a specialized part.

Second, we may mean the aggregate of laws or legal precepts; the body of authoritative grounds of judicial and administrative action established in such a society. We may mean the body of received and established materials on which judicial and administrative determinations proceed. We use the term in this sense when we speak of "systems of law" or of "justice according to law."

Third, we may mean what Mr. Justice Cardozo has happily styled "the judicial process." We may mean the process of determining controversies, whether as it actually takes place, or as the public, the jurists, and the practitioners in the courts hold it ought to take place. To this, perhaps, we shall have to add what may well be called "the administrative process," that is, the process of administrative determination whether as it takes place or as it is conceived it ought to take place. The term "law" is used in this sense in most neo-realist writing of to-day, for example, in Frank's Law and the Modern Mind and much of Mr. Frank's other writing, and in such pronouncements as that of Professor Llewellyn that he includes under "law" all that is done officially.

An excellent commentary on the law is made in a case involving an attack on the constitutionality of the Military Service Act. In upholding the Act against a charge of discrimination based upon the fact that the Act only applied to males within certain age categories and excluded females, the court stated:

The law may be defined as the rule of reason applied to existing conditions * * *. Its very foundation rests upon the reasonableness of men and women in their activities, and it is presumed that all legislation is reasonable and no absurd intention will be ascribed to Congress. For without this presumption, no government, commerce or society could exist. U. S. v. Cook, 311 F.Supp. 618 (W.D.Pa., 1970).

Methodology of Law

As previously noted, law is clearly not an exact science such as the inductive physical sciences. Cardozo said that "the more we study law in its making, at least in its present stages of development, the more we gain the sense of a gradual striving toward an end, shaped by a logic which eschewing the quest for certainty, must be satisfied if its conclusions are rooted in the probable." An exact science is descriptive, stating "what is," while law is prescriptive, stating "what should be."

Nevertheless, as noted by Cardozo, the methodology of law combines the techniques of three major methods of learning.

Science and the Inductive Method. Insofar as science relies upon inductive reasoning which builds upon experience in reaching tentative conclusions for further testing, the law is a science. Holmes said that "the life of the law has not been logic: it has been experience" and that a "page of history is worth a volume of logic." Cardozo noted that "the effect of history is to make the path of logic clear." The law relies for its knowledge upon experience, history, tradition and custom. It employs the inductive method and to that extent is a science.

Reason and the Deductive Method. The law also employs reason and logic in combination with knowledge learned through observation and study of numerous instances or cases as premises for new deductions.

Cardozo termed this technique as the "method of philosophy."

Arts and the Intuitive Method. Cardozo's final category was the method of "sociology," by which he meant that the law was also formed by more or less intuitive forces such as morals, ethics, justice, social welfare, public policy and religion. Within the intuitive category fall such other creative devices as "common sense" and a sense of artistry. Jerome Frank said that "Judges, like musical performers, are to some extent creative artists."

Law and Morals

The law is greatly affected by moral concepts. Morals and law are, however, not synonymous but may be considered as two circles, one partially superimposed upon the other. The area covered by both the morality circle and the legal circle includes the vast body of ideas which are both moral and legal. For instance, "thou shall not kill" and "thou shall not steal" are both moral precepts and legal constraints.

On the other hand, the part of the legal circle not covering the morality circle includes many rules of law that are completely unrelated to morals, such as, you must drive on the right side of the road or you must register before you can vote. Likewise, the part of the morality circle not also covered by the legal circle includes moral precepts which are not enforced by law, such as, you should not silently stand by and watch a blind man walk off a cliff, or you should not foreclose a poor widow's mortgage. Or, if Brown, a private citizen, while walking along a pier, sees Jones drowning in deep water only ten feet from the pier, the law generally imposes no legal duty on Brown to attempt a rescue. If Brown is an excellent swimmer, the mores of the community may condemn the failure to rescue but the law does not presently impose a duty upon the stranger to attempt a rescue under the circumstances set forth above.

Law and Justice

The law is no guarantee of justice, and these terms represent separate and distinct concepts. If the law is regarded as the sum total of the rules enforced and administered by courts and other agencies of government, the disparity between law and justice becomes apparent. Law is inseparable from a politically organized society. In a government by a dictatorship, its laws might be oppressive, harsh, and calculated chiefly to maintain the control and domination of the dictator. A rule, regulation, edict or order is no less a law because it is harsh, unwise, or unjust. Alexander Hamilton regarded justice as the "great cement of society." Justice is an ideal which good law continually strives to achieve. Law is ever changing and its change should be in the direction of fair, reasonable, and impartial treatment of competing interests and desires of individuals with due regard for the common good. To the extent that it fails to do so, it fails to achieve justice.

On the portico of the Supreme Court Building in Washington, D. C. is inscribed in stone "Equal Justice under Law." These words express not only an ideal, but the relative position of law and justice. Without law and order there can be no justice. The present and future welfare of mankind depends upon the administration of justice according to law.

Roscoe Pound, in his treatise on Jurisprudence, Vol. 2, pp. 380–381, postulates six advantages of the administration of justice according to law:

1. Law makes it possible to predict the course which the administration of justice will take.
2. Law secures against errors of individual judgment.

3. Law secures against improper motives on the part of those who administer justice.
4. Law provides the magistrate with standards on which the ethical ideas of the community are formulated.
5. Law gives the magistrate the benefit of all the experience of his predecessors.
6. Law prevents the sacrifice of ultimate interests, social and individual, to the more obvious and immediately pressing but less weighty immediate interests.

In a sense, equality is the root of justice. However, to achieve this ideal is not a simple task. One need only look at the school desegregation area to confirm this observation. Brown v. Board of Education (page 55) is a landmark case holding in no uncertain terms that separate educational facilities for children of different races are inherently unequal, and that racial discrimination by State law is a violation of the Fourteenth Amendment and unconstitutional. This decision of the Supreme Court stands as a beacon light illuminating the road to the achievement of equal justice under law.

Development of the Law

An additional reason why the law is respected is that its principles, precepts, ideals, and their implementation have been developed and refined over a period of centuries, although not at a uniform rate. The law did not spring full blown from the mind of any person nor the minds of any combination of persons at any one time. It evolved slowly, and it contains the seed of future change and development as new conditions and new needs arise in an era of technology and a rapidly expanding population. The law has improved by change, and will continue to change.

The common law can be traced back to the blood feuds of primitive societies and private warfare among consanguinial kindred groups such as families, tribes, or clans, resulting in continuing killings and counterkillings. Vengeance generated by a feud could be halted only by the exaction of a "blood-fine" against the killer's clan payable to the victim's clan. The buying off of a feud was known as a composition. At first the composition was optional with the slain man's kin but later it became compulsory. It was required that the feud terminate upon the payment of the sum determined in some societies by a fixed schedule and in others by disinterested arbitrators. When the state intervened to arbitrate, a portion of the fine was payable to the state, not as a penalty for a crime but as a fee for its time and trouble.

Legal Sanctions

A primary function of the legal system is to insure that legal rules are enforced. Sanctions are the means by which the law enforces the judgments and decrees of the courts. Laws without sanctions would be ineffectual and unenforceable.

Examples of sanctions to enforce a court's judgment include the seizure and sale of the debtor's real estate and personal property. In equity actions the court may enforce its orders and decrees by finding the offender in contempt of court and sentencing him to jail, whereupon he will be arrested by a deputy sheriff and put in jail until such time as he purges himself of the contempt. The sanctions for convictions of a crime are the imposition and collection of a fine, imprisonment, and capital punishment.

The mere existence of sanctions is not enough. It is essential that there be a widespread willingness on the part of individuals in the community to submit to law. Important attitudes which make the law respected and obeyed without the necessity of the state invoking legal sanctions are: fear of displeasure of one's fellow men, public sentiment and opinion, habits of obedience to law, and desire to conform to societal standards.

Classification of Law

The study of law is vast, and it is therefore beneficial to classify the law into categories. There are a number of ways in which this can be done, but the most useful is (1) substantive and procedural, (2) public and private, and (3) civil and criminal.

Substantive Law and Procedural Law. A common classification divides substantive law from adjective or procedural law. The former includes laws which create, define and regulate legal rights and obligations. Thus, the rule in contracts that an offer must be communicated to the offeree is a rule of substantive law. Adjective law, also called procedural or remedial law, prescribes the methods of enforcing rights which exist by reason of the substantive law. One turns to procedural law, found for the most part in codes of procedure, to ascertain the method by which to obtain redress in court.

Public Law and Private Law. Public law is that branch of law which deals with the rights and powers of the state in its political or sovereign capacity, and its relation to individuals or groups. Public law comprises constitutional, administrative, and criminal law. Private law is that which governs individuals and legal entities in their relations with one another. Business law is primarily private law.

Civil and Criminal Law. The civil law defines duties the violation of which constitutes a wrong against the injured party. In contrast, the criminal law establishes duties the violation of which is a wrong against the whole community. Civil law is a part of private law, while criminal law is a part of public law. In a civil action the injured party sues to recover compensation for the damage and injury that he has sustained as a result of defendant's wrongful conduct. The party bringing a civil action (the plaintiff) has the burden of proof which he must sustain by a preponderance (greater weight) of the evidence. The purpose of the civil law is to compensate the aggrieved party, not to punish the wrongdoer as in the case of criminal law. The principal relief afforded by the civil law are a judgment for money damages and a decree ordering the defendant to specifically perform a contract or to desist from specified conduct.

Of course, the same conduct may, and often does, constitute both a crime and a tort, which is one type of civil wrong. But an act may be criminal without being tortious, and by the same token, an act may be a tort but not a crime. The closest that tort law comes to an implementation of the objectives of the criminal law is in certain cases where courts may award "punitive" or "exemplary" damages. Where the defendant's tortious conduct has been intentional and deliberate, exhibiting "malice" or a fraudulent or evil motive, many courts permit a jury to award damages over and above the amount necessary to compensate the plaintiff. The allowance of punitive damages is designed to punish and make an example of the defendant and thus deter others from similar conduct.

A crime is any act or omission prohibited by public law in the interest of protection of the public and made punishable by the State in a judicial proceeding brought by it. Crimes are prohibited and punished upon the ground of public policy, which may include the protection and safeguarding of government (as in treason), human life (as in murder), private property (as in larceny). Additional purposes of the criminal law include deterrence and rehabilitation.

Within recent times the scope of the criminal law has increased substantially. Traditional crimes have been augmented by a multitude of regulations and laws to which are attached criminal penalties. These pertain to nearly every phase of modern living. Typical examples in the business law field are those respecting the li-censing and conduct of a business, and the so-called "Blue-Sky Laws" governing the sale of securities.

In general, a crime consists of two elements: (1) the wrongful or overt act and (2) the criminal intent. For example, it is not enough in order to sustain a larceny conviction to show that the defendant appropriated another's goods; it must also be established that he intended to steal the goods. The mens rea (guilty mind), as it is called, is a requisite of most crimes. Moreover, as is well known, criminal guilt must be proven beyond a reasonable doubt. Under Anglo-American law, guilt is never presumed. Indeed, the law presumes the innocence of the accused, and this presumption is not diminished by his failure to testify in his own defense. The State still has the burden of affirmatively proving the guilt of the accused.

Historically, crimes were classified *mala in se* (wrongs in themselves or morally wrong, such as murder) or *mala prohibita* (not morally wrong but declared wrongful by law, such as the prohibition against making a U-turn).

From the standpoint of the seriousness of the offense, crimes are usually classified as (1) treason (levying war against the United States or giving aid and comfort to its enemies); (2) felony (any crime punishable by death or imprisonment in the penitentiary); and (3) misdemeanor (any crime punishable by a fine or imprisonment in a local jail). Under Federal law, there is another category known as (4) petty crime (any misdemeanor punishable by fine or imprisonment of six months or less).

Although each State has its own criminal code or law, examples of felonies are arson; rape; robbery (stealing from a person by force or intimidation); burglary (entering any building for purpose of committing a felony); mayhem (disfigurement); grand larceny (theft of goods above a certain stated value); and inexcusable homicide, such as murder (with malice aforethought), voluntary manslaughter (with rage), or involuntary manslaughter (with criminal negligence). Misdemeanors usually include assault (threat to injure); battery (beating another); false imprisonment (restricting a person's freedom of movement without lawful authority); criminal libel (written defamation); and petty larceny (theft of goods below a stated value).

SOURCES OF LAW

The sources of the law of the American legal system are the Federal and State constitutions, Federal treaties, interstate compacts, Federal and State statutes, the ordinances of countless local municipal governments, Federal and State executive orders, the rules and regulations of Federal and State administrative agencies, and an increasing volume of reported Federal and State court decisions.

The supreme law of the land is the United States Constitution. The Constitution also provides that treaties made under the authority of the United States shall be the supreme law of the land. Federal treaties are, therefore, paramount to State constitutions and statutes. Federal legislation is of major significance as a source of law. The importance and complexity of new bills enacted at each Congressional session results from the interplay of tremendous economic and social forces within this nation. Federal activity having the force of law is also manifest in the promulgation of executive orders by the President and in the rules and regulations of Federal administrative officials, agencies, and commissions. The federal courts also contribute considerably to the body of law in the United States.

The same pattern exists in every State. The paramount law of each State is contained in its written constitution. Subordinate to this are the statutes passed by its legislature and the case law developed by its judiciary. Likewise, State administra-

tive agencies issue rules and regulations having the force of law as do executive orders promulgated by the Governor. In addition, cities, towns and villages have limited legislative powers within their respective municipal areas to pass ordinances and resolutions. The total annual volume of legislative law is enormous.

These sources of law will be considered under the headings of constitutional, judicial, legislative, and administrative law.

Constitutional Law

Constitutions are the organic law of a particular jurisdiction and serve a number of critical functions. They establish the governmental structure and allocate power among the levels of government, thereby defining political relationships. They also impose restrictions upon the powers of government and enumerate the rights and liberties of the people. For example, the framers of the Constitution of the United States deemed it imperative to state precisely what rights and authority were vested in the people's creation—the national government; but that it was unnecessary to list those liberties the people reserved to themselves, which the government could not restrict nor officials ignore. Alexander Hamilton, a co-author of The Federalist, put it this way: "Here in strictness the people surrender nothing; and as they retain everything, they have no need of particular reservations."

All law in the United States, whether case law, statutory law, or administrative law is subject to the Federal constitution, which is the "supreme law of the land." No statute, Federal or State, is valid if it violates the Federal constitution. The final arbiter as to constitutionality is the Supreme Court of the United States.

One of the fundamental principles upon which the government is founded is that of separation of powers, a doctrine which can be traced back to Baron Montesquieu and to John Locke. As incorporated into our Constitution it means that there are three distinct and independent branches of government, of which the Federal judiciary is one. The principle of judicial review is thus one of the basic ideas incorporated in the Federal Constitution which William Gladstone once characterized as "the greatest [document] ever struck off at one time by the brain and purpose of man."

The Constitution in Article III states "The judicial power shall extend to all cases, in law and equity, arising under this Constitution, the laws of the United States, and treaties made, or which shall be made, under their authority." This provision together with the one in regard to the judicial power of the United States being vested in the courts unmistakably gives the courts the power to test the validity of Acts of Congress. Alexander Hamilton forcefully expressed the idea when he stated: "The interpretation of the laws is the proper and peculiar province of the courts. A constitution is, in fact, and must be regarded by the judges, a fundamental law. It therefore belongs to them to ascertain its meaning as well as the meaning of any particular act or proceeding from the legislative body. If there should happen to be an irreconcilable variance between the two, that which has the superior obligation and validity ought of course to be preferred; or in other words, the Constitution ought to be preferred to the statute, the intention of the people to the intention of their agents." (The Federalist, No. 78, Lodge Ed., pp. 485–6.)

The principle stated by Hamilton was adopted by the Supreme Court in Marbury v. Madison (page 20) and reiterated with respect to the claim of executive privilege. U.S. v. Nixon (page 51).

Judicial Law

The American legal system relies heavily upon the judiciary as a source of law and upon the adversary method for adjudication of disputes. In an adversary system it is generally incumbent upon the parties, not the court, to initiate and to conduct litigation. This approach is predicated upon the belief that the truth is more likely to emerge from the investigation and presentation of evidence by two opposing parties both motivated by self-interest than from judicial investigation motivated only by official duty. The common law system is utilized by other English-speaking countries, among them England, Canada, and Australia.

Common Law. In reported opinions in litigated cases which express the reasoned legal basis for their decisions, the courts have developed a body of law which serves as precedent for determination of later controversies. This law is called "case law," "judge-made law," or "common law." In this sense, common law is distinguished from other sources of law, such as legislation and administrative rulings.

The principle of *stare decisis* (to stand by the decisions), whereby rules of law announced and applied by courts in prior decisions are later adhered to and relied upon in deciding cases of a similar nature, upholds the stability of the common law. Judicial decisions have two uses: first, to determine with finality the case decided; and, second, to indicate to the public how similar cases will be decided if and when they arise. Thus, as defined by Jerome Frank, the law, "as to any given situation is either (a) actual law, i.e., a specific past decision, as to that situation, or (b) probable law, i.e., a guess as to a specific future decision."

Stare decisis does not preclude correction of erroneous decisions or judicial choice among conflicting precedents. Thus, the doctrine allows sufficient flexibility for the common law to change. For example, prior to 1965 the long established law in Pennsylvania was that charitable hospitals were immune from tort liability based upon negligence of their employees. However, in that year, the Supreme Court of Pennsylvania, in Flagiello v. Pennsylvania Hospital, 417 Pa. 486, 208 A.2d 193 (1965), overruled its prior decisions and held a charitable hospital liable for negligence of its employees which resulted in personal injuries to a patient. In declining to be bound by precedent in this instance, the court paid tribute to the doctrine of *stare decisis* and in the words of Justice Musmanno stated:

Without *stare decisis,* there would be no stability in our system of jurisprudence.

Stare Decisis channels the law. It erects lighthouses and flys the signals of safety. The ships of jurisprudence must follow that well-defined channel which, over the years, has been proved to be secure and trustworthy. But it would not comport with wisdom to insist that, should shoals rise in a heretofore safe course and rocks emerge to encumber the passage, the ship should nonetheless pursue the original course, merely because it presented no hazard in the past. The principle of *stare decisis* does not demand that we follow precedents which shipwreck justice.

Stare decisis is not an iron mold into which every utterance by a Court—regardless of circumstances, parties, economic barometer and sociological climate—must be poured, and, where, like wet concrete, it must acquire an unyielding rigidity which nothing later can change.

The history of law through the ages records numerous inequities pronounced by courts because the society of the day sanctioned them. Reason revolts, humanity shudders, and justice recoils before much of what was done in the past under the name of law. Yet, we are urged to retain a forbidding incongruity in the law simply because it is old.

While age adds venerableness to moral principles and physical objects, it sometimes becomes necessary, and it is not sacrilegious to do so, to scrape away the moss of the years to study closely the thing which is being accepted as authoritative, inviolable, and untouchable. When a rule offends against reason, when it is at odds with every precept of natural justice, and when it cannot be defended on its own merits, but has

to depend alone on a discredited genealogy, courts not only possess the inherent power to repudiate, but, indeed, it is required, by the very nature of judicial function, to abolish such a rule.

The genius of the common law is its ability to adapt to change without losing its sense of direction. As Cardozo said: "The inn that shelters for the night is not the journey's end. The law, like the traveler, must be ready for the morrow. It must have a principle of growth."

Equity. As the common law developed, it had a tendency to become overly rigid and beset with technicalities. As a consequence, for many wrongs no remedies were provided, the judges insisting that a claim be within the scope of one of the recognized forms of action. Moreover, in every case in a court of law the major type of relief obtainable was a money judgment. There could be nothing like the injunction which is an order requiring a party to do or to refrain from doing a specified act or engaging in specified conduct. Disappointed subjects began to petition the king directly for justice. He, in turn, came to delegate these petitions to his Chancellor, who was president of the King's Council, chief secretary, head of the King's Chaplains and keeper of the royal seal. In the early period he was always a bishop and came to be known as the "keeper of the king's conscience."

Gradually, there evolved what was in effect a new and supplementary system of needed judicial relief to those who had no adequate remedy at common law. It was called Equity and was administered by a Court of Chancery presided over by the Chancellor. The latter, deciding cases on "equity and good conscience," afforded relief in many instances in which the common-law judges refused to act, or "where the remedy at law was inadequate." Thus, there grew up, side by side, two systems within the framework of the law administered by different tribunals, the common-law courts and courts of equity. Alexander Hamilton stated "that great advantages result from the separation of the equity from the law jurisdiction, and that the causes which belong to the former would be improperly committed to juries. The great and primary use of a court of equity is to give relief in extraordinary cases, which are exceptions to general rules."

An important difference between law and equity is that the chancellor had the power, and could and did order a defendant personally to do or refrain from doing a specific act. If the defendant did not comply with the order, he could be adjudged in contempt of court and punished by fine or imprisonment. This power of compulsion available in a court of equity opened the door to many needed remedies not available in a court of law.

Equity jurisdiction, in some cases, recognized rights which were enforceable at common law but provided more efficacious remedies. For example, for breach of a land contract the buyer could obtain specific performance in a court of equity. The defendant seller would be commanded to perform his part of the contract by conveying title to the land. Another powerful and effective remedy available only in the Court of Chancery was the injunction, a device to prevent future wrongs. No comparable remedies were available in the common law courts. There were other remedies in equity, which were not available elsewhere, among them the remedy of reformation, whereby upon the ground of mutual mistake an action could be brought to reform or change the language of a written agreement to conform to the actual intention of the contracting parties. Another was an action for rescission of a contract by the party who had been induced to enter into it because of the fraud or duress of the other party. Equity opened up altogether new fields, including those untouched by the common-law courts. The most notable was

the recognition and enforcement of trusts. Equity is also the genesis of such fields of law as matrimonial and family law, and probate law (all of which were earlier administered by ecclesiastical courts).

Equity courts over the years have formulated general equitable principles which are called "maxims." A few of these familiar maxims of equity are: Equity will not suffer a wrong to be without a remedy. Equity regards the substance rather than the form. Equity abhors a forfeiture. Equity delights to do justice and not by halves. He who comes into equity must come with clean hands. He who seeks equity must do equity.

In nearly every jurisdiction there has been a union of courts of law and equity into a single court which administers both systems of law. However, vestiges of the old division continue. The right to a trial by jury applies only to actions at law and not to suits filed in equity.

Restatements of Law. The common law of the United States results from the independent decisions of the state and federal courts. The rapid increase in the number of decisions by these courts led to the establishment of the American Law Institute in 1923, composed of a distinguished group of lawyers, judges, and law teachers who assumed the immediate task of preparing "an orderly restatement of the general common law of the United States, including in that term not only the law developed solely by judicial decision, but also the law that has grown from the application by the courts of statutes that were generally enacted and were in force for many years." Wolkin, "Restatements of the Law: Origin, Preparation, Availability", 21 Ohio B.A. Rept. 663 (1940).

The Restatements cover many of the important areas of the common law including torts, contracts, agency, property, and trusts. Although not law by themselves, they are highly persuasive and have frequently been cited by courts in support of their opinions. The Restatements are becoming regarded as the authoritative statement of the common law of the United States. Because they provide a concise and clear statement of much of the common law, relevant portions of the Restatements are frequently cited or quoted in this book.

Legislative Law

Since the end of the nineteenth century, legislation has become the primary source of new law and ordered social change in the United States. Justice Felix Frankfurter's remarks to the New York City Bar in 1947 are even more appropriate today:

. . . Inevitably the work of the Supreme Court reflects the great shift in the center of gravity of law-making. Broadly speaking, the number of cases disposed of by opinions has not changed from term to term. But even as late as 1875 more than 40% of the controversies before the Court were common-law litigation, fifty years later only 5%, while today cases not resting on statutes are reduced almost to zero. It is therefore accurate to say that courts have ceased to be the primary makers of law in the sense in which they "legislated" the common law. It is certainly true of the Supreme Court that almost every case has a statute at its heart or close to it.

This modern emphasis upon statutory law has occurred because case law develops evolutionarily and haphazardly; thus it is not well suited for making drastic or comrehensive changes in prior law. Moreover, courts tend to be circumspect about overruling prior decisions, while it is a common practice for legislatures to repeal prior enactments. In addition, legislatures are independent and able to choose the issues they wish to address. On the other hand, courts may deal only with those issues presented by actual cases. As a result, legislatures are better equipped to make the dramatic, sweeping, and relatively rapid changes in the law that are needed to respond to the myriad and vast technological, social, and economic innovations that arise.

Administrative Law

This branch of public law deals with various regulatory functions and activities of the government in its executive capacity as performed, supervised, and regulated by public officials, departments, boards, and commissions, and with controversies arising between individuals and such public officials and agencies. Administrative functions and activities concern such important matters of national safety, welfare, and convenience, as the establishment and maintenance of military forces, police, citizenship and naturalization, taxation, coinage of money, elections, environmental protection, the regulation of transportation, interstate highways, watercourses, television, radio, trade and commerce, and, in general, public health, safety, and welfare.

Because of the increasing complexity of the social, economic, and industrial life of the nation, the scope of administrative law has expanded enormously. Justice Jackson stated in 1952 that "the rise of administrative bodies has been the most significant legal trend of the last century, and perhaps more values today are affected by their decisions than by those of all the courts, review of administrative decisions apart." Federal Trade Commission v. Ruberoid Co., 343 U.S. 470. This is evidenced by the great increase in the number and activities of Federal government boards, commissions, and other agencies. Certainly, agencies create more legal rules and adjudicate more controversies than all the legislatures and all the courts.

The first important administrative agency was the Interstate Commerce Commission created in 1887. This was followed by the Federal Trade Commission in 1914. Beginning in 1934, the following Federal agencies, among others, have been created:

National Railroad Retirement Board, Federal Communications Commission, Securities and Exchange Commission, Social Security Administration, National Labor Relations Board, Federal Power Commission, Environmental Protection Agency, Maritime Commission, Civil Aeronautics Board, and the Occupational Safety and Health Administration. These regulatory agencies have been created by Congress to implement legislation that is beyond the flexibility, expertise, and resources of the legislative and judicial branches.

Among the more important boards and commissions in the several States are those supervising and regulating banking, insurance, communications, transportation, public utilities, pollution control, and Workmen's Compensation Boards for the administration of employers' liability laws.

So extensive and numerous have become the activities of these administrative agencies that, in their entirety, such activities are referred to as the administrative process. This term is used in contradistinction to the term "judicial process." The former term implies the administration of law by non-judicial agencies; the latter, the administration of law by judicial bodies or courts. Since these boards are not judicial bodies, but only quasi-judicial, an appeal from their rulings or orders may be taken to the courts.

The courts have held that Congress can delegate its power to administrative agencies if Congress sets up standards within which such agencies may operate. These agencies are expert bodies which regulate or supervise complicated areas of our economy. They exercise legislative power (rule-making), executive power (regulation and supervision), and judicial power (adjudication procedures). The courts have held that they may adjudicate (by administrative process) subject to review by the courts of their decisions. Their rules and decisions constitute administrative law. They administer statutes which apply to specific areas of governmental control, enacted by the Federal or by a State legislature.

The scope of judicial review of administrative agencies is limited to determining whether the agency has (1) exceeded its authority, (2) properly interpreted the applicable law, (3) violated any constitutional provision, (4) acted contrary to the procedural requirements of the law, (5) acted arbitrarily or capriciously, or (6) reached conclusions that are not supported by substantial evidence.

One of the chief complaints against administrative agencies has been that the same persons who establish the rules act as prosecutor and as judge to determine whether the rules have been violated. Congress has passed the Administrative Procedure Act to separate the functions of prosecutor and judge, yet questions arise whether Congress has granted too much authority and powers to certain administrative agencies.

Codification of Commercial Law

The entire body of laws pertaining to commercial dealings is commonly referred to as business or commercial law. The broad scope of this category appears from a mere naming of the subjects considered in this text: contracts, agency, bailments, carriers, sales, products liability, partnerships, corporations, unfair competition, secured transactions, property, commercial paper, insurance, securities regulation, antitrust, and bankruptcy.

Before the advent of common-law courts, a system of mercantile courts existed in England which administered a law known generally as Lex mercatoria, the "law merchant." This law, predicated on customs of the merchants, was important, particularly at the time of a fair, when men came with their merchandise from all over Europe. A characteristic of the merchant courts was the dispatch with which they adjudicated disputes. Adapted to the needs of the litigants, the courts sought to prevent undue delay of the itinerant merchants. Eventually, the law merchant was absorbed into the common law, and thus it became a part of American law.

At present, a number of business law topics are still governed principally by the common law, such as contracts and agency. Most areas of commercial law, however, have become largely statutory, including partnerships, corporations, sales, commercial paper, and secured transactions. Since most states enacted statutes dealing with these branches of law, a great diversity in commercial law developed among the states and hampered the conduct of business on a national scale. The increased need for greater uniformity brought about the codification of large parts of commercial law.

The Uniform Commercial Code was prepared under the joint sponsorship and direction of the National Conference of Commissioners on Uniform State Laws and the American Law Institute with the assistance of hundreds of practicing lawyers, judges, law teachers, bankers, and business men.

Work on drafting began in 1942 and by 1952 a finished draft was published for submission to the States. The entire Official Text of the Code is set forth in Appendix A of this book.

In 1961 the American Law Institute and the National Conference of Commissioners of Uniform State Laws jointly established a Permanent Editorial Board for the Uniform Commercial Code consisting of eleven members. The function of this Permanent Board is to keep abreast of the manner and extent to which the Code, as reflected in judicial decisions and amendments by legislative bodies, is fulfilling its avowed purposes, to suggest from time to time clarifying amendments where necessary, and to discourage amendments which are merely a change in language and not of substance, but which may introduce doubt and uncertainty. The Board endeavors to keep informed on new commercial practices which

may cause provisions of the Code to become obsolete or make new provisions desirable.

All fifty states (although Louisiana has adopted only Articles 1, 3, 4, and 5) the District of Columbia and the Virgin Islands, have adopted the Uniform Commercial Code.

The Code consists of ten Articles, namely:

1. General provisions.
2. Sales.
3. Commercial Paper.
4. Bank Deposits and Collections.
5. Letters of Credit.
6. Bulk Transfers.
7. Documents of Title.
8. Investment Securities.
9. Secured Transactions.
10. Effective Date and Repealer.

The Code repeals numerous statutes, including the Uniform Negotiable Instruments Law, Uniform Sales Act, Uniform Conditional Sales Act, Uniform Bills of Lading Act, Uniform Warehouse Receipts Act, Uniform Trust Receipts Act, Uniform Stock Transfer Act, Bulk Sales Act, and Factors Lien Act.

As stated in Section 1–102 the underlying purposes and policies of the Code are:

(a) to simplify, clarify and modernize the law governing commercial transactions; (b) to permit the continued expansion of commercial practices through custom, usage and agreement of the parties; (c) to make uniform the law among the varous jursidictions.

The basic principles of commercial law are not radically changed by the Code but expanded in order to clarify and liberalize the rules and state definitely the legal relationships of the parties in various types of modern commercial transactions. The Code is transaction oriented rather than legal concept oriented. It defines the rights and duties of parties as they develop in commercial situations and describes what events or acts of the parties will alter or modify them. The 168 definitions of terms, many of them well known to business men but heretofore not defined by statute, illustrate the purpose of the Code to conform the rules to modern commercial usages and understandings.

CASE AND LEGAL ANALYSIS

Trial court decisions are not generally reported, i.e., published. The weight of the precedent set by a trial court is not sufficient to warrant permanent reporting for, as has been observed, *stare decisis* does not make the decision of a trial court binding upon the reviewing courts of that or any other jurisdiction nor, indeed, any other trial court within the same jurisdiction. Except for the Federal courts, New York, and a few other States, wherein selected opinions of trial courts are published, decisions in trial courts are simply filed in the office of the clerk of the court where they are available for public inspection.

The reported appellate decisions are published in volumes called "reports" which are numbered consecutively. Most State court decisions are found in the State reports of that particular State. In addition, the State reports are published in regional reporters published by West Publishing Company and called the National Reporter System, comprised of the following: Atlantic (A. or A.2d); Southeastern (S.E.2d); Southwestern (S.W.2d); New York Supplement (N.Y.S.): Northwestern (N.W.2d); Northeastern (N.E.2d); Southern (So.2d); and Pacific (P.2d). An opinion of a State reviewing court may be published in at least two sets of books. After they are published, these opinions or "cases" are referred to ("cited") by giving the name of the case, the volume, name and page of the official State report, if any, in which it is published; the volume, name and page of the particular set and series of the National Reporter System; and the volume, name and page of any other

selected case series. For instance, the case of Lefkowitz v. Great Minneapolis Surplus Store, Inc. (page 142 of this book) indicates that the opinion in this case may be found in Volume 251 of the Official Minnesota Reports at page 188; and in Volume 86 of the Northwestern Reporter, Second Series, at page 689. The Federal Court decisions are found in the Federal Reporter (F. or F.2d); Federal Supplement (F.Supp.); Federal Rules Decisions (F.R.D.); and United States Supreme Court Reports (U.S.), Supreme Court Reporter (S.Ct.) and Lawyers Edition (L.Ed.).

The study of cases is one of the best methods of learning the law. Although reported or published cases (sometimes paradoxically called "unwritten law" in contradiction to "written" or statutory law) have been written and published since about the year 1200, for many centuries law was studied principally by means of textbooks. About 1870 Harvard Law School began having its students read and analyze the reports of decided cases. Today, most law schools use the so-called "case method" for presentation of subject matter. The study of cases is the inductive method of learning, that is, it commences with the raw materials (cases) which contain specific fact situations and application of legal principles, and encourages the student to reason from there.

In reading the title of a case, such as "Jones v. Brown," the "v" or "vs" means versus or against. In the trial court, Jones is the plaintiff, the person who filed the suit, and Brown is the defendant, the person against whom the suit was brought. When the case is appealed, some, but not all, appellate courts place the name of the party who appeals, or the appellant, first, so that "Jones v. Brown" in the trial court becomes, if Brown loses and is the appellant, "Brown v. Jones" in the appellate court. Since some appellate courts retain the trial court order of names, it is not always possible to determine from the title itself who was the plaintiff and who the defendant. The student must carefully read the facts of each case and clearly identify each party in his mind in order to understand the discussion by the appellate court.

Study of the reported cases requires an understanding and application of legal analysis. Normally, the reported opinion in a case sets forth (a) essential facts, nature of the action, the parties, what happened to precipitate the controversy, what happened in the lower court, and what pleadings are material to the issues; (b) the issues of law or fact; (c) the legal principles involved; (d) the application of these principles; and (e) the decision.

A serviceable method of analyzing and briefing cases after a careful reading and comprehension of the opinion is for the student to write in his own language a brief containing:

(a) The facts of the case;

(b) The issue or question involved;

(c) The decision of the court;

(d) The reasons for the decision.

The following excerpt from Professor Karl Llewellyn's *The Bramble Bush* contains a number of useful suggestions for reading cases:

The first thing to do with an opinion, then, is read it. The next thing is to get clear the actual decision, the judgment rendered. Who won, the plaintiff or defendant? And watch your step here. You are after in first instance the plaintiff and defendant *below,* in the trial court. In order to follow through what happened you must therefore first know the outcome *below;* else you do not see what was appealed from, nor by whom. You now follow through in order to see exactly what *further* judgment has been rendered on appeal. The stage is then cleared of form—although of course you do not yet know all that these forms mean, that they imply. You can turn now to what you want peculiarly to know. Given the actual judgments below and above as your indispensable framework—what has the case decided, and what can you derive from it as to what will be decided later?

You will be looking, in the opinion, or in the preliminary matter plus the opinion, for the following: a statement of the facts the court assumes; a statement of the precise way the question has come before the court—which includes what the plaintiff wanted below, and what the defendant did about it, the judgment below, and what the trial court did that is complained of; then the outcome on appeal, the judgment; and, finally the reasons this court gives for doing what it did. This does not look so bad. But it is much worse than it looks.

For all our cases are decided, all our opinions are written, all our predictions, all our arguments are made, on certain four assumptions. They are the first presuppositions of our study. They must be rutted into you till you can juggle with them standing on your head and in your sleep.

1) *The court must decide the dispute that is before it.* It cannot refuse because the job is hard, or dubious, or dangerous.

2) *The court can decide* only *the particular dispute which is before it.* When it speaks to that question it speaks ex cathedra, with authority, with finality, with an almost magic power. When it speaks to the question before it, it announces *law,* and if what it announces is new, it legislates, it *makes* the law. But when it speaks to any other question at all, it says mere words, which no man needs to follow. Are such words worthless? They are not. We know them as judicial *dicta;* when they are wholly off the point at issue we call them *obiter dicta—* words dropped along the road, wayside remarks. Yet even wayside remarks shed light on the remarker. They may be very useful in the future to him, or to us. But he will not feel bound to them, as to his ex cathedra utterance. They came not hallowed by a Delphic frenzy. He may be slow to change them; but not so slow as in the other case.

3) *The court can decide the particular dispute only according to a general rule which covers a whole class of like disputes.* Our legal theory does not admit of single decisions standing on their own. If judges are free, are indeed forced, to decide new cases for which there is no rule, they must at least make a new rule as they decide. So far, good. But how wide, or how narrow, is the general rule in this particular case? That is a troublesome matter. The prac-

tice of our case-law, however, is I think fairly stated thus: it pays to be suspicious of general rules which look too wide; it pays to go slow in feeling *certain* that a wide rule has been laid down at all, or that, if seemingly laid down, it will be followed. For there is a fourth accepted canon:

4) *Everything, everything, everything, big or small, a judge may say in an opinion, is to be read with primary reference to the particular dispute, the particular question before him.* You are not to think that the words mean what they might if they stood alone. You are to have your eye on the case in hand, and to learn how to interpret all that has been said *merely* as a reason for deciding *that* case *that* way.

Cases

Importance of the Common Law

COMMONWEALTH v. CHAPMAN

(1848) 54 Mass. 68.

SHAW, C. J.

* * *

To a very great extent, the unwritten law constitutes the basis of our jurisprudence, and furnishes the rules by which public and private rights are established and secured, the social relations of all persons regulated, their rights, duties, and obligations determined, and all violations of duty redressed and punished. Without its aid, the written law, embracing the constitution and statute laws, would constitute but a lame, partial, and impracticable system. Even in many cases, where statutes have been made in respect to particular subjects, they could not be carried into effect, and must remain a dead letter, without the aid of the common law. In cases of murder and manslaughter, the statute declares the punishment; but what acts shall constitute murder, what manslaughter, or what justifiable or excusable homicide, are left to be decided by the rules and principles of the common law. So, if an act is made criminal, but no mode of prosecution is directed, or no punishment provided, the common law furnishes its ready aid, prescribing the mode of prosecution by indictment, the common law punishment of fine and imprisonment. Indeed, it seems to be too obvious to require argument, that without the common law, our legislation and jurisprudence would be impotent, and wholly deficient in completeness and symmetry, as a system of municipal law.

It will not be necessary here to consider at large the sources of the unwritten law, its authority as a binding rule, derived from long and general acquiescence, its provisions, limits, qualifications, and exceptions, as established by well authenticated usage and tradition. It is sufficient to refer to 1 Bl.Com. [Blackstone's Commentories] 63 & seq.

If it be asked, "how are these customs or maxims, constituting the common law, to be known, and by whom is their validity to be determined?" Blackstone furnishes the answer; "by the judges in the several courts of justice. They are the depositaries of the laws, the living oracles, who must decide in all cases of doubt, and who are bound by oath to decide according to the law of the land. Their knowledge of that law is derived from experience and study," "and from being long personally accustomed to the judicial decisions of their predecessors." 1 Bl.Com. 69.

Of course, in coming to any such decision, judges are bound to resort to the best sources of instruction, such as the records of courts of justice, well authenticated histories of trials, and books of reports, digests, and brief statements of such decisions, prepared by suitable persons, and the treatises of sages of the profession, whose works have an established reputation for correctness.

Growth of the Common Law

PENNY v. LITTLE
(1841) 4 Ill. 301.

DOUGLASS, J.
* * *

The common law is a beautiful system; containing the wisdom and experience of ages. Like the people it ruled and protected, it was simple and crude in the infancy, and became enlarged, improved, and polished, as the nation advanced in civilization, virtue, and intelligence. Adapting itself to the condition and circumstances of the people, and relying upon them for its administration, it necessarily improved as the condition of the people was elevated.
* * *

The inhabitants of this country always claimed the common law as their birthright, and at an early period established it as the basis of their jurisprudence. Slight changes and modifications were found necessary, and consequently adopted by common consent, from time to time, to adapt it to our peculiar institution, and the habits and customs of the people. These changes, modifications, and customs having, for a long course of years, been acquiesced in by the people, and sanctioned by the courts, have acquired the force of law, and become incorporated into and made part of the common law of the land. The legislation of the territory and of our state was adopted with reference to the law as it thus existed in the country. Upon this principle and none other, can we account for the numerous cases in which the common law has been changed by statute in England, since the fourth year of James I., and those changes adopted by the courts in this country, with-

out having been first reenacted by our legislatures.

*Division of Power between
the States and the Federal
Government*

MARTIN v. HUNTER'S LESSEE
(1816) 14 U.S. (1 Wheat) 304, 4 L.Ed. 97.

MR. JUSTICE STOREY:
* * *

The Constitution of the United States was ordained and established, not by the States in their sovereign capacities, but emphatically as the preamble of the Constitution declares, by "the people of the United States." There can be no doubt that it was competent to the people to invest the general government with all the powers which they might deem proper and necessary; to extend or restrain these powers according to their own good pleasure, and to give them a paramount and supreme authority. As little doubt can there be, that the people had a right to prohibit to the States the exercise of any powers which were, in their judgment, incompatible with the objects of the general compact; to make the powers of the State governments, in given cases, subordinate to those of the nation, or to reserve to themselves those sovereign authorities which they might not choose to delegate to either. The Constitution was not, therefore, necessarily carved out of existing State sovereignties, nor a surrender of powers already existing in State institutions, for the powers of the States depend upon their own constitutions; and the people of every State had the right to modify and restrain them, according to their own views of policy or principle. On the other hand, it is perfectly clear that the sovereign powers vested in the State governments, by their respective constitutions, remained unaltered and unimpaired, except so far as they were granted to the government of the United States.

These deductions do not rest upon general reasoning, plain and obvious as they seem to be. They have been positively recognized by one of the articles in amendment of the Constitution, which declares that "the powers not delegated to the United States by the Constitution, nor prohibited by it to the States, are reserved to the States respectively, or to the people." Const.Amend. 10.

*Supremacy of
the U.S. Supreme Court*

MARBURY v. MADISON

(1803) 5 U.S. (1 Cranch) 137, 2 L.Ed. 60.

MR. CHIEF JUSTICE MARSHALL
* * *

The question whether an Act [of the Congress] repugnant to the Constitution can become the law of the land, is a question deeply interesting to the United States; but, happily, not of an intricacy proportioned to its interest. It seems only necessary to recognize certain principles, supposed to have been long and well established, to decide it.

That the people have an original right to establish, for their future government, such principles as, in their opinion, shall most conduce to their own happiness, is the basis on which the whole American fabric has been erected. The exercise of this original right is a very great exertion; nor can it nor ought it be frequently repeated. The principles, therefore, so established, are deemed fundamental. And as the authority from which they proceed is supreme, and can seldom act, they are designed to be permanent.

This original and supreme will organizes the government, and assigns to different departments their respective powers. It may either stop here, or establish certain limits not to be transcended by those departments.

The government of the United States is of the latter description. The powers of the legislature are defined and limited; and that those limits may not be mistaken, or forgotten, the Constitution is written. To what purpose are powers limited, and to what purpose is that limitation committed to writing, if these limits may, at any time, be passed by those intended to be restrained? The distinction between a government with limited and unlimited powers is abolished, if those limits do not confine the persons on whom they are imposed, and if acts prohibited and acts allowed are of equal obligation. It is a proposition too plain to be contested, that the Constitution controls any legislative Act repugnant to it; or, that the legislature may not alter the Constitution by an ordinary Act.

Between these alternatives there is no middle ground. The Constitution is either a superior paramount law, unchangeable by ordinary means, or it is on a level with ordinary legislative Acts, and, like other Acts, is alterable when the legislature shall please to alter it.

If the former part of the alternative be true, then a legislative Act contrary to the Constitution is not law; if the latter part be true, then written constitutions are absurd attempts, on the part of the people, to limit a power in its own nature illimitable.
* * *

If an Act of the Legislature, repugnant to the Constitution, is void, does it, notwithstanding its invalidity, bind the courts, and oblige them to give it effect? Or, in other words, though it be not law, does it constitute a rule as operative as if it was a law? This would be to overthrow in fact what was established in theory; and would seem, at first view, an absurdity too gross to be insisted on. It shall, however, receive a more attentive consideration.

It is emphatically the province and duty of the judicial department to say what the law is. Those who apply the rule to particular cases, must of necessity expound and interpret that rule. If two laws conflict with each other, the courts must decide on the operation of each.

So if a law be in opposition to the Constitution; if both the law and the Constitution apply to a particular case, so that the court must either decide that case conformably to the law, disregarding the Constitution; or conformably to the Constitution, disregarding the law; the court must determine which of these conflicting rules governs the case. This is of the very essence of judicial duty.

If, then, the courts are to regard the Constitution and the Constitution is superior to any ordinary Act of the Legislature, the Constitution, and not such ordinary Act, must govern the case to which they both apply.

Supremacy of the Constitution

McCULLOCH v. MARYLAND
(1819) 17 U.S. (4 Wheat) 316, 4 L.Ed. 579.

MR. CHIEF JUSTICE MARSHALL
* * *

This great principle is, that the Constitution and the laws made in pursuance thereof are supreme; that they control the Constitution and laws of the respective states, and cannot be controlled by them. From this, which may be almost termed an axiom, other propositions are deduced as corollaries, on the truth or error of which, and on their application to this case, the cause has been supposed to depend. There

are, 1st. That a power to create implies a power to preserve. 2d. That a power to destroy, if wielded by a different hand, is hostile to, and incompatible with, these powers to create and to preserve. 3d. That where this repugnancy exists, that authority which is supreme must control, not yield to that over which it is supreme.

*Power of Courts
to Interpret Statutes*

HEYDON'S CASE
(1584) 3 Co. 7a, 76 Eng.Rep. 637.

* * * And it was resolved by them, that for the sure and true interpretation of all statutes in general (be they penal or beneficial, restrictive or enlarging of the common law,) four things are to be discerned and considered:—

1st. What was the common law before the making of the Act.

2nd. What was the mischief and defect for which the common law did not provide.

3rd. What remedy the Parliament hath resolved and appointed to cure the disease of the commonwealth.

And, 4th. The true reason of the remedy; and then the office of all the Judges is always to make such construction as shall suppress the mischief, and advance the remedy, and to suppress subtle inventions and evasions for continuance of the mischief, and *pro privato commodo,* and to add force and life to the cure and remedy, according to the true intent of the makers of the Act, *pro bono publico.* * * *

Chapter
2

LEGAL PROCESS

Students of business law and owners and operators of a business enterprise will benefit from an understanding of legal process, including the manner in which court trials are conducted. Rules of procedure are needed as much to control the judge presiding at a trial as they are to keep within proper bounds the opposing lawyers who represent the litigants. The rules are also beneficial in determining the issues in a case as to its facts and as to the applicable law.

Every court has its own rules which govern its procedure and which are separate for civil law cases and for criminal law cases. A rule of great assistance in ascertaining the precise basis upon which the judge reached his decision in a case requires the judge to set forth in his order of final judgment (1) his findings of fact, and (2) his conclusions of law.

THE COURT SYSTEM

Courts are impartial tribunals established by governmental bodies to settle disputes.

A court may render a binding decision only when it has jurisdiction over the dispute and the parties to that dispute. The United States has a dual court system: each of the fifty states plus the District of Columbia has its own system as does the federal government.

The Federal Courts

Article III of the United States Constitution states that the judicial power of the United States shall be vested in one Supreme Court and such inferior courts as Congress may from time to time ordain and establish. Congress has established a federal court system consisting of a number of special courts, district courts, and courts of appeal. The federal court system is staffed by judges who receive lifetime appointments from the President.

District Court. The district courts are the trial courts of general jurisdiction in the federal system. Most cases begin in the district court and it is here that issues of fact are decided.

Congress has established ninety-eight judicial districts, each of which is located entirely in a particular state. Certain states contain more than one district. For instance, New York has four districts, Illinois has three, Wisconsin has two, while a number of less populated states comprise a single district.

Courts of Appeals. Congress has established twelve judicial circuits, each having a court known as the Court of Appeals, which primarily hears appeals from the district courts located within its circuit. In addition, they review orders of certain administrative agencies. The United States Courts of Appeals generally hear cases in panels of three judges.

The Courts of Appeals do not hear witnesses. The function of appellate courts is to examine the record of a case on appeal and to determine whether the trial court committed prejudicial error and, if so, either to reverse or to modify the judgment of the lower court, to remand it back to the lower court for further proceeding, or to affirm it.

The Supreme Court. The nation's highest tribunal is the United States Supreme Court, consisting of nine justices (a Chief Justice and eight Associate Justices), who sit as a group in Washington, D.C. The United States Supreme Court has original jurisdiction in the types of cases described in the second paragraph of Section 2 of Article III of the United States Constitution:

In all Cases affecting Ambassadors, other public Ministers and Consuls, and those in which a State shall be a Party, the supreme Court shall have original Jurisdiction. In all other Cases before mentioned, the supreme Court shall have appellate Jurisdiction, both as to Law and Fact, with such Exceptions, and under such Regulations as the Congress shall make.

The Court's principal function is to review decisions of the federal courts of appeals and, in some instances, those of the highest state courts or other tribunals. Cases reach the Supreme Court under its appellate jurisdiction by one of two routes. A relatively few come by way of appeal by right, which cases the Court must hear. Appeal by right to the United States Supreme Court is available from the United States Courts of Appeals if that court declares a state statute to be in violation of the Constitution, treaties, or laws of the United States. Appeal by right from the highest court of a state is available in two situations: (1) the state court declares a federal statute or treaty invalid, or (2) the state court upholds the validity of a state statute against a challenge that it is repugnant to the Constitution, treaties, or laws of the United States.

The second way in which a decision of a lower court may be reviewed by the Supreme Court is by the discretionary *writ of certiorari*. The vast majority of cases reaching the Supreme Court come to it by means of writs of certiorari. Writs are granted when there is a federal question of substantial importance or a conflict in the decisions of the U.S. Circuit Courts of Appeals.

Special Courts. The special courts in the federal judicial system include the Court of Claims, Tax Court, Customs Court, and Court of Customs and Patent Appeals. These courts have jurisdiction over particular subject matters. The Court of Claims was created by Congress in 1855 and hears claims against the United States. The Tax Court has jurisdiction over certain cases involving federal taxes. The Customs Court was established in 1926 to hear appeals from the decisions of customs officials. The Court of Custom and Patent Appeals reviews decisions of the Customs Court and the Patent and Trademark Office.

State Courts

Each of the 50 states and the District of Columbia has its own court system. In most states the judges are elected by the voters for a term consisting of a stated number of years. State courts have general jurisdiction which includes all cases arising under the common law and by virtue of a statute of the state.

At the summit is the state's highest tribunal, a reviewing court which is generally called the Supreme Court of the State. Except for those cases in which review by the U.S. Supreme Court is available, the decision of the highest state tribunal is final. In most states the large volume of cases in which review is sought has necessitated the creation of intermediate appellate courts. Where there is an intermediate appellate court, there is usually a provision for appeal to it by right, with further review in most cases a matter of the highest court's discretion.

Jurisdiction and Venue

Jurisdiction simply means the power or authority of a court with respect to a given case. There are two kinds of jurisdiction, both of which a court must have in order to proceed with a lawsuit. The first is jurisdiction over the subject matter of the lawsuit. Where a court lacks jurisdiction over the subject matter of a case, any action taken by it in the case is void.

The second kind of jurisdiction is over the parties to a lawsuit. In order to obtain jurisdiction over the defendant named in a lawsuit, a proper summons issued by the court must be personally served upon him.

Venue pertains to the place where the action is filed or has to be tried. Most statutes provide that the venue is in the county in which the defendant is a resident.

Article III, Section 2(1), of the Federal Constitution sets forth the subject matter jurisdiction of the federal courts, as follows:

The judicial Power shall extend to all Cases, in Law and Equity, arising under this Constitution, the Laws of the United States, and Treaties made, or which shall be made, under their Au-

thority;—to all Cases affecting Ambassadors, other public Ministers and Consuls;—to all Cases of admiralty and maritime Jurisdiction;—to Controversies to which the United States shall be a party;—to Controversies between two or more States;—between a State and Citizens of another State;—between Citizens of different States;—between Citizens of the same State claiming Lands under Grants of different States, and between a State, or the Citizens thereof, and foreign States, Citizens or Subjects.

The state courts have jurisdiction over all matters that have not been exclusively given to the federal courts or expressly taken away by the Constitution or Congress.

Exclusive Federal Jurisdiction. The federal courts have exclusive jurisdiction over Federal criminal prosecutions, admiralty, bankruptcy, anti-trust, patent, trade-mark and copyright cases, suits against the United States and cases arising under certain federal statutes that expressly provide for exclusive federal jurisdiction.

Concurrent Federal Jurisdiction. All instances of federal jurisdiction other than exclusive are concurrent and thus may be heard either by state or federal courts. Federal concurrent jurisdiction may be classified into two basic categories. The first arises whenever there is a federal question over which the federal courts do not have exclusive jurisdiction and the amount in controversy exceeds $10,000. In numerous instances the jurisdictional dollar requirement has been eliminated by Congress. A federal question is any case arising under the Constitution, statutes, or treaties of the United States.

Second, where there is "diversity of citizenship" and the amount in controversy exceeds $10,000, an action between private litigants may be brought in a federal district court or a state court. Diversity of citizenship exists when the plaintiff or plaintiffs are all citizens of a state or states different from the state or states of which the defendants are citizens; when a foreign country is bringing an action against citizens of the United States; and when the controversy is between citizens of the United States and citizens of a foreign country. The citizenship of an individual litigant is the state of his residence or domicile, while that of a corporate litigant is both (a) the State of incorporation, and (b) the state in which its principal place of business is located. When a federal district court hears a case solely under diversity of citizenship jurisdiction, there is no federal question involved and accordingly the federal courts must apply state law.

In any case involving concurrent jurisdiction the plaintiff has the choice of bringing the action in either an appropriate federal court or state court. However, if the plaintiff brings the case in a state court the defendant usually may have it removed to a federal court for the district in which the state court is located.

A case of diversity of citizenship where the amount in controversy does not exceed $10,000 must be heard in a state court. A federal question case where the amount in controversy does not exceed $10,000 must be heard in a state court unless, as noted above, Congress has eliminated the dollar requirement.

Stare Decisis in the Dual Court System. The doctrine of *stare decisis* presents certain problems when there are two parallel court systems. As a consequence, in the United States *stare decisis* functions approximately as follows:

1. The United States Supreme Court has never held itself to be rigidly bound by its own decisions, and lower federal courts and state courts have followed that course in respect to their own decisions.
2. A decision of the U.S. Supreme Court on federal questions is binding on all other courts, federal or state.

3. While a decision of a federal court other than the Supreme Court may be persuasive in a state court on a federal question, it is nevertheless not binding, since the state court owes obedience insofar as it has jurisdiction over a case involving federal law to only one federal court, namely, the Supreme Court.
4. A decision of a state court may be persuasive in the federal courts but it is not binding, except where federal jurisdiction is based on diversity of citizenship, in which case the federal courts are required to apply local state law as determined by the highest state tribunal and not by a trial or intermediate appellate court.
5. Decisions of the federal courts (other than the Supreme Court) are not binding upon other federal courts of coordinate rank, or of inferior rank, unless the latter owe obedience to the court rendering the decision.

DUE PROCESS OF LAW

Due process of law is basically the requirement of a fair trial. Every person is entitled to have charges or complaints against him, whether in civil or criminal proceedings, made publicly and in writing, and be given the opportunity to defend against them. In criminal prosecutions, it includes the right to counsel, to confront and to cross-examine adverse witnesses, to testify in his own behalf if desired, to produce witnesses and offer other evidence, and to be free from any and all prejudicial conduct and statements.

The right to due process had developed and existed under the common law of England for centuries prior to the American Revolution. In drafting the U.S. Constitution the founding fathers, with a clear and painful recollection of the hardships and injustices inflicted upon the colonies by the mother country as set forth in the Declaration of Independence in 1776, were fearful of creating a national government with too much power over the people.

The answer was the Bill of Rights, consisting of the first ten Amendments to the Constitution, which are restrictions upon the power of the national government. The draftsmen knew well the importance of "due process of law" when they inserted it in the Fifth Amendment:

No person shall be held to answer for a capital, or otherwise infamous crime, unless on a presentment or indictment of a Grand Jury, except in cases arising in the land or naval forces, or in the Militia, when in actual service in time of War or public danger; nor shall any person be subject for the same offense to be twice put in jeopardy of life or limb; nor shall be compelled in any criminal case to be a witness against himself, nor be deprived of life, liberty, or property, without due process of law; nor shall private property be taken for public use, without just compensation.

The obligation of providing due process of law for every person was also imposed upon state governments by the adoption of the Fourteenth Amendment to the Constitution following the Civil War. Section 1 of this Amendment provides:

All persons born or naturalized in the United States, and subject to the jurisdiction thereof, are citizens of the United States and of the State wherein they reside. No State shall make or enforce any law which shall abridge the privileges or immunities of citizens of the United States; nor shall any State deprive any person of life, liberty, or property, without due process of law; nor deny to any person within its jurisdiction the equal protection of the laws.

CIVIL PROCEDURE

Civil disputes that enter the judicial system are subject to the rules of civil procedure which are designed to effect a just, prompt, and inexpensive resolution of the dispute.

Journey of a Case Through the Courts

To acquaint the student with civil procedure, it will be helpful to carry a hypothet-ical action through the trial court to the highest court of review in the state. Although there are technical differences in trial and appellate procedure among the several states, the following illustration will serve to provide a general understanding of the trial and appeal of cases. Assume that A, a pedestrian, while crossing a street in Chicago, is struck by an automobile driven by B. A suffers serious personal injuries, incurs heavy medical and hospital expenses, and is unable to work for several months. A desires that B pay him for the loss and damages that he sustained. Attempts at settlement failing, A brings an action at law against B. A is the plaintiff, and B the defendant. Each is represented by a lawyer. Let us follow the progress of the case.

The Pleadings. The purpose of pleadings is to establish the issues of fact and law presented. In this case, it is by complaint and answer. A lawsuit is commenced by A, the plaintiff, filing with the clerk of the trial court a *complaint* against B which alleges: (1) the relevant facts, (2) the existence of a duty owing by the defendant to the plaintiff by reason of the facts, (3) a breach of that duty by the defendant, (4) loss and damage sustained by the plaintiff proximately resulting from that breach, and (5) prayer for relief and for judgment for money damages or decree.

The sheriff of the county, or one of his deputies, serves a summons and a copy of the complaint upon B, the defendant, commanding him to file his appearance and answer with the clerk of the court within a specific time, usually thirty days from the date of service of the summons. The summons serves the important function of notifying the defendant that a suit has been commenced against him. Proper service of the summons establishes the court's jurisdiction over the person of the defendant.

In this example A's complaint alleges that while in the exercise of due and reasonable care for his own safety, he was struck by B's automobile, which was negligently being driven by B, causing personal injuries and damages of $50,000 for which A requests judgment.

At this point B, the defendant, has several options. He may make motions contesting the court's jurisdiction over him or asserting that the action is barred by the Statute of Limitations, which requires suits to be brought within a specified time. B may also move that the complaint be made more definite and certain, or B may instead move that the complaint be dismissed for failure to state a claim upon which relief may be granted. Such a motion is sometimes called a demurrer and essentially asserts that even if all of A's allegations are true, A would nevertheless not be entitled to the relief he seeks and therefore there is no need for a trial of the facts.

Most likely, B will respond to the complaint by filing an answer which may contain admissions, denials, affirmative defenses, and counterclaims. Thus, B might answer the complaint by denying its allegations of negligence and averring, on the other hand, that he, B, was driving his car at a low rate of speed and with reasonable care (a denial) when his car struck A (an admission) who had dashed across the street in front of B's car without looking in any direction to see whether cars or other vehicles were approaching; that, accordingly, A's injuries were occasioned by his own negligence (an affirmative defense) and therefore he should not be permitted to recover any damages. B might further state that A caused damages to his car and request a judgment for $2,000 (a counterclaim). An issue of fact is thus made by the pleadings as to whether A or B, or both, had failed to exercise due and reasonable care under the circumstances, and were thus negligent and liable for their carelessness.

If the defendant counterclaims, the plaintiff must respond by a reply in which he may admit, deny, or assert an affirmative defense.

After the pleadings, either party may move for judgment on the pleadings which requests the judge to rule as a matter of law whether the facts as alleged in the pleadings, which for the purpose of the motion are taken to be as alleged by the non-moving party, form a sufficient basis to grant the requested relief.

Discovery of Evidence. Modern statutes and rules of court provide such liberal rights to a litigant to discover the evidence of the opposing party prior to trial that a trial lawyer has no excuse for being surprised by any evidence offered at the trial by his opponent.

The Rules of Civil Procedure for the United States District Courts authorize the use of seven different methods of discovery:

1. Depositions before Action or Pending Appeal.
2. Depositions upon Oral Examination.
3. Depositions upon Written Questions.
4. Interrogatories to Parties.
5. Production of Documents and Things, and Entry upon Land for Inspection and Other Purposes.
6. Physical and Mental Examination of Persons.
7. Requests for Admission of Facts.

Depositions consist of testimony under oath taken out of court, usually in the office of the lawyer taking the deposition, upon due notice to the opposing counsel in the case. The questions and the answers of the deponent are recorded by a court reporter, then transcribed, signed by the deponent, and filed with the clerk of the court for use at the trial, if desired by either party.

The evidence disclosed by discovery may be so clear that a trial to determine the facts becomes unnecessary. Thus, after discovery, either party may move for a summary judgment which requests the judge to rule that, since there are no issues of fact to be determined by trial, as a matter of law that party should prevail.

Trial. Either by statute or court rule, either party desiring trial by jury, in cases in which one is available, must file a written jury demand not later than the date when his first written pleading is due. Assuming a timely jury demand has been made, the trial begins by selection of a jury, followed by opening statements of each attorney concerning the facts that he expects to prove upon the trial. Plaintiff and his witnesses then testify upon direct examination. Each is subject to cross-examination by defendant's attorney. Plaintiff and his witnesses testify that the traffic light at the street intersection where A was struck was green for traffic in the direction in which A was crossing but changed to orange when A was about one-third way across. Defendant and his witnesses testify that B was driving his car at a low rate of speed when it struck A, and that B at the time had the green light at the intersection.

In the course of the trial, the judge rules upon the admission and exclusion of evidence. If the judge refuses to allow certain evidence to be introduced or certain testimony to be given, the only way the attorney can preserve for review on appeal the question of its admissibility is by making an offer of proof. This is not regarded as evidence and the offer, which is made outside of the presence of the jury, consists of oral statements of counsel or of witnesses for the purpose of the record to show the substance of the evidence which the judge has ruled inadmissible.

After cross-examination, followed by redirect examination of each of his witnesses, plaintiff rests his case. At this point the defendant may move for a directed verdict in his favor. If the judge concludes that the evidence introduced by the plaintiff, which is assumed to be true, would not be sufficient for the jury to find in favor of the plaintiff, then the judge will grant the directed verdict in favor of the defendant.

If the judge denies the motion for a directed verdict, then the defendant has the opportunity to present evidence. After the defendant has presented his evidence and both parties have rested, then each party may move for a directed verdict. If these motions are denied, then the plaintiff's attorney makes an argument to the jury, reviewing the evidence and urging a verdict in favor of his client, A, followed by defendant's attorney, who summarizes the evidence in the light most favorable to his client, B. A's attorney is permitted to make a short argument in rebuttal.

The attorneys have previously tendered written jury instructions on the applicable law to the trial judge, who gives those which he approves and denies those which he considers incorrect. The judge may also give the jury instructions of his own. These instructions (called "charges" in some states) are for the purpose of advising the jury of the particular rules of law which it is to apply to the facts as determined by it from the evidence. The jury then retires to the jury room to deliberate and to reach its verdict in favor of one party or the other. If it finds the issues in favor of defendant, its verdict is that the defendant is not liable. If, however, it finds the issues for the plaintiff and against defendant, its verdict is that the defendant is liable and specifies the amount of plaintiff's damages, in this case, $35,000. Upon returning to the jury box, the foreman either announces the verdict or hands it in written form to the clerk, who then gives it to the judge, who reads the verdict in open court. The unsuccessful party may then file a written motion for a new trial or for judgment notwithstanding the verdict (also referred to as a judgment n.o.v.). This motion is similar to a motion for a directed verdict, only it is made after the jury's verdict. Upon denial of these motions, the judge enters judgment on the verdict for $35,000 in favor of the plaintiff.

In the event that B does not appeal, or of affirmance by the reviewing court if he does appeal, and B does not pay the judgment, the task of enforcement remains. A requests the clerk to issue a writ of execution which is served by the sheriff upon defendant demanding payment of the judgment. Upon return of the writ "unsatisfied," A may post bond or other security and order a levy on and sale of specific property belonging to defendant which is then seized by the sheriff, advertised for sale, and sold at public sale under the writ of execution. If the proceeds of the sale do not produce sufficient funds to pay the judgment, plaintiff A's attorney may institute a supplementary proceeding in an attempt to locate money or other property belonging to defendant. He may also proceed by garnishment against B's employer or a bank in which B has an account in an attempt to collect the judgment.

Appeal. Assume that B directs his attorney to appeal. A notice of appeal is filed with the clerk of the trial court within the prescribed time. Later B, the appellant, files in the reviewing court the record on appeal which contains the pleadings, transcript of the testimony, rulings by the judge on motions made by the parties, arguments of counsel, jury instructions, verdict, post-trial motions, and the judgment order from which the appeal is taken. In states where there is an intermediate court of appeals, it will usually be the reviewing court. In states where there are no intermediate courts of appeal, a party may appeal directly from the trial court to the State Supreme Court.

B, as appellant, is required to prepare a condensation of the record, known as an abstract, or pertinent excerpts from the record, which he files together with brief and argument with the reviewing court. His brief contains a statement of the facts, the issues, the rulings by the trial court which B contends are erroneous and prejudicial, grounds for reversal of the judgment, statement of the applicable law, and argument on his behalf. A, the appellee, files an an-

swering brief and argument. B may, but is not required to, file a reply brief. The case is now ready for consideration by the reviewing court.

The appellate court does not hear any evidence. It takes the case upon the record, abstracts, and briefs. After oral argument by the attorneys, if the court elects to hear one, the case is taken under advisement. The appellate court then makes a decision based upon majority rule. The court prepares a written opinion containing the reasons for its decision, the rules of law which apply, and its judgment. The judgment may affirm the judgment of the trial court, or if it finds that reversible error was committed, the judgment may be reversed or the case may be reversed and remanded for a new trial. The losing party may file a petition for rehearing, which is usually denied.

If the reviewing court is an intermediate appellate court, the party losing in that court may decide to seek a reversal of its judgment by filing within a prescribed time a notice of appeal if the appeal is by right, or a petition for leave to appeal to the State Supreme Court, if the appeal is by discretion. This petition corresponds to a petition for a writ of certiorari in the United States Supreme Court. The party winning in the appellate court may file an answer to the petition for leave to appeal. If the petition is granted, or if the appeal is by right, the record is certified to the higher court and each party files a new brief and argument in the Supreme Court. Oral argument may be held and the case is taken under advisement. If the Supreme Court concludes that the judgment of the appellate court is correct, it affirms. If it decides otherwise, it reverses the judgment of the appellate court and enters a reversal or an order of remand. The unsuccessful party may again file a petition for a rehearing which is likely to be denied. Barring the remote possibility of an application for still further review by the United States Supreme Court, the case has either reached its terminus or upon remand is about to start its second journey through the courts, beginning as originally in the trial court.

Arbitration

Arbitration is a means whereby matters in dispute may be decided by a neutral person or persons (arbitrators) selected by the parties. The presentation of the case is informal and the arbitrator is not bound to adhere to established rules of evidence.

The decision of the arbitrator (called an *award*) is binding upon the parties. Nevertheless, it is subject to limited judicial review for such matters as lack of due process, excess of the arbitrator's jurisdiction, or violation of law.

In commercial cases, resolution by arbitration normally comes about by reason of (1) the inclusion of a provision in a contract which requires that any controversy pertaining to a matter or matters covered by the agreement shall be determined by arbitration; or (2) a written agreement called a "submission agreement" by which the parties to a dispute agree to submit the controversy to arbitration rather than to a court. The increasing popularity of arbitration stems from congestion and delay in the courts and the cost of a court trial. However, arbitration is not a panacea for these problems. Depending upon the type of case, arbitration is not always faster or less expensive.

The National Commissioners on Uniform State Laws adopted in 1955 the Uniform Arbitration Act, which has been adopted in about one-half the States and provides:

A written agreement to submit any existing controversy to arbitration or a provision in a written contract to submit to arbitration any controversy thereafter arising between the parties is valid, enforceable, and irrevocable save upon such grounds as exist at law or in equity for the revocation of any contract.

Both federal and state statutes have been widely used to enforce arbitration agreements in labor disputes and in commercial disputes. For instance, many states have enacted compulsory uninsured motorists statutes which require automobile public liability insurance policies to include uninsured motorist coverage, which provides that if the insured motorist is involved in an automobile accident with an uninsured owner or operator of an automobile, he may recover from his own insurance carrier up to a specified amount for bodily injuries for which the uninsured motorist is liable. An arbitration clause is customarily incorporated into this type of coverage. Moreover, a number of states have enacted compulsory arbitration statutes requiring arbitration of unresolved labor disputes involving policemen and firemen.

CRIMINAL SUITS

Prosecution is initiated for less serious crimes by the issuance of a warrant which is served upon the accused together with an "information" of the charge at the time of his arrest; serious crimes are prosecuted by an indictment or "true bill" after presentment to a grand jury, which determines only whether or not a criminal action should be brought. A person indicted by the grand jury is brought before the court for an "arraignment." He is informed of the charge against him and he enters his plea. If his plea is "not guilty," he must stand trial. He is entitled to a jury trial, but if he chooses, he may have his guilt or innocence determined by the court sitting without a jury, which is called a "bench trial."

At the conclusion of the testimony, the jury is instructed as to the applicable law and retires to arrive at a verdict. In most states the verdict must be unanimous. If the verdict is "not guilty," the matter ends there. The state has no right to appeal from an acquittal, and the accused having been placed in "jeopardy," cannot be tried a second time for the same offense. If the verdict is "guilty" and judgment is entered thereon, the defendant has further recourse. He may make a motion for a new trial, asserting that prejudicial error occurred at the trial, necessitating a retrial of the cause. Or he may assert that the evidence was insufficient upon which to predicate guilt beyond any reasonable doubt and ask for his discharge. He may perfect an appeal to a reviewing court, alleging error by the trial court and asking either his discharge or a remandment of the case for a new trial. There may be other proceedings in a criminal case, including, for example, a request for probation.

Historically, juries consisted of twelve jurors, but in the Federal courts and in the courts of certain states the number has been reduced to six. In Williams v. Florida, 399 U.S. 78, 90 S.Ct. 1893, 26 L.Ed.2d 446 (1970) p. 37, the Supreme Court held that the use of a six-member jury in a criminal case does not violate a defendant's right to a jury trial under the Sixth Amendment. The Supreme Court recognized that there was no discernible difference between the results reached by a jury of twelve or by a jury of six, nor was there any evidence to suggest that a jury of twelve is more advantageous to a defendant.

Cases

Due Process of Law

GOSS v. LOPEZ

(1975) 419 U.S. 565, 95 S.Ct. 729, 42 L.Ed.2d 725.

WHITE, J.

* * *

"Once it is determined that due process applies, the question remains what process is due." [Citation.] We turn to that question, fully realizing as our cases regularly do that the interpretation and application of the Due Process Clause are intensely practical matters and that "[t]he very nature of due process negates any concept of inflexible procedures universally applicable to every imaginable situation." [Citation.]
* * *

* * * At the very minimum, * * * students facing suspension and the consequent interference with a protected property interest must be given *some* kind of notice and afforded *some* kind of hearing. "Parties whose rights are to be affected are entitled to be heard; and in order that they may enjoy that right they must first be notified." [Citation.]

It also appears from our cases that the timing and content of the notice and the nature of the hearing will depend on appropriate accommodation of the competing interests involved. [Citations.] The student's interest is to avoid unfair or mistaken exclusion from the educational process, with all of its unfortunate consequences. The Due Process Clause will not shield him from suspensions properly imposed, but it disserves both his interest and the interest of the State if his suspension is in fact unwarranted. The concern would be mostly academic if the disciplinary process were a totally accurate, unerring process, never mistaken and never unfair. Unfortunately, that is not the case, and no one suggests that it is. Disciplinarians, although proceeding in utmost good faith, frequently act on the reports and advice of others; and the controlling facts and the nature of the conduct under challenge are often disputed. The risk of error is not at all trivial, and it should be guarded against if that may be done without prohibitive cost or interference with the educational process.

* * *

* * * [D]ue process requires, in connection with a suspension of 10 days or less, that the student be given oral or written notice of the charges against him and, if he denies them, an explanation of the evidence the authorities have and an opportunity to present his side of the story. The Clause requires at least these rudimentary precautions against unfair or mistaken findings of misconduct and arbitrary exclusion from school.

There need be no delay between the time "notice" is given and the time of the hearing. In the great majority of cases the disciplinarian may informally discuss the alleged misconduct with the student minutes after it has occurred. We hold only that, in being given an opportunity to explain his version of the facts at this discussion, the student first be told what he is accused of doing and what the basis of the accusation is. * * * [T]here are recurring situations in which prior notice and hearing cannot be insisted upon. Students whose presence poses a continuing danger to persons or property or an ongoing threat of disrupting the academic process may be immediately removed from school. In such cases, the necessary notice and rudimentary hearing should follow as soon as practicable.
* * *

* * *

We stop short of construing the Due Process Clause to require, countrywide, that hearings in connection with short suspensions must afford the student the opportunity to secure counsel, to confront and cross-examine witnesses supporting the charge, or to call his own witnesses to verify his version of the incident. Brief disciplinary suspensions are almost countless. To impose in each such case even truncated trial-type procedures might well overwhelm administrative facilities in many places and, by diverting resources, cost more than it would save in educational effectiveness. Moreover, further formalizing the suspension process and escalating its formality and adversary nature may not only make it too costly as a regular disciplinary tool but also destroy its effectiveness as part of the teaching process.

On the other hand, requiring effective notice and informal hearing permitting the student to give his version of the events will provide a meaningful hedge against erroneous action. At least the disciplinarian will be alerted to the existence of disputes about facts and arguments about cause and effect. He may then determine himself to summon the accuser, permit cross-examination, and allow the student to present his own witnesses. In more difficult cases, he may permit counsel. In any event, his discretion will be more informed and we think the risk of error substantially reduced.

Requiring that there be at least an informal give-and-take between student and disciplinarian, preferably prior to the suspension, will add little to the factfinding function where the disciplinarian himself has witnessed the conduct forming the basis for the charge. But things are not always as they seem to be, and the student will at least have the opportunity to characterize his conduct and put it in what he deems the proper context.

We should also make it clear that we have addressed ourselves solely to the short suspension, not exceeding 10 days. Longer suspensions or expulsions for the remainder of the school term, or permanently, may require more formal procedures. Nor do we put aside the possibility that in unusual situations, although involving only a short suspension, something more than the rudimentary procedures will be required.

* * *

[Held, plaintiff student's denial of evidentiary hearing violated the Due Process Clause of the Fourteenth Amendment.]

Due Process of Law

JACKSON v. METROPOLITAN EDISON CO.
(1974) 419 U.S. 345, 95 S.Ct. 449, 42 L.Ed.2d 477.

REHNQUIST, J.

Respondent Metropolitan Edison Co. is a privately owned and operated Pennsylvania corporation which holds a certificate of public convenience issued by the Pennsylvania Public Utility Commission empowering it to deliver electricity to a service area which includes the city of York Pa. As a condition of holding its certificate, it is subject to extensive regulation by the Commission. Under a provision of its general tariff filed with the Commission, it has the right to discontinue service to any customer on reasonable notice of nonpayment of bills.

Petitioner Catherine Jackson is a resident of York, who has received electricity in the past from respondent. [Her account with respondent was terminated in 1970 because of alleged delinquency in payments, but a new account was opened for her residence in the name of James Dodson, another occupant of the residence. In August 1971 Dodson moved away and no payments were subsequently made to the account. Finally, in October 1971 Catherine Jackson's service was disconnected without any prior notice. She brought suit in federal court, claiming that her electric service couldn't be terminated without notice and hearing.]

* * *

She urged that under state law she had an entitlement to reasonably continuous electrical service to her home and that Metropolitan's termination of her service for alleged nonpayment, action allowed by a provision of its general tariff filed with the Commission, constituted "state action" depriving her of property in violation of the Fourteenth Amendment's guarantee of due process of law.

* * *

* * * In 1883, this Court in the Civil Rights Cases [citation] affirmed the essential dichotomy set forth in [the Fourteenth] Amendment between deprivation by the State, subject to scrutiny under its provisions, and private conduct, "however discriminatory or wrongful," against which

the Fourteenth Amendment offers no shield. [Citation.]

* * * While the principle that private action is immune from the restrictions of the Fourteenth Amendment is well established and easily stated, the question whether particular conduct is "private," on the one hand, or "state action," on the other, frequently admits of no easy answer. [Citations.]

Here the action complained of was taken by a utility company which is privately owned and operated, but which in many particulars of its business is subject to extensive state regulation. The mere fact that a business is subject to state regulation does not by itself convert its action into that of the State for purposes of the Fourteenth Amendment. [Citation.] Nor does the fact that the regulation is extensive and detailed, as in the case of most public utilities do so. [Citation.] It may well be that acts of a heavily regulated utility with at least something of a governmentally protected monopoly will more readily be found to be "state" acts than will the acts of an entity lacking these characteristics. But the inquiry must be whether there is a sufficiently close nexus between the State and the challenged action of the regulated entity so that the action of the latter may be fairly treated as that of the State itself. [Citation.] * * *

* * *

All of petitioner's arguments taken together show no more than that Metropolitan was a heavily regulated privately owned utility enjoying at least a partial monopoly in the providing of electrical service within its territory, and that it elected to terminate service to petitioner in a manner which the Pennsylvania Public Utility Commission found permissible under state law. Under our decision this is not sufficient to connect the State of Pennsylvania with respondent's action so as to make the latter's conduct attributable to the State for purposes of the Fourteenth Amendment.

We conclude that the State of Pennsylvania is not sufficiently connected with respondent's action in terminating petitioner's service so as to make respondent's conduct in so doing attributable to the State for purposes of the Fourteenth Amendment.

* * *

[Judgment for defendant Metropolitan Edison Company upheld.]

*Jurisdiction over Foreign
Corporation by Long Arm Statute*

CLEMENTS v. BARNEY'S SPORTING GOODS STORE

(1980) 84 Ill.App. 600, 40 Ill.Dec. 342, 406 N.E.2d 43.

LORENZ, J.

This appeal raises the frequently litigated question of when has a foreign corporation submitted itself to the jurisdiction of our courts by the transaction of business within this State. [Citation.] Plaintiff, Thomas Clements, brought this action to recover damages for breach of warranty against defendant, Signa Corporation. According to plaintiff's complaint, he purchased a motor boat from Barney's Sporting Goods, an Illinois corporation, in 1974. The boat was manufactured by defendant, and defendant has allegedly breached its warranty of fitness for a particular purpose. Plaintiff further alleges that defendant, an Indiana corporation, is subject to the jurisdiction of Illinois courts under the "transaction of business" section of the Illinois Long-Arm Statute [citation], because of its sale of this boat to Barney's Sporting Goods in Illinois. Although defendant was served with summons, it failed to enter an appearance in this case. A default order was entered against defendant and, subsequently an ex-parte judgment of $6,220 was entered against defendant. Approximately one month later, defendant filed a special and limited appearance and affidavit contesting the jurisdiction of the trial court to enter a default judgment against defendant. A counter-affidavit was filed by the plaintiff.

The affidavit of defendant's authorized agent, M. M. Loman, states that defendant is an Indiana corporation with its principal place of business in Decatur, Indiana. Defendant has no office in Illinois and no agent authorized to do business on its behalf within Illinois. All shipments of merchandise sold by defendant are F.O.B. Decatur, Indiana.

Plaintiff's affidavit states that in 1974 he saw defendant's boats on display at the Chicago Boat Show. In addition, literature on defendant's boats was distributed at the Chicago Boat Show. Several boating magazines, delivered to plaintiff in Illinois, contained advertisements for defendant's boats. Plaintiff has also seen defendant's boats on display at Barney's Sporting Goods Store in Palatine, Illinois, where he eventually purchased the boat. A written warranty issued by defendant was delivered to plaintiff in Illinois.

After a hearing on defendant's motion, the trial court ruled for defendant. Plaintiff moved for a rehearing, and at the rehearing, the trial court reversed its earlier ruling. Defendant's subsequent motion for rehearing was denied by the trial court. Defendant now appeals.

Plaintiff seeks to sustain jurisdiction over defendant under the Illinois Long-Arm Statute. [Citation.] Section 17 provides in perinent part:

(1) Any person, whether or not a citizen or resident of this State, who in person or through an agent does any of the acts hereinafter enumerated, thereby submits such person, and, if an individual, his personal representative, to the jurisdiction of the courts of this State as to any cause of action arising from the doing of any such acts:

(a) The transaction of any business within this State;

* * *

(3) Only causes of action arising from acts enumerated herein may be asserted against a

defendant in an action in which jurisdiction over him is based upon this Section. [Citation.]

The purpose of section 17 is to exert in personam jurisdiction over non-resident defendants to the extent permitted by the due process clause of the fourteenth amendment to the United States Constitution. [Citation.] Due process requires the existence of sufficient "minimum contacts" between the forum state and the non-resident defendant so that the exercise of personal jurisdiction is consistent with traditional notions of fair play and substantial justice. [Citations.] This determination is to be made on the facts of each case and turns on an assessment of the quality and nature of defendant's activities. [Citations.] Thus, we must decide whether defendant has by some voluntary act or conduct purposely availed itself of the privilege of conducting business within Illinois and thereby invoked the benefits and protection of Illinois law. [Citations.]

After examining the affidavits submitted by both parties, we believe the defendant has intentionally and consistently engaged in practices designed to promote sale of its boats in Illinois. By displaying its boats and distributing literature at the Chicago Boat Show, advertising in magazines which have Illinois subscribers, and selling its boats to Illinois retailers, defendant has entered the Illinois marketplace and invoked the benefits and protection of Illinois law. Defendant's conduct constitutes direct solicitation of Illinois customers. Solicitation of business inside the State of Illinois has been found sufficient to sustain personal jurisdiction over a non-resident defendant. [Citations.] Additionally, defendant has indirectly entered the Illinois marketplace through the sale of its boat to the Illinois corporation, Barney's Sporting Goods Store. Although defendant was not a participant in the sale of this boat to the plaintiff, we believe defendant cannot insulate itself from the jurisdiction of our

courts by using an intermediary or by professing ignorance of the ultimate destination of his goods. [Citation.] In *Gray v. American Radiator & Standard Sanitary Corp.* (1961), 22 Ill.2d 432, 176 N.E.2d 761, our supreme court said:

As a general proposition, if a corporation elects to sell its products for ultimate use in another State, it is not unjust to hold it answerable there for any damage caused by defects in those products. Advanced means of distribution and other commercial activity have made possible these modern methods of doing business, and have largely effaced the economic significance of State lines. By the same token, today's facilities for transportation and communication have removed much of the difficulty and inconvenience formerly encountered in defending lawsuits brought in other States.

Unless they are applied in recognition of the changes brought about by technological and economic progress, jurisdictional concepts which may have been reasonable enough in a simpler economy lose their relation to reality, and injustice rather than justice is promoted. Our unchanging principles of justice, whether procedural or substantive in nature, should be scrupulously observed by the courts. But the rules of law which grow and develop within those principles must do so in the light of the facts of economic life as it is lived today. Otherwise the need for adaptation may become so great that basic rights are sacrificed in the name of reform, and the principles themselves become impaired. [Citation.]

Although the *Gray* court was applying the "commission of a tortious act" section of the Long-Arm Statute [citation], we believe its analysis is equally applicable to the "transaction of business" section of that statute. [Citations.] Accordingly, we believe that defendant has transacted business as provided in section 17(1)(a) of the Civil Practice Act.

Section 17(3) of the Long-Arm Statute mandates that plaintiff's cause of action arose from the jurisdictional acts of defendant. A cause of action arises from a defendant's jurisdictional acts where it lies in the wake of defendant's commercial activities by which defendant submitted to the jurisdiction of the Illinois courts. [Citations.] We have previously held that "[w]here the jurisdictional activities consist of the solicitation of sales, a cause of action arising from the consequences of such a sale comes within the statutory definition of section 17(3)." [Citations.] In this case, plaintiff's purchase of the defective boat was, at least in part, a result of defendant's solicitation in Illinois. Therefore, we hold that defendant has submitted itself to the jurisdiction of our courts under section 17(1)(a) of the Illinois Long-Arm Statute. The order of the circuit court denying defendant's motion to reconsider is hereby affirmed.

Affirmed.

Discovery of Evidence:
Summary Judgment

VETTE CO. v. AETNA CAS. & SUR. CO.

(1980, C.A.8) 612 F.2d 1076.

MCMANUS, J.

In this removed action, corporate plaintiffs Vette Company (Vette) and Kansas City Boneless Beef, Inc. (Boneless) appeal from summary judgment below denying Vette recovery for lack of an insurable interest under a fire insurance policy issued to it by defendant, The Aetna Casualty & Surety Company (Aetna), covering the contents of a building in Raymore, Missouri destroyed by fire March 2, 1975. We reverse and remand.

At the outset, we recognize that in reviewing a decision of a district court to grant a summary judgment, we apply the same standard as the trial court. [Citation.] Summary judgment should not be entered unless the pleadings, stipulations, affidavits and admissions in the case show that there exists no genuine issue as to any material fact. [Citations.] It is an extreme and treacherous remedy, not to be entered unless the movant has established its right to a judgment with such clarity as to leave no room for controversy and unless the other party is not entitled to recover under any discernible circumstances. [Citations.]

In passing upon a motion for summary judgment the court is required to view the facts in the light most favorable to the party opposing the motion and to give that party the benefit of all reasonable inferences to be drawn from the underlying facts disclosed in pleadings and affidavits filed in the case. [Citations.]

The entire record, including a lengthy stipulation, discloses the following undisputed facts. The corporate plaintiffs have interlocking ownership. All the common stock of Vette was owned by Dwight "Jack" Rice (Rice) and his wife. Rice was president and chief executive officer of Vette. The common stock of Boneless was owned 50% by Rice and 50% by Harold Lambrecht (Lambrecht). Rice and Lambrecht were president and vice president-manager respectively of Boneless. Vette operated a chili plant at Lee's Summit, Mo., and until the fall of 1973, Boneless operated a meat boning plant in the Missouri Bottoms at Guinotte.

Prior to 1973, Vette purchased a building at 234 N. Madison in Raymore, Mo., and it was decided that Boneless would expand its operation and move into the newly purchased building. In October, 1973, after extensive remodeling, Boneless occupied the Raymore plant. Boneless purchased all the equipment needed to make the building usable as a boning plant.

On August 31, 1974, Aetna issued fire policy # 30 FP 801960 (FP60) with $200,000 coverage on the building and $100,000 on the contents with Boneless the named insured. On December 6, 1974, at Lambrecht's request, Aetna reduced the building coverage to $100,000 retroactive to August 31, 1974. When Rice learned of the reduction, he requested and received policy # 30 FP 26627 (FP27) from Aetna with $200,000 coverage on the building and $100,000 on the contents with Vette the named insured, effective January 21, 1975.

After the fire Lambrecht prepared an inventory of the contents including all equipment and meat in the plant. On April 22 at a meeting attended by Aetna's claim representative, Rice and Lambrecht, it was agreed that Lambrecht's inventory belonged to Boneless and the damage figures for the contents were reasonable. Thereafter, upon receiving $154,779.92, Boneless executed a release to Aetna of all its claims under policy FP60. Additionally, at the meeting, after receiving a total of $176,884.07 from Aetna, Vette agreed that the building coverage of its policy had been fully satisfied. However, Aetna refused to pay Vette on the contents portion of its policy on the ground of no insurable interest. It is with respect to this dispute concerning whether Vette had an insurable interest in the contents of the building that we find the record insufficient to conclude that no genuine issue of material fact exists.

* * *

Vette bases its claimed insurable interest in the contents solely on a cancelled check dated February 1, 1974 from Vette to Boneless for $162,227.03. The 14-page stipulation of facts makes no reference to it. Since there has been no agreement on what the check was written for, we believe this issue is a proper subject of factual inquiry on remand. Whether the check was in fact paid for equipment in and contents of the Raymore plant is a disputed issue that must be resolved by the trier of fact. For, if it can be found that Vette had a direct pecuniary interest in any of the destroyed contents, it had an insurable interest in them.

Moreover, other relevant evidence of record must also be considered in resolving this issue. For example, while the check carried the memorandum "For equipment,

labor and material that was paid by Kansas City Boneless Beef for Raymore plant," Vette's tax returns show that it never took a depreciation deduction nor an investment credit on any equipment in the building through 1975. * * *

Thus, although Aetna, the movant, provided ample evidence to infer that Vette had no direct pecuniary interest, and impliedly no insurable interest, in the contents of the burned building, Vette has also provided sufficient evidence—the check with accompanying memorandum—to put in dispute this material and factual issue. As the party opposing the motion for summary judgment, Vette was entitled to the benefit of all reasonable inferences and to a review of the facts in the light most favorable to it. That we have done, and that the trial court should have done.

Accordingly, we reverse and remand for further proceedings not inconsistent herewith.

Trial by Jury

WILLIAMS v. FLORIDA
(1970) 399 U.S. 79, 90 S.Ct. 1893, 26 L.Ed.2d 446.

MR. JUSTICE WHITE delivered the opinion of the Court.
* * *
In Duncan v. Louisiana, 391 U.S. 145, 88 S.Ct. 1444, 20 L.Ed.2d 491 (1968), we held that the Fourteenth Amendment guarantees a right to trial by jury in all criminal cases which—were they to be tried in a federal court—would come within the Sixth Amendment's guarantee. Petitioner's trial for robbery on July 3, 1968, clearly falls within the scope of that holding. [Citations.] The question in this case then is whether the constitutional guarantee of a trial by "jury" necessarily requires trial by exactly 12 persons, rather than some lesser number—in this case six. We hold that the 12-man panel is not a necessary ingredient

of "trial by jury," and that respondent's refusal to impanel more than the six members provided for by Florida law did not violate petitioner's Sixth Amendment rights as applied to the States through the Fourteenth.

* * *

We do not pretend to be able to divine precisely what the word "jury" imported to the Framers, the First Congress, or the States in 1789. It may well be that the usual expectation was that the jury would consist of 12, and that hence, the most likely conclusion to be drawn is simply that little thought was actually given to the specific question we face today. But there is absolutely no indication in "the intent of the Framers" of an explicit decision to equate the constitutional and common law characteristics of the jury. Nothing in this history suggests, then, that we do violence to the letter of the Constitution by turning to other than purely historical considerations to determine which features of the jury system, as it existed at common law, were preserved in the Constitution. The relevant inquiry, as we see it, must be the function which the particular feature performs and its relation to the purposes of the jury trial. Measured by this standard, the 12-man requirement cannot be regarded as an indispensable component of the Sixth Amendment.

The purpose of the jury trial, as we noted in *Duncan,* is to prevent oppression by the Government. "Providing an accused with the right to be tried by a jury of his peers gave him an inestimable safeguard against the corrupt or overzealous prosecutor and against the compliant, biased, or eccentric judge." Duncan v. Louisiana, *supra,* 391 U.S., at 156, 88 S.Ct., at 1451. Given this purpose, the essential feature of a jury obviously lies in the interposition between the accused and his accuser of the common-sense judgment of a group of laymen, and in the community participation and shared responsibility which results

from that group's determination of guilt or innocence. The performance of this role is not a function of the particular number of the body which makes up the jury. To be sure, the number should probably be large enough to promote group deliberation, free from outside attempts at intimidation, and to provide a fair possibility for obtaining a representative cross section of the community. But we find little reason to think that these goals are in any meaningful sense less likely to be achieved when the jury numbers six, than when it numbers 12—particularly if the requirement of unanimity is retained. And, certainly the reliability of the jury as a fact-finder hardly seems likely to be a function of its size.

* * *

We conclude, in short, as we began: the fact that the jury at common law was composed of precisely 12 is an historical accident, unnecessary to effect the purposes of the jury system and wholly without significance "except to mystics." [Citation.] To read the Sixth Amendment as forever codifying a feature so incidental to the real purpose of the Amendment is to ascribe a blind formalism to the Framers which would require considerably more evidence than we have been able to discover in the history and language of the Constitution or in the reasoning of our past decisions. We do not mean to intimate that legislatures can never have good reasons for concluding that the 12-man jury is preferable to the smaller jury, or that such conclusions—reflected in the provisions of most States and in our federal system—are in any sense unwise. Legislatures may well have their own views about the relative value of the larger and smaller juries, and may conclude that, wholly apart from the jury's primary function, it is desirable to spread the collective responsibility for the determination of guilt among the larger group. In capital cases, for example, it appears that no State provides for less than 12 jurors—a fact which suggests implicit recognition of the value of the larger body as a means of legitimating society's decision to impose the death penalty. Our holding does no more than leave these considerations to Congress and the States, unrestrained by an interpretation of the Sixth Amendment which would forever dictate the precise number which can constitute a jury. Consistent with this holding, we conclude that petitioner's Sixth Amendment rights, as applied to the States through the Fourteenth Amendment, were not violated by Florida's decision to provide a six-man rather than a 12-man jury. The judgment of the Florida District Court of Appeal is

Affirmed.

Chapter
3

RIGHTS AND
RESPONSIBILITIES
OF INDIVIDUALS

It is fitting that every person occasionally reflect upon the individual benefits of freedom, liberty, and protection of person and property afforded citizens of the United States. These rights carry responsibilities which should be gladly accepted in exchange for the benefits. The major premises of democracy are toleration, justice, and participation. Toleration of the rights and beliefs of others is essential to cooperation and to equality of treatment. Justice requires a constant dedication to the ideal of rendering unto every person his due. Equality is even-handed justice. The fundamental purpose of a democratic form of government is achievement of the common good. This can be accomplished only by the intelligent participation of those affected.

SECURING INDIVIDUAL AND SOCIETAL INTERESTS

Types of Interests

Individual interests may be subdivided into (1) interests of personality, those which relate to the physical and spiritual integrity and life of the individual; (2) domestic interests, those which extend beyond the individual personality into family life and include companionship, affection, and conjugal relationship protection, health and welfare of a spouse, and custody, care, affection, protection, and education of children; (3) interests of substance, those involved in the economic life of the individual such as claims to the use and ownership of property, freedom of contract, and liberty to engage in enterprises, callings, trades, and professions and to undertake employment. This interest also includes claims to promised performances of pecuniary value as in contracts, credit transactions, and commercial paper; and non-interference by outsiders with relations with others which are economically advantageous, whether contractual, social, business, official, or domestic. These three classes of interests are not mutually exclusive, and some of them may fall within more than one class.

Public interests are claims, demands, or desires of individuals for group protection and welfare. Social interests are claims, demands, and desires of individuals relating to the maintenance, activity, and functioning of life in a politically organized society.

Role of Government

The adjustment and harmonizing of conflicting and overlapping private, public and social interests requires the force of a politically organized society to determine which of such interests, within fair and feasible limitation, shall be recognized and enforced as legal rights.

Since legal rights and duties depend for their creation and enforcement upon a state or government, the importance and absolute necessity of the continuing existence of the state to the welfare and security of its people is obvious. In exchange for the protection and security which it affords, the state is completely dependent upon its people for their loyal support and assurance of its continuity.

George Washington said, "The very idea of the power and the right of the people to establish a government presupposes the duty of every individual to obey the established government."

The responsibility of individuals is not only to comply with the laws which impose upon them duties to other individuals, but also to accept and perform fully their duties to the state, in order that it may survive as a viable institution. There is no guaranty of any kind that any state will exist in perpetuity. The lessons of history are that nations rise, flourish, decay, and ultimately die. Decay comes always from within, insidiously and sometimes painlessly, without any awareness by the sufferer of its presence until it is too late. National pride, love of country, and patriotism are highly desirable, but added to these deeply felt emotions should be an understanding and appreciation of the purpose of the law, a keenly felt commitment to the country's le-

gal system, a profound gratitude to the forefathers who established it and to their successors who improved and strengthened it, and to the innumerable men and women whose heroic sacrifices in times of war and adversity have preserved it. A strong, enduring, and deep devotion by alert and thinking people is necessary to enable a government of sound principles to resist moral decay and survive against external aggression, while complacency, commitment to individual or group selfish purposes, and failure to maintain moral standards and values, unless corrected in time, is a sure route to its extinction.

It is not difficult for an individual to understand that of necessity the law imposes standards of conduct upon himself and all others. This understanding comes more readily to an aggrieved person, although even individuals charged with wrongdoing generally do not deny that a rule of law is applicable although perhaps not the rule which the opposite party seeks to apply. The rules of law defining rights and duties between individuals are innumerable, and the principal ones relating to business law are discussed in remaining chapters of this book.

The threat to society and the legal system lies not in the area of private lawsuits between individuals, but may come about by failure of individuals to understand and fulfill their duties and responsibilities to maintain the State as a socially effective institution. The basic responsibility of every individual is to respect, uphold, and maintain the State upon which depends the existence of order and security and an operative legal system.

Rights of Individuals

A right is a legally protected interest. An interest is a need, desire, or expectation. Interests are not created by the legal order. The law finds them pressing for recognition and security, and they would exist if there were no legal order. Claims and demands of human beings to obtain and peacefully keep something, or to be permitted to do something, exist whenever a number of them come into contact.

Enforceable rights are legally protected interests which necessarily require a system of law for their formulation and enforcement. Such system can exist only in a politically organized society with the power and authority of a state or government.

Rights and duties legally exist only by reason of some form of responsible government. When a government declares, establishes, and fairly and evenly enforces laws and rules of conduct which are adapted to the common welfare of the people, the legal system thus created and in operation ably fulfills its purpose in safeguarding those interests of individuals which merit protection.

For example, an individual has a legally protected interest against other individuals for repayment of a loan of money, for the return of goods which he owns, for compensatory damages upon the breach of a contractual promise, and upon sustaining personal injury or damages to his property resulting from intentional or negligent wrongdoing.

An individual also has rights which are guaranteed by the Constitution including freedom of speech, press, religion, and peaceable assembly; freedom from self-incrimination, and from deprivation of life, liberty, or property without due process of law; and freedom from the taking of his property for public use without just compensation.

Rights and duties are correlative, which means that the extent of one is measured by the scope of the other. The right of one person to receive a certain performance from another is exactly correlative to the corresponding duty of the other to render the performance.

There are many rights and their correlative duties. There are also responsibilities which may be moral, religious, ethical, family, fraternal, or self-assumed as amenities of civilization. However, only legal rights, those interests which are legally protected and enforced by the courts, are here considered.

Responsibilities of Individuals

The Oxford Universal Dictionary defines "responsibility" as "The state or fact of being responsible; answerable or accountable to another for something." The word is frequently used as synonomous with legal duty, which is a proper usage. However, it has a broader meaning than legal duty, as it applies to obligations which are not legally enforceable. In this discussion it will be used to refer to obligations that are not legal duties, and to situations in which a person to whom responsibility of some sort may be regarded as owing has no legal redress or legal remedy in the event of a failure to fulfill the responsibility.

Does a person have a legal duty (1) to make an earnest effort to bring joy or happiness into the lives of others; (2) to be polite, courteous, and considerate of the feelings of others; (3) to be grateful for unsolicited but useful favors or benefits received from others; (4) to offer sympathy and consolation to persons bereaved by the death of a member of their family; (5) to be helpful in a tactful manner to young neighborhood children in obvious need of simple training in health care; (6) to warn others who are planning a trip or excursion of perils and dangers personally encountered on such a trip, of which they have no knowledge; (7) to attempt the rescue of another close by who is suddenly and unexpectedly discovered to be in imminent danger of drowning; (8) to attend with some regularity religious services conducted by any church or religious denomination; (9) to contribute to charitable causes amounts which he can reasonably afford; or (10) to love his country, and be a genuinely concerned, loyal, and patriotic citizen?

The answer to each of the foregoing questions is "No." If any of them involve an obligation at all, it is a responsibility, not a legal duty.

A person subject to a legal duty which he fails to perform may have a court judgment entered against him. There are no similar sanctions for failure to assume and perform a responsibility, in the sense in which the term is here used. But there are consequences of a different dimension.

Responsibilities are the lubricants of a civilized society. They add a quality to human life which would be sorely missed if people limited their relationships with one another simply to the creation of legal rights and discharge of legal duties. Human beings are fundamentally social and inescapably concerned and affected to a greater or lesser degree by what happens to others.

The nation and its government which makes, administers, and enforces the laws, are controlled and kept in operation by individuals elected by the people and assisted by those in civil service. These individuals have both statutory legal duties and responsibilities, and the citizens who vote and elect the government officials also have responsibilities.

When Pericles was ruler of the City-State of Athens (461–429 B.C.), in an era described as the "Golden Age" of ancient Greek civilization, responsible citizens of Athens took the following oath which expresses a deep feeling of individual responsibility, and concludes with a classic statement of its purposefulness:

THE ATHENIAN OATH

We will never bring disgrace to this, our City, by any act of dishonesty or cowardice, nor ever desert our suffering comrades in the ranks. We will fight for the ideals and sacred things of the City, both alone and with many. We will revere and obey the City's laws and do our best to incite a like respect in those above us who are prone to annul or set them at naught. We will strive unceasingly to quicken the public's sense of civic

duty. Thus, in all these ways we will transmit this City, not only not less, but greater, and more beautiful than it was when transmitted to us.

GOVERNMENTALLY PROTECTED RIGHTS

Natural law has been expounded through the centuries by philosophers and jurists such as Sophocles, the Stoics, Aristotle, Cicero, Justinian, St. Paul, St. Augustine, Thomas Aquinas, Bracton, Coke, Grotius, Locke, Blackstone, Marshall and Story.

Locke described the natural law as a rule "of common reason and equity which is that measure God has set to the actions of men for their mutual security." When men enter into a civil society, "the law of nature stands as an eternal rule to all men, legislators as well as others." In this sense, the natural law serves to help regulate and give direction to legislative enactments.

Natural law is based upon the assumption that all civilized persons of normal conscience throughout the world can agree that the first principle of human behavior is to do good and to avoid evil. It recognizes that man is a being invested with human dignity in whom reside basic rights, such as the right to existence and life, the right to personal freedom, the right to the pursuit of happiness, the right to keep one's body whole, the right to private ownership of material goods, the right to marry according to one's choice and to raise a family which will be assured of the liberties due it, and the right of association. The above enumerated rights of each person are inseparable from correlative duties of every other person.

Down through the ages, man has been considered endowed with natural rights. While science, technology, industry and social institutions change and develop, these fundamental rights remain constant. The precepts of natural law as a basis of individual liberty are embodied in the Magna Carta. Natural law concepts cradled the thinking which led to the American and

French revolutions and are found in the Declaration of Independence, the Bill of Rights, and the Constitutions of the States.

Declaration of Independence

Although dated and published July 4, 1776, and joyously celebrated each year on the anniversary of that date, the Declaration of Independence was adopted by the Second Continental Congress upon the affirmative vote of 12 States on July 2, 1776, with New York abstaining, which vote became unanimous one week later when New York signified its adherence.

The Declaration, an unrivalled document expressing the rights of people to self-government, written by Thomas Jefferson in deeply moving, carefully measured, and provocative language, bears the signature of John Hancock of Massachusetts, president, and 55 other representatives in the Congress.

In addition to stating a long list of unremedied and continuing grievances of the people against King George III, it declares:

When in the Course of human events it becomes necessary for one people to dissolve the political bands which have connected them with another, and to assume among the powers of the earth, the separate and equal station to which the Laws of Nature and of Nature's God entitle them, a decent respect to the opinions of mankind requires that they should declare the causes which impel them to the separation.

We hold these truths to be self-evident, that all men are created equal, that they are endowed by their Creator with certain unalienable Rights, that among these are Life, Liberty and the pursuit of Happiness.

That to secure these rights, Governments are instituted among Men, deriving their just powers from the consent of the governed.

That whenever any Form of Government becomes destructive of these ends, it is the Right of the People to alter or abolish it, and to institute new Government, laying its foundation on such principles and organizing its powers in such

form, as to them shall seem most likely to effect their Safety and Happiness.

Prudence, indeed, will dictate that Governments long established should not be changed for light and transient causes; and accordingly all experience hath shewn that mankind are more disposed to suffer, while evils are sufferable, than to right themselves by abolishing the forms to which they are accustomed. But when a long train of abuses and usurpations, pursuing invariably the same Object, evinces a design to reduce them under absolute Despotism, it is their right, it is their duty, to throw off such Government, and to provide new Guards for their future security.

Such has been the patient sufferance of these Colonies; and such is now the necessity which constrains them to alter their former Systems of Government.

(Lengthy list of abuses omitted)

WE, THEREFORE, the Representatives of the UNITED STATES OF AMERICA, in General Congress, Assembled, appealing to the Supreme Judge of the world for the rectitude of our intentions, do, in the Name, and by Authority of the good People of these Colonies, solemnly publish and declare, That these United Colonies are, and of Right ought to be FREE AND INDEPENDENT STATES; that they are Absolved from all Allegiance to the British Crown, and that all political connection between them and the State of Great Britain, is and ought to be totally dissolved; and that as Free and Independent States, they have full Power to levy War, conclude Peace, contract Alliances, establish Commerce, and to do all other Acts and Things which Independent States may of right do.

And for the support of this Declaration, with a firm reliance on the protection of divine Providence, we mutually pledge to each other our Lives, our Fortunes and our sacred Honor.

(56 signatures.)

Rights of Individuals Guaranteed by Constitutions

Bill of Rights Guaranteed by the United States Constitution. The Constitution of the United States was adopted on September 17, 1787, at Philadelphia by representatives of the thirteen newly created States (formerly colonies of Great Britain). Its purpose is stated in the preamble:

We the People of the United States, In Order to form a more perfect Union, establish Justice, insure domestic Tranquility, provide for the common defense, promote the general Welfare, and secure the Blessings of Liberty to ourselves and our Posterity, do ordain and establish this Constitution for the United States of America.

At the time of its adoption, all of the representatives at the Convention understood and were agreed that it would contain a Bill of Rights which should guarantee protection of individuals from oppression by the newly formed federal government which it created. The men who debated its provisions throughout the summer of 1787 were keenly conscious of the suffering and hardships imposed by King George III and by laws enacted by the English Parliament which they endured prior to 1776, and which brought on the Revolution. They wanted no possible repetition of any part of such tyranny by the new government.

To understand the Bill of Rights which consists of the first ten amendments to the Constitution, adopted December 15, 1791, it should be remembered that its provisions were insisted upon by the States as curbs and restrictions of the power and authority of the United States. Having won their independence after seven long hard years of warfare, the founding fathers were not about to run the risk of losing the liberties and freedom for which the Revolution had been fought and won. The long list of injustices, abuses, oppressions, and grievances contained in the Declaration of Independence served as a constant reminder, and was still fresh in their minds. The First Amendment provides:

Congress shall make no law respecting an establishment of religion, or prohibiting the free exercise thereof; or abridging the freedom of speech, or of the press; or the right of the people peaceably to assemble, and to petition the Government for a redress of grievances.

Second Amendment:

A well regulated Militia, being necessary to the security of a free State, the right of the people to keep and bear arms, shall not be infringed.

Third Amendment:

No Soldier shall, in time of peace be quartered in any house, without the consent of the Owner, nor in time or war, but in a manner to be prescribed by law.

Fourth Amendment:

The right of the people to be secure in their persons, houses, papers, and effects, against unreasonable searches and seizures, shall not be violated, and no Warrants shall issue, but upon probable cause, supported by Oath or affirmation, and particularly describing the place to be searched, and the persons or things to be seized.

Fifth Amendment:

No person shall be held to answer for a capital, or otherwise infamous crime, unless on a presentment or indictment of a Grand Jury, except in cases arising in the land or naval forces, or in the Militia, when in actual service in time of War or public danger; nor shall any person be subject for the same offence to be twice put in jeopardy of life or limb; nor shall be compelled in any criminal case to be a witness against himself, nor be deprived of life, liberty, or property, without due process of law; nor shall private property be taken for public use, without just compensation.

Sixth Amendment:

In all criminal prosecutions, the accused shall enjoy the right to a speedy and public trial, by an impartial jury of the State and district wherein the crime shall have been committed, which district shall have been previously ascertained by law, and to be informed of the nature and cause of the accusation; to be confronted with the witnesses against him; to have compulsory process for obtaining witnesses in his favor, and to have the Assistance of Counsel for his defence.

Seventh Amendment:

In Suits at common law, where the value in controversy shall exceed twenty dollars, the right of trial by jury shall be preserved, and no fact tried by jury, shall be otherwise re-examined in any Court of the United States, than according to the rules of the common law.

Eighth Amendment:

Excessive bail shall not be required, nor excessive fines imposed, nor cruel and unusual punishments inflicted.

Ninth Amendment:

The enumeration in the Constitution, of certain rights, shall not be construed to deny or disparage others retained by the people.

Tenth Amendment:

The powers not delegated to the United States by the Constitution, nor prohibited by it to the States, are reserved to the States respectively, or to the people.

State Constitutions. Each state has its own Constitution as the fundamental law of the State. Many of the provisions contained in the state constitutions are simply a reaffirmation of the provisions in the United States Constitution. On the other hand, state constitutions may include specific guarantees not mentioned in the U.S. Constitution. For example, the Illinois Bill of Rights adopted on December 15, 1970, contains the following provisions:

17. No Discrimination in Employment and the Sale or Rental of Property

All persons shall have the right to be free from discrimination on the basis of race, color, creed, national ancestry, and sex in the hiring and promotion practices of any employer or in the sale or rental of property.

These rights are enforceable without action by the General Assembly, but the General Assembly by law may establish reasonable exemptions relating to these rights and provide additional remedies for their violation.

18. No Discrimination on the Basis of Sex

The equal protection of the laws shall not be denied or abridged on account of sex by the State or its units of local government and school districts.

19. No Discrimination against the Handicapped

All persons with a physical or mental handicap shall be free from discrimination in the sale or rental of property and shall be free from discrimination unrelated to ability in the hiring and promotion practices of any employer.

ILLUSTRATIVE SUPREME COURT DECISIONS

Illustrating the role of the Supreme Court of the United States in defining and upholding the rights of individuals guaranteed by the U.S. Constitution are the following cases:

In MEYER V. NEBRASKA, 262 U.S. 390, 43 S.Ct. 625, 67 L.Ed. 1042 (1923) the Court states:

While this Court has not attempted to define with exactness the liberty * * * guaranteed (by the Fourteenth Amendment), the term has received much consideration and some of the included things have been definitely stated. Without doubt, it denotes not merely freedom from bodily restraint, but also the right of the individual to contract, to engage in any of the common occupations of life, to acquire useful knowledge, to marry, establish a home and bring up children, to worship God according to the dictates of his own conscience, and generally to enjoy those privileges long recognized * * * as essential to the orderly pursuit of happiness by free men.

In POLICE DEPARTMENT V. MOSLEY, 408 U.S. 92, 33 L.Ed.2d 212 (1972), the Court held unconstitutional a Chicago ordinance prohibiting picketing within 150 feet of any primary or secondary school building, except peaceful picketing of any school involved in a labor dispute, on the ground that this was a selective exclusion of peaceful picketing people from a public place, and therefore a denial of equal protection of the laws. The Court states:

Necessarily, then, under the Equal Protection Clause, not to mention the First Amendment itself, government may not grant the use of a forum to people whose views it finds acceptable, but deny use to those wishing to express less favored or more controversial views. And it may not select which issues are worth discussing or debating in public facilities. There is an "equality of status in the field of ideas," and government must afford all points of view an equal opportunity to be heard. Once a forum is opened up to assembly or speaking by some groups, government may not prohibit others from assembling or speaking on the basis of what they intend to say. Selective exclusions from a public forum may not be based on content alone, and may not be justified by reference to content alone.

The Supreme Court has held that refusal by a State to permit women welfare recipients to file suits for divorce except upon payment of the usual filing fees and costs of service of summons, which they were unable to pay, is a denial of due process of law. The Court stated that access to the courts in order to have fundamental rights and duties determined in an ordinary manner under a rule of law is a constitutionally guaranteed right which is not to be denied solely by reason of poverty. The fee requirement was not held unconstitutional, but only its application to indigents whereby they were denied access to the courts. Bod-

die v. Connecticut, 401 U.S. 371, 28 L.Ed.2d 113 (1971).

Two years later, the Supreme Court held that its decision in the *Boddie* case did not apply to indigents seeking to file a voluntary petition in bankruptcy, without payment of a filing fee. U. S. v. Kras, 409 U.S. 434, 34 L.Ed.2d 626 (1973).

The Court distinguished *Boddie* on the ground that marriage involves interests of basic importance to society, and court access is the exclusive means of obtaining a divorce, whereas possible debtor-relief in bankruptcy is not the only means available for adjusting a debtor's legal relationship with his creditors. The Court pointed out that for different periods of time in the 19th century, this country had no bankruptcy law, and that a person has no guaranteed constitutional right to obtain a discharge of his debts in bankruptcy.

A similar result was reached with respect to indigent recipients of old age welfare assistance who were not permitted to appeal from a decision which reduced the amount of their monthly allowance, because of nonpayment of the filing fee on the grounds that, as held in the *Kras* case, the matter of amount of monthly welfare assistance and the right to appeal from an adverse decision are of less constitutional significance than the right to dissolution of marriage which was the issue involved in the *Boddie* case. Ortwein v. Schwab, 410 U.S. 656, 35 L.2d 572 (1973).

In GIDEON V. WAINWRIGHT, 372 U.S. 335, 9 L.Ed. 799 (1963), the defendant charged with the commission of a felony was unable to provide a lawyer for his defense, and the trial court denied his request to appoint one. The Court held that depriving the defendant of the assistance of a lawyer in a felony trial is a denial of due process of law, and reversed the conviction.

In POWELL V. ALABAMA, 287 U.S. 45, 77 L.Ed. 158 (1932), the Supreme Court states:

What, then, does a hearing include? Historically and in practice, in our own country at least, it has always included the right to the aid of counsel when desired and provided by the party asserting the right. The right to be heard would be, in many cases, of little avail if it did not comprehend the right to be heard by counsel. Even the intelligent and educated layman has small and sometimes no skill in the science of law. If charged with crime, he is incapable, generally, of determining for himself whether the indictment is good or bad. He is unfamiliar with the rules of evidence. Left without the aid of counsel he may be put on trial without a proper charge, and convicted upon incompetent evidence, or evidence irrelevant to the issue or otherwise inadmissible. He lacks both the skill and knowledge adequately to prepare his defense, even though he has a perfect one. He requires the guiding hand of counsel at every step in the proceedings against him. Without it, though he be not guilty, he faces the danger of conviction because he does not know how to establish his innocence. If that be true of men of intelligence, how much more true is it of the ignorant and illiterate, or those of feeble intellect. If in any case, civil or criminal, a state or federal court were arbitrarily to refuse to hear a party by counsel, employed by and appearing for him, it reasonably may not be doubted that such a refusal would be a denial of a hearing, and, therefore, of due process in the constitutional sense.

In LOPER V. BETO, 405 U.S. 473, 31 L.Ed. 374 (1972), upon the trial of a criminal case the prosecuting attorney, in an effort to impeach defendant's credibility, offered evidence of four prior felony convictions of defendant over a period of several years, the most recent of which was 25 years prior to the trial. Following his conviction, defendant presented a petition of habeas corpus alleging that these four prior convictions were invalid because all of them were obtained after denial of defendant's request for assistance of counsel, and that he had no lawyer in any of these prior cases. The denial of habeas corpus was reversed by the Supreme Court which held that the use of any record of prior convictions, which were constitutionally invalid, to impeach the credibility of a defendant was a denial of due process.

In JACKSON V. INDIANA, 406 U.S. 715, 32 L.Ed.2d, 435 (1972) a mentally defective deaf-mute, age 27, with the mental level of a pre-school child, who could not read, write or otherwise communicate except through limited sign language, was indicted by the State on two charges of robbery, one of a purse containing four dollars; the other of five dollars. Following an examination by two court appointed psychiatrists, at a competency hearing, the court held that the defendant lacked sufficient comprehension to make a defense to the charges and ordered him committed to the State Department of Mental Health until such time as the Department should certify to the court that the defendant is sane. Although defendant had pleaded insanity as a defense, his guilt or innocence of the crimes charged was not determined, but only his competency to stand trial. The Supreme Court held that under this commitment, defendant would probably never be entitled to a release at any time because of the extreme unlikelihood of improvement in his condition, and that such commitment therefore was a denial of due process of law. The Court reversed the order and remanded the case with directions that the state either institute civil proceedings applicable to indefinite commitment of those not charged with crime, or release the defendant.

An Illinois statute providing that illegitimate children upon the death of their mother become dependent wards of the State, thus depriving the unwed father of their custody without a hearing with respect to his parental fitness for their custody, and without any showing or proof of neglect, was held unconstitutional as a denial of equal protection of the laws and due process of the law. Stanley v. Illinois, 405 U.S. 645, 31 L.Ed.2d 551 (1972). The court states:

The private interest here, that of a man in the children he has sired and raised, undeniably warrants deference and, absent a powerful countervailing interest, protection.

In DUREN V. STATE OF MISSOURI, 99 S.Ct. 664 (1979), the question was the constitutionality of a Missouri statute which granted an exemption from jury service to women who so requested. The plaintiff claimed that the statute violated his constitutional right to a jury constituted from a fair cross section of the community. The Supreme Court held that the statute was unconstitutional in that it violated the "fair cross section" requirement of the Sixth Amendment as made applicable to the State by the Fourteenth Amendment.

In OWEN V. CITY OF INDEPENDENCE, MISSOURI, 100 S.Ct. 1398 (1980), the plaintiff, a former police chief, brought an action under the Civil Rights Act against the defendant city, the city manager, and members of the city council, alleging that he was discharged in violation of his substantive and procedural due process rights. The court of appeals held that although the city had violated plaintiff's rights under the Fourteenth Amendment, all of the defendants, including the city, were entitled to qualified immunity from liability based on the good faith of the city officials involved. The Supreme Court reversed the Court of Appeals on the ground that a municipality has no immunity from liability under the Civil Rights Acts flowing from its constitutional violations and may not assert the good faith of its officers as a defense to such liability.

In WOOLEY V. MAYNARD, 97 S.Ct. 1428 (1977), the plaintiffs brought suit against officials of New Hampshire, to enjoin enforcement against them of a 1969 New Hampshire statute which required noncommercial motor vehicles to bear a license plate embossed with the state motto "Live Free or Die" and made it a misdemeanor to obscure the motto. The plaintiffs placed a covering over the motto on their automobile license plates and were arrested and fined for violating the statute. The U.S. District Court entered an injunction against enforcement of the statute against plaintiffs, and its order was affirmed by the Supreme Court. The Court held that a state could not constitutionally require an individual to participate in dissemination of an ideological message by displaying it on his private property in this manner and for the express purpose that it be observed and read by the public. The plaintiffs could not be required to display the motto.

Cases

Equal Protection of the Law

YICK WO v. HOPKINS

(1886) 118 U.S. 356, 6 S.Ct. 1064, 30 L.Ed. 220.

[The ordinances of the city of San Francisco gave the board of supervisors authority, at their discretion, to refuse permission to carry on laundries, except where located in buildings of brick or stone. The appellants applied for and were refused permission, and thereafter they were convicted of a violation of the above ordinances, and sentenced to imprisonment.]

MATTHEWS, J.

In the case of the petitioner, brought here by writ of error to the supreme court of California, our jurisdiction is limited to the question whether the plaintiff in error has been denied a right in violation of the constitution, laws, or treaties of the United States. * * *

We are * * * constrained, at the outset, to differ from the supreme court of

California upon the real meaning of the ordinances in question. That court considered these ordinances as vesting in the board of supervisors a not unusual discretion in granting or withholding their assent to the use of wooden buildings as laundries, to be exercised in reference to the circumstances of each case, with a view to the protection of the public against the dangers of fire. We are not able to concur in that interpretation of the power conferred upon the supervisors. There is nothing in the ordinances which points to such a regulation of the business of keeping and conducting laundries. They seem intended to confer, and actually do confer, not a discretion to be exercised upon a consideration of the circumstances of each case, but a naked and arbitrary power to give or withhold consent, not only as to places, but as to persons; so that, if an applicant for such consent, being in every way a competent and qualified person, and having complied with every reasonable condition demanded by any public interest, should, failing to obtain the requisite consent of the supervisors to the prosecution of his business, apply for redress by the judicial process of *mandamus* to require the supervisors to consider and act upon his case, it would be a sufficient answer for them to say that the law had conferred upon them authority to withhold their assent, without reason and without responsibility. The power given to them is not confided to their discretion in the legal sense of that term, but is granted to their mere will. It is purely arbitrary, and acknowledges neither guidance nor restraint. * * *

The rights of the petitioners, as affected by the proceedings of which they complain, are not less because they are aliens and subjects of the emperor of China. * * * The fourteenth amendment to the constitution is not confined to the protection of citizens. It says: "Nor shall any state deprive any person of life, liberty, or property without due process of law; nor deny to any person within its jurisdiction the equal protection of the laws." These provisions are universal in their application, to all persons within the territorial jurisdiction, without regard to any differences of race, of color, or of nationality; and the equal protection of the laws is a pledge of the protection of equal laws. * * *

It is contended on the part of the petitioners that the ordinances for violations of which they are severally sentenced to imprisonment are void on their face, as being within the prohibitions of the fourteenth amendment, and, in the alternative, if not so, that they are void by reason of their administration, operating unequally, so as to punish in the present petitioners what is permitted to others as lawful, without any distinction of circumstances,—an unjust and illegal discrimination, it is claimed, which, though not made expressly by the ordinances, is made possible by them.

When we consider the nature and the theory of our institutions of government, the principles upon which they are supposed to rest, and review the history of their development, we are constrained to conclude that they do not mean to leave room for the play and action of purely personal and arbitrary power. Sovereignty itself is, of course, not subject to law, for it is the author and source of law; but in our system, while sovereign powers are delegated to the agencies of government, sovereignty itself remains with the people, by whom and for whom all government exists and acts. And the law is the definition and limitation of power. It is, indeed, quite true that there must always be lodged somewhere, and in some person or body, the authority of final decision; and in many cases of mere administration, the responsibility is purely political, no appeal lying except to the ultimate tribunal of the public judgment, exercised either in the pressure of opinion, or by means of the suffrage. But the fundamental rights to life, liberty, and the pursuit of happiness, considered as individual possessions, are secured by those maxims of constitutional law which are the monuments showing the victorious progress of the race in securing to men the blessings of civilization under the reign of just and equal laws, so that, in the famous language of the Massachusetts bill of rights, the government of the commonwealth "may be a government of laws and not of men." For the very idea that one man may be compelled to hold his life, or the means of living, or any material right essential to the enjoyment of life, at the mere will of another, seems to be intolerable in any country where freedom prevails, as being the essence of slavery itself. * * *

In the present cases, we are not obliged to reason from the probable to the actual, and pass upon the validity of the ordinances complained of, as tried merely by the opportunities which their terms afford, of unequal and unjust discrimination in their administration; for the cases present the ordinances in actual operation, and the facts shown establish an administration directed so exclusively against a particular class of persons as to warrant and require the conclusion that, whatever may have been the intent of the ordinances as adopted, they are applied by the public authorities charged with their administration, and thus representing the state itself, with a mind so unequal and oppressive as to amount to a practical denial by the state of that equal protection of the laws which is secured to the petitioners, as to all other persons, by the broad and benign provisions of the fourteenth amendment to the constitution of the United States. Though the law itself be fair on its face, and impartial in appliance, yet, if it is applied and administered by public authority with an evil eye and an unequal hand, so as practically to make unjust and illegal discriminations between persons in similar circumstances, material to their rights, the denial of equal justice is still within the prohibition of the constitution. * * *

The present cases, as shown by the facts disclosed in the record, are within this class. It appears that both petitioners have complied with every requisite deemed by the law, or by the public officers charged with its administration, necessary for the protection of neighboring property from fire, or as a precaution against injury to the public health. No reason whatever, except the will of the supervisors, is assigned why they should not be permitted to carry on, in the accustomed manner, their harmless and useful occupation, on which they depend for a livelihood; and while this consent of the supervisors is withheld from them, and from 200 others who have also petitioned, all of whom happen to be Chinese subjects, 80 others, not Chinese subjects, are permitted to carry on the same business under similar conditions. The fact of this discrimination is admitted. No reason for it is shown, and the conclusion cannot be resisted that no reason for it exists except hostility to the race and nationality to which the petitioners belong, and which in the eye of the law, is not justified. The discrimination is therefore illegal, and the public administration which enforces it is a denial of the equal protection of the laws, and a violation of the fourteenth amendment of the constitution. The imprisonment of the petitioners is therefore illegal, and they must be discharged. To this end the judgment of the supreme court of California in the Case of Yick Wo, and that of the circuit court of the United States for the district of California in the Case of Wo Lee, are severally reversed, and the cases remanded, each to the proper court, with directions to discharge the petitioners from custody and imprisonment.

Claim of Executive Privilege

UNITED STATES v. NIXON

(1974) 418 U.S. 683, 94 S.Ct. 3090, 41 L.Ed. 1039.

[In March, 1974 a grand jury indicted seven individuals charging them with various offenses, including conspiracy to defraud the United States and obstruction of justice.

On motion of the Special Prosecutor, a subpoena duces tecum was issued to Richard M. Nixon, President of the United States, requiring the production of certain tapes, memoranda, papers, transcripts and other writings. The President filed his appearance and a motion to quash the subpoena on the ground of Executive privilege, which was denied by the District Court. The President appealed to the Court of Appeals, and upon the Supreme Court granting certiorari before judgment, review by the Court of Appeals was bypassed.

The Supreme Court held first, that the dispute between the Special Prosecutor and the President was a justiciable controversy although wholly within the executive branch of the government, and secondly, that the order for production of evidence would be treated as final and appealable, although ordinarily such an order is not appealable until after a refusal to comply therewith has been followed by an order of contempt. The Court stated as reasons for dispensing with this requirement for review that (1) it would be unseemly as placing a federal judge in the position of issuing a contempt citation against the President and thus creating a constitutional confrontation between two branches of the government simply in order to make review possible; and (2) it would further delay both a review on the merits of the claim of privilege and the ultimate termination of the underlying criminal proceedings. Lastly, the Court denied the claim of executive privilege which was the heart of the controversy, and affirmed the order of the District Court.]

BURGER, C. J.
* * *

Having determined that the requirements of Rule 17(c) were satisfied, we turn to the claim that the subpoena should be quashed because it demands "confidential conversations between a President and his close advisors that it would be inconsistent with the public interest to produce." The first contention is a broad claim that the separation of powers doctrine precludes judicial review of a President's claim of privilege. The second contention is that if he does not prevail on the claim of absolute privilege, the court should hold as a matter of constitutional law that the privilege prevails over the subpoena *duces tecum*.

In the performance of assigned constitutional duties each branch of the Government must initially interpret the Constitution, and the interpretation of its powers by any branch is due great respect from the others. The President's counsel, as we have noted, reads the Constitution as providing an absolute privilege of confidentiality for all presidential communications. Many decisions of this Court, however, have unequivocally reaffirmed the holding of Marbury v. Madison, 1 Cranch. 137, 2 L.Ed. 60 (1803), that "it is emphatically the province and duty of the judicial department to say what the law is."

No holding of the Court has defined the scope of judicial power specifically relating to the enforcement of a subpoena for confidential presidential communications for use in a criminal prosecution, but other exercises of powers by the Executive Branch and the Legislative Branch have been found invalid as in conflict with the Constitution. [Citations.] Since this Court has consistently exercised the power to construe and delineate claims arising under express powers, it must follow that the Court has authority to interpret claims with respect to powers alleged to derive from enumerated powers.

Our system of government "requires that federal courts on occasion interpret the Constitution in a manner at variance with the construction given the document by another branch." [Citations.] Notwithstanding the deference each branch must accord the others, the "judicial power of the United States" vested in the federal courts by Art. III, § 1 of the Constitution can no more be shared with the Executive Branch than the Chief Executive, for example, can share with the Judiciary the veto power, or the Congress share with the Judiciary the power to override a presidential veto. Any other conclusion would be contrary to the basic concept of separation of powers and the checks and balances that flow from the scheme of a tripartite government.

* * *

In support of his claim of absolute privilege, the President's counsel urges two grounds one of which is common to all governments and one of which is peculiar to our system of separation of powers. The first ground is the valid need for protection of communications between high government officials and those who advise and assist them in the performance of their manifold duties; the importance of this confidentiality is too plain to require further discussion. Human experience teaches that those who expect public dissemination of their remarks may well temper candor with a concern for appearances and for their own interests to the detriment of the decisionmaking process. Whatever the nature of the privilege of confidentiality of presidential communications in the exercise of Art. II powers the privilege can be said to derive from the supremacy of each branch within its own assigned area of constitutional duties. Certain powers and privileges flow from the nature of enumerated powers; the protection of the confidentiality of presidential communications has similar constitutional underpinnings.

* * *

However, neither the doctrine of separation of powers, nor the need for confidentiality of high level communications, without more, can sustain an absolute, unqualified presidential privilege of immunity from judicial process under all circumstances. The President's need for complete candor and objectivity from advisers calls for great deference from the courts. However, when the privilege depends solely on the broad, undifferentiated claim of public interest in the confidentiality of such conversations, a confrontation with other values arises. Absent a claim of need to protect military, diplomatic or sensitive national security secrets, we find it difficult to accept the argument that even the very important interest in confidentiality of presidential communications is significantly diminished by production of such material for *in camera* inspection with all the protection that a district court will be obliged to provide.

The impediment that an absolute, unqualified privilege would place in the way of the primary constitutional duty of the Judicial Branch to do justice in criminal prosecutions would plainly conflict with the function of the courts under Art. III. In designing the structure of our Government and dividing and allocating the sovereign power among three coequal branches, the Framers of the Constitution sought to provide a comprehensive system, but the separate powers were not intended to operate with absolute independence.

* * *

To read the Art. II powers of the President as providing an absolute privilege as against a subpoena essential to enforcement of criminal statutes on no more than a generalized claim of the public interest in confidentiality of nonmilitary and nondiplomatic discussions would upset the constitutional balance of "a workable government" and gravely impair the role of the courts under Art. III.

Since we conclude that the legitimate needs of the judicial process may outweigh presidential privilege, it is necessary to resolve those competing interests in a manner that preserves the essential functions of each branch. The right and indeed the duty to resolve that question does not free the judiciary from according high respect to the representations made on behalf of the President. [Citations.]

The expectation of a President to the confidentiality of his conversations and correspondence, like the claim of confidentiality of judicial deliberations, for example, has all the values to which we accord deference for the privacy of all citizens and added to those values the necessity for protection of the public interest in candid, objective, and even blunt or harsh opinions in presidential decisionmaking. A President and those who assist him must be free to explore alternatives in the process of shaping policies and making decisions and to do so in a way many would be unwilling to express except privately. These are the considerations justifying a presumptive privilege for presidential communications. The privilege is fundamental to the operation of government and inextricably rooted in the separation of powers under the Constitution. * * *

In this case the President challenges a subpoena served on him as a third party requiring the production of materials for use in a criminal prosecution on the claim that he has a privilege against disclosure of confidential communications. He does not place his claim of privilege on the ground they are military or diplomatic secrets. As to these areas of Art. II duties the courts have traditionally shown the utmost deference to presidential responsibilities.

* * *

No case of the Court, however, has extended this high degree of deference to a President's generalized interest in confidentiality. Nowhere in the Constitution, as we have noted earlier, is there any explicit reference to a privilege of confidentiality, yet to the extent this interest relates to the effective discharge of a President's powers, it is constitutionally based.

The right to the production of all evidence at a criminal trial similarly has constitutional dimensions. The Sixth Amendment explicitly confers upon every defendant in a criminal trial the right "to be confronted with the witnesses against him" and "to have compulsory process for obtaining witnesses in his favor. Moreover, the Fifth Amendment also guarantees that no person shall be deprived of liberty without due process of law. It is the manifest duty of the courts to vindicate those guarantees and to accomplish that it is essential that all relevant and admissible evidence be produced.

In this case we must weigh the importance of the general privilege of confidentiality of presidential communications in performance of his responsibilities against the inroads of such a privilege on the fair administration of criminal justice. The interest in preserving confidentiality is weighty indeed and entitled to great respect.
* * *

On the other hand, the allowance of the privilege to withhold evidence that is demonstrably relevant in a criminal trial would cut deeply into the guarantee of due process of law and gravely impair the basic function of the courts. A President's acknowledged need for confidentiality in the communications of his office is general in nature, whereas the constitutional need for production of relevant evidence in a criminal proceeding is specific and central to the fair adjudication of a particular criminal case in the administration of justice. Without access to specific facts a criminal prosecution may be totally frustrated. The President's broad interest in confidentiality of communications will not be vitiated by disclosure of a limited number of conversations preliminarily shown to have some bearing on the pending criminal cases.

We conclude that when the ground for asserting privilege as to subpoenaed materials sought for use in a criminal trial is based only on the generalized interest in confidentiality, it cannot prevail over the fundamental demands of due process of law in the fair administration of criminal justice. The generalized assertion of privilege must yield to the demonstrated, specific need for evidence in a pending criminal trial.

* * *

If a President concludes that compliance with a subpoena would be injurious to the public interest he may properly, as was done here, invoke a claim of privilege on the return of the subpoena. Upon receiving a claim of privilege from the Chief Executive, it became the further duty of the District Court to treat the subpoenaed material as presumptively privileged and to require the Special Prosecutor to demonstrate that the presidential material was "essential to the justice of the [pending criminal] case." [Citation.] Here the District Court treated the material as presumptively privileged, proceeded to find that the Special Prosecutor had made a sufficient showing to rebut the presumption and ordered an *in camera* examination of the subpoenaed material. On the basis of our examination of the record we are unable to conclude that the District Court erred in ordering the inspection. Accordingly we affirm the order of the District Court that subpoenaed materials be transmitted to that court. * * *

Statements that meet the test of admissibility and relevance must be isolated; all other material must be excised. * * * It is elementary that *in camera* inspection of evidence is always a procedure calling for scrupulous protection against any release or publication of material not found by the court, at that stage, probably admissible in evidence and relevant to the issues of the trial for which it is sought. That being true of an ordinary situation, it is obvious that the District Court has a very heavy responsibility to see to it that presidential conversations, which are either not relevant or not admissible, are accorded that high degree of respect due the President of the United States. * * * Moreover, a President's communications and activities encompass a vastly wider range of sensitive material than would be true of any

"ordinary individual." It is therefore necessary in the public interest to afford presidential confidentiality the greatest protection consistent with the fair administration of justice. The need for confidentiality even as to idle conversations with associates in which casual reference might be made concerning political leaders within the country or foreign statesmen is too obvious to call for further treatment. * * * This burden applies with even greater force to excised material; once the decision is made to excise, the material is restored to its privileged status and should be returned under seal to its lawful custodian.

* * *

Affirmed.

School Desegregation

BROWN v. BOARD OF EDUC. OF TOPEKA

(1954) 347 U.S. 686, 74 S.Ct. 686, 98 L.Ed.2d 873.

WARREN, C. J.

These cases come to us from the States of Kansas, South Carolina, Virginia, and Delaware. They are premised on different facts and different local conditions, but a common legal question justifies their consideration together in this consolidated opinion.

In each of the cases, minors of the Negro race, through their legal representatives, seek the aid of the courts in obtaining admission to the public schools of their community on a nonsegregated basis. In each instance, they have been denied admission to schools attended by white children under laws requiring or permitting segregation according to race. This segregation was alleged to deprive the plaintiffs of the equal protection of the laws under the Fourteenth Amendment. In each of the cases other than the Delaware case, a three-judge federal district court denied relief to the plaintiffs on the so-called "separate but equal" doctrine announced by this Court in Plessy v. Ferguson, 163 U.S. 537, 16 S.Ct. 1138, 41 L.Ed. 256. Under that doctrine, equality of treatment is accorded when the races are provided substantially equal facilities, even though these facilities be separate. In the Delaware case, the Supreme Court of Delaware adhered to that doctrine, but ordered that the plaintiffs be admitted to the white schools because of their superiority to the Negro schools.

The plaintiffs contend that segregated public schools are not "equal" and cannot be made "equal" and that hence they are deprived of the equal protection of the laws. Because of the obvious importance of the question presented, the Court took jurisdiction. * * *

Reargument was largely devoted to the circumstances surrounding the adoption of the Fourteenth Amendment in 1868. It covered exhaustively consideration of the Amendment in Congress, ratification by the states, then existing practices in racial segregation, and the views of proponents and opponents of the Amendment. This discussion and our own investigation convince us that, although these sources cast some light, it is not enough to resolve the problem with which we are faced. At best, they are inconclusive. The most avid proponents of the post-War Amendments undoubtedly intended them to remove all legal distinctions among "all persons born or naturalized in the United States." Their opponents, just as certainly, were antagonistic to both the letter and the spirit of the Amendments and wished them to have the most limited effect. What others in Congress and the state legislatures had in mind cannot be determined with any degree of certainty.

An additional reason for the inconclusive nature of the Amendment's history, with respect to segregated schools, is the status of public education at that time. In the South, the movement toward free common schools, supported by general taxation, had not yet taken hold. Education of white children was largely in the hands of private groups. Education of Negroes was almost nonexistent, and practically all of the race were illiterate. In fact, any education of Negroes was forbidden by law in some states. Today, in contrast, many Negroes have achieved outstanding success in the arts and sciences as well as in the business and professional world. It is true that public school education at the time of the Amendment had advanced further in the North, but the effect of the Amendment on Northern States was generally ignored in the congressional debates. Even in the North, the conditions of public education did not approximate those existing today. The curriculum was usually rudimentary; ungraded schools were common in rural areas; the school term was but three months a year in many states; and compulsory school attendance was virtually unknown. As a consequence, it is not surprising that there should be so little in the history of the Fourteenth Amendment relating to its intended effect on public education.

In the first cases in this Court construing the Fourteenth Amendment, decided shortly after its adoption, the Court interpreted it as proscribing all state-imposed discriminations against the Negro race. The doctrine of "separate but equal" did not make its appearance in this Court until 1896 in the case of Plessy v. Ferguson, supra, involving not education but transportation. American courts have since labored with the doctrine for over half a century. In this Court, there have been six cases involving the "separate but equal" doctrine in the field of public education. In Cumming v. Board of Education of Richmond County, 175 U.S. 528, 20 S.Ct. 197, 44 L.Ed. 262, and Gong Lum v. Rice, 275 U.S. 78, 48 S.Ct. 91, 72 L.Ed. 172, the validity of the doctrine itself was not challenged. In more recent cases, all on the graduate school level, inequality was found in that specific benefits enjoyed by white students were denied to Negro students of the same educational qualifications. [Citations.] In none of these cases was it necessary to re-examine the doctrine to grant relief to the Negro plaintiff. And in Sweatt v. Painter, 339 U.S. 629, 70 S.Ct. 848, 94 L.Ed. 1114, the Court expressly reserved decision on the question whether Plessy v. Ferguson should be held inapplicable to public education.

In the instant cases, that question is directly presented. Here, unlike Sweatt v. Painter, there are findings below that the Negro and white schools involved have been equalized, or are being equalized, with respect to buildings, curricula, qualifications and salaries of teachers, and other "tangible" factors. Our decision, therefore, cannot turn on merely a comparison of these tangible factors in the Negro and white schools involved in each of the cases. We must look instead to the effect of segregation itself on public education.

In approaching this problem, we cannot turn the clock back to 1868 when the Amendment was adopted, or even to 1896 when Plessy v. Ferguson was written. We must consider public education in the light of its full development and its present place in American life throughout the Nation. Only in this way can it be determined if segregation in public schools deprives these plaintiffs of the equal protection of the laws.

Today, education is perhaps the most important function of state and local governments. Compulsory school attendance laws and the great expenditures for education both demonstrate our recognition of the importance of education to our democratic society. It is required in the performance of our most basic public responsibilities, even service in the armed forces. It is the very foundation of good citizenship. Today it is a principal instrument in awakening the child to cultural values, in preparing him for later professional training, and in helping him to adjust normally to his environment. In these days, it is doubtful that any child may reasonably be expected to succeed in life if he is denied the opportunity of an education. Such an opportunity, where the state has undertaken to provide it, is a right which must be made available to all on equal terms.

We come then to the question presented: Does segregation of children in public schools solely on the basis of race, even though the physical facilities and other "tangible" factors may be equal, deprive the children of the minority group of equal educational opportunities? We believe that it does.

In Sweatt v. Painter, [339 U.S. 629, 70 S.Ct. 850], in finding that a segregated law school for Negroes could not provide them equal educational opportunities, this Court relied in large part on "those qualities which are incapable of objective measurement but which make for greatness in a law school." In McLaurin v. Oklahoma State Regents, supra [339 U.S. 637, 70 S.Ct. 853], the Court, in requiring that a Negro admitted to a white graduate school be treated like all other students, again resorted to intangible considerations: " * * * his ability to study, to engage in discussions and exchange views with other students, and, in general, to learn his profession." Such considerations apply with added force to children in grade and high schools. To separate them from others of similar age and qualifications solely because of their race generates a feeling of inferiority as to their status in the community that may affect their hearts and minds in a way unlikely ever to be undone. The effect of this separation on their educational opportunities was well stated by a finding in the Kansas case by a court which nevertheless felt compelled to rule against the Negro plaintiffs:

"Segregation of white and colored children in public schools has a detrimental effect upon the colored children. The impact is greater when it has the sanction of the law; for the policy of separating the races is usually interpreted as denoting the inferiority of the Negro group. A sense of inferiority affects the motivation of a child to learn. Segregation with the sanction of law, therefore, has a tendency to [retard] the educational and mental development of Negro children and to deprive them of some of the benefits they would receive in a racial[ly] integrated school system."

Whatever may have been the extent of psychological knowledge at the time of Plessy v. Ferguson, this finding is amply supported by modern authority. Any language in Plessy v. Ferguson contrary to this finding is rejected.

We conclude that in the field of public education the doctrine of "separate but equal" has no place. Separate educational facilities are inherently unequal. Therefore, we hold that the plaintiffs and others similarly situated for whom the actions have been brought are, by reason of the segregation comlained of, deprived of the equal protection of the laws guaranteed by the Fourteenth Amendment. This disposition makes unnecessary any discussion whether such segregation also violates the Due Process Clause of the Fourteenth Amendment.

Because these are class actions, because of the wide applicability of this decision, and because of the great variety of local conditions, the formulation of decrees in these cases presents problems of considerable complexity. On reargument, the consideration of appropriate relief was necessarily subordinated to the primary question—the constitutionality of segregation in public education. We have now announced that such segregation is a denial of the equal protection of the laws. In order that we may have the full assistance of the parties in formulating decrees the cases will be restored to the docket, and the parties are requested to present further argument on * * * entry of appropriate decrees.

PART

TWO

Torts

4

TORTS: INTENTIONAL INFLICTION OF INJURY

The word "tort" is derived from the Latin "tortus" meaning twisted or crooked and from the French word for injury or wrong. At the time the common law was developing, "tort" was in common English usage as a synonym for a wrong. A tort may be defined as an invasion of a legally protected interest in freedom from personal injury and property loss or damage. A tort is committed when (1) a duty owing by one person to another, (2) is breached or violated, and (3) results in injury or damage to the owner of the right.

In a tort action the injured party sues to recover compensation for the damage and injury that he has sustained as a result of the defendant's wrongful conduct. The purpose of tort law is to compensate the aggrieved party, not to punish the wrongdoer as in the case of criminal law.

Harms or injuries may be inflicted (1) intentionally or (2) negligently or (3) without fault. This chapter will discuss intentional torts. The following chapter will cover negligence and strict liability.

TYPES OF INTENTIONAL TORTS

Intent, as used in tort law, does not require a hostile or evil intent but rather is concerned with the intent to cause certain immediate consequences which invade the rights of another in a way that the law does not permit. The Restatement of Torts, Second, Section 8A, states that "the word 'intent' is used * * * to denote that the actor desires to cause consequences of his act, or that he believes that the consequences are substantially certain to result from it."

The Restatement provides the following examples to clarify the definition of intent: (1) If A fires a gun in the middle of the Mojave Desert, he intends to fire the gun, but when the bullet hits B who is in the desert without A's knowledge, A does not intend that result. (2) A throws a bomb into B's office in order to kill B. A knows that C is in B's office and that the bomb is substantially certain to injure C, although

A has no desire to do so. A is nonetheless liable to C for any injury caused C. A's intent to injure B is "transferred" to C.

Infants (i.e., persons who have not reached the age of majority) are held liable for their intentional torts. Lord Kenyon once said, "If an infant commit an assault, or utter slander, God forbid that he should not be answerable for it in a court of justice." Jennings v. Randall, 1799, 8 Term.Rep. 335, 337, 101 Eng.Rep. 1419. The infant's age and knowledge, however, are critical in determining whether the infant had sufficient intelligence to form the requisite intent. Incompetents, like infants, are generally held liable for their intentional torts.

INTENTIONAL INFLICTION OF INJURY OR DAMAGE TO THE PERSON

The most common intentional torts involve an interference with personal rights and include the following: (1) Battery, (2) Assault, (3) False Imprisonment, (4) Malicious Prosecution, (5) Outrageous Conduct, (6) Defamation, and (7) Invasion of Privacy. These torts will be separately discussed in that order.

Battery

Battery is an intentional infliction of offensive bodily touching. It may cause serious injury, as a gunshot wound, or a blow on the head with a club, or it may cause little or no physical injury, such as knocking a hat off of a man's head, or flicking a glove in his face. Bodily contact is offensive if it is harmful or would offend a reasonable person's sense of dignity. Restatement, Torts, 2nd, Section 19. Touching or contact may be accomplished by the use of objects, such as A's throwing a rock at B with the intention of hitting him. If the rock hits B, A has committed a battery. Another example is A's using his dog to attack and bite B; if the dog bites B, it is a battery.

Assault

Assault is intentional action or conduct by one person directed at another which places him in apprehension of immediate bodily harm or offensive contact. It is usually committed immediately preceding a battery, but if the intended battery fails, the assault remains. An essential element of this tort is that the person in danger of immediate bodily harm have knowledge of the danger and be apprehensive of its imminent threat to his safety. For example, A aims a loaded gun at B's back but is subdued by C before B becomes aware of the danger. A has not committed an assault upon B.

False Imprisonment

The tort of false imprisonment is the intentional confining of a person within fixed boundaries if such person is conscious of the confinement or harmed by it. Merely obstructing a person's freedom of movement is not false imprisonment so long as there is a reasonable alternative exit available.

Merchants occasionally have a problem when they seek to question a suspected shoplifter. If the merchant detains an innocent person, he may be facing a lawsuit for false imprisonment. Most states have statutes which protect the merchant, provided he detains the suspect in a reasonable manner, for not more than a reasonable time, and upon probable cause.

Malicious Prosecution

The tort of malicious prosecution or wrongful use of civil proceedings consists in bringing about a criminal proceeding or filing and maintaining a civil suit against another person if the proceeding or civil suit is initiated (1) without probable cause, (2) for an improper purpose, and (3) results in the case of a criminal proceeding in a finding of not guilty, and in the case of a civil suit in a judgment for the defendant. Restatement,

Torts, Second, Sections 653, 674. A public prosecutor acting in his official capacity in bringing about and maintaining a criminal proceeding is cloaked with absolute immunity from liability for malicious prosecution. Restatement, Torts, Second, Section 656.

Outrageous Conduct

The law is not static, and the most recent type of wrongdoing recognized as tortious and imposing liability upon the wrongdoer for money damages is that of outrageous conduct. William L. Prosser, principal author of the Restatement of Torts, states in his book, *Law of Torts,* pp. 49–50:

Notwithstanding its early recognition in the assault cases, the law has been slow to accept the interest in peace of mind as entitled to independent legal protection, even as against intentional invasions. It is not until comparatively recent years that there has been any general admission that the infliction of mental distress, standing alone, may serve as the basis of an action, apart from any other tort. In this respect, the law is clearly in a process of growth, the ultimate limits of which cannot as yet be determined.

Various reasons have been advanced for this reluctance to redress mental injuries. One is the difficulty of proof, or of measurement of the damages. "Mental pain or anxiety," said Lord Wensleydale in a famous English case, "the law cannot value, and does not pretend to redress, when the unlawful act causes that alone." It was regarded as something "metaphysical," "too subtle and speculative to be capable of admeasurement by any standard known to the law." But mental suffering is scarcely more difficult of proof, and certainly no harder to estimate in terms of money, than the physical pain of a broken leg, which never has been denied compensation; and the courts have been quite willing to allow large sums as damages for such "mental anguish" itself, where it accompanies a slight physical injury.

The Restatement of Torts, Second, Section 46 states the rule as follows:

One who by extreme and outrageous conduct intentionally or recklessly causes severe emotional distress to another is subject to liability for such emotional distress, and if bodily harm to the other results from it, for such bodily harm.

This cause of action does not protect a person from abusive language or rudeness, but from atrocious, intolerable conduct beyond all bounds of decency. Examples of this tort include leading to plaintiff's home, when he is present, a noisy demonstrating mob yelling threats to lynch him unless he leaves town, and placing a rattlesnake in another's bed as a practical joke.

A defendant is liable to a plaintiff for infliction of emotional distress where the defendant's outrageous conduct is directed at a member of the plaintiff's immediate family, provided the plaintiff is present at the time and is known by the defendant to be present. For example, C notices A and his pregnant wife, B, walking down the street and intentionally drives his car into A. As a consequence of viewing this, B suffers severe mental distress resulting in a miscarriage. C is liable to B for intentional infliction of mental distress. If B, however, was not walking with A but instead observed, without C's knowledge, the accident through a window in her home, C would not be liable to B for the tort of emotional distress.

Defamation

Libel and Slander. The tort of defamation is a communication which injures a person's good name by holding him up to hatred, contempt, or ridicule. If the defamatory communication is handwritten, typewritten, printed, pictorical, or by other means with like communicative power, such as television or radio, it is designated libel. If it is spoken or oral, it is designated slander. In either case it must be communicated to another person or persons. This is referred to as its publication. If A writes a defamatory letter about B's character which he hands or mails to B, this is not a publication as it is intended only for B. If B shows the letter to C or other persons, this is a publication of the letter by B, for which A is not liable. Defamation is the publication of a defamatory statement, in writing or orally, to a third person that injures the plaintiff's reputation by disgracing him and diminishing the respect in which he is held. An example would be the publication of a statement that a person had committed a crime or had a loathsome disease.

In Beckman v. Dunn, (1979, Pa.Super.) 419 A.2d. 583, the court stated:

A communication is defamatory if it tends to harm the reputation of another so as to lower him in the estimation of the community or deter third persons from associating or dealing with him, and necessarily involves the idea of disgrace.

Defenses. Truth and privilege are complete defenses to a defamation suit. In most states truth is a defense without regard to the purpose or intent in publishing the defamation. The law presumes that all defamation is false and places the burden upon the defendant of proving its truth.

There are three types of privileges: (1) absolute, (2) conditional, and (3) constitutional. As with the defense of truth, absolute privilege protects the defendant regardless of his motive or intent.

Absolute immunity has been confined to those few situations where public policy clearly favors complete freedom of speech and includes: (1) statements made which are germane to a judicial proceeding; (2) statements made by members of Congress on the floor of Congress; (3) statements made by certain executive officers in the discharge of their governmental duty; and (4) statements made between spouses when they are alone.

Conditional or qualified privilege is an immunity granted to the defendant conditioned upon his proper use of the privilege. A defendant has a conditional privilege to publish defamatory matter to protect his own legitimate interests, or in some cases the interests of another person. Thus, he may publish in an appropriate manner statements reasonably necessary to defend his own reputation against the defamation of another. Conditional privilege extends to many cases where the publisher and the recipient have a common interest as with letters of reference. Conditional privilege is forfeited by the publisher if he acts in an excessive manner, without probable cause or for an improper purpose.

The First Amendment to the United States Constitution guarantees freedom of speech and freedom of press. The courts have recently applied these rights to the law of defamation by extending a form of conditional privilege to comment regarding public officials or figures so long as it is done without malice. Restatement, Section 580A. For these purposes "malice" is not ill will but proof of the defendant's knowledge of falsity or reckless disregard of the truth.

Invasion of Privacy

The tort of invasion of privacy may be committed in any of four ways: (a) appropriation of a person's name or likeness; (b) unreasonable intrusion upon the seclusion of another; (c) unreasonable publication of private facts; (d) unreasonable publication which places another in a false light in the public eye. Restatement, Torts, Second, Section 652A.

Appropriation. Appropriation is the use of plaintiff's name or likeness for the benefit of the defendant. Restatement, Section 652C. Most frequently, this category of invasion of privacy has been utilized to impose liability for the use of another's name, picture, or likeness to promote or advertise a product or service. This form of invasion of privacy seeks to protect the individual's right to the exclusive use of his identity.

Intrusion. This type of invasion is the unreasonable and highly offensive interference with the solitude or seclusion of another. Restatement, Section 652B. Such unreasonable interference would include improper entry into another's dwelling, unauthorized eavesdropping upon another's private conversations and unauthorized examination of another's private papers and records. The intrusion must be offensive or objectionable to a reasonable person and must involve matters which are private. Thus, there is no liability if the defendant examines public records or observes the plaintiff in a public place. This form of invasion of privacy is committed once the intrusion occurs as publication is not required.

Public Disclosure of Private Facts. The law of privacy imposes liability for the offensive publication of private information about another. As with intrusion, this tort only applies to private, not public, information regarding the plaintiff, but unlike intrusion it requires publicity. The publicity required differs in degree from "publication" as used in the law of defamation. Under this tort, the private facts must be communicated to the public at large or become public knowledge, whereas publication of a defamatory statement need only be made to a single third party. Thus, A, a creditor of B, will not invade B's privacy by writing a letter to B's employer informing the employer of B's failure to pay the debt, but A would be liable if he posted in the window of his store a statement that B will not pay a debt owed to A. Also unlike defamation, this tort applies to truthful private information if the matter published would be offensive and objectionable to a reasonable person of ordinary sensibilities.

Placing One in False Light. This invasion of privacy imposes liability for publicity which places another in a false light that is highly offensive if the defendant knew or should have known that the matter publicized was false or placed the other in a false light. Restatement, Section 652E. For example, A includes B's name and photograph in a public "rogues gallery" of convicted crimimals. B has never been convicted of any crime. A is liable to B for placing him in a false light.

As with defamation, the matter must be untrue, but unlike defamation it must be "publicized" not merely "published." Although the matter must be objectionable to a reasonable person, it need not be defamatory. In many instances, the same facts will give rise to both an action for defamation and false light.

Defenses. Absolute, conditional, and constitutional privilege apply to the same extent to the torts of disclosure of private facts and false light as they do to defamation.

INTERFERENCE WITH PROPERTY RIGHTS

Real Property

Real property is land and anything attached thereto such as minerals, trees, and buildings. The law protects the rights of the possessor of land to its exclusive use and quiet enjoyment.

Trespass. Section 158 of the Restatement, Torts, Second, provides:

One is subject to liability to another for trespass, irrespective of whether he thereby causes harm to any legally protected interest of the other, if he intentionally

(a) enters land in the possession of the other, or causes a thing or a third person to do so, or

(b) remains on the land, or

(c) fails to remove from the land a thing which he is under a duty to remove.

It is no defense that the intruder acted upon the mistaken belief of law or fact that he was not trespassing. If the intruder intended to be upon the particular property, it is irrelevant that he reasonably believed tht he owned the land or had permission to enter upon the land. Restatement, Torts, Second, Section 164. An intruder is not liable if his presence on the land of another is not caused by his own actions. For example, if A is thrown onto B's land by C, A is not liable to B for trespass, but C is. By the same token, if a heavy gust of wind carries A's garbage can onto B's land, A is not liable to B for trespass.

A trespass may be committed on, beneath, or above the surface of the land. Although it has been stated, *cujus est solum, ejus est usque ad coelum* (he who owns the soil owns upward unto heaven), the advent of aviation has made this legal proposition obsolete. The law now regards the upper air, above the prescribed minimum altitude of flight, as a public highway. There is no trespass unless the aircraft enters into the immediate reaches of the air space and substantially interferes with the landowner's use and enjoyment of it. Restatement, Torts, Second, Section 159.

Nuisance. "A private nuisance is a nontrespassory invasion of another's interest in the private use and enjoyment of land." Restatement, Torts, Second, Section 821D. In contrast with trespass, nuisance does not require interference with another's right to exclusive possession of land but rather imposes liability for significant harm to another's use or enjoyment of land. Examples of private nuisances include the emission of unpleasant odors, smoke, dust, or gas as well as the pollution of a stream, pond, or undergound water supply.

A public nuisance is the unreasonable interference with a right common to the public in general. Restatement, Torts, Second, Section 821B. For example, the maintenance of a malarial pond or the obstruction of a public highway are public nuisances because they affect an interest common to

the general public rather than that of one or several individuals.

Personal Property

A chattel or personal property is any type of property other than an interest in land. The law protects a number of interests in the possession of chattels including an interest in their physical condition and usability, an interest in the retention of possession and an interest in their availability for future use.

Trespass. Trespass to personal property or chattels consists of the intentional dispossession or unauthorized use of the chattel of another. The interference with the right to exclusive use and possession may be direct or indirect, but liability is limited to instances in which the trespassor (a) dispossesses the other of the chattel, (b) substantially impairs the condition, quality, or value of the chattel, (c) deprives the possessor of the use of the chattel for a substantial time, or (d) causes bodily harm to the possessor or harm to some person or thing in which the possessor has some legal interest. Restatement, Torts, Second, Section 218.

Conversion. Conversion is the intentional exercise of dominion or control over another's chattel which so seriously interferes with the other's right of control as to justly require the payment of full value for the chattel. Restatement, Torts, Second, Section 222A. The Restatement considers the following factors in determining whether justice requires the wrongdoing actor to pay full value:

1. the extent and duration of the actor's exercise of dominion or control;
2. the actor's intent to assert a right in fact inconsistent with the other's right of control;
3. the actor's good faith;
4. the extent and duration of the resulting interference with the other's right of control;

5. the harm done to the chattel;
6. the inconvenience and expense caused to the other.   Section 222A.

Conversion may consist of the intentional destruction of a chattel or the use of a chattel in an unauthorized manner.   For example, A entrusts an automobile to B, a dealer, for sale.   B drives the car 2,000 miles on his own business.   B is liable to A for conversion.

A major distinction between trespass to personal property and conversion is the measure of damages.   In trespass, the possessor recovers damages for the actual harm to the chattel or as compensation for the loss of possession.   In conversion, the possessor recovers the full value of the chattel and the convertor takes possession of it upon payment of the judgment.

INTERFERENCE WITH ECONOMIC INTERESTS

Interference with Contractual Relations

Section 766 of the Restatement provides:

One who intentionally and improperly interferes with the performance of a contract (except a contract to marry) between another and a third person by inducing or otherwise causing the third person not to perform the contract, is subject to liability to the other for the pecuniary loss resulting to the other from the failure of the third person to perform the contract.

Section 766B imposes similar liability for intentional and improper interference with another's prospective contractual relation.

In either case, the rule applies whenever the defendant acts with the purpose or motive of interfering with the plaintiff's contract or with the knowledge that such interference is substantially certain to occur as a natural consequence of his actions. The interference may be by prevention through the use of physical force or by threats.   Frequently, it is accomplished by inducement such as the offer of a better contract.   For instance, A may offer B, an employee of C, a yearly salary of $5,000 per year more than the contractual arrangement between B and C.   If A is aware of the contract between B and C and that his offer to B interferes with that contract, then A is liable to C for intentional interference with contractual relations.   However, if the employment contract between B and C was at will, there would be no tort, for C had no legal right to have the relation continued.

Disparagement

Disparagement is defined as statements intended by the party making them to cast doubt upon the title or quality of another's property or products.   If the statements are so understood by the person to whom made and are untrue, the property or goods to which they relate are disparaged.

Thus, A, while contemplating the purchase of a stock of merchandise which belongs to B, reads an advertisement in a newspaper in which C falsely asserts he has a lien upon the merchandise.   C has disparaged B's property in the goods.

An untrue expression of opinion, dishonestly made, which is disparaging, is wrongful and actionable.   However, no action lies to recover damages resulting from an honest statement of opinion, one actually held by the party making it and clearly expressed as such.

Fraudulent Misrepresentation

Section 525 of the Restatement provides:

One who fraudulently makes a misrepresentation of fact, opinion, intention, or law for the purpose of inducing another to act or to refrain from action in reliance upon it, is subject to liability to the other in deceit for pecuniary loss caused to him by his justifiable reliance upon the misrepresentation.

Although intentional or fraudulent misrepresentation is a tort action, it is closely connected with contractual negotiations and is discussed in Chapter 8.

DEFENSES TO INTENTIONAL TORTS

Even though the defendant has intentionally invaded the interests of the plaintiff, the defendant will not be liable if such conduct was privileged. A defendant's conduct is privileged if it furthers an interest of such social importance that the law confers immunity from tort liability for damage to others. Examples of privilege include self-defense, defense of property, and defense of others. In addition, the plaintiff's consent to the defendant's conduct is a defense to intentional torts.

CONSENT

If one consents to conduct resulting in damage or harm done to his own person or property, no liability will generally attach to the intentional infliction of injury. This fundamental principle of the common law finds expression in the phrase *volenti non fit injuria*—to one who is willing, no wrong is done. Consent to an act is the willingness that it shall occur. It may be manifested expressly or impliedly, by words or by conduct. For example, A states that he wishes to kiss B. Although B does not wish A to do so, she does not object or resist by word or act. A kisses B. A is not liable to B for battery since A has impliedly consented to B's conduct.

Consent must be given by an individual with capacity to do so. Consent given by a minor, mental incompetent, or intoxicated individual is invalid.

The defendant's privilege is limited to the conduct to which the plaintiff consents. For example, A consents to an exploratory operation by B, a surgeon, but refuses to have any further operation performed. While A is under ether, B discovers a condition which indicates that an operation is needed and proceeds to operate. B is sub-

ject to liability to A, even though the operation is properly and successfully performed, because B exceeded the consent given. On the other hand, assume that A consents to a particular operation to be performed by B. A submits to anesthesia. Upon opening A's body, B discovers conditions which make it necessary to extend the operation in order to save A's life. A reasonable man would consent to the operation if he knew of the conditions discovered by B. B performs the operation. B is not liable to A.

Consent to Participate in a Game

By agreeing to participate in a game, one consents to encounter such bodily contact and limitations upon freedom of movement as is permitted by or general to the game. However, such consent does not extend to intentional acts of violence or restrictions beyond the rules and usages of the game. Thus, if A participates in a game of ice hockey, he does not consent to be intentionally attacked by B, another player, wielding his hockey stock as a weapon.

Consent Obtained by Mistake

Consent given under a mistake as to the nature or character of the defendant's conduct is nevertheless effective unless the defendant knew of the mistake or obtained the consent through misrepresentation. Thus, A gives B a soft drink with a decomposed mouse in it, the presence of which B is reasonably unaware. If A is also unaware of the foreign substance in the beverage, he would not be liable for battery; however, if A was aware of the foreign matter, then A would be liable for battery as B's consent would be vitiated.

Consent to a Criminal Act

The jurisdictions are divided as to whether consent to conduct that constitutes a crime is a valid defense to an intentional tort.

The Restatement takes the position that such consent should effectively eliminate tort liability, except in instances where the statute making the conduct criminal is designed to protect a certain class of individuals, irrespective of their consent. Sections 60, 61, and 892C. Thus, Illustration 1 to Restatement, Section 61, provides:

A statute makes it rape to have intercourse with a girl under the age of eighteen even with her consent. B, with A's assent (or at her solicitation), has intercourse with her. A's assent does not prevent B from being liable to her.

The majority of states, however, hold that consent to mutual combat and similar batteries will not relieve the participants from liability in tort.

PRIVILEGE

Self-Defense

The law permits an individual to take appropriate action to prevent harm to himself where time does not allow resort to the law. Section 63 of the Restatement provides:

(1) An actor is privileged to use reasonable force, not intended or likely to cause death or serious bodily harm, to defend himself against unprivileged harmful or offensive contact or other bodily harm which he reasonably believes that another is about to inflict intentionally upon him.

The privilege of self-defense exists whether or not the danger actually exists, provided that the defendant reasonably believed that self-defense was necessary. The reasonableness of the defendant's actions is based upon what a person of average courage would have thought under the circumstances.

Self-defense is warranted even if the defendant reasonably believed that he could avoid the threatened contact by retreating, giving up a right, or complying with an unprivileged demand from the plaintiff.

However, the defendant is not privileged to retaliate, as revenge is not self-defense. The defendant, to protect himself from offensive or non-serious bodily contact, is limited to reasonable force: "that is, it must not be disproportionate in extent to the harm from which the actor is seeking to protect himself. A degree of force may be privileged to ward off a blow which threatens substantial harm, where the same degree of force would not be privileged merely to prevent touching in an insulting manner." Restatement, Section 63, Comment j.

The defendant is privileged to defend by the use of force intended or likely to cause death or serious bodily harm if he reasonably believes that the plaintiff is about to inflict death, serious bodily harm, or ravishment upon the defendant. Most states limit the right to use deadly force in self-defense to those situations in which the defendant does not have a completely safe means of escape. If the defendant, however, has the slightest doubt, if reasonable, as to the safety of his escape, he may stand his ground. One may also stand his ground and use deadly force if the attack occurs in his own residence, even though a reasonable means of escape exists. Restatement, Section 65.

Defense of Others

An individual is privileged to defend third persons from harmful or offensive contact to the same extent that he is privileged to protect himself, provided that the defendant correctly or reasonably believes that the third person possesses the privilege of self-defense and that the defendant's intervention is necessary for the safety of the third person. Restatement, Section 76. Thus, A sees B about to strike A's friend C. B is in fact privileged to do so to repel C's attack. A has no reason to suspect that C is the aggressor and intercedes to assist C. A is privileged to use reasonable force to assist C against B.

Defense of Property

A possessor of property is permitted to use reasonable force, not intended or likely to cause death or serious bodily harm, to protect his real and personal property. Such force can only be employed if the possessor reasonably believes that the intrusion can only be terminated or prevented by use of force and the intruder has disregarded requests to cease. Restatement, Section 77. For example, A sees B walking across his vacant lot. A is not privileged to use even the mildest of force to eject B until A has requested B to leave and B has disregarded the warning. Once reasonable force has been used, the defendant may use such greater force as is necessary to protect himself and his property. The intruder is not entitled to invoke the privilege of self-defense.

The defendant may not through indirect means, such as mechanical devices, employ deadly force to protect his property unless he would, if present, have been privileged to employ such force. Restatement, Section 85. This section applies to spring guns, electrified fences, and other traps that are intended or likely to cause death or serious bodily harm.

Cases

Assault and Battery

CAPUNE v. ROBBINS

(1968) 273 N.C. 581, 160 S.E.2d 881.

Plaintiff instituted this civil action August 17, 1965, to recover $7,500.00 compensatory damages and $25,000.00 punitive damages on account of an alleged wilful, wanton, intentional and malicious assault by defendant on plaintiff.

Plaintiff, then about 22, was attempting a trip from Seagate, Coney Island, New York, to Florida, on an eighteen-foot-long paddleboard, without mast or sail. Plaintiff testified: "I would paddle it with my hands and steer with my feet. Paddling, I placed my arms in front of me and pulled down alongside the board. The total length of the trip I had planned was approximately 1,154 miles, paddling all the way." He came "down the entire coast on the paddleboard."

The trip was being covered by "Associated Press, United Press International, and television media, along with radio and local news coverage * * * plus coverage back on the West Coast" where plaintiff had completed a similar trip. Plaintiff testified that the publicity "enables me to make contracts with different sponsors." He testified further that, "in doing these trips I put myself as an endorser for various products that I use as you have seen with golf clubs, with baseball, that baseball players endorse. They get a certain percentage and this is what I hoped to achieve."

Plaintiff arrived at the Oceanana Motel on Atlantic Beach, N. C., on August 14, 1965, and spent the night there. The next morning, August 15th, he left the Oceanana about 9:00 o'clock a.m. on his paddleboard and "headed south under the Oceanana pier behind the surf line and * * * went under the next pier, which is Sportsmans' Pier." He then proceeded west and landed "near the Morehead Ocean pier," about two miles from the Oceanana pier. He intended to "go to the concession stand to buy something to eat and go to the rest room, * * *"

On August 15, 1965, defendant was the owner and operator of the Morehead Ocean Pier, on Bogue Banks in Carteret County. This pier, constructed pursuant to a permit issued by the U.S. Army Corps of Engineers on January 10, 1958, to Morehead Pier, Inc., from whom defendant purchased, extends out into the Atlantic Ocean for one thousand feet and is located approximately in the middle of the three hundred feet of water frontage land owned by defendant.

The pier, which is "about 20 feet above the water," was operated "for the purpose of sport fishing only." Defendant charged fishermen a fee of $1.00 a day to fish from the pier. On August 15th, a Sunday, there were "approximately 90 to 100 fishermen on the pier." Defendant operated "a concession stand and tackle shop" on the shore end of the pier. Nearby, on the shore, there was a picnic area. To avoid interference with the fishermen, defendant did not permit surf casting or bathing on his premises and undertook to prohibit boating and surfboarding in the waters 150 feet each side of the center of the pier. A sign facing those approaching from the road was in these words: "No soliciting and boats allowed on these premises." There was posted on each side of the pier a sign in these words: "No fishing or swimming near the pier."

Plaintiff and defendant were strangers. According to plaintiff's testimony, plaintiff approached defendant's premises from the ocean by paddleboard, his only means of travel, and was unaware of defendant's attempted restrictions on the use of the ocean waters alongside defendant's pier. According to defendant's testimony, defendant had no knowledge of plaintiff's sporting and publicity venture and assumed the paddleboard had been brought to his premises by land transportation.

Upon landing on defendant's premises, plaintiff put his paddleboard on the sand and walked towards the pier. Defendant came running up, told plaintiff to leave, and to get his surfboard off defendant's property, and that "for many reasons he didn't allow surfboards around the fishing pier." Thereupon defendant went back "to his business" and out of plaintiff's sight. Plaintiff took his paddleboard "out in the ocean again, starting out a little bit to sea

and * * * towards the middle of the pier." Plaintiff testified: "I saw there were a lot of fishermen on the end of the pier and didn't want to get in their way * * * I figured I would go through the center of the pier where there wasn't any or many fishermen and go on my way. * * * As I approached the pier, Mr. Robbins came running out on the pier, yelling and screaming, telling me not to go under the pier, so I stopped and said O.K., I'll go around it, and he threw a bottle at me and it came pretty close and I was trying to turn the board around to go around the pier. He told me not to go around, but to go back where I came from. I said I would, and then he threw another bottle and I had to get off in the water; I was afraid. The only place I could hide was under the water to avoid being hit, and I asked him if I could come up and get the board and turn it around and leave, and as I got the board to turn around and leave (by turning it around I mean it was sort of broadside to the pier. It's a big board and you have to head it where you are going), and I started to paddle away from the pier to go around and he got me, hit me in the head with a third bottle. He hit me on the right side of my forehead." The next thing plaintiff remembered was that somebody pulled him out of the water and helped him get on his board and took him on his board to the shore. Thereafter he was taken to the Oceanana Motel and later to the hospital in Morehead City where "(i)t took approximately 24 sutures to close the wound" on his head. There was other testimony as to plaintiff's injuries. Too, there was testimony tending to show plaintiff suffered loss of income by being forced to give up his publicized venture.

Defendant was at the tackle shop when he saw plaintiff standing "beside the boat" on defendant's property. Defendant, going down to the shore, told plaintiff: "Take your boat and get out of here; we don't allow them to operate this close to the pier and don't allow them on our property." Defendant then "rushed back" to the tackle shop. It was about fifteen or thirty minutes later when he next saw plaintiff. At that time, "(H)e (plaintiff) was on the paddleboard paddling out about 40 feet from the pier parallel with the pier going out from the shore and was about half-way out with regard to the pier about 400 feet, and he was on the east side of the pier about 40 feet away and he was paddling. * * * When I saw Capune out in the water as I have described, I went out on the pier and asked him to leave and asked him to turn away from the pier. When I saw Capune out in the water, I ran out on the pier and got almost straight in line with him, about 40 feet from him, and told him to turn away and leave. There were other people there. There were four or five fishermen standing there close by. When I told him to turn away from the pier, he turned towards the pier. I didn't hear him say anything. If he said anything to me, I didn't hear it. When he turned towards the pier, he started paddling and it looked like he was trying to go under the pier. There were fishermen there where he was trying to go under the pier. They had their lines in the water and were fishing. I told him three different times to turn away from the pier and leave. He paid no attention to it. I picked up a pop bottle beside the bench and threw it in his direction hoping that he would turn away. It hit the water about ten feet from the surfboard. He kept coming and I threw another one at him. Throwing the first two bottles had no effect on him whatsoever. I threw a third bottle at him and it hit him. I did not intend to hit him; I merely intended to frighten him to the extent that he would turn away from the pier. He fell off the surfboard. He and the surfboard separated. He was paddling around out in the water and a wave hit the board and one knocked it away from him and a fellow on the fishing pier who had a line that got tangled in the surfboard threw down his rod and reel and jumped overboard and swam

to the surfboard, paddled out to Capune and both of them got on the board and came back to shore. Capune's head did not go under the water any time. He was on top of the water paddling."

The court submitted and the jury answered the following issues: "1. Did the defendant John S. Robbins assault the plaintiff, as alleged in the Complaint? Answer: Yes. 2. What damages, if any, is the plaintiff entitled to recover from the defendant? Answer: $1,000.00. 3. What amount of punitive damages, if any, is the plaintiff entitled to recover from the defendant? Answer: $10,000.00."

"NOW, THEREFORE, IT IS ORDERED, ADJUDGED AND DECREED that the plaintiff have and recover of the defendant the sum of Eleven Thousand ($11,000.00) Dollars, together with the costs of this action."

Defendant excepted and appealed.

BOBBITT, J.
* * *

Defendant having failed to show prejudicial error, the verdict and judgment of the court below will not be disturbed.

No error.

False Imprisonment

NATIONAL BOND AND INV. CO. v. WHITHORN

(1939) 276 Ky. 204, 123 S.W.2d 263.

FULTON, J.

Appellee, William Whithorn, brought this action for false imprisonment against the appellant, National Bond and Investment Company, in the Jefferson circuit court and on a trial before a jury verdict was rendered in his favor for $700 compensatory damages and $900 punitive damages. Judgment was entered on this verdict and from that judgment this appeal is prosecuted.

* * *

The evidence discloses that the appellant had, or at least claimed to have, a conditional sales contract on a car in possession of appellee, and that payments due under this contract had not been made. Appellant desired to repossess the car and assigned its employees, O'Brien and Baer, to this task. Baer appears to have been a high-powered repossessor in the employ of appellant in Chicago and was imported to Louisville for some special work along this line. These employees, after making inquiry from a relative of appellee, and after a little "fast work" connected with this inquiry, learned where appellee lived and by so doing managed to find him driving the car on a street in Louisville. In their car they followed appellee in his car for some distance and hailed him down for the purpose of making a repossession.

There is considerable conflict in the testimony as to what occurred between appellee and these two employees of appellant on the occasion of this repossession, but the jury evidently accepted appellee's version of the melee * * *.

* * * When O'Brien and Baer hailed appellee he thought they were officers and stopped his car, whereupon O'Brien got out of his car, walked up to appellee's car, and invited him to get out and come back and talk to Baer. This appellee refused to do, so finally Baer also came to appellee's car and from that time things began to move rapidly. Appellee was informed that these employees desired to repossess the car and was notified to get out and take his personal belongings. Appellee demanded evidence of their authority, which they assured him they had, but their assurance did not satisfy appellee and the argument as to authority continued for some time. The repossessors became impatient at being balked of their quarry and finally one of them said, "Don't you move this machine, I will have an officer here in about two minutes." * * * After O'Brien came back he made

the statement that "the officers will be here any minute." Shortly after O'Brien returned, a wrecker, which had been called by O'Brien, pulled up and one of the appellant's employees motioned for the wrecker to pull in front of appellee's car to hook on, whereupon appellee started the motor in his car for the purpose of driving off, but O'Brien raised the hood of the car and jerked loose the distributor wire. Appellee, not desiring to see his car put hors du combat, opened the door of his car and started out after him. When appellee opened the door of his car and started out, Baer attempted to reach through the window of the car on the other side and get the car key, but appellee sensing what was in the wind, beat Baer to the key, and this seemed to "peeve" the repossessors very much. O'Brien then said, "He has acted so smart I will have him put in jail," and got in his machine and left. He came back in a short while and it does not clearly appear whether or not he called the police officers, but at any rate a police officer pursuant to a telephone call from some one, showed up a while afterwards.

When O'Brien returned from this second departure Baer directed the driver operating the wrecker to hook to appellee's car and pull out with it, but in view of appellee's vehement protests the driver of the wrecker hesitated to act, but after repeated demands by O'Brien finally coupled up with appellee's car and hoisted the front wheels off the ground. Baer then climbed in appellee's car and the wrecker started pulling the car down the street, whereupon appellee put on the emergency brake and threw the car into reverse, thereby managing to stall the wrecker and bring the car to a stop after it had been pulled down the street something like 75 to 100 feet. During the progress down the street, appellee who says he tried to prevent Baer from getting in the car with him, attempted to eject Baer from the car by kicks on the shins, which Baer says in his testimony were rather forcefully administered, but his attempts to dislodge this Chicago repossessor were wholly unavailing.

While all this was occurring numerous cars were passing up and down the street; some of them stopping and looking and then driving on. In other words, the passing public seemed to realize that a good act was being put on and did not miss the opportunity to enjoy at least a portion of it. After appellee had managed to bring the procession to a halt by stalling the wrecker, a policeman came up and inquired as to the meaning of the controversy, and the contestants on the respective sides stated their case. The policeman says that he refused to pass on the merits of the controversy, but he did demand appellee's driver's license, which it appears appellee had but had left at home. Appellee seemed to think the policeman was taking sides with the repossessors and became rather angry, demanding the policeman's badge number and name, whereupon the policeman placed him under arrest. The drama of repossession ended with the policeman departing with appellee in tow and O'Brien and Baer departing with appellee's car in tow, the result being a complete and satisfying repossession, at least satisfying in its results to appellant's employees, O'Brien and Baer, but highly unsatisfactory to appellee.

* * *

If appellant had a valid conditional sales contract on appellee's car, and he was behind in the payments, appellant had the right to repossess the car if it could do so peaceably, but, of course, had no right to create a breach of the peace in doing so, or to put appellee under any kind of restraint, or to use any force directed against him in making the repossession. [Citation.]

Appellant contends the transaction above recited did not amount to false imprisonment, its theory being that appellee was in no wise restrained or impeded, and

that he was perfectly at liberty at any time to go his way * * *.

We are unable to agree with appellant's contention * * *. A reading of the evidence we have quoted above makes it immediately apparent that appellee, in the present case, was placed under restraint by O'Brien and Baer. They had him in his car under forcible control, being pulled down the street some 75 to 100 feet, against his vehement protest, and we are firmly of the opinion that such conduct on their part was a false imprisonment.

It is true, as appellant argues, that appellee was at liberty to depart and these employees were not preventing him from doing so, but the result of his departure would have been an automatic parting with his automobile, which he did not desire to part with, and which he did not have to part with, and which O'Brien and Baer had no right to take over his protests. While he was in the car he was in a place he had a legal right to be, and in which neither O'Brien or Baer had a legal right to be, by force, and when these men hooked the wrecker on and hoisted the front wheels in the air, forcibly dragging appellee down the street in his car, this was unquestionably a restraint imposed upon him and a detention of his person, such as constitutes a false imprisonment.

* * *

Wherefore, the judgment is affirmed.

Outrageous Conduct

LaBRIER v. ANHEUSER FORD CO.

(1981, Mo.App.) 612 S.W.2d 790.

WEIER, J.

This is a suit for damages for injury caused by outrageous conduct. From a directed verdict in favor of defendants at the close of plaintiff's evidence, plaintiff appeals.

The question presented is whether plaintiff's evidence made a case of outrageous conduct. If the elements of such a case have been established by some of the evidence, then plaintiff is entitled to a reversal and remand of the case for retrial so that the issues of liability and damages can be presented to the jury. If not, then the lower court must be affirmed.

Plaintiff Mary Jane LaBrier is the wife of James LaBrier, a former employee of Anheuser Ford, Inc. Prior to April 17, 1975, Mr. LaBrier had been employed as a used car salesman by the company for about seven years. On that date he discussed his need for time away from his duties with his superiors. A doctor had advised him to take four to six weeks away from his employment. He first spoke to the general manager Mr. Zeiser who told him that if he needed rest he had some three weeks' vacation due. He then came back the next day and talked to Mr. Gilmour who was his immediate superior. The discussion centered around whether he should take sick leave or vacation time. He had some three weeks coming to him on vacation but company rules required thirty days' notice prior to taking a vacation and it was also policy that he receive his check for the time off before he left. To avoid any complications he requested that it be considered sick leave.

It had apparently been the custom to allow employees to take their demonstrator car with them on vacation but not on sick leave. On this matter after some discussion, Mr. Zeiser the manager talked to a Mr. Fritz at the company office. Zeiser then returned and told LaBrier that the company did not want him to take the car on vacation or on sick leave. But after discussing the matter with a union representative, Mr. LaBrier decided to take the automobile.

LaBrier left home the next morning about 5:30 in the demonstrator. That afternoon Mr. Zeiser and Mr. Gilmour came to the home where Mr. and Mrs. LaBrier resided. Plaintiff Mary Jane LaBrier came to the front porch and the men asked her repeatedly where her husband had gone and where the car was located. They told her that he had stolen the car and if it was not returned there would be an all-points bulletin sent to the State Highway Patrol. He would be detained and the car brought back. They kept repeating these questions and statements for approximately twenty to twenty-five minutes in a loud and angry tone of voice. Mrs. LaBrier, who had been under the care of a doctor and had been hospitalized for emotional problems for approximately two weeks in October of the preceding year, became very upset and she began to cry. Her eyes became swollen and itching and she developed a rash over her body. She had not been taking any medication prior to this event for several months. After this occurrence, however, she had to return to taking the medicine and was prevented from taking care of her household duties for several months. LaBrier returned within a day or two after he found out about the occurrence at the home and returned the automobile to the defendants.

Two other witnesses testified with regard to the confrontation on the porch between the two employees of Anheuser Ford and Mrs. LaBrier. A next door neighbor Annie McKay testified that she and her little son were sitting on the steps of her house when the two men drove up, got out of the car and walked up on the LaBrier porch. When they got real loud she could hear the conversation. One of the men kept asking where Mr. LaBrier had gone and then she heard him say: "Well, he stole the car and we are going to put an all-points bulletin out to get it back." She characterized these statements as being loud and angry. She noticed as they kept repeating the questions and asking them in a loud and angry fashion, Mrs. LaBrier became very nervous and her voice was trembling. Another neighbor Sandra Lee Rishar was in the LaBrier residence in the kitchen visiting with Mrs. LaBrier when the men came to the door. She also overheard the conversation and related that the questions and remarks of the two men became loud and she heard them say: "We need our car, we want it back, we are going to put out an all-points bulletin." She also heard them tell Mrs. LaBrier that her husband stole the car and that they wanted it. In reply Mrs. LaBrier informed them she didn't know exactly where he was and then one of them told her: "Oh, yes you do, and we want to know where he is, and we want our car."

Since the opinion in *Pretsky v. Southwestern Bell Telephone Company*, 396 S.W.2d 566 (Mo.1965), Missouri has recognized the tort of outrageous conduct as defined by § 46 of the Restatement (Second) of Torts wherein it is said: "One who by extreme and outrageous conduct intentionally or recklessly causes severe emotional distress to another is subject to liability for such emotional distress, and if bodily harm to the other results from it, for such bodily harm." The elements of this tort are set out clearly in *Leonard v. Pioneer Finance Company*, 568 S.W.2d 937, 940[2] (Mo.App.1978). Simply stated they are: (1) Defendant's conduct must be extreme and outrageous; (2) the defendant acts in an intentional or reckless manner; and (3) by reason of said acts, plaintiff is caused to suffer severe emotional distress from which bodily harm results.

We first consider whether the two employees of Anheuser Ford acted in a manner that could be characterized as extreme or outrageous. If in the favorable view of plaintiff's evidence, giving plaintiff all the benefit of favorable inferences to be drawn therefrom, the question is reasonably debatable, then the issue should go to the jury. "Mere insults, indignities, inconsiderations or petty oppressions do not rise to the level of the outrageous conduct essential to plaintiff's right of recovery." [Citation.] As

stated in *Golston v. Lincoln Cemetery, Inc.*, 573 S.W.2d 700, 705[2] (Mo.App.1978), generally a case of outrageous conduct "is one in which the recitation of the facts to an average member of the community would arouse his resentment against the actor, and lead him to exclaim, 'Outrageous!' ". [Citation.] Even though the facts may be scarcely overwhelming in establishing the negligent character of the act; that is, in the instant case that the conduct was overwhelmingly outrageous, if the characterization is reasonably debatable, a court cannot substitute its judgment on the facts for that of a jury. [Citation.]

We believe that the action of the employees of Anheuser Ford in appearing at plaintiff's residence in the presence of two neighbors and in a loud and threatening voice attempting to harass and humiliate plaintiff by repeatedly questioning her as to the whereabouts of her husband and the demonstrator automobile and threatening to have her husband arrested by the issuance of an "all-points bulletin" to the police could be characterized as "extreme and outrageous." Defendants suggest they had a legitimate interest in determining the whereabouts of the demonstrator. We have no doubt that this is a legitimate interest, but in light of the prior condition of plaintiff as a highly emotional and easily distraught individual who had suffered severe emotional problems before this episode that had caused her to be hospitalized, a condition known to defendants, it would appear that Mr. Gilmour and Mr. Zeiser may have exceeded the bounds of normal human conduct to such a point that the jury could find them and through them defendant Anheuser Ford guilty of outrageous conduct. As is stated in Restatement (Second) of Torts, *supra*, Comment (f) to § 46, [t]he extreme and outrageous character of the conduct may arise from the actor's knowledge that the other is peculiarly susceptible to emotional distress, by reason of some physical or mental condition or peculiarity. The conduct may become heartless, flagrant, and outrageous when the actor proceeds in the face of such knowledge, where it would not be so if he did not know. It must be emphasized again, however, that major outrage is essential to the tort; and the mere fact that the actor knows that the other will regard the conduct as insulting, or will have his feelings hurt, is not enough." Mrs. LaBrier had previously lost her father and her daughter. Because of this and several other crises in the family, she had been hospitalized for two weeks because of emotional problems. Defendants Zeiser and Gilmour were both aware that she had been in the hospital. She had received a house plant from defendant Anheuser Ford when she was in the hospital. The knowledge of her prior condition was clear.

We next test the evidence to determine whether the jury could find that the acts of Zeiser and Gilmour could be determined by the jury to be intentional or reckless as required in the second standard hereinabove set out. The requirements of what the evidence must show in justifying infliction of punitive damages for the commission of a tort were set out in *Sharp v. Robberson,* 495 S.W.2d 394, 397 (Mo.banc 1973). There the court points out that an act of negligence may manifest such reckless indifference to the rights of others that the law will imply an injury resulting from it was intentionally inflicted. It is also true that in some circumstances there may be conscious negligence that is the equivalent of intentional wrongdoing such as where the person doing the act must be conscious of his conduct and though having no specific intent to injure, must be conscious from his knowledge of the surrounding circumstances and existing conditions that his conduct will naturally or probably result in injury. It was suggested that this same standard could be applied to outrageous conduct negligence in *Golston v. Lincoln Cemetery, Inc., supra* at 705. Knowing that Mrs. LaBrier had previously had emotional problems as was

shown here, it can easily be seen that defendants could be charged with intentional commission of an outrageous act or such a reckless disregard of a previously known condition so as to supply the necessary element of intentional infliction of an emotional crisis resulting in physical harm.

The last element, that of causation, would seem to be supplied by the evidence that was given by Mrs. LaBrier and by the neighbors to the effect that following the ordeal plaintiff was nervous, upset, confused and crying. During this time, the plaintiff continually dug at her face as a result of an itch that occurred under her skin. Thereafter, Mrs. Rishar a neighbor visited plaintiff almost daily to aid her in caring for her children. During that time plaintiff would break down and cry and begin scratching her face. Mr. LaBrier also related that when he arrived home he found plaintiff in bed. She had blotches over her entire body and her eyes were swollen.

After examining the evidence and considering the case law, we have concluded that plaintiff by her evidence made a jury case. As expressed in Comment (h) of § 46, Restatement (Second) of Torts at p. 77, "[w]here reasonable men may differ, it is for the jury, subject to the control of the court, to determine whether, in the particular case, the conduct has been sufficiently extreme and outrageous to result in liability." We are therefore constrained to reverse the judgment of the court sustaining the motion for directed verdict at the close of plaintiff's case and remand the case for new trial.

The case is reversed and remanded.

Defamation

HUTCHINSON v. PROXMIRE

(1979) 443 U.S. 111, 99 S.Ct. 2675, 61 L.Ed.2d. 411.

BURGER, CHIEF JUSTICE.

We granted certiorari [citation] to resolve three issues: (1) Whether a Member of Congress is protected by the Speech or Debate Clause of the Constitution, Art. I, § 6, against suits for allegedly defamatory statements made by the Member in press releases and newsletters; (2) Whether petitioner Hutchinson is either a "public figure" or a "public official," thereby making applicable the "actual malice" standard of *New York Times v. Sullivan,* 376 U.S. 254, 84 S.Ct. 710, 11 L.Ed.2d 686 (1964); and (3) Whether respondents were entitled to summary judgment.

Ronald Hutchinson, a research behavioral scientist, sued respondents, William Proxmire, a United States Senator, and his legislative assistant, Morton Schwartz, for defamation arising out of Proxmire's giving what he called his "Golden Fleece" award. The "award" went to federal agencies that had sponsored Hutchinson's research. Hutchinson alleged that in making the award and publicizing it nationwide, respondents had libeled him, damaging him in his professional and academic standing, and had interfered with his contractual relations. The District Court granted summary judgment for respondents and the Court of Appeals affirmed, 7 Cir., 579 F.2d 1027.

* * *

I

Respondent Proxmire is a United States Senator from Wisconsin. In March 1975 he initiated the "Golden Fleece of the Month Award" to publicize what he perceived to be the most egregious examples of wasteful governmental spending. The second such award, in April 1975, went to the National Science Foundation, the National Aeronautics and Space Administration, and the Office of Naval Research for spending almost half a million dollars during the preceding seven years to fund Hutchinson's research.

At the time of the award, Hutchinson was director of research at the Kalamazoo State Mental Hospital. Before that he had held a similar position at the Ft. Custer State Home. * * *

The bulk of Hutchinson's research was devoted to the study of emotional behavior. In particular, he sought an objective measure of aggression, concentrating upon the behavior patterns of certain animals, such as the clenching of jaws when they were exposed to various aggravating stressful stimuli. The National Aeronautics and Space Agency and the Navy were interested in the potential of this research for resolving problems associated with confining humans in close quarters for extended periods of time in space and undersea exploration.

The Golden Fleece Award to the agencies that had sponsored Hutchinson's research was based upon research done for Proxmire by Schwartz. While seeking evidence of wasteful governmental spending, Schwartz read copies of reports that Hutchinson had prepared under grants from NASA. Those reports revealed that Hutchinson had received grants from the Office of Naval Research, the National Science Foundation, and the Michigan State Department of Mental Health. Schwartz also learned that other federal agencies had funded Hutchinson's research. After contacting a number of federal and state agencies, Schwartz helped to prepare a speech for Proxmire to present in the Senate on April 18, 1975; the text was then incorporated into an advance press release, with only the addition of introductory and concluding sentences. Copies were sent to a mailing list of 275 members of the news media throughout the United States and abroad.

Schwartz telephoned Hutchinson before releasing the speech to tell him of the award; Hutchinson protested that the release contained an inaccurate and incomplete summary of his research. Schwartz replied that he thought the summary was fair.

In the speech Proxmire described the federal grants for Hutchinson's research, concluding with the following comment:

The funding of this nonsense makes me almost angry enough to scream and kick or even clench my jaws. It seems to me it is outrageous.

Dr. Hutchinson's studies should make the taxpayers as well as his monkeys grind their teeth. In fact, the good doctor has made a fortune from his monkeys and in the process made a monkey out of the American taxpayer.

It is time for the Federal Government to get out of this "monkey business." In view of the transparent worthlessness of Hutchinson's study of jaw-grinding and biting by angry or hard-drinking monkeys, it is time we put a stop to the bite Hutchinson and the bureaucrats who fund him have been taking of the taxpayers. 121 Cong.Rec. 10803 (1975).

In May 1975, Proxmire referred to his Golden Fleece Awards in a newsletter sent to about 100,000 people whose names were on a mailing list that included constituents in Wisconsin as well as persons in other states. The newsletter repeated the essence of the speech and the press release. Later in 1975, Proxmire appeared on a television interview program where he referred to Hutchinson's research, though he did not mention Hutchinson by name.

The final reference to the research came in a newsletter in February 1976. In that letter Proxmire summarized his Golden Fleece Awards of 1975. The letter did not mention Hutchinson's name, but it did report:

—The NSF, the Space Agency, and the Office of Naval Research won the "Golden Fleece" for spending jointly $500,000 to determine why monkeys clench their jaws.

All the studies on why monkeys clench their jaws were dropped. No more monkey business.

* * *

II

On April 16, 1976, Hutchinson filed this suit in United States District Court in Wisconsin. In Count I he alleges that as a result of the actions of Proxmire and Schwartz he has "suffered a loss of respect in his profession, has suffered injury to his feelings, has been humiliated, held up to public scorn, suffered extreme mental anguish and physical illness and pain to his person. Further, he has suffered a loss of income and ability to earn income in the future."

* * *

The District Court granted respondents' motion for summary judgment. [Citation.] * * * It reasoned that the Speech or Debate Clause afforded absolute immunity for respondents' activities in investigating the funding of Hutchinson's research, for Proxmire's speech in the Senate, and for the press release covering the speech. The court concluded that the investigations and the speech were clearly within the ambit of the Clause. The press release was said to be protected because it fell within the "informing function" of Congress.

* * *

The District Court then turned to the First Amendment to explain the grant of summary judgment on the claims arising from the newsletters and interviews. It concluded that Hutchinson was a public figure for purposes of determining respondents' liability:

Given Dr. Hutchinson's long involvement with publicly-funded research, his active solicitation of federal and state grants, the local press coverage of his research, and the public interest in the expenditure of public funds on the precise activities in which he voluntarily participated, the court concludes that he is a public figure for the purpose of this suit. As he acknowledged in his deposition, "Certainly, any expenditure of public funds is a matter of public interest." 431 F.Supp., at 1327.

* * *

The Court of Appeals affirmed, holding that the Speech or Debate Clause protected the statements made in the press release and in the newsletters. 579 F.2d 1027 (CA7 1978). It interpreted *Doe v. McMillan,* 412 U.S. 306, 93 S.Ct. 2018, 36

L.Ed.2d 912 (1973), as recognizing a limited protection for the "informing function" of Congress and concluded that distribution of both the press release and the newsletters did not exceed what was required for legislative purposes. 579 F.2d at 1033. The follow-up telephone calls and the statements made by Proxmire on television and radio were not protected by the Speech or Debate Clause; they were, however, held by the Court of Appeals to be protected by the First Amendment. It reached that conclusion after first finding that, based on the affidavits and pleadings of record, Hutchinson was a "public figure." *Id.*, at 1034–1035. The Court then examined the record to determine whether there had been a showing by Hutchinson of "actual malice." It agreed with the District Court "that, upon this record, there is no question that [respondents] did not have knowledge of the actual or probable 'falsity' of their statements." *Id.*, at 1035.

* * *

III

* * *

The purpose of the Speech or Debate Clause is to protect Members of Congress "not only from the consequences of litigation's results but also from the burden of defending themselves." [Citations.] If the respondents have immunity under the Clause, no other questions need be considered for they may "not be questioned in any other place."

* * *

IV

In support of the Court of Appeals holding that newsletters and press releases are protected by the Speech or Debate Clause, respondents rely upon both historical precedent and present-day congressional practices. They contend that impetus for the Speech or Debate Clause privilege in our Constitution came from the history of parliamentary efforts to protect the right of members to criticize the spending of the Crown and from the prosecution of a Speaker of the House of Commons for publication of a report outside of Parliament. Respondents also contend that in the modern day very little speech or debate occurs on the floor of either House; from this they argue that press releases and newsletters are necessary for Members of Congress to communicate with other Members. For example, in his deposition Proxmire testified:

I have found in 19 years in the Senate that very often a statement on the floor of the Senate or something that appears in the Congressional Record misses the attention of most members of the Senate, and virtually all members of the House, because they don't read the Congressional Record. If they are handed a news release, or something, that is going to call it to their attention. * * *

Respondents also argue that an essential part of the duties of a Member of Congress is to inform constituents, as well as other Members, of the issues being considered.

* * * Literal reading of the Clause would, of course, confine its protection narrowly to a "Speech or Debate *in* either House." But the Court has given the Clause a practical rather than a strictly literal reading which would limit the protection to utterances made within the four walls of either Chamber. Thus, we have held that committee hearings are protected, even if held outside the Chambers; committee reports are also protected. [Citations.]

The gloss going beyond a strictly literal reading of the Clause has not, however, departed from the objective of protecting only legislative activities. In Thomas Jefferson's view,

[The privilege] is restrained to things done in the House in a Parliamentary course, * * *. For [the Member] is not to have privilege contra morem parliamentarium, to exceed the bounds and limits of his place and duty. [Citation.]

* * *

Whatever imprecision there may be in the term "legislative activities," it is clear that nothing in history or in the explicit language of the Clause suggests any intention to create an absolute privilege from liability or suit for defamatory statements made outside the Chamber. In [citation] we observed:

The immunities of the Speech or Debate Clause were not written into the Constitution simply for the personal or private benefit of Members of Congress, but to protect the integrity of the legislative process by insuring the independence of individual legislators.

Claims under the Clause going beyond what is needed to protect legislative independence are to be closely scrutinized. In [citation] we took note of this:

The authors of our Constitution were well aware of both the need for the privilege *and the abuses that could flow from two* [sic] *sweeping safeguards.* In order to preserve other values, they wrote the privilege so that it tolerates and protects behavior on the part of Members not tolerated and protected when done by other citizens, *but the shield does not extend beyond what is necessary to preserve the integrity of the legislative process.* [Citation.]

Indeed, the precedents abundantly support the conclusion that a Member may be held liable for republishing defamatory statements originally made in either House. We perceive no basis for departing from that long-established rule.

* * *

A speech by Proxmire in the Senate would be wholly immune and would be available to other Members of Congress and the public in the Congressional Record. But neither the newsletters nor the press

release was "essential to the deliberations of the Senate" and neither was part of the deliberative process.

* * *

Newsletters and press releases * * *, are primarily means of informing those outside the legislative forum; they represent the views and will of a single Member. It does not disparage either their value or their importance to hold that they are not entitled to the protection of the Speech or Debate Clause.

V

Since *New York Times v. Sullivan*, 376 U.S. 254, 84 S.Ct. 710, 11 L.Ed.2d 686 (1964), this Court has sought to define the accommodation required to assure the vigorous debate on public issues that the First Amendment was designed to protect while at the same time affording protection to the reputations of individuals. [Citations.] In *Gertz v. Robert Welch, Inc.*, the Court offered a general definition of "public figures":

For the most part those who attain this status [of public figure] have assumed roles of especial prominence in the affairs of society. Some occupy positions of such persuasive power and influence that they are deemed public figures for all purposes. More commonly, those classed as public figures have thrust themselves to the forefront of particular public controversies in order to influence the resolution of the issues involved. In either event, they invite attention and comment. [Citation.]

It is not contended that Hutchinson attained such prominence that he is a public figure for all purposes. Instead, respondents have argued that the District Court and the Court of Appeals were correct in holding that Hutchinson is a public figure for the limited purpose of comment on his receipt of federal funds for research projects. That conclusion was based upon two factors: first, Hutchinson's successful application for federal funds and the reports in local newspapers of the federal grants; second, Hutchinson's access to the media, as demonstrated by the fact that some newspapers and wire services reported his response to the announcement of the Golden Fleece Award. Neither of those factors demonstrates that Hutchinson was a public figure prior to the controversy engendered by the Golden Fleece Award; his access, such as it was, came after the alleged libel.

On this record Hutchinson's activities and public profile are much like those of countless members of his profession. His published writings reach a relatively small category of professionals concerned with research in human behavior. To the extent the subject of his published writings became a matter of controversy it was a consequence of the Golden Fleece Award. Clearly those charged with defamation cannot, by their own conduct, create their own defense by making the claimant a public figure. [Citation.]

Hutchinson did not thrust himself or his views into public controversy to influence others. Respondents have not identified such a particular controversy; at most, they point to concern about general public expenditures. But that concern is shared by most and relates to most public expenditures; it is not sufficient to make Hutchinson a public figure. If it were, everyone who received or benefited from the myriad public grants for research could be classified as a public figure—a conclusion that our previous opinions have rejected. The "use of such subject-matter classifications to determine the extent of constitutional protection afforded defamatory falsehoods may too often result in an improper balance between the competing interests in this area." [Citation.]

Moreover, Hutchinson at no time assumed any role of public prominence in the broad question of concern about expenditures. Neither his applications for federal grants nor his publications in professional journals can be said to have invited that degree of public attention and comment on his receipt of federal grants essential to meet the public figure level.

* * *

Finally, we cannot agree that Hutchinson had such access to the media that he should be classified as a public figure. Hutchinson's access was limited to responding to the announcement of the Golden Fleece Award. He did not have the regular and continuing access to the media that is one of the accouterments of having become a public figure.

* * *

Reversed and remanded.

Invasion of Privacy

NADER v. GENERAL MOTORS CORP.

(1970) 25 N.Y.2d 560, 307 N.Y.S.2d 647, 255 N.E.2d 765.

FULD, C. J.

On this appeal, taken by permission of the Appellate Division on a certified question, we are called upon to determine the reach of the tort of invasion of privacy as it exists under the law of the District of Columbia.

The complaint, in this action by Ralph Nader, pleads four causes of action against the appellant, General Motors Corporation, and three other defendants allegedly acting as its agents. The first two causes of action charge an invasion of privacy, the third is predicated on the intentional infliction of severe emotional distress and the fourth on interference with the plaintiff's economic advantage. This appeal concerns only the legal sufficiency of the first two causes of action, which were upheld in the courts below as against the appellant's motion to dismiss * * *.

The plaintiff, an author and lecturer on automotive safety, has, for some years, been an articulate and severe critic of General

Motors' products from the standpoint of safety and design. According to the complaint—which, for present purposes, we must assume to be true—the appellant, having learned of the imminent publication of the plaintiff's book "Unsafe at any Speed," decided to conduct a campaign of intimidation against him in order to "suppress plaintiff's criticism of and prevent his disclosure of information" about its products. To that end, the appellant authorized and directed the other defendants to engage in a series of activities which, the plaintiff claims in his first two causes of action, violated his right to privacy.

Specifically, the plaintiff alleges that the appellant's agents (1) conducted a series of interviews with acquaintances of the plaintiff, "questioning them about, and casting aspersions upon [his] political, social * * * racial and religious views * * *; his integrity; his sexual proclivities and inclinations; and his personal habits"; (2) kept him under surveillance in public places for an unreasonable length of time; (3) caused him to be accosted by girls for the purpose of entrapping him into illicit relationships; (4) made threatening, harassing and obnoxious telephone calls to him; (5) tapped his telephone and eavesdropped, by means of mechanical and electronic equipment, on his private conversations with others; and (6) conducted a "continuing" and harassing investigation of him.

* * *

Turning, then, to the law of the District of Columbia, it appears that its courts have not only recognized a common-law action for invasion of privacy but have broadened the scope of that tort beyond its traditional limits. [Citations.] Thus, in the most recent of its cases on the subject, [citation], the Federal Court of Appeals for the District of Columbia declared:

We approve the extension of the tort of invasion of privacy to instances of *intrusion,* whether by physical trespass or not, into spheres from which an ordinary man in a plaintiff's position could reasonably expect that the particular defendant should be excluded.

It is this form of invasion of privacy—initially termed "intrusion" by Dean Prosser in 1960 [citation]—on which the two challenged causes of action are predicated.

Quite obviously, some intrusions into one's private sphere are inevitable concomitants of life in an industrial and densely populated society, which the law does not seek to proscribe even if it were possible to do so. "The law does not provide a remedy for every annoyance that occurs in everyday life." (Kelley v. Post Pub. Co., 327 Mass. 275, 278, 98 N.E.2d 286, 287.) However, the District of Columbia courts have held that the law should and does protect against certain types of intrusive conduct, and we must, therefore, determine whether the plaintiff's allegations are actionable as violations of the right to privacy.

* * *

The classic article by Warren and Brandeis (The Right to Privacy, 4 Harv.L.Rev. 193) * * * was premised, to a large extent, on principles originally developed in the field of copyright law. The authors thus based their thesis on a right granted by the common law to "each individual * * * of determining, ordinarily, to what extent his thoughts, sentiments and emotions shall be communicated to others" (4 Harv.L.Rev., at p. 198). Their principal concern appeared to be not with a broad "right to be let alone" [citation] but, rather, with the right to protect oneself from having one's private affairs known to others and to keep secret or intimate facts about oneself from the prying eyes or ears of others.

* * *

Quoting from the Restatement, Torts (§ 867), the [District of Columbia] court * * * has declared that "[l]iability attaches to a person 'who unreasonably and seriously interferes with another's interest in *not having his affairs known to others.*' "

It should be emphasized that the mere gathering of information about a particular individual does not give rise to a cause of action under this theory. Privacy is invaded only if the information sought is of a confidential nature and the defendant's conduct was unreasonably intrusive. Just as a common-law copyright is lost when material is published, so, too, there can be no invasion of privacy where the information sought is open to public view or has been voluntarily revealed to others. [Citations.]

In order to sustain a cause of action for invasion of privacy, therefore, the plaintiff must show that the appellant's conduct was truly "intrusive" and that it was designed to elicit information which would not be available through normal inquiry or observation.

The majority of the Appellate Division in the present case stated that *all of "[t]he activities complained of"* in the first two counts constituted actionable invasions of privacy under the law of the District of Columbia [citation]. We do not agree with that sweeping determination. At most, only two of the activities charged to the appellant are, in our view, actionable as invasions of privacy.

* * *

Turning, then, to the particular acts charged in the complaint, we cannot find any basis for a claim of invasion of privacy, under District of Columbia law, in the allegations that the appellant, through its agents or employees, interviewed many persons who knew the plaintiff, asking questions about him and casting aspersions on his character. Although those inquiries may have uncovered information of a personal nature, it is difficult to see how they may be said to have invaded the plaintiff's privacy. Information about the plaintiff

which was already known to others could hardly be regarded as private to the plaintiff. Presumably, the plaintiff had previously revealed the information to such other persons, and he would necessarily assume the risk that a friend or acquaintance in whom he had confided might breach the confidence. If, as alleged, the questions tended to disparage the plaintiff's character, his remedy would seem to be by way of an action for defamation, not for breach of his right to privacy. [Citation.]

* * * the complaint contains allegations concerning other activities by the appellant or its agents which do satisfy the requirements for such a cause of action. The one which most clearly meets those requirements is the charge that the appellant and its codefendants engaged in unauthorized wiretapping and eavesdropping by mechanical and electronic means.

* * *

There are additional allegations that the appellant hired people to shadow the plaintiff and keep him under surveillance. In particular, he claims that, on one occasion, one of its agents followed him into a bank, getting sufficiently close to him to see the denomination of the bills he was withdrawing from his account. From what we have already said, it is manifest that the mere observation of the plaintiff in a public place does not amount to an invasion of his privacy. But, under certain circumstances, surveillance may be so "overzealous" as to render it actionable. [Citation.] Whether or not the surveillance in the present case falls into this latter category will depend on the nature of the proof. A person does not automatically make public everything he does merely by being in a public place, and the mere fact that Nader was in a bank did not give anyone the right to try to discover the amount of money he was withdrawing. On the other hand, if the plaintiff acted in such a way as to reveal that fact to any casual observer, then, it may not be said that the appellant intruded into his private sphere. In any event, though, it is enough for present purposes to say that the surveillance allegation is not insufficient as a matter of law.

The order appealed from should be affirmed, with costs, and the question certified answered in the affirmative.

Defense of Property

KATKO v. BRINEY

(1971, Iowa) 183 N.W.2d 657.

MOORE, C. J.

The primary issue presented here is whether an owner may protect personal property in an unoccupied boarded-up farm house against trespassers and thieves by a spring gun capable of inflicting death or serious injury.

We are not here concerned with a man's right to protect his home and members of his family. Defendants' home was several miles from the scene of the incident to which we refer * * *.

Plaintiff's action is for damages resulting from serious injury caused by a shot from a 20-gauge spring shotgun set by defendants in a bedroom of an old farm house which had been uninhabited for several years. Plaintiff and his companion, Marvin McDonough, had broken and entered the house to find and steal old bottles and dated fruit jars which they considered antiques.

* * * The jury returned a verdict for plaintiff and against defendants for $20,000 actual and $10,000 punitive damages. [The defendants appealed.]

Most of the facts are not disputed. In 1957 defendant Bertha L. Briney inherited her parents' farm land in Mahaska and Monroe Counties. Included was an 80-acre tract in southwest Mahaska County where her grandparents and parents had lived. No one occupied the house thereafter. Her husband, Edward, attempted to care for the land. He kept no farm machinery thereon. The outbuildings became dilapidated.

For about 10 years, 1957 to 1967, there occurred a series of trespassing and housebreaking events with loss of some household items, the breaking of windows and "messing up of the property in general." The latest occurred June 8, 1967, prior to the event on July 16, 1967, herein involved.

Defendants through the years boarded up the windows and doors in an attempt to stop the intrusions. They had posted "no trespass" signs on the land several years before 1967. The nearest one was 35 feet from the house. On June 11, 1967, defendants set "a shotgun trap" in the north bedroom. After Mr. Briney cleaned and oiled his 20-gauge shotgun, the power of which he was well aware, defendants took it to the old house where they secured it to an iron bed with the barrel pointed at the bedroom door. It was rigged with wire from the doorknob to the gun's trigger so it would fire when the door was opened. Briney first pointed the gun so an intruder would be hit in the stomach but at Mrs. Briney's suggestion it was lowered to hit the legs. He admitted he did so "because I was mad and tired of being tormented" but "he did not intend to injure anyone". He gave no explanation of why he used a loaded shell and set it to hit a person already in the house. Tin was nailed over the bedroom window. The spring gun could not be seen from the outside. No warning of its presence was posted.

Plaintiff lived with his wife and worked regularly as a gasoline station attendant in Eddyville, seven miles from the old house. He had observed it for several years while hunting in the area and considered it as being abandoned. He knew it had long been uninhabited. In 1967 the area around the house was covered with high weeds. Prior to July 16, 1967, plaintiff and McDonough had been to the premises and found several old bottles and fruit jars which they took and added to their collection of antiques. On the latter date about 9:30 p.m. they made a second trip to the Briney property. They entered the old house by removing a board from a porch window which was without glass. While McDonough was looking around the kitchen area plaintiff went to another part of the house. As he started to open the north bedroom door the shotgun went off striking him in the right leg above the ankle bone. Much of his leg, including part of the tibia, was blown away. Only by McDonough's assistance was plaintiff able to get out of the house and after crawling some distance was put in his vehicle and rushed to a doctor and then to a hospital. He remained in the hospital 40 days.

Plaintiff's doctor testified he seriously considered amputation but eventually the healing process was successful. Some weeks after his release from the hospital plaintiff returned to work on crutches. He was required to keep the injured leg in a cast for approximately a year and wear a special brace for another year. He continued to suffer pain during this period.

There was undenied medical testimony plaintiff had a permanent deformity, a loss of tissue, and a shortening of the leg.

The record discloses plaintiff to trial time had incurred $710 medical expense, $2056.85 for hospital service, $61.80 for orthopedic service and $750 as loss of earnings. In addition thereto the trial court submitted to the jury the question of damages for pain and suffering and for future disability.

* * *

The main thrust of defendants' defense in the trial court and on this appeal is that "the law permits use of a spring gun in a dwelling or warehouse for the purpose of preventing the unlawful entry of a burglar or thief." * * *

In the statement of issues the trial court stated plaintiff and his companion committed a felony when they broke and entered defendants' house. In instruction 2 the court referred to the early case history of the use of spring guns and stated under the law their use was prohibited except to prevent the commission of felonies of violence and where human life is in danger. The instruction included a statement breaking and entering is not a felony of violence.

Instruction 5 stated: "You are hereby instructed that one may use reasonable force in the protection of his property, but such right is subject to the qualification that one may not use such means of force as will take human life or inflict great bodily injury. Such is the rule even though the injured party is a trespasser and is in violation of the law himself."

Instruction 6 stated: "An owner of premises is prohibited from willfully or intentionally injuring a trespasser by means of force that either takes life or inflicts great bodily injury; and therefore a person owning a premise is prohibited from setting out 'spring guns' and like dangerous devices which will likely take life or inflict great bodily injury, for the purpose of harming trespassers. The fact that the trespasser may be acting in violation of the law does not change the rule. The only time when such conduct of setting a 'spring gun' or a like dangerous device is justified would be when the trespasser was committing a felony of violence or a felony punishable by death, or where the trespasser was endangering human life by his act."

* * *

The overwhelming weight of authority, both textbook and case law, supports the trial court's statement of the applicable principles of law.

Prosser on Torts, Third Edition, pages 116–118, states:

"* * * the law has always placed a higher value upon human safety than upon mere rights in property, it is the accepted rule that there is no privilege to use any force calculated to cause death or serious bodily injury to repel the threat to land or chattels, unless there is also such a threat to the defendant's personal safety as to justify a self-defense. * * * spring guns and other man-killing devices are not justifiable against a mere trespasser, or even a petty thief. They are privileged only against those upon whom the landowner, if he were present in person would be free to inflict injury of the same kind."

Restatement of Torts, section 85, page 180, states: "The value of human life and limb, not only to the individual concerned but also to society, so outweighs the interest of a possessor of land in excluding from it those whom he is not willing to admit thereto that a possessor of land has, as is stated in § 79, no privilege to use force intended or likely to cause death or serious harm against another whom the possessor sees about to enter his premises or meddle with his chattel, unless the intrusion threatens death or serious bodily harm to the occupiers or users of the premises. * * *

Judgment affirmed.

Problems

1. The Penguin intentionally hits Batman with his umbrella. Batman, stunned by the blow, falls backwards, knocking Robin down. Robin's leg is broken in the fall, and he cried out, "Holy broken bat bones! My leg is broken." Who, if anyone, has liability to Robin? Why?

2. Push, while walking down an extremely crowded sidewalk, deliberately but not discourteously or harshly, pushes against B in order to pass her. B sues Push for battery. What result?

3. For the purpose of frightening N. C. Kure, Bob comes up behind Kure in the desert and sounds a buzzer which is an excellent imitation of a rattlesnake. Kure, believing that he is about to be bitten, is frightened, but suffers no bodily harm. May Kure recover from Bob for (a) the tort of assault? (b) the tort of intentional infliction of mental distress?

4. A kisses B while she is asleep but does not waken or harm her. B sues A for battery. Decision?

5. Cole Lect, a creditor, seeking to collect a debt, calls on Over Due and demands payment in a rude and insolent manner. When Due says that he cannot pay, Cole calls Due a deadbeat and says that he will never trust Due again. Is Cole liable to Due? If so, for what tort?

6. A, a 10-year old child, is run over by a car negligently driven by B. A, at the time of the accident, was acting reasonably and without negligence. C, a newspaper reporter, photographs A while she is lying in the street in great pain. Two years later, D, the publisher of a newspaper, prints C's picture of A in his newspaper as a lead to an article concerning the negligence of children. The caption under the picture reads: "They ask to be killed." A, who has recovered from the accident, brings suit against C and D. What result?

7. In 1963 the Saturday Evening Post featured an article entitled "The Story of a College Football Fix," characterized in the sub-title as "A Shocking Report of How Wally Butts and Bear Bryant Rigged a Game Last Fall." Butts was athletic director of the University of Georgia and Bryant was head coach of the University of Alabama. The article was based on a claim by one George Burnett that he had accidentally overheard a long distance telephone conversation between Butts and Bryant in the course of which Butts divulged information on plays Georgia would use in the upcoming game against Alabama. The writer assigned to the story by the Post was not a football expert and did not interview either Butts or Bryant, nor did he personally see the notes Burnett had made of the telephone conversation. Butts admitted that he had a long distance telephone conversation with Bryant but denied that any advance information on prospective football plays was given. Butts brought a libel suit against the Post. Decision?

8. A and B engage in an altercation. Infuriated with B's conduct, A writes a defamatory letter to B but leaves it on his desk. The letter is in plain sight and can easily be seen by the numerous people who pass by A's desk. C and D, without permission from A, read the letter. B brings a suit against A for defamation. Decision?

9. A is a patient confined in a hospital with a rare disease that is of great interest to public. B, a television reporter, requests A to consent to an interview. A refuses, but B nonetheless enters A's room over her objection and photographs her. A brings a suit against B. Decision?

10. Prop T. Owner has a place on his land where he piles trash. The pile has been there for a period of three months. John, a neighbor of Owner, without Prop's consent or knowledge, throws trash onto the trashpile. Prop learns that John has done this and sues him. What tort, if any, has John committed?

11. A builds an irrigation ditch which causes water to back up onto B's property. B brings a cause of action against A. Decision?

12. Chris leaves his car parked in front of a store. There are no signs that say Chris cannot park there. The store owner, however, needs the car moved to enable a delivery truck to unload. He releases the brake and pushes Chris's car three or four feet, doing no harm to the car. Chris returns and sees that his car has been moved and is very angry. He threatens to sue the store owner for trespass of his personal property. Can he recover?

13. N. O. Carr borrowed John's brand new Ford Pinto for the purpose of going to the store. He told John he would be right back. N. O. then decided, however, to go to the beach while he had the car. Can John recover from N. O. the value of the automobile? If so, for what tort?

TORTS:
NEGLIGENCE
AND STRICT
LIABILITY

The failure to exercise reasonable care under the circumstances for the safety of another person or his property, which proximately causes injury to such person or damage to his property, or both, is the basis of liability for negligence. All types and forms of liability are either (1) voluntarily assumed, as by contract, or (2) involuntarily imposed by law independent of contract. Negligence and strict liability are of the second type. Strict liability is not based upon negligence or intent, but rather upon the nature of the activity of a person which causes personal injury to another or damage to his property. Both negligence and strict liability are the subject matter of this chapter.

NEGLIGENCE

The Restatement of Torts, Second, Section 282, defines negligence as "conduct which falls below the standard established by law for the protection of others against unreasonable risk of harm." The standard established by law is the conduct of a reason-able man acting prudently and with due care under the circumstances. Negligence involves conduct that creates an unreasonable risk of harm, whereas intentional torts deal with conduct that has a substantial certainty of causing harm. Thus, if the driver of an automobile runs down a person intending to do so, he has committed the intentional tort of battery. However, if the driver hits and injures a person while driving unreasonably for the safety of others, he is negligent.

A person is not liable for injury caused to another by an unavoidable accident, which Prosser defines as "an occurrence which was not intended, and which, under all the circumstances, could not have been foreseen or prevented by the exercise of reasonable precautions." Thus, no liability results from the sudden loss of control of an automobile because the driver is suddenly and unforeseeably stricken with a heart attack, stroke, or fainting spell. If the driver, however, had warning of the imminent heart attack or other infirmity, it would be negligent for him to drive at all.

An action for negligence consists of four elements, each of which must be proved by the plaintiff:

1. a legal duty requiring the defendant to conform to the standard of conduct established by law for the protection of others,
2. a failure of the defendant to conform to the required standard of conduct,
3. that the injury and harm sustained by the plaintiff was proximately caused by defendant's failure to conform to the required standard of conduct, and
4. that the extent and amount of loss and money damages sustained by the plaintiff was by reason of the defendant's conduct.

DUTY OF CARE

Reasonable Man Standard

The duty of care imposed by law is measured by the degree of carefulness which a reasonable man would exercise in a given situation. The reasonable man is a fictitious character who is always careful, prudent, and never negligent. What the judge or jury determines that a reasonable man would have done in the light of the facts brought out by the evidence in a particular case sets the standard of conduct for that case. The reasonable man standard is external and objective, as described by Justice Holmes:

If, for instance, a man is born hasty and awkward, is always hurting himself or his neighbors, no doubt his congenital defects will be allowed for in the courts of Heaven, but his slips are no less troublesome to his neighbors than if they sprang from guilty neglect. His neighbors accordingly require him, at his peril, to come up to their standard, and the courts which they establish decline to take his personal equation into account. Holmes, *The Common Law.*

Children. "If the actor is a child, the standard of conduct to which he must conform to avoid being negligent is that of a reason-able person of like age, intelligence, and experience under like circumstances." Restatement, Torts, Second, Section 283A. The law applies an individualized test because children are incapable of exercising the judgment, intelligence, knowledge, and experience of an adult. Moreover, children as a general rule do not engage in activities entailing high risk to others and their conduct does not involve the same magnitude of harm. However, a child who engages in an adult activity, such as flying an airplane or driving a boat or car, is held to the standard of care applicable to adults.

Physical Disability. If the defendant is ill or otherwise physically disabled, the standard of conduct to which he must conform to avoid being negligent is that of a reasonable man under like disability. The reasonable man is viewed as having the same physical characteristics as the defendant. Thus, a blind man must act as a reasonable man who is blind.

Mental Deficiency. The law makes no allowance for the insanity or other mental deficiency of the defendant in a negligence case. The Restatement, Torts, Second, Section 283B, justifies this rule as follows:

1. The difficulty of drawing any satisfactory line between mental deficiency and those variations of temperament, intellect, and emotional balance which cannot, as a practical matter, be taken into account in imposing liability for damage done.
2. The unsatisfactory character of the evidence of mental deficiency in many cases, together with the ease with which it can be feigned, the difficulties which the triers of fact must encounter in determining its existence, nature, degree, and effect, * * *
3. The feeling that if mental defectives are to live in the world, they should pay for the damage they do, and that it is better that their wealth, if any, should be used to compensate innocent victims than that it should remain in their hands.

4. The belief that their liability will mean that those who have charge of them or their estates will be stimulated to look after them, keep them in order, and see that they do not do harm.

Superior Skill or Knowledge. Persons who are qualified and who practice a profession or trade which requires special skill and expertise are required to exercise that care and skill which are normally possessed by members of their profession or trade. This standard applies to such professionals as physicians, surgeons, dentists, attorneys, pharmacists, architects, accountants, and engineers, and to such skilled trades as airline pilots, electricians, carpenters, and plumbers. If a member of a profession or skilled trade possesses greater skill than that common to the profession or trade, he is required to exercise that skill.

Emergencies. In determining whether a defendant's conduct is reasonable, the fact that he was at the time confronted with a sudden emergency is taken into consideration. Restatement, Torts, Second, Section 296. An emergency is a sudden, unexpected event which calls for immediate action and does not permit considered reflection. The standard is still that of a reasonable man under the circumstances— the emergency is simply part of the circumstances. However, an emergency is not helpful to a defendant if his own negligent or tortious conduct created the emergency.

Violation of Statute

The reasonable man standard of conduct may be established by legislation. Restatement, Torts, Second, Section 285. Some statutes expressly impose civil liability upon violators. Absent such a provision, courts may adopt the requirements of the statute as the standard of conduct required to avoid liability for negligence. The Restatement, Torts, Second, Section 286, provides:

The court may adopt as the standard of conduct of a reasonable man the requirements of a legislative enactment or an administrative regulation whose purpose is found to be exclusively or in part

(a) to protect a class of persons which includes the one whose interest is invaded, and

(b) to protect the particular interest which is invaded, and

(c) to protect that interest against the kind of harm which has resulted, and

(d) to protect that interest against the particular hazard from which the harm results.

The Supreme Court of North Carolina has stated:

It is well settled law in this jurisdiction that when a statute imposes upon a person a specific duty for the protection of others, a violation of such statute is negligence per se. Of course, to make out a case of actionable negligence the additional essential element of proximate cause is required. Lutz Industries v. Dixie Home Stores, 242 N.C. 332, 88 S.E.2d 333 (1955).

Duty of Affirmative Action

Absent special circumstances, no one is under an affirmative duty to aid another in peril. As Prosser has explained, "[b]ecause of [the] reluctance to countenance 'nonfeasance' as a basis of liability, the law has persistently refused to recognize the moral obligation of common decency and common humanity, to come to the aid of another human being who is in danger, even though the outcome is to cost him his life." For example, A, an adult standing along the edge of a steep cliff, observes a baby carriage with a crying infant in it slowly heading toward the edge and certain doom. A could easily prevent the baby's fall at no risk to his own safety. Nonetheless, A does nothing and the baby falls to its death. A is under no legal duty to act and therefore incurs no liability for failing to do so.

Section 314 of the Restatement, Torts, Second, reflects this position: "The fact that the actor realizes or should realize that action on his part is necessary for another's aid or protection does not of itself impose upon him a duty to take such action." However, special relations between the parties may exist that impose a duty upon the defendant to aid or protect the other. Thus, if in the example above, A were the baby's parent or babysitter, A would be under a duty to act and would therefore be liable for not taking action. The special relations giving rise to the duty to aid or protect another include: common carrier—passenger, innkeeper—guest, employer—employee, parent—child, and husband—wife.

A duty of affirmative action is also imposed upon those whose conduct, whether tortious or innocent, has injured another and left him helpless and in danger of further harm. For example, A drives his car into B who is rendered unconscious. A leaves B lying in the middle of the road where he is run over by a second car driven by C. A is liable to B for the additional injuries inflicted by C. Moreover, a person incurs a duty to exercise care by voluntarily coming to the assistance of another in need of aid. In such instance, the actor is liable if his failure to exercise reasonable care increases the risk of harm, causes harm to be suffered by reliance upon the undertaking, or leaves the other in a worse position. For example, A finds B drunk and stumbling along a dark sidewalk. A leads B halfway up a steep and unguarded stairway where he abandons B. B attempts to climb the stairs but trips and falls, suffering serious injury. A is liable to B for having left him in a worse position.

Special Duties of Possessors of Land

Duty to Trespassers. A trespasser is a person who enters or remains on the land of another without permission or privilege to do so. The lawful possessor of the land is not liable to trespassers for his failure to maintain the land in a reasonably safe condition. However, the trespasser is not a criminal, and the lawful possessor is not free to inflict intentional injury upon him. Some courts have held that the lawful possessor is required to exercise reasonable care for the safety of the trespasser upon discovery of his presence on the land.

The law, however, extends greater protection to a child who trespasses by imposing upon a possessor of land the liability for physical harm caused by artificial conditions upon the land if:

(a) the place where the condition exists is one upon which the possessor knows or has reason to know that children are likely to trespass, and

(b) the condition is one of which the possessor knows or has reason to know and which he realizes or should realize will involve an unreasonable risk of death or serious bodily harm to such children, and

(c) the children because of their youth do not discover the condition or realize the risk involved in intermeddling with it or in coming within the area made dangerous by it, and

(d) the utility to the possessor of maintaining the condition and the burden of eliminating the danger are slight as compared with the risk to children involved, and

(e) the possessor fails to exercise reasonable care to eliminate the danger or otherwise to protect the children. Restatement, Torts, Second, Section 339.

Duty to Licensees. A licensee is a person who is privileged to enter or remain upon land only by virtue of the consent of the lawful possessor. Restatement, Torts, Second, Section 330. Licensees include members of the possessor's household and social guests. A licensee will become a trespasser if he enters a portion of the land to which he is not invited or remains upon the land after his invitation has expired.

The possessor owes a higher duty of care to licensees than to trespassers. The

Restatement, Torts, Second, Section 342 provides:

A possessor of land is subject to liability for physical harm caused to licensees by a condition on the land if, but only if,

(a) the possessor knows or has reason to know of the condition and should realize that it involves an unreasonable risk of harm to such licensees, and should expect that they will not discover or realize the danger, and

(b) he fails to exercise reasonable care to make the condition safe, or to warn the licensees of the condition and the risk involved, and

(c) the licensees do not know or have reason to know of the condition and the risk involved.

Duty to Invitees. An invitee is either a public invitee or a business visitor. A person who enters upon land which is open to the public, such as a public park, beach, swimming pool, or governmental facility where business with the public is transacted openly (e.g., a post office or office of the Recorder of Deeds) is a public invitee. A business visitor is a person who enters upon the premises to engage in private business, such as one who enters a store with the expectation of purchasing goods or a workman who enters a residence to make repairs.

The duty of the possessor of land to invitees with respect to the condition of the premises is that he is liable to an invitee for physical harm caused thereby if, and only if, he

(a) knows or by the exercise of reasonable care would discover the condition, and should realize that it involves an unreasonable risk of harm to such invitees, and

(b) should expect that they will not discover or realize the danger, or will fail to protect themselves against it, and

(c) fails to exercise reasonable care to protect them against the danger. Restatement, Torts, Second, Section 343.

For example, A Supermarket has in its store a large glass front door, which is well lighted and plainly visible. B, a customer, mistakes the glass for an open doorway and walks into the glass injuring himself. A is not liable to B. If, on the other hand, the glass was difficult to see and it was foreseeable that a person might mistake the glass for an open doorway, then A would be liable to B if B crashed into the glass while exercising reasonable care.

Res Ipsa Loquitur

A rule has developed which permits the jury to infer both negligent conduct and causation from the mere occurrence of certain types of events. This rule is called *res ipsa loquitur,* which means "the thing speaks for itself." Section 328D of the Restatement, Torts, Second, provides as follows:

(1) It may be inferred that harm suffered by the plaintiff is caused by negligence of the defendant when

(a) the event is of a kind which ordinarily does not occur in the absence of negligence;

(b) other responsible causes, including the conduct of the plaintiff and third persons, are sufficiently eliminated by the evidence; and

(c) the indicated negligence is within the scope of the defendant's duty to the plaintiff.

The doctrine originated in an 1863 English case in which a barrel of flour rolled out of a warehouse window and landed upon a pedestrian.

PROXIMATE CAUSE

One of the requirements of imposing liability for the negligent conduct of a defendant is that it not only caused injury to the plaintiff, but that it was the proximate cause of the injury. Referring to proximate cause, Dean Prosser has stated, "[t]here is perhaps nothing in the entire field of law which has called forth more disagreement, or upon which the opinions are in such a welter of confusion." Most simply expressed, proximate cause consists of the judicially imposed limitations upon a person's liability for the consequences of his negligence. As a matter of social policy, legal responsibility has not been permitted to follow all the consequences of a negligent act. Responsibility has been limited to those persons and results which are closely connected with the negligent conduct.

Causation in Fact

In order to support a finding that the defendant's negligence was the proximate cause of the plaintiff's injury, it is first necessary that defendant's conduct was the actual cause or had a causal relation to the injury. A widely applied test for causation in fact is the 'but for" or "sine qua non" rule: A person's conduct is a cause of an event if the event would not have occurred *but for* the person's negligent conduct. Under this test, an act or omission to act is *not* a cause of an event if that event would have occurred regardless of the act or omission. For instance, A fails to erect a barrier around an excavation. B is driving a truck when its accelerator becomes stuck. A's negligence is not a cause in fact of B's death if the runaway truck would have crashed through the barrier even it it had been erected. Similarly, failure to install a proper fire escape to a hotel is not the cause in fact of the death of a person who is suffocated in bed by the smoke.

The "but for" test is not useful where there are two or more forces actively operating, each of which is sufficient to bring about the harm in question. For example, A stabs C with a knife while B fractures C's skull with a rock. Either wound would be fatal and C dies from both. Under the "but for" test, either A or B, or both, could argue that C would have died from the wound inflicted by the other and therefore he is not liable. The "substantial factor" test addresses this problem: "[t]he actor's negligent conduct is a legal cause of harm to another if his conduct is a substantial factor in bringing about the harm * * *" Restatement, Torts, Second, Section 431. Under this test the conduct of either A or B would be found to be a cause in fact of C's death.

Limitations upon Causation in Fact

As a matter of policy, the law imposes limitations upon the causal connection between the defendant's negligence and the plaintiff's injury. Two of the factors that it takes into consideration in the determination of such limitation are (a) unforeseeable consequences and (b) superseding causes.

Unforeseeable Consequences. The liability of a negligent defendant for unforeseeable consequences has proven to be troublesome and controversial. The Restatement has adopted the following position:

(1) If the actor's conduct is a substantial factor in bringing about harm to another, the fact that the actor neither foresaw nor should have foreseen the extent of the harm or the manner in which it occurred does not prevent him from being liable.

(2) The actor's conduct may be held not to be a legal cause of harm to another where after the event and looking back from the harm to the actor's negligent conduct, it appears to the court highly extraordinary that it should have brought about the harm. Section 435.

Proximate cause involves a recognition of the risk of harm to the plaintiff individually or to a class of persons of which the plaintiff is a member. If the defendant's conduct is a cause in fact of harm to a person of another class, to which the defendant could not have reasonably anticipated injury, the defendant is not liable to such persons. Restatement, Torts, Second, Section 281, Comment c.

For example, A, while negligently driving an automobile, collides with a car which is carrying dynamite. A is unaware of the contents of the other car and had no reason to know about it. The collision causes the dynamite to explode, shattering glass in a building a block away. The shattered glass injures B, who was inside the building. The explosion also injures C, who was walking on the sidewalk near the collision. A would be liable to C because A should have realized that his negligent driving might result in a collision that would endanger pedestrians nearby and the fact that the actual harm resulted in an unforeseeable manner does not affect his liability. B, however, was beyond the zone of danger and A, accordingly, is not liable to B. A's negligent driving is not deemed to be the "proximate cause" of B's injury because, looking back from the harm to A's negligence, it appears highly extraordinary that A's conduct should have brought about the harm to B.

The majority of the courts have taken the Restatement's view of proximate cause, which is enunciated in the classic case of Palsgraf v. Long Island R.R. at page 111.

Superseding Cause. A superseding cause is an intervening event or act which occurs subsequently to the defendant's negligent conduct and relieves him of liability for harm to the plaintiff caused in fact by both the defendant's negligence and the *intervening* event or act. Section 442 of the Restatement, Torts, Second, provides the following list of considerations that are of importance in determining whether an intervening force is a superseding cause that relieves the defendant of liability:

(a) the fact that its intervention brings about harm different in kind from that which would otherwise have resulted from the actor's negligence;

(b) the fact that its operation or the consequences thereof appear after the event to be extraordinary rather than normal in view of the circumstances existing at the time of its operation;

(c) the fact that the intervening force is operating independently of any situation created by the actor's negligence, or, on the other hand, is or is not a normal result of such a situation;

(d) the fact that the operation of the intervening force is due to a third person's act or to his failure to act;

(e) the fact that the intervening force is due to an act of a third person which is wrongful toward the other and as such subjects the third person to liability to him;

(f) the degree of culpability of a wrongful act of a third person which sets the intervening force in motion.

For example, A negligently runs down a cow which is left lying stunned in the road. Several minutes later the cow regains consciousness, takes fright, and charges into B, a bystander. The cow's conduct is an intervening, but not a superseding, cause of harm to B because it is a normal consequence of the situation caused by A's negligence. In contrast, A negligently leaves an excavation in a public sidewalk into which B intentionally hurls C. A is not liable to C because B's conduct is a superseding cause that relieves A of liability.

INJURY

The plaintiff must prove that the defendant's negligent conduct caused harm to a legally protected interest. Certain interests receive little or no protection from negligent interference, while others receive full protection. The extent of protection for a particular interest is determined by the courts as a matter of law on the basis of social policy and expediency. For example, negligent conduct that is the proximate cause of harmful contact with the person of another is actionable. Thus, if A negligently runs into B, a pedestrian, who is carefully crossing the street, A is liable for physical injuries sustained by B as a result of the collision. On the other hand, if A's careless driving causes only offensive contact with B's person, A is not liable. Negligently inflicted confinement of another is likewise not actionable if it is merely transitory but otherwise harmless. Thus, if A negligently locks B in a cold storage vault for several moments, A is not liable to B. If, however, A negligently locks B in the vault for several hours, A would be liable for any injury suffered by B.

The courts have traditionally been reluctant to allow recovery for negligently inflicted emotional distress. This view has gradually changed during this century and the majority of courts have adopted the Restatement's position:

(1) If the actor's conduct is negligent as violating a duty of care designed to protect another from a fright or other emotional disturbance which the actor should recognize as involving an unreasonable risk of bodily harm, the fact that the harm results solely through the internal operation of the fright or other emotional disturbance does not protect the actor from liability.

(2) If the actor's conduct is negligent as creating an unreasonable risk of causing bodily harm to another otherwise than by subjecting him to fright, shock, or other similar and immediate emotional disturbance, the fact that such harm results solely from the internal operation of fright or other emotional disturbance does not protect the actor from liability.

(3) The rule stated in Subsection (2) applies where the bodily harm to the other results from his shock or fright at harm or peril to a member of his immediate family occurring in his presence. Section 436.

If the defendant's conduct merely results in emotional disturbance without resultant bodily harm, the defendant is not liable. Restatement, Torts, Second, Section 436A.

DEFENSES

Although a plaintiff has established by the preponderance of the evidence, all the required elements of a negligence action, he may nevertheless be denied recovery if the defendant proves a valid defense. As a general rule, any defense to an intentional tort is also available in an action in negligence. In addition, there are defenses available in negligence cases that are not defenses to intentional torts.

Contributory Negligence

Contributory negligence is defined as "conduct on the part of the plaintiff which falls below the standard to which he should conform for his own protection, and which is a legally contributing cause co-operating with the negligence of the defendant in bringing about the plaintiff's harm." Restatement, Torts, Second, Section 463.

If negligence of the plaintiff in conjunction with negligence of the defendant proximately caused the injury and damage sustained by the plaintiff, at common law he cannot recover any damages from the defendant. It does not matter whether the plaintiff's contributory negligence was slight or extensive.

Notwithstanding the contributory negligence of the plaintiff, if the defendant had a last clear chance to avoid injury to him but did not avail himself of such chance, the contributory negligence of the plaintiff does not bar his recovery of damages.

The Restatement, Torts, Second, Section 479, provides:

A plaintiff who has negligently subjected himself to a risk of harm from the defendant's subsequent negligence may recover for harm caused thereby if, immediately preceding the harm,
(a) the plaintiff is unable to avoid it by the exercise of reasonable vigilance and care, and
(b) the defendant is negligent in failing to utilize with reasonable care and competence his then existing opportunity to avoid the harm, when he
(i) knows of the plaintiff's situation and realizes or has reason to realize the peril involved in it or
(ii) would discover the situation and thus have reason to realize the peril, if he were to exercise the vigilance which it is then his duty to the plaintiff to exercise.

For example, A negligently stops his car on the highway without lights. B, who is driving along, sees A's car in sufficient time to stop. However, B negligently puts his foot on the accelerator instead of the brake and runs into A's car. Because B had the last clear chance to stop his car before striking A's car, A's contributory negligence is inoperative.

Comparative Negligence

The harshness of the contributory negligence doctrine has caused an ever-increasing majority of the states to reject the all-or-nothing rule of contributory negligence and to substitute the doctrine of comparative negligence. Under comparative negligence, damages are apportioned between the parties in proportion to the degree of fault or negligence found against the parties. For instance, B negligently drives his automobile into A, who is crossing against the light. A sustains damages in the amount of $10,000 and sues B. If the trier of fact determines that B's negligence contributed 70% to A's injury and that A's contributory negligence contributed 30% to his injury, then A would recover $7,000.

The majority of states that have adopted the doctrine of comparative negligence have enacted statutes that do not permit the plaintiff any recovery if his contributory negligence was "as great as" or "greater than" that of the defendant.

Assumption of Risk

A plaintiff who has voluntarily assumed the risk of harm arising from the negligent or reckless conduct of the defendant cannot recover from such harm. Such assumption of risk or consent is expressed in the ancient maxim "Volenti non fit injuria" (to one who is willing no wrong is done).

Considerable confusion has arisen by reason of the use of the term "assumption of risk" in several different senses. Comment c to Section 496A of the Restatement,

Torts, Second, explains four of these meanings:

1. In its simplest form, assumption of risk means that the plaintiff has given his express consent to relieve the defendant of an obligation to exercise care for his protection, and agrees to take his chances as to injury from a known or possible risk. The result is that the defendant, who would otherwise be under a duty to exercise such care, is relieved of that responsibility, and is no longer under any duty to protect the plaintiff. * * *

2. A second, and closely related, meaning is that the plaintiff has entered voluntarily into some relation with the defendant which he knows to involve the risk, and so is regarded as tacitly or impliedly agreeing to relieve the defendant of responsibility, and to take his own chances. Thus a spectator entering a baseball park may be regarded as consenting that the players may proceed with the game without taking precautions to protect him from being hit by the ball. Again the legal result is that the defendant is relieved of his duty to the plaintiff. * * *

3. In a third type of situation the plaintiff, aware of a risk created by the negligence of the defendant, proceeds or continues voluntarily to encounter it. * * * The same policy of the common law which denies recovery to one who expressly consents to accept a risk will, however, prevent his recovery in such a case. * * *

4. To be distinguished from these three situations is the fourth, in which the plaintiff's conduct in voluntarily encountering a known risk is itself unreasonable, and amounts to contributory negligence. There is thus negligence on the part of both plaintiff and defendant; and the plaintiff is barred from recovery, not only by his implied consent to accept the risk, but also by the policy of the law which refuses to allow him to impose upon the defendant a loss for which his own negligence was in part responsible.

STRICT LIABILITY

The law imposes strict liability for harm or damage resulting from the carrying on of certain activities independently of the tort of intentional infliction of injury and of negligence. The areas of strict liability will be considered under the following headings: (1) Abnormally Dangerous Activities, (2) Keeping of Animals, (3) Products Liability, and (4) Common Carriers.

ABNORMALLY DANGEROUS ACTIVITIES

Strict liability is imposed for harm resulting from extraordinary, unusual, abnormal, or exceptional activities, as determined in light of the place, time, and manner in which the activity is conducted. Activities to which the rule has been applied include collecting water in such quantity and location as to make it dangerous; storing explosives or flammable liquids in large quantities; blasting or pile driving; crop dusting; drilling for or refining oil in populated areas; and emitting noxious gases or fumes into a settled community. On the other hand, courts have refused to apply the rule where the activity is a "natural" use of the land, such as drilling for oil in the oil fields of Texas, collecting water in a stock watering tank, and transmitting gas through a gas pipe or electricity in electric wiring.

Sections 519 and 520 of the Restatement, Torts, Second, impose strict liability for abnormally dangerous activities which are to be determined by considering the following six factors:

1. whether the activity involves a high degree of risk of some harm to the person, land, or chattels of others;
2. whether the gravity of the harm which may result from it is likely to be great;
3. whether the risk cannot be eliminated by the exercise of reasonable care;
4. whether the activity is not a matter of common usage;
5. whether the activity is inappropriate to the place where it is carried on; and
6. the value of the activity to the community.

KEEPING OF ANIMALS

Strict liability for harm caused by animals existed at common law and continues today with some modification. As a general rule, those who possess animals for their own purposes do so at their peril and must protect against harm to people, crops, or other animals.

Trespassing Animals

Keepers of animals are generally held liable for any damage done by their animals trespassing on the property of another. There are three exceptions to this rule: (a) keepers of cats and dogs are liable only for negligence; (b) keepers of animals are not strictly liable for animals straying from a highway on which they are being lawfully driven, although the owner may be liable for negligence if he fails to properly control them; and (c) keepers of farm animals, typically cattle, in some Western states are not strictly liable for harm caused by their trespassing animals which are allowed to freely graze.

Non-trespassing Animals

Keepers of dangerous animals are strictly liable for harm caused by such animals whether or not they are trespassing. Dangerous or wild animals are defined as those which in the particular region are known to be likely to inflict serious damage and cannot be considered safe no matter how domesticated. Animals included in this category are bears, lions, elephants, monkeys, tigers, deer, and raccoons.

Domestic animals are those which are traditionally devoted to the service of mankind and as a class are considered safe. Examples of domestic animals are dogs, cats, horses, cattle, sheep, bulls, and honey bees. Keepers of domestic animals are liable if they knew, or should have known, of the animal's dangerous propensity. The dangerous propensity of the animal must be the cause of the harm. A keeper is not liable for a dog which bites a human merely because he knows that the dog has a propensity to engage in combat with other dogs. On the other hand, if a person's 150-pound sheep dog has a propensity to enthusiastically jump on visitors, the animal's keeper would be liable for any damage done by the dog's playfulness.

PRODUCTS LIABILITY

A recent and important trend in the law is the imposition of strict liability upon manufacturers and merchants who sell goods in a defective condition unreasonably dangerous to the user or consumer. Restatement, Torts, Second, Section 402A. This section of the Restatement has been widely adopted and applied by the courts. Liability is imposed under Section 402A regardless of the seller's due care, and applies to all merchant sellers. This topic is covered in Chapter 25, Products Liability.

COMMON CARRIERS

A common carrier offers its services and facilities to the public upon terms and under circumstances which indicate that the offering is made indifferently to all persons and is not casual or individual in its character. One who carries the goods of another on isolated occasions, or one who serves a limited number of customers under individual long-term contracts without offering the same or similar contracts to the public at large, is a private or contract carrier—not a common carrier. At common law, if the goods are lost or damaged during carriage, the common carrier is liable in full for the loss or damage, notwithstanding that it has exercised due care or that the loss or damage was due to an unavoidable cause such as fire or theft.

There are five situations in which a common carrier is not subject to strict liability for loss or damage to goods it has accepted for transportation; namely, (1) Acts of God, (2) Acts of the Public Enemy, (3) Acts or Negligence of the Shipper, (4) Inherent Nature of the Goods, and (5) Acts of Public Authority.

Acts of God

A common carrier is not liable for loss or damage to goods in its possession for carriage caused by Acts of God such as lightning, earthquakes, sudden floods, tornadoes, hurricanes, or other sudden violent natural phenomena.

Acts of the Public Enemy

A common carrier is not liable for loss or damage to goods caused by the public enemy, meaning the military forces and troops of a hostile nation in time of war or invasion. This exception from liability does not apply to loss or damage to goods caused by mobs, rioters, or strikers, nor to the acts of lawless individuals such as robbers or burglars.

Acts or Negligence of the Shipper

If the shipper provides the common carrier with erroneous directions as to shipment of the goods, resulting in loss of the goods, the carrier is not liable. Likewise, if the goods are defectively packed by the shipper and as a result become damaged while in transit.

Inherent Nature of the Goods

If the goods deteriorate due to natural spoilage while in transit, not due to unjustifiable delay or negligence of the carrier, the carrier is not liable. However, some courts have held that a carrier which knows that the goods are of a kind which may spoil, notwithstanding reasonable precautions, should not accept the goods for transportation and that if it does, it is liable for the resulting loss.

Acts of Public Authority

If goods such as young trees for transplanting are shipped into a state which bans their importation, and the state seizes and destroys them, the carrier is not liable. Similarly, a shipper is not liable for shipping cattle, which are found upon inspection by state officials to have hoof and mouth disease and are promptly destroyed by the state.

When delay in the delivery of the goods by the carrier is caused by tardy inspection by public health officials or by customs officials, the carrier is not liable unless the delay was caused by its negligence.

Cases

Negligence

CALDWELL v. BECHTEL, INC.
(1980, C.A.D.C.) 631 F.2d 989.

MacKINNON, J.

We are here concerned with a claim for damages by a worker who allegedly contracted silicosis while he was mucking in a tunnel under construction as part of the metropolitan subway system [WMATA]. The basic issue is whether a consultant engineering firm owed the worker a duty to protect him against unreasonable risk of harm.

* * *

In attempting to convince the court that it owes no duty of reasonable care to protect appellant's safety, Bechtel argues that by its contract with WMATA it assumed duties only to WMATA. Appellant has not brought action, however, for breach of contract but rather seeks damages for an asserted breach of the duty of reasonable care. Unlike contractual duties, which are imposed by agreement of the parties to a contract, a duty of due care under tort law is based primarily upon social policy. The law imposes upon individuals certain expectations of conduct, such as the expectancy that their actions will not cause foreseeable injury to another. These societal expectations, as formed through the common law, comprise the concept of duty.

Society's expectations, and the concomitant duties imposed, vary in response to the activity engaged in by the defendant. If defendant is driving a car, he will be held to exercise the degree of care normally exercised by a reasonable person in like circumstances. Or if defendant is engaged in the practice of his profession, he will be held to exercise a degree of care consistent with his superior knowledge and skill. Hence, when defendant Bechtel engaged in consulting engineering services, the company was required to observe a standard of care ordinarily adhered to by one providing such services, possessing such skill and expertise.

A secondary but equally important principle involved in a determination of duty is to whom the duty is owed. The answer to this question is usually framed in terms of the foreseeable plaintiff, in other words, one who might foreseeably be injured by defendant's conduct. This secondary principle also serves to distinguish tort law from contract law. While in contract law, only one to whom the contract specifies that a duty be rendered will have a cause of action for its breach, in tort law, society, not the contract, specifies to whom the duty is owed, and this has traditionally been the foreseeable plaintiff.

It is important to keep these differences between contract and tort duties in mind when examining whether Bechtel's undertaking of contractual duties to WMATA created a duty of reasonable care toward Caldwell. Dean Prosser expressed the relationship in this terse fashion:

[B]y entering into a contract with A, the defendant may place himself in such a relation toward B that the law will impose upon him an obligation, sounding in tort and not in contract, to act in such a way that B will not be injured. The incidental fact of the existence of the contract with A does not negative the responsibility of the actor when he enters upon a course of affirmative conduct which may be expected to affect the interests of another person.

* * *

Analyzing the common law, Prosser noted that courts have found a duty to act for the protection of another when certain relationships exist, such as carrier—passenger, innkeeper—guest, shipper—seaman, employer—employee, shopkeeper—visitor, host—social guest, jailor—prisoner, and school—pupil. These holdings suggest that courts have been eroding the general rule that there is no duty to act to help another in distress, by creating exceptions based upon a relationship between the actors.

* * *

We find that case law provides many such analogous situations from which the principles deserving of application to this case may be culled. The foregoing concepts of duty converge in this case, as the facts include both the WMATA-Bechtel contractual relationship from which it was foreseeable that a negligent undertaking by Bechtel might injure the appellant, and a special relationship established between Bechtel and the appellant because of Bechtel's su-

perior skills, knowledge of the dangerous condition, and ability to protect appellant.

* * *

We reverse the summary judgment of the district court, and hold that as a matter of law, on the record as we are required to view it at this time, Bechtel owed Caldwell a duty of due care to take reasonable steps to protect him from the foreseeable risk of harm to his health posed by the excessive concentration of silica dust in the Metro tunnels. We remand so that Caldwell will have an opportunity to prove, if he can, the other elements of his negligence action.

Superior Skill

WAYNICK v. REARDON
(1952) 236 N.C. 116, 72 S.E.2d 4.

Civil action to recover damages for alleged injury caused by the negligence of the defendants.

For convenience in narration, the defendant, Marc J. Reardon, will be referred to in the statement of facts and in the opinion as Dr. Reardon, and the term, Duke Hospital, will be used to designate the hospital service of the defendant, Duke University, Inc., and will include within its scope said corporate defendant.

On August 18, 1947, plaintiff, suffering with fallen arches and pain in his feet, entered the orthopedic clinic of Duke Hospital, where he received shoe supports and instructions to use specified home treatments. He was requested to return for further observation and accordingly returned to the clinic on September 3, 1947. At that time all significant symptoms were restricted to his left foot. Upon further examination, plaintiff was referred to the surgical department, where an operation was suggested. He had never undergone surgery and greatly feared an operation. No hospital bed was then available and plaintiff returned to his home. He was notified of the availability of a bed and on September 8, 1947 entered Duke Hospital as a patient and was assigned to a bed in Halstead Ward. At this time, the plaintiff was able to perform his usual work and to walk without apparent distress.

At the time plaintiff became a patient in Duke Hospital, Drs. Marc J. Reardon, S. S. Ambrose and J. W. Kelley were not engaged in private practice, but were pursuing post-graduate training at Duke Hospital and their duties in this capacity included the care and treatment of patients assigned to Halstead Ward. Dr. Reardon was classified as Assistant Resident in Surgery and in addition to his maintenance was paid a salary of $41.67 per month. Drs. Ambrose and Kelley were internes and aides or assistants to Dr. Reardon. The operative procedure at Duke Hospital was carried out by what is known as operating teams consisting of the doctor who actually uses the surgical tools and two or more assistants or helpers who aid him in the operation. Plaintiff, as a patient in Halstead Ward, had no choice of doctors.

The diagnostic considerations of plaintiff's condition ranged all the way from Buerger's disease to arteriosclerosis. No definite diagnosis was ever reached. It was, however, concluded that plaintiff had some type of occlusive vascular or peripheral vascular disease. One of the accepted forms of treatment for such a condition is a lumbar sympathectomy. This involves the removal by surgery of nerve tissue and ganglia which control the muscles of the blood vessels, thereby reducing the spasms of the blood vessels by paralyzing the muscles. This allows the vessels to open up and increases the flow of blood. The blood supply is controlled largely by the sympathetic nervous system. Whatever may have been the cause of plaintiff's trouble, his disease appeared to have been in the early stages. Of the non-operative treatments developed

for plaintiff's condition, only pavorin was used.

Without a complete and satisfactory diagnosis, plaintiff was persuaded by agents of Duke Hospital to submit to what was described to him as a minor or simple operation requiring only a small incision in his back and the clipping of a nerve, which operation would necessitate his being in the operating room only 40 to 45 minutes. Instead, an incision 8 inches in length, extending from the 9th rib to the rectus sheath was made in the body cavity through which all internal organs were lifted out of the way for the purpose of exposing the left lumbar sympathetic nerve and ganglia. These are located along and in front of the backbone or spinal column. The operation proceeded without apparent difficulty and as the nerve and three ganglia were being removed, the nerve chain snapped and the fourth ganglion disappeared behind a mass of tissue. While exploring for the fourth ganglion, Dr. Reardon discovered that the two large vessels which control the flow of blood to and from the left lower extremities were bound together by a mass of fibrous tissue and he inadvertently punctured one of these large vessels. Profuse, massive and uncontrolled bleeding followed. The mass of fibrous tissue made these large vessels easy to tear and more difficult to separate and repair, and in his effort to part this mass of fibrous tissue, Dr. Reardon perforated or produced fissures in the vessels in a number of other places. The bleeding became more profuse and plaintiff's condition became precarious. Dr. Reardon then made an incision in plaintiff's left thigh, up near the groin, and from that point followed a blood vessel as close as possible to the point of bleeding and there tied off and ligated that vessel. This procedure failed to control the bleeding and it was discovered that both the big artery and the big vein had been damaged by several punctures or tears. Due to the protracted operative procedure and the great loss of blood, plaintiff was in a critical condition and in a state of shock. Dr. Reardon had undertaken this difficult operation when there was no supervisory surgeon available in the hospital for consultation, advice and aid. Dr. K. S. Grimson, who developed the most extensive operation which might be performed upon the sympathetic nervous system and who was the head of that branch of the surgical service of Duke Hospital, was not available. Dr. Deryl Hart, Chief of the Surgical Service of the hospital, was called from his home in an effort to save the patient's life. Dr. Hart had not undertaken a lumbar sympathectomy in five years.

When Dr. Hart arrived at the hospital, all operative procedure was at a standstill and the bleeding was temporarily controlled by means of a pack. Upon discovering the condition of the patient, Dr. Hart abandoned all efforts to repair the damaged blood vessels and directed all his attention toward saving the patient's life. In this emergency, Dr. Hart, with the aid of Dr. Reardon and his associates, tied off the fibrous tissue which included the torn blood vessels and clipped them en masse. With these main vessels severed, the blood supply to that area of patient's body was greatly diminished, and upon reacting from the anesthetic about 9 o'clock that night, plaintiff discovered he was paralyzed from his hips down. The only hope of an adequate blood supply to his lower left leg and thigh was the development of a collateral circulation by means of smaller blood vessels. This collateral circulation did not materialize and as a result, gangrene developed and Dr. Reardon amputated plaintiff's left leg below the knee. Because of defects in this amputation, plaintiff suffered and sustained another operation by Dr. Reardon whereby his left leg stump was debrided. Later, it was necessary for Dr. Hart to reamputate plaintiff's left leg removing the knee joint. Plaintiff next developed a myocardial infarction of the heart. Then, a blood clot in his right leg resulted in gangrene and plaintiff's right leg was amputated by Dr. Hart. From these operations and the suffering incident thereto, plaintiff acquired a drug habituation.

Excerpts from the pleadings received in evidence tend to show that the plaintiff neither authorized nor consented to the operations performed on him on September 13, 1947 and that he "did not need or require any operation" at that time.

Plaintiff, for the first operations, was taken to the operating room before 9 o'clock in the morning and remained there until about 4:30 in the afternoon, during which time he was given by transfusions from 14 to 17 pints of blood. When pressed by plaintiff for an explanation of what happened during the operation, Dr. Reardon gave as his only comment, "I played hell; that is what happened."

Upon admission to the hospital, plaintiff weighed between 180 and 185 pounds. When discharged on January 15, 1948, he weighed 94 pounds. Plaintiff was not a charity patient and all expenses of his hospitalization were fully paid.

At the close of plaintiff's evidence, the court overruled the motions of the defendants for judgment as of nonsuit, but such motions at the close of all the evidence were allowed to both defendants. From the judgment entered, plaintiff excepted and appealed, assigning errors.

VALENTINE, JUSTICE

The decisive question presented by this appeal is whether the evidence sufficeth to take the case to jury.

* * *

It appears from the evidence, including excerpts from the pleadings, that at all times material to this litigation Dr. Reardon was an agent, servant and employee of Duke Hospital and was acting within the scope of his duty as such agent. It follows, therefore, if Dr. Reardon was guilty of actional negligence, such negligence is imputable to his co-defendant and both are liable.

The plaintiff contends that the evidence supports many inferences of negligence, among which are these:

(a) That Dr. Reardon, without plaintiff's permission, made haste to perform a serious operation without having first obtained a fixed and definite diagnosis, and when there was no necessity for such an operation.

(b) That Dr. Reardon should not have undertaken such a serious operation without first determining that there was available in the hospital a more experienced and capable surgeon upon whom he could call for consultation and aid in case of difficulty.

(c) That Dr. Reardon extended the operative procedure too long and neglected to call for experienced surgical aid when he encountered a situation requiring skill outside the scope of his experience and beyond the range of his training.

(d) That the severe damage done to plaintiff's venal structure by Dr. Reardon resulted in so much loss of blood that Dr. Hart when summoned was unable to repair the damage, but directed his attention immediately toward saving the patient's life, with the result that plaintiff survived but suffered disastrous results.

(e) That Dr. Reardon performed a defective amputation of plaintiff's left leg.

(f) That Dr. Reardon's statement to the plaintiff, "I played hell; that is what happened," indicated a consciousness of carelessness in the performance of the operation.

We are constrained to agree with the plaintiff that whether Dr. Reardon proceeded with that degree of ordinary care required of him under the circumstances and conditions shown by the record was a question of fact for the jury. [Citations.]

"The absence of expert medical testimony, disapproving the treatment or lack of it, is not perforce fatal to the case. There are many known and obvious facts in the realm of common knowledge which speak for themselves, sometimes even louder than witnesses, expert or otherwise." Gray v. Weinstein, 227 N.C. 463, 42 S.E.2d 616, 617.

Hospitals and members of the medical profession are held in high esteem and in most cases enjoy the general affection of the public. They are, of course, entitled to every reasonable consideration, but there should not be drawn around them unnatural or artificial immunities to shield them against acts of negligence. They are not guarantors of effective cures or of perfect operative results. Nevertheless, the law of negligence holds a physician or surgeon liable for an injury to a patient proximately resulting from a want of that degree of knowledge and skill ordinarily possessed by other members of his profession, or for a failure to use reasonable care and diligence in the practice of his art, or for his failure to exercise his best judgment in the treatment of his patient. [Citation.] Every negligence case, like the proverbial tub, "must stand on its own bottom."

We, of course, express no opinion as to the truth or falsity of the evidence, but viewing it with that liberality required under the circumstances here presented, we reach the conclusion that the permissible inferences are such as to make the issue of liability one for the jury. Therefore, the judgment of nonsuit must be

Reversed.

Emergency

CORDAS v. PEERLESS TRANSP. CO.
(1941, City Court of N.Y.) 27 N.Y.S.2d 198.

CARLIN, J.

This case presents the ordinary man— that problem child of the law—in a most bizarre setting. As a lowly chauffeur in defendant's employ he became in a trice the protagonist in a breath-bating drama with a denouement almost tragic. It appears that a man, whose identity it would be indelicate to divulge was feloniously relieved of his portable goods by two nondescript highwaymen in an alley near 26th Street and Third Avenue, Manhattan; they induced him to relinquish his possessions by a strong argument ad hominem couched in the convincing cant of the criminal and pressed at the point of a most persuasive pistol. Laden with their loot, but not thereby impeded, they took an abrupt departure and he, shuffling off the coil of that discretion which enmeshed him in the alley, quickly gave chase through 26th Street toward 2d Avenue, whither they were resorting "with expedition swift as thought" for most obvious reasons. Somewhere on that thoroughfare of escape they indulged the stratagem of separation ostensibly to disconcert their pursuer and allay the ardor of his pursuit. He then centered on for capture the man with the pistol whom he saw board defendant's taxicab, which quickly veered south toward 25th Street on 2d Avenue where he saw the chauffeur jump out while the cab, still in motion, continued toward 24th Street; after the chauffeur relieved himself of the cumbersome burden of his fare the latter also is said to have similarly departed from the cab before it reached 24th Street. The chauffeur's story is substantially the same except that he states that his uninvited guest boarded the cab at 25th Street while it was at a standstill waiting for a less colorful fare; that his "passenger" immediately advised him "to stand not upon the order of his going but to go at once" and added finality to his command by an appropriate gesture with a pistol addressed to his sacroiliac. The chauffeur in reluctant acquiescence proceeded about fifteen feet, when his hair, like unto the quills of the fretful porcupine, was made to stand on end by the hue and cry of the man despoiled accompanied by a clamourous concourse of the law-abiding which paced him as he ran; the concatenation of "stop thief",

to which the patter of persistent feet did maddingly beat time, rang in his ears as the pursuing posse all the while gained on the receding cab with its quarry therein contained. The hold-up man sensing his insecurity suggested to the chauffeur that in the event there was the slightest lapse in obedience to his curt command that he, the chauffeur, would suffer the loss of his brains, a prospect as horrible to an humble chauffeur as it undoubtedly would be to one of the intelligentsia. The chauffeur apprehensive of certain dissolution from either Scylla, the pursuers, or Charybdis, the pursued, quickly threw his car out of first speed in which he was proceeding, pulled on the emergency, jammed on his brakes and, although he thinks the motor was still running, swung open the door to his left and jumped out of his car. He confesses that the only act that smacked of intelligence was that by which he jammed the brakes in order to throw off balance the hold-up man who was half-standing and half-sitting with his pistol menacingly poised. Thus abandoning his car and passenger the chauffeur sped toward 26th Street and then turned to look; he saw the cab proceeding south toward 24th Street where it mounted the sidewalk. The plaintiff-mother and her two infant children were there injured by the cab which, at the time, appeared to be also minus its passenger who, it appears, was apprehended in the cellar of a local hospital where he was pointed out to a police officer by a remnant of the posse, hereinbefore mentioned. He did not appear at the trial. The three aforesaid plaintiffs and the husband-father sue the defendant for damages predicating their respective causes of action upon the contention that the chauffeur was negligent in abandoning the cab under the aforesaid circumstances. Fortunately the injuries sustained were comparatively slight. Negligence has been variously defined but the common legal acceptation is the failure to exercise that care and caution which a reasonable and prudent person ordinarily would exercise under like conditions or circumstances. It has been most authoritatively held that "negligence in the abstract, apart from things related, is surely not a tort, if indeed it is understandable at all." Cardozo, C. J., in Palsgraf v. Long Island Railroad Co., 248 N.Y. 339, 345, 162 N.E. 99, 101, 59 A.L.R. 1253. In Steinbrenner v. M. W. Forney Co., 143 App.Div. 73, 127 N.Y.S. 620, 622 it is said, "The test of actionable negligence is what reasonably prudent men would have done under the same circumstances"; Connell v. New York Central & Hudson River Railroad Co., 144 App.Div. 664, 129 N.Y.S. 666, 669, holds that actionable negligence must be predicated upon "a breach of duty to the plaintiff. Negligence is 'not absolute or intrinsic,' but 'is always relevant to some circumstances of time, place or person.' " In slight paraphrase of the world's first bard it may be truly observed that the expedition of the chauffeur's violent love of his own security outran the pauser, reason, when he was suddenly confronted with unusual emergency which "took his reason prisoner". The learned attorney for the plaintiffs concedes that the chauffeur acted in an emergency but claims a right to recovery upon the following proposition taken verbatim from his brief: "It is respectfully submitted that the value of the interests of the public at large to be immune from being injured by a dangerous instrumentality such as a car unattended while in motion is very superior to the right of a driver of a motor vehicle to abandon same while it is in motion even when acting under the belief that his life is in danger and by abandoning same he will save his life". To hold thus under the facts adduced herein would be tantamount to a repeal by implication of the primal law of nature written in indelible characters upon the fleshy tablets of sentient creation by the Almighty Law-giver, "the supernal Judge who sits on high". There are those who stem the turbulent current for bubble fame, or who bridge the yawning chasm with a

leap for the leap's sake or who "outstare the sternest eyes that look, outbrave the heart most daring on the earth, pluck the young sucking cubs from the she-bear, yea, mock the lion when he roars for prey" to win a fair lady and these are the admiration of the generality of men; but they are made of sterner stuff than the ordinary man upon whom the law places no duty of emulation. The law would indeed be fond if it imposed upon the ordinary man the obligation to so demean himself when suddenly confronted with a danger, not of his creation, disregarding the likelihood that such a contingency may darken the intellect and palsy the will of the common legion of the earth, the fraternity of ordinary men,—whose acts or omissions under certain conditions or circumstances make the yardstick by which the law measures culpability or innocense, negligence or care. If a person is placed in a sudden peril from which death might ensue, the law does not impel another to the rescue of the person endangered nor does it condemn him for his unmoral failure to rescue when he can; this is in recognition of the immutable law written in frail flesh. Returning to our chauffeur. If the philosophic Horatio and the martial companions of his watch were "distilled almost to jelly with the act of fear" when they beheld "in the dead vast and middle of the night" the disembodied spirit of Hamlet's father stalk majestically by "with a countenance more in sorrow than in anger" was not the chauffeur, though unacquainted with the example of these eminent men-at-arms, more amply justified in his fearsome reactions when he was more palpably confronted by a thing of flesh and blood bearing in its hand an engine of destruction which depended for its lethal purpose upon the quiver of a hair? When Macbeth was cross-examined by Macduff as to any reason he could advance for his sudden despatch of Duncan's grooms he said in plausible answer "Who can be wise, amazed, temperate and furious, loyal and neutral, in a moment? No man". Macbeth did not by a "tricksy word" thereby stand justified as he criminally created the emergency from which he sought escape by indulgence in added felonies to divert suspicion to the innocent. However, his words may be wrested to the advantage of the defendant's chauffeur whose acts cannot be legally construed as the proximate cause of plaintiff's injuries, however regrettable, unless nature's first law is arbitrarily disregarded. * * * "That the duties and responsibilities of a person confronted with such a danger are different and unlike those which follow his actions in performing the ordinary duties of life under other conditions is a well-established principle of law. * * * 'The law presumes that *an act or omission done or neglected under the influence of pressing danger was done or neglected involuntarily.'* It is there said that this rule seems to be founded upon the maxim that self-preservation is the first law of nature, and that, where it is a question whether one of two men shall suffer, each is justified in doing the best he can for himself". Kolanka v. Erie Railroad Co., 215 App.Div. 82, 86, 212 N.Y.S. 714, 717, says: "The law in this state does not hold one in an emergency to the exercise of that mature judgment required of him under circumstances where he has an opportunity for deliberate action. He is not required to exercise unerring judgment, which would be expected of him, were he not confronted with an emergency requiring prompt action". The circumstances provide the foil by which the act is brought into relief to determine whether it is or is not negligent. If under normal circumstances an act is done which might be considered negligent it does not follow as a corollary that a similar act is negligent if performed by a person acting under an emergency, not of his own making, in which he suddenly is faced with a patent danger with a moment left to adopt a means of extrication. The chauffeur— the ordinary man in this case—acted in a split second in a most harrowing experience.

To call him negligent would be to brand him a coward; the court does not do so in spite of what those swaggering heroes, "whose valor plucks dead lions by the beard", may bluster to the contrary. The court is loathe to see the plaintiffs go without recovery even though their damages were slight, but cannot hold the defendant liable upon the facts adduced at the trial. Motions, upon which decision was reserved, to dismiss the complaint are granted with exceptions to plaintiffs. Judgment for defendant against plaintiffs dismissing their complaint upon the merits. * * *

Violation of Statute

VANCE v. UNITED STATES
(1973, D.Alaska) 355 F.Supp. 756.

PLUMMER, C. J.

This case comes before the court on defendant's second motion for summary judgment. Plaintiff is seeking recovery in this action for injuries to John C. Vance and his dependents resulting from injuries sustained by Mr. Vance while he was intoxicated. Plaintiff's action is brought against the United States under the Federal Tort Claims Act, 28 U.S.C.A. §§ 1346(b) and 2674, on the theory that Mr. Vance was negligently served intoxicating liquors at the Non-Commissioned Officers' Club at Clear Air Force Station, Alaska.

* * *

It is necessary to begin with an examination of the effect on this case of A.S. [Alaska Statute] 04.15.020(a), which makes it a crime to give or sell liquor to minors or intoxicated persons. Plaintiff does not contend that this statute creates a new civil cause of action. [Citations.] Rather, plaintiff contends that this statute sets a minimum standard of care for purposes of the common law cause of action based upon ordinary negligence. That is, plaintiff is contending that a violation of this statute is negligence *per se*.

* * *

Under the Restatement rule * * * [Sections 286 and 288], an unexcused violation of a statute or regulation is negligence in itself if the court adopts the statute as defining the conduct of a reasonable man. (If the statute is not so adopted, a violation may be considered as evidence of negligence.) The court may and usually must adopt the statute as the minimum standard of care if the purpose of the statute is at least in part: (a) to protect a class of persons which includes the one whose interest is invaded, and (b) to protect the particular interest which is invaded, and (c) to protect that interest against the kind of harm which has resulted, and (d) to protect that interest against the particular hazard from which the harm results.

Applying this test to the statute in question, it is clear that requirements (b), (c) and (d) are satisfied; the statute unquestionably is designed at least in part to protect against personal injuries caused by intoxication. The principal issue is whether requirement (a) is met; that is, whether the consumer himself is within the protected class.

* * *

Turning to the nub of the issue, it is apparent that, although the principal purpose of the statute may have been to protect innocent third parties from the negligence of an intoxicated consumer, the purpose at least in part was also to protect the consumer himself. If the consumer involved in this case were a minor rather than an alleged intoxicated person, it would be logical to conclude that the statute was enacted by the Legislature to protect minors. The statute does not purport to discriminate between minors and intoxicated persons and therefore it should logically follow that both are protected. Accordingly, the court adopts A.S. 04.15.020(a) as the minimum standard of conduct for defendant's agent in the present case.

Since plaintiff's claim if grounded upon the alleged negligence of defendant's agent, contributory negligence would ordinarily be a defense. This is true even though the negligence may be proved by comparing the defendant's conduct to a statutory norm rather than to the hypothetical conduct of a reasonable man. See Restatement (2d) of Torts section 483. However, as section 483 also points out, there are exceptional statutes which are intended to protect persons from their own misconduct and to place the entire responsibility for the harm upon the one who has violated the statute. The Restatement cites the following example:

Thus a statute which prohibits the sale of firearms to minors may be clearly intended, among other purposes, to protect them against their own inexperience, lack of judgment, and tendency toward negligence, and to make the seller solely responsible for any harm to them resulting from the sale. In such a case the purpose of the statute would be defeated if the contributory negligence of the minor were permitted to bar his recovery.

A.S. 04.15.020(a) presents an even more compelling example of a statute intended to place the entire responsibility for resulting harm upon the violator, for it is virtually impossible for the statute to be violated without contributory negligence on the part of the plaintiff-consumer. Also, like the example in the Restatement, the statute is clearly intended to protect minors from their own misconduct. Since the statute does not purport to treat sales to minors differently from sales to intoxicated persons, it should logically follow that both are protected to the same extent.

* * *

In summary, the court holds as follows. Defendant had a duty to Mr. Vance to exercise reasonable care in dispensing intoxicants, and a breach of this duty may be found to have been the proximate cause of plaintiff's injuries. Such a breach occurred if defendant violated A.S. 04.15.020(a), but a breach may also be found if defendant failed to take additional reasonable precautions. Contributory negligence is a defense only if the statute was not violated.

The court expresses no opinion on whether Mr. Vance was contributorily negligent, for to do so would be premature at this point. Nor does the court express an opinion on whether the statute was violated, whether defendant was otherwise negligent, or whether defendant's conduct was a proximate cause of plaintiff's injuries under the circumstances of this case.

It is hereby ordered that defendant's second motion for summary judgment is denied.

*Special Duties
of Possessors of Land*

H. E. BUTT GROCERY CO. v. HAWKINS

(1980, Ct. of Civil Appeals of Texas) 594 S.W.2d 187.

NYE, C. J.

This is a slip-and-fall * * * case. Lucille Hawkins brought suit against defendant, H. E. Butt Grocery Company, for personal injuries she allegedly sustained when she slipped and fell in the defendant's grocery store in Bay City, Matagorda County, Texas. After hearing evidence, the trial judge overruled defendant's [motion for verdict] * * *, and this appeal resulted.

* * *

In a slip-and-fall suit, such as the one that is before us, the plaintiff must establish that: 1) the defendant placed the substance on the floor; or 2) the defendant knew that the substance was on the floor and willfully or negligently failed to remove it; or 3) the substance had been on the floor for such a period of time that it would have been discovered and removed by defendant in the exercise of ordinary care. [Citations.]

Plaintiff testified by deposition that she entered the H. E. B. store at approximately 3:30 or 3:35 p.m. on the occasion in question. She described the door which opened automatically and stated in essence that she had taken approximately one or two steps off of the mat which was located on the inside of the store next to the door when she slipped and fell in some rain water that had accumulated there. The water on the floor was approximately one-half inch deep and covered approximately two feet of floor space. Plaintiff testified that she did not see anything on the floor until she fell. It was undisputed that she was injured as a result of her fall.

Kaiser, the manager on duty at the time plaintiff fell, testified in substance that he was aware that the combination of a heavy rainfall and a North wind, on prior occasions, had caused water to be tracked into the store by customers and had caused water to be blown through the door as it opened and to accumulate in dangerous quantities on the floor near the door mat inside. He further testified to the effect that: 1) such weather conditions existed on the day in question; 2) water accumulated so rapidly that he and another employee had to mop the floor in that area at least four or five times during the hour or so immediately preceding the time plaintiff fell; 3) at the time of each mopping, several minutes were required to remove such accumulation and 4) he spent about the same amount of time to remove the water which had accumulated when he mopped the floor immediately after plaintiff fell. Kaiser testified specifically:

Q. Did it surprise you that someone fell at that time?
 A. No.
 Q. I am sorry?
 A. No, sir.
 Q. It didn't surprise?
 A. No, sir.

Kaiser also testified concerning his knowledge of the short length of time required for the water to accumulate under the particular weather conditions then existing. Kaiser admitted that no signs were erected to warn store patrons of the wet condition of the floor, nor was anybody posted at the door to tell people there was a water hazard. He stated that "we usually kept it (the water) mopped up."

Appellant, as an occupier of premises, had the duty to use ordinary care to keep its premises in a reasonably safe condition for its invitees or to warn them of the hazard. [Citations.] What constitutes a hazard or danger depends upon the facts or circumstances of each case. As stated by our Supreme Court in *Rosas v. Buddies Food Store*, 518 S.W.2d 534, 537 (Tex. Sup.1975):

Whether a condition constitutes a danger is a function of reasonableness. That is, if the ordinarily prudent man could foresee that harm was a likely result of a condition, then it is a danger.

[Citation.]

We are of the opinion that the direct and circumstantial evidence adduced at the * * * hearing was sufficient for the able trial judge (sitting as a fact finder) to conclude that, at the time of plaintiff's fall, defendant's employees knew or should have known that water was present and continuing to accumulate on the floor, and they negligently failed to remove the water.

The trial court's order * * * is affirmed.

Res Ipsa Loquitur

ESCOLA v. COCA COLA BOTTLING CO. OF FRESNO

(1944) 24 Cal.2d 453, 150 P.2d 436.

GIBSON, C. J.

Plaintiff, a waitress in a restaurant, was injured when a bottle of Coca Cola broke in her hand. She alleged that defendant company, which had bottled and delivered the alleged defective bottle to her employer, was negligent in selling "bottles containing said beverage which on account of excessive pressure of gas or by reason of some defect in the bottle was dangerous * * * and likely to explode." This appeal is from a judgment upon a jury verdict in favor of plaintiff.

Defendant's driver delivered several cases of Coca Cola to the restaurant, placing them on the floor, one on top of the other, under and behind the counter, where they remained at least thirty-six hours. Immediately before the accident, plaintiff picked up the top case and set it upon a near-by ice cream cabinet in front of and about three feet from the refrigerator. She then proceeded to take the bottles from the case with her right hand, one at a time, and put them into the refrigerator. Plaintiff testified that after she had placed three bottles in the refrigerator and had moved the fourth bottle about 18 inches from the case "it exploded in my hand." The bottle broke into two jagged pieces and inflicted a deep five-inch cut, severing blood vessels, nerves and muscles of the thumb and palm of the hand. Plaintiff further testified that when the bottle exploded, "It made a sound similar to an electric light bulb that would have dropped. It made a loud pop." Plaintiff's employer testified, "I was about twenty feet from where it actually happened and I heard the explosion." A fellow employee, on the opposite side of the counter, testified that plaintiff "had the bottle, I should judge, waist high, and I know that it didn't bang either the case or the door or another bottle * * * when it popped. It sounded just like a fruit jar would blow up * * *." The witness further testified that the contents of the bottle "flew all over herself and myself and the walls and one thing and another."

* * *

One of the defendant's drivers, called as a witness by plaintiff, testified that he had seen other bottles of Coca Cola in the past explode and had found broken bottles in the warehouse when he took the cases out, but that he did not know what made them blow up.

Plaintiff then rested her case, having announced to the court that being unable to show any specific acts of negligence she relied completely on the doctrine of res ipsa loquitur.

* * *

Res ipsa loquitur does not apply unless (1) defendant had exclusive control of the thing causing the injury and (2) the accident is of such a nature that it ordinarily would not occur in the absence of negligence by the defendant. [Citations.]

Many authorities state that the happening of the accident does not speak for itself where it took place some time after defendant had relinquished control of the instrumentality causing the injury. Under the more logical view, however, the doctrine may be applied upon the theory that defendant had control at the time of the alleged negligent act, although not at the time of the accident, *provided* plaintiff first proves that the condition of the instrumentality had not been changed after it left the defendant's possession. [Citation.] As said in Dunn v. Hoffman Beverage Co., 126 N.J.L. 556, 20 A.2d 352, 354, "defendant is not charged with the duty of showing affirmatively that something happened to the bottle after it left its control or management; * * * to get to the jury the plaintiff must show that there was due care during that period." Plaintiff must also prove that she handled the bottle carefully. The reason for this prerequisite is set forth in Prosser on Torts, supra, at page 300, where the author states: "Allied to the condition of exclusive control in the defendant is that of absence of any action on the part of the plaintiff contributing to the accident.

Its purpose, of course, is to eliminate the possibility that it was the plaintiff who was responsible. If the boiler of a locomotive explodes while the plaintiff engineer is operating it, the inference of his own negligence is at least as great as that of the defendant, and res ipsa loquitur will not apply until he has accounted for his own conduct." [Citation.] It is not necessary, of course, that plaintiff eliminate every remote possibility of injury to the bottle after defendant lost control, and the requirement is satisfied if there is evidence permitting a reasonable inference that it was not accessible to extraneous harmful forces and that it was carefully handled by plaintiff or any third person who may have moved or touched it. [Citation.]

* * *

Upon an examination of the record, the evidence appears sufficient to support a reasonable inference that the bottle here involved was not damaged by any extraneous force after delivery to the restaurant by defendant. It follows, therefore, that the bottle was in some manner defective at the time defendant relinquished control, because sound and properly prepared bottles of carbonated liquids do not ordinarily explode when carefully handled.

The next question, then, is whether plaintiff may rely upon the doctrine of res ipsa loquitur to supply an inference that defendant's negligence was responsible for the defective condition of the bottle at the time it was delivered to the restaurant. Under the general rules pertaining to the doctrine, as set forth above, it must appear that bottles of carbonated liquid are not ordinarily defective without negligence by the bottling company. In 1 Shearman and Redfield on Negligence (Rev.Ed.1941), page 153, it is stated that: "The doctrine * * * requires evidence which shows at least the probability that a particular accident could not have occurred without legal wrong by the defendant."

An explosion such as took place here might have been caused by an excessive internal pressure in a sound bottle, by a defect in the glass of a bottle containing a safe pressure, or by a combination of these two possible causes. The question is whether under the evidence there was a probability that defendant was negligent in any of these respects. If so, the doctrine of res ipsa loquitur applies.

The bottle was admittedly charged with gas under pressure, and the charging of the bottle was within the exclusive control of defendant. As it is a matter of common knowledge that an overcharge would not ordinarily result without negligence, it follows under the doctrine of res ipsa loquitur that if the bottle was in fact excessively charged an inference of defendant's negligence would arise. If the explosion resulted from a defective bottle containing a safe pressure, the defendant would be liable if it negligently failed to discover such flaw. If the defect were visible, an inference of negligence would arise from the failure of defendant to discover it. Where defects are discoverable, it may be assumed that they will not ordinarily escape detection if a reasonable inspection is made, and if such a defect is overlooked an inference arises that a proper inspection was not made. A difficult problem is presented where the defect is unknown and consequently might have been one not discoverable by a reasonable, practicable inspection.

* * *

It thus appears that there is available to the industry a commonly-used method of testing bottles for defects not apparent to the eye, which is almost infallible. Since Coca Cola bottles are subjected to these tests by the manufacturer, it is not likely that they contain defects when delivered to the bottler which are not discoverable by visual inspection.

* * *

Although it is not clear in this case whether the explosion was caused by an excessive charge or a defect in the glass there is a sufficient showing that neither cause would ordinarily have been present if due care had been used. Further, defendant had exclusive control over both the charging and inspection of the bottles. Accordingly, all the requirements necessary to entitle plaintiff to rely on the doctrine of res ipsa loquitur to supply an inference of negligence are present.

It is true that defendant presented evidence tending to show that it exercised considerable precaution by carefully regulating and checking the pressure in the bottles and by making visual inspections for defects in the glass at several stages during the bottling process. It is well settled, however, that when a defendant produces evidence to rebut the inference of negligence which arises upon application of the doctrine of res ipsa loquitur, it is ordinarily a question of fact for the jury to determine whether the inference has been dispelled. [Citations.]

The judgment is affirmed.

Proximate Cause

PALSGRAF v. LONG ISLAND R. CO.
(1928) 248 N.Y. 339, 162 N.E.99.

CARDOZO, C. J.

Plaintiff was standing on a platform of defendant's railroad after buying a ticket to go to Rockaway Beach. A train stopped at the station, bound for another place. Two men ran forward to catch it. One of the men reached the platform of the car without mishap, though the train was already moving. The other man, carrying a package, jumped aboard the car, but seemed unsteady as if about to fall. A guard on the car, who had held the door open, reached forward to help him in, and another guard on the platform pushed him from behind.

In this act, the package was dislodged, and fell upon the rails. It was a package of small size, about fifteen inches long, and was covered by a newspaper. In fact it contained fireworks, but there was nothing in its appearance to give notice of its contents. The fireworks when they fell exploded. The shock of the explosion threw down some scales at the other end of the platform many feet away. The scales struck the plaintiff, causing injuries for which she sues.

The conduct of the defendant's guard, if a wrong in its relation to the holder of the package, was not a wrong in its relation to the plaintiff, standing far away. Relatively to her it was not negligence at all. Nothing in the situation gave notice that the falling package had in it the potency of peril to persons thus removed. Negligence is not actionable unless it involves the invasion of a legally protected interest, the violation of a right. "Proof of negligence in the air, so to speak, will not do." [Citations.] "Negligence is the absence of care, according to the circumstances." [Citations.]

* * *

If no hazard was apparent to the eye of ordinary vigilance, an act innocent and harmless, at least to outward seeming, with reference to her, did not take to itself the quality of a tort because it happened to be a wrong, though apparently not one involving the risk of bodily insecurity, with reference to some one else. "In every instance, before negligence can be predicated of a given act, back of the act must be sought and found a duty to the individual complaining, the observance of which would have averted or avoided the injury." [Citations.]

* * *

A different conclusion will involve us, and swiftly too, in a maze of contradictions. A guard stumbles over a package which has been left upon a platform. It seems to be a bundle of newspapers. It turns out to be a can of dynamite. To the eye of ordinary vigilance, the bundle is abandoned waste, which may be kicked or trod on with impunity. Is a passenger at the other end of the platform protected by the law against the unsuspected hazard concealed beneath the waste? If not, is the result to be any different, so far as the distant passenger is concerned, when the guard stumbles over a valise which a truckman or a porter has left upon the walk? The passenger far away, if the victim of a wrong at all, has a cause of action, not derivative, but original and primary. His claim to be protected against invasion of his bodily security is neither greater nor less because the act resulting in the invasion is a wrong to another far removed. In this case, the rights that are said to have been violated, the interests said to have been invaded, are not even of the same order. The man was not injured in his person nor even put in danger. The purpose of the act, as well as its effect, was to make his person safe. If there was a wrong to him at all, which may very well be doubted, it was a wrong to a property interest only, the safety of his package. Out of this wrong to property, which threatened injury to nothing else, there has passed, we are told, to the plaintiff by derivation or succession a right of action for the invasion of an interest of another order, the right to bodily security. The diversity of interests emphasizes the futility of the effort to build the plaintiff's right upon the basis of a wrong to some one else. The gain is one of emphasis, for a like result would follow if the interests were the same. Even then, the orbit of the danger as disclosed to the eye of reasonable vigilance would be the orbit of the duty. One who jostles one's neighbor in a crowd does not invade the rights of others standing at the outer fringe when the unintended contact casts a bomb upon the ground. The wrongdoer as to them is the man who carries the bomb, not the one who explodes it without suspicion of the danger. Life will have to be made over, and human nature transformed, before prevision so extravagant can be accepted as the norm of conduct, the customary standard to which behavior must conform.

* * *

The judgment of the Appellate Division and that of the Trial Term should be reversed, and the complaint dismissed, with costs in all courts.

Proximate Cause

PETITION OF KINSMAN TRANSIT CO.

(1964, C.A.2d) 338 F.2d 708.

FRIENDLY, J.

We have here six appeals, [citation], from * * * [a] decree in admiralty adjudicating liability. The litigation, in the District Court for the Western District of New York, arose out of a series of misadventures on a navigable portion of the Buffalo River during the night of January 21, 1959. The owners of two vessels petitioned for exoneration from or limitation of liability; numerous claimants appeared in these proceedings and also filed libels against the Continental Grain Company and the City of Buffalo, which filed cross-claims. The proceedings were consolidated for trial before Judge Burke. We shall summarize the facts as found by him:

The Buffalo River flows through Buffalo from east to west, with many turns and bends, until it empties into Lake Erie. Its navigable western portion is lined with docks, grain elevators, and industrial installations; during the winter, lake vessels tie up there pending resumption of navigation on the Great Lakes, without power and with only a shipkeeper aboard. About a mile from the mouth, the City of Buffalo maintains a lift bridge at Michigan Avenue. Thaws and rain frequently cause freshets to develop in the upper part of the river and its tributary, Cazenovia Creek; currents

then range up to fifteen miles an hour and propel broken ice down the river, which sometimes overflows its banks.

On January 21, 1959, rain and thaw followed a period of freezing weather. The United States Weather Bureau issued appropriate warnings which were published and broadcast. Around 6 P.M. an ice jam that had formed in Cazenovia Creek disintegrated. Another ice jam formed just west of the junction of the creek and the river; it broke loose around 9 P.M.

The MacGilvray Shiras, owned by The Kinsman Transit Company, was moored at the dock of the Concrete Elevator, operated by Continental Grain Company, on the south side of the river about three miles upstream of the Michigan Avenue Bridge.

* * *

None of her anchors had been put out. From about 10 P.M. large chunks of ice and debris began to pile up between the Shiras' starboard bow and the bank; the pressure exerted by this mass on her starboard bow was augmented by the force of the current and of floating ice against her port quarter. The mooring lines began to part, and a "deadman," to which the No. 1 mooring cable had been attached, pulled out of the ground—the judge finding that it had not been properly constructed or inspected. About 10:40 P.M. the stern lines parted, and the Shiras drifted into the current. During the previous forty minutes, the shipkeeper took no action to ready the anchors * * *.

Careening stern first down the S-shaped river, the Shiras, at about 11 P.M., struck the bow of the Michael K. Tewksbury, owned by Midland Steamship Line, Inc. The Tewksbury was moored in a relatively protected area flush against the face of a dock on the outer bank just below a hairpin bend so that no opportunity was afforded for ice to build up between her port bow and the dock. * * * The collision caused the Tewksbury's mooring lines to part; she too drifted stern first down the river, followed by the Shiras. The collision caused damage to the steamer Druckenmiller which was moored opposite the Tewksbury.

Thus far there was no substantial conflict in the testimony; as to what followed there was. Judge Burke found, and we accept his findings as soundly based, that at about 10:43 P.M., Goetz, the superintendent of the Concrete Elevator, telephoned Kruptavich, another employee of Continental, that the Shiras was adrift; Kruptavich called the Coast Guard, which called the city fire station on the river, which in turn warned the crew on the Michigan Avenue Bridge, this last call being made about 10:48 P.M. Not quite twenty minutes later the watchman at the elevator where the Tewksbury had been moored phoned the bridge crew to raise the bridge. Although not more than two minutes and ten seconds were needed to elevate the bridge to full height after traffic was stopped, assuming that the motor started promptly, the bridge was just being raised when, at 11:17 P.M., the Tewksbury crashed into its center. The bridge crew consisted of an operator and two tenders; a change of shift was scheduled for 11 P.M. The inference is rather strong, despite contrary testimony, that the operator on the earlier shift had not yet returned from a tavern when the telephone call from the fire station was received; that the operator on the second shift did not arrive until shortly before the call from the elevator where the Tewksbury had been moored; and that in consequence the bridge was not raised until too late.

The first crash was followed by a second, when the south tower of the bridge fell. The Tewksbury grounded and stopped in the wreckage with her forward end resting against the stern of the Steamer Farr, which was moored on the south side of the river just above the bridge. The Shiras ended her journey with her stern against the Tewksbury and her bow against the north side of the river. So wedged, the two

vessels substantially dammed the flow, causing water and ice to back up and flood installations on the banks with consequent damage as far as the Concrete Elevator, nearly three miles upstream. Two of the bridge crew suffered injuries. Later the north tower of the bridge collapsed, damaging adjacent property.

Judge Burke concluded that Continental and the Shiras had committed various faults discussed below; * * *; that the Tewksbury and her owner were entitled to exoneration; and that the City of Buffalo was at fault for failing to raise the Michigan Avenue Bridge.

* * *

For the damages sustained by the Tewksbury and the Druckenmiller in the collisions at the Standard Elevator dock, Judge Burke allowed those vessels to recover equally from Continental and from Kinsman, * * *. He held the City, Continental and Kinsman equally liable * * * for damages to persons and property sustained by all others as a result of the disaster at the bridge. But, on the basis of the last clear chance rule, he held the City solely liable for damages sustained by the other tort-feasors, to wit, the Shiras and Continental as operator of the Concrete Elevator, and refused to allow recovery by the City against them.

* * *

The very statement of the case suggests the need for considering Palsgraf v. Long Island RR., [citation], and the closely related problem of liability for unforeseeable consequences.

* * *

We see little similarity between the Palsgraf case and the situation before us. The point of Palsgraf was that the appearance of the newspaper-wrapped package gave no notice that its dislodgement could do any harm save to itself and those nearby, and this by impact, perhaps with consequent breakage, and not by explosion. In contrast, a ship insecurely moored in a fast flowing river is a known danger not only to herself but to the owners of all other ships and structures down-river, and to persons upon them. No one would dream of saying that a shipowner who "knowingly and wilfully" failed to secure his ship at a pier on such a river "would not have threatened" persons and owners of property downstream in some manner. The shipowner and the wharfinger in this case having thus owed a duty of care to all within the reach of the ship's known destructive power, the impossibility of advance identification of the particular person who would be hurt is without legal consequence. [Citations.] Similarly the foreseeable consequences of the City's failure to raise the bridge were not limited to the Shiras and the Tewksbury. Collision plainly created a danger that the bridge towers might fall onto adjoining property, and the crash of two uncontrolled lake vessels, one 425 feet and the other 525 feet long, into a bridge over a swift ice-ridden stream, with a channel only 177 feet wide, could well result in a partial damming that would flood property upstream.

* * *

All the claimants here met the Palsgraf requirement of being persons to whom the actors owed a "duty of care," * * *. But this does not dispose of the alternative argument that the manner in which several of the claimants were harmed, particularly by flood damage, was unforeseeable and that recovery for this may not be had— whether the argument is put in the forthright form that unforeseeable damages are not recoverable or is concealed under a formula of lack of "proximate cause."

So far as concerns the City, the argument lacks factual support. Although the obvious risks from not raising the bridge were damage to itself and to the vessels the danger of a fall of the bridge and of flooding would not have been unforeseeable under

the circumstances to anyone who gave them thought. And the same can be said as to the failure of Kinsman's shipkeeper to ready the anchors after the danger had become apparent. * * *

Continental's position on the facts is stronger. It was indeed foreseeable that the improper construction and lack of inspection of the "deadman" might cause a ship to break loose and damage persons and property on or near the river—that was what made Continental's conduct negligent. With the aid of hindsight one can also say that a prudent man, carefully pondering the problem, would have realized that the danger of this would be greatest under such water conditions as developed during the night of January 21, 1959, and that if a vessel should break loose under those circumstances, events might transpire as they did. But such *post hoc* step by step analysis would render "foreseeable" almost anything that has in fact occurred; if the argument relied upon has legal validity, it ought not be circumvented by characterizing as foreseeable what almost no one would in fact have foreseen at the time.

* * *

Foreseeability of danger is necessary to render conduct negligent; where as here the damage was caused by just those forces whose existence required the exercise of greater care than was taken—the current, the ice, and the physical mass of the Shiras, the incurring of consequences other and greater than foreseen does not make the conduct less culpable or provide a reasoned basis for insulation. [Citation.] The oft encountered argument that failure to limit liability to foreseeable consequences may subject the defendant to a loss wholly out of proportion to his fault seems scarcely consistent with the universally accepted rule that the defendant takes the plaintiff as he finds him and will be responsible for the full extent of the injury even though a latent susceptibility of the plaintiff renders this far more serious than could reasonably have been anticipated. See Prosser, Torts, 260.

The weight of authority in this country rejects the limitation of damages to consequences foreseeable at the time of the negligent conduct when the consequences are "direct," and the damage, although other and greater than expectable, is of the same general sort that was risked.

* * *

Here it is surely more equitable that the losses from the operators' negligent failure to raise the Michigan Avenue Bridge should be ratably borne by Buffalo's taxpayers than left with the innocent victims of the flooding; yet the mind is also repelled by a solution that would impose liability solely on the City and exonerate the persons whose negligent acts of commission and omission were the precipitating force of the collision with the bridge and its sequelae. We go only so far as to hold that where, as here, the damages resulted from the same physical forces whose existence required the exercise of greater care than was displayed and were of the same general sort that was expectable, unforeseeability of the exact developments and of the extent of the loss will not limit liability. Other fact situations can be dealt with when they arise.

* * *

Judgment accordingly.

Contributory Negligence—
Assumption of Risk

HUNN v. WINDSOR HOTEL CO.
(1937) 119 W.Va. 215, 193 S.E. 57.

HATCHER, J.

Damages for personal injuries are sought in this action. A trial was had, and, after both sides rested, the court directed a verdict for defendant.

* * * The defendant operates a hotel in the city of Wheeling and plaintiff has lodged at the hotel for the last eight years.

The day before the injury complained of, defendant replaced the treads on a short flight of marble steps which leads down from the hotel lobby to the Main street entrance. The new treads were attached to the steps with cement, and heavy planks were placed on top of the treads to protect the cement while hardening. The planks were approximately eight feet long, two inches thick, and twelve inches wide. They were "not new" and were not entirely firm under foot. At each end of the planks was about a fourteen-inch space on the steps, not covered by the treads or the planks. Plaintiff walked up the planks a few hours after the steps were repaired. She received the impression then that the planks were dangerous. Next morning she walked down the planks, "slipped" on one and fell, fracturing her ankle. She said of that plank: "It seemed the board slipped and with that it threw me * * * I think it moved and made me slip * * * Yes, it moved and made me slip, * * * looked like it was slick, I noticed that while I was sitting there on the floor." There were other exits from the hotel which she could have used, though not as direct for her purpose, as the one to Main street. The evening before plaintiff's accident, three other guests of the hotel fell on the stairway, and another stumbled on it. One of those falls was reported immediately to the hotel clerk then on duty, and the hotel manager admitted receiving that information prior to plaintiff's fall. There were no cautionary signs on the steps, and they were not roped or in any other way excluded from use.

The law in such cases is settled. It is the duty of a hotel keeper to exercise reasonable care to have the public passageways of his hotel safe for the use of lodgers. However, he is not an insurer of a lodger's safety. Where a lodger is injured on such a way, which he knows to be dangerous, he may be barred from a recovery by contributory negligence, or by voluntary assumption of the risk. [Citation.]

* * *

The doctrines of contributory negligence and of assumption of risk are not identical, yet the distinction between them has not always been closely observed in our opinions. This failure, sofar, has not affected the integrity of the decisions; but approach to these doctrines will be more orderly if the distinction be marked. The essence of contributory negligence is carelessness; of assumption or risk, venturousness. Thus an injured person may not have acted carelessly; in fact, may have exercised the utmost care, yet may have assumed, voluntarily, a known hazard. If so, he must accept the consequence. * * * The doctrine rests on two premises: First, that the nature and extent of the risk are fully appreciated; and, second, that it is voluntarily incurred. * * * "Where a person has knowledge of and fully appreciates a danger, and under such circumstances, without any special exigency compelling him, he exposes himself to such danger or peril, his act in the premises may be deemed to have been voluntary. Contributory negligence in such a case cannot properly be said to be an element therein, for certainly the voluntary act of a party in exposing himself to a known and appreciated danger is wholly incompatible with an act of negligence or carelessness, for it must be manifest that carelessness in regard to a matter is not the same as the exercise of a deliberate choice in respect thereto. Freedom of the will, in fact, is the thing emphasized by the principle asserted in the maxim *volenti non fit injuria*."

Plaintiff's use of the steps, though she was conscious of their danger, would not alone make her conduct legally negligent. [Citation.] She testified of noticing a board on the steps when she got to the top step, of observing the bare spaces on the steps at the ends of the planks, of being mindful while descending the steps that she considered them dangerous, and of descending them in her "usual walk." A legal infer-

ence of carelessness does not arise from that testimony. But, bearing in mind there were other ways, unattended by danger and reasonably convenient, which she could have used, her testimony does demonstrate that, with full appreciation of the danger on the steps, she voluntarily accepted the risk.

* * *

The judgment is affirmed.

Comparative Negligence

CAMERON v. UNION AUTO. INS. CO.

(1933) 210 Wis. 659, 246 N.W. 420, rehearing denied 210 Wis. 659, 247 N.W. 453.

Action commenced March 18, 1932, against Price county and its insurer for the death of the plaintiff's husband resulting from a collision with a county truck of the automobile in which he was riding, alleged to have been caused by negligence of employees of the defendant county in leaving the truck standing on the highway and in failing to equip it with clearance lights and a sufficient tail-light or reflector, all in violation of statutes. From a judgment entered June 7, 1932, in favor of the plaintiff, the defendants appeal.

The plaintiff's husband was killed in a collision with a highway truck belonging to the defendant county. He was riding in an automobile driven by James Funfar, who was plaintiff's agent, and who ran the automobile into the rear of the truck. The jury found that Funfar was 20 per cent. negligent; that the county was 10 per cent. negligent for not having proper clearance lights or a properly adjusted reflector at the rear of the truck as required by statute, and 70 per cent. negligent for leaving the truck standing on the highway with less than 15 feet to the left of it in violation of statute. They assessed plaintiff's pecuniary loss at $7,500 and her damages for loss of her husband's society at $2,500. Judgment was entered for 80 per cent. of the total amount.

FOWLER, J.

* * *

The comparative negligence statute, section 331.045, provides that: "* * * Contributory negligence shall not bar recovery in an action by any person or his legal representatives to recover damages for negligence resulting in death or in injury to person or property, if such negligence was not as great as the negligence of the person against whom recovery is sought, but any damages allowed shall be diminished by the jury in the proportion to the amount of negligence attributable to the person recovering." The contention that this statute does not apply to the instant case is based upon the idea that under the facts here involved the negligence of Funfar was at least as great as that of the county employees in charge of the truck; in other words, the court should have ruled as matter of law that Funfar's negligence was as great as or greater than the defendants' negligence and dismissed the case because of his contributory negligence. The learned trial judge, although apparently of the opinion that Funfar's negligence was as great as that of the county, considered that the question of comparative negligence was for the jury and that the jury's finding should stand. There was an automobile approaching from the opposite direction whose lights were burning. The driver of the automobile was watching this automobile. The truck was painted gray and it was dusk, when visibility is poorest. The driver testified that the lights of the approaching automobile did not blind him, but that they rays past the rear of the truck combined with the color of the truck and the twilight hour to prevent him from seeing the truck until the headlights of the car had passed the rear of the truck, and that the presence of the truck was then first disclosed by his own lights and it was then too late to avoid the truck by turning left and applying his brakes, both of which he did as quickly and as much as he could. We have recently said in three cases that the question of comparative negligence is ordinarily for the jury. [Citations.]

* * *

The judgment of the circuit court is affirmed.

On Rehearing

PER CURIAM.

A motion for rehearing is made herein on the ground that the plaintiff's recovery was reduced by 20 per cent, whereas, as it is claimed, it should have been reduced by a fourth, or 25 per cent. The contention is based upon the language of this court in the opinion in the case of Paluczak v. Jones, 245 N.W. 655, 656. The statement is there made that, "Under this statute [the Comparative Negligence Statute, § 331.045], where both parties to a collision are negligent and there is a counterclaim, one of the parties may recover when there is a finding that his negligence is less than that of the other, but his recovery must be reduced in such ratio as his negligence bears to the other's."

The language "in such ratio as his negligence bears to the other's" was inadvertently used, and is withdrawn. Instead of the language last quoted, the words "in proportion to his negligence" should have been used. This would have brought the statement in strict accord with the language of the statute (St. 1931, § 331.045), which is: "But any damages allowed shall be diminished by the jury in the proportion to the amount of negligence attributable to the person recovering."

* * *

The motion for rehearing is denied, * * *.

Keeping of Animals

ZAREK v. FREDERICKS

(1943, C.A.3d) 138 F.2d 689.

GOODRICH, J.

The defendant appeals from a judgment against him in the District Court rendered

in favor of the minor plaintiff, Vincent Zarek, and a second judgment in favor of the
minor's mother.   The basis of each recovery
is the damage claimed to the respective interests of each plaintiff when Vincent was
bitten by a dog owned and kept by the defendant at his summer resort hotel in Monroe County, Pennsylvania, where the mother
and son were vacation guests.   There is no
dispute concerning the defendant's ownership and possession of the dog, nor the fact
that the dog bit the minor plaintiff as the
boy leaned over to pet the dog while it lay
near the hotel, shortly after midday.
* * *

The underlying rule of law governing
the case is not in doubt.   Pennsylvania decisions enunciate with only slightly varying
phraseology, the well known rule of the
common law that one who keeps a domestic
animal which he has reason to know has
vicious propensities abnormal to its class is
liable for the harm the animal causes to
others.   [Citations.]

* * *

The question, so far as it concerns the
libility, is limited to the sufficiency of the
proof that the dog was vicious and that the
defendant knew or had reason to know that
fact.   The jury, under instructions from the
trial judge, of which no complaint is made,
found in favor of the plaintiffs.

* * *

The dog was six years old at the time
he attacked the boy.   The defendant had
owned him from infancy.   The animal's
mother was a collie or German shepherd;
father unknown.   He had, so far as the evidence shows, never bitten anyone before,
and the only evidence of an attack on anyone is that given in the mother's testimony
and admitted by the defendant, mentioned
below.   But, the notion that a dog is entitled to one bite before it becomes a source
of liability to its owner has been repudiated
in Pennsylvania.   [Citations.]

It is enough that facts are shown from
which the vicious propensities may be found.

Were sufficient facts shown here to support
the verdict which the jury reached?

The evidence most favorable to the
plaintiffs was their own testimony.   Mrs.
Zarek testified that the defendant kept and
trained the dog as a watch-dog.   She said
that the defendant had told her that in order
to try out the dog, he, on one occasion, raised
his hand to strike his wife and the dog
leaped at him and tore the shirt off his back.
Unlike another dog owned by the defendant
"Sport," who is the actor in this drama, was
not allowed to roam around during the day,
but was kept in or near the kitchen.   At
night the dog would be allowed out, near
the guests at the hotel, although the plaintiffs' testimony was equivocal as to whether
on such occasions the dog was always accompanied, either by the defendant or his
wife.   When the guests petted the dog he
snarled, showed his teeth and backed away.
The defendant did not want guests to pet
the animal since, so he supposedly stated,
"you would never know when a dog will turn
on you."   Vincent stated that when he went
in the kitchen of the hotel Mr. Fredericks
would hold the dog.

There was testimony denying or explaining all of the above statements but we
must at this stage of the case take them at
their face value after the jury's verdict.
Each individual fact is not, perhaps, very
strong against the defendant.   Taken together they lend support to the conclusion
that the defendant knew and feared the consequences of vicious propensities in "Sport"
and had taken precautions against them.
The plaintiffs are entitled at this stage of
the matter, at any rate, to have them considered together and not to have their cable
broken by snapping the individual strands
which make it up.   We cannot say that the
finding of the jury in the plaintiffs' favor
was so unreasonable that it should be set
aside.

* * *

Affirmed.

Problems

1. A statute, which requires railroads to fence their tracks, is construed as intended solely to prevent injuries to animals, straying onto the right of way, who may be hit by trains. B. & A. Railroad Company fails to fence its tracks. Two of C's cows wander onto the track. Nellie is hit by a train. Elsie is poisoned by weeds growing beside the track. For which cows, if any, is B. & A. Railroad liable to C? Why?

2. M leaves his car parked on a hill. Two minutes later, the car runs down the hill and damages D's dumpster. Though no other evidence exists, it is possible that someone could have tampered with the car. Is M liable for damages to D's dumpster? Why?

3. Martha invites John to come to lunch. Martha knows that her private road is dangerous to travel, having been guttered by recent rains. She doesn't warn John of the condition, reasonably believing that he will notice the gutters and exercise sufficient care. John's attention, while driving over, is diverted from the road by the screaming of his child, who has been stung by a bee. He fails to notice the condition of the road, hits a gutter, and skids into a tree. If John is not contributorily negligent, is Martha liable to John?

4. N is run over by a car and left lying in the street. Samaritan Sam, seeing N's helpless state, takes him in his car for the purpose of taking him to the hospital. Sam drives negligently into a ditch, causing additional injury to N. Is Sam liable to N?

5. Led Foot drives his car carelessly into another car. The second car contains dynamite which Led had no way of knowing. The collision causes an explosion which shatters a window of a building half a block away on another street. The flying glass inflicts serious cuts on Sally, who is working at a nearby desk. The explosion also harms Vic Jones, who is walking on the sidewalk near the point of the collision. Toward whom is Led Foot negligent?

6. A statute requires all vessels traveling on the Great Lakes to provide lifeboats. One of W Steamship Company's boats is sent out of port without a lifeboat. P, a sailor, falls overboard in a storm so heavy that had there been a lifeboat it could not have been launched. P drowns. Is W liable to P's estate?

7. L is negligently driving an automobile at excessive speed. R's negligently driven car crosses the center line of the highway and scrapes the side of L's car, damaging its fenders. As a result, L loses control of his car, which goes into the ditch, where L's car is wrecked and L suffers personal injuries. What can L recover?

8. a. E, the owner of a baseball park, is under a duty to the entering public to provide a reasonably sufficient number of screened seats to protect those who desire it against the risk of being hit by batted balls. E fails to do so. F, a customer entering the park, is unable to find a screened seat, and although fully aware of the risk, sits in an unscreened seat. F is struck and injured by a batted ball. Is E liable?
b. G, F's wife, has just arrived from Germany and is viewing baseball for the first time. Without asking any questions, she follows F to a seat. After the batted ball hits F, it caroms into G, injuring her. Is E liable to G?

9. C C Railroad is negligent in failing to give warning of the approach of its train to a crossing, and thereby endangers L, a blind man who is about to cross. M, a bystander, in a reasonable effort to save L, rushes onto the track to push L out of danger. Although M acts as carefully as possible, he is struck and injured by the train. Can M recover from L and/or the Railroad?

10. I, constructing a building, operates pile-driving machinery that causes excessive vibrations abnormally dangerous to buildings in the vicinity. Cy, in an adjoining building, is conducting scientific experiments with extremely delicate instruments. Although the vibration causes no other harm to Cy or to the building, it ruins the instruments and prevents the experiments. Is I liable for the harm caused Cy?

11. T keeps a pet chimpanzee, which is thoroughly tamed and accustomed to playing with its owner's children. The Chimpanzee escapes, notwithstanding every precaution to keep it upon its owner's premises. It approaches a group of children. I, the mother of one of the children, erroneously thinking the chimpanzee is about to attack the children, rushes to her child's assistance; and in her hurry and excitement, she stumbles and falls, breaking her leg. Can I recover for her personal injuries?

THREE

Contracts

INTRODUCTION TO CONTRACTS

Every business enterprise, whether large or small, must necessarily enter into contracts with its employees, its suppliers of goods and services, and its customers in order to conduct its business operations. The study of contract law is therefore a most important subject for the student of business law. Contract law is also basic to other fields of law which are treated in other parts of this book, such as agency, bailments, sales of personal property, commercial paper, and secured transactions. The law of contracts underlies each of these fields of law.

Even the most common transaction may involve a multitude of contracts. In a typical contract for the sale of land, the seller promises to convey title to the land, and the buyer promises to pay an agreed-upon purchase price. In addition, the seller may promise to pay certain accrued taxes or assessments; the buyer may promise to assume a mortgage on the property, may promise to reconvey the property to the seller upon the occurrence of a specified event, or may promise to pay the purchase price to a creditor of the seller. There may also be an assignment of a fire insurance policy, which in itself is a contract. A por-

tion of the purchase price may consist of the buyer's promissory note, which is a contract containing the buyer's written promise to pay a sum certain in money. If the parties are represented by counsel, they very likely have contracts with their attorneys. If the seller deposits the proceeds of the sale in a bank, he enters into a contract with the bank. If the buyer leases the property, he enters into a contract with the tenant. When one of the parties leaves his car in a parking lot to attend to any of these matters, he assumes a contractual relationship with the proprietor of the lot. In short, nearly every business transaction is based upon contract, and the expectations created by the agreed-upon promises. It is therefore essential to know what the law requires in order that a promise or set of promises is binding on the promisor.

DEVELOPMENT OF THE LAW OF CONTRACTS

Common Law

Contracts are primarily governed by state common law. An orderly presentation of this law is found in the Restatements of the Law of Contracts. The first Restatement was adopted and promulgated on May 6, 1932, by the American Law Institute. On May 17, 1979, the Institute adopted and promulgated a revised edition of the Restatement, hereinafter cited as the Restatement, Second, Contracts. For more than 50 years the Restatements have been regarded as a valuable authoritative reference work and extensively cited and quoted in reported judicial opinions.

The Uniform Commercial Code

The Uniform Commercial Code (herein referred to as the Code or U.C.C.) was prepared under the joint sponsorship and direction of the National Conference of Commissioners on Uniform State Laws and the American Law Institute. Work on drafting the Code started in 1942, and in 1952 a finished draft was published and submitted to all of the state legislatures for adoption into law. Article 2 of the U.C.C. has been enacted by all states except Louisiana and applies to sales of goods which are a type of contract involving the transfer of title to goods from seller to buyer for a price. Section 2–106. The Code essentially defines goods as movable, tangible personal property. Section 2–105(1). For example, the purchase of a television set, automobile or textbook is considered a sale of goods. All such transactions are governed by Article 2 of the Code but, where general contract law has not been specifically modified by the Code, contract common law continues to apply. "Unless displaced by the particular provisions of this Act, the principles of law and equity [including contract law] shall supplement its provisions." Section 1–103.

Types of Contracts Outside the Code

General contract law governs all contracts outside the scope of the Code. Such contracts play a significant role in commercial activities. For example, the Code does not apply to employment contracts, service contracts, insurance contracts, contracts involving real property, and contracts for the sale of intangibles such as patents and copyrights. These transactions continue to be governed by general contract law.

DEFINITION OF CONTRACT

Blackstone defined a contract as "an agreement, upon sufficient consideration, to do or not to do a particular thing." A more specific approach is to define contract in terms of the element which is common to all contracts: a promise. Accordingly, a brief but acceptable definition is a promise enforceable by law. The Restatement, Second, Contracts states in Section 1:

A contract is a promise or a set of promises for the breach of which the law gives a remedy, or the performance of which the law in some way recognizes as a duty.

The Restatement defines a promise as:

(1) A promise is a manifestation of intention to act or refrain from acting in a specified way, so made as to justify a promisee in understanding that a commitment has been made.

The Code definition of a contract is:

"Contract" means the total legal obligation which results from the parties' agreement as affected by this Act and any other applicable rules of law. Section 1–201(11).

The Code definition of agreement is:

"Agreement" means the bargain of the parties in fact as found in their language or by implication from other circumstances including course of dealing or usage of trade or course of performance as provided in this Act. Whether an agreement has legal consequences is determined by the provisions of this Act, if applicable; otherwise by the law of contracts. Section 1–201(3).

It is clear from the Restatement and the Code that a promise or an agreement may be binding (contractual) or not binding (non-contractual). Thus, the words, "promise" and "agreement" have a much broader scope and meaning than "contract."

But what precisely is *the* contract? In common speech the document or writing containing the parties' promises is spoken of as the contract. But this is obviously inadequate, since contracts may be oral, written, or implied from the parties' conduct. The contract might be regarded as those events leading up to the formation of the contract, such as the offer and the acceptance. Yet while these are among the requisites for the formation of the contract, they can hardly be said to be the contract itself. Rather, the contract is the legal relationship that consists of the rights and duties of the contracting parties. The rights and duties of the parties are correlative, which means, for example, that the right of the seller of land to receive the purchase price is another way of expressing the duty of the buyer to pay the price, while the duty of the seller to convey the land is the right of the buyer to obtain the conveyance.

CLASSIFICATION OF CONTRACTS

Contracts have been classified from various standpoints such as their method of formation, their content, and their legal effect. The standard classifications are: (1) Formal or Informal Contracts; (2) Express or Implied Contracts; (3) Unilateral or Bilateral Contracts; (4) Void, Voidable or Unenforceable Contracts; (5) Executed or Executory Contracts.

Formal and Informal Contracts

A formal contract depends upon a particular form, or mode of expression, for its legal efficacy. For example, at common law a promise under seal was enforceable without anything more. Another formal contract is the negotiable instrument, where a promissory note or other instrument has certain legal attributes resulting solely from the special form in which it is cast. Recognizances, formal acknowledgments of indebtedness made in court, are another example of formal contracts. All other contracts, whether oral or written, are informal contracts, since they do not depend upon mere formality for their legal existence.

Express and Implied Contracts

At the time of contracting the parties manifest their willingness either by express language or by conduct from which such willingness is implied. For instance, a man might pick up an item at a drug store, simply show it to the clerk and walk out. Yet this is a perfectly valid contract. The clerk knows from the customer's conduct that the latter is buying the item at the stipulated price and wants it charged to his account. His actions speak as effectively as words. A contract in which the parties manifest assent in words is called an express contract; a contract formed by conduct is an implied contract. Both are genuine contracts, equally enforceable. The difference between them is merely the manner in which assent is manifested.

Unilateral and Bilateral Contracts

In the typical contractual transaction, each party makes at least one promise. For example, A says to B, "If you promise to mow my lawn, I will give you ten dollars" and B agrees to mow A's lawn. A and B have made mutual promises, each undertaking to do something in exchange for the promise of the other. When a contract comes into existence by the exchange of promises, each is under a duty to the other. This kind of contract is called *bilateral,* because each party is both a promisor and a promisee, and has rights and is subject to duties under it.

But suppose that only one of the parties makes a promise. A says to B, "If you will mow my lawn, I will give you ten dollars." A contract will be formed when B has finished mowing the lawn and not before. At that time A becomes contractually bound to pay ten dollars to B. A's offer was in exchange for B's act of mowing the lawn, and not for a promise of B to mow it. B was under no duty to mow the lawn. This is a *unilateral* contract because only one of the parties makes a promise.

Thus, a bilateral contract results from the exchange of a promise for a counter-promise. A unilateral contract results from the exchange of a promise for an act or for a forbearance to act. Where it is not clear whether a unilateral or bilateral contract has been formed, the courts presume that the parties intended a bilateral contract.

Void, Voidable, and Unenforceable Contracts

By definition a contract is an enforceable promise or agreement. Thus, a void contract is no contract at all. It is merely a promise or agreement which has no legal effect. An example of a void agreement is an agreement entered into by an adjudicated incompetent.

A voidable contract, on the other hand, is not wholly lacking in legal effect. It is a contract, but because of the manner or method in which it was brought about, the law permits one or more of the parties to avoid his duties thereunder. For instance, A through fraud induces B to enter into a contract. B may, upon discovery of the fraud, notify A that by reason of the fraud he will not perform his promise, and the law will support B. The contract induced by fraud is not void, but is voidable at the elec-

tion of the defrauded party. A, the fraudulent party, has no such election.

A contract may be neither void nor voidable, yet may be unenforceable. For example, a contract may be unenforceable because of a failure to satisfy the requirements of the Statute of Frauds, which requires certain kinds of contracts to be in writing in order to be enforceable. Also, the right to bring a lawsuit for breach of contract may be barred by running of the time within which such a suit may be filed, as provided in the Statute of Limitations. After the time period has run, the contract is referred to as unenforceable, rather than void or voidable.

Executed and Executory Contracts

If a contract has been fully performed by all of the parties, it is an executed contract. Strictly, an executed contract is no contract in the present tense, as all duties under it have become discharged, but it is useful to have a term for the completed or fully performed contract. The term "executory contract" means unperformed and applies to situations where there are one or more unperformed promises by any party to the contract, or the contract is wholly unperformed by one or more of the parties.

Quasi Contracts

In addition to implied-in-fact contracts, there are implied-in-law contracts or quasi contracts which were not mentioned in the foregoing classification of contracts for the reason that a quasi (meaning "as if") contract is not a contract at all.

This is because it is not based either upon an express or an implied promise. For example, A by mistake delivers to B a plain unaddressed envelope containing $100 intended for C. B is under no contractual obligation to return it. However, historically, A was permitted to recover the $100 from B through the use of a legal remedy, an action of assumpsit that was also used for the enforcement of contracts. The law imposes an obligation upon B in order to prevent his unjust enrichment at the expense of A.

In Bradkin v. Leverton, 26 N.Y.2d 192, 309 N.Y.S.2d 192, 257 N.E.2d 643 (1970), the Court states:

Quasi contracts are not contracts at all, although they give rise to obligations more akin to those stemming from contract than from tort. The contract is a mere fiction, a form imposed in order to adapt the case to a given remedy. * * * Briefly stated, a quasi-contractual obligation is one imposed by law where there has been no agreement or expression of assent, by word or act, on the part of either party involved.

The law creates it, regardless of the intention of the parties, to assure a just and equitable result.

ESSENTIALS OF A CONTRACT

The four essential ingredients of a binding promise are:

1. Manifestation of mutual assent.
2. Consideration.
3. Legality of object.
4. Capacity of the parties.

If all of these essentials are present, the promise is contractual. If any of them is lacking, the promise is non-contractual. These essentials will be separately considered in succeeding chapters.

Cases

*Definition and
Essentials of Contract*

STEINBERG v. CHICAGO MEDICAL SCHOOL

(1976) 41 Ill.App.3d 804, 354 N.E.2d 586.

DEMPSEY, J.
* * *

A contract is an agreement between competent parties, based upon a consideration sufficient in law, to do or not do a particular thing. It is a promise or a set of promises for the breach of which the law gives a remedy, or the performance of which the law in some way recognizes as a duty. [Citation.] A contract's essential requirements are: competent parties, valid subject matter, legal consideration, mutuality of obligation and mutuality of agreement. Generally, parties may contract in any situation where there is no legal prohibition, since the law acts by restraint and not by conferring rights. [Citation.] However, it is basic contract law that in order for a contract to be binding the terms of the contract

must be reasonably certain and definite. [Citation.]

A contract, in order to be legally binding, must be based on consideration. [Citation.] Consideration has been defined to consist of some right, interest, profit or benefit accruing to one party or some forbearance, disadvantage, detriment, loss or responsibility given, suffered or undertaken by the other. [Citation.] Money is a valuable consideration and its transfer or payment or promises to pay it or the benefit from the right to its use, will support a contract.

In forming a contract, it is required that both parties assent to the same thing in the same sense [citation] and that their minds meet on the essential terms and conditions. [Citation.] Furthermore, the mutual consent essential to the formation of a contract, must be gathered from the language employed by the parties or manifested by their words or acts. The intention of the parties gives character to the transaction and if either party contracts in good faith he is entitled to the benefit of his contract no matter what may have been the secret purpose or intention of the other party. [Citation.]

* * *

Quasi Contracts

PUTTKAMMER v. MINTH
(1978) 83 Wis.2d 686, 266 N.W.2d 361.

HANSEN, J.

On November 20, 1974, Victor Puttkammer, d/b/a Asphalt Spraying Co., plaintiff-appellant, commenced this action against the defendant-respondent, Arthur Minth, seeking compensation for improvements made to certain real property owned by Minth. The complaint was subsequently amended, and the material facts alleged in the amended complaint and assumed to be true for purposes of this appeal, are as follows:

The defendant, Minth, is the owner of the Hiawatha Supper Club in Eagle River, Wisconsin, which he leased during 1972 and 1973 to James Piekarski. During the period of the lease, the plaintiff, at the request of Piekarski, resurfaced the access and service areas of the supper club, providing labor and materials with a reasonable value of $2,540, and increasing the value of the property by the same amount.

The defendant was aware that this work was being done and "stood by and acquiesced" in its completion. Piekarski did not pay for the work and was subsequently adjudged bankrupt, with no assets in his estate for the payment of plaintiff. The defendant now has the benefit of the improvements but refuses to pay for them, and the plaintiff has not been paid for any portion of the work.

The complaint further alleges that the plaintiff has exhausted his remedy against Piekarski and that if the defendant is not required to pay for the improvements, he will be unjustly enriched at the plaintiff's

expense. The amended complaint therefore prays for damages in the amount of $2,540, plus costs and disbursements.

The defendant demurred to this amended complaint on the ground that it failed to state a cause of action. The trial court sustained the demurrer and denied the plaintiff leave to further amend the complaint.

The issues on this appeal are whether the complaint alleges facts sufficient to state a cause of action * * *.

* * *

The plaintiff maintains that the complaint states a cause of action in equity for unjust enrichment. The elements of such a cause of action are: (1) a benefit conferred upon the defendant by the plaintiff; (2) an appreciation or knowledge by the defendant of the benefit; and (3) acceptance or retention by the defendant of the benefit under circumstances making it inequitable for the defendant to retain the benefit without payment of its value. [Citations.]

The amended complaint in the present case alleges facts sufficient to satisfy the first and second of these requirements. The complaint alleges that a benefit has been conferred on the defendant in that the value of his property has been enhanced by $2,540. The complaint also alleges appreciation by the defendant of the fact of the benefit, since it is alleged the defendant was aware the work was being performed and stood by and acquiesced in its completion.

The question is whether the complaint alleges facts sufficient to establish, either expressly or by inference, the third requirement: that the benefit was accepted or retained under such circumstances as to make retention of the benefit of the resurfacing, without payment therefor, inequitable.

In an action for unjust enrichment, " ' . . . [r]ecovery is based upon the universally recognized moral principle that one who has received a benefit has the duty to make restitution when to retain such benefit would be unjust.' . . . " [Citations.] It is not enough to establish that a benefit was conferred and retained; the retention must be inequitable.

The law in this state thus recognizes the principle set forth in the Restatement, *Restitution,* sec. 1, Comment c., p. 13, that:

. . . Even where a person has received a benefit from another, he is liable to pay therefor only if the circumstances of its receipt or retention are such that, as between the two persons, it is unjust for him to retain it. The mere fact that a person benefits another is not of itself sufficient to require the other to make restitution therefor . . .

* * *

In the instant case the complaint does not allege or reasonably imply that the work was ordered or ratified by the defendant; that the plaintiff performed the work expecting to be paid by the defendant; that the plaintiff was prejudiced by any miscon-

duct or fault on the part of the defendant; or that the interests of Piekarski and the defendant were so related or intermingled that it can be said that the contract was executed for the defendant's benefit. The most that can be said from the complaint is that the defendant knowingly acquiesced in the performance of the work. This is insufficient basis to impose liability on one who did not request the work and may not have desired it. The trial court was correct in ruling that the complaint fails to state a cause of action.

* * *

We agree with the holding of the trial court that this complaint, as presently constituted, even given a liberal construction, does not state a cause of action against this defendant. The demurrer was properly sustained.

* * *

[Judgment reversed and remanded on other grounds.]

Chapter
7

MANIFESTATION
OF MUTUAL
ASSENT

While each requirement for the formation of a contract is essential to its existence, mutual assent is so basic that frequently a contract is referred to as the agreement between the parties. When the contract is enforced, it is the agreement that is enforced. The agreement between the parties is the very core of the contract.

A contractual agreement always involves either a promise exchanged for a promise (bilateral contract), or a promise exchanged for an act or forbearance to act (unilateral contract) as manifested by what the parties communicated to one another. To effect the formation of a contract, the agreement must be objectively manifested. The Restatement, Second, of Contracts, Section 3, has this definition: "An agreement is a manifestation of mutual assent on the part of two or more persons." The manner in which parties usually manifest a mutual assent is by offer and acceptance.

The important thing is what the parties manifest to one another by spoken or written words or by conduct. The law applies an objective standard and is concerned only with the assent, agreement, or intention of a party as it reasonably appears from his words or actions. The law of contracts is not concerned with what a party may have actually thought or the meaning that he intended to convey, in so far as his subjective understanding or intention differed from the meaning objectively manifested. If A offers to sell to B his white horse but intends to offer and believes that he is offering his black horse, and B accepts the offer reasonably believing it to be for the white horse, a contract has been formed for the sale of the white horse. Subjectively, there is no agreement as to the subject matter, but objectively there is a manifestation by agreement, and this is binding.

OFFER TO CONTRACT

An offer is a definite proposal or undertaking made by one person to another which is effective upon an act, forbearance, or return promise being given in exchange. The person making the proposal is the offeror. The person to whom it is made is the offeree.

An offer always contains a promise. Upon receipt it confers upon the offeree the power of acceptance, which is an expression of willingness to comply with the terms of the offer. If unequivocal, the expression of willingness is an acceptance.

ESSENTIALS OF AN OFFER

An offer need not take any particular form to have legal effect. However, (1) it must be communicated to the offeree; (2) it must manifest an intent to enter into a contract; and (3) it must be sufficiently definite and certain. If these essentials are present, an offer which is open, i.e., has not terminated, confers upon the offeree the power to form a contract by accepting the offer.

Communication

In order to have the mutual assent requisite to a contract, which in practically every case is manifested by an offer and an acceptance, the offeree must have knowledge of the offer and the offer must have been communicated by the offeror. An offeree cannot agree to something of which he has no knowledge.

Assume that A signs a letter containing an offer to B and leaves it on top of the desk in his office. Later that day, B, without prearrangement, goes to A's office, discovers that A is away, notices the letter on A's desk, reads it, and then writes thereon an acceptance of the offer which he dates and signs. No contract is formed because the offer never became effective for the reason that it was never communicated by A to B. If A had mailed the letter, and it had gone astray in the mails, the offer contained therein would likewise never have become effective. The offer must be communicated to the offeree and the communication must be made or authorized by the offeror. If Jones tells Black that he is going to offer $600 to White for the latter's piano, and Black promptly informs White of this ex-

pressed intention of Jones, no offer has been made. There was no authorized communication of any offer by Jones to White. By the same token, if X should offer to sell to Y his diamond ring, an acceptance of this offer by Z would not be effective, as X made no offer to Z.

An offer need not be stated or communicated by words. Conduct from which a reasonable person may infer a promise in return for an act or a promise will amount to an offer. For example, A owns a house which is enclosed by a picket fence sadly in need of paint. One day B applied a coat of fresh white paint to the picket fence. A is not obligated to pay B for this paint job, as he did not order it or have any knowledge of it. If, however, A were present, observed B painting the fence, knew that B's occupation was that of a painter, and said nothing to B, he would then be obligated to pay B the reasonable value of the paint job if B acted in good faith. Under the circumstances, A as a reasonable man ought to have known that B in doing the work expected to be compensated for it. A's liability would be based upon an implied contract.

An offer may be made generally or to the public. However, no person can accept such an offer until and unless he has knowledge that the offer exists. If a person, without knowledge of the existence of an advertised reward for information leading to the arrest of a particular criminal, gives information which leads to such arrest, he is not entitled to the reward. His act was not an acceptance of the offer because he could not accept something of which he had no knowledge.

Intent

To have legal effect an offer must also manifest an intent to enter into a contract. Some proposals lack such intent and are therefore not deemed offers. As a result, an acceptance does not bring about a contract but operates only as an offer.

Invitations Seeking Offers. A businessman desirous of selling merchandise is interested in informing potential customers about the goods, the terms of sale, and price. But if he makes widespread promises to sell to each person on his mailing list, it is conceivable that the number of acceptances and resulting contracts might exceed his ability to perform. Consequently, he might refrain from making offers by merely announcing that he has goods for sale, describing the goods, and quoting prices. He thereby invites his customers, and in the case of published advertisements, the public, to become interested by making offers to him to buy the goods. His advertisements, circulars, quotation sheets, and display of merchandise are not offers because (1) they do not contain a promise, and (2) they leave unexpressed many terms which would be necessary to the making of a contract. Accordingly, the responses are not acceptances because no promise or offer to sell has been made. It is important to distinguish language which constitutes an offer from that which merely solicits or invites offers.

However, it should be noted that a seller is not free to advertise goods at one price and then raise the price once demand has been stimulated. Although as far as contract law is concerned no offer has been made, such conduct is prohibited by the Federal Trade Commission as well as legislation in many states. Moreover, it should be borne in mind that a public announcement or advertisement may constitute an offer. This is so if the advertisement or announcement contains a promise of something in exchange for something else, as in the case of the typical offer of a reward. In Lefkowitz v. Great Minneapolis Surplus Store, Inc. (page 142) the court held that a newspaper advertisement was an offer because it contained a promise of performance in definite terms in return for a requested act.

Communications between the parties in many cases take the form of preliminary negotiations. The parties are either requesting or supplying the terms of an offer which may or may not be given. A statement which may indicate a willingness to offer is not itself an offer. If A writes to B "Will you buy my automobile for $3000?", and B replies "Yes.", there is no contract. A has not made an offer to sell his automobile to B for $3000.

Objective Standard for Intent. Occasionally, a person exercises his sense of humor by speaking or writing words which taken literally and without regard to context or surrounding circumstances could be construed as an offer. However, the promise is intended as a joke, and the promisee as a reasonable man understands it to be such. Therefore it is not an offer. It does not create a sense of reasonable expectancy in the mind of the person to whom it is made because of his realization that it is not being made in earnest. There is no contractual intent on the part of the promisor, and the promisee is or reasonably ought to be aware of that fact. However, the success of a joke or prank is measured by the extent to which it deceives the one upon whom it is practiced. The words in jest must be spoken with a straight face or appearance of seriousness, else they are fatuous. If the intended jest is so successful that the promisee as a reasonable man under all the circumstances reasonably believes that it has been made as an offer, and so believing accepts, the objective standard applies and the parties have entered into a contract.

A promise made under circumstances of obvious excitement or emotional strain is likewise not an offer. For example, A, after having his month-old Cadillac break down for the third time in two days, screams in disgust "I will sell this car to anyone for $10.00." B hears A and hands him a ten-dollar bill. Under the circumstances, A's statement was not an offer, if a reasonable person in B's position would have not so considered it.

Definiteness

The terms of the contract which are formed upon the acceptance of an offer must be definite and certain, as otherwise it would be impossible to describe the obligations created in terms which would permit a court to determine whether or not a breach had occurred, and if so, the measure or extent of the resulting damages. For this reason, the terms of an offer, which upon acceptance become the terms of the contract, must be definite and certain. With respect to agreements for the sale of goods, the Code provides standards by which omitted essential terms may be ascertained and such deficiency supplied, provided the parties intended a binding agreement. Sections 2–204(3); 2–207(3).

To be definite an offer must define or describe its subject matter and set forth all material terms such as quality, quantity, and price or refer to some standard whereby these terms may be ascertained and made certain. A reference to the market value on a specific date by which to determine the price, if there is a market, or to reasonable value if there is no ready market, is a sufficient standard by which to determine the price. A statement in the offer that the price shall be determined by appraisers or a designated third person is also a sufficient standard. A reference to the amount of goods or supplies which a certain industrial plant requires for its normal operations during a stated period of time is sufficient for determination of the quantity offered. An offer is also sufficiently definite if it contains a minimum and a maximum and requires the offeree to state in his acceptance an amount within these limits. Thus, A writes to B that he will sell to B between 2,000 and 3,000 tons of steel at $200 per ton. B replies that he accepts for 2,400 tons of the steel. A contract is formed for 2,400 tons.

Open Terms Under the Code. The Code has relaxed the common law's requirements of definiteness in a number of ways, so long as the parties clearly indicate an intent to make a contract. The Code provides built-in standards and permits an offer, otherwise fatally indefinite because one or more of its terms are left open, to result in a contract if the parties intended to make a contract. Sections 2–204, 2–305, 2–311.

An offer for the purchase or sale of goods may leave open particulars of performance to be specified by one of the parties. The indefiniteness of such offer is cured by the requirement of the Code that "Any such specification must be made in good faith and within limits set by commercial reasonableness." Section 2–311(1). "Good faith" is defined as "honesty in fact in the conduct or transaction concerned." Section 1–201(19). "Commercial reasonableness" is a standard measured by the business judgment of reasonable men familiar with the customary practices in the type of transaction involved, and with regard to the facts and circumstances of the case.

A contract formed by acceptance of an offer which in certain respects is indefinite is reinforced by the obligation of good faith which the Code makes generally applicable in Section 1–203: "Every contract or duty within this Act imposes an obligation of good faith in its performance or enforcement." Commercial standards and reasonable practices of business supply those terms omitted by parties who have reached an agreement intended by them to be mutually binding.

Consequently, the parties may enter into a contract for the sale of goods even though they have reached no agreement on the price. A contract for the sale of goods may contain an open price term. Under Section 2–305, the price is a reasonable one at the time for delivery where the agreement (a) says nothing as to price, or (b) provides that the parties shall agree later on the price and they fail to so agree, or (c) fixes the price in terms of some agreed market or other standard or as set by a third person or agency, and the price is not so set. An agreement that the price is to be fixed by the seller or buyer means that it must be fixed in good faith. If the price is to be fixed otherwise than by agreement and is not so fixed through the fault of one of the parties, the other party has an option to treat the contract as cancelled or to fix a reasonable price in good faith for the goods. However, where the parties intend not to be bound unless the price is fixed or agreed upon as provided in the agreement, and it is not so fixed or agreed upon, the Code provides in accordance with the parties' intent that there is no contractual liability. In such case the seller must refund to the buyer any portion of the price received, and the buyer must return the goods to the seller or if unable to do so, pay the reasonable value thereof. Section 2–305(4).

Offers in the Alternative. An offer is not uncertain or indefinite because it is made in the alternative. Thus, A offers to sell to B a certain radio for $75 or a certain television set for $300. B accepts the offer. The resulting contract obligates A to sell and B to buy either the radio for $75 or the television set for $300. B has the election to determine which of the two he will take. If he refuses to take either, after having accepted the offer, he is liable to A in damages measured by his refusal to take the radio and pay for it, as the law will hold a contracting party only for the least that he has promised if such would constitute full performance under the contract. By taking and paying for the radio B would have

completely fulfilled his contractual obligation.

Output, Requirements, and Exclusive Dealings. An agreement of a buyer to purchase the entire output of a seller's factory for a stated period, or an agreement of a seller to supply a buyer with all his requirements of certain goods used in his business operations, may appear to lack definiteness and mutuality of obligation. The exact quantity of goods is not specified, and the seller may have some degree of control over his output, and the buyer over his requirements. However, such agreements are enforceable by the application of an objective standard based upon good faith of both parties. The seller cannot operate his factory twenty-four hours a day and insist upon the buyer taking all of the output where he did not do so before the agreement was made. Nor can the buyer expand his business abnormally and insist that the seller supply all of his requirements. Section 2–306(1).

An agreement between buyer and seller for exclusive dealing in a certain kind of merchandise, unless otherwise agreed, imposes an obligation upon the seller to use best efforts to supply the goods, and upon the buyer to use best efforts to promote the sale of the goods. Section 2–306(2).

DURATION OF OFFERS

An offer confers a power upon the offeree to create rights and duties by merely manifesting his acceptance, which power continues until the offer terminates. Upon termination the offeree no longer has such power, that is, the offer may no longer be accepted. The ways in which an offer may be terminated, other than by acceptance, are: (1) Lapse of time; (2) Revocation; (3) Rejection; (4) Counter-offer; (5) Death or insanity of the offeror or offeree; (6) Destruction of the specific subject matter to which the offer relates; and (7) Subsequent illegality of the type of contract contemplated by the offer.

Lapse of Time

The offeror may specify the time within which the offer is to be accepted, just as he may specify any other term or condition in the offer. Unless otherwise terminated, the offer remains open for the specified time period. After the expiration of that time, the offer no longer exists and cannot be accepted.

If no time is stated in the offer within which the offeree may accept, the offer will terminate upon the expiration of a reasonable period of time. The offeree has the power to create a contract by accepting the offer within this time period. What is a reasonable period of time is a question of fact, depending on the nature of the contract proposed, the usages of business and other circumstances of the case which the offeree at the time of his acceptance either knows or has reason to know. Restatement, Contracts, Section 41. For instance, an offer to sell a perishable good would be open for a shorter period of time than an offer to sell undeveloped real estate.

Revocation

Prior to acceptance, the offeror generally may cancel or revoke it at any time. If the offeror originally promises that the offer would be open for thirty days, but after five days wishes to terminate it, he may nonetheless do so by merely giving the offeree notice that he is withdrawing the offer. This notice may be given by any means of communication and effectively terminates the offer when received by the offeree. However, an offer made to the general public is only revoked by giving publicity to the revocation equivalent to that given the offer.

Notice of revocation may be indirectly communicated to the offeree, as where he receives reliable information from a third person that the offeror has disposed of the goods which he has offered for sale or has otherwise placed himself in a position which indicates an unwillingness or inability to perform the promise contained in the offer. For example, A offers to sell his portable television set to B and tells B that he has ten days in which to accept. One week later B observes the television set in C's house and is informed that C had purchased it from A. The next day B sends to A an acceptance of the offer. There is no contract, as A's offer was effectively revoked when B learned of A's inability to sell the television set to B by reason of his having sold it to C.

Certain limitations, however, have been imposed upon the offeror's power to revoke the offer at any time prior to its acceptance. These limitations pertain to the following four situations.

Option Contracts. An option is a contract in which the offeror is bound to hold open an offer for a specified period of time. It complies with all of the requirements of a contract, including consideration being given to the offeror by the offeree. For example, if in consideration of $100 paid to A by B, A gives B an option to buy Blackacre at a price of $20,000 exercisable at any time within thirty days, A's offer is irrevocable. A is legally bound to keep the offer open for thirty days and any communication by A to B of notice of withdrawal of the offer is ineffective. B is not bound to accept the offer, but the option contract entitles him to thirty days in which to consider acceptance.

Firm Offers. The Code provides that a merchant is bound to keep an offer open, for a stated period not in excess of three months, if the merchant gives assurance in a signed writing that it will be held open. Section 2–205. The Code therefore makes a merchant's written promise not to revoke an offer for a stated period of time enforceable even though no consideration is given the offeror for that promise.

Statutory Irrevocability. Certain offers are made irrevocable by statute, such as bids for the construction of a building or some public work made to the State, municipality, or other governmental body. Another example is pre-incorporation stock subscription agreements which are irrevocable for a period of six months under many state corporation statutes.

Irrevocable Offers of Unilateral Contract. Where the offer contemplates a unilateral contract, that is, a promise for an act, injustice to the offeree may result if revocation is permitted after the offeree has started to perform the act requested in the offer and has substantially but not completely accomplished it. Normally, such an offer is not accepted and no contract is formed until the offeree has completed the requested act. By commencing performance the offeree does not bind himself to complete performance nor does he bind the offeror to keep the offer open. Thus, the offeror could revoke the offer at any time prior to the offeree's completion of performance. For example, A offers B $300 if B will climb to the top of the flagpole in the center of campus. B commences his ascent and when he is five feet from the top A yells to him, "I revoke."

Some courts have attempted to solve this difficulty by treating the offer as if it were an offer for a bilateral contract, that is, a promise for a promise, which is accepted by the offeree's commencing performance. Such construction does violence to the terms of the offer, and causes the offeree as well as the offeror to become bound, which may not have been within the contemplation of the parties. Other courts have held that where the performance of the requested act necessarily requires time and effort to be expended by the offeree, an obligation not to revoke the offer for a reason-

able time arises. It is reasoned that the offeree's commencement of performance is tantamount to consideration being given to keep the offer open. Restatement, Second, Contracts, Section 45, provides:

(1) Where an offer invites an offeree to accept by rendering a performance and does not invite a promissory acceptance, an option contract is created when the offeree tenders or begins the invited performance or tenders a beginning of it.
(2) The offeror's duty of performance under any option contract so created is conditional on completion or tender of the invited performance in accordance with the terms of the offer.

This rule, however, presents another difficulty for it does not require the offeree to give notice to the offeror that performance has been commenced or is being given by the offeree. Where the offeror is not informed or notified that performance has been undertaken by the offeree, the situation is one in which the offeree knows that a contract has been formed, but the offeror does not know. To alleviate this hardship upon the offeror, the Code provides, Section 2–206(2):

Where the beginning of a requested performance is a reasonable mode of acceptance an offeror who is not notified of acceptance within a reasonable time may treat the offer as having lapsed before acceptance.

Rejection

Just as the acceptance of an offer is a manifestation of the willingness of the offeree to accept, a rejection of an offer is a manifestation by the offeree of his unwillingness to accept. The power of acceptance is terminated by a communicated rejection. After the effective moment of rejection, which is the receipt of the rejection by the offeror, the offeree may no longer accept the offer. Rejection by the offeree may consist of express language, or may be implied from language or from conduct.

Counter-offer

A counter-offer is a counter-proposal from the offeree to the offeror and indicates a willingness to contract with reference to the subject matter of the offer but upon terms or conditions different from those contained in the offer. It is not an unequivocal acceptance and by indicating an unwillingness to agree to the terms of the offer it operates as a rejection. Assume that A writes B a letter stating that he will sell to B a second-hand color television set for $300. B replies that he will pay A $250 for the set. This is a counter-offer which upon receipt by A terminates the original offer. However, if B in his reply states that he wishes to consider the $300 offer but is willing to pay $250 at once for the set, this is a counter-offer which does not terminate A's offer. In the first instance, after making the $250 counter-offer, B may not thereafter accept the $300 offer. In the second instance he may do so, as the counter-offer was stated in such a manner as not to indicate an unwillingness to accept the original offer and B therefore did not terminate it. With respect to the U.C.C. treatment of acceptances containing terms that vary from the offer, see U.C.C., Section 2–207, Appendix A.

Death or Insanity of Offeror or Offeree

The death or insanity of either the offeror or the offeree ordinarily terminates an offer. An offer embodies the willingness of the offeror to enter into a contract upon the terms stated in the offer. Upon his death or insanity the offeror no longer has legal capacity to enter into a contract and thus all outstanding offers are terminated. Death or insanity of the offeree likewise terminates the offer, because an ordinary offer is not assignable and can be accepted only by the person to whom it was made (the offeree). When the offeree ceases to be a person or ceases to have legal capacity to enter into a contract, there is in effect no one who can accept the offer. Therefore, the offer necessarily terminates.

The death or insanity of the offeror or offeree, however, does not terminate an offer contained in an option. An option is a contract and upon the death or insanity of the offeror becomes the obligation of his estate. If during the option period the offeree possessing the option, should die or become incompetent, his personal representative would possess the right to exercise the option within the option time period.

Destruction of Subject Matter

Destruction of the specific subject matter of an offer terminates the offer. The impossibility of performance prevents a contract from being consummated and thus terminates all outstanding offers with respect to the destroyed property.

Subsequent Illegality

One of the four essential ingredients of a contract, as previously mentioned, is legality of purpose or subject matter. If performance of a valid contract is subsequently made illegal, the obligations of both parties under the contract are discharged. Illegality taking effect after the making of an offer but prior to acceptance has the same effect. The offer is legally terminated.

ACCEPTANCE OF OFFER

The acceptance of an offer is essential to the formation of a contract. Acceptance of an offer for a bilateral contract is some overt act by the offeree which manifests his assent to the terms of the offer, such as speaking, or sending a letter, a telegram, or other communication to the offeror. If the offer is for a unilateral contract, acceptance is the performance of the requested act or forbearance with the intention of accepting. For example, if A publishes an offer of a reward to anyone who returns the diamond ring which he has lost (a unilateral contract offer), and B with knowledge of the offer finds and returns the ring to A but in doing so disclaims the reward and says that he does not accept the offer, there is no contract. Merely doing the act requested by the offeror is not sufficient to form a contract where it is not done with the intention of accepting the offer.

DEFINITENESS OF ACCEPTANCE

An acceptance must be positive and unequivocal. It may not change any of the terms of the offer, not add to, subtract from, or qualify in any way, the provisions of the offer. It must be the "mirror image" of the offer. Except as modified by the Code, any communication by the offeree which attempts to do so is not an acceptance, but is a mere counter-offer. If the offer is for a bilateral contract, the acceptance must contain a promise expressly or by implication. If the offer is for a unilateral contract, the requested act or forbearance must be precisely performed by the offeree in order to be an acceptance. Once an acceptance has been given, the contract is formed.

The "mirror image" rule is modified by the Code with respect to transactions in goods, as provided in Section 2–207(1) and (2).

(1) A definite and seasonable expression of acceptance or a written confirmation which is sent within a reasonable time operates as an acceptance even though it states terms additional to or different from those offered or agreed upon, unless acceptance is expressly made conditional on assent to the additional or different terms.
(2) The additional terms are to be construed as proposals for addition to the contract. Between merchants such terms become part of the contract unless: (a) the offer expressly limits acceptance to the terms of the offer; (b) they materially alter it; or (c) notification of objection to them has already been given or is given within a reasonable time after notice of them is received.

This section is necessitated by the realities of modern business practices. A tremendous number of business transactions are accomplished by use of standardized business forms. For example, a buyer sends to a seller on buyer's order form a purchase order for 200 bicycles at $50 per bicycle with delivery by October 1, 1982, at buyer's place of business. On the reverse side of this standard form are 25 numbered paragraphs containing provisions generally favorable to the buyer. When the seller receives the purchase order, he sends to the buyer on his acceptance form an unequivocal acceptance of the offer. However, despite the fact that seller agrees to buyer's quantity, price and delivery terms, on the back of his acceptance form the seller has 32 numbered paragraphs generally favorable to himself and in significant conflict with buyer's form. Clearly, under the "mirror image" rule, no contract would exist for there has not been an unequivocal acceptance of all of the material terms of the buyer's offer.

The Code alleviates this "Battle of the Forms" problem by focusing upon the intent of the parties. If the seller definitely and seasonably expresses his acceptance of the offer and does not expressly make his acceptance conditional upon the buyer's assent to the additional or different terms a contract is formed. Section 2–207(1). The issue then becomes whether seller's additional or different terms become part of the contract. If the contract is between merchants (both buyer and seller are merchants), the terms will be part of the contract, provided they do not materially alter the agreement and are not objected to either in the offer itself or within a reasonable period of time.   Section 2–207(2).

EFFECTIVE MOMENT OF ACCEPTANCE

As previously discussed, an offer, a revocation, a rejection, and a counter-offer are effective when they are communicated, that is, when received.   An acceptance, on the other hand, is generally effective upon dispatch.   This is true unless the offer specifically provides otherwise or the offeree uses an unauthorized means of communication.

Authorized Means

Historically, an authorized means of communication is the means expressly authorized by the offeror in the offer or, if none is authorized, it is the means utilized by the offeror.   For example, if in reply to an offer by mail, the offeree places in the mail a letter of acceptance properly stamped and addressed to the offeror, a contract is formed at the time and place that the offeree mails the letter.   This assumes, of course, that the offer at that time was open and had not been terminated by any of the methods previously discussed.   The reason for this rule is that the offeror by using the mail, impliedly authorized the offeree to use the same channel of communication and his mailing of an acceptance is an overt act of manifestation of assent.   If the offer is by telegram, a telegraphic acceptance is effective when dispatched.   It is immaterial if the telegram of acceptance is delayed in transmission, or if the letter of acceptance goes astray in the mails and is never received.   Likewise if the offeree after mailing a letter of acceptance, succeeds in withdrawing it from the mails by complying with postal regulations, a contract has been formed by the act of mailing, even though the offeror may never learn about it.

The Restatement, Second, Contracts, and the Code provide that where the language in the offer or the circumstances do not otherwise indicate, an offer to make a contract shall be construed as inviting acceptance in any reasonable manner.   Restatement, Sections 30, 65; U.C.C. Section 2–206(1)(a).   These provisions are intended to allow flexibility of response and the ability to keep pace with new modes of communication.

Unauthorized Means

When the medium of communication used by the offeree is unauthorized the traditional rule is that acceptance is effective when and if received by the offeror, provided that it is received within the time the authorized means would have arrived.   The Restatement, Second, Contracts, Section 67, provides that if these conditions are met the acceptance is effective upon dispatch.

Specific Provisions in the Offer

If the offer specifically stipulates the means of communication to be utilized by the offeree, the acceptance to be effective must conform to that specification.   Moreover, the rule that an acceptance is effective when dispatched or sent does not apply to the case where the offer provides that the acceptance must be received by the offeror.   If the offeror states that a reply must be received by a certain date or that he must hear from the offeree, or uses other language indicating that the acceptance must be received by him, the effective moment of the acceptance is when it is received by the offeror and not when it is sent or dispatched by the offeree.

Acceptance Following a Prior Rejection

To be effective to terminate an offer, a rejection must be communicated by the offeree to the offeror.   For example, A in New York sends by air mail to B in San Francisco an offer which is expressly stated to be open for one week.   On the fourth day B sends to A by air mail a letter of rejection which is delivered on the morning of the sixth day. At noon on the fifth day B dispatches a telegram of acceptance which is received by A before the close of business on that day.

The act of mailing the letter of rejection was not effective to terminate the offer until it was received. However, it did immediately have one effect, namely, to deprive the offeree of the power to cause a contract to be formed by the act of sending an acceptance. After dispatching a rejection, an acceptance is not effective when sent by the offeree but only when and if received by the offeror prior to his receipt of the rejection. Therefore, a contract was formed when B's telegram of acceptance was received by A for the reason that the offer was not then terminated, inasmuch as B's rejection had not at that time been received by A. Thus, when an acceptance follows a prior rejection the first communication to be received by the offeror is the effective one.

Defective Acceptances

A late acceptance or defective acceptance does not create a contract. After the offer has expired there can be no acceptance of it. However, a late or defective acceptance does manifest a willingness on the part of the offeree to enter into a contract and therefore constitutes a new offer. The offeror who receives a late or defective acceptance may not by silence or inaction regard it as effective. In order to create a contract the original offeror must accept the new offer by manifesting his assent to the original offeree.

MODE OF ACCEPTANCE

Silence as Acceptance

An offeree is generally under no legal duty to reply to an offer. His silence or inaction is therefore not an acceptance of the offer. However, by custom, usage, or course of dealing, silence or inaction by the offeree may operate as an acceptance.

Salesmen employed by a manufacturing company or by a distributor to solicit orders for its merchandise from its customers usually have no authority to bind their employer by contract. The order forms usually recite that no contract is formed until the order of the buyer is accepted at the home office of the seller. Upon receipt of purchase orders, the manufacturer or distributor is under a duty to notify the customer within a reasonable time of its non-acceptance in the event of its inability or unwillingness to ship the merchandise ordered. Silence or inaction by the soliciting company is treated as an acceptance of the order.

Silence or inaction of an offeree who fails to reply to an offer also operates as an acceptance and causes a contract to be formed where by previous dealings or otherwise the offeree has given the offeror reason to understand that silence or inaction by the offeree is intended by the offeree as a manifestation of assent, and the offeror does so understand.

Finally, if an offeror sends unordered or unsolicited merchandise to a person with an offer stating that the goods are sent for examination, that the addressee may purchase the goods at a specified price, and that unless the goods are returned within a stated period of time the offer will be deemed to have been accepted, the offer is one for an inverted unilateral contract (i.e., an act for a promise). However, this practice led to abuse, which has prompted the Federal government as well as most States to enact statutes which provide that in such cases the offeree-recipient of the goods may keep them as a gift and is under no obligation either to return them or to pay for them. See Federal Postal Reorganization Act, Section 3009.

Contract Formed by Conduct

Under the Code an express contract for the sale of goods may be made by conduct of the parties. There may be no definite offer and acceptance, or definite acceptance of an offer, yet a contract exists if both of the parties have acted in a manner which manifests a recognition by each of them of the existence of a contract. Recognition may result from the cumulative effect of a number of occurrences or incidents which bespeak reliance of both parties upon the existence of a contract. Section 2–207(3). Thus, it may be impossible to determine the exact moment when such a contract formed by conduct was made. Section 2–204.

Auction Sales

The auctioneer at an auction sale does not make offers to sell the property which is being auctioned, but invites offers to buy. The classic statement by the auctioneer is "How much am I offered?" The persons attending the auction may make progressively higher bids for the property, and each bid or statement of a price or a figure is an offer to buy at that figure. If the bid is accepted, which is customarily by the fall of the hammer in the hands of the auctioneer, a contract results. A bidder is free to withdraw his bid at any time prior to its acceptance. The auctioneer is likewise free to withdraw the goods from sale unless the sale is advertised or announced to be "without reserve."

If the auction sale is advertised or announced in explicit terms to be "without reserve," the auctioneer may not withdraw an article or lot put up for sale unless no bid is made within a reasonable time. Unless so advertised or announced the sale is with reserve. Whether with or without reserve, a bidder may retract his bid at any time prior to acceptance by the auctioneer. Such retraction does not revive any previous bid.

If the auctioneer knowingly receives a bid by or on behalf of the seller, and notice has not been given that the seller reserves the right to bid at the auction sale, any such bid by or on behalf of the seller gives the bidder to whom the goods are sold an election either (1) to avoid the sale, or (2) to take the goods at the price of the last good faith bid before the sale. Section 2–328.

Cases

Invitations Seeking Offers

LEFKOWITZ v. GREAT MINNEAPOLIS SURPLUS STORE, INC.

(1957) 251 Minn. 188, 86 N.W.2d 689.

MURPHY, J.

This is an appeal from an order of * * * judgment award[ing] the plaintiff the sum of $138.50 as damages for breach of contract.

This case grows out of the alleged refusal of the defendant to sell to the plaintiff a certain fur piece which it had offered for sale in a newspaper advertisement. It appears from the record that on April 6, 1956, the defendant published the following advertisement in a Minneapolis newspaper:

"Saturday 9 A.M. Sharp
3 Brand New
Fur
Coats
Worth to $100.00
First Come
First Served
$1
Each"

On April 13, the defendant again published an advertisement in the same newspaper as follows:

"Saturday 9 A.M.
2 Brand New Pastel
Mink 3-Skin Scarfs
Selling for $89.50
Out they go

Saturday. Each . . . $1.00
1 Black Lapin Stole
Beautiful,
worth $139.50 . . . $1.00
First Come
First Served"

The record supports the findings of the court that on each of the Saturdays following the publication of the above-described ads the plaintiff was the first to present himself at the appropriate counter in the defendant's store and on each occasion demanded the coat and the stole so advertised and indicated his readiness to pay the sale price of $1. On both occasions, the defendant refused to sell the merchandise to the plaintiff, stating on the first occasion that by a "house rule" the offer was intended for women only and sales would not be made to men, and on the second visit that plaintiff knew defendant's house rules. * * *

The defendant contends that a newspaper advertisement offering items of merchandise for sale at a named price is a "unilateral offer" which may be withdrawn without notice. He relies upon authorities which hold that, where an advertiser publishes in a newspaper that he has a certain quantity or quality of goods which he wants to dispose of at certain prices and on certain terms, such advertisements are not offers which become contracts as soon as any person to whose notice they may come signifies his acceptance by notifying the other that he will take a certain quantity of them. Such advertisements have been construed as an invitation for an offer of sale on the terms stated, which offer, when received, may be accepted or rejected and which therefore does not become a contract of sale until accepted by the seller; and until a contract has been so made, the seller may modify or revoke such prices or terms. [Citations.] * * *

On the facts before us we are concerned with whether the advertisement constituted an offer, and, if so, whether the plaintiff's

conduct constituted an acceptance. * * *

The test of whether a binding obligation may originate in advertisements addressed to the general public is "whether the facts show that some performance was promised in positive terms in return for something requested." 1 Williston, Contracts (Rev.ed.) § 27. * * *

Whether in any individual instance a newspaper advertisement is an offer rather than an invitation to make an offer depends on the legal intention of the parties and the surrounding circumstances. [Citations.] We are of the view on the facts before us that the offer by the defendant of the sale of the Lapin fur was clear, definite, and explicit, and left nothing open for negotiation. The plaintiff having successfully managed to be the first one to appear at the seller's place of business to be served, as requested by the advertisement, and having offered the stated purchase price of the article, he was entitled to performance on the part of the defendant. We think the trial court was correct in holding that there was in the conduct of the parties a sufficient mutuality of obligation to constitute a contract of sale.

* * *

Affirmed.

Objective Standard for Intent

LUCY v. ZEHMER
(1954) 196 Va. 493, 84 S.E.2d 516.

BUCHANAN, J.

This suit was instituted by W. O. Lucy and J. C. Lucy, complainants [plaintiffs], against A. H. Zehmer and Ida S. Zehmer, his wife, defendants, to have specific performance of a contract by which it was alleged the Zehmers had sold to W. O. Lucy a tract of land owned by A. H. Zehmer in Dinwiddie county containing 471.6 acres, more or less, known as the Ferguson farm, for $50,000. J. C. Lucy, the other complainant, is a brother of W. O. Lucy, to whom W. O. Lucy transferred a half interest in his alleged purchase.

The instrument sought to be enforced was written by A. H. Zehmer on December 20, 1952, in these words: "We hereby agree to sell to W. O. Lucy the Ferguson Farm complete for $50,000.00, title satisfactory to buyer," and signed by the defendants, A. H. Zehmer and Ida S. Zehmer.

The answer of A. H. Zehmer admitted that at the time mentioned W. O. Lucy offered him $50,000 cash for the farm, but that he, Zehmer, considered that the offer was made in jest; that so thinking, and both he and Lucy having had several drinks, he wrote out "the memorandum" quoted above and induced his wife to sign it; that he did not deliver the memorandum to Lucy, but that Lucy picked it up, read it, put it in his pocket, attempted to offer Zehmer $5 to bind the bargain, which Zehmer refused to accept, and realizing for the first time that Lucy was serious, Zehmer assured him that he had no intention of selling the farm and that the whole matter was a joke. Lucy left the premises insisting that he had purchased the farm. * * *

Mrs. Zehmer testified that when Lucy came into the restaurant he looked as if he had had a drink. When Zehmer came in he took a drink out of a bottle that Lucy handed him. She went back to help the waitress who was getting things ready for the next day. Lucy and Zehmer were talking but she did not pay too much attention to what they were saying. She heard Lucy ask Zehmer if he had sold the Ferguson farm, and Zehmer replied that he had not and did not want to sell it. Lucy said, "I bet you wouldn't take $50,000.00 cash for that farm," and Zehmer replied, "You haven't got $50,000 cash." Lucy said, "I can get it." Zehmer said he might form a company and get it, "but you haven't got $50,000.00 cash to pay me tonight." Lucy asked him if he would put it in writing that he would sell him this farm. Zehmer then

wrote on the back of a pad, "I agree to sell the Ferguson Place to W. O. Lucy for $50,000.00 cash." Lucy said, "All right, get your wife to sign it." Zehmer came back to where she was standing and said, "You want to put your name to this?" She said "No," but he said in an undertone, "It is nothing but a joke," and she signed it. * * *

In his testimony Zehmer claimed that he "was high as a Georgia pine," and that the transaction "was just a bunch of two doggoned drunks bluffing to see who could talk the biggest and say the most." That claim is inconsistent with his attempt to testify in great detail as to what was said and what was done. * * * It was in fact conceded by defendants' counsel in oral argument that under the evidence Zehmer was not too drunk to make a valid contract. * * *

The mental assent of the parties is not requisite for the formation of a contract. If the words or other acts of one of the parties have but one reasonable meaning, his undisclosed intention is immaterial except when an unreasonable meaning which he attaches to his manifestations is known to the other party. Restatement of the Law of Contracts, Vol. I, § 71, p. 74.

" * * * The law, therefore, judges an agreement between two persons exclusively from those expressions of their intentions which are communicated between them. * * *." Clark on Contracts, 4 ed., § 3, p. 4.

An agreement or mutual assent is of course essential to a valid contract but the law imputes to a person an intention corresponding to the reasonable meaning of his words and acts. If his words and acts, judged by a reasonable standard, manifest an intention to agree, it is immaterial what may be the real but unexpressed state of his mind. [Citations.]

So a person cannot set up that he was merely jesting when his conduct and words would warrant a reasonable person in believing that he intended a real agreement. [Citations.]

Whether the writing signed by the defendants and now sought to be enforced by the complainants was the result of a serious offer by Lucy and a serious acceptance by the defendants, or was a serious offer by Lucy and an acceptance in secret jest by the defendants, in either event it constituted a binding contract of sale between the parties. * * *

Reversed and remanded.

Revocation of Offers

CUSHING v. THOMSON
(1978) 118 N.H. 292, 386 A.2d 805.

PER CURIAM.

This is a bill in equity brought by five members of an antinuclear protest group called the Portsmouth Area Clamshell Alliance against Governor Meldrim Thomson, Jr., and John Blatsos, adjutant general of the State of New Hampshire. The bill seeks specific performance of a contract allegedly entered into by the parties for the use of the New Hampshire National Guard armory in Portsmouth.

* * *

The [trial] court ruled that a binding contract existed, granted the plaintiffs specific performance, and enjoined the defendants from any and all acts that would impede performance.

* * *

On or about March 30, 1978, the adjutant general's office received an application from plaintiff Cushing for the use of the Portsmouth armory to hold a dance on the evening of April 29, 1978. On March 31 the adjutant general mailed a signed contract offer agreeing to rent the armory to the Portsmouth Clamshell Alliance for the evening of April 29. The agreement required acceptance by the renter affixing his signature to the accompanying copy of the

agreement and returning the same to the adjutant general within five days after its receipt. On Monday, April 3, plaintiff Cushing received the contract offer and signed it on behalf of the Portsmouth Clamshell Alliance. At 6:30 on the evening of Tuesday, April 4, Mr. Cushing received a telephone call from the adjutant general advising him that the Governor had ordered withdrawal of the rental offer, and accordingly the offer was being withdrawn. During that conversation Mr. Cushing stated that he had already signed the contract. A written confirmation of the withdrawal was sent by the adjutant general to the plaintiffs on April 5. On April 6 defendants received by mail the signed contract dated April 3, postmarked April 5.

The first issue presented is whether the trial court erred in determining that a binding contract existed. Neither party challenges the applicable law. "To establish a contract of this character . . . there must be . . . an offer and an acceptance thereof in accordance with its terms . . . . [W]hen the parties to such a contract are at a distance from one another and the offer is sent by mail . . . the reply accepting the offer may be sent through the same medium, and the contract will be complete when the acceptance is mailed . . . properly addressed to the party making the offer and beyond the acceptor's control." [Citation.] Withdrawal of the offer is ineffectual once the offer has been accepted by posting in the mail. [Citation.]

* * *

Plaintiffs introduced the sworn affidavit of Mr. Cushing in which he stated that on April 3, he executed the contract and placed it in the outbox for mailing. Moreover plaintiffs' counsel represented to the court that it was customary office practice for outgoing letters to be picked up from the outbox daily and put in the U.S. mail. * * * Thus the representation that it was customary office procedure for the letters to be sent out the same day that they are placed in the office outbox, together with the affidavit, supported the implied finding that the completed contract was mailed before the attempted revocation. [Citation.]

[Decree affirmed.]

Counter-offer

ZELLER v. FIRST NATIONAL BANK AND TRUST, ETC.

(1979) 79 Ill.App.3d 170, 34 Ill. Dec. 473, 398 N.E.2d 148.

McNAMARA, J.

Plaintiff filed a complaint * * * alleging a contract to sell real estate to him. * * * The trial court entered summary judgment against plaintiff * * * and he appeals.

The property in question is held in trust. Defendant First National Bank and Trust Company of Evanston was trustee. William Jennings, who is not party to these proceedings, was beneficiary of the trust and executor of the estate containing the trust property. Austin L. Wyman, Jr., an attorney, and the law firm of Tenney & Bentley represented the estate.

In November, 1977, plaintiff and Jennings began negotiations with respect to the sale of the property. On December 23, 1977, Wyman wrote plaintiff, stating that he had been instructed by his principals to offer plaintiff the building for $240,000. The letter also recited interest rates and loan fees. Following receipt of this letter, plaintiff met with his attorney, Roger Jamma, and instructed him to communicate a counter-offer to Wyman. Accordingly, on January 10, 1978, Jamma sent Wyman a written counter-offer offering $230,000 and suggesting varying interest and loan arrangements.

On the same day, Jamma telephoned Wyman, and the two men discussed the offer and counter-offer. In his discovery deposition, Jamma stated that he might have mentioned the contents of the counter-offer to Wyman. Wyman testified at his deposition that Jamma informed him that a counter-offer of $230,000 had been sent and detailed the substance of the counter-offer.

* * *

On review, we deem it necessary to consider only the finding that the contract under which relief is sought was never properly formed.

It is elementary that for a contract to exist, there must be an offer and acceptance. [Citations.] Moreover, to create a binding contract, an acceptance must comply strictly with the terms of the offer. An acceptance requesting modification or containing terms which vary from those offered constitutes a rejection of the original offer, and becomes a counterproposal which must be accepted by the original offeror before a valid contract is formed. [Citations.]

On December 23, 1977, Wyman offered to sell plaintiff the property for $240,000. In a telephone conversation with Wyman on January 10, 1978, plaintiff's attorney discussed the counter-offer of $230,000. This counter-offer, containing terms varying from the original offer, operated as a rejection and terminated plaintiff's power to accept Wyman's offer. There was no suggestion that Wyman, the offeror, assented to the price modification in plaintiff's counter-offer so as to create a contract. Once having rejected Wyman's offer, plaintiff could not revive the offer by later telegraphing acceptance. [Citation.]

Plaintiff urges, however, that the counter-offer which was disclosed in the telephone conversation had no legal significance because it was oral rather than written. We do not agree. It is clear that the language of an offer may govern the mode of acceptance required. [Citation.] Where an offer requires a written acceptance, no other mode of acceptance may be used. [Citation.] Since the offer in the present case did not require acceptance or other communications regarding the sale to be in writing, verbal communication of the counter-offer was an effective rejection. Thus, contrary to plaintiff's contention, it is not determinative that the subsequent written acceptance arrived prior to the written counter-offer. In view of plaintiff's rejection prior to acceptance, no binding contract was created.

* * *

Judgment affirmed.

Definiteness of Acceptance

McAFEE v. BREWER

(1974) 214 Va. 579, 203 S.E.2d 129.

PANSON, J.

Don D. McAfee, plaintiff, instituted this action against the defendants, Jack R. Brewer and his wife, Virginia Brewer, to recover the balance due on an alleged contract between the parties for the sale of certain furniture. The case was tried without a jury, and the trial judge held for the defendants on the ground that they had not accepted plaintiff's offer to sell, since there was no "meeting of the minds" of the parties on the exact furniture items to be purchased. * * *

Plaintiff contends that the trial court erred in not holding that his offer to sell was accepted by the defendants, and in denying him recovery on the contract.

The evidence shows that plaintiff and another were co-owners of the Dower House in McLean, Virginia, which the defendants had contracted to buy. Several weeks prior to the May 7, 1971, settlement date for purchase of the property, the defendants began negotiations with the plaintiff for the purchase of certain items of furniture in the house.

On April 30, 1971, plaintiff sent the defendants a letter containing the following: a list of furnishings to be purchased by the defendants at specified prices; a pay-

ment schedule of $3,000 due upon acceptance, $3,000 due 60 days after the acceptance date, and $2,635 due 120 days after the acceptance date; a blank space for the defendants' signatures and the date the signatures were affixed; and a clause reading, "If the above is satisfactory please sign and return one copy with the first payment."

The delivery of the furniture was to be accomplished by leaving the items in the house; in fact, the items remained in the house after the settlement date.

One June 3, 1971, the defendants sent the following letter to plaintiff:

"Exams were horrible but Florida was great! Enclosing a $3,000 ck.—I've misplaced the contracts. Can the secretary send another set? We're moving into Dower House on June 12—please include the red secretary on the contract for entrance foyer. I'll have to stop by sometime during the month & order a coffee table.

"Hope all is well—

Sincerely—
/s/Va. & Jack"

Plaintiff, in turn, sent the defendants a letter dated June 8, 1971, in which he enumerated the various items of furniture purchased by them. Except for several additionally approved items, the list on the June 8 letter corresponded precisely with the list in the April 30th letter. Believing he had a contract with the Brewers to sell them the listed items of furniture, the plaintiff purchased new furniture to furnish his new home.

The defendants moved into Dower House around the middle of June 1971. Shortly thereafter the defendants made a number of telephone calls to plaintiff's office in an attempt to advise him that there had been a misunderstanding relating to their purchase of the listed items. Their calls were not returned. After unsuccessful efforts to settle the matter, the defendants refused to send plaintiff any more money, and this action was instituted.

Defendants testified that no agreement ever existed on what furniture was to be purchased. Defendant Jack R. Brewer further testified that he sent the $3,000 check only to buy several of the listed items, which totaled approximately $2,600, not to accept plaintiff's offer comprising all of the items listed. Brewer said he was not concerned about the overpayment because plaintiff was a friend, and he desired to buy some additional items from him.

Plaintiff argues that the defendants accepted his April 30th offer by their letter of June 3rd, the accompanying $3,000 check, and the request that the red secretary be included on the contract. We agree.

It is elementary that an agreement based on mutual assent is essential to a valid contract.

* * *

Code § 2–207 of the UCC provides, in pertinent part:

"(1) A definite and seasonable expression of acceptance or a written confirmation which is sent within a reasonable time operates as an acceptance even though it states terms additional to or different from those offered or agreed upon, unless acceptance is expressly made conditional on assent to the additional or different terms.

"(2) The additional terms are to be construed as proposals for addition to the contract. * * *"

Here the defendants' letters of June 3rd constituted a definite and seasonable acceptance or written confirmation sent within a reasonable time after receipt of plaintiff's offer to sell. The enclosure of the $3,000 check, the amount due upon acceptance of the contract, and the request to "include the red secretary on the contract," manifested defendants' assent or confirmation of the specific items enumerated in the April 30th letter. The reference to the red secretary was not expressed in language making acceptance conditional upon inclusion of the secretary. This item was merely a proposal for an addition to the contract.

While it is true that defendants did not sign and return one copy of the contract in the manner requested by plaintiff, their acceptance of the offer by letter was reasonable under the circumstances because they had misplaced the contract and the copy thereof. Moreover, there was no indication by the plaintiff that if the offer was not accepted in the suggested manner it would not be acceptable to him. Section 2–206 of the UCC rejects the technical rules of acceptance in providing that "an offer * * * shall be construed as inviting acceptance in any manner and by any medium reasonable in the circumstances." [Citation.]

For the reasons stated, the judgment of the court below is reversed and final judgment in the amount of $5,635 is here entered for the plaintiff.

Effective Moment of Acceptance

MORRISON v. THOELKE

(1963, Fla.App.) 155 So.2d 889.

ALLEN, C. J.
* * *

A number of undisputed facts were established by the pleadings, including the facts that appellees are the owners of the subject [real] property, located in Orange County; that on November 26, 1957, appellants, as purchasers, executed a contract for the sale and purchase of the subject property and mailed the contract to appellees who were in Texas; and that on November 27, 1957, appellees executed the contract and placed it in the mails addressed to appellants' attorney in Florida. It is also undisputed that after mailing said contract, but prior to its receipt in Florida, appellees called appellants' attorney and cancelled and repudiated the execution and contract. Nonetheless, appellants, upon receipt of the contract caused the same to be recorded.
* * *

On the basis of the foregoing facts, the lower court entered summary decree for the appellees, quieting [awarding] title in them. The basis of this decision was, in the words of the able trial judge:

"The contract executed by the parties hereto * * * constituted a cloud on the title of Plaintiffs. * * * The Court finds said contract to have been cancelled and repudiated by Plaintiffs prior to its receipt by Defendants * * * and that on this basis there was no legal contract binding on the parties * * *."

* * * The question is whether a contract is complete and binding when a letter of acceptance is mailed, thus barring repudiation prior to delivery to the offeror, or when the letter of acceptance is received, thus permitting repudiation prior to receipt. Appellants, of course, argue that posting the acceptance creates the contract; appellees contend that only receipt of the acceptance bars repudiation.

* * *

A * * * statement of the general rule is found in 1 Williston, Contracts § 81 (3rd ed. 1957):

"Contracts are frequently made between parties at some distance and therefore it is of vital importance to determine at what moment the contract is complete. If the mailing of an acceptance completes the contract, what happens thereafter, whether the death of either party, the receipt of a revocation or rejection, or a telegraphic recalling of the acceptance, though occurring before the receipt of the acceptance, will be of no avail; whereas, if a contract is not completed until the acceptance has been received, in all the situations supposed no contract will arise.

"It was early decided that the contract was completed upon the mailing of the acceptance. The reason influencing the court was evidently that when the acceptance was mailed, there had been an overt manifestation of assent to the proposal. The court failed to consider that since the proposed contract was bilateral, as is almost invariably any contract made by mail, the

so-called acceptance must also have become effective as a promise to the offeror in order to create a contract. The result thus early reached, however, has definitely established the law not only in England but also in the United States, Canada and other common law jurisdictions. It is, therefore, immaterial that the acceptance never reaches its destination."

The same work, in Section 86, negatives the possible effect of a power to recall an acceptance after mailing. In the author's words:

"By the United States Postal Regulations, the sender of a letter may regain it by complying with certain specified formalities, and yet a contract is completed by mailing an acceptance in the authorized channel. Since the acceptance is binding when it is mailed, the fact that the sender of a letter may regain possession of it should have no effect on the validity of the acceptance. * * *"

* * *

The rule that a contract is complete upon deposit of the acceptance in the mails, hereinbefore referred to as "deposited acceptance rule" and also known as the "rule in Adams v. Lindsell," had its origin, insofar as the common law is concerned, in Adams v. Lindsell, 1 Barn. & Ald. 681, 106 Eng.Rep. 250 (K.B.1818). In that case, the defendants had sent an offer to plaintiffs on September 2nd, indicating that they expected an answer "in course of post." The offer was misdirected and was not received and accepted until the 5th, the acceptance being mailed that day and received by defendant-offerors on the 9th. However, the defendants, who had expected to receive the acceptance on or before the 7th, sold the goods offered on the 8th of September. It was conceded that the delay had been occasioned by the fault of the defendants in initially misdirecting the offer.

* * * As [Professor] Corbin indicated, there must be a choice made, and such choice may, by the nature of things,

seem unjust in some cases. Weighing the arguments with reference not to specific cases but toward a rule of general application and recognizing the general and traditional acceptance of the rule as well as the modern changes in effective long-distance communication, it would seem that the balance tips, whether heavily or near imperceptively, to continued adherence to the "Rule in Adams v. Lindsell." This rule, although not entirely compatible with ordered, consistent and sometime artificial principles of contract advanced by some theorists, is, in our view, in accord with the practical considerations and essential concepts of contract law. [Citation.] * * *

In choosing to align this jurisdiction with those adhering to the deposited acceptance rule, we adopt a view contrary to that of the very able judge below, * * *.

In the instant case, an unqualified offer was accepted and the acceptance made manifest. Later, the offerees sought to repudiate their initial assent. Had there been a delay in their determination to repudiate permitting the letter to be delivered to appellant, no question as to the invalidity of the repudiation would have been entertained. As it were, the repudiation antedated receipt of the letter. However, adopting the view that the acceptance was effective when the letter of acceptance was deposited in the mails, the repudiation was equally invalid and cannot alone, support the summary decree for appellees.

The summary decree is reversed and the cause remanded for further proceedings.

Auction Sales

DREW v. JOHN DEERE CO. OF SYRACUSE, INC.

(1963) 19 A.D.2d 308, 241 N.Y.S.2d 267.

HALPERN, J.
* * *
The theory of the complaint is that a contract by the corporate defendant to sell a certain tractor to the plaintiff had come into existence as the result of an auction sale conducted by the defendant and that the defendant breached the contract by refusing to deliver the tractor upon the tender of the purchase price.

* * * The defendant advertised the auction sale, stating that the property would be sold to the highest bidder at the sale. The plaintiff bid $1500 at the sale but the auctioneer did not accept the bid; instead he announced that the defendant itself had bid $1600 and accordingly the property was struck down to the defendant.

* * *

The plaintiff's whole case rests upon the theory that the auction was one "without reserve." At such an auction, the owner of the property has no right to withdraw the property after bidding has commenced. It is also necessarily implicit in an auction "without reserve", that the owner of the property may not himself bid in the property, as this would be equivalent to withdrawing it from sale (Restatement of Contracts, § 27). Various legal theories have been advanced for the holding that the announcement that the auction would be "without reserve" imposes a binding legal obligation upon the owner, but the best view seems to be that the owner, by making such an announcement, enters into a collateral contract with all persons bidding at the auction that he will not withdraw the property from sale, regardless of how low the highest bid might be [citations]. Therefore, the highest bona fide bidder at an auction "without reserve" may insist that the property be sold to him or that the owner answer to him in damages [citations].

On the other hand, in an auction sale not expressly announced to be "without reserve", the owner may withdraw the property at any time before it is actually "knocked down" to a bidder by the auctioneer. There is no contract until the offer made by the bidder is accepted by the auctioneer's "knocking down" the property to him (Personal Property Law, § 102, subd. 2). "An auction 'with reserve' is the normal procedure" (Comment 2 to section 2–328, Uniform Commercial Code).

In our case, there was no express statement that the auction would be "without reserve". The statement that the sale would be made to the highest bidder is not the equivalent of an announcement that the auction would be "without reserve" (cf. Personal Property Law § 102(2); Uniform Commercial Code, § 2–328, subd. 3). "An announcement that a person will sell his property at public auction to the highest bidder is a mere declaration of intention to hold an auction at which bids will be received" [citations].

Corbin writes that the auctioneer at an auction sale in asking for bids, does not make an operative offer. "This is true even though the seller or his representative has issued advertisements or made other statements that the article will be sold to the highest bidder, or is offered for sale to the highest bidder. Such statements are merely preliminary negotiation, not intended and not reasonably understood to be intended to affect legal relations. When such is the case, the seller or his representative is as free to reject the bids, highest to lowest, as are the bidders to withdraw them. The

seller may at any time withdraw the article from sale, if he has not already accepted a bid. He need give no reasons; indeed, he rejects all bids by merely failing to accept them—by doing nothing at all. It is not necessary for him to say that 'the privilege is reserved to reject any and all bids.' Such a statement is merely evidence that the goods are not being offered 'without reserve'" (1 Corbin on Contracts, § 108, pp. 338–340).

Since, upon the present record, the auction sale appears to have been "with reserve", no contract of sale came into existence, even if we assume that the plaintiff was the highest lawful bidder [citation]. Concededly, the plaintiff's bid was never accepted. Therefore, the plaintiff's papers upon his motion for summary judgment fail to make out a cause of action for breach of contract.

* * *

The plaintiff has failed to show that the sale was one "without reserve".

The plaintiff's motion for summary judgment was therefore properly denied. * * * As we have seen, the announcement was insufficient of itself for that purpose but the plaintiff should be given an opportunity to produce any other evidence he may have on that subject. * * *

Problems

1. Ames, seeking business for his lawn maintenance firm, posted the following notice in the meeting room of the Antlers, a local lodge: "To the members of the Antlers—Special this month. I will resod your lawn for 30 cents per square foot using Fairway brand sod. This offer expires July 15."

The notice also included Ames's name, address, and signature and specified that the acceptance was to be in writing.

Bates, a member of the Antlers, and Cramer, the janitor, read the notice and became interested. Bates wrote a letter to Ames saying he would accept the offer if Ames would use Putting Green brand sod. Ames received this letter

July 14, and wrote to Bates saying he would not use Putting Green sod. Bates received Ames's letter on July 16, and promptly wrote Ames that he would accept Fairway sod. Cramer wrote to Ames on July 10, saying he accepted Ames's offer.

By July 15, Ames had found more profitable ventures and refused to resod either lawn at the specified price. Bates and Cramer brought an appropriate action against Ames for breach of contract. Decision as to the respective claims of Bates and Cramer?

2. In which, if any, of the following four situations described was a contract formed?

(a) A owned four speedboats named Porpoise, Priscilla, Providence and Prudence. On April 2, A made written offers to sell the four boats in the order named, for $2,200 each to C, D, E and F, respectively, allowing ten days for acceptance. Five days later, C received notice from A that he had contracted to sell Porpoise to M. The next day, April 8, C notified A that he accepted A's offer.

(b) On the third day, April 5, D mailed a rejection to A which reached A on the morning of the fifth day. At 10:00 A.M., on the fourth day, D sent an acceptance by telegram to A who received it at noon on the same day.

(c) E, on April 3, replied that he was interested in buying Providence but declared the price asked appeared slightly excessive and wondered if, perhaps, A would be willing to sell the boat for $1,900. Five days later, having received no reply from A, E, by letter, accepted A's offer and enclosed a certified check for $2,200.

(d) F was accidently killed in an automobile accident on April 9. The following day, the executor of F's will mailed an acceptance of A's offer to A.

3. Alpha Rolling Mill Corporation, by letter dated June 8 offered to sell Brooklyn Railroad Company 2,000 to 5,000 tons of 50-pound iron rails upon certain specified terms adding that, if the offer was accepted, Alpha Corporation would expect to be notified prior to June 20. Brooklyn Company, on June 16, by telegram, referring to Alpha Corporation's offer of June 8, directed Alpha Corporation to enter an order for 1,200 tons of 50-pound iron rails on the terms specified. The same day, June 16, Brooklyn Company, by letter to Alpha Corporation, confirmed the telegram. On June 18, Alpha Corporation by telegram, declined to fulfill the order. Brooklyn Company, on June 19, telegraphed Alpha Corporation: "Please enter an order for 2,000 tons rails as per your letter of the eighth. Please forward written contract. Reply." To Brooklyn Company's repeated inquiries whether the order for 2,000 tons of rails had been entered, Alpha denied the existence of any contract between Brooklyn Company and itself. Thereafter, Brooklyn Company sues Alpha Corporation for breach of contract. Decision?

4. On April 8, X received a telephone call from A, a truck dealer, who told X that a new Model truck in which X was interested would arrive in one week. Although A initially wanted $4,500 the conversation ended after A agreed to sell and X to purchase the truck for $4,000, with $1,000 down payment and the balance upon delivery. The next day, X sent A a check for $1,000 which A promptly cashed.

One week later, when X called A and inquired about the truck, A informed X he had several prospects looking at the truck and would not sell for less than $4,500. The following day A sent X a properly executed check for $1,000 with the following notation thereon: "Return of down payment on sale of truck."

After notifying A that he will not cash the check, X sues A for damages. Decision?

5. On November 15, 1982, I. Sellit, a manufacturer of crystalware, mailed to Benny Buyer a letter stating that Sellit would sell to Buyer 100 crystal "A" goblets at $100 per goblet and that "the offer would remain open for fifteen (15) days." On November 18, 1982, Sellit, noticing the sudden rise in the price of crystal "A" goblets, decided to withdraw his offer to Buyer and so notified Buyer. Buyer chose to ignore Sellit's letter of revocation and gleefully watched as the price of crystal "A" goblets continued to skyrocket. On November 30, 1982, Buyer mailed to Sellit a letter accepting Sellit's offer to sell the goblets. The letter was received by Sellit on December 4, 1982. Buyer demands delivery of the goblets, what result?

6. On May 1, 1982, Melforth Realty Company offered to sell Greenacre to Dallas, Inc., for $1,000,000. The offer was made by telegraph and stated that the offer would expire on May 15, 1982. Dallas decided to purchase the property and sent a registered letter to Melforth on May 10, 1982, accepting the offer. Due to unexplained delays in the postal service the letter was not received by Melforth until May 22. Melforth wishes to sell Greenacre to another buyer, who is offering $1,200,000 for the tract of land. Has a contract resulted between Melforth and Dallas?

7. Rowe advertised in newspapers of wide circulation and otherwise made known that he would pay $5,000 for a complete set consisting of ten volumes of certain rare books. Ford, not knowing of the offer, gave Rowe all but one of

the set of rare books as a Christmas present. Ford later learned of the offer, obtained the one remaining book, tendered it to Rowe and demanded the $5,000. Rowe refused to pay. Is Ford entitled to the $5,000?

8. Scott, manufacturer of a carbonated beverage, entered into a contract with Otis, owner of a baseball park, whereby Otis rented to Scott a large signboard on top of the center field wall. The contract provided that Otis should letter the sign as desired by Scott and would change the lettering from time to time within 48 hours after receipt of written request from Scott. As directed by Scott, the signboard originally stated in large letters that Scott would pay $100 to any ball player hitting a home run over the sign.

In the first game of the season, Hume, the best hitter in the League, hit one home run over the sign. Scott immediately served written notice on Otis instructing Otis to replace the offer on the signboard with an offer to pay $50 to every pitcher who pitched a no hit game in the park. A week after receipt of Scott's letter, Otis had not changed the wording on the sign and on that day Perry, a pitcher for a scheduled game, pitched a no hit game while Todd, one of his teammates, hit a home run over Scott's sign.

Scott refuses to make any payment to any of the three players. What are the rights of Scott, Hume, Perry and Todd?

9. B accepted C's offer to sell to him a portion of C's coin collection. C forgot that his prized $20 gold piece at the time of the offer and acceptance was included in the portion which he offered to sell to B. C did not intend to include the gold piece in the sale. B, at the time of inspecting the offered portion of the collection, and prior to accepting the offer, saw the gold piece. Is B entitled to the $20 gold piece?

10. Small, admiring Jasper's watch, asked Jasper where and at what price he had purchased it. Jasper replied: "I bought it at West Watch Shop about two years ago for around $85, but I am not certain as to that." Small then said: "Those fellows at West are good people and always sell good watches. I'll buy that watch from you." Jasper replied: "It's a deal." The next morning Small telephoned Jasper and said he had changed his mind and did not wish to buy the watch.

Jasper sued Small for breach of contract. In defense, Small has pleaded that he made no enforceable contract with Jasper (a) because the parties did not agree on the price to be paid for the watch; and (b) because the parties did not agree on the place and time of delivery of the watch to Small. Are either, or both, of these defenses good?

Chapter
8

CONDUCT INVALIDATING MANIFESTED ASSENT

The preceding chapter considered one of the essential requirements of a contract, namely, the objective manifestation of mutual assent by each party to the other. This chapter deals with situations in which the manifested consent by one of the parties to the contract has been induced by conduct of the other party that violates principles of fair dealing or in which consent is based upon a mistake of material fact. These situations are considered under the headings of duress, undue influence, fraud, misrepresentation, and mistake.

DURESS

A person should not be held to an agreement which he made because of wrongful force or threats exerted by the other party. For example, if A, a landlord, induces B, an infirm bedridden tenant, to enter into a new lease on the same premises at a greatly increased rent by wrongfully threatening to terminate B's lease and evict him, B can avoid the new lease by reason of the duress exerted upon him.

Duress has been defined as follows: "(1) If conduct that appears to be a manifestation of assent by a party who does not intend to engage in that conduct is physically compelled by duress, the conduct is not effective as a manifestation of assent." Restatement, Second, Contracts, Section 174. "(2) If a party's manifestation of assent is induced by an improper threat by the other party that leaves the victim no reasonable alternative, the contract is voidable by the victim." Restatement, Second, Contracts, Section 175(1). Such contracts are voidable at the option of the coerced party, who entered into the contract under duress and not under his own free will. In the most extreme instances of duress, however, such as where B puts a gun ot A's back and threatens to shoot him unless he signs, the contract is rendered void.

The fact that the act or threat would not affect a person of average strength and intelligence is not determinative if it places the particular person in fear and induces an action against his will. The test here is subjective. In Silsbee v. Webber, 171 Mass.

378, 50 N.E. 555 (1898), the defendant was the employer of the plaintiff's son whom he accused of stealing money. He threatened the plaintiff that if she did not transfer a share in her father's estate to make good the losses, he would tell her husband (the boy's father) of the theft. The plaintiff feared that this would be very detrimental to her husband, who was in a weakened condition because of illness, all of which was known to the defendant. The Supreme Judicial Court of Massachusetts said a jury would have been warranted in finding that the defendant obtained the assignment by duress, "solely by inspiring the plaintiff with fear of what he threatened to do."

The rule and its rationale are summarized in the Restatement, Second, Contracts, Section 175, Comment c:

In order to constitute duress, the improper threat must induce the making of the contract. The rule for causation in cases of misrepresentation stated in § 167 is also applied to analogous cases of duress. No special rule for causation in cases of duress is stated here because of the infrequency with which the problem arises. A party's manifestation of assent is induced by duress if the duress substantially contributes to his decision to manifest his assent. The test is subjective and the question is, did the threat actually induce assent on the part of the person claiming to be the victim of duress. Threats that would suffice to induce assent by one person may not suffice to induce assent by another. All attendant circumstances must be considered, including such matters as the age, background and relationship of the parties. Persons of a weak or cowardly nature are the very ones that need protection; the courageous can usually protect themselves. Timid and inexperienced persons are particularly subject to threats, and it does not lie in the mouths of the unscrupulous to excuse their imposition on such persons on the ground of their victims' infirmities.

Ordinarily, the acts or threats constituting duress are themselves crimes or torts. But this is not true in all cases. The acts need not be criminal or tortious in order to be "wrongful"; they merely need be contrary to public policy or morally reprehensible. An example of this point is the Massachusetts case discussed above. It would not have been a criminal or civil wrong for the employer to have told the woman's husband of the son's theft. But, under the circumstances of the case, the court did consider it wrongful to so threaten, since the employer knew of the husband's weakened condition and knew that this threat would induce the woman to execute the transfer regardless of her belief in the merits of his claim.

Moreover, it has generally been held that contracts induced by threats of criminal prosecution are voidable, regardless of whether the coerced party had committed an unlawful act. As Justice Cardozo observed:

The principle thus vindicated is simple and commanding. *There is to be no traffic in the privilege of invoking the public justice of the state. One may press a charge or withhold it as one will. One may not make action or inaction dependent on a price.* Union Exchange Nat. Bank of New York v. Joseph, 231 N.Y. 250, 131 N.E. 905 (1921).

To be distinguished are threats to resort to ordinary civil remedies in order to recover a debt due from another. It is not wrongful to threaten to bring a civil suit against an individual to recover a debt. It is the inducement of the payment by the threat to use criminal prosecution that is proscribed.

The applicable law has been succinctly summarized by Professor Corbin, as follows:

One who has been injured by the criminal act of another, as when his money has been embezzled or goods stolen, may lawfully threaten prosecution for the offense. * * * *The settlement agreement is made illegal only when a consideration is given in exchange for actual forbearance to prosecute or for a promise of such forbearance.*

Nevertheless, it is not safe to threaten prosecution as a means of inducing settlement of a civil claim. This is especially true when the settlement is made, not by the guilty party himself but by the parent or other close relative. When threats have been made it is easy to infer that the settlement was in exchange for forbearance or a promise thereof; and the bargain is just as illegal when the agreement is implied as when it is express. * * * (Corbin on Contracts, Section 1421, pp. 701–703.)

UNDUE INFLUENCE

The law has traditionally scrutinized very carefully contracts between those in a relationship of trust and confidence which is likely to permit unfair persuasion being exerted by one party upon the other. Examples are the relationships of guardian and ward, trustee and beneficiary, principal and agent, husband and wife, parent and child, attorney and client, physician and patient, and pastor and parishioner.

Where one party is under the domination of another, or by virtue of the relation between them is justified in assuming that the other party will not act in a manner inconsistent with his welfare, a transaction induced by unfair persuasion of the latter, is induced by undue influence and is voidable. Restatement, Second, Contracts, Section 177. The ultimate question in undue influence cases is whether the transaction was induced by influencing a freely exercised and competent judgment, or by dominating the mind or emotions of a submissive party. Obviously, the weakness or dependence of the person persuaded is a strong circumstance tending to show that persuasion may have been unfair. For example: "A, who is without business experience, has for years been accustomed to rely in business matters on the advice of B, who is experienced in business. B, without making any false representations of fact, induced A to enter into a contract with B's confederate, C, that is disadvantageous to A, as B and C know. The transaction is

voidable." Restatement, Second, Contracts, Section 177. Illustration 1.

Undue influence generally arises in the context of the relationships in which one person is in a position of dominance over another, or is likely to be. Where such a relationship exists at the time of the transaction and it appears that the dominant party has gained at the expense of the other party, the transaction is presumed to be voidable. For example, in a legally challenged contract between a guardian and his ward, the law presumes that advantage was taken by the guardian. It is, therefore, incumbent upon the guardian to rebut this presumption. Important factors in determining whether the contract is fair are (1) whether the guardian made full disclosure of all relevant information known to him, (2) whether the consideration was adequate, and (3) whether the ward had competent and independent advice before completing the transaction. Without limitation, in every situation in which a confidential relationship exists between persons who occupy a relation of trust and confidence, the dominant party is held to utmost good faith in his dealings with the other.

FRAUD

Another type of conduct that invalidates manifestation of assent is fraud, a misrepresentation of material fact by one party to the other which induces his reliance. It differs from duress and undue influence in that fraud is based upon deceit, whereas duress is based upon threats or force causing fear of harm or injury which induces manifestation of assent, while undue influence is taking unfair advantage of a person by reason of a dominant position based upon a relationship of trust and confidence.

Fraud may be defined as "A false representation of a material fact made with knowledge of its falsity or culpable ignorance of its truth with intention that it be acted on by the party deceived and inducing him to contract to his injury." (17 Corpus Juris Secundum, Contracts, Section 153.) There are two kinds of fraud, namely, fraud in the execution and fraud in the inducement.

Fraud in the Execution

This type of fraud consists in a misrepresentation which deceives the defrauded person as to the very essence of the contract he is entering into. For example, A delivers a package to B, requests B to sign a receipt for it, holds out a simple printed form headed "Receipt" and indicates the line upon which B is to sign. This line appears to B to be the bottom line of the form, but instead it is the bottom line of a promissory note cleverly concealed underneath the receipt. B signs where directed without knowing that he is signing a note. This is fraud in the execution. The note is void and of no effect. The reason is simply that, although the signature is genuine and appears to be a manifestation of assent to the terms of the note, there is no assent to be manifested. The nature of A's fraud precluded consent to the signing of the note because it prevented B from knowing what he was signing.

Fraud in the Inducement

This kind of fraud is a misrepresentation of material fact by one party to the other who consents to enter into a contract in reliance upon the misrepresentation. For example, A in offering to sell his dog to B tells B that the dog won first prize in its class in the recent National Dog Show. In fact, the dog had not even been entered in the show. This statement induces B to accept the offer and pay a fancy price for the dog. There is a contract, but it is voidable by B because of A's fraud which induced his assent. Each party knew and assented to the terms of the agreement induced by A's fraud. Another instance of fraud in the inducement is a sale of land in Texas by A to B which A misrepresented as located in an area where drilling for oil had recently commenced, which A knew was not true. The sale is voidable by B.

The requisite elements of fraud in the inducement are: (1) a false representation (2) of a fact (3) that is material (4) and made with knowledge of its falsity and the intention to deceive (5) which is justifiably relied upon.

False Representation. A basic element of fraud is a false representation. There must be some positive statement or conduct that misleads. As a general rule, silence alone does not amount to fraud. There is no obligation on the part of a seller to tell a purchaser everything he knows about the subject of the sale, although if there is a latent (hidden) defect of a substantial character, one that would not be discovered by an ordinary examination, the seller is obliged to reveal it. Moreover, one may have a duty of disclosure because of prior representations innocently made but which are later discovered to be untrue before making a contract. The Restatement, Second, Contracts, Section 161 gives this illustration: "A makes to B, a credit rating company, a true statement of his financial condition, intending that its substance be published to B's subscribers. B summarizes the information and transmits the summary to C, a subscriber. Shortly thereafter, A's financial condition becomes seriously impaired, but he does not disclose this to B. C makes a contract to lend money to A. A's nondisclosure is equivalent to an assertion that his financial condition is not seriously impaired, and this assertion is a misrepresentation."

A fiduciary, one who is in a relationship of trust and confidence with another, owes a duty to make full disclosure of all facts relevant to any transaction that he enters into with the other party to the relationship. His duty exceeds that of one who is dealing with another at "arm's length."

Active concealment can likewise form the basis for fraud, as where the seller put heavy oil or grease in an engine to conceal a knock. Truth may be suppressed by concealment quite as much as by active misrepresentation. An express denial of knowledge of a fact which a party knows to exist, or the statement of misleading half-truth, can be fraudulent. Such conduct is clearly more than mere silence and is considered the equivalent of a false representation.

Fact. The basic element of fraud is the misrepresentation of a *material fact;* actionable fraud can rarely be predicated upon what is merely a statement of opinion. The line between fact and opinion is not an easy one to draw, and in close cases presents an issue for the jury. Suppose that A induces B to purchase shares in a company unknown to B at a price of $100 per share by representing that he had the preceding year paid $150 per share for them, when in fact he had paid but $50. This is a representation of a past event, definitely ascertainable, verifiable, and fraudulent. If, on the other hand, A said to B that the shares were "a good investment," he is merely stating his opinion, and in the usual case B ought to regard it as no more than that. Suppose, however, that A said the company "had a good year last year," when in fact it failed to show a profit. Is this opinion or fact? It is difficult, if not impossible, to decide without additional evidence. The solution will often turn upon the superior knowledgeability of the person making the statement and the information available to the other party. Usually, when representations have to do with the volume of business, and the facts are peculiarly within the knowledge of the seller, buyers are not bound to make an independent investigation. If the representor is a professional broker advising a client, the courts are more likely to regard an untrue statement as actionable. It is the expression of opinion of

one holding himself out as having expert knowledge, and the tendency is to grant relief to those who have sustained loss by reasonable reliance upon expert evaluation.

Statements of fact and opinion are also considered in connection with sales of goods in distinguishing between "sales talk" or "puffing" and factual representations with respect to ascertaining the existence and extent of a seller's warranties. Statements of "value" such as "This is the best car for the money in town," or "This deluxe model will give you twice the wear of a cheaper model," are not grounds for the avoidance of a contract. Such exaggerations and commendations of articles offered for sale are to be expected from dealers who are merely puffing their wares.

Also to be distinguished from a representation of fact is a prediction of the future. Predictions are closely akin to opinions, as one cannot know with certainty what will happen in the future, and normally they are not regarded as factual statements. Promissory statements ordinarily do not constitute a basis of fraud, as a breach of contract does not indicate that the promise of performance was fraudulently made. However, by the majority view in this country, a promise which the promisor at the time of making had no intention of keeping is fraudulent as a misrepresentation of fact. Most courts take the position that the state of a person's mind, which is being misrepresented, "is as much a fact as the state of a person's digestion." Edgigton v. Fitzmaurice (1885), 29 Ch.D. 459. If a dealer promises "I will service this machine free for the next year," but at the time has no intention of doing so, his conduct is actionable if the other elements of fraud are present.

Misrepresentations of law are also generally distinguished from those of fact. Suppose that the vendor of land induces a sale by misrepresenting that a certain zoning classification, properly construed, will permit the type of commercial activity contemplated by the purchaser, or that the zoning ordinance is unconstitutional as applied to the property. Has he made a misrepresentation of fact? Practically all courts will agree that he has not. Rather, he has misrepresented the state of the law, and since everyone is presumed to know the law, the purchaser is not justified in relying upon the vendor's representation of this type, and the sale is not fraudulent. There are, however, a few exceptions to this rule. If the vendor occupies a fiduciary or confidential relationship with the purchaser, the latter will be able to avoid the transaction. A misrepresentation by one who is learned in the law, as a practicing attorney, may under certain circumstances be fraudulent. It is not unreasonable to rely upon a legal expert's statement of the law.

Materiality. In addition to the requirement that the misrepresentation be one of fact, it is necessary that it be material. It must relate to something of sufficient substance to induce reliance. In the sale of a race horse it may not be material whether the horse was ridden in its most recent race by a certain jockey, but its running time for the race probably would be. In determining the materiality of a representation, courts look to the impression made upon the mind of the party to whom it was made. It is usually material if, but for the representation, he would not have entered into the transaction. Many courts deem the misrepresentation to be material if to a substantial degree it influenced the making of a decision, even though it was not the decisive factor.

Knowledge of Falsity and Intention to Deceive. To establish fraud the misrepresentation must have been known by the one making it to be false and must be made with an intention to deceive. Knowledge of falsity can consist of (a) actual knowledge, (b) lack of belief in the statement's truthfulness, or (c) reckless indifference as to its truthfulness.

Moreover, many courts have implied knowledge to the representor and have held him strictly responsible where the special situation or his means of knowledge were such as to make it his duty to know the truth or falsity of his representation. This frequently happens in business dealings or cases relating to sales of land or stock where the superior knowledge of the seller is made apparent.

Justifiable Reliance. One is not entitled to relief unless he has justifiably relied upon the misrepresentation to his detriment or injury. If the complaining party's decision was in no way influenced by the misrepresentation, he must abide by the terms of the contract. He is not deceived if he does not rely. Moreover, if the complaining party knew or should have known that the representation of the defendant was untrue, but still entered into the contract, the courts will not permit rescission (cancellation of the contract) or recovery of damages. For example, A, seeking to purchase a six-passenger car, was told by the salesman that a two-seat sports car was appropriate and took A for a test drive. If A nevertheless relied on the salesman's statement, such reliance would not be justified, and A would not have been legally defrauded.

Remedies. It may turn out, however, that even though fraud was perpetrated, the bargain is an advantageous one for the defrauded party. He may have purchased a painting in reliance upon the seller's statement that it was the work of a certain famous artist, only to discover later that it was the work of an even more famous artist, worth a great deal more than the purchase price. In legal contemplation he has not been injured; accordingly, he would not be entitled to recover a judgment for damages, although he would be entitled to a rescission and a return of the price. The fraudulent seller, however, presumably would be pleased to rescind and receive back the painting upon a refund of the price.

At common law there are two courses open to a party who has been induced to enter into a contract by fraud: he may either affirm or disaffirm (rescind) the contract. These remedies are mutually exclusive.

Affirmation occurs where the defrauded party with full knowledge of the facts, either declares his intention to proceed with the contract or takes some other action from which such intention may reasonably be inferred. Thus, suppose that A was induced to purchase a ring from B through the latter's fraudulent misrepresentation. If, after learning the truth, A undertakes to sell the ring to C or otherwise does something which is consistent only with his ownership of the ring, he may no longer rescind the transaction.

If a defrauded party does not desire to go through with the contract, and it is still executory, he may assert the fraud as a defense to an action by the other. If the contract is executed, he may rescind the contract, and, upon returning or making a tender of the consideration that he received, reacquire that which he parted with—be it money, goods, or other property. If a defrauded party, in lieu of rescission, desires to retain the consideration which he has received, he may do so and maintain an action in tort for the damages sustained, provided that the fraudulent representation results in injury to the deceived party.

There are important limitations upon the right of the defrauded party to rescind. First, the power of avoidance is lost if after acquiring knowledge of the fraud he unreasonably delays giving notice to the other party of his intention to avoid the transaction. To illustrate, a defrauded purchaser of stock cannot wait unduly to see if the market price or value of the stock appreciates sufficiently to justify his retention of it. Second, in order to rescind, the defrauded party must restore or offer to restore everything that he has received under the contract. If he cannot make this restoration, as where the goods are destroyed or consumed, he cannot rescind. The purpose of this limitation is expressed as follows in an English case: "Though the defendant has been fraudulent, he must not be robbed, nor must the plaintiff be unjustly enriched, as he would be if he both got back what he had parted with and kept what he had received in return. The purpose of the relief is not punishment but compensation." Spence v. Crawford, 3 All E.R. 271, 288–9 (1939). This requirement prompted one judicial wit to give the example of one fraudulently induced to buy a cake. He said the buyer could return the cake and recover the price, but "cannot both eat your cake—and return your cake." Clarke v. Dickson (1858), E.B. & E. 148, 152.

Third, if a third party, good-faith purchaser acquires an interest in the subject matter of the contract before the defrauded party has elected to rescind, no rescission is permitted. In the ordinary case of fraud in the inducement, the transaction is voidable. A fraudulent buyer therefore acquires a voidable title to the goods. Upon a sale of the goods by him to a third person who is a purchaser in good faith and for value, the latter having obtained title is allowed to keep the goods. Section 2–403(1). Since both the defrauded seller and the good-faith purchaser are innocent, the law will not disturb the title in the good-faith purchaser. In this case, as in all cases where rescission is not available to a defrauded party, his only recourse is to recover damages against the fraudulent party in a tort action.

The Code liberalizes the common-law rule with respect to contracts for the sale of goods by not restricting the defrauded party to an election of remedies. That is, he may both rescind the contract by restoring the status quo and, in addition, recover damages, if any, resulting from the fraud. Section 2–721 of the Code provides:

Remedies for material misrepresentation or fraud include all remedies available under this Article for non-fraudulent breach. Neither rescission or a claim for rescission of the contract for sale nor rejection or return of the goods shall bar or be deemed inconsistent with a claim for damages or other remedy.

INNOCENT MISREPRESENTATION

At common law it was necessary for the injured party plaintiff in a fraud action, whether asking rescission or damages, to prove an intention by the defendant to deceive. Hence, the necessity for showing knowledge of the falsity, or at least culpable ignorance. The absence of an honest belief was essential; the misrepresentation alone insufficient. Today, a majority of courts permit a rescission, but not a recovery, of damages for innocent misrepresentation, provided, of course, that all of the remaining elements of fraud are present. In Hodgeson v. Brant, 156 Cal.App.2d 610, 319 P.2d 684 (1958), plaintiff sued for rescission of a sale of motel premises alleging false representation by defendants as to the condition of the property. The court found that the defendants did not know that certain walls were structurally insufficient and susceptible to collapse. However, their representations that the property was in A-1 condition were relied upon by plaintiff who was held entitled to rescission when the representations proved to be false. The structural defects materially affected the value of the property. "While the defendants were under no duty to speak as to the condition of the property, they were bound by the representations made."

MISTAKE

Mistake is an erroneous understanding or an inaccurate concept which if acted upon may produce an unfortunate result for the actor. An elusive branch of the law is that which is concerned with the effect of "mistake" upon the formation of a contract. Certain problems have been settled, but many have not been. There is, however, one concept that runs through the cases and which will at least help to place the issues in a meaningful context as well as assist in predicting results. In the chapter on "Manifestation of Mutual Assent" attention was given to the standard by which the assent of the parties is to be tested. The courts favor an objective approach. A person is bound by the reasonable impression which he has created in the mind of the other party, even if this differs from his own subjective intention.

An illustration is the offer in language manifesting an intention different from that actually intended by the offeror, a mistake resulting from carelessness, inattention, or failure to double check. This occurs in the case of A offering to sell his Chevrolet when he intended to offer his Ford automobile. If the offer is accepted before it is corrected, A is bound by the intention that he manifested. In the absence of duress, fraud, or breach of fiduciary duty by the buyer, he has no legal remedy.

The problem is how far can the objective theory be extended in mistake cases? At what point is there a lack of "real consent"? The law grants relief in a situation involving mistake only where there has been a *mutual mistake of material fact* by both parties to the contract.

Mistake as to Existence or Identity of Subject Matter

Suppose A offers to sell B a certain boat but unknown to both parties the boat has been destroyed. If B accepts, is he entitled to damages upon A's failure to deliver the boat as promised? He is not. Section 2–613 of the Code provides in part that where the contract requires for its performance goods identified when the contract is made, and the goods suffer casualty without fault of either party before the risk of loss passes to the buyer, then, if the loss is total the contract is avoided.

The rationale of this rule is based upon the presumed intention of the parties in ordinary transactions; that is, no subject matter, no contract. To be distinguished is the case in which the parties are mutually mistaken, but the contract contemplates an assumption of the risk. For instance, a ship at sea may be sold "lost or not lost." In such case the buyer is liable whether the ship was lost or not lost at the time of the making of the contract. "There is no mistake; instead, there is conscious ignorance." Corbin on Contracts, Section 600.

Possibly the most famous decision involving mutual mistake is Raffles v. Wichelhaus, 2 Hurlstone & Coltman 906 (1864), popularly known as the "Peerless Case." A contract of purchase was made for "certain goods, to-wit, 125 bales of Surat Cotton * * * to arrive ex Peerless from Bombay." It happened, however, that there were two ships by the name of "Peerless," each sailing from Bombay, one in October and the other in December. The buyer had in mind the ship that sailed in October, while the seller reasonably believed the agreement referred to the Peerless sailing in December. Neither party was at fault, but both believed in good faith that a different ship was intended. The English court held that no contract existed. The Restatement, Second, Contracts, Section 20 is in accord: "(1) There is no manifestation of mutual assent to an exchange if the parties attach materially different meanings to their manifestations and (a) neither party knows or has reason to know the meaning attached by the other; or (b) each party knows or each party has reason to know the meaning attached by the other. (2) The manifestations of the parties are operative in accordance with the meaning attached to them by one of the parties if (a) that party does not know of any different meaning at-

tached by the other, and the other knows the meaning attached by the first party; or (b) that party has no reason to know of any different meaning attached by the other, and the other has reason to know the meaning attached by the first party." However, if blame can be ascribed to either party, he will be held responsible. Thus, if the seller knew of the sailing from Bombay of two ships by the name of Peerless, then he would be at fault and the contract would be for the ship sailing in October as the buyer expected. If neither is to blame or both are to blame, there is no contract at all.

Mistake as to Nature of Subject Matter

If B contracts to purchase A's automobile under the belief that he can sell it at a profit to C, he obviously is not excused from liability if he is mistaken in this belief. Nor can he rescind the agreement simply because he was mistaken as to his estimate of what the automobile was worth. These are the ordinary risks of business, and courts do not undertake to relieve against them. But suppose that the parties contract upon the assumption that the automobile is a 1979 Cadillac, with 15,000 miles use, when, in fact, the engine is that of a cheaper model and has been run in excess of 50,000 miles? Here, a court would likely allow a rescission because of mutual mistake respecting a material fact. Another example of mutual mistake of fact was presented in a California case where a noted violinist purchased two violins from a collector for $8,000, the bill of sale reading: " * * * I have on this date sold to Mr. Efrem Zimbalist one Joseph Guarnerius violin and one Stradivarius violin dated 1717." Actually, unknown to either party, neither violin was genuine. Taken together they were worth no more than $300. The purchaser was successful in contesting the seller's suit for the unpaid balance. In a New Zealand case, the plaintiff purchased a "stud bull" at an auction. There were no express warranties as to "sex, condition or otherwise." Actually, the bull was sterile. Rescission was allowed, the court observing that it was a "bull in name only."

The foregoing cases are to be contrasted with situations in which the parties are aware that they do not know the character or value of the item sold. For example, the Supreme Court of Wisconsin refused to set aside the sale of a stone for which the purchaser paid one dollar, but which was subsequently discovered to be an uncut diamond valued at $700. The parties did not know at the time of sale what the stone was, and knew they did not know. Each consciously assumed the risk that the value might be more or less than the selling price.

A mistake unknown to the party making it, however, becomes mutual if the other party recognizes it as a mistake. For example, suppose a building contractor submits a bid for a job that is one-half of what it should be, because he made a serious error in his computations. If the other party knows that he made such an error, or reasonably should have known of it, he cannot, as a general rule, take advantage of the other's mistake and "snap up" the offer. In one case the plaintiff in computing his bid on a city sewer project, by mistake omitted the cost of one item, the steel. Accordingly, his bid was substantially lower than the others. He bid $429,444.20; the next higher bid was $671,600. All other bids were even higher. An estimate made by the city engineers, undisclosed to the bidders prior to the submission of the bids, was $632,000. The plaintiff received a sympathetic ear from the Oregon Supreme Court which stated in the course of its opinion: "It is our belief that although the plaintiff alone made the mistake, the City was aware of it. When it accepted the plaintiff's bid, with knowledge of the mistake, it sought to take an unconscionable advantage of an inadvertent error." Rushlight Automatic Sprinkler Co. v. City of Portland,

189 Or. 194, 219 P.2d 732 (1950). Some courts refer to a case of this type as one of "palpable unilateral mistake," to distinguish it from the situation where the other had no suspicion, nor any good reason to suspect that an error had been committed. In the latter type of case no judicial relief from the unilateral mistake is available.

Mistake by Failure to Read Document

As a general proposition, a party is held to what he signs. His signature authenticates the writing, and he cannot repudiate that which he has voluntarily approved. As a Louisiana court expressed it: "Signatures to obligations are not mere ornaments." Accordingly, the Restatement of the Law of Contracts, Second, 157, comment b, provides as follows: "Generally, one who assents to a writing is presumed to know its contents and cannot escape being bound by its terms merely by contending that he did not read them; his assent is deemed to cover unknown as well as known terms." This view has been stated as follows by the Court of Appeals of New York: "When a party to a written contract accepts it as a contract, he is bound by the stipulations and conditions expressed in it whether he reads them or not. Ignorance through negligence or inexcusable trustfulness will not relieve a party from his contractual obligations. He who signs or accepts a written contract, in the absence of fraud or other wrongful act on the part of another contracting party, is conclusively presumed to know its contents and to assent to them." Metzger v. Aetna Ins. Co., 227 N.Y. 411, 125 N.E. 814 (1920). However, there are instances where one is relieved of obligations to which he has apparently assented; namely, where the character of the writing was misrepresented by the other party or where the writing was such that a reasonable person would not think it contained contractual provisions. An example of the latter would be a hat-check stub containing in fine print a limitation of the proprietor's liability in case of loss or damage to the item checked. Ordinarily, stubs of this type are used for identification purposes only; hence, in the usual case one is not held to have assented to the limitation of proprietor liability merely by accepting the stub.

Mistake of Law

In the absence of fraud, one cannot obtain a release from contract liability upon the ground that he did not understand the legal effect of the contract. Courts will not grant relief from a mistake of law. By the majority view in this country, one paying money to another under a mistake of law cannot recover that money even though it was not legally due, provided the payee's claim was asserted in good faith. There are however, some exceptions. Payments made by governmental agencies or payments made to a court or court official under mistake of law are recoverable. The general reluctance to grant relief for mistake of law has been subjected to serious criticism, and has been abrogated by statute in a few States. In these States relief for mistake of law is placed upon the same basis as mutual mistake of a material fact.

Cases

Duress

INTERNATIONAL UNDERWATER CONTRACTORS, INC. v. NEW ENGLAND TELEPHONE AND TELEGRAPH CO.

(1979) ⸺ Mass.App. ⸺ , 393 N.E.2d 968.

BROWN, J.

The plaintiff, International Underwater Contractors, Inc. (IUC), appeals from the entry of summary judgment for the defendant, New England Telephone and Telegraph Company (NET).

The plaintiff, which had entered into a written contract with the defendant to assemble and install certain conduits under the Mystic River for a lump sum price of $149,680, to be paid semimonthly in installments in proportion to the progress of the work, seeks additional compensation in a total amount of $811,816.73 for a major change in the system from that specified in the contract. The plaintiff asserts that the change, which was necessitated by delays caused by the defendant, forced the work to be performed in the winter months instead of during the summer, as originally bid, making the equipment originally specified unusable. This major change was made, the plaintiff alleges, at the direction of the defendant, and upon the defendant's assurances that it would pay the resulting additional costs.

The defendant moved for summary judgment with a supporting affidavit, wherein it argued in defense a release signed by the plaintiff settling the additional claim for a total sum of $575,000. The plaintiff, which submitted countervailing affidavits in opposition to the motion, argues that the release is not binding because it was signed under economic duress.

A special master appointed to hear summary judgment motions found that "as a matter of law, the economic duress required to vitiate the subject release was not present." Summary judgment was entered for the defendant, and the plaintiff's motions for reconsideration and to vacate judgment were denied. The instant appeal ensued.

* * *

A release signed under duress is not binding. [Citation.] "Coercion sufficient to avoid a contract need not, of course, consist of physical force or threats of it. Social or economic pressure illegally or immorally applied may be sufficient." [Citations.]

To show economic duress (1) a party "must show that he has been the victim of a wrongful or unlawful act or threat, and (2) such act or threat must be one which deprives the victim of his unfettered will." Williston, Contracts § 1617, at 704 (3d ed. 1970). "As a direct result of these elements, the party threatened must be compelled to make a disproportionate exchange of values." *Ibid.*

The elements of economic duress have also been described as follows: "(1) that one side involuntarily accepted the terms of another; (2) that circumstances permitted no other alternative; and (3) that said circumstances were the result of coercive acts of the opposite party." [Citations.] "Merely taking advantage of another's financial difficulty is not duress. Rather, the person alleging financial difficulty must allege that it was contributed to or caused by the one accused of coercion." *Williston, supra,* § 1617, at 708. Thus "[i]n order to substantiate the allegation of economic duress or business compulsion . . . [t]here must be a showing of acts on the part of the defendant which produced [the financial embarrassment]. The assertion of duress must be proved by evidence that the duress resulted from defendant's wrongful and oppressive conduct and not by plaintiff's necessities." [Citation.]

* * *

[T]he affidavits show a dispute as to whether NET gave assurances to IUC that if IUC made the change in installation of equipment and continued to perform that work to completion, NET would pay the additional costs and would not permit IUC to lose money. The affidavits also raise a question whether IUC's financial difficulties were attributable to such acts of the defendant and whether the plaintiff was forced because of such difficulties to accept a disproportionately small settlement which it would not otherwise have accepted.

Such allegations are material and, if true, would make out a case for duress. Here, if the plaintiff's allegations are true, the defendant's acts in (1) insisting on a deviation from the contract and repeatedly assuring the plaintiff that it would pay the additional cost, which was substantially greater than the original, if the plaintiff would complete the work and (2) then refusing to make payments for almost a year caused the plaintiff's financial difficulties. Such acts could be considered "wrongful" acts and indications of bad faith.

* * *

The unequal bargaining power of the two parties (both in terms of their comparative size and resources as well as the financial difficulties into which the plaintiff had fallen, allegedly because of the defendant's acts) is a factor to be considered in determining whether the transaction involved duress. [Citations.] In addition, the disparity between not only the plaintiff's alleged costs ($811,816) but also the amount NET's engineers had recommended in November, 1974, to the board for settlement ($775,000) and the amount offered on a "take-or-leave-it" basis in December and accepted in settlement ($575,000) raises the possibility there may have been a disproportionate exchange of values and should be considered in determining whether the release was signed under duress. Williston, *supra* § 1617, at 704.

The defendant argues that it did not have to settle the case but could have "exercised its lawful right to litigate the rights of the parties under the agreement" and that "[d]oing or threatening to do what a party has a legal right to do cannot form the basis of a claim of economic duress." [Citation.] However, if the assertions of the plaintiff are true, the defendant did more than assert a legal right, as its acts created the financial difficulties of the plaintiff, of which it then took advantage. The defendant also argued that the plaintiff cannot be found to have acted under duress because it had an adequate remedy at law. [Citation.] However, "if recourse to courts of law is not quick enough to save the victim's business or property interests, there is no adequate legal remedy." Williston, *supra* § 1617, at 709. Here, if the allegations of the plaintiff are true, the plaintiff, as a result of the defendant's wrongful acts, was not "free either to rely on [its] legal rights or . . . voluntarily to accept the terms proposed . . . ." [Citation.]

* * *

In summary, we find, that the affidavits raise issues of material fact, and we are therefore unable to say as matter of law that the signing of the release was voluntary. Accordingly, it was error to enter summary judgment.

Judgment reversed.

Duress

GREAT AMERICAN INDEMNITY CO. v. BERRYESSA

(1952) 122 Utah 243, 248 P.2d 367.

WADE, J.

The Great American Indemnity Company, appellant herein, brought this suit against Frank Berryessa and W. S. Berryessa, the obligors [debtors] on a joint promissory note. * * * W. S. Berryessa pleaded as defenses duress and lack of consideration and also counterclaimed for the return of $1,500 paid by him and the cancellation of a personal check given by him and not cashed at time of suit. This appeal is from a jury verdict and judgment thereon in favor of respondent W. S. Berryessa.

Viewing the evidence in the light most favorable to respondent, * * * it discloses that Frank Berryessa, a son of W. S. Berryessa, misappropriated some funds of his employer the Eccles Hotel Company, which operates the Ben Lomond Hotel in Ogden, Utah. When the father first learned

of this, it was thought that the sum involved was approximately $2,000 and he agreed to repay this amount if the bonding company would not be notified and no publicity given to the matter, and gave the hotel his promissory note for $2,186 to cover the shortage. Before this note became due, it was discovered that the shortage would probably be over $6,000 and therefore the manager of the hotel called W. S. Berryessa in for a conference. W. S. Berryessa knew he couldn't pay this larger sum and it was decided that the bonding company, the appellant herein, should be advised of the shortages. The hotel didn't try to collect the note for $2,186 after the bonding company was notified apparently expecting that company to reimburse the hotel for the entire shortage discovered. After the bonding company was notified, its agent had several conferences with the Berryessas and the hotel management in which there was ascertained that the total shortage amounted to $6,865.28 and Frank Berryessa signed a statement that he had misappropriated that amount. Frank Berryessa had stated that he had given a brother-in-law some of the money he had embezzled and it was suggested that he sign a note along with the Berryessas. The brother-in-law did not sign the note and at a further meeting of the Berryessas with the agent W. S. Berryessa indicated that he did not think his son Frank would be able to make the payments of $250 quarterly suggested and that he was sure that he personally would not be able to do so and therefore did not want to sign the note. Mr. Berryessa then testified, although this was denied by the agent, that the agent thereupon swore, pounded his fists on his desk, and told him, "You can't come here and tell me what you will do," and then told them that if W. S. Berryessa would pay $2,000 in cash and sign a note with Frank Berryessa for $4,865.20, payable at the rate of $50 a month, that Frank would not be prosecuted but that if he did not sign Frank would have to be prosecuted.

Thereupon, W. S. Berryessa agreed to do this and a couple of days later signed the note sued upon herein and about a month later, having secured a loan by mortgaging his home, gave the agent a cashier's check in the amount of $1,500 and a personal check in the amount of $500 as payment for the $2,000 cash agreed upon. Mr. Berryessa asked the agent not to cash the $500 check for about a month until he could get some more funds to pay it. This is the check which was never presented for payment by the appellant.

* * *

It is well settled that a note given to suppress a criminal prosecution is against public policy and is not enforceable between the parties. * * *

In this case respondent relied on two separate defenses, duress and illegal consideration, either one of which is sufficient to nullify this note. So if the jury found that the note was the result of duress or that respondent signed the note because appellant promised to refrain from criminal prosecution of his son, either one would be sufficient to invalidate the note and would constitute a defense thereto.

The uncashed check and the payment of $1,500 cash, present a different problem. Respondent had given the hotel a note for slightly over $2,000 to pay for the son's defalcations. At the time this note was given, there can be no question that no coercion was exercised against respondent and that his act was voluntary and at his own suggestion. There is nothing in the record to indicate that this note was given under duress or a promise to suppress prosecution.

* * *

The judgment against appellant on its complaint [to collect on the $4,865.20 promissory note] is affirmed. The judgment in favor of the respondent on his counterclaim [to recover the $2,000 paid the appellant] is reversed.

Undue Influence

SCHANEMAN v. SCHANEMAN

(1980) 206 Neb. 113, 291 N.W.2d 412.

CLARK, J.

This is an action in equity to set aside and cancel a deed executed by Conrad Schaneman, Sr., hereinafter called Conrad, in favor of his eldest son, the defendant, Laurence Schaneman.

* * *

By his answer, the defendant admitted the execution of the deed but alleged that the conveyance was pursuant to an oral understanding and agreement between Conrad and the defendant.

The District Court for Scotts Bluff County, Nebraska, found that the execution of the deed was a result of fraud and undue influence, set aside the deed, and quieted title in Conrad. Defendant appeals.

* * *

We affirm the judgment of the District Court.

The property in question was purchased in January 1945 for a price of $23,500. Defendant helped arrange the purchase and loaned his father $10,500 toward the purchase price. The grantees were Conrad and the defendant as joint tenants. There is some testimony that another son, Conrad, Jr., loaned his father $2,500 toward the purchase price also. In any event, it is agreed that Conrad was the real purchaser. By October 1946, Conrad had repaid the loans to his sons * * *.

Conrad, who was born in Russia, could not read or write the English language. He was the father of eight sons and five daughters, * * *.

Over the years, the family had been closeknit, especially the father and the sons. It had been customary for Conrad and his sons to help one another financially in the purchase of farms. Conrad helped his sons; the sons helped Conrad; and the brothers helped one another in this fashion.

After Conrad's retirement from farming, all the children had frequent contact with Conrad and helped him with his personal needs, although defendant, as the oldest son, perhaps had more contact and a closer relationship with Conrad.

* * *

[T]he defendant was the primary person who advised Conrad and handled Conrad's business matters, although the other sons did continue to help Conrad to some extent.

On March 18, 1975, Conrad deeded the farm in question to the defendant for a stated consideration of $23,500, which was the original purchase price of the property in 1945. The value of the farm in March 1975 was between $145,000 and $160,000.

In March of 1975, Conrad was a man 82 years of age whose health had been deteriorating since at least 1971. He had numerous periods of hospitalization and suffered from heart problems, diabetes with extremely high and uncontrollable blood sugar levels at times, and obesity. He weighed between 325 and 350 pounds, had difficulty breathing, could not walk more than 15 feet, and was no longer able to drive an automobile. He was unable to shave himself and a special jackhoist had to be utilized to get him in and out of the bathtub. He was, for all intents and purposes, an invalid, completely dependent on others for most of his personal needs and for transportation, banking, and other business matters.

Conrad's children, other than the defendant, testified that during early 1975 Conrad had some days when he was sharper and more alert mentally than on other days, that at times he was confused, had difficulty communicating and, on occasion, seemed to lapse into times long past. * * *

In about the spring of 1977, one of Conrad's sons discovered by accident that defendant's name was on Conrad's bank account as a joint tenant with right of survivorship. At about the same time, it was discovered that defendant had bought, with Conrad's money, a $20,000 certificate of deposit and that this also listed defendant as joint owner with right of survivorship. It was also later discovered that Conrad had executed a power of attorney in favor of defendant on August 20, 1975.

* * *

At trial, defendant testified that in March 1975 his father trusted and relied on the defendant; that defendant held a "special place" with his father, and that Conrad had complete trust and confidence in defendant. He did not recall any period that he and Conrad were not speaking and said that he and his father had never had a falling out. He further stated that, in March 1975, he was handling Conrad's business affairs generally.

* * *

An examination of the evidence reflects, in our opinion, that from the fall of 1974 until the conservatorship proceedings were commenced, there existed between the defendant and Conrad a confidential relationship and that, during that period, Conrad relied on the defendant for advice in his business affairs.

"[A confidential] relationship exists between two persons if one has gained the confidence of the other and purports to act or advise with the other's interest in mind." [Citation.]

"In a confidential or fiduciary relationship in which confidence is rightfully reposed on one side and a resulting superiority and opportunity for influence is thereby created on the other, equity will scrutinize the transaction critically, especially where age, infirmity, and instability are involved, to see that no injustice has occurred." [Citation.]

Here the evidence reflects that, due to age and physical infirmities, Conrad was, for all intents and purposes, an invalid at the time of the conveyance. It further supports a finding that Conrad's mental acuity was impaired at times and that he sometimes suffered from disorientation and lapse of memory. Considering all the evidence, we find that, in March 1975, Conrad was subject to the influence of the defendant, who was acting in a confidential relationship; that the opportunity to exercise undue influence existed; that there was a disposition on the part of the defendant to exercise such undue influence; and that the conveyance appears to be the effect of such influence. These findings establish a prima facie case of undue influence and cast upon the defendant the burden of going forward with the evidence.

A prima facie case of undue influence is made out in case of a deed where it is shown by clear and satisfactory evidence (1) that the grantor was subject to such influence; (2) that the opportunity to exercise it existed; (3) that there was a disposition to exercise it; and (4) that the result appears to be the effect of such influence. . . . . In an action based on undue influence, when a confidential relationship exists between the parties, and a prima facie case is established, the burden of proof remains on the plaintiff, but the burden of going forward with the evidence shifts to the defendants.

* * *

We find that the defendant has not rebutted the presumption of undue influence which was raised by the plaintiff's prima facie case.

The judgment of the trial court was correct and is affirmed.

AFFIRMED.

Undue Influence

FRANCOIS v. FRANCOIS

(1979, 3rd Cir.) 599 F.2d 1286.

ROSENN, J.

We are asked in this appeal to assess whether the district court properly relieved a husband from the disastrous financial con-

sequences of a "Property Settlement and Separation Agreement" (agreement) entered into with his wife. The plaintiff, Victor H. Francois, instituted an action in the district court against his wife, A. Jane Francois, seeking rescission of the agreement and various real and personal property transfers made pursuant to that agreement. The district court declared the agreement and the conveyances to be null and void on the grounds * * * that Jane Francois had exerted undue influence over her husband. * * * From the final order of the district court, Jane Francois appeals alleging that the district court improperly invalidated the agreement and reconveyed properties to her husband. We affirm.

I.

The controversy before us arises out of the troubled and relatively brief marriage of the parties. Victor H. Francois (Victor) and A. Jane Francois (Jane) were married on May 13, 1971 after a brief courtship of several months. At the time of the wedding, Victor was fifty years old, a bachelor residing with his elderly mother. Jane was thirty years old, twice divorced and the mother of two minor children, one approximately sixteen years old, and the other, thirteen. Victor was relatively secure financially, possessing an acre lot, Lilliendal and Marienhoj, St. Thomas, V.I. (Lilliendal), with a two story, five bedroom building containing two apartments, a one-fourth interest in his family's hardware business, thirty shares of a family close corporation (Francois Realty), four shares of stock in a multi-family close corporation (21 Queen's Quarter), a portfolio of publicly held stock valued at between $18,000 and $19,000, and two bank accounts. Victor also received income from his job as manager of the family hardware business. Jane was gainfully employed at the time of the marriage but ceased working shortly thereafter. She apparently brought no money or property to the marriage.

The couple began to experience difficulties not long after the marriage. A series of events over the next four years centering on financial disputes led to the deterioration and eventual collapse of the marital relation. Within months of the wedding, Jane began to express anxiety over her financial security in the event that Victor died. To allay his wife's fears, Victor opened a joint savings account into which he deposited $5,000 for her use.

Jane also expressed a continuing desire for a marital homestead. In response, in March of 1972, Victor purchased a fairly large house with a swimming pool (Misgunst) for a sum of $107,000. Victor supplied a $37,000 downpayment from his assets and undertook the responsibility for the monthly mortgage payments in excess of $860 per month. Title was [jointly] taken
* * *

In the fall of 1973, the couple's finances became further consolidated. Victor conveyed all of his interest in his Lilliendal property to Jane and assigned to her a half interest in both his thirty shares of Francois Realty stock and four shares of 21 Queen's Quarter stock. He also gave Jane a power of attorney over his portfolio of publicly held stock. Jane also insisted on having a boat. Victor sold $18,000 of his stock in order to purchase a boat for Jane in her name at the cost of $17,000. Jane sold this boat approximately a year later for $16,000 and personally invested the proceeds for herself. The couple also executed reciprocal wills leaving the entirety of the marital estate to the surviving spouse or, if no spouse survived, to the children.

In September of 1974 a domestic quarrel precipitated the demise of the marriage. The dispute centered on an incident in which Victor allegedly embarrassed Jane by his behavior in front of one of Jane's friends. As a result of the incident, Jane determined to divorce Victor and on October 8, 1974, contacted an attorney, Harold Monoson, to draw up divorce papers. Victor

was unaware of his wife's decision to terminate the marriage. Two days later, Jane, without any explanation, invited Victor to accompany her to Monoson's office where Victor, to his complete surprise, was presented for his signature a "Property Settlement and Separation Agreement." Monoson advised Victor that he would need an attorney, but Victor's choice was vetoed by his wife's insistence that this attorney was unacceptable. Monoson then asked a lawyer with an office in the same building, Gregory Ball, to come into the office. Ball read the agreement, which interestingly already had his name on it as Victor's counsel. Ball strenuously advised Victor not to sign the agreement because it would commit him to "financial suicide." When Victor persisted in his determination to sign, Ball informed him that he could not represent him in the matter, and left the office.

Victor, relying on representations made to him by Monoson and Jane, was persuaded that only by signing the agreement could he preserve his marriage. Victor signed the agreement and several related documents apparently in hope of saving his marriage. He conveyed to Jane his one-half interest in the marital home, Misgunst, and assigned to her his stock portfolio and his remaining stock interest in both close corporations. In addition, the agreement required Victor to pay $300 per month in alimony to his wife.

After signing the agreement, however, the parties resumed cohabitation for approximately one year. But early in 1975, Jane informed Victor that she had sold the entire portfolio of publicly held stock for around $20,000. In October of 1975, Jane informed Victor that she had sold the Misgunst and Lilliendal properties in exchange for properties owned in California by AD'M Enterprises, a limited partnership. In mid-October Jane also summarily informed Victor that she was leaving him permanently and promptly left the Virgin Islands. AD'M took title to the properties by a single deed dated October 15, 1975 but before it could record the deed, Victor instituted these proceedings. Apparently when AD'M learned of this litigation, it never recorded the deed but instead sued Jane for rescission of the conveyance.

* * *

We turn then to the issue of undue influence.

* * *

The key inquiry in the case before us is whether Jane and Victor Francois, as husband and wife, also enjoyed a confidential relationship. The marital relation does not automatically give rise to a confidential relation, but it "arises when one party places confidence in the other with a resulting superiority and influence on the other side." [Citation.] Thus, each marriage must be examined on its own facts to determine if a confidential relation exists.

The district court unequivocally found that a confidential relationship existed between Jane and Victor Francois and that Jane was clearly the dominant partner. The district court found the evidence to be "replete with instances" in which Jane was able to secure her wishes simply by badgering Victor into submission. The record reveals that Victor, very early in the marriage, began to turn over the management of his finances to Jane who subsequently used her position to gain control incrementally over most of Victor's assets. The evidence supports the district court's findings that the relationship between the parties was one in which Victor reposed total trust and confidence in Jane who used her superior position in the marriage to Victor's financial detriment.

* * *

Undue influence is not a concept susceptible of unitary definition. The essence of the idea is the subversion of another person's free will in order to obtain assent to an agreement.

If a party in whom another reposes confidence misuses that confidence to gain his own advantage while the other has been made to feel that the party in question will not act against his welfare, the transaction is the result of undue influence. The influence must be such that the victim acts in a way contrary to his own best interest and thus in a fashion in which he would not have operated but for the undue influence.

Williston on Contracts, § 1625 at 776–77 (3d ed. 1970) (footnotes omitted).

The degree of persuasion that is necessary to constitute undue influence varies from case to case. The proper inquiry is not just whether persuasion induced the transaction but whether the result was produced by the domination of the will of the victim by the person exerting undue influence. Restatement of Contracts § 497, Comment c. Hence, the particular transaction must be scrutinized to determine if the agreement was truly the product of a free and independent mind. In this respect, the fairness of the agreement must be shown by clear and convincing evidence. [Citation.]

* * *

[Affirmed.]

Fraud:
False Representation of Fact

VOKES v. ARTHUR MURRAY, INC.

(1968, Fla.App.) 212 So.2d 906.

[Audrey E. Vokes, plaintiff, appeals from a final order dismissing her complaint, for failure to state a cause of action.]

PIERCE, J.

Defendant Arthur Murray, Inc., a corporation, authorizes the operation throughout the nation of dancing schools under the name of "Arthur Murray School of Dancing" through local franchised operators, one of whom was defendant J. P. Davenport whose dancing establishment was in Clearwater.

Plaintiff Mrs. Audrey E. Vokes, a widow of 51 years and without family, had a yen to be "an accomplished dancer" with the hopes of finding "new interest in life". So, on February 10, 1961, a dubious fate, with the assist of a motivated acquaintance, procured her to attend a "dance party" at Davenport's "School of Dancing" where she whiled away the pleasant hours, sometimes in a private room, absorbing his accomplished sales technique, during which her grace and poise were elaborated upon and her rosy future as "an excellent dancer" was painted for her in vivid and glowing colors. As an incident to this interlude, he sold her eight ½-hour dance lessons to be utilized within one calendar month therefrom, for the sum of $14.50 cash in hand paid, obviously a baited "come-on".

Thus she embarked upon an almost endless pursuit of the terpsichorean art during which, over a period of less than sixteen months, she was sold fourteen "dance courses" totalling in the aggregate 2302 hours of dancing lessons for a total cash outlay of $31,090.45, all at Davenport's dance emporium.

* * *

These dance lesson contracts and the monetary consideration therefor of over $31,000 were procured from her by means and methods of Davenport and his associates which went beyond the unsavory, yet legally permissible, perimeter of "sales puffing" and intruded well into the forbidden area of undue influence, the suggestion of falsehood, the suppression of truth, and the free exercise of rational judgment, if what plaintiff alleged in her complaint was true. From the time of her first contact with the dancing school in February, 1961, she was influenced unwittingly by a constant and continuous barrage of flattery, false praise, excessive compliments, and panegyric encomiums, to such extent that it would be not only inequitable, but unconscionable, for a Court exercising inherent chancery power to allow such contracts to stand.

She was incessantly subjected to overreaching blandishment and cajolery. She was assured she had "grace and poise"; that she was "rapidly improving and developing in her dancing skill"; that the additional lessons would "make her a beautiful dancer, capable of dancing with the most accomplished dancers"; that she was "rapidly progressing in the development of her dancing skill and gracefulness", etc., etc. She was given "dance aptitude tests" for the ostensible purpose of "determining" the number of remaining hours instructions needed by her from time to time.

At one point she was sold 545 additional hours of dancing lessons to be entitled to award of the "Bronze Medal" signifying that she had reached "the Bronze Standard", a supposed designation of dance achievement by students of Arthur Murray, Inc.

Later she was sold an additional 926 hours in order to gain the "Silver Medal", indicating she had reached "the Silver Standard", at a cost of $12,501.35.

At one point, while she still had to her credit about 900 unused hours of instructions, she was induced to purchase an additional 24 hours of lessons to participate in a trip to Miami at her own expense, where she would be "given the opportunity to dance with members of the Miami Studio".

She was induced at another point to purchase an additional 126 hours of lessons in order to be not only eligible for the Miami trip but also to become "a life member of the Arthur Murray Studio", carrying with it certain dubious emoluments, at a further cost of $1,752.30.

At another point, while she still had over 1,000 unused hours of instruction she was induced to buy 151 additional hours at a cost of $2,049.00 to be eligible for a "Student Trip to Trinidad", at her own expense as she later learned.

Also, when she still had more than 1,000 unused hours to her credit, she was prevailed upon to purchase an additional 347 hours at a cost of $4,235.74, to qualify her to receive a "Gold Medal" for achievement, indicating she had advanced to "the Gold Standard".

On another occasion, while she still had over 1200 unused hours, she was induced to buy an additional 175 hours of instruction at a cost of $2,472.75 to be eligible "to take a trip to Mexico".

Finally, sandwiched in between other lesser sales promotions, she was influenced to buy an additional 481 hours of instruction at a cost of $6,523.81 in order to "be classified as a Gold Bar Member, the ultimate achievement of the dancing studio".

All the foregoing sales promotions, illustrative of the entire fourteen separate contracts, were procured by defendant Davenport and Arthur Murray, Inc., by false representations to her that she was improving in her dancing ability, that she had excellent potential, that she was responding to instructions in dancing grace, and that they were developing her into a beautiful dancer, whereas in truth and in fact she did not develop in her dancing ability, she had no "dance aptitude", and in fact had difficulty in "hearing the musical beat". The complaint alleged that such representations to her "were in fact false and known by the defendant to be false and contrary to the plaintiff's true ability, the truth of plaintiff's ability being fully known to the defendants, but withheld from the plaintiff for the sole and specific intent to deceive and defraud the plaintiff and to induce her in the purchasing of additional hours of dance lessons". It was averred that the lessons were sold to her "in total disregard to the true physical, rhythm, and mental ability of the plaintiff". In other words, while she first exulted that she was entering the "spring of her life", she finally was awakened to the fact there was "spring" neither in her life nor in her feet.

* * *

It is true that "generally a misrepresentation, to be actionable, must be one of fact rather than of opinion". Tonkovich v.

South Florida Citrus Industries, Inc., Fla.App.1966, 185 So.2d 710. [Citation.] But this rule has significant qualifications, applicable here. * * * As stated by Judge Allen of this Court in Ramel v. Chasebrook Construction Company, Fla.App. 1961, 135 So.2d 876:

"A statement of a party having * * * superior knowledge may be regarded as a statement of fact although it would be considered as opinion if the parties were dealing on equal terms."

It could be reasonably supposed here that defendants had "superior knowledge" as to whether plaintiff had "dance potential" and as to whether she was noticeably improving in the art of terpsichore. And it would be a reasonable inference from the undenied averments of the complaint that the flowery eulogiums heaped upon her by defendants as a prelude to her contracting for 1944 additional hours of instruction in order to attain the rank of the Bronze Standard, thence to the bracket of the Silver Standard, thence to the class of the Gold Bar Standard, and finally to the crowning plateau of a Life Member of the Studio, proceeded as much or more from the urge to "ring the cash register" as from any honest or realistic appraisal of her dancing prowess or a factual representation of her progress.

Even in contractual situations where a party to a transaction owes no duty to disclose facts within his knowledge or to answer inquiries respecting such facts, the law is if he undertakes to do so he must disclose the *whole truth*. [Citations.] From the face of the complaint, it should have been reasonably apparent to defendants that her vast outlay of cash for the many hundreds of additional hours of instruction was not justified by her slow and awkward progress, which she would have been made well aware of if they had spoken the "whole truth".

* * *

Reversed.

Fraud: Misrepresentation of Fact

SUNDERHAUS v. PEREL & LOWENSTEIN

(1965) 215 Tenn. 619, 388 S.W.2d 140.

HOLMES, J.

The Chancellor sustained a demurrer to the original bill [complaint] in this case as amended. The appellant, Virginia Sunderhaus, has perfected an appeal to this Court.

The original bill alleges that on February 10, 1958 complainant [plaintiff] purchased a diamond ring from the defendant, Perel & Lowenstein, for the sum of $699.25 and received from the defendant a written warranty guaranteeing to complainant the perfection of the ring, its value, style, and trade-in value. * * *

It is further alleged in the original bill that thereafter complainant desired to trade this ring for another ring and found that one jeweler appraised the ring as having a value of $300.00, and another jeweler appraised the ring at a value of $350.00.

* * *

Later, on April 10, 1964, a further amendment to the original bill was filed in which complainant alleged that at the time of the purchase of this ring from the defendant the defendant's agent, David L. Richman, represented to her that the diamond was worth the amount of money she paid, that the defendant's agent misrepresented to her the true value of the diamond and that this representation was a fraudulent representation, that she was unfamiliar with the value of diamonds and relied upon the statement made by the agent of the defendant as to value, that the defendant's agent knew at the time of the sale that the price she paid was not the true retail value of the diamond which she purchased, that this amounted to a fraud on the purchaser and that the defendant through its agent took advantage of complainant's trust in his

statements. This amendment prays for rescission of the contract, or, in the alternative, for a judgment for the difference between the sale price and the actual retail value of the ring.

* * *

The alleged false representations of the appellee's agent relate to the value of the diamond purchased by appellant. We find the general rule to be that ordinarily representations of value made by one seeking to dispose of property commercially are to be regarded as expressions of opinion or commendatory trade statements not constituting a basis of fraud. There are, however, a number of exceptions to this general rule. In 23 Am.Jur., Fraud and Deceit, § 59, at Page 830, it is stated:

"* * * Likewise, a statement of value may be of such a character, so made and intended, and so received, as to constitute fundamental misrepresentation; and if it is made as an assertion of fact, and with the purpose that it shall be so received, and it is so received, it may amount to a fraud. Moreover, a statement of value involving and coupled with a statement of a material fact is fraud.

* * *

"Under various circumstances, it has been held that representations as to market price or market value are not mere statements of opinion, but are representations of fact which, if false, will support an action for fraud or deceit. Thus, it has been held that a false representation as to the market value of bank stock, which has an ascertainable market value, is not the mere expression of an opinion, but a misrepresentation of fact on which fraud may be based to sustain an action for deceit." * * * 23 Am.Jur., Fraud and Deceit, § 62, Page 834.

The rule is stated as follows in 3 Pomeroy, Equity Jurisprudence, § 878b (5th ed. 1941):

"There is still another and perhaps more common form of such misrepresentation. Wherever a party states a matter, which might otherwise be only an opinion, and does not state it *as the mere expression of his own opinion,* but affirms it *as an existing fact* material to the transaction, so that the other party may reasonably treat it as a fact, and rely and act upon it as such, then the statement clearly becomes an affirmation of fact within the meaning of the general rule, and may be a fraudulent misrepresentation. * * *"

* * *

Of necessity, in the purchase of a diamond or other precious stone, the purchaser must rely upon the integrity of the jeweler from whom he purchases. The layman is in no position to weigh the stone and make his own determination as to its true value, but must rely upon statements of value made to him by the jeweler. Here, the bill charges the agent of the appellee falsely represented the value of the diamond to the complainant, knowing the falsity of the representation, that the appellant was not familiar with the value of the diamond and relied upon the false representation of the appellee's agent. These averments contain all of the elements necessary to state a cause of action for fraud and deceit.

* * *

[Decree reversed and the cause is remanded for further proceedings.]

Misrepresentation

WHIPP v. IVERSON

(1969) 43 Wis.2d 166, 168 N.W.2d 201.

HALLOWS, C. J.

The complaint alleges the defendants were the owners of a business known as the Iverson Motor Company at Amery, Wisconsin. The company was engaged in general automobile and farm implement repair work and the sale of Oldsmobile, Rambler and International Harvester Scout automobiles. The Oldsmobile agency consisted of 40 percent of the volume of sales and net earnings. On October 18, 1966, the plaintiffs and the defendant Robert Iverson discussed the sale of the business. The complaint alleges Iverson falsely represented the sale included the Oldsmobile agency and franchise and he was selling the business to the plaintiffs as he was operating it. It is alleged this representation and others Iverson knew or ought to have known were false and the plaintiffs, relying on them, were induced to enter into an agreement to purchase the business and to lease the real estate occupied by the business.

In December, 1966, the Oldsmobile division of General Motors refused to transfer the franchise to the plaintiff Blaine Whipp who returned possession of the business and property to the defendants and demanded the return of the down payment and the amount of capital invested in the business. The defendants demurred to the complaint and argue it states no cause of action because it fails to allege the defendants made the false representation intentionally for the purpose of inducing the plaintiffs to sign the agreements. We think the trial court was correct in overruling the demurrer.

Rescission of a contract in equity may be grounded on misrepresentations not intentionally made for the purpose of defrauding or inducing a person to act to his detriment for the speaker's economic benefit.

At law in the action for deceit the basis of responsibility for misrepresentation was intention, generally called scienter or the intent to deceive. [Citations.] This elusive state of mind may be proved by proof the speaker believes his statement to be false or the representation is made without any belief as to its truth. [Citations.] As Prosser puts it, "A defendant who asserts a fact as of his own knowledge, or so positively as to imply that he has knowledge, under circumstances where he is aware that he will be so understood when he knows that he does not in fact know whether what he says is true is found to have the intent to deceive. * * *"

* * *

It is not necessary for rescission of a contract "that the party making a misrepresentation should have known that it was false." Recovery is allowed even though misrepresentation is innocently made because "It would be unjust to allow one who has made false representations, even innocently, to retain the fruits of a bargain induced by such representations." 5 Williston on Contracts, (Rev.Ed., 1937), p. 4189, s. 1500. This statement of law is adopted by the Restatement of Contracts, s. 476, which states "Where a party is induced to enter into a transaction with another party that he was under no duty to enter into by means of the latter's fraud or material misrepresentation, the transaction is voidable as against the latter and all who stand in no better position, subject to" certain qualifications. A misrepresentation may be innocent, negligent, or known to be false, Restatement, 2 Contracts, p. 890, s. 470, Comment a, and if innocently made is voidable, s. 476(2). See also Restatement, Restitution, p. 123, s. 28(b).

* * *

We think an express allegation of scienter is not required for rescission which is asked for in this complaint. The defendants are alleged to have known or ought to have known the Oldsmobile franchise could not be sold as part of the business. Iverson was the owner of the franchise he was purporting to sell and should know whether he could or could not sell the franchise. There is no question of Iverson's economic interest in the sale and his lack of intent to deceive is not material to the cause of action. We think therefore a cause of action is stated for rescission * * *

Order affirmed.

Mistake

BOYD v. AETNA LIFE INS. CO.

(1941) 310 Ill.App. 547, 35 N.E.2d 99.

STONE, P. J.

This suit grows out of the cancellation and surrender of a life insurance policy issued by the Aetna Life Insurance Company, appellee (hereinafter designated as defendant), on the life of one Jimmie Boyd, who, at the time the policy was issued, was the husband of Christine Boyd, appellant (hereinafter designated as plaintiff). The policy insured against permanent total disability at the rate of $50 per month during the life of the insured, beginning six months after the beginning of such permanent total disability, together with abatement of premiums and $5,000 to be paid in the event of death, with no deduction from the face of the policy on account of payments made under the total disability clause. Plaintiff was designated as beneficiary, both for the total disability benefits and the death benefit.

After the policy had been in force for a number of years, plaintiff and her husband separated. Plaintiff continued to live in Carmi, Illinois, but her husband left there and traveled as advance agent for shows that were traveling about the country, so that it was impossible for plaintiff to keep informed as to his whereabouts or his state of health.

Following their separation plaintiff paid the premiums on the insurance policy, up until about the month of August, 1938, when, owing to her financial circumstances, she felt that she could no longer afford to pay the premiums and notified the insurance company that she desired to surrender the policy and receive its cash surrender value. A loan had previously been made on this policy, which, with accrued interest, amounted to the sum of $1,039, so that when plaintiff surrendered the policy she received but $4.19 in money, that being the balance of the cash surrender value above the loan and interest.

Shortly after the policy had been surrendered and cancelled, plaintiff learned the insured had been permanently and totally disabled more than six months before the surrender of said policy. Neither plaintiff nor defendant knew of the physical condition of the insured at the time the policy was surrendered. Upon learning of the permanent total disability of the insured, plaintiff requested the reinstatement of the insurance policy she had surrendered, and the payment of the disability benefits provided therein. Afterwards, on April 8, 1939, the insured, Jimmie Boyd, died and plaintiff then requested of defendant, the payment of the death benefit, in addition to the disability benefits, claimed to have previously accrued. This was not paid, whereupon suit was instituted.

* * *

[The plaintiff appealed based upon a mutual mistake of fact, that] the cancellation or rescission of the insurance policy in question was made under such mutual mistake of fact.

It is defendant's earnest contention that at the time plaintiff decided to surrender the policy and asked for the cash surrender value, she knew that she did not know the condition of health of her husband, the insured. It is stressed that there was no unconscious ignorance on the part of plaintiff as to the health of insured, so it is claimed that the allegations of the amended complaint failed to show any mistake of fact in the legal sense upon her part; that notwithstanding her conscious want of ignorance of the condition of health of her husband she had elected to surrender the policy in question and take the cash surrender value thereof, in lieu of paying any further premiums on the policy and by such action waived any rights she had under the policy of insurance.

* * *

The decisive and practically sole question for the consideration of this court is whether the facts alleged in the amended complaint, set forth a sufficient mistake of fact, in the legal acceptation of the term, as to justify the intervention of a court of equity, and relieve against the consequences of that alleged mistake of fact, in the entering into the contract of rescission.

"Mistake of fact" has been defined to be a mistake, not caused by the neglect of a legal duty on the part of the person making the mistake, and consisting in an unconscious ignorance or forgetfulness of a fact past or present material to the contract, or belief in the present existence of a thing material to the contract which does not exist, or in the past existence of a thing which has not existed. [Citations.] It has also been defined as that which gives rise to a right of recovery, existing either when some fact which really exists is unknown or when some fact is supposed to exist, which really does not exist. [Citation.]

* * *

In the instant case, the insured's state of health was not merely incidental, nor was it a matter that would merely enhance the amount of damages. The subject matter of the mistake was intrinsic to the transaction. As set forth in plaintiff's amended complaint, "if she had known the true facts as to said Jimmie Boyd's total permanent disability * * * she would not have surrendered same (the policy) to the defendant." This policy was in full force and effect at the time of total permanent disability. Upon that contingency coming to pass the liability of defendant was fixed. The cancellation was not intended to reach back and absolve defendant from any liability which it had already incurred. * * * In the instance case both parties believed Jimmie Boyd in good health, and contracted with reference to that supposed state of facts. We are of the opinion, therefore, that the facts alleged show ground for equitable relief, and that the court erred in dismissing the amended complaint for want of equity.

[Order and judgment of Circuit Court reversed and cause remanded with directions.]

Problems

1. A and B were negotiating and A's attorney prepared a long and carefully drawn contract which was given to B for examination. Five days later and prior to its execution, B's eyes became so infected that it was impossible for him to read. Ten days thereafter and during the continuance of the illness A called upon B and urged him to sign the contract, telling him that time was running out. B signed the contract despite the fact he was unable to read it. In a subsequent action by A, B claimed that the contract was not binding upon him because it was impossible for him to read it and he did not know what it contained prior to his signing it. Decision?

2. (a) A tells B that he paid $50,000 for his farm in 1975, and that he believes it is worth twice that at the present time. Relying upon these statements, B buys the farm from A for $75,000. A did pay $50,000 for the farm in 1975, but its value has increased only slightly and it is presently not worth $100,000. On discovering this, B offers to reconvey the farm to A and sues for the return of his $75,000. Result?

(b) Modify the facts in (a) by assuming that A had paid $35,000 for the property in 1975, what result?

3. On September 1, A in Portland, Oregon, wrote a letter to B in New York City offering to sell to B 1,000 tons of chromite at $48 per ton, to be shipped by S. S. Malabar sailing from Portland, Ore., to New York City via the Panama Canal. Upon receiving the letter on September 5, B immediately mailed to A a letter stating that he accepted the offer. There were two ships by the name of S. S. Malabar sailing from Portland to New York City via the Panama Canal, one sailing in October, and the other sailing in December. At the time of mailing his letter of acceptance B knew of both sailings and further knew that A knew only of the December sailing. Is there a contract? If so, to which S. S. Malabar does it relate?

4. On March 1, A sold to B 50 acres of land in Oregon which A at the time represented to be fine, black loam, high and dry, and free of stumps. B paid A the agreed price of $5,000, and took from A a deed to the land which B subsequently discovered to be low, swampy, and not entirely free of stumps. B nevertheless undertook to convert the greater part of the land into cranberry bogs. After one year of cranberry culture, B became entirely dissatisfied, tendered the land back to A, and demanded from A the return of the $5,000. Upon A's refusal to repay the money, B brings an action at law against him to recover the $5,000. What judgment?

5. A owes B, a police captain, $500. A threatens B that unless B gives him a discharge from the debt, A will disclose the fact that B has on several occasions become intoxicated and has been seen in the company of certain disreputable persons. B, induced by fear that such a disclosure would cost him his position, and in any event lead to social disgrace, gives A a release, but subsequently sues to set it aside and recover on his claim. Decision?

6. A owned a farm which was worth about $60 an acre. By false representations of fact A induced B to buy the farm at $250 an acre. Shortly after taking possession of the farm, B discovered oil under the land. A, on learning this, sues to have the sale set aside on the ground that it was voidable because of fraud. Decision?

7. On February 2, A induced B to purchase from him fifty (50) shares of stock in the XYZ Corporation for $10,000, representing that the actual book value of each share was $200. A certificate for fifty (50) shares was delivered to B. On February 16, B discovered that the book value was only $50 per share on February 2. Thereafter, B sues A. Decision?

8. D mistakenly accused P's son, S, of negligently burning D's barn. P believed that his son, S, was guilty of the wrong, and that he, P, was personally liable for the damage, since S was only 15 years old. Upon demand made by D, P paid D $2,500 for the damage to D's barn. After making this payment, P learned that his son, S, had not caused the burning of D's barn and was in no way responsible for its burning. P then sued D to recover $2,500 which he had paid D. Decision?

9. Jones, a farmer, found an odd-looking stone in his fields. He went to Smith, the town jeweler, and asked him what he thought it was. Smith said he did not know, but thought it might be a ruby. Jones asked Smith what he would pay for it and Smith said $50; whereupon Jones sold it to Smith for $50. The stone turned out to be an uncut diamond worth $2,000. Jones brought an action against Smith to recover the stone. On trial, it was proved that Smith actually did not know the stone was a diamond when he bought it, but thought it might be a ruby. Decision?

10. Decedent, a bedridden, lonely woman of 86 years, owned outright Greenacre, her ancestral estate. F, her physician and friend, visited her weekly and was held in the highest regard by Decedent. Decedent was extremely fearful of pain and suffering and depended upon F to ease her anxiety and pain. Several months before her death Decedent deeded Greenacre to F for $5,000. The fair market value of Greenacre at this time was $125,000. Decedent was survived by two children and six grandchildren. Decedent's children challenge the validity of the deed. Decision?

Chapter

9

CONSIDERATION

In order for a promise or agreement to be binding, the requirement of legally sufficient consideration must be satisfied. If consideration is absent, neither party can enforce the promise or agreement. Historically, the doctrine of consideration has been used to ensure that promises are enforced only where the parties have received something of value in the eye of the law. Gratuitous promises, accordingly, are not legally enforceable. The requirement of legally sufficient consideration reflects the market economy that helped to shape the law of contracts.

DEFINITION OF CONSIDERATION

Consideration is whatever is given in exchange for something else and is present only when the parties intend an exchange, whether it be a promise exchanged for a promise, a promise for an act, or a promise exchanged for a forbearance to act.

Section 71 of the Restatement, Second, Contracts, defines consideration for a promise as (a) an act other than a promise, or (b) a forbearance, or (c) the creation, modification, or destruction of a legal relation, or (d) a return promise bargained for and given in exchange for the promise. The

consideration may be given to the promisor or to some other person. It may be given by the promisee or by some other person.

Bargained for Exchange

The central idea is that the parties have intentionally entered into a bargained exchange with one another, and have each given to the other something in exchange for his promise or performance. Bargain as used in this context does not mean making an advantageous deal, or buying something at a price less than its fair market value. "Bargain" as used in the phrase "bargained for exchange" means simply that the parties have negotiated and mutually agreed upon the terms of what each party is giving to the other party in exchange for what he is receiving. Thus, a promise to give someone a birthday present is without consideration, as the promisor receives nothing in exchange for his promise of a present.

Legal Sufficiency

For consideration to be effective, it is not enough for the parties to have entered into a bargained exchange. To be valid, consideration must also meet the test of legal sufficiency. The definition of legal sufficiency is technical, and in certain cases its application produces a result which is artificial. To be legally sufficient, the consideration for the promise must be either a legal detriment to the promisee or a legal benefit to the promisor. To illustrate, in order for A's promise to B to be binding, it must be supported by legally sufficient consideration, which requires that the promise or performance received from B in exchange provide either a legal benefit to A (the promisor) or a legal detriment to B (the promisee). In most cases where there is legal detriment to the promisee, a legal benefit to the promisor will also be found. However, the presence of either one is sufficient. Legal detriment is not necessarily actual detriment, nor does legal benefit necessarily mean actual benefit. These terms are words of art and have specific technical meanings.

Legal sufficiency has nothing to do with adequacy of consideration. The subject matter which the parties respectively have exchanged need not have approximately the same value. The law will treat the parties as having considered them adequate by reason of having freely agreed to the exchange. The requirement of legally sufficient consideration is therefore not at all concerned with whether the bargain was good or bad, or whether one party received disproportionately more or less than what he gave or promised in exchange for it. Such an inquiry might be relevant if a question of fraud, duress, or undue influence were involved. However, the instant requirement is simply (1) that the parties have agreed to an exchange; and (2) that with respect to each party the subject matter exchanged, or promised in exchange, either imposed a legal detriment upon the promisee or conferred a legal benefit upon the promisor.

Legal detriment is a technical concept, not to be confused with actual detriment, and means the doing (or undertaking to do) that which the promisee was under no prior legal obligation to do, or the refraining from

doing (or undertaking to refrain from doing) that which he was previously under no legal obligation to refrain from doing. On the other hand, legal benefit means the obtaining by the promisor of that which he had no prior legal right to obtain.

To illustrate, suppose that A promises B, a high school graduate, that if B will attend the XYZ College and graduate therefrom, A will pay to B upon graduation the entire cost of his college education. B enters XYZ College and duly graduates. The college education which he received is undeniably an actual benefit to B, but legally he suffered a detriment in graduating from XYZ College in that he gave up his freedom to attend any other college, or to not attend college at all, in consideration for A's promise. Consequently, the consideration which B gave for A's promise, although not actually detrimental, was legally detrimental to the promisee B. It is therefore legally sufficient and A's promise is enforceable by B. Furthermore, A may have received no actual benefit from B having obtained a college education at XYZ College, yet A received a legal benefit in that he obtained from B something that he had no previous right to have, namely, B's attendance at XYZ College and his graduation therefrom. This legal benefit may be of no value or usefulness to A, but nevertheless A's promise resulted in A obtaining a performance from B which A was not otherwise entitled to have. Thus, in this illustration the promisor (A) received a legal benefit and the promisee (B) suffered a legal detriment, although either one of these would satisfy the test of legal sufficiency.

In Devecmon v. Shaw & Devries, 69 Md. 199, 14 A. 464 (1888), a man promised his nephew that if the latter would take a trip to Europe, the uncle would reimburse and repay to the nephew all expenses of the trip. The nephew took the trip, and the court held that he was entitled to recover all of his expenses. The nephew was not previously obligated to take the trip and therefore suffered a legal detriment in making it, although the trip may have been actually beneficial to him culturally, educationally and in other respects.

In a unilateral contract, a promise is exchanged for an act or a forbearance to act. The two preceeding examples illustrate such contracts; they each involve a promise exchanged for an act. If the promisor or offeror requests a *forbearance,* such as non-smoking, non-drinking, or withholding the filing of a lawsuit, and the offeree accepts the offer by forbearing as requested, there is no question of consideration in fact. The consideration is legally sufficient because the offeree has refrained from doing that which he was under no legal obligation to refrain from doing, thereby incurring a legal detriment.

BARGAINED FOR EXCHANGE

Past Consideration

The element of exchange is absent where a promise is given for a past transaction. Hence, past consideration is no consideration. A promise made on account of something which the promisee has already done is not enforceable. Thus, on June 1, A sells B a horse for $500. On June 15 B asks A if he warrants the horse to be sound, and A tells B that he so warrants it. There is no consideration for A's warranty since B has given nothing in return for this promise. There is no bargained for exchange. Consideration is the inducement for a promise or performance. Therefore, unbargained for past events are not consideration, despite their designation as "past consideration."

Moral Obligation

A promise made in order to satisfy a pre-existing moral obligation is unenforceable for lack of consideration. Instances involving such moral obligation include promises

to pay for board and lodging previously furnished to a needy relative of the promisor, promises to pay debts owed by a relative of the promisor, and promises of an employer to pay a completely disabled former employee a sum of money in addition to the amount of an award made under a Workmen's Compensation statute. Although in many cases the moral obligation may be strong by reason of the particular facts and circumstances, no liability attaches to the promise.

LEGAL SUFFICIENCY

The doctrine of consideration requires that the promises or performance of *both* parties be legally sufficient. If the requisite mutuality of consideration does not exist, the contract is void. To be legally sufficient, the promise must be something of "value in the eye of the law"; a benefit to the promisor or a detriment to the promisee. Promises which are not legally sufficient, such as illusory promises and promises to perform a pre-existing obligation, do not constitute valid consideration.

Mutuality of Obligation

Illusory Promises. It is fundamental to the formation of a bilateral contract that if one party is not bound, neither party is bound. A promise by its literal terms may impose no obligation upon the promisor. Thus, a promise to purchase such quantity of goods as the promisor may "desire" or "want" or "wish to buy" imposes no obligation to buy any goods, as its performance is entirely optional. Thus, if A offers to sell to B as many barrels of oil as B shall choose at $40 per barrel, there is no contract for lack of consideration. B may wish or desire to buy none of the oil, and in buying none would fulfill his promise. An offer containing such a promise, although accepted by the offeree, does not create a contract because the promise is illusory—there is no constraint placed upon B's freedom. He is not bound to do anything nor can A reasonably expect to receive any performance. Thus, B, by his promise, suffers no legal detriment and confers no legal benefit. Consequently, B's promise does not provide legally sufficient consideration for A's promise.

Output and Requirement Contracts. An agreement to sell the entire production of a particular plant, factory, or mine is called an output contract. It affords the seller an assured market for his product. An agreement to purchase all materials of a particular kind for a particular use is called a requirements contract. It assures a buyer of a ready source of inventory or supplies. These contracts when made may or may not be accompanied by an estimate of the quantity to be sold or to be purchased.

Assume that A promises to supply B who promises to buy from A at an agreed price per ton all of the coal which may be required to operate B's factory for one year. These promises are not illusory. The amount of coal which B has agreed to buy is not subject to his whim or caprice. His promise is not to buy such coal as he may desire or wish to buy, but rather to buy such amount of coal as is needed for a given purpose, namely, the operation of his factory. The contract is valid although B may decide not to operate the factory in which event he would need no coal and would not be required to take or pay for any. B's promise involves at least two alternatives, each of which is a legal detriment to him. The alternative of not operating the factory whereby he requires no coal involves a legal detriment to B, as he is free to operate or not operate it. The alternative of operating and buying all coal needed from A is also a legal detriment. The possibility that B may change the type of fuel to oil or gas, or even convert to electricity, does not change the result as each of these alternatives would also involve a legal detriment to him.

The Code imposes a good faith limitation upon the quantity to be sold or purchased under an output or requirements contract, as provided in Section 2–306(1):

(1) A term which measures the quantity by the output of the seller or the requirements of the buyer means such actual output or requirements as may occur in good faith, except that no quantity unreasonably disproportionate to any stated estimate or in the absence of a stated estimate to any normal or otherwise comparable prior output or requirements may be tendered or demanded.

Exclusive Dealing Contracts. Where a manufacturer of goods grants an exclusive franchise or license to a distributor to sell his products in a designated territory, unless otherwise agreed, an implied obligation is imposed on the manufacturer to use his best efforts to supply the goods and on the distributor to use his best efforts to promote their sale. As Justice Cardozo stated in Wood v. Lucy, Lady Duff-Gordon, page 191, the exclusive privilege is "instinct with an obligation." This obligation which arises upon acceptance of the exclusive franchise is sufficient consideration for the grant of the franchise.

Conditional Contracts. The fact that the obligation to perform a contract may not arise until the happening of a specified event does not invalidate the contract. This is so, even though the specified event may never occur. The requisite mutuality of obligation nonetheless exists, since neither party need perform if the event does not occur. The same result obtains where the obligation to perform terminates upon the occurrence of a specified event.

Thus, if A offers to pay B $1,000 for B's horse, provided that A receives such amount as distributee of the estate of his deceased uncle, and B accepts the offer and delivers the horse to A, the duty of A to pay $1,000 to B is conditioned upon his receiving $1,000 from his deceased uncle's estate. The consideration moving from B to A is the transfer of title to the horse. The consideration moving from A to B is the promise of $1,000 subject to the condition. Although the contract is conditional, it is complete, definite, and certain. If the express condition was an event the occurrence of which was impossible, then no contract would exist because the agreement would be illusory.

Performance of a Pre-existing Obligation

The law does not regard the performance of, or promise to perform, a pre-existing legal duty as either a legal detriment to the party under the prior legal obligation or as a benefit to the other party.

Pre-existing Public Obligation. A public duty is one which does not arise out of a contract but is imposed upon all members of society by force of the common law or by statute. Illustrations are found in the law of torts, such as the duty not to commit an assault, battery, false imprisonment, or defamation. The criminal law also imposes upon everyone numerous duties of a public nature. Thus, if A promises to pay B, the village ruffian, $100 not to abuse him physically, A's promise is unenforceable since B is under a pre-existing obligation imposed by both tort and criminal law to refrain from so acting.

Public officials, such as the mayor of a city, members of a city council, policemen, and firemen, are under a pre-existing obligation to perform their duties by virtue of their public office. If A's house catches fire and A telephones the head of the city fire department and promises him $500 if he will immediately send a fire truck and firemen to A's house to put out the fire, and he does so, the promise is not enforceable. A public official will not be allowed to gain privately by performing his duty. In cases involving a pre-existing public duty, there is no legally sufficient consideration because there is no legal detriment in per-

forming what is already a legal obligation nor legal benefit in receiving what is already legally owed.

Pre-existing Contractual Obligation. The performance of a pre-existing contractual duty is also legally insufficient consideration because the doing of what one is legally bound to do is neither detriment to the promisee nor benefit to the promisor. For example, if A employs B for one year at a salary of $1,000 per month, and at the end of six months promises B that in addition to the salary he will pay B $3,000 if B remains on the job for the remainder of the period originally agreed upon, A's promise is not binding for lack of legally sufficient consideration. However, if B's duties were by agreement changed even to a small extent in nature or amount, A's promise would be binding.

In a case involving a building contract, the parties entered into an oral contract in June, 1969, whereby plaintiff agreed to construct a building for defendant on a time and materials basis, at a maximum cost of $56,146, plus sales tax and extras ordered by defendant. When the building was 90 percent completed defendant told plaintiff he was unhappy with the whole job as "the thing wasn't just being run right." The parties thereupon on October 17 signed a written agreement lowering the maximum cost to $52,000 plus sales tax. Plaintiff thereafter completed the building at a cost of $64,155. The maximum under the June oral agreement, plus extras and sales tax, totalled $61,040. Defendant contended that he was obligated to pay only the lower maximum fixed by the October 17 agreement. The Supreme Court of Washington held that the October 17 modification agreement was not binding for lack of consideration and plaintiff was entitled to recover under the original agreement, stating:

Applying our holding to the facts in this case, we must conclude that no consideration existed to support the October 17th agreement. Under the oral contract plaintiff had an antecedent duty to complete the building; defendant had an antecedent duty to pay a maximum of $56,146 plus extras, plus sales tax. Under the October 17th agreement plaintiff had the same duty while defendant had a lesser duty, unsupported by consideration. This is not a case of the mutual surrender of rights constituting consideration. Rosellini v. Banchero, 83 Wash.2d 268, 272, 517 P.2d 955, 958 (1974).

To be enforceable, a modification of an existing contract must be supported by mutual consideration. The key is that the modification be supported by some new consideration beyond that which is already owing. For example, A and B agree that A shall put in a gravel driveway for B at a cost of $2,000. Subsequently, B agrees to pay an additional $1,000 if A will blacktop the driveway. Since A was not bound by the original contract to provide blacktopping, he would incur a legal detriment in doing so and is therefore entitled to the additional $1,000.

The U.C.C. has modified the common law rule by providing that a contract for the sale of goods can be effectively modified by the parties without new consideration provided they so intend and act in good faith. Section 2–209(1).

Settlement of a Liquidated Debt. A liquidated (undisputed) debt is an obligation to pay a sum certain in money, or to pay an amount which by computation can be reduced to a sum certain in money. If the debtor has made an express promise to pay a specific sum of money, e.g., $100, the debt is liquidated. If he has agreed to pay $3 per bushel for apples delivered, and 50 bushels of apples have been delivered, the debt is liquidated in the amount of $150.

The payment of a sum of money in consideration of a promise to discharge a fully matured liquidated undisputed debt in an amount larger than the sum paid is legally insufficient to support the promise of discharge. Assume that B owes A $100, and

in consideration of B paying A $50, A agrees to accept the lesser sum in full satisfaction of the debt. B pays A $50, and A writes "paid in full" on an invoice for $100 and signs and delivers this receipt to B. In a subsequent suit by A against B to recover the remaining $50, at common law A is entitled to judgment for $50 on the ground that the promise of discharge is not binding for the reason that B's payment of $50 was no legal detriment to the promisee B as he was under a pre-existing legal obligation to pay that much and more. By the same token the receipt of $50 was no legal benefit to the promisor A. Consequently, the consideration for A's promise of discharge was legally insufficient, and A is not bound on his promise. However, if A had accepted from B any new or different consideration, such as the sum of $40 and a fountain pen worth $10 or less, or even the fountain pen with no payment of money, in full satisfaction of the $100 debt, the consideration moving from B would be legally sufficient inasmuch as B was under no legal obligation to give a fountain pen to A. In this example, consideration would also exist if A had agreed to accept $75 *before* the debt became due in full satisfaction of the debt. B was under no legal obligation to pay any of the debt before its due date. Consequently, B's early payment is a legal detriment to B as well as a legal benefit to A. The law is not concerned with the amount of the discount, as that is simply a question of adequacy. Likewise, B's payment of a lesser amount on the due date at an agreed-upon different place of payment would be legally sufficient consideration.

Settlement of an Unliquidated Debt. A disputed debt involves a definite obligation to pay, but the amount of money to be paid has not been agreed upon by the parties. Implied contracts frequently create obligations to pay unliquidated amounts. For example, where a person has requested professional services from a doctor or a dentist and no agreement was made with respect to the amount of the fee to be charged, the doctor or dentist is entitled to receive from his patient a reasonable fee for the services which have been rendered. As no definite amount has been agreed upon, the obligation of the patient is unliquidated. The legal obligation of the patient is to pay the reasonable worth of the services that were performed. When the doctor or dentist sends the patient a bill for his services, the amount stated in the bill is his estimate of the reasonable value of the services, but the debt does not in this manner become liquidated until and unless the patient agrees to pay the amount of the bill. If the patient honestly disputes the amount that is owing, and tenders in full settlement an amount less than the bill, acceptance of the lesser amount by the creditor discharges the debt. Consideration has been given in resolving the dispute and thereby abandoning the right to have a court settle the conflict. This is usually accomplished by the debtor sending to the creditor a check for the lesser amount marked "payment in full." The creditor may accept the check only upon the terms upon which it is offered. By cashing it, he accepts the offer of the debtor. By holding the check beyond a reasonable time, without rejecting the offer, the creditor is deemed by some courts to have accepted it, because the debtor sustains a detriment in being obligated to keep in his account at the bank at all times an amount sufficient to pay the check upon presentation. Thus, if A sends to B, an architect, a check for $120 in payment of his debt to B for services rendered, which services A considered worthless but for which B billed A $600, B's acceptance of the check releases A from any further liability. A has given up his right to further dispute the billing, while B has forfeited his right to further collection. Thus, there is mutuality of consideration.

In order for the giving up of a disputed claim to constitute legally sufficient consideration, the dispute must be honest and not frivolous. Where the dispute is based upon contentions which are non-meritorious or not made in good faith, giving up such contentions by the debtor is no legal detriment to him. The dispute must have been a reasonable one and made in good faith.

Substituted Contract Distinguished. A substituted contract occurs when the parties to a contract mutually agree to rescind their original contract and enter into a new one. Substituted contracts are perfectly valid and effective to discharge the original contract and to impose obligations under the new contract. The rescission is binding in that each party by giving up his rights under the original contract has provided consideration to the other, as long as each party still has rights under the original contract.

EXCEPTIONS TO THE REQUIREMENT FOR CONSIDERATION

New Promise to Pay a Debt Barred by the Statute of Limitations

Every State has in effect statutes which provide that suits to enforce debts must be commenced within a prescribed period of time after the debts become due. Suits not commenced within the time period prescribed will be dismissed. The periods of time vary among the States, and also vary with the nature of the claim sought to be enforced. These statutes are known as Statutes of Limitations.

A new promise by the debtor to pay the debt renews the running of the Statute of Limitations for the statutory period. This new promise requires no consideration. An unqualified acknowledgment of the debt by making part payment implies a promise to pay, and thereby extends the statutory period. The new promise to pay or acknowledgment is sufficient whether made before or after the statute has run.

The question sometimes arises whether the new promise is itself the binding obligation or whether it merely revives the old debt. The better view would seem to be that the new promise constitutes a new obligation inasmuch as the obligation thus created is measured by the terms of the new promise. If A's indebtedness to B in the amount of $500 is barred by the Statute of Limitations, and A makes a new promise to B to pay only $250, B can recover from A only the sum of $250. Furthermore, if B promises to pay $250 at the rate of $10 per month, B can only recover the amount which has accrued at this monthly rate. If A's new promise is conditional, such as a promise to pay $250 when he is able to do so, B's right to recover $250 is subject to proof of A's ability to pay this sum of money. Thus the scope and extent and conditions imposed by the new promise measure the creditor's rights thereon.

New Promise to Pay a Debt Discharged in Bankruptcy

Another exception to the requirement that consideration be given in exchange for a promise in order to make it binding is a promise to pay a debt that has been discharged in bankruptcy. Prior to October 1, 1979, the effective date of the Bankruptcy Reform Act of 1978, such a promise was binding not only without consideration but without an order of the Bankruptcy Court.

The Bankruptcy Reform Act of 1978 imposes a number of new requirements before a promise to pay a debt discharged in bankruptcy may be enforced. Section 524(c) of this Act provides the following requirements:

1. The debtor's promise must be made before the discharge of the debt is granted;
2. The debtor does not revoke the promise within thirty days after the promise becomes enforceable;

3. The debtor, if an individual, must be informed by the bankruptcy court of his legal rights and the effects of his new promise; and
4. The debtor's promise, if the debtor is an individual and the debt is a consumer obligation, must be approved by the bankruptcy court as being in the best interests of the debtor.

Although these new limitations do not prohibit promises to pay a debt discharged in bankruptcy, they should reduce the frequency of such promises, especially in cases involving consumer debts.

Promissory Estoppel

A promise may be binding even though the promisor may have received nothing by way of an agreed upon exchange. When a promise is made under circumstances which should lead the promisor reasonably to expect that the promisee will be induced by the promise to take definite and substantial action in reliance on the promise, and the promisee does take such action, the promisor is estopped from denying his promise. The basis of the promisor's liability is the doctrine of promissory estoppel, and consideration for the promise is not required.

Section 90 of the Restatement, Second, Contracts provides:

(1) A promise which the promisor should reasonably expect to induce action or forbearance on the part of the promisee or a third person and which does induce such action or forbearance is binding if injustice can be avoided only by enforcement of the promise. The remedy granted for breach may be limited as justice requires.

Promissory estoppel does not mean that every gratuitous promise is binding simply because it is followed by a change of position on the part of the promisee. The liability is created by the change of position in justifiable reliance on the promise.

Charitable Subscription Promises

The most frequently occurring application of the doctrine of promissory estoppel is to charitable subscriptions. Numerous churches, memorials, college buildings, stadia, hospitals, and other structures used for religious, educational, and charitable purposes have been built with the assistance of contributions made through fulfillment of pledges or promises to contribute to particular worthwhile causes. The pledgor regards himself as making a gift for a charitable purpose. Gift promises are not enforceable, yet the courts generally enforce charitable subscription promises. Although various reasons and theories have been advanced in support of liability, the one most generally accepted is that the subscription has induced a change of position by the promisee, the church, school, or charitable organization in reliance on the promise. As a result of the total pledges and the amount pledged, the promisee has employed architects, made plans, entered into building contracts, and in other ways changed its position. Liability is most frequently based upon the doctrine of promissory estoppel and thus the pledges are binding. Other courts, however, have held that the promise of each subscriber is given in exchange for the promises of the other subscribers and that these promises mutually support one another. The difficulty with this theory is that it does not accord with the facts. The subscribers do not in fact bargain with each other. The requirement of consideration has been stretched and pulled in many ways by the courts which, impelled by the desirability of enforcing this type of promise, have found various ways of holding charitable subscriptions binding without expressly abrogating the doctrine of consideration.

Contracts under Seal

In the early days of the common law, before the development of the law of contracts, many important persons of means and substance could neither read nor write. In the middle ages, reading and writing was an art confined mostly to the monasteries and to men of learning in universities. When a person desired to bind himself by bond or deed, or solemn promise, he executed his promise under seal. He did not have to sign the document. His delivery of a document to which he had affixed his seal was sufficient. No consideration for his promise was necessary. It is still the law today, except where changed by statute, that a promise under seal is binding without consideration.

A seal was originally an impression on a piece of wax, wafer, or other substance, affixed to the paper or other material on which was written the promise, release, conveyance, or covenant. Later, by statutes, the requirements of a seal were relaxed so that any impression or mark on a writing intended as a seal is sufficient. The written or printed word "Seal", or the initials "L.S." (Locus Sigilli, place of the seal) following the signature on a document, is the most common form of seal used today.

In most States the distinction between contracts under seal and written unsealed contracts is abolished by statute. The U.C.C. makes seals inoperative with respect to contracts for the sale of goods or an offer to buy or sell goods by providing in Section 2–203:

The affixing of a seal to a writing evidencing a contract for the sale or an offer to buy or sell goods does not constitute the writing a sealed instrument and the law with respect to sealed instruments does not apply to such a contract or offer.

Promises Which Require No Consideration under the Code

The U.C.C., as already discussed, expressly provides that no consideration is required in certain instances, as follows:

1. Any claim or right arising out of an alleged breach of contract can be discharged

in whole or in part without consideration by a written waiver or renunciation signed and delivered by the aggrieved party.   Section 1–107.

2. A written offer signed by a merchant offeror to buy or sell goods is not revocable for lack of consideration, during the time stated that it is open, not to exceed three months, or if no time is stated, for a reasonable time. Section 2–205.

3. A good faith agreement modifying a contract for the sale of goods needs no consideration to be binding.   Section 2–209(1).

Cases

Legal Sufficiency of Consideration

DEDEAUX v. YOUNG

(1965) 251 Miss. 604, 170 So.2d 561.

RODGERS, J.

The issue in this case is two-fold.   First, it is the contention of appellee K. L. Young that appellant Curtis O. Dedeaux agreed to pay him a broker's fee of five percent on the sale of property from William B. Bosworth, Jr., to appellant.   Appellant admits that he agreed to pay expenses that Young might have incurred because of the transaction but denied that he intended to pay a five percent commission on the sale price.   This is an issue of fact, and we are of the opinion that there is ample evidence in the record to substantiate the finding of the chancellor on this issue.   The finding of the chancellor on disputed issues of fact will not be disturbed on appeal unless it appears that his finding is manifestly wrong.   [Citation.]

Second, it is the contention of appellant Dedeaux that, assuming he promised to pay appellee Young a small commission, the promise was not a contract because there was no consideration moving to Dedeaux, therefore such a promise, if made, was not binding.   The testimony shows, however, that at the time appellant made the promise to pay the commission, he did so to prevent appellee from filing a suit, which could have prevented the culmination of the sale of the property.   The chancellor held, as a matter of law, that Young's agreement not to file suit was sufficient consideration moving from Young to Dedeaux to make the contract binding.   A request to forbear to exercise a legal right has been generally accepted as sufficient consideration to support a contract, by this and other Supreme Courts, for many years.   [Citations.]

We are of the opinion that the chancellor was correct in his ruling on both questions of law and fact, and that this case should be, and is, affirmed.

Affirmed.

Moral Obligation

ORSBORN v. OLD NATIONAL BANK OF WASHINGTON

(1973) 10 Wash.App. 169, 516 P.2d 795.

BARNETT, J.

Plaintiff in the trial court and appellant herein brought this action individually and as executrix of the estate of her late husband [to cancel a promissory note dated November 15, 1968, payable to defendant and a mortgage of real estate.]

The [trial] court specifically found as follows:

V

That prior to the death of Albert G. Orsborn [on January 18, 1968], the corporation of A. G. Orsborn & Sons, Inc. had incurred substantial indebtedness with the defendant as a result of the borrowing of funds from defendant; that said corporation indebtedness had been personally guaranteed by the decedent, Albert G. Orsborn, in his lifetime.   That Albert G. Orsborn had also borrowed individually from the said defendant.

VII

That on or about November 15, 1968, *the plaintiff, as president* of A. G. Orsborn & Sons, Inc., *and as executrix of the Estate* and of the Will of A. G. Orsborn, *signed and executed a promissory note* to the defendant in the amount of $8,513.99, and at the same time and place, as security for said note, executed an assignment of a vendor's interest in real estate contract wherein the plaintiff and her late husband were selling certain real estate to Joe G. Kobes and Marie Kobes, husband and wife. Also, at the same time, she signed a security agreement on certain fam [sic] equipment to the defendant.

XIII

That the promissory note was given to extend and renew the obligation; that no new different or additional consideration was received by plaintiff or the Estate of Albert G. Orsborn as a consequence of the execution of the promissory note of November 15, 1968; that the consideration for said note was moral consideration *only*.

The court found that the promissory note and documents executed November 15, 1968, by the plaintiff were of her own free will, without any threats, coercion, undue influence or fraud practiced upon her and that there was no reason the plaintiff should have been dealt with as a person of limited abilities except as to any legal capacity as executrix.

* * *

Assignment of error No. 2 claims that the court, after finding no monetary or legal consideration, erroneously concluded as a matter of law that moral consideration only was sufficient.

It is generally held that a mere moral obligation or conscientious duty arising wholly from ethical motives or a mere inducement of conscience unconnected with any legal obligation, perfect or imperfect, or with the receipt of benefit by the promisor of a material or pecuniary nature will not furnish a consideration for an executory promise. Detriment to the promisee alone is held to be insufficient even though the promisor is morally obligated to the person benefited. The rule that a moral obligation unconnected with a legal obligation, liability or benefit is insufficient consideration for a subsequent promise is illustrated by various cases such as those involving agreements made in consideration of past cohabitation or to pay for the support of an illegitimate child. It seems clear both upon principle and authority that mere moral obligation will not support an executory promise to pay another's debt or to alleviate any supposed hardship or injustice in the distribution of decedent's estate. [Citation.]

In 1 S. Williston, Contracts § 148 (3d ed. 1957), we find the following:

Most of the States of the United States, and England, have rejected the principle of moral consideration, even though some exceptional cases of liability on promises made without present consideration may still exist as in the case of promises to pay debts barred by the Statute of Limitations, or by a discharge in bankruptcy. Such cases are now rested on other grounds and moral consideration as such is held insufficient to support a promise.

In 1 S. Williston, Contracts § 147 (3d ed. 1957), we also find the following statement at page 635:

At the present day there can be no doubt that the doctrine of moral consideration is almost uniformly held to have been discarded, and "moral consideration" to have no obligatory effect.

However, the general rule is well settled that a moral obligation arising from or connected with what was once a legal liability, which has since become suspended or barred by operation of a positive rule of law or statute, will furnish consideration for a subsequent executory promise. Accordingly, where there was at one time a legal duty, which by operation of law has become unenforceable, a subsequent promise to perform the duty is binding. The familiar and uncontradicted rule that upholds a new promise after the bar of the statute of limitations has often been expressly put upon the ground that although the debt is not legally enforceable, there is still a moral obligation which comes within the exception of the rule and is sufficient to sustain the new promise. A like rule has been applied with a new promise to pay a debt discharged in bankruptcy or insolvency proceedings. [Citation.]

In the instant case, at the time the notes and security agreements were executed on November 15, 1968, the bank had no legal claim against the estate as the claim had been outlawed. Neither did the estate at the time the documents in question were executed receive any benefit from such transactions.

In Opitz v. Hayden, 17 Wash.2d 347, at page 368, 135 P.2d 819, at page 827 (1943) we find the following:

If, at the time of the execution of the contract, respondent had no existing legal claim against Anderson, then the assurances made by him in the written agreement would amount simply to an executory promise on his part, and the question would arise as to whether such promise could in any event be enforced. It has become well established by an almost unanimous current of modern authority that a mere moral obligation or conscientious duty arising solely from ethical motives or the promptings of conscience, unconnected with any legal obligation or with the receipt of material benefits to the promisor, will not furnish a consideration for an executory promise, and this rule has been very emphatically applied to promises made wholly on account of past cohabitation where no element of consideration other than moral is present. But it is equally well established that moral obligations arising from, or connected with, what was once a legal liability which has since become suspended or barred by the operation of a positive rule of law will furnish a consideration for a subsequent executory promise.

* * *

Counsel for the appellant has made other assignments of error, but in view of the fact that we hold that the decision of the trial court should be reversed because there was no consideration in the transactions noted * * *, we refrain from discussing the other assignments of error.

Reversed.

Exclusive Dealing Contracts

OTIS F. WOOD v. LUCY, LADY DUFF-GORDON

(1917) 222 N.Y. 88, 118 N.E. 214.

CARDOZO, J.

The defendant styles herself "a creator of fashions." Her favor helps a sale. Manufacturers of dresses, millinery and like articles are glad to pay for a certificate of her approval. The things which she designs, fabrics, parasols and what not, have a new value in the public mind when issued in her name. She employed the plaintiff to help her turn this vogue into money. He was to have the exclusive right, subject always to her approval, to place her indorsements on the designs of others. He was also to have the exclusive right to place her own designs on sale, or to license others to market them. In return, she was to have one-half of "all profits and revenues" derived from any contracts he might make. The exclusive right was to last at least one year from April 1, 1915, and thereafter from year to year unless terminated by notice of ninety days. The plaintiff says that he kept the contract on his part, and that the defendant broke it. She placed her indorsement on fabrics, dresses and millinery without his knowledge, and withheld the profits. He sues her for the damages, and the case comes here on demurrer.

The agreement of employment is signed by both parties. It has a wealth of recitals. The defendant insists, however, that it lacks the elements of a contract. She says that the plaintiff does not bind himself to anything. It is true that he does not promise in so many words that he will use reasonable efforts to place the defendant's indorsements and market her designs. We think, however, that such a promise is fairly to be implied. The law has outgrown its primitive stage of formalism when the precise word was the sovereign talisman, and every slip was fatal. It takes a broader view today. A promise may be lacking, and yet the whole writing may be "instinct with an obligation," imperfectly expressed (Scott, J., in McCall Co. v. Wright, 133 App.Div. 62, 117 N.Y.S. 775. Moran v. Standard Oil Co., 211 N.Y. 187, 198, 105 N.E. 217). If that is so, there is a contract.

The implication of a promise here finds support in many circumstances. The defendant gave an *exclusive* privilege. She was to have no right for at least a year to place her own indorsements or market her own designs except through the agency of the plaintiff. The acceptance of the exclusive agency was an assumption of its duties. [Citations.] We are not to suppose that one party was to be placed at the mercy of the other. [Citations.] Many other terms of the agreement point the same way. We are told at the outset by way of recital that "the said Otis F. Wood possesses a business organization adapted to the placing of such indorsements as the said Lucy, Lady Duff-Gordon has approved." The implication is that the plaintiff's business organization will be used for the purpose for which it is adapted. But the terms of the defendant's compensation are even more significant. Her sole compensation for the grant of an exclusive agency is to be one-half of all the profits resulting from the plaintiff's efforts. Unless he gave his efforts, she could never get anything. Without an implied promise, the transaction cannot have such business "efficacy as both parties must have intended that at all events it should have" (Bowen, L.J., in The Moorcock, 14 P.D. 64, 68). But the contract does not stop there.

The plaintiff goes on to promise that he will account monthly for all moneys received by him, and that he will take out all such patents and copyrights and trademarks as may in his judgment be necessary to protect the rights and articles affected by the agreement. It is true, of course, as the Appellate Division has said, that if he was under no duty to try to market designs or to place certificates of indorsement, his promise to account for profits or take out copyrights would be valueless. But in determining the intention of the parties, the promise *has* a value. It helps to enforce the conclusion that the plaintiff *had* some duties. His promise to pay the defendant one-half of the profits and revenues resulting from the exclusive agency and to render accounts monthly, was a promise to use reasonable efforts to bring profits and revenues into existence. For this conclusion, the authorities are ample. * * *

Judgment reversed.

Performance of a Pre-Existing Obligation

DENNEY v. REPPERT
(1968 Ky.) 432 S.W.2d 647.

R. L. MYRE, SR., SPECIAL COMMISSIONER.

The sole question presented in this case is which of several claimants is entitled to an award for information leading to the apprehension and conviction of certain bank robbers.

* * *

On June 12th or 13th, 1963, three armed men entered the First State Bank, Eubank, Kentucky, and with a display of arms and threats robbed the bank of over $30,000. Later in the day they were apprehended by State Policemen Garret Godby, Johnny Simms and Tilford Reppert, placed under arrest, and the entire loot was recovered. Later all of the prisoners were convicted and Garret Godby, Johnny Simms and Tilford Reppert appeared as witnesses at the trial.

The First State Bank of Eubank was a member of the Kentucky Bankers Association which provided and advertised a reward of $500.00 for the arrest and conviction of each bank robber. Hence the outstanding reward for the three bank robbers was $1,500.00. Many became claimants for the reward and the Kentucky State Bankers Association being unable to determine the merits of the claims for the reward asked the circuit court to determine the merits of the various claims and to adjudge who was entitled to receive the reward or share in it. All of the claimants were made defendants in the action.

At the time of the robbery the claimants Murrell Denney, Joyce Buis, Rebecca McCollum and Jewell Snyder were employees of the First State Bank of Eubank and came out of the grueling situation with great credit and glory. Each one of them deserves approbation and an accolade. They were vigilant in disclosing to the public and the peace officers the details of the crime, and in describing the culprits, and giving all the information that they possessed that would be useful in capturing the robbers. Undoubtedly, they performed a great service. It is in the evidence that the claimant Murrell Denney was conspicuous and energetic in his efforts to make known the robbery, to acquaint the officers as to the personal appearance of the criminals, and to give other pertinent facts.

The first question for determination is whether the employees of the robbed bank are eligible to receive or share in the reward? The great weight of authority answers in the negative. In Re Waggoner, 47 S.D. 401, 199 N.W. 244, 245 (1924) states the rule thusly:

"To the general rule that, when a reward is offered to the general public for the performance of some specified act, such reward may be claimed by any person who performs such act, is the exception of agents, employes and public officials who are acting within the scope of their employment or official duties. * * *."

Or, as the rule was set forth in Forsythe v. Murnane et al., 113 Minn. 181, 129 N.W. 134, 135 (1911):

" * * * The defendant Delaney is and during all the times herein mentioned has been, employed by defendant Great Northern Railway Company * * * and by virtue of such employment it was his duty to do and perform all the things that were done and performed by him in the matter of the arrest, identification, and prosecution * * *.

"It is clear that defendant Delaney is not, in view of * * * his contractual relations and the duties in the premises * * * entitled to any part of the reward. * * *."

In Stacy v. President, etc., of State Bank of Ill., 4 Scam., Ill., 91 (1842) it was held that a director of a bank was not entitled to share in the reward offered by the bank for the arrest of a robber because it was his duty as a director to further the best interests of the bank, and apprehending one who had robbed the bank was in the best interest of the bank. [Citations.]

At the time of the robbery the claimants Murrell Denney, Joyce Buis, Rebecca McCollum, and Jewell Snyder were employees of the First State Bank of Eubank. They were under duty to protect and conserve the resources and moneys of the bank, and safeguard every interest of the institution furnishing them employment. Each of these employees exhibited great courage, and cool bravery, in a time of stress and danger. The community and the county have recompensed them in commendation, admiration and high praise, and the world looks on them as heroes. But in making known the robbery and assisting in acquainting the public and the officers with details of the crime and with identification of the robbers, they performed a duty to the bank and the public, for which they cannot claim a reward.

The claims of Corbin Reynolds, Julia Reynolds, Alvie Reynolds and Gene Reynolds also must fail. According to their statements they gave valuable information to the arresting officers. However, they did not follow the procedure as set forth in the offer of reward in that they never filed a claim with the Kentucky Bankers Association. It is well established that a claimant of a reward must comply with the terms and conditions of the offer of reward. [Citation.]

State Policemen Garret Godby, Johnny Simms and Tilford Reppert made the arrest of the bank robbers and captured the stolen money. All participated in the prosecution. At the time of the arrest, it was the duty of the state policemen to apprehend the criminals. Under the law they cannot claim or share in the reward and they are interposing no claim to it.

This leaves the defendant, Tilford Reppert the sole eligible claimant. The record shows that at the time of the arrest he was a deputy sheriff in Rockcastle County, but the arrest and recovery of the stolen money took place in Pulaski County. He was out of his jurisdiction, and was thus under no legal duty to make the arrest, and is thus eligible to claim and receive the reward. In Kentucky Bankers Ass'n et al. v. Cassady, 264 Ky. 351, 94 S.W.2d 622, 624, it was said:

It is * * * well established that a public officer with the authority of the law to make an arrest may accept an offer of reward or compensation for acts or services performed outside of his bailiwick or not within the scope of his official duties. * * *.

The claimant Tilford Reppert was present with Garret Godby and Johnny Simms at the time of the arrest and all cooperated in its consummation. The claimant Tilford Reppert personally recovered the stolen money. He recovered $2,000.00 more than the bank records show was stolen. This record does not reveal what became of the $2,000.00 excess.

It is manifest from the record that Tilford Reppert is the only claimant qualified and eligible to receive the reward. Therefore, it is the judgment of the circuit court that he is entitled to receive payment of the $1,500.00 reward now deposited with the Clerk of this Court.

The judgment is affirmed.

Pre-existing Public Duty

HALE v. BREWSTER
(1970) 81 N.M. 342, 467 P.2d 8.

MOISE, C. J.

Appellant, Jerry Lee Brewster, appeals from an order refusing to vacate a default judgment entered against appellant and Mrs. W. E. Brewster, appellant's mother.

The record discloses a complaint filed by appellee against appellant and Mrs. W. E. Brewster, seeking judgment for $900.53, being the unpaid balance on a promissory note for $1,000.00, plus interest and attorney fees. * * *

Appellant * * * asserts a defense to the complaint in that the note sued on was lacking in consideration. The question presented concerns the right and propriety of an attorney taking compensation for representation of an indigent charged with a crime when he has been appointed by the court to represent the indigent and has been paid by the court for the services rendered.

* * *

The right of the courts to impose the duty on lawyers to defend indigent persons accused of crime without compensation has been upheld in all jurisdictions except four— Indiana, Iowa, New Jersey and Wisconsin. See Annot., 21 A.L.R.3d 819, 830. Be this as it may, we have a statute, quoted above, providing for pay, and appellant asserted in his motion that appellee had in fact been paid a fee of $85.00 by the State. Although the motion was overruled, it appears that appellant was given credit for this amount on the judgment previously entered.

However, this does not resolve the question raised by this appeal. We must decide if payment of a fee by the State, makes the note executed by appellant invalid because lacking consideration. We have found only one case directly in point. It is Commonwealth v. Wormsley, 294 Pa. 495, 144 A. 428 (1928), where the court said:

"* * * Petitioners, having been appointed by the court to represent defendant, had a duty to appeal, if they considered that course essential to protect his rights and the fee paid them by the county must be their exclusive compensation. Under the circumstances, they had no right to contract with others for fees and expenses."

That this rule is correct would seem to follow from the duty of appellee to represent to the best of his ability plus the payment and receipt of a fee from the State. Where can the consideration be found for appellant's promise to pay an additional amount? We do not see how appellant received anything that he was not entitled to receive without payment of any amount, and accordingly there is no consideration. Compare In re Quantius' Will, 58 N.M. 807, 277 P.2d 306 (1954), where we held that "the promise to do what a person is already obligated by law or contract to do is not sufficient consideration for a promise made in return." This rule is one of almost universal general application. [Citations.] It follows from what has been said that if the note was given to appellee as a fee for services, which he was already bound to perform by virtue of his appointment by the court, the appellant had a good and valid defense which he could have presented if the default judgment had been vacated.

The cause must be reversed and remanded with instructions to proceed in a manner consistent herewith. It is so ordered.

Modification of an Existing Contract

GRAHAM v. JONNEL ENTERPRISES, INC.

(1969) 435 Pa. 396, 257 A.2d 256.

O'BRIEN, J.

Appellants, Jonnel Enterprises, Inc. [Jonnel] and Arenze, Inc., are the general contractor and owner of the real estate, respectively, which was involved in the construction of a dormitory to house students of Clarion State College. Both corporations are controlled by Elmer Jonnett, who was their agent. Appellees, John F. Graham and Roy C. Long, are electrical contractors.

On May 6, 1966, appellees and Jonnel entered into a written agreement by which appellees, in return for $70,544.66 were to perform electrical work and supply materials for the dormitory at Clarion State. According to appellees, they were under the impression that the May 6 agreement obligated them to perform the electrical work on only one building or only one wing of a building, and they had no knowledge of any second wing. They discovered the second wing only after three or four days' work, and informed Elmer Jonnett at that time that they would not wire both wings for $70,544.66. They further testified that a new contract was agreed upon orally and prepared. Under the new contract, appellees were to wire both wings and were to be paid only $65,000, but they were relieved of the obligation to supply entrances and a heating system. Appellees testified that Jonnett approved the prepared contract and stated that he would take it to Pittsburgh and have it signed. It was never signed.

Acting on Jonnett's alleged agreement with regard to the second contract, appellees resumed work. Payment was to be made in eight 90% progress payments. Seven were made in accordance with the terms of the second contract, but appellants failed to pay the last 90% progress payment. Appellees then brought suit for the last 90% progress payment, the 10% retained by appellants, and some extra work allegedly agreed to by appellants, the entire amount sought totalling $15,629.88. Appellants in their answer averred that the written contract of May 6 was operative and that appellees had breached it causing them damages of more than $20,000.00. Further, appellants counter-claimed for an amount "in excess of $10,000."

The jury returned a verdict in favor of appellees in the amount they sought, $15,629.88.

* * *

Appellants' main contention on this appeal is that the jury was improperly permitted to find an amendment to the written contract, because no consideration could have existed for such an amendment. Reliance is placed on our recent decision in Nicolella v. Palmer, 432 Pa. 502, 248 A.2d 20 (1968), in which we discussed an alleged oral amendment calling for additional compensation to the plaintiff: "The only possible consideration would be appellant's agreement to proceed with the work. Yet appellant was already obligated to do so. The general rule is stated in 17 C.J.S. Contracts § 112a: 'The promise of a person to carry out a subsisting contract with the promisee or the performance of such contractual duty is clearly no consideration, as he is doing no more than he was already obliged to do, and hence has sustained no detriment, nor has the other party to the contract obtained any benefit. Thus, a promise to pay additional compensation for the performance by the promisee of a contract which the promisee is already under obligation to the promisor to perform is without consideration, and this rule has been applied to building and construction contracts.' "

However, that case is clearly distinguishable from the instant one. Without even passing on the various possible sources of consideration cited by the court below, such as the compromise of a disputed claim, we note that the amendment here called for appellees to receive *less* money than they would have received under the written contract. Appellants respond that appellees would receive only about $5,000.00 less while performing about $26,000.00 less work. Yet the function of a court is merely to determine whether consideration existed, not to examine into the adequacy of that consideration. [Citation.] Appellees suffered a detriment in contracting for some $5,000.00 less under the amendment, and thus consideration surely existed.

The judgment is affirmed.

Charitable Subscription Promises

MOUNT SINAI HOSPITAL OF GREATER MIAMI, INC. v. JORDAN

(1974 Fla.) 290 So.2d 484.

MCCAIN, J.

* * *

The salient facts establish that Harry M. Burt executed two pledges of $50,000.00 each in 1968. These pledges were delivered to the petitioner and provided in pertinent part:

In consideration of and to induce the subscriptions of others, I (We) promise to pay to Mount Sinai Hospital of Greater Miami, Inc. or order the sum of *Fifty Thousand and no/100 dollars* $5,000.00 payable herewith: Balance in *nine* equal annual installments commencing on *January* [sic] 1 of * * *.

Mr. Burt made payments totalling $20,000.00, which were applied equally to the two pledges and upon his death on November 18, 1969, there remained an unpaid balance of $80,000.00. Upon Mr. Burt's death, the petitioner filed a claim for the unpaid balance of the pledges against his estate. The respondents, executors, objected to this claim. On the basis of these facts, the trial court held in favor of the charities and the respondents appealed.

There being no claim that the petitioner had suffered any material detriment or that any substantial liability had been incurred in reliance upon the subscriptions, the District Court proceeded to reverse and answered negatively the question certified to this Court. That question is:

[W]hether the recitation in a charitable pledge that it is given in consideration of and to induce the subscription of others constitutes consideration rendering it enforceable by the promisee against the promisor, in the absence of any reliant action thereon by the promisee such as would create promissory estoppel.

* * *

A mere gratuitous promise of a future gift, lacking consideration, is simply unenforceable as a nudum pactum. When the gratuitous promise is coupled with an inducement for others to subscribe, the promise is no longer void on its face. This is the situation in this case. The pledge specifically recites that the subscription is made "[in] consideration * * * to induce the subscriptions of other, * * *."

The District Court was eminently correct when it recited the law that:

For the doctrine of promissory estoppel to be applicable, the promisor must make a promise which he should reasonably expect to induce action or forbearance of a substantial character on the part of the promisee, * * *

Therefore, in order for a pledge to survive the death of the donor and be considered a valid claim against the estate, two elements must coincidentally exist. First, the document stating the conditions of the pledge must recite with particularity the specific purpose for which the funds are to be used. It would, for example, be insufficient if the pledge designated the general operating fund. The rationale for such a decision is obvious. While the donor is alive, he has the opportunity to monitor the use of the pledged funds and, to some extent, manifest his intent as to their proper disposition. However, upon his death, and in the absence of an express written intention, the donee would have unfettered discretion as to the expenditures of these pledged monies and could spend it in a manner which might have offended the donor had he still been alive. Therefore, the donative intent as to the specific material plan, for example, for the establishment of an engineering school as in Rouff v. Washington & Lee University, 48 S.W.2d 483 (Tex.Civ.App. 1932), must be made an integral part of the pledge instrument, limiting the exercise of discretion by the donee within the boundaries set forth by the instrument.

* * *

Secondly, the donee must affirmatively show actual reliance of a substantial character in furtherance of the specified purpose set forth in the pledge instrument before the claim may be honored by the estate. Text writers have expressed a similar view:

* * * The view most commonly held is that such a subscription is an offer to contract which becomes binding as soon as the work towards which the subscription was promised has been done or begun, or liability incurred in regard to such work on the faith of the subscription.

Since the subscription in its inception is regarded as an offer, until the work has been done or liability incurred, the subscription is revokable by the death, insanity, or otherwise." 1 Williston on Contracts, Sec. 116, pp. 250–51 (1st ed. 1920).

In the light of this pronouncement we must view the facts in this case to see if the doctrine of promissory estoppel should be applied to enforce the pledge against the estate of the donor.

A review of the record reveals that the pledge in question was not made for any specified purpose, clearly was not used to induce others to subscribe and the Hospital undertook no work in reliance upon Burt's subscription.

The District Court correctly intepreted the facts when it stated:

Neither can the appellee find solace in the doctrine of promissory estoppel. The record is devoid of any evidence that the promisee was induced in reliance upon decedent's promise to take any substantial action, or to forego any material right, so that an injustice could only be avoided by applying this equitable doctrine. [Citations.]

Courts should act with restraint in respect to the public policy arguments endeavoring to sustain a mere charitable subscription. To ascribe consideration where there is none, or to adopt any other theory which affords charities a different legal rationale than other entities, is to approve fiction.

[Judgment for defendant affirmed.]

Problems

1. In consideration of $100 paid to him by Joyce, Hill gave Joyce a written option to purchase his house for $10,000 on or before April 1. Prior to April 1, Hill verbally agreed to extend the option until July 1. On May 18, Hill, known to Joyce, sold the house to Gray, who was ignorant of the unrecorded option. Joyce brought suit against Hill. Decision?

2. A owed $500 to B for services B rendered to A. The debt was due June 30, 1980. In March, 1981, the debt was still unpaid. B was in urgent need of ready cash and told A that if he would pay $150 on the debt at once, B would release him from the balance. A paid $150 and stated to A that all claims had been paid in full. In August, 1981, B demanded the unpaid balance and subsequently sued A for $350. Decision?

3. (a) Modify the facts in (2) by assuming that B gave A a written receipt which stated that all claims had been paid in full. Result?
(b) Modify the facts in (2) by assuming that A owed B the $500 on A's purchase of a motorcycle from B. Result?

4. A owed B $800 on a personal loan. Neither the amount of the debt nor A's liability to pay the $800 was disputed. B had also rendered services as a carpenter to A without any agreement as to the price to be paid. When the work was completed, an honest and reasonable difference of opinion developed between A and B with respect to the value of B's services. Upon receiving B's bill for the carpentry services for $800, A mailed in a properly stamped and addressed envelope his check for $800 to B. In an accompanying letter, A stated that the enclosed check was in full settlement of both claims. B indorsed and cashed the check. Thereafter, B unsuccessfully sought to collect from A an alleged unpaid balance of $800. B then sued A for $800. Decision?

5. Carter engaged Hughes to do plumbing work for him without any agreement with respect to the price or amount to be charged for the services. Upon completion of the work, Hughes submitted a bill for $325, to which Carter objected as being excessive. He requested an itemized bill, and thereafter received such a bill for $345.67. Carter again protested, stating that $175 would be a reasonable price. Although Hughes told Carter he would not accept a proffered check for $175 in settlement of his claim, Carter sent a check for $175 to Hughes, payable to his order, bearing the legend on both the face and back "Payment in full for services rendered." Hughes struck out the quoted words on the back of the check and deposited it. The check was paid. Hughes then sued Carter to recover $170.67 for work performed. Decision?

6. The Snyder Mfg. Co., being a large user of coal, entered into separate contracts with several coal companies, in each of which it was agreed that the coal company would supply coal during the year 1981 in such amounts as the manufacturing company might desire to order, at a price of $9.00 per ton. In February, 1981, the Snyder Company ordered 1,000 tons of coal from Union Coal Company, one of the contracting parties. Union Coal Company delivered 500 tons of the order and then notified Snyder Company that no more deliveries would be made and that it denied any obligation under the contract. In an action by Union Coal to collect $9.00 per ton for the 500 tons of coal delivered, Snyder files a counterclaim, claiming damages of $1,500 for failure to deliver the additional 500 tons of the order and damages of $4000 for breach of the agreement to deliver coal during the balance of the year. Decision?

7. On February 5, D entered into a written agreement with P whereby P agreed to drill a well on D's property for the sum of $5000 and to complete the well on or before April 15. Before entering into the contract, P made test borings and had satisfied himself as to the character of the subsurface. After two days of drilling P struck hard rock. On February 17, P removed his equipment and advised D that the project had proved unprofitable and that he would not continue. On March 17, D went to P and told P that he would assume the risk of the enterprise and would pay P $100 for each day required to drill the well, as compensation for labor, the use of P's equipment and P's services in supervising the work, provided P would furnish certain special equipment designed to cut through hard rock. P said that the proposal was satisfactory. The work was continued by P and completed in an additional 58 days. Upon completion of the work D failed to pay and P brought an action to recover $5800. D answered that he had never become obligated to pay $100 a day and filed a counterclaim for damages in the amount of $500 for the month's delay based on an alleged breach of contract by P. Decision?

8. Discuss and explain whether there is valid consideration for each of the following promises:

(a) A and B entered into a contract for the purchase and sale of goods. A subsequently promised to pay a higher price for the goods upon B's refusal to deliver at the contract price.

(b) A promised in writing to pay a debt, which was due from B to C, upon C's agreement to extend the time of payment for one year.

(c) A executed a promissory note to his son, B, solely in consideration of past services rendered to A by B, for which there had been no agreement or request to pay.

9. A purchased shoes from B on open account. B sent A a bill for $10,000. A wrote back that 200 pairs of the shoes were defective and offered to pay $6,000 and give B his promissory note for $1,000. B accepted the offer and A sent his check for $6,000, and his note conformably to the agreement. B cashed the check, collected on the note and, one month later, sued A for $3,000. Decision?

10. B owed A $1,500 but A did not initiate a law suit to collect the debt within the time period prescribed by the statute of limitations. Nevertheless, B promises A that he will pay the barred debt. Thereafter, B refuses to pay. A brings suit to collect on this new promise. Decision?

ILLEGAL BARGAINS

An essential ingredient of a binding promise or agreement is legality of objective. When the formation or performance of an agreement is criminal, tortious, or otherwise opposed to public policy, the agreement is illegal and unenforceable. In this connection, it is preferable to use the term "illegal bargain" or "illegal agreement" rather than an "illegal contract," for the reason that the word "contract," by definition, denotes a legal and enforceable agreement. Discussion of this subject will be in terms of agreements (a) in violation of a statute and (b) contrary to public policy.

VIOLATIONS OF STATUTES

An agreement declared illegal by statute will not be enforced by the courts. For example, "wagering contracts" are often expressly declared unenforceable. Likewise, an agreement which is induced by criminal conduct will not be enforced. For example, in a New York case the plaintiff sued for the purchase price, $1,555, of certain hosiery and wrappers delivered to defendant's store. The defense was that the order for the goods was obtained through the bribing of defendant's purchasing agent, to whom the plaintiff paid five per cent of the purchase price. This type of commercial bribery constituted a criminal offense. There was no showing that the price of the goods was excessive, nor did the defendant return them or offer to do so. Under these circumstances, the court denied recovery, stating that in view of the purpose of the statute to eradicate commercial bribery, a refusal to aid the plaintiff who obtained the sale by a secret bribe of defendant's employee would contribute to that end.

Licensing Statutes

In every jurisdiction there are laws requiring a license for those who engage in certain trades, professions or businesses. Common examples are licensing statutes which apply to lawyers, doctors, dentists, accountants, brokers, plumbers and contractors. Can one recover for services rendered if he has failed to comply with a licensing requirement?

The statute itself may expressly provide that an unlicensed person engaged in a business or profession for which a license is required shall not recover for his services rendered or goods sold. Where there is no such statutory provision, the courts commonly distinguish between those statutes or ordinances which are *regulatory* in character and those which are enacted merely to raise *revenue*. If the statute is regulatory, there can be no recovery for professional services rendered by a person not having the required license; if the law is for revenue purposes only, agreements for such services are enforceable.

A regulatory measure is one designed for the protection of the public against unqualified persons, such as statutes prescribing standards for those who seek to practice law or medicine. A revenue measure, on the other hand, does not seek to protect against the incompetent or unqualified, but to furnish revenue. An example is a statute requiring a license of plumbers but not establishing standards of competence for those who seek to follow the trade. It is regarded as a taxing measure and lacking in any expression of legislative intent to preclude plumbers from enforcing their business contracts.

These licensing requirements sometimes trap the unwary. In Bonasera v. Roffe, 8 Ariz.App. 1, 442 P.2d 165 (1968), the court held that the Arizona real estate brokers licensing statutes precluded plaintiff, who was not a licensed broker, from recovering a commission for finding a buyer for defendant even though his activity was a single isolated transaction. In another case a broker who was licensed in Illinois undertook to sell Illinois land, but the brokerage contract was executed in New York, where he was not licensed. The Illinois Supreme Court denied recovery in his action to collect the promised fee. Frankel v. Allied Mills, Inc., 369 Ill. 578, 17 N.E.2d 570 (1938). The result was that the plaintiff lost a $17,000 fee. In these cases the statutes expressly or impliedly provided that an unlicensed person cannot enforce his brokerage agreements. But in a few instances, where there was no such express prohibition, and none could reasonably be implied, the broker has been able to recover, the courts holding the statutes to be revenue measures only.

Gambling Statutes

All States have legislation pertaining to gambling and American courts generally refuse to recognize the enforceability of a gambling agreement. Thus, if A makes a bet with B upon the outcome of a ball game, the agreement is void. The loser need not pay and in a few States may recover back any payment that he has made.

In a wager the parties stipulate that one shall win and the other lose depending upon the outcome of an event in which they have no "interest" other than that arising from the possibility of such gain or loss. To be distinguished, therefore, are ordinary insurance contracts in which the insured having an "insurable interest" pays a certain sum of money or premium in exchange for a promise of the company to pay a larger amount upon the occurrence of some event such as a fire which causes loss to the insured. Here, the agreement is one which compensates for loss under an existing risk, rather than one which creates an entirely new risk. In a wager the parties contemplate gain through mere chance, whereas in an insurance contract they seek to distribute possible loss.

Obviously, the existence of a risk element in a business contract does not make it a gambling contract. For example, a "futures contract" is legal, provided a bona fide sale is intended, with actual delivery if required. The fact that the seller does not have the merchandise at the time of the sale does not render such an agreement illegal, nor does the transaction become a wager because one or both of the parties do not believe actual delivery will ever be demanded or made.

In the past, lotteries which are a form of wager, were generally prohibited by statute. Now many States operate lotteries for revenue producing purposes. A common statutory definition of lottery is as follows: "a scheme for the distribution of property by chance among persons who have paid or agreed to pay a valuable consideration for the chance, whether called a lottery, a raffle, a gift enterprise, or by some other name." Most gas station games and grocery store drawings have been held not to be lotteries because the participants need not make a purchase to be eligible for the prize.

Sunday Statutes

At common law a valid contract may be entered into on Sunday as on any other day. Some States have legislation referred to as "Blue Laws" modifying this common-law rule and prohibiting certain types of commercial activity on Sunday. The modern tendency is to permit week-day "ratification" or "adoption" of a contract executed on Sunday. Even in a State which prohibits contracts on Sunday, a court will enforce a subsequent week-day ratification of a loan made on Sunday or a promise to pay for goods sold and delivered on Sunday. Activities of "necessity" and "charity" are usually exempted from the application of Blue Laws.

Usury Statutes

Historically, every State has a "usuary law," a statute establishing a maximum rate of permissible interest which may be contracted for between a lender and borrower of money. Recently, however, there has been a trend to limit or relax usury statutes. Maximum rates permitted vary greatly from State to State, and among types of transactions. These statutes typically are general in their application, although certain specified types of transactions are exempted. For example, about half of the States impose no limit on the rate of interest which may be charged on loans to corporations. Furthermore, some States permit the parties to contract for any rate of interest on loans made to individual proprietorships or partnerships for the purpose of carrying on a business.

In addition to the exceptions accorded certain designated types of borrowers, a number of States have exempted specific lenders. For example, the great majority of the States have enacted installment loan laws, which permit eligible lenders a higher return on installment loans than would otherwise be permitted under the applicable general interest statute. These laws also vary greatly.

In order for a transaction to be usurious, courts usually require evidence of the following factors: (a) a loan or forbearance; (b) of money; (c) which is repayable absolutely and in all events; (d) for which an interest charge is exacted in excess of the interest rate allowed by law. Transactions which, in fact, are loans may not be clothed with the trappings of a sale for the purpose of avoiding the usury laws.

Assuming that it is established that the arrangement is for a loan, certain expenses or charges are permitted in addition to the maximum legal interest. Payments made by a borrower to the lender for expenses incurred, or for services rendered in good faith in making a loan or in obtaining security for its repayment are generally not included in determining whether the loan is usurious, but, payments made to the lender or from which he derives an advantage if they exceed the reasonable value of services actually rendered are included. Ordinary expenses by the lender which are permissible include costs of examining title, investigating the credit rating of the borrower, drawing necessary documents, and inspecting the property. If not excessive, they are not considered in determining the rate of interest with respect to usury statutes.

The legal effect to be given a usurious loan varies from State to State. In a few States both principal and interest are forfeited. In some jurisdictions the lender can recover the principal but forfeits all interest. In other States only that portion of interest exceeding the maximum permitted is forfeited. In several States the amount forfeited is a multiple (double or treble) of the interest charged. Disposition of usurious interest already paid also varies. Some States do not allow any recovery of usurious interest paid; others allow a recovery of a multiple of the usurious interest paid. An action to recover usurious interest paid is required to be filed within a certain time, the Statutes of Limitations provide time periods ranging from one year to four years from date of payment.

VIOLATIONS OF PUBLIC POLICY

The reach of a statute may extend beyond its language as courts by analogy use the statute and the policy sought to be served by it as a guide in determining the private contract rights of one in violation of the statute. In addition, the courts are frequently called upon to articulate the "public policy" of the State without significant help from statutory sources. This judicially declared public policy is very broad in scope, it often being said that agreements which have "a tendency to be injurious to the public or the public good" are contrary to public policy. Examples to be considered are agreements that involve tortious conduct, restrain trade, tend to obstruct the administration of justice, exempt a party from liability for his own negligence, tend to corrupt public officials, or impair the legislative process.

Tortious Conduct

An agreement which calls for or requires the commission of tortious conduct is an unenforceable illegal agreement. The courts will not permit contract law to contravene the law of torts. Any agreement attempting to do so is considered contrary to public policy.

Common Law Restraint of Trade

At early common law any restraint upon an individual's right to engage in his trade or calling was illegal. Such restraints were viewed with disfavor because of the belief that they would diminish the individual's means of earning a living, deprive the public of useful services, adversely affect competition, and otherwise be harmful to the welfare of the community. But this strict view has been modified so that *reasonable* restraints of trade are enforceable.

Today an agreement to refrain from a particular trade, profession or business is enforceable if (1) the purpose of the restraint is to protect a property interest of the promisee and (2) the restraint is no more extensive than is reasonably necessary to protect that interest.

Typical restraints arise in two situations. The first usually involves the sale of a business, including its good will. As part of the sales agreement, the seller promises not to compete in the particular business in a defined area for a stated period of time. The purchaser is regarded as having a property interest which is entitled to protection. In order to protect the good will, an asset which he has purchased, it is necessary that he be allowed to enforce a covenant by the vendor not to compete with the purchaser within reasonable limitations. Most of the litigation has involved the requirement that the restraint be no greater than is reasonably necessary. The reasonableness of the restraint depends upon the geographic area covered and the time period for which the restraint is to be effective.

The promise of one selling a service station business in Detroit not to enter the service station business in Michigan for the ensuing 25 years is unreasonable, both as to area and time. The business interest to be protected would not be co-extensive with the State, so it is not necessary to the protection of the purchaser that the seller be precluded from engaging in the service station business in the entire State, or perhaps for that matter, the entire city of Detroit. Limiting the area to the neighborhood, or within a radius of a few miles would probably be adequate protection. If the business were a city-wide business, such as a laundry or cleaning establishment with neighborhood outlets, a covenant restraining competition anywhere in the city might well be reasonable.

The same type of inquiry must be made with respect to time limitations. In the sale of a service station, 25 years would be unreasonable, but one year probably would not. Each case must be considered on its own facts, with the court determining what is reasonable under the particular circumstances. In Desselle v. Petrossi, 207 So.2d 190 (Ct.App.La.1968), the court held that a restrictive covenant prohibiting sellers of a seafood restaurant and bar business from opening such a business anywhere in the metropolitan New Orleans area for a period of five years was reasonable.

The second type of restraint involves employment contracts. Salesmen, management personnel, and other employees are frequently required to sign employment contracts prohibiting them from competing with their employers during the time of employment and for some additional stated period after termination. The courts readily enforce a covenant not to compete during the period of employment. The promise not to compete after termination of employment, however, is subjected to an even stricter test of reasonableness than that applied to non-competition covenants ancillary to the sale of a business. A court order enjoining the former employee from competing in a described territory for a stated period of time is the usual method by which the employer seeks enforcement of the covenant by the employee. Before granting such injunctions, the courts insist that the employer demonstrate that the restriction is necessary to protect his legitimate interests, such as trade secrets or customer lists. Because issuance of the injunction may have the practical effect of placing the defendant out of work, the courts must carefully balance the public policy favoring the employer's right to protect his business interests against the public policy favoring full opportunity for individuals to gain employment.

Thus, one court has held that a covenant in a contract that a travel agency employee after termination of his employment would not engage in a like business in any capacity in either of two named towns or within a radius of sixty miles thereof for a period of two years was unreasonable. There was no indication that the employee had such dominion over customers as would cause them to move their business to her new agency and it was not shown that any trade secrets were involved.

Some courts, instead of refusing to enforce an unreasonable covenant, will if considered justifiable under the circumstances of the particular case, reform the agreement to make it reasonable and enforceable. This is an extension of the familiar "blue pencil" rule whereby courts have upheld reasonable restrictions in a contract while deleting the unreasonable ones. In a 1970 case in which a former employer sought to enforce the non-competitive agreement of a former employee, the Supreme Court of New Jersey refused to declare the covenant invalid. It said that, "we are entirely satisfied that the time is well due for the abandonment of New Jersey's void per se rule in favor of the rule which permits the total or partial enforcement of noncompetitive agreements to the extent reasonable under the circumstances."

Obstructing the Administration of Justice

Agreements which are harmful to the administration of justice are illegal and void. For example, a promise by an employer not to press criminal charges against an embezzling employee who restores the stolen funds is not enforceable. Similarly, a promise to conceal evidence or to give false testimony tends to obstruct the adminstration of justice and for that reason is illegal and unenforceable.

Corrupting Public Officials or Impairing the Legislative Process

Agreements which have a tendency to affect adversely the public interest through the corruption of public officials or the impairment of the legislative process are unenforceable. Examples are improper means to influence legislation, secure some official action, or procure a government contract.

A bargain by a candidate for public office to make a certain appointment following his election is illegal. In addition, an agreement to pay a public officer something extra for performing his official duty, as a promise to a policeman for strictly enforcing the traffic laws on his beat, is illegal. The same is true of an agreement whereby a citizen promises to perform, or to refrain from performing, duties imposed upon him by citizenship. A promise by X to pay five dollars to Y if he will register and vote is opposed to public policy and illegal.

Exculpatory Clauses

Some contracts for work or services contain an exculpatory clause which excuses one party from liability for his own negligence. This type of clause is generally looked upon with disfavor since there is a policy to dis-

courage overreaching and to assure that wrongdoers will pay the damages caused by their negligence. Accordingly, an exculpatory clause on the reverse side of a parking lot claim check which attempts to relieve the parking lot operator of liability for negligently damaging the customer's automobile is void as against public policy. On the other hand, the policy of freedom of contract is also a factor in determining the validity of contractual clauses exempting a party from liability for his negligence, and thus not all such clauses are held to be against public policy.

Where a public service or a specific legal duty is involved, an exculpatory clause is generally held to be violative of public policy and, therefore, unenforceable. Thus, a public service company cannot by contract insulate itself from liability for negligence in performing its duties of public service, nor may a common carrier exempt itself from liability for negligence in the performance of its duties as a carrier.

Further, where one party has a superior bargaining position which has enabled him to impose upon the other party such a provision, the courts are inclined to nullify the provision. Such a situation may arise in residential leases exempting a landlord from liability for his negligence.

Unconscionable Contracts

Every contract of sale may be scrutinized by the court to determine whether in its commercial setting, purpose, and effect, it is unconscionable. The court may refuse to enforce an unconscionable contract or any part thereof found to be unconscionable. Section 2–302 provides:

If the court as a matter of law finds the contract or any clause of the contract to have been unconscionable at the time it was made the court may refuse to enforce the contract, or it may enforce the remainder of the contract without the unconscionable clause, or it may so limit the application of any unconscionable clause as to avoid any unconscionable result.

The Code does not define "unconscionable". However, the Oxford Universal Dictionary (3rd ed.) definition is: "Monstrously extortionate, harsh, showing no regard for conscience."

U.C.C. Section 2–302 denies or limits enforcement of an unconscionable contract for the sale of goods in the interest of fairness and decency, and to correct harshness in contracts resulting from unequal bargaining positions of the parties. Although the principle is not novel, its embodiment in a statute dealing with commercial transactions is novel.

In Henningsen v. Bloomfield Motors, Inc., 32 N.J. 358, 161 A.2d 69 (1960), the Supreme Court of New Jersey in a pre-Code decision refused to enforce a harsh disclaimer of warranty in a contract for the purchase of an automobile, saying, "An instinctively felt sense of justice cries out against such a sharp bargain."

In many cases a contract between a necessitous buyer in an unequal bargaining position with the seller has been held unconscionable by reason of the exorbitant price of the goods. For instance, a price of $749 ($920 on time) for a vacuum cleaner which cost the seller $140 was held unconscionable. In another case, the buyers, welfare recipients, purchased by time payment contract a home freezer unit for $900 which added to time credit charges, credit life insurance, credit property insurance and sales tax amounted to $1,235. The purchase resulted from a visit to the buyer's home by a salesman representing Your Shop At Home Service, Inc., and the maximum retail value of the freezer unit at time of purchase was $300. The court held the contract unconscionable, and reformed it by changing the price to the total payment ($620) made by the buyers.

EFFECT OF ILLEGALITY

Unenforceability

Assuming that an agreement is illegal, what are the consequences? With but few exceptions, neither party can sue the other for breach nor recover for any performance rendered. The statement is often made that where parties are in pari delicto (in equal fault) a court will leave them where it finds them. The law will provide neither with any remedy.

Exceptions

This strict rule of unenforceability is subject to certain exceptions:

Party Withdrawing Before Performance: Locus Poenitentiae. Under some circumstances one who is party to an illegal agreement may, prior to performance, withdraw from the transaction and recover whatever he has contributed. Restatement, Second, Contracts, Section 199, provides:

A party has a claim in restitution for performance that he has rendered under or in return for a promise that is unenforceable on grounds of public policy if he did not engage in serious misconduct and

    (a) he withdraws from the transaction before the improper purpose has been achieved, or

    (b) allowance of the claim would put an end to a continuing situation that is contrary to the public interest.

A common example is recovery of money left with a stakeholder pursuant to a wager before it is paid over to the winner, but the rule has also been applied to more serious misconduct.

Party Protected by Statute. Sometimes an agreement is illegal because it violates a law designed to protect persons in the position of one of the parties. For example,

State "Blue Sky Laws" prohibiting the sale of unregistered securities are designed primarily for the protection of investors. In such case, even though there is an unlawful agreement, the statute usually expressly gives the purchaser a right to rescind the sale and recover the money paid.

Party Not In Pari Delicto. Suppose one is induced to enter into an illegal bargain through the fraud, duress, or undue influence of the other. Here the courts are inclined to regard the parties as not in pari delicto and the general rule as inapplicable.

Party Ignorant of Facts Making Bargain Illegal. An agreement which appears to be entirely permissible on its face may nevertheless be illegal by reason of facts and circumstances of which one of the parties is completely unaware. For example, a man and woman make mutual promises to marry, but unknown to the woman, the man is already married. This is an agreement to commit the crime of bigamy. It is illegal and the marriage, if entered into, is void. In such case the courts permit the party who is ignorant of the vitiating fact to maintain a lawsuit against the other party for damages.

This exception was recognized in a Massachusetts case where an employee sued successfully to recover for services rendered in a business which was unlawful by reason of the employer's failure to procure a license, the plaintiff being justifiably ignorant of this fact.

Partial Illegality. Ordinarily, the entire agreement is void and unenforceable if any part of the consideration for a promise is illegal or any part of the promise is illegal. For example, a promise to pay $1,000 for the delivery of two different kinds of goods, one type legal and the other illegal, is unenforceable. The seller may not recover payment for any of the goods delivered of either type. But, if within the same agreement there is a separate price allocation for the different goods, as $250 for the legal and $750 for the illegal, a successful action may be maintained for the legal goods costing $250. Even though the agreement is tainted with illegality, there is a tendency to disregard this if the legal and illegal portions can be "severed" and to permit recovery for the legal portion.

Cases

Licensing Statutes

MANUEL TOVAR v. PAXTON COMMUNITY MEMORIAL HOSPITAL

(1975) 29 Ill.App.3d 218, 330 N.E.2d 247.

CRAVEN, J.

Plaintiff appeals the dismissal of his amended complaint which contained a count for breach of an employment contract and a count alleging the tort of misrepresentation. The trial court granted a motion to dismiss the complaint * * *.

Plaintiff's amended complaint alleges he was informed of the defendant hospital's desire to hire a full-time resident physician. He responded in a letter in which he inquired about the position and informed the defendant hospital he was presently employed by the department of mental health for the State of Kansas. He claims this letter fully described the nature and extent of his education, training and licensing as a physician. Plaintiff then personally appeared at the office of the defendant and informed its agents that he was employed in a full-time position and would only be interested in a position of resident physician if it would provide for permanent employment. Plaintiff alleges defendant's agents represented to him that the position would last for plaintiff's natural life or for so long as the defendant hospital required the services of a resident physician, and plaintiff was willing and able to do such work competently. Plaintiff alleges he thoroughly described the nature and extent of his academic background, professional experience, and licensing to defendant's agents during this interview, and that these agents then and there told and assured plaintiff that his professional credentials were satisfactory for the employment.

Plaintiff further claims that as a result of defendant's promise of permanent employment he resigned his position in Kansas and entered into defendant's service as a resident physician on August 1, 1972. However, on or about August 15, 1972, defendant discharged plaintiff. Plaintiff's complaint alleges that the defendant hospital wrongfully breached the employment contract and also misrepresented to plaintiff that his professional credentials were fully satisfactory to the defendant hospital for employment as a resident physician. Plaintiff seeks damages for the period following the termination of his employment.

In response to the defendant hospital's request to admit facts, plaintiff denies that he has never held a license to practice medicine as required under section 2 of the Medical Practice Act (Ill.Rev.Stat. 1973, ch. 91, ¶ 2), but admits he has never been licensed to practice medicine in Illinois. Plaintiff denied that he had not passed an examination of his qualifications as is required by section 3 of the Medical Practice Act because "plaintiff feels he has passed an examination of his qualifications that Illinois would accept from another state." He admitted he had taken the examination called for in section 3 of the Medical Practice Act and had never passed it in Illinois.

The trial court found plaintiff's amended complaint to be substantially insufficient at law because he had not complied with sections 2 and 3 of the Act, had not obtained a license pursuant to licensing requirements of that Act, and that it would be against public policy to enforce an employment contract where the plaintiff had not obtained the requisite license. The court found the employment contract to be in violation of public policy, illegal and void.

Section 2 of the Medical Practice Act provides:

License as prerequisite to practice.] § 2. No person shall practice medicine, or any of its branches, or midwifery, or any system or method of treating human ailments without the use of drugs or medicines and without operative surgery, without a valid, existing license so to do. [Citation.]

* * *

It has long been the law of Illinois that one who has failed to comply with the licensing provisions of the Medical Practice Act cannot maintain an action for fees or services as a physician or surgeon. [Citations.] The purpose of the statutes establishing a licensing requirement is not to generate revenue, but rather to protect the public by assuring them of adequately trained practitioners. [Citation.] Any agreement the purpose of which is to induce a breach of one of these licensing statutes is illegal. [Citation.] A person who practices medicine without obtaining the required license cannot maintain an action for his promised compensation or *in quantum meruit*. [Citations.] While the action on the employment contract involved here is not to recover for services rendered but rather for claimed wrongful termination of the employment contract, the same doctrine applies. The agreement sued upon is unenforceable as contrary to public policy.

In Count II of his amended complaint, plaintiff asked for damages from the date of termination of his employment as a result of the defendant hospital's alleged misrepresentation that his credentials were satisfactory to them. However, as plaintiff could not be a resident physician for the defendant hospital under the law of this State, public policy will not allow him to sue on the tort of misrepresentation when the alleged misrepresentations concerned the unauthorized practice of medicine. Our courts will not lend their aid to a man who founds his cause of action upon an illegal act. [Citation.] A plaintiff is not permitted to profit by his own wrong by recovering damages. [Citation.] This rule applies to a complaint that alleges the same acts amounted to a breach of contract and a tort. [Citation.] The trial court was correct in dismissing Count II of plaintiff's amended complaint.

The judgment of the circuit court dismissing both counts of plaintiff's amended complaint is affirmed.

Judgment affirmed.

Usury Statutes

ABRAMOWITZ v. BARNETT BANK OF WEST ORLANDO

(1981, Fla.App.) 394 So.2d 1033.

SHARP, J.

Abramowitz appeals from a judgment denying him any relief in his suit against the Barnett Bank of West Orlando, appellee, in which he sought damages for an allegedly "usurious" loan.

* * *

The record established that Abramowitz filed three or more loan applications with the bank from February 1973 throgh October 1973. Originally he sought a construction loan to build a building to be leased to Ford Motor Company on land he owned near the John Young Parkway. C. Lee Maynard, president of the bank, wanted the loan for his bank, although the $300,000 to $400,000 loan requests considerably ex-

ceeded the bank's lending limits. In anticipation of making the loan, Maynard made "inspections" of the site and building being constructed, although Ford was financing the construction itself and the bank had made no loan commitment.

When the building was completed in November of 1973, the parties rushed into a mortgage loan closing without the benefit of a written loan commitment and without a carefully prepared loan closing statement. Maynard had verbally promised Abramowitz a $400,000 loan for one year, at 9% interest, with a 1% "point" or "service fee." The $4,000 "service fee" was shown on the closing statement as a "discount," but everyone agreed no "discount" was involved because the bank was not purchasing a mortgage loan from another party at less than face value.

The $4,000 service fee was deducted in full from the loan proceeds, and it was immediately received by the bank as income. During the one year term of this loan, Abramowitz was charged and he paid $36,347.78 in "interest." If the $4,000 charge was also "interest," Abramowitz paid more than $40,000 or 10% of his $400,000 loan in total interest charges. If viewed as a "discount" loan where interest is paid in advance, the rate should be properly gauged on the amount of principal actually disbursed to the borrower plus legitimate expenses— ($396,000 or a somewhat larger figure if any part of the $4,000 were attributable to a legitimate expense of the lender.)

Maynard testified that the $4,000 charge was meant to be a "service charge" or "points." He was the only mortgage loan officer at his bank, so he made "in-house" inspections of the construction of the building and a final inspection. He reported verbally to the bank's loan committee. He admitted that part of the $4,000 went to pay the bank's normal overhead expenses, such as salaries and utilities. Another expense attributed to this loan was Maynard's contacting other Barnett banks to obtain the participation of other lenders, and the preparation of loan participation agreements.

The other banker witnesses at trial testified that their banks normally imposed "service fees" or "points" on real estate loans in addition to interest, but they were careful not to exceed the usury limits when the two amounts were combined. Sometimes inspection fees were paid to architects or engineers for which the customer was charged; sometimes the inspections were done "in-house," and the borrower was charged a small amount, or was not charged at all.

* * *

A lender will not be allowed to impose any miscellaneous fees or service charges on the front end of a loan when that sum, added to the interest charged, exceeds the maximum legal rate of interest allowable. [Citations.] Application of such fees to pay the general overhead of a lender or the cost of participating out the loan are not sufficient to alter the characterization of these charges as interest. [Citation.]

It is also well established that a borrower can be charged the actual reasonable expenses of making a particular loan. [Citations.] However "bogus" charges for services not actually rendered will not be allowed to cloak the extraction of illegal interest. [Citation.]

The only basis to characterize the "service fee" in this case as something other than interest, is to allocate part of it as an "inspection" fee performed "in-house" by the bank's president. Such fees are usually paid to third-parties, and are documented on the mortgage loan closing statement. We are not prepared to say, however, that in all cases the inspection must be done by a third-person or that it must be documented on the closing statement, although that obviously is the better practice. The fact that Maynard himself performed the inspection does not flaw the charges although any charge for this "service" is inconsistent with his testimony that he did

the inspection "in-house" to save the borrower money.

It is fundamental that the charges must be "reasonable." [Citations.] This loan was not a "construction" loan which requires more inspections to insure the lender's construction funds are being properly used as the building progresses. Rather, it was a loan on a completed building, and similar to a "take-out" loan for a permanent lender, only a final inspection fee is required. The only testimony in the record on this point established that $300 was the maximum a third party expert would have charged.

The conclusion thus follows inescapably that Abramowitz was charged in excess of 10% interest on this one-year loan.

"Service Fee"	$ 4,000.00
Less "Reasonable Expenses"	− 300.00
"Hidden Interest"	$ 3,700.00
Principle of Loan	$400,000.00
Less Prepaid Interest	− 3,700.00
Actual Principal	$396,300.00
Maximum legal amount of interest collectible on this loan (10%) of actual principal	$ 39,630.00
Actual interest charged and billed	36,347.78
Plus "hidden interest"	+ 3,700.00
	$ 40,047.78
Amount of over-charge	$ 40,047.78
	− 39,630.00
	$ 417.78

The lower court found there was no "corrupt" intent on the part of the bank to charge a usurious rate of interest because the bank did not deliberately charge more than 10%. It charged 9% on the loan plus 1% in points only. The difficulty here was that the 1% was taken up-front, resulting in a reduction in principal received, and an increase in the rate paid. [Citation.] The "intent" to exceed the legal rate of interest need not be to consciously decide to charge a borrower greater than the legal rate, when the lender consciously intends and does in fact make the charges which add up to usury. [Citations.]

In this case, the closing statement showing a 1% point or service fee was prepared by the bank; and it calculated and billed the borrower interest throughout the year. No errors were shown to have occurred in the billing. In fact during 2 quarters, the lender billed on a 360 day year basis, which for a 10% or maximum rate loan, was usurious in and of itself. [Citation.] We conclude the bank had the requisite intent to make the usurious charges. [Citation.]

Accordingly, the judgment is reversed and this case is remanded for imposition of damages against the bank, pursuant to section 687.04 and other appropriate charges.
REVERSED and REMANDED.

Common Law Restraint of Trade:
Sale of Business

HAYNES v. MONSON
(1974) 301 Minn. 327, 224 N.W.2d 482.

SCOTT, J.

In this action for breach of contract plaintiffs appeal from a summary judgment dismissing their action, but preserving for trial defendants' counterclaim for breach of a convenant not to compete. We affirm.

Plaintiffs entered into a contract for the sale of Haynes Bookkeeping and Tax Service in Austin, Minnesota, on March 18, 1970. The total purchase price agreed upon was to be $20,000, with $3,500 down, $2,500 to be paid at a later date, and the balance payable in 36 equal monthly installments of $425.91. On February 1, 1972, defendant purchasers discontinued payment of the monthly installments, leaving a balance of approximately $7,000. This action for breach of contract was commenced in March 1972, and defendants counterclaimed for breach of a convenant

not to compete set out in the contract. Summary judgment was entered for defendants and plaintiffs appeal.

Paragraph 3 of the contract for sale provided as follows:

The Sellers agree that they will not within five (5) years from date hereof, either solely or jointly, with or as manager or agent of any person or corporation, directly or indirectly, carry on or be engaged or interested in the business of bookkeeping, accounting, or tax practice, or pemit his name to be used in connection with any such business within fifty (50) miles of Austin, Minnesota.

Following the sale of the business, plaintiff Paul E. Haynes worked for the defendants for approximately 1½ years. In July 1971, he moved to Red Wing, Minnesota, 100 miles from Austin, and opened his new office. However, he neither sold his Austin residence nor disconnected the telephone service and returns to his home every week or two.

Evidence from Haynes' deposition indicates that he continued to furnish bookkeeping and tax services for residents of the city of Austin and that he further filed tax returns for residents of Austin from his Red Wing office. Although he testified that he did work for 45–50 Austin clients through his Red Wing office, he admitted that only two actually came to his office.

The deposition also illuminates the various methods utilized by Haynes to continue his contact with former clients. The information necessary for him to provide his services was either mailed to Red Wing, delivered to Haynes' Austin residence, or left with Haynes' relatives for delivery to him. In an affidavit, Duane Grafe indicated that he had telephoned Haynes' Austin residence, at the suggestion of defendant Gerhard A. Monson, to arrange to have some tax work done. Someone identifying himself as Haynes returned Grafe's call and agreed to do the necessary work. The caller further agreed either to pick up the information or to have Grafe deliver it to the Austin home.

* * *

The basic issue for our determination is whether the lower court erred in granting summary judgment in favor of defendants. This court has construed covenants not to compete so as to effectuate the purpose for their inception, i.e., to protect purchasers of a going concern from an infringement upon their investment and the continuation of the business for a profit. To allow one to sell his business, with its accompanying customer lists and files, and then allow him to compete for the patronage of these former customers would be contrary to the covenant, and would frustrate the intent of the parties.

This court has long held that where the restraint is for a "just and honest purpose, for the protection of a legitimate interest of the party in whose favor it is imposed, reasonable as between the parties, and not injurious to the public," that restraint is valid. [Citations.] Under these standards, covenants, such as the one before us, should be strictly construed. [Citation.]

Furthermore, covenants with rather specific geographic and economic limitations have been enforced. [Citation.]

Plaintiffs contend that the absence of the element of solicitation should be controlling. [Citation.] We, however, are of the opinion that when one has conducted a business in the same area for many years and has built a sizable clientele, active solicitation on his part is unnecessary to compete so as to defeat the covenant. Solicitation by mere reputation and past business practices is more than sufficient.

Therefore, we conclude that on the basis of the record before us, there existed no genuine issue of material fact, and that the defendants were entitled to judgment as a matter of law.

Affirmed.

Common Law Restraint of Trade: Employment Contract

POST v. MERRILL, LYNCH, PIERCE, FENNER & SMITH, INC.

(1979) 48 N.Y.2d 84, 421 N.Y.S.2d 847, 397 N.E.2d 358.

WACHTLER, J.

The narrow issue presented by this appeal from a grant of summary judgment for the defendant is the efficacy of a private pension plan provision permitting the employer to forfeit pension benefits earned by an employee who competes with the employer after being involuntarily discharged.

We begin with the premise that "powerful considerations of public policy * * * militate against sanctioning the loss of a man's livelihood." [Citation.] So potent is this policy that covenants tending to restrain anyone from engaging in any lawful vocation are almost uniformly disfavored and are sustained only to the extent that they are reasonably necessary to protect the legitimate interests of the employer and not unduly harsh or burdensome to the one restrained. [Citations.]

Merrill Lynch employed Post and Maney as account executives at its Rochester offices beginning April 20, 1959 and May 15, 1961, respectively. Both men elected to be paid a salary and to participate in the firm's pension and profit-sharing plans rather than take a straight commission, which would have returned approximately twice the amount they earned in salary during the period in question.

The employment of both plaintiffs by Merrill Lynch terminated August 30, 1974. On September 4, 1974 both began working for Bache & Company, admittedly a competitor of Merrill Lynch, in Rochester. Merrill Lynch learned about their new employment in September, 1974.

Fifteen months after their termination, and following repeated inquiries by the plaintiffs into the status of their pensions, the plaintiffs were informed by Merrill Lynch that all of their rights in the company-funded pension plan had been forfeited pursuant to a provision of the plan which permitted forfeiture in the event that an employee directly or indirectly competed with the firm.

Plaintiffs brought this action against Merrill Lynch for conversion and breach of contract, to recover amounts allegedly owed them on account of the pension plan and for punitive damages. They aver that they were discharged by Merrill Lynch without cause. Merrill Lynch does not, for the purpose of this motion, dispute plaintiffs' version, contending, rather, that for this purpose the reason for termination is irrelevant.

The Appellate Division granted Merrill Lynch's motion for summary judgment and dismissed the complaint, relying principally on the Appellate Division decision in *Kristt v. Whelan*, 4 A.D.2d 195, 199, 164 N.Y.S.2d 239, 243, affd. 5 N.Y.2d 807, 181 N.Y.S.2d 205, 155, N.E.2d 116 to sustain the validity of the forfeiture provision. As the Appellate Division in *Kristt* held: "It is no unreasonable restriction of the liberty of a man to earn his living if he may be relieved of the restriction by forfeiting a contract right or by adhering to the provisions of his contract. The provision for forfeiture here involved did not bar plaintiff from other employment. He had the choice of preserving his rights under the trust by refraining from competition with (his former employer) or risking forfeiture of such rights by exercising his right to compete with (him)."

Now, in determining the effect to be accorded a forfeiture-for-competition provision in an employees' pension, we are for the first time invited to distinguish between voluntary and involuntary termination of employment of the affected employee. Examination of our cases discloses no prior instance in which enforcement of such a forfeiture clause has been sought in circumstances where the employment has been terminated by the employer without cause. Rather, as in *Kristt*, they have involved claims by an employee who sought pension benefits from his former employer despite having voluntarily left the employer and joined forces with a competitor. In such situations effect has been given to the forfeiture-for-competition provision, and the employee's claim has been rejected.

Not only do we find no dispositive judicial precedent in our State where the employee has been terminated by the employer without cause. * * *

* * * confronted with no decisions which command a contrary result, we now conclude that our own policies—those in favor of permitting individuals to work where and for whom they please, and against forfeiture—preclude the enforcement of a forfeiture-for-competition clause where the termination of employment is involuntary and without cause.

In the case at bar we note that the particular provision in the pension plan was not drawn explicitly to cover employees whose employment had been involuntarily terminated; it indiscriminately mandates forfeiture by any "Participant who enters employment or engages directly or indirectly in any business deemed by the Committee to be competitive". Therefore we need not consider now what would have been our decision had the draftsman of this pension plan manifested an unmistakable intention to impose the heavy penalty of forfeiture for engaging in competition even after discharge of an employee without cause.

Acknowledging the tension between the freedom of individuals to contract, and the reluctance to see one barter away his freedom, the State enforces limited restraints on an employee's employment mobility where a mutuality of obligation is freely bargained for by the parties. An essential aspect of that relationship, however, is the employer's continued willingness to employ the party covenanting not to compete. Where the employer terminates the employment relationship without cause, however, his action necessarily destroys the mutuality of obligation on which the covenant rests as well as the employer's ability to impose a forfeiture. An employer should not be permitted to use offensively an anticompetition clause coupled with a forfeiture provision to economically cripple a former employee and simultaneously deny other potential employers his services.

Under the circumstances of the case at bar it would be unconscionable to tolerate a forfeiture, precipitated as it is by the unwarranted action of the employer. We find, therefore, that in the case of an involuntary discharge, the rule stated in *Kristt v. Whelan, supra* does not apply. Further, we hold, that where an employee is involuntarily discharged by his employer without cause and thereafter enters into competition with his former employer, and where the employer, based on such competition, would forfeit the pension benefits earned by his former employee, such a forfeiture is unreasonable as a matter of law and cannot stand.

ORDERED. Lower Court's dismissal of complaint reversed, motion for summary judgment denied, and complaint reinstated.

Corrupting Public Officials

WOMACK v. MANER

(1957) 227 Ark. 786, 301 S.W.2d 438.

ROBINSON, J.

The complaint in this case alleges: "From time to time, and at various intervals, * * * the plaintiff has paid to the defendant the sum of $1,675 * * * for the consideration of the defendant, as the Judge of the Circuit Court of Saline County giving to the plaintiff whatever protection was necessary to prevent the plaintiff from being prosecuted or suffering punishment in said court for engaging in the unlawful business of gambling in Saline County which the plaintiff was engaged in with the full knowledge, consent and approval of the said defendant as the Judge of said Court. Plaintiff alleges, that the consideration for his paying to the defendant the said sum of money * * * is void and unlawful and was void and unlawful when said money was paid by him to defendant, * * *. Wherefore, plaintiff prays, that he have judgment against the defendant * * * in the sum of Sixteen Hundred and Seventy Five Dollars; * * *."

The defendant demurred to the complaint on the ground that a cause of action is not stated. The demurrer was sustained by the trial court, presided over by a judge on exchange. The plaintiff, Womack, has appealed.

* * *

It is firmly established that in a situation such as is set out in the complaint the law will not aid either party to the alleged illegal and void contract. According to the allegations in the complaint the parties are *pari delicto,* hence, the plaintiff cannot recover.

* * *

"The general rule is that, where an illegal contract has been made, neither courts of law nor of equity will interpose to grant any relief to the parties, but will leave them where it finds them, if they have been equally cognizant of the illegality." Shattuck v. Watson, 53 Ark. 147, 13 S.W. 516, 517, 7 L.R.A. 551.

* * *

The United States Supreme Court said, in Clark v. United States, 102 U.S. 322, 26 L.Ed. 181 "Clearly this was bribery, and placed the claimants and the man they corrupted *in pari delicto.* They could not recover back from him the money they paid, * * *."

* * *

Affirmed.

Exculpatory Clauses

HENRIOULLE v. MARIN VENTURES, INC.

(1978) 20 Cal.3d 512, 143 Cal.Rptr. 247, 573 P.2d 465.

BIRD, CHIEF JUSTICE.

Appellant, John Henrioulle, seeks to set aside orders of the superior court granting his landlord, respondent Marin Ventures, Inc., a judgment notwithstanding the jury's verdict and a new trial. Appellant contends that the exculpatory clause in his lease could not relieve the landlord of liability for the personal injuries appellant sustained in a fall on a common stairway in the apartment building. This court agrees.

* * *

From the record, it appears that on April 3, 1974, appellant entered into a lease agreement with respondent for an apartment in San Rafael, California. At that time, appellant was an unemployed widower with two children who received public assistance in the form of a rent subsidy from the Marin County Department of Social Services. There was also evidence of a shortage of housing accommodations for person of low income in Marin County.

The printed form lease agreement which appellant signed contained the following exculpatory clause: "INDEMNIFICATION: Owner shall not be liable for any damage or injury to Tenant, or any other person, or to any property, occurring on the premises, or any part thereof, or in the common areas thereof, and Tenant agrees to hold Owner harmless from any claims for damages no matter how caused."

On May 22, 1974, appellant fractured his wrist when he tripped over a rock on a common stairway in the apartment building. At the time of the accident the landlord had been having difficulty keeping the common areas of the apartment building clean. An on-site manager, whose duties included keeping these areas clean, had proven unsatisfactory and had been terminated in the month prior to the accident. The landlord had also employed an additional person to do maintenance work, but he had worked only a few hours at the apartment building in the month preceding the accident.

* * *

In *Tunkl v. Regents of the University of California* (1963) 60 Cal.2d 92, 32 Cal.Rptr. 33, 383 P.2d 441, this court held invalid a clause in a hospital admission form which released the hospital from liability for future negligence. This court noted that although courts have made "diverse" interpretations of Civil Code section 1668, which invalidates contracts which exempt one from responsibility for certain wilful or negligent acts, all the decisions were in accord that exculpatory clauses affecting the public interest are invalid. [Citation.]

In *Tunkl,* six criteria are used to identify the kind of agreement in which an exculpatory clause is invalid as contrary to public policy. "[1] It concerns a business of a type generally thought suitable for public regulation. [2] The party seeking exculpation is engaged in performing a service of great importance to the public, which is often a matter of practical necessity for some members of the public. [3] The party holds himself out as willing to perform this service for any member of the public who seeks it, or at least any member coming within certain established standards. [4] As a result of the essential nature of the service, in the economic setting of the transaction, the party invoking exculpation possesses a decisive advantage of bargaining strength against any member of the public who seeks his services. [5] In exercising a superior bargaining power the party confronts the public with a standardized adhesion contract of exculpation, and makes no provision whereby a purchaser may pay additional fees and obtain protection against negligence. [6] Finally, as a result of the transaction, the person or property of the purchaser is placed under the control of the seller, subject to the risk of carelessness by the seller or his agents." [Citation.]

The transaction before this court, a residential rental agreement, meets the *Tunkl* criteria.

* * *

In holding that exculpatory clauses in residential leases violate public policy, this court joins an increasing number of jurisdictions. [Citations.]

* * *

The orders of the superior court granting respondent's motions for judgment notwithstanding the jury's verdict and a new trial are reversed, and the cause is remanded with direction to enter judgment for appellant on the verdict.

Unconscionable Contracts

WILLIAMS v. WALKER-THOMAS FURNITURE CO.

(1965) C.A.D.C.) 350 F.2d 445.

See page 383.

Problems

1. A and B were the principal shareholders in XYZ Corporation located in the city of Jonesville, Wisconsin. This corporation was engaged in the business of manufacturing paper novelties which were sold over a wide area in the Middle West. The corporation also was in the business of binding books. A purchased B's shares of the XYZ Corporation and, in consideration thereof, B agreed that for a period of two years he would not: (a) manufacture or sell in Wisconsin any paper novelties of any kind which would compete with those sold by the XYZ Corporation, (b) engage in the book binding business in the city of Jonesville. Discuss the validity and effect, if any, of his agreement.

2. Wilkins, a resident of, and licensed by, the State of Texas as a certified public accountant, rendered service in his professional capacity in Louisiana to Coverton Cosmetics Company. He was not registered as a certified public accountant in Louisiana. His service under his contract with the cosmetics company was not the only occasion on which he had practiced his profession in that State. The company denied liability and refused to pay him relying upon a Louisiana statute declaring it unlawful for any person to perform or offer to perform services as a CPA for compensation until he has been registered by the designated agency of the State and holds an unrevoked registration card. Provision is made for issuance of a certificate as a CPA without examination to any applicant who holds a valid unrevoked certificate as a CPA under the laws of any other State. The statute provides further that rendition of services of the character performed by Wilkins, without registration, is a misdemeanor punishable by a fine or imprisonment in the county jail, or by both fine and imprisonment. Wilkins brought an action against Coverton seeking to recover a fee in the amount of $1,500 as the reasonable value of his services. Decision?

3. A is interested in promoting the passage of a bill in a State legislature. He agrees with B, an attorney, to pay B for his services in drawing the required bill, procuring its introduction in the legislature and making an argument for its passage before the legislative committee to which it will be referred. B renders these services. Subsequently, upon A's refusal to pay B, B sues A for damages for breach of contract. Decision?

4. Anthony promises to pay McCarthy $10,000 if McCarthy reveals to the public that Washington is a Communist. Washington is not a Communist and never has been. McCarthy successfully persuades the media to report that Washington is a Communist and now seeks to recover the $10,000 from Anthony, who refuses to pay. McCarthy initiates a lawsuit against Anthony. What result?

5. The XYZ Company was engaged in the business of making and selling harvesting machines. It sold everything pertaining to the business to the ABC Company agreeing "not again to go into the manufacture of harvesting machines anywhere in the United States." The seller had a national and international good will in its business. It now begins the manufacture of such machines contrary to its agreement. Should the court enjoin it?

6. Charles Leigh, engaged in the industrial laundry business in Central City, employed Tim Close, previously employed in the home laundry business, as a route salesman on July 1, 1980. Leigh rents linens and industrial uniforms to commercial customers; the soiled linens and uniforms are picked up at regular intervals by the routemen and replaced with clean ones. Every employee is assigned a list of customers whom he services. The contract of employment stated that in consideration of being employed, upon termination of the employment, Close would not "directly or indirectly engage in the linen supply business or any competitive business within Central City, State of X, for a period of one year from the date when his employment under this contract ceases." On May 10, 1981, Close's employment was terminated by Leigh for valid reasons. Thereafter, Close accepted employment with Ajax Linen Service, a direct competitor of Leigh in Central City. He commenced soliciting former customers whom he had called on for Leigh, and obtained some of them as customers for Ajax.

Leigh brings an action to enforce the provisions of the contract. Decision?

7. A Dairy and B Dairy, the only dairies in Centerville, a town of 6,000 population, entered into an agreement which provided that A Dairy would solicit only customers who lived on the north side of Main Street, and B Dairy would solicit only customers who lived on the south side of Main Street. The agreement contained no provisions with respect to prices. B Dairy, in violation of the agreement, began to solicit customers who lived on the north side of Main Street at prices less than those quoted by A Dairy. A Dairy sues to enjoin B Dairy from so doing. Result?

8. On July 5, 1980, Billy and Nancy entered into a bet on the outcome of the 1980 presidential election. On January 28, 1981 Nancy, who bet on Ronald Reagan, approached Billy seeking to collect the $3,000 which Billy had wagered on Jimmy Carter. Billy paid Nancy the wager and now seeks to recover the funds from Nancy. Result?

9. C, a salesman for S, comes to B's home and sells him a complete set of "gourmet cooking utensils," which are worth approximately $300. B, a man of 80 years, lives alone in a one-room efficiency apartment. B signs a contract to buy the utensils for $1450 plus a credit charge of $145 and to make payment in ten equal monthly installments. After C leaves with the signed contract, B decides he cannot afford, and has no use for, cooking utensils. What can B do?

10. A rents a bicycle from B. The bicycle rental contract which A signed provides that B is not liable for any injury to the renter caused by any defect in the bicycle or the negligence of B. A is injured when he is involved in an accident due to B's improper maintenance of the bicycle. A sues B for his damage. Decision?

Chapter
11

CONTRACTUAL CAPACITY

A binding promise or agreement requires that the parties to the agreement have contractual capacity. Everyone is regarded as having such capacity unless the law for reason of public policy or historical tradition holds that the individual lacks such capacity. Therefore, this essential ingredient of a contract will be discussed by considering those classes and conditions of persons who are legally limited in their capacity to contract.

The contracting capacity of persons will be discussed in the following order: (1) minors; (2) incompetent persons; (3) intoxicated persons; and (4) other persons with impaired capacity.

MINORS

A minor (or infant) at common law was a male who had not attained the age of twenty-one years, or a female the age of eighteen, and each could avoid liability upon contracts. Today the age limit has been changed in some jurisdictions by stat-ute, usually reduced to age eighteen for both sexes. Almost without exception, a minor's contract is voidable at his option. Even an "emancipated" minor, one who by reason of marriage or otherwise is no longer subject to strict parental control, may avoid contractual liability in most jurisdictions. Consequently, businessmen deal with minors at their peril.

Liability for Necessaries

Contractual immunity does not excuse a minor from an obligation to pay for necessaries, those things which suitably and reasonably supply his personal needs, such as food, shelter, and clothing. But even here the minor is not liable for the agreed price but, instead, the reasonable value of the items furnished. Recovery is not based upon contract, but quasi-contract. If a clothier sells a minor a suit which the latter needs, he can successfully sue the minor and recover the reasonable value of the suit.

But he is limited to this amount even if it is substantially less than the selling price.

Determining what are necessaries is a difficult problem. In general, those things are regarded as necessary which the minor needs to maintain himself in his particular station in life. Items necessary for subsistence and health are obviously included, such as food, lodging, clothing, medicine and medical services. But others less essential may be included as well, such as text books, school instruction, and legal advice. Further, there may be a tendency to enlarge the concept of necessaries to include such articles of property and services as are reasonably necessary to enable minors to earn the money required to provide the necessities of life, such as the reasonable fee of an employment agency seeking to find an emancipated minor a job so he can provide proper support for himself and his dependents.

Ordinarily, luxury items, such as cameras, tape recorders, phonographs, television sets, and motor boats, seldom qualify as necessaries. Whether automobiles and trucks are necessaries has caused considerable controversy, but some courts have recognized that under certain circumstances an automobile may be a necessary where it is used by the minor for his business activities. Rose v. Sheehan Buick, Inc., (See page 227).

Life insurance has traditionally been viewed as not a necessary; the general rule is that an insurance contract of a minor is voidable by him, although subject to ratification after attaining his majority. In some jurisdictions, by statute, a minor, at varying ages, may contract for life, health and accident insurance on his own life, and cannot, by reason of his minority, rescind, avoid, or repudiate his contract. Money as such will seldom be viewed as a necessary. At the very least the money must be expended for necessaries, and it is probably incumbent upon the lender to see personally that the money is so spent.

Liability on Contracts

A minor's contract is not entirely void and of no legal effect, but rather it is voidable at the minor's option. He has a power of avoidance. His exercise of this power is called a disaffirmance, and he is thereby released from any liability on the contract. On the other hand, after the minor becomes of age, he may choose to adopt or ratify the contract, in which case he becomes bound.

Ratification. Suppose that a minor makes a contract to buy land from an adult. The contract is voidable by the minor and he can escape liability. But, suppose that after reaching his majority, he promises to go through with the purchase. His promise is binding, and the adult can sue for breach upon his failure to perform. He has expressly ratified the contract entered into when he was a minor.

A ratification need not be express, it may be implied from the minor's conduct. If, for example, the minor should, after attaining his majority, go into possession of the property, or undertake to sell it to someone else, or perform other acts showing an intention to affirm the contract, he may not thereafter disaffirm but is liable on the contract.

Ordinarily, mere silence after becoming of age does not amount to a ratification. Yet this is not always so, since it might appear that, under the circumstances, the minor had a duty to speak. For instance, suppose the minor is the vendor of land of which the purchaser has taken possession. If, after becoming of age, he stands by knowingly while the purchaser makes improvements on the property, he will be estopped from disaffirming the contract.

Perhaps the most common form of implied ratification occurs when the minor, after attaining his majority, continues to use the property which he purchased as a minor. This use is obviously inconsistent with the nonexistence of the contract, and whether the contract is performed or still partly executory, it will amount to a ratification and preclude a disaffirmance by the minor. Although there is a division of authority, payments by the minor either upon principal or interest, or upon the purchase price of goods have been held to amount to a ratification. Some courts state that it is necessary that there be some additional evidence of an intention to abide by the contract, such as an express promise to that effect or the use of the subject matter of the contract. Mere retention of the goods for an unreasonable time after attaining majority has been construed as a ratification.

It should be noted that a minor has no power to ratify a contract while he remains a minor. A ratification cannot be predicated upon words or conduct occurring while he is still under age, for his ratification at that time would be no more effective than his original contractual promise. The ratification must take place after the individual has acquired complete contractual capacity by attaining his majority.

Disaffirmance. As stated, a minor's contract is voidable at his option, thereby conferring upon him a power to avoid liability. He may exercise his power to disaffirm through words or conduct manifesting an intention not to abide by it. Aspects of this power will be considered in the following order: (1) When can the minor disaffirm? (2) How can he disaffirm? (3) What, if anything, must he do upon a disaffirmance?

In general, a minor may disaffirm a contract at any time, either before or after he becomes of age. A notable exception is that a conveyance of land by a minor cannot be disaffirmed until after he reaches his majority. But must his disaffirmance come immediately upon his becoming an adult? In the case of a sale of land, there is strong authority for a view that the minor may wait until the expiration of the period of the Statute of Limitations in the absence of circumstances sufficient to raise questions of fairness and equity. It is otherwise with an executed contract for the sale of a chattel (tangible personal property) or other types of contracts. There the disaffirmance must come either during his minority or within a reasonable time after reaching majority, the precise period varying with the circumstance and the local law.

As is true of ratification, a disaffirmance may be either express or implied. No particular form of words is essential, so long as they show an intention not to be bound. This intention may be manifested by acts or by conduct, e.g., where the minor-vendor sells the property which is the subject matter of the contract.

A troublesome, and at the same time very important problem, in this area pertains to the minor's duty of restitution upon a disaffirmance. There is no unanimity of opinion on this question. By the majority view, it is only necessary that the minor return the chattel itself, provided he has it in his possession at the time of disaffirmance. Nothing more. If the minor is disaffirming the purchase of an automobile and the vehicle has been wrecked, he need only return the wrecked vehicle. His only duty is one of restoration in specie. A few States, either by statute or common law, recognize a duty upon the part of the minor to make restitution, i.e., return an equivalency of what has been received in order to place the seller in approximately the same position he would have occupied had the sale not occurred. Others not going so far require at least the payment of a reasonable amount for the use of the property, or the amount of its depreciation while in the hands of the minor.

Finally, can a minor disaffirm and recover property which has been transferred by his buyer to a bona fide purchaser for value without notice? At one time he could avoid the contract and recover the property, despite the fact that the third person gave value for it and had no notice of the minority. This has been changed by Section

2–403 of the U.C.C., which provides that a person with voidable title, e.g., the person buying goods from a minor, has power to transfer valid title to a good faith purchaser for value. For example, a minor sells his car to an individual who resells it to a used car dealership, an innocent purchaser for value. The used car dealer would acquire legal title even though he bought the car from a seller who had only voidable title. However, in the case of the sale of real estate, a minor's deed of conveyance may be rescinded even as against a good faith purchaser of the land who did not know of the minority.

Liability for Misrepresentation of Age

The law is not uniform on the effect to be given a fraudulent misrepresentation by a minor with respect to his age at the time of entering into a contract. Suppose a minor says that he is eighteen years of age (or twenty-one if that is the year of attaining majority) and actually looks that old or even older? By the prevailing view in this country the minor may nevertheless disaffirm the contract. However, some States have enacted statutes which prohibit disaffirmance if a minor misrepresents his age and the adult, in good faith, reasonably relied upon the misrepresentation. Other states not following the majority rule either (a) require the minor to restore the other party to the position he occupied before the making of the contract or (b) allow the defrauded party to recover damages against the minor in tort.

Return of Consideration. Some courts of equity have denied relief to minors by holding that a minor is estopped to avoid a transaction in which he has made a fraudulent representation unless he can restore any consideration received by him. In Haydocy Pontiac, Inc. v. Lee, 19 Ohio App.2d 217, 250 N.E.2d 898 (1969) the court stated that:

At a time when we see young persons between 18 and 21 years of age demanding and assuming more responsibilities in their daily lives; when we see such persons emancipated, married, and raising families; when we see such persons charged with the responsibility for committing crimes; when we see such persons being sued in tort claims for acts of negligence; when we see such persons subject to military service; when we see such persons engaged in business and acting in almost all other respects as an adult, it seems timely to re-examine the case law pertaining to contractual rights and responsibilities of infants to see if the law as pronounced and applied by the courts should be redefined.

To allow infants to avoid a transaction without being required to restore the consideration received where the infant has used or otherwise disposed of it causes hardship on the other party. We hold that where the consideration received by the infant cannot be returned upon disaffirmance of the contract because it has been disposed of the infant must account for the value of it, not in excess of the purchase price, where the other party is free from any fraud or bad faith and where the contract has been induced by a false representation of the age of the infant. Under this factual situation the infant is estopped from pleading infancy as a defense where the contract has been induced by a false representation that the infant was of age.

Tort Action. Even where the principle of estoppel is not used, in some states there is another remedy available to the other party as noted by the Court in Keifer v. Fred Howe Motors, Inc., 39 Wis.2d 20, 158 N.E.2d 288 (1968):

The 19th-century view was that a minor's lying about his age was inconsequential because a fraudulent representation of capacity was not the equivalent of actual capacity. This rule has been altered by time. There appear to be two possible methods that now can be employed to bind the defrauding minor: He may be estopped from denying his alleged majority, in which case the contract will be enforced or contract damages will be allowed; or he may be allowed to disaffirm his contract but be liable in tort for damages. Wisconsin follows the latter approach.

Liability for Tort Connected with Contract

It is well settled that minors are, as a general proposition, liable for their torts, including assault, battery, libel, fraud, and negligence. There is, however, a doctrine in the law that if the tort and the contract are so connected or "interwoven" that to enforce a tort action the court must enforce the contract, the minor is not liable in tort. Thus, if a minor rents an automobile from an adult, he enters into a contractual relationship obliging him to exercise reasonable care and diligence to protect the property from injury. By negligently damaging the automobile, he breaches that contractual undertaking. But his contractual immunity protects him from an action by the adult predicated on the contract. However, can the adult sue for damages on a tort theory? By the majority view he cannot. For, it is reasoned, a tort recovery would, in effect, be an enforcement of the contract and would defeat the protection which contract law affords the minor. This rationale has been stated by the Supreme Court of Michigan as follows:

But it is also a general rule that if the tort with which an infant is charged is so connected with the contract that commission of the tort constitutes a breach of the contract, or if the tort is predicated on a transaction with the infant based upon contract, so that holding the infant liable in tort would in effect enforce a liability arising out of his contract, then, since the infant cannot be held ex contractu, he cannot be held liable for his tort. The injured party is not permitted to enforce against the infant indirectly by an action in tort a liability which he could not enforce directly against the infant by an action upon contract. Brown v. Wood, 293 Mich. 148, 291 N.W. 255, 127 A.L.R. 1436 (1940).

A different result obtains, however, when the minor departs from the terms of the agreement, as by using a rental automobile for an unauthorized purpose, and in so doing negligently causes the damage complained of. In that event most courts would hold that the tort is independent and there should be a recovery. This would not involve the breach of a duty flowing from the contractual status, but, rather, the commission of a tort during the course of an activity which is a complete departure from the rental agreement.

INCOMPETENT PERSONS

Since a contract is a consensual transaction, it is, of course, necessary to a valid contract that the parties have requisite mental capacity. If one is lacking in such capacity, or mentally incompetent, he may avoid liability under the agreement.

A person who is lacking in sufficient mental capacity to enter into a contract is one unable to comprehend the subject of the contract, its nature and probable consequences. To vitiate the contract it is not necessary that he be proved permanently insane, still less that he be so adjudged by a court. If, indeed, he has been so adjudged, his contracts are void and of no legal effect whatever. On the other hand, it must be something more than a weakness of intellect or a lack of average intelligence. In short, a person is competent unless he is unable to understand the nature and effect of his act.

As in the case of a minor, an incompetent person is liable for necessaries furnished on the principle of quasi contract, the measure of recovery being the reasonable value of the goods or services. Moreover, an insane person's voidable contract can be ratified or disaffirmed by him when he becomes sane, or during a lucid period, or by his guardian during insanity, or by his representative after his death.

The predominant view in this country respecting an insane person's responsibility upon disaffirmance varies somewhat from that of a minor. Although a few cases can be found upholding an insane person's contract where the other party did not reasonably suspect his mental impairment and did not take advantage of him, the majority permit a disaffirmance here if there is a return of the consideration received (restoration in specie) or its equivalence in money (restitution).

INTOXICATED PERSONS

If, at the time of entering into an agreement, a party is so intoxicated as not to be able to comprehend the nature and effect of the transaction, it is voidable at his option. In most states it does not matter that the intoxication was due to his own voluntary conduct; he may still avoid liability. Slight intoxication will not, of course, destroy his contractual capacity, but neither is it essential that he be so drunk as to be totally without reason or understanding. A minority of states permit an intoxicated person to avoid his contracts only if the intoxication was involuntary.

The effect of intoxication on contractual capacity is generally the same as that given to contracts that are voidable because of insanity. The options of ratification or disaffirmance remain, although the courts are even more strict with respect to the requirement of restitution upon disaffirmance than they are in the area of an insane person's agreements. The rule is only relaxed where the person dealing with the intoxicated person fraudulently took advantage of him. As with insane persons, intoxicated persons are liable in quasi contract for necessaries furnished during their incapacity.

OTHER PARTIES WITH IMPAIRED CAPACITY

Aliens

Although some States undertake to prohibit aliens from owning land, no effective effort has been made to impair substantially an alien's contractual power in other types of transactions. An alien lawfully in this country can generally contract freely and utilize the courts for enforcement of contractual obligations. Aliens illegally in this country have, however, been denied access to our courts for the purpose of asserting contract rights. Enemy aliens, citizens or subjects of a country with which the United States is at war, will not be able to enforce their contracts in this country if such action will afford aid to the enemy country.

Convicts

For the most part convicts are accorded full contractual capacity. While limited in several respects as regards the exercise of civil rights (e.g., right to vote and hold public office), the imprisoned party is not denied the right to make contracts and to use the courts for their enforcement.

Married Women

The common law denied to married women the power to make contracts. Today, by virtue of State statutes, usually called Married Women's Property Acts, substantially all of the old disabilities have been removed. Consequently, a married woman is free to contract the same as any other person.

Private Corporations

A private corporation is a creature of the State in which it is incorporated, and its power including that of contracting, are limited to those which are conferred upon it by law. In its corporate charter and the statute under which it was formed will be found express grants of power from the State. In addition, a corporation has implied powers, those which are reasonably necessary and incidental to the accomplishment of its express powers. If it purports to act beyond the scope of its powers, its actions are *ultra vires* and ineffective at common law. However, modern statutes generally permit their enforcement. See Section 7 of the Model Business Corporation Act, Appendix D.

Public Corporations

Public corporations, such as cities, villages, towns, school districts, sanitary districts, and other municipal corporations, may not contract in excess of the power granted them by their parent authority, the State. Although in many instances there may still be redress against a private corporation acting *ultra vires,* there can be no recovery against a public corporation which exceeds its legal limitations. Hence, caution should be exercised by those contracting with such units to ascertain that the corporation has the power to enter into the proposed contract and that those who act on its behalf have the lawful authority to bind the municipal corporation. Typically, public contracts are subject to detailed laws and regulations respecting authorized terms; and only by careful perusal of these may one safely proceed to contract with public corporations.

Cases

Minors: Contractual Incapacity

ROBERTSON v. KING

(1955) 225 Ark. 276, 280 S.W.2d 402.

ROBINSON, J.

The principal issue here is whether appellant, a minor, may rescind a contract to purchase a pick-up truck. On the 20th day of March, 1954, L. D. Robertson, a minor, entered into a conditional sales agreement whereby he purchased from Turner King and J. W. Julian, doing business as the Julian Pontiac Company, a pick-up truck for the agreed price of $1,743.85. On the day of the purchase, Robertson was 17 years of age, and did not have his 18th birthday until April 8th. Robertson traded in a passenger car for which he was given a credit of $723.85 on the purchase price, leaving a balance of $1,020 payable in 23 monthly installments of $52.66 plus one payment of $52.83. He paid the April installment of $52.66.

It appears that Robertson had considerable trouble with the wiring on the truck. He returned it to the automobile dealers for repairs, but the defective condition was not remedied. On May 2nd, the truck caught fire and was practically destroyed. He no-tified the automobile concern and they stated that they would send the insurance man to see him. It appears that the insurance representative, upon finding out that Robertson was only 17 years of age, refused to deal with him.

On June 7th, appellees filed suit to replevy [recover] the damaged truck from Robertson. By his father and next friend, Robertson filed a cross-complaint in which he alleged that he is a minor and asked that the contract of purchase be rescinded and sought to recover that part of the purchase price he had paid, which he alleges is the amount of $723.85, allowed by the dealers on the car traded in, plus the one monthly payment of $52.66 totalling $776.51. A jury was waived and the cause was submitted to the court. There was a judgment for King and Julian on the complaint and the cross-complaint. On appeal, Robertson contends that he was 17 years of age at the time of the alleged purchase and that he has a right under the law to rescind the contract and to recover the portion of the purchase price he has paid.

Appellees contend * * * that the judgment should be sustained because Robertson did not return the damaged truck to the automobile dealers. However, the judgment of the court states: "The court further finds the proof to be that the plaintiff has possession of the said GMC pick-up truck." Hence, there is no merit to this contention. * *. *

Appellees further contend that the minor is bound by the contract because the automobile was a necessary. The record does not contain any substantial evidence to support this contention. The only evidence on this issue is that the boy quit school in 1951 and has been earning his own living since that time, and that he has been working for a construction company and traveling around the country to different jobs with his father in his father's truck. The boy lives at home with his parents and there is no showing whatever that he needed the truck in connection with any work he was doing. One of the witnesses for the appellees testified that the boy stated he wanted to use the truck in a farming operation. The record contains no evidence that he was engaged in farming at any time. * * * He was allowed a sum on the car which he traded in, amounting to more than one-third of the purchase price of the new truck, and he was to make substantial monthly payments for the balance. It is a matter of common knowledge that the plan under which the boy bought the truck is the usual method of making purchases of automobiles. In a suit by a minor to rescind a contract the burden is on the defendant to show that the article was a necessary. [Citation.]

It is our conclusion that the evidence does not sustain a finding that the truck was a necessary to Robertson. * * * The law is settled in this State that a minor may rescind a contract to purchase where the property involved is not a necessary. [Citations.]

The automobile dealers have disposed of the car they received in the trade, and cannot restore it to the minor. In a situation of this kind, the weight of authority is that the actual value of the property given as part of the purchase price by the minor is the correct measure of damages. Neither side is bound by the agreement reached as to the value of the car at the time the trade was made. This is true because the contract has been rescinded and there is no contract fixing the value. It is said in 43 C.J.S., Infants, § 47, p. 117: "While it is generally held that, where property traded in by the infant as part of the price is beyond reach of the seller, the infant is entitled to the reasonable value of the property at the time of the purchase, rather than the value fixed in the purchase agreement, it has also been held that he is entitled to receive the value fixed in the agreement."

In support of the rule that a reasonable value of the property at the time of purchase governs, C.J.S. cites Collins v. Norfleet-Baggs, Inc., 197 N.C. 659, 150 S.E. 177, 178, where the court said: "Where the infant parts with personal property, he may, upon disaffirmance, recover the value of such property, as of the date of the contract, but he is neither bound by, nor entitled to be awarded, the price fixed by the contract, for its real value may be more or less than the amount so stipulated." * * *

In the case at bar, although the minor was allowed over $700 on his car in the trade, there is evidence to the effect that it was actually worth about $350. Although there is conflict among the authorities as pointed out above, we believe the better rule holds that the value of an article given in trade by a minor as a part of the purchase price is the reasonable market value of the article at the time of the purchase, and that neither party is bound by the value fixed in the purchase agreement.

Young Robertson is a minor; the truck was not a necessary. * * * Hence, the court erred in finding for the automobile dealers, and the cause is therefore reversed and remanded for a new trial.

Minors: Contractual Incapacity

LANGSTRAAT v. MIDWEST MUTUAL INSURANCE CO.

(1974, Iowa) 217 N.W.2d 570.

LeGrand, J.

This case presents for the first time the question whether a minor may avoid his written rejection of uninsured motorist coverage because of his minority. Upon defendant's application for summary judgment, this issue was resolved against plaintiffs. We affirm that judgment.

Since 1967, our law has required that every policy of automobile or motor vehicle liability insurance include coverage for the protection of the purchaser of such insurance for "bodily injury, sickness or disease, including death" resulting from the negligence of the owner or operator of an uninsured motor vehicle or a hit-and-run motor vehicle. [Citation.]

The same code section permits the insured to refuse such coverage in the following manner:

However, the named insured shall have the right to reject such coverage by written rejection signed by the named insured. If such rejection is made on a form or document furnished by an insurance company or insurance agent, it shall be on a separate sheet of paper which contains only such rejection and information directly related thereto. * * *

* * *

The petition was filed by Richard P. Langstraat as father of his two minor sons, Terry Langstraat, 17 years of age, and Timothy Langstraat, 13 years of age. For convenience we refer to Terry Langstraat as though he were the sole plaintiff. Plaintiff owned a motorcycle which he insured against liability with defendant insurance company. In connection with this insurance, plaintiff signed what is designated as "Notice of Rejection of Uninsured Motorist Coverage." The rejection is here set out in full:

The undersigned hereby states that he is aware that the Iowa statute requires that the uninsured motorist coverage be attached to every motor vehicle liability policy in this state, but hereby serves notice of rejection and does not desire to purchase uninsured motorist coverage from Midwest Mutual Insurance Company.

-------- ------------

This notice was on a separate sheet of paper and was signed by plaintiff, as required by § 516A.1, The Code.

While this policy of insurance was in force, plaintiff was involved in an accident with another motorcycle owned and operated by Jack Welch, who was uninsured. Both plaintiff and his young brother sustained personal injuries for which they seek recovery from defendant company under the uninsured motorist clause which plaintiff says was part of the policy he purchased.

The issue is clearly drawn. Defendant admits it issued a policy of insurance covering plaintiff's motorcycle. Plaintiff admits he signed the notice of rejection heretofore set out. In reply to defendant's answer setting up the affirmative defense that plaintiff had rejected uninsured motorist coverage, plaintiff alleged his rejection was not a valid rejection * * * because of his minority.

This is not a case in which a minor seeks to disaffirm a contract. He may, of course, do so under § 599.2, The Code. [Citation.] Such a course, however, would leave plaintiff with *no* insurance. What he seeks here, by whatever name it is called, is to retain the benefits of the policy but to avoid the one provision which has become burdensome. There is no rule permitting such a selective choice. Disaffirmance, if asserted, goes to the whole contract. [Citations.]

Our conclusion that the trial court was right in finding for defendant is limited to the circumstances of this case. As already mentioned, plaintiff relied solely on his minority to avoid the notice of rejection. He did not assert failure to understand what he signed; he did not claim defendant had a duty to explain uninsured motorist coverage to him; he did not allege fraud, misrepresentation, deceit or other artifice. The extent to which any of these circumstances might affect a rejection of the coverage offered under the statute—whether to infant or adult—is not now considered because it is not now here. We decide only that a written rejection of uninsured motorist coverage is not invalid on the sole ground the assured is a minor.

* * *

Affirmed.

Minors: Liability for Necessaries

ROSE v. SHEEHAN BUICK, INC.

(1967 Fla.App.) 204 So.2d 903.

BARKDULL, J.

The appellant seeks review of an adverse final decree in an action seeking a rescission or disaffirmance of a contract.

The record reveals that on or about August 11, 1965, the appellee sold a 1965 Buick Riviera to the appellant for a cash sales price of $5,176.87. At the time of the sale, the appellant was a minor. On March 1, 1966, while still a minor under the age of 21 years, the appellant elected to disaffirm the purchase and notified the appellee of his intention, offering to return the vehicle upon a refund of the purchase price in full. The appellee refused to accept the return of the vehicle or to refund the purchase price thereof, so the appellant [who reached the age of 21 years on April 11, 1966] brought the instant action seeking invalidation of the contract and refund of the purchase price in full. The appellee answered admitting the sale and value of the vehicle, but denying the appellant had ever disaffirmed the contract while still a minor. The answer further alleged the vehicle was purchased as a necessity for the minor appellant; that the appellant was estopped

from avoiding the purchase because his demands for rescission were in excess of that to which he was entitled, and that the appellee was entitled to deterioration in the event of disaffirmance by the appellant. The court's decree in favor of defendant made findings that: * * * The Plaintiff, at age twenty, gave all the appearance of being of legal age. He acted and negotiated for the purchase of the car as an experienced adult. He traded, as part of the purchase price of the new car, his personal car titled in his father's name. His mother advanced part of the cash purchase price. Both his mother and father ratified and confirmed the sale. The car has been used by the Plaintiff since August 11, 1965, to carry on his school, business and social activities. The car is a necessity for this Plaintiff. The attempted disaffirmance of the sale by the Plaintiff was made for trivial claimed defects in the car. If the disaffirmance were to be allowed, the Defendant would be entitled to an allowance or set-off for the use and depreciation of the car while in the possession of the Plaintiff. However, equity and good conscience will not allow a rescission or disaffirmance of this contract by the Plaintiff. * * *

* * *

The appellant has preserved five points for review on this appeal. * * *

The second point contends that the chancellor erred in finding that the vehicle was a necessity for the plaintiff. This was a finding of fact, amply supported by the record [citations] and, therefore, this court will not disturb the decree on this basis.

* * *

The appellant also urges that the chancellor erred in holding that even if the plaintiff were entitled to rescission or disaffirmance, the defendant would be entitled to depreciation or depletion in value as of the date of the disaffirmance. This is an equity court and one who seeks equity must do equity. [Citations.] We concur with the chancellor's decision and, in the event the plaintiff were permitted to disaffirm the agreement, we hold that the defendant would be entitled to take into account depreciation on the returned chattel as of the date of the election to disaffirm.

* * *

Affirmed.

Minors: Liability for Necessaries

GASTONIA PERSONNEL CORP. v. ROGERS

(1970) 276 N.C. 279, 172 S.E.2d 19.

[Court of Appeals affirmed a judgment of nonsuit entered by the District Court at the close of plaintiff's (Gastonia Personnel Corporation's) evidence, holding that the services of a professional employment agency were not a "necessary" expense of a minor. Plaintiff appeals.]

Defendant had graduated from high school in 1966. On May 29, 1968, he was nineteen years old, emancipated and married. He needed only "one quarter or 22 hours" for completion of the courses required at Gaston Tech for an A.S. degree in civil engineering. His wife was employed as a computer programmer at First Federal Savings and Loan. He and she were living in a rented apartment. They were expecting a baby in September. Defendant had to quit school and go to work.

For assistance in obtaining suitable employment, defendant went to the office of plaintiff, an employment agency, on May 29, 1968. After talking with Maurine Finley, a personnel counselor, defendant signed a contract containing, *inter alia*, the following: "If I ACCEPT employment offered me by an employer as a result of a lead (verbal or otherwise) from you within twelve (12) months of such lead even though it may not be the position originally discussed with you, I will be obligated to pay you as per the terms of the contract." * * * He was to become obligated to plaintiff only if he

accepted employment from an employer to whom he was referred by plaintiff.

After making several telephone calls to employers who might need defendant's services as a draftsman, Mrs. Finley called Spratt-Seaver, Inc., in Charlotte, North Carolina. It was stipulated that defendant, as a result of his conversation with Mrs. Finley, went to Charlotte, was interviewed by Spratt-Seaver, Inc., and was employed by that company on June 6, 1968, at an annual salary of $4,784.00. The contract provided that defendant would pay plaintiff a service charge of $295.00 if the starting annual salary of accepted employment was as much as $4,680.00.

* * *

Plaintiff sued to recover a service charge of $295.00. In his answer, defendant * * * pleaded his infancy.

The sole question presented is whether plaintiff offered evidence sufficient to withstand defendant's motion for nonsuit.

BOBBITT, C. J.

Under the common law, persons, whether male or female, are classified and referred to as *infants* until they attain the age of twenty-one years. [Citations.]

"By the fifteenth century it seems to have been well settled that an infant's bargain was in general void at his election (that is voidable), and also that he was liable for necessaries." 2 Williston, Contracts § 223 (3rd ed. 1959).

An early commentary on the common law, after the general statement that contracts made by persons (infants) before attaining the age of twenty-one "may be avoided," sets forth "some exceptions out of this generality," to wit: *"An infant may bind himselfe to pay for his necessary meat, drinke, apparell, necessary physicke, and such other necessaries,* and likewise for his good teaching or instruction, whereby he may profit himself afterwards." (Our italics.) Coke on Littleton, 13th ed. (1788), p. 172. * * * If the infant married, "necessaries" included necessary food and clothing for his wife and child. [Citation.]

In accordance with this ancient rule of the common law, this Court has held an infant's contract, unless for "necessaries" or unless authorized by statute, is voidable by the infant, at his election, and may be disaffirmed during infancy or upon attaining the age of twenty-one. [Citations.]

* * *

It is noted that, under "The Family Law Reform Act 1969" (1969, c. 46, Part I), applicable to England and Wales, a person attains full age "on attaining the age of eighteen instead of attaining the age of twenty-one." Halsbury's Statutes of England, Third Edition, Interim Service re 1969 Statutes.

This statement commands respect and approval: "Society has a moral obligation to protect the interests of infants from overreaching adults. But this protection must not become a straitjacket, stifling the economic and social advancement of infants who have the need and maturity to contract. Nor should infants be allowed to turn that protective legal shield into a weapon to wield against fair-dealing adults. It is in the interest of society to have its members contribute actively to the general economic and social welfare, if this can be accomplished consistently with the protection of those persons unable to protect themselves in the market place." [Citations.]

* * *

In general, our prior decisions are to the effect that the "necessaries" of an infant, his wife and child, include only such necessities of life as food, clothing shelter, medical attention, etc. In our view, the concept of "necessaries" should be enlarged to include such articles of property and such services as are reasonably necessary to enable the infant to earn the money required to provide the necessities of life for himself and those who are legally dependent upon him.

The evidence before us tends to show that defendant, when he contracted with plaintiff, was nineteen years of age, emancipated, married, a high school graduate, within "a quarter or 22 hours" of obtaining his degree in applied science, and capable of holding a job at a starting annual salary of $4,784.00. To hold, as a matter of law, that such a person cannot obligate himself to pay for services rendered him in obtaining employment suitable to his ability, education and specialized training, enabling him to provide the necessities of life for himself, his wife and his expected child, would place him and others similarly situated under a serious economic handicap.

In the effort to protect "older minors" from improvident or unfair contracts, the law should not deny to them the opportunity and right to obligate themselves for articles of property or services which are reasonably necessary to enable them to provide for the proper support of themselves and their dependents. The minor should be held liable for the reasonable value of articles of property or services received pursuant to such contract.

Applying the foregoing legal principles, which modify *pro tanto* the ancient rule of the common law, we hold that the evidence offered by plaintiff was sufficient for submission to the jury for its determination of issues substantially as indicated below.

To establish liability, plaintiff must satisfy the jury by the greater weight of the evidence that defendant's contract with plaintiff was an appropriate and reasonable means for defendant to obtain suitable employment. If this issue is answered in plaintiff's favor, plaintiff must then establish by the greater weight of the evidence the reasonable value of the services received by defendant pursuant to the contract. Thus, plaintiff's recovery, if any, cannot exceed the reasonable value of its services to defendant.

[Judgment of Court of Appeals reversed and cause remanded to that Court with di-

230

rection to award a new trial to be conducted in accordance with the legal principles stated herein.]

Incompetent Persons

G. A. S. v. S. I. S.
(1978, Del.Fam.Ct.) 407 A.2d 253.

JAMES, J.

Action by petitioner to rescind the separation agreement he and his former wife, respondent S.I.S., executed on February 20, 1975.

Petitioner and respondent were married on January 19, 1957, and four children were born of this marriage. Petitioner's mental health problems began in 1970 when he was hospitalized at the Delaware State Hospital for eight weeks. Similar illnesses occurred in 1972 and the early part of 1974, with petitioner suffering such symptoms as acceleration of the mind followed by paranoia and loss of a sense of reality. During the two to three day onset of the illness, petitioner generally becomes violent toward himself, but not other people. After commitment, and drug therapy, petitioner slowly comes down from this state of aggressiveness, begins to communicate with others and, according to psychiatric testimony, becomes extremely dependent. After release from the hospital, petitioner usually continues to take medication for thirty to ninety days. Petitioner has been diagnosed as suffering from schizophrenia, paranoid type, and manic-depression.

On December 23, 1974, petitioner suffered a reoccurrence of this illness and was committed again to the Delaware State Hospital by police after being called by respondent. At this time, petitioner was employed by Hercules as a design engineer at a yearly salary of approximately $21,000. Although petitioner claims there had been no marital discord prior to the December 23, 1974 mental breakdown, respondent testified that she consulted an attorney in March of 1974, during petitioner's previous reoccurrence of this illness, for the purpose of securing a legal separation. However, petitioner pleaded with her to stay with him and she agreed if he promised to take his medication. In any event, respondent filed for a divorce in Superior Court alleging the mental illness of petitioner as the sole ground for the action, and petitioner was personally served with the divorce summons on January 10, 1975, while still committed to the Delaware State Hospital.

Petitioner told respondent that he did not want the divorce and he was referred, by the hospital's patient advocate, to an attorney with whom he had a very brief consultation on January 16, 1975, the details of which are the subject of some dispute. However, all parties agree that petitioner was primarily concerned with returning to the marital home and reconciling with respondent. While there may have been some discussion as to what property petitioner owned, he did not discuss with the attorney any type of proposed written separation agreement between petitioner and respondent. Although the attorney indicated he was willing to take the case, petitioner never followed up on the initial visit.

The separation agreement which is the subject of the current dispute was prepared by respondent's attorney and signed by petitioner on February 20, 1975 at her attorney's office, at her request. Petitioner never spoke with respondent's attorney about the contents of the agreement, nor did petitioner read it in the office prior to signing the document. It is clear that petitioner was not independently represented by counsel when he executed this agreement, although at the time he was still committed to the Delaware State Hospital in the night hospital program, under which he left during working hours to attend his job and returned to the hospital at night for continuing treatment.

* * *

The Court must answer the following questions in order to resolve the issue of the validity of the February 20, 1975 separation agreement: first, whether petitioner had the legal capacity to contract on that date; * * *

Only competent persons can make a contract, and where there is no capacity to understand or agree, there can be no contract. [Citations.]

Although petitioner was still under commitment to Delaware State Hospital at the time of execution of the separation agreement, he had not been judicially adjudicated mentally incompetent, and therefore the agreement is not void but may be voidable. [Citations.]

The mental incapacity sufficient to permit the cancellation of an agreement must render the afflicted individual incapable of understanding the nature and effect of the transaction. [Citation.] The Court must determine whether his mental faculties have been impaired to such an extent that he is unable to properly, intelligently and fairly protect and preserve his property rights. *Monroe v. Shrives,* 29 Ohio App. 109, 162 N.E. 780 (1927).

At the time of the execution of the separation agreement not only was petitioner a diagnosed paranoid schizophrenic still receiving in-patient treatment, but he was also receiving significant amounts of "antipsychotic" medication. The only psychiatrist to testify, Dr. S, treated petitioner in February of 1978, and based his testimony upon direct knowledge of petitioner and a review of the existing medical records. Dr. S's opinion, based upon reasonable medical certainty, was that when petitioner executed the separation agreement on February 20, 1975, he would not have been fully able to understand or comprehend what he was signing nor the implications thereof.

* * *

Delaware courts have held that mental incapacity, resulting from the use of drugs, may furnish a ground for voiding a contract, *Poole v. Hudson,* Del.Super., 83 A.2d 703 (1951); however,

[I]f no circumstances of unfairness, fraud, duress or undue influence appear, the reasoning powers must be so impaired as to render the person actually incapable of comprehending and acting rationally in the particular transaction. *Warwick v. Addicks,* 5 W.W.Harr. 43, 157 A. 205 (1931); 17 C.J.S. *Contracts,* § 133, page 479." *Poole v. Hudson, supra,* at 704.

The facts of this case do not require this Court to make the extremely difficult decision as to whether petitioner was, in fact, incapable of comprehending and acting rationally in executing the separation agreement. For even if the mental weakness of the petitioner in this case did not rise to the level of contractual incapacity, such weakness is a circumstance that operates to make the separation agreement voidable when coupled with the evidence of lack of independent counsel, undue influence and unfairness in the transaction that is present in this case.

Intoxicated Persons

WILLIAMSON v. MATTHEWS

(1980, Ala.) 379 So.2d 1245.

PER CURIAM

This is an appeal from an order denying appellant Williamson injunctive relief seeking to cancel a deed and to set aside a sale of property from Williamson to the Matthews. We reverse and remand.

The Matthews learned from members of their family that Williamson wanted to sell her home. Her mortgage was in default, and the mortgagee was threatening foreclosure. There was some evidence to the effect that Williamson wanted to get enough equity to help her finance a mobile home. When they went to Williamson's house to inquire about it, Williamson showed the Matthews through the house. Bobby

Matthews asked Williamson how much she wanted for it. Williamson told the Matthews to come back the next day. It is at this point that the parties are in disagreement. The Matthews contend that Williamson offered to sell her equity for $1,700, and Williamson contends that she offered to sell her equity for $17,000, and that the Matthews agreed to pay off the mortgage. It is undisputed that on September 27, 1978, the parties went to attorney Arthur J. Cook's office to execute a contract for the sale of the property. The contract of sale stated the purchase price to be $1,800 ($100 increase reflecting an agreement between the parties concerning some of the furniture in the home) plus the unpaid balance of the mortgage. Attorney Cook testified that he read the terms of the sale to both parties.

The parties then met on October 10, 1978, at attorney Larry Keener's office to sign the deed and to close a loan from appellee Family Savings Federal Credit Union to the Matthews so that the Matthews could buy the property from Williamson. Appellee The Brooklyn Savings Bank was about to foreclose the mortgage on Williamson's property. Keener disbursed part of the loan proceeds to Williamson. Williamson signed the deed to the property.

* * *

Immediately after the sale, Williamson became concerned that she had not received her full consideration and consulted an attorney.

Two days later, on October 12, 1978, Williamson filed a petition for injunctive relief alleging inadequate consideration and mental weakness. * * *

Williamson contends that the "something else" in the case at bar is mental weakness, either due to some form of permanent mental incapacity or due to intoxication. * * * Williamson, however, is not contending that she was insane at the time of the contract, but rather is contending that she had a mental incapacity, which

coupled with inadequacy of consideration requires the setting aside of the transaction.

Our rule in such a case is that a party cannot avoid, free from fraud or undue influence, a contract on the ground of mental incapacity, unless it be shown that the incapacity was of such a character that, at the time of execution, the person had no reasonable perception or understanding of the nature and terms of the contract. *Weaver v. Carothers,* 228 Ala. 157, 160, 153 So. 201 (1934).

Our rule regarding incapacity due to intoxication is much the same. The drunkenness of a party at the time of making a contract may render the contract voidable, but it does not render it void; and to render the contract voidable, it must be made to appear that the party was intoxicated to such a degree that he was, at the time of the contracting, incapable of exercising judgment, understanding the proposed engagement, and of knowing what he was about when he entered into the contract sought to be avoided. *Snead v. Scott,* 182 Ala. 97, 104, 62 So. 36 (1913). Proof merely that the party was drunk on the day the sale was executed does not per se, show that he was without contractual capacity; there must be some evidence of a resultant condition indicative of that extreme impairment of the faculties which amounts to contractual incapacity. *Snead v. Scott,* supra.

The burden was therefore cast on Williamson to show, by clear and convincing evidence, that she was incapable, at the time of execution, of executing the contract for sale and of executing the deed. *Snead v. Scott,* supra.

We hold that Williamson met this burden.

* * *

Indulging the usual presumption due the trial court, we nevertheless hold that, under the facts of this case, it appears to us that Williamson was not, at the time of execution, capable of fully and completely understanding the nature and terms of the contract and of the deed. *Cross v. Maxwell*, 263 Ala. 509, 83 So.2d 211 (1955). Williamson's contention that she was intoxicated supports this holding. Testimony was admitted from various witnesses to the effect that Williamson had a history of drinking, that she still had the problem at the time she executed the contract, and that she had in fact taken a couple of drinks before leaving for the meeting in attorney Arthur Cook's office. We do not hold that Williamson was so intoxicated as to render her incapable of contracting. However, numerous factors combine to warrant the conclusion that she was operating under diminished capacity. Testimony showed that Williamson's capacity to transact business was impaired, that she had a history of drinking, that she had been drinking the day she conducted negotiations, and that she had an apparent weakened will because she was pressured by the possibility of an impending foreclosure. Moreover, Williamson made complaint to an attorney only hours after the transaction. These factors are combined with a gross inadequacy of consideration. [The property was appraised twice, once at $16,500 and once at $19,500.]

REVERSED AND REMANDED.

Problems

1. M, a minor, operates a one-man automobile repair shop. A, having heard of M's good work on other cars, takes his car to M's shop for a thorough engine overhaul. M, while overhauling A's engine, carelessly fits an unsuitable piston ring on one of the pistons, with the result that A's engine is seriously damaged. M offers to return the sum which A paid him for his work, but refuses to make good the damage. A sues M in tort for the damage to his engine. Decision?

2. (a) On March 20, Andy Small became 17 years old, but he appeared to be at least 21. On April 1, he moved into a rooming house in Chicago where he orally agreed to pay the landlady $100 a month for room and board, payable at the end of each month for services and room during that month. (b) On April 4, he went to Honest Hal's Carfeteria and signed a contract to buy a used car on time with a small down payment. He made no representation as to his age, but Honest Hal represented the car to be in A-1 condition, which it subsequently turned out not to be. (c) On April 7 Andy sold and conveyed to Adam Smith a parcel of real estate which he owned. On April 30, he refused to pay his landlady for his room and board for the month of April, he returned the car to Honest Hal and demanded his down payment be given back, and he demanded that Adam Smith reconvey the land although the purchase price, which Andy received in cash, had been spent in riotous living. Decisions as to each claim?

3. Jones, a minor, owned a 1980 automobile. He traded it to Stone for a 1981 car. Jones went on a three-week trip and found that the 1981 car was not as good as the 1980 car. He asked Stone to return the 1980 car but was told that it had been sold to Tate. Jones thereupon sued Tate for the return of the 1980 car. Decision?

4. On May 7, Roy, a minor, a resident of Smithton, purchased an automobile from Royal Motors, Inc., for $2,750 in cash. On the same day he bought a motor scooter from Marks, also a minor, for $750 and paid him in full. On June 5, two days before attaining his majority, Roy disaffirmed the contracts and offered to return the car and the motor scooter to the respective sellers. Royal Motors, Inc., and Marks each refused the offers. On June 16, Roy brought separate appropriate actions against Royal Motors, Inc., and Marks, to recover the purchase price of the car and the motor scooter. By agreement on July 30, Royal Motors, Inc., accepted the automobile. Royal filed a counterclaim against Roy for the reasonable rental value of the car between June 5 and July 30. The car was not damaged during this period. Royal knew that Roy lived 25 miles from his place of employment in Smithton and that he would probably drive the car, as he did, to provide himself necessary transportation.

Decision as to (a) Roy's action against Royal Motors, Inc., and its counterclaim against Roy; (b) Roy's action against Marks?

5. George Jones on October 1, being then a minor, entered into a contract with Johnson Motor Company, a dealer in automobiles, to buy a car for $2,600. He paid $1,100 down and, under the agreement, was to make monthly payments thereafter of $125 each. After making the first payment on November 1, he failed to make any more payments. Jones was 17 years old at the time he made the contract. He represented to the company that he was 21 years old and the reason he made the representation was because he was afraid that if the company knew his real age, it would not sell the car to him. His appearance was that of a man of 21 years of age. On December 15, the company repossessed the car under the terms provided in the contract. At that time, the car had been damaged and was in need of repairs. On December 20, George Jones became of age and at once disaffirmed the contract and demanded the return of the $1,225 paid on the contract. On refusal of the company to do so, George Jones brought an action to recover the $1,225 and the company set up a counterclaim for $1,500 for expenses to which it was put in repairing the car. Decision?

6. A entered into a written contract to sell certain real estate to M, a minor, for $10,000, payable $2,000 upon the execution of the contract and $200 on the first day of each month thereafter until paid. M paid the $2,000 down payment and 8 monthly installments before attaining his majority. Thereafter, M made two additional monthly payments, and caused the contract to be recorded in the county in which the real estate was located. M was then advised by his attorney that his contract was voidable. Immediately upon being so advised, M tendered the contract to A, together with a quitclaim deed reconveying all of M's interest in the property to A. Also, M demanded that A return to him the money which he had paid under the contract. A refused the tender and declined to repay any portion of the money paid to him by M. M then brought an action to cancel the contract and recover the amount paid to A. Decision?

7. A sold and delivered a horse to B, a minor. B during his minority, returned the horse to A, saying that he disaffirmed the sale. A accepted the horse and said he would return the purchase price to B the next day. Later in the day, without A having paid B, he (B) changed his mind, took the horse without A's knowledge and sold it to C. Upon what theory, if any, can A recover from B?

8. N in 1978 had been found innocent of a criminal offense based upon his insanity, had been released from the hospital for the criminally insane during the summer of 1979, and has since that time been a reputable and well-respected citizen and businessman. On October 1, 1980, N and S enter into a contract whereby N would sell his farm to S for $100,000. N seeks to void the contract. S insists that N is fully competent and has no right to avoid the contract. Who will prevail? Why?

9. I, while under the influence of alcohol, agreed to sell to B his 1980 automobile for $8,000. The next morning when B went to I's house with the $8,000 in cash, I stated that he did not remember the transaction but "a deal is a deal." One week after completing the sale I decides that he wishes to avoid the contract. What result?

10. A, an Australian citizen, contracts with D to purchase a diamond ring for $5,000. Prior to the delivery date the price of diamonds rises significantly and D refuses to perform the contract. In a subsequent suit by A, D alleges that A does not have contractual capacity. Decision?

Chapter

12

STATUTE OF FRAUDS

The Statute of Frauds requires that certain designated types of contracts be evidenced in a particular manner in order to be enforceable. The original statute became law in 1677 when the English Parliament adopted "An Act for Prevention of Frauds and Perjuries," commonly referred to as the Statute of Frauds. From the early days of American history practically every state has and continues to have a Statute of Frauds patterned upon Sections 4 and 17 of the original English statute.

Section 4 of the English Statute specified five classes of contracts which had to comply with its provisions in order to be enforceable. The sole method of compliance was by a writing signed by the party to be charged. Section 17 of the Statute dealt only with contracts for the sale of goods and specifies three means of compliance, namely: (1) a writing signed by the party to be charged; (2) delivery and acceptance; or (3) payment for the goods.

The reason for enactment of the original Statute of Frauds three centuries ago has long ceased to exist. At that time the law of England did not permit a person to testify as a witness in a lawsuit in which he had an interest in its outcome. The law regarded both the plaintiff and the defendant as incompetent to testify.

In Azevedo v. Minister, 86 Nev. 576, 471 P.2d 661 (1970), the court comments on the rationale and development of the statute as follows:

The development of the action of *assumpsit* in the fourteenth century gave rise to the enforceability of the oral promise. Although parties to an action could not be witnesses, the alleged promise could be enforced on the strength of oral testimony of others not concerned with the litigation. Because of this practice, a party could readily suborn perjured testimony, resulting in marked injustice to innocent parties who were held legally obligated to promises they had never made. [Citation.] The statute of frauds was enacted to preclude the practice. [Citation.] The passage of the statute did not eliminate the problem, but rather, has precipitated a controversy as to the relative merits of the statute. Those favoring the statute of frauds insist that it prevents fraud by prohibiting the introduction of perjured testimony. [Citation.]

They also suggest that it deters hasty action, in that the formality of a writing will prevent a person from obligating himself without a full appreciation of the nature of his acts. [Citation.] Moreover, it is said, since business customs almost entirely conform to the mandates of the statute, an abolition of the statute would seriously disrupt such affairs. [Citation.]

On the other hand, in England the statute of frauds has been repealed. [Citation.] The English base their position upon the reasoning that the assertion of the technical defense of the statute aids a person in breaking a contract and effects immeasurable harm upon those who have meritorious claims. [Citations.]

It is further maintained by the advocates of the English position that the rationale for the necessity of the statute has been vitiated because parties engaged in litigation today may testify as witnesses and readily defend against perjured testimony. [Citation.]

CONTRACTS WITHIN THE STATUTE OF FRAUDS

There are many more types of contracts that are not subject to the Statute of Frauds than those that are subject to it. Most oral contracts are in every way as enforceable and valid as a written contract. If a given contract is subject to the Statute of Frauds, the contract is said to be "within" the Statute; it must, therefore, comply with the requirements of the Statute in order to be enforceable. All other types of contracts are said to be "not within" or "outside" the Statute and, of course, need not comply with its requirements to be enforceable.

The following five types of contracts are within the original Section 4 of the English Statute and remain within most state statutes. Compliance requires a writing signed by the party to be charged.

1. Promises of an executor or administrator to pay debts of the estate out of his own personal funds;
2. Promises to answer for the debt of another;
3. Agreements upon consideration of marriage;
4. Agreements for the sale of land or an interest therein; and
5. Agreements not to be performed within one year.

A sixth type of contract within the Statute was originally contained in Section 17 and applies to contracts for the sale of goods. The enforceability of contracts of this type is now governed by Section 2–201 of the U.C.C., which is in effect in every state except Louisiana.

In addition to those contracts specified in the original statute, some modern statutes require that others be written; for example, a contract to make a will, to authorize an agent to sell real estate, or to pay a commission to a real estate broker. Nonetheless, the general rule is that unless a statute requires a particular contract to be in writing, it is entirely enforceable even though it is oral.

Promise by Executor or Administrator

This clause applies to promises of an executor of a decedent's will, or the administrator of his estate if he dies without a will, to pay debts of the estate he is administering out of his own funds. An executor or administrator is a person appointed by a court to carry on, subject to order of court, the administration of the estate of a deceased person. If the will of a decedent nominates a certain person as executor, the court customarily appoints such person. If an executor or administrator promises to pay a debt of the decedent out of his own funds, the promise is unenforceable unless in writing. For example, A, who is B's son and executor of B's will, recognizes that B's estate will not have sufficient funds to pay all of the decedent's debts and orally promises C, one of B's creditors, that he will personally pay all of his father's creditors in full. A's oral promise is not enforceable.

Promise to Answer for the Debt of Another

This provision applies to a contractual promise to a creditor to pay the debts or obligations of a third person, the debtor. Thus, if a father tells a merchant to extend credit to his son, and says "If he doesn't pay, I will," the promise must be in writing to be enforceable. The factual situation can be reduced to the simple "If X doesn't pay, I will." The promise is said to be "collateral," in that the promisor is not the one who is primarily liable. He does not promise to pay in any event; his promise is to pay only upon the default of the one primarily obligated.

Promise Must Be Collateral to the Debt of Another. It is sometimes difficult to ascertain whether a promise is "collateral" ("I'll pay if X doesn't"), as above, or whether the promisor undertakes to become primarily liable, or, as the courts say, makes an "original" promise ("I'll pay"). For example, a father tells a merchant to deliver certain items to his son, and says "I will pay for them." The Statute of Frauds does not apply, and the promise may be oral. Here, the father is not promising to answer for the debt of another; he is making the debt his own. It is to the father, and to the father alone, that the merchant extends credit and looks for payment. Similarly, where the son, without authority from the father, secures credit from the merchant upon the assurance that "if father does not pay, I will," the son's promise is enforceable, though oral, for here there is no underlying debt of another which the son is promising to pay. The father is not indebted for these goods, and the son's promise is regarded as an original promise.

Main Purpose Doctrine. The courts have developed an exception to the above promise to answer for the debt of another which is based on the asserted purpose or object of the promisor, called the "main purpose doctrine" or "leading object rule." Where the object of the promisor is to obtain a benefit which he did not previously enjoy, the promise is not within the Statute. Suppose that a supply company has refused to furnish materials upon the credit of a building contractor. Faced with a possible slow-down which he is desirous of avoiding, the owner promises the supplier that if he will extend credit to the contractor, the owner will pay if the contractor does not. Here, a court would be likely to view this as a situation where the purpose of the promisor was to subserve a pecuniary interest of his own, even though the performance of the promise would discharge the debt of another. The intent to benefit the contractor was at most incidental, and courts will uphold oral promises of this type by a judicial interpretation which does not follow the literal language of the statute. The courts regard this type of transaction as one against which Section 4 of the Statute of Frauds was not aimed. Another application of the rule is shown in the following excerpt from the Restatement of the Law of Contracts: "D owes C $1000. C is about to levy an attachment on D's factory. S, who is also a creditor of D, fearing that the attachment will ruin D's business and thereby destroy his own chance of collecting his claim, orally promises C that if C will forbear to take legal proceedings against D for three months, S will pay D's debt if D fails to do so. S's promise is enforceable." Restatement, Second, Contracts, Section 116, Illustration 2.

Promise Made to Debtor

Courts do not regard promises made to a *debtor* as being within the Statute. For example, D owes a debt to C. S promises

D to pay this debt. Courts do not hold that the "debt of another" which the promisor undertakes to pay can be the promisee's own debt. Accordingly, the promise may be oral. For this reason also, contracts of "indemnity," as where S says to D, "Buy goods from C and I will indemnify you against loss," are not required to be in writing.

Agreement upon Consideration of Marriage

The notable feature of this section is that it does not apply to the one case where there is perhaps the most danger of fraud and perjured testimony, namely, mutual promises to marry. Judicial interpretation has established that mutual promises to marry do not have to be in writing. The section does apply to the ordinary "marriage settlement" or antenuptial contract, as for example, where a man orally promises a woman to convey title to a certain farm to her if she accepts his proposal of marriage.

The following are additional examples of the promises which are within this section of the Statute of Frauds: "In consideration of a woman's promise to marry him, a man promises to make a settlement of money or other property in trust for her. In consideration of Mary's promising to marry or actually marrying John, John promises to pay her an allowance or to execute a will leaving Mary some or all of John's property at death. In consideration of Mary's marrying John, Peter promises to convey property or to pay her an annuity. John and Mary mutually agree that their marriage shall not affect the existing property rights of each. Mary marries John in return for John's promise to give Sarah a share in his estate, or to adopt and care for Sarah. Mary promises to release a money judgment against John in consideration of his marrying her." Corbin on Contracts, Section 462.

Contract for Sale of Land or an Interest Therein

To ascertain the subject matter covered by this section, "land or an interest therein," courts consider precedents taken from the law of property. A distinction is made between real property (land) and personal property (goods, chattels). In addition to the ordinary "estates in land," real property includes leases among which are oil and mineral leases, mortgages, and easements such as a right of way or a right to draw water from a stream.

Goods to be Severed from Realty. The Uniform Commercial Code provides that a contract for the sale of timber, minerals or the like, or of a structure or its materials to be removed from the land is considered a contract for the sale of personal property if they are to be severed by the seller. Section 2–107(1). If the buyer is to sever, such contracts are considered contracts affecting land. A contract for the sale apart from the land of growing crops or other things not enumerated above, which are capable of severance without material harm to the land, is deemed to be a contract for the sale of personal property, irrespective of whether the buyer or seller is to sever the goods from the land. Section 2–107(2).

The Part Performance Doctrine. Assume that a seller and a purchaser make an oral contract for the sale of a certain tract of land. In reliance upon his contract the purchaser takes possession of the property, pays a part of the purchase price and erects valuable improvements. If the seller refuses to go through with the deal, asserting the Statute of Frauds land clause, may the purchaser obtain redress in the courts? Upon the basis of the literal language of the Statute, he clearly could not. There are no exceptions—for "hardship" or anything else.

However, there is a "part performance doctrine," developed by courts of equity which sometimes grants relief to a buyer under these and similar circumstances. Simply expressed, the courts deem it inequitable and unjust to permit the Statute to be interposed by the seller after the purchaser has relied in good faith upon the seller's promise. Often it is said that the seller is "estopped" to assert the defense of the Statute of Frauds. The Restatement, Second, Contracts, Section 129 provides:

A contract for the transfer of an interest in land may be specifically enforced notwithstanding failure to comply with the Statute of Frauds if it is established that the party seeking enforcement, in reasonable reliance on the contract and on the continuing assent of the party against whom enforcement is sought, has so changed his position that injustice can be avoided only by specific enforcement.

Agreements Not to be Performed within One Year

The Statute requires all contracts not to be performed within one year of the making of the contract to be in writing.

The Possibility Test. The test here is not whether the agreement is one which is likely to be performed within one year from the date of the making of the contract, or whether the parties contemplate that performance will be within the year, but whether it is *possible* for the contract to be performed within a year. The enforceability of the contract does not depend upon probabilities or on the actuality of subsequent events. For example, an oral contract between A and B for A to build a bridge, which should reasonably take three years, in one year, is enforceable, since it is possible, although extremely unlikely and difficult, for A to perform the contract in one year. Similarly, if A agrees to support B for life, the contract is not within the Statute of Frauds. It is possible that B may die within the year, in which case the contract would be com-

pletely performed. The contract is therefore one which is *fully performable* within a year. However, an oral contract to support another person for thirteen months is not possible of performance within a year and is unenforceable.

Computation of Time. It should be observed in these cases that the year runs from the time the agreement is made, not from the time when the performance is to begin. Hence, a contract for a year's performance which is to begin three days from the date of the making of the contract is within the Statute, and if oral is unenforceable. If, however, the performance is to begin the following day, or consistently with the terms of the agreement could have begun the following day, it is not within the Statute, and need not be in writing, as the one year's performance would be completed on the anniversary date of the making of the contract, and the law disregards fractions of a day.

As simple as the foregoing test might appear, it is sometimes difficult to apply. In Sinclair v. Sullivan Chevrolet Co., 45 Ill.App.2d 10, 195 N.E.2d 250 (1964), affirmed 31 Ill.2d 507, 202 N.E.2d 516 (1964), an action was brought on an alleged oral agreement between plaintiff and defendant made on May 30, 1960, whereby plaintiff was to start work for defendant on June 6, 1960, and be employed for at least one year as sales manager of defendant corporation. It was alleged that acting upon the defendant's promises to pay a stipulated salary, a bonus based on profits but not to be less than a fixed amount each year, provide plaintiff with a car, and to reduce the agreement to writing, plaintiff resigned a good job in St. Louis, Missouri, and moved his place of residence to Champaign, Illinois. Plaintiff worked until March 18, 1961, then left defendant because of defendant's failure to keep its promises. In holding the Statute of Frauds applicable, the Illinois Appellate court observed:

Plaintiff argues that the contract could have been concluded by many conditions, all occurring within one year. Other than the death of plaintiff, we find nothing within the record and nothing is brought to the court's attention to show the contract could have been "performed" within one year. In every employment contract the contract is subject to termination at the death of the employed party, but this does not mean the contract has been performed in full. If we were to hold termination and performance synonymous, the act would be rendered useless. * * * Where the contract extends to a point in time, be it death or some other circumstance, at which time the full service contemplated will have been rendered, and that point in time could occur within one year, the Statute of Frauds will not be a bar to enforcement of the action.

Hence, an employment contract for more than one year must be in writing to be enforceable, whereas an employment contract for life need not be.

Full Performance by One Party. The courts have at times developed a rule to "take cases out of the Statute of Frauds," as, for instance, the "part performance doctrine" in the land contract cases and the "main purpose doctrine" in promises to answer for the debt of another. A judicially constructed exception has been engrafted upon this one-year section as well. Where a bilateral contract has been fully performed on one side, most courts hold that the promise of the other party is enforceable even though by its terms its performance was not possible within the period of a year. For example, A borrows $4,800 from B. A orally promises C to pay B $4,800 in three annual installments of $1,600. A's promise is enforceable notwithstanding the one-year clause, because B has fully performed.

Sales of Goods

Section 17 of the original Statute of Frauds applied to contracts for the sale of goods and has been used as a prototype for the U.C.C. Article 2 Statute of Frauds provision. Section 2–201 provides:

(1) Except as otherwise provided in this Section a contract for the sale of goods for the price of $500 or more is not enforceable by way of action or defense unless there is some writing sufficient to indicate that a contract for sale has been made between the parties and signed by the party against whom enforcement is sought or by his authorized agent or broker. A writing is not insufficient because it omits or incorrectly states a term agreed upon but the contract is not enforceable under this paragraph beyond the quantity of goods shown in such writing.

(2) Between merchants if within a reasonable time a writing in confirmation of the contract and sufficient against the sender is received and the party receiving it has reason to know its contents, it satisfies the requirements of subsection (1) against such party unless written notice of objection to its contents is given within 10 days after it is received.

(3) A contract which does not satisfy the requirements of subsection (1) but which is valid in other respects is enforceable

(a) if the goods are to be specially manufactured for the buyer and are not suitable for sale to others in the ordinary course of the seller's business and the seller, before notice of repudiation is received and under circumstances which reasonably indicate that the goods are for the buyer, has made either a substantial beginning of their manufacture or commitments for their procurement; or

(b) if the party against whom enforcement is sought admits in his pleading, testimony or otherwise in court that a contract for sale was made, but the contract is not enforceable under this provision beyond the quantity of goods admitted; or

(c) with respect to goods for which payment has been made and accepted or which have been received and accepted.

Section 2–201 covers a contract for the sale of "goods." Section 2–105(1) of the Code defines "goods" to include all things, including specially manufactured goods, which are movable at the time of identification to the contract for sale. It expressly includes growing crops and unborn animals.

Other U.C.C. Statute of Frauds Provisions

Sale of Securities. Section 8–319 of the Code is a separate Statute of Frauds applicable to contracts for the sale of securities (stocks and bonds). Such contracts are not enforceable unless there is a writing signed by the party against whom enforcement is sought or by his authorized agent or broker sufficient to indicate that a contract has been made and stating the parties, the quantity, the price, and a description of the securities.

Every contract for the sale of securities is within the Statute as no minimum amount in terms of price is excluded. Delivery and acceptance of the security or payment of the price satisfies the Statute, but the contract is enforceable only to the extent of such delivery or such payment. The Code also provides that a written confirmation of the sale or purchase within a reasonable time, and sufficient against the sender, is compliance with the Statute unless the other party sends written objection within ten days after receipt. This is similar to Section 2–201(2), except there is no requirement that the transaction be "between merchants."

An admission in a pleading, testimony, or otherwise in court will also satisfy the requirements of the Code and make the contract enforceable.

Sales of Other Kinds of Personal Property. Section 1–206 of the U.C.C. is a catch-all Statute of Frauds applicable to contracts for the sale of personal property, other than goods, securities or security agreements in amount or value beyond $5,000. This section makes such contracts unenforceable by way of action or defense unless there is some writing which indicates that a contract for sale has been made between the parties at

a defined or stated price, reasonably identifies the subject matter, and is signed by the party against whom enforcement is sought or by his authorized agents. This section of the Code covers rights under bilateral contracts, royalty rights, patent rights, and "general intangibles," as defined in Section 9–106.

Security Interest in Personal Property. Section 9–203 of the U.C.C. requires that agreements which create or provide a nonpossessory security interest in personal property be contained in a signed writing to be effective.

Modification or Rescission of Contracts within the Statute of Frauds

Oral contracts modifying previously existing contracts are unenforceable if the modification is within the Statute of Frauds. The reverse is also true, that is, an oral modification of a prior contract which oral modification is not within the Statute of Frauds is enforceable. Both of these statements are true for general contract law and under the U.C.C. Thus, an oral promise to guarantee additional debts of another and an oral agreement to substitute different land for that described in the original contract are both examples of unenforceable oral contracts. On the other hand, an oral promise to modify an employee's contract from one year to six months at a higher salary is not within the Statute of Frauds and is enforceable. Under the U.C.C., if the parties enter into an oral contract to sell an automobile for $450 to be delivered to the buyer and later, prior to delivery, orally agree that the seller shall paint the car and install new tires and the buyer pay a price of $550, the modified contract is unenforceable and the original contract will probably be held to be rescinded. Similarly, if the parties have a written contract for the sale of 500 bushels of wheat at a price of $1.50

per bushel and later upon oral agreement decrease the quantity to 200 bushels at the same price per bushel, the agreement, as modified, is enforceable. Section 2–209(3).

METHODS OF COMPLIANCE

A Writing or Memorandum

Section 4 Provisions. Section 4 of the original Statute of Frauds and most modern Statutes of Frauds require that the agreement be in writing to be enforceable. Such writing or memorandum (1) must be signed by the party to be charged or by his agent; (2) must specify the parties to the contract; and (3) must specify the subject matter and any material or special terms and conditions with reasonable certainty. The note or memorandum may be extremely informal; all that is necessary is that it contain the required information and be signed by the party to be charged. The "signature" may be by initials, or even typewritten or printed, so long as the party intended thereby to authenticate the writing. Furthermore, it need not be at the bottom of the page or at the customary place for a signature.

The memorandum may be such that the parties view it as having no legal significance, whatever, as for example, a personal letter between the parties or a third person, an inter-departmental communication, an advertisement, or handbill, or the minutes or record books of a business. The writing need not have been delivered to the party who seeks to take advantage of it, and it may even contain a repudiation of the oral agreement.

The memorandum may consist of several papers or documents, no one of which would be sufficient by itself. The several memoranda, however, must together satisfy all of the requirements of a writing to comply with the Statute of Frauds and must clearly indicate that they pertain to the same transaction. Restatement, Second,

Contracts, Section 132. The latter requirement can be satisfied if (a) the writings are physically attached, (b) the writings refer to each other, or (c) an examination of the writings shows them to be in reference to each other.

U.C.C. Provisions. The Statute of Frauds provisions under the U.C.C. are more liberal. The Code requires merely some writing sufficient to indicate that a contract has been made between the parties and signed by the party against whom enforcement is sought or by his authorized agent or broker. The writing is not insufficient because it omits or incorrectly states a term agreed upon but the contract can in such case be enforced only to the extent of the quantity of goods shown in the writing. Its non-insistence that the writing contain all of the terms, other than quantity, is consistent with other provisions of the Code that contracts may be enforced, although material terms are omitted, as in Section 2–305 (Open Price Contracts), Section 2–306 (Output, Requirements, and Exclusive Dealing Contracts), and Section 2–311 (Particulars of Performance to be specified by one of the parties). Given proof that a contract was intended and a signed writing describing the goods, the quantity thereof, and names of parties, the Court, under the Code, can supply omitted terms such as price or terms necessary to determine what performance is required. As with general contracts, several related documents may satisfy the writing requirement.

Concerning the signature of "the party to be charged," or "the party against whom enforcement is sought" (Section 2–201(1)), most courts hold that both parties need not have signed, only the one against whom the contract is sought to be enforced. The party "to be charged" is always the defendant. Moreover, the "signature" may be by initials, or even typewritten or printed, so long as the party intended thereby to authenticate the writing. Furthermore, it need not be at the bottom of the page or at the customary place for a signature.

Other Methods
of Compliance
Under the U.C.C.

An oral contract for the sale of goods may comply with the requirements of the Code in the following instances: (1) where written confirmation of a contract between merchants is sent and no objection is made within ten days; (2) where the party defending against the contract admits it by pleading, testimony or otherwise in court; (3) under certain circumstances, where the goods are to be specially manufactured; and (4) where there has been payment or delivery and acceptance.

Written Confirmation. The Code provides relief to a merchant who has confirmed an oral agreement for the sale of goods by letter or signed writing to the other party if he, too, is a merchant. As between merchants, the written confirmation, if sufficient against the sender, is also sufficient against the recipient of the confirmation unless the recipient gives written notice of his objection within ten days after receiving the confirmation. Section 2–201(2).

Admission. The Code permits an oral contract for the sale of goods to be enforced against a party who in his pleading, testimony, or otherwise in court, admits that a contract was made, but limits enforcement to the quantity of goods so admitted. Section 2–201(3)(b). The language "otherwise in court" may include compulsory pre-trial discovery depositions of the defendant.

Specially Manufactured Goods. The Code permits enforcement of an oral contract for goods specially manufactured for the buyer only if there is extrinsic evidence indicating that the goods were made for the buyer and if the seller can show that he has made a substantial beginning of their manufacture or commitments for their procurement prior to receipt of any notice of repudiation. If the goods, although manufactured on special order, are readily marketable in the ordinary course of the seller's business, the contract is within the statute.

If B brings an action against A alleging that pursuant to a contract A ordered from B three million balloons with A's trademark imprinted thereon at a price of $30,000, the action is not subject to the defense of the statute, unless A can show (1) that the balloons are suitable for sale to other buyers, which is highly improbable in view of the trademark, or (2) that notice of repudiation was received by B before he had made a substantial start on the production of the balloons or had otherwise substantially committed himself for their procurement.

Delivery or Payment and Acceptance of the Goods. Prior to the Code delivery and acceptance of part of the goods or payment of part of the price made enforceable the entire oral contract against the buyer who had received part delivery or against the seller who had received part payment. Under the Code, such "partial performance," as a substitute for the required memorandum, validates the contract only for the goods which have been accepted or for which payment has been accepted. Receipt and acceptance either of the goods or of the price constitutes an admission by both parties that some contract exists between them. If the court can make a just apportionment, the agreed price of any goods delivered under an oral contract can be recovered, or, if the price has been paid, the seller can be forced to deliver an apportionable part of the goods.

But what if the contract is indivisible, such as one for the sale of an automobile, so that if part payment is made there is only a choice between not enforcing the contract or enforcing the contract as a whole? Presently, there is a division of authority on this issue, although the better rule appears to be that such part payment and acceptance makes the entire contract enforceable.

EFFECT OF NONCOMPLIANCE WITH THE STATUTE OF FRAUDS

The original statute provided that "no action shall be brought" upon a contract to which the Statute of Frauds applied and which did not comply with its requirements. The Code states that the contract "is not enforceable by way of action or defense." Despite the difference in language the basic legal effect is the same: a contracting party has a defense to an action by the other for enforcement of an oral contract which is within the Statute and does not comply with its requirements. In short, the oral contract is unenforceable.

If A, a painter, and B, a home owner, make an oral contract whereby B is to give A a certain tract of land in return for the painting of B's house, the contract is unenforceable under the Statute of Frauds. It is a contract for the sale of an interest in land. Either party can repudiate and has a defense to an action by the other to enforce the contract.

If the painter has already performed a part of the work is he completely without a remedy? Clearly, he cannot enforce the contract, but courts may still permit a recovery in quasi contract to prevent an unjust enrichment. The remedy of restitution allows the painter to recover damages equal to the amount of the benefit that he has conferred upon the home owner. Thus, all may not be lost to a party unable to enforce an oral contract. However, this possibility should impel a contracting party to use the utmost caution to assure compliance with the Statute. Only by complying with the Statute of Frauds can one be reasonably certain of obtaining the benefit of the bargain that has been made.

Cases

*Promise to Answer
for the Debt of Another*

PETERSON v. ROWE

(1957) 63 N.M. 135, 314 P.2d 892.

COMPTON, J.

Appellee brought this action to recover for professional services rendered appellants' father. * * * The cause was tried to the court and the judgment went against appellants, M. H. Rowe and William W. Rowe, and they appeal. The pertinent findings are:

"(2) That between the approximate dates of July 26, 1955, and September 11, 1955, plaintiff provided hospital care, laboratory facilities and medication to patient William H. Rowe at the special instance and request of his sons, M. H. Rowe and William W. Rowe.

"(3) That the statement for services rendered totaled $3,144.25, but defendants, M. H. Rowe and William W. Rowe paid on account $245.00, and the Southwest Blood Bank credited $160.00 to this account, leaving a balance of $2739.25.

"(4) That defendants, M. H. Rowe and William W. Rowe, made direct, independent, unqualified and unconditional promises to pay for the hospital services rendered by plaintiff to William H. Rowe.

"(5) That plaintiff, in reliance upon the promises of defendants M. H. Rowe and William W. Rowe, did perform his part of the agreement."

Appellants contend (a) that the findings are not supported by substantial evidence, and, (b) that the contract, being oral, is within the statute of frauds. These contentions require a determination whether appellants are original promisors or mere guarantors. If the former, they are liable; if the latter, the statute is a complete defense. A review of the evidence convinces us that appellants are original promisors and not guarantors. It follows, both contentions must be rejected.

On July 26, 1955, when William H. Rowe was admitted to appellee's hospital, he was suffering from the effects of a severe gastric hemorrhage. He was first given emergency treatment, and later prepared for surgery, which was performed July 31, 1955. He was discharged from the hospital September 11, 1955. The hospital services, medicines, treatments, laboratory facilities, etc., amounted to $3,144.25, which amount was later reduced to $2,739.25 by appellants and Southwest Blood Bank.

The evidence discloses at least four conversations between the parties concerning payment for services to be furnished the patient. Appellants were at the hospital the day after William H. Rowe was admitted, and while there, discussed with appellee the matter of making financial arrangements. Appellee explained to appellants that the patient was very ill and would require extensive treatment. Appellants informed appellee that their father had no financial means, nevertheless, appellant, M. H. Rowe, stated that appellants themselves would pay for such services. * * * Subsequently on July 29, appellants, accompanied by their wives, came to the hospital, and again appellant, W. H. Rowe, stated to appellee: "Well, we want you to do everything you can to save his life and we don't want to to spare any expense because whatever he needs, doctor, you go ahead and get it and I will pay you." On July 31, the date of the operation, appel-

lants were at the hospital, and again the question of payment of expenses was renewed. At that time, M. H. Rowe voluntarily authorized the services of special nurses, stating: "because whatever he needs, I want him to have it and I will pay you for it." To which appellant William W. Rowe assented as follows: "That is correct, anything that—any expense." "Do not spare any expense on my father and I will pay you for it." The testimony of both Dr. Kinne and Dr. Andrews lends strong support to appellee. This evidence is substantial. Further, some three weeks later the business manager of the hospital phoned appellants and advised them that the expenses were continuing to mount, and asked them to come in and discuss the matter. They did, but stated they were just then short of cash. Appellant, M. H. Rowe, said: "We will pay you $200 now and then we will pay you $200 every month." He stated further: "My father has some property back in Missouri and we will put it on the market for sale and that when we sell the property why we will pay the entire balance off in full." Appellant, William W. Rowe, spoke up, saying, "that is correct". They then paid $200 and $45 later when threatened with litigation.

Of course, in the absence of an expressed contract, appellants would have been under no legal obligation to pay for the services rendered to their father. [Citations.] But it was at appellants' request, and for their benefit, that the services were furnished; hence, the promise to pay was an original undertaking and is without the statute. [Citations.]

Appellants argue the point that appellee did not release the patient, William H. Rowe, from liability. True, but that is not important. Appellants, having contracted for the services, are in no position to complain that the father had not been released. [Citations.]

[Judgment affirmed.]

Main Purpose Doctrine

STUART STUDIO, INC. v. NATIONAL SCHOOL OF HEAVY EQUIPMENT, INC.

(1975) 25 N.C.App. 544, 214 S.E.2d 192.

In this action plaintiff seeks to recover of the defendant, National School of Heavy Equipment, Inc., (hereafter School), and the individual defendants the sum of $18,010.02 under a contract whereby it produced catalogues for use by the School in promoting its services. The School has been adjudged a bankrupt corporation, and plaintiff has obtained a judgment against the School in the sum claimed, plus interest. By amended complaint plaintiff seeks to recover of individual defendant, Gilbert S. Shaw, the sum of $17,828.02 for purchasing and supervising the printing of the catalogues, claiming that Shaw promised, when the contract was made on 6 March 1972, to stand behind or guarantee payment.

It was stipulated that all work pursuant to the contract was completed and catalogues delivered to and accepted by the School on 7 July 1972.

It appeared from the evidence that Gilbert S. Shaw was Chairman of the Board of Directors of the School and drew a salary of $2,000 per month. He held 100% of the voting stock and 49% of the Class B stock of the School; he employed various members of his family in the operation of the School, including his son, Donald T. Shaw, as President.

Plaintiff is an art studio. Its president, Keith Stuart, had a conversation with Gilbert Shaw and Donald Shaw in August 1971, about the preparation of a new catalogue for the School, and in September, 1971, all agreed that plaintiff was to produce the camera-ready art for the catalogue. Plaintiff completed this work and the School accepted the format. There was a discussion between Stuart and the Shaws about the printing. Plaintiff does not do printing but in some cases purchased the printing

for its clients. In a meeting on 6 March 1972, when the camera-ready art work was virtually finished, Gilbert Shaw requested Stuart to purchase and supervise the printing of 25,000 catalogues. They discussed payment of printing costs, and Gilbert Shaw told Stuart that payment would be made within ten days after billing and that if the *National School could not pay the full total that he would stand good for the entire bill.*

Plaintiff then contracted in its name for the printing. The School made an advance payment of $2,000 to plaintiff on 23 March 1972. Plaintiff delivered the catalogues to the School on 7 July 1972 with its invoice. To requests for payment thereafter, Donald T. Shaw, Gilbert S. Shaw being overseas, replied that the School did not have the money but expected to get it.

At the completion of plaintiff's evidence, the individual defendants moved for directed verdicts, and from judgment granting the motions, the plaintiff appeals. It appears from the amended complaint, filed after entry of judgment, that plaintiff has elected to proceed only against the individual defendant, Gilbert S. Shaw.

CLARK, J.
* * *

The North Carolina Statute of Frauds, a substantial prototype of the historic English statute, 29 Charles II (1676) Ch. 3, Sec. 4, contains the provision that "no action shall be brought * * * upon a special promise to answer the debt * * * of another person, unless the agreement upon which such action shall be brought, or some memorandum or note thereof, shall be in writing, and signed by the party charged therewith or some other person thereunto by him lawfully authorized." [Citations.]

The promise of Gilbert S. Shaw to stand good for the debt of National School of Heavy Equipment, Inc., to be incurred for the printing of catalogues was not in writing and was within the Statute of Frauds unless plaintiff has offered evidence to invoke the application of the "main purpose rule", which is a well-known exception to the rule requiring that such promises be evidenced by a written memorandum.

The "main purpose rule" is stated in Burlington Industries v. Foil, 284 N.C. 740, 748, 202 S.E.2d 591, 597 (1974), as follows:

* * * [W]henever the main purpose and object of the promisor is not to answer for another, but to subserve some pecuniary or business purpose of his own, involving either a benefit to himself, or damage to the other contracting party, his promise is not within the statute, although it may be in form a promise to pay the debt of another, and although the performance of it may incidentally have the effect of extinguishing that liability.

The transaction between plaintiff and the defendants involved two separate and distinct operations in the production of catalogues for the School: (1) the camera-ready art, which plaintiff prepared, and (2) the printing, which was outside the scope of plaintiff's business and was purchased from and done by printers under the supervision of plaintiff. The cost of printing was several times that of the camera-ready art. At the 6 March 1972 meeting, plaintiff's President, Keith Stuart, sought assurances that the cost of printing would be paid within ten days after billing; then Gilbert S. Shaw made the promise that if the School "could not pay the full total that he would stand good for the balance or for the entire bill."

This promise of Gilbert S. Shaw was supported by a new consideration, the agreement to purchase and supervise the printing of the catalogues, which plaintiff had not previously agreed to do. Shaw's personal and pecuniary interest in the transaction was evident; he was the founder of the School, owned 100% of the Class A voting stock and 49% of the Class B stock, was Chairman of the Board of Directors, and as an officer drew a monthly salary of

$2,000. At this time, 6 March 1972, it is reasonable to assume that the School was facing financial difficulty; Shaw personally advanced $12,000 to the School during this period of financial distress. The School went into receivership in December 1972, and bankruptcy in March 1973. Apparently, Shaw sought, in a final effort to avoid the School's financial ruin, to attract new students through an advertising campaign, which included the production and circulation of new catalogues.

Burlington Industries v. Foil, supra, a 1974 decision, culminates a line of cases which have developed the "main purpose rule" and prescribed its limitations. The *Foil* case holds that the benefit accruing to a party merely by virtue of his position as a stockholder, officer, or director is not alone such personal, immediate and pecuniary benefit as to invoke the main purpose rule, and that Foil's evidence failed to establish the required *direct interest* on the part of *Foil*.

In *Foil*, supra, the Court cited with approval the cases of May v. Haynes, 252 N.C. 583, 114 S.E.2d 271 (1960) and Warren v. White, 251 N.C. 729, 112 S.E.2d 522 (1960). In Warren v. White, supra, defendant promisor was the principal investor and owned most of the capital stock, and during a period of financial difficulty advanced in excess of $23,000 to the corporation. In May v. Haynes, supra, the defendant and his wife owned the entire capital stock of the corporation, and he was its president, managing officer and controlling stockholder. In both of these cases it was held that the evidence was sufficient to invoke the main purpose rule and in doing so it is obvious that the significant, if not controlling, factor was the extent of the promisor's control over the corporation.

In this case the evidence offered by the plaintiff tends to show that Gilbert S. Shaw had a personal and direct interest in the School; and the evidence is clearly sufficient to raise an issue for jury determination. We find that the trial court improvidently granted defendant's motion for directed verdict and the judgment is modified and the cause remanded for trial on the issue of the liability of Gilbert S. Shaw on the printing contract of 6 March 1972.

Modified and remanded.

*Agreements Not to Be
Performed within One Year*

CO–OP DAIRY, INC. v. DEAN

(1968) 102 Ariz. 573, 435 P.2d 470.

MCFARLAND, VICE C.J.

Plaintiff-appellee Charles W. Dean, hereinafter referred to as Dean, sued defendant-appellant Co-Op Dairy, Inc., hereinafter referred to as Dairy, for damages for breach of an oral contract to employ Dean and to reimburse him for his moving expenses from Ardmore, Oklahoma, to Phoenix, Arizona. From a judgment on a jury verdict in Superior Court, Dairy has appealed.

The facts, stated most favorably to Dean, are as follows:

On Februrary 12, 1962, Dairy's general manager, Gerald J. Patsey, hired Dean as sales manager at a guaranteed salary of $1,000 per month. The employment period was to be "for a minimum period of one year," and the agreement provided for the payment of Dean's moving expenses. The day after Dean was hired, he signed a one-year lease on a Phoenix apartment. He then went to Oklahoma, picked up his family, arranged to have household goods moved to Phoenix, and, on February 26, 1962, he "reported for active work." After he had worked a few days, all the delivery and supervisory personnel of Dairy resigned, and refused to return to work unless and until Patsey and Dean were fired. In order to avoid a massive loss of customers from lack of service, and a large loss of milk from spoilage, Dairy capitulated to the drivers' demands and fired the two men. For the

approximately nine days that he worked, Dean was paid $1,000 "for the period ending March 8, 1962." He sued for his salary for the year, less what he was paid, and less what he earned in another job after being fired, plus his moving expenses. It was conceded that what work Dean did for Dairy was eminently satisfactory.

The jury, in addition to bringing in a general verdict for $6,000.38 for wages and $776.53 for moving expense, answered two special interrogatories by finding that there was an agreement between the parties to hire Dean for one year, and that Dairy agreed to pay Dean's moving expenses. The evidence was ample to justify the verdict and special findings.

Dairy contends that a contract of employment to start in the future, and to continue for one year, is within the Statute of Frauds, and that therefore this action cannot be maintained. As a general rule of law this is true. A.R.S. § 44–101 provides that no action shall be brought upon any oral agreement "which is not to be performed within one year from the making thereof." [Citations.]

Dean contends that a contract for one year's employment, to commence the day following the making of the contract, is not within the Statute of Frauds, [citation.] We agree. So does Dairy in its brief. The difficulty in the instant case is that the facts are not entirely clear, and the special interrogatories submitted to the jury contained no requirement that they find when the employment contract was to begin. We know that the contract was made, orally, between Patsey and Dean on February 12, 1962. We know that the contract was to guarantee Dean $1,000 per month, and that it was to run for one year. But, nowhere in the record is there a scintilla of evidence from which one can determine when the contract was to start. It is undisputed that Dean reported for work February 26th, after having gone back to Oklahoma to get his family and to arrange for the transportation of his household goods. On cross-examination, Dean was asked whether there was any specific time that he was to start working, and he answered that there was not. However, he was also asked: "When you left * * * Mr. Patsey on February 12th it was understood that you would not start work until you had moved your family out from Ardmore, Oklahoma?" and the answer was "That is correct, sir."

We need not take this statement literally. That could mean that he did not *have* to come to work until he had moved his family. It could mean that he would not come to work until he had *arranged* to move his family. However, it does not show they agreed he *could not* commence work until he had returned to Oklahoma and personally made all the arrangements. It did not mean that he could not call his wife that night, tell her to arrange for shipping the furniture and to take a plane or bus to Phoenix, so that he could start work the next day.

The conversations between Dean and Patsey, leading up to the contract of hiring, show that Dean was somewhat timid about nailing down the term of the contract. Patsey testified that Dean inquired about a contract, and Patsey told him:

"Any man that comes in on a job like this has always got a year to prove himself. I pointed out that I had no contract with Coop Dairy. I said that I have never been too much for contracts."

* * * Clearly, Dean's leasing of an apartment is no proof that the contract had begun to operate. At the same time, Dean's failure to report to work until February 26 does not prove that he could not have reported for work on February 13th.

* * * One principle that generally has been upheld is that the words "not to be performed within one year" mean *"impossible to be performed within one year."*

"In its actual application, however, the courts have been perhaps even less friendly to this provision than to the other provisions of the statute. * * * In general, the cases indicate that there must not be the *slightest possibility* that it can be fully performed within one year. It makes no difference how long the agreed performance may be delayed or over how long a period it may in fact be continued. It makes no difference how long the parties expect performance to take, or how reasonable and accurate those expectations are, if the agreed performance can *possibly* be completed within one year." [Italics ours.] 2 Corbin on Contracts 534

[Citations.]

* * *

We are inclined to agree with the court in Farmer v. Arabian American Oil Company, 277 F.2d 46, 85 A.L.R.2d 1321 (cert. denied, 364 U.S. 824, 81 S.Ct. 60, 5 L.Ed.2d 53) in which it said that the Statute of Frauds, applied to an employment contract, "is an anachronism in modern life and we are not disposed to expand its destructive force." We therefore hold that there was nothing to prevent Dean from turning over the moving details to his wife and going to work the next day. Had he done so, the Statute of Frauds would not be applicable. Though he did not do so, the mere fact that he could have done so takes the contract out of the Statute of Frauds.

Judgment affirmed.

A Writing or Memorandum

ALICE v. ROBETT MANUFACTURING CO.

(1970, D.C.Ga.) 328 F.Supp. 1377.

SIDNEY O. SMITH, JR, C. J.

* * * The complaint * * * for breach of contract * * *. Plaintiff seeks recovery of a judgment in excess of $10,000. The defendant's motion for summary judgment triggers this order.

Plaintiff alleges that in response to an invitation to bid from the General Services

Administration, he solicited an offer from the defendant to manufacture certain clothing, which plaintiff intended to supply to the Government. It is undisputed that on April 29, 1969, the defendant offered to produce 3,500 shirts at $4.00 each, and 3,500 pairs of pants at $3.00 each for the plaintiff. Plaintiff asserts that he accepted the offer and informed the defendant that its price quotation would be the basis for his bid to GSA.

On or about May 8, 1969, defendant having received the same invitation to bid as had plaintiff, the defendant submitted its own bid go GSA, offering to produce 3,500 "uniforms" at $7.78 each. On June 10, 1969, the defendant was awarded the contract for the production of this clothing. Eleven months later plaintiff filed this action. The thrust of Count I is that having entered a binding sub-contract with plaintiff for the production of this clothing for the Government, the defendant breached that contract by bidding directly with GSA for the same job.

* * *

The thrust of defendant's motion as to Count I of the complaint is that since plaintiff never accepted the defendant's offer, there was never any contract between them.

Apparently, the defendant contends that its offer was in writing. But plaintiff argues, and defendant's letter * * * shows that on the same day the letter was written the parties had a telephone conversation concerning the defendant's production of clothing for the plaintiff. It is the plaintiff's contention, supported by his affidavit, that during that conversation the defendant made an oral offer which was immediately accepted in the same fashion. Under such a theory, the defendant's letter would serve as a memorandum of the telephonic agreement. In order to recover on this theory, that memorandum would have to satisfy the statute of frauds, since the

alleged transaction involved a sale of goods for more than $500.

Under Georgia law prior to the adoption of the Uniform Commercial Code, a writing was not sufficient to comply with the requirements of the statute of frauds unless it contained *all* the terms of the agreement. [Citations.] It is clear, however, that Ga.Code Ann. § 109A–2–201 (1962) changes that rule of law. First, the Legislature repealed the old statute of frauds relating to the sale of goods * * * in adopting the Uniform Commercial Code. [Citation.] Secondly, according to the Official Comments:

The changed phraseology of this section is intended to make it clear that:
1. The required writing need not contain all the material terms of the contract and such material terms as are stated need not be precisely stated. All that is required is that the writing afford a basis for believing that the offered oral evidence rests on a real transaction. It may be written in lead pencil on a scratch pad. It need not indicate which party is the buyer and which the seller. The only term which must appear is the quantity term which need not be accurately stated but recovery is limited to the amount stated. The price, time and place of payment or delivery, the general quality of the goods, or any particular warranties may all be omitted.

* * *

Only three definite and invariable requirements as to the memorandum are made by this subsection. First, it must evidence a contract for the sale of goods; second, it must be "signed" a word which includes any authentication which identifies the party to be charged; and third, it must specify a quantity." U.C.C. § 2–201, Comment 1.

The courts of other states have given effect to the changes which this Comment states were intended. *E.g.*, Areuri v. Weiss, 198 Pa.Super. 506, 184 A.2d 24 (1962) (§ 2–201(1) doesn't require a writing which embodies all the essential terms of the contract); Azevedo v. Minister, 471 P.2d 661 (Nev.1970); and Southwest Engineering Co. v. Martin Tractor Co., 205 Kan. 684, 473 P.2d 18 (1970) (the memorandum need contain only the three elements specified in the Comment).

But it does not appear that the letter upon which the plaintiff must rely is a sufficient memorandum to satisfy even the minimal requirements of Ga.Code Ann. § 2–201. The letter states:

Confirming our telephone conversation, we are pleased to offer the 3500 shirts at $4.00 each and the trousers at $3.00 each with delivery approximately ninety days after receipt of order. We will try to cut this to sixty days if at all possible.

This, of course, is quoted f. o. b. Atlanta and the order will not be subject to cancellation, domestic pack only.

Thanking you for the opportunity to offer these garments, we are

Very truly yours,
ROBETT MANUFACTURING CO.,
INC.

Although it is not signed, the defendant admits its authenticity. Nevertheless, it does not evidence a contract for the sale of goods, but very clearly is only an offer.

* * *

Accordingly, the defendant's motion for summary judgment must be, and hereby is, granted.

It is so ordered.

Written Confirmation

CAMPBELL v. YOKEL

(1974) 20 Ill.App.3d 702, 313 N.E.2d 628.

CREBS, J.

This is an appeal from an order of the Circuit Court of Edwards County granting defendants' motion for a summary judgment and dismissing plaintiffs' complaint.

Plaintiffs, owners and operators of the Campbell Grain and Seed Company, alleged in the complaint that they had reached an oral agreement on February 7, 1973 with the defendant farmers. It was alleged that the defendants agreed to sell and the plaintiffs agreed to purchase 6,800 to 7,200 bushels of yellow soybeans at a price of $5.30 per bushel. Defendants admit that such an agreement was reached but maintain that the agreement was tentative and was not intended to be binding unless a written contract was signed. After the conversation between plaintiffs and defendants on February 7, 1973, the plaintiffs signed and mailed to the defendants a written confirmation of the oral agreement. Defendants received the written confirmation but did not sign it or give any notice of objection to its contents to the plaintiffs.

* * *

Defendants refused to deliver any soybeans to the plaintiffs and on April 30, 1973, informed the plaintiffs that, since the defendants did not sign the written confirmation, they did not feel bound by any agreement.

Plaintiffs' complaint requested damages or, in the alternative, specific performance of the alleged contract. Defendants' motion for summary judgment was based upon the pleadings and asserted the statute of frauds as a defense. The circuit court granted the summary judgment motion holding that, because the statute of frauds was a defense to the complaint, there was no genuine issue as to any material fact and that the defendants were not "merchants" within the meaning of Ill.Rev.Stat. ch. 26, sec. 2–201(2).

* * *

Plaintiffs contend that the court erred in finding that the defendant farmers were not "merchants" and that section 2–201(2) was not applicable. We agree.

Very few reviewing courts have attempted to resolve the question of whether a farmer is a "merchant" within the meaning of the various provisions of the Uniform

Commercial Code. In Cook Grains, Inc. v. Fallis, 239 Ark. 962, 395 S.W.2d 555, a case factually similar to the instant case, the Arkansas Supreme Court held that a farmer is not a "merchant" when he is acting in the capacity of a farmer and that he is acting in such a capacity when he is attempting to sell the commodities that he has raised. In Oloffson v. Coomer, 11 Ill.App.3d 918, 296 N.E.2d 871 the appellate court stated, by dictum, that a farmer in the business of growing grain is not a "merchant" with respect to the merchandising of that grain.

We disagree with the decisions in *Cook Grains* and *Oloffson* and feel that the reviewing courts in those cases failed to properly interpret the Uniform Commerical Code definition of "merchant." Ill. Rev.Stat. ch. 26, sec. 2–104(1) states:

(1) "Merchant" means a person who deals in goods of the kind or otherwise by his occupation holds himself out as having knowledge or skill peculiar to the practices or goods involved in the transaction or to whom such knowledge or skill may be attributed by his employment of an agent or broker or other intermediary who by his occupation holds himself out as having such knowledge or skill.

Growing crops are "goods" within the meaning of Article 2 of the Commercial Code [Citation]. The above definition of "merchant" leads us to the conclusion that a farmer may be considered a merchant in some instances and that one of those instances exists when the farmer is a person "who deals in goods of the kind * * * involved in the transaction."

The defendants in the instant case have admitted in discovery depositions that they have grown and sold soybeans and other grains for several years. They have sold to the plaintiffs and to other grain companies in the past. We believe that a farmer who regularly sells his crops is a person "who deals in goods of that kind."

The authors of the comments to the Uniform Commercial Code state that the term "merchant" applies to a "professional in business" rather than to a "casual or inexperienced seller or buyer." [Citation.] The defendants admittedly were not "casual or inexperienced" sellers. We believe that farmers who regularly market their crops are "professionals" in that business and are "merchants" when they are selling those crops.

Our decision does not place a great burden on farmers. As the comments to section 2–104 point out, the provisions in Article 2 of the Commercial Code dealing with "merchants" involve "normal business practices which are or ought to be typical of and familiar to any person in business." The practices involved are "non-specialized business practices such as answering mail." [Citation.] Placing this small burden upon farmers in certain instances lessens the possibility that the statute of frauds would be used as an instrument of fraud. For example, assuming that an oral agreement had been reached in the instant case, that the farmers had received the written confirmation signed by the plaintiffs and that the farmers were not "merchants," the farmers would be in a position to speculate on a contract to which the grain company was bound. If the market price fell after the agreement had been reached, the farmers could produce the written confirmation and enforce the contract. If the market price rose, the farmer could claim the protection of the statute of frauds and sell his crop on the open market. Our holding reduces the possibility of this type of practice in cases in which the farmer is a person who regularly sells crops of the kind involved in the transaction at hand.

In Ohio Grain Company v. Swisshelm, Ohio App. (Court of Appeals of Greene County, Rendered Dec. 5, 1973) the court held that a farmer was a "merchant" when he sold his soybean crop to a grain company.

* * * The defendants were in the business of growing soybeans and other grains and selling their crops to grain companies. They should be considered merchants, therefore, with respect to such sales.

For the foregoing reasons, we hold that the court erred when it determined that the defendants were not merchants. Our decision is not tantamount to a finding that a contract did exist between the plaintiffs and defendants. We hold merely that, since the defendants were merchants, section 2–201(2) operates to bar the defendants from asserting the defense of the statutes of frauds. The burden of pursuading the trier of fact that an oral contract was in fact made prior to the written confirmation is unaffected. * * *

[Reversed and remanded, with directions to proceed in accordance with view herein expressed.]

Admission/Payment and Acceptance

PRESTI v. WILSON

(1972 N.D.N.Y.) 348 F. Supp. 543.

Memorandum and Order

JUDD, J.

A motion by defendant seller in this diversity contract action asks summary judgment against plaintiff buyer on the basis of the statute of frauds. The action is one for damages for failure to complete the sale of a race horse.

Facts. The complaint asserts that plaintiff made an oral agreement with the defendant by a telephone call in October 1970 to buy a thoroughbred "Goal Line Stand" for the sum of $60,000, that he sent defendant a form of bill of sale and a check for the $60,000, post-dated December 1, 1970, and that defendant retained the check. It is asserted that defendant told plaintiff in a later conversation that he wished not to consummate the transaction until after January 1, 1971 for tax reasons, and that he would send the foal certificate in February 1971. The check was neither deposited nor negotiated, but plaintiff asserts that he kept money in his account to meet it.

Defendant asserts by answer and by affidavit that he never agreed to sell "Goal Line Stand" to plaintiff, that he never received a check from plaintiff for "Goal Line Stand," and that he never received the bill of sale which plaintiff describes.

Plaintiff's claim is supported by a copy of his check stub and by the affidavit of his executive assistant, who says that he monitored both telephone calls and prepared and mailed the bill of sale and the check.

The Law. The sale of a horse is governed by the Uniform Commercial Code covering sales of goods. The statute of frauds contained therein, U.C.C. § 2–201, states:

(1) * * * a contract for the sale of goods for the price of $500 or more is not enforceable by way of action or defense unless there is some writing sufficient to indicate that a contract for sale has been made between the parties and signed by the party against whom enforcement is sought or by his authorized agent or broker * * *.

* * *

(3) A contract which does not satisfy the requirements of subsection (1) but which is valid in other respects is enforceable * * *

    (b) if the party against whom enforcement is sought admits in his pleading, testimony or otherwise in court that a contract for sale was made * * *.

           or

    (c) with respect to goods for which payment has been made and accepted or which have been received and accepted.

Plaintiff seeks to avoid the statute of frauds on the basis of the two exceptions quoted, first that the statute would not apply if defendant admits that the contract was made and second that it does not apply where payment was made and accepted.

The cases are not consistent on the right to enforce an oral contract if the adversary can be induced to admit that the contract was made. There is New York law indicating that an admission in a deposition is involuntary and does not take the case out of the statute of frauds. Smith v. Muss, 203 Misc. 356, 117 N.Y.S.2d 501 (1952). There is contrary law in New Jersey. Cohn v. Fisher, 118 N.J.Super. 286, 287 A.2d 222 (1972). The New York decision dealt only with the question whether a deposition was a "memorandum" of the sale, since the Uniform Commercial Code, with its express exception for an admission of the contract, had not yet been adopted. [Citation.]

In any event, the exception for a party who admits the making of a contract is not applicable here, since the defendant has denied under oath that any agreement for sale was ever made with plaintiff.

Plantiff's second argument depends on establishing that the receipt and retention of a post-dated check constitutes payment and acceptance, even though the seller denies receiving the check and never negotiated it, and the check was stale before the suit was brought.

The statute of frauds permits a party to welch on an oral bargain, in order to avoid the risk that an oral contract may be proved by fraudulent testimony. The exceptions for part performance or payment and acceptance both involve mutual participation and not unilateral acts.

Defendant's liability should be tested by the rule set forth by the New York Court of Appeals in Young v. Ingalsbe, 208 N.Y. 503, 507, 102 N.E. 590, 591 (1913), that

The design of the statute requires that neither party can create the evidence which shall prove the unwritten contract as against the other.

The cases indicate that both the copy of plaintiff's check stub and the assertions of plaintiff and his executive assistant are ineffective as evidence which could be created by the plaintiff.

Issuance and acceptance of a check has been treated as payment and acceptance, permitting suit by the seller, even if the buyer subsequently stopped payment. [Citations.] The result may be different where the check does not show on its face that it constituted payment for the goods. [Citations.] * * *

Cases where the seller sues do not necessarily govern suits by a buyer. As against the buyer, his check may constitute a memorandum of the sale, if it refers to the goods in question. As against the seller, his endorsement of the check gives some objective evidence of receipt and acceptance of payment, even if the check is subsequently dishonored. * * * Where the seller has not endorsed or negotiated the check, however, there is no objective evidence of his assent to the sale.

Both payment and part performance, as exceptions to the statute of frauds, are based on the requirement of objective evidence of the assent of both parties. [Citation.]

Two threads run throughout the cases considering part performance or payment as an escape from the statute of frauds. First, payment without acceptance of the payment is not sufficient; tender alone does not constitute payment. [Citations.] Second, there must be some objective manifestation referable to payment and acceptance. [Citation.]

Assuming here that plaintiff made a tender of payment, the only alleged act by defendant which would manifest an acceptance of the payment is his statement that the check would be held until 1971 to gain a tax advantage. This is evidence which the plaintiff could create, and therefore is not an objective manifestation of assent to the contract.

The policy justification for the statute of frauds is hotly contested by legal scholars. The statute of frauds has been attacked in this country as an anachronism, and it was repealed in 1954 in England. [Citation.]

Problems

1. A was the principal shareholder in X Corporation, and, as a result, he received the lion's share of X Corporation's dividends. X Corporation was anxious to close an important deal for iron ore products to use in its business. A written contract was on the desk of Z Corporation for the sale of the iron ore to X Corporation. Z Corporation, however, was cautious about signing the contract, and it was not until A called Z Corporation on the telephone and stated that if X Corporation did not pay for the ore, he would, that Z Corporation signed the contract. Business reverses struck X Corporation and it failed. Z Corporation sues A. What defense, if any, has A?

2. Green was the owner of a large department store. On Wednesday, January 26, he talked to Smith and said, "I will hire you to act as sales manager in my store for one year at a salary of $18,000, you are to begin work next Monday." Smith accepted and started work on Monday, January 31. At the end of three months, Smith was discharged by Green. On May 15, Smith brings an action against Green to recover the unpaid portion of the $18,000 salary. Decision?

3. A, while driving, ran into B, injuring B and rendering him unconscious. There was some doubt as to who was at fault. A took B to a hospital, where he remained unconscious for twenty-four hours. On arriving at the hospital, A told the official in charge to treat B for his injuries, and stated that he would pay the bill. B was duly treated and cured by the hospital, but A refused to pay the bill. On being sued by the hospital, A pleads the Statute of Frauds as a defense. Decision?

4. Ames, Bell, Cain and Dole each orally ordered color television sets from Marvel Radio Company which accepted the orders. Ames's set was to be specially designed and encased in an ebony cabinet. Bell, Cain and Dole ordered standard sets described as "Alpha Omega Theatre." The price of Ames's set was $1,800 and of the sets ordered by Bell, Cain and Dole, $700 each. Bell paid the radio company $75 to apply on his purchase; Ames, Cain and Dole paid nothing. The next day, Marvel Radio Company sent Ames, Bell, Cain and Dole written confirmations captioned "Purchase Memorandum," numbered 12345, 12346, 12347 and 12348, respectively, containing the essential terms of the oral agreements. Each memorandum was sent in duplicate with the request that one copy be signed and returned to the company. No one of the four purchasers returned a signed copy, as requested. Ames promptly sent the radio company a repudiation of the oral contract which it received before beginning manufacture of the set for Ames or making commitments to carry out the contract. Cain sent the radio company a letter reading in part, "Referring to your Contract No. 12347, please be advised I have cancelled this contract. Yours truly, (Signed) Cain." The four television sets were duly tendered by Marvel Radio Company to Ames, Bell, Cain and Dole, all of whom refused to accept delivery. Marvel Radio Company brings four separate actions against Ames, Bell, Cain and Dole for breach of contract.

Decide each claim.

5. On March 2, Muir, a clothing manufacturer, received an order by telephone from Rice, the owner of a retail store, for 500 medium size Brand X shirts to be delivered March 23, at a price of $1,500, with payment due April 1. On March 3, Rice received from Muir a signed written confirmation which specified the above terms and also contained the following additional terms: "I have the shirts in stock and can deliver earlier if requested. A service charge will be imposed at the rate of one percent per month on any payments not received on or before April 1." On March 23, Muir tendered delivery of the shirts to Rice who refused to accept any of them because the shirts had recently gone out of style. As a result Muir had to sell the shirts elsewhere at the current market price, at a loss of $500, for which Muir sues Rice.

Decision?

6. A and B enter into an oral contract by which A promises to sell and B promises to buy Blackacre for $10,000. A repudiates the contract by writing a letter to B in which he states accurately the terms of the bargain, but adds "our agreement was oral. It, therefore, is not binding upon me, and I shall not carry it out." Thereafter, B sues A for specific performance of the contract. A interposes the defense of the Statute of Frauds, arguing that the contract is within the State and, hence, void and unenforceable. Decision?

7. On March 1, 1982, Lucas called Craig on the telephone and offered to pay him $50,000 for a house and lot which Craig owned. Craig accepted the offer immediately on the telephone. Later in the same day, Lucas told Annabelle that if she would marry him, he would convey to her the property then owned by Craig which was the subject of the earlier agreement. On March 2, Lucas called Penelope and offered her $6,000 if she would work for him for the year commencing March 15, and she agreed. Lucas and Annabelle were married on June 25. By this time Craig had refused to convey the house to Lucas. Thereafter, Lucas renounced his promise to convey the property to Annabelle. Penelope, who had been working for Lucas, was discharged without cause on July 5; Annabelle left Lucas and instituted divorce proceedings in July, 1982.

What rights, if any, have (a) Lucas against Craig for his failure to convey the property; (b) Annabelle against Lucas for failure to convey the house to her; (c) Penelope against Lucas for discharging her before the end of the agreed term of employment?

8. Ogle owned Clearview, a large dwelling with extremely odd shaped windows situated on 30 acres of land. Ogle became concerned with the high cost of oil and his high heating bills. After seeing an advertisement in a newspaper for "weather-tight" aluminum window sash, Ogle telephoned Robb Sash Co. and asked for an estimate. Ashby, owner of Robb Sash Co., convinced Ogle that "weather-tight" sash would greatly reduce oil consumption. Ashby offered to install such sash throughout Clearview for $3,400. Ashby stated that installation would be made by December 1, explaining that the order for manufacture must be sent to the factory in Ohio. Ogle told Ashby to go ahead with it.

The sash was manufactured and shipped to Ashby's plant, arriving there November 15. When Ashby telephoned Ogle's office to fix the time for installation, he learned that an electrical storm had killed Ogle and reduced Clearview to rubble. Ashby then telephoned Lucas, Ogle's executor, told him about the sash contract, and asked Lucas to see that the price was paid. Lucas refused to pay.

The manufacturer had billed Ashby for $2,200 for the sash, and he is obligated under the terms of the franchise to pay this sum to the manufacturer. What rights, if any, does Ashby have against Ogle's estate?

9. A orally promises B to sell him five crops of potatoes to be grown on Blackacre, a farm in Minnesota, and B promises to pay a stated price for them on delivery. Is the contract enforceable?

13

CONTRACTS IN
WRITING: PAROL
EVIDENCE RULE
AND
INTERPRETATION
OF CONTRACTS

The manifestation of mutual assent necessary to the formation of a contract may be oral, implied from conduct, or written. There is no legal requirement that any agreement must be in writing in order to be contractual. As noted in the preceding chapter, non-compliance with the Statute of Frauds does not nullify a contract, but simply makes it unenforceable.

It is good business practice to have all important contracts in writing and signed by the parties. The writing should express the terms of the agreement clearly, completely, and unambiguously. This will eliminate or reduce the area of possible future dispute between the parties. Furthermore, in the event of a lawsuit, proof of the existence of a contract and its terms will not depend upon the oral testimony of witnesses at the trial, some of which may be conflicting, but upon the introduction in evidence of a signed writing.

This chapter will consider contracts in writing from the standpoint of (1) the Parol Evidence Rule whereby a court may not change, alter, or vary the terms of an un-

ambiguous written contract; and (2) Interpretation of Contracts, which deals with the rules and guidelines whereby courts ascertain the meaning of words contained in ambiguous written contracts.

THE PAROL
EVIDENCE RULE

The word "parol" literally means "speech" or "words." The term "parol evidence" refers to any evidence consisting of words, either spoken or written, which are not contained in a written contract or incorporated therein by reference.

THE RULE

The parol evidence rule applies only to an integrated agreement or contract, that is, one in which the parties have assented to a certain writing or writings as the statement of the agreement or contract between them. When there is such an integration of an agreement or contract, parol evidence of any prior agreement will not be permitted to vary, change, alter, or modify any of the terms or provisions of the written agreement.

The reason for the rule is that the parties, by reducing their agreement to writing, are regarded as having intended the writing which they signed to include the whole of their agreement. The terms and provisions contained in the writing are there because the parties intended them to be in their contract. Any provision not in the writing is regarded as having been omitted because the parties intended that it should not be a part of their contract. The rule excluding evidence which would tend to change, alter, vary, or modify the terms of the written agreement is therefore a rule which safeguards the contract as made by the parties.

SITUATIONS TO WHICH
THE RULE DOES NOT APPLY

The parol evidence rule, in spite of its name, is not an exclusionary rule of evidence, nor is it a rule of construction or interpretation. It is a rule of substantive law which defines the limits of a contract. Bearing this in mind, as well as the reason underlying the rule, it will be readily understood that the rule does not apply to any of the following:

1. A contract which is partly written and partly oral. Where a written offer is accepted orally, there is no integration of the contract in a writing.
2. A receipt for goods or merchandise. This is not a contract.
3. A clerical or typographical error which obviously does not represent the agreement of the parties. Where a written contract for the services of a skilled mining engineer provides that his rate of compensation is to be $1.00 per day, a court of equity would permit reformation of the contract to correct the mistake upon a showing that both parties intended the rate to be $100 per day.
4. The lack of contractual capacity of one

of the parties, such as proof of minority or insanity. Such evidence would not tend to vary, change, or alter any of the terms of the written agreement, but merely to show that the written agreement was voidable or void.
5. A defense of fraud, duress, undue influence, or illegality. Evidence establishing any of these defenses would not purport to vary, change, or alter any of the terms of the written agreement, but merely to show such agreement to be voidable or unenforceable.
6. A condition agreed upon orally at the time of the execution of the written agreement and to which the entire agreement was made subject. If A signs a subscription agreement to buy stock in a corporation to be formed, and delivers it to B with the mutual understanding that the agreement is not to be operative unless ten other responsible persons shall each agree to buy at least an equivalent amount of such stock, A is permitted to show by parol evidence this condition. Such evidence does not tend to vary, alter, or change any of the terms of the stock subscription, but merely to show that the entire written agreement, unchanged and unaltered, never became effective.
7. A subsequent oral mutual rescission or agreed modification of the written contract. Parol evidence of a later agreement does not tend to show that the integrated writing did not represent the contract between the parties at the time it was made.
8. Parol evidence of usage and custom which is not inconsistent with the terms of the written agreement is admissible to define the meaning of the language in the agreement, where both parties knew or should have known of the existence of the usage or custom in the particular trade or locality. Such evidence does not alter, change, or vary any of the terms or language of the written contract, but simply shows the meaning which the parties attached to the particular language.

9. Parol evidence is admissible to explain ambiguous terms in the contract. To enforce a contract, it is necessary to understand its intended meaning. Such interpretation is not to alter, change, or vary the terms of the contract.

SUPPLEMENTAL EVIDENCE

Under the Code although a written agreement may not be contradicted by evidence of a prior agreement or of a contemporaneous oral agreement, a written contract for the sale of goods may be explained or supplemented by (1) course of dealing between the parties, (2) usage of trade, (3) course of performance, or (4) evidence of consistent additional terms unless the writing was intended by the parties as a complete and exclusive statement of their agreement.

A course of dealing is a sequence of previous conduct between the parties which may fairly be regarded as establishing a common basis of understanding for interpreting their expressions and other conduct. U.C.C. 1–205(1).

A usage of trade is a practice or method of dealing regularly observed and followed in a place, vocation or trade. U.C.C. 1–205(2).

"Course of performance" refers to the manner and extent to which the respective parties to a contract have accepted successive tenders of performance by the other party without objection.

Section 2–202 permits supplemental consistent evidence to be introduced into a court proceeding. Such evidence is only admissible if it does not contradict a term or terms of the original agreement and would probably not have been included in the original contract.

INTERPRETATION
OF CONTRACTS

The parties may differ as to the proper or intended meaning of language contained in the written agreement, where such language is ambiguous or susceptible of different interpretations. To ascertain the proper meaning requires a construction of the contract. This does not involve any change, alteration, modification, addition to, or elimination of any of the words, figures, or punctuation in the written agreement, but is merely a construing of the language in order to ascertain its meaning. While the parol evidence rule precludes either party from introducing any evidence in a lawsuit involving the written agreement which would change, alter, or vary the language or provisions thereof, rules of interpretation or construction permit the introduction of evidence in order to resolve ambiguity and to show the meaning of the language employed and the sense in which both parties used it.

FUNDAMENTAL RULES
OF INTERPRETATION

While the written words or language in which the parties embodied their agreement or contract may not be changed by parol evidence, the ascertainment of the meaning to be given to the written language is outside the scope of the parol evidence rule. The written words embody the terms of the contract. However, words are but symbols. If their meaning is not clear, it may be made clear by the application of rules of interpretation or construction, and by the use of extrinsic evidence for this purpose where necessary. As stated in one case:

The great object of construction is to collect from the terms or language of the instrument, the manner and extent to which the parties intended to be bound. To facilitate this, the law has devised certain rules which are not merely conventional, but are the canons by which all writings are to be construed, and the meaning and intention of men to be ascertained. These rules are to be applied with consistency and uniformity. They constitute a part of the common law, and the application of them, in the interpretation and construction of dispositive writings, is not discretionary with courts of justice, but an imperative duty. Johnson County v. Wood, 84 Mo. 489 (1884).

Section 200 of the Restatement, Second, Contracts, defines interpretation as the ascertainment of the meaning of a promise or agreement or a term thereof. Where the language in a contract is clear and unambiguous, extrinsic evidence tending to show a meaning different from that which the words clearly import will not be received by a court. It is the function of the court to interpret and construe written contracts and documents. Rules of interpretation are adopted in order to apply a legal standard to the words contained in the agreement by which to determine their sense or meaning. Among these rules which aid interpretation are:

1. Words and other conduct are interpreted in the light of all the circumstances, and if the principal purpose of the parties is ascertainable it is given great weight.
2. A writing is interpreted as a whole, and all writings that are part of the same transaction are interpreted together.
3. Unless a different intention is manifested, where language has a generally prevailing meaning, it is interpreted in accordance with that meaning.
4. Unless a different intention is manifested, technical terms and words of art are given their technical meaning.
5. Wherever reasonable, the manifestations of intention of the parties to a promise or agreement are interpreted as consistent with each other and with any relevant course of performance, course of dealing, or usage of trade.
6. An interpretation which gives a reasonable, lawful, and effective meaning to all the terms is preferred to an interpretation which leaves a part unreasonable, unlawful, or of no effect.

7. Specific terms and exact terms are given greater weight than general language.
8. Separately negotiated or added terms are given greater weight than standardized terms or other terms not separately negotiated. Restatement, Second, Contracts, Sections 228 and 229.

For example, in an action for breach of a written sales contract the subject matter was described as "Season's output of cotton linters for season 1915–1916, about four hundred (400) bales." The defendant seller shipped to the plaintiff buyer 155 bales of linters which was the total output of its mill for the season. The buyer sued for failure to deliver 245 bales. Cotton linters were a by-product of defendant's cottonseed oil mill. The Court construed the contract as one for season's output and not for 400 bales, upon the ground that the specific language controlled the general, and held for defendant. Kenan, McKay & Spier v. Yorkville Cotton Oil Co., 109 S.C. 462, 96 S.E. 524 (1917).

In addition, words contained in a document prevail over inconsistent figures and numerals. In Schorzman v. Kelly, 71 Wash.2d 457, 429 P.2d 217 (1967), the plaintiffs on September 20, 1955, leased from defendant landlord certain farm lands. The lease recited that "the landlord hereby leases to the tenants for ten years commencing on January 1, 1956, and ending December 31, 1966." On February 3, 1965, the landlord gave plaintiffs written notice that the lease would expire on December 31, 1965, and would not be renewable thereafter, and in April, 1965, leased the land to defendant Schorzman who in the fall of 1965 commenced plowing and seeding for a crop to be harvested in 1966. Plaintiffs filed suit to enjoin defendants landlord and the successor tenant from using the land for a 1966 crop on the ground that the lease did not terminate until December 31, 1966. The Court held for defendants stating that the words of the commencing date "January

1, 1965", and of the term "ten years" would prevail over the figures "December 31, 1966". The Court therefore concluded that plaintiffs had a ten-year lease which commenced with the 1956 crop year and terminated with the 1965 crop year.

A determination of the scope of coverage provided by a public liability automobile policy may involve distinquishing the word "use" from the word "occupy". Allstate Insurance Company had issued a policy to Edwin Boesken which covered both Boesken and his daughter Carol. Employer's Group Insurance Company had issued its policy to William O'Brien covering an automobile owned by O'Brien which while being driven one evening by Carol Boesken collided with another car causing injury and damage to third persons. O'Brien had given permission to his daughter Mary to drive his car that night, and knowing that Carol would be a passenger in the car told Mary not to let Carol drive. Contrary to this instruction Mary allowed Carol to take the wheel. Allstate admitted that its policy protected the Boeskens while driving another car, but contended that this coverage was abated to the extent of the liability of Employer's under its policy issued to O'Brien and covering the O'Brien car. The question was whether Carol was within the coverage of Employer's policy. This policy protected O'Brien, the named insured, and any other person "using" the car with his permission. Although Carol had O'Brien's permission to "occupy" the car as a passenger, she did not have his permission to "use" it in the sense of operating it. The Court held that Mary had no authority to delegate permission to use the car to Carol, and Carol was therefore not within the protection of Employer's policy. Allstate Ins. Co. v. Employer's Group Ins. Co., 18 Ohio Misc. 62, 246 N.E.2d 924 (1969).

In an action by the owner of truck-tractors and trailers to recover from defendant common carrier additional compensation for the transportation of freight pursuant to a written contract, the court held that the terms of a written contract may be changed by subsequent oral agreement between the parties. The contract provided that plaintiff would furnish trailer and tractor, employees for the unit, and pay all license fees and taxes, and would receive a certain percentage of the revenue received by defendant carrier on the hauls. During the period of the contract plaintiff made 28 trips hauling missiles or high-explosive radioactive materials which defendant had accepted for transportation under a contract with the government. On all regular hauls the plaintiff was furnished a bill of lading which indicated the revenue being paid to defendant carrier. There were no bills of lading on any of the 28 trips. These trips required a special trailer which plaintiff was unable to furnish and which was provided either by defendant or the government. Plaintiff contended that no new agreement was made with respect to his compensation for making these 28 trips. Defendant's office manager testified that before the first such trip was made, plaintiff agreed on $1 per loaded-mile. Plaintiff accepted compensation at this rate on the 28 trips over a period of 15 months, and did not complain of any underpayment on any of the trips until four months after the last trip was made. He then ascertained the amount of revenue which defendant had received for the 28 hauls and claimed the percentage thereof specified in the written contract, an additional $14,390. The Court held for defendant on the ground that under the evidence the 28 trips were not included within the written contract but were handled pursuant to subsequent oral agreement. Jenkins v. Watson-Wilson Transportation System, Inc., 183 Neb. 634, 163 N.W.2d 123 (1968).

U.C.C. PROVISIONS

To the above rules of interpretation should be added the Code provisions applicable to contracts for the sale of goods, namely, course of performance, course of dealing between the parties, and usage of trade, where these are not inconsistent with the express terms of the agreement.

By their actions in performing under the contract their respective duties the parties manifest a practical interpretation and indicate the meaning which they attribute to the terms of the contract. Course of performance is therefore an active recognition by conduct of the parties of the import of the contract and controls both course of dealing and usage of trade. It does not control a clear express term of the contract. Section 2–208.

A course of performance acquiesced in by the parties which differs from the express terms of the contract may result in a waiver of such express terms. A waiver of the express requirements of a contract to the extent that it remains unperformed may be retracted by reasonable notice provided that the party in whose favor the waiver would operate has not changed his position materially in reliance upon the waiver. Section 2–209(5) provides:

A party who has made a waiver affecting an executory portion of the contract may retract the waiver by reasonable notification received by the other party that strict performance will be required of any term waived, unless the retraction would be unjust in view of a material change of position in reliance on the waiver.

Through the application of the parol evidence rule, where it is properly applicable, and the above rules of interpretation and construction, it may be observed that the law not only enforces a contract but in doing so exercises great care that the contract being enforced is the one which the parties made, and that the sense and meaning of the manifested intentions of the parties is carefully ascertained and given effect.

Cases

The Rule

MITCHILL v. LATH

(1928) 247 N.Y. 377, 160 N.E. 646, 68 A.L.R. 239.

[The plaintiff brought an action seeking to compel specific performance by the defendants of an alleged oral contract to remove an ice house. The trial court entered a decree for the plaintiff. Defendants appeal.]

ANDREWS, J.

In the fall of 1923 the Laths owned a farm. This they wished to sell. Across the road, on land belonging to Lieutenant-Governor Lunn, they had an ice house which they might remove. Mrs. Mitchill looked over the land with a view to its purchase. She found the ice house objectionable. Thereupon "the defendants orally promised and agreed, for and in consideration of the purchase of their farm by the plaintiff to remove the said ice house in the spring of 1924." Relying upon this promise, she made a written contract to buy the property for $8,400, for cash and a mortgage and containing various provisions usual in such papers. Later receiving a deed, she entered into possession and has spent considerable sums in improving the property for use as a summer residence. The defendants have not fulfilled their promise as to the ice house and do not intend to do so. We are not dealing, however, with their moral delinquencies. The question before us is whether their oral agreement may be enforced in a court of equity.

This requires a discussion of the parol evidence rule—a rule of law which defines the limits of the contract to be construed. * * * It applies, however, to attempts to modify such a contract by parol. It does not affect a parol collateral contract distinct from and independent of the written agreement. It is, at times, troublesome to draw the line. Williston, in his work on Contracts (sec. 637) points out the difficulty. "Two entirely distinct contracts," he says, "each for a separate consideration may be made at the same time and will be distinct legally. Where, however, one agreement is entered into wholly or partly in consideration of the simultaneous agreement to enter into another, the transactions are necessarily bound together. * * * Then if one of the agreements is oral and the other is written, the problem arises whether the bond is sufficiently close to prevent proof of the oral agreement." That is the situation here. It is claimed that the defendants are called upon to do more than is required by their written contract in connection with the sale as to which it deals.

The principle may be clear, but it can be given effect by no mechanical rule. As so often happens, it is a matter of degree, for as Professor Williston also says where a contract contains several promises on each side it is not difficult to put any one of them in the form of a collateral agreement. If this were enough written contracts might always be modified by parol. Not form, but substance is the test.

In applying this test the policy of our courts is to be considered. We have believed that the purpose behind the rule was a wise one not easily to be abandoned. Notwithstanding injustice here and there, on the whole it works for good. Old precedents and principles are not to be lightly cast aside unless it is certain that they are an obstruction under present conditions. * * *

Under our decisions, before such an oral agreement as the present is received to vary the written contract, at least three conditions must exist. (1) The agreement must in form be a collateral one; (2) it must not contradict express or implied provisions of the written contract; (3) it must be one that

parties would not ordinarily be expected to embody in the writing; or put in another way, an inspection of the written contract, read in the light of surrounding circumstances must not indicate that the writing appears "to contain the engagements of the parties, and to define the object and measure the extent of such engagement." Or again, it must not be so clearly connected with the principal transaction as to be part and parcel of it.

* * * At least, however, an inspection of this contract shows a full and complete agreement, setting forth in detail the obligations of each party. On reading it one would conclude that the reciprocal obligations of the parties were fully detailed. Nor would his opinion alter if he knew the surrounding circumstances. The presence of the ice house, even the knowledge that Mrs. Mitchill thought it objectionable, would not lead to the belief that a separate agreement existed with regard to it. Were such an agreement made it would seem most natural that the inquirer should find it in the contract. Collateral in form it is found to be, but it is closely related to the subject dealt with in the written agreement—so closely that we hold it may not be proved. * * *

Judgment reversed.

Invalidated Consent

GANLEY BROS., INC. v. BUTLER BROS. BUILDING CO.

(1927) 170 Minn. 373, 212 N.W. 602, 56 A.L.R. 1.

[The defendant had three contracts for highway construction. It sublet all of the work in one of the contracts to the plaintiff who brought an action to recover damages for fraud. The contract between the plaintiff and defendant provided:

"The contractor [plaintiff] has examined the said contracts of December 7, 1922, and the specifications and plans forming a part thereof, and is familiar with the location of said work and conditions under which the same must be performed, and knows all the requirements, and is not relying upon any statement made by the company in respect thereto."

The trial court sustained a motion by defendant for judgment on the pleadings holding in effect that the plaintiff would not be permitted to prove fraud by reason of the above quoted provision in the contract. From an order denying its motion for a new trial, plaintiff appeals.]

WILSON, C. J.

* * * Parol evidence is admissible to show that the making of the contract was procured by fraudulent representations. This does not vary the terms of the contract. It is merely to show the presence of fraud which permits an avoidance of the contract. Established fraud impeaches its validity. A contract resting on fraud, when under attack, cannot stand. The fact that the contract has been reduced to writing does not change the rule. The contract as written was induced by the fraud. The evidence in proof of the fraud establishes the inducing or influencing cause and in no way varies or contradicts the terms of the contracts. This rule cannot be curtailed or destroyed by writing in the contract: "This contract was not procured by fraud." If so, a party could take advantage of his own fraud if he could succeed, by fraud if necessary, in getting into the instrument a clause negativing fraud. The evidence relates to an inducing cause, which is entirely distinct from the terms of the contract which are in no sense varied or modified. [Citations.] * * *

The authorities will not permit a distinction so as to allow the contract to be valid and binding to the extent that the defrauded party has agreed and unalterably committed himself to the fact that he has not relied upon any statements or representations of his adversary, but upon his own knowledge and information. Moreover this limitation would effectually destroy the general rule because in the absence of reliance there is seldom actionable fraud. Such theory would permit a party to do indirectly what he could not do directly. The contract as written may be an important factor to be considered in the determination of the facts.

The law should not and does not permit a covenant of immunity to be drawn that will protect a person against his own fraud. Such is not enforceable because of public policy. [Citation.] Language is not strong enough to write such a contract. Fraud destroys all consent. It is the purpose of the law to shield only those whose armor embraces good faith. Theoretically, if there is no fraud the rule we announce is harmless. If there is fraud the rule we announce is wholesome. Whether the rule is effective depends upon the facts. Public interest supports our conclusion. 2 Williston, Contr. par. 811, says:

"It seems clear that no agreement of the parties can preclude this defense, for fraud in the inception of the agreement renders voidable the very agreement not to set up fraud, and, aside from this technical but sound argument, such an agreement would obviously be against public policy."
* * *

Judgment reversed.

Interpretation

PHELPS DODGE CORP. v. BROWN

(1975) 112 Ariz. 179, 540 P.2d 651.

STRUCKMEYER, VICE CHIEF JUSTICE

This is an appeal from a judgment for the appellee, Louie E. Brown, against the appellant, Phelps Dodge Corporation, for $1,950.00.

The relevant facts reveal that appellant terminated appellee's employment on April 26, 1968. Prior to his termination, appellee had worked for appellant under an oral contract for approximately twenty-three years. In 1967, appellee was suspended from work forty-five days for unauthorized possession of tires belonging to the company, and in 1968, upon discovering that appellee was constructing a trailer on company time and using company property without authorization, appellant fired appellee. Appellee brought suit for damages for wrongful discharge, for a pension and for benefits under an Unemployment Benefit Plan (hereinafter referred to as the Plan). The only issue remaining for trial was whether or not appellee was entitled to recover under the Plan. The jury found for appellee. Reversed.

* * *

[The Plan provides]:

In order to be eligible for unemployment benefits, a laid-off employee must:

1. Have completed two or more years of continuous service with the company, and

2. Have been laid off from work because the company had determined that work was not available for him.

* * *

The trial court ruled, in denying appellant's Motion for Directed Verdict, that an ambiguity existed in the Plan as to who was eligible for the benefits since the requirement "Have been laid off from work because the company had determined that work was not available for him" was open to at least two possible interpretations. The trial court noted that the two possible interpretations were (1) that the company had determined it would not hire or continue to employ appellee under any circumstance and, therefore, work was not available for him, individually, and (2) it could be interpreted that the work category was not available for appellee or anyone else in his category. Because of the ambiguity, the trial court construed the contract against the party who chose the wording, in this case appellant.

It then determined that appellee was eligible for the payments since by firing appellee, appellant was saying that there was no work for appellee individually. The only issue thus left for the jury was whether appellant acted arbitrarily, capriciously, and without good faith in denying appellee eligibility to receive benefits under the Plan.

The object of all rules of interpretation is to arrive at the intention of the parties as it is expressed in the contract. [Citation.] There are many rules of interpretation which can be utilized in reaching the intent of the parties. These include giving words their ordinary meaning, giving technical terms their technical meaning, reading the contract as a whole, giving effect to the main purpose of the instrument, and interpreting the contract so as to make it effective and reasonable. [Citation.]

We believe the trial court, in construing the terms most strongly against the party who chose the wording, without first utilizing other rules of construction, acted contrary to standard principles. [Citation.]

Professor Corbin, criticizing the rules of construction used by the trial court, said:

It is frequently said that this rule is to be applied only as a last resort. It should not be applied until other rules of interpretation have been exhausted; nor should it be applied unless there remain two possible and reasonable interpretations. The rule is hardly to be regarded as truly a rule of interpretation; its application does not help to determine the meaning that the two parties gave to the words, or even the meaning that a reasonable person would have given to the language used." 3 Corbin on Contracts § 559 (1960).

From a reading of the entire contract, it becomes obvious that no ambiguity exists. It is clear that the contract was not meant to apply to someone who was dismissed for cause.

The Purpose of the Plan, Article III, specifically states who the Plan covers. This Article reads:

It is the purpose of this Plan to provide unemployment payments for laid-off employees to the extent and in the manner prescribed hereunder.

Article V, Part A, Eligibility for and Payment of Benefits, was quoted by the trial court in its instructions to the jury. Part B of that Article reads:

B. Determination of Eligibility.

When an employee is laid off the Company shall determine whether he is eligible for a Benefit. * * *

From a reading of the Plan as a whole, it is clear that it was to cover employees who were laid-off and not employees who were dismissed for cause.

The words "lay-off" and "discharge" have a normal and understood meaning in both common and industrial usage and the use of one instead of the other is sufficient to escape the charge of ambiguity. [Citation.]

* * *

The distinction has been recognized by other courts. For example, in Conner v. Phoenix Steel Corporation, 249 A.2d 866 (Del.1969), the court said:

Thus, 'discharge' normally means the termination of the employment relationship with no expectation of return, while 'lay off' normally means a temporary cessation of employment with an expectation of eventual return." 249 A.2d at 869.

In support of the finding that appellant had failed to specifically state who was eligible for benefits under the Plan, the trial court also noted that the terms "a quit", "discharge", "lay off", "disciplinary lay-off", and "laid off" were all used in the Plan but that none was defined. By reading the Plan as a whole and noting the context within which each of the terms was used, it becomes obvious that no ambiguity exists merely because the different terms were used but not defined.

The three terms, "a quit" "discharge" and "lay off" were used in defining what is meant by a break in employment. The Plan, in defining "Continuous Service", Article XIII, reads in part:

* * * The employment of an Employee shall be deemed to have been broken (a) by a quit, discharge or failure to return to work upon recall, or (b) except as otherwise provided in this definition, by a lay-off, absence for sickness, or leave of absence, of one year or more. * * *

* * *

The term "disciplinary lay-off" is included in the terms that signify why an employee is not actively at work. All the reasons apply to people who are on the payroll of the company and who are expected to return to work. An employee such as appellee, whose employment is terminated for cause, is not one who would still be on the payroll, nor would the company expect him to return to work. The term "disciplinary lay-off" must be understood to mean a situation where a person, while still an employee, is refused work for a temporary period of time because of wrongdoings. It cannot be construed to mean an employee in appellee's position.

The terms "laid-off" and "lay-off" are used in other places in the Plan. The context in which they are used support our construction.

* * *

Since as a matter of law no ambiguity existed and appellee was not entitled to recover under the Plan, it follows that there were no issues left for the jury to decide.

Judgment reversed with directions that judgment be entered for appellant.

Problems

1. A executes a written contract with B for the sale of A's building to B. Just before the parties sign the contract the parties agree orally that B will retain A as janitor for six months at a salary of $800 per month. One month later after B has taken possession of the building he discharges A. In an action by A against B, B raises the parol evidence rule to exclude evidence of the contract. Discuss B's defense. Decision?

2. On June 1, A entered into a written contract with B for the sale to B of A's entire cotton crop at thirty-five cents per pound. On September 1, A, B, and C orally agreed that C would be the buyer of A's cotton crop at a price of thirty-five cents per pound in lieu of B. C did not perform this agreement. In an action by A against B for breach of the contract of June 1, does the parol evidence rule exclude B's defense of the oral agreement of September 1?

3. A leased an apartment to B for the term May 1, 1981, to April 30, 1982, at $150 a month "payable in advance on the first day of each and every month of said term". At the time the lease was signed, B told A that he received his salary on the 10th of the month, and that he would be unable to pay the rent before that date each month. A replied that that would be satisfactory. Thereafter B paid his rent regularly on the 10th of each month through November 10, A making no complaint. On December 2, B not having paid the December rent A sued B for such rent. At the trial, B offered to prove the oral agreement as to the date of payment each month, and also that he had paid his rent regularly on the 10th of the month for the preceding seven months without any complaint by A. Decision?

4. A bought a car from the B Used Car Agency under a written contract. He purchased the same in reliance on B's agent's oral representations that the car had never been in a wreck and could be driven at least 2,000 miles without adding oil. Thereafter A discovered that the car had, in fact, been previously wrecked and rebuilt, that it used excessive quantities of oil, and that B's agent was aware of these facts when the car was sold. A brings an action to rescind the contract and recover the purchase price. B objects to the introduction of oral testimony concerning representations of its agent, contending that the written contract alone governed the rights of the parties. Decision on the objection?

5. A, a restaurant owner, entered into a written contract with Air Conditioning Company to purchase an air conditioning system and to have it installed in his restaurant. So far as material here, the written contract speaks of sale and installation of "air conditioning apparatus" described as "one G. E. warm air conditioning L. B. 4; one complete set of duct work; all controls for heating; complete installation for winter air conditioning; one oil tank." After the Company had installed the system, A refused to pay the agreed price. Air Conditioning Company sued A for the agreed price and A defended upon the ground that he signed the contract after being assured by the Company's agents that the installation would remove smoke, kitchen odors, purify the air and heat the premises, and that it had failed to do this. Air Conditioning Company contended that A was not permitted to prove what its agents may have told him, under the parol evidence rule. The contract recited: "This contract contains the entire agreement of the parties, and no representations or promises or warranties of any kind have been made except as contained in this written agreement". What are the rights of the parties?

6. In a contract drawn up by X Company, it agreed to sell and Y Contracting Company agreed to buy wood shingles at $3.25. After the shingles were delivered and used, X Company billed Y Company at $3.25 per bunch of 900 shingles. Y Company refused to pay because it thought the contract meant $3.25 per thousand shingles. X Company brought action to recover on the basis of $3.25 per bunch. The evidence showed that there was no applicable custom or usage in the trade and that each party held its belief in good faith. Decision?

7. On June 1, Owens and Price signed an agreement for Price to plant 3,000 apple tree seedlings between September 15 and October 15 on Owen's land. Owen was to supply the seedlings and Price was to receive $2,000. Before signing the agreement, Price and Owen agreed orally that the contracts would not be binding on Price until approved by Allen, his attorney. On September 15, Price started to plant. After he had planted 150 seedlings, his planter caught fire. He was unable to locate another one although the seedlings could have been planted by hand. On September 15, Allen informed Owen that the agreement was unacceptable.

(a) During trial of Owen vs. Price, may Price introduce testimony of the oral understanding? (b) Who prevails?

ASSIGNMENTS AND CONTRACTS FOR THE BENEFIT OF THIRD PARTIES

Prior chapters considered situations in which essentially only two parties were involved. This chapter deals with the rights of third parties, namely, persons who are not parties to the contract but have acquired a right to its performance.

These rights exist either by reason of (1) an assignment of the rights of a party to the contract or (2) the express terms of a contract entered into for the benefit of a third person. We shall consider these two situations in that order.

ASSIGNMENTS

HISTORICAL DEVELOPMENT OF THE LAW OF ASSIGNMENT OF CONTRACTUAL RIGHTS

A contract right to the performance of a promise is intangible. This is true whether the promise is oral or in writing. It is called a chose in action (thing in action) because the only way that the owner of the right can realize something from it is by maintaining an action at law against the obligor and reducing the claim to judgment.

At early common law, contract rights were not assignable. At that time the law regarded the personal identity of the obligor and obligee as vital parts of the obligations created by the contract. If B owed A 100 English pounds, and A assigned the claim to C, B did not have to pay C. He could take the position that his promise was to pay A, and only payment to A could amount to performance. It is still the law today that a revocable offer to contract is not assignable by the offeree.

The non-assignability of choses in action was very distressing and damaging to assignees who had acted innocently, in good faith, and in ignorance of the law. Numerous petitions of assignees were presented to the Lord High Chancellor requesting relief from the failure of the law courts to provide a remedy. Courts of equity, under the supervision of the Lord High Chancellor, were created to take jurisdiction of cases for which the courts of law provided either no remedy or an inadequate remedy. Thus, the rights of assignees became enforceable in equity. Their rights, however, were limited to and measured by the terms of the contract between the assignor and the obligor. They were subject to all defenses which would be available to the obligor if an action were brought against him by the assignor.

After courts of equity had taken jurisdiction, ultimately the rights of assignees became enforceable in courts of law. When this became established, courts of equity ceased to have jurisdiction. In the law courts, however, the cases were required to be brought in the name of the assignor for the use of the assignee. Most states have enacted a Real Party in Interest statute which permits such suits now to be brought in the name of the assignee, who is the real party in interest.

DEFINITION OF ASSIGNMENT

Frequently an assignment is referred to as a transfer. This should cause no misunderstanding on the part of anyone who knows the operation and effect of an assignment. Transfer usually connotes a passing of title or possession. As assignment is completely different from a transfer of goods, wares, and merchandise or of other tangible personal property. It is more precisely defined as a grant of an irrevocable power of attorney to collect a debt or the amount due upon a claim, together with the right of the assignee to retain the proceeds when collected.

The Restatement, Second, Contracts, Section 317(1), defines an assignment as:

A manifestation of the assignor's intention to transfer [a right] by virtue of which the assignor's right to performance by the obligor is extinguished in whole or in part and the assignee acquires a right to such performance.

What Amounts to an Assignment

No special form or particular words are necessary to create an assignment. Any words which fairly indicate an intention to make the assignee the owner of the claim are sufficient, and the assignment may be oral or written.

An Option Contract is Assignable

An option is a contract whereby an offeror is bound to keep an offer open for a stated period of time. Ordinarily, only the offeree may accept an offer. However, if performance by any person is equivalent to performance by the offeree, as in a contract which does not involve personal service or credit, an irrevocable offer to enter into such type of contract is assignable. Thus, if A gives B a thirty-day option to buy Blackacre for $25,000, B may assign this option to C, who, upon timely acceptance of the offer, enters into a contract with A for the purchase of Blackacre.

TYPES OF ASSIGNMENTS

Assignment of Future Rights

An assignment of rights expected to accrue in the future under a contract is enforceable to the extent that the rights arise. It is not operative as an assignment at the time of execution as the rights sought to be assigned do not then exist.

Wage Assignments

A wage-earner may assign future wages or salary as security for the payment of an existing debt, or as part of the consideration for a loan, or to secure payment of the price of goods purchased. Assignments of future wages are subject to statutes, some of which prohibit them altogether while others require them to be in writing and subject to certain restrictions.

Partial Assignments

The owner of a claim may assign portions of it or fractional interests in it to different assignees. He thus makes partial assignments of his claim. An assignee of a part of a claim has no right to sue the debtor in an action at law. The debtor or obligor is not required to perform in installments unless he has expressly or impliedly agreed to do so. Where his promise is to render a single performance, breaking it into piecemeal parts imposes a greater duty than he undertook. However, a partial assignee may sue in equity by naming as defendants not only the debtor or obligor but also all other partial assignees or persons having an interest in the claim. In such suit, the court of equity may enforce the liability of the obligor upon the entire claim as it has before it all parties in interest. It would be an undue hardship on the debtor to cause him to raise the same defenses in a number of suits brought in different courts by partial assignees.

Gift Assignments

A gift of property is ineffective without delivery of the property to the donee. An intangible contract right cannot be delivered in the sense that tangible property may be physically delivered. Nevertheless, the gift of a contract right may be accomplished by assignment, the donee acquiring a power of attorney to collect. A gift assignment, however, is revocable by the assignor, and is revoked by the death of the assignor. Revocation is ineffective if prior thereto the donee assignee has received payment of the claim from the debtor or has obtained judgment against the debtor. Where a contract right is identified with a document, such as a savings bank book, a policy of life insurance, a negotiable note of a third person, or a certificate of stock, a delivery of the document to the donee with the intention of making a gift is an irrevocable and effective assignment of both the document and the rights represented by it.

RIGHTS THAT ARE NOT ASSIGNABLE

Assignments Which Materially Increase Burden or Risk

An assignment is ineffective where performance by the obligor to the assignee would be different from performance to the assignor and would change the nature and extent of the duty of the obligor. Thus, a public liability automobile policy issued to A is not assignable by A to B. The risk assumed by the insurance company was liability for A's negligent operation of the automobile. Liability for operation of the same automobile by B would be an entirely different risk and one which the insurance company had not assumed. However, a bilateral contract for the purchase of coal in which no credit is extended to the buyer, may be assigned by either seller or buyer to a third person. If by the former, the seller assigns the right to the price and delegates the duty of delivering the coal. If by the latter, the buyer assigns the right to receive the coal and delegates the duty to pay the price. The respective performances, namely, delivery of the coal and payment of the price are essentially the same whether performed by the seller or buyer, or by a third person.

Assignment of Personal Rights

Where the rights and duties under a contract are of a highly personal nature, neither the rights can be assigned, nor the duties delegated. An extreme example of such contract is a contract of two persons to marry one another. A more common example of contracts of a personal character is a contract for the personal services of one of the parties. Whether the service is simple manual labor or is highly skilled or professional, the party having the right to the other's service cannot assign such right to another. One has the right to serve or work for whom he will, and cannot have another thrust upon him without his consent.

Express Prohibition against Assignment

At common law a contract may contain an express prohibition against any assignment of the rights created under it. The promisor may make his promise as narrow as he pleases and if the language in the contract clearly limits the rights thereunder solely to the promisee, an assignment by the promisee is ineffectual. The assignee of such a promise has a remedy only against the assignor for failure of consideration and breach of implied warranty.

Such prohibitions are now strictly construed. Most courts interpret a general prohibition against assignments as a mere promise not to assign. This construction allows the parties to effectively assign their rights under the contract, although by so doing the assignor would have breached the contract. The breach of contract, however, is regarded as not material and generally no damages will be awarded. In this way, most jurisdictions permit a party to assign the rights under the contract despite an express contractual prohibition to the contrary, unless the prohibition states that such an assignment will render the contract void.

Under the U.C.C., a provision in a contract which prohibits assignment of an account (as defined in Article 9) is ineffective. Section 9–318(4). Such a provision in a contract for the sale of goods, while ineffective to prohibit the assignment of rights, is construed, unless the circumstances indicate the contrary, as prohibiting delegation to the assignee of the assignor's duty of performance under the contract. Section 2–210(3).

A right of action arising out of the breach of an entire contract or out of complete performance by the assignor is assignable, notwithstanding an agreement to the contrary. Section 2–210(2).

RIGHTS OF THE ASSIGNEE

The assignee of a chose in action or claim stands in the shoes of the assignor. He acquires no new rights by reason of the assignment and takes the assigned claim with all of the defenses, defects, and infirmities to which it would be subject in a suit against the debtor by the assignor. This distinguishes an assignment from the negotiation of a negotiable instrument whereby new rights may be acquired by a negotiation of the instrument. In a suit by the assignee against the debtor, the latter may plead fraud, duress, no contract, failure of consideration, breach of contract, or any other defense which he may have against the assignor. The debtor may also assert rights of set-off or counterclaim arising out of entirely separate matters which he may have against the assignor provided they arose prior to his obtaining notice of the assignment. The debtor may also set off claims which he has against the assignee for the reason that the latter is before the court as plaintiff in the suit.

The U.C.C. permits the buyer under a contract of sale to agree as part of the contract that he will not assert against an assignee who takes an assignment for value and in good faith any claim or defense which the buyer may have against the seller. Such provision in an agreement affords greater marketability to the rights of the seller which thereby become analogous to the rights of a holder in due course of a negotiable instrument, who takes the instrument free of all claims and most defenses. Section 9–206. The Federal Trade Commission in 1977 invalidated waiver of defense provisions in consumer credit transactions. The rule is discussed more fully in Chapter 29.

Section 9–318(1) of the U.C.C. provides that unless a debtor has made an enforceable agreement not to assert defenses or claims as provided in Section 9–206, the rights of an assignee are subject to: (a) all the terms of the contract by the account debtor and assignor and any defense or claim arising therefrom; and (b) any other defense or claim of the account debtor against the assignor which accrues before the account debtor receives notification of the assignment.

An assignee will lose his rights against the debtor if the latter pays the assignor without notice of the assignment. The right of the assignee is essentially equitable and it would be unfair to compel a debtor to pay a claim a second time when he has paid it once to the only person whom he knew to be entitled to receive payment.

Notwithstanding notice of an assignment and except for a right to payment under an assigned contract which has already become an account receivable, a modification of, or substitution for the contract made between the debtor and the assignor in good faith and in accordance with reasonable commercial standards is effective against the assignee unless the account debtor has otherwise agreed. The assignee acquires corresponding rights under the modified or substituted contract. The assignment may provide that such modification or substitution is a breach by the assignor. Section 9–318(2).

Standing in the shoes of the assignor permits the assignee to have the benefit of any outstanding securities for the claim, even though not expressly assigned. If the claim has any right of priority in the hands of the assignor, such as a wage claim in bankruptcy, the assignee is entitled to the same priority as he is enforcing the right of the assignor.

IMPLIED WARRANTIES OF ASSIGNOR

In the absence of an expressed intention to the contrary, an assignor who receives value makes certain implied warranties to the assignee with respect to the assigned claim. The assignor does not guarantee that the debtor will pay the assigned debt or that the obligor will perform, but he does warrant that the right exists and is free of defenses except those which are disclosed to the assignee.

If an assignment is for value, unless a contrary intention is shown, the assignor warrants to the assignee:

1. that he will do nothing to defeat or impair the assignment,
2. that the assigned right actually exists, and is subject to no limitations or defenses other than those stated or apparent at the time of the assignment,
3. that any writing or evidence of the right delivered to the assignee or exhibited to him as an inducement to accept the assignment, is genuine and what it purports to be, and
4. that he has no knowledge of any fact that would impair the value of the assignment.

MULTIPLE ASSIGNMENTS

Sub-assignments

A chose in action or contract claim may be reassigned by the assignee. This is known as a sub-assignment. The sub-assignee may, in turn, become a sub-assignor and make a further reassignment of the claim. Every assignee or sub-assignee seeking to enforce the claim is subject to all of the defenses and rights of setoff which the obligor may assert against the original assignor. In this respect, the position of any sub-assignee is similar to that of the original or first assignee.

The right of an assignee under his assignor's warranties are not assigned to a sub-assignee by the mere assignment of the right against the obligor, but the rights under such warranties may be expressly assigned. Restatement, Second, Contracts, Section 333(4).

Successive Assignments of Same Right

The owner of a claim may conceivably make successive assignments of the same claim to different persons. Although morally reprehensible, the question is what are the rights of the successive assignees. Assume that B owes A $1,000. On June 1, A for value assigns the debt to C. Thereafter, on June 15, A for value assigns it to D, a bona fide purchaser who has no knowledge of the prior assignment by A to C. The first assignee C is in a position to give the debtor notice of his assignment before the second assignee D may do so. However, it is possible that the debtor B may receive notice of the second assignment before being notified of the first. The majority rule in the United States is that the first assignee in point of time prevails over subsequent assignees. In England, and in a minority of the States, priority of notice of the assignment to the obligor determines which assignee prevails. Even under the majority rule whereby the first assignee C prevails, if the second assignee D in good faith collects the amount of the claim from the obligor B, he will be allowed to retain the money thus collected; or if the second assignee D, acting in good faith, obtains judgment against the obligor B, he may enforce the judgment and retain the money collected thereon, although after the entry of the judgment but before collection he and the obligor were notified of the prior assignment to C. In any case payment by the obligor to the assignor, without notice of the assignment, completely discharges the obligor.

The Restatement, Second, Contracts, Section 342, adopts the majority American rule and provides that a prior assignee is entitled to the assigned right and its proceeds, to the exclusion of a subsequent assignee, except where (1) the prior assignment is revocable or voidable by the assignor; or (2) the subsequent assignee obtains payment or satisfaction of the obligor's duty; or (3) the subsequent assignee obtains judgment against the obligor; or (4) a new contract is entered into between the subsequent assignee and the obligor by means of a novation; or (5) the subsequent assignee obtains delivery of a tangible token or writing, the surrender of which is required by the obligor's contract for its enforcement.

DELEGATION OF DUTIES

Only rights under a contract are assignable. Duties may never be assigned, but their performance may be delegated to a third person if they are not of a type which involves the personal service or individual attention of the obligor, an attribute known as delectus personae (choice of person). Duties to perform personal services are not delegable if the obligee has a substantial interest in having that particular obligor's performance.

An obligor, moreover, may never rid himself of the duties under a contract without the consent of the obligee. Any delegation of a duty to a third person leaves the obligor bound to perform it. If the obligor desires to be discharged of the duty, it may be possible for him to enter into a third-party contract and obtain the consent of the obligee to substitute a third person in his place. This is a *novation* whereby the original obligor is discharged and the third party becomes directly bound upon his promise to the obligee.

At common law the mere assignment of a contract right does not impose upon the assignee any duty of performance. He is regarded as having an irrevocable power of attorney to collect the proceeds of the assigned claim or right and to retain them for himself. Unless he expressly assumes the obligations of the assignor, he is not liable for any breach of the contract out of which the assigned right arose.

Under the Code, however, with respect to transactions in goods, an assignment of "the contract" or of "all my rights under the contract" or an assignment in similar broad general terms is also a delegation of performance of the duties under the contract, and unless the language or circumstances indicates the contrary an acceptance of the rights under the assignment constitutes a promise by the assignee to perform such duties. This promise may be enforced either by the assignor or by the other party to the original contract. Section 2–210(4).

THIRD PARTY BENEFICIARY CONTRACTS

A contract in which a party promises to render a certain performance not to the promisee but to a third person is called a third party beneficiary contract. The third person is not a party to the contract but is a beneficiary of a promise contained in it. Such contracts may be divided into three types: (1) donee beneficiary; (2) creditor beneficiary; and (3) incidental beneficiary. A great majority of courts enforce both the donee beneficiary and the creditor beneficiary type of third party contract, but no court enforces the incidental beneficiary type.

DONEE BENEFICIARY

A third person is a donee beneficiary if the purpose of the promisee in bargaining for and obtaining the promise was to make a gift to the beneficiary.

Generally, the rights of a donee beneficiary vest at the time of the making of the contract, whether he has knowledge of it or not and he may not be divested without his consent.

The ordinary life insurance policy is an illustration. The insured makes a contract with an insurance company which promises, in consideration of premiums paid to it by the insured, to pay upon the death of the insured a stated sum of money to a ben-eficiary named in the policy. The beneficiary need not even know of the existence of the policy in order to have rights under it. If the policy does not reserve to the insured the right to change the beneficiary, the beneficiary has vested rights under the policy of which he may not be deprived without his consent. In most policies, however, a reservation by the insured of the right to change the beneficiary is a standard provision.

The desirability of allowing donee beneficiaries to recover on contracts made for their benefit is manifest. Upon breach by the promisor and a suit against him by the promisee, the damages which could be established by the promisee would be nominal. Unless the donee beneficiary is given the right to recover against the promisor, even though he furnished no consideration and is not in privity of contract with the promisor, the purpose of the parties to the contract is defeated and the content of the promisor's consideration loses its value. The donee beneficiary has no right of action against the promisee, who is his donor, and a denial of his right of recovery against the promisor would frustrate the agreement between the promisee and promisor.

An owner of property which was damaged as a result of blasting operations by defendants was held entitled to recover damages as third party beneficiary under a contract between defendants and Duluth, Minnesota, for certain sewer construction work which necessitated the blasting. The contract provided that defendants would be "liable for any damages done to the work or other structure of public or private property and injuries sustained by persons" resulting from the use by defendants of explosives. LaMourea v. Rhude, 209 Minn. 53, 295 N.W. 304 (1940).

It has been held that a Totten Trust created by deposit of funds in a bank savings account in the name of "Charles Wright, Pay on death to Mary Lowe" is enforceable not only as a trust but as a third party donee beneficiary contract between the donor depositor Wright and the depository bank, and entitles the donee to the funds in the account upon the death of the donor. Estate of Wright, 17 Ill.App.3d 894, 308 N.E.2d 319 (1974).

CREDITOR BENEFICIARY

A third person is a creditor beneficiary if no intention to make a gift appears in the contract and the performance of the promise will satisfy a duty owing by the promisee to the beneficiary. In this type of case the beneficiary is a creditor of the promisee, and the contract involves consideration moving from the promisee to the promisor in exchange for the promise to pay some debt or discharge some obligation of the promisee to a named third person. The making of the contract does not in any way change or affect the obligation of the promisee to the beneficiary as it previously existed. The creditor beneficiary has rights against both the promisee, based upon the original obligation, and against the promisor based upon the third party beneficiary contract. If neither performs, the third person can maintain separate suits against both and obtain judgments against both, although he can obtain satisfaction of only one of the judgments.

As to the creditor beneficiary's vesting of rights the general rule is that the parties to the contract may rescind or make a variation in the contract if the creditor beneficiary has not learned of it or assented to it. If the creditor beneficiary has not brought suit upon the promise nor otherwise changed his position in reliance upon it before the parties to the contract have rescinded or altered it by agreement, such rescission or variation of the contract is effective in all respects. Where the third party creditor beneficiary contract is executory on both sides a mutual rescission by the parties to the contract may be made at any time, and the creditor beneficiary has no ground for complaint.

The sale of real estate upon which there is an outstanding mortgage may be made to a purchaser who expressly assumes to pay the mortgage debt, or to one who merely acquires title to the land subject to the mortgage. Thus, A the owner of Blackacre which is encumbered by a mortgage securing A's note to B in the amount of $15,000, sells Blackacre to C who assumes the mortgage debt. B is a third party creditor beneficiary of the contract between A and C and has a right to enforce payment from C. A remains liable on the mortgage note but as surety because C should pay the debt and save A harmless. If C, instead of assuming the mortgage, had merely accepted a deed subject to the mortgage, he would not have become personally liable to pay B, and although C may lose his investment in Blackacre by a foreclosure sale, he is not in such case liable for any deficiency in the event the proceeds of such sale are not sufficient to pay the amount due on the mortgage.

INCIDENTAL BENEFICIARY

An incidental third party beneficiary is a person whom the parties to a contract did not intend to benefit, but who nevertheless would derive some benefit by its performance. For instance, a contract to raze an old, unsightly building and replace it with a costly modern house would benefit the owner of the adjoining property by increasing its value. However, he would have no rights under the contract as the benefit to him is unintended and incidental.

A third person who may be incidentally benefited by the performance of a contract to which he is not a party has no rights under such contract. It was not the intention of either the promisee or the promisor that the third person be benefited. Assume that for a stated consideration B promises A that he will purchase and deliver to A a brand new Buick automobile of the latest model. A performs. B does not. C, the local exclusive Buick dealer, has no rights under the contract although performance by B would produce a sale from which C would derive a benefit. C is only an incidental beneficiary.

In Northwest Airlines, Inc. v. Crosetti Bros. Inc., 483 P.2d 70 (Or.1971), plaintiff Northwest leased space in the terminal building at the Portland Airport from the Port of Portland. Defendant Crosetti entered into a contract with the Port to furnish janitorial services for the building which required Crosetti to keep the floor clean, to indemnify the Port against loss due to claims or lawsuits based upon its lack of performance, and to provide public liability insurance for the Port and Corsetti. A patron of the building who was injured by a fall caused by a foreign substance on the floor at Northwest's ticket counter brought suit for damages against Northwest, the Port, and Crosetti. Upon settlement of this suit, Northwest sued Crosetti to recover the amount of its contribution to the settlement and other expenses on the ground that Northwest was a third party beneficiary of Crosetti's contract with the Port to keep the floors clean and therefore within the protection of its indemnification agreement. The Court held that only two types of third party beneficiaries are entitled to recover; and that Northwest was not a creditor beneficiary as it was not a creditor of the Port since its lease contained no agreement by the Port to indemnify it; nor was it a donee beneficiary as there was no evidence of any intention of the Port in its contract with Crosetti to make a gift to Northwest or confer upon Northwest a right to indemnity. At most, Northwest was an incidental beneficiary, and as such had no right of recovery.

Cases

Rights of the Assignee

WISCOMBE v. LOCKHART CO.

(1980, Utah) 608 P.2d 236.

WILKINS, J.

This is an appeal from a judgment of the District Court quieting [establishing] title to certain real property in Plaintiffs and Respondents J. Elmer and Naomi B. Wiscombe (hereafter "Wiscombe") as against Defendant and Appellant Lockhart Company (hereafter "Lockhart"). We affirm.
* * *

On January 1, 1976, one Beardall, not a party to this appeal, purchased by Uniform Real Estate Contract certain real property located in Mapleton, Utah County, from Wiscombe. The Contract called for annual payments of $15,000 payable on the first day of January of each year with an initial payment of $15,000 made at the time of execution. The $15,000 payment due on January 1, 1977, was not received by Wiscombe. By Notice of Default dated January 31, 1977, and served on Beardall on February 2, 1977, Wiscombe gave Beardall five days in which to remedy his default. Beardall did not do so and quit the premises on or before February 7, 1977.

Unknown to Wiscombe, Beardall had on November 5, 1976, executed and delivered to Lockhart a promissory note secured in part by an Assignment of Contract whereby Beardall assigned to Lockhart all of his rights, title and interest in and to the Uniform Real Estate Contract of January 1, 1976. Lockhart subsequently recorded the Assignment.

Wiscombe first became aware of the existence of the Assignment by way of an abstractor's letter [a brief history of ownership of a parcel of real property] he had ordered prepared on the property. Shortly after learning about the Assignment—the letter report was dated February 14, 1977—Wiscombe's attorney wrote to Lockhart demanding that the Assignment be removed from the title to the subject real property. On March 1 and 2, 1977, Lockhart tendered Wiscombe $15,000 representing the payment due on January 1, 1977, under the Contract in question together with a tender of such additional costs and attorney's fees as had been incurred by Wiscombe. * * * By letter dated March 7, 1977, Wiscombe rejected Lockhart's tender. Lockhart refused to remove the Assignment and so Wiscombe brought suit against Lockhart * * * and to quiet title in Wiscombe.

After trial held June 8, 1978, the District Court issued its Memorandum Decision on August 1, 1978, quieting title in Wiscombe * * *. Lockhart then brought this appeal.

Lockhart maintains that the District Court erred in not recognizing Lockhart's interest in the real property in question, which interest Lockhart declares arose as a result of the Assignment. We think the District Court was correct in its decision for the following reasons.

Fundamental to the law of assignments is the concept that an assignee takes nothing more by his assignment than his assignor had. In *Tanner v. Lawler,* we stated:

An assignment merely sets over or transfers the interest of one party in certain property to another. Such an assignment does not have the effect of canceling any rights which other persons have in connection with such property.

The Uniform Real Estate Contract between Wiscombe and Beardall was properly foreclosed by Wiscombe in accordance with the terms of the Contract after Beardall's default. Beardall quit the premises in question on or before February 7, 1977, and

so certainly after February 7, the Uniform Real Estate Contract had no further viability of its own. Title to the property remained in Wiscombe no longer subject to the Contract.

Lockhart's tender on March 1 and 2, 1977, was therefore wholly ineffectual because it came almost three weeks after the Contract terminated. There was nothing which could be performed by Lockhart by way of its tender.

* * *

[Affirmed.]

Successive Assignments

BOULEVARD NAT. BANK OF MIAMI v. AIR METAL INDUS.
(1965 Fla.) 176 So.2d 94.

Willis, Cir. J.

* * * The "question" which was passed upon by the certifying court is whether the law of Florida requires recognition of the so-called "English" rule or "American" rule of priority between assignees of successive assignments of an account receivable or other similar chose in action. Stated in its simplest form, the American rule would give priority to the assignee first in point of time of assignment, while the English rule would give preference to the assignment of which the debtor was first given notice. Both rules presuppose the absence of any estoppel or other special equities in favor of or against either assignee. The English rule giving priority to the assignee first giving notice to the debtor is specifically qualified as applying "unless he takes a later assignment with notice of a previous one or without a valuable consideration". [Citations.]

* * *

The American rule for which petitioner contends is based upon the reasoning that an account or other chose in action may be assigned at will by the owner; that notice to the debtor is not essential to complete the assignment; and that when such assignment is made the property rights become vested in the assignee so that the assignor no longer has any interest in the account or chose which he may subsequently assign to another. [Citations.]

* * *

It is undoubted that the creditor of an account receivable or other similar chose in action arising out of contract may assign it to another so that the assignee may sue on it in his own name and make recovery. Formal requisites of such an assignment are not prescribed by statute and it may be accomplished by parol, by instrument in writing, or other mode, such as delivery of evidences of the debt, as may demonstrate an intent to transfer and an acceptance of it. * * *

It seems to be generally agreed that notice to a debtor of an assignment is necessary to impose on the debtor the duty of payment to the assignee, and that if before receiving such notice he pays the debt to the assignor, or to a subsequent assignee, he will be discharged from the debt. [Citation.] To regard the debtor as a total non-participant in the assignment by the creditor of his interests to another is to deny the obvious. An account receivable is only the right to receive payment of a debt which ultimately must be done by the act of the debtor. For the assignee to acquire the right to stand in the shoes of the assigning creditor he must acquire some "delivery" or "possession" of the debt constituting a means of clearly establishing his right to collect. The very nature of an account receivable renders "delivery" and "possession" matters very different and more difficult than in the case of tangible personalty and negotiable instruments which are readily capable of physical handling and holding. However, the very principles which render a sale of personal property with possession remaining in the vendor unexplained fraudulent

and void as to creditors applies with equal urgency to choses in action which are the subject of assignment. It would seem to follow that the mere private dealing between the creditor and his assignee unaccompanied by any manifestations discernable to others having or considering the acquiring of an interest in the account would not meet the requirement of delivery and acceptance of possession which is essential to the consummation of the assignment. Proper notice to the debtor of the assignment is a manifestation of such delivery. It fixes the accountability of the debtor to the assignee instead of the assignor and enables all involved to deal more safely.

* * *

We thus find that the so-called English rule which the trial and appellate court approved and applied is harmonious with our jurisprudence, whereas the so-called American rule is not. * * *

Donee Beneficiary

SAYLOR v. SAYLOR

(1965 Ky.) 389 S.W.2d 904.

PALMORE, J.

This is a declaratory judgment action to determine the ownership of a bank savings account. The facts are stipulated. The contest is between the administrator and the widow of Adrian M. Saylor. The trial court found in favor of the widow, and the administrator appeals.

The account was opened by Mr. Saylor on March 19, 1962; with the deposit of $6,540.65 derived from the sale of government bonds owned exclusively by him. The pass book issued by the bank to Mr. Saylor on March 19, 1962, was made out in the names of "Mr. or Mrs. Adrian M. Saylor," and the bank's ledger card for the account was established and thenceforth maintained in the names of "Adrian M. Saylor or Kathleen B. Saylor." Kathleen is the widow.

* * *

On June 15, 1963, Mr. Saylor deposited $2,132.60 of his own money in the account, and the deposit was entered in the pass book. There were no other deposits, and for purposes of this opinion it may be assumed that there were no withdrawals whatever, prior to the death of Mr. Saylor on May 15, 1964.

The question is whether the balance of the account at Mr. Saylor's death is payable wholly to the administrator, wholly to the widow, or half to each. The trial court held it was a survivorship account, passing wholly to the widow.

It is recognized in this state that a person may be depositing his own money in the names of himself and another create the equivalent of a tenancy in common or a tenancy by the entirety, depending upon his intent. [Citations.] As in the case of other intangibles such as bonds or stock certificates, the right gratuitously conferred on the other party is recognized and is enforceable on the theory of third party beneficiary contract. It is not necessary that such a contract be supported by a consideration moving from the beneficiary, and it is not necessary that a "gift" be proved. [Citation.]

"The prevailing modern view is that a donee-beneficiary has a right of action to enforce a promise made for his benefit. In this respect, the courts so holding have rejected any requirement of consideration, privity, or obligation as between the promisee and the third person." [Citation.]

"In this jurisdiction a party beneficiary of a contract may look to the promisor directly and sue him in his own name to enforce a promise made for plaintiff's benefit, even though he is a stranger, it being sufficient that there is a consideration between the parties who made the agreement for the benefit of the third party." [Citation.]

"It is not essential, in order to enable a third person to recover on a contract made and intended for his benefit, that he knew of the contract at the time it was made." [Citation.] A fortiori, that Mrs. Saylor did not sign the signature card or otherwise participate in the establishment of the account is immaterial.

By his deposit of money a contract was created between Mr. Saylor and the bank. By causing the account to be established and maintained in the names of himself and his wife, in the absence of evidence to the contrary there is a rebuttable presumption that Mr. Saylor intended to and did make his wife a third party beneficiary of the contract. * * *

That Mr. Saylor did not have Mrs. Saylor sign the signature card may indicate that he did not wish her to make any withdrawals. If so, that circumstance is consistent with a purpose to give her the right of survivorship, because otherwise there would have been no reason at all for him to establish a joint account.

The judgment is affirmed.

Creditor Beneficiary

LAWRENCE v. FOX
(1859) 20 N.Y. 268.

[Action by plaintiff against defendant to recover $300 and interest. The evidence showed that one Holly, in November, 1857, at the request of defendant, loaned and advanced to him $300, stating at the time that he, Holly, owed that sum to plaintiff, and had agreed to pay it to plaintiff next day; that the defendant, in consideration thereof, at the time of receiving the money promised Holly to pay it to plaintiff next day. Defendant failed to pay plaintiff. From a judgment for $344.66 for plaintiff, defendant appeals.]

H. GRAY, J.

* * *

In Hall v. Marston, 17 Mass. 575, the court says: "It seems to have been well settled that if A promises B for a valuable consideration to pay C, the latter may maintain assumpsit for the money;" and in Brewer v. Dyer, 7 Cush. 337, the recovery was upheld, as the court said, "Upon the principle of law long recognized and clearly established, that when one person, for a valuable consideration, engages with another by a simple contract, to do some act for the benefit of a third, the latter, who would enjoy the benefit of the act, may maintain an action for the breach of such engagement; that it does not rest upon the ground of any actual or supposed relationship between the parties as some of the earlier cases would seem to indicate, but upon the broader and more satisfactory basis, that the law operating on the act of the parties creates the duty, establishes a privity, and implies the promise and obligation on which the action is founded." * * *

Affirmed.

Problems

1. On December 1, A, a famous singer, contracted with B to sing at B's theatre on December 31st for a fee of $25,000 to be paid immediately after the performance. (a) A, for value received, assigns this fee to C. (b) A, for value received, assigns this contract to sing to D, an equally famous singer. (c) B sells his theatre to E, and assigns his contract with A to E.

State the effect of each of these assignments.

2. The Smooth Paving Company entered into a paving contract with the city of Chicago. The contract contained the clause "contractor shall be liable for all damages to buildings resulting from the work performed." In the process of construction one of the bulldozers of the Smooth Paving Company struck a gas main, breaking the main causing an explosion and a fire which destroyed the house of John Puff. Puff brought an appropriate action against the Smooth Paving Company to recover damages for the loss of this house. Decision?

3. A, who was unemployed, registered with the X Employment Agency. A contract was then made whereby A, in consideration of such position as the Agency would obtain for A, agreed to pay the Agency one-half of his first month's salary. The contract also contained an assignment by A to the Agency of one-half of such first month's salary. Two weeks later, the Agency obtained a permanent position for A with the B Co. at a monthly salary of $900. The agency also notified the B Co. of the assignment by A. At the end of the first month, the B Co. paid A his salary in full. A then quit and disappeared. The Agency now sues the B Co. for $450 under the assignment. Decision?

4. B purchased an option on Blackacre from S for $1,000. The option contract contained a provision by which B promised not to assign the option contract without S's permission. B, without S's permission, assigns the contract to A. A seeks to exercise the option and S refuses to sell Blackacre to him. Decision?

5. B contracts to sell to A, an ice cream manufacturer, the amount of ice A may need in his business for the ensuing three years to the extent of not more than 250 tons a week at a stated price per ton. A makes a corresponding promise to B to buy such an amount of ice. A sells his ice cream plant to C and assigns to C all A's rights under the contract with B. Upon learning of the sale, B refused to furnish ice to C. C sues B for damages. Decision?

6. Brown enters into a written contract with Ideal Insurance Company whereby, in consideration of the payment of the premiums, the Insurance Company promises to pay XYZ College the face amount of the policy, $100,000, on Brown's death. Brown pays the premiums until his death. Thereafter, XYZ College makes demand for the $100,000 of Insurance Company, which refuses to pay upon the ground that XYZ College was not a party to the contract. Decision?

7. A and B enter into a contract binding A personally to do some delicate cabinet work. A assigns his rights and delegates performance of his duties to C. On being informed of this, B agrees with C in consideration of C's promise to do the work that B will accept C's work, if properly done, instead of the performance promised by A. Later, without cause, B refuses to allow C to proceed with the work, though C is ready to do so, and makes demand on A that A perform. A refuses. Can C recover damages from B? Can B recover from A?

8. A, a homeowner, enters into a valid, written contract with B, a carpenter for the construction of various book shelves and cabinets in A's house. Prior to the commencement of the work B assigns his interest in the contract to C, another carpenter. A refuses to permit C to do the work, employs another carpenter, and brings an action against B claiming as damages the difference between the contract price and the cost to employ the other carpenter. Decision?

9. S hired G in the Spring, as he had for many years, to set out in beds the flowers S had grown during the winter in his greenhouses. The work was to be done, in S's absence for $300. G became ill the day after S departed and requested his friend, B, to set out the flowers, promising to pay him the $250 when he was paid; B agreed. Upon completion of the planting, an agent of S's who had authority to dispense the money, paid G and G paid B. Within two days it became obvious that the planting was a disaster. Everything set out by B had died of water rot, due to his inability to properly operate S's automatic watering system.

May S recover damages from B? May S recover damages from G, and, if so, does G have an action over against B?

10. Caleb, operator of a window washing business, dictated a letter to his secretary addressed to Apartments, Inc. stating: "I will wash the windows of your apartment buildings at $4.10 per window to be paid upon completion of the work." The secretary typed the letter, signed Caleb's name and mailed it to Apartments, Inc. Apartments, Inc. replied: "Accept your offer."

Caleb wrote back: "I will wash them during the week commencing July 10, and direct you to pay the money you will owe me to my son, Bernie. I am giving it to him as a wedding present." Caleb sent a signed copy of the letter to Bernie.

Caleb washed the windows during the time stated, and demanded payment to him of $8,200 (2,000 windows at $4.10 each) informing Apartments, Inc. that he had changed his mind about having the money paid to Bernie.

What are the rights of the parties?

Chapter

15

DISCHARGE OF CONTRACTS

The subject of discharge of contracts pertains to the termination of contractual duties. In earlier chapters we have seen how parties may become bound to their promises by a contract. It may be equally desirable for a person to know how he may become unbound from a contract. When a contract is made, it is not intended by either party that the duties created shall exist forever. Contractual promises are made for a purpose, and the parties reasonably expect this purpose to be fulfilled by performance. However, performance of a contractual duty is only one method of discharge. It is important also to know the others, which are numerous.

Whatever causes a binding promise to cease to be binding is a discharge of the contract. In general, there are two types of discharge: (a) by act or agreement of the parties and (b) by operation of law. In addition, there are various ways in which each type of discharge may occur. Closely allied to discharge is an excuse for non-performance of a contractual duty.

Many contractual promises are not absolute and unconditional promises to perform but are conditional promises. Their performance is dependent upon the happening or non-happening of a specified event. This makes necessary a brief discussion of the subject of conditions.

CONDITIONS

A condition is any operative event the happening or non-happening of which affects a duty of performance under a contract. Some conditions must be satisfied before any duty to perform arises; others terminate the duty to perform; still others either limit or modify the duty to perform. A condition is therefore the natural enemy of a promise. It is inserted for the protection and benefit of the promisor. The more conditions to which a promise is subject, the less content the promise has. A promise to pay $4,000 provided that such sum is realized from the sale of an automobile, provided the automobile is sold within 60 days, and provided that the automobile which has been stolen can be found, is manifestly different from and worth considerably less than an unconditional promise by the same promisor to pay $4,000.

A fundamental distinction exists between the breach or non performance of a promise, and the failure or non-happening of a condition. A breach of contract subjects the promisor to liability. It may or may not, depending upon its materiality, excuse non-performance by the other party, the promisee, of his duty under the contract. The happening or non-happening of a condition prevents the promisee from acquiring a right, or deprives him of a right, but subjects neither party to any liability, unless the party has promised that the event of the condition shall, or shall not occur.

Conditions may be either (1) express, (2) implied-in-fact, or (3) implied-in-law. They are also classified as (4) conditions concurrent, (5) conditions precedent, and (6) conditions subsequent.

These conditions are not external to the contract, that is, they do not relate to the formation or existence of the contract, but are either part and parcel of the contract as entered into between the parties, or arise by reason of events occurring subsequent to its formation. Consequently, none of the essentials to the existence of a contract, discussed in earlier chapters, are treated as conditions.

Express Conditions

A condition is express when it is set forth in language usually preceded by such words as "provided that," "on condition that," "while," "after," "upon," or "as soon as." While no particular form of words is necessary to create an express condition, the operative event to which the performance of the promise is made subject is in some manner clearly expressed. An illustration is the provision frequently found in building contracts to the effect that before the owner

is required to pay the price, or the final installment thereof, the builder shall furnish a certificate of the architect that the building has been constructed according to the plans and specifications. The price is being paid for the building, not for the certificate, yet before the owner is obliged to pay, he must have both the building and the certificate, as the duty of immediate payment was made expressly conditional upon the presentation of the certificate. This condition is excused if the architect dies, or becomes insane, or capriciously refuses to give a certificate, or if there is collusion between the owner and the architect.

The parties to a contract may also agree that performance by one of them shall be to the *satisfaction* of the other who shall not be obligated to pay for it unless he is satisfied. This is an express condition to the duty to pay for the performance. It is a valid condition. Assume that tailor A contracts to make a suit of clothes to B's satisfaction, and that B promises to pay A $250 for the suit if he is satisfied with it when completed. A completes the suit using materials ordered by B. The suit fits B beautifully, but B tells A that he is not satisfied with it and refuses to accept or pay for it. A is not entitled to recover $250 or any amount from B by reason of the non-happening of the express condition. This is so, even if the dissatisfaction of B, although honest and sincere, is unreasonable. Where satisfaction relates to a matter of personal taste, opinion or judgment, the law applies the subjective standard, and the condition has not occurred if the promisor is *actually* dissatisfied. The condition relates to the individual satisfaction of B and no one else, including a reasonable man. However, if the contract does not clearly indicate that satisfaction is subjective or if the performance contracted for relates to mechanical fitness or utility, the condition of satisfaction would be regarded as applying an objective standard. For example, the sale of a building, coal, or goods would apply the objective standard of satisfaction: It would be assumed that the satisfaction standard applies to the marketability, utility, or mechanical fitness of the item being sold. In such cases, the question would not be whether the promisor was actually satisfied with the performance tendered to him by the other party, but whether as a reasonable man, he ought to be satisfied.

Implied-in-Fact Conditions

Such conditions are similar to express conditions, in that they are understood by the parties to be part of the agreement, although not found in express language. They are necessarily inferred from the promise contained in the contract. Thus, if A for $750 contracts to paint B's house any color desired by B, it is necessarily implied in fact that B will inform A of the desired color before A shall commence to paint. The notification of choice of color is an implied-in-fact condition, an operative event which must occur before A is subject to the duty of painting the house. Likewise, a promise to do plumbing or repair work at another's house is subject to the implied-in-fact condition that the promisor be given access to the house.

Implied-in-Law Conditions

A condition implied-in-law differs from an express condition and a condition implied-in-fact in that it is not contained in the language of the contract, or necessarily implied therefrom, but is imposed by law in order to accomplish a just and fair result. For example, if A contracts to sell a certain horse to B for $1800, and the contract is silent as to the time of delivery of the horse and payment of the price, the law will imply that the respective performances are not independent of one another. The law will treat the promises as mutually dependent, and therefore that a delivery or tender of the horse by A to B is a condition to the

duty of B to pay the price and, conversely, payment or tender of $1800 by B to A is a condition to the duty of A to deliver the horse to B. If the contract specified a sale on credit, and A gave B 30 days after delivery within which to pay the price, these conditions would not be implied as the parties by their contract have made their respective duties of performance independent of each other.

Concurrent Conditions

Where the proposed reciprocal and agreed performances of two mutual promisors are to take place at the same time, such performances are concurrent conditions. In the absence of agreement to the contrary, the law assumes that the respective performances under a contract are concurrent conditions. Such conditions can only exist where complete performance by both promisors can take place simultaneously. If A has contracted to sell B a watch for $100, with delivery and payment to take place concurrently, neither party may maintain an action against the other without first performing on his side or tendering performance. The party who is suing must have first placed the other party in default. Where the conditions are concurrent, a tender of performance need not be absolute but may be made conditional upon receiving performance by the other party.

Condition Precedent

A condition precedent is an operative event the happening of which must precede the creation of a duty of performance under a contract. Where the immediate duty of one party to perform is subject to the condition that some event must first occur, such event is a condition precedent. For instance, if A is to deliver coal to B on June 1, with A's duty to pay for the coal on July 15, A's delivery of the coal is a condition precedent to B's performance. Similarly, if A promises to buy B's land for $50,000, provided A can obtain financing in the amount of $40,000 at 13% or less for ten years within sixty days of signing the contract, A's obtaining the specified financing is a condition precedent to A's duty. If the condition is met, A is bound to perform; if it does not occur, A is not bound to perform. A is under an implied-in-law duty to use his best efforts to obtain financing under these terms.

Condition Subsequent

A condition subsequent is an operative event which terminates an existing duty of immediate performance under a contract. Where goods are sold under terms of "sale or return," the buyer has the right to return the goods to the seller within a stated period, but is under an immediate duty to pay the price unless credit has been agreed upon. The duty to pay the price is terminated by a return of the goods which thereby operates as a condition subsequent. Insurance policies often contain a provision that in the event of loss and after due notice thereof has been given to the insurer, the insured must bring suit on the policy within twelve months from the date of the loss or be barred from recovery. The giving of proper notice of loss is a condition precedent, and upon its occurrence the insurer is under an immediate duty to pay the amount of the loss. The failure to bring suit within the stated period operates as an express condition subsequent which terminates the existing liability of the insurer.

DISCHARGE BY PERFORMANCE

Undoubtedly, this is the most frequent method of discharging a contractual duty. If a promisor exactly performs his duty under the contract, he is no longer subject to that duty. Less than exact performance, but substantial performance, does not fully discharge a promisor, but substantial performance by one party deprives the other party of an excuse for non-performance of his promise.

Where the contract is bilateral, a tendered or offered performance by one party to the other which is refused or rejected may be treated as a repudiation which excuses or discharges the tendering party from further duty of performance under the contract. However, a tender of payment of a debt past due does not discharge the debt if the creditor refuses to accept the tender. The effect of such refusal is to stop further accrual of interest on the debt and to deprive the creditor of court costs in a subsequent suit by him to recover the amount due.

If a debtor owes money on several accounts and tenders to his creditor less than the total amounts due, the debtor has the right to designate the account or debt to which the payment is to be applied. This direction by the debtor must be accepted by the creditor. If the debtor does not direct the application of the payment, the creditor may apply it to any account owing to him by the debtor or distribute it among several such accounts. Once the debtor has made payment without specifying its application, he may not subsequently direct its application. The payment was unconditionally made by him and may not thereafter become conditional. The application of payment may be a matter of importance, as where one of several debts is secured and the others not, or where one is barred by the Statute of Limitations and the others are not barred.

DISCHARGE RESULTING FROM BREACH

Breach by One Party as a Discharge of the Other

Breach of contract always gives rise to a cause of action by the aggrieved party. It may, however, have a more important effect. Because of the rule that one party need not perform unless the other party performs, a breach by one party operates as an excuse for non-performance by the other party, and if the breach is material and goes to the essence of the contract, it discharges the other party from any further duty under the contract.

The Code greatly alters the common law doctrine of material breach by adopting what is known as the "Perfect Tender Rule." This rule essentially provides that any deviation from the promised performance in a sales contract constitutes a material breach of the contract and discharges the aggrieved party of his duty of performance. U.C.C., Section 2–601.

In an installment sales contract, however, a slight breach, such as a delay of three days by the buyer of goods to pay the tenth installment under a twelve-installment contract, operates as a dilatory excuse for nonperformance. The seller may rightly take the position that he will not deliver any more goods until the buyer's breach is cured. He may not for such trivial breach take the position that he will not deliver any more goods under the contract, although an extended delay in payment could be a material breach and entitle him to do so. If the seller fails to deliver the first installment, or completely misses two or three consecutive installments, the breach is more serious. This would be a material breach, and the buyer may assert it as an absolute excuse for nonperformance discharging him from any duty to accept further deliveries of goods under the contract. U.C.C., Section 2–612. The seller, however, is not discharged from his duty to make compensation to the buyer for breach of the entire contract.

A material breach of contract was held to excuse non-performance by the other party in Ebco, Inc. v. Bechtold, 251 Or. 543, 446 P.2d 120 (1968), in which the plaintiff had sold a laundry business under a contract whereby plaintiff agreed to cause two hotels, which were under common control with the seller plaintiff, to have their laundering, dry cleaning, and linen supply service performed by the buyer defendant. In an action by the seller to recover the balance of the purchase price, the court held that the failure of the hotels to give all of their laundry business to the buyer was a breach of the seller's contract which discharged the buyer.

The U.C.C. uses the term "cancellation" in connection with an excuse for nonperformance by one party as the result of a material breach by the other party, and distinguishes between "cancellation" and "termination" in Section 2–106(3) and (4) as follows:

(3) "Termination" occurs when either party pursuant to a power created by agreement or law puts an end to the contract otherwise than for its breach. On "termination" all obligations which are still executory on both sides are discharged but any right based on prior breach or performance survives.

(4) "Cancellation" occurs when either party puts an end to the contract for breach by the other and its effect is the same as that of "termination" except that the cancelling party also retains any remedy for breach of the whole contract or any unperformed balance.

Termination, which occurs otherwise than by breach of contract, discharges executory duties on both sides while preserving rights based on prior breach or prior performance. On the other hand, cancellation is the right which one party has by reason of a material breach committed by the other. It discharges only the executory duties of the cancelling party while preserving his remedy against the other party for breach of the entire contract to the extent unperformed. At the time of cancellation it would be well for him to so advise the breaching party in order not to confuse the cancellation with a possible offer of mutual rescission.

Prevention of Performance

If one party to a contract substantially interferes with or prevents performance by the other, such action generally constitutes a material breach which discharges the other party to the contract. For instance, A prevents an architect from giving a certificate which is a condition to A's liability to pay B a certain sum of money. A may not set up B's failure to produce a certificate as an excuse for A's nonpayment. Likewise, if A has contracted to grow a certain crop for B and after A has planted the seed, B plows the field and destroys the seedling plants, his interference with A's performance discharges A from his duty under the contract. It does not, however, discharge B from his duty under the contract.

Anticipatory Repudiation

A breach of contract is simply a failure to perform it. It is logically and physically impossible to fail to perform a duty in advance of the date that performance is due. A party, however, may announce prior to such date that he will not perform. This is a repudiation of the contract, informing the other party that a breach is imminent. Nevertheless, it cannot be an immediate breach, for if the repudiating party should later change his mind and fully perform on the appointed date, the contract would then be both breached and performed. A repudiation of a contract prior to the date fixed by the contract for performance is called an anticipatory breach. The courts allow it to be treated as a breach and permit the non-repudiating party to bring suit immediately as if it were a breach. This rule was first clearly announced in Hochster v. De La Tour (page 000) in which Lord Campbell reasoned that since the defendant's repudiation prior to the date for performance gave the plaintiff an excuse for non-performance and enabled the plaintiff to change his position and plans, and since a breach by the defendant would have the same effect, the plaintiff may, therefore, treat the repudiation as a breach.

The U.C.C. provides that an anticipatory repudiation of a contract for the sale of goods entitles the aggrieved party to suspend performance on his part and to maintain an action for breach. Section 2–610.

Material Alteration of Written Contract

An alteration or change of any of the material terms or provisions of a written contract or document is a discharge of the entire contract. The alteration to operate as a discharge must be material and must be the act of a party to the contract or someone acting on his behalf. An unauthorized change in the terms of a written contract by one who is a stranger to the contract is not an alteration but a spoliation which does not discharge the contract.

A material alteration is defined in Section 286 of the Restatement, Second, Contracts as follows:

(1) If one to whom a duty is owed under a contract alters a writing that is an integrated agreement or that satisfies the Statute of Frauds with respect to that contract, the duty is discharged if the alteration is fraudulent and material.

(2) An alteration is material if it would, if effective, vary any party's legal relations with the maker of the alteration or adversely affect that party's legal relations with a third person. The unauthorized insertion in a blank space in a writing is an alteration.

DISCHARGE BY AGREEMENT OF THE PARTIES

Mutual Rescission

A rescission is an agreement between the parties to a contract to terminate their respective duties under the contract. It is a contract to end a contract. All of the essentials of a contract must be present. Each party furnishes consideration in giving up his rights under the contract in exchange for the other party's relinquishment of his rights under the contract. An oral agreement of mutual rescission is valid and will discharge a written contract unless the contract to rescind involves the retransfer of a subject matter which is within the Statute of Frauds, or unless under the U.C.C. the written contract provides that it cannot be modified or rescinded except by a signed writing. Section 2–209(2). In such case, under the Code, an oral rescission or modification would be ineffective. A contract containing a provision which is contrary to or inconsistent with a provision in a prior contract between the same parties is a mutual rescission of the inconsistent provision in the prior contract. Whether the later contract completely supersedes and discharges all of the provisions of the prior contract is a matter of interpretation.

Accord and Satisfaction

An accord is a contract between an obligee and his obligor whereby the former agrees to accept and the latter agrees to render a substituted performance in satisfaction of an existing contractual duty. Thus, if B owes A $500, and the parties agree that B shall paint A's house in satisfaction of the debt, the agreement is an executory accord. The debt is not discharged by the accord. However, when B has performed the accord by painting A's house, the $500 debt is discharged by accord and satisfaction.

Release and Covenant Not to Sue

A release is technically a discharge under seal of an existing obligation. The term is also applied to any formal writing supported by sufficient consideration which recites a present relinquishment and termination of the rights therein described. A covenant or promise not to sue does not effect a discharge of the obligation, as does a release. It may, however, be interposed as a bar to any suit brought in violation of the covenant and to this extent has the effect of a release. Covenants not to sue are usually employed

where an obligee of joint obligors makes a settlement with one of them and wishes to preserve his rights against the others. A release of one joint obligor releases all of them. A covenant not to sue one or more but less than all obligors does not release the remaining ones.

Novation

A novation involves three parties and an agreement between them to substitute a new obligee in place of an existing obligee, or to replace an existing obligor with a new one. The effect is to discharge the old obligation by the creation of a new one in which there is either a new obligee or a new obligor. Thus, if B owes A $500 and A, B, and C agree that C will pay the debt and B will be discharged, the novation is the substitute of the new debtor C for B. If the three parties agree that B will pay $500 to C instead of to A, the novation is the substitution of a new creditor C for A. In each instance the debt owing by B to A is discharged.

In Ophuls and Hill, Inc. v. Carolina Ice and Fuel Co., 160 S.C. 441, 158 S.E. 824 (1931), the Court states:

"Novation" may be broadly defined as a substitution of a new contract or obligation for an old one which is thereby extinguished. More specifically, it is the substitution by mutual agreement of one debtor or of one creditor for another, whereby the old debt is extinguished, or the substitution of a new debt or obligation for an existing one, which is thereby extinguished. A novation is a mode of extinguishing one contract or obligation by another, that is, the substitution, not of a new paper or note, but of a new obligation in lieu of an old one, the effect of which is to pay, dissolve, or otherwise discharge it. (66 C.J.S. Novation § 1a).

Novation of debtors, which is the most frequent form of novation, means the substitution of one debtor for another, and takes place whenever a creditor agrees to release and extinguish his claim against his debtor and to accept in lieu thereof the promise of a third person to discharge the obligation. Thus, a novation of debtors is effected where a creditor, in release and satisfaction of his original debt, accepts the note or other security of a third person or the promise of a third person who has assumed the obligations, as where the creditor in a contract of sale accepted the obligation of a transferee of the contract in release of the original purchaser, or in the case of a mortgage, where the mortgagee agrees to release the original mortgagor and accepts in his stead a transferee of the latter.

In order to accomplish a novation by substitution of debtors there must be a mutual agreement among three parties, the creditor, his immediate debtor, and the intended new debtor, by which the liability of the new debtor is accepted in the place of the original debtor in discharge of the original debt. The agreement may be orally made.

Renunciation

A duty to pay compensation in unliquidated damages for breach of a bilateral contract which is unperformed on both sides may be discharged by a manifestation by the obligee to treat his excuse for non-performance as a termination of the contract. Thus, if A contracts to employ B to work for one year at an agreed salary commencing July 1, and B on June 25 repudiates the contract by informing A that he will not work for him, A has an excuse for non-performance and may promptly fill the job by employing C. If this is all that happens, B would remain liable to A for breach of the contract. However, if when B repudiates, A tells B that he is satisfied and will regard the contract as terminated, both B and A are discharged by this act of mutual renunciation.

Cancellation or Surrender of Formal Contract

A contractual duty which is embodied in a contract under seal, or formal document, or negotiable instrument, may be discharged by a cancellation or surrender of the document or writing or instrument. Cancella-

tion at common law refers to an act of the obligee which physically destroys or mutilates the document or consists in writing the word "cancelled" or a similar word on the face of the document. Surrender means a redelivery of the document by the obligee to the obligor or to someone on his behalf with the intention of relinquishing all rights therein.

DISCHARGE BY OPERATION OF LAW

Subsequent Illegality

Performance of a contract which was legal when formed may become illegal by reason of a subsequently enacted law. In such case the duty of performance is discharged. For example, A contracts to sell and deliver to B ten cases of a certain whiskey each month for one year. A subsequent prohibition law makes unlawful the manufacture, transportation, or sale of intoxicating liquor. The contract, to the extent unperformed by A, is discharged.

War is another illustration of supervening illegality. If a contract for the sale of goods is made between citizens of two countries which subsequently are at war with one another, each country prohibits trading with the enemy. This discharges the contract upon the ground of subsequent illegality.

Impossibility

It may be impossible for a promisor to perform his contract because he is financially unable or because he personally lacks the capability or competence. This is subjective impossibility and does not excuse the promisor from liability for breach of contract. On the other hand, performance may be impossible not because the particular promisor is unable to perform, but because no one is able to perform. This is objective impossibility which in a great number of situations will be held to excuse the promisor or discharge his duty to perform. The death or illness of a person who has contracted to render personal services is a discharge of his contractual duty. If a jockey contracts to ride a certain horse in the Kentucky Derby and the horse dies prior to the Derby, the contract is discharged. It is objectively impossible for any one to perform this contract. Also, if A contracts to lease to B a certain ballroom for a party on a scheduled future date, destruction of the ballroom by fire before the scheduled event discharges the contract. Destruction of the subject matter or of the contracted for means of performance of a contract is excusable impossibility.

Where the purpose of a contract has been frustrated by fortuitous circumstances which deprive the performance of the value attached to it by the parties, although performance is not impossible, the courts generally regard the frustration as a discharge. This rule developed from the so-called "coronation cases." When Edward VII became King of England upon the death of his mother Queen Victoria, impressive coronation ceremonies were planned including a procession along a designated route through certain streets in London. Contracts were made by owners and lessees of buildings along the route to permit the use of rooms with a view on the date scheduled for the procession. The King became ill and the procession did not take place. The purpose for using the rooms having failed, the rooms were not used. Numerous suits were filed, some by landowners seeking to hold the would-be-viewers liable on their promises, and some by the would-be-viewers seeking to recover back money paid in advance for the rooms. The principle involved was novel, but from these cases evolved the frustration of purpose doctrine whereby a contract is discharged if supervening circumstances make fulfillment of the purpose which both parties had in mind possible.

In Transatlantic Financing Corporation v. United States (1966) 124 U.S.App.D.C. 183, 363 F.2d 312, the plaintiff, operator of the S. S. Christos, on October 2, 1956, entered into a voyage charter contract with defendant United States for the carriage of a full cargo of wheat from a U. S. Gulf port to Iran. The contract specified no route for the voyage, although the usual and customary route was by way of the Suez Canal. On July 26, 1956, the Egyptian Government had nationalized the Suez Canal Company and taken over operation of the Canal. On October 27, 1956, the S. S. Christos with cargo sailed from Galveston, Texas, for Iran on a course which would have taken her through the Suez Canal. Two days later Israel invaded Egypt, followed by Great Britain and France invading the Canal Zone, and on November 2, the Egyptian Government obstructed the Suez Canal and closed it to all traffic. On November 7, plaintiff contacted an employee of defendant seeking instructions for disposition of the cargo and an agreement for additional compensation for a voyage around the Cape of Good Hope. The employee advised plaintiff that defendant expected it to perform the contract according to its terms, and that he did not believe that plaintiff would be entitled to such additional compensation, but was free to file a claim. The S. S. Christos changed its course for the Cape of Good Hope and eventually arrived in Iran with the cargo. Plaintiff filed a claim against defendant for expense of approximately $44,000 in excess of the contract price of $305,842, which it had incurred by extending the contemplated voyage of 10,000 miles an additional 3,000 miles. The basis of plaintiff's claim was that the closure of the Suez Canal had made impossible the performance of the charter contract by use of the usual and customary route. The Court stated that in legal contemplation impossibility of performance means impracticability, and that a thing is impracticable when it can only be done at an excessive and unreasonable cost. It then noted that in order to construct a condition to performance based upon impossibility due to changed circumstances, it is required that (1) a contingency, something unexpected, must have occurred; (2) the risk of such occurrence must not have been allocated between the parties either by agreement or by custom; and (3) the occurrence must have rendered performance commercially impracticable. The Court held that the first two requirements had been met, but not the third. The impracticability was solely on the basis of added expense, and to justify relief there must be a greater variation between the expected cost and the cost of performing by an alternative route than existed in this case. The Court therefore held plaintiff's performance not impracticable, and affirmed judgment for defendant. The Court observed that impossibility of performance is ordinarily used as a defense in an action for breach of contract, as a shield and not as a sword, and noted that even if it were to be adjudged impracticable in this case, the relief sought by plaintiff was untenable. Upon learning of the Canal closing, plaintiff might have returned the ship to an appropriate port and unloaded its cargo. Where a contract is held to be a nullity through no fault of either party, and one party has performed, a Court will permit recovery of the reasonable value of the performance on the basis of quantum meruit, and not on the contract. Plaintiff here was seeking to recover the contract price which included its profit, plus the added expense, rather than quantum meruit for the entire trip, which would be the measure of recovery if a finding of impossibility on the basis of commercial impracticability were justified.

The modern and Code view of impossibility is that performance need not be actually or literally impossible, but that commercial impracticability will excuse non-performance. This does not mean mere hardship, or that the cost of performance would be more than expected. Impracticability refers to performance at a greatly excessive cost due to some event not contemplated by the parties, as where the cost of performance would have been much larger than reasonably contemplated.

Likewise, serious risk to life or health will excuse non-performance of a contract. A man having paid $24,812 for 2,734 hours of dancing lessons was severely injured in an automobile collision and thereby rendered incapable of continuing the lessons. This impossibility was held as a ground for rescission entitling him to a refund for lessons that he was physically unable to take. Parker v. Arthur Murray, Inc., 10 Ill.App.3d 1000, 295 N.E.2d 487 (1973).

Bankruptcy

Bankruptcy is a method of discharge of a contractual duty by operation of law available to one who is adjudicated bankrupt and who, by compliance with the requirements of the Bankruptcy Act, obtains an order of discharge by the bankruptcy court. It is applicable only to obligations which the statute provides are dischargeable in bankruptcy. The subject of bankruptcy is treated in Chapter 40.

Statute of Limitations

At common law a plaintiff was subject to no time limitation within which to bring a suit. All States now have statutes which provide such a limitation. The courts hold that the running of the period of the Statute of Limitations does not operate as a discharge but merely bars the remedy. The debtor is not discharged, but the creditor cannot maintain an action against him after the Statute has run. This distinction may be important, as in a situation where the creditor applies a payment by the debtor to a barred debt.

Exercise of a Power of Avoidance in a Voidable Contract

If a contract has been induced by fraud, misrepresentation, undue influence, mutual mistake of fact, or duress, it is voidable. The contract of a party that lacks contractual capacity is also voidable. A voidable contract has two aspects. In one, the party having the power of avoidance need take no action in order to exercise his power. He may sit back and wait until he is sued and then successfully plead his defense. The second kind of voidable contract requires affirmative action by the party having the power of avoidance in order to be relieved of a duty of performance. For example, if A fraudulently induces B to purchase goods which A delivers to B, the contract and the sale is voidable by B. But if B after learning of the fraud does not within a reasonable time take affirmative action to rescind the contract, he may not thereafter disaffirm it. He may sue A and receive damages as a result of the fraud, or he may assert such damages defensively if A sues him. However, in order to rescind the voidable contract, he must demand that A refund the purchase price, return or tender the goods to A, and state his reason for doing so.

Merger

Where a contractual duty or a duty to make compensation is replaced by an obligation of a different and higher degree, the former is merged into the latter and is discharged. A contract under seal, or formal contract, is an obligation of higher degree than one which arises informally such as a promise of the buyer to pay for goods delivered to him. If, after such a debt has arisen, the buyer should execute and deliver to the seller or creditor a promise under seal to pay the amount of it, the debt would be discharged by merger in the contract under seal. An account payable or informal debt may be discharged by merger in a negotiable instrument executed by the debtor and delivered to the creditor.

Cases

Concurrent Conditions

MONROE STREET PROPERTIES, INC. v. CARPENTER

(1969, 9th Cir.) 407 F.2d 379.

HUFSTEDLER, C. J.

Appellant, Monroe Street Properties, Inc. ("Monroe"), appeals from a judgment in favor of the defendant Carpenter entered after Carpenter's motion for a summary judgment was granted. Carpenter is a party in his capacity as a trustee for Western Equities, Inc. ("Western"). Federal jurisdiction is based upon diversity of citizenship.

Monroe's action is for claimed breach of a written contract between Monroe and Western in which Western agreed to buy from Monroe ten insured first mortgages and notes having a face value of $1,250,000 in exchange for $1,000,000 worth of Western's common stock. The District Court granted summary judgment on the ground that the uncontroverted facts showed that Monroe neither performed nor tendered performance on its side and, therefore, Western was not in breach of contract.

* * *

The following facts are undisputed. On March 27, 1962, Western submitted its written offer to Monroe to buy the ten first mortgages and notes. Monroe promptly accepted the offer. Western's offer was expressly subject to "verification by Union Title Company that the ten first mortgages

"* * * are valid first mortgages."
* * *

Pursuant to the contract the parties opened an escrow with Union Title Company on March 30, 1962. The escrow agreement provided that the terms and conditions of the agreement were to be complied with "on or before the date upon which [Western] stock has been listed on the American Stock Exchange, and delivered to Union Title Company." The Western stock was listed on the American Stock Exchange sometime before June 29, 1962, although the precise date of the listing is not clearly stated in the affidavits filed in connection with the motion for summary judgment. Monroe never deposited into escrow ten valid first mortgages or the policy of title, and Western never deposited its stock. Monroe did deposit the mortgage instruments in the escrow, but a preliminary title report received by Western on May 7, 1962, revealed that the properties subject to the ten mortgages were also subject to heavy prior encumbrances. After Monroe deposited those instruments in escrow, Monroe sent a demand to Western to deposit the stock. Western did not comply with the demand. Nothing further was done by either of the parties to perform the agreement and Monroe brought this action in October 1966.

* * *

The District Court correctly decided that Monroe never made an adequate tender of its own performance. Monroe's duty to deposit the insured first mortgages and Western's duty to deposit its stock were concurrent conditions. [Citations.] Neither party could place the other in breach for failure to perform without a tender of its own performance. "Tender" as used in this connection means " 'a readiness and willingness to perform in case of the *concurrent* performance by the other party, with present ability to do so, and notice to the other party of such readiness.' " (Emphasis added.

6 Williston, Contracts (3d ed. 1962) § 833, p. 105.) Monroe's offer to perform its concurrent condition upon condition that Western perform first was not an adequate tender and could not be relied upon by Monroe to place Western in breach of contract.

The judgment is affirmed.

Discharge by Breach:
Prevention of Performance

JACOBS v. JONES
(1967) 161 Colo. 505, 423 P.2d 321.

KELLEY, J.

Velma Jacobs, owner of an improved farm, entered into a contract with Earl Walker in which he agreed to paint the improvements on the farm. Walker purchased the paint from Charles Jones, doing business as Chas. Jones Lumber Company. Before the work was completed, Jacobs ordered Walker to stop because she was dissatisfied with the results. Offers were made by Jones and Walker to complete the job but Jacobs declined to permit Walker to fulfill his contract.

* * *

Jacobs, by her order to Walker to cease work and by refusing to permit either Walker or Jones to complete the work, which the trial court found they were willing to do, breached the contract, and excused further performance on the part of Walker. Under the circumstances the law implies a promise on the one party not to prevent, hinder or delay the performance of the other party. [Citations.]

Under the facts, as found by the trial court, Jones was entitled to be paid for the value of the paint furnished for use and used upon Jacobs' barns and improvements, and Walker was entitled to recover for the reasonable value of the work completed by him in accordance with the contract. [Citations.]

The court, with sufficient evidence to support each of its findings, entered a money judgment in favor of Jones and against Walker * * *. It also entered a money judgment in favor of Walker and against Jacobs.

The judgment is affirmed.

Anticipatory Breach

HOCHSTER v. DE LA TOUR

Court of Queen's Bench (England).
(1853) 2 Ellis and Blackburn Reports 678.

[Plaintiff brought an action against defendant on May 22, 1852, for breach of a contract of employment whereby the plaintiff was to enter the service of defendant in the capacity of a courier and travel with defendant on the continent of Europe for three months commencing June 1, 1852, at an agreed salary. The contract was made on April 12, 1852, and on May 11, 1852, defendant notified the plaintiff that he had changed his mind and declined plaintiff's services. The defendant refused to pay any compensation to the plaintiff. The plaintiff between the date of commencing the action, May 22, and June 1, obtained an engagement to act as courier for Lord Ashburton, on equally good terms, but not commencing until July 4. The jury returned a verdict for the plaintiff. Defendant made a motion for the court to overturn the jury's judgment.]

LORD CAMPBELL, C. J.

On this motion in arrest of judgment, the question arises, Whether, if there be an agreement between A. and B., whereby B. engages to employ A. on and from a future day for a given period of time, to travel with him into a foreign country as a courier, and to start with him in that capacity on that day, A. being to receive a monthly salary during the continuance of such service, B. may, before the day, refuse to perform the agreement and break and renounce it, so as to entitle A. before the day to commence an action against B. to recover damages for breach of the agreement; A. having been ready and willing to perform it, till it was broken and renounced by B. The defendant's counsel very powerfully contended that, if the plaintiff was not contented to dissolve the contract, and to abandon all remedy upon it, he was bound to remain ready and willing to perform it till the day when the actual employment as courier in the service of the defendant was to begin; and that there could be no breach of the agreement, before that day, to give a right of action. But it cannot be laid down as a universal rule that, where by agreement an act is to be done on a future day, no action can be brought for a breach of the agreement till the day for doing the act has arrived. * * *

If the plaintiff has no remedy for breach of the contract unless he treats the contract as in force, and acts upon it down to the 1st June, 1852, it follows that, till then, he must enter into no employment which will interfere with his promise "to start with the defendant on such travels on the day and year," and that he must then be properly equipped in all respects as a courier for a three months' tour on the continent of Europe. But it is surely much more rational, and more for the benefit of both parties, that, after the renunciation of the agreement by the defendant, the plaintiff should be at liberty to consider himself absolved from any future performance of it, retaining his right to sue for any damage he has suffered from the breach of it. Thus, instead of remaining idle and laying out money in preparations which must be useless, he is at liberty to seek service under another employer, which would go in mitigation of the damages to which he would otherwise be entitled for a breach of the contract. It seems strange that the defendant, after renouncing the contract, and absolutely declaring that he will never act under it, should be permitted to object that faith is given to his assertion, and that an opportunity is not left to him of changing his mind. If the plaintiff is barred of any remedy by entering into an engagement inconsistent with starting as a courier with the defendant on the 1st June, he is prejudiced by putting faith in the defendant's assertion: and it would be more consonant with principle, if the defendant were precluded from saying that he had not broken the contract when he declared that he entirely renounced it. * * * The man who wrongfully renounces a contract into which he has deliberately entered cannot justly complain if he is immediately sued for a compensation in damages by the man whom he has injured: and it seems reasonable to allow an option to the injured party, either to sue immediately, or to wait till the time when the act was to be done, still holding it as prospectively binding for the exercise of this option, which may be advantageous to the innocent party, and cannot be prejudicial to the wrongdoer. An argument against the action before the 1st of June is urged from the difficulty of calculating the damages: but this argument is equally strong against an action before the 1st of September, when the three months would expire. In either case, the jury in assessing the damages would be justified in looking to all that had happened, or was likely to happen, to increase or mitigate the loss of the plaintiff down to the day of trial. * * *

Judgment for plaintiff.

Discharge by Agreement
of the Parties

WATTS CONSTRUCTION CO. v. CULLMAN COUNTY

(1980 Ala.) 382 So.2d 520.

SHORES, J.

This is a contract case. Appellant Watts Construction Company submitted the low bid on a County Water Works Improvement Project and was awarded the contract in May of 1976. In July, Robert L. Harbison, chairman of the Cullman County Commission, executed a construction contract for the project, separate copies of which had earlier been executed by Watts. Item V, Section II, of the contract provides that "[t]his contract shall not be effective unless and until approved by the State Director of the Farmers Home Administration, U.S. Department of Agriculture or his delegated representative." FHA approval for the project was not obtained. However, when a portion of the project which was being funded by the city, rather than the county, was deleted during the summer, the change order was signed by a representative of the State Director of the FHA.

Construction on the project was delayed until the fall, allegedly due to the lowering of the county's debt limit. In September, construction still had not been authorized, and Watts requested a 5% increase in the contract price due to seasonal and inflational price increases. The county countered with an offer of 3.5%. By a letter dated September 21, 1976 * * *, Watts notified the commission that he could not accept less than a 5% increase, and concluded: "If this is not agreeable with you, please consider this letter a withdrawal of our bid." This letter was discussed at a meeting of the county commission on September 24, 1976, where it was agreed that the county could not pay a 5% increase. Negotiations were begun with the next lowest bidder to take the project on at the low bid price. On October 4, 1976, the commission re-awarded the contract to Tucker Brothers Construction Company at the low bid made by Watts. Watts alleges that the award to Tucker Brothers included project specification changes which reduced the cost of the project and which were not offered to Watts. He was notified by letter dated October 14, 1976, that his withdrawal of the bid had been accepted by the commission. On October 19, 1976, Watts informed the commission that he was willing to perform the contract at bid price with certain modifications in specifications. His offer was not accepted.

Watts then brought this action to recover damages for breach of contract, * * *. The trial court granted the county's motion for summary judgment, and this appeal followed. For the reasons discussed herein, we affirm.

* * *

We find it unnecessary to discuss the issue of whether FHA approval was a condition precedent to creation of a valid contract. Watts's letter of September 21 withdrawing his bid and the commission's letter of October 14 accepting that withdrawal effectively rescinded any contract that might have existed. Parties to a written contract may by mutual consent and without other consideration rescind the contract. [Citation.] Where the acts and conduct of one party inconsistent with the existence of a contract are acquiesced in by the other, such contract will be treated as abandoned or rescinded. [Citation.] Watts's demand for an increase in the contract price demonstrated his intention not to be bound by the original contract. The commission acquiesced in his desire not to be so bound, and the contract was rescinded. Once a party to a contract has repudiated or broken it, he cannot reinstate the contract by an offer to perform. [Citation.] Where the parties have by mutual agreement rescinded a contract, one of the parties thereto cannot recover damages in an action for breach of contract. [Citation.] Where parties agree to rescind the contract, each gives up the provisions for its benefit, and the parties are then competent to contract with others. [Citation.]

* * *

The judgment appealed from is affirmed.

AFFIRMED.

Impossibility

CHRISTY v. PILKINTON
(1954) 224 Ark. 407, 273 S.W.2d 533.

GEORGE ROSE SMITH, J.

This is a suit for specific performance, brought by the appellee as vendor in a contract for the sale of real property. In appealing from a decree for the plaintiff the defendants contend only tht the court erred in ordering them to perform a promise which the proof shows to be beyond their financial resources.

It is conceded that the parties executed a valid written contract by which the Christys agreed to buy an apartment house from Mrs. Pilkinton for $30,000. The vendor's title is admittedly good. When the time came for performance the purchasers, although not insolvent, were unable to raise enough money to carry out their contract. Mrs. Pilkinton, after having tendered a deed to the property, brought this suit. At the trial the defendants' evidence tended to show that, as a result of a decline in Christy's used car business, they do not possess and cannot borrow the unpaid balance of $29,900.

Proof of this kind does not establish the type of impossibility that constitutes a defense. There is a familiar distinction between objective impossibility, which amounts to saying, "The thing cannot be done," and subjective impossibility—"I cannot do it." Rest., Contracts, § 455; Williston on Contracts, § 1932. The latter, which is well illustrated by a promisor's financial inability to pay, does not discharge the contractual duty and is therefore not a bar to a decree for specific performance.

Much of the appellants' brief is devoted to a discussion of the difficulty that the chancellor may have in enforcing his decree; but that problem is not now before us. By the decree the defendants were allowed a period of twenty days in which to perform their obligation. If their default continues it will of course be for the chancellor to say whether further relief should be granted, as by a foreclosure of the vendor's lien or by other process available to a court of equity. At present it is enough to observe that foreseeable obstacles to the enforcement of a judgment are not a sufficient reason for denying the relief to which the plaintiff is entitled.

Affirmed.

Impossibility

NORTHERN CORP. v. CHUGACH ELECTRIC ASS'N

(1974, Alaska) 518 P.2d 76.

[Plaintiff Northern Corporation (Northern) on August 3, 1966, entered into a contract with defendant Chugach Electric Association (Chugach) to repair and upgrade the upstream face of Cooper Lake Dam in Alaska which required it to furnish all labor, equipment and materials, and to quarry at a designated site riprap and filter layer stone which it would haul and place on the upstream face of the dam according to plans and specifications. After work was commenced, the parties discovered that the rock at the designated quarry site was not suitable and therefore the parties amended their contract to designate a new quarry site at the opposite end of the lake where rock would be blasted, stockpiled, and then transported to the dam during the winter across the ice on the lake. By reason of the additional cost incurred and to be incurred on account of this change, the contract price of $63,655 was increased by $42,000. In December, 1966, plaintiff cleared a road on the ice to permit deeper freezing, but thereafter water overflowed on the ice preventing its use. Northern complained of unsafe conditions of the lake ice, but Chugach insisted on performance.

In March, 1967, one of Northern's loaded trucks broke through the ice and sank. Northern continued to encounter difficul-

ties and ceased operations on March 31, 1967, with the approval of Chugach. On January 8, 1968, Chugach notified Northern that it would be in default unless all rock was hauled by April 1. Northern advised Chugach that it was returning to Cooper Lake and would start hauling on January 31. On February 1, Northern started hauling with half-loaded trucks and within the first few hours two trucks broke through the ice causing the death of the drivers and loss of the trucks. Northern thereupon ceased operations and notified Chugach it would make no more attempts to haul across the lake.

On March 28, 1968, Northern advised Chugach it considered the contract terminated for impossibility of performance, and in September, 1968, commenced suit to recover the costs incurred in attempting completion of the contract, less payments received. Chugach counterclaimed alleging overpayment for the work performed, and seeking damages for the period between the date of completion specified in the amended contract and the date of termination by Northern. The lower court held that both parties were discharged from the contract, and denied both parties' claims for damages. Upon appeal by Northern, and cross-appeal by Chugach, the Court affirmed as to impossibility of performance, but reversed and remanded as to damages.]

BOOCHEVER, J.

*   *   *

The focal question is whether the amended contract was impossible of performance. The September 27, 1966 directive specified that the rock was to be transported "across Cooper Lake to the dam site when such lake is frozen to a sufficient depth to permit heavy vehicle traffic thereon," and the formal amendment specified that the hauling to the dam site would be done during the winter of 1966–67. It is therefore clear that the parties contemplated that the rock would be transported across the frozen lake by truck. Northern's repeated efforts to perform the contract by this method during the winter of 1966–67 and subsequently in Feburary 1968, culminating in the tragic loss of life, abundantly support the trial court's finding that the contract was impossible of performance by this method.

Chugach contends, however, that Northern was nevertheless bound to perform, and that it could have used means other than hauling by truck across the ice to transport the rock. The answer to Chugach's contention is that, as the trial court found, the parties contemplated that the rock would be hauled by truck once the ice froze to a sufficient depth to support the weight of the vehicles. The specification of this particular method of performance presupposed the existence of ice frozen to the requisite depth. Since this expectation of the parties was never fulfilled, and since the provisions relating to the means of performance was clearly material, Northern's duty to perform was discharged by reason of impossibility.

There is an additional reason for our holding that Northern's duty to perform was discharged because of impossibility. It is true that in order for a defendant to prevail under the original common law doctrine of impossibility, he had to show that no one else could have performed the contract. However, this harsh rule has gradually been eroded, and the Restatement of Contracts has departed from the early common law rule by recognizing the principle of "commercial impracticability". Under this doctrine, a party is discharged from his contract obligations, even if it is technically possible to perform them, if the costs of performance would be so disproportionate to that reasonably contemplated by the parties as to make the contract totally impractical in a commercial sense. * * * Removed from the strictures of the common law, "impossibility" in its modern context has become a coat of many colors, including among its hues the point argued here—namely, im-

possibility predicated upon "commercial impracticability." This concept—which finds expression both in case law * * * and in other authorities * * * is grounded upon the assumption that in legal contemplation something is impracticable when it can only be done at an excessive and unreasonable cost. As stated in Transatlantic Financing Corp. v. United States, 124 U.S.App.D.C. 183, 363 F.2d 312 (1966). * * *:

* * * The doctrine ultimately represents the ever-shifting line, drawn by courts hopefully responsive to commercial practices and mores, at which the community's interest in having contracts enforced according to their terms is outweighed by the commercial senselessness of requiring performance . . .

Sec. 465 of the Restatement also provides that a serious risk to life or health will excuse nonperformance.

* * *

In Merl F. Thomas Sons, Inc. v. State, 396 P.2d 76 (Alaska, 1964), we quoted with approval Professor Williston's analysis of the concept of impossibility:

The true distinction is not between difficulty and impossibility. As has been seen, a man may contract to do what is impossible, as well as what is difficult. The important question is whether an unanticipated circumstance, the risk of which should not fairly be thrown upon the promisor, has made performance of the promise vitally different from what was reasonably to be expected (footnote omitted).

In the case before us the detailed opinion of the trial court clearly indicates that the appropriate standard was followed. There is ample evidence to support its findings that "[t]he ice haul method of transporting riprap ultimately selected was within the contemplation of the parties and was part of the basis of the agreement which ultimately resulted in amendment No. 1 in October 1966," and that that method was

not commercially feasible within the financial parameters of the contract. We affirm
the court's conclusion that the contract was
impossible of performance.

* * *

Affirmed in part, reversed in part and
remanded.

Problems

1. A–1 Roofing Co. entered into a written contract with Jaffe to put a new roof on the latter's
residence for $900 with a specified type of roof-
ing, and to complete the job without unreasonable delay. A–1 undertook the work within a
week thereafter, and when all the roofing material was at the site and the labor 50 percent
completed, the premises were totally destroyed
by fire caused by lightning. A–1 submitted a
bill to Jaffe for $600 for materials furnished and
labor performed up to the time of the destruction
of the premises. Jaffe refused to pay the bill
and A–1 sued Jaffe. Decision?

2. By contract dated January 5, 1982, A agreed
to sell to B and B agreed to buy from A a certain
parcel of land then zoned commercial. The specific intent of B, which was known to A, was to
erect a storage plant on the land. The contract
stated that the agreement was conditioned upon
B's ability to construct a storage plant upon the
land. The closing date for the transaction was
set for April 1, 1982. On February 15, 1982,
the city council rezoned the land from commercial to residential, which precluded the erection
of the storage plant intended by B. As the closing date drew near, B made it known to A that
he did not intend to go through with the purchase because the land could no longer be used
as intended. On April 1, 1982, A tendered the
deed to B, who refused to pay A the agreed purchase price. A brought an action against B for
breach of their contract. Decision?

3. The Perfection Produce Company entered
into a written contract, dated March 21, 1982,
with Hiram Hodges for the purchase of 200 tons
of potatoes to be grown on Hodge's farm in
Maine, at a stipulated price per ton. The land
would ordinarily produce 1,000 tons. Although
the planting and cultivation were properly done,
Hodges was able to deliver only 100 tons because
of a partial crop failure owing to an unprecedented drought. Hodges sued the produce com-

pany to recover an unpaid balance of the agreed
price for 100 tons of potatoes. The produce company, by an appropriate counterclaim against
Hodges, sought damages for his failure to deliver
the additional 100 tons. Decision?

4. On November 23, S agrees to sell to B his
Pontiac automobile for $7,000, delivery and pay-
ment to be made on December 1. On November
26, B informs S that he wishes to rescind the
contract and will pay S $350 if S agrees. S
agrees and takes the $350 cash. On December
1, B tenders to S $6,650 and demands that S
deliver the automobile. S refuses and B initiates a law suit. Decision?

5. S dealt in automobile accessories at wholesale. Although manufacturing a few items in
his own factory, among them windshield wipers,
S purchased most of his supplies from a large
number of other manufacturers. In January,
S entered into a written contract to sell B 2,000
windshield wipers for $1900, delivery to be made
June 1. In April, S's factory burned to the
ground and S failed to make delivery on June
1. B, forced to buy windshield wipers elsewhere
at a higher price, brings an action against S for
breach of contract. Decision?

6. On May 15, the Hughes Electric Company
and the Moss Coal Company entered into a written contract whereby the coal company agreed
to sell and deliver to the electric company 500
tons of coal at a stipulated price, on or before
November 1. By September 1, the market price
of coal had increased considerably and, on that
date, the coal company notified the electric company that it would not make delivery of the coal,
as agreed. By its reply, mailed on September
2, the electric company notified the coal company
that it would expect performance in full by the
coal company on November 1. On September
30, the electric company closed its plant temporarily because of a slump in the sales of elec-

tric equipment. On November 1, the coal company delivered 500 tons of coal to the electric company. The electric company refused to accept any part of the coal delivered. Thereafter, the coal company sues the electric company for damages for breach of contract. Decision?

7. Green owed White $3,500, which was due and payable on June 1. White owed Brown $3,500, which was due and payable on August 1. On May 25, White received a letter signed by Green stating: "If you will cancel my debt to you, in the amount of $3,500, I will pay, on the due date, the debt you owe Brown, in the amount of $3,500." On May 28, Green received a letter signed by White stating: "I received your letter and agree to the proposals recited therein. You may consider your debt to me cancelled as of the date of this letter." On June 1, White, needing money to pay his income taxes, made a demand upon Green to pay him the $3,500 due on that date. Is Green obligated to pay the money demanded by White?

8. By written contract Ames agreed to build a house on Bowen's lot for $45,000 commencing within 90 days of the date of the contract. Prior to the date for beginning construction, Ames informed Bowen that he was repudiating the contract and would not perform. Bowen refused to accept the repudiation and demanded fulfillment of the contract. Eighty days after the date of the contract, Bowen entered into a new contract with Curd for $42,000. The next day without knowledge or notice of Bowen's contract with Curd, Ames began construction. Bowen ordered Ames from the premises and refused to allow him to continue.

Ames sued Bowen for damages. Decision?

9. A agreed in writing to work for B for three years as superintendent of B's manufacturing establishment, and to devote himself entirely to the business, giving it his whole time, attention, and skill, for which he was to receive $24,000 per annum, in monthly installments of $2,000. A worked and was paid for the first twelve months, when through no fault of his own or B's, he was arrested and imprisoned for one month. It became imperative for B to employ another and he treated the contract with A as breached and abandoned, refusing to permit A to resume work upon his release from jail. What rights, if any, does A have under the contract?

10. The Park Plaza Hotel awarded the valet and laundry concession to Larson for a three-year term. The contract contained the following provision: "It is distinctly understood and agreed that the services to be rendered by Larson shall meet with the approval of the Park Plaza Hotel, which shall be the sole judge of the sufficiency and propriety of the services." After seven months, the hotel gave a month's notice to discontinue services based on the failure of the services to meet its approval. Larson brought an action against the hotel, alleging that its dissatisfaction was unreasonable. The hotel defended upon the ground that subjective or personal satisfaction may be the sole justification for termination of the contract. Decision?

16

REMEDIES FOR BREACH OF CONTRACT

When one party to a contract defaults and does not respond to demands for performance of his contractual promises, the law provides a remedy. However, it is impossible for any remedy to equal the promised performance. The promisee has a primary right to exact performance by the promisor. His right to a judgment for money damages in a court of law or to a decree of specific performance in a court of equity is a secondary right. The only relief that any court can give the contractual promisee is what it regards as an equivalent of the promised performance. Even a decree of specific performance does not give the promisee what he was entitled to receive by the terms of the contract. The remedy comes at the end of a lawsuit many months or even years after the performance was due. Time may have been a matter of great importance to the promisee. A time interval between the date when a party to a contract is entitled to have his primary right fulfilled and when he receives fulfillment of his secondary right cannot be avoided. We are a government of laws, not of men.

The law of sales of personal property, such as goods, wares, and merchandise, a specialized branch of the law of contracts, is governed by Article 2 of the U.C.C. The remedies of sellers and buyers of goods are too particularized to warrant discussion in this chapter, but are treated in Chapter 26.

MONEY DAMAGES

Compensatory Damages

The right to recover compensatory money damages for breach of contract is always available to the injured party. The purpose in allowing damages is to provide compensation to the plaintiff which will place him in as nearly good a position as if the defendant had performed under the contract. In the case of a unilateral contract, the plaintiff is not a promisor and the measure of damages is the value of the performance promised by the defendant. In the case of a bilateral contract which is either wholly or partly unperformed by the plaintiff, that is, executory on both sides, the measure of damages is the amount of loss sustained by the plaintiff by reason of the defendant's non-performance.

A leading case on the subject of compensatory damages is Hadley v. Baxendale, decided in England in 1854. In this case the plaintiffs operated a flour mill and conducted an extensive milling business at Gloucester. Their mill was compelled to cease operating because of a broken crank shaft attached to the steam engine which furnished power to the mill. It was necessary to send the broken shaft to a foundry located at Greenwich so that a new shaft could be made that would fit the other parts of the engine. The plaintiffs delivered the broken shaft to the defendants, who were common carriers, for transportation from Gloucester to Greenwich and informed defendants that the shaft must be sent immediately. The defendants received the shaft, collected the freight charges in advance, and promised the plaintiffs to deliver the shaft at Greenwich the following day. The defendants neglected to make prompt delivery as promised, and as a result the resumption of the operation of the mill was delayed for several days and the plaintiffs lost profits which they otherwise would have received. The defendants contended that the loss of profits was too remote to be recoverable. In awarding damages to the plaintiffs, the jury was permitted to take into consideration the loss of these profits. The Court of Exchequer ordered a new trial on the ground that the special circumstances which caused the loss of profits, namely, the continued stoppage of the mill while awaiting the return of the repaired crank shaft, had never been communicated by the plaintiffs to the defendants. Unless given express notice of these circumstances, a common carrier would not reasonably foresee that the plaintiffs' mill would be shut down as a result of delay in transporting the broken crank shaft.

The Restatement, Second, Contracts, Section 351, expresses the rule as follows:

(1) Damages are not recoverable for loss that the party in breach did not have reason to foresee as a probable result of the breach when the contract was made.

(2) Loss may be foreseeable as a probable result of a breach because it follows from the breach
    (a) in the ordinary course of events, or
    (b) as a result of special circumstances, beyond the ordinary course of events, that the party in breach had reason to know.

(3) A court may limit damages for foreseeable loss by excluding recovery for loss of profits, by allowing recovery only for loss incurred in reliance, or otherwise if it concludes that in the circumstances justice so requires in order to avoid disproportionate compensation.

Consequential or Special Damages

A seller of goods who expressly or impliedly warrants the goods to have a certain quality may be liable for special damages sustained by the buyer which were the readily foreseeable consequences of a breach of the warranty. Unwholesome food sold for human consumption may involve the seller in extensive liability. A seller of livestock who warrants the animals to be sound when, in fact, they are diseased and communicate the disease to other animals belonging to the buyer, is liable not only for the expense of a veterinarian and medicine, but for all of the damages inflicted upon the other animals. If the seller of a horse expressly warrants it to be gentle, as he may have reason to believe, and the horse, when hitched to a buggy, runs away with the buyer causing the buggy to overturn and to break the buyer's leg, the special damages recoverable against the seller, including the medical and hospital expenses of the buyer and the property damage to the buggy, may be far in excess of the value or price of the horse. Where a farmer buys seeds with a warranty, he may recover the loss or diminished value of the crop resulting from a breach of the warranty. Special damages are designated consequential damages and are recoverable under the U.C.C. Sections 2–714, 2–715.

The above instances of special damages are to be distinguished from the ordinary measures of damages in the case of a breach of warranty which is the difference between the value of the goods if they had been as warranted and the value of the goods in their actual condition when received by the buyer (see Chapter 24).

Nominal Damages

An action to recover damages for breach of contract may be maintained even though the plaintiff has not sustained or cannot prove any injury or loss resulting from the breach. In such case he will be permitted to recover nominal damages, such as $1.00 and costs. Because of his inability to show a loss, the plaintiff is not entitled to compensatory damages.

Punitive Damages

The usual purpose in allowing damages is to compensate the plaintiff for the loss which he has sustained by reason of the defendant's breach of contract or wrongful conduct. In a case in which the plaintiff has established a breach of contract and evidence of loss or damage, the court will award him a judgment in an amount it deems sufficient to place him in the position in which he would have been if the defendant had not breached the contract. In a tort case the objective is to compensate the plaintiff in an amount commensurate with the injury sustained based upon his condition and position prior to the injury.

In certain situations involving willful, wanton or malicious torts, the courts have allowed exemplary or punitive damages, sometimes referred to as "smart money." The purpose is to punish the defendant and thereby discourage him and others from similar wrongful conduct. Damages assessed by way of punishment to the wrongdoer are in addition to the amount of compensatory damages and are imposed to make an example of the defendant and to deter others from such conduct.

The Restatement, Second, Contracts, Section 355, provides: "Punitive damages are not recoverable for a breach of contract unless the conduct constituting the breach is also a tort for which punitive damages are recoverable."

A willful breach of fiduciary duty may also result in the imposition of punitive damages where the defendant has held himself out to the public as experienced and competent in some business or professional field of activity, and has grossly violated the trust reposed in him by the plaintiff. In one case, the defendant, a licensed real estate broker, suggested to the plaintiff that he enter into an "exchange contract" whereby he would sell his old house and purchase a new one with the proceeds of the sale. To accomplish this, the broker obtained a conveyance to himself of the old house in which the plaintiff had an equity of $9,000. The broker thereupon obtained for plaintiff a new house with no equity value. When the plaintiff hesitated entering into this transaction and suggested that he obtain a lawyer, the broker advised that he was a lawyer and would take care of him. The Court sustained a jury finding of compensatory damages of $7,000 and punitive damages of $7,500. Brown v. Coates, 253 F.2d 36, 67 A.L.R.2d 943 (C.A.D.C.1958).

Liquidated Damages

A contract may contain a provision whereby one of the parties promises to pay to the other a fixed sum of money, or a fixed rate for each day of delayed performance, in the event of his breach. Such a liquidated damage provision will be enforced if it amounts to a reasonable forecast of just compensation for the loss which may result from the breach. If, however, the sum agreed upon as liquidated damages does not bear a reasonable relationship to the amount of probable loss which may result from breach, it will be treated as an invalid penalty. The law abhors a penalty and will look at the substance of the provision, the nature of the contract, and extent of probable harm to the promisee which may reasonably be expected to be caused by a breach, in order to determine whether the agreed amount is proper as liquidated damages or unenforceable as a penalty. It is immaterial what name or label the parties to the contract attach to the provision. A reasonable provision for liquidated damages whereby the parties substitute their concept of the amount of loss for that of a court or jury may be especially useful in a situation where the loss caused by a breach may be extremely difficult of accurate estimation.

RESTITUTION

Return of Consideration

One of the remedies which may be available to a party to a contract for a breach by the other is restitution. This remedy is an alternative to recovery of damages for breach of contract. A party may not have both restitution and damages. Restitution is a return to the aggrieved party of the consideration, or its value, which he gave to the other party. An action for damages seeks to recover the value of the performance promised by the defendant. The object of restitution is to restore the injured party to the position he was in before the contract was made. However a seller of goods on credit, upon failure of the buyer to pay for them, is not permitted to rescind the sale and sue the buyer either to recover the possession of the goods or their value. But, a seller who has tranferred to the buyer a parcel of real estate or a unique chattel, or exclusive privileges such as patents or copyrights, in the event of total failure of consideration by the buyer, may rescind the sale and obtain a cancellation of the deed of conveyance, a return of the unique chattel, or a reassignment of the patents or copy-

rights, provided the buyer has not transferred them to a bona fide purchaser for value.

Restitution Not Available to Party in Default

A person who is in default for failure to perform or tender his promised performance and has no excuse for non-performance, is not entitled to recover for a breach by the other party. If the plaintiff having only partially performed is permitted to recover, the court is enforcing a contract different from that which the parties made in allowing the plaintiff to sell his partial performance at a value fixed by a court or jury to a defendant who has agreed to pay only for a complete performance. However, in certain situations, a denial of recovery to the plaintiff who has not completely performed would result in unfairly benefiting the defendant and would impose a forfeiture on the plaintiff. The doctrine of substantial performance, as applied to a building contract, is an illustration of the principle involved. A contractor who has substantially performed the contract may recover the contract price less the cost of completion of the building.

REMEDIES IN EQUITY

Specific Performance

While in most cases an action at law to recover money damages for breach of contract is both an adequate remedy and the only one available to the plaintiff, there are certain contracts in which the promised performance is specifically enforceable. Only a court of equity may decree specific performance. Contracts to buy and sell land are specifically enforceable, as each parcel of land is unique and by location and nature differs from every other parcel. Money damages are inadequate relief to a buyer of land who needs the specific land for a home or for the location or expansion of a business. Contracts for the purchase of personal property may be specifically enforced if the property is unique, such as a particular painting by Rembrandt, a famous race horse, a patent, or an invention.

To be specifically enforceable, the promise must be clear, unambiguous, and relate to a specific identifiable item. A court of equity will not enter a decree which is impossible of performance or which would involve the court in the supervision of details of performance. The decree of specific performance is an order requiring the defendant to perform a certain act or to refrain from certain conduct, and the court has power to enforce compliance with its decree by finding the defendant in contempt of court for non-compliance and by imprisoning him for such contempt.

A court will not decree specific performance of a building contract, as enforcement of the decree would require minute supervision of the details and progress of construction. A court will also not decree specific performance of a contract for personal services. However, a court of equity will enforce negative covenants in a contract for personal services where damages for a breach would be inadequate. If a concert pianist has contracted that he will not perform publicly during a certain period of time in order to provide added attractiveness to an advertised and scheduled performance, the court will enforce this promise specifically by an injunction. It is much easier for the court to enforce a negative covenant, a promise to refrain from doing something, by enjoining the defendant from doing that which would constitute a breach, than to enforce a promise of affirmative performance. A court would not decree that the concert pianist must appear at a certain time and place and play a certain program.

Contracts within the Statute of Frauds but not in compliance with its provisions are specifically enforceable by reason of part performance. The Restatement, Contracts, Section 197, referred to at the beginning of this chapter, provides:

Where, acting under an oral contract for the transfer of an interest in land, the purchaser with the assent of the vendor

    (a) makes valuable improvements on the land, or

    (b) takes possession thereof or retains a possession thereof existing at the time of the bargain, and also pays a portion or all of the purchase price,

the purchaser or the vendor may specifically enforce the contract.

Injunctions

The injunction is a powerful arm of a court of equity. It is a formal order of the court commanding a person or persons to do a specific act or acts, or to refrain from doing a specific act or acts, or to refrain from engaging in specified conduct. A person who violates an injunctive order may be held guilty of contempt of court and fined or imprisoned until released by court order.

A court of equity, as previously noted, will by injunction enforce negative covenants in a contract for personal services, although not affirmative convenants. Thus, if an aspiring boxer enters into a contract to box the world's champion in a championship match which provides that prior to the match he will not engage in any other boxing match, a court of equity will not order him to box with the champion but will enjoin him from taking part in any other boxing match prior to the championship match.

LIMITATIONS ON REMEDIES

Election of Remedies

If a party is aggrieved by a breach of contract and has more than one remedy available to him, his manifestation of a choice of one of them by bringing suit or otherwise is not a bar to another remedy unless the remedies are inconsistent and the other party materially changes his position in reliance on the manifestation. Restatement, Second, Contracts, Section 378. For example, a party who seeks specific performance, an injunction or restitution may be entitled to incidental damages such as delay in performance. However, damages for total breach are inconsistent with the remedies of specific performance, an injunction or restitution.

Damages for Breach of Alternative Promises

A contract may contain alternative promises. The promisee may be given the election as to which of these promises he desires the promisor to perform. If the contract is silent as to which party has the election, the promisor has the right to determine which of the alternative promises he will perform. In such event his failure to perform either promise will cause him to be liable upon the lesser of his promises, that is, the one which will result in the smallest recovery by the promisee. Thus, A contracts to build for B either a boat for $2,000 or a barge for $1,000, each according to stated specifications. In the event of a breach, A is liable to B for the damages which result from his failure to build the barge, assuming this to be the lesser of the alternative promises and to subject him to the least liability.

Mitigation of Damages

Where a breach of contract occurs, the injured party is required to take such steps as may be reasonably calculated to lessen or mitigate the damages that he may sustain. Where a buyer receives inferior goods furnished to him under a contract, he may not enhance his damages by continuing to use the goods after learning of their unfitness. Similarly, a buyer who does not receive goods or services promised to him under a contract cannot recover damages resulting from his doing without such goods or services where it is possible for him to substitute other goods or services which he can obtain elsewhere. Where A is under a contract to manufacture goods for B who repudiates the contract after A has commenced performance, A will not be allowed to recover loss which he sustains by continuing to manufacture the goods, if to do so would increase the amount of his damages. If the goods were almost completed when B repudiated, the completion of the goods might mitigate the damages as the finished goods may be resalable whereas the unfinished goods may not. If A contracts to work for B for one year for a weekly salary and after two months is wrongfully discharged by B, A must use reasonable efforts to mitigate his damages by seeking other employment. If he cannot obtain other employment of the same general character, he is entitled to recover full pay for the contract period that he is unemployed. He is not obliged to accept a radically different type of employment or to accept work at a distant place. A person who is employed as a school teacher or accountant and is wrongfully discharged is not obliged in order to mitigate damages to accept available employment as a chauffeur or truck driver.

Cases

Compensatory Damages;
Mitigation of Damages

COPENHAVER v. BERRYMAN

(1980, Tex.Civ.App.) 602 S.W.2d 540.

NYE, C. J.

Appellants filed a motion for rehearing bringing to our attention certain matters that warrant elaboration. Although we adhere to our original determination of this case, in order to respond to appellants' complaints on motion for rehearing in an orderly fashion, we withdraw our original opinion and substitute the following opinion in its place.

Kent L. Copenhaver and Earl T. Platt, d/b/a Valley Laundry Service, filed suit against John W. Berryman, Sr., John W.

Berryman, Jr., and Joel William Ellis, d/b/a The Village Apartments, seeking damages for defendants' breach of a written contract between the parties. After a non-jury trial, the trial judge entered a judgment awarding plaintiffs damages in the amount of $3,525.84. The trial judge filed findings of fact and conclusions of law supportive of this judgment. The plaintiffs appeal, contending that the express terms of the contract and the undisputed evidence, entitled them to more damages than were awarded by the trial court.

The defendants own a large apartment complex in Harlingen, Texas. The plaintiffs are in the business of owning and operating laundry facilities which are located in various apartment complexes, condominiums, and trailer parks in several cities in the Rio Grande Valley. In December, 1975, plaintiffs purchased eight washing machines and four driers from Mr. B. O. Hooks, who owned the machines and operated the laundry facility located at the defendants' apartment complex. Thereafter, on January 21, 1976, plaintiffs and defendants executed a contract which is now in question.

The parties operated under the terms of the five-year contract until October, 1976, when defendants, who had purchased their own laundry equipment, desired to terminate the contract. By a letter dated November 10, 1976, defendant Ellis advised plaintiffs that the contract was being terminated as of December 1, 1976. Defendants protested and an exchange of correspondence between the parties ensued. After failing to reach an agreement concerning defendants' expressed intention to terminate the contract, plaintiffs were informed on March 10, 1977, that their laundry equipment had been removed from the premises. The next day, plaintiff Copenhaver drove to the apartment complex and recovered the laundry equipment.

Plaintiffs filed suit, alleging that they had complied with all of the duties pursuant to the contract and that defendants had wrongfully repudiated and breached the contract by removing plaintiffs' equipment and installing other equipment, thus, making it impossible for plaintiffs to continue their operation under the contract. Plaintiffs alleged that they were entitled to conduct the laundry operations for an additional forty-seven months, and by such, would have earned a profit of $13,886.58, after deducting defendants' share of the gross receipts and other operating expenses. Defendants answered, alleging, in part, that plaintiffs had suffered no damages from the removal of their laundry equipment because plaintiffs had placed such equipment into immediate use in other laundry facilities they operated and were earning as much or more now than when the equipment was located in defendants' facilities.

After a non-jury trail, the trial judge entered a judgment awarding plaintiffs damages in the amount of $3,525.84. In support of this judgment, the trial judge entered the following relevant findings of fact: 1) "[T]he Equipment Lease Agreement" executed by the parties was "for the purpose of leasing laundry equipment" by the plaintiffs to the defendants; 2) defendants had breached such agreement on March 10, 1977; 3) plaintiffs suffered damages caused by such breach for the six-month period from March 10, 1977, until September 10, 1977, in the amount of $3,525.84; 4) after September 10, 1977, plaintiffs leased the equipment covered by the agreement to others and received more rental income from the same machines; 5) plaintiffs did not suffer any loss or damage after September 10, 1977, by reason of defendants' breach of the contract in question.

Plaintiffs' appeal is based upon the trial court's failure to award damages for the entire duration of the forty-seven month period remaining under the terms of the contract.

Before addressing the merits of plaintiffs' specific points, however, a brief review of some of the principles relating to damages and mitigation of damages is necessary to gain the proper appellate perspective of the contentions advanced by the respective parties. As a general rule, damages for breach of contract seek to allow the injured party to have just compensation for the damages or loss actually sustained. [Citations.] The burden is upon the complaining party to establish his right to recover compensatory damages by proving he suffered a pecuniary loss as a result of the breach. [Citations.]

Here plaintiffs sought to recover damages measured by loss of profits they sustained due to defendants' breach of the contract. As a general rule, where it is shown that a loss of profit is a natural and probable consequence of the act or omission complained of, and the amount is shown with sufficient certainty, recovery of lost profits is permitted. Anticipated profits, however, cannot be recovered where they are dependent upon uncertain and changing conditions, such as market fluctuations or a change of business, or where there is no evidence from which they may be intelligently estimated. Evidence to establish profits must not be uncertain or speculative. It is not neccessary that profits should be susceptible of exact calculation. It is sufficient that there be data from which they may be ascertained with a reasonable degree of certainty and exactness. [Citations.] The term, "net profits" is, " 'to a large degree, self-explanatory and implies, generally speaking, what remains in the conduct of a business after deducting from its total receipts all of the expenses incurred in carrying on the business.' " [Citations] In the calculation of net profits, allowance should be made for expenditures that the plaintiff would have been compelled to make, and also for the value of the plaintiff's time. 17 Tex.Jur.2d, Damages, § 144 (1960).

* * *

While the defendant is liable for the pecuniary loss sustained by the party injured by the breach, the party so injured must exercise, as a general rule, reasonable efforts in an attempt to minimize his damages. As stated by our Supreme Court in *Walker v. Salt Flat Water Co.*, 128 Tex. 140, 96 S.W.2d 231, 232 (1936):

Where a party is entitled to the benefits of a contract and can save himself from the damages resulting from its breach at a trifling expense or with reasonable exertions, it is his duty to incur such expense and make such exertions.

Although the injured party has a duty to minimize his loss, the burden of proof as to the extent to which the damages were or could have been mitigated lies with the party who has breached the contract.

* * *

Plaintiffs testified that all of the equipment in question was in use in other locations within six months after such equipment had been removed from defendants' premises. There is some testimony to indicate that plaintiffs could not determine the exact location of these machines nor the sum of money the machines generated in their new locations. There is other testimony to indicate that plaintiffs had this information available to them but that plaintiffs would have to search their records to obtain the information, which plaintiffs had not done as of the time of trial. Plaintiffs agreed that all of the equipment in question as relocated was "earning money," and "are still earning money." Plaintiffs testified that they did not pay for the utilities in any of their laundry contracts. It was probable that the equipment was relocated under contracts allowing plaintiffs at least the same percentage of the gross receipts (60%) as plaintiffs received from the equipment when it was located on defendants' premises. The cost to the consumer, however, had increased by 35% from the date of the breach to the date of the trial.

There is evidence that plaintiffs experienced an increase in the size of their business between the time of the breach and the time of trial by adding approximately 350 machines and at least fourteen to fifteen new locations. Plaintiffs testified in substance that the major factor in expanding their business was obtaining desirable locations. According to plaintiffs, equipment was comparatively easy to obtain. Plaintiffs admitted the profitability of a particular location was dependent upon some fluctuating factors which were beyond their control such as seasonal fluctuations and the percent of occupancy. There is little or no evidence concerning these factors as they related to the laundry location in question or to any other laundry locations containing plaintiffs' equipment.

Plaintiffs presented somewhat contradictory and confusing testimony concerning the manner in which "profits" were determined. There is testimony that the service for all of the equipment was done by one man who was compensated by a fixed salary and that the only variable expenses were the cost of repair parts and mileage reimbursement expenses. Although plaintiffs testified in substance that their fixed expenses or overhead did not increase when they added defendants' laundry facility to their business, they also testified that fixed expenses represented an amount of approximately 30% of their gross income, a variable figure.

We are of the opinion that there is evidence in the record to support the finding of fact that the plaintiffs suffered no damage from September 10, 1977, to the date of trial. After September 10, all of the equipment was in use in other locations. There is also some evidence in the record from which the trial judge, sitting as fact-finder, reasonably could conclude that plaintiffs were generating at least as much income, if not more, from the operation of the machines in question after September 10, 1977.

* * *

Plaintiffs, however, apparently contend the case before us is different because of the nature of their over-all business. In effect, plaintiffs contend the proof established, as a matter of law, that they were capable of performing a number of concurrent laundry facility contracts which performance is limited solely by the availability of facilities for the placement of such equipment. Implicit in this contention is the assumption that, when defendants breached the contract in question, the expansion of plaintiffs' business was thereby limited because they were forced to place the equipment in question into a location they would have acquired anyway.

The testimony concerning the plaintiff's over-all business is vague, speculative, and conclusory. The only evidence we can find to substantiate this contention is some general testimony to the effect that plaintiffs acquired some 14 to 15 new locations after the breach. Plaintiffs admitted they did not even know where the machines in question were ultimately placed. Nor, did plaintiffs introduce evidence from which it could be reasonably concluded that they would have expanded to each new location even had defendants not breached the contract in question and that defendants' breach somehow limited their expansion.

We are of the opinion that the trial judge could reach no reasonable conclusion other than to find plaintiffs had not proved they were damaged beyond the six-month period, after which all the machines were in use in other locations.

* * *

The judgment of the trial court is affirmed.

Liquidated Damages

CITY OF RYE v. PUBLIC SERVICE MUTUAL INSURANCE CO.

(1974) 34 N.Y.2d 470, 358 N.Y.S.2d 391, 315 N.E.2d 458.

[Defendant developers under a plan approved by the City of Rye Planning Commission had constructed six luxury cooperative apartment buildings, and were to construct six more. In order to obtain certificates of occupancy for the six completed buildings, they were required to post a bond with the city to ensure completion of the six remaining buildings. They posted a $100,000 bond, upon which defendant Insurance Company was surety, and agreed to pay $200 for each day after April 1, 1971 that the six remaining buildings were not completed, up to the aggregate amount of the bond. More than 500 days passed without completion of the buildings within the time limit. In a suit by the city to recover $100,000 on the bond, the court held that the amount of the bond was not a reasonable estimate of probable monetary harm or damage to the city, but a penalty. Recovery was therefore denied. On appeal, affirmed.]

BREITEL, C. J.

* * *

Concededly, no statute authorizes the city to exact a penalty or forfeiture from the developers. If there were such a statute, the statutory penalty would undoubtedly be upheld. [Citations.] Hence, general principles of contract law governing the enforceability of liquidated damage clauses should apply. [Citations.] The sole issue, then, becomes whether the agreement exacted from the developers and the conditional bond supplied provide for a penalty or for liquidated damages. If the agreement provides for a penalty or forfeiture without statutory authority, it is unenforceable. Where, however, damages flowing from a breach are difficult to ascertain, a provision fixing the damages in advance will be upheld if the amount is a reasonable measure of the anticipated probable harm. [Citations.] If, on the other hand, the amount fixed is grossly disproportionate to the anticipated probable harm or if there were no anticipatable harm, the provision will not be enforced.

The harm which the city contends it would suffer by delay in construction is minimal, speculative, or simply not cognizable. The city urges that its inspectors and employees will be required to devote more time to the project than anticipated because it has taken extra years to complete. It also urges that it will lose tax revenues for the years the buildings are not completed. It contends, too, that it is harmed by a continuing violation of the height restrictions of its zoning ordinance. This is entailed because the 12 buildings in the entire complex vary in height between two and four stories; the ordinance sets a maximum average height of 30 feet for the complex; and the taller buildings, those higher than the allowable average, were built first. Only after all of the structures in the complex are built will the project comply with the average height requirement of the ordinance.

The most serious disappointments in expectation suffered by the city are not pecuniary in nature and therefore not measurable in monetary damages. The effect on increased inspectorial services or on tax revenue are not likely to be substantial and, in any event, are not developed in the record on summary judgment. There is nothing to show that either the sum of $200 per day or the aggregate amount of the bond bear any reasonable relationship to the pecuniary harm likely to be suffered or in fact suffered.

There is, as noted, no statutory authority for the city to exact harsh penal bonds from developers who are perforce dependent on approvals by local officials at the various stages of construction, and after construction for certificates of occupancy. For municipalities, without statutory authorization or restriction, to condition perhaps arbitrarily the grant of building permits or certificates of occupancy on large penalty bonds raises potential for grave abuse. A developer, especially an outside developer, is rarely in a position to bargain on an equal basis with local officials, after completion of buildings rendered useless and an economic drain without a certificate of occupancy. Whether, and under what circumstances, the drastic remedy of penal bonds may be exacted is a matter best left to legislated authority, standards, and limitations.

There is no suggestion in this case that the developers' delay was purposeful. Apparently, the mortgage market "dried up" and the developers could not obtain additional financing for the remaining six buildings in the time planned.

* * *

[Judgment for defendant affirmed.]

Equitable Remedies

FELCH v. FINDLAY COLLEGE

(1963) 119 Ohio App. 357, 200 N.E.2d 353.

GUERNSEY, J.

This is an appeal on questions of law and fact from a judgment of the Common Pleas Court for the defendant, Findlay College, a private nonprofit corporation.

Plaintiff, William E. Felch, alleges, among other things, that he was employed by the defendant as a member of its faculty on a continuing basis and that contrary to and without compliance with the provisions for dismissal contained in administrative memoranda purporting to require certain hearings the board of trustees of defendant on August 22, 1961, approved the action of its president on July 20, 1961, dismissing the plaintiff effective August 11, 1961. Plaintiff prays that "defendant be enjoined from carrying into effect the dismissal of this plaintiff as a member of the faculty * * * and that the defendant may be ordered to continue plaintiff as such member of the faculty of Findlay College, Findlay, Ohio, and that defendant be ordered to pay to this plaintiff the salary agreed upon."

In essence and in legal effect plaintiff seeks by injunction the specific performance of an employment contract. There are no Ohio statutes which purport to entitle plaintiff to the relief prayed for, and plaintiff's rights must be determined by general equitable principles.

* * *

In 81 C.J.S. Specific Performance § 82, p. 591, the rule is stated as follows:

"In general, specific performance does not lie to enforce a provision in a contract for the performance of personal services requiring special knowledge, ability, experience, or the exercise of judgment, skill, taste, discretion, labor, tact, energy, or integrity, *particularly where the performance of such services would be continuous over a long period of time.* This rule is based on the fact that mischief likely to result from an enforced continuance of the relationship incident to the service after it has become personally obnoxious to one of the parties is so great that the interests of society require that the remedy be denied, and on the fact that the enforcement of a decree requiring the performance of such a contract would impose too great a burden on the courts. * * *

However, it is claimed by the plaintiff * * * that the provisions of the plaintiff's contract require a hearing before dismissal and that the same constitutes a negative covenant, i.e., that the defendant has agreed not to dismiss the plaintiff without following such dismissal procedure. It is recognized under the law of injunctions and specific performance that notwithstanding that a personal service contract may not ordinarily be ordered specifically performed, a negative covenant in such contract may, under some circumstances, be enforced by injunction. However, there are limitations on such enforcement. As stated in 2 Restatement of the Law of Contracts, 704, Section 380:

"(1) An injunction against the breach of a contractual duty that is negative in character may be granted either "(a) to prevent harm for which money damages are not an adequate remedy caused by the breach of the negative promise itself, even though there are accompanying affirmative promises by either party that will not be specifically enforced, *unless such partial enforcement will lead to unjust or harmful results:* or

"(b) as an indirect mode of specifically enforcing an accompanying affirmative promise, if it is likely to be effective for that purpose *and if the affirmative promise is itself one that would be enforced by affirmative decree* except for the mere practical difficulties of such enforcement." (Emphasis added.)

Thus, even if the provisions for a hearing are, as claimed by plaintiff, a negative covenant, the enforcement of same would still lead to the same "unjust or harmful results" which constitute reasons for denying specific performance of the affirmative promise to employ plaintiff, and the enforcement of the negative covenant may not be used indirectly to specifically enforce the accompanying affirmative promise to employ for the reason that the affirmative promise is *not* "itself one that would be enforced by affirmative decree."

For these reasons it is the opinion and judgment of this court that the remedy of specific performance, either in itself or by means of the injunctive process, is not available to the plaintiff to enforce the provisions of the employment contract which he claims to exist between himself and defendant private college.

Judgment affirmed.

Injunctions

MADISON SQUARE GARDEN CORP., ILL. v. CARNERA

(1931 2nd Cir.) 52 F.2d 47.

Suit by plaintiff, Madison Square Garden Corporation, against Primo Carnera, defen-

dant. From an order granting an injunction against defendant, defendant appeals.

CHASE, CIRCUIT JUDGE.

On January 13, 1931, the plaintiff and defendant by their duly authorized agents entered into the following agreement in writing:

"1. Carnera agrees that he will render services as a boxer in his next contest (which contest, hereinafter called the 'First Contest,' shall be with the winner of the proposed Schmeling-Stribling contest, or, if the same is drawn, shall be with Schmeling, and shall be deemed to be a contest for the heavyweight championship title; provided, however, that, in the event of the inability of the Garden to cause Schmeling or Stribling, as the case may be, to perform the terms of his agreement with the Garden calling for such contest, the Garden shall be without further liability to Carnera,) exclusively under the auspices of the Garden, in the United States of America, or the Dominion of Canada, at such time, not, however, later than midnight of September 30, 1931, as the Garden may direct. * * *

"9. Carnera shall not, pending the holding of the First Contest, render services as a boxer in any major boxing contest, without the written permission of the Garden in each case had and obtained. A major contest is understood to be one with Sharkey, Baer, Campolo, Godfrey, or like grade heavyweights, or heavyweights who shall have beaten any of the above subsequent to the date hereof. If in any boxing contest engaged in by Carnera prior to the holding of the First Contest, he shall lose the same, the Garden shall at its option, to be exercised by a two weeks' notice to Carnera in writing, be without further liability under the terms of this agreement to Carnera. Carnera shall not render services during the continuance of the option referred to in paragraph 8 hereof for any person, firm or corporation other than the Garden. Carnera shall, however, at all times be permitted to engage in sparring exhibitions in which no decision is rendered and in which the heavyweight championship title is not at stake, and in which Carnera boxes not more than four rounds with any one opponent. * * *"

Thereafter the defendant, without the permission of the plaintiff, written or otherwise, made a contract to engage in a boxing contest with the Sharkey mentioned in paragraph 9 of the agreement above quoted, and by the terms thereof the contest was to take place before the first contest mentioned in the defendant's contract with the plaintiff was to be held.

The plaintiff then brought this suit to restrain the defendant from carrying out his contract to box Sharkey, and obtained the preliminary injunction order, from which this appeal was taken. Jurisdiction is based on diversity of citizenship and the required amount is involved.

The District Court has found on affidavits which adequately show it that the defendant's services are unique and extraordinary. A negative covenant in a contract for such personal services is enforceable by injunction where the damages for a breach are incapable of ascertainment. [Citations.]

The defendant points to what is claimed to be lack of consideration for his negative promise, in that the contract is inequitable and contains no agreement to employ him. It is true that there is no promise in so many words to employ the defendant to box in a contest with Stribling or Schmeling, but the agreement read as a whole binds the plaintiff to do just that, providing either Stribling or Schmeling becomes the contestant as the result of the match between them and can be induced to box the defendant. The defendant has agreed to "render services as a boxer" for the plaintiff exclusively, and the plaintiff has agreed to pay him a definite percentage of the gate receipts as his compensation for so doing. The promise to employ the defendant to enable him to earn the compensation agreed upon is implied to the same force and effect as though expressly stated. * * * [Citations.]

As we have seen, the contract is valid and enforceable. It contains a restrictive covenant which may be given effect. Whether a preliminary injunction shall be issued under such circumstances rests in the sound discretion of the court. [Citations.] The District Court, in its discretion, did issue the preliminary injunction and required the plaintiff as a condition upon its issuance to secure its own performance of the contract in suit with a bond for $25,000 and to give a bond in the sum of $35,000 to pay the defendant such damages as he may sustain by reason of the injunction. Such an order is clearly not an abuse of discretion.

Order affirmed.

Election of Remedies

BILLY WILLIAMS BUILDERS & DEVELOP. INC. v. HILLERICH
(1969 Ky.) 446 S.W.2d 280.

EDWARD P. HILL, J.

Appellees (hereinafter Hillerich) sued appellant (hereinafter Williams) for specific performance of a contract to convey a house and a lot, for damages growing out of the defective construction of the house, and for damages due to delay in performance.

* * *

The main thrust of Williams' argument concerns the right of the buyer to have two remedies (1) specific performance of a contract to purchase real estate (a house and a lot) and (2) damages for defective construction and for delay in performance. Williams argues that by complying with the judgment for specific performance and by accepting the deed to the property, Hillerich elected to have one of two inconsistent remedies; and by so doing, he cannot back up to the "forks of the road" and take a road different from the one on which he "first embarked."

In a proper case there can be little doubt that one may be entitled to the specific performance of a contract to purchase real estate and damages for delay in performance. [Citation.] But damages for deficiency of quantity or quality present a more complex question, on which there is some conflict among the authorities.

* * *

We find in Thompson on Real Property, volume 8A, chapter 57, § 4482, at page 487, the remedies available to both vendor and purchaser clearly defined in this fashion:

"Whether the vendor or purchaser is the plaintiff there are three alternatives presented when the vendor is able to give only a performance nonconforming in quantity, *quality* or value: (1) to refuse the remedy of specific performance; (2) to enforce the contract without any regard to the partial failure; (3) to decree a conveyance and allow the vendee an abatement from price equal to the value of the deficiency in the performance. If the vendor cannot convey the agreed quantity of the estate the vendee may have specific performance with pro tanto abatement of purchase price." (Emphasis ours.)

* * *

In Pomeroy's Specific Performance of Contracts, 3 ed., § 438, p. 903, it is said:

"The general doctrine if firmly settled, both in England and in this country, that a vendor whose estate is less than or different from that which he agreed to sell, or who cannot give the exact subject-matter embraced in his contract, will not be allowed to set up his inability as a defense against the demand of a purchaser who is willing to take what he can get with a compensation. The vendee may, if he so elect (sic), enforce a specific performance to the extent of the vendor's ability to comply with the terms of the agreement, and may compel a conveyance of the vendor's deficient estate, or defective title or partial subject-matter, and have compensation for the difference between the actual performance, and the performance which would have been an exact fulfillment of the terms of their contract."

* * *

We can see no reason for a distinction between a deficiency in quantity (short acreage or lack of title) and deficiency of quality (defective construction).

We conclude that appellees' remedies were not inconsistent so as to require an election of remedies and that the chancellor did not err in granting specific performance and directing that damages be ascertained by the common law division of the court.

* * *

Judgment affirmed.

Problems

1. A contracted to buy and B to sell to A, 1,000 barrels of sugar. B failed to deliver and A could not buy any sugar in the market, so that he was compelled to shut down his candy factory. (a) What damages is A entitled to recover? (b) Would it make any difference if B had been told by A that he wanted the sugar to make candies for the Christmas trade and that he had accepted contracts for the delivery by certain dates?

2. A agreed to erect an apartment building for B for $225,000, A to suffer deduction of $100 per day for every day of delay. A was twenty days late in finishing the job, losing ten days because of a strike and ten days by reason of delay on the part of the material men in furnishing A with material. A claims that he is entitled to payment in full (a) because the agreement as to $100 a day is a penalty; (b) because B had not shown that he has sustained any damage. Discuss each contention and decide.

3. A contracted with B, a shirtmaker, for 1,000 shirts for men. B manufactured and delivered 500 shirts which were paid for by A, who at the same time notified B that he could not use or dispose of the other 500 shirts and directed B not to manufacture any more under the contract. B proceeded to make up the other 500 shirts, tendered them to A, who refused to accept, and B then sued for the purchase price. Decision?

4. A contracts to act in a comedy for B and to comply with all theater regulations for four seasons. B promises to pay A $800 for each performance and to allow A one benefit performance each season. It is expressly agreed that "A shall not be employed in any other production for the period of the contract." A and B, during the first year of the contract, engaged in a terrible quarrel. Thereafter, A signed a contract to perform in C's production and ceased performing for B. B seeks (a) to prevent A from performing for C and (b) to require A to perform his contract with B. What result?

5. A leases a building to B for five years at a rental of $1,000 per month, commencing July 1, 1981, B depositing $10,000 as security for performance of all his covenants in the lease, to be retained by A in case of any breach on B's part, otherwise to be applied in payment of rent for the last ten months of the term of the lease. B defaulted in the payment of rent for the months of May and June, 1982. After proper notice to B of the termination of the lease for nonpayment of rent, A sued B for possession of the building and recovered a judgment for possession. Thereafter, B sues A to recover the $10,000 less the amount of rent due A for May and June, 1982. Decision?

6. (a) A and B enter into a written agreement under which A agrees to sell and B agrees to buy 100 shares of the 300 shares outstanding of the capital stock of the Infinitesimal Steel Corporation, whose shares are not listed on any exchange and are closely held, for $10 per share. A refused to deliver when tendered the $1,000 and B sues in equity for specific performance, tendering the $1,000. Decision?

(b) Modifying (a) above, assume that the subject matter of the agreement is stock of the United States Steel Corporation, which is traded on the New York Stock Exchange. Decision?

(c) Modifying (a) above, assume that the subject matter of the agreement is undeveloped farm land of little commercial value. Decision?

Agency

Chapter
17

RELATIONSHIP OF PRINCIPAL AND AGENT

Agency is a relationship between two persons whereby one of them (the agent) is authorized to act for and on behalf of the other (the principal). Within the scope of the authority granted to him by his principal, the agent may negotiate the terms of contracts with others and bind his principal to such contracts. An agent may be an employee of the principal, but this is not necessary to the existence of the relationship. The negligence of an agent in conducting the business of his principal exposes the principal to tort liability for injury and loss to third persons and judgment for money damages. A duly authorized agent may effect a transfer of his principal's title to real estate or personal property. The old maxim "Qui facet per alium, facet per se" (Who acts through another, acts himself) accurately describes the relationship of principal and agent.

If the law should require each party to a business transaction personally and directly to participate in effecting the transaction, the ability of any person to conduct

a business enterprise would be limited by the number of transactions that he could personally negotiate. This would severely curtail the size and operation of every business unit and practically paralyze commercial activity. Furthermore, it would make impossible the conduct of business by a corporation, which as an artificial legal entity can act only through its agents, officers, and employees. Moreover, it would radically change the fundamental rule of the law of partnership whereby every partner is an agent of the partnership with respect to the conduct of its business. The agency concept is therefore indispensable to modern trade and commerce. Through the use of agents, one person may enter into any number of business transactions with the same effect as if done by him personally, and in no more time than he would normally require to negotiate a single contract. A person may thus multiply and expand his business activities. If the law of agency were to be abolished, a substitute would have to be devised and made effective immediately in order for modern business to continue.

CREATION OF AGENCY

Scope of Agency Purposes

As a general rule, whatever business activity a person may accomplish personally he may do through an agent, and conversely, whatever he cannot legally do himself, he cannot authorize another to do for him. Thus a person may not validly authorize another to commit on his behalf an illegal or unlawful act or crime. Any such agreement is void, and all parties participating in the planning or commission of a crime or unlawful act are co-conspirators, and in effect, principals. Also a person may not appoint an agent to perform acts which are so peculiarly personal that their performance may not be delegated to another, as in the case of a contract for personal services.

Formalities

Agency is a consensual relationship that may arise by contract or agreement between principal and agent, by estoppel, or by ratification. Agency may result from a direction given by one person to another to act on his behalf with or without a promise by such other to act or any understanding that he is to receive compensation for his services if he acts. Because the relationship of principal and agent is consensual and not necessarily contractual, it may exist although the element of consideration is lacking. However, agency by contract or agreement is the most usual method of creating the relationship.

Agency by estoppel exists when a person by his conduct clothes another with apparent authority which reasonably induces a third person in reliance thereon to deal with such other person as his agent.

Ratification is an affirmance of the unauthorized act of an agent, or of the act of a purported agent, which relates back to the commission of the act with the same effect as if the act had been originally authorized.

Capacity

Capacity to Be a Principal. The capacity to act through an agent depends upon the capacity of the principal to do the act himself. For example, contracts entered into by a minor or an insane person are voidable. Consequently, the appointment of an agent by a minor or insane person and any resulting contracts are voidable, regardless of the agent's contractual capacity.

Capacity to Be an Agent. As the act of the agent is considered the act of the principal, the incapacity of an agent to bind himself by contract does not disqualify him from making a contract which is binding on his principal. Thus, minors and insane persons may act as agents. Although the contract of agency between the principal and the agent may be voidable, the contract between the principal and the third person who dealt with the agent is valid. Nonetheless, some mental capacity is necessary in an agent; therefore, minors of tender years and mental incompetents, under certain fact situations, may not have the capacity to act as agents.

CLASSIFICATION OF AGENCIES

Types of Principals

The identity of a principal may be disclosed, partially disclosed, or undisclosed. A principal is disclosed if "at the time of the transaction conducted by an agent, the other party has notice that the agent is acting for a principal and of the principal's identity." Restatement, Agency, Second Section 4(1). A principal is partially disclosed if "the other party has notice that the agent is or may be acting for a principal but has no notice of the principal's identity." Restatement, Agency, Second, Section 4(2). A principal is undisclosed if "the other party has no notice that the agent is acting for a principal." Restatement, Agency, Second, Section 4(3).

Types of Agents

Agents may be actual or ostensible. An actual agent is one to whom the principal has given express or implied authority to act. An ostensible agent is one to whom the principal has given no authority but by conduct has induced others to believe reasonably that he has authority to act.

Agents may also be classified as general or special. A general agent is one employed to transact all of the business of his principal, or all of his principal's business of a particular kind or in a particular place. A special agent is one employed to act for his principal only in a special transaction or for a particular purpose or class of work. He is not given entire control of a particular business operation.

A subagent is a person employed or appointed by an agent, with the knowledge and consent of the principal, to assist the agent in transacting the affairs of the principal. A subagent is an agent of the agent, and since the agent has the authority to appoint a subagent, the latter has authority to bind the principal and is in a fiduciary relationship with the principal and the agent.

Other Legal Relations

Two other legal relationships are closely related to agency: master-servant and principal-independent contractor. Historically, in a master and servant relationship, the servant generally performed duties of a ministerial nature. Therefore, a servant had very limited authority, if any, to enter into contracts on behalf of the master. A

significant element in distinguishing a master and servant relationship is the right of the master to control the physical conduct of the servant.

A person who engages an independent contractor to do a specific job does not have the right to control the conduct and activities of the independent contractor in the performance of his contract. This distinguishes an independent contractor from an agent and excludes responsibility of a person for the conduct of an independent contractor.

These relationships are summarized in the Restatement, Second, Agency, Section 2, as follows:

(1) A master is a principal who employs another to perform service in his affairs and who controls or has the right to control the physical conduct of the other in the performance of the service.

(2) A servant is an agent employed by a master to perform service in his affairs whose physical conduct in the performance of the service is controlled or is subject to the right to control by the master.

(3) An independent contractor is a person who contracts with another to do something for him but who is not controlled by the other nor subject to the other's right to control with respect to his physical conduct in the performance of the undertaking. He may or may not be an agent.

DUTIES OF AGENT TO PRINCIPAL

In addition to the express duties arising under any contract between the parties, an agent owes his principal the duties of obedience, diligence, providing information and an accounting, and loyalty as a fiduciary.

Duty of Obedience

The duty of obedience requires the agent to act in the principal's affairs only as authorized by the principal and to obey all reasonable instructions and directions of the principal in regard to the manner of performing the service that the agent has undertaken to perform.

Duty of Diligence

An agent must diligently act with reasonable care and skill in the performance of the work for which he is employed as well as exercise any special skill that he may have.

Duty to Inform

An agent must use reasonable efforts to give the principal information which is relevant to the affairs entrusted to him and which, as the agent knows or should know, the principal would desire to have.

Duty to Account

The agent is under a duty to maintain and render to the principal a true and complete account of money or other property which the agent has received or expended on behalf of the principal.

Fiduciary Duties

A fiduciary duty is one which arises out of a relationship of trust and confidence. It is a duty imposed by law which a trustee owes to a beneficiary of the trust, an officer or director of a corporation owes to the corporation and its shareholders, a lawyer owes to his clients, an employee owes to his employer, and an agent owes to his principal. Fiduciary duties are not limited to these situations but exist in every relationship where one person reposes trust and confidence in another.

The fiduciary duty is one of utmost loyalty and good faith. An agent must act solely in the interest of his principal and not in his own interest or in the interest of another. An agent may not represent his principal in any transaction in which he has a personal interest, nor take a position in conflict with the interest of his principal, unless the principal, with full knowledge of all of the facts, consents. The agent owes his principal at all times the duty of full disclosure. He does not deal with his principal at arm's length.

The fiduciary duty of an agent prevents him from competing with his principal concerning the subject matter of the agency, or acting on behalf of a competitor or for persons whose interests conflict with those of the principal. An agent who is employed to buy may not buy from himself. An agent who is employed to sell may not become the purchaser, nor may he act as agent for the purchaser. The agent's loyalty must be undivided and his actions devoted exclusively to represent and promote the interests of his principal.

An agent may not use for his own benefit, and contrary to the interest of his principal, information obtained in the course of the agency. For example, if an agent in the course of his employment discovers a defect in his principal's title to certain property, he may not use the information to acquire the title for himself. Or, if an employee prior to the expiration of his employer's lease, secretly obtains a lease of the property for his own benefit, he may be compelled to transfer it to his employer.

An agent is not permitted to make a secret profit out of the subject matter of the agency. All such profits belong to the principal to whom the agent must account. Thus, if an agent authorized to sell certain property of his principal for $1,000 sells it for $1,500, he may not secretly pocket the additional $500. Suppose A employs real estate broker B to sell his land for a commission of six percent of the sales price. B, knowing that A is willing to sell for $20,000, agrees secretly with a prospective buyer who is willing to pay $22,000 for the land that he will endeavor to obtain the consent of A to sell for $20,000 in which event the buyer will pay B $1,000, or one-half of the amount which the buyer believes he is saving on the price. The broker has violated his fiduciary duty and would not be allowed to retain the secret profit of $1,000 but must pay it to A. Furthermore, B loses the right to any commission on the transaction. The result is that the seller, who willingly sold the land for $20,000 expecting to pay a commission of $1,200 and net $18,800, receives $21,000 free of commission. B's breach of fiduciary duty produces an unexpected windfall for A. However, this is incidental to the prophylactic effect of the rule requiring a faithless fiduciary to account for any gain or profit from his acts of disloyalty.

DUTIES OF PRINCIPAL TO AGENT

The duties of a principal to his agent may be either in contract or in tort. Tort duties generally arise out of the employer-employee relationship. The principal is also under the duty to perform his contract with the agent, which include payment of an agreed salary or commission, or reasonable compensation where no amount is fixed by agreement.

Contractual Duties

Unless an agreement between the principal and the agent provides otherwise, the following contractually based duties are implied:

(1) A principal by contracting to employ an agent does not thereby promise to provide him with an opportunity for work. However, such a promise may arise by implication by reason of the circumstances under which the agreement was made or the nature of the employment. In such event, the principal has a duty to refrain from unreasonable interference with the agent's work.

(2) A principal has a duty to maintain and render to the agent a true and complete account of money or property due from him to the agent.

(3) A principal is under a duty to indemnify and reimburse his agent for authorized payments made by the agent on behalf of the principal, for expenses incurred by or resulting from authorized acts of the agent, and generally for payments beneficial to the principal made by the agent under such circumstances that it would be inequitable for indemnity not to be made.

(4) If the agreement does not specify a definite amount or rate of compensation, a principal is under a duty to pay the fair value of services which he requests or permits another to perform for him as his agent.

Restatement, Second, Agency, Sections 433–443.

Tort Duties

In addition to his contractual duties, an employer owes certain tort duties to his employees. Among these is the duty to provide an employee reasonably safe conditions of employment and to warn the employee of any unreasonable risk involved in the employment, if the employer should realize that it exists and that the employee is likely not to become aware of it. An employer is also liable to his employees for injury caused by the negligence of other employees and of other agents doing work for him, subject to the "fellow servant rule" and other defenses of the employer hereinafter discussed.

Common Law Duties. The duty of an employer as to working conditions for his employees extends to the maintenance, inspection, and repair of the premises under his control and of the tools or implements which his employees use. He is also under a duty to supply competent supervisors of the operative details of the business where this is reasonably necessary to prevent undue risk of harm to the employees. Where work is dangerous to employees unless rules are made for its conduct, the employer is also under a duty to promulgate and enforce suitable rules. The employer is under a duty to provide his employees with a reasonably safe place in which to work, and if the employee comes into a position of imminent danger of serious harm which is or should be known to the employer or to the person having the duties of management, the employer is liable for a failure to exercise reasonable care to protect against the threatened harm.

The basis of most tort actions by an employee against his employer is the failure of the employer to use reasonable care under the circumstances for the safety of the employee. The failure to measure up to this standard of due care is negligence. In order to recover for breach of this duty, the employee must establish by evidence the facts showing negligence of the employer.

In an action by an injured employee against his employer to recover damages resulting from the breach of any of the employer's tort duties, the employer has several well-established defenses available to him at common law. These include the defense of the fellow servant rule; contributory negligence on the part of the employee; and the doctrine of assumption of risk by the employee.

The fellow servant rule is that an employer is not liable for injuries sustained by an employee caused by the negligence of a fellow servant. Fellow servants are employees of the same employer engaged at the same level of employment and are held to assume the risk of negligence by one another. This defense does not apply in a suit for injury caused by the negligence of a supervisor.

Another common law defense is contributory negligence. If an employer establishes by evidence that the negligence of an injured employee contributed to the injury he sustained in the course of his employment, in many jurisdictions the employee cannot recover damages from the employer. In these states, if the negligence of both the employer and the employee con-

tributed to the injury, the employer is not liable.

At common law an employer is not liable to an employee for harm or injury caused by the unsafe condition of the premises if the employee, with knowledge of the facts and understanding the risks involved, voluntarily enters into or continues in the employment. This is regarded as a voluntary assumption of risk by the employee.

Worker's Compensation Acts. In order to provide speedier and more certain relief to injured employees, all States have adopted Worker's Compensation Acts. These statutes create commissions or boards which determine whether an injured employee is entitled to receive compensation and, if so, how much. The common-law defenses discussed above are not available to employers in proceedings under these statutes. Such defenses are abolished, and the only requirement is that the employee be injured and that the injury "arise out of and in the course of his employment." The amounts recoverable are fixed by statute for each type of injury and are on a scale which is less than a court or jury would probably award in an action at common law. However, actions at law are not permitted to injured employees who come within the Worker's Compensation Acts. The courts do not have jurisdiction over such cases except to review decisions of the board or commission, and then only to determine whether such decisions are in accordance with the statute.

TERMINATION OF AGENCY

Since the authority of an agent is predicated upon consent of the principal, when such consent is withdrawn or otherwise ceases to exist, the agency is terminated. Upon revocation by the principal, the power of the agent to bind the principal to contracts with third persons with whom the agent has previously dealt will continue until such persons have been notified or have knowledge of the revocation. Upon termination the agent's actual authority ends and he is not entitled to compensation for services thereafter rendered, although his fiduciary duties may continue. Termination of the agent's authority may take place by acts of the parties or by operation of law.

Acts of the Parties

Mutual Agreement of the Parties. The agency relationship is created by agreement and may be terminated at any time by mutual agreement of the principal and the agent.

Fulfillment of Purpose. The authority of an agent to perform a specific act or to accomplish a particular result is terminated when the act is performed or the result is accomplished by the agent. Thus, if A authorizes B to sell or lease A's land, and B leases the land to C, his authority is terminated and he may not thereafter lease the land without new authorization.

Revocation of Authority. A principal may revoke an agent's authority at any time. If such revocation is wrongful and constitutes a breach of contract by the principal, the agent may recover damages from the principal, but nevertheless the revocation effectively terminates the agency.

Renunciation by the Agent. The agent also has the power to put an end to the agency by notice to the principal that he renounces the authority given him by the principal. However, if the parties have contracted that the agency continue for a specified time, an unjustified renunciation prior to the expiration of the time is a breach of contract.

Operation of Law

Bankruptcy. Bankruptcy is a proceeding in a Federal court affording relief to finan-

cially distressed debtors. Under Chapter 7 of the Bankruptcy Reform Act of 1978, sometimes referred to as "straight bankruptcy," the assets of the debtor's estate are liquidated, and funds remaining after expenses of administration are distributed to creditors of the debtor who filed claims in the proceeding. The filing of the petition in bankruptcy, which initiates the proceedings, also terminates all of the debtor's then existing agency relationships. However, in a proceeding under Chapter 11 of the Bankruptcy Reform Act of 1978, under which business corporations and railroad companies may be reorganized, the treatment of the relationship between the debtor and its agents will be treated, if at all, under the plan of reorganization confirmed by the court and put into effect. Likewise, in a proceeding under Chapter 13 of the Bankruptcy Act, which deals with Adjustment of Debts of an Individual with Regular Income, the relationship of the debtor with his agents would depend upon the provisions of the plan of adjustment confirmed by the court and put into effect.

Death. As a dead person cannot act, no one can act for him. Consequently, the death of the principal terminates the authority of the agent. Similarly, the authority given to an agent by a principal is strictly personal, and the agent's death likewise terminates the agency.

Incapacity. Incapacity of the principal, by insanity or otherwise, which occurs after the formation of the agency, terminates the agent's authority. Likewise, subsequent incapacity of an agent to perform the acts authorized by the principal terminates the agent's authority.

Change in Business Conditions. The authority of an agent is terminated by notice or knowledge of a change in the value of the subject matter, or of a change in business conditions from which the agent should reasonably infer that the principal would not consent to an exercise of the authority given him. Thus, A authorizes B to sell his 80 acres of farm land for $800 per acre. Subsequently, oil is discovered on nearby land which causes A's land to increase substantially in value. B knows of this, but A does not. B's authority to sell the land is terminated.

Loss or Destruction of the Subject Matter. Where the authority of the agent relates to a specific subject matter which becomes lost or destroyed, such authority is thereby terminated. This is analogous to the rule that loss or destruction of the subject matter of an offer terminates the offer.

Loss of Qualification of Principal or Agent. When the authority given the agent relates to the conduct of a certain business, the operation of which requires a license from the government or a regulatory agency, the failure to acquire, or the loss or revocation of such license, terminates the authority of the agent. Thus, A, who holds a retail liquor license, employs B to sell liquor at retail in A's store. A's license is revoked. B's authority to sell A's liquor at retail is terminated.

Disloyalty of Agent. If an agent, without the knowledge of his principal, acquires interests which are adverse to those of the principal or is otherwise guilty of a serious breach of his duty of loyalty to the principal, such as double dealing, his authority to act on behalf of the principal is terminated. Thus, A employs B, a realtor, to sell A's land. Unknown to A, B has been authorized by C to purchase this land from A. B is not authorized to sell the land to C.

Change of Law. Subsequent to the employment of the agent, a change in the law may cause the performance of the authorized act to be illegal or criminal, or may impose sanctions which the agent should realize would be injurious to the principal. Such a change in the law terminates the authority of the agent. Thus, A directs his agent B to ship young elm trees from State X to State Y. In order to control elm disease, a quarantine is established by State X upon the shipment into any other State of elm trees, and any such shipment is punishable by fine. B's authority to ship the elm trees is terminated.

Outbreak of War. Where the outbreak of war places the principal and agent in the position of alien enemies, the authority of the agent is terminated because its exercise is illegal. Where the principal and agent are citizens of the same country and the outbreak of war or a revolution makes the originally authorized transaction unexpectedly hazardous or impracticable, as the agent knows or should know, the agent's authority is terminated.

Irrevocable Agencies

In the foregoing discussion of the various ways in which the authority of an agent may be terminated, the agency relationship was assumed to be the ordinary one in which the agent does not have a security interest in the power conferred upon him by the principal. Where the agency is coupled with an interest of the agent in the subject matter, as where the agent has advanced funds on behalf of the principal and his power to act is given as security therefor, the authority of the agent is irrevocable by the principal. In such case, neither the death, insanity or bankruptcy of the principal terminates the authority or the power of the agent.

Cases

Creation of Agency

WASHINGTON v. COURTESY MOTOR SALES, INC.

(1964) 48 Ill.App.2d 380, 199 N.E.2d 263.

MURPHY, P. J.

This is an action of fraud and deceit. The trial court struck the amended complaint and dismissed the action as to defendant Ford Motor Company, on the ground that the amended complaint, as to Ford, was "substantially insufficient in law." Plaintiff appeals.

In substance, the fraud alleged is that while plaintiff negotiated and paid for a new car, the automobile which was delivered to her had been previously used, and its speedometer had been set back. Charging fraud and deceit in the sale, plaintiff seeks damages totaling $50,018—being $1,018 compensatory and $49,000 exemplary.

The determinative question is whether the amended complaint alleges sufficient facts in law to support plaintiff's allegation that, for the purpose of selling a new Ford automobile to plaintiff, defendant Courtesy Motor Sales was an agent of the defendant Ford Motor Company.

* * *

We think it is a matter of common knowledge that the term "Authorized Ford Dealer" is in the nature of a trade-mark sign, which is used by independent dealers [citation] and means nothing more than a dealer who sells products which have a trade name carrying substantial good will. As stated in Westerdale v. Kaiser-Frazer Corp., 6 N.J. 571, 80 A.2d 91, 94 (1951):

Nor does the fact that when a sale is made by a dealer to the ultimate purchaser a manufacturer's warranty goes with the automobile spell out the dealer as the agent of the manufacturer. It is merely incidental to the sale and in no wise by itself gives apparent authority or agency to

the dealer. * * * The owner's service policy simply provided that defective material or workmanship would be replaced free by an authorized Frazer dealer or distributor without charge. This was an undertaking of the distributor, not the Kaiser-Frazer Corporation, and spelled out no agency existing between them.

We conclude that, absent the pleading of other facts which directly or circumstantially establish an agency relationship, plaintiff has failed to allege facts to show in law that an "authorized" or "franchised" dealer, in the sale of a new car, is an agent of the manufacturer rather than an independent merchant. [Citations.]

For the reasons given, the order of the trial court is affirmed.

Capacity of Principal

GOLDFINGER v. DOHERTY

(1934) 153 Misc. 826, 276 N.Y.S. 289.

SHIENTAG, J.

The plaintiff sued the defendant Doherty, disaffirming certain purchases of stock, made in her behalf by her duly authorized agent, alleging that she was an infant at the time of the transactions, and that she now elected to rescind and offered to return the stock, together with the stock and cash dividends received thereon. The defendant Doherty thereupon obtained an order permitting him to serve a supplmental summons and complaint on the agent Samuel Goldfinger. * * * The supplemental pleading alleged, in substance, that the agent purchased the stock from Doherty on behalf of the alleged infant "without disclosing the infancy of his principal." It further alleged that, if plaintiff should recover against Doherty, then the defendant Goldfinger, plaintiff's agent, will be liable to defendant Doherty for damages sustained through the rescission of the contracts by plaintiff, "on the ground that defendant Samuel Goldfinger has breached his implied warranty that he was authorized to enter into binding contracts for the plaintiff."

* * *

An infant's appointment of an agent is not void; it is merely voidable, like any other contract he makes. "Notwithstanding numerous general statements in the books, sound principles compel the conclusion that no satisfactory distinction can be drawn between a sale and delivery by the infant and a sale and delivery by an agent for him. * * * Dicta and general statements to the contrary are no longer respectable authority." [Citation.]

There is, therefore, no basis for the contention of the appellant that disaffirmance by the infant of a contract entered into on his behalf by his agent renders the transaction void ab initio, so that the agent is deemed to have acted without any authority. The infant, without questioning the authority of his agent, may disaffirm the contract entered into on his behalf, in the same manner as if he had made the contract directly. The infant may disaffirm the contract of agency; he may disaffirm the contract entered into by his agent. Either contract is voidable; neither is void.

* * *

"The agent does not warrant the capacity of the principal." Hall v. Lauderdale, 46 N.Y. 70, 75. "An agent does not warrant that his principal has full contractual capacity, any more than he warrants that his principal is solvent. Thus an agent for one not of legal age is not necessarily liable if the infant avoids the obligation of the contract made on his account." Comment (a) on section 332, Restatement of the Law of Agency. An agent who misrepresents the capacity of his principal to contract is liable as for any other misrepresentation, and this whether he misrepresents tortiously or innocently.

In the absence of misrepresentation, under what circumstances, if any, is an agent acting for an infant, who subsequently disaffirms, not the agency, but the transaction of the agent, liable to the other contracting party? It must appear that the agent knew or had reason to know of his principal's lack of full capacity, and it must further appear that the other contracting party was in ignorance thereof. The theory of breach of warranty of authority is that one dealing with an agent has been misled by him. * * *

Assuming that the agent knows or has reason to know of his principal's lack of full capacity, and of the other party's ignorance thereof, what, if any, is the agent's liability? * * *

The basis of the liability of an agent, in a situation such as we are here considering, is that he has produced "a false impression upon the mind of the other party; and, if this result is accomplished, it is unimportant whether the means of accomplishing it are words or acts of the defendant, or his concealment or suppression of material facts not equally within the knowledge or reach of the plaintiff." [Citation.] We believe that the correct rule is that set forth in the Restatement of the Law of Agency as follows: "par. 332. Agent of partially incompetent principal. An agent making a contract for a disclosed principal whose contracts are voidable because of lack of full capacity to contract, or for a principal who, although having capacity to contract generally, is incompetent to enter into the particular transaction, is not thereby liable to the other party. He does not become liable by reason of the failure of the principal to perform, unless he contracts or represents that the principal has capacity or unless he has reason to know of the principal's lack of capacity and of the other party's ignorance thereof." * * *

If, therefore, the liability of the agent is to be based on his failure to disclose facts in connection with his principal's lack of full capacity to the other contracting party, it must appear (1) that the agent knew or had reason to know the facts indicating his principal's lack of full capacity; (2) that the other contracting party was in ignorance thereof and the agent had reason so to believe; (3) that the transaction is one in which lack of full capacity was a material fact.

* * *

The order dismissing the supplemental complaint is affirmed. * * *

Agent's Duty of Diligence

BICKNELL, INC. v. HAVLIN

(1980)   Mass.App.   , 402 N.E.2d 116.

NOLAN, J.

The plaintiff (Bicknell) claims to be aggrieved by the direction of verdicts for the defendants John J. Havlin and Corcoran & Havlin Insurance Agency, Inc. (Corcoran and Havlin), on counts one and three of its complaint alleging negligence in failing to place proper insurance coverage on two buildings leased to Bicknell and located in Middleton. As to count two, which alleges a breach of contract, the trial judge ordered judgment notwithstanding a verdict for the plaintiff in the amount of $40,000.00. At oral argument, the parties stipulated that the damages assessed by the jury on count two constitute the only recoverable damages under all counts. We reverse the judgment on count two.

* * * Bicknell had been in the business of distributing swimming pools and their accessories and supplies since 1957. Havlin, treasurer of Corcoran & Havlin, and Corcoran & Havlin were independent insurance agents. Bicknell had been doing business with an insurance agency which was purchased by Corcoran & Havlin in 1969. At that time, Havlin met with the principals of Bicknell with a view toward a continuation of business with Bicknell.

Havlin described himself as experienced in the insurance business. He told the representatives of Bicknell that he wanted "to handle [the Bicknell] account in a highly professional manner." Bicknell decided to retain Corcoran & Havlin and, thereafter, Havlin devoted himself to the Bicknell account. He procured from various insurance carriers all the insurance required by Bicknell—casualty, liability, automobile, surety, fidelity bonds, workmen's compensation and other coverages, except life insurance. Havlin made recommendations for particular types of coverage and gave advice freely to Bicknell. One of the earliest recommendations which was adopted was for the purchase of a multiperil policy for Bicknell's commercial stock. At the end of each month, Bicknell sent Corcoran & Havlin a report disclosing the value of commercial stock at each warehouse location. Corcoran & Havlin would then review the report to make sure that Bicknell was reporting in accordance with the policy. If the report was in order, Corcoran & Havlin would transmit it to the carrier.

* * *

When Bicknell submitted its monthly report of inventory and its value on March 6, 1974, Havlin took notice that the value of the commercial stock at the warehouse in Middleton was $758,600.00. The limit of insurance coverage at that time for stock at this location was $540,000.00. Havlin telephoned Smith [who represented Bicknell] to inquire about new limits, and Smith agreed that new limits should be purchased. As a result, Havlin increased the coverage at Middleton to $750,000.00, effective immediately. During this telephone conversation, Smith told Havlin that two new warehouses, in the style of Quonset huts, were then under construction in Middleton and that Bicknell would lease them from the owner of the Middleton real estate.

Approximately ten days later, Havlin called Smith and discussed the insurance provisions of the draft of the lease. Smith informed Havlin that the two new warehouses in Middleton were just about ready for use. After Smith told Havlin the value of certain heaters which would be stored in the new warehouses. Havlin asked Smith if he thought that $50,000.00 would cover the stock in each building. When Smith indicated that this would be sufficient "at this point," Havlin said, "Let's slap fifty-thousand on each building." Havlin did not indicate that he meant specific coverage. Smith thought that the total limits of coverage were being increased by $100,000.00, consistent with the blanket type of coverage in force on the commercial stock in both Framingham and Middleton. Havlin placed specific, limited coverage of $50,000.00 on the stock in each building, effective April 4, 1974. Corcoran & Havlin on May 8, 1974, submitted its invoice to Bicknell for several changes in coverage, including the new specific coverage on the two buildings in Middleton. The language of the invoice did not distinguish the specific coverage on the contents of the two new buildings from the blanket coverage lately purchased for the contents of the other building in Middleton.

Bicknell transmitted to Corcoran & Havlin on May 6, 1974, its monthly report of stock for April, 1974. The report revealed the value at Middleton to be $839,000.00. Without Bicknell's knowledge, Havlin assigned $739,000.00 in value to the old warehouse and $50,000.00 each to the two new warehouses. He sent the report to the carrier.

A fire broke out on June 3, 1974, in one of the two new warehouses in Middleton. The fire loss to the commercial stock amounted to $103,275.91. The carrier paid Bicknell $50,000.00, the amount of the endorsement of April 4, 1974.

In a letter dated June 10, 1974, from Havlin to the carrier concerning Bicknell, Havlin admitted making "a technical error of judgment due to unfamiliarity with the advantage of blanket, versus specific, coverage on contents." In the same letter Havlin confessed to "an obvious element of confusion" regarding the different types of coverage.

The evidence warranted a finding that Havlin was the agent of Bicknell. [Citation.] An agent is bound to use due care in the implementation of the agency, [citation,] and in carrying out instructions of the principal-client. *Rayden* 337 Mass. at 660, 151 N.E.2d 57. See also Restatement (Second) of Agency § 379(1) (1958). The nature and extent of the duty of care owed by an independent insurance agent to his client depends in part, at least, upon the degree of skill which he represents himself to possess.

If he holds himself out to the world as possessing certain skill, or if his business is such as to carry with it an implication that he possesses particular skill in effecting insurances, as in [the] case of an insurance broker, then his principal is justified in relying upon the knowledge which he professes to possess, and he is bound to exercise the skill and to use the knowledge which the business requires . . . . 3 Couch, Insurance § 25:37 at 335–336 (2d ed. 1960).

Havlin undertook to advise Bicknell and to make recommendations. It was Havlin, not Smith, who suggested "slapping" $50,000.00 on each building. The jury could find that this was one of many recommendations made by Havlin over a considerable period of time and that these were "special circumstances of assertion, representation and reliance" for which Havlin may be liable. *Rapp v. Lester L. Burdick, Inc.,* 336 Mass. 438, 442, 146 N.E.2d 368, (1957), quoted with approval in *McCue v. Prudential Ins. Co. of America,* 371 Mass. 659, 661, 358 N.E.2d 799 (1976).

There is no merit to Havlin's argument that the issue of his failure to use due care required the introduction of expert testimony. Havlin's admission of "a technical error of judgment" was sufficient to raise an inference of negligence. See *Manzoni v.*

Hamlin, 348 Mass. 770, 202 N.E.2d 264 (1964), and a breach of contract.

The judgment on count two is reversed, and judgment is to be entered for the plaintiff on the verdict returned by the jury on that count.

So ordered.

Agent's Fiduciary Duty

SIERRA PAC. INDUSTRIES v. CARTER

(1980) 104 Cal.App.3d 579, 163 Cal.Rptr. 764.

RHODES, J.

Joseph H. Carter, a licensed California real estate broker for the past 26 years, appeals an order of the trial court granting respondent Sierra Pacific Industries' motion for a new trial in an action involving the sale of real property.

During the fall of 1975, Sierra Pacific purchased, for a lump sum, various timberlands and six other pieces of real property, including the subject of this dispute, a ten acre parcel in Willow Creek on which five duplexes and two single family units are located.

After the acquisition, Sierra Pacific requested Carter's assistance in selling the non-timberland properties, including the Willow Creek parcel. Carter was familiar with the property, having participated in efforts to sell it to others prior to its purchase by Sierra Pacific. Acting in reliance on Carter's representation as to the value of the Willow Creek parcel, Sierra Pacific commissioned him to sell it for an asking price of $85,000, of which Sierra Pacific would receive $80,000 and Carter, $5,000. The trial testimony was in conflict over whether, if Carter were able to find a buyer willing to pay more than $85,000, the excess was to be equally divided or whether it would go entirely to Carter under a net listing agreement.

* * *

Pursuant to the agreement, appellant showed the Willow Creek property to several prospective buyers but was for a time unable to secure a sale at the asking price of $85,000. Finally, in June of 1976, Carter sold the property for that amount to his daughter and son-in-law, Debbie and David Benson and, by his own admission, retained a $5,000 commission without informing respondent of his relationship to the buyers.

Sierra Pacific instituted a fraud action against Carter based on the foregoing facts. The jury impaneled to hear the matter returned a general verdict in Carter's favor. Judgment was entered accordingly. Thereafter Sierra Pacific moved for a new trial. The motion was granted as to all issues and on all grounds asserted: inadequacy of damages, insufficient evidence and verdict against the law. Carter appeals, claiming that the order granting the new trial cannot be sustained on any of the grounds enumerated.

We begin with a review of the substantive law. An agent bears a fiduciary relationship to his or her principal which requires, among other things, disclosure of all information in the agent's possession relevant to the subject matter of the agency (1 Witkin, Summary of Cal. Law (8th ed. 1973) p. 704). An agent may not compete with the principal, nor may he or she act as agent for another whose interests conflict with those of the principal. (*Id.,* at 705–06.)

In the context of an agreement to sell land on another's behalf, the general duties inherent in every agency become more specific. A real estate agent must refrain from dual representation in a sale transaction unles he or she obtains the consent of both principals after full disclosure. [Citation.] This means under most circumstances that if the agent is related to the buyer in a way which suggests a reasonable possibility that the agent him or herself could indirectly be acquiring an interest in the subject property, the relationship is a "material fact" which must be disclosed. [Citation.]

There is no question that Carter concealed information material to this transaction from his principal, Sierra Pacific. * * *

It thus is evident that Carter owed a duty of disclosure to his principal, Sierra Pacific. It is equally evident that the duty was breached. Given duty and breach, a minimum of $5,000 in damages to Sierra Pacific flows automatically. Apart from any actual and proximately caused loss on the price it received for its property, Sierra Pacific was entitled to recover the commission it paid to Carter. ". . . [A] real estate broker must act in good faith in the discharge of his duties as agent . . . [B]y misconduct, breach of conduct [sic] or wilful disregard, in a material respect, of an obligation imposed upon him by the law of agency he may forfeit his right to compensation." (*Baird v. Madsen* (1943) 57 Cal.App.2d 465 at p. 475, 76, 134 P.2d 885 at p. 891.) In a case closely analogous to the one at bar, for example, breach of the duty of full disclosure was held to deprive respondent real estate brokers of their right to a commission. (*Bate v. Marsteller* (1959) 175 Cal.App.2d 573, 583, 346 P.2d 903. See also Rest.2d Agency (1958) § 469.)

We thus are led to the inescapable conclusion that Carter is liable to Sierra Pacific as a matter of law for a minimum of $5,000 and that the jury's verdict to the contrary was in error. * * *

The order granting a new trial is therefore affirmed with instructions to the court below to direct a verdict against defendant as to both duty and breach. The only triable issue remaining concerns the extent of plaintiff's damages.

Contractual Duties
of Principal to Agent

HILGENDORF v. HAGUE

(1980 Iowa) 293 N.W.2d 272.

[Harvey C. Hilgendorf, a licensed real estate broker, brought action against vendors, the Hagues, for breach of listing contract. The district court entered judgment for broker and vendors appealed.]

UHLENHOPP, J.

I. *Right to terminate listing.* Since agency is a consensual relationship, a principal has *power* to terminate an agency which is not coupled with an interest, although the contract is for a period which has not expired. Ordinarily the agent's authority thereupon ceases. Absent some legal ground, however, the principal does not have a *right* to terminate an unexpired agency contract, and may subject himself to damages by doing so. *Knudson & Richardson v. Laurent,* 159 Iowa 189, 192, 140 N.W. 392, 393 (1913); Restatement (Second) of Agency § 386 (1958).

The whole question regarding liability here turns on whether the Hagues had a legal ground for terminating Hilgendorf's agency before the expiration of the year. All agree that they had power to terminate, but they contend they also had a right to do so. They say PCA [Hagues' principal creditor] would not renew their loan, they had to sell the 80 acres in addition to their other land, and the best way to sell the 80 acres was with the 160 acres. Did these circumstances give them a "right" to terminate the listing contract they had signed on the 160 acres, and cast on Hilgendorf a "duty" to give up his listing contract as a matter of an agent's loyalty to his principal?

The Hagues appear to confuse the two roles an agent occupies. In performing agency functions for the principal an agent does indeed occupy a fiduciary position, and his duty of loyalty requires him to place the principal's interests first. Restatement (Second) of Agency § 387. But in the contract of agency itself between the agent and principal, neither of the parties is acting for the other; each is acting for himself.

This case involves the latter role. * * *

We may assume that after PCA refused to renew the loan, the Hagues did have to liquidate all the real estate. But financial strictures do not constitute a legal ground for terminating contractual obligations, otherwise contracts would have little or no value. * * *

Several circumstances are given in the texts as grounds for terminating fixed-term agencies, but coming upon hard times is not among them. [Citations.] We agree with the trial court that the Hagues did not have a right to terminate the one-year listing contract on the 160 acres, and that Hilgendorf did not have a duty to give up his listing contract.

II. *Damages.* Hague terminated the listing on August 13, 1976. Since Hague had the power to do so, Hilgendorf no longer had authority to sell the 160 acre parcel. For that reason, he cannot recover a commission *as such,* although he thereafter and within the year produced a ready, willing, and able buyer for the price in the listing. Nonetheless, since Hague breached the listing agreement by terminating it, Hilgendorf can recover damages. [Citation.]

The question here relates to the *measure* of damages Hilgendorf is entitled to recover. The editors state the measure thus in 12 Am. Jur. 2d *Brokers* § 64 (1964):

The courts generally support the principle that a broker whose employment or authority is wrongfully revoked may consider his contract of employment as rescinded and sue for damages, in which event he is entitled to have his recovery include the value of the services he has already rendered, his disbursements, and *such prospective profits as he can establish would have been his but for such revocation.* . . .

* * *

Where as here the principal terminates an exclusive listing within the term, the agent may endeavor to show that he would, but for the termination, have sold the property within the unexpired period at the listed price. If he is successful in his proof, his lost profits are ordinarily measured by the commission he would have earned. He does not recover the commission itself, but his damages are measured by the commission. As stated in section 445 of the Restatement, Comment *a:*

If the principal, in breach of contract, prevents the agent from accomplishing the result upon which the agreed compensation is conditioned, the agent is entitled to damages for such breach or, as an alternative, the fair value of his services in attempting to accomplish it. The amount of recovery for damages in such a case is not the specified compensation as such, but the damages which the agent suffers by reason of the breach of contract. *Such damages may coincide in amount with the agreed compensation*; if, however, the agent would have had to incur further expense in order to earn such compensation, and these expenses have been saved to him, he is entitled only to a sum equal to the agreed compensation minus the expenses he has thereby saved.

(Emphasis added.)

* * *

Here Hilgendorf proceeded on the damage issue by showing "the gains prevented" by Hague's breach of the listing contract. He established beyond question that he would have sold the 160 acre parcel for the full asking price within the listing period. His lost profit was the offered price times the six percent commission rate, and this is the amount the trial court allowed him.

We agree with the trial court's decision. AFFIRMED.

Problems

1. A, the owner of certain unimproved real estate in Chicago, employed B, a real estate agent, to sell the property for a price of $25,000 or more and agreed to pay B a commission of 6% for mak-

ing a sale. B negotiated with C who was interested in the property and willing to pay as much as $28,000 for it. B made an agreement with C that if B could obtain A's signature to a contract to sell the property to C for $25,000, C would pay B a bonus of $1,000. B prepared and A and C signed a contract for the sale of the property to C for $25,000. C refuses to pay B the $1,000 as promised. A refuses to pay B the 6% commission. In an action by B against A and C, what judgment?

2. P employed A to sell a parcel of real estate at a fixed price without knowledge that D had previously employed A to purchase the same property for him. P gave A no discretion as to price or terms and A entered into a contract of sale with D, upon the exact terms authorized by P. After accepting a partial payment P discovered that A was employed by D and brought an action to rescind. D resisted on the ground that admittedly P had suffered no damage for the reason that A had been given no discretion and the sale was made upon the exact basis authorized by P. Decision?

3. P owned and operated a fruit cannery in Southton, Illinois. He stored a substantial amount of finished canned goods in a warehouse in East St. Louis, Illinois, owned and operated by A in order to have goods readily available for the St. Louis market. On March 1, he had 10,000 cans of peaches and 5,000 cans of apples on storage with A. On the day named, he borrowed $5,000 from A, giving A his promissory note for this amount due June 1 together with a letter authorizing A, in the event the note was not paid at maturity, to sell any or all of his goods on storage, pay the indebtedness and account to him for any surplus. P died on June 2, without having paid the note. On June 8, A told T, a wholesale food distributor, that he had for sale as agent of the owner, 10,000 cans of peaches and 5,000 cans of apples. T said he would take the peaches and would decide later about the apples. A contract for the sale of 10,000 cans of peaches for $6,000 was thereupon signed. "A, agent for P, seller; T, buyer." Both A and T knew of the death of P. Delivery of the peaches and payment therefor were made on June 10. On June 11, A and T signed a similar contract covering the 5,000 cans of apples, delivery and payment to be made June 30.

On June 23, P's executor, having learned of these contracts, wrote A and T stating that A had no authority to make the contracts, demanding that T return the peaches and directing A not to deliver the apples. Discuss the correctness of the contentions of P's executor.

4. Green, a licensed real estate broker in Illinois, and Jones, also an Illinois resident, while both were in New York, signed a contract whereby Green agreed to endeavor to find a buyer for certain real estate located in Illinois owned by Jones who agreed to pay Green a commission of $10,000 in the event of a sale. Green found a buyer, a resident of New York, to whom the land was sold. Thereafter, Jones refused to pay the commission. Green commenced an action in Illinois to recover the commission. Jones defended on the sole ground that the brokerage contract was unenforceable because Green was not a licensed real estate broker in New York. For whom should judgment be rendered?

Relevant provisions of the applicable New York statute forbid any person from holding himself out or acting temporarily as a real estate broker or saleman without first procuring a license. A violation is declared to be a misdemeanor, and the commission of a single prohibited act is a violation for which the statute provides a penalty.

5. B made a valid contract with A whereunder A was to sell B's goods on commission during the period from January 1 to June 30. A made satisfactory sales up to May 15, and was then about to close an unusually large order when B suddenly and without notice revoked A's authority to sell. Can A continue to sell B's goods during the unexpired term of his contract?

6. Pluto Company employed two research engineers, A and B, for terms of five years "to make or cause to be made, improvements in the Pluto garden-type tractor, such improvements when made to belong to Pluto." Later C was hired orally for six months with the general understanding that he was to make garden-tractor improvements. During such employment, using the facilities and material of Pluto, A and C made garden tractor improvements and B invented a corn planting machine. After some controversy, Pluto brought actions against A, B

and C to compel each to assign pending patent applications to Pluto or, in the alternative, to give Pluto irrevocable, royalty-free licenses for the use of the improvements. What results, as to each, A, B and C?

7. A Electric Co. gave a list of delinquent accounts to B, an employee, with instructions to discontinue electric service to delinquent customers. Among those listed was C Hatchery, which was then in the process of hatching chickens in a large, electrically heated incubator. C Hatchery told B that it did not consider its account delinquent, but B nevertheless cut the wires leading to the hatchery. Subsequently, C Hatchery recovered a judgment of $5,000 against B in action brought against B for the loss resulting from the interruption of the incubation process. B has paid the judgment and brings a cause of action against A Electric Co. Decision?

8. In October, 1976, Black, the owner of the Grand Opera House, and Harvey entered into a written agreement leasing the Opera House to Harvey for five years at a rental of $30,000 a year. Harvey engaged Day as manager of the theatre at a salary of $175 per week plus 10 per cent of the profits. One of the duties of Day was to determine each night the amount of money taken in and, after deducting expenses, to divide the profits between Harvey and the Manager of the particular attraction which was playing at the theatre. In September, 1982, Day went to Black and offered to rent the Opera House from Black at a rental of $37,500 per year, whereupon Black entered into a lease with Day for five years at this figure. When Harvey learned of and objected to this transaction, Day offered to assign the lease to him for $60,000 per year. Harvey refused, and brought an appropriate action seeking to have Day declared a trustee of the Opera House on behalf of Harvey. Decision?

18

RELATIONSHIPS OF PRINCIPAL AND AGENT WITH THIRD PERSONS

The purpose of an agency relationship is to allow a person to increase his business activities by authorizing another person to enter into transactions on his behalf with third persons. The relationship of a principal with third persons resulting from the activities of his agent is based either in contract or in tort. Contract liability of the principal is predicated upon acts of the agent which the principal authorized, while his liability in tort usually results from unauthorized conduct of the agent. The agent may incur personal liability to third persons either in contract or torts by reason of his acts or omissions.

RELATIONSHIP OF PRINCIPAL AND THIRD PERSONS

CONTRACT LIABILITY OF THE PRINCIPAL

It is fundamental that a principal is liable on contracts made for him by his authorized agent, including those in which his identity is not disclosed. Conversely, he is not liable in contract upon unauthorized acts of an agent unless he subsequently ratifies them. To bind the principal, the agent must act strictly within the limits of the authority granted to him by the principal.

Types of Authority

There are two basic types of authority: actual and apparent. Actual authority depends upon consent manifested by the principal to the agent. It may be either express or implied. In either case it is binding and confers upon the agent both the power and the right to create or affect legal relations of the principal with third persons. Apparent authority is based upon acts or conduct of the principal which manifests to a third person that actual authority of the agent exists, and upon which the third person justifiably relies. Such manifestation can consist of words or actions of the principal as well as other facts and circumstances, which induce in the third person reasonable reliance upon the existence of an agency relationship. To the extent that things are as represented, there is both actual and apparent authority. Whether the authority of an agent is express, implied, or apparent, it is effective to bind the principal in contract by acts of the agent or supposed agent within its scope.

Express Authority. The express authority of an agent is found in the words of the principal, spoken or written, and communicated to the agent. It is actual authority embodied in language directing or instructing the agent to do something specific. Thus, if A orally or in writing requests his agent B to sell A's automobile for $2500, B's authority to sell the car for this sum is actual and express.

Implied Authority. Implied authority is also actual, based upon the consent of the principal manifested to the agent. However, it is not found in express or explicit words of the principal, but is inferred from words or conduct manifested to the agent by the principal. Authority granted to an agent to accomplish a particular purpose necessarily includes authority to employ means reasonably required for its accomplishment. For example, A authorizes B to manage his 82-apartment complex for a commission upon rents collected. Nothing is said by A about expenses. In order to manage the building, B must employ a janitor, purchase fuel for heating, and arrange for ordinary maintenance and occasional redecorating. The authority to incur these expenses, while not expressly granted, is implied from the express authority to manage the building as they are required for its proper management. Whatever may be reasonably necessary to complete the task assigned to the agent is impliedly authorized.

Certain rules have been developed with reference to what authority is implied in particular types of agencies. Unless otherwise agreed, authority to buy or to sell property for the principal includes authority to agree upon the terms, to demand or make the usual representations and warranties, to receive or execute the instruments usually required, to pay or receive so much of the purchase price as is to be paid at the time of the transfer, and to receive possession of the goods if a buying agent, or to surrender possession of them if a selling agent.

Authority of an agent to receive payment due his principal will be implied when it is the usual incident of the business transacted. An agent in possession of his principal's goods or documents of title to the goods, with authority to sell them, is impliedly authorized to receive payment upon delivery of the goods or transfer of the documents. A salesman or sales representative who is employed only to solicit and take orders for goods to be shipped by the principal directly to the customer does not have implied authority to receive payment for the goods.

General authority to manage or operate a business for a principal impliedly confers authority upon the agent to buy and sell property for the principal to the extent usual and customary in such operation. The authority of an agent employed to manage a business is set forth in the Restatement, Second, Agency, Section 73, as follows:

Unless otherwise agreed, authority to manage a business includes authority:

(a) to make contracts which are incidental to such business, are usually made in it, or are reasonably necessary in conducting it;

(b) to procure equipment and supplies and to make repairs reasonably necessary for the proper conduct of the business;

(c) to employ, supervise, or discharge employees as the course of business may reasonably require;

(d) to sell or otherwise dispose of goods or other things in accordance with the purposes for which the business is operated;

(e) to receive payment of sums due the principal and to pay debts due from the principal arising out of the business enterprise; and

(f) to direct the ordinary operations of the business.

Apparent Authority. Apparent authority is ostensible authority which arises out of words or conduct of a *disclosed* principal manifested to third persons whereby they are reasonably induced to rely upon the assumption that actual authority exists. It is authority created by estoppel, that is imposed by law upon the principal whose conduct under the circumstances has estopped or precluded him from denying the existence of actual authority.

For example, A writes a letter to B authorizing him to sell his automobile, and sends a copy of the letter to C, a prospective purchaser. On the following day, A writes a letter to B revoking the authority to sell the car, but does not send a copy of the second letter to C, who is not otherwise informed of the revocation. Although B has no actual authority to sell the car, as to C he continues to have apparent authority. Or, suppose that B, in the presence of A, tells C that B is A's agent to buy lumber. Although this statement is not true, A does not deny it, as he could easily have done. C, in reliance upon the statement, ships lumber to A on B's order, for which A is obligated to pay. This apparent authority of B exists only with respect to C. If B were to give D an order for a shipment of lumber to A, D would not be able to hold A liable. No actual authority existed, and as to D there was no apparent authority.

Delegation of Authority

The appointment of an agent reflects confidence and reliance by the principal upon his personal skill, integrity, and other qualifications. The agent has been selected because of his supposed fitness to perform the task assigned to him, and therefore ordinarily has no power to delegate his authority or to appoint a subagent. This is the basis of the legal maxim *"Delegata potestas non potest delegari"* (delegated authority cannot be delegated). Thus, A employs B to collect his accounts. B may not delegate this authority to C as A reposed trust and confidence in B and not in C.

However, in certain situations, it is clear that the principal intended to permit the agent to delegate the authority granted to him, as where the authority contains an express power of substitution. Such an intention may also be gathered from the character of the business, the usages of trade, or the prior conduct of the parties. For example, if a check is deposited in a bank for collection at a distant place, authority to the bank to employ another bank at the place of payment is necessarily implied.

If an agent is authorized to appoint or select other persons or subagents to perform or assist in the performance of the agent's duties, the acts of the subagent are binding on the principal to the same extent as if they had been done by the agent. The subagent is an agent of both the principal and the agent and owes a fiduciary duty to each.

If no authorization exists to delegate the agent's authority, but the agent nevertheless does so, the acts of the subagent do not impose any obligation or liability upon the principal to third persons. Likewise, the principal acquires no rights against such third persons except by ratification, upon which the principal also becomes bound to the third party. The subagent, in this instance, is responsible only to the agent who is his employer since the principal did not authorize the delegation.

Effect of Termination of Agency Upon Authority

Upon the termination of an agency, the agent's actual authority ceases. When the termination is by operation of law, the agent's apparent authority also expires. However, when termination results from acts of the parties, apparent authority continues with respect to third parties with whom the agent had previously dealt until they receive *actual* notice by letter, telegram, telephone call or other means of communication. All other third parties need only be given *constructive* notice such as publication in a newspaper of general circulation in the area where the agent has been employed.

An analogy is found in the rule of partnership law that each partner is an agent of the partnership. Section 35 of the Uniform Partnership Act deals with the power of a partner to bind the partnership after dissolution:

(1) After dissolution a partner can bind the partnership

(b) By any transaction which would bind the partnership if dissolution had not taken place, provided the other party to the transaction

(I) Had extended credit to the partnership prior to dissolution and had no knowledge or notice of the dissolution; or

(II) Though he had not so extended credit, had nevertheless known of the partnership prior to dissolution, and, having no knowledge or notice of dissolution, the fact of dissolution had not been advertised in a newspaper of general circulation in the place (or in each place if more than one) at which the partnership business was regularly carried on.

Ratification

The adoption or confirmation by the principal of an unauthorized act or contract made by an agent on his behalf is a ratification of such act or contract which binds the principal and the third party as if the agent had been initially authorized. As defined in the Restatement, Second, Agency, Section 82:

Ratification is the affirmance by a person of a prior act which did not bind him but which was done or professedly done on his account, whereby the act, as to some or all persons, is given effect as if originally authorized by him.

Ratification may relate to the acts of an agent which have exceeded the authority granted to him, as well as to acts of a stranger who is without any authority, but made on behalf of an alleged principal. The act, however, must indicate to the third person that it is on behalf of the alleged principal in order that it may be ratified. To effect a ratification the principal must manifest an intent to do so with knowledge of all material facts concerning the transaction. However, it is not necessary that such intent be communicated either to the purported agent or to the third person. It may be manifested by express language or implied from conduct of the principal, such as his acceptance of the benefits of the transaction. In any event, the principal must ratify the entire act or contract.

A ratification relates back to the time of performance of the unauthorized act. For example, B, without authority from A, represents to C that he is A's agent and on June 1 enters into a bilateral executory contract with C on behalf of A. Since B acted without authority, neither A nor C is bound to the supposed contract. On June 15, A ratifies the act of B. Both A and C thereupon become bound to the contract, effective as of June 1, to which date the ratification relates back. However, suppose that on June 12, C learned of B's lack of authority and notified A that he withdrew from the contract, or otherwise repudiated it. C's ratification on June 15 would not relate back or cause a contract to be formed. The doctrine of relation back is a convenient fiction of the law of agency which treats ratification as supplying the requisite authority at the time the unauthorized act was done, which was when the third person manifested his consent. It does not apply when the third person gives notice to the principal of his non-consent before ratification. In such event there would be no consent of the third person at the time the principal gave his consent, and therefore no contract for lack of mutual consent of both parties. The Restatement, Second, Agency, Section 88 provides:

To constitute ratification, the affirmance of a transaction must be before the other party has manifested his withdrawal from it either to the purported principal or to the agent, and before the offer or agreement has otherwise terminated or been discharged.

TORT LIABILITY OF THE PRINCIPAL

In addition to contract liability to third persons, a principal may be liable in tort to third persons as a consequence of the acts of his agent. Tort liability may arise directly or indirectly from authorized or unauthorized acts of the agent.

Direct Liability of Principal

All individuals are liable for their own tortious conduct. Consequently, a principal may be held liable in damages for his own negligence or recklessness in carrying on an activity by means of servants or agents. For example, if A lends to his employee, B, a company car to run a business errand knowing that B is incapable of driving the vehicle, A would be liable for his own negligence to anyone injured by B's negligent driving. The Restatement, Second, Agency, Section 213 provides:

A person conducting an activity through servants or other agents is subject to liability for harm resulting from his conduct if he is negligent or reckless:
    (a) in giving improper or ambiguous orders or in failing to make proper regulations; or
    (b) in the employment of improper persons or instrumentalities in work involving risk of harm to others;
    (c) in the supervision of the activity; or
    (d) in permitting, or failing to prevent, negligent or other tortious conduct by persons, whether or not his servants or agents, upon premises or with instrumentalities under his control.

Vicarious Liability of Principal for Authorized Acts of Agent

A principal who authorizes his agent to commit a wrongful or tortious act with respect to the property or person of another is liable for the injury or loss sustained by such person. The authorized act is that of the principal. Thus, if A directs his agent, B, to enter upon C's land and cut timber which neither A nor B has any right to do, the cutting of the timber is a trespass and A is liable to C. Or, suppose A instructs his agent B to make certain representations as to A's property which B is authorized to sell. A knows these representations are false but B does not. Such representations by B to C who buys the property in reliance thereon is a deceit by A practiced on C, for which A is liable to C.

Vicarious Liability of Principal for Unauthorized Acts of Agent

A principal may be liable for a tort committed by his agent which he did not authorize, even one which is in flagrant disobedience of his instructions to the agent, where the tort was committed by the agent in the course of his employment. This is a form of liability without fault and is based upon the doctrine of respondeat superior, i.e., let the superior respond. The rationale of this doctrine is that one who multiplies his business activities through the use of agents and employees, is liable for their negligence in carrying out the business purposes for which they were employed. It is the price which the employer pays for thus enlarging the scope of his business activities. It does not matter how carefully the employer selected the employee, if in fact the latter negligently injured a third person while engaged in the business of the employer.

The Doctrine of Respondeat Superior. The liability of the principal under *respondeat superior* is vicarious or derivative and depends upon proof of wrongdoing by the agent in the course of his employment. Frequently both principal and agent are joined as defendants in the same suit. If the agent is not held liable, the principal is not liable. A principal who is held liable for his agent's tort has a right of indemnification against the agent, which is the right to be reimbursed the amount that he was required to pay by reason of the agent's wrongful act. However, frequently an agent is not sufficiently solvent to reimburse his employer, resulting in the principal bearing the brunt of the liability.

The wrongful act of the agent or employee must be connected with his employment and within its scope in order that the principal be held liable for resulting injuries or damage to third persons. For example, A is delivering gasoline for P. He lights his pipe and negligently throws the blazing match into a pool of gasoline which has dripped upon the ground during the delivery and which ignites. For the resulting harm, P is subject to liability because the negligence of the employee delivering the gasoline relates directly to the manner in which he is handling the goods in his custody and his conduct with respect to the gasoline which is under his control. However, if a chauffeur while driving his employer's car on an errand for his employer suddenly decided to use his pistol and shoot at pedestrians on the sidewalk for target practice, the employer would not be liable to the pedestrians. This willful and intentional misconduct is not related to the performance of the services for which the chauffeur was employed.

The same rule applies to negligent misconduct of an employee unrelated to his employment. If A employs B to deliver merchandise in a given city to A's customers, and while driving a delivery truck in going to or returning from a place of delivery B negligently causes the truck to hit and injure C, A is liable to C for the injuries sustained. But if, after making the scheduled deliveries, B drives the truck to a neighboring city to visit a friend and while so doing negligently causes the truck to hit and injure D, A is not liable. In such case, B is said to be on a "frolic of his own." He has deviated from the purpose of his employment and was using A's truck to accomplish purposes of his own and not the business of his employer. Of course, in all of these situations the wrongdoing agent is personally liable to the injured persons as a tortfeasor.

The effect of *respondeat superior* is that the negligence of the agent is imputed to the principal. An interesting question is whether negligence of an agent will be imputed as contributory negligence of the principal. For example, A's automobile, while being driven by B in the course of his duties as agent of A, is heavily damaged upon being struck by a truck negligently driven by C. In a suit by A against C to recover the amount of his damages, the defense is that B at the time of the collision was guilty of contributory negligence. If this is so, and it is imputed to A, it is a valid defense to the lawsuit. The courts are not entirely in accord on this question.

Torts of Independent Contractor. An independent contractor is not the agent or servant of the person for whom he is performing work or rendering services. Hence, the doctrine of respondeat superior does not apply to torts committed by an independent contractor. Nevertheless, certain duties imposed by law are non-delegable and a person may not escape the consequences of their non-performance by contract with an independent contractor. A landowner who permits an independent contractor to maintain a dangerous condition on his premises, such as an excavation adjoining a public sidewalk which is unprotected by a guard rail or by lights at night, is liable to a member of the public who is injured as a result of falling into the excavation. Or, in the case of the erection of a faulty or defective scaffolding on a building by an independent contractor, the owner of the building is liable by statute in certain States for injuries to employees of the independent contractor who are injured as a result of using the defective scaffolding.

CRIMINAL LIABILITY OF THE PRINCIPAL

A principal is not ordinarily liable for the unauthorized criminal acts of his agents. One of the elements of a crime is a guilty mind, and this element is not present where the act of the agent was not authorized, so far as criminal responsibility of the principal is concerned. The act of an agent may be both tortious and criminal. If connected to and committed in the course of the agent's employment, the principal will be liable civilly in damages but not criminally. However, as to certain offenses, a principal may be liable criminally for the acts of his agent as in the case of the publication of a criminal libel in a newspaper, or with respect to certain statutory crimes relating to a subject matter as to which a person is compelled at his peril to see that the law is not disobeyed, such as the sale of liquor to minors or to intoxicated persons, or the sale of unwholesome or adulterated food.

RELATIONSHIP OF AGENT AND THIRD PERSONS

The function of an agent is to assist in the conduct of the business of his principal by carrying out his orders. The agent is not normally a party to the contract which he makes with a third person on behalf of a disclosed principal. The third person gen-

erally is aware of the fact that he is dealing with an agent who is not personally undertaking to perform the contract which he is negotiating on behalf of his principal. The resulting contract, if within the agent's actual or apparent authority, is between the third person and the principal, and the agent incurs no liability thereon.

An agent, however, may be personally liable to the third person in certain situations:

1. by acting without authority or exceeding the scope of the authority granted;
2. upon entering into a contract on behalf of an undisclosed or partially disclosed principal;
3. upon knowingly entering into a contract on behalf of a non-existent principal;
4. by guaranteeing performance of a contract by the principal; or
5. by committing a tortious or wrongful act.

CONTRACT LIABILITY OF AGENT

Unauthorized Contracts

If an agent exceeds his actual and apparent authority, the principal is not bound. However, the fact that the principal is not bound does not of itself make the agent a party to the contract. The agent's liability, if any, arises from express or implied representations made by the agent to the third party concerning the agent's authority.

Agent's Implied Warranty of Authority. A person who undertakes to contract as agent impliedly warrants that he is in fact authorized to make the contract on behalf of the party whom he purports to represent. If the agent does not have authority to bind the principal, the agent is liable to the third party for damages unless the principal ratifies the contract. However, no implied warranty exists if the contract expressly provides that the agent shall not be responsible for any lack of authority, or if the agent, acting in good faith, discloses to the third person all of the facts upon which his authority rests. For example, agent B has received a letter of instruction from his principal A which is ambiguous. He shows it to C stating that it represents all of the authority that he has to act, and both B and C rely upon its sufficiency. In this case, there is no implied warranty or any warranty by B to C of his authority. The interpretation of the letter of instruction may present a question of law, but the agent did not assume the risk that it was sufficient to bind the principal.

Misrepresentation. If a purported agent falsely represents to a third person that he has authority to make a contract on behalf of a principal whom he has no power to bind, he is liable in a tort action of deceit to the third person for the loss sustained in reliance upon such misrepresentation.

Undisclosed or Partially Disclosed Principal

An agent acts for an undisclosed principal when he appears to be acting in his own behalf and the third person with whom he is dealing has no knowledge that he is acting as an agent. The instructions of the principal to the agent are not only to conceal the identity of the principal but also not to disclose the agency relationship. Ostensibly, the third person is dealing with the agent as though he were a principal. A partially disclosed principal is one whose existence is known but whose identity is unknown. The third person is aware that the agent is acting on behalf of another but he is not informed of the name or identity of the principal.

Liability of the Parties. The agent is personally liable upon a contract which he enters into with a third person on behalf of an undisclosed principal or a partially dis-

closed principal, unless the third person after discovery of the existence and identity of such principal elects to hold the principal to the contract. The reason for the liability of the agent is that the third person has placed reliance upon the agent individually and has accepted the agent's personal undertaking to perform the contract. Obviously, where the principal is wholly undisclosed the third person does not know of the interest of anyone in the contract other than himself and the agent. The reason for the liability of the undisclosed or partially disclosed principal is that the concealment by the agent is pursuant to the instructions of the principal, and having received the benefits of the agent's acts, he should assume and be responsible for the burdens thereof.

After the third person has become informed of the identity of the undisclosed or partially disclosed principal, he may hold either the principal or the agent to performance of the contract, but not both. He has the choice of disregarding the principal and requiring performance only by the agent, or of requiring performance only by the principal. Having once made an election, he is irrevocably bound by it. What constitutes an election is a question of fact. After the third person has demanded performance by both the agent and the principal, he may bring suit against both as he does not wish to incur the risk that upon a trial the evidence may fail to establish the agency relationship. Bringing suit and proceeding to trial against both is not an election, but before the entry of any judgment the third person is compelled to make an election as he is not entitled to a judgment against both.

Rights of Undisclosed or Partially Disclosed Principal. An undisclosed or partially disclosed principal acquires rights and may maintain an action in his own name against the third person with whom the agent entered into a contract in the agent's name.

The undisclosed principal is not prevented by the parol evidence rule from establishing his rights under a written contract entered into by his agent. The agent is not excused from liability by the subsequent disclosure of the principal, and evidence of the agency relationship merely introduces another person, the principal, who is bound by the contract. However, if the agent represents to the third person that he is not acting on behalf of another but solely for himself as principal, the undisclosed principal would have no rights upon the contract.

Liability of Agent Where Principal Is Non-Existent

A person who professes to act as agent for a fictitious or non-existent principal is personally liable on a contract entered into with a third person on behalf of such a principal. A promoter of a corporation who enters into contracts with third persons in the name of a corporation to be organized is personally liable on such contracts. The corporation is not liable as it did not authorize the contracts. If the corporation after coming into existence affirmatively adopts a pre-incorporation contract made in its behalf, it thereupon becomes bound along with the promoter. However, if the corporation enters into a new contract with such a third person, the prior contract between the promoter and the third person is discharged and the liability of the promoter is terminated. This is a novation.

Where an agent enters into a contract with a third person on behalf of a principal who unknown to both the agent and the third person had died prior to the making of the contract, it is generally held that the existence of the principal at the time of the making of the contract is an implied condition precedent to the contract, and that neither the agent, the third person, nor the estate of the decedent principal, is liable thereon.

TORT LIABILITY OF AGENT

An agent is personally liable for his wrongful acts which injure or damage third persons, whether or not such acts are authorized by the principal, and whether or not the principal may also be liable.

An agent who commits a wrong at the direction or under instructions of his principal is also personally liable therefor. An agent is personally liable if he converts the goods of a third person to this principal's use. An agent is also liable for making representations which he knows to be false and fraudulent to a third person who in reliance thereon sustains a loss.

RIGHTS OF AGENT AGAINST THIRD PERSON

An agent who makes a contract with a third person on behalf of a disclosed principal has no right of action against the third person for breach of the contract. The agent is not a party to the contract nor a promisee of the third person. However, an agent for an undisclosed principal or partially disclosed principal may maintain in his own name an action against the third person for breach of contract. In such case, the agent is also individually liable on the contract.

Cases

Types of Authority

SCHOENBERGER v. CHICAGO TRANSIT AUTHORITY

(1980) 84 Ill.App.3d 1132, 39 Ill.Dec. 941, 405 N.E.2d 1076.

CAMPBELL, J.

The plaintiff, James Schoenberger, brought a small claims action pro se in the Municipal Department of the circuit court of Cook County against the defendant, Chicago Transit Authority (hereinafter C.T.A.)

to recover contract damages. The trial court ruled in favor of the defendant and against the plaintiff. The plaintiff appeals from this judgment. At issue is whether the C.T.A. may be held liable under agency principles of a promise allegedly made by an employee of the C.T.A. to the plaintiff at the time that he was hired to the effect that he would receive a $500 increase in salary within a specified period of time. We affirm.

Schoenberger was employed by the C.T.A. from August 16, 1976, to October, 1976, at a salary of $19,300. The facts surrounding his employment with the C.T.A. are controverted. The plaintiff's position at the trial was that he took the job with the C.T.A. at a salary of $19,300 upon the condition that he would receive a $500 salary increase, above and beyond any merit raises, within a year. Schoenberger testified at trial that, after filling out a job application and undergoing an initial interview with a C.T.A. Placement Department interviewer, he met several times with Frank ZuChristian, who was in charge of recruiting for the Data Center. At one of the meetings with ZuChristian, the Director of Data Center Operations, John Bonner, was present. At the third meeting held between ZuChristian and the plaintiff, ZuChristian informed the plaintiff that he desired to employ him at $19,800 and that he was making a recommendation to this effect. Schoenberger told ZuChristian that he would accept the offer. ZuChristian informed him that a formal offer would come from the Placement Department within a few days. However, when the offer was made, the salary was stated at $19,300. Schoenberger did not accept the offer immediately. Rather, he called ZuChristian for an explanation of the salary difference. After making inquiries, ZuChristian informed Schoenberger that a clerical error had been made and that it would take a number of weeks to have the necessary paperwork reapproved because several people were on vacation. To expedite matters, ZuChristian suggested Schoenberger take the job at the $19,300 figure and that he would see that the $500 would be made up to him at the April, 1976, October, 1976, or at the latest, the April, 1977 performance and salary review. The $500 increase was to be prospective and not retroactive in nature. John Hogan, the head of the Data Center, was aware of this promise ZuChristian informed Schoenberger. Because the defendant was found to be ineligible for the October, 1976 performance evaluation and the April, 1976 review was cancelled, the April, 1977 evaluation was the first evaluation at which the issue of the salary increase was raised. When the increase was not given at that time, the plaintiff resigned and filed this suit.

* * *

The trial court, after hearing the evidence and reviewing the exhibits, ruled in favor of the defendant. The trial court ruled: (1) that it was inconceivable that the plaintiff thought ZuChristian had final authority in regard to employment contracts; and (2) that it was not shown that a commitment or promise was made to the plaintiff by an authorized agent of the C.T.A.

* * *

The main question before us is whether ZuChristian, acting as an agent of the C.T.A., orally contracted with Schoenberger for $500 in compensation in addition to his $19,300 salary. The authority of an agent may only come from the principal and it is therefore necessary to trace the source of an agent's authority to some word or act of the alleged principal. [Citations.] The authority to bind a principal will not be presumed, but rather, the person alleging authority must prove its source unless the act of the agent has been ratified. [Citations.] Moreover, the authority must be founded upon some word or act of the principal, not on the acts or words of the agent. [Citations.]

* * * Both Hogan and Bonner, ZuChristian's superiors, testified that ZuChristian had no actual authority to either make an offer of a specific salary to Schoenberger or to make any promise of additional compensation. Furthermore, ZuChristian's testimony corroborated the testimony that he lacked the authority to make formal offers. From this evidence, it is clear that the trial court properly determined that ZuChristian lacked the actual authority to bind the C.T.A. for the additional $500 in compensation to Schoenberger.

Nor can it be said that the C.T.A. clothed ZuChristian with the apparent authority to make Schoenberger a promise of compensation over and above that formally offered by the Placement Department. The general rule to consider in determining whether an agent is acting within the apparent authority of his principal was stated in *Wing v. Lederer* (1966), 77 Ill.App.2d 413, 222 N.E.2d 535, in this way:

Apparent authority in an agent is such authority as the principal knowingly permits the agent to assume or which he holds his agent out as possessing—it is such authority as a reasonably prudent man, exercising diligence and discretion, in view of the principal's conduct, would naturally suppose the agent to possess.

[Citations.]

* * *

Here, Schoenberger's initial contact with the C.T.A. was with the Placement Department where he filled out an application and had his first interview. There is no evidence that the C.T.A. did anything to permit ZuChristian to assume authority nor did they do anything to hold him out as having the authority to hire and set salaries. ZuChristian was not at a management level in the C.T.A. nor did his job title of Principal Communications Analyst suggest otherwise. The mere fact that he was allowed to interview prospective employees does not establish that the C.T.A. held him out as possessing the authority to hire employees or set salaries. Moreover, ZuChristian did inform Schoenberger that the formal offer of employment would be made by the Placement Department.

The plaintiff maintains that a principal who clothes an agent with apparent authority will be bound by the acts of his agent even where the agent acts in contravention of secret instructions. [Citation.] We agree. However, we do not find that principle controlling here. A third party who deals with an assumed agent has the obligation to verify both the fact and extent of the agent's authority. [Citations.]

* * *

Our final inquiry concerns the plaintiff's contention that irrespective of ZuChristian's actual or apparent authority, the C.T.A. is bound by ZuChristian's promise because it ratified his acts. Ratification may be express or inferred and occurs where "the prinicpal, with knowledge of the material facts of the unauthorized transaction, takes a position inconsistent with nonaffirmation of the transaction." [Citations.] Ratification is the equivalent to an original authorization and confirms that which was originally unauthorized. [Citation.] Ratification occurs where a principal attempts to seek or retain the benefits of the transaction. [Citations.]

Upon review of the evidence, we are not convinced that the C.T.A. acted to ratify ZuChristian's promise. According to Bonner's testimony, when he took over the supervision of ZuChristian's group in the fall of 1976 and was told of the promise, he immediately informed ZuChristian that the promise was unauthorized and consequently would not be honored. Subsequently, he informed Schoenberger of this same fact. Mere delay in telling Schoenberger does not, as the plaintiff contends, establish the C.T.A.'s intent to ratify. [Citations.]

* * *

For the reasons we have indicated, the judgment of the circuit court of Cook County granting judgment in favor of the defendant, C.T.A., is affirmed.

Effect Upon Authority of
Termination of Agency

ZUKAITIS v. AETNA CASUALTY & SURETY CO.

(1975) 195 Neb. 59, 236 N.W.2d 819.

BLUE, J.

This is an action for a declaratory judgment brought to determine whether defendant-appellee, the Aetna Casualty and Surety Company, was obligated under its professional liability insurance policy to defend plaintiff-appellant, Raymond R. Zukaitis, in a medical malpractice suit.

The case was tried to the court under a stipulation of facts which can be summarized as follows: Raymond R. Zukaitis was a physician practicing medicine in Douglas County, Nebraska. Aetna issued Dr. Zukaitis a policy of professional liability insurance through its agent, the Ed Larsen Insurance Agency, Inc. This policy was for a period from August 31, 1969, to August 31, 1970.

On August 7, 1971, Dr. Zukaitis received a written notification of a claim for malpractice which allegedly occurred on September 27, 1969. On August 10, 1971, Dr. Zukaitis telephoned the Ed Larsen Insurance Agency. At the request of the agency the written claim was forwarded to it by Dr. Zukaitis. This was received on August 11, 1971, and was erroneously referred to the St. Paul Fire and Marine Insurance Company on that date by the agency.

Dr. Zukaitis was insured with St. Paul Fire and Marine Insurance Company from August 31, 1970, to August 31, 1971. But on the date of the alleged malpractice, he was insured with Aetna. Apparently without notice to Dr. Zukaitis, the agency contract between Ed Larsen Insurance Agency

and Aetna had been canceled effective August 1, 1970. At that time the agency placed Dr. Zukaitis' insurance with St. Paul.

On November 22, 1971, a malpractice action was brought against Dr. Zukaitis based on the alleged malpractice of September 27, 1969. Attorneys for St. Paul undertook the defense of the lawsuit. On January 25, 1974, St. Paul discovered that it was not the insurance carrier for Dr. Zukaitis on September 27, 1969, the date of the alleged malpractice, and advised Aetna of this at that time. Dr. Zukaitis was also advised of this, and the attorney retained for St. Paul to represent Dr. Zukaitis withdrew. Dr. Zukaitis made demand upon Aetna on May 28, 1974, for it to undertake the defense of Dr. Zukaitis, but this demand was refused.

Dr. Zukaitis retained his own attorney to represent him in the malpractice case. A motion for summary judgment was filed by Dr. Zukaitis in that case, which motion was sustained. This action for a declaratory judgment against Aetna therefore resolved itself into an effort to recover attorney's fees and costs. The District Court found for Aetna. Dr. Zukaitis' motion for new trial was overruled, and this appeal followed.

Aetna contends that it is relieved from its obligation to Dr. Zukaitis since notice was not given as required by paragraph 4(b) of the policy which provides: "If claim is made or suit is brought against the insured, the insured shall immediately forward to the company every demand, notice, summons or other process received by him or his representative."

Dr. Zukaitis contends that under the circumstances, notice to Aetna was given within a reasonable period in that the agent who wrote the policy was given notice, and further that a delay in giving notice does not defeat policy obligations unless the insurer is prejudiced by the delay.

* * *

Ordinarily notice to a soliciting agent who countersigns and issues policies of insurance is notice to the insurance company. Restatement, Agency 2d, § 127, p. 324; 13 Couch on Insurance 2d, § 49:27, p. 652 et seq.; §§ 44–328 and 44–329, R.R.S. 1943. This is also true even if the agent forwards the notice to the wrong company. At 44 Am.Jur.2d, Insurance, § 1468, p. 336, it is stated: "Also, an insured who has promptly given notice of an accident to the general agent that issued the policy, and has also promptly delivered process to him, has been held not required to do anything further, although in each instance the agent by mistake forwarded the papers to the wrong company."

The question then is whether this is true after the agency contract between the insurance company and the agent has been terminated as it was in this case. To answer this, it is necessary to refer to the general law of agency.

The rule is that a revocation of the agent's authority does not become effective as between the principal and third persons until they receive notice of the termination. [Citations.]

Here, Dr. Zukaitis did what most reasonable persons would do in this situation; he notified the agent who sold him the policy. There is no evidence that notice of the termination was sent to him or that he knew the agency contract had been canceled.

It is stated in 3 Couch on Insurance 2d, § 26:50, p. 513: "When the insurer terminates the agency contract, it is its duty to notify third persons, such as the insureds with whom the agent dealt, and inform them of such termination. If it does not so notify and such third persons or insureds deal with the agent without notice or knowledge of the termination, and in reliance on the apparently continuing authority of the agent, the insurer is bound by the acts of the former agent."

The following appears in 3 Couch on Insurance 2d, § 26:50, p. 515: "The princi-ple of the carrying over of the authority of an agent after termination with respect to third persons having no notice or knowledge thereof has been applied so as to bind the insurer when the third person dealt with the apparent agent by contracting with him, or by forwarding or delivering to him suit papers and proofs of loss." [Citation.]

We conclude that under the facts and circumstances of this case, the notice given by the plaintiff to the agent of the defendant constitutes notice to the defendant and would obligate defendant to carry out the terms of its insurance contract with plaintiff. The District Court was in error when it determined to the contrary.

* * *

Reversed and remanded with directions.

Ratification

DAVID v. SERGES

(1964) 373 Mich. 442, 129 N.E.2d 882.

SOURIS, J.

When an agent purporting to act for his principal exceeds his actual or apparent authority, the act of the agent still may bind the principal if he ratifies it. The Restatement of Agency 2d, § 82, defines ratification thusly:

"Ratification is the affirmance by a person of a prior act which did not bind him but which was done or professedly done on his account, whereby the act, as to some or all persons, is given effect as if originally authorized by him."

"Affirmance" is defined in § 83 of the Restatement:

"Affirmance is either

"(a) a manifestation of an election by one on whose account an unauthorized act has been done to treat the act as authorized, or

"(b) conduct by him justifiable only if there were such an election."

* * * Paragraph (d) of the comment to § 82 of the Restatement, supra, discusses the matter in these terms:

"That the doctrine of ratification may at times operate unfairly must be admitted, since it gives to the purported principal an election to blow hot or cold upon a transaction to which, in contract cases, the other party normally believes himself to be bound. But this hardship is minimized by denying a power to ratify when it would obviously be unfair. See §§ 88–90. Further, if the transaction is not ratified normally the pseudoagent is responsible; if not, it is because the third party knew, or agreed to take the risk, of lack of authority by the agent. In many cases, the third person is a distinct gainer as where the purported principal ratifies a tort or a loan for which he was not liable and for which he receives nothing. This result is not, however, unjust, since although the creation of liability against the ratifier may run counter to established tort or contract principles, the liability is self-imposed. Even one who ratifies to protect his business reputation or who retains unwanted goods rather than defend a law suit, chooses ratification as preferable to the alternative. * * *"

In this case the only testimony taken was plaintiff's, who testified that defendant's managing agent had borrowed from him $3,500 upon defendant's behalf and for use in defendant's business a retail meat market. Plaintiff further testified that defendant subsequently had paid to him $200 on the alleged loan and had upon several occasions stated to plaintiff that the full sum would eventually be paid. With this testimony in the record plaintiff rested his case and defendant, without likewise resting, moved for a judgment of no cause on the theory that plaintiff had failed to prove a *prima facie* case.

The trial court erred in granting defendant's motion. * * *

Even if borrowing money were not within the agent's actual or apparent authority, plaintiff's evidence, viewed favorably, was legally sufficient to establish defendant's liability for the alleged loan upon a theory of ratification. Thus, plaintiff's evidence was sufficient to require defendant to be put to his proofs.

Reversed and remanded.

Respondeat Superior

JOEL v. MORISON
(1833) Court of Exchequer (England),
6 Carrington & Payne Reports 501.

The declaration stated, that, on the 18th of April, 1833, the plaintiff was proceeding on foot across a certain public and common highway, and that the defendant was possessed of a cart and horse, which were under the care, government, and direction of a servant of his, who was driving the same along the said highway, and that the defendant by his said servant so carelessly, negligently, and improperly drove, governed, and directed the said horse and cart, that, by the carelessness, negligence, and improper conduct of the defendant by his servant, the cart and horse were driven against the plaintiff, and struck him, whereby he was thrown down and the bone of one of his legs was fractured, and he was ill in consequence, and prevented from transacting his business, and obliged to incur a great expense in and about the setting the said bone, &c., and a further great expense in retaining and employing divers persons to superintend and look after his business for six calendar months. Plea—Not guilty.

From the evidence on the part of the plaintiff it appeared that he was in Bishopsgatestreet, when he was knocked down by a cart and horse coming in the direction from Shoreditch, which were sworn to have been driven at the time by a person who was the servant of the defendant, another of his servants being in the cart with him. The injury was a fracture of the fibula.

On the part of the defendant witnesses

were called, who swore that his cart was for weeks before and after the time sworn to by the plaintiff's witnesses only in the habit of being driven between Burton Crescent Mews and Finchley, and did not go into the City at all.

Thesiger, for the plaintiff, in reply, suggested that either the defendant's servants might in coming from Finchley have gone out of their way for their own purposes, or might have taken the cart at a time when it was not wanted for the purpose of business, and have gone to pay a visit to some friend. He was observing that, under these circumstances, the defendant was liable for the acts of his servants.

PARKE, B.

He is not liable, if, as you suggest, these young men took the cart without leave; he is liable if they were going extra viam in going from Burton Crescent Mews to Finchley; but if they chose to go of their own accord to see a friend, when they were not on their master's business, he is not liable.

His Lordship afterwards, in summing up said—This is an action to recover damages for an injury sustained by the plaintiff, in consequence of the negligence of the defendant's servant. There is not doubt that the plaintiff has suffered the injury, and there is no doubt that the driver of the cart was guilty of negligence, and there is no doubt also that the master, if that person was driving the cart on his master's business, is responsible. If the servants, being on their master's business, took a detour to call upon a friend, the master will be responsible. If you think the servants lent the cart to a person who was driving without the defendant's knowledge, he will not be responsible. Or, if you think that the young man, who was driving took the cart surreptitiously, and was not at the time employed on his master's business, the defendant will not be liable. The master is only liable where the servant is acting in the course of his employment. If he was going

out of his way, against his master's implied commands, when driving on his master's business, he will make his master liable; but if he was going on a frolic of his own, without being at all on his master's business, the master will not be liable. As to the damages, the master is not guilty of any offence, he is only responsible in law, therefor the amount should be reasonable.

Verdict, for the plaintiff—Damages, 30£.

Undisclosed Principal

PORETTA v. SUPERIOR DOWEL CO.

(1957) 153 Me. 308, 137 A.2d 361, 71 A.L.R.2d 898.

DuBORD, J.

* * * The issue thus raised presents a problem of novel impression in this State The issue is:

"Is an undisclosed principal absolved from liability to his agent's vendor who has sold goods to the agent upon the credit of the agent who has received payment or advances or a settlement of accounts, from his undisclosed principal before discovery of the undisclosed principal by the agent's vendor?"

There are two different rules bearing upon the issue. The first one, which appears to be supported by the weight of authority is that an undisclosed principal is generally relieved of his liability for his agent's contracts to the extent that he has settled with his agent prior to the discovery of the agency. The other rule is, that an undisclosed principal is discharged only where he has been induced to settle with the agent by conduct on the part of the third person leading him to believe that such person has settled with the agent.

The decisions appear to be in a state of hopeless confusion.

"The rule that an undisclosed principal, when discovered, may be held liable upon a contract made in his behalf will not be enforced for the advantage of a third party, if it will work injustice to the principal. An undisclosed principal may be relieved from liability by reason of a changed state of accounts between him and the agent, the rule formerly laid down in England and now very generally followed in the United States being that where the principal, acting in good faith, has settled with the agent so that he would be subjected to loss where he compelled to pay the third person, he is relieved from liability to the latter, and this doctrine is, in at least one jurisdiction, in effect prescribed by statute. This doctrine is now held in England, and in a few cases in the United States, to be too broad, and the better rule is stated to be that the principal is discharged only where he has been induced to settle with the agent by conduct on the part of the third person leading him to believe that such person has settled with the agent or has elected to hold the latter. In any event the principal is relieved from liability, where he has been induced by the conduct of the third person to settle with the agent." [Citations.]

"It is often said that persons dealing in their own names are presumed to deal for themselves as principals, yet if one authorized by another to act as his agent, in acting on behalf of the principal, fails to disclose the principal to the third person, or to disclose that he is acting as agent, the principal, when discovered, may become liable for the acts done in his behalf, and may be sued thereon just as if, at the time the transaction was entered into, the agent had disclosed the fact of his agency and the identity of the principal, unless the principal and the agent have so adjusted their accounts that to hold the principal liable would work an injustice to him." [Citation.]

The expression "unless the principal and the agent have so adjusted their accounts that to hold the principal liable would work an injustice to him," is qualified by 2 Am. Jur. § 399, which reads as follows:

"The general rule which allows a third person to have recourse against an undisclosed principal is subject to the qualification that the principal shall not be prejudiced by being made personally liable because he has in good faith relied upon the conduct of the third person and has paid or settled with the agent; conversely, the rule is that a third person who deals with the agent of an undisclosed principal can, upon discovering the principal, resort to the latter for payment, unless by his conduct he has led the principal in the meanwhile to pay or settle with the agent. The comparable expression of the American Law Institute is that an undisclosed principal is discharged from liability to the other party to the contract if he has paid or settled accounts with his agent, reasonably relying upon conduct of the other party, not induced by the agent's misrepresentations, which indicates that the agent has paid or otherwise settled the accounts. Thus, if the principal has settled with his agent on the basis of receipts or other documents furnished the agent by the seller, the principal cannot be held liable for the price."

The American Law Institute, as of May 4, 1933, adopted and promulgated the following rule:

"An undisclosed principal is discharged from liability to the other party to the contract if he has paid or settled accounts with an agent reasonably relying upon conduct of the other party, not induced by the agent's misrepresentations, which indicates that the agent has paid or otherwise settled the account." 1 Am.Law Inst. Restatement of Agency, § 208.

* * * The adoption of this doctrine by this court will establish a clear cut and explicit rule of law free from the confusion, complications and perplexities which have existed throughout the years.

We, therefore, adopt the rule as laid down in the Restatement of the Law of Agency.

Problems

1. A was P's traveling salesman, and was also authorized to collect accounts. Prior to the agreed termination of the agency, P wrongfully discharged A. A then called on T, an old customer, and collected an account from T. He also called on X, a new prospect, as P's agent, secured a large order, collected the price of the order, sent the order to P, and disappeared with the collections. P delivered the goods to X as per the order.

(a) P sues T for his account. Decision?

(b) P sues X for the agreed price of the goods. Decision?

2. (a) P instructed A, his agent, to purchase a quantity of hides. A bought the hides from T in his own (A's) name and delivered the hides to P. T, learning later that P was the principal, sends the bill to P, who gives A the money to pay to T. A absconds with the money. T sues P. Decision?

(b) Assume instead, that on discovering that P is A's principal, T sues A and P for the purchase price. Decision?

3. A sold goods to B in good faith, believing him to be a principal. B in fact was acting as agent for C and within the scope of his authority. The goods were charged to B, and on his refusal to pay, A sued B for the purchase price. While this action was pending, A learned of B's relationship with C. Nevertheless, thirty days after learning of that relationship, A obtained judgment against B and had an execution issued which was never satisfied. Three months after rendition of the judgment, A sued C for the purchase price of the goods. Decision?

4. Oldham owned and operated a store in Centerville under the name of the Fair Store. Sims was the manager of this store. On June 28, 1982, Oldham sold the store to Sims. While Sims was manager he ordered merchandise from Brice-Burton Dry Goods Company for the account of Oldham, and after he purchased the store he continued to order goods from Brice-Burton for the account of Oldham. Beginning in December, 1975, Betz, a salesman in the employ of Brice-Burton sold goods to the Fair Store. Sims made the purchases and the goods were billed to Oldham. No notice was given to Brice-Burton Company or Betz of the sale of the store to Sims. There was no difference in the operation of the store before June 28, 1982, and thereafter. When Brice-Burton learned of the sale of the Fair Store, it discontinued selling its merchandise to Sims, and unsuccessfully attempted to collect from Oldham the balance of $2,856 due on its merchandise account. Thereafter, Brice-Burton Company sued Oldham for $2,856 for merchandise sold subsequent to June 28, 1982. Decision?

5. X Grocery Company employed Jones as its manager. Jones was given authority by X Company to purchase supplies and goods for resale and had conducted business for several years with Brown Distributing Company. Purchases by Jones from Brown Distributing Company had been limited to groceries. Jones then contacted Brown Distributing Company and had it deliver a color television set to his home, advising Brown Company the set was to be used in promotional advertising, the object of which was to increase X Grocery Company's business. The advertising did not develop. Jones disappeared from the area, taking the television set with him. Brown Company sued X Company for the purchase price of the set. Decision?

6. Stone was the authorized agent to sell stock of the X Company at $10, per share, the par value, and was authorized, in case of sale, to fill in the blanks in the certificates with the name of the purchaser, the number of shares and the date of sale. He sold 100 shares to Barrie, and without the knowledge or consent of the company and without reporting the same, he indorsed on the back of the certificate the following:

It is hereby agreed that X Company shall, at the end of three years after the date, repurchase the stock at $11.00 per share on thirty days' notice. X Company, by Stone.

After three years, demand was made on X Company to re-purchase, which was refused and the company repudiated the agreement on the ground that the agent had no authority to make the agreement for re-purchase. Barrie sued X Company. Decision?

7. Helper, a delivery boy for Gunn, delivered two heavy packages of groceries to Reed's porch, and, as instructed by Gunn, Helper rang the bell to let Reed know the groceries had arrived. Mrs. Reed came to the door and asked Helper if he would deliver the groceries into the kitchen as the bags were heavy. Helper did so, and upon leaving he observed Mrs. Reed having difficulty in moving a cabinet in the dining room. He undertook to assist her, but being more interested in watching Mrs. Reed than the cabinet, he failed to observe a small, valuable antique table which he smashed into with the cabinet and totally destroyed.

Does Reed have a cause of action against Gunn for the value of the destroyed antique?

8. Driver picked up Friend to accompany him on an out-of-town delivery for his employer, Speedy Service. A "No Riders" sign was prominently displayed on the windshield of the truck, and Driver violated specific instructions of his employer by permitting an unauthorized person to ride in the vehicle.

While discussing a planned fishing trip with Friend, Driver ran a red light and collided with an automobile driven by Motorist. Both Friend and Motorist were injured. Is Speedy Service liable to either Friend or Motorist for the injuries they sustained?

9. X Department Store advertises that it maintains a barber shop in its store managed by Y. Actually, Y is not an employee of the store but merely rents space in the store. Y, while shaving Z in the barber shop, negligently cut off one of Z's ears. Z sues X Department Store for damages. Decision?

10. The following contract was executed on August 22:

"Ray agrees to sell and Shaw, the representative of Todd and acting in his behalf, agrees to buy 10,000 pounds of $0.32 \times 1\frac{5}{8}$ stainless steel strip type 410.

(Signed) Ray
(Signed) Shaw"

On August 26, Ray informs Shaw and Todd that the contract was signed by him as agent for Upson. What are the rights of Ray, Shaw, Todd and Upson, in the event of a breach of the contract?

11. Harris, owner of certain land known as Red Bank, mailed a letter to Byron, a real estate broker in City X, stating: "I have been thinking of selling Red Bank. I have never met you but a friend has advised that you are an industrious and honest real estate broker. I therefore employ you to find a purchaser for Red Bank at a price of $35,000." Ten days after receiving the letter, Byron mailed the following reply to Harris: "Acting pursuant to your recent letter requesting me to find a purchaser for Red Bank, this is to advise that I have sold the property to Sims for $35,000. I enclose your copy of the contract of sale signed by Sims. Your name was signed to the contract by me as your agent."

Is Harris obligated to convey Red Bank to Sims?

PART

FIVE

Bailments and Sales of Personal Property

Chapter

19

BAILMENTS, CARRIERS, AND INNKEEPERS

The term "bailment" describes a situation in which there is a delivery of possession of personal property, without transfer of title, by the owner or rightful possessor (bailor) to another person (bailee) for the accomplishment of some particular purpose, after which the property is to be returned to the bailor or to a person designated by the bailor.

Bailments are of great commercial importance in their own right. For example, the warehousing and carriage of goods, both of which are common types of bailments, involve billions of dollars worth of goods each year. In addition, bailments define the rights and duties of parties to a number of other transactions, such as sales on approval and pledges.

BAILMENTS

Bailments are commonly classified as bailments for mutual benefit, bailments for the sole benefit of the bailee, and bailments for the sole benefit of the bailor. Mutual ben-

efit bailments include the ordinary commercial bailments such as when goods are delivered to a repairman, or jewels to a pawnbroker, or when a hat or coat is checked in a restaurant, or an automobile delivered to a parking lot attendant. A bailment for the sole benefit of the bailee most commonly involves the gratuitous loan of personal property, such as when A permits his neighbor, B, to use his lawn mower or automobile. A bailment for the sole benefit of the bailor includes the gratuitous storage or carriage of personal property. For example, B's storage without charge of A's piano or transportation of A's furniture, is a bailment for the sole benefit of the bailor A.

ESSENTIAL ELEMENTS OF A BAILMENT

The essential elements of a bailment are (1) the delivery of lawful possession of (2) specific personal property by or with the consent of its owner (the bailor) to another person (the bailee) without transfer of title

(3) for a determinable time (4) at the end of which the bailee is obligated to return the property either to the bailor or to a person having a superior right to its possession.

Delivery of Possession

Possession by a bailee in a bailment relationship may be said to involve: (1) power to control and (2) either an intention to control or an awareness on the part of the bailee that the rightful possessor has lost physical control of the personal property. Thus, where a customer in a restaurant hangs his hat or coat on a hook furnished for that purpose, the hat or coat is within an area which is under the physical control of the restaurant owner; however, the restaurant owner is not a bailee of the hat or coat unless he clearly signifies that he intends to exercise the power to control the hat or coat. On the other hand, where a clerk in a store helps a customer remove his coat in order to try on a new one, it is generally held that the owner of the store becomes a bailee of the old coat through the clerk, his employee. Here, the clerk has signified an intention to exercise control over the coat by taking it from the customer and a bailment results.

Traditionally, the courts have analyzed the "possession" question by seeking to determine whether there has been a delivery. They have said that the customer in the restaurant does not "deliver" the coat or hat to the restaurant owner when he hangs it on a hook while the customer in the store "delivers" his coat to the clerk. This concept of delivery, however, does not account for many cases where a bailment is said to exist. For example, suppose that the customer in the restaurant hangs his hat on a hook and then forgets and leaves it behind. If the restaurant owner then notices the hat and realizes that it has been left behind by one of his customers, he becomes a bailee of the hat. What has happened is not that some mysterious delivery has suddenly taken place, but that the restaurant owner, hav-

ing physical control of the area in which the hat is found, becomes aware that the rightful possessor has relinquished the power to control it, that he now has both the power to control and the intent to control, and therefore possession of the hat. This is similar to the position of all finders of personal property.

A finder on the street is not a bailee merely because he has observed a billfold lying there. He becomes a bailee as soon as he evidences an intent to assume control over the property) i.e., picks up the billfold). The reason for the difference between the finder in the street and the restaurant owner is that the finder in the street does not have physical control of the area in which the billfold is found; therefore, he must assume physical control of the billfold before he can become a bailee. Pursuing the inquiry into the meaning of possession for purposes of bailment we come to several troublesome situations.

Parking Lot Transactions. The "parking lot cases" fall generally into three categories: (1) where an owner parks his car in a parking lot, pays a charge and receives a claim check, but locks the car and takes the keys away; (2) where an owner leaves his car with an attendant who assumes control of the car and parks it, and the owner pays a charge and receives a ticket as a means of identifying the car on redelivery; and (3) where the status of the parties falls in between the above two categories and is controlled by the nature of the circumstances.

The first class of cases is generally held to be a lease or license, whereas the second class is held to be a bailment. The third class covers cases where, even though the owner parks his car and keeps the keys, the parking lot operator maintains sufficient control to consitute a bailment. In analyzing this third class of cases, the amount of free access permitted by the parking lot operator is material. Where a parking lot is so constructed and manned that it is clearly impossible for anyone not authorized to enter and leave except through the parking lot operator's failure to carry out the obvious scheme of his operations, this may be sufficient to constitute him a bailee, even though the owner of the car parked it and retained the keys. The question is really how much control does the parking lot operator hold himself out to the public to be exercising?

The significance of the keys is that ordinarily the car cannot be driven without them. While a thief demonstrates that this is not always true, the parking lot operator should not be permitted to escape liability on the ground that he did not have sufficient control of the car because he could not cause it to move without "jumping" the ignition, especially where it appears by the physical structure of the lot and the way it was manned that he had assumed sufficient control to prevent the automobile from being moved.

Safe Deposit Companies. Normally, when a person rents a safe deposit box, the bank or safe deposit company has a master key to the box and the renter's access to the box is dependent upon the simultaneous use of both his own key and the key retained by the bank or safe deposit company. It should be fairly clear from what has been said about "control" in the parking lot situations, that the bank or the safe deposit company is a bailee. The conceptual difficulty experienced is due to the fact that what the depositor is concerned about is not the safe deposit box but its contents.

The general rule is that a bailee is not liable for the contents of a closed container, or, to put it more correctly, for things which are not visible when the container is bailed to him, unless, from the nature of the container itself or from the surrounding circumstances, he ought, as a reasonable man, to have anticipated the presence of such contents, or unless he had express notice of what the contents were. For example, in parking lot bailment situations, the parking lot owner is generally not held liable for items stolen from the trunk of the car unless he knew or reasonably should have known of the trunk's contents.

This rule pertains to the question of the bailee's liability and not to his possession, but it is discussed here because of its bearing upon the safe deposit situation. The safe deposit company is liable as bailee for the contents of the safe deposit box regardless of the value of the things contained in it, because it has a high degree of control in *preventing* unauthorized access and because, in view of the circumstances, it ought to anticipate that a safe deposit box may contain *any* kind of valuable thing which will fit into it.

Personal Property

The bailment relation can only exist with respect to personal property. The delivery of possession of real property by the owner to another is covered by real property law. It is not necessary that the bailed property be tangible. Intangible property such as promissory notes and corporate bonds, being evidenced by written instruments and so capable of delivery, may be and frequently are the subject matter of bailments. This is also true of such documents of title as warehouse receipts and bills of lading.

Possession for a Determinable Time

To establish a bailment relationship the person receiving possession must be under a duty to return the personal property and must not obtain title to it. This brings us to a discussion of the distinction between bailments and transactions involving transfers of title, such as sales.

Sales. Whether a particular transaction constitutes a bailment or a sale must be determined by the particular factual situation presented. The substance of the agreement, and its form or the particular expressions employed in it, is controlling. A sale always involves a transfer to the buyer of title to specific property. If the identical property transferred is to be returned, even though in altered form, the transaction is a bailment; however, if other property of equal value, or the money value, may be returned, there is a transfer of title and the transaction is a sale.

Conditional Sales. In a conditional sale the contract contains a reservation of title to the goods in the seller until the purchase price is paid in full. But title is reserved in the seller for security purposes only. For all other purposes, including risk of loss, beneficial ownership is in the buyer. The position of the buyer under a conditional sales contract is not the same as that of a bailee in any respect. He has no option to return the goods, but must pay the contract price. On the other hand, a bailee *must* return the goods or be liable to the bailor for their value. The fact that the goods are damaged or destroyed without his fault will not relieve the buyer from payment of the contract price because the goods are at his risk.

Other Transfers of Title. Whenever a person intentionally abandons all his interest in certain personal property, the relation between him and a person who takes possession of the property will not be that of bailor and bailee. A loser and finder are bailor and bailee because, although the loser may abandon hope that he will ever find the property, he does not abandon his interest in it. One who intentionally throws his property away, however, cannot be bailor because he has abandoned his interest in it. Likewise, one who gives his property to another is not a bailor. The finder of intentionally abandoned property and the donee of a gift are not bailees.

Restoration of Possession to the Bailor

The bailee is legally obligated to restore possession of the property when the period of the bailment has come to an end. A bailment for the mutual benefit of both parties ordinarily terminates when the purpose of the bailment is fully accomplished or when the time expires for which the bailment was created. Such bailment may, of course, be terminated earlier by mutual consent of the parties. A breach by the bailee of any of his obligations gives the bailor the privilege of terminating the bailment. A bailment is also terminated by destruction of the bailed goods because there can be no bailment without goods, yet if the loss is due to the bailee's fault he is liable under his bailment obligation.

Bailments for the benefit of the bailee alone or for the benefit of the bailor alone are ordinarily for a definite time or purpose. Such bailments do not terminate until the specified time expires or the purpose is accomplished. In practice, however, such bailments are often terminated at will. For example, one who has gratuitously undertaken to store his neighbor's piano for six months will most likely be able to return the piano before the expiration of that period with impunity. It is unlikely that litigation will ensue. However, if he dumps it in the neighbor's garage before the six months expire, while his neighbor is away on vacation, and the piano is damaged, he may well be liable.

Normally, the bailee is required to return the identical goods bailed although the goods may be in a changed condition due to the work which the bailee was required to perform upon them. An exception to this rule obtains in the case of fungible goods, such as grain, where, for all practical purposes, every particle is the equivalent of every other particle, and which the bailee is expected to mingle with other such like goods during the bailment. In such a case, obviously the bailee cannot be required to return the identical goods bailed. His obligation is simply to return goods of the same quality and quantity out of the common mass. Where fungible goods belonging to several bailees are properly stored in a common mass, for example, grain in an elevator, and a portion of the common mass is destroyed without fault upon the part of the bailee, each of the bailors whose goods make up the common mass will bear the loss in proportion to his share of the common mass.

The very nature of a bailment requires a bailee to return the goods when the purpose of the bailment has been accomplished to the bailor or to a person designated by the bailor at the proper time or place. The bailee has a strict duty to return the goods to the correct person. The bailor to whom the goods are restored must be either the owner or a person who has the superior right to possession.

A person having lawful possession of property for the time being may validly bail the property to another. Thus, an agent may bail his principal's property, if he is authorized to do so. A person having lawful right to possession under some agreement with the owner may bail the property, if he does not thereby violate the agreement. If such an agent or other person having lawful possession bails the property in violation of his authority from, or agreement with, the owner, he loses his right to possession and the right to possession will vest in the owners. The bailee then is justified in delivering the property to the owner instead of to his bailor. But the bailee is not justified in delivering the property to the owner if the bailor has not exceeded his authority or violated any agreement with the owner, and where, by the terms of his authority from, or agreement with, the owner he continues to be entitled to the possession of the property as against the owner. Thus, a bailee may assume a risk when he delivers property to its owner merely because he happens to be the owner. The bailee must

restore the possession of the property, when his lawful possession comes to an end, to the bailor, who is either the owner or a person who has the superior right to possession.

RIGHTS AND DUTIES OF BAILOR AND BAILEE

The bailment relationship creates rights and duties on the part of the bailor and the bailee. The bailee is under a duty to exercise due care for the safety of the goods and to return them to the right person. The bailee has the exclusive right to possess the goods for the term of the bailment. Depending upon the nature of the transaction, a bailee may have the right to compensation and reimbursement of expenses.

The law does not permit certain bailees, namely, common carriers, public warehousemen and innkeepers, to limit their liability for breach of their duties to the bailor, except as provided by statute. Other bailees, however, may vary their duties and liabilities by contract with the bailor. Where liability is limited by contract, the law requires that any such limitation be properly brought to the attention of the bailor before the goods are bailed by him. This is especially true in the case of "professional bailees," such as repair garages, who make it their business to act as bailees and who deal with the public on a uniform rather than an individualized basis. Thus, a variation or limitation in writing contained in a check or stub given to the bailor or posted on the walls of the bailee's place of business will not ordinarily bind the bailor unless (a) the bailee draws his attention to the writing and (b) informs him that it contains a limitation or variation of liability. The bailee is not required, however, to read and interpret the limitation or variation to the bailor.

Bailee's Duty to Exercise Due Care

The bailee must exercise due care not to permit injury to or destruction of the property by himself or third parties. The degree of care depends upon the nature of the bailment relationship and the character of the property.

Ordinarily, a bailee is not an insurer of the subject of the bailment. Since negligence or failure to exercise due care for the property, or intentional wrongdoing, is the basis of his liability, in the absence of negligence, the bailee is not liable where the goods are lost, or stolen, or destroyed.

In the context of a commercial bailment, from which both parties derive a benefit, the law requires the bailee to exercise the care which a reasonably prudent person would exercise under the same circumstances. Where the bailment is one which benefits the bailee alone, as in the case of one who gratuitously borrows a truck from another, the law has required more than reasonable care of him. On the other hand, where the bailee accepts the goods to accommodate the bailor, without himself deriving any economic benefit from this, the law has required a lesser degree of care.

It should be remembered, however, that the amount of care required to satisfy any of the standards will vary with the character of the property. A bailee required to take only slight care under the foregoing general rules may be liable if he does not take greater care of a $500 bracelet than he would have of a $10 watch. In practice, therefore, the distinctions are blurred by the fact that whatever degree of care is required in the abstract, a bailee must respond to the magnitude of the consequences which reasonably ought to have been foreseen if the property were lost or destroyed.

When the goods are lost, damaged or destroyed while in the possession of the bailee, it is often impossible for the bailor to obtain enough information to show that the loss or damage was due to the bailee's negligence. The law aids the bailor in this respect by setting up a presumption that the bailee was negligent. The bailor is merely required to show that certain goods were delivered by way of bailment and that the bailee has failed to return them or that they were returned in damaged condition. Upon introduction of this proof, the law raises a presumption that the loss or damage was due to the bailee's negligence and the burden then rests upon the bailee to prove that he exercised the degree of care required of him.

Bailee's Duty to Return Bailed Property

Where the bailee has an obligation by express agreement with the bailor or by custom to insure the goods against certain risks, but fails to do so and the goods are destroyed or damaged through such risk, he is liable for the damage or non-delivery, even though he has exercised due care.

Where the bailee uses the bailed property in a manner not authorized by the bailor or by the character of the bailment, and during the course of such use the property is damaged or destroyed, without fault on the part of the bailee, the bailee is absolutely liable for the damage or destruction. The reason for this is that wrongful use by the bailee automatically terminates his lawful possession, and he becomes a trespasser as to the property. That is what was earlier referred to as the requirement that the possession must be "lawful" to constitute a bailment. A trespasser is not a bailee, and he is liable for all damage to the property which would not have occurred but for his trespass, regardless of fault. To illustrate the last rule, suppose a garage mechanic, after repairing A's care, takes it out for a road test, and the car is damaged in an accident which is solely the fault of someone other than the mechanic. The proprietor of the garage will not be liable as bailee for such damage, a road test being a normal incident to this type of bailment. But where the mechanic takes A's car for a joy ride or on independent business, and the car is damaged solely through the fault of someone other than the mechanic, the proprietor will be liable as bailee for such damage.

The garage operator cannot escape liability upon the ground that his mechanic was acting outside the scope of his employment, since liability in such case is based upon breach of contract rather than in tort.

A bailee has a duty to return the property to the right person. He is not excused by delivering the property to the wrong person by mistake, even where such mistake was induced by negligence on the part of the bailor. The bailee is liable for misdelivery, regardless of fault, except: (a) Where the person to whom he delivers the property is better entitled to its possession than the bailor. However, it is not sufficient that the bailee thinks that such person is so entitled. (b) Where the property is taken from the bailee under valid legal process, as by a sheriff under a writ of execution. But, in all such cases, the bailee must take care to notify the bailor before he surrenders the property, and if he fails to do so, and the bailor is thereby deprived of some legal remedy to avert the seizure of the property, the bailee will be liable to the bailor.

If the bailee, by mistake or intentionally, misdelivers the property to someone other than the bailor, someone who has no right to its possession, he is guilty of conversion and is liable to the bailor.

Rights of Bailor and Bailee Against Third Party Who Damages Goods

If a third party negligently damages the goods, both the bailor and the bailee have a right of action against him. The law permits either the bailor or the bailee to sue alone for the entire damage. In such case, whichever one sues, he is required to account to the other for that portion of the entire recovery which represents the other's interest in the goods.

Where the bailee is guilty of contributory negligence and contributory negligence is a complete bar to an action, the question arises whether the bailor may nevertheless recover from the third party. Certainly, where the bailee has a substantial interest in the goods, the bailor should not be permitted to recover the entire damages against the third party. If he were, and if he then accounted to the bailee for that portion of the recovery which represented the bailee's interest, the bailee would be indirectly compensated by the third party despite his contributory negligence. Thus, most courts deny full recovery to the bailor under these circumstances although recovery for the damage done to the bailor's interest in the goods is permitted. The bailee, of course, is also liable to the bailor for such damage.

Bailee's Rights to Compensation and Reimbursement for Expenses

A bailee who by express or implied agreement undertakes to perform work upon, or render services in connection with, the bailed goods is entitled to reasonable compensation for those services or work. In most cases, of course, the agreement between bailor and bailee fixes the amount of compensation and provides how it shall be paid. In the absence of a contrary agreement, the compensation is payable upon completion of the work or the performance of the services by the bailee. If, after such completion or performance, and before the goods are redelivered to the bailor, the goods are lost or damaged without fault on the part of the bailee, the bailee is still entitled to compensation for his work and services.

The bailee who performs work or services on the bailed chattel is, of course, entitled to compensation for those expenses incident to his performance. Where the bailment does not involve the performance of work or services by the bailee, the question arises as to who is to bear the expenses incident to such bailment, such as the expenses incident to the bailment involved in the rental of an automobile. The rule in these situations is that, unless the agreement between the parties provides otherwise, the bailee bears all the ordinary expenses of maintenance, i.e., he has to pay for gas, oil, and ordinary repairs and replacements. Ordinary repairs and replacements, in this context, are those normally incident to the operation of an automobile of comparable age in reasonable condition. The bailor, however, bears the cost of all extraordinary repairs and replacements, i.e., those not normally incident to the operation of an automobile of comparable age in reasonable condition.

Most bailees who are entitled to compensation for work and services performed in connection with bailed goods acquire a lien upon the goods to secure the payment of such compensation. By statute in most jurisdictions the bailee is given the right to obtain a judicial foreclosure of his lien and sale of the goods. A substantial number of statutes provide, also, that the bailee does not lose his lien upon redelivery of the goods to the bailor—as was the case at common-law. Instead, the lien continues for a specified period after redelivery by timely recording with the proper authorities an instrument claiming such lien.

SPECIAL KINDS OF BAILMENTS

Pledges

A pledge is a bailment for security whereby the owner gives possession of his goods to another (the pledgee) to secure a debt or the performance of some obligation. A pledge is similar to a lien, in that both the pledgee and the lienholder have no title to the goods involved but merely a possessory interest to secure a debt or some other obligation. The pledgee can usually transfer and assign

his special interest in the goods to others, even without the consent of the pledgor. Pledges of most types of personal property for security purposes are governed by Article 9 of the Uniform Commercial Code which is discussed in Chapter 00. In most respects, the pledgee's duties and liabilities are the same as those of the bailee for compensation.

Warehousing

A warehouseman is a bailee who receives goods to be stored in his warehouse for compensation. His duties and liabilities under the common law were in all respects the same as those of the ordinary bailee for compensation. Because the activities of warehousemen are affected by a public interest, they are subject to extensive regulation by State and Federal authorities. Statutes changing the rule as to acceptance of goods properly tendered for storage and imposing extensive regulations involving structural safety and health measures are in force in all jurisdictions. Federal statutes govern warehousemen who store goods in interstate and foreign commerce. Warehousemen must also be distinguished from ordinary bailees in that the receipts they issue for storage have acquired a special status in commerce. These receipts are regarded as "documents of title" and are governed by Article 7 of the Uniform Commercial Code.

CARRIERS OF GOODS

Carriers which undertake to transport the goods of others from place to place are also bailees of such goods. Thus, unless the contract of carriage provides otherwise, both common carriers and contract carriers owe to the person for whom they undertake to transport goods the duties which a bailee owes to his bailor. The common law, however, imposes an extraordinary liability upon the common carrier because of the public nature of its services.

COMMON CARRIERS AND PRIVATE CARRIERS DISTINGUISHED

A common carrier offers its services and facilities to the public upon terms and under circumstances which indicate that the offering is made indifferently to all persons. One who carries the goods of another on isolated occasions, or who serves a limited number of customers under individual contracts without offering the same or similar contracts to the public at large, is a private or contract carrier—not a common carrier.

Stated somewhat differently, the criteria for determining whether a carrier is subject to the rules applicable to common carriers are: (1) the carriage must be a part of its business; (2) the carriage must be for remuneration; and (3) the carrier must represent to the general public that it is willing to serve the public in the transportation of property.

DUTY TO CARRY

A common carrier is under a duty to serve the public to the limits of its capacity and, within those limits, to accept for carriage goods of the kind which it normally transports. A private carrier has no duty to accept goods for carriage except where it is bound to do so by contract.

LIABILITY OF THE CARRIER FOR LOSS OR DAMAGE

A private carrier, in the absence of special contract terms, is liable as a bailee with respect to the goods it undertakes to carry. The common carrier, on the other hand, is under a stricter liability which approaches that of an insurer of the safety of the goods.

CARRIER'S DUTY TO DELIVER TO THE RIGHT PERSON

The carrier is under an absolute duty to deliver the goods to the person to whom they are consigned by the shipper. This duty is not peculiar to common carriers but applies also to private carriers. Essentially, this is the duty which renders an ordinary bailee liable for misdelivery. The person to whom delivery must be made is controlled by the form of the bill of lading or other contract of carriage.

LIMITATION OF LIABILITY

In most jurisdictions, the carrier is permitted to limit its liability by contract with the shipper. However, a carrier may not absolve itself of liability for its own negligence. Section 7–309 of the U.C.C. Where not prohibited by statute, the carrier may limit its liability by excepting particular hazards, such as fire or strikes, or may limit its liability to a certain value of the goods agreed upon with the shipper, or to an amount declared by the shipper. To avail itself of such limitation, the carrier is required to offer to the shipper a choice between limited and unlimited liability, and may charge different rates to reflect the extent of liability assumed. Interstate rates and the contracts offered under them are subject to regulation and approval by the Interstate Commerce Commission and many States have similar requirements for intrastate shipments.

In order that a carrier may avail itself of a limitation of liability it must show that the shipper knew of and assented to the limitation. This is particularly true of limitations contained in mere shipping receipts. Moreover, a shipper is placed upon notice of limitations contained in published tariffs filed by the carrier and approved by the appropriate State or Federal agency. Pursuant to powers vested in it by Congress, the Interstate Commerce Commission has approved standard forms for bills of lading. These I.C.C. approved forms contain a number of conditions and limitations which are generally printed on the back of the forms, but this is not required. A shipper who accepts such a form is taken prima facie to have assented to the terms and conditions of the relevant uniform bill, although not printed on the back of the form. The reason is that the terms and conditions of the uniform bill are a matter of public record.

INNKEEPERS

At common law, innkeepers (today better known as hotel owners or operators), are held to the same strict liability with regard to their guests' belongings as are common carriers with regard to the goods they carry. This rule of strict liability applies only to those who furnish lodging to the public for compensation as a regular business, and such liability extends only to the belongings of lodgers who are "guests." To qualify as a "guest," within this rule, a person must be on travel status, and persons who intend to become and are accepted as permanent lodgers are not guests.

Today, in almost all jurisdictions, the old common-law strict liability of the "innkeeper" has been substantially modified by case law and statute. The statutes vary as to detail but they all have certain features in common. They provide that the innkeeper may avoid strict liability for loss of his guests' valuables or money by providing a safe where they may be kept and by posting adequate notice of its availability. To avoid liability, the innkeeper must comply strictly with the statutory prescribed mode of posting such notices. With regard to articles which are not placed in a safe provided for this purpose, or which are not articles of the kind normally kept in a safe, the statutes often limit recovery to a maximum figure which, while it differs from State to State, is generally insubstantial. However, these statutory limitations are generally applicable to the innkeeper as an insurer and do not apply where the loss is due to the fault of the innkeeper or his employees. In the case of loss due to his own fault or that of his employees, the innkeeper is liable for the full value of the lost property.

The liability of an innkeeper for his guest's automobile deserves special mention. The hotel or motel owner ordinarily assumes no responsibility for the safety of the guest's car since the guest customarily retains possession and control. However, if the innkeeper provides parking facilities and the guest's car is entrusted to him or his employees, the innkeeper may be liable under the rules previously considered in this chapter with respect to parking lot bailees.

Cases

Delivery of Possession

LAVAL v. LEOPOLD
(1965) 47 Misc.2d 624, 262 N.Y.S.2d 820.

BERNARD NADEL, J.

Plaintiff brings this action to recover $1,725, the value of plaintiff's coat, which she claims she delivered into defendant's care and custody and which was not returned.

Defendant moves for summary judgment, asserting that there are no triable issues of fact and that plaintiff, as a matter of law, was guilty of contributory negligence and therefore may not have a recover against him. Plaintiff cross-moves for summary judgment in her favor.

Defendant is a practicing psychiatrist, who, at the time, when plaintiff was his patient, maintained his office with two associates or colleagues, also practicing in the same field. No receptionist or other employee attended the office.

Plaintiff claims that on one of her professional visits to defendant's office, in accordance with her usual custom she deposited her coat in a clothes closet in the office reception room. When plaintiff's professional consultation was complete and she was ready to leave defendant's office, her coat was missing.

The maintenance of the closet in defendant's office created an implied invitation to plaintiff to deposit her coat there.

In Webster v. Lane, 125 Misc. 868, 212 N.Y.S. 298, which involved the loss of a coat in a dentist's office, the court took judicial notice of the fact that patients of a dentist are not placed in a dental chair with their wraps on. This court likewise takes judicial notice that it is not custom for a patient to lie on the couch or sit in the chair in a psychiatrist's office wrapped in her fur coat.

The plaintiff cannot be said to be contributorily negligent as a matter of law because she placed her coat in a clothes closet in defendant's reception room.

Implicit in the relationship between the parties, the defendant became a bailee of plaintiff's coat, and it is for the trier of the facts to determine whether under the circumstances then prevailing at the time and place of this happening, reasonable care was exercised by the defendant with reference to plaintiff's coat which was temporarily deposited in the reception room closet preliminary to treatment by the defendant.

Accordingly, the motion and cross-motion are denied.

Parking Lot Transactions

SEWALL v. FITZ-INN AUTO PARKS, INC.

(1975) 3 Mass.App. 380, 330 N.E.2d 853.

ARMSTRONG, J.

The plaintiff seeks recovery of the value of his automobile, which was left by him on the defendant's parking lot early on the morning of April 15, 1970, and was gone when he returned for it early that evening, having apparently been stolen by an unidentified third person. The declaration is in two counts, one based on a theory of breach of the defendant's contractual duty to safeguard the automobile and the other based on principles of ordinary negligence. At the conclusion of the evidence the trial judge directed verdicts for the defendant on both counts. The propriety of that action is the sole issue raised by the plaintiff's bill of exceptions.

The facts do not appear to be in dispute. The defendant's parking lot was approximately 100 by 200 feet in size. A chain link fence had been erected along its rear boundary, separating the lot from a facility of the Massachusetts Bay Transportation Authority. The normal entrance and exit to the lot were located at the front, but it was also possible to leave the lot from the sides, each of which bordered on a small street. Upon entering the lot on the morning of April 15, the plaintiff paid the attendant on duty a fee of twenty-five cents, a flat rate for which he was permitted to park all day or for a shorter period, as he chose. He parked his car in a space designated by the attendant, locked it and took the keys with him. The attendant remained on duty until 10:30 or 11:00 A.M. on April 15, after which time the lot was unattended, apparently pursuant to a practice followed by the defendant. The plaintiff had never been expressly informed of that practice, but he had regularly parked in the lot for several years and had never seen an attendant when he returned for his car in the evening.

The case turns on whether those facts warranted a finding that the transaction between the parties constituted a bailment for hire of the plaintiff's automobile, rather than a mere letting of parking space. [Citations.] The existence of a bailment is a prerequisite to the plaintiff's right to recover, either in contract or in tort, as the defendant would not otherwise by under any duty to sfeguard the plaintiff's car against theft. [Citations.] We are of the opinion that no bailment has been shown and that the trial judge was correct in directing verdicts on both counts.

A bailment, by definition, arises only upon delivery of possession of the property sought to be bailed, and at least some degree of control over that property, to the putative bailee. [Citations.] Once possession and control of an automobile have been transferred to the operator of a parking facility for a fee, the owner (in the absence of any warning or understanding to the contrary) is justified in concluding that the operator has assumed responsibility to safeguard the automobile, and the operator has a legally enforceable duty to exercise reasonable care in the fulfillment of that responsibility. [Citation.] But if there has been no such delivery of possession or control to the operator, nor any acceptance thereof by him, he cannot, without more, be regarded as having undertaken to protect the car and owes the owner no duty to do so. [Citation.]

It has long been held that the surrender of the car keys to the parking facility attendant is a sufficient delivery of possession and control to create a bailment for hire, whether the keys are left at the attendant's request [Citation] or with his knowledge and acquiescence in the absence of such a request. [Citation.] The same result has recently been reached where the owner parked and locked his car, without surrendering the keys, in an enclosed parking facility whose sole means of egress was manned by an attendant responsible for stopping and checking each car leaving the facility. [Citation.] * * *

The plaintiff in effect is asking us to extend the principle applied in the *Hale* and subsequent cases. In those cases the garage, while not exercising the degree of control possible through possession of the keys, did exercise (or purport to exercise) control over the departure of vehicles from its facility. In the present case neither type of control was actually or apparently exercised or asserted by the defendant. The role of the attendant, so far as known to the plaintiff, was confined to collecting a uniform twenty-five cent fee from motorists as they entered the lot and directing them to parking spaces. The plaintiff knew that he could remove his car from the lot at any time without interference by any employee of the defendant. Indeed, it should have been obvious to him, because of the open character of the lot and the absence of any attendant on all the evenings when he had removed his car, that any control exercised by the defendant over his car, and any correlative responsibility assumed with respect thereto, came to an end once he had paid the fee and parked the car. [Citation.]

Exceptions overruled.

*Bailee's Duty to
Exercise Due Care*

HAYNIE v. A & H CAMPER SALES, INC.

(1975) 233 Ga. 654, 212 S.E.2d 825.

HILL, J.

This case is before the court on certiorari. [Citation.] The plaintiff, Mr. Haynie, delivered his 1972 Holiday Rambler trailer to the defendant, A & H Camper Sales, Inc., for the purpose of having the defendant make some repairs. At the time the trailer was delivered to the defendant plaintiff signed a work authorization which contained the following language:

Not responsible for loss or damage to vehicles or articles left in vehicles in case of fire, theft or any other cause beyond our control.

That night, plaintiff's trailer was removed from defendant's premises. Plaintiff filed suit against the defendant as bailee for the value of the trailer and personalty therein, alleging the removal to have resulted from defendant's negligence. Relying on the above quoted disclaimer, defendant moved for a summary judgment, which was granted by the trial court.

Plaintiff appealed, and the Court of Appeals affirmed.

At common law, the bailee generally was under a duty to return the chattel to the bailor at the termination of the bailment. [Citations.]

The common law rules relating to bailment have been codified and sometimes modified. The following sections of our Code are pertinent to our consideration. Code § 12–403 provides: "The relation of the owner of an automobile and the owner of the garage in which the automobile is stored is that of bailor and bailee. Such bailee is bound to use ordinary care for the safe-keeping and return of the automobile." Code § 12–408 provides: "In all such cases, the bailee is not only bound to exercise skill in the labor and work bestowed, but it is a *part of the contract* that he shall exercise ordinary care and diligence in keeping and protecting the articles intrusted to him." (Emphasis supplied.)

More pertinent however is Code Sec. 12–106, which provides: "In order for a bailee to avail himself of the act of God or *exception under the contract* as a defense, *he must establish not only that the* act of God or *excepted fact ultimately occasioned the loss*, but that his *own negligence did not contribute thereto*." (Emphasis supplied.)

Limitations of liability written by bailees undertaking to limit their common law responsibilities have been accepted by the courts. Such contractual limitations have become so frequent that the lawmakers have made provision for them. In order for a bailee to avail himself of an exception under the contract, he must establish (1) that the loss was occasioned by the exception, and (2) that his own negligence did not contribute thereto. [Citation.]

In the base before us, plaintiff alleged that the defendant negligently allowed the trailer to be removed by an unauthorized person or persons. Thus, although defendant need not necessarily prove that the loss was occasioned by one of his exceptions, to wit: theft, defendant must establish that his own negligence did not contribute thereto. [Citation.] * * *

The defendant's motion for summary judgment should have been denied. The evidence submitted by defendant in support of its motion for summary judgment did not establish that defendant's negligence did not contribute to the loss.

Judgment reversed.

Bailee's Duty to
Return Bailed Property

MIESKE v. BARTELL DRUG CO.

(1979) 92 Wash.2d 40, 593 P.2d 1308.

BRACHTENBACH, J.

This case determines the measure of damages for personal property, developed movie film, which is destroyed, and which cannot be replaced or reproduced. It also decides the legal effect of a clause which purports to limit the responsibility of a film processor to replacement of film.

We will detail the facts later, but the heart of the matter is that plaintiffs delivered already developed movie film to a retail store for the sole purpose of having the film spliced onto larger reels. The film was lost or destroyed by the retailer's processing agent. A jury verdict of $7,500 was returned against the retailer and the agent-processor. Those defendants appeal. We affirm.

The facts are that over a period of years the plaintiffs had taken movie films of their family activities. The films started with the plaintiffs' wedding and honeymoon and continued through vacations in Mexico, Hawaii and other places, Christmas gatherings, birthdays, Little League participation by their son, family pets, building of their home and irreplaceable pictures of members of their family, such as the husband's brother, who are now deceased.

Plaintiffs had 32 50-foot reels of such developed film which they wanted spliced together into four reels for convenience of viewing. Plaintiff wife visited defendant Bartell's camera department, with which she had dealt as a customer for at least 10 years. She was told that such service could be performed.

The films were put in the order which plaintiffs desired them to be spliced and so marked. They were then placed in four separate paper bags which in turn were placed in one large bag and delivered to the manager of Bartell. The plaintiff wife explained the desired service and the manner in which the films were assembled in the various bags. The manager placed a film processing packet on the bag and gave plaintiff wife a receipt which contained this language: "We assume no responsibility beyond retail cost of film unless otherwise agreed to in writing." There was no discussion about the language on the receipt. Rather, plaintiff wife told the manager, "Don't lose these. They are my life."

There was no discussion or agreement about who was going to perform the splicing service.

Bartell sent the film package to defendant GAF Corporation, which intended to send them to another processing lab for splicing. Plaintiffs assumed that Bartell did this service and were unaware of the involvement of two other firms.

The bag of films arrived at the processing lab of GAF. The manager of the GAF lab described the service ordered and the packaging as very unusual. Yet it is undisputed that the film was in the GAF lab at the end of one day and gone the next morning. The manager immediately searched the garbage disposal dumpster which already had been emptied. The best guess is that the plaintiff's film went from GAF's lab to the garbage dumpster to a truck to a barge to an up-Sound landfill where it may yet repose.

After several inquiries to Bartell, plaintiff wife was advised to call GAF. Not surprisingly, after being advised of the com-

plete absence and apparent fatality of plaintiffs' films, this lawsuit ensued.

At trial defendants Bartell and GAF denied liability. The janitorial service company which aparently removed the film was a defendant. The verdict was against Bartell and GAF but not against the janitorial service company. It is not a party to the appeal. For purposes of appeal, Bartell and GAF admit liability for negligence.

Two main issues are raised: (1) the measure of damages and (2) the effect of the exclusionary clause appearing on the film receipt.

On damages, the defendants assign error to (a) the court's damages instruction and (b) the court's failure to give their proposed damages instruction.

The standard of recovery for destruction of personal property was summarized in *McCurdy v. Union Pac. R.R.,* 68 Wash.2d 457, 413 P.2d 617 (1966). We recognized in *McCurdy* that (1) personal property which is destroyed may have a market value, in which case that market value is the measure of damages; (2) if destroyed property has no market value but can be replaced or reproduced, then the measure is the cost of replacement or reproduction; (3) if the destroyed property has no market value and cannot be replaced or reproduced, then the value to the owner is to be the proper measure of damages. However, while not stated in *McCurdy,* we have held that in the third *McCurdy* situation, damages are not recoverable for the sentimental value which the owner places on the property. [Citations.]

The defendants argue that plaintiffs' property comes within the second rule of *McCurdy, i.e.,* the film could be replaced and that their liability is limited to the cost of replacement film. Their position is not well taken. Defendants' proposal would award the plaintiffs the cost of acquiring film without pictures imposed thereon. That is not what plaintiffs lost. Plaintiffs lost not merely film able to capture images by exposure but rather film upon which was recorded a multitude of frames depicting many significant events in their lives. Awarding plaintiffs the funds to purchase 32 rolls of blank film is hardly a replacement of the 32 rolls of images which they had recorded over the years. Therefore the third rule of *McCurdy* is the appropriate measure of damages, *i.e.*, the property has no market value and cannot be replaced or reproduced.

The law, in those circumstances, decrees that the measure of damages is to be determined by the value to the owner, often referred to as the intrinsic value of the property. Restatement of Torts § 911 (1939).

Necessarily the measure of damages in these circumstances is the most imprecise of the three categories. Yet difficulty of assessment is not cause to deny damages to a plaintiff whose property has no market value and cannot be replaced or reproduced. [Citations.]

The fact that damages are difficult to ascertain and measure does not diminish the loss to the person whose property has been destroyed. Indeed, the very statement of the rule suggests the opposite. If one's destroyed property has a market value, presumably its equivalent is available on the market and the owner can acquire that equivalent property. However, if the owner cannot acquire the property in the market or by replacement or reproduction, then he simply cannot be made whole.

The problem is to establish the value to the owner. Market and replacement values are relatively ascertainable by appropriate proof. Recognizing that value to the owner encompasses a subjective element, the rule has been established that compensation for sentimental or fanciful values will not be allowed. [Citations.] That restriction was placed upon the jury in this case by the court's damages instruction.

* * *

Under these rules, the court's damages instruction was correct. In essence it al-

lowed recovery for the actual or intrinsic value to the plaintiffs but denied recovery for any unusual sentimental value of the film to the plaintiffs or a fanciful price which plaintiffs for their own special reasons, might place thereon.

* * *

The next issue is to determine the legal effect of the exclusionary clause which was on the film receipt given plaintiff wife by Bartell. As noted above, it read: "We assume no responsibility beyond retail cost of film unless otherwise agreed to in writing."

Is the exclusionary clause valid? Defendants rely upon 2–719(3), a section of the Uniform Commercial Code, which authorizes a limitation or exclusion of consequential damages unless the limitation is unconscionable.

Plaintiffs, on the other hand, argue that the Uniform Commercial Code is not applicable to this transaction. Their theory is that article 2 applies only to sales and not to a bailment as was present in this case. Plaintiffs read article 2 too narrowly. While article 2 is entitled "Sales," the declared scope is more comprehensive. 2–102 sets the parameters of the article by its declaration that it applies to *transactions in goods,* excluding security transactions. If article 2 were limited to sales it would not be directly applicable to this bailment transaction as 2–106(1) defines "Sales" as the passing of title from a seller to a buyer, a factor not present here. Obviously "transactions in goods"—the scope of article 2—is broader than "sales." Had the drafters of the code intended to limit article 2 to sales they could have easily so stated. They did not.

Our analysis seems commonly accepted. See for example 3 Bender's U.C.C. Service, R. Duesenberg & L. King, *Sales and Bulk Transfers* ¶ 103[4], at 1–35 (1977), which states:

It is now clearly established that the reach of Article 2 goes considerably beyond the confines of that type transaction which the Code itself defines to be a "sale"; namely, the passing of title from a party called the seller to one denominated a buyer for a price. Chief opportunity for this expansion is found in Section 2–102, which states that the article applies to "transactions in goods." Article 2 sections are finding their way into more and more decisions involving transactions which are not sales, but which are used as substitutes for a sale or which to a court appear to have attributes to which sales principles—or at least some of them—seem appropriate for application. . . .

. . . Most important of these is the application of the Article's warranty provisions to leases, *bailments,* or construction contracts. Of growing importance is the tendency of courts to find the Section on unconscionability, Section 2–302, appropriate to nonsales deals.

[Citations.]

While there are cases to the contrary, [citations] we do not find them persuasive. In fact we have held already that article 2 declares a public policy as to disclaimers and, at least by analogy, applied it to a bailment. *Baker v. Seattle,* 79 Wash.2d 198, 484 P.2d 405 (1971). (Article 2's provisions apply to lease of golf cart.)

We do not think that a distinction can be drawn between a bailment arising from a service transaction, as is the case here, and one arising from a leasing transaction, as was the case in *Baker.* [Citation.] Nor do we think, for this purpose, that a proper distinction can be drawn between the lease or rental of a chattel and the sale of a chattel.

* * *

In determining conscionability, the parties are to be provided "a reasonable opportunity to present evidence as to its commercial setting, purpose and effect to aid the court in making the determination." RCW 62A.2–302(2). Defendants concede that there was adequate compliance with that requirement in this case. The court had before it testimony and documents as

to each element it was required to consider.
* * *

Judgment affirmed.

Warehousing

RIO GRANDE CITY RY. CO. v. GUERRA

(1930 Tex.Civ.App.) 26 S.W.2d 360.

FLY, C. J.

Horace P. Guerra and Virginia C. Guerra, doing business under the firm name of M. Guerra & Son, sued appellant to recover the sum of $2,094.01, alleged to be due as damages arising from the negligent destruction of twenty-three bales of cotton weighing 11,319 pounds in the aggregate. The cause was tried by jury, which returned a verdict for appellees in the sum of $2,094.01.

The facts are, that appellees delivered appellant twenty-nine bales of cotton, for shipment, when seventy-one more bales were delivered, so as to constitute a shipment of one hundred bales of cotton. The remaining bales were in the possession of appellees and were to be delivered to appellant at another time.

When the twenty-nine bales were brought to the agent of appellant he instructed the employees of appellees to place them on a certain platform used for shipping purposes. The platform was not the one nearest to the depot, but was the one designated by the agent. The first night the cotton was on the platform twenty-three bales were destroyed by fire.

It is the contention of appellant that the relation of shipper and carrier had not arisen between the parties, and that, if appellant was liable, it was not as a carrier, but as a warehouseman.

When the cotton was delivered it was the distinct understanding that the delivery was not for immediate transportation, but that the bales delivered were to be held until the number delivered by appellees had reached one hundred bales, and, from the fact that only twenty-nine bales were delivered on the first day, it may be inferred or presumed that it would take at least two more days to deliver the remaining seventy-one bales. Evidently the twenty-nine bales of cotton were delivered and received for storage until the time fixed by appellees for shipment; that is when one hundred bales had been placed on the platform. It is the ordinary rule that, where goods are delivered to be held by the carrier for a certain time before shipment, the liability of the carrier is that of a warehouseman. There was an implied agreement between the parties that the cotton should be held by appellant as a warehouseman until the remaining cotton was delivered. Elliott on Railroads, Sec. 1464.

The facts of this case place appellant in the position of a warehouseman; indeed, it is not contended by appellees, in their brief, that appellant is liable other than as a warehouseman. In such case appellant was not an insurer of the cotton, and is not liable for its destruction, unless it appears that its negligence contributed to the loss of the property. It was liable as a bailee and owed the duty to exercise ordinary care and diligence in protecting the property of appellees, and unless a breach of the exercise of ordinary care and diligence is reasonably apparent from all the facts and circumstances, its liability does not attach. [Citations.]

The court instructed a verdict for appellees, whether on the assumption that appellant occupied the position of carrier to the cotton, or upon the assumption that it was incumbent upon appellant to show that it was not guilty of negligence as a warehouseman, we know not. The cotton was not delivered for immediate shipment, and for that reason the company could be held liable only as a warehouseman, and not as a common carrier. Elliott on Railroads, Sec. 1409. The shipment was not to be made at once, but depended on further acts by appellees. So it was necessary to show negligence upon the part of appellant, and if it could be held that placing the cotton on the platform, or failure to have a watchman, if there was such failure, or any other circumstances, none nor all of them constituted negligence per se, and the question of negligence, if any was shown, should have been sumitted to a jury. The verdict should not have been instructed. [Citations.]

The judgment will be reversed, and the cause remanded.

Innkeepers

DIPLOMAT RESTAURANT, INC. v. TOWNSEND

(1968) 118 Ga.App. 694, 165 S.E.2d 317.

BELL, P. J.

Dr. Robert Townsend, Dianne Townsend and Sherry Fitts brought this suit against Diplomat Restaurant, Inc., to recover the value of personal property stolen while plaintiffs were guests in defendant's restaurant. The property was taken from an automobile which one plaintiff had delivered to defendant's employee to be parked in facilities operated by defendant. Defendant contends on appeal that the judgment for each plaintiff was excessive because its liability to each was limited to $100 by Code § 52–111. *Held:*

The pertinent portions of Code § 52–111 (Ga.L.1922, p. 52) are: "The liability of the innkeeper for loss of or injury to personal property placed by any guest under his care * * * shall not exceed the sum of $100: Provided * * * that the innkeeper shall post a copy of this section printed in distinct type on the inside of the door of the guest's room." We think it is clear from the quoted proviso that the Act of 1922 was intended to apply only to houses of public entertainment furnishing lodging to a guest. [Citation.] Obviously, as defendant merely operated a restaurant and a bar for serving liquors, it could not introduce evidence of the notice required by Code § 52–111. This Code section was not effective to limit defendant's liability.

Judgment affirmed.

Problems

1. A was the owner of a herd of 20 highly bred dairy cows. He was a prosperous farmer, but his health was very poor. On the advice of his doctor, A decided to winter in Arizona. Before he left he made an agreement with Y, whereby Y was to keep the cows on Y's farm through the winter, pay A the sum of $800, and return to A the 20 cows at the close of the winter. For reasons that Y thought were good farming, Y sold six of the cows and replaced them with six other cows. After the winter was over, A returned from Arizona. When he saw that Y had replaced six cows out of the 20 originally given, he sued Y for the conversion of the original six cows. Decision?

2. O left his automobile at R's garage for repairs and storage, stating that he would pick it up in ten days. R agreed to park the car in the lot adjacent to his garage after the repairs were completed. O had left a valuable wrist watch in the glove compartment, but R had no knowledge of the presence of the wrist watch. R loaned O's car to F while F's car was being repaired by R. F returned the car in three days. When O returned he found that the wrist watch was missing and also that one fender of the car was damaged. O sued R and F for damage to the car and the loss of the wrist watch. Decision?

3. Hines stored his furniture, including a grand piano in Arnett's warehouse. Needing more space, Arnett stored Hine's piano in Butler's warehouse next door. As a result of a fire, which occurred without any fault of Arnett or Butler, both warehouses and contents were destroyed. Hines sues Arnett for the value of his piano and furniture. Decision?

4. B rented a safe deposit box from X Safe Deposit Company in which he deposited valuable securities and $4,000 in currency. Subsequently, B went to the box and found that $1,000 was missing. B brought an action against X and upon the trial, the company showed that its customary procedure was as follows: That there were two keys for each box furnished to each renter; that if the key was lost the lock was changed; also, that new keys were provided for each lock each time a box was rented; that there were two clerks in charge of the vault; and that one of the clerks was always present to open the box. X Safe Deposit Company also proved two keys were given to B at the time he rented his box; that his box could not be opened without the use of one of the keys in his possession, and the company had issued no other keys to B's box. Decision?

5. A, B, and C each stored 5,000 bushels of yellow corn in the same bin in X's warehouse. X wrongfully sold 10,000 bushels of this corn to Y. A contends that inasmuch as his 5,000 bushels of corn were placed in the bin first, the remaining 5,000 bushels belong to him. What are the rights of the parties?

6. (a) On April 1, Mary Rich, at the solicitation of Super Fur Company, delivered a $3,000 mink coat to the company at its place of business for storage in its vaults until November 1. On the same day, she paid the company its customary charge of $20 for such storage. After Mary left the store, the general manager of the company, upon finding that its storage vaults were already filled to capacity, delivered Mary's coat to Swift Trucking Company for shipment to Fur Storage Company. En route, the truck in which Mary's coat was being transported was totally damaged by fire caused by negligence on the part of the driver of the truck, and Mary's coat was totally destroyed. Is Super Fur Company liable to Mary for the value of her coat?

Would your answer be the same if Mary's coat had been safely delivered to Fur Storage Company and had been stolen from its storage vaults without negligence on its part?

7. Rich, a club member, left his golf clubs with Bogan, pro at the Happy Hours Country Club, to be refinished at Bogan's pro shop. The refinisher employed by Bogan, suddenly left town taking Rich's clubs with him. The refinisher had theretofore been above suspicion, although Bogan had never checked on the man's character references. A valuable sand wedge which Bogan had borrowed from another member, Smith, for his own use in an important tournament match was also stolen by the refinisher, as well as several pairs of golf shoes which Bogan had checked for members without charge as an accommodation. The club members concerned each made claims against Bogan for their losses. Can (a) Rich, (b) Smith and the other members compel Bogan to make good their respective losses?

8. B drove an automobile into T's garage and requested him to make repairs for which the charge would be $125. B never returned to get the automobile, and two months later C saw it in T's garage. C claimed it as his own and asserted that it had been stolen from him. T told C that he could have the automobile upon paying for the repairs and storage. C paid him, took the automobile, and disappeared. 'A week later O appeared and proved that the autombile was his, that it had been stolen from him, and that neither B nor C had any rights in it.

O brings an action against T for conversion of the automobile to his (T's) own use. Decision?

9. Poe, without comment, left a briefcase and a sample case with the attendant in the check stand in Doe's hotel and received and pocketed immediately two claim checks; on the back of each check was stated a $50 limitation of liability for loss of the article received or any damage to it. No charge was made for keeping articles less than 24 hours. Customarily, patrons left tips when the articles were returned. The attendant was out of the stand for a few minutes after the cases were deposited when called to a telephone. Later the same day, Poe presented the two checks but the attendant could locate and, hence, returned only the briefcase. Poe was neither staying at, eating in, nor meeting anyone in the hotel. Poe sued Doe to recover $12,000 for loss of the sample case and the jewels in it. Decision?

10. On June 1, Cain delivered his 1974 automobile to Barr, operator of a repair shop, for necessary repairs. Barr put the car in his lot on Main Street which is fenced on all sides except that along Main Street. The lot accommodates 100 cars, and is unguarded at night although the police make periodic checks. The lot is well illuminated. The cars do not have the keys in them when left out overnight. Some time during the night of June 4, the hood, starter, alternator and gear shift were removed by theft from Cain's car. The car remained on the lot and during the evening of June 5 the transmission was stolen from the car. The cost of replacement of the parts stolen in the first theft was $300 and in the second theft $400.

Cain sued Barr to recover $700. Decision?

SALES AND
CONTRACTS TO SELL

One of the oldest branches of the law is that which pertains to sales of goods. Before the use of money as a medium of exchange, people exchanged goods by way of barter, which is the exchange of goods for other goods. Under the U.C.C. a barter of goods is a sale. Section 2–304(1) provides:

The price can be made payable in money or otherwise. If it is payable in whole or in part in goods, each party is a seller of the goods which he is to transfer.

The law of sales is an important subject because the buying and selling of goods, wares, and merchandise is the principal activity of most business enterprises. Everyone in our economy is a buyer of goods which are required or useful in everyday living. And where there is a buyer, there must be a seller.

A sale is defined as a transfer of title to goods for a consideration known as the price. A contract to sell goods is not a sale but a contractual promise to transfer title to goods in the future, and at the time of making the contract, the subject matter may be either goods in existence or goods which are to be manufactured or grown in the future. In a contract to sell goods, the sale does not take place until title to the goods is transferred by the seller to the buyer.

DEFINITION OF GOODS

The Code defines "goods" as all things, including those specially manufactured, which are movable at the time of identification to the contract for sale, excluding money, investment securities, and choses in action. "Goods" include the unborn young of animals, growing crops, and certain identified things such as timber, minerals, or a structure or its materials attached to realty and to be removed therefrom by the seller. Section 2–105(1). Before any interest in goods can be transferred, the goods must be both existing and identified. Goods which are not both existing and identified are "future" goods. Section 2–105(2).

A purported present sale of future goods operates as a contract to sell.

Goods Not in Existence

As a matter of definition, since a sale is a present transfer of the title to goods, and no one owns or can transfer goods which do not exist it is impossible to make a sale of goods which are not in existence.

Contract to Sell Future Goods. Goods which are to be grown or manufactured by the seller or to be acquired by the seller after he has made a contract to sell them are known as future goods. While it is impossible to make a present sale of future goods, it is possible to make a contract to sell them.

The Code, as previously noted, provides that goods must be both existing and identified to the contract before any interest in them can pass; and goods which are not both existing and identified are "future" goods. Section 2--105. A contract for the sale of goods not in existence at the time of making is a contract for future goods.

Doctrine of Potential Possession. At common law, where a person was the owner or lessee of land, he could by using language of present transfer make a sale of future crops grown upon the land. The same rule applied to the owner of animals with respect to future offspring. Of course, no title to the future crops or unborn animals could pass at the time the parties used language of present transfer as the goods were not then in existence. But under the doctrine of potential possession, ownership of the crops or of the offspring was regarded as in the transferee as of the moment the crops matured or the offspring was born.

The doctrine was never applied in a case where the grantor of future crops did not have a present interest in the land upon which the crops were to be grown at the time of the grant, nor to the future offspring of animals which did not belong to the grantor at the time of the grant.

The Code does not deal with the problem of growing crops and unborn young of animals in terms of potential possession but approaches it directly and realistically by enlarging the concepts of property interests and by establishing rules to determine whether goods are identified to the contract. Growing crops and the unborn young of animals, in the absence of explicit agreement, are identified to the contract respectively when the crops are planted and when the young are conceived. Section 2–501. Thereupon the buyer obtains a special property and an insurable interest in these future goods. Upon becoming identified to the contract these future goods exist as planted seed, but the contract is not for planted seed. It is for matured crops and offspring of animals. Consequently, title cannot pass until the crops have fully matured and the animals are born. The Code does not change the common-law rule that title passes to the buyer at that time.

Fungible Goods

Goods of which each particle or unit of measurement is the equivalent of every other particle or like unit of the same goods, such as grain, cereals, flour, oil, and wine, are fungible goods. The goods just named are fungible by nature. Other goods, such as hogsheads of molasses, or bales of cotton, may be fungible by commercial usage. Each hogshead may not be exactly alike in volume to every other, nor each bale of cotton be the exact weight of every other bale, but if the parties or the usage of trade so regard them they are deemed fungible. Section 1–201 of the Code contains this definition:

"Fungible" with respect to goods or securities means goods or securities of which any unit is, by nature or usage of trade, the equivalent of any other like unit. Goods which are not fungible shall be deemed fungible for the purposes of this Act to the extent that under a particular agreement or document unlike units are treated as equivalents.

Where the subject matter of a contract of sale is the undivided portion of a mass of fungible goods, an ownership or property interest may pass to the buyer without a separation of the portion from the mass. The buyer becomes the owner of an undivided fractional interest in the mass as a tenant in common with the owners of the remaining fractional interests. A warehouseman or bailee may commingle different lots of fungible goods without violating his duty to keep separate the goods covered by each warehouse receipt.

Sale of Undivided Shares

A joint owner or tenant in common of specific personal property may sell his undivided interest in the property. The buyer becomes a tenant in common with the other owners.

There may be a sale of a part interest in existing identified goods, including a bulk of fungible goods, although the quantity of goods in the bulk is undetermined. A proportion of the bulk may be agreed upon, or the undivided share may be measured by reference to number, weight, or count, to the extent of the seller's interest in the bulk. The buyer becomes an owner in common of an undivided interest in the mass or bulk. Section 2–105.

There is an obvious difference in ownership of an undivided one-third interest in a horse and of an undivided one-third interest in 300 bushels of wheat. In the latter case, severance may be had and by agreement of the parties the undivided interest in 300 bushels may be exchanged for complete ownership of 100 bushels of the wheat which have been separated from the mass. The wheat is fungible; the horse is neither fungible nor divisible.

Assume that A owns a large pile of nut size coal of uniform quality containing 500 tons. A executes a bill of sale to B which recites that in consideration of $800 paid by B to A, A sells and transfers to B 100 tons of coal in the pile. It is obvious that B does not obtain title to 100 tons of the coal. The reason is that 100 tons of the coal as such does not exist. The pile of coal is specific, and the goods to which the contract refers are identified, but title to 100 tons of the coal cannot be transferred until this quantity is separated from the mass. However, since the parties intended to create in the buyer an immediate ownership interest, under Section 2–105(4) of the Code the buyer becomes a tenant in common with the seller and owns an undivided fractional interest or share in the mass of coal. This interest is measured by the fraction of which the number of tons of coal purchased is the numerator and the number of tons in the mass is the denominator.

SALES DISTINGUISHED FROM OTHER TRANSACTIONS

In order to understand clearly what is meant by a sale of goods, it is well to distinguish it from certain other transactions, such as a gift, bailment, lease, chattel mortgage, pledge, and conditional sale.

Gift

A gift is a transfer of title to property but differs from a sale in that the transferor neither bargains for nor receives anything in exchange for the goods. A promise to make a gift is unenforceable for lack of consideration. To be effective, a gift requires a delivery of the property to the donee with donative intent. Delivery of the property is not necessary in order to transfer title by way of sale.

Bailment

A bailment is a transfer of the possession of personal property without a transfer of the title. Transfer of title is essential to a sale, although transfer of possession is not.

Lease

A lease of goods is a contract whereby the owner of the goods (the lessor) agrees with another person (the lessee) that he will transfer to the lessee the possession and right to use the goods for a period of time in consideration of a specified payment. A lease of goods does not involve a transfer of title to the goods.

Security Agreement

A sale is distinguished from a security agreement in that a sale transfers to the buyer all of the ownership rights of the seller in the goods, whereas under a security agreement both the creditor and the debtor have ownership rights in the goods. The right of the secured creditor in the goods is to realize upon their value in the event of default by the debtor.

Chattel Mortgage. At common law a chattel mortgage is the transfer of title to goods as security for the payment of a debt. The Code, Article 9, treats it as a security agreement whereby the creditor obtains a security interest in the goods. The debtor retains possession of the goods. To be valid against other creditors of the debtor, the security interest must be perfected by filing a financing statement in a designated public office.

Pledge of Goods. A pledge is a transfer of the possession of goods, but not the title, as security for the payment of a debt. Its purpose is different from that of a sale, and possession of the goods by the creditor gives him a security interest in them which is valid against other creditors without a filing. Section 9–305.

Conditional Sale. A conditional sale is a transfer of title to specific goods for a consideration upon the happening of a certain operative event or condition. The parties by their contract may provide that title shall pass to the buyer upon the happening of any event or condition, but the event which is usually of the greatest interest to the seller is payment of the price. Consequently, the term conditional sale, in ordinary usage, refers to a contract whereby the seller has delivered possession of the goods to the buyer, the buyer has agreed to pay the price, and title is not to pass to the buyer until the price is completely paid. Since its purpose is to secure payment of the price, it is also a security agreement. To obtain protection against other creditors perfection is required by filing a financing statement under the provisions of the Code, except in the case of a purchase money security interest in consumer goods. Section 9–302(1)(d).

PRICE

The price is the consideration which the buyer pays or promises to pay to the seller for the goods. It is usually expressed in terms of money, but it may be made payable in any personal property. Section 2–304.

Ascertainment of the Price

Under the Code, if the parties intend to be bound, they may enter into a contract for the sale of goods even though the agreement contains no price provision. In such case, the price is a reasonable one at the time for delivery of the goods, if (1) nothing is said as to price; or (2) the price is left to later agreement and the parties fail to agree; or (3) the price is to be set according to some agreed market or other standard, or as recorded by a third person or agency, and it has not been so set or recorded. Section 2–305(1).

If the parties manifested an intention not to be bound unless the price were fixed in the manner agreed upon, and it was not so fixed, there is no contract. In such case, the buyer must return to the seller any goods received, or if unable to do so, must pay their reasonable value; and, the seller must refund to the buyer any portion of the price paid on account. Section 2–305(4).

Sale at a Valuation

The seller and buyer may enter into a sale or contract to sell whereby the price of the goods or the terms of sale are to be fixed by a third person. At common law if the third person, without the fault of the seller or the buyer, does not or cannot fix the price or terms, the contract is avoided and neither party is liable to the other. Under the Code, in such case, the contract is not avoided and the price for the goods is the reasonable price at the time for delivery. Section 2–304(1)(c).

An agreement which provides that the price is to be fixed by the seller or by the buyer means a price which such party shall fix in good faith. Section 2–305(2).

Where the price is left to be fixed otherwise than by subsequent agreement of the parties and the price fails to be fixed through the fault of one of the parties, the other party has the option to treat the contract as cancelled or as enforceable at a reasonable price fixed by himself. Section 2–305(3).

The price of the goods fixed by valuers which the parties have agreed upon is conclusive upon the parties, in the absence of fraud, collusion, or mistake.

TITLE AND OWNERSHIP

The concept of legal title is generally well understood. It is the concept of ownership, a legally protected interest in specific property good against the entire world. The law regards specific property as owned by some person or persons at all times.

Absolute ownership means that there is only one legally protected interest in the goods. However, it is possible for different property interests to exist in the same goods at the same time, as in the case of a security agreement. The security interest of the creditor is a defined property interest, while the debtor owns all other property rights in the goods.

Knowledge of the identity of the owner of goods is important in many respects. In the event of destruction of the goods, risk of loss ordinarily falls upon the owner, except where otherwise provided in the code. Sections 2–509, 2–510. A levy upon or attachment of goods by a judgment creditor is unavailing unless the judgment debtor owns the goods and is effective only to the extent of such ownership. Goods which are subject to a contract of sale may not be attached by creditors of the seller if the ownership has been transferred to the buyer, nor by creditors of the buyer if the ownership remains in the seller. The obligation to pay personal property taxes assessed against the goods rests upon the owner who may be the buyer or the seller depending upon whether title has been transferred.

The Code recognizes that several property interests may be held by different persons in the same goods, and particularizes these various interests by referring to or defining: (1) title, (2) security interest, (3) special property, (4) insurable interest, (5) right to goods, and (6) risk of loss. The Code is transaction oriented and does not attach to the concept of title all of the legal incidents of the common law. It provides for specific property rights and interests which the parties may have in the goods, as well as the right which the seller may have to recover the price for the goods, independently of transfer of title.

As an anti-theft measure, a substantial majority of the States have statutes which provide in essence that the Secretary of State or other proper State official shall not issue or renew the registration of any motor vehicle unless the owner thereof shall have a certificate of title to the motor vehicle duly issued to him by the State in which registration is sought or by another State in which the motor vehicle was purchased or previously registered. The statute also provides that the owner of a motor vehicle who sells or transfers his interest therein shall endorse a sworn assignment and warranty of title upon the certificate of title thereto and deliver it to the purchaser or transferee at the time of delivering to him the motor vehicle. A failure to comply with the statute is a misdemeanor and subjects the offender upon conviction to a fine or imprisonment, or both. With respect to the validity of the sale of the motor vehicle, where the owner does not comply with the certificate of title law, the rules differ in the various jurisdictions. The majority rule is that non-compliance with the statute does not invalidate the sale.

Acceptance of Goods

The word "acceptance" means a willingness to agree and includes overt acts or conduct which manifest such willingness. In the law of contracts, acceptance is a manifestation by the offeree of his willingness to abide by the terms of the offer. In the law of sales, acceptance is a manifestation by the buyer of his willingness to become owner of specific goods offered, tendered or delivered by the seller. Acceptance is independent of possession, delivery or payment for the goods. Acceptance may be indicated by express words, by the presumed intention of the buyer or by conduct of the buyer with respect to specific goods inconsistent with the seller's ownership thereof.

Acceptance occurs when the buyer after a reasonable opportunity to inspect the goods, (1) signifies to the seller that the goods conform to the contract, or (2) signifies to the seller that he will take the goods or retain them in spite of their non-conformity to the contract, or (3) fails to make an effective rejection of the goods. Section 2–606.

The buyer must pay at the contract rate for any goods accepted. Section 2–607.

Revocation of Acceptance

The buyer may revoke his acceptance of goods which are non-conforming to the contract and the non-conformity substantially impairs their value to him if (a) his acceptance was on the reasonable assumption that the non-conformity could and would be cured by the seller, and it was not reasonably cured; or (b) without discovery of the non-conformity and acceptance was reasonably induced by the difficulty of discovery before acceptance or by the seller's assurances. Section 2–608(1).

Revocation of acceptance must occur within a reasonable time after the buyer discovers or should have discovered the non-conformity, and is not effective until the buyer notifies the seller of it. Section 2–608(2). Upon revocation, the rights and duties of the buyer with regard to the goods are the same as if he had rejected them. Section 2–608(3).

Rejection of Goods

Rejection is a manifestation by the buyer of his unwillingness to become owner of the goods. It must be within a reasonable time after the goods have been tendered or delivered. It is not effective unless the buyer seasonably notifies the seller. Section 2–601(1).

Rejection of the goods may be rightful or wrongful, depending on whether the goods tendered or delivered conform to the contract.

After rejection of the goods, any exercise of ownership by the buyer with respect to them is wrongful as against the seller. If the buyer does not have a security interest in the goods he is under a duty after rejection to hold them, and to exercise reasonable care with respect to their safekeeping, for a time sufficient to permit the seller to remove them. If the buyer's rejection is rightful, he has no further obligations with regard to the goods unless he is a merchant in which case he is subject to the duties imposed by Section 2–603 of the Code. If wrongful, the seller has remedies as provided in Section 2–703.

Casualty to Identified Goods

A purported sale of nonexistent goods is void, as in the case of a seller who purports to make a sale of specific goods which unknown to him and the buyer have been wholly destroyed.

If the contract is for goods which are specified and identified when the contract was made, and these goods are totally lost or damaged without fault of either party and before risk of loss passes to the buyer, the contract is voided. Section 2–613(a).

A different situation is presented where the seller purports to sell specific or identified goods and without the knowledge of the parties a portion of them has been destroyed. Thus, A purports to make a sale to B of a specific lot of wheat containing 1,000 bushels at a price of $3 per bushel. Unknown to A, fire had destroyed or damaged 300 bushels of the wheat. The contract is divisible. B does not have to take the remaining 700 bushels of wheat, but he has the option to do so upon paying $2,100, the price of 700 bushels. Section 2–613(b). In the case of a partial destruction or deterioration of the goods, the buyer has the option to avoid the contract or to accept the undestroyed or deteriorated goods with due allowance or deduction from the contract price. The rights of the buyer do not depend upon whether the contract or sale is divisible or indivisible.

If the destruction or casualty to the goods, total or partial, occurs after risk of loss has passed to the buyer, the buyer has no option but must pay the contract price of the goods.

UNCONSCIONABLE CONTRACTS

Every contract of sale may be scrutinized by the court to determine whether in its commercial setting, purpose, and effect, it is unconscionable. The court may refuse to enforce an unconscionable contract or any part of the contract found to be unconscionable. Section 2–302 provides:

If the court as a matter of law finds the contract or any clause of the contract to have been unconscionable at the time it was made the court may refuse to enforce the contract, or it may enforce the remainder of the contract without the unconscionable clause, or it may so limit the application of any unconscionable clause as to avoid any unconscionable result.

The Code does not define "unconscionable". However, the Oxford Universal Dictionary (3rd ed.) definition is: "Monstrously extortionate, harsh, showing no regard for conscience."

Section 2–302 denies or limits enforcement of an unconscionable contract for the sale of goods in the interest of fairness and decency, and to correct harshness in contracts resulting from unequal bargaining positions of the parties. Although the principle is not novel, its embodiment in a statute dealing with commercial transactions is novel.

In Henningsen v. Bloomfield Motors, Inc., 32 N.J. 358, 161 A.2d 69 (1960), the Supreme Court of New Jersey in a pre-Code decision refused to enforce a harsh disclaimer of warranty in a contract for the purchase of an automobile, saying, "An instinctively felt sense of justice cries out against such a sharp bargain."

In many cases a contract between a necessitous buyer in an unequal bargaining position with the seller has been held unconscionable by reason of the exorbitant price of the goods. A price of $749 ($920 on time) for a vacuum cleaner which cost the seller $140 was held unconscionable. In another case, the buyers, welfare recipients, purchased by time payment contract a home freezer unit for $900 which added to time credit charges, credit life insurance, credit property insurance and sales tax amounted to $1,235. The purchase resulted from a visit to the buyer's home by a salesman representing Your Shop At Home Service, Inc., and the maximum retail value of the freezer unit at time of purchase was $300. The court held the contract unconscionable, and reformed it by changing the price to the total payment ($620) made by the buyers. Jones v. Star Credit Corp., 59 Misc.2d 189, 298 N.Y.S.2d 264 (1969).

Section 2–715(2) of the Code defines consequential damages resulting from a seller's breach as including (a) loss resulting from the general or particular requirements or needs of the buyer which the seller had reason to know and which could not be prevented by cover (obtaining the goods elsewhere); and (b) injury to person or property resulting from any breach of warranty. Section 2–719(3) provides that consequential damages may by contract be limited or excluded unless the limitation or exclusion is unconscionable. Such limitation or exclusion of damages for injury to the person in the case of consumer goods is prima facie unconscionable, but limitation or exclusion of commercial loss or property damage is not. K & C, Inc. v. Westinghouse Electric Corp., 437 Pa. 303, 263 A.2d 390 (1970).

SALES BY AND BETWEEN MERCHANTS

A novel feature of the Code is the introduction into the law of sales of standards of commercial reasonableness which it wisely leaves undefined, and the establishment of separate rules which apply to transactions between merchants or involving a merchant as a party.

A "merchant" is defined, as a person (1) who is a dealer in the goods, or (2) who by his occupation holds himself out as having knowledge or skill peculiar to the goods or practices involved, or (3) who employs an agent or broker whom he holds out as having such knowledge or skill. Section 2–104.

Sixteen sections of the Code contain special rules which apply to transactions between merchants or in which a merchant is a party. These rules do not apply to nonmerchants and exact a higher standard of conduct from merchants because of their knowledge of trade and commerce, and because merchants as a class generally set the standards.

1. Good faith in the case of a merchant means honesty in fact plus the observance of reasonable commercial standards of fair dealing in the trade. Section 2–103(1)(b).

2. A contract for the sale of goods for the price of $500 or more requires a writing to be enforceable (Statute of Frauds). Where such a contract between merchants is oral, a confirmatory writing by one to the other satisfies the statute unless the recipient within 10 days objects in writing. Section 2–201(2).

3. A written offer by a merchant to buy or sell goods is irrevocable during the period of time it is stated to remain open, or if no time is stated, for a reasonable time, not to exceed 3 months, without consideration. Section 2–205.

4. Between merchants, terms contained in an offeree's acceptance which add to or differ from those in the offer become part of the contract unless (a) the offer expressly limits acceptance to the terms of the offer; or (b) the different terms materially alter the offer; or (c) the offeror objects to such

additional or different terms within a reasonable time.   Section 2–207(2).

5. A signed agreement cannot be modified or rescinded except by a signed writing where it expressly so requires.   However, where the signed agreement is not between merchants such requirement on a form supplied by a merchant party must be separately signed by the non-merchant party. Where the signed agreement is between merchants such requirement on a form supplied by one of them need not be signed by the other.   Section 2–209(2).

6. A seller who is a merchant impliedly warrants that goods of the kind in which he regularly deals shall be delivered free of any rightful claim of any third person by way of infringement.   Section 2–312(3).

7. A seller who is a merchant impliedly warrants the merchantability of the goods that he sells, unless such warranty is expressly excluded or modified.   Section 2–314(1).

8. Where goods are delivered for sale to a merchant who maintains a place of business where he deals in goods of the kind involved, under a name other than the name of the person making delivery, the goods are deemed to be on sale or return with respect to creditors of the merchant.   Section 2–326(3).

9. Under a sale on approval unless otherwise agreed, a merchant-buyer after giving notice of his election to return the goods must follow any reasonable instructions of the seller in order that the return be at the seller's risk and expense.   Section 2–327(1)(c).

10. Where retention of possession of goods by the seller would be fraudulent as to creditors of the seller under any rule of law, such retention by a merchant-seller in good faith and in the current course of trade for a commercially reasonable time is not fraudulent. Section 2–402(2).

11. Any entrusting of the possession of goods to a merchant who deals in goods of that kind gives him power to transfer all rights of the entruster to a buyer in the ordinary course of business.   Section 2–403(2).

12. Except where the contract requires or authorizes the seller to ship the goods by carrier, and except where the goods are held by a bailee to be delivered to the buyer without being moved, the risk of loss passes to the buyer upon his receipt of the goods if the seller is a merchant.   In such case, if the seller is not a merchant, the risk of loss passes to the buyer on tender of delivery. Section 2–509(3).

13. Where a merchant-buyer has rightfully rejected goods in his possession, and the seller has no agent or place of business at the market of rejection, the merchant-buyer is under a duty to follow any reasonable instructions of the seller with respect to the goods, and in the absence of such instructions to make reasonable efforts to sell them for the seller's account if they are perishable.   Section 2–603(1).

14. When a merchant-buyer sells goods pursuant to section 2–603(1), he is entitled to a selling commission and to reimbursement of his reasonable expenses out of the proceeds.   Section 2–603(2).

15. Between merchants, a buyer who has rejected goods is precluded from relying upon any unstated defect to justify such rejection or to establish a breach by the seller where the seller has made a request in writing for a full and final written statement of all defects upon which the buyer proposes to rely.   Section 2–605(1)(b).

16. When reasonable grounds for insecurity arise with respect to the performance of either party to a contract for the sale of goods, the other party may in writing demand adequate assurance of due performance and may suspend performance until such assurance is received.   Between merchants, the reasonableness of grounds for insecurity and the adequacy of any assurance offered is determined according to commercial standards.   Section 2–609(1)(2).

Cases

*Sales Distinguished
from Other Transactions*

OSTERHOLT v. ST. CHARLES DRILLING CO.

(1980 D.C.Mo.) 500 F.Supp. 529.

[Property owner brought action against contractor for misrepresentation and for breach of contract to install well and water system. The District Court held that the evidence established that contractor breached contract to install well and water system by failing to bury pipe at depth of 36 inches at two locations, by failing to dig well where it had originally been staked, by installing two 120-gallon tanks instead of one 315-gallon tank, by installing "float-type" squat tank rather than bladder-type tank, and by failing to install water system that had physical capacity to provide 12 houses with 12 gallons per minute each and to provide such quantity of water at 30# to 50# pressure at each house.]

FILIPPINE, J.

* * *

The parties have not addressed the possibility that the Uniform Commercial Code, as adopted by Illinois, governs this case. The Court has given strong consideration to that possibility, but has concluded that the contract at issue was primarily a service contract, with a sale of goods incidental thereto, rather than vice versa. [Citation.] At least one Illinois appellate court has adopted a "predominant factor in the contract" test, [citation] to determine the applicability of the U.C.C. [citation.] *Bonebrake v. Cox*, 499 F.2d 951 involved a contract to sell and install specified items of used equipment in a bowling alley that had been damaged by fire. The Court held that the contract fell within the (Iowa) Uniform Commercial Code, rejecting the decision below that because the contract was "mixed"

(for goods and services), the U.C.C. did not govern. The Court held that the U.C.C. did apply because the items to be installed fell within the U.C.C.'s definition of "goods" and because the language of the contract was essentially that of a sales contract. The Court formulated the following general test of the U.C.C.'s applicability: "The test for inclusion or exclusion is not whether [contracts] are mixed, but, granting that they are mixed, whether their predominant factor, their thrust, their purpose, reasonably stated, is the rendition of service, with goods incidentally involved (e.g., contract with artist for painting) or is a transaction of sale, with labor incidentally involved (e.g., installation of a water heater in a bathroom)." [Citation.] The Seventh Circuit, in a case governed by Illinois law, approved the *Bonebrake* test and held that a contract for the construction of a one-million-gallon water tank fell within the U.C.C. [Citation.]

This Court finds that the transaction between the parties in the instant case falls on the "service" side of the *Bonebrake* test, for two reasons: with two exceptions discussed below, the parties had no agreement specifying the various component parts of the "water system" which were to be installed. The defendant was not bound to use specified items of "goods" in the water system. Neither party has suggested that the estimate sheet (plaintiff's Exhibit 8) prepared by defendant the day before the contract was signed, was a part of the parties' contract. Essentially, defendant undertook to install a "water system" of indefinite description but with a certain warranted capacity, rather than to install a detailed list of specific "goods." Therefore, not only was the contract essentially for defendant's services, but the component parts did not become identified to the contract until they were actually installed on plaintiff's property, and thus it is doubtful that they fell within the definition of "goods" contained in Ill.Rev.Stat., ch. 26, para. 2–105.

Secondly, the language of the instant contract is unmistakably that of service rather than of sale. Defendant is identified as the "contractor," and the contract acknowledges "an express mechanics lien . . . to secure the amount of contract or repairs." Plaintiff's Exhibit 9, General Terms & Conditions no. 9.

Thus, the Court concludes that the U.C.C. does not, strictly speaking, govern this case.

* * *

[Judgment for plaintiff.]

Unconscionable Contracts

WILLIAMS v. WALKER-THOMAS FURNITURE CO.

(1965 C.A.D.C.) 350 F.2d 445.

WRIGHT, C. J.

Appellee, Walker-Thomas Furniture Company, operates a retail furniture store in the District of Columbia. During the period from 1957 to 1962 each appellant in these cases purchased a number of household items from Walker-Thomas, for which payment was to be made in installments. The terms of each purchase were contained in a printed form contract which set forth the value of the purchased item and purported to lease the item to appellant for a stipulated monthly rent payment. The contract then provided, in substance, that title would remain in Walker-Thomas until the total of all the monthly payments made equaled the stated value of the item, at which time appellants could take title. In the event of a default in the payment of any monthly installment, Walker-Thomas could repossess the item.

The contract further provided that "the amount of each periodical installment payment to be made by [purchaser] to the Com-

pany under this present lease shall be inclusive of and not in addition to the amount of each installment payment to be made by [purchaser] under such prior leases, bills or accounts; *and all payments now and hereafter made by [purchaser] shall be credited pro rata on all outstanding leases, bills and accounts* due the Company by [purchaser] at the time each such payment is made." (Emphasis added.) The effect of this rather obscure provision was to keep a balance due on every item purchased until the balance due on all items, whenever purchased, was liquidated. As a result, the debt incurred at the time of purchase of each item was secured by the right to repossess all the items previously purchased by the same purchaser, and each new item purchased automatically became subject to a security interest arising out of the previous dealings.

On May 12, 1962, appellant Thorne purchased an item described as a Daveno, three tables, and two lamps, having total stated value of $391.10. Shortly thereafter, he defaulted on his monthly payments and appellee sought to replevy all the items purchased since the first transaction in 1958. Similarly, on April 7, 1962, appellant Williams bought a stereo set of stated value of $514.95. She too defaulted shortly thereafter, and appellee sought to replevy all the items purchased since December, 1957. The Court of General Sessions granted judgment for appellee. The District of Columbia Court of Appeals affirmed, and we granted appellants' motion for leave to appeal to this court.

Appellants' principal contention, rejected by both the trial and the appellate courts below, is that these contracts, or at least some of them, are unconscionable and, hence, not enforceable. * * *

Unconscionability has generally been recognized to include an absence of meaningful choice on the part of one of the parties together with contract terms which are unreasonably favorable to the other party. Whether a meaningful choice is present in a particular case can only be determined by consideration of all the circumstances surrounding the transaction. In many cases the meaningfulness of the choice is negated by a gross inequality of bargaining power. The manner in which the contract was entered is also relevant to this consideration. Did each party to the contract, considering his obvious education or lack of it, have a reasonable opportunity to understand the terms of the contract, or were the important terms hidden in a maze of fine print and minimized by deceptive sales practices? Ordinarily, one who signs an agreement without full knowledge of its terms might be held to assume the risk that he has entered a one-sided bargain. But when a party of little bargaining power, and hence little real choice, signs a commercially unreasonable contract with little or no knowledge of its terms, it is hardly likely that his consent, or even an objective manifestation of his consent, was ever given to all the terms. In such a case the usual rule that the terms of the agreement are not to be questioned should be abandoned and the court should consider whether the terms of the contract are so unfair that enforcement should be withheld.

In determining reasonableness or fairness, the primary concern must be with the terms of the contract considered in light of the circumstances existing when the contract was made. The test is not simple, nor can it be mechanically applied. The terms are to be considered "in the light of the general commercial background and the commercial needs of the particular trade or case." Corbin suggests the test as being whether the terms are "so extreme as to appear unconscionable according to the mores and business practices of the time and place." [Citation.] We think this formulation correctly states the test to be applied in those cases where no meaningful choice was exercised upon entering the contract.

Because the trial court and the appellate court did not feel that enforcement could be refused, no findings were made on the possible unconscionability of the contracts in these cases. Since the record is not sufficient for our deciding the issue as a matter of law, the cases must be remanded to the trial court for further proceedings.

Reversed and remanded.

Sales By and Between Merchants

CBS, INC. v. AUBURN PLASTICS, INC.
(1979) 67 A.D.2d 811, 413 N.Y.S.2d 50.

MEMORANDUM:

In September, 1973 defendant submitted price quotations to plaintiff for the manufacture of eight cavity molds to be used in making parts for plaintiff's toys. The quotations were apparently based on drawings or samples which plaintiff had previously submitted to defendant.

The face of each price quotation was headed by the word "PROPOSAL" and specified, inter alia, the mold and tool charge, the number of cavities per mold, and the material to be used. The quotations further specified as to when sample parts could be submitted, when shipment could commence, and stated that "[u]nless accepted within 15 days from date, the proposal is not binding except at our option". Also imprinted on the face of each quotation was the following underlined sentence: "Please note that the conditions on the reverse side are made a part of this proposal and all subsequent orders". On the reverse side condition 8 stated, in part, that: "In consideration of the engineering services necessary in the designing of molds and tools, the customer hereby agrees to pay Auburn Plastics, Inc., an additional charge of thirty per cent above the quoted price of sale molds and tools when and if the customer demands delivery thereof."

Thereafter, in December, 1973 and January, 1974 plaintiff sent detailed purchase orders to defendant for the eight molds. The orders recited on their face that "[a]cceptance of this purchase order by the Vendor means that the Vendor understands and accepts all stipulations noted above". One such stipulation provided that plaintiff reserved the right to remove the molds from the defendant at any time without a withdrawal charge. The reverse side of the purchase orders similarly recited that the molds will be subject to removal without additional cost to the buyer, and also that no modification of the conditions of the contract shall be binding upon the buyer unless made in writing and signed by the buyer's representative.

In response to the purchase orders, defendant sent acknowledgements which described the molds, the price and the terms of payment and delivery essentially as contained in the purchase orders. However, the acknowledgements also stated that "[t]his sale subject to the terms and conditions of our quotation pertinent to this sale."

Thereafter plaintiff paid for the molds and ordered toy parts from the defendant which were fabricated from the molds. In May, 1978, however, as a result of defendant's announcement of a price increase, plaintiff requested delivery of the molds. Defendant refused to do so on the ground that it was entitled to a 30% engineering charge. Plaintiff obtained an order directing the sheriff to seize the molds. Defendant moved to quash that order and appeals from the denial of its motion.

The earliest communications between the parties shown in this record are defendant's price quotations. While it appears that the quotations were sufficiently detailed and specific so as to constitute offers [citations], plaintiff did not respond to them until months after 15 days had passed. Thus the purchase orders submitted by plaintiff did not create enforceable contracts since they had no binding effect upon defendant [citation].

In our view then, plaintiff's purchase orders constituted offers to buy the molds, and defendant's acknowledgements of those orders represented its acceptance of the offers. While the acknowledgements incorporate the conditions contained in the price quotations and therefore conflict with the terms of the offers with respect to the mold acquisition charge, the acknowledgements are nonetheless operable as acceptances since they are not expressly made conditional on plaintiff's assent to the different terms (Uniform Commercial Code, § 2–207, subd. 1 [citations]).

Whether the condition in defendant's acknowledgements calling for an additional 30% charge became a part of the contracts requires the application of subdivision 2 of section 2–207. The parties are clearly merchants (see Uniform Commercial Code, § 2–104) and, therefore, since the purchase orders expressly limited acceptance to their terms (Uniform Commercial Code, § 2–207, subd. 2, par. [a]) and also because notification of objection to a withdrawal charge was implicitly given by plaintiff (Uniform Commercial Code, § 2–207, subd. 2, par. [c]; [citations]) the provision for such a charge did not become a part of the contracts.

Order unanimously affirmed, with costs.

Problems

1. "I hereby bargain, sell, assign, and set over unto the Meadow Museum at $400 each, all specimens of ovis poli which I shall bring back from the hunting expedition in Mongolia and Tibet on which I am starting today, May 1, 1980. (Signed) James Nimrod." The Meadow Mu-

seum paid Nimrod $800 on account. He went on the expedition as planned, collected five specimens of the ovis poli and brought them home. Did the quoted instrument in accordance with its terms transfer to the Museum the title to the specimen?

2. a. A orders 1,000 widgets at $5 per widget from International Widget to be delivered within 60 days. After the contract is consummated and signed, A requests that International deliver the widgets within 30 days rather than 60 days. International agrees. Is the contractual modification binding?

b. In part a, what affect, if any, would the following telegram have:

International Widget:

In accordance with our agreement of this date you will deliver the 1,000 previously ordered widgets within 30 days. Thank you for your cooperation in this matter.

A

3. A, a San Francisco company, orders from U.S. Electronics, a New York company, 10,000 electronic units. A's order form provides that any dispute would be resolved by an arbitration panel located in San Francisco. U.S. Electronics executes and delivers to A its acknowledgment form which accepts the order and contains the following provision: "All disputes will be resolved by the state courts of New York." A dispute arose concerning the workmanship of the parts and A wishes the case to be arbitrated in San Francisco. What result?

4. A executed a written contract with B to purchase an assorted collection of shoes for $3,000. A week before the agreed shipment date, B called A and said, "We cannot deliver at $3,000; unless you agree to pay $4,000, we will cancel the order." After considerable discussion, A agreed to pay $4,000 if B would ship as agreed in the contract. After the shoes had been delivered and accepted by A, A refused to pay $4,000 and insisted on paying only $3,000. Decision?

5. On November 23, A, a dress manufacturer, mailed to B a written and signed offer to sell 1,000 sun dresses at $50 per dress. The offer stated that "it would remain open for 10 days and that it could not be withdrawn prior to that date."

Two days later, A, noting a sudden increase in the price of sun dresses changed his mind. A therefore sent B a letter revoking the offer. The letter was sent on November 25 and received by B on November 28.

B chose to disregard the letter of November 25; instead, he happily continued to watch the price of sun dresses rise. On December 1, B sent a letter accepting the original offer. The letter, however, was not received by A until December 9, due to a delay in the mails.

B has demanded delivery of the goods according to the terms of the offer of November 23, but A has refused. Decision?

6. Plaintiff, an insurance agent, contracted to place several advertisements in the Flint classified telephone directory. The defendant, Michigan Bell Telephone Company, accepted the order and agreed to publish the listings in its 1981 yellow pages—but failed to do so. Upon plaintiff's suit for damages, the defendant Bell Telephone asserted the following clause of their contract as an affirmative defense:

Telephone Company (a) will not be bound by any verbal agreements or (b) will not be liable to Advertiser for damages resulting from failure to include all or any of said items of advertising in the Directories or from errors in the advertising printed in the Directories, in excess of the agreed prices for such advertising for the issue in which the error or omission occurs.

Decision?

21

TRANSFER OF TITLE, RISK OF LOSS AND DOCUMENTS OF TITLE

At common law the risk of loss or damage to goods identified under a contract of sale fall upon the person who had title or ownership of the goods at the time of their loss or damage. The rule was that simple. The court had only to determine who had title to the goods. Under both the common law and the U.C.C., the law is that title to the goods passes to the buyer at the time and place that the parties to the contract intend that it shall pass. The ascertainment of such intent, which is a question of fact to be determined upon evidence, may not be so simple. The U.C.C., Section 2–401, states that subject to the provisions of Article 2 and of Article 9 (Secured Transactions) of the Code, title to identified goods "passes from the seller to the buyer in any manner and on any condition explicitly agreed on by the parties."

However, the U.C.C. differs from the common law in its treatment of risk of loss or damage to identified goods. It does not treat such risk as invariably placed upon the party who has title or ownership of the goods. The Code contains specific rules which impose the risk of loss or damage as determined by the situation and the circumstances, irrespective of which of the parties had title or ownership of the goods.

TRANSFER OF TITLE AND OTHER PROPERTY RIGHTS

TITLE

A sale of goods is defined as the transfer of title from the seller to the buyer for a consideration known as the price. Transfer of title is, therefore, fundamental to the existence of a sale of goods.

Title passes when the parties intend it to pass, but in many cases such intention is difficult to ascertain by reason of conflicting testimony, or because the negotiation between the parties leading up to formation of the contract involved no discussion or mention of title. The parties may have considered such matters as price, credit terms, discounts, quality, quantity, delivery schedule, warranties, and inspection, but not title. However, the parties do explicitly agree, and usually in writing, upon transfer of title in a conditional sales contract. Such a contract always expressly states that title to the goods is reserved in the seller until the entire purchase price is paid.

A determination of the location of title to goods can be very important in such situations as liability for payment of taxes, duties created by statute, insurance coverage, loss or damage in situations not specifically covered by the U.C.C., and situations involving the rights or duties of third parties.

Where the parties have no explicit agreement as to transfer of title, the Code provides in Section 2–401 rules that determine when title passes to the buyer.

Physical Movement of the Goods

When delivery is to be made by moving the goods, title passes at the time and place at which the seller completes his performance with reference to delivery of the goods, despite any reservation of a security interest or any agreement that a document of title is to be delivered to the buyer at a different time or place, more specifically:

(a) At the time and place of shipment, if the contract authorizes shipment but does not require the seller to deliver the goods to the buyer at destination; or
(b) Upon tender of the goods to the buyer at destination, if the contract requires delivery at destination.

No Movement of the Goods

When delivery is to be made without moving the goods, title passes:

(a) Upon delivery of a document of title where the contract calls for delivery of such document; or
(b) At the time and place of contracting where the goods at that time are identified

to the contract and no documents are to be delivered.

Re-transfer of Title Back to Seller

By acceptance of the goods the buyer becomes owner of them. A buyer having once accepted goods which conform to the contract may not thereafter reject them and revest title in the seller. Section 2–607. Any such attempt at rejection is wrongful.

A buyer, however, may reject goods which he has not accepted. He may also revoke his acceptance of non-conforming goods provided (1) he accepted them on the reasonable assumption that the non-conformity would be cured, and it has not been seasonably cured, or (2) his acceptance having been made prior to discovery of non-conformity was reasonably induced by the difficulty of discovery before acceptance or by the seller's assurances. Section 2–608(1).

Revocation of acceptance is not effective until the buyer notifies the seller of it. Such notice must be given within a reasonable time after the buyer has discovered or should have discovered that the goods are non-conforming, and before the condition of the goods has changed by any cause other than inherent defects. Section 2–608(2).

Upon a rightful revocation of acceptance the buyer has the same rights and duties with respect to the goods as if he had rejected them. Section 2–608(3).

A revocation of acceptance does not revest title in the seller unless the revocation is justified. A revesting of title in the seller in the manner here discussed occurs by operation of law and is not a "sale" of the goods. Section 2–401(4).

SPECIAL PROPERTY OF THE BUYER IN IDENTIFIED GOODS

The Code creates a new property interest in goods which is unknown at common law. It is described as a special property which the buyer obtains by the identification of existing goods as goods to which the contract of sale refers. Sections 2–401(1), 2–501(1).

Identification of goods to the contract may take place by agreement of the parties, by act of the seller alone, or by act of the buyer alone. Where it is accomplished by unilateral action of the seller, the buyer may acquire a special property in goods without knowledge of the fact.

In order for the buyer to acquire a special property in the goods it is essential that the goods be identified to the contract of sale. After formation of the contract it is normal for the seller to take steps to obtain, manufacture, prepare, or select goods with which to fulfill his obligation under the contract. At some stage in the process the seller will have identified the goods which he intends to ship or deliver or hold for the buyer. These goods may or may not conform to the contract. This identification of goods to the contract is extremely important as it immediately creates for the buyer a special property right in the goods so identified and an insurable interest in them, even though the goods so identified are nonconforming and the buyer has an option to return or reject them. Section 2–501(1).

Identification of the goods to the contract does not shift the risk of loss. The risk of loss provisions of the Code still apply. After identification, the seller may under the contract have duties to perform with respect to the goods and his remedies depend upon his not defaulting under the contract.

Identification may be made by either the seller or the buyer, and can be made at any time and in any manner agreed upon by the parties. In the absence of explicit agreement identification takes place, as provided in Section 2–501(1):

1. upon the making of the contract if it is for goods already existing and identified;
2. if the contract is one for future goods other than crops to be grown or unborn animals, when the seller ships, marks, or otherwise designates the goods as those to which the contract refers;
3. if the contract is for crops to be grown within 12 months or the next normal harvest, or for the offspring of animals to be born within 12 months, when the crops are planted or become growing, or when the young animals are conceived.

Where the goods have been identified to the contract by the seller alone he may substitute other goods for those so identified until such time as he (a) defaults, or (b) becomes insolvent, or (c) notifies the buyer that the identification is final. Section 2–501(2).

This Code created interest designated as a special property in goods identified to the contract has specific incidents which give rise to the following rights in the buyer:

1. The buyer has an insurable interest in the goods. Section 2–501.
2. Where the buyer has paid all or part of the price of goods he may reclaim them from the seller who has become insolvent within 10 days after receiving the first installment on the price. If the identification creating the special property was made by the buyer alone he may reclaim the goods only if they conform to the contract of sale. Section 2–502.
3. The buyer has the right to inspect identified goods at any reasonable time and place. Section 2–513(1).
4. The buyer has the right to replevin goods identified to the contract if he is unable to effect cover for such goods. Section 2–716.
5. The buyer may maintain an action and recover damages against a third party for conversion of identified goods or for loss or injury to the goods caused by a third party. Section 2–722.

INSURABLE INTEREST IN THE GOODS

In order for a contract or policy of insurance to be valid the insured must have an insurable interest in the subject matter. At common law only a person with title or a lien could insure his interest in specific goods. The Code extends this right to a buyer's interest in goods which have been identified as goods to which the contract of sale refers. This interest enables the buyer to purchase insurance protection on goods which he does not own but which he may own upon delivery by the seller. Section 2–501(1).

The seller also has an insurable interest in the goods so long as he has title to them or any security interest in them. Section 2–501(2). There is nothing to prevent both seller and buyer at the same time carrying insurance on goods in which they both have a property interest, whether it be title, security interest or special property.

SECURITY INTEREST IN THE GOODS

A "security interest" is defined in the Code as an interest in personal property or fixtures which secures payment or performance of an obligation. Section 1–201(37). Security interests in goods are governed by Article 9 of the Code, except that so long as the buyer does not have or lawfully obtain possession of the goods (a) no security agreement is necessary, (b) no filing is required, and (c) the rights of the seller on default by the buyer are governed by Article 2. Section 9–113.

Any reservation by the seller of title to goods delivered to the buyer, as in the case of a conditional sales contract, is the reservation of a security interest. Section 2–401.

The special property in the goods created by Sections 2–401(1) and 2–501(1) is not a security interest, but the buyer may acquire a security interest therein by complying with Article 9, Section 1–201(37).

RISK OF LOSS

It has been observed that according to the common law the risk of loss or damage to goods without the fault of either the seller or buyer is borne by the person who is the owner at the time of the loss or damage. Where risk of loss is on the buyer and the seller has a security interest, it is unrealistic to state that a destruction of the goods does not involve loss to the seller. Destruction or damage to goods results in loss to every one who has an interest in them. The seller has lost his right to resell the goods upon the buyer's default, his right to reclaim them, his right to a security interest. He has lost all of the rights he might have even where both title and risk of loss were in the buyer, such as the right to stop delivery of the goods.

It is all right to ask "For Whom the Bells Toll," but the answer is that they toll for every one who had an interest in the subject matter that is lost, to the extent of his interest.

Risk of loss, as the term is used in the law of Sales, means placement of the ultimate loss upon the buyer or the seller. If placed upon the buyer, he is under a duty to pay the price for lost or damaged goods even though he never received them or became owner of them. If upon the seller, he has no right to recover the purchase price from the buyer.

In determining the location of risk of loss by definite rules for specific situations, the Code departs sharply from the common law concept of risk of loss determined by ownership of the goods which depended upon whether title had been transferred. In its transactional approach, the Code is necessarily detailed, and for this reason is probably more understandable and meaningful than the common law's reliance upon the abstract concept of title.

RISK OF LOSS IN ABSENCE OF A BREACH

The Code contains specific rules which impose risk of loss upon the buyer or the seller irrespective of title or ownership of the goods. These rules apply to particularized situations where there has been no breach of contract, as follows:

Agreement of the Parties

The parties by agreement may not only shift the allocation of risk of loss but may also divide the risk between them. Such agreement is controlling. Under Section 2–509(4) the rules of the Code are expressly subject to a contrary agreement of the parties. Section 2–303 provides:

Where this Article allocates a risk or a burden as between the parties "unless otherwise agreed," the agreement may not only shift the allocation but may also divide the risk or burden.

Trial Sales

Sale on Approval. In a sale on approval possession, but not title to the goods, is transferred to the buyer for a stated period of time or, if none is stated, for a reasonable time, during which period the buyer may use the goods to determine whether he wishes to buy them. Both title and risk of loss are in the seller until "approval" or acceptance of goods by the buyer. Section 2–326.

Use of the goods consistent with the purpose of approval by the buyer is not acceptance, but failure of the buyer to notify the seller of his election to return the goods seasonably is an acceptance. The buyer's approval may also be manifested by exercising any dominion or control over the goods inconsistent with the seller's ownership. Upon approval, risk of loss and title passes to the buyer who thereupon becomes liable to the seller for the price of the goods.

Sale or Return. In a sale or return, the goods are sold and delivered to the buyer with an option to return them to the seller. The risk of loss is on the buyer who has title until he revests it in the seller by a return

of the goods. The return of the goods is at the buyer's risk and expense.

It is frequently difficult to determine from the facts of a particular transaction whether the parties intended a sale on approval or a sale or return. The consequences are, of course, drastically different with respect to transfer of title and risk of loss. The Code provides a test which is neat, sensible, and easily applied, namely, unless otherwise agreed, if the goods are delivered primarily for the buyer's use the transaction is a sale on approval; if they are delivered primarily for resale by the buyer, it is a sale or return. Section 2–326(1).

Under the Code, a sale on *consignment* is regarded as a sale or return and attaching creditors of the consignee (an agent who receives the merchandise for sale) or his trustee in bankruptcy prevail over the consignor, if the consignee maintains a place of business where he deals in goods of the kind involved under a name other than the name of the consignor, unless the consignor:

(a) complies with an applicable law requiring a consignor's interest to be evidenced by a sign, or

(b) establishes that the consignee is generally known by his creditors to be substantially engaged in selling the goods of others, or

(c) complies with the filing provisions of Article 9 (Secured Transactions). Section 2–326(3).

Contracts Involving Carriers

If the contract does not require the seller to deliver the goods at a particular destination but merely to the carrier (a *shipment contract*), risk of loss passes to the buyer upon delivery of the goods to the carrier. If the seller is required to deliver them to a particular destination (a *destination contract*), risk of loss passes to the buyer at destination upon tender of the goods to the buyer. Section 2–509(1).

Sales contracts frequently contain terms which indicate the agreement of the parties as to delivery. These terms designate whether the contract is a shipment contract or a destination contract and, thereby, when the risk of loss passes.

F.O.B.—F.A.S. Shipments. The initials "F.O.B." mean "free on board"; "F.A.S." means "free alongside." Under the Code these are delivery terms and not price terms when used in a contract of sale. Section 2–319(1)(2). Where the contract provides that the sale is F.O.B. place of destination, the seller must at his own expense and risk transport the goods to that place and there tender delivery of them to the buyer.

Where the contract is F.A.S. at a named port, the seller is obligated at his own expense and risk to deliver the goods alongside the vessel in the manner usual in that port or to deliver them on a dock designated by the buyer and also to obtain and tender to the buyer a receipt for the goods in exchange for which the carrier is under a duty to issue a bill of lading. Section 2–319(2).

C.I.F. and C. & F. Shipments. The initials C.I.F. mean "cost, insurance, and freight"; C. & F. means simply "cost and freight."

Under a C.I.F. contract, in consideration for an agreed unit price for the goods the seller pays all costs of transportation, insurance, and freight to destination. The amount of the agreed unit price of the goods will, of course, reflect these costs. The unit price in a C. & F. contract is understandably less than in a C.I.F. contract as it does not include the cost of insurance.

Under the Code, both C.I.F. and C. & F. contracts are regarded as shipment and not destination contracts. In a shipment contract, as previously noted, title and risk of loss pass to the buyer upon delivery of the goods to the carrier. Section 2–509. If the seller has properly performed all of his obligations with respect to the goods, title and risk of loss under either a C.I.F. or a C. &

F. contract pass to the buyer upon delivery of the goods to the carrier. Section 2–320.

C.O.D. Shipments. These initials mean "Collect on Delivery," and are instructions to the carrier not to deliver the goods at destination until it has collected the price and transportation charges from the buyer. In this manner the seller retains control over the possession of the goods by preventing the buyer from obtaining delivery unless he pays the price. It does not prevent title from passing to the buyer upon delivery of the goods to the carrier. Under the usual rule, where the buyer pays or agrees to pay the freight, title and risk of loss pass to the buyer upon delivery to the carrier. A shipment C.O.D. deprives the buyer of the right of inspection to which he would otherwise be entitled under Section 2–513(3)(a) of the Code.

Delivery "Ex-Ship" Contract. Where the contract provides for delivery "ex-ship," or from the ship, it is not only a destination contract but title and risk of loss do not pass to the buyer until the goods are unloaded from the carrier at destination. Section 2–322.

"No Arrival, No Sale" Contract. Where the contract contains terms of "no arrival, no sale," the title and risk of loss do not pass to the buyer until the seller makes a tender of the goods after their arrival at destination. These terms excuse the seller from any liability to the buyer for failure of the goods to arrive, unless the seller has caused their non-arrival.

Section 2–324 of the Code provides:

Under a term "no arrival, no sale" or terms of like meaning, unless otherwise agreed, (a) the seller must properly ship conforming goods and if they arrive by any means he must tender them on arrival but he assumes no obligation that the goods will arrive unless he has caused the non-arrival; and (b) where without fault of the seller the goods are in part lost or have so deteriorated as no longer to conform to the contract or arrive after the contract time, the buyer may proceed as if there had been casualty to identified goods.

In emphasizing the location of risk of loss with definite rules for specific situations, the Code departs sharply from the common law, which treated risk of loss as an incident to ownership of the goods.

Goods in Possession of Bailee

In some sales, the goods at the time of the contract are held by a bailee and are to be delivered without being moved. For instance, a seller may contract with a buyer to sell grain which is located in a grain elevator and which the buyer intends to leave in the same elevator. The risk of loss passes to the buyer on his receipt of a negotiable document of title covering the goods, or an acknowledgment by the bailee of the buyer's right to possession, or receipt of a non-negotiable document of title or other written direction to deliver the goods unless the buyer seasonably objects. Section 2–509(2).

All Other Sales

If the goods are in the possession of the buyer at the time of the making of the contract, risk of loss passes to the buyer at that time, as the buyer is in "receipt of the goods." Section 2–509(3). Title would also pass to the buyer at that time, as the seller would have no performance to complete "with reference to the physical delivery of the goods." Section 2–401(2).

However, if the contract of sale is not on approval and does not provide expressly for the passage of risk of loss and if at the time the contract was formed, the goods were not in the possession of the buyer, were not to be shipped by carrier, and were not in the possession of a bailee, the situation is one of frequent occurrence in which a seller is required to tender or deliver the goods to the buyer. In such case, risk of loss depends upon whether the seller is a merchant. If the seller is a merchant, risk of loss passes to the buyer upon delivery and receipt of the goods. If the seller is not a merchant, it passes on tender of the goods by the seller to the buyer. Section 2–509(3).

Suppose B goes to A's furniture store, selects a particular set of dining room furniture and pays A the agreed price of $800 for it upon A's agreement to stain the set a darker color and deliver it. A stains the furniture, transports it by truck to B's residence, and there tenders it to B who refuses to accept it. The furniture is then returned to A's store where shortly thereafter it is accidentally destroyed by fire. B can recover from A the $800 payment less the amount of A's damages resulting from B's breach of contract. The risk of loss is on seller A as he is a merchant and the goods were not delivered and received but only tendered.

However, if X, an accountant, upon moving to a different city contracts to sell his household furniture to Y for $1000 by written agreement signed by Y, and thereafter loads the furniture on a rented truck which is driven to Y's residence where the goods are tendered to Y who refuses to accept or pay for them, and on the return trip the truck is smashed and the furniture destroyed, X may recover from Y the $1000 purchase price. The risk of loss is on buyer Y as the seller is not a merchant and tender is sufficient to transfer the risk. Section 2–509(3).

RISK OF LOSS
WHERE THERE IS A BREACH

Breach by the Seller

If the seller ships non-conforming goods to the buyer, the risk of loss remains on the seller until the buyer has accepted the goods, and the buyer is under no duty to accept them.   Section 2–510(1) provides:

Where a tender or delivery of goods so fails to conform to the contract as to give a right of rejection the risk of their loss remains on the seller until cure or acceptance.

Where the buyer has accepted non-conforming goods, and thereafter by timely notice to the seller rightfully revokes his acceptance, he may treat the risk of loss as resting on the seller from the beginning to the extent of any deficiency in the buyer's effective insurance coverage.   Section 2–510(2).   For example, S delivers to B defective goods which B accepts.   Subsequently, B discovers a hidden defect in the goods and rightfully revokes his prior acceptance.   If the goods are destroyed through no fault of either party, and B has insured the goods for 60% of their fair market value of $10,000, then the insurance company will cover $6,000 of the loss and S will bear the loss of $4,000.   If the buyer's insurance coverage had been $10,000, then the seller would not bear any of the loss.

Breach by the Buyer

Where conforming goods have been identified to a contract which the *buyer repudiates or breaches* before risk of loss has passed to him, the seller may treat the risk of loss as resting on the buyer "for a commercially reasonable time" to the extent of any deficiency in the seller's effective insurance coverage.   Section 2–510(3).   For example, S agrees to sell 40,000 pounds of plastic resin to B, f.o.b. B's factory, delivery by March 1. On February 1, B wrongfully repudiates the contract by telephoning S and telling him that he does not want the resin.   S immediately seeks out another buyer but before he is able to locate one, and within a commercially reasonable time, the resin is destroyed by a fire through no fault of S.   The fair market value of the resin is $35,000.

S's insurance only covers $15,000 of the loss. B is liable for $20,000.

In a case involving the question of a commercially reasonable time, the seller had manufactured 40,000 pounds of plastic resin pellets specially for the buyer who agreed to accept them at the rate of 1000 pounds per day upon his issuance of shipping instructions.   Despite numerous requests by the seller, the buyer issued no such instructions.   On August 18, the seller, after warehousing the goods for 40 days, demanded by letter that buyer issue instructions.   Buyer agreed to issue them beginning August 20, but never did.   On September 22, a fire destroyed seller's plant containing the goods which were not covered by insurance.   The court fixed the date of the breach as August 20, and held that since the goods were conforming and manufactured for the buyer, it was reasonable for the seller to believe that the buyer would soon take them off his hands, so as to forego obtaining insurance, and from that date to September 22 was therefore a commercially reasonable time for the risk of loss to rest on the buyer.   Judgment for the seller for the contract price was affirmed.   Multiplastics, Inc. v. Arch Industries, Inc., 166 Conn. 280, 348 A.2d 618 (1974).

DOCUMENTS OF TITLE

In discussing transfer of title and other property rights and the passage of risk of loss, documents of title figured prominently. Documents of title serve a very important function in facilitating the transfer of title to goods and the creation of a security interest in goods.   Sales frequently involve the storage and transport of goods, both of which are commonly accomplished through the use of documents of title.   Article 7 of the U.C.C. has consolidated and revised the Uniform Warehouse Receipts Act and the Uniform Bills of Lading Act and now governs the negotiation of documents of title.

TYPES OF DOCUMENTS OF TITLE

Section 1–201(45) states:

"Document of title" includes bill of lading dock warrant, dock receipt, warehouse receipt or order for the delivery of goods, and also any other document which in the regular course of business or financing is treated as adequately evidencing that the person in possession of it is entitled to receive, hold and dispose of the document and the goods it covers. To be a document of title a document must purport to be issued by or addressed to a bailee and purport to cover goods in the bailee's possession which are either identified or are fungible portions of an identified mass.

Warehouse Receipts

A warehouse receipt means a receipt issued by a person engaged in the business of storing goods for hire. Section 1–204(45).

Duties of Warehouseman. A warehouseman is liable for damages for loss or injury to the goods caused by his failure to exercise such care in regard to them as a reasonably careful man would exercise under the circumstances. Section 7–204(1).

A warehouseman must keep separate the goods covered by each receipt issued by him although different lots of fungible goods may be commingled. Section 7–207.

The warehouseman must deliver the goods to the person entitled to receive them under the terms of the warehouse receipt. If he has already delivered the goods to another, the burden is on him to establish that such delivery was rightful as against the holder of the document. Similarly, if the goods have become damaged, lost, or destroyed, the burden is on the warehouseman to prove by evidence the facts and circumstances which establish his non-liability. Section 7–403(1).

If a warehouseman issues a negotiable warehouse receipt in blank, and the blank is subsequently filled in without authority, a purchaser of the receipt for value without notice of the lack of authority may treat the insertion as authorized. The warehouseman is liable to such purchaser upon the terms of the document as filled in. However, if a receipt has been altered without authority it is enforceable against the warehouseman issuer only according to its original tenor. Section 7–208.

Contractual Limitation of Liability of Warehouseman. The extent of the liability of a warehouseman may be limited by a provision in the warehouse receipt fixing a specific maximum liability per article, or item, or unit of weight. This limitation does not apply in the event of a conversion of the goods by the warehouseman to his own use. Section 7–204(2).

Bona Fide Purchaser of Fungible Goods from Warehouseman. The Code protects bona fide purchasers of fungible goods from a warehouseman-dealer in such goods. If a warehouseman is in the business of buying and selling fungible goods, a buyer of such goods from him in the ordinary course of business takes them free of any claim under an outstanding warehouse receipt even though duly negotiated. Section 7–205. The protection of the buyer of the goods as against the holders of negotiable warehouse receipts is consistent with the warehouseman's right of commingling fungible goods and the reasonable commercial expectations of bailors in this type of situation.

Thus, the owner or grower of wheat delivers it to a grain elevator either by way of sale or bailment. If it is a sale, the warehouseman becomes the owner of an undivided fractional interest in the mass of grain in the elevator as tenant in common; and if a bailment, the bailor acquires such interest in lieu of his former complete ownership of specific wheat. Where the operator of the elevator (bailee warehouseman) is also buying and selling grain on his own account, the bailor or holder of a receipt should recognize the possibility of loss by reason of a sale of grain by the warehouseman to third parties in the ordinary course of business.

Termination of Storage. A warehouseman is not required to keep the goods indefinitely. At the termination of the period of storage stated in the document, the warehouseman may notify the person on whose account the goods are held to pay accrued storage charges and remove the goods. If no period of time is stated in the document, the warehouseman is required to give 30 days notice to pay charges and remove the goods. A shorter time, which must be reasonable, is permitted if the goods are about to deteriorate or decline in value to less than the amount of the warehouseman's lien, or if the quality or condition of the goods cause them to be a hazard to other property or to persons. Section 7–206.

Lien of Warehouseman. To enforce the payment of his charges and necessary expenses in connection with keeping and handling the goods a warehouseman has a lien on the goods which enables him to sell them at public or private sale after notice, and to apply the net proceeds of the sale to the amount of his charges.

As against the holder of a negotiable warehouse receipt to whom it has been duly negotiated, this lien is limited to charges at the rate specified in the receipt, and if none are specified, to a reasonable charge for storage of the goods subsequent to the date of the receipt. Section 7–209(1).

The Code provides a definite procedure for enforcement of the lien of a warehouseman against the goods stored and in his possession. Section 2–710.

Bills of Lading

A bill of lading is a document issued by a carrier upon receipt of goods for transpor-

tation. It serves a threefold function: (1) as a receipt for the goods, (2) as evidence of the contract of affreightment, and (3) as a document of title.

Under the Code bills of lading may be issued not only by common carriers, but by contract carriers, freight forwarders, or any person engaged in the business of transporting or forwarding goods, and the term includes an airbill. Section 1–201(6).

A bill of lading is negotiable if by its terms the goods are deliverable to bearer or to the order of a named person. Any other document is non-negotiable. Section 7–104.

Duties of Issuer of Bill of Lading. The Code treats the duties of a carrier and those of a warehouseman in separate sections of Article 7. Their functions, namely, transportation and storage, are different, and in addition common carriers of goods are extraordinary bailees under the law and subject to a greater degree of liability than an ordinary bailee such as a warehouseman.

The carrier is liable to the consignee of a non-negotiable bill who has given value in good faith or a holder to whom a negotiable bill has been duly negotiated for damages caused by misdating the bill or by non-receipt or misdescription of the goods, unless the document indicates that the issuer does not know whether the goods were in fact received or conform to the kind, quantity or condition described. In such case the carrier may qualify its obligation by stating on the document: "contents or condition of contents of packages unknown," or "said to contain," or "shipper's weight, load and count," or words of similar import. Section 7–301.

While its broad duty of care is similar to that of a warehouseman, the extraordinary liability at common law of the common carrier as an insurer of the goods, with five exceptions, as discussed in Chapter 5, is preserved in Section 7–309(1).

A carrier is not in the business of buying and selling goods, as a warehouseman may be, and therefore no special rule is required as to buyers of fungible goods from warehousemen, as provided in Section 7–205.

The carrier must deliver the goods to the person entitled to receive them under the terms of the bill of lading. The carrier's duty in this respect is similar to that of the warehouseman. Section 7–403(1).

Any unauthorized alteration of a bill of lading or the unauthorized filling in of a blank in a bill of lading leaves the bill enforceable only according to its original tenor. Section 7–306. The carrier thus has greater protection than the warehouseman in the case of an unauthorized filling in of a blank. Section 7–208.

Contractual Limitation of Liability of Carrier. The Code allows a carrier to limit its liability by contract in all cases where its rates are dependent upon value and the shipment is given an opportunity to declare a higher value. The limitation does not apply to a conversion of the goods by the carrier to its own use. Section 7–309(2).

Through Bills of Lading. A bill of lading may provide that the issuer deliver the goods to a connecting carrier for further transportation to destination. Manifestly, the carrier accepting goods for shipment does not itself provide service to every place of destination. It will endeavor to route the shipment in such manner as will give the initial carrier the longest haul on its line in order to obtain maximum freight revenue, before delivery to a connecting carrier which may or may not be the destination carrier. A bill of lading which specifies one or more connecting carriers is called a "through bill of lading."

The initial or originating carrier which receives the goods from the shipper and issues a through bill of lading is liable to the holder of the document for loss or damage to the goods caused by any connecting or delivering carrier. Section 7–302(1). A carrier, however, is not required to issue through bills of lading.

Unlike the initial carrier, the liability of a connecting carrier is limited to the period while the goods are in its possession.

The carrier issuing a through bill of lading is entitled to recover from the connecting or delivering carrier in possession of the goods when loss or damage occurred the amount of damages that it has been obliged to pay to any one entitled to recover under the document, together with the reasonable expenses of defending any action brought against it in connection with such loss or damage. Section 7–302(3).

Diversion or Reconsignment of Goods. A shipment of goods may be diverted or reconsigned during the course of transportation. For instance, this may occur when the shipper has no buyer of the goods at the time of shipment. If the goods are perishable, such as fruits and vegetables, they are usually loaded in refrigerated cars at the local market where grown and shipped immediately to a metropolitan market. The carrier issues a shipper's order bill of lading, or a straight bill naming the shipper or his agent as consignee. While the goods are moving on the rails or on the highways, the shipper makes a contract for their sale and accordingly instructs the carrier to reconsign them or divert them to the buyer.

Section 7–303 authorizes the carrier to deliver the goods to a person or at a destination other than that stated in the bill of lading on instructions from (a) the holder of the negotiable bill of lading; (b) the consignor on a non-negotiable bill, despite contrary instructions from the consignee; (c) the consignee on a non-negotiable bill in the absence of contrary instructions from the consignor.

If the goods are moving under a negotiable bill of lading, a person to whom the bill has been duly negotiated can hold the carrier according to its original terms. Section 7–303(2).

If the carrier has issued a non-negotiable bill of lading covering the goods, a diversion of them or change in shipping instructions by the consignor whereby the carrier does not deliver the goods to the consignee defeats all rights of the consignee against the carrier. Section 7–504(3).

Destination Bills of Lading. A novel provision in the Code designed to facilitate the use of negotiable bills in connection with fast shipments permits the carrier to issue the bill at destination or any other place requested by the consignor. The carrier is under no duty to issue a destination bill.

However, such a bill may be useful where goods shipped overnight by fast truck, rail, or air service are scheduled to arrive before a document issued at the place of origin could be received by mail, and the carrier has inadequate terminal facilities for holding the goods. The seller may request the carrier to issue the bill of lading to the order of a bank located in the city of destination and deliver the bill to the bank. The seller sends to the bank by telegraph a draft drawn on the buyer. Upon honoring the draft, the bank indorses and delivers the bill of lading to the buyer. Section 7–305.

Lien of Carrier. Upon goods in its possession covered by a bill of lading the carrier has a lien for its charges, including demurrage and terminal charges, and expenses necessary for preservation of the goods. As against a purchaser for value of a negotiable bill of lading this lien is limited to charges stated in the bill or in the applicable published tariff, and if no charges are so stated, to a reasonable charge. Section 7–307(1).

If the consignor had no authority of the owner of the goods to ship them or subject them to such charges and expenses, the lien is nevertheless effective unless the carrier had notice of the lack of authority. Section 7–307(2).

The enforcement of the lien of the carrier is by public or private sale of the goods after notice to all persons known to the carrier to claim an interest in them. The sale must be on terms which are "commercially reasonable," and must be conducted in a "commercially reasonable manner." Section 7–308(1).

A purchaser in good faith of goods sold to enforce the lien takes free of any rights of persons against whom the lien was valid, even though the enforcement of the lien does not comply with the requirements of the Code. This rule applies to both carrier's and warehouseman's liens. Section 7–308(4), 7–310(5).

NEGOTIABILITY OF DOCUMENTS OF TITLE

The concept of negotiability has long been established in law and is well known to bankers, business men, lawyers and the courts. It is important not only in connection with documents of title, but also in commercial paper, and investment securities including corporate stock certificates treated in other chapters of this book.

Negotiability is a characteristic which the law confers upon instruments and documents which comply with the requisite statutory form. The magic words are "bearer" or "order." Obviously a promise to deliver goods to a named person is manifestly different from a promise to deliver the goods to bearer or to the order of a named person. The first promise may be safely performed by the promisor by delivery of the goods to the person named in the promise. This is typical of a straight bill of lading, i.e. one issued by a carrier whereby it undertakes to deliver the goods at destination to a named consignee. In such case, it is not necessary for the carrier to obtain surrender of the bill of lading upon delivery of the goods at destination. The only concern of the carrier is to make sure that the person to whom it delivers the goods at destination is the person named in the straight bill of lading as consignee. Such a bill of lading is non-negotiable.

If the promise of the carrier in the bill of lading is to deliver the goods to bearer or to the order of a person named in the bill, the carrier may not safely deliver the goods to anyone at destination without surrender of the original bill of lading. Anyone in possession of a bearer form document is entitled to receive the goods from the carrier. Anyone in possession of an order form document, properly indorsed, is likewise entitled to receive possession of the goods from the carrier. A bearer or order form document of title is negotiable. By the terms of the promise contained on its face it was intended to go to market, to pass from hand to hand, and to circulate freely in the channels of commerce.

A non-negotiable document such as a straight bill of lading or a warehouse receipt whereby the goods are deliverable to a person named in the bill and not to the order of any person or to bearer, may be transferred by assignment, but may not be negotiated. Only a negotiable document or instrument may be negotiated.

Section 7–104 of the Code provides that a warehouse receipt, bill of lading, or other document of title is negotiable if by its terms the goods are to be delivered to bearer or to the order of a named person, or where in overseas trade, it runs to a named person or assigns. Any other document is non-negotiable.

Due Negotiation

The manner in which a negotiable document of title may be negotiated and the requirements of "due negotiation" are set forth in Section 7–501 of the Code. An order form negotiable document of title running to the order of a named person is negotiated by his indorsement and delivery. After such indorsement in blank or to bearer, the document may be negotiated by delivery alone. A special indorsement by which the document is indorsed over to a specified person requires the indorsement of the special indorsee as well as delivery in order to accomplish a further negotiation.

The naming in a negotiable document of a person to be notified upon the arrival of the goods does not limit the negotiability of the bill of lading nor serve as notice to any purchaser of the document that such person has any interest in the goods. The indorsement of a non-negotiable document neither makes it negotiable nor adds to the rights of any transferee.

It will be observed that "due negotiation" is a term peculiar to Article 7, Part 5, and requires not only that the purchaser of the negotiable document must take it in good faith without notice of any adverse claim or defense and pay value, but also that he must take it in the regular course of business or financing, and value does not include the settlement or payment of a pre-existing debt. Thus, a transfer for value of a negotiable document of title to a non-business man or non-banker, such as a college professor or student, would not be a due negotiation.

Rights Acquired by Due Negotiation

Negotiation is a form of transfer whereby the transferee acquires not merely the rights which the transferor had but also direct rights based upon the language of the promise contained in the instrument or document. Where a property right is merely assigned, the assignee takes only such rights as the assignor had. He stands in the shoes of the assignor, and his rights are subject to all defects and infirmities in the title of the assignor. However, where a document is negotiable and is transferred by due negotiation, the transferee is one to whom the promise of the issuer runs and he thereby acquires the direct obligation of the issuer. Thus, if A issues a warehouse receipt to B wherein he promises to deliver the goods to bearer, and subsequently X presents the document to A and demands the goods, X is the bearer and therefore the very person to whom A promised to deliver the goods. The same is true with respect to a properly indorsed order form warehouse receipt or bill of lading.

The effect of due negotiation is that it creates new rights in the holder of the document. Upon due negotiation the transferee does not stand in the shoes of his transferor. Defects and defenses available against the transferor are not available against the new holder. His rights are newly created by the negotiation and free of such defects and defenses. This enables bankers and business men to extend credit upon documents of title without concern about possible adverse claims or the rights of third parties.

The rights of a holder of a negotiable document of title to whom it has been duly negotiated are that he has (a) title to the document; (b) title to the goods; (c) all rights accruing under the law of agency or estoppel including rights to goods delivered to the bailee after the document was issued; and (d) the direct obligation of the issuer to hold or deliver the goods according to the terms of the document. Section 7–502.

The indorsement of a document of title does not make the indorser liable for any default by the bailee or by previous indorsers. Section 7–505.

If an order form document of title is transferred without a requisite indorsement, the transferee has the right to compel his transferor to supply any necessary indorsement. This right is specifically enforceable in a court of equity. The transfer becomes a negotiation only as of the time the indorsement is supplied. Section 7–506.

Rights Acquired in the Absence of Due Negotiation

If a non-negotiable document is transferred or a negotiable document is transferred without due negotiation, the transferee of the document acquires all of the title and rights which the transferor had or had actual authority to convey. He does not as such transferee acquire title or ownership to the goods as he would in the case of the negotiation of a negotiable document. Prior to notification received by the bailee of the transfer, the rights of the transferee may be defeated by the creditors of the transferor or by a buyer from the transferor in the ordinary course of business, if the bailee has delivered the goods to the buyer, or as against the bailee by good faith dealings of the bailee with the transferor. Section 7–504.

Warranties on Negotiation or Transfer

A person who either negotiates or transfers a document of title for value other than a collecting bank or other intermediary incurs certain warranty obligations unless otherwise agreed as provided in Section 7–507. Such transferor warrants to his immediate purchaser: (a) that the document is genuine; (b) that he has no knowledge of any fact that would impair its validity or worth; and (c) that his negotiation or transfer is rightful and fully effective with respect to the document of title and the goods it represents.

Ineffective Documents of Title

It is fundamental that a thief or finder of goods may not by delivery of them to a warehouseman or carrier and issuance to the thief or finder of a negotiable document of title defeat the rights of the owner by a negotiation of the document. While such document would be genuine and its indorsement by the thief or finder not a forgery, it would in such case not represent title to the goods.

In order that a person obtain title to goods by a negotiation to him of a document, the goods must have been delivered to the issuer of the document by the owner of the goods or by one to whom the owner has delivered or entrusted them with actual or apparent authority to ship, store, or sell them. Section 7–503(1).

Protection of Warehousemen and Carriers Who Deliver Goods Pursuant to Document of Title

A warehouseman or carrier may deliver goods according to the terms of the document which it has issued, or otherwise dispose of the goods as provided in the Code, without incurring liability even though the document did not represent title to the goods. It must have acted in good faith and complied with reasonable commercial standards in both the receipt and delivery or other disposition of the goods. The bailee has no liability even though the person from whom it received the goods had no authority to obtain the issuance of the document or dispose of the goods, and even though the person to whom it delivered the goods had no authority to receive them. Section 7–404.

This protection accorded the issuer of a document of title does not apply generally to a person acting in good faith and in the ordinary course of business who resells goods which he has received or purchased from a thief or person with no authority to dispose of them. Thus, a factor who in good faith receives goods from a thief or finder and resells them in the ordinary course of business is liable to the true owner for conversion of the goods.

A carrier or warehouseman who receives goods from a thief or finder and later delivers them to a person to whom the thief or finder ordered them to be delivered is not liable to the true owner of the goods. Even a sale of the goods by the carrier or warehouseman to enforce a lien for transportation or storage charges and expenses would not subject it to liability.

Warehousemen and carriers are regarded as furnishing a service necessary to trade and commerce. They are not a link in the chain of title, and do not purport to represent the owner in transactions affecting title to the goods. Consequently, it is a sound rule which relieves them from liability upon delivery of the goods pursuant to their contract under the document of title even though the document is ineffective against the true owner of the goods.

Lost or Missing Documents of Title

If a document has been lost, stolen, or destroyed, a claimant of the goods may apply to a court for an order directing delivery of the goods or the issuance of a substitute document. Compliance of the carrier or warehouseman with the order of court relieves it of liability. Section 7–601(1).

The claimant must provide security approved by the court if the missing document is negotiable.

If the carrier or warehouseman without a court order delivers goods to a person claiming them under a missing negotiable document, it is liable to any person who is thereby injured. Delivery to such person in good faith is not a conversion of the goods if security is posted in an amount at least double the value of the goods to indemnify any person injured by the delivery who files notice of claim within one year. Section 7–601(2).

Cases

Concept of Title

MEINHARD–COMMERCIAL CORP. v. HARGO WOOLEN MILLS

(1972) 112 N.H. 500, 300 A.2d 321.

[A receiver was appointed for defendant Hargo, a manufacturer of woolen cloth, in proceedings brought by plaintiff. Prior to the proceedings Shabry Trading Company, a trader in card waste material and supplier to Hargo for many years, shipped to Hargo 24 bales of card waste which it had not ordered and did not wish to purchase. Hargo intended to return the bales but Shabry, wishing to avoid the cost of warehouse storage, offered to let Hargo retain possession and buy such merchandise as Hargo would give notice that it intended to use. On one occasion, Hargo notified Shabry that it would use eight bales, for which it was invoiced. The goods were stored separately from Hargo's other goods, and the remaining 16 bales continued in such storage until the receiver took possession. Shabry thereupon filed a claim in the proceedings as owner of the 16 bales and requested their return. By order of court the goods were sold by the receiver for $7,500 which was held in a bank account pending determination of Shabry's claim. Judgment in favor of Shabry.]

GRIMES, J.
* * *

The utilization of the concept of title in sales transactions is not novel, nor is the misconception and the misuse of it. Learned Hand has said: " '[T]itle' is a formal word for a purely conceptual notion; I do not know what it means and I question whether anybody does, except perhaps legal historians." [Citation.] Prior to the Uniform Commercial Code, the Uniform Sales Act accepted the common-law notion that title determination was the main solvent of sales problems. The U.C.C. deliberately deemphasizes this view. 2–101, Uniform Law Comments. The code supplants many title-determined issues with specific code provisions to determine the rights and duties of the buyer and seller, such as risk of loss (2–509, 2–510), insurable interest (2–501), suit of third parties (2–722), buyer's rights on seller's insolvency (2–709), and buyer's right to replevy identified goods (2–716). Despite its minimization of the title concept, the code does recognize situations where the lack of any other legal tool requires the courts to fall back on the eternal title question of mine or thine. The code therefore provides a catch-basin rule

(2–401) that applies only when the more specific code provisions fail to deal with the issue. The case before us was decided below with resort to this catch-basin rule, the pertinent portion of which reads as follows: "Any retention or reservation by the seller of the title (property) in goods shipped or delivered to the buyer is limited in effect to a reservation of a security interest. *Subject to these provisions* * * *, title to goods passes from the seller to the buyer in any manner and on any conditions explicitly agreed on by the parties." 2–401(1) (emphasis added).

* * *

However, since 2–401 speaks only in terms of buyers and sellers, we believe it does not apply to the transaction between these parties. 2–103(1)(d) defines seller as "unless the context otherwise requires * * * (1)(d) 'Seller' means a person who sells or contracts to sell goods." A buyer is defined in 2–103(1)(a) as "unless the context otherwise requires * * *, (a) 'Buyer' means a person who buys or contracts to buy goods." To determine the meaning of these sections, we refer to the definition of sale and contract for sale in 2–106(1). " 'Contract for sale' includes both a present sale of goods and a contract to sell goods at a future time. A 'sale' consists in the passing of title from the seller to the buyer for a price. (See 2–401)." For 2–401(1) to apply, we must therefore first find that the transaction between the supplier, Shabry, and the manufacturer, Hargo, was a sale. [Citation.]

Whether this transaction was a sale or some other type of transaction is a question of the intent of the parties, which is a question for the trier of fact to determine. [Citation.] Under the code, there must still be a meeting of minds between the parties before there is a contract. [Citation.] The master found in the parties' requests for findings and rulings that the factual understanding between Hargo and Shabry contemplated no passage of title until Shabry was notified of Hargo's intention to use the goods and Shabry thereafter invoiced the goods to Hargo. The master also found that Hargo was never obligated to purchase and Shabry could have sold the goods to other buyers.

Given these findings, it is clear that the parties' agreement concerning the delivered card waste created no contract for sale by the passage of title for a price. The parties showed no intent to pass title. No title may pass for a price without commitment of the buyer to pay the price. [Citations.] The mere fact that goods are delivered to the premises of a prospective buyer does not in and of itself create a sale, where neither party considered it a sale. [Citation.]

The parties did agree as to the placement of the goods on Hargo's premises and Shabry did make an offer on the pro-forma invoice of a price if Hargo wished to buy. The parties' course of dealings in card waste helps us interpret the meaning of this agreement. 1–205(1), 1–205(3). The record shows that Shabry's previous dealings with Hargo involved completed sales when the goods were delivered. When Shabry sent Hargo the contested card waste, Hargo, already possessing a card waste surplus, did not want to buy. Hargo, in accord with their prior course of dealing, intended to return the card waste; but Shabry, wishing to avoid the high cost of warehouse storage of card waste, offered to let Hargo retain possession of the goods and buy them only as Hargo had use for them at the price of the pro-forma invoice. Hargo accepted this storage offer and marked and stored Shabry's card waste independent of its other goods. This agreement contravened the old sale-on-delivery course of dealing between the parties and indicated this was a special new deal that did not purport to be a sale until further action by Hargo on Shabry's offer. Hargo was nothing more than

a bailee with an option to buy if the goods were not sold to others. [Citation.]

The performance of the parties also sheds light on their agreement. Cf. 2–208(1). When Hargo needed eight bales of the card waste, he notified Shabry, who separately invoiced the eight bales to Hargo at the pro forma invoice price, and Hargo thereafter paid for the goods. The clear notification and separate invoicing show that Shabry had not previously relinquished ownership of the bales to Hargo. All that Shabry had relinquished was possession of goods for his own benefit to save storage costs and for the benefit of Hargo if it should need the goods. This course of performance also shows Shabry had made Hargo an offer at the pro-forma invoice price with specific instructions as to how Hargo could accept this offer. When Hargo decided to buy the eight bales they were invoiced as of that time instead of as of the date the twenty-four bales were stored with Hargo.

We find from the master's finding of the express terms of the parties' agreement, from the parties' course of dealing, and from the parties' course of performance, that the parties agreed only as to storage of the goods with Hargo for their mutual benefit. No sale was made until Shabry's offer was accepted by Hargo through notification of intent to use. No such acceptance occurred with respect to the sixteen bales at issue here.

* * *

We therefore hold that, since there was no sale, title to these goods cannot be determined by 2–401 and, since no other provisions of the code apply, the rights of the parties are determined by the law of contracts. *See* 2–102, 1–103.

The master found the parties' stated intentions to be that title to these sixteen bales never passed to Hargo. We therefore hold that title remained in Shabry and that the receiver wrongfully withheld return of the sixteen bales to Shabry.

Exceptions of Shabry Trading Co. sustained.

Risk of Loss:
Seller Not a Merchant

MARTIN v. MELLAND'S INC.

(1979, N.D.) 283 N.W.2d 76.

ERICKSTAD, C. J.

The narrow issue on this appeal is who should bear the loss of a truck and an attached haystack mover that was destroyed by fire while in the possession of the plaintiff, Israel Martin (Martin), but after certificate of title had been delivered to the defendant, Melland's Inc. (Melland's). The destroyed haymoving unit was to be used as a trade-in for a new haymoving unit that Martin ultimately purchased from Melland's. Martin appeals from a district court judgment dated September 28, 1978, that dismissed his action on the merits after it found that at the time of its destruction Martin was the owner of the unit pursuant to Section 41–02–46(2), N.D.C.C. (Section 2–401 U.C.C.). We hold that Section 2–401 is inapplicable to this case, but we affirm the district court judgment on the grounds that risk of loss had not passed to Melland's pursuant to Section 41–02–57, N.D.C.C. (Section 2–509 U.C.C.).

On June 11, 1974, Martin entered into a written agreement with Melland's, a farm implement dealer, to purchase a truck and attached haystack mover for the total purchase price of $35,389. Martin was given a trade-in allowance of $17,389 on his old unit, leaving a balance owing of $18,000 plus sales tax of $720 or a total balance of $18,720. The agreement provided that Martin "mail or bring title" to the old unit to Melland's "this week". Martin mailed the certificate of title to Melland's pursuant to the agreement, but he was allowed to retain the use and possession of the old unit

"until they had the new one ready." The new unit was not expected to be ready for two to three months because it required certain modifications. During this interim period, Melland's performed minor repairs to the trade-in unit on two occasions without charging Martin for the repairs.

Fire destroyed the truck and the haymoving unit in early August, 1974, while Martin was moving hay. The parties did not have any agreement regarding insurance or risk of loss on the unit and Martin's insurance on the trade-in unit had lapsed. Melland's refused Martin's demand for his new unit and Martin brought this suit. The parties subsequently entered into an agreement by which Martin purchased the new unit, but they reserved their rights in any lawsuit arising out of the prior incident.

The district court found "that although the Plaintiff [Martin] executed the title to the . . . [haymoving unit], he did not relinquish possession of the same and therefore the Plaintiff was the owner of said truck at the time the fire occurred pursuant to Section 2–401.

Martin argues that the district court erroneously applied Section 2–401 regarding passage of title, to this case and that Section 2–509, which deals with risk of loss in the absence of breach, should have been applied instead. Martin argues further that title (apparently pursuant to Section 2–401) and risk of loss passed to Melland's and the property was then merely bailed back to Martin who held it as a bailee. Martin submits that this is supported by the fact that Melland's performed minor repairs on the old unit following the passage of title without charging Martin for the repairs. Melland's responds that Section 2–401(2), governs this case and that the district court's determination of the issue should be affirmed.

One of the hallmarks of the pre-Code law of sales was its emphasis on the concept of title. The location of title was used to determine, among other things, risk of loss, insurable interest, place and time for measuring damages, and the applicable law in an interstate transaction. This single title or "lump" title concept proved unsatisfactory because of the different policy considerations involved in each of the situations that title was made to govern. Furthermore, the concept of single title did not reflect modern commercial practices, *i.e.* although the single title concept worked well for "cash-on-the-barrelhead sales", the introduction of deferred payments, security agreements, financing from third parties, or delivery by carrier required a fluid concept of title with bits and pieces held by all parties to the transaction.

Thus the concept of title under the U.C.C. is of decreased importance. The official comment to Section 2–101 U.C.C. provides in part:

The arrangement of the present Article is in terms of contract for sale and the various steps of its performance. The legal consequences are stated as following directly from the contract and action taken under it without resorting to the idea of when property or title passed or was to pass as being the determining factor. The purpose is to avoid making practical issues between practical men turn upon the location of an intangible something, the passing of which no man can prove by evidence and to substitute for such abstractions proof of words and actions of a tangible character."

Section 41–02–46, N.D.C.C. (§ 2–401 U.C.C.), which the district court applied in this case, provides in relevant part:

Each provision of this chapter with regard to the rights, obligations and remedies of the seller, the buyer, purchasers or other third parties applies irrespective of title to the goods except where the provision refers to such title. Insofar as situations are not covered by the other provisions of this chapter and matters concerning title become material the following rules apply . . . ."

Section 41–02–57, N.D.C.C. (§ 2–509 U.C.C.), is an "other provision of this chapter" and is applicable to this case without regard to the location of title. Comment one to Section 2–509 U.C.C. [§ 41–02–57, N.D.C.C.] provides that "the underlying theory of these sections on risk of loss is the adoption of the contractual approach rather than an arbitrary shifting of the risk with the 'property' in the goods."

The position that the Code has taken, divorcing the question of risk of loss from a determination of title, is summed up by Professor Nordstrom in his hornbook on sales:

No longer is the question of title of any importance in determining whether a buyer or seller bears the risk of loss. It is true that the person with title will also (and incidentally) often bear the risk that the goods may be destroyed or lost; but the seller may have title and the buyer the risk, or the seller may have the risk and the buyer the title. In short, title is not a relevant consideration in deciding whether the risk has shifted to the buyer." R. Nordstrom, Handbook of the Law of Sales, 393 (1970).

* * *

Thus, the question in this case is not answered by a determination of the location of title, but by the risk of loss provisions in Section 41–02–57, N.D.C.C. (§ 2–509 U.C.C.). Before addressing the risk of loss question in conjunction with Section 41–02–57, N.D.C.C. (§ 2–509 U.C.C.), it is necessary to determine the posture of the parties with regard to the trade-in unit, *i.e.* who is the buyer and the seller and how are the responsibilities allocated. It is clear that a barter or trade-in is considered a sale and is therefore subject to the Uniform Commercial Code. [Citations.] It is also clear that the party who owns the trade-in is considered the seller. Section 41–02–21, N.D.C.C. (§ 2–304 U.C.C.), provides that the "price can be made payable in money or otherwise. If it is payable in whole or in part in goods each party is a seller of the goods which he is to transfer." [Citations.]

Martin argues that he had already sold the trade-in unit to Melland's and, although he retained possession, he did so in the capacity of a bailee (apparently pursuant to Section 41–02–57(2), N.D.C.C. (§ 2–509(2) U.C.C.)). White and Summers in their hornbook on the Uniform Commercial Code argue that the seller who retains possession should not be considered bailee within Section 2–509.

* * *

The courts that have addressed this issue have agreed with White and Summers. [Citations.]

It is undisputed that the contract did not require or authorize shipment by carrier pursuant to Section [2–509(1)] therefore, the residue section, subsection 3, is applicable:

In any case not within subsection 1 or 2, the risk of loss passes to the buyer on his receipt of the goods if the seller is a merchant; otherwise the risk passes to the buyer on tender of delivery.

Martin admits that he is not a merchant; therefore, it is necessary to determine if Martin tendered delivery of the trade-in unit to Melland's. Tender is defined in Section 41–02–51(1), N.D.C.C. (§ 2–503 U.C.C.), as follows:

41–02–51. (2–503) *Manner of seller's tender of delivery.*—1. Tender of delivery requires that the seller put and hold conforming goods at the buyer's disposition and give the buyer any notification reasonably necessary to enable him to take delivery. The manner, time and place for tender are determined by the agreement and this chapter, and in particular

a. tender must be at a reasonable hour, and if it is of goods they must be kept available for the period reasonably necessary to enable the buyer to take possession; but

b. unless otherwise agreed the buyer must furnish facilities reasonably suited to the receipt of the goods.

It is clear that the trade-in unit was not tendered to Melland's in this case. The parties agreed that Martin would keep the old unit "until they had the new one ready."

* * *

We hold that Martin did not tender delivery of the trade-in truck and haystack mover to Melland's pursuant to Section 41–02–57, N.D.C.C. (§ 2–509 U.C.C.); consequently, Martin must bear the loss.

We affirm the district court judgment.

Risk of Loss: F.O.B. Shipment

NINTH STREET EAST, LTD. v. HARRISON

(1968) 5 Conn.Cir. 597, 259 A.2d 772.

NORTON M. LEVINE, J.

This is an action to recover the purchase price of merchandise sold to defendant by plaintiff. Plaintiff is a manufacturer of men's clothing, with a principal place of business in Los Angeles, California. Defendant is the owner and operator of a men's clothing store, located in Westport, Connecticut, known as "The Rage."

Pursuant to orders received by plaintiff in Los Angeles on November 28, 1966, defendant ordered a variety of clothing items from plaintiff. On November 30, 1966, plaintiff delivered the merchandise in Los Angeles to a common carrier known as Denver-Chicago Trucking Company, Inc., hereinafter called Denver, and received a bill of lading from the trucker. Simultaneously, plaintiff mailed defendant four invoices, all dated November 30, 1966, covering the clothing, in the total sum of $2216. All the invoices bore the notations that the shipment was made "F.O.B. Los Angeles" and "Via Denver-Chicago." Further, all four invoices contained the printed phrase, "Goods Shipped at Purchaser's Risk." Denver's bill of lading disclosed that the shipment was made "collect," to wit, that defendant was obligated to pay the freight charges from Los Angeles to Westport. Denver subsequently transferred the shipment to a connecting carrier known as Old Colony Transportation Company, of South Dartmouth, Massachusetts, hereinafter called

Old Colony, for ultimate delivery at defendant's store in Westport. The delivery was attempted by Old Colony at defendant's store on or about December 12, 1966. A woman in charge of the store, identified as defendant's wife, requested the Old Colony truck driver to deliver the merchandise inside the door of defendant's store. The truck driver refused to do so. The dispute not having been resolved, Old Colony retained possession of the eight cartons comprising the shipment, and the truck thereupon departed from the store premises.

Defendant sent a letter, dated December 12, 1966, and received by plaintiff in Los Angeles on December 20, 1966, reporting the refusal of the truck driver to make the delivery inside defendant's store. This was the first notice to plaintiff of the nondelivery. The letter alleged that defendant needed the merchandise immediately for the holidays but that defendant nevertheless insisted that the merchandise must be delivered inside his store, as a condition of his acceptance. Plaintiff tried to reach defendant by phone, but without success. Similarly, its numerous attempts to locate the shipment were fruitless. Plaintiff filed a claim against Denver for the lost merchandise, but up to the date of trial had not been reimbursed, in whole or in part, by the carrier. Defendant never recovered possession of the merchandise at any time following the original refusal.

The sole special defense pleaded was, "The Plaintiff refused to deliver the merchandise into the Defendant's place of business." Therefore defendant claimed that he is not liable for the subsequent loss or disappearance of the shipment, or the purchase price thereof, and that the risk of loss remained with plaintiff.

* * * The use of the phrase "F.O.B.," meaning free on board, made this portion of the agreement not only a price term covering defendant's obligation to pay freight charges between Los Angeles and Westport but also a controlling factor as to risk of loss of the merchandise upon delivery to Denver and subsequently to Old Colony as the carriers. [Citations.] Title to the goods, and the right to possession, passed to defendant at Los Angeles, the F.O.B. point. [Citations.] Upon delivery to the common carrier at the F.O.B. point, the goods thereafter were at defendant's sole risk. [Citations.] * * *

The arrangements as to shipment were at the option of plaintiff as the seller. § 2–311(1). Plaintiff duly placed the goods in possession of a carrier, to wit, Denver, and made a reasonable contract for their transportation, having in mind the nature of the merchandise and the remaining circumstances. Notice of the shipment, including the F.O.B. provisions, was properly given to defendant, as required by law, pursuant to the four invoices. § 2–504; Uniform Commercial Code § 2–504, comment 5.

The law erects a presumption in favor of construing the agreement as a "shipment" contract, as opposed to a "destination" contract. § 2–503; Uniform Commercial Code § 2–503, comment 5. Under the presumption of a "shipment" contract, plaintiff's liability for loss or damage terminated upon delivery to the carrier at the F.O.B. point, to wit, Los Angeles. * * * A disagreement arose between defendant's wife and the truck driver, resulting in nondelivery of the merchandise, retention thereof by the carrier, and finally, disappearance of the shipment. The ensuing dispute was fundamentally a matter for resolution between defendant and the carriers, as his agents. Nothing in the outcome of that dispute could defeat or impair plaintiff's recovery against defendant.

In view of defendant's wrongful rejection, following the shifting of the risk of loss to him, he is liable to plaintiff for the entire purchase price of the merchandise. Thus, § 2–709 provides in part: "(1) When the buyer fails to pay the price as it becomes due the seller may recover * * * the price (a) * * * of conforming goods lost or damaged within a commercially reasonable time after risk of their loss has passed to the buyer." In Lewis v. Scoville, [citation] the court said: "Refusal by the defendant to receive the goods did not revest title in the plaintiff, and he is * * * entitled to recover the contract price." [Citations.]

The issues are found for plaintiff. Judgment may therefore enter for plaintiff to recover of defendant the sum of $2216, plus taxable costs.

Risk of Loss
on Merchant Seller
Until Buyer Accepts Goods

RAMOS v. WHEEL SPORTS CENTER

(1978) 96 Misc.2d 646, 409 N.Y.S.2d 505.

MERCORELLA, J.

In this non-jury action plaintiff/purchaser is seeking to recover from defendant/vendor the sum of $893, representing the payment made by plaintiff for a motorcycle.

The parties entered into a sales contract wherein defendant agreed to deliver a motorcycle to plaintiff by June 30, 1978, for the agreed price of $893. The motorcycle was subsequently stolen by looters during the infamous power blackout of July 11, 1977.

It is uncontroverted that plaintiff paid for the motorcycle in full; was given the papers necessary for registration and insurance and did in fact register the cycle and secure liability insurance prior to the loss although license plates were never affixed to the vehicle. It is also conceded that the loss occurred without any negligence on defendant's part.

Plaintiff testified that defendant's salesman was informed that plaintiff was leaving on vacation and plaintiff would come for the cycle when he returned. He further testified that he never saw or rode the vehicle. From the evidence adduced at trial it is apparent that plaintiff never exercised dominion or control over the vehicle.

* * *

The sole issue presented to the Court is which party, under the facts disclosed bears the risk of loss?

It is the opinion of this Court that defendant must bear the risk of loss under the provisions of Section 2–509(3) of the Uniform Commercial Code.

This section provides that " . . . the risk of loss passes to the buyer on his receipt of the goods if the seller is a merchant . . . ." Section 2–103(1)(c) states that receipt of goods means taking physical possession of them.

The provision tends more strongly to hold risk of loss on the seller than did the former Uniform Sales Act (1955 Law Revision Commission Report, p. 489). Whether the contract involves delivery at the seller's place of business or at the situs of the goods, a merchant seller cannot transfer risk of loss and it remains on him until actual receipt by the buyer, even though full payment has been made and the buyer notified that the goods are at his disposal. The underlying theory is that a merchant who is to make physical delivery at his own place continues meanwhile to control the goods and can be expected to insure his interest in them [citation].

The Court is also of the opinion that no bailee/bailor relationship, constructive or otherwise, existed between the parties.

Accordingly, let judgment be entered in favor of plaintiff for the sum of $893, together with interest, costs and disbursements.

Document of Title

CAPITOL PACKING CO. v. SMITH

(1967 D.C.Mass.) 270 F.Supp. 36.

WYZANSKI, C. J.

1. Capitol Packing Company, a Colorado corporation, filed a complaint against

(1) Smith and Kirk, citizens of Connecticut and Massachusetts, who are trustees of the property of the New York, New Haven and Hartford Railroad Company, a debtor in reorganization, (2) Mt. Vernon Motor Transportation Co., Inc., a Massachusetts corporation, and (3) Consolidated Packing Co., Inc., another Massachusetts corporation. Thereafter Smith and Kirk, trustees as aforesaid, filed a third-party complaint against The Travelers Indemnity Company, a Connecticut corporation.

2. In the principal action Capitol claimed in count 1 that the trustees of the railroad are liable for the railroad's delivery of Capitol's goods covered by an order bill of lading without receipt of that bill, in count 2 that Mt. Vernon is liable for not having carefully guarded the goods, and in count 3 that Consolidated is liable for the beef which it bought and of which it received delivery.

* * *

October 14 or 15, 1965, Consolidated by telephone agreed to buy from Capitol 235 hind quarters of fresh beef. In accordance with their earlier dealings, the parties impliedly agreed that Capitol would ship the meat on an order-notify bill of lading.
* * *

* * *

October 20, 1965 Capitol shipped 235 fresh beef hinds having a value of $16,414.40 by delivering them to Curtis, Inc., a common carrier by motor vehicle, for it to carry the shipment from Denver to Chicago, and there to transfer it to the Erie-Lackawanna Railroad Company for carriage by it and the N. Y., N. H. & H. R. Co. from Chicago to Boston. Curtis, Inc., placed the 235 hinds in what is called "Curtis Box 907." To cover this shipment in Curtis Box 907, Capitol's agent and an agent acting for both Curtis and E.L.R. Co. executed an order-notify bill of lading upon a uniform domestic order of bill of lading form adopted by car-

riers in Official, Southern, Western and Illinois Classification territories.

On its face the bill recited that "The surrender of this Original ORDER Bill of Lading properly indorsed shall be required before the delivery of the property." That bill names Curtis, Inc. and Erie-Lackawanna as the receiving parties, and Capitol as shipper and as consignee. The bill then recites that the destination is "Boston", that the carrier is to "Notify Consolidated Packing Co."; that the "Route" is "CURTIS TO CHICAGO, EL NY NH–H TOFC PLAN 2½% MT. VERNON TRANS."; and that the freight is "to be prepaid."

* * *

In accordance with the aforesaid agreement, bond, and rider, the N. Y., N. H. & H. R. Co. shortly after 6 A.M. on Tuesday, November 2, 1965 made delivery of the shipment of 235 hinds contained in Curtis Box 907 to Ernest R. Miller, a driver of a Mt. Vernon truck, acting as agent for Consolidated. At the time he accepted delivery, Miller did not have or surrender to the railroad the order-notify bill of lading covering those 235 hinds.

Miller trucked Curtis Box 907 to the side of a platform at 132 Newmarket Square. This platform ran in front of several adjoining places of business, called "bays", leased by different enterprises. At about 6:30 P.M. Miller deposited Box 907 at a place less than 50 feet from the entrance to the premises or bay leased by Consolidated, and as close as was then practical.

Almost simultaneously, Sampson, another Mr. Vernon employee who was not only a truck driver but also Miller's foreman, arrived at 132 Newmarket Square. He was trucking a shipment that came in "Curtis Box 508", pursuant to a sale and a bill of lading which are not relevant to this case.

At about 7 A.M., Sampson informed Harold Stone, who was the treasurer of Consolidated and authorized to act for it in connection with the receipt of merchandise, that "Both your trailers are here." Stone acknowledged this message by stating "That's good." Stone having acknowledged the presence of the trailer, in effect acknowledged the delivery of the contents of Box 907. * * *

Stone forgetting about Curtis 907, which remained loaded with beef in an unguarded place in front of the platform, left Consolidated's premises at 9 P.M. on November 2. During the night, Curtis 907 was taken, presumably by thieves. Since the putative larceny, the hinds have not been recovered.

Consolidated never paid the draft which Capitol made upon it, nor did it otherwise pay for the 235 hinds of beef. Capitol received back from its bank the order-notify bill of lading and has never received payment for the 235 hinds of beef. November 22, 1965 Capitol made written demand upon the N. Y., N. H. & H. R. Co. for $16,414.40, as the value of the shipment covered by the bill of lading. This demand was timely. * * *

The foregoing findings of fact and conclusions of law can be summarized in three paragraphs.

(a) Capitol agreed to sell to Consolidated 235 hinds, Capitol to pay the freight from Denver to Boston ramp of the N. Y., N. H. & H. R. Co., and Consolidated to use its own agent, Mt. Vernon as its contract carrier to pick up the shipment at the Boston ramp. Pursuant to the agreement, Capitol shipped the hinds on an order-notify bill of lading, under which the last common carrier was the N. Y., N. H. & H. R. Co. When the shipment reached its Boston ramp, the railroad notified Consolidated which sent to the Boston ramp its agent Mt. Vernon to accept delivery. The railroad made delivery to Consolidated's agent Mt. Vernon without receiving the order-notify bill of lading. Mt. Vernon in turn delivered the beef to its principal, Consolidated. Then the beef was stolen. Capitol has not been paid for the beef. It has the bill of lading.

(b) Consolidated as principal and The Travelers Indemnity Company as surety had executed a bond to the N. Y., N. H. & H. R. Co. as obligee agreeing to hold the railroad harmless for the railroad's liability for delivering shipments to Consolidated without surrender of the covering bills of lading.

(c) On the basis of these facts Consolidated is liable to Capitol for goods sold and delivered; the N. Y., N. H. & H. R. Co. trustees are liable to Capitol [citation]; and the trustees are entitled to indemnification from Travelers. Mt. Vernon is not liable to Capitol.

Problems

1. A who had 100 bushel baskets of peaches in his fruit shed offered to sell them to B for $6.00 per bushel. B accepted the offer. At this time the peaches were fully packed and in the baskets. At the end of the day upon which A had received B's acceptance of his offer, A placed 50 of the baskets of peaches on a wagon which was standing inside the shed. During the night the fruit shed accidentally caught fire. A rushed to the scene and was able to pull the loaded wagon out of the burning shed and save the 50 baskets which were on the wagon but was unable to save the other 50 baskets which were destroyed with the shed. What are the rights of the parties?

2. Stein, a mechanic, and Beal, a life insurance agent, entered into a written contract for the sale of Stein's tractor to Beal for $750 cash. It was agreed that stein would tune the motor on the tractor. Stein fulfilled this obligation and on the night of July 1 telephoned Beal that the tractor was ready to be picked up on making payment. Beal responded, "I'll be there in the morning with the money." On the next morning, however, Beal was approached by an insurance prospect and decided to get the tractor at a later date. On the night of July 2, the tractor was destroyed by fire of unknown origin. Neither Stein nor Beal had any fire insurance. Who must bear the loss?

3. Regan received a letter from Chase, the material portion of which stated: "Chase hereby places an order with you for 50 cases of Red Top Tomatoes, Ship them C.O.D." Promptly upon receipt of the letter Regan shipped the tomatoes to Chase. While en route, the railroad car carrying the tomatoes was wrecked. Upon Chase's refusal to pay for the tomatoes, Regan commenced an action to recover the purchase price. Chase defended on the ground that as the shipment was C.O.D., neither title to the tomatoes nor risk of loss passed until their delivery to Chase. Decision?

4. On May 10, the A Company, acting through one Brown, entered into a contract with C for the installation of a milking machine at C's farm. Following the enumeration of the articles to be furnished, together with the price of each article, the written contract provided: "This outfit is subject to thirty days' free trial and is to be installed about June 1." Within thirty days after installation, the entire outfit, excepting the double utility unit, was destroyed by fire through no fault of C. The A Company sued C to recover the value of the articles destroyed. Decision?

5. A contracted to buy sixty cases of X Brand canned corn from B at a contract price of $600. Pursuant to the contract, B selected and set aside sixty cases of X Brand canned corn and tagged them "For A." The contract required B to ship the corn to A via T Railroad, F.O.B. Toledo. Before B delivered the corn to the railroad, the sixty cases were stolen from B's warehouse.

(a) Who is liable for the loss of the sixty cases of corn, A or B?
(b) Suppose B had delivered the corn to the railroad in Toledo. After the corn has been loaded on a freight car, but before the train left the yard, the car was broken open and its contents, including the corn, stolen. As between A and B, who is liable for the loss?
(c) Would your answer in question (b) be the same if this were a F.O.B. A's warehouse contract, all other facts remaining the same?

6. A, in Chicago, pursuant to a contract with B in New York, ships to B goods conforming to the contract, and takes from the carrier a shipper's order bill of lading which A indorses in blank and forwards by mail to C, his agent in New York, with instructions to deliver the bill of lading to B upon receipt of payment of the price for the goods. X, a thief, steals the bill of lading from C and transfers it for value to Y, a bona fide purchaser. Before the goods arrive in New York, B is petitioned into bankruptcy. What are the rights of the parties?

7. A owned a quantity of corn which was contained in a corn crib located on A's farm. On March 12, A wrote a letter to B stating that he would sell to B all of the corn in this crib, which he estimated at between 900 and 1000 bushels, for $2.60 per bushel. B received this letter on March 13, and immediately wrote and mailed on the same day a letter to A stating that he would buy the corn. The corn crib and contents were accidentally destroyed by fire which broke out about 3 o'clock a.m. on March 14. What are the rights of the parties? What difference, if any, in result if A is a merchant?

8. A, a New York dealer, purchased 25 barrels of specially graded and packed apples from a producer at Hood River, Oregon. These apples he afterwards resold to B under a contract which specified an agreed price on delivery at B's place of business in New York. The apples were shipped to A from Oregon but, through no fault of either A or B, were totally destroyed before reaching New York. Is there any liability resting upon A?

9. A, a New York merchant, purchased merchandise from B in Chicago. The contract of sale provided that the merchandise was sold f. o. b., Chicago, payment to be made 60 days after delivery. B delivered the goods to the railroad carrier in Chicago, took an order bill of lading in the name of A and forwarded it to A. Before the goods arrived at New York, B learned that A had become insolvent, and exercised a right of stoppage in transit by proper notice to the railroad company. Thereafter, and before the shipment reached New York, A indorsed and delivered the bill of lading to C, an innocent purchaser for value. C claimed the goods by reason of holding the bill of lading. To whom should the goods be awarded?

SALE OF GOODS BY NON-OWNER

Most sales of goods are accomplished by duly authorized agents of dealers in goods, such as merchants, chain stores, department stores, corporations, and other business enterprises which employ sales personnel. The salesmen are non-owners of the goods which they sell but act under the instruction and authority of the owner of the goods. This chapter does not deal with such sales, but deals with sales of goods which are not authorized by their owner, nor made by an agent of the owner for the benefit of the owner. It also considers sales of goods in bulk which comprise the entire inventory of a going concern in business which has trade creditors, and the necessity of complying with the provisions of Article 6 of the Code, Bulk Transfers

SALE OF GOODS WITHOUT CONSENT OF THE OWNER

Two Competing Policies of the Law

The venerable rule of property law protecting existing ownership of goods is the start-

ing point and background in any discussion of a sale of goods by a non-owner. It is elementary that a purchaser of goods obtains such title as his transferor had or had power to transfer, and the Code expressly so states. Section 2–403. Likewise, the purchaser of a limited interest in goods acquires rights only to the extent of the interest which he purchased. By the same token, no one can transfer what he does not have. A purported sale by a thief, or finder, or ordinary bailee of goods does not transfer title to the purchaser, even to a bona fide purchaser for value without notice or knowledge of lack of title in the transferor.

The reasons underlying the policy of the law in protecting existing ownership of goods are obvious. A person should not be required to retain possession or control at all times of all the goods that he owns in order to maintain his ownership of them. One of the valuable incidents of ownership of goods is the freedom of the owner to make a bailment of his goods as he pleases, and the mere possession of goods by a bailee does not establish any authority of the bailee to sell them.

A policy of the law in competition with that which protects existing ownership is protection of the good faith purchaser based upon the needs of trade and commerce in protecting the security of good faith transactions in goods. To encourage and make secure good faith acquisitions of goods it is necessary that bona fide purchasers for value under certain circumstances be protected. For example, an entrusting by the owner of his goods to a merchant who deals in goods of that type is a bailment which is peculiarly dangerous to bona fide purchasers from the merchant. In such case the Code protects the bona fide purchaser, and the rights of the owner are defeated. Section 2–403(2).

The problems presented in this portion of the chapter and the rules for their solution should be considered in the light of these two competing policies of the law. Both policies are sound, salutary, and worthy of enforcement. One protects existing property rights; the other protects the stability of good faith transactions in the market place. In the area of sales of goods by a non-owner, these policies come into conflict. In every such conflict only one may prevail. As between innocent parties, the law must either protect existing ownership and defeat the interests of bona fide purchasers for value, or vice versa.

The rules discussed herein apply only to transactions in goods, not in other kinds of property such as money, and bearer form or properly endorsed negotiable commercial paper, negotiable documents of title, or investment securities. Such items are intended to circulate freely in the market place, and other specialized rules of law apply to them. Code Article 3—Commercial Paper; Article 7—Documents of Title; Article 8—Investment Securities.

Void and Voidable Title to Goods

Common Law. A void title is no title. A person claiming ownership of goods by virtue of a bill of sale bearing the forged signature of the true owner has a void title. A thief or a finder of goods has no title to them, and can transfer none. Where a thief or a finder delivers the goods to a carrier or warehouseman and receives a negotiable document of title which he subsequently indorses and delivers to a bona fide purchaser for value, the bona fide purchaser of the document acquires no title to the goods. Section 7–503.

A voidable title is one acquired under circumstances which permit the former owner to rescind the transfer and re-vest himself with title. The title of a buyer may be subject to rescission by the seller, as in a case of mistake, duress, undue influence, fraud in the inducement, or sale by a person without contractual capacity. In these situations, the buyer has acquired legal title to the goods of which he may be divested by action taken by the seller. If, before the seller has rescinded the transfer of title, the buyer should resell the goods to a bona fide purchaser for value and without notice of any infirmity in his title, the equity of rescission in the seller is cut off, and the bona fide purchaser acquires good title.

The distinction between a void and voidable title is extremely important in determining the rights of bona fide purchasers of goods. The bona fide purchaser always believes tht he is buying the goods from the owner or from one with authority to sell. Otherwise he would not be acting in good faith. In each situation the party selling the goods appears to be the owner whether his title is valid, void, or voidable. As between two innocent persons, the true owner who has done nothing wrong and the bona fide purchaser who has done nothing wrong, the law will not disturb the legal title but will rule in favor of the one who has it. Thus, where A transfers possession of goods to B under such circumstances that B acquires no title or a void title, and B thereafter sells the goods to C, a bona fide purchaser for value, B has nothing except possession to transfer to C.   In a lawsuit between A and C involving the right to the goods, A will win because he has the legal title.   However, if B acquired a voidable title from A and resold the goods to C, in a suit between A and C over the goods, C would win.   In this case, B had title, although it was voidable, which he transferred to the bona fide purchaser.   The title thus acquired by C will be protected.   The voidable title in B is title until it has been avoided.   After transfer to a bona fide purchaser, it may not be avoided.

The common law permitted an infant seller of goods to disaffirm the contract and the sale, and to recover the goods from a third person who had purchased them in good faith and for value from the immediate vendee of the infant.   Thus, A, a minor, sells certain goods to B who in turn resells them to C, a bona fide purchaser for value.   Upon disaffirmance, A may recover the goods from C.

Uniform Commercial Code.   The Code enlarges the rights of bona fide purchasers of goods by changing the common law rule.   The fraudulent buyer or a purchaser at a "cash sale" is in the position of one having voidable title and such person under the Code has the "power to transfer a good title to a good faith purchaser for value."   Section 2–403(1) provides that when goods have been delivered under a transaction of purchase, the purchaser has such power even though:

(a) the transferor was deceived as to the identity of the purchaser, or
(b) the delivery was in exchange for a check which is later dishonored, or
(c) it was agreed that the transaction was to be a "cash sale," or
(d) the delivery was procured through fraud punishable as larcenous under the criminal law.

A "good faith purchaser for value" is one who acts honestly in taking the goods by way of sale, discount, negotiation, pledge, lien or other voluntary transaction creating an interest in the property (Section 1–201(32)); who takes without notice or knowledge of any defect or infirmity in the title of his transferor; and who gives value.

"Value" is defined to include (1) purchases in return for a binding commitment to extend credit; (2) taking the goods as security for or in total or partial satisfaction of a pre-existing claim; (3) accepting delivery under a pre-existing purchase contract; and (4) generally, any consideration sufficient to support a simple contract. Section 1–201(44).

The Code does not permit the minor seller to prevail over the bona fide purchaser for value, as the vendee of the minor acquired a voidable title which he had power to transfer to the bona fide purchaser. Section 2–403.

Entrusting of Goods

Entrusting Possession to a Merchant.   The Code establishes a broad rule protecting good faith acquisitions of goods in the ordinary course of business from merchants who deal in goods of that kind, where the owner has entrusted possession of the goods to the merchant.   Section 2–403(2) provides:

Any entrusting of possession of goods to a merchant who deals in goods of that kind gives him power to transfer all rights of the entruster to a buyer in ordinary course of business.

This section does not go so far as to protect the bona fide purchaser from a merchant to whom the goods have been entrusted by a thief or finder, or by a completely unauthorized person.   It merely grants the good faith buyer in the ordinary course of business the rights of the entruster.

The Code defines "buyer in ordinary course of business" as "a person who in good faith and without knowledge that the sale to him is in violation of the ownership rights or security interest of a third party in the goods buys in ordinary course from a person in the business of selling goods of that kind but does not include a pawnbroker." Section 1–201(9).

Sales by a Merchant Seller in Possession of Goods Already Sold. Where the buyer of goods to whom title has passed leaves the seller in possession of the goods the buyer has "entrusted the goods" with the seller. It makes no difference whether the buyer has paid the seller the price of the goods, if the seller is a merchant who resells and delivers the goods to a bona fide purchaser for value, this second buyer acquires good title to the goods. The Code defines "entrusting" as including "any acquiescence in retention of possession." Section 2–403(3).

The rule applies to a third purchaser of the goods where the first and second buyers have each left the seller in possession. Thus, A sells certain goods to B who pays the price but allows possession to remain with A. A thereafter sells the same goods to C who pays the price and also leaves possession with A. A then sells the goods to D, a bona fide purchaser for value without notice of the prior sales to B and C. D takes delivery of the goods. Neither B nor C have any rights against D or to the goods.

Rights of Seller's Creditors against Goods Sold. The Code treats more favorably the rights of bona fide purchasers under Section 2–403 than the rights of attaching creditors under Section 2–402 which deals with the rights of creditors of the seller in goods sold but left in the possession of the seller. Section 2–402(2) provides:

A creditor of the seller may treat a sale or an identification of goods to a contract for sale as void if as against him a retention of possession by the seller is fraudulent under any rule of law of the state where the goods are situated, except

that retention of possession in good faith and current course of trade by a merchant-seller for a commercially reasonable time after a sale or identification is not fraudulent.

The facility with which a debtor in embarrassed or failing financial circumstances may transfer title to his property to a friend or favored person in order to defraud his creditors by trying to place the property beyond their reach has led every State to enact a Fraudulent Conveyance statute based upon the early English statute of 13 Eliz.c. 5. The early statutes provided that the retention of possession by the seller made the transfer fraudulent and void as to his creditors. The creditors, therefore, could proceed to attach and levy upon the goods as if no transfer had occurred.

It is the purpose of the Code not to change the local law as to the rights of creditors with respect to goods sold but left in the possession of the seller. The statutes in the various States contain different provisions regarding the fraudulent effect of retention of possession by the seller or a transfer of both title and possession with intent to defraud, and each State has well-settled rules on this subject embodied in its court decisions. Each case involves questions of fact such as, whether the transfer was for value or gratuitous, the good faith of the transferor and his financial circumstances, the intent of the transferee and his knowledge of the circumstances and of the intent of the transferor, and the standing of the particular creditor seeking to set aside the transfer.

In some States, retention of possession by the transferor is merely evidence to be considered by the court with all of the other evidence, and does not give rise to a presumption of fraud. In other States, the courts hold that retention of possession is presumptively fraudulent, that is, *prima facie* evidence of fraud which may be rebutted by other evidence tending to show that the transfer was for value and in good faith. A third rule enforced in other States is that retention of possession by the seller creates a conclusive presumption of fraud. A presumption which is conclusive is not rebuttable by any amount or any quality of evidence to the contrary. These various rules of local State law are not changed by the Code.

Estoppel of the Owner

The principle of estoppel is applied to the situation where the owner of certain goods by words or conduct represents that a person in possession of the goods is the owner, and a third party in reliance therein and in good faith purchases the goods for value from the possessor. The owner of the goods is precluded by his conduct from denying the possessor's authority to sell.

The owner of goods may entrust their possession, together with some evidence or indicia of title, to a person which will enable him to transfer title to a bona fide purchaser. Thus, where an owner of grain permits his agent to store the grain in an elevator in the name of the agent, and the books and records of the elevator company show apparent ownership in the agent, a bona fide purchaser from the agent relying upon this indicia of title will be protected.

Similarly, the owner of an automobile who permits registration or the issuance of a certificate of title in the name of another, provides such person with indicia of title, and a bona fide purchaser acting in reliance thereon will be protected. The owner of a wagon who permits his employee to paint his name thereon and to use it publicly has provided the employee with indicia of ownership. However, if a thief should steal the wagon, and repaint it with only the name of the thief appearing thereon, a bona fide purchaser from the thief, although deceived by such indicia of ownership, would not be protected. The thief was not clothed by the owner with indicia of ownership, and no estoppel would apply.

SALES OF GOODS IN BULK

In order to protect the creditors of dealers and merchants who sell all or the major part of their merchandise or inventory in bulk and not in the usual and ordinary course of business, every State has a statute which makes such sales or transfers in bulk invalid against creditors of the transferor unless certain procedures are followed and the creditors are duly notified in advance of the proposed sale or transfer. The danger to creditors is that the debtor may secretly liquidate all or a major part of his tangible assets by a bulk sale not in the ordinary course of business and conceal or divert the proceeds of the sale without paying his creditors.

Article 6 of the Code relates to such sales and defines a bulk transfer as "any transfer in bulk and not in the ordinary course of the transferor's business of a major part of the materials, supplies, merchandise, or other inventory (Section 9–109) of an enterprise subject to this Article." The transfer of a substantial part of equipment is a bulk transfer only if made in connection with a bulk transfer of inventory. The enterprises subject to Article 6 of the Code are those whose principal business is the sale of merchandise from stock, including those who manufacture what they sell. Section 6–102.

Requirements of Article 6

The Code provides that a bulk transfer of assets is ineffective against any creditor of the transferor, unless four requirements are met, namely:

(a) The transferor furnishes to the transferee a sworn list of his existing creditors, including those whose claims are disputed, stating names, business addresses, and amounts due and owing when known. Section 6–104(1)(a).

(b) The transferor and transferee prepare a schedule or list of the property being transferred, sufficient to identify it. Section 6–104(1)(b).

(c) The transferee preserve the list of creditors and schedule of property for six months and permit inspection thereof by any creditor of the transferor, or file the list and schedule in a designated public office; (Section 6–104(1)(c)), and

(d) Notice of the proposed transfer in bulk be given by the transferee to each creditor of the transferor at least 10 days before the transferee takes possession of the goods or makes payment for them, whichever happens first. Section 6–105.

If all of the above steps are taken, the transfer in bulk complies with the statute and the transferee acquires the goods free of all claims of creditors of the transferor. The transferor is responsible for the completeness and accuracy of the sworn list of his creditors. Errors or omissions in this list do not impair the validity of the bulk transfer unless the transferee has knowledge of such errors or omissions. Section 6–104(3).

Contents of Notice to Creditors

The Code requires that the notice from the buyer in bulk to the creditors of the transferor in bulk shall contain specific information: (1) that a bulk transfer is about to be made; (2) the names and business addresses of the seller in bulk and buyer in bulk; (3) whether all debts of the seller in bulk are to be paid in full as a result of the transaction and if so the address to which creditors should send their bills. Section 6–107(1).

If the debts of the seller in bulk are not to be paid in full as they fall due, the notice to creditors shall also state:

(a) The location and general description of the property to be transferred;

(b) The estimated total debts of the seller in bulk;

(c) The address where the schedule of property and list of creditors may be inspected;

(d) Whether the transfer is to pay existing debts and if so, the amount of such debts and to whom owing;

(e) Whether the transfer is for new consideration and if so the amount of such consideration and the time and place of payment, and

(f) If the transfer is for new consideration, the time and place where creditors of the seller in bulk are to file their claims. Section 6–107(2).

If the debts of the transferor are to be paid in full as they fall due, only a short form of notice to creditors is required as provided in Section 6–107(1).

Exempted Bulk Transfers

Certain transfers in bulk are exempt and need not comply with Article 6 of the Code, such as:

(a) Transfers by way of security;

(b) General assignments for the benefit of the creditors of the seller in bulk;

(c) Transfers in settlement or realization of a lien or security interest;

(d) Sales by executors, administrators, receivers, trustees in bankruptcy or any public officer under judicial process;

(e) Sales in the course of proceedings for the dissolution or reorganization of a corporation in a court proceeding where notice is given to creditors;

(f) Transfers to a person who maintains a known place of business in the State who agrees to become bound to pay in full the debts of the seller in bulk, gives public notice of that fact, and who is solvent after becoming so bound;

(g) Transfers to a new business enterprise organized to take over and continue the business of the seller in bulk, where public notice is given, the new enterprise assumes the debts of the seller in bulk who receives nothing from the transaction except an interest in the new enterprise which is junior to the claims of creditors; and

(h) Transfers of property which is exempt from execution under exemption statutes. Section 6–103.

Effect of Failure to Comply with Article 6

The effect of a failure to comply with the requirements of Article 6 of the Code is that the goods in the possession of the transferee continue to be subject to the claims of unpaid creditors of the transferor. These creditors may proceed against the goods by levy or attachment and by sheriff's sale, or by causing the involuntary bankruptcy of the transferor and the appointment of a trustee in bankruptcy to take over the goods from the transferee.

Where the title of the transferee is subject to the defect of non-compliance with the Code, a bona fide purchaser of the goods from the transferee who pays value in good faith and takes the property without notice of such defect acquires the goods free of any claim of creditors of the transferor. A purchaser of the property from the transferee who pays no value or who takes with notice of non-compliance with the Code acquires the goods subject to the claims of creditors of the transferor.

Optional Provisions of Article 6

In the case of bulk transfers for which new consideration is payable, except those made at auction sales, the Code imposes in optional Section 6–106 a personal duty upon the transferee to apply the new consideration to the payment of the debts of the transferor, and if it is insufficient to pay them in full, to make distribution to creditors pro rata.

In Code States which do not adopt optional subsection (4) of Section 6–106, there is no duty on the transferee owing to the creditors of the transferor. In the event of noncompliance with the Code, except for sales at auction, the creditors merely proceed to enforce their claims against the property transferred as though it belonged to the transferor. This is what is meant by the language of the Code that the bulk transfer "is ineffective against any creditor of the transferor." The transferee loses the property but does not assume any obligation to pay the debts of the transferor.

Optional subsection (4) of Section 6–106 provides that the transferee may discharge his duty to pay the creditors of the transferor out of the proceeds by payment of the consideration into court within 10 days after taking possession of the goods, and by giving notice to all of the creditors that such payment has been made and that they should file their claims with the court.

Auction Sales

The Code has special provisions with respect to auction sales of goods which represent a transfer in bulk not in the ordinary course of the transferor's business where the goods offered for sale are a major part of the materials, supplies, merchandise, or inventory used in the business. In such an auction sale Section 6–108 requires that:

(a) The transferor furnish the auctioneer a sworn list of his creditors and assist in the preparation of a schedule of the property to be sold.

(b) The auctioneer receive and retain the list of creditors and schedule of property for six months and permit inspection thereof by any creditor.

(c) The auctioneer give notice by registered or certified mail at least 10 days before the auction to all creditors named in the list as well as all other persons known to him to have any claims against the transferor.

(d) The auctioneer apply the net proceeds of the auction sale to payment of all debts of the transferor as provided in Section 6–106.

A failure of the auctioneer to perform his duties does not affect the validity of the sale or the title of the purchasers of the goods at the auction sale. The auctioneer is personally liable to creditors of the transferor as a class to the extent of the net proceeds of the auction.

Cases

Void Title

MARVIN v. CONNELLY

(1979) ____ S.C. ____, 252 S.E.2d 562.

RHODES, J.

Respondent, J. T. Marvin, instituted this action, based on breach of warranty of title and misrepresentation of material facts, to recover the price of a refrigeration trailer which he had purchased from the appellant, Connelly. The lower court resolved the issue favorably to respondent. We affirm.

The primary question to be determined is whether appellant breached an implied warranty of title by selling respondent a trailer which, unknown to both parties, had been stolen from its rightful owner.

The undisputed facts reveal that appellant originally obtained possession of the trailer when an unknown individual employed him to make certain repairs on it. After the repairs were made, the vehicle remained unclaimed. In order to satisfy his mechanic's lien for repairs and storage, the appellant brought a foreclosure action in the magistrate's court. At the magistrate's sale on April 7, 1972, appellant was the successful bidder and consummated the purchase. On April 10, 1972, respondent purchased the trailer from appellant for $6,045.52.

It is established that the vehicle was stolen from its rightful owner at some point prior to appellant's original possession of it. This fact, however, was admittedly unknown to both parties until September 14, 1973, at which time the trailer was attached by Northland Insurance Company, which, upon payment of the theft claim to the rightful owner, had been assigned the true title.

Relying upon U.C.C. § 36–2–403(1), appellant initially asserts that he acquired at least a voidable title from the judicial sale which would have ripened into an indefeasible title after sale to respondent. We disagree.

Section 36–2–403(1) states the basic common law rule that a purchaser acquires all of the interest of his transferor. This U.C.C. section also recognizes that a person with voidable title has power to transfer a good title to a good faith purchaser for value. The concept of "voidable title", however, turns on whether the original owner assented to the transfer. *See* § 36–2–403, S.C. Reporter's Comments. As such, the section was intended to cover such factual situations as involve the severance of property from a rightful owner who intended to sell, as where there has been a fraudulent impersonation of the purchaser of the property [§ 36–2–403(1)(a)]; or a fraudulent check is given for the purchase price of the property [§ 36–2–403(1)(b)]; or when the sale is induced by fraudulent misrepresentation [§ 36–2–403(1)(d)]. Since the record is devoid of any evidence showing assent by the rightful owner, the appellant failed to show that he purchased the trailer under any of the circumstances contemplated and can not take refuge under the theory of "voidable title". Therefore, the appellant purchased only the title rights belonging to his predecessor, the thief, thereby obtaining no title.

This conclusion is also supported by the common law principle that a person can pass to his successor no greater title than he acquired and, therefore, a thief or even one in the subsequent chain of title cannot grant good title to stolen property even to a bona fide purchaser. *Sun Ins. Office v. Foil,* 187 S.C. 183, 197 S.E. 683 (1938). *See also* 67 Am.Jur.2d, Sales § 257 (1973). Annot. 71 A.L.R.2d 221 (1960). The law in our state is well settled that where property is sold at a judicial sale, there is no warranty of title flowing to the purchaser and he buys only the interest which the debtor, or in this case, the thief, had in the property. *Gulf Refining Co. v. Mc-Candless,* 118 S.C. 6, 109 S.E. 801 (1921). *Long v. McKissick,* 50 S.C. 218, 27 S.E. 636 (1897).

* * *

AFFIRMED.

Voidable Title: Estoppel

UNITED ROAD MACHINERY CO. v. JASPER
(1978, Ky. App.) 568 S.W.2d 242.

WHITE, J.

Appellant seeks reversal of a Laurel Circuit Court order dismissing the complaint against appellees Ethard Jasper individually and d/b/a Jasper Wrecking or Junk Yard, Jasper & Jasper Coal Co., Inc. and Clyde Jasper. * * *

Appellant United Road Machinery Co. is a dealer in heavy road equipment, including truck scales, with its principal place of business in Memphis, Tennessee. Its supplier for such truck scales is Thurman Scale Company in Columbus, Ohio. Appellant received a phone call on July 21, 1975, from James R. Durham, an officer of Consolidated Coal Co., seeking acquisition of truck scales for his coal-mining operation. A lease-purchase agreement was entered into by the parties at this time providing for monthly payments of $608 over a 24-month period with an option to purchase for one dollar consideration, exercisable at the termination of the lease. * * *

Appellant subsequently notified its supplier, Thurman Scale Company, that Consolidated Coal would take possession of the scales from the supplier. Appellant paid for the machinery at that time. On July 28, 1975, Consolidated Coal obtained the scales without signing a contract with appellant at that time; rather, the contract papers were forwarded to Consolidated by appellant but never returned. The scales were taken to Consolidated's place of business in Laurel County where decking was added, increasing the value of the scales to approximately $16,000. Appellant has never received any consideration, either in rental payments or purchase price, on this equipment.

On September 20, 1975, Consolidated Coal, through its agent and officer J. R. Durham, sold the truck scales to Kentucky Mobile Homes, whose president is Ethard Jasper, for a purchase price of $8,500. Before purchase, Ethard Jasper checked Laurel and Pulaski County records for any possible lien, mortgage or other encumbrance on the property. Such search revealed no encumbrance of any kind. Ethard Jasper contends that Consolidated Coal appeared to have good title to the scales and he further denies any knowledge of the dispute between appellant and Consolidated Coal.

On September 22, 1975, Kentucky Mobile Homes sold the truck scales to Clyde Jasper, individually, for $8,500 in cash. Before purchasing the equipment, Clyde Jasper also conducted a search of Laurel and Pulaski County records, which revealed no evidence of any lien, mortgage or encumbrance on said machinery. Clyde Jasper also denies any knowledge of the dispute between appellant and Consolidated Coal Company or appellant and Kentucky Mobile Homes. The scales are presently in the possession of Clyde Jasper. * * *

Three possible situations exist under which appellees received possession of the scales, any one and/or all three of the possibilities conferring good title in appellees.

The first possibility is that Consolidated Coal Company had good title to the truck scales. Under both Common Law and the Uniform Commercial Code, a purchaser acquires all title the seller had or, if a limited interest is transferred, all title to the extent of that interest. [U.C.C. 2–403(1)]. Thus if Consolidated Coal possessed good title to the truck scales, appellees in turn gained good title upon transfer.

The second possibility occurs if Consolidated Coal had voidable title. [U.C.C.] 2–403(1) provides: "A person with voidable title has power to transfer a good title to a good faith purchaser for value." Assuming that Consolidated Coal had voidable title, appellees, to obtain good title, must be found to be good faith purchasers for value. [U.C.C.] 1–201(19) defines "good faith" as ". . . honesty in fact in the conduct or transaction concerned." "Purchaser" is defined as ". . . a person who takes by purchase." [U.C.C.] 1–201(33). "Purchase" in turn ". . . includes taking by sale, discount, negotiation, mortgage, pledge, lien, issue or reissue, gift or any other voluntary transaction creating an interest in property." [U.C.C.] 1–201(32). Lastly, ". . . a person gives 'value' for rights if he acquires them (d) generally, in return for any consideration sufficient to support a simple contract." [U.C.C.] 1–201(44)(d). As the circuit court aptly put it: "A 'good faith purchaser for value' can be defined as one who takes by purchase getting sufficient consideration to support a simple contract, and who is honest in the transaction of the purchase." It is the opinion of this court that appellees meet this criteria.

Concerning voidable title, [U.C.C.] 2–403(1) goes on to state that good title may be transferred under certain circumstances:

When goods have been delivered under a transaction of purchase the purchaser has such power even though (a) the tranferor was deceived as to the identity of the purchaser, or (b) the delivery was in exchange for a check which is later dishonored, or (c) it was agreed that the transaction was to be a "cash sale," or (d) the delivery was procured through fraud punishable as larcenous under the criminal law.

Assuming that Consolidated Coal's actions toward appellant fall within one of the four enumerated circumstances, a "transaction of purchase" is still requisite before the statute becomes operative allowing transfer of good title. Appellant argues that no transaction of purchase occurred, that the agreement between appellant and Consolidated Coal was not a purchase transaction but merely a lease, and that the law concerning landlord-tenant, and not the Uniform Commercial Code, governs. Therefore the concept of voidable title has no application in this case.

This court feels there was a "transaction of purchase" per the code definition (see above). "The purpose, rather than the name given a contract by the parties controls, and the court will give effect to the real and dominant intention of the parties when definitely ascertained." *Trinity Temple Charities, Inc. v. City of Louisville*, 300 Ky. 172, 188 S.W.2d 91, 94 (1945).

Even if Consolidated Coal Company had no title in the truck scales to convey, this court finds appellant estopped from asserting his proper title against the appellees as bona fide purchaser. The Common Law rule generally allowed a purchaser to obtain that title possessed by the seller and ". . . one who had no title could convey none." 67 Am.Jur.2d *Sales* § 259, at 394. Exceptions to the general rule were shaped by equity courts and under certain circumstances the true owner of the property was estopped from asserting title. The doctrine of estoppel was applied to circumstances where the seller possessed indicia of ownership sufficient to indicate to the purchaser that he had power to convey.

And it has been stated that no buyer was bound to assume that the seller with whom he dealt was a wrongdoer, and if the seller presented property the title to which was apparently valid and there were no circumstances disclosed which cast suspicion upon the title, the buyer might rightfully deal with him, and, paying full value of the same, acquire the rights of a purchaser in good faith. *Id.* at 395.

In the present case, there was nothing to suggest that Consolidated Coal was not the owner of the scales. J. R. Durham in fact held himself out to be such owner. Furthermore, a search of county records revealed no encumbrances upon the machinery, and appellees had no knowledge of or reason to suspect a dispute between appellant and Consolidated Coal. [U.C.C.] 1–201(37); [U.C.C.] 9–102(1)(a). Under these circumstances, appellees are found to be bona fide purchasers in good faith.

Bona fide purchasers are favorites of the law, and they should only be required to pay for another's negligence or mistake when the circumstances are so unusual as to justify a finding that they took unfair advantage of a transaction initiated by the complaining party.

It is unfortunate that [appellant was] defrauded. It is inequitable to require a blameless third party to pay for their mistake. Both parties being innocent, the loss must be borne by the party whose initial conduct puts it in the power of another to cause the loss. *Dudly v. Lovins,* 310 Ky. 491, 220 S.W.2d 987, 980 (1949).

For the foregoing reasons, the judgment is affirmed.

Estoppel of the Owner

ZENDMAN v. HARRY WINSTON, INC.

(1953) 305 N.Y. 180, 111 N.E.2d 871.

FULD, J.

On November 28, 1947, plaintiff Jane Zendman, bought a diamond ring for $12,500, at an auction held at the gallery of Brand, Inc., on the Boardwalk in Atlantic City, New Jersey. Harry Winston, Inc., a dia-

mond merchant located in New York City, claims ownership of the ring.

Brand and Winston had done business together for years. It was the custom of Harold Brand, the owner and proprietor of Brand, Inc., to visit Winston's premises in New York several times a month and select articles that were later sold at the gallery in Atlantic City. In October of 1947, Brand chose the ring—later purchased by Miss Zendman—advising that he wished to show it to a customer, and, at his request, that one item was mailed to the gallery in New Jersey. Accompanying it was a memorandum, reciting that "the goods" were only for Brand's examination and that no title was to pass "until you have made you selection, notified us of your agreement to pay the indicated price [$11,000] and we have indicated our acceptance thereof by sending to you a bill of sale."

Upon the receipt of the ring, Brand placed it in one of his public show windows, such display being with the knowledge and acquiescence of the owner Winston. And there the ring remained on display until, more than a month later, it was put up at auction and, after some bidding, "knocked down" and sold to plaintiff for $12,500. She received a bill of sale from Brand and knew nothing about the written memorandum or the circumstances under which Brand had obtained possession. Sometime in January, 1948, Winston discovered that Brand had sold the ring to plaintiff and, on February 2d, demanded its return. On the following day, an involuntary petition in bankruptcy was filed against Brand.

The record established that delivery of merchandise "on memorandum" similar to that here involved, had been the regular course of dealing between Winston and Brand for some years, and "hundreds" of such memoranda were found in Brand's files. Every week or so—evidence, admitted without objection, disclosed—one of Winston's salesmen and officers, Raticoff, would visit Brand's gallery, and, after checking items that had been sent to Brand, would settle Winston's account, collecting either cash or Brand's check or the checks of those customers who had bought Winston articles.

The court at Special Term, * * * rendered judgment in favor of plaintiff on defendant Winston's counterclaim for replevin. * * * Upon appeal, the Appellate Division, deciding that there was no basis for an "estoppel," reversed and directed judgment for defendant.

* * *

Generally, we seek a proper balance between the competing interests of an owner who has entrusted his property to another for purposes other than sale, and of an innocent purchaser who has in good faith bought that property from the latter without notice of the seller's lack of title or authority to sell. In resolving this conflict, the courts have evolved certain principles "akin to estoppel", 2 Williston, op. cit., § 311, p. 242, based on the maxim that "As between two innocent victims of the fraud, the one who made possible the fraud on the other should suffer." [Citation.]

Thus, on the one hand, it is settled that simply delivering possession of an article of property to another as depository, pledgee or agent "is clearly insufficient to preclude the real owner from reclaiming his property, in case of an unauthorized disposition of it by the person so intrusted." [Citations.] "Neither is it sufficient, to work an estoppel, that the person to whose possession the owner intrusts chattels is a dealer in similar merchandise." [Citations.] Nor, finally, is an estoppel created merely by the addition of the circumstance "that the possessor of the chattel is authorized by the owner to exhibit the same for the purpose of obtaining offers of purchase." [Citations.]

On the other hand, it is equally settled that "but slight additional circumstances may turn the scale" against the true owner,

2 Williston, op. cit., § 315, p. 249, and estop him from asserting title against one who has purchased the property in good faith. [Citations.] As this court noted, some eighty years ago, in McNeil v. Tenth Nat. Bank, 46 N.Y. 325, 329, the rule that a vendor can convey no greater title to property than he possesses "is a truism, predicable on a simple transfer from one party to another where no other element intervenes." However, continued the court, "It does not interfere with the well-established principle, that where the true owner holds out another, or allows him to appear, as the owner of, or as having full power of disposition over the property, and innocent third parties are thus led into dealing with such apparent owner, they will be protected. Their rights in such cases do not depend upon the actual title or authority of the party with whom they deal directly, but are derived from the act of the real owner, which precludes him from disputing, as against them, the existence of the title or power which, through negligence or mistaken confidence he caused or allowed to appear to be vested in the party making the conveyance. [Citations.]"

Adopting that principle, the courts have generally acknowledged that "The rightful owner may be estopped by his own acts from asserting his title. If he has invested another with the usual evidence of title, *or an apparent authority to dispose of it,* he will not be allowed to make claim against an innocent purchaser dealing on the faith of such apparent ownership." [Citations.]

* * *

We realize, of course, that "The law takes into account not simply the deception of the subsequent buyer by the appearance of title in the possessor of the goods, but also whether this appearance of title was created by the original owner for a purpose so essential and proper that the original title must be protected irrespective of the injury to the subsequent buyer". 2 Williston, op.

cit., § 312, p. 243. The task in each case is, therefore to balance the probability of deception with the necessity for adopting the particular mode of entrusting chosen. In this case, we fail to see how defendant's mode of operation is "so essential" to the conduct of its business as to warrant placing upon an innocent purchaser the burden and consequences of the very fraud which defendant made possible.

An owner must be fully aware of the potentialities for fraud created when, for purposes of sale, he entrusts merchandise to a retail dealer, regularly engaged in selling such goods, and the dangers are many times multiplied if that dealer happens to be an auctioneer. It ill behooves the owner to complain if he is not permitted to rely upon his private and secret agreement, when he himself has failed to require strict adherence to its terms and has thus become responsible for the dealer's apparent authority to sell.

The judgment of the Appellate Division should be reversed and that of Special Term affirmed, with costs in this court and the Appellate Division.

Entrusting Possession to a Merchant

MEDICO LEASING CO. v. SMITH

(1969 Okl.) 457 P.2d 548.

HODGES, J.

Plaintiff, Medico Leasing Company, sought in this action below to replevin an automobile from the defendants, W. C. and Dorene Carter. Plaintiff had turned over possession of the automobile to a used car dealer named Smith to sell. Smith, representing himself as owner, sold the automobile to the defendant Wessell Buick Company who later resold it to Country Cousins Motors, Inc. Smith did not remit the purchase money to the plaintiff. Subsequently Carters purchased the car from Country

Cousins Motors. No redelivery bond was posted and plaintiff took possession of the automobile. Defendants, W. C. and Dorene Carter and Country Cousins Motors each filed cross petitions against the plaintiff seeking damages for wrongful taking.

* * * The jury returned a verdict in favor of the Carters in the amount of $741.00 and in favor of Country Cousins Motors in the amount of $2100.00.

The principal issue presented by this appeal is the trial court's ruling that the defendant, Wessell Buick Company, was a "buyer in the ordinary course of business" in good faith as defined by Sections 1–201(9) and 2–403(2) of the Oklahoma Uniform Commercial Code when they purchased the automobile from defendant Smith, a used car dealer, to whom plaintiff had entrusted possession of the car. The trial court found that Wessell Buick acquired sufficient legal title even though the sale was made without the actual transfer of the automobile's Certificate of Title, and therefore the defendants, Carters and Country Cousins Motors, were entitled to damages for the wrongful taking.

The evidence shows substantially the following facts: Plaintiff corporation was engaged in the business of leasing various items of equipment and had leased a 1962 Buick automobile for a period of two years. Subsequent to the termination of the lease the car was offered for sale by means of advertising in the newspaper. In answer to the ad the defendant Smith telephoned the treasurer of the corporation, hereinafter referred to as Raskin, who had placed the ad and informed him that he could sell the car. Raskin informed Smith that he could have the car to show to a prospect, however, he did not give Smith the certificate of title. Smith testifying for the plaintiff contradicted the testimony of Raskin in that he stated that the only instructions he got from Raskin was that he wanted $2200.00 for the car. Raskin was later warned by the president of plaintiff corporation to be careful of Smith. Smith was engaged in the used car business and had been for some time prior to this transaction. This fact was known to both the president of the corporation and to Raskin. In addition to showing the car to the prospect, Smith took the car to defendant Wessell Buick Co., sold it to them and retained the money himself. Some three weeks following the sale Smith gave Raskin a check for $600.00 with the notation thereon, "partial payment 62 Buick, hold for cashiers check." Raskin testified that he accepted this check on the date that it bears. This check was never cashed, however, as there were insufficient funds deposited in the bank to cover it.

Some time following the sale of the car to defendant Wessell an employee of Wessell designated as the title clerk called Smith for the certificate of title and was informed by him that the certificate had been left with her previously. Subsequent to that conversation the clerk again contacted Smith and was informed that he did not have the certificate but that he would try to get it. Not receiving the certificate, the clerk made application to the Tax Commission for a lost certificate of title and in time received it. Prior to making application for lost title defendant Wessell sold the Buick to the defendant Country Cousins Motors, who subsequently sold the car to defendants W. C. and Dorene Carter.

Meanwhile, plaintiff had not received any money for its car and further, could not find the car. Through the Tax Commission it traced the ownership registration of the car and found it to be in the possession of W. C. and Dorene Carter. Plaintiff then filed a suit in replevin, posted bond, took possession of the car from the Carters and sold it to a third party.

Plaintiff does not contest the fact that Smith is their agent, but they maintain that he was a limited agent and did not have title to the automobile or authority to convey title. They assert that Smith could not convey any better title than he had, and as

he had no title, none was conveyed. It is further asserted by plaintiff that defendant Wessel was not a buyer in good faith as required by our Uniform Commercial Code, because they purchased the car without a certificate of title under facts and circumstances which would have put an ordinarily prudent businessman on inquiry.

The provisions of the code pertinent to the issues in this case are in part set out:

"12A O.S. § 2–403(2) Any entrusting of possession of goods to a merchant who deals in goods of that kind gives him power to transfer all rights of the entruster to a buyer in ordinary course of business.

"12A O.S. § 1–201(9) 'Buyer in ordinary course of business' means a person who in good faith and without knowledge that the sale to him is in violation of the ownership rights or security interest of a third party in the goods buys in ordinary course from a person in the business of selling goods of that kind but does not include a pawnbroker. 'Buying' may be for cash or by exchange of other property or on secured or unsecured credit and includes receiving goods or documents of title under a pre-existing contract for sale but does not include a transfer in bulk or as security for or in total or partial satisfaction of a money debt."

The "entruster" in the instant case, the plaintiff, had good title to the Buick, which was a used car. The one to whom the automobile was entrusted, Smith, as a used car dealer, is a "merchant who deals in goods of that kind" within the meaning of the statute. Smith was known by the plaintiff to be a used car dealer. The Uniform Commercial Code has not changed the law in this state regarding clothing an agent with apparent authority to convey title, especially if the agent is one who ordinarily deals in the goods which the principal has entrusted to him. A recognized principle of estoppel consistently followed by this court is that if a principal or owner of an automobile permits a dealer in automobiles to have an automobile under circumstances indicating authority to sell, he is estopped to assert title against a bona fide purchaser for value without notice. [Citations.]

Since Smith had apparent authority to convey legal title, the question then arises as to whether Wessell was a buyer in good faith when they purchased the car without a certificate of title.

It has long been held by this court that a certificate of title to an automobile issued under the motor vehicle act is not a muniment of title which establishes ownership, but is merely intended to protect the public against theft and to facilitate recovery of stolen automobiles and otherwise aid the state in enforcement of its regulation of motor vehicles. [Citations.] This rule was not changed with the passage of the Uniform Commercial Code. Under Section 1–201(15) the certificate of title of an automobile is not listed as a "document of title". It was not necessary for the defendant Smith to deliver the certificate of title before he conveyed ownership of the Buick Automobile, and the absence of a certificate does not invalidate the sale or prevent title from passing. [Citation.] The sale of the automobile was complete upon delivery of the car with the intent to sell. Title 12A O.S. Section 2–401(2) states:

"Unless otherwise explicitly agreed title passes to the buyer at the time and place at which the seller completes his performance with reference to the physical delivery of the goods, despite any reservation of a security interest and even though a document of title is to be delivered at a different time or place; * * *"

* * *

Judgment affirmed.

*Entrusting Possession
to a Merchant*

MATTEK v. MALOFSKY

(1969) 42 Wis.2d 16, 165 N.W.2d 406.

HALLOWS, C. J.

Two issues are presented on this appeal: (1) Whether the provisions of sec. 402.403, Stats. are applicable to sales between merchants; and (2) whether an automobile dealer who buys a used car from another automobile dealer, who has lawful possession of the car, without obtaining or inquiring about the certificate of title to the used car is a "buyer in the ordinary course of business" within the meaning of sec. 402.403.

We think the provisions of sec. 402.403 are applicable to sales between merchants. We come to this conclusion because the purpose of sec. 402.403(2) and (3) is to protect a person from a third-party interest in goods purchased from the general inventory of a merchant regardless of that merchant's actual authority to sell those goods. This section does not expressly or by implication restrict such protection of a sale by a merchant to a member of the consumer public. If the policy of negotiability of goods held in the inventory of a merchant is to be promoted, it would seem to apply between merchants where merchants buy from one another in the ordinary course of business. The protection is afforded to "a buyer in the ordinary course of business," and by other provisions of the Uniform Commercial Code the term "buyer" includes a merchant.

In sec. 401.201(9), Stats., a buyer in the ordinary course of business is defined as "a person who in good faith and without knowledge that the sale to him is in violation of the ownership rights or security interest of a third party in the goods buys in ordinary course from a person in the business of selling goods of that kind but does not include a pawn broker." Good faith is defined in sec. 401.201(19), Stats., to mean "honesty in fact in the conduct or transaction concerned." This definition applies to a member of the consumer public only, because in sec. 402.103(1)(b) " 'good faith' in the case of a merchant" is defined to mean "honesty in fact and the observance of reasonable commercial standards of fair dealing in the trade." In addition, sec. 402.104(3), Stats., relating to the general standard applicable to transactions between merchants charges each merchant with the "knowledge or skill of merchants."

Consequently, a merchant may be a buyer in the ordinary course of business under sec. 402.403 from another merchant if he meets four elements: (1) Be honest in fact, (2) be without knowledge of any defects of title in the goods, (3) pay value, and (4) observe reasonable commercial standards. In the observance of reasonable commercial standards, however, a merchant is chargeable with the knowledge or skill of a merchant.

We think Malofsky was not the buyer in the ordinary course of business within the meaning of sec. 402.403, Stats. Although the delivery of the automobile to Frakes, a used-car dealer, constituted an entrustment, Frakes could by subsequent sale pass title to a buyer in the ordinary course of business. However, Malofsky as a merchant was not a buyer in the ordinary course of business because he was chargeable with the knowledge that the registration law, sec. 342.19(2), Stats. of 1963, which provides that while a dealer need not apply for a certificate of title for a vehicle in stock or acquired for stock purposes, he shall upon the transfer of such vehicle give the transferee evidence of title, and in the case of a vehicle which has a certificate of title, the certificate of title shall be reassigned and delivered to the transferee. Malofsky should have known the used automobile had a certificate of title outstand-ing and that Frakes was required to give him such certificate of title. Under the standards set forth in sec. 402.104(3), Stats., applicable to transactions between merchants, Malofsky is chargeable with this knowledge and his failure to procure a certificate of title or some evidence of title was unreasonable as a matter of law. Evidence of custom or usage of automobile dealers contrary to the statute cannot be used to defeat the rights of a third party whatever the value of such evidence may be in adjusting disputes between dealers.

* * *

A case from a lower court, almost on all fours with the present case, is Atlas Auto Rental Corp. v. Weisberg (1967), 54 Misc.2d 168, 281 N.Y.S.2d 400, where the court held the provisions of the U.C.C. 2–403 applied to transactions between merchants but a dealer who purchased a used car without any bill of sale or owner's registration took the risk that his transferor was not the owner. We think sec. 342.19(2), Stats. of 1963, of the Motor Vehicle Code must be construed with the Uniform Commercial Code and it is proper to refer to the Motor Vehicle Code to determine what a used-automobile dealer is supposed to know or what knowledge he is chargeable with when he claims to be a buyer in the ordinary course of business.

Judgment affirmed.

Problems

1. Adams Jewelry Company employed Brown as a jewelry salesman and delivered to him a sample line of watches, diamonds and rings, which he was to show to customers. He was authorized to sell for cash and was to report each sale promptly to the jewelry company and remit the cash proceeds. Brown took one of the diamond rings which was delivered to him by the jewelry company and pawned it with a pawnbroker for $200. The jewelry company later discovered that the pawnbroker had the ring and made a demand upon him, and upon his failure to deliver the ring, brought an action against him for its value. The pawnbroker defended upon the ground that the jewelry company having put it in the power of Brown, the salesman, to represent himself as the owner of the property, the jewelry company, and not he, should suffer the loss. Decision?

2. Smith was approached by a man who introduced himself as Brown of Brown and Co.

Brown was not known to Smith, but Smith asked Dun & Bradstreet for a credit report and obtained a very favorable report on Brown. He thereupon sold Brown some expensive gems and billed Brown & Co. "Brown" turned out to be a clever jewel thief, who later sold the gems to Brown & Co. for valuable consideration. Brown & Co. was unaware of "Brown's" transaction with Smith. Smith sued Brown & Co. for the return of the gems or the price thereof as billed to Brown & Co. Decision?

3. Z, the owner of a 1982 Cadillac automobile, agreed to loan the car to Y for the month of February of 1982 while he (Z) went to Florida for a winter vacation. It was understood that Y, who was a small town Cadillac dealer, would merely place Z's car in his showroom for exhibition and sales promotion purposes. While Z was away, Y sold the car to B. Upon Z's return from Florida, he sued to recover the car from B. Decision?

4. A was indebted to B and also to C. On April 2, he gave B a bill of sale of certain farm implements but did not deliver possession. On April 7, he executed and delivered to C a bill of sale covering the same implements and also delivered possession of the implements to C. C had no prior knowledge of B's bill of sale. B and C both claim title to the farm implements. Decision?

5. A offered to sell his used automobile to B for $2,600 cash. B agreed to buy the car, gave A a check for $2,600, and drove away in the car. The next day B sold the car for $3,000 to C, a bona fide purchaser. The $2,600 check was returned to A by the bank in which he had deposited it for the reason that there were insufficient funds in the drawer's account in the drawee bank. A brings an action against C to recover the automobile. What judgment?

6. B told S he wished to buy S's automobile. He drove the car for about ten minutes, returned to S, stated he wanted to take the automobile to show it to his wife, and then left with the automobile and never returned. B sold the automobile in another State to T and gave him a bill of sale. S sued T to recover the automobile. Decision?

7. P owned a cameo pin which had recently been appraised for $6,000. P's granddaughter

X was to be married and asked P if she (X) could wear the cameo on her wedding dress. Pleased, P loaned the pin to X, informing her that it was insured against theft so X "need not worry if it is stolen."

As X was throwing her bridal bouquet her sleeve caught on the pin and bent the clasp. Without telling P, she took the pin to Jay, who owned a store which repaired and sold jewelry, to have the pin repaired. One week later X returned and was advised that through error the pin had been sold by Jay to B for $3,800. Jay immediately called B, offered to return the $3,800, and requested that the pin be returned. B refused, claiming that he had purchased the pin in good faith and without knowing of P's ownership.

What are P's rights against Jay and B? What are B's rights against P and Jay? P wants her pin returned.

8. Altman and his wife spend each winter at Miami Beach, including the period around January 30, which was his wife's birthday. For several years Altman had the habit of purchasing jewelry as a birthday gift from a retail store on Collins Avenue known as Malcolm of Miami. On January 28, Altman bought a diamond bracelet for his wife for $4,000. He paid Malcolm by check and received a receipt, a bill of sale and a written appraisal, valuing the bracelet at $4,775. On April 15, Altman received a letter from a jeweler in New Jersey known as Thomas of Trenton. Thomas demanded return of the diamond bracelet or its value of $4,775 in cash. He advised Altman that he was the owner of the bracelet and had sent it to Malcolm in accordance with a consignment agreement which contained the following provision: "A sale of merchandise can only be effected and title will pass only if, as and when Thomas of Trenton shall agree to such sale and a bill of sale rendered therefor by him." When Altman refused to return the bracelet or pay Thomas, Thomas brought an action against Altman. Decision?

9. On January 3, A entered into an agreement with B, whereby A agreed to purchase a grocery business owned by B in Chicago, including the stock of merchandise and all equipment and fixtures. It was agreed that the transfer would take place on February 15 and that the purchase price would be paid at that time. At A's request,

B furnished to him an affidavit, setting forth the names and addresses of all of B's creditors and the amounts owing to them. On January 15, A sent registered letters to the creditors listed, notifying them that he was purchasing the business and advising them of the price, terms and conditions of the sale. On February 15 the sale was consummated and the purchase price paid. Subsequently, three business creditors of the former owner made demand upon A for payment of their indebtedness: (a) X, who was not listed in the affidavit furnished by B; (b) Y, who was listed in the affidavit, but who received no notice of the sale, because his name was overlooked by A; and (c) Z, who was listed in the affidavit, and who received the notice sent by A. What is the liability of A, if any, with respect to each of these creditors?

10. Avery was the owner of a race horse named Secretary. Boner was the owner of a stable of race horses and trained, bought, sold and raced horses at Upson Downes race track. Avery arranged with Boner to train the horse and delivered it to Boner, who entered it without Avery's knowledge or permission in a race with Boner listed as Secretary's owner on the racing program. Secretary won and on the following day was sold by Boner to Craig for $10,000 cash. Craig took possession of the horse. Upon learning these facts, Avery brought an appropriate action against Craig to recover the horse. Decision?

11. Price was engaged in the business of buying and selling automobiles at wholesale. In February, Price sold a used Ford sedan on a conditional sales contract to Hunt who was known to him to be a retail dealer in new and used cars. Hunt signed a note for the amount of the purchase price. The conditional sales contract provided that title was to remain in Price until the note was paid in full.

A statute in effect provides that the owner of a motor vehicle who sells the same shall supply the purchaser with a certificate of title. No certificate of title was delivered to Hunt.

Day saw this Ford in Hunt's garage and purchased it from him, paying the purchase price in full. No certificate of title was delivered to Day. Thereafter, Hunt defaulted on his conditional sales contract, and Price brings an appropriate action to recover possession of the Ford from Day, who for the first time learned of Price's claim of ownership. Decision?

Chapter
23

PERFORMANCE OF
SALES CONTRACTS

Performance of a contract is a realization of the expectations of the parties and a discharge of the duties created by the contract. The obligations of the parties are determined in accordance with their contractual agreement. If the contract does not sufficiently cover the particulars of performance, these terms will be supplied by the Code, common law, course of dealings, usage of trade and course of performance. In all events, both parties to the sales contract must perform their contractual obligations in good faith. Section 1–203.

BASIC DUTIES
OF PERFORMANCE

The basic obligations of the buyer and seller in a contract for the sale of goods are set forth in Section 2–301:

The obligation of the seller is to transfer and deliver and that of the buyer is to accept and pay in accordance with the contract.

The contract of sale may expressly provide whether the seller must deliver the goods before receiving payment of the price or whether the buyer must pay the price before receiving the goods. The rights of the parties are fixed by the terms of the contract. For example, if the seller has agreed to sell goods on 60 or 90 days' credit, he is required to perform his part of the contract in advance of performance by the buyer. Likewise, if the buyer has agreed to pay for the goods in advance of delivery either to the buyer or to a carrier, his duty to perform is not conditional upon performance or a tender of performance by the seller.

Where the contract does not expressly provide that the sale is on credit, or that one party must perform before the other performs, delivery of the goods and payment of the price are said to be concurrent conditions. Sections 2–507(1) and 2–511. In fairness to both parties, neither is required to perform until the other performs or tenders performance. This is based upon the assumption that delivery and payment are acts which are each capable of simultaneous performance, and it is unfair that one party to a contract should be compelled to part with the consideration which he has promised unless he receives at the same time the consideration promised by the other party.

Under the Code the seller must be ready and willing to deliver the goods to the buyer in exchange for the price, and the buyer must be ready and willing to pay the price in exchange for possession of the goods. It is not enough for both parties merely to stand ready, able and willing to perform. In order for either party to maintain against the other an action upon the contract, he must put the other party in default. This is accomplished either by (a) performance according to the contract, (b) tender of performance according to the contract, or (c) being excused from tender of performance.

Assume that A enters into a contract to sell to B 100 tons of coal at $9 per ton, delivery to be made on February 1, and the price to be paid by B on February 15. If A fails to deliver the coal on February 1, B may properly start an action against him on February 2, or any date up to and including February 14, to recover damages for breach of contract without first making a tender of the price. A has breached the contract, and no act is required on B's part to put A in default as the respective performances are not concurrent conditions by reason of the terms of the contract. However, when the time for B's performance arrives on February 15, he must tender the price to A, in order to maintain an action against A, unless A by words or conduct has excused tender. While originally the respective duties of performance on the part of buyer and seller were independent of one another, by lapse of time and inaction of the parties they have become mutually dependent.

Section 2–611(1) provides:

Until the repudiating party's next performance is due he can retract his repudiation unless the aggrieved party has since the repudiation cancelled or materially changed his position or

otherwise indicated that he considers the repudiation final.

PERFORMANCE BY THE SELLER

The Code is explicit in requiring a tender of performance by one party as a condition to performance by the other party. Section 2–507(1). Tender of conforming goods by the seller entitles him to acceptance thereof by the buyer and to payment of the price according to the contract.

Tender of delivery requires that the seller put and hold goods which conform to the contract at the buyer's disposition and that he give the buyer notification reasonably necessary to enable him to take delivery. Section 2–503.

TIME AND MANNER OF DELIVERY

Tender must be at a reasonable hour, and the goods tendered must be kept available for the period reasonably necessary to enable the buyer to take possession of them. Unless otherwise agreed the buyer must furnish facilities reasonably suited to the receipt of the goods. Section 2–503.

If no definite time for delivery is fixed by the terms of the contract, the seller is allowed a reasonable time after the making of the contract within which to deliver the goods to the buyer, or have them available for delivery at the required place. Likewise, the buyer has a reasonable time within which to accept delivery. What length of time is reasonable is a question of fact, and depends upon the facts and circumstances of each case. If the goods are capable of immediate delivery, a reasonable time would be very short. Where the goods must be constructed or manufactured, obviously a reasonable time would be longer and would depend upon the usual length of time required to make the goods, together with other factors.

Unless the parties so agree, a contract is not performable piecemeal or in installments. All of the goods called for by a contract must be tendered in a single delivery and payment is due on such tender. However, where the circumstances give either party the right to make or demand delivery in lots, the price if it can be apportioned may be demanded for each lot. Section 2–307.

PLACE OF TENDER

If the contract is silent as to the place for delivery of the goods, the place for delivery is the seller's place of business; or if he has none, his residence. If the contract is for the sale of identified goods which the parties know at the time of making the contract are located elsewhere than the seller's place of business or residence, the location of the goods is the place for delivery. Section 2–308. For example, A, a boat builder in Chicago, contracts to sell to B a certain yacht which both parties know is anchored at Milwaukee. The place of delivery would be Milwaukee. On the other hand, if the contract provides that A shall overhaul the motor at A's shipyard in Chicago, A would have to return the yacht to Chicago, and the place of delivery would be A's Chicago shipyard.

If the contract of sale contains delivery terms such as F.O.B., F.A.S., C.I.F., C.F. or C.O.D. at a specified destination, the seller must tender delivery of the goods at such destination.

Shipment Contracts

The delivery terms F.O.B. place of shipment, F.A.S. seller's port, C.I.F., C.F., and C.O.D. are all "shipment contracts." Under a shipment contract the seller is required or authorized to send the goods to the buyer, but the contract does not obligate him to deliver them at a particular destination. In these cases the seller's tender of performance occurs at the point of shipment, provided the seller meets certain specified conditions which are designed to protect the interests of the absent buyer.

Under a shipment contract, the seller is required to: (1) deliver the goods to a carrier; (2) make a contract for their transportation which is reasonable according to the nature of the goods and other circumstances of the case; (3) obtain and promptly deliver or tender to the buyer a document in due form necessary to enable the buyer to obtain possession of the goods from the carrier; and (4) promptly notify the buyer of the shipment. Section 2–504.

Destination Contracts

The delivery terms "F.O.B. at city of buyer," "ex-ship," and "no arrival, no sale" are destination contracts. Since a destination contract requires the seller to tender delivery of conforming goods at a specified destination, the seller must place the goods at the buyer's disposition and give the buyer reasonable notice to enable him to take delivery. In addition, if the destination contract involves documents of title, the seller must tender the necessary documents. Section 2–503.

Goods Held by Bailee

Where goods are in the possession of a bailee and are to be delivered without being moved, in most instances the seller may either tender a document of title or obtain an acknowledgement by the bailee of the buyer's right to possess the goods. Section 2–503(4).

QUALITY OF TENDER

Perfect Tender Rule

The Code imposes upon the seller the obligation that his tender of goods conform strictly to the requirements of the contract and does not deviate in any way from the terms of the contract.   Section 2–601 of the Code provides:

Subject to the provisions of this Article on breach in installment contracts (Section 2–612) and unless otherwise agreed under the sections on contractual limitations of remedy (Sections 2–718 and 2–719), if the goods or the tender of delivery fail in any respect to conform to the contract, the buyer may (a) reject the whole; or (b) accept the whole; or (c) accept any commercial unit or units and reject the rest.

Thus, a buyer may rightfully reject the delivery of 110 dozen shirts under an agreement calling for the delivery of 100 dozen shirts.   The size or extent of the breach does not affect the right to reject.

Modifications of the Perfect Tender Rule

There are two basic modifications of the buyer's right to reject the goods upon the seller's failure to comply with the perfect tender rule: (a) installment contracts and (b) cure by the seller.

Installment Contracts. Unless the parties have otherwise agreed, the buyer does not have to pay any part of the price of the goods until the entire quantity specified in the contract has been delivered or tendered to him.   Section 2–307.   An installment contract is an instance where the parties have otherwise agreed.   It expressly provides for delivery of the goods in separate lots or installments and usually for payment of the price in installments.   Section 2–612.

The buyer may reject any installment which is non-conforming if the non-conformity substantially impairs the value of that installment and cannot be cured.   Section 2–612(2).   When the installment does substantially impair the value of the installment but not the value of the entire contract, if the seller gives adequate assurance of the installment's cure, then the buyer cannot reject the installment.   Sec-

tion 2–612(2).   Whenever non-conformity or default with respect to one or more installments substantially impairs the value of the whole contract, there is a breach of the whole contract.   Section 2–612(3).

It should be observed that under Section 2–612 of the Code a party to an installment contract loses his right to treat a material breach as one which entitles him to cancel the entire contract if he (1) accepts a nonconforming installment without seasonably notifying the other party of cancellation, or (2) brings an action to recover only for past installments, or (3) demands performance as to future installments.   "Cancellation" occurs when either party puts an end to the contract for breach by the other, and in such case the cancelling party retains any remedy for breach of the whole contract or any unperformed balance.   Section 2–106(4).

For example, A makes a contract to deliver to B 50 tons of coal each month for one year, delivery to be made on the first day of each month commencing with January; B agrees to pay a certain price for each installment on the twentieth day of the month of delivery.   A delivers to B 50 tons of coal on January 1.   B does not pay for this coal on January 20.   May A on January 21 treat this breach of contract by B as completely excusing A from any further duty to perform under the contract and entitling him to recover damages against B for breach of the entire contract?   A one-day delay in making payment would not substantially impair the value of the whole contract and therefore would not be a material breach. A delay of a week or ten days in payment of the January installment might well be a material breach substantially impairing the value of the whole contract and thereby excuse the seller from any further duty under the contract, whereas an equal delay in payment of the July installment, by which time the contract has been one-half performed on both sides, would probably not be a material breach.

The test is therefore the materiality of the breach. This involves a weighing of all relevant factors among which are the terms of the contract, its subject matter, the nature and extent of the breach, the reason for delay in performance, the time when the breach occurred, whether in the beginning or after partial or substantial performance on both sides, and the effect of the delay upon the party from whom performance has been withheld. Conceivably, a delay in delivery of an installment of the goods might be more serious than an equal delay in the payment of an installment of the price.

Cure by the Seller. Where the buyer refuses to accept a tender of goods which do not conform to the contract, the seller by acting promptly and within the time allowed for performance may make a proper tender or delivery of conforming goods and thereby "cure" his defective tender or performance. Section 2–508. For example, A is to deliver to B 25 blue shirts and 50 white shirts by October 15. On October 1, A delivers 29 blue shirts and 46 white shirts which B rejects as not conforming to the contract. B notifies A of his rejection and the reasons for it. A has until October 15 to cure the defect by making a perfect tender if he seasonably notifies B of his intention to do so.

If the buyer refuses a tender of goods or rejects them as non-conforming without disclosing to the seller the nature of the defect, he may not assert such defect as an excuse for not accepting the goods or as a breach of contract by the seller if the defect is one which is curable. The buyer must act in good faith and state his reasons for refusing to accept the goods or be precluded from later relying upon such reasons. Section 2–605.

The Code also provides:

Where the buyer rejects a non-conforming tender which the seller had reasonable grounds to believe would be acceptable with or without money allowance the seller may if he seasonably notifies the buyer have a further reasonable time to substitute a conforming tender. Section 2–508(2).

PERFORMANCE BY THE BUYER

The obligation of the buyer is to accept conforming goods and to pay for them according to the contract terms. Tender of payment or payment by the buyer, unless otherwise agreed, is a condition to the seller's duty to tender and to complete any delivery. Tender of payment in the form of a check in the ordinary course of business is sufficient unless the seller demands legal tender and allows the buyer a reasonable time within which to obtain it. However, payment by personal check is defeated as between seller and buyer by dishonor of the check on due presentment. Section 2–511(3).

BUYER'S RIGHT OF INSPECTION

Unless otherwise agreed between the parties, the buyer has a right to inspect the goods before payment or acceptance. Section 2–513. This enables him before payment or acceptance to satisfy himself that goods tendered or delivered conform to the contract. If the contract requires payment before acceptance, non-conformity unless apparent without inspection does not excuse the buyer from making payment, and payment in such case is not an acceptance of the goods. Section 2–512. This is the situation where the contract requires payment upon presentation of a bill of lading, or provides for shipment C.O.D. If the contract does not provide for shipment C.O.D. the buyer may rightfully refuse to accept such a shipment if the carrier does not permit inspection.

The buyer is allowed a reasonable time to inspect the goods and may lose the right to reject or revoke acceptance of non-conforming goods by failing to inspect them within a reasonable time. A plumbing contractor defendant entered into a contract with plaintiff supplier to purchase four kitchen units per specifications. They were to be installed by defendant in a building under construction. Plaintiff delivered the units enclosed in shipping crates to the construction site where defendant stored them without opening the crates or inspecting the contents. Three months later the crates were opened and the units installed when they were then found to be of defective quality and not to comply with the contract specifications. Defendant notified plaintiff of rejection and shipped them back to plaintiff who refused to accept them. A dismissal of plaintiff's action for the price was reversed on appeal on the ground that defendant had lost his right to reject or revoke acceptance as three months was not a reasonable time under Section 2–608(2) within which to inspect the goods, or discover their condition and notify the seller that they were non-conforming. The case was remanded with directions to enter judgment for plaintiff for the price, subject to defendant's right to damages for breach of contract. Cervitor Kitchens Inc. v. Chapman, 7 Wash.App. 520, 500 P.2d 783 (1972).

The buyer must bear the expense of inspection but incurs no liability for the value of the goods necessarily destroyed in making the test. If the goods do not conform to the contract and are rejected, the buyer may recover from the seller the necessary expenses of inspection. Section 2–513(2).

BUYER'S RIGHTS
UPON IMPROPER DELIVERY

The buyer is not obliged to accept a tender or delivery of goods which do not conform to the contract. Upon such tender or delivery by the seller, the buyer has the choice of three alternatives. He may (1) reject all of the goods; or (2) accept all of the goods; or (3) accept any commercial unit or units of the goods and reject the rest. Section 2–601.

Where the seller delivers goods of a different description mixed with the goods ordered or contracted for, he is in effect making an offer to sell all of the goods so delivered. The buyer may therefore accept the entire lot, or he may make a separation of the goods, retain the part which is in accordance with the contract, and reject the rest.

Acceptance of any part of a commercial unit is acceptance of the entire unit. Section 2–606(2). Commercial unit is defined in Section 2–105(6):

"Commercial unit" means such a unit of goods as by commercial usage is a single whole for purposes of sale and division of which materially impairs its character or value on the market or in use. A commercial unit may be a single article (as a machine) or a set of articles (as a suite of furniture or an assortment of sizes) or a quantity (as a bale, gross, or carload) or any other unit treated in use or in the relevant market as a single whole.

The buyer must pay at the contract rate for such commercial units as he accepts. However, after giving the seller timely notice of the breach, he is entitled to recover from the seller or deduct from the purchase price the amount of damages for non-conformity of the commercial units accepted and for non-delivery of the commercial units rejected. Section 2–717.

BUYER'S RIGHT
OF REJECTION

Rejection is a manifestation by the buyer of his unwillingness to become owner of the goods. It must be within a reasonable time after the goods have been tendered or delivered. It is not effective unless the buyer seasonably notifies the seller. Section 2–602(1).

Rejection of the goods may be rightful or wrongful, depending on whether the goods tendered or delivered conform to the contract. The buyer's rejection of non-conforming goods is rightful.

After the buyer has rejected the goods any exercise of ownership of the goods by him is wrongful as against the seller. If the buyer has possession of the rejected goods but no security interest in them, he is obliged to hold them with reasonable care for a time sufficient to permit the seller to remove them. The buyer who is not a merchant is under no further obligation with regard to goods rightfully rejected. Section 2–602.

A merchant buyer of goods who has rightfully rejected them is obligated to follow reasonable instructions from the seller with respect to the disposition of the goods in his possession or control, when the seller has no agent or place of business at the market of rejection. Section 2–603(1). If the merchant buyer receives no instructions from the seller within a reasonable time after notice of the rejection, and the rejected goods are perishable or threaten to decline in value speedily, he is obligated to make reasonable efforts to sell them for the seller's account. Otherwise, he may (1) store the goods for the seller's account, or (2) reship them to the seller; or (3) resell them for the seller's account. Such action is not an acceptance or conversion of the goods. Section 2–604.

When the buyer sells the rejected goods, he is entitled to reimbursement from the seller or out of the proceeds for reasonable expenses of caring for and selling them and a reasonable selling commission not to exceed ten per cent of the gross proceeds. Section 2–603(2).

ACCEPTANCE OF GOODS

The word "acceptance" means a willingness by the buyer to become the owner of the goods tendered or delivered to him by the seller. It includes overt acts or conduct which manifest such willingness. Acceptance is independent of possession, delivery, or payment for the goods. Acceptance may be indicated by express words, by the presumed intention of the buyer, or by conduct of the buyer with respect to specific goods inconsistent with the seller's ownership thereof. Acceptance of the goods precludes any rejection of the goods accepted. Section 2–607(2).

Acceptance occurs when the buyer, after a reasonable opportunity to inspect the goods, (1) signifies to the seller that the goods conform to the contract, or (2) signifies to the seller that he will take the goods or retain them in spite of their non-conformity to the contract, or (3) fails to make an effective rejection of the goods. Section 2–606.

The buyer must pay at the contract rate for any goods accepted but may recover damages for any non-conformity of the goods provided the buyer reasonably notifies the seller of any breach. Sections 2–607 and 2–714.

With regard to goods rejected by the buyer, the burden is on the seller to establish their conformity to the contract; but the burden is on the buyer to establish any breach of contract or warranty with regard to goods accepted. Section 2–607(4).

REVOCATION OF ACCEPTANCE

The buyer may revoke his acceptance of goods which do not conform to the contract and such non-conformity substantially impairs the value of the goods to the buyer, provided that his acceptance was: (1) on the reasonable assumption that the non-conformity would be cured by the seller, and it was not seasonably cured; or (2) without discovery of the non-conformity and such acceptance was reasonably induced by the difficulty of discovery before acceptance or by assurances of the seller. Section 2–608(1).

Revocation of acceptance is not effective until notification is given to the seller which must be within a reasonable time after the buyer discovers or should have discovered the grounds for revocation and before the goods have undergone any substantial change which was not caused by their own defects. Section 2–608(2).

Upon revocation of acceptance, the buyer is in the same position with respect to the goods and has the same rights and duties with regard to them as if he had rejected them. Section 2–608(3).

The test of substantial impairment of the value to the buyer of non-conforming goods is subjective rather than objective. Plaintiffs, buyers of a new mobile home on an installment contract, after moving in discovered water and air leaks and defects in doors, cabinets, vents, and walls. Defendant seller repaired some of the defects, but leakage continued creating other problems. After giving notice of revocation of acceptance, plaintiffs continued to live in the mobile home for approximately one year. The revocation was upheld on the grounds (1) that substantial impairment of value to the buyers justifying revocation of acceptance was not to be measured objectively by the relatively small cost of repairs, but subjectively by plaintiffs' deprivation of a home for a substantial period of time; and (2) that continued occupancy of the home was not inconsistent with revocation as plaintiffs had a security interest for the down payment, and occupancy was a feasible method of preserving their collateral. Jorgensen v. Pressnall, 274 Or. 285, 545 P.2d 1382 (1976).

OBLIGATION OF PAYMENT

The terms of the contract may expressly state the time and place that the buyer is obligated to pay for the goods. If so, these terms are controlling. In the absence of agreement, payment is due at the time and place at which the buyer is to receive the goods even though the place of shipment is the place of delivery. Section 2–310(a).

This rule is understandable in view of the right of the buyer to inspect the goods before being obliged to pay for them, in the absence of agreement to the contrary.

Where the sale is on credit the buyer is not obligated to pay for the goods when he receives them. The credit provision in the contract will control the time of payment. Unless the contract specifies the time when the credit period commences to run, the time commences on the date of the shipment of the goods. However, post-dating the invoice or delaying its dispatch will correspondingly delay the starting of the credit period. Section 2–310(d).

EXCUSES FOR NON-PERFORMANCE

CASUALTY TO IDENTIFIED GOODS

A purported sale of nonexistent goods is void, as in the case of a seller who purports to make a sale of specific goods which unknown to him and the buyer have been wholly destroyed.

If the contract is for goods which are specified and identified when the contract was made, and these goods are totally lost or damaged without fault of either party and before risk of loss passes to the buyer, the contract is avoided. Section 2–613(a).

A different situation is presented where the seller purports to sell identified goods and without the knowledge of the parties a portion of them has been destroyed. In the case of a partial destruction or deterioration of the goods, the buyer has the option to avoid the contract or to accept the undestroyed or deteriorated goods with due allowance or deduction from the contract price. The rights of the buyer do not depend upon whether the contract or sale is divisible or indivisible.

Thus, A purports to make a sale to B of a specific lot of wheat containing 1,000 bushels at a price of $4 per bushel. Unknown to A, fire had destroyed or damaged 300 bushels of the wheat. The contract is divisible. B does not have to take the remaining 700 bushels of wheat, but he has the option to do so upon paying $2,800, the price of 700 bushels. Section 2–613(b).

If the destruction or casualty to the goods, total or partial, occurs after risk of loss has passed to the buyer, the buyer has no option but must pay the entire contract price of the goods.

NON-HAPPENING OF PRESUPPOSED CONDITIONS

The ability to perform a contract for the sale of goods is subject to a number of possible hazards, such as strikes, lock-outs, unforeseen shutdown of sources of supply, loss of plant or machinery by fire or other casualty, or embargoes or other governmental regulations. Ordinarily these do not operate as an excuse on the ground of impossibility of performance, unless the contract expressly so provides. However, both parties may have understood at the time the contract was made that its performance depended upon the existence of certain facilities, or that the purpose of the contract and the value of performance depended entirely upon the happening of a specific future contemplated event.

Unless the seller has expressly assumed the risk, the Code provides that the seller is excused from his duty of performance upon the non-occurrence of presupposed conditions which were a basic assumption of the contract. Section 2–615(a).

Increased production cost *alone* does not excuse performance by the seller, nor does a collapse of the market for the goods excuse the buyer. Comment 4 to Section 2–615. However, a contract for the sale of programs for a scheduled yacht regatta which is called off; or for the sale of tin horns for export to Cuba which become subject to embargo; or for the production of goods at a designated factory which becomes damaged or destroyed by fire would be an excuse for non-performance.

Although the seller may be relieved of his contractual duty by the non-happening of presupposed conditions, if the contingency affects only a part of the seller's capacity to perform, he must to the extent of his remaining capacity allocate delivery and production among his customers.

Where delay in delivery or non-delivery, in whole or in part, results from the happening of such contingency, the seller must give seasonable notice thereof to the buyer and, in the event that allocation of goods is required, must also provide the buyer with an estimate of the quota of goods which will be made available to him.

When the buyer receives notice of such delay in delivery or of an allocation of goods to him, he may by written notice to the seller where the prospective deficiency is material either (1) terminate the contract and discharge any portion of it which is executory, or (2) modify the contract by agreement to accept his quota of the goods. Section 2–616(1).

If the buyer, after receiving notice from the seller of such delay in delivery or of an allocation of goods, fails to modify the contract by written notice to the seller within a reasonable time not exceeding 30 days, the contract lapses with respect to any deliveries affected. Section 2–616(2).

SUBSTITUTED PERFORMANCE

The Code provides that where neither party is at fault and the agreed manner of delivery of the goods becomes commercially impracticable, as by reason of the failure of berthing, loading, or unloading facilities, or unavailability of an agreed type of carrier, or similar cause, a substituted manner of performance, if commercially reasonable, must be tendered and accepted. Section 2–614(1).

The goods must be delivered or tendered where reasonable, practical, commercial facilities are available for delivery. Neither seller nor buyer is excused on the ground that delivery in the express manner provided in the contract is impossible where a practical alternative or substitute exists.

If the means or manner in which the buyer is to make payment becomes impossible by reason of supervening governmental regulation, the seller may withhold or stop delivery of the goods unless the buyer provides payment which is commercially a substantial equivalent to that required by the contract. If delivery has already been made, payment as provided by the governmental regulation discharges the buyer unless the regulation is "discriminatory, oppressive or predatory." Section 2–614(2). The Code does not define these terms, and presumably the burden of establishing such character of the regulation would rest upon the seller.

Cases

Requirement of Tender

VIDAL v. TRANSCONTINENTAL & WESTERN AIR, INC.

(1941 C.A.3d) 120 F.2d 67.

GOODRICH, C. J.

This action for breach of contract was tried by the court below without a jury. This appeal by the plaintiffs is from the action of the trial court in dismissing their complaint. By the terms of the contract, which bears date of April 14, 1937, the defendant agreed to sell and the plaintiff agreed to buy four used airplanes of a specified type belonging to the seller. The price was stipulated and payment was to be made by certified check upon delivery of the airplanes to the buyer at the Municipal Airport, Kansas City, Missouri. The date for delivery was stated to be June 1, 1937. * * *

The trial court found as a fact that on June 1 the defendant was ready, able and willing to deliver one of the planes described in the contract to the plaintiffs at Municipal Airport in Kansas City, Missouri, and that after June 1 and on and prior to July 10 the defendant was ready, able and willing to deliver all of the four airplanes at the place specified. It was also found as a fact that the plaintiffs did not on June 1 or any other date either tender payment on any or all of the machines nor request delivery. Plaintiffs' action for damages was begun in the United States District Court for the District of Delaware on October 8, 1938.

What are the respective rights and duties of the parties in a contract of this kind? Assume, for the moment, that there had been no qualifying clause with regard to time of delivery and there was a simple contract promising delivery by the seller to the buyer of specified goods at a definite time and place and neither party demanded performance from the other or tendered his own. Has either a right against the other? Payment and delivery are concurrent conditions since both parties are bound to render performance at the same time. Restatement, Contracts, § 251. In such a case, as Williston points out, neither party can maintain an action against the other without first making an offer of performance himself. Otherwise, if each stayed at home ready and willing to perform each would have a right of action against the other. " * * * to maintain an action at law the plaintiff must not only be ready and willing but he must have manifested this before bringing his action, by some offer of performance to the defendant, * * *. It is one of the consequences of concurrent conditions that a situation may arise where no right of action ever arises against either party * * * so long as both parties remain inactive, neither is liable * * *." This statement by the learned author not only has the force of his authority and that of many decisions from many states, but is also sound common sense. It is not an unfair requirement that a party complaining of another's conduct should be required to show that the other has fallen short in the performance of a legal obligation.

* * *

The conclusion is, therefore, that the defendant is not in default. Neither side having demanded performance by the other, neither side is in a position to complain or to assert any claim in an action of law against the other. This view of the case makes it unnecessary to examine the testimony which asserts that the buyers either abandoned or repudiated the contract prior to the time of the performance.

The judgment is affirmed.

Perfect Tender Rule

MOULTON CAVITY & MOLD INC. v. LYN-FLEX IND.

(Me. 1979) 396 A.2d 1024.

DELAHANTY, J.

Defendant, Lyn-Flex Industries, Inc., appeals from a judgment entered after a jury trial by the Superior Court, York County, in favor of plaintiff, Moulton Cavity & Mold, Inc. The case concerns itself with an oral contract for the sale of goods which, as both parties agree, is governed by Article 2 of the Uniform Commercial Code, 11 M.R.S.A. §§ 2–101 *et seq.* For the reasons set forth below, we agree with defendant that the presiding Justice committed reversible error by instructing the jury that the doctrine of substantial performance applied to a contract for the sale of goods. * * *

An examination of the record discloses the following sequence of events: On March

19, 1975, Lynwood Moulton, president of plaintiff, and Ernest Sturman, president of defendant, orally agreed that plaintiff would produce, and defendant purchase, twenty-six innersole molds capable of producing saleable innersoles. The price was fixed at $600.00 per mold. Whether or not a time for delivery had been established was open to question. In his testimony at trial, Mr. Moulton admitted that he was fully aware that defendant was in immediate need of the molds, and he stated that he had estimated that he could provide suitable molds in about five weeks' time. * * *

In apparent conformity with standard practice in the industry, plaintiff set about constructing a sample mold and began a lengthy series of tests. These tests consisted of bringing the sample mold to defendant's plant, fitting the mold to one of defendant's plastic-injecting machines, and checking the innersole thus derived from the plaintiff's mold to determine if it met the specifications imposed by defendant. After about thirty such tests over a ten-week period, several problems remained unsolved. * * *

It was plaintiff's contention at trial, supported by credible evidence, that at one point during the testing period officials of defendant signified that in their judgment plaintiff's sample mold was turning out innersoles correctly configured so as to fit the model last supplied by defendant's customer. Allegedly relying on this approval, plaintiff went ahead and constructed the full run of twenty-six molds.

For its part, defendant introduced credible evidence to rebut the assertion that it had approved the fit of the molds. It also noted that Moulton's allegation of approval extended only to the fit of the mold; as Moulton conceded, defendant had never given full approval since it considered the flashing problem, among others, unacceptable.

* * *

At trial, plaintiff's basic theory of recovery was that it had received approval with regard to the fit of the sample mold, that in reliance on that approval it had constructed a full run of twenty-six molds, and that defendant had, in effect, committed an anticipatory breach of contract within the meaning of Section 2–610 by demanding that the fit of the molds be completely redesigned. On its counterclaim, and in response to plaintiff's position, defendant advanced the theory that plaintiff had breached the contract by failing to tender conforming goods within the five-week period mentioned by both parties.

After the presiding Justice had charged the jury, counsel for plaintiff requested at side bar that the jury be instructed on the doctrine of substantial performance. Counsel for defendant entered a timely objection to the proposed charge which objection was overruled. The court then supplemented its charge as follows:

The only point of clarification that I'll make, ladies and gentlemen, is that I've referred a couple of times to performance of a contract and you, obviously, have to determine no matter which way you view the contract to be, and there might even be a possible third way that I haven't even considered, whether the contract whatever it is has been performed and there is a doctrine that you should be aware of in considering that. That is the doctrine of substantial performance.

It is not required that performance be in any case one hundred percent complete in order to entitle a party to enforcement of their contractual rights. That is not to say within the confines of this case that the existence of flashing would be excused or not be excused. It is just a recognition on the part of the law when we talk about performance, probably if we took any contract you could always find something of no substance that was not completed one hundred percent. It is for you to determine that whether it has been substantially performed or not and what in fact constitutes substantial performance.

In your consideration, and as I say in this case, that's not to intimate that something like flashing is to be disregarded or to be considered. It's up to you based upon facts.

The jury returned a verdict in favor of plaintiff in the amount of $14,480.82.

I

In *Smith, Fitzmaurice Co. v. Harris*, 126 Me. 308, 138 A. 389 (1927), a case decided under the common law, we recognized the then-settled rule that with respect to contracts for the sale of goods the buyer has the right to reject the seller's tender if in any way it fails to conform to the specifications of the contract. We held that "[t]he vendor has the duty to comply with his order in kind, quality and amount." *Id.* at 312, 138 A. at 391. Thus, in *Smith,* we ruled that a buyer who had contracted to purchase twelve dozen union suits could lawfully refuse a tender of sixteen dozen union suits. Various provisions of the Uniform Sales Act, enacted in Maine in 1923, codified the common-law approach. R.S. (1954) ch. 185, §§ 11, 44. The so-called "perfect tender" rule came under considerable fire around the time the Uniform Commercial Code was drafted. No less an authority than Karl Llewellyn, recognized as the primum mobile of the Code's tender provisions, [citations] attacked the rule principally on the ground that it allowed a dishonest buyer to avoid an unfavorable contract on the basis of an insubstantial defect in the seller's tender. Llewellyn, *On Warranty of Quality and Society,* 37 Colum.L.Rev. 341, 389 (1937). Although Llewellyn's views are represented in many Code sections governing tender, the basic tender provision, Section 2–601, represents a rejection of Llewellyn's approach and a continuation of the perfect tender policy developed by the common law and carried forward by the draftsmen of the Uniform Sales Act. [Citations.] Thus, Section 2–601 states that, with certain exceptions not here applicable, the buyer has the right to reject "if the goods or the tender of delivery fail *in any respect* to conform to the contract . . ." (emphasis supplied). Those few courts that have considered the question agree that the perfect tender rule has survived the enactment of the Code. [Citations.] We, too, are convinced of the soundness of this position.

In light of the foregoing discussion, it is clear that the presiding Justice's charge was erroneous and, under the circumstances, reversibly so.

* * *

Appeal sustained.
New trial ordered.

*Right of Seller
to Cure Tender of
Nonconforming Goods*

WILSON v. SCAMPOLI

(1967 D.C.App.) 228 A.2d 848.

MYERS, A. J.

This is an appeal from an order of the trial court granting rescission of a sales contract for a color television set and directing the return of the purchase price plus interest and costs.

Appellee purchased the set in question on November 4, 1965, paying the total purchase price in cash. The transaction was evidenced by a sales ticket showing the price paid and guaranteeing ninety days' free service and replacement of any defective tube and parts for a period of one year. Two days after purchase the set was delivered and uncrated, the antennae adjusted and the set plugged into an electrical outlet to "cook out." When the set was turned on, however, it did not function properly, the picture having a reddish tinge. Appellant's delivery man advised the buyer's daughter, Mrs. Kolley, that it was not his duty to tune in or adjust the color but that a service representative would shortly call at her house for that purpose. After the departure of the delivery men, Mrs. Kolley unplugged the set and did not use it.

On November 8, 1965, a service representative arrived, and after spending an hour in an effort to eliminate the red cast from the picture advised Mrs. Kolley that he would have to remove the chassis from the cabinet and take it to the shop as he could not determine the cause of the difficulty from his examination at the house. He also made a written memorandum of his service call, noting that the television "Needs Shop Work (Red Screen)." Mrs. Kolley refused to allow the chassis to be removed, asserting she did not want a "repaired" set but another "brand new" set. Later she demanded the return of the purchase price, although retaining the set. Appellant refused to refund the purchase price, but renewed his offer to adjust, repair, or, if the set could not be made to function properly, to replace it. Ultimately, appellee instituted this suit against appellant seeking a refund of the purchase price. After a trial, the court ruled that "under the facts and circumstances the complaint is justified. Under the equity powers of the Court I will order the parties put back in their original status, let the $675 be returned, and the set returned to the defendant."

Appellant does not contest the jurisdiction of the trial court to order rescission in a proper case, but contends the trial judge erred in holding that rescission here was appropriate. He argues that he was always willing to comply with the terms of the sale either by correcting the malfunction by minor repairs or, in the event the set could not be made thereby properly operative, by replacement; that as he was denied the opportunity to try to correct the difficulty, he did not breach the contract of sale or any warranty thereunder, expressed or implied.

D.C.Code § 28:2–508 (Supp. V, 1966) provides:

(1) Where any tender or delivery by the seller is rejected because non-conforming and the time for performance has not yet expired, the seller may seasonably notify the buyer of his intention to cure and may

then within the contract time make a conforming delivery.

(2) Where the buyer rejects a nonconforming tender which the seller had reasonable grounds to believe would be acceptable with or without money allowance the seller may if he seasonably notifies the buyer have a further reasonable time to substitute a conforming tender.

A retail dealer would certainly expect and have reasonable grounds to believe that merchandise like color television sets, new and delivered as crated at the factory, would be acceptable as delivered and that, if defective in some way, he would have the right to substitute a conforming tender. The question then resolves itself to whether the dealer may conform his tender by adjustment or minor repair or whether he must conform by substituting brand new merchandise. The problem seems to be one of first impression in other jurisdictions adopting the Uniform Commercial Code as well as in the District of Columbia.

* * *

While these cases provide no mandate to require the buyer to accept patchwork goods or substantially repaired articles in lieu of flawless merchandise, they do indicate that minor repairs or reasonable adjustments are frequently the means by which an imperfect tender may be cured. In discussing the analogous question of defective title, it has been stated that:

The seller, then, should be able to cure [the defect] under subsection 2–508(2) in those cases in which he can do so without subjecting the buyer to any great inconvenience, risk, or loss. [Citations.]

Removal of a television chassis for a short period of time in order to determine the cause of color malfunction and ascertain the extent of adjustment or correction needed to effect full operational efficiency presents no great inconvenience to the buyer. In the instant case, appellant's expert witness testified that this was not infrequently necessary with new televisions. Should the set be defective in workmanship or parts, the loss would be upon the manufacturer who warranted it free from mechanical defect. Here the adamant refusal of Mrs. Kolley, acting on behalf of appellee, to allow inspection essential to the determination of the cause of the excessive red tinge to the picture defeated any effort by the seller to provide timely repair or even replacement of the set if the difficulty could not be corrected. The cause of the defect might have been minor and easily adjusted or it may have been substantial and required replacement by another new set—but the seller was never given an adequate opportunity to make a determination.

We do not hold that appellant has no liability to appellee, but as he was denied access and a reasonable opportunity to repair, appellee has not shown a breach of warranty entitling him either to a brand new set or to rescission. We therefore reverse the judgment of the trial court granting rescission and directing the return of the purchase price of the set.

Reversed.

Acceptance of Goods

F. W. LANG CO. v. FLEET

(1960) 193 Pa.Super. 365, 165 A.2d 258.

PER CURIAM.

The order of the court below is affirmed on the opinion of Judge Boyle, of the Municipal Court of Philadelphia.

The opinion of Judge Boyle follows:

* * *

On April 30, 1957, the defendants purchased from the plaintiff an ice cream freezer and a refrigeration compressor unit. A written installment sales contract was executed wherein the defendants agreed to pay a total sale price of $2160; the sum of $860 was to be paid as a down payment and the balance including finance charges was to be paid in 18 equal installments of $78.72.

Actually the defendants paid only the sum of $200 at the time of receiving the freezer and compressor and made no further payments. On July 30, 1959, the plaintiff caused a writ of replevin to issue in this court as of July Term, 1959, No. 3911, and the equipment was seized by the sheriff and delivered to the plaintiff. * * *

The plaintiff sold the equipment for $500, the highest price then obtainable and there is no averment by the defendants that this sale was not a fair and equitable resale of the equipment in accordance with accepted commercial practices. * * *

The defendants filed a complaint in assumpsit in this court as of September Term, 1959, No. 3198, alleging there that the equipment was defective and was wholly unusable for the purpose intended. The defendants demanded damages for the return of the down money, the cost of maintenance of the equipment while it was in the possession of the defendants and the court costs incurred in defending the replevin action.

The plaintiff obtained judgment * * * pursuant to the written installment sales contract on January 4, 1960.

* * *

[The defendants' complaint is] based on an alleged rescission of the contract by the defendants. But the depositions establish that the defendants have forfeited any right of rescission, if such right did exist in fact. About one year after the equipment was installed the defendants moved to a new location and took the equipment with them without notifying the plaintiff. In May or June of 1959 the defendants disconnected the compressor from the freezer and connected it to an air conditioner where it was used by the defendants to operate the air conditioner until the equipment was replevied by the plaintiff.

The Uniform Commercial Code, Sec. 2–602, 12A P.S. § 2–602 provides:

"(1) Rejection of goods must be within a reasonable time after their delivery or tender.

"It is ineffective unless the buyer seasonably notifies the seller.

"(2) * * * (a) after rejection any exercise or ownership by the buyer with respect to any commercial unit is wrongful as against the seller."

Section 2–606 provides:

"(1) Acceptance of goods occurs when the buyer * * *

"(c) does any act inconsistent with the seller's ownership; but if such act is wrongful as against the seller it is an acceptance only if ratified by him.

"(2) Acceptance of a part of any commercial unit is acceptance of that entire unit."

In the instant case the defendants exercised dominion over the compressor unit by using it to operate an air conditioner. This is completely inconsistent with the seller's ownership. The seller in this case by entering judgment for the unpaid balance ratified the sale as represented by the installment sales contract. The seller never accepted or agreed to a rescission by the defendants. Therefore under the cited provisions of the Commercial Code the buyer is deemed to have accepted the goods and is precluded from unilaterally asserting a rescission of the sales contract.

A rescission based on breach of warranty must be made within a reasonable time and cannot be made if the buyer exercises an act of dominion over the goods or permits the goods to be altered or changed while in his exclusive possession—[Citations].

* * *

We are convinced that there is no valid defense to the plaintiff's claim * * *.

Revocation of Acceptance

PECKHAM v. LARSEN CHEVROLET

(1978) 99 Idaho 675, 587 P.2d 816.

SHEPARD, C. J.

This is an appeal from a summary judgment in an action by plaintiff-appellant John Peckham seeking a rescission of a contract under which he had purchased a new automobile from the defendant-respondents Larsen Chevrolet and General Motors. Summary judgment was entered in favor of defendants. We reverse on the basis that genuine issues of material fact remain for resolution.

Although the action was brought for "rescission," we treat it as one for revocation of acceptance under the Uniform Commercial Code. Peckham asserts that the action is not one for rejection of goods pursuant to I.C. §§ 28–2–601 and 28–2–602, and hence we decline to discuss the potential application of the remedy of rejection to a factual situation similar to that presented here. On March 17, 1976, Peckham purchased a new automobile for the sum of $6,400.85, by entering into an installment sale and security agreement with Larsen Chevrolet.

* * *

During the first month and one-half after the purchase of the automobile, Peckham discovered that there was a dent in the hood, the gas tank contained no baffles, the emergency brake was inoperable, that the automobile did not contain a jack or spare tire, and that the clock and speedometer were inoperable. He asserts that despite repeated attempts to have those defects repaired, they were not finally completed until June 11, 1976. Larsen Chevrolet, on the other hand, argues that all of the alleged defects were known by Peckham at the time of purchase.

On July 15, 1976, a fire occurred in the dashboard of the automobile, resulting in damage to it and the carpeting, and also rendering the vehicle inoperable. Peckham has stated in an affidavit in opposition to the motion for summary judgment that the automobile was thereafter returned to Larsen Chevrolet and he informed Larsen Chevrolet that they had the responsibility of repairing the vehicle at their expense and otherwise he would either rescind the contract or demand a new automobile. There appears to have ensued a discussion relating to the damage from the fire being the responsibility of Peckham's insurance company. Peckham contends that at the conclusion of that discussion he orally informed Larsen Chevrolet that he was electing to rescind the contract and was demanding the return of the purchase price. Larsen Chevrolet denies having received that alleged oral notice of rescission.

* * *

On October 12, 1976, Peckham's written notice of rescission was sent to Larsen Chevrolet and General motors and Peckham's complaint was filed on January 26, 1977. * * *

Sale of the automobile here is a sale of goods governed by Article 2 of the Uniform Commercial Code. I.C. § 28–2–711 sets forth in general a buyer's remedies. It is provided therein that a buyer may cancel the contract if the seller's delivery is such that it gives the buyer a right to reject or a right to revoke acceptance of the goods.

As noted, this action was originally brought as one for "rescission" and Larsen Chevrolet and General Motors argue that because there is no provision in the Uniform Commercial Code for this remedy, it is unavailable to the buyer. The Code has, in most instances, abandoned the use of the term "rescission" in favor of terms such as "cancellation or termination." However, it has been held, and the commentators agree, that rescission and revocation of acceptance amount to the same thing under the Uniform Commercial Code, particularly since cancellation is a remedy available to a buyer who has established justifiable grounds for revocation of acceptance. I.C. § 28–2–711(1); [citations.] We, therefore, view and treat Peckham's action for "rescission" as one for "revocation of acceptance" under I.C. § 28–2–608. The principal issue in this case is whether Peckham has sufficiently established the elements necessary for a revocation of acceptance under I.C. § 28–2–608, so as to avoid a summary judgment in favor of the defendants.

Before a buyer may revoke acceptance under § 28–2–608, he must first show that the goods are nonconforming and that the nonconformity substantially impairs the value of the goods to the buyer. In that regard, it is provided:

28–2–608. Revocation of acceptance in whole or in part.—(1) The buyer may revoke his acceptance of a lot or commercial unit whose nonconformity substantially impairs its value to him if he has accepted it (a) on the reasonable assumption that its nonconformity would be cured and it has not been seasonably cured; or (b) without discovery of such nonconformity if his acceptance was reasonably induced either by the difficulty of discovery before acceptance or by the seller's assurances.

(2) Revocation of acceptance must occur within a reasonable time after the buyer discovers or should have discovered the ground for it and before any substantial change in condition of the goods which is not caused by their own defects. It is not effective until the buyer notifies the seller of it.

(3) A buyer who so revokes has the same rights and duties with regard to the goods involved as if he had rejected them.

Thereafter, if the buyer knew of the nonconformity when he accepted the goods, it is necessary that he show he acted with a reasonable assumption that the nonconformity would be cured, but that it was not seasonably cured. I.C. § 28–2–608(1)(a). If the buyer did not know of the noncon-

formity when he accepted, he must show that his acceptance was reasonably induced, either by the difficulty of discovering the nonconformity before acceptance or by the seller's assurances. I.C. § 28–2–608(1)(b); [citation.] Finally, the revocation of acceptance by the buyer must occur within a reasonable time after the buyer discovers the defect or should have discovered it, and before any substantial change in condition of the goods which is not caused by their own defects. Such revocation of acceptance is not effective until the buyer notifies the seller. I.C. § 28–2–608(2).

* * *

Considering the requisite elements for a revocation of acceptance and the facts construed most favorably toward Peckham, a factual dispute exists as to whether Peckham orally notified Larsen Chevrolet of his desire to cancel or rescind the contract (revocation of acceptance) immediately following the fire. Such is denied by Larsen Chevrolet. Depending upon the resolution of that disputed fact, also unresolved is whether Peckham's alleged oral or written notice of cancellation of the contract took place within a reasonable time.

As explained by comment 4 to § 28–2–608(2) of the Uniform Commercial Code, revocation of acceptance is required within . . . a reasonable time after discovery of the grounds for such revocation. Since this remedy will be generally resorted to only after attempts at adjustment have failed, the reasonable time period should extend in most cases beyond the time in which notification of breach must be given, beyond the time for discovery of non-conformity after acceptance and beyond the time for rejection after tender. The parties may by their agreement limit the time for notification under this section, but the same sanctions and considerations apply to such agreements as are discussed in the comment on manner and effect of rightful rejection.

It would appear that no particular form or content of notice of revocation of acceptance is required if the notice is sufficient to inform the seller that the buyer has revoked and identify the particular goods as to which he has revoked. [Citations.]

A further factual issue appears to remain regarding the conformity of the goods. Here there appears to be a dispute as to whether the goods were accepted by Peckham in a defective nonconforming condition or whether he accepted the goods upon assurance by the seller that the defects would be remedied. As stated by I.C. § 28–2–608, comment 2:

[r]evocation of acceptance is possible only where the nonconformity substantially impairs the value of the goods to the buyer. For this pur-

pose, the test is not what the seller had reason to know at the time of contracting; the question is whether the nonconformity is such as will in fact cause a substantial impairment of value to the buyer though the seller had no advance knowledge as to the buyer's particular circumstances.

An exhaustive discussion of what constitutes substantial impairment to a buyer is unnecessary since it is held each case must be examined on its own merits to determine what is a substantial impairment of value to the particular buyer.

* * *

The cause is reversed and remanded for further proceedings consistent with this opinion.

Problems

1. A contracted with B to manufacture, sell, and deliver to B and put in running order a certain machine. A set up the machine and put it in running order. B found it unsatisfactory and notified A that he rejected the machine. He continued to use it for three months, but continually complained of its defective condition. At the end of the three months he notified A to come and get it. Has B lost his right (a) to reject the machine? (b) to revoke acceptance of the machine?

2. Smith, having contracted to sell to Beyer 30 tons of described fertilizer, shipped to Beyer by carrier 30 tons of fertilizer which he stated conformed to the contract, taking from the carrier a shipper's order bill of lading. Nothing was stated in the contract as to time of payment, but Smith demanded payment as a condition of handing over to Beyer the properly indorsed bill of lading. Beyer refused to pay unless he were given the opportunity to inspect the fertilizer. Smith sues Beyer for breach of contract. Decision?

3. A and B entered into a contract for the sale of 100 barrels of flour. No mention was made

of any place of delivery. Thereafter, B demanded that A should deliver the flour at B's place of business, and A demanded that B should come and take the flour from A's warehouse. Neither party acceded to the demand of the other. Has either one a right of action against the other?

4. A, a manufacturer of air conditioning units, makes a written contract with B to sell and deliver to B 40 units at a price of $200 each and to deliver them at a certain apartment building owned by B for installation by B. Upon the arrival of A's truck for delivery at the apartment building, B examines the units on the truck, counts only 30 units and asks the driver if this is the total delivery. The driver replies that it is as far as he knows. B tells the driver that he will not accept delivery of the units. The next day A telephones B and inquires why delivery was refused. B states that the units on the truck were not what he ordered in that he ordered 40 units and that only 30 were tendered, and that he was going to buy air conditioning units elsewhere. In an action by A against B for breach of contract, B defends upon the ground that the tender of 30 units was improper as the contract called for delivery of 40 units. Is this a valid defense?

5. S sells a sofa to B for $800. S and B both know that the sofa is in S's warehouse located approximately ten miles further from B's home. The contract did not specify the place of delivery and B insists that the place of delivery is either B's house or S's store. Is B correct?

6. On November 4, S contracted to sell to B 500 sacks of flour at $4.00 each to be shipped in November to B in X City. On November 27, S shipped the flour. By December 5, when the car arrived, containing only 450 sacks, the market price of flour had fallen. The usual time required for shipment was 5 to 12 days. B refused to accept delivery or to pay. S shipped 50 more sacks of flour which arrived December 10. B refused delivery. S resold the flour for $3.00 per sack. What are S's rights against B?

7. A and B enter into a written contract whereby A agrees to sell and B to buy 6,000 bushels of wheat at $3.75 per bushel, deliverable at the rate of 1,000 bushels a month commencing June 1, the price for each installment being payable ten days after delivery thereof. A delivered and received payment for the June installment. A defaulted by failing to deliver the July and August installments. By August 15, the market price of wheat had increased to $4.00 per bushel. B thereupon entered into a contract with C to purchase 5,000 bushels of wheat at $4.00 per bushel deliverable over the ensuing four months. In late September, the market price of wheat commenced to decline and by December 1 was $3.25 per bushel. B brings an action against A for breach of contract. Decision?

8. Bain ordered from Marcum a carload of lumber which he intended to use in the construction of small boats for the U.S. Navy pursuant to contract. The order specified that the lumber was to be free from knots, wormholes, and defects. The lumber was shipped and immediately upon receipt Bain looked into the door of the fully loaded car, ascertained that there was a full carload of lumber, and acknowledged to Marcum that the carload had been received. On the same day, Bain moved the car to his private siding and sent to Marcum full payment in accordance with the terms of the order.

A day later, the car was moved to the work area and unloaded in the presence of the Navy inspector, who refused to allow three-fourths of it to be used because of excessive knots and wormholes in the lumber. Bain then informed Marcum that he was rejecting the order and requested refund of the payment and directions as to disposition of the lumber. Marcum replied that since Bain had accepted the order and unloaded it, he was not entitled to return of the purchase price. Bain thereupon brought an action against Marcum to recover the purchase price. Decision?

Chapter
24

WARRANTIES

The concept of warranty as an obligation of the seller to the buyer with respect to the title, quality, quantity, condition or performability of goods sold or to be sold, is an ancient one. Historically, the remedy of the buyer for breach of warranty was an action in tort for fraud. However, today the liability of a seller for breach of warranty is universally recognized as contractual.

In the law of sales, a warranty creates a duty on the part of the seller for breach of which the buyer may recover a judgment against the seller for damages. In addition by timely notice, the buyer may reject or revoke acceptance of the goods. Although the word "warranty" has different meanings as used in other branches of the law, under the law of sales warranties arise out of (1) the mere fact that the transaction is a sale of goods, such as a warranty of title; (2) affirmations of fact or promises by the seller to the buyer, which are express warranties; or (3) circumstances under which the sale is made, as in the case of implied warranties of merchantability and of fitness for the buyer's particular purpose. Implied

warranties are obligations of the seller which he has not assumed by express language.

A seller is not required to warrant the goods, and in general he may, by appropriate words, exclude, negate, or modify a particular warranty or even all warranties. Moreover, he may carefully refrain from making an express warranty. With respect to implied warranties he must act affirmatively, and in the manner prescribed by the Code in order effectively to disclaim liability. The seller will be guided in each case by his personal honesty, business judgment, the sales resistance of the particular customer, and his earnestness and desire to make the sale.

This chapter will examine the various types of warranties as well as the obstacles to a cause of action based on warranty.

TYPES OF WARRANTIES

Express Warranties

Under Section 2–313 of the Code, express warranties of the seller are that: (1) The goods shall conform to any affirmation of fact or promise made by the seller to the buyer which relates to the goods and becomes part of the basis of the bargain. (2) The goods shall conform to any description of them which is made part of the basis of the bargain. (3) The whole of the goods shall conform to any sample or model of the goods which is made part of the basis of the bargain.

An express warranty is an explicit undertaking by the seller with respect to the quality, description, condition, or performability of the goods. The Code does not require that affirmations of fact or promises by the seller be relied upon by the buyer but only that they constitute a part of the basis of the bargain. If they are basic to the bargain, reliance by the buyer is implicit.

Affirmations of fact by the seller with respect to the goods are usually a part of the description of the goods. The seller expressly warrants that the goods shall conform to the description. The use of a sample or model is a means of describing the goods, and the seller expressly warrants that the entire lot of goods sold shall conform to the sample or model.

In order to create an express warranty it is not necessary that the seller have a specific intention to make a warranty or use formal words such as "warrant" or "guarantee". Statements or promises made by the seller to the buyer prior to the sale may be express warranties, as they may form a part of the basis of the bargain just as much as statements made at the time of the sale. Each case presents a question of fact whether statements of the seller prior to the formation of the contract should reasonably be considered as basic to the bargain.

It is not necessary that a seller have knowledge of the falsity of a statement made by him in order to be liable for breach of express warranty. The seller may be acting in good faith and relying upon secondhand inaccurate information. To be liable for fraud, on the other hand, a person must make a misrepresentation of fact with knowledge of its falsity.

At common law statements or promises by the seller made subsequent to the contract or sale are not binding on the seller in the absence of new consideration from the buyer. Such statements were regarded not only as unsupported by consideration from the buyer but also as not inducing the contract or sale because it had already taken place.

Under the Code, statements or promises made by the seller subsequent to the contract of sale may become express warranties even though no new consideration is given. Section 2–209(1) provides that, "An Agreement modifying a contract within this Article needs no consideration to be binding." Thus, a statement, or promise, or assurance with respect to the goods made by the seller to the buyer at the time of delivery may be a binding modification of the prior contract of sale and held to be an express warranty as basic to the bargain. It requires no consideration from the buyer to be binding on the seller.

The Code further provides that a mere affirmation of the value of the goods or a statement purporting merely to be the seller's opinion or commendation of the goods does not create a warranty. Section 2–313(2). Such statements do not deceive the ordinary buyer. They are accepted merely as opinions or as puffing statements. If the seller genuinely believes the goods to be more valuable than the price at which he is willing to sell them, he probably would not sell. However, a statement of value may be an express warranty where the seller states the price at which the goods were purchased from a former owner, or where he gives market figures relating to sales of similar goods. These are affirmations of facts. They are statements of events and not mere opinions, and the seller is liable for breach of warranty if they are untrue.

While ordinarily a statement of opinion by the seller is not a warranty, if the seller is an expert and gives his opinion as such, he may be liable for breach of warranty. Thus, an art expert who states that a certain painting is a genuine Rembrandt, which is the basis of the bargain, warrants the accuracy of his opinion.

A seller may also be liable if he misrepresents his opinion. Thus, a seller may say, "This horse is sound," or he may say, "In my opinion, this horse is sound." In the first instance he has made an express warranty of the soundness of the horse. In the second, he has made no warranty if he actually believed the horse to be sound. But if he knew that the horse was unsound at the time of stating his opinion to the contrary, he has misrepresented his opinion as a factual matter. This is not only fraud, but also a breach of warranty.

Another manner in which a statement of opinion may become an affirmation of fact is illustrated by Section 539 of the Restatement of Torts:

A statement of opinion in a business transaction upon facts not disclosed or otherwise known to the recipient may reasonably be interpreted as an implied statement that the maker knows of no fact incompatible with his opinion.

Warranty of Title and Warranty against Infringement

Warranty of Title. Under the early English common law, there was no implied warranty of title by the seller. The principle applied was that of *caveat emptor,* let the buyer beware. A seller was held liable for fraud where he knew that he did not have title and concealed this fact from the buyer, but otherwise he assumed no risk as to title unless he made an express warranty. The law subsequently developed to the point where a seller in possession of the goods impliedly warranted title, but if he were not in possession at the time of the contract or sale it was to be assumed that he was merely selling such interest in the goods, if any, as he might have.

Later the common law developed and enforced an implied warranty of title and implied warranty of quiet possession regardless of the location of the goods at the time of the sale.

The Code abolishes the implied warranty of quiet possession and imposes upon the seller the obligation of a warranty of title without designating it either as express or implied. Disturbance of quiet possession is merely one way in which a breach of warranty of title may be shown.

Under the Code the seller warrants that (1) the title conveyed is good and its transfer rightful, and (2) the goods are not encumbered by any security interest or other lien of which the buyer had no knowledge at the time of contracting. Section 2–312.

Warranty against Patent Infringement. A seller who is a merchant makes an additional warranty in sales of goods of the kind in which he regularly deals that such goods shall be delivered free of the rightful claim of any third person by way of infringement of any existing patent. Section 2–312(3).

This warranty does not run in favor of a buyer who furnishes specifications to the seller. In such case it is the buyer who must hold the seller harmless against any claim of infringement by a third person arising out of the seller's compliance with the buyer's specifications.

If the buyer is sued for infringement by a third person he must notify the seller within a reasonable time after he receives notice of the litigation or be barred from any remedy against the seller by reason of any liability established by the litigation. Section 2–607(3)(b). The same requirement of notice applies to the seller with respect to the obligation of the buyer to hold the seller harmless against claims for infringement. Section 2–607(6).

Implied Warranties

An implied warranty arises out of the situation of the parties, the type of contract or sale, and the circumstances of the case. It has been developed by the law, not as something to which the parties have agreed, but as a departure from the early rule of *caveat emptor*. In its early formative period of development, the law of sales was influenced more by the pressures and demands of sellers as a class rather than those of buyers as a class. However the law has developed more solicitude for buyers as a class and has imposed implied warranties upon the seller unless he expressly stipulates against them.

Implied Warranty of Merchantability. At early common law a seller was not held to any implied warranty as to the quality of the goods, particularly in the case of a sale of specific goods. However, under the Code a seller who is a merchant impliedly warrants the merchantability of goods that are of the kind in which he deals.

The implied warranty of merchantability is an obligation of the merchant-seller that the goods are reasonably fit for the general purpose for which they are manufactured and sold, and also that they are of fair, average, merchantable quality. Under Section 2–314 of the Code, the minimum requirements of merchantability are that the goods must:

(a) pass without objection in the trade under the contract description, and
(b) in the case of fungible goods, be of fair average quality within the description, and
(c) be fit for the ordinary purposes for which the goods are used, and
(d) run, within variations permitted by the agreement, of even kind, quality and quantity within each unit and among all units involved, and
(e) be adequately contained, packaged, and labeled as the agreement may require, and

(f) conform to the promises or affirmations of fact made on the container or label, if any.

The term "merchantable" has come to mean fair, average, medium quality. The seller is not required to supply the finest or highest quality of goods, nor is the buyer obliged to accept the lowest quality or dregs of goods which comply with the contract description. Between the two extremes is a medium or average quality. If the goods described in the contract have a brand name, they must have the quality of that brand which is fairly salable.

The official Comment to Section 2–314 states that a contract for the sale of second-hand goods "involves only such obligation as is appropriate to such goods for that is their description." It has been held that "such obligation" includes an implied warranty of merchantability. In defining this warranty the price, age, and condition of the goods must be considered. For example, the defendant purchased in June, 1970, a used 1965 model automobile from plaintiff retail dealer. The day after the purchase, the transmission fell out of the car while being driven by defendant on an expressway. A week after repairs were made, the brakes went out completely on another expressway. The court held that any car without adequate transmission and proper brakes is not fit for the ordinary purpose of driving, that the implied warranty of merchantability was therefore breached, and that defendant had justifiably revoked his acceptance of the car. Overland Bond & Investment Corp. v. Howard, 9 Ill.App.3d 348, 292 N.E.2d 168 (1972).

Implied Warranty of Fitness for Particular Purpose. Any seller, whether or not he is a merchant, impliedly warrants that the goods, whether they are new or used, are reasonably fit for the particular purpose of the buyer for which the goods are required, if at the time of contracting the seller has reason to know such particular purpose and that the buyer is relying upon the seller's skill and judgment to furnish suitable goods. Section 2–315 provides:

Where the seller at the time of contracting has reason to know any particular purpose for which the goods are required and that the buyer is relying on the seller's skill or judgment to select or furnish suitable goods, there is unless excluded or modified under the next section an implied warranty that the goods shall be fit for such purpose.

A particular purpose of the buyer may differ from the ordinary purpose for which the goods are usually purchased. A particular purpose may be a specific use or relate to a special situation in which the buyer intends to use the goods. Thus, if the seller has reason to know that the buyer is purchasing a pair of shoes for mountain climbing and that the buyer is relying upon the seller's judgment to furnish suitable shoes for this purpose, a sale of shoes suitable only for ordinary walking purposes would be a breach of this implied warranty.

The buyer need not specifically inform the seller of his particular purpose. It is sufficient if the seller has reason to know it. However, the buyer must rely upon the seller's skill or judgment in selecting or furnishing suitable goods in order that this implied warranty exist.

In the sale of food products for human consumption, the particular purpose of the buyer and the ordinary purpose for which the goods are used are the same. Hence, both the implied warranty of merchantability under Section 2–314 and of fitness under Section 2–315 apply. The Code provides that the serving for value of food or drink to be consumed on the premises or elsewhere is a sale. Section 2–314(1).

Where injuries have been caused by a nonedible substance in food, an implied warranty may not exist if the substance is natural to the food. Some courts distinguish between natural objects in food, such

as fish bones in fish, and objects which are foreign, as a pebble, piece of wire, or glass. For example, a person injured by a fish bone becoming lodged in her throat while eating fish chowder served in a restaurant was denied recovery on the ground that fish bones are a proper ingredient of fish chowder and therefore are to be reasonably expected. Webster v. Blue Ship Tea Room, Inc., 347 Mass. 421, 198 N.E.2d 309 (1964). However, under this test, damages are recoverable for a broken tooth and lacerated gums caused by a piece of metal in a serving of maple walnut ice cream.

The modern test is not the natural relation of the injurious substance to the food, but the reasonable expectation of the consumer upon eating it. A substance natural to a product in one stage of preparation does not necessarily imply that the consumer will reasonably anticipate or expect it to be in the final product served. In one case the plaintiff, upon being served a martini cocktail, removed the olive, observed that it had a hole in the end, and bit down upon it thereby breaking a tooth upon the olive pit. The court held it was a question of fact for the jury to determine whether he had acted reasonably in expecting that the olive contained no pit. If this was a reasonable expectation, he was entitled to recover damages. Hochberg v. O'Donnell's Restaurant, Inc., 272 A.2d 846 (D.C.App., 1971).

OBSTACLES TO WARRANTY ACTIONS

Disclaimer or Modification of Warranties

Subsection 2–316(1) calls for a reasonable construction of words or conduct tending to negate or limit warranties. In addition, subsection 2–316(4) provides that remedies and recovery of damages for breach of warranty may be contractually limited under Sections 2–718 and 2–719.

The Code makes clear that the seller should not rely upon a time-honored formula of words and expect to obtain a disclaimer which may go unnoticed by the buyer. Disclaimers should be positive, explicit, unequivocal and conspicuous.

Express Exclusions. Warranty of title may be excluded or modified only by specific language or by certain circumstances, Section 2–312(2), including a judicial sale or sales by sheriffs, executors, or foreclosing lienors. In such cases the seller is manifestly offering to sell only such right or title as he or a third person might have in the goods, as it is apparent that the goods are not the property of the person selling them.

Express warranties may be excluded upon the seller carefully refraining from making any promise or affirmation of fact relating to the goods, or description of the goods, or a sale by means of a sample or model. Section 2–313. The seller may also negate an express warranty by clear, specific, unambiguous language in the contract to that effect. Section 2–316(1) provides:

Words or conduct relevant to the creation of an express warranty and words or conduct tending to negate or limit warranty shall be construed wherever reasonable as consistent with each other; but subject to the provisions of this Article on parol or extrinsic evidence (Section 2–202) negation or limitation is inoperative to the extent that such construction is unreasonable.

To exclude or to modify an *implied warranty of merchantability,* the language of disclaimer or modification must mention merchantability and in the case of a writing must be conspicuous. Section 2–316(2).

To exclude or to modify an *implied warranty of fitness* for the particular purpose of the buyer, the language of disclaimer must be in writing and conspicuous. Section 2–316(2), subject to 2–316(3).

Notwithstanding the express requirements of Section 2–316(2) *all implied war-*

ranties, unless the circumstances indicate otherwise, are excluded by expressions like "as is," "with all faults," or other language plainly calling the buyer's attention to the exclusion of warranties. Section 2–316(3)(a). They may also be excluded by the buyer's examination of the goods or by his refusal to examine them, Section 2–316(3)(b); or by course of dealing, course of performance, or usage of trade, Section 2–316(3)(c).

Buyer's Examination or Refusal to Examine the Goods. If the buyer inspects the goods, implied warranties do not apply to obvious defects which are apparent upon examination. It may be noted that Section 2–316(3)(b) provides not only that there is no implied warranty as to defects which an examination ought to have revealed where the buyer has examined the goods as fully as he desired, but also where the buyer has refused to examine the goods.

A mere failure or omission to examine the goods is not a refusal to examine them. It is not enough that the goods were available for inspection and the buyer did not see fit to inspect them. In order for the buyer to have "refused to examine the goods," the seller must have first made a demand upon the buyer that he examine them. Such demand is necessary.

Trade Usage. If a well-recognized trade usage or custom exists, of which both of the parties to a contract or sale have knowledge, in the absence of evidence of a contrary intention, the law will regard the parties as having intended the usage to apply to their contract or sale, and they are each bound by it.

Thus, where the seller of a new automobile failed to lubricate it before delivery to the buyer, and the evidence established that it was the regular custom and usage of new car dealers to do so, the seller was held liable to the buyer for the resulting damages to the automobile in an action for breach of implied warranty. (Davis Motors, Dodge & Plymouth Co. v. Avett, 294 S.W.2d 882, Texas Civ.App.1956).

The Code in Section 2–314(3) expressly provides that implied warranties may arise from course of dealing or usage of trade. An implied warranty can also be excluded or modified by course of dealing or course of performance or usage of trade. Section 2–316(3)(c).

Cumulation and Conflict of Warranties. In a contract for the sale of goods it is possible to have both express warranties and implied warranties. All warranties are to be construed as consistent with each other and cumulative, unless such construction is unreasonable.

The intention of the parties is controlling, and in ascertaining that intention the Code sets forth the following rules: (a) Exact or technical specifications displace an inconsistent sample, or model, or general language of description; (b) A sample from an existing bulk displaces inconsistent general language of description; and (c) Express warranties displace inconsistent implied warranties other than an implied warranty of fitness for a particular purpose. Section 2–317.

Federal Legislation Relating to Warranties of Consumer Products. In order to afford protection to purchasers of consumer products (defined as "tangible personal property normally used for personal, family or household purposes"), the Congress in 1974 enacted the Magnuson-Moss Warranty Act. The purpose of the Act is to make available to consumer purchasers adequate information with respect to warranties and to prevent deception.

Administration and enforcement of the Act is by the Federal Trade Commission. The statutory guidelines for rules and regulations of the Commission with respect to the type of information required to be set forth in warranties of consumer products are contained in Title 15, U.S. Code, Section 2302, as follows:

(1) The clear identification of the names and addresses of the warrantors.

(2) The identity of the party or parties to whom the warranty is extended.

(3) The products or parts covered.

(4) A statement of what the warrantor will do in the event of a defect, malfunction, or failure to conform with such written warranty—at whose expense—and for what period of time.

(5) A statement of what the consumer must do and expenses he must bear.

(6) Exceptions and exclusions from the terms of the warranty.

(7) The step-by-step procedure which the consumer should take in order to obtain performance of any obligation under the warranty, including the identification of any person or class of persons authorized to perform the obligation set forth in the warranty.

(8) Information respecting the availability of any informal dispute settlement procedure offered by the warrantor and a recital, where the warranty so provides, that the purchaser may be required to resort to such procedure before pursuing any legal remedies in the courts.

(9) A brief, general description of the legal remedies available to the consumer.

(10) The time at which the warrantor will perform any obligations under the warranty.

(11) The period of time within which, after notice of a defect, malfunction, or failure to conform with the warranty, the warrantor will perform any obligation under the warranty.

(12) The characteristics or properties of the products, or parts thereof, that are not covered by the warranty.

(13) The elements of the warranty in words or phrases which would not mislead a reasonable, average consumer as to the nature or scope of the warranty.

In addition, the Act provides that a written warrantor cannot disclaim any implied warranty. For a more complete discussion of the Act, see Chapter 43.

Privity of Contract

By reason of the association of warranties with contracts, a principle of law became established in the nineteenth century whereby recovery for breach of warranty would not be allowed unless the plaintiff was in a contractual relationship with the defendant. This relationship is known as privity of contract.

Under this rule a warranty by seller A to buyer B who resells the goods to purchaser C under a similar warranty gives C no rights against A. There is no privity of contract between A and C. In the event of breach of warranty, C may recover only from his seller B who in turn may recover from A.

Suppose A sells a horse to B with a warranty that it is sound. B resells the horse to C with no warranty. The horse is not sound. C has no cause of action against B who made no warranty, nor against A because no privity of contract exists between A and C, and A's warranty does not run with the horse.

One reason for the rule which requires privity of contract is that by merely selling goods the seller does not thereby necessarily also intend that the buyer shall be a transferee of a right of action which he may have against the person from whom he had previously bought the goods. Thus, B buys a horse from A with a warranty of soundness. The horse is not sound. B has both the horse and a cause of action against A for breach of warranty. These are both assets of B and he may wish to sell one and not the other. The fact that he sells the horse to C does not mean that he is also selling to C his cause of action against A. He could assign this cause of action to C or to any one.

A second reason for the rule is that a warranty is similar to a personal indemnity. An accrued right of action for breach of warranty is assignable, but to permit the buyer to assign the warranty itself would be an enlargement of the scope of the seller's undertaking to include the indemnification of persons to whom it was not made.

The requirement of privity of contract may have had some merit in an economy where the retailers of goods were the sole source of representations as to the quality of the goods purchased by users and consumers. A century ago it was common practice for retailers to purchase goods in bulk and upon resale to package or bag separately for each customer the desired quantity purchased. The retailer had an opportunity to become familiar with the condition, quality, and purity of the merchandise which he sold to the public. However, where the retailer buys and resells goods which are packaged by the manufacturer, to open the package would greatly impair their merchantability.

Today the affirmations, promises and representations with respect to goods are made directly to retail purchasers by persons remote in the distributive chain through widespread advertising use of television, radio, newspapers, magazines and direct mail. There is no privity of contract between the person making the representations and the person induced thereby to purchase the goods. This has caused most courts, including those in leading commercial States, to abolish the requirement of privity of contract.

Since privity requires that the plaintiff and defendant stand in direct contractual relationship in order for the plaintiff to maintain his contractually based warranty action, there are two broad categories of privity problems which arise. The first of these, *horizontal privity*, pertains to noncontracting parties who are injured by the defective goods; this group would include users, consumers, and bystanders who are not the contracting purchaser. The second type of privity problem, *vertical privity*, applies to remote sellers within the chain of distribution with whom the consumer purchaser has not dealt.

The Code relaxes the requirement of horizontal privity of contract to the extent of permitting recovery on a seller's warranty to members of the family or household of the buyer or guests in his home. Section 2–318 provides three alternative sections from which the states may select:

Alternative A A seller's warranty whether express or implied extends to any natural person who is in the family or household of his buyer or who is a guest in his home if it is reasonable to expect that such person may use, consume or be affected by the goods and who is injured in person by breach of the warranty. A seller may not exclude or limit the operation of this section.

Alternative B A seller's warranty whether express or implied extends to any natural person who may reasonably be expected to use, consume or be affected by the goods and who is injured in person by breach of the warranty. A seller may not exclude or limit the operation of this section.

Alternative C A seller's warranty whether express or implied extends to any person who may reasonably be expected to use, consume or be affected by the goods and who is injured by breach of the warranty. A seller may not exclude or limit the operation of this section with respect to injury to the person of an individual to whom the warranty extends.

The Code, however, was not intended to establish outer boundaries as to which third parties may recover for injuries caused by defective goods, but rather it sets a minimum beyond which the states may expand through case law. The official Comment to Section 2–318 states:

The first alternative expressly includes as beneficiaries within its provisions the family, household and guests of the purchaser. Beyond this, the section *in this form* is neutral and is not intended to enlarge or restrict the developing case law on whether the seller's warranties, given to his buyer who resells, extend to other persons in the distributive chain. *The second alternative is designed for states where the case law had already developed further and for those*

that desire to expand the class of beneficiaries. The third alternative goes further, following the trend of modern decisions as indicated by Restatement of Torts 2d (Tentative Draft No. 10, 1965) in extending the rule beyond injuries to the person.

This comment also presents the "neutral" position the Code has taken regarding vertical privity.

In the great majority of states, the courts have accepted the Code's invitation to relax the requirements of privity and, for all practical purposes, have eliminated the requirements of both vertical and horizontal privity in warranty cases.

Requirement of Notice of Breach

Where the buyer has accepted a tender of goods which are warranted by the seller, he is required to notify the seller of any breach of warranty, express or implied, as well as any other breach, within a reasonable time after he has discovered or should have discovered it.

If the buyer fails to notify the seller of any breach within such reasonable time, he shall be barred from remedy against the seller. Section 2–607(3)(a).

Contributory Negligence

By reason of the development of warranty liability in the law of sales and contracts, contributory negligence of the buyer is no defense to an action against the seller for breach of warranty.

Voluntary Assumption of the Risk

If the buyer after discovery of a defect in the goods which may cause injury, and being aware of the danger, nevertheless proceeds to make use of the goods, he will not be permitted to recover damages from the seller for loss or injuries caused by such use.

This is not contributory negligence, but voluntary assumption of a known risk.

Thus, a buyer may not recover damages for breach of an implied warranty of fitness for a particular purpose where he uses the goods after discovering their unfitness. For example, a contractor planning to lay a water pipe line gave plans for the job to defendant supplier who prescribed the needed materials which the contractor purchased from him. Through an error, the supplier delivered sewer pipe glue instead of glue for water pipe line. Upon commencing the work, the man in charge reported to the contractor his dissatisfaction with the glue as it "didn't bond" the pipe sections. The project supervisor telephoned the supplier who checked his records and said they had shipped the right material. Use of the glue was then continued and after completion of the pipe line, tests disclosed numerous leaks. The contractor had to dig up the line and reconstruct it at a cost of $9,000. The court held that the seller was not liable as the buyer's continued use of the glue after knowledge of its unfitness for the purpose was unreasonable under Section 2–607(3)(a). Davis v. Pumpco, Inc., 519 P.2d 557 (Okl.App. 1974).

No Warranty Exists
Apart from Sale or
Contract for Sale of Goods

Under the Code, as under pre-Code law, a warranty of goods exists only in connection with a sale or contract to sell.

In a modern self-service store, the usual practice is that a customer selects the goods that he wishes to buy from a wide variety displayed on shelves with prices marked, then takes these goods to the check-out counter where he pays for them before taking them from the store.

It may become critical to determine at what precise moment a sale or contract of sale occurs, as in the event that a customer after picking up goods with intent to buy them, but before check-out and payment, is injured by a defect in the goods. If a sale or contract were made prior to the occurrence of the injuries, the seller's warranties are operative, and the customer may recover damages for breach of implied warranty of merchantability. If there were no sale or contract of sale at the time of the injuries, he may recover only upon proof of negligence of the retailer or of the manufacturer which may be difficult to establish.

The few reported decisions are in conflict as to whether a sale or contract is made before closing at the check-out counter. The Maryland case of Sheeskin v. Giant Foods, Inc. (page 462), cites three pre-Code cases which hold that in such situation no sale or contract is made. Most cases, including *Sheeskin,* decided under the Code reach the opposite conclusion.

In *Sheeskin* the court unequivocally holds that at the moment the customer picks up the goods with intent to buy them, an executory bilateral contract of sale by offer and acceptance is entered into between the retailer and the customer, and from that moment forward the implied warranties of the Code apply. The reasoning of the Court in support of its finding of manifestation of mutual assent required by the law of contracts is tenuous, and appears to be based more upon judicial importation than factual realities. The lay-out of the floor of a self-service store consists usually of numerous parallel aisles formed by tall rows of shelving holding priced items of merchandise. Some of the personnel re-stock the shelves as needed, while other employees at check-out counters total the prices of items brought there by customers and receive payment. The acts of customers at the time they take physical possession of goods with intent to buy is seldom noticed or observed or made manifest to any employee. No one is employed to be attentive to these acts which generally occur outside of the range of vision of otherwise occupied employees. There was no evidence in *Sheeskin* that the plaintiff's act of picking up the six-pack carton was manifested to any agent or employee of the defendant retailer. However, imposition of liability upon the retailer in *Sheeskin* does not seem unjust or shocking. Recovery may be justified on the basis of the public policy discouraging the marketing of products having defects that are a menace to the public, as expressed in Embs v. Pepsi-Cola Bottling Company (page 491) which also involved injuries caused by the explosion of a bottle of carbonated beverage in a self-service store.

No Warranty of Goods Supplied Incidental to a Service

A warranty is part and parcel of a sale or contract to sell. Express warranties must be part of the basis of the bargain which is the contract of sale. Both at common law and under the Code, a sale is defined as the passing of title to goods from the seller to the buyer for a price. Section 2–106.

In certain transactions goods are used up or consumed. A question may arise whether the use or consumption involved a sale or whether the goods are merely incidental to a service being furnished.

Patients in hospitals have contracted hepatitis resulting from blood transfusions administered in connection with operations. This is a serious illness which may cause death. The problem is that blood transfusions are sometimes necessary to the success of an operation, and hepatitis virus is not effectively excludable or its presence detectable in whole blood, plasma, or blood components, by known methods of medical testing. In actions against hospitals and suppliers of whole blood or its components for use in transfusions, liability has been imposed upon a finding that there was a sale of the blood and a breach of implied war-

ranty of merchantability, and substantial consequential damages were recovered. The great majority of States have statutes which expressly provide that blood supplied for transfusions is a service and not a sale, some stating that the supplier is not liable except for negligence or wilful misconduct.

These statutes generally preclude warranty liability, and their effect is salutary as they relieve hospitals and suppliers of blood from the risk of a potential liability which they have no capability of guarding against except by discontinuing transfusions, an option not favorable to the patient.

The use of disclaimers of warranty is frequently impractical, and impossible in emergency operations on unconscious patients. Such statutes have been held constitutional as not arbitrary or discriminatory, and not a denial of due process or equal protection of the law, on the ground that they apply equally and fairly to all who engage in like transactions and affect alike all persons pursuing the same business under the same conditions. Heirs of Fruge v. Blood Services, 506 F.2d 841 (C.A.5, 1975).

It has been held that the doctrine of *res ipsa loquitur* does not apply in an action for damages caused by hepatitis following a blood transfusion, as no presumption of negligence arises from the mere fact that hepatitis was contracted following the transfusion. Morse v. Riverside Hospital, 44 Ohio App.2d 422, 339 N.E.2d 846 (1974).

It has also been held that blood should be considered "unavoidably unsafe," that is, not "unreasonably dangerous," and not a proper subject for application of the rule of strict liability in tort. McMichael v. American Red Cross, 532 S.W.2d 7 (Ky.1975). One court has stated that strict liability does not apply to a business of supplying the public with "an apparently useful and desirable product, attended with a known and apparently reasonable risk." McDaniel v. Baptist Memorial Hospital, 352 F.Supp. 690 (W.D.Tenn.1971).

Cases

Types of Warranties

DONALD v.
CITY BANK OF DOTHAN

(1976, Ala.) 329 So.2d 92.

SHORES, J.

The plaintiff filed suit against City National Bank of Dothan claiming damages for alleged breach of warranty on the sale of a boat. The bank denied the allegations of the complaint and filed a motion for summary judgment supported by testimony of Robert G. Donald, the plaintiff, Jesse S. Doyle and James H. Eason, officers of the bank. The plaintiff filed a brief in opposition to the motion but filed no affidavits or other testimony in opposition thereto. The court granted summary judgment and the plaintiff appealed. The only question presented is whether any genuine issue of material fact exists according to the depositions.

An officer of the bank told the plaintiff that the bank had repossessed a boat and was interested in selling it. The plaintiff says in deposition:

* * * I told him that I was possibly interested in one, because I was thinking about buying a boat to put into charter service out of Destin, Florida.

The boat was located at Tibbetts Marina at Panama City. The plaintiff went to Panama City to "look at the boat" and says Tibbetts was in the process of making repairs on it. Prior to purchasing the boat the plaintiff hired Willings Detroit Diesel of Birmingham to inspect it. He said Willings was unable to make a "running test" because the engines would not start, but reported to him that it needed repiping, new tubes and lines, but otherwise "everything appeared okay." In addition, and again prior to the purchase of the boat, the plain-

tiff hired Tibbetts Boat Works to do a vessel survey and install new batteries. This report described the specifications of the boat and stated that the topsides, decking bilges and water tanks were in "good" condition.

The plaintiff contended that Tibbetts advised him that the generator was being repaired but would be shipped later.

The bank claims that no evidence was offered establishing any warranties; and, in addition, that summary judgment was proper since the plaintiff failed to file any affidavits or other testimony in opposition to its motion.

The plaintiff contends that there were issues of material fact requiring the court to overrule the bank's motion. He summarizes these issues as follows:

1. Whether the bank is a merchant with regard to the goods sold, giving rise to an implied warranty of merchantability under Title 7A, § 2–314, Code;
2. whether the bank had reason to know of any particular purpose to which the boat would be put, thereby creating an implied warranty for a particular purpose under Title 7A, § 2–315; and
3. whether the bank breached its express agreement to include a generator with the boat.

* * *

We turn now to the evidence.

Two officers of the bank testified that the bank made absolutely no representations whatever concerning the boat; that the plaintiff was told that all the bank wanted was to get rid of the boat and was not willing to finance the purchase; and that it wanted " ' * * * to sell the boat as it sits at Mr. Tibbetts['] dock. * * *'"

The depositions of the bank's officers state unequivocally that no officer or employee of the bank ever made any representation of any kind about the boat, other than there were no liens or encumbrances against it. The plaintiff offered no evidence of any express warranty or representation other than as to the inclusion of a generator with the boat. He does contend on appeal that an implied warranty of merchantability was made under the provisions of Title 7A, § 2–314, which provides, in part:

* * * a warranty that the goods shall be merchantable is implied in a contract for their sale if the seller is a merchant with respect to goods of that kind. * * *

§ 2–314(c) provides that goods to be merchantable must be at least such as "are fit for the ordinary purposes for which such goods are used; * * *"

A merchant is defined by Title 7A, § 2–104(1), as:

* * * a person who deals in goods of the kind or otherwise by his occupation holds himself out as having knowledge or skill peculiar to the practices or goods involved in the transaction * * *

A merchant is defined in Anderson, Uniform Commercial Code, Vol. 1, § 2–104:4 (2d ed. 1970), as follows:

(a) Dealer. He may be a person who deals in goods of the kind involved. Whether he deals in other goods is immaterial. He must deal in goods of the kind involved in the transaction in order to come within the first category.
(b) Representation. He may be a person who by his occupation holds himself out as having knowledge or skill peculiar to the practices or goods involved in the transaction. Whether he actually has such knowledge or skill is immaterial if he so holds himself out.

Obviously, a bank may be a merchant under the U.C.C. definitions (see Official Comments to § 2–104); but absolutely no evidence was offered in this case to bring the bank within either of the definitions. No evidence was offered that the City National Bank of Dothan deals in the kind of goods involved in this transaction—boats—or that it holds itself out as having knowledge or skill peculiar to such goods.

The record before the trial court and here indicates that the sale of the boat was no more than an isolated transaction by the bank.

Prince v. LeVan, Alaska 1971, 486 P.2d 959 (9 U.C.C. Reporting Service 367), also involved a sale of a boat. In treating the same issue the court said:

In the present case we deal with a single isolated transaction. Defendants were not shown to deal in vessels or to possess peculiar knowledge or skill in relation to vessels. Defendants were therefore not merchants [under U.C.C., § 2–104(1)] and a warranty of merchantability may not be implied [under U.C.C., § 2–314]. At 964 (9 U.C.C. Reporting Service at 375)

The plaintiff next argues that an implied warranty of fitness was made within Title 7A, § 2–315, which provides:

Where the seller at the time of contracting has reason to know any particular purpose for which the goods are required and that the buyer is relying on the seller's skill or judgment to select or furnish suitable goods, there is unless excluded or modified under the next section an implied warranty that the goods shall be fit for such purpose.

This provision of the U.C.C. deals with an implied warranty of fitness for a *particular* purpose as opposed to ordinary purpose under the warranty of merchantability. This warranty is implied if:

1. The seller has reason to know the buyer's particular purpose; *and*
2. the seller has reason to know that the buyer is relying on the seller's skill or judgment to furnish appropriate goods; *and*
3. the buyer, in fact, relied upon the seller's

skill or judgment.   J. White & R. Summers, Handbook of the Law under the Uniform Commercial Code, § 9–9 (1972).

Although the plaintiff's deposition indicates that he told the bank officer that he "was thinking about buying a boat to put into charter service out of Destin, Florida," the record is devoid of any evidence that the plaintiff in anywise relied upon the bank's skill or judgment (or indeed that it possessed such skill or judgment) that the boat was fit for a particular purpose, here, charter service.

* * *

No evidence was presented to establish an implied warranty of fitness for a particular purpose under Title 7A, § 2–315.

* * *

The only question remaining concerns the generator, which the plaintiff says was not on the boat and which he says he has yet to receive.   In his deposition, the plaintiff says " * * * when I first asked the bank about the boat, they said, yes, it had a generator on it."   We think this testimony establishes a scintilla of controversy as to whether the defendant made a warranty with respect to the generator.   Since, on this issue, a genuine issue of material fact was established, summary judgment was improper as to this issue.

* * *

Since there is a scintilla of evidence in support of the claim involving the generator and since that claim is separate from the claims involving the alleged warranty of merchantability, and warranty of fitness for a particular purpose, partial summary judgment * * * was appropriate; but the plaintiff is entitled to a trial insofar as his claim that the bank told him the boat included a generator.

Affirmed in part, reversed in part and remanded.

Implied Warranties

SHEESKIN v. GIANT FOODS, INC.

(1974) 20 Md.App. 611, 318 A.2d 874.

[While shopping with his wife at defendant's retail Giant Food Store (Giant), plaintiff, age 73, was carrying a six-pack carton of Coca Cola taken from a display bin at Giant to a shopping cart in the store when one or more of the bottles exploded, causing plaintiff to lose his footing, fall to the floor, and sustain injuries.   Plaintiff sued Giant and Washington Coca Cola Bottling Company (Bottler) for damages on the grounds of negligence and breach of implied warranty.   At the conclusion of the trial, the court directed a verdict for each defendant.   On appeal, the Maryland Court of Special Appeals stated that the evidence was sufficient to show a greater likelihood that plaintiff's injury was caused by Giant's negligence than by any other cause, and therefore res ipsa loquitur (the thing speaks for itself) applied and plaintiff was entitled to have the jury pass on the question of Giant's negligence.   On the issue of negligence, the Court summarily reversed the judgment in favor of Giant, and affirmed the judgment in favor of the Bottler.   The Court then considered the question of the liability of each defendant upon an implied warranty of merchantability.]

DAVIDSON, J.
* * *

The retailer, Giant Food, Inc., contends that appellant failed to prove that an implied warranty existed between himself and the retailer because he failed to prove that there was a sale by the retailer to him or a contract of sale between the two.   The retailer maintains that there was no sale or contract of sale because at the time the bottles exploded Mr. Seigel had not yet paid for them.   We do not agree.

Code (1957), Art. 95B, § 2–314(1) states in pertinent part:

Unless excluded or modified (§ 2–316), a warranty that the goods shall be merchantable is implied *in a contract for their sale* if the seller is a merchant with respect to goods of that kind. (Emphasis added.)

Thus, in order for the implied warranties of § 2–314 to be applicable there must be a "contract for sale." In Maryland it has been recognized that neither a completed "sale" nor a fully executed contract for sale is required. It is enough that there be in existence an executory contract for sale. [Citation.]

* * *

Here, the plaintiff has the burden of showing the existence of the warranty by establishing that at the time the bottles exploded there was a contract for their sale existing between himself and the Giant. [Citations.] Mr. Titus, the manager of the Giant, testified that the retailer is a "self-service" store in which "the only way a customer can buy anything is to select it himself and take it to the checkout counter." He stated that there are occasions when a customer may select an item in the store and then change his mind and put the item back. There was no evidence to show that the retailer ever refused to sell an item to a customer once it had been selected by him or that the retailer did not consider himself bound to sell an item to the customer after the item had been selected. Finally, Mr. Titus said that an employee of Giant placed the six-pack of Coca Cola selected by Mr. Seigel on the shelf with the purchase price already stamped upon it. Mr. Seigel testified that he picked up the six-pack with the intent to purchase it.

We think that there is sufficient evidence to show that the retailer's act of placing the bottles upon the shelf with the price stamped upon the six-pack in which they were contained manifested an intent to offer them for sale, the terms of the offer being that it would pass title to the goods when Mr. Seigel presented them at the check-out counter and paid the stated price in cash. We also think that the evidence is sufficient to show that Mr. Seigel's act of taking physical possession of the goods with the intent to purchase them manifested an intent to accept the offer and a promise to take them to the check-out counter and pay for them there.

* * *

In our view the manner by which acceptance was to be accomplished in the transaction herein involved was not indicated by either language or circumstances. The seller did not make it clear that acceptance could not be accomplished by a promise rather than an act. Thus it is equally reasonable under the terms of this specific offer that acceptance could be accomplished in any of three ways: 1) by the act of delivering the goods to the check-out counter and paying for them; 2) by the promise to pay for the goods as evidenced by their physical delivery to the check-out counter; and 3) by the promise to deliver the goods to the check-out counter and to pay for them there as evidenced by taking physical possession of the goods by their removal from the shelf.

The fact that customers, having once selected goods with the intent to purchase them, are permitted by the seller to return them to the shelves does not preclude the possibility that a selection of the goods, as evidenced by taking physical possession of them, could constitute a reasonable mode of acceptance. Section 2–106(3) provides:

"Termination" occurs when either party pursuant to a power created by agreement or law puts an end to the contract otherwise than for its breach. On "termination" all obligations which are still executory on both sides are discharged but any right based on prior breach or performance survives.

Here the evidence that the retailer permits the customer to "change his mind" indicates only an agreement between the parties to permit the consumer to end his contract with the retailer irrespective of a breach of the agreement by the retailer. It does not indicate that an agreement does not exist prior to the exercise of this option by the consumer.

Moreover, the absence of evidence to show that the retailer ever refused to sell an item to a customer once it had been selected by him or that the retailer did not consider himself bound to sell an item to a customer after the customer had made a selection supports an inference that the selection of the goods, as evidenced by the consumer's taking physical possession of them, could constitute a reasonable mode of acceptance. We believe that under the circumstances surrounding this transaction reasonable men could conclude that Mr. Seigel's act of taking physical possession of the goods with the intent to pay for them constituted a reasonable mode of acceptance; that at that moment a contract for the sale of the goods (that is, a bilateral executory agreement to transfer title to the goods for a price) came into being; and that from that moment forward the implied warranties of Code (1957), Art. 95B, § 2–314 were applicable. Accord, Day v. Grand Union Co., 280 App.Div. 253, 113 N.Y.S.2d 436, 439 (1952) (Brewster, J., concurring); Sanchez-Lopez v. Fedco Food Corp., 27 Misc.2d 131, 211 N.Y.S.2d 953, 956–957 (N.Y. City Court 1961).

* * *

Appellant contends that the evidence was sufficient to show that the retailer breached an implied warranty of merchantability and that he suffered loss as a result of that breach. We agree.

It is axiomatic that a buyer may recover for breach of warranty without proving negligence on the part of the seller. [Citations.] In order to recover on a warranty, the plaintiff need show only that the article sold did not conform to the representation of the warranty at the time it left the control of the defendant. [Citations.]

Here Mr. Seigel testified that all of the circumstances surrounding his selection of the bottles were normal; that the carton in which the bottles came was not defective; that in lifting the carton from the shelf and moving it toward his basket the bottles neither touched nor were touched by anything other than his hand; that they exploded almost instantaneously after he removed them from the shelf; and that as a result of the explosion he fell injuring himself. It is obvious that Coca Cola bottles which would break under normal handling are not fit for the ordinary use for which they were intended and that the relinquishment of physical control of such a defective bottle to a consumer constitutes a breach of warranty. Thus the evidence was sufficient to show that when the bottles left the retailer's control they did not conform to the representations of the warranty of merchantability, and that this breach of the warranty was the cause of the loss sustained.

* * *

The Bottler

Appellant contends that the bottler also breached the implied warranties of merchantability found in Code (1957), Art. 95B, § 2–314. The bottler concedes that an implied warranty of merchantability exists with respect to appellant, the ultimate consumer, but asserts that appellant failed to prove that the warranty was broken because he failed to prove that a defect existed in the bottles at the time of their delivery to the retailer. We agree with the bottler.

* * *

Effective 1 July 1969, § 2–314 was amended so as to include within the meaning of the term "seller" the "manufacturer, distributor, dealer, wholesaler or other middleman and/or the retailer." The section was also amended to provide, in pertinent part, that "any previous requirement of privity is abolished as between the buyer and any of the aforementioned parties in any action brought by the buyer." In addition, § 2–318 was amended to extend a "seller's" express or implied warranty not only to any natural person who is in the family or household of his buyer or a guest in his home, but also to "any other ultimate consumer or user of the goods or person affected thereby if it is reasonable to expect that such person may use, consume or be affected by the goods and who is injured in person by breach of the warranty."

These amendments establish that protection under the implied warranty of merchantability provided in § 2–314 extends not only to the person buying for resale to the ultimate consumer (that is, the retailer) but also to the ultimate consumer. [Citation.]

While privity between the bottler and the ultimate consumer is not required, a "sale" or "contract for sale" is required in order to make the warranty implied by § 2–314 applicable. Thus, there must be a sale or contract for sale from the bottler to some individual in the distributive chain in order for the implied warranties to arise in favor of the ultimate consumer. Here there was evidence that prior to Mr. Seigel's injuries, the bottler sold the bottles of Coca Cola selected by Mr. Seigel to the retailer, Giant Food, Inc. This evidence was sufficient to show that there was a warranty in existence which extended from the bottler to Mr. Seigel, the ultimate consumer.

* * *

Judgment in favor of Bottler affirmed.

Judgment in favor of retailer Giant reversed, and case remanded for a new trial.

Disclaimer or Modification of Warranties

O'NEIL v. INTERNATIONAL HARVESTER CO.

(1978 Colo.App.) 575 P.2d 862.

RULAND, J.

The plaintiff, Albert M. O'Neil, appeals from a summary judgment dismissing his complaint against the defendants, International Harvester Company and International Harvester Credit Corporation, and from a summary judgment in favor of the defendants on their first counterlcaim. * * * We affirm in part, reverse in part, and remand for further proceedings.

The pleadings, interrogatories, and depositions in this case disclose the following pertinent facts. On August 22, 1975, O'Neil entered into a "Retail Installment Contract" with the defendant, International Harvester Company, for the purchase of a used diesel tractor and trailer. International Harvester Company assigned its interest in the contract to the defendant, International Harvester Credit Corporation. The contract provided, *inter alia*:

Each USED motor vehicle covered by this contract is sold AS IS WITHOUT WARRANTY OF ANY CHARACTER expressed or implied, unless purchaser has received from seller a separate written warranty executed by seller.

No written warranties were received by O'Neil. The contract also provided:

Purchaser agrees that this contract . . . which he has read and to which he agrees contains the entire agreement relating to the installment sale of said property and supersedes all previous contracts and agreements between purchaser and seller relating to the order or sale of said property except as to any written agreements between purchaser and seller concerning warranty.

Pursuant to the contract, O'Neil paid $1,700 as a down payment, but failed to make any of the required monthly payments.

According to O'Neil's deposition, shortly after the purchase his employee drove the truck to a location in the mountains for the purpose of hauling firewood to Denver. He had numerous problems with the truck, causing delays which resulted in the loss of his permit to cut and remove firewood, as well as loss of business. A representative of International Harvester agreed to pay one-half of the cost of certain repairs. After several attempts to have the defendants repair the truck during the next month, O'Neil returned it to the defendants, but the defendants refused to rescind the sale.

O'Neil admitted reading the contract, including the warranty exclusion provision. He stated, however, that he understood the provision to mean that the tractor and trailer would be in the condition represented by the defendant's salesman. According to O'Neil, the salesman represented that the truck had been recently overhauled and would be suitable for operation in the mountains; later, when he returned the truck, O'Neil overheard another employee of the defendant International Harvester Company say to the salesman, *inter alia,* "I told you not to sell him Inman's truck— Inman took every piece of used equipment off his other fleet of trucks and stuck it on that one."

In his complaint O'Neil sought both rescission of the contract and damages, alleging that International Harvester was liable for breach of express warranties, an implied warranty of fitness for a particular purpose, and fraud. Defendants answered denying that any warranties were made to O'Neil or that any fraud was committed in the sale and, insofar as pertinent here, defendants counterclaimed for the balance due under the contracts.

O'Neil first contends that the trial court improperly granted summary judgment against him on his claim that the defendants breached an implied warranty of fitness for a particular purpose relative to the capability of the truck. In response, the defendants assert that summary judgment was proper because this warranty was effectively disclaimed in the contract. We agree with the defendants.

Pursuant to the Uniform Commercial Code, one way an implied warranty of fitness for a particular purpose can be excluded is by a conspicuous writing which states generally that there are no warranties extending beyond the description in the contract. § 2–316(2). O'Neil admits reading the warranty disclaimer provision. Thus, we need not decide whether as a matter of law it was "conspicuous." See § 1–201(10). And, we hold that the language "AS IS WITHOUT WARRANTY OF ANY CHARACTER expressed or implied" was sufficient to inform O'Neil that there was no implied warranty in effect for the truck. See § 2–316(2). [Citation.]

Even though express warranties are also included in the above quoted language, still O'Neil asserts that summary judgment was improvidently granted against him on his claim that International Harvester breached the express warranties. The defendants argue that the trial court's ruling was correct. We agree with O'Neil.

Section 2–316 provides that "[w]ords or conduct relevant to the creation of an express warranty *and* words or conduct tending to negate or limit warranty shall be construed wherever reasonable as consistent with each other . . . ." Here, the oral warranties relied upon by O'Neil are totally inconsistent with the warranty exclusion clause of the contract. Section 2–316 further provides that, under these circumstances (but subject to the provisions of the Code governing the admission of parol evidence), a provision limiting an express warranty is inoperative.

Turning to the applicable parol evidence rule as set forth in § 2–202, one finds that:

Terms with respect to which the confirmatory memoranda of the parties agree or which are otherwise set forth in writing intended by the parties as a final expression of their agreement with respect to such terms as are included therein, may not be contradicted by evidence of any prior agreement or of a contemporaneous oral agreement . . . .

Various commentators have noted the difficulty in applying §§ 2–316 and 2–202 when, as here, the buyer alleges oral warranties by the seller, but the written contract contains both a warranty disclaimer clause and an "integration" provision. See 3 R. Duesenberg & L. King, Bender's Uniform Commercial Code Service § 6.06; J. White & R. Summers, Uniform Commercial Code § 12.4; Broude, The Consumer and the Parol Evidence Rule: Section 2–202 of the Uniform Commercial Code, 1970 Duke L.J. 881. While the courts divide on whether testimony as to the oral warranties may be admitted under these circumstances, [citations] we do not reach that issue in this case.

Where, as here, the buyer alleges the existence of oral warranties prior to execution of the written contract, as well as conduct following the sale (such as a commitment to pay for certain repairs) which tends to show that warranties were in fact made, there is a material issue of fact for resolution. That issue is whether the parties intended the written contract to be a final expression of their agreement, and if not, what the terms actually agreed upon by the parties consisted of. Further, we hold that, under such circumstances, evidence of both oral warranties and the conduct of the parties subsequent to signing the contract is admissible for purpose of resolving this issue. Thus, entry of summary judgment on this issue was error. [Citations.]

* * *

That part of the judgment dismissing O'Neil's claim for breach of implied warranty is affirmed. The balance of the judgment is reversed and the cause remanded for further proceedings consistent with this opinion.

Privity of Contract—
Requirement of Notice of Breach

L. A. GREEN SEED CO. OF ARKANSAS v. WILLIAMS

(1969 Ark.) 438 S.W.2d 717.

HOLT, J.

Appellee is a commercial grower of tomatoes and appellant is a distributor and seller of tomato seed. Appellee brought this action to recover damages for breach of warranty by appellant in the sale of tomato seed. When the trial court overruled appellant's demurrer to appellee's complaint, as amended, the appellant refused to plead further. Thereupon the trial court, sitting as a jury, proceeded to award damages to the appellee, after taking evidence upon this issue.

The appellant first contends that it was error for the trial court to overrule its demurrer to the complaint as amended. This contention is based upon the premise that appellee did not purchase a product sold by the appellant. In his complaint appellee asserts that appellant packaged, labeled and sold tomato seed as "Green's Pink Shipper" variety, knowing the seed would be purchased by the public to raise and sell "Pink Shipper Tomatoes" for a profit; that this seed was so represented and sold to Brown Seed Store, which retailer then so represented and sold the seed to Guy Jones (who is engaged in the business of growing tomato seedlings and selling the plants to commercial tomato growers); that appellee purchased, from Jones, plants grown from this particular seed, transplanted and raised them "in accordance with accepted standards of farming" on three-fourths of an acre of his farm; that appellant represented and warranted the seed from which the tomato plants were grown as being "Green's Pink Shipper" tomato seed, when, in fact, it was some unknown variety of tomato seed which produced an inferior tomato; that appellant expressly and impliedly warranted to appellee, through Brown and Jones, that its product was "Pink Shipper" variety of merchantable quality and fit for intended purposes; and that because of breach of warranty, the appellee was unable to market his tomatoes which spoiled in the field, resulting in a crop loss of $900 caused by the alleged breach of warranty.

* * *

A cause of action exists, based upon a breach of warranty, where one sells seed to an immediate purchaser upon a misrepresentation of a certain variety and fitness, and the purchaser, who relied upon the warranty, is entitled to recover damages from the seller for the breach of warranty. [Citation.] And the same is true where inferior plants are sold and the purchaser relies upon a warranty of fitness. [Citation.]

Appellant, however, argues that appellee's cause of action, if any, is against the seller of the tomato plants and cannot reach the appellant because it sold appellee nothing. Appellant contends that it has made no warranty, express or implied, with respect to the tomato plants purchased by appellee and that its warranty, with respect to the seed, does not extend to and reach appellee, a remote purchaser, because appellee is a purchaser of the tomato plant and not the seed which was distributed by the appellant. We think appellant's argument is without merit.

The defense or shield of lack of privity is now removed where an action is brought against a seller of goods to recover damages for breach of warranty.

* * * Plainly, a seller of tomato seed might reasonably expect a commercial grower of tomatoes (as appellee in the case at bar) to use or be affected by the seeds distributed and sold on the market by the seller. The appellee is an integral part of the distributive chain for production purposes.

According to the allegations, which are admitted as being true, appellee purchased tomato plants and raised tomatoes from plants which were grown from the very seed distributed, warranted and sold by appellant as "Green's Pink Shipper" variety, when, in fact, the seed was of an inferior and unknown variety. To be sure, the seed changed in natural form into plants after appellant placed it into channels of commerce. Yet, such transformation was an expected result by the laws of nature and not by the hand of man. We hold that when a seller of tomato seed warrants it to be of

particular fitness and variety, the warranty extends in the distributive chain to a purchaser of tomato plants which are grown from the seed for commercial purposes.

Appellant next asserts that the complaint is defective because it does not contain an allegation of notice to the appellant with respect to the claimed breach of warranty. This contention is based upon Ark.Stat.Ann. § 85–2–607(3)(a) (Add.1961) which requires a buyer to give notice of a breach of warranty to the seller within a reasonable time after the buyer discovers, or should have discovered, the alleged breach. We must agree with the appellant that the appellee's complaint is subject to a demurrer since it does not contain an allegation of notice.

The issue of allegation of notice, under this section, seems to be one of first impression in our state. However, it appears that in jurisdictions which have had occasion to interpret this section, the giving of notice must be pleaded as a condition precedent to recovery. * * * In Smith v. Pizitz of Bessemer, Inc., 271 Ala. 101, 122 So.2d 591 (Ala.1960), the court said:

" * * * it appears that a majority of the American Courts which have considered the problem have held the notice requirement applicable in a case of the nature now before this court and that such notice should be alleged in the complaint as a condition precedent to recovery." [Citations.]

The Committee Comment following § 85–2–607 reflects that it also intended that notice be a condition precedent to any recovery since it refers to the notice as the "notification which saves the buyer's rights." The purpose of the statutory requirement of notice to the seller of breach of warranty is to enable the seller to minimize damages in some manner, such as correcting the defect, and also to give the seller some immunity against stale claims. Of course, the sufficiency of notice and what is considered to be a reasonable time within which to give notice of breach of warranty are ordinarily questions of fact for the jury, based upon the circumstances in each case.

* * *

The case at bar is a breach of warranty action. We have held, in an action based upon a breach of warranty, that where a notice of defect is required, it is necessary for a buyer to allege and prove, as a condition precedent to a recovery, that there was compliance with the requirement of notice. [Citations.]

We hold that the giving of reasonable notice is a condition precedent to recovery in this action and that the giving of notice must be alleged in the complaint in order to state a cause of action.

* * *

The judgment is reversed and the cause remanded with the right of the appellee to amend his complaint to contain the allegation of notice. Otherwise, the demurrer will be sustained.

Voluntary Assumption of the Risk

GUARINO v. MINE SAFETY APPLIANCE CO.

(1969) 25 N.Y.2d 460, 306 N.Y.S.2d 942, 255 N.E.2d 173.

JASEN, J.

These consolidated actions arose out of an accident wherein three men died and five others were injured.

On October 2, 1957, one John J. Rooney, an engineer employed by the Bureau of Sewage Disposal of the City of New York, died of gas asphyxiation after descending into an interceptor sewer located 30 or 40 feet below the ground in the Borough of Queens to ascertain the source of water in the bulkhead. At the time of the accident, he was wearing an oxygen-type protective mask manufactured by the defendant herein. The estate of John J. Rooney recovered a judgment against the defendant on a theory of breach of implied warranty of merchant-

ability, in "that the mask did not work because the plunger was defective." [Citation.]

The two other decedents, and the surviving plaintiffs, were all sewage treatment workers and members of Rooney's work team at the time of the accident. Plaintiff Fattore entered the sewer tunnel with Rooney after testing for gas and finding none. Decedent Guarino was stationed at the bottom level of the shaft, decedent Messina was at the next level, and a survivor, Mirabile, was at the upper level. After correcting the water leakage problem, Rooney and Fattore began to recross the tunnel and return to the shaft, at which time Fattore felt Rooney slump behind him. He attempted to drag Rooney from the sewer tunnel, but finding himself having difficulty breathing, he released Rooney, ripped off his own mask, and hollered for help. Guarino and Messina were fatally stricken by the lethal gas present in the sewer when they left their posts in the sewer shaft and entered the sewer tunnel without masks in answer to Fattore's call for help. The other surviving plaintiffs were injured as they also descended into the sewer in response to Rooney's plight.

This appeal presents for our review the "danger invites rescue" doctrine.

In New York the rescue doctrine had its historical genesis in Eckert v. Long Is. R.R. Co. (43 N.Y. 502 [1871]), which stated that the plaintiff's intestate, who was killed while attempting to rescue a child on the railroad tracks was not to be found contributorily negligent unless acting rashly or recklessly. The purpose of the doctrine, we said, was to prevent a plaintiff from being found contributorily negligent, as a matter of law, when he voluntarily placed himself in a perilous situation to prevent another from suffering serious injury.

The doctrine has been most frequently applied when a defendant through his negligence either injured or imperilled another and a third person was injured in attempting to rescue the person in jeopardy. [Citations.] * * *

In these actions plaintiffs seek application of the "danger invites rescue" doctrine to a situation where a breach of warranty endangers a person so as to invite rescue by a third party. It is significant to note that all of the cases that have invoked the rescue doctrine since it was first promulgated by this court have been negligence actions. This is, we believe, the first instance in which the doctrine has been invoked in an action where the gravamen of the wrong complained of has been breach of warranty.

We do not believe that the theory of the action, whether it be negligence or breach of warranty, is significant where the doctrine of "danger invites rescue" applies. A breach of warranty and an act of negligence are each clearly wrongful acts. Both terms are synonymous as regards fixation of liability, differing primarily in their requirements of proof.

As we recently held in Provenzo v. Sam (23 N.Y.2d 256, 260, 296 N.Y.S.2d 322, 325, 244 N.E.2d 26, 28), the rescue doctrine should be applied when "one party *by his culpable act* has placed another person in a position of imminent peril which invites a third person, the rescuing plaintiff, to come to his aid." (Emphasis supplied.)

* * *

Here the defendant committed a culpable act against the decedent Rooney, by manufacturing and distributing a defective oxygen-producing mask, for which it has been held accountable in damages. (Rooney v. Healy Co., 20 N.Y.2d 42.) By virtue of this defendant's culpable act, Rooney was placed in peril, thus inviting his rescue by the plaintiffs who were all members of Rooney's sewage treatment crew. There was no time for reflection when it became known

that Rooney was in need of immediate assistance in the dark tunnel some 30 to 40 feet below the street level. These plaintiffs responded to the cries for help in a manner which was reasonable and consistent with their concern for each other as members of a crew. To require that a rescuer answering the cry for help make inquiry as to the nature of the culpable act that imperils someone's life would defy all logic.

As Judge Cardozo so eloquently stated in Wagner v. International Ry. Co.: "Danger invites rescue. The cry of distress is the summons to relief. * * * The *wrong* that imperils life is a wrong to the imperilled victim; it is a wrong also to his rescuer." (232 N.Y. 176, 180, 133 N.E. 437 [emphasis added].)

"[T]hese judgments," the Appellate Division correctly held, "while nominally premised on a breach of warranty theory as applied to a user, rest fundamentally on the rescue doctrine, a concept unaffected by the exact label put upon the wrong which created the danger to the imperiled victim. For the same reason, the rescuer's status as a user or non-user of the defective instrumentality is not directly relevant to our analysis. It is enough that the plaintiffs attempted to rescue a user with respect to whom a breach of warranty or 'tortious wrong' had been committed." (31 A.D.2d 261, 297 N.Y.S.2d 644.)

We conclude that a person who by his culpable act, whether it stems from negligence or breach of warranty, places another person in a position of imminent peril, may be held liable for any damages sustained by a rescuer in his attempt to aid the imperilled victim.

* * *

Accordingly, the order and judgment appealed from should be affirmed.

Problems

1. B, having read in the manufacturer's advertising of the Model 3-Z Zenmac Heater, asked

S, a contractor, to deliver and install one in B's machine shop. S was intimately familiar with the shop. The heater was installed but, because of its design and capacity, and not due to defect in its mechanical operation, proved entirely inadequate to heat B's shop. B refused to pay for the heater, and S sued him for the sale price. B defended upon the ground of breach of warranty of fitness for the particular use. Decision?

2. At the advent of the social season Aunt Lavinia purchased a Hula skirt in Sadie's dress shop. The saleslady told her: "This superior garment will do things for a person." Aunt Lavinia's house guest, her niece, Florabelle, asked and obtained her aunt's permission to wear the skirt to a masquerade ball. In the midst of the festivity at which there was much dancing, drinking and smoking, the long skirt brushed against a glimmering cigarette butt. Unknown to Aunt Lavinia and Florabelle, its wearer, the garment was made of a fine unwoven fiber which is highly flammable. It burst into flames and Florabelle suffered severe burns. Aunt Lavinia notified Sadie of the accident and of Florabelle's intention to recover from Sadie. Florabelle seeks to recover damages in an action against Sadie, the proprietor of the dress shop, and Exotic Clothes, Inc., the manufacturer from which Sadie purchased the skirt. Decision?

3. The X Company, manufacturer of a widely advertised and expensive perfume, sold a quantity of this product to Y, a retail druggist. A and B visited the store of Y, and A, desiring to make a gift to B, purchased from Y a bottle of this perfume, asking for it by its trade name. Y wrapped up the bottle so purchased and handed it directly to B. The perfume contained an injurious foreign chemical substance which, upon the first use of the perfume by B, severely burned the face of B and caused a permanent facial disfigurement. What are the rights of B, if any, against A, Y, and the X Company, respectively?

4. Jane Doe, a housewife, purchased a bottle of "Bleach-All", a well-known brand, from Roe's combination service station and grocery store. When Jane Doe used the "Bleach-All" the clothes severely deteriorated due to an error made in mixing the chemicals during manufacture of "Bleach-All." Jane Doe brings an action against Roe to recover damages. Decision?

5. B brings an action to recover for injuries suffered while eating a dinner purchased and served on January 15, at a restaurant owned and operated by A. B alleges that as part of the dinner A furnished for drinking purposes water that was contaminated with bacteria and unfit for human consumption. He further alleges that he drank the water and became ill therefrom. At the trial it was established that A had employed ordinary and reasonable care in obtaining the water from a faucet through which the water was supplied by the city, and that A had no knowledge, nor by the exercise of due care could have had knowledge, that the water was contaminated. What judgment?

6. A route salesman for Ideal Milk Company delivered a one-half gallon glass jug of milk to Allen's home. The next day when Allen grasped the milk container by its neck to take it out of his refrigerator, it shattered in his hand and caused serious injury. Allen paid Ideal on a monthly basis for the regular delivery of milk. Ideal's milk bottles each contained the legend "Property of Ideal—to be returned" and the route salesman would pick up the empty bottles when he delivered milk. Allen brought an action against Ideal Milk Company, charging breach of warranty. Decision?

7. While Butler and his wife Wanda were browsing through Sloan's used car lot, Butler told Sloan that he was looking for a safe but cheap family car. Sloan said, "That old Cadillac hearse ain't hurt at all, and I'll sell it to you for $950." Butler said, "I'll have to take your word for it because I don't know a thing about cars." Butler asked Sloan whether he would guarantee the car and Sloan replied, "I don't guarantee used cars." Then Sloan added, "But I have checked that Caddy over and it will run another 10,000 miles without needing any repairs." Butler replied, "It has to because I won't have an extra dime for any repairs." Butler made a down payment of $100 and signed a printed form contract furnished by Sloan which contained a provision, "Seller does not warrant the merchandise's condition or performance of any used automobile described herein."

As Butler drove the car out of Sloan's lot, the left rear wheel fell off and Butler lost control of the vehicle. It veered over an embankment, causing serious injuries to Wanda. What is Sloan's liability to Butler and Wanda?

8. Pace was employed by Ray to sell Ray's automobile and instructed by Ray not to give the buyer any warranties. Ray was not mechanically inclined and did not know the difference between a carburetor and a muffler. Pace knew of this indifference of Ray to matters mechanical. In the process of selling the car to Davis, Pace warranted that the car was in first class condition. Ray's prior cavalier use of the car had resulted in its having scored cylinders, gears which meshed infrequently, and other mechanical defects, many of which could not be detected by casual inspection. Davis paid $4,000 to Pace, who deducted his commission and remitted the balance to Ray.

What are Davis's rights, if any?

9. John purchased for cash a Revenge automobile manufactured by Japanese Motors, Ltd. from an authorized franchised dealer in the United States. The dealer told John that the car had a "24 months—24,000 miles warranty." Two days after John accepted delivery of the car, he received an 80 page fine-print manual which stated, among other things, on page 72:

The warranties herein are expressly in lieu of any other express or implied warranty, including any implied warranty of merchantability or fitness, and of any other obligation on the part of the company or the selling dealer.

Japanese Motors, Ltd. and the selling dealer warrant to the owner each part of this vehicle to be free under use and service from defects in material and workmanship for a period of 24 months from the date of original retail delivery of first use, or until it has been driven for 24,000 miles, whichever first occurs.

Within nine months after the purchase, John has been forced to return the car for repairs to the dealer on 30 different occasions, and the car has been in the dealer's custody for over 70 days during these nine months. The dealer has been forced to make major repairs of the engine, transmission and steering assembly. The car is now in the custody of the dealer for further major repairs, and John has demanded that it keep the car and refund his entire purchase price. The dealer has refused on the ground that it has not breached its contract and is willing to continue repairing the car during the remainder of the "24–24" period.

What are the rights and liabilities of the dealer and John?

10. Harry, a middle-aged bachelor and playboy, became concerned with the amount of his gray hair that was beginning to show. He consulted his barber who recommended that he use "Youthful Tint" to conceal his gray hair. The barber sold "Youthful Tint" which was manufactured by X Corporation. The barber told him to follow the directions on the bottle and by using it his hair would have the appearance of the hair of a 20-year old man. The barber said he had many satisfied customers.

Upon this recommendation, Harry selected a bottle of "Youthful Tint" from the barber's stock on display and paid for it. That night he applied "Youthful Tint" to his hair, following the directions on the bottle in every respect. The next morning upon awakening Harry discovered to his horror that all of his hair had fallen out.

Does Harry have a cause of action against the barber and against X Corporation, or either of them?

Chapter
25

PRODUCTS LIABILITY

This chapter considers the liability of manufacturers and vendors of goods to buyers, users, consumers, and bystanders for damages caused by defective goods. The rapid and expanding development of case law has established products liability as a separate and distinct field of law, combining and enforcing rules and principles of contract, sales, warranty, negligence, torts, and statutory law.

An impetus to the expansion of such liability has been the modern practice whereby the retailer serves principally as a conduit of pre-packaged goods in sealed containers which are widely advertised by the manufacturer or distributor on television and radio, in newspapers, magazines, brochures, and by direct mail. This has hastened the extension of product liability coverage to include manufacturers and other parties within the chain of distribution. The extension of products liability to manufacturers, however, has not lessened the exposure of a vendor to liability to his immediate purchaser. It has broadened and extended the base of liability by the devel-

opment and application of new principles of law.

The cost of products liability is a major concern for business. Between 1975 and 1978 the cost of products liability insurance paid by manufacturers and retailers rose by over 100%, from $1.13 billion to $2.75 billion.

LEGAL GROUNDS UPON WHICH PRODUCT LIABILITY IS BASED

The liability of manufacturers and sellers of goods by reason of a defect or condition in a product, or its failure to perform adequately, may be based upon one or more of the following: (1) express warranty, (2) implied warranty, (3) fraudulent misrepresentation, (4) non-fraudulent misrepresentation, (5) negligence, (6) violation of statutory duty, (7) strict liability in tort. The first six grounds shall be briefly discussed in the above order. Strict liability in tort, the most frequently used ground upon which product liability is based, shall be treated at greater length and under a separate heading.

Liability Based on Express Warranty

This type of liability is predicated upon a promise, affirmation of fact, or description of the goods made by the vendor to his vendee.   Section 2–313.

Liability Based on Implied Warranty

Except for implied warranties arising from course of dealing or usage of trade, the three warranties imposed upon the seller by the Code, unless properly disclaimed, are (1) warranty of title, Section 2–312; (2) implied warranty of merchantability, Section 2–314; (3) implied warranty of fitness for the buyer's particular purpose, Section 2–315.

Although a seller's warranty of title does not extend beyond liability to his immediate vendee, any other warranty, express or implied, extends, at a minimum, to members of the buyer's family or household, or persons who are guests in his home, if it is reasonable to expect that such persons may use, consume or be affected by the goods and are injured in person by breach of warranty.   Section 2–318, Alternative A.

Both express and implied warranties are discussed in the preceding chapter.

Fraudulent Misrepresentation

Fraud is available as a remedy to the injured user or consumer of a product to whom a misrepresentation of fact has been made to induce action and who in reliance thereon has sustained loss and damage.   Fraud may consist either of intentional misrepresentation, such as the mislabeling of packaged drugs or cosmetics, or concealment of defects as where a wooden stepladder is made of defective wood and the defects are concealed by paint.

Non-fraudulent Misrepresentation

The Restatement, Second, Torts, provides for liability on the part of a person engaged in the business of selling goods who makes to the public a misrepresentation as to the character or quality of the goods, even though such misrepresentations are not made fraudulently or negligently and even though there is no privity of contract.   Section 402B reads as follows:

One engaged in the business of selling chattels who, by advertising, labels, or otherwise, makes to the public a misrepresentation of a material fact concerning the character or quality of a chattel sold by him is subject to liability for physical harm to a consumer of the chattel caused by justifiable reliance upon the misrepresentation, even though (a) it is not made fraudulently or negligently, and (b) the consumer has not bought the chattel from or entered into any contractual relation with the seller.

This rule is one of strict liability for personal injuries sustained by a consumer resulting from a misrepresentation of the goods even though innocently made.

The manufacturer of a drug product known as "talwin" was held liable in an action for wrongful death resulting from its continuing use by decedent who had become addicted to it.   Defendant manufacturer innocently made untrue representations to the medical profession that the drug would not cause physical dependence or addiction. In reliance upon this misrepresentation, a physician prescribed the drug for his patient (decedent) who developed an addiction to it which was fatal.   The Court found that decedent's addiction was an "abreaction", defined as an unusual reaction resulting from a person's unusual susceptibility to the product or its intended effect and different from that of a normal person.   Crocker v. Winthrop Laboratories, Division of Sterling Drug, Inc., 514 S.W.2d 429 (Tex. 1974).

Liability Based upon Negligence

Conduct involving an unreasonable or foreseeable risk of harm is negligence. The failure to exercise reasonable care under the circumstances which proximately causes loss or damage to the person or property of another is the basis of liability for negligence. A manufacturer or assembler of goods must exercise due care to make his product safe for the purpose for which it is intended to be used. This requires care in the design of the product, selection of materials, selection and fabrication of component parts, inspection and testing, and may require an adequate warning of dangers in the use of the product of which the ordinary person might not be aware. The duty of the manufacturer extends to inspection and testing of products fabricated by others and incorporated into his product.

In a landmark case decided in 1916, the manufacturer of an automobile was held liable for personal injuries sustained by the plaintiff who had purchased it from a retail dealer and while driving it was injured as the result of the collapse of a wheel due to the crumbling of the spokes which had been made of defective wood. The wheels had been purchased by the automobile manufacturer from a third person who was not a defendant in the case. The basis of liability was negligence of the automobile manufacturer and its duty to foresee that the finished product, if negligently constructed or built of defective component parts, would be inherently or imminently dangerous. MacPherson v. Buick Motor Co., 217 N.Y. 382, 111 N.E. 1050 (1916).

Recoveries have been sustained against manufacturers of motor cars on behalf of buyers, users, passengers and bystanders, based upon negligence, for damages and injuries resulting from defective steering apparatus, wheels, axles, brakes, tires, and other operating components. A right of action based upon negligence does not require privity of contract between the injured plaintiff and the negligent defendant manufacturer or seller.

The Restatement, Second, Torts, § 395 provides:

A manufacturer who fails to exercise reasonable care in the manufacture of a chattel, which, unless carefully made, he should recognize as involving an unreasonable risk of causing substantial bodily harm to those who lawfully use it for a purpose for which it is manufactured and to those whom the supplier should expect to be in the vicinity of its probable use, is subject to liability for bodily harm caused to them by its lawful use in a manner and for a purpose for which it is manufactured.

Section 401 provides:

A seller of a chattel manufactured by a third person who knows or has reason to know that the chattel is, or is likely to be, dangerous when used by a person to whom it is delivered or for whose use it is supplied, or to others whom the seller should expect to share in or be endangered by its use, is subject to liability for bodily harm caused thereby to them if he fails to exercise reasonable care to inform them of the danger or otherwise to protect them against it.

Section 401 liability applies to any seller of a chattel manufactured by a third person. The chattel does not have to be in a defective condition. The seller must have "reason to know" and is not under a duty to ascertain unknown facts. This duty is less strict than one imposed by the words "should know". The liability is based upon the dangerous character of the product and the duty is to exercise reasonable care to inform the purchaser or user of the danger or otherwise to protect him against it. The extent of the liability is for damages resulting from personal injuries.

Section 402 excuses from liability the seller of goods manufactured by a third person who neither knows nor has reason to know of their dangerous character, for failure to inspect or test the goods before selling them, and provides:

A seller of a chattel manufactured by a third person, who neither knows nor has reason to know that it is, or is likely to be, dangerous, is not liable in an action for negligence for harm caused by the dangerous character or condition of the chattel because of his failure to discover the danger by an inspection or test of the chattel before selling it.

This section protects a retailer who sells goods that are pre-packaged or placed in sealed containers by the manufacturer, from liability based upon negligence. The retailer, however, may be liable upon express or implied warranties to his purchaser or to a member of the family or household, or guest in the home of the purchaser.

Thus, A, a wholesale distributor, sells to B, a retail dealer, a defective gas heater manufactured by X, a reputable manufacturer, which both A and B believed to be in perfect condition, although neither of them have inspected it. C purchases the gas heater from B and is injured by reason of the emission of poisonous fumes. Neither A nor B is liable to C for negligence although B may be liable to C upon an implied warranty of merchantability, and in turn A may be liable to B upon an identical implied warranty.

Violation of Statutory Duty

State and Federal statutes impose duties upon manufacturers of food, drugs, cosmetics, flammable materials and toxic substances, with respect to branding, labeling, description of contents, advertising, and the selling or offering for sale of adulterated, contaminated or unwholesome products. Included among these statutes are The Federal Food, Drug and Cosmetics Act, 15 U.S.C.A. §§ 301–392; Federal Flammable Fabrics Act, 15 U.S.C.A. §§ 1191–1200; Federal Hazardous Substances Labeling Act, 15 U.S.C.A. §§ 1261–1273; Federal Insecticide, Fungicide and Rodenticide Act, 7 U.S.C.A. §§ 135–135(k).

These statutes provide for enforcement by criminal sanctions, seizure of goods and injunctions. They do not expressly impose civil liability based upon injuries to the user or consumer of a product which has been sold in violation of the statute. However, in a civil action for damages, a violation of statutory duty, if established by evidence, is held by many courts to constitute negligence *per se*.

A wholesome seed merchant who sold mislabelled seed to a retailer who resold it in the original package to a farmer for planting, was held liable in damages to the farmer. The label on the seed was false and misleading in violation of a Florida statute which provided penal sanctions but no civil remedies. The Supreme Court of Florida reversed a judgment in favor of the wholesale merchant stating:

Where one violates a penal statute imposing upon him a duty designed to protect another he is negligent as a matter of law, therefore responsible for such damage as is proximately caused by his negligence. Hoskins v. Jackson Grain Co., 63 So.2d 514 (Fla.1953).

A non-statutory safety code may impose a duty of care upon a manufacturer of goods. In a case in which the plaintiff was injured by a fall resulting from the breaking of a stepladder while using it, the evidence showed that the defendant manufacturer had adopted the American Standard Safety Code for Portable Wood Ladders sponsored by the American Ladder Institute and two other national associations and that the construction of the stepladder did not comply with this Safety Code. In affirming a judgment for the plaintiff the Court stated:

The voluntary adoption of a safety code as the guide to be followed for protection of the public is at least some evidence that a reasonably prudent person would adhere to the requirements of the code. Wilson v. Lowe's Asheboro Hardware, Inc., 259 N.C. 660, 131 S.E.2d 501 (1963).

STRICT LIABILITY IN TORT

The most recent, significant and far-reaching development in the field of products liability is that of strict liability in tort. It imposes liability only upon a person who is in the business of selling the product involved; applies to a product in a defective condition unreasonably dangerous, and extends both to personal injuries and property damage suffered by the ultimate user or consumer of the product. It does not apply to an occasional seller who is not in the business of selling the product, such as a person who trades in his used car, or who sells his lawn mower to a neighbor. It is similar in this respect to the implied warranty of merchantability under Section 2–314 of the Code which applies only to sales by a merchant with respect to goods of the type in which he deals. It also does not apply to sales of the stock of merchants not in the usual course of business, such as execution sales, bankruptcy sales, and bulk sales. Subject to the foregoing, it applies to all sellers engaged in business including manufacturers, wholesalers, distributors, retailers and operators of restaurants.

Section 402A, imposing strict liability in tort, provides:

(1) One who sells any product in a defective condition unreasonably dangerous to the user or consumer or to his property is subject to liability for physical harm thereby caused to the ultimate user or consumer, or to his property, if
(a) the seller is engaged in the business of selling such a product, and
(b) it is expected to and does reach the user or consumer without substantial change in the condition in which it is sold.
(2) The rule stated in Subsection (1) applies although
(a) the seller has exercised all possible care in the preparation and sale of his product, and
(b) the user or consumer has not bought the product from or entered into any contractual relation with the seller.

In Dippel v. Sciano, 37 Wis.2d 443, 155 N.W.2d 55 (1967), the Supreme Court of Wisconsin summarized the requirements of strict liability in tort as follows:

From a reading of the plain language of the rule, the plaintiff must prove (1) that the product was in defective condition when it left the possession or control of the seller, (2) that it was unreasonably dangerous to the user or consumer, (3) that the defect was a cause (a substantial factor) of the plaintiff's injuries or damages, (4) that the seller engaged in the business of selling such product or, put negatively, that this is not an isolated or infrequent transaction not related to the principal business of the seller, and (5) that the product was one which the seller expected to and did reach the user or consumer without substantial change in the condition it was when he sold it.

This liability is imposed by law as a matter of public policy and does not depend upon contract either express or implied. It does not require reliance by the injured user or consumer upon any statements made by the manufacturer or seller. The liability is not limited to persons in a relationship of buyer and seller. No notice of defect is required to have been given by the injured user or consumer. The liability is not ordinarily subject to disclaimer, exclusion or modification by contractual agreement. The liability is strictly in tort and arises out of the common law. It is not governed by the provisions of the Uniform Commercial Code.

It is to be emphasized that negligence is not the basis of this liability which applies although "the seller has exercised all possible care in the preparation and sale of his product." However, the seller is not an insurer of the goods which he manufactures or sells and the essential requirements for this type of liability are: (1) that defendant sold the product in a defective condition; (2) that defendant was engaged in the business of selling such a product; (3) that the defective condition was one which made the product unreasonably dangerous to the user or consumer or to his property; (4) that the defect in the product existed at the time it left the hands of the defendant; (5) that the plaintiff sustained physical harm or property damage by use or consumption of the product; and (6) that the defective condition was the proximate cause of such injury or damage.

In an action against a defendant manufacturer or seller to recover damages under the rule of strict liability in tort, the plaintiff must prove a defective condition in the product, but he is not required to prove how or why or in what manner the product became defective. On the issue of liability, the reason or cause of the defect is not material as it would be in an action based upon negligence. The plaintiff, however, must show that at the time he was injured the condition of the product was not substantially changed from what it was at the time it was sold by the defendant manufacturer or seller.

The reasons asserted in support of imposing strict liability in tort upon manufacturers and assemblers of products are: (1) maximum protection should be given consumers against dangerous defects in products; (2) manufacturers are in the best position to prevent or reduce the hazards to life and health in defective products; (3) manufacturers realize the most profit from the total sales of their goods and are best able to carry the financial burden of such liability by distributing it among the public as a cost of doing business; (4) manufacturers utilize wholesalers and retailers merely as conduits in the marketing of their products and should not be permitted to avoid liability simply because they have no contract with the user or consumer; and (5) since the manufacturer is liable to his vendee who may be a wholesaler who in turn is liable to the retailer who in turn is liable to the ultimate purchaser, time and expense would be saved by making the li-

ability a direct one rather than a chain reaction.

Defective Condition

In an action against a defendant manufacturer or seller to recover damages under the rule of strict liability in tort, the plaintiff must prove a defective condition in the product, but he is not required to prove how or why or in what manner the product became defective. On the issue of liability, the reason or cause of the defect is not material as it would be in an action based upon negligence. The plaintiff, however, must show that at the time he was injured the condition of the product was not substantially changed from what it was at the time it was sold by the defendant manufacturer or seller. The defect may arise through faulty manufacturing; through faulty product design; or through inadequate warning, labelling, or instructions.

Manufacturing Defect. A manufacturing defect occurs when the product is not properly made, such as failing to meet its own manufacturing specifications. For instance, suppose a chair is manufactured with legs designed to be attached by four screws and glue. If such a chair were produced without inserting the appropriate screws, this would constitute a manufacturing defect.

Design Defect. A product contains a design defect when it is produced as specified but is dangerous or hazardous because its design is inadequate. Design defects can result from a number of causes, including poor engineering and poor choice of materials. An example of a design defect that received great notoriety was the Ford Pinto. A number of courts found the car to be inadequately designed in that its fuel tank had been placed too close to its rear axle, causing the fuel tank to rupture upon impact from the rear.

Inadequate Warning or Instructions. A seller is under a duty to provide adequate warning of danger and to provide appropriate directions for safe use. Nevertheless, inadequate and dangerous products, regardless of their warning, will be held to be defective, especially if there are superior alternative designs or manufacturing procedures. Typically, warning or instructions are needed to insure that appropriately designed and manufactured products are properly utilized. Comment J to Section 402A provides that in some instances "in order to prevent the product from being unreasonably dangerous, the seller may be required to give directions or warning, on the container, as to its use." In one case a drug company was found liable for inadequately warning of the dangerous and not infrequent side-effects of one of its drugs (MER-29). Toole v. Richardson-Merrell, Inc., 251 Cal.App.2d 689, 60 Cal.Rptr.398 (1967).

Almost any product may be used or misused in a manner which involves danger of physical harm. The blow of a poorly-aimed hammer may crush a thumb. The inhaling of a feather may damage a lung. The use of a sled on a busy street may endanger the child using it. The excessive drinking of liquor is dangerous. Allowing children to play with firearms is also dangerous. These hazards arise out of the use of products in a manner or to the extent that they were not intended by the supplier to be used, and generally no duty is imposed upon the manufacturer or seller to give warning against the possible dangers that might arise from such misuse of the product.

The duty to give a warning arises out of a foreseeable danger of physical harm arising out of the normal use or probable use of the product and the likelihood that unless warned, the user or consumer will not ordinarily be aware of such danger or hazard.

In Spruill v. Boyle-Midway Incorporated, 308 F.2d 79 (C.A.4, 1962), the defendants were manufacturers and distributors of furniture polish, containing 98% mineral seal oil, the remaining ingredients consisting of cedar oil, a trace of turpentine, and some red dye. The label on the bottle in which the product was sold stated in red letters about ⅛ inch in height "CAUTION, COMBUSTIBLE MATERIAL." Beneath this in red letters 1/16 inch in height were the words "DO NOT USE NEAR FIRE OR FLAME." This warning was followed by seven lines of directions printed in letters about 1/32 inch in height following which was a statement in letters of the same height: "Contents refined petroleum distillate, may be harmful if swallowed, especially by children."

A baby, 14 months old, died as the result of chemical pneumonia caused by swallowing a small quantity of this furniture polish. The defendants were held liable for failure to give adequate notice of its poisonous nature. Mineral seal oil is extremely toxic, and the warning against combustibility overshadowed and made more inconspicuous the toxicity warning in smaller print.

Unreasonably Dangerous

Section 402A imposes liability only if the defective product is unreasonably dangerous to the user or consumer. An unreasonably dangerous product is one which contains a danger beyond that which would be contemplated by the ordinary consumer who purchases it with the common knowledge of its characteristics.

Obstacles to Recovery

Disclaimers and Notice. Comment m to Section 402A makes it clear that the basis of strict liability rests solely in tort and is not subject to contractual defenses. The comment specifically states that strict product liability is not governed by the Code, that it is not affected by contractual limitations or disclaimers and that it is not subject to any requirement that notice be given to the seller by the injured party within a reasonable time.

Horizontal Privity. The strict liability in tort of manufacturers and other seller extends not only to buyers, users and consumers, but also to injured bystanders. Illustrative cases are: occupants of automobile injured in collision with another car due to such other car having defective brakes, or defective drive shaft, or defective accelerator, or defective steering mechanism; golfer killed by runaway car which started due to faulty transmission system; bystander injured by runaway truck started by short circuit; bystander injured by explosion of defective beer keg; neighbor injured by explosion of propane gas tank; and bystander injured by explosion of shotgun barrel caused by defective shell.

Vertical Privity. The rule of strict liability in tort, as formulated in Section 402A of the Restatement, Second, Torts, imposes liability upon the seller for physical harm to the ultimate user or consumer of the defective product. Such liability extends to any seller who is engaged in the business of selling the product, including a wholesaler or distributor as well as the manufacturer and retailer.

The rule of strict liability in tort also applies to the manufacturer of a defective component part which has been incorporated into the larger product where no essential change has been made in it by the manufacturer of the finished product, and such manufacturer is not excused from liability by reason of the failure of the manufacturer of the finished product to discover the defect by testing or inspection. The manufacturer of the finished product is also liable for damages caused by a defective condition of the goods resulting exclusively from a defective component part.

Although liability for personal injuries caused by the defective condition of goods which makes them unreasonably dangerous

is usually associated with sales of goods, such liability also exists with respect to leases of such goods or chattels. The extension of liability to lessors of chattels is not surprising in view of the rationale developed by the courts in imposing strict liability in tort upon manufacturers of products and component parts. The danger to which the public is exposed by defectively manufactured cars and trucks traveling on the highways is not greatly different from the hazards of defectively maintained cars and trucks leased to operators.

The Restatement, Second, Torts § 408, provides:

One who leases a chattel as safe for immediate use is subject to liability to those whom he should expect to use the chattel, or to be endangered by its probable use, for physical harm caused by its use in a manner for which and by a person for whose use, it is leased, if the lessor fails to exercise reasonable care to make it safe for such use or to disclose its actual condition to those who may be expected to use it.

In a case in which the plaintiff, a passenger and employee of the lessee of a truck, was injured due to the defendant lessor's failure to maintain the vehicle in a safe operating condition, the Court held that the leasing agreement gave rise to "a continuing implied promissory warranty that the leased trucks would be fit for plaintiff's employer's use for the duration of the lease." The Court also applied the rule of strict liability in tort and held that the plaintiff had a cause of action. Cintrone v. Hertz Truck Leasing & Rental Service, 45 N.J. 434, 212 A.2d 769 (1965).

Contributory Negligence. At common law in an action based on negligence, contributory negligence of the plaintiff either completely bars recovery or diminishes the amount of recovery under the rule of comparative negligence adopted in certain states.

Negligence and contributory negligence are immaterial in an action based upon strict liability in tort which is a separate and distinct form of tort liability. It is a form of liability without fault arising out of the sale of "any product in a defective condition unreasonably dangerous to the user or consumer". Negligence involves reasonable foreseeability of harm, whereas strict liability assumes that the particular danger presented was foreseeable by the manufacturer.

In Johnson v. Clark Equipment Co., Or., 547 P.2d 132 (1976) the Oregon Supreme Court states:

Foreseeability is a negligence concept; a standard for assessing culpability. As such, it is not an appropriate consideration when determining whether a manufacturer should be held liable without fault. If, however, we assume foreseeability of the danger and ask only whether it would be reasonable to market the product in that condition with full knowledge of the risks involved, then that inquiry will reflect the proper focus of the law of products liability and center on the condition of the product rather than on the culpability of the particular manufacturer.

Assumption of Risk. Assumption of risk is a defense in an action based on strict liability in tort. The user or consumer who voluntarily uses the goods in an unusual, inappropriate or improper manner for which they were not intended, and which under the circumstances is unreasonable, assumes the risk of injuries which result from such use.

To establish such defense the burden is on the defendant to show that (1) the plaintiff subjectively and actually knew and appreciated the particular risk or danger created by the defect; (2) the plaintiff voluntarily encountered the risk while realizing the danger; and (3) the plaintiff's decision to encounter the known risk was unreasonable.

Misuse or Abuse of the Product. Closely connected to voluntary assumption of the risk is the defense of misuse or abuse of the product by the injured party. The major difference is that misuse or abuse includes actions which the injured party does not know to be dangerous, while assumption of the risk does not. The courts, however, have significantly limited this defense by requiring that the misuse or abuse not be foreseeable by the seller. If a use is foreseeable, then the seller must take measure to guard against it. Thus, a manufacturer has been held liable for injuries to a stevedore who was injured while walking on cargo for failing to package its cargo so as to avoid such injury. It was foreseeable that stevedores would indeed walk on the cargo.

Subsequent Alteration. Section 402A provides that liability only exists if the product reaches "the user or consumer without substantial change in the condition in which it is sold." Accordingly, most but not all courts would not hold a manufacturer liable for a faulty carburetor if the retailer were to remove the part and make significant changes in it prior to re-inserting it into the automobile.

Cases

Strict Liability in Tort

VICTORSON v. BOCK LAUNDRY MACHINES CO.

(1975) 37 N.Y.2d 395, 373 N.Y.S. 39, 335 N.E.2d 275.

[Separate suits were filed by three plaintiffs to recover damages for personal injuries sustained while using defective laundry centrifuge extractors manufactured by defendant and installed in commercial laundromats. In the case of one injured plaintiff, the extractor had been sold in 1948 and the injury occurred in 1969; in another, the sale was in 1959, the injury in 1967; in the third case, the sale was in 1955, the injury

in 1965. In each case liability was predicated upon strict liability in tort. The
Court held that each suit was timely commenced within three years from the date of
injury as provided in the statute of limitations applicable to actions for personal injury and property damage. Judgments
against the manufacturer in each case,
affirmed.]

JONES, J.

These three cases arise out of claims
asserted against the manufacturer of allegedly defective products by remote users;
the theory of liability is that which we have
called strict products liability. [Citation.]
We now hold that the period of limitation
with respect to these claims begins to run
at the date of injury and that the duration
of such period is that found in CPLR 214
(subds. 4, 5) under which there is a limitation of three years in actions for personal
injury and property damage. [Citation.]
Accordingly, our court's holding to the contrary in Mendel v. Pittsburgh Plate Glass
Co., 25 N.Y.2d 340, 305 N.Y.S.2d 490, 253
N.E.2d 207, must be overruled.

Defendant Bock Laundry Machine
Company manufactured and marketed a
centrifuge extractor for use in apartment
house laundry rooms and commercial laundromats to spin water out of laundry after
washing and preparatory to its being placed
in a dryer. In *Victorson* the extractor was
sold in 1948 and the injury occurred in 1969;
in *Rivera* the sale was in 1959, the injury
in 1967; and in *Brown* the sale was in 1955
and the injury in 1965. The Appellate Di-
visions have properly unraveled the procedural complexities, presenting for our determination, on motions addressed to the
pleadings, the questions as to when the
Statute of Limitations began to run and for
what period it continued.

Preliminarily we observe as a matter
of analysis that, while one seeking to recover from a manufacturer for injuries sustained in consequence of an alleged defect

in its product may be said to have but a
single claim, that claim may be grounded
in one or more of four causes of action or
theories of liability. Depending on the factual context in which the claim arises, the
injured plaintiff, and those asserting derivative claims, may state a cause of action in
contract, express or implied, on the ground
of negligence, or, as here, on the theory of
strict products liability. In these cases now
before us we are concerned only with claims
based on the last theory. What we say
here, therefore, should not be understood as
in any way referring to the liability of a
manufacturer of a defective product under
familiar but different doctrines of the law
of contracts for injuries sustained by a customer or other person with whom or for
whose benefit the manufacturer previously
has made a warranty or other agreement,
express or implied. As indicated, it may
be open to a particular plaintiff to base his
case on contract liability or negligence or
strict products liability, or on some combination thereof.

* * *

Initially we recognize the general distinction between these two areas of the law.
"The fundamental difference between tort
and contract lies in the nature of the interests protected. Tort actions are created to
protect the interest in freedom from various
kinds of harm. The duties of conduct which
give rise to them are imposed by the law,
and are based primarily upon social policy,
and not necessarily upon the will or intention of the parties." [Citation.]

* * *

In a simplistic sense it is obvious that
this liability does not arise out of contract
concepts if such concepts be thought of as
the means for analyzing the jural relationship between two parties who have entered
into a contractual relationship prior to the
date on which injury is sustained. Here
none of these plaintiffs had had any association with the manufacturer of the cen-

trifuge extractors prior to being injured. Nor are these claims grounded in any contention that the liability of the manufacturer stems from its nonperformance of an obligation to plaintiffs arising out of an agreement, express or implied. Rather than arising out of the "will or intention of the parties", the liability imposed on the manufacturer under strict products liability, whether it be to purchaser, user, or innocent bystander, is predicated largely on considerations of sound social policy. [Citation.]

* * *

Whatever may have been earlier doubt and confusion, the authorities are now in general agreement that strict products liability sound in tort rather than in contract. "It has been said over and over again that this warranty—if that is the name for it— is not the old sales warranty, it is not the warranty covered by the Uniform Sales Act or the Uniform Commercial Code. It is not a warranty of the seller to the buyer at all, but it is something separate and distinct which sounds in tort exclusively, and not at all in contract; which exists apart from any contract between the parties; and which makes for strict liability in tort." [Citations.]

* * *

Restrictions of time on claim assertion involve two aspects—how long shall the period be within which the claim may be asserted, and as of what date shall that period begin to run?

On principle, there having been no prior relationship between the parties in strict products liability cases, the cause of action if any there be, should accrue at the time the injury is sustained. To hold that it somehow came into being prior thereto would defy both logic and experience. "[I]t is all but unthinkable that a person should be time-barred from prosecuting a cause of action before he ever had one." [Citation.] In this perspective the analogy in principle

is to "tort" claims, that is claims for injury to person or property, as to most of which, although not all, the statute runs from the date of injury. [Citations.] By contrast, in contract actions the statute runs from the date of the breach of performance of the contractual obligation, in the present context, the date of sale of the defective product. (CPLR 213, subd. 2; Uniform Commercial Code, § 2–725, subd. [2].)

Then over how long a period thereafter should the injured party be allowed to assert his claim? As in other instances in which periods of limitation must be fixed, the answer depends on a nice balancing of policy considerations. "Any Statute of Limitations reflects a policy that there must come a time after which fairness demands that a defendant should not be harried; the duration of the period is chosen with a balancing sense of fairness to the claimant that he shall not unreasonably be deprived of his right to assert his claim." [Citation.]
* * *

One argument of policy is pressed on us by appellants in these cases. Is it fair or reasonable, they ask, to hold a manufacturer liable for a defect in production many years after the product has left the manufacturer's plant? The predicament of the manufacturer is not then significantly different whether its liability in tort be grounded in theories of negligence or of strict products liability. One can observe that while passage of time may work a deterioration of the manufacturer's capability to defend, by similar token it can be expected to complicate the plaintiff's problem of proving, as he must, that the alleged defect existed at the time the product left the manufacturer's plant. [Citation.]
* * *

Again the authorities are now in general agreement that Statute of Limitations governing injuries to person or property are those properly applicable to strict products liabilities claims. [Citations.] * * *

Judgments affirmed.

Strict Liability in Tort

PRICE v. SHELL OIL CO.

(1970) 85 Cal.Rptr. 178, 466 P.2d 722.

SULLIVAN, J.

We hold in this case that the doctrine of strict liability in tort which we have heretofore made applicable to sellers of personal property is also applicable to bailors and lessors of such property. As appears * * * we find substantial evidence in the record that the lessor in the present matter falls within the reach of the doctrine. We therefore affirm the judgment entered on the verdicts in favor of plaintiff Merton Price and plaintiff in intervention Pacific Employers Insurance Company (Pacific) and against defendant Shell Oil Company (Shell). On a secondary issue, presented by Shell's cross-complaint against cross-defendant Flying Tiger Line, Inc. (Flying Tiger) we hold that Shell's aforementioned liability as lessor does not fall within the indemnity provisions of its lease so as to impose on Flying Tiger an obligation to indemnify. We therefore affirm the judgment of nonsuit in favor of Flying Tiger dismissing Shell's cross-complaint for indemnity. In sum, we uphold the judgments of the trial court.

Plaintiff is an aircraft mechanic employed by Flying Tiger. In 1958 Flying Tiger leased from defendant Shell a gasoline tank truck with a movable ladder mounted upon the tank for refueling certain types of aircraft. Under the terms of the lease Flying Tiger was obligated to maintain the equipment in safe operating condition and to make specified repairs not here relevant. All other repairs were to be made by Shell at the request of Flying Tiger.

In 1962 Shell, at Flying Tiger's request, removed the original ladder from the truck. A replacement, built by an undisclosed manufacturer, was furnished and installed under Shell's direction. Both Shell and Flying Tiger participated in the inspection of the new ladder. On March 12, 1964, about two years later, while plaintiff was climbing the ladder onto the wing of an aircraft, both of its legs split into segments. Plaintiff fell against the gasoline tank, hanging by his leg which was caught between the rungs of the upper segment of the ladder still attached to the aircraft wing. As a result he sustained serious personal injuries.

Plaintiff brought the instant action for damages against Shell. His complaint was in two counts: the first based on Shell's alleged negligence in manufacturing and maintaining a gasoline tank truck; the second based on an alleged breach of warranties that the tank truck and all its parts were free from defects, of merchantable quality and fit for the purpose for which they were intended to be used.

As we have already indicated, Shell cross-complained against Flying Tiger for indemnity but was nonsuited. On defendant's motion the trial court also nonsuited plaintiff on both of his pleaded causes of action but on its own motion submitted the case to the jury on the theory of strict liability in tort. The jury returned a verdict in favor of plaintiff and against Shell in the sum of $40,000, and in favor of plaintiff in intervention Pacific, the workman's compensation insurance carrier of Flying Tiger, and against Shell for $1,859.24 for medical and indemnity benefits paid by Pacific in connection with Price's injuries. Shell appeals both from the judgment entered on the above verdicts and the judgment of nonsuit dismissing its cross-complaint against Flying Tiger for indemnity. * * *

The rule is now settled in California that "A manufacturer is strictly liable in tort when an article he places on the market, knowing that it is to be used without inspection for defects, proves to have a defect that causes injury to a human being." [Citations.] We have given this rule of strict liability a broad application. Recently in the *Elmore* case, 70 Cal.2d 578, 451 P.2d 84 (1969) we extended its protection to injured bystanders, a category not covered by the Restatement which limited its application to harm caused "to the ultimate user or consumer." [Citation.] We there observed that the doctrine of strict liability may not be limited either "on a theory of privity of contract" or "on the theory that no representation of safety is made to the bystander." [Citation.] * * *

Such a broad philosophy evolves naturally from the purpose of imposing strict liability which "is to insure that the costs of injuries resulting from defective products are borne by the manufacturers that put such products on the market rather than by the injured persons who are powerless to protect themselves." [Citation.] Essentially the paramount policy to be promoted by the rule is the protection of otherwise defenseless victims of manufacturing defects and the spreading throughout society of the cost of compensating them. Thus the court in Kriegler v. Eichler Homes, Inc., 269 Cal.App.2d 224, 74 Cal.Rptr. 749 (1969) while noting that the rule of strict liability had theretofore been applied in California only to manufacturers, retailers and suppliers of personal property, found no difficulty in extending its application to builders engaged in the mass production and sale of homes.

Similarly we can perceive no substantial difference between *sellers* of personal property and *non-sellers,* such as bailors and lessors. In each instance, the seller or non-seller "places [an article] on the market, knowing that it is to be used without inspection for defects, * * *." (*Greenman,* 59 Cal.2d at p. 62, 27 Cal.Rptr. at p. 700, 377 P.2d at p. 900.) In the light of the policy to be subserved, it should make no difference that the party distributing the article has retained title to it. Nor can we see how the risk of harm associated with the use of the chattel can vary with the legal form under which it is held. Having in mind the market realities and the widespread use of the lease of personalty in today's business world, we think it makes

good sense to impose on the lessors of chattels the same liability for physical harm which has been imposed on the manufacturers and retailers. The former, like the latter, are able to bear the cost of compensating for injuries resulting from defects by spreading the loss through an adjustment of the rental.

* * *

For the above reasons, we are of the opinion that the doctrine of strict liability in tort should be made applicable to bailors and lessors of personal property in the same manner as we have held it applicable to sellers of such property. * * *

However, since we reason by analogy, we make clear that the doctrine should be made applicable to lessors in the same way as we have made it applicable to sellers. In *Greenman,* we fastened liability on a manufacturer "when an article *he places on the market,* * * * proves to have a defect * * *." [Citation.] In *Vandermark* we again emphasized the necessity for a continuous course of business as a condition to application of the rule: "Retailers like manufacturers are *engaged in the business* of distributing goods to the public. * * * Strict liability * * * works no injustice to the defendants, *for they can adjust the costs of such protection between them in the course of their continuing business relationship.*" (61 Cal.2d at pp. 262–263, 37 Cal.Rptr. at pp. 899–900, 391 P.2d at pp. 171–172.) * * * Our analysis of these authorities leads to the conclusion that for the doctrine of strict liability in tort to apply to a lessor of personalty, the lessor should be found to be in the business of leasing, in the same general sense as the seller of personalty is found to be in the business of manufacturing or retailing.

* * *

In view of the foregoing we are satisfied that there is substantial evidence showing, or from which it can be reasonably inferred, that Shell was a commercial lessor within the rule of strict liability applicable to this case.

The Shell lease provides in relevant part: "Lessee shall indemnify Shell against any and all claims and liability for injury or death of persons or damage to property caused by or happening in connection with the equipment or the condition, maintenance, possession, operation or use thereof." Shell's cross-complaint against Flying Tiger was grounded on the above indemnity clause and prayed that if plaintiff recovered damages against Shell, the court enter judgment on the cross-complaint against Flying Tiger in a like amount plus the amount of Shell's attorney fees, court costs and investigation expenses. * * *

In the indemnity clause before us in the instant case, there is no language "expressly and unequivocally" requiring Flying Tiger to indemnify Shell for liability or damages caused by Shell's own act in furnishing a defective tank truck or its equipment. No language of such essential specificity indicates that the lessee is to be held responsible for the negligent acts of the lessor, much less for the strict liability in tort imposed upon the lessor for placing on the market a defective article. Indeed it would do violence to the doctrine of strict liability and thwart its basic purpose, if we were to interpret so general a clause as transferring the liability for a defective article from the party putting the article in the stream of commerce, to the user or consumer of the article who is within the class the doctrine was designed to protect.

The judgments are affirmed.

Design Defect—
Obstacles to Recovery

THIBAULT v.
SEARS ROEBUCK & CO.

(1978) 118 N.H. 802, 395 A.2d 843.

DOUGLAS, J.

This is an action to recover damages for harm sustained by the plaintiff when a lawn mower manufactured by the defendant injured the plaintiff's foot. Trial by jury on tort counts sounding in negligence and strict liability before *Flynn,* J., resulted in verdicts for the defendant. The plaintiff's exceptions concerning his strict liability claim were reserved and transferred. We affirm.

The plaintiff bought a "Craftsman" rotary power mower from the Sears, Roebuck & Company outlet in 1968. He had used similar mowers for over fifteen years and was thoroughly familiar with them. The rear of the housing of plaintiff's mower is embossed with the warning, "Keep Hands & Feet From Under Mower." The instruction booklet twice advises the operator to mow slopes lengthwise, not up and down. Although this advice is not highlighted, the type throughout the booklet is easily readable.

Despite this advice, the plaintiff thought that a long steep slope on his property could be mowed more safely if it were mowed up and down. While mowing in this manner, he lost his balance and fell. He instinctively gripped the handle of the mower as he fell and when he came to rest at the bottom of the slope, his foot was under the housing. Although there was conflicting testimony at the trial, the plaintiff contended that his foot slipped under the housing because the mower lacked a rear trailing guard. The defendant contended that the plaintiff lifted the mower from the ground when he fell, thus bringing the blade down on his foot. The defendant therefore argued that the lack of a guard did not contribute to the accident. Alternatively, the defendant contended that the plaintiff was "contributorily negligent" in mowing up and down contrary to the explicit written instructions.

Before the adoption of the doctrine of strict liability, the injured consumer's recourse at law was "to bring an action based either on the negligence of the manufacturer or, additionally or alternatively, on breach of warranty." Cassidy, *Strict Liability in New Hampshire,* 18 N.H.B.J. 3, 4 (1976). Consumers may now maintain actions based upon strict liability. [Citations.] Some commentators have suggested that strict liability is in reality a tool of social engineering, and that manufacturers should be required to bear the entire risk and costs of injuries caused by products. "If redistribution [of costs] is desired, there is no reason why the law should retain the requirements of causation and product defect; to the extent that any defendant can rely upon those requirements to defeat a plaintiff's cause of action, this 'policy' of tort law will be defeated." Epstein, *Products Liability: The Search for the Middle Ground,* 56 N.C.L.Rev. 643, 659 (1978).

We disagree with this approach to the doctrine of strict liability. Unlike workmen's compensation and no-fault automobile insurance, strict liability is not a no-fault system of compensation. The common-law principle that fault and responsibility are elements of our legal system applicable to corporations and individuals alike will not be undermined or abolished by "spreading" of risk and cost in this State. Viewed as a system of spreading the risk, the doctrine of strict liability has had economic consequences. In the fifteen years since *Greenman v. Yuba Power Products, Inc.,* 59 Cal.2d 57, 27 Cal.Rptr. 697, 377 P.2d 897 (1963), some writers have noted that the doctrine "has led to a decline in consumer 'freedom of choice.' Consumers willing to assume risk, and who want to avail themselves of lower product prices, are less able to do so." Sachs, *Products Liability: An Economic View,* 14 Trial 48, 51 (1978).

The "Fortune 500" companies suffer less economically because they can develop adequate statistics, purchase insurance, and employ expensive experts and legal counsel. For thousands of small manufacturers, the high cost of self-protection or insurance can be prohibitive so as to force them out of business. [Citation.] The resultant economic concentration lessens the consumer's choices in the marketplace. * * *

The present case concerns the elements of and defenses to a strict liability action alleging defective *design*. We are not here involved with an action alleging a *manufacturing* defect, where the defect is an accidental variation caused by a mistake in the manufacturing process; that is, where the product does not "conform to the great majority of products manufactured in accordance with that design." [Citations.] A design defect occurs when the product is manufactured in conformity with the intended design but the design itself poses unreasonable dangers to consumers. [Citation.]

In a strict liability case alleging defective design, the plaintiff must first prove the existence of a "defective condition unreasonably dangerous to the user." [Citations.] In determining unreasonable danger, courts should consider factors such as social utility and desirability. [Citations.] The utility of the product must be evaluated from the point of view of the public as a whole, because a finding of liability for defective design could result in the removal of an entire product line from the market. Some products are so important that a manufacturer may avoid liability as a matter of law if he has given proper warnings. [Citations.] In weighing utility and desirability against danger, courts should also consider whether the risk of danger could have been reduced without significant impact on product effectiveness and manufacturing cost. For example, liability may attach if the manufacturer did not take available and reasonable steps to lessen or eliminate the danger of even a significantly useful and desirable product. [Citation.]

Another factor to be considered is the presence or absence of a warning. Of course, some products, such as carving knives, are obviously and inherently dangerous. When a risk is not apparent, however, the user must be adequately and understandably warned of concealed dangers. We do not agree, however, with such cases as *Davis* [citation] in which the Ninth Circuit held that in the absence of adequate warning a one-in-a-million risk of adverse reaction to a vaccine, known to the manufacturer, was a sufficient basis on which to impose strict liability. We also reject cases that demand that a manufacturer warn against uses which were neither intended by the manufacturer nor within the reasonably foreseeable use of the product. *Cf. Moran v. Faberge, Inc.*, 273 Md. 538, 332 A.2d 11 (1975) (perfume manufacturer liable for burns to teenage girl whose companion used cologne to scent a lit candle); *Spruill v. Boyle-Midway, Inc.*, 308 F.2d 79 (4th Cir. 1962) (manufacturer in failure-to-warn case liable when child drank furniture polish). These decisions fail to recognize that individual consumers have certain responsibilities. Manufacturers cannot foresee and warn of all absurd and dangerous uses of their product. Such decisions may harm our economy and unnecessarily encourage legislative intervention. * * *

The duty to warn is concomitant with the general duty of the manufacturer, which "is limited to foreseeing the probable results of the normal use of the product or a use that can reasonably be anticipated." [Citation.] Nevertheless, when an unreasonable danger could have been eliminated without excessive cost or loss of product efficiency, liability may attach even though the danger was obvious or there was adequate warning. [Citations.] A manufacturer "is not obliged to design the safest possible product, or one as safe as others make or a safer product than the one he has designed, so long as the design he has adopted is reasonably safe." *Mitchell v. Ford Motor Co.*, 533 F.2d 19, 20 (1st Cir. 1976). The obviousness of the danger should be evaluated against the reasonableness of the steps which the manufac-

turer must take to reduce the danger. [Citations.]

The plaintiff in a defective design case must also prove causation and foreseeability. He must show that the unreasonably dangerous condition existed when the product was purchased, [citation] and that the dangerous condition caused the injury. [Citation.] The plaintiff must further prove that the purpose and manner of his use of the product was foreseeable by the manufacturer. This requirement is predicated on the manufacturer's duty to design his product reasonably safely for the uses which he can foresee. Foreseeability of use, however, extends beyond the consumer's actual use of the product; for example, a failure to read or follow instructions for product use may not be fatal to the plaintiff's case if he can show that such failure was reasonably foreseeable. [Citation.]

Inquiry into the dangerousness of a product requires a multifaceted balancing process involving evaluation of many conflicting factors. A court will rarely be able to say as a matter of law that a product has no social utility, or that the purpose or manner of its use that caused the injury was not foreseeable. [Citations.] The jury must decide whether the potentiality of harm is open and obvious. [Citations.] Reasonableness, foreseeability, utility, and similar factors are questions of fact for jury determination. We now turn to defenses.

The Restatement (Second) of Torts §§ 402A, Comment n (1965) states in part that:

. . . [t]he form of contributory negligence which consists in *voluntarily and unreasonably proceeding* to encounter a *known* danger, and commonly passes under the name of *assumption of the risk, is a defense* under this Section as in other cases of strict liability. If the user or consumer discovers the defect and is aware of the danger, and nevertheless proceeds to make use of the product and is injured by it, he is barred from recovery.

* * *

Of course, product misuse and abnormal uses are defenses to strict liability, [citation].

The [New Hampshire] legislature passed a comparative negligence statute effective August 12, 1969. That statute requires a comparison of defendant's negligence with plaintiff's contributory negligence. Thus contributory negligence is no longer an absolute bar to a negligence action; a comparing process is now used by the jury. A plaintiff can recover if the jury does not find that his negligence was greater "than the causal negligence of the defendant." [Citation.]

* * * We now hold, however, that the comparative negligence statute, RSA 507:7–a, does not apply to strict liability cases because it is confined by its terms to actions for negligence. However, strict liability is a judicially created doctrine, to which the principle of comparative causation will be applied as hereinafter described.

* * *

We judicially recognize the comparative concept in strict liability cases parallel to the legislature's recognition of it in the area of negligence.

* * *

In the present case the jury returned a verdict for the defendant and the trial judge entered judgment. There is evidence to support the verdict. [Citation.] Even though the jury could have found that the plaintiff's actual use of the lawn mower that caused the injury was foreseeable, a jury could also have found that the warning was adequate, or that the design was not the cause of the accident, or that the plaintiff's misconduct was more than fifty percent responsible for the injury.

* * *

[Affirmed.]

Design Defect

HECKMAN v. FEDERAL PRESS CO.

(1978 3rd Cir.) 587 F.2d 612.

WEIS, J.

In this products liability case, a jury found that a power press manufactured by defendant without a guarding device was unreasonably dangerous, and awarded plaintiff damages for the injuries he sustained while operating the machine. Although the question of liability was for the jury, the judgment must be vacated because of error in permitting expert testimony that included a "growth factor" in projecting future loss of earnings. Admission of such evidence being impermissible under applicable Pennsylvania law, we grant a new trial.

Plaintiff's left hand was severely injured when it was caught in a power press he was operating in the course of his employment with the Clark Equipment Company. He brought suit against The Federal Press Company, the manufacturer of the machine, alleging defective design because of the lack of an adequate safety device. A jury returned a verdict in favor of the plaintiff in the amount of $750,000 against Federal, with a verdict over against the employer Clark, joined by Federal on a claim for contribution.

The accident occurred on September 24, 1972, at the Clark factory in Reading, Pennsylvania as Heckman was using a foot pedal to operate the press. The machine functions by dropping a heavy ram onto a die, cutting or shaping the metal which rests on the lower surface. As plaintiff placed a piece of metal in the machine to be cut, the ram came down on his hand, resulting in the amputation of several fingers and other damage.

The press had been purchased by Clark in 1970. It could be operated in two different ways: with hand controls requiring the use of both hands on switches away from the point of operation, or, alternatively, by the use of a foot pedal, an optional item ordered by Clark. When the manual operation was used, the employee's hands necessarily were protected. However, when the foot pedal was utilized without a guard, there was nothing to prevent the hands from being placed in the operating area directly under the descending ram.

Federal did not provide safety appliances other than the dual buttons for manual operation except upon the customer's specific request and at its expense. When ordered, the guards were secured from other sources and attached by Federal. On delivery of the equipment to Clark, Federal sent a letter suggesting, *inter alia,* that the customer "obtain, install, and use 'point of operation' guarding for greater operator safety." In addition, the press itself had a warning plate with similar instructions for use.

Various types of safeguards designed to protect the operator were available on the market, including some designed to accommodate specific uses of the multi-purpose machine. Clark did in fact purchase a point-of-operation guard for $100, but it was not on the press at the time the injury occurred, and, in any event, its efficacy was challenged. Plaintiff produced expert testimony to establish that at least one type of appliance would be effective in about 95% of the customary uses of the press, and that the failure to supply such a device made the press defective within the meaning of Restatement (Second) of Torts § 402A (1965).

Federal contended it was not customary in the trade to furnish guards except upon request, and the multitude of uses to which the machine could be put made it impracticable to designate any one device as standard equipment. Moreover, Clark's failure to heed Federal's warning was said to be a superseding cause absolving defendant from all liability. Finally, Federal relied upon state regulations placing responsibility for the safe operation of presses upon employers and employees.

* * *

In answer to interrogatories, the jury found that Federal had sold a press in a defective condition, Clark Equipment Company was negligent, and plaintiff Heckman had not assumed the risk. It awarded Heckman damages of $750,000. Motions for judgment n.o.v., and for a new trial were filed by both Federal and Clark, and Federal also asked in the alternative for a remittitur. After argument, all motions were denied without opinion by the district court. Only Federal has appealed.

* * * In *Webb v. Zern,* 422 Pa. 424, 427, 220 A.2d 853, 854 (1966), Pennsylvania adopted the strict liability provisions of § 402A of the Restatement (Second) of Torts. Cases interpreting this section have held that lack of proper safety devices can constitute a defective design which may subject the manufacturer of machinery to liability. [Citations.]

We find the present case quite similar on its facts to *Capasso v. Minster Machine Co.,* 532 F.2d 952 (3d Cir. 1976), which also discussed a power press injury. There, as here, a two button system provided protection in manual operation, but no guard was provided when the optional foot control pedal was used. The manufacturer failed to provide any proposals for a safety guard and a device of the customer's own design proved to be ineffective. We held that since the original purchase included the optional foot switch, its use did not as a matter of law constitute a "substantial change" in the machinery within the scope of § 402A(1)(b) absolving the manufacturer; nor did the use of the inadequate shield act as a superseding cause as a matter of law.

[Citations.] We concluded that the issue of a defect in the press at delivery was for the jury.

Similarly here, plaintiff's expert maintained that the defendant should have provided safeguards to be used in connection with the foot pedal operation, and that effective implements were available at a reasonable cost. [Citation.]

Federal asserts that the bolster plate which Clark had installed blocked the operator's view of the machine's warning plate, and that this screening constituted a superseding cause insulating the manufacturer from liability. Thus, Federal's theory is that when Clark obscured the warning sign it effected a substantial change that became a superseding cause of the accident. But it cannot be said that as a matter of law the decreased visibility of the plaque was such a major departure from the original design of the machine as to cut off the manufacturer's obligations. [Citation.] Particularly is this so when the sign was addressed to a condition that was not latent. We are unwilling to accept the proposition that the warning plate in and of itself absolved Federal as a matter of law. As we observed in *Schell v. AMF, Inc.,* [citation]:

[A]s a matter of policy, it is questionable whether a manufacturer which produces a machine without minimal available safeguards is entitled to escape liability by warning of a dangerous condition which could reasonably have been avoided by a better design.

In the circumstances here, the warning issue was for the jury as was the defense of assumption of the risk. [Citation.]

Federal also maintains that it was exculpated as a matter of law because regulations of the Pennsylvania Department of Labor and Industry requiring the use of point-of-operation devices placed the responsibility upon the employer and employee. We do not accept this premise. Whatever effect the regulations might have

as between employer and employee does not extend to relieve the manufacturer of its liability under § 402A as a matter of law. If a manufacturer fails to provide reasonable safety devices for a product and thus creates an unreasonable risk of harm to the user, the fact that the manufacturer may expect the user to provide a protective appliance is not sufficient to preclude liability in most circumstances. [Citations.] The issue is one which should be decided by a jury in light of such matters as the feasibility of incorporating safety features during manufacture of the machine, the likelihood that users will not secure adequate devices, whether the machinery is of a standard make or built to the customer's specifications, the relative expertise of manufacturer and customer, the extent of risk to the user, and the seriousness of injury which may be anticipated.

* * *

We conclude that the questions of liability were for the jury's consideration and it was not error to deny Federal's motion for judgment n.o.v.

[A new trial is granted due to a reversible error in the award of damages.]

Defective Condition—Privity

EMBS v. PEPSI-COLA BOTTLING CO. OF LEXINGTON, KENTUCKY, INC.

(1975 Ky.) 528 S.W.2d 703.

LUKOWSKY, J.

This is an appeal from a judgment entered by the Clark Circuit Court dismissing the claim of plaintiff-appellant pursuant to a directed verdict granted at the completion of her proof. We reverse and remand.

On the afternoon of July 25, 1970 plaintiff-appellant entered the self-service retail store operated by the defendant-appellee, Stamper's Cash Market, Inc., for the purpose of "buying soft drinks for the kids."

She went to an upright soft drink cooler, removed five bottles and placed them in a carton. Unnoticed by her, a carton of Seven-Up was sitting on the floor at the edge of the produce counter about one foot from where she was standing. As she turned away from the cooler she heard an explosion that sounded "like a shotgun." When she looked down she saw a gash in her leg, pop on her leg, green pieces of a bottle on the floor and the Seven-Up carton in the midst of the debris. She did not kick or otherwise come into contact with the carton of Seven-Up prior to the explosion. Her son, who was with her, recognized the green pieces of glass as part of a Seven-Up bottle.

She was immediately taken to the hospital by Mrs. Stamper, a managing agent of the store. Mrs. Stamper told her that a Seven-Up bottle had exploded and that several bottles had exploded that week. Before leaving the store Mrs. Stamper instructed one of her children to clean up the mess. Apparently, all of the physical evidence went out with the trash. The location of the Seven-Up carton immediately before the explosion was not a place where such items were ordinarily kept.

The defendant-appellee, Arnold Lee Vice, was the distributor of Seven-Up in the Clark County area. As such, he supplied Stamper's Cash Market, Inc. with its entire stock of Seven-Up. He would deliver it with his truck to the store and place it in the store and the cooler. Employees of the store would also place Seven-Up in the cooler from other locations in the store. His truck was loaded with Seven-Up by the bottler at the plant.

The defendant-appellee, Pepsi-Cola Bottling Co. of Lexington, Kentucky, Inc., was the bottler who produced and supplied Vice with his entire stock of Seven-Up.

* * *

In Dealers Transport Co. v. Battery Distributing Co., Ky., 402 S.W.2d 441 (1966) we adopted the view of strict product lia-bility in tort expressed in Section 402A of the American Law Institute's Restatement, Second, Torts.

* * *

Our expressed public policy will be furthered if we minimize the risk of personal injury and property damage by charging the costs of injuries against the manufacturer who can procure liability insurance and distribute its expense among the public as a cost of doing business; and since the risk of harm from defective products exists for mere bystanders and passersby as well as for the purchaser or user, there is no substantial reason for protecting one class of persons and not the other. The same policy requires us to maximize protection for the injured third party and promote the public interest in discouraging the marketing of products having defects that are a menace to the public by imposing strict liability upon retailers and wholesalers in the distributive chain responsible for marketing the defective product which injures the bystander. The imposition of strict liability places no unreasonable burden upon sellers because they can adjust the cost of insurance protection among themselves in the course of their continuing business relationship. [Citation.]

We must not shirk from extending the rule to the manufacturer for fear that the retailer or middleman will be impaled on the sword of liability without regard to fault. Their liability was already established under Section 402A of the Restatement of Torts 2d. As a matter of public policy the retailer or middleman as well as the manufacturer should be liable since the loss for injuries resulting from defective products should be placed on those members of the marketing chain best able to pay the loss, who can then distribute such risk among themselves by means of insurance and indemnity agreements. [Citation.]
* * *

The result which we reach does not give the bystander a "free ride." When products and consumers are considered in the aggregate, bystanders, as a class, purchase most of the same products to which they are exposed as bystanders. Thus, as a class, they indirectly subsidize the liability of the manufacturer, middleman and retailer and in this sense do pay for the insurance policy tied to the product.

Public policy is adequately served if parameters are placed upon the extension of the rule so that it is limited to bystanders whose injury from the defect is reasonably foreseeable. [Citation.]

For the sake of clarity we restate the extension of the rule. The protections of Section 402A of the Restatement, Second, Torts extend to bystanders whose injury from the defective product is reasonably foreseeable.

* * *

It matters not that the evidence be circumstantial for as Thoreau put it "Some circumstantial evidence is very strong, as when you find a trout in the milk." There are some accidents, as where a beverage bottle explodes in the course of normal handling, as to which there is common experience that they do not ordinarily occur without a defect; and this permits the inference of a defect. Prosser on Torts, 4th Ed., 673. This is particularly true when there is evidence in the case of the antecedent explosion of other bottles of the same product. [Citation.]

In cases involving multiple defendants the better reasoned view places the onus of tracing the defect on the shoulders of the dealers and the manufacturer as a policy matter, seeking to compensate the plaintiff and to require the defendants to fight out the question of responsibility among themselves. [Citation.]

The motions for a directed verdict should have been denied.

Judgment reversed, and cause remanded.

Problems

1. A purchased from a local dealer a truck manufactured by M, which was one of a fleet of trucks operated by A in its business. B, employed by A, while driving the truck in a reasonable manner at a lawful speed was seriously injured when it suddenly became uncontrollable, veered sharply to the right, and overturned. Prior to this occurrence the truck had been driven only 1,637 miles, and B, the truck driver who drove it regularly, had experienced no mechanical difficulties nor noticed anything unusual about it.

The accident was caused by the sudden separation of the right front spring hanger bracket from the frame of the truck to which it had been fastened with defective rivets. This separation allowed the right front wheel to be displaced rearward and make contact with the inside of the right front wheel well, forcing the vehicle into a sharp right turn.

Prior to the accident, M learned that defective rivets had been used in the manufacture of this particular model truck, and notified A by letter of such fact, stating that this condition could interfere with steering control of the vehicle, and requesting A to contact promptly the dealer who had sold the truck and arrange for the necessary corrections. The letter enclosed a customer notification and authorization form for verification to the dealer that this service was to be performed at no charge to A. As A had purchased a number of trucks of this same model manufactured by M, conferences and negotiations ensued between A and representatives of M as to whether repairs to the fleet of trucks would be made by the dealer, or by A with cost and expense reimbursed by M.

In an action against M, B sues to recover for the personal injuries he sustained, and A sues to recover for the damage to the truck, its contents, and refrigerating equipment installed in it. Decision?

2. Plaintiff Holly purchased from defendant Store, Inc. a raw pork roast which was sliced into pork chops. Holly prepared them for the family dinner by frying them on each side in a skillet for 15 minutes until browned, then adding water, putting a cover on the skillet, and boiling them for an hour and ten minutes over a medium flame on a gas stove. After eating them, Holly and others in the family contracted trichinosis in varying degrees, with Holly, the most severely affected, requiring hospitalization. Trichinosis is a disease caused by parasitic worms known as trichinae which are sometimes present in raw or undercooked pork.

Although there is no method of detecting the presence of trichinae in raw pork, it is generally known that this parasite infests pork and that pork must be well cooked before being eaten. Thorough cooking at a temperature of 137 or more degrees Fahrenheit destroys the parasite and makes the meat safe for human consumption.

Plaintiff's complaint against Store, Inc. is based upon strict liability in tort. How should the case be decided?

3. William Joyce purchased a refrigerator manufactured by Acorn Company which was installed in his residence and plugged into an electrical outlet in the wall directly behind the refrigerator. There were no other outlets on the refrigerator circuit which had a circuit breaker manufactured by King Electric Company.

Two years after the installation, Joyce's residence was completely destroyed by fire, the origin of which was found to have been in the immediate vicinity of the refrigerator. There was evidence of considerable interior fire damage to the refrigerator. Joyce sues both Acorn and King Electric to recover his loss totaling $200,000. Each defendant blames the product manufactured by the other as the cause of the fire. There was no direct proof of any defect in the refrigerator or of any causal connection between any specific part of the refrigerator and the damages sustained by Joyce. The testimony as to liability was by expert witnesses, and Acorn offered no evidence. The jury brought in a verdict against Acorn for the full amount of the loss, and held King Electric not liable.

May the verdict of the jury be sustained as a matter of law?

4. Fred Lyon of New York, while on vacation in California, rented a 1982 model Home Run automobile from Hurts Drive-A-Car. The car was manufactured by Itsu-Bitsu Motor Company, and was purchased by Hurts from Katz & Jammer, Inc., an automobile importer. Lyon was driving the car on a street in San Jose when, due to a defect in the steering mechanism, it suddenly became impossible to steer. The speed of the car at the time was 30 miles per hour, but before Lyon could bring it to a stop, the car jumped a low curb and struck Peter Wolf standing on the sidewalk, breaking both of his legs and causing other injuries. Wolf sues Hurts Drive-A-Car, Itsu-Bitsu Motor Company, Katz & Jammer, Inc. and Lyon. Decision?

5. Plaintiff brings this cause of action against a manufacturer for the loss of one leg below the hip. The leg was lost when caught in the gears of a screw auger machine sold and installed by the defendant. Shortly before the accident, plaintiff's co-employees had removed a covering panel from the machine by use of sledgehammers and crowbars in order to do repair work. When finished, they replaced the panel with a single piece of cardboard instead of restoring the equipment to its original condition. The plaintiff stepped on the cardboard in the course of his work and fell, catching his leg in the moving parts. Decision?

6. The plaintiff, while driving a van manufactured by the defendant, was struck in the rear by another motor vehicle. Upon impact, the plaintiff's head was jarred backward against the rear window of the cab, causing the plaintiff serious injury. The van was not equipped with a headrest, and none was required at the time. Should the plaintiff prevail on a cause of action based upon strict liability in tort? Why?

7. Plaintiff, while dining at Defendant's Restaurant, ordered a chicken-pot pie. While he was eating the food, he swallowed a sliver of chicken bone, which became lodged in his throat causing him serious injury. Plaintiff brings a cause of action based upon strict liability in tort. Should he prevail? Why?

8. Plaintiff brought this action against the defendant, claiming that he suffered physical and mental distress when he partially consumed the contents of a bottle of soda containing a decomposed mouse. Decision?

9. Plaintiff, a homeowner, brings this cause of action against defendant, a water meter manufacturer, for damage done to plaintiff's property allegedly caused by the breaking of the meter. The meter was initially purchased by the city in 1962 and installed in the plaintiff's home in 1970. The meter broke in 1981. Assuming plaintiff can prove that the product was defectively manufactured and that the manufactur-ing defect was the cause of plaintiff's injury, should the plaintiff prevail? Why?

10. Mother, while cleaning her home, places a closed can of cleaner on a table next to her baby's crib. The family's cat jumps onto the table and accidently knocks the cleanser into the crib causing the can to open upon impact. Baby, seeing the pretty colors, begins to play with the powerful crystals causing severe injury to herself. In a suit brought on behalf of the baby based upon faulty packaging of the cleanser, what result? Why?

REMEDIES OF
SELLER
AND OF BUYER

The performance of a contract for the sale of goods may require part performance in stages, and at any stage one of the parties may breach or repudiate the contract, or insolvency of one of the parties may occur. The goods may be in the possession of the seller and identified to the contract, or in the possession of a bailee of the buyer, or in transit to the buyer, or in the possession of the buyer. The goods may be conforming or non-conforming to the contract. The buyer may have justifiably or unjustifiably rejected the goods on tender or delivery or revoked his acceptance of them. Remedies are necessary not only for a breach of the contract but also relating to the factual situation with respect to the goods. Consequently, the Code provides separate and distinct remedies for the seller and for the buyer, each specifically keyed to the factual situation respecting the goods. In all events, the avowed purpose of the Code is to put the aggrieved party in as good a position as if the other party had fully performed. Section 1–106.

REMEDIES OF THE SELLER

When a buyer defaults in any of his contractual obligations, the seller has been deprived of the rights for which he bargained. The buyer's default may consist of any of the following acts: the buyer wrongfully rejects the goods, the buyer wrongfully revokes acceptance of the goods, the buyer fails to make a payment due on or before delivery, or the buyer repudiates the contract in whole or in part. Section 2–703 catalogs the seller's remedies for each of these defaults. These remedies are: (1) to withhold delivery of the goods; (2) to stop delivery of the goods by a carrier or other bailee; (3) to identify conforming goods to the contract not already identified; (4) to resell the goods and recover damages; (5) to recover damages for non-acceptance of the goods or repudiation of the contract; (6) to recover the price; (7) to recover incidental damages; (8) to cancel the contract; and (9) to reclaim the goods upon the buyer's insolvency as provided by Section 2–702(2).

To Withhold Delivery of the Goods

A seller may withhold delivery to a buyer who has wrongfully rejected or revoked acceptance of the goods or has failed to make a payment due on or before delivery or has repudiated the contract.

Where the contract calls for installments, any breach of an installment which impairs the value of the whole contract (Section 2–612) will permit the seller to withhold the entire undelivered balance of the goods. Section 2–703. In addition, upon discovery of the buyer's insolvency, the seller may refuse to deliver the goods except for cash including payment for all goods previously delivered under the contract. Section 2–702.

This right is essentially that of a seller to withhold or discontinue performance of his side of the contract by reason of the buyer's breach.

To Stop Delivery of the Goods by a Carrier or Other Bailee

An extension of the right to withhold delivery is the right of an aggrieved seller to stop delivery of the goods in transit to the buyer or in the possession of a bailee upon discovery of the buyer's insolvency. The seller accomplishes this by timely notification to the carrier or other bailee to stop delivery of the goods. After such notification the carrier or bailee must hold and deliver the goods according to the directions of the seller who is liable to the carrier or bailee for any ensuing charges or damages. Section 2–705(3).

If the seller discovers the buyer to be insolvent, then the seller may stop any de-

livery. If the buyer repudiates or fails to make a payment due before delivery, the seller may stop only shipments by carload, truckload, planeload, or larger shipments. The right applies not only to carriers but to other bailees.

The right of the seller to stop delivery ceases when (1) the buyer receives the goods; or (2) the bailee of the goods, except a carrier, acknowledges to the buyer that he holds them for the buyer; or (3) the carrier acknowledges to the buyer that he holds them for the buyer by reshipment or as warehouseman; or (4) a negotiable document of title covering the goods is negotiated to the buyer. Section 2–705(2).

Insolvency, as it applies to the right to stop delivery and to other rights of the seller and the buyer when pertinent, is defined in Section 1–201(23) of the Code as follows:

A person is "insolvent" who either has ceased to pay his debts in the ordinary course of business or cannot pay his debts as they become due, or is insolvent within the meaning of the federal bankruptcy law.

Insolvency is thus defined to include both its equity meaning and its bankruptcy meaning. The equity meaning of insolvency is the inability of a person to pay his debts as they mature. The bankruptcy meaning is that his total liabilities exceed the total value of all his assets.

To Identify Goods to the Contract

Upon a breach of the contract by the buyer, the seller may proceed to identify to the contract conforming goods in his possession or control which were not so identified at the time he learned of the breach. Section 2–704. He may also treat as the subject of resale unfinished goods which have demonstrably been intended for fulfillment of the particular contract. With respect to such unfinished goods, the seller in the exercise of reasonable commercial judgment for the purpose of mitigating loss may either complete their manufacture and identify them to the contract or cease their manufacture and resell the unfinished goods for scrap or salvage value. Section 2–704.

For example, if at the time of the buyer's breach or repudiation the goods in the process of manufacture are 90% finished, in order to avoid loss and obtain maximum realization of value a seller may be justified in completing their manufacture and reselling them as finished goods. On the other hand, if at such time the manufacturing process has only just commenced, sound business judgment may require that the manufacture be halted in order to mitigate loss and damage.

To Resell the Goods

Under the same circumstances which permit the seller to withhold delivery of goods to the buyer, the seller may resell the goods concerned or the undelivered balance thereof. The resale must be in good faith and in a commercially reasonable manner, and the seller may recover from the buyer the difference between the resale price and the contract price, together with any incidental damages such as reasonable charges and expenses incurred in stopping delivery, in the transportation, care, and custody of the goods after the buyer's breach, and in connection with the return or resale of the goods, less expenses saved in consequence of the buyer's breach. Section 2–706(1).

For example, A agrees to sell goods to B for a contract price of $8,000 due on delivery. B wrongfully rejects the goods and refuses to pay A anything. A resells the goods in strict compliance with the Code for $6,000 and incurs incidental damages for sales commissions of $500 but saves $200 in transportation costs. A would recover from B the contract price ($8,000) minus the resale price ($6,000) plus incidental damages ($500) minus expenses saved ($200) which equals $2,300.

The resale may be at public or private sale and the goods may be sold as a unit or in parcels. The goods resold must be identified as those related to the contract, but it is not necessary that the goods be in existence or that they have been identified to the contract before the buyer's breach. Section 2–706(2).

Where the resale is at private sale the seller must give the buyer reasonable notice of his intention to resell.

Where the resale is at public sale only identified goods can be sold except where there is a recognized market for a public sale of future goods of the kind involved. The public sale must be made at a usual place or market for public sale if one is reasonably available. The seller must give the buyer reasonable notice of the time and place of the resale unless the goods are perishable or threaten to decline in value speedily. Prospective bidders at the sale must be given an opportunity for reasonable inspection of the goods before the sale. The seller may be a purchaser of the goods at the public sale. Section 2–706(3).

The seller is not accountable to the buyer for any profit made on any resale of the goods.

A bona fide purchaser at a resale takes the goods free of any rights of the original buyer, even though the seller has failed to comply with one or more of the requirements of the Code with respect to making the resale. Section 2–706(5).

To Recover Damages for Non-acceptance or Repudiation

The seller in the event of a repudiation, non-acceptance, wrongful rejection or revocation of the goods by the buyer may maintain an action at law and recover damages from the buyer measured by the difference between the market price at the time and place of tender of the goods and the unpaid contract price, plus incidental damages, less expenses saved in consequence of the buyer's breach. Section 2–708(1). This remedy is an alternative to the remedy of resale under Section 2–706.

For example, A in Seattle agrees to sell goods to B in Chicago for $20,000 F.O.B. Chicago, delivery on June 15. B wrongfully rejects the goods. The market price would be ascertained as of June 15 in Chicago because F.O.B. Chicago is a destination contract in which the place of tender would be Chicago. The market price of the goods on June 15 in Chicago is $15,000. A incurred $1,000 in incidental expenses while saving $500 in expenses. A's recovery from B would be the contract price ($20,000) minus the market price ($15,000) plus incidental damages ($1,000) minus expenses saved ($500), which equals $5,500.

If the difference between the market price and the contract price is inadequate to place the seller in as good a position as performance would have done, then the measure of damages is the profit, including reasonable overhead, which the seller would have realized from full performance by the buyer, plus any incidental damages less expenses saved in consequence of the buyer's breach. Section 2–708(2).

For example, A, an automobile dealer, enters into a contract to sell a large, luxury, fuel inefficient car to B for $14,000. The price of gasoline increases 20% and B repudiates. The market value of the car is still $14,000 but because A cannot sell as many cars as he can obtain, A's sales volume has decreased by one due to B's breach. Section 2–708(2) would apply and permit A to recover the profits he lost on the sale to B (computed as the contract price minus what the car costs A plus an allocation of overhead) plus any incidental damages.

To Recover the Price

At common law, an action by the seller to recover the price depended upon a transfer of title to the buyer. The Code permits the seller to recover the price in three situations: (1) where the buyer has accepted the goods; (2) where conforming goods have been lost or damaged after the risk of loss has passed to the buyer; and (3) where the goods have been identified to the contract and there is no ready market available for their resale at a reasonable price. Section 2–709(1).

A seller who sues for the price must hold for the buyer any goods which have been identified to the contract and are still in his control. If resale becomes possible, the seller may resell the goods at any time prior to the collection of the judgment and the net proceeds of such resale must be credited to the buyer. Payment of the judgment entitles the buyer to any goods not resold. Section 2–709(2).

If the buyer has wrongfully rejected or revoked acceptance of the goods or has repudiated or failed to make a payment due, a seller who is held not entitled to recover the price shall be awarded damages for non-acceptance of the goods. Section 2–709(3).

To Recover Incidental Damages

In addition to recovering damages for the difference between the resale price and the contract price (Section 2–706), or recovering damages for non-acceptance or repudiation (Section 2–708), or recovering the price (Section 2–709), the seller may also recover in the same action his incidental damages which are defined in Section 2–710 of the Code as follows:

Incidental damages to an aggrieved seller include any commercially reasonable charges, expenses or commissions incurred in stopping delivery, in the transportation, care and custody of goods after the buyer's breach, in connection with return or resale of the goods or otherwise resulting from the breach.

To Cancel the Contract

Where the buyer wrongfully rejects or revokes acceptance of the goods, or fails to make a payment due, or repudiates the contract in whole or in part, the seller may cancel the contract with respect to the goods directly affected, and if the breach is of an installment contract which substantially impairs the whole contract, he may cancel the entire contract. Section 2–703(f).

A material breach is one going to the essence of the contract. It is a failure to perform wholly or a partial failure of performance which substantially impairs the value of the whole contract to the aggrieved party. The materiality of a breach depends upon all of the circumstances. A breach in limine, that is, at the beginning or threshold of the performance due under an installment contract, is more serious than a breach after acceptance and payment for a number of installments.

Section 2–106 of the Code defines cancellation as the putting an end to the contract by one party by reason of a breach by the other. The obligation of the cancelling party for any future performance under the contract is discharged, although he retains any remedy for breach of the whole contract or any unperformed balance.

To Reclaim the Goods
Upon Buyer's Insolvency

In addition to the right of an unpaid seller to withhold and stop delivery of the goods, he may reclaim them from an insolvent buyer by demand upon the buyer within ten days after the buyer has received the goods. Section 2–702(2). Where the buyer has committed fraud by a misrepresentation of his solvency made to the seller in writing within three months prior to delivery of the goods, the ten-day limitation does not apply. The seller's right to reclaim is subject to the rights of a purchaser of the goods from the buyer in ordinary course or other good faith purchaser. Upon a successful recla-

mation of the goods from an insolvent buyer, the seller thereby obtains preferential treatment over other creditors of the buyer. The Code therefore provides that after thus recovering the goods, the seller is excluded from all other remedies with respect to them. Section 2–702(3).

REMEDIES OF THE BUYER

Where the seller fails to make delivery or repudiates, or the buyer rightfully rejects or justifiably revokes acceptance, the buyer may with respect to any goods involved, or with respect to the whole if the breach goes to the whole contract, (1) cancel *and* (2) recover payments made. In addition, the buyer may (3) "cover" and have damages *or* (4) recover damages for non-delivery. Section 2–711(1). Where the seller fails to deliver or repudiates, the buyer where appropriate may also (5) recover identified goods if the seller is insolvent, *or* (6) obtain specific performance *or* (7) replevy the goods. Section 2–711(2). Moreover, upon rightful rejection or justifiable revocation of acceptance, the buyer (8) has a security interest in the goods. Section 2–711(3). Where the buyer has accepted goods and given notification to the seller of their non-conformity, the buyer may (9) recover damages for breach of warranty. Section 2–714. Finally, in addition to the remedies listed above, the buyer may, where appropriate, (10) recover incidental damages, and (11) recover consequential damages. Section 2–715.

Cancellation of the Contract

Where the seller fails to make delivery or repudiates the contract, or where the buyer rightfully rejects or justifiably revokes acceptance of goods tendered or delivered to him, the buyer may cancel the contract with respect to any goods involved, and if the breach by the seller is material and goes to the whole contract, the buyer may cancel the entire contract. Section 2–711(1).

The materiality of a breach depends upon the same factors discussed in reference to the seller's right to cancel.

The buyer must give the seller notice of his cancellation of the contract and is not only excused from further performance or tender on his part but also may "cover" and have damages or recover damages from the seller for nondelivery of the goods. Section 2–711(1).

Recover Payments Made

Where the seller fails to make delivery or repudiates the contract or where the buyer rightfully rejects or justifiably revokes acceptance of the goods, the buyer may recover so much of the price as has been paid. Section 2–711(1). For example, A and B enter into a contract for a sale of goods for a contract price of $3,000 and B, the buyer, has made a downpayment of $600. A delivers non-conforming goods to B who rightfully rejects them. B may cancel the contract and recover the $600 plus whatever other damages B may prove, as discussed later in this chapter.

The Right of "Cover"

Where a seller repudiates the contract or fails to make delivery or where the buyer rightfully rejects or justifiably revokes an acceptance of the goods the buyer may protect himself by a "cover." This means that the buyer may in good faith and without unreasonable delay proceed to purchase goods or make a contract to purchase goods in substitution for those due under the contract from the seller. This right enables the buyer to assure himself of a needed source of supply of the goods.

Upon making a reasonable contract of cover the buyer may recover from the seller the difference between the cost of cover and the contract price, plus any incidental and consequential damages as defined in Sec-

tion 2–715, less expenses saved in consequence of the seller's breach. Section 2–712.

The buyer is not required to effect "cover" and his failure to do so does not bar him from any other remedy provided by the Code (Section 2–712). However, the buyer may not recover consequential damages resulting from his general or particular requirements or needs which he could have prevented by cover. Section 2–715(2)(a).

A farmer who made a contract in April, 1970, to sell to a grain dealer 40,000 bushels of corn deliverable in October, unequivocally informed the buyer on June 3 that he was not going to plant any corn, that he would not fulfill the contract, and that if the buyer had commitments to resell the corn he should make other arrangements. This was an anticipatory repudiation of the contract. Under Section 2–610(a) the aggrieved party may await performance for a commercially reasonable time, or under 2–610(b) resort to any remedy for breach. The court held that a commercially reasonable time expired on June 3, as the buyer had no reasonable expectation of performance by the seller, and "cover" was available. The buyer was therefore denied the consequential damages that he could have prevented by cover (Section 2–715(2)(a)), and was allowed to recover from the seller only the difference between the contract price and the June 3 futures market price for corn to be delivered in October. This was substantially less than the actual loss sustained by the grain dealer buyer who in vain had awaited performance of the repudiated contract until October and then had to buy corn at a greatly increased price on the market in order to fulfill commitments to his vendees. Oloffson v. Coomer, 11 Ill.App.3d 918, 296 N.E.2d 871 (1973).

Recovery of Damages for Non-delivery or Repudiation

In the event that the seller repudiates the contract or fails to deliver the goods or the

buyer rightfully rejects or justifiably revokes acceptance of the goods, the buyer is
entitled to recover damages from the seller
measured by the difference between the
market price at the time when the buyer
learned of the breach and the contract price,
together with incidental and consequential
damages, less expenses saved in consequence of the seller's breach. The market
price is to be determined as of the place for
tender, or, in the event that the buyer has
rightfully rejected the goods or has justifiably revoked his acceptance of them, the
market price is to be determined as of the
place of arrival. Sections 2–713 and
2–711(1).

For example, A agrees to sell goods to
B for $7,000 C.O.D. delivery by November
15. A fails to deliver. As a consequence
B suffered incidental damages of $1,500 and
consequential damages of $1,000. In the
case of non-delivery or repudiation, market
price is determined as of the place of tender.
Since C.O.D. is a shipment contract, the
place of tender would be the seller's city.
Therefore, the market price must be determined in the seller's city and on November
15, when B learned of the breach. At this
time and place the market price is $8,000.
B would recover the market price ($8,000)
minus the contract price ($7,000) plus in-
cidental damages ($1,500) plus consequen-
tial damages ($1,000) less expenses saved
($0 in this example) which equals $3,500.

In the example above, if A had instead
delivered non-conforming goods which B
rejected, then the market price would be
determined at B's place of business; if instead A repudiated the contract on November 1, then the market price would be determined on that date.

Recovery of Identified Goods upon the Seller's Insolvency

Where existing goods are identified to the
contract of sale, the buyer acquires a special

property in the goods. Section 2–501.
This special property exists even though the
goods are nonconforming and the buyer has
the right to return or reject them. Identification of the goods to the contract may
be made either by the buyer or by the seller.

The Code gives the buyer a right which
does not exist at common law to recover
from an insolvent seller the goods in which
the buyer has a special property and for
which he has paid a part or all of the price.
This right exists where the seller who is in
possession or control of the goods becomes
insolvent within 10 days after receipt of the
first installment of the price. To exercise
it the buyer must tender to the seller any
unpaid portion of the price. If the special
property exists by reason of an identification made by the buyer, he may recover the
goods only if they conform to the contract
for sale. The buyer does not have the right
to recover from an insolvent seller nonconforming goods which only the buyer has
identified to the contract. Section 2–502.

Suit for Specific Performance

In an action at law the buyer can recover
only a money judgment against a seller who
refuses or fails to perform, and ordinarily
compensatory money damages are an adequate remedy. However, where the contract is for the purchase of a unique item
such as a work of art, or a famous race horse,
heirloom, patent right, copyright, or shares
of stock in a closely held corporation, money
damages may not be an adequate remedy,
and in such case a court of equity has jurisdiction to order the seller specifically to
deliver to the buyer the goods described in
the contract upon payment of the price. If
the seller refuses to comply with such an
order or decree of a court of equity, he is
subject to the contempt powers of the court
which include the power to fine and im-
prison.

The Code provides that the buyer may
have specific performance of a contract for

the sale of goods where the goods are unique or in other proper circumstances. In addition, a decree for specific performance may include terms and conditions as to payment of the price, damages or other relief. Section 2–716.

Right of Replevin

Replevin is a form of action to recover specific goods in the possession of a defendant which are being unlawfully withheld from the plaintiff.

The buyer may maintain against the seller an action of replevin for goods which have been identified to the contract where the seller has repudiated or breached the contract, if (1) the buyer after a reasonable effort is unable to effect cover for such goods, or (2) the goods have been shipped under reservation of a security interest in the seller and satisfaction of this security interest has been made or tendered. Section 2–716.

Buyer's Security Interest in the Goods

A buyer who has rightfully rejected or justifiably revoked his acceptance of goods which remain in his possession or control has a security interest in these goods to the extent of any payment of the price which he has made and for any expenses reasonably incurred in their inspection, receipt, transportation, care, and custody. The buyer may hold such goods and resell them in the same manner as an aggrieved seller may resell goods. Section 2–711(3). He has the same rights as an unpaid seller to withhold delivery, or to stop delivery of the goods by a carrier or other bailee upon learning of the seller's insolvency, or to resell the goods. Section 2–706(6). In the event of resale the buyer is required to account to the seller for any excess of the net proceeds of the resale over the amount of his security interest. Section 2–706(6).

Recovery of Damages for Breach of Warranty in Regard to Accepted Goods

Where the buyer has accepted non-conforming goods and has given timely notification to the seller of the breach of contract, the buyer is entitled to maintain an action at law to recover from the seller the damages resulting from the seller's breach. Section 2–714.

In the event of breach of warranty, the measure of damages is the difference at the time and place of acceptance between the value of the goods which have been accepted and the value that the goods would have had if they had been as warranted. Special circumstances may entitle the buyer to recover damages proximately resulting from the breach of warranty in a different amount as well as incidental and consequential damages. Section 2–714.

The price of the goods does not figure in this computation, as the buyer is entitled to the benefit of his bargain which was to receive goods that were as warranted. For example, the price is $1,000. The value of the goods accepted is $800 but if they had been as warranted their value would have been $1,200. The buyer's damages for breach of warranty are $400, which he may deduct from any unpaid balance due on the purchase price upon notice to the seller of his intention to do so. Section 2–717.

Recovery of Incidental Damages

Section 2–715 of the Code defines the buyer's incidental damages as follows:

(1) Incidental damages resulting from the seller's breach include expenses reasonably incurred in inspection, receipt, transportation and care and custody of goods rightfully rejected, any commercial reasonable charges, expenses or commissions in connection with effecting cover and any other reasonable expense incident to the delay or other breach.

For example, the buyer of a racehorse justifiably revokes acceptance because the horse does not conform to the contract. The buyer will be allowed to recover as incidental damages the cost of caring for the horse from the date the horse was delivered until it is returned to the seller. It should be noted that the incidental damages listed in Section 2–715(1) are not intended to be exhaustive but merely illustrative of typical kinds of incidental damages. Comment 1 to Section 2–715.

Recovery of Consequential Damages

In many cases the remedies discussed above will not fully compensate the aggrieved buyer for his losses. For example, nonconforming goods that are accepted may explode and destroy the buyer's warehouse and its contents. Goods that are not delivered may have been the subject of a lucrative contract of resale, the profits from which are lost. The Code responds to this problem by providing the buyer with the opportunity to recover such damages in Section 2–715(2):

Consequential damages resulting from the seller's breach include
(a) any loss resulting from general or particular requirements and needs of which the seller at the time of contracting had reason to know and which could not reasonably be prevented by cover or otherwise; and
(b) injury to person or property proximately resulting from any breach of warranty.

An example of consequential damages would be a case in which the seller delivered to the buyer non-conforming goods which exploded, destroying the buyer's warehouse and its contents. Included in the contents were goods which had been stored pending delivery to a customer of the buyer in performance of a lucrative contract. The value of the warehouse and its contents, and the amount of profit lost due to the inability of the buyer to fulfill his lucrative contract

with his customer are consequential damages.

CONTRACTUAL PROVISIONS AFFECTING REMEDIES

Liquidation or Limitation of Damages

The parties may provide in their contract for liquidated damages by specifying the amount or measure of damages which either party may recover in the event of a breach by the other party. The amount of such damages must be reasonable and commensurate with the anticipated or actual loss resulting from a breach. A provision in a contract fixing unreasonably large liquidated damages is void as a penalty. Section 2–718.

Modification or Limitation of Remedy by Agreement

The contract between the seller and buyer may expressly provide for remedies in addition to or in lieu of those provided in the Code and may limit or change the measure of damages recoverable in the event of breach. Section 2–719.

The contract may validly limit the remedy of the buyer to a return of the goods and a refunding of the price, or to the replacement of non-conforming goods or parts.

A remedy provided by the contract is optional unless it is expressly agreed to be exclusive of other remedies, in which event it is the sole remedy. However, where circumstances cause an exclusive remedy to fail of its essential purpose, resort may be had to the remedies provided by the Code. Section 2–719(2).

The contract may expressly limit or exclude consequential damages unless such limitation or exclusion would be unconscionable. Limitation of consequential damages for personal injuries resulting from breach of warranty in the sale of consumer goods is prima facie unconscionable, whereas limitation of such damages where the loss is commercial is not. Section 2–719(3).

Cases

Seller's Right to Recover Damages

JAGGER BROTHERS, INC. v. TECHNICAL TEXTILE CO.

(1964) 202 Pa.Super. 639, 198 A.2d 888.

MONTGOMERY, J.

This appeal concerns the measure of damages * * * based on a written contract under which appellant agreed to purchase, at $2.15 per pound, 20,000 pounds of yarn to be manufactured by appellee. Appellee manufactured 3,723 pounds of the yarn and delivered it to appellant, who accepted and paid for it. The remaining 16,277 pounds were never manufactured because appellant advised appellee by letter, dated August 12, 1960, that it repudiated the contract and would refuse any future delivery of yarn.

Appellee was awarded $4,069.25 in a nonjury trial, which award was based on testimony offered by appellee that the market price of the yarn was $1.90 per pound on August 12, 1960. The award represents 16,277 times the difference between the contract price and the market price ($.25 per pound). No evidence was offered as to the cost of manufacturing the yarn.

Appellant contends that the proper measure of damages in such cases is the difference between the cost of manufacturing and the contract price; and, therefore, since appellee did not prove its cost of manufacture, it is entitled only to nominal damages.

Appellee contends that it has properly proved its damages under section 2–708 of the Uniform Commercial Code, [citation], which reads as follows:

"Seller's Damages for Non-Acceptance or Repudiation—(1) Subject to subsection (2) and to the provisions of this Article with respect to proof of market price (Section 2–723) the measure of damages for non-acceptance or repudiation by the buyer is the difference between the market price at the time and place for tender and the unpaid contract price together with any incidental damages provided in this Article (Section 2–710), but less expenses saved in consequence of the buyer's breach.

"(2) If the measure of damages provided in subsection (1) is inadequate to put the seller in as good a position as performance would have done then the measure of damages is the profit (including reasonable overhead) which the seller would have made from full performance by the buyer, together with any incidental damages provided in this Article (Section 2–710), due allowance for costs reasonably incurred and due credit for payments or proceeds of resale."

* * *

Section 2–723 of the Uniform Commercial Code * * * contains the following provisions for establishing market price:

"Proof of Market Price: Time and Place—(1) If an action based on anticipatory repudiation comes to trial before the time for performance with respect to some or all of the goods, any damages based on market price (Section 2–708 or Section 2–713) shall be determined according to the price of such goods prevailing at the time when the aggrieved party learned of the repudiation.

"(2) If evidence of a price prevailing at the times or places described in this Article is not readily available the price prevailing within any reasonable time before or after the time described or at any other place which in commercial judgment or under usage of trade would serve as a reasonable substitute for the one described may be used, making any proper allowance for the cost of transporting the goods to or from such other place.

"(3) Evidence of a relevant price prevailing at a time or place other than the one described in this Article offered by one party is not admissible unless and until he has given the other party such notice as the court finds sufficient to prevent unfair surprise."

* * *

In view of our conclusion that appellant properly based its measure of damages on the difference between the contract price and the current market price and satisfactorily established the proper market price, there is no need to engage in any further discussion of appellant's other contentions, other than to refer to the case of C. P. Mayer Brick Company, v. D. J. Kennedy Company, 230 Pa. 98, 79 A. 246 (1911), which was relied on heavily by appellant. We find that case to be in accord with our views as previously stated. The measure of damages in the Mayer case was the difference between the contract price and the cost of manufacturing the brick because there was no market price proved in that case. * * * An existing market price was proved in the present case.

Judgment affirmed.

Seller's Right
to Recover the Price

FRENCH v. SOTHEBY & CO.
(1970 Okl.) 470 P.2d 318.

DAVISON, J.
* * *

Plaintiff is located in London, England. Defendant is a resident of Ardmore, Oklahoma, but was in Europe most of the time, where her children were in school.

Plaintiff's petition (filed July 19, 1965) and amendment thereto alleged that defendant was indebted to plaintiff on open account in the sum of $24,886.27 for merchandise purchased by defendant on March 22, 1965, and March 25, 1965. The attached statement of account stated Sotheby & Co. were Auctioneers of Works of Art in London, England, and showed that the merchandise consisted of eight ancient or antique guns bought (bid in) for 10,480 pounds, on which there had been credited on May 6, 1965, the amount of 1571 pounds, 2 shillings, and 3 pence, leaving a balance due of 8908 pounds, 17 shillings, and 9 pence. It was alleged that the value of the British pound at the time the debt was made was $2.7937.

* * *

Defendant contends that regardless of all other questions, it was error of law to render judgment for the price of the guns. It is defendant's position that under the circumstances reflected by the record the defendant's liability, if any, would be only for the difference between the market price and the unpaid contract price.

Sec. 2–703, of Uniform Commercial Code, provides in part that where the buyer wrongfully rejects acceptance of goods, the aggrieved seller may:

"(d) resell and recover damages as hereafter provided (Section 2–706);

"(e) recover damages for non-acceptance (Section 2–708) or in a proper case the price (Section 2–709);"

* * * Plaintiff did not proceed under Subd. (d) and elected to seek recovery of the price.

Sec. 2–708 referred to in Subd. (d) * * * provides that the measure of damages for non-acceptance or repudiation by the buyer is the difference between the market price at the time and place for tender and the unpaid contract price together with any incidental damages, but less expenses saved in consequence of the buyer's breach.

Defendant did not accept the guns, they are still in the possession of plaintiff. The remedy provided by Sec. 2–708 and Subd.

(e) of Sec. 2–703, is clearly and distinctly described therein. This measure of damages is essentially the same as that announced in our decisions prior to the adoption of the Uniform Commercial Code. [Citations.] This remedy was available to plaintiff, but plaintiff sought recovery of the price.

This leaves for consideration the statutory provisions governing actions to recover the price of goods.

Sec. 2–709 states in part as follows:

"(1) When the buyer fails to pay the price as it becomes due the seller may recover, together with any incidental damages under the next section, the price:

"(a) of goods accepted or of conforming goods lost or damaged within a commercially reasonable time after risk of their loss has passed to the buyer; and

"(b) of goods identified to the contract if the seller is unable after reasonable effort to resell them at a reasonable price or the circumstances reasonably indicate that such effort will be unavailing."

* * * Our previous law, 23 Okl. St.Ann. Sec. 31, now repealed, permitted the seller to recover the purchase price when title to the goods had passed to the buyer, even though the seller was still in possession. This is not the meaning or purpose of Sec. 2–709. The "Uniform Commercial Code Comment" immediately following Sec. 2–709, and Anderson's Uniform Commercial Code, Vol. 1, Sec. 2–709.1, pp. 433, 434, state that the purpose of the changes was to make it clear that the passing of title was not material to a price action, but that the section is intended to be exhaustive in its enumeration of cases where an action for the price lies.

Applying the provisions of Sec. 2–709 to the present situation, there is nothing in the record to show that the goods were accepted, or that they were lost after risk thereof had passed to defendant, or that plaintiff was unable to resell them at a reasonable price. The record lacked an essential fact, the presence of which was necessary to entitle plaintiff to recover the balance of the price of the goods.

* * *

Judgment [for plaintiff] reversed and cause remanded.

Buyer's Right
to Cancel the Contract

GARFINKEL v. LEHMAN FLOOR COVERING CO.

(1969) 60 Misc.2d 72, 302 N.Y.S.2d 167.

DONOVAN, J.

Plaintiff seeks to recover the sum of $1,363.63 which was paid to the defendant for floor covering. The covering was installed on the floors March 8, 1967. Immediately the plaintiff noticed an unsightly condition and called it to the attention of the defendant.

On two occasions representatives of the defendant called at the plaintiff's home and worked on the carpet in an attempt to correct the condition.

The expert who testified on behalf of the defendant, described the condition as pressure bands caused by pressure when the carpeting was on the roller.

* * * On April 12, 1967 plaintiff's attorney wrote to the defendant rejecting the merchandise and demanding its removal.

* * * The merchandise is substantially defective and the plaintiff is entitled to have the purchase price refunded unless he has in some way prejudiced that right by retaining the carpet which is still on his floor and in use.

* * * Section 2–602 of the Uniform Commercial Code provides that the buyer, if he has possession of the goods, is under a duty after rejection to "hold them with reasonable care at the seller's disposition for a time sufficient to permit the seller to remove them; but the buyer has no further obligations with regard to goods rightfully rejected." It follows that the plaintiff was then permitted to retain the goods at his

home awaiting removal by the seller and had no further obligation if the rejection was within a reasonable time and he had notified the seller.

The court finds as a fact that the rejection was justified; that it was made within a reasonable time and that proper notification was given to the seller.

The need for this provision of the Uniform Commercial Code has been apparent in this court for some time. Many cases were brought where a merchant delivered defective merchandise, bulky in character, expensive to transport and store. He then left the defective merchandise and refused to remove it. This placed the consumer in a dilemma. If the consumer removes and returns the goods, it is an expensive proposition. He is out of pocket money, in addition to the loss of his purchase price, in exchange for the gamble of recovering some of it by court action. On the other hand, if he retains the merchandise in his home, he loses the right to rescind the contract and his purchase money is gone. In return he has to seek the right to damage for which he will need expensive expert testimony.

It is the opinion of the court that one of the beneficial purposes intended by the new commercial code was to put the burden on the merchant where the goods are defective and he is given proper notice of the defect. He delivered the goods and it is fair that he should remove them or let them remain at his peril.

Judgment for plaintiff for the sum of $1363.63 with interest from March 8, 1967.

Buyer's Right
to Recover Damages

STATE v. TRAVELERS INDEM. CO.

(1968) 250 Or. 356, 442 P.2d 612.

Goodwin, J.

Plaintiff, an unpaid seller of materials used in a highway construction project, brought action for $31,961, the contract price of the goods, and for attorney fees. Defendant paid into court the sum of $24,143. Plaintiff appeals from a judgment in the amount paid into court.

There are numerous assignments of error, but it is necessary to discuss only one. The trial court submitted to the jury the defendant's theory that the plaintiff had substituted inferior materials for those called for in the contract. There was evidence to support such a theory. However, the record contained no evidence by which the jury could measure the damages for the breach of warranty if they found one. The evidence showed that the volume of material called for by the contract has been accepted and used by the purchaser. The purchaser had protested the invoices and had asserted that there were defects in the materials, but the purchaser did not reject the goods. Under such circumstances, the rights of the parties are controlled by [U.C.C. Section 2–607] and [Section 2–714]. Neither statute appears to have been called to the trial court's attention. Had the court's attention been directed to the controlling statutes, the trial undoubtedly would have produced the necessary evidence or the case would not have been submitted to the jury. The burden was upon the defendant to prove the amount of the alleged damage. [2–607(4)].

The correct measure of damages under [2–714] is the difference in value between the goods accepted and the value they would have had if they had been as warranted. The evidence is barren of any testimony on the difference in value. Since there was no foundation in the pleadings for such evidence, the omission is understandable. The record left the case without support, however, for the verdict which the jury was allowed to return. The jury was allowed to speculate from the generalities in the pleadings, and from estimates of "damages" that had no discernible connection with a difference in value between substituted goods and ordered goods. The defendant did not even disclose to the jury how it had arrived at the amount of money it had tendered into court but which the jury nonetheless decided was a proper sum for the plaintiff to recover.

Reversed and remanded.

Limitation of Remedies

WILSON TRADING CORP. v. DAVID FERGUSON, LTD.

(1968) 23 N.Y.2d 398, 297 N.Y.S.2d 108, 244 N.E.2d 685.

JASEN, J.

The plaintiff, Wilson Trading Corporation, entered into a contract with the defendant, David Ferguson, Ltd., for the sale of a specified quantity of yarn. After the yarn was delivered, cut and knitted into sweaters, the finished product was washed. It was during this washing that it was discovered that the color of the yarn had "shaded"—that is, "there was a variation in color from piece to piece and within the pieces." This defect, the defendant claims, rendered the sweaters "unmarketable".

This action for the contract price of the yarn was commenced after the defendant refused payment. As a defense to the action and as a counterclaim for damages, the defendant alleges that "[p]laintiff has failed to perform all of the conditions of the contract on its part required to be performed, and has delivered * * * defective and unworkmanlike goods".

The sales contract provides in pertinent part:

"2. No claims relating to excessive moisture content, short weight, count variations, twist, quality or shade shall be allowed *if made after weaving, knitting, or processing,* or more than 10 days after receipt of shipment. * * * The buyer shall within 10 days of the receipt of the merchandise by himself or agent examine the merchandise for any and all defects." (Emphasis supplied.)

* * *

Special Term granted plaintiff summary judgment for the contract price of the yarn sold on the ground that "notice of the alleged breach of warranty for defect in shading was not given within the time expressly limited and is not now available by way of defense or counterclaim." The Appellate Division affirmed, without opinion.

The defendant on this appeal urges that the time limitation provision on claims in the contract was unreasonable since the defect in the color of the yarn was latent and could not be discovered until after the yarn was processed and the finished product washed.

Defendant's affidavits allege that its sweaters were rendered unsaleable because of latent defects in the yarn which caused "variation in color from piece to piece and within the pieces." * * * Indeed, the plaintiff does not seriously dispute the fact that its yarn was unmerchantable, but instead, like Special Term, relies upon the failure of defendant to give notice of the breach of warranty within the time limits prescribed by paragraph 2 of the contract.

Subdivision (3) (par. [a]) of section 2–607 of the Uniform Commercial Code expressly provides that a buyer who accepts goods has a reasonable time after he discovers or should have discovered a breach to notify the seller of such breach. (Cf. 5 Williston, Contracts [3d ed.], § 173.) Defendant's affidavits allege that a claim was made immediately upon discovery of the breach of warranty after the yarn was knitted and washed, and that this was the earliest possible moment at which the defects could reasonably be discovered in the normal manufacturing process. * * *

However, the Uniform Commercial Code allows the parties, within limits established by the code, to modify or exclude warranties and to limit remedies for breach of warranty. * * *

We are, therefore, confronted with the effect to be given the time limitation pro-

vision in paragraph 2 of the contract.
* * *

Parties to a contract are given broad latitude within which to fashion their own remedies for breach of contract (Uniform Commercial Code, § 2–316, subd. [4]; §§ 2–718–2–719). Nevertheless, it is clear from the official comments to section 2–719 of the Uniform Commercial Code that it is the very essence of a sales contract that at least minimum adequate remedies be available for its breach. "If the parties intend to conclude a contract for sale within this Article they must accept the legal consequence that there be at least a fair quantum of remedy for breach of the obligations or duties outlined in the contract. Thus any clause purporting to modify or limit the remedial provisions of this Article in an *unconscionable manner* is subject to deletion and in that event the remedies made available by this Article are applicable as if the stricken clause had never existed." (Uniform Commercial Code, § 2–719, official comment 1; emphasis supplied.)

It follows that contractual limitations upon remedies are generally to be enforced unless unconscionable. * * *

However, it is unnecessary to decide the issue of whether the time limitation is unconscionable on this appeal for section 2–719 (subd. [2]) of the Uniform Commercial Code provides that the general remedy provisions of the code apply when "circumstances cause an exclusive or limited remedy to fail of its essential purpose". As explained by the official comments to this section: "where an apparently fair and reasonable clause because of circumstances fails in its purpose or operates to deprive either party of the substantial value of the bargain, it must give way to the general remedy provisions of this article." (Uniform Commercial Code, § 2–719, official comment 1.) Here, paragraph 2 of the contract bars all claims for shade and other specified defects made after knitting and processing. Its effect is to eliminate any remedy for shade defects not

reasonably discoverable within the time limitation period. It is true that parties may set by agreement any time not manifestly unreasonable whenever the code "requires any action to be taken within a reasonable time" (Uniform Commercial Code, § 1–204, subd. [1]), but here the time provision eliminates all remedy for defects not discoverable before knitting and processing and section 2–719 (subd. [2]) of the Uniform Commercial Code therefore applies.

Defendant's affidavits allege that sweaters manufactured from the yarn were rendered unmarketable because of latent shading defects not reasonably discoverable before knitting and processing of the yarn into sweaters. If these factual allegations are established at trial, the limited remedy established by paragraph 2 has failed its "essential purpose" and the buyer is, in effect, without remedy. The time limitation clause of the contract, therefore, insofar as it applies to defects not reasonably discoverable within the time limits established by the contract, must give way to the general code rule that a buyer has a reasonable time to notify the seller of breach of contract after he discovers or should have discovered the defect. (Uniform Commercial Code, § 2–607, subd. [3], par. [a].) * * *

The result reached under the Uniform Commercial Code is, therefore, similar to the pre-code case law holding unreasonable contractual provisions expressly limiting the time for inspection, trial or testing of goods inapplicable or invalid with respect to latent defects. [Citations.] * * *

In sum, there are factual issues for trial concerning whether the shading defects alleged were discoverable before knitting and processing, and, if not, whether notice of the defects was given within a reasonable time after the defects were or should have been discovered. If the shading defects were not reasonably discoverable before knitting and processing and notice was given within a reasonable time after the defects were or should have been discovered, a further factual issue of whether the sweaters were rendered unsaleable because of the defect is presented for trial.

The order of the Appellate Division should be reversed, with costs, and plaintiff's motion for summary judgment should be denied.

Problems

1. A contracts to sell 1,000 bushels of wheat to B at $4.00 per bushel. Just prior to the time A was to deliver the wheat, B notified him that he would not receive or accept the wheat. A sold the wheat for $3.60 per bushel, the market price, and, later, sued B for the difference of $400. B claims he was not notified by A of the resale and, hence, not liable. Decision?

2. On December 15, 1981, A wrote a letter to B stating that he would sell to B all of the mine run coal that B might wish to buy during the calendar year 1982 for use at B's factory, delivered at the factory at a price of $7.00 per ton. B immediately replied by letter to A stating that he accepted the offer, that he would purchase all of his mine run coal from A, and that he would need 200 tons of coal during the first week in January 1982. During the months of January, February, and March, A delivered to B a total of 700 tons of coal for all of which B made payment to A at the rate of $7.00 per ton. On April 10, B ordered 200 tons of mine run coal from A who replied to B on April 11, that he could not supply A with any more coal except at a price of $8.00 per ton delivered. B thereafter purchased elsewhere at the market price namely $8.00 per ton, all of the requirements of his factory of mine run coal for the remainder of the year, amounting to a total of 2,000 tons of coal. B now brings an action against A to recover damages at the rate of $1.00 per ton for the coal thus purchased amounting to $2,000. Decision?

3. On January 10, B, of Emanon, Missouri, visited the show rooms of the X Piano Company in St. Louis and selected a piano. A sales memorandum of the transaction signed both by B and by the salesman of the X Piano Company read as follows: "Sold to B one new Andover piano, factory number 46832, price $1,300 to be shipped to the buyer at Emanon, Missouri, freight prepaid, before February 1. Prior to shipment seller will stain the case a darker color in ac-

cordance with buyer's directions and will make the tone more brilliant." On January 15, B repudiated the contract by letter to the X Piano Company. The Company subsequently stained the case, made the tone more brilliant, and offered to ship the piano to B on January 26. B persisted in his refusal to accept the piano. In an action by the X Piano Company against B to recover the contract price, what judgment?

4. Sims contracted in writing to sell Blake 100 electric motors at a price of $100 each, freight prepaid to Blake's warehouse. By the contract of sale Sims expressly warranted that each motor would develop 25 brake horse power. The contract provided that the motors would be delivered in lots of 25 per week beginning January 2, that Blake should pay by draft for each lot of 25 motors as delivered; but that Blake was to have right of inspection upon delivery.

Immediately upon delivery of the first lot of 25 motors on January 2, Blake forwards Sims a draft for $2,500, but upon testing each of the 25 motors Blake determines that none of the 25 motors will develop more than 15 brake horse power.

State all of the remedies available to Blake.

5. A and B entered into a written contract whereby A agreed to sell and B agreed to buy a certain automobile for $3,500. A drove the car to B's residence and properly parked it on the street in front of B's house where he tendered it to B and requested payment of the price. B refused to take the car or pay the price. A informed B that he would hold him to the contract and before A had time to enter the car and drive it away, a fire truck, answering a fire alarm and traveling at a high speed, crashed into the car and demolished it. A brings an action against B to recover the price of the car. Who is entitled to judgment? Would there be any difference in result if A were a dealer in automobiles?

6. A sells and delivers to B on June 1 certain goods and receives from B at the time of delivery B's check in the amount of $900 for the goods. The following day B is petitioned into bankruptcy and the check is dishonored by the drawee bank. On June 5, A serves notice upon B and the trustee in bankruptcy that he reclaims the goods. The trustee is in possession of the goods and refuses to deliver them to A. What are the rights of the parties?

7. The ABC Company, located in Chicago, contracted to sell a carload of television sets to Dodd in St. Louis, Missouri, on 60 days' credit. ABC Company shipped the carload, consigned to Dodd, and forwarded the bill of lading to Dodd. Upon arrival of the car at St. Louis, Dodd presented the bill of lading to XYZ Railroad Company, paid the freight charges and reconsigned the car to Hines at Little Rock, Arkansas, to whom he had previously contracted to sell the television sets. While the car was in transit to Little Rock, Dodd was adjudged a bankrupt. ABC Company was informed of this at once and immediately telegraphed XYZ Railroad Company to withhold delivery of the television sets. What should the XYZ Railroad Company do?

8. S in Chicago entered into a contract to sell certain machines to B, in New York. The machines were to be manufactured by S and shipped f. o. b. Chicago not later than March 25. On March 24, when S is about to ship the machines, he receives a telegram from B wrongfully repudiating the contract. The machines cannot readily be resold for a reasonable price being of a special kind used only in B's manufacturing processes. S sues B to recover the agreed price of the machines. What are the rights of the parties?

9. Egyptian Livestock, Inc. of Topeka, Kansas, pursuant to a written order dated November 15, 1981, shipped by rail a carload of cattle to Southern Cattle Co. The shipment was f. o. b. at the point of delivery to the carrier. The purchase money was due and payable two days after receipt of the shipment by the buyer. The carrier issued a straight bill of lading for the shipment. While the shipment was enroute, the seller learned that the buyer was insolvent and had filed a voluntary petition in bankruptcy. Before the shipment reached its destination the carrier, upon directions of the seller, delivered the carload of cattle back to the seller. The Trustee in Bankruptcy brought an action claiming he was entitled ot take possession of the cattle and to sell them and apply the proceeds of the sale ratably among the general creditors of Southern Cattle Company. Decision?

PART
SIX

Commercial Paper

Chapter

27

FORM AND
CONTENT

As stated in Chapter 6, the operation of a trade or business would not be possible without the law of contracts. Similarly, modern business, commerce, and finance could not be conducted without the use of commercial paper, which facilitates the creation and transfer of rights to the payment of money. Commercial paper is frequently referred to collectively as negotiable instruments, or bills and notes. Most commercial paper is negotiable. This enables it to fulfill its usefulness in the marketplace by being capable of transfer in a manner which may create in the transferee greater rights to payment of the instrument than the transferor possessed.

The starting point for an understanding of negotiable instruments is to recognize that four or five centuries ago in England a contract right to the payment of money was not assignable. The reason was that a contractual promise ran to the promisee and required that performance be rendered to him and to no one else. This was a hardship on the owner of the right as it prevented him from selling or disposing of it.

Development of the law, with the needed assistance of courts of equity, ultimately permitted recovery upon an assignment by the assignee against the debtor of the assignor, although the assignee acquired no new rights but only those of his assignor. In a suit by an innocent assignee against the debtor he was subject to all defenses available to the debtor as if the suit were brought against the debtor by the assignor. Thus, a contract right became assignable but not very marketable, as merchants and traders who otherwise might be willing to acquire it in the course of business had no interest in buying into a possible lawsuit. That is still the law of assignments; that the assignee stands in the shoes of his assignor.

With the flourishing of trade and commerce in the fifteenth and sixteenth centuries, it became inevitable that a means would be developed whereby contractual rights to money could readily and dependably be traded. A merchant who sells goods for cash may use the cash to buy more goods for resale. If he makes a sale on credit in exchange for a promise to pay money, why should he not be permitted to market the promise and trade it for cash with which to carry on his business. One difficulty was that the buyer of the goods gave the seller only a promise to pay money to him. He was the only person to whom performance or payment was promised. However, if the seller obtained from the buyer a promise in writing to pay money to the bearer of the paper or to the order of a named payee, the obligation of the buyer is owing directly to the bearer or to the person named therein as payee or to whom the payee has ordered it to be paid. The ready marketability of the paper enables the seller of the goods to sell it or to use it as collateral for a loan in order to obtain cash necessary in the operation of his business.

This chapter and the three chapters that follow examine the requirements of (1) form and content, (2) transfer and negotiation, (3) holder in due course, and (4) liability of parties on negotiable instruments.

THE CONCEPT OF NEGOTIABILITY

The quality of negotiability is imparted to commercial paper by law. It was devised by the law to meet the needs of traders, merchants, and businessmen who wanted promises and orders to pay money to circulate freely in the marketplace, not as money, but as a ready substitute for money in business transactions.

A negotiable instrument has been called a "courier without luggage," a promise or order to pay money designed and intended for movement in the channels of commerce. To have the full benefit of negotiability, an instrument must not only fulfill all of the requirements specified in the U.C.C., Section 3–104, but must also be in the hands of a "holder in due course" defined in the U.C.C., Section 3–302, and discussed in chapter 29.

The concept of negotiability applies not only to commercial paper which meets the requirements of Article 3, but also to other types of documents, namely, warehouse receipts, bills of lading, and documents of title (defined in Section 1–201 (15)), as provided in Article 7, Section 7–104; and investment securities (defined in Section 8–102) as provided in Article 8, Section 8–105. An investment security which meets the requirements of Article 3 is nevertheless governed by Article 8 and not by Article 3. Section 8–102(1)(b).

FORMAL REQUIREMENTS OF NEGOTIABLE INSTRUMENTS

The U.C.C., Section 3–104, provides:

(1) Any writing to be a negotiable instrument within this Article must
    (a) be signed by the maker or drawer; and
    (b) contain an unconditional promise or order to pay a sum certain in money and no other promise, order, obligation or power given by the maker or drawer except as authorized by this Article; and
    (c) be payable on demand or at a definite time; and
    (d) be payable to order or to bearer.
(2) A writing which complies with the requirements of this section is
    (a) a "draft" ("bill of exchange") if it is an order;
    (b) a "check" if it is a draft drawn on a bank and payable on demand;
    (c) a "certificate of deposit" if it is an acknowledgment by a bank of receipt of money with an engagement to repay it;
    (d) a "note" if it is a promise other than a certificate of deposit.

The requirements of negotiability will each be considered separately.

The Instrument Must Be a Writing

The requirement that the instrument be a writing is broadly construed. Printing, typewriting or any other intentional reduction to tangible form is sufficient to satisfy the requirement. Section 1–201(46). Pen, pencil, or paint are equally valid. Most negotiable instruments, of course, are written on paper, but this is not required. Since negotiable instruments are designed to serve a credit and currency function, it would seem that they must be prepared on a material capable of retaining the writing, thus permitting them to remain outstanding for a period of time.

The Instrument Must Be Signed

A note or certificate of deposit must be signed by the maker; a draft or check must be signed by the drawer. As in the case of a writing, extreme latitude is granted in determining what constitutes a signature. Any symbol executed or adopted by a party with present intention to authenticate a writing is sufficient. Section 1–201(39). It may be printed, stamped or typed, although it would behoove the recipient of the instrument to insist on a written signature as a matter of proof of genuineness or authority. It may consist of any word or mark used in lieu of a written signature (Section 3–401(2)), such as initials, an X or a thumb print. It may be a trade name or assumed name (Section 3–401(2)), however fictitious. Parol evidence is admissible to identify the signer, and when identified, the signature is effective. It may be made on behalf of the maker or drawer by an agent or other representative. Section 3–403(1).

The Instrument Must Contain a Promise or Order to Pay Money

A negotiable instrument must contain a promise to pay money, in the case of a note or certificate of deposit, or an order to pay, in the case of a draft or check.

A promise is an undertaking and must be more than the mere acknowledgment or

recognition of the existing obligation. Section 3–102(1)(c).

An order is a direction to pay which must be more than an authorization or request and must identify the person to pay with reasonable certainty. Section 3–102(1)(b).

The so-called "due bill" or "I.O.U." is not a promise, but a mere acknowledgment of indebtedness. Accordingly, an instrument reciting, "due Adam Brown $100" or "I.O.U., Adam Brown, $100" is not negotiable because it does not contain a promise to pay. Similarly, it was held in a celebrated case that the following request did not amount to an order, and hence the instrument was not negotiable: "Mr. Little— Please let the bearer have seven pounds and place it to my account, and you will oblige your humble servant R. Slackford." Little v. Slackford, Moody & M. 171 (1828).

The Instrument Must Be Unconditional

The requirement that the promise or order be unconditional is to preclude any provision that could diminish the obligation. The currency and credit functions of such instruments would be defeated by conditions limiting the promise, since costly and time consuming investigations would become necessary to ascertain the degree of risk imposed by the condition. Moreover, if the holder had to take an instrument subject to certain conditions his risk factor would be substantial and this would lead to high discounting. Substitutes for money must be capable of rapid circulation at minimum risks and credit instruments are feasible only when low discounting prevails.

A promise or order is conditional: (a) Where the instrument states that it is subject to or governed by any other agreement; and (b) Where the instrument states that it is to be paid only out of a particular fund or source. Section 3–105(2). In an effort to define what provisions an instrument may contain without making conditional an otherwise unconditional promise or order, the U.C.C. includes very specific language in Section 3–105(1).

Reference to Other Agreements. The restriction against reference to another agreement is to enable the holder of an instrument to ascertain his right to payment as provided therein without having to look beyond its four corners. If such right is made subject to the terms of another document, the instrument is non-negotiable. However, it may be clear from the reference that the other document is one which does not impair the obligation. For instance, an instrument may refer to a mortgage securing its payment without affecting its negotiability.

In United States v. Farrington, 172 F.Supp. 797 (D.C.Mass.1959), the court held non-negotiable a note containing the following provision: "This note evidences a borrowing made under and is subject to the terms of loan agreement dated Jan. 3, 1952 between the undersigned and the payee thereof."

A statement in a note such as:

This note is given in partial payment for a color T.V. set to be delivered two weeks from date in accordance with a contract of this date between the payee and the maker

does not impair negotiability. It merely is a description of the transaction giving rise to the note and describes the consideration. It does not place any restriction or condition on the maker's obligation to pay. The holder does not have to concern himself as to whether or not the payee delivers or has delivered the color T.V. set on the date specified. The promise is not made subject to any implied or constructive condition. Added words which *would* impair negotiability are:

and in the event such set is not delivered, then the maker's obligation hereunder shall be null and void.

If such a condition were contained in the underlying contract, but not in the note, it would not affect the negotiability of the note. However, if the note stated:

in accordance with a contract of this date between the payee and the maker and subject to such contract

it would not be negotiable, no matter what the underlying contract provided, because a subsequent holder would have to examine the contract before knowing the extent of the maker's obligation. Terms such as "As per our contract, I promise to pay * * *" or "In accordance with our contract, I promise to pay * * *" are not regarded as making the instrument subject to the contract, and hence do not impair negotiability. Section 3–105(1)(b).

A distinction is to be made between a mere recital of the *existence* of a separate agreement (this does not destroy negotiability) and a recital which makes the instrument *subject* to the terms of another agreement (this does destroy negotiability).

The Particular Fund Doctrine. An order or promise to pay out of a particular fund is conditional and destroys negotiability, because payment is made dependent upon the existence and sufficiency of the particular fund. On the other hand, a promise or order to pay, coupled with a mere indication of a particular fund out of which reimbursement is to be made, or a particular account to be debited with the amount, does not impair negotiability since the drawer's or maker's general credit is relied upon and charging a particular account is merely a bookkeeping entry to be followed after payment. Thus there is a difference between a recital which says: "Sixty days after date pay to the order of John Jones $500 out of the proceeds of the sale of the contents of freight car No. 1234" and "Sixty days after date pay to the order of John Jones $500 and charge to proceeds of sale of the contents of freight car No. 1234." In the first case, payment would be made only if such contents were sold and then only to the extent of the proceeds. In the second case, the instrument contains an unqualified order to pay, with merely bookkeeping instructions to the drawee of the draft.

An instrument reciting that the makers promised to pay to the payee "within the next sixty days the sum of Five Thousand ($5,000) * * * from the jobs now under construction" was held non-negotiable because it did not contain an unconditional promise. Webb & Sons, Inc. v. Hamilton, 30 A.D.2d 597, 290 N.Y.S.2d 122 (1968).

The U.C.C. creates two exceptions to the particular fund rule, however, in the interest of promoting marketability of instruments. The first exception permits governmental agencies to draw short-term commercial paper in which payment is restricted to a particular fund. Statutes in many States and ordinances in municipalities may authorize the issuance of instruments to pay for public improvements, and these instruments are generally payable only out of funds raised from special assessments levied against the property benefited. To aid municipalities and States, and to prevent investors from disappointment, Section 3–105(1)(g) provides that an instrument is not rendered non-negotiable solely because payable out of a particular fund "if the instrument is issued by a government or governmental agency or unit."

The other exception is in favor of persons and organizations generally regarded in commercial circles as business entities. Trustees, executors and administrators commonly limit payment to the assets of the trust or estate they are administering. Partners tend to limit payment to the assets of the partnership. Other unincorporated organizations such as associations, joint stock companies and Massachusetts Trusts or business trusts issue instruments limited to payment from the entire assets of the organization, expressly providing that the members are not to be personally liable thereon. Section 3–105(1)(h) of the U.C.C. specifies that none of these limitations impair negotiability of an instrument despite the fact that its payment is limited to a particular fund. In fact, the limitation is no more than that present in the case of a corporate promissory note. A corporation's note does not lack negotiability because payable only from its assets which is true of all its obligations.

The Instrument Must Specify a Sum Certain in Money

The holder must be able to determine from the face of the instrument the amount which he is entitled to receive in any event, so that he can ascertain the present and future value of the instrument indispensable to discounting.

"Money." The term "money" means a medium of exchange authorized or adopted by a domestic or foreign government as part of its currency. Section 1–201(24). Consequently, even though local custom may make gold dust, uncut diamonds, beaver pelts or wampum, a medium of exchange, an instrument payable in such commodities would be non-negotiable because of the lack of governmental sanction of such media as legal tender. A sum certain payable in French francs, German marks, Italian lira, Japanese yen or other foreign currency, would not impair its negotiability. Unless otherwise specified, such an instrument may be satisfied by payment of the market exchange equivalent of such foreign currency as of the date the instrument is payable, or, if payable on demand, as of the date of demand. An instrument payable in "currency" or "current funds" is deemed to be payable in money. Section 3–107.

"Sum Certain." The requirement that payment be of a "sum certain" must be considered from the point of view of the holder, not the obligor. The holder must be as-

sured of a determinable minimum payment, although provisions of the instrument may augment the recovery under certain circumstances. Thus, a frequent provision of a note is that the maker will pay, in addition to the face amount and specified interest, if any, costs of collection or attorney's fees or both upon default in payment. Such provision is designed to make the paper more attractive without lessening the certainty of the amount due.

An instrument payable with a stated rate of interest is an obligation for a sum certain. The rates may be different before and after default, or before and after a specified date. In fact, if the instrument merely provides that the principal amount is payable "with interest," the statutory legal rate of interest applies. But if interest is payable "at the current rate," (which means current banking rate) it is non-negotiable because this is not a matter that can be determined without reference to any outside source.

Where no date is specified from which interest is to run, interest accrues from the date of the instrument, and if the instrument is undated, from the time the possession of it is first transferred to the payee or the first holder.

A sum payable is a sum certain, even though it is payable in installments, or with a fixed discount if paid before maturity or a fixed addition if paid thereafter. Again, the minimum sum receivable is ascertainable, although additional amounts may be added in the event the instrument is not paid before or at maturity. In addition, it is always possible to make the necessary computations from the face of the instrument to determine the amount due at any given time.

The U.C.C. does not render any of these provisions legal where they would otherwise be illegal under State law, such as a statute with respect to usury. It merely provides that any such provision does not affect negotiability.

The Instrument Must Contain No Other Promise or Order

A negotiable instrument must contain a promise or order to pay money, but it may not contain any other promise, order, obligation or power given by the maker or drawer, except as otherwise specifically authorized under Section 3–104(1)(b). Accordingly, if an instrument contains an order or promise to do an act in addition to the payment of money, it is not negotiable. For example, a promise to pay $100 "and a ton of coal" wold be non-negotiable. The reason for the limitation is obvious. The concept of negotiability requires that an instrument be made payable in money because this makes it possible to determine its present value. Where the promise requires something in addition to money, its present value is more difficult to compute, and such promises, therefore, are not suitable in instruments which must be highly certain as to present value to serve the credit and currency functions for which they are created.

In view of this reason for the rule, the courts draw a distinction between "additional" acts which destroy certainty of present value, thereby rendering the instrument non-negotiable, and those acts, though technically additional to the payment of money, which better secure its payment and are therefore held not to render the instrument non-negotiable. In First Nat. Bank of Bridgeport v. Blackman, 249 N.Y. 322, 164 N.E. 113 (1928), the New York Court of Appeals observed:

The question in every case is not whether the act is technically 'additional' to the payment of money but whether it is substantively so. If its real purpose is to aid the holder to secure the payment of money and protect him from the risks of insolvency, if it steadies the value of the note, and makes it circulate more readily, then it should not be fatal to negotiability.

The U.C.C. sets out in Section 3–112 a list of terms and provisions which may be included in instruments without adversely affecting negotiability. Among these are: a promise or power to maintain, protect or increase collateral and to sell it in case of default in payment of principal or interest on the instrument; a term authorizing confession of judgment on the instrument if it is not paid when due; a term purporting to waive the benefit of any law intended for the advantage or protection of any obligor, such as a homestead exemption; and a term in a draft providing that the payee, by indorsing or cashing it acknowledges full satisfaction of an obligation of the drawer. It is important to note that the U.C.C. does not render any of these terms legal or effective; it merely provides that their inclusion will not affect negotiability. Many States forbid waiver of laws for the protection of debtors. In such a State, a waiver in the instrument would be ineffective, but it would not affect negotiability.

The rule that the instrument may contain no promise, order, obligation or power other than for the payment of money does not prevent incorporation of such matters into a separate agreement, so long as the instrument is not made subject to such agreement. The terms of such other agreement, however, while binding on the parties thereto cannot limit the rights of a holder in due course who takes without notice of the limitation. Section 3–119.

The Instrument Must Be Payable on Demand or at a Definite Time

Section 3–104(1)(c) requires, for purposes of negotiability, that the instrument "be payable on demand or at a definite time." This requirement, like the other formal requisites of negotiability, is designed to promote certainty in ascertaining the present value of a negotiable instrument.

Demand paper always has been considered sufficiently certain as to time of payment to satisfy the requirements of negotiability, because it is the holder who makes the demand and thus sets the time for payment. An instrument such as a check in which no time for payment is stated is payable on demand. An instrument qualifies as being payable on demand if it is payable "at sight" or "on presentation." Section 3–108. The discount rate of demand paper can be determined, because the holder may plan on presentment at a particular time. Indeed, demand paper may be valuable to holders, because it gives them an opportunity to demand payment at an earlier time than planned, for instance if the obligor shows signs of financial weakness.

Instruments payable at a definite time, other than on demand, are called *time paper*. When the date of payment is stated, discounts and risks may be evaluated with that in mind.

Various types of provisions which may be regarded as fixing a definite time for payment of an instrument are detailed in Section 3–109 and will be considered separately.

"On or before" Clauses. Section 3–109(1)(a) provides that an instrument is payable at a definite time if it is payable "on or before a stated date." Obligors, with bargaining strength, frequently insist on the use of the "on or before" clause. For example, in 1981 a person desires to borrow money and have five years within which to repay the loan. There is a possibility that he might be able to repay it sooner, and he would like to have the legal right to do so in order to reduce interest payments if there should be a drastic decline in rates. He therefore insists that the promissory language of the note take the following form: "On or before September 1, 1986, I promise to pay to the order of * * *." The holder is thus assured that he will have his money, at the latest, by the maturity date of September 1, 1986, although he may receive it sooner. This right of anticipation enables the maker to pay the note in advance of the stated maturity date (prepayment) and thereby stop

the further accrual of interest or in the event of a decline in interest rates to refinance at a lower rate of interest. It constitutes sufficient certainty so as not to impair negotiability.

At a Fixed Period after a Stated Date. Frequently, instruments are made payable at a fixed period after a stated date. For example, the instrument may be made payable "thirty days after date." This means it is payable thirty days after the date of issuance which is recited on the instrument. Such an instrument is payable at a definite time, for its exact maturity date can be reckoned by simple arithmetic. It is consistent with negotiability.

An undated instrument payable "thirty days after date" is not payable at a definite time, since the date of payment cannot be determined from its face. It is therefore non-negotiable. It is, however, an incomplete instrument, and, according to rules considered below, will meet the payable at a definite time standard when completed as authorized, or, in the hands of a holder in due course, when completed even in an unauthorized manner. Sections 3–115 and 3–407.

At a Fixed Period after Sight. This clause is frequently used in trade acceptances. A trade acceptance is a draft, drawn by the seller of goods on and accepted by the purchaser. Usually the draft is accompanied by a bill of lading ("bill of lading with draft attached") and the purchaser is not given the bill of lading until he accepts the draft. The bill of lading enables the purchaser to obtain the goods from the carrier. If the time of maturity of the draft signed by the purchaser is payable "60 days after sight," a 60-day credit period has been given the purchaser, for "60 days after sight" means sixty days after the drawee accepts. An instrument payable a fixed period after sight is negotiable, for a slight mathematical calculation, makes the maturity date certain.

At a Definite Time Subject to Acceleration. An instrument payable at a fixed time subject to acceleration satisfies the requirement of being payable at a definite time. Indeed, such an instrument would seem to have a more certain maturity date than a demand instrument, because it at least states a definite maturity date. For this reason, the U.C.C. specifies that such a provision does not adversely affect the certainty of the time of payment.

At a Definite Time Subject to Extension. A provision permitting the acceptor of a draft to extend the maturity date to a further definite time does not affect negotiability. For example, a provision in a note, payable one year from date, that the maker may extend the maturity date six months does not impair negotiability.

However, if the maker is given an option to extend the maturity of the note for an indefinite period of time, his promise is illusory and there is no certainty of time of payment. Such a note is non-negotiable. If the maker's right to extend is limited to a definite time, the extension clause is no more indefinite than an acceleration clause with a time limitation. Section 3–109(1)(d). Moreover, a provision in a note granting the holder an option to extend the maturity of the note for an indefinite period does not impair its negotiability.

In addition, extension may be made automatic upon or after a specified act or event, provided a definite time limit is stated. An example of such an extension clause is, "I promise to pay to the order of John Doe the sum of $2,000 on December 1, 1982, but it is agreed that if the crop of sections 25 and 26 of Twp. 145 is below eight bushels per acre for the 1982 season, this note shall be extended for one year."

An Instrument Payable Only upon an Act or Event Uncertain as to Time of Occurrence is Not Payable at a Definite Time. Section 3–109(2) provides that an instrument which by its terms is otherwise payable only upon an act or event uncertain as to time of occurrence is *not* payable at a definite time even though the act or event has occurred. Familiar examples include notes providing for payment to the payee or order "thirty days after my marriage" or "when he (payee) is twenty-one years old." Such promises in instruments otherwise negotiable in form destroy the negotiable character of the paper. The notes are not payable at a definite time. Nor does the fact that the maker of the note may marry or the payee becomes twenty-one years of age after the execution of the notes change the result. Negotiability is determined from the face of the instrument.

If an instrument provides: "Upon the sale of my house, I promise to pay * * * ," a holder would have no certainty as to whether it would ever become payable. If it provides: "Six weeks after the death of my Uncle George Doe, I promise to pay * * * " the holder would be sure that the note would become payable, but the time when payment would become due could not be ascertained with sufficient definiteness. Hence, each instrument is non-negotiable.

Since it is necessary that the negotiability of an instrument be determinable from its face, the fact that an act or event specified has occurred will not confer negotiability upon an instrument. U.C.C. Section 3–109(2) provides: "An instrument which by its terms is otherwise payable only upon an act or event uncertain as to time of occurrence is not payable at a definite time even though the act or event has occurred."

It would seem possible to circumvent Section 3–109(2) of the Code quoted above by a definite maturity date provision in a promissory note subject to acceleration. Thus, if the instrument were to provide on its face: "I promise to pay Richard Roe $6,000 on September 1, 1999, but the time for payment shall be accelerated by the death of my uncle George Doe to a point of time six months after his death," it would appear to be payable at a sufficiently certain time to comply with Section 3–109(1)(c).

The Instrument Must Be Payable to Order or to Bearer

A negotiable instrument must contain words indicating that the maker or drawer intends that it may pass into the hands of someone other than the payee. This requires language clearly providing either that it will be paid to such party as the person to whom it was issued may direct or order, or that it will be paid to the person who is the holder and bearer of the instrument. The "magic words" of negotiability are thus "to the order of" or "to bearer," but other words which are clearly equivalent to these may be regarded as fulfilling this requirement. The use of synonyms, however, only invites trouble.

This requirement should not be confused with the requirement that the instrument contain an order or promise to pay. An order to pay is a direction to a third party to pay the instrument as drawn. An "order instrument," on the other hand, pertains to the transferability of the instrument rather than specifying which party is to pay.

Payable to Order. Section 3–110 clarifies the meaning of "payable to order." In addition to the eminently correct "Pay to the order of John Jones," the maker or drawer may state: "Pay to John Jones or his order"; or "Pay to John Jones or his assigns." A statement frequently found on certificates of deposit: "payable upon return of this instrument properly indorsed" does not render it payable to order. Section 3–110(2). It means merely that the maker is entitled to have the payment of the instrument receipted by indorsement.

In every instance, the person to whose order the instrument is payable must be designated with reasonable certainty. Within this limitation, a broad range of payees is possible, including an individual, the maker or drawer, the drawee, two or more payees, an office (such as "The Swedish Consulate"), an estate, trust, or fund, a partnership or unincorporated association, and a corporation.

Payable to Bearer. Section 3–111 states that an instrument fulfills the requirements of being payable to bearer if by its terms it is payable (1) to bearer or the order of bearer; or (2) to the order of a specified person or "bearer"; or (3) to "cash" or to the order of "cash" or any other indication which does not purport to designate a specific payee. It should be noted, however, that Section 3–110(3) provides that an instrument made payable both to order and to bearer is payable to order unless the bearer words are handwritten or typewritten. This Section is primarily designed to cover the situation where a maker or drawer has filled in a payee's name on a printed form without noticing it is payable to bearer.

Terms and Omissions and Their Effect on Negotiability

Frequently the negotiability of an instrument is questioned because of omission of certain provisions or ambiguity of language. Problems also arise in connection with interpretation of instruments whether or not negotiability is called into question. Section 3–118 of the Code contains rules of construction which apply to every instrument.

Absence of Statement of Consideration. Consideration is required to support a contract at common law. However, Section 3–112(1)(a) provides that the negotiability of an instrument is not affected by the omission of a statement of consideration. The giving of consideration is presumed, and want or failure thereof must be raised as an affirmative defense. If the holder proves he has the rights of a holder in due course, the defense is not available. If he is not, it then becomes incumbent upon him to prove that consideration was given.

Absence of Statement of Where the Instrument Is Drawn or Payable. To determine what law applies to the issuance and form of an instrument, the place of issue must be known. To determine the law applicable to matters of payment, the place of payment must be known. But the omission of a statement of either of these on the face of the instrument does not affect its negotiability. Section 3–112(1)(a). These matters may be shown by other evidence. But if a place is stated, it is conclusive in favor of a holder in due course, irrespective of the facts.

Sealed Instruments. The fact that an instrument is under seal has no effect on its negotiability, whatever other effect the seal might have under common law. Section 3–113.

Dating of the Instrument. The negotiability of an instrument is not affected by the fact that it is undated, antedated or postdated. Section 3–114.

If the instrument is antedated, that is, carries a date prior to its actual issue, the stated date controls. Hence, a note dated October 1, 1982, payable thirty days after date, and issued on November 1, 1982, is due and payable the day before its issue. This would prevent anyone from becoming a holder in due course of this note (Section 3–302(1)(c)), because it could not be negotiated before maturity. Furthermore, any indorser would be deprived of the right to require presentment, notice of dishonor, or protest, as a condition to his liability on the instrument. Section 3–501.

If the instrument is postdated, that is, carries a date later than the day on which it was issued, the date stated on the instrument is conclusive. A demand instrument by postdating becomes a time instrument; and a postdated check is a time instrument as payment by the drawee bank will not be made until the date shown on the check. For example, if on January 2, 1982, the drawer issues a check and dates it January 21, 1982, the drawer's bank is not authorized to pay the instrument until January 21. Thus, a time instrument payable thirty days from date may become payable sixty days from date by postdating.

An undated instrument payable at a fixed time "after date" is uncertain as to time of payment and therefore non-negotiable, subject to the special rules applicable to incomplete instruments.

Incomplete Instruments. On occasion, a party will sign a paper the contents of which show that it is intended to become an instrument, but which, either by intention or through oversight, is incomplete in some necessary respect, such as the omission of promise or order, designation of the payee, amount payable, or time for payment. Section 3–115 provides that such a paper cannot be enforced until completed. If it is completed in accordance with authority given, it is effective as completed. If it is completed without authorization, the unauthorized completion is a defense except that a subsequent holder in due course may enforce the instrument as completed. Section 3–407(3). This is not the same as a forgery or material alteration which are discussed in a subsequent chapter.

If an undated instrument is delivered on November 1, 1982, payable "thirty days after date," the payee has implied authority to fill in "November 1, 1982." Until he does so, however, the instrument is not negotiable because it is not payable at a definite time. If the payee completes the instru-

ment by inserting an erroneous date, such date will control, unless the maker or drawer in a lawsuit establishes the correct date.

Ambiguous Instruments. Rather than commit the parties to the use of parol evidence to establish the interpretation of an instrument, Section 3–118 establishes rules to resolve common ambiguities. This tends to promote negotiability by providing a degree of certainty to the holder which would otherwise be lacking.

Where it is doubtful whether the instrument is a draft or note, the holder may treat it as either and present it for payment to the drawee or the person signing it. For example, an instrument reading

To X: On demand I promise to pay $500 to the order of Y.

/s/Z

may be presented for payment to X as a draft or to Z as a note.

A draft drawn on the drawer is, of course, effective as a note. An instrument naming no drawee but stating

On demand, please pay $500 to the order of Y

/s/Z

although in the form of a draft, may be treated as a note and presented to Z for payment.

If a printed form of note or draft is used and the party signing it inserts hand written or typewritten language which is inconsistent with the printed words, the handwritten words control the typewritten and the printed words, and the typewritten words control the printed.

If the amount payable is set forth on the face of the instrument in both figures and words which differ, the words control the figures. It is presumed that the maker or drawer would be more careful with words.

If an instrument omits to provide for any interest, no interest accrues until after maturity, at which time the unpaid principal will begin to bear interest at the rate that applies to unpaid money judgments under the law of the place where the instrument is payable. If an instrument states that it is payable "with interest" but does not designate any rate, the judgment rate under the law at the place of payment applies from the date of the instrument.

The U.C.C., Section 3–118(c), provides: "Unless the instrument otherwise specifies, two or more persons who sign as maker, acceptor or drawer or indorser and as part of the same transaction are jointly and severally liable even though the instrument contains such words as 'I promise to pay.' "

FORM OF NEGOTIABLE INSTRUMENTS

The four forms of negotiable instruments are drafts, checks, certificates of deposit, and notes. U.C.C., Section 3–104(2). The first two each contain orders to pay money, while the last two entail promises to pay money.

A check is a specialized form of draft, namely, an order to pay money drawn on a bank and payable on demand. A certificate of deposit is a specialized form of promise to pay money given by a bank or savings and loan association.

Order to Pay Money

Drafts. A draft involves three parties, each in a distinct capacity. One party, the drawer, orders a second party, the drawee, to pay a sum certain in money to a third party, the payee. The same party may appear in more than one capacity, for instance, the drawer may also be the payee .

Drafts may be either "time" or "sight." A time draft is one payable at a specified future date whereas a sight draft is payable immediately upon presentation to the drawee.

A form of time draft, known as a trade acceptance, is frequently used as a credit device in a commercial transaction. For example, Ben Buyer wishes to purchase goods from Sam Seller. Seller needs cash immediately, but Buyer cannot pay for the goods until he has resold them, or processed and sold them, which will require time. Therefore, Seller draws a draft on Buyer ordering Buyer to pay the amount of the purchase price to the order of Seller at a specified future date. Seller presents this draft to Buyer, who "accepts" it thereby

FIGURE 27–1. TRADE ACCEPTANCE

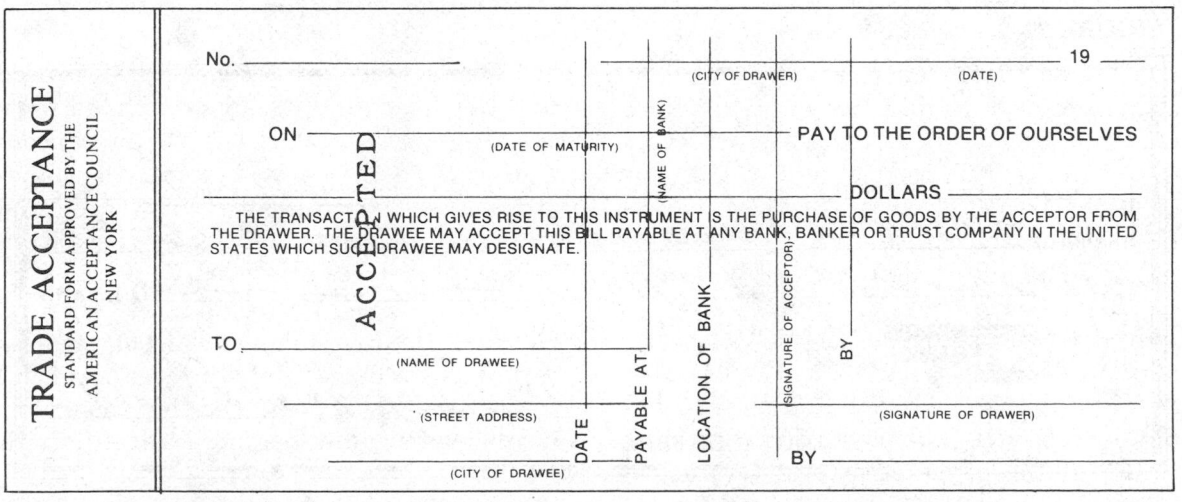

agreeing to make payment according to its terms, and returns the accepted draft to seller.

A sight draft, sometimes called customer's draft, is used by the seller of goods who desires immediate payment for the goods upon delivery of a bill of lading. Upon shipment of the goods, the seller would obtain from the carrier an order bill of lading which he would attach to a customer's draft drawn on the buyer and would send to his local bank for handling. The local bank would send the paper to a bank located in the city where the goods were to be delivered. That bank would then notify the buyer upon arrival of the goods. In order to obtain the bill of lading and thus the goods, the buyer would pay the amount of the seller's draft, which would be forwarded to the seller's bank and there credited to his account.

Checks. Checks, as already noted, are drafts drawn on a bank and payable on demand. Once again, there are parties involved in three distinct capacities: the *drawer,* who orders the *drawee,* a bank, to pay the *payee* on demand.

A cashier's check is a check drawn by a bank upon itself to the order of the named payee. It is accepted in advance by the act of its issuance, and upon presentment for payment by the payee or a holder in due course, the bank must honor the check.

Promises to Pay Money

Negotiable instruments containing promises to pay money are either notes or certificates of deposit. The most frequently used and in greater volume are notes.

Notes. A promissory note is an instrument involving parties in two capacities. One party, the *maker,* promises to pay to the order of a second party, the *payee,* a stated sum of money, either on demand or at a stated future date. The note may range from a simple "I promise to pay $X to the order of Y," form to more complex legal instruments such as installment notes, collateral notes, mortgage notes, and judgment notes.

Certificates of Deposit. A certificate of deposit is a written acknowledgment by a bank of the receipt of a specific sum of money which it engages to pay on demand or at a stated future date, with interest at a stated rate, to a person named in the certificate and upon the terms thereof. The issuing party, the *maker,* who is always a bank or savings and loan association, promises to pay a second party, the *payee.*

FIGURE 27–2. CHECK

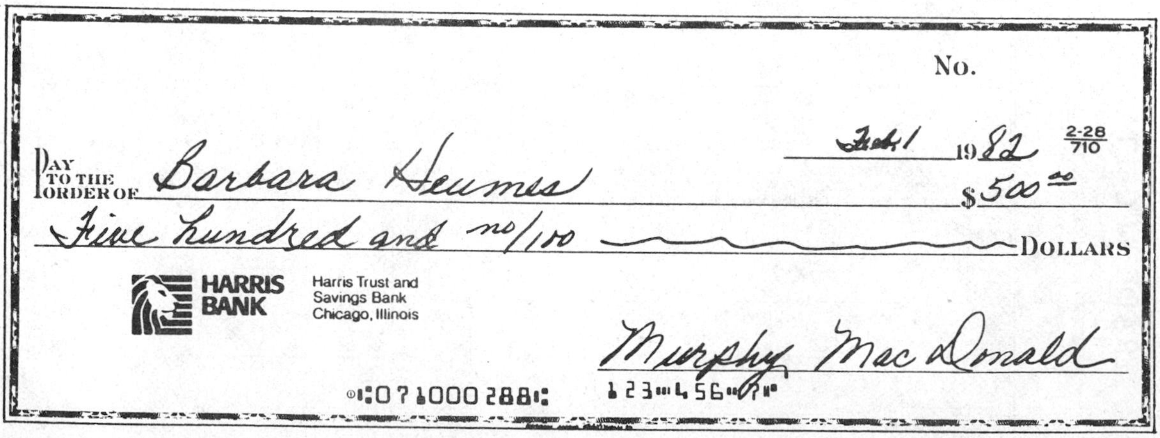

No.

Feb. 1 19 82 2-28/710

PAY TO THE ORDER OF Barbara Heumes $500.00

Five hundred and no/100 DOLLARS

HARRIS BANK Harris Trust and Savings Bank Chicago, Illinois

Murphy MacDonald

⑆0710002881⑆ 123⑈456⑈7⑈

FIGURE 27–3.   NOTE AND SECURITY AGREEMENT

 **HARRIS BANK**

SIMPLE INTEREST INSTALLMENT NOTE AND SECURITY AGREEMENT

Disbursed on _____, 19 _____

FOR VALUE RECEIVED, the undersigned (the "Borrower") promises to pay to the order of Harris Trust and Savings Bank at its office at 111 West Monroe Street, Chicago, Illinois: (i) the Amount financed shown in item 1 below; (ii) the interest on the principal balance remaining unpaid hereon from time to time determined at the Annual Percentage Rate specified in item 4 below; and (iii) the charges for group credit life insurance at the rate shown below, if such insurance has been requested by the Borrower (as indicated below), such amounts to be payable in the installments and on the dates set forth in the Payment Schedule (item 6) shown below. All payments on this Note shall be applied first to the charge for group credit life insurance accrued to the date of payment, then to accrued and unpaid interest and the balance, if any, shall be applied toward payment of the Amount Financed. Any partial prepayment of the Amount Financed may be applied at the option of the Bank to the unpaid installments hereunder in the inverse order of their maturity. The Borrower authorizes the Bank to disburse the proceeds of the loan evidenced hereby as set forth below and to date this Note as of the date of disbursement.

DISCLOSURE STATEMENT

SECURITY. This loan is secured by a security interest created under

☐ A Uniform Commercial Code security agreement covering the following personal property: _____
_____
_____

☐ A Mortgage or Deed of Trust covering the real estate commonly known as: _____
_____

which security interest will attach to any additions or attachments thereto. In addition to that collateral, if any, this loan will also be secured by any other property of the Borrower delivered to the Bank as security for this or any other loan. The Bank has the right to set off any deposit balances owing by the Bank to the Borrower against this loan, before as well as after maturity. The Bank has the right to require that the Borrower furnish to the Bank a security interest in additional property of a type and amount satisfactory to the Bank. All other present and future debt of the Borrower to the Bank will also be secured by the personal property described or referred to above. The Bank has the right to receive any insurance proceeds payable in the event the security is lost, damaged or destroyed.

FINANCE CHARGE. The Finance Charge shall begin to accrue on the date that this loan is disbursed by the Bank, which is expected to be _____, 19 ____.

PREPAYMENT. The Borrower has the right to prepay the loan in full or in part an any time. Interest and charges for credit life insurance shall cease to accrue on any portion of the Amount Financed which is prepaid.

DEFAULT CHARGES. Interest and the charge for credit life insurance continue to accrue on the principal amount of each installment which is not paid on its scheduled payment date. Upon default the entire unpaid balance of this Note may be declared due and payable, and the Borrower may be required to pay reasonable attorneys' fees and other costs incurred because of the Borrower's default.

PROPERTY INSURANCE. Insurance against loss or damage to property or against liability arising out of the use or ownership of property, which may be obtained by the Borrower in connection with this loan is not available from the Bank, even though the Bank may extend credit to finance premiums for such insurance. Therefore, the Borrower has the responsibility and opportunity to choose the person through whom the insurance is to be obtained and to determine the cost of such insurance.

CREDIT LIFE INSURANCE IS NOT REQUIRED BY THE BANK IN CONNECTION WITH THIS LOAN. Such insurance is available through the Bank at a rate of 0.9% per year which shall accrue daily on the unpaid balance of the Amount Financed. The cost of such insurance for the scheduled term of this loan is $ _____. Such insurance may be terminated by the insured Borrower at any time.

GROUP CREDIT LIFE INSURANCE IS HEREBY REQUESTED.

_____   _____
       Date   Signature of Insured Borrower

CREDIT LIFE INSURANCE, IF INCLUDED, COVERS ONLY THE PERSON SIGNING ABOVE.

BORROWER(S): _____
                        Name
_____
                        Name
_____
                        Address
_____
                    City, State, Zip Code

1. Amount Financed $_____

2. Charge for optional Group Credit Life Insurance $_____
    (If all installments are paid on time)

3. **FINANCE CHARGE** (Interest if all installments $_____
    are paid on time)

4. **ANNUAL PERCENTAGE RATE**   _____ %

5. Total of Payments (Sum of Items 1, 2 and 3) $_____

6. Payment Schedule
    Number of Consecutive Monthly Installments   _____
    Amount of each installment

          $ _____ $ _____
            ALL BUT FINAL   FINAL

Payment of monthly installments will begin on _____.
19 ____, and will continue thereafter on the same day of each succeeding calendar month to and including _____, 19 _____ which shall be the due date of any Amount Financed and Finance Charges then remaining unpaid. A monthly installment will not be considered in default as long as it is received by the last day of the month in which it is due, but a delay in making any payment will result in the accrual of additional Finance Charges.

7. Fees (Itemize and Describe)

    _____ $ _____
    _____ $ _____
    _____ $ _____
    _____ $ _____
                                        $ _____

BLANK SPACES. Any spaces which are not filled in in this Disclosure Statement call for information which is not pertinent to this transaction and therefore should be read as though "None" or "Not Applicable" has been inserted in such spaces.

THE BORROWER ACKNOWLEDGES RECEIPT OF A COMPLETED COPY OF THIS NOTE AND DISCLOSURE STATEMENT AND, IF CREDIT LIFE INSURANCE IS OBTAINED THROUGH THE BANK, A GROUP CERTIFICATE OF INSURANCE PRIOR TO SIGNING THIS NOTE. THIS NOTE INCLUDES ALL OF THE ADDITIONAL PROVISIONS ON THE REVERSE SIDE HEREOF.

SIGNATURES   Signed by the Borrower on _____, 19 _____

X _____   X _____

FIGURE 27–4. NON-RENEWABLE CERTIFICATE OF DEPOSIT

The Wilmette Bank
1200 Central Avenue, Wilmette, Illinois 60091

CERTIFICATE OF DEPOSIT
NON-RENEWABLE/NOT TRANSFERABLE

NON-NEGOTIABLE
No. 13900

Date August 3,1982 Soc. Sec. No. 123-5-7809

..... Adam Romeiser, III ..... HAS DEPOSITED IN THIS BANK

..... One Thousand ..... DOLLARS $ 1,000 .....

This Certificate shall be payable to the Registered Holder(s), or to the survivor(s), in current funds upon surrender properly endorsed by the Registered Holder(s) on August 3,1983 with interest at 14 per cent per annum. This Certificate is non-negotiable and no assignment shall affect the rights or liabilities of the Bank unless and until notice thereof, signed by the assignor(s), and the assignee(s), is received and acknowledged by the Bank.

This Certificate of Deposit constitutes a contract whereby the depositor agrees that no part of the deposit may be withdrawn before maturity. In the event the Bank at its option permits payment of any part or all of this deposit prior to the maturity thereof, Federal laws and regulations require that three month/six months of interest hereon be forfeited. In case of the Depositor's death or mental incompetency the bank is required to honor a request for withdrawal prior to maturity without penalty.

THIS CERTIFICATE WILL NOT BEAR INTEREST AFTER MATURITY

NOT SUBJECT TO CHECK
Member F.D.I.C.

William Murphy
AUTHORIZED SIGNATURE

FIGURE 27–5. AUTOMATICALLY RENEWABLE CERTIFICATE OF DEPOSIT

The Wilmette Bank
1200 Central Avenue, Wilmette, Illinois 60091

CERTIFICATE OF DEPOSIT
AUTOMATICALLY RENEWABLE

NON-NEGOTIABLE
No. 4199

Date June 15,1982 Soc. Sec. No. 321-6-8790

... Mary MacDonald ..... HAS DEPOSITED IN THIS BANK

.... Two Thousand ..... DOLLARS $ 2,000 .....

This Certificate shall be payable to the Registered Holder(s), or to the survivor(s), in current funds upon surrender properly endorsed by the Registered Holder(s) on June 15,1984 with interest at 13 per cent per annum. Interest payments will be mailed to the Registered Holder(s) at the address appearing on the books of the Bank unless otherwise directed. This Certificate shall be automatically renewed for an additional period of time equal to the original term and thereafter for additional successive periods of time equal to such original term, unless the Registered Holder(s) shall present this Certificate for payment within ten days after any maturity date, or unless the Bank shall indicate its desire to redeem this Certificate by mailing written notice thereof to the Registered Holder(s) at least thirty days prior to any maturity date.

The interest rate to be paid in future renewal periods may be changed effective the next maturity date by mailing to the Registered Holder(s) at least thirty days advance notice of such change. This Certificate is non-negotiable and no assignment shall affect the rights or liabilities of the Bank unless and until notice thereof, signed by the assignor(s), and the assignee(s), is received and acknowledged by the Bank.

This Certificate of Deposit constitutes a contract whereby the depositor agrees that no part of the deposit may be withdrawn before maturity. In the event the Bank at its option permits payment of any part or all of this deposit prior to the maturity thereof, Federal laws and regulations require that three months of interest hereon be forfeited on Certificates of Deposit with a maturity of one year and six months interest forfeited on Certificates of Deposit with a maturity in excess of one year.

Member F.D.I.C.

NOT SUBJECT TO CHECK

William Murphy
AUTHORIZED SIGNATURE

Cases

The Concept of Negotiability

FIRST STATE BANK AT GALLUP v. CLARK

(1977) 91 N.M. 117, 570 P.2d 1144.

EASLEY, J.

First State Bank of Gallup (First State), Plaintiff-Appellee sued M. S. Horne (Horne), Defendant-Appellant on a promissory note. The trial court granted summary judgment against defendant and we affirm.

Facts. Horne had executed a $100,000 note in favor of R. C. Clark which contained a restriction that the note could not be transferred, pledged or assigned without the written consent of Horne. As part of the transaction between Horne and Clark, Horne gave Clark a separate letter authorizing Clark to pledge the note as collateral for a loan of $50,000 which Clark anticipated making with First State. Clark did make the loan and pledged the note, which was accompanied by Horne's letter authorizing the note to be used as collateral. First State also called Horne to verify that he was in agreement that his note could be accepted as collateral. First State attempted to collect from Horne on Horne's note to Clark which had been pledged as collateral. Horne refused to pay and this suit resulted.

Issues. The issues raised on appeal include (1) whether the note was a negotiable instrument for purposes of Article 3 of the Uniform Commercial Code (U.C.C.) * * *. Article 3 of the U.C.C. defines a certain type of readily transferable instrument and lays down certain rules for the treatment of that instrument and rules concerning the rights, remedies and defenses of persons dealing with it.

In order to be a "negotiable instrument" for Article 3 purposes the paper must precisely meet the definition set out in § 3–104, since § 3–104 itself states that, to be a negotiable instrument, a writing "must" meet the definition therein set out. Moreover, it is clear that in order to determine whether an instrument meets that definition *only the instrument itself* may be looked to, *not* other documents, even when other documents are referred to in the instrument. [Citations.] As Hart & Willier, 2 Bender's U.C.C. Service, *Commercial Paper,* § 2.03[1] points out in its text and in footnote 3:

The applicability of Article 3 must be determined from the instrument itself, without reference to other documents or oral agreements. The "four-corners test" is still applicable: the determination of negotiability under Article 3 must be made by inspecting only the instrument itself. . . .

This is clear from the mandatory language of U.C.C. § 3–104, and from the following language from the Official Comment to U.C.C. § 3–105 found under the heading "Purposes of Changes": "The section is intended to make it clear that, so far as negotiability is affected, the conditional or unconditional character of the promise or order is to be determined by what is expressed in the instrument itself. . . .

We recognize the Official Comments to the U.C.C. as persuasive, though they are not controlling authority. [Citation.]

Section 3–104 thus requires that, in order to be a negotiable instrument for Article 3 purposes, one must be able to ascertain without reference to other documents that the instrument:

(a) [is] signed by the maker or drawer; and (b) contain[s] an unconditional promise or order to pay a sum certain in money and no other promise, order, obligation or power given by the maker or drawer except as authorized by [Article 3]; and (c) [is] payable on demand or at a definite time; and (d) [is] payable to order or to bearer.

The note in question here failed to meet the requirements of § 3–104, since the promise to pay contained in the note was not unconditional. Moreover, the note was expressly drafted to be non-negotiable since it stated:

This note may not be transferred, pledged, or otherwise assigned without the written consent of M. S. Horne.

These words, even though they appeared on the back of the note, effectively cancelled any implication of negotiability provided by the words "Pay to the order of" on the face of the note. Notations and terms on the back of a note, made contemporaneously with the execution of the note and intended to be part of the note's contract of payment, constitute as much a part of the note as if they were incorporated on its face. [Citation.]

* * *

The whole purpose of the concept of a negotiable instrument under Article 3 is to declare that transferees in the ordinary course of business are only to be held liable for information appearing in the instrument itself and will not be expected to know of any limitations on negotiability or changes in terms, etc., contained in any separate documents. The whole idea of the facilitation of easy transfer of notes and instruments requires that a transferee be able to trust what the instrument says, and be able to determine the validity of the note and its negotiability from the language in the note itself. [Citation.] * * *

Since the note in question is not negotiable for Article 3 purposes, First State cannot be a holder in due course under Article 3, and we need not discuss that issue.

* * *

The summary judgment of the district court is hereby affirmed for the stated reasons, although we reject the trial court's conclusion that the note in question was a negotiable instrument as contemplated by Article 3.

The Instrument
Must Be Unconditional

RESERVE PLAN, INC. v. SCHLEIDER

(1955) 208 Misc. 805, 145 N.Y.S.2d 122.

BENNETT, J.

It appears that the action was brought to recover the unpaid balance of an alleged promissory note. The plaintiff contends that it is a holder for value in due course and that as such the defenses of general denial, breach of warranty and breach of agreement are not available against it. The instrument on which the action is predicated was executed by the defendant on May 5, 1954 and was given to secure payment for dental work to be performed by the payee. These payments were to be made in monthly installments of $20 each beginning June 5, 1954 for a total sum of $480. Two days after the execution of said instrument the same was negotiated to the plaintiff.

The defendant contends that the payee did not perform his agreement and that he still is in serious need of dental care which the payee has neglected and refused to furnish him; that he was not informed that the instrument he signed was a negotiable document but only a contract for installment payments.

The question arises as to whether the agreement is in fact a negotiable instrument. If it is then the defenses asserted would not be available against this plaintiff. However, if the instrument does not conform to the requirements of the Negotiable Instruments Law of the State of New York, such defenses may be asserted against the present holder.

[The applicable] Negotiable Instruments Law provides * * * as follows: "Must contain an unconditional promise or order to pay a sum certain in money", in setting forth the elements of a promissory note.

Examination of the instrument in suit discloses that the same contains this proviso, "In case of death of maker all payments not due at date of death are cancelled". Can it then be said that the form of the instrument sets forth an unconditional promise to pay a sum certain? It appears to this Court that such essential element is definitely lacking. * * *

It is obvious * * * that the document herein does not meet the required standards * * * for although the sum specified as payable is stated to be $480, such payment would be contingent on the maker continuing to live during the twenty-four months during which the installments were payable. By the terms of the said agreement, the contingency was always present during the said twenty-four months that a lesser amount would be payable in the event of death of the maker.

For the foregoing reasons the Court finds that the instrument does not constitute a negotiable promissory note and that the defendant is entitled to assert his defenses which raise issues of fact that can only be determined by a trial.　Accordingly the motion is denied.

Reference to Other Agreements

HOLLY HILL ACRES, LTD. v. CHARTER BANK OF GAINESVILLE

(1975 Fla.App.) 314 So.2d 209.

SCHEB, J.

* * *

Appellant/defendant appeals from a summary judgment in favor of appellee/plaintiff Bank in a suit wherein the appellee sought to foreclose a note and mortgage given by appellant.

The appellee Bank was the assignee from appellees Rogers and Blythe of a promissory note and purchase money mortgage executed and delivered by the appellant. The note, executed April 28, 1972, contains the following stipulation:

This note with interest is secured by a mortgage on real estate, of even date herewith, made by the maker hereof in favor of the said payee, and shall be construed and enforced according to the laws of the State of Florida. *The terms of said mortgage are by this reference made a part hereof.* (Emphasis supplied.)

* * *

The note having incorporated the terms of the purchase money mortgage was not negotiable. * * *

The note, incorporating by reference the terms of the mortgage, did not contain the unconditional promise to pay required by [U.C.C. §] 3–104(1)(b). Rather, the note falls within the scope of [U.C.C. §] 3–105(2)(a). Although negotiability is now governed by the Uniform Commercial Code, this was the Florida view even before the U.C.C. was adopted. *E.g.,* the Supreme Court in Brown v. Marion Mortgage Co., 1932, 107 Fla. 727, 145 So. 413, held that certain bonds which were "to be received

and held subject to" a certain mortgage were non-negotiable.　[Citations.]

Appellee Bank relies upon Scott v. Taylor, 63 Fla. 612, 58 So. 30, 1912, as authority for the proposition that its note is negotiable. *Scott,* however, involved a note which stated: "this note secured by mortgage." Mere reference to a note being secured by mortgage is a common commercial practice and such reference in itself does not impede the negotiability of the note.　There is, however, a significant difference in a note stating that it is "secured by a mortgage" from one which provides, "the terms of said mortgage are by this reference made a part hereof." In the former instance the note merely refers to a separate agreement which does not impede its negotiability, while in the latter instance the note is rendered nonnegotiable.　*See* [U.C.C. §] 3–105(2)(a); [U.C.C. §] 3–119.[4]

As a general rule the assignee of a mortgage securing a non-negotiable note, even though a bona fide purchaser for value, takes subject to all defenses available as against the mortgagee.　[Citation.] Appellant raised the issue of fraud as between himself and other parties to the note, therefore, it was incumbent on the appellee Bank, as movant for a summary judgment, to prove the non-existence of any genuinely triable issue.　[Citation.]

Accordingly, the entry of a summary final judgment is reversed and the cause remanded for further proceedings.

---

4. Official Comment 5 to Fla.Stat. § 673.119 provides: Subsection (2) rejects decisions which have carried the rule that contemporaneous writings must be read together to the length of holding that a clause in a mortgage affecting a note destroyed the negotiability of the note. The negotiability of an instrument is always to be determined by what appears on the face of the instrument alone, and if it is negotiable in itself a purchaser without notice of a separate writing is in no way affected by it. *If the instrument itself states that it is subject to or governed by any other agreement, it is not negotiable under this Article;* but if it merely refers to a separate agree-

ment or states that it arises out of such an agreement, it is negotiable. (Emphasis supplied.)

The Instrument
Must Be Payable on Demand
or at a Definite Time

FERRI v. SYLVIA

(1965) 100 R.I. 270, 214 A.2d 470.

JOSLIN, J.

This action * * * based upon a promissory note was tried before a justice of the superior court sitting without a jury and resulted in a decision for the plaintiff of $2,600. The defendants [appeal.]

The note, which is dated May 25, 1963, obligates defendants to pay to plaintiff or her order $3,000 "within ten (10) years after date." The trial justice determined that the maturity of the note was uncertain, admitted testimony of the parties as to both their intentions and prior agreements, and premised upon such extrinsic evidence found that plaintiff "could have the balance that may be due at any time she needed it and that she could call for and demand the full payment of any balance that may be due or owing her at the time of her demand."

The question is whether the note is payable at a fixed or determinable future time. If the phrase "within ten (10) years after date" lacks explicitness or is ambiguous then clearly parol evidence was admissible for the purpose of ascertaining the intention of the parties. [Citations.] Moreover, if it was apparent from an inspection of the note that it did not include the entire agreement of the parties then it was permissible to accept extrinsic evidence of their prior agreements relative to its due date in supplementation and explanation of the writing; provided, however, that the collateral terms were consistent therewith and such as would normally have been excluded by the parties from the note. [Citations.] While the trial justice in admitting and accepting the extrinsic evidence apparently relied on these principles, neither is applicable because the payment provisions of the note are not uncertain nor are they incomplete.

At the law merchant it was generally settled that a promissory note or a bill of exchange payable "on or before" a specified date fixed with certainty the time of payment. [Citations.] The same rule has been fixed by statute first under the negotiable instruments law, G.L.1956, § 6–18–10, subd. 2, and now pursuant to the uniform commercial code. The code in § 6A–3–109(1) reads as follows: "An instrument is payable at a definite time if by its terms it is payable (a) on or before a stated date or at a fixed period after a stated date * * *."

The courts in the cases we cite were primarily concerned with whether a provision for payment "on or before" a specified date impaired the negotiability of an instrument. Collaterally, of course, they necessarily considered whether such an instrument was payable at a fixed or determinable future time for unless it was, an essential prerequisite to negotiability was lacking.

They said that the legal rights of the holder of an "on or before" instrument were clearly fixed and entitled him to payment upon an event that was certain to come, even though the maker might be privileged to pay sooner if he so elected. They held, therefore, that the due date of such an instrument was fixed with certainty and that its negotiability was unaffected by the privilege given the maker to accelerate payment. Professor Chafee referred to it as providing "the simplest form of acceleration provision," 32 Harv.L.Rev. 747, 757, and Judge Cooley in Mattison v. Marks, 31 Mich. 421, observing that notes of this kind were common in commercial transactions, said 31 Mich. at page 423:

"It seems to us that this note is payable at a time certain. It is payable certainly, and at all events, on a day particularly named; and at that time, and not before, payment might be enforced against the maker. * * * The legal rights of the holder are clear and certain; the note is due at a time fixed, and it is not due before. True, the maker may pay sooner if he shall choose, but this option, if exercised, would be a payment in advance of the legal liability to pay, and nothing more."

On principle no valid distinction can be drawn between an instrument payable "on or before" a fixed date and one which calls for payment "within" a stipulated period. This was the holding in Leader v. Plante, 95 Me. 339, where the court said at page 341, 50 A. 54:

" 'Within' a certain period, 'on or before' a day named and 'at or before' a certain day, are equivalent terms, and the rules of construction apply to each alike."

* * *

We follow the lead of the Maine court and equate the work "within" with the phrase "on or before." So construed it fixes both the beginning and the end of a period, and insofar as it means the former it is applicable to the right of a maker to prepay, and insofar as it means the latter it is referable to the date the instrument matures. We hold that the payment provision of a negotiable instrument payable "within" a stated period is certain as well as complete on its face and that such an instrument does not mature until the time fixed arrives.

For the foregoing reasons it is clear that the parties unequivocally agreed that the plaintiff could not demand payment of the note until the expiration of the ten-year period. It is likewise clear that any prior or contemporaneous oral agreements of the parties relevant to its due date were so merged and integrated with the writing as to prevent its being explained or supplemented by parol evidence. [Citations.]

The defendants' exception to the trial justice's decision is sustained, and on November 29, 1965 the plaintiff may appear in this court to show cause, if any she has, why the case should not be remitted to the superior court with direction to enter judgment for the defendants.

The Instrument
Must Be Payable to Order
or to Bearer

BROADWAY MANAGEMENT CORP. v. BRIGGS

(1975) 30 Ill.App.3d 403, 332 N.E.2d 131.

CRAVEN, J.

Conan Briggs appeals from a circuit court's refusal to vacate an allegedly void judgment by confession against him, * * *

The note on which the confession of judgment was based reads in part: "Ninety Days after date, I, we, or either of us, promise to pay to the order of Three Thousand Four Hundred Ninety Eight and 45/100 .... Dollars." (The underlined words and symbols have been typed in; the remainder is printed.) There are no blanks on the face of the instrument, any unused space having been filled in with hyphens. The note contains clauses permitting acceleration in the event the holder deems itself insecure and authorizes confession of judgment "if this note is not paid at any stated or accelerated maturity."

The trial court determined this instrument to be non-negotiable paper, yet applied certain elements of the law of negotiable instruments in arriving at its conclusion. We believe the instrument to be negotiable. Uniform Commercial Code, section 3–109 establishes that an acceleration clause does not affect negotiability; neither, under Uniform Commercial Code, section 3–112(d) is negotiability impaired by a clause confessing judgment on an instrument "if it is not paid when due." Since the operation of the acceleration clause would have made the note due (that is, mature) as of the time of its operation, [citation] the note does not, as suggested by the trial court, authorize confession of judgment prior to maturity.

Thus, the critical question of whether this is order or bearer paper is to be determined by section 3 of the Uniform Commercial Code, which governs negotiable instruments. If this is bearer paper, the plaintiff's possession was sufficient to make it a holder (Uniform Commercial Code, section 1–201(20)) and this note on its face authorizes the holder to confess judgment against the maker.

On the other hand, if the instrument is order paper, it becomes apparent that the payee cannot be determined upon the face of the instrument. The power to confess judgment must be clearly given and strictly pursued. [Citation.] The warrant of authority having been given in favor of a named person, that warrant may be exercised only by the person named. [Citation.] If the warrant in this case cannot be read to extend to "bearer", then it may not be exercised, since the strict construction mandated by Illinois decisions will not allow a court to guess in whose name such a power may be exercised.

Under the Code, an instrument is payable to bearer only when by its terms it is payable to:

(a) bearer or the order of bearer; or (b) a specified person or bearer; or (c) 'cash' or the order of 'cash', or any other indication which does not purport to designate a specific payee. (U.C.C., § 3–111.)

The official comments to the section note that an instrument made payable "to the order of _____" is not bearer paper, but an incomplete order instrument unenforceable until completed in accordance with authority. U.C.C., § 3–115.

The instrument here is not bearer paper. We cannot say that it "does not purport to designate a specific payee." Rather, we believe the wording of the instrument is clear in its implication that the payee's name is to be inserted between the promise and the amount, so that the literal absence of blanks is legally insignificant.

Since the holder could not be determined from the face of the instrument, the trial court was in error in allowing plaintiff Broadway Management Corporation to exercise the warrant of attorney granted by this instrument to its holder. The judgment by confession therefore must be vacated.

* * *

Reversed and remanded with directions to allow the motion to vacate the confession of judgment * * *

Problems

1. State whether the following provisions in a note, draft, or certificate of deposit or other instrument impair or preclude negotiability, the instrument in each instance being otherwise in proper form. Answer each statement with either the word "Negotiable" or "Non-negotiable," and explain why.

(a) A note for $2,000 payable in twenty monthly installments of $100 each, providing: "In case of death of maker all payments not due at date of death are cancelled."

(b) A note stating, "this note is secured by a chattel mortgage of even date herewith on personal property located at 351 Maple Street, Smithton, Illinois."

(c) A certificate of deposit reciting, "John Jones has deposited in the Citizens Bank of Emanon, Illinois, Two Thousand Dollars, to the credit of himself, payable upon the return of this instrument properly indorsed, with interest at the rate of 10¾% per annum from date of issue upon 90 days written notice."

(d) An instrument reciting "I.O.U., Mark Noble, $1,000.00."

(e) A note stating "In accordance with our

contract of December 13, 1981, I promise to pay to the order of Sam Stone $100 on March 13, 1982."

(f) A draft drawn by Brown on the Acme Publishing Company for $500, payable to the order of the Sixth National Bank of Erewhon directing the bank to "Charge this draft to my royalty account."

(g) A note executed by Pierre Janvier, a resident of Chicago, for $2,000, payable in Swiss francs.

(h) An undated note for $1,000 payable "six months after date."

(i) A note for $500 payable to the order of Ray Rodes six months after the death of Albert Olds.

(j) A note for $500 payable to the assigns of Levi Lee.

2. State whether the following provisions in a note impair or preclude negotiability, the instrument in each instance being otherwise in proper form.   Answer each statement with either the word "Negotiable" or "Non-negotiable" and explain why.

(a) A note signed by Henry Brown in the trade name of the Quality Store.

(b) A note for $450, payable to the order of TV Products Company, "If, but only if, the color television set for which this note is given proves entirely satisfactory to me."

(c) A note executed by Adams, Burton and Cady Company, a partnership, for $1,000, payable to the order of Davis, payable only out of the assets of the partnership.

(d) A note promising to pay $500 to the order of Leigh and to deliver ten tons of coal to Leigh.

(e) A note for $10,000 executed by Eaton payable to the order of the First National Bank of Emanon in which Eaton promises to give additional collateral if the bank deems itself insecure and demands additional security.

(f) A note reading, "I promise to pay to the order of Richard Roe $2,000 on January 31, 1982, but it is agreed that if the crop of Blackacre falls below ten bushels per acre for the 1981 season, this note shall be extended indefinitely."

(g) A note payable to the order of Ray Rogers 50 years from date but providing that

payment shall be accelerated by the death of Silas Hughes to a point of time four months after his death.

(h) A note for $4,000 calling for payments of installments of $250 each and stating, "In the event any installment hereof is not paid when due this note shall immediately become due at the holder's option."

(i) An instrument dated September 17, 1981, in the handwriting of John Henry Brown which reads in full: "Sixty days after date, I, John Henry Brown, promise to pay to the order of William Jones $500."

(j) A note reciting: "I promise to pay Ray Reed $100 on December 24, 1982."

3. On March 10, 1982, Tolliver Tolles, also known as Thomas Towle, delivered to Alonzo Craig and Abigail Craig the following instrument, written by him in pencil:

For value received, I, Thomas Towle, promise to pay to the order of Alonzo Craig or Abigail Craig One Thousand Seventy-Five ($1,000.75) Dollars six months after my mother, Alma Tolles, dies with interest at the rate of six per cent from date to maturity and after maturity at the rate of seven per cent.   I hereby waive the benefit of all laws exempting real or personal property from levy or sale.

Is this instrument negotiable?   Explain.

4. Henry Hughes, who operates a department store, executed the following instrument:

$2,600   Chicago, March 5, 1982
    On July 1, 1982, I promise to pay Daniel Dalziel, or order, the sum of Twenty-Six Hundred Dollars, for the privilege of one framed advertising sign, size 24 × 36 inches, at one end of each of two hundred sixty motor coaches of the New Omnibus Company for a term of three months, from May 15, 1982.
                                     Henry Hughes.

Is this instrument negotiable?   Explain.

5. P agreed to lend M $500.   Thereupon M made and delivered his note for $500 payable to P or order "ten days after my marriage."   P, however, made no part of the agreed loan to M.

Shortly thereafter M was married. Is the instrument negotiable? Explain.

6. On June 1, A executed a note for $1,000 payable to the order of B, which contained the clause: "This note is payable when this year's corn crop is harvested." Is the instrument negotiable? Explain.

7. M employs A to work for him for one year from January 1, 1982, to December 31, 1982, at a salary of $800 a month payable monthly. On January 2, M delivers to A twelve promissory notes in otherwise negotiable form, maturing respectively on the last day of successive calendar months throughout the year 1982. On the first note there is the statement "For January 1982 salary"; on the second note "For February 1982 salary"; and so on for each note. On January 3, 1982, A sold and indorsed the twelve notes to XYZ Bank and on January 4, 1982, quit work. Are these notes negotiable? Explain.

8. For the balance due on the purchase of a tractor, Henry Brown executed and delivered to John Jones his promissory note containing the following language:

January 1, 1982, I promise to pay to the order of John Jones the sum of $1,000 to be paid only out of my checking account at the XYZ National Bank in Pinckard, Illinois, in two installments of $500 each, payable on May 1, 1982, and on July 1, 1982, provided that if I fail to pay the first installment on the due date, the entire sum shall become immediately due. (Signed) Henry Brown.

Is the note negotiable? Explain.

9. Sam Sharpe executed and delivered to Don Dole the following instrument:

Knoxville, Tennessee
May 29, 1982

Thirty days after date I promise to pay Don Dole or order, Five Thousand Dollars. The holder of this instrument shall have the election to require the assignment and delivery to him of my 100 shares of Brookside Iron Works Corporation stock in lieu of the payment of Five Thousand Dollars in money.

(Signed) Sam Sharpe.

Is this statement negotiable? Explain.

28

TRANSFER AND NEGOTIATION

The essential utility of commercial paper is in its transferability. Both negotiable and non-negotiable instruments are transferable by assignment, but only negotiable instruments are transferable by negotiation. This distinction is highly significant. If the transferee of a negotiable instrument is by its terms entitled to payment, he is a holder of the instrument. Section 3–202(1). Only holders may be holders in due course and thus entitled to greater rights in the instrument than the transferor may have possessed. These rights are discussed in the next chapter and are the reason why negotiable instruments move freely without luggage in the market place. The transfer of a non-negotiable instrument and of a negotiable instrument otherwise than by negotiation operates only as an assignment.

TRANSFER

Whether a transfer is by assignment or negotiation, the transferee acquires such rights as his transferor had. Section 3–201(1). The transfer need not be for value: if the instrument is transferred as a gift, the donee acquires all the rights of the donor. If the transferor was a holder in due course, the transferee acquires the rights of a holder in due course, which rights he in turn may transfer. This rule which is sometimes referred to as the "shelter rule," existed at common law and exists under the U.C.C., Section 3–201(1).

Any transfer for value of an instrument not payable to bearer gives the transferee the specifically enforceable right to have the unqualified indorsement of the transferor, unless the parties otherwise agreed. Section 3–201(3). The parties may agree that the transfer is to be an assignment rather than a negotiation, in which case no indorsement is required. Absent such agreement, it is presumed when value is given that negotiation was intended, and if the instrument is not payable to bearer, the right of the transferee to an unqualified indorsement is enforceable by court order. Where a transfer is not for value, the transaction is normally not commercial in nature, and such presumption is not appropriate. Until the necessary indorsement has been supplied, the transferee has nothing more than the contract rights of an assignee. Negotiation takes effect only when a proper indorsement is made, as it is not until then, notwithstanding possession, that the transferee becomes a holder of the instrument.

NEGOTIATION

Negotiation is the transfer of a negotiable instrument in such a manner that the transferee becomes a holder of it. Negotiation of bearer paper requires only voluntary delivery of the instrument, while order paper requires both delivery and all indorsements necessary to make the transferee a holder. Section 3–202(1). A holder is defined in Section 1–201(20) as "a person who is in possession of an instrument drawn, issued or indorsed to him or to his order or to bearer or in blank."

Anyone in possession of bearer paper is a holder even though he did not receive possession by voluntary transfer, as in the case of a thief or a finder in possession. For example, an instrument payable to bearer and issued to P is lost by P. It is found by F who sells and delivers it to B, who thus receives it by negotiation and is a holder. F also qualifies as a holder under Section 1–201(20). As a holder, F has the power to negotiate the instrument, Section 3–301, and the transferee may be a holder in due course if he meets the Code's requirements for such a holder.

INDORSEMENTS

An indorsement is the signature of a payee, drawee, accommodation indorsor, or holder of an instrument. An indorsement must be written on the instrument or on a paper, called an allonge, so firmly affixed to the instrument as to become a part thereof. The use of an allonge is required when there are so many indorsements that there is no room for additional signatures. A purported indorsement on a separate piece of paper, clipped or pinned to the instrument, is not valid.

Customarily, indorsements are made on the back or reverse side of the instrument, starting at the top and continuing down the back. The liability of indorsers, unless otherwise agreed, is presumed to be the order in which their signatures appear. Section 3–414(2). Occasionally, however, a signature may appear on an instrument in such a way that it is impossible to tell with certainty the nature of the liability undertaken by the signer. In such an event, Section 3–402 specifies that the signer is to be treated as an indorser. An indorsement which shows that it is not in the chain of title is notice of its accommodation character. Section 3–415(4).

An accommodation indorser receives no money or value for his indorsement but signs in order to add his liability and thereby accommodate, or assist, another party who might otherwise be unable to obtain funds. In keeping with the rule that a transferee must be able to determine his rights from the face of the instrument, the person who signed in an ambiguous capacity may not introduce parol evidence to establish that he intended to be something other than an indorser.

An indorsement may be complex or simple. It may be dated and may indicate where it is made, but neither date nor place are required to be shown. The simplest type is merely the signature of the indorser. Since the indorser undertakes certain obligations, as explained later, an indorsement consisting of merely a signature may be said to be the shortest contract known to the law. A forged or otherwise unauthorized signature necessary to negotiation is inoperative and thus breaks the chain of title to the instrument. Section 3–404(1).

If the name of the payee or indorsee is misspelled, or is a name different from the holder, as for example, a trade name, he may indorse the instrument in that name or in his own or both. Section 3–203. A check payable to "Crescent Pizza Palace," a sole proprietorship, may be quite properly indorsed by the owner in either his own name, John Doe, or in that of his business, Crescent Pizza Palace. To assure the highest degree of security and to facilitate subsequent negotiation, a person paying or giving value for such an instrument may require indorsement in both names. Section 3–203.

An indorsement which conveys less than the entire instrument or any unpaid residue thereon is ineffective as a negotiation. Section 3–202(3). For example, an indorsement containing a direction to pay A "one-half of the within note" or "$500 of the within note", or to pay "two-thirds to A, one-third to B" constitutes only an assignment in whole or in part, as the case may be. But an indorsement "to A and B" is effective as a negotiation because it transfers the entire interest to A and B as tenants in common. Words such as "I hereby assign all my right, title and interest in the within note" are also sufficient to support a negotiation, and will not cause the transfer to be regarded as a mere assignment. Section 3–302(4).

TYPES OF INDORSEMENTS

The type of indorsement used in negotiating an instrument affects its subsequent negotiation. Every indorsement is (1) either blank or special (Section 3–204), and (2) either restrictive or non-restrictive (Section 3–205 and Section 3–206), and (3) either qualified or unqualified (Section 3–414).

These indorsements are not mutually exclusive. Indeed, all indorsements may be sorted into three of these six categories. This is true because all indorsements disclose three things: (1) The method to be employed in making subsequent negotiations. This depends upon whether the indorsement is blank or special. (2) The kind of interest that is being transferred. This depends upon whether the indorsement is restrictive or non-restrictive. (3) The liability of the indorser. This depends upon whether the indorsement is qualified or unqualified. An indorser who merely signs his name on the back of an instrument is making a blank, non-restrictive, unqualified indorsement.

Blank Indorsements

A blank indorsement is one specifying no indorsee and consists of merely the signature of the indorser. A blank indorsement converts order paper into bearer paper. Thus, an instrument indorsed in blank may be negotiated by manual delivery without further indorsement. Hence, the holder should treat it with the same care as cash. He may protect himself, however, by converting the blank indorsement to a special indorsement by writing over the signature of the indorser any contract consistent with the character of the indorsement. For example, on the back of a negotiable instrument appears the blank indorsement "Sam Seller." Harry Holder, who received the instrument from Seller, may convert this bearer instrument into order paper by inserting above Seller's signature "Pay Harry Holder" or other words of like effect.

Special Indorsements

A special indorsement specifically designates the person to whom or to whose order the instrument is to be payable. Thus, M makes a note payable to bearer and delivers it to P. The note may be changed from a bearer instrument to an order instrument by P indorsing it: "Pay to the order of A," or even "Pay to A." Words of negotiability are not required in an indorsement. Any further negotiation of the instrument requires A's indorsement. This is appropriate because P, as the owner of the instrument, should have the right to direct the payment and require the indorsement of A, his indorsee, as evidence of the satisfaction of P's obligation to A.

Restrictive Indorsements

As the term implies, a restrictive indorsement attempts to restrict the rights of the indorsee in some fashion designed to protect the rights of the indorser. Section 3–205 of the U.C.C. defines four types of indorsements as restrictive: conditional indorsements, indorsements prohibiting further transfer, indorsements for deposit or collection, and indorsements in trust.

Conditional Indorsements. A conditional indorsement is one by which the indorser makes the rights of the indorsee subject to the happening or non-happening of a specified event. Suppose M makes a note payable to P's order. P indorses it "Pay A, but only if the good ship Jolly Jack arrives in Chicago harbor by November 15, 1981." If M had used this language in the instrument, it would be non-negotiable, because his promise to pay must be unconditional to satisfy the formal requisites of negotiability. But indorsers are permitted to condition the rights of their indorsees without destroying negotiability.

If the good ship Jolly Jack does not arrive in Chicago harbor by November 15, 1981, A has no rights in the instrument. If he presents the instrument to M for payment, M must dishonor the instrument or be required to pay it again to P. Under Section 3–603(1)(b), M is not discharged when he pays an instrument which has been restrictively indorsed, unless he pays in a manner consistent with the indorsement. Since the Jolly Jack did not arrive in port by November 15, 1981, it would be inconsistent with P's restrictive indorsement to pay to A or any transferee of A the amount due on the instrument.

Indorsements Prohibiting Further Transfer. Under Section 3–104(1)(d), to be negotiable, an instrument not payable to bearer must be payable to the order of a payee. If the instrument reads merely "Pay A" it is not negotiable and the only method of transfer would be by assignment. The requirements of negotiability are not imposed upon indorsements. An indorsement reading "Pay A" or even "Pay A only" is interpreted as meaning "Pay to the order of A." Such indorsements, or any other purporting to prohibit further transfer, are designed to be a restriction on the rights of the indorsee. To remove any doubt as to the effect of such a provision, Section 3–206(1) provides that no restrictive indorsement prevents further transfer or negotiation of the instrument. The net result of this provision is that an indorsement which purports to prohibit further transfer of the instrument is given the same effect as an unrestricted indorsement.

Indorsements for Deposit or Collection. The most frequently used form of restrictive indorsement is that designed to lodge the instrument in the banking system for deposit or collection. Indorsements of this type include those "for collection," "for deposit" and "pay any bank." Such indorsements put all non-banking persons on notice as to who has a valid interest in the paper.

Indorsements in Trust. Another common kind of restrictive indorsement is that in which the indorser creates a trust for the benefit of himself or others. If an instrument is indorsed "Pay T in trust for B" or "Pay T for B" or "Pay T for account of B" or "Pay T as agent for B," T is a fiduciary, subject to liability for any breach of his obligation. Trustees commonly and legitimately sell trust assets, and as a consequence, a trustee has power to negotiate an instrument. The first indorsee under an indorsement to him in trust is under the duty to pay or apply all funds given by him consistently with the indorsement, or risk having to pay twice. Subsequent indorsees or transferees are not bound by such indorsement unless they have notice that the negotiation to the first taker was in breach of fiduciary duty.

Qualified Indorsements

Indorsers, except those indorsing "without recourse," engage that they will pay the instrument according to its tenor at the time of their indorsement to the holder or to any subsequent indorser who takes it up. Section 3–414(1). In short, an unqualified indorser guarantees payment of the instrument if certain conditions are met. An indorser may disclaim his liability on the contract of indorsement, but only if the indorsement so declares and the disclaimer is written on the instrument. The customary manner of disclaiming the indorser's liability is to add the words "without recourse," either before or after his signature. A "without recourse" indorsement is called a qualified indorsement. A qualified indorsement and delivery is a negotiation and transfers legal title to the indorsee but does not guarantee payment of the instrument. A qualified indorsement does not destroy negotiability nor prevent further negotiation of the instrument.

For example, assume that an attorney receives a check payable to his order in payment of a client's claim. He may indorse the check to the client without recourse, thereby disclaiming liability as a guarantor of payment of the check. The qualified indorsement plus delivery would transfer title to the client.

Sample Indorsements

Examples of the various kinds of indorsements are:
(1) "John Doe"—Blank—unqualified—non-restrictive

(2) "Pay to Richard Roe, John Doe"—Special—unqualified—non-restrictive
(3) "Without recourse, John Doe"—Blank—qualified—non-restrictive
(4) "Pay to Richard Roe, without recourse, John Doe"—Special—qualified—non-restrictive
(5) "John Doe, without recourse, for collection only"—Blank—qualified—restrictive
(6) "Pay to XYZ Bank for collection and deposit only, without recourse on me, John Doe"—Special—qualified—restrictive.

WARRANTIES OF INDORSERS

The Code imposes upon an unqualified indorser the following warranties: (1) that he has a good title to the instrument; (2) that all signatures are genuine or authorized; (3) that the instrument has not been materially altered; (4) that no defense of any party is good against him; and (5) that he has no knowledge of any insolvency proceeding instituted with respect to the maker or acceptor or the drawer of an unaccepted instrument. Section 3–417(2).

The qualified indorser is subject to the same warranties except that with respect to number (4) above. Instead of warranting that no defense of any party is good against him, the qualified indorser warrants that he has no knowledge of any defense of any party against him. Section 3–417(3).

For breach of any of the warranties imposed by the Code upon both the unqualified indorser and the qualified indorser, the indorser is liable to his indorsee and subsequent holders for resulting damages. The warranty liability of an indorser is more fully discussed in chapter 30.

Cases

Indorsements

WATERTOWN FEDERAL SAV. & LOAN ASS'N v. SPANKS

(1963) 346 Mass. 398, 193 N.E.2d 333.

CUTTER, J.
The plaintiff (the bank) seeks to recover from the defendants, husband and wife, upon a promissory note, dated June 24, 1959, payable to "Greenlaw & Sons Roofing & Siding Co.," indorsed to Colony Distributors, Inc. (Colony), by an indorsement signed "Greenlaw & Sons by George M. Greenlaw," and then indorsed by Colony to the bank. The defendants denied the genuineness of their purported signatures and

of all indorsements and filed a declaration in set-off to recover their payments to the bank on the note.

At the trial, the defendants admitted signing the note and also a completion certificate which they had given to the bank. This certificate recited that the siding material, paid for by the note, had been attached to the defendants' house and that the work was satisfactory. The bank presented evidence of the balance due on the note.

The defendants requested the trial judge to rule that their "demand for proof * * * of their supposed signatures and of the supposed endorsements * * * is constructively broad enough to come within" G.L. c. 106, § 3–203.[1] The judge denied this request "not because as an abstract statement of law it may not be correct, but because, upon the facts as found by me * * * it has no bearing." Apart from an offer of proof mentioned later in this opinion, the defendants offered no evidence.

The trial judge found for the bank both as plaintiff and as defendant in set-off. The case is here on the defendant's bill of exceptions.

1. The trial judge correctly denied the defendants' requested ruling as immaterial. It does not appear that Greenlaw & Sons and Greenlaw & Sons Roofing & Siding Co. are not the same company. The indorsement by Greenlaw was not shown to have been in a name other than his own, nor is it shown that the name of the payee, as stated in the note, was not a name under which Greenlaw individually did business, identifiably repeated in the indorsement. Section 3–203 purports to give only an indorsee for value, and not the maker of a

note, the power to require indorsement in both names in the circumstances stated in the section. No evidence was introduced with respect to the indorsement. It comes within G.L. c. 106, § 3–307 (and see the official comments on that section), which reads in part, "(1) * * * When the effectiveness of a signature is put in issue (a) the burden of establishing it is on the party claiming under the signature; but (b) the signature is presumed to be genuine or authorized [with an exception not here pertinent]. (2) When signatures are * * * established, production of the instrument entitles a holder to recover on it unless the defendant establishes a defense." There was no evidence whatsoever to counter the presumption of the indorsement's regularity existing under § 3–307(1)(b). Thus the signature of Greenlaw was established under § 3–307(2), and the bank, as the holder of the note, see G.L. c. 106, § 1–201(20), is entitled to recover.

* * *

Exceptions overruled.

Blank Indorsements

PALMER & RAY DENTAL SUPPLY OF ABILENE, INC. v. FIRST NAT'L BANK

(1972 Tex.Civ.App.) 477 S.W.2d 954.

WALTER, J.

* * * Palmer and Ray Dental Supply Company of Abilene, Inc. filed suit against First National Bank of Abilene for conversion of the proceeds of thirty-five checks presented to the Bank by its bookkeeper Mrs. Wilson on which she received cash. The court granted the Bank's motion for summary judgment and Palmer and Ray Dental Supply have appealed.

* * *

James Frank Ray, President and manager of the dental supply company testified

---

1. [Footnote by the Court.] As inserted by St.1957, c. 765, § 1 (the Uniform Commercial Code), § 3–203 reads, "Where an instrument is made payable to a person under a misspelled name or one other than his own he may indorse in that name or his own or both; but signature in both names may be required by a person paying or giving value for the instrument."

substantially as follows: Mrs. Wilson was employed as our office manager. In February 1970, our auditor found a discrepancy in our inventory and we started looking for the leak. After we had worked on it for about two weeks, Mrs. Wilson called me one Saturday night and told me she would like to talk to me. I met her at the office and she told me she had been stealing by cashing checks that she was supposed to deposit. She was employed to answer the phone, take orders, invoice merchandise, order merchandise and to perform the general office duties. She also made deliveries and looked after the internal workings of the office. We do a credit business and the customers pay by check. I generally take the checks from the mail and place them in Mrs. Wilson's desk and she deposited them. We try to do our banking business everyday. She made out the deposit slips in our office. At the time Mrs. Wilson was working for us we had a rubber stamp which we used to endorse our checks. The stamp read:

Palmer & Ray Dental Supply
Inc. of Abilene
Box 2894
3110 B N. 1st
Abilene, Texas 79603

I authorized and directed Mrs. Wilson to endorse the checks with this rubber stamp. During the time Mrs. Wilson worked for us this was the only endorsement stamp we used. We had no stamp which read "for deposit only".

Most of the time she would go to the bank in our van. All deposits were made at the First National Bank and she would bring the deposit slips back to the office. She made the deposits about 75% of the time.

We will try to follow the rules set forth in [citations] in disposing of this summary judgment case.

In its trial petition appellant alleges that Mrs. Wilson made the deposits for it at First National Bank but instead of depositing the thirty-five checks which are listed in appellant's petition as she was instructed to do, she drew cash on them and did not account to the company for such money. It further alleged: "and by means of an unauthorized endorsement by said Dinah Wilson, the defendant First National paid cash to the *plaintiff* (Mrs. Wilson?) for the amount of the checks". It further alleged that by giving Mrs. Wilson cash instead of depositing the checks to its account the Bank converted its funds. Its cause of action against the Bank was predicated on the theory of wrongful conversion.

Article 3.204, Tex. Uniform Commercial Code, U.T.C.A., defines a blank endorsement as one that specifies no particular endorsee and may consist of a mere signature. Article 3.205 of the U.C.C. defines a restrictive endorsement to include one that uses the words "for deposit". Section 1.201(43), U.C.C., defines an unauthorized signature or endorsement as one made without actual implied or apparent authority and includes a forgery.

The summary judgment proof establishes that each of the checks has affixed thereto the blank rubber stamp endorsement of the appellant. We hold that such blank endorsement constitutes an authorized endorsement. When the Bank delivered cash to Mrs. Wilson instead of depositing the proceeds from the checks to appellant's account, the Bank was not guilty of conversion. [Citation].

The judgment is affirmed.

Special Indorsements

TUBIN v. RABIN

(1965 C.A. 5) 533 F.2d 255.

PER CURIAM:

This is a diversity of citizenship claim predicated on the Uniform Commercial Code (U.C.C.). Max Triplett sought to acquire a $2,850,000 loan for the acquisition and development of a New Mexico ghost town.

Triplett attempted to arrange the financing through Meyer Rabin and Consumers Investment Company (CIC). CIC issued a commitment letter conditioned on the payment of a $14,250 commitment fee and the personal guarantee of C. D. Wyche. Because Triplett lacked the personal resources to fund the commitment fee, he sought to secure an additional loan. Melvin Rueckhaus, a New Mexico attorney, arranged a meeting between Triplett and E. S. Tubin to discuss the transaction. Tubin agreed to provide the $14,250 if the money would be "safe" pending the closing of the $2,850,000 loan and if he would receive $4,500 for the use of his money. Triplett agreed and Tubin purchased a $14,250 cashier's check from First National Bank of Albuquerque payable to Rueckhaus.

Rueckhaus typed the following restrictive endorsement on the back of the check:

PAY TO THE ORDER—CONSUMERS INVESTMENT CO. and CHARLES D. WYCHE, SR., of 1631 Rachelle Road, Irving, Texas, the same C. D. WYCHE mentioned in commitment letter 11/6/67 by CONSUMERS to Max Triplett. Endorsement constitutes acknowledgement by endorsees that the money represented by this check is the only remaining condition to funding the loan committee (sic commitment) and that endorsees will return the $14,250.00 to Melvin E. Rueckhaus, Attorney for E. S. Tubin, within 30 days if the loan is not funded as per agreement before that time.

Rabin presented the check to Fair Park National Bank for deposit and immediate credit to CIC's account. Wyche's signature was forged, but Fair Park National Bank was unaware of the forgery and immediately credited $14,250 to CIC and Rabin's account. Rabin depleted the CIC account, including the $14,250 attributable to the credit for Tubin's cashier's check.

The loan was never closed, but the $14,250 was never returned to Tubin or Rueckhaus.

Tubin sued Fair Park National Bank for breach of warranty and conversion of the cashier's check. After a non-jury trial, Judge Taylor filed two opinions in favor of Tubin. [Citations.] Essentially, in his memorandum opinion Judge Taylor held:

Under § 3.202 [of the U.C.C.], negotiation of an 'order' instrument occurs when delivery, together with any necessary endorsements, is accomplished so that the transferee becomes a qualified 'holder' of that instrument. In the present case, Fair Park could not stand in the shoes of either a 'holder' or a 'holder in due course' because C. D. Wyche's special endorsement was forged. According to § 3.204(a) a special endorsement is one which specifies the person to whose order the instrument is made payable. Reuckhaus, in endorsing the check as the original payee, required that in order for further negotiation of the check to occur, a collecting bank should 'pay to the order of Consumer's Investment Company and Carles D. Wyche, Sr.' Thus, the $14,250.00 cashier's check became a specially endorsed instrument and could only be negotiated by both Wyche's and C.I.C.'s special endorsements together. The forgery of Wyche's signature rendered both special endorsements inoperative under § 3–404(a) and insofar as § 3–204(a) is concerned prevented the attempted negotiation.

By specially endorsing the check, the payee Reuckhaus in effect was saying that he desired only his enumerated endorsees or those persons who they desired by further negotiation, to receive the proceeds of the check. When the defendant collecting bank [Fair Park National Bank] paid the proceeds to a forger, the payee's [Reuckhaus] specific wishes were not carried out and under § 3–419(1)(c) it converted the payee's funds. Placing the funds received into the C.I.C. account, an account owned by one of its customers, does not alter this conclusion insofar as the collecting bank is concerned. When a payee specially endorses a check, he remains the rightful and deserving owner until his designated special endorsees—in this case, Wyche and C.I.C.—endorse.

The Court is of the opinion that Fair Park National Bank is liable to plaintiff upon the conversion theory. [Citation.]

* * *

Finding no reversible error, we AFFIRM the judgment of the district court.

*Indorsements for
Deposit or Collection*

FULTZ v. FIRST NAT'L BANK IN GRAHAM

(1965 Tex.) 338 S.W.2d 405.

STEAKLEY, J.

This suit was brought by W. B. Fultz, Petitioner here, against the First National Bank in Graham, Respondent, to recover the sum of $13,060.00 representing "less cash" sums, in amounts ranging between $50.00 and $300.00, paid by the bank to Mrs. Fern McCoy, an employee of Fultz, in "for deposit only" transactions to the account of Fultz over a period of time between February, 1960, and April, 1963. The sums so paid to Mrs. McCoy were misappropriated to her personal use. Mrs. McCoy had not signed a signature card at the bank and was not authorized by Fultz either to check on his account or to withhold cash amounts from the deposits made for him. The full endorsement which was stamped on each of the checks read: "Pay to the order of the First National Bank, Graham, Texas—For deposit only—W. B. Fultz."

Both parties moved for summary judgement and the trial court granted the motion of Fultz. The Court of Civil Appeals held that the alleged negligence on the part of Fultz in not examining his bank statements and other records and discovering the defalcations so as to notify the bank would, if found to be true, constitute a defense to his suit against the bank. Consequently, that Court held that in these respects there were issues of fact to be determined by the trier of facts and the summary judgment for Fultz was improper. * * * We reverse the judgment of the Court of Civil Appeals and affirm that of the trial court.

Smith et al. Bus.Law 5th Ed.—13

The key to the first problem is the undisputed fact that the bank violated the written instructions of Fultz, and hence breached its deposit contract with him in each deposit transaction. In the exercise of care by Fultz, all of the checks which were deposited were endorsed "For Deposit Only." This was an unqualified direction to the bank to place the full amount of the checks to the account of Fultz. This instruction was violated when part of the amount of the checks was paid to Mrs. McCoy in cash. The bank had knowledge of its acts in violation of the instruction. Fultz as a depositor had the right to rely on the bank to honor the "For Deposit Only" instructions he had established as the regular deposit routine for his employee and the bank to follow; he was under no duty to exercise further care to ascertain if the bank had followed his instructions, and it is not asserted that Fultz had actual knowledge that the bank had not done so. The instruction carried in the restricted endorsement, "For Deposit Only," if followed, afforded absolute protection to both the bank and the depositor in the check deposit transactions and would have rendered the misappropriations impossible. The bank was in no way misled. Fultz had not filed a signature card for his defalcating employee and had not authorized his employee to sign checks on his account or make cash withdrawals in connection with deposits to his account. The "For Deposit Only" endorsements in the latter transactions were positively to the contrary.

The decisions which consider the question of the liability of a bank for the payment of forged checks recognize the principle stated by the Supreme Court of the United States in Leather Manufacturers' National Bank v. Morgan, 117 U.S. 96, 6 S.Ct. 657, 29 L.Ed. 811 (1885), and quoted with approval in Southwest National Bank of Dallas v. Underwood, 120 Tex. 83, 36 S.W.2d 141 (1931), that "If the bank's officers, before paying forged or altered checks, could by proper care and skill have detected the forgeries, then it cannot receive a credit for the amount of these checks, even if the depositor omitted all examination of his account."

So it is here. The Respondent bank had only to exercise proper care by following the specific instructions of Fultz, the depositor, the doing of this required no skill. Its course of action in failing to do so resulted in liability to Fultz "even if" he "omitted all examination of his account." This distinguishes the decisions in the cases which are premised upon a duty of the depositor to examine his statements from the bank, which examination would have revealed the defalcations. [Citations.]

* * *

Since Fultz owed no duty to the bank to examine his bank statements and other records, he was, for that reason, not guilty of negligence in not doing so, and in not discovering the defalcations of his employee. For the same reason he is not estopped to assert the liability of the bank. There existed no genuine issue of fact between the parties in such respects.

The judgment of the Court of Civil Appeals is reversed and that of the trial court is affirmed.

Qualified Indorsements

COULTER v. STEWART

(1963) 93 Ariz. 242, 379 P.2d 910.

UDALL, VICE CHIEF JUSTICE.

Appeal was taken from a summary judgment for plaintiff in an action on a promissory note. Suit was brought in Maricopa County Superior Court.

The promissory note was executed in the state of Colorado by Richard L. and Rebecca H. Sardou to Clyde H. and Caroline Harvey for the amount of $54,271.47. The Harveys were the original appellants on this appeal. (Subsequent to the bringing of this appeal Clyde H. Harvey died and

Rufus C. Coulter, Jr., as ancillary administrator with the will annexed of the estate of Clyde H. Harvey, was substituted as an appellant in the place of Clyde H. Harvey.) September 10, 1956, at Colorado Springs, Colorado, Clyde H. and Caroline Harvey transferred the note to W. O. Stewart, the appellee, by use of the following statement on the back of the note:

"September 10, 1956

"FOR VALUABLE CONSIDERATIONS, we hereby assign all of our right, title and interest in the within installment note to W. O. STEWART.

"/s/ Clyde H. Harvey
"/s/ Caroline Harvey"

Payments on the note became delinquent and a foreclosure proceeding in Colorado on certain security resulted in the reduction of principal to $43,499.36. Stewart then brought this action against the Sardous, the makers, who were not served and whose residence was alleged in the complaint to be unknown, and against the Harveys as endorsers of the note. The suit resulted in a summary judgment against the Harveys. From this the appeal is taken upon the following assignments of error:

* * *

The transfer of the instrument from the Harveys to the appellee occurred in Colorado. Therefore, the law of that state should govern the effect of the transaction. * * * The parties base their arguments upon Colorado Revised Statutes, § 95–1–38 (1953) which * * * reads:

"A qualified [e]ndorsement constitutes the [e]ndorser a mere assignor of the title to the instrument. It may be made by adding to the [e]ndorser's signature the words *'without recourse' or any words of similar import.* Such an [e]ndorsement does not impair the negotiable character of the instrument." (Emphasis supplied.) [A.R.S. 44–438 employs this identical language.]

* * *

We are of the view that the language used to transfer the note in the case at bar is not language of limitation and the signers are merely generally endorsers. The principal reason for this position is found in the Uniform Negotiable Instruments Law § 63 which has the same wording as A.R.S. § 44–463 and Colorado Revised Statutes § 95–1–63 (1953). It reads:

"A person placing his signature upon an instrument otherwise than as maker, drawer or acceptor, is deemed to be an [e]ndorser, unless he clearly indicates by appropriate words his intention to be bound in some other capacity."

This section should be read in conjunction with Uniform Negotiable Instruments Law § 38, which is the same wording as A.R.S. § 44–438 and Colorado Revised Statutes § 95–1–38 (1953), supra. By doing so we conclude that words used in this transaction are not words of "similar import" to the words "without recourse" and do not convey clearly that the Harveys meant to be bound as mere assignors. The words "We assign all our right, title and interest" are not appropriate words that clearly indicate an intention by the signers to be bound in some other capacity than that of an endorser.

It was said in Prichard v. Strike, 66 Utah 394, 243 P. 114, 117, 44 A.L.R. 1348 (1926) where statutes identical to those we are considering were in force:

" * * * We think that one endorsing a negotiable promissory note and desiring to disclaim the responsibility of an endorser must, by appropriate words, clearly indicate such an intention or an intention to be bound in some other capacity, and that he does not do so by language as here assigning and delivering all his right, title, and interest in the note *which is nothing more than what the law implies from a blank or general [e]ndorsement* without words creating the implication, and hence is but the expression of a clause which the law implies, and works nothing." (Emphasis supplied.)

See also McCullough v. Stepp, 91 Ga.App. 103, 85 S.E.2d 159, 160 (1954) where it was said:

"The words, 'I hereby transfer my right to this note over to W. E. McCullough,' are not words of similar import to 'without recourse.' "

Furthermore, the view we take more adequately insures the free circulation of negotiable paper. This is of vital importance to the commercial world and any language likely to hamper it must be strictly construed. [Citations.]

* * *

Judgment affirmed.

Problems

1. Roy Rand executed and delivered to Seth Sims the following note: "Chicago, Illinois, June 1, 1982. I promise to pay to the order of Seth Sims or bearer, on or before July 1, 1982, the sum of $3,000. This note is given in consideration of Sims transferring to the undersigned title to his 1980 Buick automobile. (signed) Roy Rand." Rand and Sims agreed that delivery of the car be deferred to July 1, 1982. On June 15, Sims sold and delivered the note to Karl Kaye for $2,500. What rights, if any, has Kaye acquired?

2. M executed and delivered his negotiable promissory note for $1,000, payable to the order of Hettie Hope. Before maturity, Hettie Hope wrote on the back of the note: "Pay $500 of this note to Betty Blue, or order Hettie Hope" and delivered the note to Betty Blue. M refused to pay $500 to Betty Blue upon demand at maturity. Betty Blue then brought an action against M to recover $500. Decision?

3. Lavinia Lane received a check from Wilmore Enterprises, Inc., drawn on the Citizens Bank

of Erehwon, in the sum of $10,000. Mrs. Lane indorsed the check "Mrs. Lavinia Lane for deposit only, Account of Lavinia Lane," placed it in a "Bank by Mail" envelope addressed to the First National Bnk of Emanon, where she maintained a checking account, and placed the envelope over a tier of mailboxes in her apartment building along with other letters to be picked up by the postman the next day.

Flora Fain stole the check, went to the Bank of X, where Mrs. Lane was unknown, represented herself to be Lavinia Lane, opened an account in that name and deposited $200 in currency. The next day Flora Fain withdrew $100 and deposited the check for $10,000. It was forwarded for collection, paid in due course and thereafter Flora Fain cashed a $4,000 check in the account with the Bank of X, and purchased a cashier's check for $6,000, which she also cashed, leaving a balance of $100 in the account. Has Bank X taken the check by negotiation? Why or why not?

4. What type of indorsement are the following:
(a) "Pay to M without recourse."
(b) "Pay to A for collection.
(c) "I hereby assign all my right, title, and interest in this note to F in full."
(d) "Pay to the Southern Trust Company."
(e) "Pay to the order of the Farmers Bank of Nicholasville for deposit only."
Indicate whether the indorsement is (1) blank or special, (2) restrictive or non-restrictive, and (3) qualified or unqualified.

5. Explain whether the following transactions result in a valid negotiation:
(a) A gives a negotiable check payable to bearer to B without indorsing it.
(b) G indorses a negotiable, promissory note payable to the order of G, "Pay to M and N, (signed) G."

(c) X lost a negotiable check payable to his order. Y found it and indorsed the back of the check: "Pay to Z, (signed) Y."
(d) C indorsed a negotiable promissory note payable to the order of C, "(signed) C" and delivered it to D. D then wrote above C's signature, "Pay to D."

6. Alpha issues a negotiable check to Beta payable to the order of Beta in payment of an obligation Alpha owed Beta. Beta delivers the check to Gamma without indorsing it in exchange for 100 shares of General Motors stock owned by Gamma. How has Beta transferred the check? What rights, if any, does Gamma have against Beta?

7. M executed and delivered to P a negotiable promissory note payable to the order of P as payment for 100 bushels of wheat P had sold to M. P indorsed the note "Pay to R only, (signed) P" and sold it to R. R then sold the note to S after indorsing it "Pay to S, (signed) R." What rights, if any, does S acquire in the instrument?

8. Simon Sharpe executed and delivered to Ben Bates a negotiable promissory note payable to the order of Ben Bates for $500. Bates indorsed the note "Pay to Carl Cady upon his satisfactorily repairing the roof of my house, (signed) Ben Bates," and delivered it to Cady as a downpayment on the contract price of the roofing job. Cady then indorsed the note and sold it to Timothy Tate for $450. What rights, if any, does Tate acquire in the promissory note?

9. Debbie Dean issued a check to Betty Brown payable to the order of Cathy Cain and Betty Brown. Betty indorsed the check "Pay to Elizabeth East, (signed) Betty Brown." What rights, if any, does Elizabeth acquire in the check?

Chapter
29

HOLDER IN DUE COURSE

The law of commercial paper exists for the purpose of encouraging and facilitating trade and commerce by making it possible for the purchaser of a negotiable instrument, under certain conditions, to acquire rights in the instrument greater than those possessed by the person from whom he purchased it. The law has conferred this preferred position upon such a purchaser in order to encourage the free negotiability of commercial paper by minimizing the risks assumed by an innocent purchaser of the instrument. In determining in a particular transaction whether this has occurred, all of the legal requirements and aspects of negotiability and negotiation must be considered.

Chapter 27 discusses the formal requirements of negotiability and the forms of negotiable instruments. An instrument which is in compliance with all of these requirements can freely travel in the channels of trade and commerce.

In order to travel easily, expeditiously, and most advantageously in the marketplace, an instrument must (1) be negotiable;

(2) be transferred to a holder; and (3) be held by a holder in due course or one who has acquired the rights of a holder in due course. Although these three requirements are considered separately in the two preceding chapters and in this one, it is important to recognize that they operate simultaneously and together in providing the benefits desired by the transferee, namely, freedom from claims and defenses of third parties.

If a non-negotiable instrument is transferred or a negotiable instrument is transferred without negotiation, or if the transferee is not a holder in due course or does not possess the rights of one under the shelter rule, the transaction is merely an assignment of the right, title, and interest of the transferor in the instrument. Consequently, the infirmities of the assignor are not cut off and the assignee acquires the paper subject to all of the claims and defenses to which the assignor would be subject if he were bringing the lawsuit.

Having considered the formal requirements of negotiability (Chapter 27) and the manner in which a negotiable instrument may be negotiated (Chapter 28), this chapter discusses what the law requires of a transferee to whom an instrument has been negotiated in order for him to become a holder in due course.

HOLDER IN DUE COURSE STATUS

REQUIREMENTS OF A HOLDER IN DUE COURSE

To acquire the preferential rights of a holder in due course, the holder must meet the requirements of Section 3–302 or he must "inherit" these rights under Section 3–201, the shelter provision. Section 3–302 requires a holder in due course to

(1) be a holder who takes the instrument;
(2) for value;
(3) in good faith; and
(4) without notice
    (a) that it is overdue or has been dishonored or
    (b) of any defense against or claim to it on the part of any person.

Holder of the Instrument

In order to become a holder in due course, one must first be a holder. A "holder" is a person who is in possession of an instrument drawn or issued to his order or to bearer, or indorsed to him or in blank. Section 1–201(20). He is therefore a person in possession who by the terms of the instrument is entitled to payment. Whether or not the holder is the owner of the instrument he may transfer it, negotiate it, or (with certain exceptions specified in Section 3–603) discharge it or enforce payment in his own name. Section 3–301.

The significance of being a "holder" is brought out in the following factual situation. Poe indorsed his paycheck in blank and cashed it at a tavern where he was a well known customer. Shortly thereafter, a burglar stole the check from the tavern.

The tavernkeeper immediately notified Poe's employer who gave the drawee bank a stop-payment order. The burglar indorsed the check in a false name and passed it to a grocer who took it in good faith and for value. The check was dishonored upon presentment to the drawee. The paycheck became bearer paper when Poe indorsed it in blank. It retained this character in the hands of the tavernkeeper, in the hands of the burglar and in the hands of the grocer who became a holder in due course even though he had received it from a thief who had indorsed it with a false name. An indorsement is not necessary to the negotiation of bearer paper. The forged indorsement was therefore immaterial. The thief was a "holder" of the check, within the definition of Section 1–201(20) of the U.C.C. and under Section 3–301 a holder may negotiate a check "whether or not he is the owner." Accordingly, one who, like the grocer, takes from a "holder" for value and in good faith becomes a holder in due course.

This rule does not apply to a stolen order instrument. In the example above assume that the thief had stolen the paycheck from Poe prior to indorsement. The thief then forged Poe's signature and passed the check to the grocer who again took it in good faith and for value. Negotiation of an order instrument requires a valid indorsement by the person to whose order the instrument is payable, in this case Poe. Since the forged indorsement is not effective as Poe's, there has been no valid indorsement by Poe. Consequently, the grocer has not taken the instrument with all necessary indorsements and therefore he could not be a holder nor be a holder in due course.

Value

The law requires a holder in due course to have given value. The obvious case of failure to give value is the one in which the holder makes a gift of the instrument to a third person. For example, assume M executes a note payable to the order of P, who indorses the note and gives it to his fiancee, W. Since W had not given value for the note, she is not a holder in due course.

The concept of value in the law of negotiable instruments is not the same as that of consideration under the law of contracts. An executory promise, clearly valid consideration to support a contract, is not the giving of value to support a holder in due course status. A purchaser of a note or draft who has not yet given value may rescind the transaction and avoid it if a defense becomes known to him. A person who has given value, however, needs and deserves the protection given to a holder in due course. For example, M executes and delivers a $1,000 note payable to the order of P, who negotiates it to H who promises to pay P for it a month later. During the month, H learns that M has a defense against P. H can rescind the agreement with P and return or tender the note back to P. This makes him whole. He has no need to cut off M's defense. Assume, on the other hand, that H has paid P for the note before he learns of M's defense. It may not be possible for H to recover his money from P. H then needs the holder-in-due-course protection which permits him to recover on the instrument from M.

Section 3–303(a) establishes this principle by providing in part that a holder takes an instrument for value only to the extent that the agreed consideration has been given. Assume that in the foregoing case, H had agreed to pay P $850 for the note. If H had paid P $600, he could be a holder in due course only to the extent of $600, and if a defense were available, it would be valid against him to the extent of the balance. When H paid the $250 balance to P, he would become a holder in due course as to the full $1,000 face value of the note. A holder in due course, to give value, is not required to pay the face amount of the instrument, but only the amount he agreed to pay.

The U.C.C. provides exceptions to the executory promise rule in two situations: the giving of a negotiable instrument and the making of an irrevocable commitment to a third party. Section 3–303(c). Suppose that M makes a note for $1,000 payable to the order of P which P indorses and delivers to H who gives P in exchange for it his personal check for $1,000. H met the requirement of giving value for the note when he gave P his check, not when the check was paid by the drawee bank. The check might pass into the hands of a holder in due course against whom H would have no valid defense in a suit on the check. Value would likewise be given if H made any other irrevocable commitment if the commitment was to a third party rather than to P. An example of an irrevocable commitment is the issuance by a bank of a letter of credit, under which it agrees to pay amounts advanced to the person to whom it is issued, up to a stated limit. The bank has no way of stopping payment on such a letter of credit.

In the case of an instrument given as security for an obligation, the lender is regarded as having given value to the extent of his security interest, as provided in Section 3–302(4):

A purchaser of a limited interest can be a holder in due course only to the extent of the interest purchased.

For example, P is the holder of a $1,000 note payable to his order, executed by M, and due in twelve months. P uses the note as security for a $700 loan made to him by H. Since H has advanced $700, with respect to the requirement of value, he qualifies as a holder in due course of M's note to this extent. If P does not repay the loan, H may recover on the note by collecting the $700 from M.

At common law an antecedent debt is not sufficient consideration to support a promise to pay the debt or a lesser amount in full satisfaction. However, under Section 3–303(b) of the Code a holder gives value when he takes an instrument in payment of or as security for an antecedent debt. Thus, M makes and delivers a note for $1,000 to the order of P which P sells by indorsement and delivery to H in payment of or security for a debt owing to H by P. H has thereby met the value requirement.

Good Faith

Prior to the Uniform Commercial Code, American courts were divided over the definition of "good faith." They first adopted a subjective test, following the early English cases. Under this test, if the purchaser was actually innocent, he was held to have bought the paper in good faith, even though a prudent man under the circumstances would have known that something was wrong with it. A second approach was the "suspicious circumstances" test: if the holder bought the paper under circumstances which a reasonably prudent man would regard as "suspicious" he was considered as not having purchased it in good faith, although his actual state of mind was one of innocence. Under this test, a person buying a $10,000 note from an obvious tramp would not be held to be a good-faith purchaser, even though he may have bought in innocence. The first test is *subjective*: it measures good faith by what the purchaser knows or believes. He may be empty-headed, but if his heart is pure, he can pass muster on good faith grounds. On the other hand, the second test is *objective*: it measures good faith by what a reasonably prudent purchaser would have done under the circumstances. This requires the holder to act diligently and prudently.

The U.C.C. defines good faith as "honesty in fact in the conduct or transaction concerned." Section 1–201(19). This appears to be an adoption of the subjective test, an interpretation borne out by the judicial decisions applying this section.

Lack of Notice

To become a holder in due course, a holder must also take the instrument without notice that it is overdue, dishonored, or subject to any defense or claim. Notice of any of these matters should alert the purchaser that he may be buying a lawsuit and therefore should refuse to take the instrument. "Notice" is defined in Section 1–201(25) as follows: "A person has 'notice' of a fact when (a) he has actual knowledge of it; or (b) he has received a notice or notification of it; or (c) from all the facts and circumstances known to him at the time in question he has reason to know that it exists." The first two clauses of this definition impose a wholly subjective standard. The last clause provides a partially objective one: the fact that suspicious circumstances are present does not adversely affect the purchaser, unless he has the reason to recognize them as suspicious.

Section 3–304(6) deals with the question of a prospective holder learning of a defense before he has purchased the instrument, but the knowledge comes too late for him to act upon it. Suppose that the bank upon which a check is drawn is notified one minute before the teller cashes it that payment is stopped because of fraud. The acquisition of this notice does not prevent the bank from being a holder in due course. Section 3–304(6) provides:

To be effective, notice must be received at such time and in such manner as to give a reasonable opportunity to act on it.

Of course, notice acquired *after* the holder has purchased an instrument does not impair his status as a holder in due course.

Notice of a Claim or Defense. Section 3–304 establishes detailed rules which state when a purchaser is deemed to have notice of a claim or defense. Section 3–304(1)(a) provides that "The purchaser has notice of a claim or defense if the instrument is so incomplete, bears such visible evidence of forgery or alteration, or is otherwise so irregular as to call into question its validity, terms or ownership or to create an ambiguity as to the party to pay."

Suppose that D draws a check on the XYZ Bank for $100, payable to the order of P. P crudely raises the amount of the check to $1,000 and negotiates it to H. H cannot be a holder in due course. He is charged with information which he can learn from the face of the instrument. The instrument is irregular, and the alteration is so manifest on its face that H would be held to have notice of it.

Suppose there is an obvious change on the face of the instrument which would not indicate wrongdoing. The date is changed from January 2, 1980 to January 2, 1981, and it might be reasonable to assume that the drawer, out of force of habit, wrote "1980" rather than "1981." This would not be considered a material alteration that would give notice of a defense or claim.

Section 3–304(1)(b) provides that "The purchaser has notice of a claim or defense if the purchaser has notice that the obligation of any party is voidable in whole or in part, or that all parties have been discharged." The fact that the holder knows that one or more but not all the parties have been discharged, however, does not have the same consequences as knowledge of other defenses. For example, M issues a negotiable promissory note to P who endorses it in blank and delivers it to A. The instrument then passes by blank indorsements to B, C, and D. D strikes out C's indorsement and negotiates it for value to H. H would have notice that C's liability had been discharged. This would not prevent H from being a holder in due course with respect to M, P, A, B, and D because their liability is not discharged. Section 3–304(1) applies only when a purchaser has notice that all the parties have been discharged.

Section 3–304(4) provides a listing of facts the knowledge of which does not of itself give the purchaser notice of a defense or claim. Subparagraph (4)(a) provides that knowledge of the fact that the instrument is antedated or postdated does not of itself give the purchaser notice of a defense or claim. This accords with Section 3–114(1) that antedating or postdating does not affect negotiability. Subparagraph (b) of Section 3–304(4) provides that the mere fact that the purchaser of an instrument knows that it was originally given or negotiated for an executory promise or was accompanied by a separate agreement does not impair his good faith, unless he knows that the promise has not been kept. Suppose M makes and delivers a note to the order of P which recites that it was given "As per our contract of even date." This recital does not impair negotiability because it does not burden the note with the extraneous contract. Section 3–105(1)(b). The recital notifies prospective purchasers that the note was given pursuant to a contract which may or may not have been performed. Subparagraph (c) states that mere knowledge of the fact that one party has signed for the accommodation of another does not give the purchaser notice of any claim or defense. Suppose that M makes a note payable to the order of P and W also signs as maker to accommodate M. If a purchaser of the note from P knows the relationship between M and W, he has knowledge of the possibility of a defense by W based upon some conduct by P, but if he does not know of any such defense he is not deprived of the status of holder in due course. Subparagraph (d) provides that knowledge of the fact that an incomplete instrument has been completed does not of itself constitute notice of a defense or claim unless the purchaser also has knowledge that the completion was improper.

Notice an Instrument Is Overdue. To be a holder in due course the purchaser must take the instrument without notice that it is overdue. This requirement is based on the idea that overdue paper conveys a suspicion that something is wrong. Under this requirement, the holder is bound to know what the instrument itself reveals. Thus, if an instrument is payable on July 1, a purchaser cannot become a holder in due course by buying it on July 2.

In the case of an installment note, or of several notes issued as part of the same transaction with successive maturity dates, there is a natural question as to the effect of notice of default in payment of an installment or of a note in the same series. Section 3–304(3)(a) answers this by providing that the purchaser has notice that an instrument is overdue if he has reason to know that any part of the principal amount is overdue or that there is an uncured default in payment of another instrument of the same series.

Demand paper is not overdue for purposes of preventing one from becoming a holder in due course unless the purchaser has notice that he is taking it after demand has been made, or until it has been outstanding an unreasonable length of time. Section 3–304(3)(c).

The U.C.C. does not state what constitutes a reasonable time. Usually, in the case of a demand note, this means about 60 days. The time is somewhat shorter for drafts, and is considerably shorter for checks. With regard to checks, Section 3–304(3)(c) provides that a reasonable time is presumed to be thirty days. But the particular situation, business custom, and other relevant factors are important factors in making the determination, and no hard-and-fast rules are possible.

Acceleration clauses have also caused trouble. If an instrument's maturity date has been automatically accelerated, the holder may be unaware that it is past due. A prospective purchaser may similarly be unaware of this fact. Section 3–304(3)(b) provides that the latter can be a holder in due course, unless he has reason to know that the acceleration has occurred.

Notice an Instrument Has Been Dishonored. If a transferee has notice that an instrument has been dishonored by the refusal of a party to pay or accept it, he cannot become a holder in due course. He knows the instrument may not be paid.

A PAYEE MAY BE A HOLDER IN DUE COURSE

Section 3–302(2) provides that "A payee may be a holder in due course." This does not mean that the payee will always be a holder in due course but merely that he *may* be if he satisfies all the requirements for a holder to become a holder in due course. For example, if a seller delivers goods to a buyer and accepts a current check in payment, the seller will be a holder in due course if he acted in good faith and had no notice of defenses or claims. However, the seller takes the check *subject* to all claims and defenses because a holder in due course takes free of defenses only as to persons with whom he had not dealt. Section 3–305(2).

There are a number of situations, however, in which the payee is not an immediate party. For example, R, upon purchasing goods from P, fraudulently obtains a bank draft payable to the order of P and forwards it to P. P takes it for value and without any knowledge that R had defrauded the bank into issuing the draft. In such a case, the payee, P, is held to be a holder in due course, free and clear of the defense. There are a number of other ways in which a payee may be a holder in due course, but they are rather infrequent. In every instance there are three parties involved in the transaction, and the defense exists between the parties other than the payee.

THE SHELTER RULE

Section 3–201 provides that the transferee of an instrument acquires such rights therein as the transferor had. Therefore, even if a holder does not comply with all the requirements for being a holder in due course, he nevertheless acquires all the rights of that status if some previous holder of the instrument had been a holder in due course. This rule whereby a transferee who is not a holder in due course acquires the rights of one by taking from a holder in due course, is referred to as the "shelter rule," and existed under statute and the common law prior to its codification in Section 3–201(1). The purpose of the shelter provision is not to benefit the transferee but to assure the holder in due course of a free market for commercial paper he acquires.

Thus, P induces M by fraud to make a note payable to his order and then negotiates it to A, a holder in due course. After the note is overdue, A gives it to B, who has notice of the fraud. B is not a holder in due course, since he has taken the instrument when overdue, did not pay value, and has notice of M's defense. Nonetheless, through the operation of the shelter rule B acquires A's rights as a holder in due course, and M cannot successfully assert his defense against B.

The rule, however, provides that a person who is not a holder in due course cannot wash the paper clean in his hands by later re-acquiring it from a subsequent holder in due course or person having the rights of one. Section 3–201(1). For example, P induces M by fraud to make an instrument payable to the order of P who negotiates it to H, a holder in due course, and later re-acquires it from H. P does not succeed to H's rights as a holder in due course and remains subject to the defense of fraud. Similarly, if H upon taking the instrument from P had notice of the fraud and would therefore not be a holder in due course, he could not improve his position by transferring it to a holder in due course and later re-acquiring it, no matter how many intermediate transfers occur.

SPECIAL CIRCUMSTANCES DENYING HOLDER IN DUE COURSE STATUS

In keeping with the theory that the purpose of negotiability is to facilitate the flow of commerce, when an instrument is acquired in a way other than the ordinary flow of commerce, there is no reason to accord the transferee holder in due course status. Section 3–302(3) defines the situations to which this rule applies:

A holder does not become a holder in due course of an instrument:

(a) by purchase of it at judicial sale or by taking it under legal process; or

(b) by acquiring it in taking over an estate; or

(c) by purchasing it as a part of a bulk transaction not in regular course of business of the transferor.

In each of these situations, the transferee takes under unusual circumstances which indicate he is merely a successor in interest to the prior holder. As such, he should acquire no better rights. But if his transferor was a holder in due course, under the shelter provision of Section 3–201, the transferee acquires the rights of a holder in due course.

THE PREFERRED POSITION OF A HOLDER IN DUE COURSE

Section 3–305 sets forth succinctly the rights of a holder in due course: He takes the instrument free from all claims on the part of any person and free from all defenses of any party with whom he has not dealt except for a limited number of defenses which are available against anyone, including a holder in due course. Such defenses are referred to as "real defenses", as opposed to defenses which may not be asserted against a holder in due course and which are referred to as "personal defenses."

Defenses to an instrument may arise in many ways, either at the time of its issuance or later. In general, defenses to liability on a negotiable instrument are of the kind which may be raised in the case of any action for breach of contract. They are numerous. Section 3–306 provides that they are available against any holder of the instrument unless he has the rights of a holder in due course.

REAL DEFENSES

The real defenses listed in Sections 3–305(2), 3–404, and 3–407, are:

1. infancy (minority), to the extent that it is a defense to a simple contract;
2. such other incapacity, or duress, or illegality of the transaction, as renders the obligation of the party a nullity;
3. such misrepresentation as has induced the party to sign the instrument with neither knowledge nor reasonable opportunity to obtain knowledge of its character or its essential terms (fraud in the execution);
4. discharge in insolvency proceedings;
5. any other discharge of which the holder has notice when he takes the instrument;
6. forgery; and
7. material alteration.

Minority

All States have a firmly entrenched public policy of protecting minors from persons who might take advantage of them through contractual dealings. The exact application of this policy may differ from State to State. The U.C.C. does not state when minority is available as a defense or the conditions under which it may be asserted. Rather, Section 3–305(2) provides that minority is a defense available against a holder in due course to the extent that it is a defense to a simple contract under the laws of the State involved.

Void Obligations

Where the obligation on an instrument originates in such a way that under the law of the State involved it is void from the beginning, the U.C.C. authorizes the interposition of this defense against a holder in due course. This follows from the fact that where the party was never obligated, it is unreasonable to permit an event over which he has no control—negotiation to a holder in due course—to convert a nullity into a valid claim against him. The purchaser has bought a valueless item and should look to his transferor for reimbursement.

Incapacity, other than minority, duress and illegality of the transaction are defenses which may render the obligation of a party voidable or void, depending upon the law of the State involved as applied to the facts of a transaction. To the extent the obligation is rendered void, the defense may be asserted against a holder in due course. To the extent it is voidable only, the defense is not available against a holder in due course.

Fraud in the Execution

Fraud in the execution of the instrument renders the instrument void and therefore is a defense valid against a holder in due course. Section 3–305(2)(c) describes this type of fraud as such misrepresentation as has induced the party to sign the instrument with neither knowledge nor reasonable opportunity to obtain knowledge of its character or its essential terms. For example, M is asked to sign a receipt, and does so without realizing or having the opportunity of learning that his signature is going on a form of promissory note cleverly concealed under the receipt. M's signature procured under these circumstances does not involve M's consent to the instrument upon which it appears, and the courts treat it as no consent and therefore no contract.

Discharge in Insolvency Proceedings

If a party becomes bankrupt and the instrument represents an indebtedness discharged in the bankruptcy proceedings, he has a defense that is valid in any suit brought aginst him on the instrument including one by a holder in due course.

Discharge of Which the Holder Has Notice When He Takes the Instrument

Any holder, including a holder in due course, takes the instrument subject to any discharge of which the holder has notice when he takes the instrument. For example, a cancelled instrument is discharged, and cancellation prevents anyone from becoming a holder in due course because the condition of the instrument manifests its having been discharged. Where a cancellation, however, does not put the purchaser on such notice, he may be a holder in due course against whom the defense is not available. In Ingham v. Primrose, 7 C.B. (N.S.) 82, 141 Eng.Rep. 745 (1859), the instrument was torn up by the primary party in order to cancel the instrument and was discarded in the street. It was picked up and pasted together so carefully that a reasonable inspection would not reveal that it had been destroyed. It was sold to the plaintiff in this condition. The court held that the plaintiff was a holder in due course, and not subject to the defense of discharge.

No discharge of any party provided by this Article is effective aginst a subsequent holder in due course unless he has notice thereof when he takes the instrument.

If a holder acquires an instrument with notice that *all* prior parties have been discharged, he cannot become a holder in due course. Section 3–304(1)(b). However, if only some, but not all, of the parties to the instrument have been discharged, this fact does not preclude a purchaser from being a holder in due course. Those parties of whose discharge the holder in due course had notice, however, possess a real defense.

Forgery and Unauthorized Signature

Closely akin to the defense of void obligation is the defense of unauthorized signature. A party's signature to an instrument is a forgery when it is made without actual, implied, or apparent authority. A person whose signature is forged cannot be held liable on it, in the absence of estoppel or ratification, even if the instrument is negotiated to a holder in due course. He has not made a contract. Similarly, if A's signature were forged on the back of an instrument, A could not be held as an indorser. A has not made a contract. In keeping with these principles, Section 3–404(1) provides that any unauthorized signature is wholly inoperative as that of the person whose name is signed unless he ratifies it or is precluded from denying it; the unauthorized signature operates only as the signature of the unauthorized signer. This provision makes forgery a real defense.

It is well settled that a person may be estopped from asserting a defense, because his conduct in the matter has caused reliance thereon by a third party to his loss or damage. Suppose D's son forges D's name to a check which the drawee bank cashes. When the returned check reaches D he learns of the forgery. Rather than subject his son to trouble, possibly criminal prosecution, D says nothing. Thereafter, D's son continues to forge checks and cashes them at the drawee bank. The bank may be suspicious of the signature, but the fact that D has not complained may induce it to believe that the signatures are all right. Finally, D does complain, seeking to compel the bank to re-credit his account for all the forged checks. D will not succeed, as he is precluded by his conduct from denying that his son had authority to sign his name.

A party is similarly precluded from denying the validity of his signature if his negligence substantially contributes to the making of the unauthorized signature. The most obvious case is that of the drawer who makes use of a mechanized or other automatic signing device and is negligent in looking after it. In such an instance the drawer would not be permitted to assert the unauthorized signature as a defense against a holder in due course. The rule extends to negligence which contributes to a forgery of the signature of another, as in the case where a check is negligently mailed to the wrong person having the same name as the payee.

Material Alteration

Section 3–407 makes a material alteration a real defense. Any alteration is material which changes the contract of any party thereto in any respect, including any such change in (a) the number or relations of the parties; (b) an incomplete instrument by completing it otherwise than as authorized; or (c) any writing as signed, by adding to it or by removing any part of it. Subsection 2 provides that as against any person other than a subsequent holder in due course (a) alteration by the holder which is both fraudulent and material discharges any party whose contract is thereby changed unless that party assents or is precluded from asserting the defense; (b) no other alteration discharges any party and the instrument may be enforced according to its original tenor, or as to incomplete instruments according to the authority given. Subsection 3 states that a subsequent holder in due course may always enforce the instrument according to its original tenor, and when an incomplete instrument has been completed, he may enforce it as completed.

Since alteration is material only as it may change the contract of a party to the instrument, the addition or deletion of words which do not in any way affect the contract of any previous signer is not material. For example, where there is a discrepancy between words and figures on a check, the words being "twenty-five hundred dollars" and the figures "$25," a change of the figures to $2,500 is not a material change. But even a slight change in the contract of a party is a material alteration; the addition of one cent to the amount payable, or an advance of one day in the date of payment, will operate as a discharge if it is fraudulent.

Where an instrument contains blanks or is otherwise incomplete, it may be completed in accordance with the authority given and is then valid and effective as completed. If, however, the completion is unauthorized and has the effect of changing the contract of any previous signer, it is considered a material alteration which operates as a discharge.

A material alteration does not discharge any party unless it is made for a fraudulent purpose. There is no discharge where a blank is filled in the honest belief that it is as authorized.

If the alteration is not material or if not made for a fraudulent purpose, there is no discharge, and the instrument may be enforced according to its original tenor. Where blanks are filled or an incomplete instrument is otherwise completed there is no original tenor, but the instrument may be enforced according to the authority actually given. The maker or drawer, by leaving the blank, must bear the responsibility for making the unauthorized completion possible. Section 3–406.

Thus, a party is discharged from liability on a negotiable instrument by an alteration if the alteration is (1) made by a holder (2) with fraudulent intent and (3) is material. If one or more of these requirements is not met, no party is discharged and a holder may recover the original tenor of the altered instrument or the authorized amount where the instrument was incomplete. In keeping with the preferential position accorded a holder in due course, he may enforce any altered instrument according to its original terms and may enforce an incomplete instrument as completed. The following illustrations may explain the operation of these rules.

1. M executes and delivers a note to P for $2,000 which P subsequently indorses and transfers to A for $1900. A intentionally and skillfully raises the note to $20,000 and then negotiates it to B who takes it in good faith and without notice of any wrongdoing for $19,500. B is a holder in due course and therefore can collect the amount of the original tenor ($2,000) from M or P and the full amount ($20,000) from A, less the amount paid by the other parties.

2. Assume the facts in (1) except that B is not a holder in due course, M and P are both discharged by A's fraudulent and material alteration. B's only recourse is against A for the full amount ($20,000).

3. M issues his blank check to P who is to complete it when the exact amount is determined. P wrongfully fills in $4,000 when the correct amount should be $2,000. P then negotiates the check to H. If H is a holder in due course, he can collect the amount as completed ($4,000) from either M or P. However, if H is not a holder in due course, he has no recourse against M but may recover the full amount ($4,000) from P.

Material alterations frequently are made possible by the negligent manner in which the instrument is drawn or made. Suppose that M makes a note, writing it out in lead pencil. A party raises the amount. M has a real defense, based on the material alteration, but he may be precluded from raising it because of his own negligence. Section 3–406 provides a rule for guidance:

Any person who by his negligence substantially contributes to a material alteration of the instrument or to the making of an unauthorized signature is precluded from asserting the alteration or lack of authority against a holder in due course or against a drawee or other payor who pays the instrument in good faith and in accordance with reasonable commercial standards of the drawee's or payor's business.

Section 3–406 adopts the doctrine of Young v. Grote, 4 Bing. 253 (1827), which held that a drawer who so negligently draws an instrument as to facilitate its material alteration is liable to a drawee who pays the altered instrument in good faith. The rule requires that the negligence must "substantially" contribute to the alteration.

The U.C.C. does not define negligence which contributes to an alteration. The question is left to the court or the jury for determination upon the particular factual situation presented. Negligence usually has been found where spaces are left in the body of the instrument in which words or figures may be inserted. Unusual precautions are not required. Specifically, the drawer of a draft is under no duty to use sensitized paper, indelible ink or a protectograph, and it has not been considered negligence to leave spaces between the lines or at the end of the instrument in which a provision for interest or the like can be written. It is only where the negligence contributes to the alteration that the Section applies. It must afford an opportunity of which advantage was taken.

The Section only protects parties who act in good faith (Section 1–201) and in observance of reasonable business standards. For example, a bank which pays an altered check which ordinary banking standards would require it to dishonor cannot take advantage of the drawer's negligence.

Section 3–406 applies the same rule to negligence which contributes to a forgery or other unauthorized signature, as defined in Section 1–201.

PERSONAL DEFENSES

Among the personal defenses which are valid against any holder except a holder in due course or those who acquire the rights of a holder in due course under the shelter rule are: (1) lack of consideration; (2) failure of consideration; (3) breach of contract; (4) fraud in the inducement; (5) illegality which does not render the transaction a nullity; (6) duress or undue influence which does not render the transaction a nullity; (7) set-off or counterclaim; (8) discharge of which the holder in due course does not have notice; (9) non-delivery of an instrument, whether complete or incomplete; (10) unauthorized completion of an incomplete instrument; (11) payment without obtaining surrender of the instrument; (12) lack of authority of a corporate officer or an agent or partner as to the particular instrument, where such officer, agent or partner had general authority to issue negotiable paper for his principal or firm.

These twelve situations are the most common examples, but others exist. Indeed, the U.C.C. does not attempt to detail defenses which may be cut off. It is content to state that a holder in due course takes free and clear of all defenses except those listed in Section 3–305(2) and forgery and material alteration, which are separately covered in Sections 3–404 and 3–407.

JUS TERTII: DEFENSE THAT THIRD PARTY HAS CLAIM

Jus tertii defenses are those not possessed by a defendant in a suit on an instrument but are possessed by a third party. Suppose that M makes and delivers a note payable to the order of P who indorses and delivers it to H, in return for which H undertakes certain contractual obligations to P. H does not perform these obligations. P thereupon directs M not to pay the note when H presents it. M has no defense of his own. If H sues M on the note M's assertion of P's defense is called *jus tertii*. Section 3–306(d) denies the right of *jus tertii*, except where the instrument has been

stolen or restrictively indorsed by providing:

Unless he has the rights of a holder in due course any person takes the instrument subject to * * * (d) the defense that he or a person through whom he holds the instrument acquired it by theft, or that payment or satisfaction to such holder would be inconsistent with the terms of a restrictive indorsement. The claim of any third party to the instrument is not otherwise available as a defense to any party liable thereon unless the third person himself defends the action for such party.

The *jus tertii* situation seldom arises where the plaintiff is a holder in due course as the defense is a personal one and not available against such a holder. Where H is not a holder in due course, he may nevertheless be able to recover against M, where M does not have a defense of his own but asserts a defense which P would have in an action by H against P. Under the U.C.C., M cannot set up P's defenses against H. P must intervene in the action and assert his own defense. P might be prompted to intervene by way of asserting an equitable claim of ownership to the note upon rescission of his contract with H for non-performance by H. P would ask that H take nothing in his suit against M and that judgment be entered in favor of P against M on the note.

PROCEDURE IN RECOVERING ON INSTRUMENT

A frequent misconception is that only a holder in due course may recover on an instrument and that the plaintiff's lack of holder-in-due-course status is a defense. Nothing could be further from the truth. If the maker of a negotiable note has no defense it does not matter whether the plaintiff is or is not a holder in due course.

In the normal law suit in which recovery on an instrument is sought, the question of whether the plaintiff is a holder in due course may never arise. Section 3–307 describes the step by step procedure.

When the holder brings an action to collect, he relies upon Section 3–301, which provides that the holder of an instrument, whether or not he is a holder in due course, may, among other things, enforce payment in his own name. Upon filing of suit, it is assumed that all signatures are valid and effective unless the defendant denies this. At this point it is not pertinent whether the plaintiff is a holder in due course, since the defense of unauthorized signature is valid against any holder.

If the signatures are admitted, or proved valid, the plaintiff is entitled to recover merely upon production of the instrument and proof of the amount of the unpaid principal due. Up to this point there has been no occasion for the plaintiff to allege that he is a holder in due course. If no defense is asserted, he obtains judgment without more. If the defense asserted is a real defense, it is effective against a holder in due course. However, a party claiming to be a holder in due course has the burden of proof to show by evidence the facts necessary to establish his holder in due course status. Section 3–307(3).

LIMITATIONS UPON HOLDER IN DUE COURSE RIGHTS

The preferential position enjoyed by a holder in due course has been severely circumscribed by a recent Federal Trade Commission rule, which purports to limit the rights of a holder in due course of an instrument which evidences a debt arising out of a consumer credit contract. The rule, entitled "Preservation of Consumers' Claims and Defenses," applies to sellers and lessors of goods, and defines consumer credit contracts in terms which include negotiable instruments. The rule is intended to prevent situations in which consumer purchase transactions have been financed in such manner that the purchaser is legally obligated to make full payment of the price to a third party, although the dealer from whom he bought the goods had committed fraud, or the goods were defective. This occurs when the purchaser executes and delivers to the seller his negotiable instrument which the seller negotiates to a holder in due course. The buyer's defense that the goods were defective or that the seller had committed fraud although valid against the seller, is not valid against a holder in due course of the instrument.

The Federal Trade Commission in order to correct this situation by preserving and making available claims and defenses of consumer buyers and borrowers against holders in due course, amended its Trade Regulation Rules as provided in Title 15, U.S.Code, Sections 41 *et seq.* by adding to the Rules a new part designated Section 433 which became effective May 14, 1976.

The Rule provides that is is an unfair or deceptive act or practice within the meaning of Section 5 of the Federal Trade Commission Act (and a violation of the Act), for a seller, directly or indirectly, in connection with any sale or lease of goods or services to consumers, to: (a) take or receive a consumer credit contract, or (b) accept, as full or partial payment for such sale or lease, the proceeds of any purchase money loan made in connection with any consumer credit contract, if the consumer credit contract in either (a) or in (b) fails to contain the following provision in at least ten point, bold face, type:

NOTICE
ANY HOLDER OF THIS CONSUMER CREDIT CONTRACT IS SUBJECT TO ALL CLAIMS AND DEFENSES WHICH THE DEBTOR COULD ASSERT AGAINST THE SELLER OF GOODS OR SERVICES OBTAINED PURSUANT HERETO OR WITH THE PROCEEDS HEREOF. RECOVERY HEREUNDER BY THE DEBTOR SHALL NOT EXCEED AMOUNTS PAID BY THE DEBTOR HEREUNDER.

The purpose of this conspicuous notice which the FTC Rule requires to be contained in consumer credit contracts is to inform any holder upon acquisition thereof that it is subject to all claims and demands which the debtor could assert against the promisee or payee named therein, and thereby place a holder in due course of the paper or negotiable instrument in the position of an assignee.

A more simple and direct approach to the problem which the FTC is endeavoring to resolve, with two worthwhile competing public policies involved, and one which would not affect the rights of holders in due course, would be to provide by FTC Rule, Congressional legislation, or Uniform State law, if found to be constitutionally permissible, that all consumer credit contracts and notes given in connection with consumer purchase money loans be required to be non-negotiable. Instruments and contracts which are non-negotiable may be assigned and transferred, but lacking the quality of negotiability they can not be negotiated. The concept of holder in due course is inseparable from the negotiation of a negotiable instrument, and there can be no such holder of non-negotiable commercial paper.

At common law, upon the assignment by a creditor of a contractual right, the debtor may assert against the assignee all defenses which would be available to him if he were sued by the assignor. This is essentially all that is sought to be accomplished by FTC Rule 433. Non-negotiability might have the effect of chilling the marketability of consumer credit contracts, but perhaps to no greater extent than may be the ultimate effect of FTC Rule 433.

Cases

Requirement of Value

KORZENIK v. SUPREME RADIO, INC.

(1964) 347 Mass. 309, 197 N.E.2d 702.

WHITTEMORE, J.

The plaintiffs, as indorsees, brought an action in the District Court of Western Hampden to recover $1,900 on two "note[s] in the form of * * * trade acceptance[s]" given by Supreme Radio, Inc. (Supreme), to Southern New England Distributing Corporation (Southern), dated October 16, 1961, and due, respectively, on November 1, 1961, and December 1, 1961. The plaintiffs are partners in the practice of law. The trade acceptances in suit and others, all of a total face value of about $15,000, were transferred to them on October 31, 1961, by their client Southern "as a retainer for services to be performed" by the plaintiff Korzenik. The trade acceptances in suit and two others given by Supreme had been obtained by fraud. Southern had retained Korzenik on October 25, 1961, in connection with certain anti-trust litigation. Korzenik did some legal work between October 25 and October 31, but there was no testimony as to the value of the services and the trial judge was unable to determine their value. He found for the defendant. Korzenik did not know that the acceptances were obtained by fraud. "He has paid co-counsel retained in the anti-trust case part of the money he has collected" on the assigned items.

The Appellate Division dismissed the report of the trial judge.

Decisive of the case, as the Appellate Division held, is the correct ruling that the plaintiffs are not holders in due course under * * * § 3–302; they have not shown to what extent they took for value under § 3–303. That section provides: "A holder takes the instrument for value (a) to the extent that the agreed consideration has been performed or that he acquires a security interest in or a lien on the instrument otherwise than by legal process; or (b) when he takes the instrument in payment of or as security for an antecedent claim against any person whether or not the claim is due; or (c) when he gives a negotiable instrument for it or makes an irrevocable commitment to a third person."

Under clause (a) of § 3–303 the "agreed consideration" was the performance of legal services. It is often said that a lawyer is "retained" when he is engaged to perform services, and we hold that the judge spoke of "retainer" in this sense. The phrase that the judge used, "retainer *for services*" (emphasis supplied), shows his meaning as does the finding as to services already performed by Korzenik at the time of the assignments. Even if the retainer had been only a fee to insure the attorney's availability to perform future services [citation] there is no basis in the record for determining the value of this commitment for one week.

The Uniform Laws Comment to § 3–303 points out that in this article "value is divorced from consideration" and that except as provided in paragraph (c) "[a]n executory promise to give value is not * * * value. * * * The underlying reason of policy is that when the purchaser learns of a defense * * * he is not required to enforce the instrument, but is free to rescind the transaction for breach of the transferor's warranty."

[U.C.C.] § 3–307(3), provides: "After it is shown that a defense exists a person claiming the rights of a holder in due course has the burden of establishing that he or some person under whom he claims is in all respects a holder in due course." The defence of fraud having been established this section puts the burden on the plaintiffs. The plaintiffs have failed to show "the extent * * * [to which] the agreed consideration * * * [had] been performed."

* * *

Order dismissing report affirmed.

Good Faith/
Lack of Notice

FRANTZ v. FIRST NAT'L BANK OF ANCHORAGE

(1978 Alaska) 584 P.2d 1125.

MATTHEWS, J.

This case arises under the commercial paper article of the Uniform Commercial Code as enacted in Alaska. A section of that article provides that the drawer of a check which is dishonored is liable to its holder. [Section 3–413.] If the holder is not a holder in due course he takes the check subject to all defenses which the drawer has against any other party to the check. [Section 3–306.] A holder in due course, on the other hand, takes the check free from all but a very limited class of defenses. [Section 3–305.] In this case the court determined that the First National Bank of Anchorage was a holder in due course of a dishonored check drawn by Jack Frantz and granted summary judgment in favor of the bank. Frantz now appeals. We hold that summary judgment was properly granted.

The relevant facts are as follow. Frantz wrote a check for $35,776.15 on his account at Alaska National Bank of the North, payable to Wilson & Son, as partial payment for building a house. Wilson deposited it in his account at First National Bank of Anchorage. First National cashed the check and covered $10,504.86 in overdrafts on Wilson's account, credited $24,495.14 to his account and paid him $776.15 in cash. The following day Frantz filed a stop payment order with Alaska National which dishonored the check when First National presented it for payment. Frantz decided to stop payment of the check after he learned that Wilson had not paid certain subcontractors who might lien his property. His decision was made after First National had cashed the check.

About a month before the transaction in question, First National had received information from a Fairbanks contractor that Wilson was planning to leave Alaska without paying his bills. Since the bank was a creditor of Wilson, two of its officers, Renfrew and Harris, questioned him concerning the report, and he denied it.

There was also evidence that First National's normal practice was to withhold credit on a check until five days after its deposit. Where the bank knew the drawer to be a responsible person, however, it would waive the waiting period and extend immediate credit to the depositor.

On the morning of the day of the disputed transaction, Renfrew had been on the verge of dishonoring the overdrafts on Wilson's account. Before he did so, Wilson deposited Frantz' check, and the deposit was brought immediately to Renfrew's attention. Renfrew ascertained that the bank had extended immediate credit on Frantz' checks in the past. He also requested verification of the check from Alaska National, and testified that it had informed his teller that the check was "good at this time." Frantz, on the other hand, asserts that First National merely inquired into Frantz' credit rating. For the purposes of this appeal we accept as true the version advanced by Frantz. [Citations.]

First National sued Frantz to recover $11,281.01, the funds it had disbursed before it received notice of the stop payment order.

A holder in due course is a holder who takes a check for value, in good faith, and without notice that it is overdue or has been dishonored or of any defense against it or claim to it on the part of any person. [Section 3–302(1).] In his appeal Frantz does not dispute the fact that First National gave value for the check, but argues that there are factual questions concerning the existence of good faith and notice which preclude the entry of summary judgment.

The Code defines "good faith" as "honesty in fact in the conduct or transaction concerned." [Section 1–201(19).] A de-

termination of whether a depositary has acted in good faith involves a subjective inquiry as to whether the bank extended credit on a check having knowledge of facts which suggest that the check would eventually be dishonored. [Citations.]

Frantz set forth no facts indicating that First National had any basis for believing that he would not honor the check that he wrote to Wilson. Absent such subjective knowledge, the extension of immediate credit on a check does not manifest bad faith. While the Uniform Commercial Code does not require a depositary to give immediate credit on a check, it encourages this practice by granting the bank rights against the drawer of the check on which immediate credit is extended. [Citations.]

Assuming that the bank departed from its customary practice in extending immediate credit on Frantz' check, we fail to see how such a departure has any tendency to prove that the bank did not honestly expect that the check would be paid. At the time the bank honored the check, even Frantz had no intention of stopping payment. Whether or not First National's conduct conformed to a standard of reasonableness is immaterial, for the draftsmen of the Uniform Commercial Code expressly rejected the idea of including a concept of objective commercial reasonableness within the meaning of good faith. [Citation.]

Frantz also contends that questions of fact exist as to whether or not First National had notice which disqualified it from becoming a holder in due course. Frantz points out that First National knew of Wilson's overdrafts, and that the bank had heard a month before the transaction that Wilson was planning to leave Alaska.

The Code states that "a person has 'notice' of a fact when (A) he has actual knowledge of it; (B) he has received a notice or notification of it; or (C) from all the facts and circumstances known to him at the time in question he has reason to know that it exists." Section 1–201(25). Subjective and objective tests are therefore used to determine whether a depositary had notice of a defense to a check, i.e., whether it knew or should have known of a defense against a particular instrument at the time it was negotiated for value. [Citation.] Absent actual knowledge or reason to know, a bank has no affirmative duty to inquire whether a defense exists. [Citation.]

Frantz did not demonstrate the existence of facts showing that First National had notice of any defenses to his check. At the time Wilson was given credit on the check, Frantz did not even know of the defenses which subsequently caused him to file a stop payment order; it stretches credulity to assert that First National either knew or should have known of them. First National's awareness of Wilson's overdrafts or rumored plans to depart is not probative because knowledge of a depositor's financial problems does not impart notice of a defense to a check issued to him by a third party. [Citation.]

* * *

Affirmed * * *.

A Payee May Be
a Holder in Due Course

ELDON'S SUPER FRESH STORES, INC. v. MERRILL LYNCH, PIERCE, FENNER & SMITH, INC.

(1973) 296 Minn. 130, 207 N.W.2d 282.

O. RUSSELL OLSON, J.

Plaintiff, drawer of a check payable to defendant Merrill Lynch, Pierce, Fenner & Smith, Inc., appeals from a summary judgment entered in favor of defendant. The appeal raises the issue of whether the payee was, as a matter of law, a holder in due course and thus not subject to the drawer's claim that the check, possession of which it gave to its agent, was wrongfully delivered to defendant-payee in payment of the agent's own personal obligation to de-

fendant rather than for the benefit of plaintiff-drawer.

Elson's Super Fresh Stores, Inc. (hereafter Eldon's) is a closely held corporation headquartered in Faribault, Minnesota, and engaged in the retail grocery business. Merrill Lynch, Pierce, Fenner & Smith, Inc. (hereafter Merrill Lynch) is a national stock brokerage firm with offices in St. Paul, Minnesota. William E. Drexler was the attorney for and corporate secretary of Eldon's and the personal attorney of Eldon Prinzing, the corporation's president and sole shareholder.

The relevant facts are not in dispute. From January 1968 through January 1970, Drexler maintained a trading account in his name with Merrill Lynch by which he purchased and sold stock at various times. Eldon's, on the other hand, maintained no trading account with Merrill Lynch at any time relevant herein. On August 12, 1969, Drexler purchased 100 shares of Clark Oil & Refining Company stock through his stockbroker at Merrill Lynch for $41.50 per share. A confirmation statement was mailed to Drexler by the stockbroker, and Drexler then mailed the $4,150 check here involved, together with the confirmation statement, to Merrill Lynch in payment for the stock purchase. The check was drawn by the corporation, Eldon's Super Fresh Stores, Inc., on the Security National Bank and Trust Company of Faribault, Minnesota, and contained corporate identification. * * * The check, in the exact amount of the purchase price of the 100 shares of stock (not including commission charge of $39.75) and payable to Merrill Lynch, was dated August 12, 1969, and signed for the corporation by E. C. Prinzing, its president. The check contained no other designation or directive as to its use. On August 15, 1969, Merrill Lynch accepted the check in payment of Drexler's stock purchase, treating Drexler as the remitter. * * * There was no communication between Drexler and Merrill Lynch except the stock purchase order for Drexler's personal account on August 12, the mailing of the confirmation statement to Drexler, and the receipt by Merrill Lynch on August 15 of the check and confirmation statement. * * * There was no communication between Eldon's and Merrill Lynch until November 1970, 15 months after the issuance of the check, at which time Eldon's inquired of Merrill Lynch relative to the stock certificate and asserted a claim to its ownership.

* * *

The narrow issue * * * is whether under the recited factual circumstances Merrill Lynch, as payee of the check, was a holder in due course. Since defendant, as payee, took as a holder and obviously took for full value, decision turns on whether the payee, which received the check from the drawer's agent who in turn had received possession with the drawer's consent, took it "without notice * * * of any defense against or claim to it on the part of any person," Minn.St. 336.3–302(1)(c), and thus became a holder in due course free of any claim of the drawer that the delivery to the payee was wrongful.

* * *

The law governing checks is now codified in Article 3 of the Uniform Commercial Code (hereafter U.C.C.), Minn.St. 336.3–101 to .3–805. * * * By § 336.3–102(1)(e) the word "instrument" for purposes of Article 3 means "negotiable instrument" as defined in § 336.3–104. That section embodies the traditional requirements for negotiable checks, drafts, and notes.

Section 336.3–102(1)(a) defines "issue" as "the first delivery of an instrument to a holder or a remitter." Section 336.1–201(20), which contains general definitions for the U.C.C., defines "holder" as "a person who is in possession of * * * an instrument * * * drawn, issued or endorsed to him or to his order or to bearer or in blank." The facts in this case are un-

disputed that Eldon's, the drawer of the check, placed the check in the hands of its agent, Drexler, for the purpose of delivery to the payee, Merrill Lynch.

It follows from those facts and those two code definitions (while somewhat circular) of "issue" and "holder" that Merrill Lynch was a holder of the instrument. * * * For the purposes of this case then, we treat the instrument as "issued" to Merrill Lynch, the payee and the holder * * *.

We next consider the requirements for a "holder" to become a "holder in due course" (hereafter HDC).

Minn.St. 336.3–302 sets out the requirements for being a HDC of negotiable instruments as follows:

(1) A holder in due course is a holder who takes the instrument (a) for value; and (b) in good faith; and (c) *without notice* that it is overdue or has been dishonored or *of any defense against or claim to it on the part of any person.* (2) A payee may be a holder in due course. (Italics supplied.)

The U.C.C. has thus made it clear that a payee may be a HDC. § 336.3–302(2). A payee who fulfills the requirements of § 336.3–302(1) acquires the rights of a HDC as set forth in § 336.3–305 with respect to the unknown claims or defenses of parties with whom he has not dealt even though he has become a holder as payee by delivery from a remitter or the drawer's agent rather than by negotiation from a prior holder.

* * *

It is the third and critical requirement—taking "without notice * * * of any defense against or claim to it on the part of any person"—with which we must deal.

The holder of an instrument has the burden of proving that he is a HDC when defenses or claims are shown. [Citations.]

"Notice" is defined in § 336.1–201(25) as follows:

A person has 'notice' of a fact when (a) he has *actual knowledge* of it; or (b) he has received a notice or notification of it; or (c) from all the facts and circumstances known to him at the time in question he has *reason to know* that it exists.

A person 'knows' or has 'knowledge' of a fact when he has actual knowledge of it." (Italics supplied.)

The Minnesota Code Comment to Minn.St. 336.1–201(25), 21A M.S.A. 76, points out that "notice" (as with "notice" in other recited uniform acts) is restricted—

* * * to actual knowledge of the fact, receipt of notification of it, or knowledge of facts from which the fact in question is inferable; and they all exclude the situation in which a person does not have actual or inferable knowledge but merely *could discover* the fact by reasonable investigation. In the latter situation it is sometimes said that when a person has a duty to another to investigate a matter he has 'notice' of what he could have discovered, but the U.C.C. does not employ 'notice' in that sense under this definition except in the case covered by paragraph (b) where one has *received notification* but may not have read or understood it.

The knowledge which a person has that constitutes "notice" according to § 336.1–201(25) could, then, be termed "inferable" knowledge.

In addition to Minn.St. 336.1–201(25), § 336.3–304 describes circumstances which do and do not constitute notice for the purpose of being a HDC. Paragraphs (2) and (4)(e) of § 336.3–304, which refer specifically to a fiduciary, speak in terms of "negotiating" whereas in the instant case we treat the instrument as "issued" to the payee without reaching the question of negotiation. However, the law on "notice"—actual or inferable—is precisely the same whether the instrument is issued to a holder or negotiated to a holder. Therefore, the Minnesota Code Comment to § 336.3–304, 21B M.S.A. 231, is pertinent. The comments to paragraphs (2) and (4)(e) make

clear that the test of "notice" is the existence of actual knowledge of a fact or of facts from which one can infer the fact in question. Under the "notice" test, the question then becomes: (a) Did Merrill Lynch have actual knowledge of Eldon's claim, or (b) did Merrill Lynch have "inferable knowledge" of the claim, i.e., did Merrill Lynch have actual knowledge of facts from which it could reasonably infer the probable existence of the drawer's claim?

Facts or circumstances from which a purchaser could infer that a claim exists on the part of any person are referred to in Minnesota as "danger signals" and knowledge of such facts is the "red light" test. * * * We have in Minnesota several cases applying this test to facts similar to the case at hand. In applying the test, this court has rather consistently held that having notice by way of the "inferable knowledge" test is something more than failure to make inquiry about an unknown fact. Failure to make such inquiry may be negligence and lack of diligence, but it is not "notice" of what he might discover. [Citations.]

* * *

Applying the "inferable knowledge" test to the instant case, this court concludes that Merrill Lynch did not have notice of any claim of the drawer, Eldon's, simply by virtue of its receipt of the check and confirmation notice from Drexler. The fact that Merrill Lynch was the named payee on the check drawn by Eldon's did not in and of itself constitute "notice" that Drexler was using the check improperly. Significantly, there were no other identification or designation marks on the check to indicate or give notice that it was drawn in payment for stock for Eldon's. Furthermore, and equally as significant, Eldon's had no account with Merrill Lynch. The designation on the check that the corporate maker was doing business as Prinzing's Markets is not by itself sufficient to constitute such "notice." Merrill Lynch was entitled to conclude that Drexler, known to be an attorney, had lawfully obtained and was delivering the instrument to discharge the debt incurred by his own stock purchase. Merrill Lynch was not required to surmise that the check, rather than being a payment for Drexler's legal services, was being misused.

* * *

Under the circumstance of this case, namely, where (1) a bank check was delivered to the payee by the drawer's agent with the drawer's consent and knowledge, (2) the check itself contained no restrictions or designations as to its use, and (3) the payee, a stock brokerage firm, had no trading account with, or indebtedness to, the drawer, we hold that the payee took the check without notice of the drawer's claims. Thus, the payee became a holder in due course of the instrument.

This court is not deciding in this case whether, as between Drexler and Eldon's, Drexler was authorized to deliver the check to Merrill Lynch in payment of his personal stock purchase.

* * *

Affirmed.

Real Defenses:
Fraud in the Execution

EXCHANGE INT'L LEASING CORP. v. CONSOLIDATED BUSINESS FORMS CO., INC.

(1978 W.D.Pa.) 462 F.Supp. 626.

DIAMOND, J.

Plaintiff, Exchange International Leasing Corporation, (hereinafter Exchange) brought the instant suit to recover rental payments from defendant, Consolidated Business Forms, (hereinafter Consolidated) arising out of defendant's leasing of a Phillips business computer. Plaintiff is the named lessor of said computer by virtue of an assignment from the original lessor.
* * *

It has been established through the ruling on a prior motion for summary judgment filed by plaintiff that the aforesaid assignment conferred upon plaintiff the status of a holder in due course under § 3–302 of the Uniform Commercial Code (hereinafter UCC), and that the defendant's only plausible defense was misrepresentation under § 3–305(2)(c) of the UCC. The matter now before the court is plaintiff's second motion for summary judgment in which it claims that no genuine issue of misrepresentation exists. For the reasons set forth below, we conclude that there is no genuine issue of a material fact regarding the misrepresentations defense and that the defendant was not the victim of misrepresentation within the meaning of § 3–305(2)(c) and, therefore, grant the motion.

* * *

In order to rule on the instant motion we must consider (1) the meaning of "misrepresentation" under § 3–305(2)(c); (2) the factual basis in support of the allegations of misrepresentation relied on by Consolidated; and (3) whether or not there exists a genuine issue of a material fact which if true would constitute a defense.

Turning first to the meaning of "misrepresentation," § 3–305(2)(c) states:

To the extent that a holder is a holder in due course he takes the instrument free from

. . . . . .

(2) all defenses of any party to the instrument with whom the holder has not dealt except

. . . . . .

(c) such misrepresentation as has induced the party to sign the instrument with neither knowledge nor reasonable opportunity to obtain knowledge of its character or its essential terms . . .

Thus, to establish the defense, one must not only have had no knowledge of a document's character or essential terms, but also have had no "reasonable opportunity" to acquire such knowledge. Comment 7 to § 3–305 elaborates by stating that in determining what constitutes a "reasonable opportunity" factors such as the age, intelligence, and business experience of the signator, his ability to read English, and the representations made to him and his reason to rely on them are to be considered.

The reported Pennsylvania decisions interpreting § 3–305(2)(c) while few in number are nonetheless uniform in holding that only fraud in the factum, as opposed to fraud in the inducement, is a defense under § 3–305. [Citations.] This view is in accord with comment 7 and also the view expressed by certain scholars in the area. [Citations.]

As comment 7 notes, the classic example of fraud in the factum is that of a person who is tricked into signing a note on the pretense that it is a mere receipt of some sort. Pennsylvania is apparently hesitant to expand the defense and afford relief to less obvious victims. For example, in [citation], defendants agreed to permit a company to install and demonstrate a water softening machine in defendants' home in order to promote sales to defendants' neighbors. The defendants signed a document which was represented by the company to be a bond securing against damage to the equipment. In reality, the document was a note securing the purchase price of the equipment. The court refused to hold that defendants had been the victims of misrepresentation within the purview of § 3–305(2)(c), for the reason that defendants had established no basis from which it could be concluded that they had reason to rely on the statements of the company's representative and, that they had the opportunity, time, and ability to read the document before signing it. * * *

With the foregoing in mind we consider the specific misrepresentations relied on by Consolidated. In its brief Consolidated contends that "Mr. Spohn was precluded from examining the contents of the agree-ment by the representations made to him" by employees of Phillips and Benchmark. Although defendant's brief does not disclose the specifics of those representations, Spohn's deposition indicates that they were in the nature of assurances that the computer would be removed with a complete refund if it failed to function properly. * * *

Assuming without deciding that the statements referred to by Spohn could form the basis of a misrepresentation, nevertheless the court is of the opinion that genuine issue exists as to the presence of a § 3–305(2)(c) defense. For, even if it be true that Spohn did not have actual knowledge of the essential terms of the lease, it can hardly be said that he lacked a "reasonable opportunity" to acquire that knowledge—an essential element of a § 3–305(2)(c) defense. Spohn testified unequivocally that O'Connor in no way prevented him from reading the instrument before he signed it, that he could have read the document in its entirety had he so desired, and that he was not busy or otherwise distracted at the time of execution. Spohn further testified that he read part of the lease but simply chose not to read the "fine print" because he had trust in O'Connor.

Consolidated argues for a contrary result by emphasizing that portion of comment 7 which states that in determining what constitutes a "reasonable opportunity" one is to consider the representations made to the signator and "his reason to rely on them or to have confidence in the person making them." The court does not find this argument persuasive because it simply ignores the other facts to be considered in determining whether one had reasonable opportunity to obtain knowledge of the instrument's character and essential terms. When these other factors; viz., age, intelligence, business experience, ability to read the document, necessity for acting speedily, are considered in the light of Spohn's deposition it is clear that there is no legal justification for the blind reliance which Spohn contends he had on the statements of O'Connor.

An appropriate Order will be entered granting plaintiff's motion for summary judgment.

Limitations Upon Holder
in Due Course Rights

JEFFERSON BANK & TRUST CO. v. STAMATIOU

(1980 La.) 384 So.2d 388.

CALOGERO, J.

Defendant's [answer] asserting a defense to plaintiff's suit on a promissory note given plaintiff's assignor for the purchase of a truck was dismissed. The trial judge held in favor of the plaintiff bank, granting its exception of no cause of action upon finding the bank to be a holder in due course. The Court of Appeal affirmed the trial court judgment. [Citation.] We granted writs upon application of defendant, vendee and maker of the promissory note.

Defendant, Christos G. Stamatiou, purchased a truck from Key Dodge, Inc. At the time of purchase, defendant and an agent of Key Dodge signed an instrument designated Sale and Chattel Mortgage. The instrument or contract is on a single sheet of paper, front and back. It consists of provisions relative to the Sale and Chattel Mortgage with a promissory note at the bottom of this same page. The note portion of the contract bears language indicating that it is an unconditional promise to pay $10,774.44 on prescribed terms. The preceding Sale and Chattel Mortgage portion of the instrument has numerous provisions including the following which preserves for the purchaser his defenses against a future holder:

NOTICE: ANY HOLDER OF THIS CONSUMER CREDIT CONTRACT IS SUBJECT TO ALL CLAIMS AND DEFENSES WHICH THE DEBTOR COULD ASSERT AGAINST THE SELLER OF GOODS OR SERVICES OB-TAINED PURSUANT HERETO OR WITH THE PROCEEDS HEREOF. RECOVERY HEREUNDER SHALL NOT EXCEED AMOUNTS PAID BY THE DEBTOR HEREUNDER.

Defendant's signature appears twice on the instrument, once following the sale and chattel mortgage and once at the conclusion of the promissory note. The purchaser is shown on the contract as "Christos G. Stamatiou" and no provision of the sale and chattel mortgage/promissory note indicates the purpose of the purchase, or the use to which the truck is to be put. Nor does any provision of the instrument indicate that Stamatiou purchased anything other than an ordinary truck. Near the top of the contract there is a "Disclosure Statement" by which "Buyer acknowledges that the Promissory Note secured by Sale and Chattel Mortgage will be assigned to JEFFERSON BANK, as Assignee and CREDITOR within the meaning of the Federal Truth-In-Lending Act."

Key Dodge assigned this contract to plaintiff, Jefferson Bank and Trust Co., as contemplated. Defendant alleges that the truck became inoperable and unusable a short time after purchase and that he notified Key Dodge and Jefferson Bank of the problem and demanded rescission of the sale. * * * Later, Jefferson Bank filed an ordinary petition against Stamatiou for the unpaid balance on the note (after separating or cutting the note off from the remainder of the contract).

Defendant answered the suit * * * seeking rescission of the sale and judgment for return of the purchase price.

Plaintiff bank filed an exception of no cause of action * * * contending that because defendant purchased the truck for use in his tow truck business, the instrument is not a "consumer credit contract" and that therefore the above quoted language of the contract is not applicable.

* * *

Our writ grant requires that we determine whether the inclusion of the preservation of defenses language (federally required in all "consumer credit contracts") in a contract which is not a consumer credit contract, allows the defendant to present his defense against a party who would otherwise be a holder in due course; in effect, whether the language, specifically countering the primary effect of holder in due course status is applicable to this holder, Jefferson Bank.

Under authority of 15 U.S.C. § 41, et seq., the Federal Trade Commission, a United States regulatory agency, requires the inclusion of the exact same language as was included in the present contract in all "consumer credit contracts" for the sale of goods or services. 16 CFR 433. The federal regulations define a consumer as "a natural person who seeks or acquires goods or services for *personal, family or household use.*" Therefore in any contract for the sale of goods or services where credit is being extended to the purchaser, and the purchaser is acquiring the item for personal, family, or household use, * * * language identical to that language used in the contract and quoted above, must be contained in the contract.

* * *

The express purpose of the FTC regulation is to prevent the seller, in a consumer credit transaction, from separating the buyer's duty to pay from the seller's duty to perform as promised, by the seller's assigning the buyer's promissory note to a financing institution, as against whom, because of holder status, defenses would otherwise not be available.

Plaintiff makes the following argument; that the preservation of defenses language is included in all credit contracts to insure compliance with federal regulations but is only intended to apply to the appropriate transactions even though there is no notation to the effect that the clause is pos-sibly inapplicable; absent inclusion in all credit contracts, the vendor and/or finance company would be required to have two different forms and to hire a staff attorney to instruct them each time which to use; and that the sale of the truck to defendant for use in his tow truck business takes the transaction out of the consumer credit contract category as defined by the FTC, and thus the provision, although there in the contract, was not applicable to this transaction and should be ignored.

Defendant on the other hand claims that the preservation of defenses language (whether federally required in this contract or not) was included in the contract and as such becomes a part of that contract.

* * *

We conclude that defendant's argument is the more persuasive and is more supported by the law. Under the provisions of the Civil Code, parties are free to govern their relationships through their contracts, and the contractural provisions have the effect of law on the parties. The contract between Stamatiou and Key Dodge, as assigned to plaintiff, provided "Any holder of this . . . contract it subject to all claims and defenses which the debtor could assert against the seller." That the parties to the contract mistakenly asserted that it was a consumer credit contract ("any holder of this consumer credit contract") is of little consequence. In looking at the contract, there was nothing on the face of the instrument to indicate that this was not a "consumer contract." The assignee/holder was put on notice that all defenses were available to the buyer against him at the time he acquired the instrument. In looking at the face of the instrument, plaintiff could not have expected to be a holder in due course, and is not now entitled to be so treated. At best the contract is ambiguous and is surely not to be construed against the purchaser who did not confect it. [Citations.]

* * *

For these reasons we conclude that the preservation of defenses language is applicable to the contract. Plaintiff bank is subject to defendant purchaser's claims or defenses and the contract provision takes precedence over the rights plaintiff would otherwise have been legally entitled to under R.S. 10:3–305 as a holder in due course.

* * *

REVERSED; REMANDED TO DISTRICT COURT.

Problems

1. On November 1, 1981, P installed a burglar alarm system in M's store. M executed and delivered to P a negotiable promissory note payable to the order of P for $1,100, the purchase price, due on December 1, 1981. On November 8, P returned to M's store and told M that he needed money and would accept $1,000 as payment in full. M immediately paid P $1,000 but forgot to obtain the note from P.

On November 10, P indorsed the note in blank and transferred it to H for value. Two days later, H learned that M had already paid P for the note, whereupon he gave the note to X, his mother-in-law, as a going away present, without further indorsement. X was not aware of M's prior payment of the note.

What are the rights of X, if any, against M? Explain.

2. M issues a negotiable promissory note payable to the order of P for the amount of $3,000. P raises the amount to $13,000 and negotiates it to H for $12,000.

(a) If H is a holder in due course, how much can he recover from M? How much from P? If M's negligence substantially contributed to the making of the alteration, how much can H recover from M and P, respectively?
(b) If H is not a holder in due course, how much can he recover from M? How much from P? If M's negligence substantially contributed to the making of the alteration, how much can H recover from M and P, respectively?

3. On December 2, 1981, Miles executed and delivered to Proctor a negotiable promissory note for $1,000, payable to Proctor or order, due March 2, 1982, with interest at 14% from maturity, in partial payment of a printing press. On January 3, 1982, Proctor, in need of ready cash, indorsed and sold the note to Hughes for $800. Hughes paid $600 in cash to Proctor on January 3 and agreed to pay the balance of $200 one week later, namely, on January 10. On January 6, Hughes learned that Miles claimed a breach of warranty by Proctor and, for this reason, intended to refuse to pay the note when it matured. On January 10, Hughes paid Proctor $200, conformably to their agreement of January 3. Following Mile's refusal to pay the note on March 2, 1982, Hughes sues Miles for $1,000. Decision?

4. X fraudulently represented to D that he would obtain for him a new car for $2,800 from P Motor Company. D thereupon executed his personal check for $2,800, payable to the order of P Motor Company, and delivered the check to X, who immediately delivered it to the Motor Company in payment of his own prior indebtedness. The Motor Company had no knowledge of the representations made by X to D. P Motor Company now brings an action on the check against D, who defends on the ground of failure of consideration. Decision?

5. Adams reads with difficulty. He arranged to borrow $200 from Bell. Bell prepared a note which Adams read laboriously. As Adams was about to sign it, Bell diverted Adams's attention and substituted the following paper, which was identical with the note Adams had read except that the amounts were different:

On June 1, 1982, I promise to pay Ben Bell or order Two Thousand Dollars with interest from date at 17%. This note is secured by certificate No. 13 for 100 shares of stock of Brookside Mills, Inc.

Adams did not detect the substitution, signed as maker, handed the note and stock certificate to Bell, and received from Bell $200. Bell indorsed and sold the paper to Fore, a holder in due course, who paid him $2,000. Fore presented the note at maturity to Adams who refused to pay. Fore gave notice of dishonor to Bell. What are Fore's rights, if any, against Adams?

6. John Ford sold a valuable painting to Max Moore who owned an art gallery. Ford took in payment Moore's negotiable promissory note dated March 1, 1982, for $1,000, payable to the order of Ford on April 1, 1982. Ford had stolen the painting from the Vale Museum. On March 19, Ford indorsed and delivered the note to Ronald Roy, who had no knowledge of Ford's improprieties, and who paid Ford $950 for the note. On April 20, Roy indorsed and delivered the note to his friend, Paul Peel, as a birthday present. Peel accepted the note as a gift, secretly knowing that Moore had executed it in reliance upon fraudulent misrepresentations of Ford. On April 21, Peel presented the note to Moore for payment, which was refused. Thereupon, Peel brought an appropriate action on the note against Moore. Decision?

7. On January 2, 1982, Martin, 17 years of age, as a result of Dealer's fraudulent misrepresentation, bought a used motor boat to use in his fishing business for $2,000 from Dealer, signed an installment contract for $1,500, and gave Dealer the following instrument as down payment:

> Dated: 1982
> I promise to pay to the order of Dealer, six months after date, the sum of $500 without interest. This is given as a down payment on installment contract for motor boat.
>
> (signed) Martin

Dealer, on July 1, sold his business to Henry, and included this note in the transaction. Dealer wrote on the back of the note the following: "Collection guaranteed. (signed) Dealer" and handed it to Henry. Henry left the note in his office safe. On July 10, Sharpie, an employee of Henry, without authority, stole the note and sold it to Bert for $300, indorsing the note "Sharpie." At the time, in Bert's presence, Sharpie filled in the date on the note as February 2, 1982. Bert demanded payment from Martin, who refused to pay.

What are Bert's rights against Martin? Please discuss.

8. M borrowed $1,000 from A. A, disturbed about M's ability to pay, demanded security. M indorsed and delivered to A a negotiable promissory note executed by T for $1,200 payable to M's order in 12 equal monthly installments. The note did not contain an acceleration clause, but it recited that the consideration for the note was M's promise to paint and shingle T's barn. At the time M transferred the note to A, the first installment was overdue and unpaid. A was unaware that the installment had not been paid. T did not pay any one of the installments on the note. When the last installment became due, A presented the note to T for payment. T refused upon the ground that M had not painted or reshingled his barn.

What are A's rights, if any, against T on the note?

9. M purchased a refrigerator for his home from P Appliance Store for $700. M paid $200 in cash and signed an installment contract for $500, which in its entirety stated:

> January 15, 1982
> I promise to pay to the order of P Appliance Store the sum of $500 in 10 equal monthly installments.
> (Signed) M

P negotiated the installment contract to H, who took the instrument for value in good faith and without notice of any claim or defense of any party. After paying two installments, the refrigerator ceased operating and M wishes to recover his downpayment, his first two monthly payments, and to discontinue further payments. What outcome?

10. Joseph Higbee executed and delivered to Robert Dudley the following instrument:

On September 19, 1982, I promise to pay $15,000 to Robert Dudley. (signed) Joseph Higbee.

This note was secured by a mortgage on Higbee's real property. Dudley altered the note and mortgage by changing the amount to $25,000 and the date to September 17, 1982. Dudley then sold the note and mortgage for $25,000 less 2% discount to Citizens Bank which was unaware of the alterations. Dudley assigned the mortgage to Citizens Bank and signed the reverse side of the note as follows: "I hereby assign this note to the order of Citizens Bank. (signed) Robert Dudley."

On September 8, 1982, Citizens Bank demanded payment of the note from Higbee. Higbee refused. On September 22, Citizens Bank notified Higbee that the note was in default and demanded payment from him. Higbee again refused. Citizens Bank thereupon brought an action against Higbee to recover $25,000 on the note. No action was taken by Citizens Bank to foreclose the mortgage.

What defenses, if any, may Higbee properly assert in this action?

11. Adams, by fraudulent representations, induced Barton to purchase 100 shares of the capital stock of the Evermore Oil Company. The shares were worthless. Barton executed and delivered to Adams a negotiable promissory note for $5,000 dated May 5, in full payment for the shares, due six months after date. On May 20, Adams indorsed and sold the note to Cooper for $4,800. On October 21, Barton, having learned that Cooper now held the note, notified Cooper of the fraud and stated he would not pay the note. On December 1, Cooper negotiated the note to Davis who, while not a party to had full knowledge of the fraud perpetrated on Barton. Upon refusal of Barton to pay the note, Davis sues Barton for $5,000. Decision?

Chapter
30

LIABILITY OF
PARTIES

The preceding chapters discussed the negotiability of commercial paper, the transfer of negotiable instruments, and the preferred position of a holder in due course. This chapter examines the liability of parties arising out of negotiable instruments and the ways in which liability may be terminated.

There are two types of potential liability associated with commercial paper: contractual liability and warranty liability. The basis for contract liability is provided in Section 3–401(1), which states that "[n]o person is liable on an instrument unless his signature appears thereon." Contractual liability is imposed by the operation of law upon those who sign a negotiable instrument. Some parties to a negotiable instrument never sign it and consequently never assume contractual liability.

On the other hand, warranty liability does not depend upon a party's signing the instrument and thus may be imposed upon both signers and non-signers. Warranty liability applies (1) to persons who transfer an insrument and (2) to persons who receive payment or acceptance of an instrument.

LIABILITY ON
THE INSTRUMENT

All parties whose signatures appear on a negotiable instrument, unless they disclaim liability, incur certain contractual obligations. The maker of a promissory note and the acceptor of a draft assume an absolute obligation to pay according to the tenor of the instrument at the time of their engagement. Drawers of drafts and checks order a drawee to pay their instruments without indicating their own liability in the event of non-payment. Indorsers may merely sign their names on the back of negotiable instruments, and these signatures, standing alone, do not fully reveal the indorsement contract. The contractual obligations of the maker, drawer, indorser, and acceptor are codified by the U.C.C.

SIGNATURE

The word "signature" is broadly defined to include any name, word, or mark, whether handwritten, typed, printed, or made in any other manner, if it is done with the present intention of authenticating the instrument. Section 3–401(2) and 1–201(39). The signature may be signed by the individual himself or on his behalf by the individual's authorized agent.

Authorized Signatures

Negotiable instruments are frequently executed by authorized agents or other representatives with a view to binding their principals only. Where the execution is done skillfully (e.g., "P, principal, by A, agent") and the agent is authorized to execute the instrument, the principal is liable and the agent is not liable. Occasionally, however, the agent, although fully authorized, uses a careless form of signature, and holders or prospective holders may be misled as to the identity of the party to be held.

Careless forms of signatures by agents are myriad, but they can be conveniently sorted into three groups. The first is where the agent signs his own name to an instrument intending to bind his principal, but neither the fact that the agent is signing in a representative capacity nor the name of the principal is revealed. For example, Adams, the agent of Prince, makes a note on behalf of Prince but signs it "Adams." The signature does not indicate that Adams has signed in a representative capacity or that he has made the instrument on behalf of Prince. In this situation the courts have universally held the agent alone is liable on the instrument. Prince may be liable to Adams or to a third party, but not on the instrument because his name does not appear on it.

The second type is that in which the authorized agent indicates that he is signing in a representative capacity, but does not disclose the name of his principal. For example, Adams, executing an instrument on behalf of Prince, merely signs it "Adams, agent." As between the immediate parties to the instrument, if the payee knows that Adams represents Prince, Prince is liable.

As to any subsequent party and to the payee if he does not know that Adams represents Prince, Prince is not liable and Adams alone is personally liable.

The third type of careless signatures involves signatures by agents which reveal their principal's name, but do not indicate that the agent has signed in a representative capacity. For example, Adams, signing an instrument on behalf of Prince, signs it "Adams and Prince." A holder might well think that Adams and Prince were comakers, and it would be unfair to let Adams exonerate himself from liability as against remote parties. Consequently, he is fully liable as to them. If the party who dealt with Adams knew he was acting on behalf of Prince without intending to incur personal liability, Adams may prove this fact by parol evidence and exonerate himself from liability as to this immediate party.

Unauthorized Signatures

A purported agent lacks authority to bind his principal but executes a negotiable instrument in the name of the principal and clearly reveals his own representative capacity. For example, Adams, without authority, signs Prince's name to an instrument, "Prince, by Adams, agent." Who is liable on such an instrument? Clearly not Prince. As to him, an unauthorized signature is no more binding than a forgery. Section 3–404(1) provides:

Any unauthorized signature * * * operates as the signature of the unauthorized signer in favor of any person who in good faith pays the instrument and takes it for value.

An unauthorized signature includes both a forgery and a signature made by an agent exceeding his actual or apparent authority. Notice the rule is broad enough to make an unauthorized signer liable whether or not his own name appears on the instrument. Thus, if Adams, without authority, merely signed Prince's name to an instrument, Adams would be liable on the instrument. The rule represents, therefore, an exception to the principle that only those whose names appear on a negotiable instrument can be liable thereon.   But the rule is consistent with the principle that someone must be liable on a negotiable instrument, a principle which would be defeated if a forger or unauthorized agent were permitted to escape liability on the instrument simply because his name did not appear on it.   Surely no public policy is violated in holding such a person personally liable on the instrument, and the rule has the advantage of supporting the concept of negotiability, for a holder at least has the assurance of knowing that someone will be liable on the instrument.

LIABILITY OF PRIMARY PARTIES

There is a primary party on every note: the maker.   The maker's commitment is unconditional.   No one, however, is primarily liable on a draft as issued; the drawer, the payee if he indorses it, and other indorsers are secondarily liable.   This is because their liability is subject to the conditions of presentment, dishonor, and notice of dishonor.   They do not unconditionally promise to pay the instrument, but expect the drawee-acceptor to pay.   The drawee is not liable on the instrument unless he accepts it.   He is free to pay or accept it as he sees fit, although by refusing to accept or pay it he may be liable to the drawer for breach of contract.   For example, a bank is not obligated to pay any check drawn upon it. To do so would be to obligate a bank to pay an instrument regardless of whether the drawer had an account at that bank or sufficient funds in his account.   On the other hand, if the drawer does have sufficient funds to cover the check, the drawee may nevertheless refuse to honor the instrument, but such dishonor will constitute a

breach of its contract of deposit with the drawer.

The refusal of the drawee to pay or accept the draft causes the drawer to become liable on the instrument upon receiving proper notice of dishonor.   If, on the other hand, the drawee accepts the draft, after which he is known as the acceptor, he becomes primarily liable on the instrument. Acceptance, or in the case of a check, certification, is the drawee's signed engagement to honor the draft as presented to him. Section 3–410(1).

Since the maker of a note and the acceptor of a draft are primarily liable, presentment (that is, a demand for payment) is not a condition to the right of the holder to recover from them.   While the holder usually makes a demand, there is no such requirement, nor need one be timely, and he may prefer to hold on to a "good" instrument for a period of time, thus accumulating interest.   Unless the maker knows the identity and address of the holder, or the note specifies a place of payment, he has no way to pay or tender payment of the instrument so as to avoid liability for the accruing interest.   Unlike parties who are secondarily liable, such as indorsers, he cannot claim discharge or excuse by the failure of the holder to present, because presentment and demand for payment is not a condition precedent to his liability.   He is liable absolutely.

Makers

Makers engage that they will pay the instrument according to its tenor at the time of their engagement.   Section 3–413(1).

Acceptors

A drawee has no liability on the instrument until he accepts it, at which time he becomes an acceptor and primarily liable.   Upon acceptance the acceptor becomes liable on the draft according to its terms at the time of the acceptance, Section 3–413.

The form or method of acceptance is related to the type of instrument. The holder of a sight draft ordinarily has no occasion to have the draft accepted rather than paid by the drawee when presented. The holder of a time draft, on the other hand, is entitled to the undertaking of the drawee to pay it when due. Some time drafts specifically require presentation for acceptance within a stated time.

Checks may be accepted by the drawee bank. Certification is the bank's promise to honor the check when subsequently presented for payment. Since a check is in essence a sight draft, the bank has no obligation to certify it. Section 3–411(2). The order upon the bank is to pay and if the bank is willing to pay, refusal to certify is not dishonor of the check.

Section 3–410 provides that an acceptance must be written on the draft. No writing separate from the draft, and no oral statement or conduct of the drawee will convert the drawee into an acceptor. The acceptance may take many forms. It may be printed on the face of the draft, ready for the drawee's signature. It may consist of a rubber stamp, with the signature of the drawee added. It may be the drawee's signature, preceded by a word or phrase such as "Accepted," "Certified" or "Good." It must not, however, bear any words indicating an intent to refuse to honor the draft. It has been held that a drawee's signature accompanied by the words "Kiss my foot" is not an acceptance. Norton v. Knapp, 64 Iowa 112, 19 N.W. 867 (1884). It may consist of nothing more than the drawee's signature. Normally, but by no means necessarily, an acceptance is written vertically across the face of the draft.

An acceptance is effective although the draft has not been signed by drawer or is otherwise incomplete or is overdue or has been dishonored. Section 3–410(2). It is as though the draft became a note on which the acceptor is the maker.

Where a check is certified at the request of the holder, the drawer and all prior indorsers are discharged. Section 3–411. The liability of indorsers subsequent to certification is not affected. Upon certification the bank withholds from the drawer's account sufficient funds to pay the check. Since the bank is primarily liable on its certification and has the funds and the drawer does not, the discharge is reasonable.

Certification at the request of the drawer does not relieve him of secondary liability on the instrument. For example, the drawer may have a check certified before using it to close a business transaction such as the purchase of a house. The seller requires that a bank be primarily liable, but since the drawer is then obtaining the benefit of the transaction, he should bear the risk of the bank's credit, rather than the payee.

Assume that Moe, a depositor in the Last National Bank, had $3,000 on deposit when the bank ceased operations because of insolvency. The bank proved to be 60% solvent. Two weeks prior to the bank's closing, Hume received two checks for $1,000 each from Moe drawn on the bank. Check No. 1 was certified by the bank at the request of Moe prior to Moe's delivery of the check to Hume. Check No. 2 was taken by Hume to the bank which certified it at Hume's request. When the bank went into receivership, Hume was the holder of both checks.

Since check No. 1 was certified at the request of Moe, the drawer, he remains secondarily liable on the instrument. The bank having certified the instrument is primarily liable. Hume may recover judgment against Moe for $1,000. Either Hume or Moe, or both, may file a claim in the insolvency proceedings against the bank for $1,000 upon which $600 is ultimately distributable. If Moe pays the judgment he is entitled to the $600 distribution. If he fails to do so, Hume will receive it and credit the amount against the unpaid judgment.

Since Hume, the holder, obtained the bank's certification of check No. 2, the drawer Moe is released from liability on that check. The bank is primarily liable. Hume is a general creditor of the bank to the extent of $1,000 and his only right is to file a claim and receive through the insolvency proceedings 60% ($600).

LIABILITY OF SECONDARY PARTIES

Indorsers and Drawers

Conditions precedent to the liability of secondary parties are presentment, prompt notice of dishonor, and in some situations, protest. If the instrument is not paid by a primary party and these conditions are satisfied, a secondary party who is not a qualified drawer or indorser is liable. The drawer engages that he will pay the amount of the draft to the holder, or any indorser who takes it up, unless he has disclaimed this liability by drawing without recourse. Section 3–413(2). Unless the indorsement otherwise specifies, as by using such words as "without recourse," every indorser engages that he will pay the instrument according to its tenor at the time of his indorsement to the holder or any subsequent indorser who takes it up. Section 3–414(1). The consequences of failing to comply with the condition precedents varies greatly between indorsers and drawers.

Conditions Precedent to Liability

Presentment. Presentment is a demand for acceptance or payment made upon the maker, acceptor, or drawee by the holder. Section 3–504. If there are two or more makers, acceptors, or drawees, presentment to one is sufficient. Section 3–504(3)(a).

Presentment may be made in any reasonable manner. The only specific requirement is that an accepted draft or a note made payable at a bank in the United States must be presented at such bank. Section 3–504(4). Otherwise, presentment may be made by mail, through a clearing house in a proper case, or at the place specified in the instrument, or if none is specified, at the place of business or residence of the acceptor or payor. Section 3–504(2).

When presentment is to be made is set forth in detail in Section 3–503. An instrument with a specified maturity date is due for presentment on that date. In any other case presentment is due within "a reasonable time". What is "a reasonable time" depends upon all the facts of the particular case, including the nature of the instrument and any usage of banking or trade.

In the case of an uncertified check, Section 3–503(2) is specific: a reasonable time for presentment for payment or to initiate the bank collection process is presumed to be:

(a) with respect to the liability of the drawer, thirty days after date or issue, whichever is later; and (b) with respect to the liability of an indorser, seven days after his indorsement.

A delay in presentment discharges the indorser; however, the drawer is discharged only to the extent of any loss suffered by reason of the delay. The difference in treatment between indorsers and drawers is based upon the simple fact that the drawer always expects to have to pay the check and the indorser has no reason to expect that he will ever be called upon to do so. Consequently, the latter should be given prompt notice of dishonor so that he may take immediate steps to assert his rights against other parties that he may charge with liability.

The discharge of one indorser, of course, does not mean that all are discharged. Assume that D draws a check payable to the order of P on March 1. P indorses it to A on March 3 and A indorses it to B on March 6. B must present the check by the 10th to hold P, but if he presents by the 13th he can hold A. If he waits until after the 13th, both parties are discharged unless B, who is now unaided by the presumption can show by affirmative evidence that the presentment was within a reasonable time. B, however, has thirty days within which to present it in order to hold D liable, this period being presumptively reasonable as to the drawer. If he did not present the check for payment until after March 31, D would be discharged only to the extent of any loss he might have suffered as the result of the delay, but not otherwise. The indorsers P and A, however, would be completely discharged by B's failure to make presentment within a reasonable time, irrespective of any showing of loss.

Presentments are of two types: presentment for acceptance and presentment for payment. Section 3–501(1).

Presentment of a draft for acceptance is necessary to charge secondary parties where the draft so provides, or is payable elsewhere than at the residence or place of business of the drawee, or its date of payment depends on such presentment, as in the case of a draft providing: "Seven days after acceptance pay * * *." Presentment for acceptance is also authorized in the case of any other time draft, although it is not required.

Presentment of any instrument for payment is necessary to charge any indorser, although an exception exists in the case of an instrument indorsed after maturity. Failure to present for payment does not discharge the drawer, however, except to the extent, as indicated above, that there was unreasonable delay in presenting a draft to a bank where funds were available for its payment and the bank became insolvent in the interim.

Although the drawee may be willing to accept the draft in strict accordance with its terms, he nevertheless has certain rights which he is entitled to exercise before he commits himself. These rights, the exercise of which in no sense constitutes a dishonor, are set out in Sections 3–505 and 3–506. He may require exhibition of the instrument, its production at a proper place, reasonable identification of the person mak-

ing presentment, and upon payment, a signed receipt, with surrender of the instrument if it is paid in full. Failure to comply with any of these requests invalidates the presentment, and consequently there can be no dishonor. The person making presentment is entitled to a reasonable opportunity to comply with any such requests, and the time for making presentment is extended accordingly.

Acceptance may be deferred until the close of the next business day following a proper presentment, thereby giving the drawee the opportunity to check back with the drawer or to take any other steps he may desire to assure himself of the propriety of acceptance. Conversely, the holder is authorized to allow postponement of acceptance for an additional business day in a good faith effort to obtain acceptance. For example, the drawee may refuse to accept without verification from the drawer and be unable to get in touch with him. He would either have to dishonor the instrument or ask the holder for an additional day. If the holder grants it, there is no dishonor.

Payment of an instrument may be deferred without dishonor pending reasonable examination to determine whether the instrument is properly payable, but payment must be made in any event before the close of business on the day of presentment.

Notice of Dishonor. An instrument is dishonored when presentment has been duly made and acceptance or payment is refused or cannot be obtained within the prescribed time, or presentment is excused and the instrument is not duly accepted or paid. Section 3–507(1). Return for lack of a proper indorsement is not dishonor.

Upon proper presentment and dishonor, and subject to any necessary notice of dishonor and protest, the holder has an immediate right of recourse against drawers and indorsers upon giving them seasonable notice of presentment and dishonor.

Such notice is necessary to charge any indorser. It is also necessary with respect to any drawer or the acceptor of a draft payable at a bank who because of insolvency of the bank is deprived of funds which he maintained at the bank to cover the instrument. Section 3–502(1)(b).

Notice of dishonor is normally given by the holder or by an indorser who has himself received notice. For example, M makes a note payable to the order of P; P indorses it to A; A indorses it to B; B indorses it to H, the last holder; H timely presents it to M, who refuses payment. H may give notice of dishonor to all secondary parties: P, A, and B. If he is satisfied that B will pay him, he may only notify B. B then must see to it that A or P is notified, or B will have no recourse. He may notify either or both. If he notifies A only, A will have to see to it that P is notified, or A will have no recourse.

If, in this hypothetical problem, H notifies P alone, A and B are discharged. P cannot complain, because he has no claim against A or B who indorsed subsequently to him. It cannot matter to P that he is compelled to pay H rather than A, and therefore subsequent parties are permitted to skip intermediate indorsers if they want to discharge them and are willing to look solely to prior indorsers for recourse.

Section 3–508(1) further permits any party who may be compelled to pay the instrument to notify any party who may be liable on it. Thus an indorser who has not himself received notice may give notice, and one may notify another who is not liable to him.

Section 3–508(2) provides that any necessary notice must be given by a bank before midnight on the next banking day following the banking day on which it receives notice of dishonor, and by any other person before midnight of the third business day after dishonor or receipt of notice of dishonor. Written notice is effective when sent regardless of whether it is received. Suppose that D draws a check on Y bank payable to the order of P; P indorses to A; A deposits it to his account in X bank; X bank properly presents it to Y bank, the drawee; Y bank dishonors it because the drawer, D, has insufficient funds on deposit to cover it. Y bank has until midnight of the following day to notify X bank A, P, or D of the dishonor. X bank has until midnight of the day after receipt of notice of dishonor to notify A, P, or D of the dishonor. That is, if X received the notice of dishonor on Monday, it would have until midnight of Tuesday to notify A, P, or D. If it failed to notify A, it could not charge the item back to him. But A has until midnight of the third business day after receipt of notice of dishonor to notify P or D. If he received notice on Tuesday, he would have until midnight on Friday to notify P or D. P would also have three business days in which to notify D.

Parties other than banks are given additional time to give notice of dishonor because they are normally not in the business of handling commercial paper, whereas banks are. Consequently, other parties are given additional time to find out what they need to do, and under most circumstances they will have time to take care of the matter by an ordinary business letter.

Frequently, notice of dishonor is given by returning the unpaid instrument with a stamp, ticket or memorandum attached stating that the item was not paid and requesting that the recipient make good on it. Section 3–508(3). But since the purpose of notice is to give knowledge of dishonor and to inform the secondary party that he may be held on the instrument, any kind of notice which so informs is sufficient. No formal requisites are imposed—notice may be given in any reasonable manner. An oral notice is sufficient, but it may be difficult to prove. Consequently, one is not advised to use it, and oral notification has little place in the business world, except as a mere preliminary to be followed by a more formal statement in writing.

If the person notified is not misled, a misdescription of the instrument does not defeat the notice. Section 3–508(3). Thus, if a payee of a promissory note executed on January 3 by Mike Maker is told that the "note of January 5 made by Mike Maker" has been dishonored, this would constitute a sufficient notice if the recipient knew that the dishonor related to Mike Maker's note dated January 3. Furthermore, notice operates for the benefit of all parties who have rights against the party notified. Section 3–508(8). For example, M makes a note payable to the order of P; P indorses it to A; A indorses it to H. H duly presents the note to M who dishonors it. H notifies both P and A of the dishonor, and then asks A to pay him. A does so. Can A now hold P? The answer is yes. A does not have to notify P of the dishonor. P already has been notified of it by H.

Protest. A protest is a certificate of dishonor made under the hand and seal of a United States consul or vice consul or a notary public or other person authorized to certify to a dishonor by the law of the place where the dishonor occurred. It may be made upon information satisfactory to such person. It must identify the instrument and certify either that due presentment has been made or the reason why it is excused and that the instrument has been dishonored by non-acceptance or non-payment. The protest may also certify that notice of dishonor has been given to all parties or to specified parties. Protest, or the noting for protest, must be made at a point of time proximate to the time of dishonor, so that the facts are fresh in the mind of the notary or the one making it. Therefore, subsections 3–509(4) and (5) require the protest to be made or noted within the time allowed for giving notice of dishonor. Protest is only required where the draft is drawn or payable outside the United States. In addition, any holder may, at his option make protest of any dishonor. Since protest is basically eviden-

tiary in character, it may dispense with the necessity for depositions and other expensive means of obtaining evidence.

When Presentment, Notice of Dishonor, and Protest Are Excused. Section 3–511(1) outlines two situations in which presentment, notice and protest are excused. The first excuses a delay where the holder does not have notice that the instrument is due, for example, an instrument may provide that its maturity shall be automatically accelerated upon the happening of a particular event. If the holder does not know that this event has happened, he is excused from presentment until he learns of the acceleration, and secondary parties are not discharged because of the delay. Once the holder learns that the event has occurred, he must present the note within a reasonable time and give prompt notice of dishonor to hold the indorsers liable.

The second situation excuses the holder's delay where it is caused by circumstances beyond his control. For example, suppose the holder cannot present the instrument to the primary party because a storm has disrupted all means of communication and transportation. He should be excused, in such a case, until the effect of the storm is over, at which time he must exercise reasonable diligence to present it. The circumstances need not make presentment impossible. It is enough if they are of the degree and character which would deter men of ordinary prudence, energy, and courage from encountering them in the pursuit of business.

Section 3–511(2)(b) entirely excuses the holder from presentment, notice, or protest if the secondary party to be charged has himself dishonored the instrument or has countermanded payment, or if the holder otherwise has no reason to expect the instrument to be accepted or paid. If, for example, D draws a check on a bank with which he has no account, or has closed his account, or has stopped payment on the check, he is not entitled to a due presentment and notice of dishonor. These matters are entirely excused so far as he is concerned. But they would not be excused as to intermediate indorsers who did not have any reason to expect that the instrument would not be accepted or paid.

Subsection 3–511(2)(c) entirely excuses a presentment, notice or protest, as the case may be, if these things cannot be accomplished by reasonable diligence. For example, if the maker of a note has "departed for places unknown" and cannot be located by reasonable diligence, the holder has no way of making a presentment to him. In such case, presentment is entirely excused, and the holder should treat the instrument as dishonored and give prompt notice of dishonor to indorsers. If one of the indorsers cannot be located by reasonable diligence, notice of dishonor would not have to be given to him—it would be entirely excused.

Subsection 3–511(3) sets out some additional situations in which *presentment* is entirely excused. These situations, which do not excuse notice or protest, include the following: (1) The maker, acceptor or drawee (except in the case of a documentary draft) is dead or in insolvency proceedings; or (2) the primary party refuses payment or acceptance for reasons not relating to presentment, making it clear that a subsequent presentment would be a useless ceremony.

Waiver of Presentment, Notice, and Protest. Presentment, notice and protest may also be waived. Section 3–511(2)(a). A drawer or indorser who waives all of these conditions becomes almost indistinguishable from a primary party, such as a maker, who has no conditions precedent to his liability.

Waivers are of two types, express and implied. Express waivers have not caused much difficulty. Usually, they are stated in terms such as "Presentment, notice and protest waived" or "Protest waived." Where such language appears on the face of the

instrument it is deemed to bind all parties. Where it is written above the signature of an indorser, it binds him only. Section 3–511(6). Waivers are customarily provided for in standard forms of notes used by banks and other financial institutions.

It is possible to waive all conditions or only some conditions. For example, an indorser could waive notice of dishonor, but require the holder to make a due presentment to hold him. Most of the difficulty with express waivers has involved an interpretation of the language to determine which conditions have or have not been waived.

Under Section 3–511(5) of the U.C.C. it is provided that a waiver of protest is also a waiver of presentment and of notice of dishonor even though protest is not required. This rule is based upon the common commercial understanding of the term "Protest waived."

Disclaimer of Liability by Secondary Parties

Both drawers and indorsers may disclaim their normal secondary liability by drawing or indorsing instruments "without recourse." Sections 3–413(2), 3–414(1). The use of the words "without recourse," is understood in commercial circles to place purchasers on notice that they may not rely on the credit of the person using this language, but may look only to the other parties to the instrument. A person drawing or indorsing an instrument in this manner does not incur the normal contractual liability of a drawer or indorser to pay the instrument but, as will appear later, he may be liable for breach of warranty under certain circumstances.

LIABILITY OF ACCOMMODATION PARTIES

Accommodation parties are those who sign a negotiable instrument for the purpose of lending their credit to another party to it.

Section 3–415. They may be makers or co-makers, drawers or co-drawers, or indorsers. When an instrument has been taken for value before it is due, the accommodation party is liable in the capacity in which he signed. It is immaterial that the taker knew of the accommodation.

Frequently, one or more persons indorse an instrument to accommodate another party, rather than sign as maker. Suppose M wants to borrow money from P, and P insists that M procure the signatures of A, B, C, and D before the loan is made. M asks these parties to accommodate him, and, pursuant to the agreement with P, M makes the note and A, B, C, and D sign their names on the back of it in that order. A, B, C, and D by reason of signing on the back are liable to P as indorsers. M is liable to P and to A, B, C, and D, if these accommodating parties pay the instrument.

Suppose M becomes insolvent so that the reimbursement rights that A, B, C, and D have against him are meaningless. Suppose that P enforces the note against D. Can D pass the loss on to C? May C shift it to B? Would A ultimately be out-of-pocket simply because he signed first? Parol evidence would be admissible to show that the indorsers had agreed to share the loss equally or in some other proportion, if that is the case. If they made no agreement among themselves the rule of indorsers-liability-in-order-of-signature should not apply. The law of suretyship which applies to accommodation parties is based upon concepts of equity and fairness which would not be consistent with having the rights of these sureties among themselves depend upon the accidental or fortuitous order in which they signed the instrument. Although each is liable to the holder for the full amount, they should share the loss equally, and one who is required to pay more than his share is entitled to recover ratably from the others. Accommodation parties are sureties, and the law of suretyship has long recognized the right of contribution among co-sureties.

LIABILITY OF PARTIES FOR CONVERSION

"Conversion" is a tort whereby a person becomes liable in damages by reason of his wrongful exercise of dominion over the personal property of another. If the latter suffers loss as a result, he may recover in an action at law.

Section 3–419 provides that a conversion occurs in three situations: (a) when a drawee to whom a draft is delivered for acceptance refuses to return it on demand; (b) when any person to whom an instrument is delivered for payment refuses on demand either to pay or to return it; and (c) when an instrument is paid on a forged indorsement. Situations (a) and (b) involve wilful action on the part of the party guilty of the conversion, whereas in situation (c) the payor's action was in all probability completely innocent as his dominion over the instrument resulted in an unrecognized break in the chain of title. Nevertheless, the liability is the same in all three cases: good faith is completely immaterial.

Where the action in conversion is brought against the drawee, the measure of liability is the face amount of the instrument. In any other action for conversion of commercial paper, the measure of liability is presumed to be the face amount of the instrument, but the defendant may establish a lesser liability if he can.

SPECIAL SITUATIONS AFFECTING LIABILITY

If a drawee on a draft or check pays it, the drawer is under a duty to make reimbursement. Usually, the drawer has funds in the hands of the drawee, and the drawee honoring a draft or check reimburses itself immediately by charging the drawer's account or his funds. The drawee can be reimbursed, however, only if it acts in accordance with the drawer's order as it appears on the draft. Thus, if Davis draws a check to the order of Jones, the drawee bank to whom the instrument is addressed acquires no right of reimbursement by paying Roe, unless Jones has indorsed the check to Roe. In short, it is up to the drawee to determine whether the one presenting the item for payment or acceptance has rights in it, for if it pays the wrong party, it is the drawee's loss and not the drawer's. Two situations involving these principles have been especially troublesome.

The Imposter Rule

Usually, this rule comes into play in situations involving a confidence man who impersonates a respected citizen and who deceives a third party into delivering a negotiable instrument to the imposter in the name of the respected citizen. For instance, John Doe, falsely representing himself as Richard Roe, a creditor of Ray Davis, induces Davis to draw a check payable to the order of Richard Roe and to deliver it to him. Doe then forges Roe's name to the check and presents it to the drawee for payment. The drawee pays it. Subsequently, the drawer denies the drawee's right of reimbursement upon the ground that the drawee did not pay in accordance with his order: the drawer ordered payment to Roe, or to Roe's order. Roe did not order payment to anyone; therefore, the drawee would not acquire a right of reimbursement against the drawer Davis. This is the argument in favor of the drawer and is supported by the general rule governing unauthorized signatures.

However, Section 3–405(1)(a) provides that the indorsement of the imposter or of any other person, in the name of the named payee is effective if an imposter has induced the maker or drawer to issue the instrument to him or his confederate using the name of the payee. It is as if the named payee had indorsed the instrument. The reason for this rule is that the drawer or maker is to blame for failing to detect the impersona-

tion by the impostor. Thus, in the above example, the drawee would be able to debit the drawer's account.

The Fictitious Payee Rule

The second situation is similar, only it involves a faithless agent rather than an impostor. For instance, the drawer's agent falsely tells the drawer that money is owed to X, and the drawer draws a check payable to the order of X and hands it to the agent for delivery to X. The agent forges X's name to the check and obtains payment from the drawee bank.

The drawer then denies the bank's claim to reimbursement upon the ground that the latter did not comply with his order; that the drawer had ordered payment to X or order; that the drawee did not make payment either to X or as ordered by X inasmuch as the forgery of X's signature is wholly inoperative; that the drawee paid in accordance with the scheme of the faithless agent, and not in compliance with the drawer's order.

Once again, the drawee bank will be able to debit the drawer's account. Section 3–405(1)(c) provides that "an indorsement by any person in the name of a named payee is effective if * * * an agent or employee of the maker or drawer has supplied him with the name of the payee intending the latter to have no such interest." The risk of employee fraud presents business risks which the Code imposes upon the party employing the agent.

Section 3–405(1)(b) deals with the analogous situation in which "a person signing as or on behalf of a maker or drawer intends the payee to have no interest in the instrument." In such situations any person's indorsement in the name of the named payee is effective. For instance, P gives A, his employee, authority to write checks in order to pay P's debts. A writes a check for $2,000 to F, a fictitious payee, which A takes and indorses in F's name to A. A cashes the check at P's bank.   P's bank can debit P's account.   P should bear the risk of his unscrupulous employees.

LIABILITY BASED ON WARRANTY

A draft or note is not only the written evidence of contract liability but it is also a special kind of property intended for trading and having marketability.   Just as certain implied warranties under the Code attach to the sale of goods, certain warranties imposed by the Code attach to the sale of commercial paper.   These warranties are effective whether or not the transferor or presenter signs the instrument, although as will be seen, the extent of the warranty to subsequent holders does depend upon whether they have indorsed the instrument. There are two types of warranties: (a) transferor's warranties and (b) presenter's warranties.

WARRANTIES ON TRANSFER

Any person who transfers an instrument, whether by negotiation or assignment, and receives value makes certain warranties. Section 3–417(2).   The requirement that he receive value is intended to eliminate the warranty liability of an accommodation party and of a donor.

Warranties on transfer run to the immediate transferee only if transfer is by delivery alone, but if the transfer is made by indorsement, whether qualified or unqualified, the warranties run to "any subsequent holder who takes the instrument in good faith."

Section 3–417(2)(a)–(e) lists the warranties of the transferor whether the indorsement is qualified or unqualified or the transfer is by mere delivery.

Good Title

Subsection (a) imposes a warranty that the transferor has good title to the instrument or is authorized to obtain payment or acceptance on behalf of one who has good title and the transfer is otherwise rightful.   Under this rule, if M makes a note payable to the order of P which is stolen from the latter and the thief forges P's indorsement and sells the instrument to A, A does not have good title.   The break in the indorsement chain prevents him from acquiring title. If A indorses the instrument over to B for value, B can hold A for breach of warranty. The warranty action is important to B, because it enables him to hold A liable, even if A has indorsed the note "without recourse."

Signatures Genuine

In the foregoing situation the warranty imposed by subsection (b) that *all* signatures are genuine or authorized would also be breached.   However, if the signature of a maker, drawer, drawee, acceptor, or indorser not in the chain of title is unauthorized, there is a breach of this warranty but no breach of the warranty of title.

Material Alteration

Subsection (c) provides a warranty against material alteration.   Suppose that M makes a note payable to the order of the payee in the amount of $100.   The payee, without authority, raises the note so that it appears to be drawn for $1,000 and negotiates the instrument to A, who buys it innocent of the alteration.   A, indorsing "without recourse," negotiates the instrument to B for value.   B presents the instrument to M, who refuses to pay more than $100 on it. B can collect the difference from A.   While A is not liable to B on the indorsement contract due to his qualified indorsement, he is liable to him upon the warranty.   If A had not qualified his indorsement, B would be able to recover against A on either the basis of warranty or the indorsement contract.

No Defenses

Subsection (d) imposes a warranty that no defense of any party is good against the transferor. Under this subsection, a transferor who indorses "without recourse" stands in a better position than an unqualified indorser. His warranty is only that he has no knowledge of any such defense. Section 3–417(3). Suppose that M, a minor, a resident of a State where minors' contracts for non-necessaries are void, in payment of a motorcycle, makes a note payable to bearer; P, the first holder, negotiates it to A by mere delivery; A indorses it "without recourse" (qualified indorsement) and negotiates it to B; B unqualifiedly indorses it to H. H cannot recover upon the instrument against M because of M's minority (a real defense). H therefore recovers against B on either the breach of warranty that no valid defenses exist to the instrument or the indorsement contract, after giving him prompt notice of dishonor. B cannot recover against A upon A's qualified indorsement. Can B hold A for breach of warranty? Since A indorsed without recourse, he does not warrant that the instrument is defenseless; he only warrants that he knows of no defense which is good against him. Assuming that A did not know that M was a minor, B cannot hold A for breach of warranty. Can B hold P? Surely P is not liable as an indorser, because he did not indorse the instrument. While he must warrant as a transferor that there are no defenses good against him, this warranty only extends to his immediate transferee, A. Therefore, B cannot hold P. This illustration shows the interplay between indorsement and warranty liability and the relationship between the liability imposed under the various warranties and the individuals who can or cannot claim protection under a particular warranty.

No Knowledge of Insolvency

Any person who transfers a negotiable instrument warrants that he has no knowledge of any insolvency proceedings instituted with respect to the maker or acceptor or the drawer of an unaccepted instrument. Section 3–417(2)(e). Thus, if M makes a note payable to bearer, and the first holder, P, negotiates it without indorsement to A, who then negotiates it by qualified indorsement to B, both P and A make a warranty that they do not know that M is in bankruptcy. However, B could not hold P for breach of warranty, since P's warranty runs only in favor of his immediate transferee, A. If B should hold A liable on his warranty, A could thereupon hold P, his immediate transferor, liable.

WARRANTIES ON PRESENTMENT

All parties called upon to pay or accept an instrument must do so strictly in compliance with the order given. The drawee bank agrees to pay checks as ordered by the depositor so long as his account is sufficient to cover them. If the bank pays other than pursuant to the depositor's order, it cannot charge the payment to the depositor's account.

If a drawee pays an instrument which has been forged or altered, he has the initial loss, for he cannot charge this amount to the drawer. May the drawee shift this loss to a holder in due course who received the payment? With respect to instruments on which the drawer's signature has been forged, the answer is "no." The drawee can, however, recover from a holder or even a holder in due course to whom it made payment any loss incurred because of a forged indorsement or an alteration of the instrument.

For example, suppose D's (drawer's) name is forged to a check so as to make it appear that it was drawn by him. If the bank pays this check, it cannot charge D's account, nor recover from a holder in due course to whom it made the payment. Similarly, if a drawee pays a draft purportedly drawn by D, it cannot seek reimbursement from D if D's signature is forged. The justification for the rule is that the drawee is supposed to know the drawer's signature. On the other hand, if D draws a check to P or order, and P's indorsement is forged, the bank does not follow D's order in paying such an item, and hence cannot charge his account (except in the impostor or faithless employee situations discussed above). The bank, however, can recover from a holder in due course of the check the payment made to him. The bank should not be required to bear this loss, because it should not be expected to know the signature of payees of checks although it should know the signatures of its own customers (drawers).

The same rationale applies to raised instruments. If D makes a check to P's order in the amount of $3 and it is raised so as to appear to be in the amount of $300, the bank cannot charge the $300 it pays out on such an item to the drawer's account. It can only charge the account to the extent of $3, because that is all the drawer ordered it to pay. On the other hand, the bank can charge back the difference against the presenting party who received payment from it.

The examples to this point have involved drawees. Suppose that it is the maker of a note who pays on a forged indorsement or an altered item. The maker, like the drawee, cannot know everyone's signature, and where the indorser's signature is forged, the maker can recover any money paid to the presenting party. The situation is different where the amount of the note has been raised. Suppose that the maker makes a note in the amount of $300 and it is raised to $3,000. If he pays this note, he is not permitted to recover from an innocent presenting party, because the maker—unlike a drawee—has a way of knowing the original principal amount of the instrument. Similarly, suppose that a check or draft is raised *after* it has been accepted or certified by the drawee. If the

drawee pays the raised amount to an innocent presenting party, the drawee is not entitled to recover the amount by which the instrument was raised because it has a way of knowing the proper amount of this item.

The rule of Price v. Neale and all its modifications and developments as described above have been incorporated in Section 3–417(1) as limitations on the warranties given to a party who in good faith pays or accepts an instrument. These warranties, as so limited, run not only from the person who obtains payment or acceptance, but also from any prior transferor. These presentment warranties are as follows.

Good Title

Subsection (a) of Section 3–417(1) extends the same warranty of good title to persons who pay or accept as is granted to transferees under subsection (a) of Section 3–417(2). Moreover, the warranty extends to the genuineness of the indorsers' signatures, but *not* to the signature of the drawer or maker.

Genuineness of Signature of Maker and Drawer

A person who presents an instrument knowing that the signature of the maker or drawer is forged or unauthorized is committing an obvious fraud and consequently subsection (b) imposes a warranty that the presenter has no knowledge that the signature of the maker or drawer is unauthorized. To protect a person who takes an instrument in good faith and later learns it was forged, and in keeping with Price v. Neale, certain exceptions to the warranty of subsection (b) are specified. A holder in due course acting in good faith does not give such a warranty to the maker of a note, to the drawer of a draft, even if he is also the drawee, or to the acceptor of a draft if such holder took the draft after acceptance or obtained the acceptance without knowledge of the unauthorized signature. Only a holder in due course can avail himself of these exceptions.

Material Alteration

Subsection (c) imposes a warranty against material alteration, but again it is not given by a holder in due course to a maker, or drawer, whether or not the drawer is also the drawee. Further, the holder in due course does not give this warranty to the acceptor of a draft with respect to an alteration made prior to acceptance if such holder took after acceptance, even though the acceptance included a term such as "payable as originally drawn." The acceptor had the first opportunity to detect the alteration. To permit the acceptor to shift the responsibility for a prior material alteration to a subsequent party would defeat the entire purpose of acceptance and certification. An acceptance or certification must constitute a definite commitment to honor a definite instrument.

This rule should not be confused with that which applies where the alteration is made *after* the acceptance or certification. In such a situation, the drawee knows the amount of the original acceptance or certification and he should not be able to charge back against an innocent party if he pays out more than that amount. Hence, a holder in due course does not warrant against post-acceptance or post-certification alterations.

DAMAGES FOR BREACH OF WARRANTY

Damages for breach of warranty are computed by determining the difference between the value of the instrument in its present state and the value it would have had if the warranty had not been breached. Usually warranty damages equal the face amount of the instrument, but this is not always the case.

For example, F forges M's name to a $1,000 note payable to the order of P and sells it to P. P indorses the note "without recourse" to A. Upon presentment, M refuses to pay A, setting up the defense of forgery. A cannot sue P on the indorsement contract, because it has been disclaimed by the qualified indorsement. The instrument is not genuine, however, and P has therefore breached his warranty of genuineness. A can recover $1,000 from P, because this represents the difference between the value of the note as it is (worthless) and the value it would have had if the warranty had not been breached—that is, the value it would have had if M's signature were genuine ($1,000).

Suppose, however, that M had become insolvent as of the time of presentment, so that, even if his signature had been genuine, A could only have collected $300 on it (M is able to pay only 30 cents on the dollar to creditors). In such a case A can collect from P only $300. The point was well illustrated in the case of McNaghten Loan Co. v. Sandifer, 137 Kan. 353, 20 P.2d 523 (1933). The maker's signature had been forged in that case, and he subsequently became insolvent and could pay his creditors only part of their claims. The court refused to allow a holder to recover the full amount of the instrument against an indorser by reason of the breach of warranty of genuineness, but limited recovery to the amount that the holder could have collected from the maker had the latter's signature not been forged.

TERMINATION OF LIABILITY

Sooner or later, every commercial transaction must come to rest, with the potential liabilities of the parties to the instrument terminated. One aspect of this is covered by Section 3–418. Except for the presentment warranties, a holder in due course has no further liability to an acceptor or payor after acceptance or payment: The payment or acceptance is final. The payor or acceptor cannot thereafter recover even though he discovers he has paid or accepted an instrument with a forged drawer's or maker's signature, or he has paid a check over a stop order. The provisions of this section also run in favor of a person who in good faith has changed his position in reliance on the payment or acceptance.

The Code specifies the various methods and extent whereby the liability of any party, primary or secondary, and of all parties, is discharged. Section 3–601. However, no discharge of a party is effective against a subsequent holder in due course unless he has knowledge thereof when he takes the instrument. Section 3–602.

PAYMENT OR SATISFACTION

The most obvious way for a party to discharge his liability on an instrument is to pay the holder. Section 3–603. Such a payment results in a discharge even though it is made with knowledge of the claim of another person to the instrument unless such other person either supplies adequate indemnity or obtains an injunction in a proceeding to which the holder is made a party. The person making payment is not required to decide at his peril whether the claim to the instrument is valid or not. Such a claim may arise, for example, where the prior holder contends the instrument was stolen from him.

The person making payment should, of course, take up the instrument so that it cannot pass into the hands of a subsequent holder in due course, against whom his discharge would be ineffective.

TENDER OF PAYMENT

Any party liable on an instrument who makes tender of full payment to a holder when or after payment is due is discharged to the extent of all subsequent liability for interest, costs and attorney's fees. Section 3–604(1). He does not, however, relieve himself of his liability for the face amount of the instrument or any interest accrued thereon to that time. The maker or acceptor may, however, have no way of seeking out a holder so as to make tender to stop the running of interest. Subsection (3) of Section 3–604 solves this problem by providing that if such party is ready and able to pay a time instrument when it is due at the place of payment specified in the instrument, it is the equivalent of tender. This remedy is not available in the case of demand paper or paper which does not specify a place of payment.

Occasionally a holder will refuse a tender of payment for reasons known only to himself. It may be that he believes he has rights over and beyond the amount of the tender, or because he desires to enforce payment against another party. In any event, his refusal of the tender has the effect of wholly discharging every party who has a right of recourse against the party making tender. Section 3–604(2). For example, a note executed by M in favor of P is negotiated by indorsement successively to A, B and H. M defaults, and H perfects his rights against indorsers P, A, and B. If P tenders full payment to H and H refuses to accept it, desiring to collect from M, A and B are wholly discharged. The reason is that both A and B would have rights of recourse against P if they were required to pay.

CANCELLATION
AND RENUNCIATION

Section 3–605 provides that a holder may discharge the liability of any one or more parties to an instrument, or that of all parties in any manner apparent on the face of the instrument or the indorsement, by cancelling the instrument or the signature of the party or parties to be discharged, by destruction or mutilation of the instrument, or by striking out a party's signature.

Since the instrument itself constitutes the obligation, intentional cancellation of it by the holder results in a discharge of all parties. Accidental destruction of an instrument does not have such an effect, nor does cancellation in any form by anyone other than the holder.

If the holder wishes to discharge one, but not all parties, he may merely strike out that party's signature. He must be careful, however, that he does not discharge other parties as well by impairing their rights of recourse, as discussed below.

A holder may also renounce his rights by a writing signed and delivered, or by surrender of the instrument, to the party to be discharged. As in the case of other discharges, however, a written renunciation is of no effect as against a subsequent holder in due course who takes without knowledge of it.

Cancellation or renunciation is effective, even without consideration.

IMPAIRMENT OF RECOURSE OR COLLATERAL

If the holder collects the amount of an instrument from an indorser, the latter normally has a right of recourse against parties primarily liable, prior indorsers, if any, the drawer, in the case of a draft, or any one or more of them. At the time such indorser accepted the instrument, he relied upon the credit of the prior parties, the strict nature of their liability, and, in the case of an instrument secured by collateral, on the value of that collateral.

If any of these rights is adversely affected by the action or inaction of the holder, the indorser should not be required to pay the instrument, for when he thereafter seeks reimbursement, he will not possess the rights he bargained for at the time he accepted the instrument. The same rule applies to an accommodation maker or acceptor known to the holder to be such.

Section 3–606 provides that the holder discharges any party to the instrument to the extent that without his consent the holder

1. Releases or agrees not to sue any person against whom such party, to the knowledge of the holder, has a right of recourse;
2. Agrees to suspend the right to enforce against such person the instrument or collateral;
3. Otherwise discharges such person; or
4. Unjustifiably impairs any collateral given by or on behalf of the party or any person against whom such party has a right of recourse.

As indicated above, striking out the signature of a prior indorser discharges subsequent indorsers who have a right of recourse against the indorser discharged.

Similarly, if the holder suspends the right to enforce the instrument, as by granting an unauthorized extension of time to pay, the subsequent indorsers are discharged. Their undertaking is only to pay if the maker or drawee does not pay on demand or on the date specified in a time instrument. They have not contracted for any extension of the time for payment. The discharge of the indorser is based upon principles of suretyship law.

The holder may, however, take any of the first three steps indicated above without discharging a party with a right of recourse if at the same time he expressly reserves his rights against such party. In so doing, he cannot, of course, impair any rights of recourse which such party may possess against others.

OTHER METHODS OF DISCHARGE

Other methods by which a party's liability may be discharged include:

1. Discharge of intervening parties upon reacquisition of an instrument by a prior holder.   Section 3–208.

2. Fraudulent and material alteration.   Section 3–407.

3. Discharge of the drawer and prior indorsers by a check certification procured by a holder.   Section 3–411.

4. Acceptance varying a draft.   Section 3–412.

5. Unexcused delay in presentment, notice of dishonor or protest.   Section 3–502.

Any party may also be discharged as against another party by an act or agreement with such party which would discharge a simple contract for the payment of money.

Cases

Signature

NATIONAL BANK OF GEORGIA v. AMENT

(1973) 27 Ga.App. 838, 195 S.E.2d 202.

STOLZ, J.

* * *

The payee bank sued R & A Concrete Contractors, Inc. and John Ament on a promissory note allegedly executed by the defendant corporation and personally indorsed by defendant Ament.   On the face of the note (attached as an exhibit) the first two lines provided for the makers are filled in with "R & A Concrete" (handwritten) on the first line, and "By: Grover Roberts" (signature) with the name typed thereunder on the second line.   The third line is blank, except that the typed in "Grover Roberts" partially fills that space.   On the reverse side of the note, the following appears: "X John Ament Sec. & Treas."

The trial judge granted defendant Ament's motion to dismiss on the ground that the qualified signature on the reverse side of the note in no way makes him personally liable thereon, from which judgment the plaintiff bank appeals.   *Held*:

Even though the instrument may name the person represented, the one who signs in a representative capacity may still be personally liable on the instrument if, by his manner of signing in a representative capacity, he does not clearly indicate that he is signing in a representative capacity. [Citation.]   Although defendant Ament's indorsement was followed by the notation "Sec. & Treas.," apparently connoting his representative capacity, a jury should consider all of the circumstances of his signing, including the facts that the complete, correct name of the corporate defendant maker was not utilized; that Ament indorsed the note on its reverse side, rather than on the line for maker on the face of the note; and that he (or someone else) may have considered there to have been insufficient space in which to indorse on the face of the note.

* * *

Judgment reversed.

Acceptors

LAWLESS v. TEMPLE

(1926) 254 Mass. 395, 150 N.E. 176, 48 A.L.R. 758.

PIERCE, J.

This is an action by the payee of a bill of exchange against the drawee.   The bill is as follows:

Natick, Sept. 24, 1923.

Maurice E. Temple

Please pay to the order of Hazel Lawless $351.50/100 three hundred and fifty one dollars & 50/100

Norris J. Temple

Maurice E. Temple

The answer raised the question of the sufficiency of the acceptance under G.L., c. 107, sec. 155, which is as follows: "The acceptance of a bill is the signification by the drawee of his assent to the order of the drawer. The acceptance must be in writing and signed by the drawee. It must not express that the drawee will perform his promise by any other means than the payment of money." The specific contention of the defendant is that the mere signature of the name of the drawee on the bill cannot fulfill the requirement of the statute that the signification of the assent of the drawee must be in writing and must also be signed. Before the passage of the negotiable instruments act, an oral acceptance of an existing bill of exchange was generally valid in this country and formerly was so in England. [Citation.] The reason for the adoption of the rule requiring acceptance in writing, like the underlying reason for the statute of frauds and similar statutes, "is that sound policy requires some substantial evidence of the contract and more reliable in its nature than the statement or recollection of witnesses." [Citations.]

The common practice before the act was to write the word "accepted" on the face of the bill, followed by the signature of the acceptor. [Citation.] But such was not necessary, as Sewall, J., said in Storer v. Logan, 9 Mass. 55 at page 59: "An acceptance entered upon a bill generally, or the blank endorsement of the name of the drawee, holds him absolutely as the acceptor; and no conditions or stipulations, which he may have connected with his acceptance, unless expressed upon the bill, will avail him against an endorsee or payee, to whom the bill has been negotiated, and who had received the bill as accepted, without notice of the conditions."

* * *

We are of the opinion that under G.L. c. 107, sec. 155, a drawee may be charged as acceptor although he writes merely his name upon the bill, and that any one taking the bill has the right to fill up a blank acceptance on the same principle that any holder may fill up a blank indorsement. [Citation.]

The instrument in question was legally accepted. It follows in accordance with the terms of the stipulation that judgment is to be "entered for the plaintiff for the full amount of the bill and interest thereon from the date of demand as set forth in the second count."

So ordered.

Conditions Precedent to Secondary Liability

HANE v. EXTEN

(1969) 255 Md. 668, 259 A.2d 290.

SINGLEY, J.

John B. Hane is the assignee of the note of Theta Electronic Laboratories, Inc. (Theta) in the stated amount of $15,377.07, with interest at six per cent per annum. The note was dated 10 August 1964; stipulated that the first monthly payment of $320.47 would be due five months from date, or on 10 January 1965; and that "In the event of the failure to pay the interest or principal, as the same becomes due on this Note the entire debt represented hereby shall at the end of thirty (30) days become due and demandable * * *." The note was assigned without recourse to Hane by George B. and Marguerite F. Thomson, the original payees, on 26 November 1965. A default having occurred in the making of the monthly payments, Hane took judgments by confession in the Circuit Court for Montgomery County on 7 June 1967 against Theta and three individuals, Gerald M. Exten, Emil L. O'Neal, and James W. Hane, and their wives, who had endorsed Theta's note. On motion of the Extens, the judgment was vacated as to them and the case came on for trial on the merits before the court without a jury. From a judgment for the Extens for costs, Hane has appealed.

This case raises the familiar question: Must Hane show that the Extens were given notice of presentment and dishonor before he can hold them on their endorsement?

The court below, in finding for the Extens, relied on the provisions of Uniform Commercial Code (the U.C.C.), Maryland Code (1957, 1964 Repl.Vol.) Art. 95B, § 3–414(1) of the U.C.C. provides:

"Unless the indorsement otherwise specifies (as by such words as 'without recourse') every indorser engages that upon dishonor and any necessary notice of dishonor and protest he will pay the instrument according to it tenor at the time of his indorsement to the holder or to any subsequent indorser who takes it up, even though the indorser who takes it up was not obligated to do so."

§ 3–501(1)(b) provides that "Presentment for payment is necessary to charge any indorser" and § 3–501(2)(a) that "Notice of any dishonor is necessary to charge any indorser," in each case subject, however, to the provisions of § 3–511 which recite the circumstances under which notice of dishonor may be waived or excused, none of which is here present. § 3–502(1)(a) makes it clear that unless presentment or notice of dishonor is waived or excused, unreasonable delay will discharge an indorser. [Citations.]

There was testimony from which the trier of facts could find as he did that presentment and notice of dishonor were unduly delayed.

It is clear that Hane held the note from November, 1965, until some time in April 1967 before he made demand for payment. U.C.C. § 3–503(1)(d) provides that "Where an instrument is accelerated presentment for payment is due within a reasonable time after the acceleration." "Reasonable time" is not defined in § 3–503, except that § 3–503(2) provides, "A reasonable time for

presentment is determined by the nature of the instrument, any usage of banking or trade and the facts of the particular case." But § 1–204(2) characterizes it. "What is a reasonable time for taking any action depends on the nature, purpose and circumstances of such action."

Reasonableness is primarily a question for the fact finder. [Citations.] We see no reason to disturb the lower court's finding that Hane's delay of almost 18 months in presenting the note "was unreasonable from any viewpoint." [Citation.]

As regards notice of dishonor, § 3–508(2) requires that notice be given by persons other than banks "before midnight of the third business day after dishonor or receipt of notice of dishonor." Exten, called as an adverse witness by Hane, testified that his first notice that the note had not been paid was the entry of the confessed judgment on 7 June 1967. Hane's brother testified that demand had been made about 15 April 1967. He was uncertain as to when he had given Exten notice of dishonor, but finally conceded that it was "within a week." The lower court found that the ambiguity of this testimony, coupled with Exten's denial that he had received *any* notice before 7 June fell short of meeting the three day notice requirement of the U.C.C. The date of giving notice of dishonor is a question of fact, solely for determination by the trier of facts. [Citation.] We cannot say that the court erred in its finding.

In the absence of evidence that presentment and notice of dishonor were waived or excused, Hane's unreasonable delay discharged the Extens, § 3–502(1)(a).

* * *

Whether Hane was or was not a holder in due course has no relevance to the issue here presented. In either case timely presentment and notice of dishonor were required to hold the Extens. Whether Hane was or was not a holder in due course is of no significance unless there was a defense which could have been asserted against the payee. [Citations.]

Judgment affirmed, * * *.

The Imposter Rule

PHILADELPHIA TITLE INS. CO. v. FIDELITY-PHILADELPHIA TRUST CO.

(1965) 419 Pa. 78, 212 A.2d 222, 23 A.L.R.3d 925.

[Edmund Jezemski, estranged and living apart from his wife, Paula, was administrator and sole heir-at-law of his deceased mother's estate, one asset of which was real estate in Philadelphia. Without Edmund's knowledge or consent, and with the assistance of John M. McAllister, an attorney, and Anthony DiBenedetto, a real estate broker, Paula arranged for a mortgage on the property through Philadelphia Title Insurance Company. Shortly before settlement, Paula represented to McAllister and DiBenedetto that her husband would be unable to attend the closing on the mortgage. She appeared at McAllister's office in advance of the closing, accompanied by a man, whom she introduced to McAllister and DiBenedetto as her husband. She and this man, in the presence of McAllister and DiBenedetto, executed a deed conveying the property from the estate to her husband and herself as tenants by the entireties and also executed the mortgage. McAllister and DiBenedetto were witnesses. Thereafter, McAllister, DiBenedetto and Paula met at the office of the Title Company on the closing date, produced the signed deed and mortgage, and Paula obtained from Title Company its check for the mortgage loan proceeds of $15,640.82, payable to the order of Edmund Jezemski and Paula Jezemski individually and to Edmund as administrator.

In the absence of Edmund at the closing, Title Company's representative accepted the word of McAllister and DiBenedetto that Edmund had signed the deed and mortgage. The representative then signed as a witness to the signatures on the instruments and, as a notary public, acknowledged execution of the deed. Paula collected the check, bearing the purported indorsements of all the payees, at Penns Grove National Bank and Trust Company, N.J. Edmund received none of the proceeds, either individually or as administrator. His purported indorsements were forgeries. In the collection process the check was presented to and paid by the drawee bank, Fidelity-Philadelphia Trust Company, and charged against Title Company's account. Upon discovery of the existence of the mortgage, Edmund brought an action which resulted in the setting aside of the deed and mortgage and the repayment of the amount advanced by the mortgagee. Title Company thereupon sued the drawee bank to recover the amount of the check, $15,640.82.]

COHEN, J.

* * *

The complaint alleged that the endorsement of one of the payees had been forged and that, therefore, Fidelity should not have paid the check. Fidelity joined the Philadelphia National Bank as an additional defendant claiming that if Fidelity were liable to plaintiff, PNB was liable over to Fidelity for having guaranteed the endorsements. PNB joined the Penn's Grove National Bank and Trust Company as a second additional defendant claiming that if PNB were liable to Fidelity, Penn's Grove was liable to PNB for having cashed the check and guaranteed the endorsements. By way of defense all of the banks asserted that none of them were liable because the issuance of the check by the Title Company was induced by an impostor and delivered by the

Title Company to a confederate of the impostor thereby making the forged endorsement effective.

* * * Judgment was entered against the Title Company and in favor of the banks.

* * *

"There is no question that the man whom Mrs. Jezemski introduced to McAllister and DiBenedetto was not Edmund Jezemski, her husband. It was sometime later that Edmund Jezemski, when he tried to convey the real estate, discovered the existence of the mortgage. When he did so he instituted an action in equity which resulted in the setting aside of the deed and mortgage and the repayment of the fund advanced by the mortgagee."

The parties do not dispute the proposition that as between the payor bank (Fidelity-Philadelphia) and its customer (Title Company), ordinarily, the former must bear the loss occasioned by the forgery of a payee's endorsement (Edmund Jezemski) upon a check drawn by its customer and paid by it. [Citations.] Uniform Commercial Code—Commercial Paper, Act of April 6, 1953, P.L. 3, § 3–404, as amended, 12A P.S. § 3–404. The latter provides, inter alia, that "(1) Any unauthorized signature [Edmund Jezemski's] is wholly inoperative as that of the person whose name is signed unless he ratifies it or is precluded from denying * * *."

However, the banks argue that this case falls within an exception to the above rule, making the forged indorsement of Edmund Jezemski's name effective so that Fidelity-Philadelphia was entitled to charge the account of its customer, the Title Company, who was the drawer of the check. The exception asserted by the banks is found in § 3–405(1)(a) of the Uniform Commercial Code—Commercial Paper which provides:

"An indorsement by any prson in the name of a named payee is effective if (a) an impostor by use of the mails or otherwise has induced the maker or drawer to issue the instrument to him or his confederate in the name of the payee; * * *."

The lower court found and the Title Company does not dispute that an impostor appeared before McAllister and DiBenedetto, impersonated Mr. Jezemski, and, in their presence, signed Mr. Jezemski's name to the deed, bond and mortgage; that Mrs. Jezemski was a confederate of the impostor; that the drawer, Title Company, issued the check to Mrs. Jezemski naming her and Mr. Jezemski as payees; and that some person other than Mr. Jezemski indorsed his name on the check. In effect, the only argument made by the Title Company to prevent the applicability of Section 3–405(1)(a) is that the impostor, who admittedly played a part in the swindle, *did not "by the mails or otherwise" induce the Title Company* to issue the check within the meaning of Section 3–405(1)(a). The argument must fail.

* * *

Both the words of Section 3–405(1)(a) and the official Comment thereto leave no doubt that the impostor can induce the drawer to issue him or his confederate a check within the meaning of the section even though he does not carry out his impersonation before the very eyes of the drawer. Section 3–405(1)(a) says the inducement might be by "the mails or otherwise." The Comment elaborates:

"2. Subsection (1)(a) is new. It rejects decisions which distinguish between face-to-face imposture and imposture by mail and hold that where the parties deal by mail the dominant intent of the drawer is to deal with the name rather than with the person so that the resulting instrument may be negotiated only by indorsement of the payee whose name has been taken in vain. The result of the distinction has been under some prior law, to throw the loss in the mail imposture forward to a subsequent holder or to the drawee. Since the drawer believes the two to be one and the same, the two intentions cannot be separated, and the 'dominant intent' is a fiction. The position here taken is that the loss, regardless of the type of fraud which the particular impostor has committed, should fall upon the drawer."

* * * For purposes of imposing the loss on one of two "innocent" parties, either the drawer who was defrauded or the drawee bank which paid out on a forged indorsement, we see no reason for distinguishing between the drawer who is duped by an impersonator communicating directly with him through the mails and a drawer who is duped by an impersonator communicating indirectly with him through third persons. Thus, both the language of the Code and common sense dictates that the drawer must suffer the loss in both instances.

* * *

Judgment affirmed.

The Fictitious Payee Rule

TRAVCO CORP. v. CITIZENS FEDERAL SAV. & LOAN ASS'N OF PORT HURON

(1972) 42 Mich.App. 291, 201 N.W.2d 695.

R. B. BURNS, J.

Defendant Frank Mitchell, while assistant treasurer of plaintiff Travco Corporation, caused two checks, each payable to a fictitious company, to be drawn on his employer's account with the defendant Brown City Savings Bank (hereinafter Brown City). The first check was payable to "L. & B. Dist., C/O F. & B. Mitchell." It was indorsed "F. Mitchell" and "B. Mitchell" and was cashed at defendant Citizens Federal Savings & Loan Association of Port Huron (hereinafter Citizens). The second check was payable to "L. & B. Distr. Sales, 19704 West Seven Mile Road, Detroit, Michigan 48219." This latter check was indorsed "For deposit only F. Mitchell" and was also cashed at Citizens. Both checks were cleared through normal banking channels and charged against Travco's account with Brown City. Thereafter Travco discovered the embezzlement and demanded that its account be reimbursed. Brown City refused, and Travco initiated this suit against Citizens and Brown City.

Travco alleged that payment of the two checks by Brown City was improper because payment was not made according to the order of Travco and because neither check bore the authorized indorsement of the payee. Brown City's answer alleged, as an affirmative defense, that any loss was due to the negligence of Citizens and that, therefore, Citizens was liable to Brown City for any judgment which might be entered against Brown City.

The trial judge entered judgments in favor of Travco against Brown City and Citizens, in favor of Brown City against Citizens, and in favor of Brown City and Citizens against Frank and Bernice Mitchell. Only Citizens has appealed.

Citizens argues that M.C.L.A. § 440.3405(1); M.S.A. § 19.3405(1) relieves it of liability because Frank Mitchell was an employee of Travco at the time he caused the checks to issue. The cited section of the Uniform Commercial Code provides:

An indorsement by any person in the name of a named payee is effective if * * * (c) an agent or employee of the maker or drawer has supplied him with the name of the payee intending the latter to have no such interest.

Indeed, at the time the checks at issue herein were drawn, Frank Mitchell was an employee of the drawer and had supplied the drawer with the names of fictitious payees. However, neither check was indorsed "in the name of a named payee." Consequently, the indorsements were not effective.

Affirmed.

Warranties on Presentment

PRICE v. NEALE

(1762) 3 Burrow's 1355 (Court of King's Bench).

This was a special case reserved at the sittings at Guildhall after Trinity term 1762, before Lord Mansfield.

It was an action upon the case brought by Price against Neale; wherein Price declares that the defendant Edward Neale was indebted to him in 80 pounds for money had and received to his the plaintiff's use; and damages were laid to 100 pounds. The general issue was pleaded; and issue joined thereon.

It was proved at the trial, that a bill was drawn as follows—"Leicester, 22d November 1760. Sir, Six weeks after date pay Mr. Rogers Ruding or order forty pounds, value received for Mr. Thomas Ploughfor; as advised by, Sir, your humble servant Benjamin Sutton. To Mr. John Price in Bush-lane Cannon-street, London;" indorsed "R. Rudding; Antony Topham, Hammond and Laroche. Received the contents, James Watson and son: witness Edward Neale."

That this bill was indorsed to the defendant for a valuable consideration; and notice of the bill left at the plaintiff's house, on the day it became due. Whereupon the plaintiff sent his servant to call on the defendant, to pay him the said sum of 40 pounds and take up the said bill; which was done accordingly.

That another bill was drawn as follows—"Leicester, 1st February 1761. Sir, Six weeks after date pay Mr. Rogers Ruding or order forty pounds, value received for Mr. Thomas Ploughfor; as advised by, Sir, your humble servant Benjamin Sutton. To Mr. John Price in Bush-lane, Cannon-street, London." That this bill was indorsed, "R. Ruding, Thomas Watson and son." Witness for "Smith, Right and Co." That the plaintiff accepted this bill, by writing on it, "accepted John Price:" and that the plaintiff wrote on the back of it.—"Messieurs,

Freame and Barclay, pray pay forty pounds for John Price."

That this bill being so accepted was indorsed to the defendant for a valuable consideration, and left at his bankers for payment; and was paid by order of the plaintiff and taken up.

Both these bills were forged by one Lee, who has been since hanged for forgery.

The defendant Neale acted innocently and bona fide, without the least privity or suspicion of the said forgeries or of either of them; and paid the whole value of those bills.

The jury found a verdict for the plaintiff; and assessed damages 80 pounds and costs 40 shillings subject to the opinion of the court upon this question—

"Whether the plaintiff, under the circumstances of the case, (a) can recover back, from the defendant, the money he paid on the said bills, or either of them."

Mr. Stowe, for the plaintiff, argued that he ought to recover back the money, in this action; as it was paid by him by mistake only, on supposition "that these were true genuine bills;" and as he could never recover it against the drawer, because in fact no drawer exists; nor against the forger, because he is hanged.

He owned that in a case at Guild-hall, of Jenys v. Fawler et al., (an action by an indorsee of a bill of exchange brought against the acceptor,) Lord Raymond would not admit the defendants to prove it a forged bill, by calling persons acquainted with the hand of the drawer, to swear "that they believed it not to be so:" and he even strongly inclined, "that actual proof of forgery would not excuse the defendants against their own acceptance, which had given the bill a credit to the indorsee."

But he urged, that in the case now before the court, the forgery of the bill does not rest in belief and opinion only; but has been actually proved, and the forger executed for it.

Thus it stands even upon the accepted bill. But the plaintiff's case is much stronger upon the other bill which was not accepted. It is not stated "that that bill was accepted before it was negotiated;" on the contrary, the consideration for it was paid by the defendant, before the plaintiff had seen it. So that the defendant took it upon the credit of the indorsers, not upon the credit of the plaintiff; and therefore the reason, upon which Lord Raymond grounds his inclination to be of opinion "that actual proof of forgery would be no excuse," will not hold here.

Mr. Yates, for the defendant, argued that the plaintiff was not entitled to recover back this money from the defendant.

He denied it to be a payment by mistake: and insisted that it was rather owing to the negligence of the plaintiff; who should have inquired and satisfied himself "whether the bill was really drawn upon him by Sutton, or not." Here is no fraud in the defendant; who is stated "to have acted innocently and bona fide, without the least privity or suspicion of the forgery; and to have paid the whole value for the bills."

Lord Mansfield stopped him from going on; saying that this was one of those cases that could never be made plainer by argument.

It is an action upon the case, for money had and received to the plaintiff's use. In which action, the plaintiff can not recover the money, unless it be against conscience in the defendant, to retain it: and great liberality is always allowed, in this sort of action.

But it can never be thought unconscientious in the defendant, to retain this money, when he has once received it upon a bill of exchange indorsed to him for a fair and valuable consideration, which he had bona fide paid, without the least privity or suspicion of any forgery.

Here was no fraud: no wrong. It was incumbent upon the plaintiff, to be satisfied "that the bill drawn upon him was the drawer's hand," before he accepted or paid it: but it was not incumbent upon the defendant, to inquire into it. Here was notice given by the defendant to the plaintiff of a bill drawn upon him: and he sends his servant to pay it and take it up. The other bill he actually accepts; after which acceptance, the defendant innocently and bona fide discounts it. The plaintiff lies by, for a considerable time after he has paid these bills; and then found out "that they were forged;" and the forger comes to be hanged. He made no objection to them, at the time of paying them. Whatever neglect there was, was on his side. The defendant had actual encouragement from the plaintiff himself, for negotiating the second bill, from the plaintiff's having without any scruple or hesitation paid the first: and he paid the whole value, bona fide. It is a misfortune which has happened without the defendant's fault or neglect. If there was no neglect in the plaintiff, yet there is no reason to throw off the loss from one innocent man upon another innocent man; but, in this case, if there was any fault or negligence in any one, it certainly was in the plaintiff, and not in the defendant.

Per Cur'.

Rule—That the postea be delivered to the Defendant.

Problems

1.

$800.00   Smalltown, Illinois
                                            November 15, 1981
The undersigned promises to pay to the order of John Doe, Nine Hundred Dollars with interest from date of note. Payment to be made in five monthly install-ments of One Hundred Eighty Dollars, plus accrued interest beginning on December 1, 1981. In the event of default in the payment of any installment or interest on installment date the holder of this instrument may declare the entire obligation due and owing and proceed forthwith to collect the balance due on this instrument.

(Signed) Acton, agent.

On December 18, no payment having been made on the note, Doe indorsed and delivered the instrument to Todd to secure a pre-existing debt in the amount of $800.

On January 18, 1982, Todd brought an action against Acton and Phi Corporation, Acton's principal, to collect the full amount of the instrument, with interest. Acton defended on the basis that he signed the instrument in a representative capacity and that Doe had failed to deliver the consideration for which the instrument had been issued. Phi Corporation defended on the basis that it did not sign the instrument and that its name does not appear thereon.

What is the liability, if any, of Acton and Phi Corporation?

2. Cole was supervisor of the shipping department of Machine Mfg. Inc. In February Cole found himself in need of funds and, at the end of that month, submitted to Ames, the treasurer of the corporation, a payroll listing which showed as an employee, among others, "Ben Day," to whom was allegedly owed $800 for services rendered during February. Actually, there was no employee named Day. Relying upon the word of Cole, Ames drew and delivered to him a series of corporate payroll checks, drawn upon the corporate account in the Capital Bank, one of which was made payable to the order of "Ben Day" for $800. Cole took the check, indorsed on its back "Ben Day," cashed it at the Capital Bank and pocketed the proceeds. He repeated the same procedure at the end of March, April and May. In Mid-June, Machine Mfg., Inc. learned of Cole's fraudulent conduct, fired him and brought an appropriate action against Capital Bank seeking a judgment for $3,200. Decision?

3. While employed as a night watchman at the place of business of A. B. Cate Trucking Company, Fred Fain observed that the office safe had been left unlocked. It contained 50 payroll checks which were ready for distribution to employees two days later. The checks had all been signed by the sole proprietor, Cate. Fain removed five of these checks and took two blank checks which were also in the safe. Fain forged the indorsements of the payees on the five payroll checks and cashed them at local supermarkets. He then filled out one of the blank checks, making himself payee, and forged Cate's sig-

nature as drawer. After cashing that check at a supermarket, Fain departed by airplane to Jamaica. The six checks were promptly presented for payment to the drawee bank, the Bank of Emanon, which paid each of the checks. When Cate learned about the missing payroll checks and forgeries, he demanded that the Bank of Emanon credit his account with the amount of the six checks.

Must the Bank comply with Cate's demand? What are the Bank's rights, if any, against the supermarkets? You may assume that the supermarkets cashed all of the checks in good faith.

4. A negotiable promissory note executed and delivered by B to C passed in due course to and was indorsed in blank by C, D, E and F. G, the present holder, strikes out D's indorsement. What is the liability of C, D, E and F on their respective indorsements?

5. On June 15, 1977, J, for consideration, executed a negotiable promissory note for $10,000 payable to R on or before June 15, 1982. J suffered financial reverses, and in January of 1982, R on two occasions told J that he knew that J was having a difficult time and that he, R, did not need the money and the debt should be considered as completely cancelled with no other act or payment being required of R. These conversations were witnessed by three persons, including L. On March 15, 1982, R changed his mind and indorsed the note for value to L. The note was not paid by June 15, 1982, and L sued J for the amount of the note. J defended upon the ground that T had cancelled the debt and renounced all rights against J and that L had notice of this fact. Decision?

6. Tate and Fitch were longtime friends. Tate was a man of considerable means; Fitch had encountered financial difficulties. In order to bolster his failing business, Fitch desired to borrow $6,000 from Farmers Bank of Erehwon. To accomplish this, he persuaded Tate to aid him in the making of a promissory note by which it would appear that Tate had the responsibility of maker, but with Fitch agreeing to pay the instrument when due. Accordingly, they executed the following instrument:

December 1, 1981

Thirty days after date and for value received, I promise to pay to the order of Frank Fitch the sum of $6,000.

/s/ Timothy Tate

On the back of the note, Fitch indorsed: "Pay to the order of Farmers Bank of Erehwon /s/ Frank Fitch" and delivered it to the Bank in exchange for $6,000.

The note not having been paid at maturity, the Bank, without first demanding payment by Fitch, brought an action on the note against Tate. (a) Decision? (b) If Tate voluntarily pays the note to the Bank, may he then recover on the note against Fitch who appears as an indorser?

7. On December 8, 1981, A, who owed C $200 on a past due debt, drew his check upon B Bank payable to the order of C for $200 and delivered it to C. The next day, C took the check to B Bank and at C's request, B Bank certified the check by stamping it "Certified December 9, 1981, B Bank by (signed) D. Eaton, Cashier." That afternoon C erased the amount of the check as written and filled in a new amount in words and figures of $2,000 instead of $200. The fact that the check had been altered could not be detected upon inspection, nor was the certification erased or physically altered in any way.

The following day C bought a second hand car from F for $2,000 and in payment indorsed the check, "Pay to the order of F, (signed) C", and delivered it to F. That evening F indorsed the check, "Pay to the order of G, without recourse (signed) F" and delivered it to G, his nephew, as a wedding present.

The next day G presented the check to B Bank for payment. B Bank checked its records, discovered that the check had been altered and refused payment. G immediately gave notice of dishonor to A and F. C cannot be found.

What are the rights, if any, of G against A, B Bank and F?

8. Alpha orally appointed Omega as his agent to find and purchase for him a 1930 Dodge automobile in good condition. Omega located such a car. The car's owner, Roe, agreed to sell and deliver the car on January 10, 1982, for $5,000. To evidence the purchase price, Omega mailed to Roe the following instrument:

December 1, 1981

$5,000.00

We promise to pay to the order of bearer Five Thousand Dollars with interest from date of this instrument on or before January 10, 1982. This note is given in consideration of John Roe transferring title to and possession of his 1930 Dodge automobile

(Signed) Omega, agent.

Smith stole the note from Roe's mailbox, indorsed Roe's name on the note and promptly discounted it with Sunset Bank for $4,700. Not having received the note, Roe sold the car to a third party. On January 10, 1982, the bank having discovered all the facts demanded payment of the note from Alpha and Omega. Payment was refused by both.

Is this note negotiable? What are Sunset Bank's rights with regard to Omega; its rights with regard to Roe and Smith?

9. In payment of the purchase price of a used motor boat which had been fraudulently misrepresented, Y signed and delivered to A his negotiable note in the amount of $2,000 due October 1, 1981, with S as an accommodation comaker. Y intended to use the boat for his fishing business. A indorsed the note in blank preparatory to discounting it. T stole the note from A and delivered it to M on July 1, 1981, in payment of a past due debt owing by T to M in the amount of $600, with M making up the difference by giving T his check for $800 and an oral promise to pay T an additional $600 on October 1, 1981.

When M demanded payment of the note on December 1, 1981, both Y and S refused to pay the note because it had not been presented for payment on its due date and because A had fraudulently misrepresented the motor boat for which the note has been executed.

What are M's rights, if any, against Y; S; T; and A, respectively?

10. On July 1, 1981, A sold D, who is a jeweler, a necklace containing imitation gems which A fraudulently represented to be diamonds. In payment for the necklace D executed and delivered to A his promissory note for $25,000 dated July 1, 1981, and payable on July 1, 1982 to A's order with interest at 14 percent per annum.

The note was thereafter successively indorsed in blank and delivered by A to B, B to C, and by C to S, who became a holder in due course on May 10, 1982. On June 1, 1982, D discovered A's fraud and immediately notified A, B, C and S that he would not pay the note when it became due. B, a friend of S, requested that S release him from liability on the note and S, as a favor to B and for no other consideration, struck out B's indorsement.

On June 15, 1982, S, who was solvent and had no creditors, indorsed the note to the order of F, his father, and delivered it to F as a gift. At the same time, S told F of D's statement that D would not pay the note when it became due. F presented the note to D for payment on July 1, 1982, but D refused to pay. Thereafter F gave due notice of dishonor to A, B and C.

What are F's rights, if any, against A, B, C and D on the note?

11. Mayo, on January 3, 1981, prepared and signed a negotiable promissory note for $1,000 payable to the order of Peel one year after date, intending to satisfy a debt owed by him to Peel. The same day, during a visit to Mayo's house, Allen, a mutual friend of Mayo and Peel, saw the note on Mayo's desk and having heard Mayo's promise for over a year to pay the debt to Peel, took the note while Mayo was out of the room without telling him that he had done so and gave the note to Peel that evening. Allen told Peel that he took the note so that Mayo could not change his mind about paying the debt. Mayo, assuming that he had mislaid the note, gave it no further thought.

The next day Peel, in need of immediate cash, indorsed the note in blank and sold it to Tate, at a slight discount. Two weeks later, Tate indorsed the note and sold it back to Peel for the face amount. Peel drew a line in ink through Tate's indorsement on the note.

On June 18, 1981, Peel gave the note to Howe as collateral security for a $1,000 loan from Howe. Peel subsequently defaulted on his obligation to Howe and Howe kept the note in satisfaction of Peel's debt.

On January 3, 1982, Howe presented the note to Mayo with a demand for payment. Mayo refused to pay the note. Howe gave prompt notice of Mayo's dishonor of the note to Peel and to Tate.

Can Howe recover on the note from (a) Mayo, (b) Tate, (c) Peel?

Chapter
31

BANK DEPOSITS AND COLLECTIONS

In our society, goods and services are in substantial measure sold and paid for with some form of credit and without a physical transfer of "money." The wide acceptance of credit cards, charge accounts and various deferred payment plans have made the cash sale increasingly rare. But even credit sales must ultimately be settled and a check, rather than cash, is the vehicle by which payment is usually made. If the parties to a sales transaction happen to have accounts at the same bank, a transfer of credit is easily accomplished. In the vast majority of cases, however, the parties do business at different banks. Then the buyer's check must journey from the seller-payee's bank (*depositary bank*), where the check is deposited by the seller for credit to his account, to the buyer-drawer's bank (*payor bank*), for payment. In this collection process, the check frequently passes through one or more other banks (*intermediary banks*) so that it may be collected and the appropriate entries recorded.

Our banking system has developed a network to handle the collection of checks and other instruments. The thirteen Federal Reserve Banks located across the country form the main arteries of this system. When a check is drawn on a bank located in one Federal Reserve district and is deposited at a bank in another, it customarily is routed through the "Fed." Traffic through the "Fed." is heavy. To handle more local traffic, banks in the major cities have formed clearing house associations. Through such clearing houses, a member bank is able to obtain payment of checks deposited by its customers drawn on other banks in the metropolitan area and to receive in one package checks drawn by its depositors which have been deposited with other banks using the same clearing house. Only one settlement is made by a clearing bank for all checks handled on a given day. If the total amount of checks drawn on a member bank exceeds the total amount of all checks it is collecting from other members, it pays a sum to the clearing house equal to the difference. Conversely, if a member's collections total more than its payables, it receives the difference from the clearing house.

603

Another method of collecting checks is through the so-called "correspondent bank" arrangement. Larger banks in major urban centers have accounts on their books from many other banks, primarily those located in smaller communities in the area. An item received for deposit by such an outlying or "country" bank may be forwarded to its big city correspondent, which will then collect it through its clearing house, or from a correspondent of its own, or by sending it directly to the payor bank. In reverse, an item drawn on a country bank may be collected through its big city correspondent. In either case, settlement is made through appropriate adjustment to the account of the country bank on the books of the city bank.

Article 4 of the U.C.C., entitled "Bank Deposits and Collections," provides the principal rules which govern the bank collection process. Since items in the bank collection process are essentially those covered by Article 3, "Commercial Paper," and to a lesser extent by Article 8, "Investment Securities," these Articles may have application to a bank collection problem.

COLLECTION OF ITEMS

Upon the deposit of a check by the payee in his bank, the account of the payee is given a credit in the amount of the check which is characterized as *"provisional."* Normally, a bank will not permit a customer to draw against a provisional credit. When the amount of the check has been collected from the payor bank (drawee), the credit becomes *final*.

If the check is not paid for any reason, such as a stop payment order or insufficient funds in the drawer's account the provisional credit to the payee's account is reversed, his account is debited for that amount, and the check is returned to him with a statement of the reason for nonpayment. If, in the meantime, he has been permitted to draw against the provisional credit, the bank may recover the payment from him.

In the case just described, it was assumed that the bank involved was both the "depositary bank"—the bank in which the payee deposited the check for credit to his account and the "payor bank"—the bank on which the drawer wrote his check. It is only where the depositary and payor banks are different that the bank collection aspects of Article 4 come into play. Where the depositary and payor banks are different, it is necessary for the item to pass from one to the other, either directly, through a clearing house, if both are members, or through one or more "intermediary banks."

Depositary and Collecting Banks

In the usual situation where the depositary and payor banks are different, the depositary bank gives a provisional credit to its customer, transfers the item to the next bank in the chain, receiving a provisional credit or "settlement" from it, and so on to the payor bank which gives a provisional settlement to its transferor. When the item is paid, all the provisional settlements given by the respective banks in the chain become final and the particular transaction has been completed. No adjustment is necessary on the books of any of the banks involved. This procedure simplifies the bookkeeping processes of all the banks involved because only one entry is necessary if the item is paid.

If an item is not paid by the payor, it is returned to whence it came and each intermediary or collecting bank reverses the provisional settlement or credit previously given by it to its forwarding bank. Ultimately, the depositary bank will charge the account of its customer that deposited the item, and he must seek recovery from the indorsers or the drawer.

A collecting bank, any bank handling the item for collection other than the payor bank—Section 4–105(d), is an agent or sub-agent of the owner of the item until the settlement which it gave the owner becomes final. Section 4–201(1). Clearly, then, unless otherwise provided, any credit given for the item initially is provisional. Once it is firmed up into a final settlement, the agency relationship changes to one of debtor-creditor. The effect of this agency rule is that the risk of loss remains with the owner and any chargebacks go to him, not to the collecting bank.

All collecting banks have certain responsibilities and duties in collecting an item. These will be discussed in this section.

Duty of Care. A collecting bank must use ordinary care in handling an item transferred to it for collection. Section 4–202(1). Of particular importance are the steps it takes in presenting an item or sending it for presentment. It must act within a reasonable time after receipt of the item and must choose a reasonable method of forwarding the item for presentment. It is also responsible for using care with respect to routing and in the selection of intermediary banks or other agents.

The proper method of presenting an item drawn on or payable by a non-bank payor is in person by a representative of the collecting bank. To simplify procedures and save time, it is specified by Section 4–210 that unless otherwise instructed, the collecting bank may send a written notice to the drawee or maker that the bank holds the item for acceptance or payment. When presentment has been made by notice and neither honor nor request for compliance with a requirement under Section 3–505, such as exhibiting the item or establishing its authority to present it, is received by the close of business on the day after maturity in the case of a time item, or by the close of business on the third banking day after notice was sent, in the case of a demand item, the presenting bank may treat the item as dishonored and charge secondary parties by sending appropriate notice.

Duty to Act Seasonably. Closely related to the collecting bank's duty of care is its duty to act seasonably. In this connection it is necessary to understand the concept of the "midnight deadline" introduced by Article 4. One of the important elements in determining liability in numerous situations is whether action was taken before a bank's midnight deadline. This means midnight of a bank's next banking day following the banking day on which it receives the relevant item or notice or from which the time for taking action commences to run, whichever is later. Section 4–104(1)(h). Thus, if the time for a bank to take action of some sort commences to run on a Monday, the midnight deadline applicable is midnight of the next banking day, or Tuesday. A banking day means that part of any day on which a bank is open to the public for carrying on substantially all of its banking functions. Section 4–104(1)(c). If the bank is open for only limited functions, as for example on a Friday evening or a Saturday to receive deposits and cash checks, but with loan, bookkeeping and other departments closed, it is not part of a banking day.

A further problem is presented by the fact that it necessarily takes time to process an item through a bank, whether it be the depositary, an intermediary or the payor. If the various steps in connection with a day's transaction are to be completed without overtime work, either the bank must close early or it must fix a cutoff time for the day's work. Recognizing this problem, Section 4–107 provides that for the purpose of allowing time to process items, prove balances and make the necessary entries on its books to determine its position for the day, a bank may fix an afternoon hour of 2:00 P.M. or later as a cutoff hour for the handling of money and items and the making of entries on its books. Items received after the cutoff hour so fixed or after the close of the banking day may be treated as having been received at the opening of the next banking day, and the time for taking action and for determining the bank's midnight deadline with respect to the item involved begins to run from that point.

Recognizing that if an item is not paid, everyone involved will be greatly inconvenienced, Section 4–108 provides that unless otherwise instructed, a collecting bank in a good faith effort to secure payment may, in the case of specific items, waive, modify or extend the time limits specified in Article 4, but not in excess of one additional banking day. Such an extension may be made without the approval of the parties involved, and, despite the provisions of Article 3, without discharging secondary parties. The Section also authorizes delay in the case of interruption of communications, as by blizzard, flood, hurricane or other disaster or "Act of God," suspension of payments by another bank, war, emergency conditions or other circumstances beyond the control of the bank. Delay for such causes will be excused only if the bank exercises such diligence as the circumstances require.

A collecting bank acts seasonably in any event if it takes proper action, such as forwarding or presenting an item before its midnight deadline following receipt of the item, notice or payment, as the case may be. Section 4–202(2). If the bank adheres to this standard, the timeliness of its action cannot be challenged.

Indorsements. When an item is restrictively indorsed with words such as "pay any bank," it is locked into the bank collection system and only a bank may acquire the rights of a holder.

When a bank forwards an item for collection, it normally indorses it "pay any bank," irrespective of the type of indorsement, if any, which the item carried at the time of receipt. This serves to protect the collecting bank by making it impossible for the item to stray from regular collection channels.

If the item had no indorsement when received by the depositary bank, it may supply any indorsement of its customer which is necessary to title unless the item contains the words "payee's indorsement required" or the like, as is the case with certain government, pension and insurance checks. Section 4–205(1). This rule speeds up the collection process by eliminating the necessity of returning checks for indorsement when the depositary bank knows they came from its customers. The usual form of such an indorsement reads "Deposited to the account of the within named payee." This will be followed by the bank's own "pay any bank" indorsement. Each intermediary bank will in turn place a similar restrictive indorsement on the item, since no bank in the collection chain other than a depositary bank is given notice or otherwise affected by the restrictive indorsement of any person except its immediate transferor. Sections 4–205(2) and 3–206. This rule is necessary to keep the collection process moving smoothly and rapidly. The depositary bank has the responsibility of examining the item for prior restrictive indorsements. Subsequent intermediary banks and the payor bank need check only one indorsement, and may rely on the fact that the depositary bank performed its required function. It would be unnecessarily time consuming to require each bank to examine all the indorsements on each item.

Warranties. Section 4–207 provides that customers and collecting banks give substantially the same warranties as those given by parties under Article 3, Sections 3–417 and 3–414, upon presentment and transfer, which are discussed at pages 586–589.

Settlements. As has been indicated previously, as an item passes through the bank collection system, the normal procedure is for a transferee, whether it be the payor bank, an intermediary bank or a non-bank payor, to give a settlement to its transferor bank. Settlements may be either provisional or final, depending on whether they are subject to being reversed. Section 4–211(1) specifies certain types of settlements which a collecting bank may accept without liability in the event of ultimate nonpayment of an item.

Final Payment. The provisional settlements made in the collection chain are all pointed toward final payment of the item by the payor bank. This is one terminus of the collection process—the turn-around point from which the proceeds of the item begin the return flow, and the initiation of the process of firming provisional settlements into final ones. For example, a customer of the California Country State Bank may deposit a check on the State of Maine Country National Bank. The check may then take a course such as follows: to a correspondent bank in San Francisco, to the Federal Reserve Bank of San Francisco, to the Federal Reserve Bank of Boston, to the payor bank. At each step, provisional settlements were made. When the payor bank finally paid the item, the proceeds began a return flow over the same course.

The critical question is the point in time when the item has been paid by the payor bank, since this not only commences the payment process but also has a bearing on questions of priority between the item on the one hand and actions such as the filing of a stop order against the item or some notice with respect to the item or legal process or setoff affecting the amount available in the drawer's account at the payor bank. It is clear that final payment occurs at some moment during the processing of the item by the payor bank. This moment may be difficult to ascertain. An item may be received by a bank in many ways: over the counter, through the mail from a customer, in a collection letter from another bank or through a clearing house. Under some of these circumstances a receipt may be given or an entry made in a passbook. The item then normally moves through the sorting and proving departments. Still later it goes to the bookkeeping department, where it is examined for form and signature. It is then matched against the ledger for the customer's account to see if funds are sufficient or whether there is a stop order or some other reason why the item should not be paid. If everything is in good order, the item will be posted to the drawer's account either then or later. The item will be stamped or punched "Paid" and filed with the other items paid from the customer's account. When did final payment occur? Section 4–213 establishes rules for determining when that point in time has been reached.

Traditionally, when a bank pays an item in cash, it is deemed to have made a final payment. This rule is reaffirmed in subsection (1)(a) of Section 4–213. Equivalent to cash payment in making final payment is a final settlement for the item. If the payor bank has not reserved the right to revoke the settlement, or does not have such right through agreement, statute or clearing house rule, final payment has been made. Section 4–213(1)(b).

A provisional settlement also becomes a final payment if the payor bank does not revoke it in the time and manner permitted by statute, clearing house rule or agreement. Section 4–213(1)(d).

More importantly, however, final payment is made when the payor bank has completed the process of posting the item to the account of the drawer or maker. Section 4–213(1)(c). Essentially, this means the point in time when the decision is made to pay the item. The question then arises: when is the process of posting completed?

To clarify the steps legitimately involved in posting an item, Section 4–109 provides as follows:

The "process of posting" means the usual procedure followed by a payor bank in determining to pay an item and in recording the payment including one or more of the following or other steps as determined by the bank:

(a) verification of any signature;

(b) ascertaining that sufficient funds are available;

(c) affixing a "paid" or other stamp;

(d) entering a charge or entry to a customer's account;

(e) correcting or reversing an entry or erroneous action with respect to the item.

Normally, all of these steps must be taken before the "process of posting" is completed, and an item may be regarded as finally paid.

Payor Banks

Due to the tremendous increase in volume of bank collections as well as the improved methods of processing items by payor banks, it has become necessary to adopt production line methods for handling checks to assure an even flow of items on a day to day basis. This is necessary if work is to be conducted without abnormal peak loads and overtime. The solution has been the institution of deferred posting procedures whereby items are sorted and proved on the day of receipt, but are not posted to customers' accounts or returned until the next banking day. Part 3 of Article 4 of the U.C.C. not only gives approval to this procedure, but sets up specific standards to govern its application to the actions of payor banks.

When a payor bank which is not a depositary bank receives a demand item other than a documentary draft otherwise than for immediate payment over the counter, it must either return the item or give its transferor a provisional settlement before midnight of the banking day on which the item is received. Otherwise it becomes liable to its transferor for the amount of the item unless it has a valid defense. Section 4–302(a).

If it gives the provisional settlement as required, it then has until its midnight deadline to return the item or, if it is held for protest or is othrwise unavailable for return, to send written notice of dishonor or nonpayment. Section 4–301(1). Upon so doing, it is entitled to revoke the settlement and recover any payment made. If the payor bank fails to return the item or send notice before its midnight deadline, it becomes accountable for the amount of the item unless it has a valid defense for its inaction.

There are innumerable reasons why a bank may dishonor an item and return it or send notice where appropriate. Among these are, of course, that the drawer or maker either has no account or has insufficient funds to cover the item; that the signature on the item is forged; or that payment of the item has been stopped by the drawer or maker.

As to priority between items, where the customer's account is not sufficient to pay them all, the bank may charge them against the account in any order it deems convenient. Items against an account may reach the bank in several different ways on the same day. It would be unreasonable to require the bank to determine their order of arrival. Items received at the same time, but passing through different channels may be posted to the customer's account hours apart. Consequently, a person presenting an item to a payor bank may not object that the bank paid other items received the same day and left his unpaid. He is properly relegated to seeking his remedy against the maker, drawer or other secondary parties. The owner of the account from which the item was payable also has no basis for complaint that one item, rather than another, was paid. It is his responsibility to have enough funds on deposit to pay all items chargeable to his account at any time.

RELATIONSHIP BETWEEN PAYOR BANK AND ITS CUSTOMER

Payment of an Item

When a payor bank receives an item properly payable from a customer's account but there are insufficient funds in the account to pay it, the bank may (1) dishonor the item and return it or (2) pay the item and charge its customer's account even though an overdraft is created as a result. The item authorized or directed the bank to make the payment, and hence carries with it an enforceable implied promise to reimburse the bank. Further, the customer may be liable to the bank to pay a service charge for the bank's handling of the overdraft or may be liable to pay interest on the amount of the overdraft.

A check or draft is not an assignment of funds in the hands of the drawee available for its payment, and the drawee is not liable on an instrument until he accepts it. Section 3–409(1). The holder of a check has no right to require the drawee bank to pay it, whether or not there are sufficient funds in the drawer's account. But if an item is presented to a payor bank and the bank improperly refuses payment it will incur a liability to its customer from whose account the item should have been paid. Section 4–402. If the item is not more than six months old and regular in form, if the customer had adequate funds on deposit and there is no other valid basis for the refusal to pay, the bank is liable to its customer for any reasonably expectable damages which the customer may incur. Such damages may include, for example, damages for arrest or prosecution under a statute which makes the issuance of a check against insufficient funds in exchange for goods a misdemeanor punishable by fine or imprisonment.

A payor bank is under no obligation to its customer to pay an uncertified check which is over six months old. Section 4–404. This rule reflects the usual banking practice of consulting a depositor before paying a stale item on his account. The bank is not required to dishonor such an item, however, and if payment is made in good faith, it may charge the amount of the item to its customer's account.

Stop Payment Orders

A check drawn on a bank is an order to pay a sum of money and an authorization to charge the amount to the drawer's account. The drawer may countermand this order, however, by means of a stop payment order. If such order does not come too late, the bank is bound by it and must assume the risk of loss. An oral stop order is binding on the bank for only fourteen calendar days. Therefore, the normal practice is for a customer to confirm an oral stop order in writing, and such an order is effective for six months, and may be renewed in writing.

The fact that a drawer has filed a stop payment order does not automatically relieve him of liability. If the bank honors the stop payment order and returns the check, the holder may bring an action against the drawer. If the holder qualifies as a holder in due course, personal defenses that the drawer might have to such an action would be of no avail.

If the bank inadvertently pays a check over a valid stop order, it is prima facie liable to the customer, but only to the extent of the customer's loss resulting from the payment. The burden of establishing the fact and amount of loss is on the customer.

Effect of Customer's Death or Incompetence

The general rule is that death or incompetence revokes all agency agreements. Furthermore, adjudication of incompetency by a court is regarded as notice to the world of that fact. Actual notice is not required. Section 4–405 modifies these stringent rules with respect to bank deposits and collections in several ways.

First, a payor bank's authority to accept, pay or collect an item or to account for proceeds of its collection is not rendered ineffective by the incompetence of a customer of either bank at the time the item is issued or its collection undertaken if the bank does not in fact know of the adjudication of incompetence. The item may be paid without the bank incurring any liability.

Second, neither death nor adjudication of incompetence of a customer revokes such authority until the bank knows of it and has a reasonable opportunity to act on such knowledge.

Finally, even though a bank knows of the death of its customer, it may for ten days after the date of his death pay or certify checks drawn by the customer unless a person claiming an interest in the account, such as an heir, legatee or executor or administrator of his estate, orders the bank to stop making such payments. Section 4–405(2). This rule facilitates matters for all concerned. There is almost never any reason why such checks should not be paid and if there is, the personal representative of the deceased customer would have a claim against the person receiving payment. If the check is not paid, the holder will be required to file a claim in the probate proceeding and the personal representative will have the duty of processing it for payment.

Customer's Duty to Discover and Report Unauthorized Signatures and Alterations

In order to terminate a bank's open liability for paying an item with a forged signature or indorsement or an item which has been altered, Section 4–406 imposes certain affirmative duties on bank customers and fixes time limits within which they must assert their rights. The duties arise and the time starts to run from the time the bank either sends or makes available to its customer a statement of account accompanied by the items paid against the account. The customer is required to exercise reasonable care and promptness to examine the bank statement and items to discover his unauthorized signature of any alteration on an item. Since he is not presumed to know the signatures of payees or indorsers, this duty of prompt and careful examination applies only to the customer's own signature and alterations, both of which he should be able to detect immediately. If he discovers an unauthorized signature or an alteration, he must notify the bank promptly.

If the customer fails to discharge these duties of prompt examination and notice, Section 4–406(2) precludes him from asserting against the bank his unauthorized signature and alteration if the bank establishes that it suffered a loss by reason of such failure.

Furthermore, he will lose his rights in a potentially more important situation. Occasionally a forger will embark upon a series of transactions involving the account of the same individual. Perhaps he is an employee who has access to his employer's check book. He may forge one or more checks each month until he is finally detected. The bank, on the other hand, having paid one or more of the customer's checks bearing such signatures without objection, may be lulled into a false sense of security. Suddenly the forgery is detected by the customer after many months or even years. Is the bank to be held liable for all such items? Section 4–406(2) answers this in the negative. The bank is liable on all items with unauthorized signatures or alterations by the same wrongdoer which accompany the statement with which the first such item is returned. The customer had no way of knowing such items were being cashed. But once the statement and items become available to him, he must examine them within a reasonable period, which in no event may exceed fourteen calendar days, but may, under the circumstances, be less, and notify the bank. Any alterations or unauthorized signatures on instruments by the same wrongdoer and paid by the bank during that period will still be the responsibility of the bank, but any paid thereafter but before the customer notifies the bank may not be asserted against it. This rule is based on the concept that the loss involved is directly traceable to the customer's negligence and, as a result, he should stand the loss.

The two rules under Section 4–406(2)

depend on the bank exercising ordinary care in paying the items involved. If it does not, it properly loses its right to require prompt action on the part of its customer. But whether the bank exercised due care or not, the customer must in all events report an alteration or his unauthorized signature within one year from the time the statement and items were made available to him or be precluded from asserting them against the bank. Section 4–406(4). Any unauthorized indorsement must be asserted within three years from the time the bank statements and items containing such indorsements are made available to the customer.

Cases

Warranties

BIRMINGHAM TRUST NAT'L BANK v. CENTRAL BANK & TRUST CO.

(1973) 49 Ala.App. 630, 275 So.2d 148.

WRIGHT, P. J.

The Birmingham Trust National Bank brought suit for breach of warranty against Central Bank & Trust Company.

The facts out of which the suit arose are briefly as follows: On July 21, 1969, one Boehmer, a customer of Birmingham Trust, secured a loan from Birmingham Trust for the principal sum of $5500.00. The loan was granted for the purchase of a boat allegedly being manufactured for Boehmer by A. C. Manufacturing Company, Inc., of Florida. Upon signing of a note and security instruments by Boehmer granting them a mortgage upon the boat, Birmingham Trust issued its cashier's check to Boehmer and A. C. Manufacturing Company as payees. The check was given into the possession of Boehmer.

Apparently Boehmer immediately went to Central Bank and deposited the check in an account which he had established there

and to which he was the only authorized signatory. It is stipulated that the endorsement of A. C. Manufacturing Company on the check was a forgery and was upon the check when it was presented to Central Bank. The account of Boehmer was credited with the amount of the check. Central placed its legend "P.E.G." meaning in the banking business "Prior Endorsements Guaranteed" on the check on July 21, 1969, and it was received by Birmingham Trust and paid by them on July 22, 1969, to Central.

After some difficulty in collecting payments on the loan, and after it ultimately became delinquent, Birmingham Trust in the latter part of March 1970 contacted A. C. Manufacturing Company in Florida attempting to learn the location of the boat. They learned at that time that the boat had never been purchased by Boehmer. At about the same time it was learned that Boehmer had died or killed himself on January 24, 1970.

* * *

On May 1, 1970, Birmingham Trust called upon Central for reimbursement under its warranty of prior endorsements.

Central refused repayment. Thus, this suit.

* * *

The cause of action brought here by Birmingham Trust arose under the provisions of Title 7A, § 4–207 which in pertinent part are as follows:

§ 4–207. Warranties of customer and collecting bank on transfer or presentment of items; time for claims.—(1) Each customer or collecting bank who obtains payment or acceptance of an item and each prior customer and collecting bank warrants to the payor bank or other payor who in good faith pays or accepts the item that (a) he has a good title to the item or is authorized to obtain payment or acceptance on behalf of one who has a good title; and * * * (3) The warranties and the engagement to honor set forth in the two preceding subsections arise notwithstanding the absence of indorsement or words of guaranty or warranty in the transfer or presentment and a collecting bank remains liable for their breach despite remittance to its transferor. Damages for breach of such warranties or engagement to honor shall not exceed the consideration received by the customer or collecting bank responsible plus finance charges and expenses related to the item, if any. (4) Unless a claim for breach of warranty under this section is made within a reasonable time after the person claiming learns of the breach, the person liable is discharged to the extent of any loss caused by the delay in making claim. (1965, No. 549, effective midnight Dec. 31, 1966).

The above quoted provisions of the Uniform Commercial Code codifies the theory of implied warranty of the genuineness of prior endorsements which was the accepted general rule as to transactions between collecting banks and drawee banks prior to the Uniform Commercial Code. This provision of the Code places the burden directly upon the first bank in the collection chain to make sure that endorsements on a check are valid. The reason for such requirement is that the first bank is in a better position to insure that the one presenting the check

has good title than subsequent banks or the payor bank. [Citation.]

This is different from the rule of Price v. Neal, 3 Burrows 1254, which is that the drawee bank is presumed to know the signature of his customer, the drawer. This is the principle contended for by appellee in brief—that is, that in spite of the warranty of the collecting bank (Central) that it had good title to the check and all signatures and endorsements thereon were genuine and authorized, there yet remained a duty on the payor or drawee (Birmingham Trust National), to check or verify the genuineness of all endorsements before it paid the check.

Such principle does not apply to endorsements on a check as it may to a drawer's signature or to the drawees' signature. There is no duty either under law merchant or under Uniform Commercial Code for a drawee bank to verify the endorsement of a payee on a check which comes to it from a collecting bank under a warranty of endorsement. [Citations.]

It is stated in the *Clearfield Trust* case [Clearfield Trust Co. v. United States, 318 U.S. 363, 744, 63 S.Ct. 573, 87 L.Ed. 838] that the drawee's right to recover from the collecting bank accrues when the drawee makes payment. The warranty of the endorsements is breached at that time. The court said in *Clearfield* "there is no other barrier to the maintenance of the cause of action."

It was the payment of the check to Central, who had no legal right to collect it, (because of the forged endorsement) which constituted Birmingham Trust's loss. It was the responsibility of Central to determine that the endorser and the payee were one and the same. Central's warranty, and the requirement of § 4–207, even in the absence of such express warranty, were designed to protect Birmingham Trust from the failure of Central to fulfill its responsibility. [Citations.]

It is clear that there was no duty upon Birmingham Trust to discover the forgery of the endorsement, either prior or subsequent to payment of the check to Central. A plea or evidence of negligence in that respect is no defense to the action on the breach of warranty.

Appellee attempted to plead that the failure of Birmingham Trust to promptly, or within a reasonable time after discovery of the forgery, notify Central of the forged endorsement was a defense of contributory negligence and a bar to recovery by Birmingham Trust. The trial court gave written charges requested by appellee to that effect. Such defense is not available as a bar to recovery.

* * *

[Judgment for collecting bank and against drawee bank reversed and cause remanded.]

Payment of an Item:
Wrongful Dishonor by Payor Bank

BANK OF LOUISVILLE ROYAL v. SIMS

(1968 Ky.) 435 S.W.2d 57.

CLAY, COMMISSIONER

Appellee [Mrs. Sims] recovered $631.50 for the wrongful dishonor of two small checks. This sum included the following items of damage: $1.50 for a telephone call; $130 for two weeks' lost wages; and $500 for "illness, harassment, embarrassment and inconvenience". The trial court, trying the case without a jury, found that the dishonor was due to a mistake and was not malicious.

KRS 355.4–402 provides:

"A payor bank is liable to its customers for damages *proximately caused* by the wrongful dishonor of an item. *When the dishonor occurs through mistake liability is limited to actual damages proved.* If so proximately caused and proved damages may include damages for an arrest or prosecution of the customer or *other consequential damages*. Whether any consequential damages are proximately caused by the wrongful dishonor is a question of fact to be determined in each case." (Emphasis added.)

This statute does not define "consequential" damages but it is clear they must be proximately caused by the wrongful dishonor. It appears this statute codifies the common law measure of damages as it heretofore existed in Kentucky. [Citations.] As in other cases of breach of contract, "proximately caused" damages, whether direct or consequential, would be those which could be reasonably foreseeable by the parties as the natural and probable result of the breach. [Citations.]

The plaintiff deposited for her account with appellant a check for $756, drawn on an out-of-town bank. In order to permit such a check to clear, it was apparently customary for the bank to delay crediting the account for a period of three days. By mistake one of appellant's clerks posted a ten-day hold on this check, and during that period two of plaintiff's checks were dishonored and returned with the notation "Drawn Against Uncollected Funds". Apparently she had some difficulty getting the matter straightened out.

The plaintiff had respiratory trouble and, because of it and a case of "nerves", her doctor advised her to take a two-week leave of absence from her place of employment, which she did. She testified she was embarrassed, humiliated and mortified, but her principal complaint seems to be of the difficulty and delay in getting the bank to correct its mistake.

In American Nat. Bank v. Morey, 113 Ky. 857, 69 S.W. 759, 58 L.R.A. 956, it was held that if there was no basis for punitive damages for the dishonor of a check, recovery cannot be had for humiliation or mortification. It was also held that plaintiff's "nervous chill" was not the natural result of the dishonor or such a thing as could be reasonably anticipated. In Berea Bank and Trust Co. v. Mokwa, 194 Ky. 556, 239 S.W. 1044, it was recognized that loss of time could be a proper item of damages provided it was the direct and proximate result of the bank's refusal to honor a check.

On the authority of Morey, the plaintiff was not entitled to recover for her hurt feelings or for her "nerves". It follows, therefore, that she was likewise not entitled to recover for her two weeks' lost time from work even if her mental state actually contributed to this loss. From the proximate cause standpoint, these nebulous items of damage bore no reasonable relationship to the dishonor of her two checks and consequently they could not be classified as "actual damages proved". (Had the action of the bank been willful or malicious, justifying a punitive award, damages of this kind might have been recoverable as naturally flowing from this type of tortious misconduct, but we do not have that question here.)

The charge for the telephone call was a proper item of damages.

The judgment is reversed, with directions to enter judgment for the plaintiff in the sum of $1.50.

Payment of an Item:
Good Faith Payment
of Stale Check

ADVANCED ALLOYS, INC. v. SERGEANT STEEL CORP.

(1973) 72 Misc.2d 614, 340 N.Y.S.2d 266.

CHARLES H. COHEN, J.

The question presented is whether a bank has a duty of inquiry before paying a check which is stale in that it was presented for payment 14 months after issuance. Prior to the enactment of the Uniform Commercial Code, such a duty existed. [Citation.] However, U.C.C. 4–404 states that:

A bank is under no obligation to a customer having a checking account to pay a check, other than a certified check, which is presented more than six months after its date, but it may charge its customer's account for a payment made thereafter in good faith.

This statute appears to change the common law rule. See New York Annotations (McKinney's Cons.Laws of N. Y., Book 62½, Uniform Commercial Code § 4–404) stating that "This is new law." [Citation.]

Under this statute, it must be determined whether this payment was made "in good faith." Since no evidence was presented on this point and since both plaintiff and defendant The Chase Manhattan Bank, N.A. agree that there are no issues of fact— the case having been presented to the Court on affidavits prepared for a summary judgment motion—the Court must simply decide whether a payment of a check by a drawee bank 14 months after issuance is a payment "in good faith" when made without inquiry of the depositor. U.C.C. 1–201(19) defines "good faith" as "honesty in fact in the conduct or transaction concerned." Under this definition, to which the Official Comment to U.C.C. 4–404 makes reference, it appears that the payment of the stale check, without making such inquiry constitutes a payment "in good faith." [Citation.]

Apparently, when the Code intends to apply a concept of "good faith" beyond "honesty in fact", a broader definition is provided. Thus, with respect to dealings of merchants, U.C.C. 2–103(1)(b) states:

'Good faith' in the case of a merchant means honesty in fact and the observance of reasonable commercial standards of fair dealing in the trade.

Presumably, if it were intended to place a duty of inquiry upon a bank before it could safely pay a stale check, a broader definition of "good faith" would have been made applicable to this situation. It may very well be that in enacting the Code consideration was given, as defendant argues, to the vast number of checks being issued and the requirement that a bank accept or refuse to honor a check within a short, prescribed time limit (U.C.C. 4–301, 302), leading to the conclusion that a bank should not be liable for paying stale checks as long as the bank was honest in fact.   *   *   *

The court realizes that a determination that there is no duty of inquiry puts a substantial burden upon one who issues a check, and then, even for a good reason—as in this case—does not want it to be paid. Since a stop payment order is good for only six months (U.C.C. 4—403(2)), it means that the issuer must, in order to protect himself, either continue to renew the stop payment order every six months or close the account.   Apparently, in balancing the problems of the issuer and the bank in this situation, the Code resolved the matter in favor of the bank.

The court notes the statement in the Official Comment (McKinney's Cons.Laws of N. Y., Book 62½, Uniform Commercial Code, § 4–404) that normally a bank will not pay a stale check without consulting the depositor and, further that U.C.C. 4–404 does not require a bank to pay a stale check but the bank " *   *   * is given the option to pay because it may be in a position to know, as in the case of dividend checks, that the drawer wants payment made." Plaintiff argues that this option to pay is given only when the drawee bank is in a position to know that the drawer wants the check to be paid; and in this case the bank could only know this if it made inquiry—something it did not do.   However, the language of the Code itself, as indicated above, does not support this argument and does not impose a duty of inquiry upon the bank in the situation presented herein.

Judgment is directed in favor of the defendant the Chase Manhattan Bank, N.A. against plaintiff; and any claim over by that defendant against Long Island Trust Company is dismissed.

Judgment is directed in favor of plaintiff against defendant Sergeant Steel Corporation, the payee of the check, in the amount of $2500 with interest thereon from April 5, 1971 plus cost.

Stop Payment Orders

SINISCALCHI v. VALLEY BANK OF NEW YORK
(1974) 79 Misc.2d 64, 359 N.Y.S.2d 173.

ELI H. MELLAN, J.

This action was tried before me in a Small Claims Part of this Court and involved a claim by the plaintiff against the defendant bank for the sum of $200 based upon the fact that he had issued a check dated June 11, 1974, which incidentally was a Tuesday and that on Monday following, namely, on June 17, 1974, bright and early as he testified, at 9 A.M. he appeared at the bank and asked them to place a stop payment on the check.   The plaintiff testified that in speaking to the employee of the bank when he appeared in person as stated, the bank's employee detained the plaintiff for approximately 25 minutes or more while she checked the records to see if in fact this instrument had cleared the bank and, thereafter, at 9:45 A.M. gave him a printed notice confirming his request to stop payment and charging his account $5 for this stop payment   *   *   *.

Nevertheless, it appears from the testimony in this matter that this bank has evening hours on Fridays and morning hours on Saturdays so that on June 14, 1974, Friday evening the bank was open for business, received deposits, made payments on checks and similarly on Saturday morning June 15, 1974.   The bank transacted such business, but those transactions were not recorded or processed through the bookkeeping system of the bank until Monday June 17, 1974, the date on which the plaintiff appeared to stop payment the first thing in the morning.   Thus, although the bank employee checked early that morning, the activities of Saturday morning had not yet been reflected and it appeared at that time that the check had not yet cleared.

The testimony shows, however, that on Saturday morning, June 15, 1974, the check had been cashed so that the cashing of the check preceded the actual stop order. It is significant that the check was outstanding for nearly a full week before the stop order payment came in.

Section 4–403 of the Uniform Commercial Code provides for the customer's right to stop payment on a check, but specifically provides that the stop payment order must be received at such time and in such manner as to afford the bank a reasonable opportunity to act on the stop payment order prior to other action normally taken by the bank as described in Section 4–303 of the Uniform Commercial Code. Furthermore, the law thus provides that the burden is upon the depositor or customer of the bank to establish the amount of loss which may result from the payment by the bank of an item contrary to a binding stop payment order.

A payment in violation of an effective direction to stop payment is an improper payment even though it is made by mistake or inadvertence. This, however, does not appear to have been the case in this instance since the payment actually anteceded the stop payment order.

It may have been difficult for most depositors without special knowledge of banking practices to realize the multiple details involved in the handling of checks and other banking instruments, but it is clear that the bank must have a reasonable opportunity to act upon stop payment orders. [Citation.] In the case of knowledge, notice and stop orders the effective time for determining whether they were received too late to affect the payment of an item and a charge to the customer's account by reason of such payment is receipt plus a reasonable time for the bank to act on any of these communications. Usually a relatively short time is required to communicate to the bookkeeping department advice of these specific notices, but certainly some time is necessary. In the instant case with the weekend activities all being reflected on the records on the Monday following, the bank certainly did not have a reasonable time to act upon the plaintiff's stop payment order. [Citation.]

Under Section 4–303 of the Uniform Commercial Code a stop payment order comes too late to modify the bank's right or duty to pay a check after the bank has already paid the item in cash. Such is the case in the instant matter and for these reasons I find that the defendant is entitled to judgment.

Customer's Duty to Discover and Report Unauthorized Signatures and Alterations

MICHIGAN NAT'L BANK v. AMERICAN NAT'L BANK & TRUST CO.

(1975) 34 Ill.App. 30, 339 N.E.2d 375.

McGLOON, P. J.

This appeal involves a lawsuit and a third party action generated by the forgery of a payee's indorsement. The drawee, Michigan National Bank, reimbursed the drawer and sued the collecting bank, American National Bank & Trust Company, in the circuit court of Cook County upon American's warranty of good title and guarantee of prior indorsements. American filed a third party claim against the depositary bank, the Valley Bank of Nevada, on the same grounds. The trial court granted summary judgments for plaintiff Michigan against defendant American, and for third party plaintiff American against third party defendant Valley. The Valley Bank of Nevada argues on appeal that the trial court erred by granting the motions for summary judgments because there were genuine issues of material fact.

We affirm.

The pleadings reveal the following pertinent facts. On July 12, 1968, Max Larsen drew a check for $10,000 on his account at the Michigan National Bank in Battle Creek, Michigan, and then mailed the check to Edward B. Stanton. The check was deposited into the account of a customer in the Valley Bank of Nevada in Las Vegas, Nevada. Valley sent the check to American for collection, and American presented the check to Michigan for payment. Michigan, the drawee bank, paid the check on July 19, 1968.

The drawer's affidavit states that in February 1970, he was notified by the payee that the check was never received. The drawer searched through his cancelled checks and found the paid check in question. Six months later, on August 6, 1970, the drawer notified his bank that the payee never received the check and the letter of notification alluded to the forgery of the payee's indorsement. Five months later, on January 13, 1971, the payee executed an affidavit of forgery. Thereafter, Michigan made a claim against American on American's warranty of good title under U.C.C. § 4–207(1) and guarantee of prior indorsements. [Citation.] American similarly proceeded against Valley. Lawsuits were filed and various motions for summary judgment were presented to the trial court, which ruled in favor of the respective plaintiffs. * * *

It is a settled rule of commercial law that the drawer of a check who has notice of a forged indorsement has the duty to exercise reasonable care to investigate and to inform the drawee bank. (U.C.C. § 4–406, Official Comment No. 6.) Should the drawer unreasonably delay in giving notice, the person liable for the breach of warranty of good title is "discharged to the extent of any loss caused by the delay in making claim." U.C.C. § 4–207(4); [Citation.]

In the case at bar, Valley argues that the drawer unreasonably delayed in notifying the drawee of the suspected forgery. Assuming that the facts indicate that the delay of six months was unreasonable, the question must be whether any party sustained a loss caused by the delay. The pleadings and affidavits presented to the trial court at the proceedings below do not mention or even allude to any losses caused by the delay. Valley attempts for the first time on appeal to introduce facts which show that it may have sustained a loss due to the delay, but we cannot take cognizance of such facts. [Citation.] Valley had an opportunity to submit affidavits on this point below, but did not do so. We must conclude that based upon the pleadings and affidavits filed, there was no genuine issue as to any material fact and the respective plaintiffs were entitled to judgment as a matter of law so that the trial court did not err in granting the motions for summary judgment. [Citations.]

Valley's argument concerning Michigan's delay in notifying American is raised for the first time on appeal, and will therefore not be considered.

* * *

Judgment affirmed.

Problems

1. On December 9, John Jones writes a check for $500 payable to Ralph Rodgers in payment for goods to be received later in the month. Before the close of business on the 9th John notifies the bank by telephone to stop payment on the check. On the 19th of December Ralph gives the check to Bill Briggs for value and without notice. On the 20th Bill deposits the check in his account at Bank A. On the 21st Bank A sends the check to its correspondent Bank B. On the 22nd Bank B presents the check through the clearing house to Bank C. On the 23rd

Bank C presents the check to Bank P, the payor bank. On the 28th of December the payor bank makes payment of the check final. John Jones sues the payor bank. Decision?

2. Howard Harrison, a long time customer of Western Bank, operates a small department store, Harrison's Store. Since his store has few experienced employees, Harrison frequently travels throughout the United States on buying trips, although he also runs the financial operations of the business. On one of his buying trips Harrison purchased a gross of sport shirts from Well-Made Shirt Company and paid for the transaction with a check on his store account with Western Bank in the amount of $1,000. Adams, an employee of Well-Made who deposits its checks in Security Bank, raised the amount of the check to $10,000 and indorsed the check, "Pay to the order of Adams from Pension Plan Benefits, Well-Made Shirt Company by Adams". He cashes the check and cannot be found. The check is processed and paid by the Western Bank and is sent to Harrison's Store with the monthly statement. After brief examination of the statement, Harrison leaves on another buying trip for three weeks.

(a) Assuming the bank acted in good faith and the alteration is not discovered and reported to the bank until an audit conducted 13 months after the statement was received by Harrison's Store, who must bear the loss on the raised check?

(b) Assuming that Harrison, because he was unable to examine his statement promptly due to his buying trips, left instructions with the bank to notify him of any item over $5,000 to be charged to his account and the bank paid the item anyway in his absence, who bears the loss if the alteration is discovered one month after the statement was received by Harrison's Store?

3. Tom Jones owed Bank Y $10,000 on a note due November 17, with a 1% interest due the bank for each day delinquent in payment. Tom Jones issued a check to Bank Y and delivered it via night vault the evening of November 17. Several days later he received a letter saying he owed one day's interest on the payment because of one day delinquency in payment on the original $10,000. Jones refused because he said he

had put it in the vault on the 17th of November. What action?

4. Assume that D draws a check on Y Bank payable to the order of P; that P indorses to A; that A deposits it to his account in X Bank; that X Bank presents it to Y Bank, the drawee; that Y Bank dishonors it because of insufficient funds. X Bank has until midnight of the day after presentment to notify A of the dishonor. That is, if X Bank received the dishonor on Monday, it would have until midnight of Tuesday to notify A. Assume that X Bank, because of an interruption of communication facilities, fails to notify A by midnight Tuesday. Is A, the secondarily liable party, now discharged?

5. A presented a check for $1,000 to B Bank. A was not a customer of the bank. There was an agreement that B Bank would take the check and send it through for collection and that A could come back, to receive his cash or the check if it was dishonored, in five days. B Bank maintains its account with C Bank, and at the close of each business day sends its checks to C Bank by railway. B Bank sent its checks together with A's collection item in this usual manner that same evening. Due to a derailment the item was delayed one day before finally reaching the payor bank. The B Bank had not received any notice whether the check had been paid or dishonored within the time set. A came back to B Bank on the agreed day and demanded his money or the check.

Would A be able to hold B Bank to the agreement?

6. Jones, a food wholesaler whose company carries an account with B Bank in New York City, is traveling in California on business. He comes upon a particularly attractive offer and decides to buy a carload of oranges for delivery in New York. He gives S, the seller, his company's check for $25,000 to pay for the purchase. S places the check, with others he received that day, with his bank, the C Bank. C Bank sends the check to D Bank in Los Angeles which, in turn, deposits with the Los Angeles Federal Reserve Bank. The L. A. Fed. sends the check, with others, to the N. Y. Fed. The N. Y. Fed. forwards the check to B Bank, Jones's bank for collection.

(a) Is B Bank a depository bank? A collecting bank? A payor bank?

(b) Is C Bank a depository bank? A presenting bank?

(c) Is the N. Y. Fed. a remitting bank? An intermediary bank?

(d) Is D Bank a collecting bank? A remitting bank?

7. On April 1, M gave P a check properly drawn by M on Z Bank for $500 in payment of a painting to be framed and delivered the next day. P immediately indorsed the check and gave it to Y Bank as payment in full of his indebtedness to the Bank on a note he previously had signed. Y Bank cancelled the note and returned it to P.

On April 2, upon learning that the painting had been destroyed in a fire at P's studio, M promptly went to Z Bank, signed a printed form of stop payment order and gave it to the cashier. The stop payment order contained a provision releasing Z Bank from responsibility if the check should be paid through inadvertence, accident, or oversight.

Z Bank refused payment on the check upon proper presentment by Y Bank.

(a) What are the rights of Y Bank against Z Bank?

(b) What are the rights of Y Bank against M?

(c) Assuming that Z Bank by inadvertence had paid the amount of the check to Y Bank and debited M's account, what are the rights of M against Z Bank?

8. On Monday, December 20, 1981, G drew two checks on his account at X Bank, each for $1,500, one payable to his grandson, A, age 17, the other to his grandson, B, age 22, and immediately delivered the checks to A and B as Christmas gifts. On the same day, A indorsed his check to D, a used car dealer, in full payment for a used car reasonably worth $1,500 which A, a college student, intended to use solely to commute to college. A presented a very mature physical appearance and D had no reason to believe that A was a minor.

G died suddenly on Wednesday, December 22. Although X Bank knew of G's death, it cashed B's check when B presented it to X Bank at noon on December 23. However, X Bank refused to cash the check held by D when D presented it to X Bank later in the afternoon of December 23. D gave due notice of dishonor to A.

E has duly qualified as executor of G's will. E, as executor, has commenced an action against X Bank to recover the $1,500 paid to B from G's account by X Bank after G's death.

D, the used car dealer, has commenced an action against E, as executor, and X Bank to recover on the check indorsed to D by A.

What are the rights, if any, of: (1) E in his action against X Bank? (2) D in his action against E and X Bank?

9. As payment in advance for services to be performed, Acton signed and delivered the following instrument:

December 1, 1981

LAST NATIONAL BANK
MONEYVILLE, STATE X

Pay to the order of Olaf Owen $1,500.00 _____ Fifteen Hundred Dollars _____ For services to be performed by Olaf Owen starting on December 6, 1981, (signed) Arthur Acton

Owen requested and received Last National Bank's certification of the check, even though Acton had only $900 on deposit. Owen indorsed the check in blank and delivered it to Dan Doty in payment of a pre-existing debt.

When Owen failed to appear for work, Acton gave a written stop payment order to the bank ordering the bank not to pay the check. Doty presented the check to Last National Bank for payment. The bank refused payment.

What are the Bank's rights and liabilities relating to the transactions described?

10. Jones drew a check for $1,000 on The First Bank, and mailed it to the payee, T, Inc. C stole the check from T, Inc., chemically erased the name of the payee and inserted the name of H as payee. C also increased the amount of the check to $10,000, and by using the name of H, negotiated the check to W. W then took the check to The First Bank and obtained its certification on the check. W then negotiated the check to G who deposited the check in The Second National Bank for collection. The Second National forwarded the check to the D Trust Company for collection from The First Bank which honored the check. G exhausted his account in the Second National Bank and the account was closed. Shortly thereafter, The First Bank learned that it had paid an altered check.

What are the rights of each of the parties? Assume that all parties (except C) are respectively holders in due course.

Chapter

32

NATURE, FORMATION, AND PROPERTY

A business enterprise may be operated or conducted by a sole proprietor, a partnership, a limited partnership, a corporation or by some other form of business organization. The selection of the particular form of business unit to be employed is a matter for the owner or owners of the enterprise to determine. It is not unusual for a business to have a small beginning as a sole proprietorship, later expand into a partnership, and ultimately be incorporated. When a new enterprise is started, various factors will affect the decision to use one medium rather than another, not the least of which will be the current or prospective incidence of Federal and State income tax laws.

The Uniform Partnership Act, since its promulgation in 1914 by the National Conference of Commissioners on Uniform State Laws, has been adopted by forty-eight States, all except Georgia and Louisiana, and also by the District of Columbia, the Virgin Islands, and Guam. It contains forty-five Sections which are set forth in Appendix B

of this book. It is sometimes referred to herein as the "U.P.A."

The Uniform Limited Partnership Act, consisting of thirty-one Sections, is set forth in Appendix C. Prior to 1976 it was adopted in forty-eight States, all except Delaware and Louisiana, and also in the District of Columbia and the Virgin Islands. It is sometimes referred to herein as the "U.L.P.A."

In August, 1976, the National Conference of Commissioners on Uniform State Laws adopted the Revised Uniform Limited Partnership Act and submitted it to the States for enactment. It contains eleven Articles and is much more comprehensive than the U.L.P.A., which it is intended to replace. It is set forth in Appendix D in this book. By August, 1981, ten States had adopted the Revised Uniform Limited Partnership Act, namely, Arkansas, Colorado, Connecticut, Maryland, Minnesota, Montana, Nebraska, Washington, West Virginia, and Wyoming.

622

NATURE OF PARTNERSHIP

Definition of Partnership

General Partnership. A partnership, or co-partnership, as it is sometimes called, has been variously defined, although the best definition is that contained in Section 6 of the U.P.A.:

A partnership is an association of two or more persons to carry on as co-owners a business for profit.

The U.P.A. broadly defines "person" to include "individuals, partnerships, corporations, and other associations." Section 2. A business is defined by the Act to include every trade, occupation, or profession.

Limited Partnership. A limited (or special) partnership is defined by Section 1 of the U.L.P.A.:

A limited partnership is a partnership formed by two or more persons under the provisions of Section 2, having as members one or more general partners and one or more limited partners. The limited partners as such shall not be bound by the obligations of the partnership.

Entity Theory

An entity is anything which possesses the quality of oneness and may therefore be regarded as a single unit. A legal person or legal entity is such a unit which has the recognized capacity of possessing legal rights and being subject to legal duties. A legal entity may acquire, own and dispose of property. It may enter into contracts, commit wrongs, sue and be sued. It is a juristic (legal) person. Each human being is a legal entity of natural origin. Each business corporation is a legal entity created by the act of a legislature.

A partnership is a relationship or association of persons which has the quality of oneness, but the common law regarded it not as an entity but as an aggregation of individuals. Unlike a corporation, a partnership is not an artificial person having a distinct legal existence separate from its members. The U.P.A., however, has basically, but not totally, rejected the common law view of partnerships. The U.P.A. treats partnerships as a legal entity for most purposes, although for some purposes it still treats them as an aggregate.

Partnership as a Legal Entity. A partnership is recognized as a legal entity in the following respects:

1. The assets, liabilities and business transactions of the firm are treated as those of a business unit and are considered separate and distinct from the individual assets, liabilities and nonpartnership business transactions of its members. Section 25.
2. In the marshalling of assets, the assets and liabilities of the firm and those of the respective individual members are considered separate and distinct. Partnership creditors have a prior right to partnership assets, while creditors of the individual members have a prior right, respectively, to the separate assets of their individual debtors. Section 40(h).
3. Title to real estate may be acquired by a partnership in the partnership name, and if so acquired can be conveyed only in the partnership name. Section 8(3).
4. Every partner is considered an agent of the partnership. Section 9(1).
5. In certain States by statute, and in the Federal courts, a partnership may sue and be sued in the partnership name.
6. A partnership is defined as a person in such statutes as the Uniform Commercial Code (Sections 1–201(28), (30)) and the Bankruptcy Reform Act (Section 101(30)).

This listing is by no means exhaustive. It may therefore be observed that a partnership is a unit and in most transactions is regarded as a business unit distinct from each of its component members. It is manifest that a partnership could be endowed by the law with full legal personality and thereby become a full legal entity. It is so regarded by the law of Louisiana and of certain foreign countries.

Partnership as a Legal Aggregate. As a result of the legal characterization of a partnership as an aggregate for some purposes, a partnership can neither sue nor be sued in the firm name in the absence of a permissive statute. Similarly, the debts of the partnership are ultimately the debts of the individual partners, and any one partner may be held liable for the partnership's entire indebtedness. Section 15.

In addition, a partnership lacks continuity of existence: whenever any partner ceases to be associated with the partnership, it is dissolved. Section 29. However, the U.P.A. does grant partnership continuity of existence in circumstances the common law would not.

Most significantly, the Internal Revenue Code treats a partnership as an aggregate. A partnership is not required to pay Federal income tax but must file an information return setting forth the name of each partner and the amount of income derived from the partnership. It is the responsibility of each partner to include his share of partnership income in his individual tax return and to pay the tax thereon. Partnership income is taxed to the individual partners regardless of whether the income is actually distributed.

Types of Partners

A *general partner* is a partner whose liability for partnership indebtedness is unlimited, who has full management powers, and who shares in the profits.

A *special or limited partner* is one who, as a member of a limited partnership, is liable for firm indebtedness only to the ex-

tent of the capital which he has contributed or agreed to contribute.

An *ostensible partner* is one who has consented to be held out as a partner whether he is a real partner or not. The term is more commonly applied to one who is a partner by estoppel: although not an actual partner, he is liable to those who, in good faith, have extended credit on the reasonable assumption that he was a partner.

A *silent partner* is a real partner who has no voice, and takes no part, in the partnership business.

A *secret partner* is a real partner whose membership in the firm is not disclosed to the public.

A *dormant partner* is a real partner who is both a silent and a secret partner.

A *sub-partner* is one who is not a partner at all but has a contractual arrangement with a partner which entitles him to a share of the profits realized by such partner. The relationship calls for no continuous acts or the performance of any duty by the sub-partner.

Delectus Personae

A partnership is manifestly a highly personal relationship. Each partner has a right to take part in the management of the business, to handle the partnership assets for partnership purposes, and to act as agent of the partnership. Accordingly, a partner, by his negligence, injudiciousness or dishonesty, may bring financial loss or ruin to his co-partners. Because of the close relationship involved, partnerships must necessarily be founded on mutual trust and confidence. While occasionally a person may be chosen as a partner because of his ability to make a needed capital contribution, the mutual choice of partners is based largely on desirable personal traits such as business ability, good health, experience, sound judgment, good reputation and integrity. All this finds expression in the term *delectus personae*, which means literally choice of the person and indicates the right one has to choose or select his partners. This principle is embodied in Section 18(g) of the U.P.A. which provides: "No person can become a member of a partnership without the consent of all the partners."

FORMATION OF A PARTNERSHIP

The formation of a partnership is simple and may be done consciously or unconsciously. Needless to say, a partnership which is formed consciously and carefully has a greater likelihood of success. A partnership may result from an oral or written agreement between the parties, or from an informal arrangement not definitely articulated but left to subsequent expression. Persons become partners by associating themselves in business together as co-owners. Whether their agreement is simple or elaborate, definite or indefinite, fully understood and fair, or obscure and productive of discord, is of importance principally to the partners. The existence of the relationship depends upon the agreement and the association in business as co-owners, and not upon the degree of care, intelligence, study or investigation which preceded its formation.

Articles of Partnership

In the interest of achieving a more clear, definite, and complete understanding between the partners, it is preferable that their partnership agreement be reduced to writing. A written agreement creating a partnership is referred to as the partnership agreement or articles of partnership, and should include:

1. The firm name and the identity of the partners;
2. The nature and scope of the partnership business;
3. Duration of the partnership;
4. The capital contributions of each partner and whether in money or specifically described property;
5. The division of profits and sharing of losses;
6. The amount of time that each partner agrees to devote to the business and the duties of each partner in the management;
7. A provision for salaries and drawing accounts of partners, if desired;
8. Restrictions, if any, upon the authority of particular partners to bind the firm;
9. The right, if desired, of a partner to withdraw from the firm and the terms, conditions and notice requirements in the event of such withdrawal;
10. A provision for continuation of the business by the remaining partners, if desired, in the event of the death of a partner or dissolution otherwise caused, and a statement of the method or formula for appraisal and payment of the interest of the deceased or former partner.

Who May Become Partners

Any natural person having full contractual capacity may enter into a partnership. Inasmuch as a minor has capacity to act as principal or agent, he may become a partner, although he has the privilege of disaffirming the partnership agreement at any time before reaching majority, and of avoiding personal liability to partnership creditors. Upon disaffirmance and withdrawal from the partnership, a minor is entitled to the return of his capital contribution and his accrued and unpaid share of the profits except to the extent that such funds are necessary to pay partnership creditors.

The position of an incompetent person is substantially the same as that of a minor except that his insanity may afford his copartners a ground for seeking dissolution by court decree as provided in Section 32 of the Uniform Partnership Act.

A corporation is defined as a "person" in Section 2 of the Uniform Act and is therefore legally capable of entering into a partnership. Section 4(p) of the Model Business Corporation Act authorizes a corporation to be a partner. (Appendix E).

Tests of Partnership Existence

The existence of a community of interest for business purposes is one of the fundamental tests of the existence of a partnership. By this is meant a community of interest in the capital employed in the business, a community of interest in profits and losses, and a community of authority to conduct the business operations.

In the typical contract of partnership, the parties expressly agree to become partners and co-owners of a business for profit, to contribute certain capital to their mutual enterprise, to devote their personal services to the conduct of the business, and to share the profits and losses in stated proportions. Not infrequently, persons become associated in the conduct of a business with only an informal or incomplete agreement as to the extent of their rights and duties and the nature of their relationship. In other situations, the express contract between the parties may purport to be a loan, a lease, or a contract of employment, and yet contain certain elements of a partnership.

Co-ownership alone does not establish a partnership. The co-ownership must relate to a business. Conversely, granting the existence of a business, a person financially interested in or participating in the operation of the business is not a partner unless his interest in participation in the enterprise is that of a co-owner of the business. The existence of a business being relatively easy to ascertain, most of the tests of the partnership relation pertain to the issue of co-ownership. In this connection the incidents of partnership, such as the sharing of profits, the sharing of losses, and the right to manage and control the business, are helpful in determining the element of co-ownership.

Business Element. Section 7(2) of the Uniform Partnership Act provides that joint tenancy, tenancy in common, tenancy by the entireties, joint property, common property or part-ownership does not of itself establish a partnership, even though the co-owners share the profits derived from use of the property. In addition to property there must be a business. An intention to acquire profits being essential to the conduct of a business enterprise, it is clear that an unincorporated nonprofit association, such as a social club, literary society, or fraternal or political organization, is not a business and therefore not a partnership. Where persons are associated together for mutual financial gain on a temporary or limited basis involving a single transaction or a relatively few isolated transactions, no partnership results because the parties are not engaged in a continuous series of commercial activities necessary to constitute a business. Thus, a contract between four farmers whereby they purchase a threshing machine for their mutual use and agree to rent the machine to others and divide the profits does not create a partnership. Co-ownership of the means or instrumentality of accomplishing a single business transaction or a limited series of transactions may result in a joint venture but not a general partnership.

To illustrate: A and B are joint owners of shares of the capital stock of a corporation, have a joint bank account, and have inherited or purchased real estate as joint tenants or tenants in common. They share the dividends paid on the stock, the interest on the bank account, and the net proceeds from the sale or lease of the real estate. A and B are not partners. Although they are co-owners and share profits, they are not engaged in the carrying on of a business, and hence no partnership results. On the other hand, if A and B were engaged in continuous transactions of buying and selling real estate over a period of time and were carrying on a business of trading in real estate, a partnership relation would exist betwen them, irrespective of whether they regarded one another as partners.

A, B, and C each inherit an undivided one-third interest in a hotel and instead of selling the property decide, by an informal and incomplete agreement, to continue operation of the hotel. The operation of a hotel is a business, and, as co-owners of a hotel business, A, B, and C are partners and are subject to all of the rights, duties and incidents arising from the partnership relation.

Co-ownership. The receipt by a person of a share of the profits of a business is prima facie evidence that he is a partner in the business, but Section 7(4) of the Uniform Partnership Act further provides that no inference of the existence of a partnership relation shall be drawn where the profits are received in payment:

1. of a debt by installments or otherwise;
2. of wages of an employee or rent to a landlord;
3. of an annuity to a widow or representative of a deceased partner;
4. of interest on a loan, though the amount of payment vary with the profits of the business, or
5. as consideration for the sale of the good will of a business or other property by installments, or otherwise.

These transactions do not give rise to a presumption that the party is a co-owner because the law assumes it more likely that the creditor, employee, or landlord is not a co-owner. However, it is possible to establish that such a person was a partner by proof of other facts and circumstances. For example, the payment of money or the transfer of title to property in exchange for a share of the profits may be either the cap-

ital contribution of a partner or a loan or sale on credit by a creditor. Outside of the usual incidents of a loan or a sale on credit, the test most frequently employed in doubtful situations is whether an obligation has been created to pay for property received or to repay money advanced in any event. If the party sought to be charged as a partner is entitled at some time to receive payment for the money or property which he advanced, he is generally not a partner but a creditor.

An agreement to share in or contribute to the losses of a business affords strong evidence of an ownership interest. Few jurisdictions insist upon an express agreement of loss sharing for a partnership to exist, but all consider such an agreement compelling proof of the existence of a partnership.

Evidence as to participation in the management or control of a business, standing alone, does not constitute conclusive proof of a partnership relation. A voice in management and control of a business may be accorded, in a limited degree, to an employee, a lessor, or a creditor. On the other hand, one who is actually a partner may take no active part in the affairs of the firm and, indeed, may, by agreement with his copartners, forego all right to exercise any control over the ordinary affairs of the business. In any event, the right to participate in control is an important factor considered by the courts in conjunction with other factors, in particular, profit sharing.

Incidence of Statute of Frauds

The Statute of Frauds does not expressly apply to a contract for the formation of a partnership, and therefore no writing is required in order to create the relationship. The promise of an incoming partner to assume existing debts incurred in the prior operation of the business is not within Section 4 of the Statute as a promise to answer for the debt or default of another, because such promise is made not to the creditors but to the debtor or debtors. It is a third party creditor beneficiary type of contract. However, a contract to form a partnership to continue for a period longer than one year is within the statute and requires a writing in order to be enforceable.

A contract for the transfer of an interest in real estate to or by a partnership, or by a member or prospective member thereof, is governed by the Statute of Frauds and requires a writing to be enforceable. However, the statute does not bar an accounting suit brought by a partner to recover his share of the proceeds of fully consummated transactions in real estate carried on pursuant to an orally constituted partnership or joint venture.

Firm Name

In the interest of acquiring and retaining good will a partnership should have a firm name. It is more desirable for the partners to provide their business enterprise with a name than to have the public provide one for them. The name selected by the partners should not be identical with or deceptively similar to the name of any other existing business concern. It may be the name of the partners or of any one of them, or the partners may decide to operate the business under a fictitious or assumed name, such as "Peachtree Restaurant" or "Globe Theater," or "Paradise Laundry." A partnership may not use a name which would be likely to indicate to the public that it is a corporation.

Nearly all of the States have enacted statutes which require any person or persons conducting or transacting any business under an assumed or fictitious name to file in a designated public office a certificate setting forth the name under which the business is conducted and the true or real names and addresses of all persons conducting the business as partners or proprietors. The purpose of such a statute is to disclose and make available to the public the real names of all parties who see fit to deal or trade with the public under an assumed or fictitious name. The statutes generally provide penalties of fine or imprisonment, or both, for violations. Some statutes provide that no action upon contract can be maintained by an individual or a partnership which has failed to comply with the statute. Other statutes provide that the failure to file the required certificate may be cured, with respect to the right to institute a suit, provided that the certificate is filed prior to the institution of suit even though it was not filed at the time the cause of action arose.

When a person ceases to be a member of a partnership operating under an assumed name, or a new member is added, and the partnership continues to use the assumed name, a new certificate must be filed.

Partnership Capital

The sum total of the money and property contributed by the partners and dedicated to permanent use in the enterprise is the partnership capital. Except upon dissolution no partner may withdraw any part of his capital contribution without the consent of all the partners. Partnership property is the sum of all of the partnership assets including capital contributions, and may vary in amount from day to day or even from hour to hour, while partnership capital is a fixed amount.

A partner, by the terms of the agreement, may contribute no capital but only his skill and services, or a partner may contribute the use of certain property rather than the property itself. For example, a partner who owns a store building may contribute to the partnership the use of the building but not the building itself. The building is therefore not partnership property, and the amount of capital contributed by this partner is the capitalized value of the reasonable annual rental of the building for the duration of the partnership agreement or for the remaining economic life of the building, whichever is the lesser.

Although in accounting practice partnership profits are frequently included in the capital amount, a clear differentiation should be made between capital and profits. Likewise, a loan by a partner to the firm should be distinguished from capital. A partner is entitled to his share of the profits and to repayment of money advanced as a loan without any new agreement with his co-partners, but a withdrawal of capital requires a new agreement. Furthermore, upon dissolution, a debt owing to a partner by the partnership has priority over the rights of partners to return of capital.

Title to real estate which is properly a partnership asset, as where purchased with partnership funds or specifically made a capital contribution, may stand in the name of the partnership, an individual partner, or a third party. Section 8 of the U.P.A. alters the common law by permitting title to real estate to be conveyed to a partnership in the partnership name.

A question may arise whether property owned by a partner before formation of the partnership and used in the partnership business is a capital contribution and an asset of the partnership. Whether it is a partnership asset determines the rights of creditors and partners in the property. The fact that legal title to the property remains unchanged is not conclusive evidence that it has not become a partnership asset. An intention that property is partnership property may be inferred from any of the following facts: (1) the property was improved with partnership funds; (2) the property was carried on the books of the partnership as an asset; (3) taxes, liens or expenses, such as insurance, were paid by the partnership; (4) income or proceeds of the property were treated as partnership funds; or (5) admissions or declarations by the partners.

FORMATION OF LIMITED PARTNERSHIP

Under the Uniform Limited Partnership Act

A limited partnership is one composed of one or more general partners and one or more limited partners. It is sometimes called a special partnership in contrast to a general partnership. It differs from a general partnership in several respects, three of which are basic: (1) there must be a statute in effect providing for the formation of limited partnerships; (2) the limited partnership must fully comply with the requirements of such statute; and (3) the liability of a limited partner for partnership debts or obligations is limited to the extent of the capital which by the limited partnership agreement he has contributed or agreed to contribute.

The Uniform Limited Partnership Act (Appendix C) provides, as to the formation of a limited partnership, that two or more persons desiring to form such a partnership shall sign and swear to a certificate, which shall contain pertinent information including the name of the partnership; the character of the business; the location of the principal place of business; the name and place of residence of each member, general and limited partners being respectively designated; the term for which the partnership is to exist; the amount of cash and a description, and the agreed value, of any other property contributed by each limited partner; the additional contributions, if any, to be made by each limited partner and the times at which or events on the happening of which they shall be made; the time, if agreed upon, when the contribution of each limited partner is to be returned; the share of the profits or the other compensation by way of income which each limited partner is entitled to receive.

This certificate must be filed or caused to be recorded in the office of a designated public official, usually in the county in which the principal office of the limited partnership is located. In some States there is the further requirement that a copy of the certificate shall be published in some newspaper for a designated period. Members of the public dealing with a limited partnership are held to have knowledge of the limited liability of limited partners and of the contents of such certificate upon public notice thereof having been given in the manner prescribed by the statute.

The contribution of a limited partner may be cash or other property but not services. The inclusion of the surname of a limited partner in the partnership name is prohibited unless it is also the surname of a general partner. A violation of this provision renders the limited partner liable as a general partner to any creditor who did not know that he was a limited partner. A limited partner is also liable as a general partner if he takes part in the control of the business. If the certificate contains a false statement, any one who suffers loss by reliance on such statement may hold liable any party to the certificate who knew the statement to be false.

A limited partner occupies a position similar in some respects to that of a shareholder in a corporation. He is primarily an investor. Except at the risk of incurring unlimited liability, he can take no part in the management or operation of the business. He is not an agent of the partnership. Unlike a general partner, he knows in advance the exact extent of his possible loss.

Under the Revised
Uniform Limited Partnership Act

The Revised Uniform Limited Partnership Act, adopted by the National Conference of Commissioners on Uniform State Laws in August 1976, is more modern and comprehensive than the Uniform Limited Partnership Act promulgated in 1916. The Revised Act provides that a limited partnership is formed when the Certificate of Limited Partnership required under the Act is filed in the office of the Secretary of State of the State in which the limited partnership has its principal office.

The Revised Act contains eleven Articles and a total of sixty-four Sections which are set forth in Appendix D of this book. These Articles are:

1. General Provisions (Sections 101–107)
2. Formation; Certificate of Limited Partnership (Sections 201–209)
3. Limited Partners (Sections 301–305)
4. General Partners (Sections 401–405)
5. Finance (Sections 501–504)
6. Distributions and Withdrawal (Sections 601–608)
7. Assignment of Partnership Interests (Sections 701–705)
8. Dissolution (Sections 801–804)
9. Foreign Limited Partnerships (Sections 901–908)
10. Derivative Actions (Sections 1001–1004)
11. Miscellaneous (Sections 1101–1105)

OTHER TYPES OF UNINCORPORATED BUSINESS ASSOCIATIONS

Joint Stock Company

A joint stock company, or joint stock association, as it is sometimes called, is technically a form of general partnership having some of the attributes of a corporation yet differing in several important respects from the ordinary partnership. It is dissimilar to a partnership in that its capital is divided into shares represented by certificates which are transferable; its business and affairs are managed by directors or managers elected by the members, and who alone have the authority to represent and bind it; its members as such are not its agents; and a transfer of shares by a member, or his death, insanity or other incapacity, does not dissolve it or afford a ground for dissolution. It is similar to a partnership, but unlike a corporation, in that it is formed by contract and not by State authority.

Joint Venture

A joint venture or joint adventure is a form of temporary partnership organized to carry out a single or isolated business enterprise for profit, and usually, although not necessarily, of short duration. It is an association of persons who combine their property, money, efforts, skill and knowledge for the purpose of carrying out a single business operation for profit. An example is a securities underwritings syndicate. Another is a syndicate formed to acquire a certain tract or land for subdivision and resale. A joint venture differs from a partnership which is formed to carry on a business over a considerable or indefinite period of time. A joint venturer, as such, is not an agent of his co-venturers and does not necessarily have authority to bind them, although in a given case a joint venturer may have real or apparent authority to bind his co-venturers. Usually the management and operation of the enterprise is placed by agreement in the hands of one member designated as manager. The death of a partner dissolves the partnership, while the death of a joint venturer does not necessarily dissolve the joint venture. A partner cannot sue a co-partner or the firm at law, but must go into equity for relief. On the other hand, a court of law will take jurisdiction over disputes betwen joint venturers. Except for these principal differences, a joint venture is generally governed by the law of partnerships.

Mining Partnerships

A mining partnership is an association of the several owners of the mineral rights in land for the purpose of operating a mine and extracting minerals of economic value for their mutual profit. Although mining partnerships are governed to a considerable extent by the law of general partnerships, there are certain important differences between them. For example, a mining partner has the right to sell his interest in the partnership, and death of a partner does not dissolve a mining partnership.

Limited Partnership Associations

This form of business unit, known as a limited partnership association, is permitted by statute in certain States. It is a legal hybrid. Although called a partnership association, it closely resembles a corporation. It is a legal entity separate and distinct from its members who are not personally responsible for its debts, their liabilities being limited to their capital contribution, except in the event of violation of some statutory provision. An important difference between this type of association and a corporation pertains to the transfer of shares. Although the shares in a limited partnership association are freely transferable, the transferee does not, however, become a member in the association unless so elected by the other members. If membership is refused, he may recover the value of his shares from the association.

Business Trusts

A trust is a transfer of the legal title to certain specific property to one person for the use and benefit of another. Where an express trust results from contract, the agreement is commonly known as a declaration of trust which customarily sets forth a designation of the property or trust res, the duration of the trust, the exact functions and duties of the trustees with respect to the management of the property, the persons to whom the income of the trust is to be paid and the share to be received by each, the method of winding up the trust, and the person or persons entitled to share in the trust property upon termination.

Although trusts are almost as old as the law of equity itself, it was not until late in the nineteenth century that lawyers and business men perceived that the trust concept was capable of being utilized as a method of conducting a commercial enterprise. The business trust, sometimes called a Massachusetts trust, was devised to avoid the burdens of corporate regulation, and particularly the formerly widespread prohibition denying to corporations the power to own and deal in real estate. Like an ordinary trust between living persons, a business trust may be created by a voluntary agreement without the necessity of any authorization or consent of the State.

There are three distinguishing characteristics of a business trust: (1) the trust estate is devoted to the conduct of a business; (2) by the terms of the agreement each beneficiary is entitled to a certificate evidencing his ownership of a beneficial interest in the trust which he is free to sell or otherwise transfer; and (3) the trustees must have the exclusive right to manage and control the business free from control of the beneficiaries, otherwise the trust may fail and the beneficiaries become personally liable for the obligations of the business as partners.

The trustees are personally liable for the debts of the business unless, in entering into contractual relations with others, it is expressly stipulated or definitely understood between the parties that the obligation is incurred solely upon the responsibility of the trust estate. The trustee, in order to escape personal liability on the contractual obligations of the business, must obtain the agreement or consent of the other contracting party to look solely to the assets of the trust. The personal liability of the trustees for their own torts or the torts of their agents and servants employed in the operation of the business stands on a different footing. While this liability cannot be avoided, the risk involved may be reduced substantially or eliminated altogether by insurance.

Unincorporated Associations

With regard to contracts of an unincorporated association, and torts committed by its agents, members of the association who have not authorized the contract or participated in commission of the tort are not personally liable. However, managers of the association entering into contracts on its behalf are personally liable on such contracts; and managers who negligently supervise or conduct an association affair or social event are liable in tort for injuries caused by such negligence.

Cases

Partnership as Legal Entity

HORN'S CRANE SERV. v. PRIOR

(1967) 182 Neb. 94, 152 N.W.2d 421.

WHITE, C. J.

The district court sustained a general demurrer and a motion to dismiss an amended petition, dismissed the action, and plaintiff appeals. We affirm the judgment.

Plaintiff, a seller of equipment and supplies, in two causes of action in his amended petition seeks a personal judgment against the defendants, and each of them, for liability arising out of specific sums due under a written contract with (first cause of action) and for supplies and services furnished (second cause of action) a partnership or joint adventure comprised of the two defendants, Wendell H. Prior and Orie Cook, and one C. E. Piper, the manager who, being a resident of Colorado, was not joined in the action. The partnership or joint adventure was formed for the purpose of operating a quarry and rock-crushing business for profit, and the written contract was entered into and the supplies and services furnished pursuant thereto. Defendants' ultimate liability for personal judgment flowed out of the partnership's or joint adventure's original liability as a separate entity in the transactions. * * *

In neither the original nor amended petition is it alleged, either directly or by inference, that the partnership or joint adventure property was insufficient to satisfy its debts, or that there was no partnership property, and there is no allegation of dissolution or insolvency of said joint adventure or partnership. This was fatal.

In an action seeking a personal judgment against the individual members of a partnership or a joint adventure the petition does not state a cause of action if it fails to state that there is no partnership property or that it is insufficient to satisfy the debts of the partnership of joint adventure. [Citations.] * * *

In State v. Pielsticker, 118 Neb. 419, 225 N.W. 51, this court said: "This court is committed to the doctrine that a partnership is a legal entity by a long line of cases. * * * However, the partnership relation is such that the separate property of a partner cannot be subjected to the payment of partnership debts until the property of the firm is exhausted. [Citation.] Firm property must also be subjected to the payment of the firm debts before it can be applied to the debts of the individual members of the firm. [Citations.] The partners are personally, jointly, and severally responsible for partnership liabilities. But the benefits and liabilities of a partner arise from and are the result of the partnership relation. Therefore in this state a partnership is an entity, distinct and apart from the members composing it, for the purpose for which the partnership exists. [Citations.]

"There are several reasons for the rule. One of the most obvious is that credit having been extended to the partnership or firm, the members ought to have a right to insist that the partnership property be exhausted first. And to permit a firm creditor to bypass the partnership property and exhaust the assets of an individual member leaving the partnership property extant, would be an obvious injustice, permit the other partners to profit at his expense, and place him in an adverse position with relation to his copartners.

"No problem arises out of the plaintiff's allegation that this is a joint adventure. Both parties consider it as a partnership in their briefs. Plaintiff alleges that the defendants and Piper jointly entered into an enterprise for the purpose of acquiring and operating a business; that they contributed money and property thereto; that they all exercised control but that Piper was the manager; and that the plaintiff entered into said contracts on the representation of the defendants that they were an existing partnership. The substance of plaintiff's theory, which he affirms in his brief, is that defendants were members of a partnership and individually and jointly liable on that basis. We further note that section 67–306, R.R.S.1943, defines a partnership as "an association of persons organized as a separate entity to carry on a business for profit." Under the facts alleged and the theory presented by the plaintiff, the law of partnership applies. With reference to joint adventures, this court, in Soulek v. City of Omaha, 140 Neb. 151, 299 N.W. 368, said as follows: "The principal distinction between a partnership and a joint adventure is that the latter may relate to a single transaction. * * * The law of partnership applies to the questions arising between the parties and among the parties in relation to third parties." The district court was correct in sustaining the demurrer and dismissing the action on the ground that the petition did not state a cause of action.

Judgment affirmed.

Test of Partnership Existence

CHAIKEN v.
EMPLOYMENT SEC. COMM'N

(1971) Del.Super., 274 A.2d 707.

[The Delaware Employment Security Commission ordered unemployment compensation contributions assessed against the plaintiff for two barbers in his barber shop upon its determination that they were his employees. Plaintiff maintained they were not employees but partners pursuant to written partnership agreements. As partners, plaintiff would not be liable for contributions under the statute. Upon appeal from the Commission's order, affirmed.]

STOREY, J.

* * *

Chaiken contends that he and his "partners":

(1) properly registered the partnership name and names of partners in the Prothonotary's office, in accordance with 6 Del.C. § 3101,

(2) properly filed federal partnership information returns and paid federal taxes quarterly on an estimated basis, and

(3) duly executed partnership agreements.

Of the three factors, the last is most important. Agreements of "partnership" were executed between Chaiken and Mr. Strazella, a barber in the shop, and between Chaiken and Mr. Spitzer, similarly situated. The agreements were nearly identical. The first paragraph declared the creation of a partnership and the location of business. The second provided that Chaiken would provide barber chair, supplies, and licenses, while the other partner would provide tools of the trade. The paragraph also declared that upon dissolution of the partnership, ownership of items would revert to the party providing them. The third paragraph declared that the income of the partnership would be divided 30% for Chaiken, 70% for Strazella; 20% for Chaiken

and 80% for Spitzer. The fourth paragraph declared that all partnership policy would be decided by Chaiken, whose decision was final. The fifth paragraph forbade assignment of the agreement without permission of Chaiken. The sixth paragraph required Chaiken to hold and distribute all receipts. The final paragraph stated hours of work for Strazella and Spitzer and holidays.

The mere existence of an agreement labeled "partnership" agreement and the characterization of signatories as "partners" does not conclusively prove the existence of a partnership. Rather, the intention of the parties, as explained by the wording of the agreement, is paramount. [Citation.]

A partnership is defined as an association of two or more persons to carry on as co-owners a business for profit. [Citation.] As co-owners of a business, partners have an equal right in the decision making process. [Citation.] But this right may be abrogated by agreement of the parties without destroying the partnership concept, provided other partnership elements are present. [Citation.]

Thus, while paragraph four reserves for Chaiken all right to determine partnership policy, it is not standing alone, fatal to the partnership concept. Co-owners should also contribute valuable consideration for the creation of the business. Under paragraph two, however, Chaiken provides the barber chair (and implicitly the barber shop itself), mirror, licenses and linen, while the other partners merely provide their tools and labor—nothing more than any barber-employee would furnish. Standing alone, however, mere contribution of work and skill can be valuable consideration for a partnership agreement. [Citations.]

Partnership interests may be assignable, although it is not a violation of partnership law to prohibit assignment in a partnership agreement. [Citation.] Therefore, paragraph five on assignment of partnership interests does not violate the partnership concept. On the other hand, distribution of partnership assets to the partners upon dissolution is only allowed after all partnership liabilities are satisfied. [Citation.] But paragraph two of the agreement, in stating the ground rules for dissolution, makes no declaration that the partnership assets will be utilized to pay partnership expenses before reversion to their original owners. This deficiency militates against a finding in favor of partnership intent since it is assumed Chaiken would have inserted such provision had he thought his lesser partners would accept such liability. Partners do accept such liability, employees do not.

Most importantly, co-owners carry on "a business for profit." The phrase has been interpreted to mean that partners share in the profits and the losses of the business. The intent to divide the profits is an indispensable requisite of partnership. [Citations.] Paragraph three of the agreement declares that each partner shall share in the income of the business. There is no sharing of the profits, and as the agreement is drafted, there are no profits. Merely sharing the gross returns does not establish a partnership. [Citation.] Nor is the sharing of profits prima facie evidence of a partnership where the profits received are in payment of wages. [Citation.]

The failure to share profits therefore, is fatal to the partnership concept here.

Evaluating Chaiken's agreement in the light of the elements implicit in a partnership, no partnership intent can be found. The absence of the important right of decision making or the important duty to share liabilities upon dissolution individually may not be fatal to a partnership. But when both are absent, coupled with the absence of profit sharing, they become strong factors in discrediting the partnership argument. * * *

In addition, the total circumstances of the case taken together indicate the employer-employee relationship between Chaiken and his barbers. The agreement set forth the hours of work and days off—unusual subjects for partnership agreements. The barbers brought into the relationship only the equipment required of all barber shop operators. And each barber had his own individual "partnership" with Chaiken. Furthermore, Chaiken conducted all transactions with suppliers, and purchased licenses, insurance, and the lease for the business property in his own name. Finally, the name "Richard's Barber Shop" continued to be used after the execution of the so called partnership agreements.

* * *

[Decision of Commission affirmed.]

Test of Partnership Existence

CUTLER v. BOWEN

(1975, Utah) 543 P.2d 1349.

CROCKETT, J.

Plaintiff, alleging a partnership with defendant, sued to recover half of $10,000 paid by the Salt Lake City Redevelopment Agency as compensation for the disruption of their tavern business known as The Havana Club at the corner of Second South and West Temple Streets. The district court made findings and entered judgment in favor of the plaintiff. Defendant appeals.

The Havana Club had been operated for some years at the location mentioned under a lease running to defendant Dale Bowen, who owned the equipment, furnishings and inventory. He did not himself work in operating the club. In June, 1968, he discussed with the plaintiff Frances Cutler, who had been working for him as a bartender, that she take over the management of the club. They arrived at an oral agreement which included these conditions: that the plaintiff was to have the authority and the responsibility for the entire active management and operation: to purchase the supplies, pay the bills, keep the books, to hire and fire employees; and do whatever else was necessary to run the business. As to compensation, the arrangement was for a down-the-middle split; each was to receive $100 per week, plus one half of the net profits.

The business was operated under this arrangement for four years, until the lessor's building was taken over by the Redevelopment Agency in 1972. * * * On the basis of the regulations it was ascertained that for such displacement the Havana Club should be entitled to the maximum allowable amount of $10,000. The parties made some effort to find a suitable new location for the Havana Club, but failing to do so, decided to terminate that business in April, 1972.

The dispute giving rise to this lawsuit arose because the defendant contended that he was the sole owner of the entire business; and that the plaintiff's status was merely that of an employee, so defendant was entitled to the whole $10,000. Whereas, plaintiff took the position that, conceding the defendant was the owner of the physical assets of the business as above stated, insofar as the going concern and goodwill value, as a partner in the business, she was entitled to one half of the relocation fund.

One of the primary matters to consider in determining whether a partnership exists is the nature of the contribution each party makes to the enterprise. It need not be in the form of tangible assets or capital, but, as is frequently done, one partner may make such a contribution, and this may be balanced by the other's performance of services and the shouldering of responsibility.

When parties join in an enterprise, it is usually in contemplation of success and making profits, and is often without much concern about who will bear losses. However, when they so engage in a venture for their mutual benefit or profit, that is generally held to be a partnership, in which the law imposes upon them both liability for debts or losses that may occur. This basic principle of partnership law is set forth in our Uniform Partnership Act, Title 48 of U.C.A. 1953:

Sec. 48–1–4. Rules for determining the existence of a partnership.—In determining whether a partnership exists these rules shall apply:

* * *

(4) The receipt by a person of a share of the profits of a business is prima facie evidence that he is a partner in the business, but no such inference shall be drawn if such profits were received in payment:

* * *

(b) As wages of an employee or rent to a landlord.

On the question whether profits shared should be regarded simply as wages, it is important to consider the degree to which a party participates in the management of the enterprise and whether the relationship is such that the party shares generally in the potential profits or advantages and thus should be held responsible for losses or liability incurred therein.

* * *

It is not shown here that any occasion arose where the plaintiff's responsibility for debts or other liabilities of the business was tested. However, throughout the four years in which she operated and managed the Club, apparently with competence and efficiency, it was her responsibility to see that all bills were paid, including the rental on the lease, employees' salaries, the costs of all purchases, licenses and other expenses of the business. During that time she saw the defendant Bowen only infrequently for the purpose of rendering an accounting and dividing the profits. It is further pertinent that the parties reported their income tax as a partnership.

Under the arrangement as shown and as found by the trial court, a good case can be made out that it was largely through the capability, experience, and efforts of the plaintiff that, in addition to the physical plant, there existed a separate asset in the value of the "going concern and goodwill" of the business, which was being lost by its displacement. On the basis of what has been said above, we see nothing to persuade us to disagree with the view taken by the trial court: that the plaintiff's involvement in this business was such that she would have been liable for any losses that might have occurred in its operation; and that, concomitantly, she was entitled to participate in any profits or advantages that inured to it.

* * *

From the circumstances shown in evidence as discussed herein, there appears to be a reasonable basis for the trial court's view that, except for the physical assets, which belonged to the defendant and to which the plaintiff makes no claim, the further asset of the business: that is, the value of what is called going concern and goodwill belonged to the two of them as partners in the enterprise; and that when the business could not be relocated, the $10,000 should properly be regarded as compensation for the loss by the forced relocation (which turned out to be a termination) of the business; and that the partners having lost their respective equal shares in the going business operation, they should also share equally in the compensation for its loss. * * *

Affirmed.

Formation of Limited Partnership

VIDRICKSEN v. GROVER

(1966, C.A.9) 333 F.2d 372.

CHAMBERS, CIRCUIT J.

Dr. Vidricksen intended, when he turned over to Thom $25,000 in July, 1952, to become a limited partner with Thom, the general partner, in a Chevrolet car agency business at Dunsmuir, California. Thus, the shoemaker strayed from his last.

Articles of partnership were drawn up but no effort was made to comply with the California statutory requirement of recording a certificate of limited partnership.

Bankruptcy overtook Thom in September, 1961. And the issue here is whether Dr. Vidricksen is a general partner for the purposes of bankruptcy. The referee held he was. On review, the district court sustained the referee. Here on appeal, we affirm.

Apparently the agency developed financial difficulties in March, 1961, and the doctor consulted successively two different lawyers. From them, although they could not represent him because of conflict of interest, he did learn he had a problem, to-wit, whether in his venture he had attained a real limited partnership and therefore limited liability under California law. The Uniform Limited Partnership Act has been adopted in California with some modification.

On the issue before us, no significant facts occurred until August, 1961, when, through another set of attorneys, he filed a complaint against Thom which seemed to seek an accounting. In it, Vidricksen said:

"That due to the lack of filing and recordation of [the] Limited Partnership Agreement, all as is required under law, * * * said plaintiff [Vidricksen] and said defendant [Thom] have become general partners, insofar as their relationship with third party creditors is concerned."

On September 19, 1961, (eight days after the bankruptcy proceedings started) Dr. Vidricksen filed in the bankruptcy proceedings a renunciation under Section 15511 of the Corporations Code of California. That section reads as follows:

"A person who has contributed to the capital of a business conducted by a person or partnership erroneously believing that he has become a limited partner in a limited partnership, is not, by reason of his exercise of the rights of a limited partner, a general partner with the person or in the partnership carrying on the business, or bound by the obligations of such person or partnership; provided, that on ascertaining the mistake he promptly renounces his interest in the profits of the business, or other compensation by way of income."

Was such renunciation timely? We think not.

Appellant would count the time on "promptly" in "promptly renounces" only from August 7, 1961, to September 19, 1961, or a period of 43 days. We disagree. In our view "promptly" began to run when he learned in March, 1961, that something was wrong with the organizational setup.

No California case is of help to us in construing the code section, so we must use our best judgment as to what California courts would hold. We do not think Dr. Vidricksen needed a bonded opinion to start the time running. Knowledge that he was probably in trouble was enough. Thus, we conclude that six months from the time he had notice something was wrong until the actual renunciation is not a prompt renunciation. Even in August when he sued, the doctor was not renouncing, but was apparently accepting the fate of a general partner. It is possible that that action on his part could be held an abandonment of the limited partnership and acceptance of general partnership status. But we do not find it necessary to so hold. Certainly, though, the act went in the wrong direction. And we do not reach the question of his status had he renounced on August 7, 1961, when he instead affirmed general partnership. We simply hold the attempted renunciation was not timely. Thus, the doctor must be held to the pains of a general partner.

* * *

Affirmed.

Problems

1. A and B are joint owners of shares of stock of a corporation, have a joint bank account and have purchased and own as tenants in common a piece of real estate. They share equally the dividends paid on the stock, the interest on the bank account, and the rent from the real estate. Without the knowledge of A, B makes a trip to inspect the real estate and on his way runs over X. X sues A and B for his personal injuries, joining A as defendant on the theory that A was B's partner. Is A liable?

2. Smith, Jones and Brown were creditors of White, who operated a grain elevator known as White's Elevator. White was heavily involved and was about to fail when the three creditors mentioned agreed to take a conveyance of his elevator property and pay all the debts. It was also agreed that White should continue as manager of the business at a salary of $500 per month and that all profits of the business were to be paid to Smith, Jones and Brown. It was further agreed that they could dispense with White's services at any time and he was also at liberty to quit when he pleased. White accepted the proposition and continued to operate the business as before, buying and selling grain, incurring obligations and borrowing money at the bank in his own name for the business. He did, however, tell the banker of the transaction with Smith, Jones and Brown and other former creditors of the business knew of it. It worked successfully and for several years paid substantial profits, enough so that Smith, Jones and Brown had received back nearly all that they had originally advanced. Were Smith, Jones and Brown partners?

3. John Palmer and Henry Morrison formed the partnership of Palmer & Morrison for the management of the Huntington Hotel. The partnership agreement provided that Palmer would contribute $40,000 and be a general partner and Morrison would contribute $30,000 and be a limited partner. Palmer was to manage the dining and cocktail rooms and Morrison was to manage the rest of the hotel. Nanette, a popular French singer, who knew nothing of the partnership affairs, appeared for four weeks in the Blue Room at the hotel and was not paid her salary of $8,000. Subsequently, Palmer and Morrison had a difference of opinion and Palmer bought

Morrison's interest in the partnership for $20,000. Palmer later went into bankruptcy. Nanette sued Morrison for $8,000. For how much, if anything, is Morrison liable?

4. A and B engaged in the grocery business as partners. In one year they earned considerable money and at the end of the year, after due deliberation, they decided to and did invest a part of the profits in oil land. Title to the land was taken in their names as tenants in common. The investment was fortunate for oil was discovered near the land and its value increased many times. A died, leaving a wife and one child. At the time of A's death both he and the partnership were heavily involved financially and there was a contest between his creditors and the partnership creditors for a prior claim against the oil land. Which should succeed?

5. A owned an old roadside building which he believed could be easily converted into an antique shop. He talked to his friend B, an antique fancier, and they executed the following written agreement:

(a) A would supply the building, all utilities, and $10,000 capital for purchasing antiques.

(b) B would supply $3,000 for purchasing antiques, A to repay him at the time the business terminates.

(c) B would manage the shop, make all purchases, and receive a salary of $100 per week plus five percent of the gross receipts.

(d) Fifty percent of the net profits would go into the purchase of new stock. The balance of the net profits would go to A.

(e) The business would operate under the name "Roadside Antiques."

Business went poorly and the result after one year is a debt of $4,000 owing to Old Fash-

ioned, Inc., the principal supplier of antiques purchased by B in the name of "Roadside Antiques." Old Fashioned, Inc. sues "Roadside Antiques", and A, and B as partners. Decision?

6. Clark owned a vacant lot. Bird was engaged in building houses. An oral agreement was entered into between Clark and Bird whereby Bird was to erect a house on the lot. Upon the sale of the house and lot, Bird was to have his money first. Clark was then to have the agreed value of the lot, and the profits were to be equally divided. Did a partnership exist?

7. X, Y, and Z formed a partnership for the purpose of betting on boxing matches. X and Y would become friendly with various boxers and offer them bribes to lose certain bouts. Z would then place large bets, using money contributed by all three, and would collect the winnings. After Z had accumulated a large sum of money, X and Y demanded their share but Z refused to make any split. X and Y then brought suit in a court of equity to compel Z to account for the profits of the partnership. What decision?

8. A, B, C, and D, residents of the State of X, were partners doing business under the trade name of Morning Glory Nursery. A owned a one-third interest and B, C, and D, two-ninths each. The partners acquired three tracts of land in the State of X for the purpose of the partnership. Two of the tracts were acquired in the names of the four partners, "trading and doing business as Morning Glory Nursery." The third tract was acquired in the names of the individuals, the trade name not appearing in the deed. This third tract was acquired by the partnership out of partnership funds and for partnership purposes. Who owns each of the three tracts? Why?

RELATIONSHIPS BETWEEN PARTNERS AND WITH THIRD PERSONS; DISSOLUTION, WINDING UP, AND TERMINATION

The relationship of partners to one another is considered separately from the relationship of partners to third persons. The rights and duties of the partners among themselves are determined by the partnership agreement and as provided in the U.P.A., Part IV, Sections 18–23. The relations of partners to third persons dealing with the partnership are governed by the U.P.A., Part III, Sections 9–17.

Before commencing the study of the text in this chapter the student should carefully read Sections 18–23 and Sections 9–17 of the U.P.A. in Appendix B of this book.

RELATIONSHIPS OF PARTNERS TO ONE ANOTHER

When parties enter into a partnership or other business association, the law imposes certain obligations upon the parties as well as providing them with specific rights. So long as the rights of third parties are not affected and standards of fairness are maintained, the parties may by agreement vary these rights and obligations.

DUTIES AMONG PARTNERS

Fiduciary Duty

A fiduciary relationship exists among the members of a partnership based upon the high standard of trust and confidence which they have a right to repose in one another. Each partner owes a duty of good faith and utmost loyalty to his co-partners, and only upon such basis may so intimate a business relationship fairly function. The requirement of the law of agency that the agent shall not make a profit other than his agreed compensation, and shall not compete with his principal, or otherwise profit from the relationship at the expense of his principal, appears in partnership law as the fiduciary duty that each partner owes to his co-partners.

Section 21 of the Uniform Act provides that every partner must account to the partnership for any benefit, and hold as trustee for it any profits derived by him without the consent of the other partners from any transaction connected with the formation, conduct, or liquidation of the partnership or from any use by him of its property. This rule also applies to the representatives of a deceased partner engaged in the liquidation of the affairs of the partnership as the personal representative of the last surviving partner. A partner may not deal at arm's length with his co-partners. He may not prefer himself over the firm. His duty is one of undivided and continuous loyalty to his co-partners.

The extent of this fiduciary duty, which binds all fiduciaries and not just partners, has been most eloquently expressed by the often quoted words of Judge (later Justice) Cardozo:

Joint adventurers, like co-partners, owe to one another, while the enterprise continues, the duty of the *finest loyalty*. Many forms of conduct permissible in a workaday world for those acting at arm's length, are forbidden to those bound by fiduciary ties. A trustee is held to something stricter than the morals of the market place. *Not honesty alone, but the punctilio of an honor the most sensitive, is then the standard of behavior*. As to this there has developed a tradition that is unbending and inveterate. Upcompromising rigidity has been the attitude of courts of equity when petitioned to undermine the rule of undivided loyalty by the "disintegrating erosion" of particular exceptions. Only thus has the level of conduct for fiduciaries been kept at a level higher than that trodden by the crowd. It will not consciously be lowered by any judgment of this court. Meinhard v. Salmon, 249 N.Y. 458, 459, 164 N.E. 545, 546 (1928) [emphasis added].

Duty of Obedience

A partner owes his partners a duty to act in obedience to the partnership agreement and to any business decisions properly made by the partnership. Any partner violating this duty will be individually liable for any resulting loss. Thus, a partner who in violation of an express agreement not to extend credit to relatives, advanced money from partnership funds and sold goods on credit to an impecunious relative, was held personally liable for the unpaid debt to his partners.

Duty of Care

A partner must manage the partnership affairs without culpable negligence. Culpable negligence is something more than ordinary negligence, yet short of gross negligence. Thus, a partner does not breach his duty of care if he makes honest errors of judgment or fails to use ordinary skill in transacting partnership business, so long as he is not culpably negligent.

As with fiduciary duty, the law does not distinguish between the duty of care owed by a general partner to a general partnership and that owed by a general partner to a limited partnership. This results in part from Section 6 of the U.P.A. which provides that "the act will apply to limited partnerships except in so far as it is inconsistent with the statutes relating to such partnerships." On the other hand, a limited partner owes no duty of care to a limited partnership as long as he remains a limited partner.

RIGHTS AMONG PARTNERS

Rights in Specific Partnership Property

A partner's ownership interest in any specific item of partnership property is that of a tenant in partnership. Section 25. This species of ownership exists only in a partnership, and the principal characteristics of a tenancy in partnership are:

1. Each partner has an equal right with his co-partners to possess partnership property for partnership purposes, but he has no

right to possess it for any other purpose without the consent of his co-partners.

2. A partner may not make an individual assignment of his right in specific partnership property.

3. A partner's interest in specific partnership property is not subject to attachment or execution at the instance of his individual creditors. It is subject to attachment or execution only on a claim against the partnership.

4. Upon the death of a partner, his right in specific partnership property vests in the surviving partner or partners. Upon the death of the last surviving partner, his right in such property vests in his legal representative.

Partner's Interest in the Partnership

In addition to owning as a tenant in partnership every specific item of partnership property, each partner has an interest in the partnership which is defined as his share of the profits and surplus, and is expressly stated to be personal property. Section 26.

Assignability. A partner may sell or assign his interest in the partnership, but this does not cause dissolution. The new owner, however, does not become a partner, does not succeed to the partner's rights to participate in the management and does not have access to the information available to a member of the firm as a matter of right. He is merely entitled to receive the share of profits and participation in any liquidation to which the assigning partner would otherwise be entitled. Section 27. The assigning partner remains a partner with all the usual rights and duties.

A limited partner may assign his interest. If he does so, the assignee may become a substituted limited partner if all the others consent, or if the assigning partner, having such power as provided in the cer-

tificate, gives the assignee this right. Upon the death of a limited partner, his executor or administrator has all the rights of such partner for the purpose of settling his estate, and such power as the deceased partner had to constitute his assignee a substituted limited partner.

Creditors' Rights. A partner's interest is subject to the claims of that partner's creditors who may obtain a charging order against the partner's interest. Section 28. A creditor who has charged the interest of a partner with a judgment debt may apply for the appointment of a receiver. The court may appoint a receiver for the partner's interest who will receive and hold for the benefit of the creditor the share of profits which ordinarily would be paid to the partner. Neither the judgment creditor nor the receiver is entitled to participation in the management or to have access to information.

Right to Share in Profits

As a partnership is an association to carry on a business for profit, each partner is entitled to a share of the profits, and conversely, must contribute toward the losses. Section 18(a). In the absence of an agreement among the partners with regard to division of profits, the partners share the profits equally, regardless of the ratio of their financial contributions and advancements or the degree of their participation in the management. Unless the partnership agreement provides otherwise, the partners bear losses in the same proportion in which they share profits. The agreement may, however, validly provide for bearing losses in some different proportion than that in which profits are shared.

A limited partner is entitled to his share of the profits as stipulated in the certificate before the general partners receive their share of the profits. A limited partner does not share in the losses of the partnership beyond his capital contribution. U.L.P.A., Section 7.

Right to Return of Capital

Subject to the rights of the partnership creditors, upon termination of the firm each partner is entitled to be repaid his capital contribution. Unless otherwise agreed, a partner is not entitled to interest on his capital contribution. His share of the profits of the partnership may be considered as earnings on his investment of capital. However, if there is a delay in return of his capital contribution, he is entitled to interest at the legal rate from the date when it should have been repaid.

If a partner makes advancements from time to time over and above his agreed capital contribution, he is entitled to repayment of the loan plus interest thereon. Section 18(d). His position as a creditor of the firm is subordinate to the claims of creditors who are not partners. A partner who has reasonably and necessarily incurred personal liabilities in the ordinary and proper conduct of the business of the firm or who has made payments on behalf of the partnership is entitled to indemnification or repayment. Section 18(b).

A limited partner is entitled to his capital contribution before any general partner and upon six months' demand so long as there are sufficient partnership assets to pay all liabilities owed to third party creditors and limited partners. U.L.P.A., Sections 16 and 23. If a limited partner makes a loan to the partnership, he is entitled to repayment of the loan on a pro rata basis with general creditors of the partnership.

Right to Compensation

The Uniform Act provides that, unless otherwise agreed, no partner is entitled to remuneration for acting in the partnership business. Section 18(f). This represents the common-law viewpoint that whatever a partner does for the partnership, he is doing for himself. If the partnership agreement contemplates that one partner shall perform a substantial or disproportionate share of the work of conducting the business, such partner may, by agreement among all of the partners, receive a salary or, in lieu of salary, an increased percentage of the profits. In the absence of agreement, he is entitled to no salary but only his share of the profits. The only exception to the rule is that provided in Section 18(f) whereby a surviving partner is entitled to reasonable compensation for his services in winding up the partnership affairs.

Right to Participate in Management

Although each of the partners may carve out for himself or have delegated to him a certain sphere of activity within the business, each of them has an equal voice in its management. When a difference of opinion develops, the majority prevails, both at common law and under the U.P.A. Section 18(h). There is conflict among the authorities as to what should be done in the event of an equal division of opinion resulting in a stalemate. Some courts hold that, in such case, a partner may go ahead and deal with third parties with impunity. Others hold to the contrary.

Unanimous agreement of the partners is necessary if a matter involves contravention of the agreement between them, such as the addition of a new business activity or the dropping of an old one. In addition, Section 9(3) of the U.P.A. requires unanimous consent for changing the location of the business, compromising a firm debt, agreeing to an arbitration, or a disposition of so much of the firm's assets that it would be impossible to continue the business.

Although limited partners are not barred from management, they forfeit their limited liability if they take part in control of the business.

Right to Information and Inspection of the Books

Each partner is entitled to full information as to all partnership matters upon demand at any time, and each has a duty to supply such information as he may possess. The right to demand information extends also to the legal representative of a deceased partner for a reasonable time following the dissolution of the partnership. Section 20.

Unless the partners agree otherwise, the books of the partnership are to be kept at the principal place of business at all times, and each partner has an absolute right to have access to them, to inspect them, and to copy any of them. This right may be exercised by a duly authorized attorney or accountant on behalf of a partner. The right continues after dissolution of the partnership, although the courts are loath to require that records be maintained for an extended period, with the attendant expense, after the partnership no longer has a place of business.

Right to Choose Associates

No partner may be forced to accept any person as a partner whom he does not choose. This is because of the fiduciary relationship between the parties. When a partner sells his interest to another, the purchaser does not become a partner and is not entitled to participate in the management. He is entitled only to receive the profits and rights upon liquidation accruing to the share which he has bought. If the purchaser is admitted to the firm as a partner by agreement of all of the parties, the old partnership is ended and a new one has been formed.

A partner need not acquiesce in efforts of his partners to bring a new partner into the business. He may choose to dissolve the partnership, and, if this is necessary because of the insistence of the others, he may be entitled to an accounting for damages against them. On the other hand, the partners cannot prevent a partner withdrawing although in breach of the agreement, as a court will not decree specific performance of a partnership contract. The wrongfully withdrawing partner is subject to damages in a suit against him by his co-partners for breach of the partnership contract.

Right to an Accounting

At common law and under the U.P.A., a partner is entitled to an accounting and may invoke the power of a court of equity to decree an accounting whenever he is wrongfully excluded from the partnership business or possession of its property by his co-partners, or whenever other circumstances render it just and reasonable. Section 22. A partner may not be permitted to sue the partnership at law, as he would be suing himself, but he may sue in equity in an action for an accounting. The suit will be against his co-partners individually, as there is no legal entity involved.

RELATIONSHIP BETWEEN PARTNERS AND THIRD PARTIES

Under the law of agency, a principal is liable upon contracts made on his behalf by his duly authorized agents and is liable in tort for the wrongful acts of his agents committed in the course of their employment. A large part of the law of partnership is the law of agency and most problems arising between partners and third persons require the application of principles of agency law. This relationship is made explicit by Section 4(3) of the U.P.A.: "The law of agency shall apply under this act."

Section 9 of the U.P.A. further states:

Every partner is an agent of the partnership for the purpose of its business, and the act of every partner, including the execution in the partnership name of any instrument, for apparently carrying on in the usual way the business of the partnership of which he is a member binds the partnership, unless the partner so acting has in fact no authority to act for the partnership in the particular matter, and the person with whom he is dealing has knowledge of the fact that he has no such authority.

Thus, the act of every partner binds the partnership with respect to transactions within the scope of the partnership business unless the partner does not have actual or apparent authority to so act. If the partnership is bound, then each partner has unlimited, personal liability for that partnership obligation.

CONTRACTS OF PARTNERSHIP

Contract Liability of Partners

The U.P.A. provides (Section 15) that partners are jointly liable on all debts and contract obligations of the partnership. The consequences of joint liability are as follows:

1. In a suit upon a joint obligation, each living joint obligor must be made a party defendant in the action.
2. A judgment based upon a joint obligation must be against all of the obligors or none. The death of an obligor terminates his liability.
3. A release of one joint obligor releases all. A covenant not to sue may be given to one of serveral joint obligors and will have the effect of releasing that one while preserving rights against the others.

Authority to Bind Partnership

A partner may bind the partnership by his act (a) if he has actual authority, express or implied, to perform the act; or (b) if he has apparent authority to perform the act, his lack of actual authority being unknown to the third person, and the act apparently carries on in the usual way the business of the partnership. If the act is not apparently

within the scope of the partnership business, then the partnership is bound only where the partner has actual authority, and the third person dealing with the partner assumes the risk of the existence of such actual authority.

Express Actual Authority. This authority may be specifically set forth in the partnership agreement or in a collateral agreement between the partners, written or oral. In addition, it may arise from decisions made by a majority of the partners regarding ordinary matters connected with the partnership business. Section 18(h).

Section 9 of the U.P.A. provides that the following acts do not bind the partnership unless authorized by *all* of the partners: (1) assignment of partnership property for the benefit of its creditors; (2) disposal of the good will of the business; (3) any act which would make it impossible to carry on the ordinary business of the partnership; (4) confession of a judgment; (5) submission of a partnership claim or liability to arbitration or reference.

In addition to the foregoing, a partner who does not have actual authority from each of his co-partners may not bind the partnership by any of the following acts inasmuch as they are clearly outside of the scope of the partnership under ordinary circumstances: (1) execution of contracts of guaranty and suretyship in the firm name; (2) sale of partnership property not held for sale in the usual course of business, and (3) payment of individual debts out of partnership assets.

Implied Actual Authority. This authority includes authority which is neither expressly granted nor expressly denied but is reasonably deduced from the nature of the partnership, the terms of the partnership agreement, and the relations of the partners. For example, a partner has implied authority to hire and fire employees whose services are necessary to carry on the business of the partnership. In addition, a partner has implied authority to purchase property necessary for the business.

Apparent Authority. Apparent authority, which may or may not be actual, is such authority as may, in view of the circumstances and the conduct of the parties, be reasonably considered to exist by a third person who has no knowledge or notice of the lack of actual authority. A third person may not rely upon apparent authority in any situation where he is put on notice or has knowledge that the partner does not, or may not, have actual authority. In such case, the third person must ascertain the actual authority of the partner or assume the risk of the absence of such authority.

Partnership by Estoppel

Partnership is a voluntary relationship founded upon contract, express or implied. The meaning of "partnership by estoppel" is not that a partnership may be created by any method other than agreement, but that a person who is actually not a partner may be held liable as a partner for a partnership obligation by reason of a representation which estops or precludes him from later asserting that in truth no partnership existed.

Partnership by estoppel imposes partnership duties and liabilities upon a person who is not a partner in an existing partnership by reason of his making or consenting to a representation that he is a partner. It extends to a third person to whom such representation is made who gives credit to the partnership in reliance thereon. It existed at common law, and is codified in the U.P.A. Section 16(1) as follows:

When a person, by words spoken or written or by conduct, represents himself, or consents to another representing him to anyone, as a partner in an existing partnership or with one or more persons not actual partners, he is liable to any such person to whom such representation has been made, who has, on the faith of such representation, given credit to the actual or apparent partnership, and if he has made such representation or consented to its being made in a public manner he is liable to such person, whether the representation has or has not been made or communicated to such person so giving credit by or with the knowledge of the apparent partner making the representation or consenting to its being made.

For example, A and B are sole partners doing business as A and Company. A introduces C to T, describing C as a member of the partnership. Believing that C is a member, T sells goods on credit to A and Company. In an action by T against A, B, and C as partners to recover the price of the goods, C is liable although not a partner in A and Company. T had relied upon the representation to which C by his silence consented. However, if T at the time had knowledge that C was not a partner, his reliance on the representation would not have been justified and C would not be liable.

Except where the representation of membership in a partnership has been made in a public manner, no person is entitled to rely upon a representation of partnership unless it is made directly to him. For example, C falsely tells D that he is a member of the partnership A and Company. D casually relays this statement to T who in reliance thereon sells goods on credit to A and Company. T cannot hold C liable, as he was not justified in relying on the representation made privately by C to D which C did not consent to have repeated to T.

However, where C knowingly permits his name to appear publicly in the firm name or a list of partners, or used in public announcements or advertisements in a manner which indicates that he is a partner in the firm, C is liable to any member of the public dealing with the partnership whether or not the representations have been made or communicated to such person by or with the knowledge of C. Section 16(1).

Admissions of a Partner

An admission or representation by any partner concerning partnership affairs, within the scope of his authority, is evidence against the partnership. An admission by one person that a partnership exists does not prove its existence. But once the partnership is established by competent evidence, the admission of one partner may be used against the partnership provided the partner is acting within the scope of the partnership business.

Notice to and Knowledge of a Partner

A partnership is bound by notice to any partner of any matter relating to partnership affairs, and by the knowledge of the partner acting in a particular matter acquired while he was a partner or then present in his mind, and the knowledge of any other partner who reasonably could and should have communicated it to the acting partner. U.P.A. Section 12. If the knowledge was then present in the mind of the acting partner or other partner, it is immaterial when either one acquired it.

A demand upon one partner as representative of the firm constitutes a demand upon the partnership.

TORTS OF PARTNERSHIP

The liability of partners for a tort or breach of trust committed by any partner or by an employee of the firm in the course of partnership business is joint and several. All of the partners may be sued jointly in one action based upon tort liability, or separate actions may be maintained against each of them and separate judgments obtained. Section 15. Judgments obtained are enforceable only against property of the defendant or defendants named in the suit. However, payment of any one of the judgments operates as a satisfaction of all of them.

Section 13 of the U.P.A. provides:

Where, by any wrongful act or omission of any partner acting in the ordinary course of the business of the partnership or with the authority of his co-partners, loss or injury is caused to any person not being a partner in the partnership or any penalty is incurred, the partnership is liable therefor to the same extent as the partner so acting or omitting to act.

This liability is comparable to the vicarious liability imposed upon a principal for the torts of an agent by the doctrine of respondeat superior. The partner committing the tort is directly liable to the third party and must also indemnify the partnership for any damages it pays to the third party. Tort liability of the partnership may include not only the negligence of the partners but also trespass, fraud, defamation, and breach of fiduciary duty, so long as the tort is committed in the course of business.

LIABILITY OF INCOMING PARTNER

A person admitted as a partner into an existing partnership is liable for all of the obligations of the partnership arising before his admission as though he had been a partner when such obligations were incurred, although this liability may be satisfied only out of partnership property, as provided in Section 17 of the Uniform Partnership Act. In substance, the liability of an incoming partner upon antecedent debts and obligations of the firm is limited to his capital contribution. This restriction does not apply, of course, to obligations arising subsequent to his admission into the partnership as to which his liability is unlimited.

DISSOLUTION AND TERMINATION

There are three steps leading to the extinguishment of a partnership: (1) dissolution; (2) winding up or liquidation, and (3) termination.

The U.P.A. defines dissolution as the change in the relation of the partners caused by any partner ceasing to be associated in the carrying on, as distinguished from the winding up, of the business. Section 29. Upon dissolution, the partnership is not terminated but continues until the winding up of the partnership affairs is completed. Section 30.

Between dissolution and termination there is a twilight period, called winding up or liquidation, during which the business affairs are put in order, receivables collected, accountings had, payments made to creditors according to their respective contractual preferences and distribution made of the remaining assets to the partners as provided in Section 40 of the U.P.A.

DISSOLUTION

Causes of Dissolution

Dissolution by Act of the Parties. As a partnership is a personal relationship, a partner always has the *power* to dissolve it, but whether he has the *right* to do so is determined by the partnership agreement. A partner who has withdrawn in violation of the partnership agreement is liable to the remaining partners for damages resulting from the wrongful dissolution.

A partnership is rightfully dissolved by the act of the parties, that is, without violation of the agreement between the partners: (1) when they expressly agree to dissolve the partnership; (2) upon expiration of the period of time provided in the agreement or accomplishment of the purpose for which the partnership was formed; (3) when a partner withdraws from a partnership at will; or (4) by the expulsion of a partner in accordance with a power to expel conferred by the partnership agreement.

Dissolution by Operation of Law. A partnership is dissolved by operation of law

upon (1) the death of a partner; (2) the bankrupcty of a partner or of the partnership; or (3) the subsequent illegality of the partnership, which includes any event which makes it unlawful for the business of the partnership to be carried on or for the members to carry on such business in partnership form. For example, a partnership formed to manufacture liquor would be dissolved by a law prohibiting the production and sale of alcoholic beverages. A partnership of lawyers would be dissolved if one of its members were disbarred from the practice of law.

Dissolution by Court Order. When controversies develop between partners which they are unable to settle by agreement, one of the partners usually petitions a court of equity for an accounting. This brings the matter before the court, which may decide as a matter of fact that the parties have by their own acts dissolved the partnership. The court will thereupon supervise liquidation, and, after all creditors have been paid or provision has been made for payment, will determine a proper accounting between the parties.

Upon application by a partner, a court will order a dissolution if it finds that (a) a partner is insane or suffers some other incapacity preventing him from functioning as a partner; (b) a partner is guilty of conduct prejudicial to the business or has wilfully and persistently breached the partnership agreement; (c) the business can only be carried on at a loss; or (d) other circumstances render it inequitable for the partnership to continue. Section 32.

An assignee of a partner's interest and a partner's personal creditor who has obtained a charging order against the partner's interest may petition the court to dissolve a partnership. Application for a court ordered dissolution may be made at any time if the partnership was at will when the interest was assigned or the charging order was issued but, if the partnership was not at will, only after the termination of the specified term or particular undertaking.

Effects of Dissolution

On Authority. Upon dissolution, the actual authority of a partner to act for the partnership terminates, except so far as may be necessary to wind up partnership affairs. Actual authority to wind up includes completing existing contracts, reducing partnership assets to cash, and paying partnership obligations.

Although actual authority terminates upon dissolution, apparent authority persists and binds the partnership for acts within the scope of the partnership business unless notice of the dissolution is given to the third party. A third party who had extended credit to the partnership prior to dissolution may hold the partnership liable for any transaction which would bind the partnership if dissolution had not taken place unless the third party has knowledge or *actual* notice of the dissolution. Actual notice requires a verbal statement to the third party or actual delivery of a written statement. Section 3(2). On the other hand, a third party, who prior to dissolution had not extended credit to the partnership but nevertheless knew of the partnership, can hold the partnership liable unless he has knowledge or *constructive* notice of dissolution. Constructive notice consists of advertising a notice of dissolution in a newspaper of general circulation in the places at which partnership business was regularly conducted. Section 35(1)(b)(II).

On Existing Liability. The dissolution of the partnership does not of itself discharge the existing liability of any partner. But in some instances the cause of dissolution may result in discharging an executory contract. For example, if the contract called for the personal services of one of the partners, the death of that partner usually will discharge the contract as well as bring about the dissolution of the partnership.

A retiring partner may be discharged from his existing liabilities by a novation with the continuing partners and the creditors. A creditor must agree to the novation, although such consent may be inferred from his course of dealing with the partnership after dissolution. Whether such dealings with the continuing partnership constitutes an implied novation is a factual question of intent.

WINDING UP

Whenever a dissolved partnership is not to be continued, the partnership must be liquidated. The process of liquidation is called *winding up* and involves completing unfinished business, collecting debts, reducing assets to cash, taking inventory, auditing the partnership books, paying creditors and distributing the remaining assets to the partners.

The Right to Wind Up

Upon dissolution any partner has the right to insist upon the winding up of the partnership unless the partnership agreement provides otherwise or the dissolution was caused by expulsion of a partner pursuant to the partnership agreement. Unless otherwise agreed, all non-bankrupt partners who have not wrongfully dissolved the partnership have the right to wind up the partnership affairs.

Where the partnership agreement contains no provision for winding up the affairs of the partnership upon dissolution, and the partners are unable to agree upon control, management, or procedures during the winding up period, a court upon the petition of a partner may appoint a receiver of all of the property and assets of the partnership with authority to operate the business subject to the direction of the court for such time as may be reasonably necessary. The appointment of a receiver is discretionary with the court and its discretion may be exercised upon such grounds as dissension among the partners or waste, fraud, mental incompetence, misconduct, or other breach of duty by a partner.

Distribution of Assets

After all the partnership assets have been collected and reduced to cash, they are then distributed to the creditors and partners. When the partnership has been profitable, the order of distribution is not critical; however, when liabilities are greater than assets, the order assumes great importance.

Distribution of Assets in a General Partnership. Section 40 of the U.P.A. sets forth the rules to be observed in settling accounts between the parties after dissolution. As provided in Section 40(b), the order in which the liabilities of a partnership are ranked for payment out of partnership assets is as follows:

I. Amounts owing to creditors other than partners;
II. Amounts owing to partners other than for capital and profits;
III. Amounts owing to partners in respect of capital;
IV. Amounts owing to partners in respect of profits.

The partners may by agreement change the internal priorities of distribution (II, III, and IV) but not the preferred position of third parties (I). Section 40(a) defines partnership assets to include all partnership property as well as the contributions necessary for the payment of all partnership liabilities, which consists of I, II, and III.

In addition, Section 18(a) of the U.P.A. provides that in the absence of any contrary agreement each partner shall "share equally in the profits and surplus remaining after all liabilities, including those to partners,

are satisfied; and must contribute towards the losses, whether of capital or otherwise, sustained by the partnership according to his share in the profits."

The proportion in which the partners bear losses, whether of capital or otherwise, does not depend upon their relative capital contributions. It is determined by their agreement, and absent agreement, losses are borne in the same proportion in which profits are shared.

If the partnership is insolvent, the partners individually are obliged to contribute their respective share of the losses in order to make the creditors whole. Furthermore, if one or more of the partners is insolvent or bankrupt or, being out of the jurisdiction, refuses to contribute, the other partners are obliged to contribute the additional amount necessary to pay the firm's liabilities, in the relative proportions in which they share the profits. When any partner has paid an amount in excess of his proper share of the losses, he has a right of contribution against the other partners who have not paid their share. Section 40(d).

To illustrate the operation of these rules, consider the following examples.

1. *Solvent Partnership:* Assume that A, B and C form the ABC Company, a partnership, with A contributing $6,000 capital, B contributing $4,000 capital, and C contributing services but no capital. A also loaned the partnership $3,000 which has not been repaid. There is no agreement as to the proportions in which profits and losses are to be shared. After a few years of operations, the partnership is liquidated. At this time the assets of ABC Company are $54,000 and its liabilities to creditors are $26,000. The partnership is thus solvent and has enjoyed a profit of $15,000 which is calculated by subtracting from the total assets ($54,000) the total liabilities ($39,000), which reepresents the sum of the amounts owed to creditors ($26,000) plus amounts owed to partners other than for capital and

profits ($3,000 owed to A for his loan) plus the amounts owed to partners in respect of capital ($6,000 to A and $4,000 to B). Since A, B, and C have not explicitly agreed upon a profit sharing ratio, they share equally, in this case $15,000 ÷ 3 = $5,000. After the creditors have been paid in full A will receive $14,000 ($3,000 for repayment of the loan, $6,000 for capital and $5,000 for share of profits); B will receive $9,000 ($4,000 for capital and $5,000 for share of profits); and C will receive $5,000 (for share of profits).

2. *Insolvent Partnership:* Assume the same partnership had instead experienced financial adversity. While still owing creditors $26,000, its total assets only amount to $12,000. In this case the partnership has sustained an aggregate loss of $27,000, which is calculated by subtracting from the total assets ($12,000) the total liabilities ($39,000), calculated in the same manner as the solvent partnership example. In the absence of an agreement, the losses are shared as the profits are, which in this case is equally. Accordingly, each partner's share of the loss will be $9,000 ($27,000 ÷ 3 = $9,000). After the creditors are paid ($26,000), A will receive nothing ($3,000 owed for the loan plus $6,000 for capital *minus* $9,000 for share of loss); B must make an additional *contribution* of $5,000 to make good his share of the loss ($4,000 owed for capital *minus* $9,000 for his share of losses); and C must contribute $9,000 (his share of losses).

3. *Contribution of Partner upon Insolvency:* In the insolvent partnership example above, if A were individually insolvent, the results would not be changed, since A was not required to contribute any additional moneys. However, if A and B were solvent and C were individually insolvent, C would be unable to pay any of his share of the loss. Then A and B must contribute equally, since that is the relative proportion in which they share profits, in order to make good the amount of C's share. As C's share

of the loss is $9,000, A and B are each required to contribute an additional $4,500. This means that in total A will have to contribute $4,500 and B $9,500 in order to satisfy the unpaid claims of partnership creditors. Suppose further that A and C individually are insolvent while B is solvent. B would be required to pay the entire balance of $14,000 due to partnership creditors, representing his unpaid share of the loss plus a contribution of the full amount of C's unpaid share of the loss.

Distribution of Assets in a Limited Partnership. The priorities in distributing the assets of a limited partnership are set forth in Section 23 of the U.L.P.A.:

In setting accounts after dissolution the liabilities of the partnership shall be entitled to payment in the following order: (a) Those to creditors, in the order of priority as provided by law, except those to limited partners on account of their contributions, and to general partner., (b) Those to limited partners in respect to their share of the profits and other compensation by way of income on their contributions, (c) Those to limited partners in respect to the capital of their contributions, (d) Those to general partners other than for capital and profits, (e) Those to general partners in respect to profits, (f) Those to general partners in respect to capital.

A limited partner shares pro rata with general creditors with respect to advancements beyond his capital contribution. U.L.P.A., Section 13.

Marshalling of Assets. The doctrine of marshalling of assets is applicable only where the assets of a partnership and of its respective members are being administered by a court of equity. Marshalling means segregating and considering separately the assets of the partnership and the respective assets of the individual partners, as well as the respective liabilities of the partnership and of the several partners. Partnership creditors are entitled to be satisfied first out of partnership assets. They have a right to recover any deficiency out of the individually owned assets of the partners, subordinate however to the rights of nonpartnership creditors to those assets.

Conversely, the non-partnership creditors have first claim to the individually-owned assets of their respective debtors, and a claim junior to that of partnership creditors to participate in partnership assets to the extent of the interest therein of their respective individual debtors.

When the partnership and several or all of the partners are insolvent, the partnership creditors are entitled to prior participation in the partnership assets and non-partnership creditors are entitled to prior participation in the individually owned assets of their respective debtors. When a partner is insolvent, the order of distribution of his assets is, as follows: (1) debts and liabilities owing to non-partnership creditors; (2) debts and liabilities owing to partnership creditors, and (3) contributions owing to other partners by reason of payments by them to partnership creditors in excess of their respective share of the liabilities of the firm. Section 40(i).

This rule, however, is *no longer* followed if the partnership is a debtor under the Bankruptcy Reform Act of 1978. In a proceeding under the federal bankruptcy law, a trustee is appointed to administer the estate of the debtor. If the partnership property is insufficient to pay all the claims against the partnership, then the trustee is directed by the Act to seek recovery of the deficiency first from the general partners who are not bankrupt. Then, the trustee may seek recovery against the estates of bankrupt partners on the same basis as other creditors of the bankrupt partner. Bankruptcy Reform Act, Section 723. This provision, although contrary to the U.P.A.'s doctrine of marshalling of assets, governs whenever the assets of a partnership are being administered by a bankruptcy court.

CONTINUATION OF PARTNERSHIP AFTER DISSOLUTION

When a partnership is liquidated after dissolution, the value of a going concern is sacrificed. Continuation of the partnership after dissolution avoids this loss. The U.P.A., however, gives each partner the right to have the partnership liquidated except (1) when the partnership has been dissolved in contravention of the partnership agreement, (2) when a partner has been expelled in accordance with the partnership agreement, or (3) when all the partners agree to continue the business.

Partners' Right to Continue Partnership

Continuation after Wrongful Dissolution. Because of the personal element in a partnership, courts will not decree specific performance of a partnership agreement. However, a partner who wrongfully withdraws cannot force the liquidation of the firm. The aggrieved partners have the option of either liquidating the firm and recovering damages for the breach of the partnership agreement or continuing the partnership by buying out the withdrawing partner. The withdrawing partner is entitled to realize his interest in the partnership less the amount of the damages which the other partners have sustained as the result of his breach. However, his interest is computed without reference to the good will of the business. In addition, the remaining partners are entitled, if they so desire, to use the capital contributions of the wrongdoing partner for the unexpired period of the partnership agreement. They must, however, indemnify the former partner against all present and future partnership liabilities. Section 38(2).

Continuation after Expulsion. A partner expelled pursuant to the partnership agreement also cannot force the liquidation of the partnership. He is only entitled to be discharged from all partnership liabilities by either payment or a novation with the creditors and to receive in cash the net amount due him from the partnership.

Continuation per Agreement of the Parties. By far the best and most reliable way of assuring the preservation of a partnership business after dissolution is a continuation agreement. Professor Bromberg clearly explains the reasons for this:

Without an agreement, the alternatives at dissolution may be bleak. If the business is liquidated, there is typically a sacrifice of economic values in a going concern, not to mention the livelihood of the other partners. Recognizing this, an outgoing partner may demand an exorbitant price to forego his liquidation right. If the business is continued too long after dissolution pending negotiations for an agreement, the continuing partners are at the mercy of the outgoing interest's election to be paid its full value at dissolution, plus either profits or interest on that amount until final settlement. On the other hand, if the outgoing partner is ill or dead, it is in practice all too easy for the other partners to take advantage of the situation. Crane and Bromberg on Partnership, Bromberg, Section 90A, p. 509.

Continuation agreements are frequently used to insure continuity in the event of death or retirement of one of the partners. Otherwise, when a partner dies or retires and the business is continued by the surviving partner or partners with or without third persons as new partners, and without any settlement of accounts with the retired partner or the legal representative of the deceased partner, the retired partner or such legal representative is entitled to have the value of his interest as of the date of the dissolution ascertained and to be paid the amount thereof as an ordinary creditor of the partnership. In addition, he is entitled to receive interest on this amount, or at his option, in lieu of interest, the profits of the business attributable to the use of his right in the property of the dissolved partnership. His rights, however, are subordinate to those of creditors of the dissolved partnership. Section 42.

Rights of Creditors with Respect to a Reconstituted Partnership

Whenever a partnership undergoes any change in membership, it is dissolved, and a new partnership is formed even though a majority of the old partners are present in the new combination. This is true whether the change consists in dropping one or more members, adding one or more members, or both. The creditors of the old partnership have claims against the new partnership and may also proceed to hold personally liable all of the members of the dissolved partnership. If a withdrawing partner has made arrangements with those who continue the business whereby they assume and pay all debts and obligations of the firm, and the accounting between the partners has reflected this undertaking, the withdrawing partner is nevertheless liable to creditors whose claims arose prior to the dissolution. Upon being compelled to pay such debts, he immediately has a right of indemnity against his former partners who had agreed to pay them but failed to do so.

A withdrawing partner may protect himself against liability upon contracts which were entered into by the firm subsequent to his withdrawal by giving notice that he is no longer a member of the firm. Otherwise, he is liable for debts thus incurred and due and owing to a creditor who had no notice or knowledge of the partner having withdrawn from the firm. Actual notice is required to be given to the persons with whom the partnership regularly does business, while notice by newspaper publication will be sufficient for the general business community. Section 35. The basis of liability is estoppel. In the absence of notice, the outgoing partner is estopped to deny his membership in the firm in an ac-

tion at law against him by a creditor who sold merchandise to the firm in the reasonable belief that he was still a member.

Cases

Fiduciary Duty

CLEMENT v. CLEMENT

(1970) 436 Pa. 466, 260 A.2d 728.

ROBERTS, J.

Charles and L. W. Clement are brothers whose forty year partnership had ended in acrimonious litigation. The essence of the conflict lies in Charles' contention that L. W. has over the years wrongfully taken for himself more than his share of the partnership's profits. Charles discovered these misdeeds during negotiations with L. W. over the sale of Charles' interest in the partnership in 1964. He then filed an action in equity, asking for dissolution of the partnership, appointment of a receiver, and an accounting. Dissolution was ordered and a receiver appointed. After lengthy hearings on the issue of the accounting the chancellor decided that L. W., who was the brighter of the two and who kept the partnership books, had diverted partnership funds. The chancellor awarded Charles a one-half interest in several pieces of property owned by L. W. and in several insurance policies on L. W.'s life on the ground that these had been purchased with partnership assets.

The court en banc then heard the case and reversed the chancellor's decree in several material respects. The reversal was grounded on two propositions: that Charles' recovery could only be premised on a showing of fraud and that this burden was not met, and that the doctrine of laches foreclosed Charles' right to complain about the bulk of the alleged misdeeds.

We disagree with the court en banc's statement of the applicable law and therefore reverse. Our theory is simple. There is a fiduciary relationship between partners. Where such a relationship exists actual fraud need not be shown. There was ample evidence of self-dealing and diversion of partnership assets on the part of L. W.— more than enough to sustain the chancellor's conclusion that several substantial investments made by L. W. over the years were bankrolled with funds improperly withdrawn from the partnership. Further, we are of the opinion that the doctrine of laches is inapplicable because Charles' delay in asserting his rights was as much a product of L. W.'s concealment and misbehavior as of any negligence on his part. In all this we are strongly motivated by the fact that the chancellor saw and heard the various witnesses for exhausting periods of time and was in a much better position than we could ever hope to be to taste the flavor of the testimony.

The Act of 1915, March 26, P.L. 18, part IV, § 21, 59 P.S. § 54, very simply and unambiguously provides that partners owe a fiduciary duty one to another. [Citation]. One should not have to deal with his partner as though he were the opposite party in an arms-length transaction. One should be allowed to trust his partner, to expect that he is pursuing a common goal and not working at cross-purposes. This concept of the partnership entity was expressed most ably by Mr. Justice, then Judge, Cardozo in Meinhard v. Salmon, 249 N.Y. 458, 164 N.E. 545, 62 A.L.R. 1 (1928):

"Joint adventurers, like copartners, owe to one another, while the enterprise continues, the duty of the finest loyalty. Many forms of conduct permissible in a workaday world for those acting at arm's length, are forbidden to those bound by fiduciary ties. A trustee is held to something stricter than the morals of the marketplace. Not honesty alone, but the punctilio of an honor the most sensitive, is then the standard of behavior. As to this there has developed a tradition that is unbending and inveterate. Uncompromising rigidity has been the attitude of courts of equity when petitioned to undermine the rule of undivided loyalty by the 'disintegrating erosion' of particular exceptions. * * * Only thus has the level of conduct for fiduciaries been kept at a level higher than that trodden by the crowd. It will not consciously be lowered by any judgment of this court." 249 N.Y. at 463–464, 164 N.E. at 546.

It would be unduly harsh to require that one must prove actual fraud before he can recover for a partner's derelictions. Where one partner has so dealt with the partnership as to raise the probability of wrongdoing it ought to be his responsibility to negate that inference. It has been held that "where a partner fails to keep a record of partnership transactions, and is unable to account for them, every presumption will be made against him." [Citation]. Likewise, where a partner commingles partnership funds with his own and generally deals loosely with partnership assets he ought to have to shoulder the task of demonstrating the probity of his conduct.

In the instant case L. W. dealt loosely with partnership funds. At various times he made substantial investments in his own name. He was totally unable to explain where he got the funds to make these investments. The court en banc held that Charles had no claim on the fruits of these investments because he could not trace the money that was invested therein dollar for dollar from the partnership. Charles should

not have had this burden. He did show that his brother diverted substantial sums from the partnership funds under his control. The inference that these funds provided L. W. with the wherewithal to make his investments was a perfectly reasonable one for the chancellor to make and his decision should have been allowed to stand.

* * *

The decree is vacated and the case remanded for further proceedings consistent with this opinion.

*Partner's Interest
in Partnership Property*

BOHONUS v. AMERCO

(1979) 124 Ariz. 88, 602 P.2d 469.

HAYS, J.

Appellee Amerco, plaintiff below, secured a judgment against appellant Bohonus, defendant below, and sought to enforce that judgment by judicial sale of Bohonus' interest in a partnership. * * *

The first issue before us is: *May the trial court order the sale of partnership property to satisfy the individual debt of a partner?*

The appellee, Amerco, after it secured a judgment against the appellant, Bohonus, sought a charging order from the court pursuant to A.R.S. § 29–228, a provision embodied in the Uniform Partnership Act. The court granted the request for a charging order and as a part of that order mandated the sale of appellant's interest in the assets and property of the partnership business, including a spiritous liquor license. The sheriff proceeded with the sale and filed his return.

We now look at the partnership statute. A.R.S. § 29–225(B)(3) says:

A partner's right in specific partnership property is not subject to attachment or execution, except on a claim against the partnership. * * *

A.R.S. § 29–224 sets forth the extent of the property rights of the partner:

"The property rights of a partner are:

1. His rights in specific partnership property.
2. His interest in the partnership.
3. His right to participate in the management."

A.R.S. § 29–226 defines "a partner's interest":

A partner's interest in the partnership is his share of the profits and surplus, and the same is personal property.

A.R.S. § 29–228 reads, in pertinent part, as follows:

A. On due application to a competent court by any judgment creditor of a partner, the court which entered the judgment, order, or decree, or any other court, may charge the interest of the debtor partner with payment of the unsatisfied amount of such judgment debt with interest thereon; and may then or later appoint a receiver of his share of the profits, and of any other money due or to fall due to him in respect of the partnership, and make all other orders, directions, accounts and inquiries which the debtor partner might have made, or which the circumstances of the case may require.

With the foregoing statutes in mind, we note that it is only a partner's interest in the partnership which may be charged and, in some jurisdictions, sold. It cannot be overemphasized that "interest in the partnership" has a special limited meaning in the context of the Uniform Partnership Act and hence in the Arizona statutes.

The appellee urges that somehow A.R.S. § 29–228(A), *supra,* authorizes the sale of partnership assets and property. We note that the record reflects that pursuant to the provisions of the same statute a receiver was appointed in this case. The fact of the receivership provision enforces the conclu-

sion that only the "interest in the partnership" may be charged and we find no provision therein for sale of assets or property of the partnership.

Appellee seeks aid and comfort in the language of A.R.S. § 29–232(B) which provides for dissolution of the partnership upon application of the purchaser of a partner's interest under §§ 29–227 or 29–228. No decree of dissolution however has been asked for here.

We concur with appellee's position that the charged interest of a debtor-partner can be sold, but further enforcement of the creditor's rights must be pursuant to statute. *See* A.R.S. § 29–232(B) and *Tupper v. Kroc,* 88 Nev. 146, 494 P.2d 1275 (1972). However, this in nowise makes the sale of the partnership assets valid.

* * *

For the foregoing reasons, we reverse and remand to the trial court for proceedings consistent with this opinion.

Right to an Accounting

CENTRAL TRUST & SAFE CO. v. RESPASS

(1902) 112 Ky. 606, 66 S.W. 421, 56 L.R.A. 479.

[Action for the settlement of partnership accounts by J. B. Respass against the trust company, as executor of the will of his deceased partner, S. L. Sharp. The partners owned and managed a racing stable and, in addition, were engaged in bookmaking, or accepting wagers on race horses. At the time Sharp died, $4,724, representing the undistributed profits of the bookmaking business, was on deposit in Sharp's personal bank account. The trial court held that Respass was entitled to one-half of the profits from the bookmaking business and the executor appeals.]

DURELLE, J.
* * *

A closer question is presented by the claim for a division of the "bank roll." This

$4,724 was, as found by the chancellor, earned by the firm composed of Respass and Sharp in carrying on an illegal business—that of "bookmaking"—in the State of Illinois. But though this amount had been won upon horse races in Chicago, it is claimed that, though secured illegally, "the transaction has been closed, and the appellee Respass is only seeking his share from the realized profits from the illegal contracts, if they are illegal." On the other hand, it is claimed for appellant, the executor, that, as to the bank roll, this proceeding is a bill for an accounting of profits from the business of gambling.

It does not seem to be seriously contended that the business of "bookmaking," whether carried on in Chicago or in this Commonwealth, was legal, for by the common law of this country all wagers are illegal. [Citation.] One of the most interesting cases upon this subject is that of Everet v. Williams—the celebrated Highwaymen's Case—an account of which is given in 9 Law Quart. Rev., 197 [England]. That was a bill for an accounting of a partnership in the business of highwaymen, though the true nature of the partnership was veiled in ambiguous language. The bill set up the partnership between defendant and plaintiff, who was "skilled in dealing in several sorts of commodities;" that they "proceeded jointly in the said dealing with good success on Hounslow Heath, where they dealt with a gentleman for a gold watch;" that defendant had informed plaintiff that Finchley "was a good and convenient place to deal in," such commodities being "very plenty" there, and if they were to deal there "it would be almost all gain to them"; that they accordingly "dealt with several gentlemen for divers watches, rings, swords, canes, hats, cloaks, horses, bridles, saddles, and other things, to the value of £2000 and upwards"; that a gentleman of Blackheath had several articles which defendant thought "might be had for a little or no money in case they could prevail on the said gentleman to part with the said things;" and that, "after some small discourse with the said gentleman," the said things were dealt for "at a very cheap rate." The dealings were alleged to have amounted to £2,000 and upward. This case, while interesting, from the views it gives of the audacity of the parties and their solicitors, sheds little light upon the legal questions involved, for the bill was condemned for scandal and impertinence; the solicitors were taken into custody, and "fyned" £50 each for "reflecting upon the honor and dignity of this court"; the counsel whose name was signed to the bill was required to pay the costs; and both the litigants were subsequently hanged, at Tyburn and Maidstone, respectively; while one of the solicitors was transported. [Citations.] * * *

In Watson v. Fletcher, 7 Grat., 1, the business of the firm had been the operation of a faro bank. One of the partners having died, the survivor sought an accounting of profits earned. The syllabus reads: "A court of equity will not lend its aid for the settlement and adjustment of the transactions of a partnership for gambling. Nor will it give relief to either partner against the other, founded on transactions arising out of such partnership, whether for profits, losses, expenses, contribution, or reimbursement. * * *"

We conclude that in this country, in the case of a partnership in a business confessedly illegal, whatever may be the doctrine where there has been a new contract in relation to, or a new investment of, the profits of such illegal business, and whatever may be the doctrine as to the rights or liabilities of a third person who assumes obligations with respect to such profits, or by law becomes responsible therefor, the decided weight of authority is that a court of equity will not entertain a bill for an accounting.

The judgment of the chancellor is therefore reversed, and the cause remanded, with directions to enter a judgment in accordance with this opinion.

Authority to Bind Partnership

NATIONAL BISCUIT v. C.N. STROUD

(1959) 249 N.C. 467, 106 S.E.2d 692.

[Proceeding by seller of bread against former partners who had operated food store for value of goods sold and delivered. The Superior Court rendered judgment for seller, and partner appealed.]

PARKER, J.

C. N. Stroud and Earl Freeman entered into a general partnership to sell groceries under the firm name of Stroud's Food Center. There is nothing in the agreed statement of facts to indicate or suggest that Freeman's power and authority as a general partner were in any way restricted or limited by the articles of partnership in respect to the ordinary and legitimate business of the partnership. Certainly, the purchase and sale of bread were ordinary and legitimate business of Stroud's Food Center during its continuance as a going concern.

Several months prior to February 1956 Stroud advised plaintiff that he personally would not be responsible for any additional bread sold by plaintiff to Stroud's Food Center. After such notice to plaintiff, it from 6 February 1956 to 25 February 1956, at the request of Freeman, sold and delivered bread in the amount of $171.04 to Stroud's Food Center.

* * *

The General Assembly of North Carolina in 1941 enacted a Uniform Partnership Act, which became effective 15 March 1941. G.S. Ch. 59, Partnership, Art. 2.

G.S. § 59–39 is entitled "Partner Agent of Partnership as to Partnership Business," and subsection (1) reads: "Every partner is an agent of the partnership for the purpose of its business, and the act of every partner, including the execution in the partnership name of any instrument, for apparently carrying on in the usual way the business of the partnership of which he is a member binds the partnership, unless the partner so acting has in fact no authority to act for the partnership in the particular matter, and the person with whom he is dealing has knowledge of the fact that he has no such authority." G.S. § 59–39(4) states: "No act of a partner in contravention of a restriction on authority shall bind the partnership to persons having knowledge of the restriction."

G.S. § 59–45 provides that "all partners are jointly and severally liable for the acts and obligations of the partnership."

G.S. § 59–48 is captioned "Rules Determining Rights and Duties of Partners." Subsection (e) thereof reads: "All partners have equal rights in the management and conduct of the partnership business." Subsection (h) hereof is as follows: "Any difference arising as to ordinary matters connected with the partnership business may be decided by a majority of the partners; but no act in contravention of any agreement between the partners may be done rightfully without the consent of all the partners."

Freeman as a general partner with Stroud, with no restrictions on his authority to act within the scope of the partnership business so far as the agreed statement of facts shows, had under the Uniform Partnership Act "equal rights in the management and conduct of the partnership business." Under G.S. § 59–48(h) Stroud, his co-partner, could not restrict the power and authority of Freeman to buy bread for the partnership as a going concern, for such a purchase was an "ordinary matter connected with the partnership business," for the purpose of its business and within its scope, because in the very nature of things Stroud was not, and could not be, a majority of the partners. Therefore, Freeman's purchases of bread from plaintiff for Stroud's Food Center as a going concern bound the partnership and his co-partner Stroud. * * *

In Crane on Partnership, 2d Ed., p. 277, it is said: "In cases of an even division of the partners as to whether or not an act within the scope of the business should be done, of which disagreement a third person has knowledge, it seems that logically no restriction can be placed upon the power to act. The partnership being a going concern, activities within the scope of the business should not be limited, save by the expressed will of the majority deciding a disputed question; half of the members are not a majority."

The judgment of the court below is affirmed.

Torts of Partnership

PHILLIPS v. COOK

(1965) 239 Md. 215, 210 A.2d 743.

MARBURY, J.

This is an appeal by Daniel Phillips individually, and trading as "Dan's Used Cars", one of the defendants below, from a judgment in favor of Delores Cook and Marshall Cook, her husband, plaintiffs below, entered upon the verdict of a jury in favor of the plaintiffs against the defendants, Isadore Harris and Daniel Phillips, individually and as co-partners trading as Dan's Used Cars, in the Superior Court of Baltimore City. The verdict was rendered in an action by the Cooks to recover damages for injuries sustained by them as a result of a collision involving a partnership automobile operated by Harris and bearing dealer plates issued to Dan's Used Cars by the Department of Motor Vehicles.

The Cooks sued Harris and Phillips, individually, and as co-partners trading as Dan's Used Cars. The accident in question occurred on January 7, 1960, at about 6:50 p.m., when a partnership automobile operated by Harris struck the rear of a vehicle driven by one Smith, which in turn hit an automobile operated by Delores Cook, at the intersection of Reisterstown Road and Quantico Avenue in Baltimore. Harris was on his way home from the used car lot when the accident occurred. He was using the most direct route from the partnership lot and was only five blocks from his home at the time of the incident.

In October 1959, Harris and Phillips entered into a partnership on an equal basis under the name of "Dan's Used Cars" for the purpose of buying and selling used automobiles. * * * This partnership agreement was oral and it was agreed between the partners that each would have an equal voice in the conduct and management of the business.

Neither of the partners owned a personal automobile or had one titled in his individual name. It was agreed as a part of the partnership arrangement that Harris would use a partnership vehicle for transportation to and from his home. Under this agreement, he was authorized to demonstrate and sell such automobiles, call on dealers for the purpose of seeing and purchasing used cars, or go to the Department of Motor Vehicles on partnership business after leaving the lot in the evening and before returning the next day. Both Harris and Phillips could use a partnership automobile as desired. Such vehicles were for sale at any time during the day or night and at various times and places they had "for sale" signs on the windshields. Harris had no regular hours to report to the used car lot but could come and go as he saw fit. Phillips testified that it was essential that Harris have a partnership automobile for his transportation to and from his home, and that it was the most practical way to operate. * * *

* * * It is clear that the partnership is bound by the partner's wrongful act if done within the scope of the partnership's business. Code (1957), Article 73A, Section 13 provides:

Where, by any wrongful act or omission of any partner acting in the ordinary course of the business of the partnership, or with the authority of his copartners, loss or injury is caused to any person, not being a partner in the partnership, or any penalty is incurred, the partnership is liable therefor to the same extent as the partner so acting or omitting to act.

The test of the liability of the partnership and of its members for the torts of any one partner is whether the wrongful act was done within what may reasonably be found to be the scope of the business of the partnership and for its benefit. The extent of the authority of a partner is determined essentially by the same principles as those which measure the scope of an agent's authority. [Citation.] Partnership cases may differ from principal and agent and master and servant relationships because in the non-partnership cases, the element of control or authorization is important. This is not so in the case of a partnership for a partner is also a principal, and control and authorization are generally within his power to exercise.

* * *

Here, the fact that the defendant partners were in the used car business; that the very vehicle involved in the accident was one of the partnership assets for sale at all times, day or night, at any location; that Harris was on call by Phillips or customers at his home—he went back to the lot two or three times after going home; that he had no set time and worked irregular hours, coupled with the fact that he frequently stopped to conduct partnership business on the way to and from the lot; that he drove partnership vehicles to the Department of Motor Vehicles, and to dealers in Baltimore to view and buy used cars while on his way to or from his home; that one of the elements of the partnership arrangement was that each partner could have full use of the vehicles; that the uses of the automobile by Harris for transportation to and from his home was admittedly "essential" to the partnership arrangement and the most practical and convenient way to operate; and that Harris conducted partnership business both at the used car lot and from his home requires that the question of whether the use of the automobile at the time of the accident was in the partnership interest and for its benefit be submitted to the jury.

* * *

Judgment affirmed.

Dissolution

McCLENNEN v. COMMISSIONER OF INTERNAL REVENUE

(1943 C.C.A.1st) 131 F.2d 165, 144 A.L.R. 1127.

[George R. Nutter, a partner in the law firm of Nutter, McClennen & Fish, was entitled to eight per cent of the net profits. The partnership agreement also contained the following provision: "On the retirement of a partner or on his death—the others continuing the business—the retiring partner or his estate in the case of his death shall, in addition to his percentage of net profits of the Firm received by it in cash up to the date of such death or retirement, also receive the same percentage of net profits of the Firm received by it in cash until the expiration of the eighteen (18) calendar months next after such retirement, or death, and this shall be in full of the retiring or deceasing member's interest in the capital, the assets, the receivables, the possibilities and the good will of the Firm." Following Nutter's death in February, 1937, the surviving partners continued the business. During the course of the next eighteen months, eight per cent of the profits, amounting to $34,069.99, were paid over to the executors of Nutter's will. In filing a Federal estate tax return the only item included pertaining to the partnership was the sum of $6,136.21, representing Nutter's share in undistributed profits of the firm as of date of death.   Beyond this nothing was included with respect to the value of decedent's interest in the partnership.]

MAGRUDER, J.
* * *

In his notice of deficiency the Commissioner determined that $34,069.99 should have been included in the gross estate as the value of decedent's "interest in partnership Nutter, McClennen & Fish."   The Board has upheld the Commissioner in this determination.   We think the Board was right.

In the absence of a controlling agreement in the partnership articles the death of a partner dissolves the partnership.   The survivors have the right and duty, with reasonable dispatch, to wind up the partnership affairs, to complete transactions begun but not then finished, to collect the accounts receivable, to pay the firm debts, to convert the remaining firm assets into cash, and to pay in cash to the partners and the legal representative of the deceased partner the net amounts shown by the accounts to be owing to each of them in respect of capital contributions and in respect of their shares of profits and surplus.   The representative of a deceased partner does not succeed to any right to specific partnership property. In substance the deceased partner's interest, to which his representative succeeds, is a chose in action, a right to receive in cash the sum of money shown to be due him upon a liquidation and accounting.   These substantive results may be rationalized upon a theory of the partnership "entity."   [Citation.]   The same substantive results are reached under the Uniform Partnership Act which, in form at least, proceeds on the aggregate theory.   [Citation.]   That act, which is law in Massachusetts, conceives of the partner as a "co-owner with his partners of specific partnership property holding as a tenant in partnership;" but provides that on the death of a partner "his right in specific partnership property vests in the sur-

viving partner or partners."   Another enumerated property right of a partner, "his interest in the partnership," is described as "his share of the profits and surplus, and the same is personal property," regardless of whether the firm holds real estate or personalty or both.   [Citations.]   * * *

In the case at bar, if there had not been the controlling provision in the partnership articles, above quoted, or if the survivors had not come to some agreement otherwise with the executors of Mr. Nutter, the survivors would have had to proceed to wind up the affairs of the partnership, to conclude all unfinished legal business on hand at the date of the death, to realize upon all of the assets of the firm, tangible or intangible, to pay the debts, to return to Mr. Nutter's estate his contribution of capital, if any, and to pay to his estate in cash the amount shown to be due in respect of his "interest in the partnership," that is, his "share of the profits and surplus", as determined upon an accounting.   Among other things to be taken into account, "the earned proportion of the unfinished business" would have had "to be valued to determine the decedent's interest in the partnership assets."   [Citations.]

To obviate the necessity of a liquidation, or to eliminate accounting difficulties in determining the value of the deceased partner's interest, partners often make specific provision in the partnership articles.

Sometimes the partnership agreement merely provides for the postponement of liquidation, say, to the end of the term for which the partnership was created.   Thus, a partnership agreement between A, B and C might provide that "should any partner die during the term of said co-partnership the firm shall not be dissolved thereupon, but the business shall be continued by the survivors until the expiration of said partnership term, the estate of the deceased partner to bear the same share in profits and losses as would have been received and borne by the deceased partner had he lived."

Under such an agreement, if A dies, B and C do not buy out A's interest in the partnership. Unless more appears, A's executor does not become personally liable as a general partner. [Citation.] Nor is A's general estate in the executor's hands liable as a partner for new debts created by B and C in continuing the business. [Citation.] For the remainder of the term, A's share already embarked in the business remains in, subject to the risks of the business. It would seem not improper to describe the continuing business as now being owned by B and C as general partners, with A's estate (or A's executor as trustee under the will of A) as a limited partner therein, sharing in the profits, but not liable beyond the amount or interest already embarked in the business.

In the case at bar the partnership agreement contains another familiar arrangement, whereby no liquidation and final accounting will ever be necessary in order to satisfy the claim of the deceased partner. In place of the chose in action to which Mr. Nutter's executor would have succeeded in the absence of specific provision in the partnership articles, that is, a right to receive payment in cash of the amount shown to be due the deceased partner upon a complete liquidation and accounting, a different right is substituted, a right of the estate to receive a share of the net profits of the firm for 18 calendar months after the partner's death.

The language of the partnership agreement in the present case is couched in terms of a purchase of the deceased partner's interest. What the estate is to receive "shall be in full of the retiring or deceasing member's interest in the capital, the assets, the receivables, the possibilities and the good will of the Firm." There is to be an extinguishment of the decedent's interest in the totality of the firm assets, tangible and intangible, as they stood at the moment of death, and the interests therein of the surviving partners are to be correspondingly

augmented. Decision in the estate tax case now before us does not turn on the question whether the effect of the partnership agreement may be characterized with entire accuracy as a "purchase" and "sale" of the deceased partner's interest in the partnership.

The decision of the Board of Tax Appeals is affirmed.

*Distribution of Assets
in a General Partnership*

HANSON v. HANSON
(1979) 125 Ariz. 553, 611 P.2d 557.

HOWARD, J.

This is an appeal from an action for an accounting after dissolution of a partnership which resulted inter alia, in the trial court ordering appellants to pay the sum of $66,230 to appellees. * * * Donald Hanson and Joseph Hanson are brothers who in 1972 became partners in a synthetic marble manufacturing and installation business. The trial court found that Joseph had contributed the whole of his pre-existing tile contracting business to the partnership. When the partnership dissolved, after 1973, Joseph separated the tile business from the marble business and sought an accounting from Donald, who continued in the marble business. * * *

The court valued the land owned by the partnership as of the date of the trial. This was error. The value of partnership assets for purposes of settlement should be determined as of the date of dissolution. [Citations.]

* * *

We agree with Donald's contention that the trial court's computation and division of the partnership good will was erroneous. The only testimony as to its value was from Lois Bradley, a CPA hired by the parties. She testified that the good will was $78,600, which in her opinion was a conservative figure. She also testified that the value of this good will could not be broken down between the tile business and the marble business. The trial court nevertheless attributed a separate good will value to each business and arrived at a total figure of $125,772. There is no basis in the record for this figure and no reason appears for the court's rejection of the figure stated by Lois Bradley. It is the only evidence. In the absence of an agreement to the contrary, good will is a partnership asset which should be accounted for on the termination of the partnership. [Citations.] The good will of a partnership is an asset which the partner appropriating it to his own use must account for. [Citation.] When the partner seeking an accounting has in effect received the benefit of his interest in the good will an accounting has been denied. [Citations.] The record clearly demonstrates here that when Joseph took the tile business, he in effect received his share of the good will. Donald therefore did not appropriate a portion of the good will for which he must account.

Each partner is entitled to a return of his capital amount and one-half of the remaining assets after creditors are first paid. See A.R.S. Sec. 29–240.

Based on the evidence, the trial court should have concluded as follows:

PARTNERSHIP ASSETS

Cash	$10,541.91
Land	48,000.00
	$58,541.91
Less mortgage due	− 8,400.00
	$50,141.91

CAPITAL ACCOUNTS

Joseph	$27,199.00	= 51.01%
Donald	26,121.00	= 48.99%
	$53,320.00	

SHARE OF ASSETS

Joseph — 51.01% of $50,141.91 = $25,577.38
Donald — 48.99% of 50,141.91 = 24,564.52

ASSETS IN POSSESSION AFTER DISSOLUTION

Joseph		Donald
	Cash	$10,541.91
	Land	+48,000.00
NONE		58,541.91
	Less Mortgage	−8,400.00
		$50,141.91

DUE TO JOSEPH $25,577.38 $20,199.96
less set-off of $5,377.42[1]

[1]Percentage share of cash account.

The judgment in favor of appellees is modified to the sum of $20,199.96 and is affirmed as modified.

Problems

1. A, B and C own and operate the Roy Lumber Company, each contributing one third of the capital and sharing equally in the profits and losses. Their agreement provides that all firm purchases over $500 must be authorized in advance by two partners, and that only A is authorized to draw checks. Unknown to A or C, B purchases on the firm account a $2,500 diamond bracelet and a $5,000 fork lift truck, and orders $2,000 worth of logs, all from D who operates a jewelry store and is engaged in various activities connected with the lumber business. A has told D prior to these purchases that B is not the log buyer. A refuses to pay D for these purchases. D calls at the mill to collect and A again refuses to pay him. D calls A an unprintable name, and A thereupon punches D in the nose. While D is lying unconscious on the ground, an employee of Roy Lumber Company negligently drops a log on D's leg breaking three bones. The firm and the three partners are completely solvent.

What are the rights of D?

2. A, B and C agree that A and B will form and conduct a partnership business and that C will become a partner in two years. C agrees to lend the firm $5,000 and take 10% of the profits in lieu of interest. Without C's knowledge A and B tell X that C is a partner and X, relying on C's sound financial status, gives the firm credit. Later the firm becomes insolvent and X seeks to hold C liable as a partner. Should X succeed?

3. X and Y had been partners for many years in a mercantile business. Their relationship deteriorated, however, to the point where X threatened to bring an action for an accounting and dissolution of the firm. Thereupon, Y offered to buy X's interest in the partnership for $25,000. X refused the offer and told Y that he would take no less than $36,000. Shortly thereafter, Z approached Y and advised him he had inside information that a proposed street change would greatly benefit the business and that he, Z, would buy the entire business for $100,000 or buy a one-half interest for $50,000. Y made a final offer of $35,000 to X for his interest. X accepted this offer, and the transaction was completed. Thereafter, Y sold the one-half interest to Z for $50,000. Several months later, X learned for the first time of the transaction between Y and Z.

What rights, if any, does X have against Y?

4. A and B were partners doing business as the Petite Garment Company. C owned a dye plant which did much of the processing for the Company. A and B decided to offer C an interest in their Company in consideration for which C would contribute his dye plant to the partnership. C accepted the offer and was duly admitted as a partner.

Unknown to C, at the time he was admitted as a partner, was the fact that the partnership was on the verge of insolvency. Numerous debts had been incurred which A and B had been unable to meet. About three months after C was admitted to the partnership, a textile firm obtained a judgment against the partnership in the amount of $50,000. This debt represented an unpaid balance which had existed before C was admitted as a partner.

The textile firm brought an action to subject the partnership property, including the dye plant, to the satisfaction of its judgment. The complaint also prayed that, in the event the judgment was unsatisfied by sale of the partnership property, C's home be sold and the proceeds applied to the balance of the judgment. A and B owned nothing but their interest in the partnership property.

What should be the result (a) with regard to the dye plant, and (b) with regard to C's home?

5. Jones and Ray formed a partnership in October 1980 known as JR Construction Co. to engage in the construction business, each partner owning a one-half interest. On December 27, 1980, while conducting partnership business, Jones negligently injured Ware who brought an action against Jones, Ray, and JR Construction Co., and obtained judgment for $25,000 against them on March 1, 1981. On April 15, 1981, Muir joined the partnership by contributing $10,000 cash and, by agreement, each partner was entitled to a one-third interest. In July 1981, the partners agreed to purchase new construction equipment for the partnership and Muir was authorized to obtain a loan from XYZ Bank in the partnership name for $20,000 to finance the purchase. On July 10, 1981, Muir signed a $20,000 note on behalf of the partnership, and the equipment was purchased.

In November 1981 the partnership was in financial difficulty, its total assets amounting to $5,000. The note was in default, with a balance of $15,000 owing to XYZ Bank. Muir has substantial resources, while Jones and Roy each individually have assets of $2,000.

What is the extent of Muir's personal liability, and the personal liability of Jones and Ray, as to (a) the judgment obtained by Ware and (b) the debt owing to XYZ Bank?

6. A, B, and C were partners under a written agreement made in 1974 that it should continue for 10 years. During 1980, C being indebted to X sold and conveyed his interest in the partnership to X. A and B paid X $5,000 as C's share of the profits for the year 1980, but refused X permission to inspect the books or to come into the managing office of the partnership. X brings an action setting forth the above facts and asks for an accounting and an order to inspect the books and to participate in the management of the partnership business.
(a) Does C's action dissolve the partnership?
(b) To what is X entitled with respect (1) partnership profits, (2) inspection of partnership books, (3) accounting by the partnership and (4) participation in the partnership management?
(c) In case of a dissolution to what is X entitled with respect to C's interest and an accounting?

7. Adams, a consulting engineer, entered into a partnership with three others for the practice of their profession. The only written partnership agreement is a brief document specifying

that Adams is entitled to 55% of the profits and the others to 15% each.

The venture is an utter failure. Creditors are pressing for payment, and some have filed suit. The partners are in fundamental disagreement as to future course of action.

How many of the partners must agree to achieve each of the following objectives:

(a) To add Jones, also an engineer, as a partner, Jones being willing to contribute a substantial amount of new capital.

(b) To sell a vacant lot held in the partnership name, which had been acquired as the site of a future office for the partnership.

(c) To move the offices of the partnership to less expensive quarters.

(d) To demand a formal accounting.

(e) To dissolve the partnership.

(f) To confess judgment in amounts owing to certain creditors who are threatening court action, and thereby avoid incurring the cost of litigation.

(g) To agree to submit certain disputed claims to arbitration which Adams believes will prove less expensive than litigation.

(h) To sell all of the partnership personal property, Adams having what he believes to be a good offer for the property from a newly formed engineering firm.

(i) To alter the respective interests of the parties in the profits and losses by decreasing Adams share to 40% and increasing the others accordingly.

(j) To assign all the assets to a bank in trust for the benefit of creditors, hoping to work out satisfactory arrangements without formal bankruptcy.

8. A and B orally agreed to become partners in a small tool and die business. A, who had experience in tool and die work, was to operate the business. B was to take no active part but was to contribute the entire $50,000 capitalization. A worked 10 hours a day at the plant for which he was paid nothing. Despite A's best efforts, the business failed. The $50,000 capital was depleted, and the partnership owed $50,000 in debts. Prior to the failure of the partnership business B became personally insolvent through private investments, so that the creditors of the partnership collected the entire $50,000 indebtedness from A, who was forced to sell his home and a farm to satisfy the indebtedness. Sub-

sequently, B regained his financial responsibility and A brought an appropriate action against B for (a) one-half of the $50,000 he had paid to partnership creditors; and (b) one-half of $18,000, the reasonable value of his (A's) services during the operation of the partnership. Decision?

9. Simmons, Hoffman, and Murray were partners doing business under the firm name of Simmons & Co. The firm borrowed money from a bank and gave the bank the firm's note for the loan. In addition, each partner guaranteed the note individually. The firm became insolvent and a receiver was appointed. The bank claims that it has a right to file its claim as a firm debt and also that it has a right to participate in the distribution of the assets of the individual partners before partnership creditors receive any payment from such assets.

(a) Explain the principle involved in this case.

(b) Is the bank correct?

10. A, B and C form a partnership, A contributing $10,000, B, $5,000, and C his time and skill. Nothing was said as to the division of profits. The firm becomes insolvent, and after payment of all firm debts, the remaining assets realize $6,000. A claims that he is entitled to the entire $6,000. B contends that the distribution is $4,000 to A and $2,000 to B. C claims the $6,000 should be divided equally between the partners. Who is correct?

11. Martin, Mark and Marvin formed a retail clothing partnership by the name of "M" Clothiers and conducted a business for many years, buying most of their clothing from Hill, a wholesaler. On January 15 Marvin retired from the business, but Martin and Mark decided to continue it. As part of the retirement agreement, Martin and Mark agreed in writing with Marvin that Marvin would not be responsible for any of the partnership debts, either past or future. A news item concerning Marvin's retirement appeared in the local newspaper on January 15.

Prior to January 15, Hill was a creditor of "M" Clothiers to the extent of $10,000 and, on January 30, extended additional credit of $5,000. Hill was not advised and did not, in fact, know of Marvin's retirement and the change of the partnership. On January 30, Ray, a competitor of Hill, extended credit for the first time to "M" Clothiers in the amount of $3,000.

On February 1, Martin and Mark left for parts unknown and left no partnership assets with which to pay the described debts. What is Marvin's liability, if any, (a) to Hill, and (b) to Ray?

12. A, B and C were partners sharing profits in proportions of one-fourth, one-third, and five-twelfths, respectively. Their business failed and the firm was dissolved. At the time of dissolution no financial adjustments between the partners were necessary with reference to their respective capital contributions, but the firm's liabilities to creditors exceed its assets by $24,000. Without contributing any amount toward the payment of the liabilities, B has moved to South America, where he is not subject to the service of legal process. A and C are financially responsible. How much must each contribute?

13. Indicate which of the following statements are true and which are false:

(a) Creditors having claims based upon torts committed by partners in the course of business of the partnership are preferred over creditors with claims based upon contracts.

(b) Partners who wish to continue the business have a prior right to purchase the assets.

(c) In the absence of a contract providing otherwise, the distribution to partners of accrued profits should be in equal parts regardless of the fact that the partners had contributed to the firm unequally.

(d) Advances in the nature of loans made by the various partners to the partnership share in the firm assets on the same basis as debts due other creditors.

(e) As between the partners the assets of the partnership must be applied to pay the claims of partners in respect of capital ahead of the claims of partners in respect to profits.

(f) Debts owing to partners (other than for the capital and profits) rank ahead of debts owing to partners in respect to capital and profits.

(g) The capital contributed by a limited partner must be repaid before any other claims or debts are paid out of partnership assets.

NATURE, FORMATION, AND POWERS OF CORPORATIONS

A corporation is an entity created by law and existing separate and distinct from the individuals whose contributions of initiative, property, and control make it possible for it to function.   In the opinion of the Supreme Court in Dartmouth College v. Woodward, 4 Wheat. (U.S.) 518, 636, 4 L.Ed. 629 (1819), Chief Justice Marshall stated:

A corporation is an artificial being, invisible, intangible, and existing only in contemplation of law.   Being the mere creature of law, it possesses only those properties which the charter of its creation confers upon it, either expressly or as incidental to its very existence.   These are such as are supposed best calculated to effect the object for which it was created.   Among the most important are immortality, and, if the expression may be allowed, individuality; properties by which a perpetual succession of many persons are considered as the same, so that they may act as a single individual.   A corporation manages its own affairs, and holds property without the hazardous and endless necessity, of perpetual conveyances for the purpose of transmitting it from hand to hand.   It is chiefly for the purpose of clothing bodies of men, in succes-

sion, with these qualities and capacities, that corporations were invented, and are in use.   By these means, a perpetual succession of individuals are capable of acting for the promotion of the particular object, like one immortal being.

The corporation is the dominant form of business organization in the United States. Use of the corporation as an instrument of commercial enterprise has made possible the vast concentrations of wealth and capital which have largely transformed this country from an agrarian to an industrial economy.

NATURE OF CORPORATIONS

Historical Development

In order to obtain the advantages of conducting a business enterprise in corporate form, a charter or franchise granted by the legislative branch of the government is required.   Prior to the middle of the nineteenth century, it was not uncommon for the legislatures of the several States and for the English Parliament to pass special Acts creating corporations. The early railroad companies in this country were formed under special Acts of the legislature of their respective States of incorporation.

It would be an intolerable burden on State legislatures if the formation of each corporation required a special statute. Incorporation would be more difficult, less speedy, more politicized, and the corporate birth rate substantially reduced. Domestic corporations currently doing business in the United States number well over one million.

In order to avoid a special privileged class of corporations, state legislatures began enacting during the nineteenth century general statutes authorizing the Secretary of State to issue a certificate of incorporation or charter upon compliance with its provisions. Presently, all states have such general incorporation statutes.

In 1946 a committee of the American Bar Association after careful study and research submitted a draft of a Model State Business Corporation Act patterned largely upon the Illinois Business Corporation Act which had been adopted in that State in 1933. The Model Act has been revised and improved from time to time and is the product of the best thinking of the leading practitioners and professors of corporation law in the United States. The Model Act as revised in 1979 is set forth in Appendix E of this book.

The provisions of the Model Act do not become law until enacted by a State, but its influence has been widespread and it has been adopted in whole or in part by a majority of the States. As a recommended model statute, it sets a standard for the statutory law of business corporations.

Partnerships and Corporations Contrasted

The essential differences between a partnership and a corporation are summarized in Figure 34–1.

FIGURE 34–1 PARTNERSHIP AND CORPORATION COMPARED

	Partnership	**Corporation**
Creation	By agreement of the parties.	By statutory authorization.
Entity	A legal entity for some, but not all purposes.	A legal entity.
Duration	Dissolved by death, bankruptcy, or withdrawal of a partner.	May be perpetual.
Limitation of Liability	Partners are subject to unlimited liability upon the contracts, debts and torts of the partners.	Shareholders are not generally liable for the contracts, debts, or torts of the corporation.
Transferability of Interest	Interest of a partner in a partnership is not transferable without the consent of all of the other partners.	Shares of stock in a corporation are freely transferable.
Management and Control	Each partner is entitled to an equal voice in the management and control of the business.	The business of the corporation is managed by a board of directors elected by the shareholders.
Agency	Each partner is an agent of the partnership.	A shareholder is neither a principal nor an agent of the corporation.
Suits by and Against	In actions brought by or against the partnership, all partners are generally necessary parties.	The corporation may sue and be sued in its own name.

CORPORATE ATTRIBUTES

The principal attributes of a corporation are that (1) it is a legal entity, (2) it owes its existence to a state which also regulates it, (3) it provides limited liability to its shareholders, (4) its shares of stock are freely transferable, (5) it has perpetual existence, (6) its management is centralized, and it is considered, for some purposes, (7) a person and (8) a citizen.

The Corporation as a Legal Entity

A corporation is a legal entity separate and apart from its members or shareholders, with rights and liabilities entirely distinct from theirs. It may sue, or be sued by, or contract with any other party including any one of its members. A transfer of stock in the corporation from one individual to another has no effect upon the legal existence of the corporation. Title to corporate property belongs not to such shareholder but to the corporation. Even where a single individual owns all of the stock of the corporation, the shareholder and the corporation are not the same but have separate and distinct existences.

The Corporation as a Creature of the State

A corporation may only be formed by compliance with a state incorporation statute. A corporation's charter and the provisions of the statute under which it is formed constitute a contract between it and the State. Article I, Section 10, of the Federal constitution provides that no State shall pass any law "impairing the obligation of contracts" and this prohibition applies to contracts between a State and a corporation.

The incorporation of Dartmouth College by charter granted by King George III in 1769 provided for its creation, corporate structure, and administration and control by a self-perpetuating board of trustees.

In 1816 New Hampshire enacted a statute creating a board of 25 overseers of the College to be appointed by the State and empowered to have access to the books and records of Dartmouth College; to appoint and remove its president, faculty members, and administrative personnel; to establish departments and professorships; to provide for the erection of new buildings; and in other ways to exercise control over the affairs of the College given by its charter to the board of trustees. In Dartmouth College v. Woodward, previously cited, the Supreme Court held the statute unconstitutional as impairing the obligations of contract.

To avoid the impact of this decision incorporation statutes reserve to the State the power to prescribe such regulations, provisions, and limitations as it shall deem advisable, and to amend, repeal or modify the statute at its pleasure. Section 149. As such reservation is a material part of the contract between the State and a corporation formed under the statute, any amendment or modification regulating or altering the structure of the corporation does not impair the obligation of contract because expressly permitted by the contract.

Limited Liability

A corporation is a legal entity and as such is liable out of its own assets for its debts. The shareholders generally are not personally liable for the corporation's debts beyond the amount of their investment. By the same token, the corporation is not liable for the personal obligations of its shareholders.

Free Transferability of Corporate Shares

In the absence of contractual restrictions, shares in a corporation may be freely transferred by way of sale, gift, or pledge. Transfers of shares of stock are governed by Article 8 of the Uniform Commercial Code,

Investment Securities, and are discussed in Chapter 35.

The Corporation
May Have Perpetual Existence

A corporation may have perpetual existence: "Each corporation shall have power to have perpetual succession by its corporate name unless a limited period of duration is stated in its articles of incorporation." Section 4(a). As a consequence, the death or withdrawal of a shareholder, director, or officer does not terminate the existence of the corporation.

The Corporation Has
Centralized Management

The shareholders of a corporation elect the board of directors which manages the business affairs of the corporation. It is then incumbent upon the board to appoint officers to run the day-to-day operations of the business. Since neither the directors nor the officers (collectively referred to as "management") generally need be shareholders, it is entirely possible, and in large corporations quite typical, for the ownership of the corporation to be separated from the management of the corporation.

The Corporation as a Person

Whether a corporation is a "person" within the meaning of a constitution or statute is a matter of construction based upon the intention of the lawmakers in using the word, as ascertained from the legislative history of the particular provision and the understood aim and purpose of the document. A corporation is a person within the provision in the Fifth and Fourteenth Amendments to the Federal constitution that no "person" shall be "deprived of life, liberty or property without due process of law"; and the provision in the Fourteenth Amendment that no State shall "deny to any person within

its jurisdiction the equal protection of the laws." On the other hand, a corporation is not considered to be a person within the clause of the Fifth Amendment which protects a "person" against self-incrimination.

The Corporation as a Citizen

A corporation is not deemed to be a citizen as that term is used in the Fourteenth Amendment which provides "No state shall make or enforce any law which shall abridge the privileges or immunities of citizens of the United States."

A corporation, however, is regarded as a citizen of the State of its incorporation and of the State in which it has its principal office, for the purpose of determining whether diversity of citizenship exists between the parties to a lawsuit as a basis for jurisdiction of the federal courts.

CLASSIFICATION
OF CORPORATIONS

Corporations may be classified as public or private; profit or non-profit; domestic or foreign; closely held; and professional.

Public or Private

A public corporation is one which is created to administer a unit of local civil government such as a School District, Park District, or Sanitary District; or one created by the United States to conduct a public business such as the Tennessee Valley Authority or the Federal Deposit Insurance Corporation.

A private corporation is one organized to conduct a privately owned business enterprise for profit, or a non-profit corporation organized for community benefit or enjoyment.

Profit or Non-profit

A profit corporation is one found for the purpose of operating a business for profit from which payments are made to its shareholders in the form of dividends.

A non-profit corporation may make profits but they may not be distributed to its members, but must be used exclusively for the charitable, educational, or scientific purpose for which it was organized. Examples of non-profit corporations are private schools, library clubs, athletic clubs, fraternities, sororities, and hospitals.

Domestic or Foreign

A corporation is domestic in the state in which it is incorporated. It is foreign in every other state or jurisdiction.

Closely Held

A corporation is described as closely held when its outstanding shares of stock are held by a small number of persons, frequently family relatives. The shareholders frequently enter into a buy-sell agreement with one another at the time of incorporation in order to prevent the stock from getting into the hands of persons outside the original group of shareholders.

Professional Corporations

Practically all of the States have a "Professional Association Act" which permits the practice of professions by duly licensed individuals under corporate form. These statutes do not change the rule that a corporation may not be permitted to practice a profession, as the professional practice involved is allowed only to licensed individuals. The purpose of the statute in authorizing the formation of this type of corporation under specified limitations is to permit duly licensed professionals to obtain tax advantages not allowable to individuals or partnerships.

FORMATION OF A CORPORATION

Selection of Name

A corporation must have a name and, as Blackstone stated, "by that name alone it must sue and be sued, and do all legal acts, though a very minute variation therefrom is not material. Such name is the very being of its constitution, without which it could not perform its corporate functions."

The general incorporation laws of the various States have differing provisions in regard to the corporate name. Most acts require that the name contain a word or words which clearly indicate that it is a corporation, such as "corporation," "company," "incorporated," "limited," "Corp.," "Co.," "Inc.," or "Ltd." In some States, it is required that "Company" not be preceded by "and" lest a partnership be implied.

Practically every incorporation statute provides that no corporate name shall be the same as, or deceptively similar to, the name of an existing corporation doing business within the State.

Selection of State for Incorporation

A corporation is usually incorporated in the state in which it is intended to be located and transact all or the principal part of its business. However, a corporation may be formed in one State and have its principal place of business and conduct all or most of its operations in another State or States by duly qualifying and obtaining a certificate of authority to transact business in such other States. The principal criteria useful in selecting a State for incorporation include the flexibility accorded management, the rights granted to shareholders, the limitations imposed upon the issuance of shares, the restrictions placed upon the payment of dividends, and the organizational costs such as fees and taxes.

Promoters

A promoter is a person who brings about the "birth" of a corporation. The promoter arranges for the capital and financing of the corporation, including stock subscriptions. In addition, the promoter will assemble the necessary assets, equipment, licenses, personnel, leases, and services. He will also attend to the actual legal formation of the corporation. Upon incorporation, the promoter's organizational task is finished.

Promoters' Contracts. In addition to procuring subscriptions and preparing the incorporation papers, promoters often enter into contracts in anticipation of the creation of the corporation. The contracts may be ordinary agreements necessary for the eventual operation of the business, such as leases, purchase orders, employment contracts, and sales contracts, or the promoter may obtain a particularly advantageous contract outside of the routine business requirements of the incipient corporation, such as a valuable selling franchise. If these contracts are executed by the promoter in his own name and there is no further action, the promoter is liable on such contracts, and the corporation, when created, is not liable. A pre-incorporation contract made by promoters does not bind the corporation even though made in the name of the corporation and in its behalf, except where so provided by statute. The promoter, in executing such contracts, may do so in the corporate name although incorporation has not yet taken place. Prior to its formation, a corporation has no capacity to enter into contracts or to employ agents or representatives. Upon being formed, it is not liable at common law upon any prior contract, even one made in its name, unless it adopts or ratifies the contract expressly, impliedly, or by knowingly accepting benefits under it.

Promoters' Fiduciary Duty. The promoters of a corporation occupy a fiduciary relationship among themselves as well as to the corporation, to its subscribers, and to its initial shareholders. This duty requires good faith, fair dealing, and full disclosure. Accordingly, the promoters are under a duty to account for any secret profit realized by them at the expense of those to whom such duty is owing.

Subscribers of Shares

A subscription is an offer to purchase capital stock in a corporation yet to be formed. The offeror is called a "subscriber." Sometimes the term subscription is used loosely to include a contract to purchase stock in an existing corporation, but this latter type of agreement is an executory contract of purchase and sale rather than a subscription. The distinction is important since a subscriber becomes a shareholder, with all of the rights and liabilities attached thereto as soon as the corporation is formed, whereas a purchaser of stock does not become a shareholder until the certificate of stock is issued to him.

Courts have viewed subscriptions in two ways. The majority regards a subscription as a continuing offer to purchase stock from a non-existing entity, which is incapable of accepting the offer until created. Under this view, a subscription may be revoked at any time prior to its acceptance. A minority of jurisdictions treat a subscription as a contract between the various subscribers and therefore irrevocable except with the consent of all of the subscribers. Most courts agree that the subscription is accepted by the corporation immediately upon its coming into existence. Thus, the general common-law rule is that a subscription may be revoked by the subscriber at any time prior to the incorporation of the corporation but may not be revoked thereafter. Modern incorporation

statutes, however, have taken an intermediate position in resolving this issue. The
Model Business Corporation Act, Section
17, provides that a subscription is irrevocable for a period of six months, unless otherwise provided in the subscription agreement or unless all of the subscribers consent
to the revocation of the subscription.

The valuation of porperty to be contributed by subscribers in payment for shares
is determined by the pre-incorporation subscription agreement subject to statutory
limitations. The time for payment may be
set forth in the agreement, but if not, is
determined by the board of directors upon
making a call on the subscribers for payment in full or in stated installments.
Upon default in payment the corporation
may proceed to collect it in the same manner
as any debt due the corporation.

Incorporators

The incorporators are the persons who sign
the articles of incorporation which is filed
with the Secretary of State of the state of
incorporation. Although they perform a
necessary function, their services as incorporators are perfunctory and short-lived,
ending with the organizational meeting of
the initial board of directors following the
issuance of the certificate of incorporation.
Accordingly, modern statutes have greatly
relaxed the qualifications of incorporators
and reduced the number required. The
Model Act, for example, provides that one
or more persons, or a domestic or foreign
corporation, may act as incorporators. Section 53.

Articles of Incorporation

The articles of incorporation or charter
must be signed and filed with the Secretary
of State in order to form a corporation. The
articles of incorporation then become the
basic governing document of the corporation, so long as its provisions are consistent

with state and federal law. Although requirements differ in the several States, the
Model Act (Section 54) requires articles of
incorporation to set forth the following:

1. Name of the corporation.
2. Address of the corporation's initial registered office and the name of its registered
agent for service of process and receipt of
notice or demand upon the corporation.
3. Duration, which may be perpetual or
for a limited period of time.
4. Names and addresses of each incorporator.
5. Purpose or purposes for which the corporation is formed, which may be any lawful
purpose except for the purpose of banking
or insurance.
6. Number of authorized shares of stock
and the par value of each share or a statement that the shares are without par value.
7. If the shares are to be divided into
classes, the designation, preferences, limitations, and relative rights in respect of the
shares of each class.
8. If the corporation is to issue any preferred or special stock in series, the provisions thereof.
9. Number of directors constituting the
initial board of directors, and the names and
addresses of those who are to serve as directors until the first annual meeting of
shareholders or until their successors are
elected and qualify.
10. If any pre-emptive right is to be granted
to shareholders, the provisions thereof.
11. Any provision not inconsistent with law
which the incorporators choose to insert for
the regulation of the internal affairs of the
corporation.

Organization Meeting

The Model Act requires that an organization meeting be held to adopt the by-laws,
elect officers, and transact "such other business as may come before the meeting."
Section 57. This business typically in-

cludes authorization to issue shares of stock, approval of pre-incorporation contracts made by promoters, selection of a bank as well as approval of a corporate seal and the form of stock certificate.

By-laws

The by-laws of a corporation are the rules and regulations which govern its internal management. They are necessary to its organization, and the adoption of by-laws is one of the first items of business at the organization meeting held promptly after incorporation. Section 57.

Under the Model Business Corporation Act, the by-laws may provide for:

1. penalties for failure to pay installments or calls on subscriptions for shares (Section 17);
2. the place of shareholders' meetings (Section 28);
3. the calling of special meetings of shareholders (Section 28);
4. the qualifications of directors (Section 35);
5. an increase or decrease in the number of directors (Section 36);
6. classification of directors (Section 37);
7. the number of directors necessary for a quorum, not less than a majority (Section 40);
8. an executive committee of the board of directors (Section 42);
9. the notice to be given for meetings of the board of directors (Section 43); and
10. the duties of each of the officers.

The by-laws may contain provisions other than those just enumerated. However, nothing contained in the by-laws may be contrary to or inconsistent with any provision in the statute or in the articles of incorporation, and nothing in the articles may be repugnant to the statute. Section 27. In contrast to the certificate of incorporation which embodies the articles of in-

corporation, the by-laws do not have to be publicly filed and may be changed without shareholder approval: "The power to alter, amend, or repeal the by-laws or adopt new by-laws shall be vested in the board of directors unless reserved to the shareholders by the articles of incorporation." Section 27.

Qualification and Issuance of Stock

Almost every state now has a statute providing regulation for the issuance and sale of corporate stock and other securities, popularly known as "Blue Sky Laws." Certain State statutes are of the licensing or qualification type and others are of the notification or description type. In no case, however, does any state by qualifying an issue of stock or other security for sale, give any endorsement of the merits of the security.

In 1933, Congress passed the first Federal statute providing regulation of securities offered for sale and sold through the use of the mails or instrumentalities of interstate commerce. This statute, often called the "Truth in Securities Act," is administered by the Securities and Exchange Commission (S.E.C.). It is a disclosure type of statute, and the S.E.C. does not examine into the merits of the security proposed to be offered but only into the truthfulness, accuracy, and completeness of the information given and required to be given in a registration statement and prospectus. Regulation of the issuance and sale of securities is sanctioned by anti-fraud provisions, and by requirements for registration of broker-dealers, agents, and investment advisers, as well as by registration of securities.

An exemption from the requirement of registration under the Blue Sky Laws of most States and the Securities Act of 1933 may be available under certain conditions upon compliance with the rules and regulations of the appropriate State agency and of the S.E.C. If no exemption is available, a corporation offering for sale or selling its shares of stock or other securities, as well as any person selling such securities, is subject to court injunction, possible criminal prosecution and civil liability in damages to the persons to whom the shares or securities are sold in violation of the regulatory statute.

A more detailed discussion of Federal regulation of securities appears in Chapter 42.

RECOGNITION AND DISREGARD OF CORPORATENESS

Defectively Organized Corporations

Corporation de Jure. A corporation *de jure* is one which is not defectively organized but formed in strict compliance with the incorporation statute and the required organizational procedure. Once formed, the existence of a *de jure* corporation may not be challenged by anyone, even the State in a direct proceeding for this purpose.

Corporation de Facto. A failure to form a *de jure* corporation may result in the formation of a *de facto* corporation if the following requirements are met: (1) existence of a general corporation statute; (2) a bona fide attempt to comply with that law in organizing a corporation thereunder; and (3) actual exercise of corporate power by conducting a business in the belief that a corporation has been formed. The existence of a *de facto* corporation can be challenged only by the State. If such corporation sues to collect a debt, it is no defense to such suit that the plaintiff corporation is not *de jure*. Not even the State can collaterally question *de facto* corporation existence in a proceeding involving some other issue. The State must bring an independent suit against the corporation for this

express purpose, known as an action of *quo warranto* (by what right).

The Illinois statute provides that "a certificate of incorporation shall be conclusive evidence, except against the State, that all conditions precedent required to be performed by the incorporators have been complied with and that the corporation has been incorporated under this Act." The Model Act has a similar provision in Section 56.

Corporation by Estoppel. A person who has dealt with a defectively organized corporation may be precluded or estopped from denying its corporate existence, where the necessary elements of holding out and reliance are present. The doctrine of corporation by estoppel is different and distinct from that of corporation *de facto*. Estoppel does not create a corporation. It only operates to prevent a person or persons under the facts and circumstances of a particular case from raising the question of a corporation's existence or its capacity to act or to own property.

Defective Corporation. If the associates fail to comply with the requirements of the incorporation statute to such an extent that neither a *de jure* nor a *de facto* corporation is formed and the circumstances do not justify the application of the corporation by estoppel doctrine, then the courts generally deny the associates the benefits of incorporation. With respect to the attribute of limited liability, the Model Act provides that "All persons who assume to act as a corporation without authority to do so shall be jointly and severally liable for all debts and liabilities incurred or arising as a result thereof." Section 146.

Piercing the Corporate Veil

The courts will disregard the corporation entity when it is used to defeat public convenience, commit wrongdoing, protect fraud, or circumvent the law. Going behind the corporate entity in order to prevent its use by individuals seeking to insulate themselves from personal accountability and the consequences of their wrongdoing is referred to as *piercing the corporate veil.* Courts are quick to pierce the corporate veil where deemed necessary to remedy wrongdoing and have done so most frequently with close corporations and in parent-subsidiary relationships.

Close Corporations. The joint and active management by all the shareholders of close corporations frequently results in a tendency to forgo adherence to all of the niceties of corporate formalities, such as holding meetings of the board and shareholders, while the small size of close corporations often results in creditors who are unable to satisfy fully their claims against the corporation. Accordingly, the frustrated creditor will likely invoke the court to disregard the organization's corporateness and impose personal liability for the corporate obligations upon the shareholders. Courts have responded by piercing the corporate veil where the shareholders (1) have not conducted the business on a corporate basis or (2) have not provided an adequate financial basis for the business. Conducting the business on a corporate basis involves maintaining the corporation's funds separate from the shareholders' funds, maintaining separate financial records, holding regular directors' meetings and generally observing corporate formalities. Adequate capitalization requires that the shareholders invest sufficient capital to meet the reasonably anticipated requirements of the enterprise. The difficulty in determining adequacy of capitalization is well illustrated by the following two cases:

In New York City it is not an uncommon practice for persons in the taxicab industry to place the ownership and operation of a fleet of taxicabs in many corporations each owning and operating only one or two cabs. The stock of such multiple shell corporations is owned by one or a few shareholders. The purpose of this fragmentation is to avoid exposing the entire fleet and all of the assets of the combined corporations to a money judgment based upon liability for personal injuries or property damage resulting from the negligent operation of one of the cabs, and to take advantage of the minimum permissible public liability insurance for taxicabs. This would, of course, not be possible if the entire fleet were owned and operated by one corporation. In Mull v. Colt Co., 31 F.R.D. 154 (D.C.S.D.N.Y.1962) a Federal court pierced the corporate veil and imposed personal liability upon the various cab corporations and their controlling shareholders for injuries resulting from the negligent operation of a cab owned by one of such corporations. One of the reasons for the decision is that the fragmented corporation was inadequately capitalized considering the size of the entire business enterprise and the public responsibility. However, in the later case of Walkovszky v. Carlton, 18 N.Y.2d 414, 276 N.Y.S.2d 585, 223 N.E.2d 6 (1966), the Court of Appeals of New York held that a controlling shareholder of multiple corporations each owning and operating one or two cabs was not individually liable for personal injuries resulting from the negligent operation of a cab owned by one of such corporations unless the shareholder was using the control of the corporation to further his own business as distinguished from the business of the corporation. The State court regarded fragmented corporate ownership of a fleet of taxicabs, standing alone, as not a sufficient basis for piercing the corporate veil. The decision was by a 5 to 2 vote of the members of the Court. The rationale of this decision is not reconcilable with that of the Federal court in New York. Since Federal courts are required to apply the law of the State in cases where Federal jurisdiction is based on diversity of citizenship, as in Mull v. Colt Company, that case will no longer be followed by Federal courts in New York. However, a number of other states do follow the rule of the Federal decision.

Parent-Subsidiary. A corporation may choose to risk only a portion of its assets in a particular enterprise by forming a subsidiary. Courts will pierce the corporate veil in this situation if

1. both corporations are not adequately capitalized, or
2. the formalities of separate corporate procedures are not observed, or
3. each corporation is not held out to the public as separate enterprises, or
4. the funds of the two corporations are commingled.

So long as these pitfalls are avoided, the courts will recognize the separateness of the subsidiary even though the parent owns all the stock of the subsidiary and the two corporations have common directors and officers.

CORPORATE POWERS

A corporation derives its existence and all of its powers from the State of incorporation, and therefore has only such powers as the State has conferred upon it. These powers are those expressly set forth in the statute and articles of incorporation, and powers reasonably implied from them.

The word "power" as applied to corporations means legally authorized; the absence of power does not connote physical incapability. A corporation may by its agents actually engage in business activities and perform acts that are beyond its corporate powers, or *ultra vires.* To declare such acts null and void is merely to deal with the legal effect of them and not to dispute their existence. It cannot be maintained that a corporation does not have the physical ability to engage in activities and transactions which transgress the limits of its authorized

powers. If that were so, *ultra vires* acts would never occur.

Sources of Corporate Powers

Statutory Powers. Typical of the general powers granted by incorporation statutes are those provided by Sections 4 and 5 of the Model Act, which include the following:

1. To have perpetual succession.
2. To sue and be sued in its corporate name.
3. To acquire, own, mortgage, and dispose of real and personal property.
4. To lend money and use its credit to assist its employees.
5. To acquire, own, vote, and dispose of shares or obligations of other business entities.
6. To make contracts, incur liabilities and issue notes, bonds, or other obligations.
7. To invest surplus funds and acquire its own shares.
8. To conduct its business and carry on its operations within or without the State of incorporation.
9. To elect or appoint officers and agents, define their duties, and fix their compensation.
10. To make and alter by-laws for the administration and regulation of its affairs.
11. To make donations for the public welfare or for charitable, scientific, or educational purposes.
12. To establish pension, profit sharing and other incentive plans for its directors, officers, and employees.
13. To be a promoter, partner, member, associate, or manager of any partnership, joint venture, trust, or other enterprise.
14. To amend its articles of incorporation.
15. To effect a merger or consolidation with one or more other corporations.
16. To indemnify against personal liability officers, directors, employees, and agents of the corporation who act on behalf of the corporation in good faith and without negligence.

Express Charter Powers. The objects or purposes for which a corporation is formed are expressly stated in its articles of incorporation, which delineate in general language the type of business activities in which the corporation proposes to engage. This serves (1) to advise the shareholders of the nature and kind of particular business activity in which their investment is being risked, (2) to guide the officers, directors and management as to the extent of the corporation's authority to act, and (3) to inform any person who may contemplate dealing with the corporation of the extent of its legally authorized power.

The express powers must relate to a legitimate business activity or industry within the purview of the general statute. Thus, a state may provide that a bank, savings and loan association, insurance company or railroad company may not be organized under its general corporation law but may be organized under a separate statute. In such case, the power to engage in any of these businesses is not granted to a corporation formed under the general statute.

Implied Powers. A corporation has the authority to do any act which is necessary or convenient to and consistent with the execution of any of its express powers and the operation of the business which it was formed to conduct. This power exists by implication and does not depend upon express language in the charter or statute but upon reasonable inference as to the proper scope and content of such language, taking into consideration the facts and circumstances of the particular case. Thus, a railroad corporation is not ordinarily authorized to operate a hotel, but at a junction point of two of its intersecting lines a particular railroad company was held to have the implied power to build, own, and manage a hotel to accommodate its transfer passengers who would otherwise be without such facilities.

The express powers of a corporation may and should be stated in general language, and it is not necessary to set forth in detail every particular type of act which the corporation is empowered to perform. A general statement of corporate purpose or object is sufficient to give rise to all of the powers necessary, incidental, or convenient to accomplish that purpose. Section 4(q). For instance, a corporation organized "to buy and sell goods, wares and merchandise" has implied power to (a) purchase or lease store premises, (b) employ salesmen, (c) buy or rent trucks, (d) spend money for advertising, (e) open and manage a bank account, (f) employ buyers and pay their salaries and traveling expenses, and (g) purchase insurance on the lives of officers as well as other powers necessary or incidental to such stated purpose.

Effect of *Ultra Vires*

Since a corporation has authority to act only within the limitation of its express and implied powers, any action taken or contract made by it which goes beyond these powers is *ultra vires*. *Ultra vires* does not mean without power or capability, but rather without legal authorization, because the act is not within the scope and type of acts which the corporation is legally empowered to perform.

Traditionally, *ultra vires* contracts were unenforceable as null and void. Under the modern common law approach, courts allow the *ultra vires* defense where the contract is wholly executory on both sides. A corporation having received full performance from the other party to the contract is not permitted to escape liability by a plea of *ultra vires*. Conversely, where a corporation is suing for breach of a contract which has been fully performed on its side, the defense of *ultra vires* is unavailing.

Most statutes now have abolished the defense of *ultra vires* in an action for breach of contract by or against a corporation.

No act of a corporation and no conveyance or transfer of real or personal property to or by a corporation shall be invalid by reason of the fact that the corporation was without capacity or power to do such act or to make or receive such conveyance or transfer.   Section 7, Model Act.

While *ultra vires* under modern statutes may no longer be used defensively as a shield against liability, corporate activities which are *ultra vires* may be redressed in any of the three following ways as provided in Section 7 of the Model Act:

(a) In an injunction proceeding brought by a shareholder against the corporation to restrain and enjoin the commission of the *ultra vires* act.
(b) In a suit by the corporation or through shareholders in a representative suit against the officers or directors of the corporation.
(c) In a proceeding by the Attorney General of the State of incorporation to dissolve the corporation or to enjoin it from the transaction of unauthorized business.

In some jurisdictions officers and directors are absolutely liable for losses to the corporation resulting from *ultra vires* transactions.   In other jurisdictions officers and directors acting in good faith and without negligence are not personally liable for having caused the corporation to engage in an activity which is beyond its powers.   However, officers and directors who wilfully manifest disregard for limitations upon the corporation's authority to act, and apply corporate funds to unauthorized purposes, become individually liable for losses thereby sustained by the corporation in all jurisdictions.

The doctrine of *ultra vires* is of less significance today because modern statutes permit incorporation for any lawful purpose and most articles of incorporation do not limit the powers of the corporation.   As a consequence, far fewer acts are *ultra vires*.

Liability for Torts and Crimes

A corporation is liable for the torts and crimes committed by its agents in the course of their employment.   The doctrine of *ultra vires,* even in those jurisdictions where it is permitted as a defense, has no application to wrongdoing by the corporation.   The doctrine of respondeat superior imposes full liability upon a corporation for the torts of its agents and employees while engaged in company business.   For example, X, a truck driver employed by the ABC Corporation, while on a business errand, negligently runs over Y, a pedestrian.   Both X and the ABC Corporation are liable to Y in an action by him to recover damages for the injuries sustained.

A corporation may also be found guilty of fraud, false imprisonment, malicious prosecution, libel, and other torts.

One of the essential elements of most crimes is a guilty mind or criminal intent, and it has been argued that since a corporation is artificial, intangible and incorporeal, it cannot have either a mind or a soul and is therefore incapable of committing a crime.   This is a tenuous argument and overlooks the fact that a corporation never acts except through the minds, eyes, and hands of human agents, and that some corporations command and are commanded by the finest executive minds in this country.   As a juristic fiction, a corporation is theoretically immortal.   It may not have a soul to save, but the absence of a soul in its incorporeal body does not noticeably inhibit or prevent a corporation from transgressing the laws of man which exist for the welfare and safety of the community and the State.   Corporations do not go to heaven because no business is transacted there.   Corporations are amenable to the criminal law for violations of which they may be indicted and punished.   The punishment necessarily is by fine and not imprisonment.

Cases

Promoters' Fiduciary Duty

GOLDEN v. OAHE ENTERPRISES, INC.

(1980, S.D.) 295 N.W.2d 160.

WOLLMAN, C. J.

* * *

Emmick is the major figure in the story of Oahe. In years past, Emmick has been involved in the sale of industrial chemicals, the promotion of nursing homes, and the management of various farming activities. Emmick approached one J. B. Morris (now deceased) with a plan whereby Morris' Sully County, South Dakota, ranch would be incorporated and through Emmick's managerial skills made to show a profit. At approximately the same time, Emmick approached Golden, who was then operating the Silver Spur Bar in Ft. Pierre, and proposed that Golden contribute some farm machinery and livestock to Oahe. Golden was not, however, present on October 26, 1966, when Oahe was incorporated at a meeting in the office of George Qualley, Emmick's lawyer, in Sioux City, Iowa.

At this meeting, it was concluded that Oahe shares would be given a $50 par value. Officers of the corporation were elected: Chairman and Secretary-Treasurer, J. B. Morris; President, Emmick; and Vice-President, Milton Morris (J. B. Morris' son). An agreement was signed whereby J. B and Mary Morris transferred their ranch to Oahe Enterprises. It was concluded that the Morris ranch was worth $168,000.00 Of this amount, Morris' equity was determined to be $120,000.00. As his contribution, Emmick transferred 6,315 shares of Colonial Manors, Inc., stock (CM stock) to Oahe.

Colonial Manors, Inc., is an Iowa corporation that is involved in the promotion and management of nursing homes throughout the Midwest. There is serious disagreement concerning the value this stock had at the time Emmick exchanged it for Oahe stock. Emmick represented to the Morrises that the stock was worth $19 per share. At the March 1966 meeting of the CM Corporation, the board of directors set the value of CM stock for internal stock-option purposes at $19 per share. This figure represented $1 for each nursing home the CM Corporation was involved with. At the September 1966 meeting, the value of the CM stock was reduced by the board of directors to $9.50 per share. Emmick knew of the reduction in value of the CM stock prior to the October 26, 1966, meeting at which Oahe was incorporated. There is, however, no evidence that would suggest that this knowledge was disclosed to the Morrises.

* * *

Courts faced with the situation in which a promoter benefits from a violation of his fiduciary duty at the expense of the corporation or its members often characterize the promoter's gain as "secret profit." Such profit is not secret if all interested parties know of and assent to it. But where a promoter through, for example, overvaluation of property exchanged for stock and failure to disclose all material facts regarding such exchange, takes more from the corporation than he transfers in, he is held liable for what courts term secret profit. [Citations.]

As a promoter of Oahe, Emmick stood in a fiduciary relationship to both the corporation and its stockholders and was bound to deal with them in the utmost good faith. "The obtaining of a secret profit by a promoter through the sale of property to a corporation is uniformly held to be a fraud on the corporation and stockholders, and the promoter may be required to account for such profit." [Citation.]

The valuation of the CM stock was based on Emmick's self-serving estimate of matters well known to him as a CM insider and was warped by Emmick's self-interest. Emmick was not trading stock that had an easily ascertainable value; he was not dealing with people experienced in transactions of this type. He failed to make known facts of which he, as an insider of CM, was aware. It is true that Emmick was not the only member on the Oahe board of directors. He was, however, the controlling member and the one in possession of information pertinent to the value of his CM stock not generally available to the public or to the other Oahe board members. In addition to being an insider of CM, he was both a director of and the dominant and controlling force in Oahe. We hold, therefore, that he failed in his duty to the corporation to disclose information regarding stock he intended to transfer into Oahe for Oahe shares and is therefore liable for the shortfall to the corporation therefrom.

* * *

Because the total value of the CM stock Emmick transferred to Oahe was less than the value Emmick received in Oahe stock, the difference can be equalized by canceling the number of Oahe shares held by Emmick that is proportional to the overevaluation. [Citations.] We note that this Court has upheld the cancellation of stock under circumstances where original issue stock was transferred for the worthless stock of another corporation or for services to be performed in the future.

* * *

The judgment is reversed, and the case is remanded to the circuit court with directions to redetermine the fair market value of the CM stock exchanged by Emmick for Oahe stock * * *.

Stock Subscriptions

LITTLE SWITZERLAND BREWING CO. v. OXLEY

(1973) 260 W.Va. 504, 197 S.E.2d 301.

[Proceedings on behalf of creditors of Little Switzerland Brewing Company, a corporation, to recover money owing by defendants on stock subscription agreements. The trial court entered summary judgment for defendants. On appeal, reversed.]

BERRY, PRESIDENT:
* * *

Little Switzerland Brewing Company was incorporated and a charter was issued by the Secretary of State on January 28, 1968. The company had authorized capital stock of $200,000 consisting of 2,000,000 shares at the par value of ten cents a share. On February 18, 1968 Fred Ellison and Charles A. Oxley were made directors of the company after they purchased 5,000 shares at $5 per share. On the same date the company entered into an agreement with Valanco, Inc. to underwrite the sale of 100,000 shares of Little Switzerland common stock at $10 per share with $1.50 of the $10 going to Valanco, Inc. as its underwriting commission.

* * *

Little Switzerland contends that 275 citizens throughout the State of West Virginia subscribed for shares in the company prior to September 22, 1968. On September 25, 1968 Charles E. Oxley and Fred J. Ellison signed stock subscription agreements to purchase 5,000 shares of stock at $10 a share. At the bottom of each agreement were three boxes, one of which was to be marked depending on whether the subscriber was tendering cash, check or a money order with the agreement. Oxley and Ellison did not mark any of the boxes but wrote the word "Note" in a blank space which was to be filled in with the amount of money that was being tendered with the subscription. The "Note" that accompanied the stock subscription agreement was titled "Noninterest Bearing-Nonobligatory Note" and merely stated that Oxley and Ellison would pay "at their discretion" $50,000 to Little Switzerland Brewing Company.

* * *

On March 24, 1970, eight of the ten directors of the company met and passed a resolution 7 to 1 to cancel the stock subscription agreements of Ellison, Oxley, * * * Mr. Ellison was not present at that meeting. * * *

Two questions are presented on this appeal for the decision of this Court: (1) Should the defendants be allowed to escape liability under the provisions of the stock subscription agreements signed by them by tendering a non-interest bearing non-obligatory note as payment for said subscriptions? (2) Did the board of directors have the right and power to release the defendants from liability under the subscription agreements?

* * *

* * * It is the appellees' contention that the stock subscription agreements signed by them are not valid because the non-obligatory notes were a part of the stock subscription agreements and the notes did not obligate them to pay for the stock in question although the subscription agreements themselves said it was paid for at the time it was signed. This contention is without merit because it was held by this Court in the case of Pittsburg, Wheeling & Kentucky R.R. Co. v. Applegate & Son, 21 W.Va. 172, that a subscriber to the stock of a corporation cannot escape liability to pay for his subscription on the grounds that he did not pay the sum required to be paid by the statute at the time he subscribed.

It should be noted that the appellees in the instant case were not only stockholders but were also directors of the company and it is their contention that the stock subscription agreements were only options to buy stock. However, the agreements were used to assure the Commissioner of Securities that the public offering had been fully subscribed and to free the other stock of the Little Switzerland Brewing Company for over-the-counter trading. The contention of the appellees would appear to be that the subscription agreements in question were merely fictitious or colorable subscriptions; but if this were done to induce others to subscribe and there was an understanding that there was to be no liability on the part of the appellees, the subscriptions are nevertheless just as binding on the subscribers as if they were made in good faith. 4 M.J., Corporations, § 78. * * *

It has been held that a corporation has no authority to accept subscriptions to its capital stock upon special terms, where the terms are such as to constitute a fraud upon other subscribers, or upon persons who become creditors of the corporation, and the invalidity of such terms or conditions will not release the subscriber from liability upon his subscription. [Citations.]

* * *

The authorities appear to be uniform in holding that a subscriber to corporate stock based upon the subscription is liable for such subscription of stock regardless of any extrinsic agreement between the subscriber and the corporation. [Citations.]

The Supreme Court of the United States has consistently held since the case of Sawyer v. Hoag, 17 Wall. 610, 21 L.Ed. 731, that the capital stock of an insolvent corporation is a trust fund for the payment of its debts; that the law implies a promise by the subscribers of stock who did not pay for it to make such payment when demanded by the creditors of the corporation; and that any extrinsic agreement limiting the subscriber's liability therefor is void against creditors. [Citations.]

* * *

It is clear from the authorities that the appellees in the instant case are liable for their stock subscriptions.

The answer to the second question involved in the case presented here is that the directors of the corporation did not have the authority in any event to release the appellees from liability on their stock subscription agreements. In the first place the directors of a solvent corporation have no authority to release any stockholder from liability on stock subscription agreements unless authorized by the stockholders of the corporation. [Citation.] Then, too, where a corporation is insolvent such action by the corporation is prohibited by statute. Code, 31–1–35. This statute not only provides that the appellees, as stockholders of the Little Switzerland Brewing Company, shall be liable for the benefit of the creditors of Little Switzerland for the amount of their stock subscriptions, but also that in the event of insolvency of Little Switzerland all such liability of the stockholders shall be considered as assets of the corporation and may be enforced by the proper person notwithstanding any release agreement or arrangement which may have been made between the corporation and the stockholders.

* * *

Judgments reversed; remanded with directions.

Piercing the Corporate Veil: Close Corporations

FELSENTHAL CO. v. NORTHERN ASSUR. CO., LTD.

(1918) 284 Ill. 343, 120 N.E. 268.

[Action by plaintiff, D. I. Felsenthal Company, against defendant, the Northern Assurance Company, Ltd. of London, on a fire insurance policy issued in favor of plaintiff. Defendant resisted liability on the grounds, among others, that gasoline kept on the premises was fraudulently, knowingly and purposely ignited by plaintiff, its officers, agents and employees in such manner as to cause the fire and for the purpose of causing the fire and destroying the property. Judgment rendered on the verdict in favor of defendant. The Appellate Court affirmed the judgment. The cause is here upon a certificate of importance granted by the Appellate Court.

Plaintiff was an Illinois corporation capitalized at $15,000. The corporation was engaged in the wholesale business of dealing in tailors' clippings, and had its warehouse and assorting rooms in leased buildings located at 902–904 South Morgan street, Chicago, consisting of a three-story brick building with a small barn in the rear. Morris L. Fox was the beneficial owner of practically all of the 150 shares of capital stock, was its president, a director and, also, a creditor of the company in the amount of approximately $30,000—a sum greater than the total loss caused by the fire. On March 7, 1912, about three or four o'clock A.M., plaintiff's property, consisting of loose and bailed tailors' clippings, was destroyed or damaged by fire. The total amount of insurance then carried on the property was $31,500; the total cash value of the property $30,721.42; the total loss and damage $29,471.73.

Evidence adduced by defendant tended strongly to prove, in substance, that Fox and David I. Felsenthal, about two months prior to the fire, went to the saloon of Moe Rosenberg, and from there went with Rosenberg into the restaurant adjoining the saloon and had dinner. Fox and Felsenthal told Rosenberg they were going out of business and were planning to have a fire at their place. Fox had known Rosenberg from his early boyhood. Rosenberg told them that Ben Fink, who was in the saloon with him, was in the business of firing and destroying buildings and property insured.

Rosenberg saw Fink for them and gave them his terms for firing the building and its contents, namely, ten per cent of the amount of insurance collected from the insurance company, $500 to be paid in advance. They told Rosenberg they had $32,000 or $33,000 of insurance; that they had shipped out some of the stock but had not cancelled any of the insurance, and that they did not know whether any of the policies would hold. Rosenberg then told them he would take up the matter with Fink and have Fink, in turn, take it up with Nathan Spira, an insurance adjuster, and who was at the fire when it occurred and afterwards appeared as a representative of the plaintiff in adjusting the loss. The burning of the building was agreed to upon these terms and about ten days later Fox paid Rosenberg $500 advance deposit. The agreement was carried out.

Upon the basis of the facts narrated, the Supreme Court observed that the jury was warranted in finding that the building was destroyed at the instigation of Fox beyond all reasonable doubt, and that the loss by the fire was the loss of Fox himself as every dollar of insurance money recovered would ultimately be paid to Fox.]

DUNCAN, C. J.
* * *

It is true, as contended by appellant [plaintiff], that the general rule of law is that the willful burning of property by a stockholder in a corporation is not a defense against the collection of the insurance by the corporation, and that the corporation cannot be prevented from collecting the insurance because its agents willfully set fire to the property without the participation or authority of the corporation or of all of the stockholders of the corporation. When, however, the beneficial owner of practically all of the stock in a corporation, and who has the absolute management and control of its affairs and its property and is its president and a director, sets fire to the property of a corporation or causes it to be done, there is no sound reason to support the contention of appellant that the corporation should be allowed to recover on a policy for the destruction of the corporate property by a fire so occasioned. Every principle of insurance law and sound reasoning would seem to be against such contention. * * *

It certainly cannot be said that a corporation can recover on a fire insurance policy where the property insured is destroyed by a fire at the instance of all of the stockholders and of all of the creditors of the corporation. That is substantially the fact found by the jury as disclosed by this record, as Fox is sole creditor and equitable owner, and the trial court held, and so instructed the jury, that the charge of incendiarism must be proved beyond a reasonable doubt. * * *

No matter from what angle this case may be viewed, to allow appellant (plaintiff) to recover in this case would be to go against the established rule of law that the assured may not profit by his own criminal act, which is at the same time an act committed with a criminal intent to defraud the insurance company. While the money collected from appellee (defendant) on this insurance policy would not be paid directly to Fox, still, ultimately, the amount collected would all go, under the showing in this record, in the settlement of the affairs of the corporation to Fox. It is therefore certainly good law to hold that an incendiary cannot by a circuity of action recover from an insurance company a loss occasioned by his own willful conduct, which loss he could not recover by a direct suit against the company on a policy made direct to him. We cannot allow the corporation in this case to be used as a cloak to protect Fox and to aid him in his designs to defraud the insurance company and at the same time to profit by his own wrong or fraud. * * *

Judgment affirmed.

Piercing the Corporate Veil:
Parent-Subsidiary

BERGER v. COLUMBIA BROADCASTING SYSTEM, INC.

(1972, C.A.5) 453 F.2d 991.

[Plaintiff, who was planning to produce in Las Vegas a show called International Fashion Festival consisting of a display of "*haute couture*" fashions and models to match, entered into a written licensing agreement in April, 1965, with CBS Films, Inc. ("Films") for presentations of the show. Films is a wholly owned subsidiary of defendant Columbia Broadcasting System, Inc., ("CBS").

In the fall of 1966 Stewart Cowley, operator of a model agency in New York City, developed the idea of producing a fashion spectacular similar to plaintiff's and entered into a contract with CBS for television broadcasts of his show if he could obtain sponsorship, which he succeeded in doing. CBS broadcast Cowley's show on television in 1967 and 1968. Plaintiff sued CBS to recover damages for breach of plaintiff's 1965 contract with Films alleging that CBS was liable thereon as Films was its instrumentality or alter ego.

The trial court applied the instrumentality rule, and held that CBS by developing, producing and televising Cowley's fashion show had breached the implied covenant of good faith and fair dealing in the contract between plaintiff and Films. Judgment was entered against CBS in excess of $200,000. The Court of Appeals held that the facts did not justify application of the instrumentality rule and reversed the judgment.]

GOLDBERG, J.
* * *

On appeal, the defendant complains (1) that the plaintiff failed to adduce sufficient ~~of~~ so as to justify invocation of New ~~k's~~ instrumentality rule in order to disard the corporate identity of Films, (2)

that the court below erroneously interpreted the 1965 contract, and (3) that the trial court erred in its computation of damages. Finding ourselves in complete agreement with the defendant's first assertion, we reverse the judgment of the district court. Because we conclude that neither the findings of the district court nor the evidence introduced at trial will support corporate monism, we do not reach the issues involving contractual interpretation and computation of damages.

It is elemental jurisprudence that a corporation is a creature of the law, endowed with a personality separate and distinct from that of its owners, and that one of the principal purposes for legal sanctioning of a separate corporate personality is to accord stockholders an opportunity to limit their personal liability. There does exist, however, a large class of cases in which the separateness of a corporate entity has been disregarded and a parent corporation held liable for the acts of its subsidiary because the subsidiary's affairs had been so controlled as to render it merely an instrument or agent of its parent. [Citation.] But the dual personality of parent and subsidiary is not lightly disregarded, since application of the instrumentality rule operates to defeat one of the principal purposes for which the law has created the corporation. [Citation.] Therefore, to justify judicial derogation of the separateness of a corporate creature, an aggrieved party must prove something more than a parent's mere ownership of a majority or even all of the capital stock and the parent's use of its power as an incident of its stock ownership to elect officers and directors of the subsidiary. [Citations.]

In formulating a basis for predicating liability of a parent corporation for the acts of its subsidiary, courts have developed various legal theories and descriptive terms to explain the relationship between a subsidiary and its dominating parent. For example, under the "identity" theory the separate corporate entity of the dominated subsidiary is disregarded and the parent and subsidiary are treated as one corporation. [Citation.] Furthermore, a dominated subsidiary has been labeled an instrument, agent, adjunct, branch, dummy, department, or tool of the parent corporation. [Citation.] In Lowendahl v. Baltimore & O. R. R., 1936, 247 App.Div. 144, 287 N.Y.S. 62, aff'd, 272 N.Y. 360, 6 N.E.2d 56, a New York court analyzed the various terms and legal theories and concluded that the instrumentality rule furnished the most practical theory for toppling a parent corporation's immunity. The court in *Lowendahl* then postulated the following three elements as the quantum of proof necessary to sustain application of the instrumentality rule:

(1) Control, not mere majority or complete stock control, but complete domination, not only of finances, but of policy and business practice in respect to the transaction attacked so that the corporate entity as to this transaction had at the time no separate mind, will or existence of its own; and (2) Such control must have been used by the defendant to commit fraud or wrong, to perpetrate the violation of a statutory or other positive legal duty, or a dishonest and unjust act in contravention of plaintiff's legal rights; and (3) The aforesaid control and breach of duty must proximately cause the injury or unjust loss complained of.

Applying these three elements to the relationship between the defendant and Films in the case at bar, we first turn to the lower court's factual determinations. The district court held that at all relevant times Films was merely an instrumentality of the defendant based on the following findings: (1) the board of directors of Films consisted solely of employees of the defendant; (2) the organization chart of CBS, Inc. included Films; and (3) all lines of employee authority from Films passed through employees of the defendant and other subsidiaries to the chairman of the board of CBS, Inc.

In addition, the trial judge was greatly influenced by the fact that several witnesses, including a comptroller of one of the defendant's subsidiaries, testified that Films was a "division" of CBS, Inc. Comparing these several facts to the requisite quantum of proof necessary to satisfy *Lowendahl's* "control" element, we think it is obvious that these factual determinations, standing alone, are insufficient to sustain application of the instrumentality rule. Moreover, an independent examination of the record in this case convinces us that the evidence adduced below concerning the relationship between the defendant and Films could not sustain any finding that the defendant completely dominated not only the finances, but the policy and business practice of Films.

* * * In our opinion complete stock ownership, common officers and directors, and the use of organizational charts illustrating lines of authority are all business practices common to most parent-subsidiary relationships, and such proof of a parent's potential to dominate its subsidiary is precisely the kind of evidence that New York courts have consistently rejected as insufficient in proving a community of management between corporations. [Citations.] Furthermore, with respect to the testimony concerning Films' status as a division of the defendant, we think this evidence under New York law is equally unpersuasive. Affixing labels to corporate relationships for purposes of showing a parent's complete domination of a subsidiary is a dangerous business. As Justice Cardozo, speaking for the New York Court of Appeals [citation], stated: * * *

Metaphors in law are to be narrowly watched, for starting as devices to liberate thought, they end often by enslaving it. We say at times that the corporate entity will be ignored when the parent corporation operates a business through a subsidiary which is characterized as an 'alias' or a "dummy." All this is well enough if the picturesqueness of the epithets does not lead us to forget that the essential term to be defined is the act of operation.

      * * * But when a lay witness testifies that one corporation is a division of another, then individual thought indeed becomes enslaved for a court to assume that the use of a descriptive term, by some process of testimonial osmosis, automatically introduces into evidence a composite of facts tending to show a community of management. Just as siamesing is a biological fact, so must corporate umbilication be anatomically demonstrated under New York law. For purposes of application of the instrumentality rule, descriptive characterization is simply not an adequate alternative to a factual showing of the essential "act of operation."

Our prerequisition of the record in this case reveals that the evidence concerning the defendant's "act of operation" is totally insufficient to sustain any possible finding that, with respect to the transaction attacked, Films possessed at the time no separate mind, will, or existence of its own. The only evidence tending to show the defendant's actual participation in the business of its subsidiary is the deposition testimony of Films' general manager. As stated in plaintiff's brief, the general manager admitted that "he answers directly to the President of CBS Television Services Division who answers directly to the President of the CBS/COMTEC Group who answers directly to the Vice President of CBS

who answers directly to the President of CBS." In our opinion, however, all of this "answering" is insignificant. This testimony relates to the present-day relationship between the defendant and Films, and New York law requires "that the unlawful control must be shown to have been exercised at the time the acts complained of took place."

      * * *

Faced with both this testimony and the total absence of any evidence showing the defendant's actual domination of its subsidiary Films during the period in which the plaintiff's contract was executed and allegedly breached, this court has no alternative but to reverse the decision of the district court on the simple basis that plaintiff has failed to prove, in accordance with New York law, that Films was the alter ego of the defendant. We reiterate that under the substantive law of the State of New York a parent's potential to dominate its subsidiary is insufficient to justify application of the instrumentality rule. New York law respects corporate identity, and its destruction by piercing or surrogation requires substantiation of facts, not just organizational charts and labels. The instrumentality referred to in New York cases requires a specific kinetic result, and muscularity to effectuate such result must be demonstrated. Plaintiff's omission in proving such muscularity constitutes his failing.

The judgment of the district court is reversed.

Problems

1. After part of the shares of a proposed corporation had been successfully subscribed, A, the promoter, hired a carpenter to repair a building. The promoters subsequently secured subscriptions to the balance of the shares, and completed the organization, but the corporation declined to use the building or pay the carpenter for the reason that it was not suitable to the purposes of the company, whereupon the carpenter brought

suit against it for the amount agreed to be paid him by the promoter. Was the corporation liable?

2. C. A. Nimocks was a promoter engaged in effecting the organization of the Times Printing Company. On September 12, on behalf of the proposed corporation, he made a contract with McArthur for his services as comptroller for the

period of one year beginning October 1. The Times Printing Company was incorporated October 16, and on that date McArthur commenced his duties as comptroller. No formal action with reference to his employment was taken by the board of directors or by any officer, but all the shareholders, directors and officers knew of the contract made by Nimocks. On December 1, McArthur was discharged without cause. Has he a cause of action against the Times Printing Company?

3. A and B obtained an option upon a building which had been used for manufacturing pianos. They acted as the promoters for a corporation and turned over the building to the new corporation for $100,000 worth of stock. As a matter of fact, their option on the building called for a purchase price of only $60,000. The other shareholders desire to have $40,000 of the common stock cancelled. Can they succeed in an action to have it cancelled?

4. S signed a subscription agreement for 10 shares of stock having a par value of $100 per share of the proposed ABC Company. Two weeks later the company was incorporated. A certificate was duly tendered to S but he refused to accept it. He was notified of all shareholders' meetings but he never attended. A dividend check was sent to him but he returned it. ABC Company brings an action against S to recover $1,000. He defends upon the ground that his subscription agreement was an unaccepted offer and that he had done nothing to ratify it and that he was therefore not liable upon it. Decision?

5. A, B, and C petitioned for a corporate charter for the purpose of conducting a retail shoe business. All the statutory provisions were complied with, except that they failed to have their charter recorded. This was an oversight on their part, and they felt that they had fully complied with the law. They operated the business for three years, after which time it became insolvent. The creditors desire to hold the members personally and individually liable. May they do so?

6. In June, A, who had been engaged in the toy manufacturing business at a plant he leased, orally agreed with B and C that, commencing July 1, they would organize a corporation, to be

Smith et al. Bus.Law 5th Ed.—16

known as M Corporation to conduct the toy business, each of the three to provide $15,000 toward capital and to give full time to the business. They agreed upon a capitalization of 450 shares of no par value stock, each to receive 150 shares in return for his $15,000 investment.

Approval of the proposed corporate name was obtained from the Secretary of State and articles of incorporation were prepared and signed on a form purchased by A at a law stationery store, but no papers were ever filed. At a meeting held July 1, A was elected president, B vice president, and C secretary and treasurer; the agreed capital was paid in, and beginning that day the business was carried on as M Corporation at the plant previously occupied by A.

The toy business required considerable sheet tin and on August 1, A, in the presence of B and C, signed a contract "as President of M Corporation" to purchase approximately three months' supply from X, a dealer in tin, for $14,000, a reasonable price, delivery by August 30, payment on November 1.

X delivered the tin on August 30. Payment not having been made, X would like to sue A, B, C and M Corporation. What are X's rights?

7. A, B, C, and D decided to form a corporation for bottling and selling apple cider. A, B and C were to operate the business and D was to supply the necessary capital but was to have no voice in the management. They went to John Lawyer who agreed to organize a corporation for them under the name, A-B-C Inc., and sufficient funds were paid to him to accomplish the incorporation. Lawyer promised that the corporation would definitely be formed by May 3. On April 27, A telephoned Lawyer to inquire how the incorporation was progressing, and Lawyer said he had drafted the articles of incorporation and would send them to the Secretary of State that very day. He assured A that A, B, C and D would be incorporated before May 3.

Relying on Lawyer's assurance, A, with the approval of B and C, on May 4, entered into a written contract with Grower for the latter's entire apple crop. The contract was executed by A in behalf of "A-B-C Inc." Grower delivered the apples as agreed. Unknown to A, B, C, D or Grower the articles of incorporation were never filed, through Lawyer's negligence. The business subsequently failed.

What are Grower's rights, if any, against A, B, C and D as individuals?

8. The AB Corporation has outstanding 20,000 shares of common stock without par value, of which 19,000 are owned by Peter B. Arson, 500 shares are owned by Elizabeth Arson, his wife, and 500 shares are owned by Joseph Q. Arson, his brother. These three individuals are the officers and directors of the corporation. The AB Corporation obtained a $10,000 fire insurance policy covering a certain building owned by it. Thereafter, Peter B. Arson set fire to the building which was wholly destroyed by the fire. The corporation now brings an action against the fire insurance company to recover on the $10,000 fire insurance policy. What judgment?

9. A corporation is formed for the purpose of manufacturing, buying, selling and dealing in drugs, chemicals and similar products. The corporation, under authority of its board of directors, contracted to purchase the land and building occupied by it as a factory and store. S, a shareholder, sues in equity to restrain the corporation from completing the contract, claiming that as the certificate of incorporation contained no provision authorizing the corporation to purchase real estate, the contract was *ultra vires*. Decision?

10. The Board of Directors of X, a business corporation, at a regular meeting, unanimously and in good faith, adopted a resolution that X pay to the widow of its deceased president, until further ordered by the directors, the sum of $1,000 a month, in recognition of the long and valued services rendered to the corporation by the late president. The statute under which the corporation was organized and functioned provided that a business corporation shall have the same capacity to act as that possessed by natural persons and shall have authority to accomplish its purposes which are not repugnant to law. After several payments had been made to the widow, pursuant to the resolution, a minority shareholder of X brought an action against the corporation, its Board of Directors and the widow to enjoin further payments to the widow and to compel restitution by the widow of all payments made to her. Decision?

Chapter
35

CAPITAL STOCK, DIVIDENDS, AND TRANSFER OF SHARES

Capital is necessary for any business to function. An initial, and often continuing, source of corporate funds derives from the sale of equity securities or capital stock. Capital stock represents an ownership interest in the corporation and includes both common and preferred stock. Owners of capital stock acquire a number of rights including the right to participate in the earnings of the corporation. This participation occurs through the declaration and payment of dividends.

This chapter will discuss capital stock, the payment of dividends, and the manner in which shares of capital stock and other investment securities are transferred.

CAPITAL STOCK

Probably no term in the law of corporations has caused as much confusion and misunderstanding as the phrase "capital stock." In decisions and in commercial usage, the terms "capital stock," "capital" and "stock" are sometimes treated as synonymous. Likewise, the words "stock" and "shares"

are used interchangeably to indicate the same concept. The fundamental idea of capital stock is that it is the property or consideration which the corporation has obtained from its shareholders, whether in the form of cash, services rendered, or property, which is dedicated to use in the business and represented by shares of stock. While capital stock may be authorized by the charter but not issued, the term has practical significance only with respect to shares of stock which have been sold and issued. Where par value stock has been sold at a premium, that is, at a price greater than par, the amount of the excess over par is allocated to a paid-in surplus account and sometimes referred to as capital surplus.

Capital stock should not be confused with the assets of a corporation nor, on the other hand, with the certificates representing shares of capital stock. The value of corporate assets and the aggregate value of shares outstanding may fluctuate from day to day, or they may have different values attributed to them at any given time, depending upon the purpose for which the valuation is sought. Capital stock, however, has a fixed and predetermined stated value as fixed by the charter or by the directors or shareholders in the manner prescribed by law. This dollar amount attributed to the capital stock cannot be changed except in compliance with the requirements of the statute.

Certain states have discarded the term "capital stock" and have replaced it in their statutes with phraseology more precise. The Model Act does not speak of "capital stock" but uses instead "stated capital" which it defines as the sum of the consideration received by the corporation for its issued stock, excepting therefrom that part of the consideration properly allocated to capital surplus and including therein any amount transferred to stated capital upon issuance of shares by way of stock dividend. Section 2(j).

Shares of capital stock are property, but unlike the certificates representing them, are intangible and incorporeal and cannot be seized or reduced to physical possession. Shares are a method of describing a proportionate interest in a corporate enterprise, and they do not in any way vest their owner with title to any property of the corporation.

Classes of Shares

Corporations are generally authorized by statute to issue two or more classes of stock which differ according to their respective rights and interests. Thus, classes may vary with respect to their rights to dividends, their voting rights, and their right to share in the assets of the corporation upon liquidation. The most usual classification of stock is into common and preferred shares.

Common Stock. Common stock is that class of stock which does not have any special contract rights or preferences. Frequently it is the only class of stock outstanding. It generally represents the greatest proportion of the corporation's capital structure and bears the greatest risk of loss in the event of failure of the enterprise. If the business is profitable, its holders may receive the largest dividends, while upon failure they stand to lose their entire investment. In return for supplying the equity capital and bearing this risk, holders of common stock have the predominant voice in selecting the corporate management.

Preferred Stock. Although the stock of a corporation other than its common is generally referred to as "preferred stock," such description, standing alone, means only that the stock has one or more preferential contractual rights or powers over some other class or classes of stock of the same corporation. Frequently, an issue of preferred provides that its holders shall receive dividends at a stated annual rate before any dividend may be paid to holders of common stock, and that upon liquidation of the corporation they shall receive the par value of the stock, or par value plus a premium, prior to any distribution of assets upon the common.

The description is relative or comparative, and the nature and extent of such preferences must be stated in the articles of incorporation. Section 15 and 54. The contractual rights and preferences of an issue of preferred differs from those of any other issue of preferred stock by the same or any other corporation; and the variations and combinations of contract rights which find expression usually are determined by the requirements of financing the issue.

Preferred stock may provide that dividends thereon are "cumulative" or "non-cumulative." If cumulative, upon failure of the board to declare regular dividends on the preferred, such omitted dividends cumulate and no dividend may be declared on the common until all dividend arrearages on the preferred are declared and paid. If "non-cumulative," regular dividends do not cumulate upon failure of the board to declare them, and all rights to a dividend for the period omitted are gone forever. Unless the dividends on preferred stock are made expressly non-cumulative, the courts generally hold them to be cumulative.

The Supreme Court of the United States has held that even when earnings and earned surplus are adequate and available, the holders of non-cumulative preferred are not entitled to a dividend unless the board of directors declares one. Wabash Railway Co. v. Barclay, 280 U.S. 197, 74 L.Ed. 368. This is the majority rule. However, New Jersey holds that dividends on non-cumulative preferred cumulate to the extent earned in a particular year, and although not declared for that year in which earned nevertheless constitute a cumulative charge for that year which must be paid prior to any dividend on the common. Sanders v. Cuba Railroad Co., 21 N.J. 78, 120 A.2d 849 (1956).

Preferred stock may also be "participating." The nature and extent of such participation on a specified basis with the common stock must be stated in the articles of incorporation. For example, a class of participating preferred stock could be entitled to share at the same rate with the common in any additional distribution of earnings for a given year *after* provision has been made for payment of the prior preferred dividend and payment of dividends on the common at a rate equal to the fixed rate of the preferred.

Preferred stock may have additional rights, designations, and limitations. It may be expressly denied voting rights if permitted by the statute. It may be redeemable by the corporation, or convertible into shares of another class.

The power of a corporation to effect changes in an issue of its preferred stock depends upon the contract with the preferred shareholders and the applicable law. No change may be made which will impair vested contractual rights because any State statute or action taken thereunder which impairs the obligation of contract violates Article I, Section 10 of the Constitution of the United States. However, the statute in effect at the time of the issuance of the preferred stock is considered part and parcel of the contract, and therefore subsequent changes in the redemption, dividend rate, or other rights of the preferred shareholders which are effected strictly in accordance with the statute are binding upon all of the shareholders.

Notwithstanding the special rights and preferences which distinguish preferred from common, preferred stock, similar to the common, represents a contribution of capital. Preferred stock is no more a debt than common, and, until a dividend is declared, the holder of preferred shares is not a creditor of the corporation. Preferred shareholders do not have liens on specific corporate assets or priorities over creditors. Their rights are subordinate to the rights of all of the creditors of the corporation.

Amount of Consideration for Shares

Shares are deemed fully paid and nonassessable when the corporation receives full payment of the consideration for which the shares are issued. The amount of that consideration depends upon the type of shares being issued.

Par Value Stock. Par value shares may be issued for any amount, not less than par, as set by the board of directors or shareholders. The par value of a share of stock can be an arbitrary value selected by the corporation and may or may not reflect either the actual value of the share or the actual price paid to the corporation. It only indicates the minimum price which the corporation must receive for it. The par value of stock must be stated in the articles of incorporation.

The consideration received constitutes stated capital to the extent of the par value of the shares; any consideration in excess of par value constitutes capital surplus.

The practice of placing a par value on a share of stock has been criticized as misleading to shareholders who may mistakenly assume that the market value or the book value of stock should be the same as its par value.

No Par Value Stock. Shares without par value may be issued for any amount set by the board of directors or shareholders. The entire consideration received constitutes stated capital unless within sixty days after issuance the board of directors allocates a portion of the consideration to capital surplus. Section 21. The directors are free to allocate any or all of the consideration received, unless the no par stock has a liquidation preference. In that event, only the consideration in excess of the amount of liquidation preference may be allocated to capital surplus. Section 21. For this reason preferred stock is usually issued with a par value. Thus, no par shares provide the directors with great latitude in establishing capital surplus, which can in some jurisdictions provide greater flexibility for subsequent distributions to shareholders. Another advantage of utilizing no par value stock is to lessen the confusion between par, book, and market values. Many states, however, tax no par shares at a higher rate than par value shares. As a result, corporations most frequently issue shares with a low par value. This enables them as a practical matter to issue the shares for whatever price the market will pay and to allocate a substantial portion of the consideration to capital surplus, yet at the same time to enjoy the benefits of a more favorable tax rate.

One court has explained the lack of practical significance between par and no par stock by observing that "if the assets received are one thousand dollars in money, it is of no consequence whether five shares or ten shares, or one thousand shares are

given for it. Each share has its one-fifth or one-tenth or one one-thousandth aliquot part of the thousand dollars as the case may be, and no one is damaged because everyone knows that under each share is simply its proportionate part of the total assets, unexpressed in terms of money." Bodell v. General Gas & Electric Corporation, 15 Del.Ch. 119, 130, 132 A. 442.

Treasury Shares. A corporation may acquire its own shares by purchase, gift, or otherwise, without reduction of its stated capital. Such shares, unless cancelled, are referred to as treasury shares and must be so noted on the corporation's balance sheet. A corporation may purchase its own shares only out of surplus, and may distribute treasury shares as a stock dividend, or may resell them for a type and amount of consideration not permissible upon their original issuance. Sections 18, 19. Treasury shares may not be voted, nor any dividend be paid upon them, nor do they have any pre-emptive rights.

Treasury shares may be cancelled at any time by resolution of the board of directors and filing a statement of cancellation with the Secretary of State. The effect of cancellation is to reduce stated capital by the amount represented by the shares cancelled and to restore such cancelled shares to the status of authorized but unissued shares. Section 68.

Issuance of Capital Stock

Amount of Issuance. The amount of capital stock to be initially issued is determined by the promoters or incorporators and is generally governed by practical business considerations and financial exigencies. Once the amount which the corporation is *authorized* to issue has been established and specified in the charter, it cannot be increased or decreased without amendment to the charter. This means that the shareholders have the residual authority over increases or decreases in the amount of authorized capital stock. It is a frequent practice to authorize initially more shares than are immediately to be issued, which may have practical consequences with respect to control over the affairs of the corporation. The directors alone may have the power to issue additional shares if all the authorized shares are not already issued and outstanding.

Pre-emptive Rights. At common law, a shareholder has the right to purchase a pro rata share of every offering of stock by the corporation in order to preserve his proportionate interest in the equity. This right may be denied or limited by the articles of incorporation, as permitted by statute, or it may be subject to a statutory right of the corporation to make an offering of stock to its employees without first offering the stock to its shareholders. In the absence of a pre-emptive right, a shareholder may be unable to prevent a dilution of his ownership interest in the corporation.

For example, X owns 200 shares of stock of the ABC Company, which has a total of 1,000 shares outstanding. The company determines to increase its capital stock to 2,000 shares. If X has pre-emptive rights, he and every other shareholder will be offered one share of the newly issued stock for every share they own. Upon accepting the offer and buying the stock, he will have 400 shares out of a total of 2,000 outstanding, and his relative interest in the corporation is unchanged. However, without pre-emptive rights, he may have only 200 out of the 2,000 shares outstanding and instead of owning 20% of the stock, would own 10%.

Payment for Newly Issued Shares. With respect to the issuance of capital stock, there are two paramount questions: (a) What type of consideration may be validly accepted in payment for shares, and (b) who shall determine whether valid consideration has been paid and what limits are placed upon the discretion of those making the decision.

With very few exceptions, and in the absence of any charter limitation, cash, property, and services rendered are generally acceptable as valid consideration for the issuance of shares (Camden v. Stuart, 144 U.S. 104, 36 L.Ed. 363), and this general rule has been recognized by statute. Section 19, Model Act. Because the capital of a corporation is a measure of solvency and an important source for payment of corporate debts, the courts have frequently refused to accept as "property" certain items which for other purposes might be so considered. In most jurisdicitons, promissory notes or future services are not acceptable. Section 19. Patents, good will, merchandise, leases and the assets of a business are acceptable consideration. The good will of a business which has been operating at a loss, or an unpatented formula, however, have been held not to constitute adequate payment.

The determination of the value to be placed on property which is exchanged for shares is the responsibility of the directors. The ultimate consequence of issuing stock for over-valued property may be to impose liability upon the shareholder to creditors or to other shareholders even though the stock purports to be fully paid and non-assessable. Certain jurisdictions hold that notwithstanding good faith and the absence of fraud in the valuation, a subscriber is liable for the difference between the actual value of the property and the stated or par value of the shares issued. The majority of jurisdictions, however, hold that valuation is a matter of opinion and that, if the parties making the valuation have exercised good faith and no actual fraud is present in the transaction, the shareholder is not liable even though the actual value of the property proves to be considerably less than the dollar amount of the stock issued in exchange for it. Section 19 of the Model Act provides: "In the absence of fraud in the transaction, the judgment of the board of directors or the shareholders, as the case may be, as to the value of the consideration received for shares shall be conclusive."

What constitutes "actual fraud" depends, of course, upon the facts and circumstances of the particular case. Evidence of gross undervaluation alone may be enough to permit a court to find that there was fraud. Payment for shares having an aggregate par value of $999,800 by a patent worth not over $50,500 has been held to constitute a fraudulent over-valuation. On the other hand, no fraud was found where a long-established business with a record of annual earnings between $25,000 and $50,000 was exchanged for $150,000 of stock even though recent earnings had declined and actual losses were experienced. Where a going business is exchanged for shares of stock, a wide divergence of honest opinion as to value is not unusual.

Redemption, Acquisition, and Cancellation of Its Shares

Redemption is the repurchase by the corporation of its own shares. Shares of common stock ordinarily are not subject to redemption. Preferred shares, however, are frequently redeemable by the corporation at a call price stated in the stock certificate. This power of redemption must be expressly provided for in the articles of incorporation, pursuant to authorization by statute, and the redemption or call price must be specified together with all of the other special rights and limitations of the preferred shares.

Redemption of preferred shares when the business is in financial straits may be harmful to those who extended credit in reliance upon the capital represented by such shares. Generally, however, creditors are held to have no right to complain as the redemption provisions are recited in the charter. To protect creditors and holders of other classes of preferred shares, in most

States there are statutory restrictions upon redemption.

A corporation may not redeem or purchase its redeemable shares when insolvent or when such redemption or purchase would render it insolvent or reduce its net assets below the aggregate amount payable upon shares having prior or equal rights to the assets of the corporation upon involuntary dissolution. Section 66. "Insolvent" means the inability of a corporation to pay its debts as they become due in the usual course of its business. Section 2(n).

The redemption or purchase of redeemable shares by the corporation effects a cancellation of such shares, and in such case a statement of cancellation must be filed as provided in the statute. Section 67. After this is done, the shares are restored to the status of authorized but unissued shares.

In addition to redeeming shares, a corporation may acquire its own shares by purchase, gift, or otherwise without reduction of its stated capital. Section 6. A corporation may purchase its own shares only out of earned surplus or, if the articles of incorporation permit or if the shareholders approve, out of capital surplus. As with redemption, no purchase of shares may be made at a time when the corporation is insolvent or when such purchase would make it insolvent. Section 6.

Directors who vote for or assent to the redemption or repurchase of shares contrary to the statutory provisions restricting such reacquisitions are jointly and severally liable to the corporation for the unlawful amount of the consideration paid for the shares. Directors are entitled to contribution from other directors who voted for or assented to the unlawful reacquisition and from shareholders who knowingly received the unlawful payment. Section 48.

DIVIDENDS

The objective of every private, for-profit business corporation is to operate profitably, and it is a fundamental desire of most shareholders to share in the profits through the receipt of dividends. The declaration of dividends, however, is within the discretion of the board of directors subject to certain restrictions and limitations.

The conditions under which the earnings of a business may be paid out in the form of dividends will depend upon the contractual rights of the holders of the particular shares involved, the provisions in the charter and by-laws of the corporation, and the statute of the State of incorporation which is designed to protect creditors and shareholders from dissipation of corporate assets. More significant protection of creditors is provided by contractual restrictions typically included in their loan agreements as well as state fraudulent conveyance laws and federal bankruptcy law.

Types of Dividends

Cash Dividends. The most customary type of dividend is the cash dividend declared and paid at regular intervals depending in amount upon the policy of the board of directors and the earnings of the enterprise. References to "regular" dividends in a charter or contract are considered as referring to a distribution of the earned surplus in the form of cash. While dividends are almost invariably paid in cash, in a few instances a distribution of earnings has been made to shareholders in the form of property and has been termed a *property dividend.* On one occasion, a distillery declared and paid a dividend in bonded whiskey.

Stock Dividends. A stock dividend is a ratable distribution of additional shares of the capital stock of the corporation to its shareholders. It is reflected on the books of the corporation by a reduction in the surplus account equal to the amount of the stock dividend and a corresponding increase in the stated capital account. The practical and legal significance of a stock dividend differs greatly from a dividend payable in cash or property. Following the payment of a stock dividend, the assets of the corporation are no less than they were before, and the shareholder does not have any greater relative interest in the net worth of the corporation than he had before except possibly where the dividend is paid in shares of a different class. His shares will each represent a smaller proportionate interest in the assets of the corporation, but by reason of the increase in the number of shares his total investment will remain the same. The declaration and payment of a stock dividend means that surplus which may have been previously available for distribution or other uses is thereafter frozen in stated capital.

A stock dividend should not be confused with a stock split. By the latter, each of the issued and outstanding shares is simply broken up into a greater number of shares, each representing a proportionately smaller interest in the corporation. A stock split effects no change in the stated capital or in the surplus account. Where there is more than one class of shares outstanding it is possible for either a stock dividend or a stock split in one class to alter the relative voting strength of the different classes.

Liquidating Dividends. While dividends ordinarily are identified with the distribution of profits, a distribution of capital assets to shareholders upon termination of the business is considered a form of dividend and is referred to as a liquidating dividend. A distribution to common shareholders of paid-in surplus or capital surplus, or a distribution to shareholders of funds taken from a proper reserve for depreciation of assets, is also a liquidating dividend and should be specifically identified as such. The statute usually requires that the shareholder be informed when a distribution is a liquidating dividend. It is not taxable to the recipient as income but as a return of capital.

Legal Restrictions on Cash Dividends

The board of directors in its discretion determines when to declare dividends and in what amount. The corporation's working capital requirements, expectations of shareholders, tax consequences, and other factors influence the board in its formation of dividend policy. Nonetheless, the board is constrained as to the amount of dividends it may declare by a number of legal restrictions. All states have statutes restricting the funds that are legally available for dividends. In many instances contractual restrictions imposed by lenders provide even more stringent limitations upon the declaration of dividends.

States restrict in one way or another the payment of dividends in order to protect creditors. All states impose the insolvency test which prohibits the payment of a dividend when the corporation is insolvent or when the payment of the dividend would render the corporation insolvent. Section 45. In addition, each state imposes further restrictions as to what funds are legally available to pay dividends. Some states permit dividends to be paid only out of earned surplus while others are more permissive by allowing dividends to come from any kind of surplus. Moreover, some states permit dividends to be paid from current earnings even in the absence of the required surplus. Such dividends are called "nimble dividends."

Since, in most instances, dividends may only be paid out of the excess of assets over liabilities, including capital stock, the proper valuation of assets is sometimes a troublesome problem. An overvaluation of assets due to inadequate depreciation charges, insufficient reserve for bad debts, unjustified appraisal of questionable accounts receivable, or unrealized appreciation of fixed assets, may cause a dividend to constitute an illegal invasion of capital. This possibility is reflected in the rule that those responsible for the declaration of dividends must likewise be responsible for a bona fide valuation of the assets.

The legal restrictions upon the payment of dividends involve the concepts of earned surplus, surplus, net assets, stated capital and capital surplus. Earned surplus consists of the undistributed net profits, income, gains, and losses from the date of incorporation. See Section 2 (l) of the Model Act for an elaborate definition.

Surplus means the excess of the net assets of a corporation over its stated capital.

Net assets are the amount by which the total assets of a corporation exceed the total debts of the corporation.

Stated capital is defined as the sum of the consideration received by the corporation for its issued stock, excepting therefrom that part of the consideration properly allocated to capital surplus, and including therein any amount transferred to stated capital upon issuance of shares by way of stock dividend. Section 2(i), (j) and (k). In the case of par value shares, the amount of the capital stock or stated capital is the aggregate par value of all the issued shares. In the case of no par stock, it is the consideration received by the corporation for all the no par shares which have been issued, except such part thereof as may have been allocated in a manner permitted by law, to an account designated as capital surplus or paid-in surplus. Without further issuance or cancellation of shares, stated capital may be increased or reduced by adjustments between that account and the paid-in surplus account in the manner permitted by the statute. A reduction of stated capital not accompanied by a cancellation of shares, or by any action requiring an amendment to the articles of incorporation, requires a resolution by the board of directors and approval of the shareholders at an annual or special meeting by majority vote of the shares entitled to vote at such meeting. Section 69.

Capital surplus may result from an allocation of part of the consideration received for no-par shares, or from any consideration in excess of par value received for par shares or from a reappraisal upward of certain corporate assets.

Earned Surplus Test. Unreserved and unrestricted earned surplus is available for dividends in all jurisdictions. An increasing number of states permit dividends to be paid only from earned surplus: "Dividends may be declared and paid in cash or property only out of the unreserved and unrestricted earned surplus of the corporation." Section 45(a). Thus, dividends in these jurisdictions may not be paid out of capital surplus or stated capital.

Surplus Test. A number of states are less restrictive and permit dividends to be paid out of any surplus—earned or capital. Some of these states express this test by prohibiting dividends that impair stated capital.

Nimble Dividends. Although dividends are properly payable only out of earnings or earned surplus and are generally not payable when the corporation has an accrued earned deficit, the statutes of a number of states permit payment of dividends out of current earnings notwithstanding the existence of such deficit. For example, Alternate Section 45(a) of the Model Act permits dividends to be paid out of the unreserved and unrestricted net earnings of the current fiscal year as a single period. Some states, such as Delaware, permit dividends to be paid out of earnings of the current or next preceding year but stated capital represented by shares having a liquidation preference may not be thus impaired. A board of directors in these states is permitted by timely action to declare a dividend in a year when the corporation has no earnings, provided it had earnings for the year immediately preceding. Because of the time limitation within which such dividends must be declared, they are sometimes called "nimble dividends."

Legal Restrictions on Liquidating Dividends

Even those states that do not permit dividends to be paid from capital surplus usually will permit "distributions" or dividends in partial liquidation from that source. A dividend paid out of such surplus is a return to the shareholders of a part of their investment.

No such distribution may be made, however, when the corporation is insolvent or would be rendered insolvent by the distribution. Distributions from capital surplus are also restricted to protect the liquidation preference of preferred shareholders.

Unless provided for in the articles of incorporation, a liquidating dividend must be authorized not only by the board of directors but also by the affirmative vote of the holders of a majority of the outstanding shares of stock of each class. Section 46(b). A careful balance should be maintained between the interests of shareholders and those of creditors in connection with the occasional necessity or advisability of such a distribution of capital by a going business.

Declaration and Payment of Dividends

The declaration of dividends is the responsibility of the directors of the corporation. This duty cannot be delegated, and an attempt by shareholders to usurp the power is ineffective, although, in some instances, informal distribution of corporate profits has been sustained where all shareholders consent and creditor interests are not affected. It is well settled that there can be no discrimination in the declaration of dividends among shareholders of the same class.

Once properly declared, a cash dividend is considered a debt owing by the corporation to the shareholders, and in the event of failure to pay or insolvency, the shareholder may enforce his claim as an unsecured creditor in a court of law or in a bankruptcy court. If a separate fund is established at the time of declaration out of which the dividend is to be paid, courts have regarded the fund as having the characteristics of a trust to which the shareholders have a preferential claim.

It follows from the debtor-creditor relationship created by the declaration of a cash dividend that once declared it cannot be rescinded as against non-assenting shareholders. However, a stock dividend may be revoked unless actually distributed.

The time, place and manner of payment are in the discretion of the directors. It is not uncommon for the resolution declaring a dividend to fix a cut-off date by providing that the dividend shall be paid to the shareholders of record as of the close of business on a specified future date, usually about two weeks earlier than the date fixed for payment.

A problem may arise as to which of two successive owners of shares is entitled to a particular dividend. The general rule is that, in the absence of a special agreement, the owner of the shares at the time the dividend is declared is entitled to the dividend even though prior to the time for payment the ownership has changed hands. Where the resolution declaring a dividend fixes a cutoff date, the shareholder of record as of that date is entitled to the dividend. Sales of stock between the cut-off date and the date of payment are said to be "ex-dividend."

Right to Dividends

A shareholder may not maintain an action at law against the corporation to recover a dividend until and unless the dividend has been formally declared by resolution of the board of directors. A proper dividend so declared becomes a debt of the corporation, and enforceable at law as any other debt.

Where the directors have failed to declare a dividend, a shareholder may bring a suit in equity against them and the corporation seeking a mandatory injunction requiring the directors to declare a dividend. Courts of equity are reluctant to order an injunction of this kind which involves substituting the business judgment of the court for that of the directors elected by the shareholders. A court of equity will grant an injunction and require the directors to declare a dividend where (1) a demand has been made upon the directors before commencement of the suit; (2) corporate earnings or surplus are available out of which a dividend may be declared; (3) the earnings or surplus is in the form of available cash, and (4) the directors have acted so unreasonably in withholding a dividend that their conduct clearly amounts to an abuse of discretion.

The existence of a large accumulated surplus will not alone justify compelling the directors to distribute funds which, in their opinion, should be retained for plant expansion, technological research and development, reserve for cost of environmental protection, or other bona fide corporate purposes. However, where the evidence shows noncorporate motives or personal animosity as the basis for a refusal to declare dividends, a court may require the directors to distribute what appears to be a reasonable portion of the earnings. Thus, personal philanthropic convictions are no basis for refusal to pay dividends out of substantial amounts of earned surplus.

The fact that a preferred shareholder has prior rights with respect to dividends does not make his position different from that of the holder of common shares with respect to the discretion of the directors as to the declaration of dividends. The holders of preferred stock, in the absence of special contract or statute, must likewise abide by the decision of the directors, although provisions for change of management control in an issue of preferred stock in the event dividends are omitted may go a long way to assure the declaration and payment of dividends to the holders of such stock.

Wrongful or Illegal Dividends

Section 48 of the Model Act imposes joint and several liability upon the directors of a corporation who vote for or assent to the declaration of a dividend or the distribution of corporate assets (a) when the corporation is insolvent or when its net assets are less than its stated capital, or (b) when the declaration of such a dividend would render the corporation insolvent or reduce its net assets below its stated capital. The directors may not escape liability by delegation of the power to declare dividends to an executive committee. The measure of damages in the first instance is the amount of the dividend, whereas in the second instance the directors are liable only to the extent that the corporation is rendered insolvent or its net assets are reduced below its stated capital.

The liability of directors is generally to the corporation or to its creditors. The Model Act expressly provides that the directors who vote for or assent to an illegal dividend are jointly and severally liable to the corporation. Section 48(a).

Where an illegal dividend has been declared but not yet paid, a shareholder or creditor may by speedy action obtain a court injunction against the payment. Where the directors have improperly discriminated between various classes of stock in the declaration of a dividend, a shareholder may likewise by prompt action restrain the payment.

The obligation of a shareholder to repay an illegally declared dividend depends upon a variety of factors which may include the good or bad faith on the part of the shareholder in accepting the dividend, his knowledge of the facts, the solvency or insolvency of the corporation, and, in some instances, special statutory provisions. The existence of a statutory liability on the part of directors does not relieve shareholders from the duty to make repayment. A shareholder who receives illegal dividends either as a result of his own fraudulent act or with knowledge of their unlawful character is under a duty to refund them to the corporation.

Where the corporation is insolvent, a dividend may not be retained by the shareholder even though received by him in good faith. The assets of an insolvent corporation are regarded as a trust fund for its creditors.

Where an unsuspecting shareholder receives an illegal dividend from a solvent corporation, the majority rule is that he cannot be compelled to make a refund. The Maryland Supreme Court has rationalized this doctrine, as follows:

We are disposed to follow the federal decisions as being more in accord with modern conditions and with the realities of life. In these days stocks of corporations are so widely held that it would be practically impossible for stockholders generally to know whether each semi-annual dividend paid in regular course was earned. Whatever their position may be theoretically, practically they are in no better position than creditors to know the condition of the company, and it would be an unfair and unreasonable burden to require them to pay back, years after they have spent, dividends received in good faith from a solvent corporation in regular course of business. *Bartlett v. Smith, 162 Md. 478, 482, 160 A. 440, 441.*

In the event that the shareholder recipient of an illegal dividend is held liable to make restitution, the party or parties to whom the refund is owing depends in part upon the theory of liability. If an innocent shareholder is obliged to make a refund because the capital is regarded as a trust fund, the creditors of the corporation are the logical claimants, and this doctrine has in some cases been extended to grant relief even to creditors whose claims arose after the illegal payment. However, even where the statute expressly gives creditors the right to recover, it has been held that the corporation itself may hold the shareholder liable on the theory that the illegal dividends constitute property of the corporation unlawfully in the possession of the shareholders.

TRANSFER OF SHARES

An investor has the right to transfer by way of sale, gift, or pledge his securities just as he has the inherent right to transfer any other property he may own. The right to transfer securities is a valuable one and the ease with which it may be done adds to their value and marketability. The availability of a ready market for any security affords liquidity and makes the security attractive to investors and useful as collateral.

The statutory rules applicable to transfers of securities are contained in the Uniform Commercial Code, Article 8, Investment Securities, which establishes rules similar to those in Article 3. Article 8 applies not only to shares but also to bonds, debentures, voting trust certificates, certificates of beneficial interest in business trusts, and any other "interest in property of or an enterprise of the issuer or an obligation of the issuer" which is of a "class or series" and "issued or dealt in as a medium for investment." Section 8–102.

A number of aspects of the transfer of securities are also regulated by the federal securities laws, discussed in Chapter 42.

Record Ownership

A security is intangible personal property and exists independently of a certificate. The name and address of the owner is usually recorded on the books of the corporation or of a transfer agent employed by the corporation, but these records are not determinative of ownership. Article 8 now permits the issuance and transfer of "uncertificated securities," which are securities not represented by a certificate, and the transfer of which is registered on books maintained for that purpose by or on behalf of the issuer. Section 8–102(1)(b). The loss or destruction of a certificate does not

deprive the owner of his title to the security represented by the certificate, although it does prevent the owner from making an effective transfer or pledge of the securities. In order to sell or otherwise dispose of certificated securities, an owner must have possession of the certificate and must indorse and deliver it to the transferee.

It is uniformly held that a shareholder has the right to demand a certificate from the corporation representing the shares of which he is the owner. A shareholder has the right to have his name and address entered on the records of the corporation so that he may receive dividends, notices of meetings, and the reports of operations and financial condition which the corporation distributes to its shareholders. So long as the corporate records reflect his ownership of stock, a shareholder does not need a certificate for the purpose of receiving notices or dividends or in order to vote or execute a proxy.

The 1979 Revision to the Model Business Corporation Act provide that "the shares of a corporation shall be represented by certificates or shall be uncertificated shares." Section 23. The rights and obligations of holders of uncertificated shares and certificated shares of the same class and series are identical.

Manner of Transfer

Under the Code, a transfer of certificated securities is made by delivery of the certificate alone if it is in bearer form or indorsed in blank or, if in registered form, which is more usual, by delivery of the cetificate with either (1) the indorsement thereof by "an appropriate person," or (2) a separate document of assignment and transfer signed by "an appropriate person." The term "appropriate person," as defined in Section 8–308, includes the person specified in the certificate or entitled to it by special indorsement, their successors in interest, or the authorized agent of a person so specified or so entitled. Unlike commercial paper, the indorser of a stock certificate assumes no obligation other than the warranties of a transferor. Sections 8–308(4) and 8–306(2).

Prior to presentment for registration of transfer of a certificated security in registered form, the corporation may treat the registered owner as the person entitled to vote, to receive notices, and otherwise to exercise all of the rights and powers of the owner. Section 8–207.

The delivery of an unindorsed certificate by the owner with the intention of transferring title to the securities represented thereby gives the intended transferee as against the transferor complete rights in the certificate and in the certificated securities, including the right to compel indorsement. He becomes a bona fide purchaser of the certificated securities, however, only as of the time the indorsement is supplied. Section 8–307.

Bona Fide Purchasers

A "bona fide purchaser" is a purchaser for value in good faith and without notice of any adverse claim who takes delivery of a certificated security in bearer form or in registered form issued to him or indorsed to him or in blank. Section 8–302. The negotiation and transfer of a security to a bona fide purchaser passes title to him free of all adverse claims not conspicuously noted on the certificate. Section 8–204. Adverse claims include a claim that a transfer was or would be wrongful or that a particular adverse person is the owner of or has an interest in the security. Section 8–302(2). Thus, the bona fide purchaser from a thief, finder or other unauthorized person, is protected.

Transfer Warranties

A person by transferring certificated securities to a purchaser for value warrants that

1. the transfer is effective and rightful;
2. the security is genuine and has not been materially altered; and
3. he knows of no fact which might impair the validity of the security. Section 8–306(2).

A person who presents a certificated security for registration of transfer or for payment or exchange warrants to the issuer that he is entitled to the registration, payment or exchange, but a purchaser for value and without notice of adverse claims who receives a new, reissued, or reregistered certificated security on registration of transfer warrants only that he has no knowledge of any unauthorized signature in a necessary indorsement. Section 8–306(1).

Forged or Unauthorized Indorsement

The owner of securities represented by a certificate is not deprived of his title by a transfer of the certificate bearing a forged or unauthorized indorsement. The purchaser of a security bearing a forged or unauthorized indorsement who resells and transfers it to a bona fide purchaser is liable to him for the value of the securities at the time of sale, as he has breached his warranty that the transfer is effective and rightful. Section 8–306(2). Neither party is owner of the securities, as title cannot be transferred through a forged or unauthorized indorsement.

Unless the owner has ratified an unauthorized indorsement or is otherwise precluded from asserting its ineffectiveness, he may assert its ineffectiveness against the issuer and against any purchaser, other than a bona fide purchaser, who has in good faith received a new, re-issued, or re-registered certificated security on registration of transfer. Section 8–311(a). An issuer who registers the transfer of a certificated security upon an unauthorized indorsement is subject to liability for improper registration. Section 8–311(b).

Example: A lost by theft or in some other manner his unindorsed certificate of stock, and within a reasonable time gave notice of the loss to the issuing corporation. X, a thief or finder, forges A's signature on the reverse side of the certificate, or without authority signs A's name by X, as agent. X thereafter sells and delivers the certificate to B, a bona fide transferee who pays value and takes the certificate without knowledge of the theft or loss or of the forged or unauthorized indorsement. A is still the owner of the shares, and B is liable to A for their value.

If B surrenders the certificate to the issuing corporation which cancels it and issues a new one in B's name, B is now owner of the shares represented by the certificate registered in his name. Section 8–311. However, A is entitled on demand to receive from the corporation a new certificate for the same number of shares. Section 8–404(2). If all of its authorized shares are outstanding, any additionally issued shares would be illegal as an overissue of stock. The corporation must therefore buy the replacement shares on the market, or if no shares are available for purchase must pay A the price that he or the last purchaser for value paid for the stock, with interest from the date of the demand. Section 8–104.

Duty of Issuer to Register Transfer of Security

The issuing corporation is under a duty to register transfer of its certificated securities and issue new certificates to the new owner. Section 8–401. The owner or purchaser is entitled to registration in order to vote and to receive dividends, notices, and periodic reports of the corporation, and to receive a new certificate, as the only way that he can sell or pledge or dispose of the certificated securities is by a transfer of the certificate.

Under Section 8–401, if a certificated security in registered form is presented to the issuer with a request to register transfer, the issuer shall register the transfer as requested if:

1. the certificate is indorsed by the appropriate person or persons (Section 8–308);
2. reasonable assurance is given that those endorsements are genuine and effective (Section 8–402);
3. the issuer has no duty as to adverse claims or has discharged the duty (Section 8–403);
4. any applicable law relating to the collection of taxes has been complied with; and
5. the transfer is in fact rightful or is to a bona fide purchaser.

Lost, Destroyed, or Stolen Certificated Securities

If a certificated security has been lost, apparently destroyed, or wrongfully taken, the owner is entitled to a new certificate to replace the missing one provided he (1) requests it before the issuer has notice that the "missing" certificate has been acquired by a bona fide purchaser, (2) files with the issuer a sufficient indemnity bond, and (3) satisfies other reasonable requirements of the issuer such as furnishing a sworn statement of the facts in connection with the loss. Section 8–405(2).

The owner of a lost, destroyed, or stolen certificate may be deprived of the right to a replacement certificate by failing to notify the issuing corporation within a reasonable time after learning of the loss, if the corporation has registered a transfer of the certificate before receiving such notification. Section 8–405(1).

Cases

Payment for Newly Issued Shares

UNITED STEEL INDUS., INC. v. MANHART

(1966, Tex.Civ.App.) 405 S.W.2d 231, ref. n. r. e.

McDONALD, C. J.

This is an appeal by defendants, United Steel Industries, Inc., J. R. Hurt and W. B. Griffitts, from a judgment declaring void and cancelling 5000 shares of stock in United Steel Industries, Inc. issued to Hurt, and 4000 shares of stock in such corporation issued to Griffitts.

Plaintiffs Manhart filed this suit individually and as major stockholders against defendants United Steel Industries, Inc., Hurt, and Griffitts, alleging the corporation had issued Hurt 5000 shares of its stock in consideration of Hurt agreeing to perform CPA and bookkeeping services for the corporation for one year in the future; and had issued Griffitts 4000 shares of its stock in consideration for the promised conveyance of a 5 acre tract of land to the Corporation, which land was never conveyed to the Corporation. Plaintiffs assert the 9000 shares of stock were issued in violation of Article 2.16 Business Corporation Act, V.A.T.S. and prayed that such stock be declared void and cancelled.

Trial was before the Court without a jury which, after hearing, entered judgment declaring the 5000 shares of stock issued to Hurt and the 4000 shares issued to Griffitts, issued without valid consideration, void, and decreeing such stock cancelled.

* * *

The trial court found (on ample evidence) that the incorporators of the Corporation made an agreement with Hurt to issue him 5000 shares in consideration of Hurt's agreement to perform bookkeeping and accounting services for the Corporation

for the first year of its operation. The Corporation minutes reflect the 5000 shares issued to Hurt "in consideration of labor done, services in the incorporation and organization of the Corporation." The trial court found (on ample evidence) that such minutes do not reflect the true consideration agreed upon, and that Hurt performed no services for the Corporation prior to February 1, 1965. The Articles of Incorporation were filed on January 28, 1965, and the 500 shares were issued to Hurt on May 29, 1965. There is evidence that Hurt performed some services for the Corporation between January and May 29, 1965; but Hurt himself testified the "5000 (shares) were issued to me for services rendered or to be rendered for the first year in keeping the books * * *."

The situation is thus one where the stock was issued to Hurt both for services already performed and for services to be rendered in the future.

The trial court concluded the promise of future services was not a valid consideration for the issuance of stock under Article 2.16 Business Corporation Act; that the issuance was void; and that since there was no apportionment of the value of future services from the value of services already rendered, the entire 5000 shares were illegally issued and void.

Article 12, Section 6, Texas Constitution, Vernon's Ann.St. provides: "No corporation shall issue stock * * * except for money paid, labor done, or property actually received * * *." And Article 2.16 Texas Business Corporation Act provides: "Payment for Shares.

"A. The consideration paid for the issuance of shares shall consist of money paid, labor done, or property actually received. Shares may not be issued until the full amount of the consideration, fixed as provided by law, has been paid. * * *

"B. Neither promissory notes nor the promise of future services shall constitute payment or part payment for shares of a corporation.

"C. In the absence of fraud in the transaction, the judgment of the board of directors * * * as to the value of the consideration received for shares shall be conclusive."

* * *

The 5000 shares were issued before the future services were rendered. Such stock was illegally issued and void.

Griffitts was issued 10,000 shares partly in consideration for legal services to the Corporation and partly in exchange for the 5 acres of land. The stock was valued at $1 per share and the land had an agreed value of $4000. The trial court found (upon ample evidence) that the 4000 shares of stock issued to Griffitts was in consideration of his promise to convey the land to the Corporation; that Griffitts never conveyed the land; and the issuance of the stock was illegal and void.

The judgment of the board of directors "as to the value of consideration received for shares" is conclusive, but such does not authorize the board to issue shares contrary to the Constitution, for services to be performed in the future (as in the case of Hurt), or for property not received (as in the case of Griffitts).

The judgment is correct. Defendants' points and contentions are overruled.

Affirmed.

Preferred Stock

IN RE OLYMPIC NAT'L LIQUIDATION AGENCIES, INC.
(1968) 74 Wash.2d 1, 442 P.2d 246.

HUNTER, J.

This is an appeal from a decree instructing the liquidating trustee to distrib-ute the assets of Olympic National Agencies, Inc., after the preference of the preferred stock is satisfied, to the common and preferred stockholders on a pro rata basis.

Olympic National Agencies, Inc., (hereinafter referred to as Agencies), was organized as Olympic Mutual Agencies, Inc., in 1935 with an authorized capitalization of 1,980 shares of preferred stock ($50 par value) and 2,000 shares of common stock (no par value). The initial capital of the corporation after formation consisted chiefly of (1) an exclusive agency contract with Olympic Mutual Life Insurance Company (now Olympic National Life Insurance Company) with a remaining term of 4 years, and (2) certain guaranty notes of Olympic Mutual Life Insurance Company. These assets were exchanged by the organizers for Agencies stock. After being formed, Agencies renegotiated the exclusive agency contract with Olympic National Life Insurance Company for a 20-year term and as a result the appraised value of that asset increased from $10,050 to $50,000.

In 1938, Agencies amended its articles of incorporation to increase the number of authorized preferred shares to 19,800 and the number of authorized common shares to 20,000 in connection with a 10 for 1 stock split. The par value of preferred shares was accordingly reduced to $5. Agencies stock has been issued and sold to the public and traded on the open market, and all of the authorized shares are now outstanding. Preferred stock has been offered and sold by the corporation at par, except for certain shares sold under a 1935 application to sell stock filed with the state. A 7 per cent dividend has been paid on the preferred stock each year since 1936, with a total return of $10.40 for each $5 of par value to date of liquidation. Dividends have been paid on common stock each year since 1943, totaling $4.91 per share at the date of liquidation.

The shareholders of Agencies passed a resolution of dissolution on September 8,

1965, and elected a liquidating trustee and an alternative liquidating trustee. The assets of the corporation considerably exceed its liabilities. These assets consist of 249,580 shares of Class B common stock of Olympic National Life Insurance Company. The liquidating trustee (one of the respondents on this appeal) petitioned the trial court for instructions on October 27, 1965. One of the issues raised by the petition, and the one which concerns us on this appeal, was the matter of the respective rights, upon dissolution, of the preferred and common shareholders of Agencies.

After due notice to the interested parties and a hearing at which the appellant, the holder of the largest number of common shares, and the additional respondents, who own chiefly preferred shares, appeared, the trial court entered findings of fact, conclusions of law and a decree, which provided that the liquidating trustee should first pay $5 to each share of preferred stock, then $5 to each share of common stock and should then distribute any surplus pro rata to both classes of stock. The court based its conclusion on article V of Agencies' articles of incorporation, which reads:

The preferred stock shall be entitled to a preferred non-cumulative dividend of seven percent (7%) per annum before any dividend shall be declared or paid on common stock. Dividends shall be out of the net earnings or surplus of the company, and shall be in such amount and payable at such times as shall be declared by the Board of Directors. The preferred stock shall further be preferred as to the assets of the corporation up to par value.

The court also considered, in interpreting the effect and intent of this language, acts of the organizers, incorporators, directors and officers of the corporation, both before and after Agencies was formed. The court's finding of fact No. 6 concluded that these acts were for the most part consistent with an interpretation that all shares, both preferred and common, should participate

in the assets of the company on dissolution on a *pro rata* basis * * *.

The appellant contends that the trial court erred in ruling that the preferred stock could share in the distribution of assets in excess of its stated preference. He argues that the language of article V, of the articles of incorporation, supra, is clearly a restriction on the preferred stock's right to participate in the corporation's assets, and that the majority of American courts which have considered the question have held that when the articles of incorporation grant a class of stock a preference as to assets this preference is presumed to be exhaustive of the stock's rights. We agree with this contention.

The articles of incorporation are a contract, and govern, save as statute may otherwise provide, the rights of the parties. [Citation.] The articles should be read in the context of the usages and practices of businessmen. * * *

It is generally recognized that a dividend preference precludes the preferred stock from participating in dividend distributions beyond the stated preference, when nothing to the contrary appears in the articles of incorporation. [Citations.] A prominent authority comments that:

It seems a reasonable implication that in consideration of his preferential rights, the preferred shareholder agrees to accept his priority as to dividends as a fixed rate in lieu of further participation with the common. Such is the common understanding of the investing public * * *. Ballantine on Corporations § 216 (Rev.1946).

The analogous question before us is whether a preference precludes the preferred stock from participating in the distribution of assets byond the stated preference upon liquidation. In Squires v. Balbach Co., 177 Neb. 465, at 478, 129 N.W.2d 462, at 470 (1964), the court said:

We conclude that provisions in corporate articles and memoranda that holders of preferred stock shall be paid the par value of their stock before any liquidation dividends are paid to the holders of common stock is exhaustive and means that the preferred stock shall have its par preference on liquidation and nothing more.

* * *

We hold that, under facts such as in the instant case, where one class of stock is afforded a stated preference as to assets on liquidation, and the articles of incorporation are silent as to any further participation, the clear implication is that the rights of the preferred stock are exhausted once the preference has been satisfied. [Citations.]

The decree of the trial court is reversed, and the cause is remanded for further proceedings with directions that a decree be entered in conformity with our views expressed herein.

Right to Dividends

DODGE v. FORD MOTOR CO.

(1919) 204 Mich. 459, 170 N.W. 668.

[Action in equity by John F. and Horace E. Dodge, plaintiffs, against the Ford Motor Company and its directors to compel the declaration of dividends and for an injunction restraining a contemplated expansion of the business. The complaint was filed in November, 1916. Since 1909, the capital stock of the company has been $2,000,000, divided into 20,000 shares of the par value of $100 each of which plaintiffs held 2,000. As of the close of business of July 31, 1916, the end of the company's fiscal year, the surplus above capital was $111,960,907.53 and the assets included cash on hand of $52,550,771.92.

For a number of years the company had paid regularly quarterly dividends equal to sixty percent annually on the capital stock of $2,000,000. In addition, from December, 1911, to October, 1915, inclusive, eleven special dividends totalling $41,000,000 had been paid and in November, 1916, after this action was commenced, a special dividend of $2,000,000 was paid.

Plaintiffs' complaint alleged that Henry Ford, president of the company and a member of its board of directors, had declared it to be the settled policy of the company not to pay any special dividends in the future, but to put back into the business all future earnings in excess of the regular quarterly dividend. Plaintiffs sought an injunction restraining the carrying out of the alleged declared policy of Henry Ford and a decree requiring the directors to pay a dividend of at least seventy-five per cent of the accumulated cash surplus.

In December, 1917, the trial court entered a decree requiring the directors to declare and pay a dividend of $19,275,385.96 and enjoining the corporation from using its funds for a proposed smelting plant and certain other planned projects. From this decree, defendants have appealed.]

OSTRANDER, J.
* * *

The case for plaintiffs must rest upon the claim, and the proof in support of it, that the proposed expansion of the business of the corporation involving the further use of profits as capital, ought to be enjoined because inimical to the best interests of the company and its shareholders, and upon the further claim that in any event the withholding of the special dividend asked for by plaintiffs is arbitrary action of the directors requiring judicial interference.

The rule which will govern courts in deciding these questions is not in dispute.
* * * In 1 Morawetz on Corporations (2d Ed.), sec. 447, it is stated:

Profits earned by a corporation may be divided among its shareholders; but it is not a violation of the charter if they are allowed to accumulate and remain invested in the company's business. The managing agents of a corporation are impliedly invested with a discretionary power with regard to the time and manner of distributing its profits. They may apply profits in payment of floating or funded debts, or in development of the company's business; and so long as they do not abuse their discretionary powers, or violate the company's charter, the courts cannot interfere.

But it is clear that the agents of a corporation, and even the majority, cannot arbitrarily withhold profits earned by the company, or apply them to any use which is not authorized by the company's charter. The nominal capital of a company does not necessarily limit the scope of its operations; a corporation may borrow money for the purpose of enlarging its business, and in many instances it may use profits for the same purpose. * * *

When plaintiffs made their complaint and demand for further dividends the Ford Motor Company had concluded its most prosperous year of business. The demand for its cars at the price of the preceding year continued. It could make and could market in the year beginning August 1, 1916, more than 500,000 cars. Sales of parts and repairs would necessarily increase. The cost of materials was likely to advance, and perhaps the price of labor, but it reasonably might have expected a profit for the year of upwards of $60,000,000. It had assets of more than $132,000,000, a surplus of almost $112,000,000, and its cash on hand and municipal bonds were nearly $54,000,000. Its total liabilities, including capital stock, was a little over $20,000,000. It had declared no special dividend during the business year except the October, 1915, dividend. It had been the practice, under similar circumstances, to declare larger dividends. Considering only these facts, a refusal to declare and pay further dividends appears to be not an exercise of discretion on the part of the directors, but an arbitrary refusal to do what the circumstances required to be done. These facts and others call upon the directors to justify their action, or failure or refusal to act. In justification, the defendants have offered testimony tending to prove, and which does prove, the following facts. It had been the policy of the corporation for a considerable time to annually reduce the selling price of cars, while keeping up, or improving, their quality. As early as in June 1915 a general plan for the expansion of the productive capacity of the concern by a practical duplication of its plant had been talked over by the executive officers and directors and agreed upon, not all of the details having been settled and no formal action of directors having been taken. The erection of a smelter was considered, and engineering and other data in connection therewith secured. In consequence, it was determined not to reduce the selling price of cars for the year beginning August 1, 1915, but to maintain the price and to accumulate a large surplus to pay for the proposed expansion of plant and equipment, and perhaps to build a plant for smelting ore. It is hoped, by Mr. Ford, that eventually 1,000,000 cars will be annually produced. The contemplated changes will permit the increased output.

The plan, as affecting the profits of the business for the year beginning August 1, 1916, and thereafter, calls for a reduction in the selling price of cars. * * * In short, the plan does not call for and is not intended to produce immediately a more profitable business but a less profitable one; not only less profitable than formerly but less profitable than it is admitted it might be made. The apparent immediate effect will be to diminish the value of shares and the return to shareholders.

It is the contention of plaintiffs that the apparent effect of the plan is intended to be the continued and continuing effect of it and that it is deliberately proposed, not of record and not by official corporate declaration, but nevertheless proposed, to continue the corporation henceforth as a semi-eleemosynary institution and not as a business institution. In support of this contention they point to the attitude and to the expressions of Mr. Henry Ford.

Mr. Henry Ford is the dominant force in the business of the Ford Motor Company.

No plan of operations could be adopted unless he consented, and no board of directors can be elected whom he does not favor. One of the directors of the company has no stock. One share was assigned to him to qualify him for the position, but it is not claimed that he owns it. A business, one of the largest in the world, and one of the most profitable, has been built up. It employs many men, at good pay.

"My ambition", said Mr. Ford, "is to employ still more men, to spread the benefits of this industrial system to the greatest possible number, to help them build up their lives and their homes. To do this we are putting the greatest share of our profits back in the business." * * *

The record, and especially the testimony of Mr. Ford, convinces that he has to some extent the attitude towards shareholders of one who has dispensed and distributed to them large gains and that they should be content to take what he chooses to give. His testimony creates the impression, also, that he thinks the Ford Motor Company has made too much money, has had too large profits, and that although large profits might still be earned, a sharing of them with the public, by reducing the price of the output of the company, ought to be undertaken. We have no doubt that certain sentiments, philanthropic and altruistic, creditable to Mr. Ford, had large influence in determining the policy to be pursued by the Ford Motor Company—the policy which has been herein referred to. * * *

These cases, after all, like all others in which the subject is treated, turn finally upon the point, the question, whether it appears that the directors were not acting for the best interest of the corporation. * * * The difference between an incidental humanitarian expenditure of corporate funds for the benefit of the employees, like the building of a hospital for their use and the employment of agencies for the betterment of their condition, and a general

purpose and plan to benefit mankind at the expense of others, is obvious. * * * A business corporation is organized and carried on primarily for the profit of the stockholders. The powers of the directors are to be employed for that end. The discretion of directors is to be exercised in the choice of means to attain that end and does not extend to a change in the end itself, to the reduction of profits or to the nondistribution of profits among stockholders in order to devote them to other purposes. * * *

We are not, however, persuaded that we should interfere with the proposed expansion of the business of the Ford Motor Company. In view of the fact that the selling price of products may be increased at any time, the ultimate results of the larger business cannot be certainly estimated. The judges are not business experts. It is recognized that plans must often be made for a long future, for expected competition, for a continuing as well as an immediately profitable venture. The experience of the Ford Motor Company is evidence of capable management of its affairs. * * *

Defendants say, and it is true, that a considerable cash balance must be at all times carried by such a concern. But, as has been stated, there was a large daily, weekly, monthly, receipt of cash. The output was practically continuous and was continuously, and within a few days, turned into cash. Moreover, the contemplated expenditures were not to be immediately made. The large sum appropriated for the smelter plant was payable over a considerable period of time. So that, without going further, it would appear that, accepting and approving the plan of the directors, it was their duty to distribute on or near the first of August, 1916, a very large sum of money to stockholders. * * *

The decree of the court below fixing and determining the specific amount to be distributed to stockholders is affirmed. In other respects, except as to the allowance of costs, the said decree is reversed.

Liability of Shareholders to
Repay Improper Dividends

WOOD v. CITY NAT'L BANK

(1928, C.C.A.2d) 24 F.2d 661.

[Action by Wood, ancillary receiver of the Stanton Oil Company, a Delaware corporation, to recover from the defendants, shareholders in the corporation, dividends paid to them in the years 1917, 1918 and 1919. The plaintiff alleged that at the time the dividends were declared the corporation "was in fact insolvent and unable to pay its debts, and had not then, nor had it ever had, any reserve over and above its capital stock, or any surplus or net profits of any kind, and each and all of the said dividends were paid wholly from and out of the capital of said corporation". On motion of defendants, the complaint was dismissed for insufficiency on its face and plaintiff appeals.]

L. HAND, JR, J.

* * *

We have not to do with the liability commonly imposed by statute, because, whatever that may be in Delaware, the plaintiff does not invoke it here. He depends upon the fact that the directors have paid, and the defendants received, dividends when the corporation was insolvent. Merely because this impairs the capital stock, it is commonly regarded as a wrong to creditors on the directors' part, and it is often made such by statute. We may, without discussion, assume that it would be a wrong in the case at bar. Even so, it is primarily only the wrong of those who commit it, like any other tort, and innocent participants are not accomplices to its commission. Hence it has been settled, at least for us, that when the liability is based merely on the depletion of the capital, a stockholder must be charged with notice of that fact. McDonald v. Williams, 174 U.S. 397, 19 S.Ct. 743, 43 L.Ed. 1022. This has become a thoroughly fixed principle in the federal courts. [Citiations.]

It is apparent that this result could not have been reached if the capital of the corporation were regarded as a trust fund for its creditors, because a stockholder is not a purchaser, but a donee, and his bona fides would not protect him, in the absence of some further equity, in detaining the proceeds of a trust. So it became necessary to decide that the capital was not such a fund, and McDonald v. Williams did expressly so decide. The so-called "trust fund" doctrine had, indeed, earlier been repudiated by the Supreme Court [citation]; but it was a hardy weed and would not die at the first uprooting. It is apparent, therefore, that the bill does not set forth a cause of suit based upon the impairment of the capital, because the stockholders are not alleged to have been privy to the directors' tort. This is not a defense which must be pleaded, like that of a bona fide purchaser; it is necessary positively to allege the stockholders' complicity in the wrong to set forth any case at all.

However, there is quite another theory, and quite another liability, if the payments not only impair the capital, but are taken out of assets already too small to pay the existing debts. The situation then strictly is not peculiar to corporation law, but merely an instance of a payment from an insolvent estate. Since, we have said, a stockholder is a donee, he receives such payments charged with whatever trust they were subject to in the hands of the corporation. In that situation it can indeed be said with some truth that the corporate assets have become a "trust fund." [Citation.] Hence it has never been doubted, so far as we can find, at least in any federal court, that if the dividends are paid in fraud of creditors the stockholder is so liable. [Citations.] * * *

If the bill be regarded as presenting only an instance of a payment in fraud of creditors, the question arises whether it is enough merely to allege that the payment was made while the corporation was insolvent. It is agreed with substantial unanimity that, when an insolvent makes a voluntary payment out of his assets, it is regarded as at least presumptively in fraud of his creditors. [Citations.] We shall assume, for argument, in accordance with the language of some of the foregoing decisions, that such a transfer is fraudulent per se. In Hayden v. Williams, (C.C.A.2) 96 F. 279, no more is mentioned than that the corporation was insolvent, and apparently no more was thought necessary. Even so, the bill is bad, because, when the invalidity of the gift depends only upon the fact of the donor's insolvency, regardless of his intent, it is voidable only at the demand of creditors existing when it is made. [Citations.] Hummell v. Harrington, 92 Fla. 87, 109 So.

320, if holding otherwise, is an exception; it probably meant no more than that, if there be actual intent to defraud subsequent creditors, they also may avoid the gift. [Citation.] In the case at bar the bill does not allege that any of the creditors in existence when the receiver was appointed were creditors when the dividends were declared. Only in case the bill had alleged this, would the question arise whether insolvency per se avoids the gift. For this reason, and this alone, the decree was right.

[Decree affirmed without prejudice to file an amended complaint alleging the dividends were paid in fraud of creditors and that some of the present creditors were also creditors when the dividends were paid.]

Problems

1. Frank McAnarney and Joseph Lemon entered into an agreement to promote a corporation to engage in the manufacture of farm implements. Prior to the organization of the corporation McAnarney and Lemon solicited subscriptions to the stock of the corporation and presented a written agreement for signatures of the subscribers.

The agreement provided that subscribers pay $100 per share for stock in the corporation in consideration of McAnarney's and Lemon's agreement to organize the corporation and advance the pre-incorporation expenses. Thomas Jordan signed the agreement making application for 100 shares of stock. Subsequent to the filing of the articles of incorporation with the Secretary of State, but prior to the issuance of a charter to the corporation, Jordan died. The administrator of Jordan's estate notified McAnarney and Lemon that the estate would not honor Jordan's subscription.

After the formation of the corporation, Franklin Adams signed a subscription agreement making application for 100 shares of stock. Before acceptance by the corporation Adams advised the corporation that he was cancelling his subscription.

(a) The corporation brings an appropriate action against Jordan's estate to enforce Jordan's stock subscription. Decision?

(b) The corporation brings an appropriate action to enforce Adams' stock subscription. Decision?

2. The XYZ Corporation was duly organized on July 10. Its certificate of incorporation provides for a total authorized capital of $100,000, consisting of 1,000 shares of common stock, par value $100 per share. The corporation issues for cash a total of 50 certificates, numbered 1 to 50 inclusive, representing various amounts of shares in the names of various individuals. Payment for the shares having been made in advance, the certificates are all dated and mailed on the same day to the individuals, respectively, whose names appear thereon. The 50 certificates of stock represent a total of 1,050 shares. Certificate No. 49 for 30 shares was issued to John Smith. Certificate No. 50 for 25 shares was issued to William Jones. Is there any question concerning the validity of any of the stock thus issued? What are the rights of Smith and Jones?

3. D subscribed for 200 shares of 8 percent cumulative, participating, redeemable, convertible, preferred shares of the X Hotel Company of the par value of $100 per share. The subscription agreement provided that he was to receive a bonus of one share of common stock of $100 par value for each share of preferred stock. D fully paid his subscription agreement of $20,000 and received the aforementioned 200 shares of preferred and the bonus stock of 200 shares of the par value common. Subsequently, the Hotel Co. becomes insolvent. R, the receiver of the corporation, brings suit for $20,000, the par value of the common stock. What judgment?

4. A, B, and C organized the Wistful Vista Corporation for the purpose of subdividing and selling 100 acres of land located on the outskirts of a certain city. The authorized capital of the corporation consisted of 2,000 shares of common stock of $100 par value. A conveyed to the corporation in exchange for 500 shares of stock 50 acres of land which he had purchased that year for $5,000. B conveyed to the corporation in exchange for 400 shares of stock 25 acres of land for which he had paid $4,000 that year. C conveyed to the corporation in exchange for 300 shares of stock 25 acres of land for which he had paid $3,000 that year. The remaining 800 shares of stock were sold to the public at par for a total of $80,000. After two years of unsuccessful operations the corporation has spent the $80,000, and has incurred debts aggregating $50,000. What are the rights of its creditors?

5. The X Company has an authorized capital stock of 1,000 shares of the par value of $100 per share, of which 900 shares, all fully paid, are outstanding. Having an ample surplus, the X Company purchases from its shareholders 100 shares at par. Subsequently, the X Company, needing additional working capital, issues the 200 shares in question to S at $80 per share. Two years later the X Company is forced into bankruptcy. The trustee in bankruptcy now sues S for $4,000, being the difference between the par value of 200 shares and the amount he paid for them. Decision?

6. For five years, B and C had been engaged as partners in building homes. They owned the necessary equipment to conduct the business and had an excellent reputation for competence.

In March, D, who had previously been in the same kind of business, proposed that B, C and D form a corporation for the purpose of constructing medium price houses. They engaged attorney A who did all the work required and caused the business to be incorporated under the name of X Corp.

The certificate of incorporation authorized 100 shares of $100 par value stock. At the organization meeting of the incorporators, B, C and D were elected directors and X Corp. issued a total of 65 shares of its stock. B and C each received 20 shares in consideration of transferring to X Corp. the equipment and good will of their partnership having a value of over $4,000. D received 20 shares as an inducement to work for X Corp. in the future and A received 5 shares as compensation for the legal services rendered in forming X Corp.

Later that year X Corp. had a number of financial setbacks and in December ceased operations. What rights, if any, does X Corp. have against B, C, D, and A in connection with the original issuance of its shares?

7. Paul Bunyan is the owner of non-cumulative 8% preferred stock in the Broadview Corporation which had no earnings or profits in 1979. In 1980 the corporation had large profits and a surplus from which it might properly have declared dividends. The directors refused to do so, but used the surplus to purchase goods necessary for their expanding business.

In view of the large profits made in 1980, the directors at the end of 1981 declared a 10% dividend on the common stock and an 8% dividend on the preferred stock, without paying preferred dividends for 1980. The corporation earned a small profit in 1981.

(a) Is Bunyan entitled to dividends for 1979? and 1980?

(b) Is Bunyan entitled to a dividend of 10% rather than 8% in 1981?

8. A corporation has outstanding 400 shares of $100 par value common stock which has been issued and sold at $105 per share for a total of $42,000. At a time when the assets of the corporation amount to $65,000, and the liabilities to creditors total $10,000, the directors learn that S, who holds 100 of the 400 shares of stock, is planning to sell his shares on the open market for $10,500. Considering that this will not be to the best interest of the corporation, the directors enter into an agreement with S whereby S sells to the corporation itself the 100 shares in exchange for a corporate note for $10,500, payable one year from date. About six months later, when the assets of the corporation have decreased to $50,000 and its liabilities, exclusive of its liability to S, have increased to $20,000, the directors use $10,000 to pay a dividend to all of the shareholders. Subsequently, the corporation becomes insolvent.

(a) Is the corporation liable to S on the note for $10,500?

(b) Was the payment of the $10,000 dividend proper?

9. Almega Corporation, organized under the laws of State S, has outstanding 20,000 shares of $100 par value non-voting preferred stock calling for non-cumulative dividends of $5 per year; 10,000 shares of voting preferred $50 par value, calling for cumulative dividends of $2.50 per year, and 10,000 shares of no par common. In 1977 the corporation had net earnings of $170,000; in 1978, $135,000; in 1979, $60,000; in 1980, $210,000; and 1981, $120,000. The board of directors passed over all dividends during the four years 1977–1980, since the company needed working capital for expansion purposes. In 1981 the directors declared a dividend on the non-cumulative preferred shares of $5 per share, on the cumulative preferred of $12.50 and on the common a dividend of $30. The board submitted their declaration to the voting shareholders and they ratified it. Before the dividends were paid, Payne, the record holder of 500 shares of the non-cumulative preferred stock, brought an appropriate action to restrain any payment to the cumulative preferred or common shareholders until a full dividend for the five years stated should be paid to non-cumulative preferred shareholders.

Decision?

10. Sayre learned that Adams, Boone, and Chase were planning to form a corporation for the purpose of manufacturing and marketing a line of novelties to wholesale outlets. Sayre had patented a self-lock gas tank cap, but lacked the financial backing to market it profitably. He negotiated with Adams, Boone and Chase, who agreed to purchase the patent rights for $5,000 in cash and 200 shares of $100 par value preferred stock in a corporation to be formed.

The corporation was formed and Sayre's stock issued to him but the corporation has refused to be bound by the agreement for the cash payment. It has refused to declare dividends, although the business has been very profitable due to the value of Sayre's patent, and has a substantial earned surplus with a large cash balance on hand. It is selling the remainder of the originally authorized issue of preferred shares, ignoring Sayre's demand to purchase a proportionate share of the stock so sold. What are Sayre's rights, if any?

11. A by-law of Betma Corporation provides that no shareholder can sell his shares unless he first offers them for sale to the corporation or its directors. The by-law also stated that this restriction shall be printed or stamped upon each stock certificate and will thereupon bind all present or future owners or holders. Betma Corporation did not comply with this latter provision. Shaw, having knowledge of the by-law restriction, purchased 20 shares of the corporation's stock from Rice, but these shares were not first offered for sale to the corporation or its directors by Shaw or Rice. When Betma Corporation refused to effectuate a transfer of the shares to him, Shaw sued to compel a transfer and the issuance of a new certificate to him.

Decision?

12. A certificate for 100 shares of stock of General Motors Corporation was issued to Jones & Co. The certificate was misappropriated from the portfolio of Jones & Co. by X who by forged indorsement transferred and delivered it for value to Y, a bona fide purchaser. Y subsequently delivered the certificate to his stock broker, Bond & Share Co., with instructions to sell the shares represented thereby. Bond & Share Co. sold it upon the open market, remitting the proceeds of the sale to Y less the usual brokerage commission. Jones & Co. learns the facts, and brings an action in conversion against Bond & Share Co. to recover the value of the shares. What judgment?

36

MANAGERIAL AND FIDUCIARY DUTIES OF OFFICERS AND DIRECTORS

The business and affairs of a corporation are managed by its officers who are appointed to office and managed by the board of directors, the members of which are elected by and responsible to the shareholders of the corporation. Officers and directors have both managerial and fiduciary duties.

The board of directors, as the shareholders' elected representatives, are delegated the power to manage the business and affairs of a corporation. Directors exercise dominion and control over the corporation, have access to inside information, hold positions of trust and confidence, and determine questions of operating policy. Directors are not ordinarily expected to devote full time to the affairs of the corporation and have broad authority to delegate power to officers and agents. The officers of the corporation hold their office at the will of the board. The officers, in turn, hire and fire the clerical staff, agents, salesmen, employees, workers, and all necessary operating personnel and run the day-to-day affairs of the corporation.

THE BOARD OF DIRECTORS

Section 35 of the Model Act states that "[a]ll corporate powers shall be exercised by or under the authority of, and the business and affairs of a corporation shall be managed under the direction of, a board of directors." The board is supposed to determine corporate policy in a number of areas, including (1) selection and removal of the officers, (2) determining the capital structure, (3) initiating organic changes, (4) declaring dividends, and (5) setting management compensation.

Qualification, Election, and Tenure of Directors

Qualification of Members. The governing statute, articles of incorporation, and by-laws determine the qualifications which individuals must possess in order to be eligible as directors of the corporation. There are no common law requirements. The statute may require that directors be shareholders or residents of the State of incorporation, although most states have eliminated such requirements.

Number of Members and Tenure in Office. The number of directors on a board shall consist of one or more as fixed by the articles of incorporation or by-laws, except as to the number constituting the initial board of directors which number shall be fixed by the articles of incorporation. Section 36.

Directors are elected at the annual meeting of the shareholders to hold office for one year or until their successors are duly elected and qualified. If the shares represented at a meeting in person or by proxy are not sufficient to constitute a quorum, the incumbent board continues in office as "hold-over" directors until an election is held.

Where the board consists of nine or more, the by-laws may provide for a classification of directors, that is, a division into two or three classes to be as nearly equal in number as possible. If into two classes, the members of each class are elected once a year in alternate years for a two-year term; if into three classes, for three-year terms. This permits one-half of the board to be elected every two years, or one-third to be elected every three years, thus providing an element of continuity of membership. Section 37.

Vacancies and Removal of Directors. The Model Act provides that a vacancy in the board may be filled by the affirmative vote of a majority of the remaining directors, although less than a quorum of the board, and the director so elected shall hold office for the unexpired term of his predecessor. A directorship to be filled by reason of an increase in the number of directors may be filled by the board for a term continuing until the next election of directors by the shareholders. Section 38.

Some States have no statutory provision for removal of directors, although a common-law rule permits removal for cause by action of the shareholders. The Model Act is liberal in permitting removal of one or more of the directors, or of the entire board by the shareholders with or without cause at a special meeting called for that purpose. Section 39A.

Compensation of Directors. Traditionally, directors did not receive salaries for their services as directors, although it was usual for them to be paid a fee or honorarium for attendance at meetings. The Model Act and other incorporation statutes now expressly authorize the board of directors to fix the compensation of directors absent a contrary provision in the articles of incorporation. Section 35.

Meetings of the Board of Directors

Directors by reason of their office do not have the power to bind the corporation when acting individually, but only when acting as a board. When an individual acts as a director it is at a meeting with other directors, or without a meeting by a written consent signed by all of the directors, provided that this manner of action is authorized by the statute and not contrary to the charter or by-laws.

The board is presumably representative of the shareholders. Its members usually are people of experience in various fields of business and professions, who may represent and speak for diverse interests among the shareholders. A minority interest having representation on the board is entitled to have its viewpoint presented and considered by the board in meeting assembled.

Meetings are held either regularly at a time and place fixed in the by-laws, or specially or periodically as they may be called. Notice of meetings must be given as prescribed in the by-laws. Attendance of a director at any meeting is a waiver of such notice, unless the director attends for the express purpose of objecting to the transaction of any business on the ground that the meeting is not lawfully called or convened. Most modern statutes provide that meetings of the board may be held either within or without the State. Section 43.

Quorum. A majority of the members of the board of directors constitutes a quorum, the minimum number of members necessary to be present at a meeting in order to transact business. The articles of incorporation or by-laws may, however, require a number greater than a simple majority. If a quorum is present at any meeting, the act of a majority of the directors in attendance at such meeting is the act of the board, unless the act of a greater number is required by the articles of incorporation or by-laws. In any event, directors may not vote by proxy.

Action Taken by the Board without a Meeting. The Model Act provides that, unless otherwise provided by the articles of incorporation or by-laws, any action required by the statute to be taken at a meeting of the board, or any act which may be taken at such meeting or a meeting of a committee, may be taken without a meeting if a consent in writing is signed by all of the directors, or by all of the members of the committee, as the case may be. Such consent shall have the same effect as a unanimous vote. Section 44.

Powers of the Board of Directors

A summary of the statutory powers of a typical board of directors may be obtained from an examination of the Model Business Corporation Act. Under this Act the board has power to:

1. Authorize a change of the registered office or registered agent. Section 13.
2. If expressly authorized by the articles, divide special or preferred stock into series

and fix the rights and preferences of the shares of any series. Section 16.

3. Determine the method of payment of subscriptions for shares, whether in full or in installments, and the terms thereof. Section 17.

4. Fix the selling price of newly issued par value shares at not less than par. Section 18.

5. Fix the stated value and selling price of no par shares, unless the power to do so is reserved to the shareholders by the articles. Section 18.

6. Determine the value of the consideration in the form of property, or labor or services actually performed, received by the corporation in payment for shares issued. Section 19.

7. Determine, subject to statutory limitations, what part of the consideration received by the corporation for its newly issued shares shall be stated capital and what part shall be capital surplus. Section 21.

8. Increase stated capital by transfer of all or a part of capital or other surplus, and allocate the increased amount of stated capital in respect to any designated class of shares. Section 21.

9. Direct the issuance of scrip or other evidence of ownership of fractional shares, and impose a condition that the scrip shall become void if not exchanged for share certificates within a specified time, or a condition whereby the corporation may sell the shares for which the scrip is exchangeable and distribute the proceeds thereof to the holders of the scrip. Section 24.

10. Make, alter, amend or repeal the by-laws, unless this power is reserved to the shareholders by the articles. Section 27.

11. Provide for closing of stock transfer books, and fix a record date for the purpose of determining the shareholders who are entitled to receive notice, to vote, or to receive a dividend. Section 30.

12. Manage the business and affairs of the corporation. Section 35.

13. Elect a director to fill a vacancy occur-

ring in the board of directors. Section 38.

14. Declare dividends, subject to statutory limitations. Sections 45, 46.

15. Remove any officer or agent of the corporation at any time, without prejudice, however, to the contract rights, if any, of the person so removed. Section 51.

16. Initiate proceedings to amend the articles of incorporation. Section 59.

17. Initiate proceedings to reduce the stated capital. Section 69.

18. Apply any part or all of the capital surplus to the reduction or elimination of a deficit. Section 70.

19. Initiate proceedings for a merger or consolidation. Sections 71, 72.

20. Sell, lease, exchange or mortgage assets of the corporation in the usual and regular course of business. Section 78.

21. Initiate proceedings for the sale, lease, exchange or mortgage of assets of the corporation other than in the usual and regular course of business. Section 79.

22. Initiate proceedings to dissolve the corporation. Section 84.

Delegation of Board Powers

If provided for by the articles of incorporation or by-laws, the board of directors may by majority vote of the full board appoint executive and other committees, all of whose members must be directors. Committees may exercise all of the authority of the board except for certain matters specified in the statute such as the declaration of dividends, amending the by-laws, approving a merger, and authorizing the sale of stock. Delegation of authority to a committee does not relieve any board member of his duties to the corporation.

The board of directors acts independently of the shareholders, and a contract or agreement or understanding whereby a director subordinates his will and judgment to the dictates of a shareholder or group of shareholders is generally held to be contrary to public policy and illegal. However,

such agreements between all the shareholders of a close corporation are not illegal where neither the public nor the rights of creditors are affected.

OFFICERS

The officers of a corporation are those appointed to hold the offices provided in the by-laws which sets forth the respective duties of each officer. Statutes generally require as a minimum that they consist of a president, one or more vice-presidents as prescribed by the by-laws, a secretary, and a treasurer. Section 50. The by-laws may provide for other officers such as assistant to the president, assistant secretary, assistant treasurer, comptroller, cashier, auditor, and general counsel. A person may hold more than one office, except that the same person may not hold the office of president and secretary at the same time.

Selection and Removal of Officers

Most State statutes provide that the officers are appointed by the board of directors and serve at the pleasure of the board. Accordingly, officers may be removed by the board with or without cause. Section 51. Of course, if the officer has a valid employment contract for a specified period of time, removal of the officer without cause before the contract expires would constitute a breach of the employment contract. The board also determines the compensation of officers.

Role of Officers

The officers are, like the directors, fiduciaries to the corporation. On the other hand, unlike the directors, they are agents of the corporation. The roles of officers are set forth in the corporate by-laws, typical of which is the following description drawn from model by-laws:

President. The president is the principal executive officer of the corporation and, subject to the control of the board of directors, in general supervises and controls all of the business and affairs of the corporation. He presides at all meetings of the shareholders and of the board of directors. He may sign for the corporation any deeds, mortgages, bonds, contracts, or other instruments which the board of directors has authorized to be executed.

Vice-President. In the absence of the president or in the event of his death, inability or refusal to act, the vice-president shall perform the duties of the president, and when so acting, shall have all the powers of and be subject to all the restrictions upon the president.

Secretary. The secretary keeps the minutes of the proceedings of the shareholders and of the board of directors; sees that all notices are duly given; is custodian of the corporate records and of the seal of the corporation; signs with the president certificates for shares of the corporation, the issuance of which shall have been authorized by resolution of the board of directors; and has general charge of the stock transfer books of the corporation.

Treasurer. The treasurer has charge and custody of and is responsible for all funds and securities of the corporation; receives and gives receipts for and deposits moneys due and payable to the corporation.

Authority of Officers

Actual Express Authority. Actual express authority arises from the incorporation statute, the articles of incorporation, the by-laws and resolutions of the board of directors. Section 50. The principal source of actual express authority is the resolutions of the board of directors.

Actual Implied Authority. Officers, as agents of the corporation, have implied authority to do what is reasonably necessary to perform their actual, delegated authority. In addition, the question arises whether officers possess implied authority merely by virtue of their positions. The courts have been circumspect in granting such implied or inherent authority. Traditionally, the courts tended to hold that the president had no implied authority by virtue of his office, although the more recent decisions tend to recognize his authority to bind the corporation in ordinary business transactions. However, any act requiring board approval, such as issuing stock, is clearly beyond the implied authority of the president or any other officer. In most jurisdictions, implied authority of position does not extend to any other officer.

Apparent Authority. Apparent authority arises from acts of the principal that lead third parties to believe reasonably and in good faith that an officer has the requisite authority. Apparent authority might arise when a third party relies on the fact that an officer has exercised the same authority in the past with the consent of the board of directors.

Ratification. A corporation may ratify the unauthorized acts of its officers. Ratification is equivalent to the corporation's having granted the officer prior authority. Ratification relates back to the original transaction and may be express or implied from the corporation's acceptance of the benefits of the contract with full knowledge of the facts. Restatement, Second, Agency, Sections 84–104.

Compensation of Officers

Compensation of executives takes a number of forms in addition to straight salaries. For example, it is common for management to also receive cash bonuses, stock options, phantom stock (which provide the financial benefits of participating in earnings of the company and appreciation in value of its stock without stock ownership), deferred compensation and a host of other "fringe benefits," such as pension plans and various kinds of insurance. Because the amount of management compensation is typically determined by management, the question may arise as to the reasonableness of the amount. As a general rule, courts are reluctant to find management compensation excessive.

DUTIES OF
DIRECTORS AND OFFICERS

A corporation may not recover damages from its directors and officers for losses resulting from their poor business judgment, or honest mistake of judgment. It is a corporation's good fortune if its directors and officers are intelligent, conscientious, industrious people possessed of business acumen, and its misfortune if they prove to be mediocre or worse. The directors and officers are not insurers of business success. They are required only to be obedient, honest, loyal, and reasonably careful. These duties of obedience, diligence, and loyalty are for the most part judicially imposed. State statutes supplement the common law by imposing liability upon directors and officers for specific acts, but the common law still remains the most significant source of duties.

Shareholders who own a sufficient number of shares to have effective control over the corporation are termed "controlling shareholders." In some instances, controlling shareholders are held to the same duties as directors and officers. Moreover, in close corporations some courts impose upon all the shareholders a fiduciary duty similar to that imposed upon partners.

Duty of Obedience

When the directors or officers permit assets of the corporation to be diverted to purposes and objectives that are not within the charter or statutory powers, express or implied, they may not only be enjoined from a continuation of such activities, but also may be held liable in damages to the corporation or to a receiver or trustee appointed for the corporation, or to the shareholders in a representative suit.

Directors are jointly and severally liable for issuing shares of the corporation at a discount and for declaring a dividend which is paid when the corporation is insolvent or in violation of the state incorporation statute. They are liable for any distribution of the assets to shareholders, after the filing of a statement of intent to dissolve, without adequate provision for payment of all of the debts and obligations of the corporation. They are also liable for voting or assenting to a purchase by the corporation of its own shares in violation of the statute. Section 48.

A director is not liable for any of the acts mentioned in the preceding paragraph if in assenting to them he acted in good faith and in reliance upon information, reports, or financial statements of the corporation represented to him to be correct by an officer or employee of the corporation having charge of its books of account, or public accountant, or by a board committee. Nor is he liable if in good faith he considered the assets of the corporation to be of their book value in determining the amount available for a dividend or other distribution to shareholders. Section 35.

If a director is present at a meeting of the board at which action on any corporate matter is taken, he is presumed to have assented to such action unless in addition to dissenting therefrom he (1) has his dissent entered of record in the minutes of the meeting, or (2) files his written dissent to such action with the person acting as secretary before the meeting adjourns, or (3) forwards his written dissent by registered mail to the secretary of the corporation immediately after the adjournment of the meeting. Section 35.

Directors and officers also must act within their respective authority. Some jurisdictions hold officers and directors absolutely liable if they act beyond their authority, while others hold them liable only if they intentionally or negligently exceed their authority.

Duty of Diligence

In the discharge of their duties, directors and officers must exercise ordinary care and prudence. Some states interpret this standard as providing that directors and officers must exercise "the same degree of care and prudence that men promoted by self-interest generally exercise in their own affairs." Hun v. Cary, 82 N.Y. 65. Most states, however, hold that the test requires that "[a] director shall perform his duties as a director . . . with such care as an ordinarily prudent person in a like position would use under similar circumstances." Section 35.

Directors and officers are permitted to entrust important work to others, and, if employees have been selected with care, are not personally liable for the negligent acts or willful wrongs of such employees. A reasonable amount of supervision is required, and an officer or director will be held liable for the losses resulting from an employee's carelessness, theft, or peculations if he knew or ought to have known or suspected that such losses were being incurred.

So long as the directors and officers act in good faith and with due care, the courts will not substitute their judgment for the board's or officer's judgment—the so-called "business judgment rule." Directors and officers will, nonetheless, be held liable for bad faith or negligent conduct. For instance, a director of a bank, who in the five and a half years that he had been on the board had never attended a board meeting or made any examination of the books and records, was held liable for the losses resulting from the unsupervised acts of the president and cashier who had made various improper loans and had permitted large overdrafts. McCormick v. King, 241 F. 737, affirmed sub nom. Bowerman v. Hamner, 250 U.S. 504, 63 L.Ed. 1113.

Fiduciary Duties

The officers and directors of a corporation owe a fiduciary duty to the corporation and to its shareholders. The essence of a fiduciary duty is the subordination of self-interest to the interest of the person or persons to whom the duty is owing. It requires undeviating loyalty on the part of officers and directors to the corporation which they both serve and control. It prohibits an officer or director from making secret profits for himself or for others by the use of inside information which is available to him by reason of his position. It prohibits such a person from accepting bribes or secret favors even though it may not be demonstrated that the judgment of the officer or director was thereby influenced in the slightest degree. As Bowen, C. J., stated in Archer's Case, 1892, 1 Ch. at 341: "The director is really a watch dog, and the watch dog has no right, without the knowledge of his master, to take a sop from a possible wolf."

An officer or director is required to make full disclosure to the corporation of any financial interest which he may have in any contract or transaction to which the corporation is a party. Section 41. This is a corollary to the rule which forbids fiduciaries from making secret profits. His business conduct must be insulated from self-interest, and he may not avail himself of opportunities to advance his personal interest at the expense of the corporation. He may not represent conflicting interests, and his duty is one of strict allegiance to the corporation.

The remedy for breach of fiduciary duty is a suit in equity by the corporation, or more often a derivative suit instituted by a shareholder, to require the fiduciary to pay to the corporation the secret profits which he has obtained through breach of his fiduciary duty. It need not be shown that the corporation could otherwise have made the profits which the fiduciary has realized. The object of the rule is to discourage breaches of duty by a fiduciary and this is achieved by taking from the fiduciary all of the profits he has made. The enforcement of the rule may result in a windfall to the corporation but this is incidental to the prophylactic effect of the rule.

Conflict of Interests. A contract between an officer or a director and the corporation is not void, but voidable. A rule which would preclude such a contract would be unreasonable because it would prevent directors from entering into contracts that are beneficial to the corporation. Therefore, if such a contract is honest and fair, it will be upheld.

In the case of contracts between corporations having an interlocking directorate, or having one or more persons who are members of both boards of directors, the courts subject the contracts to the severest scrutiny and are quick to set them aside unless the transaction is shown to have been entirely fair and entered into in good faith. The Supreme Court of the United States has aptly stated the rule in Geddes v. Anaconda Copper Mining Co., 254 U.S. 590, 599, 41 S.Ct. 209, 212, 65 L.Ed. 425:

The relation of directors to corporations is of such a fiduciary nature that transactions between boards having common members are regarded as jealously by the law as are personal dealings between a director and his corporation; and where the fairness of such transactions is challenged, the burden is upon those who would maintain them to show their entire fairness; and where a sale is involved the full adequacy of the consideration. Especially is this true where a common director is dominating in influence or in character. This court has been consistently emphatic in the application of this rule, which, it has declared, is founded in sound-

est morality, and we now add, in the soundest business policy.

The Model act addresses both of these related problems as follows:

No contract or other transaction between a corporation and one or more of its directors or any other corporation, firm, association or entity in which one or more of its directors are directors or officers or are financially interested, shall be either void or voidable because of such relationship or interest or because such director or directors are present at the meeting of the board of directors or a committee thereof which authorizes, approves or ratifies such contract or transaction or because his or their votes are counted for such purpose, if:

(a) the fact of such relationship or interest is disclosed or known to the board of directors or committee which authorizes, approves or ratifies the contract or transaction by a vote or consent sufficient for the purpose without counting the votes or consents of such interested directors; or

(b) the fact of such relationship or interest is disclosed or known to the shareholders entitled to vote and they authorize, approve or ratify such contract or transaction by vote or written consent; or

(c) the contract or transaction is fair and reasonable to the corporation. Section 41.

Corporate Opportunity. An officer or director of a corporation which has extensive properties and substantial operations is frequently confronted with an opportunity to use his position of trust and confidence for self-advantage and thereby reap huge profits for himself. Officers and directors are managing property and operating a business which belongs to others, and they are entrusted with power and responsibility because of their presumed integrity. When they exercise this power for selfish purposes, the courts uniformly hold that they must account for all the profits which they have thereby realized.

Directors and officers may not usurp any corporate opportunity that in all fairness should belong to the corporation. A corporate opportunity is an opportunity in which the corporation has a right, property interest, or expectancy and depends upon the facts and circumstances of each case. For instance, a party proposes a business arrangement to X Corporation through its vice president who personally accepts it without offering it to the corporation. The vice president has usurped a corporate opportunity.

Purchases and Sales of Stock by Insiders. Officers and directors have access to inside advance information not available to the public which may affect the future market value of the shares of the corporation. This position gives them a trading advantage. If the information indicates an unpublicized loss, or a reduction in dividends, or reflects adversely on prospective earnings, the officer or director may sell his shares through a broker in the open market, or even sell the stock short. Conversely, if the information pertains to some potential profit or lucrative contract in the offing or unpublicized substantial earnings, the officer or director may purchase stock in the open market or approach a shareholder and negotiate a purchase of his stock on the basis of current market quotations without disclosure of the factors which will increase the market value of the shares upon becoming public knowledge.

Federal statutes have defined and extended the liability of officers and directors who purchase shares of stock of their corporation without adequate disclosure of all material facts in their possession that may affect the value or potential value of the stock. Under the Securities Exchange Act of 1934, the Securities and Exchange Commission adopted Rule 10b–5 which requires disclosure in such purchases where use has been made of the mails or an instrumentality of interstate commerce, such as the telephone or telegraph. In addition, Section 16(b) of the same statute requires insiders to disgorge to the corporation any profit realized by their short-swing speculation in its stock.

Although state law has not consistently imposed liability upon officers and directors for secret and selfishly profitable use of inside information, the trend is toward holding them liable for breach of fiduciary duty to shareholders from whom they purchase stock without making disclosure to them of facts which give the stock added value potential; and liable to the corporation for profits realized upon a sale of the stock when undisclosed conditions of the corporation make a substantial decline in value practically inevitable.

For example, a shareholders' derivative action was filed in New York against officers and directors of Management Assistance, Inc. (MAI) to compel an accounting to the corporation for profits resulting from their sale of personally held shares of stock of the corporation shortly prior to a severe decline in its market value. MAI was in the business of financing computer installations through sale and lease back arrangements with commercial and industrial users. Lacking the capacity to maintain and repair the computers, MAI engaged IBM, the manufacturer, to service the machines. Due to a sharp increase by IBM of its charges for the service, MAI's expenses in August, 1966, rose and its net earnings declined from $262,000 in July to $66,000 in August, a 75% decrease. This information was not made public until October, 1966, although it was known earlier by the defendants. Prior to public release of the information, the president and chairman of the board of MAI sold 56,500 shares of their MAI stock at the current market price of $28 a share. In October, 1966, after the release, the market price declined to $11 a share. These defendants thus realized $800,000 more for their securities than they could have realized if the inside information had not been available to them. Although MAI sustained no loss nor suffered any damage by this sale of stock, the court in Diamond v. Oreamuno, 24 N.Y.2d 494, 301 N.Y.S.2d 78, 248 N.E.2d 910 (1969) held these defendants liable to the corporation for the profits which they had realized, stating:

Just as a trustee has no right to retain for himself the profits yielded by property placed in his possession but must account to his beneficiaries, a corporate fiduciary, who is entrusted with potentially valuable information, may not appropriate that asset for his own use even though, in so doing, he causes no injury to the corporation. The primary concern, in a case such as this, is not to determine whether the corporation has been damaged but to decide, as between the corporation and the defendants, who has a higher claim to the proceeds derived from the exploitation of the information. In our opinion, there can be no justification for permitting officers and directors, such as the defendants, to retain for themselves profits which, it is alleged, they derived solely from exploiting information gained by virtue of their inside position as corporate officials.

Duty Not to Compete. As fiduciaries, directors and officers owe to the corporation the duty of undivided loyalty which does not permit them to compete with the corporation. Although directors and officers may engage in their own business interests, courts will closely scrutinize any interest that competes with the business of the corporation. For instance, they cannot use corporate personnel, resources, or facilities nor hire away personnel for their own business.

Sale of Control. A special problem arises when controlling shareholders sell their shares in a block because such a sale necessarily and unavoidably conveys control to the purchaser. Such sales are required by the courts to be made with due care. The controlling shareholders must make a reasonable investigation so as not to transfer control to purchasers who plan to wrongfully convert or "loot" the assets of the corporation or to act contrary to the best interests of the corporation.

Additionally, purchasers are willing to pay a premium for a block of shares that also conveys control. Although some courts require this so-called "control premium" to inure to the benefit of the corporation, other courts permit the controlling shareholders to retain the full amount of the control premium. Where recoverable, the courts are divided over whether to permit the corporation to retain the premium or to require the corporation to distribute the premium ratably among the shareholders.

TORT LIABILITY OF OFFICERS AND DIRECTORS

Although officers and directors are insulated from personal liability on contracts of the corporation, unless performance is individually guaranteed or assumed, they are subject to personal liability in tort for their intentional wrongdoing or negligent conduct even while engaged in corporate business activities.

For instance, four persons brought an action against a corporation and its president individually to recover damages resulting from defective construction of the basement in each of their new homes. They had entered into separate contracts with the defendant corporation for construction of a residence similar to a model home exhibited on a tract of land being developed. A year or so after completion and occupancy of the new homes, water commenced to seep into each basement through cracks in the floor and at the junction of the floor and the basement walls. Upon removal of the water, it would soon return and cover the floor to a depth of approximately one inch. This occurred repeatedly. The seepage would cease in the fall but re-appear in March and continue throughout most of the summer.

Plaintiffs' actions against the corporation were based upon breach of contract and implied warranty of habitability; and against the president individually for negligence in that while supervising the construction of the houses he failed (1) to properly test the water table of the homesites prior to commencing construction, and (2) to install lateral drainage lines in compliance with the F.H.A. and V.A. specifications or to use alternative means to prevent leakage into the basements. Judgment was entered by the trial court in favor of each plaintiff in varying amounts against both defendants, and on appeal, affirmed.

McFeeters v. Renollet, and Renollet Homes, Inc., 210 Kan. 158, 500 P.2d 47 (1972). In its opinion the Court stated:

It is true, as defendants suggest, that a director or officer of a corporation does not incur personal liability for its torts merely by reason of his official character. If, however, an officer commits or participates in the commission of a tort, whether or not it is also by or for the corporation, he is liable to third persons injured thereby, and it does not matter what liability attaches to the corporation for the tort.

Cases

Selection and Removal of Officers

STOTT v. STOTT REALTY CO.

(1929) 246 Mich. 267, 224 N.W. 623.

[Bill by Stott, plaintiff, against the Stott Realty Company, defendant, to enjoin the removal of the secretary of the defendant corporation. The president and secretary of the company were directed by the board of directors to sign certain mortgage papers. Julia Stott Orloff, secretary, (and also a director) of the company, refused to sign them. Shortly thereafter she was removed from the office of secretary at a full meeting of the board of directors, and T. P. Danahey was appointed to fill the vacancy. From a decree dismissing the bill plaintiff appeals.]

FELLOWS, J.

* * *

Cases will be found holding that the board of directors may remove fellow directors, but the weight of authority is against the proposition. Mrs. Orloff was continued as director. The office of secretary is a ministerial office, may be filled by one not a director, and its occupant, unless a director, has nothing to say about the management of the company. The selection is made by the board of directors (section 5, chap. 1, pt. 2, Act No. 335, Pub.Acts 1927).

This distinction between a director and a secretary should be kept in mind. The director, being selected by the stockholders, may only be removed by them, while the secretary, being selected by the directors, may be removed by them. The rule is thus stated in 3 Thompson on Corporations (3d Ed.) sec. 1926:

Below the grade of director and such other officers as are elected by the corporation at large, the general rule is that the officers of private corporations hold their offices during the will of the directors, and are hence removable by the directors without assigning any cause for the removal, except so far as their power may be restrained by contract with the particular officer,—just as any other employer may discharge his employee. Speaking generally, it may be said that the power to appoint carries with it the power to remove. * * * Applying the foregoing principles, it has been held that the directors, unless specially authorized, have no power to remove an officer or agent elected or employed by the stockholders; and that the president has no power to remove an officer appointed by the board of directors. The ordinary ministerial and other lesser officers, however, hold their offices during the pleasure of the directors and may be removed at will, without assigned cause. Of this class of officers and agents are the secretary and treasurer of the corporation.

Without quoting from them, the text-writers generally state the same rule although in different language. * * *

The removal of Mrs. Orloff as secretary of the company was validly accomplished, and we have left only the question of the validity of the election of Mr. Danahey as her successor. The board has power under the bylaws of the company to fill vacancies. Mr. Danahey was a member of the board of directors. We need not consider whether he could validly vote for himself, as there was a quorum present without him, and a majority of that quorum voted for his election. With his vote he received a majority of the full board; without it he received the vote of a majority of the quorum which was present after Mrs. Orloff had left the meeting. The rule is recognized by this court and elsewhere that a quorum may act, and a majority vote of such quorum binds the corporation.

Decree affirmed.

Directors' Duty of Diligence

NEESE v. BROWN

(1964) 218 Tenn. 686, 405 S.W.2d 577.

BURNETT, C. J.

The bill, as amended and supplemented, was filed by G. Royal Neese as Trustee in Bankruptcy of the First Trust Company, Bankrupt, against the defendants who were directors of said company, for losses sustained by that company as the result of the failure of the defendants to use due care and diligence in the discharge of their duties as such directors.

* * *

Briefly the acts of negligence charged are: (a) failure to give as much time and attention to the affairs of the corporation as the care of its business interests required; (b) virtual abdication of their control of the corporation by turning the entire management of the corporation over to its president,

Scott N. Brown; (c) failure to inform themselves of the affairs, condition and management of the corporation; (d) ignored their duties as directors and paid no attention to the company's affairs; (e) took no action to direct or control the company, its officers and agents; (f) permitted large, open unsecured loans to be made by the company to affiliated companies which were dominated, controlled and owned by the said Scott N. Brown, and said companies were not financially sound; (g) failed to examine the financial reports on the company prepared by a firm of public accountants, which financial reports the defendants knew existed, and which on examination by them would have disclosed the continuing unsound and disastrous financial practices of the company; (h) reliance on selected portions of said reports read to them by the said Brown, and failed to insist on being furnished with said reports, and failure to examine the same, which reports and an examination thereof would have disclosed the illegal diversions of the company's funds and waste of its assets; (i) failure to exercise proper oversight and supervision of the officers and directors of the company.

The bill likewise averred that the negligence, malfeasance, misfeasance and nonfeasance on the part of these directors was the direct and proximate cause of large losses suffered by the company.

The bill also alleges that the affiliated companies to whom the loans were made are insolvent, that two of them are in bankruptcy, that the Trustee has obtained judgments against two of them but the judgments are uncollectible, and that the loans cannot be collected.

* * *

It is generally held that the liability of the directors and other officers of a corporation is not limited to wilful breaches of trust or excessive power but also extends to negligence. What constitutes such negligence? In Fletcher's Private Corporations,

Vol. 3, 1947 Rev.Ed., § 1029, page 541, the author after discussing the question at some length says this:

"The fact remains, however, that, except as already stated, the courts are practically unanimous in their general statements that directors and other corporate officers must be diligent and careful in performing their duties; that the directors must be something more than mere figureheads, etc. And in recent years, courts have in general held directors of corporations to a higher standard of duty than was formerly the rule. A stricter rule has become necessary by a growing inclination on the part of officers and directors of large corporations to consider their personal interests and profits to the exclusion of the rights and interests of a large and uninformed body of stockholders. Whether or not a court will act must be determined by the facts developed on the trial, with the complaining stockholders carrying the burden of proof. Accordingly, it is held that liability may result from mere inaction on their part, where such inaction is the proximate cause of a loss. Likewise, a director is chargeable with knowledge actually possessed or which he might have possessed had he diligently discharged his functions. Ignorance of performance of illegal acts which is the result of inattention does not exculpate."

* * *

After very carefully reading and rereading this bill we think that it does state a cause of action against the directors for nonfeasance and mismanagement of the corporate affairs, including the standard of care and duties imposed upon the directors as hereinabove set forth.

* * *

Most courts hold that a director, or other officer, of a corporation, although not responsible for errors of judgment is a fiduciary charged with the duty of caring for property of the corporation and managing its affairs honestly and in good faith. [Citation.] From our very thorough study of the matter we have concluded that there is no appreciable conflict of opinion among the courts as to the liability of directors as hereinabove set forth.

* * *

We do not think that a Trustee in Bankruptcy must await the outcome of all these involved transactions to see whether or not this money can be collected when it is alleged in this bill that these judgments are uncollectible. It seems to us that such suits are not premature. * * *

It seems to us that the Chancellor was clearly correct in overruling the pleas in bar filed herein. This appellee, complainant below, as Trustee in Bankruptcy of this corporation should not be barred or estopped to sue these allegedly defaulting directors because they have, under the allegations of this bill, been given a blanket ratification by the stockholders. The substance of these pleas is that the action of the stockholders at the annual meetings from 1959 to 1962, inclusive, approved the acts of these directors, etc., in the furtherance of the business of the corporation for the preceding year. Certainly such does not estop this Trustee from maintaining this suit, because the very allegations of negligence and wrongdoing on the part of these directors in itself is the allegation that these wrongs, through Scott Brown, were done in approving all acts at these meetings. In other words if the directors were going to sit by and allow one man to run this corporation without doing their duty by it, it is a natural and easy thing for the stockholders who had confidence in the directors to ratify their acts, the stockholders not knowing what was going on inside this corporation.

* * *

Our conclusion is, under the action as it now reaches us, that the directors of a corporation have to see to it that the corporation had the benefit of their best judgment and act solely and always with reasonable care in good faith to promote its welfare.

The decree of the Chancellor in all things is affirmed. * * * The case will be remanded to the Chancery Court of Hamilton County for further proceedings consistent with this opinion.

Officers' Fiduciary Duty

WILSHIRE OIL CO. OF TEXAS v. RIFFE

(1969, C.A.10) 406 F.2d 1061.

SETH, C. J.

This is an appeal by the plaintiff-appellant from a portion of the judgment of the trial court in this action which was commenced by the plaintiff corporation against one of its former corporate officers. The suit was to recover profits made by the corporate officer by participating in competitive enterprises, in receiving personally commissions for corporate construction work, and to recover the compensation paid to the officer by the corporation during the period he was interested in a competitive corporation.

This is the second appeal. This court on the first appeal reversed and remanded the case, holding that the defendant had breached his duty to the corporation and had engaged in activities contrary to the terms of his contract of employment (Wilshire Oil Co. of Texas v. Riffe, 381 F.2d 646). On remand the trial court entered judgment on the claims for recovery of the profits made through participating in a competitive corporation, but denied the corporation recovery of the compensation it paid to the defendant for this period.

The nature and extent of the fiduciary duties owed by a corporate officer to the corporation he serves have been long established. This matter was considered at some length in the previous opinion in this case as it related to these facts and need not

be repeated here. As stated in the first opinion the acts of the appellee also constituted a breach of his contract of employment. On the prior appeal all the basic and determinative issues were thus decided.

When a corporate officer engages in activities which constitute a breach of his duty of loyalty or if it is a wilful breach of his contract of employment, he is not entitled to compensation for services during such a period of time although part of his services may have been properly performed. In the Restatement (Second), Agency § 469 the above doctrine is set forth, and this is followed by the comment which states in part:

"An agent, who, without the acquiescence of his principal, acts for his own benefit or for the benefit of another in antagonism to or in competition with the principal in a transaction is not entitled to compensation which otherwise be due him."

The comment continues and states that the agent is not entitled to compensation although the acts may not actually harm his principal and even if he thinks his actions will benefit the principal or he is otherwise "justified" in "so acting." [Citations.]

This rule is applicable to the case before us, and it is not necessary to again describe the several breaches of duty involved which were clearly established in the record. The record shows, as to one of the principal events, that the failure commenced on or before May 31, 1962, and continued to the end of the year when the officer's employment terminated. It was then also that the particular division which he was responsible for was sold by the corporation. The record thus sets out the period of this violation, and this is sufficient to apply the above doctrine. Thus we hold that the appellee was not entitled to compensation of any kind from May 31, 1962, to December 31, 1962.

The appellee argues that the corporate division he was responsible for made money during the period in question, and that the division was itself sold at a profit to appellant corporation. However, under the authorities or on any other basis, this is no answer to the established violation of duty. The fact that the division may have made money does not prove that no breach took place nor does it excuse one any more than a failure to make money demonstrates a breach of duty. The same may be said about whether the officer considered that he was acting properly or in good faith.

The case is reversed and remanded to the trial court with directions to enter judgment for appellant against appellee in an amount equal to seven-twelfths of all compensation (both salary and bonus) paid to appellee for services during the calendar year 1962. * * *

Reversed and remanded.

Fiduciary Duty of
Controlling Shareholder

PEPPER v. LITTON

(1939) 308 U.S. 295, 60 S.Ct. 238, 84 L.Ed. 281.

[In a bankruptcy proceeding the District Court disallowed either as a secured or as an unsecured claim, a judgment by confession obtained by the dominant shareholder of the bankrupt corporation on alleged salary claims. The Court of Appeals for the Fourth Circuit reversed the District Court. Certiorari was granted.]

DOUGLAS, J.
* * *

The mere fact that an officer, director, or stockholder has a claim against his bankrupt corporation or that he has reduced that claim to judgment does not mean the bankruptcy court must accord it pari passu treatment with the claims of other creditors. Its disallowance or subordination may be necessitated by certain cardinal principles of equity jurisprudence. A director is a fiduciary. [Citation.] So is a dominant or controlling stockholder or group of stock-

holders. [Citation.] Their powers are powers in trust. [Citation.] Their dealings with the corporation are subjected to rigorous scrutiny and where any of their contracts or engagements with the corporation is challenged the burden is on the director or stockholder not only to prove the good faith of the transaction but also to show its inherent fairness from the viewpoint of the corporation and those interested therein. [Citation.] The essence of the test is whether or not under all the circumstances the transaction carries the earmarks of an arm's length bargain. If it does not, equity will set it aside. While normally that fiduciary obligation is enforceable directly by the corporation, or through a stockholder's derivative action, it is, in the event of bankruptcy of the corporation, enforceable by the trustee. For that standard of fiduciary obligation is designed for the protection of the entire community of interests in the corporation-creditors as well as stockholders.

As we have said, the bankruptcy court in passing on allowance of claims sits as a court of equity. Hence, these rules governing the fiduciary responsibilities of directors and stockholders come into play on allowance of their claims in bankruptcy. In the exercise of its equitable jurisdiction the bankruptcy court has the power to sift the circumstances surrounding any claim to see that injustice or unfairness is not done in administration of the bankrupt estate. And its duty so to do is especially clear when the claim seeking allowance accrues to the benefit of an officer, director, or stockholder. That is clearly the power and duty of the bankruptcy courts under the reorganization sections. In Taylor v. Standard Gas & Electric Co., 306 U.S. 307, 59 S.Ct. 543, 83 L.Ed. 669, this Court held that the claim of Standard against its subsidiary (admittedly a claim due and owing) should be allowed to participate in the reorganization plan of the subsidiary only in subordination to the preferred stock of the subsidiary. This was based on the equities of the case—the history of spoliation, mismanagement, and faithless stewardship of the affairs of the subsidiary by Standard to the detriment of the public investors. Similar results have properly been reached in ordinary bankruptcy proceedings. Thus, salary claims of officers, directors, and stockholders in bankruptcy of "one-man" or family corporations have been disallowed or subordinated where the courts have been satisfied that allowance of the claims would not be fair or equitable to other creditors. And that result may be reached even though the salary claim has been reduced to judgment. It is reached where the claim is void or voidable because the vote of the interested director or stockholder helped bring it into being or where the history of the corporation shows dominancy and exploitation on the part of the claimant. It is also reached where on the facts the bankrupt has been used merely as a corporate pocket of the dominant stockholder, who, with disregard of the substance or form of corporate management, has treated its affairs as his own. And so-called loans or advances by the dominant or controlling stockholder will be subordinated to claims of other creditors and thus treated in effect as capital contributions by the stockholder not only in the foregoing types of situations but also where paid-in capital is purely nominal, the capital necessary for the scope and magnitude of the operations of the company being furnished by the stockholder as a loan. * * *

On such a test the action of the District Court in disallowing or subordinating Litton's claim was clearly correct. Litton allowed his salary claims to lie dormant for year and sought to enforce them only when his debtor corporation was in financial difficulty. Then he used them so that the rights of another creditor were impaired. Litton as an insider utilized his strategic position for his own preferment to the damage of Pepper. Litton as the dominant influence over Dixie Splint Coal Company used his power not to deal fairly with the creditors of that company but to manipulate its affairs in such a manner that when one of its creditors came to collect her just debt the bulk of the assets had disappeared into another Litton company. Litton, though a fiduciary, was enabled by astute legal manoeuvring to acquire most of the assets of the bankrupt not for cash or other consideration of value to creditors but for bookkeeping entries representing at best merely Litton's appraisal of the worth of Litton's services over the years.

This alone would be a sufficient basis for the exercise by the District Court of its equitable powers in disallowing the Litton claim. But when there is added the existence of a "planned and fraudulent scheme," as found by the District Court, the necessity of equitable relief against that fraud becomes insistent. No matter how technically legal each step in that scheme may have been, once its basic nature was uncovered it was the duty of the bankruptcy court in the exercise of its equity jurisdiction to undo it. Otherwise, the fiduciary duties of dominant or management stockholders would go for naught; exploitation would become a substitute for justice; and equity would be perverted as an instrument for approving what it was designed to thwart. * * *

[Judgment of the Court of Appeals reversed and that of the District Court affirmed.]

Problems

1. Brown was the president and director of a corporation engaged in owning and operating a chain of motels. Brown was advised, upon what seemed to be good authority, that a super-high-

way was to be constructed through the town of X, which would afford a most desirable location for a motel. Brown represented these facts to the board of directors of the motel corporation and recommended that the corporation build a motel in the town of X at the location described. The board of directors agreed, and the new motel was constructed. It developed that the super-highway plans were changed after the motel was constructed. The highway was never built. Later, a packing house was built on property adjoining the motel and as a result the corporation sustained a considerable loss.

The shareholders brought an appropriate action against Brown charging that his representation had caused a substantial loss to the corporation. Decision?

2. A, B, C, D, and E constituted the board of directors of the X Corporation. While D and E were out of town, A, B, and C held a special meeting of the board. Just as the meeting began, C became ill. He then gave a proxy to A and went home. A resolution was then adopted directing and authorizing the purchase by the X Corporation of an adjoining piece of land, owned by S, as a site for an additional factory building. A and B voted for the resolution, and A, as C's proxy, cast C's vote in favor of the resolution. A contract was then made by the X Corporation with S for the purchase of the land. Upon the return of D and E, another special meeting of the board was held, with all five directors present. A resolution was then unanimously adopted to cancel the contract with S. S was so notified, and now sues X Corporation for damages for breach of contract. Decision?

3. Bernard Koch was president of United Corporation, a close corporation. Koch, James Trent, and Henry Phillips comprised the three-man board of directors. At a meeting of the board of directors, Trent was elected president, replacing Koch. At the same meeting, Trent attempted to have the salary of the president increased. He was unable to obtain board approval of the increase because, while Phillips voted for the increase, Koch voted against it. Trent was disqualified from voting.

As a result the directors, by a two-to-one vote, amended the by-laws to provide for the appointment of an executive committee, composed of three reputable business men, to pass upon

and fix all matters of salary for employees of the corporation. Subsequently, the executive committee consisting of John Jones, James Black and William Johnson, increased the salary of the president.

Koch brought an appropriate action against the corporation, Trent and Phillips to enjoin them from paying the increased compensation to the president above that fixed by the board of directors.

What decision?

4. Zenith Steel Company operates a prosperous business. Its president, Roe, who is also a director, in January 1982 was voted a $100,000 bonus by the board of directors for his valuable services to the company in 1981. Roe receives an annual salary of $25,000 from the company. In January 1982 the board of directors also voted to spend $20,000,000 of the surplus funds of the company to purchase a majority of the stock of two other companies—the Green Insurance Company and the Blue Trust Company. The Green Insurance Company is a thriving business whose stock is an excellent investment at the price at which it will be sold to Zenith Steel Company. The principal reasons for the purchase of the Green Insurance stock by the Steel Company are as an investment of surplus funds and as a diversification of its business. The Blue Trust Company owns a controlling interest in Zenith Steel Company. The main purpose for the purchase of the Blue Trust Company stock by Zenith Steel Company is to enable the present management and directors of Zenith Steel Company to perpetuate their management of the company.

Black, a minority shareholder in Zenith Steel Company, brings an appropriate action to enjoin any payment by the company of the $100,000 bonus to its president, Roe, and to enjoin the purchase by Zenith Steel Company of the stock of either the Green Insurance Company or of the Blue Trust Company.

You may assume that the articles of incorporation and the applicable statute authorize the purchase of shares in another corporation, and that Black has standing to bring the action. Decision?

5. (a) Smith, a director of the Sample Corporation, sells a piece of vacant land to the Sample Corporation for $25,000, which land cost him

$10,000.

(b) Jones, a shareholder of the Sample Corporation, sells a used truck to the Sample Corporation for $2,800, which truck was worth $2,400.

Raphael, a minority shareholder of the Sample Corporation, claims that the above sales are void and should be annulled. Is he correct?

6. The X Corporation manufactures machine tools. Its two principal competitors are Y Corporation and Z Corporation. The five directors of X Corporation are Black, White, Brown, Green, and Crimson. At a duly called meeting of the board of directors of X Corporation in January, all five directors were present. They transacted the following business and voted as indicated.

A contract for the purchase of $1,000,000 worth of steel from the D Company of which Black, White, and Brown are directors, was discussed and approved by a unanimous vote. There was a lengthy discussion about entering into negotiations for the purchase of Q Corporation, which allegedly was about to be sold for around $15,000,000. By a 3 to 2 vote it was decided not to open such negotiations.

Three months later Green purchased Q Corporation for $15,000,000. Shortly thereafter, a new board of directors for X Corporation took office. X Corporation brings actions to rescind its contracts with D Company and to compel Green to assign to X Corporation his contract for the purchase of Q Corporation.

Decisions as to each action?

7. T, a director and officer of Deep Hole Oil Company, approached R for the purpose of buying 200 shares of Deep Hole Company stock owned by R. During the period of negotiations, T concealed his identity and did not disclose the fact that earlier in the day he had received a report of two rich oil "strikes" on the oil company's property. R sold his 200 shares to T for $10 per share. Taking into consideration the new strikes, the fair value of the stock was approximately $20 per share. R sues T to recover damages. Decision?

RIGHTS, POWERS, AND REMEDIES OF SHAREHOLDERS AND CREDITORS

Many corporations have issued and have outstanding different classes of stock, all of which are equity securities. In addition to common stock, a corporation may have issued one or more classes of preferred stock. All classes of stock are subordinate to the rights of creditors of the corporation to participate in its assets; and the rights of holders of the common stock to participate in such assets is junior to any and all classes of preferred stock.

RIGHTS, POWERS, AND REMEDIES OF SHAREHOLDERS

Shareholders have definite established rights. Among them are (1) the right to have their ownership of shares evidenced by a tangible stock certificate, (2) the right to vote, (3) the right to inspect the books and records of the corporation, (4) the right to receive dividends, (5) the right to the appointment of a receiver, and (6) the right to participate in the assets of the corporation upon dissolution.

Right to Stock Certificate

A share of stock is intangible personal property, and exists independently of a stock certificate. The name and address of the owner is usually recorded on the books of the corporation or of a transfer agent employed by the corporation, but these records are not determinative of ownership. The loss or destruction of a certificate of stock does not deprive the owner of his title to the shares of stock represented by the certificate, although it does prevent the owner from making an effective transfer or pledge of the shares. In order to sell or otherwise dispose of his shares of stock, a shareholder must have possession of the certificate and must indorse and deliver it to the transferee. It is uniformly held that a shareholder has the right to demand a certificate from the corporation representing the shares of which he is the owner. A shareholder has the right to have his name and address entered on the records of the corporation so that he may receive dividends, notices of meetings, and the reports of operations and financial condition which the corporation distributes to its shareholders.

So long as the corporate records reflect his ownership of stock, a shareholder does not need a certificate for the purpose of receiving notices or dividends or in order to vote or execute a proxy. He has a right to a certificate in order to make a transfer of his shares. If his certificate of stock has been accidentally lost or destroyed, the shareholder is entitled to have a new certificate issued to him by the corporation upon furnishing the corporation an indemnity bond and otherwise complying with Section 8–405 of the U.C.C., to protect it against loss in the event the certificate should reappear at some future date in the hands of a bona fide purchaser for value.

It is possible for a shareholder to lose the right to a certificate where the interest is a fraction of a share, as occurred in Teschner v. Chicago Title and Trust Company, 59 Ill.2d 452, 322 N.E.2d 54 (1974). The corporation had outstanding 223.321 common shares of a par value of $63\frac{2}{3}$ each of which the plaintiff owned 63 shares and Lincoln National Corporation owned more than 99 per cent of the remaining shares. The corporation duly amended its charter to authorize a reverse split and reclassification of the 223.321 common shares into 3,722 shares each having a par value of $4,000. Plaintiff's 63 shares were thus convertible into $^{63}/_{4000}$th of a share of a par value of $4,000. Section 52 of the Illinois Act provides that a corporation may amend its charter "To exchange, classify, reclassify, or cancel all or any part of its shares, whether issued or unissued." Section 22 provides that a corporation may but is not obliged to issue a certificate for a fractional share, and may in lieu thereof pay cash equal to the value of such fractional share. In an action to compel the corporation to issue to the plaintiff a stock certificate, the court held that the plaintiff was not entitled to a certificate representing her interest in

the corporation, but only its cash equivalent.

Voting Rights of Shareholders

The shareholder's right to vote is fundamental to the concept of the corporation and its pyramidal management structure. In most States today a shareholder is entitled to one vote for each share of stock that he owns. Statutes generally permit the issuance of one or more classes of non-voting stock. Section 33. The denial of a right to vote is occasionally found in an issue of preferred stock, frequently coupled with a provision that upon the happening of a certain condition, such as the omission of dividends or the failure to maintain a specified working capital ratio, the holders of the preferred stock shall be permitted to vote.

Formalities. Shareholders can exercise their voting rights at the annual and special shareholder meetings. Annual meetings are required and must be held at a time fixed by the by-laws. If the annual shareholder meeting is not held within a thirteen-month period, any shareholder may petition and obtain a court order requiring such meeting to be held. Section 28. Special meetings may be called by the board of directors, holders of at least 10% of the shares, or such other persons authorized in the articles of incorporation. Section 28. Written notice stating the place, day, and hour of the meeting and, in the case of a special meeting the purposes for which it is called, must be given in advance of the meeting. Notice, however, may be waived in writing by any shareholder entitled to notice. Section 144.

In order to effectuate corporate business, a quorum of shares must be represented at the meeting, either in person or by proxy. Unless otherwise provided in the articles of incorporation, a majority of shares entitled to vote constitutes a quorum but under no circumstances may a quorum consist of less than one-third of the shares entitled to vote. Section 32. Unissued shares and treasury stock may not be voted nor counted in determining whether a quorum exists.

Most states require shareholder actions to be approved by a majority of shares represented at the meeting and entitled to vote. Nonetheless, many states permit the articles of incorporation to increase the percentage of shares required to take any action subject to shareholder approval. Section 143.

A number of states permit shareholders to conduct business without a meeting if all the shareholders consent in writing to the action taken. Section 145. A few states, including Delaware, have further relaxed the formalities of shareholder action by permitting shareholders to act without a meeting with written consent of only the number of shares required to act on the matter.

Cumulative Voting. Directors are elected each year at the annual meeting of the shareholders. Normally, each shareholder has one vote for each share owned. However, in certain States by statute, shareholders have the right of cumulative voting for the election of directors of the corporation. In most of these states cumulative voting is permissive and not mandatory. Section 33.

Cumulative voting entitles each shareholder, who has one vote for each share owned, to cumulate his votes and give one candidate as many votes as the number of directors to be elected multiplied by the number of shares owned, or to distribute such number of votes among as many candidates as he wishes. Cumulative voting permits a minority shareholder, or group of minority shareholders acting together, to obtain minority representation on the board if they own a certain minimum number of shares. Without cumulative voting, the

holder or holders of 51% of the voting shares can elect all of the members of the board.

The formula for determining how many shares a minority shareholder with cumulative voting rights must own or have proxies to vote, in order to secure representation on the board is as follows:

$$X = \frac{ac}{b + 1} + 1$$

a = number of shares voting.

b = number of directors to be elected.

c = number of directors desired to be elected.

X = number of shares necessary to elect the number of directors desired to be elected.

For example, X corporation has two shareholders, A with 64 shares and B with 36 shares. The board of directors of X corporation consists of three directors. Under "straight" or non-cumulative voting, A could cast 64 votes for each of his three candidates and B could cast 36 votes for this three candidates. As a result, all three of A's candidates would be elected. On the other hand, if cumulative voting were in force, B could elect one director:

$$X = \frac{ac}{b + 1} + 1$$

$$X = \frac{100\ (1)}{3 + 1} + 1 = 26 \text{ shares}$$

Since B has the right to vote more than 26 shares, he would be able to elect one director. A, of course, with his 64 shares, could elect the remaining two directors:

$$X = \frac{ac}{b + 1} + 1$$

$$X = \frac{100\ (2)}{3 + 1} + 1 = 51 \text{ shares}$$

To elect all three directors A would need 76 shares $(\frac{100\,(3)}{3+1} + 1)$.

Regarding the removal of a director from the Board, shareholders may remove, with or without cause, any director or the entire board of directors in a meeting called for that purpose. However, in the case of a corporation having cumulative voting, removal of a director requires sufficient votes to prevent his election. Section 39.

Approval of Extraordinary Matters. The board of directors manages the ordinary business affairs of the corporation. Extraordinary matters require shareholder approval and include such matters as amendments of the articles of incorporation, sale or lease of assets not in the regular course of business, mergers, consolidations and dissolution.

Proxies. A shareholder may vote either in person or by written proxy. A proxy is simply the authorization by a shareholder to an agent to vote his shares at a particular meeting or on a particular question. Generally, proxies must be in writing to be effective. The duration of proxies are typically limited by statute to no more than eleven months, unless the proxy specifically provides otherwise. Section 33. Since a proxy is the appointment of an agent, it is revocable, as all agencies are, unless coupled with an interest, such as when shares are held as collateral.

Voting Trusts. All or part of the stock of a corporation may, by written agreement among the shareholders, be issued to a trustee or trustees who thereupon hold legal title to the stock and have all of the voting rights possessed by the stock. The voting trustee or trustees issue to the former shareholders certificates of beneficial interest which represent units, comparable to shares, of the equitable and beneficial ownership of the stock. A voting trust differs from a proxy in that a proxy is revocable at any time and ordinarily expires at the end of eleven months, while a voting trust is terminable as provided by the statute or in the voting trust agreement. Under the Model Act, its term may not exceed ten years. Section 34. In addition, the holder of the proxy does not have title to the stock nor possession of the stock certificates, as do voting trustees.

Voting trusts are devices designed to concentrate corporate control in one or more persons and have been used in both publicly held and close corporations. Voting trusts have been sometimes used for wrongful purposes, and their validity has been successfully attacked where the object of the trust was to combine voting strength in a few persons who thereby obtained control of the management which they utilized for their individual benefit. Voting trusts were once considered illegal regardless of their purpose, but the general view today at common law is that if the purpose is not unlawful, the voting trust will be sustained. In most States, voting trusts are permitted by statute.

Shareholder Agreements. In most jurisdictions, shareholders may agree in advance to vote in a specified manner for the election or removal of directors, or on any other matter subject to shareholder approval. Section 34. Shareholder agreements are used frequently in close corporations, especially in conjunction with restrictions on the transfer of shares. These restrictions typically require that the shares be offered to the corporation or other shareholders before offering them to an outsider, thereby enabling the shareholders in closely held corporations to achieve the equivalent of *delectus personae* in partnerships. Such control over choice of associates is critical in close corporations in which shareholders also serve as officers and directors.

Right to Examine
Books and Records

The right of a shareholder to inspect for a proper purpose the books and records of the corporation, in person or by his attorney, agent, or accountant, and to make transcriptions therefrom, is provided by statute in practically every State. By examination of the books and records, a shareholder may determine the financial condition of the corporation, the profits realized or loss sustained, the propriety of certain items reflected in the profit and loss statement or balance sheet, the amount of executive salaries and administrative overhead and the possible existence of causes of action based upon fraud or breach of fiduciary duty by officers or directors. The shareholder may also learn the names and addresses of other shareholders with whom he may wish to communicate in their common interest, and whether officers or directors have made purchases or sales of stock of the corporation. The right of inspection is therefore valuable and may be enforced by an action of mandamus. However, it is subject to abuse and will be denied a shareholder who is seeking information for an improper purpose, such as use by a competing company, or to embarrass or cause loss to the corporation or its shareholders, or to obtain a list of the shareholders in order to offer it for sale.

The Model Act provides that any officer or agent of a corporation who refuses to allow a shareholder, or his agent or attorney, to examine and make extracts from its books and records of account, corporate minutes, and record of shareholders for a proper purpose shall be liable to such shareholder in a penalty of ten per cent of the value of the shares owned by him, in addition to any other damages or remedy afforded him by law. Section 52.

Right to Dividends

A shareholder may not maintain an action at law against the corporation to recover a dividend until and unless the dividend has been formally declared by resolution of the board of directors. A proper dividend so declared becomes a debt of the corporation, and enforceable at law as any other debt.

Right to the
Appointment of a Receiver

A shareholder is not required to sit idly by and suffer a board of directors dominated by the majority to misapply or waste the assets of the corporation, or to permit a deadlock in the management to cause or threaten irreparable injury to the corporation. He may apply to a court of equity, which has full power to appoint a receiver and to liquidate the assets and business of the corporation in an action instituted by any shareholder when it appears (1) that the directors are deadlocked in the management of the corporate affairs and the shareholders are unable to break the deadlock, and that irreparable injury to the corporation is being suffered or is threatened by reason thereof; (2) that the acts of the directors or those in control of the corporation are illegal, oppressive, or fraudulent; or (3) that the corporate assets are being misapplied or wasted. Section 97.

Rights upon Dissolution

When a corporation is dissolved, its assets liquidated, and claims of all of its creditors have been satisfied, the remaining assets are distributable pro rata among the shareholders according to the priority of their contractual rights. Preferred stock usually has priority over common to the extent of the par value of the stock, and in some instances, par value plus a premium. In the event that preferred stock does not expressly provide for a preference of any kind upon dissolution and liquidation, the holders of the preferred share ratably with the common in the assets remaining after all creditors have been paid. If the dissolved corporation has assets which are not sold, levied upon by creditors, or distributed to shareholders, the title to these assets passes to the shareholders as tenants in common.

RIGHTS, POWERS, AND REMEDIES OF CREDITORS

Unsecured Creditors

The creditors of a corporation include persons who have made a loan to a corporation which has not been repaid; who have sold to it property or rendered services creating debts that are unpaid; who have unpaid salary or wages due; who have a right of action or obtained a judgment which is unpaid; or who are the holders of notes, bonds, or other evidences of indebtedness of the corporation. The rights of creditors of a corporation are enforceable in the same manner as the rights of creditors of an individual. A court judgment may be entered against a corporation for breach of contract or commission of a tort. The creditor may cause a writ of execution to be issued on the judgment, served upon the corporation, and a levy or attachment made upon its property which is sold at a judicial sale and the net proceeds paid to the creditor.

These are the ordinary remedies of an unsecured creditor. In an action against a corporation to recover a debt, the corporation may not plead usury as a defense. A corporation also does not have the advantage or benefit of any homestead or exemption laws.

Secured Creditors

The financing of a corporation is sometimes partially accomplished by conditional sales contracts, equipment trust certificates, or other security agreements with respect to personal property, and by real estate mortgages, or trust indentures in the nature of a mortgage, with respect to real estate. The rights and remedies of a secured cred-itor are usually set forth at length in the document which creates his security.

A secured creditor is one whose claim against the corporation is enforceable not only against the general assets of the corporation but is also a lien upon certain specific property. The holder of a first mortgage bond not only has the contractual promise of the corporation to pay the face amount of the bond but also, as security for the performance of this promise, has a lien upon certain real estate which is prior to the claim of any other class of creditor except a claim for taxes. Enforcement of the rights of bondholders by foreclosure is in the hands of the trustee, and a common provision in trust indentures is one which denies to an individual bondholder the right to institute foreclosure proceedings. The duties of an indenture trustee are greater upon default by the corporate obligor than prior to a default.

Likewise, a creditor who holds a security interest in property under a security agreement enjoys the right to have his claim first satisfied out of the specific property to which his security interest attaches. The secured creditor in order to have priority over claims of third persons must perfect his security interest as provided in Article 9 of the U.C.C. Realization upon the security is usually accomplished by repossession and resale of the property.

Creditors' Rights against Shareholders

Creditors' Rights with Respect to Unpaid Stock Subscriptions. An unpaid balance due upon a stock subscription is an asset of the corporation. In the event of bankruptcy of the corporation, this asset passes to the trustee in bankruptcy, who may properly bring an action at law against the subscriber and obtain judgment for the balance due. If there is no bankruptcy, a creditor of the corporation who has exhausted his legal remedies by reducing his claim to judgment and having an execution issued thereon and returned not satisfied, may proceed by a bill in equity on behalf of himself and other creditors against those shareholders who owe a balance upon their respective stock subscriptions. A transferee of stock is also liable for call or assessments on the stock until the par value of the stock has been fully paid, unless the certificate transferred to him recites that it is fully paid and non-assessable. The liability of the shareholders is several, not joint, and it is not necessary that all shareholders who are indebted upon their stock subscriptions be made defendants in the creditor's bill. The corporation, however, is a necessary party to the suit.

If a shareholder who owes a balance due upon his subscription is also a creditor of the corporation, he may not, when the corporation is insolvent, set off the amount due to him from the corporation against his liability upon the unpaid stock subscription. He is required to pay the full amount due upon his stock subscription, and is permitted as a creditor to share ratably with other creditors in the assets of the corporation. The reason for this rule is that the capital stock of a corporation is the basis of credit extended to the corporation. It would also amount to an unlawful preference to allow the claim of the shareholder as a creditor to be paid in full by permitting it to be set off against his shareholder's liability. Likewise, a corporation may not defeat the claims of creditors by releasing subscribers from their obligations upon stock subscriptions.

Creditors' Rights with Respect to Watered Stock. A corporation is said to have issued bonus or watered stock when it issues fully paid up shares upon receiving no consideration therefor or consideration worth less than the par or stated value of the shares. In the case of bonus stock where no consideration is received for the shares, or in the case of shares sold at a cash discount, it is easy to discern both the existence and extent of the water in the stock. However, when stock is issued in exchange for property or for services rendered, and the board of directors or shareholders have fixed a value for the property or services equivalent to the value of the stock, a determination that the stock is watered depends upon whether the property or services have been overvalued.

In certain jurisdictions, the courts apply the "true value" rule which requires that the actual value of property received by, or of services rendered to, a corporation upon issuance of its stock be not less than the par or stated value of the shares issued. In other jurisdictions the standard of "good faith" is applied, and if the board of directors does not act fraudulently in placing a valuation upon the consideration received by the corporation for its shares, the judgment of the board as to such valuation is conclusive. Section 19 of the Model Act adopts the "good faith" rule.

The liability of shareholders on bonus or watered stock is enforceable by creditors of the corporation. At common law, persons who became creditors before the issuance of the bonus or watered stock have no ground for complaint, as they did not extend credit in reliance upon the stock being outstanding. Also, a creditor who participated in the issuance of bonus or watered stock, or who consented thereto, or who dealt with the corporation with full knowledge thereof, had no standing to maintain a suit against the persons to whom such stock was issued. The common-law rule has been changed by statutes in certain States which impose liability upon shareholders who have received bonus or watered stock without regard to any distinction between prior and subsequent creditors, or between creditors with knowledge and those without.

Remedies of Employees. By statute in some States employees of corporations are given rights that other creditors of the corporation do not have, such as the right to recover from shareholders unpaid wages and salaries owing to them.

Creditors' Rights with Respect to Insolvent Corporations

Creditors' Rights to the Appointment of a Receiver for the Corporation. Apart from the rights of bondholders or secured creditors to have a receiver appointed for property of the corporation in connection with the foreclosure of a mortgage, any creditor of the corporation may, pursuant to statute, maintain a suit in equity for the appointment of a receiver of the property of the corporation and for the purpose of having the assets and business of the corporation liquidated upon a showing that (1) the corporation has become unable to pay its debts and obligations as they mature in the regular course of its business, and (2) the creditor has reduced his claim to a judgment and an execution issued thereon has been returned unsatisfied, or the corporation has admitted in writing that the claim of the creditor is due and owing.   Section 97.

Trust Fund Doctrine. In the case of Wood v. Drummer, Fed.Cas. No. 17,944, 3 Mason 308 (1824), Judge Story, by way of hyperbole, stated that "the capital stock of banks is to be deemed a pledge or trust fund for the payment of the debts contracted by the bank." This language was unnecessary to the decision in the case but nevertheless has been so often repeated in subsequent opinions that it has become almost regarded as axiomatic. It is not true that the capital stock of a bank or any other corporation is a trust fund for its creditors. The assets of a corporation represented by its capital stock are owned by it completely and entirely. It does not hold legal title to its assets in trust for its creditors, as would be the situation if a trust fund existed.

However, the assets of an insolvent corporation are treated as a trust fund for its creditors, and probably this is all that was intended by the expression of Judge Story. If the total assets of a corporation are less in value than the amount of its total indebtedness to creditors, there is no equity or value in these assets for shareholders. The officers and directors are managing property in which the shareholders have no interest, and the equity in the corporate assets is not in the shareholders but in the creditors of the corporation. In this situation the trust fund doctrine is applicable.

In the event of bankruptcy or receivership, the assets of a corporation constitute a trust estate administered under court supervision primarily for the benefit of creditors and, if the corporation is not insolvent, for the benefit of its shareholders also. It is not inappropriate to refer to the assets of an insolvent corporation or assets in the hands of a court trustee or receiver as a trust fund.

Cases

Shareholder Agreements

GALLER v. GALLER
(1965) 32 Ill.2d 16, 203 N.E.2d 577.

[Benjamin and Isadore Galler, brothers, were equal partners in a wholesale drug business from 1919 to 1924, when the business was incorporated under Illinois law as the Galler Drug Company with each brother owning one-half of the outstanding 220 shares of stock. In 1945, each of them contracted to sell 6 shares of his stock to Rosenberg, an employee of the company.

The corporation prospered, and in July, 1955, Benjamin and Isadore and their wives entered into a carefully prepared written agreement among themselves and the corporation, the purpose of which was to provide for their families after the death of either brother equal control of the corporation.

Benjamin died in 1957, and shortly after his death his widow Emma requested Isadore, the surviving brother, to comply with the terms of the 1955 agreement, which he refused to do. Isadore proposed modifications of the agreement that were unacceptable to Emma, who thereupon brought suit against Isadore Galler and his wife Rose for specific performance of the July, 1955, agreement.

During the pending of the suit, Rosenberg sold to Isadore and Rose the 12 shares of stock in the company that he owned, and Emma asserted a claim to 6 of the shares. The trial court entered a decree of specific performance in favor of the plaintiff Emma. On appeal, the decree was reversed by the Appellate Court on the ground that the July, 1955, agreement was void as contrary to the Illinois Business Corporation Act and as against public policy. On further appeal, the Supreme Court reversed the Appellate Court.]

UNDERWOOD, J.
* * *
During the last few years of Benjamin's life both brothers drew an annual salary of $42,000. * * * In 1957, 1958, and 1959 a $40,000 annual dividend was paid. Plaintiff has received her proportionate share of the dividend.

The July, 1955, agreement in question here, entered into between Benjamin, Emma, Isadore and Rose, recites that Benjamin and Isadore each own 47½% of the issued and outstanding shares of the Galler Drug Company, an Illinois corporation, and that Benjamin and Isadore desired to provide income for the support and maintenance of their immediate families. No reference is made to the shares then being purchased by Rosenberg. The essential features of the contested portions of the agreement are substantially as set forth in the opinion of the Appellate Court: (2) that the bylaws of the corporation will be amended to provide for a board of four directors; that the necessary quorum shall be three directors; and that no directors' meeting shall be held without giving ten days notice to all directors. (3) The shareholders will cast their votes for the above named persons (Isadore, Rose, Benjamin and Emma) as directors at said special meeting and at any other meeting held for the purpose of electing directors. (4, 5) In the event of the death of either brother his wife shall have the right to nominate a director in place of the decedent. (6) Certain annual dividends will be declared by the corporation. The dividend shall be $50,000 payable out of the accumulated earned surplus in excess of $500,000. If 50% of the annual net profits after taxes exceeds the minimum $50,000, then the directors shall have discretion to declare a dividend up to 50% of the annual net profits. If the net profits are less than $50,000, nevertheless the minimum $50,000 annual dividend shall be declared, providing the $500,000 surplus is maintained. Earned surplus is defined. (9) The certificates evidencing the said shares of Benjamin Galler and Isadore Galler shall bear a legend that the shares are subject to the terms of this agreement. (10) A salary continuation agreement shall be entered into by the corporation which shall authorize the corporation upon the death of Benjamin Galler or Isadore Galler, or both, to pay a sum equal to twice the salary of such officer, payable monthly over a five-year period. Said sum shall be paid to the widow during her widowhood, but should be paid to such widow's children if the widow remarries within the five-year period. (11, 12) The parties to this agreement further agree and hereby grant to the corporation the authority to purchase, in the event of the death of either Benjamin or Isadore, so much of the stock of Galler Drug Company held by the estate as is necessary to provide sufficient funds to pay the federal estate tax, the Illinois inheritance tax and other administrative expenses of the estate. If as a result of such purchase from the estate of the decedent the amount of dividends to be received by the heirs is reduced, the parties shall nevertheless vote for directors so as to give the estate and heirs the same representation as before (2 directors out of 4, even though they own less stock), and also that the corporation pay an additional benefit payment equal to the diminution of the dividends. In the event either Benjamin or Isadore decides to sell his shares he is required to offer them first to the remaining shareholders and then to the corporation at book value, according each six months to accept the offer.

The Appellate Court found the 1955 agreement void because "the undue duration, stated purpose and substantial disregard of the provisions of the Corporation Act outweigh any considerations which might call for divisibility" and held that "the public policy of this state demands voiding this entire agreement".

* * *

The power to invalidate the agreements on the grounds of public policy is so far reaching and so easily abused that it should be called into action to set aside or annul the solemn engagement of parties dealing on equal terms only in cases where the corrupt or dangerous tendency clearly and unequivocally appears upon the face of the agreement itself or is the necessary inference from the matters which are expressed, and the only apparent exception to this general rule is to be found in those cases where the agreement, though fair and unobjectionable on its face, is a part of a corrupt scheme and is made to disguise the real nature of the transaction. [Citation.]

* * *

At this juncture it should be emphasized that we deal here with a so-called close corporation. Various attempts at definition of the close corporation have been made. [Citation.] For our purposes, a close corporation is one in which the stock is held in a few hands, or in a few families, and wherein it is not at all, or only rarely, dealt in by buying or selling. [Citation.] Moreover, it should be recognized that shareholder agreements similar to that in question here are often, as a practical consideration, quite necessary for the protection of those financially interested in the close corporation. While the shareholder of a public-issue corporation may readily sell his shares on the open market should management fail to use, in his opinion, sound business judgment, his counterpart of the close corporation often has a large total of his entire capital invested in the business and has no ready market for his shares should he desire to sell. He feels, understandably, that he is more than a mere investor and that his voice should be heard concerning all corporate activity. Without a shareholder agreement, specifically enforceable by the courts, insuring him a modicum of control, a large minority shareholder might find himself at the mercy of an oppressive or unknowledgeable majority. Moreover, as in the case at bar, the shareholders of a close corporation are often also the directors and officers thereof. With substantial shareholding interests abiding in each member of the board of directors, it is often quite impossible to secure, as in the large public-issue corporation, independent board judgment free from personal motivations concerning corporate policy. For these and other reasons too voluminous to enumerate here, often the only sound basis for protection is afforded by a lengthy, detailed shareholder agreement securing the rights and obligations of all concerned. For a discussion of these and other considerations, see Note, "A Plea for Separate Statutory Treatment of the Close Corporation", 33 N.Y.U.L.Rev. 700 (1958).

* * *

* * * While limiting voting trusts in 1947 to a maximum duration of 10 years, the legislature has indicated no similar policy regarding straight voting agreements although these have been common since prior to 1870. In view of the history of decisions of this court generally upholding, in the absence of fraud or prejudice to minority interests or public policy, the right of stockholders to agree among themselves as to the manner in which their stock will be voted, we do not regard the period of time within which this agreement may remain effective as rendering the agreement unenforceable.

The clause that provides for the election of certain persons to specified offices for a period of years likewise does not require invalidation. * * *

We turn next to a consideration of the effect of the stated purpose of the agreement upon its validity. The pertinent provision is: "The said Benjamin A. Galler and Isadore A. Galler desire to provide income for the support and maintenance of their immediate families." Obviously, there is no evil inherent in a contract entered into for the reason that the persons originating the terms desired to so arrange their property as to provide post-death support for those dependent upon them. Nor does the fact that the subject property is corporate stock alter the situation so long as there exists no detriment to minority stock interests, creditors or other public injury.

* * *

The terms of the dividend agreement require a minimum annual dividend of $50,000, but this duty is limited by the subsequent provision that it shall be operative only so long as an earned surplus of $500,000 is maintained. It may be noted that in 1958, the year prior to commencement of this litigation, the corporation's net earnings after taxes amounted to $202,759 while its earned surplus was $1,543,270, and this was increased in 1958 to $1,680,079 while earnings were $172,964. The minimum earned surplus requirement is designed for the protection of the corporation and its creditors, and we take no exception to the contractual dividend requirements as thus restricted. [Citation.]

The salary continuation agreement is a common feature, in one form or another, of corporate executive employment. It requires that the widow should receive a total benefit, payable monthly over a five-year period, aggregating twice the amount paid her deceased husband in one year. This requirement was likewise limited for the protection of the corporation by being contingent upon the payments being income tax-deductible by the corporation. The charge made in those cases which have considered the validity of payment to the widow of an officer and shareholder in a corporation is that a gift of its property by a noncharitable corporation is in violation of the rights of its shareholders and *ultra vires*. Since there are no shareholders here other than the parties to the contract, this objection is not here applicable, and its effect, as limited, upon the corporation is not so prejudicial as to require its invalidation.

* * *

Accordingly, the judgment of the Appellate Court is reversed except insofar as it relates to fees, and is, as to them affirmed. * * *

Affirmed in part and reversed in part, and remanded with directions.

Right to Examine
Books and Records

APPLICATION OF LOPEZ
(1979) 420 N.Y.S.2d 225, 71 A.D.2d 976.

MEMORANDUM DECISION.

Order and judgment, Supreme Court, New York County, entered August 30, 1979, denying application for disclosure of respondent's shareholder lists, unanimously reversed on the law and the facts, with costs, and the petition is granted to the extent of disclosure of all record and beneficial ownership of shares as of September 7, 1979.

Respondent is currently defending a multimillion dollar lawsuit brought in federal court by one Muller over the latter's unsuccessful negotiations for purchase of SCM assets abroad. Muller formed the "SCM Corporation Shareholders Committee", consisting of himself, his corporation (MacMuller Industries) and two other officers of his corporation, to challenge the position of respondent's management in this controversy. Up until August 6, 1979, this committee controlled 269,900 of the more than 9½ million outstanding shares of SCM stock. In order to wage a proxy battle for management control at the next meeting for election of directors, scheduled for October 25, 1979, the committee was anxious to obtain the list of shareholders eligible to vote as of the record date of September 7, 1979. However, BCL § 624(b) allows for the availability of such information only to shareholders of record in the corporation for at least six months. As of August 5, 1979, Muller's committee consisted of shareholders of record whose longevity of holdings in the corporation ranged from one month to four months and 23 days. On August 6 petitioner, a former SCM executive and record holder of 38 shares of stock since 1977, joined the committee. That same day, petitioner, on behalf of the committee, demanded inspection of minutes of respondent's shareholder proceedings, as well as current lists of shareholders' names and addresses, updated by daily transfer sheets to reflect those eligible to vote at the next election of directors. The stated purpose of the demand was to communicate with shareholders for solicitation of proxies in support of the committee's nominees for directors. Respondent's rejection of this request inspired the instant proceeding.

The purpose of petitioner's demand was clearly set forth in his letter of August 6, so there is no procedural basis for respondent's rejection. [Citation.] Further, the inspection of shareholder lists to facilitate a proxy challenge to incumbent directors is a valid purpose. [Citation.] The burden is on respondent to show an improper purpose for the demand. [Citation.] Petitioner's association with Muller is certainly no indication of impropriety, in light of the otherwise valid stated purpose of the demand. Petitioner alleges without challenge that he has independently concluded that change in the management of SCM in the interest of its shareholders is warranted, and that in this respect his views and those of the committee are similar. Where the demand is facially valid, good faith is assumed, obviating the necessity for a hearing on this issue. [Citation.] The mere fact that Muller and his companies are engaged in litigation with SCM does not demonstrate lack of good faith. Nor would there be an improper purpose or bad faith if communications with shareholders discussed such litigation. [Citation.]

Petitioner is entitled to access to available transfer sheets, at his expense, showing the daily status of record and beneficial ownership through September 7, 1979 [Citation].

Creditors' Rights With
Respect to Watered Stock

RHODE v. DOCK-HOP CO.

(1920) 184 Cal. 367, 194 P. 11.

OLNEY, J.

This is an action by the judgment creditor of a corporation against certain of its stockholders, seeking to collect from them what are claimed to be unpaid balances on the par value of their shares. The plaintiff had judgment, and the defendants appeal.

No contention is made that the plaintiff's claim against the corporation is not valid. The sole point in the case is as to whether or not the defendants are required, because of that claim, to make up any difference which may exist between what was actually paid in on their stock and its par value. Upon this point, the complaint alleged simply that the defendants were subscribers and stockholders of the corporation in amounts specified and that only 25 cents on the dollar had been paid in on the par value of their shares. The answers of the defendants, in addition to some other defenses, denied that they were either subscribers or stockholders, or that the full par value of their stock had not been paid.

* * *

It is apparent that, when one accepts partially paid stock, which does not purport to be anything else, he does so, or must be taken to do so, upon the understanding that it is answerable upon call for the unpaid balance upon it, and that he as its owner must respond to such a call. When he enters into relationship with the corporation as one of its stockholders owning stock of that character, he assumes as an incident of the relationship, the obligation to respond to calls upon him for further contributions to the capital of the company until such capital is fully paid in. [Citations.]

But where a person accepts the ownership of stock which purports to be fully paid, a very different situation is presented. It cannot be said of him for a moment that he accepts the stock and enters upon the relation of stockholder to the corporation upon any understanding that his stock is liable for further calls on capital account, or that he, as an incident of his ownership and consequent relationship, assumes any such obligation. On the contrary, it is evident that he accepts the ownership of the stock and enters upon the relationship of stockholder with just the contrary understanding. What then, is the principle upon which the holder of watered stock is, under any circumstances, obligated to supply substance instead of water, to make good what it is pretended the corporation received but did not? The answer to this question is not in doubt. The stockholder is held upon the

principle that one giving credit to a corporation is entitled to rely upon its ostensible capitalization as the basis for the credit given, and that, when the corporation issues watered stock and thereby assumes an ostensible capitalization in excess of its real assets, the transaction necessarily involves the misleading of subsequent creditors, and, whether done with that purpose actually in mind or not, is at least a constructive fraud upon such creditors. In other words the essence of the right of the creditor to brush aside the issuance of the stock as fully paid, and to show that it was not such and to compel the payment of the balance upon it, is that its issuance as fully paid was as to him a fraud. This is now the view generally accepted in this country. [Citation.]

It must be taken, then, that the right of a creditor of a corporation, which knowingly issued shares as fully paid when they are not, to compel payment on them in full, proceeds upon the ground of fraud. This ground is entirely different from the ground upon which proceeds his right in the case of shares only partially paid up and issued as such, and it follows that a recovery may be had in the latter case, when it cannot be in the former. In the case of partially paid shares issued as such, the stockholder does so, as we have said, upon the condition that his shares are subject to call for the unpaid balance upon them, and that he, as their owner, will respond to such call. This obligation is an asset of the corporation which it may enforce, and which, if it does not itself do so, its unpaid creditors may themselves enforce if it be necessary for the full discharge of their debt. It makes no difference, therefore, in such a case, whether any particular stockholder against whom a recovery is sought was a party to the original transaction whereby the stock was issued or is only a transferee of some such party. He is liable simply as the owner of the stock and because of the relationship with the corporation which he voluntarily assumed when he accepted such ownership.

Such, however, is not the situation of the stockholder owning shares ostensibly fully paid but not so in fact. He owes the corporation no duty to make good the difference, and there is no obligation on his part which is an asset of the corporation or which the corporation may enforce. [Citation.] He is liable only because of the original transaction whereby the stock was issued for a fictitious consideration, and then only to those who were defrauded thereby. His liability, in other words, is not based upon his relationship to the corporation as a stockholder but upon a fraudulent transaction. Upon the plainest principles, therefore, he cannot be held liable unless he was either a party to the transaction in the first instance or has in effect in some manner made himself a party since. It is not sufficient to justify a recovery against him that it be pleaded, proven, and found only that he be a stockholder owning watered stock. Upon those facts alone the full elements necessary to make a cause of action against him do not appear. * * *

Judgment reversed.

Shareholders' Derivative Suit

McMENOMY v. RYDEN
(1970) 286 Minn. 358, 176 N.W.2d 876.

[Plaintiffs are minority shareholders of Midwest Technical Development Corporation ("Midwest"), a closed-end investment company owning assets consisting principally of securities in companies in technological fields. In June, 1962, plaintiffs filed a shareholders derivative suit against 18 individuals and Midwest, as nominal defendant, to recover on behalf of Midwest the profits realized by the individuals through dealing in stock held in the portfolio of Midwest in breach of their fiduciary duty as officers and directors of Midwest.

In October, 1965, a new corporation, Midtex, Inc. was organized to acquire the assets of Midwest. The transfer of assets to Midtex, Inc., was completed in December, 1965, and the shareholders of Midwest received shares of Midtex, Inc. The transfer included all assets owned by Midwest of every kind and nature "whether or not disclosed, on Midwest's books and records, including any contingent assets or claims arising out of Midwest's operations prior to the Closing Date * * * subject, however, to all of the liabilities or obligations of Midwest."

Plaintiffs' motion to join Midtex, Inc. as a party defendant in the suit was denied by the trial court. On appeal, order of the trial court reversed, and case remanded.]

KNUTSON, C. J.
* * *

A stockholders' derivative action of the type that we have here is an invention of equity to permit stockholders to seek relief for breach of fiduciary duty by officers or directors when the corporation itself refuses to bring such action. In Koster v. Lumbermens Mutual Cas. Co., 330 U.S. 518, 522, 67 S.Ct. 828, 830, 91 L.Ed. 1067, 1072, the court said:

"The stockholder's derivative action * * * is an invention of equity to supply the want of an adequate remedy at law to redress breaches of fiduciary duty by corporate managers. Usually the wrongdoing officers also possess the control which enables them to suppress any effort by the corporate entity to remedy such wrongs. Equity therefore traditionally entertains the derivative or secondary action by which a single stockholder may sue in the corporation's right when he shows that the corporation on proper demand has refused to pursue a remedy, or shows facts that demonstrate the futility of such a request. * * *

"The cause of action which such a plaintiff brings before the court is not his own but the corporation's. It is the real party in interest and he is allowed to act in protection of its interest, somewhat as a 'next friend' might do for an individual, because it is disabled from protecting itself."

* * *

That being so, it should not be possible to frustrate this remedy created by equity by the simple expedient of creating a new corporation and assigning the assets of one for whose benefit suit is brought to the newly created entity. Someone should have the continuing right to seek relief from those guilty of breach of fiduciary duty, if there has been such. The stockholders of Midwest, if there was a breach of fiduciary duty by the managing officers, did not lose the right to recover simply because the assets were transferred to a new corporation.

* * *

It has been argued that inasmuch as Midtex, after procuring legal advice from independent attorneys, decided not to continue the suit or to join it, plaintiffs are thereby barred from continuing the suit. * * *

* * *

Here the members of the board of directors of Midtex, only one of whom was a member of the board of Midwest at the time

plaintiffs commenced this action, have exercised their judgment in deciding not to join the lawsuit or to continue with it. This they had a right to do. By refusing to become a party to the lawsuit, they undoubtedly have chosen a course that will eliminate liability on the part of Midtex for the payment of expenses of the litigation. However, this should not preclude the joining of Midtex as an involuntary defendant if it is in fact the real party in interest as the assignee of the cause of action brought for the benefit of Midwest.

It may be possible to determine prior to trial whether it was the intention of the parties to assign this cause of action to Midtex. If so, the action should proceed for the benefit of the corporation that will receive the benefit of the recovery, if there is one. Unless that issue is determined before trial, Midtex should be joined as an involuntary defendant and the case proceed with both Midwest and Midtex named as defendants. If there is a recovery, the question as to who shall receive the benefit of it can then be determined after the trial.

The case is therefore remanded to the trial court for disposition in conformity with this opinion.

Problems

1. Gore had been the owner of one per cent of the outstanding shares of the Webster Company, a corporation, since its organization in 1961. Ratliff, the president of the Company, was the owner of seventy per cent of the outstanding shares. In May 1981, Ratliff used the shareholders' list to submit to the shareholders an offer of $50 per share for their stock. Gore, upon receiving the offer, called Ratliff and told him that the offer was inadequate and advised that he was willing to offer $60 per share, and for that purpose demanded a shareholders' list. Ratliff was informed that Gore was willing and able to supply the funds necessary to purchase the stock but he nevertheless refused to supply the list to Gore. Further, he did not offer to

transmit Gore's offer to the shareholders of record. Gore then filed an action in mandamus to compel the corporation to make the shareholders' list available to him.

Decision?

2. Union Corporation is capitalized for $75,000, represented by 750 shares of capital stock at the par value of $100 each, of which Smith owns 250 shares. At a properly called shareholders' meeting, the owners of the other 500 shares vote, over Smith's objections, to amend the articles of incorporation by increasing the capital stock to 1,000 shares and further vote to sell the new shares, at par value, to Jones, a person not previously interested in the corporation. Smith

now seeks an injunction to restrain the corporation from issuing the new shares over his objection as a minority shareholder. There is no provision in the charter or by-laws of the corporation concerning the issuance of additional shares of stock and it is conceded by all parties that par value is a fair price for the shares. What result?

3. In 1978, at a duly called meeting of the shareholders of Commerce Corporation, the holders of a majority of the outstanding stock adopted a by-law prohibiting any shareholder from selling or transferring his stock without first giving the corporation a thirty-day option to purchase such stock at its book value. Nothing further was done to implement the by-law.

In 1982, Karl Boone, a shareholder, without first offering his stock to the company, sold and assigned his certificate of stock to Fred Marberry who was not a shareholder. Marberry bought Boone's stock at par, although the book value was considerably below par value. Commerce Corporation refused to transfer the stock to Marberry on its books. Marberry brought an appropriate action against Commerce Corporation to compel the corporation to transfer the stock to him.

What decision?

4. X, Y and Z each own one third of the stock of XYZ Corporation. On Friday, X received an offer to merge XYZ into Buyer Corporation. X agreed to call a shareholders' meeting to discuss the offer on the following Tuesday. X telephoned Y and Z, and informed them of the offer and the scheduled meeting. Y agreed to attend. However, Z, unable to attend because he was leaving on a trip on Saturday, asked if the three of them could meet Friday night to discuss the offer. X and Y agreed. The three shareholders met informally Friday night and agreed to accept the offer only if they received preferred stock of Buyer Corporation for their shares. Z then left on his trip. On Tuesday, at the time and place appointed by X, X and Y convened the shareholders' meeting. After discussion, they concluded that the preferred stock payment limitation was unwise and passed a formal resolution to accept Buyer Corporation's offer without any such condition.

Z files suit to enjoin X, Y, and the XYZ Corporation from implementing this resolution. Decision?

5. (a) May shareholders of a corporation at their meeting restrict the directors in the management of the corporation? May the shareholders, by vote, compel the directors to declare a dividend?

(b) What is a voting trust of corporate stock?

6. M, N, O, and P, experts in manufacturing baubles, each owned 15 out of 100 authorized shares of Baubles, Inc., a corporation of State X which does not permit cumulative voting. On July 7, 1978, the corporation sold 40 shares to Q, an investor, for $150,000 which it used to purchase a factory building for $150,000. On July 8, 1978, M, N, O, and P contracted as follows:

All parties will act jointly in exercising voting rights as shareholders. In the event of a failure to agree, the question shall be submitted to George Yost, whose decision shall be binding upon all parties.

Until a meeting of shareholders on April 17, 1982, when a dispute arose, all parties to the contract had consistently and regularly voted for N, O, and P as directors.

At that meeting Yost considered the dispute and decided and directed that M, N, O, and P vote their shares for the latter three as directors. N, O, and P so voted. M and Q voted for themselves and Mrs. Q as directors.

(a) Is the contract of July 8, 1978, valid and, if so, what is its effect?

(b) Who were elected directors of Baubles, Inc. at the meeting of its shareholders on April 17, 1982?

7. X Corporation's articles of incorporation require cumulative voting for the election of its directors. The board of directors of X Corporation consists of nine directors, each elected annually.

(a) A owns 25% of the outstanding shares of X Corporation. How many directors may he elect with his votes?

(b) If X Corporation were to classify its board into three classes, each consisting of three directors elected every three years, how many directors would A be able to elect?

8. A, who was a promoter of a corporation, was issued fully paid up shares for services and property that were greatly overvalued. He transferred these shares to B, who knew nothing of the overvaluation. The corporation and its

creditors now seek to recover the difference between the value of the property and the value of the shares from B. Decision? What if B knew of the overvaluation, but relied on the statement on the face of the stock certificate that it was "fully paid and nonassessable" in purchasing it?

9. John Brown paid $10,000 for 100 shares of the preferred stock of Y Corporation of a par value of $100 per share. The corporation in accordance with its usual practice delivered to him as a bonus one share of common stock of the par value of $100 for each share of preferred purchased. As a result of business recession, the corporation became insolvent and a suit on behalf of creditors was instituted against Brown under the statute in force in the State of incorporation to compel payment by him of "the unpaid portion of his stock." Brown interposed the defense that he had never contracted to pay anything for the common stock; that there was no evidence of its value; that therefore there was no basis on which to determine the amount of the unpaid portion of his stock; and that, accordingly there could be no recovery. Decision?

Chapter

38

MERGER, CONSOLIDATION, AND DISSOLUTION; FOREIGN CORPORATIONS

Certain extraordinary changes affect a corporation in such a fundamental manner that they are outside the ambit of the board of directors and require shareholder approval. Changes, such as charter amendments, various forms of corporate combinations and dissolution, are extraordinary in nature because they alter the basic structure of the corporation. The legal aspects of extraordinary changes will be discussed in the first part of this chapter. The chapter will then proceed to cover the important topic of foreign corporations and, in particular, what must a corporation do in order to legally transact business outside its state of incorporation.

MERGERS, CONSOLIDATION, AND DISSOLUTION

Shareholders have delegated to the board of directors the authority to manage the ordinary business affairs of the corporation. Extraordinary matters that produce organic changes in the corporation, however,

are not delegated to the board of directors but require shareholder approval. Extraordinary changes include charter amendments, sale or lease of all or substantially all the corporation's assets, mergers, consolidations, and dissolution. Although each of these actions are authorized by state incorporation statutes which impose specific procedural requirements, they are also subject to equitable limitations imposed by the courts.

The requirement of shareholder approval is entirely appropriate, since the articles of incorporation may be viewed as a three-party contract among the State, the corporation, and the shareholders. The State has consented in advance to amendments to the charter by prescribing amendment procedures in the incorporation statute. The shareholders, as the other party to the contract, must also consent to any change in the charter. This contract argument is also applicable to other fundamental changes.

Since shareholder approval for extraordinary changes usually needs not be unanmous, such changes will frequently be approved despite opposition by minority shareholders. In some instances, these shareholders are accorded the right to dissent and recover the fair value of their shares if they follow the prescribed procedure. This right is called the appraisal remedy.

CHARTER AMENDMENTS

Modern statutes permit the articles of incorporation to be freely amended. The amended articles of incorporation, however, may contain only such provisions as might be lawfully contained in the original articles of incorporation. The Model Act is extremely comprehensive in its authorization for amendments and includes very broad powers. The following listing is illustrative of the powers granted by Section 58:

1. To change its corporate name.
2. To change its period of duration.
3. To change, enlarge, or diminish its corporate purposes.
4. To increase or decrease the number or par value of shares.
5. To reclassify shares and change the preferential rights of shares.
6. To create new classes of shares.
7. To limit, deny, or grant preemptive rights.

Since articles of incorporation now rarely limit the duration or powers of the corporation, the most common amendments relate to changes in the capital structure of the corporation.

The typical procedure under modern statutes for amending the articles of incorporation requires the board of directors to adopt a resolution setting forth the proposed amendment, which must then be approved by a majority vote of the shareholders, although older statutes required a two-thirds shareholder vote. In most states dissenting shareholders are *not* given an appraisal remedy. After the amendment is approved by the shareholders, articles of amendment are executed and filed with the Secretary of State. The amendment becomes effective upon the issuance of the certificate of amendment by the Secretary of State but does not affect the existing rights of nonshareholders.

COMBINATIONS

It may be desirable and profitable for a corporation to enlarge its plant, increase its property holdings, extend or diversify its operations, acquire assured markets or supplies, gain new technology, enjoy economies of scale, or employ idle capital. To do so, the corporation may wish to acquire all or substantially all of the assets, including good will, of another corporation or corporations, and combine them with its own. This may be accomplished by (1) a purchase or lease of such assets, (2) a purchase of a controlling stock interest in such other corporation or corporations, (3) a merger or consolidation with such corporation.

The appraisal rights of dissenting shareholders in connection with such a sale or lease and in the case of a merger or a consolidation are subsequently discussed. When any of these methods of combination involves the issuance of shares, proxy solicitations or tender offers, it may be subject to federal securities regulation, as discussed in Chapter 42. Moreover, when a combination may have a detrimental effect on competition the federal antitrust laws, as discussed in Chapter 41, may apply.

Purchase or Lease of All or Substantially All of the Assets

When one corporation purchases or leases all, or substantially all, of the assets of another corporation, no change is effected in the legal personality of either corporation. The purchaser or lessee corporation has simply acquired ownership or control of additional physical assets. The selling or lessor corporation, in lieu of its physical properties, has cash or other property, or a stipulated rental. Each corporation continues its separate existence with only the form or extent of its assets altered.

If such sale or lease of all or substantially all of its assets is in the usual course of business of the selling or lessor corporation, approval by its board of directors is necessary, but no shareholder authorization is required. Section 78. Shareholder approval is necessary only if such a sale or lease is not in the usual and regular course of business. The selling corporation by liquidation of its assets, or the lessor corporation by placing its physical assets beyond its control, have each changed its position and perhaps its ability to carry on the type of business contemplated by its charter. For this reason, such sale or lease must be approved not only by action of the directors but also by the affirmative vote of the holders of a majority of its shares entitled to vote at a meeting of shareholders called for this purpose. Section 79. The board of directors may abandon any such sale or lease of assets, subject to the contract rights of third parties, without shareholder approval. Section 79.

Purchase of Shares

An alternative to the purchase of the assets of another corporation is the purchase of its stock. When one corporation acquires all of the stock or a controlling interest in the stock of another corporation, no change is wrought in the legal existence of either corporation. The acquiring corporation acts through its board of directors, while the corporation which becomes a subsidiary does not act at all, as the sale of stock is by its shareholders. There is no state statutory procedure to be followed except for public utility or quasi-public corporations. The capital structure of the subsidiary remains unchanged, and that of the parent is usually not altered unless required in connection with financing the acquisition of the stock.

Merger

A merger of two or more corporations is the combination of all of their total assets, title to which is vested in one of them, known as the surviving corporation. The other party or parties to the merger, known as the merged corporation or corporations, are merged into the surviving corporation and cease to exist as a separate entity. Thus, if A Corporation and B Corporation combine into the A Corporation, A is the surviving corporation and B the merged corporation. All debts and other liabilities of the merged corporation are assumed by the surviving corporation by operation of law. The shareholders of the merged corporation receive stock or other securities issued by the surviving corporation, as provided in the plan of merger. A merger requires the approval of the board of directors of each corporation, as well as the affirmative vote of the holders of a majority of the shares entitled to vote of each corporation party to the merger. Section 73.

A corporation that owns at least 90% of the outstanding shares of a subsidiary may merge the subsidiary into itself without approval by the shareholders of either corporation. All that is required is a resolution by the board of directors of the parent corporation. Section 75. The dissenting shareholders of the subsidiary would have the right to obtain payment from the parent for their shares; the shareholders of the parent do not have this appraisal remedy. Section 80(c).

Consolidation

A consolidation of two or more corporations is the combination of all of their total assets, title to which is taken by a newly created corporation known as the consolidated corporation. Each of the constituent corporations ceases to exist, and all of their debts and liabilities of every kind are assumed by the new corporation. The shareholders of each of the constituent corporations receive stock or other securities, not necessarily of the same class, issued to them by the new corporation pursuant to the plan of consolidation. A consolidation requires the approval of the boards of directors of each constituent corporation as well as the affirmative vote of the holders of a majority of the shares entitled to vote of each constituent corporation. Section 73.

Rights of Dissenting Shareholders

While the consent of creditors is not requisite to a merger or a consolidation, nor to a sale or lease of all or substantially all of the assets of a corporation not in the usual and regular course of business, shareholder approval is required with respect to each corporation which is party to a merger or consolidation (Section 73), and by the shareholders of the selling or lessor corporation. Section 79.

A shareholder may prefer not to participate in a proposed plan of merger or consolidation or in such a sale or lease of assets of the corporation, and he has a right to dissent. Section 80. If he dissents and strictly complies with the provisions of the statute (Section 81), he is entitled to receive the fair value of his shares. In order to perfect his right to payment for his shares, a dissenting shareholder must:

1. File with the corporation a written objection to the proposed corporate action prior to the vote of the shareholders.
2. Refrain from voting in favor of the proposed corporate action either in person or by proxy.
3. Make a written demand upon the corporation on a form provided by that corporation within the time period set by the corporation, which may not be less than thirty days after the corporation mails the form. Section 81.

Unless written demand is made within the prescribed time period, the dissenting shareholder is bound by the terms of the proposed corporate action. For example, A is the owner of 10% of the outstanding stock of the X Corporation which has proposed a merger or consolidation with the Y Corporation. A files a written notice of intent to dissent with the corporation before the shareholder meeting. At the meeting of the shareholders, A files written objections, makes a vehement speech in opposition to the proposed merger or consolidation, and casts a dissenting vote. However, the holders of a majority of the outstanding stock vote in favor of it. Thereafter, at every opportunity A loudly proclaims his disagreement and dissent. Nevertheless, he forgets and fails to file a written demand for payment within the required time period. Despite his protests to the contrary, A has legally assented to the merger or consolidation and is bound by the terms thereof. A is in precisely the same position as if he had favored the merger or consolidation from the start and had voted in favor of it.

The purpose of the statutory procedure is to fix a not too remote date at which time the corporation may be apprised of the number of shares for which it is required to pay cash in order to carry through the merger or consolidation. If dissenting shareholders in sufficient numbers perfect their right to be paid, the lack of sufficient cash or the inability of the surviving or new corporation to raise funds for this purpose may make the merger or consolidation impracticable at this stage.

A dissenting shareholder who complies with all of these requirements is entitled to an appraisal remedy which is payment by the corporation of the fair value of his shares. The Model Act defines fair value to mean their value immediately before the effectuation of the merger, the consolidation, or the sale or lease of assets excluding any appreciation or depreciation in anticipation of such corporate action unless such exclusion would be inequitable. Section 81(a)(3). The corporation may pay dissenting shareholders out of *any* funds, so long as such payment is not made when the corporation is insolvent or when such payment would make it insolvent. Section 6(c).

DISSOLUTION

Although a corporation may have perpetual existence, its life may be terminated in a number of ways. Incorporation statutes usually provide both for dissolution without judicial proceedings (nonjudicial dissolution) and for dissolution with judicial proceedings (judicial dissolution).

Nonjudicial Dissolution

Nonjudicial dissolution may be brought about by:

1. An act of the legislature of the State of incorporation.
2. Expiration of the period of time for which the corporation was formed.
3. Voluntary action on the part of all of the holders of all of the outstanding shares of stock. Section 83.
4. Voluntary action by the corporation, pursuant to a resolution of the board of directors which is approved by the affirmative vote of the holders of a majority of the shares of the corporation entitled to vote at a meeting of the shareholders duly called for this purpose. Section 84.

Involuntary Judicial Dissolution

Involuntary dissolution by judicial proceeding may be instituted by the state, the shareholders, or the creditors and may occur by:

1. Court action taken at the instance of the Attorney General of the State of incorporation when it is established as provided in Section 94 that the corporation has failed to file its annual report with the Secretary of State, failed to pay its annual franchise tax, procured its articles of incorporation through fraud, continued to exceed or abuse the authority conferred upon it by law, failed for thirty days to appoint and maintain a registered agent in the State, or failed for thirty days after a change of its registered office or registered agent to file a statement of such change.
2. Shareholders when it is established that the directors are deadlocked in the management of the corporate affairs and the shareholders are unable to break the deadlock and that irreparable injury to the corporation is being suffered or is threatened; that the acts of the directors or those in control of the corporation are illegal, oppressive, or fraudulent; that the corporate assets are being misapplied or wasted; or that the shareholders are deadlocked and cannot elect directors. Section 97(a).
3. A creditor upon a showing that the corporation has become unable to pay its debts and obligations as they mature in the regular course of its business and either the creditor has reduced his claim to a judgment and an execution issued thereon has been returned unsatisfied, or that the corporation has admitted in writing that the claim of the creditor is due and owing. Section 97(b).

Liquidation

Upon dissolution, the assets of a corporation are liquidated and used first to pay the expenses of liquidation and its creditors according to their respective contract or lien rights, and any remainder is distributed to shareholders ratably according to their respective contract rights, preferred stock having priority over common. When liquidation is voluntary, it is carried out by the board of directors who serve as trustees; but when liquidation is involuntary, it is conducted by a court appointed receiver.

FOREIGN CORPORATIONS

A corporation is domestic in its State of incorporation and foreign in every other State. However, in the treatment in prior chapters of corporate existence, structure, function and scope of activities, no consideration was given to the problems of foreign corporations which transact business in one or more States other than the State of their incorporation.

Except for acts in interstate commerce, a corporation may not do business in a State other than the State of its incorporation without the permission and authorization of such State. Every State, however, provides for the issuance to foreign corporations of a certificate to do business within its borders and for the taxation of such foreign businesses. In addition, the doing or transacting of business within a particular state is a determinant of whether that state's courts have jurisdiction over a foreign corporation. The powers conferred upon a corporation by the State of incorporation may be exercised in other States which grant it a license or certificate of authority to do so. The nature of the business which a foreign corporation may transact depends upon its charter powers, the laws of the States in which the business is transacted, and the rights granted and obligations and limitations imposed by such laws upon foreign corporations.

DOING BUSINESS

The question of whether a corporation is or is not present in a State other than the State of incorporation is generally raised in connection with local statutes imposing obligations upon foreign corporations that are "doing business" or "transacting business" within the State. Although the phrase "doing business" is so common as to have become almost a term of art, it is a term for which no satisfactory legal definition can be given

for the reason that whether or not a foreign corporation is doing business in a particular State is essentially a question of fact. A number of jurisdictions have attempted to define the phrase in their statutes, but the necessity of litigating close questions of fact has not been noticeably lessened by statutory definitions.

No two jurisdictions may necessarily agree upon whether a given set of facts constitutes doing business. The problem is further complicated by the different meanings attached to the phrase in the same jurisdiction, depending upon the particular local regulation which is sought to be imposed upon the foreign corporation. There are three principal types of statutes which apply to a foreign corporation doing business within the State:

1. Statutes requiring foreign corporations to qualify or register and to subject themselves to regulations pertaining to their operations in the State.
2. Statutes imposing taxes upon foreign corporations.
3. Statutes providing for service of process upon foreign corporations.

This chapter is concerned with the first of these.

What may constitute doing sufficient business in the State to subject a foreign corporation to valid service of process may not be sufficient to require the foreign corporation to obtain a certificate of authority from the State. Furthermore, the qualifying statutes are limited in their application by the constitutional provision that the regulation of commerce between the States is within the power of the Congress of the United States.

Although it is fundamental that a State may not impose regulations which constitute a burden upon or interfere with interstate commerce, it is not always clear whether a particular business activity or transaction is solely intrastate or local in character, or is interstate commerce. For example, a shipment of goods into a State to fill an order solicited in the State and accepted only at the home office outside of the State is generally considered to be interstate commerce, and a local statute regulating corporations which do business in the State would not apply to foreign corporations making such shipments. A different situation exists when goods are shipped into the State, stored there by the foreign corporation, and after an interval of time are sold to local customers. If later offered for sale to the general public, the usual rule is that they have lost their interstate status.

Similar problems arise when a contract provides not only for the sale of goods but also for local installation services by the foreign vendor. The contract may be held to be separable and the sale to be in interstate commerce, but the installation is local and subjects the corporation to local control. The line of demarcation is further illustrated by two Illinois decisions involving correspondence schools. In one, the school maintained a local distributing office and was held to have been doing business within the State. In a later case where no local distributing office was maintained and the educational materials were mailed directly to the students, the school was held to have been engaged in interstate commerce.

It is considerably easier to say what does not constitute doing business than to say what does, and this negative approach is reflected in the statutes, the textbooks and the welter of judicial decisions dealing with the subject. In nearly every jurisdiction, an isolated transaction will not constitute doing business so as to subject it to local qualification statutes. The courts have held that acts preliminary to the commencement of business, or acts solely for the purpose of winding up the corporation's affairs, do not constitute doing business

within the state. The holding of title to real estate does not of itself constitute doing business in most states, and a few states have recognized this by statute.

The Model Act, Section 106, provides a nonexclusive list of activities in which a foreign corporation may engage without being considered to have transacted intrastate business:

(a) Maintaining or defending any action or suit or any administrative or arbitration proceeding, or effecting the settlement thereof or the settlement of claims or disputes.

(b) Holding meetings of its directors or shareholders or carrying on other activities concerning its internal affairs.

(c) Maintaining bank accounts.

(d) Maintaining offices or agencies for the transfer, exchange and registration of its securities, or appointing and maintaining trustees or depositaries with relation to its securities.

(e) Effecting sales through independent contractors.

(f) Soliciting or procuring orders, whether by mail or through employees or agents or otherwise, where such orders require acceptance without this State before becoming binding contracts.

(g) Creating evidences of debt, mortgages or liens on real or personal property.

(h) Securing or collecting debts or enforcing any rights in property securing the same.

(i) Transacting any business in interstate commerce.

(j) Conducting an isolated transaction completed within a period of thirty days and not in the course of a number of repeated transactions of like nature.

QUALIFICATION PROCEDURES

An obvious corollary to the rule that a State may refuse to permit a foreign corporation to transact any intrastate business within its borders is that the State may impose reasonable conditions precedent to the granting of permission to carry on such business.

In order to protect its citizens in their dealings with foreign corporations and, incidentally, to obtain additional revenue, every State provides by statute that foreign corporations must obtain a license or certificate of authority before they may transact intrastate business or have access to the local courts to enforce rights arising out of such business. Obtaining a certificate usually involves filing certain information with the Secretary of State and the payment of prescribed fees.

Conditions may be imposed upon granting the certificate of authority. Nevertheless, a State cannot by statute require as a condition to a foreign corporation doing business within the State that it surrender rights guaranteed a corporation by the Federal constitution, such as resort to the Federal courts, due process, or equal protection. Moreover, States typically will not deny qualification because the corporate laws of the jurisdiction in which the foreign corporation was incorporated differ from that State's laws. Section 106.

Most jurisdictions require that foreign corporations upon obtaining a certificate of authority to transact business in the State designate a local registered agent upon whom service of summons and other notices may be had. An additional requirement is the filing of annual reports which will give some evidence of financial condition and also afford a basis for determining the amount of whatever franchise or license taxes is levied by the State. The State may, in order to protect domestic corporations, restrict the use of certain corporate names or, on the grounds of local public policy, the type of business in which a foreign corporation may engage.

A few jurisdictions require the posting of bond by a foreign corporation to insure performance of its contracts, and certain States require a foreign corporation to comply with standards of financial responsibility before a certificate of authority to transact intrastate business will be issued.

SCOPE OF REGULATION

A foreign corporation must comply with those local laws which are expressly designed to regulate foreign corporations. A problem occasionally arises whether local statutes relating to corporations in general apply to foreign as well as to domestic corporations. Where the statutes relate to internal corporate affairs, they will not be held to apply to foreign corporations. For example, statutes governing the rights of shareholders, or the consequences of insolvency, will be applied exclusively to domestic corporations, while those relating primarily to commerce and trade, such as local usury laws, will be applicable both to foreign and domestic corporations.

In the absence of express statutory prohibition, foreign corporations are generally accorded the fundamental commercial rights extended to domestic corporations with regard to contracts, commercial paper, and the acquisition of property. This general right may be specifically denied or limited in instances where public policy reflects an intent to restrict certain powers to organizations more amenable to local sanction. Thus, it is not uncommon for foreign corporations to be denied the power to act as trustees or in other fiduciary capacities.

It is a common and accepted principle that local courts will not interfere with the internal affairs of a foreign corporation. This principle may have developed because of the obvious difficulties in attempting to enforce a judgment in cases where the books, records and principal officers may be outside the jurisdiction, or because of general considerations of public policy and comity. Whatever the rationale underlying the rule, a court of any State other than the

State of incorporation almost invariably refuses relief when the issues involved are solely matters of administrative or managerial policy. The Model Act states that "nothing in this Act contained shall be construed to authorize the State to regulate the organization or internal affairs of [a foreign] corporation." Section 106.

There is no clear line of demarcation between the internal affairs and the other affairs of a corporation. Litigation raising questions of shareholders' right is generally considered outside the province of a foreign jurisdiction. Contests over the election of directors or officers or the issuance of capital stock should also be brought before a court of the State of incorporation. However, courts have ordered a foreign corporation to transfer shares of stock on its books and to permit inspection of its books and records by a shareholder. Where a corporation has its principal office and principal assets in a State in which it is not incorporated and its directors, officers, and most of its agents reside in such State, the reluctance of a local court to inquire into its internal affairs may be tempered by a recognition that the corporation is domesticated if not domestic.

SANCTIONS FOR
FAILURE TO QUALIFY

A foreign corporation that transacts business without having first qualified may be subject to a number of penalties. One of the most common penalties is to deny the corporation access to local courts and treat any contract between it and a local resident as unenforceable by the corporation. In many instances the foreign corporation is not permitted to enforce a contract until it has obtained a certificate of authority to do business. Section 124 of the Model Act reflects the prevailing current view that qualification is primarily a matter between the State and the foreign corporation and that a failure to obtain a certificate of authority to transact business in the State does not impair the validity of a contract entered into by the corporation nor prevent such corporation from defending any action or proceeding brought against it in the State. This section provides that an unlicensed foreign corporation doing business in the State shall not be entitled to maintain a suit in the State courts until such corporation shall have obtained a certificate of authority.

In addition, many states impose fines upon the corporation, while a few states also impose fines upon the corporation's officers and directors as well as holding them personally liable in contracts made within the State. A State may also specify conditions under which a license or certificate of authority shall be revoked. Upon revocation, the foreign corporation is denied the right to transact further local business in the State. In general, the statutes provide that a failure to pay taxes, file reports, or maintain a registered agent or registered office in the State will justify revocation of a license.

Cases

Rights of Dissenting Shareholders

ENDICOTT JOHNSON
CORP. v. BADE

(1975) 37 N.Y.2d 585, 376 N.Y.S.2d 103, 338 N.E.2d 614.

FUCHSBERG, J.

This proceeding was brought pursuant to section 623 of the Business Corporation Law to fix the fair value of the stock of respondent stockholders, who had dissented from a proposed merger as a result of which petitioner Endicott Johnson Corporation was to become a wholly-owned subsidiary of McDonough Corporation. Special Term, confirming and adopting the report of the appraiser it had appointed, fixed, *inter alia,* the fair value of the common stock at $45.75. The Appellate Division having modified the order of Special Term by reducing the valuation of the stock to $42.77 per share and having increased the amount of fees allowed to one of respondent's counsel, both sides now appeal.

At the heart of the issues involved are the weight required to be given to the market price of the stock * * *.

The general principles applicable here are clear. Dissenting stockholders were entitled to be paid the "fair value" of their Endicott common stock, excluding any appreciation or depreciation due to the merger or its proposal. (Business Corporation Law, § 623.) Although the statute itself is silent as to how fair value is to be determined, it is well established by case law that, in our State, the elements which are to enter into such an appraisal are net asset value, investment value and market value. [Citations.] While, in order to provide the elasticity deemed necessary to reach a just result, all three factors are to be considered, the weight to be accorded to each varies with the facts and circumstances in a particular case. [Citations.]

* * *

It follows that all three elements do not have to influence the result in every valuation proceeding. It suffices if they are all considered. Compelling the consideration of all of them, including those which may turn out to be unreliable in a particular case, has the salutary effect of assuring more complete justification by the appraiser of the conclusion he reaches. It also provides a more concrete basis for court review.

The three elements are not always discrete: definitionally, they may even flow into one another. For instance, in this very case, by their general concurrence that it would here be inappropriate, no estimation of net asset value was attempted by the parties or the appraiser. Since the corporation was not being liquidated, but was to continue to operate as part of the surviving parent McDonough Corporation, that made business and legal sense. For, in cases of nonliquidation, to the extent that the net

asset value might include elements such as good will and potential earnings, these are invariably taken into account, in any event, among the numerous tangible and intangible factors that enter into judgment of the investment value of going concerns, whether by experienced appraisers or prudent investors. [Citations.]

Indeed, in this case investment value, for all practical purposes, became the sole determinant of fair value when the appraiser eliminated market value as a meaningful factor by reporting as follows:

"My opinion is that little weight should be given to the past history of market value prior to 1969 because I believe that there was a radical enough change in the management of the company so that it had 'turned around', and that the pre-1969 market is not particularly helpful.

"I agree with the thinking of the text writers that a dramatic change in leadership for the good may be valid grounds for disregarding company's [sic] past history of weakness.

"Subsequent to 1969 I believe the market became so thin because of the control of McDonough and the subsequent delisting that it is fairly meaningless."

Endicott, pointing to an average market price of $26.25 per share in public trading of the stock for the six months immediately preceding the announcement of the merger, argues that market value was required to be given substantial weight and that the lower courts acted contrary to law in adopting that part of the appraiser's report which had failed to do so. In further support of its position, Endicott, among other things, asserts that, during the premerger period it regards as relevant, McDonough controlled only 31.8% of the common shares, the remainder constituting a large enough public float in the hands of over two thousand stockholders to ensure a free and active market. On the other hand, the stockholders, relying heavily on such facts as the stock's delisting from the New York Stock Exchange, its relegation for a year before the merger to being traded on the over-the-counter market and, by then, the ownership by McDonough of 70% of the stock, claim the marketplace was no longer "a fair reflection of the judgment of the buying and selling public" as to Endicott common. [Citation.]

Under the circumstances, the weight of market value, whether great or small or none, was for the fact-finding tribunals, and there is no reason to disturb the Appellate Division's conclusion, on the facts and in its discretion, that in this case the appraiser was not required to rely "to any large degree" on the market value of Endicott's common stock.

* * *

In addition, the right of dissenting stockholders to obtain fair value rather than market value for their stock protects them from being forced to sell at unfair values arbitrarily and unilaterally fixed by those who may dominate a corporation. The obligation to accept fair value is an accepted risk of public stock ownership for, in some instances market price at the time of a merger may have been pushed to levels in excess of fair value, and the automatic right to it in a valuation proceeding could bring a windfall. Either way, market price is but an ingredient that must enter into the calculation for what it is worth, no more and no less. [Citation.]

* * *

Accordingly, the order should be affirmed.

Involuntary Judicial Dissolution

CALLIER v. CALLIER
(1978) 61 Ill.App.3d 1011, 18 Ill.Dec. 941, 378 N.E.2d 405

WINELAND, J.

This is an appeal from a judgment of the Circuit Court of St. Clair County order-ing liquidation of the assets and business of All Steel Pipe and Tube, Inc., an Illinois corporation, pursuant to Section 86(a)(1) of the Business Corporation Act of 1933, as amended (Ill.Rev.Stat.1975, ch. 32, par. 157.86(a)(1)).

* * *

All Steel Pipe and Tube is a close corporation formed in 1969 to engage in the business of selling steel pipes and tubes. The two equal shareholders, plaintiff-appellee Leo Callier and defendant-appellant Scott Callier, each made an initial investment of $500 in the corporation. Scott is Leo's uncle. Defendant-appellant Felix Callier, one of the two directors of the corporation, is Scott's father and Leo's grandfather. It is undisputed that Felix, who is in his 80's, is the "nominee" of Scott on the board of directors, and that he has never taken an active role in the day-to-day management of the business. Leo is the other director, and is president of the corporation. Scott's title is general manager; he was appointed to that position by unanimous resolution of the board, and can only be removed by the board.

Increasingly over the years of their business association, Scott and Leo had differences of opinion about various aspects of the operation of the company. Despite the steady deterioration of the owners' relationship, the company flourished. From about $200,000 in 1970, gross sales had increased to $25,000,000 a year in 1974.

In early 1975, the series of events leading to this litigation took place. Scott was involved in preparing and sending to each employee of the corporation, and each employee's spouse, a letter warning that "social and/or emotional and/or physical relationships between male and female employees for other than business purposes" would thenceforth be grounds for immediate dismissal. This so called "fraternization letter" created a furor within the company, and resulted in Leo's informing

Scott that he no longer wanted to be associated with him.

Negotiations looking towards the redemption of Scott's shares by Leo began immediately, but despite the diligent efforts of their attorneys the parties could not reach an agreement. In April 1975, the discussion turned to voluntary dissolution and liquidation of the corporation, but still no agreement could be reached.

On April 30, 1975, Leo sent a telegram to Scott purporting to fire him as general manager. On the next day, without any prior notice, Leo called all the employees together and announced that the business was being closed down immediately. During the next month, Leo began to wind down the business of All Steel. On May 5 he formed a new Delaware corporation, Callier Steel Pipe and Tube, Inc. On May 30, all operations at All Steel ceased. Callier Steel opened for business on June 2, employing about 40 of All Steel's previous employees. On June 11, Leo filed the complaint in the instant cause.

The issue on this appeal is whether the plaintiff sustained his burden of proof under Section 86(a)(1) of the Business Corporation Act. The defendants contend that there was insufficient proof of either a deadlock or irreparable injury within the meaning of the Act to justify dissolution and liquidation of the corporation.

Corporations, which are creatures of statute, can only be dissolved according to statute. (Central Standard Life Insurance Co. v. Davis, 10 Ill.App.2d 245, 134 N.E.2d 653 (3d Dist. 1956), aff'd 10 Ill.2d 566, 141 N.E.2d 45 (1957).) As our Supreme Court said in the Davis case, "Corporate dissolution is a drastic remedy, and the teachings of generations of chancellors admonish us that it must not be lightly invoked." [Citations.]

The statute at issue here is as follows:

Circuit courts have full power to liquidate the assets and business of a corporation:

(a) In an action by a shareholder when it appears:

(1) That the directors are deadlocked in the management of the corporate affairs and the shareholders are unable to break the deadlock, and that irreparable injury to the corporation is suffered or threatened by reason thereof * * *. (Ill.Rev.Stat.1975, ch. 32, par. 157–86(a)(1).)

Section 86(a)(1) has not been a frequently used basis for dissolution, presumably because of the "substantial problems of interpretation" connected with its provisions. [Citation.] The terms *deadlock* and *irreparable injury* are both undefined and troublesome. It has been said that mere dissension among stockholders is not a ground for dissolution unless it is of such serious proportions as to defeat the end for which the corporation is organized. [Citations.] * * *

After a careful review of the entire record, we have concluded that plaintiff's proof was insufficient to show either deadlock in the management of corporate affairs or the threat of irreparable injury to the corporation. What the evidence shows, instead, is two equal shareholders who were unable to get along and unable to reach agreement within a four-month period as to the redemption of one's shares by the other or to the terms of voluntary dissolution. This is not equivalent to an inability of the corporation to perform the functions for which it was created. Without adopting the position of defendants that the threat of irreparable injury can never be shown under this statute so long as a corporation is making a profit, we must agree with defendants that such a threat was not proved here.

It appears to us that Leo Callier simply decided that he was not going to have anything more to do with Scott Callier, and when their redemption-liquidation negotiations stalled, he made a unilateral decision—without consulting the other director or shareholder—to shut down the corporation. On the day that he informed the employees of the closing of the corporation, corporate affairs were being managed, and quite successfully. In fact, the company appeared on its way to the second best year of its history, despite a general downturn in the pipe industry. Neither Scott nor Felix Callier was interfering with the management of the corporation; Scott had in fact intentionally stayed away from the company and allowed Leo to run things alone while the redemption discussions were going on.

Thus, absent sufficient proof of the jurisdictional facts of deadlock and irreparable injury, the court below erred in ordering liquidation of the corporate assets.

* * *

For the foregoing reasons the judgment of the Circuit Court of St. Clair County is reversed, and this cause is remanded to that court for further proceeding consistent with this opinion.

Reversed and Remanded.

Foreign Corporations:
Doing Business

REISMAN v. MARTORI, MEYER, HENDRICKS, & VICTOR

(1980) 155 Ga.App. 551, 271 S.E.2d 685.

BANKE, J.

Appellee sued appellant for fees for legal services. Appellant Reisman is a medical doctor and general surgeon. The appellee is an Arizona professional association comprised of approximately 18 lawyers. In November of 1977, Dr. Reisman contacted Edwin Hendricks, a partner of appellee, seeking legal advice and representation in a dispute between himself and the Floyd County Medical Center (hospital). The hospital had restricted Dr. Reisman's privilege to use its facilities by requiring him to consult with another surgeon before scheduling a patient for surgery and to have another surgeon present during surgery. In addition to vindicating his reputation, Dr. Reisman sought advice as to bringing an action against the doctors who were responsible for having the restrictions imposed.

Hendricks flew to Atlanta and associated local counsel, who was hired with Dr. Reisman's approval and was to be paid for his services directly by Dr. Reisman. A hearing was obtained before the hospital authority resulting in affirmance of the restrictions of Dr. Reisman's privileges. Working through the Christmas holidays, Hendricks obtained an injunction in federal court on due process grounds, ordering the hospital to refrain from enforcing the restrictions. Before the order was entered, however, the hospital authority reinstituted disciplinary proceedings against Dr. Reisman, this time in apparent accordance with due process requirements. In the second proceeding, the hospital's investigating committee recommended that Dr. Reisman's privileges be completely revoked, rather than restricted. Revocation of privileges requires notification of the State Board of Medical Examiners, and Dr. Reisman feared he could lose his license to practice medicine. Accordingly, he decided after consultation with Hendricks and local counsel that it would be to his advantage to negotiate a dismissal of the administrative proceeding in return for his resignation from the hospital staff.

Hendricks negotiated this compromise and was preparing to pursue an action for damages against the doctors who had instituted the disciplinary proceedings against Dr. Reisman, when Dr. Reisman requested that the case be abandoned and a final bill presented. The total bill for Hendricks' services, including travel costs and professional services of several of Hendricks' associates who also worked on the case, was $21,438.14. Dr. Reisman had made advances of $15,000 but failed and refused to pay the balance. In the subsequent action on the debt, Dr. Reisman contended that appellee's services left him in the same position as if he had not had legal representation at all and that a failure of consideration had thus occurred. A jury awarded appellee the full amount of the unpaid portion of the bill, and Dr. Reisman appeals. Held:

Dr. Reisman urges that the trial court erred in denying his motion for directed verdict based upon appellee's failure to register as a foreign corporation in accordance with Code Ann. § 22–1421(b) for the purpose of maintaining this suit. We do not agree. Assuming, without deciding, that the appellee professional association was required under Code Ann. § 22–1421(a) to procure a certificate of authority from the Secretary of State in order to transact business in Georgia, its activities in this state have not been sufficiently extensive to invoke the statute here. " 'In most jurisdictions it has been held that single or isolated transactions do not constitute doing business within the meaning of such statutes, although they are a part of the very business for [sic] which the corporation is organized to transact, if the action of the corporation in engaging therein indicated no purpose of continuity of conduct in that respect.' [Citation.]" Winston Corp. v. Park Elec. Co., 126 Ga.App. 489, 493, 191 S.E.2d 340, 344, 90 A.L.R.3d 929 (1972).

Winston held that "the question of 'doing business' is to be considered a matter of fact to be resolved on an ad hoc or case-by-case basis * * * [and] * * * the meaning of 'isolated transaction' in our corporation code is to be determined in the same way as the term 'doing business.'" Id. at p. 495–96, 191 S.E.2d at p. 345. Winston also makes it clear that the purpose of Code Ann. § 22–1401 is to require registration of foreign corporations which intend to conduct business in Georgia on a continuous basis, not as a temporary matter. Activity related to a single transaction or contract is thus not contemplated.

The evidence here showed that the appellee's activities were concentrated in Arizona, although various attorneys in the firm had handled litigation (or "transacted business") outside the state of incorporation. Hendricks had represented clients in Georgia on two prior occasions, but these had nothing to do with his representation of Dr. Reisman. Under these circumstances, there is ample basis for the court's conclusion that the appellee had neither extended its business into Georgia on a continuous basis nor engaged "in the course of a number of repeated transactions of like nature" within the state. Code Ann. § 22–1401(b)(11); Cf. Van Bergen &c., Inc. v. Exec. Equities, Inc., 139 Ga.App. 319, 320, 228 S.E.2d 356 (1976). The trial court correctly held that the appellee's representation of Dr. Reisman amounted to an isolated transaction and therefore properly denied the motion for directed verdict.

Judgment affirmed.

Foreign Corporations:
Qualification Procedures

TERRAL v. BURKE CONSTRUCTION CO.

(1922) 257 U.S. 529, 42 S.Ct. 188, 66 L.Ed. 352.

TAFT, C. J.

This is an appeal by Terral, defendant, from the District Court under sec. 238 of the Judicial Code, in a case in which the law of a State is claimed to be in contravention of the Consitution of the United States.

The Burke Construction Company, a corporation organized under the laws of the State of Missouri, filed its bill against Terral, Secretary of State of Arkansas, averring that it had been licensed to do business in the State of Arkansas under an act of the Arkansas Legislature approved May 13, 1907; that it was organized for the purpose of doing construction work, and carrying on interstate commerce, and was actually so engaged in Arkansas; that the right to do business in the State was a valuable privilege, and the revocation of the license would greatly injure it; that it had brought an original suit in the federal court of Arkansas and had removed a suit brought against it to the same federal court; that the Secretary of State was about to revoke the license because of such suit and such removal, acting under the requirement of Sec. 1 of the Act of the Legislature of Arkansas on May 13, 1907, reading as follows:

"If any company shall, without the consent of the other party to any suit or proceeding brought by or against it in any court of this State, remove said suit or proceeding to any Federal court, or shall institute any suit or proceeding against any citizen of this State in any Federal court, it shall be the duty of the Secretary of State to forthwith revoke all authority to such company and its agents to do business in this State, and to publish such revocation in some newspaper of general circulation published in this State; and if such corporation shall thereafter continue to do business in this State, it shall be subject to the penalty of this Act for each day it shall continue to do business in this State after such revocation."

The penalty fixed is not less than $1,000 a day. The Construction Company avers that this act is in contravention of Sec. 2, Article III, i.e., the judiciary article of the Federal Constitution, and of Sec. 1 of the Fourteenth Amendment. * * *

The sole question presented on the record is whether a state law is unconstitutional which revokes a license to a foreign corporation to do business within the State because, while doing only a domestic business in the State, it resorts to the federal court sitting in the State.

The cases in this court in which the conflict between the power of a State to exclude a foreign corporation from doing business within its borders, and the federal constitutional right of such foreign corporation to resort to the federal courts has been considered, can not be reconciled. [Citations.]

The principle established by the more recent decisions of this court is that a State may not, in imposing conditions upon the privilege of a foreign corporation's doing business in the State, exact from it a waiver of the exercise of its constitutional right to resort to the federal courts, or thereafter withdraw the privilege of doing business because of its exercise of such right, whether waived in advance or not. The principle does not depend for its application on the character of the business the corporation does, whether state or interstate, although that has been suggested as a distinction in some cases. It rests on the ground that the Federal Constitution confers upon citizens of one State the right to resort to federal courts in another, that state action, whether legislative or executive, which is necessarily calculated to curtail the free exercise of the right thus secured, is void because the sovereign power of a State in excluding foreign corporations, as in the exercise of all others of its sovereign powers, is subject to the limitations of the supreme fundamental law. It follows that the cases of Doyle v. Continental Insurance Co., 94 U.S. 535, 24 L.Ed. 148, and Security Mutual Life Insurance Co. v. Prewitt, 202 U.S. 246, 26 S.Ct. 619, 50 L.Ed. 1013, 6 Ann.Cas. 317, must be considered as overruled and that the views of the minority judges in those cases have become the law of this court. The appellant in proposing to comply with the statute in question and revoke the license was about to violate the constitutional right of the appellee. In enjoining him the District Court was right, and its decree is affirmed.

Problems

1. The stock in Hotel Management, Inc., a hotel management corporation, was divided equally between two families. For several years the two families had been unable to agree or coop-

erate in the management of the corporation. As a result of this dissension no meeting of shareholders or directors had been held for five years. There had been no withdrawal of profits for five years and the hotel had been operated at a loss for the year prior to the suit hereinafter mentioned. While the corporation was not insolvent such a state was imminent due to the fact that the business was poorly managed and its properties in need of repair. As a result the owners of one-half of the stock brought an action in equity for dissolution of the corporation. What decision?

2. (a) When may a corporation sell, lease, exchange, mortgage, or pledge all, or substantially all of its assets in the usual and regular course of its business?

(b) When may a corporation sell, lease, exchange, mortgage, or pledge all, or substantially all, of its assets otherwise than in the usual and regular course of its business?

(c) What are the rights of a shareholder who dissents from a proposed sale or exchange of all or substantially all, of the assets of a corporation otherwise than in the usual and reguluar course of its business?

3. The X Company was duly merged into the Y Company. S, a shareholder of the former X Company, having paid in only one-half of his subscription, is now sued by the Y Company for the balance of such subscription. S, who took no part in the merger proceedings, denied liability on the ground that inasmuch as the X Company no longer exists, all his rights and obligations in connection with the X Company have been terminated. Decision?

4. Smith, while in the course of his employment with the Bee Corporation, negligently ran the company's truck into X, injuring him very severely. Subsequently, the Bee Corporation, and the Sea Corporation, consolidated, forming the SeaBee Corporation. X filed suit against the SeaBee Corporation for damages and the SeaBee Corporation interposed the defense that the injuries sustained by X were not caused by any of SeaBee's employees, that the SeaBee was not even in existence at the time of the injury, and that, therefore, the SeaBee Corporation was not liable. What decision?

5. The Business Corporation Act of the State of X, after prescribing the procedure for the con-

solidation of two or more corporations, provides that "such surviving or new corporation shall thenceforth be responsible and liable for all the liabilities and obligations of each of the corporations so merged or consolidated."

The A Company, a corporation organized under the laws of the State of X, duly authorized by the shareholders, sold its entire assets to the B Company, also an X Corporation. T, an unpaid creditor of the A Company, sues the B Company upon his claim. Decision?

6. X Corporation, organized under the laws of State S, sends traveling salesmen into State M to solicit orders which are accepted only at the Home Office of X Corporation in State S. D, a resident of State M, places an order which is accepted by X Corporation and the goods are shipped to D from the office of X Corporation in State S. The Corporation Act of State M provides that "no foreign corporation transacting business in this state without a certificate of authority shall be permitted to maintain an action in any court of this state until such corporation shall have obtained a certificate of authority." D fails to pay for the goods and when X Corporation sues D in a court of State M, D defends on the ground that X Corporation has never had such a certificate of authority from State M. Result?

7. The Emanon Corporation was a Delaware corporation having its executive officer in Philadelphia, Pa. Jones, its vice-president was served with a summons in Trenton, N.J. The corporation had not procured a license to do business in New Jersey. It appeared that Jones had an office in Trenton in which he devoted his time to research work on matters affecting the Emanon Corporation, to the editing of printed literature for the corporation, and to the training of employees for it. Do these facts constitute doing business within New Jersey to such an extent as to require the Emanon Corporation to qualify?

8. The X Company, of Pennsylvania, manufactures articles and merchandise used all over the United States. Its business in Massachusetts was handled through the A Company, a large jobbing house, which purchased from the X Company in Pennsylvania and resold to retailers in Massachusetts. The X Company maintained no office in Massachusetts, was never licensed to do business in Massachusetts and paid no taxes to that State. Four times a year salesmen from the home office of the X Company canvassed the retail trade in Massachusetts, educating the trade in the use of the X Company's products and taking orders. Such orders were immediately turned over to the A Company by the salesmen, the A Company filling the orders from its own stock purchased from the X Company. The State of Massachusetts imposed heavy penalties against the X Company on the ground that the X Company was doing business in Massachusetts without having obtained the necessary license. Decision?

9. (a) X Corporation was an Illinois corporation. The Illinois legislature passed a statute exempting all stock in Illinois corporations from personal property tax. Y Corporation was a foreign corporation doing 75% of its business in the State of Illinois. As a result of the tax savings made possible by the above statute to persons owning stock in Illinois corporations, Y Corporation was at a great disadvantage in securing proper financing through stock sales. In a proper suit, Y Corporation challenged the con-

stitutionality of the statute.
(b) Illinois likewise passed a tax law providing that a personal property tax shall be levied on *all* the railroad cars owned by a railroad corporation, operating in Illinois, whether such cars ever come into Illinois or not. About 5% of X Railroad Corporation's cars were operated in Illinois. In a proper suit the X Railroad Corporation challenged the constitutionality of the statute.

Decide the issues involved in the above fact situations.

10. The A Corporation organized under the laws of New Jersey, had its general office and factory in New York and opens up a branch office in Illinois, from which contracts are closed and goods are delivered to purchasers. It also has a traveling salesman in Massachusetts who solicits orders and sends them in to be approved and filled. It also purchases land in Ohio, and then, deciding not to open an office there, resells the land and takes back a mortgage. In which of these States must it comply with the foreign corporation law?

Chapter

39

SECURED TRANSACTIONS IN PERSONAL PROPERTY

A secured transaction includes two elements: (1) a debt or obligation to pay money, and (2) an interest of the creditor in specific property which secures performance of the obligation. An obligation or debt needs no security in order to exist. A vast amount of entirely satisfactory indebtedness is unsecured, such as accounts payable, promissory notes, drafts, traveler's checks, and United States bonds, treasury notes and bills. The integrity, reputation for prompt payment, and net worth of the debtor are deemed adequate by the creditor. However, a security interest in property cannot exist apart from the debt which it secures, and upon a discharge of the debt in any manner, the security interest in the property is terminated.

In many situations, businessmen or other individuals cannot obtain credit without giving adequate security. Sometimes an unsecured loan can be obtained, but giving security may result in a lower interest rate. Financing transactions involving security in personal property are governed by Article 9 of the U.C.C., Secured Transac-

tions, which does not apply to liens on real estate. The official comment to Section 9–101 states:

The aim of this Article is to provide a simple and unified structure within which the immense variety of present-day secured financing transactions can go forward with less cost and with greater certainty.

* * *

The Article's flexibility and simplified formalities should make it possible for new forms of secured financing, as they develop, to fit comfortably under its provisions * * *.

ESSENTIALS OF SECURED TRANSACTIONS

Secured transactions in personal property occur generally in situations where a person wants to buy goods and does not have either the cash price or sufficient credit standing to obtain the goods on open credit. The seller obtains a security interest in the goods to secure payment of all or part of the price. Alternatively, the buyer may borrow the purchase price from a third party and pay the seller in cash. The third party lender then takes a security interest in the goods to secure repayment of the loan. In every financing transaction of this type, there is a debtor, a secured party, collateral, a security agreement, and a security interest. These are all defined terms in the U.C.C., but in most instances are self-explanatory.

As defined in Section 9–105(1), a "debtor" is a person who owes payment or performance of an obligation. A "secured party" is the creditor-lender, seller, or other person who owns the security interest in the collateral. "Collateral" is the property subject to the security interest. "Security Agreement" is the agreement which creates or provides for a security interest. Section 1–207(37) defines "security interest" which, in its broadest sense, is an interest in personal property or fixtures which secures payment or performance of an obligation. Thus, a security interest is created when an automobile dealer sells and delivers a car to an individual (debtor) under a retail installment contract (security agreement) whereby the dealer (secured party) obtains a security interest in the car (collateral) until the price is paid. This type of security agreement is also referred to as a conditional sale contract.

Attachment

The term "attachment" is basically synonymous with "enforceable between the parties." The security interest created by a security agreement attaches to the collateral described therein upon (1) the giving of value by the secured party, (2) the debtor acquiring rights in the collateral, and (3) either the collateral is in the possession of the secured party or the security agreement is in a writing which contains a description of the collateral and is signed by the debtor. Section 9–203. Attachment occurs as soon as all of these described events have taken place.

Perfection

In order to have a valid security interest which is effective against other creditors of the debtor, his trustee in bankruptcy, and transferees of the debtor, the security interest must be perfected. "A security interest is perfected when it has attached and when all of the applicable steps required for perfection have been taken." Section 9–303(1).

A security interest may be perfected by filing a financing statement signed by the debtor, or by retention of possession of the collateral by the secured party, but neither is required in the case of a purchase money security interest in consumer goods. Section 9–302(1)(d).

Possession. A pledge is the delivery of possession of personal property to a creditor as security for the payment of a debt. Perhaps the most common pledge is that of a borrower who pledges corporate stock by delivery of the certificates to a bank in order to secure a loan. The delivery of the collateral (stock certificates properly indorsed or accompanied by a stock power) to the bank (secured party) is the essential element of the pledge. Since delivery is made, the security interest is "perfected" without filing. In a pledge, it is not legally required that the debtor sign a security agreement, but it is customary. In any situation other than a pledge, a security agreement is required by the Code.

Filing a Financing Statement. Where the secured party does not have possession of the collateral, the filing of a financing statement with the Secretary of State or other official as provided in the Code constitutes a perfection of the security interest. The form of the financing statement, which is filed to give public notice of the security interest, may vary from State to State. The financing statement does not contain details, but the names and addresses of the secured party and the debtor, a description of the collateral, and the signature of the debtor is required. Section 9–402(1). Where fixtures are being financed, a description of the real estate upon which they are located is required. The Code provides that any description of the real estate or personal property is sufficient if it reasonably identifies them. Section 9–110. A financing statement should indicate the types, or describe the items, of collateral. Section 9–402(1). It is obviously easier to be more specific in describing certain items, such as a cutting machine or a computer, than in describing others, such as a manufacturer's raw materials or work in process, or a retail store's inventory.

In order to ascertain the terms of a financing transaction between the parties, resort must be had to the security agreement or the collateral note or preferably both. It is possible that the maturity date of the obligation will not appear on the financing statement, nor the amount of the obligation secured. Where no maturity date is stated on a financing statement, the statement is effective for five years from the date of filing. Section 9–403(2).

Automatic Perfection. A seller of goods retaining a security interest in them by a security agreement has a *purchase money security interest*. Similarly, a third party which advances funds to enable the debtor to purchase goods has a purchase money security interest if it has a security agreement and the debtor in fact uses the funds to purchase the goods. Section 9–107. A purchase money security interest is perfected without the necessity of filing a financing statement with respect to consumer goods. Section 9–302(1)(d). Prior to the 1972 amendments, automatic perfection also occurred with respect to a purchase money security interest in farm equipment having a purchase price not in excess of $2,500.

Motor Vehicle Title. In most States security interests in motor vehicles must be perfected by a notation on the certificate of title rather than by filing a financing statement.

CLASSIFICATION OF COLLATERAL

The Code classifies collateral as: (a) goods, (b) collateral involving "indispensable paper," and (c) intangibles.

An item of goods may fall into different classifications depending on its use or purpose. A refrigerator purchased by a physician to store medicines in his office is classified as equipment, while the same refrigerator would classify as consumer goods if purchased for use in his home, or classify as inventory in the hands of a refrigerator dealer or manufacturer.

Goods

Goods are subdivided into (1) consumer goods, (2) equipment, (3) farm products, (4) inventory, and (5) fixtures.

Consumer Goods. Goods are consumer goods if they are used or bought for use primarily for personal, family, or household purposes. Section 9–109(1).

Equipment. Goods are classified as equipment if they are used or purchased for use primarily in business (including farming or a profession), and if they are not included in the definition of inventory, farm products, or consumer goods. Section 9–109(2). This category is broad enough to include a lawyer's library, a physician's office furniture, or machinery in a factory.

Farm Products. Section 9–109(3) defines farm products as "crops or livestock or supplies used or produced in farming operations or if they are products of crops or livestock in their unmanufactured states * * *"

Inventory. The term "inventory" includes goods held for sale or lease, as well as raw materials, work in process, or materials used or consumed in a business. Thus, a retailer's or wholesaler's merchandise as well as a manufacturer's materials are inventory. Section 9–109(4). The purchase of inventory by a retailer or manufacturer may require financing, and buyers of goods from the retailer or manufacturer in the ordinary course of business must be able to take them free of the financier's security interest.

Inventory is the stock in trade of a retailer. It is also the materials required by a manufacturer in the course of his daily production. It is constantly changing, being turned over, and renewed. An inventory financier is necessarily interested in the use and disposition of the proceeds from the sale of inventory in which he has a security interest. These proceeds may be in the form of cash, checks, accounts, chattel paper (probably installment or conditional sale contracts), or traded-in goods. It is possible that one financier may finance inventory, and another finance the accounts receivable or chattel paper resulting from sale of the inventory. If different financiers are involved at these two levels of financing, the inventory financier will be concerned about his right to the proceeds arising when accounts receivable or chattel paper are sold or assigned as security for further financing. The Code accommodates the legitimate interests of both financiers by allowing a perfected security interest in after-acquired property where the security agreement specifically so provides. Section 9–204. This permits a valid "floating lien" on after-acquired items of inventory, as well as after-acquired accounts receivable.

The term "floating lien" is descriptive of a security interest in changing collateral. While all collateral changes to some extent—an automobile deteriorates, a crop grows and is harvested—the above description applies particularly to collateral that is inventory, the proceeds from its sale, and the stock of fresh inventory acquired by way of replacement; and also to accounts receivable, the proceeds from their collection, and subsequently created accounts receivable generated by future sales. In the case of a merchant's inventory, the security interest in any specific item of inventory terminates upon its sale in the ordinary course of business, but attaches to the new inventory which replaces or replenishes the stock. The constant changes and turnover of inventory and receivables in the operation of a mercantile business may be likened to the flow of a stream or river. Although the specific water in the stream at any particular time and place changes from hour to hour, the stream remains the same. The Code permits a security interest to be perfected to a stream of changing collateral of this type by the inclusion of an "after acquired property" clause in the security agreement and the financing statement. Section 9–306.

Fixtures. The term "fixtures" refers to personal property or goods which have become so related to particular real property that an interest in them arises under real estate law. Section 9–313(1). In essence, the law of the State other than the Code shall determine whether and when goods become fixtures. In general terms, goods become fixtures when firmly affixed or attached to real estate in such manner that they are considered part of the real estate, yet may be detached without destroying the structure. Examples are furnaces, air-conditioning units, and plumbing fixtures. In some States a gas stove may be a fixture, whereas an electric stove generally is not.

Most disputes concerning fixture financing under the Code have arisen between real estate financiers and chattel financiers. If a mortgagee finances a complete building, he expects the furnace to stay in place if necessary to foreclose the mortgage. On the other hand, furnaces wear out, and debtors replace them by purchasing new furnaces on a time payment plan from sellers who retain security interests and, if the buyers do not pay, the sellers expect to be able to repossess the furnaces.

Under the 1962 Code, a security interest which attaches to goods before they become fixtures took priority over real estate interests, including an earlier recorded mortgage. Section 9–313(2), as limited, by Section 9–313(4). This supposedly eliminated windfalls to prior real estate mortgage interests. The 1972 version governing security interests in fixtures is extremely complex and is governed by Section 9–313(3) through (7).

Collateral Involving "Indispensable Paper"

Three kinds of collateral involve rights evidenced by "indispensable paper": (1) chattel paper, (2) instruments, and (3) documents.

Chattel Paper. "Chattel paper" is a writing or writings which evidence both a monetary obligation and a security interest in, or a lease of, specific goods. Section 9–105(1)(b). Frequently, to satisfy his own capital requirements a secured party may borrow against or sell the security agreement of his debtor along with his interest in the collateral. The secured party's collateral in this type of transaction is described by the term "chattel paper". Comment 4 to U.C.C. 9–105 provides the following illustration:

A dealer sells a tractor to a farmer on conditional sales contract or purchase money security interest. The conditional sales contract is a "security agreement", the farmer is the "debtor", the dealer is the "secured party" and the tractor is the type of "collateral" defined in Section 9–109 as "equipment". But now the dealer transfers the contract to his bank, either by outright sale or to secure a loan. Since the conditional sales contract is a security agreement relating to specific equipment, the conditional sales contract is

now the type of collateral called "chattel paper". In this transaction between the dealer and his bank, the bank is the "secured party", the dealer is the "debtor", and the farmer is the "account debtor".

Instrument. The term "instrument" includes negotiable instruments, stocks, bonds, and other investment securities. Section 9–105(1)(i). It is the usual type of paper transferable by delivery with any necessary indorsement or assignment, which is not of itself a security agreement or lease.

With two exceptions, the only means of perfecting a security interest in instruments is by taking possession of them. Filing does not constitute notice of the security interest to bona fide purchasers or holders in due course. The two exceptions are: (1) when the security interest in instruments is created for new value under a written security agreement, the interest is perfected without filing or taking possession for a period of 21 days from the time it attaches; and (2) if the interest has been previously perfected by taking possession, it continues to be perfected for a period of 21 days where the secured party delivers the instruments to the debtor for the purpose of sale or exchange, presentation, collection, renewal, or registration of transfer. Section 9–304. There are legitimate business reasons for allowing the debtor to have the collateral for short periods. It would serve no particular purpose to require filing for short-term transactions, and in long-term transactions, it is the custom for the secured party to take possession of the collateral. However, the secured party runs the risk of loss or impairment of his security interest during the 21-day period, for although his interest is temporarily perfected, a holder in due course of a negotiable instrument or a bona fide purchaser of the instrument will take priority over the security interest. Section 9–309.

Document. The term "document" includes bills of lading and warehouse receipts (Sections 9–105(1)(f), 1–201 (15)), which may be either negotiable or non-negotiable. A document of title is negotiable if by its terms the goods it covers are deliverable to bearer or to the order of a named person. Any other document is non-negotiable. (Section 7–104.)

A security interest in goods represented by a negotiable document is perfected by negotiation of the document. A security interest in goods in the possession of a bailee other than one who has issued a negotiable document therefor is perfected by the issuance of a document in the name of the secured party, by notification to the bailee of the secured party's interest, or by a filing as to the goods. Section 9–304(3). This provision covers the traditional area of field warehousing.

A security interest in a negotiable document may be perfected either by filing or by taking possession of the document. However, filing is not notice to a holder to whom a negotiable document has been duly negotiated. There are 21-day "trust receipt privileges" provided in Section 9–304(5) during which period a perfected interest continues to be perfected without filing or without possession by the secured party who, however, runs the risk that the debtor may negotiate the document to a bona fide purchaser who will take priority over the secured party. Sections 9–304, 9–309.

Intangible Collateral

The Code also recognizes two kinds of collateral which are neither goods nor "paper" collateral, namely, accounts, and general intangibles. These types of intangible collateral are not evidenced by any indispensable paper, such as a stock certificate or a negotiable bill of lading.

Account. The term "account" or "accounts receivable" refers to the right to payment for goods sold or leased, or for services rendered, which is not evidenced by an instru-

ment or chattel paper, whether or not it has been earned by performance. Section 9–106. The 1972 Code deletes from Section 9–106 the term "contract right" but includes contract rights in the expanded definition of account.

General Intangibles. The term "general intangibles" applies to any personal property (including things in action) other than goods, accounts, chattel paper, documents, instruments, and money. Section 9–106. This is a catch-all category for interests not otherwise covered or specifically excluded. It leaves room for the utilization of new kinds of collateral for financing purposes. It includes good will, literary rights, rights to performance of a contract, and interests in patents, trademarks, and copyrights to the extent they are not regulated by Federal statute. Since there is no indispensable paper which evidences rights in general intangibles, perfection is by filing a financing statement.

PRIORITIES

As previously noted, in order to have a valid security interest which is effective against other creditors of the debtor, the debtor's trustee in bankruptcy and transferees of the debtor, the security interest must be perfected. Article 9 establishes a complex set of rules that determine the relative priorities among these parties. These rules of priority may be summarized as follows:

1. A creditor with a perfected security interest has greater rights in the collateral than either a creditor with an unperfected security interest or an unsecured creditor. Section 9–201.

2. As between two parties each with a perfected security interest, Section 9–312(5)(a) provides:

(a) Conflicting security interests rank according to priority in time of filing or perfection. Priority dates from the time a filing is first made covering the collateral or the time the security interest is first perfected, whichever is earlier, provided that there is no period thereafter when there is neither filing nor perfection.

For example, D Store and S Bank enter into a loan agreement under the terms of which S agrees to lend $5,000 upon the security of D's existing store equipment. A financing statement is filed but no funds are advanced. One week later D enters into a loan agreement with R Bank, and R Bank agrees to lend $5,000 on the security of the same store equipment. The funds are advanced and a financing statement is filed. One week later S Bank advances the agreed sum of $5,000. D Store defaults on both loans. As between S Bank and R Bank, S has priority. When both security interests are perfected by filing, priority is determined in the order of filing. Section 9–312(5)(a). R Bank could have checked the financing statements on file and would have learned that S Bank claimed a security interest in the equipment. Once S's financing statement was on file, with no prior secured party of record, S was not required to check the files prior to advancing funds to D Store in accordance with its loan commitment.

Assume that X grants a security interest in a Chagall painting to S Bank, and in accordance with a loan agreement, the Bank advances funds to X. A financing statement is filed. Later X wishes more money and goes to C, an art dealer, who advances funds to X upon a pledge of the painting. X defaults on both loans. As between S and C, S has priority because its security interest was filed prior to C's perfection by possession. Section 9–312(5)(a). By checking the financing statements on file C could have discovered that S had a prior security interest in the painting.

3. If neither security interest is perfected then Section 9–312(5)(b) governs:

(b) So long as conflicting security interests are unperfected, the first to attach has priority.

4. Where there is a purchase money security interest in the collateral, the rules depend upon whether the collateral is non-inventory or inventory.

(a) A purchase money security interest in non-inventory collateral takes priority over conflicting security interest if the purchase money security interest is perfected at the time the debtor receives possession of the collateral or within ten days of receipt. Section 9–312(4).

For example, D Manufacturing Co. entered into a loan agreement with S Bank which lent money to D upon the security of D's existing and future equipment. A financing statement was filed reciting that the collateral is "all equipment presently owned and subsequently acquired" by D. At a later date D buys new equipment from X Supply Co., paying 25% of the purchase price with X retaining a security interest in the equipment to secure the remaining balance. If X files a financing statement within 10 days after D obtains possession of the equipment, X's purchase money security interest in the new equipment has priority over S's interest under Section 9–312(4). If X filed on the eleventh day after D received the equipment, X's interest would be subordinated to S's interest.

(b) A purchase money security interest in inventory has priority over conflicting security interests provided that the purchase money security holder perfects his interest in the inventory at the time the debtor receives the inventory and notifies in writing all holders of conflicting security interests who have filed a financing statement covering the same type of inventory of his acquisition of a purchase money security interest and a description of the secured inventory. Section 9–312(3).

D Store and S Bank enter into a loan agreement under the terms of which S agrees to finance D's entire inventory of stoves, refrigerators, and kitchen furniture. A financing statement is filed, and S advances funds to D. Subsequently, D enters into an agreement under which R Stove Co.

will supply D with stoves, retaining a purchase money security interest in this inventory. Under Section 9–312(3), R will have priority as to the inventory it supplies to D provided that before delivery of the stoves to D, a financing statement is filed and R notifies S that it is going to engage in this purchase money financing of the described stoves. If R fails to give the required notice or fails to file a financing statement before delivery of the stoves to D, S will have priority over R as to the stoves supplied by R to D. Section 9–312(3). The Code adopts a system of notice filing, and secured parties proceed at their peril in failing to check the financing statements on file.

5. A buyer in the ordinary course of business takes free of any security interest created by *his seller,* even if the security interest is perfected and the buyer knows of its existence. Section 9–307(1).

6. In the case of consumer goods, a buyer who buys without knowledge of a security interest, for value and for his own personal, family, or household use takes free of any purchase money security interest, automatically perfected under Section 9–302(1)(d), but takes the goods subject to a security interest perfected by filing. Section 9–307(2).

7. A perfected security interest has priority over lien creditors. Section 9–301(1). A lien creditor means a creditor who has acquired a lien in the property by attachment and a trustee in bankruptcy. Section 9–301(3).

8. It is possible, under Section 9–316, for a secured party entitled to priority to subordinate his interest to that of another secured creditor. This may be done by agreement between the secured parties, and nothing need be filed.

DEFAULT

After default, the rights and remedies of the parties are governed by the security agreement and by the applicable provisions of Article 9, Part 5. In general, the secured party may reduce his claim to judgment, foreclose, or otherwise enforce the security interest by available judicial procedure. Section 9–501. Unless the parties have agreed otherwise, the secured party may take possession of the collateral on default without judicial process if it can be done without a breach of the peace. Without removing it, the secured party may render equipment unusable and dispose of it on the debtor's premises. Section 9–503. The secured party may sell, lease, or otherwise dispose of any collateral in its condition existing at the time of repossession, or following any commercially reasonable preparation or processing. Section 9–504(1). The debtor is entitled to any surplus and is liable for any deficiency, except that in the case of a sale of accounts, or chattel paper, he is not entitled to any surplus or liable for a deficiency unless the security agreement so provides. Section 9–504(2).

The collateral may be disposed of at public or private sale, so long as all aspects of its disposition are "commercially reasonable." Unless the collateral is perishable or threatens to decline speedily in value or is of a type customarily sold on a recognized market, reasonable notice must be given to the debtor of a public sale or of the time after which a private disposition will be made, and except in the case of consumer goods, to other secured parties who have filed or who are known by the secured party to have security interests in the collateral. The secured party may buy at a public sale, and at a private sale if the collateral is customarily sold in a recognized market or is the subject of widely distributed standard price quotations. Section 9–504(3).

The secured party may, after default, and repossession, send written notice to the debtor and, except in the case of consumer goods, to other secured parties that he proposes to retain the collateral in satisfaction of the obligation, and if no objection is received within twenty-one days, the secured party may retain the collateral; but if objection is received, the collateral must be disposed of as provided in the Code. In the case of consumer goods, if the debtor has paid sixty per cent of the purchase money security obligation and has not, after default, signed a statement renouncing his rights, the secured party who has taken possession of the collateral must dispose of it by sale within ninety days after repossession or the debtor may recover in conversion or under the Code not less than the credit service charge plus ten per cent of the principal amount of the debt or the time price differential plus ten per cent of the cash price. Sections 9–505, 9–507(1).

Unless the debtor has waived his rights in the collateral after default, he has a right of redemption at any time before the secured party has disposed of the collateral or entered into a contract to dispose of it. Section 9–506.

Cases

Essentials of Secured Transactions

MATTER OF AMEX-PROTEIN DEVELOPMENT CORPORATION

(1974 C.A.9th) 504 F.2d 1056.

PER CURIAM:

This is an appeal filed pursuant to § 24 of the Bankruptcy Act (11 U.S.C. § 47) from a judgment of the district court holding that a valid and enforceable security interest was created under the provisions of the Uniform Commercial Code.

We adopt the following opinion of the Honorable George B. Harris, United States District Judge for the Northern District of California:

"This matter is on review from an Order of the Referee which declared invalid a security interest claimed by petitioner Plant Reclamation, a creditor of the bankrupt, in certain personal property in the possession of the bankrupt.

"Plant Reclamation had sold equipment to the bankrupt on open account, but on October 16, 1972, substituted a promissory note for the open account indebtedness and caused a financing statement to be signed and filed. The parties intended to create a security interest in the property sold as collateral for the note, and the Referee so found.

"The promissory note included the following line: 'This note is secured by a Security Interest in subject personal property as per invoices.' The words 'subject * * * as per invoices' were handwritten in an otherwise typewritten sentence; the testimony before the Referee established that such words were added by an officer of the bankrupt in order to tie the security interest to the personal property that had been sold to the bankrupt by Plant Reclamation. The invoices referred to in the promissory note were the only ones submitted by Plant Reclamation.

"The financing statement named Plant Reclamation as the secured party and recited that it covered the following types or items of property:

1—Door Oliver 100 Sq. Ft. Vacuum Filter
1—Chicago Pheumatic [sic] Vacuum Compression
1—Stainless Steel Augar [sic] and Drive
1—Nichols Micro 7″ dryer
1—Tolhurst Centerfuge [sic] 26 inch

Discussion
I. Did the Promissory Note 'Create or Provide for' a Security Interest?

* * *

"No magic words or precise form are necessary to create or provide for a security interest so long as the minimum formal requirements of the Code are met. [Citations.] This liberal approach is mandated by an expressed purpose of the secured transaction provisions of the Code:

The aim of this Article is to provide a simple and unified structure within which the immense variety of present-day secured financing transactions can go forward with less cost and with greater certainty.

* * *

The Article's flexibility and simplified formalities should make it possible for new forms of secured financing, as they develop, to fit comfortably under its provisions * * *. Comment to U.C.C. and Cal.Com.C. § 9101.

"The court in In re Center Auto Parts, 6 U.C.C.Rep. 398 (C.D.Cal.1968) upheld the validity of a promissory note as a security agreement by reading the two together. The promissory note merely recited that, 'This note is secured by a certain financing statement,' and the court found that such was sufficient to 'create or provide for' a security interest within the meaning of § 9105(1)(h).

* * *

"Accordingly, the promissory note herein qualifies as a security agreement which by its terms 'creates or provides for' a security interest.

II. Adequacy of Description of the Collateral

"The trustee urges a second ground for sustaining the Order of the Referee complained of here, namely the inadequacy of the description of the collateral in the promissory note and hence the failure to comply with Cal.Com.C. § 9203(1)(b) [citation].

* * *

"Although the promissory note does not describe the collateral within the four corners of the document such description is provided (1) through incorporation by reference of the subject invoices, as well as (2) through reference to the more specific description of the collateral contained in the financing statement.

"The use of such extrinsic aids is clearly permissible to identify the collateral:

Under the Uniform Commercial Code there is no reason why parol evidence may not be admitted in aid of the description of the collateral, even where the collateral has been reasonably and sufficiently identified in the security agreement. In many instances, a description in a security agreement may be in general terms; parol evidence should therefore be admissible to explain or supplement the general description, or to resolve ambiguities. [Footnotes omitted.] 44 Cal.Jur.2d Rev. Secured Transactions § 107 at 386.

"The doctrine of incorporation by reference is likewise available in this area:

There is nothing in the Uniform Commercial Code to prevent reference in the security agreement to another writing for particular terms and conditions of the transaction. There is also nothing in the Uniform Commercial Code to prevent reference in the Security Agreement to another writing for a description of the collateral, so long as the reference in the security agreement is sufficient to identify reasonably what it described. In other words, it will at times be expedient to give a general description of the collateral in the security agreement and refer to a list or other writing for more exact description. In addition, the security agreement could itself consist of separate parts, one a general description of the obligation secured and the rights and duties of the parties, and the other a description of the collateral, both such writings being signed by the debtor and stated to comprise a single security agreement or referring to each other. [Footnotes omitted.] Id. § 109 at 387–388.

"Thus there is no requirement that the description of the collateral be complete within the four corners of the security agreement or other single document. The description in the security agreement is sufficient, however, if it provides such information as would lead a reasonable inquirer to the identity of the collateral. [Citations.]

"It is manifest that the reference to the invoices in the subject promissory note, coupled with the existence of a financing statement containing a more specific description, satisfies the requirements of Cal.Com.C. §§ 9203(1)(b) and 9110.

* * *

Conclusion
"For the reasons stated above, the petition of Plant Reclamation is hereby granted, and the Order of the Referee Declaring Lien Invalid, dated April 10, 1973, is hereby reversed. It is so ordered."

The judgment is affirmed.

Priorities: Purchase
Money Security Interest

MATTER OF ULTRA PRECISION INDUSTRIES, INC.

(1974 C.A.9th) 503 F.2d 414.

EAST, Senior District Judge:

The Appeal
National Acceptance Company of California (National) appeals from the two several orders of the District Court denying its Petition for Review and affirming the referee's two several rulings or orders that the security interest held by Community Bank (Bank) and Wolf Machinery Company (Wolf) in three large Rigid Hydro Copy Profiling Machines, numbered 5890 and 5910 (Bank) and machine numbered 5934 (Wolf), respectively, had priority over a conflicting security interest held by National. § 9312(4) of the Uniform Commercial Code of California (Code). We affirm.

Facts
The pertinent facts are:

National loaned Ultra Precision Industries, Inc. (Ultra) $692,000, and to secure the repayment of that sum, Ultra on or about March 7, 1967, executed in favor of National a Chattel Mortgage Security Agreement covering specifically described equipment of Ultra. National perfected its security interest by timely filing a Financing Statement. The Chattel Mortgage Security Agreement and the Financing Statement contained the usual after-acquired equipment security clauses; however, without reference to any specific property.

Subsequent to the acquisition of National's security interest and during 1967 and 1968, Ultra placed orders with Wolf for two of the machines, later identified as machines numbered 5890 and 5910. It was agreed between Ultra and Wolf that after those machines had been shipped to Ultra and installed, Ultra would be given an opportunity to test them in their operations during a reasonable testing period, and, further, that arrangements satisfactory to Ultra for outside financing was a condition precedent to the ultimate purchase of those machines. The machines were delivered to Ultra on April 30, 1968 and June 20, 1968, respectively, satisfactory testing was accomplished, outside financing obtained, and on July 31, 1968, Ultra nad Wolf executed a Purchase Money Security Interest Conditional Sales Agreement (Security Interest Agreement) covering the sale of those two machines by Wolf to Ultra, and as a part of the outside financing arrangement, Wolf in consideration of the payment of $128,122.20 assigned the Security Interest Agreement to Bank. Bank's security interest was perfected by the filing of a Financing Statement on August 5, 1968.

In June, 1968, Ultra placed another order with Wolf for a similar machine, later identified as machine numbered 5934, under identical terms of testing and purchase as those for the purchase of the above numbered machines 5890 and 5910. The machine was delivered to Ultra on August 7, 1968, satisfactory testing was accomplished, outside financing obtained, and on October 23, 1968, Ultra and Wolf executed a similar Security Interest Agreement covering the sale of the machine numbered 5934 by Wolf to Ultra, and as a part of the outside financing arrangement, Wolf, for value received, assigned the Security Interest Agreement to C.I.T. Corporation. C.I.T. Corporation's security interest was perfected by the filing of a Financing Statement on October 30, 1968. On October 7, 1969, C.I.T. Corporation reassigned the Security Interest Agreement to Wolf when Ultra became bankrupt.

Issue

The priorities among the three security interests involved are determined by the application of § 9312(4), which reads:

A purchase money security interest in collateral other than inventory has priority over a conflicting security interest in the same collateral *if the purchase money security interest is perfected at the time the debtor receives possession of the collateral or within 10 days thereafter. (emphasis added):*

The sole issue presented by the facts and the contention of the parties on appeal is: On what dates did Ultra become "the debtor [receiving] possession of the collateral [the three respective machines]" within the meaning of § 9312(4)?

Discussion

Briefly stated, National contends that Ultra was its "debtor" in "possession of the collateral" at the moment it received physical delivery of the respective three machines, without regard to any agreement to the contrary between Wolf and Ultra as to the terms and conditions of the ultimate sale and purchase of the machines respectively; hence, the machines were within the grasp of the after-acquired property clause. Since the Security Interest Agreements held by Bank and Wolf were not perfected within ten days "thereafter" as commanded by § 9312(4), they are unenforceable as against National's perfected security interest.

Bank and Wolf each contend that Ultra did not become their "debtor" in "possession of the collateral" (the three respective machines) until the terms and conditions of the

proposed sales and purchases thereof had been met and the Security Interest Agreement had been executed and delivered. We subscribe to that contention.

Section 9105(1) of the Code provides:

(1) In this division unless the context otherwise requires:

(d) "Debtor" means the person who owes payment or other performance of the obligation secured * * *.

National urges that the term "debtor" as used in § 9312(4) means the debtor under its "conflicting security interest." Such an interpretation does violence to the clear language of the section, and such a thesis is inherently rejected under the rationale and holdings in Brodie Hotel Supply, Inc. v. United States, 431 F.2d 1316 (C.A.9 1970), and In Re Automated Bookbinding Sevices, Inc., 471 F.2d 546 (C.A.4 1972). To us, the word "debtor" in § 9312(4) means the debtor of the seller or holder of the "purchase money security interest in collateral" (the thing sold).

It is manifest that Ultra was not a "debtor" of Wolf and did not owe payment or other performance of the obligation secured unto Wolf until the moment of the execution and delivery of the Security Interest Agreements on July 31, 1968, and October 23, 1968, respectively. Suffice to say that prior to those dates, (a) Wolf held no definitive security interest in the machines which could be perfected by the filing of a Financing Statement, and (b) Ultra held no assignable legal interest in the machines which could fall into the grasp of National's after-acquired property security clause.

We hold that Ultra became the purchase money security interest "debtor [receiving] possession of the collateral [the three respective machines]" at the instant of the execution and delivery of the Security Interest Agreements, respectively, and not before; and, further, that since each of the

Security Interest Agreements were timely perfected, the security interests of Wolf and Bank, respectively, are each prior and superior to the conflicting security interest held by National. [Citation.]

* * *

The record as a whole reveals good faith, above board, uninvolved commercial credit transactions, without any withholding on the part of or secret equities among the parties. National was in no way misled by any acts of Wolf or Bank giving rise to an estoppel, and National advanced no money or credit on the strength of Ultra's pre-Security Interest Agreement possession of the machines. Wolf was entitled to abide with the terms and conditions of the proposed sales and purchases of its machines and to perfect its ultimate Security Interest Agreements in accordance with § 9312(4).

Affirmed.

Priorities: Buyer in the Ordinary Course of Business

CESSNA FINANCE CORP. v. SKYWAYS ENTERPRISES, INC.

(1979, Ky.) 580 S.W.2d 491.

LUKOWSKY, J.

Cessna Finance seeks a reversal of a decision of the Court of Appeals affirming a judgment of the Fayette Circuit Court. The trial court held that Cessna Finance's perfected security interest in a Cessna 414 aircraft could not be enforced against Skyways, a subsequent purchaser of the aircraft in the ordinary course of business from Du Page, a Cessna dealer, and First Security which subsequently acquired a perfected security interest in the aircraft from Skyways. We affirm.

Cessna Finance bank-rolled the sale of a Cessna 414 by Aviation Activities, a Cessna distributor, to Central States, a Cessna dealer, controlled by Brooks. Central States gave Cessna Finance a mortgage supported by a promissory note to se-cure the loan. The mortgage provided that Central States could not sell the aircraft without the prior consent of Cessna Finance. Cessna Finance recorded its mortgage with the Federal Aviation Administration (F.A.A.) pursuant to 49 U.S.C. Sec. 1403, which provides for the centralized recording of all title and security documents for civil aircraft.

On June 18, 1973, Central States transferred the aircraft without consideration to Du Page, another Cessna dealer controlled by Brooks [footnotes omitted]. Cessna Finance was not notified of nor did it consent to this transfer. On the same day Du Page sold the aircraft to Skyways, a recently formed aircraft dealership, which failed to make a title search of F.A.A. records and did not have actual knowledge of the Cessna Finance security interest. Skyways recorded its title to the aircraft with the F.A.A. on November 8, 1973, nearly five months after the sale.

In January, 1974 First Security acquired a security interest in the aircraft from Skyways. First Security had no actual knowledge of the Cessna Finance security interest and also failed to make a title search of F.A.A. records. On April 12, 1974, First Security perfected its security interest by filing with the F.A.A. First Security was aware of the F.A.A. records facility. Skyways was not.

Cessna Finance did not consent to the sale of the aircraft by Du Page to Skyways. However, Cessna Finance was notified of a proposed sale by Du Page of the Cessna 414 to Skyways on May 23, 1973. It was the practice of the parties to treat such a notification as a commitment to sell the aircraft to the named buyer within four (4) months and during this period the loan would run interest free. Cessna Finance also knew that Du Page was selling other aircraft in which it held a security interest without its consent, and without satisfaction of the security interest until after consummation of the sale.

* * *

In November, 1973, Cessna Finance became aware of the sale of this aircraft out of trust without pay-off of its security interest. Cessna Finance made several searches of the title of the Cessna 414 before discovering on November 27, 1974, that Skyways had been sold the aircraft. Cessna Finance informed Skyways of its security interest and requested that Skyways surrender the aircraft to it, because Central States had defaulted on its note. Skyways refused to comply with the request. Cessna Finance filed suit in April, 1974, to replevy the aircraft. First Security intervened in a timely manner to protect its security interest in the aircraft.

Cessna Finance contends that the Federal Aviation Act, 49 U.S.C. Sec. 1403, preempts all state laws governing priorities among perfected security interests. We do not agree. * * *

Kentucky has adopted the Uniform Commercial Code and its provisions govern priorities between conflicting security interests. [U.C.C.] 1–101—10–102. The general rule under the Uniform Commercial Code is that a perfected security interest "continues in collateral notwithstanding sale, exchange, or other disposition by the debtor unless his action was authorized by the secured party in the security agreement or *otherwise* * * *." 9–306(2). However, there are many cases where by operation of statute a purchaser of collateral will take free of a perfected security interest under the "or otherwise" exception in 9–306(2) and the secured party's only right will be to proceeds of the sale held by the debtor. U.C.C. Sec. 9–306, comment 3 (1962).

9–307(1) is one of the statutory "or otherwise" exceptions to 9–306(2). U.C.C. Sec. 9–306, comment 3 (1962). It provides that a buyer in the ordinary course of business takes free of a security interest created by the seller even though the secured party has perfected its interest and the buyer knows of it and even though the disposition was not authorized. U.C.C. Sec. 9–306, comment 3 (1962). A buyer in the ordinary course of business is defined as a "person who in good faith and without knowledge that the sale to him is in violation of the ownership rights or security interest of a third party in the goods buys in ordinary course from a person in the business of selling goods of that kind but does not include a pawnbroker." 1–201(9). Under these two statutory provisions a buyer will purchase goods free of any security interest created by the seller if he knows that there is a security interest which covers the goods, but will be subject to the claims of the secured party if he knows, in addition, that the sale is in violation of some term in the security agreement not waived by the words or conduct of the secured party. U.C.C. Sec. 9–307, comment 2 (1962).

Du Page was in the business of selling aircraft. The sale to Skyways occurred in the ordinary course of its business. Clearly, Skyways was a buyer in the ordinary course of business. It purchased the aircraft in good faith without knowledge that the sale was in violation of any security interest held by Cessna Finance. Contrary to the contention of Cessna Finance the fact that Skyways was also a dealer in aircraft does not prevent it from being a buyer in the ordinary course of Du Page's business. The only person excluded from being a buyer in the ordinary course of business by the character of his business is a pawnbroker. A dealer may be a buyer in the ordinary course of business from another dealer in the same goods provided he meets the other requirements of 1–201(9). [Citation.]

Because Skyways was a buyer of the aircraft in the ordinary course of business from Du Page, a person in the business of selling aircraft, and did not know of the restriction on the sale of the aircraft in Cessna Finance's mortgage, it took title to the Cessna 414 free of the security interest held by Cessna Finance. 9–307(1); U.C.C. Sec.

9–307, comment 2 (1962). First Security has a superior security interest in the aircraft because Cessna Finance no longer had a valid security interest in the aircraft after its sale to Skyways. 9–307(1).

The decision of the Court of Appeals and the judgment of the Circuit Court are affirmed.

Priorities: Buyer in the Ordinary Course of Business

EXCHANGE BANK OF OSCEOLA v. JARRETT

(1979, Mont.) 588 P.2d 1006.

SHEEHY, J.

Plaintiff appeals from an order entered by the District Court, Custer County, granting defendant's motion to dismiss for failure to state a claim upon which relief could be granted. We reverse.

The material facts are not in dispute. On September 8, 1976, Daniel F. Holland purchased a Michigan tractor-scraper through the Exchange Bank of Osceola (bank), located in Kissimmee, Florida. The bank retained a security interest in the tractor to insure full payment of the $13,000.00 purchase price. The bank took the necessary steps to perfect its security interest under Florida's Commercial Code.

On February 1, 1977, Daniel F. Holland, without plaintiff's permission and in violation of the security agreement, sold the tractor-scraper to C. B. and O. Equipment Co. of Council Bluffs, Iowa. C. B. and O., an Iowa merchant dealing in farm implements, transported the tractor-scraper from Florida to Council Bluffs, Iowa. The record shows that the tractor arrived in Iowa on February 7, 1977.

On February 21, 1977, defendant, a Montana contractor, purchased the tractor-scraper from C. B. and O. for a good and valuable consideration. Defendant took possession of the tractor-scraper on or about February 21, 1977 and returned to Montana. The record indicates the tractor-

scraper arrived in Miles City, Montana on March 9, 1977.

On April 4, 1977 (within four months from the date the tractor arrived in Iowa) the bank filed a financing statement in Iowa, pursuant to Iowa Code § 9–401. Thereafter, plaintiff filed the same financing statement with the Montana Secretary of State.

When Daniel F. Holland defaulted on his obligation to the bank, the bank instituted this action in the District Court, Custer County, to foreclose its security interest.

On November 4, 1977, the District Court entered the following order, dismissing plaintiff's complaint:

* * *

The defendant's motion to dismiss is based upon the following factual premise: An Iowa dealer sold certain equipment to the defendant, a Montana resident. The equipment was supplied to the Iowa dealer by a Florida company, who had given plaintiff a security interest, which was filed in Florida. The security interest agreement of plaintiff was filed in Iowa after the Iowa dealer had sold and delivered the equipment to the Montana purchaser.

The Court agrees with defendant's contention that Sections 87–A–9–307(1) [87A–9–307(1)], 87–A–1–201(9) [87A–1–201(9)] and 87–A–2–403(2) control and gives the purchaser title free of the security agreement filed in Iowa.

It Is Ordered that defendant's motion to dismiss be granted.

* * *

Judgment finalizing the dismissal was signed on November 29, 1977. This appeal followed.

The sole issue for our determination is whether Spencer Jarrett purchased the tractor-scraper "free of" or "subject to" the bank's security interest.

It is agreed that the bank perfected its security interest in the tractor-scraper by filing the financing statement required by Fla.Stat. § 9–302. The Uniform Commercial Code contemplates the continued perfection of a security interest if there has been no intervening period when it was unperfected. Fla.Stat. § 9–303. A perfected security interest is generally not destroyed by the sale, exchange or other disposition of the collateral:

(2) Except where this chapter otherwise provides, a security interest continues in collateral notwithstanding sale, exchange or other disposition thereof by the debtor unless his action was authorized by the secured party in the security agreement or otherwise, and also continues in any identifiable proceeds including collections received by the debtor. Fla.Stat. § 9–306(2).

Since Daniel Holland sold the tractor without plaintiffs permission and in violation of the security agreement, it is clear that C. B. and O. purchased the tractor-scraper "subject to" the bank's security interest.

When C. B. and O. transported the tractor from Florida to Iowa, the continued existence of the bank's security interest was contingent on the provisions of Iowa's Commercial Code. Iowa Code § 9–103, provides:

d. When collateral is brought into and kept in this state while subject to a security interest perfected under the law of the jurisdiction from which the collateral was removed, the security interest remains perfected, but if action is required by Part 3 of this Article to perfect the security interest,

i. if the action is not taken before the expiration of the period of perfection in the other jurisdiction or the end of four months after the collateral is brought into this state, whichever period first expires, the security interest becomes unperfected at the end of that period and is thereafter deemed to have been unperfected as against a person who became a purchaser after removal;

ii. *if the action is taken before the expiration of the period specified in subparagraph (i), the security interest continues perfected thereafter*;

The courts uniformly hold that Section 9–103 gives a secured party a four-month

grace period during which his security interest is protected without any further action on his part. * * *

Applying the provisions of Iowa Code § 9–103 to our fact pattern, it is obvious that the bank's security interest was viable at the time defendant purchased the tractor-scraper from C. B. and O. Equipment Company. The bank fully complied with section 9–103 by filing its financing statement in Iowa on April 4, 1977, well within the four-month period. Therefore, plaintiff's security interest continued unless Article 9 provides otherwise.

Defendant contends that Iowa Code § 9–307 allowed him to purchase the tractor-scraper "free of" plaintiffs security interest. Section 9–307 provides:

Protection of buyers of goods. 1. A buyer in ordinary course of business (subsection 9 of Section 1–201) other than a person buying farm products from a person engaged in farming operations takes free of a security interest *created by his seller* even though the security interest is perfected and even though the buyer knows of its existence.

In the present case, defendant Jarrett purchased in good faith and without knowledge that the sale to him was in violation of the bank's security interest. Defendant also purchased the tractor in the ordinary course from a person in the business of selling tractors, therefore, he was a "buyer in the ordinary course of business". Iowa Code § 1–201(9).

However, section 9–307 contains the further limitation that the security interest must be "created by his [defendant's] seller". This Court has never interpreted the "created by his seller" limitation. However, the landmark case in this area is *National Shawmut Bank of Boston v. Jones* (1967), 108 N.H. 386, 236 A.2d 484.

Shawmut was a replevin action instituted to recover possession of a 1964 Dodge station wagon. The station wagon was originally purchased by a man named Robert Wever. To obtain the car, Wever had secured a loan from the plaintiff bank and had executed a security agreement using the car as collateral. Sometime thereafter, Wever traded or sold the wagon to a reputable dealer engaged in the business of selling new and used cars to the public. The dealer then sold the car to defendant. Neither the dealer nor the defendant knew of plaintiff's security interest.

While the defendant in Shawmut was obviously a "buyer in the ordinary course", the Court nonetheless allowed the bank to recover the automobile from him. The Shawmut Court held:

* * * defendant purchased in good faith without knowledge that the sale was in violation of the security interest of another and bought in the ordinary course from a person in the business of selling automobiles, he was a "buyer in the ordinary course of business" * * *. However, s. 307(1) permits him to take free only of "a security interest created by his seller". The security interest of the plaintiff was not created by * * * the defendants seller, but by Wentworth Motor Co., Inc. *Defendant, therefore, does not take free of the plaintiffs security interest under this section.* Shawmut, supra, 236 A.2d 486 at 485–486. (Emphasis added.)

As in Shawmut, defendant's seller *did not* create plaintiff's security interest, therefore, defendant does not take the tractor "free of" plaintiff's security interest under Iowa Code § 9–307.

* * *

This Court recognizes that this is a harsh result, since the purchaser, on the date of purchase in Iowa, had no means to learn in Iowa that the property he purchased was subject to a security interest. It may be that legislative action is necessary to prevent such results in the future. Since we are bound by the enacted laws, and must give full faith and credit to the laws of our sister states, no other course is open to us here.

For the foregoing reasons, this cause is reversed and remanded to the District Court for further proceedings consistent with this decision.

Default

EGGMAN v. WESTERN NAT. BANK

(1979, Wyo.) 596 P.2d 318.

ROONEY, J.

This is an appeal from an order denying a motion of appellant-defendant to vacate a sheriff's sale of defendant's real and personal property, which was made pursuant to a foreclosure action brought by appellee-plaintiff. We will reverse and order vacation of the sale.

On January 15, 1973, defendant and his wife gave plaintiff a promissory note in the principal amount of $41,000, and they secured the debt by a mortgage on two adjoining tracts of land near Lovell. The two tracts were purchased at different times. On one was a building, which was used by defendant in his business, known as Lovell Machine. The other tract was vacant.

On April 25, 1975, defendant gave plaintiff another note in the principal amount of $8,625, which was secured by collateral described only as "inventory and accounts receivable" in the note, and as follows in the security agreement:

(a) All of debtor's inventory including all goods, merchandise, raw materials, goods in process, finished goods and all other tangible personal property now owned or hereafter acquired and held for sale or lease or furnished or to be furnished under contracts of service or used or consumed in debtor's business, * * * and in contract rights with respect thereto and proceeds of both. * * *

(b) All accounts, notes, drafts, chattel paper, acceptances and other forms of obligations and receivables now or hereafter received by or belonging to debtor for goods sold by it or for services rendered by it, all guaranties and securities thereof, hereinafter called the "receivables", all right, title and interest of debtor in the merchandise which gave rise thereto including the right of stoppage in transit, and all rights of debtor earned or yet to be earned under contracts to sell goods or render services and in the proceeds thereof, including all accounts receivable listed and described on Exhibit A attached hereto and by this reference made a part hereof.

There was no Exhibit A.

Defendant defaulted in payments on both notes, and plaintiff filed a complaint containing two claims for relief. One was against defendant for judgment on the balance due on the $8,625 note and requesting sale of the collateral in satisfaction thereof. The other was against defendant and his wife on the balance due on the $41,000 note and requesting sale of the mortgaged real property in satisfaction thereof. * * *

The judgment recited that "it appearing to the Court" that defendant and his wife "authorized" their counsel to stipulate to the entry of judgment in the amount of $42,197.04 against them, specifically: (1) in amount of $38,431.05 against defendant and his wife, and that the "premises covered by the mortgage * * * be decreed sold *according to law*; that the proceeds of the sale be brought into the Court and applied * * * [to] the amount due Plaintiff; and that Plaintiff have judgment *and execution* against the Defendants, and each of them, for any deficiency * * *"; and (2) in the amount of $3,765.99 against defendant, and that "the lien represented by the security agreement * * * be foreclosed; that the collateral listed in the security agreement be sold *under and pursuant to the judgment of this Court* and the proceeds of such sale be applied toward the satisfaction and payment of the lien"; and judgment for deficiency to be rendered against defendant. There was no reference to the disposition to be made of any amount received from the sale in excess of the debt.

* * *

A Notice of Foreclosure Sale of defendant's property was duly published. It read in part:

* * * on January 20, 1978, at 11:00 o'clock A.M., at the front door of the courthouse at Basin, Big Horn County, Wyoming, the Sheriff of Big Horn County will sell the above-described real property, inventory and accounts receivable or so much thereof as may be necessary to satisfy Plaintiff Western National Bank's judgment with interest and costs, to the highest bidder.

The two tracts of real property were described separately in this notice—as they were in the mortgage.

At the sale, both tracts of real property and the inventory and the accounts receivable were offered only as a whole and in one group. They were sold in that fashion for the high bid of James T. Frost in the amount of $67,500.

* * *

The inventory and accounts receivable were never listed or itemized. A list of the items taken into Frost's possession was attached to an affidavit of defendant. Most of the items listed thereon were equipment and supplies rather than inventory and accounts receivable. The term "inventory" does not include "equipment." Section 9–109(2) and (4).

Defendant contends that the remedy taken by plaintiff with reference to the default of the $8,625 note and of the security agreement was not pursuant to law, and he contends that the sale of the real property was illegal inasmuch as each tract was not separately offered for bid. Plaintiff contends that the sale was proper as a *judicial* sale, wherein the several requirements of a sale by execution under a judgment are not applicable.

Sale of Inventory and Accounts Receivable

Under law, there are five principal remedies given to the secured party on default of the terms of a security agreement by the debtor. Since none of the remedies were properly used in this case, the sale of the personal property was not proper. The five remedies are:

1. Use of the real estate mortgage foreclosure procedures if the security agreement covers both real and personal property.[2] Although both real and personal property were involved in this action, the security agreement does not cover real property. Therefore, this remedy is not available to plaintiff.

2. With reference to accounts receivable, as here, collect the same from those obligated thereon.[3] Plaintiff did not choose to pursue this remedy.

3. Any special remedy provided in the security agreement.[4] This security agreement did not set forth any special remedy.

4. Take possession of the collateral without judicial process[6] and either accept it in full satisfaction[7] or sell it.[8] The notice required for acceptance in full satisfaction was not here given. Here possession was not taken without judicial process, and the sale was made before plaintiff took possession. A

sale under this remedy must be commercially reasonable. Section 9–504(3). This is the remedy most commonly used. The usual reasons for not using it are: (a) inability to secure peaceable possession of the collateral, and (b) desire to be able to proceed against assets of the debtor, other than the collateral. Plaintiff did not use this remedy.

5. Take a judgment on the underlying obligation, and proceed under the judgment.[9] This seems to be the remedy attempted in this case. The procedure for this remedy is not set out in the Uniform Commercial Code, i.e., § 1–101, et seq. The usual procedure for enforcement of judgments for money is set out in § 1–17–101, et seq., W.S.1977. Usually the judgment is executed on by issuance of a writ of execution. The sheriff levies the writ upon the goods and chattels of the debtor, taking them actually or constructively into his possession. The various items levied upon are then identified and are subject to valuation and inspection. If necessary, the sheriff then holds an execution sale. Such procedure is anticipated by the Uniform Commercial Code.[10]

---

2. Section 9–501(4) "(4) If the security agreement covers both real and personal property, the secured party may proceed under this part as to the personal property or he may proceed as to both the real and the personal property in accordance with his rights and remedies in respect of the real property in which case the provisions of this part do not apply."

3. Section 9–502(1), reads in part: "(1) * * * on default the secured party is entitled to notify an account debtor or the obligor on an instrument to make payment to him whether or not the assignor was theretofore making collections on the collateral * * *."

4. Section 9–501(2) reads in part: "(2) After default, the debtor has the rights and remedies provided * * * in the security agreement * * *."

6. Section 9–503 reads in part: "Unless otherwise agreed a secured party has on default the right to take possession of the collateral. In taking possession a secured party may proceed without judicial process if this can be done without breach of the peace or may proceed by action. * * *."

7. Section 9–505(2) reads: "(2) In any other case involving consumer goods or any other collateral a secured party

in possession may, after default, propose to retain the collateral in satisfaction of the obligation. Written notice of such proposal shall be sent to the debtor and except in the case of consumer goods to any other secured party who has a security interest in the collateral and who has duly filed a financing statement indexed in the name of the debtor in this state or is known by a secured party in possession to have a security interest in it. If the debtor or other person entitled to receive notification objects in writing within thirty (30) days from the receipt of the notification or if any other secured party objects in writing within thirty (30) days after the secured party obtains possession the secured party must dispose of the collateral under section 9–504. In the absence of such written objection the secured party may retain the collateral in satisfaction of the debtor's obligation."

8. Section 9–504(1) reads in part: "(1) A secured party after default may sell, lease or otherwise dispose of any or all of the collateral * * *."

9. Section 9–501(1) reads in part: " * * * He may reduce his claim to judgment, foreclose or otherwise enforce the security interest by any available judicial procedure. * * * "

A writ of execution was not issued or levied in this case. The sheriff did not take possession of the goods, actually or constructively, and they were not otherwise specifically identified or evaluated. The usual execution and levy procedure was not followed.

But plaintiff contends that a judicial sale, as distinguished from an execution sale, was here held. A judicial sale is proper under the Code [11] and under the remedy here under discussion. However, the judicial sale attempted in this case was not properly mandated or conducted. Inasmuch as the property to be sold was not definitely or accurately described in the judgment and at the sale; inasmuch as it was not taken into the sheriff's possession prior to the sale or was not otherwise specifically identified or made subject to evaluation as to quantity and quality prior to the sale, a jurisdictional defect existed and the sale was void.

* * *

The judgment in this case only directed that the sale be "pursuant to judgment of this court." It did not prescribe the terms and mode of sale as is required for a fair and proper judicial sale.

The distinctive characteristics of a judicial sale are that it must be the result of a judicial proceeding; it must be based upon an order, decree, or judgment directing that the property be sold, as distinguished from a judicial assent to the sale of property under statutory provisions authorizing certain sales by fiduciaries; and it must be made by the court or by its direction upon the terms and in the mode provided by the decree or order, which of course must conform with any pertinent statutory provisions regulating judicial sales * * *.

* * *

A judicial sale cannot be held in a "grab bag" fashion. Such would not be commercially reasonable. All parties to the sale must have an opportunity to see and evaluate the goods being sold. [Citations.] The judgment can direct that the sale be held at the place where the items are located, or it can direct a time and place before the sale at which the items can be inspected. Some means must be provided by which the items to be sold can be identified specifically, or the items must be identified specifically and not generically in the judgment.

Since this judgment and the sale resulting therefrom were deficient in these respects, the sale of personal property was void and must be vacated.

* * *

Reversed and remanded.

---

10. Section 9–501(5) reads: "(e) When a secured party has reduced his claim to judgment the lien of any levy which may be made upon his collateral by virtue of any execution based upon the judgment shall relate back to the date of the perfection of the security interest in such collateral. A judicial sale, *pursuant to such execution,* is a foreclosure of the security interest by judicial procedure within the meaning of this section, and the secured party may purchase at the sale and thereafter hold the collateral free of any other requirements of this article." 11. See footnote 10.

Problems

1. A sells to B a refrigerator under a conditional sales contract for $600 payable in monthly installments of $30 for 20 months. The refrigerator is installed in the kitchen of B's apartment. There is no filing of any financing statement. Assume that after B has made the first three monthly payments:

(1) B moves from his apartment and sells the refrigerator in place to the new occupant for $350 cash. What are the rights of A?

(2) B is adjudicated bankrupt, and his trustee in bankruptcy claims the refrigerator. What are the rights of the parties?

2. On January 2, Burt asked Logan to loan him money "against my diamond ring." Logan agreed to do so if a credit check proved Burt to be solvent. To guard against intervening liens Logan received permission to record his interest, and Burt and Logan signed a security agreement giving Logan an interest in the ring which security agreement Logan filed with the Recorder of Deeds of the county of Burt's residence on January 3. On January 4, Burt borrowed money from Tillo pledging his ring to secure the debt. Tillo took possession of the ring and paid Burt the money on the same day. The next day, January 5, Logan received a favorable credit report on Burt and loaned him the money under the assumption that Burt still had the ring.

Who has priority, Logan or Tillo?

3. A takes a security interest in the equipment in X Store and files a financing statement claiming "equipment and all after acquired equipment." B later sells X Store a cash register on conditional sale and (a) files 9 days after X receives the register or (b) files 15 days after X receives the register. If X fails to pay both A and B and they foreclose their security interests, who has priority as to the cash register?

4. X Motor Company sells an automobile to A on conditional sale. The automobile is insured and X is named loss payee. The automobile is totally destroyed in an accident, and three days later A files a petition in bankruptcy. As between X and A's trustee in bankruptcy, who is entitled to the insurance proceeds?

5. On September 5, 1982, W, a widow who occasionally teaches piano and organ in her home, purchased an electric organ from M's music store for $4,800, trading in her old organ for $1,200 and promising in writing to pay the balance at $120 per month, and granting to M a security interest in the property in terms consistent with and incorporating provisions of the U.C.C. A financing statement relative to the transaction was also properly filled out and signed, and M properly filed it. W did not make the December or January payments and M went to her home

to collect the payments or take the organ. Finding no one home and the door unlocked, he went in and took the organ. Two hours later, T, a third party, and the present occupant of the house, who had purchased the organ for his own use, stormed into M's store demanding return of the organ, exhibiting a bill of sale from W to T dated December 15, 1982, listing the organ and other furnishing in the house.

What are the rights of M, T and W?

6. Would your answer to number five (5) change if M did not file a financing statement? Why?

7. On May 1, A lends B $20,000 and receives from B his promissory note for this amount due in two years and takes a security interest in the machinery and equipment in B's factory. A proper financing statement is filed with respect to the security agreement. On August 1, upon A's request B executes an addendum to the security agreement covering after acquired machinery and equipment in B's factory. A second financing statement is filed covering the addendum. In September B acquires $5,000 worth of new equipment which he installs in his factory. In December C, a judgment creditor of B, causes an attachment to issue against the new equipment. What are the rights of the parties?

8. A bought a television set from B for his own personal use. B was out of conditional sales contracts and showed A a form B had executed with C, another consumer. A and B orally agree to the terms of the form. A subsequently defaults on payment and B seeks to repossess the television. Decision? Would the result differ if B had filed a financing statement?

9. A bought a television set for his own personal use from B. A properly signed a security agreement and paid B $25 down as required by their agreement. B did not file and subsequently A sells the television to C, A's neighbor, for $300 for C to use in his den. When A fails to make the January and February payments, may B repossess the television from C?

10. What if, in question 9, instead of A selling the television set to C a judgment creditor levied (sought possession) of the television. Who would prevail?

Chapter

40

BANKRUPTCY AND
RELIEF OF DEBTORS

A debt is an obligation to pay money owing by a person referred to as a "debtor" to a person referred to as a "creditor". Debts are created daily in countless instances by purchases of goods at the consumer level, by retailers of goods executing promissory notes and trade acceptances for purchases of inventory and upon buying merchandise on open account from a manufacturer, wholesaler, or distributor, and at the level of financing in larger amounts by obtaining funds through the issuance and sale of debentures, corporate mortgage bonds, and other types of securities representing indebtedness.

An enormous volume of business transactions is entered into daily on a credit basis, and usually the trust and confidence of the creditors is not misplaced. Trust in others which is essential to conducting a business involves the extension of credit and the creation of debts. Commercial activity would be restricted and greatly diminished if credit were not readily obtainable, or needed funds not available for lending. Debts are a necessary part of ordinary life in an urban, industrial society.

Fortunately, most debts are paid when due, thereby justifying the extension of credit and encouraging its continuation. Defaults may create credit and collection problems, although normally the total amount in default represents a very small percentage of the total amount of outstanding indebtedness. However, widespread continuing defaults by reason of business failures resulting from and contributing to a decline in production, sales, employment, and personal and corporate income, cause a shrinkage of credit which if persistent and unremedied may result in an economic depression. Credit has the perverse and elusive quality of being absent when most needed.

In good times, bad times, and with or without blame, both individuals and corporations encounter financial crises and business misfortune. An individual or a business unit may be confronted by an accumulation of debts the amount of which exceeds total assets, or may have assets in excess of total indebtedness but a large amount of which is in such non-liquid form that the debtor is unable to pay his debts as they mature. Relief from pressing debt and from the threat of impending lawsuits by creditors is frequently necessary for economic survival.

Out of the conflict between creditor rights and debtor relief various solutions have developed, such as voluntary adjustments and compromises requiring payment in installments to creditors over a period of time during which they agree to withhold legal action. Other voluntary methods include compositions and assignments of his assets by a debtor to a trustee or assignee for the benefit of his creditors. Equity receiverships or insolvency proceedings are sometimes filed by creditors in a State court pursuant to statute. However, the most adaptable and frequently employed method of debtor relief which also affords protection to creditors is by a proceeding in a Federal court under the Bankruptcy Act.

CREDITORS' RIGHTS AND DEBTOR RELIEF OUTSIDE OF BANKRUPTCY

In the area of creditors' rights and debtor relief, there are several inherent conflicts: (1) The right of the diligent creditor to pursue his claim to judgment and to satisfy that judgment by levy and sale of property of the debtor; (2) The right of the unsecured creditor who has refrained from suing the debtor; and (3) The social policy of affording relief to a debtor who has contracted debts beyond his ability to pay, and who may be confronted by a lifetime burden. A resolution of these conflicts necessarily involves a compromise whereby the debtor will disclose and surrender all his assets to a trustee or other person for the benefit of his creditors, and the creditors will receive fair and equal treatment.

Various forms of compromises have been developed to provide relief to debtors, some of which are non-legal in form, such

as those effected by the hundreds of credit agencies and adjustment bureaus. Of the legal compromises, some are founded in common law and involve simple contract and trust principles, such as compositions and assignments; others are statutory, such as statutory assignments. Some involve the intervention of a court and its officers, such as equity receiverships, while others do not.

COMPOSITIONS

A common law or non-statutory composition is an ordinary contract or agreement between the debtor on the one hand and his creditors on the other, whereby the creditors receive pro rata a part, but not the whole amount, of their claims and the debtor is discharged from the balance of the claims, since the whole amount is deemed satisfied by payment of the part.

As a contract, it requires the formalities of a contract, such as offer, acceptance and consideration. For example, debtor D owing debts of $5,000 to A, $2,000 to B, and $1,000 to C, offers to settle these claims by paying $4,000 to A, B and C. If A, B and C accept the offer, a composition results with A receiving $2,500, B $1,000, and C $500. The consideration for the promise of A to forgive the balance of his claim, consists of the promises of B and C, respectively, to forgive the balance of their claims. All the creditors benefit since a race of diligence among creditors to obtain the debtor's limited assets is avoided. Thus, a composition differs from an accord and satisfaction, involving a single debtor and a single creditor, in which case some additional consideration from D is necessary before the balance of a liquidated debt will be deemed satisfied by payment of only a part of the debt.

It should be noted, however, that, in accordance with fixed contract principles, the debtor in a composition is discharged from liability only upon the claims of creditors who voluntarily consent to the composition and thereby voluntarily release the balance of their claims. If, in the above illustration, C refused to accept the offer of composition and refused to take the $500, he could later attempt to collect the full $1,000 claim. Likewise, if D owed additional debts to X, Y and Z, these creditors would not be bound by the agreement between D and A, B and C. Another disadvantage of the composition is the fact that any creditor can attach the assets of the debtor during the usual period of bargaining and negotiation which precedes the execution of the composition agreement. For instance, once D advised A, B and C that he was negotiating or offering to compose the claims, any one of the creditors could seize D's property.

A variation of the composition is an extension agreement worked out by the debtor with his creditors providing for payment of his debts either in full or proportionately scaled down over a period of time.

ASSIGNMENTS FOR BENEFIT OF CREDITORS

A common law or non-statutory assignment for the benefit of creditors or general assignment, as it is sometimes called, is a voluntary transfer by the debtor of some or all of his property to an assignee in trust, or trustee, who applies the property to the payment of all of the debtor's debts. For instance, debtor D transfers title to his property to trustee T, who converts the property into money and pays it to all of the creditors on a pro rata basis.

STATUTORY ASSIGNMENTS

Because of the benefit to creditors of assignments by immunizing the debtor's assets from attachments, there have been many statutory attempts to retain the idea

of the assignment and, at the same time, to give a corresponding benefit to the debtor by discharging him from the balance of his debts. Since the United States Constitution prohibits a State from impairing the obligation of a contract between private citizens, it is impossible for a State to force all creditors to discharge a debtor upon a pro rata distribution of assets, although, as pointed out hereafter, the Federal government *does* have such power and exercises it in the Bankruptcy Act. Accordingly, the States have generally enacted two different types of assignment statutes, one type providing that any person who voluntarily accepts a dividend or part payment *automatically* discharges the debtor from the balance of the claim, the creditor having the privilege of refusing to participate and retaining his claim in full, and the other type permitting the debtor to exact *voluntary* releases of the balance of claims from creditors who accept part payments, thus combining the advantages of common law compositions and assignments. Statutes of the first type have generally been superseded by the Federal Bankruptcy Act but statutes of the second type continue in effect.

EQUITY RECEIVERSHIPS

One of the oldest remedies in equity is the appointment of a receiver by the court. The receiver is a disinterested person who collects and preserves the debtor's assets and the income therefrom, and disposes of the assets and income at the direction of the court which appointed him.

A receiver will be appointed upon the petition (1) of a secured creditor seeking foreclosure of his security; (2) of a judgment creditor bringing a creditor's bill in equity after exhausting legal remedies to satisfy the judgment, or (3) of a shareholder of a corporate debtor where it appears that the assets of the corporation will be dissipated by fraud or mismanagement, as distinguished from mere differences of opinion or errors of judgment. The appointment of a receiver always rests within the sound discretion of the court. Insolvency, in the equity sense of inability by the debtor to pay his debts as they mature, is one of the factors considered by the court in appointing a receiver.

Once the receiver is appointed and takes over the possession of the debtor's assets all of his future actions are governed by the court of appointment which may instruct him either (1) to liquidate the assets by public or private sale; (2) to operate the business as a going concern temporarily; or (3) to conserve the assets until final disposition of the matter before the court. A receiver has been aptly described as a liquidator, manager, and custodian.

FEDERAL BANKRUPTCY LAW

The most important method of protecting creditor rights and granting debtor relief is Federal Bankruptcy law, which is largely statutory and involves court supervision. The word "bankrupt" is derived from the Latin *banque*, meaning bench or table, and *ruptus*, meaning broken. There is some authority for the legend that, upon bankruptcy, the customary place of business of a merchant in medieval times, his bench or table, was literally broken. In any event, it was figuratively broken since bankruptcy meant commercial failure.

Bankruptcy legislation serves a dual purpose: (1) to effect an equitable distribution of the debtor's property among his creditors and (2) to discharge the debtor from his debts and enable him to rehabilitate himself and start afresh. Other subsidiary purposes are to provide uniform treatment of creditors, preserve existing business relations, stabilize commercial usages, and effect a speedy, as well as equitable, distribution of the debtor's assets.

HISTORY, COVERAGE, AND COURTS OF BANKRUPTCY

Historical Perspective

The first English Bankruptcy Act in 1542 applied only to traders since, according to Blackstone, "that class of men are, generally speaking, the only persons liable to accidental losses, and to an inability to pay their debts, without any fault of their own," whereas "if persons in other situations of life run into debt, they must take the consequences of their own indiscretion." Until the passage of the English Bankruptcy Act of 1861, the English acts applied only to traders or merchants, persons who bought and sold merchandise.

The Constitution of the United States provides that "The Congress shall have power * * * to establish * * * uniform Laws on the subject of Bankruptcies throughout the United States." Article I, Section 8, clause 4. Federal bankruptcy law has generally superseded state insolvency laws.

The first Bankruptcy Act, enacted by Congress on April 4, 1800, applied only to traders. It was repealed in 1803, and during the ensuing 38 years no Bankruptcy Act was in effect in the United States. The second Bankruptcy Act, enacted August 19, 1841, was repealed in 1843. Following the Civil War and during a post-war period of severe inflation, Congress passed a third Bankruptcy Act on March 2, 1867, which was repealed in 1878. Between 1878 and 1898, when no Bankruptcy Act was in effect, many states enacted Insolvency Acts granting relief by statutory assignments. The Bankruptcy Act of 1898, as amended from time to time, remained in effect until 1938 when Congress overhauled the bankruptcy law by enactment of the Chandler Act which largely retained the straight bankruptcy provisions of the 1898 Act, as amended, but introduced new statutory types of debtor relief.

In 1978 Congress again enacted a major revision of the Bankruptcy Act. The Bankruptcy Reform Act of 1978 became effective on October 1, 1979, and will be discussed in the remainder of this chapter.

Bankruptcy Reform Act of 1978

The Bankruptcy Reform Act consists of eight odd-numbered chapters:

CHAPTER	TITLE
1	General Provisions
3	Case Administration
5	Creditors, The Debtor and the Estate
7	Liquidation
9	Adjustment of Debts of a Municipality
11	Reorganization
13	Adjustment of Debts of an Individual with Regular Income
15	United States Trustees

Chapters 7, 9, 11, and 13 provide four different types of proceedings, while Chapters 1, 3, and 5 apply to all four proceedings. Straight, or ordinary, bankruptcy (Chapter 7) provides for liquidation and termination of the business of the debtor, whereas the other proceedings provide for reorganization and continuance of the business of the debtor.

Chapter 7 applies to all debtors with the exception of railroads, insurance companies, banks, savings and loan associations, homestead associations, and credit unions. Moreover, Chapter 7 has special provisions for the liquidation of the estates of stockbrokers and commodity brokers. Any person that may be a debtor under Chapter 7 (except stockbrokers and commodity brokers) as well as railroads may be a debtor under Chapter 11. Chapter 9, however, applies only to a municipality that is generally authorized to be a debtor under that chapter, is insolvent, and desires to effect a plan to adjust its debts. Chapter 13 applies to individuals with regular income who owe liquidated unsecured debts of less than $100,000 and secured debts of less than $350,000.

Bankruptcy Courts

The Bankruptcy Reform Act provides for a new Bankrutpcy Court effective April 1, 1984. At that time there will be established in each judicial district, as an adjunct to the district court, a United States Bankruptcy Court for that district. Section 151. Appeals from all final judgments, orders, and decrees of the bankruptcy court will go to the district court or, where established, a panel of three bankruptcy judges. Section 1334. The Circuit Court of Appeals will have jurisdiction over appeals from the district court or panel. However, if all parties agree, direct appeal to the circuit court from the bankruptcy court's final judgment, order, or decree may be had. Section 1293.

The Bankruptcy Reform Act provides that the courts of bankruptcy, as defined and created by the previous Bankruptcy Act, shall continue to be the courts of bankruptcy for the purposes of the Reform Act through March 31, 1984. Under the old Bankruptcy Act, the District Courts of the United States served as bankruptcy courts with exclusive original jurisdiction over bankruptcy proceedings. Section 2a of that Act sets forth the jurisdictional powers of bankruptcy courts. The Supreme Court of the United States has held that "courts of bankruptcy are essentially courts of equity, and their proceedings inherently proceedings in equity." Thus, the District Courts, when functioning as bankruptcy courts, primarily administer the bankruptcy statute and secondarily exercise equitable powers to further bankruptcy proceedings in all matters not expressly covered by the bankruptcy statute.

Under the Reform Act, each bankruptcy court is to be staffed by a bankruptcy judge appointed by the President with the advice and consent of the Senate for a term of 14 years.   Until then, referees will continue to serve unless found not qualified.   Section 404(b).   Presently, upon the filing of a petition, the clerk refers the case to a referee who thereafter, with certain exceptions, conducts all proceedings.   The referee is for all practical purposes the judge in a bankruptcy proceeding.   However, the referee's orders, findings of fact, and conclusions of law, are subject to review by the judge of the bankruptcy court.

CASE ADMINISTRATION (CHAPTER 3)

Chapter 3 of the Bankruptcy Reform Act contains provisions dealing with the commencement of cases, the officers that administer the case, the meetings of creditors, and the administrative powers of the various officers.

Commencement of the Case

The jurisdiction of the bankruptcy court and the operation of the bankruptcy laws are commenced by the filing of a voluntary or involuntary petition.

Voluntary Petitions. The great majority of petitions are voluntarily filed.   Any person eligible to be a debtor under a given bankruptcy proceeding may file a voluntary petition under that chapter.   Moreover, he need not be, although virtually all are, insolvent to file the petition.   The commencement of a voluntary case constitutes an automatic order for relief.

Involuntary Cases. An involuntary petition in bankruptcy may be filed only under Chapter 7 or 11 by (1) any three or more creditors who have unsecured claims at the time of the filing against the debtor, which claims are not contingent as to liability and total in the aggregate $5,000 or more, or, (2) if all of the creditors of the debtor are less than twelve in number, then, by one or more of such creditors whose claim equals $5,000 or more.   Section 303(b).   An involuntary petition may not be filed against a farmer or a corporation that is not a moneyed, business, or commercial corporation.   Section 303(a).

If the debtor does not contest the petition, the court will enter an order for relief against the debtor.   However, if the debtor opposes the petition, the court may enter an order of relief only if (1) the debtor is generally not paying his debts as they become due, or (2) within 120 days before the filing of the petition a custodian, receiver, or agent took possession of the debtor's property to enforce a lien against that property.   Section 303(h).   The court otherwise will dismiss the petition.

Automatic Stays

The filing of a voluntary or involuntary petition operates as a stay against attempts by creditors to begin or continue to recover claims against the debtor, to enforce judgments against the debtor, or to create or enforce liens against property of the debtor.   Section 362.   This stay applies to both secured and unsecured creditors.   Nonetheless, a secured creditor may petition the court to terminate the stay as to his security upon the showing that the secured party lacks adequate protection in his property.

Trustees

The trustee is the representative of the estate and has the capacity to sue and be sued.   The trustee is responsible for collecting, liquidating, and distributing the debtor's estate.

In proceedings under Chapter 7, trustees are selected by a vote of the creditors; in all other proceedings the trustee is appointed by the court.   Within five days of his selection, the trustee must file a bond conditioned on the faithful performance of his official duties. The duties and powers of the trustee include:

1. After notice and a hearing, to use, sell, or lease other than in the ordinary course of business, property of the estate (Section 363(b));
2. If the business of the debtor is authorized to be operated and unless the court orders otherwise, to use, sell, or lease the property of the estate and to obtain credit in the ordinary course of business (Sections 363(c)(1) and 364);
3. To deposit or invest the money of the estate so as to yield the maximum reasonable net return, taking into account the safety of such deposit or investment (Section 345);
4. Subject to court approval to employ disinterested professionals such as attorneys, accountants, appraisers, or auctioneers and to act himself as attorney or accountant for the estate (Section 327); and
5. Subject to the court's approval, to assume or reject any executory contract or unexpired lease of the debtor (Section 365).

Meetings of Creditors

Within a reasonable time after relief is ordered, a meeting of creditors must be held. The court may not preside at nor attend this meeting. The debtor must appear and submit to examination under oath of his financial situation. Creditors, indenture trustees and the trustee may examine the debtor. In a proceeding under Chapter 7, qualified creditors at this meeting elect the permanent trustee who succeeds the interim trustee appointed by the court when relief was ordered.

CREDITORS, THE DEBTOR, AND THE ESTATE (CHAPTER 5)

Creditors

The Reform Act defines creditors to include any entity that has a claim against the debtor that arose at the time of or before the order for relief. A claim means a "right to payment, whether or not such right is reduced to judgment, liquidated, unliquidated, fixed, contingent, matured, unmatured, disputed, undisputed, legal, equitable, secured, or unsecured." Section 101(4).

Proof of Claims. Creditors may file a proof of claim. If a creditor does not do so in a timely manner, then the debtor or trustee may file a proof of such claim. Claims that are filed are allowed unless a party in interest objects. If an objection to a claim is made, the court determines after a hearing the amount and validity of the claim. The court may not allow any claim that (1) is unenforceable against the debtor and his property, (2) is for unmatured interest, (3) may be offset against a debt owing the debtor, or (4) is for services of an insider or attorney in excess of the reasonable value of such services. Section 502.

Secured Claims. An allowed claim of a creditor who has a lien on property of the estate is a secured claim to the extent of the value of the creditor's interest in the property. The creditor's claim is unsecured to the extent the value of his interest is less than the allowed amount of his claim. Thus, if A has an allowed claim of $5,000 against the estate of debtor B and has a security interest in property of the estate that is valued at $3,000, A has a secured claim in the amount of $3,000 and an unsecured claim for $2,000.

Priority of Claims. Certain classes of claims have a priority, which means that they must be paid in full out of the debtor's estate before any distribution is made to claims of lesser rank. Every claim of each preceding class must be paid in full before claims of the next succeeding class may be paid. The prior claims and the order of their payment are as follows (Section 507):

1. Expenses of administration of the debtor's estate, including the expenses of preserving the estate subsequent to the commencement of the case; the filing fees paid by creditors in involuntary cases; the expenses of creditors in recovering concealed assets for the benefit of the bankrupt's estate; the trustee's necessary expenses; the fees and mileage payable to witnesses; and reasonable compensation to receivers, trustees, and their attorneys as allowed by the court.

2. Unsecured claims in an involuntary case arising in the ordinary course of the debtor's business after the commencement of the case but before the earlier of the appointment of the trustee or the order for relief. Such claimants are referred to as "gap" creditors.

3. Allowed, unsecured claims up to $2,000 for wages, salaries, or commissions earned within ninety days before the filing of the petition or the date of cessation of the debtor's business, which ever comes first.

4. Allowed, unsecured claims for contributions to employee benefit plans arising from services rendered within 180 days before the filing of the petition or the cessation of the debtor's business, whichever occurs first, but limited to $2,000 multiplied by the number of employees covered by the plan.

5. Allowed, unsecured claims up to $900 for moneys deposited in connection with the purchase, lease, or rental of property or the purchase of services, for personal, family, or household use.

6. Specified taxes owed to governmental units for certain income, property, employment, or excise taxes.

After creditors with secured claims and creditors with claims having a priority have been satisfied, creditors with allowed, unsecured claims share proportionately in any remaining assets.

Debtors

Debtor's Duties. The Act imposes a number of duties upon the debtor. He must file a list of creditors, a schedule of assets and liabilities, and a statement of his financial affairs. In any case in which a trustee is serving, he must cooperate with the trustee and surrender to the trustee all property of the estate and all records relating to property of the estate.

Debtor's Exemptions. Section 522 of the Reform Act exempts specified property of the debtor from the bankruptcy proceedings including the following:

1. Up to $7,500 in equity in property used as a residence or burial plot.
2. Up to $1,200 in equity in one motor vehicle.
3. Up to $200 for any particular item of household furnishings, household goods, wearing apparel, appliances, books, animals, crops, or musical instruments that are held primarily for personal, family, or household use.
4. Up to $500 in jewelry.
5. Any property up to $400 plus any unused amount of the first exemption.
6. Up to $750 in implements, professional books, or tools of the debtor's trade.
7. Unmatured life insurance contracts owned by debtor other than a credit life insurance contract.
8. Professionally prescribed health aids.
9. Social security, veterans, and disability benefits.
10. Unemployment compensation.
11. Alimony and support payments including child support.
12. Payments from pension, profit sharing, and annuity plans.
13. Payments from an award under a crime victim's reparation law, a wrongful death award, and up to $7,500, not including pain and suffering, or compensation for actual pecuniary loss, from a personal injury award.

The debtor has the option of using either the exemptions provided by the Bankruptcy Reform Act or those available under State law. Nevertheless, a State may by specific legislative action deny to its citizens the use of the federal exemptions and thereby limit them to the exemptions provided by State law.

Discharge. Discharge is the termination of all debts of the debtor for allowed claims, except those which are non-dischargeable under the Statute. A discharge of a debt in a case brought under Chapters 7, 9, 11, or 13 voids any judgment obtained at any time with respect to that debt and operates as an injunction against the commencement or continuation of any action to recover that debt. An agreement between a debtor and a creditor permitting the creditor to enforce a discharged debt is enforceable to the extent applicable state law permits but only if (1) the agreement was made before the discharge has been granted; (2) the debtor has not rescinded the agreement within 30 days after it becomes enforceable; (3) the court has informed a debtor who is an individual that he is not required to enter into such an agreement and explains the legal effect of the agreement; and (4) if the debt is a consumer debt, the court approves the agreement as not imposing an undue hardship upon the debtor and in the debtor's best interest.

Section 523 sets forth the following debts that are *not* dischargeable in bankruptcy:

1. Certain taxes and customs duties;
2. Legal liabilities for obtaining money or property by false pretenses or false representations;
3. Legal liability for willful and malicious injuries to the person or property of another (that is, intentional torts but not negligent torts);
4. Alimony and support of spouse or child;
5. Debts not scheduled, unless the creditor knew of the bankruptcy;
6. Debts created by the fraud or embezzlement of the debtor while acting in a fiduciary capacity;
7. Student loans which became first due less than five years before the filing of the petition; and
8. Debts that were or could have been listed in a previous bankruptcy in which the debtor waived or was denied a discharge.

The Estate

The commencement of a case creates an estate comprised of all legal and equitable interests of the debtor in property at the time of commencement of the case wherever located. The estate also includes property that the debtor acquires within 180 days after the commencement of the case by bequest, devise, inheritance, or as a beneficiary of a life insurance policy. The estate consists of any proceeds, rents, and profits from property of the estate but *not* earnings from services performed by an individual debtor. The estate includes property that the trustee recovers under his powers (1) as a lien creditor, (2) to avoid voidable preferences, and (3) to avoid fraudulent transfers.

Trustee as Lien Creditor. Section 544(a) provides that the trustee shall have, as of the commencement of the case, the rights and powers of any creditor with a judicial lien or an execution against the debtor that is returned unsatisfied whether or not such creditor exists. This section makes the trustee an "ideal creditor * * * armed cap-a-pie with every right and power which is conferred by the law of the state upon its most favored creditor who has acquired a lien by legal or equitable proceedings." In re Waynesboro Motor Co., 60 F.2d 688 (1932). Section 544(a) does not require the trustee to locate an actual existing lien creditor, for the trustee assumes the rights and powers of a purely hypothetical lien creditor.

For example, A, the debtor, grants a security interest in goods purchased on credit to B, the seller. B fails to perfect the security interest before A files a voluntary petition. C, the trustee, by virtue of Section 544(a) would assume the status of a lien creditor who has priority over an unperfected security interest. U.C.C. Section 9–301. As a consequence, A would be denied standing as a secured creditor and be relegated to the ranks of the unsecured creditors.

Voidable Preferences. The Bankruptcy Reform Act invalidates certain preferential transfers from the debtor to favored creditors before the date of bankruptcy. Section 547 empowers the trustee to avoid any transfer of property of the debtor—

1. to or for the benefit of a creditor;
2. for or on account of an antecedent debt owed by the debtor before such transfer was made;
3. made while the debtor was insolvent;
4. made on or within 90 days before the date of the filing of the petition; and
5. that enables such creditor to receive more than he would have received under Chapter 7.

However, if the creditor was an "insider" and had reasonable cause to believe the debtor was insolvent at the time of the transfer, then the transfer is voidable if made within one year of the date of the filing of the petition. An insider includes a relative or general partner of a debtor as well as a partnership in which the debtor is a general partner or a corporation of which the debtor is a director, officer, or person in control. Section 101(25).

A transfer is any mode, direct or indirect, voluntary or involuntary, of disposing with property or an interest in property including the retention of title as a security interest. For the purposes of this section, the debtor is presumed to have been insolvent on and during the ninety days imme-

diately preceding the date of the filing of the petition.

It should be noted that not all transfers made within ninety days of bankruptcy are voidable. For example, if sixty days before the petition is filed the debtor purchases an automobile for $6,000, this transfer of property (i.e., the $6,000) is *not* voidable because it was not made for an antecedent debt but rather as a contemporaneous exchange for new value. Section 547(c)(1). Similarly, if within ninety days of the filing of the petition the debtor purchases a refrigerator on credit and grants the seller a security interest in the refrigerator, the transfer of that interest is not voidable if the secured party perfects within ten days after the security interest attaches. Section 547(c)(3).

Fraudulent Transfers. Section 548 permits the trustee to avoid fraudulent transfers made on or within one year before the date of the filing of the petition. One type of fraudulent transfer consists of the debtor's transferring property with the actual intent to hinder, delay, or defraud any of his creditors. Another instance of a fraudulent transfer is the transfer by the debtor of property for less than a reasonably equivalent consideration while he is insolvent or would become insolvent because of the transfer. For example, A, who is in debt, transfers title to his home to B, his father, without any payment by B to A and with the understanding that when the home is no longer in danger of seizure by creditors, B will reconvey it to A.

A fraudulent transfer, therefore, differs from a preference, which is a transfer of property in payment of an antecedent debt by a debtor to one creditor at a time when other creditors of like standing will not be paid in full. Debtor A while insolvent pays creditor C, an old friend, but does not pay creditors D, E, or F. This is a preference, not a fraudulent transfer.

LIQUIDATION (CHAPTER 7)

Proceedings

Chapter 7 of the Reform Act provides for liquidation and termination of the business of the debtor, distribution of his assets, and usually a discharge of all dischargeable debts of the debtor. Upon entering an order for relief, the court appoints an interim trustee who serves until a permanent trustee is selected by the creditors. Under Chapter 7, the trustee performs the following duties:

1. collect and reduce to money the property of the estate for which such trustee serves, and close up such estate as expeditiously as is compatible with the best interests of parties in interest;
2. be accountable for all property received;
3. investigate the financial affairs of the debtor;
4. if a purpose would be served, examine proofs of claims and object to the allowance of any claim that is improper;
5. if advisable, oppose the discharge of the debtor;
6. unless the court orders otherwise, furnish such information concerning the estate and the estate's administration as is requested by a party in interest;
7. if the business of the debtor is authorized to be operated, file with the court and with any governmental unit charged with responsibility for collection or determination of any tax arising out of such operation periodic reports and summaries of the operation of such business, including a statement of receipts and disbursements, and such other information as the court requires; and
8. make a final report and file a final account of the administration of the estate with the court. Section 704.

The creditors may also elect a committee of not fewer than three nor more than eleven unsecured creditors which committee may consult with the trustee, make recommendations to him, and submit questions to the court.

Distribution of the Estate

After the trustee has collected all the assets of the debtor's estate, he distributes them to the creditors and, if any assets remain, to the debtor. First, those creditors entitled to a priority receive payment in the order provided. Second, payment is made to unsecured creditors who file their claims on time. Third, payment is made to unsecured creditors who filed their claims tardily. Fourth, claims for multiple, exemplary or punitive damages are paid. Fifth, interest at the legal rate from the date of the filing of the petition is paid to all of the above claimants. Sixth, whatever property remains is distributed to the debtor. Claims of the same rank are paid pro rata.

Discharge

Upon distribution of the estate, the court will grant the debtor a discharge unless the debtor:

1. Is not an individual;
2. Has destroyed, falsified, concealed, or failed to keep books of account and records;
3. Has knowingly and fraudulently made a false oath or account, presented or used a false claim, or given or received bribes;
4. Transferred, removed, destroyed, or concealed any of his property with intent to hinder, delay, or defraud his creditors within twelve months preceding the filing of the bankruptcy petition;
5. Has, within six years prior to bankruptcy been granted a discharge;
6. Refused to obey any lawful order of, or to answer any material question approved by, the court in the course of bankruptcy proceedings;
7. Has failed to explain satisfactorily any

losses of assets or deficiency of assets to meet his liabilities; or

8. Has executed a written waiver of discharge approved by the court. Section 727.

Upon the request of the trustee or a creditor and after notice and a hearing, the court may revoke a discharge within one year if it was obtained through the fraud of the debtor.

REORGANIZATION (CHAPTER 11)

Reorganization is the means by which a distressed business enterprise and its value as a going concern are preserved through the correction or elimination of those factors which brought about its distress. Chapter 11 of the Bankruptcy Reform Act governs reorganization of eligible debtors, including corporations, and permits restructuring of their capital structure. The main objective of a reorganization proceeding is to develop and consummate a fair, equitable, and feasible plan of reorganization. After a plan has been prepared and filed, a hearing is held before the court to determine whether or not it shall be confirmed.

Proceedings

Any person that may be a debtor under Chapter 7 (except stockbrokers and commodity brokers) and railroads may be a debtor under Chapter 11. Petitions may be voluntary or involuntary.

As soon as practicable after the order for relief, the court will appoint a committee of unsecured creditors ordinarily consisting of persons that hold the seven largest claims against the debtor. In addition, the court may appoint additional committees of creditors or of equity security holders if necessary to assure adequate representation. Section 1102. The committee may, with the court's approval, employ attorneys, accountants, and other agents to represent or perform services for the committee. The committee should consult with the debtor or trustee concerning the administration of the case and may investigate the debtor's affairs and participate in the formulation of a plan. Section 1103.

The debtor will remain in possession and management of the property of the estate unless the court appoints a trustee. The court will appoint a trustee only for cause (including fraud, dishonesty, incompetence, or gross mismanagement of the debtor's affairs) or if such appointment is in the interests of creditors or equity security holders. Section 1104. If the court does not appoint a trustee upon the request of a party in interest, the court will appoint an examiner to conduct investigations into any allegations of fraud, dishonesty, incompetence, misconduct, or mismanagement if (1) such appointment is in the interests of creditors or equity security holders or (2) the debtor's fixed, liquidated, unsecured debts exceed $5,000,000. At any time before confirmation of a plan, the court may terminate the trustee's appointment and restore the debtor to possession and management of the property of the estate. Section 1105.

The duties of a trustee in a case under Chapter 11 include:

1. to be accountable for all property received;

2. to examine proof of claims;

3. to furnish information to all parties in interest;

4. to provide the court and taxing authorities with financial reports of the business operations;

5. to make a final report and account of the administration of the estate;

6. to investigate the financial condition of the debtor and the desirability of the continuance of the debtor's business; and

7. to file a plan or a report as to why there will be no plan or to recommend conversion of the case to Chapter 7.

The trustee also may operate the debtor's business. If the debtor remains in possession, he has essentially the same rights, duties, and powers as a trustee.

The Securities and Exchange Commission may raise, appear, and be heard on any issue but may not appeal from any judgment, order, or decree entered in the case. Section 1109.

The debtor may convert a case to Chapter 7 unless (1) the debtor is not in possession, (2) the case is an involuntary case begun under Chapter 11, or (3) the case was converted to Chapter 11 by the request of a party other than the debtor. The court may convert a case to Chapter 7 or dismiss it, whichever is in the best interest of creditors and the estate, but only for cause. Cause includes continuing loss to the estate, inability to effectuate a plan, or unreasonable delay by the debtor. Section 1112(b). The court may not convert a case to Chapter 7 if the debtor is a farmer or not-for-profit corporation unless the debtor requests such conversion.

Plan of Reorganization

The debtor may file a plan at any time and has the exclusive right to file a plan during the 120 days after the order for relief. Any party in interest (including the debtor, the trustee, a creditors' committee, an equity security holders' committee, a creditor, an equity security holder, or any indenture trustee) may file a plan but only if (1) a trustee has been appointed, or (2) the debtor has not filed a plan within 120 days, or (3) the debtor has not filed a plan that has been accepted by those creditors whose rights are impaired by the plan within 180 days.

After a plan has been filed, the plan, or a summary of it approved by the Court, and a written disclosure statement approved by the court as containing adequate information must be transmitted to each holder of a claim before soliciting acceptance or rejection of the plan. "Adequate informa-

tion" means information of a kind and in sufficient detail that would enable a hypothetical reasonable investor to make an informed judgment about the plan. Section 1125.

Acceptance of Plan

A class of *claims* has accepted a plan if it has been accepted by creditors that hold at least two-thirds in amount and more than one-half of the allowed claims of such class. Acceptance of a plan by a class of *interests,* such as shareholders, requires acceptance by holders of at least two-thirds in amount of the allowed interests of such class.

A class that is not impaired under a plan is deemed to have accepted the plan. Basically, a class is not impaired if the plan leaves unaltered the legal, equitable, and contractual rights to which such claim or interest entitles the holder of that claim or right. Section 1124.

Confirmation of Plan

A plan must be confirmed by the court before the plan is binding upon any parties. A court may confirm a plan only if it meets all of the requirements set forth in Section 1129. The most important of these requirements are the following.

Good Faith. The plan must have been proposed in good faith and not by any means forbidden by law. It must comply with all applicable provisions of the Reform Act as must its proponent. Section 1129(a)(1), (2) and (3).

Feasibility. The court must find that confirmation of the plan is not likely to be followed by the liquidation, or the need for further financial reorganization, of the debtor. Section 1129(a)(11). The reorganized debtor must have adequate working capital, sufficient earning power to meet fixed lien charges, fairly good credit prospects, ability to retire or refund its proposed debt over the period of extended maturity, must be soundly capitalized with no disproportionate ratio of debt to total value of assets, and must have assurance of reasonably good management. The essence of feasibility is that the reorganization entity will be able to operate economically and efficiently, will be able to compete upon fairly equal terms with other companies within the industry, and is not likely to require liquidation or a second reorganization within the foreseeable future.

The cornerstone of the feasibility of a plan of reorganization is a proper valuation of the debtor's assets. A valuation for reorganization purposes does not mean physical appraisal, book value, original cost less depreciation, reproduction cost less depreciation, reimbursement cost, or aggregate current market prices of outstanding security issues, but means *going concern value.* The proper method of determining this value is by ascertaining the reasonably prospective earnings of the reorganized debtor and by applying to these prospective earnings a proper rate of capitalization which will reflect all of the elements of risk inherent in the ability of the reorganized entity to realize the estimated earnings.

Cash Payments. Certain classes of creditors must have their allowed claims paid in full in cash immediately or, in some instances, upon a deferred basis. Section 1129(a)(9). These classes include the expenses of administration, gap creditors, claims for wages and salaries, and employee benefits and consumer deposits.

Acceptance by Creditors. To be confirmed, the plan must be accepted by at least *one* class of claims and with respect to *each* class each holder must either accept the plan *or* receive not less than the amount he would have received under Chapter 7. In addition, each class must accept the plan or be unimpaired by the plan. However, if the last requirement is not met, i.e., less than all classes accept the plan, the court may nonetheless "cram down" the plan if the plan does not discriminate unfairly and is fair and equitable. Section 1129(b)(1).

"Fair and equitable" with respect to secured creditors requires that they either retain their security interest and receive deferred payments at least equal to their claims or that they realize the "indubitable equivalent" of their claims. Fair and equitable with respect to unsecured creditors means that such creditors receive property of value equivalent to the full amount of their claim *or* that no junior claim or interest receive anything at all. With respect to a class of interests, a plan is fair and equitable if the holders receive full value or if no junior interest receives anything at all.

Effect of Reorganization

The reorganized debtor of the new entity succeeding to the debtor's properties emerges from the proceedings and begins life anew with only such obligations as are imposed upon it by the plan. It is entitled to injunctive relief to insure its freedom from all prior debts, obligations, and duties of every kind except those which have been preserved in the plan. The plan binds the debtor, any creditor, equity security holder, or general partner of the debtor. Upon the entry of a final decree closing the proceedings, the debtor, as provided in Section 524 is discharged from all of its debts and liabilities except those that are not dischargeable. All persons who are entitled to participate in the plan of reorganization have a period of not less than five years from the date of the final decree within which to exchange their old securities for the new, as provided in the plan.

It should be observed that the liability of a surety or guarantor of any of the outstanding indebtedness of the debtor is not altered or affected by a plan of reorganization, and an action at law by a creditor against such surety or guarantor will not be enjoined.

ADJUSTMENT OF DEBTS OF INDIVIDUALS (CHAPTER 13)

Proceedings

Chapter 13 provides a procedure for the adjustment of debts of an individual with regular income who owes liquidated, unsecured debts of less than $100,000 and secured debts of less than $350,000. So long as the debt limitations are met, sole proprietorships are also eligible. A case under Chapter 13 may only be initiated by a voluntary petition and may not be commenced by the court converting a Chapter 7 or Chapter 11 case except by request of the debtor. Sections 301, 303, 706, and 1112. On the other hand, the court may convert a case under Chapter 13 to Chapter 7 for cause or upon the request of the debtor or to Chapter 11 at any time before confirmation but after notice and a hearing.

The Plan

The debtor files the plan and may modify it at any time before confirmation. The plan must meet three requirements under Section 1322:

1. It must provide for submission of all or any portion of future earnings or income of the debtor, as is necessary for the execution of the plan, to the supervision and control of the trustee.

2. It must provide for full payment on a deferred basis of all claims entitled to a priority unless a holder of a claim agrees to a different treatment of such claim.

3. If the plan classifies claims, it must provide the same treatment for each claim in the same class.

In addition, the plan *may* modify the rights of unsecured creditors and the rights of secured creditors except those secured only by a security interest in the debtor's principal residence. A plan may provide for payments on any unsecured claim to be made concurrently with payments on any secured claim.

The plan may *not* provide for payments over a period that is longer than three years, unless the court approves for cause a longer period not to exceed five years.

Confirmation

The plan will be confirmed by the court if certain requirements have been met. First, the plan must comply with applicable law and be proposed in good faith. Second, the value of the property to be distributed to unsecured creditors, as of the effective date of the plan, must be not less than the amount that would be paid them under Chapter 7. Third, either the secured creditors must accept the plan *or* the plan must provide that the debtor will surrender to the secured creditors the collateral *or* the plan must permit the secured creditors to retain their security interest and the value of property to be distributed to them is not less than the allowed amount of their claim. Fourth, the debtor must be able to make all payments and comply with the plan.

Discharge

After a debtor completes all payments under the plan, the court will grant him a discharge of all debts except long-term debts whose maturity extends beyond the expiration of the plan and nondischargeable debts for alimony, maintenance, and support. This discharge is considerably more extensive than that granted under Chapter 7

Even if all payments have *not* been made, the court may, after a hearing, grant a discharge if the debtor's failure to complete such payments is due to circumstances for which the debtor should not justly be held accountable, the value of property actually distributed is not less than what would have been received under Chapter 7, and modification of the plan is not practicable.   Section 1328(b).

UNITED STATES TRUSTEES SYSTEM (CHAPTER 15)

Chapter 15 of the Act provides for a five year pilot project program known as the United States Trustees System, which utilizes the services of U.S. trustees appointed by the U.S. Attorney General.   Unless extended by Congress the pilot program will terminate on April 1, 1984.   Chapter 15 is therefore "sunset legislation" because the United States Trustees program will cease to exist at sunset on a specified date without requiring any action by Congress.   The pilot program is operative in only 18 specified judicial districts located in 10 areas of the United States:

1. District of Maine, District of New Hampshire, District of Massachusetts, and District of Rhode Island.
2. Southern District of New York.
3. District of Delaware and District of New Jersey.
4. Eastern District of Virginia and District of Columbia.
5. Northern District of Alabama.
6. Northern District of Texas.
7. Northern District of Illinois.
8. District of Minnesota, District of North Dakota, District of South Dakota.
9. Central District of California.
10. District of Colorado and District of Kansas.

These judicial districts have been selected on the basis of the kind and number of cases that predominate in these areas. This mix is necessary in order to determine at the end of the five-year trial period whether or not the system should be implemented throughout the entire country or be abandoned entirely.

The United States trustees are not intended to replace private trustees in bankruptcy cases, but rather to perform the supervisory and appointing powers handled by the bankruptcy judges under the Act and to monitor trustee performance in more detail than under current practice.   The primary function of the United States trustee is to establish, maintain, and supervise panels of private trustees in cases under Chapter 7 and to serve as trustee or to appoint standing trustees in Chapter 13 cases.

Under the bankruptcy law in effect prior to October 1, 1979, bankruptcy judges were required to both resolve disputes and supervise the administration of bankruptcy cases.   The main purpose of the U.S. trustee is to remove administrative duties from the bankruptcy judge leaving him free to resolve disputes.   The U.S. trustee, rather than the court, in each pilot district will appoint trustees, supervise administration of bankruptcy cases, and exercise all other functions prescribed by the Attorney General, such as presiding at first meetings of creditors, related to bankruptcy administration.   Moreover, in no-asset cases, where private trustees may be unwilling to serve, or in Chapter 13 cases, where no standing trustee may be willing to serve, the U.S. trustee is required to serve as a trustee or standing trustee in that case.

The duties of each United States trustee, within his district, are to:

1. establish, maintain, and supervise a panel of private trustees that are eligible and available to serve as trustees in cases under Chapter 7 of the Reform Act;
2. serve as and perform the duties of a trustee in a case under the Bankruptcy Reform Act when required under the Act to serve as trustee in such a case;
3. supervise the administration of cases and trustees in cases under Chapter 7, 11 or 13 of the Bankruptcy Reform Act;
4. deposit or invest under section 345 of the

Bankruptcy Reform Act money received as trustee in cases under the Act;

5. perform the duties prescribed for the United States trustee under the Bankruptcy Reform Act; and

6. make such reports as the Attorney General directs.

Each United States trustee shall be under the general supervision of the Attorney General, who shall provide general coordination and assistance to the United States trustees.

Not later than January 3, 1984, the Attorney General is required to report to the Congress, to the President, and the Judicial Conference of the United States on the feasibility, projected annual cost and effectiveness of the United States trustee system, as determined on the basis of the studies and surveys respecting the operation of the United States trustee system in the districts, together with recommendations as to the desirability and method of proceeding with implementation of the United States trustee system in all judicial districts of the United States.

Cases

Voidable Preferences

IN RE CONN

(1981 Bkrtcy. N.D.Ohio) 9 B.R. 431.

WHITE, Bankruptcy Judge.

A complaint to recover property transferred pursuant to an avoided preference was filed by Marc P. Gertz, trustee of the estate of Freelin Alva Conn, debtor herein, against BancOhio National Bank, hereinafter referred to as creditor, on December 9, 1980.

An answer admitting that the disputed transfers of property of the debtor to the creditor amounting to $439.17 were made within 90 days preceding the filing of debtor's petition, on account of an antecedent debt, while the debtor was insolvent and denying the remaining allegations of the complaint was filed by creditor on January 12, 1981.

A trial on said complaint was held on February 19, 1981. From the testimony of the debtor and the exhibits admitted into evidence, the court makes the following finding of fact and law.

Finding of Fact

1. A voluntary petition under Chapter 7 of

the Bankruptcy Code was filed by Freelin Alva Conn on September 30, 1980.

2. Marc P. Gertz was appointed interim trustee of debtor's estate on September 30, 1980 and became trustee, pursuant to 11 U.S.C. § 702(d), subsequent to the meeting of creditors on November 4, 1980.

3. BancOhio National Bank was listed by debtor on his Schedule A-2 as having a claim incurred in October of 1979, in the amount of $4,000.00 secured by a 1978 Oldsmobile Omega having a market value of $3,500.00.

4. During the period from June 30, 1980 to September 30, 1980 the following payments were made by debtor to creditor:

August 9, 1980	—$148.39
August 22, 1980	—$145.39
September 10, 1980	—$145.39

* * *

5. The net payoff balance on creditor's installment loan to debtor was $4,015.91 at the time debtor's bankruptcy petition was filed on September 30, 1980. * * *

6. The debtor was insolvent with liabilities of $19,775.00 and assets of $6,010.00 for the entire period in question.

7. The debtor was granted a discharge on January 20, 1981.

Issue

Do the transfers of property of the Debtor to the creditor constitute voidable preferences under 11 U.S.C. § 547(b)?

Discussion of Law

A trustee may avoid a transfer of property of the debtor to a creditor as a preference if the trustee proves that the five elements of a preference under 11 U.S.C. § 547(b) are met.   11 U.S.C. § 547(b) provides that:

Except as provided in subsection (c) of this section, the trustee may avoid any transfer of property of the debtor—

    (1) to or for the benefit of a creditor;

    (2) for or on account of an antecedent debt owed by the debtor before such transfer was made;

    (3) made while the debtor was insolvent;

    (4) made—

(A) on or within 90 days before the date of the filing of the petition; or

(B) between 90 days and one year before the date of the filing of the petition, if such creditor at the time of such transfer—

(i) was an insider; and

(ii) had reasonable cause to believe the debtor was insolvent at the time of such transfer; and

    (5) that enables such creditor to receive more than such creditor would receive if—

(A) the case were a case under chapter 7 of this title;

(B) The transfer had not been made; and

(C) such creditor received payment of such debt to the extent provided by the provisions of this title.

In the instant case, debtor, during the period from June 30, 1980 to September 30, 1980, made three transfers of property to creditor.   Creditor admits that said transfers meet the first four elements of a preference under § 547(b).

The existence of the fifth and final element of a preferential transfer is denied by creditor.   * * *

In order to determine whether a transfer allows a creditor to receive a greater percentage of his claim than otherwise receivable under the distributive provisions of the Code, the court must determine the status of the creditor's claim; i.e., whether the creditor's claim is a secured claim or an undersecured claim.   The Court must also consider the classes of creditors as provided for under Sections 507 and 506.   The provision of the Bankruptcy Code that governs the determination of secured status is 11 U.S.C. § 506(a).   Under § 506(a), a creditor's claim is secured to the extent of the value of his collateral.   If the amount of a creditor's claim is greater than the value of his collateral, the creditor is undersecured and his claim is broken down into two parts: he has a secured claim to the extent of the value of his collateral; and he has an unsecured claim for the balance of his claim. [Citations.]

The claim of the creditor herein was secured by a 1978 Oldsmobile Omega automobile.   The amount of creditor's claim on the date of the filing of debtor's petition was $4,015.91.   The market value of creditor's collateral was listed by debtor on his Schedule A-2 at $3,500.00.   At the trial upon the instant matter, debtor testified that he did not believe that $3,500.00 was a fair value of what the car was worth at the time he filed bankruptcy.

Debtor testified that the car was in excellent condition, except for a few stone marks around the rear wheel wells, at the time he filed his petition in bankruptcy.   Debtor had purchased the car in October of 1979 for $4,250.00.

Trustee failed to carry his burden of establishing what the value of the collateral car was on the date of the filing of debtor's petition.   There was no evidence presented by the trustee to prove that the amount of creditor's claim was greater than the value of creditor's collateral. Therefore, the court finds that the amount of creditor's claim was equivalent to the value of the collateral car and thus, creditor had a fully secured claim.

A trustee may only avoid as a preference a pre-bankruptcy transfer which enables one creditor to recover more on his claim than other creditors of the same class. The greater percentage test under § 547(b)(5) serves the prime bankruptcy policy of equality of distribution among creditors of the debtor. The legislative history describes the purpose of the preference section as follows:

The purpose of the preference section is two-fold. First, by permitting the trustee to avoid pre-bankruptcy transfers that occur within a short period before bankruptcy, creditors are discouraged from racing to the courthouse to dismember the debtor during his slide into bankruptcy * * * Second, and more important, the preference provisions facilitate the prime bankruptcy policy of equality of distribution among creditors of the debtor. Any creditor that received a greater payment than others of his class is required to disgorge so that all may share equally * * * H.R.Rep.No. 595, 95th Cong., 1st Sess., 177–78 (1977), U.S. Code Cong. & Admin. News 1978, p. 6138.

Trustee, herein, has failed to carry his burden of proving that the effect of the payments was to enable creditor to obtain a greater percentage of its debt than it would receive under the distributive provisions of the Code. If any one of the elements of a preference under § 547(b), is wanting, a preference has not been established. [Citation.]

Therefore, it is the conclusion of this Court that the transfers of property of the debtor to the creditor do not constitute voidable preferences under 11 U.S.C. § 547(b) as the trustee failed to prove that the effect of the transfers was to enable the creditor to obtain a greater percentage of its debt than it would receive under the distributive

provisions of the Code. Trustee's complaint to recover the amount of the August 9, 1980, August 22, 1980, and September 10, 1980 payments in the total sum of $439.17 should be denied as said payments do not meet all five elements necessary for a preference under 11 U.S.C. § 547(b).

Reorganization (Chapter 11):
Confirmation of Plan

MATTER OF LANDMARK AT PLAZA PARK, LTD.

(1980 Bktcy. D.N.J.) 7 B.R. 653.

HILL, Bankruptcy Judge.

This opinion constitutes the Court's findings of fact and conclusions of law with respect to a Chapter 11 confirmation hearing held on debtor's plan of reorganization, as modified. The opinion explains the November 3, 1980, letter decision of the Court.

Debtor, Landmark at Plaza Park, Ltd., is a limited partnership whose only substantial asset is a 200-unit garden apartment complex located in Morrisville, Pennsylvania. City Federal (hereafter City) holds a first mortgage on this property in the face amount of $2,250,000. The mortgage bears an interest rate of 9.5% and is due and payable on October 1, 1986. * * * This opinion deals with debtor's plan as it affects City, the only objecting class of creditors. As to all other classes of creditors, there is no dispute and the Court is satisfied that the confirmation standards specified in 11 *U.S.C.* Section 1129 have been met.

* * *

The Plan as Modified
Crucial to an understanding of the Court's decision is a discussion of the plan and how it affects City. Contractually, City is a first mortgagee without recourse. It has possession of the property and is collecting the rents pursuant to a rent assignment

agreement. The mortgage has been in default since at least December, 1979. City is undersecured and wants to complete its foreclosure action.

The debtor has proposed in substance the following plan:

1. City is to redeliver possession of the property to the debtor.
2. On the 16th month after the effective date of the plan and through the 36th month debtor will commence monthly interest payments at the rate of 12.5% computed on the value of the property—$2,260,000.
3. Debtor will deliver to City a non-recourse note, payable in three years in the face amount of $2,705,820.31, in substitution of all existing liabilities.
4. The existing mortgage will secure the note set forth in paragraph 3, except to the extent that it is inconsistent with or modified by the plan.
5. City is the only member of the class of creditors to which it has been assigned.

The face amount of the note is derived as follows:

a. Current value of collateral
$2,260,000.00
b. Unpaid interest: months 1–15
@ 12.5%   353,125.00
c. Interest on unpaid interest:
21 months @ 15%

92,695.31
Face amount of note $2,705,820.31

The debtor's principal theory is that the note will be paid off at the end of 36 months by a combination of refinancing and accumulation of cash from the project, all of which will subsequently be discussed at length. The key to the debtor's plan is a proposal to obtain a new first mortgage in three years in the face amount of $2,400,000.

It is undisputed that pursuant to this plan City is impaired within the meaning of Section 1124 of the Code. City has rejected the plan.

The Issues
Confirmation standards under the Code are set forth in Section 1129. Clearly, the debtor has complied with all provisions of that section except for the following subsections: * * * (a)(11), (b)(1) and (b)(2). Subsection (a)(11) of Section 1129 is the feasibility requirement and, in a general sense, deals with whether the debtor can and will accomplish what it has proposed. Subsection (b) of Section 1129 is the "cram-down" provision of the Code. It describes those circumstances in which a class of creditors or interests may over its objection be involuntarily subjected to the provisions of a plan. Each of these sections will be discussed at length. The provisions of subsection (b) will be discussed first because certain determinations made there bear on the feasibility determination required by subsection (a)(11).

The Requirements of
Section 1129(b)(1) and (2)
The provisions of Section 1129(b) specify the circumstances under which a class of creditors or interests may be involuntarily subjected to a plan of reorganization. * * *

Given the present posture of this case the Court is satisfied that the factors set forth in Section 1129(b)(2)(A)(i), dealing with the cram down of a secured creditor, adequately deal with the question of whether the plan, as to City, is fair and equitable, and the Court will limit its consideration to those factors.

To meet the requirements of Section 1129(b)(2)(A)(i) the debtor's plan must do three things. First, it must provide for retention by the creditor of its lien. Second, the total stream of deferred cash payments proposed by the plan must at least total the amount of the secured claim. Third, the total stream of payments must have a value equal to the value of the property. The plan before the Court satisfies the first two requirements, but may not satisfy the third.

* * *

Conceptually, the modified plan seeks to force City to make a $2,260,000 loan, repayable in three years, with the first 15 months of interest deferred. There is no amortization over the term of the loan. Since there is currently no equity in the property the debtor is asking City to make a 100% loan. The rate of interest on a loan of this type should correspond to the rate of interest which would be charged or obtained by a creditor making a loan to a third party with similar terms, duration, collateral and risk. 5 *Collier on Bankruptcy* at para. 1129.03 (15th ed. 1980). Although the rate of interest may be identical to the market rate of interest, this will often not be the case because of the particular risk involved. 5 *Collier, supra* at para. 1129.03.

It appears clear to the Court that the forced loan proposed by the debtor includes terms less favorable to City than would typically be found in the market and that any confirmable plan must compensate City for this deficiency. * * * Thus, if a note and interest payments were offered to City by debtor at a 15% rate debtor would appear to meet the requirement that the discounted stream of payments equal the value of the property. Because the 12.5% rate proposed by debtor is below the 15% minimum rate established by the Court the plan as presented does not comply with Section 1129(b)(2)(A)(i)(II) and, therefore, cannot be confirmed. Since the plan could be readily modified, however, the Court must determine whether the plan is feasible if funded at a 15% rate. * * *

The Requirements
of Section 1129(a)(11)
* * *

Section 1129(a)(11) of the Code, which for the most part incorporates the policy of the Act, requires the Court to scrutinize the plan proposed by a debtor to determine whether it offers a reasonable prospect of success and whether it is workable. Specifically Section 1129(a)(11) requires the Court to find that:

Confirmation of the plan is not likely to be followed by the liquidation, or the need for further financial reorganization, of the debtor or any successor to the debtor under the plan, unless such liquidation or reorganization is proposed in the plan. 11 U.S.C. Section 1129(a)(11).

Collier states that the purpose of Section 1129(a)(11) is to prevent confirmation of visionary schemes that promise creditors and equity security holders more under a proposed plan than the debtor could possibly attain after confirmation. 5 *Collier on Bankruptcy*, para. 1129.02 (15th ed. 1980). Thus, if the facts indicate that the plan will ultimately lead to liquidation, it is not feasible and cannot be confirmed even if the debtor is sincere and has made a best effort to perform according to the terms of the plan. 5 *Collier, supra* at para. 1129.02. The factors courts should generally consider in making the above determination are (1) the adequacy of the capital structure; (2) the earning power of the business; (3) economic conditions; (4) the ability of management; (5) the probability of the continuation of the same management; and (6) any other related matters which determine the prospects of a sufficiently successful operation to enable performance of the provisions of the plan. 5 *Collier, supra* at para. 1129.02.

* * *

It is clear, then, that debtor's projections of income and expense are not realistic. In response to this conclusion the Court has formulated its own judgment as to what income and expenses should properly be over a three-year period. * * * Given these figure and the 15% interest factor previously derived the final question for the Court is whether debtor can realistically carry out its plan, as required by 1129(a)(11).

Fulfillment of the Plan
As stated earlier, fulfillment of the plan contemplates the ability of the debtor to cure certain deferred maintenance items, to make certain interest payments to City, and

to pay off a note to City in three years.
* * *

* * *

The Court has discussed the cost of curing deferred maintenance and the income and expenses of the project over the next three years. In the Court's opinion fulfillment of the plan by the debtor is not possible if its "best judgment" figures are utilized. Furthermore, even assuming a 10% income increase, fulfillment of the plan's conditions is highly doubtful. In the Court's judgment it is more probable than not that confirmation of a plan would likely be followed either by a liquidation or further reorganization proceedings. Thus, the debtor has not fulfilled the requirements of Section 1129(a)(11) and confirmation of the debtor's plan, as modified, must be denied.

Comparison of
Chapter 7 with Chapter 13

IN RE YEE

(1980 Bkrtcy. E.D.N.Y.) 7 B.R. 747.

GOETZ, Bankruptcy Judge:

In both of these cases, as in a substantial percentage of the other cases now being filed in this judicial district, beneficiaries of generous student loans are invoking Chapter 13 of the new bankruptcy law (11 U.S.C. §§ 1301–1330) to escape the obligation to repay student loans that would not be dischargeable in ordinary bankruptcy, except where hardship could be demonstrated. Chapter 13 was intended to provide a means whereby individuals could repay their debts over a period of time. Typically, the two cases now before the Court involve minimal payments which in their totality are far less than the debtors' outstanding student loans. The question before the Court is whether the plans of these debtors qualify for confirmation. This Court holds that they do not; that they do not satisfy the requirement of § 1325(a)(3) because they have not been proposed in good faith.

JOHN YEE

Mr. Yee is employed as a financial analyst by Columbia Broadcasting Systems and last year earned $16,836.37. He supports only himself; he has no dependents. He holds a bachelor's degree in accounting from the Bernard M. Baruch College of the City University of New York, which he secured with the assistance of a National Direct Student Loan. There is now owing on that student loan, with interest, the sum of $2,583.62. Among Mr. Yee's other debts which total about $10,790, the Parking Violations Bureau of the City of New York is owed $380.

Mr. Yee has no assets; were his estate to be liquidated, his creditors would receive nothing.

Under the Chapter 13 plan submitted for confirmation, Mr. Yee would pay the Chapter 13 trustee $30 per month for 36 months, for a total of $1,020, or less than half what he owes on his student loan alone. A partially secured creditor will be paid the value of its secured interest, with the balance to go to unsecured creditors. After deduction of administrative expenses, there will be left for distribution among Mr. Yee's creditors about $918. This represents approximately 7 percent of the total amount owed, including his student loan.

At the confirmation hearing on July 23, 1980, the Court found that, in view of the debtor's excellent education, substantial income, and lack of dependents, the minimal payment plan he proposed was not filed in good faith, and denied it confirmation. "Good faith," the Court said, does not necessarily mean "best efforts," but, rather a bona fide effort to discharge outstanding obligations. The token payments offered by the debtor do not represent a bona fide effort.

The debtor, John Yee, has filed a motion requesting reconsideration, and in the event such reconsideration is denied, that the proceeding be converted to a case under Chapter 7 pursuant to § 1307(a).

DENA M. COYE

Dena M. Coye is a resident alien who arrived in the United States in 1977. In 1978, she applied for, and secured, a student loan in the amount of $5,600 with which she pursued and obtained a master's degree in social work from the Graduate School of Social Services at Fordham University in June, 1978.

In 1979, Miss Coye received a second loan in the same amount, with which she began to pursue a second graduate degree in the New School for Social Research. In May, 1980, she decided to discontinue, at least temporarily, her pursuit of graduate degrees. She is currently employed as a vocational counselor at a salary of $14,500 annually.

Student loans normally do not become payable until nine months after a student has either graduated or permanently terminated her education. It is unclear whether Miss Coye's loans have yet become due. No one has as yet asked her to pay these loans, nor has she received a bill for them. She believes that no payments will be due for a year or more. Nevertheless, promptly upon deciding to discontinue her education, she filed this petition on May 20, 1980. In addition to her student loans totaling $11,200, Miss Coye owes various New York City department stores and other creditors a total of $6,348.

Her budget shows that her monthly income exceeds her expenses by only $19. She proposes to pay her creditors $15 a month for 36 months. After deducting her attorney's fees and the commissions of the Chapter 13 trustee, her creditors would receive $390, or 2 percent.

At the hearing on her plan, it developed that the figures furnished the Court by Miss Coye in her Chapter 13 Statement were incorrect. Her budget did not show $30 a month she sends her parents in Jamaica. Furthermore, since filing her petition, she has moved into a more expensive apartment, raising her monthly cost for rent and utilities from $393 a month to $418.85 per month. Including these expenses in her budget would eliminate any surplus for the repayment of her debts.

Her creditors, too, would receive nothing if her estate were liquidated.

The New York State Higher Education Services Corporation opposed confirmation of her plan and requested that the case be converted to one under Chapter 7 on the grounds: (a) that since in straight bankruptcy its debt would be nondischargeable, it would receive payment in full in Chapter 7, and that, accordingly, Miss Coye's plan did not satisfy 11 U.S.C. § 1325(a)(4); and (b) that the plan was not proposed in good faith (§ 1325(a)(3)).

Discussion

The issue before the Court is one of statutory construction. Stated simply, it is whether there is authority in the bankruptcy court to deny confirmation to a Chapter 13 plan which proposes minimal, or token, payments to creditors, and which would result in the discharge of student loans of substantial magnitude. Under § 1328 of the Code, upon completion of all payments under a Chapter 13 plan, a debtor is discharged from all debts, other than long-term obligations extending beyond the life of the plan, and those owed the debtor's family for alimony, maintenance, and support. See 11 U.S.C. §§ 1322(b)(5), 523(a)(5). Unlike the discharge available in Chapter 7, the Chapter 13 discharge includes student loans.

* * *

In approaching the task at hand, it is important to bear in mind that Chapter 13 was part of a wholesale revision of the bankruptcy laws in which a number of separate objectives were independently pursued, resulting in a statute, the separate parts of which mesh only imperfectly.

All aspects of the laws governing bankruptcy were revised. Many changes were made respecting conventional, or straight, bankruptcy, now Chapter 7 of the Code. At the same time, Congress sought to encourage the use of the type of debt relief afforded by former Chapter XIII, under which wage earners had paid off their debts out of current income.

In revising the law with respect to what is now Chapter 7, the exceptions to discharge were a major focus of concern, and none more so than the treatment to be given student loans.

* * *

As the Code now reads, all loans owing a governmental unit or a nonprofit institution of higher education are not dischargeable in a Chapter 7 proceeding for five years after they first become due, unless excepting such debts from discharge would impose "an undue hardship on the debtor and the debtor's dependents."

At the same time as Congress was revising what became Chapter 7, it was also reworking Chapter XIII into the present Chapter 13.

* * *

Persuaded of the superiority from every point of view of encouraging debtors to pay their debts, where possible, Congress set out to eliminate the obstacles which it believed the prior statute had placed in the way of the fullest utilization of Chapter XIII. Congress believed that most people, given the opportunity, wanted to pay off their obligations, rather than otherwise.

* * *

The changes made in Chapter XIII were designed to eliminate what experience with predominantly extension plans had shown to be the defects of that chapter. Relatively little attention appears to have been paid to other aspects of the new law. [Citations.]

* * *

But while Congress may have legis-

lated in the expectation that most Chapter 13 plans would provide for repayment in full, or in large measure, of outstanding debts, it fixed no minimum, either percentage-wise or in absolute terms, respecting the size of the payments to be made under a Chapter 13 plan. While certain conditions are imposed, they can be satisfied in many cases by nominal or even zero payment. See 11 U.S.C. § 1325(a).

All that Chapter 13 requires is that a plan provide that priority creditors, if any, be paid in full, that secured creditors, who neither accept the plan nor receive back their collateral, are paid the "allowed amount" of their claims, and that unsecured creditors receive "not less than the amount that would be paid" on their claims "if the estate of the debtor were liquidated under chapter 7." 11 U.S.C. § 1325(a)(4).

For the bulk of the debtors requiring relief under the bankruptcy laws, this last requirement imposes no minimum monetary limit. In most cases, it can be satisfied by zero payments, i.e., by the payment of no money whatsoever to unsecured creditors. This is because most persons having recourse to debt relief do not own property having a value higher than the generous exemption allowed by the Code before any estate becomes available to general creditors.

This means that invocation of Chapter 13 involves no greater cost to the debtor than filing under Chapter 7. But the difference to the debtor between filing under Chapter 7 as compared with filing under Chapter 13 can be enormous.

A Chapter 7 discharge does not release a debtor from all outstanding obligations. As previously noted, it will not release him from student loans, in the absence of hardship, for five years after they first become due. There are eight other exceptions, including debts arising out of willful or malicious injury, or fines, penalties, or forfeitures payable to or for the benefit of a governmental unit, or debts fraudulently incurred. See 11 U.S.C. § 523(a).

However, a Chapter 13 discharge is different. Only if a debtor fails to complete his payments under his plan, but, nevertheless, is allowed a discharge, is such discharge subject to the same exceptions as a Chapter 7 discharge. See 11 U.S.C. § 1328(c). Otherwise, only two types of debts are specifically excluded from a Chapter 13 discharge. First, the debtor is not discharged from long-term obligations, i.e., debts respecting which the last payment is due after the date on which the final payment under the plan is due. 11 U.S.C. § 1328(a)(1). The reasons for this exception are obvious: to the extent the debt has a life longer than the plan, it was not covered by the plan. See 11 U.S.C. § 1322(b)(5). The other exceptions are the debtor's obligations to his family, i.e., to his spouse, former spouse, or child for alimony, maintenance, or support created by a separation agreement, divorce decree, or property settlement. 11 U.S.C. § 1328(a)(2). See 11 U.S.C. § 523(a)(5). Like long-term obligations, such obligations would appear to fall into the category of continuing debts, which are not necessarily satisfied in full during the life of the plan. Further, familial obligations have always enjoyed a special position under the bankruptcy laws. [Citations.]

Another critical difference between Chapter 13 and Chapter 7 is that a debtor who receives a discharge under Chapter 7 cannot obtain a discharge again under that Chapter for six years, 11 U.S.C. § 727(a)(8); whereas a debtor seeking relief under Chapter 13 is not subject to the same bar, or, indeed, to any explicit statutory bar. [Citations.]

To these advantages should be added the fact that a Chapter 13 discharge, unlike a Chapter 7 discharge, cannot be denied for misconduct. There is no section in Chapter 13 paralleling 11 U.S.C. § 727, which applies only to cases under Chapter 7. See 11 U.S.C. § 103(b).

* * *

The difference between the discharge granted under Chapter 13 when a plan is completed, and that made available when it is not, strongly suggests that Congress anticipated that plans that paid less than 100 percent would be the exception rather than the rule. But experience under Chapter 13 in this judicial district, as elsewhere, has turned out to be markedly different. As Bankruptcy Judge Radoyevich has noted, "Plans which would provide for the repayment of more than 50% of unsecured debt are few and far between." [Citations.]

Debtors have seen in Chapter 13 an opportunity at little cost to escape burdensome obligations from which straight bankruptcy would not free them. Persons owing large debts for student loans, or other obligations not dischargeable in ordinary bankruptcy, are filing plans which are intended to result in the discharge of these debts in exchange for minimal, or token, payments to their creditors. They want the benefits Congress intended for debtors trying to pay their bills, but without the burden of payment.

However, before a Chapter 13 plan can be confirmed, it must pass the scrutiny of the Court. In this respect, Chapter 13 differs markedly from Chapter 7. The Court has virtually no role to play in straight bankruptcy or liquidation under Chapter 7. A Chapter 7 proceeding, from filing to discharge, is processed almost entirely by clerical personnel carrying out largely ministerial functions. The Court's role is limited to ensuring that the debtor understands the significance of the discharge he receives, and that he does not diminish its value imprudently. 11 U.S.C § 524(d).

Chapter 13 is quite different. A Chapter 13 plan must be confirmed by the Court.

Before the Court confirms a plan, it must make various affirmative findings. See 11 U.S.C. § 1325(a). Among other things, the Court must find that "the plan has been proposed in good faith and not by any means forbidden by law." 11 U.S.C. § 1325(a)(3).

The term "good faith" is not defined in the Code and its meaning is not clarified by the legislative history of the new statute. It is a phrase well known to the law, and characteristically derives its meaning from the context in which it is found. It is not new to bankruptcy law; it was present in the Bankruptcy Act of 1898. It was interpreted as calling for an inquiry as to "whether or not there has been an abuse of the provisions, purpose or spirit" of the chapter involved. [Citations.]

The meaning of the term "good faith" has assumed great significance in the interpretation of Chapter 13. The bankruptcy courts are split on the question of whether the need to find "good faith" empowers them to refuse to confirm plans where to do so would produce a result incompatible with the overall structure of the bankruptcy laws.

* * *

Only if the bankruptcy courts are given a discretionary role to play in determining under what circumstances a debtor may claim the benefits of Chapter 13 is Chapter 13 reconcilable with Chapter 7. No rational legislative policy would totally bar student loans from discharge in straight bankruptcy but permit their avoidance automatically upon payment of a pittance to creditors. The difference in treatment between student loans in Chapter 7 and in Chapter 13 is defensible only if the Chapter 13 plan either calls for payments of all debts in full, as Congress thought most plans would do, or, if it calls for less than full

payment, that a court determine that, in light of the surrounding circumstances, including the substantiality of the payments made, that it merits confirmation, nevertheless.

Looking to all the guides to legislative intent, i.e., to the history of the law, statements, and committee reports at the time it was enacted, and the overall structure of the Code, the construction which best carries out the legislative intent is one which finds in the direction to the bankruptcy court to assess the good faith of a Chapter 13 plan the authority to deny confirmation to a plan which has as a principal objective the discharge of student loans.

Applying that standard to the two plans here involved, the Court finds that neither was filed in good faith. Neither debtor has invoked Chapter 13 for its intended purpose, and that is, to pay off, rather than escape, debts which have become too burdensome to meet without the help of the bankruptcy laws. Both are seeking the advantages of Chapter 13 without its drawbacks.

Mr. Yee offers to pay his creditors no more each month than he spends for cigarettes; Miss Coye proposes to pay about fifty cents per day, less than the cost of a subway ride. Miss Coye, who has obtained an education most Americans would envy, is seeking to shift the burden of repayment off her own shoulders even before her debt is due.

These Chapter 13 plans have as their objective, not the payment of debts, but the discharge of student loans; they represent an abuse of the provisions, purpose, and spirit of Chapter 13. Accordingly, they lack good faith and cannot be confirmed because they do not satisfy § 1325(a)(3).

* * *

Problems

1. (a) B goes into bankruptcy. His estate has no assets. Are B's taxes discharged by the proceedings?

(b) B obtains property from A on credit by representing that he is solvent when in fact he knows he is insolvent. Is B's debt to A discharged by B's discharge in bankruptcy?

2. B goes into bankruptcy owing $5,000 as wages to his four employees. There is enough in his estate to pay all costs of administration and enough to pay his employees but nothing will then be left for general creditors. Do the employees take all the estate? Under what conditions? If the general creditors received nothing at all, would these debts be discharged?

3. A sold goods to B for $2,500 and retained a security interest in them. Three months later B filed a petition in bankruptcy under Chapter 7. At this time B still owed A $2,000 for the purchase price of the goods whose value was $1,500.

(a) May the trustee invalidate A's security interest. If so, under what provision?

(b) If the security interest is invalidated, what is A's status in the bankruptcy proceeding?

(c) If the security interest in *not* invalidated, what is A's status in the bankruptcy proceeding?

4. A debtor went through bankruptcy and received his discharge. Which of the following debts were completely discharged and which remain debts against him in the future:

(a) Claims of $900 each by X and Y for wages earned within three months immediately prior to bankruptcy.

(b) A judgment of $3,000 against the debtor by C for breach of contract.

(c) Sales taxes of $1,800.

(d) $1,000 in past alimony and support money owed to his divorced wife for herself and their child.

(e) A judgment of $4,000 for injuries received because of the debtor's negligent operation of an automobile.

5. Rosinoff and his wife, who were business partners, entered bankruptcy. Objection was made to their discharge in bankruptcy by a creditor, Baldwin, on the grounds that:

(a) The partners had obtained credit from Baldwin on the basis of a false financial statement;

(b) The partners had failed to keep books of account and records from which their financial condition would be ascertained;

(c) Rosinoff had falsely sworn that he had taken $7 from the partnership account when the correct amount was $700.

Were the debtors entitled to a discharge?

6. X Corporation is a debtor in reorganization proceeding under Chapter 11 of the Bankruptcy Reform Act. By fair and proper valuation its assets are worth $100,000. The indebtedness of the corporation is $105,000, it has outstanding preferred stock of par value of $20,000, and common stock of par value of $75,000. The plan of reorganization submitted by the trustees would eliminate the common shareholders and give bonds of the face amount of $5,000 to the creditors, common stock in the ratio of 84% to the creditors, and 16% to the preferred shareholders. Should this plan be confirmed?

7. A is a wage earner with a regular income. He has unsecured debts of $42,000 and secured debts owing to B, C, D and E totaling $120,000. E's debt is secured only by a mortgage on A's home. A files a petition under Chapter 13 and a plan providing payment as follows:

(a) 60% of all taxes owed,

(b) 35% of all unsecured debts, and

(c) $100,000 in total to B, C, D and E.

Should the court confirm the plan? If not, how must the plan be modified and/or what other conditions must be satisfied?

Regulation
of Business

Chapter
41

UNFAIR
COMPETITION
AND
ANTITRUST LAW

The economic community is best served in normal times by free competition in trade and industry. It is in the public interest that quality, price, and service, in an open competitive market for goods and services be determining factors in the business rivalry for the customer's dollar.

Practices such as imitation of a competitor's trade mark, passing or palming off one's products as those of another, betrayal of trade secrets, disloyalty of employees, interference with contracts, false advertising, and product disparagement are injurious to free and fair competition. To preserve fairness and to protect freedom of competition by preventing businessmen from taking unfair advantage of their competitors, certain rules and principles have been developed by the courts. Generally referred to as the law of unfair competition, they are basically rules of fair play, the rules of the game applied to the world of business.

Antitrust laws are similarly designed to protect free competition by insuring that such competition is fair. These statutes seek to prevent unreasonable aggregation of economic power which would stifle or weaken competition. This chapter after first exploring the area of unfair competition will examine the major antitrust statutes.

UNFAIR COMPETITION

PALMING OFF GOODS

One of the earliest forms of unfair competition is the fraudulent marketing of one person's goods as those of another. This unlawful practice is sometimes referred to as "passing off" or "palming off." It may involve infringement of another's trademark or appropriation of another's trade name, or a conscious imitation of the physical appearance of another's goods deceptive to the purchaser. It is basically a "cashing in" on the good will, good name, and reputation of a competitor and of his products. It results in deception of the public and loss of trade by honest businessmen.

TRADE SECRETS

Every business has secret information including lists of customers as well as contracts with suppliers and customers. Some have secret formulas, processes, and methods used in the production of goods that are vital to successful operation of the business. These are sometimes designated as "trade secrets", involving information received and held in confidence by employees which they are required to have in order to perform their duties.

An employee is under a duty of loyalty to his employer which includes the non-disclosure of trade secrets to competitors. It is wrongful for a competitor to obtain vital secret trade information of this type from an employee by bribery or otherwise. The faithless employee also commits a tort by divulging secret trade information. Contracts of employment frequently contain restrictive covenants whereby the employee agrees that for a stated period of time and within a specific territory he will not directly or indirectly engage in competition with his former employer, or become employed by a competitor of his former employer. These restrictive agreements, if reasonable with respect to time and area limitations, are enforced by the courts, although in some jurisdictions enforcement depends upon the employee having acquired trade secrets of his employer during the course of his employment.

In the absence of contract restriction, an employee is under no duty upon termination of his employment to refrain from competing or working for a competitor of his former employer. During the period of employment he is under such a duty whether or not provided by contract. An example of unfair competition would be the inducement by one company of employees of another company possessed of certain unique technical skills and secret knowledge acquired by them in the course of such employment, to terminate their employment and to use such skills and secret information for its benefit. Thus, A and B, who have been employees of the X Company for 15 years, have developed in the course of their employment highly specialized knowledge and skills in the manufacture of space suits for astronauts. There are few, if any, persons who have equivalent skill and knowledge. Y Company, desirous of obtaining a contract with the government for the manufacture of space suits, approaches A and B and offers them employment. There is no contract which prohibits A and B from leaving the X Company and going to work for the Y Company. However, if they do so, the X Company is entitled to an injunction restraining A, B and the Y Company from the use of trade secrets and methods for manufacturing space suits which were developed by A and B while in the employ of the X Company.

DISPARAGEMENT OF ANOTHER'S PROPERTY

An unprivileged statement which is untrue and disparaging to the title or quality of another's property, and which adversely affects the conduct of a third person as prospective purchaser or lessee of the property, subjects the person making the statement to liability. He is liable to the person whose property is disparaged even though he did not intend to influence the conduct of a third person, and although he neither knew nor believed that the disparaging matter was false.

Disparagement is defined as statements intended by the party making them to be understood, or which are reasonably understood, as casting doubt upon the title or quality of another's property, if the statements are so understood by the person to whom made. Thus, A, while contemplating the purchase of a stock of merchandise which belongs to B, reads an advertisement in a newspaper in which C falsely asserts he has a lien upon the merchandise. C has disparaged B's property in the goods.

A person who publishes disparaging matter is liable for loss sustained by the owner of the property disparaged as a result of repetition of the disparaging matter by a third person if the repetition was either authorized or reasonably foreseeable. For instance, Jones makes an offer to purchase Smith's farm which has been represented free and clear of encumbrances. Tattle tells Mrs. Jones that the farm is mortgaged up to its full value. Mrs. Jones, as she is privileged to do, repeats this to her husband who withdraws his offer for the farm. Tattle is liable to Smith.

An untrue expression of opinion, dishonestly made, which is disparaging, is wrongful and actionable. However, no action lies to recover damages resulting from an honest statement of opinion, one actually held by the party making it, and clearly expressed as such.

The pecuniary loss which may be recovered by an injured person is that which directly and immediately results from impairment of the marketability of the property disparaged. Thus, A publishes an untrue statement in a magazine that cranberries grown during the current season in a particular area are unwholesome. B is a jobber who has contracted to buy the entire output of cranberries grown in this area. B's business falls off 50%. If there are no other facts which account for this falling off of B's business, B is entitled to recover the amount of his loss from A.

TRADE-MARKS, MARKS, AND TRADE NAMES

Trade-Marks

A trade-mark is a distinctive mark, word, letter, number, design, picture or combination thereof in any form of arrangement which is affixed to goods and is adopted or used by a person identifying goods which he manufactures or sells. Generic and descriptive designations cannot be used as trademarks. Thus, a word which is descriptive of the ingredients, quality, purpose, function, or uses of a product, may not be monopolized by a person as his proprietary trademark. The word "Plow" cannot be a trade-mark for plows, although it may be a trade-mark for shoes.

A geographical name may not be used as a trade-mark if the name is likely to be understood as representing that the goods were produced or processed in the place designated by the name, or if they are of the same distinct kind or quality as goods produced, processed, or used in that place, unless the person using the name is the owner, or acts with the consent of the owner of the geographical place, or is the sole source of supply of goods originated in the place indicated by the name.

At common law a trade-mark was required to be affixed to the goods it identified. The Lanham Act, Trade-Mark Act of 1946, relaxes this requirement by permitting trademark registration and protection of a mark placed "on the goods or their containers or the displays associated therewith or on the tags or labels affixed thereto."

Trade-marks may be registered in the United States Patent Office. If infringed, the owner is entitled to injunctive relief and damages.

Service Marks, Certification Marks, Collective Marks

Similar in function to the trade-mark which identifies tangible goods and products, a service mark is used to identify and distinguish the services of one person from those of others. A service mark need not be affixed to goods and when registered in the Patent Office is entitled to the same protection as a registered trade-mark. Service marks were not registerable prior to the Lanham Act of 1946.

A certification mark is a mark used

upon or in connection with goods or services of one or more persons other than the owner of the mark to certify regional or other origin, material, mode of manufacture, quality, accuracy, or other characteristics of the goods or services, or that the work or labor in the goods or services were performed by members of a union or other organization.

A collective mark is a distinctive mark or symbol used to identify, or indicate membership in a trade union, trade association, fraternal society, or other organization.

Trade-marks, service marks, certification marks, and collective marks, are protected against misuse or infringegment by injunctive relief and a right of action for damages against the infringer. An infringement is a form of passing off one's goods or services as those of the owner of the mark, is deceptive of the public, and constitutes unfair competition.

Trade Names

A trade name, like a trademark, is serviceable as an indentification of the product of a particular manufacturer or distributor. It may also designate a service or be the name under which a business is conducted. Trade names, therefore, have broader scope than trade-marks which only identify goods.

Descriptive and generic words, and personal and generic names, although not proper trademarks, may become protected as trade names upon acquiring a special significance in the trade. This special significance is frequently referred to as a "secondary meaning" of the name acquired as the result of continuing and extended use in connection with specific goods or services whereby the name has lost its primary meaning to a substantial number of purchasers or users of the goods or services. A trade name for a product may be coined, such as "Kodak" or "Nylon," or it may be a popularly accepted nickname as "Coke."

Trade names are protected, and a person who palms off his goods or services by using the trade name of another is liable in damages and also may be enjoined from doing so.

COPYRIGHTS AND PATENTS

Copyrights

A copyright is the exclusive right to print, reprint, publish, copy, and sell books, periodicals, newspapers, dramatic and musical compositions, lectures, works of art, photographs, pictorial illustrations, and motion pictures, for a period of the author's life plus an additional fifty years.

Applications for copyright are filed with the Register of Copyrights, Copyright Office, Library of Congress, Washington, D.C. Registration of the copyright is not required, but is a condition of certain remedies for copyright infringement. The right is protected by the Federal Copyright Act, and infringements are remediable in the Federal courts.

Patents

A patent is the grant by the government of a monopoly right to an inventor to exclude others from making, using, or selling his invention for a period of 17 years.

The owner of the patent may also profit by licensing others to use the invention on a royalty basis. A patent is issued by the United States Patent Office upon the basis of an application containing specific claims relating to the invention, process, product, or design.

Before granting a patent, the Patent Office makes a careful and thorough examination of the prior art and determines that the submitted invention has novelty and does not conflict with a prior pending application or a previously issued patent. An application for a patent is confidential and its contents will not be divulged by the Patent Office. This confidentiality ends upon the granting of the patent.

The granting of a patent is no guaranty of exclusive rights to make, use, or sell the alleged invention. The Patent Office is not a court and does not determine the rights of holders of patents. It may be necessary for the patentee to bring an action in the Federal court for infringement in order to determine the validity of his patent. If the court finds that the idea or invention is not novel, or is fully covered by the prior art, or that someone else had reduced the idea to practice before conception date by the patentee, the patent may be ruled invalid.

ANTITRUST STATUTES

The common law has traditionally favored free and open competition in the market place and has held illegal and unenforceable agreements and contracts in restraint of trade. Implementing this policy are antitrust statutes adopted in most of the States to prohibit local anticompetitive practices. There is no Federal common law against restraint of trade, but only statutory law enacted by the Congress. In the latter half of the 19th century, it became apparent that concentrations of economic power in the form of "trusts" and "combinations" were too powerful and widespread to be effectively curbed and controlled by State action. This prompted the Congress in 1890 to enact the first Federal statute in this field known as the Sherman Antitrust Act. Since then, Congress has enacted other antitrust statutes including the Clayton Act, the Robinson-Patman Act, and the Federal Trade Commission Act.

SHERMAN ANTITRUST ACT

Section 1 of the Sherman Act prohibits contracts, combinations, and conspiracies in restraint of trade while Section 2 proscribes monopolization and attempts to monopolize. Violators of either section are subject to fine or imprisonment, or both. The Federal district courts are empowered to issue injunc-

tions restraining violations, and anyone injured by a violation is entitled to recover in a civil action treble damages, three times the amount of his actual loss sustained. It is the duty of United States district attorneys, under the supervision of the Attorney General, and of the Federal Trade Commission, to institute appropriate enforcement proceedings other than treble damage actions.

Contracts, Combinations, and Conspiracies in Restraint of Trade

Section 1 of the Sherman Act provides that "[e]very contract, combination in the form of trust or otherwise, or conspiracy, in restraint of trade or commerce among the several states, or with foreign nations is hereby declared to be illegal." Taken literally, this prohibition would invalidate every unperformed contract. In order to avoid such a broad and impractical application, the courts have interpreted this section to invalidate only *unreasonable* restraints of trade:

The true test of legality is whether the restraint imposed is such as merely regulates and perhaps thereby promotes competition or whether it is such as may suppress or even destroy competition. To determine that question the courts must ordinarily consider the facts peculiar to the business to which the restraint is applied; its condition before and after the restraint was imposed; the nature of the restraint and its effect, actual or probable. The history of the restraint, the evil believed to exist, the reason for adopting the particular remedy, the purpose or end sought to be attained, are all relevant facts. This is not because a good intention will save an otherwise objectionable regulation or the reverse; but because knowledge of intent may help the court to interpret facts and to predict consequences. Chicago Bd. of Trade v. United States, 246 U.S. 231 (1918).

This standard, known as the *rule of reason test*, however, presented several problems of its own. By mandating that courts balance the anticompetitive effects against the procompetitive effects of every questioned restraint, this standard placed a substantial burden upon the judicial system. The United States Supreme Court accordingly responded by declaring certain categories of restraints to be unreasonable by their very nature and thus illegal *per se*:

[T]here are certain agreements or practices which because of their pernicious effect on competition and lack of any redeeming virtue are conclusively presumed to be unreasonable and therefore illegal without elaborate inquiry as to the precise harm they have caused or the business excuse for their use. This principal of *per se* unreasonableness not only makes the type of restraints which are proscribed by the Sherman Act more certain to the benefit of everyone concerned, but it also avoids the necessity for an incredibly complicated and prolonged economic investigation into the entire history of the industry involved, as well as related industries, in an effort to determine at large whether a particular restraint has been unreasonable—an inquiry so often wholly fruitless when undertaken. Northern Pacific Railway Co. v. United States, 345 U.S. 1 (1958).

Those restraints not categorized as *per se* illegal are judged by the rule of reason test.

In addition, restraints may be classified as either horizontal or vertical. A restraint is *horizontal* if it involves collaboration among competitors at the same level in the chain of distribution. For example, an agreement among manufacturers or wholesalers or retailers would be horizontal. On the other hand, an agreement is *vertical* if made by parties not in direct competition at the same level of distribution. Thus, an agreement between a manufacturer and a wholesaler is vertical. Although the distinction between horizontal and vertical restraints can become blurred, it is often determinative of whether a restraint is illegal *per se* or judged by the rule of reason. For instance, horizontal market allocations are

illegal *per se*, whereas vertical market allocations are not.

Finally, Section 1 does not prohibit unilateral conduct; rather, it forbids concerted action. Thus, one person or business cannot violate the section alone. Although concerted action usually takes the form of explicit agreements, combinations or conspiracies, less overt conduct has on occasion been found to violate Section 1. For example, in Interstate Circuit, Inc., v. United States, 306 U.S. 208 (1939), eight motion pictures distributors received identical letters from a movie theatre chain requesting that they deal exclusively with theatres that charged a specified minimum price for first-run movies and did not run double features. The Supreme Court found this conduct violative of Section 1, based upon the fact that all eight responded with identical and intricate counteroffers, that all eight knew that each of the others had been approached, that all eight had the opportunity to directly communicate with each of the others, and that the proposal would be advantageous only if all eight agreed. Thus, the courts may find concerted action in ostensibly interdependent conduct where there is sufficient circumstantial evidence to warrant such a finding. However, it should be understood that conscious parallelism by itself does not violate Section 1; there must be corroborative, direct or circumstantial evidence in addition to price leadership or other forms of conscious parallelism.

Those restraints which are considered *per se* illegal include the following:

Price Fixing. Any horizontal agreement that has "the effect of raising, depressing, fixing, pegging, or stabilizing the price of a commodity in interstate or foreign commerce" is considered illegal *per se*. United States v. Socony-Vacuum Oil Co., at page 827. This prohibition covers any agreements between sellers to establish maximum prices at which certain commodities or services are offered for sale as well as minimum prices. The law also prohibits sellers agreements to simultaneously change the prices of certain commodities or services or not to advertise their prices.

Similarly, it is illegal *per se* for a seller to fix the price at which its purchasers must resell the product. This vertical form of price fixing—usually called retail price maintenance—was allowed in some states under the "Fair Trade Laws." However, in 1975 Congress repealed the statute authorizing these laws and now resale price maintenance is considered a *per se* violation of Section 1.

Market Allocations. Direct price fixing is not the only method by which prices can be controlled. Competitors may agree not to compete with each other in specified markets, which may be defined by geographic area, type of customer, or class of product. Because their effects are similar to price fixing, all horizontal agreements to divide markets have been declared illegal *per se*.

However, vertical territorial and customer restrictions are no longer illegal *per se* but are now judged by the rule of reason. This change in approach has resulted from a recent United States Supreme Court decision, Continental T.V., Inc. v. GTE Sylvania, Inc., at page 831, directing the trial courts to balance the positive effect of such restrictions upon inter-brand competition against the negative effects upon intrabrand competition. Consequently, in some situations vertical territorial restrictions will be found legitimate if they, on balance, increase competition.

Boycotts. Section 1 of the Sherman Act, as previously noted, does not apply to unilateral action but only to agreements or combinations. Accordingly, the refusal of a seller to deal with any particular buyer does not violate the Act. Thus, a manufacturer can refuse to sell to a retailer who persists in selling below the manufacturer's sug-

gested retail price. On the other hand, concerted refusals to deal—group boycotts—are prohibited. Therefore, a manufacturer would violate Section 1 if it were to induce wholesalers to refuse to deal with retailers that disobeyed a suggested retail price.

Tying Arrangements. A seller of a product may condition its sale upon the buyer's purchasing a second product from the seller. For example, in International Salt Co. v. United States, 332 U.S. 392 (1947), the defendant, the largest producer of commercially used salt, required that anyone that leased its patented industrial salt machines (the "tying" product) also to purchase all of its salt (the "tied" product) from the defendant. Because tying arrangements limit the freedom of choice of buyers and may exclude competitors, the law closely scrutinizes such agreements. When the seller has considerable economic power in the tying product *or* when a not insubstantial amount of interstate commerce is affected in the tied product, the tying arrangement will be *per se* illegal.

Monopolies

Economic analysis indicates that a monopolist will utilize its power to limit production and increase prices. Accordingly, a monopolistic market will produce fewer goods at a higher price than a competitive market. Addressing the problem of monopolization, Section 2 of the Sherman Act prohibits monopolies, attempts to monopolize and conspiracies to monopolize. Thus, Section 2 prohibits both agreements among businesses and, unlike Section 1, unilateral conduct by one firm.

Monopolization. Although the language of Section 2 appears to prohibit *all* monopolization, the courts have declined to interpret it in that manner. Rather, they have required more than the mere possession of market power: either the unfair attainment of the monopoly power or the abusive use of that power once attained.

It is extremely rare to find an unregulated industry with only one firm, so the issue of monopoly power involves defining what degree of market dominance constitutes monopoly power. The courts have grappled with this question and have developed a number of approaches, but the prevelant test is market share. A market share greater than 75% generally indicates monopoly power, a share less than 50% does not, while a 50 to 75% share is inconclusive.

Market concentration is the fractional share possessed by a firm of the total relevant product and geographic markets, but defining the relevant markets is often a difficult and subjective project for the courts. The relevant product market includes products that are substitutable for the firm's product on the basis of price, quality, and cross-elasticity. For example, in the landmark case of the United States v. E. I. Du Pont de Nemous & Co., 351 U.S. 377 (1956), it was decided that the relevant product market for cellophane was the entire flexible packaging market, which included wrapping paper, wax paper, Saran wrap, aluminum foil, and polyethelene, among others. According to this broad market definition, du Pont's market share was less than 20%. Had the market been defined as just cellophane, du Pont's market share would have been 75%.

Assuming sufficient monopoly power has been proven, it must then be shown that the firm has engaged in unfair conduct. Precisely what constitutes unfair conduct has not yet been prescribed by the courts. One judicial approach is that a firm possessing monopoly power has the burden of proving that it acquired such power passively or that it had the power "thrust" upon it. An alternative view is that monopoly power when coupled with conduct designed to exclude competitors, violates Section 2.

A third approach requires monopoly power plus some type of predatory practice such as pricing below marginal costs.

To date, however, the United States Supreme Court has not provided a definitive answer to the basic question of exactly what conduct, beyond the mere possession of monopoly power, violates Section 2. To do so, the Court must resolve the complex and conflicting policies involved. On the one hand, condemning fairly acquired monopoly power—that acquired "merely by virtue of superior skill, foresight and industry"—penalizes firms that compete effectively. On the other hand, permitting firms with monopoly power to continue provides them the opportunity to lower output and raise prices, thereby injuring consumers.

Attempts to Monopolize. Section 2 also prohibits attempts to monopolize. As with monopolization, the courts have experienced difficulty in developing a standard that distinguishes undesirable conduct likely to lead to monopoly from healthy competitive conduct. The standard test applied by the courts requires proof of a specific intent to monopolize plus a dangerous probability of success. This standard leaves unanswered numerous questions, such as what conduct constitutes an attempt and how much power must be achieved. Recent cases suggest that the greater the power acquired, the less egregious the conduct must be to constitute an attempt. These cases, however, do not specify any threshold level of market power.

CLAYTON ACT

In 1914 Congress strengthened the Sherman Act by adopting the Clayton Act which was expressly designed "to supplement existing laws against unlawful restraints and monopolies." Section 2 as amended in 1936, prohibits price discrimination, and is commonly referred to as the Robinson-Patman Act.

Section 3 of the Clayton Act prohibits "tying contracts" and exclusive selling and leasing arrangements preventing purchasers from dealing with the seller's competitors, where the effect may be to substantially lessen competition or tend to create a monopoly. This section is intended to attack anti-competitive practices in their incipiency before they ripen into violations of Section 1 or 2 of the Sherman Act.

Section 7 of the Clayton Act, as amended, prohibits the acquisition by a corporation of stock in another corporation or assets of another corporation where the effect may be to substantially lessen competition or tend to create a monopoly. Interlocking directorates in competing corporations engaged in interstate commerce (except banks, banking associations, trust companies and common carriers) where the aggregate capitalization is a million dollars or more, are prohibited by Section 8.

Finally, the Clayton Act exempts labor, agricultural, and horticultural organizations from antitrust laws. Section 6.

ROBINSON-PATMAN ACT

In 1936 the Congress amended Section 2 of the Clayton Act by adopting the Robinson-Patman Act which prohibits price discrimination in interstate commerce of commodities of like grade and quality. In order to constitute a violation, the price discrimination must substantially lessen competition or tend to create a monopoly, or injure, disturb, or prevent competition with any person who either grants or knowingly receives the benefit of such discrimination, or with customers of either the party claiming or receiving a price discrimination.

The Federal Trade Commission is empowered after due investigation and hearing to establish quantity limits as to particular commodities where it finds that available purchasers in greater quantities are so few as to render differentials on account of quantities allotted to customers unjustly discriminatory or promoting monopoly.

Under this Act sellers of goods are prevented from granting discounts to buyers and from making any payments or furnishing any services or facilities connected with the processing, handling, sale, or offering for sale of commodities, including allowances for radio and newspaper advertising, counter displays and samples, unless offered to all other purchasers on proportionately equal terms. The Act, moreover, also outlaws other types of discounts, rebates, and allowances and makes it unlawful to sell goods at unreasonably low prices for the purpose of destroying competition or eliminating a competitor. The Act makes it unlawful for one knowingly to "induce or receive" an illegal discrimination in price, thus creating buyer, as well as seller, liability.

Price differentials are permitted when justified by proof of either a cost savings to the seller or a good faith price reduction to meet the lawful price of a competitor.

FEDERAL TRADE COMMISSION ACT

In 1914 the Congress enacted the Federal Trade Commission Act creating the Federal Trade Commission and charging it with the duty to prevent "unfair methods of competition in commerce, and unfair or deceptive acts or practices in commerce." To this end the five member Commission is empowered to conduct appropriate investigations and hearings. It may issue "cease and desist" orders against violators enforceable in the Federal courts. Its broad power has been described as follows by the United States Supreme Court:

The "unfair methods of competition," which are condemned by * * * the Act, are not confined to those that were illegal at common law or that were condemned by the Sherman Act * * *. It is also clear that the Federal Trade Commission Act was designed to supplement and bolster the Sherman Act and the Clayton Act * * * *to stop in their incipiency acts and practices which, when full blown, would violate those Acts.* F.T.C. v. Motion Picture Adv. Service Co., 344 U.S. 392, 73 S.Ct. 361, 97 L.Ed. 426 (1953). (Emphasis supplied).

Complaints may be instituted by the Commission which after a hearing "has wide latitude for judgment and the courts will not interfere except where the remedy selected has no reasonable relation to the unlawful practices found to exist." Jacob Siegel v. FTC, 327 U.S. 608 (1946). Although the Commission most frequently enters a cease and desist order having the effect of an injunction, it may order other relief such as affirmative disclosure, corrective advertising, and the granting of licenses to patents on a reasonable royalty basis. Appeals may be taken from orders of the Commission to the United States Courts of Appeals which have exclusive jurisdiction to enforce, set aside, or modify, orders of the Commission.

The work of the Federal Trade Commission includes not only investigation of possible violations of the antitrust laws but also unfair methods of competition, such as false and misleading advertisements, false or inadequate labeling of products, passing or palming off goods as those of a competitor, lotteries, gambling schemes, discriminatory offers of rebates and discounts, false disparagement of a competitor's goods, false or misleading descriptive names of products, use of false testimonials, and other unfair trade practices.

Illustrative of price advertising which the Federal Trade Commission considered deceptive is the case of a manufacturer and distributor of paint sold under the trade name of "Mary Carter." This company in advertising its product stated: "Buy one, get one free"; "Every Second Can Free of Extra Cost"; "Every Second Can Free." While this might not deceive a sophisticated purchaser, the Commission found that inasmuch as the manufacturer had no history of selling single cans of paint but was marketing twins, its allocation of what in fact was the price of two cans to one can, and calling one "free," was a misrepresentation. The Commission entered a cease and desist order. The Court of Appeals reversed the Commission, 333 F.2d 654, (5th Cir., 1964), but was reversed by the Supreme Court. Federal Trade Commission v. Mary Carter Paint Co., 382 U.S. 46, 86 S.Ct. 219, 15 L.Ed. 128 (1965).

Cases

Horizontal Price Fixing

UNITED STATES v. SOCONY-VACUUM OIL CO.

310 U.S. 150, 60 S.Ct. 811 (1940)

DOUGLAS, J.

Respondents were convicted by a jury under an indictment charging violations of § 1 of the Sherman Anti-Trust Act. The Circuit Court of Appeals reversed and remanded for a new trial. * * *

The Indictment

* * *

The methods of marketing and selling gasoline in the Mid-Western area are set forth in the indictment in some detail. * * * Each defendant major oil company owns, operates or leases retail service stations in this area. It supplies those stations, as well as independent retail stations, with gasoline from its bulk storage plants. All but one sell large quantities of gasoline to jobbers in tank car lots under term contracts. In this area these jobbers exceed 4,000 in number and distribute about 50% of all gasoline distributed to retail service stations therein, the bulk of the jobbers' purchases being made from the defendant companies. The price to the jobbers under those contracts with defendant companies is made dependent on the spot market price, pursuant to a formula. * * * And the spot market tank car prices of gasoline directly and substantially influence the retail prices in the area. In sum, it is alleged that defendants by raising and fixing the tank car prices of gasoline in these spot markets could and did increase the tank car prices and the retail prices of gasoline sold in the Mid-Western area. * * *

Background of the Alleged Conspiracy

Evidence was introduced (or respondents made offers of proof) showing or tending to show the following conditions preceding the commencement of the alleged conspiracy in February 1935. * * *

Beginning about 1926 there commenced a period of production of crude oil in such quantities as seriously to affect crude oil and gasoline markets throughout the United States. Overproduction was wasteful, reduced the productive capacity of the oil fields and drove the price of oil down to levels below the cost of production from pumping and stripper wells. When the price falls below such cost, those wells must be abandoned. Once abandoned, subsurface changes make it difficult or impossible to bring those wells back into production. Since such wells constitute about 40% of the country's known oil reserves, conservation requires that the price of crude oil be maintained at a level which will permit such wells to be operated. As Oklahoma and Kansas were attempting to remedy the situation through their proration laws, the largest oil field in history was discovered in East Texas. That was in 1930.

The supply of oil from this field was so great that at one time crude oil sank to 10 to 15 cents a barrel, and gasoline was sold in the East Texas field for 2⅛¢ a gallon. Enforcement by Texas of its proration law was extremely difficult. Orders restricting production were violated, the oil unlawfully produced being known as "hot oil" and the gasoline manufactured therefrom, "hot gasoline." Hot oil sold for substantially lower prices than those posted for legal oil. Hot gasoline therefore cost less and at times could be sold for less than it cost to manufacture legal gasoline. The latter, deprived of its normal outlets, had to be sold at distress prices. The condition of many independent refiners using legal crude oil was precarious. In spite of their unprofitable operations they could not afford to shut down, for if they did so they would be apt to lose their oil connections in the field and their regular customers. Having little storage capacity they had to sell their gasoline as fast as they made it. As a result their gasoline became "distress" gasoline—gasoline which the refiner could not store, for which he had no regular sales outlets and which therefore he had to sell for whatever price it would bring. Such sales drove the market down.

In the spring of 1933 conditions were acute. The wholesale market was below the cost of manufacture. As the market became flooded with cheap gasoline, gasoline was dumped at whatever price it would bring. On June 1, 1933, the price of crude oil was 25¢ a barrel; the tank car price of regular gasoline was 2⅝¢ a gallon. * * *

Meanwhile the retail markets had been swept by a series of price wars. These price wars affected all markets—service station, tank wagon, and tank car. Early in 1934 the Petroleum Administrative Board tried to deal with them—by negotiating agreements between marketing companies and persuading individual companies to raise the price level for a period. * * *

The Alleged Conspiracy

* * *

It was estimated that there would be between 600 and 700 tank cars of distress gasoline produced in the Mid-Continent oil field every month by about 17 independent refiners. These refiners, not having regular outlets for the gasoline, would be unable to dispose of it except at distress prices. Accordingly, it was proposed and decided that certain major companies (including the corporate respondents) would purchase gasoline from these refiners. The Committee would assemble each month information as to the quantity and location of this distress gasoline. Each of the major companies was to select one (or more) of the independent refiners having distress gasoline as its "dancing partner," and would assume responsibility for purchasing its distress supply. In this manner buying power would be coordinated, purchases would be effectively placed, and the results would be much superior to the previous haphazard purchasing. There were to be no formal contractual commitments to purchase this gasoline, either between the major companies or between the majors and the independents. Rather it was an informal gentlemen's agreement or understanding whereby each undertook to perform his share of the joint undertaking. Purchases were to be made at the "fair going market price." * * *

Application of the Sherman Act

The court charged the jury that it was a violation of the Sherman Act for a group of individuals or corporations to act together to raise the prices to be charged for the commodity which they manufactured where they controlled a substantial part of the interstate trade and commerce in that commodity. The court stated that where the members of a combination had the power to raise prices and acted together for that purpose, the combination was illegal; and

that it was immaterial how reasonable or unreasonable those prices were or to what extent they had been affected by the combination. It further charged that if such illegal combination existed, it did not matter that there may also have been other factors which contributed to the raising of the prices. In that connection, it referred specifically to the economic factors which we have previously discussed and which respondents contended were primarily responsible for the price rise and the spot markets' stability in 1935 and 1936, * * *. The court then charged that, unless the jury found beyond a reasonable doubt that the price rise and its continuance were "caused" by the combination and not caused by those other factors, verdicts of "not guilty" should be returned. It also charged that there was no evidence of governmental approval which would exempt the buying programs from the prohibitions of the Sherman Act; and that knowledge or acquiescence of officers of the government or the good intentions of the members of the combination would not give immunity from prosecution under that Act.

The Circuit Court of Appeals held this charge to be reversible error, since it was based upon the theory that such a combination was illegal per se. In its view respondents' activities were not unlawful unless they constituted an unreasonable restraint of trade.

* * *

In United States v. Trenton Potteries Co., 273 U.S. 392, this Court sustained a conviction under the Sherman Act where the jury was charged that an agreement on the part of the members of a combination, controlling a substantial part of an industry, upon the prices which the members are to charge for their commodity is in itself an unreasonable restraint of trade without regard to the reasonableness of the prices or the good intentions of the combining units.

* * *

Therefore the sole remaining question of this phase of the case is the applicability of the rule of the Trenton Potteries case to these facts. Respondents seek to distinguish the Trenton Potteries case from the instant one. * * *

But we do not deem those distinctions material. In the first place, there was abundant evidence that the combination had the purpose to raise prices. And likewise, there was ample evidence that the buying programs at least contributed to the price rise and the stability of the spot markets, and to increases in the price of gasoline sold in the Mid-Western area during the indictment period. That other factors also may have contributed to that rise and stability of the markets is immaterial. * * *

Secondly, the fact that sales on the spot markets were still governed by some competition is of no consequence. For it is indisputable that that competition was restricted through the removal by respondents of a part of the supply which but for the buying programs would have been a factor in determining the going prices on those markets. * * *

The elimination of so-called competitive evils is no legal justification for such buying programs. The elimination of such conditions was sought primarily for its effect on the price structures. Fairer competitive prices, it is claimed, resulted when distress gasoline was removed from the market. But such defense is typical of the protestations usually made in price-fixing cases. Ruinous competition, financial disaster, evils of price cutting and the like appear throughout our history as ostensible justifications for price-fixing. If the so-called competitive abuses were to be appraised here, the reasonableness of prices would necessarily become an issue in every price-fixing case. In that event the Sherman Act would soon be emasculated; its philosophy would be supplanted by one which is wholly alien to a system of free competition; it would not be the charter of freedom which its framers intended.

The reasonableness of prices has no constancy due to the dynamic quality of the business facts underlying price structures. Those who fixed reasonable prices today would perpetuate unreasonable prices tomorrow, since those prices would not be subject to continuous administrative supervision and readjustment in light of changed conditions. Those who controlled the prices would control or effectively dominate the market. And those who were in that strategic position would have it in their power to destroy or drastically impair the competitive system. But the thrust of the rule is deeper and reaches more than monopoly power. Any combination which tampers with price structures is engaged in an unlawful activity. Even though the members of the price-fixing group were in no position to control the market, to the extent that they raised, lowered, or stabilized prices they would be directly interfering with the free play of market forces. The Act places all such schemes beyond the pale and protects that vital part of our economy against any degree of interference. Congress has not left us the determination of whether or not particular price-fixing schemes are wise or unwise, healthy or destructive. It has not permitted the age-old cry of ruinous competition and competitive evils to be a defense to price-fixing conspiracies. * * *

Nor is it important that the prices paid by the combination were not fixed in the sense that they were uniform and inflexible. * * * That price-fixing includes more than the mere establishment of uniform prices is clearly evident from the Trenton Potteries case itself, where this Court noted with approval Swift & Co. v. United States, 196 U.S. 375, in which a decree was affirmed which restrained a combination from "raising or lowering prices or fixing uniform prices" at which meats will be sold. Hence prices are fixed within the meaning of the

Trenton Potteries case if the range within which purchases or sales will be made is agreed upon, if the prices paid or charged are to be at a certain level or on ascending or descending scales, if they are to be uniform, or if by various formulae they are related to the market prices. They are fixed because they are agreed upon.

* * *

Under the Sherman Act a combination formed for the purpose and with the effect of raising, depressing, fixing, pegging, or stabilizing the price of a commodity in interstate or foreign commerce is illegal per se. Where the machinery for price-fixing is an agreement on the prices to be charged or paid for the commodity in the interstate or foreign channels of trade, the power to fix prices exists if the combination had control of a substantial part of the commerce in that commodity.

* * *

Accordingly, we conclude that the Circuit Court of Appeals erred in reversing the judgments on this ground. A fortiori the position taken by respondents in their cross petition that they were entitled to directed verdicts of acquittal is untenable.
* * *

Reversed.

Vertical Market Allocation

CONTINENTAL T.V. v. GTE SYLVANIA

433 U.S. 36, 97 S.Ct. 2549, 53 L.Ed.2d 568 (1977)

POWELL, J.

Franchise agreements between manufacturers and retailers frequently include provisions barring the retailers from selling franchised products from locations other than those specified in the agreements. This case presents important questions concerning the appropriate antitrust analysis of these restrictions under § 1 of the Sherman Act and the Court's decision in United States v. Arnold, Schwinn & Co., 388 U.S. 365 (1967).

I.

Respondent GTE Sylvania, Inc. (Sylvania) manufactures and sells television sets through its Home Entertainment Products Division. Prior to 1962, like most other television manufacturers, Sylvania sold its televisions to independent or company-owned distributors who in turn resold to a large and diverse group of retailers. Prompted by a decline in its market share to a relatively insignificant 1 to 2% of national television sales Sylvania conducted an intensive reassessment of its marketing strategy, and in 1962 adopted the franchise plan challenged here. Sylvania phased out its wholesale distributors and began to sell its televisions directly to a smaller and more select group of franchised retailers. An acknowledged purpose of the change was to decrease the number of competing Sylvania retailers in the hope of attracting the more aggressive and competent retailers thought necessary to the improvement of the company's market position. To this end, Sylvania limited the number of franchises granted for any given area and required each franchisee to sell his Sylvania products only from the location or locations at which he was franchised. A franchise did not constitute an exclusive territory, and Sylvania retained sole discretion to increase the number of retailers in an area in light of the success or failure of existing retailers in developing their market. The revised marketing strategy appears to have been successful during the period at issue here, for by 1965 Sylvania's share of national television sales had increased to approximately 5%, and the company ranked as the Nation's eighth largest manufacturer of color television sets.

This suit is the result of the rupture of a franchisor-franchisee relationship that had previously prospered under the revised Sylvania plan. Dissatisfied with its sales in the city of San Francisco, Sylvania decided in the spring of 1965 to franchise Young Brothers, an established San Francisco retailer of televisions, as an additional San Francisco retailer. The proposed location of the new franchise was approximately a mile from a retail outlet operated by petitioner Continental T.V., Inc. (Continental), one of the most successful Sylvania franchisees. Continental protested that the location of the new franchise violated Sylvania's marketing policy, but Sylvania persisted in its plans. Continental then cancelled a large Sylvania order and placed a large order with Phillips, one of Sylvania's competitors.

During this same period, Continental expressed a desire to open a store in Sacramento, Cal., a desire Sylvania attributed at least in part to Continental's displeasure over the Young Brothers decision. Sylvania believed that the Sacramento market was adequately served by the existing Sylvania retailers and denied the request. In the face of this denial, Continental advised Sylvania in early September 1965, that it was in the process of moving Sylvania merchandise from its San Jose, Cal., warehouse to a new retail location that it had leased in Sacramento. Two weeks later, allegedly for unrelated reasons, Sylvania's credit department reduced Continental's credit line from $300,000 to $50,000. In response to the reduction in credit and the generally deteriorating relations with Sylvania, Continental withheld all payments owed to John P. Maguire & Co., Inc. (Maguire), the finance company that handled the credit arrangements between Sylvania and its retailers. Shortly thereafter, Sylvania terminated Continental's franchises, and Maguire filed this diversity action in the United States District Court for the Northern District of California seeking recovery of money owed and of secured merchandise held by Continental.

The antitrust issues before us originated in cross-claims brought by Continental against Sylvania and Maguire. Most important for our purposes was the claim that Sylvania had violated § 1 of the Sherman Act by entering into and enforcing franchise agreements that prohibited the sale of Sylvania products other than from specified locations. At the close of evidence in the jury trial of Continental's claims, Sylvania requested the District Court to instruct the jury that its location restriction was illegal only if it unreasonably restrained or suppressed competition. Relying on this Court's decision in United States v. Arnold, Schwinn & Co., the District Court rejected the proffered instruction in favor of the following one: "Therefore, if you find by a preponderance of the evidence that Sylvania entered into a contract, combination or conspiracy with one or more of its dealers pursuant to which Sylvania exercised dominion or control over the products sold to the dealer, after having parted with title and risk to the products, you must find any effort thereafter to restrict outlets or store locations from which its dealers resold the merchandise which they had purchased from Sylvania to be a violation of Section 1 of the Sherman Act, regardless of the reasonableness of the location restrictions." In answers to special interrogatories, the jury found that Sylvania had engaged "in a contract, combination or conspiracy in restraint of trade in violation of the antitrust laws with respect to location restrictions alone," and assessed Continental's damages at $591,505, which was trebled. * * *

On appeal, the Court of Appeals for the Ninth Circuit, sitting en banc, reversed by a divided vote. * * * Contrasting the nature of the restrictions, their competitive impact, and the market shares of the franchisors in the two cases, the court concluded that Sylvania's location restriction had less potential for competitive harm than the restrictions invalidated in Schwinn and thus should be judged under the "rule of reason" rather than the per se rule stated in Schwinn.

* * *

II.

A

We turn first to Continental's contention that Sylvania's restriction on retail locations is a per se violation of § 1 of the Sherman Act as interpreted in Schwinn.

* * *

Schwinn produced sharply contrasting results depending upon the role played by the distributor in the distribution system. With respect to that portion of Schwinn's sales for which the distributors acted as ordinary wholesalers, buying and reselling Schwinn bicycles, the Court held that the territorial and customer restrictions challenged by the Government were per se illegal. But, with respect to that larger portion of Schwinn's sales in which the distributors functioned under the Schwinn Plan [manufacturer's representatives or sales agents] and under the less common consignment and agency arrangements, the Court held that the same restrictions should be judged under the rule of reason.

* * *

B

In the present case, it is undisputed that title to the televisions passed from Sylvania to Continental. Thus, the Schwinn per se rule applies unless Sylvania's restriction on locations falls outside Schwinn's prohibition against a manufacturer attempting to restrict a "retailer's freedom as to where and to whom it will resell the products." As the Court of Appeals concluded, the language of Schwinn is clearly broad enough to apply to the present case. Unlike the Court of Appeals, however, we are unable to find a principled basis for distinguishing Schwinn from the case now before us.

* * *

III.

Sylvania argues that if Schwinn cannot be distinguished, it should be reconsidered. Although Schwinn is supported by the principle of stare decisis [citation] we are convinced that the need for clarification of the law in this area justifies reconsideration. Schwinn itself was an abrupt and largely unexplained departure from White Motor Co. v. United States, 372 U.S. 253 (1963), where only four years earlier the Court had refused to endorse a per se rule for vertical restrictions. Since its announcement, Schwinn has been the subject of continuing controversy and confusion, both in the scholarly journals and in the federal courts. The great weight of scholarly opinion has been critical of the decision, and a number of the federal courts confronted with analogous vertical restrictions have sought to limit its reach. In our view, the experience of the past 10 years should be brought to bear on this subject of considerable commercial importance.

The traditional framework of analysis under § 1 of the Sherman Act is familiar and does not require extended discussion. * * * [The "rule of reason" is] the prevailing standard of analysis. [Citation.] Under this rule, the factfinder weighs all of the circumstances of a case in deciding whether a restrictive practice should be prohibited as imposing an unreasonable restraint on competition. Per se rules of illegality are appropriate only when they relate to conduct that is manifestly anticompetitive. As the Court explained in Northern Pac. R. Co. v. United States, 356 U.S. 1, 5 (1958), "there are certain agreements or practices which because of their pernicious effect on competition and lack of redeeming virtue are conclusively presumed to be unreasonable and therefore illegal without elaborate inquiry as to the precise harm they have caused or the business excuse for their use."

In essence, the issue before us is whether

Schwinn's per se rule can be justified under the demanding standards of Northern Pac. R. Co. The Court's refusal to endorse a per se rule in White Motor Co. was based on its uncertainty as to whether vertical restrictions satisfied those standards. Addressing this question for the first time, the Court stated: "We need to know more than we do about the actual impact of these arrangements on competition to decide whether they have such a 'pernicious effect on competition and lack * * * any redeeming virtue' [citation] and therefore should be classified as per se violations of the Sherman Act." Only four years later the Court in Schwinn announced its sweeping per se rule without even a reference to Northern Pac. R. Co. and with no explanation of its sudden change in position. We turn now to consider Schwinn in light of Northern Pac. R. Co.

The market impact of vertical restrictions is complex because of their potential for a simultaneous reduction of intrabrand competition and stimulation of interbrand competition. Significantly, the Court in Schwinn did not distinguish among the challenged restrictions on the basis of their individual potential for intrabrand harm or interbrand benefit. Restrictions that completely eliminated intrabrand competition among Schwinn distributors were analyzed no differently than those that merely moderated intrabrand competition among retailers. The pivotal factor was the passage of title: All restrictions were held to be per se illegal where title had passed, and all were evaluated and sustained under the rule of reason where it had not. The location restriction at issue here would be subject to the same pattern of analysis under Schwinn.

* * *

Vertical restrictions reduce intrabrand competition by limiting the number of sellers of a particular product competing for the business of a given group of buyers. Location restrictions have this effect because of practical constraints on the effective marketing area of retail outlets. Although intrabrand competition may be reduced, the ability of retailers to exploit the resulting market may be limited both by the ability of consumers to travel to other franchised locations and, perhaps more importantly, to purchase the competing products of other manufacturers. * * *

Vertical restrictions promote interbrand competition by allowing the manufacturer to achieve certain efficiencies in the distribution of his products. These "redeeming virtues" are implicit in every decision sustaining vertical restrictions under the rule of reason. Economists have identified a number of ways in which manufacturers can use such restrictions to compete more effectively against other manufacturers. [Citation.] For example, new manufacturers and manufacturers entering new markets can use the restrictions in order to induce competent and aggressive retailers to make the kind of investment of capital and labor that is often required in the distribution of products unknown to the consumer. Established manufacturers can use them to induce retailers to engage in promotional activities or to provide service and repair facilities necessary to the efficient marketing of their products. Service and repair are vital for many products, such as automobiles and major household appliances. The availability and quality of such services affect a manufacturer's good will and the competitiveness of his product. Because of market imperfections such as the so-called "free rider" effect, these services might not be provided by retailers in a purely competitive situation, despite the fact that each retailer's benefit would be greater if all provided the services than if none did. [Citation.]

* * *

Certainly, there has been no showing in this case, either generally or with respect to Sylvania's agreements, that vertical restrictions have or are likely to have a "pernicious effect on competition" or that they "lack * * * any redeeming virtue." Accordingly, we conclude that the per se rule stated in Schwinn must be overruled. In so holding we do not foreclose the possibility that particular applications of vertical restrictions might justify per se prohibition under Northern Pac. R. Co. But we do make clear that departure from the rule of reason standard must be based upon demonstrable economic effect rather than— as in Schwinn—upon formalistic line drawing.

In sum, we conclude that the appropriate decision is to return to the rule of reason that governed vertical restrictions prior to Schwinn. When anticompetitive effects are shown to result from particular vertical restrictions they can be adequately policed under the rule of reason, the standard traditionally applied for the majority of anticompetitive practices challenged under § 1 of the Act. Accordingly, the decision of the Court of Appeals is affirmed.

Monopolization

UNITED STATES v. UNITED SHOE MACHINERY CORP.

110 F.Supp. 295 (D.Mass.1953), aff'd per curiam, 347 U.S. 521, 74 S.Ct. 699, 98 L.Ed. 910 (1954).

WYZANSKI, J.
* * *

There are 18 major processes for the manufacturing of shoes by machine. Some machine types are used only in one process, but others are used in several; and the relationship of machine types to one another may be competitive or sequential. The approximately 1460 shoe manufacturers themselves are highly competitive in many respects, including their choice of processes and other technological aspects of production. Their total demand for machine services, apart from those rendered by dry thread sewing machines in the upper-fitting room, constitutes an identifiable market

which is a "part of the trade or commerce among the several States." § 2 of the Sherman Act.

United, the largest source of supply, is a corporation, lineally descended from a combination of constituent companies, adjudged lawful by the Supreme Court of the United States in 1918. United States v. United Shoe Machinery Co. of N.J., 247 U.S. 32. It now has assets rising slightly over 100 million dollars and employment rolls around 6,000. In recent years it has earned before federal taxes 9 to 13.5 million dollars annually.

Supplying different aspects of that market are at least 10 other American manufacturers and some foreign manufacturers, whose products are admitted to the United States free of tariff duty. Almost all the operations performed in the 18 processes can be carried out without the use of any of United's machines, and (at least in foreign areas, where patents are no obstacle,) a complete shoe factory can be efficiently organized without a United machine.

Nonetheless, United at the present time is supplying over 75%, and probably 85%, of the current demand in the American shoe machinery market, as heretofore defined. This is somewhat less than the share it was supplying in 1915.

* * *

Although at the turn of the century, United's patents covered the fundamentals of shoe machinery manufacture, those fundamental patents have expired. Current patents cover for the most part only minor developments, so that it is possible to "invent around" them, to use the words of United's chief competitor. However, the aggregation of patents does to some extent block potential competition. It furnishes a trading advantage. It leads inventors to offer their ideas to United, on the general principle that new complicated machines embody numerous patents. And it serves as a hedge or insurance for United against unforeseen competitive developments.

In the last decade and a half, United has not acquired any significant patents, inventions, machines, or businesses from any outside source, and has rejected many offers made to it. Before then, while it acquired no going businesses, in a period of two decades it spent roughly $3,500,000 to purchase inventions and machines. Most of these were from moribund companies, though this was not true of the acquisitions underlying the significant Littleway process and the less significant heel seat fitting machines and patents, each of which was from an active enterprise and might have served as a nucleus of important, though, at least initially, not extensive competition.

In supplying its complicated machines to shoe manufacturers, United, like its more important American competitors, has followed the practice of never selling, but only leasing. Leasing has been traditional in the shoe machinery field since the Civil War. So far as this record indicates, there is virtually no expressed dissatisfaction from consumers respecting that system; * * *. Under the system, entry into shoe manufacture has been easy. The rates charged for all customers have been uniform. The machines supplied have performed excellently. United has, without separate charge, promptly and efficiently supplied repair service and many kinds of other service useful to shoe manufacturers. These services have been particularly important, because in the shoe manufacturing industry a whole line of production can be adversely affected, and valuable time lost, if some of the important machines go out of function, and because machine breakdowns have serious labor and consumer repercussions. The cost to the average shoe manufacturer of its machines and services supplied to him has been less than 2% of the wholesale price of his shoes.

However, United's leases, in the context of the present shoe machinery market, have created barriers to the entry by competitors into the shoe machinery field.

First, the complex of obligations and rights accruing under United's leasing system in operation deter a shoe manufacturer from disposing of a United machine and acquiring a competitor's machine. * * * The lessee is now held closely to United by the combined effect of the 10-year term, the requirement that if he has work available he must use the machine to full capacity, and by the return charge which can in practice, through the right of deduction fund, be reduced to insignificance if he keeps this and other United machines to the end of the periods for which he leased them.

Second, when a lessee desires to replace a United machine, United gives him more favorable terms if the replacement is by another United machine than if it is by a competitive machine.

Third, United's practice of offering to repair, without separate charges, its leased machines, has had the effect that there are no independent service organizations to repair complicated machines.

* * *

On the foregoing facts, the issue of law is whether defendant in its shoe machinery business has violated that provision of § 2 of the Sherman Act. * * *

[In] recent authorities there are discernible at least three different, but cognate, approaches.

The approach which has the least sweeping implications really antedates the decision in Aluminum. But it deserves restatement. An enterprise has monopolized in violation of § 2 of the Sherman Act if it has acquired or maintained a power to exclude others as a result of using an unreasonable "restraint of trade" in violation of § 1 of the Sherman Act. * * *

A more inclusive approach was adopted by Mr. Justice Douglas in United States v. Griffith. He * * * concluded that an enterprise has monopolized in violation of § 2 if it (a) has the power to exclude competition, and (b) has exercised it, or has the purpose to exercise it. The least that this conclusion means is that it is a violation of § 2 for one having effective control of the market to use, or plan to use, any exclusionary practice, even though it is not a technical restraint of trade. But the conclusion may go further.

Indeed the way in which Mr. Justice Douglas used the terms "monopoly power" and "effective market control" and cited Aluminum suggests that he endorses a third and broader approach, which originated with Judge Hand. It will be recalled that Judge Hand said that one who has acquired an overwhelming share of the market "monopolizes" whenever he does business, apparently even if there is no showing that his business involves any exclusionary practice. But, it will also be recalled that this doctrine is softened by Judge Hand's suggestion that the defendant may escape statutory liability if it bears the burden of proving that it owes its monopoly solely to superior skill, superior products, natural advantages, (including accessibility to raw materials or markets), economic or technological efficiency, (including scientific research), low margins of profit maintained permanently and without discrimination, or licenses conferred by, and used within, the limits of law (including patents on one's own inventions, or franchises granted directly to the enterprise by a public authority).

In the case at bar, the Government contends that the evidence satisfies each of the three approaches to § 2 of the Sherman Act, so that it does not matter which one is taken.

If the matter were res integra, this Court would adopt the first approach, and, as a preliminary step to ruling upon § 2, would hold that it is a restraint of trade under § 1 for a company having an overwhelming share of the market, to distribute its more important products only by leases which have provisions that go beyond assuring prompt, periodic payments of rentals, which are not terminable cheaply, which

involve discrimination against competition, and which combine in one contract the right to use the product and to have it serviced. But this inferior court feels precluded from so deciding because of the overhanging shadows of United States v. United Shoe Machinery Co. of N.J., 247 U.S. 32, and United Shoe Machinery Corp. v. United States, 258 U.S. 451, the Sherman and Clayton Act cases involving this company's predecessor and itself. Though these cases may ultimately be overruled by the Supreme Court, they have not yet lost all authority. * * *

This Court finds it unnecessary to choose between the second and third approaches. For, taken as a whole, the evidence satisfies the tests laid down in both Griffith and Aluminum. The facts show that (1) defendant has, and exercises, such overwhelming strength in the shoe machinery market that it controls that market, (2) this strength excludes some potential, and limits some actual, competition, and (3) this strength is not attributable solely to defendant's ability, economies of scale, research, natural advantages, and adaptation to inevitable economic laws.

In estimating defendant's strength, this Court gives some weight to the 75 plus percentage of the shoe machinery market which United serves. But the Court considers other factors as well. In the relatively static shoe machinery market where there are no sudden changes in the style of machines or in the volume of demand, United has a network of long-term, complicated leases with over 90% of the shoe factories. These leases assure closer and more frequent contacts between United and its customers than would exist if United were a seller and its customers were buyers. Beyond this general quality, these leases are so drawn and so applied as to strengthen United's power to exclude competitors. Moreover, United offers a long line of machine types, while no competitor offers more than a short line. Since in some parts of its line United faces no important competition, United has the power to discriminate, by wide differentials and over long periods of time, in the rate of return it procures from different machine types. Furthermore, being by far the largest company in the field, with by far the largest resources in dollars, in patents, in facilities, and in knowledge, United has a marked capacity to attract offers of inventions, inventors' services, and shoe machinery businesses. And finally, there is no substantial substitute competition from a vigorous second-hand market in shoe machinery.

* * *

Not only does the evidence show United has control of the market, but also the evidence does not show that the control is due entirely to excusable causes. The three principal sources of United's power have been the original constitution of the company, the superiority of United's products and services, and the leasing system. The first two of these are plainly beyond reproach. The original constitution of United in 1899 was judicially approved in United States v. United Shoe Machinery Company of New Jersey, 247 U.S. 32. It is no longer open to question, and must be regarded as protected by the doctrine of res judicata, which is the equivalent of a legal license. Likewise beyond criticism is the high quality of United's products, its understanding of the techniques of shoemaking and the needs of shoe manufacturers, its efficient design and improvement of machines, and its prompt and knowledgeable service. These have illustrated in manifold ways that "superior skill, foresight and industry" of which Judge Hand spoke in Aluminum.

But United's control does not rest solely on its original constitution, its ability, its research, or its economies of scale. There are other barriers to competition, and these barriers were erected by United's own business policies. Much of United's market power is traceable to the magnetic ties in-

herent in its system of leasing, and not selling, its more important machines.

* * *

In one sense, the leasing system and the miscellaneous activities just referred to * * * were natural and normal, for they were, in Judge Hand's words, "honestly industrial." They are the sort of activities which would be engaged in by other honorable firms. And, to a large extent, the leasing practices conform to long-standing traditions in the shoe machinery business. Yet, they are not practices which can be properly described as the inevitable consequences of ability, natural forces, or law. They represent something more than the use of accessible resources, the process of invention and innovation, and the employment of those techniques of employment, financing, production, and distribution, which a competitive society must foster. They are contracts, arrangements, and policies which, instead of encouraging competition based on pure merit, further the dominance of a particular firm. In this sense, they are unnatural barriers; they unnecessarily exclude actual and potential competition; they restrict a free market. While the law allows many enterprises to use such practices, the Sherman Act is now construed by superior courts to forbid the continuance of effective market control based in part upon such practices. Those courts hold that market control is inherently evil and constitutes a violation of § 2 unless economically inevitable, or specifically authorized and regulated by law.

It is only fair to add that the more than 14,000 page record, and the more than 5,000 exhibits, representing the diligent seven year search made by Government counsel aided by this Court's orders giving them full access to United's files during the last 40 years, show that United's power does not rest on predatory practices. Probably few monopolies could produce a record so free from any taint of that kind of wrongdoing.

The violation with which United is now charged depends not on moral considerations, but on solely economic considerations. United is denied the right to exercise effective control of the market by business policies that are not the inevitable consequences of its capacities or its natural advantages. That those policies are not immoral is irrelevant.

Defendant seems to suggest that even if its control of the market is not attributable exclusively to its superior performance, its research, and its economies of scale, nonetheless, United's market control should not be held unlawful, because only through the existence of some monopoly power can the thin shoe machinery market support fundamental research of the first order, and achieve maximum economies of production and distribution.

To this defense the shortest answer is that the law does not allow an enterprise that maintains control of a market through practices not economically inevitable, to justify that control because of its supposed social advantage. [Citation.] It is for Congress, not for private interests, to determine whether a monopoly, not compelled by circumstances, is advantageous. And it is for Congress to decide on what conditions, and subject to what regulations, such a monopoly shall conduct its business.

* * *

Defendant, having willed the means, has willed the end.

* * *

Robinson-Patman Act

GREAT ATLANTIC & PACIFIC TEA COMPANY v. FEDERAL TRADE COMMISSION

440 U.S. 69, 99 S.Ct. 925, 59 L.Ed.2d 153 (1979)

STEWART, J.

The question presented in this case is whether the petitioner, the Great Atlantic and Pacific Tea Company (A&P), violated § 2(f) of the Robinson-Patman Act, as amended, [citation], by knowingly inducing or receiving illegal price discriminations from the Borden Company (Borden).

The alleged violation was reflected in a 1965 agreement between A&P and Borden under which Borden undertook to supply "private label" milk to more than 200 A&P stores in a Chicago area that included portions of Illinois and Indiana. This agreement resulted from an effort by A&P to achieve cost savings by switching from the sale of "brand label" milk (milk sold under the brand name of the supplying dairy) to the sale of "private label" milk (milk sold under the A&P label).

To implement this plan, A&P asked Borden, its longtime supplier, to submit an offer to supply under private label certain of A&P's milk and other dairy product requirements. After prolonged negotiations, Borden offered to grant A&P a discount for switching to private label milk provided A&P would accept limited delivery service. Borden claimed that this offer would save A&P $410,000 a year compared to what it had been paying for its dairy products. A&P, however, was not satisfied with this offer and solicited offers from other dairies. A competitor of Borden, Bowman Dairy, then submitted an offer which was lower than Borden's.

At this point, A&P's Chicago buyer contacted Borden's chain store sales manager and stated, "I have a bid in my pocket. You [Borden] people are so far out of line it is not even funny. You are not even in the ball park." When the Borden representative asked for more details, he was told nothing except that a $50,000 improvement in Borden's bid "would not be a drop in the bucket."

Borden was thus faced with the problem of deciding whether to rebid. A&P at the time was one of Borden's largest customers in the Chicago area. Moreover, Borden had just invested more than five million dollars in a new dairy facility in

Illinois. The loss of the A&P account would result in underutilization of this new plant. Under these circumstances, Borden decided to submit a new bid which doubled the estimated annual savings to A&P, from $410,000 to $820,000. In presenting its offer, Borden emphasized to A&P that it needed to keep A&P's business and was making the new offer in order to meet Bowman's bid. A&P then accepted Borden's bid after concluding that it was substantially better than Bowman's.

I.

* * *

[T]he Court of Appeals for the Second Circuit * * * held that * * * as a matter of law A&P could not successfully assert a meeting competition defense because it, unlike Borden, had known that Borden's offer was better than Bowman's.[6] * * *

II.

* * *

Liability under § 2(f) * * * is limited to situations where the price discrimination is one "which is prohibited by this section." While the phrase "this section" refers to the entire § 2 of the Act, only subsections (a) and (b) dealing with seller-liability involve discriminations in price. Under the plain meaning of § 2(f), therefore, a buyer cannot be liable if a prima facie case could not be established against a seller or if the seller has an affirmative defense. In either situation, there is no price discrimination "prohibited by this section." The legislative history of § 2(f) fully confirms the conclusion that buyer liability under § 2(f) is dependent on seller liability uner § 2(a). * * *

III.

The petitioner, relying on this plain meaning of § 2(f) and the teaching of the Automatic Canteen case, argues that it cannot be liable under § 2(f) if Borden had a valid meeting competition defense. The respondent, on the other hand, argues that the petitioner may be liable even assuming that Borden had such a defense. The meeting competition defense, the respondent contends, must in these circumstances be judged from the point of view of the buyer. Since A&P knew for a fact that the final Borden bid beat the Bowman bid, it was not entitled to assert the meeting competition defense even though Borden may have honestly believed that it was simply meeting competition. Recognition of a meeting competition defense for the buyer in this situation, the respondent argues, would be contrary to the basic purpose of the Robinson-Patman Act to curtail abuses by large buyers.

A

The short answer to these contentions of the respondent is that Congress did not provide in § 2(f) that a buyer can be liable even if the seller has a valid defense. The clear language of § 2(f) states that a buyer can be liable only if he receives a price discrimination "prohibited by this section." If a seller has a valid meeting competition defense, there is simply no prohibited price discrimination. * * *

B

* * *

In a competitive market, uncertainty among sellers will cause them to compete for business by offering buyers lower prices. Because of the evils of collusive action, the Court has held that the exchange of price information by competitors violates the Sherman Act. United States v. Container Corp., 893 U.S. 333. Under the view advanced by the respondent, however, a buyer, to avoid liability, must either refuse a seller's bid or at least inform him that his bid had beaten competition. Such a duty of affirmative disclosure would almost inevitably frustrate competitive bidding and, by reducing uncertainty, lead to price matching and anticompetitive cooperation among sellers.

* * *

As in the Automatic Canteen case, we decline to adopt a construction of § 2(f) that is contrary to its plain meaning and would lead to anticompetitive results. Accordingly, we hold that a buyer who has done no more than accept the lower of two prices

competitively offered does not violate § 2(f) provided the seller has a meeting competition defense.

* * *

Since Borden had a meeting competition defense and thus could not be liable under § 2(b) the petitioner who did no more than accept that offer cannot be liable under § 2(f).

Accordingly, the judgment is reversed.

Problems

1. Discuss the validity and effect of each of the following:

a. A, B, and C, manufacturers of radios, orally agree that due to the disastrous, cutthroat competition in the market, they would establish a reasonable price to charge their purchasers.

b. A, B, C, and D, newspaper publishers, agree not to charge their customers more than thirty cents per newspaper.

c. A, a distiller of liquor, and B, A's retail distributor, agree that B should charge a price of $5 per bottle.

2. Discuss the validity of the following:

a. An agreement between two manufacturers of the same type of products to allocate territories whereby neither will sell its products in the area allocated to the other.

b. An agreement between manufacturer and distributor not to sell a dealer a particular product or parts necessary for repair of the product.

3. Universal Video sells $40,000,000 worth of video recording equipment in the United States. The total sales of such equipment in the United States is $100,000,000. One-half of Universal's sales is to Giant Retailer, a company which possesses 50% of the retail market. Giant is presently seeking (1) to obtain an exclusive dealing arrangement with Universal or (2) to acquire Universal. Please advise Giant as to validity of their alternatives.

4. Z sells cameras to A, B, C, and D for $60.00 per camera. Y, one of Z's competitors, sells a comparable camera to A for $58.50. Z in response to this competitive pressure from Y lowers its price to A to $58.50. B, C, and D insist

that Z lowers its price to them to $58.50, but Z refuses. B, C, and D sue Z for unlawful price discrimination. Decision. Would your answer differ if Z reduced its price to A to $58.00?

5. Discount is a discount appliance chain store which continually sells goods at a price below the manufacturers' suggested retail prices. A, B, and C, the three largest manufacturers of appliances, agree that unless Discount ceases from its discount pricing, they will no longer sell to Discount. Discount refuses and A, B, and C refuse to sell to Discount. Discount sues A, B, and C. Decision?

6. Company X produces 77% of all of the coal utilized in the United States. Coal provides 25% of all of the energy used in the United States. In a suit brought by the United States against X for violation of the antitrust laws, what result?

7. A conceived a secret process for the continuous freeze drying of food stuffs and related products and constructed a small pilot plant which practiced the process. A lacked the financing necessary to develop the commercial potential of the process and hoping to obtain a contract for its development and the payment of royalties, disclosed it in confidence to B, a coffee manufacturer, who signed an agreement not to disclose it to anyone else. At the same time, A signed an agreement not to disclose the process to any other person as long as A and B were considering a contract for its development. Upon disclosure, B became extremely interested and offered to pay A the sum of $1,750,000 if, upon further development, the process proved to be commercially feasible. While negotiations between A and B were in progress, C, a competitor of B, learned of the existence of the process and requested a disclosure from A who informed C that the process could not be disclosed to anyone unless negotiations with B were broken off. C offered to pay A $2,500,000 for the process provided it met certain defined objective performance criteria. A contract was prepared and executed between A and C on this basis without any prior disclosure of the process to C. Upon the making of this contract, A rejected the offer of B. The process was thereupon disclosed to C and demonstration runs of the pilot plant in the presence of representatives of C were conducted under varying conditions. After three weeks of experimental demonstrations, compiling of data and analysis of results, C informed A that the process did not meet the performance criteria in the contract and that for this reason C was rejecting the process. Two years later C placed on the market freeze-dried coffee which resembled in color, appearance, and texture the product of A's pilot plant. What are the rights of the parties.

8. B, a chemist, was employed by A, a manufacturer, to work on a secret process for A's product under an exclusive three-year contract. C, a salesman, was employed by A on a week-to-week basis. B and C resigned the employment with A and accepted employment in their respective capacities with D, a rival manufacturer. C began soliciting patronage from A's former customers who names he had memorized. What are the rights of the parties in (1) a suit by A to enjoin B from working for D; and (2) a suit by A to enjoin C from soliciting A's customers?

9. George McCoy of Florida has been manufacturing and distributing a cheese cake for over five years, labeling his product with a picture of a cheese cake which serves as a background for a Florida bathing beauty under which is written the slogan "McCoy All Spice Florida Cheese Cake." George McCoy has not registered his trade-mark. Subsequently, Leo McCoy of California begins manufacturing a similar product on the West coast using a label in appearance similar to that of George McCoy, containing a picture of a Hollywood star, and the words "McCoy's All Spice Cheese Cake." Leo McCoy begins marketing his products in the Eastern United States, using labels with the word "Florida" added as in George McCoy's label. Leo McCoy has registered his product under the Federal Trademark Law. To what relief, if any, is George McCoy entitled?

10. X, having filed locally an affidavit required under the "Assumed Name" statute, has been operating and advertising his exclusive toy store for 20 years in Centerville, Illinois. His advertising has consisted of large signs on his premises reading "The Toy Mart". B, after operating a store in Chicago under the name of "The Chicago Toy Mart" relocated in Centerville, Illinois, and erected a large sign reading "TOY MART" with the word "Centerville" being written underneath in substantially smaller letters. Thereafter, the sales of X declined, and many of X's customers patronized B's store thinking it to be a branch of B's business. What are the rights of the parties?

Chapter

42

SECURITIES REGULATION

There was no well defined, separate branch of law regulating the offering and sale of securities, the national stock exchanges, and the operations of brokers and dealers in securities until Congress enacted the Securities Act of 1933, also known as the "Truth-in-Securities Act" (herein the 1933 Act) and the Securities Exchange Act of 1934 (herein the 1934 Act).

The 1933 Act has two basic objectives: (1) to provide investors with financial material and other information concerning securities offered for sale to the public; and (2) to prohibit misrepresentation, deceit, and other fraudulent acts and practices in the sale of securities generally, whether or not they are required to be registered.

The 1934 Act extended protection for investors to regulation of the national stock exchanges and to companies whose stocks are listed for trading on these exchanges. In 1964 this Act was amended to apply its disclosure and reporting requirements to the equity securities of companies traded over-the-counter that have assets in excess of $1,000,000 and a class of equity securities with 500 or more shareholders.

In addition to the Federal laws regulating the sale of securities, most of the States have their own laws regulating such sales within the State. Thus, any person selling securities must comply with the Federal securities laws and those of each State in which it intends to offer its securities.

Because of the diversity among the State securities laws, and the more efficient enforcement of the Federal statutes, this chapter will discuss only the 1933 Act and the 1934 Act.

THE SECURITIES ACT OF 1933

The 1933 Act, administered by the Securities and Exchange Commission (herein SEC), requires that a registration statement be filed with the SEC and become effective before any securities, other than those which are exempt from registration as provided in the Act, may be offered for sale to the public. The purpose of registration is to provide disclosure of financial and other information about the issuer and those in control of it, on the basis of which potential investors may appraise the merits of the securities. The Act provides that such investors must be furnished with a prospectus containing the salient data set forth in the registration statement.

Regardless of whether the securities are exempt from the registration and disclosure requirements of the Act, the anitfraud provisions of the Act apply to all sales of securities involving interstate commerce or the mails. Civil and criminal liability may be imposed for violations of the provisions of the Act.

Definition of a Security

For the purposes of the securities laws, a security is an investment of money, property, or other valuable consideration made in expectation of receiving a financial return involving no effort on the part of the investor. The most common types of securities are (1) written evidences of an obligation to pay a specified sum of money at a definite future date upon stated terms, such as corporate notes, bonds, and debentures; and (2) written evidences of ownership of an equity interest in a corporation, such as certificates of preferred or common stock.

Section 2(1) of the 1933 Act defines the term security to mean:

any note, stock, treasury stock, bond, debenture, evidence of indebtedness, certificate of interest or participation in any profit-sharing agreement, collateral-trust certificate, preorganization certificate or subscription, transferable share, investment contract, voting-trust certificate, certificate of deposit for a security, fractional undivided interest in oil, gas, or other mineral rights, or, in general, any interest or instrument commonly known as a "security," or any certificate of interest or participation in, temporary or interim certificate for, receipt for, guarantee of, or warrant or right to subscribe to or purchase, any of the foregoing.

This definition expansively incorporates the numerous types of instruments that fall within the ordinary concept of a security. Accordingly, the ultimate task of determining which of the myriad financial transactions constitutes a security has fallen to the SEC and the federal courts. Even though a transaction is evidenced by an instrument labeled "stock," it may not be considered a security under the Securities Act. For example, the Supreme Court has held that shares of stock entitling a purchaser to lease an apartment in a state subsidized and supervised non-profit housing cooperative are not securities. United Housing Foundation, Inc. v. Forman, 421 U.S. 837, 95 S.Ct. 2051, 44 L.Ed.2d 621 (1975).

The courts, however, have generally interpreted the statutory definition, in particular, the term "investment contract," so as to expand its coverage to non-traditional forms of investments. In the landmark case of SEC v. Howey, 328 U.S. 293, 66 S.Ct. 1100, 90 L.Ed.2d 1244 (1970) (page 853), the Court defined an investment contract as

a contract, transaction or scheme whereby a person invests his money in a common enterprise and is led to expect profits solely from the efforts of the promoter or a third party. * * * [This definition] embodies a flexible rather than a static principle, one that is capable of adaptation to meet the countless and variable schemes devised by those who seek the use of money of others on the promise of profit.

Under this test, such investments as the sale of limited partnership interests, citrus groves, whiskey warehouse receipts, real estate condominiums, beef cattle, franchises, and pyramid schemes have been held in certain circumstances to be securities.

Registration of Securities

Section 5 of the Securities Act prohibits the offer or sale through the use of the mails or any means of interstate commerce of any security, unless a registration statement is in effect as to that security or an exemption from registration is secured. The purpose of registration is to provide disclosure of financial and other information upon which investors may appraise the merits of the securities. Registration does not insure investors against loss, as the SEC does not pass on the financial merits of any security nor does it guarantee the accuracy of the facts presented in the registration statement.

In general, the registration forms call for disclosure of information such as (1) a description of the registrant's properties and business, (2) a description of the significant provisions of the security to be offered for sale and its relationship to the registrant's other capital securities, (3) information about the management of the registrant, and (4) financial statements certified by independent public accountants.

The registration statement and prospectus become public immediately on filing with the Commission; but it is unlawful to sell the securities until the effective date. After the filing of the registration statement, the securities may be offered orally or by certain summaries of the information in the registration statement as permitted by rules of the SEC.

Section 3 Exemptions

Section 3 of the Securities Act exempts a number of securities from the registration requirements of the Act. These exemptions fall into two categories: (1) those which apply to the securities themselves and may be resold without registration and (2) those which relate to the transaction in which the securities are issued. Securities that are sold pursuant to the second type of exemption are considered "restricted securities" which may be resold only by registration or in a transaction exempt from registration.

Section 3(a) exempts specific securities including short-term commercial paper and intra-state transactions. Section 3(b) of the Act authorizes the SEC to establish regulations exempting securities not to exceed five million dollars from registration when it determines that registration is not necessary by reason of the small amount or limited character of the offering. The SEC has utilized this provision in three instances: (a) Regulation A, (b) Rule 240, and (c) Rule 242.

Regulation A. This regulation permits an issuer to offer up to 1.5 million dollars of securities in any twelve-month period without registering them provided that the issuer files a notification and an offering circular with the SEC's regional office. The circular must also be provided to offerees and purchasers. Regulation A filings are less detailed and time consuming than full registration statements and the required financial statements are simpler and need not be audited. Because each purchaser must be supplied with an offering circular, securities sold under Regulation A may be freely traded after issuance.

Closely Held Issuers. Rule 240 of the SEC provides closely held issuers with a further exemption from registration for extremely small issues. The exemption requires that: (1) the securities are offered and sold without general advertising or commissions; (2) the aggregate sales within twelve months do not exceed $100,000; (3) the securities of the issuer are owned by 100 or fewer persons; (4) the issuer takes precautions against non-exempt, unregistered resales; and (5) the issuer notifies the SEC of sales under the rule.

Securities sold under this exemption are restricted securities and may be resold only by registration or in a transaction exempt from registration. In order to assure against non-exempt, unregistered resales of these restricted securities, Rule 240 (as well as Rule 242 and 146 discussed below) provide that *reasonable precautions* must be taken that include but are not limited to the following: (a) making a reasonable inquiry into whether the purchaser is acquiring the securities for his own account or for the account of others; (b) informing the purchaser of the restrictions on resale; and (c) placing a legend on the securities certificate stating that the securities have not been registered and that they are restricted securities.

Small Business Exemption. In order to facilitate small business capital formation, the SEC has promulgated Rule 242 pursuant to its authority under Section 3(b). Effective February 25, 1980, the rule exempts from registration offerings by qualified, corporate issuers that do not exceed $2,000,000 per issue. In computing the dollar limit, an issuer must include the aggregate gross proceeds from all Section 3(b) sales (e.g., Regulation A and Rule 240) in the six months preceding the commencement and during the Rule 242 issue. Securities sold under this exemption are restricted securities and may be resold only by registration or in a transaction exempt from registration. General advertising and promotion are not permitted. The issue may be purchased by an unlimited number of "accredited" purchasers and by no more than thirty-five other purchasers. The term "accredited person" includes banks, insurance companies, investment companies, executive officers or directors of the issuer, and any person who purchases $100,000 or more of the securities issued under the exemption in cash or its equivalent. If the sale involves any non-accredited persons, all purchasers must be furnished prior to the sale with information material to an understanding of the issuer, its business, and the securities being offered; otherwise, such information is not required to be disclosed. The issuer must take precautions, as discussed under Rule 240, against non-exempt unregistered resales and must notify the SEC of sales made pursuant to the exemption.

Short-term Commercial Paper. The Act exempts any note, draft, bill of exchange, or bankers' acceptance which arises out of a current transaction or from which the proceeds are used for current transactions and which has a maturity at the time of issuance of not more than nine months. Section 3(a)(3). However, the SEC has adopted the position that the exemption is not available if the proceeds are to be used for permanent purposes such as the acquisition of a plant or if the paper is sold in relatively small denominations to the public.

Intra-state Issues. Section 3(a)(11) exempts from registration "any security which is a part of an issue offered and sold only to persons resident within a single state * * * where the issuer of such security is a person resident and doing business within, or, if a corporation, incorporated by and doing business within, such state." This exemption is intended to apply to issues local in character representing local financing by local persons and carried out through local investments. The exemption is inapplicable if merely one offeree, who need not be a purchaser, is not a resident of the state in which the issuer is resident.

The SEC has promulgated Rule 147, which is a "nonexclusive safe harbor" for securing the intra-state exemption: Satisfying the rule assures the exemption but there is no presumption that the exemption provided by Section 3(a)(11) is not available for transactions which do not comply with the rule. Rule 147 requires that:

1. the issuer is incorporated or organized in the state in which the issuance occurs;
2. the issuer is principally doing business in that state, which means that 80% of its gross revenues must be derived from that state, 80% of its assets must be located in that state, and 80% of the net proceeds from the issue must be used in that state;

3. all of the *offerees* and purchasers are residents of that state;

4. during the period of sale and for nine months after the last sale, no resales to non-residents are made; and

5. precautions are taken against inter-state distribution which include placing on the certificate evidencing the security a legend which states that the securities have not been registered and that resales can only be made to persons resident within the state in accordance with Paragraph 4 as well as obtaining from each purchaser a written statement as to his residence.

Other Exempt Securities. Section 3 also exempts from registration the following types of securities:

1. Securities of domestic governments.
2. Securities of domestic banks and savings and loans associations.
3. Securities of not-for-profit, charitable organizations.
4. Securities of issuers where the issuance is regulated by the Interstate Commerce Commission.
5. Certificates issued by a receiver or trustee in bankruptcy with court approval.
6. Insurance policies and annuity contracts issued by regulated insurance companies.
7. Securities issued solely for exchange by the issuer with its existing security holders where no commission is paid.
8. Reorganization securities issued and exchanged with court or other governmental approval.

Section 4 Exemptions

Section 4 of the Act exempts certain transactions from registration. As with exempted sales by closely held issuers (Rule 240) and small businesses (Rule 242), the transaction-based exemptions from registration do not necessarily exempt a subsequent transaction in the same securities.

Rather, those who acquire securities under Rule 240, Rule 242, or Section 4 of the Act must register any resales or find an exemption from registration.

Private Placements. The most important exemption for issuers wishing to raise money without registration is Section 4(2) of the Act which exempts "transactions by an issuer not involving any public offering." Rule 146 of the SEC establishes a non-exclusive, safe harbor for securing this exemption. The rule requires the following:

1. The securities are offered and sold only to persons that either have such knowledge and experience in financial and business matters that they are capable of evaluating the merits and risks of the investment or are able to bear the risk of the investment and have the services of a representative who has the requisite knowledge and experience to make such an evaluation.
2. Each offeree either has access to or is furnished the same kind of information that registration would disclose.
3. There is no general advertising or general solicitation.
4. The securities are purchased by not more than 35 persons excluding those who purchase $150,000 or more of securities.
5. Reasonable precautions are taken against non-exempt, unregistered resales and to insure that no purchaser is an underwriter. These precautions include, in addition to those detailed in Rule 240, that the issuer provides stop transfer instructions to its transfer agent with respect to the securities and obtains from all purchasers a written signed agreement that the securities will not be sold without registration under the Act or exemption from it.

Transactions by Non-issuers. The requirement that any offer or sale of a security be registered unless exempt applies not only to issuers but to any other person offering or selling a security. Accordingly, ordinary investors need an exemption from registration or they must register the security prior to offering it for sale. Section 4(1), which exempts "transactions by any person other than an issuer, underwriter, or dealer," provides such an exemption for most sales. If the non-issuer is a dealer or a broker, Sections 4(3) and 4(4) respectively provide a qualified exemption. Thus, essentially only underwriters are left without an exemption.

The Act broadly defines an underwriter as "any person who has purchased from an issuer with a view to * * * the distribution of any security. * * * As used in this paragraph, the term 'issuer' shall include * * * any person directly or indirectly controlling or controlled by the issuer * * *." Section 2(11). This definition applies to purchasers of unregistered, restricted securities acquired from an issuer or control person under Rules 240, 242, and 146. To resell these securities under the exemption afforded by Section 4(1), the reseller must show that he did not acquire them with a view toward distribution.

Rule 144 of the SEC sets forth conditions, which if met by any person selling restricted securities, demonstrate that the person is not engaged in a distribution and therefore is not an underwriter. The rule requires that there must be adequate current public information with respect to the issuer, that the person selling under the rule must have owned the securities for at least two years, that he sell them only in limited amounts in unsolicited brokers' transactions, and that notice of the sale must be provided to the SEC. These limitations are imposed to assure that the sale is a routine trading transaction and not a distribution. The rule is designed to make certain that the seller has held the securities long enough to show that he has not acquired them with a view to distribution

and that the sale does not disrupt the trading markets.

Where there is no public market for securities Rule 144 is unavailable. Rule 237, however, provides an exemption for sales of restricted securities by non-control persons of up to the lesser of $50,000 or 1% of the outstanding securities in any one-year period. The issuer must be organized or incorporated in the United States and have been actively engaged in business for at least the last five years. The securities sold pursuant to this exemption must have been owned for at least five years and must be bona fide sold in negotiated transactions otherwise than through a broker or dealer.

Regulation A, in addition to providing an exemption for issuers from registration for securities up to 1.5 million dollars, also provides an exemption of up to $300,000 in any twelve-month period for non-issuers. Use of this exemption requires compliance with all of the conditions imposed upon issuers by Regulation A, as discussed above.

Liability

In order to implement the statutory objectives of providing full disclosure and preventing fraud in the sale of securities, the Act imposes a number of sanctions for non-compliance with its requirements. The sanctions include administrative remedies by the SEC, civil liability to injured investors, and criminal penalties.

Section 12(1). Section 12(1) imposes civil liability for any violation of Section 5 of the Act. Thus, the sale of an unregistered security which is required to be registered, the sale of a registered security without delivery of a prospectus, the sale of a security by use of a non-current prospectus, the offer of a sale prior to the filing of the registration statement, or the sale of a security while a stop order is in effect would subject the seller to civil liability. Liability under Section 12(1) is absolute, as there are no defenses. The person who purchases a security sold in violation of this section has the right to tender it back to the seller and recover the purchase price plus interest less income received. If the purchaser no longer owns the security, he may recover monetary damages from the seller. An action under Section 12(1) must be brought within one year after the violation but no more than three years after the security was bona fide offered to the public.

Section 11. Section 11 applies to securities that have been sold subject to a registration statement. It imposes liability for the inclusion in the registration statement of any untrue statement or omission of material fact. Liability is imposed upon (1) the issuer; (2) all persons who signed the registration statement; (3) every person who was, or who consents to be named as being or about to become, a director or partner; (4) every accountant, engineer, appraiser, or expert who prepared or certified any part of the registration statement; and (5) all underwriters. These persons are jointly and severally liable to any person who acquires the security without knowledge of the untruth or omission for the amount paid for the security less either its value at the time of suit or the price for which it was sold. However, an expert is only liable for misstatements or omissions in the portion of the registration that he prepared or certified. Moreover, any defendant, other than the issuer, may assert the defense of due diligence. This defense generally requires a showing that the defendant had reasonable grounds to believe that there were no untrue statements or material omissions. In some instances due diligence requires that a reasonable investigation be made. In determining what constitutes a reasonable investigation and reasonable ground for belief, the standard of reason-

ableness shall be that required of a prudent man in the management of his own property. Section 11 actions must be brought within one year after the discovery of the misstatement or omission was made or should have been made, but no more than three years after the security was bona fide offered to the public.

Section 12(2). Section 12(2) is a broad antifraud provision which applies to all securities, whether registered or exempt, with the exception of bank and governmental securities. It imposes liability upon any person who offers or sells a security by means of a prospectus or oral communication which includes an untrue statement of material fact or an omission of a material fact. Liability under Section 12(2) extends only to the immediate purchaser provided he did not know of the untruth or omission. The seller may avoid liability by proving that he did not know, and in the exercise of reasonable care could not have known, of the untrue statement or omission. The seller is liable to the purchaser for the amount paid plus interest less income received upon tender of the security. If the purchaser no longer owns the security, he may recover damages from the seller. An action under Section 12(2) must be brought within one year after the discovery of the misstatement or omission was made or should have been made, but no more than three years after the sale.

Section 17(a). This section makes it unlawful for any person in the offer or sale of any securities by the use of any means of transportation or communication in interstate commerce or by the use of the mails, directly or indirectly—

1. to employ any device, scheme, or artifice to defraud, or
2. to obtain money or property by means of any untrue statement of a material fact or

any omission to state a material fact necessary in order to make the statements made not misleading, or

3. to engage in any transaction, practice, or course of business which operates or would operate as a fraud or deceit upon the purchaser.

There is some doubt whether the courts may imply a private right of action for persons injured by violations of this section. The Supreme Court has reserved this question and the lower courts are divided on the issue.

Section 24. Section 24 imposes criminal sanctions upon any person who willfully violates any of the provisions of the 1933 Act or the rules and regulations promulated by the SEC pursuant to the Act. Conviction may carry a fine of not more than $10,000 or imprisonment of not more than five years or both.

THE SECURITIES EXCHANGE ACT OF 1934

The Securities Exchange Act of 1934 deals principally with the secondary distribution of securities. It provides protection for the holders of securities listed on national exchanges as well as equity securities of companies traded over the counter if their assets exceed $1 million and they have a class of equity securities with 500 or more shareholders. Companies must register such securities and are also subject to the Act's periodic reporting requirements, the short swing profits provision, the tender offer provisions, the proxy solicitation provisions and the internal control and record keeping requirements of the Foreign Corrupt Practices Act. In addition, issuers of securities, whether registered or not, must comply with the anti-fraud provisions of Section 10(b) and the anti-bribery provisions of the Foreign Corrupt Practices Act.

Registration and Periodic Reporting Requirements

Section 12 of the 1934 Act requires all regulated publicly held companies to register with the SEC. These registrations are one-time registrations which apply to an entire class of securities and differ from registrations under the Securities Act of 1933 which relate only to securities involved in a specific offering.

The SEC has promulgated rules which prescribe the nature and content of these registration statements which are similar to that required in a 1933 Act registration statement but less extensive. Following registration, an issuer must file specified annual and periodic reports to update the information contained in the original registration. The required reports include the annual Form 10–K report and the interim quarterly Form 10–Q reports. Within fifteen days after the occurrence of certain events, such as changes in control or disposition of significant amounts of assets, a Form 8–K report must be filed.

The 1934 Act imposes penalties for filing false statements and reports with the SEC as well as providing liability to investors who suffer losses in the purchase or sale of registered securities in reliance on such false reports. Sections 18 and 32.

Short Swing Profits

The 1934 Act, Section 16(b), imposes liability upon directors, officers, and any person owning 10% or more of the stock of the corporation which is listed upon a national stock exchange or registered with the SEC, for all profits resulting from their "short swing" trading in such stock. If any of the above described "insiders" sells such stock within six months from the date of its purchase or purchases such stock within six months from the date of a sale of the stock, the corporation is entitled to recover any and all profit realized by the insider from such transactions. If the corporation does not receive such profit or fails to file suit to recover it, any shareholder of the corporation may file and maintain such a suit for the benefit of the corporation. The "profit" recoverable is calculated by matching the highest sale price against the lowest purchase price, within six months of each other. Losses cannot be offset against profits.

Officers, directors, and persons owning 10% or more of an equity security that is listed or registered are required to report periodically to the Securities and Exchange Commission their purchases and sales of stock of the corporation. In this way information with respect to trading by insiders in the stock of the corporation is made available to the public.

Anti-fraud Provision

Section 10(b) makes it unlawful for any person by use of the mails or facilities of interstate commerce to use or employ, in connection with the purchase or sale of any security, any manipulative or deceptive device or contrivance in contravention of such rules and regulations as the Commission may prescribe as necessary or appropriate in the public interest or for the protection of investors. In 1942 the SEC promulgated Rule 10b–5 which provides:

It shall be unlawful for any person, directly or indirectly, by the use of any means or instrumentality of interstate commerce, or of the mails, or of any facility of any national securities exchange,
  (1) to employ any device, scheme, or artifice to defraud,
  (2) to make any untrue statement of a material fact or to omit to state a material fact necessary in order to make the statements made, in the light of circumstances under which they were made, not misleading, or
  (3) to engage in any act, practice, or course of business which operates or would operate as a fraud or deceit upon any person,
in connection with the purchase or sale of any security.

Despite the fact that the rule is worded as a prohibition, it has been construed as creating implicit civil liability and has been applied in varied and numerous situations.

Rule 10b–5 applies to any purchase or sale of *any* security, whether it is registered under the Exchange Act or not, whether it is publicly traded or closely held, whether it is listed on an exchange or sold over the counter. There are *no* exemptions. Unlike Sections 11, 12, and 17(a) of the Securities Act, Rule 10b–5 applies to misconduct of purchasers as well as sellers and thereby allows both defrauded sellers and buyers to recover.

Recovery under Rule 10b–5 requires proof of several elements including (1) a misstatement or omission, (2) that is material, (3) made with *scienter,* and (4) relied upon (5) in connection with the purchase or sale of a security. A misstatement or omission is material if there is a substantial likelihood that a reasonable investor would consider it important in deciding whether to purchase or sell the security. Unlike common law fraud, Rule 10b–5 imposes an affirmative duty of disclosure. For example, when any person possesses material information regarding a security, which information is non-public and that person has reason to know it is non-public, he may not buy or sell that security without first disclosing the "inside information" or waiting until the information becomes public. The affirmative duty of disclosure extends beyond executives and directors to all employees and any person who receives inside information—the so-called "tippees," as discussed in the Texas Gulf Sulphur case, page 868.

Recently, the United States Supreme Court decided that in an action for damages under Rule 10b–5, it must be shown that the violation was committed with *scienter,* which is intentional misconduct. In its decision, the Court did not address the questions whether recklessness would constitute *scienter* or whether *scienter* is a necessary element in an action for injunctive relief. The Court did hold that negligence would not be sufficient. (See Ernst & Ernst v. Hochfelder, page 865.)

Proxy Soliciions

A proxy is a writing signed by a shareholder of a corporation authorizing a named person or persons to vote his shares of stock at a specified annual or special meeting of the shareholders. Section 14 of the 1934 Act makes it unlawful for any person to solicit any proxy with respect to any registered security "in contravention of such rules and regulations as the Commission may prescribe." The rules of the SEC require the issuer to furnish security holders with a proxy statement describing all material facts concerning the matters being submitted to their vote together with a proxy form on which the security holders can indicate their approval or disapproval of each proposal to be presented. Preliminary proxy materials must be filed with the SEC for comment at least ten days before mailing them to shareholders. When proxies are solicited for the annual election of directors, the proxy statement must be accompanied by an annual report. Even if a company does not solicit proxies from its shareholders but submits a matter to a shareholder vote, it must provide them with information substantially equivalent to that which would appear in a proxy statement.

Where management makes a solicitation, any security holder entitled to vote has the opportunity to communicate with other security holders. Upon written request, the corporation must mail the communication or, at its option, promptly furnish to that security holder a current list of security holders.

If any security holder entitled to vote timely submits a proposal for action at a forthcoming meeting, management must include the proposal in its proxy statement and provide security holders with an opportunity to vote for or against it. If management opposes the proposal, it must include in its proxy materials a statement by the security holder of not more than 200 words. However, management may omit a proposal if, among other things, it (1) is under state law not a proper subject for shareholder action, (2) is not significantly related to the business of the issuer or is beyond the issuer's power to effectuate, or (3) relates to the conduct of the ordinary business operations of the issuer.

An issuer who distributes a false or misleading proxy statement to its security holders may be liable under Section 18 to any person who suffers a loss caused by purchasing or selling a security in reliance upon the statement. An implied private right of action for any violation of the proxy regulations also exists. J. I. Case Co. v. Borak, 377 U.S. 426 (1964).

Tender Offers

In 1968 Congress amended the 1934 Act to extend reporting and disclosure requirements to attempts to acquire control through a tender offer. A tender offer has been defined as "a general invitation to all of the shareholders of a company to purchase their shares at a specified price, sometimes subject to a minimum and/or a maximum that the offeror will accept, communicated to the shareholders by means of newspaper ads * * *." Jennings and Marsh, *Securities Regulation.*

Section 13(d) requires any person or group that acquires more than 5% of any registered equity security to file within ten days a statement containing (1) the person's background, (2) the source of the funds used to acquire the securities, (3) the purpose of the acquisition, (4) the number of shares owned, and (5) any relevant contracts, arrangements or understandings.

Section 14(d) requires any person who makes a tender offer that would result in the acquisition of more than 5% of a class of registered equity securities to file with the SEC and to furnish to each offeree a statement containing the information required under Section 13(d) as well as several additional items relating to the terms of the offer. Section 14(d) requires that the tender offeror prorate his purchases if more securities are tendered than will be accepted. The section also requires the tender offeror to pay equal consideration to all those who have tendered even though the bid price may be raised during the tender offer.

Section 14(e) makes it unlawful for any person to make any untrue statement of material fact or omit to state any material fact or to engage in any fraudulent, deceptive, or manipulative practices in connection with any tender offer. An implied, private right of action exists for violations of Section 14(e), although the Supreme Court has limited its application by denying standing to sue to an unsuccessful tender offeror who alleged that a successful competitor had violated Section 14(e). Piper v. Chris-Craft Industries, Inc., 430 U.S. 1, 97 S.Ct. 926, 51 L.Ed.2d 124 (1977).

Foreign Corrupt Practices Act

In 1977 Congress enacted the Foreign Corrupt Practices Act as an amendment to the 1934 Act. The Act imposes internal control requirements upon companies with registered securities and prohibits all U.S. corporations from bribing foreign governmental or political officials.

Accounting Requirements. The 1977 Act amended Section 13(b) of the 1934 Act to require every issuer which has a class of registered securities to:

1. make and keep books which, in reasonable detail, accurately and fairly reflect the transactions and disposition of the assets of the issuer and

2. devise and maintain internal controls to assure that transactions are executed as authorized and recorded in conformity with generally accepted accounting principles so as to provide accountability for assets, and that access to assets is permitted only in accordance with management's authorization.

Anti-bribery Provisions. Sections 103 and 104 of the Foreign Corrupt Practices Act make it unlawful for *any* domestic concern or any of its officers, directors, employees, or agents to give directly or indirectly anything of value to any foreign official, political party, or political official for the purpose of (1) influencing any act or decision of such person or party in his or its official capacity or (2) inducing such person or party to use his or its influence to affect a decision of a foreign government, in order to assist such domestic concern in obtaining or retaining business. Violation of this provision can result in fines of up to one million dollars for companies; individuals may be fined a maximum of $10,000 and imprisoned up to five years, or both. Fines imposed upon individuals may not be paid directly or indirectly by the issuer.

Cases

Definition of a Security

SECURITIES & EXCHANGE COMM'N v. W. J. HOWEY CO.

(1970) 328 U.S. 293, 66 S.Ct. 1100, 90 L.Ed. 1244.

MURPHY, J.

This case involves the application of § 2(1) of the Securities Act of 1933 to an offering of units of a citrus grove development coupled with a contract for cultivating, marketing and remitting the net proceeds to the investor.

The Securities and Exchange Commission instituted this action to restrain the respondents from using the mails and instrumentalities of interstate commerce in the offer and sale of unregistered and non-exempt securities in violation of § 5(a) of the Act. The District Court denied the injunction, * * * and the Fifth Circuit Court of Appeals affirmed the judgment * * *.

* * *

Most of the facts are stipulated. The respondents, W. J. Howey Company and Howey-in-the-Hills Service, Inc., are Florida corporations under direct common control and management. The Howey Company owns large tracts of citrus acreage in Lake County, Florida. During the past several years it has planted about 500 acres annually, keeping half of the groves itself and offering the other half to the public "to help us finance additional development." Howey-in-the-Hills Service, Inc., is a service company engaged in cultivating and developing many of these groves, including the harvesting and marketing of the crops.

Each prospective customer is offered both a land sales contract and a service contract, after having been told that it is not feasible to invest in a grove unless service arrangements are made. While the purchaser is free to make arrangements with other service companies, the superiority of Howey-in-the-Hills Service, Inc., is stressed. Indeed, 85% of the acreage sold during the 3-year period ending May 31, 1943, was covered by service contracts with Howey-in-the-Hills Service, Inc.

The land sales contract with the Howey Company provides for a uniform purchase price per acre or fraction thereof, varying in amount only in accordance with the number of years the particular plot has been planted with citrus trees. Upon full payment of the purchase price the land is conveyed to the purchaser by warranty deed. Purchases are usually made in narrow strips of land arranged so that an acre consists of a row of 48 trees. During the period between February 1, 1941, and May 31, 1943, 31 of the 42 persons making purchases bought less than 5 acres each. The average holding of these 31 persons was

1.33 acres and sales of as little as 0.65, 0.7 and 0.73 of an acre were made. These tracts are not separately fenced and the sole indication of several ownership is found in small land marks intelligible only through a plat book record.

The service contract, generally of a 10-year duration without option of cancellation, gives Howey-in-the-Hills Service, Inc., a leasehold interest and "full and complete" possession of the acreage. For a specified fee plus the cost of labor and materials, the company is given full discretion and authority over the cultivation of the groves and the harvest and marketing of the crops. The company is well established in the citrus business and maintains a large force of skilled personnel and a great deal of equipment, including 75 tractors, sprayer wagons, fertilizer trucks and the like. Without the consent of the company, the land owner or purchaser has no right of entry to market the crop; thus there is ordinarily no right to specific fruit. The company is accountable only for an allocation of the net profits based upon a check made at the time of picking. All the produce is pooled by the respondent companies, which do business under their own names.

The purchasers for the most part are non-residents of Florida. They are predominantly business and professional people who lack the knowledge, skill and equipment necessary for the care and cultivation of citrus trees. They are attracted by the expectation of substantial profits.

* * *

Section 2(1) of the Act defines the term "security" to include the commonly known documents traded for speculation or investment. This definition also includes "securities" of a more variable character, designated by such descriptive terms as "certificate of interest or participation in any profit-sharing agreement," "investment contract" and "in general, any interest or instrument commonly known as a 'security.'" The legal issue in this case turns upon a determination of whether, under the circumstances, the land sales contract, the warranty deed and the service contract together constitute an "investment contract" within the meaning of § 2(1). An affirmative answer brings into operation the registration requirements of § 5(a), unless the security is granted an exemption under § 3(b). The lower courts, in reaching a negative answer to this problem, treated the contracts and deeds as separate transactions involving no more than an ordinary real estate sale and an agreement by the seller to manage the property for the buyer.

The term "investment contract" is undefined by the Securities Act or by relevant legislative reports. But the term was common in many state "blue sky" laws in existence prior to the adoption of the federal statute * * *.

By including an investment contract within the scope of § 2(1) of the Securities Act, Congress was using a term the meaning of which had been crystallized by this prior judicial interpretation. It is therefore reasonable to attach that meaning to the term as used by Congress, especially since such a definition is consistent with the statutory aims. In other words, an investment contract for purposes of the Securities Act means a contract, transaction or scheme whereby a person invests his money in a common enterprise and is led to expect profits solely from the efforts of the promoter or a third party, it being immaterial whether the shares in the enterprise are evidenced by formal certificates or by nominal interests in the physical assets employed in the enterprise. Such a definition * * * permits the fulfillment of the statutory purpose of compelling full and fair disclosure relative to the issuance of "the many types of instruments that in our commercial world fall within the ordinary concept of a security." H.Rep.No. 85, 73d Cong., 1st Sess., p. 11. It embodies a flexible rather than a static principle, one that is capable of adaptation to meet the countless and variable schemes devised by those who seek the use of the money of others on the promise of profits.

The transactions in this case clearly involve investment contracts as so defined. The respondent companies are offering something more than fee simple interests in land, something different from a farm or orchard coupled with management services. They are offering an opportunity to contribute money and to share in the profits of a large citrus fruit enterprise managed and partly owned by respondents. They are offering this opportunity to persons who reside in distant localities and who lack the equipment and experience requisite to the cultivation, harvesting and marketing of the citrus products. Such persons have no desire to occupy the land or to develop it themselves; they are attracted solely by the prospects of a return on their investment. Indeed, individual development of the plots of land that are offered and sold would seldom be economically feasible due to their small size. Such tracts gain utility as citrus groves only when cultivated and developed as component parts of a larger area. A common enterprise managed by respondents or third parties with adequate personnel and equipment is therefore essential if the investors are to achieve their paramount aim of a return on their investments. Their respective shares in this enterprise are evidenced by land sales contracts and warranty deeds, which serve as a convenient method of determining the investors' allocable shares of the profits. The resulting transfer of rights in land is purely incidental.

Thus all the elements of a profit-seeking business venture are present here. The investors provide the capital and share in the earnings and profits; the promoters manage, control and operate the enterprise. It follows that the arrangements whereby the investors' interests are made manifest involve investment contracts, regardless of the legal terminology in which such contracts are clothed. The investment contracts in this instance take the form of land sales contracts, warranty deeds and service contracts which respondents offer to prospective investors. And respondents' failure to abide by the statutory and administrative rules in making such offerings, even though the failure result from a bona fide mistake as to the law, cannot be sanctioned under the Act.

This conclusion is unaffected by the fact that some purchasers choose not to accept the full offer of an investment contract by declining to enter into a service contract with the respondents. The Securities Act prohibits the offer as well as the sale of unregistered, non-exempt securities. Hence it is enough that the respondents merely offer the essential ingredients of an investment contract.

* * *

Reversed.

The Securities Act of 1933:
Section 11

ESCOTT v. BARCHRIS CONST. CO.

(1968, S.D.N.Y.) 283 F.Supp. 643.

McLean, J.

This is an action by purchasers of 5½ per cent convertible subordinated fifteen year debentures of BarChris Construction Corporation (BarChris). * * *

The action is brought under Section 11 of the Securities Act of 1933. Plaintiffs allege that the registration statement with respect to these debentures filed with the Securities and Exchange Commission, which became effective on May 16, 1961, contained material false statements and material omissions.

Defendants fall into three categories: (1) the persons who signed the registration statement; (2) the underwriters, consisting of eight investment banking firms, led by Drexel & Co. (Drexel); and (3) BarChris's

auditors, Peat, Marwick, Mitchell & Co. (Peat, Marwick).

The signers, in addition to BarChris itself, were the nine directors of BarChris, plus its controller, defendant Trilling, who was not a director. Of the nine directors, five were officers of BarChris, *i.e.*, defendants Vitolo, president; Russo, executive vice president; Pugliese, vice president; Kircher, treasurer; and Birnbaum, secretary. Of the remaining four, defendant Grant was a member of the firm of Perkins, Daniels, McCormack & Collins, BarChris' attorneys. He became a director in October 1960. Defendant Coleman, a partner in Drexel, became a director on April 17, 1961, as did the other two, Auslander and Rose, who were not otherwise connected with BarChris.

Defendants, in addition to denying that the registration statement was false, have pleaded the defenses open to them under Section 11 of the Act, * * *. On the main issue of liability, the questions to be decided are (1) did the registration statement contain false statements of fact, or did it omit to state facts which should have been stated in order to prevent it from being misleading; (2) if so, were the facts which were falsely stated or omitted "material" within the meaning of the Act; (3) if so, have defendants established their affirmative defenses?

* * *

In December 1959, BarChris sold 560,000 shares of common stock to the public at $3.00 per share. This issue was underwritten by Peter Morgan & Company, one of the present defendants.

By early 1961, BarChris needed additional working capital. The proceeds of the sale of the debentures involved in this action were to be devoted, in part at least, to fill that need.

The registration statement of the debentures, in preliminary form, was filed with the Securities and Exchange Commission on March 30, 1961. A first amendment was filed on May 11 and a second on May 16. The registration statement became effective on May 16. The closing of the financing took place on May 24. On that day BarChris received the net proceeds of the financing.

By that time BarChris was experiencing difficulties in collecting amounts due from some of its customers. Some of them were in arrears in payments due to factors on their discounted notes. As time went on those difficulties increased. Although BarChris continued to build alleys in 1961 and 1962, it became increasingly apparent that the industry was overbuilt. Operators of alleys, often inadequately financed, began to fail. Precisely when the tide turned is a matter of dispute, but at any rate, it was painfully apparent in 1962.

In May of that year BarChris made an abortive attempt to raise more money by the sale of common stock. It filed with the Securities and Exchange Commission a registration statement for the stock issue which it later withdrew. In October 1962 BarChris came to the end of the road. On October 29, 1962, it filed in this court a petition for an arrangement under Chapter XI of the Bankruptcy Act.

* * *

Summary
For convenience, the various falsities and omissions which I have discussed in the preceding pages are recapitulated here. They were as follows:

1. *1960 Earnings*
   (a) *Sales*

As per prospectus	$9,165,320
Correct figure	8,511,420
Overstatement	$ 653,900

   (b) *Net Operating Income*

As per prospectus	$1,742,801
Correct figure	1,496,196
Overstatement	$ 246,605

   (c) *Earnings per Share*

As per prospectus	$.75
Correct figure	.65
Overstatement	$.10

2. *1960 Balance Sheet*
   Current Assets

As per prospectus	$4,524,021
Correct figure	3,914,332
Overstatement	$ 609,689

3. *Contingent Liabilities as of December 31, 1960 on Alternative Method of Financing*

As per prospectus	$ 750,000
Correct figure	1,125,795
Understatement	$ 375,795
Capitol Lanes should have been shown as a direct liability	$ 325,000

4. *Contingent Liabilities as of April 30, 1961*

As per prospectus	$ 825,000
Correct figure	1,443,853
Understatement	$ 618,853
Capitol Lanes should have been shown as a direct liability	$ 314,166

5. *Earnings Figures for Quarter ending March 31, 1961*
   (a) *Sales*

As per prospectus	$2,138,455
Correct figure	1,618,645
Overstatement	$ 519,810

   (b) *Gross Profit*

As per prospectus	$ 483,121
Correct figure	252,366
Overstatement	$ 230,755

6. *Backlog as of March 31, 1961*

As per prospectus	$6,905,000
Correct figure	2,415,000
Overstatement	$4,490,000

7. *Failure to Disclose
Officers' Loans
Outstanding and
Unpaid on May 16,
1961* $ 386,615

8. *Failure to Disclose
Use of Proceeds in
Manner not Revealed
in Prospectus*
    Approximately $1,160,000

9. *Failure to Disclose
Customers'
Delinquencies In May
1961 and BarChris's
Potential Liability
with Respect Thereto*   Over $1,350,000

10. *Failure to Disclose the
Fact that BarChris
was Already Engaged
and was about to be
More Heavily
Engaged, in the
Operation of Bowling
Alleys*

* * *

The "Due Diligence" Defenses
Section 11(b) of the Act provides that:
"* * * no person, other than the issuer, shall be liable * * * who shall sustain the burden of proof—

* * *

"(3) that (A) as regards any part of the registration statement not purporting to be made on the authority of an expert * * * he had, after reasonable investigation, reasonable ground to believe and did believe, at the time such part of the registration statement became effective, that the statements therein were true and that there was no omission to state a material fact required to be stated therein or necessary to make the statements therein not misleading; * * * and (C) as regards any part of the registration statement purporting to be made on the authority of an expert (other than himself) * * * he had no reasonable ground to believe and did not believe, at the time such part of the registration statement became effective, that the statements therein were untrue or that there was an omission to state a material fact required to be stated therein or necessary to make the statements therein not misleading. * * *"

Section 11(c) defines "reasonable investigation" as follows:
"In determining, for the purposes of paragraph (3) of subsection (b) of this section, what constitutes reasonable investigation and reasonable ground for belief, the standard of reasonableness shall be that required of a prudent man in the management of his own property."

Every defendant, except BarChris itself, to whom, as the issuer, these defenses are not available, and except Peat, Marwick, whose position rests on a different statutory provision, has pleaded these affirmative defenses. Each claims that (1) as to the part of the registration statement purporting to be made on the authority of an expert (which, for convenience, I shall refer to as the "expertised portion"), he had no reasonable ground to believe and did not believe that there were any untrue statements or material omissions, and (2) as to the other parts of the registration statement, he made a reasonable investigation, as a result of which he had reasonable ground to believe and did believe that the registration statement was true and that no material fact was omitted. As to each defendant, the question is whether he has sustained the burden of proving these defenses. Surprising enough, there is little or no judicial authority on this question. No decisions directly in point under Section 11 have been found.

Before considering the evidence, a preliminary matter should be disposed of. The defendants do not agree among themselves as to who the "experts" were or as to the parts of the registration statement which were expertised. Some defendants say that

Peat, Marwick was the expert, others say that BarChris's attorneys, Perkins, Daniels, McCormack & Collins, and the underwriters' attorneys, Drinker, Biddle & Reath, were also the experts. On the first view, only those portions of the registration statement purporting to be made on Peat, Marwick's authority were expertised portions. On the other view everything in the registration statement was within this category, because the two law firms were responsible for the entire document.

The first view is the correct one. To say that the entire registration statement is expertised because some lawyer prepared it would be an unreasonable construction of the statute. Neither the lawyer for the company nor the lawyer for the underwriters is an expert within the meaning of Section 11. The only expert, in the statutory sense, was Peat, Marwick, and the only parts of the registration statement which purported to be made upon the authority of an expert were the portions which purported to be made on Peat, Marwick's authority.

* * *

I turn now to the question of whether defendants have proved their due diligence defenses. The position of each defendant will be separately considered.

* * *

Kircher. Kircher was treasurer of BarChris and its chief financial officer. He is a certified public accountant and an intelligent man. He was thoroughly familiar with BarChris's financial affairs. He knew the terms of BarChris's agreements with Talcott. He knew of the customer's delinquency problem. He participated actively with Russo in May 1961 in the successful effort to hold Talcott off until the financing proceeds came in. He knew how the financing proceeds were to be applied and he saw to it that they were so applied. He arranged the officers' loans and he knew all the facts concerning them.

Moreover, as a member of the executive committee, Kircher was kept informed as to those branches of the business of which he did not have direct charge. He knew about the operation of alleys, present and prospective.

* * *

Knowing the facts, Kircher had reason to believe that the expertised portion of the prospectus, *i.e.,* the 1960 figures, was in part incorrect. He could not shut his eyes to the facts and rely on Peat, Marwick for that portion.

As to the rest of the prospectus, knowing the facts, he did not have a reasonable ground to believe it to be true. On the contrary, he must have known that in part it was untrue. Under these circumstances, he was not entitled to sit back and place the blame on the lawyers for not advising him about it.

Kircher has not proved his due diligence defenses.

* * *

Birnbaum. Birnbaum was a young lawyer, admitted to the bar in 1957, who, after brief periods of employment by two different law firms and an equally brief period of practicing in his own firm, was employed by BarChris as house counsel and assistant secretary in October 1960. Unfortunately for him, he became secretary and a director of BarChris on Aril 17, 1961, after the first version of the registration statement had been filed with the Securities and Exchange Commission. He signed the later amendments, thereby becoming responsible for the accuracy of the prospectus in its final form.

Although the prospectus, in its description of "management," lists Birnbaum among the "executive officers" and devotes several sentences to a recital of his career, the fact seems to be that he was not an executive officer in any real sense. He did not participate in the management of the company. As house counsel, he attended to legal matters of a routine nature.

* * *

One of Brinbaum's more important duties, first as assistant secretary and later as fullfledged secretary, was to keep the corporate minutes of BarChris and its subsidiaries. This necessarily informed him to a considerable extent about the company's affairs. Birnbaum was not initially a member of the executive committee, however, and did not keep its minutes at the outset. According to the minutes, the first meeting which he attended, "upon invitation of the Committee," was on March 22, 1961. He became a member shortly thereafter and kept the minutes beginning with the meeting of April 24, 1961.

It seems probable that Birnbaum did not know of many of the inaccuracies in the prospectus. He must, however, have appreciated some of them. In any case, he made no investigation and relied on the others to get it right. * * * As a lawyer, he should have known his obligations under the statute. He should have known that he was required to make a reasonable investigation of the truth of all the statements in the unexpertised portion of the document which he signed. Having failed to make such an investigation, he did not have reasonable ground to believe that all these statements were true. Birnbaum has not established his due diligence defenses except as to the audited 1960 figures.

Auslander. Auslander was an "outside" director, *i.e.*, one who was not an officer of BarChris. He was chairman of the board of Valley Stream National Bank in Valley Stream, Long Island. In February, 1961, Vitolo asked him to become a director of BarChris. Vitolo gave him an enthusiastic account of BarChris's progress and prospects. As an inducement, Vitolo said that when BarChris received the proceeds of a forthcoming issue of securities, it would deposit $1,000,000 in Auslander's bank.

In February and early March 1961, before accepting Vitolo's invitation, Auslan-

der made some investigation of BarChris. He obtained Dun & Bradstreet reports which contained sales and earnings figures for periods earlier than December 31, 1960. He caused inquiry to be made of certain of BarChris's banks and was advised that they regarded BarChris favorably.

* * *

In considering Auslander's due diligence defenses, a distinction is to be drawn between the expertised and non-expertised portions of the prospectus. As to the former, Auslander knew that Peat, Marwick had audited the 1960 figures. He believed them to be correct because he had confidence in Peat, Marwick. He had no reasonable ground to believe otherwise.

As to the non-expertised portions, however, Auslander is in a different position. He seems to have been under the impression that Peat, Marwick was responsible for all the figures. This impression was not correct, as he would have realized if he had read the prospectus carefully. Auslander made no investigation of the accuracy of the prospectus. He relied on the assurance of Vitolo and Russo, and upon the information he had received in answer to his inquiries back in February and early March. These inquiries were general ones, in the nature of a credit check. The information which he received in answer to them was also general, without specific reference to the statements in the prospectus, which was not prepared until some time thereafter.

It is true that Auslander became a director on the eve of the financing. He had little opportunity to familiarize himself with the company's affairs. The question is whether, under such circumstances, Auslander did enough to establish his due diligence defense with respect to the nonexpertised portions of the prospectus.

* * *

Section 11 imposes liability in the first instance upon a director, no matter how new he is. He is presumed to know his responsibility when he becomes a director. He can escape liability only by using that reasonable care to investigate the facts which a prudent man would employ in the management of his own property. In my opinion, a prudent man would not act in an important matter without any knowledge of the relevant facts, in sole reliance upon representations of persons who are comparative strangers and upon general information which does not purport to cover the particular case. To say that such minimal conduct measures up to the statutory standard would to all intents and purposes, absolve new directors from responsibility merely because they are new. This is not a sensible construction of Section 11, when one bears in mind its fundamental purpose of requiring full and truthful disclosure for the protection of investors.

* * *

Grant. Grant became a director of BarChris in October 1960. His law firm was counsel to BarChris in matters pertaining to the registration of securities. Grant drafted the registration statement for the stock issue in 1959 and for the warrants in January 1961. He also drafted the registration statement for the debentures. In the preliminary division of work between him and Ballard, the underwriters' counsel, Grant took initial responsibility for preparing the registration statement, while Ballard devoted his efforts in the first instance to preparing the indenture.

Grant is sued as a director and as a signer of the registration statement. This is not an action against him for malpractice in his capacity as a lawyer. Nevertheless, in considering Grant's due diligence defenses, the unique position which he occupied cannot be disregarded. As the director most directly concerned with writing the registration statement and assuring its accuracy, more was required of him in the way of reasonable investigation than could fairly

be expected of a director who had no connection with this work.

* * *

Grant was entitled to rely on Peat, Marwick for the 1960 figures. He had no reasonable ground to believe them to be inaccurate. But the matters which * * * were not within the expertised portion of the prospectus * * * Grant was obliged to make a reasonable investigation. I am forced to find that he did not make one. After making all due allownaces for the fact that BarChris's officers misled him, there are too many instances in which Grant failed to make an inquiry which he could easily have made which, if pursued, would have put him on his guard. In my opinion, this finding on the evidence in this case does not establish an unreasonably high standard in other cases for company counsel who are also directors. Each case must rest on its own facts. I conclude that Grant has not established his due diligence defenses except as to the audited 1960 figures.

The Underwriters. The underwriters other than Drexel made no investigation of the accuracy of the prospectus. One of them, Peter Morgan, had underwritten the 1959 stock issue and had been a director of BarChris. He thus had some general familiarity with its affairs, but he knew no more than the other underwriters about the debenture prospectus. They all relied upon Drexel as the "lead" underwriter.

Drexel did make an investigation. The work was in charge of Coleman, a partner of the firm, assisted by Casperson, an associate. Drexel's attorneys acted as attorneys for the entire group of underwriters. Ballard did the work, assisted by Stanton.

* * *

The underwriters say that the prospectus is the company's prospectus, not theirs. Doubtless this is the way they customarily regard it. But the Securities Act makes no such distinction. The underwriters are just as responsible as the company if the prospectus is false. And prospective investors rely upon the reputation of the underwriters in deciding whether to purchase the securities.

There is no direct authority on this question, no judicial decision defining the degree of diligence which underwriters must exercise to establish their defense under Section 11.

* * *

The purpose of Section 11 is to protect investors. To that end the underwriters are made responsible for the truth of the prospectus. If they may escape that responsibility by taking at face value representations made to them by the company's management, then the inclusion of underwriters among those liable under Section 11 affords the investors no additional protection. To effectuate the statute's purpose, the phrase "reasonable investigation" must be construed to require more effort on the part of the underwriters than the mere accurate reporting in the prospectus of "data presented" to them by the company. It should make no difference that this data is elicited by questions addressed to the company officers by the underwriters, or that the underwriters at the time believe that the company's officers are truthful and reliable. In order to make the underwriters' participation in this enterprise of any value to the investors, the underwriters must make some reasonable attempt to verify the data submitted to them. They may not rely solely on the company's officers or on the company's counsel. A prudent man in the management of his own property would not rely on them.

It is impossible to lay down a rigid rule suitable for every case defining the extent to which such verification must go. It is a question of degree, a matter of judgment in each case. In the present case, the underwriters' counsel made almost no attempt to verify management's representations. I hold that that was insufficient.

On the evidence in this case, I find that the underwriters' counsel did not make a reasonable investigation of the truth of those portions of the prospectus which were not made on the authority of Peat, Marwick as an expert. Drexel is bound by their failure. It is not a matter of relying upon counsel for legal advice. Here the attorneys were dealing with matters of fact. Drexel delegated to them, as its agent, the business of examining the corporate minutes and contracts. It must bear the consequences of their failure to make an adequate examination.

The other underwriters, who did nothing and relied solely on Drexel and on the lawyers, are also bound by it. It follows that although Drexel and the other underwriters believed that those portions of the prospectus were true, they had no reasonable ground for that belief, within the meaning of the statute. Hence, they have not established their due diligence defense, except as to the 1960 audited figures.

* * *

Peat, Marwick
Section 11(b) provides:

"Notwithstanding the provisions of subsection (a) no person * * * shall be liable as provided therein who shall sustain the burden of proof—

* * *

"(3) that * * * (B) as regards any part of the registration statement purporting to be made upon his authority as an expert * * * (i) he had, after reasonable investigation, reasonable ground to believe and did believe, at the time such part of the registration statement became effective, that the statements therein were true and that there was no omission to state a material fact required to be stated therein or necessary to make the statements therein not misleading * * *."

This defines the due diligence defense for an expert. Peat, Marwick has pleaded it.

The part of the registration statement purporting to be made upon the authority of Peat, Marwick as an expert was, as we have seen, the 1960 figures. But because the statute requires the court to determine Peat, Marwick's belief, and the grounds thereof, "at the time such part of the registration statement became effective," for the purposes of this affirmative defense the matter must be viewed as of May 16, 1961, and the question is whether at that time Peat, Marwick, after reasonable investigation, had reasonable ground to believe and did believe that the 1960 figures were true and that no material fact had been omitted from the registration statement which should have been included in order to make the 1960 figures not misleading. In deciding this issue, the court must consider not only what Peat, Marwick did in its 1960 audit, but also what it did in its subsequent "S–1 review."

* * *

The 1960 Audit. Peat, Marwick's work was in general charge of a member of the firm, Cummings, and more immediately in charge of Peat, Marwick's manager, Logan. Most of the actual work was performed by a senior accountant, Berardi, who had junior assistants, one of whom was Kennedy.

Berardi was then about thirty years old. He was not yet a C.P.A. He had had no previous experience with the bowling industry. This was his first job as a senior accountant. He could hardly have been given a more difficult assignment.

After obtaining a little background information on BarChris by talking to Logan and reviewing Peat, Marwick's work papers on its 1959 audit, Berardi examined the results of test checks of BarChris's accounting procedures which one of the junior accountants had made, and he prepared an "internal control questionnaire" and an "audit program." Thereafter, for a few days subsequent to December 30, 1960, he inspected BarChris's inventories and examined cer-

tain alley construction. Finally, on January 13, 1961, he began his auditing work which he carried on substantially continuously until it was completed on February 24, 1961. Toward the close of the work, Logan reviewed it and made various comments and suggestions to Berardi. It is unnecessary to recount everything that Berardi did in the course of the audit. We are concerned only with the evidence relating to what Berardi did or did not do with respect to those items which I have found to have been incorrectly reported in the 1960 figures in the prospectus. More narrowly, we are directly concerned only with such of those items as I have found to be material.

Capitol Lanes. First and foremost is Berardi's failure to discover that Capitol Lanes had not been sold. The error affected both the sales figure and the liability side of the balance sheet. Fundamentally, the error stemmed from the fact that Berardi never realized that Heavenly Lanes and Capitol were two different names for the same alley.

* * *

In any case, he never identified this mysterious Capitol with the Heavenly Lanes which he had included in his sales and profit figures. The vital question is whether he failed to make a reasonable investigation which, if he had made it, would have revealed the truth.

Certain accounting records of BarChris, which Berardi testified he did not see, would have put him on inquiry. One was a job cost ledger card for job no. 6036, the job number which Berardi put on his own sheet for Heavenly Lanes. This card read "Capitol Theatre (Heavenly)." In addition, two accounts receivable cards each showed both names on the same card, Capitol and Heavenly. Berardi testified that he looked at the accounts receivable records but that he did not see these particular cards. He testified that he did not look on the job cost ledger cards because he took the costs from another record, the costs register.

The burden of proof on this issue is on Peat, Marwick. Although the question is a rather close one, I find that Peat, Marwick has not sustained that burden. Peat, Marwick has not proved that Berardi made a reasonable investigation as far as Capitol Lanes was concerned and that his ignorance of the true facts was justified.

Howard Lanes Annex. Berardi also failed to discover that this alley was not sold. Here the evidence is much scantier. Berardi saw a contract for this alley in the contract file. No one told him that it was to be leased rather than sold. There is no evidence to indicate that any record existed which would have put him on notice. I find that his investigation was reasonable as to this item.

* * *

The S–1 Review
The purpose of reviewing events subsequent to the date of a certified balance sheet (referred to as an S–1 review when made with reference to a registration statement) is to ascertain whether any material change has occurred in the company's financial position which should be disclosed in order to prevent the balance sheet figures from being misleading. The scope of such a review, under generally accepted auditing standards, is limited. It does not amount to a complete audit.

Peat, Marwick prepared a written program for such a review. I find that this program conformed to generally accepted auditing standards.

* * *

Berardi made the S–1 review in May 1961. He devoted a little over two days to it, a total of 20½ hours. He did not discover any of the errors or omissions pertaining to the state of affairs in 1961 which I have previously discussed at length, all of which

were material. The question is whether, despite his failure to find out anything, his investigation was reasonable within the meaning of the statute.

What Berardi did was to look at a consolidating trial balance as of March 31, 1961, which had been prepared by BarChris, compare it with the audited December 31, 1960, figures, discuss with Trilling certain unfavorable developments which the comparison disclosed, and read certain minutes. He did not examine any "important financial records" other than the trial balance. As to minutes, he read only what minutes Birnbaum gave him, which consisted only of the board of directors' minutes of BarChris. He did not read such minutes as there were of the executive committee. He did not know that there was an executive committee, hence he did not discover that Kircher had notes of executive committee minutes which had not been written up. He did not read the minutes of any subsidiary.

In substance, what Berardi did is similar to what Grant and Ballard did. He asked questions, he got answers which he considered satisfactory, and he did nothing to verify them.

* * *

Accountants should not be held to a standard higher than that recognized in their profession. I do not do so here. Berardi's review did not come up to that standard. He did not take some of the steps which Peat, Marwick's written program prescribed. He did not spend an adequate amount of time on a task of this magnitude. Most important of all, he was too easily satisfied with glib answers to his inquiries.

This is not to say that he should have made a complete audit. But there were enough danger signals in the materials which he did examine to require some further investigation on his part. Generally accepted accounting standards required such further investigation under these circumstances. It is not always sufficient merely to ask questions.

Here again, the burden of proof is on Pcat, Marwick. I find that that burden has not been satisfied. I conclude that Peat, Marwick has not established its due diligence defense.

* * *

Defendants' motions to dismiss this action, upon which decision was reserved at the trial, are denied. * * *

Pursuant to Rule 52(a), this opinion constitutes the court's findings of fact and conclusions of law with respect to the issues determined herein.

So ordered.

The Securities Exchange Act of 1934: Anti-Fraud Provision

ERNST & ERNST v. HOCHFELDER

(1976) 425 U.S. 185, 96 S.Ct. 1375, 47 L.Ed.2d 668.

POWELL, J.

The issue in this case is whether an action for civil damages may lie under § 10(b) of the Securities Exchange Act of 1934 (1934 Act), * * *, and Securities and Exchange Commission Rule 10b–5, * * * in the absence of an allegation of intent to deceive, manipulate, or defraud on the part of the defendant.

I

Petitioner, Ernst & Ernst, is an accounting firm. From 1946 through 1967 it was retained by First Securities Company of Chicago (First Securities), a small brokerage firm and member of the Midwest Stock Exchange and of the National Association of Securities Dealers, to perform periodic audits of the firm's books and records. In connection with these audits Ernst & Ernst prepared for filing with the Securities and Exchange Commission (Commission) the annual reports required of First Securities under § 17(a) of the 1934 Act. It also prepared for First Securities responses to the financial questionnaires of the Midwest Stock Exchange (Exchange).

Respondents were customers of First Securities who invested in a fraudulent securities scheme perpetrated by Leston B. Nay, president of the firm and owner of 92% of its stock. * * *

This fraud came to light in 1968 when Nay committed suicide, leaving a note that described First Securities as bankrupt and the escrow accounts as "spurious." Respondents subsequently filed this action for damages against Ernst & Ernst in the United States District Court for the Northern District of Illinois under § 10(b) of the 1934 Act. The complaint charged that Nay's escrow scheme violated § 10(b) and Commission Rule 10b–5, and that Ernst & Ernst had "aided and abetted" Nay's violations by its "failure" to conduct proper audits of First Securities. As revealed through discovery, respondents' cause of action rested on a theory of negligent nonfeasance. The premise was that Ernst & Ernst had failed to utilize "appropriate auditing procedures" in its audits of First Securities, thereby failing to discover internal practices of the firm said to prevent an effective audit.

* * *

II

Federal regulation of transactions in securities emerged as part of the aftermath of the market crash in 1929. The Securities Act of 1933 (1933 Act), [citation] was designed to provide investors with full disclosure of material information concerning public offerings of securities in commerce, to protect investors against fraud and, through the imposition of specified civil liabilities, to promote ethical standards of honesty and fair dealing. See H.R. Rep.No.85, 73d Cong., 1st Sess., 1–5 (1933). The 1934 Act was intended principally to protect investors against manipulation of stock prices through regulation of transactions upon securities exchanges and in over-the-counter markets, and to impose regular reporting requirements on companies whose stock is listed on national securities exchanges. See S.Rep.No.792, 73d Cong., 2d Sess., 1–5 (1934). Although the Acts contain numerous carefully drawn express civil remedies and criminal penalties, Congress recognized that efficient regulation of securities trading could not be accomplished under a rigid statutory program. As part of the 1934 Act Congress created the Commission, which is provided with an arsenal of flexible enforcement powers. [Citations.]

Section 10 of the 1934 Act makes it "unlawful for any person * * * (b) [t]o use or employ, in connection with the purchase or sale of any security * * * any manipulative or deceptive device or contrivance in contravention of such rules and regulations as the Commission may prescribe as necessary or appropriate in the public interest or for the protection of investors." [Citation.] In 1942, acting pursuant to the power conferred by § 10(b), the Commission promulgated Rule 10b–5.

* * *

Although § 10(b) does not by its terms create an express civil remedy for its violation, and there is no indication that Congress, or the Commission when adopting Rule 10b–5, contemplated such a remedy, the existence of a private cause of action for violations of the statute and the Rule is now well established. [Citation.] During the 30-year period since a private cause of action was first implied under § 10(b) and Rule 10b–5, a substantial body of case law and commentary has developed as to its elements. Courts and commentators long have differed with regard to whether scienter is a necessary element of such a cause of action, or whether negligent conduct alone is sufficient.

* * *

Although the extensive legislative history of the 1934 Act is bereft of any explicit explanation of Congress' intent, we think the relevant portions of that history support our conclusion that § 10(b) was addressed to practices that involve some element of scienter and cannot be read to impose liability for negligent conduct alone.

* * *

There is no indication * * * that § 10(b) was intended to proscribe conduct not involving scienter. The extensive hearings that preceded passage of the 1934 Act touched only briefly on § 10, and most of the discussion was devoted to the enumerated devices that the Commission is empowered to proscribe under § 10(a). The most relevant exposition of the provision that was to become § 10(b) was by Thomas G. Corcoran, a spokesman for the drafters. Corcoran indicated:

Subsection (c) [§ 9(c) of H.R. 7852—later § 10(b)] says, "Thou shalt not devise any other cunning devices."

* * *

Of course subsection (c) is a catch-all clause to prevent manipulative devices. I do not think there is any objection to that kind of clause. The Commission should have the authority to deal with new manipulative devices. Hearings on H.R. 7852 and H.R. 8720 before the House Committee on Interstate and Foreign Commerce, 73d Cong., 2d Sess., 115 (1934).

This brief explanation of § 10(b) by a spokesman for its drafters is significant. The section was described rightly as a "catchall" clause to enable the Commission "to deal with new manipulative [or cunning] devices." It is difficult to believe that any lawyer, legislative draftsman, or legislator would use these words if the intent was to create liability for merely negligent acts of omissions. Neither the legislative history nor the briefs supporting respondents identify any usage or authority for construing "manipulative [or cunning] devices" to include negligence.

* * *

The 1933 and 1934 Acts constitute interrelated components of the federal regulatory scheme governing transactions in securities. [Citation.] As the Court indicated in SEC v. National Securities, Inc., 393 U.S. 453, 466, 89 S.Ct. 564, 571, 21 L.Ed.2d 668 (1969), "the interdependence of the various sections of the securities laws is certainly a relevant factor in any interpretation of the language Congress has chosen * * *." Recognizing this, respondents and the Commission contrast § 10(b) with other sections of the Acts to support their contention that civil liability may be imposed upon proof of negligent conduct. We think they misconceive the significance of the other provisions of the Acts.

The Commission argues that Congress has been explicit in requiring willful conduct when that was the standard of fault intended, * * *.

* * *

The structure of the Acts does not support the Commission's argument. In each instance that Congress created express civil liability in favor of purchasers or sellers of securities it clearly specified whether recovery was to be premised on knowing or intentional conduct, negligence, or entirely innocent mistake. [Citations.] For example, § 11 of the 1933 Act unambiguously creates a private action for damages when a registration statement includes untrue statements of material facts or fails to state material facts necessary to make the statements therein not misleading. Within the limits specified by § 11(e), the issuer of the securities is held absolutely liable for any damages resulting from such misstatement or omission. But experts such as accountants who have prepared portions of the registration statement are accorded a "due diligence" defense. In effect, this is a negligence standard. An expert may avoid

civil liability with respect to the portions of the registration statement for which he was responsible by showing that "after reasonable investigation" he had "reasonable ground[s] to believe" that the statements for which he was responsible were true and there was no omission of a material fact. § 11(b)(3)(B)(i). See e.g., Escott v. Barchris Const. Corp., 283 F.Supp. 643, 697–703 (S.D.N.Y.1968). The express recognition of a cause of action premised on negligent behavior in § 11 stands in sharp contrast to the language of § 10(b), and significantly undercuts the Commission's argument.

We also consider it significant that each of the express civil remedies in the 1933 Act allowing recovery for negligent conduct, see §§ 11, 12(2), 15, [citations] is subject to significant procedural restrictions not applicable under § 10(b). Section 11(e) of the 1933 Act, for example, authorizes the court to require a plaintiff bringing a suit under § 11, § 12(2), or § 15 thereof to post a bond for costs, including attorneys' fees, and in specified circumstances to assess costs at the conclusion of the litigation. Section 13 specifies a statute of limitations of one year from the time the violation was or should have been discovered, in no event to exceed three years from the time of offer or sale, applicable to actions brought under § 11, § 12(2), or § 15. These restrictions, significantly, were imposed by amendments to the 1933 Act adopted as part of the 1934 Act.

* * *

We have addressed, to this point, primarily the language and history of § 10(b). The Commission contends, however, that subsections (b) and (c) of Rule 10b–5 are cast in language which—if standing alone—could encompass both intentional and negligent behavior. These subsections respectively provide that it is unlawful "[t]o make any untrue statement of a material fact or to omit to state a material fact necessary in order to make the statements made, in the light of the circumstances under which they were made, not misleading * * * " and "[t]o engage in any act, practice, or course of business which operates or would operate as a fraud or deceit upon any person * * *."

Viewed in isolation the language of subsection (b), and arguably that of subsection (c), could be read as proscribing, respectively, any type of material misstatement or omission, and any course of conduct, that has the effect of defrauding investors, whether the wrongdoing was intentional or not.

We note first that such a reading cannot be harmonized with the administrative history of the Rule, a history making clear that when the Commission adopted the Rule it was intended to apply only to activities that involved scienter. More importantly, Rule 10b–5 was adopted pursuant to authority granted the Commission under § 10(b). The rulemaking power granted to an administrative agency charged with the administration of a federal statute is not the power to make law. Rather, it is " 'the power to adopt regulations to carry into effect the will of Congress as expressed by the statute.' " [Citations.] Thus, despite the broad view of the Rule advanced by the Commission in this case, its scope cannot exceed the power granted the Commission by Congress under § 10(b). For the reasons stated above, we think the Commission's original interpretation of Rule 10b–5 was compelled by the language and history of § 10(b) and related sections of the Acts. [Citations.] When a statute speaks so specifically in terms of manipulation and deception, and of implementing devices and contrivances— the commonly understood terminology of intentional wrongdoing—and when its history reflects no more expansive intent, we are quite unwilling to extend the scope of the statute to negligent conduct.

* * *

The judgment of the Court of Appeals is Reversed.

Insider Trading

SECURITIES AND EXCHANGE COMM'N v. TEXAS GULF SULPHUR CO.
(1968, 2nd Cir.) 401 F.2d 833, *cert. denied*, 394 U.S. 976, 89 S.Ct. 1454, 22 L.Ed.2d 756.

WATERMAN, J.

This action was commenced in the United States District Court for the Southern District of New York by the Securities and Exchange Commission (the SEC) pursuant to Sec. 21(e) of the Securities Exchange Act of 1934 (the Act) against Texas Gulf Sulphur Company (TGS) and several of its officers, directors and employees, to enjoin certain conduct by TGS and the individual defendants said to violate Section 10(b) of the Act and Rule 10b–5 (the Rule), promulgated thereunder, and to compel the rescission by the individual defendants of securities transactions assertedly conducted contrary to law. The complaint alleged (1) that defendants Fogarty, Mollison, Darke, Murray, Huntington, O'Neill, Clayton, Crawford, and Coates had either personally or through agents purchased TGS stock or calls thereon from November 12, 1963 through April 16, 1964 on the basis of material inside information concerning the results of TGS drilling in Timmins, Ontario, while such information remained undisclosed to the investing public generally or to the particular sellers; (2) that defendants Darke and Coates had divulged such information to others for use in purchasing TGS stock or calls or recommended its purchase while the information was undisclosed to the public or to the sellers; (3) that defendants Stephens, Fogarty, Mollison, Holyk, and Kline had accepted options to purchase TGS stock on Feb. 20, 1964, without disclosing the material information as to the drilling progress to either the Stock Option Committee or the TGS Board of Directors; and (4) that TGS issued a deceptive press release on April 12, 1964. The case was tried at length before Judge Bonsal of the Southern District of New York, sitting without a jury. Judge Bonsal in a detailed opinion decided, *inter alia,* that the insider activity prior to April 9, 1964 was not illegal because the drilling results were not "material" until then; that Clayton and Crawford had traded in violation of law because they traded after that date; that Coates had committed no violation as he did not trade before disclosure was made; and that the issuance of the press release was not unlawful because it was not issued for the purpose of benefiting the corporation, there was no evidence that any insider used the release to his personal advantage and it was not "misleading, or deceptive on the basis of the facts then known." Defendants Clayton and Crawford appeal from that part of the decision below which held that they had violated Sec. 10(b) and Rule 10b–5 and the SEC appeals from the remainder of the decision which dismissed the complaint against defendants TGS, Fogarty, Mollison, Holyk, Darke, Stephens, Kline, Murray, and Coates.

* * *

The Factual Setting
This action derives from the exploratory activities of TGS begun in 1957 on the Canadian Shield in eastern Canada.

* * *

On October 29 and 30, 1963, Clayton conducted a ground geophysical survey on the northeast portion of the Kidd 55 segment which confirmed the presence of an anomaly and indicated the necessity of diamond core drilling for further evaluation. Drilling of the initial hole, K–55–1, at the strongest part of the anomaly was commenced on November 8 and terminated on November 12 at a depth of 655 feet. Visual estimates by Holyk of the core of K–55–1 indicated an average copper content of 1.15% and an average zinc content of 8.64% over a length of 599 feet. This visual estimate convinced TGS that it was desirable to acquire the remainder of the Kidd 55 segment, and in order to facilitate this acquisition TGS President Stephens instructed

the exploration group to keep the results of K–55–1 confidential and undisclosed even as to other officers, directors, and employees of TGS. The hole was concealed and a barren core was intentionally drilled off the anomaly. Meanwhile, the core of K–55–1 had been shipped to Utah for chemical assay which, when received in early December, revealed an average mineral content of 1.18% copper, 8.26% zinc, and 3.94% ounces of silver per ton over a length of 602 feet. These results were so remarkable that neither Clayton, an experienced geophysicist, nor four other TGS expert witnesses, had ever seen or heard of a comparable initial exploratory drill hole in a base metal deposit. So, the trial court concluded, "There is no doubt that the drill core of K–55–1 was unusually good and that it excited the interest and speculation of those who knew about it." By March 27, 1964, TGS decided that the land acquisition program had advanced to such a point that the company might well resume drilling, and drilling was resumed on March 31.

During this period, from November 12, 1963 when K–55–1 was completed, to March 31, 1964 when drilling was resumed, certain of the individual defendants * * * and persons * * * said to have received "tips" from them, purchased TGS stock or calls thereon. Prior to these transactions these persons had owned 1135 shares of TGS stock and possessed no calls; thereafter they owned a total of 8235 shares and possessed 12,300 calls.

On February 20, 1964, also during this period, TGS issued stock options to 26 of its officers and employees whose salaries exceeded a specified amount, five of whom were the individual defendants Stephens, Fogarty, Mollison, Holyk, and Kline. Of these, only Kline was unaware of the detailed results of K–55–1, but he, too, knew that a hole containing favorable bodies of copper and zinc ore had been drilled in Timmins. At this time, neither the TGS Stock Option Committee nor its Board of Directors had been informed of the results of K–55–1, presumably because of the pending land acquisition program which required confidentiality. All of the foregoing defendants accepted the options granted them.

* * *

Meanwhile, rumors that a major ore strike was in the making had been circulating throughout Canada. On the morning of Saturday, April 11, Stephens at his home in Greenwich, Conn. read in the New York Herald Tribune and in the New York Times unauthorized reports of the TGS drilling which seemed to infer a rich strike from the fact that the drill cores had been flown to the United States for chemical assay. * * * With the aid of one Carroll, a public relations consultant, Fogarty drafted a press release designed to quell the rumors which release, after having been channeled through Stephens and Huntington, a TGS attorney, was issued at 3:00 P.M. on Sunday, April 12, and which appeared in the morning newspapers of general circulation on Monday, April 13. It read in pertinent part as follows:

NEW YORK, April 12—The following statement was made today by Dr. Charles F. Fogarty, executive vice president of Texas Gulf Sulphur Company, in regard to the company's drilling operations near Timmins, Ontario, Canada. Dr. Fogarty said:

During the past few days, the exploration activities of Texas Gulf Sulphur in the area of Timmins, Ontario, have been widely reported in the press, coupled with rumors of a substantial copper discovery there. These reports exaggerate the scale of operations, and mention plans and statistics of size and grade of ore that are without factual basis and have evidently originated by speculation of people not connected with TGS.

The facts are as follows: TGS has been exploring in the Timmins area for six years as part of its overall search in Canada and elsewhere for various minerals—lead, copper, zinc, etc. During the course of this work, in Timmins as well as in Eastern Canada, TGS has conducted exploration entirely on its own, without the participation by others. Numerous prospects have

been investigated by geophysical means and a large number of selected ones have been core-drilled. These cores are sent to the United States for assay and detailed examination as a matter of routine and on advice of expert Canadian legal counsel. No inferences as to grade can be drawn from this procedure.

Most of the areas drilled in Eastern Canada have revealed either barren pyrite or graphite without value; a few have resulted in discoveries of small or marginal sulphide ore bodies.

Recent drilling on one property near Timmins has led to preliminary indications that more drilling would be required for proper evaluation of this prospect. The drilling done to date has not been conclusive, but the statements made by many outside quarters are unreliable and include information and figures that are not available to TGS.

The work done to date has not been sufficient to reach definite conclusions and any statement as to size and grade of ore would be premature and possibly misleading. When we have progressed to the point where reasonable and logical conclusions can be made, TGS will issue a definite statement to its stockholders and to the public in order to clarify the Timmins project.

* * *

The release purported to give the Timmins drilling results as of the release date, April 12. From Mollison Fogarty had been told of the developments through 7:00 P.M. on April 10, and of the remarkable discoveries made up to that time, detailed supra, which discoveries, according to the calculations of the experts who testified for the SEC at the hearing, demonstrated that TGS had already discovered 6.2 to 8.3 million tons of proven ore having gross assay values from $26 to $29 per ton. TGS experts, on the other hand, denied at the hearing that proven or probable ore could have been calculated on April 11 or 12 because there was then no assurance of continuity in the mineralized zone.

The evidence as to the effect of this release on the investing public was equivocal and less than abundant. * * * The trial court stated only that "While, in retrospect, the press release may appear gloomy or incomplete, this does not make it misleading or deceptive on the basis of the facts then known."

* * *

While drilling activity ensued to completion, TGS officials were taking steps toward ultimate disclosure of the discovery. On April 13, a previously-invited reporter for The Northern Miner, a Canadian mining industry journal, visited the drillsite, interviewed Mollison, Holyk and Darke, and prepared an article which confirmed a 10 million ton ore strike. This report, after having been submitted to Mollison and returned to the reporter unamended on April 15, was published in the April 16 issue. A statement relative to the extent of the discovery, in substantial part drafted by Mollison, was given to the Ontario Minister of Mines for release to the Canadian media. Mollison and Holyk expected it to be released over the airwaves at 11 P.M. on April 15th, but, for undisclosed reasons, it was not released until 9:40 A.M. on the 16th. An official detailed statement, announcing a strike of at least 25 million tons of ore, based on the drilling data set forth above, was read to representatives of American financial media from 10:00 A.M. to 10:10 or 10:15 A.M. on April 16, and appeared over Merrill Lynch's private wire at 10:29 A.M. and, somewhat later than expected, over the Dow Jones ticker tape at 10:54 A.M.

Between the time the first press release was issued on April 12 and the dissemination of the TGS official announcement on the morning of April 16, the only defendants before us on appeal who engaged in market activity were Clayton and Crawford and TGS director Coates.

* * *

During the period of drilling in Timmins, the market price of TGS stock fluctuated but steadily gained overall. On Friday, November 8, when the drilling began, the stock closed at 17⅜; on Friday, Novem-

ber 15, after K–55–1 had been completed, it closed at 18. After a slight decline to 16⅜ by Friday, November 22, the price rose to 20⅞ by December 13, when the chemical assay results of K–55–1 were received, and closed at a high of 24⅛ on February 21, the day after the stock options had been issued. It had reached a price of 26 by March 31, after the land acquisition program had been completed and drilling had been resumed, and continued to ascend to 30⅛ by the close of trading on April 10, at which time the drilling progress up to then was evaluated for the April 12th press release. On April 13, the day on which the April 12 release was disseminated, TGS opened at 30⅛, rose immediately to a high of 32 and gradually tapered off to close at 30⅞. It closed at 30¼ the next day, and at 29⅜ on April 15. On April 16, the day of the official announcement of the Timmins discovery, the price climbed to a high of 37 and closed at 36⅜. By May 15, TGS stock was selling at 58¼.

The Individual Defendants

* * *

Rule 10b–5 was promulgated pursuant to the grant of authority given the SEC by Congress in Section 10(b) of the Securities Exchange Act of 1934. By that Act Congress purposed to prevent inequitable and unfair practices and to insure fairness in securities transactions generally, whether conducted face-to-face, over the counter, or on exchanges. The Act and the Rule apply to the transactions here, all of which were consummated on exchanges. Whether predicated on traditional fiduciary concepts or on the "special facts" doctrine, see, e.g., Strong v. Repide, the Rule is based in policy on the justifiable expectation of the securities marketplace that all investors trading on impersonal exchanges have relatively equal access to material information. The essence of the Rule is that anyone who, trading for his own account in the securities of a corporation has "access, directly or indirectly, to information intended to be available only for a corporate purpose and not for the personal benefit of anyone" may not take "advantage of such information knowing it is unavailable to those with whom he is dealing," i.e., the investing public. Insiders, as directors or management officers are, of course, by this Rule, precluded from so unfairly dealing, but the Rule is also applicable to one possessing the information who may not be strictly termed an "insider" within the meaning of Sec. 16(b) of the Act. Thus, anyone in possession of material inside information must either disclose it to the investing public, or, if he is disabled from disclosing it in order to protect a corporate confidence, or he chooses not to do so, must abstain from trading in or recommending the securities concerned while such inside information remains undisclosed. So, it is here no justification for insider activity that disclosure was forbidden by the legitimate corporate objective of acquiring options to purchase the land surrounding the exploration site; if the information was, as the SEC contends, material, its possessors should have kept out of the market until disclosure was accomplished.

Material Inside Information. An insider is not, of course, always foreclosed from investing in his own company merely because he may be more familiar with company operations than are outside investors. An insider's duty to disclose information or his duty to abstain from dealing in his company's securities arises only in "those situations which are essentially extraordinary in nature and which are reasonably certain to have a substantial effect on the market price of the security if [the extraordinary situation is] disclosed."

Nor is an insider obligated to confer upon outside investors the benefit of his superior financial or other expert analysis by disclosing his educated guesses or predictions. The only regulatory objective is that access to material information be enjoyed equally, but this objective requires nothing more than the disclosure of basic facts so that outsiders may draw upon their own evaluative expertise in reaching their own investment decisions with knowledge equal to that of the insiders.

This is not to suggest, however, as did the trial court, that "the test of materiality must necessarily be a conservative one, particularly since many actions under Section 10(b) are brought on the basis of hindsight" in the sense that the materiality of facts is to be assessed solely by measuring the effect the knowledge of the facts would have upon prudent or conservative investors. As we stated in List v. Fashion Park, Inc., "The basic test of materiality * * * is whether a *reasonable* man would attach importance * * * in determining his choice of action in the transaction in question. (Emphasis supplied.) This, of course, encompasses any fact " * * * which in reasonable and objective contemplation *might* affect the value of the corporation's stock or securities * * *." List v. Fashion Park, Inc. quoting from Kohler v. Kohler Co. (Emphasis supplied.) Such a fact is a material fact and must be effectively disclosed to the investing public prior to the commencement of insider trading in the corporation's securities. The speculators and chartists of Wall and Bay Streets are also "reasonable" investors entitled to the same legal protection afforded conservative traders. Thus, material facts include not only information disclosing the earnings and distributions of a company but also those facts which affect the probable future of the company and those which may affect the desire of investors to buy, sell, or hold the company's securities.

In each case, then, whether facts are material within Rule 10b–5 when the facts relate to a particular event and are undisclosed by those persons who are knowledgeable thereof will depend at any given time upon a balancing of both the indicated probability that the event will occur and the anticipated magnitude of the event in light of the totality of the company activity. Here, notwithstanding the trial court's conclusion that the results of the first drill core, K–55–1, were "too 'remote' * * * to have had any significant impact on the market, i.e., to be deemed material," knowledge of the possibility, which surely was more than marginal, of the existence of a mine of the vast magnitude indicated by the remarkably rich drill core located rather close to the surface (suggesting mineability by the less expensive open-pit method) within the confines of a large anomaly (suggesting an extensive region of mineralization) might well have affected the price of TGS stock and would certainly have been an important fact to a reasonable, if speculative, investor in deciding whether he should buy, sell, or hold. After all, this first drill core was "unusually good and * * * excited the interest and speculation of those who knew about it."

* * *

When May Insiders Act? Appellant Crawford, who ordered the purchase of TGS stock shortly before the TGS April 16 official announcement, and defendant Coates, who placed orders with and communicated the news to his broker immediately after the official announcement was read at the TGS-called press conference, concede that they were in possession of material information. They contend, however, that their purchases were not proscribed purchases for the news had already been effectively disclosed. We disagree.

* * *

Before insiders may act upon material information, such information must have been effectively disclosed in a manner sufficient to insure its availability to the investing public. Particularly here, where a formal announcement to the entire financial news media had been promised in a prior official release known to the media, all insider activity must await dissemination of the promised official announcement.

* * *

The Corporate Defendant
At 3:00 P.M. on April 12, 1964, evidently believing it desirable to comment upon the rumors concerning the Timmins project, TGS issued the press release quoted in pertinent part in the text [above]. The SEC argued below and maintains on this appeal that this release painted a misleading and deceptive picture of the drilling progress at the time of its issuance, and hence violated Rule 10b–5(2). TGS relies on the holding of the court below that "The issuance of the release produced no unusual market action" and "In the absence of a showing that the purpose of the April 22 press release was to affect the market price of TGS stock to the advantage of TGS or its insiders, the issuance of the press release did not constitute a violation of Section 10(b) or Rule 10b–5 since it was not issued "in connection with the purchase or sale of any security' " and, alternatively, "even if it had been established that the April 12 release was issued in connection with the purchase or sale of any security, the Commission has failed to demonstrate that it was false, misleading or deceptive."

* * *

*The "In Connection with * * *" Requirement.* In adjudicating upon the relationship of this phrase to the case before us it would appear that the court below used a standard that does not reflect the congressional purpose that promoted the passage of the Securities Exchange Act of 1934.

* * *

Therefore it seems clear from the legislative purpose Congress expressed in the Act, and the legislative history of Section 10(b) that Congress when it used the phrase "in connection with the purchase or sale of any security" intended only that the device employed, whatever it might be, be of a sort that would cause reasonable investors to rely thereon, and, in connection therewith, so relying, cause them to purchase or sell a corporation's securities. There is no indication that Congress intended that the corporations or persons responsible for the issuance of a misleading statement would not violate the section unless they engaged in related securities transactions or otherwise acted with wrongful motives; indeed, the obvious purposes of the Act to protect the investing public and to secure fair dealing in the securities markets would be seriously undermined by applying such a gloss onto the legislative language. Absent a securities transaction by an insider it is almost impossible to prove that a wrongful purpose motivated the issuance of the misleading statement. The mere fact that an insider did not engage in securities transactions does not negate the possibility of wrongful purpose; pehaps the market did not react to the misleading statement as much as was anticipated or perhaps the wrongful purpose was something other than the desire to buy at a low price or sell at a high price. Of even greater relevance to the Congressional purpose of investor protection is the fact that the investing public may be injured as much by one's misleading statement containing inaccuracies caused by negligence as by a misleading statement published intentionally to further a wrongful purpose. We do not believe that Congress intended that the proscriptions of the Act would not be violated unless the makers of a misleading statement also participated in pertinent securities transactions in connection therewith, or unless it could be shown that the issuance of the statement was motivated by a plan to benefit the corporation or themselves at the expense of a duped investing public.

* * *

The foregoing discussion demonstrates that Congress intended to protect the in-

vesting public in connection with their purchases or sales on Exchanges from being misled by misleading statements promulgated for or on behalf of corporations irrespective of whether the insiders contemporaneously trade in the securities of that corporation and irrespective of whether the corporation or its management have an ulterior purpose or purposes in making an official public release. Indeed, the Commission has been charged by Congress with the responsibility of policing all misleading corporate statements from those contained in an initial prospectus to those contained in a notice to stockholders relative to the need or desirability of terminating the existence of a corporation or of merging it with another. To render the Congressional purpose ineffective by inserting into the statutory words the need of proving, not only that the public may have been misled by the release, but also that those responsible were actuated by a wrongful purpose when they issued the release, is to handicap unreasonably the Commission in its work. We should have in mind the wise words of Judge Learned Hand in Cawley v. United States relative to an interpretation of the words contained within a congressional statute, that " * * * unless they explicitly forbid it, the purpose of a statutory provision is the best test of the meaning of the words chosen. We are to put ourselves so far as we can in the position of the legislature that uttered them, and decide whether or not it would declare that the situation that has arisen is within what it wishes to cover. Indeed, at times the purpose may be so manifest as to override even the explicit words used."

As was pointed out by the trial court, the intent of the Securities Exchange Act of 1934 is the protection of investors against fraud. Therefore, it would seem elementary that the Commission has a duty to police management so as to prevent corporate practices which are reasonably likely fraudulently to injure investors. And, of course, as we have already emphasized, a corporation's misleading material statement may injure an investor irrespective of whether the corporation itself, or those individuals managing it, are contemporaneously buying or selling the stock of the corporation. Therefore, when materially misleading corporate statements or deceptive insider activities have been uncovered, the courts, as they should, have broadly construed the statutory phrase "in connection with the purchase or sale of any security." The court below found: "There is no evidence that TGS derived any direct benefit from the issuance of the press release or that any of the defendants who participated in its preparation used it to their personal advantage." The requirement that a statement may not be found misleading unless its issuance is actuated by a "wrongful purpose" might well have the effect of permitting the issuers of misleading statements to seek an advantage but to escape liability if the advantage fails to materialize to the degree contemplated, or cannot be demonstrated.

* * *

We conclude, then, that, having established that the release was issued in a manner reasonably calculated to affect the market price of TGS stock and to influence the investing public, we must remand to the district court to decide whether the release was misleading to the reasonable investor and if found to be misleading, whether the court in its discretion should issue the injunction the SEC seeks.

* * *

Problems

1. Acme Realty, a real estate development company, is a limited partnership organized in Georgia. It is planning to develop a 200-acre parcel of land for a regional shopping center and needs to raise $1,250,000. As part of its financing, Acme plans to offer $1,250,000 worth of limited partnership interests to about 100 prospective investors in the Southeastern United States. It anticipates that about 40 to 50 private investors will purchase the limited partnership interests. (a) Must Acme register this offering? Why or why not?
(b) If Acme must register but fails to do so, what are the legal consequences?

2. In 1981 Bigelow Corporations had total assets of $850,000, sales of $1,350,000, one class of common stock with 375 shareholders and a class of preferred stock with 250 shareholders, both of which are traded over the counter. Which provisions of the Securities Exchange Act of 1934 apply to Bigelow Corporation? Explain.

3. Capricorn, Inc., is planning to "go public" by offering its common stock which had been previously owned by only three shareholders. The company intends to limit the number of purchasers to 25 persons resident in the state of its incorporation. All of Capricorn's business and all of its assets are located in the state of incorporation. Based upon these facts, what exemptions from registration, if any, are available to Capricorn and what conditions would each of these available exemptions impose upon the terms of the offer?

4. Dryden, a CPA, audited the books of Elixir, Inc., and certified incorrect financial statements in Form 10–K which were filed with the SEC. Shortly thereafter Elixer, Inc. went bankrupt. Investigation into the bankruptcy disclosed that Kraft, the president of Elixir, had engaged in an intricate and clever embezzlement scheme that siphoned off substantial sums of money which now supports Kraft in a luxurious life style in South America. Investors who purchased shares of Elixir have brought suit against Dryden under Rule 10(b)–5. At trial Dryden produces evidence that demonstrates his failure to discover the embezzlements resulted merely from negligence on his part and that he had no knowledge of the defalcations. Decision?

5. Farthing is a director and vice president of Garp, Inc., whose common stock is listed on the New York Stock Exchange. Farthing engaged in the following transactions in 1981: On January 1 Farthing sold 500 shares at $30 per share; on January 15 he purchased 300 shares at $30 per share; on February 1 he purchased 200 shares at $45 per share; on February 15 he purchased 200 shares at $50 per share; on March 1 he purchased 300 shares at $60 per share; on March 15 he sold 200 shares at $55 per share; on April 1 he sold 200 shares at $50 per share; and on April 15 he sold 100 shares at $40 per share. Howell brings suit on behalf of Garp alleging that Farthing has violated Section 16(b) of the Securities Act of 1934. Farthing defends on the ground that he lost money on the transactions in question. Decision.

6. Intercontinental Widgets, Inc., had applied for a patent for a new state-of-the-art widget which, if patented, would increase significantly the value of Intercontinental's shares. On September 1 the Patent Office notified Jackson, attorney for Intercontinental, that the patent application had been approved. After informing Kingsley, the president of Intercontinental, of the good news, Jackson called his broker and purchased 1,000 shares at $18 per share. He also told his partner, Lucas, who immediately proceeded to purchase 500 shares at $19 per share. Lucas then called his brother-in-law, Mammon, and told him the news. On September 3 Mammon bought 4,000 shares at $21 per share. On September 4 Kingsley issued a press release which accurately reported that a patent had been granted to Intercontinental. On the next day Intercontinental's stock soared to $38 per share. A class action suit is brought against Jackson, Lucas, Mammon, and Intercontinental for violations of Rule 10b–5.

(a) Who, if anyone, is liable?

(b) For what amount, if anything?

(c) Who may be properly joined as plaintiffs in the class action suit?

7. Nova, Inc., sought to sell a new issue of common stock. It registered the issue with the SEC but included false information in both the registration statement and the prospectus. The issue was underwritten by Omega & Sons and was sold in its entirety by Periwinkle, Rameses and Sheffield, Inc., a securities broker-dealer. Telford purchased 500 shares at $6 per share. Three months later the falsity of the information contained in the prospectus was made public and the price of the shares fell to $1 per share. The following week Telford brought suit under Sections 11 and 12(2) of the Securities Act of 1933.

(a) Who is liable, if anyone, under each of these sections?

(b) What defenses, if any, are available to the various defendants?

Chapter
43

CONSUMER PROTECTION

A consumer can be defined as a person who purchases or otherwise acquires goods, services, or land for personal, family, or household use. Many State and Federal statutes have been enacted to protect consumers from unfair and deceptive trade practices and to provide for their health and safety.

Between 1968 and 1980 the Congress of the United States enacted numerous statutes protecting consumers, including the following:

— Consumer Credit Protection Act (also known as the "Truth-in Lending Act")
— Depositary Institutions Deregulation and Monetary Control Act of 1980 (Truth in Lending Simplification and Reform Act)
— Magnuson-Moss Warranty Act
— Interstate Land Sales Full Disclosure Act
— Equal Credit Opportunity Act
— Fair Credit Billing Act
— Real Estate Settlement Procedures Act
— Fair Credit Reporting Act
— Fair Debt Collection Practices Act

— Consumer Product Safety Act
— Fair Packaging and Labeling Act
— Food, Drugs, and Cosmetics Act
— Fair Products Labeling Act
— Wholesome Meat Act
— Flammable Fabrics Act
— Cigarette Labeling and Advertising Act
— Wool Products Labeling Act
— Wholesome Poultry Products Act
— Special Packaging of Household Substances for the Protection of Children Act
— Refrigerator Safety Act

This chapter will briefly discuss the provisions of some of the above-mentioned statutes.

UNFAIR AND DECEPTIVE TRADE PRACTICES

In 1914 the Congress enacted the Federal Trade Commission Act creating the Federal Trade Commission and charging it with the duty to prevent "unfair methods of competition in commerce, and unfair or deceptive acts or practices in commerce." To this end the five-member Commission is empowered to conduct appropriate investigations and hearings. Complaints may be instituted by the Commission which after a hearing may enter appropriate relief. Appeals may be taken from orders of the Commission to the United States Courts of Appeals which have exclusive jurisdiction to enforce, set aside, or modify orders of the Commission.

The Commission has established a Bureau of Consumer Protection which investigates unfair methods of competition such as false and misleading advertisements, false or inadequate labeling of products, passing or palming off goods as those of a competitor, lotteries, gambling schemes, discriminatory offers of rebates and discounts, false disparagement of a competitor's goods, false, or misleading descriptive names of products, use of false testimonials, and other unfair trade practices.

CONSUMER PURCHASES

A number of State and Federal regulations protect the consumer in his purchases of goods, services, and real property for personal, household, or family use. The Uniform Commercial Code, discussed more fully in Chapters 20–24, prohibits unconscionable contractual terms and imposes implied warranties for the protection of the purchaser.

Federal Warranty Protection

In order to provide protection to buyers of consumer products by making available to them adequate information with respect to warranties of such products, and to prevent deception, Congress in 1974 enacted the Magnuson-Moss Warranty Act, which became effective on January 4, 1975. Administration and enforcement of the Act is by the Federal Trade Commission.

The Magnuson-Moss Warranty Act was enacted in order to alleviate certain re-

ported warranty problems: (1) most warranties were not understandable; (2) most warranties disclaimed implied warranties; (3) most warranties were unfair; and (4) in some instances the warrantors did not live up to their warranties. The Act was Congress's attempt to make consumer product warranties more easily understood and to facilitate the consumer in satisfactorily enforcing his remedies. In order to accomplish this purpose the Act provides for: (1) disclosure in clear and understandable language of the warranty that is to be offered; (2) a description of the warranty as either "full" or "limited"; (3) a prohibition against disclaiming implied warranties if a written warranty is given; and (4) an optional informal settlement mechanism.

The Act is applicable when a consumer product containing a written warranty is marketed. A consumer product is defined as any item of tangible personal property which is *normally* used for family, household, or personal use and which is distributed in commerce. The exclusion of commercial purchasers from the Act's protection is to some degree based on the notion that such businessmen are sufficently knowledgeable in contracting, are able to employ their own attorneys to protect themselves, and are able to spread the cost of their injuries in the marketplace.

The Act contains pre-sale disclosure provisions, which are calculated to avert confusion and deception and to enable purchasers to make educated product comparisons. A warrantor must, "to the extent required by the rules of the Commission [Federal Trade Commission], fully and conspicuously disclose in simple and readily understood language the terms and conditions of such warranty."

The second major part of the Act pertains to the labeling requirement. The Act divides written warranties into two categories, "limited" and "full," one of which, for any product costing more than $10, must be designated on the written warranty itself.

The purpose of this provision is to alert the consumer to the relative quantum of legal rights under a certain warranty for purposes of initial comparison. In order to designate the warranty as "full," the warrantor must agree to repair without charge the product to conform with the warranty, no limitation may be placed on the duration of any implied warranty, the consumer must be given the option of a refund or replacement if repair is unsuccessful and consequential damages may be excluded only if conspicuously noted.

Most significantly, the Act provides that a written warranty, whether full or limited, can not disclaim any implied warranty. This provision strikes at the heart of the problem, for as revealed in an earlier Presidential task force report, most written warranties gave limited protection but in return took away the more valuable implied warranties. Hence, consumers were lulled into believing that the warranties they received and the warranty registration cards they promptly returned to the manufacturer were to their benefit. The Act, on the other hand, provides that a "full" warranty must not disclaim, modify or limit any implied warranty, while a "limited" warranty cannot disclaim or modify any implied warranty but can limit its duration to that of the written warranty, provided that such limitation is reasonable, conscionable, and conspicuously displayed.

For example, A sells consumer goods to B for $150 and provides a written warranty regarding the quality of the goods. A must designate the warranty as full or limited, depending upon the characteristics of the warranty, and cannot disclaim or modify any implied warranty. Nevertheless, if A had not provided B with a written warranty, then the Magnuson-Moss Act would not apply and A could disclaim any and all implied warranties.

Finally, the Act also contains a part dealing with remedies and the establishment, at the option of the warrantor, of an informal settlement procedure. However, the Act does not provide any new or expanded remedies.

Consumer Right of Rescission

In most cases, once a consumer has signed a contract he is legally obligated. In some States, however, a consumer has by statute a brief period of time—two or three days—during which he may rescind an otherwise binding credit obligation if the sale solicitation occurred in his home. Under the Federal Consumer Credit Protection Act, as amended by the Truth in Lending Simplification and Reform Act, a consumer has three days during which he may withdraw from any credit obligation secured by a mortgage on his home, unless the extension of credit was made to acquire the dwelling. The Federal Trade Commission has promulgated a Trade Regulation applicable to door-to-door sales of goods and services for $25 or more, whether the sale is for cash or on credit. The regulation permits a consumer within three days of signing to rescind the contract.

The Interstate Land Sales Full Disclosure Act applies to sales or leases of twenty-five or more lots of unimproved land as part of a common promotional plan in interstate commerce. The Act requires the filing of a detailed "statement of record" containing specified information about the subdivision and the developer with the Department of Housing and Urban Development before offering the lots for sale or lease. The developer must provide a property report, which is a condensed version of the statement of record, to each prospective purchaser or lessee.

The Act provides that any contract or agreement for sale or lease may be revoked at the option of the purchaser or lessee within seven days of signing the contract, and the contract must clearly provide this right. If the property report has not been given to the purchaser or lessee in advance of signing the contract, the contract may be revoked within two years from the date of signing.

The Act prohibits the developer from (1) employing any device, scheme, or artifice to defraud, (2) obtaining money or property by means of any untrue statement of material fact; and (3) engaging in any transaction, practice, or course of business which operates or would operate as a fraud or deceit upon the purchaser.

CONSUMER CREDIT OBLIGATIONS

In the absence of special regulation, consumer credit transactions are governed by laws regulating commercial transactions generally. A consumer credit transaction is customarily defined as any transaction the subject matter of which is to be used by one of the parties for personal, household, or family purposes, i.e., for non-business purposes. The following are illustrative: A borrows $600 from a bank to pay a dentist bill or to take a vacation; B buys a refrigerator for his home from a department store and agrees to pay the purchase price in twelve equal monthly installments; C has a credit card with an oil company which he uses to purchase gasoline and tires for his family car.

Regulation of consumer sales credit is designed to minimize abuses occurring in an essentially unregulated area of financing. Retail installment sale credit acts are in force in almost all of the states. Credit sales of automobiles are often treated differently from sales of other goods and services. Revolving charge credit and home improvement contracts may also be subject to different requirements.

Two significant developments have accelerated the legislative trend toward treating all consumer credit obligations the same: (1) the enactment in 1968 of the Federal Consumer Credit Protection Act (FCCPA), and (2) the promulgation of the Uniform Consumer Credit Code (UCCC) in the same year. The FCCPA deals with effective disclosure of interest and finance charges, credit extensions charges, and garnishment proceedings. The UCCC integrates into one document the regulation of all consumer credit transactions and gives substantially similar regulatory treatment to both credit sales and loan transactions.

Consumer credit protection has broadened considerably since the passage of the FCCPA and includes the following areas: (1) access by creditors and consumers to the consumer credit market, (2) disclosure of information to the consumer, (3) regulation of contract terms, (4) fair reportage of credit information concerning consumers, and (5) creditors' remedies.

Access to the Market

The Equal Credit Opportunity Act, enacted by Congress, prohibits all businesses that regularly extend credit from discriminating in extending credit on the basis of sex, marital status, race, color, religion, national origin, or age. The Act requires the creditor within thirty days after receipt of an application for credit to notify the applicant of action taken and to provide specific reasons for a denial of credit. The Act is administered and enforced by the Federal Reserve Board.

Disclosure Requirements

The FCCPA has superseded State disclosure requirements relating to credit terms for both loans and sales. Federal disclosure standards must be complied with in every State except those specifically exempted by the Federal Reserve Board. Such an exemption is only made if the State disclosure requirements are substantially the same as the Federal requirements, and enforcement is assured. The Federal Act does not eliminate the necessity for creditor compliance with State requirements not covered by, or more stringent than, the requirements of the FCCPA.

A creditor is required, under both State and Federal statutes, to provide certain information about contract terms to the consumer before he formally incurs the obligation. This information must be provided in a written statement presented to the consumer. Generally, disclosure is associated with the cost of credit, i.e., interest or sales finance charges. An important requirement in the FCCPA is that sales finance and interest rates must be quoted in terms of annual percentage rate (APR) and must be calculated on a uniform basis.

In addition to the cost of the credit, a creditor must inform the consumer who is opening a revolving credit account as to when the finance chage is imposed and how it is computed, what other charges may be imposed, and whether a security interest is retained or acquired by the creditor. The creditor is also required to provide a statement of account for each billing period. As to non-revolving credit, the creditor must provide the consumer with information about the total amount financed, the number, amount and due date of installments, delinquency charges, and a description of the security, if any.

In 1975 the Fair Credit Billing Act went into effect to ameliorate some of the problems and abuses associated with billing errors. The Act established procedures for the consumer to follow in making complaints about specified errors in billing and requires the creditor to explain or correct such errors. Billing errors are defined to include: (1) extensions of credit that were never made or were not made in the amount indicated on the billing statement; (2) undelivered or unaccepted goods or services; (3) incorrect recordation of payments or credits; and (4) accounting or computational errors. Until the creditor responds to the complaint, it may not (1) take any action to collect the disputed amount, (2) restrict the use of an open end credit account

because the disputed amount is unpaid, or (3) report the disputed amount as delinquent.

In 1974 Congress enacted the Real Estate Settlement Procedures Act (RESPA) in order to provide consumers who purchase a home with greater and more timely information on the nature and costs of the settlement process and with protection from unnecessarily high settlement charges. The Act applies to all federally related mortgages and requires advance disclosure to home buyers and sellers of all settlement costs including attorney fees, credit reports, and title insurance. RESPA prohibits kickbacks and referral fees and limits the amount home buyers are required to place in escrow accounts to insure payment of real estate taxes and insurance. The Act is administered and enforced by the Secretary of Housing and Urban Development.

Contract Terms

Consumer credit is marketed on a mass basis. Contract documents are frequently printed forms containing blank spaces to be filled in by the creditor. These blank spaces relate to matters usually negotiated at the time of the credit extension. Standardization and uniformity of contract terms facilitate transfer of the rights of the creditor, in most situations a seller, to a third party which is usually a bank or finance company.

Practically all of the States impose statutory ceilings on the amount that may be charged for the extension of consumer credit. The rate maximums imposed are ceiling rates.

Statutes regulating rates also specify what other charges may be made. For example, charges for insurance, official fees, and taxes are usually not considered part of the finance charge. Charges that are incidental to the extension of credit are usually considered part of the finance charge, e. g., a service charge or commission for extending credit. Any charge that does not qualify as an authorized additional charge is treated as part of the finance charge and subject to the statutory rate ceiling. Other special permitted charges include delinquency and default charges usually limited to five percent of the amount of the late installment, charges incurred in connection with storing and repairing repossessed goods for sale, reasonable attorney's fees for a lawyer who is not a salaried employee of the creditor, and court costs.

Most statutes require a creditor to permit the debtor to pay his obligation in full at any time prior to the maturity date of the final installment. In case the interest charge over the period of the loan was computed in advance and added to the principal of the loan, upon making pre-payment in full the debtor is entitled to a refund of an amount representing the interest portion of the note that is unearned by reason of the pre-payment. When interest is computed at the time of each payment on the basis of the then outstanding principal balance, no refund is necessary because no interest has been collected in advance.

Aside from provisions relating to cost, the balance of a credit contract deals with the terms of repayment and the remedies of the creditor if payments are delinquent. Usually, payments must be periodic and substantially equal in amount. Balloon payments (e.g., where the monthly installments, for example, are $50 and the final installment is $1,000) may be prohibited or, if not prohibited, the creditor may be required to refinance the loan at the same rate and with installments in the same amount as the original loan without penalty to the borrower.

Situations have arisen in which consumer purchase transactions have been financed in such manner that the purchaser is legally obligated to make full payment of the price to a third party, although the dealer from whom he bought the goods had committed fraud or the goods were defective. This occurs when the purchaser executes and delivers to the seller his negotiable promissory note which the seller negotiates to a holder in due course, a third party who purchases the note for value, in good faith, and without notice that it is overdue or of any defenses or claims to it. The buyer's defense that the goods were defective or that the seller had committed fraud, although valid against the seller, was not valid against a holder in due course of the note.

The Federal Trade Commission, in order to correct this situation by preserving and making available claims and defenses of consumer buyers and borrowers against holders in due course, amended its Trade Regulation Rules by adopting a rule, effective May 14, 1976, which limits the rights of a holder in due course of an instrument which evidences a debt arising out of a consumer credit contract. The rule applies to sellers and lessors of goods, and defines consumer credit contracts in terms which include negotiable instruments. A discussion of the rule is in Chapter 28.

A similar rule applies to credit card issuers under the Fair Credit Billing Act. The Act preserves consumers defenses against the issuer provided the consumer has made a good faith attempt to resolve the dispute with the seller, but only if (1) the seller is controlled by the issuer or under common control with the issuer; or (2) the card issuer included the seller's promotional literature in the monthly billing statement sent to the card holder; or (3) the sale involves more than $50 and the consumer's billing address is in the same state as, or within 100 miles of, the seller's place of business.

The FCCPA limits the card holder's liability for unauthorized use of a credit card to $50. The card issuer may collect up to that amount for unauthorized use only if (1) the card has been accepted; (2) the issuer has furnished adequate notice of potential liability to the cardholder; (3) the issuer has provided the cardholder with a statement of the means by which the card issuer may be notified of the loss or theft of the credit card; (4) the unauthorized use occurs before the card holder has notified the card issuer of the loss or theft; and (5) the card issuer has provided a method by which the user can be identified as the person authorized to use the card.

Fair Reportage

Since the extension of credit to consumers is usually made only after an investigation into the consumer's credit worthiness, it is essential that the information upon which such decisions are made is accurate and current. To this end, Congress enacted the Fair Credit Reporting Act in 1970, which applies to consumer reports used for purposes of securing employment, insurance, and credit. The Act prohibits the inclusion in consumer reports of obsolete information specifically listed in the statute. The Act requires that a consumer be notified in writing in advance that an investigative report may be made. The consumer may request information regarding the nature and substance of all information in the consumer reporting agency's files, the source of the information, and the names of all recipients of the consumer reports furnished for employment purposes within the preceding two years and for other purposes within the preceding six months.

If the consumer notifies the reporting agency of disagreement with the accuracy and completeness of information in the file, the agency must then re-investigate the matter within a reasonable period of time unless the complaint is frivolous or irrelevant. If re-investigation proves that the information is inaccurate, it must be promptly deleted. If after re-investigation the dispute remains unresolved, the consumer may submit a brief statement setting forth the nature of the dispute which must be incorporated into the report.

Creditors' Remedies

Of primary concern to creditors, once credit is granted, are their rights if the debtor defaults or is tardy in payment. When the credit charge is precomputed, the creditor may impose a delinquency charge for late payments, subject to statutory limits for such charges. If instead of being delinquent, the consumer defaults, the creditor may declare the entire balance of the debt immediately due and payable and sue on the debt. What other courses of action are open to him depend upon his security. Various security provisions included in consumer credit contracts are: a co-signer, an assignment of wages, a security interest in the goods sold, a security interest in other real or personal property of the debtor, and a confession of judgment clause.

Many consumer credit arrangements contain a provision in which the consumer assigns his future wages to the creditor in the event of default. Wage assignments are prohibited in some States for certain types of transactions, such as credit sales. In most States and under the FCCPA, a limitation is imposed on the amount that may be deducted from an individual's wages during any pay period. In addition, the FCCPA prohibits an employer from discharging an employee solely because of the exercise of a creditor's right by notice to the employer under an assignment of wages in connection with any one debt.

Even where assignments of wages are prohibited, the creditor may still reach the wages of the consumer through garnishment. However, garnishment is only available in a court proceeding to enforce the collection of a judgment. The FCCPA and State statutes contain exemption provisions which limit the amount of wages subject to garnishment.

In the case of sales credit, the seller may retain a security interest in the goods sold. Many States impose restrictions on other security the creditor may obtain.

A confession of judgment clause in a consumer contract permits the creditor to obtain without notice a judgment against the debtor for the amount claimed to be owing, and then proceed to enforce the judgment against the wages and property of the debtor. Certain State statutes invalidate confession of judgment clauses in promissory notes and contracts. Other States allow them and prescribe a procedure for the entry of judgments by confession, including the re-opening of such judgments with leave given to the defendant to appear and defend.

In 1977 Congress enacted the Fair Debt Collection Practices Act in order to eliminate abusive, deceptive, and unfair practices employed in collecting consumer debts by debt collection agencies. The Act does not apply to the creditors themselves. The Act provides that any debt collector who communicates with a person other than the consumer for the purpose of acquiring information about the location of the consumer may not state that the consumer owes any debt. Moreover, the Act prohibits a number of abusive collection practices including: (1) communication with the consumer at unusual or inconvenient hours, (2) communication with the consumer if he is represented by an attorney; (3) conduct that is harrassing, oppressive, or abusive such as threats of violence or obscene language; (4) false, deceptive, or misleading representation or means; and (5) any unfair or unconscionable means to collect any debt. The Act is enforced by the Federal Trade Commission and consumers may recover damages from the collection agency for violations of the Act.

CONSUMER HEALTH AND SAFETY

In 1972 Congress enacted the Consumer Product Safety Act, the purposes of which, as expressly stated in Section 2(b) of the Act, are:

1. to protect the public against unreasonable risks of injury associated with consumer products;
2. to assist consumers in evaluating the comparative safety of consumer products;
3. to develop uniform safety standards for consumer products and to minimize conflicting State and local regulations; and
4. to promote research and investigation into the causes and prevention of product-related deaths, illnesses, and injuries.

The Act creates an independent regulatory federal agency, the Consumer Product Safety Commission, consisting of five Commissioners, to carry out the Act's mandate.

There are also a number of Federal statutes that impose labelling and packaging requirements designed to provide the consumer with accurate information and adequate warnings about specific products. Such statutes include the Fair Packaging and Labeling Act, the Food, Drugs and Cosmetic Act, the Fur Products Labeling Act, the Wholesome Meat Act, the Flammable Fabrics Act, the Cigarette Labeling and Advertising Act, the Wool Products Labeling Act, the Wholesome Poultry Products Act, the Special Packaging of Household Substances for the Protection of Children Act, and the Refrigerator Safety Act.

Cases

Deceptive Trade Practices:
Corrective Advertising
Ordered by FTC

WARNER-LAMBERT CO. v. F.T.C.

(1977, C.A.D.C.) 562 F.2d 749

J. SKELLY WRIGHT, J.

The Warner-Lambert Company peti-

tions for review of an order of the Federal Trade Commission requiring it to cease and desist from advertising that its product, Listerine Antiseptic mouthwash, prevents, cures, or alleviates the common cold. The FTC order further requires Warner-Lambert to disclose in future Listerine advertisements that: "Contrary to prior advertising, Listerine will not help prevent colds

or sore throats or lessen their severity."
We affirm but modify the order to delete
from the required disclosure the phrase
"Contrary to prior advertising."

Background
The order under review represents the culmination of a proceeding begun in 1972, when the FTC issued a complaint charging petitioner with violation of Section 5(a)(1) of the Federal Trade Commission Act by misrepresenting the efficacy of Listerine against the common cold.

Listerine has been on the market since 1879. Its formula has never changed. Ever since its introduction it has been represented as being beneficial in certain respects for colds, cold symptoms, and sore throats. Direct advertising to the consumer, including the cold claims as well as others, began in 1921.

* * *

The Commission's Power
Petitioner contends that even if its advertising claims in the past were false, the portion of the Commission's order requiring "corrective advertising" exceeds the Commission's statutory power. The argument is based upon a literal reading of Section 5 of the Federal Trade Commission Act, which authorizes the Commission to issue "cease and desist" orders against violators and does not expressly mention any other remedies. The Commission's position, on the other hand, is that the affirmative disclosure that Listerine will not prevent colds or lessen their severity is absolutely necessary to give effect to the prospective cease and desist order; a hundred years of false cold claims have built up a large reservoir of erroneous consumer belief which would persist, unless corrected, long after petitioner ceased making the claims.

The need for the corrective advertising remedy and its appropriateness in this case are important issues which we will explore *infra*. But the threshold question is whether the Commission has the authority to issue such an order. We hold that it does.

Petitioner's narrow reading of Section 5 was at one time shared by the Supreme Court. In FTC v. Eastman Kodak Co. the Court held that the Commission's authority did not exceed that expressly conferred by statute. The Commission has not, the Court said, "been delegated the authority of a court of equity."

But the modern view is very different. In 1963 the Court ruled that the Civil Aeronautics Board has authority to order divestiture in addition to ordering cessation of unfair methods of competition by air carriers. The CAB statute, like Section 5, spoke only of the authority to issue cease and desist orders, but the Court said, "We do not read the Act so restrictively. * * * [W]here the problem lies within the purview of the Board, * * * Congress must have intended to give it authority that was ample to deal with the evil at hand." The Court continued, "Authority to mold administrative decrees is indeed like the authority of courts to frame injunctive decrees * * *. [The] power to order divestiture need not be explicitly included in the powers of an administrative agency to be part of its arsenal of authority * * *."

Later, in FTC v. Dean Foods Co., the Court applied Pan American to the Federal Trade Commission. In upholding the Commission's power to seek a preliminary injunction against a proposed merger, the Court held that it was not necessary to find express statutory authority for the power. Rather, the Court concluded, "It would stultify congressional purpose to say that the Commission did not have the * * * power * * *. * * * Such ancillary powers have always been treated as essential to the effective discharge of the Commission's responsibilities."

Thus it is clear that the Commission has the power to shape remedies which go beyond the simple cease and desist order. Our next inquiry must be whether a corrective advertising order is for any reason outside the range of permissible remedies.

Petitioner and *amici curiae* argue that it is because (1) legislative history precludes it, (2) it impinges on the First Amendment, and (3) it has never been approved by any court.

Legislative History. Petitioner relies on the legislative history of the 1914 Federal Trade Commission Act and the Wheeler-Lea amendments to it in 1938 for the proposition that corrective advertising was not contemplated. In 1914 and in 1938 Congress chose not to authorize such remedies as criminal penalties, treble damages, or civil penalties, but that fact does not dispose of the question of corrective advertising.

Petitioner's reliance on the legislative history of the 1975 amendments to the Act is also misplaced. The amendments added a new Section 19 to the Act authorizing the Commission to bring suits in federal District Courts to redress injury to consumers resulting from a deceptive practice. The section authorizes the court to grant such relief as it "finds necessary to redress injury to consumers or other persons, partnerships, and corporations resulting from the rule violation or the unfair or deceptive act or practice," including, but not limited to,

rescission or reformation of contracts, the refund of money or return of property, the payment of damages, and public notification respecting the rule violation or the unfair or deceptive act or practice * * *.

* * *

The First Amendment. Petitioner * * * further contends that corrective advertising is not a permissible remedy because it trenches on the First Amendment. Petitioner is correct that this triggers a special responsibility on the Commission to order corrective advertising only if the restriction inherent in its order is no greater than necessary to serve the interest involved. But this goes to the appropriateness of the order in this case.

* * *

The Supreme Court [has] expressly noted that the First Amendment presents "no obstacle" to government regulation of false or misleading advertising. The First Amendment, the Court said, as we construe it today, does not prohibit the State from insuring that the stream of commercial information flow[s] cleanly as well as freely.

* * *

Precedents. According to petitioner, "The first reference to corrective advertising in Commission decisions occurred in 1970, nearly fifty years and untold number of false advertising cases after passage of the Act." In petitioner's view, the late emergence of this "newly discovered" remedy is itself evidence that it is beyond the Commission's authority. This argument fails on two counts. First the fact that an agency has not asserted a power over a period of years is not proof that the agency lacks such power. Second, and more importantly, we are not convinced that the corrective advertising remedy is really such an innovation. The label may be newly coined, but the concept is well established. It is simply that under certain circumstances an advertiser may be required to make affirmative disclosure of unfavorable facts.

* * *

The Remedy

Having established that the Commission does have the power to order corrective advertising in appropriate cases, it remains to consider whether use of the remedy against Listerine is warranted and equitable. We have concluded that part 3 of the order should be modified to delete the phrase "Contrary to prior advertising." With that modification, we approve the order.

Our role in reviewing the remedy is limited. The Supreme Court has set forth the standard:

The Commission is the expert body to determine what remedy is necessary to eliminate the unfair or deceptive trade practices which have been disclosed. It has wide latitude for judgment and the courts will not interfere except where the remedy selected has no reasonable relation to the unlawful practices found to exist.

The Commission has adopted the following standard for the imposition of corrective advertising:

[I]f a deceptive advertisement has played a substantial role in creating or reinforcing in the public's mind a false and material belief which lives on after the false advertising ceases, there is clear and continuing injury to competition and to the consuming public as consumers continue to make purchasing decisions based on the false belief. Since this injury cannot be averted by merely requiring respondent to cease disseminating the advertisement, we may appropriately order respondent to take affirmative action designed to terminate the otherwise continuing ill effects of the advertisement.

We think this standard is entirely reasonable.

* * *

Accordingly, the order, as modified, is Affirmed.

*State Deceptive
Trade Practices Act*

SMITH v. BALDWIN

(1980, Texas) 611 S.W.2d 611

STEAKLEY, J.

On September 9, 1976, Alan Baldwin, d/b/a/ Alan Baldwin, Builder, contracted to build a house for Roland Smith. On the same day, Smith executed to Baldwin a promissory note for $31,300, payable within 180 days, Baldwin agreeing to pay all interim interest. Baldwin assigned the note to Mutual Savings Institution (Mutual) in order to obtain interim financing. The permanent financing was to be supplied by the Veteran's Administration (V.A.) which required a final V.A. inspection report prior to approval of the permanent loan. Smith began moving into the house prior to the date scheduled for completion. On March 28, 1977, the house remained incompleted and unapproved by the V.A. and Smith, who had previously occupied the house, ordered Baldwin to leave the premises. In October, 1977, Baldwin attempted to obtain V.A. approval but this was refused on the basis of construction defects and a final V.A. inspection report and approval was not obtained.

Baldwin brought suit against Smith on the contract and the note, seeking the foreclosure of his lien and claiming additional expenses in construction of the house, and for interference with its completion. Smith generally denied and counterclaimed under the [Texas] Deceptive Trade Practices Act. He alleged in his Fourth Amended Cross-Action that, among other things, Baldwin failed to obtain a V.A. inspection compliance report.

* * *

After a non-jury trial, the trial court rendered a * * * judgment against Baldwin. On the counterclaim of Smith, the court awarded him a recovery of $4,400 as actual damages sustained under the DTPA which consisted of the sum of $1,500 as the cost of remedying the defects in the house and the additional sum of $2,900 in interim interest, included in Smith's permanent financing note. The trial court trebled damages, awarding a total sum of $13,200. The court further awarded Smith the sum of $10,000 as reasonable attorney's fees and additional attorney's fees in the sum of $2,500 in the event of an appeal through the Court of Civil Appeals, the sum of $1,000 in the event of the filing of an application for writ of error, and a final sum of $500 in the event writ of error is granted.

The trial court filed findings of fact describing numerous construction defects. Further, that:

Baldwin has never obtained a final inspection report which shows full and final compliance with V.A. requirements.

The court found, however, that as a matter of fact the contract was substantially performed and this conclusion has not been challenged by Smith.

Upon appeal by Baldwin the Court of Civil Appeals held that the unchallenged finding of substantial performance precluded the application of the DTPA. The court reversed the judgment of the trial court that had awarded Smith treble damages for interim interest and attorney's fees, and treble damages for the cost of correcting the defects in the house, and reform the judgment so as to award Smith the sum of $1,500 as the cost of remedying the defects in the house. 586 S.W.2d 624. We reverse the judgment below and render judgment as later set forth.

Smith, our petitioner, contends that substantial performance of a contract does not preclude liability under § 17.46(b)(7) of the DTPA which states that the term "false, misleading or deceptive acts or practices" includes:

(7) representing that goods or services are of a particular standard, quality, or grade, or that goods are of a particular style or model, if they are of another.

Baldwin argues that to hold builders liable for treble damages and attorney's fees notwithstanding a substantial performance of the building contract places an unreasonable burden on the builder. Whether this is so or not, the Legislature in the DTPA did not provide that substantial performance is a defense to an action under the statute and directed further that "This subchapter shall be liberally construed and applied to promote its underlying purposes, which are to protect consumers against false, misleading, and deceptive business practices, unconscionable actions and breaches of warranty and to provide efficient

and economical procedures to secure such protection." § 17.44.

It is our view that the doctrine of substantial performance is not relevant to the statutory cause of action under the DTPA asserted by Smith in his counterclaim. The portions of Smith's Fourth Amended Cross-Action alleging that Baldwin had violated the DTPA by misrepresenting that the house he would build for Smith would meet the requirements for a final V.A. inspection compliance report are distinct from the pleadings of Smith complaining of Baldwin's failure to fulfill his contractual commitments. The judgment of the trial court awarding damages to Smith under the DTPA is not based on findings of a contract breach; the judgment is based on the misrepresentations of Baldwin as to the quality and standard of the goods and services in building the house, i.e., that the house when completed would qualify for V.A. approval so that Smith could obtain permanent financing.

Baldwin further argues that apart from the substantial performance defense, there has been no violation of § 17.46(b)(7) because: (1) Section 17.46(b)(7) is applicable to representations of quality of *existing* goods or services, not to representations of quality concerning goods or services not yet in existence; (2) false representations concerning future goods fall within subdivision (9), which requires intent; and (3) if subdivision (7) is applicable to the condition of goods and services in the future, there is a requirement of intent not to provide them as represented.

Section 17.46(b) declares that nine acts constitute false, deceptive or misleading practices with respect to goods and services. The thrust of Baldwin's argument is that only two, subdivisions (9) and (10), are applicable to representations made concerning the *future* quality of goods or services. These subdivisions provide:

(9) advertising goods or services with intent not to sell them as advertised; (10) advertising

goods or services with intent not to supply a reasonable expectable public demand unless the advertisements disclosed a limitation of quality;

It is noted that these subdivisions expressly require an intent not to provide goods and services as advertised and it is Baldwin's position that these are applicable here and that there is no evidence that he did not intend to provide the goods and services he promised.

Black's Law Dictionary (5th ed. 1979) defines the verb "advertise" as follows:

Advertise. To advise, announce, apprise, command, give notice of, inform, make known, publish. On call to the public attention by any means whatsoever. Any oral, written, or graphic statement made by the seller in any manner in connection with the solicitation of business and includes, without limitation because of enumeration, statements and representations made in a newspaper or other publication or on radio or television or contained in any notice, handbill, sign, catalog, or letter, or printed on or contained in any tag or label attached to or accompanying any merchandise.

[Citations.]

It is apparent that a primary purpose of subdivisions (9) and (10) is the prevention of "bait advertising," a practice by which a seller seeks to attract customers through advertising products at low prices which he does not intend to sell in more than nominal amounts. The customers who respond to the advertisement are switched to another product or service, at a higher price. [Citations.]

There is nothing in the record which suggests that Baldwin's representations involved advertising, much less "bait advertising."

* * *

Excluding the provisions on advertising previously discussed, there are seven other subdivisions which declare unlawful specific practices dealing with goods and services. Goods and services are defined by the DTPA:

§ 17.45. Definitions

As used in this subchapter:

(1) "Goods" means tangible chattels or real property purchased or leased for use.

(2) "Services" means work, labor, or service purchased or leased for use, for other than commercial or business use, including services furnished in connection with the sale or repair of goods.

There is no language in these definitions or in § 17.46(b) to indicate that the provisions were intended to be limited to existing goods and services. Goods are frequently scheduled to be manufactured at a later date and service contracts routinely involve future performance. It would be contradictory to the explicit legislative intent expressed in § 17.44 of the DTPA—see Woods v. Littleton, 554 S.W.2d 662 (Tex.1972)—to hold that consumers who have been misled by misrepresentations on future quality are, not entitled to protection from the specific provisions on goods and services, but instead must seek recovery under the general language of § 17.46(a).

[Citations.]

* * *

Subdivision (7) contains no requirement of proof of intent. By contrast, this is found in subdivisions (9) and (10), and the words "knowingly" and "fraudulently" appear in subdivisions (13) and (17) respectively. The Legislature could readily have imposed an intent requirement in subdivision (7) but did not do so. [Citation.] When the Legislature has carefully employed a term in one section of a statute, and has excluded it in another, it should not be implied where excluded. [Citations.]

* * *

[Judgment reversed and a new judgment entered in favor of Smith.]

Federal Truth in Lending Act

CHAPMAN v. MILLER

(1978, Tex.App.) 575 S.W.2d 581

KEITH, J.

Defendant below appeals from an adverse judgment rendered in a bench trial of a suit brought under * * * the Federal Truth in Lending Act and Regulation Z promulgated thereunder.

Plaintiff entered into a retail installment contract with Don Chapman Motor Sales for the purchase of a used automobile. The contract provided for a down payment of $200, six weekly payments of $25, and eighteen monthly payments of $70.47. Plaintiff made the down payment and the six weekly payments without too much difficulty. The next five monthly installments were accepted even though they were late; but, when the March 1975 payment became overdue, defendant repossessed the car notifying plaintiff that the entire balance was then due and payable. When plaintiff did not pay the balance due, defendant sold the car and determined that plaintiff was entitled to a refund of $19.69. Before the refund was made, plaintiff brought this suit alleging several violations of the cited statute and regulation. The trial court agreed and awarded damages, plus attorney's fees, and the appeal is predicated upon nineteen points of error.

Violation of Federal Regulation. In point of error three, defendant complains that the trial court erred in conclusion of law number 14 by holding that his contract violated 12 C.F.R. § 226.8(a)(1) [Regulation Z] because the description of the security interest is not on the same side of the paper as the buyer's signature.

The cited section requires that all disclosures which must be made thereunder be made together on:

(1) The note or other instrument evidencing the obligation on the same side of the page and above

or adjacent to the place for the customer's signature; or (2) One side of a separate statement which identifies the transaction.

Defendant chose to make his disclosures on the retail credit contract. However, he failed to put all the required disclosures on one side of the contract above plaintiff's signature, *i.e.*, the description of his retained security interest is located on the reverse side of the contract. Relying upon the language found in Southwestern Inv. Co. v. Mannix, 557 S.W.2d 755, 765–766 (Tex.1977), we are of the opinion that the trial court correctly found a violation of Regulation Z.

Defendant claims that he did not have to make all required disclosures on the front side because of the Interpretive Ruling of the Federal Reserve Board, 12 C.F.R. § 226.801, which allows the required disclosures to be made on both sides of a combination contract and security agreement. This interpretation, however, has a caveat:

Provided, That the amount of the finance charge and the annual percentage rate shall appear on the face of the document, and, if the reverse side is used, the printing on both sides of the document shall be equally clear and conspicuous, both sides shall contain the statement, "NOTICE: See other side for important information," *and the place for the customer's signature shall be provided following the full content of the document.*

The space provided for the plaintiff's signature is on the front page of the contract only and does not follow "the full content of the document." Therefore, defendant has violated Section 226.801. [Citation.]

Defendant rationalizes that his notices at the top and bottom of the front side allow him to incorporate by reference all disclosures and conditions from the reverse side into the front side above the signature. The notice at the top of the page provides:

BUYER HAS ELECTED TO PURCHASE FROM SELLER SUBJECT TO THE TERMS AND

CONDITIONS AS SET FORTH BELOW AND UPON THE REVERSE SIDE HEREOF, THE FOLLOWING DESCRIBED MOTOR VEHICLE, WHICH BUYER HAS THOROUGHLY INSPECTED AND WHICH MEETS WITH BUYER'S APPROVAL IN ALL RESPECTS:

The notice at the bottom of the page provides: "NOTICE: SEE REVERSE SIDE FOR IMPORTANT INFORMATION, ALL TERMS OF WHICH ARE HEREBY INCORPORATED BY REFERENCE." However, this notice was below plaintiff's signature.

The Truth in Lending Act was enacted and Regulation Z was issued "to assure a meaningful disclosure of credit terms so that the consumer will be able to compare more readily the various credit terms available to him and avoid the uninformed use of credit * * *." [Citations.] Their provisions are detailed and explicit.

As noted in Charles v. Drauss Co., Ltd., 572 F.2d 544, 546 (5th Cir. 1978):

Moreover, liability flows from even minute deviations from the requirements of the statute and of Regulation Z. The statute aims to assure a meaningful disclosure of credit terms so that consumers may shop comparatively for credit * * *. [Citations.] Therefore, the defendant may not escape liability by means of incorporation by reference. The line provided for plaintiff's signature should have been at the end of the contract; her signature so located would show that she knew to read the entire contract—front and back—for all important provisions before signing it. The fact that she did not read any of the contract is immaterial.

* * *

Finance Charge and Statutory Penalty. In defendant's point of error sixteen and plaintiff's crosspoint one, both parties contend that the trial court erred in conclusion of law number 16 by holding that the finance charge in this transaction was $326.99. Defendant claims the finance charge was $199.99, while plaintiff claims it was $423.46. We disagree with both parties.

Section 226.4 of 12 C.F.R. gives instructions on how to determine a finance charge. Applying these rules to the contract before us, we hold that the finance charge is the sum of the time price differential and the official fees, or $249.04. We are not required to include the premiums for property insurance, credit life insurance, or health and accident insurance in the finance charge because defendant has satisfied the caveats of §§ 226.4(a)(5) and (6).

In his point of error number seventeen, defendant contends the trial court erred in conclusion of law number 15 by awarding damages of $653.98 for violations of Regulation Z. We agree. The applicable statutory penalty set out in 15 U.S.C.A. § 1640(a) includes twice the amount of the finance charge, plus court costs and reasonable attorney's fees. [Citations.] In the present case, the proper statutory penalty would have been twice of $249.04, or $498.08, plus court costs and reasonable attorney's fees. Point of error seventeen is sustained.

* * *

The judgment of the trial court is reformed so that the plaintiff will recover of and from the defendant the sum of $498.08 for the violation of Regulation Z instead of the excessive amount of $652.98 mistakenly awarded by the trial court; and, as reformed, the judgment is Affirmed.

Problems

1. The FTC brings a deceptive trade practice action against Beneficial Finance Company based on Beneficial's use of its "instant tax refund" slogan. The FTC argues that Beneficial's advertising a tax refund loan or instant tax refund is deceptive in that the loan is not in any way

connected with a tax refund but is merely Beneficial's everyday loan based on the applicant's creditworthiness. Decision? If the FTC prevails, what relief is appropriate?

2. B borrows $1000 from L for one year. B agreed to pay L $200 in interest on the loan and to repay the loan in twelve monthly installments of $100. The contract which L provides and B signs specifies that the APR is 20%. B now contends that the contract violates the FCCPA. Decision?

3. A consumer entered into an agreement with Rent-It Corporation for the rental of a television set at a charge of $17 per week. The agreement also provided that if the renter chooses to rent the set for 78 consecutive weeks, title would be transferred. The consumer now contends that the agreement was really a sales agreement and not a lease and therefore was a credit sale subject to the Truth-in-Lending Act.

4. Central Adjustment Bureau allegedly threatened Consumer with lawsuit, service at his office, and attachment and sale of the property in order to collect a debt when it did not intend to do so and when it did not have the authority to commence litigation. On some notices sent to consumer, Central failed to disclose that it was attempting to collect a debt. In addition, Central, it is charged, sent dunning notices that purported to be from attorneys but were written, signed, and sent by Central. Decision?

5. The Giant Development Company undertakes a massive real estate venture to sell 9,000 one-acre unimproved lots in Utah. The company advertises the project nationally. A, a resident of New York, learns of the opportunity and requests information about the project. The company provides A with a small advertising brochure, that is devoid of information about the developer and the land. The brochure consists of vague descriptions of the joys of home ownership and nothing else. A purchases a lot. Two weeks after entering into the agreement,

A wishes to rescind the contract. Will A prevail?

6. Mrs. X applies for a credit card from Exxon, but is refused credit. Mrs. X is bewildered as to why she was turned down. What are her legal rights in this situation?

7. On a beautiful Saturday in October A decides to take the twenty-mile ride from her home in New Jersey into New York City in order to do some shopping. A finds that B Retail Sales Inc. has a terrific sale on television sets and decides to surprise her husband with a new color T.V. She purchases the set from B on her American Express credit card for $450. When the set is delivered, A discovered that it does not work. B refuses to repair or replace it or to refund the money. A therefore refuses to pay American Express for the television. American Express brings this suit against A. Decision?

8. F finds A's wallet, which contains numerous credit cards and A's identification. By using A's identification and Visa Card, F goes on a shopping spree and runs up $5000 in charges. A does not discover that he has lost his wallet until the following day when he promptly notifies his Visa bank. How much can Visa collect from A?

9. B applies to N National Bank for a loan. Prior to granting the loan, N requests that C Credit Agency provide it with a credit report on B. C reports that three years previously B had embezzled money from his employer. Based on this report, N rejects B's loan application.
a. B demands to know why, but N refuses to divulge the information arguing that it is privileged. Is B entitled to the information?
b. Assume that B obtains the information and alleges that it is inaccurate. What recourse does B have?

10. A owed B $400, which was long overdue. B decided to hire the C Collection Agency to collect the debt. After writing several letters to A, C began a campaign of calling A every hour on the hour between the hours of 8 a.m. and 8 p.m. both at work and at home. A brings suit against C and B for harassment. Decision?

Chapter

44

INTRODUCTION TO PROPERTY; PERSONAL PROPERTY

The ownership of property in the United States occupies a unique status because of the protection expressly granted it by the Federal constitution as well as by most State constitutions. The fifth amendment to the Federal constitution provides, in part, that "No person shall be * * * deprived of life, liberty, or property, without due process of law; nor shall private property be taken for public use, without just compensation." A similar injunction is contained in the fourteenth amendment: "No State shall * * * deprive any person of life, liberty, or property, without due process of law." This protection afforded to property owners is subject, however to police power regulation for the public good.

In spite of the unique place accorded property by the constitution, uncertainties arise because the term "property" is not easily defined. This should not be surprising: the term "property" includes almost every *right*, exclusive of personal liberty, that the law will protect. Property is valuable only because our law provides that certain con-sequences follow from the ownership of it. The right to use the property, to sell it, and to say to whom it shall pass on the death of the owner, are all included within the term "property." In this sense, property is not so much a thing capable of being reduced to physical possession as it is an interest, or group of interests, that is legally protected.

Thus, when a person speaks of "owning property" he may have two separate ideas in mind: (1) the physical *thing* itself, as when a home owner says, "I just bought a house in Oakland," meaning complete ownership of a physically identifiable parcel of land and structure; or (2) a right or interest in the physical object, as, for example, with respect to land, a tenant under a lease has a property interest in the leased land; the holder of a mortgage (mortgagee) has a property interest in the mortgaged premises although legal ownership is in the mortgagor; and a person who has a right-of-way over land of another has a property interest in the land although he does not "own" the land.

KINDS OF PROPERTY

Tangible and Intangible Property

A 40-acre farm, a chair, and household pet are *tangible* property. The group of rights or interests referred to as "title" or "ownership" are embodied in each of these physical objects. On the other hand, a stock certificate, a promissory note, and a deed granting X a right-of-way over the land of Y are *intangible* property. Each is a paper which represents and stands for certain rights that are not capable of reduction to physical possession, but have a *legal* reality in the sense that they will be protected.

The same item may be the object of both tangible and intangible property rights. Suppose A purchases a book published by B. On the first page, there is the statement "Copyright 1982, by B." A owns the volume he purchased. He has the right to exclusive physical possession and use of that particular copy. It is a *tangible* piece of property of which he is the owner. B, however, has the exclusive right to publish copies of the book. This is a right granted him by the copyright laws. The courts will protect this *intangible* property of B as well as A's right to the particular volume.

This distinction between "tangible" and "intangible" property can have significant consequences. The courts have frequently been called upon to decide the scope of retail sales tax laws levying taxes upon "tangible personal property." For example, several States have exempted the sale of gas and electrical energy from these laws because they are not "tangible" personal property. Other States have included both within the definition of taxable property.

Real and Personal Property

The most significant practical distinction between types of property is the classification into things real and things personal. A simple definition would be to say the land

and all interests therein are real property and every other thing or interest identified as property is personal.

For most purposes this easy description is adequate although certain physical objects that are personal property under most circumstances may, because of their attachment to land or their use in connection with land, become real property. Although this volatile characteristic may be important in certain relations such as that existing between landlord and tenant, most property always remains either real or personal.

INCIDENTS OF PROPERTY OWNERSHIP

The importance of the distinction between real and personal property stems primarily from very practical legal consequences that follow from the distinction. Some of these consequences are:

Transfer of Property During Life

As will be explained hereafter, the transfer of real property during life can only be accomplished by certain formalities, including the execution and delivery of a written instrument known as a deed. Personal property, on the other hand, may be transferred with relative simplicity and informality.

Devolution of Title on Death of Owner

In many States, if a person dies without a will, title to his real property passes directly to whomever the law declares to be his heirs while title to his personal property passes to his personal representative who, in turn, must distribute it as the law directs.

A widow's right to dower in her deceased husband's property was, by the common law, limited to a specified interest in his *real* property. Even where the old right of dower has been abolished or modified, the widow may be allowed a different percentage of the real property than of the personal property of her deceased husband. For a more detailed discussion of this topic see Chapter 51.

Taxation

Most States levy an ad valorum tax on the ownership of both real property and personal property. However, the applicable tax rate will be dependent on whether the property is classified as real property or personal property.

The Applicable Law

Although all laws in the fifty States are subject to the provisions of the Federal constitution, there is ample room for variation among the States as to the rules governing rights in property within the constitutional limits referred to at the beginning of this chapter. The governing law with respect to real property is the law of its location or situs whereas the governing law with respect to personal property is frequently the domicile of the owner, regardless of where the personal property is located. Thus, suppose A, a resident of Illinois, dies without a will, leaving real estate in Indiana and stocks and bonds in Wisconsin. Each State has its own laws prescribing who shall receive what interest in the estate of a person who dies without a will. The Indiana real estate will be distributed in accordance with the laws of Indiana, not of Illinois. The stocks and bonds, however, will be distributed according to Illinois law, not the law of Wisconsin.

TRANSFER OF TITLE TO PERSONAL PROPERTY

Title to personal property is acquired and transferred with relative ease and with a minimum of formality. The facility with which personal property may be transferred

is required by the demands of a society based upon commercial necessities. Transactions in personal property are the principal activities of trade and industry.

The law pertaining to personal property has been largely codified. The Uniform Commercial Code includes the law of sales of goods (Article 2), the law governing the transfer and negotiation of commercial paper (Article 3), and of certificates of investment securities (Article 8).

Transfer of Title by Sale

By definition, a sale of personal property is a transfer of title to specified existing goods for a consideration known as the price. Title passes when the parties intend it to pass, and transfer of possession is not requisite to a transfer of title. For a discussion of this manner of transfer of title, refer to Chapter 21.

Transfer of Title by Gift

A gift is a transfer of property from one person to another without consideration. The lack of any consideration is the basic distinction between a gift and a contract. Since a gift involves no consideration or compensation, to be effective it must be completed by delivery of the gift. A gratuitous promise to make a gift is not binding.

Delivery. Delivery is absolutely necessary to a valid gift. The term "delivery" has a very special meaning including of course, but not limited to, manual transfer of the item to the recipient, or "donee," as he is called. There can be "delivery" of a gift sufficient to make it irrevocable if the item is turned over to a third person with instructions to give it to the donee. Frequently, an item, because of its size or location, is incapable of immediate manual delivery. In such case, an irrevocable gift may be effected by delivery of something symbolic of dominion over the item. This is referred to as constructive delivery. For example, if A declares that he gives an antique desk and all its contents to B and hands B the key to the desk, in many States a valid gift has been made.

Intent. The law is also clear that there must be an intent on the part of the donor to make a present gift of the property. Thus, if A leaves a packet of stocks and bonds with B, B may or may not acquire good title to them, depending upon whether A intended to make a gift of them or simply to place them in B's hands for safekeeping. A voluntary, uncompensated delivery with intent to give the recipient title immediately constitutes a gift. If these conditions are met, the donor has no further claim to the property.

It is possible for a person to make a gift of property while still retaining the right to the income therefrom during his life. By creation of a trust a person can make a valid present gift of shares of stock and, at the same time, reserve the right to receive the dividends therefrom during his life.

Inter Vivos Gifts and Gifts Causa Mortis. In most instances, a valid gift is made during lifetime and takes effect immediately and irrevocably upon the delivery of the property.

Sometimes a gift is made in apprehension or contemplation of death. This apprehension may arise from a serious illness or the expectation of impending peril. Such gifts are frequently referred to by their Latin name, *donatio causa mortis.* The principal distinction of a gift *causa mortis* is that it is revocable in the event that the would-be donor does not die as contemplated. If A, about to undergo a serious surgical operation, and believing that he will not survive, gives B his collection of Royal Doulton china, this is a gift *causa mortis,* and should A, effect a complete recovery, he can claim back his china.

Federal Tax Law Provisions. Under Federal law prior to January 1, 1977, gifts of property to any one person in any one year, not exceeding an aggregate value of $3,000, were exempt from gift tax. In addition, the law provided a lifetime gift tax exemption of $30,000 to every person which could be used in any manner, including charges against this exemption of the value of gifts made in excess of the annual exclusion. The donor was obligated to report all gifts made by him on a quarter-annual calendar basis, and to pay any gift tax due at that time.

The Tax Reform Act of 1976, effective January 1, 1977, eliminated the separate gift tax and estate tax rate schedule, the $30,000 lifetime gift tax exemption, the $60,000 estate tax deduction, and substituted in their place a new unified tax rate schedule and a new unified tax credit applicable to Federal gift and estate taxes. The unified tax credit was initially $30,000 for the year 1977 (although on gifts made prior to July 1, 1977, only $6,000 of the credit could be used), and increased in amount for each year thereafter until it reached $47,000 in 1981, which tax credit for that and succeeding years is equivalent to a deduction of $175,625.

The unified system lessens the permissible tax savings by making lifetime gifts. Under the Tax Reform Act of 1976, all taxable gifts made after December 31, 1976, are considered as part of the donor's gross estate for Federal estate tax purposes. It is still possible to reduce in some measure estate and gift taxes by systematic use of the annual gift tax exclusion. Gift splitting is also permitted under the 1976 Act, as it was under prior laws.

If gifts to a donee in any one year do not exceed the annual exclusion of $10,000, they are not subject to gift tax, and reduce the size of the donor's estate for Federal estate tax purposes upon his death.

Gifts in any one year to the same donee having a value in excess of $10,000 (other than gifts qualifying for the gift tax marital deduction) are subject to gift tax, and the amount of such gifts is treated as part of the estate of the donor for Federal estate tax purposes when he dies. Moreover, the amount of gift taxes paid by the donor on gifts made within three years prior to his death is also added back to his adjusted gross estate for Federal estate tax purposes.

A gift of income producing property reduces the aggregate amount of the tax on income received from the property after the date of the gift. Such gifts are sometimes made in order that the income tax may be payable by the donee, who may be a child of the donor and in a lower income tax bracket. The income tax is payable by the owner of the property at the time the income therefrom is received, except for taxpayers using the accrual basis of accounting.

In August, 1981, the 97th Congress passed a bill amending the federal tax laws which was promptly signed by President Reagan. Among the provisions of this statute, known as the Economic Recovery Tax Act of 1981 and effective January 1, 1982, are the following:

1. Exemption from both gift and estate tax of all transfers of money and property between spouses, namely, 100% tax-free marital deduction.
2. Exclusion of gift tax on all transfers of money and property not exceeding a total of $10,000 per recipient per year per donor. The amount of exclusion was $3,000 per recipient per year per donor prior to January 1, 1982.
3. Reduction of the federal estate tax by increasing the deductions which are to be phased in over a five-year period in the following amounts: $225,000 in 1982; $275,000 in 1983; $350,000 in 1984; $450,000 in 1985; and $600,000 in 1986.
4. A reduction of individual income tax rates of approximately 1% in 1981; 10% in 1982; 19% in 1983; and 23% in 1984 and following years.

5. One-time exclusion of taxable gain from sale of the principal residence by an individual 55 or more years of age, increased from $100,000 to $125,000. (Effective date July 20, 1981)
6. The number of shareholders of a small business corporation qualifying as a Subchapter S Corporation increased from 15 to 25.
7. Dividends of a qualified public utility corporation reinvested in stock of the corporation under the terms of a qualified dividend reinvestment plan are tax exempt to the extent of $750 in the aggregate in any taxable year. ($1,500 in the case of a joint return)
8. An increase in the unified credit with respect to both estate taxes and gift taxes to the following amounts:

Year of death/ Year of gift	Amount of Unified Credit
1982	$ 62,800
1983	$ 79,300
1984	$ 96,300
1985	$121,800
1986	$155,800

Finally, the question may arise as to whether a transfer of property should be treated as "income" to the recipient or as a gift. Assume that A, who is the owner and holder of a valid $10,000 promissory note executed by B, without receiving any payment or other consideration, voluntarily cancels the note and the obligation. Is this a gift and taxable as such, or is it taxable income to B? Discharge of the indebtedness has the effect of a transfer of value to B, as it increases his net worth by $10,000. If this is strictly a non-business transaction, the cancellation of the debt will be treated as a gift. A is required to file a gift tax return, and B need not report the $10,000 as income. However, if B, in consideration for the cancellation of the debt, performs services for A, the $10,000 is taxable income to B as compensation for his services. If, instead of services, B conveys a vacant lot to A by way of accord and satisfaction of the debt, the transaction may result in a capital gain or loss to B.

In Commissioner v. Duberstein, 363 U.S. 278, 80 S.Ct. 1190, 4 L.Ed. 1218 (1960), petitioner Duberstein, a businessman in Dayton, Ohio, in a conversation with the president of a metal manufacturing company in New York, was asked if he would supply the names of a few companies which the president could solicit as possible customers for products of his company, providing that it would not involve any possibility of conflict with the business conducted by Duberstein. In response, petitioner sent a list of names of companies, one of which, with no further effort by Duberstein, became a customer of the New York company and provided it with a large volume of profitable business. Duberstein had known the president for several years, and over this period in their regular business contacts they had developed a personal friendship. After promoting the new business, the president telephoned Duberstein and informed him that he had purchased a new Cadillac automobile as a gift for him. Duberstein said that he did not wish to accept it, as what he had done was with no thought of being paid. However, he did accept it, and did not include its value in his Federal income tax return as he deemed it a gift and not income. The Commissioner of Internal Revenue assessed an income tax deficiency against Duberstein. The U.S. Tax Court held that the Cadillac was not a gift under the circumstances, but was taxable income. The Court of Appeals, Sixth Circuit, reversed the Tax Court on the ground that it was a gift and therefore not taxable as income (265 F.2d 28). The Supreme Court in a 5–4 decision reversed the Court of Appeals and sustained the Tax Court. The majority opinion quotes from earlier opinions of the Court that a "gift" proceeds from "detached and disinterested generosity", and that it is a transfer of property "out of affection, respect, admiration, charity, or like impulses." The decision reflects the sense of a definition attributed to Prime Minister Disraeli: "Gratitude is a lively appreciation of favors yet to be conferred."

Transfer of Title by Accession

Many of the practical problems surrounding the title to personal property stem from its principal characteristic: movability. One of these problems is identified by the phrase "title by accession" and another by the term "title by confusion."

"Accession," in its strict sense, means the right of the owner of property to any increase thereof, whether caused by natural or man-made means. The more practical problems arising under this term involve the rights between the owner of a chattel and the owner of another item of property which is attached to or made a part of the chattel when the attachment or conversion is without the consent of the owner of the item attached or converted. A takes lumber belonging to B and without B's consent builds it into a wagon. Or, A takes a silver loving cup belonging to B and without B's consent melts it down into a tray. To whom does the "new" product belong? The material, or part of it, was originally the property of B. The labor and skill necessary to create the new product were A's.

The law has evolved a set of rules to decide these and similar problems. In any case where there is a dispute concerning accession, the relative rights are measured in terms of two principles:

1. Was the taking or conversion wilful or unintentional? Did the taker know the item was not his?
2. What is the relative importance of the labor of the taker and the property taken? This standard may be expressed in any one of three ways:
    (a) What is the relative value of the property taken and the "new" item?
    (b) Is the property taken still identifiable?

(c) Is the property taken easily severable or "reconverted" from the new item?

Whatever the outcome under these tests, the owner of the converted item will be entitled to one of two forms of relief. He will either be entitled to a return of the item or to damages. Which of these two forms of relief he can claim will depend upon how the facts of the case fit into the foregoing tests.

If a taking was deliberate and with knowledge that the item was the property of another, the general rule is that the original owner can have the property returned to him except in a case where the identity has been hopelessly lost or the value of the new item is almost entirely the result of the labor of the taker and this value is far greater than the value of the original item. If A knowingly takes a piece of canvas belonging to B and on it creates a masterpiece in oil, B probably cannot claim title to the painting but, because the taking was wilful, B will be entitled to damages based upon the increase in value of the canvas. Except in such a rare instance, a wilful taking will not pass title and the owner of the taken item will be able to claim title to it or to the new property of which it forms an integral part.

The more difficult and frequent problems arise where the taking is without knowledge that the property belongs to another. In this case, the law is not aided by a sense of punishing a wrongdoer. The law must attempt to reconcile two innocent parties without injuring either. One rule is that if there is an innocent taking and the identity of the converted item has changed, then title passes to the person who applied the labor. The original owner is only able to obtain damages for the *original* value of the converted article. This rule simply moves the issue up a peg where the meaning of the phrase "change of identity" must be determined. It has been held that cloth does not lose its identity when coverted into

a coat nor timber when it is converted innocently into planks. It is apparent, however, in most cases that title passes to the innocent converter if the value of the labor is greater than the value of the converted material in its original form. In such a case, the original owner will not be entitled to the new item; his only remedy will be an award of money damages for the value of the original article.

Transfer of Title
by Confusion of Goods

The basic problem here is much the same as in a case of title by accession. For example, Hereford cattle belonging to B are mingled with Hereford cattle belonging to A and neither man's herd can be specifically identified; or grain owned by X is mixed with similar grain owned by Y. The problem arises where the goods are identical, and the confusion may have resulted from accident, mistake, wilful act, or agreement of the parties. If the goods can be apportioned, each owner proving his proportion of the whole is entitled to receive his share. If, however, the confusion results from the wilful and wrongful act of one of the parties, he will lose his entire interest if he cannot prove his share. Frequently, the real problem arises not because the original interest cannot be proved but because there is not enough left to distribute a full share to each owner. In such a case, if the confusion was due to mistake, accident or agreement, the loss will be borne by each, proportionate to his share. If caused by an intentional and unauthorized act, the wrongdoer will first bear any loss.

Where, as is frequently the case, the confusion is caused by acts of a third party, his liability will depend not only upon the character of his act, as in the foregoing instance, but also upon whether his responsibility was assumed gratuitously or for a consideration.

Title to Lost or Misplaced Personal Property

Suppose X, the owner of an apartment hotel, leases a kitchenette apartment to Y. One night, Z, who happens to be Y's mother-in-law, is invited to sleep in the Murphy bed in the living room. In the course of preparing the bed, Z finds an emerald ring caught on the springs under the mattress. The ring is turned over to the police but diligent inquiry does not turn up the true owner. Who is entitled to the ring? The law insists, as a theoretical proposition, that title be in someone and X, Y and Z each insist that he or she has title. Z will be entitled to the ring. The law says that a "finder" is entitled to lost property as against the whole world except the true owner. It might be argued that calling Z the "finder" simply begs the question. X owned the property on (or in) which the lost article was located. Was not he thereby the "finder"? Compare the situation in which X buys an old trunk because he believes it contains some letters written by Benjamin Franklin. He does not locate the letters, but, while Y is repairing the trunk at the request of X, Y comes across the correspondence in a secret compartment. In this case, X as owner of the trunk, will have a superior claim to the lost items. Since X purchased the trunk with the intention of claiming the items, he is the "finder." The general superior right of the one who first takes physical hold of the goods is limited by some courts where the object is discovered by an employee in the course of employment. If, instead of Y's mother-in-law, the maid employed to clean the apartment had found the emerald ring, then the owner of the apartment would have had a stronger claim to the property.

A different rule applies when the lost property is in the ground. Here, the owner of the land has a claim superior to that of the finder. X employs Y to excavate a lateral sewer. Y uncovers old Indian relics.

X, not Y, has the superior claim. There is, of course, no logic to this distinction between something found in a building and something found in the ground. The building is as much as part of the real estate as is the land. The only exception to the rule granting superior rights to the landowner when the property is buried is the rule governing "treasure trove." In some jurisdictions, the person who discovers bullion or coin in the soil has a claim superior to that of the owner of the land. This exception probably stems from the traditional rule that the sovereign had a right to a share of any treasure trove, and a rule encouraging discovery had a distinct financial advantage to the crown.

There is a further exception to the rule giving the "finder" first claim against all but the true owner. Most decisions hold that if property has been mislaid, not lost, then the owner of the premises, not the "finder," has first claim if the true owner is not discovered. This doctrine is involved frequently in cases where items are found on trains, buses, and airplanes. The true owner, it is said, did not lose the parcel of banknotes, he simply mislaid them. Barber shops and restaurants are a common focal point for litigation over mislaid articles. The owner of the premises has the superior right to possession if the articles were mislaid.

Many States now have statutes which provide a means of vesting title to lost property in the "finder" where a prescribed search for the owner proves fruitless. These statutes generally do not provide for the disposition of mislaid or abandoned property nor do they purport to describe or determine the right to possession against any party other than the true owner.

FIXTURES

It is not always easy to decide whether particular property is real or personal. Real property, as previously noted, may be defined as land and all things permanently affixed thereto including fixtures. Personal property may be defined as any kind of property which is not real estate. A fixture is an article or piece of personal property which has been attached in some manner to land or a building thereon. Thus, materials for a building are clearly personal property. However, when worked into a building as its construction progresses from the foundation up, they become real property because buildings are part of the land.

Even this simple illustration bristles with problems. Buildings are generally part of the land, but, as we shall see later, not all buildings are part of the land. Moreover, what is meant by materials worked into a building? Would plumbing be correctly described as "materials worked into a building"?

Consider the following list of things which, at one stage, are clearly personal property but which are used in connection with buildings: heating, lighting and air conditioning systems; ranges, refrigerators, television antennae, bathroom and kitchen cabinets, mantels, fireplaces, dishwashers, disposals, door mirrors, venetian blinds, shades, window screens, awnings, storm windows, window boxes, storm doors, screen doors and mail boxes. These items may be so firmly affixed to the land or building in a somewhat permanent fashion that they have become an actual part of the realty, or they may be annexed in such a way as to retain their character as personalty.

While the question whether these various items are personal property or real property may in certain instances be difficult to answer, it is only by obtaining the answer that conflicting claims to the ownership of such things may be determined. Unless otherwise provided by agreement, personalty remains the property of the person who placed it on the real estate. On the other hand, if the fixture has been affixed so as to become an actual part of the real estate, it becomes the property of the owner of the real estate.

Conflicting Claims

Conflicting claims to fixtures may arise in a variety of situations. The conflict may arise between the landlord and his tenant. One tenant may have built a garage on the leased premises which he intends and expects to be able to remove when the lease expires. Another may have installed heating and lighting systems in the landlord's building, expecting to take them with him when he leaves. In each case the landlord may successfully contend that these things have become part of the real estate and are no longer the property of the tenant.

The conflict may arise between the vendor and the purchaser of a house. The vendor may think that the sale did not include the refrigerator, range, venetian blinds, and screens, while the purchaser thinks otherwise.

The conflict may arise between the equity owner of an apartment building and the mortgagee. The mortgagee may regard the new refrigerators and gas stoves installed subsequent to the execution of the mortgage as part of his security, yet the owner contends that these are items which he bought with fresh capital and are not subject to the mortgage. Even more troublesome is the conflict between a conditional vendor (or chattel mortgagee) of these types of items and the subsequent purchaser of the building, or the prior or subsequent mortgagee of the building.

The conflict may also arise between a devisee and legatee under a will. A devisee of real property may claim various articles attached thereto over the objection of heirs who have been bequeathed the decedent's personalty.

Law Applicable to Fixtures

One accepted general rule is that as between parties to a valid agreement, the intention of the parties as expressed in the agreement will control. This rule removes many conflicts between the well advised landlord and tenant, and between the well advised vendor and purchaser. As between themselves, these parties may expressly provide, in the lease or in the contract of sale, with respect to the ownership of each item of property.

Absent the binding force of an agreement, the following guides are helpful in determining whether any particular item is part of the realty, and thus belongs to the landowner or the person having the title or right to the realty: (1) the physical relationship of the item to the land; (2) the intention of the person who attaches the item to the land; (3) the purpose served by the item in relation to the land and in relation to the person who brought it there; and (4) the interest of that person in the land at the time of the attachment of the item.

Although physical attachment is significant, a more important test is whether the item can be removed without material injury to the land or building on the land. If it cannot be so removed, it is generally held that the item has become part of the realty. The converse is also true but to a lesser degree. Where the item may be removed without material injury to the land or building, it is generally held that it has not become part of the realty. This test, however, is not conclusive.

In the converse situation the courts have searched for the answer in the intention of the person who brought the item upon the realty and attached it thereto. The tests of intention are objective. One of the tests developed has been to inquire into the purpose or use of the item in relation to the land and in relation to the person who brought it there. If the use or purpose of the item is unusual for the type of realty involved (e.g., small crane in the backyard of a country house) or peculiar to the particular individual who brought it there, then it may be reasonably concluded that

the individual intended to remove the item when he leaves.

However, an item is not regarded as part of the realty merely because its use or purpose is usual for the type of realty involved. For example, it is usual to have beds and dressers in the bedrooms, and dining tables in the dining rooms, but these items are not ordinarily part of the realty. The test of purpose or use becomes operative only if the item both (a) is affixed to the realty in some way, and (b) can be removed without material injury to the realty. In such a situation, if the use or purpose of the item is peculiar to the particular owner or occupant of the premises the courts will tend to let him remove the item when he leaves.

The courts, in searching for the intention of the person bringing such items upon the land, have looked to his interest in the realty. The courts have found it much easier to find an intention to remove such items on the part of occupants with a limited interest in the real estate, such as lessees, and more difficult to find such an intention on the part of absolute owners of the real estate.

Accordingly, in the law of landlord and tenant, it is settled that the tenant may remove "trade fixtures," i.e., items used in connection with his trade, provided that this can be done without material injury to the realty. This is merely another way of saying that he may remove items whose use on the premises is peculiar to him. However, if the item is a building which is merely resting on the land, the tenant may have no right to remove it merely because it is not firmly affixed to or embedded in the land. The reason for this is that buildings, of whatever kind, are legally a part of the realty. In view of this, it is extremely doubtful that a tenant would be permitted to remove a building if it is not a "trade fixture," that is, if its use on the premises is not peculiar to the tenant's trade.

A vendor of real estate who is parting

with his absolute ownership in the property is not in as favorable a position, with regard to fixtures brought onto the realty by him, as a tenant would be.   Courts find it more difficult to hold that an absolute owner of realty intended to remove the fixtures, at some future date, when he placed them on his property.   The difference between the vendor's position and that of a tenant is that the vendor is presumed to have sold all fixtures which usually go with the type of property involved, whereas the tenant generally intends to remove any of the fixtures installed by him which are removable without material injury to the real estate.

Cases

Transfer of Title by Gift

COHEN v. BAYSIDE FEDERAL SAVINGS AND LOAN ASS'N

(1970) 62 Misc.2d 738, 309 N.Y.S.2d 980.

HAROLD TESSLER, J.

The fundamental question presented to this court in an agreed statement of facts submitted by the parties is:

Can an engagement ring, given in contemplation of marriage, be recovered from a "donee", by the estate of the "donor", when the contemplated marriage fails to occur because of the death of the "donor"?

The undisputed facts can be summarized as follows: Richard Alan Rothchild became engaged to be married to Carol Sue Cohen, the defendant in this action.   Both were over 21 years of age.   Richard gave Carol a diamond "engagement" ring which is valued at $1,000.   Shortly before the wedding date, Richard was killed in an automobile accident and his estate has instituted this action to recover the ring.   The sole question for determination by this court is: "Who is entitled to the ring?"

Actions for return of engagement rings have had an interesting and confusing history in New York.   These actions were permitted at common law prior to 1935.   However, in 1935 the Legislature of this State enacted Article 2–A of the Civil Practice Act (the heart balm statute) which was later interpreted by the courts so as to bar actions for the return of engagement rings in most instances.   [Citations.]   These results were widely criticized.   [Citations.]   In response to this criticism, in 1965 the Legislature amended section 80–b of the Civil Rights Law to permit recovery of engagement rings where "justice so requires."

In Lowe v. Quinn, 32 A.D.2d 269, 301 N.Y.S.2d 361 the Appellate Division, First Department, held that the common law rules formulated before 1935 would again be applicable.   * * *

However, reference to these common law rules formulated prior to 1935 is of little help in the present instance since this case appears to be one of first impression in this State.   In the absence of any controlling authority, this court has sought help by looking to applicable decisional law in other jurisdictions, the general principles underlying engagement ring cases in general and, finally, to what justice requires in this situation.

An examination of the relevant authorities in other states indicates that they are split.   * * *

* * *

Nor does an examination of the principles underlying the gift of engagement ring cases in general clearly point the way to a particular result.   The results set forth in the decisions in gift of engagement ring cases are usually predictable and understandable.   However, the legal principles and rationales relied upon by the courts are often divergent and muddled. For example, it is settled that where a financee breaks an engagement without the fault of the donor, she must return the ring. [Citation]. It is also well settled that where the donor breaks the engagement, the ring may be kept by the donee [citation] and, generally, where the engagement is broken by mutual consent, the ring also goes back to the donor. [Citation.]

While these results are equitable, the various legal theories asserted are not always logical and persuasive. Some courts have propounded a pledge theory. [Citation.] Other courts state that principles of unjust enrichment govern [citation] and the most popular rationale is that the ring is given as a gift on condition subsequent. [Citation.] It is not always clear, however, whether it is the actual marriage of the parties or the donee's not performing any act that would prevent the marriage that is the actual condition of the "transaction."

Thus, a confusing body of law has grown up around the engagement ring and, after careful consideration of these principles, this court has decided that Carol should keep the ring because that result is equitable and because "justice so requires" for the following reasons:

While the engagement ring to some people in the "mod" world of today is just another material possession and while it has not been unknown in some circles for recipients of these rings to flaunt them, to compare their luster, number of carats, etc., with the rings of their friends, for the vast majority the ring still remains a hallowed symbol of the love and devotion that a prospective husband and wife bear for each other. In my judgment, no gift given during a lifetime can approach the meaningfulness and significance of the engagement ring. When Richard gave the ring to Carol, he obviously intended that she have it and keep it unless she affirmatively did something to prevent the marriage of the parties. While it is improbable that at the time of the gift either gave a thought to the consequences that would arise in the event of the death of one of the parties, I firmly believe that had Richard thought of these con-

sequences he would have intended that in the event of his untimely death Carol should keep the ring as a symbol of his love and affection. There appears to be no reason, in logic or morals, to prevent such a result.

This court frankly acknowledges that implicit in this determination is a recognition that the gift of an engagement ring is a special occasion interwoven with romance and mutual love. It is a meaningful act symbolic of much more than the ordinary and usual business transaction. I am convinced that it is time for a change in our approach to this area. The traditional approach of applying the sound and settled principles of business law and the law of gifts to the giving of an engagement ring has resulted in a myriad of decisional law in this area, which is, to say the least, in much confusion and determinative of little.

I can not believe that the age-old ritual of giving an engagement ring to bind the mutual premarital vows can be or is intended to be treated as an exchange of consideration as practiced in the everyday market place. Can it be seriously urged that the giving of this ring by the decedent "groom" to his loved one and bride-to-be can be treated as the ordinary commercial or business transaction requiring the ultimate in consideration and payment? I think not. To treat this special and usually once in a lifetime occasion, one as requiring quid pro quo, is a mistake and unrealistic.

Accordingly the ring shall remain with Carol and judgment shall be entered accordingly.

Title to Lost or
Misplaced Personal Property

PASET v. OLD ORCHARD BANK AND TRUST CO.

(1978) 62 Ill.App.3d 534, 19 Ill. Dec. 389, 378 N.E.2d 1264.

SIMON, J.

On May 8, 1974, the plaintiff, Brenice Paset, a safety deposit box subscriber at the defendant Old Orchard Bank (the bank), found $6,325 in currency on the seat of a chair in an examination booth in the safety deposit vault. The chair was partially under a table. The plaintiff notified officers of the bank and turned the money over to them. She then was told by bank officials that the bank would try to locate the owner, and that she could have the money if the owner was not located within 1 year.

The bank wrote to everyone who had been in the safety deposit vault area either on the day of, or on the day preceding, the discovery, stating that some property had been found and inviting the customers to describe any property they might have lost. No one reported the loss of currency, and the money remained unclaimed a year after it had been found. However, when the plaintiff requested the money, the bank refused to deliver it to her, explaining that it, was obligated to hold the currency for the owner.

The safety deposit vault area of the bank was located on a lower floor of the bank. This area was separated from a lobby by a gate, and * * * entrance to the safety deposit vault area was restricted to bank employees and customers maintaining safety deposit boxes in the vault. * * * The plaintiff sought a declaratory judgment that the Illinois estray statute [citation] was applicable to her discovery and granted her ownership of the $6,325. The circuit court judge, however, found that the money was "deemed mislaid," and concluded that despite the plaintiff's compliance with the requirements of the estray statute, that statute was not applicable. * * *

This appeal, then, requires a determination of whether a finder of cash in an examining booth in a safety deposit vault may be a keeper under the Illinois estray statute and an analysis of the extent to which the common law concepts of lost and mislaid property apply to the statute. * * * The Illinois estray statute's principle pur-

poses are to encourage and facilitate the return of property to the true owner, and then to reward a finder for his honesty if the property remains unclaimed. The statute provides an incentive for finders to report their discoveries by making it possible for them, after the passage of the requisite time, to acquire legal title to the property they have found. [Citation.] By directing the county clerk to publicize and advertise the property, the statute further enhances the opportunity of the owner to recover what he has lost.

Traditionally, the common law has treated lost and mislaid property differently for the purposes of determining ownership of property someone has found. Mislaid property is that which is intentionally put in a certain place and later forgotten; at common law a finder acquires to rights to mislaid property. The element of intentional deposit present in the case of mislaid property is absent in the case of lost property, for property is deemed lost when it is unintentionally separated from the dominion of its owner. The general rule is that the finder is entitled to possession of lost property against everyone except the true owner. We are not concerned in this case with abandoned property where the owner, intending to relinquish all rights to his property, leaves it free to be appropriated by any other person. Although at common law the finder is entitled to keep abandoned property, the plaintiff has not taken the position that the money here was abandoned. [Citation.]

As is usual in cases involving a determination of whether property is lost or mislaid, this court is not here assisted by direct evidence, for, obviously, the true owner is not available to state what his intent was. Also, because all the evidence here has been presented by affidavit or stipulation, this court is in as advantageous a position as the trial judge to determine whether the money was lost or mislaid. Our conclusion is that the estray statute should be applied, and ownership of the money vested in the plaintiff finder.

Thus, we do not accept the bank's argument that the money was mislaid rather than lost. It is complete speculation to infer, as the bank urges, that the money was deliberately placed by its owner on the chair located partially under a table in the examining booth, and then forgotten. If the money was intentionally placed on the chair by someone who forgot where he left it, the bank's notice to safety deposit box subscribers should have alerted the owner. The failure of an owner to appear to claim the money in the interval since its discovery is affirmative evidence that the property was not mislaid. [Citations.]

Because the evidence, though ambiguous, tends to indicate that the money probably was not mislaid, and because neither party contends that the money was abandoned, we conclude that the ambiguity should, as a matter of public policy, be resolved in favor of the presumption that the money was lost. This conclusion is in harmony with the above mentioned purposes of the estray statute, for it construes the statute liberally rather than technically, with the result that the statute is brought into play rather than rejected. Such an application of the statute better effectuates the legislature's goal of restoring property to a true owner; it provides incentive for a finder to report his discovery by rewarding him if the true owner does not appear within the statutorily-determined time limit.

* * *

Further, whether the property was discovered in a public or private place should not be permitted to preclude the application of the estray statute. The statute itself makes no distinction between "public" and "private" places of finding. * * *

Accordingly, the judgment of the circuit court is reversed and the case is remanded with directions to enter judgment in favor of the plaintiff finder.

Judgment reversed and remanded with directions.

Fixtures

SEARS, ROEBUCK AND COMPANY v. SEVEN PALMS MOTOR INN, INC.

(1975 Mo.) 530 S.W.2d 695.

HENLEY, J.
* * *

It involves a claim by Sears, Roebuck and Company (respondent) to recover $8,357.49 with interest, and to establish a mechanic's lien, for materials and labor including, among other items, drapes and bedspreads furnished Seven Palms Motor Inn (defendant) in connection with the construction of a motel on land then owned by it. The case was submitted on a stipulation in which * * * the only issue to be decided is whether respondent is entitled to a mechanic's lien. The trial court decided this issue for respondent and entered judgment accordingly. The court of appeals affirmed the money judgment but reversed that portion of the judgment imposing the lien, holding that the bedspreads were not lienable items and their inclusion in the statement vitiated the entire lien. While we determine the case the same as on original appeal, Mo.Const. Art. V, § 10, we ordered the transfer primarily to review the questions presented by the holding that the whole lien was vitiated. We decide that it was not.

* * *

Section 429.010, RSMo 1969 provides in part: "Every mechanic or other person, who shall do or perform any work or labor upon, or furnish any material [or], fixtures * * * for any building * * * under or by virtue of any contract with the owner * * * upon complying with the provisions of sections 429.010 to 429.340, shall have for his work or labor done, or materials [or], fixtures * * * furnished, a lien upon such building * * * and upon the land * * *."

Characterization of an item as a fixture, something otherwise personal but attached to realty under such circumstances as to become part of it, depends upon the finding of three elements: annexation to the realty, adaption to the use to which the realty is devoted, and intent of the annexor that the object become a permanent accession to the freehold. Missouri cases are uniform in requiring each of these elements to be present in some degree, however slight, before an item may be considered a fixture. [Citations.]

Appellants contend that neither the drapes nor the bedspreads are fixtures within the meaning of § 429.010 and therefore not lienable, because they are not annexed or attached to the building.

The purpose of attaching the traverse rods to the realty was to hang drapes therefrom which could be opened or drawn across a window by the motel's guest to control the light in his room or secure his privacy. Of itself, the traverse rod attached to the wall above the window in the room did not accomplish this purpose. To serve this purpose it was essential that the drapes be provided and attached to the rod. They were provided and attached, and became an integral part of the instrument designed for use in connection with the window in the guest's room. As such, the drapes were as much a fixture as the traverse rod itself. It is obvious that the rod and drapes, as a unit, were adpated to the proper use of rooms in a motel and were placed therein with the intent they would form a part of the special purpose for which the building was designed to be used.

Not so the bedspreads. Respondent admits that those items are not physically attached to the realty in any way but insists that they have been "constructively annexed." In support of this proposition, respondent argues: the rods are physically fastened to the building; the drapes are

affixed to the rods by hooks; the bedspreads match the drapes; a fortiori, the bedspreads "are at least 'constructively annexed' to the rooms * * * by their relationship with the drapes."

The doctrine of constructive annexation recognizes that a particular article, not physically attached to the land, "may be so adapted to the use to which the land is put that it may be considered an integral part of the land" and "constructively annexed" thereto. 36A C.J.S. Fixtures § 6, pp. 613–614. * * * The rule has not been applied to establishments such as hotels, restaurants, bars and apartment buildings. Thus, movable furniture, tableware and similar equipment, although necessary to the operation of a hotel, are generally not considered fixtures. [Citations.]

The bedspreads are not essential to the use of what is clearly a fixture, nor has it been shown that they cannot readily be used independently elsewhere. Respondent asserts that because the bedspreads "were designed to match and to coexist with the drapes" they must be considered part of a matched set which is essential to the use of rods which are clearly fixtures. Respondent seeks support for this contention in cases that have held easily removable parts of machines and other fixtures may not be considered as separate items. [Citations.] However, in each of these cases, the fixture would have been rendered absolutely useless by removal of the items in question, and such items could not readily be used independently elsewhere. There is no indication that the unit of rod and drapes could not serve its function, which respondent says is to "regulate the flow of light and serve the need for privacy," if the bedspreads were removed. That the decor of a guest room in a motel may be more aesthetically pleasing when bedspreads are made of the same material as drapes, falls far short of the functional relationship needed to justify "constructive annexation." Since the bedspreads were not annexed, physically or constructively, they cannot be characterized as fixtures and are, therefore, nonlienable items.

* * *

* * * Respondent's argument that both were lienable was not without some substance, even though we have determined that one, the bedspreads, was not a fixture and not lienable. In these circumstances, the inclusion in the lien statement of the nonlienable item, separable as it is from the lienable items, does not vitiate the entire lien.

Appellants do not question the money judgment in favor of respondent and against defendant, Seven Palms Motor Inn. Accordingly, that part of the judgment is affirmed. That part of the judgment imposing a lien on the property for the full amount of the money judgment is reversed and the cause is remanded with directions that the trial court enter judgment in favor of respondent imposing a lien for the amount of the balance due according to the statement after deducting therefrom the amount charged for the bedspreads.

Problems

1. In January 1982, Roger Burke loaned his favorite nephew, Jimmy White, his valuable painting by Picasso. Knowing that on May 15, 1982, Jimmy would celebrate his twenty-first birthday, Burke, on April 14, 1982, sent a letter to Jimmy stating:

Dear Jimmy,

Tomorrow I leave on my annual trip to Europe, and I want to make you a fitting birthday gift which I do by sending you my enclosed promissory note. Also I want you to keep the Picasso which I loaned you last January, and you may now consider it yours. Happy birthday!

Affectionately,
/s/ Uncle Roger

The negotiable promissory note for $5,000, sent with the letter, was signed by Roger Burke, payable to Jimmy White or bearer, and dated May 15, 1982. On May 21, 1982, Burke was killed in an automobile accident while motoring in France.

First Bank was appointed administrator of Burke's estate. Jimmy presented the note to the administrator and demanded payment, which was refused. Jimmy brought an action against First Bank as administrator seeking recovery on the note. The administrator brought an action against Jimmy seeking return of the painting by Picasso.

(a) What decision in the action on the note?
(b) What decision in the action to recover the painting?

2. Several years ago P purchased a tract of land on which there was an old, vacant house. Recently, P employed F, a carpenter, to repair and remodel the house. While F was tearing out a partition for the purpose of enlarging one of the rooms, he discovered a metal box hidden in the wall of the house. F broke open the box and discovered that it contained $2,000 in gold and silver coins and old-style bills. F then took the box and its contents to P and told him where he had found it. When F handed the box and the money over to P he said, "If you do not find the owner, I claim the money." P placed the money in an envelope and deposited it in his safe deposit box where it is at present. No one has ever claimed the money, but P refuses to give it to F.

F brings an action against P to recover the money. Decision?

3. Gable, the owner of a lumber company, was cutting trees over the boundary line of his property and property owned by Lane. Although he realized he had crossed onto Lane's property, Gable cut trees on Lane's property of the same kind as those he had cut on his own land. While on Lane's property he found a diamond ring on the ground, which he took home. All of the timber cut that day by Gable was commingled.

What are Lane's rights, if any, (a) in the timber; and (b) in the ring?

4. Decide each of the following problems.
(a) A chimney sweep found a jewel and took it to a goldsmith whose apprentice took the stone

out and refused to return it. The chimney sweep sues the goldsmith.

(b) One of several boys walking along a railroad track found a old stocking. All started playing with it until it burst in the hands of its discoverer revealing several hundred dollars. The original discoverer claims it all; the other boys claim it should be divided equally.

(c) A traveling salesman notices a parcel of bank notes on the floor of a store as he is leaving. He picks them up and gives them to the owner of the store to keep for the true owner. After three years they have not been reclaimed, and the salesman sues the storekeeper.

(d) F is hired to clean out the swimming pool at the country club. He finds a diamond ring on the bottom of the pool. The true owner can not be found. The country club sues F.

(e) A customer found a pocketbook lying on a barber's table. He gave it to the barber to hold for the true owner who failed to appear. The customer sues the barber.

5. Jones had 50 crates of oranges about equally divided between grades A, B, and C, grade A being the highest quality and C the lowest quality. Smith had 1,000 crates of oranges, about 90 per cent of which were of grade A, but some of them grade B and C, the exact quantity of each being unknown. Smith wilfully mixed Jones's crates with his own so that it was impossible to identify any particular crate. Jones seized the whole lot. Smith demanded 900 crates of grade A and 50 each of grades B and C. Jones refused to give them up unless Smith could identify particular crates. This, Smith could not do. Smith brought an action against Jones to recover what he demanded or its value. Judgment for whom, and why?

6. A, the owner and operator of Blackacre, decided to cease farming operations and liquidate his holdings. A sold 50 head of yearling Merino sheep to B and sold Blackacre to C. He executed and delivered to B a bill of sale for the sheep and was paid $40 each for the 50 sheep. It was understood that B would send a truck for the sheep within a few days. At the same time, A executed a warranty deed conveying Blackacre to C. C took possession of the farm and brought along 100 head of his yearling Merino sheep and turned them into the pasture, not knowing the sheep A sold B were still in the pasture. After

the sheep were mixed, it was impossible to identify the 50 head belonging to B. After proper demand, B sued C to recover the 50 head of sheep. Decision?

7. O permitted S to take his very old grandfather clock on the basis of S's representations that he was skilled at repairing such clocks and restoring them to their original condition and could do the job for $60. The clock had been badly damaged for years. S immediately sold it to Fixit Shop for $30. Fixit Shop was in the business of repairing a large variety of items, and also sold used articles. Three months later, O was in the Fixit Shop and clearly established that a grandfather clock Fixit Shop had for sale was the one he had given S to repair. Fixit Shop had replaced more than half of the moving parts by having exact duplicates custom made; the clock's exterior had been restored by a skilled cabinet maker; and the clock's face had been replaced by a duplicate. All materials belonged to Fixit Shop and the work was accomplished by its employees. Fixit Shop asserts it bought the clock in the normal course of business from S who represented that it belonged to him. The fair market value of the clock in its damaged condition was $30 and the value of repairs made is $220.

O sued Fixit Shop for return of the clock. Fixit Shop defended that it now had title to the clock, and, in the alternative, that O must pay the value of the repairs if he is entitled to regain possession. Decision?

8. A rented vacant lots from B for a filling station under an oral agreement and placed thereon a lightly constructed building bolted to a concrete slab and storage tanks laid on the ground in a shallow excavation. Later, a lease was prepared by A, providing that A might remove the equipment at the termination of the lease. This lease was not executed, having been rejected by B because of a renewal clause it contained, but several years later another lease was prepared which A and B signed. This lease did not mention removal of the equipment. At the termination of this lease A removed the equipment and B brought an action of replevin. What judgment?

9. A sold a parcel of real estate describing it by its legal description and making no mention of any improvements or fixtures thereon. The land had upon it a residence, a barn, a rail fence, a stack of hay, some growing corn, and a wind mill; and the residence had a mirror built into the panel, a heating system consisting of a furnace and steam pipes and coils; in the house were chairs, beds, tables, and other furniture. On the house was a lightning rod. In the basement were screens for the windows. State which of these things passed by the deed and which did not.

10. John Swan rented a safety deposit box at the Tenth Citizens Bank of Emanon, State of X. On December 17, 1981, Swan went to the Bank with stock certificates for placing in the safety deposit box. After admittance to the vault, and having placed the stock certificates in the box, Swan found lying on the floor of the vault a $5,000 negotiable bearer bond issued by the State of Wisconsin with coupons attached, due June 30, 1988. Swan picked up the bond and, observing that it did not recite the name of the owner, left the vault and went to the office of the President of the Bank. He told the President what had occurred, and delivered the bond to the President only after obtaining his promise that, should the owner not call for the bond or become known to the Bank by June 30, 1982, the Bank would redeliver the bond to Swan. On July 1, Swan learned that the owner of the bond had not called for it, nor was his identity known to the Bank. Swan thereupon asked that the bond be returned to him. The Bank refused, stating that it would continue to hold the bond until claimed by the owner.

Swan brings suit against the Bank to recover possession of the bond. Decision?

OWNERSHIP AND OCCUPANCY OF REAL PROPERTY

Rights of ownership in real property are called estates and are classified to indicate the quantity, nature, and extent of the rights. The two major categories are freehold estates (those existing for an indefinite time) and estates less than freehold (those which exist for a predetermined time), called leasehold estates.

ESTATES IN LAND

FEE ESTATES

Fee Simple Estate

The absolute right of alienability and of transmitting by inheritance are basic characteristics of a fee simple estate. The estate signifies full dominion over the property. That is, the property is owned absolutely (possibly subject to a mortgage) and it can be sold or disposed of by will. If estates are measured by the quantity of the rights possessed in the property, the fee simple signifies the greatest quantity of possible rights. In common usage, ownership of property usually refers to fee simple. A fee simple is created by any words which indicate an intent to convey absolute ownership. "To B in fee simple" will accomplish just that. "To B forever" means legally just what the grantor said. The general presumption is that a conveyance is intended to convey full and absolute title in the absence of a clear intent to the contrary.

A practical consequence of a fee simple title is that it may not only be voluntarily alienated but it also may be levied upon and sold at the instance of judgment creditors.

Base or Qualified Fee Estate

It is possible to convey or will property to a person to enjoy absolutely, subject to being taken away at a later date if a certain event takes place. The estate thus created is known as a base fee, qualified fee or fee simple defeasible. A may provide in his will that his widow is to have his house and lot in "fee simple forever so long as she does not remarry." If his widow dies without remarrying, the property is transferred to her heirs as though she owned it absolutely since the condition did not take place. Such a condition was bound to occur, if at all, during the life of the taker of the property. A condition in a deed which conveys land "to A and if he dies without children then to revert" to the grantor and his heirs, must also occur, if at all within A's lifetime. A limitation on a fee simple may, on the other hand, survive the life of the first taker. "To A as long as no commercial buildings are erected thereon," imposes a qualification which limits the fee through subsequent purchasers from A. If land is left to A forever so long as she does not remarry, and A first sells the land to B and then remarries, B thereby loses his title to the land and it reverts to the heirs of the grantor.

LIFE ESTATES

By tradition, life estates are divided into two major classes: (1) conventional life estates or those created by voluntary act and (2) those established by law, the most significant example of which is a wife's dower right in the property of her husband.

Conventional Life Estates

A grant or a devise "to A for life" creates in A an estate which terminates on his death. Such a provision may stand alone in which case the property will revert to the grantor and his heirs or, as is more likely, it will be followed by a subsequent grant to another party such as "to A for life and then to B and his heirs." A is the life tenant and B is generally described as the "remainderman." A's life may not be the measure of his life estate, as where an estate is granted "to A for the life of B." Upon B's death, A's interest terminates and, if A dies before B, A's interest passes to his heirs or as he directs in his will for the remainder of B's life.

No particular words are necessary to create a life estate. It is always a matter of determining the intent of the grantor.

Life estates arise most frequently in connection with the creation of trusts, a subject considered in Chapter 50. A man may leave his property upon death to trustees who are instructed to pay the income from the property to the widow during her life, and, upon her death, to distribute the property itself to the children. The widow has what is known as an equitable life estate. Or, a man may convey property to trustees who are instructed to pay the income therefrom to him during his life and, upon his death, to distribute it in a particular manner. The grantor has thereby reserved a life estate in the property to himself. Occasionally, life estates are created with the power given to the life tenant to dispose of the proceeds as he may direct in his will. Thus, A may leave his property to trustees "to pay the net income to my wife during her life and to distribute the principal as she may direct in her will."

The creation of a life estate creates practical problems with respect to the rights and duties of the life tenant vis-a-vis the person who is entitled to the property at the end of the life estate (the remainderman). If a ranch is left "to A for life and on his death to B," A cannot sell the ranch to the detriment of B, but what limits are there upon A's use of it? Generally, A may make such reasonable use of the property as long as he does not commit "waste." Any act or omission which does permanent injury to the realty or unreasonably changes its characteristics or value will constitute waste. For example, the failure to make repairs on a building, the unreasonable cutting of timber or the neglect of an adequate conservation policy may subject the life tenant to an action by the remainderman to recover damages for waste. Where land is involved, a life tenant can generally use the property to the extent it was being used by the former owner and such actions do not constitute waste.

The life tenant is obligated to pay the general taxes on the property but he may demand contribution from the remainder-man to pay any special assessment or tax which results in a permanent improvement.

A conveyance by the life tenant passes only his interest. The life tenant and the remainderman may, however, join in a conveyance to pass the entire fee to the property, or the life tenant may terminate his interest by conveying it to the remainder-man.

Life Estates Established by Law

Dower. Under common law, dower is a life estate which a wife surviving her husband has in one-third of all the real property the husband owned during the marriage. It arises by operation of law and exists irrespective of the intent or wishes of the parties. By statute it is generally a one-third interest in such real estate, rather than a life estate therein.

Until the death of the husband, the wife's dower is contingent or "inchoate." During his life she cannot transfer or sell her dower interest. Dower can only exist in fee simple estates or in an estate that, for practical purposes, is equivalent to a fee simple estate. There is no dower in a life estate since it is not an estate of inheritance. Likewise, although a widow has dower in property which the husband owned as a tenant in common, because each tenant's interest passes by inheritance, there is no dower in property held in joint tenancy since the survivor of the joint tenants is entitled to the entire property.

Although the widow does not realize her dower unless she survives her husband, her right in this respect is protected during the marriage. If the husband sells his property after he marries, the purchaser takes subject to the inchoate right of dower even though the purchaser did not know the seller was married. Dower also takes precedence over any claims against the husband's estate which were not reduced to judgment or made a lien against his prop-

erty before marriage, including mortgage liens (except purchase money mortgage liens as noted below). Generally, to bar dower during marriage, it is necessary that the wife expressly waive her dower and, since dower is an interest in land, such a release must be in writing. Generally, the husband is required to join in the release. In most jurisdictions, the wife can bar her dower simply by joining in a conveyance with her husband.

A mortgage lien on real estate granted during the marriage is subject to the wife's dower interest unless the wife joined in the mortgage or it is a purchase money mortgage. A purchase money mortgage is a mortgage on property purchased either in whole or in part with the proceeds of the loan which it secures. Thus, H, husband, purchases a house from V, vendor, for $60,000. He pays $24,000 down and gives V a mortgage on the house for the balance. The mortgage is a purchase money mortgage. Or suppose, H purchases a house from V for $60,000. H pays $24,000 of his own funds and $36,000 representing the proceeds of a loan from First Bank secured by a mortgage on the house. First Bank's mortgage is a purchase money mortgage. The rule is that whether or not H's wife joins in the purchase money mortgage, the mortgage is superior to her dower rights.

The incidents of dower at common law have been substantially modified by statute in most jurisdictions. In some States, the widow may elect whether to take common law dower or an alternative amount given her by statute, the widow being given a period of time within which to elect between dower and her statutory portion. In many jurisdictions, dower has been abolished and a statutory share of the husband's property is substituted in lieu thereof.

Divorce generally bars dower although this is not the case in some States if the divorce is obtained by reason of the fault of the husband. It is possible to bar dower by antenuptial contract between the husband

and wife if adequate consideration has been given the wife in exchange for her release and if she enters into the agreement with an understanding of the meaning of her rights to dower.

Curtesy. The surviving husband, at common law, had a life estate in the real property of his wife akin to, if not identical with, the widow's dower. This estate, known as curtesy, required a valid marriage and the death of the wife before the husband. As with dower, it existed only in estates of inheritance and there was no curtesy in a life estate. Unlike dower, curtesy did not exist unless a child were born of the marriage. The child need not, however, survive the wife. But, like dower, the wife could not alienate the husband's claim to curtesy without his written waiver. In many States, the estate of curtesy has been substantially modified or entirely abolished and in lieu of it the husband is given a statutory share in the estate of his deceased wife.

FUTURE INTERESTS

Not all interests in property are subject to immediate use and possession even though the right and title to the interest are absolute. Thus, where property is conveyed or devised by will "To A during his life and then to B and his heirs," B has a definite present *interest* in the property, but he is not entitled to immediate *possession*. Such and similar rights are generically referred to as future interests.

Reversions

Under the common law, the fee interest in property always had to be in someone. If A conveys property "to B for life" and makes no disposition of the remainder of the estate, A holds the reversion. This result is not as apparent when A conveys property "to B for life and then to my heirs." It is arguable that there is a remainder in the grantor's

next-of-kin. The common-law doctrine, however, was that such a reference to the heirs of the grantor placed a reversion in *him*, and his heirs took nothing except as they might inherit the reversion. This technical rule has important practical consequences where it has not been changed by statute. It means that the reversion may be attached by the grantor's creditors or it may be sold by him or devised by his will and, in any of such events, his heirs receive nothing.

Assume that H devises a life estate in farm land to his wife, W "and then to the legal heirs of my body," and that he devises the residue of his estate to W. H and W had no children, and H died without heirs of his body. The remainder to H's unborn children being necessarily limited on an event which may happen before or after, or at or after, the termination of the particular estate was contingent. Since there was no one in being to take the remainder when H died, a reversion was created by operation of law. W took this reversion which H had devised to her.

A "possibility of reverter," as the phrase suggests, exists where property may return to the grantor or his successor in interest because of the happening of an event upon which a fee simple estate was to terminate. It is the possibility of a reversion that is present in the grant of a conditional fee discussed in this chapter. Thus, A has a possibility of reverter if he dedicates property to a public use "so long as it is used as a park." If, in one hundred years, the city ceases to use the property for a park, the persons who are the heirs of A will be entitled to the property. Unlike a reversion, which is a present estate to be enjoyed in the future, a possibility of reverter is simply an expectancy.

Remainders

A remainder is an estate in property which, like a reversion, will take effect in possession, if at all, upon the termination of a prior estate created by the same instrument. Unlike a reversion, a remainder is held by a person other than the grantor or his successors. A gift to "A for his life and then to B and his heirs" creates a remainder in B. Upon the determination of the life estate, B will be entitled to possession as remainderman. A gift to A for 10 years and then to B will give B an estate to use and possess *after* the occurrence of the event that terminates A's estate. B takes his title not from A but from the original grantor.

There are two kinds of remainders, vested remainders and contingent remainders, and it is important to understand the difference between them.

Vested Remainders. A remainder is vested when the only contingency to the possession by the remainderman is the termination of the preceding estate. When B has a remainder in fee, subject only to a life estate in A, the only obstacle to the right of immediate possession by B or his heirs is A's life. A's death, no more, no less, is sufficient and necessary to place B in possession. The law considers this vested remainder as a fixed *present* interest but to be enjoyed in the future. It is an interest in property which is transferable just as much as the preceding estate in possession; and it is characteristic of a vested remainder that the owner of the preceding estate can do nothing to defeat the remainder.

By his will X devised certain property, "to my wife Y for her life, and then to my daughter Z for her life, and then to my nephew, A, and his heirs." Upon the death of X, A has at that instant a vested remainder although it may be many years before he or his heirs will enjoy possession. If the remainder is vested in fee simple the vesting does not depend upon the named remainderman surviving the owner of the intervening estate.

At common law, in order to create a fee simple, it was necessary to follow the language of a transfer to A with the phrase "and his heirs." The use of "heirs" not only was necessary to a fee simple but absolutely created a fee in A, regardless of the intention of the grantor. Under the Rule in Shelley's case, a conveyance to "A for life, remainder to the heirs of A," created a fee simple estate in A. The word "heirs" simply describes the estate given A and does not create any interest in his heirs except as they may take by inheritance if A does not dispose of the property during his life. In order to give A only a life estate, it was necessary to use a more explicit phrase such as "to A for life and then to his children," or "to A for life and then to his issue." Under a deed "to A and his heirs," the heirs took nothing by the conveyance. In many States, the Rule in Shelley's case has been abrogated by statute, giving the first taker only a life estate with a remainder to whomever are his heirs on his death.

Contingent Remainders. A remainder is contingent if the right to possession is dependent or conditional upon the happening of some event *in addition to* the termination of the preceding estate. The remainder may be conditioned upon the existence of some person not yet in being or upon the happening of an event which may never occur. A contingent remainder, by definition and unlike a vested remainder, is *not* ready to take immediate possession simply upon the termination of the preceding estate. A provision in a will "to A for life and then to his children but if he has no children then to B" creates contingent remainders both as to the children and as to B. If A marries and has a child, the remainder then vests in that child and B's expectancy is closed out. If A dies without having fathered a child, then and only then will an estate vest in B. It is, of course, possible for a contingent remainder to become vested while possession is still in the preceding life estate as evidenced by the birth of a child to A in the foregoing illustration.

A remainder may be contingent until the termination of the preceding estate. "To A for life and upon A's death to B and his heirs if B then be living in Chattanooga" will give B an estate only if he meets the condition. In such case, it is impossible to determine whether the remainder will be vested until the death of A. A gift to X "until Y returns from Mexico, and then to Z" is another illustration of a remainder (to Z) contingent upon an event which may never take place.

It is not always easy to decide whether a remainder is contingent, as in the above example, or is actually "vested" subject to being divested by a condition subsequent. If X, by his will, leaves his property to his wife for her life with the power to dispose of it by her will but, in the absence of such disposition, to their children, he creates a vested remainder in the children upon the death of X, subject to being divested by the exercise of the power.

In one sense, both vested and contingent remainders are contingent but there is an important distinction in the nature of the contingency. The grant "to A for life and then to B and his heirs" is contingent only as to the exact time when B will be entitled to possession. A grant "to A for life and then to B and his heirs if B is then a bachelor" is contingent upon the qualification of B, not just upon the death of A.

The Rule against Perpetuities

A contingent estate is void unless, by the terms of its creation, it must vest within a life or lives in being and twenty-one years thereafter. The purpose of this rule is to encourage the easy transfer of property by prohibiting the clouding of the title with future interests dependent upon uncertain contingencies which may not take place for a long period of time. A gift in a will by C to the first son of B who reaches the age of thirty years is void if B had no son at the death of C because a son might be born who would not reach the age of thirty until longer than twenty-one years after B's death, B being the "life in being" under the rule. If, on the other hand, the gift had been to the first child of B who reaches twenty-one years of age the gift is valid since such an event must take place, if at all, within twenty-one years of B's death. A "life in being" may be anyone named by the donor and need not be connected in any way with the property. Any number of persons may be the lives in being as long as the death of the last survivor can be determined. Thus, a gift to the children of B who are living upon the death of the last survivor of the present living descendents of Queen Victoria is valid. The fact that it is probable the contingent gift will vest, if at all, within the required period is not enough to avoid the rule. The rule is a strict rule which is not always governed by what appears reasonable in view of general human experience. For example, if property is deeded to A for life, remainder to his wife for life, remainder to such of his children as survive his wife, the rule requires the assumption that A's wife may die, that he may marry another woman who was not living at the date of the deed, that A may have more children by her, that she may live for more than twenty-one years after A's death and that the children's interests thus may not vest in quantity and quality within the limits of time.

Vested interests are not within the rule against perpetuities. If a future interest is vested, it is not prohibited by the rule against perpetuities no matter how long it may be before the possession will be enjoyed. A grant to X for 999 years and then to Z and his heirs creates a present vested interest in Z and his interest is not therefore subject to the rule. Thus, in any problem of future interests, the first question is always: Is the gift vested? If it is vested, the rule against perpetuities has no application. If the future interest is not vested, the second question is: Must it vest, if at all, within a named life or lives in being and twenty-one years thereafter.

Accumulation of Income

The law does not favor the indefinite accumulation of income. If a trust were established whereby the trustees were to collect and reinvest the income forever without distributing it, an ad terrorem argument could be made that, eventually, enormous amounts of capital and resources would be concentrated in a few hands. As a consequence, in most States income cannot be accumulated for a period longer than a life or lives in being and twenty-one years. In other States, the law provides that the accumulation must be limited to one of four periods; namely, during the life of the donor, during twenty-one years after the death of the donor, during the minority of anyone who is living at the donor's death, or during the minority of a person who is entitled to the income.

LEASEHOLD ESTATES

A lease is both a contract and a grant of an estate in land. It is a contract by which the owner of the fee or of a lesser estate in land, the landlord, grants to another, the tenant, an exclusive right to use and possession of the land for a definite or ascertainable period of time or term. The possessory term thus granted is an estate in land, called a *leasehold*. The landlord retains an interest in the property called a reversion. The principal characteristics of the leasehold estate are that it continues for a definite or ascertainable term and that it carries with it the obligation upon the part of the tenant to pay rent to the landlord.

CREATION AND DURATION OF THE LEASEHOLD ESTATE

By statute, in most jurisdictions, leases for a term longer than a specified period of time must be in writing. The period is fixed at one year in some jurisdictions; in others it is three years.

Definite Term

A lease for a definite term automatically expires at the end of the term by virtue of its own limitation. Such leases are frequently termed an "estate for years" even though the duration may be for one year or shorter. No notice to terminate is required.

Periodic Tenancy

A periodic tenancy is a definite term to be held over and over in indefinite succession. To illustrate, a lease "to T from month to month" or "from year to year" creates a periodic tenancy. Periodic tenancies arise frequently by implication. L leases to T without stating any term in the lease. This creates a tenancy at will. If T pays rent to L at the beginning of each month, and L accepts such payments, most courts hold that the tenancy at will has been transformed into a tenancy from month to month.

A periodic tenancy may be terminated by either party at the expiration of any one period but only upon adequate notice to the other party. In the absence of express agreement in the lease, the common law requires six months' notice in tenancies from year to year. However, this period has been shortened in most jurisdictions by statute to periods ranging between thirty and ninety days. In periodic tenancies involving periods of less than one year, the notice required at common law is one full period in advance, but, again, this may be subject to regulation by statute.

Tenancy at Will

A lease containing a provision that either party may terminate at any time creates a tenancy at will. So does a lease which does not specify any duration. At common law such tenancies were terminable without any notice but many jurisdictions now have statutes requiring a notice to terminate, usually thirty days.

Tenancy at Sufferance

One who is in possession without a valid lease is a tenant at sufferance. A tenant at sufferance is technically a trespasser and the landlord owes him no duties except to the extent that, under the common law, no landowner has a right wilfully to injure a trespasser.

The most common case of a tenancy at sufferance arises when a tenant fails to vacate the premises at the expiration of the lease. The common law gives the landlord the right to elect either to dispossess such tenant or to hold him for another term. If the expired lease was one for a year or more, or from year to year, the landlord can hold the holdover tenant for another full year. If the expired lease was for less than a year, or from month to month, the landlord can hold the holdover tenant for another full month. In the absence of express agreement, the holdover tenancy is a periodic tenancy, that is, it must be terminated by proper notice. The strict common law rule is that the landlord may elect to hold the tenant for another full period regardless of the fact that the tenant's failure to vacate on time was wholly without fault. Most courts today attempt to avoid this result if at all possible, and the rule has not been applied where the tenant's holdover is for a comparatively short time and is due to sickness or death of one of the members of his household.

TRANSFER OF INTERESTS IN A LEASEHOLD

Both the tenant's interest in the leasehold and the landlord's reversionary interest in the property may be freely transferred in the absence of contractual or statutory pro-hibition. This general rule is subject to one major exception: the tenancy at will. Any attempt by either party to transfer his interest is usually considered as an expression of the intent to terminate the tenancy.

Transfers by Landlord

After conveying the leasehold interest, a landlord is left with a reversionary interest in the property plus the right to rent and other benefits reserved under the lease. The landlord may transfer either or both of these interests. A party to whom the reversion is transferred takes the property subject to the tenant's leasehold interest if the transferee has actual or constructive notice of the lease. For example, L leases Whiteacre to T for five years and T records the lease with the Register of Deeds. L then sells Whiteacre to A. T's lease is still valid and enforceable against A whose right to possession of Whiteacre begins only after the expiration of the lease. The death of the landlord does *not* terminate the lease-hold and the reversionary interest passes to the heirs of the landlord. The landlord may also assign his right to unaccrued rent.

Transfers by Tenant

Assignment. Absent specific restrictions in the lease, leases are freely assignable. Many leases, however, prohibit assignment without the landlord's written consent. If the tenant assigns without such written consent, the assignment is not void, but it may be avoided by the landlord. In other words, the prohibition of assignment in a lease is only for the benefit of the landlord and cannot be relied upon by the assignor to terminate an otherwise valid assignment on the ground that the landlord did not consent. If, however, the landlord accepts rent from the assignee he will be held to have waived the restriction. The restriction, once waived, cannot be revived by the land-lord upon subsequent assignments.

The implied obligation to pay reasonable rent, because it arises in and out of the leasehold estate, ceases as soon as the estate is transferred by assignment. Thus, when the tenant assigns a lease which does not contain an express agreement to pay rent, the implied obligation to pay reasonable rent passes to the assignee. This is not true where the lease contains an express agreement of the tenant to pay rent. The tenant remains liable under this express covenant despite the fact that he has assigned the leasehold estate to another, unless the landlord releases him from the obligation. The assignee is also liable to the landlord for the stipulated rent. Note that the assignee of a lease which contains an express covenant to pay rent is liable for the *stipulated* rent— not for the reasonable rent. This result is obtained under the theory that certain covenants in the lease, of which the covenant to pay rent is one, *run with the land.* Such covenants pass to and obligate the assignee of the lease as if they were attached to the land covered by the lease. Covenants which have this quality of "running with the land" are covenants which "touch and concern" the land. The idea of covenants "touching and concerning" the land is an old one and is not easy of application. The following covenants have been held to "touch and concern" the land and thus to "run" with it: covenants to pay rent, covenants to pay taxes, options to renew, options to purchase, covenants to repair and restore, and covenants to keep the premises insured but only if coupled with covenants to repair and restore.

Under this doctrine, the covenant to pay rent and other covenants that run with the land pass to and obligate the assignee of the lease so long as he remains in possession of the leasehold estate. Although the assignee of the lease is thus bound to pay rent, the original tenant is not relieved of his contractual obligation to pay rent. Should the assignee fail to pay the stipulated rent, the original tenant will have to pay it. He will, of course, have a right to be reimbursed by the assignee. Thus, after an assignment of a tenant's interest, both the tenant and the assignee are primarily liable to the landlord for violations of covenants that run with the land.

Sublease. A sublease differs from an assignment in that it involves the transfer, by the tenant to another, of less than all the tenant's rights in the lease. For example, T, is a tenant under a lease which is to terminate on December 31, 1981. He enters into an agreement with S L, captioned "Assignment of Lease." The agreement provides that T "hereby assigns all his right, title and interest in the above lease to" S L, for a stated sum of money, and provides further that if S L does not pay the rent reserved in the lease to T's landlord, "then and in that event T reserves the right to reenter the said premises." Most courts hold that even though this agreement is labeled "Assignment of Lease," T has not, in fact, assigned the lease but has merely subleased. The reason is that T has reserved a right of reentry, that is, he has in fact transferred less than his whole interest in the lease. Most subleases are easily recognizable as such. The typical sublease would arise in the foregoing example if T leased the premises to S L for a shorter period than that covered by his own lease, e.g., until December 30, 1981, at a stated rental payable to T—not to T's landlord.

The legal effects of a sublease are entirely different from those of an assignment. In a sublease the sublessee, S L in the example above has no obligation to T's landlord. S L's obligations run solely to T, the original tenant. T is not relieved of any of his obligations under the lease. The doctrine that certain covenants run with the land has no application to a sublease. Thus, T's landlord has no right of action against T's sublessee S L under any covenants contained in the original lease between him and T, because that lease has not been assigned to S L. T, of course, remains liable to his landlord for the rent reserved, and upon all of the other covenants of the lessee, in the original lease between him and his landlord. Under the majority view, a covenant against assignment of a lease does not prohibit the tenant from subleasing the premises.

TENANT'S OBLIGATION TO PAY RENT

While the leasehold estate carries with it an implied obligation upon the part of the tenant to pay reasonable rent, the contract of lease almost always contains an express promise, known as a covenant, by the tenant to pay rent in specified amounts at specified times. There are several reasons for this. The most obvious is that, in the absence of such express covenant providng the amount of rental and the times for payment, the rent is a *reasonable* amount and is *payable only at the end of the term*. Aside from the economic advantage of settling the amount of the rent without recourse to the courts and of obtaining its payment in stated installments, the tenant's express covenant to pay rent serves other useful functions.

Most leases contain a provision to the effect that breach by the tenant of any of his covenants in the lease will entitle the landlord to declare the lease at an end, and will give him the right to regain possession of the premises. The tenant's express undertaking to pay rent thus becomes one of the covenants upon which this provision can operate. At common law, where there is no such provision in the lease, the tenant's failure to pay rent when due gives the landlord only the right to recover a judgment for the amount of such rent; it gives him no right to oust the tenant from the premises. This is a direct result of the common-law doctrine that the mutual covenants in a lease are independent of one another, unless the lease contains an express provision to the contrary.

In many jurisdictions today the foregoing rule has been changed by statute, to the extent that the landlord is given a right to dispossess the tenant for non-payment of rent although there is no provision for this in the lease. However, such statutes give the landlord a meaningful remedy only where the lease contains an express covenant to pay rent in stated installments or in advance. Rent which is not expressly made payable in advance or in stated installments becomes payable only at the end of the term.

The tenant is under no duty to make any repairs to the demised premises, unless the lease expressly so provides. He is not obliged to repair or restore substantial or extraordinary damage occurring without his fault, nor to repair damage caused by ordinary wear and tear. If damage occurs, the tenant continues to pay rent and to enjoy the use of the unrepaired premises.

Effect of Destruction of the Premises

The dual character of a lease as a contract and as a grant of an estate in land is particularly evident when considering the common law rule governing the destruction of the premises by fire or other fortuitous cause.

Where the tenant leases land together with a building and the building is destroyed by fire, or other fortuitous cause, the common law does not relieve him of his obligation to pay rent nor does it permit him to terminate the lease. The reason for this rule is that the common law regards the tenant's obligation to pay rent as given in exchange for the *estate* in land. The "estate" is a possessory term. The concept of an estate at common law is divorced from the economic benefits which go with it. Thus, while the destruction of a building may very well deprive the tenant of the entire economic benefit of his lease, the common law does not permit him to argue that the destruction of the builidng in fact amounted to a destruction of his "estate."

The common law rule has been modified in some States by statute, and in most States it is not applied to tenants who occupy only a portion of the building and have no interest in the building as a whole, such as apartment tenants. Most courts take the view that it would be stretching the concept of an "estate" too far to say that a tenant occupying a few rooms in a house is left with his "estate" in return for which he must pay rent, despite the total destruction of the building or his rooms.

Most leases contain clauses covering the fortuitous destruction of the premises. A typical clause provides that, upon damage by fire or other fortuitous cause, the landlord will repair and restore, and that, if the premises are wholly untenantable, the tenant's obligation to pay rent will be suspended until the premises are restored, but that if the landlord decides to demolish and reconstruct the premises, the lease will terminate.

This standard clause has several disadvantages to the business tenant. If the landlord elects to repair, the tenant remains bound under the lease although his business may be suspended long enough to cause a substantial loss of profit. Moreover, the tenant remains liable for the full rent if the premises, though partially destroyed, are not "wholly untenantable."

Effect of Public Controls

A tenant proposing to make a particular business use of the premises should be careful to check the applicable zoning ordinances before he enters into a lease. An existing zoning ordinance, prohibiting the very use which the tenant has in mind when he enters into the lease, will not relieve him of the obligation to pay rent. An exception may be made, however, in the case where the lease specifically restricts the tenant's use to a use which is subsequently outlawed

by a zoning ordinance. In such cases, the doctrine of commercial frustration is frequently applied by the courts to relieve the tenant of his obligations under the lease.

Total condemnation of the fee in the premises for public use terminates the lease and relieves the tenant from all obligations under it. Partial condemnation, however, does not relieve the tenant from his obligation to pay rent. For example, where T leases an office building for five years, and, in the first year a portion of the building is condemned for the construction of a road, T must continue to pay full rent to his landlord for the remainder of the term. He is entitled, however, to so much of the condemnation award as represents the rent he would be required to pay to the landlord for the portion condemned for the remainder of the term. Because this computation has the tendency to exhaust a substantial portion of the condemnation award, landlords prefer to insert a clause in the lease providing for a proportionate reduction of the rent, reserving to themselves the right to claim the entire condemnation award.

Effect of Eviction or Abandonment

Dispossession by Landlord for Breach of Covenant. When the tenant breaches one of the covenants in his lease, such as the covenant to pay rent, and the landlord evicts or dispossesses him pursuant to an express provision in the lease or under statute authorizing him to do so, the lease is terminated. Because the breach of the covenant to pay rent does not involve any injury to the premises and because the landlord's action in evicting the tenant terminates the lease, the tenant is not liable to the landlord for any future installments of the rent after such eviction. However, most long term business leases contain a "survival clause" providing that the eviction of the tenant for non-payment of rent will not relieve him of liability for damages measured by the difference between the rent reserved in the lease and the rent the landlord is able to obtain upon a reletting. Such a survival clause alone is not adequate protection to the landlord. It has generally been held that, because the tenant's liability is one in damages, the landlord is not entitled to sue him until the day on which the lease would have terminated if it had not been broken. This could mean that the landlord would have to wait twenty years to recover damages if that was the unexpired term of the lease. For this reason, landlords, in addition to inserting the "survival clause" mentioned, also insert a clause to the effect that the damages recoverable under it will accrue "at such times as the rent would have accrued under this lease." Such provisions have been upheld by the courts.

Wrongful Abandonment by Tenant. If the tenant wrongfully abandons the premises before the expiration of the term of the lease and the landlord re-enters the premises or relets them to another, a majority of the courts hold that the tenant's obligation to pay rent after re-entry terminates. The landlord, if he desires to hold the tenant to his obligation to pay rent, must either leave the premises vacant, or he must have available in the lease another "survival clause" covering this situation. Such survival clauses generally provide that, upon wrongful abandonment by the tenant, the landlord may relet the premises "as agent for the tenant; " and that the tenant will remain liable to the landlord for the difference between the rent reserved in the lease and the rent obtained upon such reletting minus costs of reletting. Under such a clause, the tenant remains liable for the rent, the lease is not terminated as in the case of eviction, and the landlord may sue him on the dates when installments of rent become due and payable under the original lease.

Wrongful Eviction by Landlord. If the tenant is wrongfully evicted by the landlord, his obligations under the lease are terminated. The landlord is bound to provide for the tenant quiet and peaceful enjoyment. This duty arises by implication, and is known as the landlord's covenant of "quiet enjoyment." It is the only covenant in a lease which, if breached, has the effect of terminating the lease without any express provision to this effect. The landlord breaches this covenant whenever he wrongfully evicts the tenant. He is also regarded as having breached this covenant if the tenant is evicted by someone having a better title than the landlord. The landlord is not responsible, however, for the wrongful acts of third parties unless they are done with his assent and under his direction.

LANDLORD'S OBLIGATIONS

Absent express provisions in the lease, the landlord, under the common law, has few obligations to his tenant. At the inception of the lease he must give the tenant a right to possession, but, under the majority rule, he is not required to give the tenant actual possession. Thus, if the previous tenant wrongfully holds over and refuses to move out, the landlord must bring dispossession proceedings to oust him, but he is not responsible to the new tenant for the delay thus occasioned and the new tenant is not relieved of the obligation to pay rent from the inception of his lease. A tenant may guard against such a situation by inserting a provision in the lease that, if through no fault of his own, he is kept out of possession, his obligation to pay rent will be suspended and that if the delay is longer than a specified time, the lease shall become void. In addition, the landlord may not interfere with the tenant's right to physical possession, use, and enjoyment of the premises.

Unless there is a specific undertaking in the lease, the landlord, under the common law, is under no obligation to maintain the premises in a tenantable condition or to make them fit for any purpose. Some courts, however, have recently abandoned this rule in residential leases by imposing an implied warranty that the leased premises are habitable, that is, fit for ordinary residential purposes. There courts have also held that the covenant to pay rent is conditioned upon the landlord's performance of the implied warranty of habitability. Courts reaching these results have emphasized the contractual aspects of a lease, although some have limited the warranty to leases of units in multiple-unit apartment buildings. Moreover, where the lease is of a furnished apartment, the majority of the courts hold that the landlord must maintain it in a tenantable condition.

In a few States there are statutes requiring landlords, specifically apartment landlords, to keep the premises fit for occupation. Zoning ordinances and health and safety regulations may also impose certain duties upon the landlord. Further, some States go so far as to impose duties on landlords to guarantee tenant security.

In the absence of an express provision in the lease, or statutory duty, no obligation rests upon the landlord to repair or restore the premises. The landlord does have, however, a duty to maintain, repair, and keep in safe condition, those portions of the premises which remain under his control. For example, an apartment house owner who controls the stairways, elevators, and other common areas is liable for their maintenance and repair and is responsible for injuries occurring as a result of his failure to do so. In respect to apartment buildings, the presumption obtains that any portion of the premises which is not expressly leased to the tenants remains under the landlord's control. Thus, the landlord, in such cases, is liable to make external repairs, including repairs to the roof.

While, at common law, the landlord is under no duty to repair, restore, or keep the premises in a tenantable condition, he may and often does assume those duties in the lease. When he does, the question presents itself whether breach by him of any of his undertakings under the lease entitles the tenant to abandon the premises and refuse to pay rent. Unless an express provision in the lease gives the tenant this right, the common law gives him only an action for damages. The reason for this rule is the same as the reason for the rule that a landlord has no right to dispossess the tenant for the breach of any of his covenants. The common law regards the mutual covenants in the lease as independent of one another. Thus, a breach by the landlord of any of his covenants does not operate to excuse the tenant from the duty to abide by his covenants, and vice versa. The only exception to this rule, noted earlier, is the landlord's covenant for quiet enjoyment.

In some States, statutes have changed this rule in favor of the landlord by giving him a right to evict the tenant for non-payment of rent. In practice, most leases contain express provisions giving the landlord the right to evict the tenant for breach of any of his covenants. Very few leases, however, give the tenant a correlative right. The inequality manifest in this situation has led the courts to develop the doctrine of *constructive eviction*. Under this doctrine, a failure by the landlord in any of his undertakings under the lease, which causes a substantial and lasting injury to the tenant's beneficial enjoyment of the premises, is regarded as being, in effect, an eviction of the tenant. Under such circumstances, the courts permit the tenant to abandon the premises and thereby terminate the lease. The tenant must abandon possession within a reasonable time in order to claim that there was a constructive eviction.

Cases

Vested Remainders

GRIFFIN v. MOON

(1965) 238 Ark. 692, 384 S.W.2d 243.

HOLT, J.

This case requires the interpretation of a will. The appellees instituted an action against the appellants seeking specific performance of their written agreement to purchase certain realty. The appellants' refusal to purchase was based upon their assertion that appellees did not have a merchantable title because of the ambiguous terms in a will devising the property to the appellees. The chancellor decreed specific performance of appellants' contract to purchase the lands. On appeal appellants' sole contention is that the trial court erred in finding that appellees' title to the land in question is marketable.

The appellants argue that the correctness of the decision of the chancellor depends upon the construction of a portion of the will which reads as follows:

"I give all the residue of my estate comprising a farm of twenty-four (24) acres and one lot, where I now reside, in Miller County, State of Arkansas, after fulfilling the foregoing legacies, to my wife, with the remainder thereof on her decease or marriage, to my said children and their children, respectively, share and share alike."

The testator was survived only by his widow, Maggie J. Moon, and his four sons, Ivor, Erbert, Loy and Fred Moon. These parties and the wives of the four sons are the appellees. The testator's widow is living and has never remarried. Each of his sons now has children, however, his sons had no children when the testator died. The appellants reject the title as unmarketable upon the contention that the remainder interest does not finally vest in the testator's children until the death or re-

marriage of the life tenant, the testator's widow. Further, that the testator's grandchildren, born and unborn, eventually would be entitled to an interest as remaindermen. We do not agree with the appellants and find no merit in either contention.

The real issue to be determined is whether the testator's four sons, the appellees, took a vested or contingent remainder upon the death of their father. If they took a vested remainder, then they can join with their mother, the life tenant, and convey a merchantable title; if they took only a contingent remainder, then they cannot. [Citation.] We are of the view that the questioned provisions of the will created a vested remainder in the testator's sons upon his death.

* * *

In McKinney v. Dillard & Coffin Co., 170 Ark. 1181, 283 S.W. 16, the devise involved principles applicable to the case at bar. In that case the father devised realty to his daughter for her natural life and at her death the lands were devised to her children in equal portions and if at the time of her death "any of her children be dead, leaving children, then such child or children is to have the same interest in said lands that said parent would have had, if alive." In that case we held that the remainder vested in the daughter's children as soon as born and before the death of the daughter. Further, that such vested interest, upon partition of the lands by the consent of the life tenant and vested remaindermen, was subject to a valid and enforceable mortgage. [Citations.]

In the very recent case of Gibson v. Lowry, 235 Ark. 234, 357 S.W.2d 531, we held that where a will gave a life estate to the testator's mother and stepfather and provided that at their death the farm should vest absolutely in the testator's brother, a vested remainder and not a contingent remainder was created in the brother. There we said that the interest vested "at the same instant and by the same grant as the life estate" and that although "the enjoyment of the possession of this interest was postponed until the termination of the life estate, still this right, * * * was presently fixed, and was in no wise dependent upon the happening of any event." [Citation.]

Thus, in the case at bar, appellants' contention that under the terms of the will the remainder is not vested in the testator's four sons until the death or remarriage of the life tenant is without merit. We hold that the testator's four sons now have a vested remainder and it is not subject to the happening of any future event. Their remainder interest vested at the same time that the life estate vested. [Citations.]

It is well settled that where both the life tenant and vested remaindermen join in a deed the entire estate in fee is passed to the grantee. Therefore, it follows that in the case at bar a deed by the appellees conveys a merchantable title.

The decree of the chancellor ordering specific performance of the contract is affirmed.

Periodic Tenancy: Notice
Required for Termination

MARKOE v. NAIDITCH AND SONS

(1975, Minn.) 225 N.W.2d 289.

TODD, J.

Defendant Jack Lehtinen appeals from an order denying his alternative motions for amended findings or a new trial. The district court ordered judgment for plaintiffs, J. Stuart Markoe and Richard Markoe, against defendant Naiditch and Sons, and for Naiditch and Sons on their cross-claim against appellant in an action for rent and

costs in connection with a month-to-month lease. We affirm.

Naiditch and Sons is a partnership engaged in the business of development and management of rental properties. From 1966 on, it rented, for the storage of furniture, the fourth floor of a commercial building owned by plaintiffs. The premises were rented initially under two 2-year leases and subsequently under a month-to-month oral lease.

In September 1971, the partnership sold the furniture stored on plaintiff's premises to Jack Lehtinen for use in apartment buildings that he managed. Naiditch and Sons and Lehtinen agreed that Lehtinen would pay the rent on plaintiffs' property until the furniture was removed.

Lehtinen began removing the furniture in October 1971. In October or November 1971, he told Stuart Markoe of the purchase of the furniture and indicated that he would be out of the premises as soon as possible. No written notice of termination was given by either Naiditch and Sons or Lehtinen.

After paying the rent for October and November, Lehtinen left the Markoe premises for the last time in December 1971. In April 1973, pursuant to an order of the fire marshal, Stuart Markoe had all remaining material removed from the premises and hauled away and dumped as junk. Among the items removed were couches without legs, lawn furniture, several mattresses and bed springs, some end tables, and some lamps. In May 1973, this action was tried.

Minn.St. 504.06 requires that notice of termination of a month-to-month tenancy be written. Our decisions have consistently required strict statutory compliance. [Citations.]

The actions of Naiditch and Sons and Lehtinen amount to no more than an abandonment of the leased premises. In Gruman v. Investors Diversified Services, Inc., 247 Minn. 502, 507, 78 N.W.2d 377, 380 (1956), we stated the following rule:

* * * [A] lessee's unilateral action in abandoning leased premises, *unless accepted by his lessor*, does not terminate the lease or forfeit the estate conveyed thereby, nor the lessee's right to use and possess the leased premises and, by the same token, his obligation to pay the rent due therefor. [Citations].

There is no evidence of acceptance in the facts of this case. As landlords are under no obligation in Minnesota to mitigate damages after a tenant abandons leased premises [citation], the judgment against Naiditch and Sons was proper.

The trial court found that Lehtinen assumed responsibility for the rent of the premises. * * * A careful review of the record and proceedings herein indicates that the evidence more than adequately meets this standard.

Affirmed.

Tenant's Obligation to Pay Rent

COLONIAL COURT APARTMENTS, INC. v. KERN

(1968) 282 Minn. 533, 163 N.W.2d 770.

PER CURIAM. This is an appeal from an order of the municipal court denying plaintiff's alternative motion for judgment notwithstanding the findings or for a new trial in an action for rent. The trial court found for defendant, holding that there had been a constructive eviction. Plaintiff contends that the findings are not supported by the record.

From the record it appears that plaintiff, Colonial Court Apartments, Inc., rented an apartment to defendant, Irene Kern, for a 1-year term to begin January 1, 1966. The apartment immediately above was occupied by a young couple. When Mrs. Kern leased from plaintiff, she expressed her desire for a quiet apartment and was assured that the building was well insulated and not noisy. It is agreed that the building was well constructed and well maintained. However, almost from the start of her oc-

cupancy, Mrs. Kern complained that some young neighbors interfered with her enjoyment of the apartment, alleging that they gave noisy parties twice a week, ran water early in the morning, operated a dishwasher at late hours, subjected her to insulting and abusive language, and disturbed her sleep to the point where she had to go elsewhere for rest. After she had lodged several complaints, the landlord terminated the young couple's lease, effective February 28, 1966. However, due to the pregnancy of the wife, it was agreed that they could remain in the apartment until the baby was born on condition that there would be no further disturbances and with the understanding that they would vacate as soon as possible thereafter. This agreement was explained to defendant. There were no further disturbances until shortly after the baby was born, at which time the objectionable conduct was resumed. On May 12, 1966, the landlord received a letter from the young couple expressing their intention to vacate by June 1, 1966. In response, the landlord wrote informing them that they were responsible for rent to June 30, 1966, because they had not given the full 30-day statutory notice, and went on to explain that "your notice and the first possibility to vacate, according to law, will be June 30th." They were advised that if the landlord could rerent the apartment sooner he would do so. On Memorial Day of 1966, in response to Mrs. Kern's complaint about another loud party the night before, the landlord told her that the neighbors would be out by June 1. On June 16, the young couple still being in possession, defendant vacated the apartment, feeling that she could no longer endure the continued disturbances and annoyances. The trial court found:

"That the noise emanating from the Lindgren apartment so disturbed and interfered with Defendant's rest, that she found it necessary to drive to her parents' home in Eau Claire, Wisconsin, on the average of twice a month, on week ends, to get a good night's sleep on the Friday nights of said week ends.

"That Plaintiff took no further action with respect to removing the source of Defendant's disturbance by requiring performance by Lindgrens of their agreement to vacate as soon as possible following the said birth of their child until, on May 12, 1966, Plaintiff was advised by the said Lindgrens that they intended to vacate their apartment effective June 1, 1966. Whereupon, on May 16, 1966, Plaintiff, through its authorized agent, notified the said Lindgrens that their notice of intention to vacate was insufficient and that their first possibility of vacating according to law would be June 30, 1966."

A constructive eviction is said to occur when the beneficial enjoyment of an apartment by the lessee is so interfered with by the landlord as to justify an abandonment. It does not suppose an actual ouster or dispossession by the landlord. [Citation.] Ordinarily, the rule is that the acts of one tenant do not constitute a constructive eviction of another tenant of the same landlord unless they materially disturb the latter tenant in the use, occupancy, and enjoyment of the demised premises or the natural consequence thereof is to injure the other tenant. [Citations.]

* * *

In fairness it should be said that the trial court could well have found that the landlord took such reasonable measures as were warranted under the circumstances to correct the conditions of which defendant complained. He might also have found that the landlord's letter to the tenants that their "first possibility to vacate, according to law, will be June 30," referred to liability for rent rather than a requirement to remain in possession. Nevertheless, we are not warranted in making an exception to our well-established rule that in reviewing the record the testimony must be considered in the light most favorable to the prevailing party, and if support for the findings may be found in the evidence as a whole, such findings will not be disturbed. The findings of fact by the trial court and the jury stand on equal footing and are entitled to the same weight and will not be reversed on appeal unless they are manifestly and palpably contrary to the evidence. [Citation.]

"The definition of what constitutes constructive eviction does not get us far. Usually the question whether there is a constructive eviction is one of fact with each case largely dependent upon its particular circumstances."

* * *

Affirmed.

Problems

1. Under the will of X, a farm was devised to Y, to have and to hold for and during his life and upon his death to Z. Y went into possession on the death of X. Some years thereafter, oil was discovered in the vicinity. Y thereupon made an oil and gas lease and the oil company set up its machinery to commence drilling operations. Z thereupon filed suit to enjoin the operations. Assuming an injunction to be the proper form of remedy, what decision?

2. George Cook conveyed Blackacre, as follows:

I convey and warrant to my daughter, Jane Cook, and her bodily heirs and assigns forever, all of the following described premises [legal description]."

When the deed was delivered, Jane Cook was seven years of age. Later George Cook died, at which time Jane was married and the mother of two children. After her father's death, another child was born to Jane. Subsequently, Jane conveyed all of her right, title and interest in the premises to Brooks. Brooks now contends that he is the owner in fee simple of the premises.   After the conveyance to Brooks, a fourth child was born to Jane.

Determine and explain the estate created by the conveyance and the interests, if any, of the children in the premises.

3. S owned Blackacre in fee simple.   In section 3 of a properly executed will, S devised Blackacre as follows: "I devise my farm Blackacre to my son D so long as it is used as a farm."   Sections 5 and 6 made testamentary gifts to persons other than D.   The last and residuary clause of S's will provided: "All the residue of my real and personal property not disposed of heretofore in this will, I devise and bequeath to the A B C University."

S died in 1982, survived by his son D.   S's estate has been administered.   D has been offered $100,000 for Blackacre if he can convey title to it in fee simple.

What interests in Blackacre were created by S's will?

4. By his validly executed will John Stone provided: "I give and bequeath to my son, Ray Stone, my farm known as Blackacre to have and enjoy the use of thereof during his natural life and upon his death said real estate shall be divided in equal parts among his children."   Ray Stone, recently married to a young wife, survived his father as did the only children of his first marriage, Jack and Jill, 22 and 24 years of age, respectively.

Shortly after the probate of John Stone's will had been completed, Ray and his two children had an opportunity to sell Blackacre to William Todd provided they could grant a fee simple title.   Can they convey a fee simple title?

5. On September 1, 1979, A, the owner of a 160-acre farm leased it to B.   The terms of the lease provided that the lease should continue from year to year and could be terminated upon a 60-day notice.   B remained in possession for three years, paying the agreed rental.   A desired to terminate the lease and, on June 1, 1982, gave the required 60-day notice to B, that he had elected to terminate the lease at the end of the tenant year, being September 1, 1982.   On June 15, 1982, B planted a corn crop, cultivated the same and on September 1, 1982, delivered possession of the premises to A.   On October 1, 1982, B returned to harvest the matured corn crop and was prevented from entering the land

by A.   B brought an action against A for the value of his share of the corn crop.

Decision?

6. A leased to B for a term of ten years beginning May 1, 1981, certain premises located at 527-529 Main Street in the city of X.   The premises were improved with a 3-story building, the first floor being occupied by stores and the upper stories by apartments.   On May 1, 1982, B leased one of the apartments to C for one year.   On July 5, 1982, a fire destroyed the second and third floors of the building.   The first floor was not burned but was rendered untenantable.   Neither the lease from A to B, nor the lease from B to C contained any provision in regard to the fire loss.   Discuss the liability of B and C to continue to pay rent.

7. Ames leased an apartment to Boor at $200 a month payable the last day of each month.   The term of the written lease was from January 1, 1981 through April 30, 1982.   On March 15, 1981 Boor moved out, telling Ames that he disliked all the other tenants.   Ames replied: "Well, you are no prize as a tenant; I probably can get more rent from someone more agreeable than you."   Ames and Boor then had a minor physical altercation in which neither was injured.   Boor sent the keys to the apartment to Ames by mail.   Ames wrote Boor, "It will be my pleasure to hold you for every penny you owe me.   I am renting the apartment in your behalf to Clay until April 30, 1982, at $175 a month."   Boor had paid his rent through February 28, 1981.   Clay entered the premises on April 1, 1981.

How much rent, if any, may Ames recover from Boor?

8. T, a widower, died at the age of 90, and by his will left his entire estate in trust.   Surviving T were B, a son, C, a grandson, D, a great-grandson, and E, a five year old son of D.   The trustees were directed to pay the income to B for life;   then to C for life;   then to D for life;   then to E for life;   then to the first son of E until he became 21, at which time the trust estate was to be turned over to such son of E.   An action is brought to have this trust declared void as offending Rule against Perpetuities.   Decision?

9. P and D executed a written lease on October 20, 1979, for a business property in Emanon.

The lease provided for an annual rental of $8,000 for the first year, payable in advance; an annual rental of $10,000 for the next nine years of the term, payable annually in advance, the first payment to be due on October 1,1980, and thereafter on the first day of October. D did not pay the rent of $10,000 payable on October 1, 1982. He had assigned the lease to Muir Gas, Inc., with P's consent. Muir Gas, Inc. assumed the obligation to pay the rent to P for the use of the property. It did not, however, pay the rent due on October 1, 1982. Upon D's refusal to pay him $10,000, P brought an action against D to recover this amount. Decision?

10. Jay signed a two-year lease which contained a clause which expressly prohibited subletting. After six months, Jay asked the landlord for permission to sublet the apartment for one year. The landlord refused. This angered Jay and he immediately assigned his rights under the lease to Kay. Kay was a distinguished gentleman and Jay knew that everyone would consider him a desirable tenant. Is Jay's assignment of his lease of the apartment to Kay valid?

REAL PROPERTY: CONCURRENT OWNERSHIP, EASEMENTS, AND NATURAL RIGHTS

The ownership of real property may be held by one individual or, concurrently, by two or more persons. If title is concurrently in two or more persons they are generally referred to as co-tenants, each entitled to an undivided interest in the entire property and neither having a claim to any specific portion of it. Each may have equal undivided interests or one may have a larger undivided share than the other. Regardless of the particular relationships between the co-tenants, this form of ownership must be carefully distinguished from the separate ownership of specific parts of property by different persons. Thus, it is possible, for example, for A, B and C to each own distinct and separate parts of Blackstone Manor or they may each own, as co-tenants, an undivided one-third interest in all of Blackstone Manor. Whether they are co-tenants or owners of specific portions will depend upon the manner and form in which they acquire their interests.

CONCURRENT OWNERSHIP

There are two major classifications of concurrent ownership; tenancy in common and joint tenancy. They have in common the characteristic of undivided interest in the whole, a right in both tenants to possession and the right of either to sell his interest during life, thereby terminating the original relationship. Other forms of co-ownership of real estate are community property, tenancy by the entireties, condominiums, and cooperatives.

Joint Tenancy

The most significant incident of joint tenancy is the right of survivorship. Upon the death of one of the joint tenants, title to the entire property passes by operation of law to the survivor or survivors. The heirs-at-law of the deceased joint tenant have no claim to his interest nor do his general creditors; nor can a joint tenant transfer his interest by will. Also, the undivided interest of a joint tenant is not an "estate of inheritance" so that where a husband holds property in joint tenancy with someone other than his wife, his wife cannot claim dower in her husband's interest as against the surviving joint tenant.

Because of the right of survivorship, the joint tenancy is an attractive method for holding title between husband and wife. Upon the death of either spouse, the property will go to the survivor by operation of law without recourse to a will and the necessity, together with the attendant delay and expense, of probate. For this reason, joint tenancies between husband and wife or between other members of a family, have, on occasion, been referred to as the "poor man's willl." Even in large estates, where probate is necessary, joint tenancies can perform useful functions. For example, a joint bank account can provide the survivor with an immediate source of cash for family needs.

Tax considerations and other factors, however, often make this form of ownership inadvisable as a substitute for a will. Thus, even in the case of the smaller estate, use of the joint tenancy in substitution for a will should not be lightly undertaken.

Creation of a Joint Tenancy. By statute in most States, certain words must be used to create a joint tenancy in real property. Some of those statutes provide that a grant of an estate to two or more persons in their own right shall be a tenancy in common, unless expressly declared to be in joint tenancy. Other statutes add that the deed of conveyance must expressly state that the estate is granted not in tenancy in common but in joint tenancy.

Thus, if a deed of conveyance is not drafted properly, the resulting ownership would be a tenancy in common and the deed will wholly fail in its purpose where it is intended that it act in substitution for a will. This is so because there is no right of survivorship in a tenancy in common. Instead, assuming that the deceased tenant in common leaves no will, (as may be the case where reliance was placed upon the existence of a joint tenancy) his undivided interest will descend to his heirs-at-law un-

der the statutes of descent instead of passing to the surviving co-tenant, as intended.

To sustain a joint tenancy, the common law requires the presence of what is known as the "four unities" of time, title, interest and possession. (1) The unity of time means that the interest of all tenants must vest at the same time; (2) the unity of title means that all tenants must acquire title by the same instrument; (3) the unity of interest means that all tenants must have identical interests as to duration and scope; (4) the unity of possession means that all the tenants have the same right of possession and enjoyment. The absence of any one of these four unities will prevent the creation of a joint tenancy. Failure of any one of the first three unities will result in the creation of a tenancy in common as the only unity required of a tenancy in common is the unity of possession.

The most important unity is that of time. Most would-be joint tenancies are created by the same instrument (unity 2) and purport to grant identical interests as to duration and scope (unity 3). The failure of the unity of time, however, has resulted in many disappointed expectations. Assume that H owns Blackacre. H marries W. H and W decide that they should hold all real property as joint tenants so as to assure succession between them without recourse to a will. Accordingly, H conveys Blackacre "to H and W as joint tenants and not as tenants in common." H dies and W claims Blackacre by right of survivorship. Under the common law, W's claim will not be sustained because when H conveyed Blackacre to H and W as joint tenants his interest in Blackacre was already in existence—he owned Blackacre. W's interest came into existence at a later time than H's. Because of the failure of the unity of time, H and W held as tenants in common and W takes only such interest in Blackacre as will come to her under the rules of intestate succession. Statutes in some States have changed this rule, but its existence must be borne in mind when creating a joint tenancy. In the absence of such a statute, H should convey Blackacre to a "dummy or straw man," who reconveys "to H and W as joint tenants and not as tenants in common."

The concept of unity of interest requires that the interest of a joint tenant be equal to that of his co-tenant. A deed conveying title to H to ¾ and W to ¼ as joint tenants would result in a tenancy in common and not a joint tenancy. However, two separate groups of joint tenants may hold a parcel of real estate as tenants in common with the interests of the two groups being unequal. For example, assume that H and W, as joint tenants, own an undivided ¾ interest in Blackacre, and A and B, as joint tenants, own the other ¼ interest in the property. The right of survivorship would exist between H and W only with respect to their joint tenancy, and between A and B in their joint tenancy, and the two groups would hold as tenants in common toward one another. Accordingly, if A and B should both die in a common disaster, H and W would not acquire any interest in their one-fourth, which would pass to the heirs of A and B.

Severance of Joint Tenancy. One important rule of joint tenancies is that any joint tenant may sever the joint tenancy by conveying or mortgaging his interest to a third party. Further, the interest of either co-tenant is subject to levy and sale upon execution. While the mere entry of a judgment against one of the joint tenants does not sever the joint tenancy, where a judgment has been entered against one of the joint tenants, the judgment creditor may levy upon his interest, and a sale under execution will sever the joint tenancy. "Sever" here means that the right of survivorship is lost and the tenancy becomes a tenancy in common as between the remaining joint tenant and the grantee, mortgagee or execution purchaser. In those States which still recognize tenancy by the entireties between husband and wife, a conveyance by either of the spouses does not defeat the surviving spouse's right of survivorship. Except in those States, however, a joint tenancy between husband and wife as a substitute for a will may, because of the rule permitting severance, defeat the expectations of either party.

The will of one of the joint tenants devising his interest in the joint tenancy property to a third person does not effect a severance because a will does not become effective until the death of the testator. Upon the death of a joint tenant the entire estate automatically vests in the surviving joint tenant by operation of law. Accordingly, in such case, there is no property for the will to operate upon.

Tenancy in Common

Tenants in common, like joint tenants, are persons who hold undivided interests in the same property, each having the right to possession but neither claiming any specific portion of the property. Unlike joint tenants, there is no right of survivorship and, also unlike joint tenants, the only prerequisite is the so-called unity of possession. One tenant may have acquired his interest by conveyance at a different time, and the other may have acquired his interest through inheritance. Persons may become tenants in common by operation of law as well as by the intention of a party.

A conveyance to two or more parties, "share and share alike," is a frequent method of establishing tenancy in common and, by statute in many States, a conveyance to two or more persons will be presumed to create a tenancy in common. A tenancy in common may result from an unskilled attempt to create a joint tenancy. The relationship will also arise when an owner conveys a fractional interest in his property to another person as, for example, a conveyance of a one-tenth interest in a coal mine or an oil lease.

Tenancy in common may be terminated either by transfer of all co-interests to one person or by partition of the property among the tenants, making each the exclusive owner of a specific part of the entire property. Partition is a device recognized and regulated by law for changing undivided interests into several and exclusive interests proportionate to the former undivided shares. Because of the obvious practical difficulty of making an equitable division of most real estate, the usual consequence of a partition suit instituted by a co-owner of real property is a sale of the entire tract by order of court with each co-owner receiving a share of the proceeds equivalent to his undivided interest in the property.

Community Property

In Arizona, California, Idaho, Louisiana, Nevada, New Mexico, Texas and Washington, any property acquired by the efforts of either the husband or wife belongs one-half to each spouse. This system known as "community property" originated in the civil law of continental Europe but it has been modified and affected by the common law as well as by statutes in this country.

In most instances, the only property which belongs separately to either spouse is that acquired prior to the marriage or subsequent thereto by gift or devise. Upon the death of either spouse, one-half of the community property belongs outright to the survivor and the interest of the deceased spouse in the other half may go to the heirs of the decedent or as directed by will, although, under some conditions in a few jurisdictions, the surviving spouse may also claim an interest in the decedent's one-half share of the property.

Community property is said to be liable for all "community debts," being those debts incurred by the husband during the marriage and not for his own separate benefit. It is also generally liable for the ante-nuptial debts of both husband and wife. Formerly, the husband had control over all such property during his lifetime but this doctrine has been substantially modified.

Tenancy by the Entireties

This form of concurrent ownership, less common today than formerly, was created only by a conveyance to a husband and wife and was distinguished from joint tenancy by the inability of either spouse to convey separately his or her interest during life and thus destroy the right of survivorship. Likewise, the interest of either spouse could not be attached by creditors. In some States, statutes giving the wife the right to convey her property have been construed as abolishing this form of concurrent ownership, but, in other jurisdictions, a conveyance to a husband and wife is still presumed to create a tenancy by the entireties unless a joint tenancy or a tenancy in common is clearly indicated. By the nature of the tenancy, a divorce terminates the relationship and partition would then be available as a method of creating separate interests in the property.

Condominiums

A form of coownership called "condominium" has recently gained extensive use in the United States. All states have enacted statutes authorizing the use of this form of ownership. The purchaser of a condominium acquires separate ownership to the unit and becomes a tenant in common in the common facilities such as the land upon which the project is built, recreational facilities, hallways, parking areas, and spaces between the units. The common elements are maintained by a condominium association funded by assessments levied on each unit. The transfer of a condominium conveys both the separate ownership of the unit and the share in the common elements.

Cooperatives

Cooperatives involve an indirect form of common ownership. A cooperative, usually a corporation, purchases or constructs the dwelling units. The cooperative then leases the units to the shareholders as tenants who acquire the right to use and occupy their units.

Rights and Duties of Co-owners

As a rule of general application, each co-tenant is entitled to the use of any or all of the property subject only to a similar right in his co-tenants. As a practical matter, the most common problems between co-tenants arise from the exclusive use of the property by one of the co-tenants. In such cases, the issues are (1) the extent of the duty of the possessor to account to his co-tenants for the rents or profits and (2) the extent of the duty of the co-tenants to contribute to the costs of maintaining the common property. In some instances, a third problem—that of waste—may arise due to use of the land by a co-tenant who is in sole possession.

The duty of one co-tenant to account for rents and profits over and above his fair (proportionate) share was established by statute in England at an early date. In most jurisdictions, this duty to account is only for the rents or profits actually received and not for a fair return on the property except where the possessing tenant has ousted the other tenants from the property. Thus, if A, by common consent, lives in and manages an apartment building owned jointly by himself, B and C, on which the 1970 level of rents still prevail, he will not be liable to B and C for more than two thirds of the rent received even though rents have subsequently risen for similar properties.

Non-possessing co-tenants are obligated to contribute to such costs as repairs and taxes if they have not been restrained from using the property, and if the possessing tenant in good faith has incurred the expenses which have mutually benefited all the owners. There is more doubt as to the liability of co-tenants to contribute to major or capital improvements even though the improvement may benefit the property and thus increase the value of each co-tenant's interest.

The doctrine of waste which exists with respect to life tenants, remaindermen, and landlord and tenant has application among concurrent owners. Whether or not waste has been committed by a co-tenant will depend not only upon the extent of the use but upon the nature of the property. Thus, the cutting of timber may be waste while the mining of coal would not be. The former may constitute an unreasonable use of the land while the latter would be a natural use.

It is sometimes said that co-owners share a fiduciary obligation to each other. By this, the courts generally mean that such owners cannot deal with each other as they might with strangers driving whatever bargain circumstances permit. Thus, a person must account to his co-tenants if he bids on the common property at a judicial or tax sale and they, in turn, if they wish to reacquire an interest in the property, must contribute to the bid price.

Parties dealing with co-owners must recognize the limits upon the powers of any individual co-tenant. While he may mortgage or lease his undivided interest, that is all with which he can deal. One co-owner cannot dispose of or encumber any specific portion of the common property. All must act to deal effectively with the entire property. For example, A, one of several tenants in common, gives a lease to B of all the property. Later, A and all the others lease the entire tract to C who has knowledge of the lease to B. Under these circumstances,

B has the right to use only A's interest while C has the right to the use of the entire remaining interest.

EASEMENTS

An easement may be defined as a limited right to make use of the land of another in a specific manner, created by the acts of the parties or by operation of law, and having all the attributes of an estate in the land itself. A typical easement exists where A sells a part of his land to B and expressly provides in the same or a separate document that B, as the adjoining landowner, shall have a right-of-way over a strip of A's remaining parcel of land. B's land is said to be the *dominant* parcel and A's land, which is subject to the easement, is the *servient* parcel. Easements may, of course, include a multitude of different types of uses as, for example, a right to run a ditch across another's land, to lay pipe under the surface, to erect power lines or, in the case of adjacent buildings, to use a stairway or a common or "party" wall.

Easements fall into two classes, easements *appurtenant* and easements *in gross*. Appurtenant easements are by far the more common type and, as the name indicates, the rights and duties created by such easements pertain to the land itself and not to the particular individuals who may have created them. Thus, in the foregoing illustration, if A conveys his servient parcel to C who has actual notice of the easement for the benefit of B's land or constructive notice by means of the local recording act, C takes the parcel subject to the easement. Likewise, if B conveys his dominant parcel to D, it is not necessary to refer specifically to the easement in the deed from B to D in order to give to D, as the new owner of the dominant parcel, the right to use the right-of-way over the servient parcel. Since B does not then own the dominant parcel he has no further right to use the right-of-way.

B could not, however, transfer the benefit of the easement to a party who did not acquire an interest in the dominant parcel of land. Most frequently, a deed conveying the land "together with all appurtenances" is sufficient to transfer the easement. This characteristic of an appurtenant easement is described by the statement that both the burden and the benefit of an appurtenant easement pass with the land.

The second class of easements are those which are said to be in gross or personal to the particular individual who received the right. They do not depend upon the ownership of land and, in effect, amount to little more than an irrevocable license.

Creation of Easements

Easements may be created in a number of different wasys: (a) by express grant, (b) by implied grant, (c) by necessity, (d) by dedication, and (e) by prescription.

By Express Grant or Reservation. The most common way to create an easement is to convey it by deed. For example, when A conveys part of his land to B, he may, in the same deed, expressly grant an easement to B over A's remaining property. Alternatively, A may grant an easement to B in a separate document. This document must comply with all the formalities of a deed. An easement is an interest in land subject to the Statute of Frauds. Like other instruments granting interests in land, it must be recorded, otherwise it will not be binding upon anyone who acquires A's remaining property for value and without notice of B's easement.

In other instances, when an owner of land transfers it, he may wish to retain certain rights in it. In the example given, A may want to "reserve" an easement in favor of the land retained by himself over the land granted to B. A may do this by express words to that effect in the deed of conveyance to B. Alternatively, A may "except" an easement right over the land granted to B in favor of the land retained by himself.

By Implied Grant or Reservation. In some instances the law will imply the grant or reservation of an easement where the parties have not expressly provided for one. Suppose A owns two adjacent lots, Nos. 1 and 2. There is a house on each lot. Behind each house is a garage. A has constructed a driveway along the medial line between the two lots, partly on lot 1 and partly on lot 2, which leads from the street in front of the houses to the two garages in the rear. A conveys lot 2 to B without any mention of the driveway. A is held to have *impliedly granted* an easement to B over that portion of the driveway which lies on A's lot 1, and he is held to have *impliedly reserved* an easement over that portion of the driveway which lies on B's lot 2.

Easements by implied grant or implied reservation arise whenever an owner of adjacent properties establishes an *apparent* and *permanent* use, in the nature of an easement, and then conveys one of the properties without mention of any easement. The law causes the apparent and permanent use (commonly known as a *quasi-easement*) to survive the conveyance by implying a grant or a reservation of such easement in the conveyance. In the example given, there was both an implied grant and an implied reservation when A conveyed lot 2 to B because the driveway was partly on lot 1 and partly on lot 2.

By Necessity. If A conveys part of his land to B, and the part conveyed to B is so situated that B would have no access to it except across A's remaining land, the law implies a grant by A to B of a right-of-way across A's remaining land. An easement by necessity does not depend upon the prior existence of an apparent and permanent roadway across A's remaining land; on the other hand, the circumstances which will give rise to a way by necessity must be more than mere convenience. A way by necessity will not usually arise if an alternative but circuitous approach to B's land is available. It should be noted that a way by necessity can be established only over the land of one who has conveyed the landlocked property. Thus, where A conveys a parcel of land to B which is wholly landlocked by the properties of C, D and E, no way by necessity can be established against C, D or E. A way by necessity may, however, arise by implied reservation. This would be the case where A conveys part of his land to B and A's remaining property would be wholly landlocked unless he is given a right-of-way across the land conveyed to B.

By Dedication. When an owner of land subdivides it into lots and records the plan or plat of the subdivision, he is held, both by common law and now more frequently by statute, to have dedicated *to the public* all of the streets, alleys, parks, playgrounds and beaches shown on the plat. In addition, when the subdivider sells the lots by reference to the plat, it is now generally recognized that the purchasers acquire easements by implication over the areas shown dedicated to the public.

By Prescription. An easement may arise by prescription in most States if certain required conditions are met. To obtain an easement by prescription, a person must use a portion of land owned by another in a way (1) that is adverse to the rightful owner's use, (2) that is open and notorious, and (3) that is continuous and uninterrupted for a specific period of time. If the owner gives the claimant permission to use the land, no easement by prescription is acquired.

The time period varies from State to State, but twenty years is a common statutory period. In most instances, the period is the same as is necessary in the particular jurisdiction to establish ownership of land by adverse possession. Very little is required in the way of exercise of dominion by the owner of the land to break off the "uninterrupted" adverse user and start the period running again from the beginning. One common practice in cases of paths or private roads is for the owner to block the passage for a day. Little more than symbolic assertion of ownership appears to be required.

Use and Maintenance of Easements

In the case of easements established by grant, the extent of the use which can be made of the easement will depend not only upon the terms of the grant but also, upon the circumstances surrounding the transaction. A right-of-way general in its terms may validly be used for automobiles even though only horse-drawn carriages were in style at the time of its creation. On the other hand, a way intended as access to one parcel of land may not be extended so as to afford access to other land. If a grant is for a specific purpose, the dominant owner has no right to use it for other purposes. Thus, an easement "for driveway purposes" has been held to be for ingress and egress only and does not allow for parking on the servient estate. Similarly, an easement for a pipe line does not permit the establishment of a power line nor a roadway although the owner of the easement will, of course, be entitled to have reasonable access to the pipe line for repair and maintenance.

Since the title to the servient parcel remains in the owner of the entire servient tract, he may make any use of, or allow others the use of, the tract which does not interfere with the easement. Thus, crops may be grown over an easement for a pipe line but livestock could not be pastured on an easement for a driveway. Although it is the duty of the owner of the servient parcel not to interfere with the use of the ease-

ment, it is generally the responsibility of the owner of the dominant parcel to maintain and keep in repair the easement. Conversely, the owner of the servient parcel does not have an affirmative duty to keep the property in proper condition for the use of the easement.

Since an easement is considered as benefiting all the dominant parcel, the right to use the easement will generally pass to each owner upon the sale of portions of the dominant parcel, unless the additional use is excessive to a degree not reasonably anticipated at the time the easement was created.

Extinction of Easements

Easements may be extinguished by (1) express release, (2) merger of the dominant and servient parcels, (3) abandonment, (4) misuser or change of the dominant property, and (5) destruction of the servient property.

Although easements may, of course, be removed by express release by the owner of the dominant property, there are numerous circumstances under which easements will be extinguished without any executed document in the nature of a transfer of an interest in land. For this reason title companies which issue policies to buyers of land will rarely agree to guarantee an easement appurtenant to the land.

When title to the servient and dominant tract become united in one owner, the easement is extinguished since the right formerly enjoyed by the dominant parcel becomes an ordinary incident to the ownership of the entire tract of land. The ownership of both parcels must be identical in quantity and quality, however, to effect an extinguishment. If the owner of the servient parcel acquires a lease of the dominant parcel, or if he acquires an estate for years, or holds title as trustee, the easement will not be extinguished.

It is possible that an easement may be extinguished by abandonment. A right to draw water for a mill may cease if the mill is destroyed and the use abandoned for a long period of time. Mere non-use, however, is not equivalent to abandonment. Nor is a declaration that the use is abandoned necessarily sufficient to accomplish the extinguishment of the easement. Abandonment is a question of fact in each case to be determined by all the circumstances, no one of which may be controlling. As noted, misuse or change in the character of the dominant parcel may overburden the servient parcel. This excessive user may be sufficient to terminate the easement. Finally, destruction of the servient property does not impose any duty upon its owner to rebuild and an easement which depended on the existence of a structure on the servient estate is thereby extinguished. If the servient structure is rebuilt, however, it is generally held that the easement is thereby re-established.

PROFITS A PRENDRE

The grant by B to A, an adjoining landowner, of the right to remove coal or fish or timber from B's land or to graze his cattle on B's land (thereby "removing" the grass) is said to create in A a profit a prendre in B's land. It is a right to remove the produce of another's land. Like an easement, a profit may arise by prescription but, if by act of the parties, it must be created with all the formalities of a grant of an estate in real property. Unless the right is clearly designated as exclusive, it is always subject to a similar use by the owner of the land. The right to take profits is frequently held independent of the ownership of other land. Thus, A may have a right to remove crushed gravel from B's acreage even though A lives in another part of the county. Indeed, in order for profits to be appurtenant to a dominant tenement and pass with it, the right must directly benefit the dominant parcel.

Profits are subject to extinguishment in much the same manner as easements, by release, merger or, under some circumstances, improper use.

LICENSES

It is not always easy to distinguish such real interests in property as easements or profits a prendre from an equally common right of use designated as a license. Permission to make use of one's land generally constitutes a license which creates no interest in the property and is, in most circumstances, exercised only at the will of and subject to revocation by the owner at any time. If A tells B he may cut across A's land to pick hickory nuts, B has nothing but a license subject to revocation at any time. It is possible that, upon the basis of a license, B may expend funds to exercise the right and the courts may prevent A from revoking the license simply because, under the circumstances, it would be unfair to penalize B. In such a case, B's interest is practicably indistinguishable from an easement.

The usual illustration of a typical license is a theater ticket or the use of a hotel room. No interest is acquired in the premises; simply a right of use for a given length of time, subject to good behavior. No formality is required to create a license; a shopkeeper licenses persons to enter his establishment merely by being open for business.

NATURAL RIGHTS

The ownership of land in itself carries with it certain rights in neighboring land, irrespective of any transfer of an interest by the adjoining landowner. Because these "rights" and the correlative duties are imposed by operation of law without regard to the intent of the parties, they are referred to as "natural rights." Without these "rights," a landowner might be effectively deprived of complete use and enjoyment of his land because of the acts of his neighbor. In their operation, if not their origin, these rights are similar to easements, and, because they operate to restrict the use of land, they are occasionally and loosely termed "negative easements."

These rights take many forms. The most common are, (1) right of lateral support, (2) right of riparian ownership, and (3) right to unpolluted air.

Right of Lateral Support

The enjoyment and use of land depends upon the lateral support it receives from adjacent land, and every landowner is entitled to expect that his land, in its natural condition, will receive this support. If A excavates upon his land and fails to provide adequate artificial support for the adjoining land of B, the latter may recover for any damages to the soil. There are, of course, limits upon this right of support. Damages will not usually be granted for injury to buildings caused by the excavation of adjacent land if there would have been no damage were the land unimproved by structures. An owner is entitled only to such support as will hold up the land in its natural condition. Thus, if X digs a well near the boundary of Y's land and a building on Y's land is damaged but the land is not substantially affected, Y will have no claim for damages. Obviously, it is frequently difficult to establish whether land improved with buildings would or would not have collapsed in its natural state.

This doctrine is altered in some jurisdictions by statute. Thus, under statute, the question sometimes may not be one of absolute liability for removing support but whether the landowner used reasonable care in excavating and giving the adjoining property owner notice in order that he might take necessary precautions.

Riparian Rights

The presence of water adjacent to, upon or under land, raises special problems and creates certain rights and duties in the owner of the land irrespective of any agreement between individuals. These rights and duties that are peculiar to land on which there is water are referred to as "riparian." A riparian right is a term used to describe the interest which a landowner has, for example, in a stream which flows through his property. It is not surprising that, as a general rule, it is said that a riparian landowner may make whatever use he chooses of the water provided he does not materially interfere with the rights of other riparian owners to do the same. A, living upstream from B, may appropriate the water for use in a mill, provided he does not substantially diminish the flow through B's land. A may not, however, divert the stream out of its natural course so that it no longer flows through B's land.

Separate rules apply to surface water, as distinguished from streams. The problem usually arises where one landowner drains surface water off his land causing it to flow on adjoining land or where an owner constructs walls or abutments causing surface water to back up onto adjoining property. The freedom of the landowner to do so varies in different jurisdictions.

A substantial body of law governs the rights and duties of landowners through whose property subsurface water passes. If the flow is not in a regular channel any landowner may appropriate all of it. A may sink a well drawing off percolating water, thereby causing a spring on B's land to dry up without being liable to B. If the subsurface water flows in a definite channel, the rules governing use are substantially the same as those affecting streams.

Right to Unpolluted Air

Even in the absence of local ordinance or statute, a person will not be able to establish a rendering plant on a fifty-foot lot in a residential neighborhood. The adjacent landowner has a natural right to clean air. Fumes, vapor or dust caused by a use of adjacent land will give the suffering property owner a cause of action. If the offensive use is extensive, it will give rise to a right of complaint on the part of the general public. Whether the damage is limited to a private neighbor or is offensive to the entire community, it is generally designated as a "nuisance." Such nuisances may be regulated by local ordinances governing zoning.

Zoning ordinances implement the common-law rules governing this natural right of property owners to be protected against offensive and unhealthy odors and noise and dirt caused by the commercial and industrial use of land.

Due to the constant population growth in our country with no corresponding enlargement of our natural resources, with a resulting increase in urbanization and virtually unchecked industrialization, there is widespread recognition of the pressing need for determined action on the part of Federal, State, and local governments to insure environmental protection and conservation of natural ecological values.

In enacting the Environmental Quality Inprovement Act of 1970 (U.S.Pub.L. 91–224, 84 Stat. 114), the Congress made the following express findings and declarations:

1. that man has caused changes in the environment;
2. that many of these changes may affect the relationship between man and his environment; and
3. that population increases and urban concentration contribute directly to pollution and the degradation of our environment.

On June 29, 1970, Illinois enacted a comprehensive Environmental Protection Act creating an Environmental Protection Agency and a Pollution Control Board, and entrusting them with wide powers, duties, and responsibilities.

Article XI of the 1970 Illinois constitution, entitled "Environment," contains the following two sections:

Section 1. Public Policy—Legislative Responsibility. The public policy of the State and the duty of each person is to provide and maintain a healthful environment for the benefit of this and future generations. The General Assembly shall provide by law for the implementation and enforcement of this public policy.

Section 2. Rights of Individuals. Each person has the right to a healthful environment. Each person may enforce this right against any party, governmental or private, through appropriate legal proceedings subject to reasonable limitation and regulation as the General Assembly may provide by law.

These salutary provisions incorporate one of the natural rights of mankind in the fundamental law of the State.

Cases

Concurrent Ownership

HENDRICKSON v. MINNEAPOLIS FEDERAL SAV. & L. ASS'N

(1968) 281 Minn. 462, 161 N.W.2d 688.

SHERAN, J.

Appeal from an order and decree of registration of the district court.

The Facts

On June 30, 1956, Martin Hendrickson and Solveig Hendrickson were married, and on January 3, 1957, a home previously owned by him was so conveyed as to make them owners of it as joint tenants and not as tenants in common. No part of the consideration for the premises was paid by Mrs. Hendrickson and there is no evidence to show that the creation of the joint tenancy was pursuant to an enforceable agreement.

On August 3, 1964, Martin Hendrickson duly executed a Declaration of Election to Sever Survivorship of Joint Tenancy by which he endeavored to preserve an interest in the premises for Ruth Halbert, his daughter by a previous marriage, appellant in this court. On the same day, he executed his last will and testament, by the terms of which he directed that his wife, Solveig M. Hendrickson, receive the minimum amount to which she was entitled under the laws of the State of Minnesota.

Mr. Hendrickson died testate on October 9, 1964. Thereafter, Solveig M. Hendrickson made application to register title to the premises here involved in her name as fee owner. Ruth Halbert appeared and asserted claim to the interest in the realty to which she would be entitled if the declaration was effective to make Martin Hendrickson and Solveig M. Hendrickson owners of the realty as tenants in common, i.e., an undivided one-half interest subject to the widow's life estate.[1]

Upon reference, the referee found that Martin Hendrickson did not terminate the joint tenancy by his declaration, and that Solveig M. Hendrickson became the owner of an estate in fee simple in the whole of said property as surviving joint tenant. The district court ratified the report of the referee. A decree was entered accordingly and this appeal followed.

The Issue

The issue for decision is this: Did the declaration have the effect of severing the joint tenancy, creating a tenancy in common? If it did, Ruth Halbert is the owner of an undivided one-half interest in said real estate subject to the life estate therein of Solveig M. Hendrickson. If it did not, Solveig M. Hendrickson owns the realty in fee simple absolute.

The Decision

Under the common law, there were three types of concurrent ownership: Tenancy in

common, joint tenancy, and tenancy by the entirety. A joint tenancy is distinguished from a tenancy in common by the fact that a surviving joint tenant succeeds to the person with whom he shared the joint tenancy. A tenancy by the entirety, which can exist only between husband and wife, is like a joint tenancy in that survivorship exists, but is distinguished from the joint tenancy by the fact that there can be no partition, and it cannot be converted into a tenancy in common. [Citations.]

As the common law of property developed during feudal times, there was a presumption in favor of joint tenancy due to reasons related to feudalism. As the age of feudalism ended, the reasons for this presumption also ended and survivorship came to be regarded "as an 'odious thing' that too often deprived a man's heirs of their rightful inheritance." [Citations.]

In Minnesota, the original presumption in favor of joint tenancy has been reversed by Minn.St. 500.19, subd. 2, which provides: "All grants and devises of lands, made to two or more persons, shall be construed to create estates in common, and not in joint tenancy, unless expressly declared to be in joint tenancy." Disfavor for survivorship in Minnesota is also shown by the fact that in this state the estate of tenancy by the entirety, with its indestructible survivorship, is not recognized. [Citations.]

For a joint tenancy to exist, unity of time, title, interest, and possession must concur. [Citations.] Traditionally, the survivorship feature could be destroyed and the joint tenancy converted into a tenancy in common if one of the unities was destroyed. [Citations.] This would result, for example, if one of the joint tenants conveyed his interest to a third party. [Citation.] The common-law lawyer used this principle to enable one joint tenant to unilaterally eliminate the survivorship feature and yet retain ownership in the property. A conveyance would be made to a third party or strawman, thus destroying the

---

1. Mrs. Hendrickson would be the owner in fee of the other undivided one-half interest in this realty because if the joint tenancy was severed she became with respect to it a tenant in common and owner in fee of an undivided one-half interest therein.

joint tenancy. Immediately thereafter the property would be reconveyed to the original owner. A tenancy in common would thus be created because the unities of time and interest would no longer be present. More recently the courts have come to allow joint tenants to convert their estate into a tenancy in common without the ritual of conveyance and reconveyance. It is only necessary for the joint tenants to mutually agree to sever the joint tenancy. [Citations.] We are now asked to allow one joint tenant to do unilaterally that which we allow joint tenants acting in concert to do, i.e., terminate the joint tenancy by declaration without being required to go through the ceremony of a conveyance to a strawman and a reconveyance back again.

* * *

We hold that the method chosen here is sufficient to sever a joint tenancy. Had the property involved been any property other than a homestead, the decedent could have unilaterally severed the joint tenancy. Minn.St. 507.02 and 525.145(1)(b)[7] establish a public policy to protect for the wife the continued occupancy of the place of joint abode. However, this public policy does not necessarily apply to the remainder interest, which can be disposed of without adversely affecting the right of the surviving spouse to continue in possession and enjoyment for so long as she might live. Putting the property into joint tenancy was apparently an estate-planning device. If the decedent had kept title to this real estate in his own name and executed a will by the terms of

---

7. Minn.St. 525.145(1) provides: "Where there is a surviving spouse the homestead shall descend free from any testamentary or other disposition thereof to which such spouse has not consented in writing or by election to take under the will as provided by law, as follows:

* * *

"(b) If there be children or issue of deceased children surviving, then to the spouse for the term of his natural life and the remainder in equal shares to such children and the issue of deceased children by right of representation."

which it was devised to his wife in fee simple absolute, he would have been free at any time to revoke the will unilaterally. His wife would nevertheless have the right to a life estate in the homestead upon his death, but her right would be based on the statute and not the will. § 525.145(1)(b).

* * *

If the survivor had taken some irrevocable action in reliance upon the creation or existence of the joint tenancy, or if some consideration was given or received when the joint tenancy was created, it would seem reasonable to insist that unilateral action would not be effective to deprive the passive joint tenant of the rights so created. But this is not such a case.

Our conclusion is that the trial court should be reversed.

Creation of Easements

EDWARD DeV. BUNN v. OFFUTT
(1976) 216 Va. 681, 222 S.E.2d 522.

HARRISON, J.
* * *

On July 9, 1962, Temco, Inc. conveyed to Harvey W. Wynn and Rosabelle G. Wynn property known as 900 South Wakefield Street in Arlington. Prior thereto, on January 26, 1962, the Wynns had signed a contract of purchase prepared by the seller's agent. In this contract is found the following provision: "Use of apartment swimming pool to be available to purchaser and his family." The Wynns testified that the agent, Willis L. Lawrence, told them that the use of the pool went with the ownership of the home being purchased, and that subsequent purchasers would have the right to use the pool. The pool is located in an adjoining apartment complex which was being developed by appellees at the time. The Wynns said the sales agent emphasized that use of this pool would be a desirable feature in the event they subsequently decided to sell the property. No reference was made to the pool in the deed from Temco to the Wynns.

On May 31, 1969, the Bunns contracted in writing to buy the property from the Wynns through the latter's agent, Sonnett Realty Co., Inc. While no reference to the pool was made in the contract, the Wynns and a representative of Sonnett told the Bunns that the use of the pool went with the purchase of the property. However, the deed, dated July 18, 1969, conveying the property from the Wynns to the Bunns contains no reference to the pool. After the purchase was effected, and when the Bunns requested passes from appellees showing their entitlement to the use of the pool, their request was refused.

Appellants attach significance to the close relationship which they allege existed between Offutt, Temco, Dittmar, and Sonnett. The appellees all have their offices in the same room of a building situated on the property where the pool is located, and Sonnett, which in 1969 was the exclusive sales agency for the appellees, has its office in the same building. Furthermore, the Wynns had agreed to purchase another house, then under construction, from appellees provided Sonnett could sell their Wakefield home. The Bunns testified that as an inducement for them to increase by $750 their offering price for the Wynn property, Sonnett stressed the value of using the swimming pool, and represented that pool membership in a club elsewhere would cost them an initial $300 fee plus annual dues.

Representatives of Sonnett attempted to persuade the appellees to grant pool privileges to appellants, but without success. Ultimately, on November 14, 1969, Sonnett wrote Mr. Bunn a letter advising that it had been unable to secure from appellees passes for the swimming pool, and that since the situation was beyond its control, Sonnett "would be only too happy to assume your existing trust and give you the cash you have invested in the property." This offer was refused.

We agree with the trial judge that the rights of the parties depend upon the nature of the transaction in 1962 between appellees, as sellers, and Mr. and Mrs. Wynn, as purchasers.

The dispositive issue in this case is whether the language in the contract, "Use of apartment swimming pool to be available to purchaser and his family," amounted to a grant of a mere license to the Wynns and their family; or whether the Wynns acquired thereby a private easement across the land of appellees to the swimming pool and to the use of the pool, which easement was thereafter transferred to the Bunns.

A license has been described as "a right, given by some competent authority to do an act which without such authority would be illegal, a tort, or a trespass." 12 M.J., License to Real Property, § 2, p. 148. A license is personal between the licensor and the licensee and cannot be assigned. * * * And a grant which creates any interest or estate in land is not a license. Such a grant creates an easement. * * *

An easement has been described as " 'a privilege without profit, which the owner of one tenement has a right to enjoy in respect of that tenement in or over the tenement of another person; by reason whereof the latter is obliged to suffer, or refrain from doing something on his own tenement to the advantage of the former'." Stevenson v. Wallace, 27 Gratt. (68 Va.) 77, 87 (1876).

* * *

Easements may be created by express grant or reservation, by implication, by estoppel or by prescription. The only rights acquired by the Wynns in the property of appellees were acquired by deed from Temco. The provisions of the contract were merged in this deed. However, the deed is silent as to the pool, and the contract made the use of the pool available only to "purchaser and his family." The trial court found this language consistent with appellees' theory that a mere license only was granted to the purchasers and their families, and not an interest in land or an estate of inheritance; that the absence of any provision regarding the swimming pool in the deed to the Wynns was sufficient to preclude any easement by grant or reservation; and that the evidence and exhibits failed to show that an easement was created by estoppel, necessity or prescription. The trial court further found that no easement had been created by implication for there was neither a showing of a preexisting use of the easement prior to the conveyance by Temco to the Wynns, nor any showing that the use of the swimming pool was essential to the beneficial enjoyment of the land conveyed.

* * *

In Hamlin v. Pandapas, 197 Va. 659, 664, 90 S.E.2d 829, 833 (1956), the court held:

In the construction of language contained in a deed the grantor must generally be considered as having intended to convey all that the language he employed is capable of passing to the grantee, and where the description admits of two constructions, it will be construed most favorably to the grantee. * * *

However, the deed from Temco to the Wynns did not purport to convey an easement to the swimming pool, and the language in the sales contract between the parties is not sufficient to create an express easement. The Wynns and their family were given a mere license to use the swimming pool. It was not an interest running with the land that could subsequently be transferred by them.

The decree of the lower court under review is affirmed.

Natural Rights

THRASHER v. CITY OF ATLANTA

(1934) 178 Ga. 514, 173 S.E. 817.

[Suit for injunction to restrain flight of airplanes at low altitudes over plaintiff's land that was adjacent to municipal airport. The plaintiff's petitions were dismissed, and he appeals.]

BELL, J.

* * *

The allegations with reference to flights over the land and the complaints against low flying are now to be considered. In paragraph 13 the petition averred: "That there have been frequent occasions of low flying by pilots, who have permission to arrive and depart at the said field and whose names are unknown to petitioner, but are acting by permit and under license of the defendant, City of Atlanta, and other defendants named in the bill, who arrive and depart, who have been guilty of low flying, that such low flights over adjacent property is a trespass and is a violation of the constitutional rights of plaintiff and other property owners, and that such low flying has been so frequent as to be a nuisance and is dangerous to plaintiff and his family and others in the community." * * *

The Civil Code (1910), sec. 3617, declares that "the right of an owner of lands extends downward and upward indefinitely." In section 4477 it is stated that "the owner of realty having title downwards and upwards indefinitely, an unlawful interference with his rights, below and above the surface, alike gives him a right of action." These statements as to ownership above the surface are based upon the common-law maxim, cujus est solum ejus est usque ad coelum,—who owns the soil owns also to the sky. These provisions of the code should therefore be construed in the light of the authoritative content of the maxim itself. As a matter of fact, the language of the code that the title to land extends upwards indefinitely would seem to be a limitation upon the ad coelum doctrine, indicating by implication that the title will include only such portions of the upper space as may be seized and appropriated by the owner of the soil. Such a construction of the code provisions would materially minimize the difficulties in the present case; but even if the code was intended to express the ad coelum theory in its entirety, and this we assume in the present case, it remains true that the maxim can have only such legal signification as it brings from the common law.

What is the sky? Who can tell where it begins or define its meaning in terms of the law? When can it be said that a plane is above the sky or below it? How can there be an unqualified tangible right in a thing so indeterminate and elusive? What and where is the res of which a court may assume jurisdiction in a case involving a private claim of title? Possession is the basis of all ownership [citation], and that which man can never possess would seem to be incapable of being owned. [Citations.] In order to recover for a trespass it is necessary to show title or actual possession. [Citation.] The space in the far distance above the earth is in the actual possession of no one, and, being incapable of such possession, title to the land beneath does not necessarily include title to such space. The legal title can hardly extend above an altitude representing the reasonable possibility of man's occupation and dominion, although as respects the realm beyond this the owner of the land may complain of any use tending to diminish the free enjoyment of the soil beneath. The maxim to which reference has been made is a generalization from old cases involving the title to space within the range of actual occupation, and any statement as to title beyond was manifestly a mere dictum. For instance, a court in dealing with the title to space at a given distance above the earth could make no authoritative decision as to the title at higher altitudes, the latter question not being involved. The common-law cases from which the ad coelum doctrine emanated were limited to facts and conditions close to earth and did not require an adjudication on the title to the mansions in the sky. Accordingly, the maxim imported from the ancient past consists in large measure of obiter dicta, and to that extent can not be taken as an authentic statement of any law. It follows that the literal terms of the code sections referred to must be discounted or qualified in like measure. * * *

But the space is up there, and the owner of the land has the first claim upon it. If another should capture and possess it, as by erecting a high building with a fixed overhanging structure, this alone will show that the space affected is capable of being possessed, and consequently the owner of the soil beneath the overhanging structure may be entitled to ejectment or to an action for trespass. However, the pilot of an airplane does not seize and hold the space or stratum of air through which he navigates, and can not do so. He is merely a transient, and the use to which he applies the ethereal realm does not partake of the nature of occupation in the sense of dominion and ownership. So long as the space through which he moves is beyond the reasonable possibility of possession by the occupant below, he is in free territory,—not as every or any man's land, but rather as a sort of "no man's land." As stated above, however, the occupant of the soil is entitled to be free from danger or annoyance by any use of the super-incumbent space, and for any infringement of this right he may apply to the law for appropriate redress or relief. * * *

[The court held that the plaintiff allegations were insufficient to show that the flights constituted a trespass.]

Problems

1. A and B purchased Blackacre and the deed to them conveyed the premises to "A and B, husband and wife, as joint tenants." Subsequently A made his will leaving all of his property to his

son C. D, the son of B, conveyed Blackacre by warranty deed to E. A died leaving as his only heirs, his wife B and his son C. Later B died intestate leaving as her only heir her son D.

(a) What kind of interest did the conveyance to A and B create?

(b) Upon the death of A, what interest, if any, did B, C, D, and E acquire in Blackacre?

(c) Upon the death of B, what interest, if any, did C, D, and E acquire in Blackacre?

(d) Under the deed from D to E, what interest, if any, did E acquire?

2. In 1971 Roy Martin and his wife, Alice, their son, Hiram, and the latter's wife, Myrna, acquired title to a 240-acre farm. The deed ran to Roy Martin and Alice Martin, the father and mother, as joint tenants, with the right of survivorship, and to Hiram Martin and Myrna Martin, the son and his wife, as joint tenants, with the right of survivorship. Alice Martin died in 1976, and in 1979 Roy Martin married Agnes Martin. By his will, Roy Martin bequeathed and devised his entire estate to Agnes Martin. When Roy Martin died in 1982, Hiram and Myrna Martin assumed complete control of the farm.

State the interest in the farm, if any, of Agnes, Hiram and Myrna Martin, immediately upon the death of Roy Martin.

3. A and B, who are husband and wife, acquired Redacre by a warranty deed which contained the following clause, " * * * convey and warrant to A and B with full rights of survivorship and not as tenants in common. * * * " A executed a mortgage upon his interest to C, which he subsequently paid. A died intestate, leaving as his only heirs-at-law, his widow, B and his son, D.

(a) What is the interest, if any, of B in Redacre?

(b) What is the interest, if any, of D in Redacre?

4. Robert Dudley died leaving a will in which he devised Blackacre to his sisters, Anne, Belle and Celia in joint tenancy. Anne, by quitclaim deed, conveyed all her interest in the property to Belle. Anne died the following year. Belle died five years later, and by her will she devised whatever interest she had in the realty to four nieces. The latter instituted an action to partition the property. Their complaint and Celia's answer were based upon diametrically opposing theories. The complaint of the nieces alleged that Anne's deed entirely severed the joint tenancies existing among the three sisters; that thereafter Belle owned an undivided two-thirds interest in the property and Celia an undivided one-third interest as tenants in common; and that the nieces, as successors to Belle's interest, each owned an undivided one-sixth interest as tenants in common with Celia, who owned an undivided one-third. Celia's answer averred that the nieces each owned an undivided one-twelfth interest as tenants in common with Celia, who owned an undivided two-thirds. Who is correct?

5. Henry Thornburn and Mary Thornburn, husband and wife, acquired vacant lands by warranty deed. The deed recited, " * * * do convey and warrant to Henry Thornburn and Mary Thornburn as joint tenants the (legal description)." Shortly thereafter, marital discord developed and Henry conveyed his one-half interest in the premises to his brother Jim. Mary did not join in the conveyance. Henry died intestate in 1982 leaving his widow, Mary, and no children.

What is the interest of Mary, if any, in the real estate?

6. T, having no children, died testate. His will granted a life estate to A in certain real estate, with remainder to B and C in joint tenancy. All the residue of T's estate was left to the X College. While going to T's funeral, the car in which A, B and C were driving was wrecked. B was killed, C died a few minutes later, and A died on his way to the hospital. Who is entitled to the real estate in question?

7. Otis Olson, the owner of two adjoining city lots, A and B, built a house on each. He laid a drainpipe from lot B across lot A to the main sewer pipe under the alley beyond lot A. Olson then sold and conveyed lot A to Fred Ford. The deed, which made no mention of the drainpipe, was promptly recorded. Ford had no actual knowledge or notice of the drainpipe although it would have been apparent to anyone making an inspection of the premises, having been only partially imbedded. Later, Olson sold and conveyed lot B to Luke Lane. This deed, which likewise made no reference to the drainpipe, was also promptly recorded.

A few weeks thereafter, Ford discovered the drainpipe across lot A and removed it. Did he have the right to do so?

8. At the time of his marriage to Ann, Robert owned several parcels of real estate in joint tenancy with his brother, Sam. During his marriage, Robert purchased a house, title to which he put in his name and his wife's name as joint tenants and not as tenants in common. Robert died; within a month of his death, Smith obtained a judgment against the estate of Robert. What are the relative rights of Sam, the judgment creditor, and Ann, Robert's wife?

9. In 1956, Ogle was the owner of two adjoining lots numbered 6 and 7 fronting at the north on a city street. In that year he laid out and built a concrete driveway along and two feet in from what he erroneously believed to be the west boundary of lot 7. Ogle used the driveway for access to buildings situated at the southern end of both lots. Later, in 1956 he conveyed lot 7 to Dale, and thereafter in the same year he con-

veyed lot 6 to Pace. Neither deed made any reference to the driveway, and after the conveyance Dale used it exclusively for access to lot 7. In 1982 a survey by Pace established that the driveway encroached six inches on lot 6, and he brought an appropriate action to establish his lawful ownership of the strip upon which the driveway approaches, to enjoin its use by Dale, and to require Dale to remove the overlap. Decision?

10. X, the owner of two adjoining lots, conveyed one of them, on which stood a photograph studio, to B, a photographer. The remaining lot was vacant, and subsequently X commenced the erection of a large building on it which, if completed, would obstruct the light to the building occupied by B, and render it useless for purposes of photography. B brought suit for injunction to restrain X from erecting his building on the ground that he (B) had an implied easement for light. Should the injunction be granted?

CONVEYANCES, DEEDS AND MORTGAGES OF REAL ESTATE

Ownership of real property may be acquired by a variety of methods, but the most common is by transfer for valuable consideration. Such transfers involve a contract for the sale of the land and the subsequent delivery of the deed and payment of the agreed consideration. In most cases, the purchase of real estate requires borrowing a part of the purchase price secured by the realty. This chapter will discuss these matters under the headings of (1) Contract of Sale, (2) Deeds, and (3) Secured Transactions.

CONTRACT OF SALE

A transfer of land for valuable consideration invariably involves two steps: (1) A contract for the sale of the land and (2) the delivery of the deed and payment of the agreed consideration.

There are good reasons why the two-step system has become firmly established in the law of conveyancing. Except in cases of fraud, the acceptance of a deed is an irrevocable step. Thereafter, if it should ap-

pear that the vendor's title is defective or that he has no title at all, the purchaser's sole remedy is an action for damages based upon the covenants in the deed, if any. The rule in most jurisdictions is that the damages recoverable on account of failure of title may not, in any case, exceed the purchase price paid plus the costs of defending a bad title.

Obviously, most purchasers want some assurance that they will own and be able to keep the property they are about to purchase. Such assurance may be obtained only from a thorough and competent title search. A party will not undertake the expense of a title search unless he has a contract assuring him that the transaction will be consummated.

Even where no title search is contemplated, there are other reasons why a conveyance of land for a valuable consideration will be preceded by a contract for its sale. Although in the case of a gift of land one might expect no antecedent agreement, in a sale for valuable consideration, the parties will mutually desire to reach an agreement on a number of matters before the deed is prepared.

Formation and Terms

Most real estate brokers require the purchaser to sign a binder or memorandum of sale even before the formal agreement is prepared. The Statute of Frauds requires that such binders contain the essential terms of the contract. Since an oral agreement will not be enforceable under the Statute of Frauds, the vendor, if he wants to be assured that the deed will be accepted, must also reduce the agreement to writing and have it signed by the purchaser. The simplest agreement should contain (1) the names and addresses of the parties; (2) a description of the property to be conveyed; (3) the time for the conveyance; (4) the type of deed to be given; and (5) the price and manner of payment. To avoid dispute, and to assure adequate protection of the rights of both parties, there are many other points which should be covered by a properly drawn contract for the sale of land. For example, the contract should contain careful provisions as to any and all fixtures intended to be included in the sale.

The contract should also provide for an apportionment of those charges between vendor and purchaser for taxes and assessments which have not and cannot be paid at the time of closing so that each may pay the proportion of the entire charge which is attributable to his period of ownership. Suppose that, under the applicable law, the lien for 1982 general taxes attaches on January 1, 1982, but that the amount of the taxes is not ascertained or payable until May 1, 1983. The contract calls for closing on June 1, 1982. If the taxes for 1982 are not excepted, the contract should provide for prorating the tax on the basis of the most recent available tax bill, i.e., 1981, requiring the vendor to pay so much as is attributable to the period before June 1, 1982, and the purchaser to pay the remainder.

The same situation exists in the case of advance payments of rent where the purchaser has agreed to take subject to outstanding leases. At common law, rents are not apportionable. Accordingly, unless the contract of sale provides for a credit to the purchaser by prorating the rent, he will receive no rent until the next advance payment becomes due.

Marketable Title

It is firmly established in the law of conveyancing that a contract for the sale of land carries with it an implied obligation upon the part of the vendor to convey marketable title. A marketable title is one which is free from (a) encumbrances, such as mortgages, easements, liens, leases, and restrictive covenants; (b) defects in the chain of title appearing in the land records such as a prior recorded conveyance of the same property by the vendor; (c) any defects which, while they are not sufficient to amount to encumbrances, may yet subject the purchaser to the inconvenience of having to defend his title in court. This third category of defects comes under an oft repeated principle that "no purchaser should be forced to buy a law suit."

Two important exceptions to this rule should be noted. (1) Most courts hold that the vendor's implied or express obligation to convey marketable title does not require him to convey free from existing zoning restrictions. The reasons given are (a) the buyer is charged with notice of the existing law and (b) the zoning restriction being beneficial to the community as a whole, in effect, benefits rather than encumbers the property involved. The time for a purchaser to check for zoning restrictions is *before* he signs a contract to purchase, *not after*. (2) Some courts also hold that the vendor's implied or express obligation to convey marketable title does not require him to convey free from open and visible public rights of way or easements such as public roads and sewers.

Except in those two instances, however, the purchaser's *knowledge* or constructive knowledge of an encumbrance or other title defect *never* operates to diminish the vendor's obligation to convey marketable title. In all such cases, it is conclusively presumed that by the contract of sale the vendor has undertaken to remove such defects before the date set for delivery of the deed and payment of the price known as the "closing date."

It can be seen, therefore, that if the vendor desires to establish any exceptions to this very strict duty he must do so by express language in the contract of sale. Accordingly, it is common practice for the contract of sale to provide that the vendor shall convey marketable title subject only to: (1) special taxes or assessments for improvements not yet completed; (2) installments not due at the date thereof of any special tax or assessment for improvements theretofore completed; (3) general taxes for a stated year and for subsequent years; (4) building, building line and use or occupancy restrictions, conditions and covenants of record; (5) zoning and building laws or ordinances; (6) roads and highways, if any.

If there are any existing leases not expiring before the date of closing or if there are any outstanding mortgages, subject to which the purchaser is undertaking to take the property, these must be included in the foregoing list.

Further Assurances of Title

It has been noted that the purchaser will want greater title protection than the assurance of a right of action for damages based upon the covenants in the deed. This is provided by the title search. The significance of the vendor's obligation to convey marketable title is that if the title

search reveals any flaw which has not been made an express exception to that obligation, the purchaser may refuse to take the conveyance on the date set for closing, and may sue and recover damages from the seller unless the title defect is promptly remedied.

Title Search. The title search may take several forms. In some localities and in some States it is still customary for the purchaser's attorney to conduct a search of all the relevant records. This search is aided by the recording acts which provide, in general, that any instrument affecting title which is not recorded will have no effect against subsequent purchasers who take the property for value and without notice of such an instrument.

It may be seen that the title searcher can rely largely upon the instruments of record to determine whether the vendor's title is good. There are, however, many encumbrances which will not appear of record and which are not required to be recorded. Thus, easements by implication and inchoate dower interests of spouses who are not mentioned in any conveyance in the chain of title will not appear of record, yet the purchaser will take subject to them despite his good faith and lack of notice. This is also true of the rights of persons in possession of the premises. It is possible, however, to procure title guaranty policies to cover such defects.

While the individual title search is still common, the growing practice is to rely upon searches made by abstract companies or upon title guaranty policies. The abstract or the preliminary report of title furnished by the title insurance company must still be examined by the purchaser's attorney to determine, in the one case, whether the abstract reveals any title defects and, in the other, whether the title guaranty which the title insurance company is willing to issue will cover all the defects and encumbrances that are not assumed by the purchaser.

It is customary to include a clause in the contract of sale giving the vendor a stated period of time in which to remove such defects as may be revealed in the course of title examination, or shown on a preliminary report on title furnished by the title insurance company. The purchaser should, therefore, be careful to include in the contract words to the effect that the vendor must, during such period of time, use diligent effort to remove any and all defects revealed by the title search; otherwise, the vendor may do nothing and the purchaser may find himself compelled to decide either not to take the property or to take it subject to the discovered defects of title and the possibility of a law suit against the vendor.

The Torrens System. In a number of States, it is possible to register land with the local government and make the condition of the title determinable by reference to the certificate of registration alone. This method of title registration is known as the Torrens System after its original sponsor, Sir Robert Torrens, who introduced it into Australia about the middle of the nineteenth century. Under the Torrens System, an owner of land files a petition in court to have his land registered and, after careful investigation, a certificate is issued by direction of the court confirming the owner's title and noting thereon any outstanding interests or encumbrances. One copy of the certificate is filed in the registration office; one goes to the owner. Upon subsequent sale, the owner executes a deed and delivers it with his duplicate copy of the certificate to the buyer. The buyer may inform himself as to the state of the seller's title by inspecting the certificate on file in the registrar's office. The buyer is absolutely protected against any liens or outstanding interests which have not been noted on the certificate. He does not need an abstract or a guaranty pol-

icy. The statute provides that the certificate is conclusive as to all but a very few interests. If a judgment creditor of the seller has failed to note his lien on the certificate the buyer takes the land clear of the claim. The title vests in the buyer not upon the execution of the deed but upon the delivery of the new certificate by the Torrens Office.

It is apparent that, in theory at least, the Torrens System represents a great improvement over the older methods of giving buyers assurances as to the seller's title. Under the Torrens System, there is no need to make or pay for a careful search of the history of the parcel because the certificate is conclusive evidence of the current state of the title. There have been many disputes as to why the Torrens System has not always worked better than was hoped for by its proponents. It has not been widely adopted in this country and even in States where it is authorized by statute has not made serious inroads upon the abstract or guaranty policy systems.

Risk between Contract and Closing Date

Except in a few jurisdictions which have adopted the Uniform Vendor and Purchaser Risk Law, a majority of the jurisdictions adhere to the common-law rule that, *after the contract, the risk of loss or destruction of the property is upon the purchaser.* The reason for this rule is that a contract for the sale of land is specifically enforceable in a court of equity, and therefore at the time of making the contract the purchaser is regarded as the equitable or beneficial owner of the land. It is important, therefore, to make provision in the contract that, upon payment of the purchase price, the purchaser will be entitled to the proceeds of any insurance held by the vendor. It is not advisable for the vendor to assign his policy of insurance on the date of the contract for the reason that, if the purchaser thereafter defaults and becomes insolvent, the vendor may not be able to reach the proceeds in the hands of the purchaser. A solution to the problem is to secure an indorsement of the policy making it payable to either the vendor or the purchaser "as his interest may appear." If such an indorsement cannot be secured, the purchaser usually obtains an insurance policy on his own behalf protecting his interest in the property.

The contract of sale may, of course, provide that the risk of loss or destruction shall remain upon the vendor until conveyance to the purchaser, or it may provide that the vendor shall restore any structures destroyed before closing.

DEEDS TO REAL PROPERTY

There are three ways in which title to land may be transferred: (1) by deed, (2) by will or by the law of descent upon the death of the owner, and (3) by open, continuous and adverse possession by a non-owner for a period of twenty years. We shall now consider the first method of transfer.

Types of Deeds

Warranty Deed. By a warranty deed, the seller (grantor) promises the buyer (grantee) that he has a valid title to the property and, expressly or impliedly, under such a deed, the grantor obliges himself to make the grantee whole if the latter suffers any damage because the grantor's title was defective. In most jurisdictions, a form of warranty deed is set out in the statute and the words necessary to create such a deed are specified.

Aside from the liability of the grantor for any defects in his title, a distinct characteristic of the warranty deed is that it will convey an after-acquired title. For example, on January 30, A conveys Blackacre by warranty deed to B. On January 30, A's

title to Blackacre is defective but by February 14th, A has acquired a good title. Without more, B has good title under the deed.

Special Warranty Deed. Whereas a warranty deed contains a general warranty of title, a special warranty deed is one which warrants only that the title has not been impaired, encumbered or rendered defective by reason of any act or omission of the grantor. The grantor merely warrants the title so far as acts or omissions of the grantor are concerned. He does not warrant that the title may not be defective by reason of the acts or omissions of others.

Quitclaim Deed. By a quitclaim deed, the grantor says no more, in effect, than "I make no promise as to what interest I do have in this land but whatever it be I convey it to you." Quitclaim deeds are used most frequently when it is desired to have persons who appear to, or may, have an interest in land release their interest. If one tenant in common offers to buy his co-tenant's interest a quitclaim deed is customarily the method of transfer. If, through some error in a legal description in a prior deed, A, the owner of a parcel, has innocently acquired some interest in an adjoining parcel of land belonging to B, A will be asked to execute a quitclaim deed in order to clear up B's title.

Form and Requirements

Any transfer of an interest in land is within the Statute of Frauds if it is an interest of more than a limited duration, and must therefore be in writing. Originally, leases for less than three years were excepted from this requirement. Today, in some jurisdictions, a lease for more than a year has to be in writing to create more than a tenancy at will.

Nearly all deeds, whatever the type, follow substantially the same pattern and most of the essential characteristics of deeds can be considered by analyzing the component parts of the usual deed. These parts are:

1. Names of parties.
2. Consideration.
3. Words of conveyance.
4. Description of the land conveyed.
5. Exceptions or reservations.
6. Quantity of the estate conveyed.
7. Covenants of title.
8. Execution.

Items 1 through 5 are referred to as the *premises,* and item 6 is the *habendum.*

Names of Parties. The omission of the name of the grantor from a deed is generally not as serious a flaw as the omission of the grantee's name since the grantor's signature will appear at the bottom. Omission of the grantee's name is said to void a deed but generally it can be filled in, provided it is done before delivery and with the oral authority of the grantor. A deed from a man and wife will usually read "Tom Jones and Mary Jones, his wife."

Consideration. In most instances, the law does not require consideration for a valid deed. A grantor may be bound by his gift of land if the deed is properly executed and delivered. It is, however, the custom to specify nominal consideration in deeds, presumably to protect the grantee not only from the allegation that he holds the property under a resulting trust for the grantor but also to protect him from third parties with adverse interests in the land who might allege that he was not an innocent purchaser for value. The usual practice of reciting a consideration of ten dollars even though the actual price may be many times this amount probably is due partly to custom and partly to a wish to conceal the actual sale price from those who might inspect the public records.

Words of Conveyance. The statutory forms of deeds prescribed by statute in most States suggest certain operative words of conveyance. The words used will, of course, vary depending upon whether the instrument is a warranty deed or a quitclaim deed. A common phrase for a warranty deed is "convey and warrant" although, in a number of States the phrase "grant, bargain and sell" is used together with a covenant by the seller later in the deed that he will "warrant and defend the title." A quitclaim deed will generally provide that the grantor "conveys and quitclaims" or, more simply, "quitclaims all interest" in the property. Whatever the recommended statutory form, generally any words which substantially evidence the intent of the grantor will be sufficient.

Description of the Land Conveyed. The primary requirement of any description is that it be sufficiently clear and certain to permit identification of the property conveyed. The test is frequently applied in terms of whether a subsequent purchaser or a surveyor employed by him could mark off the land from the description. This does not mean that any particular method is necessary to a valid conveyance. There is a great variety to be found in legal descriptions of property. A conveyance of "all my land in McHenry County" is sufficient, provided all the grantor's land is determinable from other records. The conveyance of "my house" will pass title to the lot although a description in a conveyance by street number is risky because of the chance of revisions in the street numbers.

Such informal descriptions may be sufficiently definite to convey property; this is not, however, the usual method. Customary descriptions generally fall into three major classes: (a) Description by reference to monuments and courses, (b) Description by reference to Rectangular Survey System, and (c) Description by reference to recorded plat.

One of the oldest methods of describing property is by reference to its boundaries in terms of physical objects. These may be metal or stone markers placed there for the specific purpose of identifying the boundary or they may be natural or man-made objects such as trees, rivers, fences or highways. The description will state the "course" of a boundary, the direction in which the line runs in terms of the compass and the line may then be described as running a certain distance or as running between two designated monuments. This method of description is sometimes colloquially referred to as "by metes and bounds."

Where there is a conflict between monuments, on the one hand, and courses or distances, the former will generally prevail since they represent more or less permanent objects on the site while a course or distance is simply someone's judgment as to the direction or length of a line.

The use of monuments is, of course, subject to the risk that they may disappear or be changed and, where alternative methods of description are feasible, description by monuments and courses is not preferred.

Most of the continental United States west of the Allegheny Mountains is included in a survey made by the Federal government and known as the Rectangular Survey System. Land in this great area is generally conveyed by use of a description which, in its entirety or in part, refers to this comprehensive rectangular survey system. The survey has for its points of beginning lines running parallel to longitudinal and latitudinal bases. A line conforming to a parallel of latitude is referred to as a "base" line and a series of lines running due North and South at right angles to the base line are called "Principal Meridians." Lines running due East and West drawn at intervals of six miles both North and South of the base line are designated as Township lines. Similar lines drawn at six-mile intervals East and West of the Principal Meridians and running due North and South are designated as Range lines. The six-mile strips of the Township lines and Range lines are numbered consecutively, extending from the base line and Principal Meridian, respectively. The six-mile square areas formed by the intersection of range and township lines are "townships" and these, in turn, are divided into thirty-six "Sections" containing one square mile and numbered consecutively from one to thirty-six. A normal section contains 640 acres but, due to the convergence of the range lines running true north, in some instances a section may contain less than 640 acres. Fractional sections may also result from natural boundaries which cut into the land.

The breakdown of a Section is shown on the chart on the following page.

Although the Section is the smallest official unit of the Survey, for the purpose of conveyancing, each section may be divided into quarters of 160 acres and each quarter, in turn, may again be quartered into 40-acre tracts. Thus, property may be described as "the Northwest Quarter of the Southeast Quarter of Section 12, Township 3 North, Range 2 West of the 3rd Principal Meridian." Frequently, even smaller parcels are described as follows:

"The north half of the Southwest Quarter of the Northeast Quarter of Section 11— being 20 acres more or less." or

"The Northwest Quarter of the Southeast Quarter of the Northwest Quarter of Section 12   *   *   *."

A third method of describing property in a deed is by reference to a survey of a larger tract which includes the parcel to be conveyed and which has been filed for record in the county in which the land is located. Sellers may thereby avoid a lengthy description by monuments or reference only to the government survey and, instead, refer to the property as "Lot 1" or "Lot 12" in an identified plat. This method is used

A SECTION OF LAND—640 Acres

A rod is 16½ feet.
A chain is 66 feet or 4 rods.
A mile is 320 rods, 80 chains or 5,280 ft.
A square rod is 272¼ square feet.
An acre contains 43,560 square feet.
  "   "   " 160 square rods.
  "   " is about 208¾ feet square.
  "   " is 8 rods wide by 20 rods long.
  or any two numbers (of rods) whose product
  is 160.
25 × 125 feet equals .0717 of an acre.

80 rods

10 chains | 330 ft.

5 acres | 5 acres

20 acres | 5 chs. | 20 rods

80 acres

40 rods | 10 acres | 660 feet

660 feet | 10 acres | 10 chains

40 acres

CENTER | 20 chains | 1,320 feet

OF SECTION

Sectional Map of a Township with adjoining Sections.

36	31	32	33	34	35	36	31
1	6	5	4	3	2	1	6
12	7	8	9	10	11	12	7
13	18	17	16	15	14	13	18
24	19	20	21	22	23	24	19
25	30	29	28	27	26	25	30
36	31	32	33	34	35	36	31
1	6	5	4	3	2	1	6

160 acres

40 chains, 160 rods, or 2,640 feet.

[Provided by the Chicago Title and Trust Company, Chicago, Illinois.] [A3021]

where, under authorization of statute, an owner has had his land surveyed and subdivided into blocks, lots and streets. In most cases, the seller is required to convey or "dedicate" the streets to the local government for public use. In most cities, villages and incorporated towns, reference to a plat is the common method of describing property. Thus, such a deed might describe the land as "Lot 1 in Block 7 of McGuire's Subdivision in the village of Bull Creek, Iowa, being part of Section 1, Township 4 North, Range 28 West of the 4th Principal Meridian."

When the boundary of a tract is described by reference to a body of water or to a street or highway, additional problems of identification may arise. Where the stream bed does not belong to the State, it is a general rule that the owner of the land "bounded by" a stream is entitled to the bed to the center of the stream, in the absence of a clear indication in the description that the grantee was only to take to the edge of the water. Similarly, unless the State owns the fee to a road bed a description of land as bounded "by" a street will be sufficient to pass title to the center of the street. An intention to exclude the road bed to the center line must be clearly indicated.

It was noted in Chapter 46 that a conveyance of land will convey easements or other rights appurtenant thereto without further reference.

Exceptions or Reservations. Immediately following the description of the property conveyed, the grantor will usually provide for any exceptions or reservations which are to be excluded from the grant. One illustration would be a deed conveying "The East one half of the Northwest Quarter of Section 11 * * * excepting therefrom one acre square in the Northeast corner of the Northeast Quarter of said Northwest Quarter." Another example would be a deed conveying "Lots 2, 3 and 4 of Laurence's Subdivision in Section 1 * * * reserving, however, to the grantors, his heirs and assigns forever, the minerals upon and underneath said land."

An exception or reservation in a deed cannot create any interest in a stranger to the transaction. A warranty deed contained the following language:

Grantors, Mary Brown and John Brown, her husband, of the City of Chicago, County of Cook and State of Illinois, for $10.00 and other valuable consideration convey and warrant the following described property (here follows property description) unto William Smith of the City of Chicago, County of Cook and State of Illinois, excepting a life estate for William White and Helen White, father and mother of grantor Mary Brown.

The father and mother of Mary Brown acquired nothing by the deed. The effect of the language was to reserve to the grantor, Mary Brown, presumed to be the owner, an interest for the lifetime of her father and mother and the grantee took title subject thereto.

Quantity of the Estate Conveyed. After the property has been described, the deed will state "to have and to hold" and then proceed to describe the *quantity* of estate conveyed to the grantee. Thus, either "to have and to hold to himself and his heirs forever" or "to have and to hold in fee simple" would vest the grantee with absolute title to the land. This part of a deed is called the *habendum* and is distinguished from the parts which come before it which are called the *premises.*

There is the possibility that in a carelessly prepared deed there will be a conflict between the size of estate granted in the premises and the quantity described in the habendum. One technical rule is that the

estate described in the granting clause takes precedence over that described in the habendum. A more reasonable rule is that the larger estate will prevail whether it appears in the granting clause of the premises or in the habendum.

Covenants of Title. It is the practice in deeds for the grantor to make certain promises concerning his title to the land. If any one of these promises or covenants is breached, the grantee is entitled to be indemnified. There are a number of these convenants, the most usual of which are of title, against incumbrances, of quiet enjoyment and of warranty. These various covenants add up to an assurance that the grantee will have undisturbed possession and will, in turn, be able to transfer the land without adverse claims of third parties. In many States, these covenants, or many of them, are implied from the words of conveyance themselves such as "warrants" or "grant, bargain and sell."

Execution. Deeds are generally concluded by the signature of the grantor, a seal and an acknowledgment before a notary public or other official authorized to attest to the authenticity of documents. The signature can be made by a person other than the grantor himself as his attorney or agent if such party has written authority from the grantor in a form required by law. The seal today has lost a great deal of its former significance and in those jurisdictions where it is required, the seal is sufficient if the word "Seal" or the letters "L. S." appear next to the signature.

Although the acknowledgment may not be required to bind the parties to the deed, it is generally a prerequisite to recording the deed and without an acknowledgment a deed may not be effective as against third parties, or a certified copy may not be admissible in evidence as a public document. In most jurisdictions, a special form of acknowledgment for deeds is specified by statute. A simple and usual notary's statement that a party "subscribed and was sworn" may not be sufficient.

Delivery of Deeds

A deed does not transfer title to land until it is delivered. "Delivery" means an *intent* that the deed shall take effect and is evidenced by the acts or statements of the grantor. Manual or physical transfer of the deed is usually the best evidence of this intent but is not necessary to effect "delivery." Thus, the act of the grantor in placing a deed in a safe deposit box may or may not constitute delivery depending upon many facts such as whether the grantee did or did not have access to the box and whether the grantor deals with the deed as though the property were the grantee's. A deed conceivably may be "delivered" even when kept in the possession of the grantor just as it would be possible that physical delivery of the deed to the grantee would not transfer title. A deed is frequently turned over to a third party to hold until the performance of certain conditions by the grantee. This is spoken of as an escrow and the third party is the escrow agent. Upon the performance of the condition, the escrow agent, or escrowee, is obliged to turn the deed over the the grantee. If, after delivery to the escrow agent, the grantor should die or become incompetent the "delivery" is said to "date back" to the time deed was placed with the escrow agent. In this way, subsequent incapacity of the grantor does not make delivery by the escrowee invalid. If a grantor dies subsequent to the execution of a deed, it is possible that questions will be raised as to whether there was "delivery" before death. This will depend upon whether the evidence shows an intent on his part to divest himself of dominion over the property and to give control to the named grantee.

In one case, the grantors, H and W, husband and wife, executed quitclaim deeds conveying their house to their granddaughters. After execution, the deeds were placed in a strongbox under the control of the grantors' son. The grantors continued to live in the house and pay taxes on the property. Further, they continuously made statements that they wanted the house to go to the girls. W died the year following execution of the deeds. H died fifteen years later. In an action by the granddaughters for a declaration that they had title to the property, the court found that there was no intent to make a present conveyance. The granddaughters did not have that dominion of the incidents of ownership requisite to a finding of transfer of title. Haasjes v. Woldring, 10 Mich.App. 100, 158 N.W.2d 777 (1968).

This case illustrates the uncertainties which arise when the intent of a deceased person is the deciding factor. It is indispensable to the delivery of a deed that the grantor should part with control over it with the intention that it will immediately become operative to convey the estate described in it. If the grantor retains any dominion and control over the deed, it is ineffectual as a conveyance. In this case, the court felt that the grantors did not intend a present conveyance as evidenced by their expressed wishes and subsequent acts of ownership.

Recordation

In all states but two, it is not necessary to record deeds in order to pass title from grantor to grantee. However, unless the grantee has the deed recorded, a subsequent good faith purchaser of the property will acquire superior title to the grantee. Recordation consists of delivery of a duly executed and acknowledged deed to the recorder's office in the county where the property is located. There a copy of the instrument is made and inserted in the current deed book and indexed.

In some states (*notice* states) unrecorded instruments are invalid against any subsequent purchaser without notice. In other states (*notice-race* states) an unrecorded deed is invalid against any subsequent purchaser without notice who records first. Finally, in a few states (*race* states) an unrecorded deed is invalid against *any* deed recorded before it.

Without going further into the law surrounding the recording acts, the importance to the purchaser of recording the deed of conveyance to him *immediately* after delivery, cannot be overemphasized.

SECURED TRANSACTIONS IN REAL ESTATE

The purchase of real estate usually involves a relatively large outlay of money so that few people are able with their own funds to pay all cash for a house or business real estate. It is then necessary to borrow a part of the purchase price or defer payment over a period of time. In such case, the realty itself is used to secure the obligation evidenced by a note and mortgage or trust deed. The debtor is referred to as the mortgagor and the creditor as the mortgagee.

A secured transaction includes two elements: (1) a debt or obligation to pay money, and (2) an interest of the creditor in specific property which secures performance of the obligation. However, a security interest in property cannot exist apart from the debt which it secures, and upon a discharge of the debt in any manner, the security interest in the property is terminated. Transactions involving the use of real estate as security for a debt are subject to real estate law consisting of statutes and rules developed by the common law relating to mortgages and trust deeds. The U.C.C. does not apply to real estate mortgages or trust deeds.

Form of Mortgages

The instrument creating a mortgage is in the form of a conveyance from the mortgagor to the mortgagee with all the necessary requirements for such documents, namely, adequate description of the property, seal and acknowledgment, and delivery. In most jurisdictions, a simple and concise form is recognized by statute but the transaction remains essentially the same whether it is a one-page document covering a house and lot or a 350-page book covering substantially all the property of an interstate railroad company.

The usual mortgage will differ from an outright conveyance of the property by virtue of a provision in the instrument that upon the performance of the promise of the mortgagor, the conveyance is void and of no effect. This condition is referred to as the "defeasance," and, while normally it appears on the face of the mortgage, it may be in a separate document. If evidence indicates that an instrument which purports to be an outright conveyance is actually a security transaction, defeasance will be implied.

The concept of a mortgage as a lien upon property as security for the payment of a debt applies with equal force to transactions having the same purpose but under a different name and form. A trust deed is fundamentally identical with a mortgage, the most striking difference being that, under a trust deed, the property is conveyed not to the creditor as security but to a third person as trustee, referred to as Indenture Trustee, for the benefit of the creditor. Trust deeds are frequently employed where the amount borrowed is substantial and has been obtained from a large number of creditors. The creditors receive bonds or certificates evidencing the indebtedness due them and their interest in the security. The trust deed creates rights substantially similar to those created by a mortgage. In some States, it is customary to use a trust deed in lieu of the ordinary form of mortgage.

As with all interest in realty, the mortgage or deed of trust should be promptly recorded to protect the mortgagee's rights against persons who acquire an interest in the mortgaged property without knowledge of the mortgage.

Property Which Can Be Mortgaged

Almost any interest in real property can be mortgaged. Rents, life estates, vested remainders and even, in some instances, options have been held to be proper subjects of a mortgage.

At common law, it was the general rule that property not yet acquired or not in existence could not be mortgaged since there could be no present conveyance. Under this rule, mortgage clauses seeking to subject after-acquired property to a mortgage were void. The majority of jurisdictions today recognize the validity of such clauses in equity and hold that the mortgage attaches to the property when acquired.

A real estate mortgage may also cover personalty. In such cases, the combination of the real estate mortgage and the "mortgage" on personalty, commonly called a "package mortgage," provides a means of financing the purchase of household appliances in place in a new house. Under a package mortgage, the lender-mortgagee provides funds for the house and the household appliances, and specifically provides in the mortgage instrument that such appliances shall be part of the security. These appliances become "fixtures" and, if subsequently replaced, may result in a conflict between the mortgagee and the seller of the appliance who has retained a purchase money security interest in the goods.

Rights and Duties of Mortgagor

The correlative rights and duties of the parties to a mortgage may depend upon whether it is viewed as creating a lien or as transferring lgal title to the mortgagee. In the majority of States, the "lien" theory has been adopted. The mortgagor retains title and, even in the absence of any stipulation in the mortgage, is entitled to possession of the premises to the exclusion of the mortgagee even in the event of default by the mortgagor. Only by foreclosure or sale or court appointment of a receiver can the right of possession be taken from the mortgagor. The minority of States have adopted the common-law "title" theory which gives the right of ownership and possession to the mortgagee. In most cases, as a practical matter, the mortgagor retains possession because the mortgagee has little interest in possession until default occurs.

In the "lien" States, the mortgagor is, for all practical purposes, the owner of the property and may lease, sell, give away, or transfer by will his interest, subject only to the outstanding mortgage. Unless expressly waived or released, dower exists in the mortgagor's interest. The mortgagor's interest known as an equity of redemption is subject to execution by his judgment creditors. If a house and lot have a market value of $70,000 and are subject to a mortgage of $50,000, the mortgagor's "equity" is $20,000, and it is this margin with which he may deal.

If the mortgagor is in possession, he is entitled to the rents and profits from the land. His obligation to the mortgagee is to pay the interest and principal when due. It is occasionally stipulated, however, that rents and profits shall be assigned to the mortgagee as additional security for the debt.

Even though the mortgagor is entitled to possession and to many of the attributes of unfettered ownership, he has a responsibility to deal with the property in such manner as not to impair the security. The general rules as to waste which apply between landlord and tenant, and life tenant and remainderman, are modified to some extent in the direction of allowing greater freedom to the mortgagor in possession. This is particularly true in the "lien" theory

States where the mortgagor is frequently allowed to deal with the property at his pleasure, so long as the security of the mortgagee is not rendered insufficient.

In most instances, "waste" (impairment of the security) results from failure of the mortgagor to prevent the action, or threatened action, of third parties against the land. Thus, a failure by the debtor to pay taxes or to discharge a prior lien may seriously impair the security of the creditor. In such cases, the creditor is generally permitted to pay the obligation and add it to his claim against the mortgagor. Similarly, although a mortgagor is not obligated to insure the premises in the absence of an agreement to do so, if he does promise to insure and fails to do so, the mortgagee may insure and charge the expense to the mortgagor.

Whether a mortgage is viewed as giving the mortgagee a legal title or simply a lien may also affect the rights of the mortgagee against third parties. In States that consider the legal title to be in the mortgagee, he does, of course, have all the remedies incident to ownership. Where he is looked upon as having only a lien, he is, nevertheless, regarded as having a sufficient interest to obtain an injunction against damage to the property although he will not always be permitted to maintain an action at law for damages.

Some of the most troublesome problems relate to the rights and duties of the mortgagee vis-a-vis a lessee of the mortgagor. A mortgage made subsequent to a lease of the premises is junior to the right of the tenant to use the property for the term of the lease, but once a mortgage has been placed on the property no subsequent lease by the mortgagor will bind the mortgagee. Thus, if A rents a farm to C on January 1 and later mortgages the same land to B, a default by A and subsequent foreclosure by B cannot disturb C's right to use the land under his lease. But, if B holds a mortgage on A's farm and A later leases the land to C, upon foreclosure, B, or any purchaser at the foreclosure sale, may either eject C or elect to treat him as a tenant. If C is ejected, he will have a right to sue A for breach of a covenant in the lease for quiet enjoyment.

Transfer of the Interests under the Mortgage

The interests of the original mortgagor and mortgagee are capable of being transferred and the rights and obligations of the assignees will depend primarily upon (1) the agreement of the parties to the assignment and (2) the rules of law protecting the interest of the one who is party to the mortgage but not to the transfer.

If the mortgagor conveys the land, the purchaser (of the equity of redemption) is not personally liable for the mortgage debt unless he expressly assumes the mortgage. If he assumes it, he is personally obligated to pay the mortgagor's debt owing to the mortgagee who can also hold the mortgagor on his promise to pay. A transfer of mortgaged property "subject to" the mortgage does not obligate the transferee to pay the mortgage debt. In such case the grantee's exposure to loss is limited to the realty.

A mortgagee has the right to assign the mortgage to another person without the consent of the mortgagor. Under the title theory the mortgage places legal title in the mortgagee, and there can be no assignment of the mortgage except by formal conveyance of the land. However, in States which have adopted the lien theory, an assignment of the *debt*, whether formal or not, effects an assignment of the mortgage. This follows from the basic principle of the lien theory that the transaction is essentially a debt with security and not a conditional conveyance of property.

An assignee of a mortgage is well advised to obtain the assignment in writing duly executed by the mortgagee, and to record it promptly with the proper public official. This will protect his rights against persons who subsequently acquire an interest in the mortgaged property without knowledge of the assignment. Failure to record an assignment may cause an assignee of a mortgage note to lose his security. For example, A buys land from B, relying upon a release executed and recorded by the mortgagee, C. C, however, had previously assigned the mortgage to D who had failed to have his assignment recorded. In the absence of actual knowledge on the part of A of the assignment by C, D has no claim against the property.

An assignee who causes his assignment to be recorded is, of course, protected against prior assignees who neglected to record their interests. The recording of an assignment does not, however, constitute notice to the mortgagor. This means that X, a mortgagor without actual notice of a recorded assignment, may discharge his debt by payment to Y, the original mortgagee, in spite of the fact that Y, by virtue of an assignment, may have absolutely no interest in the property at the date he receives payment.

Payment, Redemption, and Discharge of Mortgage

The mortgagor has the right to relieve his mortgaged property from the lien of a mortgage by payment of the indebtedness which it secures. This right of redemption is characteristic of a mortgage, and cannot be extinguished except by operation of law. The right to redeem carries with it the obligation to pay the debt, and payment in full with interest is prerequisite to redemption.

The mortgagor is not the only person with redemption rights. Any person having an interest that is affected by the mortgage may pay the mortgage debt and be subrogated to the rights of the mortgagee, that is, entitled to the security and the rights therein formerly belonging to the mortgagee. If A, one of three tenants in common with equal interests in property on which there is a $60,000 mortgage, pays the mortgage debt in full, he is entitled to contribution from his co-tenants to the extent of $20,000 each and has a lien on their respective undivided interests to that extent.

Foreclosure

The mortgagor's right to redeem the property is limited in all jurisdictions by the mortgagee's right of foreclosure. Usually, the right to foreclose arises when the mortgagor fails to pay the debt. However, the mortgagor's default by non-performance of other promises in the mortgage may also give the mortgagee this right. Thus, a mortgage may provide that failure of the mortgagor to pay taxes is a default which permits foreclosure. It is also a common provision in mortgages that default in payment of an installment of the debt makes the entire unpaid balance of the indebtedness immediately due and payable, permitting foreclosure for the entire amount.

Foreclosure has historically taken three principal forms: (1) strict foreclosure, (2) foreclosure by judicial sale, and (3) power of sale in mortgage.

Strict Foreclosure. By the time equity had developed the right of the mortgagor to redeem after his indebtedness had matured, it became apparent that there should be a time limit upon the exercise of this right. The practice arose of providing by judicial decree that the right of redemption would be cut off or "foreclosed" within a specified time. Upon the expiration of this period, an indefeasible title to the property vested in the mortgagee. This was known as "strict foreclosure" and, in effect, meant that the consequence, under the early common law, of failure to pay the debt on the precise date when it became due was the acquisition by the mortgagee of property which may have a value greatly in excess of the debt. Although this method of foreclosure is still permissible in one or two States it is no longer permitted in most jurisdictions.

Foreclosure by Judicial Sale. The most general method of terminating the right to redeem is by a suit in equity to obtain a judicial decree directing the sale of the property by an officer of the court, the debt being paid out of the proceeds of the sale and the excess, if any, paid to the mortgagor. In some jurisdictions, the mortgagor is given a statutory right to redeem from the foreclosure sale within a specified period of time thereafter. This right, in effect is a second "right of redemption" and should not be confused with the customary right of redemption before foreclosure. In most jurisdictions, a foreclosure sale is subject to approval by the court.

Power of Sale in Mortgage. In States where foreclosure is not limited to a sale under judicial decree, a clause may be inserted in mortgages permitting the mortgagee to foreclose by a sale without obtaining an order of court. This power of sale in a trust deed form of mortgage is considerably more expedient than a judicial proceeding. The power of sale usually provides for a public auction with published notice thereof, and not infrequently the mortgagee is forbidden by statute to purchase at the sale on the theory that he occupies a fiduciary relation to the mortgagor which would be breached by his buying in the property at a sale conducted by himself.

Whether foreclosure is by sale under judicial proceeding or by grant of power in the mortgage itself, the transaction retains its character of a procedure to obtain satisfaction of a debt. If the proceeds are insufficient to satisfy the debt in full, the debtor-mortgagor remains liable for payment of the balance of the debt. Generally,

the mortgagee will obtain a deficiency judgment for any unsatisfied balance of the debt, and may proceed to enforce payment of this amount out of other assets of the mortgagor.

Mechanic's Liens

At common law a person who has furnished material or labor for the construction or repair of a building or other improvement to land has no lien against the property. However, this rule has been changed by statute in practically every State whereby the laborer or materialman is given a lien upon the property for the unpaid amount due and owing for work and materials supplied, *provided* he takes the required legal steps within the time specified in the statute to "perfect" his claim. The statute protects both prime contractors and subcontractors. Consequently, the builder invariably demands waivers or releases of all such liens before final payment of all amounts due contractors and subcontractors.

A mechanic's lien, once perfected in the manner required by the statute, may be asserted against a purchaser of the property, and takes precedence over subsequent mortgages but not over mortgages executed *and recorded* prior to the attaching of a mechanic's lien. However, a mechanic's lien perfected subsequent to the recording of a prior mortgage is generally entitled to priority limited in extent to the value of the improvement or the repairs for which the lien is asserted.

ADVERSE POSSESSION

It is a possible although very rare event that title to land may be transferred *involuntarily* without any deed or other formality. Such an occurrence results from what the law calls "adverse possession" and, although the landowner should be aware of this peculiar risk, its infrequency calls for only a brief comment.

In most States, if a person openly and continuously occupies or exerts dominion over the land of another for a period of twenty years, that person will gain title to the land. The possession must be actual and not merely constructive. Living on land, farming it, or building and maintaining fences on it have been held sufficient to constitute possession. It is necessary, however, that the possession be *adverse*. By this, it is meant that any act of dominion by the true owner during the twenty years will stop the period from running. His entry on the land or the assertion of ownership by him will break the period. In such event, the period will have to commence anew from that time.

The purchasers or heirs of one occupying adversely may "tack on" the period during which the vendor or ancestor possessed the land to establish the necessary period of time. So long as the persons occupied continuously without break and had some continuity by virtue of inheritance or contract, it is not necessary that the same person remain for twenty years.

In some jurisdictions, shorter periods of adverse possession have been established by statute where there is not only possession but also some other claim such as the payment of taxes for seven years and at least a colorable claim of title.

Unless provided by statute, adverse possession cannot be asserted against the United States or against a State.

Cases

Form of Deeds

STERLING v. PARK

(1907) 129 Ga. 309, 58 S.E. 828, 13 L.R.A.,N.S., 298.

EVANS, J.

The various assignments of error raise but one question: Is it essential that a person who signs, seals and delivers a deed should be mentioned in the body of the deed, to be bound by it, and to make it an operative conveyance of his estate in the land? The case in hand was complaint for land, and one of the plaintiff's muniments of title was a deed in which M. C. Huntley was named as grantor, and R. E. Park as grantee, and which purported to convey, for a valuable consideration, a described lot of land, in fee simple. The deed was signed and sealed by M. C. Huntley, W. H. Huntley, and the defendant. Neither W. H. Huntley, nor the defendant was named in it as grantor. At the time the deed was executed the title to the land was in M. C. Huntley for life, with remainder to the others who signed the deed. The plaintiff's contention is that the deed is operative and effective as a conveyance of the estate which each maker-signer had in the land; while on the other hand, the defendant contends that as she was not named in the deed as grantor, it is not an operative conveyance of her estate in remainder.

The point in the case has been before many courts of last resort, and there is much contrariety of opinion on the subject. We believe the true rule to be that one who signs, seals, and delivers a deed, in which he is not named as grantor, is nevertheless bound by these acts as a grantor. We think an examination into the origin and reason of the contrary doctrine will demonstrate the correctness of our conclusion. At common law a deed is defined to be a writing, sealed and delivered by the parties. Coke's Lit. 171; 2 Bl.Com. 295. * * * Signing was not necessary to make a deed valid as such, at common law, and Sir William Blackstone says that "It was held in all our books that sealing alone was sufficient to authenticate a deed: and so the common form of attesting deeds—'sealed and delivered'—continues to this day notwithstanding the statute 29 Car. II, c. 3," which requires deeds to be signed by the maker. 2 Bl.Com. 307. Not only could any seal be used, but "a stick or any such like thing which doth make a print." Shep. Touch. 57. "In Termes de la Ley s. v. 'Fait,' reference is made to a charter of Edward III, of which the last two lines run in the English translation thus:

And in witness that it was sooth
He bit the wax with his foretooth.

Norton on Deeds, 6.

Thus it will be seen, from the conditions prevailing at common law, the prime importance of the grantor's name appearing in the body of the deed was to identify the deed as the act of a particular grantor. Without signature, and executed with a seal indented by the prick of a pin, or imprint of a tooth, the deed could not disclose the identity of the grantor, except by mention of his name in the grant. From the very necessity of the case grew the rule that the name of the grantor should appear in connection with apt words indicating that the deed was his grant. But even at common law a deed could be made in a very informal manner. Says Lord Coke: "I have tearmed the said parts of the deed formall or orderly parts, for that they be not of the essence of a deed of feofment; for if such a deed be without premises, habendum, tenendum, the clause of in cujus rei testimonium, the date, and the clause of hiis testibus, yet the deed is good. For if a man by deed give lands to another, and to his heires, without more saying, this is good, if he put his seale to the deede, deliver it and make lievry accordingly." 1 Coke's Inst. 7a. Thus it would seem that the requirement of a deed made before the statute of frauds was, not that the grantor's name should appear in formal context, but if the writing should identify the grantor, the deed would be considered his grant. * * *

Text writers now very generally discard as unsound the proposition that the grantor should be named as such in the deed, and approve those cases which hold that the conveyance is operative when signed by the grantor, though his name be omitted from the body of the instrument. [Citations.]

The requisites of a deed under the code are, that it must be in writing, signed by the maker, attested by at least two witnesses, and delivered to the purchaser, or some one for him, and be made on a valuable or good consideration. No prescribed form is essential to the validity of a deed, and the instrument will be deemed sufficient if it make known the transaction. [Citation.] We think that the deed under discussion measures up to these statutory essentials, and is effective as a conveyance of the defendant and her co-remainderman, though their names are not mentioned in the body of the installment. [Citation.]

Judgment affirmed.

Quantity of the Estate Conveyed

STYLECRAFT, INC. v. THOMAS

(1968) 250 S.C. 495, 159 S.E.2d 46.

LEGGE, A. A. J.

The parties have stipulated that the sole issue here is as to the quantum of the estate conveyed by a certain deed which in pertinent part reads as follows:

KNOW ALL MEN BY THESE PRESENTS, that I, T. C. Hammond in the State aforesaid, Aiken County, in consideration of the sum of Eighty & No/100 Dollars to me paid by Tom McCain, James Smith, & William Hammond as Trustee of Carys Hill School in the State aforesaid Edgefield County have granted, bargained, sold and released, and by these presents do grant, bargain, sell and release unto the said Tom McCain, James Smith and William Hammond, their successors and assigns, All that lot or parcel of land in the State & County above named containing Four (4) acres and bounded East North & West by lands of the Grantor (T. C. Hammond) and South by lands of H. W McKie.

It is specifically understood and agreed by all parties that the land is to be used for school purposes only—should it ever be used for other purposes the said property is to be reverted to him the said T. C. Hammond or his heirs and assigns forever.

Together with all and singular, the rights, members, hereditaments and appurtenances to the said premises belonging or in anywise incident or appertaining.

TO HAVE AND TO HOLD all and singular the premises before mentioned unto the said Tom McCain, James Smith and William Hammond, their successors and Assigns forever.

And I do hereby bind myself & my Heirs, Executors and Administrators, to warrant and forever defend all and singular the said premises unto the said Tom McCain, James Smith, and William Hammond, their successors and Assigns, against me and my heirs and all other persons lawfully claiming, or to claim, the same or any part thereof.

WITNESS my hand and Seal this 16th day of April in the year of our Lord one thousand nine hundred and Twenty five and in the one hundred and 49th year of the Sovereignty and Independence of the United States of America.

                                        T.C. Hammond (SEAL)

Signed, Sealed and Delivered
in the Presence of:
W. R. Swearingen
H. W. McKie

Plaintiff claimed ownership in fee simple as successor in title, through successive conveyances, of the grantees named in the foregoing deed. The defendant P. E. Thomas claimed as owner, through successive assignments, of the reversionary interest which he alleged remained in the grantor; his co-defendant Otis Robinson was in possession, at the commencement of this action, as his tenant or agent. It is stipulated that for some time prior to its acquisition by the plaintiff the property in question had ceased to be used for school purposes. The defendants have appealed from a circuit decree adjudging the plaintiff to be the owner in fee simple and ordering them to surrender possession.

In a long and unbroken line of decisions this court has approved the rule that where the granting clause in a deed purports to convey title in fee simple absolute that estate may not be cut down by subsequent words in the same instrument. [Citations.] The deed now before us falls squarely within that rule. The granting clause conveyed a fee simple absolute; the restrictive words following the description of the property were ineffectual to cut down that estate.

Appellants contend that the judgment of the lower court should be reversed because application of the rule before mentioned would defeat the grantor's plainly expressed intention. That position cannot be sustained; the intention of a grantor will not be allowed to prevail if it runs counter to an established rule of law. [Citations.]

Affirmed.

Delivery of Deeds

PARRAMORE v. PARRAMORE
(1978 Fla.App.) 371 So.2d 123.

SMITH, Acting C. J.

Appellant Alney Parramore and his brother and sisters, appellees Eudell, Bernice, and Iris, are the four surviving children of Fred Parramore of Gadsden County, who died there in November 1974. Fred Parramore's estate was almost entirely in Gadsden County lands, and his plan was to parcel and convey those lands to his children at his death. He implemented that plan by inter vivos deeds purporting to convey life estates to himself and his wife with remainder interests to his children. In May 1963, the deeds were executed and acknowledged, but not delivered to the grantees. Fred placed the deeds with his will in a safe deposit box of a Quincy bank and instructed his children to pick up their deeds at his death. Fred survived his wife, later delivered Alney's deed to him, and, six months before his death, made another conveyance to Alney, the apparent effect of which was to release Fred's life estate and merge the fee in Alney. But Fred's deeds conveying remainder interests to appellees Eudell, Bernice and Iris were never handed over to them during Fred's lifetime.

Appellant Alney, whose parcel is securely vested in him, urges that the inter vivos deeds of remainder interests to his brother and sisters failed for want of delivery, and that the affected lands pass to all four children equally by the residuary clause of Fred's will. After a trial in which the decedent's later years were explored for evidence of his intent, the circuit court held that Fred Parramore's words and acts accomplished a symbolic and constructive delivery of the deeds during his lifetime, and that the remainder estates were vested in Eudell, Bernice, and Iris before their father's death. Alney appeals. We affirm.

Delivery is "the life of a deed"; without it no deed is good, though "the intent to deliver is clear and failure to deliver due to accident." [Citation.] Yet delivery is not an exact ceremony, to be done invariably in a particular way. The clearest delivery is by "a manual tradition of the prepared deed with accompanying words or circumstances showing an appropriate intent." [Citation.] But a grantor may fully relinquish a deed, signifying a conveyance, otherwise than by placing it in the grantee's hands. The grantor may hand his deed to a person not the grantee, with directions to deliver

it; and, if an intent to relinquish the deed is shown, and the grantor's directions eventually are carried out, delivery is regarded as having been accomplished even though it cannot be proved absolutely that the grantor could never have retrieved the deed. [Citations.]

* * *

We believe there is substantial competent evidence to support the trial court's decision that Fred Parramore, during his life, vested remainder interests in his children by conduct recognizable as delivery of the deeds. * * * It is enough that Fred Parramore, unsophisticated in such matters, signed deeds creating remainder interests in his several children and put the deeds beyond his immediate reach in a place which he understandably regarded and verbally identified as the appropriate depository for instruments having practical effect at life's end; that he invariably spoke and acted to indicate that he considered the children's remainder interests vested, even to the point of declaring to a prospective buyer that he could not convey the land because it had been deeded away; and that he did not again take the deeds into his more immediate possession or otherwise disturb them. There is no reason why the grantor's evident intent, as discerned by the trial court, should not be regarded as effectuated by his conduct; nor any reason to doubt that his deeds were thereby delivered by all ceremonies that the law may sensibly require.

Affirmed.

Secured Transactions

LIGHTCAP v. BRADLEY
(1900) 186 Ill. 510, 58 N.E. 221.

[H. W. Lightcap brought an ejectment action against Lydia Bradley. Defendant, to defend her claim, proved that one of the grantors in plaintiff's chain of title had made a trust deed of the land to defendant to secure promissory notes payable to her and that this deed had been foreclosed and she had received a deed from the trustee's heirs. It was agreed that the trust deed conveyed the fee to the trustee with only the equitable right on the part of the mortgagor to redeem. Judgment for defendant, and plaintiff appeals.]

CARTWRIGHT, J.

* * *

Leaving out of consideration the effect of a mortgage in the statutory form it is true that a mortgage or trust deed like the one in question here, which purports to convey title, does, as between the mortgagor and mortgagee, convey such title; but it is only a qualified conveyance of the land, and the mortgagor parts with the title only as security to his creditor and during the existence of his debt or obligation. In the development of the law of real estate mortgages in England the mortgage was at first a pledge of land, usually requiring a judgment to complete the transfer of title and to vest it in the mortgagee. Afterward, a form of mortgage came into use which vested title of itself, and the pledge changed into an estate in fee without judicial foreclosure upon the mortgagor's default. This mortgage vested absolute title in the mortgagee upon condition broken. Courts of equity, however, recognizing the purpose of the mortgage as merely a pledge to secure a debt, established a right of the mortgagor to redeem. They created a new estate in the form of the equity of redemption and a remedy for the creditor to cut off this estate. A proceeding was devised to extinguish the mortgagor's right to redeem and to vest title in the mortgagee, and this was the proceeding now known as strict foreclosure. [Citation.] Equity assumed jurisdiction to relieve the mortgagor against a forfeiture upon default, and he was relieved from it on payment of the debt. [Citation.] Courts of law, following the lead of courts of equity, have adopted many equitable principles as

to the titles of the respective parties, and at law the title of the mortgagee can be used only for the purpose of securing his equitable rights under it. "As to all persons except the mortgagee and those claiming under him, it is everywhere the established modern doctrine that a mortgagor in possession is at law, both before and after breach of the condition, the legal owner." (1 Jones on Mortgages, sec. 11.) In many of the States a mortgage confers no title or estate upon the mortgagee, and it is nothing but a mere security for a debt or obligation. This State has adhered to the rule that at law a title vests in the mortgagee, but only for the protection of his interests. For the purpose of protecting and enforcing his security the mortgagee may enter and hold possession by virtue of his title and take the rents and profits in payment of his mortgage debt. He may maintain the possessory action of ejectment on the strength of such title, but the purpose and effect of the action are not to establish or confirm title in him, but, on the contrary, to give him the rents and profits which undermine and destroy his title. [Citation.] When the rents and profits have paid the mortgage debt, both the title and right of possession of the mortgagee are at an end. The mortgagor's interest in the land may be sold upon execution; his widow is entitled to dower in it; it passes as real estate by devise; it descends to his heirs, by his death, as real estate; he is a freeholder by virtue of it; he may maintain an action for the land against a stranger and the mortgage cannot be set up as a defense. The mortgagee has no such estate as can be sold on execution; his widow has no right to dower in it; upon his death the mortgage passes to his personal representatives as personal estate, and it passes by his will as personal property. [Citation.] The title of the mortgagee, even after condition broken, is not an outstanding title of which a stranger can take advantage, but it is available only to the mortgagee or one claiming under him.

[Citation.] The mortgagor may sell and convey his title or mortgage it to successive mortgagees, and his grantee or mortgagee will succeed to his estate and occupy his position subject to the encumbrance.

* * *

The mortgagee is the legal owner for only one purpose, while, at the same time, the mortgagor is the owner for every other purpose and against every other person. The title of the mortgagee is anomalous, and exists only between him and the mortgagor and for a limited purpose. * * * The title is never out of the mortgagor, except as between him and the mortgagee and as an incident of the mortgage debt, for the purpose of obtaining satisfaction. When the debt is barred by the Statute of Limitations the title of the mortgagee or trustee ceases at law as well as in equity. When the debt, the principal thing, is gone, the incident, the mortgage, is also gone. [Citation.] The mortgagor's title is then freed from the title of the mortgagee, and he is the owner of the premises, not by any new title, but by the title he always had. Statutes of limitation do not transfer title from one to another, and a statute of limitations which would have the effect of transferring the legal title back from the mortgagee to the mortgagor would be unconstitutional. [Citation.] The title of the mortgagor becomes perfect because the title of the mortgagee is measured by the existence of the mortgage debt or obligation and terminates with it. [Citation.] * * *

Reversed and remanded.

Adverse Possession

GERWITZ v. GELSOMIN
(1979) 69 A.D.2d 992, 416 N.Y.S.2d 127.

MEMORANDUM:

Plaintiffs reside at 317 Rita Drive, Clay, New York, property known also as Lot #24 of the Belleville Tract. They acquired the premises in 1957 and shortly thereafter they began to use the adjacent vacant Lot #25, now owned by defendant Gelsomin. At various times they have planted grass seed, flowers and shrubs on the land and used it for picnics or cookouts. In 1977 defendant Gelsomin acquired Lot #25. He constructed a foundation on it on which he attempted to move a house. Plaintiffs thereupon commenced then action claiming title to Lot #25 by adverse possession.

Before a claimant may acquire land by adverse possession, he must prove by clear and convincing evidence that his possession of the premises has been (1) hostile and under a claim of right, (2) actual, (3) open and notorious, (4) exclusive, and (5) continuous. [Citations.] The trial court found that plaintiffs had failed to prove that their occupation of these premises had been exclusive or continuous. We affirm because the possession was not hostile to the owner and under a claim of right.

The reasonable inference to be drawn from the evidence is that plaintiffs knew in 1957 that they did not own Lot #25 and they never intended to claim ownership of it. The entered the land to remedy an eyesore next to their home and use the land as they could. Thus, the proof establishes that plaintiffs had clear knowledge of the boundaries of their land by map and deed and because the other lots on the street were the same size. At the time of purchase, plaintiffs' Lot #24 was graded and improved by the contractor, but he did not grade or improve Lot #25. Plaintiffs were satisfied with this grading which established a clear boundary line between their improved property and the unimproved Lot #25 next door which was covered with debris. Plaintiffs paid the taxes on their own property regularly and received receipts for those payments. They have never paid or attempted to pay the taxes on Lot #25, even after defendant started his construction. While the failure to pay taxes is not conclusive evidence, it is a significant circumstance which weakens plaintiffs' claim that occupation of the land was under a claim of title, particularly when the failure continued for 20 years (see 2 C.J.S. Adverse Possession § 211, pp. 937–938).

Finally, the proof establishes that at various times during the prospective period "For Sale" signs were placed upon the vacant premises by the owner without objection or inquiry by plaintiffs. Upon this evidence, plaintiffs have failed to sustain their burden of proof that they occupied Lot #25 or any part of it under a claim of right.

Judgment unanimously affirmed with costs.

Problems

1. Adler was the owner of Blackacre and made and delivered his warranty deed conveying Blackacre to his son Bert. The deed provided "to have and to hold the same to the said Bert for his lifetime and upon his death leaving issue then to such issue in fee simple, but in the case of Bert without issue, then to the heirs-at-law of Adler."

Adler died intestate leaving his sons, Bert and Charles, his only heirs-at-law. Bert has a son David, who conveyed Blackacre by quitclaim deed to Edward. Bert died and Edward brings an appropriate action to obtain Blackacre. Decision?

2. A was the father of B, C and D and the owner of Redacre, Blackacre and Greenacre.

A made and executed his warranty deed to B conveying Redacre. The deed provided that "this deed shall only become effective upon the death of the grantor." A retained possession of the deed and died leaving the deed in his safe deposit box.

A made and executed his warranty deed to C conveying Blackacre. The deed provided "this deed shall only become effective upon the death of the grantor." A delivered the deed to C. A died and after A's death, C recorded the deed.

A made and executed his warranty deed to D conveying Greenacre. The deed was delivered by A to X with specific instructions to deliver the deed to D upon A's death. Upon the death of A, X delivered the deed to D.

(a) What is the interest of B in Redacre, if any?
(b) What is the interest of C in Blackacre, if any?
(c) What is the interest of D in Greenacre, if any?

3. A, the owner of Redacre, executed a real estate mortgage to the Shawnee Bank and Trust Company for $10,000. After the execution and recording of the mortgage, A constructed a dwelling on the premises and planted a corn crop. After default in the payment of the mortgage debt, the bank proceeded to foreclose the mortgage. At the time of the foreclosure sale, the corn crop was mature and unharvested. A contends: (a) the value of the dwelling should be credited to him and (b) he is entitled to the corn crop. Decision?

4. A, for a valuable consideration, executed and delivered to B a warranty deed conveying a lot improved with a bungalow. The deed was delivered on January 15. B did not record this deed, but took possession and moved into the bungalow on February 1. C, who held A's note for $1,000 which was due January 2, obtained a judgment on the note against A on February 3, and on February 4th, took out an execution and placed it in the hands of the sheriff. Did C acquire a lien on the premises?

5. Robert was the holder of the legal title of record by deed to the N½ of the SE¼ of Section 5. The legal title of record by deed to the N½ of the SW¼ of Section 5 was in Stanley.

Stanley fenced his 80 acres in 1958. He placed his east fence fifteen feet east of the east line of the N½ of the SW¼ of Section 5. Thereafter, he was in possession of this fifteen foot strip of land lying in the N½ of the SE¼ of Section 5 and kept it fenced and cultivated continuously until possession thereof was delivered by him to Nathan on March 1, 1963. Nathan took possession under deed from Stanley by which Stanley conveyed to Nathan the N½ of the SW¼ of Section 5. Nathan continued possession and cultivation of the fifteen-foot strip until May 27, 1982, when Robert, having on several occasions strenuously objected to Nathan's possession, brought suit against Nathan for trespass.

What decision?

6. A, a widower and the owner of Brown Acre, was the father of four bachelor sons, B, C, D and E. A died intestate. B conveyed an undivided one-half interest in Brown Acre by warranty deed to F. C and D died intestate, never having married. B died intestate never having married and left all of his property, real and personal, to his brother, E.

E filed his suit for partition against F asking for a division of Brown Acre.

What is the interest of E in Brown Acre?

7. A executed a mortgage of Blackacre to secure his indebtedness to Ajax Savings and Loan Association in the amount of $25,000. Later A sold Blackacre to B. The deed contained the following, "this deed is subject to the mortgage executed by the Grantor herein to Ajax Savings and Loan Association."

The sale price of Blackacre to B was $50,000. B paid $25,000 in cash, deducting the $25,000 mortgage debt from the purchase price. Upon default in the payment of the mortgage debt, Ajax brings an action against A and B to recover a judgment for the amount of the mortgage debt, and to foreclose the mortgage. Decision?

8. A who owed B $5,000 executed and delivered to B his promissory note to evidence the indebtedness. When the note became due, A was unable to pay it, A and B then entered into an oral agreement whereby A would convey Blackacre to B and upon payment of the note B would reconvey Blackacre to A. A deed was executed and recorded conveying Blackacre from A to B.

Three years later A paid the $5,000 note to B and demanded that B reconvey Blackacre to him. Upon B's refusal to reconvey, A brings an appropriate action against B to recover Blackacre. Decision?

9. On January 1, 1981, A and B owned Blackacre as tenants in common. On July 1, 1981, A made a written contract to sell Blackacre to C for $25,000. Pursuant to this contract, C paid A $25,000 on August 1, 1981, and A executed and delivered to C a warranty deed to Blackacre. On May 1, 1982, B quitclaimed his interest in Blackacre to A. C brings an action against A for breach of warranty of title. What judgment?

10. John Doe, for a valuable consideration, agreed to convey to Richard Roe 80 acres of land. He delivered a deed, the material portions of which read:

"I, John Doe, grant and convey to Richard Roe 80 acres of land [legal description]: To have and to hold unto Richard Roe, his heirs and assigns forever.

"I, John Doe, covenant to warrant and defend the premises hereby conveyed against all persons claiming the same or any part thereof by or through me."

Thereafter, Roe conveyed "all my right, title and interest" in the 80 acres to Paul Poe. It develops that Doe had no title to the land when he conveyed to Roe. Subsequently, Doe inherited an undivided one-half interest in the property.

What rights, if any, does Poe have against Doe and Roe?

Chapter

48

PUBLIC AND
PRIVATE CONTROL
OF LAND USE

A man is no stranger to mankind. The property that he owns is not his to do with as he pleases. In the exercise of its police power, the state can and does place controls upon the use of privately owned land for the benefit of the community. For loss or damage sustained by the owner by reason of such legitimate controls, the state does not pay the owner any compensation. The enforcement of zoning laws, which is a proper exercise of the police power, is not a taking of property but a regulation of its use. However, the taking of private property for a public use or purpose under its power of eminent domain is not an exercise of the police power, and the owners of the property so taken are entitled to be paid its fair and reasonable value.

There are also private controls of the use of privately owned property by means of restrictive covenants, which will be considered in this chapter.

EMINENT DOMAIN

The power to take private property for public use, known as the power of eminent do-main, is recognized as one of the inherent powers of government in the Federal constitution and in the constitutions of the States. At the same time, however, the power is carefully circumscribed and controlled. The fifth amendment to the Federal constitution provides: "Nor shall private property be taken for public use without just compensation." Similar or identical provisions are to be found in the constitutions of the States. There is, therefore, a direct constitutional prohibition against taking private property without just compensation and an implicit prohibition against taking private property for other than public use.

Moreover, under both Federal and State constitutions the individual is entitled to due process of law in connection with the taking. A Kansas statute providing for the determination of just compensation at a hearing of which notice was to be given only by publication in a newspaper was held unconstitutional upon the ground that due process requires that the property owner be served with personal notice of such hearing. Under most statutes regulating the exercise of the power, condemnation involves a judicial proceeding in a court of law, and the property owner is entitled to receive the fair market value of the property as determined by a jury.

Public Use

As noted, there is an implicit constitutional prohibition against taking private property for other than public use. "Public use," here, has been interpreted to mean the same thing as "public purpose." Thus, it was early established that the power of eminent domain may be delegated to railroad and public utility companies. The reasonable exercise of this power by such companies, to enable them to offer continued and improved service to the public is upheld as being for a public purpose.

As society grows more complex other public purposes are accepted as legitimate grounds for exercise of the power of eminent domain. One is in the area of urban renewal. Most States have legislation permitting the establishment of housing authorities with power to condemn slum, blighted and vacant areas, and to finance, construct and maintain low rental housing projects.

Just Compensation

When the power of eminent domain is exercised, just compensation must he made to the owners of the property taken. The measure of compensation is the fair market value of the property as of the time of taking. The compensation award goes to holders of vested interests in the condemned property. Future contingent interests are not compensable. For example, a wife is not entitled to compensation for her inchoate dower interest in her husband's land since she may predecease her husband.

Sometimes, in a proceeding by the Federal Government, the condemnation sought is only of a possessory interest for a number of years. If this period is less than the unexpired term of the lease, the tenant is not only entitled to the entire award but he is also entitled to the cost of removal from the premises as a separate item of damage. If the period extends beyond the term of the lease, while the tenant is entitled to his proportionate share of the entire award, he is not entitled to removal costs for the reason that he would have had these costs in any event, namely, at the time of the expiration of his lease.

ZONING

Zoning is the principal method of public control over land use. The validity of zoning is based upon the police power of the state. The police power to provide for the public health, safety, morals, and welfare, like the power of eminent domain, is one of the inherent powers of government. The Federal constitution nowhere provides for its exercise but neither does it prohibit it. It is one of the powers which is neither delegated to the United States by the Federal constitution, nor prohibited by it to the States; it is, therefore, by article X of the constitution, "reserved to the States * * *, or to the people."

The first thing to be noted is that legitimate exercise of the police power does not require payment of compensation to the property owner affected by such exercise. From this, it follows that the exercise of the police power does not result in a condemnation or "taking" of private property.

Police power can be used only to *regulate* private property, never to "take" it. It is firmly established that regulation which has no reasonable relation to public health, safety, morals, or welfare is unconstitutional as being contrary to due process of law.

Enabling Acts
and Zoning Ordinances

The power to zone, which involves an exercise of the State's police power, is delegated to local city and village authorities by statutes known as "enabling" statutes. A typical "enabling" statute grants the following powers to municipalities: (1) to regulate and limit the height and bulk of buildings thereafter to be erected; (2) to establish, regulate and limit the building or setback lines on or along any street traffic way, drive or parkway; (3) to regulate and limit the intensity of the use of lot areas, and to regulate and determine the area of open spaces, within and surrounding buildings; (4) to classify, regulate and restrict the location of trades and industries and the location of buildings designated for specified industrial, business, residential and other uses; (5) to divide the entire municipality into districts of such number, shape, area, and such different classes as may be deemed best suited to carry out the purposes of the Act; and (6) to fix standards to which buildings or structures shall conform.

The enabling statute also provides that the foregoing powers are to be exercised only "[t]o the end that adequate light, pure air, and safety from fire and other dangers may be secured; that the taxable value of land and buildings throughout the municipality may be conserved; that congestion in the public streets may be lessened and avoided, and that the public health, safety, comfort, morals, and welfare may be otherwise promoted." Many enabling statutes provide, in addition, that "such regulation shall be in accordance with a comprehensive plan."

Under these powers the local authorities may enact zoning ordinances which consist of a map and a text. The map involves an exercise of the fourth and fifth powers enumerated above, that is, it divides the municipality into districts which are designated principally as industrial, commercial, or residential, with possible sub-classifications.

A well drafted zoning ordinance will carefully define the uses permitted in each area. If a proposed use does not appear anywhere in the ordinance and its classification is doubtful, it is not safe for the property owner to rely upon an opinion of the zoning authorities or upon the issuance of a building permit, because it is well settled that a municipality is not estopped from later maintaining that the use is unlawful in the particular area. The property owner may, however, rely upon a variation granted pursuant to the provisions of the zoning ordinance.

The division of a municipality into areas of permitted use is familiar to the layman. However, comprehensive zoning ordinances include regulations regarding the height and bulk of buildings, establish setback lines and often prescribe spacing and minimum lot size for residential areas, or such provisions may be contained in the municipal Building Code. In every case the constitutional validity of a zoning ordinance or building code may be tested by its relation to public health, safety, morals, and welfare.

Variance

All enabling statutes provide that the zoning authorities shall have power to grant variances in cases of "particular hardship." There are two problems connected with this method of freeing property from unwanted restrictions: (a) there is considerable authority to the effect that the power to vary is the power to vary only the strict letter of the zoning ordinance. Thus, if the owner's proposed use can be carried on only by changing the classification of his property from "residential" to "commercial," the zoning authorities may not have statutory power to make such a change under the guise of a variance. The statutory grant of such power raises a constitutional problem of delegation of legislative power to administrative officials. Moreover, a variance which makes such a major change for the benefit of one owner encounters the constitutional prohibition against spot zoning.

(b) A variance is not available except in cases of "particular hardship." Mere failure to make a profit is not enough. It must affirmatively appear that the property as presently zoned cannot yield a reasonable return upon the owner's investment.

Non-conforming Uses

A zoning ordinance may not immediately terminate a lawful use existing prior to its enactment. Such use must be permitted to continue as a non-conforming use—at least for a reasonable time. Some ordinances which provide that non-conforming uses must be discontinued within a specified time are subject to attack by owners who maintain that the specified time is unreasonable as applied to their property. Most ordinances provide for the elimination of non-conforming uses (1) when the use is discontinued, (2) when a non-conforming structure is destroyed or substantially damaged or (3) when a non-conforming structure has been permitted to exist for the period of its useful life as fixed by municipal authorities. The last provision constitutes a sound method of eliminating non-conforming structures but it cannot be utilized in cases of non-conforming uses such as junk yards and parking lots which have no ascertainable useful life.

Judicial Review of Zoning

Although the zoning process is traditionally viewed as legislative in nature, it is subject to judicial review on a number of grounds, including: (1) invalidity of the zoning ordinance, (2) unreasonable application of the zoning ordinance, and (3) zoning ordinance amounts to a confiscation or taking of property.

Invalidity of Zoning Ordinance. A zoning ordinance may be invalid as a whole either because (a) it bears no reasonable relation to public health, safety, morals, or welfare,

or (b) it involves an exercise of powers not granted to the municipality by the "enabling" act. Assume that A owns a parcel of property located in a district which is zoned "Residence A." The ordinance provides that "Every dwelling hereafter erected or placed in a Residence A District shall have a living-floor space, as herein defined: of not less than 768 square feet for a one-story dwelling; of not less than 1,000 square feet for a two-story dwelling." A intends to build a housing development on his property and is convinced that there will be a greater demand for residential housing of smaller living-floor space than that required by the ordinance.

A may be able to convince the courts that the ordinance is unreasonable and that it bears no relation to public health, safety, morals, or welfare. His argument may be that the minimum floor space requirement is not tied to occupancy, that is, it is impossible to state whether 768 square feet for a one-story dwelling is conducive to health, safety, or morals unless one knows how many persons will live in the dwelling. He may be able to show that the only purpose of the ordinance is to prevent poorer families from living within the municipality and that, if such ordinances are upheld poor families may not be able to purchase housing at all. The question of the validity of minimum floor space requirements is not fully settled.

A may be also able to show that the statute does not authorize the adoption of such an ordinance. The enabling statute must be analyzed to determine whether such an ordinance is authorized under it.

Unreasonable Application of Zoning Ordinance. A property owner may be able to show that classification of his property as "residential" is unreasonable in the light of the character and use of the area immediately contiguous to his property. He may argue that the classification of property located on one side of the street as "residential", while property located on the other side is classified and built up as "industrial", is unreasonable. Part of his argument would be that the classification deprives him of any beneficial use of the property because there is very little incentive to build or purchase a residence opposite a factory. In most cases, the contrast and its effects are not so obvious.

A deterrent to the acceptance of this argument is the possibility that if a parcel of property within an area zoned "residential" is granted a variance for industrial use and freed from the restriction merely because it happens to front upon some industrial establishments, the adjoining parcel will have more reason to be similarly freed when the first parcel is built up as industrial. In other words, the domino effect of freeing one parcel of property is a powerful deterrent to acceptance of this form of attack upon the ordinance.

Zoning Amounts to a Taking. Another form of attack is to show that the restrictions amount to confiscation or a "taking." For this purpose, it is not sufficient for the owner to show that he will sustain a financial loss if the restriction is not lifted. In this connection, the courts have stated that what is good for the entire community cannot be bad for a particular owner. Other courts merely say that the private interest must give way to the public good. But when the property owner can show that the restriction makes it impracticable for him to use the property for any beneficial purpose, he should be entitled to prevail. Deprivation of all beneficial use is confiscation.

Suppose A owns a small lot in a residential area. The city adopts an official map which locates a proposed street through the middle of A's lot. The Official Map Statute provides that one who builds in the bed of a proposed street will not be entitled to compensation for such building when his property is condemned for a street. The street may never be built. Meanwhile, A

is effectively prevented from making any use of his property for residential purposes. This is confiscation. Other less obvious forms of confiscation have invalidated ordinances. The test in each case is whether the owner has been effectively prevented from making any beneficial use of his property—if so, the ordinance is confiscatory and invalid.

Subdivision Master Plans

A growing municipality has a special interest in regulating new housing developments so that they will harmonize with the rest of the community; that streets within the development are integrated with existing streets or planned roads; that adequate provision is made for open spaces for traffic, recreation, light and air; and that adequate provision is made for water, drainage and sanitary facilities. Accordingly, in most States there is legislation enabling local authorities to require municipality approval of every land subdivision plat. These "enabling" statutes provide penalties for failure to secure such approval where required by local ordinance. Some statutes make it a criminal offense to sell lots by reference to unrecorded plats, and provide that such plats may not be recorded unless approved by the local planning board. Other statutes provide that building permits will not be issued unless the plat is approved and recorded.

Planning Laws and the Purchaser of Real Property

All purchasers of real property, and particularly those who intend to conduct business or manufacturing activities, should determine whether or not their proposed use is permissible before signing a contract to purchase the property. This is so because an existing zoning restriction is not regarded as an encumbrance and does not render title unmarketable. A contract for the sale of land usually obligates the vendor to convey marketable title to the purchaser. If he signs the contract first, and then discovers that he is not permitted to make use of the property for the purpose he had in mind, he will not be able to rescind the contract, unless the vendor has fraudulently represented that the intended use is permissible. The vendor is not required to inform the purchaser of restrictions—he may remain silent—as the purchaser is presumed to know the law.

It may not be safe for the purchaser to rely upon the fact that the vendor is currently using the property for the same purpose as that intended by the purchaser. If the vendor's use is unlawful, i.e., constitutes a violation of the zoning or building ordinances, his title is unmarketable and, accordingly, the purchaser may refuse to take the conveyance, and sue the vendor for breach of contract. But the vendor's use may be a lawful non-conforming use which has almost reached a termination date. Furthermore, the vendor's existing use may be based upon a variance. A purchaser who relies upon the fact that his vendor is currently using the property for the same purpose as that which he intends, may find to his dismay that he is not entitled to rely upon the vendor's variance. A variance is, as observed, based on "particular hardship" to the person who obtained it. There is authority to the effect that no one may buy his way into another's hardship. However, one who purchases property which is subject to a zoning restriction is not deprived of the right to challenge the validity or constitutionality of the restriction.

PRIVATE RESTRICTIONS UPON LAND USE

The owners of lots are subject to restrictive convenants which, if actually brought to the attention of subsequent purchasers, or recorded by original deed, or by means of a recorded plat or separate agreement, bind

purchasers of lots in the subdivision as though the restriction had been inserted in their own deed.

Suppose X owns a lot in a residential subdivision of a suburban community. On the lot are a house and a garage, and the remainder of the subdivision is either similarly improved or vacant. X decides to enlarge his living room and to extend the front of the house to within twenty feet of the front line of the lot. He knows that this is not prohibited by the zoning ordinance and that there is no limitation in the deed from his seller limiting the area of the house. He will, indeed, be astounded when a neighbor, observing the excavation, informs him that he cannot build to within twenty feet of the front line. He will be only slightly less surprised to hear that the reason he cannot do so is because of a provision in the recorded deed from the original subdivider to the original purchasers of lots in the subdivision requiring front yards of at least thirty feet depth.

X will discover upon further investigation that the entire subdivision has been subjected to a general building plan designed to benefit all the lots and any lot owner in the subdivision has the right to enforce the restriction against a purchaser whose title descends from a common grantor.

Nature of Restrictive Covenants

Restrictive covenants of the foregoing type are, in a sense, easements—or at least *negative* easements—to the extent that they impose a limitation on the use of the land in favor of the owner of other land. Yet, unlike most easements they are not directly based upon any formal grant, and the ability of any number of property owners to enforce them does not suggest the usual easement that normally is enforceable by an adjoining landowner.

Restrictive covenants are a consequence of the untechnical notion that a person should not, as noted in a leading case, "be permitted to use the land in a manner inconsistent with the contract entered into by his vendor, and with notice of which he purchased." If there is a clear intent that a restriction is intended to benefit an entire tract, the fact that the covenant is not formally executed will not prevent it being enforced against a subsequent purchaser of one of the lots in the tract. Indeed, some cases have held that the restriction need not appear in the deeds at all if the intent to establish a general building scheme is evident from a plat recorded at the time of the original formation of the subdivision. As long as two requirements are met, the restriction will be enforced: First, that it is apparent that the restriction was intended to benefit the purchaser of any lot in the tract, and second, that the restriction appears somewhere in the chain of title to which the lot is subject.

Type and Construction of Restrictive Covenants

There are many types of restrictive covenants. The more common types limit the use of property to residential purposes or restrict the area of the lot on which a structure can be built or provide for a special type of architecture as, for example, the requirement that all houses must be of Early American Colonial design. Frequently a subdivider will specify a minimum cost for each house, attempting thereby to maintain a minimum standard in the neighborhood. A provision prohibiting the sale of intoxicating liquor is a common covenant which will be enforced for the benefit of owners of other lots derived from one original tract.

One difficult problem in construing these covenants is the meaning of words describing the restriction. "Dwelling," "business use" and "trade purposes" are not certain in their application. Generally, a covenant restricting the use to "private dwellings" excludes apartments. On the other hand, a doctor's or dentist's office in-

cidental to a private residence will not violate a covenant against "business or trade use." Billboards have been held prohibited by a covenant restricting property to residential use, but the sale of intoxicating liquor in the original package by a grocer has been held not to violate a covenant against the sale of liquor. A building line restriction is not violated by a fire escape that encroaches, and a porch may or may not constitute a violation of a minimum front yard restriction, depending upon whether its construction substantially blocks the view.

Termination of Restrictive Covenants

In the example of X and his desire to enlarge his living room, if he is advised to proceed with his plans it may be that the character of the neighborhood has so changed that the original purpose of the covenant (in this case, to provide front yards not less than twenty feet in depth) has no further application. If, during the preceding decade, houses, apartment buildings, and even stores have been constructed in disregard of the building line restriction, X may successfully maintain that the character of the area has so changed as no longer to justify enforcement of the covenant against him. To succeed he must convince the court that the circumstances which gave rise to the covenant no longer exist. Typical of this "abandonment" of restrictive covenants is a once fine residential area that has gradually deteriorated into a neighborhood of boarding houses and small shops. In such an area, a court would probably refuse to enforce a covenant restricting use to single-family houses. Evidence of changed conditions may be found either within the tract covered by the original covenant or in the area adjacent to or surrounding the tract.

The principal reason for not enforcing private restrictions is long acquiescence by neighbors in numerous violations in the past. Aside from the obvious failure of the original purpose of the covenant in such cases, the courts consider it unreasonable to have the covenant suddenly enforced after years of indifference to violations. Acquiescence with respect to one or two isolated violations in the entire tract will not, however, be a defense to a complaint for violation.

Validity of Restrictive Covenants

Although restrictions upon the use of land have never been popular in the law, if it appears that the restriction will operate to the general benefit of the owners of all the land intended to be affected, the restriction will be enforced. The usual method of enforcing such agreements is by injunction to restrain a violation.

For many decades, the United States Supreme Court took the position that *private* racial restrictive agreements, regardless of their moral status, did not deny any right guaranteed by the Federal constitution. It has been the law for many years, however, that a State or municipality could not, under the Fourteenth Amendment to the Federal constitution, impose any such restrictions by statute or ordinance. In 1947, the United States Supreme Court held that private racial restrictive covenants could not be enforced by State courts since the courts were an arm of the State government. This effectively invalidated racial restrictive covenants. Shelly v. Kraemer, 334 U.S. 1, 92 L.Ed. 1161, 3 A.L.R.2d 441 (1947).

Cases

*Just Compensation
for Property Taken
by Eminent Domain*

URBAN RENEWAL AGENCY v. GOSPEL MISSION CHURCH

(1979) 4 Kan.App.2d 101, 603 P.2d 209.

SPENCER, J.

At issue in this case is the proper measure of compensation for the taking by condemnation of property owned and operated exclusively for religious and educational purposes on a nonprofit basis.

The Gospel Mission Church and School was located at 1545 North Wabash in Wichita. The property taken consisted of land, a dwelling house, and a structure housing the church sanctuary and a gymnasium. There is no issue in this court as to the land or the dwelling house. The sanctuary and gymnasium consisted of a large concrete block building which had been erected in two stages. The sanctuary portion was built to accommodate approximately 200 worshipers and contained separate rooms

for the church office, choir, and restrooms. The gymnasium portion was equipped with kitchen facilities, restrooms, a storage deck, and basketball goals. The gymnasium was used on a regular basis for basketball games and served as a fellowship and banquet hall.

* * *

The sole issue on appeal is whether the trial court erred in applying the "substitute facilities" measure of compensation, i.e., the amount needed to provide an equivalent necessary replacement facility undiminished by depreciation or functional obsolescence. The Agency contends that the proper measure is the "depreciated replacement cost" approach, i.e., the cost to build an equivalent facility less depreciation as of the date of taking.

It is fundamental that private property shall not be taken or damaged for public use without just compensation. U.S. Const.Amend. 5th; K.S.A. 26–513(a). It is also the law of this state that, if the entire tract of land or interest therein is taken, the measure of compensation is the value of the property or interest at the time of the taking. K.S.A. 26–513(b).

The three generally accepted methods of valuing real property for purposes of condemnation are: (1) The market data approach based upon what comparable properties within the area have sold for at or near the time of taking; (2) the depreciated replacement cost or cost approach based upon what it would cost to acquire the land and to erect equivalent improvements, less depreciation; and (3) the income approach or capitalization of income based upon what the property taken is producing or is capable of producing in income at the time of the taking. [Citations.] As stated in [citation] the market data approach is by far the most commonly used method of appraisal and is the method which should be used when there have been sales of comparable properties in the same locale near the time of the taking. When, however, the property is so unique that is has no ascertainable market and there are no sales of reasonably similar or comparable property, the other methods (depreciated replacement cost or capitalization of income—may be used. [Citation.]

It is agreed that the value of the church sanctuary and gymnasium could not, in this instance, be determined by the traditional market data approach. Obviously, the capitalization of income method is inappropriate. However, there would appear to be no obstacle to determining value under the depreciated replacement approach advocated by the Agency. Despite this, the Church contends and the trial court ruled that when a condemnee is a "private owner of a non-profit public facility devoted to a special purpose," "just compensation" requires departure from the value standard and application of the substitute facilities method.

* * *

The rationale for departing from value as the measure of compensation in the case of a public condemnee was stated as follows:

The status of a school district deprived by condemnation of its property differs radically from that of a private condemnee. A school district exists to further the educational process, and when its school property has been condemned, it may not take its money and liquidate its operations. The district remains charged with the same public duty of providing educational facilities for its children as it had before its property was taken. And the cost of constructing substitute facilities is equally great whether those condemned were new or ancient. [Citation.]

* * *

Even though it was established that the church facilities consisted of properties not ordinarily traded on the market and the market data approach was not therefore available, the fact remains that here we are concerned with private property for which the Church is entitled to just compensation based on the value of the property at the time of the taking. K.S.A. 26–513. It may be noted that for the Church to continue to serve its congregation and community in the same manner as before the taking, a comparable facility may be necessary. However, there is no requirement beyond good intentions that it do so.

* * *

The substitute facilities approach applied to public condemnees is based on the condemnee's legal or factual obligation to replace the facilities. It does not apply to a private condemnee which is "free to allocate its resources to serve its own institutional objectives, which may or may not correspond with community needs." Awarding replacement cost on the theory that the condemnee would continue to operate for a public purpose as before the taking would provide a windfall if substitute facilities were never acquired or, if acquired, were later sold or converted to another use. * * *

Having determined that this case must be reversed on the issue of measure of compensation, we turn to the disposition of the matter on remand. * * *

We find no justification for a new trial on all issues, but rather that the trial court should receive and consider evidence on the limited issues of depreciation and functional obsolescence of the church property, if any, and reduce the jury's award of compensation accordingly.

Reversed and remanded for new trial on the limited issues of depreciation and functional obsolescence.

Zoning: Non-conforming Uses

FRANKLIN PLANNING & ZONING COMMISSION v. SIMPSON COUNTY LBR. CO.

(1965 Ky.) 394 S.W.2d 593.

HILL, J.

This appeal concerns the propriety of a judgment interpreting the rights of these litigants under a planning and zoning ordinance of the City of Franklin.

Appellee Desford Potts for about seven years owned a six-acre tract of land within the corporate limits of Franklin. It lies between Railroad and Morris Streets. During this period, Potts maintained a livestock barn on the tract in which was stored lumber and other building materials. Outside, and mostly to the rear of the barn, brick was stored in stacks four or five feet high. In 1959 the City of Franklin passed a zoning ordinance by virtue of which Potts' lot was classified as residential (R-2) property.

Shortly before this suit was instituted, Potts moved some saw logs onto his lot back of the barn where he had recently had a bulldozer level the lot. The city complained. Potts sued to enjoin interference by the city. The chancellor decided in favor of Potts.

The city contends the continued use by Potts of his property for storage of building materials is a "nonconforming" use, and under the law cannot be enlarged by storing saw logs thereon. Potts contends it is not an enlargement of the "nonconforming" use and therefore not in violation of the zoning ordinance. We should say here that a "nonconforming use" means simply a use which does not conform to the classification provided for in the ordinance, residential in this instance.

The applicable portion of the ordinance is as follows:

Section 33, Continuance of Non-Conforming Uses. Any use of land or structure existing at the time of enactment or subsequent amendment of this ordinance, but not in conformity with its use provisions may be continued * * *.

Regardless of our sadness at seeing the elimination of the "spreading chestnut tree," and the village smith, it must be admitted that in the interest of progress the law favors the gradual elimination of "nonconforming" uses of property in our cities. [Citation.] It naturally follows that such nonconforming uses as are tolerated under the law cannot be enlarged. [Citations.]

So, our question is whether the storage of saw logs in Potts' lot is an enlargement of the "nonconforming use" he enjoyed previously. The chancellor found as a matter of fact the use was not enlarged. We have numerous photographs of the stored logs, and they appear to be stacked higher than the brick, perhaps eight feet high; but it cannot be said they are unsightly, obnoxious, or a health hazard.

Admitting the saw logs were stacked higher than the brick and not so symmetrically, unless they obstruct the view or impede the natural flow of air we cannot see wherein their storage back of the barn is materially different from the storage of the stacks of brick. Accordingly, we agree with the chancellor that the "nonconforming use" by Potts of his property has not been enlarged by the storage of saw logs on the property. There is no contention Potts plans a sawmill. It goes without saying that a sawmill in such a residential community would be such an enlargement as appellants oppose.

The judgment is affirmed.

Zoning: Subdivision Master Plan

BOARD OF CTY. COM'RS v. GASTER

(1979) 285 Md. 233, 401 A.2d 666.

SMITH, J.

We granted certiorari in this case in order that we might consider the question of whether a county planning commission acting under subdivision regulations adopted by the county's legislative body might properly disapprove establishment of a proposed subdivision which met all zoning requirements but failed to comply with the master plan, also adopted by the county's legislative body. Since we conclude that approval of the subdivision plan was properly denied, we shall reverse.

* * *

Gaster presented to the Cecil County Planning Commission (the commission) a preliminary subdivision plan for what he called "Chesapeake Coves." He contemplated development of 408 lots for single-family dwelling units, together with associated roads, water and sewer facilities, and recreational areas. The commission notified Gaster that it "ha[d] disapproved said plat as not being in conformance with the Cecil County Subdivision Regulations."

* * *

Gaster appealed to the Cecil County Board of Appeals, as the commission advised him he might do. It reversed. It found the conclusions of the commission were "factually correct and would be sufficient to defeat [the] appeal if they were, in fact, applicable to the development in question." * * * The commission and the Board of County Commissioners of Cecil County appealed to the Circuit Court for Cecil County. Upon motion of Gaster, the trial judge dismissed the appeal of the commission for lack of standing to take the appeal, but denied a similar motion as to the county commissioners.

* * *

This appeal on behalf of Cecil County followed. We granted the county's petition for the writ of certiorari prior to the hearing of this case by the Court of Special Appeals because of the importance of this issue in planning matters involving noncharter counties in Maryland.

Before we get into the legal background for this particular controversy, a word should be said relative to planning and zoning generally. * * *

As we noted in Wash. Co. Taxpayers [citation] some confusion exists relative to the terms planning and zoning, which are not synonymous. Zoning is concerned with the use of property but planning is broader in its concept. 1 E. Yokley, *Zoning Law and Practice* § 1–2 (4th ed. 1978) comments:

Expressing the matter in another way, let us say that zoning is almost exclusively concerned with use regulation, whereas planning is a broader term and indicates the development of a community, not only with respect to the uses of lands and buildings, but also with respect to streets, parks, civic beauty, industrial and commercial undertakings, residential developments and such other matters affecting the public convenience and welfare as may be properly embraced within the police power. [Id. at 4.]

There are three integral parts of adequate land planning, the master plan, zoning, and subdivision regulations. The need for subdivision regulations as a part of that planning is well illustrated by the case here. As it is put in 4. R. Anderson, *American Law of Zoning* § 23.03 (2d ed. 1977), "[Z]oning ordinances are not calculated to protect the community from the financial loss which may result from imperfect development. Some of these purposes are sought through the imposition of subdivision controls." Id.

at 47. 4 A. Rathkopf, *The Law of Zoning and Planning* Ch. 71 § 2 (4th ed. 1979), gives reasons for subdivision control:

Planning enabling acts and the requirements for plat approval are based upon the realization that homes are no longer generally constructed one at a time for individual owners, resulting in a gradual development which can be controlled by zoning ordinances and local health, building, plumbing, and electrical codes alone. Vacant lots suitable for single homes in already developed communities have all but disappeared. The great increases in population and the unprecedented demand for homes has necessarily resulted in opening up undeveloped land in outlying areas, and the development thereof by large numbers of homes which may be said to be built all at one time. Where such development takes place without restriction other than zoning restrictions, it is the developer who designs the community in respect to the number, length, width, condition, and location of streets. The developer also determines where the newly arrived inhabitants of the community shall reside, without consideration of the necessity for, or existence of, schools, fire protection, parks, playgrounds, and other public facilities. If subdivisions develop too rapidly, or before the community is ready for the added burdens which an increased population imposes, and without adequate control, the result too often is the creation of deteriorating neighborhoods which create a blight upon the community and a drain upon the municipal purse. [Id. at 71–6–7.]

See also 82 Am.Jur.2d, Zoning and Planning § 163 (1976).

* * *

It is the county legislative body, the County Commissioners of Cecil County in this instance, which, pursuant to legislative authority, adopted the master plan, the zoning regulations, and the subdivision regulations, a fact which seems to have been overlooked by the trial judge. In the case at bar we see no basic conflict between the zoning regulations and the subdivision regulations. If there were a conflict, the subdivision ordinance in this instance provides

that the more restrictive provision shall prevail. Moreover, Art. 66B, § 3.08 specifies that once a master plan has been adopted by the local legislative body "no street * * * shall be constructed or authorized * * * until the location, character, and extent of such development shall have been submitted to and approved by the commission as *consistent with the plan* * * *."

* * *

In sum, Cecil County has validly used the planning tools placed in its hands by the General Assembly to provide for orderly growth for the county.

Judgment reversed and case remanded to the Circuit Court for Cecil County for passage of an order consistent with this opinion; appellees to pay the costs.

Restrictive Covenants

JOHN J. WALKER v. ROBERT V. GROSS

(1972, Mass.) 290 N.E.2d 543.

WILKINS, J.

The plaintiffs seek a determination, under G.L. c. 240, § 10A, that a deed restriction providing that no part of their premises in Waltham shall be "used for any business purpose" does not prevent the use of their premises for an apartment house. The plaintiffs' land is subject to a restriction, imposed by a 1947 deed to a predecessor in title, which reads as follows: "The premises are conveyed with the benefit of and subject to any easements of record and subject to a permanent restriction that no part of the premises shall be used for any business purpose except for raising, growing and selling live bait and for the sale at retail of fishing tackle and sporting goods, and the grantees for themselves, their heirs, executors, administrators and assigns, covenant and agree with the grantor, his heirs and assigns, not to use the premises or any part thereof in violation of the above restriction, and it is agreed that this covenant shall run with the land."

The plaintiffs contemplate the construction of an apartment building with eighty-three family units and a store. Building permits have been issued for the apartment house by the building inspector of Waltham. The defendants, landowners in the neighborhood of the plaintiffs' premises, are entitled to the benefit of the restriction by which the plaintiffs' premises are burdened.

The restriction quoted above was held to be enforceable in Walker v. Sanderson, 348 Mass. 409, 204 N.E.2d 108, where this court concluded that the purpose of the restriction was to preserve the residential character of the neighborhood (except for the limited business use specified) and that certain changes in the neighborhood did not make the restriction unenforceable. In that earlier opinion, however, the scope of the limitation against the use of the burdened premises for "any business purpose" was not considered.

The judge, who heard the present case on a statement of agreed facts and certain documents, ruled that the restriction against use of the premises for any business purpose did not prohibit the construction and operation of an apartment house. The defendants appeal.

*   *   *

The restriction itself gives no significant guidance on the question whether an apartment house use is a use for a business purpose. No extrinsic evidence has been presented to assist us in interpreting the intent of the parties in light of the material circumstances and pertinent facts known to the parties to the deed at the time it was executed. We know only that the retail sale of fishing tackle and sporting goods was regarded as a business purpose because those activities were expressly excluded from the prohibition of the restriction. In these circumstances we are guided in reaching our conclusion by the general rule that restrictions in a deed are to be strictly construed against the party seeking to enforce those restrictions. [Citation.] Thus any doubt should be "resolved in favor of the freedom of land from servitude." St. Botolph Club, Inc. v. Brookline Trust Co., 292 Mass. 430, 433, 198 N.E. 903, 904.

We hold that the use of the plaintiffs' premises for apartment house purposes does not violate the deed restriction against the use of those premises for any business purpose. The plaintiffs' apartment building will be used by its occupants for residential purposes. The fact that the apartment house may be owned for income producing purposes does not make the *use* of the premises a use for a business purpose. If we were to accept the view asserted by the defendants, the renting of a single family house and the construction of such a house for sale would seemingly be in violation of this restriction as well. We think that the language of the restriction is concerned with the physical activity carried on upon the premises and not with the presence or absence of a profit making motive on the part of the landowner.[2]

Authority in other jurisdictions supports our view that the use of premises for apartment house purposes does not violate a deed restriction against the use of premises for any business purpose. [Citations.]

The defendants basically object to the construction of an apartment house instead of single family houses. The restriction, however, does not speak in terms of allowing only single family houses, but rather it speaks in words of exclusion to prevent any use for business purposes. If use of an apartment house is, as we hold under the

---

2. Presumably a wholly owner-occupied apartment house, such as a condominium (see G.L. c. 183A), would be permissible under the defendants' view of the restriction because the ownership would be free from any profit motive, except as to the gain which even the owner of a private house hopes to derive from an increase in the value of his property.

language of the deed restriction, not a use for a business purpose, the scope of the limitation contained in the deed obviously fails to reach the proposed apartment house use. What the grantor might have done if he had anticipated present circumstances need not concern us. Construed, as it must be, strictly against the parties asserting the applicability of the restriction, the restriction simply fails to do what the defendants assert.

Decree affirmed.

Validity of Restrictive Covenants

SHELLEY v. KRAEMER

(1947) 334 U.S. 1, 68 S.Ct. 836, 92 L.Ed. 1161, 3 A.L.R.2d 441.

[Suits were commenced in Missouri and Michigan to enjoin violations of covenants in deeds restricting the use and occupancy of real estate to persons of the Caucasian race. The Supreme Courts of both States upheld the covenants, and the two cases were joined upon certiorari being granted by the United States Supreme Court.]

VINSON, C. J.

* * *

Whether the equal protection clause of the Fourteenth Amendment inhibits judicial enforcement by state courts of restrictive covenants based on race or color is a question which this Court has not heretofore been called upon to consider.

* * *

It is well, at the outset, to scrutinize the terms of the restrictive agreements involved in these cases. In the Missouri case, the covenant declares that no part of the affected property shall be "occupied by any person not of the Caucasian race, it being intended hereby to restrict the use of said property * * * against the occupancy as owners or tenants of any portion of said property for resident or other purpose by people of the Negro or Mongolian Race." Not only does the restriction seek to proscribe use and occupancy of the affected properties by members of the excluded class, but as construed by the Missouri courts, the agreement requires that title of any person who uses his property in violation of the restriction shall be divested. The restriction of the covenant in the Michigan case seeks to bar occupancy by persons of the excluded class. It provides that "This property shall not be used or occupied by any person or persons except those of the Caucasian race."

It should be observed that these covenants do not seek to proscribe any particular use of the affected properties. Use of the properties for residential occupancy, as such, is not forbidden. The restrictions of these agreements, rather, are directed toward a designated class of persons and seek to determine who may and who may not own or make use of the properties for residential purposes. The excluded class is defined wholly in terms of race or color; "simply that and nothing more."

It cannot be doubted that among the civil rights intended to be protected from discriminatory state action by the Fourteenth Amendment are the rights to acquire, enjoy, own and dispose of property.

* * *

But the present cases, unlike those just discussed, do not involve action by state legislatures or city councils. Here the particular patterns of discrimination and the areas in which the restrictions are to operate, are determined, in the first instance, by the terms of agreements among private individuals. Participation of the State consists in the enforcement of the restrictions so defined. The crucial issue with which we are here confronted is whether this distinction removes these cases from the operation of the prohibitory provisions of the Fourteenth Amendment.

Since the decision of this Court in the Civil Rights Cases, 109 U.S. 3, 3 S.Ct. 18, 27 L.Ed. 835 (1883), the principle has become firmly embedded in our constitutional law that the action inhibited by the first section of the Fourteenth Amendment is only such action as may fairly be said to be that of the States. That Amendment erects no shield against merely private conduct, however discriminatory or wrongful.

We conclude, therefore, that the restrictive agreements standing alone cannot be regarded as violative of any rights guaranteed to petitioners by the Fourteenth Amendment. So long as the purposes of those agreements are effectuated by voluntary adherence to their terms, it would appear clear that there has been no action by the State and the provisions of the Amendment have not been violated. [Citation.]

But here there was more. These are cases in which the purposes of the agreements were secured only by judicial enforcement by state courts of the restrictive terms of the agreements. * * *

We hold that in granting judicial enforcement of the restrictive agreements in these cases, the States have denied petitioners the equal protection of the laws and that, therefore, the action of the state courts cannot stand. We have noted that freedom from discrimination by the States in the enjoyment of property rights was among the basic objectives sought to be effectuated by the framers of the Fourteenth Amendment. That such discrimination has occurred in these cases is clear. Because of the race or color of these petitioners they have been denied rights of ownership or occupancy enjoyed as a matter of course by other citizens of different race or color. The Fourteenth Amendment declares "that all persons, whether colored or white, shall stand equal before the laws of the States, and, in regard to the colored race, for whose protection the amendment was primarily designed, that no discrimination shall be made against them by law because of their color." Strauder v. West Virginia, 100 U.S. 303, 25 L.Ed. 664. * * *

Upon full consideration, we have concluded that in these cases the States have acted to deny petitioners the equal protection of the laws guaranteed by the Fourteenth Amendment. Having so decided, we find it unnecessary to consider whether petitioners have also been deprived of property without due process of law or denied privileges and immunities of citizens of the United States.

For the reasons stated, the judgment of the Supreme Court of Missouri and the judgment of the Supreme Court of Michigan must be reversed.

Problems

1. (a) The city council of Urbania enacted a zoning ordinance which limited the use of A's land to residential. At the time of the enactment of the ordinance A owned and operated a tavern upon the premises in question. Urbania's building commissioner arrested A for violating the ordinance. What defenses, if any, are available to A upon his trial?

(b) As a member of Urbania's city council, could you suggest anything to alleviate the problems suggested? Would your suggestions withstand an attack based upon constitutional grounds?

2. A, the owner of the several lots in an area zoned for commercial and residential uses, conveyed one of his lots to B "so long as B shall use the said premises for private dwelling purposes only." Ten years later B sold the property to C, who proposed constructing a multi-office building on the lot. By this time the area was about 40% residential and 60% commercial. When A learned of C's plans he brought an action to enjoin C from proceeding with those plans. What decision?

3. Z, owner of a meat packing plant situated in an industrial area of the city where other packing plants are located, develops a new process for making glue which, although efficient, gives off an unusually unpleasant odor. Packing plants and other concerns in the area sue Z to enjoin the use of this odor producing process. They are able to show at the trial that 90% of their employees are made ill from the odor to the extent that their working efficiency is reduced 20%. Result of suit?

4. B operated a retail bakery, D a drug store, F a food store, G a gift shop and H a hardware store in adjoining locations along one side of a single suburban village block. As the population grew the business section developed at the other end of the village and the establishments of B, D, F, G and H were surrounded for at least a mile in each direction solely with residences. A zoning ordinance with the usual provisions was adopted by the village and the area including the five stores was declared to be a "residential district for single-family dwellings." Thereafter, B tore down the frame building which housed the bakery and commenced to construct a modern brick bakery. D found his business increasing to such an extent that he began to build an addition upon the drug store in order to extend it to the rear alley. F's building was destroyed by fire and he started to reconstruct it in order to restore it to its former condition. G changed the gift shop into a sporting goods store and after six months of operation has decided to go back into the gift shop business. H sold his hardware store to X.

The village building commissioner brings an action under the zoning ordinance to enjoin the construction work of B, D and F and to enjoin the carrying on of any business by G and X. Assume the ordinance is valid.

What result?

5. A and B are residents of Unit I of Chimney Hills Subdivision. The lots owned by A and B are subject to the following restrictive covenant: "Lots shall be for single family residence purposes only." A intends to convert the interior of her carport into a beauty shop, and B brings suit against A to enjoin her from doing so. A argues that the covenant restricts only the type of building that can be constructed, not the incidental use to which residential structures are put. Decision?

6. The City of Erewhon sought to condemn land in fee simple for use in constructing an entrance to an underground terminal for a subway. The owners of the land contend that no more than surface and subsurface easements are necessary for the terminal entrance and seek to retain air rights above 36 feet. The city argues that any building utilizing this airspace would require structural supports that would interfere with the city's plan for the terminal. The city concedes that the properties around the condemned property could be assembled and structures could be designed to span over the condemned property, in which case the air rights would be quite valuable. Decision?

Chapter
49

INSURANCE

Insurance is a contractual undertaking by one person (the "insurer") to pay a sum of money or to give something of value to another (the "insured" or a "beneficiary") upon the happening of a contingency or fortuitous event which is beyond the control of the contracting parties and in which the insured has an interest apart from the contract. Such a contract does not have to be called or labeled "insurance" in order for the law to treat it as insurance. For example, a warranty by an electric shaver manufacturer which promises repair or replacement for damage to the shaver from *any* cause for a period of one year from date of sale is insurance and subject to State regulation. This is because some potential causes of damage, such as dropping the shaver and breaking its case, are fortuitous events beyond the control of the maker. A one-year warranty against defects of material and workmanship would not be insurance, since those potential defects are within the control of the manufacturer.

The McCarran Act (Public Law 15), enacted in 1945, left the regulation of insur-ance to the States, with several exceptions not material here. Each State has its own statutes regulating its domestic insurance companies as well as setting forth standards which foreign insurance companies must meet in order to do business within the State. Most of the State legislation relates to the incorporation, licensing, supervision, and liquidation of insurers, and to licensing and supervision of agents and brokers.

KINDS OF INSURANCE

There are many kinds of insurance and many kinds of insurance policies. While the listing which follows does not pretend to be complete, it is believed to contain the most generally utilized kinds of insurance.

Life Insurance

Life insurance might be more accurately called "death insurance," since it is a contract by the terms of which the insurer will pay a specified sum of money upon the death of the insured, provided the required premiums have been paid. The payment is made either to a named beneficiary, ordinarily a third-party donee or creditor, or to the estate of the deceased. The naming of a beneficiary is a privilege of the insured, but unless the right to do so is reserved in the policy, the insured has no right to change the beneficiary. Most modern policies as part of the standard form give to the insured the express right to change beneficiaries.

Ordinary Life. This type of life insurance is often considered a form of saving or investment, since the insured has a right to borrow from the insurer an amount not to exceed the cash surrender value of the policy, which value increases the longer the policy is in force. Such a loan bears a reasonable interest rate and is secured by an assignment to the insurer of the policy proceeds to the extent necessary to pay the loan in the event of death, with the remainder going to the beneficiary.

"Ordinary" life insurance generally requires the payment of premiums until death, unless the policy is converted into a different type of policy by agreement, whereas "term" life insurance is issued for a limited number of years with premiums payable during the period of coverage. "Limited-payment" life policies require the payment of premiums only for a fixed number of years, thus eliminating the duty of paying premiums through the later years of life when such payments may be burdensome.

If the insured under an ordinary life policy is unable to continue making premium payments, he does not lose all the money he has already paid. Policies contain various non-forfeiture provisions which give the insured at least three alternatives: (1) to obtain the cash surrender value of the policy; (2) to purchase "extended term" insurance in the face amount of the policy for whatever period the cash surrender value will purchase; or (3) to reduce the principal amount by "paid-up" insurance which can

be purchased by the cash surrender value. The policy may provide that one of the alternatives is automatically chosen by the insured unless he notifies the insurer of a different election within a certain period of time, such as sixty days after the due date of the premium in default.

Term Life. Term insurance is the least expensive form of life insurance because it is in effect only for a specified period and builds up no cash surrender or loan values. Term policies are especially useful to young married persons, who cannot afford to purchase permanent insurance. Such policies may contain provisions for later renewal or for conversion to ordinary life or other types of insurance. Term policies frequently contain a right to convert to a permanent plan of insurance (ordinary life, limited-payment life, or endowment) upon payment of the premium applicable at the time of conversion; or, by suitable payment, the policyholder may elect to convert as of the date of the original policy. Usually, the conversion right must be exercised within a limited time after issuance of the policy, as during the first three years of a five-year term, to reduce the possibility of adverse selection. There are numerous variations in individual policies.

Endowment and Annuity Contracts

Either endowment or annuity contracts may contain various provisions which are customarily found in life insurance contracts, but basically an endowment contract is an agreement by the insurer to pay a lump sum of money to the insured when he reaches a certain age or to a beneficiary in the event of premature death, whereas an annuity contract is an agreement by the insurer to pay fixed sums to the insured at periodic intervals after the insured reaches a designated age. Strictly speaking, an annuity policy is not an insurance contract, but most annuity contracts contain various life insurance features, which subject them to regulation by State insurance departments. A modern version of the annuity is called the Variable Annuity. The Variable Annuity is an agreement by the company to pay to the annuitant a variable sum depending upon the effect of inflation or deflation on the company's equity investments. The formula used in computing the annuitant's interest is complex, but the principle is designed as a hedge against inflation. In the usual annuity contract, the company agrees to pay fixed sums periodically, and these sums are based on the return the company can expect to receive on a conservative investment of the premiums paid by the annuitant and his life expectancy as determined by mortality tables.

Accident and Health Insurance

Accident and health insurance is really insurance against losses due to accidents and sickness, and provides for the payment of certain benefits or the reimbursement of specified expenses in the event of illness or accidental injury, within the limits set forth in the policies.

Fire Insurance

Fire insurance protects the owner, or other person with an insurable interest such as a secured creditor or mortgagee, of real or personal property against loss resulting from damage to or destruction of the property by fire and certain related perils.

Fire insurance policies are standardized in the United States, either by statute or by order of the State insurance departments, but their coverage is frequently enlarged by an "endorsement" or "rider" to include other perils or to benefit the insured in ways not provided in the standard form. These policies are normally written for periods of one or three years.

Co-insurance is common in property insurance, and is a means of sharing the risk between insurer and insured. For example, under an 80% co-insurance clause, the insured may recover the full amount of loss not to exceed the face amount of the policy, provided the policy is for an amount not less than 80% of the insurable value of the property. If the policy is less than such 80%, he recovers that proportion of the loss which the amount of the policy bears to 80% of the insurable value. Thus, if the value of the property is $10,000, and the policy is for $8,000 or more, the insured is protected against loss not to exceed the amount of the policy. However, if the amount of the policy is less than such 80%, he does not receive the full amount of loss but only the above stated proportion. Thus, in the above example, if the fire policy was in the amount of $6,000, and the property fifty per cent destroyed, the loss would be $5,000, of which the insurer would pay $3,750, which is 6,000/8,000 of $5,000. On a total loss the recovery could not, of course, exceed the face amount of the policy.

Casualty Insurance

The term casualty insurance is broad in scope, but usually covers loss due to the damage or destruction of personal property by various causes other than fire or the elements, and is sometimes applied to personal injury or death or property loss due to accident.

Other Kinds of Insurance

Collision Insurance. This kind of insurance protects the owner of an automobile against the risk of loss or damage due to contact with other vehicles or objects, usually subject to a deductability clause.

Credit Insurance. This kind of insurance protects creditors against loss due to the insolvency of their debtors. Credit Life Insurance protects the creditor and the debtor by providing for the payment of an indebtedness of the insured in the event of his death before the indebtedness shall have been fully liquidated by time payments which the debtor is under contract to make.

Fidelity Insurance. This type of insurance protects an employer against loss due to the dishonesty or defalcation of employees.

Group Insurance. This kind covers a number of individuals, having some common interest, under a blanket or single policy. This insurance is usually either life or accident and health insurance.

Liability Insurance. Liability insurance provides indemnification against loss by reason of liability of the insured for damages resulting from injuries to another's person or property. While this kind of insurance is most generally thought of in connection with automobiles, where it is often of greater interest to the injured person than to the driver who caused the injury, it is customarily carried by owners and lessees of real property to protect against public liability for injuries arising on the premises owned or leased.

Marine Insurance. This kind of insurance originally was restricted to destruction of vessels or cargo due to perils of the sea. While it is sometimes divided into ocean marine and inland marine, the distinction is not always made, and marine insurance covers transportation risks generally, as well as personal property floater risks and other personal property coverages of almost all kinds. A floater policy is one which is variable as to the property covered, as in a personal property floater policy in which the property covered is generally described but not specifically identified at the time the policy is written.

Title Insurance. Title insurance provides indemnity against loss arising from defects in the title to real estate or due to liens or encumbrances thereon. Title insurance companies are organized under statutes different from those under which other insurance companies are organized. An owner's title insurance policy is issued in the amount of the purchase price of the property and guarantees the owner against any loss due to defects in the title to the property, or due to liens or encumbrances except for those stated in the policy as existing at the time the policy is issued. Such policies may also be issued to mortgagees or to tenants of property to protect their interests. This form of insurance is not available everywhere in the United States but is written in all major metropolitan areas. In some counties the Torrens system of land registration, which is operated by the local government, is competitive with private title insurance business.

Surplus Line Insurance. This kind of insurance is the one exception to the requirement that insurance can be written within a particular State only by companies licensed by that State. If an Illinois applicant, for instance, wants a form of insurance coverage (other than life) which a broker or agent after diligent search is unable to place with a company authorized to do business in Illinois, the insurance may be placed with an unlicensed company, provided the agent or broker fulfills certain requirements. This is called surplus line insurance and it is the source of much of the American business given to Lloyd's of London.

Re-Insurance. Re-insurance may be thought of as an insurance policy for insurance companies. This is not strictly true, but is the basic idea. Re-insurance is a contract whereby one insurer, for a consideration, agrees to indemnify another, wholly or partially, against loss or liability arising under a policy of insurance which such other insurer has issued to a third party.

A re-insurance treaty is an agreement between two insurance companies whereby one agrees to cede and the other agrees to accept re-insurance business under the terms specified in the treaty.

A re-insurance compact is an agreement between two or more insurance companies by the terms of which each agrees in advance to re-insure any policies written in certain lines by the others, in an amount equal to a fixed percentage of such lines or in the amount by which a risk exceeds a particular sum.

NATURE OF INSURANCE CONTRACTS

The basic principles of contract law are applicable to insurance policies, but although most contracts involve a fairly even exchange between the parties, this is not true of every insurance contract. Insurance companies engage in a large volume of business over wide areas, and their policies are standardized. In some States standardization is required by statute. This usually means that the insured must accept a given policy or do without desired insurance, and for this reason insurance contracts are sometimes said to be contracts of adhesion.

Offer and Acceptance

No matter how assiduously a life insurance agent has solicited a person to take out a policy, it is generally true that it is the applicant who makes the offer, and the contract is created when that offer is accepted by the company. The company's acceptance may be conditioned, for instance, upon payment of the premium or delivery of the policy while the insured is in good health. If the company writes a policy which differs from the application, then it is the company which makes a counter-offer which the applicant may or may not choose to accept. This situation arises most frequently where the company is unwilling to write the policy which the agent proposed, because of the results of a physical examination of the applicant, but is willing to write a different policy based on the particular risk involved. Some companies will not intentionally insure persons who have had certain physical ailments or a history of disease, while other companies will write such life insurance for a premium which they consider appropriate to the risk.

Life insurance agents therefore cannot generally bind the company to a contract with the insured, although on occasion a "binding receipt" may be issued by an authorized agent, acknowledging payment of the premium and providing for the issuance of a standard policy effective from the date of the medical examination, so long as the company has no bona fide reason to reject the application. In fire and casualty insurance, agents often have authority to make the insurance effective immediately, when needed, by means of a "binder." In the event of a loss before the company has actually issued a policy, the binder will be effective on the same terms and conditions the policy would have had if it had been issued.

Insurable Interest

The concept of insurable interest has been developed over many years, primarily to eliminate gambling and to lessen the moral hazard. If a person could obtain an enforceable insurance policy on the life of anyone, or a fire insurance policy on property that he did not own or in which he had no interest, he would be in a position to profit by the death of a stranger or the destruction of property which represented no loss to him. An insurable interest is such relationship which a person has to another person, or with respect to certain property, that the happening of a possible specific damage causing contingency would result in direct loss or injury to him. The purpose of insurance is protection against the risk of loss resulting from such happening, not the realization of gain or profit therefrom. Because of this interest and relationship, an insurance policy is not a gambling agreement but an aleatory contract.

In property insurance, ownership of the fee creates an insurable interest in the property, whether the ownership is sole, or by joint tenants or tenants in common. In some instances, shareholders in a close corporation have been held to have an insurable interest in the corporation's property. Lessees of property have interests which are insurable as do holders of security interests, such as mortgagees or conditional vendors. The insurable interest must exist at the time the property loss occurs.

In life insurance, those who may take out insurance on another's life are practically limited to close relatives, creditors, and business associates or employers, depending generally on the particular facts involved. The insurable interest must exist at the time the policy is taken out and need not exist at the time of death. Except for that written by fraternal benefit societies, an insured may take out a policy on his own life and name any one he chooses as beneficiary, although that particular beneficiary may have no insurable interest in the insured's life. An insured may assign the life policy proceeds to a third person who has no insurable interest.

In fire insurance policies, the recovery is usually the replacement value of the property, minus depreciation. In some States the insurer and the insured are permitted to agree in advance upon the value of the property insured (a "valued policy") and in such cases the agreed value is the recovery on a total loss. An owner or lessee of property may take out rent loss or business interruption insurance to protect himself against loss during the time that the property is unusable. Fire insurance policies are not assignable before loss occurs.

Premiums

Life insurance companies usually receive premiums from their insureds over periods of years. These premiums are fixed in amount and are such that the company will be able to pay the principal sum when the policy matures upon the death of the insured, through the accumulation of reserves. Company funds are invested to bring as high a return as the company is able to secure, commensurate with security of principal and compliance with State investment laws. Barring catastrophes, a life company can estimate quite accurately how many policyholders will die during a particular period. Some will die prematurely and some will live longer than expected, but the company can operate efficiently on actuarial averages. This enables a life company to invest its funds in long-term loans, such as mortgages and corporate bonds and debentures.

Life insurance premiums are calculated on the basis of (1) mortality, (2) interest, and (3) expense.

Mortality tables are constructed on the basis of the experience which companies have accumulated in the past, and reflect the experienced rate of death. There are many mortality tables constructed on various bases. The most famous is the "American Experience Table of Mortality," published in 1868 and standard until 1948, when it was replaced by the "Commissioners' 1941 Standard Ordinary Mortality Table," which was based on the experience of sixteen companies between 1930 and 1940. The C.S.O. table shows, for each age and sex, the number of persons living, the number dying, and the rate of mortality per thousand lives. Other mortality tables are in use. However, while premiums may be set by one table, the use of another table may be required by a State in the valuation of policy reserves.

Almost all life insurance is written on the level-premium plan, which means that the annual premium payable during the life of the insured is a fixed amount. The company will earn interest on the premiums over a period of years, and while the earned interest rate may fluctuate, the company must assume a constant rate of interest which will be sufficient, when added to the principal held in reserve, to equal the total required death payments at the assumed mortality rate.

In these calculations companies use compound, not simple, interest, because as interest is returned to the companies through their investments, this money is reinvested and in turn bears interest.

Premiums are calculated on the present value of future claims; that is, premiums are such amounts as will be sufficient, if invested at an assumed compound interest rate, to pay future claims as they become due, the number of claims being estimated on the basis of mortality tables.

The mortality and interest items just discussed enter into the calculation of the "net" premiums. These items will be the same for all companies using the same mortality and interest bases. In order to compute the gross premium, which the policyholder actually pays, an amount to cover expenses and contingencies called "loading" must be added to the net premium. A company must pay for a medical examination of the applicant, a commission or salary to the agent who brought in the business, and for the book work and office expense in setting up the policy on company records. Some of the expenses involved are just as great in writing a policy for $1,000 as one for $100,000, and certain companies therefore allow what may be called a "quantity discount," or a reduction in premium for larger amounts of insurance. Some companies include in the premium a larger expense charge than is estimated to be necessary and then return the overage to policyholders through dividends.

Under the level premium plan of life insurance, a policyholder pays more during the earlier period of the policy than the actual cost of insurance, just as he pays less than the actual cost during later years, and the excess payments which the company

receives are accumulated as the "reserve." This fund is a liability on the company's books and is not a surplus in any conventional accounting sense. Basically, a company's reserves are the funds on hand at the beginning of an accounting year (the "net" premiums received plus, after the first year, accrued interest thereon), plus interest on this fund during the year, less death claims paid or payable.

Casualty insurance policies are written only for periods of a few years at most. Long continued liability on this type of policy is the exception rather than the rule. Most casualty company investments must be such that they can quickly be converted into cash to pay losses, for the risks assumed are often large and will occur within a short time, if at all. It is the business of the underwriters to determine whether a particular risk can or should be assumed, and, if so, to set the premium. Some casualty or multiple-line companies are adventurous in the varieties of risks against which they will insure. If the event to be insured against is very likely to happen, the premium may be prohibitive, but, so long as the chances of occurrence are less than even, in most cases an underwriter may be found who is willing to issue a policy.

The rates which may be charged for fire and various kinds of casualty insurance are regulated by State law. The regulatory authorities are under a duty to require that the companies' rates be reasonable, not unfairly discriminatory, and neither excessively high nor inadequately low. The solvency of the companies must be maintained for the benefit of the policyholders.

Life insurance rates are not regulated but the mortality tables which companies may use are subject to approval.

Double Indemnity

A provision found in some life insurance contracts provides for the recovery of "double indemnity," or twice the face amount of the policy, in the event of accidental death or death which results "directly and independently of all other causes from bodily injuries sustained solely from external, violent, and accidental means." These accidental death provisions are worded in various ways and have given rise to much litigation, frequently involving the question whether a death which resulted from the unexpected consequences of an intentional act was an accidental death. The cases cannot be reconciled, but it has been held that death resulting from an infection following the intentional pulling of a hair from the nose was accidental death, whereas death resulting from sunstroke, due to voluntary but unintentional overexposure to the sun, was not. Death as a result of playing Russian roulette has been held not to be accidental, under a double indemnity clause.

Defenses of the Insurer

Representations. A representation is a statement made by or on behalf of an applicant for insurance to induce an insurer to enter into a contract. The representation is not a part of the insurance contract, but if the application containing the representation is incorporated by reference into the contract, as in liability or burglary insurance, the representation becomes a warranty. For a representation to have legal consequences, it must have been relied upon by the insurer as an inducement to enter into the contract, and it must have been substantially false when made or it must have become so, to the insured's knowledge, before the contract was created. The principal remedy of the insurer, on discovery of misrepresentation, is rescission of the contract. To rescind the contract, the insurer must tender to the insured all premiums which have been paid, since a rescission restores the parties to the position they were in before the contract was made. Rescission may or may not be available to

the life insurer, however, because of the "incontestability clause" which generally makes the policy incontestable by the insurer after a specified period of time, such as one or two years after the policy has been in effect during the lifetime of the insured.

To be effective, rescission must be made as soon as possible after discovery of the misrepresentation. Despite the presence of the incontestability clause, the insurer can always contest the policy for failure to pay the premiums, for misrepresentation of age, for lack of an insurable interest by the policy owner and for false impersonation as when the physical examination is taken by another. If the applicant for insurance misstates his age, the amount of insurance is simply reduced to that sum which the premiums paid would have purchased at the insured's correct age.

An innocent misrepresentation of a material fact (not opinion) prior to the running of the incontestability clause is a sufficient ground for avoidance of a policy by the insurer. Whether the fact is material or not depends, generally, upon whether the policy would have been issued had the truth been known. An immaterial misrepresentation, even though fraudulently made, is not a ground for avoidance of the policy.

Warranties. Warranties are of great importance in insurance contracts because they operate as conditions which must exist before the contract is effective or before the insurer's promise to pay is enforceable. Failure of the condition to exist or to occur relieves the insurer from any obligation to perform its promise. Broadly speaking, a condition is simply an event the happening of which, or its failure to happen, precedes the existence of a legal relationship, or terminates one previously existing. Conditions are either precedent or subsequent; for example, payment of the premium is a condition precedent to the enforcement of the insurer's promise, as is the happening of the insured event. A condition subsequent is an operative event the happening of which terminates an existing matured legal obligation. A provision in a policy to the effect that the insured shall not be liable unless suit is brought within twelve months from the date of the occurrence of the loss operates as a condition subsequent.

Usually, those statements in policies which the insurer looks upon as express warranties can be identified by the use of the words "warrant" or "on condition that" or "provided that" or words of similar import. Other statements which are important to the risk assumed, such as the building address in the case where personal property at a particular location is insured against fire, are sometimes held to be informal warranties. Generally, the trend is away from allowing an insurer to avoid liability on the policy for *any* breach of a warranty by an insured; the breach must usually be material to have such an effect.

The effect of warranties is frequently regulated by statute. The New York statute provides that all statements made by an applicant for life insurance shall be deemed representations and not warranties, regardless of what the policy or application may state.

Affirmative warranties state conditions which must exist at the time the insurance contract is made, while promissory warranties are undertakings to do or cause something to be done during the period of the policy. A statement in a fire insurance policy that the premises are used as a grocery store probably will be considered an affirmative warranty which need be true only at the time the policy is issued. Unless the character of use is changed to such an extent that there is a substantial increase in the hazard, the policy will remain enforceable. A statement in a burglary policy that a watchman will be on duty at all times is a promissory warranty.

Concealment. While rarely relied upon in life insurance, the doctrine of concealment has vitality in other fields of insurance. Concealment is simply the failure of an applicant for insurance to disclose material facts which the insurer does not know. For example, if an applicant telephoned an insurance company agent for a policy protecting against damage by windstorm, effective immediately, and at the same time was watching a tornado approach, he could hardly complain if the insurer objected to settling for a total loss. The non-disclosure must normally be fraudulent as well as material to invalidate the policy; that is, (1) did the applicant have reason to believe the fact was material, and (2) would its disclosure have affected the acceptance of the risk by the insurer?

Waiver and Estoppel

There are instances when an insurer would normally be entitled to deny liability under a policy because of a misrepresentation or breach of condition or concealment, but because of other facts, the insurer is said to be "estopped" to take advantage of the defense or else to have "waived" the right to rely on it.

"Waiver" and "estoppel" are terms used interchangeably, although by definition they are not synonymous. As generally defined, waiver is the intentional relinquishment of a known right, and estoppel means that a person is precluded by his own conduct from asserting a position which is inconsistent with his acts which have been relied upon by another with justification.

Since a corporation, such as an insurance company, can act only by agents, situations involving waiver invariably find root in an agent's conduct. The higher the agent's position in the company organization, the more likely his conduct to bind the company, since an agent acting within the scope of his authority binds the principal. Insureds have the right to rely on representations made by the insurer's employees and where such representations reasonably induce or cause a change of position by the insured, or prevent the insured from causing a condition to occur, the insurer may not assert the failure of the condition to occur, whether the term applied to this situation be waiver or estoppel. Companies have tried in many ways to limit the authority of local selling agents to bind the company through waiver or estoppel, but this is difficult to do effectively.

As a general rule, when a local agent delivers a policy with knowledge of the nonoccurrence of a condition precedent to the company's liability which would make the policy void or voidable at the company's option, the condition is waived. While there is always a question whether the agent had authority to waive the condition, most courts will find an effective waiver even though the condition is a delivery-in-good-health clause or the medical-treatment clause in a life insurance policy. Such clauses provide that a life insurance policy shall not take effect unless delivered to the applicant while his insurability or good health continues, and that the policy shall not take effect if the applicant has been treated by a physician or has been hospitalized between the date of the application and the date of delivery of the policy.

Performance and Termination

Most contracts of insurance are performed according to their terms, and due performance terminates the insurer's obligation. In life insurance contracts, the insurer pays the principal sum due on death, and the contract is thereby performed and discharged.

Cancellation. Cancellation of an insurance contract by mutual consent is one way of terminating it. Cancellation by the insurer alone means that the insurer is liable according to the terms of the policy until such time as the cancellation is effective. This is not always a right which is available to insurers, but where available, it is sometimes mistakenly used where rescission is preferable, from the insurer's point of view.

If an insurer under an accident policy elects to cancel after the occurrence of an insured event, where a right of rescission existed because of material misrepresentation, this will be taken as an admission of liability for events occurring before cancellation. To cancel a policy, the insurer must tender the unearned portion of the premium to the insured. To effect a rescission, all premiums received by the insurer must be returned to the insured.

Occasionally, a life insurance company will decline to pay a death benefit because of a material misrepresentation by the insured. In a suit by the beneficiary against the insurer, the company may be faced with facts pointing to waiver or estoppel due to the actions of a local agent, and the issue will ordinarily be resolved by a jury. In the event the insurer learns of a material misrepresentation during the lifetime of the insured, the proper remedy is rescission of the contract. Because of the incontestability clause in life insurance policies, the insurer's rights to rescind are restricted, but an insured may cancel the policy and recover the cash surrender value at any time. The minimum cash surrender value payable on cancellation to the insured is determined by calculations specified in the nonforfeiture statute, but, in general, this value will approximate the reserve on the policy, at least after the policy has been in effect long enough to amortize certain expenses incurred in writing it.

Notice. After the occurrence of the insured event, the insured is required to give notice to the insurer and, in the case of property insurance, proof of loss within a specified time, such as 60 days for fire insurance. In liability policies the requirement of immediate notice is construed by the courts as notice within a "reasonable" time. The period within which an insured may commence suit against the insurer upon a fire policy is limited by the policy, usually to one year.

Automobile liability policies require that the insured immediately notify the insurer of any accident or occurrence which may involve liability as well as notify the insurer of the institution of suit and forward any summons or process served upon him. These notice requirements are conditions precedent to the insurer's contractual liability, but may be waived by the insurer. If an insured under an automobile liability policy fails to forward a court summons to the insurer and a judgment by default is entered, the insurer may lose the opportunity to defend the suit. The insured's breach of condition will give the insurer a defense in any action brought to enforce the policy.

The proper procedure is for the insured to give notice as promptly as possible after the happening of an insured event and to furnish a proof of loss, if required, within the time allowed. If the terms of the policy are complied with, it is beneficial to both insured and insurer. An insurance company will rarely rely upon a strict construction of notice provisions unless the company has been prejudiced by the insured's delay, but these provisions are in policies for sufficient reasons and failure to perform a condition in a contract normally excuses performance by the other party.

INSURANCE ORGANIZATIONS

Forms of Organization

Perhaps the oldest kind of insurance organization is the fraternal society, which existed in many ancient civilizations. There are still many fraternal benefit societies which write insurance only for members of their groups.

The oldest continuously operating form of insurer is Lloyd's of London. While originally Lloyd's was restricted to marine insurance, the organization now writes every form of insurance except ordinary life, and the form of organization remains basically unchanged; the insurance is written by syndicates of individuals who are personally liable to the extent of the risk they have assumed. An American Lloyd's is recognized by statute in some States, but this plan whereby individuals act through an attorney-in-fact is not widely used.

Similar in pattern to American Lloyd's are the reciprocals or interinsurance exchanges. Here, the participants act through an attorney-in-fact, as in Lloyd's, but the distinguishing feature is that each participant is both insurer and insured. This operation is necessarily limited in scope, but it is occasionally beneficial to aggregations of businesses which individually have to pay rather large premiums for needed insurance, and by means of this device, participate in any surplus at the end of the policy period.

Most insurance is written either by mutual corporations or by stock corporations. In theory, mutual corporations are aggregations of individuals each of whom is both insurer and insured; if there is a surplus, it is divided among the members by way of a dividend; and if there is insolvency, the members are required to contribute their appropriate shares. The contribution requirement may be restricted by statute, of course, so that a member's liability is limited or may not exist at all.

Stock insurance corporations are organized along the lines of ordinary corporations and are intended to make a profit for their shareholders, although many stock life insurance companies issue participating policies by which surplus is shared with the policyholders. There is no call, however, on policyholders for contribution in the event of insolvency. Stock companies generally operate through agents who are paid commissions on insurance sold, whereas mutual companies often operate through salaried employees. As is generally true in corporation law, when we speak of a *domestic* insurance corporation, we mean one organized under the laws of the particular

State of which we are speaking; while a *foreign* insurer is one organized under the laws of any other State; and, an *alien* insurer is organized under the laws of a foreign country.

Agents and Brokers

A corporation, such as an insurance company, can act only through agents, from the president down to the salesman, and it is the local selling agent most persons mean when they refer to an insurance agent. This particular kind of agent must be appointed by the company for which he acts and must be licensed by the insurance department of the State in which he works. Licensing requirements vary from the perfunctory to written examinations and educational standards.

Brokers are required to be licensed in many States, and the requirements for a broker's license are generally higher than those for an agent's license. A broker occupies a somewhat anomalous position in that he is usually the agent for the insured to procure insurance, yet his compensation is paid by commissions from the insurance companies. To illustrate the function of a broker, the X Corporation which requires various kinds of insurance—automobile liability insurance covering a fleet of company cars, collision insurance, fire and extended coverage insurance for real estate owned, rent loss insurance for real estate rented, public liability and property damage insurance covering office locations, workmen's compensation, and fidelity bonds—calls upon a broker to place the insurance. The broker selects the companies which can write the policies which X needs and negotiates with them to secure the desired coverages. The policies are delivered to the broker for transmission to X, and the broker may be the agent of the insurers for the purpose of collecting the premiums.

The usual rules of agency law are applicable to local agents of insurance companies in their dealings with applicants and insureds. An agent binds his principal when he acts within the scope of his authority. That authority may be express, implied, or apparent, and beyond that point there is always the possibility that a company will ratify an agent's unauthorized acts or else will be estopped to deny the authority of a local agent because of the particular circumstances involved in a given case. An agent is not personally liable on a contract made in the name of the principal where the agent had any kind of authority to make the contract; but if the agent had no authority but represented that he did, the agent is liable to third parties who relied upon his representations.

Local agents of an insurance company do not always act as the company officials may desire, but the knowledge which agents receive through the exercise of their authority is usually imputed to the principal, and the principal often is bound by an agent's waiver of certain conditions in an insurance contract. Policies may contain clauses stating that no waiver of any provision will be effective unless it is in writing and attached to the policy, but the effect which courts give to this clause varies considerably. If all agents were honest, the problems of the companies would be less, as would those of insureds. The company does not ordinarily discover that an agent has waived a condition until there has been a loss under the policy. It is often difficult to determine whether the insured (or beneficiary) is telling the truth about the agent's conduct, and it is highly unlikely that the insured would admit having read in the policy that an agent could not waive compliance with an express condition upon the waiver of which the insured's recovery depends. In the event that there has been provable collusion between a local agent and an applicant or insured with the intention of defrauding the insurance company, knowledge of the agent will not be imputed to the principal, nor will his conduct bind the company.

Cases

*Insurable Interest of Purchaser
of Another's Life Policy*

GRIGSBY v. RUSSELL

222 U.S. 149, 32 S.Ct. 58, 56 L.Ed. 133 (1911).

HOLMES, J.

This is a bill of interpleader brought by an insurance company to determine whether a policy of insurance issued to John C. Burchard, now deceased, upon his life, shall be paid to his administrators or to an assignee, the company having turned the amount into court. The material facts are that after he had paid two premiums and a third was overdue, Burchard, being in want and needing money for a surgical operation, asked Dr. Grigsby to buy the policy, and sold it to him in consideration of $100 and Grigsby's undertaking to pay the premiums due or to become due; and that Grigsby had no interest in the life of the assured. The circuit court of appeals, in deference to some intimations of this court, held the assignment valid only to the extent of the money actually given for it and the premiums subsequently paid. 36 L.R.A.,N.S., 642, 94 C.C.A. 61, 168 F. 577.

Of course, the ground suggested for denying the validity of an assignment to a person having no interest in the life insured is the public policy that refuses to allow insurance to be taken out by such persons in the first place. A contract of insurance upon a life in which the insured has no interest is a pure wager that gives the insured a sinister counter interest in having the life come to an end. And although that counter interest always exists, as early was emphasized for England in the famous case of Wainewright (Janus Weathercock), the chance that in some cases it may prove a sufficient motive for crime is greatly enhanced if the whole world of the unscrupulous are free to bet on what life they choose. The very meaning of an insurable interest is an interest in having the life continue, and so one that is opposed to crime. And what, perhaps, is more important, the existence of such an interest makes a roughly selected class of persons who, by their general relations with the person whose life is insured, are less likely than criminals at large to attempt to compass his death.

But when the question arises upon an assignment, it is assumed that the objection to the insurance as a wager is out of the case. In the present instance the policy was perfectly good. There was a faint suggestion in argument that it had become void by the failure of Burchard to pay the third premium *ad diem,* and that when Grigsby paid, he was making a new contract. But a condition in a policy that it shall be void if premiums are not paid when due means only that it shall be voidable at the option of the company. [Citations.] The company waived the breach, if there was one, and the original contract with Burchard remained on foot. No question as to the character of that contract is before us. It has been performed and the money is in court. But this being so, not only does the objection to wagers disappear, but also the principle of public policy referred to, at least, in its most convincing form. The danger that might arise from a general license to all to insure whom they like does not exist. Obviously it is a very different thing from granting such a general license, to allow the holder of a valid insurance upon his own life to transfer it to one whom he, the party most concerned, is not afraid to trust. The law has no universal cynic fear of the temptation opened by a pecuniary benefit accruing upon a death. It shows no prejudice against remainders after life estates, even by the rule in Shelley's Case. Indeed, the ground of the objection to life insurance without interest in the earlier English cases was not the temptation to murder, but the fact that such wagers came to be regarded as a mischievous kind of gaming. Stat. 14 George III., chap. 48.

On the other hand, life insurance has become in our days one of the best recognized forms of investment and self-compelled saving. So far as reasonable safety permits, it is desirable to give to life policies the ordinary characteristics of property. This is recognized by the bankruptcy law, § 70, which provides that unless the cash surrender value of a policy like the one before us is secured to the trustee within thirty days after it has been stated, the policy shall pass to the trustee as assets. Of course the trustee may have no interest in the bankrupt's life. To deny the right to sell except to persons having such an interest is to diminish appreciably the value of the contract in the owner's hands. The collateral difficulty that arose from regarding life insurance as a contract of indemnity only (Godsall v. Boldero, 9 East, 72), long has disappeared (Phoenix Mut. L. Ins. Co. v. Bailey, 13 Wall. 616, 20 L.Ed. 501). And cases in which a person having an interest lends himself to one without any, as a cloak to what is, in its inception, a wager, have no similarity to those where an honest contract is sold in good faith.

Coming to the authorities in this court, it is true that there are intimations in favor of the result come to by the circuit court of appeals. But the case in which the strongest of them occur was one of the type just referred to, the policy having been taken out for the purpose of allowing a stranger association to pay the premiums and receive the greater part of the benefit, and having been assigned to it at once. Warnock v. Davis, 104 U.S. 775, 26 L.Ed. 924. On the other hand, it has been decided that a valid policy is not avoided by the cessation of the insurable interest, even as against the insurer, unless so provided by the policy itself. [Citation.] And expressions more or less in favor of the doctrine that we adopt are to be found also in Aetna L. Ins. Co. v.

France, 94 U.S. 561, 24 L.Ed. 287; Mutual L. Ins. Co. v. Armstrong, 117 U.S. 591, 29 L.Ed. 997, 6 Sup.Ct. 877. It is enough to say that while the court below might hesitate to decide against the language of Warnock v. Davis, there has been no decision that precludes us from exercising our own judgment upon this much debated point. It is at least satisfactory to learn from the decision below that in Tennessee, where this assignment was made, although there has been much division of opinion, the supreme court of that state came to the conclusion that we adopt, in an unreported case,—Lewis v. Edwards, December 14, 1903. The law in England and the preponderance of decisions in our state courts are on the same side.

Some reference was made to a clause in the policy that "any claim against the company, arising under any assignment of the policy, shall be subject to proof of interest." But it rightly was assumed below that if there was no rule of law to that effect, and the company saw fit to pay, the clause did not diminish the rights of Grigsby, as against the administrators of Burchard's estate.

Decree reversed.

Insurable Interest of Good Faith Purchaser of Stolen Automobile

SCAROLA v. INSURANCE COMPANY OF NORTH AMERICA

(1972) 31 N.Y.2d 411, 340 N.Y.S.2d 630, 292 N.E.2d 776.

BERGAN, J.

The finding of fact that plaintiff purchased the automobile insured by defendant for value and without knowledge it was stolen has been affirmed, both by the Appellate Term, 67 Misc.2d 437, 323 N.Y.S.2d 1001, and by the Appellate Division, 38 A.D.2d 1012, 331 N.Y.S.2d 340, and is not an open question here. Thus the issue of plaintiff's insurable interest must be examined on the assumption he was an innocent buyer of the vehicle insured by defendant, and subsequently stolen.

Plaintiff had a right to possession of the car against any contrary assertion except that of the true owner. This right, under general principles, ought to be regarded as an insurable interest. The New York rule was laid down by Judge Finch in National Filtering Oil Co. v. Citizens' Inc. Co. of Mo., 106 N.Y. 535, 13 N.E. 337. He noted that the cases he cited, e.g., Herkimer v. Rice, 27 N.Y. 163, "decide that an interest, legal or equitable, in the property burned, is not necessary to support an insurance upon it; that it is enough if the assured is so situated as to be liable to loss if it be destroyed by the peril insured against; that such an interest in property connected with its safety and situation as will cause the insured to sustain a direct loss from its destruction, is an insurable interest; that if there be a right in or against the property which some court will enforce upon the property, a right so closely connected with it and so much dependent for value upon the continued existence of it alone as that a loss of the property will cause pecuniary damage to the holder of the right against it, he has an insurable interest." (106 N.Y., at p. 541, 13 N.E., at p. 339)

This decision was followed in Riggs v. Commercial Mut. Ins. Co., 125 N.Y. 7, 25 N.E. 1058, in which Judge Andrews observed that although a stockholder of a corporation had neither title to corporate property nor equitable title which he could convert to a legal title, he has a sufficient interest in such property to insure it. For example, its loss might affect dividends (p. 13, 25 N.E. p. 1060). If the law recognizes the right of a purchaser of a car in good faith and for value to possession, it would seem to follow that this right to possession, limited though it may be, is insurable.

The general policy problem underlying the concept of "insurable interest" essentially is whether an insured, having no real economic interest in the subject, is actually making a wagering contract. The principle is laid down in C.J.S. (Vol. 44 Insurance § 175, subd. [b], p. 870): "An 'insurable interest' is sui generis, and peculiar in its texture and operation. In general a person has an insurable interest in the subject matter insured where he has such a relation or connection with, or concern in, such subject matter that he will derive pecuniary benefit or advantage from its preservation, or will suffer pecuniary loss or damage from its destruction, termination, or injury by the happening of the event insured against. Great liberality is indulged in determining whether a person has anything at hazard in the subject matter of the insurance, and any interest which would be recognized by a court of law or equity is an insurable interest."

Two States (New Jersey and Washington) have held under similar circumstances to those now here that the purchaser in good faith of a car has an insurable interest. [Citation].

In the latter case the court observed: "The car covered by the policy upon which the action is based was purchased by the respondent in good faith, used by him, the insurance policy issued to him and the premium paid. Even though the automobile may have been originally stolen from the rightful owner, the respondent had the title and the right to possession of it as against all the world, except the rightful owner, assuming that the car had been stolen from him" 138 Wash., at p. 675, 245 P., at p. 4.

In a recent case in the Second Department (Perrotta v. Empire Mut. Ins. Co., 35 A.D.2d 961, 371 N.Y.S.2d 779) the court treated as decisive on insurable interest whether plaintiff was "an innocent purchaser of the automobile." Holding that he was not, the court held he had no insurable interest.

* * *

The order should be affirmed.

Defenses of Insurer:
Material Misrepresentation in
Application for Insurance

HAWKEYE-SECURITY INS. CO. v. GOVERNMENT EMP. INS. CO.

(1967) 207 Va. 944, 154 S.E.2d 173.

SNEAD , J.

On August 18, 1962, Einer Carl Mattson, Jr. was operating an automobile owned by and with consent of his father, Einer Carl Mattson, Sr. It became involved in a collision with another vehicle operated by William Henry Droughn who received personal injuries. Mattson, Sr. reported the accident to Government Employees Insurance Company, appellee, which had issued to him a liability insurance policy on his car involved in the mishap. Under the terms of the policy, Mattson, Jr. was an additional insured. On November 20, 1962, after some investigation, Government Employees wrote Mattson, Sr. advising "[W]e hereby declare the captioned policy null and void and of no effect as of its inception date" because of a material misrepresentation made in his application for the insurance coverage, and it enclosed a check for a refund of premiums paid.

On September 22, 1964, Droughn recovered a judgment in the sum of $2,000 against Mattson, Jr., and on the same day Droughn assigned it to Hawkeye-Security Insurance Company, appellant, for a valuable consideration. Execution on the judgment was returned "unsatisfied."

* * *

Hawkeye, assignee, instituted an action against Government Emp Employees seeking a judgment for $2,000 against it. In its answer and grounds of defense, Government Employees denied that the Mattson vehicle was insured by it, and denied that it was liable to Hawkeye in any amount. A trial by jury was waived, and after hearing all the evidence, the court found that Mattson, Sr. had made a material misrepresentation in his application to Government Employees for the insurance policy and on November 3, 1965, rendered judgment in its behalf. We granted Hawkeye a writ of error.

* * * The crucial issue presented in this appeal is whether the insurance policy issued to Mattson, Sr. by Government Employees was in full force and effect on August 18, 1962, the date Droughn was injured, or whether it was void *ab initio* because of an alleged material misrepresentation made by Mattson, Sr. in the procurement of the policy.

The record shows that Mattson, Sr. was insured under an automobile liability policy issued by State Farm Mutual Insurance Company from January 29, 1959, until it was cancelled by the Company on August 5, 1959. Douglas R. Mays, an underwriter for State Farm, testified that the policy was cancelled for "general underwriting reasons" and that Mattson, Sr. was notified of the Company's action by registered mail.

Thereafter, Mattson, Sr. obtained another policy from Home Indemnity Insurance Company which he retained until October 20, 1960 when he was issued the policy here involved by Government Employees. This policy was twice renewed with coverage extending through October 20, 1963. All premiums were duly paid.

Mattson, Sr. testified that he contacted Government Employees by mail for the insurance and was mailed an application for him to complete and return. Above the space for his signature and the questions to be answered the application read:

"I understand and agree that if the answers to questions 7, 8, 9 or 10, or any of them, are other than 'No,' the insurance requested will not be effective until approved by the Company. * * * The Company agrees that * * * if the true answers to questions 7, 8, 9 and 10 are 'No,' the insurance applied for will be effective as of: postmarked time and date * * *

* * *

"IMPORTANT ISSUANCE OF A VALID POLICY IS DEPENDENT UPON YOUR TRUE ANSWERS."

We are here concerned only with question No. 7, which follows:

"7. Has any insurance company (including this Company) ever refused, cancelled, refused to renew, or given notice of intention to cancel or refuse, any automobile insurance for you or any member of your household? * * *. If 'yes,' see above (the quoted statement) (Give full information on separate sheet)"

The application which Mattson, Sr. admitted that he himself completed and signed, contained a "No" answer in response to question No. 7. * * *

Gerald T. Jackson, underwriting manager for Government Employees, testified that he had the responsibility of deciding whether a policy should or should not be issued by his Company to an applicant. He said that if question No. 7 had been answered "yes" without elaboration, the application of Mattson, Sr. would have been rejected; * * *

Jackson, on the other hand, testified that when an application contained a "No" answer to question No. 7, and the rest of the application showed no accidents or violations, the answer would be accepted as true and no investigation would be made.

Hawkeye concedes that the answer "No" to question No. 7 was untrue, but contends Government Employees did not clearly prove that such answer was material to the risk when assumed.

Code, 38.1–336 is applicable and provides:

"All statements, declarations and descriptions in any application for a policy of insurance * * * shall be deemed representations and not warranties, and no statement in such application * * * shall bar a recovery upon a policy of insurance * * * unless it be clearly proved that such answer or statement was material to the risk when assumed and was untrue."

Whether a representation was made and the terms upon which it was made are factual questions for the jury, but when proved its materiality becomes a question for the court to decide. Materiality of a misrepresentation is an affirmative defense, and the burden is upon the insurer to prove it. [Citation.]

"A fact is material to the risk to be assumed by an insurance company if the fact would reasonably influence the company's decision whether or not to issue a policy." [Citations.]

* * *

We have repeatedly held that under Code, § 38.1–336, supra, a misrepresentation of a fact material to the risk when assumed renders an insurance contract void. [Citations.]

Here, Government Employees carried its burden of clearly proving that the untrue answer to question No. 7 in the application for insurance made by Mattson, Sr. was material to the risk when assumed. * * *

Government Employees was entitled to know the whole truth. The false answer ("No) to question No. 7 caused the Company to forego an opportunity to investigate why the State Farm policy was cancelled and to determine whether or not the risk should be assumed as well as the premium rate applicable to the risk in the event the policy was issued. [Citation.]

* * *

Under the evidence adduced, the trial court porperly held that the misrepresentation was material to the risk when assumed and that the policy was null and void *ab initio* for that reason.

Accordingly, the judgment appealed from is

Affirmed.

Waiver and Estoppel

MARLOWE v. RESERVE LIFE INSURANCE CO.

(1973) 261 S.C. 23, 198 S.E.2d 267.

MOSS, C. J.

The appellant, Reserve Life Insurance Company, on January 15, 1970, issued a hospital insurance policy to Helen S. Marlowe, the respondent herein. By the terms of said policy, appellant agreed to pay to the insured certain hospital expenses incurred by her.

The respondent instituted this action alleging that while the aforesaid policy was in full force and effect she was hospitalized in Duke Hospital, in Durham, North Carolina, there receiving medical treatment from May 19, 1970, until May 28, 1970. She alleges that she has filed a claim for the benefits due her under said policy and the appellant has refused to pay said claim.

The appellant, by answer, * * * refused to pay the claim upon the ground that there were misrepresentations in the application of the respondent as to her medical history, which was relied upon by it, such being material to the risk involved and had the truth been known the policy would not have been issued and it has elected to rescind said policy of insurance and declare same null and void from its inception.

The facts in this case are undisputed. The respondent contacted an agent of New York Life Insurance Company for the purpose of purchasing hospital insurance coverage for herself and her children. This agent informed her that his company could not insure her in view of her medical history, but he agreed to contact an agent of another company which might possibly provide coverage. Shortly thereafter, one John Rouse, an agent of the appellant, contacted her by telephone and made an appointment with her for January 7, 1970, at her home. * * * The application was filled out by the agent himself while asking the respon-

dent questions with respect to the medical history portion of the application. She told the agent that her medical history was so long that she could not remember it all but if he would inquire of Dr. Shingleton at Duke Hospital and Dr. Smith of Conway, South Carolina, they could make such history available to him.

The respondent testified that her application for hospital insurance was filled out by the agent of the appellant and that she made no entries thereon except the affixation of her signature on the bottom line thereof. She was then asked, "Did you read the application as completed before you signed it?", and her answer thereto was, "No sir, he didn't offer it to me. He just asked me to sign it, and he asked me for a check, and I told him I felt sure he was wasting his time."

The policy in question was delivered to the respondent by mail and when asked if she read it she replied, "No sir, because he (the agent) told me what it would be and I can tell you now."

* * *

The general rule is that the knowledge of an agent acquired within the scope of his agency is imputable to his principal, and if an insurance company, at the inception of the contract of insurance has knowledge of facts which render the policy void at its option, and the company delivers the policy as a valid policy, it is estopped to assert such ground of forfeiture. * * * [Citations.]

The appellant admits that if the foregoing rule was applicable it would be estopped to rescind the contract by reason of misrepresentations in the application. However, the appellant contends that the soliciting agent, Rouse, had no authority to waive any of the appellant's rights by reason of the above quoted limitation contained in the application and that the insured was bound by such.

The rule in this State is that an insurance company cannot set up forfeiture on account of facts known by the agent of the company to be existing at the time of the making of the contract. A provision limiting the power of an agent has no sacrosanct character over any other provision, and like all of them is itself subject to waiver by the company. [Citation.]

* * *

When an agent of an insurance company, who fills out an application for an insurance policy, is duly informed of the facts and fails to state them in the application, the actual knowledge of the agent will be held to be the knowledge of the company, where there is good faith on the part of the applicant. Reserve Life Ins. Co. v. Ferebee, 202 Va. 556, 118 S.E.2d 675.

* * *

We conclude that where the insured, acting in good faith, makes truthful answers to the application questions, but those answers are incorrectly transcribed by reason of the fraud, mistake, or negligence of the insurer's soliciting agent, the insurer is estopped to set up the omissions in or the falsity of such answers, even though there is a limitation on such agent's authority in the application.

* * *

Affirmed.

Problems

1. Lile, an insurance broker, handled all insurance for X Co. Lile purchased a fire policy from Insurance Company insuring X Co.'s factory against fire in the amount of $150,000. Before the policy was delivered to X Co. and while it was in Lile's hands, X Co. advised Lile to cancel the policy. Prior to cancellation, X Co. suffered a loss and makes claim against Insurance Company on the policy. The premium had been billed to Lile but was unpaid at the time of loss. In an action by X Co. against Insurance Company, what judgment?

2. On July 15, 1982, A purchased in Chicago a 1980 Buick Sedan intending to drive it that day to St. Louis, Missouri. He telephoned a friend X who was in the insurance business and told him that he wished public liability insurance on the automobile limited in amount to $50,000 for injuries to one person and $100,000 for any one accident. X took the order and told A over the telephone that he was covered and that his policy would be written by the Y Insurance Company. Later that same day and before X had advised the Y Insurance Company of A's application, A negligently operated the automobile on the public highway and seriously injured B who brings suit against A. Is A protected by public liability insurance?

3. A owns a building having a fair market value of $120,000. He takes out a fire insurance policy in the B Company for $72,000, the policy containing an 80% co-insurance clause. The building is damaged by fire to the extent of $48,000. How much insurance is A entitled to collect?

4. The B Automobile Insurance Company issues to A, owner of a Mercury automobile, a liability policy, $30,000–60,000 limits. On April 3, as the result of A's negligent operation of his car, C, D, and E are injured in a collision. C, D, and E sue A and recover judgments of $45,000, $9,000 and $6,000, respectively. To what extent is the B Company liable?

5. Arthur Heartburn, having knowledge of a bad heart condition, arranges to have his friend, Ira Imposter, represent himself as Heartburn to the medical examiner of the Taken Life Insurance Company. Imposter, posing as Heartburn, is found to be physically sound; and the Insurance Company issues a $75,000 life insurance policy to Heartburn. The policy contains a two-year incontestable clause. Twenty-six months after the issuance of the policy Heartburn suffers a heart attack and dies. Before paying off the claim of Heartburn's widow, the beneficiary under the policy, the Insurance Company learns about Imposter's actions in helping Heartburn procure the policy. When the Taken Insurance Company refuses to pay the claim, the widow files suit on the policy. Decision?

6. Wiley, an insurance salesman, induces Glutz to purchase a $60,000 life insurance policy on the life of his best friend Doe and at the same time sells a policy to Doe insuring Glutz's life. After ten years Doe dies, and on due proof of death, the insurance company denies liability. Glutz sues the company. Decision?

7. Kay was issued a $30,000 life insurance policy by Atlantic Bell Life Insurance Company. In his application Kay truthfully warranted that he was a professional actor, and that he was not engaged in the employ of a railroad company or an airplane company. The policy provided that the company insured "the life of Kay so long as he was engaged solely in the business of a professional actor." The policy also provided:

This policy shall be incontestable for any cause after it shall have been in force during the life of the insured for two years from its date.

After the policy had been in effect for three years Kay was killed while employed as a brakeman by a railroad company. Kay was so employed without the knowledge and consent of the insurance company. The beneficiary of the policy sued the company to recover the face amount of the policy. The company defended, denying liability on the ground that Kay was employed by a railroad company at the time of his death and had been so employed for six months previously. Decision?

8. Paul Poe purchased a life insurance policy in the sum of $100,000. The policy provided: "The proceeds of this policy are payable upon the death of the insured to Penelope Poe, wife of the insured." The policy also provided that Poe had the right to change the name of the beneficiary. Four years after the policy had been purchased, Poe obtained a divorce from his wife, Penelope. One year later, Poe married Dora Doe, and this marriage continued until Poe's death two years thereafter. At Poe's death the policy remained in its original form. Penelope demanded that the insurance company pay her the proceeds of the policy. Upon its refusal, she brought an action against the company to recover $100,000. Decision?

9. Day had for some time been seeking out Short to "teach him a lesson" for taking out Day's girlfriend and Day carried a pistol for this purpose. Eventually, Day caught up with Short at a local beer parlor, and, without warning, fired a shot at Short. Day's aim was not too good, for the shot only creased Short's head. Short dove at Day and a scuffle ensued. During the scuffle Day fell to the floor, hitting his head upon the bar railing. As a direct result of this blow to his head, Day died. At the time of his death, Day had in effect a policy of accidental death insurance in which the insurance company had agreed to pay the named beneficiary, Day's mother, $7,000, upon the death of Day, if the death were "effected solely through external violent and accidental means." The insurance company refused to pay the beneficiary.

What are the beneficiary's rights, if any?

TRUSTS

The legal title to property may be held by one or more persons, while its use, enjoyment, and benefit belong to another. This situation may arise by agreement of the parties, by testamentary bequest, or by decree of court. However created, the relationship is known as a "trust." The party holding the legal title to the property is the "trustee" of the trust, and the beneficial owner of the trust is the "cestui que trust," commonly referred to as the beneficiary.

TYPES OF TRUSTS

The trust relationship can take a variety of forms. Some of them have distinguishing characteristics which merit special attention. The following types of trusts are not mutually exclusive, but are listed for simplicity of identification.

1. Express Trusts.
2. Implied Trusts.
    (a) Constructive Trusts.
    (b) Resulting Trusts.
3. Charitable Trusts.
4. Spendthrift Trusts.
5. Totten Trusts.
6. Precatory Trusts.

Express Trusts

An express trust is contained in express language of the settlor, written or oral, whereby specific property is transferred to a trustee for the use and benefit of one or more third persons.

Implied Trusts

In some cases, the courts, in the absence of any expressed trust intent, will impose a trust upon property because the acts of the parties appear to call for such a construction. An implied trust owes its existence to the law. Customarily, these implied trusts are divided into two classes, constructive trusts and resulting trusts. Although the line between these two subclasses is frequently blurred, a constructive trust is said to cover those instances where the court will impose a trust upon property to rectify a fraud or to prevent unjust enrichment.

Constructive Trusts. A constructive trust exists where a confidential relation, and the subsequent abuse of the confidence reposed are sufficient to establish such trust, or where actual fraud or duress is considered as equitable ground for raising the trust. The mere existence of such relationship prohibits the one trusted from seeking any selfish benefit for himself during the course of the relationship and affords a basis for fastening a constructive trust upon the property in his hands. In general, a fiduciary or confidential relation exists where trust and confidence are reposed by one person in another, who, as a result, gains an influence and superiority over the first. Specifically, a confidential relation exists where, by reason of kinship, business or association, disparity in age, or physical or mental condition, or other reason, the grantee occupies an especially intimate position with regard to the grantor and the latter reposes a high degree of trust and confidence in the former. Where a fiduciary relation exists, the burden rests upon the grantee or beneficiary of an instrument executed during the existence of such relatoinship to prove, by clear and convincing proof, the fairness of the transaction, that it was equitable and just, that it did not proceed from undue influence, and that he exercised good faith and did not betray the confidence reposed in him, irrespective of whether he was instrumental in causing the conveyance to be made. It is not essential that the undue influence vitiating the transfer be deemed fraudulent. It is sufficient if the influence arises out of the fiduciary or confidential relation.

Business and personal affairs provide many examples of constructive trusts. A director of a corporation who takes advantage of a "corporate opportunity" or who makes an undisclosed profit in a deal with the corporation will be treated as a trustee for the corporation with respect to the property thus acquired by him, or to the extent of the profit realized by him. A trustee under an express trust who permits a lease held by the trust to expire and then acquires a new lease of the property in his individual capacity will be required to hold the new lease in trust for the beneficiary. If an agent who is given money by his principal to purchase property in the name of the principal instead uses the funds to acquire title in himself, courts will treat him as a trustee for the principal.

Resulting Trusts. A resulting trust is said to be distinguished from a constructive trust in that while the latter is designed to rectify fraud, the former serves to carry out the true intent of the parties in those cases where the intent was inadequately expressed. The most common example of a resulting trust is where A pays the purchase price for property and title is taken in the name of B. The presumption here is that the parties intended B to hold the property for the benefit of A, and B will be treated as a trustee. The difficulty is that, in many cases, it would be equally reasonable to presume that A intended to make a gift to B, and, in the cases where the payor is a husband or a parent, a gift is generally the more favored presumption.

A resulting trust does not depend on contract or agreement but is founded on a presumed intent which arises out of the acts of the parties. Since a resulting trust is created by implication and operation of law, it need not be evidenced in writing. The trust arises, if at all, in the same transaction in which the legal title vests, on consideration advanced before or at that time, and not on acts arising thereafter. It is, of course, always possible to prove that a trust was not intended. A resulting trust is based upon the presumption of normal self interest, and courts generally require very careful proof to establish a resulting trust. The burden of proof rests on the parties seeking to establish a resulting trust and the evidence, to be effective for such purpose, must be clear, strong, unequivocal, unmistakable, and so convincing as to lead to but one conclusion. If a reasonable explanation of the evidence may be made upon any theory other than the existence of a resulting trust, a trust will not be declared and enforced.

Charitable Trusts

The legal meaning of charity is broader than that usually attributed to the word by the layman. It includes substantially any *public* purpose which will contribute to education, the advancement of science, and knowledge in general. Almost any trust which has for its purpose the improvement of mankind, or a class of mankind, will be classified as charitable, provided it is not so vague and indefinite as to be incapable of enforcement. Gifts for public museums, upkeep of parks, propagation of a particular political doctrine or religious belief have been upheld as "charitable" in character.

There are practical differences in the law depending upon whether a trust is for charitable or private purposes. In general, the rule against perpetuities does not apply to charitable trusts. For example, it is valid to provide for a gift in trust to the Middlesex Hospital, a non-profit corporation, with a provision that if the Hospital ceased to maintain free wards the property should go to the Town of Middlesex for care of the poor. If the trust had been noncharitable the contingent gift to the town would have violated the rule against perpetuities.

Secondly, the cy pres doctrine is applicable only to charitable trusts. The doctrine reflects the traditional sympathy of courts toward charitable motives whereby when it is impossible or impracticable to carry out a charitable bequest exactly as directed by the settlor, a court will apply the funds to a charity as similar as possible in purpose to that specified. One of the famous cases illustrating the doctrine of cy pres involved two trusts, one providing funds to create sentiment favoring the ab-

olition of slavery and the second establishing a fund to assist runaway slaves. The Emancipation Proclamation abolished slavery soon after the death of the settlor and the court authorized the use of the first trust fund for Negro education and the second for the aid of needy Negroes in the town where the settlor had lived. There must, however, be a general charitable intent in order to apply cy pres. A trust to encourage the propagation of a particular religious cult could not, if the cult disbanded, be applied for use by any other religion unless there was a definite indication of a non-sectarian religious purpose on the part of the settlor.

Spendthrift Trusts

A settlor frequently does not believe that a beneficiary can be relied upon to preserve even the limited rights granted him as beneficiary. He will then provide that the beneficiary cannot, by assignment, or otherwise, impair his rights to receive principal or income and that creditors of the beneficiary cannot attach the fund or the income. The term "spendthrift," as used in connection with spendthrift trusts, refers to a provision in a trust instrument whereby the trust estate is removed from the beneficiary's control and disposition and from liability for his individual debts. Of course, once income from the trust is actually received by the beneficiary, creditors may seize it or the beneficiary may do with it as he pleases.

Spendthrift provisions are generally valid. A typical provision follows:

Payments and distributions to all the beneficiaries hereunder, except to minors and persons under disability, shall be made only to such beneficiaries in person or upon their personal receipt, and no interest of any beneficiary in the income or principal of the Trust Estate shall be assignable in anticipation of payment, either by the voluntary or involuntary act of such beneficiary or by operation of law, or be liable in any way for the debts of such beneficiary.

Totten Trusts

A totten trust involves a joint bank account opened by the settlor of the trust. Typically, A deposits a sum of money in a savings account in a bank in the name of "A, in trust for B." A may make additional deposits in the account from time to time and may withdraw money from it whenever he pleases. The courts have held this to be a tentative trust which the depositor may revoke by withdrawing the fund or changing the form of the account. The transfer of ownership becomes complete only upon the depositor's death. The donee has no enforceable claim during the donor-depositor's lifetime.

It has been held that a Totten Trust created by deposit of funds in a bank savings account in the name of Charles Wright, Pay on death to Mary Lowe" is enforceable not only as a trust but as a third party donee beneficiary contract between donor depositor Wright and the depository bank, and entitles the donee to the funds in the account upon the death of the donor. Estate of Wright, 17 Ill.App.3d 894, 308 N.E.2d 319 (1974).

Precatory Trusts

It is not always easy to tell whether a settlor really intended to create a trust. Sometimes, words of request or recommendation are used in connection with a gift implying or hoping that the gift will be used for the purpose stated. Thus, instead of leaving property "to X for the benefit and use of Y," a settlor may leave property to X "in full confidence and with hope that he will care for Y." Such a "precatory expression" may be so definite and certain as to impose a trust upon the property for the benefit of Y. Whether it creates a trust or is nothing more than a gratuitous wish will depend on whether the court believes from all the facts that the settlor genuinely intended a trust. More frequently, courts are viewing such words as "request," "hope" and "rely" as cre-

ating no legal obligation upon the recipient of the gift and therefore do not create a trust.

CREATION OF TRUSTS

Each trust has (1) a creator or "settlor," (2) a "corpus" or trust property, (3) a trustee and (4) a beneficiary. A may convey property in trust to B for the benefit of C; or A may declare himself trustee for the benefit of C; or A may convey in trust to B for the benefit of himself, A.

No particular words are necessary to create a trust, provided that the intent of the settlor to establish a trust is unmistakable. A not uncommon provision is "to X, as Trustee, to have and hold upon the trusts and uses hereinafter set forth."

Trusts are employed in wills as a means of conserving property for the benefit of widows and children. These trusts are known as *testamentary trusts* because they become effective after the death of the settlor. Frequently, individuals establish trusts during their lifetime in which case they are referred to as *inter vivos* or *"living" trusts*. Such trusts are sometimes established in order to reduce the aggregate individual income taxes of a family group by placing income producing property in a trust whereby the trustee is directed and required to distribute the income to the beneficiaries who are close relatives of the settlor and in a lower income tax bracket. They are also used to facilitate estate administration and lessen the amount of probate fees and expenses. If a person dies leaving assets in a trust established during his lifetime by the terms of which the principal is distributable upon his death, the assets pass at that time immediately to the beneficiaries without the delay of probate that testamentary trusts encounter. Living trusts may be revocable or irrevocable depending upon the estate planning goals of the settlor.

Consideration is not essential to an enforceable trust. In this respect, a trust is more akin to a conveyance than a contract. It is not, however, always clear whether a person has by his actions created a trust or simply *promised* to create a trust. Since consideration is necessary to enforce such a promise, the practical importance of distinguishing between an actual declaration of trust and a statement of intent to create a trust in the future is apparent.

The Settlor

Any person legally capable of making a contract can create a trust. However, if the settlor's conveyance would be voidable or void because of infancy, insanity, or other reason, a declaration of trust is likewise voidable or void.

Subject Matter of a Trust

One of the chief characteristics which sets a trust apart from other relationships such as a debtor-creditor relationship, is the requirement of a trust *"res,"* which is property that is definite and specific and subject to the trust. A trust cannot be effective immediately with respect to property not yet in existence or to be acquired at a later date. A organizes a corporation and executes a trust instrument declaring that he holds all future dividends in trust for his children. When dividends are subsequently declared, A may keep them or set them aside as trust property. His prior declaration does not oblige him to hold the *future* unrealized profits in trust. In each succeeding year, a declaration and segregation of dividends received is necessary in order to impose the character of a trust upon them.

The requirement of a definite and certain subject matter is satisfied by the creation of a testamentary trust in A's will which provides that he leaves to B, as trustee, sufficient funds to pay $300 a month to C. The will takes effect upon the death of A.

Sometimes living trusts are established as "dry" trusts to become receptacles for cash assets whenever the assets are realized. A common example is the revocable life insurance trust wherein the trustee is named beneficiary of certain life insurance policies. When the settlor dies, the policy proceeds are paid into the trust and the trust thereby becomes activated.

The distinction between a trustee-beneficiary relationship and a debtor-creditor relationship has many important consequences in business affairs, particularly where an obligor has become insolvent. If A owes B $1,000 and A becomes insolvent, B will share ratably with A's other creditors. If, on the other hand, A opens a bank account as "A, Trustee for B," deposits the $1,000 and then becomes insolvent, B will be able to collect the full amount due him under the trust. When money is paid over to one person for the use of another, as in the case of rents paid to an agent for the owner of the premises or the purchase price paid to a commission agent for goods sold, the earmarking of the proceeds or the maintenance of a separate credit by the agent generally establishes him as a trustee, not a debtor. When a corporation declares a dividend, it becomes a debtor to the shareholders of record. If, in addition to a declaration, it sets funds aside in a special bank account to pay the dividend, it will be considered a trustee and in the event of its subsequent insolvency, the shareholders will, so far as that fund is concerned, share ahead of the corporation's general creditors. In most of these cases, the crucial issue is whether there is an identifiable subject matter separate and distinct from the obligor's other assets.

The Trustee

Anyone legally capable of holding title to and dealing with property may be a trustee. A corporation may act as trustee within the limits of its authorized powers; a public institution may act as a trustee. A substantial trust business is carried on by many banks, a function limited primarily by the statutory provision in most States that only domiciliary institutions are qualified to act as corporate trustees. The lack of a trustee will not, however, destroy the trust. If the settlor neglects to appoint one, or if a named trustee does not qualify, the court, upon request, will appoint an individual or institution to act as trustee.

Duties of the Trustee. A trustee can, of course, decline to serve, and before the property will vest in him it is necessary that he accept the trust. Acceptance is often inferred from the acts of the trustee indicative of an intent to exercise dominion over the trust estate. It is a common statutory requirement that a court appointed trustee must post a bond for the honest administration of his duties. A bond is not required of a trustee appointed by the settlor.

There are three primary duties of any trustee:

1. To carry out the purposes of the trust.
2. To act with prudence and care in the administration of the trust.
3. To exercise a high degree of loyalty toward the beneficiary.

The first of these duties needs little comment. It is obvious that the trustee is charged with following the direction of the settlor as to the manner of administration of the estate and the distribution of the property to the beneficiaries.

The second responsibility, that of using prudence and care in administration, is not as easily defined. No special skills are required of a trustee under ordinary circumstances. He is required to act with the same degree of care that a prudent man would exercise with respect to his personal affairs. What constitutes the prudence of a "prudent man" is, of course, not easy to classify in any particular case. In those cases involving disastrous investments by a trustee the advantages of hindsight often obscure the fact that, at the time of the investment, the general business community looked upon a particular security as a good risk. Generally, a trustee follows a safe course if he makes the conservation of capital his main goal and the realization of income a policy to be followed only insofar as it is consistent with the continued security of the capital entrusted to him.

The third duty of the trustee, that of loyalty, arises out of and illustrates the fiduciary character of the relationship between the trustee and the beneficiary. The trustee in all his dealings with the trust property, the beneficiary and third parties, must always act in the exclusive interest of the beneficiary. Indeed, the trustee, to protect himself from liability for misfeasance, should lean over backward to avoid any suggestion of personal advantage from the trust. He cannot act as though the beneficiary were a stranger with whom he could deal at arms length. Lack of loyalty may arise from palpable self-dealing or it may be entirely innocent; in either event the trustee can be charged with lack of loyalty. The sale of his own property to a trust or the purchase of trust property at a sale conducted by himself as trustee are common instances of a violation of this fiduciary duty. The loan of trust funds by a trustee to himself or the loan of such funds to a corporation of which he is a principal shareholder, or director or officer, would constitute a breach of this duty. The fact that the transaction is carried on through a "dummy" will not prevent a court from setting aside such a transaction. The fact that no harm may be done the trust does not excuse the transaction. It is a prophylactic rule designed to discourage temptation regardless of the outcome of any particular transaction.

A beneficiary can require that the disloyal trustee restore the status quo. A beneficiary who is legally competent may, on the other hand, ratify the disloyal act and be prevented from holding the trustee liable. In such a case, the beneficiary would be estopped, but only if full disclosure of the entire transaction had been made by the trustee.

Powers of the Trustee. The powers of a trustee are determined by (1) the rules of law in the jurisdiction in which the trust is established and (2) the authority granted him by the settlor in the instrument creating the trust. State laws affecting the powers of trustees have their greatest impact upon the investments a trustee may make with trust funds. Most States prescribe a list of types of securities qualified for trust investment. In some jurisdictions this list is permissive; in others it is mandatory. If the list is permissive, the trustee may invest in unlisted types of securities although he carries the burden of showing that he made a prudent choice. If the list is mandatory, it would appear that the trustee must confine himself to the listed types regardless of the "prudence" of an unlisted investment. Those investments usually approved, in the order of their general preference, are (1) obligations of the United States, (2) bonds of States and municipalities which meet certain standards, (3) first mortgages, if the security is adequate and, occasionally, (4) the secured-debt securities of triple-A corporations, frequently limited to public utilities. If a security does not fall within these classes, its purchase by a trustee will be disapproved except in extraordinary cases. Such improper investments would include unsecured loans, investments in a small business, loans secured by second mortgages and other junior liens and, in most instances, common and preferred stocks. In some States, statutes or court decisions have relaxed the rule with respect to certain types of stocks.

The trust instrument may give the trustee wide discretion as to investments and, in such an event, the trustee is not bound to adhere to the list deemed advisable under the statute. Thus, if a statute does not include the preferred stock of industrial corporations a trustee may so invest if given the authority by the settlor. It is not uncommon for a settlor to specifically direct the trustee to retain the stock in a family corporation and the trustee may do so whereas, otherwise, he would undoubtedly be obliged to dispose of such securities within a reasonable time. Wide discretion in a trust instrument does not, nevertheless, relieve a trustee from the general duty of prudence and care.

In the absence of specific directions, the trustee normally has the power and, indeed, sometimes the duty, to sell or exchange securities left in trust. He may also select a depositary for the funds and do what is impliedly necessary to carry out satisfactorily the purpose of the trust. But, in the absence of specific authority, there are many incidents of ownership normally exercised by the average person that a cautious trustee would hestitate to undertake. It is for this reason that a trust instrument will frequently grant very broad powers to the trustee.

The Beneficiary

There are very few restrictions on who (or what) may be a beneficiary. Dogs, cats, horses and a multitude of pets limited only by the imaginative attachments of humans have at one time or another been held to be the proper objects of a settlor's bounty. Charitable uses are a common purpose of trusts and, if the settlor's object does not outrage public policy or morals, almost any purpose which happens to strike the fancy of a settlor will be upheld. A corporation or a public institution may be a beneficiary. The settlor not infrequently makes himself beneficiary and, if this does not defraud his creditors, such action is perfectly valid.

In the absence of restrictive provisions in the trust instrument such as a spendthrift clause, a beneficiary's interest may be reached by his creditors, or the beneficiary may sell or dispose of his interest. If he held more than a life estate in the trust, his interest upon his death unless disposed of by his will passes to his heirs or personal representative.

TERMINATION OF A TRUST

Unless a power of revocation is reserved by the settlor, the general rule is that a trust, once validly created, is irrevocable. If so reserved, the trust may be terminated at the discretion of the settlor. Parents occasionally create living trusts for children and reserve a power of revocation to insure proper filial respect for parental discipline.

Normally, a trust has a termination date in the instrument and the trust terminates at the time stated without complication. A period of years may be specified or the settlor may provide that the trust shall continue during the life of a named individual. The death of the trustee or beneficiary does not terminate the trust if neither of their lives is the measure of the duration of the trust.

The ability of the settlor to control the life of a trust makes it more useful than other types of agreements whereby a person may entrust the administration of property to another. For example, a broad power of attorney may enable a person to manage the assets of the owner and make distribution as directed. However, title to the assets is not in the holder of the power of attorney which terminates upon his death or the death of the grantor.

Occasionally, the purpose for which a trust has been established may be regarded as fulfilled before the specified termination date. In such a case, a court upon petition by the trustee or beneficiary may decree a termination of the trust. A court will usually decree a trust terminated if the beneficiary acquires legal title to the trust assets, but courts will not order the termination of a trust simply because all of the beneficiaries petition the court to do so. The court will be governed by the purposes set forth in the trust instrument by the settlor, not by the wishes of the beneficiaries.

Cases

Creation of a Constructive Trust

BALLARD v. LANCE

(1969) 6 N.C.App. 24, 169 S.E.2d 199.

The Court found the following facts:

Beulah Lance died 19 July 1967 as a result of an airplane crash in Henderson County, North Carolina; she left surviving her seven infant grandchildren, namely, Michael Lance, Jackie Lance, Linda Lance, Douglas Lance, Frank Lance, Calvin Lance and Dawn Lance; prior to boarding the aircraft, Beulah purchased a contract of insurance with Mutual of Omaha Insurance Company in the amount of $40,000.00;

proof of claim has been made and said $40,000.00 has been paid to the plaintiff, Frankie Surrett Ballard, as guardian of Linda Lance and Douglas Lance; at the time of purchase of the insurance, Beulah Lance was in the presence of her daughter, Blanche Shuler, and stated, "there is not enough room to put all of the grandchildren on the insurance policy, and I'll just put on Linda and Doug. If anything happens to me, be sure and tell Frankie that half of it is to be for Linda and Doug and the rest of it is to be divided between the grandchildren"; that "Frankie" was the plaintiff, Frankie Surrett Ballard, and that Linda and Doug are the infant plaintiffs; after the policy was issued and the above statements made, Beulah Lance put the policy in an envelope and gave it to Blanche Shuler, who thereafter took the policy and gave it to Frankie Surrett Ballard. Beulah Lance had another grandchild, Martin Shuler, who accompanied her on the aircraft and came to his death in the air crash. He was the only child of Blanche Shuler, daughter of Beulah Lance.

The trial court made conclusions of law to the effect that the testimony of Blanche Shuler was competent; by virtue of the oral statement of Beulah Lance and her relationship to the parties to the action, a trust arose by operation of law and the two named beneficiaries in the insurance policy hold the proceeds of said policy as trustees for themselves and the other five minor defendants in the action in accordance with the terms of the oral statement. The court further concluded that the plaintiff, Frankie Surrett Ballard, as guardian of Linda Lance and Douglas Lance, holds the $40,000.00 proceeds of the insurance policy as trustee for her two children Linda Lance and Douglas Lance to the extent of 50% of the balance remaining after payment of the court costs, including reasonable counsel fees; that the remaining 50% of said balance should be paid to the other grandchildren (children of other children of Beulah Lance) as follows: 10% to Mary Lacy Byrd, Guardian of Frank Lance; 10% to Mary Lacy Byrd, Guardian of Calvin Lance; 10% to Mary Lacy Byrd, Guardian of Michael Lance; 10% to Mary Lacy Byrd, Guardian of Jackie Lance; 10% to Mary Lacy Byrd, Guardian of Dawn Lance.

* * *

CAMPBELL, J.
* * *
The second question presented by this appeal is whether the oral statement made by Beulah Lance at the time she filled out the application for the insurance policy created a trust in favor of the grandchildren who were not specifically named in the application and who were children of Beulah Lance's other children.

Judge Martin found as a fact, upon competent evidence, "that Beulah Lance stated at the time the insurance policy was issued that 'there was not enough room to put all of the grandchildren on the insurance policy, and I'll just put on Linda and Doug. If anything happens to me, be sure and tell Frankie that half of it is to be for Linda and Doug and the rest of it is to be divided between the Grandchildren.' "

A trust may be created although there is no mention of a trust in the policy. The fact that the trustees, namely, Linda and Doug, are under age does not affect the trust, and it remains enforceable despite their minority. [Citation.]

The mere fact that the proceeds are not payable until the death of the insured does not make the disposition testamentary. An insurance trust will be upheld even though it has not been executed with the formality necessary to constitute a will. G.S. § 36–53 provides:

"*Interest of trustee as beneficiary of policy sufficient to support inter vivos trust.*— The interest of a trustee as the beneficiary of a life insurance policy is a sufficient property interest or res to support the creation of an inter vivos trust notwithstanding the fact that the insured or any other person or persons reserves or has the right or power to exercise any one or more of the following rights or powers:

(1) To change the beneficiary,

(2) To surrender the policy and receive the cash surrender value,

(3) To borrow from the insurance company issuing the said policy or elsewhere using the said policy as collateral security,

(4) To assign the said policy, or

(5) To exercise any other right in connection with the said policy commonly known as an incident of ownership thereof. (1957, c. 1444, s. 1.)"

In Cooney v. Montana, 347 Mass. 29,

196 N.E.2d 202, a man took out a policy of life insurance for $10,000.00 with a double indemnity feature in case of death by accident. The policy named his sister as beneficiary. The sister agreed to pay $5,000.00 to one child, $2,500.00 to another, and the balance after paying the funeral expenses to a third child. The insured was accidentally killed. The court held that the entire $20,000.00 should be divided proportionately among the three children. The sister was not allowed to keep any of the proceeds, and there was not a resulting trust of the extra $10,000.00.

In the case of In re Koziell's Trust, 412 Pa. 348, 194 A.2d 230, the insured had an insurance policy naming his wife as beneficiary. He and his wife separated, and the insured changed the beneficiary in the policy from the wife to his sister without telling his sister. At the time of making the change, he stated that his reason for doing so was that he did not wish his wife to have the proceeds from the policy, and that his sister would take care of his two minor children. After the death and the collection of the proceeds of the policy, the sister claimed the money personally. The Pennsylvania Court held that a parol trust of personal property was perfectly all right, and that the insurance proceeds were impressed with the trust even though the new beneficiary did not know about the trust. To the same effect, see Ballard v. Ballard, Tex.Civ.App., 296 S.W.2d 811 where the Texas court held that a parol trust of an insurance policy proceeds was perfectly valid.

In the case *sub judice* [before the court], we have a situation where the trust relationship is created at the inception of the policy. Only two of the beneficiaries could be named in the space provided, and accordingly Beulah Lance at that time stated that all of her grandchildren were to share in the proceeds.

* * *

If Linda Lance and Douglas Lance were to retain all of the proceeds of the insurance policy as contended for by the plaintiff, the result would be contrary to the wishes of their grandmother, Beulah Lance, at the time she took out the insurance policy, and they would be unjustly enriched. In BOGERT TRUSTS AND TRUSTEES, 2d ed. § 471, p. 8, we find this quotation from Cardozo, C. J.:

"'A constructive trust is the formula through which the conscience of equity finds expression. When property has been acquired in such circumstances that the holder of the legal title may not in good conscience retain the beneficial interest, equity converts him into a trustee. * * * A court of equity in decreeing a constructive trust is bound by no unyielding formula. The equity of the transaction must shape the measure of relief.'"

BOGERT goes on to quote from Dean Roscoe Pound as follows:

"Another learned writer has referred to this trust as 'specific restitution of a received benefit in order to prevent unjust enrichment.'" * * *

Affirmed.

Constructive Trusts

SHARP v. KOSMALSKI

(1976) 40 N.Y.2d 119, 351 N.E.2d 721.

GABRIELLI, J.

Plaintiff commenced this action to impose a constructive trust upon property transferred to defendant on the ground that the retention of the property and the subsequent ejection of the plaintiff therefrom was in violation of a relationship of trust and confidence and constituted unjust enrichment. The Trial Judge dismissed plaintiff's complaint and his decision was affirmed without opinion by the Appellate Division.

Upon the death of his wife of 32 years, plaintiff, a 56-year-old dairy farmer whose education did not go beyond the eighth grade, developed a very close relationship with defendant, a school teacher and a woman 16 years his junior. Defendant assisted plaintiff in disposing of his wife's belongings, performed certain domestic tasks for him such as ironing his shirts and was a frequent companion of the plaintiff. Plaintiff came to depend upon defendant's companionship and, eventually, declared his love for her, proposing marriage to her. Notwithstanding her refusal of his proposal of marriage, defendant continued her association with plaintiff and permitted him to shower her with many gifts, fanning his hope that he could induce defendant to alter her decision concerning his marriage proposal. Defendant was given access to plaintiff's bank account, from which it is not denied that she withdraw substantial amounts of money. Eventually, plaintiff made a will naming defendant as his sole beneficiary and executed a deed naming her a joint owner of his farm. The record reveals that numerous alterations in the way of modernization were made to plaintiff's farmhouse in alleged furtherance of "domestic plans" made by plaintiff and defendant.

In September 1971 while the renovations were still in progress, plaintiff transferred his remaining joint interest to defendant. At the time of the conveyance, a farm liability policy was issued to plaintiff naming defendant and her daughter as additional insureds. Furthermore, the insurance agent was requested by plaintiff, in the presence of defendant, to change the policy to read "J. Rodney Sharp, life tenant. Jean C. Kosmalski, owner." In February 1973 the liaison between the parties was abruptly severed as defendant ordered plaintiff to move out of his home and vacate the farm. Defendant took possession of the home, the farm and all the equipment thereon, leaving plaintiff with assets of $300.

Generally, a constructive trust may be imposed "[w]hen property has been ac-

quired in such circumstances that the holder of the legal title may not in good conscience retain the beneficial interest" (Beatty v. Guggenheim Exploration Co., 225 N.Y. 380, 386, 122 N.E. 378, 380; 1 Scott, Trusts [3d ed.], § 44.2, p. 337; 4 Pomeroy's Equity Jurisprudence [5th ed.], § 1053, p. 119). In the development of the doctrine of constructive trust as a remedy available to courts of equity, the following four requirements were posited: (1) a confidential or fiduciary relation, (2) a promise, (3) a transfer in reliance thereon and (4) unjust enrichment. [Citations.]

Most frequently, it is the existence of a confidential relationship which triggers the equitable considerations leading to the imposition of a constructive trust. [Citation.] Although no marital or other family relationship is present in this case, such is not essential for the existence of a confidential relation (see Muller v. Sobol, 277 App.Div. 884, 97 N.Y.S.2d 905 [meretricious relationship]; Bogert, op. cit., § 482, pp. 136–147; 1 Scott, op. cit., p. 339). The record in this case clearly indicates that a relationship of trust and confidence did exist between the parties and, hence, the defendant must be charged with an obligation not to abuse the trust and confidence placed in her by the plaintiff. The disparity in education between the plaintiff and defendant highlights the degree of dependence of the plaintiff upon the trust and honor of the defendant.

Unquestionably, there is a transfer of property here, but the Trial Judge found that the transfer was made "without a promise or understanding of any kind." Even without an express promise, however, courts of equity have imposed a constructive trust upon property transferred in reliance upon a confidential relationship. In such a situation, a promise may be implied or inferred from the very transaction itself. As Judge Cardozo so eloquently observed: "Though a promise in words was lacking, the whole transaction, it might be found, was 'instinct with an obligation' imperfectly expressed." [Citations.] In deciding that a formal writing or express promise was not essential to the application of the doctrine of constructive trust, Judge Cardozo further observed in language that is most fitting in the instant case:

"Here was a man transferring to his sister the only property he had in the world . . . He was doing this, as she admits, in reliance upon her honor. Even if we were to accept her statement that there was no distinct promise to hold for his benefit, the exaction of such a promise, in view of the relation, might well have seemed to be superfluous" (Sinclair v. Purdy, supra, 235 N.Y. p. 254, 139 N.E. p. 258).

More recently, in Farano v. Stephanelli (7 A.D.2d 420, 425, 183 N.Y.S.2d 707, 713, supra), Chief Judge Breitel, then writing for the Appellate Division, First Department, followed the *Sinclair* approach stating that the decision to invoke the remedy of constructive trust "need not be determined exclusively by whether or not the defendant daughters expressed in so many words a promise to reconvey the properties to the father if he should ask." Indeed, in the case before us, it is inconceivable that plaintiff would convey all of his interest in property which was not only his abode but the very means of his livelihood without at least tacit consent upon the part of the defendant that she would permit him to continue to live on and operate the farm. I would therefore reject the Trial Judge's conclusion, erroneously termed a finding of fact, that no agreement or limitation may, as a matter of law, be implied from the circumstances surrounding the transfer of plaintiff's farm.

The salutary purpose of the constructive trust remedy is to prevent unjust enrichment and it is to this requirement that I now turn. The Trial Judge in his findings of fact, concluded that the transfer did not constitute unjust enrichment. In this instance also, a legal conclusion was mistakenly labeled a finding of fact. A person may be deemed to be unjustly enriched if he (or she) has received a benefit, the retention of which would be unjust (Restatement, Restitution, § 1, Comment *a*). A conclusion that one has been unjustly enriched is essentially a legal inference drawn from the circumstances surrounding the transfer of property and the relationship of the parties. It is a conclusion reached through the application of principles of equity. Having determined that the relationship between plaintiff and defendant in this case is of such a nature as to invoke consideration of the equitable remedy of constructive trust, it remains to be determined whether defendant's conduct following the transfer of plaintiff's farm was in violation of that relationship and, consequently, resulted in the unjust enrichment of the defendant. This must be determined from the circumstances of the transfer since there is no express promise concerning plaintiff's continued use of the land. Therefore, the case should be remitted to the Appellate Division for a review of the facts. In so doing I would emphasize that the conveyance herein should be interpreted "not literally or irrespective of its setting, but sensibly and broadly with all its human implications." [Citation.] This case seems to present the classic example of a situation where equity should intervene to scrutinize a transaction pregnant with opportunity for abuse and unfairness. It was for just this type of case that there evolved equitable principles and remedies to prevent injustices. Equity still lives. To suffer the hands of equity to be bound by misnamed "findings of fact" which are actually conclusions of law and legal inferences drawn from the facts is to ignore and render impotent the rich and vital impact of equity on the common law and, perforce, permit injustice. Universality of law requires equity.

Accordingly, the order of the Appellate

Division should be reversed and the case remitted to that court for a review of the facts, or, if it be so advised, in its discretion, to order a new trial in the interests of justice.

*Constructive and
Resulting Trusts*

MESKELL v. MESKELL

(1969) 355 Mass. 148, 243 N.E.2d 804.

SPALDING, J.

From interlocutory decrees sustaining the defendant's demurrer to the plaintiff's bill and denying his motion to amend, the plaintiff appealed. He also appealed from the final decree dismissing his bill.

* * *

2. We turn to the first ground, which alleges that the bill failed to state a case for equitable relief. The bill, according to the plaintiff, seeks to etablish a resulting trust in certain real estate * * *.

The allegations as to this aspect of the bill are as follows: In 1943 the plaintiff, his sister Mary, and his two brothers, Thomas and Edward, each inherited a one-quarter undivided interest in the family homestead. Thereafter the three brothers agreed to sign over their interests to Mary, who in turn agreed that the brothers could continue to live in the house as long as they lived. The four children conveyed the property to a straw, who then gave a deed back to Mary, the oldest surviving child, and Edward, the youngest, as joint tenants. The plaintiff believed that Mary was the sole owner and did not know of the joint ownership. Mary and Thomas died in 1958 and 1961, respectively. Thereafter the plaintiff did minor repairs on the premises after receiving assurances from Edward that the plaintiff owned half the house. After Edward's death in 1966 the plaintiff learned that in 1961 Edward had placed the real estate in the names of himself and his wife as tenants by the entirety. The defendant, Edward's wife, now claims to be the sole owner of this property.

The bill's allegations are not sufficient to prove the existence of a resulting trust. A resulting trust typically arises when a transfer of property is made to one person and the purchase price is paid by another; in such a case a trust results in favor of the person who furnished the consideration. [Citations.] The case at bar, however, is distinguishable, since the plaintiff voluntarily transferred an undivided interest in the realty itself, not money. By the great weight of authority no resulting trust arises in these circumstances. For example, in Howe v. Howe, 199 Mass. 598, 602, 85 N.E. 945, 947, we said that a resulting trust "cannot be implied when the conveyance is voluntary, without the payment of any purchase price." No resulting trust arises in a transfer from A to B merely because the transfer was gratuitous, even if B orally promised to hold the land in trust. Restatement 2d: Trusts, § 411, comment *o*. Scott, Trusts (3d ed.) § 411.8.

It remains to consider whether there was a constructive trust. See Restatement 2d: Trusts, §§ 44(1) and 411, comment *o*. Such a trust is imposed "in order to avoid the unjust enrichment of one party at the expense of the other where the legal title to the property was obtained by *fraud* or *in violation of a fiduciary relation* or arose where information confidentially given or acquired was used to the advantage of the recipient at the expense of the one who disclosed the information" (emphasis supplied). Barry v. Covich, 332 Mass. 338, 342, 124 N.E.2d 921, 924. See Restatement 2d: Trusts, § 44(1). The fraud required to create a constructive trust must occur at the time the property was transferred; a subsequent refusal to carry out an oral promise, standing by itself, is not fraud. [Citations.] The plaintiff's allegations are not sufficient to show that at the time of the transfer either Edward or Mary did not intend to carry out the promise.

The allegations also do not show that there was a violation of a fiduciary or confidential relationship. "Mere respect for the judgment of another or trust in his character is not enough to constitute * * * a [confidential] relation." Comstock v. Livingston, 210 Mass. 581, 584, 97 N.E. 106, 108. The allegations show that the three brothers and Mary agreed that they all could live on the premises as long as they lived. According to some authorities, this by itself might have been sufficient to establish a confidential relationship between the plaintiff and Edward since such a relationship exists when, "because of family relationship or otherwise, the transferor is in fact accustomed to be guided by the judgment of the transferee or is justified in placing confidence in the belief that the transferee will act in the interest of the transferor." Restatement 2d: Trusts, § 44, comment c. But under our decisions a confidential relationship does not arise merely because the conveyance was made between members of the family, even if the transferee promised to hold the land in trust. [Citation.] * * * We therefore hold that the allegations are not sufficient to establish either a constructive or a resulting trust in the real estate.

* * *

[Affirmed.]

Charitable Trust

WESLEY UNITED METHODIST CHURCH v. HARVARD COLLEGE

(1974, Mass.), 316 N.E.2d 620.

TAURO, C. J.

This is a bill in equity brought by the board of trustees of the Wesley United Methodist Church, as trustees under a charitable trust created by the will of one Harold E. Colson, seeking modification of the terms of the trust under the doctrine of cy pres. * * * The sole heirs at law of Harold E.

Colson, Harold C. Guppy, Sr., and Mary F. Smith, contend that the doctrine of cy pres is inapplicable and that a resulting trust should be declared in their favor. The Probate Court granted the plaintiff the requested relief, and the heirs at law have appealed. We affirm.

The case is before us on a statement of agreed material facts which may be summarized as follows. Harold E. Colson died on December 28, 1968. His will, executed in September, 1957, contained the following provision: "Fourth: All the rest, residue and remainder of my estate, of whatsoever kind and wheresoever situate, I give, devise and bequeath unto Wesley Methodist Church Salem, Massachusetts, to be used by the Board of Trustees of said church to establish a fund to be designated as the 'Frances L. Colson Memorial Scholarship Fund' and both the principal and income of such fund shall be used by said Board of Trustees to provide one five-hundred dollar scholarship each year to assist one worthy male member of the congregation or communicant of said church, to be selected each year at the discretion of said Board of Trustees, to attend Harvard College, Cambridge, Massachusetts for undergraduate education. In the event that the annual income from said fund shall exceed five hundred dollars, then the income in excess of that required for the scholarship above referred to shall be accumulated until such excess income exceeds the sum of five hundred dollars, at which time said Board of Trustees may, at its discretion, provide a second five-hundred-dollar scholarship, subject to the qualifications and limitations as above provided."

Frances L. Colson was the testator's mother. Both she and the testator had been members of the Wesley United Methodist Church, he having joined on December 29, 1907. When his will was executed in September, 1957, the decedent had a small estate, with modest investment in United States Savings Bonds. In time, his net worth increased significantly, and as of July

11, 1972, the funds given to the Wesley United Methodist Church for trust purposes exceeded $55,000, producing an annual income approximating $3,200.

To date, the church has given out no scholarships. In fact, it has not even received any applications from students or prospective students. It has only 236 members, most of whom are adults. The tuition charge at Harvard College has risen substantially since 1957, and as of 1973 was $2,600 a year. In 1957 the college did not admit women, but it does today.

The Probate Court found that "the express terms of the trust * * * are literally impracticable of operation in limiting the beneficiaries to male members or communicants of Wesley Methodist Church," and that "the testator's intention to provide scholarships for students attending Harvard College as a memorial for his mother may be fulfilled to promote and accomplish the general charitable intent of the testator under the application of cy pres." It was ordered that "the Board of Trustees of the Petitioner apply income and accumulations of the trust fund in the awarding of annual scholarships, in their discretion, unlimited in amount, to worthy male or female applicants, not restricted to members or communicants of the petitioner if there are no such applicants, for undergraduate or graduate education in Harvard University."

The defendant heirs at law argue that both the findings as to impracticability and general charitable intent are erroneous. Each is a necessary element for the application of the cy pres doctrine: "Where property is given in trust for a particular charitable purpose, and it is impossible or impracticable to carry out that purpose, the trust does not fail if the testator has a more general intention to devote the property to charitable purposes. In such a case the property will be applied under the direction of the court to some charitable purpose falling within the general intention of the testator." Scott, Abridgment of the Law of

Trusts, § 399.2 (1960). [Citations.] Cy pres will not apply, however, if the trust remains capable of meaningful application, or if, despite impracticability, there is a lack of general charitable intent on the testator's part. In the latter situation, "* * * in the absence of any limitation over or other provision, the legacy lapses." Rogers v. Attorney Gen., supra, 347 Mass. at 131, 196 N.E.2d at 860. * * *

We hold that the Probate Court's findings were warranted and the decree was not erroneous. It is true, as the respondent heirs argue, that the Colson trust is theoretically capable of application, in that (1) a male undergraduate student at Harvard might at some point in the future join the Wesley United Methodist Church; (2) an adult male member of the church might himself enroll at the college, or (3) eligible male children might be born to the present predominantly adult membership. Nevertheless, it is clear that literal compliance with the terms of the trust is now preventing, and will most likely continue to prevent, any use of the funds. Of the 236 members, only a portion are males, and most of them are adult, past college age. It is obvious that the Wesley United Methodist Church, in bringing this suit, sees very few or even no present or prospective scholarship applicants among that slim percentage of its congregation that is even eligible under the terms of the trust. This and other courts have found impracticability where a present and probably continuing lack of specified beneficiaries serves effectively to freeze disbursement of charitable funds. * * * We believe that in the instant case, in view of the size and character of the Wesley United Methodist Church membership, the Probate Court was correct in its finding that the Frances L. Colson trust is impracticable.

Moreover, we believe that the settlor displayed a general charitable intent, as distinguished from an intent "limited to * * * a specific charitable purpose."

Rogers v. Attorney Gen., 347 Mass. 126, 131, 196 N.E.2d 855, 860 (1964). * * *

We are satisfied that the settlor would have wished that the funds be applied to a like charitable purpose rather than be removed from charitable use entirely. The applicable provision establishes a $500 scholarship in his mother's name to assist "one worthy male member of the congregation or communicant of * * * [the Wesley United Methodist] church, to be selected each year at the discretion of * * * [the] Board of Trustees, to attend Harvard College * * * for undergraduate education." While "[t]he class whom * * * [the testator] sought to benefit is narrowly circumscribed," Rogers v. Attorney Gen., supra, at 133, 196 N.E.2d at 861, that fact alone does not preclude a finding that the testator was motivated by broader, overriding charitable considerations. * * *

Decree affirmed.

Problems

1. In each of the following situations state whether or not a trust is created.

(a) A declares himself trustee of "the bulk of my securities" in trust for B.

(b) A, the owner of Blackacre, purports to convey to B in trust for C "a small part" of Blackacre.

(c) A orders B, a stockbroker, to buy a thousand shares of American Steel or any part thereof at par. After the broker has bought five hundred shares but before A knows whether any shares have been bought for him, A declares himself trustee for C of such shares of American Steel as A has bought.

(d) A owns ten bonds. He declares himself trustee, for B, of such five of the bonds as B may select at any time within a month.

(e) A deposits $1000 in a savings bank. He declares himself trustee of the deposit in trust to pay B $500 out of the deposit, reserving the power to withdraw from the deposit any amounts not in excess of $500.

2. In 1967, A executed a trust agreement providing that the trust corpus of $200,000 was to be held by B, as trustee, for the benefit of A's children, C and D, aged 7 and 9, respectively. The agreement further provided that B was to invest the corpus in stocks and bonds and accumulate all income from those investments until C and D reached age 25, at which time the trust was to terminate and the property distributed to C and D, share and share alike. In 1981 B dies. D who was then 23 years of age and madly in love with Neromina, a dancer, brought an action to terminate the trust and to obtain his share of the trust. His complaint alleged that the trust must terminate because of B's death. Decision?

3. The following provision was in A's will:

"To the Solid Trust Company with the sure knowledge that it will expend the funds for the maintenance, education and comfort of my grandniece Sally."

The Solid Trust Co. brings a suit to have the will construed to determine whether or not a valid trust is established. Decision?

4. Testator gives property to T in trust for B's benefit, providing that B cannot anticipate the income by assignment or pledge. B borrows money from L, assigning his future income under the trust for a stated period. Can L obtain any judicial relief to prevent B from collecting this income?

5. Davis conveyed all of his assets to Gibralter Trust Company in trust to pay only such amounts of income to Davis as it determines in its absolute discretion during Davis's life and upon his death, to distribute the trust corpus and undistributed income to Davis's daughter, Mary. After the trust had been created, Davis became indebted to Putnam, who recovered a judgment against him for $10,000.

Can Putnam reach any interest of Davis in the trust?

6. Collins was trustee for Indolent under the will of Indolent's father. Indolent, a middle-aged doctor, gave little concern to the management of the trust fund, contenting himself with receiving the income paid him by the trustee. Among the assets of the trust were 100 shares of ABC Corporation and 100 shares of XYZ Corporation. About two years before the termination of the trust Collins, at a fair price and after full explanation to Indolent, purchased from the trust the ABC stock. At the same time, but without saying anything to Indolent, he purchased the XYZ stock at a price in excess of its then market value. At the termination of the trust both stocks had advanced in market value well beyond the prices paid by Collins, and Indolent demanded that Collins either account for this advance in the value of both stocks, or replace the stocks. What are Indolent's rights?

7. Joe Brown on September 1, 1972, furnished to his wife Mary Brown $35,000 with which to buy real property. It was orally agreed between them that title to the real property should be taken in the name of Mary Brown, but that she should hold the same in trust for Joe Brown. There were two witnesses to the oral agreement, both of whom are now living. On the following day the property was purchased and a deed to it with Mary Brown as the grantee was delivered and duly recorded.

Mary died on October 5, 1981, without a will. The real property is now worth $100,000. Joe Brown is claiming the property as the beneficiary of a trust. Mary's children are claiming that the property belongs to Mary's estate and have pleaded the Statute of Limitations and the Statute of Frauds as defenses to the claim of Joe. There is no evidence one way or the other as to whether Mary would have conveyed the property to Joe during her lifetime if she had been requested to do so.

What are Joe's ownership rights to this particular real property?

8. Plaintiff was married to Arnold Gerstenschlager in 1978 and divorced from him in 1980. During their marriage, plaintiff and Arnold acquired a parcel of real estate as tenants by the entireties. Subsequent to the divorce, Arnold in 1980 executed a quitclaim deed to the plaintiff, conveying all of his interest in the real estate to her. In May 1981 plaintiff deeded the real estate back to Arnold to hold in trust for her pending her divorce from her then husband, Paul Rivers. Plaintiff alleged that Arnold promised to re-convey the real estate to her on demand. This action was brought when Arnold failed to re-convey. Decision?

Chapter

51

WILLS, INTESTATE SUCCESSION, AND ADMINISTRATION OF DECEDENTS' ESTATES

The assets of a person who dies leaving a valid will are to be distributed according to the directions contained in the will. If he dies without leaving a will, his property will pass to his heirs and next of kin in the proportions provided in the applicable state statute. This is known as intestate (dying without a will) succession. If a person dies without a will and leaves no heirs or next of kin, his property escheats (reverts) to the state.

There is one major characteristic of a will which sets it apart from other transactions such as deeds and contracts: A will is revocable at any time during life. There is no such thing as an irrevocable will. A document binding during life may be a contract (such as a promise to make a will) or a deed (conveying a vested remainder after a life estate in the grantor) but it is not a will. A will takes effect only upon and not until the death of the testator.

Whether a will is looked upon as an inalienable right or a privilege the fact remains that the execution of a will is, in a large sense, a moral responsibility and one too frequently ignored or forgotten by persons who own property. It is indeed a strange fact that persons who exercise the most extreme caution over their affairs during life neglect to execute a will, thereby allowing the State, by default, to direct who shall inherit their property.

WILLS

In August, 1969, the National Conference of Commissioners on Uniform State Laws and the American Bar Association approved the Uniform Probate Code (UPC), an extraordinary attempt to encourage throughout the United States, in the face of widespread criticism of the present American probate institution, the adoption of a uniform, flexible, speedy, efficient, and, in most cases, less expensive system of settling a decedent's estate. The UPC is based on the major premise that the probate court's appropriate role is to be available to assist in the settlement of an estate when assistance is requested or required rather than to impose its unsolicited supervision to enforce

INSURANCE, TRUSTS, AND WILLS

every detailed formality upon completely non-contentious settlements. As of September 1, 1981, fourteen states had enacted the Uniform Probate Code, namely, Alaska, Arizona, Colorado, Idaho, Maine, Michigan, Minnesota, Montana, Nebraska, New Jersey, New Mexico, North Dakota, Pennsylvania, and Utah.

In the following discussion of decedents' estates, principles and procedures are summarized generally with a notation of the parallel principles and procedures under the UPC.

Mental Capacity

Testamentary Capacity and Power. Two qualifications are necessary for a person to be able to make a valid disposition of his property at death. In order to make a valid will, the testator must have both the "power" and the "capacity" to do so. Both of these terms refer to restrictions imposed by statute or court decision but each has a distinct and separate meaning. The power to make a will is granted by the State to persons who are of a class believed generally able to handle their affairs without regard to personal limitations. Thus, in most States, children under a certain age cannot make valid wills.

The capacity to make a will refers to the limits placed upon particular persons in the class generally granted the power to make wills because of personal mental deficiencies. The will of an insane adult is invalid because he lacks the capacity to make a will. Since capacity is a personal matter it is not easy to set down any test which will, in all cases, measure this qualification. A person adjudged insane can, in a lucid period, make a valid will. An aged and enfeebled octogenarian may have the capacity to execute a will. If one rule appears clear, it is that it takes less in the way of mental qualities to meet the test of capacity to make a will than is required for the independent management of one's affairs during lifetime. A deed from X to Y may

be set aside because of the incompetence of X, although X may validly leave the same property to Y by will. Proof that the testator held beliefs not accepted by society in general will not impinge upon his capacity.

Underlying the notion of capacity is the premise that, in order to be valid, a testator must *intend* a document to be his will. This requisite intent will be lacking if he is insane or suffers from delusions just as intent is presumed to be lacking in persons below the age at which persons generally are given the power to make wills.

Under the UPC, any person eighteen or more years of age who is of sound mind may make a will. Section 2–501.

Undue Influence, Fraud, and Mistake. The requisite testamentary intent must always be present in order to create a valid will. Any document purporting to be a will that reflects an intent other than the testator's is not a valid will. This is the basis for the rule that a will which transmits property as a result of undue influence or a fraud is no will at all. What constitutes "undue influence" cannot be generally defined. Certainly, a wife can urge her husband to leave all his property to her and, out of love and affection, he will probably accede. This influence is not "undue." Nor is a general influence over the testator sufficient to make a case of improper pressure. The influence must be directed specifically to the act of making the will. Most frequently, the charge of undue influence is made when a testator leaves his property to a person who is not a blood relative, such as a friend who took care of the testator in his last illness or during his last years.

If the evidence demonstrates that the beneficiary under the will was in close contact with the testator and that natural objects of his bounty are ignored in the will, there is a suggestion of undue influence.

The charge of fraud is similar. For example, A dies leaving all his property to B upon the representation by B that he is

A's long lost son. B in fact is not A's son. In such a case, the will may be set aside because the misrepresentation was made with the intent to deceive and that A rely upon it. Fraud sufficient to set aside a will also exists where a mother dies willing all her property to one of two daughters because the daughter who takes under the will falsely represented to the mother that the other daughter was scheming to have the mother committed to an institution. The burden of proving fraud rests upon those who make the allegation.

The law is generally not as ready to invalidate or partially revise a will because of mistake as it is to adjust a contract based on an error. A mistake as to the identity of the instrument voids a will. But a stenographic error or a mistake in drafting may be corrected by clear evidence of the testator's intent.

Formal Requirements of a Will

By statute in all jurisdictions, a will to be valid must comply with certain formalities. These are necessary not only to indicate that the testator understood what he was doing but, also, to help prevent fraud.

Writing. A basic requirement to a valid will is that it be in writing. The only notable exceptions are found in statutes permitting oral wills by soldiers and sailors and, less frequently, in statutes validating oral wills of personal property made on death bed or in extremis.

Under the UPC every will must be in writing to be effective. Section 2–502.

The writing may be informal so long as the basic formalities required by the statute are substantially met. Pencil, ink, and mimeograph are equally valid methods and valid wills have been made on scratch paper or on an envelope.

It is also valid to incorporate into a will by reference another document which in itself is not a will for lack of proper execution.

To incorporate a memorandum in a will by reference, the following four conditions must exist: (1) it must be in writing; (2) it must be in existence when the will is executed; (3) it must be adequately described in the will; and (4) it must be described in the will as being in existence. In an Illinois case, T died leaving a will which left the residue of his substantial estate in trust "to be held by the trustee for such charities" as T "shall designate to his trustee." No charities were named in the will. However, after execution of the will, T named the charities in a memorandum. The court held that the intended trust failed. In short, although a memorandum may be used to assist in the identification of beneficiaries named in the will, it may not be used as evidence to supply omitted beneficiaries. A memorandum, not a part of the will, cannot be used to establish the terms and conditions and the requirements of a trust not set forth in the will itself. Phelps v. La Moille, 52 Ill.App.2d 164, 201 N.E.2d 634.

Under the UPC any writing which was in existence when a will was executed may be incorporated therein by reference if the language of the will manifests this intent and describes the writing sufficiently to permit its identification. Section 2–510.

Signature. A will must be signed by the testator. The signature verifies that the will has been executed and is a fundamental requirement in almost all jurisdictions. The initials "A. H." or "father" at the end of a will in the handwriting of the testator are adequate if intended as an execution. On the other hand, a person who makes a couple of strokes of the pen and then stops saying "I can't sign it now" has not made a valid signature.

Most statutes require the signature to be at the end of the will and, even in jurisdictions where this is not specified, careful draftsmanship will so provide to avoid the charge that the portions of a will coming after a signature were written subsequent to the execution and, therefore, without the necessary formality of a signature. Fortunately, legibility is not a prerequisite to a valid signature.

Under the UPC, every will must be signed by the testator or in the testator's name by some other person in the testator's presence and by his direction. Section 2–502.

Attestation. With the exception of a few isolated types of wills noted later that are valid in a limited number of jurisdictions, a written will must be attested by witnesses. The number and qualification of witnesses and the manner of attestation are generally set out by statute. Usually two or three witnesses are required. It is good practice to have a will attested by one more than the legal minimum number to increase the likelihood that at least the minimum will be available when the will is offered for probate. However, the signature of a witness who has predeceased the testator may be proved by a competent witness. Although a witness generally need not be a resident of or domiciled in the jurisdiction of the testator, it is expedient to have witnesses who may be easily available. Age is no barrier to a witness, provided he is generally competent, although for obvious reasons an elderly person may be a risky witness from an actuarial point of view.

The function of witnesses is to acknowledge that the testator did execute the will and that he had the requisite intent and capacity. It is important that the testator sign first in the presence of all the witnesses, and it is usually essential that each witness sign in his presence and in the presence of one another.

Under the UPC, every will must be signed by at least two persons each of whom witnessed either the signing or the testator's acknowledgment of the will. Section 2–502.

The most common restriction is that a witness must not have any interest under the will. This requirement takes at least two forms under statutes. One type of statute disqualifies a witness who is also a beneficiary under the will. The other type voids the bequest or devise to the interested witness thereby making him a disinterested and qualified witness. What constitutes an "interest" sufficient to disqualify a witness is not always easily defined. The spouse of a beneficiary under a will has been held to be "interested" and thus not qualified. Generally, a person is not disqualified simply because he is named as executor in the will. The attorney who drafts the will is generally a qualified witness. A member of a church named as a beneficiary or a shareholder of a corporate executor or trustee under a will is not so "interested" as to be disqualified. In all cases, however, caution should dictate that the witnesses have no connection with persons or institutions entitled to share under a will.

Under the UPC, no will or any provision thereof is invalid because the will was attested by an interested witness. Section 2–505.

Publication. It is sometimes said that a testator must declare that a document is his Last Will and Testament and that this should take the form of an oral declaration to the witnesses. This idea stems from the concept that there must be "publication" of a will. It is generally an unnecessary formality. Under the UPC, there is no requirement that the testator publish the will.

Revocation of a Will

By definition, a will is revocable by the testator. Under certain circumstances, a will may be revoked by operation of law. This does not mean that certain formalities are not necessary to effect a revocation. In most jurisdictions, the methods by which a will is revoked are specified by statute. These methods fall into the following classes:

Destruction or Alteration of the Will.
Tearing, burning, or otherwise destroying
a will is a strong sign that the testator intended to revoke it and, in the absence of
a showing that the destruction was inad-
vertent, is an effective way of revoking a
will. In some States, partial revocation of
a will may be accomplished by erasure or
obliteration of a part thereof. In no case,
however, will a substituted or additional
bequest by interlineation be effective without re-execution and re-attestation.

Under the UPC, a will is revoked by
being burned, torn, cancelled, obliterated,
or destroyed with the intent and for the purpose of revoking it by the testator or by another person in his presence and by his direction. Section 2–507.

Later Will. The execution of a second will
does not in itself constitute a revocation of
an earlier will. To the extent that the second will is inconsistent with the former will,
the first will is revoked. The most certain
manner of revocation is the execution of a
later will which contains a declaration that
all former wills are revoked. In some but
not all jurisdictions, a will may be revoked
by a written declaration to this effect in a
subsequent document such as a letter, even
though the document does not meet the formal requirements of a will.

Under the UPC, a will is revoked by a
subsequent will which revokes the prior will
or part thereof expressly or by inconsistency. Section 2–507.

Operation of Law. A marriage generally
revokes a will executed prior to the marriage. This rule of law is based partly on
the reasonable presumption that a person's
intention with respect to his property change
with marriage, even though he may neglect
to alter a prior will, and partly on the belief
that marrige imposes new moral obligations
which should not be impaired by a will executed before marriage. Divorce, under
the general rule, does not revoke a provision

in the will of one of the parties for the benefit of the other party.

Under the UPC, a divorce or annulment
which occurs after the execution of a will
revokes any disposition of property made by
the will to the former spouse. No change
of circumstances other than divorce or annulment revokes a will. Thus a subsequent marriage or marriage plus the birth
of issue does not revoke a will. Section
2–508. However, if the spouse marries the
testator after the execution of the will, she
is, with certain limitations, entitled to the
same share as though the testator died
without a will. Section 2–301.

After-Born Children. The birth of a child
after execution of a will may revoke a will
at least as far as that child is concerned if
it appears that the testator omitted to make
a provision for the child.

Statutory provisions are frequently to
the effect that unless provision is made in
a will for a child of the testator born after
the will is made or unless it appears by the
will that it was the intention of the testator
to disinherit the child, the child is entitled
to receive the portion of the estate to which
he would be entitled if the testator had died
intestate.

Under the UPC, the subsequent birth
of a child will not revoke the will, but the
child is entitled to the same share as though
the testator died without a will unless it
appears from the will that the omission was
intentional. Section 2–302.

*Renunciation of Will by the Surviving
Spouse.* Statutes generally provide for a
right of renunciation of the will by a surviving spouse and set forth the method of
accomplishing it. The purpose of such statutory provisions is to enable the spouse to
elect which method of taking, e.g., under
the will or under the Statute of Descent,
would be most advantageous to him or her.
Where a spouse dies owning real and personal property, the surviving spouse has an

interest in the decedent's estate which cannot be divested by will without his or her consent. The right to renounce a will may be exercised only by persons designated by the statute, and the right conferred on the surviving spouse is personal. A surviving spouse must execute and file a written renunciation of the will within the time prescribed. The right is absolute; and approval of the renunciation or its filing is not required. Upon renunciation of the will, the law determines the share of the estate taken by the surviving spouse.

Under the UPC, the surviving spouse has the right to take an elective share of one-third of the estate. Section 2-201.

Ademption and Abatement of a Bequest. In his will, A leaves $5,000 to B, $5,000 to C and "my faithful Collie, Rex" to D. At the time of A's death, after payment of his debts, there is only $5,000 in his estate and a Siamese cat by the name of Queenie, faithful Rex having been disposed of after biting his master. B and C will each receive $2,500 and D will receive nothing, Queenie going to whomever takes the residue of A's estate. The gifts to B and C are said to have abated while the gift to D, not being in existence at the time of A's death, has "adeemed."

Abatement is an occurrence generally resulting from a reduction in the value of the estate of the testator after the execution of his will. It can have serious implications. The first items which abate in a will are all the residue or remainder after provisions for specific devises and legacies. Specific gifts must be satisfied first. Thus, if John, a widower, after making specific gifts, leaves "all the rest, residue and remainder of my estate to my daughter, Mary," Mary may receive a great deal less than her deceased father intended. For example, suppose at the time John executes his will he estimates his worth at $150,000. He leaves $20,000 to his church and $20,000 to the Salvation Army and assumes that Mary will receive approximately $110,000.

John dies five years later without changing his will but having suffered substantial business and market reverses. His executor reports that there is only $50,000 in the estate. Mary will receive $10,000 less than each of the charitable bequests and only a fraction of what her father expected her to enjoy. Unless the specific bequests are small or the testator has confidence in the stability of his estate, specific bequests to persons outside his family or to institutions should be based on a percentage of the net estate of the decedent.

Ademption may not be as serious as abatement but the consequences may be regretable. It occurs when a testator neglects to change his will after changed circumstances have rendered impossible of performance a provision in the will. X buys a farm "Blackacre" and wants it to go on his death to a favorite nephew who is studying agronomy at college. After so providing in his will, he sells "Blackacre" and, with the purchase price, buys "Greenacre." The general rule is that the nephew will not be entitled to Greenacre. Ademption is always a question of trying to determine the testator's intent. Did he want the legatee or devisee to have *that* particular item and no other? If X leaves "my 200 shares of General Motors stock" to Y and at his death he has no such securities, his executor will not be authorized to purchase 200 shares and give them to Y. But, if X leaves "my 100 shares of Southern Commonwealth stock" to Y and, upon his death, he has only 50 shares of Eastern Commonwealth, Southern having merged therewith and a 1 for 2 stock reorganization having transpired, Y will be entitled to the 50 shares.

Special Types of Wills

Nuncupative Wills. A nuncupative will is an oral declaration made before witnesses without any writing. In the jurisdictions where authorized, generally it can only be made when the testator is in his last illness. Under most statutes permitting nuncupative wills only personal property may be passed by such a will. An abortive attempt to make a written will in which the testator gives oral directions generally will not be recognized as a nuncupative will. The intent must be to make a nuncupative will. Under the UPC, all wills must be in writing. Section 2–502.

Holographic Wills. In some jurisdictions, a will entirely in the handwriting of the testator is a valid testamentary document notwithstanding the fact that the will is not witnessed. Such an instrument is referred to as a holographic will. Printing of any kind on the paper will invalidate such a will. Thus, a holographic will cannot be written on a pad of paper that has even part of a date printed on it if dating is essential to a valid will in the jurisdiction. A holographic will must comply strictly with the statutory requirements for such wills.

Under the UPC, a holographic will is valid if the signature and material provisions are in the handwriting of the testator. Section 2–503.

Soldiers' and Sailors' Wills. In the case of soldiers on active service and sailors while at sea, most statutes relax the formal requirements and permit a valid testamentary disposition regardless of the informality of the document. In most jurisdictions, however, such a will cannot pass title to real estate.

Conditional Wills. A contingent or conditional will is one which takes effect as a will only on the happening of a specified contingency which is a condition precedent to the operation of the will. If a contingency is referred to in a will as a reason for making the particular disposition that is provided for, and whether a particular will is conditional or is unconditional is largely dependent upon the factual situation presented.

For example, X executed an instrument, properly witnessed, at 2:00 A.M., reading: "I am leaving for New York State this morning, and if anything should happen to me I request that everything I own, both personal and real, be given to my sister, Z." This will was held to be unconditional.

Joint Wills—Mutual or Reciprocal Wills. A joint will is one where the same instrument is made the will of two or more persons and is signed by them jointly. Mutual or reciprocal wills are the separate instruments of two or more persons, the terms being reciprocal and by which each testator makes testamentary disposition in favor of the other.

Under the UPC, the execution of a joint will or mutual wills does not create a presumption of a contract not to revoke the will or wills. Section 2–701.

Codicil to a Will

A codicil is an addition to or revision of a will, generally by a separate instrument, in which the will is expressly referred to and, in effect, incorporated into the codicil, by reference. Codicils must be executed with all the formal requirements of a will. The most frequent problem raised by codicils is the extent to which their terms, if not absolutely clear, revoke or alter provisions in the will. For the purpose of determining the testator's intent, the codicil and the will are regarded as a single instrument.

INTESTATE SUCCESSION

When a person dies, the title to his property must pass to someone. If the decedent leaves a valid will, property will pass as he directs, subject only to certain limitations imposed by the State, such as the widow's right to dower. If, however, no valid will has been executed, the decedent is said to have died "intestate" and the State prescribes who shall be entitled to the property.

The rules set forth in statutes for determining, in case of intestacy, to whom the decedent's property shall be distributed not only assure an orderly transfer of title to property but, also, purport to carry out what would probably be the wishes of the decedent.

That the rules of descent are statutory reflects the dominant principle that inheritance is a privilege granted by the sovereign and may, therefore, be regulated by it. The State may, at any time, change the rules. If A expects to be an heir of B upon the latter's death, it is within the constitutional power of the State to change the rules *before* B's death in such a way that A would not fall within the class designated as heirs. Until the death of B, A has no vested property right that the constitution will protect. Similarly, it would be legally possible, no matter how unlikely, that a State might provide that, after payment of the debts of a decedent, all his intestate property should be public property, or that intestate property should pass to persons other than the next of kin.

Property Which Descends

All vested property interest will descend to heirs. For instance, vested remainder following a life estate will pass to the heirs of the remainderman upon his death and may be possessed by his heirs upon the death of the life tenant.

Course of Descent

The rules of descent vary widely from State to State but, as a general rule, and excepting the specific statutory or dower rights of the widow, the intestate property passes in equal shares to each child of the decedent living at the time of his death, with the share of any predeceased child to be divided equally among the children of such prede-ceased child. For example, if A dies intestate leaving a widow and children, the widow generally will receive one-third of his real estate and personal property, and the remainder passes to his children in the manner stated above. If the wife does not survive A, his entire estate passes to the children. If A dies leaving surviving two children, B and C, and grandchildren, D_1 and D_2, the children of a predeceased child D, the estate will go one-third to B, one-third to C, and one-sixth each to D_1 and D_2, the grandchildren dividing equally their parent's one-third share. This result is legally described by the statement that lineal descendants of predeceased children take "by stirpes" or by representation of their parent. If A had executed a will, he may have provided that all his lineal descendants, regardless of generation, would share equally. In such case A's estate would be divided into four equal parts and his descendants would be said to take "per capita."

If no children but only the widow and other relatives survive the decedent, a larger share is generally allotted the widow. She may receive all the personal property and one-half the real estate or, in some States the entire estate.

Regardless of who the other relatives are, whether children, brothers, parents or cousins of the deceased, a surviving spouse cannot, without his or her consent, be cut off from a dower or statutory share.

At common law, property could not lineally ascend; parents of an intestate decedent did not, in any event, share in his estate. Today, in many States, if there are no lineal descendants, the statute provides that parents are the next to share.

Most statutes make some provision for brothers and sisters in the event no spouse, parents or children survive the decedent. Brothers and sisters, together with nieces, nephews, aunts and uncles are termed collateral heirs. Beyond these limits most statutes provide that, if there are no survivors of the named classes, the property shall be distributed equally among the next of kin in equal degree.

The common law did not consider a stepchild as an heir or next of kin, that is, as one to whom property would descend by operation of law, and this rule prevails today. Legally adopted children are, however, recognized as lawful heirs of their adopting parents.

These generalities should be accepted as such; few fields of the law of property are so strictly a matter of statute, and the rights of heirs cannot be reasonably predicted without a knowledge of the exact terms of the applicable statute.

Under the UPC, the surviving spouse is entitled to (1) a homestead allowance of $5,000, (2) exempt household and personal effects of a value not to exceed $3,500, and (3) a family allowance to provide for one year after death not to exceed $6,000. Sections 2–401, 2–402, 2–403 and 2–404.

Furthermore under the UPC, if the decedent dies without a will, the surviving spouse (1) is entitled to the entire estate if there is no issue and no parent surviving; (2) if there is a parent surviving, the spouse is entitled to $50,000 plus one-half of the remaining estate; (3) if there are surviving issue all of whom are issue also of the spouse, the spouse receives $50,000 plus one-half of the remaining estate; and (4) if there are surviving issue one or more of whom are not issue of the spouse, the spouse receives one-half of the estate.

The one impression that the layman should take with him from even a brief glance at the law of intestate succession is the complete abdication of his control over disposition of his property that results from the failure to execute a will. In some cases, intestacy may result from an intelligent analysis of the consequences, but most frequently when a person dies without a will he has left to the State the decision as to the disposition of his estate.

ADMINISTRATION OF ESTATES

The rules and procedures controlling the management of the estate of a deceased are statutory and therefore vary in some respect from State to State. In all jurisdictions, the estate is managed and finally disbursed under the supervision of a court. The procedure of managing the estates of decedents is referred to as "probate" and not infrequently the court which supervises the procedure is designated as the Probate Court.

Under the UPC, a highly flexible system of administration is introduced whereby the court's assistance is utilized only when requested or needed. Each step in the administration may be formal or informal; the parties may go "in-and-out" of courts as they desire; and if the parties wish, the traditional "supervised administration" of the entire estate by the court may be utilized.

The Executor or Administrator

The first legal step after death is usually to determine whether or not the deceased left a will. His personal attorney may have the will or may know that one was executed; sometimes the existence or absence of a will is not determined until after careful search of the safe deposit box and personal papers of the deceased.

If a will exists, it is probable that in it the testator named his widow, child, relative, friend or a trust company as his executor.

If there is no will, or if there is a will which fails to name an executor, the court will, upon petition, appoint an administrator. The closest adult relative who is a resident of the State is entitled to such appointment. In the event there is no one else who qualifies as administrator, a public administrator may be appointed to fill the office.

An administrator or executor is required to post a bond to insure the faithful performance of his duties, although, if a testator directs that the executor need not post bond, this will be accepted by the court in most cases. Usually, this bond is an amount in excess of the estimated value of the personal estate of the decedent. Once approved or appointed by the court, it is the executor or administrator who holds title to all the personal property of the deceased and who accounts to the creditors and the beneficiaries. The estate is his responsibility.

Under the UPC, the term "personal representative" is used to include both executor and administrator and other such persons. Section 1–201(30).

Preliminary Steps in Probate

If there is a will, it must be proved before the court by the witnesses. They will testify to the signing of the will by all signatories and as to the mental condition of the testator at the time of the execution of the will. If the witnesses are dead, proof of their handwriting is necessary. If the court is satisfied that the will is proved, a formal decree will be entered admitting the will to probate.

Proof of heirship is required whether there is a will or whether the decedent died intestate. This step requires testimony by any relative who is acquainted with the genealogy of the family as to the heirs of the decedent. This testimony is obviously necessary where there is no will in order to establish those entitled under law to the property of the decedent. If there is a will, proof of heirship is required so that heirs may be notified in order to protect their interests. By custom, in most jurisdictions, the proof of heirship is made up partly of first-hand knowledge and partly of hearsay.

Soon after the admission of the will to probate or the issuance of letters of administration, the personal representative of the decedent (i.e., the executor or administra-

tor) must file an inventory of the estate. Frequently, independent appraisers must be appointed to value the personal assets.

A bank account will be opened in the name of the estate, and the personal representative will commence his duties of collecting the assets, paying the debts and disbursing the remainder. In his position the executor or administrator occupies a fiduciary position not unlike that of a trustee and his responsibility for investing proceeds and otherwise managing the estate is equally demanding.

Creditors; Widow's Award

One of the first duties of the personal representative is to publish a notice that all claims against the decedent's estate must be filed and proved within a certain period of time. It is the duty of the personal representative to demand proof of the claims and pay those which are valid. In most jurisdictions, certain claims are entitled to priority over general creditors of the decedent. At the top of these preferred claims are estate and inheritance taxes. By statute, the widow is entitled to a cash allowance pending final disposition of the estate and this "widow's award" is regarded as a preferred claim against the estate. After settlement of these obligations and the funeral expenses, general creditors of the decedent whose claims are filed and allowed must be satisfied before any distribution to beneficiaries or heirs.

Assets

Corporate securities, government obligations, and items of personal use are all part of the assets of the decedent which pass into the hands of the personal representative. The personal representative may exercise the same powers incident to the ownership of such property as the decedent might have exercised during his life. Thus, the personal representative may vote stock owned by the decedent or exercise conversion privileges.

Insurance on the life of the decedent passes directly to the named beneficiary and does not go into his estate unless payable to his executor or the estate itself. Thus, insurance will not be available to pay the debts of the decedent if it is payable directly to a named beneficiary other than the personal representative in his representative capacity.

Administration Expenses

In the administration of every estate, there are probate expenses as well as fees to be paid to the executor or administrator and the attorney who handles the estate. In addition, taxes are imposed at death by both the Federal and State governments. The Federal government imposes an "estate tax" which is on the transfer of property at death. The State government imposes an "inheritance tax" which is on the privilege of an heir or beneficiary to receive the property. These taxes are separate and apart from the basic income tax which the estate must pay on income received during estate administration.

Estate Planning. In view of the statutes affecting the disposition of an individual's property at death, as well as the expenses and taxes involved, it is frequently advisable to plan for this eventuality in order to: (a) make adequate provision for family members and other beneficiaries; (b) facilitate administration of the estate; (c) minimize expenses and death taxes; and (d) provide funds for the payment of expenses and taxes.

A properly drafted will may provide for these items, as well as contain appropriate trust or guardianship provisions for minor children, if deemed necessary or desirable.

Sometimes inter vivos trusts are established in order to facilitate estate distribution and minimize probate fees and expenses. Insurance policies are sometimes made payable to a trustee for the benefit of intended beneficiaries, and a "pour over" clause in a will may provide that other property owned by the testator at the time of his death be placed in such a trust or in another inter vivos trust created by the testator.

Federal Estate Tax. The Federal government imposes a tax upon the total value of the estate, after deducting debts and expenses of administration. Prior to 1977, there was a specific exemption of $60,000, but under the Tax Reform Act of 1976 this has been replaced by a unified gift and estate tax credit. The tax is upon the estate itself, not upon the beneficiaries, and it is not affected by the amount or character of any bequest or by the relationship of a beneficiary to the decedent except in two important respects: (1) a gift to a charity recognized as such by the Treasury Department is deductible from the total estate for tax purposes; (2) a bequest to the surviving spouse.

The Economic Recovery Tax Reform Act of 1981, effective in 1982, allows a 100% tax free marital deduction on both lifetime gifts and bequests by one spouse to the other.

State Inheritance Tax. Under the statutes of most States, death taxes take the form of an inheritance tax which is imposed upon the recipient of a bequest or legacy, and not upon the estate itself. The amount of exemption from such inheritance tax, and the tax rate, are graduated according to the degree of relationship of the beneficiary to the decedent. The surviving spouse and the children of the decedent have a larger exemption and a lower rate of tax than nephews and nieces, and the latter have a larger exemption and a lower rate than beneficiaries not in a consanguineous relationship to the decedent. Thus, in one jurisdiction, assuming two bequests of $50,000 each, one to the wife and the other to a nonrelative of the decedent, the bequest to the wife is subject to an inheritance tax of $200, and

the bequest to the nonrelative, $5,588.

While the state inheritance tax is in addition to the Federal estate tax, a credit is allowed upon the Federal estate tax in the amount of the state tax paid.

Cases

Undue Influence

IN RE ESTATE OF PETERSON

(1969) 283 Minn. 446, 168 N.W.2d 502.

ROGOSHESKE, J.

Appeal from a judgment affirming an order of the probate court of Hennepin County denying admission of a purported will of Grace V. Peterson, decedent, to probate.

The sole question presented for review is whether the evidence sustains the determination by the district court that a purported will of decedent, dated October 21, 1964, was procured by undue influence exerted upon the testatrix by appellant, the named executor and the attorney who drafted it and supervised its execution. We hold that it does.

In April 1961, decedent, Grace V. Peterson, a spinster then aged 74, asked Chester G. W. Gustafson, a Minneapolis attorney, to draw a will for her. Gustafson, who had probated her sister's estate, drew this first as well as six subsequent wills and codicil free of charge because, as he testified, she had no money to pay for his services. The beneficiaries of this first will were various cousins and close friends. In this will, as well as in all subsequent wills except the last, decedent bequeathed to each beneficiary specifically described household goods, wearing apparel, or personal effects, and named Howard Rhedin, a cousin, as the residual beneficiary. On December 11, 1962, and on January 14, 1963, Gustafson drew new wills for decedent, each containing sev-

eral changes in her bequests and in the beneficiaries. On May 19, 1964, Gustafson drew a fourth will for decedent. In this will, decedent for the first time included Gustafson's children, Chester G. W. Jr., then aged 20 or 21, and Jo H., then aged 18, as beneficiaries. She left each a diamond ring and also left a watch and a coffee table to Jo. Gustafson testified that the only contacts decedent ever had with his children were several chance encounters between 5 and 10 years before in the offices where she worked, when the children delivered some produce to one of decedent's employers. There is no claim that she ever saw the children after that time. They neither attended her funeral nor appeared or testified in probate or district court.

Subsequent to this fourth will, Gustafson drew two more wills and a codicil, each will increasing the specific bequests of household articles to his children. On October 21, 1964, he drew a seventh will in which decedent left all of her property, which at her death included a homestead valued at $10,000 (encumbered by a $1,000 mortgage) and personal property valued, as the court found, at $1,459, to the Gustafson children. This will was drawn and executed under Gustafson's supervision within a 1-hour period. It was witnessed by two attorneys from a nearby office. Despite the radical changes in the will, its contents were never discussed with the witnesses, and they did not read its dispositive provisions. Gustafson immediately took possession of the will. Except for the testimony of Gustafson, no evidence was submitted that decedent knew she had named the Gustafson children as sole beneficiaries.

As the trial court found, during the last 5 years of her life decedent often visited Gustafson in his office, where he joshed, kidded, and flattered her. He sent her flowers, brought her vegetables, visited in her home but never entertained her in his, was given a key to her house, and arranged a $1,000 loan for her (secured by a mortgage on her home) from a trust of which he was the trustee. Gustafson had himself appointed decedent's guardian in November 1965 following her incapacitating stroke without consulting with the relatives who arranged for her hospitalization.

Grace V. Peterson died on February 1, 1966, without ever changing the will of October 21, 1964. Gustafson, who, as in prior wills, was named as executor, sought to have it admitted to probate. The probate court refused on the ground that the will was "executed by decedent as a result of undue influence exercised upon her by * * * Chester G. W. Gustafson." Gustafson, as proponent of the will, appealed this decision to the district court. After a trial de novo, the district court found that the will was procured as the result of Gustafson's "exercising undue influence over and upon Testatrix" and affirmed the order of the probate court. Gustafson appeals.

* * *

Undue influence has been defined as influence—

" * * * such as to substitute the will of the person exercising it for that of the testator, thereby making the written result express the purpose and intent of such person, not those of the testator. It must be equivalent to moral coercion or constraint overpowering the will of the testator. *It must operate at the very time the will is made and dominate and control its making.*" In re Estate of Marsden, 217 Minn. 1, 9, 13 N.W.2d 765, 770.

By its very nature, undue influence can usually be shown only by circumstantial evidence. [Citations.] Among the factors which should be considered in determining whether the circumstantial evidence clearly and convincingly supports a finding of undue influence are whether the evidence shows (1) an opportunity to exercise undue influence; (2) a confidential relationship between the person making the will and the party allegedly exercising the undue influence; (3) active participation in the preparation of the will by the party alleged to have exercised it; (4) disinheritance of those whom the decedent would have been expected to remember in his will; (5) a singularity of the provisions of the will; and (6) the exercise of either influence or persuasion to induce decedent to make the will in question. [Citation.]

The evidence clearly shows that each one of these factors was in some degree present in this case. Gustafson had the opportunity to exert undue influence; had developed a confidential relationship with decedent; and had himself controlled the drafting of each of the series of wills which progressively disinherited all of her relatives and friends, with whom she had maintained close relationships, until finally her entire estate was left to his children, whom she had met only briefly a few times at least 4 years before she executed her final will. While the presence of any one of these facts standing alone might not have been enough to establish undue influence, taken together they clearly permit an inference of undue influence, furnish adequate evidentiary support for the court's determination, and most certainly answer the argument that the evidence is conclusive against the determination.

Once undue influence, however exerted, is established, a proffered will may not be admitted to probate even though the named beneficiaries are innocent of any wrongdoing, for such an instrument cannot thereafter be regarded as a free and voluntary declaration of the testator's intentions. [Citation.]

In addition, we held in In re Estate of Keeley, 167 Minn. 120, 124, 208 N.W. 535, 537, that—

" * * * when a beneficiary of a substantial portion of the estate sustains a fiduciary or confidential relation with the testator and acts as the scriviner [sic] in drawing the will or controls its drafting, such facts alone will make a prima facie case and will sustain a finding of undue influence."

While it was the children of decedent's attorney who were the sole beneficiaries of the will rather than the attorney himself, under the circumstances of this case surely the same rule must apply. * * * Appellant could easily have avoided the effects of this rule by referring decedent to another attorney for a discussion of her wishes, independent advice, and preparation of her will. Such adherence to what we view as a proper standard of professional conduct would have provided disinterested testimony that decedent did in fact intend his children to inherit her estate and quite probably would have avoided placing of the will in jeopardy. * * *

Affirmed.

Signature

IN RE ESTATE OF WILLIAMS
(1965 Fla.) 182 So.2d 10.

O'CONNELL, J.

The District Court of Appeal, Third District, has certified to us, as passing upon a question of great public interest, its decisions in In re Williams Estate, Fla.App. 1965, 172 So.2d 464, and In re Estate of Zarkey, Fla.App.1965, 172 So.2d 465.

In each of these cases the county judge refused to admit to probate a will signed by the testator with a mark, similar to an X, on the ground that the making of a mark was not sufficient signing of the will under the provisions of F.S. Section 731.07, F.S.A. On appeal the district court affirmed the county judge in each case. The factual circumstances in both cases are so similar as to require no discussion.

The single issue for decision is whether, under the wording of Sec. 731.07, a testator may execute his will by making his mark, as distinguished from writing his alphabetical name. The county judges and the district court held that a will could not be validly executed in this manner. We cannot agree.

The pertinent portions of the controlling statute read:

"731.07 Execution of Wills.—Every will, other than a nuncupative will, must be in writing and must be executed as follows:

"(1) The testator must sign his will at the end thereof, or some other person in his presence and by his direction must subscribe the name of the testator thereto.

"(2) The testator, in the presence of at least two attesting witnesses present at the same time, must sign his will or cause his name to be signed as aforesaid or acknowledge his signature thereto."

We are here concerned only with the requirement that the "testator must sign his will at the end thereof * * *." The county judges and the district court were of the view that in order to "sign" the testator must write his alphabetical name. The respondents, of course, agree with this, while the petitioners argue that one may "sign" by making his mark.

In the construction of any statute it is always our duty to give effect to the legislative intent where such is ascertainable. However, we find nothing in the statute itself which gives support to either of the definitions urged to be given the word "sign."

This being so, we think we must then decide in that way which gives effect to the will of the testators involved unless some countervailing factor of public policy prevents.

We are surprised that the question here presented is one of first impression in this state. The only Florida case dealing with the question of signing by mark is Bruner v. Hart, 1910, 59 Fla. 171, 51 So. 593, in which this court held that a witness to a deed could subscribe as a witness by affixing his mark, rather than by writing his alphabetical name. In so holding this court stated that a person could witness by mark unless such method was forbidden by statute and noted that the applicable statute did not forbid a witness "subscribing his name by making his mark." A witness to a will is now required to actually sign his name to the will. [Citation.]

It is interesting to note that in Bruner v. Hart, supra, the two grantors also signed the questioned deed by mark. Surprisingly the deed was not attacked on this ground. This would seem to indicate that the parties in that case conceded that a grantor could "sign" by mark, but questioned only whether a witness could "subscribe" by mark. It is not unreasonable to assume that a like and widely held concession that a testator could sign his will by mark may account for the fact that no case in point has previously been presented to the appellate courts of this state.

We have carefully read the three cases cited by this court in support of the holding in Bruner v. Hart that a witness could subscribe by mark. Two of the cited cases decided that a witness to a will could subscribe as an attesting witness by mark. Garrett v. Heflin, 1893, 98 Ala. 615, 13 So. 326; and Pridgen v. Pridgen's Heirs, 1852, 13 Ired. 259, 35 N.C. 259. In the Pridgen case that court discussed the early English cases and statutes dealing with the execution of wills, explained that the word "signum" (from which our word sign is derived) meant no more than a mark, and expressed the view that sign and subscribe meant essentially the same thing when used in a statute. This seems to be the prevailing view in this country.

There can be no doubt that the effect of this court's decision in Bruner v. Hart is that a person can meet the statutory mandate of subscribing his name by making his mark rather than writing his alphabetical name. If there is a difference in meaning in the words "sign" and "subscribe" it is that "subscribe" is more limited than "sign." This logically leads to the conclusion that if one can subscribe by making his mark he can certainly sign by the same means. We so hold.

The great majority of the courts which have dealt with cases like these involving similar statutes hold as we do here, that a mark made by the testator at the proper place on his will with the intent that it constitute his signature and evidence his assent to the will is sufficient to satisfy the statutory requirement that he "sign" his will. [Citations.]

* * *

* * * we hold, as do most jurisdictions, that a testator may "sign" his will by making a mark. It is a matter of fact to be proved in proper proceedings whether the testator made the mark with the intention that it evidence his assent to the document.

* * *

For the reasons given above the decisions of the district court are reversed and the cause remanded for further proceedings consistent herewith.

It is so ordered.

Revocation of a Will:
Lost or Destroyed Will

BARKSDALE v. PENDERGRASS
(1975) 294 Ala. 526, 319 So.2d 267.

MERRILL, J.

Mrs. Mamie C. Henry, a widow, died on October 18, 1972. She had no children, but was survived by a number of nieces and nephews.

No duly executed will was found and

Joe Barksdale, a nephew of Mrs. Henry, was appointed administrator of her estate.

Later, Rita Jan Pendergrass, formerly Rita Jan Gray, filed a petition in the Probate Court of DeKalb County to probate an alleged lost or destroyed will of Mamie C. Henry. A copy of the will was made an exhibit to the petition. According to its terms, Mrs. Henry left all of her property to Rita Jan Gray and appointed her as executrix.

Joe Barksdale and Olen Barksdale filed a contest and the case was transferred to the circuit court, where it was tried before a jury. The grounds of the contest were that the purported will was never duly executed, or, that if executed, was destroyed by Mrs. Henry prior to her death.

The jury found in favor of the proponent, Rita Jan Gray Pendergrass. Judgment was entered ordering the will admitted to probate. * * *

* * *

In a proceeding to probate an alleged lost or destroyed will, the burden is on the proponent to establish, to the reasonable satisfaction of the judge or jury trying the facts:

(1) The existence of a will—an instrument in writing, signed by the testator or some person in his presence, and by his direction, and attested by at least two witnesses, who must subscribe their names thereto in the presence of the testator. [Citations.]

* * *

(3) The nonrevocation of the instrument by the testator. [Citations.]

(4) The contents of the will in substance and effect. [Citations.]

The first question then is whether there was a validity executed will. It is not necessary that the attestation be at the personal request of the testator. It is sufficient if done in testator's presence with his knowledge and consent expressed or implied. [Citations.]

The testator does not have to tell the subscribing witnesses that the instrument is his will, or to inform them of its contents. [Citations.]

It is not necessary for the witnesses to actually see the testator sign his name. [Citations.] The testator may acknowledge to the subscribing witnesses that it is his signature on the instrument by his express words or by implication from his conduct and from the surrounding circumstances. [Citations.]

* * *

The evidence produced at trial showed that Charles M. Scott, a Ft. Payne attorney, prepared a will for Mrs. Henry in November of 1963. She did not execute the will in Scott's office because she wanted to "get her own witnesses" in Collinsville where she lived. Scott subsequently made several minor changes in the will and mailed her a final version in January of 1964. Rita Jan Gray was named as beneficiary in every version of the will.

The evidence also showed that sometime around 1964, Bill Cook, Jack Farmer and Cecil Sharp met at Sharp's funeral home and witnessed Mrs. Henry's signature on a document. The testimony adduced at trial indicated that there was some doubt as to whether each of the witnesses knew that the document was a will. Jack Farmer was deceased at the time of the trial. Witness Bill Cook thought that Mrs. Henry mentioned that the document was a will at some time, but Cecil Sharp could only say that Mrs. Henry wanted him to witness a signature. Nevertheless it is apparent that the requirements of Tit. 61, § 24, Code 1940, were met since both Cook and Sharp witnessed a signature which Mrs. Henry acknowledged as her own.

The second thing which the proponent must prove is the loss or destruction of the instrument. Billy McDowell, who rented an apartment from Mrs. Henry between 1967 and 1969, testified that Mrs. Henry showed him a will; that she said Charles M. Scott prepared it; that Cecil Sharp's name was on the will as a witness, and that Rita Jan Gray was the sole beneficiary. He also said that Mrs. Henry kept the will in a purse under a mattress in a spare room. Floyd Gray, the father of the beneficiary, testified that he saw one of Mrs. Henry's nephews at her house shortly after her death. Willard Reaves, an employee of the funeral home, testified that several of Mrs. Henry's relatives visited her house that day after she died. There was also an abundance of testimony that the will might have been lost or destroyed by accident. Finally, attorney Scott testified that several weeks after Mrs. Henry's death he searched the house himself. Proponent Rita Jan Gray Pendergrass subsequently filed an application to compel production of the will. Appellants Barksdale responded "That the said purported will, if executed, has been destroyed prior to the death of the Testatrix, and was not found in her possession nor among has [sic] effects at the time of her death, and is presumed, if ever executed, to have been destroyed in accordance with law."

The third element of proof involved the presumption of revocation. When the will is shown to have been in the possession of the testator, and is not found at his death, the presumption arises that he destroyed it for the purpose of revocation; but the presumption may be rebutted, and the burden of rebutting it is on the proponent. [Citations.]

Billy McDowell, attorney Scott, and Mildred Johnson, a former neighbor of Mrs. Henry, testified that Mrs. Henry said that she did not want her neices and nephews to have anything she had; that she had always made it abundantly clear that she wanted to select somebody other than her nieces and nephews; that she was afraid they were going to get her property; that she knew that her nieces and nephews would get her property if she died intestate;

that she wanted Rita to have it, and that this was her fixed opinion.

Finally, proponent offered the copy of the will in evidence as proof of its contents.

A jury question was adequately presented * * * and the jury found for the proponent.

* * *

In the instant case, Billy McDowell testified that Mrs. Henry showed him her will; that he remembered seeing Cecil Sharp's signature; and that Mrs. Henry told him that attorney Scott had written the will, and that Rita Jan Gray was her sole beneficiary. It would appear that there was sufficient evidence from which to identify the copy.

* * *

Affirmed.

*Ademption and
Abatement of a Bequest*

IN RE ESTATE OF WOLFE

(1973 Iowa) 208 N.W.2d 923.

LeGRAND, J.

On June 6, 1971, the decedent, Leonard Allen Wolfe, was involved in a fatal automobile accident while driving his 1969 Buick Electra automobile. The car was rendered a total loss and subsequently decedent's insurance carrier paid his executor $3,550.00 for damage to the vehicle.

This litigation involves a dispute between decedent's daughter, Carol Lynn Wolfe, (the residuary legatee under his will) and his brother, David Wolfe, (to whom he left the automobile) over who shall have this money. The case submitted on stipulated facts raising this one legal issue: Was the testamentary gift to David Wolfe adeemed by the virtual destruction of the automobile in the accident which caused decedent's death? The trial court held there was no ademption and we affirm.

The decedent's will included this provision:

Item III. To my brother, David Wolfe, * * *, I will the sum of $1,000.00 and any automobile which I may own at the time of my death to be his absolutely and forever, if he survives me, and if not this bequest shall lapse.

Put as briefly as possible, ademption means a taking away. It occurs when property which has been specifically given under a will is later destroyed or disposed of so that it does not exist as part of the estate at the testator's death. The general rule is that nothing else may be substituted for that which was originally given, and the gift is then said to have adeemed. [Citations.]

There is a split of authority over the part intent should play in resolving ademption problems. The minority view adheres to a rigid "identity" theory, concerning itself solely with the presence of the property in the estate at the time of death. If it is not among the decedent's assets, there has been an ademption, regardless of the reason for its absence. Intent is immaterial under this view. Warren, The History of Ademption, 25 Iowa L.Rev. 290, 314 (1940); In re Wright's Will, 7 N.Y.2d 365, 197 N.W.S.2d 711, 165 N.E.2d 561, 563 (1960); In re Barry's Estate (1952), 208 Okl. 8, 252 P.2d 437, 439, 440.

The majority rule gives consideration and effect to circumstances which explain why the property is not among the decedent's assets at the time of his death. This rule, like the minority, finds there has been an ademption when there has been a *voluntary* sale or other disposal of specifically devised property by the testator during his lifetime. However, when the property in question is missing from the estate because of some act or event *involuntary* as to him, there is no ademption. This is the rule we follow.

It is clear the difference in the two rules is based upon the importance attached to the testator's intent. We have referred to our rule as the "modified intention theory."

In re Estate of Bierstedt, supra, 254 Iowa at 775, 119 N.W.2d at 236. There we put it this way,

Where the testator is competent and disposes of the subject of the gift, the gift is adeemed; where the testator is incompetent and the subject of the gift is sold by a guardian with court approval, the gift is only adeemed to the extent the proceeds are used for care and maintenance of the ward. The only question of intention involved is the opportunity of the testator to change the will. This opportunity is denied the incompetent testator. No question of his intentions other than expressed in the will is involved. Where, as here, the testator is incompetent and under guardianship, a sale by the guardian does not work an ademption so far as the proceeds are traceable. This is the majority view in this country.

Both the Bierstedt case and Stake v. Cole, 257 Iowa 594, 133 N.W.2d 714, deal with judicial sales made under court order, one by an executor, the other by a guardian. We have never faced the precise problem now presented. However, we believe those two decisions clearly point the way to the proper result here.

The accident which cost decedent his life and caused destruction of the devised car was, it seems unnecessary to point out, an involuntary disposition of the automobile indicating no intention to change the terms of the will. Furthermore, like the incompetent testator mentioned in Bierstedt, decedent was denied by death any opportunity to change his will after the event occurred. The argument against ademption under these circumstances is at least as persuasive as in the Bierstedt and Stake cases.

We find surprisingly little authority from other states. Under almost identical facts the California appellate court ruled, as we do here, in favor of the specific legatee of the destroyed vehicle, basing its decision on the obvious intent of the testator. [Citation.]

In Reading v. Dixon, 10 N.C.App. 319, 178 S.E.2d 322, 324 (1971), the specific legatee again prevailed over the objection a testamentary gift of silverware had adeemed by reason of its loss or theft at a time when the testator was mentally unable to change his will. The insurance proceeds were awarded to the specific legatee of the silverware, again on a finding of testamentary intent.

We have already referred to several cases holding to the strict identity theory. In re Wright's Will and In re Barry's Estate, both supra. It is interesting to note, however, New York has refused to follow its own pronouncements in the Wright case on at least two occasions. See In re Zimmerli's Estate, (Sur.Ct.1961), 30 Misc.2d 669, 220 N.Y.S.2d 123, 126 (insurance proceeds awarded to specific devisee of damaged real estate over objection fire had worked an ademption); In re Buda's Will, (Sur.Ct.1960), 21 Misc.2d 931, 197 N.Y.S.2d 824, 825 (gift of car was not adeemed by accident resulting in death of testator and destruction of vehicle).

* * *

An interesting discussion of the question appears in Walsh v. Gillespie, (1959),

338 Mass. 278, 154 N.E.2d 906, 908. We also believe this quotation from Wilmerton v. Wilmerton, (7th Cir. 1910) 176 F. 896, 900 expresses quite well the right rule,

[W]e think that the rule, that legacies are adeemed only where such an intention appears on the part of the testator himself, ought to be followed. The question, in our judgment, is not whether, as a mere matter of accident, * * *, the thing set apart as the corpus of a special bequest has been changed in specie. The real question is whether, all things considered, the testator's testamentary disposition did, or did not, remain, with reference to the particular thing embodied in the specific bequest or its proceeds, the same as it was the last moment he was able to exercise a testamentary disposition. In that way, and in that way only, we think, can the right of the man to dispose of his property according to his own wishes, exempt from the interference, caprice or interest of others, be fully carried out. In that way only can his intention, as embodied in his will, be truly administered.

We approve that statement and adopt its rationale in holding the gift to David Wolfe was not adeemed by the accident in question.

Affirmed.

Problems

1. Jasper, who was in bed following a heart attack, properly signed his will in the presence of Alan and Ben, competent witnesses. He then asked them to sign as attesting witnesses. They walked to a table which was in full view of Jasper and only a few feet away, and there they prepared to subscribe the will. After Alan had completed his signature and as Ben was getting ready to sign his name, Jasper lapsed into unconsciousness, but Ben completed his signature. The next day, without having regained consciousness, Jasper died. Should the document be admitted to probate?

2. John Carver executed his will on March 10, 1981, which was witnessed by William Hobson

and Sam Witt. By his will Carver devised his farm, Stonecrest, to his nephew Roy White. The residue of his estate was given to his sister, Florence Carver.

A codicil to his will executed April 15, 1981, provided that $5,000 be given to Carver's niece, Mary Jordan, and $5,000 to Wanda White, Roy White's wife. The codicil was witnessed by Roy White and Harold Brown. John Carver died September 1, 1981, and the will and codicil were admitted to probate.

How should Carver's estate be distributed?

3. Edwin Fuller, a bachelor, prepared his will in his office. The will, which contained no residuary clause, provided that one-third of his

estate would go to his nephew Tom Fuller, one-third to the City of Emanon to be used for park improvements, and one-third to his brother Kurt.

He signed the will in his office and then went to the office of his nephew Tom Fuller who at Edwin's request, signed the will as a witness. Since no other persons were available in Tom's office, Edwin then went to the bank where Frank Cash, the cashier, at Edwin's request, also signed as a witness. In each instance Edwin stated that he had signed the document but did not state that it was his will.

Edwin returned to his office where he placed the will in his safe. Subsequently Edwin died, survived by Kurt, his only heir-at-law. How should the estate be distributed?

4. A executed a one-page will, wherein he devised his farm to B. Later, as the result of a quarrel with B, A wrote the words "I hereby cancel and revoke this will /s/A," and nothing more, in the margin of the will, but did not destroy the will. A then executed a deed to the property, naming C as grantee, and placed the deed and will in his safe. Shortly afterwards, A married D, by whom he had one child, E. Thereafter, A died and the deed and will were found in his safe. B, C and E claim the fee to the farm and D claims dower. Discuss the validity of each claim.

5. The following instrument was offered for probate: "I give, devise and bequeath all of my property, both real and personal, which I may have a right to dispose of at my death, unto my sister, Mary Strong, for life and after her death said property to go to and become vested in the heirs of her body when they reach the age of twenty-five years.

John Smith (seal)"
"Witnesses:
W. C. Jones
R. C. Brown"

At the hearing on the probate of the will, the two witnesses were called and testified but Mary Strong, who was the only heir-at-law of the testator, objected to the probate of the will for the following reasons: (1) there was nothing on the face of the instrument signed by the witnesses to show that the testator acknowledged said instrument as his will before them or that they saw him sign it, or that they believed him to be of sound mind at the time he signed; (2) it made no provision for the payment of the testator's debts; (3) it did not name an executor. Decide each objection.

6. A obtained a divorce from his wife, B, because she deserted him and their only child, C. He was awarded the custody of C. Later, he married D, a widow with one son, E. A and D had another child, F. A legally adopted G, the child of a deceased friend. E later married and had a son, J. A died intestate, leaving all of the above surviving him except E, who died earlier. His parents and a brother also survived A. He left a large estate comprising both real and personal property. Who will share in his estate and what fractional interest will they each receive?

7. John Walker, a widower, died testate. His will, in part, provided:

"I give and bequeath my piano to my daughter Nancy. I give and bequeath to my daughter Jennifer the sum of $1,000. I give and bequeath to my son John the sum of $1,000 to be paid out of my account at the Tenth National Bank in the city of Erehwon. All the rest and residue of my estate I give to Mary, Jennifer and John, share and share alike."

Subsequent to the execution of his will Walker sold his piano for $2,300 and deposited the proceeds in the Citizens Bank of Erehwon. He withdrew the money he had on deposit in the Tenth National Bank and purchased a new automobile.

At the time of his death, Walker had no debts. The account in the Citizens Bank of Erehwon had a balance of $2,300 which constituted his entire net estate after all expenses of administration were paid. How should Walker's estate be distributed?

8. Todd, by his will, bequeathed $25,000 to XYZ Bank in trust for such persons as Todd would name in a letter to XYZ Bank to be found with his will. On Todd's death there was found with his will a typewritten letter to XYZ Bank, signed by Todd and dated one month after the execution of his will, naming Arthur and Beatrice as beneficiaries of the trust and directing XYZ Bank to pay each of them respectively one-half of the trust corpus and accumulated income

upon reaching 35 years of age. Was a valid trust created?

9. The validly executed will of John Dane contained the following provision: "I give and devise to my daughter, Mary, Redacre for and during her natural life and, at her death the remainder to go to Wilmore College." The will also provided that the residue of his estate should go to Wilmore College. Thereafter, Dane sold Redacre and then added a validly executed codicil to his will, "Due to the fact that I have sold Redacre which I previously gave to my daughter, Mary, I now give and devise Blackacre to Mary in place and instead of Redacre."

Another clause of the codicil provided: "I give my one-half interest in the oil business which I own in common with William Steele to my son, Henry." Subsequently, Dane acquired all of the interest in the oil business from his partner, Steele, and, at the time of his death, Dane owned the entire oil business. The will and codicil have been admitted to probate.

(a) What interest, if any, does Mary acquire in Blackacre?

(b) What is the interest, if any, of Henry in the oil business?

10. Timm, a well-to-do, middle-aged widower, executed a will. Among other clauses were:

"(3) I leave $5,000 to my nephew Art's wife."

"(6) I leave Nancy Brown $1,000."

"(7) I leave my granddaughter, Julia, a mink coat."

At Timm's death it appeared: (a) Nephew Art had lived in South America for many years. Timm knew and liked his wife Abigail. Shortly before Timm's death Art divorced Abigail and married a South American girl, Carmen, who was Art's wife when Timm died. Timm did not know of this. (b) Timm knew two women named Nancy Brown. One was the wife of Timm's business partner Tom Brown. The Browns were both close friends of Timm, and he very much liked and admired Nancy. The other Nancy Brown was Timm's favorite manicurist who worked in the barbershop that Timm regularly patronized. Timm always tipped her generously and gave her a bottle of perfume or something of the sort each Christmas. (c) A year before Timm's death, and after the execution of his will, Julia moved to Panama, where her husband was in government service. Thereafter, Timm sent her a diamond ring worth $3,500 with a note: "Since you don't need a fur coat now, I thought you might rather have this ring."

Who takes under the will?

Appendix
A

THE UNIFORM COMMERCIAL CODE
1977 Official Text

(Adopted in 52 jurisdictions; all 50 States, although Louisiana has adopted only Articles 1, 3, 4, and 5; the District of Columbia, and the Virgin Islands.)

The Code consists of 10 Articles as follows:

Art.

1. GENERAL PROVISIONS

2. Sales.

3. Commercial Paper

4. Bank Deposits and Collections

5. Letters of Credit

6. Bulk Transfers

7. Warehouse Receipts, Bills of Lading and Other Documents of Title

8. Investment Securities

9. Secured Transactions: Sales of Accounts, Contract Rights and Chattel Paper

10. Effective Date and Repealer

Article 1
GENERAL PROVISIONS

Part 1 Short Title, Construction, Application and Subject Matter of the Act

§ 1—101. Short Title.

This Act shall be known and may be cited as Uniform Commercial Code.

§ 1—102. Purposes; Rules of Construction; Variation by Agreement.

(1) This Act shall be liberally construed and applied to promote its underlying purposes and policies.

(2) Underlying purposes and policies of this Act are

(a) to simplify, clarify and modernize the law governing commercial transactions;

(b) to permit the continued expansion of commercial practices through custom, usage and agreement of the parties;

(c) to make uniform the law among the various jurisdictions.

(3) The effect of provisions of this Act may be varied by agreement, except as otherwise provided in this Act and except that the obligations of good faith, diligence, reasonableness and care prescribed by this Act may not be disclaimed by agreement but the parties may by agreement determine the standards by which the performance of such obligations is to be measured if such standards are not manifestly unreasonable.

(4) The presence in certain provisions of this Act of the words "unless otherwise agreed" or words of similar import does not imply that the effect of other provisions may not be varied by agreement under subsection (3).

(5) In this Act unless the context otherwise requires

(a) words in the singular number include the plural, and in the plural include the singular;

(b) words of the masculine gender include the feminine and the neuter, and when the sense so indicates words of the neuter gender may refer to any gender.

§ 1—103. Supplementary General Principles of Law Applicable.

Unless displaced by the particular provisions of this Act, the principles of law and equity, including the law merchant and the law relative to capacity to contract, principal and agent, estoppel, fraud, misrepresentation, duress, coercion, mistake, bankruptcy, or other validating or invalidating cause shall supplement its provisions.

§ 1—104. Construction Against Implicit Repeal.

This Act being a general act intended as a unified coverage of its subject matter, no part of it shall be deemed to be impliedly repealed by subsequent legislation if such construction can reasonably be avoided.

§ 1—105. Territorial Application of the Act; Parties' Power to Choose Applicable Law.

(1) Except as provided hereafter in this section, when a transaction bears a reasonable relation to this state and also to another state or nation the parties may agree that the law either of this state or of such other state or nation shall govern their rights and duties. Failing such agreement this Act applies to transactions bearing an appropriate relation to this state.

(2) Where one of the following provisions of this Act specifies the applicable law, that provision governs and a contrary agreement is effective only to the extent permitted by the law (including the conflict of laws rules) so specified:

Rights of creditors against sold goods. Section 2—402.
Applicability of the Article on Bank Deposits and Collections. Section 4—102.
Bulk transfers subject to the Article on Bulk Transfers. Section 6—102.
Applicability of the Article on Investment Securities. Section 8—106.
Perfection provisions of the Article on Secured Transactions. Section 9—103.

§ 1—106. Remedies to Be Liberally Administered.

(1) The remedies provided by this Act shall be liberally administered to the end that the aggrieved party may be put in as good a position as if the other party had fully performed but neither consequential or special nor penal damages may be had except as specifically provided in this Act or by other rule of law.

(2) Any right or obligation declared by this Act is enforceable by action unless the provision declaring it specifies a different and limited effect.

§ 1—107. Waiver or Renunciation of Claim or Right After Breach.

Any claim or right arising out of an alleged breach can be discharged in whole or in part without consideration by a written waiver or renunciation signed and delivered by the aggrieved party.

§ 1—108. Severability.

If any provision or clause of this Act or application thereof to any person or circumstances is held invalid, such invalidity shall not affect other provisions or applications of the Act which can be given effect without the invalid provision or application, and to this end the provisions of this Act are declared to be severable.

§ 1—109. Section Captions.

Section captions are parts of this Act.

Part 2 General Definitions and Principles of Interpretation

§ 1—201. General Definitions

Subject to additional definitions contained in the subsequent Articles of this Act which are applicable to specific Articles or Parts thereof, and unless the context otherwise requires, in this Act:

(1) "Action" in the sense of a judicial proceeding includes recoupment, counterclaim, set-off, suit in equity and any other proceedings in which rights are determined.

(2) "Aggrieved party" means a party entitled to resort to a remedy.

(3) "Agreement" means the bargain of the parties in fact as found in their language or by implication from other circumstances including course of dealing or usage of trade or course of performance as provided in this Act (Sections 1—205 and 2—208). Whether an agreement has legal consequences is determined by the provisions of this Act, if applicable; otherwise by the law of contracts (Section 1—103). (Compare "Contract".)

(4) "Bank" means any person engaged in the business of banking.

(5) "Bearer" means the person in possession of an instrument, document of title, or certificated security payable to bearer or indorsed in blank.

(6) "Bill of lading" means a document evidencing the receipt of goods for shipment issued by a person engaged in the business of transporting or forwarding goods, and includes an airbill. "Airbill" means a document serving for air transportation as a bill of lading does for marine or rail transportation, and includes an air consignment note or air waybill.

(7) "Branch" includes a separately incorporated foreign branch of a bank.

(8) "Burden of establishing" a fact means the burden of persuading the triers of fact that the existence of the fact is more probable than its non-existence.

(9) "Buyer in ordinary course of business" means a person who in good faith and without knowledge that the sale to him is in violation of the ownership rights or security interest of a third party in the goods buys in ordinary course from a person in the business of selling goods of that kind but does not include a pawnbroker. All persons who sell minerals or the like (including oil and gas) at wellhead or minehead shall be deemed to be persons in the business of selling goods of that kind. "Buying" may be for cash or by exchange of other property or on secured or unsecured credit and includes receiving goods or documents of title under a pre-existing contract for sale but does not include a transfer in bulk or as security for or in total or partial satisfaction of a money debt.

(10) "Conspicuous": A term or clause is conspicuous when it is so written that a reasonable person against whom it is to operate ought to have noticed it. A printed heading in capitals (as: NON-NEGOTIABLE BILL OF LADING) is conspicuous. Language in the body of a form is "conspicuous" if it is in larger or other contrasting type or color. But in a telegram any stated term is "conspicuous". Whether a term or clause is "conspicuous" or not is for decision by the court.

(11) "Contract" means the total legal obligation which results from the parties' agreement as affected by this Act and any other applicable rules of law. (Compare "Agreement".)

(12) "Creditor" includes a general creditor, a secured creditor, a lien creditor and any representative of creditors, including an assignee for the benefit of creditors, a trustee in bankruptcy, a receiver in equity and an executor or administrator of an insolvent debtor's or assignor's estate.

(13) "Defendant" includes a person in the position of defendant in a cross-action or counterclaim.

(14) "Delivery" with respect to instruments, documents of title, chattel paper, or certificated securities means voluntary transfer of possession.

(15) "Document of title" includes bill of lading, dock warrant, dock receipt, warehouse receipt or order for the delivery of goods, and also any other document which in the regular course of business or financing is treated as adequately evidencing that the person in possession of it is entitled to receive, hold and dispose of the document and the goods it covers. To be a document of title a document must purport to be issued by or addressed to a bailee and purport to cover goods in the bailee's possession which are either identified or are fungible portions of an identified mass.

(16) "Fault" means wrongful act, omission or breach.

(17) "Fungible" with respect to goods or securities means goods or securities of which any unit is, by nature or usage of trade, the equivalent of any other like unit. Goods which are not fungible shall be deemed fungible for the purposes of this Act to the extent that under a particular agreement or document unlike units are treated as equivalents.

(18) "Genuine" means free of forgery or counterfeiting.

(19) "Good faith" means honesty in fact in the conduct or transaction concerned.

(20) "Holder" means a person who is in possession of a document of title or an instrument or a certificated investment security drawn, issued, or indorsed to him or his order or to bearer or in blank.

(21) To "honor" is to pay or to accept and pay, or where a credit so engages to purchase or discount a draft complying with the terms of the credit.

(22) "Insolvency proceedings" includes any assignment for the benefit of creditors or other proceedings intended to liquidate or rehabilitate the estate of the person involved.

(23) A person is "insolvent" who either has ceased to pay his debts in the ordinary course of business or cannot pay his debts as they become due or is insolvent within the meaning of the federal bankruptcy law.

(24) "Money" means a medium of exchange authorized or adopted by a domestic or foreign government as a part of its currency.

(25) A person has "notice" of a fact when

(a) he has actual knowledge of it; or

(b) he has received a notice or notification of it; or

(c) from all the facts and circumstances known to him at the time in question he has reason to know that it exists.

A person "knows" or has "knowledge" of a fact when he has actual knowledge of it. "Discover" or "learn" or a word or phrase of similar import refers to knowledge rather than to reason to know. The time and circumstances under which a notice or notification may cease to be effective are not determined by this Act.

(26) A person "notifies" or "gives" a notice or notification to another by taking such steps as may be reasonably required to inform the other in ordinary course whether or not such other actually comes to know of it. A person "receives" a notice or notification when

(a) it comes to his attention; or

(b) it is duly delivered at the place of business through which the contract was made or at any other place held out by him as the place for receipt of such communications.

(27) Notice, knowledge or a notice or notification received by an organization is effective for a particular transaction from the time when it is brought to the attention of the individual conducting that transaction, and in any event from the time when it would have been brought to his attention if the organization had exercised due diligence. An organization exercises due diligence if it maintains reasonable routines for communicating significant information to the person conducting the transaction and there is reasonable compliance with the routines. Due diligence does not require an individual acting for the organization to communicate information unless such communication is part of his regular duties or unless he has reason to know of the transaction and that the transaction would be materially affected by the information.

(28) "Organization" includes a corporation, government or governmental subdivision or agency, business trust, estate, trust, partnership or association, two or more persons having a joint or common interest, or any other legal or commercial entity.

(29) "Party", as distinct from "third party", means a person who has engaged in a transaction or made an agreement within this Act.

(30) "Person" includes an individual or an organization (See Section 1—102).

(31) "Presumption" or "presumed" means that the trier of fact must find the existence of the fact presumed unless and until evidence is introduced which would support a finding of its non-existence.

(32) "Purchase" includes taking by sale, discount, negotiation, mortgage, pledge, lien, issue or re-issue, gift or any other voluntary transaction creating an interest in property.

(33) "Purchaser" means a person who takes by purchase.

(34) "Remedy" means any remedial right to which an aggrieved party is entitled with or without resort to a tribunal.

(35) "Representative" includes an agent, an officer of a corporation or association, and a trustee, executor or administrator of an estate, or any other person empowered to act for another.

(36) "Rights" includes remedies.

(37) "Security interest" means an interest in personal property or fixtures which secures payment or performance of an obligation. The retention or reservation of title by a seller of goods notwithstanding shipment or delivery to the buyer (Section 2—401) is limited in effect to a reservation of a "security interest". The term also includes any interest of a buyer of accounts or chattel paper which is subject to Article 9. The special property interest of a buyer of goods on identification of such goods to a contract for sale under Section 2—401 is not a "security interest", but a buyer may also acquire a "security interest" by complying with Article 9. Unless a lease or consignment is intended as security, reservation of title thereunder is not a "security interest" but a consignment is in any event subject to the provisions on consignment sales (Section 2—326). Whether a lease is intended as security is to be determined by the facts of each case; however, (a) the inclusion of an option to purchase does not of itself make the lease one intended for security, and (b) an agreement that upon compliance with the terms of the lease the lessee shall become or has the option to become the owner of the property for no additional consideration or for a nominal consideration does make the lease one intended for security.

(38) "Send" in connection with any writing or notice means to deposit in the mail or deliver for transmission by any other usual means of communication with postage or cost of transmission provided for and properly addressed and in the case of an instrument to an address specified thereon or otherwise agreed, or if there be none to any address reasonable under the circumstances. The receipt of any writing or notice

within the time at which it would have arrived if properly sent has the effect of a proper sending.

(39) "Signed" includes any symbol executed or adopted by a party with present intention to authenticate a writing.

(40) "Surety" includes guarantor.

(41) "Telegram" includes a message transmitted by radio, teletype, cable, any mechanical method of transmission, or the like.

(42) "Term" means that portion of an agreement which relates to a particular matter.

(43) "Unauthorized" signature or indorsement means one made without actual, implied or apparent authority and includes a forgery.

(44) "Value". Except as otherwise provided with respect to negotiable instruments and bank collections (Sections 3—303, 4—208 and 4—209) a person gives "value" for rights if he acquires them

    (a) in return for a binding commitment to extend credit or for the extension of immediately available credit whether or not drawn upon and whether or not a chargeback is provided for in the event of difficulties in collection; or

    (b) as security for or in total or partial satisfaction of a pre-existing claim; or

    (c) by accepting delivery pursuant to a pre-existing contract for purchase; or

    (d) generally, in return for any consideration sufficient to support a simple contract.

(45) "Warehouse receipt" means a receipt issued by a person engaged in the business of storing goods for hire.

(46) "Written" or "writing" includes printing, typewriting or any other intentional reduction to tangible form.
Amended in 1962, 1972 and 1977.

§ 1—202. Prima Facie Evidence by Third Party Documents.

A document in due form purporting to be a bill of lading, policy or certificate of insurance, official weigher's or inspector's certificate, consular invoice, or any other document authorized or required by the contract to be issued by a third party shall be prima facie evidence of its own authenticity and genuineness and of the facts stated in the document by the third party.

§ 1—203. Obligation of Good Faith.

Every contract or duty within this Act imposes an obligation of good faith in its performance or enforcement.

§ 1—204. Time; Reasonable Time; "Seasonably".

(1) Whenever this Act requires any action to be taken within a reasonable time, any time which is not manifestly unreasonable may be fixed by agreement.

(2) What is a reasonable time for taking any action depends on the nature, purpose and circumstances of such action.

(3) An action is taken "seasonably" when it is taken at or within the time agreed or if no time is agreed at or within a reasonable time.

§ 1—205. Course of Dealing and Usage of Trade.

(1) A course of dealing is a sequence of previous conduct between the parties to a particular transaction which is fairly to be regarded as establishing a common basis of understanding for interpreting their expressions and other conduct.

(2) A usage of trade is any practice or method of dealing having such regularity of observance in a place, vocation or trade as to justify an expectation that it will be observed with respect to the transaction in question. The existence and scope of such a usage are to be proved as facts. If it is established that such a usage is embodied in a written trade code or similar writing the interpretation of the writing is for the court.

(3) A course of dealing between parties and any usage of trade in the vocation or trade in which they are engaged or of which they are or should be aware give particular meaning to and supplement or qualify terms of an agreement.

(4) The express terms of an agreement and an applicable course of dealing or usage of trade shall be construed wherever reasonable as consistent with each other; but when such construction is unreasonable express terms control both course of dealing and usage of trade and course of dealing controls usage of trade.

(5) An applicable usage of trade in the place where any part of performance is to occur shall be used in interpreting the agreement as to that part of the performance.

(6) Evidence of a relevant usage of trade offered by one party is not admissible unless and until he has given the other party such notice as the court finds sufficient to prevent unfair surprise to the latter.

§ 1—206. Statute of Frauds for Kinds of Personal Property Not Otherwise Covered.

(1) Except in the cases described in subsection (2) of this section a contract for the sale of personal property

is not enforceable by way of action or defense beyond five thousand dollars in amount or value of remedy unless there is some writing which indicates that a contract for sale has been made between the parties at a defined or stated price, reasonably identifies the subject matter, and is signed by the party against whom enforcement is sought or by his authorized agent.

(2) Subsection (1) of this section does not apply to contracts for the sale of goods (Section 2—201) nor of securities (Section 8—319) nor to security agreements (Section 9—203).

§ 1—207. **Performance or Acceptance Under Reservation of Rights.**

A party who with explicit reservation of rights performs or promises performance or assents to performance in a manner demanded or offered by the other party does not thereby prejudice the rights reserved. Such words as "without prejudice", "under protest" or the like are sufficient.

§ 1—208. **Option to Accelerate at Will.**

A term providing that one party or his successor in interest may accelerate payment or performance or require collateral or additional collateral "at will" or "when he deems himself insecure" or in words of similar import shall be construed to mean that he shall have power to do so only if he in good faith believes that the prospect of payment or performance is impaired. The burden of establishing lack of good faith is on the party against whom the power has been exercised.

§ 1—209. **Subordinated Obligations**

An obligation may be issued as subordinated to payment of another obligation of the person obligated, or a creditor may subordinate his right to payment of an obligation by agreement with either the person obligated or another creditor of the person obligated. Such a subordination does not create a security interest as against either the common debtor or a subordinated creditor. This section shall be construed as declaring the law as it existed prior to the enactment of this section and not as modifying it. Added 1966.

Note: *This new section is proposed as an optional provision to make it clear that a subordination agreement does not create a security interest unless so intended.*

Article 2
SALES

Part 1
Short Title, Construction and Subject Matter

§ 2—101. **Short Title.**

This Article shall be known and may be cited as Uniform Commercial Code—Sales.

§ 2—102. **Scope; Certain Security and Other Transactions Excluded From This Article.**

Unless the context otherwise requires, this Article applies to transactions in goods; it does not apply to any transaction which although in the form of an unconditional contract to sell or present sale is intended to operate only as a security transaction nor does this Article impair or repeal any statute regulating sales to consumers, farmers or other specified classes of buyers.

§ 2—103. **Definitions and Index of Definitions.**

(1) In this Article unless the context otherwise requires

 (a) "Buyer" means a person who buys or contracts to buy goods.

 (b) "Good faith" in the case of a merchant means honesty in fact and the observance of reasonable commercial standards of fair dealing in the trade.

 (c) "Receipt" of goods means taking physical possession of them.

 (d) "Seller" means a person who sells or contracts to sell goods.

(2) Other definitions applying to this Article or to specified Parts thereof, and the sections in which they appear are:

"Acceptance". Section 2—606.
"Banker's credit". Section 2—325.
"Between merchants". Section 2—104.
"Cancellation". Section 2—106(4).
"Commercial unit". Section 2—105.
"Confirmed credit". Section 2—325.
"Conforming to contract". Section 2—106.
"Contract for sale". Section 2—106.
"Cover". Section 2—712.
"Entrusting". Section 2—403.
"Financing agency". Section 2—104.
"Future goods". Section 2—105.
"Goods". Section 2—105.
"Identification". Section 2—501.

"Installment contract". Section 2—612.
"Letter of Credit". Section 2—325.
"Lot". Section 2—105.
"Merchant". Section 2—104.
"Overseas". Section 2—323.
"Person in position of seller". Section 2—707.
"Present sale". Section 2—106.
"Sale". Section 2—106.
"Sale on approval". Section 2—326.
"Sale or return". Section 2—326.
"Termination". Section 2—106.

(3) The following definitions in other Articles apply to this Article:
"Check". Section 3—104.
"Consignee". Section 7—102.
"Consignor". Section 7—102.
"Consumer goods". Section 9—109.
"Dishonor". Section 3—507.
"Draft". Section 3—104.

(4) In addition Article 1 contains general definitions and principles of construction and interpretation applicable throughout this Article.

§ 2—104. **Definitions: "Merchant"; "Between Merchants"; "Financing Agency".**

(1) "Merchant" means a person who deals in goods of the kind or otherwise by his occupation holds himself out as having knowledge or skill peculiar to the practices or goods involved in the transaction or to whom such knowledge or skill may be attributed by his employment of an agent or broker or other intermediary who by his occupation holds himself out as having such knowledge or skill.

(2) "Financing agency" means a bank, finance company or other person who in the ordinary course of business makes advances against goods or documents of title or who by arrangement with either the seller or the buyer intervenes in ordinary course to make or collect payment due or claimed under the contract for sale, as by purchasing or paying the seller's draft or making advances against it or by merely taking it for collection whether or not documents of title accompany the draft. "Financing agency" includes also a bank or other person who similarly intervenes between persons who are in the position of seller and buyer in respect to the goods (Section 2—707).

(3) "Between merchants" means in any transaction with respect to which both parties are chargeable with the knowledge or skill of merchants.

§ 2—105. **Definitions: Transferability; "Goods"; "Future" Goods; "Lot"; "Commercial Unit".**

(1) "Goods" means all things (including specially manufactured goods) which are movable at the time of identification to the contract for sale other than the money in which the price is to be paid, investment securities (Article 8) and things in action. "Goods" also includes the unborn young of animals and growing crops and other identified things attached to realty as described in the section on goods to be severed from realty (Section 2—107).

(2) Goods must be both existing and identified before any interest in them can pass. Goods which are not both existing and identified are "future" goods. A purported present sale of future goods or of any interest therein operates as a contract to sell.

(3) There may be a sale of a part interest in existing identified goods.

(4) An undivided share in an identified bulk of fungible goods is sufficiently identified to be sold although the quantity of the bulk is not determined. Any agreed proportion of such a bulk or any quantity thereof agreed upon by number, weight or other measure may to the extent of the seller's interest in the bulk be sold to the buyer who then becomes an owner in common.

(5) "Lot" means a parcel or a single article which is the subject matter of a separate sale or delivery, whether or not it is sufficient to perform the contract.

(6) "Commercial unit" means such a unit of goods as by commercial usage is a single whole for purposes of sale and division of which materially impairs its character or value on the market or in use. A commercial unit may be a single article (as a machine) or a set of articles (as a suite of furniture or an assortment of sizes) or a quantity (as a bale, gross, or carload) or any other unit treated in use or in the relevant market as a single whole.

§ 2—106. **Definitions: "Contract"; "Agreement"; "Contract for Sale"; "Sale"; "Present Sale"; "Conforming" to Contract; "Termination"; "Cancellation".**

(1) In this Article unless the context otherwise requires "contract" and "agreement" are limited to those relating to the present or future sale of goods. "Contract for sale" includes both a present sale of goods and a contract to sell goods at a future time. A "sale" consists in the passing of title from the seller to the buyer for a price (Section 2—401). A "present

sale" means a sale which is accomplished by the making of the contract.

(2) Goods or conduct including any part of a performance are "conforming" or conform to the contract when they are in accordance with the obligations under the contract.

(3) "Termination" occurs when either party pursuant to a power created by agreement or law puts an end to the contract otherwise than for its breach. On "termination" all obligations which are still executory on both sides are discharged but any right based on prior breach or performance survives.

(4) "Cancellation" occurs when either party puts an end to the contract for breach by the other and its effect is the same as that of "termination" except that the cancelling party also retains any remedy for breach of the whole contract or any unperformed balance.

§ 2—107. Goods to Be Severed From Realty: Recording.

(1) A contract for the sale of minerals or the like (including oil and gas) or a structure or its materials to be removed from realty is a contract for the sale of goods within this Article if they are to be severed by the seller but until severance a purported present sale thereof which is not effective as a transfer of an interest in land is effective only as a contract to sell.

(2) A contract for the sale apart from the land of growing crops or other things attached to realty and capable of severance without material harm thereto but not described in subsection (1) or of timber to be cut is a contract for the sale of goods within this Article whether the subject matter is to be severed by the buyer or by the seller even though it forms part of the realty at the time of contracting, and the parties can by identification effect a present sale before severance.

(3) The provisions of this section are subject to any third party rights provided by the law relating to realty records, and the contract for sale may be executed and recorded as a document transferring an interest in land and shall then constitute notice to third parties of the buyer's rights under the contract for sale.

Part 2 Form, Formation and Readjustment of Contract

§ 2—201. Formal Requirements; Statute of Frauds.

(1) Except as otherwise provided in this section a contract for the sale of goods for the price of $500 or more is not enforceable by way of action or defense unless there is some writing sufficient to indicate that a contract for sale has been made between the parties and signed by the party against whom enforcement is sought or by his authorized agent or broker. A writing is not insufficient because it omits or incorrectly states a term agreed upon but the contract is not enforceable under this paragraph beyond the quantity of goods shown in such writing.

(2) Between merchants if within a reasonable time a writing in confirmation of the contract and sufficient against the sender is received and the party receiving it has reason to know its contents, it satisfies the requirements of subsection (1) against such party unless written notice of objection to its contents is given within ten days after it is received.

(3) A contract which does not satisfy the requirements of subsection (1) but which is valid in other respects is enforceable

(a) if the goods are to be specially manufactured for the buyer and are not suitable for sale to others in the ordinary course of the seller's business and the seller, before notice of repudiation is received and under circumstances which reasonably indicate that the goods are for the buyer, has made either a substantial beginning of their manufacture or commitments for their procurement; or

(b) if the party against whom enforcement is sought admits in his pleading, testimony or otherwise in court that a contract for sale was made, but the contract is not enforceable under this provision beyond the quantity of goods admitted; or

(c) with respect to goods for which payment has been made and accepted or which have been received and accepted (Sec. 2—606).

§ 2—202. Final Written Expression: Parol or Extrinsic Evidence.

Terms with respect to which the confirmatory memoranda of the parties agree or which are otherwise set forth in a writing intended by the parties as a final expression of their agreement with respect to such terms as are included therein may not be contradicted by evidence of any prior agreement or of a contemporaneous oral agreement but may be explained or supplemented

(a) by course of dealing or usage of trade (Section 1—205) or by course of performance (Section 2—208); and

(b) by evidence of consistent additional terms unless the court finds the writing to have been intended also as a complete and exclusive statement of the terms of the agreement.

§ 2—203. Seals Inoperative.

The affixing of a seal to a writing evidencing a contract for sale or an offer to buy or sell goods does not constitute the writing a sealed instrument and the law with respect to sealed instruments does not apply to such a contract or offer.

§ 2—204. Formation in General.

(1) A contract for sale of goods may be made in any manner sufficient to show agreement, including conduct by both parties which recognizes the existence of such a contract.

(2) An agreement sufficient to constitute a contract for sale may be found even though the moment of its making is undetermined.

(3) Even though one or more terms are left open a contract for sale does not fail for indefiniteness if the parties have intended to make a contract and there is a reasonably certain basis for giving an appropriate remedy.

§ 2—205. Firm Offers.

An offer by a merchant to buy or sell goods in a signed writing which by its terms gives assurance that it will be held open is not revocable, for lack of consideration, during the time stated or if no time is stated for a reasonable time, but in no event may such period of irrevocability exceed three months; but any such term of assurance on a form supplied by the offeree must be separately signed by the offeror.

§ 2—206. Offer and Acceptance in Formation of Contract.

(1) Unless other unambiguously indicated by the language or circumstances

(a) an offer to make a contract shall be construed as inviting acceptance in any manner and by any medium reasonable in the circumstances;

(b) an order or other offer to buy goods for prompt or current shipment shall be construed as inviting acceptance either by a prompt promise to ship or by the prompt or current shipment of conforming or nonconforming goods, but such a shipment of non-conforming goods does not constitute an acceptance if the seller seasonably notifies the buyer that the shipment is offered only as an accommodation to the buyer.

(2) Where the beginning of a requested performance is a reasonable mode of acceptance an offeror who is not notified of acceptance within a reasonable time may treat the offer as having lapsed before acceptance.

§ 2—207. Additional Terms in Acceptance or Confirmation.

(1) A definite and seasonable expression of acceptance or a written confirmation which is sent within a reasonable time operates as an acceptance even though it states terms additional to or different from those offered or agreed upon, unless acceptance is expressly made conditional on assent to the additional or different terms.

(2) The additional terms are to be construed as proposals for addition to the contract. Between merchants such terms become part of the contract unless:

(a) the offer expressly limits acceptance to the terms of the offer;

(b) they materially alter it; or

(c) notification of objection to them has already been given or is given within a reasonable time after notice of them is received.

(3) Conduct by both parties which recognizes the existence of a contract is sufficient to establish a contract for sale although the writings of the parties do not otherwise establish a contract. In such case the terms of the particular contract consist of those terms on which the writings of the parties agree, together with any supplementary terms incorporated under any other provisions of this Act.

§ 2—208. Course of Performance or Practical Construction.

(1) Where the contract for sale involves repeated occasions for performance by either party with knowledge of the nature of the performance and opportunity for objection to it by the other, any course of performance accepted or acquiesced in without objection shall be relevant to determine the meaning of the agreement.

(2) The express terms of the agreement and any such course of performance, as well as any course of dealing and usage of trade, shall be construed whenever reasonable as consistent with each other; but when such construction is unreasonable, express terms shall control course of performance and course of performance shall control both course of dealing and usage of trade (Section 1—205).

(3) Subject to the provisions of the next section on modification and waiver, such course of performance shall be relevant to show a waiver or modification of any term inconsistent with such course of performance.

§ 2—209. **Modification, Rescission and Waiver.**

(1) An agreement modifying a contract within this Article needs no consideration to be binding.

(2) A signed agreement which excludes modification or rescission except by a signed writing cannot be otherwise modified or rescinded, but except as between merchants such a requirement on a form supplied by the merchant must be separately signed by the other party.

(3) The requirements of the statute of frauds section of this Article (Section 2—201) must be satisfied if the contract as modifed is within its provisions.

(4) Although an attempt at modification or rescission does not satisfy the requirements of subsection (2) or (3) it can operate as a waiver.

(5) A party who has made a waiver affecting an executory portion of the contract may retract the waiver by reasonable notification received by the other party that strict performance will be required of any term waived, unless the retraction would be unjust in view of a material change of position in reliance on the waiver.

§ 2—210. **Delegation of Performance; Assignment of Rights.**

(1) A party may perform his duty through a delegate unless otherwise agreed or unless the other party has a substantial interest in having his original promisor perform or control the acts required by the contract. No delegation of performance relieves the party delegating of any duty to perform or any liability for breach.

(2) Unless otherwise agreed all rights of either seller or buyer can be assigned except where the assignment would materially change the duty of the other party, or increase materially the burden or risk imposed on him by his contract, or impair materially his chance of obtaining return performance. A right to damages for breach of the whole contract or a right arising out of the assignor's due performance of his entire obligation can be assigned despite agreement otherwise.

(3) Unless the circumstances indicate the contrary a prohibition of assignment of "the contract" is to be construed as barring only the delegation to the assignee of the assignor's performance.

(4) An assignment of "the contract" or of "all my rights under the contract" or an assignment in similar general terms is an assignment of rights and unless the language or the circumstances (as in an assignment for security) indicate the contrary, it is a delegation of performance of the duties of the assign-

or and its acceptance by the assignee constitutes a promise by him to perform those duties. This promise is enforceable by either the assignor or the other party to the original contract.

(5) The other party may treat any assignment which delegates performance as creating reasonable grounds for insecurity and may without prejudice to his rights against the assignor demand assurances from the assignee (Section 2—609).

Part 3 **General Obligation and Construction of Contract**

§ 2—301. **General Obligations of Parties.**

The obligation of the seller is to transfer and deliver and that of the buyer is to accept and pay in accordance with the contract.

§ 2—302. **Unconscionable Contract or Clause.**

(1) If the court as a matter of law finds the contract or any clause of the contract to have been unconscionable at the time it was made the court may refuse to enforce the contract, or it may enforce the remainder of the contract without the unconscionable clause, or it may so limit the application of any unconscionable clause as to avoid any unconscionable result.

(2) When it is claimed or appears to the court that the contract or any clause thereof may be unconscionable the parties shall be afforded a reasonable opportunity to present evidence as to its commercial setting, purpose and effect to aid the court in making the determination.

§ 2—303. **Allocation or Division of Risks.**

Where this Article allocates a risk or a burden as between the parties "unless otherwise agreed", the agreement may not only shift the allocation but may also divide the risk or burden.

§ 2—304. **Price Payable in Money, Goods, Realty, or Otherwise.**

(1) The price can be made payable in money or otherwise. If it is payable in whole or in part in goods each party is a seller of the goods which he is to transfer.

(2) Even though all or part of the price is payable in an interest in realty the transfer of the goods and the seller's obligations with reference to them are subject to this Article, but not the transfer of the interest in realty or the transferor's obligations in connection therewith.

§ 2—305. Open Price Term.

(1) The parties if they so intend can conclude a contract for sale even though the price is not settled. In such a case the price is a reasonable price at the time for delivery if

(a) nothing is said as to price; or

(b) the price is left to be agreed by the parties and they fail to agree; or

(c) the price is to be fixed in terms of some agreed market or other standard as set or recorded by a third person or agency and it is not so set or recorded.

(2) A price to be fixed by the seller or by the buyer means a price for him to fix in good faith.

(3) When a price left to be fixed otherwise than by agreement of the parties fails to be fixed through fault of one party the other may at his option treat the contract as cancelled or himself fix a reasonable price.

(4) Where, however, the parties intend not to be bound unless the price be fixed or agreed and it is not fixed or agreed there is no contract. In such a case the buyer must return any goods already received or if unable so to do must pay their reasonable value at the time of delivery and the seller must return any portion of the price paid on account.

§ 2—306. Output, Requirements and Exclusive Dealings.

(1) A term which measures the quantity by the output of the seller or the requirements of the buyer means such actual output or requirements as may occur in good faith, except that no quantity unreasonably disproportionate to any stated estimate or in the absence of a stated estimate to any normal or otherwise comparable prior output or requirements may be tendered or demanded.

(2) A lawful agreement by either the seller or the buyer for exclusive dealing in the kind of goods concerned imposes unless otherwise agreed an obligation by the seller to use best efforts to supply the goods and by the buyer to use best efforts to promote their sale.

§ 2—307. Delivery in Single Lot or Several Lots.

Unless otherwise agreed all goods called for by a contract for sale must be tendered in a single delivery and payment is due only on such tender but where the circumstances give either party the right to make or demand delivery in lots the price if it can be apportioned may be demanded for each lot.

§ 2—308. Absence of Specified Place for Delivery.

Unless otherwise agreed

(a) the place for delivery of goods is the seller's place of business or if he has none his residence; but

(b) in a contract for sale of identified goods which to the knowledge of the parties at the time of contracting are in some other place, that place is the place for their delivery; and

(c) documents of title may be delivered through customary banking channels.

§ 2—309. Absence of Specific Time Provisions; Notice of Termination.

(1) The time for shipment or delivery or any other action under a contract if not provided in this Article or agreed upon shall be a reasonable time.

(2) Where the contract provides for successive performances but is indefinite in duration it is valid for a reasonable time but unless otherwise agreed may be terminated at any time by either party.

(3) Termination of a contract by one party except on the happening of an agreed event requires that reasonable notification be received by the other party and an agreement dispensing with notification is invalid if its operation would be unconscionable.

§ 2—310. Open Time for Payment or Running of Credit; Authority to Ship Under Reservation.

Unless otherwise agreed

(a) payment is due at the time and place at which the buyer is to receive the goods even though the place of shipment is the place of delivery; and

(b) if the seller is authorized to send the goods he may ship them under reservation, and may tender the documents of title, but the buyer may inspect the goods after their arrival before payment is due unless such inspection is inconsistent with the terms of the contract (Section 2—513); and

(c) if delivery is authorized and made by way of documents of title otherwise than by subsection (b) then payment is due at the time and place at which the buyer is to receive the documents regardless of where the goods are to be received; and

(d) where the seller is required or authorized to ship the goods on credit the credit period runs from the time of shipment but post-dating the invoice or delaying its dispatch will correspondingly delay the starting of the credit period.

§ 2—311. **Options and Cooperation Respecting Performance.**

(1) An agreement for sale which is otherwise sufficiently definite (subsection (3) of Section 2—204) to be a contract is not made invalid by the fact that it leaves particulars of performance to be specified by one of the parties. Any such specification must be made in good faith and within limits set by commercial reasonableness.

(2) Unless otherwise agreed specifications relating to assortment of the goods are at the buyer's option and except as otherwise provided in subsections (1) (c) and (3) of Section 2—319 specifications or arrangements relating to shipment are at the seller's option.

(3) Where such specification would materially affect the other party's performance but is not seasonably made or where one party's cooperation is necessary to the agreed performance of the other but is not seasonably forthcoming, the other party in addition to all other remedies

  (a) is excused for any resulting delay in his own performance; and

  (b) may also either proceed to perform in any reasonable manner or after the time for a material part of his own performance treat the failure to specify or to cooperate as a breach by failure to deliver or accept the goods.

§ 2—312. **Warranty of Title and Against Infringement; Buyer's Obligation Against Infringement.**

(1) Subject to subsection (2) there is in a contract for sale a warranty by the seller that

  (a) the title conveyed shall be good, and its transfer rightful; and

  (b) the goods shall be delivered free from any security interest or other lien or encumbrance of which the buyer at the time of contracting has no knowledge.

(2) A warranty under subsection (1) will be excluded or modified only by specific language or by circumstances which give the buyer reason to know that the person selling does not claim title in himself or that he is purporting to sell only such right or title as he or a third person may have.

(3) Unless otherwise agreed a seller who is a merchant regularly dealing in goods of the kind warrants that the goods shall be delivered free of the rightful claim of any third person by way of infringement or the like but a buyer who furnishes specifications to the seller must hold the seller harmless against any such claim which arises out of compliance with the specifications.

§ 2—313. **Express Warranties by Affirmation, Promise, Description, Sample.**

(1) Express warranties by the seller are created as follows:

  (a) Any affirmation of fact or promise made by the seller to the buyer which relates to the goods and becomes part of the basis of the bargain creates an express warranty that the goods shall conform to the affirmation or promise.

  (b) Any description of the goods which is made part of the basis of the bargain creates an express warranty that the goods shall conform to the description.

  (c) Any sample or model which is made part of the basis of the bargain creates an express warranty that the whole of the goods shall conform to the sample or model.

(2) It is not necessary to the creation of an express warranty that the seller use formal words such as "warrant" or "guarantee" or that he have a specific intention to make a warranty, but an affirmation merely of the value of the goods or a statement purporting to be merely the seller's opinion or commendation of the goods does not create a warranty.

§ 2—314. **Implied Warranty: Merchantability; Usage of Trade.**

(1) Unless excluded or modified (Section 2—316), a warranty that the goods shall be merchantable is implied in a contract for their sale if the seller is a merchant with respect to goods of that kind. Under this section the serving for value of food or drink to be consumed either on the premises or elsewhere is a sale.

(2) Goods to be merchantable must be at least such as

  (a) pass without objection in the trade under the contract description; and

  (b) in the case of fungible goods, are of fair average quality within the description; and

  (c) are fit for the ordinary purposes for which such goods are used; and

  (d) run, within the variations permitted by the agreement, of even kind, quality and quantity within each unit and among all units involved; and

  (e) are adequately contained, packaged, and labeled as the agreement may require; and

(f) conform to the promises or affirmations of fact made on the container or label if any.

(3) Unless excluded or modified (Section 2—316) other implied warranties may arise from course of dealing or usage of trade.

§ 2—315. Implied Warranty: Fitness for Particular Purpose.

Where the seller at the time of contracting has reason to know any particular purpose for which the goods are required and that the buyer is relying on the seller's skill or judgment to select or furnish suitable goods, there is unless excluded or modified under the next section an implied warranty that the goods shall be fit for such purpose.

§ 2—316. Exclusion or Modification of Warranties.

(1) Words or conduct relevant to the creation of an express warranty and words or conduct tending to negate or limit warranty shall be construed wherever reasonable as consistent with each other; but subject to the provisions of this Article on parol or extrinsic evidence (Section 2—202) negation or limitation is inoperative to the extent that such construction is unreasonable.

(2) Subject to subsection (3), to exclude or modify the implied warranty of merchantability or any part of it the language must mention merchantability and in case of a writing must be conspicuous, and to exclude or modify any implied warranty of fitness the exclusion must be by a writing and conspicuous. Language to exclude all implied warranties of fitness is sufficient if it states, for example, that "There are no warranties which extend beyond the description on the face hereof."

(3) Notwithstanding subsection (2)

(a) unless the circumstances indicate otherwise, all implied warranties are excluded by expressions like "as is", "with all faults" or other language which in common understanding calls the buyer's attention to the exclusion of warranties and makes plain that there is no implied warranty; and

(b) when the buyer before entering into the contract has examined the goods or the sample or model as fully as he desired or has refused to examine the goods there is no implied warranty with regard to defects which an examination ought in the circumstances to have revealed to him; and

(c) an implied warranty can also be excluded or modified by course of dealing or course of performance or usage of trade.

(4) Remedies for breach of warranty can be limited in accordance with the provisions of this Article on liquidation or limitation of damages and on contractual modification of remedy (Sections 2—718 and 2—719).

§ 2—317. Cumulation and Conflict of Warranties Express or Implied.

Warranties whether express or implied shall be construed as consistent with each other and as cumulative, but if such construction is unreasonable the intention of the parties shall determine which warranty is dominant. In ascertaining that intention the following rules apply:

(a) Exact or technical specifications displace an inconsistent sample or model or general language of description.

(b) A sample from an existing bulk displaces inconsistent general language of description.

(c) Express warranties displace inconsistent implied warranties other than an implied warranty of fitness for a particular purpose.

§ 2—318. Third Party Beneficiaries of Warranties Express or Implied.

Note: If this Act is introduced in the Congress of the United States this section should be omitted. (States to select one alternative.)

Alternative A

A seller's warranty whether express or implied extends to any natural person who is in the family or household of his buyer or who is a guest in his home if it is reasonable to expect that such person may use, consume or be affected by the goods and who is injured in person by breach of the warranty. A seller may not exclude or limit the operation of this section.

Alternative B

A seller's warranty whether express or implied extends to any natural person who may reasonably be expected to use, consume or be affected by the goods and who is injured in person by breach of the warranty. A seller may not exclude or limit the operation of this section.

Alternative C

A seller's warranty whether express or implied extends to any person who may reasonably be expected to use, consume or be affected by the goods and who is injured by breach of the warranty. A seller may not exclude or limit the operation of this section with respect to injury to the person of an individual to whom the warranty extends. As amended 1966.

§ 2—319. F.O.B. and F.A.S. Terms.

(1) Unless otherwise agreed the term F.O.B. (which means "free on board") at a named place, even though used only in connection with the stated price, is a delivery term under which

   (a) when the term is F.O.B. the place of shipment, the seller must at that place ship the goods in the manner provided in this Article (Section 2—504) and bear the expense and risk of putting them into the possession of the carrier; or

   (b) when the term is F.O.B. the place of destination, the seller must at his own expense and risk transport the goods to that place and there tender delivery of them in the manner provided in this Article (Section 2—503);

   (c) when under either (a) or (b) the term is also F.O.B. vessel, car or other vehicle, the seller must in addition at his own expense and risk load the goods on board. If the term is F.O.B. vessel the buyer must name the vessel and in an appropriate case the seller must comply with the provisions of this Article on the form of bill of lading (Section 2—323).

(2) Unless otherwise agreed the term F.A.S. vessel (which means "free alongside") at a named port, even though used only in connection with the stated price, is a delivery term under which the seller must

   (a) at his own expense and risk deliver the goods alongside the vessel in the manner usual in that port or on a dock designated and provided by the buyer; and

   (b) obtain and tender a receipt for the goods in exchange for which the carrier is under a duty to issue a bill of lading.

(3) Unless otherwise agreed in any case falling within subsection (1) (a) or (c) or subsection (2) the buyer must seasonably give any needed instructions for making delivery, including when the term is F.A.S. or F.O.B. the loading berth of the vessel and in an appropriate case its name and sailing date. The seller may treat the failure of needed instructions as a failure of cooperation under this Article (Section 2—311). He may also at his option move the goods in any reasonable manner preparatory to delivery or shipment.

(4) Under the term F.O.B. vessel or F.A.S. unless otherwise agreed the buyer must make payment against tender of the required documents and the seller may not tender nor the buyer demand delivery of the goods in substitution for the documents.

§ 2—320. C.I.F. and C. & F. Terms.

(1) The term C.I.F. means that the price includes in a lump sum the cost of the goods and the insurance and freight to the named destination. The term C. & F. or C.F. means that the price so includes cost and freight to the named destination.

(2) Unless otherwise agreed and even though used only in connection with the stated price and destination, the term C.I.F. destination or its equivalent requires the seller at his own expense and risk to

   (a) put the goods into the possession of a carrier at the port for shipment and obtain a negotiable bill or bills of lading covering the entire transportation to the named destination; and

   (b) load the goods and obtain a receipt from the carrier (which may be contained in the bill of lading) showing that the freight has been paid or provided for; and

   (c) obtain a policy or certificate of insurance, including any war risk insurance, of a kind and on terms then current at the port of shipment in the usual amount, in the currency of the contract, shown to cover the same goods covered by the bill of lading and providing for payment of loss to the order of the buyer or for the account of whom it may concern; but the seller may add to the price the amount of the premium for any such war risk insurance; and

   (d) prepare an invoice of the goods and procure any other documents required to effect shipment or to comply with the contract; and

   (e) forward and tender with commercial promptness all the documents in due form and with any indorsement necessary to perfect the buyer's rights.

(3) Unless otherwise agreed the term C. & F. or its equivalent has the same effect and imposes upon the seller the same obligations and risks as a C.I.F. term except the obligation as to insurance.

(4) Under the term C.I.F. or C. & F. unless otherwise agreed the buyer must make payment against tender of the required documents and the seller may not tender nor the buyer demand delivery of the goods in substitution for the documents.

§ 2—321. C.I.F. or C. & F.: "Net Landed Weights"; "Payment on Arrival"; Warranty of Condition on Arrival.

Under a contract containing a term C.I.F. or C. & F.

(1) Where the price is based on or is to be adjusted according to "net landed weights", "delivered

weights", "out turn" quantity or quality or the like, unless otherwise agreed the seller must reasonably estimate the price. The payment due on tender of the documents called for by the contract is the amount so estimated, but after final adjustment of the price a settlement must be made with commercial promptness.

(2) An agreement described in subsection (1) or any warranty of quality or condition of the goods on arrival places upon the seller the risk of ordinary deterioration, shrinkage and the like in transportation but has no effect on the place or time of identification to the contract for sale or delivery or on the passing of the risk of loss.

(3) Unless otherwise agreed where the contract provides for payment on or after arrival of the goods the seller must before payment allow such preliminary inspection as is feasible; but if the goods are lost delivery of the documents and payment are due when the goods should have arrived.

§ 2—322. **Delivery "Ex-Ship".**

(1) Unless otherwise agreed a term for delivery of goods "ex-ship" (which means from the carrying vessel) or in equivalent language is not restricted to a particular ship and requires delivery from a ship which has reached a place at the named port of destination where goods of the kind are usually discharged.

(2) Under such a term unless otherwise agreed

(a) the seller must discharge all liens arising out of the carriage and furnish the buyer with a direction which puts the carrier under a duty to deliver the goods; and

(b) the risk of loss does not pass to the buyer until the goods leave the ship's tackle or are otherwise properly unloaded.

§ 2—323. **Form of Bill of Lading Required in Overseas Shipment; "Overseas".**

(1) Where the contract contemplates overseas shipment and contains a term C.I.F. or C. & F. or F.O.B. vessel, the seller unless otherwise agreed must obtain a negotiable bill of lading stating that the goods have been loaded on board or, in the case of a term C.I.F. or C. & F., received for shipment.

(2) Where in a case within subsection (1) a bill of lading has been issued in a set of parts, unless otherwise agreed if the documents are not to be sent from abroad the buyer may demand tender of the full set; otherwise only one part of the bill of lading need be tendered. Even if the agreement expressly requires a full set

(a) due tender of a single part is acceptable within the provisions of this Article on cure of improper delivery (subsection (1) of Section 2—508); and

(b) even though the full set is demanded, if the documents are sent from abroad the person tendering an incomplete set may nevertheless require payment upon furnishing an indemnity which the buyer in good faith deems adequate.

(3) A shipment by water or by air or a contract contemplating such shipment is "overseas" insofar as by usage of trade or agreement it is subject to the commercial, financing or shipping practices characteristic of international deep water commerce.

§ 2—324. **"No Arrival, No Sale" Term.**

Under a term "no arrival, no sale" or terms of like meaning, unless otherwise agreed,

(a) the seller must properly ship conforming goods and if they arrive by any means he must tender them on arrival but he assumes no obligation that the goods will arrive unless he has caused the non-arrival; and

(b) where without fault of the seller the goods are in part lost or have so deteriorated as no longer to conform to the contract or arrive after the contract time, the buyer may proceed as if there had been casualty to identified goods (Section 2—613).

§ 2—325. **"Letter of Credit" Term; "Confirmed Credit".**

(1) Failure of the buyer seasonably to furnish an agreed letter of credit is a breach of the contract for sale.

(2) The delivery to seller of a proper letter of credit suspends the buyer's obligation to pay. If the letter of credit is dishonored, the seller may on seasonable notification to the buyer require payment directly from him.

(3) Unless otherwise agreed the term "letter of credit" or "banker's credit" in a contract for sale means an irrevocable credit issued by a financing agency of good repute and, where the shipment is overseas, of good international repute. The term "confirmed credit" means that the credit must also carry the direct obligation of such an agency which does business in the seller's financial market.

§ 2—326. **Sale on Approval and Sale or Return; Consignment Sales and Rights of Creditors.**

(1) Unless otherwise agreed, if delivered goods may

be returned by the buyer even though they conform to the contract, the transaction is

(a) a "sale on approval" if the goods are delivered primarily for use, and

(b) a "sale or return" if the goods are delivered primarily for resale.

(2) Except as provided in subsection (3), goods held on approval are not subject to the claims of the buyer's creditors until acceptance; goods held on sale or return are subject to such claims while in the buyer's possession.

(3) Where goods are delivered to a person for sale and such person maintains a place of business at which he deals in goods of the kind involved, under a name other than the name of the person making delivery, then with respect to claims of creditors of the person conducting the business the goods are deemed to be on sale or return. The provisions of this subsection are applicable even though an agreement purports to reserve title to the person making delivery until payment or resale or uses such words as "on consignment" or "on memorandum". However, this subsection is not applicable if the person making delivery

(a) complies with an applicable law providing for a consignor's interest or the like to be evidenced by a sign, or

(b) establishes that the person conducting the business is generally known by his creditors to be substantially engaged in selling the goods of others, or

(c) complies with the filing provisions of the Article on Secured Transactions (Article 9).

(4) Any "or return" term of a contract for sale is to be treated as a separate contract for sale within the statute of frauds section of this Article (Section 2—201) and as contradicting the sale aspect of the contract within the provisions of this Article on parol or extrinsic evidence (Section 2—202).

§ 2—327. **Special Incidents of Sale on Approval and Sale or Return.**

(1) Under a sale on approval unless otherwise agreed

(a) although the goods are identified to the contract the risk of loss and the title do not pass to the buyer until acceptance; and

(b) use of the goods consistent with the purpose of trial is not acceptance but failure seasonably to notify the seller of election to return the goods is acceptance, and if the goods conform to the contract acceptance of any part is acceptance of the whole; and

(c) after due notification of election to return, the return is at the seller's risk and expense but a merchant buyer must follow any reasonable instructions.

(2) Under a sale or return unless otherwise agreed

(a) the option to return extends to the whole or any commercial unit of the goods while in substantially their original condition, but must be exercised seasonably; and

(b) the return is at the buyer's risk and expense.

§ 2—328. **Sale by Auction.**

(1) In a sale by auction if goods are put up in lots each lot is the subject of a separate sale.

(2) A sale by auction is complete when the auctioneer so announces by the fall of the hammer or in other customary manner. Where a bid is made while the hammer is falling in acceptance of a prior bid the auctioneer may in his discretion reopen the bidding or declare the goods sold under the bid on which the hammer was falling.

(3) Such a sale is with reserve unless the goods are in explicit terms put up without reserve. In an auction with reserve the auctioneer may withdraw the goods at any time until he announces completion of the sale. In an auction without reserve, after the auctioneer calls for bids on an article or lot, that article or lot cannot be withdrawn unless no bid is made within a reasonable time. In either case a bidder may retract his bid until the auctioneer's announcement of completion of the sale, but a bidder's retraction does not revive any previous bid.

(4) If the auctioneer knowingly receives a bid on the seller's behalf or the seller makes or procures such a bid, and notice has not been given that liberty for such bidding is reserved, the buyer may at his option avoid the sale or take the goods at the price of the last good faith bid prior to the completion of the sale. This subsection shall not apply to any bid at a forced sale.

Part 4 Title, Creditors and Good Faith Purchasers

§ 2—401. **Passing of Title; Reservation for Security; Limited Application of This Section.**

Each provision of this Article with regard to the rights, obligations and remedies of the seller, the buyer, purchasers or other third parties applies irrespective of title to the goods except where the provision refers to such title. Insofar as situations are not covered by the other provisions of this Article and matters concerning title became material the following rules apply:

(1) Title to goods cannot pass under a contract for sale prior to their identification to the contract (Section 2—501), and unless otherwise explicitly agreed the buyer acquires by their identification a special property as limited by this Act. Any retention or reservation by the seller of the title (property) in goods shipped or delivered to the buyer is limited in effect to a reservation of a security interest. Subject to these provisions and to the provisions of the Article on Secured Transactions (Article 9), title to goods passes from the seller to the buyer in any manner and on any conditions explicitly agreed on by the parties.

(2) Unless otherwise explicitly agreed title passes to the buyer at the time and place at which the seller completes his performance with reference to the physical delivery of the goods, despite any reservation of a security interest and even though a document of title is to be delivered at a different time or place; and in particular and despite any reservation of a security interest by the bill of lading

(a) if the contract requires or authorizes the seller to send the goods to the buyer but does not require him to deliver them at destination, title passes to the buyer at the time and place of shipment; but

(b) if the contract requires delivery at destination, title passes on tender there.

(3) Unless otherwise explicitly agreed where delivery is to be made without moving the goods,

(a) if the seller is to deliver a document of title, title passes at the time when and the place where he delivers such documents; or

(b) if the goods are at the time of contracting already identified and no documents are to be delivered, title passes at the time and place of contracting.

(4) A rejection or other refusal by the buyer to receive or retain the goods, whether or not justified, or a justified revocation of acceptance revests title to the goods in the seller. Such revesting occurs by operation of law and is not a "sale".

§ 2—402. **Rights of Seller's Creditors Against Sold Goods.**

(1) Except as provided in subsections (2) and (3), rights of unsecured creditors of the seller with respect to goods which have been identified to a contract for sale are subject to the buyer's rights to recover the goods under this Article (Sections 2—502 and 2—716).

(2) A creditor of the seller may treat a sale or an identification of goods to a contract for sale as void if as against him a retention of possession by the seller is fraudulent under any rule of law of the state where the goods are situated, except that retention of possession in good faith and current course of trade by a merchant-seller for a commercially reasonable time after a sale or identification is not fraudulent.

(3) Nothing in this Article shall be deemed to impair the rights of creditors of the seller

(a) under the provisions of the Article on Secured Transactions (Article 9); or

(b) where identification to the contract or delivery is made not in current course of trade but in satisfaction of or as security for a pre-existing claim for money, security or the like and is made under circumstances which under any rule of law of the state where the goods are situated would apart from this Article constitute the transaction a fraudulent transfer or voidable preference.

§ 2—403. **Power to Transfer; Good Faith Purchase of Goods; "Entrusting".**

(1) A purchaser of goods acquires all title which his transferor had or had power to transfer except that a purchaser of a limited interest acquires rights only to the extent of the interest purchased. A person with voidable title has power to transfer a good title to a good faith purchaser for value. When goods have been delivered under a transaction of purchase the purchaser has such power even though

(a) the transferor was deceived as to the identity of the purchaser, or

(b) the delivery was in exchange for a check which is later dishonored, or

(c) it was agreed that the transaction was to be a "cash sale", or

(d) the delivery was procured through fraud punishable as larcenous under the criminal law.

(2) Any entrusting of possession of goods to a merchant who deals in goods of that kind gives him power to transfer all rights of the entruster to a buyer in ordinary course of business.

(3) "Entrusting" includes any delivery and any acquiescence in retention of possession regardless of any condition expressed between the parties to the delivery or acquiescence and regardless of whether the procurement of the entrusting or the possessor's disposition of the goods have been such as to be larcenous under the criminal law.

(4) The rights of other purchasers of goods and of lien creditors are governed by the Articles on Secured

Transactions (Article 9), Bulk Transfers (Article 6) and Documents of Title (Article 7).

Part 5 Performance

§ 2—501. Insurable Interest in Goods; Manner of Identification of Goods.

(1) The buyer obtains a special property and an insurable interest in goods by identification of existing goods as goods to which the contract refers even though the goods so identified are non-conforming and he has an option to return or reject them. Such identification can be made at any time and in any manner explicitly agreed to by the parties. In the absence of explicit agreement identification occurs

(a) when the contract is made if it is for the sale of goods already existing and identified;

(b) if the contract is for the sale of future goods other than those described in paragraph (c), when goods are shipped, marked or otherwise designated by the seller as goods to which the contract refers;

(c) when the crops are planted or otherwise become growing crops or the young are conceived if the contract is for the sale of unborn young to be born within twelve months after contracting or for the sale of crops to be harvested within twelve months or the next normal harvest season after contracting whichever is longer.

(2) The seller retains an insurable interest in goods so long as title to or any security interest in the goods remains in him and where the identification is by the seller alone he may until default or insolvency or notification to the buyer that the identification is final substitute other goods for those identified.

(3) Nothing in this section impairs any insurable interest recognized under any other statute or rule of law.

§ 2—502. Buyer's Right to Goods on Seller's Insolvency.

(1) Subject to subsection (2) and even though the goods have not been shipped a buyer who has paid a part or all of the price of goods in which he has a special property under the provisions of the immediately preceding section may on making and keeping good a tender of any unpaid portion of their price recover them from the seller if the seller becomes insolvent within ten days after receipt of the first installment on their price.

(2) If the identification creating his special property has been made by the buyer he acquires the right to recover the goods only if they conform to the contract for sale.

§ 2—503. Manner of Seller's Tender of Delivery.

(1) Tender of delivery requires that the seller put and hold conforming goods at the buyer's disposition and give the buyer any notification reasonably necessary to enable him to take delivery. The manner, time and place for tender are determined by the agreement and this Article, and in particular

(a) tender must be at a reasonable hour, and if it is of goods they must be kept available for the period reasonably necessary to enable the buyer to take possession; but

(b) unless otherwise agreed the buyer must furnish facilities reasonably suited to the receipt of the goods.

(2) Where the case is within the next section respecting shipment tender requires that the seller comply with its provisions.

(3) Where the seller is required to deliver at a particular destination tender requires that he comply with subsection (1) and also in any appropriate case tender documents as described in subsections (4) and (5) of this section.

(4) Where goods are in the possession of a bailee and are to be delivered without being moved

(a) tender requires that the seller either tender a negotiable document of title covering such goods or procure acknowledgment by the bailee of the buyer's right to possession of the goods; but

(b) tender to the buyer of a non-negotiable document of title or of a written direction to the bailee to deliver is sufficient tender unless the buyer seasonably objects, and receipt by the bailee of notification of the buyer's rights fixes those rights as against the bailee and all third persons; but risk of loss of the goods and of any failure by the bailee to honor the non-negotiable document of title or to obey the direction remains on the seller until the buyer has had a reasonable time to present the document or direction, and a refusal by the bailee to honor the document or to obey the direction defeats the tender.

(5) Where the contract requires the seller to deliver documents

(a) he must tender all such documents in correct form, except as provided in this Article with respect to bills of lading in a set (subsection (2) of Section 2—323); and

(b) tender through customary banking channels is sufficient and dishonor of a draft accompanying the documents constitutes non-acceptance or rejection.

§ 2—504. Shipment by Seller.

Where the seller is required or authorized to send the goods to the buyer and the contract does not require him to deliver them at a particular destination, then unless otherwise agreed he must

(a) put the goods in the possession of such a carrier and make such a contract for their transportation as may be reasonable having regard to the nature of the goods and other circumstances of the case; and

(b) obtain and promptly deliver or tender in due form any document necessary to enable the buyer to obtain possession of the goods or otherwise required by the agreement or by usage of trade; and

(c) promptly notify the buyer of the shipment.

Failure to notify the buyer under paragraph (c) or to make a proper contract under paragraph (a) is a ground for rejection only if material delay or loss ensues.

§ 2—505. Seller's Shipment Under Reservation.

(1) Where the seller has identified goods to the contract by or before shipment:

(a) his procurement of a negotiable bill of lading to his own order or otherwise reserves in him a security interest in the goods. His procurement of the bill to the order of a financing agency or of the buyer indicates in addition only the seller's expectation of transferring that interest to the person named.

(b) a non-negotiable bill of lading to himself or his nominee reserves possession of the goods as security but except in a case of conditional delivery (subsection (2) of Section 2—507) a non-negotiable bill of lading naming the buyer as consignee reserves no security interest even though the seller retains possession of the bill of lading.

(2) When shipment by the seller with reservation of a security interest is in violation of the contract for sale it constitutes an improper contract for transportation within the preceding section but impairs neither the rights given to the buyer by shipment and identification of the goods to the contract nor the seller's powers as a holder of a negotiable document.

§ 2—506. Rights of Financing Agency.

(1) A financing agency by paying or purchasing for value a draft which relates to a shipment of goods acquires to the extent of the payment or purchase and in addition to its own rights under the draft and any document of title securing it any rights of the shipper in the goods including the right to stop delivery and the shipper's right to have the draft honored by the buyer.

(2) The right to reimbursement of a financing agency which has in good faith honored or purchased the draft under commitment to or authority from the buyer is not impaired by subsequent discovery of defects with reference to any relevant document which was apparently regular on its face.

§ 2—507. Effect of Seller's Tender; Delivery on Condition.

(1) Tender of delivery is a condition to the buyer's duty to accept the goods and, unless otherwise agreed, to his duty to pay for them. Tender entitles the seller to acceptance of the goods and to payment according to the contract.

(2) Where payment is due and demanded on the delivery to the buyer of goods or documents of title, his right as against the seller to retain or dispose of them is conditional upon his making the payment due.

§ 2—508. Cure by Seller of Improper Tender or Delivery; Replacement.

(1) Where any tender or delivery by the seller is rejected because non-conforming and the time for performance has not yet expired, the seller may seasonably notify the buyer of his intention to cure and may then within the contract time make a conforming delivery.

(2) Where the buyer rejects a non-conforming tender which the seller had reasonable grounds to believe would be acceptable with or without money allowance the seller may if he seasonably notifies the buyer have a further reasonable time to substitute a conforming tender.

§ 2—509. Risk of Loss in the Absence of Breach.

(1) Where the contract requires or authorizes the seller to ship the goods by carrier

(a) if it does not require him to deliver them at a particular destination, the risk of loss passes to the buyer when the goods are duly delivered to the carrier even though the shipment is under reservation (Section 2—505); but

(b) if it does require him to deliver them at a particular destination and the goods are there duly tendered while in the possession of the carrier, the risk of loss passes to the buyer when the goods are there duly so tendered as to enable the buyer to take delivery.

(2) Where the goods are held by a bailee to be delivered without being moved, the risk of loss passes to the buyer

(a) on his receipt of a negotiable document of title covering the goods; or

(b) on acknowledgment by the bailee of the buyer's right to possession of the goods; or

(c) after his receipt of a non-negotiable document of title or other written direction to deliver, as provided in subsection (4) (b) of Section 2—503.

(3) In any case not within subsection (1) or (2), the risk of loss passes to the buyer on his receipt of the goods if the seller is a merchant; otherwise, the risk passes to the buyer on tender of delivery.

(4) The provisions of this section are subject to contrary agreement of the parties and to the provisions of this Article on sale on approval (Section 2—327) and on effect of breach on risk of loss (Section 2—510).

§ 2—510. Effect of Breach on Risk of Loss.

(1) Where a tender or delivery of goods so fails to conform to the contract as to give a right of rejection the risk of their loss remains on the seller until cure or acceptance.

(2) Where the buyer rightfully revokes acceptance he may to the extent of any deficiency in his effective insurance coverage treat the risk of loss as having rested on the seller from the beginning.

(3) Where the buyer as to conforming goods already identified to the contract for sale repudiates or is otherwise in breach before risk of their loss has passed to him, the seller may to the extent of any deficiency in his effective insurance coverage treat the risk of loss as resting on the buyer for a commercially reasonable time.

§ 2—511. Tender of Payment by Buyer; Payment by Check.

(1) Unless otherwise agreed tender of payment is a condition to the seller's duty to tender and complete any delivery.

(2) Tender of payment is sufficient when made by any means or in any manner current in the ordinary course of business unless the seller demands payment in legal tender and gives any extension of time reasonably necessary to procure it.

(3) Subject to the provisions of this Act on the effect of an instrument on an obligation (Section 3—802),

payment by check is conditional and is defeated as between the parties by dishonor of the check on due presentment.

§ 2—512. Payment by Buyer Before Inspection.

(1) Where the contract requires payment before inspection non-conformity of the goods does not excuse the buyer from so making payment unless

(a) the non-conformity appears without inspection; or

(b) despite tender of the required documents the circumstances would justify injunction against honor under the provisions of this Act (Section 5—114).

(2) Payment pursuant to subsection (1) does not constitute an acceptance of goods or impair the buyer's right to inspect or any of his remedies.

§ 2—513. Buyer's Right to Inspection of Goods.

(1) Unless otherwise agreed and subject to subsection (3), where goods are tendered or delivered or identified to the contract for sale, the buyer has a right before payment or acceptance to inspect them at any reasonable place and time and in any reasonable manner. When the seller is required or authorized to send the goods to the buyer, the inspection may be after their arrival.

(2) Expenses of inspection must be borne by the buyer but may be recovered from the seller if the goods do not conform and are rejected.

(3) Unless otherwise agreed and subject to the provisions of this Article on C.I.F. contracts (subsection (3) of Section 2—321), the buyer is not entitled to inspect the goods before payment of the price when the contract provides

(a) for delivery "C.O.D." or on other like terms; or

(b) for payment against documents of title, except where such payment is due only after the goods are to become available for inspection.

(4) A place or method of inspection fixed by the parties is presumed to be exclusive but unless otherwise expressly agreed it does not postpone identification or shift the place for delivery or for passing the risk of loss. If compliance becomes impossible, inspection shall be as provided in this section unless the place or method fixed was clearly intended as an indispensable condition failure of which avoids the contract.

§ 2—514. **When Documents Deliverable on Acceptance; When on Payment.**

Unless otherwise agreed documents against which a draft is drawn are to be delivered to the drawee on acceptance of the draft if it is payable more than three days after presentment; otherwise, only on payment.

§ 2—515. **Preserving Evidence of Goods in Dispute.**

In furtherance of the adjustment of any claim or dispute

(a) either party on reasonable notification to the other and for the purpose of ascertaining the facts and preserving evidence has the right to inspect, test and sample the goods including such of them as may be in the possession or control of the other; and

(b) the parties may agree to a third party inspection or survey to determine the conformity or condition of the goods and may agree that the findings shall be binding upon them in any subsequent litigation or adjustment.

Part 6 Breach, Repudiation and Excuse

§ 2—601. **Buyer's Rights on Improper Delivery.**

Subject to the provisions of this Article on breach in installment contracts (Section 2—612) and unless otherwise agreed under the sections on contractual limitations of remedy (Sections 2—718 and 2—719), if the goods or the tender of delivery fail in any respect to conform to the contract, the buyer may

(a) reject the whole; or

(b) accept the whole; or

(c) accept any commercial unit or units and reject the rest.

§ 2—602. Manner and Effect of Rightful Rejection.

(1) Rejection of goods must be within a reasonable time after their delivery or tender. It is ineffective unless the buyer seasonably notifies the seller.

(2) Subject to the provisions of the two following sections on rejected goods (Sections 2—603 and 2—604),

(a) after rejection any exercise of ownership by the buyer with respect to any commercial unit is wrongful as against the seller; and

(b) if the buyer has before rejection taken physical possession of goods in which he does not have a security interest under the provisions of this Article (subsection (3) of Section 2—711), he is under a duty after rejection to hold them with reasonable care at the seller's disposition for a time sufficient to permit the seller to remove them; but

(c) the buyer has no further obligations with regard to goods rightfully rejected.

(3) The seller's rights with respect to goods wrongfully rejected are governed by the provisions of this Article on seller's remedies in general (Section 2—703).

§ 2—603. **Merchant Buyer's Duties as to Rightfully Rejected Goods.**

(1) Subject to any security interest in the buyer (subsection (3) of Section 2—711), when the seller has no agent or place of business at the market of rejection a merchant buyer is under a duty after rejection of goods in his possession or control to follow any reasonable instructions received from the seller with respect to the goods and in the absence of such instructions to make reasonable efforts to sell them for the seller's account if they are perishable or threaten to decline in value speedily. Instructions are not reasonable if on demand indemnity for expenses is not forthcoming.

(2) When the buyer sells goods under subsection (1), he is entitled to reimbursement from the seller or out of the proceeds for reasonable expenses of caring for and selling them, and if the expenses include no selling commission then to such commission as is usual in the trade or if there is none to a reasonable sum not exceeding ten per cent on the gross proceeds.

(3) In complying with this section the buyer is held only to good faith and good faith conduct hereunder is neither acceptance nor conversion nor the basis of an action for damages.

§ 2—604. **Buyer's Options as to Salvage of Rightfully Rejected Goods.**

Subject to the provisions of the immediately preceding section on perishables if the seller gives no instructions within a reasonable time after notification of rejection the buyer may store the rejected goods for the seller's account or reship them to him or resell them for the seller's account with reimbursement as provided in the preceding section. Such action is not acceptance or conversion.

§ 2—605. **Waiver of Buyer's Objections by Failure to Particularize.**

(1) The buyer's failure to state in connection with rejection a particular defect which is ascertainable by

reasonable inspection precludes him from relying on the unstated defect to justify rejection or to establish breach

    (a) where the seller could have cured it if stated seasonably; or

    (b) between merchants when the seller has after rejection made a request in writing for a full and final written statement of all defects on which the buyer proposes to rely.

(2) Payment against documents made without reservation of rights precludes recovery of the payment for defects apparent on the face of the documents.

§ 2—606. What Constitutes Acceptance of Goods.

(1) Acceptance of goods occurs when the buyer

    (a) after a reasonable opportunity to inspect the goods signifies to the seller that the goods are conforming or that he will take or retain them in spite of their nonconformity; or

    (b) fails to make an effective rejection (subsection (1) of Section 2—602), but such acceptance does not occur until the buyer has had a reasonable opportunity to inspect them; or

    (c) does any act inconsistent with the seller's ownership; but if such act is wrongful as against the seller it is an acceptance only if ratified by him.

(2) Acceptance of a part of any commercial unit is acceptance of that entire unit.

§ 2—607. Effect of Acceptance; Notice of Breach; Burden of Establishing Breach After Acceptance; Notice of Claim or Litigation to Person Answerable Over.

(1) The buyer must pay at the contract rate for any goods accepted.

(2) Acceptance of goods by the buyer precludes rejection of the goods accepted and if made with knowledge of a non-conformity cannot be revoked because of it unless the acceptance was on the reasonable assumption that the non-conformity would be seasonably cured but acceptance does not of itself impair any other remedy provided by this Article for non-conformity.

(3) Where a tender has been accepted

    (a) the buyer must within a reasonable time after he discovers or should have discovered any breach notify the seller of breach or be barred from any remedy; and

    (b) if the claim is one for infringement or the like (subsection (3) of Section 2—312) and the buyer is sued as a result of such a breach he must so notify the seller within a reasonable time after he receives notice of the litigation or be barred from any remedy over for liability established by the litigation.

(4) The burden is on the buyer to establish any breach with respect to the goods accepted.

(5) Where the buyer is sued for breach of a warranty or other obligation for which his seller is answerable over

    (a) he may give his seller written notice of the litigation. If the notice states that the seller may come in and defend and that if the seller does not do so he will be bound in any action against him by his buyer by any determination of fact common to the two litigations, then unless the seller after seasonable receipt of the notice does come in and defend he is so bound.

    (b) if the claim is one for infringement or the like (subsection (3) of Section 2—312) the original seller may demand in writing that his buyer turn over to him control of the litigation including settlement or else be barred from any remedy over and if he also agrees to bear all expense and to satisfy any adverse judgment, then unless the buyer after seasonable receipt of the demand does turn over control the buyer is so barred.

(6) The provisions of subsections (3), (4) and (5) apply to any obligation of a buyer to hold the seller harmless against infringement or the like (subsection (3) of Section 2—312).

§ 2—608. Revocation of Acceptance in Whole or in Part.

(1) The buyer may revoke his acceptance of a lot or commercial unit whose non-conformity substantially impairs its value to him if he has accepted it

    (a) on the reasonable assumption that its non-conformity would be cured and it has not been seasonably cured; or

    (b) without discovery of such non-conformity if his acceptance was reasonably induced either by the difficulty of discovery before acceptance or by the seller's assurances.

(2) Revocation of acceptance must occur within a reasonable time after the buyer discovers or should have discovered the ground for it and before any substantial change in condition of the goods which is not caused by their own defects. It is not effective until the buyer notifies the seller of it.

(3) A buyer who so revokes has the same rights and

duties with regard to the goods involved as if he had rejected them.

§ 2—609. Right to Adequate Assurance of Performance.

(1) A contract for sale imposes an obligation on each party that the other's expectation of receiving due performance will not be impaired. When reasonable grounds for insecurity arise with respect to the performance of either party the other may in writing demand adequate assurance of due performance and until he receives such assurance may if commercially reasonable suspend any performance for which he has not already received the agreed return.

(2) Between merchants the reasonableness of grounds for insecurity and the adequacy of any assurance offered shall be determined according to commercial standards.

(3) Acceptance of any improper delivery or payment does not prejudice the aggrieved party's right to demand adequate assurance of future performance.

(4) After receipt of a justified demand failure to provide within a reasonable time not exceeding thirty days such assurance of due performance as is adequate under the circumstances of the particular case is a repudiation of the contract.

§ 2—610. Anticipatory Repudiation.

When either party repudiates the contract with respect to a performance not yet due the loss of which will substantially impair the value of the contract to the other, the aggrieved party may

(a) for a commercially reasonable time await performance by the repudiating party; or

(b) resort to any remedy for breach (Section 2—703 or Section 2—711), even though he has notified the repudiating party that he would await the latter's performance and has urged retraction; and

(c) in either case suspend his own performance or proceed in accordance with the provisions of this Article on the seller's right to identify goods to the contract notwithstanding breach or to salvage unfinished goods (Section 2—704).

§ 2—611. Retraction of Anticipatory Repudiation.

(1) Until the repudiating party's next performance is due he can retract his repudiation unless the aggrieved party has since the repudiation cancelled or materially changed his position or otherwise indicated that he considers the repudiation final.

(2) Retraction may be by any method which clearly indicates to the aggrieved party that the repudiating party intends to perform, but must include any assurance justifiably demanded under the provisions of this Article (Section 2—609).

(3) Retraction reinstates the repudiating party's rights under the contract with due excuse and allowance to the aggrieved party for any delay occasioned by the repudiation.

§ 2—612. "Installment Contract"; Breach.

(1) An "installment contract" is one which requires or authorizes the delivery of goods in separate lots to be separately accepted, even though the contract contains a clause "each delivery is a separate contract" or its equivalent.

(2) The buyer may reject any installment which is non-conforming if the non-conformity substantially impairs the value of that installment and cannot be cured or if the non-conformity is a defect in the required documents; but if the non-conformity does not fall within subsection (3) and the seller gives adequate assurance of its cure the buyer must accept that installment.

(3) Whenever non-conformity or default with respect to one or more installments substantially impairs the value of the whole contract there is a breach of the whole. But the aggrieved party reinstates the contract if he accepts a non-conforming installment without seasonably notifying of cancellation or if he brings an action with respect only to past installments or demands performance as to future installments.

§ 2—613. Casualty to Identified Goods.

Where the contract requires for its performance goods identified when the contract is made, and the goods suffer casualty without fault of either party before the risk of loss passes to the buyer, or in a proper case under a "no arrival, no sale" term (Section 2—324) then

(a) if the loss is total the contract is avoided; and

(b) if the loss is partial or the goods have so deteriorated as no longer to conform to the contract the buyer may nevertheless demand inspection and at his option either treat the contract as avoided or accept the goods with due allowance from the contract price for the deterioration or the deficiency in quantity but without further right against the seller.

§ 2—614. Substituted Performance.

(1) Where without fault of either party the agreed berthing, loading, or unloading facilities fail or an agreed type of carrier becomes unavailable or the agreed manner of delivery otherwise becomes com-

mercially impracticable but a commercially reasonable substitute is available, such substitute performance must be tendered and accepted.

(2) If the agreed means or manner of payment fails because of domestic or foreign governmental regulation, the seller may withhold or stop delivery unless the buyer provides a means or manner of payment which is commercially a substantial equivalent. If delivery has already been taken, payment by the means or in the manner provided by the regulation discharges the buyer's obligation unless the regulation is discriminatory, oppressive or predatory.

§ 2—615. Excuse by Failure of Presupposed Conditions.

Except so far as a seller may have assumed a greater obligation and subject to the preceding section on substituted performance:

(a) Delay in delivery or non-delivery in whole or in part by a seller who complies with paragraphs (b) and (c) is not a breach of his duty under a contract for sale if performance as agreed has been made impracticable by the occurrence of a contingency the non-occurrence of which was a basic assumption on which the contract was made or by compliance in good faith with any applicable foreign or domestic governmental regulation or order whether or not it later proves to be invalid.

(b) Where the causes mentioned in paragraph (a) affect only a part of the seller's capacity to perform, he must allocate production and deliveries among his customers but may at his option include regular customers not then under contract as well as his own requirements for further manufacture. He may so allocate in any manner which is fair and reasonable.

(c) The seller must notify the buyer seasonably that there will be delay or non-delivery and, when allocation is required under paragraph (b), of the estimated quota thus made available for the buyer.

§ 2—616. Procedure on Notice Claiming Excuse.

(1) Where the buyer receives notification of a material or indefinite delay or an allocation justified under the preceding section he may by written notification to the seller as to any delivery concerned, and where the prospective deficiency substantially impairs the value of the whole contract under the provisions of this Article relating to breach of installment contracts (Section 2—612), then also as to the whole,

   (a) terminate and thereby discharge any unexecuted portion of the contract; or

   (b) modify the contract by agreeing to take his available quota in substitution.

(2) If after receipt of such notification from the seller the buyer fails so to modify the contract within a reasonable time not exceeding thirty days the contract lapses with respect to any deliveries affected.

(3) The provisions of this section may not be negated by agreement except in so far as the seller has assumed a greater obligation under the preceding section.

Part 7 Remedies

§ 2—701. Remedies for Breach of Collateral Contracts Not Impaired.

Remedies for breach of any obligation or promise collateral or ancillary to a contract for sale are not impaired by the provisions of this Article.

§ 2—702. Seller's Remedies on Discovery of Buyer's Insolvency.

(1) Where the seller discovers the buyer to be insolvent he may refuse delivery except for cash including payment for all goods theretofore delivered under the contract, and stop delivery under this Article (Section 2—705).

(2) Where the seller discovers that the buyer has received goods on credit while insolvent he may reclaim the goods upon demand made within ten days after the receipt, but if misrepresentation of solvency has been made to the particular seller in writing within three months before delivery the ten day limitation does not apply. Except as provided in this subsection the seller may not base a right to reclaim goods on the buyer's fraudulent or innocent misrepresentation of solvency or of intent to pay.

(3) The seller's right to reclaim under subsection (2) is subject to the rights of a buyer in ordinary course or other good faith purchaser under this Article (Section 2—403). Successful reclamation of goods excludes all other remedies with respect to them.

§ 2—703. Seller's Remedies in General.

Where the buyer wrongfully rejects or revokes acceptance of goods or fails to make a payment due on or before delivery or repudiates with respect to a part or the whole, then with respect to any goods directly affected and, if the breach is of the whole contract (Section 2—612), then also with respect to the whole undelivered balance, the aggrieved seller may

(a) withhold delivery of such goods;

(b) stop delivery by any bailee as hereafter provided (Section 2—705);

(c) proceed under the next section respecting goods still unidentified to the contract;

(d) resell and recover damages as hereafter provided (Section 2—706);

(e) recover damages for non-acceptance (Section 2—708) or in a proper case the price (Section 2—709);

(f) cancel.

§ 2—704. **Seller's Right to Identify Goods to the Contract Notwithstanding Breach or to Salvage Unfinished Goods.**

(1) An aggrieved seller under the preceding section may

(a) identify to the contract conforming goods not already identified if at the time he learned of the breach they are in his possession or control;

(b) treat as the subject of resale goods which have demonstrably been intended for the particular contract even though those goods are unfinished.

(2) Where the goods are unfinished an aggrieved seller may in the exercise of reasonable commercial judgment for the purposes of avoiding loss and of effective realization either complete the manufacture and wholly identify the goods to the contract or cease manufacture and resell for scrap or salvage value or proceed in any other reasonable manner.

§ 2—705. **Seller's Stoppage of Delivery in Transit or Otherwise.**

(1) The seller may stop delivery of goods in the possession of a carrier or other bailee when he discovers the buyer to be insolvent (Section 2—702) and may stop delivery of carload, truckload, plane-load or larger shipments of express or freight when the buyer repudiates or fails to make a payment due before delivery or if for any other reason the seller has a right to withhold or reclaim the goods.

(2) As against such buyer the seller may stop delivery until

(a) receipt of the goods by the buyer; or

(b) acknowledgment to the buyer by any bailee of the goods except a carrier that the bailee holds the goods for the buyer; or

(c) such acknowledgment to the buyer by a carrier by reshipment or as warehouseman; or

(d) negotiation to the buyer of any negotiable document of title covering the goods.

(3) (a) To stop delivery the seller must so notify as to enable the bailee by reasonable diligence to prevent delivery of the goods.

(b) After such notification the bailee must hold and deliver the goods according to the directions of the seller but the seller is liable to the bailee for any ensuing charges or damages.

(c) If a negotiable document of title has been issued for goods the bailee is not obliged to obey a notification to stop unitl surrender of the document.

(d) A carrier who has issued a non-negotiable bill of lading is not obliged to obey a notification to stop received from a person other than the consignor.

§ 2—706. **Seller's Resale Including Contract for Resale.**

(1) Under the conditions stated in Section 2—703 on seller's remedies, the seller may resell the goods concerned or the undelivered balance thereof. Where the resale is made in good faith and in a commercially reasonable manner the seller may recover the difference between the resale price and the contract price together with any incidental damages allowed under the provisions of this Article (Section 2—710), but less expenses saved in consequence of the buyer's breach.

(2) Except as otherwise provided in subsection (3) or unless otherwise agreed resale may be at public or private sale including sale by way of one or more contracts to sell or of identification to an existing contract of the seller. Sale may be as a unit or in parcels and at any time and place and on any terms but every aspect of the sale including the method, manner, time, place and terms must be commercially reasonable. The resale must be reasonably identified as referring to the broken contract, but it is not necessary that the goods be in existence or that any or all of them have been identified to the contract before the breach.

(3) Where the resale is at private sale the seller must give the buyer reasonable notification of his intention to resell.

(4) Where the resale is at public sale

(a) only identified goods can be sold except where there is a recognized market for a public sale of futures in goods of the kind; and

(b) it must be made at a usual place or market for public sale if one is reasonably available and except in the case of goods which are perishable or threaten to decline in value speedily the seller must give the buyer reasonable notice of the time and place of the resale; and

(c) if the goods are not to be within the view of those attending the sale the notification of sale must state the place where the goods are located and provide for their reasonable inspection by prospective bidders; and

(d) the seller may buy.

(5) A purchaser who buys in good faith at a resale takes the goods free of any rights of the original buyer even though the seller fails to comply with one or more of the requirements of this section.

(6) The seller is not accountable to the buyer for any profit made on any resale. A person in the position of a seller (Section 2—707) or a buyer who has rightfully rejected or justifiably revoked acceptance must account for any excess over the amount of his security interest, as hereinafter defined (subsection (3) of Section 2—711).

§ 2—707. **"Person in the Position of a Seller".**

(1) A "person in the position of a seller" includes as against a principal an agent who has paid or become responsible for the price of goods on behalf of his principal or anyone who otherwise holds a security interest or other right in goods similar to that of a seller.

(2) A person in the position of a seller may as provided in this Article withhold or stop delivery (Section 2—705) and resell (Section 2—706) and recover incidental damages (Section 2—710).

§ 2—708. **Seller's Damages for Non-Acceptance or Repudiation.**

(1) Subject to subsection (2) and to the provisions of this Article with respect to proof of market price (Section 2—723), the measure of damages for non-acceptance or repudiation by the buyer is the difference between the market price at the time and place for tender and the unpaid contract price together with any incidental damages provided in this Article (Section 2—710), but less expenses saved in consequence of the buyer's breach.

(2) If the measure of damages provided in subsection (1) is inadequate to put the seller in as good a position as performance would have done then the measure of damages is the profit (including reasonable overhead) which the seller would have made from full performance by the buyer, together with any incidental damages provided in this Article (Section 2—710), due allowance for costs reasonably incurred and due credit for payments or proceeds of resale.

§ 2—709. **Action for the Price.**

(1) When the buyer fails to pay the price as it becomes due the seller may recover, together with any incidental damages under the next section, the price

(a) of goods accepted or of conforming goods lost or damaged within a commercially reasonable time after risk of their loss has passed to the buyer; and

(b) of goods identified to the contract if the seller is unable after reasonable effort to resell them at a reasonable price or the circumstances reasonably indicate that such effort will be unavailing.

(2) Where the seller sues for the price he must hold for the buyer any goods which have been identified to the contract and are still in his control except that if resale becomes possible he may resell them at any time prior to the collection of the judgment. The net proceeds of any such resale must be credited to the buyer and payment of the judgment entitles him to any goods not resold.

(3) After the buyer has wrongfully rejected or revoked acceptance of the goods or has failed to make a payment due or has repudiated (Section 2—610), a seller who is held not entitled to the price under this section shall nevertheless be awarded damages for non-acceptance under the preceding section.

§ 2—710. **Seller's Incidental Damages.**

Incidental damages to an aggrieved seller include any commercially reasonable charges, expenses or commissions incurred in stopping delivery, in the transportation, care and custody of goods after the buyer's breach, in connection with return or resale of the goods or otherwise resulting from the breach.

§ 2—711. **Buyer's Remedies in General; Buyer's Security Interest in Rejected Goods.**

(1) Where the seller fails to make delivery or repudiates or the buyer rightfully rejects or justifiably revokes acceptance then with respect to any goods involved, and with respect to the whole if the breach goes to the whole contract (Section 2—612), the buyer may cancel and whether or not he has done so may in addition to recovering so much of the price as has been paid

(a) "cover" and have damages under the next section as to all the goods affected whether or not they have been identified to the contract; or

(b) recover damages for non-delivery as provided in this Article (Section 2—713).

(2) Where the seller fails to deliver or repudiates the buyer may also

(a) if the goods have been identified recover them as provided in this Article (Section 2—502); or

(b) in a proper case obtain specific performance or replevy the goods as provided in this Article (Section 2—716).

(3) On rightful rejection or justifiable revocation of acceptance a buyer has a security interest in goods in his possession or control for any payments made on their price and any expenses reasonably incurred in their inspection, receipt, transportation, care and custody and may hold such goods and resell them in like manner as an aggrieved seller (Section 2—706).

§ 2—712. "Cover"; Buyer's Procurement of Substitute Goods.

(1) After a breach within the preceding section the buyer may "cover" by making in good faith and without unreasonable delay any reasonable purchase of or contract to purchase goods in substitution for those due from the seller.

(2) The buyer may recover from the seller as damages the difference between the cost of cover and the contract price together with any incidental or consequential damages as hereinafter defined (Section 2—715), but less expenses saved in consequence of the seller's breach.

(3) Failure of the buyer to effect cover within this section does not bar him from any other remedy.

§ 2—713. Buyer's Damages for Non-Delivery or Repudiation.

(1) Subject to the provisions of this Article with respect to proof of market price (Section 2—723), the measure of damages for non-delivery or repudiation by the seller is the difference between the market price at the time when the buyer learned of the breach and the contract price together with any incidental and consequential damages provided in this Article (Section 2—715), but less expenses saved in consequence of the seller's breach.

(2) Market price is to be determined as of the place for tender or, in cases of rejection after arrival or revocation of acceptance, as of the place of arrival.

§ 2—714. Buyer's Damages for Breach in Regard to Accepted Goods.

(1) Where the buyer has accepted goods and given notification (subsection (3) of Section 2—607) he may recover as damages for any non-conformity of tender the loss resulting in the ordinary course of events from the seller's breach as determined in any manner which is reasonable.

(2) The measure of damages for breach of warranty is the difference at the time and place of acceptance between the value of the goods accepted and the value they would have had if they had been as warranted, unless special circumstances show proximate damages of a different amount.

(3) In a proper case any incidental and consequential damages under the next section may also be recovered.

§ 2—715. Buyer's Incidental and Consequential Damages.

(1) Incidental damages resulting from the seller's breach include expenses reasonably incurred in inspection, receipt, transportation and care and custody of goods rightfully rejected, any commercially reasonable charges, expenses or commissions in connection with effecting cover and any other reasonable expense incident to the delay or other breach.

(2) Consequential damages resulting from the seller's breach include

(a) any loss resulting from general or particular requirements and needs of which the seller at the time of contracting had reason to know and which could not reasonably be prevented by cover or otherwise; and

(b) injury to person or property proximately resulting from any breach of warranty.

§ 2—716 Buyer's Right to Specific Performance or Replevin.

(1) Specific performance may be decreed where the goods are unique or in other proper circumstances.

(2) The decree for specific performance may include such terms and conditions as to payment of the price, damages, or other relief as the court may deem just.

(3) The buyer has a right of replevin for goods identified to the contract if after reasonable effort he is unable to effect cover for such goods or the circumstances reasonably indicate that such effort will be unavailing or if the goods have been shipped under reservation and satisfaction of the security interest in them has been made or tendered.

§ 2—717. Deduction of Damages From the Price.

The buyer on notifying the seller of his intention to do so may deduct all or any part of the damages resulting from any breach of the contract from any part of the price still due under the same contract.

§ 2—718. Liquidation or Limitation of Damages; Deposits.

(1) Damages for breach by either party may be liquidated in the agreement but only at an amount which is reasonable in the light of the anticipated or actual harm caused by the breach, the difficulties of proof of loss, and the inconvenience or nonfeasibility of otherwise obtaining an adequate remedy. A term fixing unreasonably large liquidated damages is void as a penalty.

(2) Where the seller justifiably withholds delivery of goods because of the buyer's breach, the buyer is entitled to restitution of any amount by which the sum of his payments exceeds

(a) the amount to which the seller is entitled by virtue of terms liquidating the seller's damages in accordance with subsection (1), or

(b) in the absence of such terms, twenty per cent of the value of the total performance for which the buyer is obligated under the contract or $500, whichever is smaller.

(3) The buyer's right to restitution under subsection (2) is subject to offset to the extent that the seller establishes

(a) a right to recover damages under the provisions of this Article other than subsection (1), and

(b) the amount or value of any benefits received by the buyer directly or indirectly by reason of the contract.

(4) Where a seller has received payment in goods their reasonable value or the proceeds of their resale shall be treated as payments for the purposes of subsection (2); but if the seller has notice of the buyer's breach before reselling goods received in part performance, his resale is subject to the conditions laid down in this Article on resale by an aggrieved seller (Section 2—706).

§ 2—719. Contractual Modification or Limitation of Remedy.

(1) Subject to the provisions of subsections (2) and (3) of this section and of the preceding section on liquidation and limitation of damages,

(a) the agreement may provide for remedies in addition to or in substitution for those provided in this Article and may limit or alter the measure of damages recoverable under this Article, as by limiting the buyer's remedies to return of the goods and repayment of the price or to repair and replacement of non-conforming goods or parts; and

(b) resort to a remedy as provided is optional unless the remedy is expressly agreed to be exclusive, in which case it is the sole remedy.

(2) Where circumstances cause an exclusive or limited remedy to fail of its essential purpose, remedy may be had as provided in this Act.

(3) Consequential damages may be limited or excluded unless the limitation or exclusion is unconscionable. Limitation of consequential damages for injury to the person in the case of consumer goods is prima facie unconscionable but limitation of damages where the loss is commercial is not.

§ 2—720. Effect of "Cancellation" or "Rescission" on Claims for Antecedent Breach.

Unless the contrary intention clearly appears, expressions of "cancellation" or "rescission" of the contract or the like shall not be construed as a renunciation or discharge of any claim in damages for an antecedent breach.

§ 2—721. Remedies for Fraud.

Remedies for material misrepresentation or fraud include all remedies available under this Article for non-fraudulent breach. Neither rescission or a claim for rescission of the contract for sale nor rejection or return of the goods shall bar or be deemed inconsistent with a claim for damages or other remedy.

§ 2—722. Who Can Sue Third Parties for Injury to Goods.

Where a third party so deals with goods which have been identified to a contract for sale as to cause actionable injury to a party to that contract

(a) a right of action against the third party is in either party to the contract for sale who has title to or a security interest or a special property or an insurable interest in the goods; and if the goods have been destroyed or converted a right of action is also in the party who either bore the risk of loss under the contract for sale or has since the injury assumed that risk as against the other;

(b) if at the time of the injury the party plaintiff did not bear the risk of loss as against the other party to the contract for sale and there is no arrangement between them for disposition of the recovery, his suit or settlement is, subject to his own interest, as a fiduciary for the other party to the contract;

(c) either party may with the consent of the other sue for the benefit of whom it may concern.

§ 2—723. Proof of Market Price: Time and Place.

(1) If an action based on anticipatory repudiation comes to trial before the time for performance with respect to some or all of the goods, any damages based on market price (Section 2—708 or Section 2—713) shall be determined according to the price of such goods prevailing at the time when the aggrieved party learned of the repudiation.

(2) If evidence of a price prevailing at the times or places described in this Article is not readily available the price prevailing within any reasonable time before or after the time described or at any other place which in commercial judgment or under usage of trade would serve as a reasonable substitute for the one described may be used, making any proper allowance for the cost of transporting the goods to or from such other place.

(3) Evidence of a relevant price prevailing at a time or place other than the one described in this Article offered by one party is not admissible unless and until he has given the other party such notice as the court finds sufficient to prevent unfair surprise.

§ 2—724. Admissibility of Market Quotations.

Whenever the prevailing price or value of any goods regularly bought and sold in any established commodity market is in issue, reports in official publications or trade journals or in newspapers or periodicals of general circulation published as the reports of such market shall be admissible in evidence. The circumstances of the preparation of such a report may be shown to affect its weight but not its admissibility.

§ 2—725. Statute of Limitations in Contracts for Sale.

(1) An action for breach of any contract for sale must be commenced within four years after the cause of action has accrued. By the original agreement the parties may reduce the period of limitation to not less than one year but may not extend it.

(2) A cause of action accrues when the breach occurs, regardless of the aggrieved party's lack of knowledge of the breach. A breach of warranty occurs when tender of delivery is made, except that where a warranty explicitly extends to future performance of the goods and discovery of the breach must await the time of such performance the cause of action accrues when the breach is or should have been discovered.

(3) Where an action commenced within the time limited by subsection (1) is so terminated as to leave available a remedy by another action for the same breach such other action may be commenced after the expiration of the time limited and within six months after the termination of the first action unless the termination resulted from voluntary discontinuance or from dismissal for failure or neglect to prosecute.

(4) This section does not alter the law on tolling of the statute of limitations nor does it apply to causes of action which have accrued before this Act becomes effective.

Article 3
COMMERCIAL PAPER

Part 1 Short Title, Form and Interpretation

§ 3—101. Short Title.

This Article shall be known and may be cited as Uniform Commercial Code—Commercial Paper.

§ 3—102. Definitions and Index of Definitions.

(1) In this Article unless the context otherwise requires

(a) "Issue" means the first delivery of an instrument to a holder or a remitter.

(b) An "order" is a direction to pay and must be more than an authorization or request. It must identify the person to pay with reasonable certainty. It may be addressed to one or more such persons jointly or in the alternative but not in succession.

(c) A "promise" is an undertaking to pay and must be more than an acknowledgment of an obligation.

(d) "Secondary party" means a drawer or endorser.

(e) "Instrument" means a negotiable instrument.

(2) Other definitions applying to this Article and the sections in which they appear are:
"Acceptance". Section 3—410.
"Accommodation party". Section 3—415.
"Alteration". Section 3—407.
"Certificate of deposit". Section 3—104.
"Certification". Section 3—411.
"Check". Section 3—104.
"Definite time". Section 3—109.
"Dishonor". Section 3—507.
"Draft". Section 3—104.
"Holder in due course". Section 3—302.

"Negotiation". Section 3—202.

"Note". Section 3—104.

"Notice of dishonor". Section 3—508.

"On demand". Section 3—108.

"Presentment". Section 3—504.

"Protest". Section 3—509.

"Restrictive Indorsement". Section 3—205.

"Signature". Section 3—401.

(3) The following definitions in other Articles apply to this Article:

"Account". Section 4—104.

"Banking Day". Section 4—104.

"Clearing House". Section 4—104.

"Collecting Bank". Section 4—105.

"Customer". Section 4—104.

"Depositary Bank". Section 4—105.

"Documentary Draft". Section 4—104.

"Intermediary Bank". Section 4—105.

"Item". Section 4—104.

"Midnight deadline". Section 4—104.

"Payor Bank". Section 4—105.

(4) In addition Article 1 contains general definitions and principles of construction and interpretation applicable throughout this Article.

§ 3—103. **Limitations on Scope of Article.**

(1) This Article does not apply to money, documents of title or investment securities.

(2) The provisions of this Article are subject to the provisions of the Article on Bank Deposits and Collections (Article 4) and Secured Transactions (Article 9).

§ 3—104. **Form of Negotiable Instruments; "Draft"; "Check"; "Certificate of Deposit"; "Note".**

(1) Any writing to be a negotiable instrument within this Article must

(a) be signed by the maker or drawer; and

(b) contain an unconditional promise or order to pay a sum certain in money and no other promise, order, obligation or power given by the maker or drawer except as authorized by this Article; and

(c) be payable on demand or at a definite time; and

(d) be payable to order or to bearer.

(2) A writing which complies with the requirements of this section is

(a) a "draft" ("bill of exchange") if it is an order;

(b) a "check" if it is a draft drawn on a bank and payable on demand;

(c) a "certificate of deposit" if it is an acknowledgment by a bank of receipt of money with an engagement to repay it;

(d) a "note" if it is a promise other than a certificate of deposit.

(3) As used in other Articles of this Act, and as the context may require, the terms "draft", "check", "certificate of deposit" and "note" may refer to instruments which are not negotiable within this Article as well as to instruments which are so negotiable.

§ 3—105. **When Promise or Order Unconditional.**

(1) A promise or order otherwise unconditional is not made conditional by the fact that the instrument

(a) is subject to implied or constructive conditions; or

(b) states its consideration, whether performed or promised, or the transaction which gave rise to the instrument, or that the promise or order is made or the instrument matures in accordance with or "as per" such transaction; or

(c) refers to or states that it arises out of a separate agreement or refers to a separate agreement for rights as to prepayment or acceleration; or

(d) states that it is drawn under a letter of credit; or

(e) states that it is secured, whether by mortgage, reservation of title or otherwise; or

(f) indicates a particular account to be debited or any other fund or source from which reimbursement is expected; or

(g) is limited to payment out of a particular fund or the proceeds of a particular source, if the instrument is issued by a government or governmental agency or unit; or

(h) is limited to payment out of the entire assets of a partnership, unincorporated association, trust or estate by or on behalf of which the instrument is issued.

(2) A promise or order is not unconditional if the instrument

(a) states that it is subject to or governed by any other agreement; or

(b) states that it is to be paid only out of a particular fund or source except as provided in this section.

§ 3—106. **Sum Certain.**

(1) The sum payable is a sum certain even though it is to be paid

(a) with stated interest or by stated installments; or

(b) with stated different rates of interest before and after default or a specified date; or

(c) with a stated discount or addition if paid before or after the date fixed for payment; or

(d) with exchange or less exchange, whether at a fixed rate or at the current rate; or

(e) with costs of collection or an attorney's fee or both upon default.

(2) Nothing in this section shall validate any term which is otherwise illegal.

§ 3—107. **Money.**

(1) An instrument is payable in money if the medium of exchange in which it is payable is money at the time the instrument is made. An instrument payable in "currency" or "current funds" is payable in money.

(2) A promise or order to pay a sum stated in a foreign currency is for a sum certain in money and, unless a different medium of payment is specified in the instrument, may be satisfied by payment of that number of dollars which the stated foreign currency will purchase at the buying sight rate for that currency on the day on which the instrument is payable or, if payable on demand, on the day of demand. If such an instrument specifies a foreign currency as the medium of payment the instrument is payable in that currency.

§ 3—108. **Payable on Demand.**

Instruments payable on demand include those payable at sight or on presentation and those in which no time for payment is stated.

§ 3—109. **Definite Time.**

(1) An instrument is payable at a definite time if by its terms it is payable

(a) on or before a stated date or at a fixed period after a stated date; or

(b) at a fixed period after sight; or

(c) at a definite time subject to any acceleration; or

(d) at a definite time subject to extension at the option of the holder, or to extension to a further definite time at the option of the maker or acceptor or automatically upon or after a specified act or event.

(2) An instrument which by its terms is otherwise payable only upon an act or event uncertain as to time of occurrence is not payable at a definite time even though the act or event has occurred.

§ 3—110. **Payable to Order.**

(1) An instrument is payable to order when by its terms it is payable to the order or assigns of any person therein specified with reasonable certainty, or to him or his order, or when it is conspicuously designated on its face as "exchange" or the like and names a payee. It may be payable to the order of

(a) the maker or drawer; or

(b) the drawee; or

(c) a payee who is not maker, drawer or drawee; or

(d) two or more payees together or in the alternative; or

(e) an estate, trust or fund, in which case it is payable to the order of the representative of such estate, trust or fund or his successors; or

(f) an office, or an officer by his title as such in which case it is payable to the principal but the incumbent of the office or his successors may act as if he or they were the holder; or

(g) a partnership or unincorporated association, in which case it is payable to the partnership or association and may be indorsed or transferred by any person thereto authorized.

(2) An instrument not payable to order is not made so payable by such words as "payable upon return of this instrument properly indorsed."

(3) An instrument made payable both to order and to bearer is payable to order unless the bearer words are handwritten or typewritten.

§ 3—111. **Payable to Bearer.**

An instrument is payable to bearer when by its terms it is payable to

(a) bearer or the order of bearer; or

(b) a specified person or bearer; or

(c) "cash" or the order of "cash", or any other indication which does not purport to designate a specific payee.

§ 3—112. **Terms and Omissions Not Affecting Negotiability.**

(1) The negotiability of an instrument is not affected by

(a) the omission of a statement of any consideration or of the place where the instrument is drawn or payable; or

(b) a statement that collateral has been given to secure obligations either on the instrument or otherwise of an obligor on the instrument or that in case of default on those obligations the holder may realize on or dispose of the collateral; or

(c) a promise or power to maintain or protect collateral or to give additional collateral; or

(d) a term authorizing a confession of judgment on the instrument if it is not paid when due; or

(e) a term purporting to waive the benefit of any law intended for the advantage or protection of any obligor; or

(f) a term in a draft providing that the payee by indorsing or cashing it acknowledges full satisfaction of an obligation of the drawer; or

(g) a statement in a draft drawn in a set of parts (Section 3—801) to the effect that the order is effective only if no other part has been honored.

(2) Nothing in this section shall validate any term which is otherwise illegal.

§ 3—113. **Seal.**

An instrument otherwise negotiable is within this Article even though it is under a seal.

§ 3—114. **Date, Antedating, Postdating.**

(1) The negotiability of an instrument is not affected by the fact that it is undated, antedated or postdated.

(2) Where an instrument is antedated or postdated the time when it is payable is determined by the stated date if the instrument is payable on demand or at a fixed period after date.

(3) Where the instrument or any signature thereon is dated, the date is presumed to be correct.

§ 3—115. **Incomplete Instruments.**

(1) When a paper whose contents at the time of signing show that it is intended to become an instrument is signed while still incomplete in any necessary respect it cannot be enforced until completed, but when it is completed in accordance with authority given it is effective as completed.

(2) If the completion is unauthorized the rules as to material alteration apply (Section 3—407), even though the paper was not delivered by the maker or drawer; but the burden of establishing that any completion is unauthorized is on the party so asserting.

§ 3—116. **Instruments Payable to Two or More Persons.**

An instrument payable to the order of two or more persons

(a) if in the alternative is payable to any one of them and may be negotiated, discharged or enforced by any of them who has possession of it;

(b) if not in the alternative is payable to all of them and may be negotiated, discharged or enforced only by all of them.

§ 3—117. **Instruments Payable With Words of Description.**

An instrument made payable to a named person with the addition of words describing him

(a) as agent or officer of a specified person is payable to his principal but the agent or officer may act as if he were the holder;

(b) as any other fiduciary for a specified person or purpose is payable to the payee and may be negotiated, discharged or enforced by him;

(c) in any other manner is payable to the payee unconditionally and the additional words are without effect on subsequent parties.

§ 3—118. **Ambiguous Terms and Rules of Construction.**

The following rules apply to every instrument:

(a) Where there is doubt whether the instrument is a draft or a note the holder may treat it as either. A draft drawn on the drawer is effective as a note.

(b) Handwritten terms control typewritten and printed terms, and typewritten control printed.

(c) Words control figures except that if the words are ambiguous figures control.

(d) Unless otherwise specified a provision for interest means interest at the judgment rate at the place of payment from the date of the instrument, or if it is undated from the date of issue.

(e) Unless the instrument otherwise specifies two or more persons who sign as maker, acceptor or drawer or indorser and as a part of the same transaction are jointly and severally liable even though the instrument contains such words as "I promise to pay."

(f) Unless otherwise specified consent to extension authorizes a single extension for not longer than the original period. A consent to extension, expressed in the instrument, is binding on secondary parties and accommodation makers. A holder may not exercise his option to extend an instrument over the objection of a maker or acceptor or other party who in accordance with Section 3—604 tenders full payment when the instrument is due.

§ 3—119. Other Writings Affecting Instrument.

(1) As between the obligor and his immediate obligee or any transferee the terms of an instrument may be modified or affected by any other written agreement executed as a part of the same transaction, except that a holder in due course in not affected by any limitation of his rights arising out of the separate written agreement if he had no notice of the limitation when he took the instrument.

(2) A separate agreement does not affect the negotiability of an instrument.

§ 3—120. Instruments "Payable Through" Bank.

An instrument which states that it is "payable through" a bank or the like designates that bank as a collecting bank to make presentment but does not of itself authorize the bank to pay the instrument.

§ 3—121. Instruments Payable at Bank.

Note: If this Act is introduced in the Congress of the United States this section should be omitted.
(States to select either alternative)

Alternative A—

A note or acceptance which states that it is payable at a bank is the equivalent of a draft drawn on the bank payable when it falls due out of any funds of the maker or acceptor in current account or otherwise available for such payment.

Alternative B—

A note or acceptance which states that it is payable at a bank is not of itself an order or authorization to the bank to pay it.

§ 3—122. Accrual of Cause of Action.

(1) A cause of action against a maker or an acceptor accrues

(a) in the case of a time instrument on the day after maturity;

(b) in the case of a demand instrument upon its date or, if no date is stated, on the date of issue.

(2) A cause of action against the obligor of a demand or time certificate of deposit accrues upon demand, but demand on a time certificate may not be made until on or after the date of maturity.

(3) A cause of action against a drawer of a draft or an indorser of any instrument accrues upon demand following dishonor of the instrument. Notice of dishonor is a demand.

(4) Unless an instrument provides otherwise, interest runs at the rate provided by law for a judgment

(a) in the case of a maker, acceptor or other primary obligor of a demand instrument, from the date of demand;

(b) in all other cases from the date of accrual of the cause of action.

Part 2 Transfer and Negotiation

§ 3—201. Transfer: Right to Indorsement.

(1) Transfer of an instrument vests in the transferee such rights as the transferor has therein, except that a transferee who has himself been a party to any fraud or illegality affecting the instrument or who as a prior holder had notice of a defense or claim against it cannot improve his position by taking from a later holder in due course.

(2) A transfer of a security interest in an instrument vests the foregoing rights in the transferee to the extent of the interest transferred.

(3) Unless otherwise agreed any transfer for value of an instrument not then payable to bearer gives the transferee the specifically enforceable right to have the unqualified indorsement of the transferor. Negotiation takes effect only when the indorsement is made and until that time there is no presumption that the transferee is the owner.

§ 3—202. Negotiation.

(1) Negotiation is the transfer of an instrument in such form that the transferee becomes a holder. If the instrument is payable to order it is negotiated by delivery with any necessary indorsement; if payable to bearer it is negotiated by delivery.

(2) An indorsement must be written by or on behalf of the holder and on the instrument or on a paper so firmly affixed thereto as to become a part thereof.

(3) An indorsement is effective for negotiation only when it conveys the entire instrument or any unpaid residue. If it purports to be of less it operates only as a partial assignment.

(4) Words of assignment, condition, waiver, guaranty, limitation or disclaimer of liability and the like accompanying an indorsement do not affect its character as an indorsement.

§ 3—203. **Wrong or Misspelled Name.**

Where an instrument is made payable to a person under a misspelled name or one other than his own he may indorse in that name or his own or both; but signature in both names may be required by a person paying or giving value for the instrument.

§ 3—204. **Special Indorsement; Blank Indorsement.**

(1) A special indorsement specifies the person to whom or to whose order it makes the instrument payable. Any instrument specially indorsed becomes payable to the order of the special indorsee and may be further negotiated only by his indorsement.

(2) An indorsement in blank specifies no particular indorsee and may consist of a mere signature. An instrument payable to order and indorsed in blank becomes payable to bearer and may be negotiated by delivery alone until specially indorsed.

(3) The holder may convert a blank indorsement into a special indorsement by writing over the signature of the indorser in blank any contract consistent with the character of the indorsement.

§ 3—205. **Restrictive Indorsements.**

An indorsement is restrictive which either

(a) is conditional; or

(b) purports to prohibit further transfer of the instrument; or

(c) includes the words "for collection", "for deposit", "pay any bank", or like terms signifying a purpose of deposit or collection; or

(d) otherwise states that it is for the benefit or use of the indorser or of another person.

§ 3—206. **Effect of Restrictive Indorsement.**

(1) No restrictive indorsement prevents further transfer or negotiation of the instrument.

(2) An intermediary bank, or a payor bank which is not the depositary bank, is neither given notice nor otherwise affected by a restrictive indorsement of any person except the bank's immediate transferor or the person presenting for payment.

(3) Except for an intermediary bank, any transferee under an indorsement which is conditional or includes the words "for collection", "for deposit", "pay any bank", or like terms (subparagraphs (a) and (c) of Section 3—205) must pay or apply any value given by him for or on the security of the instrument consistently with the indorsement and to the extent that he does so he becomes a holder for value. In addition such transferee is a holder in due course if he otherwise complies with the requirements of Section 3—302 on what constitutes a holder in due course.

(4) The first taker under an indorsement for the benefit of the indorser or another person (subparagraph (d) of Section 3—205) must pay or apply any value given by him for or on the security of the instrument consistently with the indorsement and to the extent that he does so he becomes a holder for value. In addition such taker is a holder in due course if he otherwise complies with the requirements of Section 3—302 on what constitutes a holder in due course. A later holder for value is neither given notice nor otherwise affected by such restrictive indorsement unless he has knowledge that a fiduciary or other person has negotiated the instrument in any transaction for his own benefit or otherwise in breach of duty (subsection (2) of Section 3—304).

§ 3—207. **Negotiation Effective Although It May Be Rescinded.**

(1) Negotiation is effective to transfer the instrument although the negotiation is

(a) made by an infant, a corporation exceeding its powers, or any other person without capacity; or

(b) obtained by fraud, duress or mistake of any kind; or

(c) part of an illegal transaction; or

(d) made in breach of duty.

(2) Except as against a subsequent holder in due course such negotiation is in an appropriate case subject to rescission, the declaration of a constructive trust or any other remedy permitted by law.

§ 3—208. **Reacquisition.**

Where an instrument is returned to or reacquired by a prior party he may cancel any indorsement which is not necessary to his title and reissue or further negotiate the instrument, but any intervening party is discharged as against the reacquiring party and subsequent holders not in due course and if his indorsement has been cancelled is discharged as against subsequent holders in due course as well.

Part 3 **Rights of a Holder**

§ 3—301. **Rights of a Holder.**

The holder of an instrument whether or not he is the owner may transfer or negotiate it and, except as otherwise provided in Section 3—603 on payment or satisfaction, discharge it or enforce payment in his own name.

§ 3—302. Holder in Due Course.

(1) A holder in due course is a holder who takes the instrument

(a) for value; and

(b) in good faith; and

(c) without notice that it is overdue or has been dishonored or of any defense against or claim to it on the part of any person.

(2) A payee may be a holder in due course.

(3) A holder does not become a holder in due course of an instrument:

(a) by purchase of it at judicial sale or by taking it under legal process; or

(b) by acquiring it in taking over an estate; or

(c) by purchasing it as part of a bulk transaction not in regular course of business of the transferor.

(4) A purchaser of a limited interest can be a holder in due course only to the extent of the interest purchased.

§ 3—303. Taking for Value.

A holder takes the instrument for value

(a) to the extent that the agreed consideration has been performed or that he acquires a security interest in or a lien on the instrument otherwise than by legal process; or

(b) when he takes the instrument in payment of or as security for an antecedent claim against any person whether or not the claim is due; or

(c) when he gives a negotiable instrument for it or makes an irrevocable commitment to a third person.

§ 3—304. Notice to Purchaser.

(1) The purchaser has notice of a claim or defense if

(a) the instrument is so incomplete, bears such visible evidence of forgery or alteration, or is otherwise so irregular as to call into question its validity, terms or ownership or to create an ambiguity as to the party to pay; or

(b) the purchaser has notice that the obligation of any party is voidable in whole or in part, or that all parties have been discharged.

(2) The purchaser has notice of a claim against the instrument when he has knowledge that a fiduciary has negotiated the instrument in payment of or as security for his own debt or in any transaction for his own benefit or otherwise in breach of duty.

(3) The purchaser has notice that an instrument is overdue if he has reason to know

(a) that any part of the principal amount is overdue or that there is an uncured default in payment of another instrument of the same series; or

(b) that acceleration of the instrument has been made; or

(c) that he is taking a demand instrument after demand has been made or more than a reasonable length of time after its issue. A reasonable time for a check drawn and payable within the states and territories of the United States and the District of Columbia is presumed to be thirty days.

(4) Knowledge of the following facts does not of itself give the purchaser notice of a defense or claim

(a) that the instrument is antedated or postdated;

(b) that it was issued or negotiated in return for an executory promise or accompanied by a separate agreement, unless the purchaser has notice that a defense or claim has arisen from the terms thereof;

(c) that any party has signed for accommodation;

(d) that an incomplete instrument has been completed, unless the purchaser has notice of any improper completion;

(e) that any person negotiating the instrument is or was a fiduciary;

(f) that there has been default in payment of interest on the instrument or in payment of any other instrument, except one of the same series.

(5) The filing or recording of a document does not of itself constitute notice within the provisions of this Article to a person who would otherwise be a holder in due course.

(6) To be effective notice must be received at such time and in such manner as to give a reasonable opportunity to act on it.

§ 3—305. Rights of a Holder in Due Course.

To the extent that a holder is a holder in due course he takes the instrument free from

(1) all claims to it on the part of any person; and

(2) all defenses of any party to the instrument with whom the holder has not dealt except

(a) infancy, to the extent that it is a defense to a simple contract; and

(b) such other incapacity, or duress, or illegality of the transaction, as renders the obligation of the party a nullity; and

(c) such misrepresentation as has induced the party to sign the instrument with neither knowledge nor reasonable opportunity to obtain knowledge of its character or its essential terms; and

(d) discharge in insolvency proceedings; and

(e) any other discharge of which the holder has notice when he takes the instrument.

§ 3—306. **Rights of One Not Holder in Due Course.**

Unless he has the rights of a holder in due course any person takes the instrument subject to

(a) all valid claims to it on the part of any person; and

(b) all defenses of any party which would be available in an action on a simple contract; and

(c) the defenses of want or failure of consideration, nonperformance of any condition precedent, non-delivery, or delivery for a special purpose (Section 3—408); and

(d) the defense that he or a person through whom he holds the instrument acquired it by theft, or that payment or satisfaction to such holder would be inconsistent with the terms of a restrictive indorsement. The claim of any third person to the instrument is not otherwise available as a defense to any party liable thereon unless the third person himself defends the action for such party.

§ 3—307. **Burden of Establishing Signatures, Defenses and Due Course.**

(1) Unless specifically denied in the pleadings each signature on an instrument is admitted. When the effectiveness of a signature is put in issue

(a) the burden of establishing it is on the party claiming under the signature; but

(b) the signature is presumed to be genuine or authorized except where the action is to enforce the obligation of a purported signer who has died or become incompetent before proof is required.

(2) When signatures are admitted or established, production of the instrument entitles a holder to recover on it unless the defendant establishes a defense.

(3) After it is shown that a defense exists a person claiming the rights of a holder in due course has the burden of establishing that he or some person under whom he claims is in all respects a holder in due course.

Part 4 **Liability of Parties**

§ 3—401. **Signature.**

(1) No person is liable on an instrument unless his signature appears thereon.

(2) A signature is made by use of any name, including any trade or assumed name, upon an instrument, or by any word or mark used in lieu of a written signature.

§ 3—402. **Signature in Ambiguous Capacity.**

Unless the instrument clearly indicates that a signature is made in some other capacity it is an indorsement.

§ 3—403. **Signature by Authorized Representative.**

(1) A signature may be made by an agent or other representative, and his authority to make it may be established as in other cases of representation. No particular form of appointment is necessary to establish such authority.

(2) An authorized representative who signs his own name to an instrument

(a) is personally obligated if the instrument neither names the person represented nor shows that the representative signed in a representative capacity;

(b) except as otherwise established between the immediate parties, is personally obligated if the instrument names the person represented but does not show that the representative signed in a representative capacity, or if the instrument does not name the person represented but does show that the representative signed in a representative capacity.

(3) Except as otherwise established the name of an organization preceded or followed by the name and office of an authorized individual is a signature made in a representative capacity.

§ 3—404. **Unauthorized Signatures.**

(1) Any unauthorized signature is wholly inoperative as that of the person whose name is signed unless he ratifies it or is precluded from denying it; but it operates as the signature of the unauthorized signer in favor of any person who in good faith pays the instrument or takes it for value.

(2) Any unauthorized signature may be ratified for all purposes of this Article. Such ratification does not of itself affect any rights of the person ratifying against the actual signer.

§ 3—405. **Impostors; Signature in Name of Payee.**

(1) An indorsement by any person in the name of a named payee is effective if

(a) an impostor by use of the mails or otherwise has induced the maker or drawer to issue the instrument to him or his confederate in the name of the payee; or

(b) a person signing as or on behalf of a maker or drawer intends the payee to have no interest in the instrument; or

(c) an agent or employee of the maker or drawer has supplied him with the name of the payee intending the latter to have no such interest.

(2) Nothing in this section shall affect the criminal or civil liability of the person so indorsing.

§ 3—406. Negligence Contributing to Alteration or Unauthorized Signature.

Any person who by his negligence substantially contributes to a material alteration of the instrument or to the making of an unauthorized signature is precluded from asserting the alteration or lack of authority against a holder in due course or against a drawee or other payor who pays the instrument in good faith and in accordance with the reasonable commercial standards of the drawee's or payor's business.

§ 3—407. Alteration.

(1) Any alteration of an instrument is material which changes the contract of any party thereto in any respect, including any such change in

(a) the number or relations of the parties; or

(b) an incomplete instrument, by completing it otherwise than as authorized; or

(c) the writing as signed, by adding to it or by removing any part of it.

(2) As against any person other than a subsequent holder in due course

(a) alteration by the holder which is both fraudulent and material discharges any party whose contract is thereby changed unless that party assents or is precluded from asserting the defense;

(b) no other alteration discharges any party and the instrument may be enforced according to its original tenor, or as to incomplete instruments according to the authority given.

(3) A subsequent holder in due course may in all cases enforce the instrument according to its original tenor, and when an incomplete instrument has been completed, he may enforce it as completed.

§ 3—408. Consideration.

Want or failure of consideration is a defense as against any person not having the rights of a holder in due course (Section 3—305), except that no consideration is necessary for an instrument or obligation thereon given in payment of or as security for an antecedent obligation of any kind. Nothing in this section shall be taken to displace any statute outside this Act under which a promise is enforceable notwithstanding lack or failure of consideration. Partial failure of consideration is a defense pro tanto whether or not the failure is in an ascertained or liquidated amount.

§ 3—409. Draft Not an Assignment.

(1) A check or other draft does not of itself operate as an assignment of any funds in the hands of the drawee available for its payment, and the drawee is not liable on the instrument until he accepts it.

(2) Nothing in this section shall affect any liability in contract, tort or otherwise arising from any letter of credit or other obligation or representation which is not an acceptance.

§ 3—410. Definition and Operation of Acceptance.

(1) Acceptance is the drawee's signed engagement to honor the draft as presented. It must be written on the draft, and may consist of his signature alone. It becomes operative when completed by delivery or notification.

(2) A draft may be accepted although it has not been signed by the drawer or is otherwise incomplete or is overdue or has been dishonored.

(3) Where the draft is payable at a fixed period after sight and the acceptor fails to date his acceptance the holder may complete it by supplying a date in good faith.

§ 3—411. Certification of a Check.

(1) Certification of a check is acceptance. Where a holder procures certification the drawer and all prior indorsers are discharged.

(2) Unless otherwise agreed a bank has no obligation to certify a check.

(3) A bank may certify a check before returning it for lack of proper indorsement. If it does so the drawer is discharged.

§ 3—412. Acceptance Varying Draft.

(1) Where the drawee's proffered acceptance in any manner varies the draft as presented the holder may refuse the acceptance and treat the draft as dishonored in which case the drawee is entitled to have his acceptance cancelled.

(2) The terms of the draft are not varied by an acceptance to pay at any particular bank or place in the United States, unless the acceptance states that the draft is to be paid only at such bank or place.

(3) Where the holder assents to an acceptance varying the terms of the draft each drawer and indorser who does not affirmatively assent is discharged.

§ 3—413. **Contract of Maker, Drawer and Acceptor.**

(1) The maker or acceptor engages that he will pay the instrument according to its tenor at the time of his engagement or as completed pursuant to Section 3—115 on incomplete instruments.

(2) The drawer engages that upon dishonor of the draft and any necessary notice of dishonor or protest he will pay the amount of the draft to the holder or to any indorser who takes it up. The drawer may disclaim this liability by drawing without recourse.

(3) By making, drawing or accepting the party admits as against all subsequent parties including the drawee the existence of the payee and his then capacity to indorse.

§ 3—414. **Contract of Indorser; Order of Liability.**

(1) Unless the indorsement otherwise specifies (as by such words as "without recourse") every indorser engages that upon dishonor and any necessary notice of dishonor and protest he will pay the instrument according to its tenor at the time of his indorsement to the holder or to any subsequent indorser who takes it up, even though the indorser who takes it up was not obligated to do so.

(2) Unless they otherwise agree indorsers are liable to one another in the order in which they indorse, which is presumed to be the order in which their signatures appear on the instrument.

§ 3—415. **Contract of Accommodation Party.**

(1) An accommodation party is one who signs the instrument in any capacity for the purpose of lending his name to another party to it.

(2) When the instrument has been taken for value before it is due the accommodation party is liable in the capacity in which he has signed even though the taker knows of the accommodation.

(3) As against a holder in due course and without notice of the accommodation oral proof of the accommodation is not admissible to give the accommodation party the benefit of discharges dependent on his character as such. In other cases the accommodation character may be shown by oral proof.

(4) An indorsement which shows that it is not in the chain of title is notice of its accommodation character.

(5) An accommodation party is not liable to the party accommodated, and if he pays the instrument has a right of recourse on the instrument against such party.

§ 3—416. **Contract of Guarantor.**

(1) "Payment guaranteed" or equivalent words added to a signature mean that the signer engages that if the instrument is not paid when due he will pay it according to its tenor without resort by the holder to any other party.

(2) "Collection guaranteed" or equivalent words added to a signature mean that the signer engages that if the instrument is not paid when due he will pay it according to its tenor, but only after the holder has reduced his claim against the maker or acceptor to judgment and execution has been returned unsatisfied, or after the maker or acceptor has become insolvent or it is otherwise apparent that it is useless to proceed against him.

(3) Words of guaranty which do not otherwise specify guarantee payment.

(4) No words of guaranty added to the signature of a sole maker or acceptor affect his liability on the instrument. Such words added to the signature of one of two or more makers or acceptors create a presumption that the signature is for the accommodation of the others.

(5) When words of guaranty are used presentment, notice of dishonor and protest are not necessary to charge the user.

(6) Any guaranty written on the instrument is enforcible notwithstanding any statute of frauds.

§ 3—417. **Warranties on Presentment and Transfer.**

(1) Any person who obtains payment or acceptance and any prior transferor warrants to a person who in good faith pays or accepts that

(a) he has a good title to the instrument or is authorized to obtain payment or acceptance on behalf of one who has a good title; and

(b) he has no knowledge that the signature of the maker or drawer is unauthorized, except that this warranty is not given by a holder in due course acting in good faith

(i) to a maker with respect to the maker's own signature; or

(ii) to a drawer with respect to the drawer's own signature, whether or not the drawer is also the drawee; or

(iii) to an acceptor of a draft if the holder in due course took the draft after the acceptance or obtained the acceptance without knowledge that the drawer's signature was unauthorized; and

(c) the instrument has not been materially altered, except that this warranty is not given by a holder in due course acting in good faith

(i) to the maker of a note; or

(ii) to the drawer of a draft whether or not the drawer is also the drawee; or

(iii) to the acceptor of a draft with respect to an alteration made prior to the acceptance if the holder in due course took the draft after the acceptance, even though the acceptance provided "payable as originally drawn" or equivalent terms; or

(iv) to the acceptor of a draft with respect to an alteration made after the acceptance.

(2) Any person who transfers an instrument and receives consideration warrants to his transferee and if the transfer is by indorsement to any subsequent holder who takes the instrument in good faith that

(a) he has a good title to the instrument or is authorized to obtain payment or acceptance on behalf of one who has a good title and the transfer is otherwise rightful; and

(b) all signatures are genuine or authorized; and

(c) the instrument has not been materially altered; and

(d) no defense of any party is good against him; and

(e) he has no knowledge of any insolvency proceeding instituted with respect to the maker or acceptor or the drawer of an unaccepted instrument.

(3) By transferring "without recourse" the transferor limits the obligation stated in subsection (2) (d) to a warranty that he has no knowledge of such a defense.

(4) A selling agent or broker who does not disclose the fact that he is acting only as such gives the warranties provided in this section, but if he makes such disclosure warrants only his good faith and authority.

§ 3—418. **Finality of Payment or Acceptance.**

Except for recovery of bank payments as provided in the Article on Bank Deposits and Collections (Article 4) and except for liability for breach of warranty on presentment under the preceding section, payment or acceptance of any instrument is final in favor of a holder in due course, or a person who has in good faith changed his position in reliance on the payment.

§ 3—419. **Conversion of Instrument; Innocent Representative.**

(1) An instrument is converted when

(a) a drawee to whom it is delivered for acceptance refuses to return it on demand; or

(b) any person to whom it is delivered for payment refuses on demand either to pay or to return it; or

(c) it is paid on a forged indorsement.

(2) In an action against a drawee under subsection (1) the measure of the drawee's liability is the face amount of the instrument. In any other action under subsection (1) the measure of liability is presumed to be the face amount of the instrument.

(3) Subject to the provisions of this Act concerning restrictive indorsements a representative, including a depositary or collecting bank, who has in good faith and in accordance with the reasonable commercial standards applicable to the business of such representative dealt with an instrument or its proceeds on behalf of one who was not the true owner is not liable in conversion or otherwise to the true owner beyond the amount of any proceeds remaining in his hands.

(4) An intermediary bank or payor bank which is not a depositary bank is not liable in conversion solely by reason of the fact that proceeds of an item indorsed restrictively (Sections 3—205 and 3—206) are not paid or applied consistently with the restrictive indorsement of an indorser other than its immediate transferor.

Part 5 **Presentment, Notice of Dishonor and Protest**

§ 3—501. **When Presentment, Notice of Dishonor, and Protest Necessary or Permissible.**

(1) Unless excused (Section 3—511) presentment is necessary to charge secondary parties as follows:

(a) presentment for acceptance is necessary to charge the drawer and indorsers of a draft where the draft so provides, or is payable elsewhere than at the residence or place of business of the drawee, or its date of payment depends upon such presentment. The holder may at his option present for acceptance any other draft payable at a stated date;

(b) presentment for payment is necessary to charge any indorser;

(c) in the case of any drawer, the acceptor of a draft payable at a bank or the maker of a note payable at a bank, presentment for payment is necessary, but failure to make presentment discharges such drawer, acceptor or maker only as stated in Section 3—502(1) (b).

(2) Unless excused (Section 3—511)

(a) notice of any dishonor is necessary to charge any indorser;

(b) in the case of any drawer, the acceptor of a draft payable at a bank or the maker of a note payable at a bank, notice of any dishonor is necessary, but failure to give such notice discharges such drawer, acceptor or maker only as stated in Section 3—502(1) (b).

(3) Unless excused (Section 3—511) protest of any dishonor is necessary to charge the drawer and indorsers of any draft which on its face appears to be drawn or payable outside of the states, territories, dependencies, and possessions of the United States, the District of Columbia and the Commonwealth of Puerto Rico. The holder may at his option make protest of any dishonor of any other instrument and in the case of a foreign draft may on insolvency of the acceptor before maturity make protest for better security.

(4) Notwithstanding any provision of this section, neither presentment nor notice of dishonor nor protest is necessary to charge an indorser who has indorsed an instrument after maturity.

§ 3—502. **Unexcused Delay; Discharge.**

(1) Where without excuse any necessary presentment or notice of dishonor is delayed beyond the time when it is due

(a) any indorser is discharged; and

(b) any drawer or the acceptor of a draft payable at a bank or the maker of a note payable at a bank who because the drawee or payor bank becomes insolvent during the delay is deprived of funds maintained with the drawee or payor bank to cover the instrument may discharge his liability by written assignment to the holder of his rights against the drawee or payor bank in respect of such funds, but such drawer, acceptor or maker is not otherwise discharged.

(2) Where without excuse a necessary protest is delayed beyond the time when it is due any drawer or indorser is discharged.

§ 3—503. **Time of Presentment.**

(1) Unless a different time is expressed in the instrument the time for any presentment is determined as follows:

(a) where an instrument is payable at or a fixed period after a stated date any presentment for acceptance must be made on or before the date it is payable;

(b) where an instrument is payable after sight it must either be presented for acceptance or negotiated within a reasonable time after date or issue whichever is later;

(c) where an instrument shows the date on which it is payable presentment for payment is due on that date;

(d) where an instrument is accelerated presentment for payment is due within a reasonable time after the acceleration;

(e) with respect to the liability of any secondary party presentment for acceptance or payment of any other instrument is due within a reasonable time after such party becomes liable thereon.

(2) A reasonable time for presentment is determined by the nature of the instrument, any usage of banking or trade and the facts of the particular case. In the case of an uncertified check which is drawn and payable within the United States and which is not a draft drawn by a bank the following are presumed to be reasonable periods within which to present for payment or to initiate bank collection:

(a) with respect to the liability of the drawer, thirty days after date or issue whichever is later; and

(b) with respect to the liability of an indorser, seven days after his indorsement.

(3) Where any presentment is due on a day which is not a full business day for either the person making presentment or the party to pay or accept, presentment is due on the next following day which is a full business day for both parties.

(4) Presentment to be sufficient must be made at a reasonable hour, and if at a bank during its banking day.

§ 3—504. **How Presentment Made.**

(1) Presentment is a demand for acceptance or payment made upon the maker, acceptor, drawee or other payor by or on behalf of the holder.

(2) Presentment may be made

(a) by mail, in which event the time of presentment is determined by the time of receipt of the mail; or

(b) through a clearing house; or

(c) at the place of acceptance or payment specified in the instrument or if there be none at the place of business or residence of the party to accept or pay. If neither the party to accept or pay nor anyone authorized to act for him is present or accessible at such place presentment is excused.

(3) It may be made

(a) to any one of two or more makers, acceptors, drawees or other payors; or

(b) to any person who has authority to make or refuse the acceptance or payment.

(4) A draft accepted or a note made payable at a bank in the United States must be presented at such bank.

(5) In the cases described in Section 4—210 presentment may be made in the manner and with the result stated in that section.

§ 3—505. Rights of Party to Whom Presentment Is Made.

(1) The party to whom presentment is made may without dishonor require

(a) exhibition of the instrument; and

(b) reasonable identification of the person making presentment and evidence of his authority to make it if made for another; and

(c) that the instrument be produced for acceptance or payment at a place specified in it, or if there be none at any place reasonable in the circumstances; and

(d) a signed receipt on the instrument for any partial or full payment and its surrender upon full payment.

(2) Failure to comply with any such requirement invalidates the presentment but the person presenting has a reasonable time in which to comply and the time for acceptance or payment runs from the time of compliance.

§ 3—506. Time Allowed for Acceptance or Payment.

(1) Acceptance may be deferred without dishonor until the close of the next business day following presentment. The holder may also in a good faith effort to obtain acceptance and without either dishonor of the instrument or discharge of secondary parties allow postponement of acceptance for an additional business day.

(2) Except as a longer time is allowed in the case of documentary drafts drawn under a letter of credit, and unless an earlier time is agreed to by the party to pay, payment of an instrument may be deferred without dishonor pending reasonable examination to determine whether it is properly payable, but payment must be made in any event before the close of business on the day of presentment.

§ 3—507. Dishonor; Holder's Right of Recourse; Term Allowing Re-Presentment.

(1) An instrument is dishonored when

(a) a necessary or optional presentment is duly made and due acceptance or payment is refused or cannot be obtained within the prescribed time or in case of bank collections the instrument is seasonably returned by the midnight deadline (Section 4—301); or

(b) presentment is excused and the instrument is not duly accepted or paid.

(2) Subject to any necessary notice of dishonor and protest, the holder has upon dishonor an immediate right of recourse against the drawers and indorsers.

(3) Return of an instrument for lack of proper indorsement is not dishonor.

(4) A term in a draft or an indorsement thereof allowing a stated time for re-presentment in the event of any dishonor of the draft by nonacceptance if a time draft or by nonpayment if a sight draft gives the holder as against any secondary party bound by the term an option to waive the dishonor without affecting the liability of the secondary party and he may present again up to the end of the stated time.

§ 3—508. Notice of Dishonor.

(1) Notice of dishonor may be given to any person who may be liable on the instrument by or on behalf of the holder or any party who has himself received notice, or any other party who can be compelled to pay the instrument. In addition an agent or bank in whose hands the instrument is dishonored may give notice to his principal or customer or to another agent or bank from which the instrument was received.

(2) Any necessary notice must be given by a bank before its midnight deadline and by any other person before midnight of the third business day after dishonor or receipt of notice of dishonor.

(3) Notice may be given in any reasonable manner. It may be oral or written and in any terms which identify the instrument and state that it has been dishonored. A misdescription which does not mislead the party notified does not vitiate the notice. Sending the instrument bearing a stamp, ticket or writing stating

that acceptance or payment has been refused or sending a notice of debit with respect to the instrument is sufficient.

(4) Written notice is given when sent although it is not received.

(5) Notice to one partner is notice to each although the firm has been dissolved.

(6) When any party is in insolvency proceedings instituted after the issue of the instrument notice may be given either to the party or to the representative of his estate.

(7) When any party is dead or incompetent notice may be sent to his last known address or given to his personal representative.

(8) Notice operates for the benefit of all parties who have rights on the instrument against the party notified.

§ 3—509. **Protest; Noting for Protest.**

(1) A protest is a certificate of dishonor made under the hand and seal of a United States consul or vice consul or a notary public or other person authorized to certify dishonor by the law of the place where dishonor occurs. It may be made upon information satisfactory to such person.

(2) The protest must identify the instrument and certify either that due presentment has been made or the reason why it is excused and that the instrument has been dishonored by nonacceptance or nonpayment.

(3) The protest may also certify that notice of dishonor has been given to all parties or to specified parties.

(4) Subject to subsection (5) any necessary protest is due by the time that notice of dishonor is due.

(5) If, before protest is due, an instrument has been noted for protest by the officer to make protest, the protest may be made at any time thereafter as of the date of the noting.

§ 3—510. **Evidence of Dishonor and Notice of Dishonor.**

The following are admissible as evidence and create a presumption of dishonor and of any notice of dishonor therein shown:

(a) a document regular in form as provided in the preceding section which purports to be a protest;

(b) the purported stamp or writing of the drawee, payor bank or presenting bank on the instrument or accompanying it stating that acceptance or payment has been refused for reasons conconsistent with dishonor;

(c) any book or record of the drawee, payor bank, or any collecting bank kept in the usual course of business which shows dishonor, even though there is no evidence of who made the entry.

§ 3—511. **Waived or Excused Presentment, Protest or Notice of Dishonor or Delay Therein.**

(1) Delay in presentment, protest or notice of dishonor is excused when the party is without notice that it is due or when the delay is caused by circumstances beyond his control and he exercises reasonable diligence after the cause of the delay ceases to operate.

(2) Presentment or notice or protest as the case may be is entirely excused when

(a) the party to be charged has waived it expressly or by implication either before or after it is due; or

(b) such party has himself dishonored the instrument or has countermanded payment or otherwise has no reason to expect or right to require that the instrument be accepted or paid; or

(c) by reasonable diligence the presentment or protest cannot be made or the notice given.

(3) Presentment is also entirely excused when

(a) the maker, acceptor or drawee of any instrument except a documentary draft is dead or in insolvency proceedings instituted after the issue of the instrument; or

(b) acceptance or payment is refused but not for want of proper presentment.

(4) Where a draft has been dishonored by nonacceptance a later presentment for payment and any notice of dishonor and protest for nonpayment are excused unless in the meantime the instrument has been accepted.

(5) A waiver of protest is also a waiver of presentment and of notice of dishonor even though protest is not required.

(6) Where a waiver of presentment or notice or protest is embodied in the instrument itself it is binding upon all parties; but where it is written above the signature of an indorser it binds him only.

Part 6 **Discharge**

§ 3—601. **Discharge of Parties.**

(1) The extent of the discharge of any party from

liability on an instrument is governed by the sections on

(a) payment or satisfaction (Section 3—603); or

(b) tender of payment (Section 3—604); or

(c) cancellation or renunciation (Section 3—605); or

(d) impairment of right of recourse or of collateral (Section 3—606); or

(e) reacquisition of the instrument by a prior party (Section 3—208); or

(f) fraudulent and material alteration (Section 3—407); or

(g) certification of a check (Section 3—411); or

(h) acceptance varying a draft (Section 3—412); or

(i) unexcused delay in presentment or notice of dishonor or protest (Section 3—502).

(2) Any party is also discharged from his liability on an instrument to another party by any other act or agreement with such party which would discharge his simple contract for the payment of money.

(3) The liability of all parties is discharged when any party who has himself no right of action or recourse on the instrument

(a) reacquires the instrument in his own right; or

(b) is discharged under any provision of this Article, except as otherwise provided with respect to discharge for impairment of recourse or of collateral (Section 3—606).

§ 3—602. Effect of Discharge Against Holder in Due Course.

No discharge of any party provided by this Article is effective against a subsequent holder in due course unless he has notice thereof when he takes the instrument.

§ 3—603. Payment or Satisfaction.

(1) The liability of any party is discharged to the extent of his payment or satisfaction to the holder even though it is made with knowledge of a claim of another person to the instrument unless prior to such payment or satisfaction the person making the claim either supplies indemnity deemed adequate by the party seeking the discharge or enjoins payment or satisfaction by order of a court of competent jurisdiction in an action in which the adverse claimant and the holder are parties. This subsection does not, however, result in the discharge of the liability

(a) of a party who in bad faith pays or satisfies a holder who acquired the instrument by theft or who (unless having the rights of a holder in due course) holds through one who so acquired it; or

(b) of a party (other than an intermediary bank or a payor bank which is not a depositary bank) who pays or satisfies the holder of an instrument which has been restrictively indorsed in a manner not consistent with the terms of such restrictive indorsement.

(2) Payment or satisfaction may be made with the consent of the holder by any person including a stranger to the instrument. Surrender of the instrument to such a person gives him the rights of a transferee (Section 3—201).

§ 3—604. Tender of Payment.

(1) Any party making tender of full payment to a holder when or after it is due is discharged to the extent of all subsequent liability for interest, costs and attorney's fees.

(2) The holder's refusal of such tender wholly discharges any party who has a right of recourse against the party making the tender.

(3) Where the maker or acceptor of an instrument payable otherwise than on demand is able and ready to pay at every place of payment specified in the instrument when it is due, it is equivalent to tender.

§ 3—605. Cancellation and Renunciation.

(1) The holder of an instrument may even without consideration discharge any party

(a) in any manner apparent on the face of the instrument or the indorsement, as by intentionally cancelling the instrument or the party's signature by destruction or mutilation, or by striking out the party's signature; or

(b) by renouncing his rights by a writing signed and delivered or by surrender of the instrument to the party to be discharged.

(2) Neither cancellation nor renunciation without surrender of the instrument affects the title thereto.

§ 3—606. Impairment of Recourse or of Collateral.

(1) The holder discharges any party to the instrument to the extent that without such party's consent the holder

(a) without express reservation of rights releases or agrees not to sue any person against whom the party has to the knowledge of the holder a right of recourse or agrees to suspend the right to enforce against such person the instrument or collateral or otherwise discharges such person, except that failure or delay in effecting any required present-ment, protest or notice of dishonor with respect to any such person does not discharge any party as to whom presentment, protest or notice of dishonor is effective or unnecessary; or

(b) unjustifiably impairs any collateral for the instrument given by or on behalf of the party or any person against whom he has a right of recourse.

(2) By express reservation of rights against a party with a right of recourse the holder preserves

(a) all his rights against such party as of the time when the instrument was originally due; and

(b) the right of the party to pay the instrument as of that time; and

(c) all rights of such party to recourse against others.

Part 7 Advice of International Sight Draft

§ 3—701. Letter of Advice of International Sight Draft.

(1) A "letter of advice" is a drawer's communication to the drawee that a described draft has been drawn.

(2) Unless otherwise agreed when a bank receives from another bank a letter of advice of an internation-al sight draft the drawee bank may immediately debit the drawer's account and stop the running of interest pro tanto. Such a debit and any resulting credit to any account covering outstanding drafts leaves in the drawer full power to stop payment or otherwise dispose of the amount and creates no trust or interest in favor of the holder.

(3) Unless otherwise agreed and except where a draft is drawn under a credit issued by the drawee, the drawee of an international sight draft owes the drawer no duty to pay an unadvised draft but if it does so and the draft is genuine, may appropriately debit the drawer's account.

Part 8 Miscellaneous

§ 3—801. Drafts in a Set.

(1) Where a draft is drawn in a set of parts, each of which is numbered and expressed to be an order only if no other part has been honored, the whole of the parts constitutes one draft but a taker of any part may become a holder in due course of the draft.

(2) Any person who negotiates, indorses or accepts a single part of a draft drawn in a set thereby becomes liable to any holder in due course of that part as if it were the whole set, but as between different holders in due course to whom different parts have been negotiated the holder whose title first accrues has all rights to the draft and its proceeds.

(3) As against the drawee the first presented part of a draft drawn in a set is the part entitled to payment, or if a time draft to acceptance and payment. Acceptance of any subsequently presented part renders the drawee liable thereon under subsection (2). With respect both to a holder and to the drawer payment of a subsequently presented part of a draft payable at sight has the same effect as payment of a check notwithstanding an effective stop order (Section 4—407).

(4) Except as otherwise provided in this section, where any part of a draft in a set is discharged by payment or otherwise the whole draft is discharged.

§ 3—802. Effect of Instrument on Obligation for Which It Is Given.

(1) Unless otherwise agreed where an instrument is taken for an underlying obligation

(a) the obligation is pro tanto discharged if a bank is drawer, maker or acceptor of the instrument and there is no recourse on the instrument against the underlying obligor; and

(b) in any other case the obligation is suspended pro tanto until the instrument is due or if it is payable on demand until its presentment. If the instrument is dishonored action may be main-tained on either the instrument or the obligation; discharge of the underlying obligor on the in-strument also discharges him on the obligation.

(2) The taking in good faith of a check which is not postdated does not of itself so extend the time on the original obligation as to discharge a surety.

§ 3—803. Notice to Third Party.

Where a defendant is sued for breach of an obligation for which a third person is answerable over under this Article he may give the third person written notice of the litigation, and the person notified may then give similar notice to any other person who is answerable over to him under this Article. If the notice states that the person notified may come in and defend and that if the person notified does not do so he will in any action against him by the person giving the notice be bound by any determination of fact common to the two litigations, then unless after seasonable receipt of the notice the person notified does come in and defend he is so bound.

§ 3—804. **Lost, Destroyed or Stolen Instruments.**

The owner of an instrument which is lost, whether by destruction, theft or otherwise, may maintain an action in his own name and recover from any party liable thereon upon due proof of his ownership, the facts which prevent his production of the instrument and its terms. The court may require security indemnifying the defendant against loss by reason of further claims on the instrument.

§ 3—805. **Instruments Not Payable to Order or to Bearer.**

This Article applies to any instrument whose terms do not preclude transfer and which is otherwise negotiable within this Article but which is not payable to order or to bearer, except that there can be no holder in due course of such an instrument.

Article 4
BANK DEPOSITS AND COLLECTIONS

Part 1 **General Provisions and Definitions**

§ 4—101. **Short Title.**

This Article shall be known and may be cited as Uniform Commercial Code—Bank Deposits and Collections.

§ 4—102. **Applicability.**

(1) To the extent that items within this Article are also within the scope of Articles 3 and 8, they are subject to the provisions of those Articles. In the event of conflict the provisions of this Article govern those of Article 3 but the provisions of Article 8 govern those of this Article.

(2) The liability of a bank for action or non-action with respect to any item handled by it for purposes of presentment, payment or collection is governed by the law of the place where the bank is located. In the case of action or non-action by or at a branch or separate office of a bank, its liability is governed by the law of the place where the branch or separate office is located.

§ 4—103. **Variation by Agreement; Measure of Damages; Certain Action Constituting Ordinary Care.**

(1) The effect of the provisions of this Article may be varied by agreement except that no agreement can disclaim a bank's responsibility for its own lack of good faith or failure to exercise ordinary care or can limit the measure of damages for such lack or failure; but the parties may by agreement determine the standards by which such responsibility is to be measured if such standards are not manifestly unreasonable.

(2) Federal Reserve regulations and operating letters, clearing house rules, and the like, have the effect of agreements under subsection (1), whether or not specifically assented to by all parties interested in items handled.

(3) Action or non-action approved by this Article or pursuant to Federal Reserve regulations or operating letters constitutes the exercise of ordinary care and, in the absence of special instructions, action or non-action consistent with clearing house rules and the like or with a general banking usage not disapproved by this Article, prima facie constitutes the exercise of ordinary care.

(4) The specification or approval of certain procedures by this Article does not constitute disapproval of other procedures which may be reasonable under the circumstances.

(5) The measure of damages for failure to exercise ordinary care in handling an item is the amount of the item reduced by an amount which could not have been realized by the use of ordinary care, and where there is bad faith it includes other damages, if any, suffered by the party as a proximate consequence.

§ 4—104. **Definitions and Index of Definitions.**

(1) In this Article unless the context otherwise requires

    (a) "Account" means any account with a bank and includes a checking, time, interest or savings account;

    (b) "Afternoon" means the period of a day between noon and midnight;

    (c) "Banking day" means that part of any day on which a bank is open to the public for carrying on substantially all of its banking functions;

    (d) "Clearing house" means any association of banks or other payors regularly clearing items;

(e) "Customer" means any person having an account with a bank or for whom a bank has agreed to collect items and includes a bank carrying an account with another bank;

(f) "Documentary draft" means any negotiable or nonnegotiable draft with accompanying documents, securities or other papers to be delivered against honor of the draft;

(g) "Item" means any instrument for the payment of money even though it is not negotiable but does not include money;

(h) "Midnight deadline" with respect to a bank is midnight on its next banking day following the banking day on which it receives the relevant item or notice or from which the time for taking action commences to run, whichever is later;

(i) "Properly payable" includes the availability of funds for payment at the time of decision to pay or dishonor;

(j) "Settle" means to pay in cash, by clearing house settlement, in a charge or credit or by remittance, or otherwise as instructed. A settlement may be either provisional or final;

(k) "Suspends payments" with respect to a bank means that it has been closed by order of the supervisory authorities, that a public officer has been appointed to take it over or that it ceases or refuses to make payments in the ordinary course of business.

(2) Other definitions applying to this Article and the sections in which they appear are:
"Collecting bank" Section 4—105.
"Depository bank" Section 4—105.
"Intermediary bank" Section 4—105.
"Payor bank" Section 4—105.
"Presenting bank" Section 4—105.
"Remitting bank" Section 4—105.

(3) The following definitions in other Articles apply to this Article:
"Acceptance" Section 3—410.
"Certificate of deposit" Section 3—104.
"Certification" Section 3—411.
"Check" Section 3—104.
"Draft" Section 3—104.
"Holder in due course" Section 3—302.
"Notice of dishonor" Section 3—508.
"Presentment" Section 3—504.
"Protest" Section 3—509.
"Secondary party" Section 3—102.

(4) In addition Article 1 contains general definitions and principles of construction and interpretation applicable throughout this Article.

§ 4—105. "Depositary Bank"; "Intermediary Bank"; "Collecting Bank"; "Payor Bank"; "Presenting Bank"; "Remitting Bank".

In this Article unless the context otherwise requires:

(a) "Depositary bank" means the first bank to which an item is transferred for collection even though it is also the payor bank;

(b) "Payor bank" means a bank by which an item is payable as drawn or accepted;

(c) "Intermediary bank" means any bank to which an item is transferred in course of collection except the depositary or payor bank;

(d) "Collecting bank" means any bank handling the item for collection except the payor bank;

(e) "Presenting bank" means any bank presenting an item except a payor bank;

(f) "Remitting bank" means any payor or intermediary bank remitting for an item.

§ 4—106. Separate Office of a Bank.

A branch or separate office of a bank [maintaining its own deposit ledgers] is a separate bank for the purpose of computing the time within which and determining the place at or to which action may be taken or notices or orders shall be given under this Article and under Article 3.

Note: *The brackets are to make it optional with the several states whether to require a branch to maintain its own deposit ledgers in order to be considered to be a separate bank for certain purposes under Article 4. In some states "maintaining its own deposit ledgers" is a satisfactory test. In others branch banking practices are such that this test would not be suitable.*

§ 4—107. Time of Receipt of Items.

(1) For the purpose of allowing time to process items, prove balances and make the necessary entries on its books to determine its position for the day, a bank may fix an afternoon hour of two P.M. or later as a cut-off hour for the handling of money and items and the making of entries on its books.

(2) Any item or deposit of money received on any day after a cut-off hour so fixed or after the close of the banking day may be treated as being received at the opening of the next banking day.

§ 4—108. Delays.

(1) Unless otherwise instructed, a collecting bank in a good faith effort to secure payment may, in the case of specific items and with or without the approval of any person involved, waive, modify or extend time limits imposed or permitted by this Act for a period not in excess of an additional banking day without

discharge of secondary parties and without liability to its transferor or any prior party.

(2) Delay by a collecting bank or payor bank beyond time limits prescribed or permitted by this Act or by instructions is excused if caused by interruption of communication facilities, suspension of payments by another bank, war, emergency conditions or other circumstances beyond the control of the bank provided it exercises such diligence as the circumstances require.

§ 4—109. **Process of Posting.**

The "process of posting" means the usual procedure followed by a payor bank in determining to pay an item and in recording the payment including one or more of the following or other steps as determined by the bank:

(a) verification of any signature;

(b) ascertaining that sufficient funds are available;

(c) affixing a "paid" or other stamp;

(d) entering a charge or entry to a customer's account;

(e) correcting or reversing an entry or erroneous action with respect to the item.

Part 2 **Collection of Items: Depository and Collecting Banks**

§ 4—201. **Presumption and Duration of Agency Status of Collecting Banks and Provisional Status of Credits; Applicability of Article; Item Indorsed "Pay Any Bank".**

(1) Unless a contrary intent clearly appears and prior to the time that a settlement given by a collecting bank for an item is or becomes final (subsection (3) of Section 4—211 and Sections 4—212 and 4—213) the bank is an agent or sub-agent of the owner of the item and any settlement given for the item is provisional. This provision applies regardless of the form of indorsement or lack of indorsement and even though credit given for the item is subject to immediate withdrawal as of right or is in fact withdrawn; but the continuance of ownership of an item by its owner and any rights of the owner to proceeds of the item are subject to rights of a collecting bank such as those resulting from outstanding advances on the item and valid rights of setoff. When an item is handled by banks for purposes of presentment, payment and collection, the relevant provisions of this Article apply even though action of parties clearly establishes that a particular bank has purchased the item and is the owner of it.

(2) After an item has been indorsed with the words "pay any bank" or the like, only a bank may acquire the rights of a holder

(a) until the item has been returned to the customer initiating collection; or

(b) until the item has been specially indorsed by a bank to a person who is not a bank.

§ 4—202. **Responsibility for Collection; When Action Seasonable.**

(1) A collecting bank must use ordinary care in

(a) presenting an item or sending it for presentment; and

(b) sending notice of dishonor or non-payment or returning an item other than a documentary draft to the bank's transferor [or directly to the depositary bank under subsection (2) of Section 4—212] *(see note to Section 4—212)* after learning that the item has not been paid or accepted as the case may be; and

(c) settling for an item when the bank receives final settlement; and

(d) making or providing for any necessary protest; and

(e) notifying its transferor of any loss or delay in transit within a reasonable time after discovery thereof.

(2) A collecting bank taking proper action before its midnight deadline following receipt of an item, notice or payment acts seasonably; taking proper action within a reasonably longer time may be seasonable but the bank has the burden of so establishing.

(3) Subject to subsection (1) (a), a bank is not liable for the insolvency, neglect, misconduct, mistake or default of another bank or person or for loss or destruction of an item in transit or in the possession of others.

§ 4—203. **Effect of Instructions.**

Subject to the provisions of Article 3 concerning conversion of instruments (Section 3—419) and the provisions of both Article 3 and this Article concerning restrictive indorsements only a collecting bank's transferor can give instructions which affect the bank or constitute notice to it and a collecting bank is not liable to prior parties for any action taken pursuant to such instructions or in accordance with any agreement with its transferor.

§ 4—204. **Methods of Sending and Presenting; Sending Direct to Payor Bank.**

(1) A collecting bank must send items by reasonably prompt method taking into consideration any relevant instructions, the nature of the item, the number of such items on hand, and the cost of collection involved and the method generally used by it or others to present such items.

(2) A collecting bank may send

(a) any item direct to the payor bank;

(b) any item to any non-bank payor if authorized by its transferor; and

(c) any item other than documentary drafts to any non-bank payor, if authorized by Federal Reserve regulation or operating letter, clearing house rule or the like.

(3) Presentment may be made by a presenting bank at a place where the payor bank has requested that presentment be made.

§ 4—205. **Supplying Missing Indorsement; No Notice from Prior Indorsement.**

(1) A depositary bank which has taken an item for collection may supply any indorsement of the customer which is necessary to title unless the item contains the words "payee's indorsement required" or the like. In the absence of such a requirement a statement placed on the item by the depositary bank to the effect that the item was deposited by a customer or credited to his account is effective as the customer's indorsement.

(2) An intermediary bank, or payor bank which is not a depositary bank, is neither given notice nor otherwise affected by a restrictive indorsement of any person except the bank's immediate transferor.

§ 4—206. **Transfer Between Banks.**

Any agreed method which identifies the transferor bank is sufficient for the item's further transfer to another bank.

§ 4—207. **Warranties of Customer and Collecting Bank on Transfer or Presentment of Items; Time for Claims.**

(1) Each customer or collecting bank who obtains payment or acceptance of an item and each prior customer and collecting bank warrants to the payor bank or other payor who in good faith pays or accepts the item that

(a) he has a good title to the item or is authorized to obtain payment or acceptance on behalf of one who has a good title; and

(b) he has no knowledge that the signature of the maker or drawer is unauthorized, except that this warranty is not given by any customer or collecting bank that is a holder in due course and acts in good faith

(i) to a maker with respect to the maker's own signature; or

(ii) to a drawer with respect to the drawer's own signature, whether or not the drawer is also the drawee; or

(iii) to an acceptor of an item if the holder in due course took the item after the acceptance or obtained the acceptance without knowledge that the drawer's signature was unauthorized; and

(c) the item has not been materially altered, except that this warranty is not given by any customer or collecting bank that is a holder in due course and acts in good faith

(i) to the maker of a note; or

(ii) to the drawer of a draft whether or not the drawer is also the drawee; or

(iii) to the acceptor of an item with respect to an alteration made prior to the acceptance if the holder in due course took the item after the acceptance, even though the acceptance provided "payable as originally drawn" or equivalent terms; or

(iv) to the acceptor of an item with respect to an alteration made after the acceptance.

(2) Each customer and collecting bank who transfers an item and receives a settlement or other consideration for it warrants to his transferee and to any subequent collecting bank who takes the item in good faith that

(a) he has a good title to the item or is authorized to obtain payment or acceptance on behalf of one who has a good title and the transfer is otherwise rightful; and

(b) all signatures are genuine or authorized; and

(c) the item has not been materially altered; and

(d) no defense of any party is good against him; and

(e) he has no knowledge of any insolvency proceeding instituted with respect to the maker or acceptor or the drawer of an unaccepted item.

In addition each customer and collecting bank so transferring an item and receiving a settlement or other consideration engages that upon dishonor and any necessary notice of dishonor and protest he will take up the item.

(3) The warranties and the engagement to honor set forth in the two preceding subsections arise notwithstanding the absence of indorsement or words of guaranty or warranty in the transfer or presentment and a collecting bank remains liable for their breach despite remittance to its transferor. Damages for breach of such warranties or engagement to honor shall not exceed the consideration received by the customer or collecting bank responsible plus finance charges and expenses related to the item, if any.

(4) Unless a claim for breach of warranty under this section is made within a reasonable time after the person claiming learns of the breach, the person liable is discharged to the extent of any loss caused by the delay in making claim.

§ 4—208. Security Interest of Collecting Bank in Items, Accompanying Documents and Proceeds.

(1) A bank has a security interest in an item and any accompanying documents or the proceeds of either

(a) in case of an item deposited in an account to the extent to which credit given for the item has been withdrawn or applied;

(b) in case of an item for which it has given credit available for withdrawal as of right, to the extent of the credit given whether or not the credit is drawn upon and whether or not there is a right of charge-back; or

(c) if it makes an advance on or against the item.

(2) When credit which has been given for several items received at one time or pursuant to a single agreement is withdrawn or applied in part the security interest remains upon all the items, any accompanying documents or the proceeds of either. For the purpose of this section, credits first given are first withdrawn.

(3) Receipt by a collecting bank of a final settlement for an item is a realization on its security interest in the item, accompanying documents and proceeds. To the extent and so long as the bank does not receive final settlement for the item or give up possession of the item or accompanying documents for purposes other than collection, the security interest continues and is subject to the provisions of Article 9 except that

(a) no security agreement is necessary to make the security interest enforceable (subsection (1) (b) of Section 9—203); and

(b) no filing is required to perfect the security interest; and

(c) the security interest has priority over conflicting perfected security interests in the item, accompanying documents or proceeds.

§ 4—209. When Bank Gives Value for Purposes of Holder in Due Course.

For purposes of determining its status as a holder in due course, the bank has given value to the extent that it has a security interest in an item provided that the bank otherwise complies with the requirements of Section 3—302 on what constitutes a holder in due course.

§ 4—210. Presentment by Notice of Item Not Payable by, Through or at a Bank; Liability of Secondary Parties.

(1) Unless otherwise instructed, a collecting bank may present an item not payable by, through or at a bank by sending to the party to accept or pay a written notice that the bank holds the item for acceptance or payment. The notice must be sent in time to be received on or before the day when presentment is due and the bank must meet any requirement of the party to accept or pay under Section 3—505 by the close of the bank's next banking day after it knows of the requirement.

(2) Where presentment is made by notice and neither honor nor request for compliance with a requirement under Section 3—505 is received by the close of business on the day after maturity or in the case of demand items by the close of business on the third banking day after notice was sent, the presenting bank may treat the item as dishonored and charge any secondary party by sending him notice of the facts.

§ 4—211. Media of Remittance; Provisional and Final Settlement in Remittance Cases.

(1) A collecting bank may take in settlement of an item

(a) a check of the remitting bank or of another bank on any bank except the remitting bank; or

(b) a cashier's check or similar primary obligation of a remitting bank which is a member of or clears through a member of the same clearing house or group as the collecting bank; or

(c) appropriate authority to charge an account of the remitting bank or of another bank with the collecting bank; or

(d) if the item is drawn upon or payable by a person other than a bank, a cashier's check, certified check or other bank check or obligation.

(2) If before its midnight deadline the collecting bank properly dishonors a remittance check or authoriza-

tion to charge on itself or presents or forwards for collection a remittance instrument of or on another bank which is of a kind approved by subsection (1) or has not been authorized by it, the collecting bank is not liable to prior parties in the event of the dishonor of such check, instrument or authorization.

(3) A settlement for an item by means of a remittance instrument or authorization to charge is or becomes a final settlement as to both the person making and the person receiving the settlement

(a) if the remittance instrument or authorization to charge is of a kind approved by subsection (1) or has not been authorized by the person receiving the settlement and in either case the person receiving the settlement acts seasonably before its midnight deadline in presenting, forwarding for collection or paying the instrument or authorization,—at the time the remittance instrument or authorization is finally paid by the payor by which it is payable;

(b) if the person receiving the settlement has authorized remittance by a non-bank check or obligation or by a cashier's check or similar primary obligation of or a check upon the payor or other remitting bank which is not of a kind approved by subsection (1) (b),—at the time of the receipt of such remittance check or obligation; or

(c) if in a case not covered by sub-paragraphs (a) or (b) the person receiving the settlement fails to seasonably present, forward for collection, pay or return a remittance instrument or authorization to it to charge before its midnight deadline,—at such midnight deadline.

§ 4—212. Right of Charge-Back or Refund.

(1) If a collecting bank has made provisional settlement with its customer for an item and itself fails by reason of dishonor, suspension of payments by a bank or otherwise to receive a settlement for the item which is or becomes final, the bank may revoke the settlement given by it, charge back the amount of any credit given for the item to its customer's account or obtain refund from its customer whether or not it is able to return the items if by its midnight deadline or within a longer reasonable time after it learns the facts it returns the item or sends notification of the facts. These rights to revoke, charge-back and obtain refund terminate if and when a settlement for the item received by the bank is or becomes final (subsection (3) of Section 4—211 and subsections (2) and (3) of Section 4—213).

[(2) Within the time and manner prescribed by this section and Section 4—301, an intermediary or payor bank, as the case may be, may return an unpaid item directly to the depositary bank and may send for collection a draft on the depositary bank and obtain reimbursement. In such case, if the depositary bank has received provisional settlement for the item, it must reimburse the bank drawing the draft and any provisional credits for the item between banks shall become and remain final.]

Note: *Direct returns is recognized as an innovation that is not yet established bank practice, and therefore, Paragraph 2 has been bracketed. Some lawyers have doubts whether it should be included in legislation or left to development by agreement.*

(3) A depositary bank which is also the payor may charge-back the amount of an item to its customer's account or obtain refund in accordance with the section governing return of an item received by a payor bank for credit on its books (Section 4—301).

(4) The right to charge-back is not affected by

(a) prior use of the credit given for the item; or
(b) failure by any bank to exercise ordinary care with respect to the item but any bank so failing remains liable.

(5) A failure to charge-back or claim refund does not affect other rights of the bank against the customer or any other party.

(6) If credit is given in dollars as the equivalent of the value of an item payable in a foreign currency the dollar amount of any charge-back or refund shall be calculated on the basis of the buying sight rate for the foreign currency prevailing on the day when the person entitled to the charge-back or refund learns that it will not receive payment in ordinary course.

§ 4—213. Final Payment of Item by Payor Bank; When Provisional Debits and Credits Become Final; When Certain Credits Become Available for Withdrawal.

(1) An item is finally paid by a payor bank when the bank has done any of the following, whichever happens first:

(a) paid the item in cash; or

(b) settled for the item without reserving a right to revoke the settlement and without having such right under statute, clearing house rule or agreement; or

(c) completed the process of posting the item to the indicated account of the drawer, maker or other person to be charged therewith; or

(d) made a provisional settlement for the item and failed to revoke the settlement in the time and manner permitted by statute, clearing house rule or agreement.

Upon a final payment under subparagraphs (b), (c) or (d) the payor bank shall be accountable for the amount of the item.

(2) If provisional settlement for an item between the presenting and payor banks is made through a clearing house or by debits or credits in an account between them, then to the extent that provisional debits or credits for the item are entered in accounts between the presenting and payor banks or between the presenting and successive prior collecting banks seriatim, they become final upon final payment of the item by the payor bank.

(3) If a collecting bank receives a settlement for an item which is or becomes final (subsection (3) of Section 4—211, subsection (2) of Section 4—213) the bank is accountable to its customer for the amount of the item and any provisional credit given for the item in an account with its customer becomes final.

(4) Subject to any right of the bank to apply the credit to an obligation of the customer, credit given by a bank for an item in an account with its customer becomes available for withdrawal as of right

(a) in any case where the bank has received a provisional settlement for the item,—when such settlement becomes final and the bank has had a reasonable time to learn that the settlement is final;

(b) in any case where the bank is both a depositary bank and a payor bank and the item is finally paid,—at the opening of the bank's second banking day following receipt of the item.

(5) A deposit of money in a bank is final when made but, subject to any right of the bank to apply the deposit to an obligation of the customer, the deposit becomes available for withdrawal as of right at the opening of the bank's next banking day following receipt of the deposit.

§ 4—214. Insolvency and Preference.

(1) Any item in or coming into the possession of a payor or collecting bank which suspends payment and which item is not finally paid shall be returned by the receiver, trustee or agent in charge of the closed bank to the presenting bank or the closed bank's customer.

(2) If a payor bank finally pays an item and suspends payments without making a settlement for the item with its customer or the presenting bank which settlement is or becomes final, the owner of the item has a preferred claim against the payor bank.

(3) If a payor bank gives or a collecting bank gives or receives a provisional settlement for an item and thereafter suspends payments, the suspension does not prevent or interfere with the settlement becoming final if such finality occurs automatically upon the lapse of certain time or the happening of certain events (subsection (3) of Section 4—211, subsections (1) (d), (2) and (3) of Section 4—213).

(4) If a collecting bank receives from subsequent parties settlement for an item which settlement is or becomes final and suspends payments without making a settlement for the item with its customer which is or becomes final, the owner of the item has a preferred claim against such collecting bank.

Part 3 Collection of Items: Payor Banks

§ 4—301. Deferred Posting; Recovery of Payment by Return of Items; Time of Dishonor.

(1) Where an authorized settlement for a demand item (other than a documentary draft) received by a payor bank otherwise than for immediate payment over the counter has been made before midnight of the banking day of receipt the payor bank may revoke the settlement and recover any payment if before it has made final payment (subsection (1) of Section 4—213) and before its midnight deadline it

(a) returns the item; or

(b) sends written notice of dishonor or nonpayment if the item is held for protest or is otherwise unavailable for return.

(2) If a demand item is received by a payor bank for credit on its books it may return such item or send notice of dishonor and may revoke any credit given or recover the amount thereof withdrawn by its customer, if it acts within the time limit and in the manner specified in the preceding subsection.

(3) Unless previous notice of dishonor has been sent an item is dishonored at the time when for purposes of dishonor it is returned or notice sent in accordance with this section.

(4) An item is returned:

(a) as to an item received through a clearing house, when it is delivered to the presenting or last collecting bank or to the clearing house or is sent or delivered in accordance with its rules; or

(b) in all other cases, when it is sent or delivered to the bank's customer or transferor or pursuant to his instructions.

§ 4—302. **Payor Bank's Responsibility for Late Return of Item.**

In the absence of a valid defense such as breach of a presentment warranty (subsection (1) of Section 4—207), settlement effected or the like, if an item is presented on and received by a payor bank the bank is accountable for the amount of

(a) a demand item other than a documentary draft whether properly payable or not if the bank, in any case where it is not also the depositary bank, retains the item beyond midnight of the banking day of receipt without settling for it or, regardless of whether it is also the depositary bank, does not pay or return the item or send notice of dishonor until after its midnight deadline; or

(b) any other properly payable item unless within the time allowed for acceptance or payment of that item the bank either accepts or pays the item or returns it and accompanying documents.

§ 4—303. **When Items Subject to Notice, Stop-Order, Legal Process or Setoff; Order in Which Items May Be Charged or Certified.**

(1) Any knowledge, notice or stop-order received by, legal process served upon or setoff exercised by a payor bank, whether or not effective under other rules of law to terminate, suspend or modify the bank's right or duty to pay an item or to charge its customer's account for the item, comes too late to so terminate, suspend or modify such right or duty if the knowledge, notice, stop-order or legal process is received or served and a reasonable time for the bank to act thereon expires or the setoff is exercised after the bank has done any of the following:

    (a) accepted or certified the item;

    (b) paid the item in cash;

    (c) settled for the item without reserving a right to revoke the settlement and without having such right under statute, clearing house rule or agreement;

    (d) completed the process of posting the item to the indicated account of the drawer, maker or other person to be charged therewith or otherwise has evidenced by examination of such indicated account and by action its decision to pay the item; or

    (e) become accountable for the amount of the item under subsection (1) (d) of Section 4—213 and Section 4—302 dealing with the payor bank's responsibility for late return of items.

(2) Subject to the provisions of subsection (1) items may be accepted, paid, certified or charged to the indicated account of its customer in any order convenient to the bank.

Part 4 **Relationship Between Payor Bank and Its Customer**

§ 4—401. **When Bank May Charge Customer's Account.**

(1) As against its customer, a bank may charge against his account any item which is otherwise properly payable from that account even though the charge creates an overdraft.

(2) A bank which in good faith makes payment to a holder may charge the indicated account of its customer according to

    (a) the original tenor of his altered item; or

    (b) the tenor of his completed item, even though the bank knows the item has been completed unless the bank has notice that the completion was improper.

§ 4—402. **Bank's Liability to Customer for Wrongful Dishonor.**

A payor bank is liable to its customer for damages proximately caused by the wrongful dishonor of an item. When the dishonor occurs through mistake liability is limited to actual damages proved. If so proximately caused and proved damages may include damages for an arrest or prosecution of the customer or other consequential damages. Whether any consequential damages are proximately caused by the wrongful dishonor is a question of fact to be determined in each case.

§ 4—403. **Customer's Right to Stop Payment; Burden of Proof of Loss.**

(1) A customer may by order to his bank stop payment of any item payable for his account but the order must be received at such time and in such manner as to afford the bank a reasonable opportunity to act on it prior to any action by the bank with respect to the item described in Section 4—303.

(2) An oral order is binding upon the bank only for fourteen calendar days unless confirmed in writing within that period. A written order is effective for only six months unless renewed in writing.

(3) The burden of establishing the fact and amount of loss resulting from the payment of an item contrary to a binding stop payment order is on the customer.

§ 4—404. Bank Not Obligated to Pay Check More Than Six Months Old.

A bank is under no obligation to a customer having a checking account to pay a check, other than a certified check, which is presented more than six months after its date, but it may charge its customer's account for a payment made thereafter in good faith.

§ 4—405. Death or Incompetence of Customer.

(1) A payor or collecting bank's authority to accept, pay or collect an item or to account for proceeds of its collection if otherwise effective is not rendered ineffective by incompetence of a customer of either bank existing at the time the item is issued or its collection is undertaken if the bank does not know of an adjudication of incompetence. Neither death nor incompetence of a customer revokes such authority to accept, pay, collect or account until the bank knows of the fact of death or of an adjudication of incompetence and has reasonable opportunity to act on it.

(2) Even with knowledge a bank may for ten days after the date of death pay or certify checks drawn on or prior to that date unless ordered to stop payment by a person claiming an interest in the account.

§ 4—406. Customer's Duty to Discover and Report Unauthorized Signature or Alteration.

(1) When a bank sends to its customer a statement of account accompanied by items paid in good faith in support of the debit entries or holds the statement and items pursuant to a request or instructions of its customer or otherwise in a reasonable manner makes the statement and items available to the customer, the customer must exercise reasonable care and promptness to examine the statement and items to discover his unauthorized signature or any alteration on an item and must notify the bank promptly after discovery thereof.

(2) If the bank establishes that the customer failed with respect to an item to comply with the duties imposed on the customer by subsection (1) the customer is precluded from asserting against the bank

(a) his unauthorized signature or any alteration on the item if the bank also establishes that it suffered a loss by reason of such failure; and

(b) an unauthorized signature or alteration by the same wrongdoer on any other item paid in good faith by the bank after the first item and statement was available to the customer for a reasonable period not exceeding fourteen calendar days and

before the bank receives notification from the customer of any such unauthorized signature or alteration.

(3) The preclusion under subsection (2) does not apply if the customer establishes lack of ordinary care on the part of the bank in paying the item(s).

(4) Without regard to care or lack of care of either the customer or the bank a customer who does not within one year from the time the statement and items are made available to the customer (subsection (1)) discover and report his unauthorized signature or any alteration on the face or back of the item or does not within three years from that time discover and report any unauthorized indorsement is precluded from asserting against the bank such unauthorized signature or indorsement or such alteration.

(5) If under this section a payor bank has a valid defense against a claim of a customer upon or resulting from payment of an item and waives or fails upon request to assert the defense the bank may not assert against any collecting bank or other prior party presenting or transferring the item a claim based upon the unauthorized signature or alteration giving rise to the customer's claim.

§ 4—407. Payor Bank's Right to Subrogation on Improper Payment.

If a payor bank has paid an item over the stop payment order of the drawer or maker or otherwise under circumstances giving a basis for objection by the drawer or maker, to prevent unjust enrichment and only to the extent necessary to prevent loss to the bank by reason of its payment of the item, the payor bank shall be subrogated to the rights

(a) of any holder in due course on the item against the drawer or maker; and

(b) of the payee or any other holder of the item against the drawer or maker either on the item or under the transaction out of which the item arose; and

(c) of the drawer or maker against the payee or any other holder of the item with respect to the transaction out of which the item arose.

Part 5 Collection of Documentary Drafts

§ 4—501. Handling of Documentary Drafts; Duty to Send for Presentment and to Notify Customer of Dishonor.

A bank which takes a documentary draft for collection must present or send the draft and accompanying documents for presentment and upon learning that the draft has not been paid or accepted in due course must seasonably notify its customer of such fact even though it may have discounted or bought the draft or extended credit available for withdrawal as of right.

§ 4—502. Presentment of "On Arrival" Drafts.

When a draft or the relevant instructions require presentment "on arrival", "when goods arrive" or the like, the collecting bank need not present until in its judgment a reasonable time for arrival of the goods has expired. Refusal to pay or accept because the goods have not arrived is not dishonor; the bank must notify its transferor of such refusal but need not present the draft again until it is instructed to do so or learns of the arrival of the goods.

§ 4—503. Responsibility of Presenting Bank for Documents and Goods; Report of Reasons for Dishonor; Referee in Case of Need.

Unless otherwise instructed and except as provided in Article 5 a bank presenting a documentary draft

(a) must deliver the documents to the drawee on acceptance of the draft if it is payable more than three days after presentment; otherwise, only on payment; and

(b) upon dishonor, either in the case of presentment for acceptance or presentment for payment, may seek and follow instructions from any referee in case of need designated in the draft or if the presenting bank does not choose to utilize his services it must use diligence and good faith to ascertain the reason for dishonor, must notify its transferor of the dishonor and of the results of its effort to ascertain the reasons therefor and must request instructions.

But the presenting bank is under no obligation with respect to goods represented by the documents except to follow any reasonable instructions seasonably received; it has a right to reimbursement for any expense incurred in following instructions and to prepayment of or indemnity for such expenses.

§ 4—504. Privilege of Presenting Bank to Deal With Goods; Security Interest for Expenses.

(1) A presenting bank which, following the dishonor of a documentary draft, has seasonably requested instructions but does not receive them within a reasonable time may store, sell, or otherwise deal with the goods in any reasonable manner.

(2) For its reasonable expenses incurred by action under subsection (1) the presenting bank has a lien upon the goods or their proceeds, which may be

foreclosed in the same manner as an unpaid seller's lien.

Article 5
LETTERS OF CREDIT

§ 5—101. Short Title.

This Article shall be known and may be cited as Uniform Commercial Code—Letters of Credit.

§ 5—102. Scope.

(1) This Article applies

(a) to a credit issued by a bank if the credit requires a documentary draft or a documentary demand for payment; and

(b) to a credit issued by a person other than a bank if the credit requires that the draft or demand for payment be accompanied by a document of title; and

(c) to a credit issued by a bank or other person if the credit is not within subparagraphs (a) or (b) but conspicuously states that it is a letter of credit or is conspicuously so entitled.

(2) Unless the engagement meets the requirements of subsection (1), this Article does not apply to engagements to make advances or to honor drafts or demands for payment, to authorities to pay or purchase, to guarantees or to general agreements.

(3) This Article deals with some but not all of the rules and concepts of letters of credit as such rules or concepts have developed prior to this act or may hereafter develop. The fact that this Article states a rule does not by itself require, imply or negate application of the same or a converse rule to a situation not provided for or to a person not specified by this Article.

§ 5—103. Definitions.

(1) In this Article unless the context otherwise requires

(a) "Credit" or "letter of credit" means an engagement by a bank or other person made at the request of a customer and of a kind within the scope of this Article (Section 5—102) that the issuer will honor drafts or other demands for payment upon compliance with the conditions specified in the credit. A credit may be either revocable or irrevocable. The engagement may be either an agreement to honor or a statement that the bank or other person is authorized to honor.

(b) A "documentary draft" or a "documentary demand for payment" is one honor of which is conditioned upon the presentation of a document or documents. "Document" means any paper including document of title, security, invoice, certificate, notice of default and the like.

(c) An "issuer" is a bank or other person issuing a credit.

(d) A "beneficiary" of a credit is a person who is entitled under its terms to draw or demand payment.

(e) An "advising bank" is a bank which gives notification of the issuance of a credit by another bank.

(f) A "confirming bank" is a bank which engages either that it will itself honor a credit already issued by another bank or that such a credit will be honored by the issuer or a third bank.

(g) A "customer" is a buyer or other person who causes an issuer to issue a credit. The term also includes a bank which procures issuance or confirmation on behalf of that bank's customer.

(2) Other definitions applying to this Article and the sections in which they appear are:

"Notation of Credit". Section 5—108.

"Presenter". Section 5—112(3).

(3) Definitions in other Articles applying to this Article and the sections in which they appear are:

"Accept" or "Acceptance". Section 3—410.

"Contract for sale". Section 2—106.

"Draft". Section 3—104.

"Holder in due course". Section 3—302.

"Midnight deadline". Section 4—104.

"Security". Section 8—102.

(4) In addition, Article 1 contains general definitions and principles of construction and interpretation applicable throughout this Article.

§ 5—104. Formal Requirements; Signing.

(1) Except as otherwise required in subsection (1) (c) of Section 5—102 on scope, no particular form of phrasing is required for a credit. A credit must be in writing and signed by the issuer and a confirmation must be in writing and signed by the confirming bank. A modification of the terms of a credit or confirmation must be signed by the issuer or confirming bank.

(2) A telegram may be a sufficient signed writing if it identifies its sender by an authorized authentication. The authentication may be in code and the authorized naming of the issuer in an advice of credit is a sufficient signing.

§ 5—105. Consideration.

No consideration is necessary to establish a credit or to enlarge or otherwise modify its terms.

§ 5—106. Time and Effect of Establishment of Credit.

(1) Unless otherwise agreed a credit is established

(a) as regards the customer as soon as a letter of credit is sent to him or the letter of credit or an authorized written advice of its issuance is sent to the beneficiary; and

(b) as regards the beneficiary when he receives a letter of credit or an authorized written advice of its issuance.

(2) Unless otherwise agreed once an irrevocable credit is established as regards the customer it can be modified or revoked only with the consent of the customer and once it is established as regards the beneficiary it can be modified or revoked only with his consent.

(3) Unless otherwise agreed after a revocable credit is established it may be modified or revoked by the issuer without notice to or consent from the customer or beneficiary.

(4) Notwithstanding any modification or revocation of a revocable credit any person authorized to honor or negotiate under the terms of the original credit is entitled to reimbursement for or honor of any draft or demand for payment duty honored or negotiated before receipt of notice of the modification or revocation and the issuer in turn is entitled to reimbursement from its customer.

§ 5—107. Advice of Credit; Confirmation; Error in Statement of Terms.

(1) Unless otherwise specified an advising bank by advising a credit issued by another bank does not assume any obligation to honor drafts drawn or demands for payment made under the credit but it does assume obligation for the accuracy of its own statement.

(2) A confirming bank by confirming a credit becomes directly obligated on the credit to the extent of its confirmation as though it were its issuer and acquires the rights of an issuer.

(3) Even though an advising bank incorrectly advises the terms of a credit it has been authorized to advise the credit is established as against the issuer to the extent of its original terms.

(4) Unless otherwise specified the customer bears as against the issuer all risks of transmission and

reasonable translation or interpretation of any message relating to a credit.

§ 5—108. "Notation Credit"; Exhaustion of Credit.

(1) A credit which specifies that any person purchasing or paying drafts drawn or demands for payment made under it must note the amount of the draft or demand on the letter or advice of credit is a "notation credit".

(2) Under a notation credit

(a) a person paying the beneficiary or purchasing a draft or demand for payment from him acquires a right to honor only if the appropriate notation is made and by transferring or forwarding for honor the documents under the credit such a person warrants to the issuer that the notation has been made; and

(b) unless the credit or a signed statement that an appropriate notation has been made accompanies the draft or demand for payment the issuer may delay honor until evidence of notation has been procured which is satisfactory to it but its obligation and that of its customer continue for a reasonable time not exceeding thirty days to obtain such evidence.

(3) If the credit is not a notation credit

(a) the issuer may honor complying drafts or demands for payment presented to it in the order in which they are presented and is discharged pro tanto by honor of any such draft or demand;

(b) as between competing good faith purchasers of complying drafts or demands the person first purchasing has priority over a subsequent purchaser even though the later purchased draft or demand has been first honored.

§ 5—109. Issuer's Obligation to Its Customer.

(1) An issuer's obligation to its customer includes good faith and observance of any general banking usage but unless otherwise agreed does not include liability or responsibility

(a) for performance of the underlying contract for sale or other transaction between the customer and the beneficiary; or

(b) for any act or omission of any person other than itself or its own branch or for loss or destruction of a draft, demand or document in transit or in the possession of others; or

(c) based on knowledge or lack of knowledge of any usage of any particular trade.

(2) An issuer must examine documents with care so as to ascertain that on their face they appear to comply with the terms of the credit but unless otherwise agreed assumes no liability or responsibility for the genuineness, falsification or effect of any document which appears on such examination to be regular on its face.

(3) A non-bank issuer is not bound by any banking usage of which it has no knowledge.

§ 5—110. Availability of Credit in Portions; Presenter's Reservation of Lien or Claim.

(1) Unless otherwise specified a credit may be used in portions in the discretion of the beneficiary.

(2) Unless otherwise specified a person by presenting a documentary draft or demand for payment under a credit relinquishes upon its honor all claims to the documents and a person by transferring such draft or demand or causing such presentment authorizes such relinquishment. An explicit reservation of claim makes the draft or demand non-complying.

§ 5—111. Warranties on Transfer and Presentment.

(1) Unless otherwise agreed the beneficiary by transferring or presenting a documentary draft or demand for payment warrants to all interested parties that the necessary conditions of the credit have been complied with. This is in addition to any warranties arising under Articles 3, 4, 7 and 8.

(2) Unless otherwise agreed a negotiating, advising, confirming, collecting or issuing bank presenting or transferring a draft or demand for payment under a credit warrants only the matters warranted by a collecting bank under Article 4 and any such bank transferring a document warrants only the matters warranted by an intermediary under Articles 7 and 8.

§ 5—112. Time Allowed for Honor or Rejection; Withholding Honor or Rejection by Consent; "Presenter".

(1) A bank to which a documentary draft or demand for payment is presented under a credit may without dishonor of the draft, demand or credit

(a) defer honor until the close of the third banking day following receipt of the documents; and

(b) further defer honor if the presenter has expressly or impliedly consented thereto.

Failure to honor within the time here specified constitutes dishonor of the draft or demand and of the credit [except as otherwise provided in subsection (4) of Section 5—114 on conditional payment].

Note: *The bracketed language in the last sentence of subsection (1) should be included only if the optional provisions of Section 5—114(4) and (5) are included.*

(2) Upon dishonor the bank may unless otherwise instructed fulfill its duty to return the draft or demand and the documents by holding them at the disposal of the presenter and sending him an advice to that effect.

(3) "Presenter" means any person presenting a draft or demand for payment for honor under a credit even though that person is a confirming bank or other correspondent which is acting under an issuer's authorization.

§ 5—113. Indemnities.

(1) A bank seeking to obtain (whether for itself or another) honor, negotiation or reimbursement under a credit may give an indemnity to induce such honor, negotiation or reimbursement.

(2) An indemnity agreement inducing honor, negotiation or reimbursement

(a) unless otherwise explicitly agreed applies to defects in the documents but not in the goods; and

(b) unless a longer time is explicitly agreed expires at the end of ten business days following receipt of the documents by, the ultimate customer unless notice of objection is sent before such expiration date. The ultimate customer may send notice of objection to the person from whom he received the documents and any bank receiving such notice is under a duty to send notice to its transferor before its midnight deadline.

§ 5—114. Issuer's Duty and Privilege to Honor; Right to Reimbursement.

(1) An issuer must honor a draft or demand for payment which complies with the terms of the relevant credit regardless of whether the goods or documents conform to the underlying contract for sale or other contract between the customer and the beneficiary. The issuer is not excused from honor of such a draft or demand by reason of an additional general term that all documents must be satisfactory to the issuer, but an issuer may require that specified documents must be satisfactory to it.

(2) Unless otherwise agreed when documents appear on their face to comply with the terms of a credit but a required document does not in fact conform to the warranties made on negotiation or transfer of a document of title (Section 7—507) or of a certificated security (Section 8—306) or is forged or fraudulent or there is fraud in the transaction:

(a) the issuer must honor the draft or demand for payment if honor is demanded by a negotiating bank or other holder of the draft or demand which has taken the draft or demand under the credit and under circumstances which would make it a holder in due course (Section 3—302) and in an appropriate case would make it a person to whom a document of title has been duly negotiated (Section 7—502) or a bona fide purchaser of a certificated security (Section 8—302); and

(b) in all other cases as against its customer, an issuer acting in good faith may honor the draft or demand for payment despite notification from the customer of fraud, forgery or other defect not apparent on the face of the documents but a court of appropriate jurisdiction may enjoin such honor.

(3) Unless otherwise agreed an issuer which has duly honored a draft or demand for payment is entitled to immediate reimbursement of any payment made under the credit and to be put in effectively available funds not later than the day before maturity of any acceptance made under the credit.

[(4) When a credit provides for payment by the issuer on receipt of notice that the required documents are in the possession of a correspondent or other agent of the issuer

(a) any payment made on receipt of such notice is conditional; and

(b) the issuer may reject documents which do not comply with the credit if it does so within three banking days following its receipt of the documents; and

(c) in the event of such rejection, the issuer is entitled by charge back or otherwise to return of the payment made.]

[(5) In the case covered by subsection (4) failure to reject documents within the time specified in sub-paragraph (b) constitutes acceptance of the documents and makes the payment final in favor of the beneficiary.]

Amended in 1977.

Note: *Subsections (4) and (5) are bracketed as optional. If they are included the bracketed language in the last sentence of Section 5—112(1) should also be included.*

§ 5—115. Remedy for Improper Dishonor or Anticipatory Repudiation.

(1) When an issuer wrongfully dishonors a draft or demand for payment presented under a credit the person entitled to honor has with respect to any documents the rights of a person in the position of a

seller (Section 2—707) and may recover from the issuer the face amount of the draft or demand together with incidental damages under Section 2—710 on seller's incidental damages and interest but less any amount realized by resale or other use or disposition of the subject matter of the transaction. In the event no resale or other utilization is made the documents, goods or other subject matter involved in the transaction must be turned over to the issuer on payment of judgment.

(2) When an issuer wrongfully cancels or otherwise repudiates a credit before presentment of a draft or demand for payment drawn under it the beneficiary has the rights of a seller after anticipatory repudiation by the buyer under Section 2—610 if he learns of the repudiation in time reasonably to avoid procurement of the required documents. Otherwise the beneficiary has an immediate right of action for wrongful dishonor.

§ 5—116. **Transfer and Assignment.**

(1) The right to draw under a credit can be transferred or assigned only when the credit is expressly designated as transferable or assignable.

(2) Even though the credit specifically states that it is nontransferable or nonassignable the beneficiary may before performance of the conditions of the credit assign his right to proceeds. Such an assignment is an assignment of an account under Article 9 on Secured Transactions and is governed by that Article except that

(a) the assignment is ineffective until the letter of credit or advice of credit is delivered to the assignee which delivery constitutes perfection of the security interest under Article 9; and

(b) the issuer may honor drafts or demands for payment drawn under the credit until it receives a notification of the assignment signed by the beneficiary which reasonably identifies the credit involved in the assignment and contains a request to pay the assignee; and

(c) after what reasonably appears to be such a notification has been received the issuer may without dishonor refuse to accept or pay even to a person otherwise entitled to honor until the letter of credit or advice of credit is exhibited to the issuer.

(3) Except where the beneficiary has effectively assigned his right to draw or his right to proceeds, nothing in this section limits his right to transfer or negotiate drafts or demands drawn under the credit.

§ 5—117. **Insolvency of Bank Holding Funds for Documentary Credit.**

(1) Where an issuer or an advising or confirming bank or a bank which has for a customer procured issuance of a credit by another bank becomes insolvent before final payment under the credit and the credit is one to which this Article is made applicable by paragraphs (a) or (b) of Section 5—102(1) on scope, the receipt or allocation of funds or collateral to secure or meet obligations under the credit shall have the following results:

(a) to the extent of any funds or collateral turned over after or before the insolvency as indemnity against or specifically for the purpose of payment of drafts or demands for payment drawn under the designated credit, the drafts or demands are entitled to payment in preference over depositors or other general creditors of the issuer or bank; and

(b) on expiration of the credit or surrender of the beneficiary's rights under it unused any person who has given such funds or collateral is similarly entitled to return thereof; and

(c) a charge to a general or current account with a bank if specifically consented to for the purpose of indemnity against or payment of drafts or demands for payment drawn under the designated credit falls under the same rules as if the funds had been drawn out in cash and then turned over with specific instructions.

(2) After honor or reimbursement under this section the customer or other person for whose account the insolvent bank has acted is entitled to receive the documents involved.

Article 6
BULK TRANSFERS

§ 6—101. **Short Title.**

This Article shall be known and may be cited as Uniform Commercial Code—Bulk Transfers.

§ 6—102. **"Bulk Transfer"; Transfers of Equipment; Enterprises Subject to This Article; Bulk Transfers Subject to This Article.**

(1) A "bulk transfer" is any transfer in bulk and not in the ordinary course of the transferor's business of a major part of the materials, supplies, merchandise or

other inventory (Section 9—109) of an enterprise subject to this Article.

(2) A transfer of a substantial part of the equipment (Section 9—109) of such an enterprise is a bulk transfer if it is made in connection with a bulk transfer of inventory, but not otherwise.

(3) The enterprises subject to this Article are all those whose principal business is the sale of merchandise from stock, including those who manufacture what they sell.

(4) Except as limited by the following section all bulk transfers of goods located within this state are subject to this Article.

§ 6—103. Transfers Excepted From This Article.

The following transfers are not subject to this Article:

(1) Those made to give security for the performance of an obligation;

(2) General assignments for the benefit of all the creditors of the transferor, and subsequent transfers by the assignee thereunder;

(3) Transfers in settlement or realization of a lien or other security interest;

(4) Sales by executors, administrators, receivers, trustees in bankruptcy, or any public officer under judicial process;

(5) Sales made in the course of judicial or administrative proceedings for the dissolution or reorganization of a corporation and of which notice is sent to the creditors of the corporation pursuant to order of the court or administrative agency;

(6) Transfers to a person maintaining a known place of business in this State who becomes bound to pay the debts of the transferor in full and gives public notice of that fact, and who is solvent after becoming so bound;

(7) A transfer to a new business enterprise organized to take over and continue the business, if public notice of the transaction is given and the new enterprise assumes the debts of the transferor and he receives nothing from the transaction except an interest in the new enterprise junior to the claims of creditors;

(8) Transfers of property which is exempt from execution.

Public notice under subsection (6) or subsection (7) may be given by publishing once a week for two consecutive weeks in a newspaper of general circulation where the transferor had its principal place of business in this state an advertisement including the names and addresses of the transferor and transferee and the effective date of the transfer.

§ 6—104. Schedule of Property, List of Creditors.

(1) Except as provided with respect to auction sales (Section 6—108), a bulk transfer subject to this Article is ineffective against any creditor of the transferor unless:

(a) The transferee requires the transferor to furnish a list of his existing creditors prepared as stated in this section; and

(b) The parties prepare a schedule of the property transferred sufficient to identify it; and

(c) The transferee preserves the list and schedule for six months next following the transfer and permits inspection of either or both and copying therefrom at all reasonable hours by any creditor of the transferor, or files the list and schedule in (a public office to be here identified).

(2) The list of creditors must be signed and sworn to or affirmed by the transferor or his agent. It must contain the names and business addresses of all creditors of the transferor, with the amounts when known, and also the names of all persons who are known to the transferor to assert claims against him even though such claims are disputed. If the transferor is the obligor of an outstanding issue of bonds, debentures or the like as to which there is an indenture trustee, the list of creditors need include only the name and address of the indenture trustee and the aggregate outstanding principal amount of the issue.

(3) Responsibility for the completeness and accuracy of the list of creditors rests on the transferor, and the transfer is not rendered ineffective by errors or omissions therein unless the transferee is shown to have had knowledge.

§ 6—105. Notice to Creditors.

In addition to the requirements of the preceding section, any bulk transfer subject to this Article except one made by auction sale (Section 6—108) is ineffective against any creditor of the transferor unless at least ten days before he takes possession of the goods or pays for them, whichever happens first, the transferee gives notice of the transfer in the manner and to the persons hereafter provided (Section 6—107).

[§ 6—106. Application of the Proceeds.

In addition to the requirements of the two preceding sections:

(1) Upon every bulk transfer subject to this Article for which new consideration becomes payable except those made by sale at auction it is the duty of the transferee to assure that such consideration is applied so far as necessary to pay those debts of the transferor which are either shown on the list furnished by the transferor (Section 6—104) or filed in writing in the place stated in the notice (Section 6—107) within thirty days after the mailing of such notice. This duty of the transferee runs to all the holders of such debts, and may be enforced by any of them for the benefit of all.

(2) If any of said debts are in dispute the necessary sum may be withheld from distribution until the dispute is settled or adjudicated.

(3) If the consideration payable is not enough to pay all of the said debts in full distribution shall be made pro rata.]

Note: *This section is bracketed to indicate division of opinion as to whether or not it is a wise provision, and to suggest that this is a point on which State enactments may differ without serious damage to the principle of uniformity. In any State where this section is omitted, the following parts of sections, also bracketed in the text, should also be omitted, namely:*
Section 6—107(2)(c).
6—108(3)(c).
6—109(2).
In any State where this section is enacted, these other provisions should be also.

Optional Subsection (4)

[(4) The transferee may within ten days after he takes possession of the goods pay the consideration into the (specify court) in the county where the transferor had its principal place of business in this state and thereafter may discharge his duty under this section by giving notice by registered or certified mail to all the persons to whom the duty runs that the consideration has been paid into that court and that they should file their claims there. On motion of any interested party, the court may order the distribution of the consideration to the persons entitled to it.]

Note: *Optional subsection (4) is recommended for those states which do not have a general statute providing for payment of money into court.*

§ 6—107. **The Notice.**

(1) The notice to creditors (Section 6—105) shall state:

(a) that a bulk transfer is about to be made; and

(b) the names and business addresses of the transferor and transferee, and all other business names and addresses used by the transferor within three years last past so far as known to the transferee; and

(c) whether or not all the debts of the transferor are to be paid in full as they fall due as a result of the transaction, and if so, the address to which creditors should send their bills.

(2) If the debts of the transferor are not to be paid in full as they fall due or if the transferee is in doubt on that point then the notice shall state further:

(a) the location and general description of the property to be transferred and the estimated total of the transferor's debts;

(b) the address where the schedule of property and list of creditors (Section 6—104) may be inspected;

(c) whether the transfer is to pay existing debts and if so the amount of such debts and to whom owing;

(d) whether the transfer is for new consideration and if so the amount of such consideration and the time and place of payment; [and]

[(e) if for new consideration the time and place where creditors of the transferor are to file their claims.]

(3) The notice in any case shall be delivered personally or sent by registered or certified mail to all the persons shown on the list of creditors furnished by the transferor (Section 6—104) and to all other persons who are known to the transferee to hold or assert claims against the transferor.

§ 6—108. **Auction Sales; "Auctioneer".**

(1) A bulk transfer is subject to this Article even though it is by sale at auction, but only in the manner and with the results stated in this section.

(2) The transferor shall furnish a list of his creditors and assist in the preparation of a schedule of the property to be sold, both prepared as before stated (Section 6—104).

(3) The person or persons other than the transferor who direct, control or are responsible for the auction are collectively called the "auctioneer". The auctioneer shall:

(a) receive and retain the list of creditors and prepare and retain the schedule of property for the period stated in this Article (Section 6—104);

(b) give notice of the auction personally or by registered or certified mail at least ten days before it occurs to all persons shown on the list of creditors and to all other persons who are known to him to hold or assert claims against the transferor; [and]

[(c) assure that the net proceeds of the auction are applied as provided in this Article (Section 6—106).]

(4) Failure of the auctioneer to perform any of these duties does not affect the validity of the sale or the title of the purchasers, but if the auctioneer knows that the auction constitutes a bulk transfer such failure renders the auctioneer liable to the creditors of the transferor as a class for the sums owing to them from the transferor up to but not exceeding the net proceeds of the auction. If the auctioneer consists of several persons their liability is joint and several.

§ 6—109. **What Creditors Protected; [Credit for Payment to Particular Creditors].**

(1) The creditors of the transferor mentioned in this Article are those holding claims based on transactions or events occurring before the bulk transfer, but creditors who become such after notice to creditors is given (Sections 6—105 and 6—107) are not entitled to notice.

[(2) Against the aggregate obligation imposed by the provisions of this Article concerning the application of the proceeds (Section 6—106 and subsection (3) (c) of 6—108) the transferee or auctioneer is entitled to credit for sums paid to particular creditors of the transferor, not exceeding the sums believed in good faith at the time of the payment to be properly payable to such creditors.]

§ 6—110. **Subsequent Transfers.**

When the title of a transferee to property is subject to a defect by reason of his non-compliance with the requirements of this Article, then:

(1) a purchaser of any of such property from such transferee who pays no value or who takes with notice of such non-compliance takes subject to such defect, but

(2) a purchaser for value in good faith and without such notice takes free of such defect.

§ 6—111. **Limitation of Actions and Levies.**

No action under this Article shall be brought nor levy made more than six months after the date on which the transferee took possession of the goods unless the transfer has been concealed. If the transfer has been concealed, actions may be brought or levies made within six months after its discovery.

Note to Article 6: *Section 6—106 is bracketed to indicate division of opinion as to whether or not it is a wise provision, and to suggest that this is a point on*

which State enactments may differ without serious damage to the principle of uniformity.
In any State where Section 6—106 is not enacted, the following parts of sections, also bracketed in the text, should also be omitted, namely:
Sec. 6—107(2)(e).
6—108(3)(c).
6—109(2).
In any State where Section 6—106 is enacted, these other provisions should be also.

Article 7
Warehouse Receipts, Bills of Lading and Other Documents of Title

Part 1 General

§ 7—101. **Short Title.**

This Article shall be known and may be cited as Uniform Commercial Code—Documents of Title.

§ 7—102. **Definitions and Index of Definitions.**

(1) In this Article, unless the context otherwise requires:

(a) "Bailee" means the person who by a warehouse receipt, bill of lading or other document of title acknowledges possession of goods and contracts to deliver them.

(b) "Consignee" means the person named in a bill to whom or to whose order the bill promises delivery.

(c) "Consignor" means the person named in a bill as the person from whom the goods have been received for shipment.

(d) "Delivery order" means a written order to deliver goods directed to a warehouseman, carrier or other person who in the ordinary course of business issues warehouse receipts or bills of lading.

(e) "Document" means document of title as defined in the general definitions in Article 1 (Section 1—201).

(f) "Goods" means all things which are treated as movable for the purposes of a contract of storage or transportation.

(g) "Issuer" means a bailee who issues a document except that in relation to an unaccepted delivery order it means the person who orders the possessor of goods to deliver. Issuer includes any person for whom an agent or employee purports to act in issuing a document if the agent or employee has real or apparent authority to issue documents, notwithstanding that the issuer received no goods or that the goods were misdescribed or that in any other respect the agent or employee violated his instructions.

(h) "Warehouseman" is a person engaged in the business of storing goods for hire.

(2) Other definitions applying to this Article or to specified Parts thereof, and the sections in which they appear are:

"Duly negotiate". Section 7—501.

"Person entitled under the document". Section 7—403(4).

(3) Definitions in other Articles applying to this Article and the sections in which they appear are:

"Contract for sale". Section 2—106.

"Overseas". Section 2—323.

"Receipt" of goods. Section 2—103.

(4) In addition Article 1 contains general definitions and principles of construction and interpretation applicable throughout this Article.

§ 7—103. Relation of Article to Treaty, Statute, Tariff, Classification or Regulation.

To the extent that any treaty or statute of the United States, regulatory statute of this State or tariff, classification or regulation filed or issued pursuant thereto is applicable, the provisions of this Article are subject thereto.

§ 7—104. Negotiable and Non-Negotiable Warehouse Receipt, Bill of Lading or Other Document of Title.

(1) A warehouse receipt, bill of lading or other document of title is negotiable

(a) if by its terms the goods are to be delivered to bearer or to the order of a named person; or

(b) where recognized in overseas trade, if it runs to a named person or assigns.

(2) Any other document is non-negotiable. A bill of lading in which it is stated that the goods are consigned to a named person is not made negotiable by a provision that the goods are to be delivered only against a written order signed by the same or another named person.

§ 7—105. Construction Against Negative Implication.

The omission from either Part 2 or Part 3 of this Article of a provision corresponding to a provision made in the other Part does not imply that a corresponding rule of law is not applicable.

Part 2 Warehouse Receipts: Special Provisions

§ 7—201. Who May Issue a Warehouse Receipt; Storage Under Government Bond.

(1) A warehouse receipt may be issued by any warehouseman.

(2) Where goods including distilled spirits and agricultural commodities are stored under a statute requiring a bond against withdrawal or a license for the issuance of receipts in the nature of warehouse receipts, a receipt issued for the goods has like effect as a warehouse receipt even though issued by a person who is the owner of the goods and is not a warehouseman.

§ 7—202. Form of Warehouse Receipt; Essential Terms; Optional Terms.

(1) A warehouse receipt need not be in any particular form.

(2) Unless a warehouse receipt embodies within its written or printed terms each of the following, the warehouseman is liable for damages caused by the omission to a person injured thereby:

(a) the location of the warehouse where the goods are stored;

(b) the date of issue of the receipt;

(c) the consecutive number of the receipt;

(d) a statement whether the goods received will be delivered to the bearer, to a specified person, or to a specified person or his order;

(e) the rate of storage and handling charges, except that where goods are stored under a field warehousing arrangement a statement of that fact is sufficient on a non-negotiable receipt;

(f) a description of the goods or of the packages containing them;

(g) the signature of the warehouseman, which may be made by his authorized agent;

(h) if the receipt is issued for goods of which the warehouseman is owner, either solely or jointly or in common with others, the fact of such ownership; and

(i) a statement of the amount of advances made and of liabilities incurred for which the warehouseman claims a lien or security interest (Section 7—209). If the precise amount of such advances made or of such liabilities incurred is, at the time of the issue of the receipt, unknown to the warehouseman or to his agent who issues it, a statement of the fact that advances have been made or liabilities incurred and the purpose thereof is sufficient.

(3) A warehouseman may insert in his receipt any other terms which are not contrary to the provisions of this Act and do not impair his obligation of delivery (Section 7—403) or his duty of care (Section 7—204). Any contrary provisions shall be ineffective.

§ 7—203. Liability for Non-Receipt or Misdescription.

A party to or purchaser for value in good faith of a document of title other than a bill of lading relying in either case upon the description therein of the goods may recover from the issuer damages caused by the non-receipt or misdescription of the goods, except to the extent that the document conspicuously indicates that the issuer does not know whether any part or all of the goods in fact were received or conform to the description, as where the description is in terms of marks or labels or kind, quantity or condition, or the receipt or description is qualified by "contents, condition and quality unknown", "said to contain" or the like, if such indication be true, or the party or purchaser otherwise has notice.

§ 7—204. Duty of Care; Contractual Limitation of Warehouseman's Liability.

(1) A warehouseman is liable for damages for loss of or injury to the goods caused by his failure to exercise such care in regard to them as a reasonably careful man would exercise under like circumstances but unless otherwise agreed he is not liable for damages which could not have been avoided by the exercise of such care.

(2) Damages may be limited by a term in the warehouse receipt or storage agreement limiting the amount of liability in case of loss or damage, and setting forth a specific liability per article or item, or value per unit of weight, beyond which the warehouseman shall not be liable; provided, however, that such liability may on written request of the bailor at the time of signing such storage agreement or within a reasonable time after receipt of the warehouse receipt be increased on part or all of the goods thereunder, in which event increased rates may be charged based on such increased valuation, but that no such increase shall be permitted contrary to a lawful limitation of liability contained in the warehouseman's tariff, if any. No such limitation is effective with respect to the warehouseman's liability for conversion to his own use.

(3) Reasonable provisions as to the time and manner of presenting claims and instituting actions based on the bailment may be included in the warehouse receipt or tariff.

(4) This section does not impair or repeal . . .

Note: *Insert in subsection (4) a reference to any statute which imposes a higher responsibility upon the warehouseman or invalidates contractual limitations which would be permissible under this Article.*

§ 7—205. Title Under Warehouse Receipt Defeated in Certain Cases.

A buyer in the ordinary course of business of fungible goods sold and delivered by a warehouseman who is also in the business of buying and selling such goods takes free of any claim under a warehouse receipt even though it has been duly negotiated.

§ 7—206. Termination of Storage at Warehouseman's Option.

(1) A warehouseman may on notifying the person on whose account the goods are held and any other person known to claim an interest in the goods require payment of any charges and removal of the goods from the warehouse at the termination of the period of storage fixed by the document, or, if no period is fixed, within a stated period not less than thirty days after the notification. If the goods are not removed before the date specified in the notification, the warehouseman may sell them in accordance with the provisions of the section on enforcement of a warehouseman's lien (Section 7—210).

(2) If a warehouseman in good faith believes that the goods are about to deteriorate or decline in value to less than the amount of his lien within the time prescribed in subsection (1) for notification, advertisement and sale, the warehouseman may specify in the notification any reasonable shorter time for removal of the goods and in case the goods are not removed, may sell them at public sale held not less than one week after a single advertisement or posting.

(3) If as a result of a quality or condition of the goods of which the warehouseman had no notice at the time of deposit the goods are a hazard to other property or to the warehouse or to persons, the warehouseman may sell the goods at public or private sale without advertisement on reasonable notification to all persons known to claim an interest in the goods. If the warehouseman after a reasonable effort is unable to sell the goods he may dispose of them in any lawful manner and shall incur no liability by reason of such disposition.

(4) The warehouseman must deliver the goods to any person entitled to them under this Article upon due demand made at any time prior to sale or other disposition under this section.

(5) The warehouseman may satisfy his lien from the proceeds of any sale or disposition under this section but must hold the balance for delivery on the demand of any person to whom he would have been bound to deliver the goods.

§ 7—207. **Goods Must Be Kept Separate; Fungible Goods.**

(1) Unless the warehouse receipt otherwise provides, a warehouseman must keep separate the goods covered by each receipt so as to permit at all times identification and delivery of those goods except that different lots of fungible goods may be commingled.

(2) Fungible goods so commingled are owned in common by the persons entitled thereto and the warehouseman is severally liable to each owner for that owner's share. Where because of overissue a mass of fungible goods is insufficient to meet all the receipts which the warehouseman has issued against it, the persons entitled include all holders to whom overissued receipts have been duly negotiated.

§ 7—208. **Altered Warehouse Receipts.**

Where a blank in a negotiable warehouse receipt has been filled in without authority, a purchaser for value and without notice of the want of authority may treat the insertion as authorized. Any other unauthorized alteration leaves any receipt enforceable against the issuer according to its original tenor.

§ 7—209. **Lien of Warehouseman.**

(1) A warehouseman has a lien against the bailor on the goods covered by a warehouse receipt or on the proceeds thereof in his possession for charges for storage or transportation (including demurrage and terminal charges), insurance, labor, or charges present or future in relation to the goods, and for expenses necessary for preservation of the goods or reasonably incurred in their sale pursuant to law. If the person on whose account the goods are held is liable for like charges or expenses in relation to other goods whenever deposited and it is stated in the receipt that a lien is claimed for charges and expenses in relation to other goods, the warehouseman also has a lien against him for such charges and expenses whether or not the other goods have been delivered by the warehouseman. But against a person to whom a negotiable warehouse receipt is duly negotiated a warehouseman's lien is limited to charges in an amount or at a rate specified on the receipt or if no

charges are so specified then to a reasonable charge for storage of the goods covered by the receipt subsequent to the date of the receipt.

(2) The warehouseman may also reserve a security interest against the bailor for a maximum amount specified on the receipt for charges other than those specified in subsection (1), such as for money advanced and interest. Such a security interest is governed by the Article on Secured Transactions (Article 9).

(3) (a) A warehouseman's lien for charges and expenses under subsection (1) or a security interest under subsection (2) is also effective against any person who so entrusted the bailor with possession of the goods that a pledge of them by him to a good faith purchaser for value would have been valid but is not effective against a person as to whom the document confers no right in the goods covered by it under Section 7—503.

(b) A warehouseman's lien on household goods for charges and expenses in relation to the goods under subsection (1) is also effective against all persons if the depositor was the legal possessor of the goods at the time of deposit. "Household goods" means furniture, furnishings and personal effects used by the depositor in a dwelling.

(4) A warehouseman loses his lien on any goods which he voluntarily delivers or which he unjustifiably refuses to deliver.

§ 7—210. **Enforcement of Warehouseman's Lien.**

(1) Except as provided in subsection (2), a warehouseman's lien may be enforced by public or private sale of the goods in bloc or in parcels, at any time or place and on any terms which are commercially reasonable, after notifying all persons known to claim an interest in the goods. Such notification must include a statement of the amount due, the nature of the proposed sale and the time and place of any public sale. The fact that a better price could have been obtained by a sale at a different time or in a different method from that selected by the warehouseman is not of itself sufficient to establish that the sale was not made in a commercially reasonable manner. If the warehouseman either sells the goods in the usual manner in any recognized market therefor, or if he sells at the price current in such market at the time of his sale, or if he has otherwise sold in conformity with commercially reasonable practices among dealers in the type of goods sold, he has sold in a commercially reasonable manner. A sale of more goods than apparently necessary to be offered to insure satisfac-

tion of the obligation is not commercially reasonable except in cases covered by the preceding sentence.

(2) A warehouseman's lien on goods other than goods stored by a merchant in the course of his business may be enforced only as follows:

(a) All persons known to claim an interest in the goods must be notified.

(b) The notification must be delivered in person or sent by registered or certified letter to the last known address of any person to be notified.

(c) The notification must include an itemized statement of the claim, a description of the goods subject to the lien, a demand for payment within a specified time not less than ten days after receipt of the notification, and a conspicuous statement that unless the claim is paid within the time the goods will be advertised for sale and sold by auction at a specified time and place.

(d) The sale must conform to the terms of the notification.

(e) The sale must be held at the nearest suitable place to that where the goods are held or stored.

(f) After the expiration of the time given in the notification, an advertisement of the sale must be published once a week for two weeks consecutively in a newspaper of general circulation where the sale is to be held. The advertisement must include a description of the goods, the name of the person on whose account they are being held, and the time and place of the sale. The sale must take place at least fifteen days after the first publication. If there is no newspaper of general circulation where the sale is to be held, the advertisement must be posted at least ten days before the sale in not less than six conspicuous places in the neighborhood of the proposed sale.

(3) Before any sale pursuant to this section any person claiming a right in the goods may pay the amount necessary to satisfy the lien and the reasonable expenses incurred under this section. In that event the goods must not be sold, but must be retained by the warehouseman subject to the terms of the receipt and this Article.

(4) The warehouseman may buy at any public sale pursuant to this section.

(5) A purchaser in good faith of goods sold to enforce a warehouseman's lien takes the goods free of any rights of persons against whom the lien was valid, despite noncompliance by the warehouseman with the requirements of this section.

(6) The warehouseman may satisfy his lien from the proceeds of any sale pursuant to this section but must hold the balance, if any, for delivery on demand to any person to whom he would have been bound to deliver the goods.

(7) The rights provided by this section shall be in addition to all other rights allowed by law to a creditor against his debtor.

(8) Where a lien is on goods stored by a merchant in the course of his business the lien may be enforced in accordance with either subsection (1) or (2).

(9) The warehouseman is liable for damages caused by failure to comply with the requirements for sale under this section and in case of willful violation is liable for conversion.

Part 3 Bills of Lading: Special Provisions

§ 7—301. Liability for Non-Receipt or Misdescription; "Said to Contain"; "Shipper's Load and Count"; Improper Handling.

(1) A consignee of a non-negotiable bill who has given value in good faith or a holder to whom a negotiable bill has been duly negotiated relying in either case upon the description therein of the goods, or upon the date therein shown, may recover from the issuer damages caused by the misdating of the bill or the non-receipt or misdescription of the goods, except to the extent that the document indicates that the issuer does not know whether any part of all of the goods in fact were received or conform to the description, as where the description is in terms of marks or labels or kind, quantity, or condition or the receipt or description is qualified by "contents or condition of contents of packages unknown", "said to contain", "shipper's weight, load and count" or the like, if such indication be true.

(2) When goods are loaded by an issuer who is a common carrier, the issuer must count the packages of goods if package freight and ascertain the kind and quantity if bulk freight. In such cases "shipper's weight, load and count" or other words indicating that the description was made by the shipper are ineffective except as to freight concealed by packages.

(3) When bulk freight is loaded by a shipper who makes available to the issuer adequate facilities for weighing such freight, an issuer who is a common carrier must ascertain the kind and quantity within a reasonable time after receiving the written request of

the shipper to do so. In such cases "shipper's weight" or other words of like purport are ineffective.

(4) The issuer may by inserting in the bill the words "shipper's weight, load and count" or other words of like purport indicate that the goods were loaded by the shipper; and if such statement be true the issuer shall not be liable for damages caused by the improper loading. But their omission does not imply liability for such damages.

(5) The shipper shall be deemed to have guaranteed to the issuer the accuracy at the time of shipment of the description, marks, labels, number, kind, quantity, condition and weight, as furnished by him; and the shipper shall indemnify the issuer against damage caused by inaccuracies in such particulars. The right of the issuer to such indemnity shall in no way limit his responsibility and liability under the contract of carriage to any person other than the shipper.

§ 7—302. **Through Bills of Lading and Similar Documents.**

(1) The issuer of a through bill of lading or other document embodying an undertaking to be performed in part by persons acting as its agents or by connecting carriers is liable to anyone entitled to recover on the document for any breach by such other persons or by a connecting carrier of its obligation under the document but to the extent that the bill covers an undertaking to be performed overseas or in territory not contiguous to the continental United States or an undertaking including matters other than transportation this liability may be varied by agreement of the parties.

(2) Where goods covered by a through bill of lading or other document embodying an undertaking to be performed in part by persons other than the issuer are received by any such person, he is subject with respect to his own performance while the goods are in his possession to the obligation of the issuer. His obligation is discharged by delivery of the goods to another such person pursuant to the document, and does not include liability for breach by any other such persons or by the issuer.

(3) The issuer of such through bill of lading or other document shall be entitled to recover from the connecting carrier or such other person in possession of the goods when the breach of the obligation under the document occurred, the amount it may be required to pay to anyone entitled to recover on the document therefor, as may be evidenced by any receipt, judgment, or transcript thereof, and the amount of any expense reasonably incurred by it in defending any action brought by anyone entitled to recover on the document therefor.

§ 7—303. **Diversion; Reconsignment; Change of Instructions.**

(1) Unless the bill of lading otherwise provides, the carrier may deliver the goods to a person or destination other than that stated in the bill or may otherwise dispose of the goods on instructions from

(a) the holder of a negotiable bill; or

(b) the consignor on a non-negotiable bill notwithstanding contrary instructions from the consignee; or

(c) the consignee on a non-negotiable bill in the absence of contrary instructions from the consignor, if the goods have arrived at the billed destination or if the consignee is in possession of the bill; or

(d) the consignee on a non-negotiable bill if he is entitled as against the consignor to dispose of them.

(2) Unless such instructions are noted on a negotiable bill of lading, a person to whom the bill is duly negotiated can hold the bailee according to the original terms.

§ 7—304. **Bills of Lading in a Set.**

(1) Except where customary in overseas transportation, a bill of lading must not be issued in a set of parts. The issuer is liable for damages caused by violation of this subsection.

(2) Where a bill of lading is lawfully drawn in a set of parts, each of which is numbered and expressed to be valid only if the goods have not been delivered against any other part, the whole of the parts constitute one bill.

(3) Where a bill of lading is lawfully issued in a set of parts and different parts are negotiated to different persons, the title of the holder to whom the first due negotiation is made prevails as to both the document and the goods even though any later holder may have received the goods from the carrier in good faith and discharged the carrier's obligation by surrender of his part.

(4) Any person who negotiates or transfers a single part of a bill of lading drawn in a set is liable to holders of that part as if it were the whole set.

(5) The bailee is obliged to deliver in accordance with Part 4 of this Article against the first presented part of a bill of lading lawfully drawn in a set. Such delivery discharges the bailee's obligation on the whole bill.

§ 7—305. **Destination Bills.**

(1) Instead of issuing a bill of lading to the consignor at the place of shipment a carrier may at the request

of the consignor procure the bill to be issued at destination or at any other place designated in the request.

(2) Upon request of anyone entitled as against the carrier to control the goods while in transit and on surrender of any outstanding bill of lading or other receipt covering such goods, the issuer may procure a substitute bill to be issued at any place designated in the request.

§ 7—306. Altered Bills of Lading.

An unauthorized alteration or filling in of a blank in a bill of lading leaves the bill enforceable according to its original tenor.

§ 7—307. Lien of Carrier.

(1) A carrier has a lien on the goods covered by a bill of lading for charges subsequent to the date of its receipt of the goods for storage or transportation (including demurrage and terminal charges) and for expenses necessary for preservation of the goods incident to their transportation or reasonably incurred in their sale pursuant to law. But against a purchaser for value of a negotiable bill of lading a carrier's lien is limited to charges stated in the bill or the applicable tariffs, or if no charges are stated then to a reasonable charge.

(2) A lien for charges and expenses under subsection (1) on goods which the carrier was required by law to receive for transportation is effective against the consignor or any person entitled to the goods unless the carrier had notice that the consignor lacked authority to subject the goods to such charges and expenses. Any other lien under subsection (1) is effective against the consignor and any person who permitted the bailor to have control or possession of the goods unless the carrier had notice that the bailor lacked such authority.

(3) A carrier loses his lien on any goods which he voluntarily delivers or which he unjustifiably refuses to deliver.

§ 7—308. Enforcement of Carrier's Lien.

(1) A carrier's lien may be enforced by public or private sale of the goods, in bloc or in parcels, at any time or place and on any terms which are commercially reasonable, after notifying all persons known to claim an interest in the goods. Such notification must include a statement of the amount due, the nature of the proposed sale and the time and place of any public sale. The fact that a better price could have been obtained by a sale at a different time or in a different method from that selected by the carrier is not of itself sufficient to establish that the sale was not made in a commercially reasonable manner. If the carrier either sells the goods in the usual manner in any recognized market therefor or if he sells at the price current in such market at the time of his sale or if he has otherwise sold in conformity with commercially reasonable practices among dealers in the type of goods sold he has sold in a commercially reasonable manner. A sale of more goods than apparently necessary to be offered to ensure satisfaction of the obligation is not commercially reasonable except in cases covered by the preceding sentence.

(2) Before any sale pursuant to this section any person claiming a right in the goods may pay the amount necessary to satisfy the lien and the reasonable expenses incurred under this section. In that event the goods must not be sold, but must be retained by the carrier subject to the terms of the bill and this Article.

(3) The carrier may buy at any public sale pursuant to this section.

(4) A purchaser in good faith of goods sold to enforce a carrier's lien takes the goods free of any rights of persons against whom the lien was valid, despite noncompliance by the carrier with the requirements of this section.

(5) The carrier may satisfy his lien from the proceeds of any sale pursuant to this section but must hold the balance, if any, for delivery on demand to any person to whom he would have been bound to deliver the goods.

(6) The rights provided by this section shall be in addition to all other rights allowed by law to a creditor against his debtor.

(7) A carrier's lien may be enforced in accordance with either subsection (1) or the procedure set forth in subsection (2) of Section 7—210.

(8) The carrier is liable for damages caused by failure to comply with the requirements for sale under this section and in case of willful violation is liable for conversion.

§ 7—309. Duty of Care; Contractual Limitation of Carrier's Liability.

(1) A carrier who issues a bill of lading whether negotiable or non-negotiable must exercise the degree of care in relation to the goods which a reasonably careful man would exercise under like circumstances. This subsection does not repeal or change any law or rule of law which imposes liability upon a common carrier for damages not caused by its negligence.

(2) Damages may be limited by a provision that the carrier's liability shall not exceed a value stated in the

document if the carrier's rates are dependent upon value and the consignor by the carrier's tariff is afforded an opportunity to declare a higher value or a value as lawfully provided in the tariff, or where no tariff is filed he is otherwise advised of such opportunity; but no such limitation is effective with respect to the carrier's liability for conversion to its own use.

(3) Reasonable provisions as to the time and manner of presenting claims and instituting actions based on the shipment may be included in a bill of lading or tariff.

Part 4 **Warehouse Receipts and Bills of Lading: General Obligations**

§ 7—401. **Irregularities in Issue of Receipt or Bill or Conduct of Issuer.**

The obligations imposed by this Article on an issuer apply to a document of title regardless of the fact that

(a) the document may not comply with the requirements of this Article or of any other law or regulation regarding its issue, form or content; or

(b) the issuer may have violated laws regulating the conduct of his business; or

(c) the goods covered by the document were owned by the bailee at the time the document was issued; or

(d) the person issuing the document does not come within the definition of warehouseman if it purports to be a warehouse receipt.

§ 7—402. **Duplicate Receipt or Bill; Overissue.**

Neither a duplicate nor any other document of title purporting to cover goods already represented by an outstanding document of the same issuer confers any right in the goods, except as provided in the case of bills in a set, overissue of documents for fungible goods and substitutes for lost, stolen or destroyed documents. But the issuer is liable for damages caused by his overissue or failure to identify a duplicate document as such by conspicuous notation on its face.

§ 7—403. **Obligation of Warehouseman or Carrier to Deliver; Excuse.**

(1) The bailee must deliver the goods to a person entitled under the document who complies with subsections (2) and (3), unless and to the extent that the bailee establishes any of the following:

(a) delivery of the goods to a person whose receipt was rightful as against the claimant;

(b) damage to or delay, loss or destruction of the goods for which the bailee is not liable [, but the burden of establishing negligence in such cases is on the person entitled under the document];

Note: The brackets in (1)(b) indicate that State enactments may differ on this point without serious damage to the principle of uniformity.

(c) previous sale or other disposition of the goods in lawful enforcement of a lien or on warehouseman's lawful termination of storage;

(d) the exercise by a seller of his right to stop delivery pursuant to the provisions of the Article on Sales (Section 2—705);

(e) a diversion, reconsignment or other disposition pursuant to the provisions of this Article (Section 7—303) or tariff regulating such right;

(f) release, satisfaction or any other fact affording a personal defense against the claimant;

(g) any other lawful excuse.

(2) A person claiming goods covered by a document of title must satisfy the bailee's lien where the bailee so requests or where the bailee is prohibited by law from delivering the goods until the charges are paid.

(3) Unless the person claiming is one against whom the document confers no right under Sec. 7—503(1), he must surrender for cancellation or notation of partial deliveries any outstanding negotiable document covering the goods, and the bailee must cancel the document or conspicuously note the partial delivery thereon or be liable to any person to whom the document is duly negotiated.

(4) "Person entitled under the document" means holder in the case of a negotiable document, or the person to whom delivery is to be made by the terms of or pursuant to written instructions under a nonnegotiable document.

§ 7—404. **No Liability for Good Faith Delivery Pursuant to Receipt or Bill.**

A bailee who in good faith including observance of reasonable commercial standards has received goods and delivered or otherwise disposed of them according to the terms of the document of title or pursuant to this Article is not liable therefor. This rule applies even though the person from whom he received the goods had no authority to procure the document or to dispose of the goods and even though the person to whom he delivered the goods had no authority to receive them.

Part 5 Warehouse Receipts and Bills of Lading: Negotiation and Transfer

§ 7—501. Form of Negotiation and Requirements of "Due Negotiation".

(1) A negotiable document of title running to the order of a named person is negotiated by his indorsement and delivery. After his indorsement in blank or to bearer any person can negotiate it by delivery alone.

(2) (a) A negotiable document of title is also negotiated by delivery alone when by its original terms it runs to bearer.

(b) When a document running to the order of a named person is delivered to him the effect is the same as if the document had been negotiated.

(3) Negotiation of a negotiable document of title after it has been indorsed to a specified person requires indorsement by the special indorsee as well as delivery.

(4) A negotiable document of title is "duly negotiated" when it is negotiated in the manner stated in this section to a holder who purchases it in good faith without notice of any defense against or claim to it on the part of any person and for value, unless it is established that the negotiation is not in the regular course of business or financing or involves receiving the document in settlement or payment of a money obligation.

(5) Indorsement of a non-negotiable document neither makes it negotiable nor adds to the transferee's rights.

(6) The naming in a negotiable bill of a person to be notified of the arrival of the goods does not limit the negotiability of the bill nor constitute notice to a purchaser thereof of any interest of such person in the goods.

§ 7—502. Rights Acquired by Due Negotiation.

(1) Subject to the following section and to the provisions of Section 7—205 on fungible goods, a holder to whom a negotiable document of title has been duly negotiated acquires thereby:

(a) title to the document;

(b) title to the goods;

(c) all rights accruing under the law of agency or estoppel, including rights to goods delivered to the bailee after the document was issued; and

(d) the direct obligation of the issuer to hold or deliver the goods according to the terms of the document free of any defense or claim by him

except those arising under the terms of the document or under this Article. In the case of a delivery order the bailee's obligation accrues only upon acceptance and the obligation acquired by the holder is that the issuer and any indorser will procure the acceptance of the bailee.

(2) Subject to the following section, title and rights so acquired are not defeated by any stoppage of the goods represented by the document or by surrender of such goods by the bailee, and are not impaired even though the negotiation or any prior negotiation constituted a breach of duty or even though any person has been deprived of possession of the document by misrepresentation, fraud, accident, mistake, duress, loss, theft or conversion, or even though a previous sale or other transfer of the goods or document has been made to a third person.

§ 7—503. Document of Title to Goods Defeated in Certain Cases.

(1) A document of title confers no right in goods against a person who before issuance of the document had a legal interest or a perfected security interest in them and who neither

(a) delivered or entrusted them or any document of title covering them to the bailor or his nominee with actual or apparent authority to ship, store or sell or with power to obtain delivery under this Article (Section 7—403) or with power of disposition under this Act (Sections 2—403 and 9—307) or other statute or rule of law; nor

(b) acquiesced in the procurement by the bailor or his nominee of any document of title.

(2) Title to goods based upon an unaccepted delivery order is subject to the rights of anyone to whom a negotiable warehouse receipt or bill of lading covering the goods has been duly negotiated. Such a title may be defeated under the next section to the same extent as the rights of the issuer or a transferee from the issuer.

(3) Title to goods based upon a bill of lading issued to a freight forwarder is subject to the rights of anyone to whom a bill issued by the freight forwarder is duly negotiated; but delivery by the carrier in accordance with Part 4 of this Article pursuant to its own bill of lading discharges the carrier's obligation to deliver.

§ 7—504. Rights Acquired in the Absence of Due Negotiation; Effect of Diversion; Seller's Stoppage of Delivery.

(1) A transferee of a document, whether negotiable or non-negotiable, to whom the document has been delivered but not duly negotiated, acquires the title

and rights which his transferor had or had actual authority to convey.

(2) In the case of a non-negotiable document, until but not after the bailee receives notification of the transfer, the rights of the transferee may be defeated

(a) by those creditors of the transferor who could treat the sale as void under Section 2—402; or

(b) by a buyer from the transferor in ordinary course of business if the bailee has delivered the goods to the buyer or received notification of his rights; or

(c) as against the bailee by good faith dealings of the bailee with the transferor.

(3) A diversion or other change of shipping instructions by the consignor in a non-negotiable bill of lading which causes the bailee not to deliver to the consignee defeats the consignee's title to the goods if they have been delivered to a buyer in ordinary course of business and in any event defeats the consignee's rights against the bailee.

(4) Delivery pursuant to a non-negotiable document may be stopped by a seller under Section 2—705, and subject to the requirement of due notification there provided. A bailee honoring the seller's instructions is entitled to be indemnified by the seller against any resulting loss or expense.

§ 7—505. Indorser Not a Guarantor for Other Parties.

The indorsement of a document of title issued by a bailee does not make the indorser liable for any default by the bailee or by previous indorsers.

§ 7—506. Delivery Without Indorsement: Right to Compel Indorsement.

The transferee of a negotiable document of title has a specifically enforceable right to have his transferor supply any necessary indorsement but the transfer becomes a negotiation only as of the time the indorsement is supplied.

§ 7—507. Warranties on Negotiation or Transfer of Receipt or Bill.

Where a person negotiates or transfers a document of title for value otherwise than as a mere intermediary under the next following section, then unless otherwise agreed he warrants to his immediate purchaser only in addition to any warranty made in selling the goods

(a) that the document is genuine; and

(b) that he has no knowledge of any fact which would impair its validity or worth; and

(c) that his negotiation or transfer is rightful and fully effective with respect to the title to the document and the goods it represents.

§ 7—508. Warranties of Collecting Bank as to Documents.

A collecting bank or other intermediary known to be entrusted with documents on behalf of another or with collection of a draft or other claim against delivery of documents warrants by such delivery of the documents only its own good faith and authority. This rule applies even though the intermediary has purchased or made advances against the claim or draft to be collected.

§ 7—509. Receipt or Bill: When Adequate Compliance With Commercial Contract.

The question whether a document is adequate to fulfill the obligations of a contract for sale or the conditions of a credit is governed by the Articles on Sales (Article 2) and on Letters of Credit (Article 5).

Part 6 Warehouse Receipts and Bills of Lading: Miscellaneous Provisions

§ 7—601. Lost and Missing Documents.

(1) If a document has been lost, stolen or destroyed, a court may order delivery of the goods or issuance of a substitute document and the bailee may without liability to any person comply with such order. If the document was negotiable the claimant must post security approved by the court to indemnify any person who may suffer loss as a result of non-surrender of the document. If the document was not negotiable, such security may be required at the discretion of the court. The court may also in its discretion order payment of the bailee's reasonable costs and counsel fees.

(2) A bailee who without court order delivers goods to a person claiming under a missing negotiable document is liable to any person injured thereby, and if the delivery is not in good faith becomes liable for conversion. Delivery in good faith is not conversion if made in accordance with a filed classification or tariff or, where no classification or tariff is filed, if the claimant posts security with the bailee in an amount at least double the value of the goods at the time of posting to indemnify any person injured by the delivery who files a notice of claim within one year after the delivery.

§ 7—602. **Attachment of Goods Covered by a Negotiable Document.**

Except where the document was originally issued upon delivery of the goods by a person who had no power to dispose of them, no lien attaches by virtue of any judicial process to goods in the possession of a bailee for which a negotiable document of title is outstanding unless the document be first surrendered to the bailee or its negotiation enjoined, and the bailee shall not be compelled to deliver the goods pursuant to process until the document is surrendered to him or impounded by the court. One who purchases the document for value without notice of the process or injunction takes free of the lien imposed by judicial process.

§ 7—603. **Conflicting Claims; Interpleader.**

If more than one person claims title or possession of the goods, the bailee is excused from delivery until he has had a reasonable time to ascertain the validity of the adverse claims or to bring an action to compel all claimants to interplead and may compel such interpleader, either in defending an action for non-delivery of the goods, or by original action, whichever is appropriate.

Article 8
INVESTMENT SECURITIES

Part 1 **Short Title and General Matters**

§ 8—101. **Short Title.**

This Article shall be known and may be cited as Uniform Commercial Code—Investment Securities.

§ 8—102. **Definitions and Index of Definitions.**

(1) In this Article, unless the context otherwise requires:

(a) A "certificated security" is a share, participation, or other interest in property of or an enterprise of the issuer or an obligation of the issuer which is

(i) represented by an instrument issued in bearer or registered form;

(ii) of a type commonly dealt in on securities exchanges or markets or commonly recognized in any area in which it is issued or dealt in as a medium for investment; and

(iii) either one of a class or series or by its terms divisible into a class or series of shares, participations, interests, or obligations.

(b) An "uncertificated security" is a share, participation, or other interest in property or an enterprise of the issuer or an obligation of the issuer which is

(i) not represented by an instrument and the transfer of which is registered upon books maintained for that purpose by or on behalf of the issuer;

(ii) of a type commonly dealt in on securities exchanges or markets; and

(iii) either one of a class or series or by its terms divisible into a class or series of shares, participations, interests, or obligations.

(c) A "security" is either a certificated or an uncertificated security. If a security is certificated, the terms "security" and "certificated security" may mean either the intangible interest, the instrument representing that interest, or both, as the context requires. A writing that is a certificated security is governed by this Article and not by Article 3, even though it also meets the requirements of that Article. This Article does not apply to money. If a certificated security has been retained by or surrendered to the issuer or its transfer agent for reasons other than registration of transfer, other temporary purpose, payment, exchange, or acquisition by the issuer, that security shall be treated as an uncertificated security for purposes of this Article.

(d) A certificated security is in "registered form" if

(i) it specifies a person entitled to the security or the rights it represents; and

(ii) its transfer may be registered upon books maintained for that purpose by or on behalf of the issuer, or the security so states.

(e) A certificated security is in "bearer form" if it runs to bearer according to its terms and not by reason of any indorsement.

(2) A "subsequent purchaser" is a person who takes other than by original issue.

(3) A "clearing corporation" is a corporation registered as a "clearing agency" under the federal securities laws or a corporation:

(a) at least 90 percent of whose capital stock is held by or for one or more organizations, none of which, other than a national securities exchange or association, holds in excess of 20 percent of the capital stock of the corporation, and each of which is

(i) subject to supervision or regulation pursuant to the provisions of federal or state banking laws or state insurance laws,

(ii) a broker or dealer or investment company registered under the federal securities laws, or

(iii) a national securities exchange or association registered under the federal securities laws; and

(b) any remaining capital stock of which is held by individuals who have purchased it at or prior to the time of their taking office as directors of the corporation and who have purchased only so much of the capital stock as is necessary to permit them to qualify as directors.

(4) A "custodian bank" is a bank or trust company that is supervised and examined by state or federal authority having supervision over banks and is acting as custodian for a clearing corporation.

(5) Other definitions applying to this Article or to specified Parts thereof and the sections in which they appear are:

"Adverse claim". Section 8—302.
"Bona fide purchaser". Section 8—302.
"Broker". Section 8—303.
"Debtor". Section 9—105.
"Financial intermediary". Section 8—313.
"Guarantee of the signature". Section 8—402.
"Initial transaction statement". Section 8—408.
"Instruction". Section 8—308.
"Intermediary bank". Section 4—105.
"Issuer". Section 8—201.
"Overissue". Section 8—104.
"Secured Party". Section 9—105.
"Security Agreement". Section 9—105.

(6) In addition, Article 1 contains general definitions and principles of construction and interpretation applicable throughout this Article.

Amended in 1962, 1973 and 1977.

§ 8—103. **Issuer's Lien.**

A lien upon a security in favor of an issuer thereof is valid against a purchaser only if:

(a) the security is certificated and the right of the issuer to the lien is noted conspicuously thereon; or

(b) the security is uncertificated and a notation of the right of the issuer to the lien is contained in the initial transaction statement sent to the purchaser or, if his interest is transferred to him other than by registration of transfer, pledge, or release, the initial

transaction statement sent to the registered owner or the registered pledgee.

Amended in 1977.

§ 8—104. **Effect of Overissue; "Overissue".**

(1) The provisions of this Article which validate a security or compel its issue or reissue do not apply to the extent that validation, issue, or reissue would result in overissue; but if:

(a) an identical security which does not constitute an overissue is reasonably available for purchase, the person entitled to issue or validation may compel the issuer to purchase the security for him and either to deliver a certificated security or to register the transfer of an uncertificated security to him, against surrender of any certificated security he holds; or

(b) a security is not so available for purchase, the person entitled to issue or validation may recover from the issuer the price he or the last purchaser for value paid for it with interest from the date of his demand.

(2) "Overissue" means the issue of securities in excess of the amount the issuer has corporate power to issue.

Amended in 1977.

§ 8—105. **Certificated Securities Negotiable; Statements and Instructions Not Negotiable; Presumptions.**

(1) Certificated securities governed by this Article are negotiable instruments.

(2) Statements (Section 8—408), notices, or the like, sent by the issuer of uncertificated securities and instructions (Section 8—308) are neither negotiable instruments nor certificated securities.

(3) In any action on a security:

(a) unless specifically denied in the pleadings, each signature on a certificated security, in a necessary indorsement, on an initial transaction statement, or on an instruction, is admitted;

(b) if the effectiveness of a signature is put in issue, the burden of establishing it is on the party claiming under the signature, but the signature is presumed to be genuine or authorized;

(c) if signatures on a certificated security are admitted or established, production of the security entitles a holder to recover on it unless the defendant establishes a defense or a defect going to the validity of the security;

(d) if signatures on an initial transaction statement are admitted or established, the facts stated in the statement are presumed to be true as of the time of its issuance; and

(e) after it is shown that a defense or defect exists, the plaintiff has the burden of establishing that he or some person under whom he claims is a person against whom the defense or defect is ineffective (Section 8—202).

Amended in 1977.

§ 8—106. Applicability.

The law (including the conflict of laws rules) of the jurisdiction of organization of the issuer governs the validity of a security, the effectiveness of registration by the issuer, and the rights and duties of the issuer with respect to:

(a) registration of transfer of a certificated security;

(b) registration of transfer, pledge, or release of an uncertificated security; and

(c) sending of statements of uncertificated securities.

Amended in 1977.

§ 8—107. Securities Transferable; Action for Price.

(1) Unless otherwise agreed and subject to any applicable law or regulation respecting short sales, a person obligated to transfer securities may transfer any certificated security of the specified issue in bearer form or registered in the name of the transferee, or indorsed to him or in blank, or he may transfer an equivalent uncertificated security to the transferee or a person designated by the transferee.

(2) If the buyer fails to pay the price as it comes due under a contract of sale, the seller may recover the price of:

(a) certificated securities accepted by the buyer;

(b) uncertificated securities that have been transferred to the buyer or a person designated by the buyer; and

(c) other securities if efforts at their resale would be unduly burdensome or if there is no readily available market for their resale.

Amended in 1977.

§ 8—108. Registration of Pledge and Release of Uncertificated Securities.

A security interest in an uncertificated security may be evidenced by the registration of pledge to the secured party or a person designated by him. There can be no more than one registered pledge of an uncertificated security at any time. The registered owner of an uncertificated security is the person in

whose name the security is registered, even if the security is subject to a registered pledge. The rights of a registered pledgee of an uncertificated security under this Article are terminated by the registration of release.

Added in 1977.

Part 2 Issue—Issuer

§ 8—201. "Issuer"

(1) With respect to obligations on or defenses to a security, "issuer" includes a person who:

(a) places or authorizes the placing of his name on a certificated security (otherwise than as authenticating trustee, registrar, transfer agent, or the like) to evidence that it represents a share, participation, or other interest in his property or in an enterprise, or to evidence his duty to perform an obligation represented by the certificated security;

(b) creates shares, participations, or other interests in his property or in an enterprise or undertakes obligations, which shares, participations, interests, or obligations are uncertificated securities;

(c) directly or indirectly creates fractional interests in his rights or property, which fractional interests are represented by certificated securities; or

(d) becomes responsible for or in place of any other person described as an issuer in this section.

(2) With respect to obligations on or defenses to a security, a guarantor is an issuer to the extent of his guaranty, whether or not his obligation is noted on a certificated security or on statements of uncertificated securities sent pursuant to Section 8—408.

(3) With respect to registration of transfer, pledge, or release (Part 4 of this Article), "issuer" means a person on whose behalf transfer books are maintained.

Amended in 1977.

§ 8—202. Issuer's Responsibility and Defenses; Notice of Defect or Defense.

(1) Even against a purchaser for value and without notice, the terms of a security include:

(a) if the security is certificated, those stated on the security;

(b) if the security is uncertificated, those contained in the initial transaction statement sent to such purchaser or, if his interest is transferred to him other than by registration of transfer, pledge, or release, the initial transaction statement sent to the registered owner or registered pledgee; and

(c) those made part of the security by reference, on the certificated security or in the initial transaction statement, to another instrument, indenture, or document or to a constitution, statute, ordinance, rule, regulation, order or the like, to the extent that the terms referred to do not conflict with the terms stated on the certificated security or contained in the statement. A reference under this paragraph does not of itself charge a purchaser for value with notice of a defect going to the validity of the security, even though the certificated security or statement expressly states that a person accepting it admits notice.

(2) A certificated security in the hands of a purchaser for value or an uncertificated security as to which an initial transaction statement has been sent to a purchaser for value, other than a security issued by a government or governmental agency or unit, even though issued with a defect going to its validity, is valid with respect to the purchaser if he is without notice of the particular defect unless the defect involves a violation of constitutional provisions, in which case the security is valid with respect to a subsequent purchaser for value and without notice of the defect. This subsection applies to an issuer that is a government or governmental agency or unit only if either there has been substantial compliance with the legal requirements governing the issue or the issuer has received a substantial consideration for the issue as a whole or for the particular security and a stated purpose of the issue is one for which the issuer has power to borrow money or issue the security.

(3) Except as provided in the case of certain unauthorized signatures (Section 8—205), lack of genuineness of a certificated security or an initial transaction statement is a complete defense, even against a purchaser for value and without notice.

(4) All other defenses of the issuer of a certificated or uncertificated security, including nondelivery and conditional delivery of a certificated security, are ineffective against a purchaser for value who has taken without notice of the particular defense.

(5) Nothing in this section shall be construed to affect the right of a party to a "when, as and if issued" or a "when distributed" contract to cancel the contract in the event of a material change in the character of the security that is the subject of the contract or in the plan or arrangement pursuant to which the security is to be issued or distributed.

Amended in 1977.

§ 8—203. **Staleness as Notice of Defects or Defenses.**

(1) After an act or event creating a right to immediate performance of the principal obligation represented by a certificated security or that sets a date on or after which the security is to be presented or surrendered for redemption or exchange, a purchaser is charged with notice of any defect in its issue or defense of the issuer if:

(a) the act or event is one requiring the payment of money, the delivery of certificated securities, the registration of transfer of uncertificated securities, or any of these on presentation or surrender of the certificated security, the funds or securities are available on the date set for payment or exchange, and he takes the security more than one year after that date; and

(b) the act or event is not covered by paragraph (a) and he takes the security more than 2 years after the date set for surrender or presentation or the date on which performance became due.

(2) A call that has been revoked is not within subsection (1).

Amended in 1977.

§ 8—204. **Effect of Issuer's Restrictions on Transfer.**

A restriction on transfer of a security imposed by the issuer, even if otherwise lawful, is ineffective against any person without actual knowledge of it unless:

(a) the security is certificated and the restriction is noted conspicuously thereon; or

(b) the security is uncertificated and a notation of the restriction is contained in the initial transaction statement sent to the person or, if his interest is transferred to him other than by registration of transfer, pledge, or release, the initial transaction statement sent to the registered owner or the registered pledgee.

Amended in 1977.

§ 8—205. **Effect of Unauthorized Signature on Certificated Security or Initial Transaction Statement.**

An unauthorized signature placed on a certificated security prior to or in the course of issue or placed on an initial transaction statement is ineffective, but the signature is effective in favor of a purchaser for value of the certificated security or a purchaser for value of an uncertificated security to whom the initial transaction statement has been sent, if the purchaser is without notice of the lack of authority and the signing has been done by:

(a) an authenticating trustee, registrar, transfer agent, or other person entrusted by the issuer with the signing of the security, of similar securities, or of initial transaction statements or the immediate preparation for signing of any of them; or

(b) an employee of the issuer, or of any of the foregoing, entrusted with responsible handling of the security or initial transaction statement.

Amended in 1977.

§ 8—206. Completion or Alteration of Certificated Security or Initial Transaction Statement.

(1) If a certificated security contains the signatures necessary to its issue or transfer but is incomplete in any other respect:

(a) any person may complete it by filling in the blanks as authorized; and

(b) even though the blanks are incorrectly filled in, the security as completed is enforceable by a purchaser who took it for value and without notice of the incorrectness.

(2) A complete certificated security that has been improperly altered, even though fraudulently, remains enforceable, but only according to its original terms.

(3) If an initial transaction statement contains the signatures necessary to its validity, but is incomplete in any other respect:

(a) any person may complete it by filling in the blanks as authorized; and

(b) even though the blanks are incorrectly filled in, the statement as completed is effective in favor of the person to whom it is sent if he purchased the security referred to therein for value and without notice of the incorrectness.

(4) A complete initial transaction statement that has been improperly altered, even though fraudulently, is effective in favor of a purchaser to whom it has been sent, but only according to its original terms.

Amended in 1977.

§ 8—207. Rights and Duties of Issuer With Respect to Registered Owners and Registered Pledgees.

(1) Prior to due presentment for registration of transfer of a certificated security in registered form, the issuer or indenture trustee may treat the registered owner as the person exclusively entitled to vote, to receive notifications, and otherwise to exercise all the rights and powers of an owner.

(2) Subject to the provisions of subsections (3), (4), and (6), the issuer or indenture trustee may treat the registered owner of an uncertificated security as the person exclusively entitled to vote, to receive notifications, and otherwise to exercise all the rights and powers of an owner.

(3) The registered owner of an uncertificated security that is subject to a registered pledge is not entitled to registration of transfer prior to the due presentment to the issuer of a release instruction. The exercise of conversion rights with respect to a convertible uncertificated security is a transfer within the meaning of this section.

(4) Upon due presentment of a transfer instruction from the registered pledgee of an uncertificated security, the issuer shall:

(a) register the transfer of the security to the new owner free of pledge, if the instruction specifies a new owner (who may be the registered pledgee) and does not specify a pledgee;

(b) register the transfer of the security to the new owner subject to the interest of the existing pledgee, if the instruction specifies a new owner and the existing pledgee; or

(c) register the release of the security from the existing pledge and register the pledge of the security to the other pledgee, if the instruction specifies the existing owner and another pledgee.

(5) Continuity of perfection of a security interest is not broken by registration of transfer under subsection (4)(b) or by registration of release and pledge under subsection (4)(c), if the security interest is assigned.

(6) If an uncertificated security is subject to a registered pledge:

(a) any uncertificated securities issued in exchange for or distributed with respect to the pledged security shall be registered subject to the pledge;

(b) any certificated securities issued in exchange for or distributed with respect to the pledged security shall be delivered to the registered pledgee; and

(c) any money paid in exchange for or in redemption of part or all of the security shall be paid to the registered pledgee.

(7) Nothing in this Article shall be construed to affect

the liability of the registered owner of a security for calls, assessments, or the like.

Amended in 1977.

§ 8—208. Effect of Signature of Authenticating Trustee, Registrar, or Transfer Agent.

(1) A person placing his signature upon a certificated security or an initial transaction statement as authenticating trustee, registrar, transfer agent, or the like, warrants to a purchaser for value of the certificated security or a purchaser for value of an uncertificated security to whom the initial transaction statement has been sent, if the purchaser is without notice of the particular defect, that:

(a) the certificated security or initial transaction statement is genuine;

(b) his own participation in the issue or registration of the transfer, pledge, or release of the security is within his capacity and within the scope of the authority received by him from the issuer; and

(c) he has reasonable grounds to believe the security is in the form and within the amount the issuer is authorized to issue.

(2) Unless otherwise agreed, a person by so placing his signature does not assume responsibility for the validity of the security in other respects.

Amended in 1962 and 1977.

Part 3 Transfer

§ 8—301. Rights Acquired by Purchaser.

(1) Upon transfer of a security to a purchaser (Section 8—313), the purchaser acquires the rights in the security which his transferor had or had actual authority to convey unless the purchaser's rights are limited by Section 8—302(4).

(2) A transferee of a limited interest acquires rights only to the extent of the interest transferred. The creation or release of a security interest in a security is the transfer of a limited interest in that security.

Amended in 1977.

§ 8—302. "Bona Fide Purchaser"; "Adverse Claim"; Title Acquired by Bona Fide Purchaser.

(1) A "bona fide purchaser" is a purchaser for value in good faith and without notice of any adverse claim:

(a) who takes delivery of a certificated security in bearer form or in registered form, issued or indorsed to him or in blank;

(b) to whom the transfer, pledge, or release of an uncertificated security is registered on the books of the issuer; or

(c) to whom a security is transferred under the provisions of paragraph (c), (d)(i), or (g) of Section 8—313(1).

(2) "Adverse claim" includes a claim that a transfer was or would be wrongful or that a particular adverse person is the owner of or has an interest in the security.

(3) A bona fide purchaser in addition to acquiring the rights of a purchaser (Section 8—301) also acquires his interest in the security free of any adverse claim.

(4) Notwithstanding Section 8—301(1), the transferee of a particular certificated security who has been a party to any fraud or illegality affecting the security, or who as a prior holder of that certificated security had notice of an adverse claim, cannot improve his position by taking from a bona fide purchaser.

Amended in 1977.

§ 8—303. "Broker".

"Broker" means a person engaged for all or part of his time in the business of buying and selling securities, who in the transaction concerned acts for, buys a security from, or sells a security to, a customer. Nothing in this Article determines the capacity in which a person acts for purposes of any other statute or rule to which the person is subject.

§ 8—304. Notice to Purchaser of Adverse Claims.

(1) A purchaser (including a broker for the seller or buyer, but excluding an intermediary bank) of a certificated security is charged with notice of adverse claims if:

(a) the security, whether in bearer or registered form, has been indorsed "for collection" or "for surrender" or for some other purpose not involving transfer; or

(b) the security is in bearer form and has on it an unambiguous statement that it is the property of a person other than the transferor. The mere writing of a name on a security is not such a statement.

(2) A purchaser (including a broker for the seller or buyer, but excluding an intermediary bank) to whom the transfer, pledge, or release of an uncertificated security is registered is charged with notice of adverse claims as to which the issuer has a duty under Section 8—403(4) at the time of registration and which are noted in the initial transaction statement sent to the purchaser or, if his interest is transferred to him other

than by registration of transfer, pledge, or release, the initial transaction statement sent to the registered owner or the registered pledgee.

(3) The fact that the purchaser (including a broker for the seller or buyer) of a certificated or uncertificated security has notice that the security is held for a third person or is registered in the name of or indorsed by a fiduciary does not create a duty of inquiry into the rightfulness of the transfer or constitute constructive notice of adverse claims. However, if the purchaser (excluding an intermediary bank) has knowledge that the proceeds are being used or the transaction is for the individual benefit of the fiduciary or otherwise in breach of duty, the purchaser is charged with notice of adverse claims.

Amended in 1977.

§ 8—305. Staleness as Notice of Adverse Claims.

An act or event that creates a right to immediate performance of the principal obligation represented by a certificated security or sets a date on or after which a certificated security is to be presented or surrendered for redemption or exchange does not itself constitute any notice of adverse claims except in the case of a transfer:

(a) after one year from any date set for presentment or surrender for redemption or exchange; or

(b) after 6 months from any date set for payment of money against presentation or surrender of the security if funds are available for payment on that date.

Amended in 1977.

§ 8—306. Warranties on Presentment and Transfer of Certificated Securities; Warranties of Originators of Instructions.

(1) A person who presents a certificated security for registration of transfer or for payment or exchange warrants to the issuer that he is entitled to the registration, payment, or exchange. But, a purchaser for value and without notice of adverse claims who receives a new, reissued, or re-registered certificated security on registration of transfer or receives an initial transaction statement confirming the registration of transfer of an equivalent uncertificated security to him warrants only that he has no knowledge of any unauthorized signature (Section 8—311) in a necessary indorsement.

(2) A person by transferring a certificated security to a purchaser for value warrants only that:

(a) his transfer is effective and rightful;

(b) the security is genuine and has not been materially altered; and

(c) he knows of no fact which might impair the validity of the security.

(3) If a certificated security is delivered by an intermediary known to be entrusted with delivery of the security on behalf of another or with collection of a draft or other claim against delivery, the intermediary by delivery warrants only his own good faith and authority, even though he has purchased or made advances against the claim to be collected against the delivery.

(4) A pledgee or other holder for security who redelivers a certificated security received, or after payment and on order of the debtor delivers that security to a third person, makes only the warranties of an intermediary under subsection (3).

(5) A person who originates an instruction warrants to the issuer that:

(a) he is an appropriate person to originate the instruction; and

(b) at the time the instruction is presented to the issuer he will be entitled to the registration of transfer, pledge, or release.

(6) A person who originates an instruction warrants to any person specially guaranteeing his signature (subsection 8—312(3)) that:

(a) he is an appropriate person to originate the instruction; and

(b) at the time the instruction is presented to the issuer

(i) he will be entitled to the registration of transfer, pledge, or release; and

(ii) the transfer, pledge, or release requested in the instruction will be registered by the issuer free from all liens, security interests, restrictions, and claims other than those specified in the instruction.

(7) A person who originates an instruction warrants to a purchaser for value and to any person guaranteeing the instruction (Section 8—312(6)) that:

(a) he is an appropriate person to originate the instruction;

(b) the uncertificated security referred to therein is valid; and

(c) at the time the instruction is presented to the issuer

(i) the transferor will be entitled to the registration of transfer, pledge, or release;

(ii) the transfer, pledge, or release requested in the instruction will be registered by the issuer free from all liens, security interests, restrictions, and claims other than those specified in the instruction; and

(iii) the requested transfer, pledge, or release will be rightful.

(8) If a secured party is the registered pledgee or the registered owner of an uncertificated security, a person who originates an instruction of release or transfer to the debtor or, after payment and on order of the debtor, a transfer instruction to a third person, warrants to the debtor or the third person only that he is an appropriate person to originate the instruction and, at the time the instruction is presented to the issuer, the transferor will be entitled to the registration of release or transfer. If a transfer instruction to a third person who is a purchaser for value is originated on order of the debtor, the debtor makes to the purchaser the warranties of paragraphs (b), (c)(ii) and (c)(iii) of subsection (7).

(9) A person who transfers an uncertificated security to a purchaser for value and does not originate an instruction in connection with the transfer warrants only that:

(a) his transfer is effective and rightful; and

(b) the uncertificated security is valid.

(10) A broker gives to his customer and to the issuer and a purchaser the applicable warranties provided in this section and has the rights and privileges of a purchaser under this section. The warranties of and in favor of the broker, acting as an agent are in addition to applicable warranties given by and in favor of his customer.

Amended in 1962 and 1977.

§ 8—307. Effect of Delivery Without Indorsement; Right to Compel Indorsement.

If a certificated security in registered form has been delivered to a purchaser without a necessary indorsement he may become a bona fide purchaser only as of the time the indorsement is supplied; but against the transferor, the transfer is complete upon delivery and the purchaser has a specifically enforceable right to have any necessary indorsement supplied.

Amended in 1977.

§ 8—308. Indorsements; Instructions.

(1) An indorsement of a certificated security in registered form is made when an appropriate person signs on it or on a separate document an assignment or transfer of the security or a power to assign or transfer it or his signature is written without more upon the back of the security.

(2) An indorsement may be in blank or special. An indorsement in blank includes an indorsement to bearer. A special indorsement specifies to whom the security is to be transferred, or who has power to transfer it. A holder may convert a blank indorsement into a special indorsement.

(3) An indorsement purporting to be only of part of a certificated security representing units intended by the issuer to be separately transferable is effective to the extent of the indorsement.

(4) An "instruction" is an order to the issuer of an uncertificated security requesting that the transfer, pledge, or release from pledge of the uncertificated security specified therein be registered.

(5) An instruction originated by an appropriate person is:

(a) a writing signed by an appropriate person; or

(b) a communication to the issuer in any form agreed upon in a writing signed by the issuer and an appropriate person.

If an instruction has been originated by an appropriate person but is incomplete in any other respect, any person may complete it as authorized and the issuer may rely on it as completed even though it has been completed incorrectly.

(6) "An appropriate person" in subsection (1) means the person specified by the certificated security or by special indorsement to be entitled to the security.

(7) "An appropriate person" in subsection (5) means:

(a) for an instruction to transfer or pledge an uncertificated security which is then not subject to a registered pledge, the registered owner; or

(b) for an instruction to transfer or release an uncertificated security which is then subject to a registered pledge, the registered pledgee.

(8) In addition to the persons designated in subsections (6) and (7), "an appropriate person" in subsections (1) and (5) includes:

(a) if the person designated is described as a fiduciary but is no longer serving in the described capacity, either that person or his successor;

(b) if the persons designated are descirbed as more than one person as fiduciaries and one or more are no longer serving in the described capacity, the remaining fiduciary or fiduciaries, whether or not a successor has been appointed or qualified;

(c) if the person designated is an individual and is

without capacity to act by virtue of death, incompetence, infancy, or otherwise, his executor, administrator, guardian, or like fiduciary;

(d) if the persons designated are described as more than one person as tenants by the entirety or with right of survivorship and by reason of death all cannot sign, the survivor or survivors;

(e) a person having power to sign under applicable law or controlling instrument; and

(f) to the extent that the person designated or any of the foregoing persons may act through an agent, his authorized agent.

(9) Unless otherwise agreed, the indorser of a certificated security by his indorsement or the originator of an instruction by his origination assumes no obligation that the security will be honored by the issuer but only the obligations provided in Section 8—306.

(10) Whether the person signing is appropriate is determined as of the date of signing and an indorsement made by or an instruction originated by him does not become unauthorized for the purposes of this Article by virtue of any subsequent change of circumstances.

(11) Failure of a fiduciary to comply with a controlling instrument or with the law of the state having jurisdiction of the fiduciary relationship, including any law requiring the fiduciary to obtain court approval of the transfer, pledge, or release, does not render his indorsement or an instruction originated by him unauthorized for the purposes of this Article.

Amended in 1962 and 1977.

§ 8—309. **Effect of Indorsement Without Delivery.**

An indorsement of a certificated security, whether special or in blank, does not constitute a transfer until delivery of the certificated security on which it appears or, if the indorsement is on a separate document, until delivery of both the document and the certificated security.

Amended in 1977.

§ 8—310. **Indorsement of Certificated Security in Bearer Form.**

An indorsement of a certificated security in bearer form may give notice of adverse claims (Section 8—304) but does not otherwise affect any right to registration the holder possesses.

Amended in 1977.

§ 8—311. **Effect of Unauthorized Indorsement or Instruction.**

Unless the owner or pledgee has ratified an unauthorized indorsement or instruction or is otherwise precluded from asserting its ineffectiveness:

(a) he may assert its ineffectiveness against the issuer or any purchaser, other than a purchaser for value and without notice of adverse claims, who has in good faith received a new, reissued, or re-registered certificated security on registration of transfer or received an initial transaction statement confirming the registration of transfer, pledge, or release of an equivalent uncertificated security to him; and

(b) an issuer who registers the transfer of a certificated security upon the unauthorized indorsement or who registers the transfer, pledge, or release of an uncertificated security upon the unauthorized instruction is subject to liability for improper registration (Section 8—404).

Amended in 1977.

§ 8—312. **Effect of Guaranteeing Signature, Indorsement or Instruction.**

(1) Any person guaranteeing a signature of an indorser of a certificated security warrants that at the time of signing:

(a) the signature was genuine;

(b) the signer was an appropriate person to indorse (Section 8—308); and

(c) the signer had legal capacity to sign.

(2) Any person guaranteeing a signature of the originator of an instruction warrants that at the time of signing:

(a) the signature was genuine;

(b) the signer was an appropriate person to originate the instruction (Section 8—308) if the person specified in the instruction as the registered owner or registered pledgee of the uncertificated security was, in fact, the registered owner or registered pledgee of the security, as to which fact the signature guarantor makes no warranty;

(c) the signer had legal capacity to sign; and

(d) the taxpayer identification number, if any, appearing on the instruction as that of the registered owner or registered pledgee was the taxpayer identification number of the signer or of the owner or pledgee for whom the signer was acting.

(3) Any person specially guaranteeing the signature of the originator of an instruction makes not only the warranties of a signature guarantor (subsection (2))

but also warrants that at the time the instruction is presented to the issuer:

(a) the person specified in the instruction as the registered owner or registered pledgee of the uncertificated security will be the registered owner or registered pledgee; and

(b) the transfer, pledge, or release of the uncertificated security requested in the instruction will be registered by the issuer free from all liens, security interests, restrictions, and claims other than those specified in the instruction.

(4) The guarantor under subsections (1) and (2) or the special guarantor under subsection (3) does not otherwise warrant the rightfulness of the particular transfer, pledge, or release.

(5) Any person guaranteeing an indorsement of a certificated security makes not only the warranties of a signature guarantor under subsection (1) but also warrants the rightfulness of the particular transfer in all respects.

(6) Any person guaranteeing an instruction requesting the transfer, pledge, or release of an uncertificated security makes not only the warranties of a special signature guarantor under subsection (3) but also warrants the rightfulness of the particular transfer, pledge, or release in all respects.

(7) No issuer may require a special guarantee of signature (subsection (3)), a guarantee of indorsement (subsection (5)), or a guarantee of instruction (subsection (6)) as a condition to registration of transfer, pledge, or release.

(8) The foregoing warranties are made to any person taking or dealing with the security in reliance on the guarantee, and the guarantor is liable to the person for any loss resulting from breach of the warranties.

Amended in 1977.

§ 8—313. When Transfer to Purchaser Occurs; Financial Intermediary as Bona Fide Purchaser; "Financial Intermediary".

(1) Transfer of a security or a limited interest (including a security interest) therein to a purchaser occurs only:

(a) at the time he or a person designated by him acquires possession of a certificated security;

(b) at the time the transfer, pledge, or release of an uncertificated security is registered to him or a person designated by him;

(c) at the time his financial intermediary acquires possession of a certificated security specially indorsed to or issued in the name of the purchaser;

(d) at the time a financial intermediary, not a clearing corporation, sends him confirmation of the purchase and also by book entry or otherwise identifies as belonging to the purchaser

(i) a specific certificated security in the financial intermediary's possession;

(ii) a quantity of securities that constitute or are part of a fungible bulk of certificated securities in the financial intermediary's possession or of uncertificated securities registered in the name of the financial intermediary; or

(iii) a quantity of securities that constitute or are part of a fungible bulk of securities shown on the account of the financial intermediary on the books of another financial intermediary;

(e) with respect to an identified certificated security to be delivered while still in the possession of a third person, not a financial intermediary, at the time that person acknowledges that he holds for the purchaser;

(f) with respect to a specific uncertificated security the pledge or transfer of which has been registered to a third person, not a financial intermediary, at the time that person acknowledges that he holds for the purchaser;

(g) at the time appropriate entries to the account of the purchaser or a person designated by him on the books of a clearing corporation are made under Section 8—320;

(h) with respect to the transfer of a security interest where the debtor has signed a security agreement containing a description of the security, at the time a written notification, which, in the case of the creation of the security interest, is signed by the debtor (which may be a copy of the security agreement) or which, in the case of the release or assignment of the security interest created pursuant to this paragraph, is signed by the secured party, is received by

(i) a financial intermediary on whose books the interest of the transferor in the security appears;

(ii) a third person, not a financial intermediary, in possession of the security, if it is certificated;

(iii) a third person, not a financial intermediary, who is the registered owner of the security, if it is uncertificated and not subject to a registered pledge; or

(iv) a third person, not a financial intermediary, who is the registered pledgee of the security, if it is uncertificated and subject to a registered pledge;

(i) with respect to the transfer of a security interest where the transferor has signed a security agreement containing a description of the security, at the time new value is given by the secured party; or

(j) with respect to the transfer of a security interest where the secured party is a financial intermediary and the security has already been transferred to the financial intermediary under paragraphs (a), (b), (c), (d), or (g), at the time the transferor has signed a security agreement containing a description of the security and value is given by the secured party.

(2) The purchaser is the owner of a security held for him by a financial intermediary, but cannot be a bona fide purchaser of a security so held except in the circumstances specified in paragraphs (c), (d)(i), and (g) of subsection (1). If a security so held is part of a fungible bulk, as in the circumstances specified in paragraphs (d)(ii) and (d)(iii) of subsection (1), the purchaser is the owner of a proportionate property interest in the fungible bulk.

(3) Notice of an adverse claim received by the financial intermediary or by the purchaser after the financial intermediary takes delivery of a certificated security as a holder for value or after the transfer, pledge, or release of an uncertificated security has been registered free of the claim to a financial intermediary who has given value is not effective either as to the financial intermediary or as to the purchaser. However, as between the financial intermediary and the purchaser the purchaser may demand transfer of an equivalent security as to which no notice of adverse claim has been received.

(4) A "financial intermediary" is a bank, broker, clearing corporation, or other person (or the nominee of any of them) which in the ordinary course of its business maintains security accounts for its customers and is acting in that capacity. A financial intermediary may have a security interest in securities held in account for its customer.

Amended in 1962 and 1977.

§ 8—314. Duty to Transfer, When Completed

(1) Unless otherwise agreed, if a sale of a security is made on an exchange or otherwise through brokers:

(a) the selling customer fulfills his duty to transfer at the time he:

(i) places a certificated security in the possession of the selling broker or a person designated by the broker;

(ii) causes an uncertificated security to be registered in the name of the selling broker or a person designated by the broker;

(iii) if requested, causes an acknowledgment to be made to the selling broker that a certificated or uncertificated security is held for the broker; or

(iv) places in the possession of the selling broker or of a person designated by the broker a transfer instruction for an uncertificated security, providing the issuer does not refuse to register the requested transfer if the instruction is presented to the issuer for registration within 30 days thereafter; and

(b) the selling broker, including a correspondent broker acting for a selling customer, fulfills his duty to transfer at the time he:

(i) places a certificated security in the possession of the buying broker or a person designated by the buying broker;

(ii) causes an uncertificated security to be registered in the name of the buying broker or a person designated by the buying broker;

(iii) places in the possession of the buying broker or of a person designated by the buying broker a transfer instruction for an uncertificated security, providing the issuer does not refuse to register the requested transfer if the instruction is presented to the issuer for registration within 30 days thereafter; or

(iv) effects clearance of the sale in accordance with the rules of the exchange on which the transaction took place.

(2) Except as provided in this section or unless otherwise agreed, a transferor's duty to transfer a security under a contract of purchase is not fulfilled until he:

(a) places a certificated security in form to be negotiated by the purchaser in the possession of the purchaser or of a person designated by the purchaser;

(b) causes an uncertificated security to be registered in the name of the purchaser or a person designated by the purchaser; or

(c) if the purchaser requests, causes an acknowledgment to be made to the purchaser that a certificated or uncertificated security is held for the purchaser.

(3) Unless made on an exchange, a sale to a broker purchasing for his own account is within subsection (2) and not within subsection (1).

Amended in 1977.

§ 8—315. Action Against Transferee Based Upon Wrongful Transfer

(1) Any person against whom the transfer of a security is wrongful for any reason, including his incapacity, as against anyone except a bona fide purchaser, may:

    (a) reclaim possession of the certificated security wrongfully transferred;

    (b) obtain possession of any new certificated security representing all or part of the same rights;

    (c) compel the origination of an instruction to transfer to him or a person designated by him an uncertificated security constituting all or part of the same rights; or

    (d) have damages.

(2) If the transfer is wrongful because of an unauthorized indorsement of a certificated security, the owner may also reclaim or obtain possession of the security or a new certificated security, even from a bona fide purchaser, if the ineffectiveness of the purported indorsement can be asserted against him under the provisions of this Article on unauthorized indorsements (Section 8—311).

(3) The right to obtain or reclaim possession of a certificated security or to compel the origination of a transfer instruction may be specifically enforced and the transfer of a certificated or uncertificated security enjoined and a certificated security impounded pending the litigation.

Amended in 1977.

§ 8—316. Purchaser's Right to Requisites for Registration of Transfer, Pledge, or Release on Books

Unless otherwise agreed, the transferor of a certificated security or the transferor, pledgor, or pledgee of an uncertificated security on due demand must supply his purchaser with any proof of his authority to transfer, pledge, or release or with any other requisite necessary to obtain registration of the transfer, pledge, or release of the security; but if the transfer, pledge, or release is not for value, a transferor, pledgor, or pledgee need not do so unless the purchaser furnishes the necessary expenses. Failure within a reasonable time to comply with a demand made gives the purchaser the right to reject or rescind the transfer, pledge, or release.

Amended in 1977.

§ 8—317. Creditors' Rights

(1) Subject to the exceptions in subsections (3) and (4), no attachment or levy upon a certificated security or any share or other interest represented thereby which is outstanding is valid until the security is actually seized by the officer making the attachment or levy, but a certificated security which has been surrendered to the issuer may be reached by a creditor by legal process at the issuer's chief executive office in the United States.

(2) An uncertificated security registered in the name of the debtor may not be reached by a creditor except by legal process at the issuer's chief executive office in the United States.

(3) The interest of a debtor in a certificated security that is in the possession of a secured party not a financial intermediary or in an uncertificated security registered in the name of a secured party not a financial intermediary (or in the name of a nominee of the secured party) may be reached by a creditor by legal process upon the secured party.

(4) The interest of a debtor in a certificated security that is in the possession of or registered in the name of a financial intermediary or in an uncertificated security registered in the name of a financial intermediary may be reached by a creditor by legal process upon the financial intermediary on whose books the interest of the debtor appears.

(5) Unless otherwise provided by law, a creditor's lien upon the interest of a debtor in a security obtained pursuant to subsection (3) or (4) is not a restraint on the transfer of the security, free of the lien, to a third party for new value; but in the event of a transfer, the lien applies to the proceeds of the transfer in the hands of the secured party or financial intermediary, subject to any claims having priority.

(6) A creditor whose debtor is the owner of a security is entitled to aid from courts of appropriate jurisdiction, by injunction or otherwise, in reaching the security or in satisfying the claim by means allowed at law or in equity in regard to property that cannot readily be reached by ordinary legal process.

Amended in 1977.

§ 8—318. No Conversion by Good Faith Conduct

An agent or bailee who in good faith (including observance of reasonable commercial standards if he is in the business of buying, selling, or otherwise dealing with securities) has received certificated securities and sold, pledged, or delivered them or has sold or caused the transfer or pledge of uncertificated securities over which he had control according to the instructions of his principal, is not liable for conversion or for participation in breach of fiduciary duty although the principal had no right so to deal with the securities.

Amended in 1977.

§ 8—319. Statute of Frauds

A contract for the sale of securities is not enforceable by way of action or defense unless:

(a) there is some writing signed by the party against whom enforcement is sought or by his authorized agent or broker, sufficient to indicate that a contract has been made for sale of a stated quantity of described securities at a defined or stated price;

(b) delivery of a certificated security or transfer instruction has been accepted, or transfer of an uncertificated security has been registered and the transferee has failed to send written objection to the issuer within 10 days after receipt of the initial transaction statement confirming the registration, or payment has been made, but the contract is enforceable under this provision only to the extent of the delivery, registration, or payment;

(c) within a reasonable time a writing in confirmation of the sale or purchase and sufficient against the sender under paragraph (a) has been received by the party against whom enforcement is sought and he has failed to send written objection to its contents within 10 days after its receipt; or

(d) the party against whom enforcement is sought admits in his pleading, testimony, or otherwise in court that a contract was made for the sale of a stated quantity of described securities at a defined or stated price.

Amended in 1977.

§ 8—320. Transfer or Pledge Within Central Depository System

(1) In addition to other methods, a transfer, pledge, or release of a security or any interest therein may be effected by the making of appropriate entries on the books of a clearing corporation reducing the account of the transferor, pledgor, or pledgee and increasing the account of the transferee, pledgee, or pledgor by the amount of the obligation or the number of shares or rights transferred, pledged, or released, if the security is shown on the account of a transferor, pledgor, or pledgee on the books of the clearing corporation; is subject to the control of the clearing corporation; and

(a) if certificated,

(i) is in the custody of the clearing corporation, another clearing corporation, a custodian bank,

or a nominee of any of them; and

(ii) is in bearer form or indorsed in blank by an appropriate person or registered in the name of the clearing corporation, a custodian bank, or a nominee of any of them; or

(b) if uncertificated, is registered in the name of the clearing corporation, another clearing corporation, a custodian bank, or a nominee of any of them.

(2) Under this section entries may be made with respect to like securities or interests therein as a part of a fungible bulk and may refer merely to a quantity of a particular security without reference to the name of the registered owner, certificate or bond number, or the like, and, in appropriate cases, may be on a net basis taking into account other transfers, pledges, or releases of the same security.

(3) A transfer under this section is effective (Section 8—313) and the purchaser acquires the rights of the transferor (Section 8—301). A pledge or release under this section is the transfer of a limited interest. If a pledge or the creation of a security interest is intended, the security interest is perfected at the time when both value is given by the pledgee and the appropriate entries are made (Section 8—321). A transferee or pledgee under this section may be a bona fide purchaser (Section 8—302).

(4) A transfer or pledge under this section is not a registration of transfer under Part 4.

(5) That entries made on the books of the clearing corporation as provided in subsection (1) are not appropriate does not affect the validity or effect of the entries or the liabilities or obligations of the clearing corporation to any person adversely affected thereby.

Added in 1962; amended in 1977.

§ 8—321. Enforceability, Attachment, Perfection and Termination of Security Interests

(1) A security interest in a security is enforceable and can attach only if it is transferred to the secured party or a person designated by him pursuant to a provision of Section 8—313(1).

(2) A security interest so transferred pursuant to agreement by a transferor who has rights in the security to a transferee who has given value is a perfected security interest, but a security interest that has been transferred solely under paragraph (i) of Section 8—313(1) becomes unperfected after 21 days unless, within that time, the requirements for transfer under any other provision of Section 8—313(1) are satisfied.

(3) A security interest in a security is subject to the provisions of Article 9, but:

(a) no filing is required to perfect the security interest; and

(b) no written security agreement signed by the debtor is necessary to make the security interest enforceable, except as provided in paragraph (h), (i), or (j) of Section 8—313(1). The secured party has the rights and duties provided under Section 9—207, to the extent they are applicable, whether or not the security is certificated, and, if certificated, whether or not it is in his possession.

(4) Unless otherwise agreed, a security interest in a security is terminated by transfer to the debtor or a person designated by him pursuant to a provision of Section 8—313(1). If a security is thus transferred, the security interest, if not terminated, becomes unperfected unless the security is certificated and is delivered to the debtor for the purpose of ultimate sale or exchange or presentation, collection, renewal, or registration of transfer. In that case, the security interest becomes unperfected after 21 days unless, within that time, the security (or securities for which it has been exchanged) is transferred to the secured party or a person designated by him pursuant to a provision of Section 8—313(1).

Added in 1977.

Part 4 **Registration**

§ 8—401. **Duty of Issuer to Register Transfer, Pledge, or Release**

(1) If a certificated security in registered form is presented to the issuer with a request to register transfer or an instruction is presented to the issuer with a request to register transfer, pledge, or release, the issuer shall register the transfer, pledge, or release as requested if:

(a) the security is indorsed or the instruction was originated by the appropriate person or persons (Section 8—308);

(b) reasonable assurance is given that those indorsements or instructions are genuine and effective (Section 8—402);

(c) the issuer has no duty as to adverse claims or has discharged the duty (Section 8—403);

(d) any applicable law relating to the collection of taxes has been complied with; and

(e) the transfer, pledge, or release is in fact rightful or is to a bona fide purchaser.

(2) If an issuer is under a duty to register a transfer, pledge, or release of a security, the issuer is also liable to the person presenting a certificated security or an instruction for registration or his principal for loss resulting from any unreasonable delay in registration or from failure or refusal to register the transfer, pledge, or release.

Amended in 1977.

§ 8—402. **Assurance that Indorsements and Instructions Are Effective**

(1) The issuer may require the following assurance that each necessary indorsement of a certificated security or each instruction (Section 8—308) is genuine and effective:

(a) in all cases, a guarantee of the signature (Section 8—312(1) or (2)) of the person indorsing a certificated security or originating an instruction including, in the case of an instruction, a warranty of the taxpayer identification number or, in the absence thereof, other reasonable assurance of identity;

(b) if the indorsement is made or the instruction is originated by an agent, appropriate assurance of authority to sign;

(c) if the indorsement is made or the instruction is originated by a fiduciary, appropriate evidence of appointment or incumbency;

(d) if there is more than one fiduciary, reasonable assurance that all who are required to sign have done so; and

(e) if the indorsement is made or the instruction is originated by a person not covered by any of the foregoing, assurance appropriate to the case corresponding as nearly as may be to the foregoing.

(2) A "guarantee of the signature" in subsection (1) means a guarantee signed by or on behalf of a person reasonably believed by the issuer to be responsible. The issuer may adopt standards with respect to responsibility if they are not manifestly unreasonable.

(3) "Appropriate evidence of appointment or incumbency" in subsection (1) means:

(a) in the case of a fiduciary appointed or qualified by a court, a certificate issued by or under the direction or supervision of that court or an officer thereof and dated within 60 days before the date of presentation for transfer, pledge, or release; or

(b) in any other case, a copy of a document showing the appointment or a certificate issued by or on behalf of a person reasonably believed by the issuer to be responsible or, in the absence of that document or certificate, other evidence reasonably deemed by the issuer to be appropriate. The issuer may adopt standards with respect to the evidence if they are not manifestly unreasonable. The issuer is not charged with notice of the contents of any document obtained pursuant to this paragraph (b) except to the extent that the contents relate directly to the appointment or incumbency.

(4) The issuer may elect to require reasonable assurance beyond that specified in this section, but if it does so and, for a purpose other than that specified in subsection (3)(b), both requires and obtains a copy of a will, trust, indenture, articles of co-partnership, by-laws, or other controlling instrument, it is charged with notice of all matters contained therein affecting the transfer, pledge, or release.

Amended in 1977.

§ 8—403. **Issuer's Duty as to Adverse Claims**

(1) An issuer to whom a certificated security is presented for registration shall inquire into adverse claims if:

(a) a written notification of an adverse claim is received at a time and in a manner affording the issuer a reasonable opportunity to act on it prior to the issuance of a new, reissued, or re-registered certificated security, and the notification identifies the claimant, the registered owner, and the issue of which the security is a part, and provides an address for communications directed to the claimant; or

(b) the issuer is charged with notice of an adverse claim from a controlling instrument it has elected to require under Section 8—402(4).

(2) The issuer may discharge any duty of inquiry by any reasonable means, including notifying an adverse claimant by registered or certified mail at the address furnished by him or, if there be no such address, at his residence or regular place of business that the certificated security has been presented for registration of transfer by a named person, and that the transfer will be registered unless within 30 days from the date of mailing the notification, either:

(a) an appropriate restraining order, injunction, or other process issues from a court of competent jurisdiction; or

(b) there is filed with the issuer an indemnity bond, sufficient in the issuer's judgment to protect the issuer and any transfer agent, registrar, or other agent of the issuer involved from any loss it or they may suffer by complying with the adverse claim.

(3) Unless an issuer is charged with notice of an adverse claim from a controlling instrument which it has elected to require under Section 8—402(4) or receives notification of an adverse claim under subsection (1), if a certificated security presented for registration is indorsed by the appropriate person or persons the issuer is under no duty to inquire into adverse claims. In particular:

(a) an issuer registering a certificated security in the name of a person who is a fiduciary or who is described as a fiduciary is not bound to inquire into the existence, extent, or correct description of the fiduciary relationship; and thereafter the issuer may assume without inquiry that the newly registered owner continues to be the fiduciary until the issuer receives written notice that the fiduciary is no longer acting as such with respect to the particular security;

(b) an issuer registering transfer on an indorsement by a fiduciary is not bound to inquire whether the transfer is made in compliance with a controlling instrument or with the law of the state having jurisdiction of the fiduciary relationship, including any law requiring the fiduciary to obtain court approval of the transfer; and

(c) the issuer is not charged with notice of the contents of any court record or file or other recorded or unrecorded document even though the document is in its possession and even though the transfer is made on the indorsement of a fiduciary to the fiduciary himself or to his nominee.

(4) An issuer is under no duty as to adverse claims with respect to an uncertificated security except:

(a) claims embodied in a restraining order, injunction, or other legal process served upon the issuer if the process was served at a time and in a manner affording the issuer a reasonable opportunity to act on it in accordance with the requirements of subsection (5);

(b) claims of which the issuer has received a written notification from the registered owner or the registered pledgee if the notification was received at a time and in a manner affording the issuer a reasonable opportunity to act on it in accordance with the requirements of subsection (5);

(c) claims (including restrictions on transfer not imposed by the issuer) to which the registration of transfer to the present registered owner was subject and were so noted in the initial transaction statement sent to him; and

(d) claims as to which an issuer is charged with

notice from a controlling instrument it has elected to require under Section 8—402(4).

(5) If the issuer of an uncertificated security is under a duty as to an adverse claim, he discharges that duty by:

(a) including a notation of the claim in any statements sent with respect to the security under Sections 8—408(3), (6), and (7); and

(b) refusing to register the transfer or pledge of the security unless the nature of the claim does not preclude transfer or pledge subject thereto.

(6) If the transfer or pledge of the security is registered subject to an adverse claim, a notation of the claim must be included in the initial transaction statement and all subsequent statements sent to the transferee and pledgee under Section 8—408.

(7) Notwithstanding subsections (4) and (5), if an uncertificated security was subject to a registered pledge at the time the issuer first came under a duty as to a particular adverse claim, the issuer has no duty as to that claim if transfer of the security is requested by the registered pledgee or an appropriate person acting for the registered pledgee unless:

(a) the claim was embodied in legal process which expressly provides otherwise;

(b) the claim was asserted in a written notification from the registered pledgee;

(c) the claim was one as to which the issuer was charged with notice from a controlling instrument it required under Section 8—402(4) in connection with the pledgee's request for transfer; or

(d) the transfer requested is to the registered owner.

Amended in 1977.

§ 8—404. Liability and Non-Liability for Registration

(1) Except as provided in any law relating to the collection of taxes, the issuer is not liable to the owner, pledgee, or any other person suffering loss as a result of the registration of a transfer, pledge, or release of a security if:

(a) there were on or with a certificated security the necessary indorsements or the issuer had received an instruction originated by an appropriate person (Section 8—308); and

(b) the issuer had no duty as to adverse claims or has discharged the duty (Section 8—403).

(2) If an issuer has registered a transfer of a certificated security to a person not entitled to it, the issuer on demand shall deliver a like security to the true owner unless:

(a) the registration was pursuant to subsection (1);

(b) the owner is precluded from asserting any claim for registering the transfer under Section 8—405(1); or

(c) the delivery would result in overissue, in which case the issuer's liability is governed by Section 8—104.

(3) If an issuer has improperly registered a transfer, pledge, or release of an uncertificated security, the issuer on demand from the injured party shall restore the records as to the injured party to the condition that would have obtained if the improper registration had not been made unless:

(a) the registration was pursuant to subsection (1); or

(b) the registration would result in overissue, in which case the issuer's liability is governed by Section 8—104.

Amended in 1977.

§ 8—405. Lost, Destroyed, and Stolen Certificated Securities

(1) If a certificated security has been lost, apparently destroyed, or wrongfully taken, and the owner fails to notify the issuer of that fact within a reasonable time after he has notice of it and the issuer registers a transfer of the security before receiving notification, the owner is precluded from asserting against the issuer any claim for registering the transfer under Section 8—404 or any claim to a new security under this section.

(2) If the owner of a certificated security claims that the security has been lost, destroyed, or wrongfully taken, the issuer shall issue a new certificated security or, at the option of the issuer, an equivalent uncertificated security in place of the original security if the owner:

(a) so requests before the issuer has notice that the security has been acquired by a bona fide purchaser;

(b) files with the issuer a sufficient indemnity bond; and

(c) satisfies any other reasonable requirements imposed by the issuer.

(3) If, after the issue of a new certificated or uncertificated security, a bona fide purchaser of the original certificated security presents it for registration of transfer, the issuer shall register the transfer unless

registration would result in overissue, in which event the issuer's liability is governed by Section 8—104. In addition to any rights on the indemnity bond, the issuer may recover the new certificated security from the person to whom it was issued or any person taking under him except a bona fide purchaser or may cancel the uncertificated security unless a bona fide purchaser or any person taking under a bona fide purchaser is then the registered owner or registered pledgee thereof.

Amended in 1977.

§ 8—406. Duty of Authenticating Trustee, Transfer Agent, or Registrar

(1) If a person acts as authenticating trustee, transfer agent, registrar, or other agent for an issuer in the registration of transfers of its certificated securities or in the registration of transfers, pledges, and releases of its uncertificated securities, in the issue of new securities, or in the cancellation of surrendered securities:

(a) he is under a duty to the issuer to exercise good faith and due diligence in performing his functions; and

(b) with regard to the particular functions he performs, he has the same obligation to the holder or owner of a certificated security or to the owner or pledgee of an uncertificated security and has the same rights and privileges as the issuer has in regard to those functions.

(2) Notice to an authenticating trustee, transfer agent, registrar or other agent is notice to the issuer with respect to the functions performed by the agent.

Amended in 1977.

§ 8—407. Exchangeability of Securities

(1) No issuer is subject to the requirements of this section unless it regularly maintains a system for issuing the class of securities involved under which both certificated and uncertificated securities are regularly issued to the category of owners, which includes the person in whose name the new security is to be registered.

(2) Upon surrender of a certificated security with all necessary indorsements and presentation of a written request by the person surrendering the security, the issuer, if he has no duty as to adverse claims or has discharged the duty (Section 8—403), shall issue to the person or a person designated by him an equivalent uncertificated security subject to all liens, restrictions, and claims that were noted on the certificated security.

(3) Upon receipt of a transfer instruction originated by an appropriate person who so requests, the issuer of an uncertificated security shall cancel the uncertificated security and issue an equivalent certificated security on which must be noted conspicuously any liens and restrictions of the issuer and any adverse claims (as to which the issuer has a duty under Section 8—403(4)) to which the uncertificated security was subject. The certificated security shall be registered in the name of and delivered to:

(a) the registered owner, if the uncertificated security was not subject to a registered pledge; or

(b) the registered pledgee, if the uncertificated security was subject to a registered pledge.

Added in 1977.

§ 8—408. Statements of Uncertificated Securities

(1) Within 2 business days after the transfer of an uncertificated security has been registered, the issuer shall send to the new registered owner and, if the security has been transferred subject to a registered pledge, to the registered pledgee a written statement containing:

(a) a description of the issue of which the uncertificated security is a part;

(b) the number of shares or units transferred;

(c) the name and address and any taxpayer identification number of the new registered owner and, if the security has been transferred subject to a registered pledge, the name and address and any taxpayer identification number of the registered pledgee;

(d) a notation of any liens and restrictions of the issuer and any adverse claims (as to which the issuer has a duty under Section 8—403(4)) to which the uncertificated security is or may be subject at the time of registration or a statement that there are none of those liens, restrictions, or adverse claims; and

(e) the date the transfer was registered.

(2) Within 2 business days after the pledge of an uncertificated security has been registered, the issuer shall send to the registered owner and the registered pledgee a written statement containing:

(a) a description of the issue of which the uncertificated security is a part;

(b) the number of shares or units pledged;

(c) the name and address and any taxpayer identification number of the registered owner and the registered pledgee;

(d) a notation of any liens and restrictions of the issuer and any adverse claims (as to which the issuer has a duty under Section 8—403(4)) to which the uncertificated security is or may be subject at the time of registration or a statement that there are none of those liens, restrictions, or adverse claims; and

(e) the date the pledge was registered.

(3) Within 2 business days after the release from pledge of an uncertificated security has been registered, the issuer shall send to the registered owner and the pledgee whose interest was released a written statement containing:

(a) a description of the issue of which the uncertificated security is a part;

(b) the number of shares or units released from pledge;

(c) the name and address and any taxpayer identification number of the registered owner and the pledgee whose interest was released;

(d) a notation of any liens and restrictions of the issuer and any adverse claims (as to which the issuer has a duty under Section 8—403(4)) to which the uncertificated security is or may be subject at the time of registration or a statement that there are none of those liens, restrictions, or adverse claims; and

(e) the date the release was registered.

(4) An "initial transaction statement" is the statement sent to:

(a) the new registered owner and, if applicable, to the registered pledgee pursuant to subsection (1);

(b) the registered pledgee pursuant to subsection (2); or

(c) the registered owner pursuant to subsection (3).

Each initial transaction statement shall be signed by or on behalf of the issuer and must be identified as "Initial Transaction Statement".

(5) Within 2 business days after the transfer of an uncertificated security has been registered, the issuer shall send to the former registered owner and the former registered pledgee, if any, a written statement containing:

(a) a description of the issue of which the uncertificated security is a part;

(b) the number of shares or units transferred;

(c) the name and address and any taxpayer identification number of the former registered owner and of any former registered pledgee; and

(d) the date the transfer was registered.

(6) At periodic intervals no less frequent than annually and at any time upon the reasonable written request of the registered owner, the issuer shall send to the registered owner of each uncertificated security a dated written statement containing:

(a) a description of the issue of which the uncertificated security is a part;

(b) the name and address and any taxpayer identification number of the registered owner;

(c) the number of shares or units of the uncertificated security registered in the name of the registered owner on the date of the statement;

(d) the name and address and any taxpayer identification number of any registered pledgee and the number of shares or units subject to the pledge; and

(e) a notation of any liens and restrictions of the issuer and any adverse claims (as to which the issuer has a duty under Section 8—403(4)) to which the uncertificated security is or may be subject or a statement that there are none of those liens, restrictions, or adverse claims.

(7) At periodic intervals no less frequent than annually and at any time upon the reasonable written request of the registered pledgee, the issuer shall send to the registered pledgee of each uncertificated security a dated written statement containing:

(a) a description of the issue of which the uncertificated security is a part;

(b) the name and address and any taxpayer identification number of the registered owner;

(c) the name and address and any taxpayer identification number of the registered pledgee;

(d) the number of shares or units subject to the pledge; and

(e) a notation of any liens and restrictions of the issuer and any adverse claims (as to which the issuer has a duty under Section 8—403(4)) to which the uncertificated security is or may be subject or a statement that there are none of those liens, restrictions, or adverse claims.

(8) If the issuer sends the statements described in subsections (6) and (7) at periodic intervals no less frequent than quarterly, the issuer is not obliged to send additional statements upon request unless the owner or pledgee requesting them pays to the issuer the reasonable cost of furnishing them.

(9) Each statement sent pursuant to this section must bear a conspicuous legend reading substantially as follows: "This statement is merely a record of the rights of the addressee as of the time of its issuance.

Delivery of this statement, of itself, confers no rights on the recipient. This statement is neither a negotiable instrument nor a security."

Added in 1977.

Article 9
Secured Transactions; Sales of Accounts and Chattel Paper

Note: *The adoption of this Article should be accompanied by the repeal of existing statutes dealing with conditional sales, trust receipts, factor's liens where the factor is given a non-possessory lien, chattel mortgages, crop mortgages, mortgages on railroad equipment, assignment of accounts and generally statutes regulating security interests in personal property.*

Where the state has a retail installment selling act or small loan act, that legislation should be carefully examined to determine what changes in those acts are needed to conform them to this Article. This Article primarily sets out rules defining rights of a secured party against persons dealing with the debtor; it does not prescribe regulations and controls which may be necessary to curb abuses arising in the small loan business or in the financing of consumer purchases on credit. Accordingly there is no intention to repeal existing regulatory acts in those fields by enactment or re-enactment of Article 9. See Section 9—203(4) and the Note thereto.

Part 1 Short Title, Applicability and Definitions

§ 9—101. Short Title.

This Article shall be known and may be cited as Uniform Commercial Code—Secured Transactions.

§ 9—102. Policy and Subject Matter of Article.

(1) Except as otherwise provided in Section 9—104 on excluded transactions, this Article applies

(a) to any transaction (regardless of its form) which is intended to create a security interest in personal property or fixtures including goods, documents, instruments, general intangibles, chattel paper or accounts; and also

(b) to any sale of accounts or chattel paper.

(2) This Article applies to security interests created by contract including pledge, assignment, chattel mortgage, chattel trust, trust deed, factor's lien, equipment trust, conditional sale, trust receipt, other lien or title retention contract and lease or consign-ment intended as security. This Article does not apply to statutory liens except as provided in Section 9—310.

(3) The application of this Article to a security interest in a secured obligation is not affected by the fact that the obligation is itself secured by a transaction or interest to which this Article does not apply. Amended in 1972.

§ 9—103. Perfection of Security Interest in Multiple State Transactions

(1) Documents, instruments and ordinary goods.

(a) This subsection applies to documents and instruments and to goods other than those covered by a certificate of title described in subsection (2), mobile goods described in subsection (3), and minerals described in subsection (5).

(b) Except as otherwise provided in this subsection, perfection and the effect of perfection or non-perfection of a security interest in collateral are governed by the law of the jurisdiction where the collateral is when the last event occurs on which is based the assertion that the security interest is perfected or unperfected.

(c) If the parties to a transaction creating a purchase money security interest in goods in one jurisdiction understand at the time that the security interest attaches that the goods will be kept in another jurisdiction, then the law of the other jurisdiction governs the perfection and the effect of perfection or non-perfection of the security interest from the time it attaches until thirty days after the debtor receives possession of the goods and thereafter if the goods are taken to the other jurisdiction before the end of the thirty-day period.

(d) When collateral is brought into and kept in this state while subject to a security interest perfected under the law of the jurisdiction from which the collateral was removed, the security interest remains perfected, but if action is required by Part 3 of this Article to perfect the security interest,

(i) if the action is not taken before the expiration of the period of perfection in the other jurisdiction or the end of four months after the collateral is brought into this state, whichever period first expires, the security interest becomes unperfected at the end of that period and is thereafter deemed to have been unperfected as against a person who became a purchaser after removal;

(ii) if the action is taken before the expiration of the period specified in subparagraph (i), the security interest continues perfected thereafter;

(iii) for the purpose of priority over a buyer of consumer goods (subsection (2) of Section 9—307), the period of the effectiveness of a filing in the jurisdiction from which the collateral is removed is governed by the rules with respect to perfection in subparagraphs (i) and (ii).

(2) Certificate of title.

(a) This subsection applies to goods covered by a certificate of title issued under a statute of this state or of another jurisdiction under the law of which indication of a security interest on the certificate is required as a condition of perfection.

(b) Except as otherwise provided in this subsection, perfection and the effect of perfection or non-perfection of the security interest are governed by the law (including the conflict of laws rules) of the jurisdiction issuing the certificate until four months after the goods are removed from that jurisdiction and thereafter until the goods are registered in another jurisdiction, but in any event not beyond surrender of the certificate. After the expiration of that period, the goods are not covered by the certificate of title within the meaning of this section.

(c) Except with respect to the rights of a buyer described in the next paragraph, a security interest, perfected in another jurisdiction otherwise than by notation on a certificate of title, in goods brought into this state and thereafter covered by a certificate of title issued by this state is subject to the rules stated in paragraph (d) of subsection (1).

(d) If goods are brought into this state while a security interest therein is perfected in any manner under the law of the jurisdiction from which the goods are removed and a certificate of title is issued by this state and the certificate does not show that the goods are subject to the security interest or that they may be subject to security interests not shown on the certificate, the security interest is subordinate to the rights of a buyer of the goods who is not in the business of selling goods of that kind to the extent that he gives value and receives delivery of the goods after issuance of the certificate and without knowledge of the security interest.

(3) Accounts, general intangibles and mobile goods.

(a) This subsection applies to accounts (other than an account described in subsection (5) on minerals) and general intangibles (other than uncertificated securities) and to goods which are mobile and which are of a type normally used in more than one jurisdiction, such as motor vehicles, trailers, rolling stock, airplanes, shipping containers, road building and construction machinery and commercial harvesting machinery and the like, if the goods are equipment or are inventory leased or held for lease by the debtor to others, and are not covered by a certificate of title described in subsection (2).

(b) The law (including the conflict of laws rules) of the jurisdiction in which the debtor is located governs the perfection and the effect of perfection or non-perfection of the security interest.

(c) If, however, the debtor is located in a jurisdiction which is not a part of the United States, and which does not provide for perfection of the security interest by filing or recording in that jurisdiction, the law of the jurisdiction in the United States in which the debtor has its major executive office in the United States governs the perfection and the effect of perfection or non-perfection of the security interest through filing. In the alternative, if the debtor is located in a jurisdiction which is not a part of the United States or Canada and the collateral is accounts or general intangibles for money due or to become due, the security interest may be perfected by notification to the account debtor. As used in this paragraph, "United States" includes its territories and possessions and the Commonwealth of Puerto Rico.

(d) A debtor shall be deemed located at his place of business if he has one, at his chief executive office if he has more than one place of business, otherwise at his residence. If, however, the debtor is a foreign air carrier under the Federal Aviation Act of 1958, as amended, it shall be deemed located at the designated office of the agent upon whom service of process may be made on behalf of the foreign air carrier.

(e) A security interest perfected under the law of the jurisdiction of the location of the debtor is perfected until the expiration of four months after a change of the debtor's location to another jurisdiction, or until perfection would have ceased by the law of the first jurisdiction, whichever period first expires. Unless perfected in the new jurisdiction before the end of that period, it becomes unperfected thereafter and is deemed to have been unperfected as against a person who became a purchaser after the change.

(4) Chattel paper.

The rules stated for goods in subsection (1) apply to a possessory security interest in chattel paper. The rules stated for accounts in subsection (3) apply to a non-possessory security interest in chattel paper, but the security interest may not be perfected by notification to the account debtor.

(5) Minerals.

Perfection and the effect of perfection or non-perfection of a security interest which is created by a debtor who has an interest in minerals or the like (including oil and gas) before extraction and which attaches thereto as extracted, or which attaches to an account resulting from the sale thereof at the wellhead or minehead are governed by the law (including the conflict of laws rules) of the jurisdiction wherein the wellhead or minehead is located.

(6) Uncertificated securities.

The law (including the conflict of laws rules) of the jurisdiction of organization of the issuer governs the perfection and the effect of perfection or non-perfection of a security interest in uncertificated securities.

Amended in 1972 and 1977.

§ 9—104. Transactions Excluded From Article.

This Article does not apply

(a) to a security interest subject to any statute of the United States, to the extent that such statute governs the rights of parties to and third parties affected by transactions in particular types of property; or

(b) to a landlord's lien; or

(c) to a lien given by statute or other rule of law for services or materials except as provided in Section 9—310 on priority of such liens; or

(d) to a transfer of a claim for wages, salary or other compensation of an employee; or

(e) to a transfer by a government or governmental subdivision or agency; or

(f) to a sale of accounts or chattel paper as part of a sale of the business out of which they arose, or an assignment of accounts or chattel paper which is for the purpose of collection only, or a transfer of a right to payment under a contract to an assignee who is also to do the performance under the contract or a transfer of a single account to an assignee in whole or partial satisfaction of a preexisting indebtedness; or

(g) to a transfer of an interest in or claim in or under any policy of insurance, except as provided with respect to proceeds (Section 9—306) and priorities in proceeds (Section 9—312); or

(h) to a right represented by a judgment (other than a judgment taken on a right to payment which was collateral); or

(i) to any right of set-off; or

(j) except to the extent that provision is made for fixtures in Section 9—313, to the creation or transfer of an interest in or lien on real estate, including a lease or rents thereunder; or

(k) to a transfer in whole or in part of any claim arising out of tort; or

(l) to a transfer of an interest in any deposit account (subsection (1) of Section 9—105), except as provided with respect to proceeds (Section 9—306) and priorities in proceeds (Section 9—312).

Amended in 1972.

§ 9—105. Definitions and Index of Definitions

(1) In this Article unless the context otherwise requires:

(a) "Account debtor" means the person who is obligated on an account, chattel paper or general intangible;

(b) "Chattel paper" means a writing or writings which evidence both a monetary obligation and a security interest in or a lease of specific goods, but a charter or other contract involving the use or hire of a vessel is not chattel paper. When a transaction is evidenced both by such a security agreement or a lease and by an instrument or a series of instruments, the group of writings taken together constitutes chattel paper;

(c) "Collateral" means the property subject to a security interest, and includes accounts and chattel paper which have been sold;

(d) "Debtor" means the person who owes payment or other performance of the obligation secured, whether or not he owns or has rights in the collateral, and includes the seller of accounts or chattel paper. Where the debtor and the owner of the collateral are not the same person, the term "debtor" means the owner of the collateral in any provision of the Article dealing with the collateral, the obligor in any provision dealing with the obligation, and may include both where the context so requires;

(e) "Deposit account" means a demand, time, savings, passbook or like account maintained with a bank, savings and loan association, credit union or like organization, other than an account evidenced by a certificate of deposit;

(f) "Document" means document of title as defined in the general definitions of Article 1 (Section 1—201), and a receipt of the kind described in subsection (2) of Section 7—201;

(g) "Encumbrance" includes real estate mortgages and other liens on real estate and all other rights in real estate that are not ownership interests;

(h) "Goods" includes all things which are movable at the time the security interest attaches or which are fixtures (Section 9—313), but does not include money, documents, instruments, accounts, chattel paper, general intangibles, or minerals or the like (including oil and gas) before extraction. "Goods" also includes standing timber which is to be cut and removed under a conveyance or contract for sale, the unborn young of animals, and growing crops;

(i) "Instrument" means a negotiable instrument (defined in Section 3—104), or a certificated security (defined in Section 8—102) or any other writing which evidences a right to the payment of money and is not itself a security agreement or lease and is of a type which is in ordinary course of business transferred by delivery with any necessary indorsement or assignment;

(j) "Mortgage" means a consensual interest created by a real estate mortgage, a trust deed on real estate, or the like;

(k) An advance is made "pursuant to commitment" if the secured party has bound himself to make it, whether or not a subsequent event of default or other event not within his control has relieved or may relieve him from his obligation;

(l) "Security agreement" means an agreement which creates or provides for a security interest;

(m) "Secured party" means a lender, seller or other person in whose favor there is a security interest, including a person to whom accounts or chattel paper have been sold. When the holders of obligations issued under an indenture of trust, equipment trust agreement or the like are represented by a trustee or other person, the representative is the secured party;

(n) "Transmitting utility" means any person primarily engaged in the railroad, street railway or trolley bus business, the electric or electronics communications transmission business, the transmission of goods by pipeline, or the transmission or the production and transmission of electricity, steam, gas or water, or the provision of sewer service.

(2) Other definitions applying to this Article and the sections in which they appear are:

"Account". Section 9—106.
"Attach". Section 9—203.
"Construction mortgage". Section 9—313(1).
"Consumer goods". Section 9—109(1).
"Equipment". Section 9—109(2).
"Farm products". Section 9—109(3).
"Fixture". Section 9—313(1).
"Fixture filing". Section 9—313(1).
"General intangibles". Section 9—106.
"Inventory". Section 9—109(4).
"Lien creditor". Section 9—301(3).
"Proceeds". Section 9—306(1).
"Purchase money security interest". Section 9—107.
"United States". Section 9—103.

(3) The following definitions in other Articles apply to this Article:

"Check". Section 3—104.
"Contract for sale". Section 2—106.
"Holder in due course". Section 3—302.
"Note". Section 3—104.
"Sale". Section 2—106.

(4) In addition Article 1 contains general definitions and principles of construction and interpretation applicable throughout this Article.

Amended in 1966, 1972 and 1977.

§ 9—106. Definitions: "Account"; "General Intangibles".

"Account" means any right to payment for goods sold or leased or for services rendered which is not evidenced by an instrument or chattel paper, whether or not it has been earned by performance. "General intangibles" means any personal property (including things in action) other than goods, accounts, chattel paper, documents, instruments, and money. All rights to payment earned or unearned under a charter or other contract involving the use or hire of a vessel and all rights incident to the charter or contract are accounts. Amended in 1966, 1972.

§ 9—107. Definitions: "Purchase Money Security Interest".

A security interest is a "purchase money security interest" to the extent that it is

(a) taken or retained by the seller of the collateral to secure all or part of its price; or

(b) taken by a person who by making advances or incurring an obligation gives value to enable the debtor to acquire rights in or the use of collateral if such value is in fact so used.

§ 9—108. When After-Acquired Collateral Not Security for Antecedent Debt.

Where a secured party makes an advance, incurs an obligation, releases a perfected security interest, or otherwise gives new value which is to be secured in whole or in part by after-acquired property his security interest in the after-acquired collateral shall be deemed to be taken for new value and not as security for an antecedent debt if the debtor acquires his rights in such collateral either in the ordinary course of his business or under a contract of purchase made pursuant to the security agreement within a reasonable time after new value is given.

§ 9—109. Classification of Goods; "Consumer Goods"; "Equipment"; "Farm Products"; "Inventory".

Goods are

(1) "consumer goods" if they are used or bought for use primarily for personal, family or household purposes;

(2) "equipment" if they are used or bought for use primarily in business (including farming or a profession) or by a debtor who is a non-profit organization or a governmental subdivision or agency or if the goods are not included in the definitions of inventory, farm products or consumer goods;

(3) "farm products" if they are crops or livestock or supplies used or produced in farming operations or if they are products of crops or livestock in their unmanufactured states (such as ginned cotton, wool-clip, maple syrup, milk and eggs), and if they are in the possession of a debtor engaged in raising, fattening, grazing or other farming operations. If goods are farm products they are neither equipment nor inventory;

(4) "inventory" if they are held by a person who holds them for sale or lease or to be furnished under contracts of service or if he has so furnished them, or if they are raw materials, work in process or materials used or consumed in a business. Inventory of a person is not to be classified as his equipment.

§ 9—110. Sufficiency of Description.

For purposes of this Article any description of personal property or real estate is sufficient whether or not it is specific if it reasonably identifies what is described.

§ 9—111. Applicability of Bulk Transfer Laws.

The creation of a security interest is not a bulk transfer under Article 6 (see Section 6—103).

§ 9—112. Where Collateral Is Not Owned by Debtor.

Unless otherwise agreed, when a secured party knows that collateral is owned by a person who is not the debtor, the owner of the collateral is entitled to receive from the secured party any surplus under Section 9—502(2) or under Section 9—504(1), and is not liable for the debt or for any deficiency after resale, and he has the same right as the debtor

(a) to receive statements under Section 9—208;

(b) to receive notice of and to object to a secured party's proposal to retain the collateral in satisfaction of the indebtedness under Section 9—505;

(c) to redeem the collateral under Section 9—506;

(d) to obtain injunctive or other relief under Section 9—507(1); and

(e) to recover losses caused to him under Section 9—208(2).

§ 9—113. Security Interests Arising Under Article on Sales.

A security interest arising solely under the Article on Sales (Article 2) is subject to the provisions of this Article except that to the extent that and so long as the debtor does not have or does not lawfully obtain possession of the goods

(a) no security agreement is necessary to make the security interest enforceable; and

(b) no filing is required to perfect the security interest; and

(c) the rights of the secured party on default by the debtor are governed by the Article on Sales (Article 2).

§ 9—114. Consignment.

(1) A person who delivers goods under a consignment which is not a security interest and who would be required to file under this Article by paragraph (3) (c) of Section 2—326 has priority over a secured party who is or becomes a creditor of the consignee and who would have a perfected security interest in the goods if they were the property of the consignee, and also has priority with respect to identifiable cash proceeds received on or before delivery of the goods to a buyer, if

(a) the consignor complies with the filing provision of the Article on Sales with respect to consignments (paragraph (3) (c) of Section 2—326) before the consignee receives possession of the goods; and

(b) the consignor gives notification in writing to the holder of the security interest if the holder has filed a financing statement covering the same types of goods before the date of the filing made by the consignor; and

(c) the holder of the security interest receives the notification within five years before the consignee receives possession of the goods; and

(d) the notification states that the consignor expects to deliver goods on consignment to the consignee, describing the goods by item or type.

(2) In the case of a consignment which is not a security interest and in which the requirements of the preceding subsection have not been met, a person who delivers goods to another is subordinate to a person who would have a perfected security interest in the goods if they were the property of the debtor. Added in 1972.

Part 2 Validity of Security Agreement and Rights of Parties Thereto

§ 9—201. General Validity of Security Agreement.

Except as otherwise provided by this Act a security agreement is effective according to its terms between the parties, against purchasers of the collateral and against creditors. Nothing in this Article validates any charge or practice illegal under any statute or regulation thereunder governing usury, small loans, retail installment sales, or the like, or extends the application of any such statute or regulation to any transaction not otherwise subject thereto.

§ 9—202. Title to Collateral Immaterial.

Each provision of this Article with regard to rights, obligations and remedies applies whether title to collateral is in the secured party or in the debtor.

§ 9—203. Attachment and Enforceability of Security Interest; Proceeds; Formal Requisites

(1) Subject to the provisions of Section 4—208 on the security interest of a collecting bank, Section 8—321 on security interests in securities and Section 9—113 on a security interest arising under the Article on Sales, a security interest is not enforceable against the debtor or third parties with respect to the collateral and does not attach unless:

(a) the collateral is in the possession of the secured party pursuant to agreement, or the debtor has signed a security agreement which contains a description of the collateral and in addition, when the security interest covers crops growing or to be grown or timber to be cut, a description of the land concerned;

(b) value has been given; and

(c) the debtor has rights in the collateral.

(2) A security interest attaches when it becomes enforceable against the debtor with respect to the collateral. Attachment occurs as soon as all of the events specified in subsection (1) have taken place unless explicit agreement postpones the time of attaching.

(3) Unless otherwise agreed a security agreement gives the secured party the rights to proceeds provided by Section 9—306.

(4) A transaction, although subject to this Article, is also subject to .... *, and in the case of conflict between the provisions of this Article and any such statute, the provisions of such statute control. Failure to comply with any applicable statute has only the effect which is specified therein.

Amended in 1972 and 1977.

Note: *At * in subsection (4) insert reference to any local statute regulating small loans, retail installment sales and the like.*

The foregoing subsection (4) is designed to make it clear that certain transactions, although subject to this Article, must also comply with other applicable legislation.

This Article is designed to regulate all the "security" aspects of transactions within its scope. There is, however, much regulatory legislation, particularly in the consumer field, which supplements this Article and should not be repealed by its enactment. Examples are small loan acts, retail installment selling acts and the like. Such acts may provide for licensing and rate regulation and may prescribe particular forms of contract. Such provisions should remain in force despite the enactment of this Article. On the other hand if a retail installment selling act contains provisions on filing, rights on default, etc., such provisions should be repealed as inconsistent with this Article except that inconsistent provisions as to deficiencies, penalties, etc., in the Uniform Consumer Credit Code and other recent related legislation should remain because those statutes were drafted after the substantial enactment of the Article and with the intention of modifying certain provisions of this Article as to consumer credit.

§ 9—204. After-Acquired Property; Future Advances.

(1) Except as provided in subsection (2), a security agreement may provide that any or all obligations covered by the security agreement are to be secured by after-acquired collateral.

(2) No security interest attaches under an after-acquired property clause to consumer goods other than accessions (Section 9—314) when given as additional security unless the debtor acquires rights in them within ten days after the secured party gives value.

(3) Obligations covered by a security agreement may include future advances or other value whether or not the advances or value are given pursuant to commitment (subsection (1) of Section 9—105). Amended in 1972.

§ 9—205. Use or Disposition of Collateral Without Accounting Permissible.

A security interest is not invalid or fraudulent against creditors by reason of liberty in the debtor to use, commingle or dispose of all or part of the collateral (including returned or repossessed goods) or to collect or compromise accounts or chattel paper, or to accept the return of goods or make repossessions, or to use, commingle or dispose of proceeds, or by reason of the failure of the secured party to require the debtor to account for proceeds or replace collateral. This section does not relax the requirements of possession where perfection of a security interest depends upon possession of the collateral by the secured party or by a bailee. Amended in 1972.

§ 9—206. Agreement Not to Assert Defenses Against Assignee; Modification of Sales Warranties Where Security Agreement Exists.

(1) Subject to any statute or decision which establishes a different rule for buyers or lessees of consumer goods, an agreement by a buyer or lessee that he will not assert against an assignee any claim or defense which he may have against the seller or lessor is enforceable by an assignee who takes his assignment for value, in good faith and without notice of a claim or defense, except as to defenses of a type which may be asserted against a holder in due course of a negotiable instrument under the Article on Commercial Paper (Article 3). A buyer who as part of one transaction signs both a negotiable instrument and a security agreement makes such an agreement.

(2) When a seller retains a purchase money security interest in goods the Article on Sales (Article 2) governs the sale and any disclaimer, limitation or modification of the seller's warranties. Amended in 1962.

§ 9—207. Rights and Duties When Collateral is in Secured Party's Possession.

(1) A secured party must use reasonable care in the custody and preservation of collateral in his possession. In the case of an instrument or chattel paper reasonable care includes taking necessary steps to preserve rights against prior parties unless otherwise agreed.

(2) Unless otherwise agreed, when collateral is in the secured party's possession

(a) reasonable expenses (including the cost of any insurance and payment of taxes or other charges) incurred in the custody, preservation, use or operation of the collateral are chargeable to the debtor and are secured by the collateral;

(b) the risk of accidental loss or damage is on the debtor to the extent of any deficiency in any effective insurance coverage;

(c) the secured party may hold as additional security any increase or profits (except money) received from the collateral, but money so received, unless remitted to the debtor, shall be applied in reduction of the secured obligation;

(d) the secured party must keep the collateral identifiable but fungible collateral may be commingled;

(e) the secured party may repledge the collateral upon terms which do not impair the debtor's right to redeem it.

(3) A secured party is liable for any loss caused by his failure to meet any obligation imposed by the preceding subsections but does not lose his security interest.

(4) A secured party may use or operate the collateral for the purpose of preserving the collateral or its value or pursuant to the order of a court of appropriate jurisdiction or, except in the case of consumer goods, in the manner and to the extent provided in the security agreement.

§ 9—208. Request for Statement of Account or List of Collateral.

(1) A debtor may sign a statement indicating what he believes to be the aggregate amount of unpaid indebtedness as of a specified date and may send it to the secured party with a request that the statement be approved or corrected and returned to the debtor. When the security agreement or any other record kept

by the secured party identifies the collateral a debtor may similarly request the secured party to approve or correct a list of the collateral.

(2) The secured party must comply with such a request within two weeks after receipt by sending a written correction or approval. If the secured party claims a security interest in all of a particular type of collateral owned by the debtor he may indicate that fact in his reply and need not approve or correct an itemized list of such collateral. If the secured party without reasonable excuse fails to comply he is liable for any loss caused to the debtor thereby; and if the debtor has properly included in his request a good faith statement of the obligation or a list of the collateral or both the secured party may claim a security interest only as shown in the statement against persons misled by his failure to comply. If he no longer has an interest in the obligation or collateral at the time the request is received he must disclose the name and address of any successor in interest known to him and he is liable for any loss caused to the debtor as a result of failure to disclose. A successor in interest is not subject to this section until a request is received by him.

(3) A debtor is entitled to such a statement once every six months without charge. The secured party may require payment of a charge not exceeding $10 for each additional statement furnished.

Part 3 Rights of Third Parties; Perfected and Unperfected Security Interests; Rules of Priority

§ 9—301. Persons Who Take Priority Over Unperfected Security Interests; Rights of "Lien Creditor".

(1) Except as otherwise provided in subsection (2), an unperfected security interest is subordinate to the rights of

(a) persons entitled to priority under Section 9—312;

(b) a person who becomes a lien creditor before the security interest is perfected;

(c) in the case of goods, instruments, documents, and chattel paper, a person who is not a secured party and who is a transferee in bulk or other buyer not in ordinary course of business or is a buyer of farm products in ordinary course of business, to the extent that he gives value and receives delivery of the collateral without knowledge of the security interest and before it is perfected;

(d) in the case of accounts and general intangibles, a person who is not a secured party and who is a transferee to the extent that he gives value without knowledge of the security interest and before it is perfected.

(2) If the secured party files with respect to a purchase money security interest before or within ten days after the debtor receives possession of the collateral, he takes priority over the rights of a transferee in bulk or of a lien creditor which arise between the time the security interest attaches and the time of filing.

(3) A "lien creditor" means a creditor who has acquired a lien on the property involved by attachment, levy or the like and includes an assignee for benefit of creditors from the time of assignment, and a trustee in bankruptcy from the date of the filing of the petition or a receiver in equity from the time of appointment.

(4) A person who becomes a lien creditor while a security interest is perfected takes subject to the security interest only to the extent that it secures advances made before he becomes a lien creditor or within 45 days thereafter or made without knowledge of the lien or pursuant to a commitment entered into without knowledge of the lien. Amended in 1972.

§ 9—302. When Filing Is Required to Perfect Security Interest; Security Interests to Which Filing Provisions of This Article Do Not Apply

(1) A financing statement must be filed to perfect all security interests except the following:

(a) a security interest in collateral in possession of the secured party under Section 9—305;

(b) a security interest temporarily perfected in instruments or documents without delivery under Section 9—304 or in proceeds for a 10 day period under Section 9—306;

(c) a security interest created by an assignment of a beneficial interest in a trust or a decedent's estate;

(d) a purchase money security interest in consumer goods; but filing is required for a motor vehicle required to be registered; and fixture filing is required for priority over conflicting interests in fixtures to the extent provided in Section 9—313;

(e) an assignment of accounts which does not alone or in conjunction with other assignments to the same assignee transfer a significant part of the outstanding accounts of the assignor;

(f) a security interest of a collecting bank (Section 4—208) or in securities (Section 8—321) or arising under the Article on Sales (see Section 9—113) or covered in subsection (3) of this section;

(g) an assignment for the benefit of all the creditors of the transferor, and subsequent transfers by the assignee thereunder.

(2) If a secured party assigns a perfected security interest, no filing under this Article is required in order to continue the perfected status of the security interest against creditors of and transferees from the original debtor.

(3) The filing of a financing statement otherwise required by this Article is not necessary or effective to perfect a security interest in property subject to

(a) a statute or treaty of the United States which provides for a national or international registration or a national or international certificate of title or which specifies a place of filing different from that specified in this Article for filing of the security interest; or

(b) the following statutes of this state; [list any certificate of title statute covering automobiles, trailers, mobile homes, boats, farm tractors, or the like, and any central filing statute.]; but during any period in which collateral is inventory held for sale by a person who is in the business of selling goods of that kind, the filing provisions of this Article (Part 4) apply to a security interest in that collateral created by him as debtor; or

(c) a certificate of title statute of another jurisdiction under the law of which indication of a security interest on the certificate is required as a condition of perfection (subsection (2) of Section 9—103).

(4) Compliance with a statute or treaty described in subsection (3) is equivalent to the filing of a financing statement under this Article, and a security interest in property subject to the statute or treaty can be perfected only by compliance therewith except as provided in Section 9—103 on multiple state transactions. Duration and renewal of perfection of a security interest perfected by compliance with the statute or treaty are governed by the provisions of the statute or treaty; in other respects the security interest is subject to this Article.

Amended in 1972 and 1977.

§ 9—303. When Security Interest Is Perfected; Continuity of Perfection.

(1) A security interest is perfected when it has attached and when all of the applicable steps required for perfection have been taken. Such steps are specified in Sections 9—302, 9—304, 9—305 and 9—306. If such steps are taken before the security interest attaches, it is perfected at the time when it attaches.

(2) If a security interest is originally perfected in any way permitted under this Article and is subsequently perfected in some other way under this Article, without an intermediate period when it was unperfected, the security interest shall be deemed to be perfected continuously for the purposes of this Article.

§ 9—304. Perfection of Security Interest in Instruments, Documents, and Goods Covered by Documents; Perfection by Permissive Filing; Temporary Perfection Without Filing or Transfer of Possession

(1) A security interest in chattel paper or negotiable documents may be perfected by filing. A security interest in money or instruments (other than certificated securities or instruments which constitute part of chattel paper) can be perfected only by the secured party's taking possession, except as provided in subsections (4) and (5) of this section and subsections (2) and (3) of Section 9—306 on proceeds.

(2) During the period that goods are in the possession of the issuer of a negotiable document therefor, a security interest in the goods is perfected by perfecting a security interest in the document, and any security interest in the goods otherwise perfected during such period is subject thereto.

(3) A security interest in goods in the possession of a bailee other than one who has issued a negotiable document therefor is perfected by issuance of a document in the name of the secured party or by the bailee's receipt of notification of the secured party's interest or by filing as to the goods.

(4) A security interest in instruments (other than certificated securities) or negotiable documents is perfected without filing or the taking of possession for a period of 21 days from the time it attaches to the extent that it arises for new value given under a written security agreement.

(5) A security interest remains perfected for a period of 21 days without filing where a secured party having a perfected security interest in an instrument (other than a certificated security), a negotiable document or goods in possession of a bailee other than one who has issued a negotiable document therefor

(a) makes available to the debtor the goods or documents representing the goods for the purpose of ultimate sale or exchange or for the purpose of loading, unloading, storing, shipping, transshipping, manufacturing, processing or otherwise dealing with them in a manner preliminary to their sale or exchange, but priority between conflicting security interests in the goods is subject to subsection (3) of Section 9—312; or

(b) delivers the instrument to the debtor for the purpose of ultimate sale or exchange or of presentation, collection, renewal or registration of transfer.

(6) After the 21 day period in subsections (4) and (5) perfection depends upon compliance with applicable provisions of this Article.

Amended in 1972 and 1977.

§ 9—305. When Possession by Secured Party Perfects Security Interest Without Filing

A security interest in letters of credit and advices of credit (subsection (2) (a) of Section 5—116), goods, instruments (other than certificated securities), money, negotiable documents, or chattel paper may be perfected by the secured party's taking possession of the collateral. If such collateral other than goods covered by a negotiable document is held by a bailee, the secured party is deemed to have possession from the time the bailee receives notification of the secured party's interest. A security interest is perfected by possession from the time possession is taken without a relation back and continues only so long as possession is retained, unless otherwise specified in this Article. The security interest may be otherwise perfected as provided in this Article before or after the period of possession by the secured party.
Amended in 1972 and 1977.

§ 9—306. "Proceeds"; Secured Party's Rights on Disposition of Collateral.

(1) "Proceeds" includes whatever is received upon the sale, exchange, collection or other disposition of collateral or proceeds. Insurance payable by reason of loss or damage to the collateral is proceeds, except to the extent that it is payable to a person other than a party to the security agreement. Money, checks, deposit accounts, and the like are "cash proceeds". All other proceeds are "non-cash proceeds".

(2) Except where this Article otherwise provides, a security interest continues in collateral notwithstanding sale, exchange or other disposition thereof unless the disposition was authorized by the secured party in the security agreement or otherwise, and also continues in any identifiable proceeds including collections received by the debtor.

(3) The security interest in proceeds is a continuously perfected security interest if the interest in the original collateral was perfected but it ceases to be a perfected security interest and becomes unperfected ten days after receipt of the proceeds by the debtor unless

(a) a filed financing statement covers the original collateral and the proceeds are collateral in which a security interest may be perfected by filing in the office or offices where the financing statement has been filed and, if the proceeds are acquired with cash proceeds, the description of collateral in the financing statement indicates the types of property constituting the proceeds; or

(b) a filed financing statement covers the original collateral and the proceeds are identifiable cash proceeds; or

(c) the security interest in the proceeds is perfected before the expiration of the ten day period.

Except as provided in this section, a security interest in proceeds can be perfected only by the methods or under the circumstances permitted in this Article for original collateral of the same type.

(4) In the event of insolvency proceedings instituted by or against a debtor, a secured party with a perfected security interest in proceeds has a perfected security interest only in the following proceeds:

(a) in identifiable non-cash proceeds and in separate deposit accounts containing only proceeds;

(b) in identifiable cash proceeds in the form of money which is neither commingled with other money nor deposited in a deposit account prior to the insolvency proceedings;

(c) in identifiable cash proceeds in the form of checks and the like which are not deposited in a deposit account prior to the insolvency proceedings; and

(d) in all cash and deposit accounts of the debtor in which proceeds have been commingled with other funds, but the perfected security interest under this paragraph (d) is

(i) subject to any right to set-off; and

(ii) limited to an amount not greater than the amount of any cash proceeds received by the debtor within ten days before the institution of the insolvency proceedings less the sum of (I) the payments to the secured party on account of cash proceeds received by the debtor during such period and (II) the cash proceeds received by the debtor during such period to which the secured party is entitled under paragraphs (a) through (c) of this subsection (4).

(5) If a sale of goods results in an account or chattel paper which is transferred by the seller to a secured party, and if the goods are returned to or are repossessed by the seller or the secured party, the following rules determine priorities:

(a) If the goods were collateral at the time of sale, for an indebtedness of the seller which is still unpaid, the original security interest attaches again to the goods and continues as a perfected security interest if it was perfected at the time when the goods were sold. If the security interest was originally perfected by a filing which is still effective, nothing further is required to continue the perfected status; in any other case, the secured party must take possession of the returned or repossessed goods or must file.

(b) An unpaid transferee of the chattel paper has a security interest in the goods against the transferor. Such security interest is prior to a security interest asserted under paragraph (a) to the extent that the transferee of the chattel paper was entitled to priority under Section 9—308.

(c) An unpaid transferee of the account has a security interest in the goods against the transferor. Such security interest is subordinate to a security interest asserted under paragraph (a).

(d) A security interest of an unpaid transferee asserted under paragraph (b) or (c) must be perfected for protection against creditors of the transferor and purchasers of the returned or repossessed goods.

Amended in 1972.

§ 9—307. **Protection of Buyers of Goods.**

(1) A buyer in ordinary course of business (subsection (9) of Section 1—201) other than a person buying farm products from a person engaged in farming operations takes free of a security interest created by his seller even though the security interest is perfected and even though the buyer knows of its existence.

(2) In the case of consumer goods, a buyer takes free of a security interest even though perfected if he buys without knowledge of the security interest, for value and for his own personal, family or household purposes unless prior to the purchase the secured party has filed a financing statement covering such goods.

(3) A buyer other than a buyer in ordinary course of business (subsection (1) of this section) takes free of a security interest to the extent that it secures future advances made after the secured party acquires knowledge of the purchase, or more than 45 days after the purchase, whichever first occurs, unless made pursuant to a commitment entered into without knowledge of the purchase and before the expiration of the 45 day period. Amended in 1972.

§ 9—308. **Purchase of Chattel Paper and Instruments.**

A purchaser of chattel paper or an instrument who gives new value and takes possession of it in the ordinary course of his business has priority over a security interest in the chattel paper or instrument

(a) which is perfected under Section 9—304 (permissive filing and temporary perfection) or under Section 9—306 (perfection as to proceeds) if he acts without knowledge that the specific paper or instrument is subject to a security interest; or

(b) which is claimed merely as proceeds of inventory subject to a security interest (Section 9—306) even though he knows that the specific paper or instrument is subject to the security interest.

Amended in 1972.

§ 9—309. **Protection of Purchasers of Instruments, Documents and Securities**

Nothing in this Article limits the rights of a holder in due course of a negotiable instrument (Section 3—302) or a holder to whom a negotiable document of title has been duly negotiated (Section 7—501) or a bona fide purchaser of a security (Section 8—302) and the holders or purchasers take priority over an earlier security interest even though perfected. Filing under this Article does not constitute notice of the security interest to such holders or purchasers.

Amended in 1977.

§ 9—310. **Priority of Certain Liens Arising by Operation of Law.**

When a person in the ordinary course of his business furnishes services or materials with respect to goods subject to a security interest, a lien upon goods in the possession of such person given by statute or rule of law for such materials or services takes priority over a perfected security interest unless the lien is statutory and the statute expressly provides otherwise.

§ 9—311. **Alienability of Debtor's Rights: Judicial Process.**

The debtor's rights in collateral may be voluntarily or involuntarily transferred (by way of sale, creation of a security interest, attachment, levy, garnishment or other judicial process) notwithstanding a provision in the security agreement prohibiting any transfer or making the transfer constitute a default.

§ 9—312. Priorities Among Conflicting Security Interests in the Same Collateral

(1) The rules of priority stated in other sections of this Part and in the following sections shall govern when applicable: Section 4—208 with respect to the security interests of collecting banks in items being collected, accompanying documents and proceeds; Section 9—103 on security interests related to other jurisdictions; Section 9—114 on consignments.

(2) A perfected security interest in crops for new value given to enable the debtor to produce the crops during the production season and given not more than three months before the crops become growing crops by planting or otherwise takes priority over an earlier perfected security interest to the extent that such earlier interest secures obligations due more than six months before the crops become growing crops by planting or otherwise, even though the person giving new value had knowledge of the earlier security interest.

(3) A perfected purchase money security interest in inventory has priority over a conflicting security interest in the same inventory and also has priority in identifiable cash proceeds received on or before the delivery of the inventory to a buyer if

(a) the purchase money security interest is perfected at the time the debtor receives possession of the inventory; and

(b) the purchase money secured party gives notification in writing to the holder of the conflicting security interest if the holder had filed a financing statement covering the same types of inventory (i) before the date of the filing made by the purchase money secured party, or (ii) before the beginning of the 21 day period where the purchase money security interest is temporarily perfected without filing or possession (subsection (5) of Section 9—304); and

(c) the holder of the conflicting security interest receives the notification within five years before the debtor receives possession of the inventory; and

(d) the notification states that the person giving the notice has or expects to acquire a purchase money security interest in inventory of the debtor, describing such inventory by item or type.

(4) A purchase money security interest in collateral other than inventory has priority over a conflicting security interest in the same collateral or its proceeds if the purchase money security interest is perfected at the time the debtor receives possession of the collateral or within ten days thereafter.

(5) In all cases not governed by other rules stated in this section (including cases of purchase money security interests which do not qualify for the special priorities set forth in subsections (3) and (4) of this section), priority between conflicting security interests in the same collateral shall be determined according to the following rules:

(a) Conflicting security interests rank according to priority in time of filing or perfection. Priority dates from the time a filing is first made covering the collateral or the time the security interest is first perfected, whichever is earlier, provided that there is no period thereafter when there is neither filing nor perfection.

(b) So long as conflicting security interests are unperfected, the first to attach has priority.

(6) For the purposes of subsection (5) a date of filing or perfection as to collateral is also a date of filing or perfection as to proceeds.

(7) If future advances are made while a security interest is perfected by filing, the taking of possession, or under Section 8—321 on securities, the security interest has the same priority for the purposes of subsection (5) with respect to the future advances as it does with respect to the first advance. If a commitment is made before or while the security interest is so perfected, the security interest has the same priority with respect to advances made pursuant thereto. In other cases a perfected security interest has priority from the date the advance is made.

Amended in 1972 and 1977.

§ 9—313. Priority of Security Interests in Fixtures.

(1) In this section and in the provisions of Part 4 of this Article referring to fixture filing, unless the context otherwise requires

(a) goods are "fixtures" when they become so related to particular real estate that an interest in them arises under real estate law

(b) a "fixture filing" is the filing in the office where a mortgage on the real estate would be filed or recorded of a financing statement covering goods which are or are to become fixtures and conforming to the requirements of subsection (5) of Section 9—402

(c) a mortgage is a "construction mortgage" to the extent that it secures an obligation incurred for the construction of an improvement on land including the acquisition cost of the land, if the recorded writing so indicates.

(2) A security interest under this Article may be created in goods which are fixtures or may continue in goods which become fixtures, but no security interest exists under this Article in ordinary building materials incorporated into an improvement on land.

(3) This Article does not prevent creation of an encumbrance upon fixtures pursuant to real estate law.

(4) A perfected security interest in fixtures has priority over the conflicting interest of an encumbrancer or owner of the real estate where

(a) the security interest is a purchase money security interest, the interest of the encumbrancer or owner arises before the goods become fixtures, the security interest is perfected by a fixture filing before the goods become fixtures or within ten days thereafter, and the debtor has an interest of record in the real estate or is in possession of the real estate; or

(b) the security interest is perfected by a fixture filing before the interest of the encumbrancer or owner is of record, the security interest has priority over any conflicting interest of a predecessor in title of the encumbrancer or owner, and the debtor has an interest of record in the real estate or is in possession of the real estate; or

(c) the fixtures are readily removable factory or office machines or readily removable replacements of domestic applicances which are consumer goods, and before the goods become fixtures the security interest is perfected by any method permitted by this Article; or

(d) the conflicting interest is a lien on the real estate obtained by legal or equitable proceedings after the security interest was perfected by any method permitted by this Article.

(5) A security interest in fixtures, whether or not perfected, has priority over the conflicting interest of an encumbrancer or owner of the real estate where

(a) the encumbrancer or owner has consented in writing to the security interest or has disclaimed an interest in the goods as fixtures; or

(b) the debtor has a right to remove the goods as against the encumbrancer or owner. If the debtor's right terminates, the priority of the security interest continues for a reasonable time.

(6) Notwithstanding paragraph (a) of subsection (4) but otherwise subject to subsections (4) and (5), a security interest in fixtures is subordinate to a construction mortgage recorded before the goods become fixtures if the goods become fixtures before the completion of the construction. To the extent that it is given to refinance a construction mortgage, a mortgage has this priority to the same extent as the construction mortgage.

(7) In cases not within the preceding subsections, a security interest in fixtures is subordinate to the conflicting interest of an encumbrancer or owner of the related real estate who is not the debtor.

(8) When the secured party has priority over all owners and encumbrancers of the real estate, he may, on default, subject to the provisions of Part 5, remove his collateral from the real estate but he must reimburse any encumbrancer or owner of the real estate who is not the debtor and who has not otherwise agreed for the cost of repair of any physical injury, but not for any diminution in value of the real estate caused by the absence of the goods removed or by any necessity of replacing them. A person entitled to reimbursement may refuse permission to remove until the secured party gives adequate security for the performance of this obligation. Amended in 1972.

§ 9—314. **Accessions.**

(1) A security interest in goods which attaches before they are installed in or affixed to other goods takes priority as to the goods installed or affixed (called in this section "accessions") over the claims of all persons to the whole except as stated in subsection (3) and subject to Section 9—315(1).

(2) A security interest which attaches to goods after they become part of a whole is valid against all persons subsequently acquiring interests in the whole except as stated in subsection (3) but is invalid against any person with an interest in the whole at the time the security interest attaches to the goods who has not in writing consented to the security interest or disclaimed an interest in the goods as part of the whole.

(3) The security interests described in subsections (1) and (2) do not take priority over

(a) a subsequent purchaser for value of any interest in the whole; or

(b) a creditor with a lien on the whole subsequently obtained by judicial proceedings; or

(c) a creditor with a prior perfected security interest in the whole to the extent that he makes subsequent advances

if the subsequent purchase is made, the lien by judicial proceedings obtained or the subsequent advance under the prior perfected security interest is made or contracted for without knowledge of the security interest and before it is perfected. A purchaser of the whole at a foreclosure sale other than the holder of a perfected security interest purchasing at his own foreclosure sale is a subsequent purchaser within this section.

(4) When under subsections (1) or (2) and (3) a secured party has an interest in accessions which has priority over the claims of all persons who have interests in the whole, he may on default subject to the provisions of Part 5 remove his collateral from the whole but he must reimburse any encumbrancer or owner of the whole who is not the debtor and who has not otherwise agreed for the cost of repair of any physical injury but not for any diminution in value of the whole caused by the absence of the goods removed or by any necessity for replacing them. A person entitled to reimbursement may refuse permission to remove until the secured party gives adequate security for the performance of this obligation.

§ 9—315. Priority When Goods Are Commingled or Processed.

(1) If a security interest in goods was perfected and subsequently the goods or a part thereof have become part of a product or mass, the security interest continues in the product or mass if

(a) the goods are so manufactured, processed, assembled or commingled that their identity is lost in the product or mass; or

(b) a financing statement covering the original goods also covers the product into which the goods have been manufactured, processed or assembled.

In a case to which paragraph (b) applies, no separate security interest in that part of the original goods which has been manufactured, processed or assembled into the product may be claimed under Section 9—314.

(2) When under subsection (1) more than one security interest attaches to the product or mass, they rank equally according to the ratio that the cost of the goods to which each interest originally attached bears to the cost of the total product or mass.

§ 9—316. Priority Subject to Subordination.

Nothing in this Article prevents subordination by agreement by any person entitled to priority.

§ 9—317. Secured Party Not Obligated on Contract of Debtor.

The mere existence of a security interest or authority given to the debtor to dispose of or use collateral does not impose contract or tort liability upon the secured party for the debtor's acts or omissions.

§ 9—318. Defenses Against Assignee; Modification of Contract After Notification of Assignment; Term Prohibiting Assignment Ineffective; Identification and Proof of Assignment.

(1) Unless an account debtor has made an enforceable agreement not to assert defenses or claims arising out of a sale as provided in Section 9—206 the rights of an assignee are subject to

(a) all the terms of the contract between the account debtor and assignor and any defense or claim arising therefrom; and

(b) any other defense or claim of the account debtor against the assignor which accrues before the account debtor receives notification of the assignment.

(2) So far as the right to payment or a part thereof under an assigned contract has not been fully earned by performance, and notwithstanding notification of the assignment, any modification of or substitution for the contract made in good faith and in accordance with reasonable commercial standards is effective against an assignee unless the account debtor has otherwise agreed but the assignee acquires corresponding rights under the modified or substituted contract. The assignment may provide that such modification or substitution is a breach by the assignor.

(3) The account debtor is authorized to pay the assignor until the account debtor receives notification that the amount due or to become due has been assigned and that payment is to be made to the assignee. A notification which does not reasonably identify the rights assigned is ineffective. If requested by the account debtor, the assignee must seasonably furnish reasonable proof that the assignment has been made and unless he does so the account debtor may pay the assignor.

(4) A term in any contract between an account debtor and an assignor is ineffective if it prohibits assignment of an account or prohibits creation of a security interest in a general intangible for money due or to become due or requires the account debtor's consent to such assignment or security interest. Amended in 1972.

Part 4 Filing

§ 9—401. Place of Filing; Erroneous Filing; Removal of Collateral.

First Alternative Subsection (1)

(1) The proper place to file in order to perfect a security interest is as follows:

(a) when the collateral is timber to be cut or is minerals or the like (including oil and gas) or accounts subject to subsection (5) of Section 9—103, or when the financing statement is filed as a fixture filing (Section 9—313) and the collateral is goods which are or are to become fixtures, then in the office where a mortgage on the real estate would be filed or recorded;

(b) in all other cases, in the office of the [Secretary of State].

Second Alternative Subsection (1)

(1) The proper place to file in order to perfect a security interest is as follows:

(a) when the collateral is equipment used in farming operations, or farm products, or accounts or general intangibles arising from or relating to the sale of farm products by a farmer, or consumer goods, then in the office of the . . . . in the county of the debtor's residence or if the debtor is not a resident of this state then in the office of the . . . . in the county where the goods are kept, and in addition when the collateral is crops growing or to be grown in the office of the . . . . in the county where the land is located;

(b) when the collateral is timber to be cut or is minerals or the like (including oil and gas) or accounts subject to subsection (5) of Section 9—103, or when the financing statement is filed as a fixture filing (Section 9—313) and the collateral is goods which are or are to become fixtures, then in the office where a mortgage on the real estate would be filed or recorded;

(c) in all other cases, in the office of the [Secretary of State].

Third Alternative Subsection (1)

(1) The proper place to file in order to perfect a security interest is as follows:

(a) when the collateral is equipment used in farming operations, or farm products, or accounts or general intangibles arising from or relating to the sale of farm products by a farmer, or consumer goods, then in the office of the . . . . in the county of the debtor's residence or if the debtor is not a resident of this state then in the office of the . . . . in the county where the goods are kept, and in addition when the collateral is crops growing or to be grown in the office of the . . . . in the county where the land is located;

(b) when the collateral is timber to be cut or is minerals or the like (including oil and gas) or accounts subject to subsection (5) of Section

9—103, or when the financing statement is filed as a fixture filing (Section 9—313) and the collateral is goods which are or are to become fixtures, then in the office where a mortgage on the real estate would be filed or recorded;

(c) in all other cases, in the office of the [Secretary of State] and in addition, if the debtor has a place of business in only one county of this state, also in the office of . . . . of such county, or, if the debtor has no place of business in this state, but resides in the state, also in the office of . . . . of the county in which he resides.

Note: *One of the three alternatives should be selected as subsection (1).*

(2) A filing which is made in good faith in an improper place or not in all of the places required by this section is nevertheless effective with regard to any collateral as to which the filing complied with the requirements of this Article and is also effective with regard to collateral covered by the financing statement against any person who has knowledge of the contents of such financing statement.

(3) A filing which is made in the proper place in this state continues effective even though the debtor's residence or place of business or the location of the collateral or its use, whichever controlled the original filing, is thereafter changed.

Alternative Subsection (3)

[(3) A filing which is made in the proper county continues effective for four months after a change to another county of the debtor's residence or place of business or the location of the collateral, whichever controlled the original filing. It becomes ineffective thereafter unless a copy of the financing statement signed by the secured party is filed in the new county within said period. The security interest may also be perfected in the new county after the expiration of the four-month period; in such case perfection dates from the time of perfection in the new county. A change in the use of the collateral does not impair the effectiveness of the original filing.]

(4) The rules stated in Section 9—103 determine whether filing is necessary in this state.

(5) Notwithstanding the preceding subsections, and subject to subsection (3) of Section 9—302, the proper place to file in order to perfect a security interest in collateral, including fixtures, of a transmitting utility is the office of the [Secretary of State]. This filing constitutes a fixture filing (Section 9—313) as to the collateral described therein which is or is to become fixtures.

(6) For the purposes of this section, the residence of an organization is its place of business if it has one or its chief executive office if it has more than one place of business. Amended in 1962 and 1972.

Note: *Subsection (6) should be used only if the state chooses the Second or Third Alternative Subsection (1).*

§ 9—402. Formal Requisites of Financing Statement; Amendments; Mortgage as Financing Statement.

(1) A financing statement is sufficient if it gives the names of the debtor and the secured party, is signed by the debtor, gives an address of the secured party from which information concerning the security interest may be obtained, gives a mailing address of the debtor and contains a statement indicating the types, or describing the items, of collateral. A financing statement may be filed before a security agreement is made or a security interest otherwise attaches. When the financing statement covers crops growing or to be grown, the statement must also contain a description of the real estate concerned. When the financing statement covers timber to be cut or covers minerals or the like (including oil and gas) or accounts subject to subsection (5) of Section 9—103, or when the financing statement is filed as a fixture filing (Section 9—313) and the collateral is goods which are or are to become fixtures, the statement must also comply with subsection (5). A copy of the security agreement is sufficient as a financing statement if it contains the above information and is signed by the debtor. A carbon, photographic or other reproduction of a security agreement or a financing statement is sufficient as a financing statement if the security agreement so provides or if the original has been filed in this state.

(2) A financing statement which otherwise complies with subsection (1) is sufficient when it is signed by the secured party instead of the debtor if it is filed to perfect a security interest in

(a) collateral already subject to a security interest in another jurisdiction when it is brought into this state, or when the debtor's location is changed to this state. Such a financing statement must state that the collateral was brought into this state or that the debtor's location was changed to this state under such circumstances; or

(b) proceeds under Section 9—306 if the security interest in the original collateral was perfected. Such a financing statement must describe the original collateral; or

(c) collateral as to which the filing has lapsed; or

(d) collateral acquired after a change of name, identity or corporate structure of the debtor (subsection (7)).

(3) A form substantially as follows is sufficient to comply with subsection (1):

Name of debtor (or assignor) ....

Address ....

Name of secured party (or assignee) ....

Address ....

1. This financing statement covers the following types (or items) of property:

     (Describe) ....

2. (If collateral is crops) The above described crops are growing or are to be grown on:

     (Describe Real Estate) ....

3. (If applicable) The above goods are to become fixtures on *

*Where appropriate substitute either "The above timber is standing on . . . . " or "The above minerals or the like (including oil and gas) or accounts will be financed at the wellhead or minehead of the well or mine located on . . . . ."

     (Describe Real Estate) ....

and this financing statement is to be filed [for record] in the real estate records. (If the debtor does not have an interest of record) The name of a record   owner is ....

4. (If products of collateral are claimed) Products of the collateral are also covered.

(use   ....

whichever   Signature of Debtor (or Assignor)

is   ....

applicable)   Signature of Secured Party

                                (or Assignee)

(4) A financing statement may be amended by filing a writing signed by both the debtor and the secured party. An amendment does not extend the period of effectiveness of a financing statement. If any amendment adds collateral, it is effective as to the added collateral only from the filing date of the amendment. In this Article, unless the context otherwise requires, the term "financing statement" means the original financing statement and any amendments.

(5) A financing statement covering timber to be cut or covering minerals or the like (including oil and gas) or accounts subject to subsection (5) of Section 9—103, or a financing statement filed as a fixture filing (Section 9—313) where the debtor is not a transmit-

ting utility, must show that it covers this type of collateral, must recite that it is to be filed [for record] in the real estate records, and the financing statement must contain a description of the real estate [sufficient if it were contained in a mortgage of the real estate to give constructive notice of the mortgage under the law of this state]. If the debtor does not have an interest of record in the real estate, the financing statement must show the name of a record owner.

(6) A mortgage is effective as a financing statement filed as a fixture filing from the date of its recording if

    (a) the goods are described in the mortgage by item or type; and

    (b) the goods are or are to become fixtures related to the real estate described in the mortgage; and

    (c) the mortgage complies with the requirements for a financing statement in this section other than a recital that it is to be filed in the real estate records; and

    (d) the mortgage is duly recorded.

No fee with reference to the financing statement is required other than the regular recording and satisfaction fees with respect to the mortgage.

(7) A financing statement sufficiently shows the name of the debtor if it gives the individual, partnership or corporate name of the debtor, whether or not it adds other trade names or names of partners. Where the debtor so changes his name or in the case of an organization its name, identity or corporate structure that a filed financing statement becomes seriously misleading, the filing is not effective to perfect a security interest in collateral acquired by the debtor more than four months after the change, unless a new appropriate financing statement is filed before the expiration of that time. A filed financing statement remains effective with respect to collateral transferred by the debtor even though the secured party knows of or consents to the transfer.

(8) A financing statement substantially complying with the requirements of this section is effective even though it contains minor errors which are not seriously misleading. Amended in 1972.

Note: *Language in brackets is optional.*

Note: *Where the state has any special recording system for real estate other than the usual grantor-grantee index (as, for instance, a tract system or a title registration or Torrens system) local adaptations of subsection (5) and Section 9—403(7) may be necessary. See Mass.Gen.Laws Chapter 106, Section 9—409.*

§ 9—403. What Constitutes Filing; Duration of Filing; Effect of Lapsed Filing; Duties of Filing Officer.

(1) Presentation for filing of a financing statement and tender of the filing fee or acceptance of the statement by the filing officer constitutes filing under this Article.

(2) Except as provided in subsection (6) a filed financing statement is effective for a period of five years from the date of filing. The effectiveness of a filed financing statement lapses on the expiration of the five year period unless a continuation statement is filed prior to the lapse. If a security interest perfected by filing exists at the time insolvency proceedings are commenced by or against the debtor, the security interest remains perfected until termination of the insolvency proceedings and thereafter for a period of sixty days or until expiration of the five year period, whichever occurs later. Upon lapse the security interest becomes unperfected, unless it is perfected without filing. If the security interest becomes unperfected upon lapse, it is deemed to have been unperfected as against a person who became a purchaser or lien creditor before lapse.

(3) A continuation statement may be filed by the secured party within six months prior to the expiration of the five year period specified in subsection (2). Any such continuation statement must be signed by the secured party, identify the original statement by file number and state that the original statement is still effective. A continuation statement signed by a person other than the secured party of record must be accompanied by a separate written statement of assignment signed by the secured party of record and complying with subsection (2) of Section 9—405, including payment of the required fee. Upon timely filing of the continuation statement, the effectiveness of the original statement is continued for five years after the last date to which the filing was effective whereupon it lapses in the same manner as provided in subsection (2) unless another continuation statement is filed prior to such lapse. Succeeding continuation statements may be filed in the same manner to continue the effectiveness of the original statement. Unless a statute on disposition of public records provides otherwise, the filing officer may remove a lapsed statement from the files and destroy it immediately if he has retained a microfilm or other photographic record, or in other cases after one year after the lapse. The filing officer shall so arrange matters by physical annexation of financing statements to continuation statements or other related

filings, or by other means, that if he physically destroys the financing statements of a period more than five years past, those which have been continued by a continuation statement or which are still effective under subsection (6) shall be retained.

(4) Except as provided in subsection (7) a filing officer shall mark each statement with a file number and with the date and hour of filing and shall hold the statement or a microfilm or other photographic copy thereof for public inspection. In addition the filing officer shall index the statement according to the name of the debtor and shall note in the index the file number and the address of the debtor given in the statement.

(5) The uniform fee for filing and indexing and for stamping a copy furnished by the secured party to show the date and place of filing for an original financing statement or for a continuation statement shall be $.......... if the statement is in the standard form prescribed by the [Secretary of State] and otherwise shall be $.........., plus in each case, if the financing statement is subject to subsection (5) of Section 9—402, $........... The uniform fee for each name more than one required to be indexed shall be $........... The secured party may at his option show a trade name for any person and an extra uniform indexing fee of $.......... shall be paid with respect thereto.

(6) If the debtor is a transmitting utility (subsection (5) of Section 9—401) and a filed financing statement so states, it is effective until a termination statement is filed. A real estate mortgage which is effective as a fixture filing under subsection (6) of Section 9—402 remains effective as a fixture filing until the mortgage is released or satisfied of record or its effectiveness otherwise terminates as to the real estate.

(7) When a financing statement covers timber to be cut or covers minerals or the like (including oil and gas) or accounts subject to subsection (5) of Section 9—103, or is filed as a fixture filing, [it shall be filed for record and] the filing officer shall index it under the names of the debtor and any owner of record shown on the financing statement in the same fashion as if they were the mortgagors in a mortgage of the real estate described, and, to the extent that the law of this state provides for indexing of mortgages under the name of the mortgagee, under the name of the secured party as if he were the mortgagee thereunder, or where indexing is by description in the same fashion as if the financing statement were a mortgage of the real estate described. Amended in 1972.

Note: *In states in which writings will not appear in the real estate records and indices unless actually recorded the*

bracketed language in subsection (7) should be used.

§ 9—404. Termination Statement.

(1) If a financing statement covering consumer goods is filed on or after ...., then within one month or within ten days following written demand by the debtor after there is no outstanding secured obligation and no commitment to make advances, incur obligations or otherwise give value, the secured party must file with each filing officer with whom the financing statement was filed, a termination statement to the effect that he no longer claims a security interest under the financing statement, which shall be identified by file number. In other cases whenever there is no outstanding secured obligation and no commitment to make advances, incur obligations or otherwise give value, the secured party must on written demand by the debtor send the debtor, for each filing officer with whom the financing statement was filed, a termination statement to the effect that he no longer claims a security interest under the financing statement, which shall be identified by file number. A termination statement signed by a person other than the secured party of record must be accompanied by a separate written statement of assignment signed by the secured party of record complying with subsection (2) of Section 9—405, including payment of the required fee. If the affected secured party fails to file such a termination statement as required by this subsection, or to send such a termination statement within ten days after proper demand therefor, he shall be liable to the debtor for one hundred dollars, and in addition for any loss caused to the debtor by such failure.

(2) On presentation to the filing officer of such a termination statement he must note it in the index. If he has received the termination statement in duplicate, he shall return one copy of the termination statement to the secured party stamped to show the time of receipt thereof. If the filing officer has a microfilm or other photographic record of the financing statement, and of any related continuation statement, statement of assignment and statement of release, he may remove the originals from the files at any time after receipt of the termination statement, or if he has no such record, he may remove them from the files at any time after one year after receipt of the termination statement.

(3) If the termination statement is in the standard form prescribed by the [Secretary of State], the uniform fee for filing and indexing the termination statement shall be $......, and otherwise shall be $......, plus in each case an additional fee of $...... for each

name more than one against which the termination statement is required to be indexed. Amended in 1972.

Note: *The date to be inserted should be the effective date of the revised Article 9.*

§ 9—405. Assignment of Security Interest; Duties of Filing Officer; Fees.

(1) A financing statement may disclose an assignment of a security interest in the collateral described in the financing statement by indication in the financing statement of the name and address of the assignee or by an assignment itself or a copy thereof on the face or back of the statement. On presentation to the filing officer of such a financing statement the filing officer shall mark the same as provided in Section 9—403(4). The uniform fee for filing, indexing and furnishing filing data for a financing statement so indicating an assignment shall be $...... if the statement is in the standard form prescribed by the [Secretary of State] and otherwise shall be $......, plus in each case an additional fee of $...... for each name more than one against which the financing statement is required to be indexed.

(2) A secured party may assign of record all or part of his rights under a financing statement by the filing in the place where the original financing statement was filed of a separate written statement of assignment signed by the secured party of record and setting forth the name of the secured party of record and the debtor, the file number and the date of filing of the financing statement and the name and address of the assignee and containing a description of the collateral assigned. A copy of the assignment is sufficient as a separate statement if it complies with the preceding sentence. On presentation to the filing officer of such a separate statement, the filing officer shall mark such separate statement with the date and hour of the filing. He shall note the assignment on the index of the financing statement, or in the case of a fixture filing, or a filing covering timber to be cut, or covering minerals or the like (including oil and gas) or accounts subject to subsection (5) of Section 9—103, he shall index the assignment under the name of the assignor as grantor and, to the extent that the law of this state provides for indexing the assignment of a mortgage under the name of the assignee, he shall index the assignment of the financing statement under the name of the assignee. The uniform fee for filing, indexing and furnishing filing data about such a separate statement of assignment shall be $...... if the statement is in the standard form prescribed by the [Secretary of State] and otherwise shall be $......, plus in each case an additional fee of $...... for each name

more than one against which the statement of assignment is required to be indexed. Notwithstanding the provisions of this subsection, an assignment of record of a security interest in a fixture contained in a mortgage effective as a fixture filing (subsection (6) of Section 9—402) may be made only by an assignment of the mortgage in the manner provided by the law of this state other than this Act.

(3) After the disclosure or filing of an assignment under this section, the assignee is the secured party of record. Amended in 1972.

§ 9—406. Release of Collateral; Duties of Filing Officer; Fees.

A secured party of record may by his signed statement release all or a part of any collateral described in a filed financing statement. The statement of release is sufficient if it contains a description of the collateral being released, the name and address of the debtor, the name and address of the secured party, and the file number of the financing statement. A statement of release signed by a person other than the secured party of record must be accompanied by a separate written statement of assignment signed by the secured party of record and complying with subsection (2) of Section 9—405, including payment of the required fee. Upon presentation of such a statement of release to the filing officer he shall mark the statement with the hour and date of filing and shall note the same upon the margin of the index of the filing of the financing statement. The uniform fee for filing and noting such a statement of release shall be $...... if the statement is in the standard form prescribed by the [Secretary of State] and otherwise shall be $......, plus in each case an additional fee of $...... for each name more than one against which the statement of release is required to be indexed. Amended in 1972.

[§ 9—407. Information From Filing Officer].

[(1) If the person filing any financing statement, termination statement, statement of assignment, or statement of release, furnishes the filing officer a copy thereof, the filing officer shall upon request note upon the copy the file number and date and hour of the filing of the original and deliver or send the copy to such person.]

[(2) Upon request of any person, the filing officer shall issue his certificate showing whether there is on file on the date and hour stated therein, any presently effective financing statement naming a particular debtor and any statement of assignment thereof and if there is, giving the date and hour of filing of each such statement and the names and addresses of each secured party therein. The uniform fee for such a certificate shall be $...... if the request for the certificate is in the standard form prescribed by the [Secretary of State] and otherwise shall be $....... Upon request the filing officer shall furnish a copy of any filed financing statement or statement of assignment for a uniform fee of $...... per page.] Amended in 1972.

Note: *This section is proposed as an optional provision to require filing officers to furnish certificates. Local law and practices should be consulted with regard to the advisability of adoption.*

§ 9—408. Financing Statements Covering Consigned or Leased Goods.

A consignor or lessor of goods may file a financing statement using the terms "consignor," "consignee," "lessor," "lessee" or the like instead of the terms specified in Section 9—402. The provisions of this Part shall apply as appropriate to such a financing statement but its filing shall not of itself be a factor in determining whether or not the consignment or lease is intended as security (Section 1—201(37)). However, if it is determined for other reasons that the consignment or lease is so intended, a security interest of the consignor or lessor which attaches to the consigned or leased goods is perfected by such filing. Added in 1972.

Part 5 Default

§ 9—501. Default; Procedure When Security Agreement Covers Both Real and Personal Property.

(1) When a debtor is in default under a security agreement, a secured party has the rights and remedies provided in this Part and except as limited by subsection (3) those provided in the security agreement. He may reduce his claim to judgment, foreclose or otherwise enforce the security interest by any available judicial procedure. If the collateral is documents the secured party may proceed either as to the documents or as to the goods covered thereby. A secured party in possession has the rights, remedies and duties provided in Section 9—207. The rights and remedies referred to in this subsection are cumulative.

(2) After default, the debtor has the rights and remedies provided in this Part, those provided in the security agreement and those provided in Section 9—207.

(3) To the extent that they give rights to the debtor and impose duties on the secured party, the rules stated in the subsections referred to below may not be waived or varied except as provided with respect to compulsory disposition of collateral (subsection (3) of Section 9—504 and Section 9—505) and with respect to redemption of collateral (Section 9—506) but the parties may by agreement determine the standards by which the fulfillment of these rights and duties is to be measured if such standards are not manifestly unreasonable:

(a) subsection (2) of Section 9—502 and subsection (2) of Section 9—504 insofar as they require accounting for surplus proceeds of collateral;

(b) subsection (3) of Section 9—504 and subsection (1) of Section 9—505 which deal with disposition of collateral;

(c) subsection (2) of Section 9—505 which deals with acceptance of collateral as discharge of obligation;

(d) Section 9—506 which deals with redemption of collateral; and

(e) subsection (1) of Section 9—507 which deals with the secured party's liability for failure to comply with this Part.

(4) If the security agreement covers both real and personal property, the secured party may proceed under this Part as to the personal property or he may proceed as to both the real and the personal property in accordance with his rights and remedies in respect of the real property in which case the provisions of this Part do not apply.

(5) When a secured party has reduced his claim to judgment the lien of any levy which may be made upon his collateral by virtue of any execution based upon the judgment shall relate back to the date of the perfection of the security interest in such collateral. A judicial sale, pursuant to such execution, is a foreclosure of the security interest by judicial procedure within the meaning of this section, and the secured party may purchase at the sale and thereafter hold the collateral free of any other requirements of this Article. Amended in 1972.

§ 9—502. Collection Rights of Secured Party.

(1) When so agreed and in any event on default the secured party is entitled to notify an account debtor or the obligor on an instrument to make payment to him whether or not the assignor was theretofore making collections on the collateral, and also to take control of any proceeds to which he is entitled under Section 9—306.

(2) A secured party who by agreement is entitled to charge back uncollected collateral or otherwise to full

or limited recourse against the debtor and who undertakes to collect from the account debtors or obligors must proceed in a commercially reasonable manner and may deduct his reasonable expenses of realization from the collections. If the security agreement secures an indebtedness, the secured party must account to the debtor for any surplus, and unless otherwise agreed, the debtor is liable for any deficiency. But, if the underlying transaction was a sale of accounts or chattel paper, the debtor is entitled to any surplus or is liable for any deficiency only if the security agreement so provides. Amended in 1972.

§ 9—503. Secured Party's Right to Take Possession After Default.

Unless otherwise agreed a secured party has on default the right to take possession of the collateral. In taking possession a secured party may proceed without judicial process if this can be done without breach of the peace or may proceed by action. If the security agreement so provides the secured party may require the debtor to assemble the collateral and make it available to the secured party at a place to be designated by the secured party which is reasonably convenient to both parties. Without removal a secured party may render equipment unusable, and may dispose of collateral on the debtor's premises under Section 9—504.

§ 9—504. Secured Party's Right to Dispose of Collateral After Default; Effect of Disposition.

(1) A secured party after default may sell, lease or otherwise dispose of any or all of the collateral in its then condition or following any commercially reasonable preparation or processing. Any sale of goods is subject to the Article on Sales (Article 2). The proceeds of disposition shall be applied in the order following to

(a) the reasonable expenses of retaking, holding, preparing for sale or lease, selling, leasing and the like and, to the extent provided for in the agreement and not prohibited by law, the reasonable attorneys' fees and legal expenses incurred by the secured party;

(b) the satisfaction of indebtedness secured by the security interest under which the disposition is made;

(c) the satisfaction of indebtedness secured by any subordinate security interest in the collateral if written notification of demand therefor is received before distribution of the proceeds is completed. If requested by the secured party, the holder of a subordinate security interest must

seasonably furnish reasonable proof of his interest, and unless he does so, the secured party need not comply with his demand.

(2) If the security interest secures an indebtedness, the secured party must account to the debtor for any surplus, and, unless otherwise agreed, the debtor is liable for any deficiency. But if the underlying transaction was a sale of accounts or chattel paper, the debtor is entitled to any surplus or is liable for any deficiency only if the security agreement so provides.

(3) Disposition of the collateral may be by public or private proceedings and may be made by way of one or more contracts. Sale or other disposition may be as a unit or in parcels and at any time and place and on any terms but every aspect of the disposition including the method, manner, time, place and terms must be commercially reasonable. Unless collateral is perishable or threatens to decline speedily in value or is of a type customarily sold on a recognized market, reasonable notification of the time and place of any public sale or reasonable notification of the time after which any private sale or other intended disposition is to be made shall be sent by the secured party to the debtor, if he has not signed after default a statement renouncing or modifying his right to notification of sale. In the case of consumer goods no other notification need be sent. In other cases notification shall be sent to any other secured party from whom the secured party has received (before sending his notification to the debtor or before the debtor's renunciation of his rights) written notice of a claim of an interest in the collateral. The secured party may buy at any public sale and if the collateral is of a type customarily sold in a recognized market or is of a type which is the subject of widely distributed standard price quotations he may buy at private sale.

(4) When collateral is disposed of by a secured party after default, the disposition transfers to a purchaser for value all of the debtor's rights therein, discharges the security interest under which it is made and any security interest or lien subordinate thereto. The purchaser takes free of all such rights and interests even though the secured party fails to comply with the requirements of this Part or of any judicial proceedings

(a) in the case of a public sale, if the purchaser has no knowledge of any defects in the sale and if he does not buy in collusion with the secured party, other bidders or the person conducting the sale; or

(b) in any other case, if the purchaser acts in good faith.

(5) A person who is liable to a secured party under a guaranty, indorsement, repurchase agreement or the

like and who receives a transfer of collateral from the secured party or is subrogated to his rights has thereafter the rights and duties of the secured party. Such a transfer of collateral is not a sale or disposition of the collateral under this Article. Amended in 1972.

§ 9—505. Compulsory Disposition of Collateral; Acceptance of the Collateral as Discharge of Obligation.

(1) If the debtor has paid sixty per cent of the cash price in the case of a purchase money security interest in consumer goods or sixty per cent of the loan in the case of another security interest in consumer goods, and has not signed after default a statement renouncing or modifying his rights under this Part a secured party who has taken possession of collateral must dispose of it under Section 9—504 and if he fails to do so within ninety days after he takes possession the debtor at his option may recover in conversion or under Section 9—507(1) on secured party's liability.

(2) In any other case involving consumer goods or any other collateral a secured party in possession may, after default, propose to retain the collateral in satisfaction of the obligation. Written notice of such proposal shall be sent to the debtor if he has not signed after default a statement renouncing or modifying his rights under this subsection. In the case of consumer goods no other notice need be given. In other cases notice shall be sent to any other secured party from whom the secured party has received (before sending his notice to the debtor or before the debtor's renunciation of his rights) written notice of a claim of an interest in the collateral. If the secured party receives objection in writing from a person entitled to receive notification within twenty-one days after the notice was sent, the secured party must dispose of the collateral under Section 9—504. In the absence of such written objection the secured party may retain the collateral in satisfaction of the debtor's obligation. Amended in 1972.

§ 9—506. Debtor's Right to Redeem Collateral.

At any time before the secured party has disposed of collateral or entered into a contract for its disposition under Section 9—504 or before the obligation has been discharged under Section 9—505(2) the debtor or any other secured party may unless otherwise agreed in writing after default redeem the collateral by tendering fulfillment of all obligations secured by the collateral as well as the expenses reasonably incurred by the secured party in retaking, holding and

preparing the collateral for disposition, in arranging for the sale, and to the extent provided in the agreement and not prohibited by law, his reasonable attorneys' fees and legal expenses.

§ 9—507. Secured Party's Liability for Failure to Comply With This Part.

(1) If it is established that the secured party is not proceeding in accordance with the provisions of this Part disposition may be ordered or restrained on appropriate terms and conditions. If the disposition has occurred the debtor or any person entitled to notification or whose security interest has been made known to the secured party prior to the disposition has a right to recover from the secured party any loss caused by a failure to comply with the provisions of this Part. If the collateral is consumer goods, the debtor has a right to recover in any event an amount not less than the credit service charge plus ten per cent of the principal amount of the debt or the time price differential plus 10 per cent of the cash price.

(2) The fact that a better price could have been obtained by a sale at a different time or in a different method from that selected by the secured party is not of itself sufficient to establish that the sale was not made in a commercially reasonable manner. If the secured party either sells the collateral in the usual manner in any recognized market therefor or if he sells at the price current in such market at the time of his sale or if he has otherwise sold in conformity with reasonable commercial practices among dealers in the type of property sold he has sold in a commercially reasonable manner. The principles stated in the two preceding sentences with respect to sales also apply as may be appropriate to other types of disposition. A disposition which has been approved in any judicial proceeding or by any bona fide creditors' committee or representative of creditors shall conclusively be deemed to be commercially reasonable, but this sentence does not indicate that any such approval must be obtained in any case nor does it indicate that any disposition not so approved is not commercially reasonable.

Article 10
EFFECTIVE DATE AND REPEALER

§ 10—101. Effective Date.

This Act shall become effective at midnight on December 31st following its enactment. It applies to transactions entered into and events occurring after that date.

§ 10—102. Specific Repealer; Provision for Transition.

(1) The following acts and all other acts and parts of acts inconsistent herewith are hereby repealed: (Here should follow the acts to be specifically repealed including the following:

Uniform Negotiable Instruments Act
Uniform Warehouse Receipts Act
Uniform Sales Act
Uniform Bills of Lading Act
Uniform Stock Transfer Act
Uniform Conditional Sales Act
Uniform Trust Receipts Act
        Also any acts regulating:
Bank collections
Bulk sales
Chattel mortgages
Conditional sales
Factor's lien acts
Farm storage of grain and similar acts
Assignment of accounts receivable)

(2) Transactions validly entered into before the effective date specified in Section 10—101 and the rights, duties and interests flowing from them remain valid thereafter and may be terminated, completed, consummated or enforced as required or permitted by any statute or other law amended or repealed by this Act as though such repeal or amendment had not occurred.

Note: *Subsection (1) should be separately prepared for each state. The foregoing is a list of statutes to be checked.*

§ 10—103. General Repealer.

Except as provided in the following section, all acts and parts of acts inconsistent with this Act are hereby repealed.

§ 10—104. Laws Not Repealed.

(1) The Article on Documents of Title (Article 7) does not repeal or modify any laws prescribing the form or contents of documents of title or the services or facilities to be afforded by bailees, or otherwise regulating bailees' businesses in respects not specifically dealt with herein; but the fact that such laws are violated does not affect the status of a document of title which otherwise complies with the definition of a document of title (Section 1—201).

[(2) This Act does not repeal . . . . *, cited as the Uniform Act for the Simplification of Fiduciary Security Transfers, and if in any respect there is any inconsistency between that Act and the Article of this Act on investment securities (Article 8) the provisions of the former Act shall control.]

Note: *At * in subsection (2) insert the statutory reference to the Uniform Act for the Simplification of Fiduciary Security Transfers if such Act has previously been enacted. If it has not been enacted, omit subsection (2).*

Article 11
(REPORTERS' DRAFT) EFFECTIVE DATE AND TRANSITION PROVISIONS

This material has been numbered Article 11 to distinguish it from Article 10, the transition provision of the 1962 Code, which may still remain in effect in some states to cover transition problems from pre-Code law to the original Uniform Commercial Code. Adaptation may be necessary in particular states. The terms "[old Code]" and "[new Code]" and "[old U.C.C.]" and "[new U.C.C.]" are used herein, and should be suitably changed in each state.

Note: *This draft was prepared by the Reporters and has not been passed upon by the Review Committee, the Permanent Editorial Board, the American Law Institute, or the National Conference of Commissioners on Uniform State Laws. It is submitted as a working draft which may be adapted as appropriate in each state.*

§ 11—101. Effective Date.

This Act shall become effective at 12:01 A.M. on _____, 19___.

§ 11—102. Preservation of Old Transition Provision.

The provisions of [here insert reference to the original transition provision in the particular state] shall continue to apply to [the new U.C.C.] and for this purpose the [old U.C.C. and new U.C.C.] shall be considered one continuous statute.

§ 11—103. Transition to [New Code]—General Rule.

Transactions validly entered into after [effective date of old U.C.C.] and before [effective date of new U.C.C.], and which were subject to the provisions of [old U.C.C.] and which would be subject to this Act as amended if they had been entered into after the effective date of [new U.C.C.] and the rights, duties and interests flowing from such transactions remain valid after the latter date and may be terminated, completed, consummated or enforced as required or permitted by the [new U.C.C.]. Security interests arising out of such transactions which are perfected when [new U.C.C.] becomes effective shall remain perfected until they lapse as provided in [new U.C.C.], and may be continued as permitted by [new U.C.C.], except as stated in Section 11—105.

§ 11—104. **Transition Provision on Change of Requirement of Filing.**

A security interest for the perfection of which filing or the taking of possession was required under [old U.C.C.] and which attached prior to the effective date of [new U.C.C.] but was not perfected shall be deemed perfected on the effective date of [new U.C.C.] if [new U.C.C.] permits perfection without filing or authorizes filing in the office or offices where a prior ineffective filing was made.

§ 11—105. **Transition Provision on Change of Place of Filing.**

(1) A financing statement or continuation statement filed prior to [effective date of new U.C.C.] which shall not have lapsed prior to [the effective date of new U.C.C.] shall remain effective for the period provided in the [old Code], but not less than five years after the filing.

(2) With respect to any collateral acquired by the debtor subsequent to the effective date of [new U.C.C.], any effective financing statement or continuation statement described in this section shall apply only if the filing or filings are in the office or offices that would be appropriate to perfect the security interests in the new collateral under [new U.C.C.].

(3) The effectiveness of any financing statement or continuation statement filed prior to [effective date of new U.C.C.] may be continued by a continuation statement as permitted by [new U.C.C.], except that if [new U.C.C.] requires a filing in an office where there was no previous financing statement, a new financing statement conforming to Section 11—106 shall be filed in that office.

(4) If the record of a mortgage of real estate would have been effective as a fixture filing of goods described therein if [new U.C.C.] had been in effect on the date of recording the mortgage, the mortgage shall be deemed effective as a fixture filing as to such goods under subsection (6) of Section 9—402 of the [new U.C.C.] on the effective date of [new U.C.C.].

§ 11—106. **Required Refilings.**

(1) If a security interest is perfected or has priority when this Act takes effect as to all persons or as to certain persons without any filing or recording, and if the filing of a financing statement would be required for the perfection or priority of the security interest against those persons under [new U.C.C.], the perfection and priority rights of the security interest continue until 3 years after the effective date of [new U.C.C.]. The perfection will then lapse unless a financing statement is filed as provided in subsection (4) or unless the security interest is perfected otherwise than by filing.

(2) If a security interest is perfected when [new U.C.C.] takes effect under a law other than [U.C.C.] which requires no further filing, refiling or recording to continue its perfection, perfection continues until and will lapse 3 years after [new U.C.C.] takes effect, unless a financing statement is filed as provided in subsection (4) or unless the security interest is perfected otherwise than by filing, or unless under subsection (3) of Section 9—302 the other law continues to govern filing.

(3) If a security interest is perfected by a filing, refiling or recording under a law repealed by this Act which required further filing, refiling or recording to continue its perfection, perfection continues and will lapse on the date provided by the law so repealed for such further filing, refiling or recording unless a financing statement is filed as provided in subsection (4) or unless the security interest is perfected otherwise than by filing.

(4) A financing statement may be filed within six months before the perfection of a security interest would otherwise lapse. Any such financing statement may be signed by either the debtor or the secured party. It must identify the security agreement, statement or notice (however denominated in any statute or other law repealed or modified by this Act), state the office where and the date when the last filing, refiling or recording, if any, was made with respect thereto, and the filing number, if any, or book and page, if any, of recording and further state that the security agreement, statement or notice, however denominated, in another filing office under the [U.C.C.] or under any statute or other law repealed or modified by this Act is still effective. Section 9—401 and Section 9—103 determine the proper place to file such a financing statement. Except as specified in this subsection, the provisions of Section 9—403(3) for continuation statements apply to such a financing statement.

§ 11—107. **Transition Provisions as to Priorities.**

Except as otherwise provided in [Article 11], [old U.C.C.] shall apply to any questions of priority if the positions of the parties were fixed prior to the effective date of [new U.C.C.]. In other cases questions of priority shall be determined by [new U.C.C.].

§ 11—108. **Presumption that Rule of Law Continues Unchanged.**

Unless a change in law has clearly been made, the provisions of [new U.C.C.] shall be deemed declaratory of the meaning of the [old U.C.C.]

Appendix

B

THE UNIFORM PARTNERSHIP ACT

(Adopted in 48 States, all except Georgia and Louisiana; the District of Columbia, the Virgin Islands, and Guam. The adoptions by Alabama and Nebraska do not follow the official text in every respect, but are substantially similar, with local variations.)

The Act consists of 7 Parts as follows:

I. Preliminary Provisions

II. Nature of Partnership

III. Relations of Partners to Persons Dealing with the Partnership

IV. Relations of Partners to One Another

V. Property Rights of a Partner

VI. Dissolution and Winding Up

VII. Miscellaneous Provisions

An Act to make uniform the Law of Partnerships Be it enacted, etc.:

Part I Preliminary Provisions

Sec. 1. Name of Act.

This act may be cited as Uniform Partnership Act.

Sec. 2. Definition of Terms.

In this act, "Court" includes every court and judge having jurisdiction in the case.

"Business" includes every trade, occupation, or profession.

"Person" includes individuals, partnerships, corporations, and other associations.

"Bankrupt" includes bankrupt under the Federal Bankruptcy Act or insolvent under any state insolvent act.

"Conveyance" includes every assignment, lease, mortgage, or encumbrance.

"Real property" includes land and any interest or estate in land.

Sec. 3. Interpretation of Knowledge and Notice.

(1) A person has "knowledge" of a fact within the meaning of this act not only when he has actual knowledge thereof, but also when he has knowledge of such other facts as in the circumstances shows bad faith.

(2) A person has "notice" of a fact within the meaning of this act when the person who claims the benefit of the notice

(a) States the fact to such person, or

(b) Delivers through the mail, or by other means of communication, a written statement of the fact to such person or to a proper person at his place of business or residence.

Sec. 4. Rules of Construction.

(1) The rule that statutes in derogation of the common law are to be strictly construed shall have no application to this act.

(2) The law of estoppel shall apply under this act.

(3) The law of agency shall apply under this act.

(4) This act shall be so interpreted and construed as to effect its general purpose to make uniform the law of those states which enact it.

(5) This act shall not be construed so as to impair the obligations of any contract existing when the act goes into effect, nor to affect any action or proceedings begun or right accrued before this act takes effect.

Sec. 5. **Rules for Cases Not Provided for in this Act.**

In any case not provided for in this act the rules of law and equity, including the law merchant, shall govern.

Part II **Nature of Partnership**

Sec. 6. **Partnership Defined.**

(1) A partnership is an association of two or more persons to carry on as co-owners a business for profit.

(2) But any association formed under any other statute of this state, or any statute adopted by authority, other than the authority of this state, is not a partnership under this act, unless such association would have been a partnership in this state prior to the adoption of this act; but this act shall apply to limited partnerships except in so far as the statutes relating to such partnerships are inconsistent herewith.

Sec. 7. **Rules for Determining the Existence of a Partnership.**

In determining whether a partnership exists, these rules shall apply:

(1) Except as provided by Section 16 persons who are not partners as to each other are not partners as to third persons.

(2) Joint tenancy, tenancy in common, tenancy by the entireties, joint property, common property, or part ownership does not of itself establish a partnership, whether such co-owners do or do not share any profits made by the use of the property.

(3) The sharing of gross returns does not of itself establish a partnership, whether or not the persons sharing them have a joint or common right or interest in any property from which the returns are derived.

(4) The receipt by a person of a share of the profits of a business is prima facie evidence that he is a partner in the business, but no such inference shall be drawn if such profits were received in payment:

(a) As a debt by installments or otherwise,

(b) As wages of an employee or rent to a landlord,

(c) As an annuity to a widow or representative of a deceased partner,

(d) As interest on a loan, though the amount of payment vary with the profits of the business.

(e) As the consideration for the sale of a good-will of a business or other property by installments or otherwise.

Sec. 8. **Partnership Property.**

(1) All property originally brought into the partnership stock or subsequently acquired by purchase or otherwise, on account of the partnership, is partnership property.

(2) Unless the contrary intention appears, property acquired with partnership funds is partnership property.

(3) Any estate in real property may be acquired in the partnership name. Title so acquired can be conveyed only in the partnership name.

(4) A conveyance to a partnership in the partnership name, though without words of inheritance, passes the entire estate of the grantor unless a contrary intent appears.

Part III **Relations of Partners to Persons Dealing with the Partnership**

Sec. 9. **Partner Agent of Partnership as to Partnership Business.**

(1) Every partner is an agent of the partnership for the purpose of its business, and the act of every partner, including the execution in the partnership name of any instrument, for apparently carrying on in the usual way the business of the partnership of which he is a member binds the partnership, unless the partner so acting has in fact no authority to act for the partnership in the particular matter, and the person with whom he is dealing has knowledge of the fact that he has no such authority.

(2) An act of a partner which is not apparently for the carrying on of the business of the partnership in the usual way does not bind the partnership unless authorized by the other partners.

(3) Unless authorized by the other partners or unless they have abandoned the business, one or more but less than all the partners have no authority to:

(a) Assign the partnership property in trust for creditors or on the assignee's promise to pay the debts of the partnership,

(b) Dispose of the good-will of the business,

(c) Do any other act which would make it impossible to carry on the ordinary business of a partnership,

(d) Confess a judgment,

(e) Submit a partnership claim or liability to arbitration or reference.

(4) No act of a partner in contravention of a restriction on authority shall bind the partnership to persons having knowledge of the restriction.

Sec. 10. Conveyance of Real Property of the Partnership.

(1) Where title to real property is in the partnership name, any partner may convey title to such property by a conveyance executed in the partnership name; but the partnership may recover such property unless the partner's act binds the partnership under the provisions of paragraph (1) of section 9 or unless such property has been conveyed by the grantee or a person claiming through such grantee to a holder for value without knowledge that the partner, in making the conveyance, has exceeded his authority.

(2) Where title to real property is in the name of the partnership, a conveyance executed by a partner, in his own name, passes the equitable interest of the partnership, provided the act is one within the authority of the partner under the provisions of paragraph (1) of section 9.

(3) Where title to real property is in the name of one or more but not all the partners, and the record does not disclose the right of the partnership, the partners in whose name the title stands may convey title to such property, but the partnership may recover such property if the partners' act does not bind the partnership under the provisions of paragraph (1) of section 9, unless the purchaser or his assignee, is a holder for value, without knowledge.

(4) Where the title to real property is in the name of one or more or all the partners, or in a third person in trust for the partnership, a conveyance executed by a partner in the partnership name, or in his own name, passes the equitable interest of the partnership, provided the act is one within the authority of the partner under the provisions of paragraph (1) of section 9.

(5) Where the title to real property is in the names of all the partners a conveyance executed by all the partners passes all their rights in such property.

Sec. 11. Partnership Bound by Admission of Partner.

An admission or representation made by any partner concerning partnership affairs within the scope of his authority as conferred by this act is evidence against the partnership.

Sec. 12. Partnership Charged with Knowledge of or Notice to Partner.

Notice to any partner of any matter relating to partnership affairs, and the knowledge of the partner acting in the particular matter, acquired while a partner or then present to his mind, and the knowledge of any other partner who reasonably could and should have communicated it to the acting partner, operate as notice to or knowledge of the partnership, except in the case of a fraud on the partnership committed by or with the consent of that partner.

Sec. 13. Partnership Bound by Partner's Wrongful Act.

Where, by any wrongful act or omission of any partner acting in the ordinary course of the business of the partnership or with the authority of his co-partners, loss or injury is caused to any person, not being a partner in the partnership, or any penalty is incurred, the partnership is liable therefor to the same extent as the partner so acting or omitting to act.

Sec. 14. Partnership Bound by Partner's Breach of Trust.

The partnership is bound to make good the loss:

(a) Where one partner acting within the scope of his apparent authority receives money or property of a third person and misapplies it; and

(b) Where the partnership in the course of its business receives money or property of a third person and the money or property so received is misapplied by any partner while it is in the custody of the partnership.

Sec. 15. Nature of Partner's Liability.

All partners are liable

(a) Jointly and severally for everything chargeable to the partnership under sections 13 and 14.

(b) Jointly for all other debts and obligations of the partnership; but any partner may enter into a separate obligation to perform a partnership contract.

Sec. 16. Partner by Estoppel.

(1) When a person, by words spoken or written or by conduct, represents himself, or consents to another representing him to any one, as a partner in an existing partnership or with one or more persons not actual partners, he is liable to any such person to whom such representation has been made, who has, on the faith of such representation, given credit to the actual or

apparent partnership, and if he has made such representation or consented to its being made in a public manner he is liable to such person, whether the representation has or has not been made or communicated to such person so giving credit by or with the knowledge of the apparent partner making the representation or consenting to its being made.

(a) When a partnership liability results, he is liable as though he were an actual member of the partnership.

(b) When no partnership liability results, he is liable jointly with the other persons, if any, so consenting to the contract or representation as to incur liability, otherwise separately.

(2) When a person has been thus represented to be a partner in an existing partnership, or with one or more persons not actual partners, he is an agent of the persons consenting to such representation to bind them to the same extent and in the same manner as though he were a partner in fact, with respect to persons who rely upon the representation. Where all the members of the existing partnership consent to the representation, a partnership act or obligation results; but in all other cases it is the joint act or obligation of the person acting and the persons consenting to the representation.

Sec. 17. **Liability of Incoming Partner.**

A person admitted as a partner into an existing partnership is liable for all the obligations of the partnership arising before his admission as though he had been a partner when such obligations were incurred, except that this liability shall be satisfied only out of partnership property.

Part IV Relations of Partners to One Another

Sec. 18. **Rules Determining Rights and Duties of Partners.**

The rights and duties of the partners in relation to the partnership shall be determined, subject to any agreement between them, by the following rules:

(a) Each partner shall be repaid his contributions, whether by way of capital or advances to the partnership property and share equally in the profits and surplus remaining after all liabilities, including those to partners, are satisfied; and must contribute towards the losses, whether of capital or otherwise, sustained by the partnership according to his share in the profits.

(b) The partnership must indemnify every partner in respect of payments made and personal liabilities reasonably incurred by him in the ordinary and proper conduct of its business, or for the preservation of its business or property.

(c) A partner, who in aid of the partnership makes any payment or advance beyond the amount of capital which he agreed to contribute, shall be paid interest from the date of the payment or advance.

(d) A partner shall receive interest on the capital contributed by him only from the date when repayment should be made.

(e) All partners have equal rights in the management and conduct of the partnership business.

(f) No partner is entitled to remuneration for acting in the partnership business, except that a surviving partner is entitled to reasonable compensation for his services in winding up the partnership affairs.

(g) No person can become a member of a partnership without the consent of all the partners.

(h) Any difference arising as to ordinary matters connected with the partnership business may be decided by a majority of the partners; but no act in contravention of any agreement between the partners may be done rightfully without the consent of all the partners.

Sec. 19. **Partnership Books.**

The partnership books shall be kept, subject to any agreement between the partners, at the principal place of business of the partnership, and every partner shall at all times have access to and may inspect and copy any of them.

Sec. 20. **Duty of Partners to Render Information.**

Partners shall render on demand true and full information of all things affecting the partnership to any partner or the legal representative of any deceased partner or partner under legal disability.

Sec. 21. **Partner Accountable as a Fiduciary.**

(1) Every partner must account to the partnership for any benefit, and hold as trustee for it any profits derived by him without the consent of the other partners from any transaction connected with the formation, conduct, or liquidation of the partnership or from any use by him of its property.

(2) This section applies also to the representatives of a deceased partner engaged in the liquidation of the affairs of the partnership as the personal representatives of the last surviving partner.

Sec. 22. **Right to an Account.**

Any partner shall have the right to a formal account as to partnership affairs:

(a) If he is wrongfully excluded from the partnership business or possession of its property by his co-partners,

(b) If the right exists under the terms of any agreement,

(c) As provided by section 21,

(d) Whenever other circumstances render it just and reasonable.

Sec. 23. **Continuation of Partnership Beyond Fixed Term.**

(1) When a partnership for a fixed term or particular undertaking is continued after the termination of such term or particular undertaking without any express agreement, the rights and duties of the partners remain the same as they were at such termination, so far as is consistent with a partnership at will.

(2) A continuation of the business by the partners or such of them as habitually acted therein during the term, without any settlement or liquidation of the partnership affairs, is prima facie evidence of a continuation of the partnership.

Part V Property Rights of a Partner

Sec. 24. **Extent of Property Rights of a Partner.**

The property rights of a partner are (1) his rights in specific partnership property, (2) his interest in the partnership, and (3) his right to participate in the management.

Sec. 25. **Nature of a Partner's Right in Specific Partnership Property.**

(1) A partner is co-owner with his partners of specific partnership property holding as a tenant in partnership.

(2) The incidents of this tenancy are such that:

(a) A partner, subject to the provisions of this act and to any agreement between the partners, has an equal right with his partners to possess specific partnership property for partnership purposes; but he has no right to possess such property for any other purpose without the consent of his partners.

(b) A partner's right in specific partnership property is not assignable except in connection with the assignment of rights of all the partners in the same property.

(c) A partner's right in specific partnership property is not subject to attachment or execution, except on a claim against the partnership. When partnership property is attached for a partnership debt the partners, or any of them, or the representatives of a deceased partner, cannot claim any right under the homestead or exemption laws.

(d) On the death of a partner his right in specific partnership property vests in the surviving partner or partners, except where the deceased was the last surviving partner, when his right in such property vests in his legal representative. Such surviving partner or partners, or the legal representative of the last surviving partner, has no right to possess the partnership property for any but a partnership purpose.

(e) A partner's right in specific partnership property is not subject to dower, curtesy, or allowances to widows, heirs, or next of kin.

Sec. 26. **Nature of Partner's Interest in the Partnership.**

A partner's interest in the partnership is his share of the profits and surplus, and the same is personal property.

Sec. 27. **Assignment of Partner's Interest.**

(1) A conveyance by a partner of his interest in the partnership does not of itself dissolve the partnership, nor, as against the other partners in the absence of agreement, entitle the assignee, during the continuance of the partnership to interfere in the management or administration of the partnership business or affairs, or to require any information or account of partnership transactions, or to inspect the partnership books; but it merely entitles the assignee to receive in accordance with his contract the profits to which the assigning partner would otherwise be entitled.

(2) In case of a dissolution of the partnership, the assignee is entitled to receive his assignor's interest and may require an account from the date only of the last account agreed to by all the partners.

Sec. 28. **Partner's Interest Subject to Charging Order.**

(1) On due application to a competent court by any judgment creditor of a partner, the court which entered the judgment, order, or decree, or any other court, may charge the interest of the debtor partner with payment of the unsatisfied amount of such judgment debt with interest thereon; and may then or later appoint a receiver of his share of the profits, and of any other money due or to fall due to him in respect

of the partnership, and make all other orders, directions, accounts and inquiries which the debtor partner might have made, or which the circumstances of the case may require.

(2) The interest charged may be redeemed at any time before foreclosure, or in case of a sale being directed by the court may be purchased without thereby causing a dissolution:

(a) With separate property, by any one or more of the partners, or

(b) With partnership property, by any one or more of the partners with the consent of all the partners whose interests are not so charged or sold.

(3) Nothing in this act shall be held to deprive a partner of his right, if any, under the exemption laws, as regards his interest in the partnership.

Part VI Dissolution and Winding up

Sec. 29. Dissolution Defined.

The dissolution of a partnership is the change in the relation of the partners caused by any partner ceasing to be associated in the carrying on as distinguished from the winding up of the business.

Sec. 30. Partnership Not Terminated by Dissolution.

On dissolution the partnership is not terminated, but continues until the winding up of partnership affairs is completed.

Sec. 31. Causes of Dissolution.

Dissolution is caused:

(1) Without violation of the agreement between the partners,

(a) By the termination of the definite term or particular undertaking specified in the agreement,

(b) By the express will of any partner when no definite term or particular undertaking is specified,

(c) By the express will of all the partners who have not assigned their interests or suffered them to be charged for their separate debts, either before or after the termination of any specified term or particular undertaking.

(d) By the expulsion of any partner from the business bona fide in accordance with such a power conferred by the agreement between the partners;

(2) In contravention of the agreement between the partners, where the circumstances do not permit a dissolution under any other provision of this section, by the express will of any partner at any time;

(3) By any event which makes it unlawful for the business of the partnership to be carried on or for the members to carry it on in partnership;

(4) By the death of any partner;

(5) By the bankruptcy of any partner or the partnership;

(6) By decree of court under section 32.

Sec. 32. Dissolution by Decree of Court.

(1) On application by or for a partner the court shall decree a dissolution whenever:

(a) A partner has been declared a lunatic in any judicial proceeding or is shown to be of unsound mind,

(b) A partner becomes in any other way incapable of performing his part of the partnership contract,

(c) A partner has been guilty of such conduct as tends to affect prejudicially the carrying on of the business,

(d) A partner wilfully or persistently commits a breach of the partnership agreement, or otherwise so conducts himself in matters relating to the partnership business that it is not reasonably practicable to carry on the business in partnership with him,

(e) The business of the partnership can only be carried on at a loss,

(f) Other circumstances render a dissolution equitable.

(2) On the application of the purchaser of a partner's interest under sections 27 or 28:

(a) After the termination of the specified term or particular undertaking,

(b) At any time if the partnership was a partnership at will when the interest was assigned or when the charging order was issued.

Sec. 33. General Effect of Dissolution on Authority of Partner.

Except so far as may be necessary to wind up partnership affairs or to complete transactions begun but not then finished, dissolution terminates all authority of any partner to act for the partnership,

(1) With respect to the partners,

(a) When the dissolution is not by the act, bankruptcy or death of a partner; or

(b) When the dissolution is by such act, bankruptcy or death of a partner, in cases where section 34 so requires.

(2) With respect to persons not partners, as declared in section 35.

Sec. 34. Right of Partner to Contribution From Copartners After Dissolution.

Where the dissolution is caused by the act, death or bankruptcy of a partner, each partner is liable to his copartners for his share of any liability created by any partner acting for the partnership as if the partnership had not been dissolved unless

(a) The dissolution being by act of any partner, the partner acting for the partnership had knowledge of the dissolution, or

(b) The dissolution being by the death or bankruptcy of a partner, the partner acting for the partnership had knowledge or notice of the death or bankruptcy.

Sec. 35. Power of Partner to Bind Partnership to Third Persons After Dissolution.

(1) After dissolution a partner can bind the partnership except as provided in Paragraph (3)

(a) By any act appropriate for winding up partnership affairs or completing transactions unfinished at dissolution;

(b) By any transaction which would bind the partnership if dissolution had not taken place, provided the other party to the transaction

(I) Had extended credit to the partnership prior to dissolution and had no knowledge or notice of the dissolution; or

(II) Though he had not so extended credit, had nevertheless known of the partnership prior to dissolution, and, having no knowledge or notice of dissolution, the fact of dissolution had not been advertised in a newspaper of general circulation in the place (or in each place if more than one) at which the partnership business was regularly carried on.

(2) The liability of a partner under paragraph (1b) shall be satisfied out of partnership assets alone when such partner had been prior to dissolution

(a) Unknown as a partner to the person with whom the contract is made; and

(b) So far unknown and inactive in partnership affairs that the business reputation of the partnership could not be said to have been in any degree due to his connection with it.

(3) The partnership is in no case bound by any act of a partner after dissolution

(a) Where the partnership is dissolved because it is unlawful to carry on the business, unless the act is appropriate for winding up partnership affairs; or

(b) Where the partner has become bankrupt; or

(c) Where the partner has no authority to wind up partnership affairs; except by a transaction with one who

(I) Had extended credit to the partnership prior to dissolution and had no knowledge or notice of his want of authority; or

(II) Had not extended credit to the partnership prior to dissolution, and, having no knowledge or notice of his want of authority, the fact of his want of authority has not been advertised in the manner provided for advertising the fact of dissolution in paragraph (1bII).

(4) Nothing in this section shall affect the liability under section 16 of any person who after dissolution represents himself or consents to another representing him as a partner in a partnership engaged in carrying on business.

Sec. 36. Effect of Dissolution on Partner's Existing Liability.

(1) The dissolution of the partnership does not of itself discharge the existing liability of any partner.

(2) A partner is discharged from any existing liability upon dissolution of the partnership by an agreement to that effect between himself, the partnership creditor and the person or partnership continuing the business; and such agreement may be inferred from the course of dealing between the creditor having knowledge of the dissolution and the person or partnership continuing the business.

(3) Where a person agrees to assume the existing obligations of a dissolved partnership, the partners whose obligations have been assumed shall be discharged from any liability to any creditor of the partnership who, knowing of the agreement, consents to a material alteration in the nature or time of payment of such obligations.

(4) The individual property of a deceased partner shall be liable for all obligations of the partnership incurred while he was a partner but subject to the prior payment of his separate debts.

Sec. 37. Right to Wind Up.

Unless otherwise agreed the partners who have not wrongfully dissolved the partnership or the legal representative of the last surviving partner, not bankrupt, has the right to wind up the partnership affairs; provided, however, that any partner, his legal representative or his assignee, upon cause shown, may obtain winding up by the court.

Sec. 38. **Rights of Partners to Application of Partnership Property.**

(1) When dissolution is caused in any way, except in contravention of the partnership agreement, each partner as against his co-partners and all persons claiming through them in respect of their interests in the partnership, unless otherwise agreed, may have the partnership property applied to discharge its liabilities, and the surplus applied to pay in cash the net amount owing to the respective partners. But if dissolution is caused by expulsion of a partner, bona fide under the partnership agreement and if the expelled partner is discharged from all partnership liabilities, either by payment or agreement under section 36(2), he shall receive in cash only the net amount due him from the partnership.

(2) When dissolution is caused in contravention of the partnership agreement the rights of the partners shall be as follows:

(a) Each partner who has not caused dissolution wrongfully shall have,

(I) All the rights specified in paragraph (1) of this section, and

(II) The right, as against each partner who has caused the dissolution wrongfully, to damages for breach of the agreement.

(b) The partners who have not caused the dissolution wrongfully, if they all desire to continue the business in the same name, either by themselves or jointly with others, may do so, during the agreed term for the partnership and for that purpose may possess the partnership property, provided they secure the payment by bond approved by the court, or pay to any partner who has caused the dissolution wrongfully, the value of his interest in the partnership at the dissolution, less any damages recoverable under clause (2aII) of the section, and in like manner indemnify him against all present or future partnership liabilities.

(c) A partner who has caused the dissolution wrongfully shall have:

(I) If the business is not continued under the provisions of paragraph (2b) all the rights of a partner under paragraph (1), subject to clause (2aII), of this section,

(II) If the business is continued under paragraph (2b) of this section the right as against his co-partners and all claiming through them in respect of their interests in the partnership, to have the value of his interest in the partnership, less any damages caused to his co-partners by the dissolution, ascertained and paid to him in cash, or the payment secured by bond approved by the court, and to be released from all existing liabilities of the partnership; but in ascertaining the value of the partner's interest the value of the good-will of the business shall not be considered.

Sec. 39. **Rights Where Partnership is Dissolved for Fraud or Misrepresentation.**

Where a partnership contract is rescinded on the ground of the fraud or misrepresentation of one of the parties thereto, the party entitled to rescind is, without prejudice to any other right, entitled,

(a) To a lien on, or right of retention of, the surplus of the partnership property after satisfying the partnership liabilities to third persons for any sum of money paid by him for the purchase of an interest in the partnership and for any capital or advances contributed by him; and

(b) To stand, after all liabilities to third persons have been satisfied, in the place of the creditors of the partnership for any payments made by him in respect of the partnership liabilities; and

(c) To be indemnified by the person guilty of the fraud or making the representation against all debts and liabilities of the partnership.

Sec. 40. **Rules for Distribution.**

In settling accounts between the partners after dissolution, the following rules shall be observed, subject to any agreement to the contrary:

(a) The assets of the partnership are:

(I) The partnership property,

(II) The contributions of the partners necessary for the payment of all the liabilities specified in clause (b) of this paragraph.

(b) The liabilities of the partnership shall rank in order of payment, as follows:

(I) Those owing to creditors other than partners,

(II) Those owing to partners other than for capital and profits,

(III) Those owing to partners in respect of capital,

(IV) Those owing to partners in respect of profits.

(c) The assets shall be applied in the order of their declaration in clause (a) of this paragraph to the satisfaction of the liabilities.

(d) The partners shall contribute, as provided by section 18(a) the amount necessary to satisfy the liabilities; but if any, but not all, of the partners are insolvent, or, not being subject to process, refuse to contribute, the other parties shall contribute their share of the liabilities, and, in the relative proportions in which they share the profits, the additional amount necessary to pay the liabilities.

(e) An assignee for the benefit of creditors or any person appointed by the court shall have the right to enforce the contributions specified in clause (d) of this paragraph.

(f) Any partner or his legal representative shall have the right to enforce the contributions specified in clause (d) of this paragraph, to the extent of the amount which he has paid in excess of his share of the liability.

(g) The individual property of a deceased partner shall be liable for the contributions specified in clause (d) of this paragraph.

(h) When partnership property and the individual properties of the partners are in possession of a court for distribution, partnership creditors shall have priority on partnership property and separate creditors on individual property, saving the rights of lien or secured creditors as heretofore.

(i) Where a partner has become bankrupt or his estate is insolvent the claims against his separate property shall rank in the following order:

(I) Those owing to separate creditors,

(II) Those owing to partnership creditors,

(III) Those owing to partners by way of contribution.

Sec. 41. **Liability of Persons Continuing the Business in Certain Cases.**

(1) When any new partner is admitted into an existing partnership, or when any partner retires and assigns (or the representative of the deceased partner assigns) his rights in partnership property to two or more of the partners, or to one or more of the partners and one or more third persons, if the business is continued without liquidation of the partnership affairs, creditors of the first or dissolved partnership are also creditors of the partnership so continuing the business.

(2) When all but one partner retire and assign (or the representative of a deceased partner assigns) their rights in partnership property to the remaining partner, who continues the business without liquidation of partnership affairs, either alone or with others, creditors of the dissolved partnership are also creditors of the person or partnership so continuing the business.

(3) When any partner retires or dies and the business of the dissolved partnership is continued as set forth in paragraphs (1) and (2) of this section, with the consent of the retired partners or the representative of the deceased partner, but without any assignment of his right in partnership property, rights of creditors of the dissolved partnership and of the creditors of the person or partnership continuing the business shall be as if such assignment had been made.

(4) When all the partners or their representatives assign their rights in partnership property to one or more third persons who promise to pay the debts and who continue the business of the dissolved partnership, creditors of the dissolved partnership are also creditors of the person or partnership continuing the business.

(5) When any partner wrongfully causes a dissolution and the remaining partners continue the business under the provisions of section 38(2b), either alone or with others, and without liquidation of the partnership affairs, creditors of the dissolved partnership are also creditors of the person or partnership continuing the business.

(6) When a partner is expelled and the remaining partners continue the business either alone or with others, without liquidation of the partnership affairs, creditors of the dissolved partnership are also creditors of the person or partnership continuing the business.

(7) The liability of a third person becoming a partner in the partnership continuing the business, under this section, to the creditors of the dissolved partnership shall be satisfied out of partnership property only.

(8) When the business of a partnership after dissolution is continued under any conditions set forth in this section the creditors of the dissolved partnership, as against the separate creditors of the retiring or deceased partner or the representative of the deceased partner, have a prior right to any claim of the retired partner or the representative of the deceased partner against the person or partnership continuing the business, on account of the retired or deceased partner's interest in the dissolved partnership or on account of any consideration promised for such interest or for his right in partnership property.

(9) Nothing in this section shall be held to modify any

right of creditors to set aside any assignment on the ground of fraud.

(10) The use by the person or partnership continuing the business of the partnership name, or the name of a deceased partner as part thereof, shall not of itself make the individual property of the deceased partner liable for any debts contracted by such person or partnership.

Sec. 42. Rights of Retiring or Estate of Deceased Partner When the Business is Continued.

When any partner retires or dies, and the business is continued under any of the conditions set forth in section 41 (1, 2, 3, 5, 6), or section 38(2b), without any settlement of accounts as between him or his estate and the person or partnership continuing the business, unless otherwise agreed, he or his legal representative as against such persons or partnership may have the value of his interest at the date of dissolution ascertained, and shall receive as an ordinary creditor an amount equal to the value of his interest in the dissolved partnership with interest, or, at his option or at the option of his legal representative, in lieu of interest, the profits attributable to the use of his right in the property of the dissolved partnership; provided that the creditors of the dissolved partnership as against the separate creditors, or the representative of the retired or deceased partner, shall have priority on any claim arising under this section, as provided by section 41(8) of this act.

Sec. 43. Accrual of Actions.

The right to an account of his interest shall accrue to any partner, or his legal representative, as against the winding up partners or the surviving partners or the person or partnership continuing the business, at the date of dissolution, in the absence of any agreement to the contrary.

Part VII Miscellaneous Provisions

Sec. 44. When Act Takes Effect.

This act shall take effect on the _____ day of _____ one thousand nine hundred and _____.

Sec. 45. Legislation Repealed.

All acts or parts of acts inconsistent with this act are hereby repealed.

Appendix
C

UNIFORM LIMITED PARTNERSHIP ACT

(Adopted in 39 States, all except Arkansas, Colorado, Connecticut, Louisiana, Maryland, Minnesota, Montana, Nebraska, Washington, West Virginia, and Wyoming.   Also adopted in the District of Columbia, and the Virgin Islands.)

Sec. 1. **Limited Partnership Defined.**

A limited partnership is a partnership formed by two or more persons under the provisions of Section 2, having as members one or more general partners and one or more limited partners. The limited partners as such shall not be bound by the obligations of the partnership.

Sec. 2. **Formation.**

(1) Two or more persons desiring to form a limited partnership shall

(a) Sign and swear to a certificate, which shall state

I. The name of the partnership,

II. The character of the business,

III. The location of the principal place of business,

IV. The name and place of residence of each member; general and limited partners being respectively designated,

V. The term for which the partnership is to exist,

VI. The amount of cash and a description of and the agreed value of the other property contributed by each limited partner,

VII. The additional contributions, if any, agreed to be made by each limited partner and the times at which or events on the happening of which they shall be made,

VIII. The time, if agreed upon, when the contribution of each limited partner is to be returned,

IX. The share of the profits or the other compensation by way of income which each limited partner shall receive by reason of his contribution,

X. The right, if given, of a limited partner to substitute an assignee as contributor in his place, and the terms and conditions of the substitution,

XI. The right, if given, of the partners to admit additional limited partners,

XII. The right, if given, of one or more of the limited partners to priority over other limited partners, as to contributions or as to compensation by way of income, and the nature of such priority,

XIII. The right, if given, of the remaining general partner or partners to continue the business on the death, retirement or insanity of a general partner, and

XIV. The right, if given, of a limited partner to demand and receive property other than cash in return for his contribution.

(b) File for record the certificate in the office of [here designate the proper office].

(2) A limited partnership is formed if there has been substantial compliance in good faith with the requirements of paragraph (1).

Sec. 3. Business Which May Be Carried On.

A limited partnership may carry on any business which a partnership without limited partners may carry on, except [here designate the business to be prohibited].

Sec. 4. Character of Limited Partner's Contribution.

The contributions of a limited partner may be cash or other property, but not services.

Sec. 5. A Name Not to Contain Surname of Limited Partner; Exceptions.

(1) The surname of a limited partner shall not appear in the partnership name, unless

(a) It is also the surname of a general partner, or

(b) Prior to the time when the limited partner became such the business had been carried on under a name in which his surname appeared.

(2) A limited partner whose name appears in a partnership name contrary to the provisions of paragraph (1) is liable as a general partner to partnership creditors who extend credit to the partnership without actual knowledge that he is not a general partner.

Sec. 6. Liability for False Statements in Certificate.

If the certificate contains a false statement, one who suffers loss by reliance on such statement may hold liable any party to the certificate who knew the statement to be false.

(a) At the time he signed the certificate, or

(b) Subsequently, but within a sufficient time before the statement was relied upon to enable him to cancel or amend the certificate, or to file a petition for its cancellation or amendment as provided in Section 25(3).

Sec. 7. Limited Partner Not Liable to Creditors.

A limited partner shall not become liable as a general partner unless, in addition to the exercise of his rights and powers as a limited partner, he takes part in the control of the business.

Sec. 8. Admission of Additional Limited Partners.

After the formation of a limited partnership, additional limited partners may be admitted upon filing an amendment to the original certificate in accordance with the requirements of Section 25.

Sec. 9. Rights, Powers and Liabilities of a General Partner.

(1) A general partner shall have all the rights and powers and be subject to all the restrictions and liabilities of a partner in a partnership without limited partners, except that without the written consent or ratification of the specific act by all the limited partners, a general partner or all of the general partners have no authority to

(a) Do any act in contravention of the certificate,

(b) Do any act which would make it impossible to carry on the ordinary business of the partnership,

(c) Confess a judgment against the partnership,

(d) Possess partnership property, or assign their rights in specific partnership property, for other than a partnership purpose,

(e) Admit a person as a general partner,

(f) Admit a person as a limited partner, unless the right so to do is given in the certificate,

(g) Continue the business with partnership property on the death, retirement or insanity of a general partner, unless the right so to do is given in the certificate.

Sec. 10 Rights of a Limited Partner.

(1) A limited partner shall have the same rights as a general partner to

(a) Have the partnership books kept at the principal place of business of the partnership, and at all times to inspect and copy any of them,

(b) Have on demand true and full information of all things affecting the partnership, and a formal account of partnership affairs, whenever circumstances render it just and reasonable, and

(c) Have dissolution and winding up by decree of court.

(2) A limited partner shall have the right to receive a share of the profits or other compensation by way of income, and to the return of his contribution as provided in Sections 15 and 16.

Sec. 11. **Status of Person Erroneously Believing Himself a Limited Partner.**

A person who has contributed to the capital of a business conducted by a person or partnership erroneously believing that he has become a limited partner in a limited partnership, is not, by reason of his exercise of the rights of a limited partner, a general partner with the person or in the partnership carrying on the business, or bound by the obligations of such person or partnership; provided that on ascertaining the mistake he promptly renounces his interest in the profits of the business, or other compensation by way of income.

Sec. 12. **One Person Both General and Limited Partner.**

(1) A person may be a general partner and a limited partner in the same partnership at the same time.

(2) A person who is a general, and also at the same time a limited partner, shall have all the rights and powers and be subject to all the restrictions of a general partner; except that, in respect to his contribution, he shall have the rights against the other members which he would have had if he were not also a general partner.

Sec. 13. **Loans and Other Business Transactions with Limited Partner.**

(1) A limited partner also may loan money to and transact other business with the partnership, and, unless he is also a general partner, receive on account of resulting claims against the partnership, with general creditors, a pro rata share of the assets. No limited partner shall in respect to any such claim

(a) Receive or hold as collateral security any partnership property, or

(b) Receive from a general partner or the partnership any payment, conveyance, or release from liability, if at the time the assets of the partnership are not sufficient to discharge partnership liabilities to persons not claiming as general or limited partners.

(2) The receiving of collateral security, or a payment, conveyance, or release in violation of the provisions of paragraph (1) is a fraud on the creditors of the partnership.

Sec. 14. **Relation of Limited Partners Inter Se.**

Where there are several limited partners the members may agree that one or more of the limited partners shall have a priority over other limited partners as to the return of their contributions, as to their compensation by way of income, or as to any other matter. If such an agreement is made it shall be stated in the certificate, and in the absence of such a statement all the limited partners shall stand upon equal footing.

Sec. 15. **Compensation of Limited Partner.**

A limited partner may receive from the partnership the share of the profits or the compensation by way of income stipulated for in the certificate; provided, that after such payment is made, whether from the property of the partnership or that of a general partner, the partnership assets are in excess of all liabilities of the partnership except liabilities to limited partners on account of their contributions and to general partners.

Sec. 16. **Withdrawal or Reduction of Limited Partner's Contribution.**

(1) A limited partner shall not receive from a general partner or out of partnership property any part of his contribution until

(a) All liabilities of the partnership, except liabilities to general partners and to limited partners on account of their contributions, have been paid or there remains property of the partnership sufficient to pay them,

(b) The consent of all members is had, unless the return of the contribution may be rightfully demanded under the provisions of paragraph (2), and

(c) The certificate is cancelled or so amended as to set forth the withdrawal or reduction.

(2) Subject to the provisions of paragraph (1) a limited partner may rightfully demand the return of his contribution

(a) On the dissolution of a partnership, or

(b) When the date specified in the certificate for its return has arrived, or

(c) After he has given six months' notice in writing to all other members, if no time is specified in the certificate either for the return of the contribution or for the dissolution of the partnership.

(3) In the absence of any statement in the certificate to the contrary or the consent of all members, a limited partner, irrespective of the nature of his contribution, has only the right to demand and receive cash in return for his contribution.

(4) A limited partner may have the partnership dissolved and its affairs wound up when

(a) He rightfully but unsuccessfully demands the return of his contribution, or

(b) The other liabilities of the partnership have not been paid, or the partnership property is insufficient for their payment as required by paragraph (1a) and the limited partner would otherwise be entitled to the return of his contribution.

Sec. 17. Liability of Limited Partner to Partnership.

(1) A limited partner is liable to the partnership

(a) For the difference between his contribution as actually made and that stated in the certificate as having been made, and

(b) For any unpaid contribution which he agreed in the certificate to make in the future at the time and on the conditions stated in the certificate.

(2) A limited partner holds as trustee for the partnership

(a) Specific property stated in the certificate as contributed by him, but which was not contributed or which has been wrongfully returned, and

(b) Money or other property wrongfully paid or conveyed to him on account of his contribution.

(3) The liabilities of a limited partner as set forth in this section can be waived or compromised only by the consent of all members; but a waiver or compromise shall not affect the right of a creditor of a partnership, who extended credit or whose claim arose after the filing and before a cancellation or amendment of the certificate, to enforce such liabilities.

(4) When a contributor has rightfully received the return in whole or in part of the capital of his contribution, he is nevertheless liable to the partnership for any sum, not in excess of such return with interest, necessary to discharge its liabilities to all creditors who extended credit or whose claims arose before such return.

Sec. 18. Nature of Limited Partner's Interest in Partnership.

A limited partner's interest in the partnership is personal property.

Sec. 19. Assignment of Limited Partner's Interest.

(1) A limited partner's interest is assignable.

(2) A substituted limited partner is a person admitted to all the rights of a limited partner who has died or has assigned his interest in a partnership.

(3) An assignee, who does not become a substituted limited partner, has no right to require any information or account of the partnership transactions or to inspect the partnership books; he is only entitled to receive the share of the profits or other compensation by way of income, or the return of his contribution, to which his assignor would otherwise be entitled.

(4) An assignee shall have the right to become a substituted limited partner if all the members (except the assignor) consent thereto or if the assignor, being thereunto empowered by the certificate, gives the assignee that right.

(5) An assignee becomes a substituted limited partner when the certificate is appropriately amended in accordance with Section 25.

(6) The substituted limited partner has all the rights and powers, and is subject to all the restrictions and liabilities of his assignor, except those liabilities of which he was ignorant at the time he became a limited partner and which could not be ascertained from the certificate.

(7) The substitution of the assignee as a limited partner does not release the assignor from liability to the partnership under Sections 6 and 17.

Sec. 20. Effect of Retirement, Death or Insanity of a General Partner.

The retirement, death or insanity of a general partner dissolves the partnership, unless the business is continued by the remaining general partners

(a) Under a right so to do stated in the certificate, or

(b) With the consent of all members.

Sec. 21. Death of Limited Partner.

(1) On the death of a limited partner his executor or administrator shall have all the rights of a limited partner for the purpose of settling his estate, and such power as the deceased had to constitute his assignee a substituted limited partner.

(2) The estate of a deceased limited partner shall be liable for all his liabilities as a limited partner.

Sec. 22. Rights of Creditors of Limited Partner.

(1) On due application to a court of competent jurisdiction by any judgment creditor of a limited partner, the court may charge the interest of the indebted limited partner with payment of the unsatisfied amount of the judgment debt; and may appoint a receiver, and make all other orders, directions, and inquiries which the circumstances of the case may require.

In those states where a creditor on beginning an action can attach debts due the defendant before he has obtained a judgment against the defendant it is recommended that paragraph (1) of this section read as follows:

On due application to a court of competent jurisdiction by any creditor of a limited partner, the court may charge the interest of the indebted limited partner with payment of the unsatisfied amount of such claim; and may appoint a receiver, and make all other orders, directions, and inquiries which the circumstances of the case may require.

(2) The interest may be redeemed with the separate property of any general partner, but may not be redeemed with partnership property.

(3) The remedies conferred by paragraph (1) shall not be deemed exclusive of others which may exist.

(4) Nothing in this act shall be held to deprive a limited partner of his statutory exemption.

Sec. 23. **Distribution of Assets.**

(1) In settling accounts after dissolution the liabilities of the partnership shall be entitled to payment in the following order:

(a) Those to creditors, in the order of priority as provided by law, except those to limited partners on account of their contributions, and to general partners,

(b) Those to limited partners in respect to their share of the profits and other compensation by way of income on their contributions,

(c) Those to limited partners in respect to the capital of their contributions,

(d) Those to general partners other than for capital and profits,

(e) Those to general partners in respect to profits,

(f) Those to general partners in respect to capital.

(2) Subject to any statement in the certificate or to subsequent agreement, limited partners share in the partnership assets in respect to their claims for capital, and in respect to their claims for profits or for compensation by way of income on their contributions respectively, in proportion to the respective amounts of such claims.

Sec. 24. **When Certificate Shall be Cancelled or Amended.**

(1) The certificate shall be cancelled when the partnership is dissolved or all limited partners cease to be such.

(2) A certificate shall be amended when
(a) There is a change in the name of the partnership or in the amount or character of the contribution of any limited partner,

(b) A person is substituted as a limited partner,

(c) An additional limited partner is admitted,

(d) A person is admitted as a general partner,

(e) A general partner retires, dies or becomes insane, and the business is continued under section 20,

(f) There is a change in the character of the business of the partnership,

(g) There is a false or erroneous statement in the certificate,

(h) There is a change in the time as stated in the certificate for the dissolution of the partnership or for the return of a contribution,

(i) A time is fixed for the dissolution of the partnership, or the return of a contribution, no time having been specified in the certificate, or

(j) The members desire to make a change in any other statement in the certificate in order that it shall accurately represent the agreement between them.

Sec. 25. **Requirements for Amendment and for Cancellation of Certificate.**

(1) The writing to amend a certificate shall

(a) Conform to the requirements of Section 2(1a) as far as necessary to set forth clearly the change in the certificate which it is desired to make, and

(b) Be signed and sworn to by all members, and an amendment substituting a limited partner or adding a limited or general partner shall be signed also by the member to be substituted or added, and when a limited partner is to be substituted, the amendment shall also be signed by the assigning limited partner.

(2) The writing to cancel a certificate shall be signed by all members.

(3) A person desiring the cancellation or amendment of a certificate, if any person designated in paragraphs (1) and (2) as a person who must execute the writing refuses to do so, may petition the [here designate the proper court] to direct a cancellation or amendment thereof.

(4) If the court finds that the petitioner has a right to have the writing executed by a person who refuses to do so, it shall order the [here designate the responsible official in the office designated in Section 2] in the office where the certificate is recorded to record the cancellation or amendment of the certificate; and where the certificate is to be amended, the court shall also cause to be filed for record in said office a certified copy of its decree setting forth the amendment.

(5) A certificate is amended or cancelled when there is filed for record in the office [here designate the office designated in Section 2] where the certificate is recorded

(a) A writing in accordance with the provisions of paragraph (1), or (2) or

(b) A certified copy of the order of court in accordance with the provisions of paragraph (4).

(6) After the certificate is duly amended in accordance with this section, the amended certificate shall thereafter be for all purposes the certificate provided for by this act.

Sec. 26. **Parties to Actions.**

A contributor, unless he is a general partner, is not a proper party to proceedings by or against a partnership, except where the object is to enforce a limited partner's right against or liability to the partnership.

Sec. 27. **Name of Act.**

This act may be cited as The Uniform Limited Partnership Act.

Sec. 28. **Rules of Construction.**

(1) The rule that statutes in derogation of the common law are to be strictly construed shall have no application to this act.

(2) This act shall be so interpreted and construed as to effect its general purpose to make uniform the law of those states which enact it.

(3) This act shall not be so construed as to impair the obligations of any contract existing when the act goes into effect, nor to affect any action on proceedings begun or right accrued before this act takes effect.

Sec. 29. **Rules for Cases Not Provided for in this Act.**

In any case not provided for in this act the rules of law and equity, including the law merchant, shall govern.

Sec. 30.[1] **Provisions for Existing Limited Partnerships.**

(1) A limited partnership formed under any statute of this state prior to the adoption of this act, may become a limited partnership under this act by complying with the provisions of Section 2; provided the certificate sets forth

(a) The amount of the original contribution of each limited partner, and the time when the contribution was made, and

(b) That the property of the partnership exceeds the amount sufficient to discharge its liabilities to persons not claiming as general or limited partners by an amount greater than the sum of the contributions of its limited partners.

(2) A limited partnership formed under any statute of this state prior to the adoption of this act, until or unless it becomes a limited partnership under this act, shall continue to be governed by the provisions of [here insert proper reference to the existing limited partnership act or acts], except that such partnership shall not be renewed unless so provided in the original agreement.

Sec. 31.[1] **Act [Acts] Repealed.**

Except as affecting existing limited partnerships to the extent set forth in Section 30, the act (acts) of [here designate the existing limited partnership act or acts] is (are) hereby repealed.

[1]Sections 30, 31, will be omitted in any state which has not a limited partnership act.

Appendix
D

REVISED UNIFORM LIMITED PARTNERSHIP ACT

(Adopted August 5, 1976, by the National Conference of Commissioners on Uniform State Laws, subject to style changes; it is intended that it will replace the existing Uniform Limited Partnership Act (Appendix C); as of publication, it has been adopted in Arkansas, Colorado, Connecticut, Maryland, Minnesota, Montana, Nebraska, Washington, West Virginia, and Wyoming.

The Act consists of 11 Articles as follows:

1. General Provisions
2. Formation; Certificate of Limited Partnership
3. Limited Partners
4. General Partners
5. Finance
6. Distribution and Withdrawal
7. Assignment of Partnership Interests
8. Dissolution
9. Foreign Limited Partnerships
10. Derivative Actions
11. Miscellaneous

Article 1
GENERAL PROVISIONS

Sec. 101. **Definitions.**

As used in this Act:

(1) "Certificate of limited partnership" means the certificate referred to in Section 201, as that certificate is amended from time to time.

(2) "Contribution" means any cash, property, or services rendered, or a promissory note or other binding obligation to contribute cash or property or to perform services, which a partner contributes to a limited partnership in his capacity as a partner.

(3) "Event of withdrawal of a general partner" means an event that causes a person to cease to be a general partner as provided in Section 402.

(4) "Foreign limited partnership" means a partnership formed under the laws of any state other than this State and having as partners one or more general partners and one or more limited partners.

(5) "General partner" means a person who has been admitted to a limited partnership as a general partner in accordance with the partnership agreement and who is named in the certificate of limited partnership as a general partner.

(6) "Limited partner" means a person who has been admitted to a limited partnership as a limited partner in accordance with the partnership agreement and who is named in the certificate of limited partnership as a limited partner.

(7) "Limited partnership" and "domestic limited partnership" mean a partnership formed by 2 or more persons under the laws of this State and having one or more general partners and one or more limited partners.

(8) "Partner" means any limited partner or general partner.

(9) "Partnership agreement" means the agreement, written or, to the extent not prohibited by law, oral or both, of the partners as to the affairs of a limited partnership and the conduct of its business.

(10) "Partnership interest" has the meaning specified in Section 701.

(11) "Person" means a natural person, partnership, limited partnership (domestic or foreign), trust, estate, association, or corporation.

(12) "State" means a state, territory, or possession of the United States, the District of Columbia, or the Commonwealth of Puerto Rico.

Sec. 102. **Name.**

The name of each limited partnership as set forth in its certificate of limited partnership:

(1) shall contain the words "limited partnership" in full;

(2) may not contain the name of a limited partner unless (i) it is also the name of a general partner or (ii) the business of the limited partnership had been carried on under that name before the admission of that limited partner;

(3) may not contain any word or phrase indicating or implying that it is organized other than for a purpose stated in its certificate of limited partnership;

(4) may not be the same as, or deceptively similar to, the name of any corporation or limited partnership organized under the laws of this State or licensed or registered as a foreign corporation or limited partnership in this State; and

(5) may not contain the following words [here insert prohibited words].

Sec. 103. **Reservation of Name.**

(a) The exclusive right to the use of a name may be reserved by:

(1) any person intending to organize a limited partnership under this Act and to adopt that name;

(2) any domestic limited partnership or any foreign limited partnership registered in this State which, in either case, intends to adopt that name;

(3) any foreign limited partnership intending to register in this State and to adopt that name; and

(4) any person intending to organize a foreign limited partnership and intending to have it registered in this State and to adopt that name.

(b) The reservation shall be made by filing with the Secretary of State an application, executed by the applicant, to reserve a specified name. If the Secretary of State finds that the name is available for use by a domestic or foreign limited partnership, he shall reserve the name for the exclusive use of the applicant for a period of 120 days. Once having reserved a name, the same applicant may not again reserve the same name until more than 60 days after the expiration of the last 120-day period for which that applicant had reserved that name. The right to the exclusive use of a name so reserved may be transferred to any other person by filing in the office of the Secretary of State a notice of the transfer, executed by the applicant for whom the name was reserved and specifying the name and address of the transferee.

Sec. 104. **Specified Office and Agent.**

Each limited partnership shall continuously maintain in this State:

(1) an office, which may but need not be a place of its business in this State, at which shall be kept the records required to be maintained by Section 105; and

(2) an agent for service of process on the limited partnership, which agent must be an individual resident of this State, a domestic corporation, or a foreign corporation authorized to do business in this State.

Sec. 105. **Records to be Kept.**

Each limited partnership shall keep at the office referred to in Section 104(1) the following: (1) a current list of the full name and last-known business address of each partner set forth in alphabetical order, (2) a copy of the certificate of limited partnership and all certificates of amendment thereto, together with executed copies of any powers of attorney pursuant to which any certificate has been executed, (3) copies of the limited partnership's federal, state, and local income tax returns and reports, if any, for the 3 most recent years, and (4) copies of any then effective written partnership agreements and of any financial statements of the limited partnership for the 3 most recent years. These records shall be available for inspection and copying at the reasonable request, and at the expense, of any partner during ordinary business hours.

Sec. 106. **Nature of Business.**

A limited partnership may carry on any business that a partnership without limited partners may carry on except [here designate prohibited activities].

Sec. 107. **Business Transactions of Partner with the Partnership.**

Except as otherwise provided in the partnership agreement, a partner may lend money to and transact other business with the limited partnership and, subject to other applicable provisions of law, has the same rights and obligations with respect thereto as a person who is not a partner.

Article 2
FORMATION; CERTIFICATE OF LIMITED PARTNERSHIP

Sec. 201. **Certificate of Limited Partnership.**

(a) Two or more persons desiring to form a limited partnership shall execute a certificate of limited partnership. The certificate shall be filed in the office of the Secretary of State and shall set forth:

(1) the name of the limited partnership;

(2) the general character of its business;

(3) the address of the office and the name and address of the agent for service of process required to be maintained by Section 104;

(4) the name and the business address of each partner (specifying the general partners and limited partners separately);

(5) the amount of cash and a description and statement of the agreed value of the other property or services contributed by each partner and which each partner has agreed to contribute in the future;

(6) the times at which or events on the happening of which any additional contributions agreed to be made by each partner are to be made;

(7) any power of a limited partner to grant an assignee of any part of his partnership interest the right to become a limited partner, and the terms and conditions of the power;

(8) if agreed upon, the time at which or the events on the happening of which a partner may terminate his membership in the limited partnership and the amount of, or the method of determining, the distribution to which he may be entitled respecting his partnership interest, and the terms and conditions of the termination and distribution;

(9) any right of a partner to receive distributions of property including cash from the limited partnership;

(10) any right of a partner to receive, or of a general partner to make, distributions to a partner which include a return of all or any part of the partner's contribution;

(11) any time at which or events upon the happening of which the limited partnership is to be dissolved and its affairs wound up;

(12) any right of the remaining general partners to continue the business on the happening of an event of withdrawal of a general partner; and

(13) any other matters the partners, in their sole discretion, determine to include therein.

(b) A limited partnership is formed at the time of the filing of the certificate of limited partnership in the office of the Secretary of State or at any later time specified in the certificate of limited partnership if, in each case, there has been substantial compliance with the requirements of this section.

Sec. 202. **Amendments to Certificate.**

(a) A certificate of limited partnership is amended by filing a certificate of amendment thereto in the office of the Secretary of State. The certificate shall set forth:

(1) the name of the limited partnership;

(2) the date of filing of the certificate; and

(3) the amendments to the certificate.

(b) Within 30 days after the happening of any of the following events an amendment to a certificate of limited partnership reflecting the occurrence of the event or events shall be filed:

(1) a change in the amount or character of the contribution of any partner, or in any partner's obligation to make a contribution;

(2) the admission of a new partner;

(3) the withdrawal of a partner; and

(4) the continuation of the business under Section 801 after an event of withdrawal of a general partner.

(c) A certificate of limited partnership must be amended promptly by any general partner upon becoming aware that any statement therein was false when made or that any arrangements or other facts described have changed, making the certificate inaccurate in any respect, but amendments to show changes of addresses of limited partners need be filed only once every 12 months.

(d) A certificate of limited partnership may be amended at any time for any other proper purpose the general partners may determine.

(e) No person shall have any liability because an amendment to a certificate of limited partnership has not been filed to reflect the occurrence of any event referred to in subsection (b) of this section if the amendment is filed within the 30-day period specified in subsection (b).

Sec. 203. **Cancellation of Certificate.**

A certificate of limited partnership shall be cancelled upon the dissolution and the commencement of winding up of the limited partnership and at any other time there are no remaining limited partners. A certificate of cancellation shall be filed in the office of the Secretary of State and shall set forth:

(1) the name of the limited partnership;

(2) the date of filing of its certificate of limited partnership;

(3) the reason for filing the certificate of cancellation;

(4) the effective date (which shall be a date certain) of cancellation if it is not to be effective upon the filing of the certificate; and

(5) any other information the general partners filing the certificate may determine.

Sec. 204. **Execution of Certificates.**

(a) Each certificate required by this Article to be filed in the office of the Secretary of State shall be executed in the following manner:

(1) each original certificate of limited partnership must be signed by each partner named therein;

(2) each certificate of amendment must be signed by at least one general partner and by each other partner who is designated in the certificate as a new partner or whose contribution is described as having been increased; and

(3) each certificate of cancellation must be signed by each general partner.

(b) Any person may sign a certificate by an attorney-in-fact, but any power of attorney to sign a certificate relating to the admission or increased contribution of a partner must specifically describe the admission or increase.

(c) The execution of a certificate by a general partner constitutes an affirmation under the penalties of perjury that the facts stated therein are true.

Sec. 205. **Amendment or Cancellation by Judicial Act.**

If the persons required by Section 204 to execute any certificate of amendment or cancellation fail or refuse to do so, any other partner, and any assignee of a partnership interest, who is adversely affected by the failure or refusal, may petition the [here designate the proper court] to direct the amendment or cancellation. If the court finds that the amendment or cancellation is proper and that the persons so designated have failed or refused to execute the certificate, it shall order the Secretary of State to record an appropriate certificate of amendment or cancellation.

Sec. 206. **Filing in the Office of the Secretary of State.**

(a) Two signed copies of the certificate of limited partnership and of any certificates of amendment or cancellation (or of any judicial decree of amendment or cancellation) shall be delivered to the Secretary of State. A person who executes a certificate as an agent or fiduciary need not exhibit evidence of his authority as a prerequisite to filing. Unless the Secretary of State finds that any certificate does not conform to law, upon receipt of all filing fees required by law the Secretary of State shall:

(1) endorse on each duplicate original the word "Filed" and the day, month, and year of the filing thereof;

(2) file one duplicate original in his office; and

(3) return the other duplicate original to the person who filed it or his representative.

(b) Upon the filing of a certificate of amendment (or judicial decree of amendment) in the office of the Secretary of State, the certificate of limited partnership shall be amended as set forth therein, and upon the effective date of a certificate of cancellation (or a judicial decree thereof), the certificate of limited partnership shall be cancelled.

Sec. 207. **Liability for False Statement in Certificate.**

If any certificate of limited partnership or certificate of amendment or cancellation contains a false statement, one who suffers loss by reliance on the statement may recover damages for the loss from:

(1) any person actually executing, or causing another to execute on his behalf, the certificate who knew, and any general partner who knew or should have known, the statement to be false at the time the certificate was executed; and

(2) any general partner who thereafter knew or should have known that any arrangements or other facts described in the certificate have changed, making the statement inaccurate in any respect, within a sufficient time before the statement was relied upon to have reasonably enabled that general

partner to cancel or amend the certificate, or to file a petition for its cancellation or amendment under Section 205.

Sec. 208. **Constructive Notice.**

The fact that a certificate of limited partnership is on file in the office of the Secretary of State is constructive notice that the partnership is a limited partnership and that the persons designated therein as limited partners are limited partners, but is not constructive notice of any other fact.

Sec. 209. **Delivery of Certificates to Limited Partners.**

Upon the return by the Secretary of State pursuant to Section 206 of any certificate marked "Filed," the general partners shall promptly deliver or mail a copy of the certificate to each limited partner unless the partnership agreement provides otherwise.

Article 3
LIMITED PARTNERS

Sec. 301. **Admission of Additional Limited Partners.**

(a) After the filing of a limited partnership's original certificate of limited partnership, a person may be admitted as a new limited partner:

(1) in the case of a person acquiring a partnership interest directly from the limited partnership, upon compliance with the partnership agreement or, if the partnership agreement does not so provide, upon the written consent of all partners; and

(2) in the case of an assignee of a partnership interest of a partner who has the power, as provided in Section 704, to grant the assignee the right to become a limited partner, upon the exercise of that power and compliance with any conditions limiting the grant or exercise of the power.

(b) In each case under subsection (a), the person acquiring the partnership interest becomes a limited partner only upon amendment of the certificate of limited partnership reflecting that fact.

Sec. 302. **Voting.**

Subject to the provisions of Section 303, the partnership agreement may grant to all or a specified group of the limited partners the right to vote (on a per capita or any other basis) upon any matter.

Sec. 303. **Liability to Third Parties.**

(a) Except as provided in subsection (d), a limited partner as such is not liable for the obligations of a limited partnership unless, in addition to the exercise of his rights and powers as a limited partner, he takes part in the control of the business. But the limited partner's participation in the control of the business is not substantially the same as the exercise of the powers of a general partner, he is liable only to persons who transact business with the limited partnership with actual knowledge of his participation in control.

(b) A limited partner does not participate in the control of the business within the meaning of subsection (a) solely by doing one or more of the following:

(1) being a contractor for or an agent or employee of the limited partnership or of a general partner;

(2) consulting with and advising a general partner with respect to the business of the limited partnership;

(3) acting as surety for the limited partnership;

(4) approving or disapproving an amendment to the partnership agreement; and

(5) voting on one or more of the following matters:

(i) the dissolution and winding up of the limited partnership;

(ii) the sale, exchange, lease, mortgage, pledge, or other transfer of all or substantially all of the assets of the limited partnership other than in the ordinary course of its business;

(iii) the incurrence of indebtedness by the limited partnership other than in the ordinary course of its business;

(iv) a change in the nature of the business; or

(v) the removal of a general partner.

(c) The enumeration in subsection (b) shall not be construed to mean that the possession or exercise of any other powers by a limited partner constitutes participation by him in the business of the limited partnership.

(d) A limited partner who knowingly permits his name to be used in the name of the limited partnership, except under circumstances permitted by Section 102(2)(i), is liable to creditors who extend credit to the limited partnership without actual knowledge that the limited partner is not a general partner.

Sec. 304. **Person Erroneously Believing Himself a Limited Partner.**

(a) Except as provided in subsection (b) a person who makes a contribution to a business enterprise and erroneously and in good faith believes that he has become a limited partner in the enterprise is not a general partner in the enterprise and is not bound by its obligations by reason of making the contribution, receiving distributions from the enterprise, or exercising any rights of a limited partner, if, on ascertaining the mistake, he:

(1) causes an appropriate certificate of limited partnership or a certificate of amendment to be executed and filed; or

(2) withdraws from future equity participation in the enterprise.

(b) Any person who makes a contribution of the kind described in subsection (a) is liable as a general partner to any third party who transacts business with the enterprise (i) before the person withdraws and an appropriate certificate if any is filed to show the withdrawal, or (ii) before an appropriate certificate is filed to show his status as a limited partner and, in the case of an amendment, after expiration of the 30-day period for filing an amendment relating to the person as a limited partner under Section 202, but in each case only if the third party actually believed in good faith that the person was a general partner at the time of the transaction.

Sec. 305. **Information.**

Each limited partner has the right to:

(1) inspect and copy any of the partnership records required to be maintained by Section 105; and

(2) obtain from the general partners from time to time upon reasonable demand (i) true and full information regarding the state of the business and financial condition of the limited partnership, (ii) promptly after becoming available, a copy of the limited partnership's federal, state, and local income tax return for each year, and (iii) any other information regarding the affairs of the limited partnership as is just and reasonable.

Article 4
GENERAL PARTNERS

Sec. 401. **Admission.**

After the filing of a limited partnership's original certificate of limited partnership, new general partners may be admitted only with the specific written consent of each partner.

Sec. 402. **Events of Withdrawal.**

Except as otherwise approved by the specific written consent at the time of all partners, a person ceases to be a general partner of a limited partnership upon the happening of any of the following events:

(1) the general partner withdraws from the limited partnership as provided in Section 602;

(2) the general partner ceases to be a member of the limited partnership as provided in Section 702;

(3) the general partner is removed as a general partner in accordance with the partnership agreement;

(4) unless otherwise provided in the certificate of limited partnership, the general partner: makes an assignment for the benefit of creditors; files a voluntary petition in bankruptcy; is adjudicated a bankrupt or insolvent; files any petition or answer seeking for himself any reorganization, arrangement, composition, readjustment, liquidation, dissolution, or similar relief under any statute, law, or regulation; files any answer or other pleading admitting or failing to contest the material allegations of a petition filed against him in any proceeding of this nature; or seeks, consents to, or acquiesces in the appointment of any trustee, receiver, or liquidator of the general partner or of all or any substantial part of his properties;

(5) unless otherwise provided in the certificate of limited partnership, [120] days after the commencement of any proceeding against the general partner seeking any reorganization, arrangement, composition, readjustment, liquidation, dissolution, or similar relief under any statute, law, or regulation, the proceeding has not been dismissed, or if, within [90] days after the appointment without his consent or acquiescence of any trustee, receiver, or liquidator of the general partner or of all or any substantial part of his properties, the appointment is not vacated or stayed, or if, within [90] days after the expiration of any stay, the appointment is not vacated;

(6) in the case of a general partner who is a natural person

(i) his death; or

(ii) the entry by a court of competent jurisdiction adjudicating him incompetent to manage his person or his property;

(7) in the case of a general partner who is acting as such in the capacity of a trustee of a trust, the

termination of the trust (but not merely the substitution of a new trustee);

(8) in the case of a general partner that is a partnership, the dissolution and commencement of winding up of the partnership;

(9) in the case of a general partner that is a corporation, the filing of a certificate of dissolution, or its equivalent, for the corporation or the revocation of its charter; and

(10) in the case of an estate, the distribution by the fiduciary of all the estate's interest in the partnership.

Sec. 403. **General Powers and Liabilities.**

Except as otherwise provided in this Act and in the partnership agreement, a general partner of a limited partnership has all the rights and powers and is subject to all the restrictions and liabilities of a partner in a partnership without limited partners.

Sec. 404. **Contributions by a General Partner.**

A general partner may make contributions to a limited partnership and share in the profits and losses of, and in distributions from, the limited partnership as a general partner. A general partner may also make contributions to and share in profits, losses, and distributions as a limited partner. A person who is both a general partner and a limited partner has all the rights and powers, and is subject to all the restrictions and liabilities, of a general partner and also has, except as otherwise provided in the partnership agreement, all powers, and is subject to the restrictions, of a limited partner to the extent he is participating in the partnership as a limited partner.

Sec. 405. **Voting.**

The partnership agreement may grant to all or a specified group of general partners the right to vote (on a per capita or any other basis), separately or with all or any class of the limited partners, on any matter.

Article 5
FINANCE

Sec. 501. **Form of Contributions.**

The contribution of a partner may be in cash, property, or services rendered, or a promissory note or other obligation to contribute cash or property or to perform services.

Sec. 502. **Liability for Contributions.**

(a) Except as otherwise provided in the certificate of limited partnership, a partner is obligated to the limited partnership to perform any promise to contribute cash or property or to perform services regardless of whether he is unable to perform because of death, disability or any other reason. If a partner does not make the required contribution of property or services, he is obligated at the option of the limited partnership to contribute cash equal to that portion of the value (as stated in the certificate of limited partnership) of the stated contribution that has not been made.

(b) Unless otherwise provided in the partnership agreement, the obligation of a partner to make a contribution or return money or other property paid or distributed in violation of this Act may be compromised only by consent of all of the partners. Notwithstanding a compromise so authorized, a creditor of a limited partnership who extends credit, or whose claim arises, after the filing of the certificate of limited partnership or an amendment thereto which, in either case, reflects the obligation and before the amendment or cancellation thereof to reflect the compromise may enforce the precompromise obligation.

Sec. 503. **Sharing of Profits and Losses.**

The profits and losses of a limited partnership shall be allocated among the partners, and among classes of partners, in the manner provided in the partnership agreement. If the partnership agreement does not so provide, profits and losses shall be allocated on the basis of the value (as stated in the certificate of limited partnership) of the contributions actually made by each partner to the extent they have not been returned.

Sec. 504. **Sharing of Distributions.**

Distributions of cash or other assets of a limited partnership shall be allocated among the partners, and among classes of partners, in the manner provided in the partnership agreement. If the partnership agreement does not so provide, distributions shall be made on the basis of the value (as stated in the certificate of limited partnership) of the contributions actually made by each partner to the extent they have not been returned.

Article 6
DISTRIBUTIONS AND WITHDRAWAL

Sec. 601. **Interim Distributions.**

Except as otherwise provided in this Article, a partner is entitled to receive distributions from a limited partnership before his withdrawal from the limited partnership and before the dissolution and winding up thereof:

(1) to the extent and at the times or upon the happening of the events specified in the partnership agreement; and

(2) if any distribution constitutes a return of any part of his contribution under Section 608(b), to the extent and at the times or upon the happening of the events specified in the certificate of limited partnership.

Sec. 602. **Withdrawal of General Partner.**

A general partner may withdraw from a limited partnership at any time by giving written notice to the other partners, but if the withdrawal violates the partnership agreement, the limited partnership may recover from the withdrawing general partner damages for breach of the partnership agreement and offset the damages against the amount otherwise distributable to him.

Sec. 603. **Withdrawal of Limited Partner.**

A limited partner may withdraw from a limited partnership at the time or upon the happening of the events specified in the certificate of limited partnership and in accordance with any procedures provided in the partnership agreement. If the certificate of limited partnership does not specify the time or the events upon the happening of which a limited partner may withdraw from the limited partnership or a definite time for the dissolution and winding up of the limited partnership, a limited partner may withdraw from the limited partnership upon not less than 6 months' prior written notice to each general partner at his address on the books of the limited partnership at its office in this State.

Sec. 604. **Distributions Upon Withdrawal.**

Except as provided in this Article, upon withdrawal any withdrawing partner is entitled to receive any distributions to which he is entitled under the partnership agreement and, if not provided, he is entitled to receive, within a reasonable time after withdrawal, the fair value of his interest in the limited partnership as of the date of withdrawal, based upon his right to share in distributions from the limited partnership.

Sec. 605. **Distributions in Kind.**

Except as provided in the certificate of limited partnership, a partner, regardless of the nature of his contribution, has no right to demand and receive any distribution from a limited partnership in any form other than cash. Except as provided in the partnership agreement, a partner may not be compelled to accept a distribution of any asset in kind from a limited partnership to the extent that the percentage of the asset distributed to him exceeds a percentage of that asset which is equal to the percentage in which he shares in distributions from the limited partnership.

Sec. 606. **Right to Distributions.**

At the time a partner becomes entitled to receive a distribution, he has the status of, and is entitled to all of the remedies available to, a creditor of the limited partnership with respect to the distribution.

Sec. 607. **Limitations on Distributions.**

A partner may not receive a distribution from a limited partnership to the extent that, after giving effect to the distribution, all liabilities of the limited partnership other than liabilities to partners on account of their partnership interests, exceed the fair value of the partnership's assets.

Sec. 608. **Liability Upon Return of Contributions.**

(a) If a partner has received the return of any part of his contribution without violation of the partnership agreement or this Act, for a period of one year thereafter he is liable to the limited partnership for the amount of his contribution returned, but only to the extent necessary to discharge the limited partnership's liabilities to creditors who extended credit to the limited partnership during the period the contribution was held by the partnership.

(b) If a partner has received the return of any part of his contribution in violation of the partnership agreement or this Act, for a period of 6 years thereafter he is liable to the limited partnership for the amount of the contribution wrongfully returned.

(c) A partner has received a return of his contribution to the extent that a distribution to him reduces his share of the fair value of the net assets of the limited partnership below the value (as set forth in the certificate of limited partnership) of his contributions which have not theretofore been distributed to him.

Article 7
ASSIGNMENT OF PARTNERSHIP INTERESTS

Sec. 701. **Nature of Partnership Interest.**

A partnership interest is a partner's share of the profits and losses of a limited partnership and the right to receive distributions of partnership assets. A partnership interest is personal property.

Sec. 702. **Assignment of Partnership Interest.**

Except as otherwise provided in the partnership agreement, a partnership interest is assignable in whole or in part. An assignment of a partnership interest does not dissolve a limited partnership nor entitle the assignee to become a partner or to exercise any of the rights thereof. An assignment only entitles the assignee to receive, to the extent assigned, any distributions to which the assignor would be entitled. Except as otherwise provided in the partnership agreement, a partner ceases to be a partner upon assignment of all his partnership interest.

Sec. 703. **Rights of Creditors.**

On due application to a court of competent jurisdiction by any judgment creditor of a partner, the court may charge the partnership interest of the partner with payment of the unsatisfied amount of the judgment debt with interest thereon. To the extent so charged, the judgment creditor has only the rights of an assignee of the partnership interest. This Act shall not be construed to deprive any partner of the benefit of any exemption laws applicable to his partnership interest.

Sec. 704. **Right of Assignee to Become Limited Partner.**

(a) An assignee of a partnership interest, including an assignee of a general partner, may become a limited partner if and to the extent that (1) the assignor gives the assignee that right in accordance with authority described in the certificate of limited partnership or, (2) in the absence of that authority, all other partners consent.

(b) An assignee who has become a limited partner has, to the extent assigned, all the rights and powers, and is subject to all the restrictions and liabilities, of a limited partner under the partnership agreement and this Act. An assignee who becomes a limited partner is also liable for the obligations of his assignor to make and return contributions as provided in Article 6, but the assignee is not obligated for liabilities unknown to the assignee at the time he became a limited partner and which could not be ascertained from the certificate of limited partnership.

(c) If an assignee of a partnership interest becomes a limited partner, the assignor is not released from the liability to the limited partnership under Sections 207 and 502.

Sec. 705. **Power of Estate of Deceased or Incompetent Partner.**

If a partner who is a natural person dies or a court of competent jurisdiction adjudges him to be incompetent to manage his person or his property, the partner's executor, administrator, guardian, conservator, or other legal representative may exercise all of the partner's rights for the purpose of settling his estate or administering his property, including any power the partner had to give an assignee the right to become a limited partner. If a partner that is a corporation, trust, or other entity other than a natural person is dissolved or terminated, those powers may be exercised by the legal representative or successor of the partner.

Article 8
DISSOLUTION

Sec. 801. **Nonjudicial Dissolution.**

A limited partnership is dissolved and its affairs shall be wound up upon the happening of the first to occur of the following:

(1) at the time or upon the happening of the events specified in the certificate of limited partnership;

(2) upon the unanimous written consent of all partners;

(3) upon the happening of an event of withdrawal of a general partner unless at the time there is at least one other general partner and the certificate of limited partnership permits the business of the limited partnership to be carried on by the remaining general partner and he does so, but the limited partnership shall not be dissolved or wound up by reason of any event of withdrawal if, within 90 days after the withdrawal, all partners agree in writing to continue the business of the limited partnership and to the appointment of one or more new general partners if necessary or desired; or

(4) upon entry of a decree of judicial dissolution in accordance with Section 802.

Sec. 802. **Dissolution by Decree of Court.**

On application by or for a partner the [here designate the proper court] court may decree a dissolution of a limited partnership whenever it is not reasonably practicable to carry on the business in conformity with the partnership agreement.

Sec. 803. **Winding Up.**

Unless otherwise provided in the partnership agreement, the general partners who have not wrongfully dissolved the limited partnership or, if none, the limited partners, may wind up the limited partnership's affairs; but any partner, his legal representative or his assignee, upon cause shown, may obtain winding up by the [here designate the proper court] court.

Sec. 804. **Distribution of Assets.**

Upon the winding up of a limited partnership, the assets shall be distributed as follows:

(1) to creditors, including partners who are creditors (to the extent otherwise permitted by law), in satisfaction of liabilities of the limited partnership other than liabilities for distributions to partners pursuant to Section 601 or 604;

(2) except as otherwise provided in the partnership agreement, to partners and ex-partners in satisfaction of liabilities for distributions pursuant to Section 601 or 604; and

(3) except as otherwise provided in the partnership agreement, to partners *first* for the return of their contributions and *second* respecting their partnership interests, in the proportions in which the partners share in distributions.

Article 9
FOREIGN LIMITED PARTNERSHIPS

Sec. 901. **Law Governing.**

Subject to the constitution and public policy of this State, the laws of the state under which a foreign limited partnership is organized govern its organization and internal affairs and the liability of its limited partners, and a foreign limited partnership may not be denied registration by reason of any difference between those laws and the laws of this State.

Sec. 902. **Registration.**

Before transacting business in this State, a foreign limited partnership shall register with the Secretary of State. In order to register, a foreign limited partnership shall submit to the Secretary of State in duplicate an application for registration as a foreign limited partnership, signed and sworn to by a general partner and setting forth:

(1) the name of the foreign limited partnership and, if different, the name under which it proposes to transact business and register in this State;

(2) the state and date of its formation;

(3) the general character of the business it proposes to transact in this State;

(4) the name and address of any agent for service of process on the foreign limited partnership whom the foreign limited partnership desires to appoint, which agent must be an individual resident of this State, a domestic corporation, or a foreign corporation authorized to do business in this State; and with a place of business in this State;

(5) a statement that the Secretary of State is appointed the agent of the foreign limited partnership for service of process if no agent has been appointed pursuant to paragraph (4) or, if appointed the agent's authority has been revoked or the agent cannot be found or served with the exercise of reasonable diligence;

(6) the address of the office required to be maintained in the state of its organization by the laws of that state or, if not so required, of the principal office of the foreign limited partnership; and

(7) if the certificate of limited partnership filed in the foreign limited partnership's state of organization is not required to include the names and business addresses of the partners, a list of the names and addresses.

Sec. 903. **Issuance of Registration.**

(a) If the Secretary of State finds that an application for registration conforms to law and all requisite fees have been paid, he shall:

(1) endorse on the application the word "Filed", and the month, day, and year of the filing thereof;

(2) file in his office one of the duplicate originals of the application; and

(3) issue a certificate of registration to transact business in this State.

(b) The certificate of registration, together with one duplicate original of the application, shall be returned to the person who filed the application or his representative.

Sec. 904. **Name.**

A foreign limited partnership may register with the Secretary of State under any name (whether or not it is the name under which it is registered in its state of organization) that includes the words "limited partnership" and that could be registered by a domestic limited partnership.

Sec. 905. **Changes and Amendments.**

If any statement in a foreign limited partnership's application for registration was false when made or any arrangements or other facts described have changed, making the application inaccurate in any respect, the foreign limited partnership shall promptly file in the office of the Secretary of State a certificate, signed and sworn to by a general partner, correcting the statement.

Sec. 906. **Cancellation of Registration.**

A foreign limited partnership may cancel its registration by filing with the Secretary of State a certificate of cancellation signed and sworn to by a general partner. A cancellation does not terminate the authority of the Secretary of State to accept service of process on the foreign limited partnership with respect to [claims for relief] [causes of action] arising out of the transaction of business in this State.

Sec. 907. **Transaction of Business Without Registration.**

(a) A foreign limited partnership transacting business in this State without registration may not maintain any action, suit, or proceeding in any court of this State until it has registered.

(b) The failure of a foreign limited partnership to register in this State does not impair the validity of any contract or act of the foreign limited partnership, and does not prevent the foreign limited partnership from defending any action, suit, or proceeding in any court of this State.

(c) A limited partner of a foreign limited partnership is not liable as a general partner of the foreign limited partnership solely by reason of the foreign limited partnership's transacting business in this State without registration.

(d) A foreign limited partnership, by transacting business in this State without registration, appoints the Secretary of State as its agent for service of process with respect to [claims for relief] [causes of action] arising out of the transaction of business in this State.

Sec. 908. **Action by [Appropriate Official].**

The [appropriate official] may bring an action to restrain a foreign limited partnership from transacting business in this State in violation of this Article.

Article 10
DERIVATIVE ACTIONS

Sec. 1001. **Right of Action.**

A limited partner may bring an action in the right of a limited partnership to recover a judgment in its favor if the general partners having authority to do so have refused to bring the action or an effort to cause those general partners to bring the action is not likely to succeed.

Sec. 1002. **Proper Plaintiff.**

In a derivative action, the plaintiff must be a partner at (1) the time of bringing the action, and (2) at the time of the transaction of which he complains or his status as a partner must have devolved upon him by operation of law or pursuant to the terms of the partnership agreement from a person who was a partner at the time of the transaction.

Sec. 1003. **Pleading.**

In any derivative action, the complaint shall set forth with particularity the effort of the plaintiff to secure initiation of the action by a general partner having authority to do so or the reasons for not making the effort.

Sec. 1004. **Expenses.**

If a derivative action is successful, in whole or in part, or anything is received by the plaintiff as a result of a judgment, compromise, or settlement of an action or claim, the court may award the plaintiff reasonable expenses, including reasonable attorney's fees, and shall direct him to account to the limited partnership for the remainder of the proceeds so received by him.

Article 11
MISCELLANEOUS

Sec. 1101. **Savings Clause.**

Sec. 1102. **Name of Act.**
This Act may be cited as the Uniform Limited Partnership Act.

Sec. 1103. **Construction and Application.**
This Act shall be so construed and applied to effect its

general purpose to make uniform the law with respect to the subject of this Act among states enacting it.

Sec. 1104. Rules for Cases Not Provided for in This Act.

In any case not provided for in this Act the provisions of the Uniform Partnership Act govern.

Sec. 1105. Act Repealed.

Except as affecting existing limited partnerships to the extent set forth in Section ——, the Act of [here designate the existing limited partnership act or acts] is hereby repealed.

THE MODEL BUSINESS CORPORATION ACT

(As amended to January 1, 1980)

§ 1. **Short Title***

This Act shall be known and may be cited as the ".......† Business Corporation Act."

§ 2. **Definitions**

As used in this Act, unless the context otherwise requires, the term:

(a) "Corporation" or "domestic corporation" means a corporation for profit subject to the provisions of this Act, except a foreign corporation.

(b) "Foreign corporation" means a corporation for profit organized under laws other than the laws of this State for a purpose or purposes for which a corporation may be organized under this Act.

(c) "Articles of incorporation" means the original or restated articles of incorporation or articles of consolidation and all amendments thereto including articles of merger.

(d) "Shares" means the units into which the proprietary interests in a corporation are divided.

(e) "Subscriber" means one who subscribes for shares in a corporation, whether before or after incorporation.

(f) "Shareholder" means one who is a holder of record of shares in a corporation. If the articles of incorporation or the by-laws so provide, the board of directors may adopt by resolution a procedure whereby a shareholder of the corporation may certify in writing to the corporation that all or a portion of the shares registered in the name of such shareholder are held for the account of a specified person or persons. The resolution shall set forth (1) the classification of shareholder who may certify, (2) the purpose or purposes for which the certification may be made, (3) the form of certification and information to be contained therein, (4) if the certification is with respect to a record date or closing of the stock transfer books within which the certification must be received by the corporation and (5) such other provisions with respect to the procedure as are deemed necessary or desirable. Upon receipt by the corporation of a

---

*[By the Editor] The Model Business Corporation Act prepared by the Committee on Corporate Laws (Section of Corporation, Banking and Business Law) of the American Bar Association was originally patterned after the Illinois Business Corporation Act of 1933. It was first published as a complete act in 1950. In subsequent years several revisions, addenda and optional or alternative provisions were added. The Act was substantially revised and renumbered in 1979.

This Act should be distinguished from the Model Business Corporation Act promulgated in 1928 by the Commissioners on Uniform State Laws under the name "Uniform Business Corporation Act" and renamed Model Business

Corporation Act in 1943. This Uniform Act was withdrawn in 1957.

The Model Business Corporation Act has been influential in the codification of corporation statutes in more than 35 states. However, there is no state that has totally adopted it in its current form. Moreover, since the Model Act itself has been substantially modified from time to time, there is considerable variation among the statutes of the states that used this Act as a model.

†Supply name of State.

certification complying with the procedure, the persons specified in the certification shall be deemed, for the purpose or purposes set forth in the certification, to be the holders of record of the number of shares specified in place of the shareholder making the certification.

(g) "Authorized shares" means the shares of all classes which the corporation is authorized to issue.

(h) "Employee" includes officers but not directors. A director may accept duties which make him also an employee.

(i) "Distribution" means a direct or indirect transfer of money or other property (except its own shares) or incurrence of indebtedness, by a corporation to or for the benefit of any of its shareholders in respect of any of its shares, whether by dividend or by purchase, redemption or other acquisition of its shares, or otherwise.

(j) "Stated capital" means, at any particular time, the sum of (1) the par value of all shares of the corporation having a par value that have been issued, (2) the amount of the consideration received by the corporation for all shares of the corporation without par value that have been issued, except such part of the consideration therefor as may have been allocated to capital surplus in a manner permitted by law, and (3) such amounts not included in clauses (1) and (2) of this paragraph as have been transferred to stated capital of the corporation, whether upon the issue of shares as a share dividend or otherwise, minus all reductions from such sum as have been effected in a manner permitted by law. Irrespective of the manner of designation thereof by the laws under which a foreign corporation is organized, the stated capital of a foreign corporation shall be determined on the same basis and in the same manner as the stated capital of a domestic corporation, for the purpose of computing fees, franchise taxes and other charges imposed by this Act.

(k) "Surplus" means the excess of the net assets of a corporation over its stated capital.

(l) "Earned surplus" means the portion of the surplus of a corporation equal to the balance of its net profits, income, gains and losses from the date of incorporation, or from the latest date when a deficit was eliminated by an application of its capital surplus or stated capital or otherwise, after deducting subsequent distributions to shareholders and transfers to stated capital and capital surplus to the extent such distributions and transfers are made out of earned surplus. Earned surplus shall include also any portion of surplus allocated to earned surplus in mergers, consolidations or acquisitions of all or substantially

all of the outstanding shares or of the property and assets of another corporation, domestic or foreign.

(m) "Capital surplus" means the entire surplus of a corporation other than its earned surplus.

(n) "Insolvent" means inability of a corporation to pay its debts as they become due in the usual course of its business.

(o) "Employee" includes officers but not directors. A director may accept duties which make him also an employee.

§ 3. Purposes

Corporations may be organized under this Act for any lawful purpose or purposes, except for the purpose of banking or insurance.

§ 4. General Powers

Each corporation shall have power:

(a) To have perpetual succession by its corporate name unless a limited period of duration is stated in its articles of incorporation.

(b) To sue and be sued, complain and defend, in its corporate name.

(c) To have a corporate seal which may be altered at pleasure, and to use the same by causing it, or a facsimile thereof, to be impressed or affixed or in any other manner reproduced.

(d) To purchase, take, receive, lease, or otherwise acquire, own, hold, improve, use and otherwise deal in and with, real or personal property, or any interest therein, wherever situated.

(e) To sell, convey, mortgage, pledge, lease, exchange, transfer and otherwise dispose of all or any part of its property and assets.

(f) To lend money and use its credit to assist its employees.

(g) To purchase, take, receive, subscribe for, or otherwise acquire, own, hold, vote, use, employ, sell, mortgage, lend, pledge, or otherwise dispose of, and otherwise use and deal in and with, shares or other interests in, or obligations of, other domestic or foreign corporations, associations, partnerships or individuals, or direct or indirect obligations of the United States or of any other government, state, territory, governmental district or municipality or of any instrumentality thereof.

(h) To make contracts and guarantees and incur liabilities, borrow money at such rates of interest as the corporation may determine, issue its notes, bonds, and other obligations, and secure any of its obligations by mortgage or pledge of all or any of its property, franchises and income.

(i) To lend money for its corporate purposes, invest and reinvest its funds, and take and hold real and personal property as security for the payment of funds so loaned or invested.

(j) To conduct its business, carry on its operations and have offices and exercise the powers granted by this Act, within or without this State.

(k) To elect or appoint officers and agents of the corporation, and define their duties and fix their compensation.

(l) To make and alter by-laws, not inconsistent with its articles of incorporation or with the laws of this State, for the administration and regulation of the affairs of the corporation.

(m) To make donations for the public welfare or for charitable, scientific or educational purposes.

(n) To transact any lawful business which the board of directors shall find will be in aid of governmental policy.

(o) To pay pensions and establish pension plans, pension trusts, profit sharing plans, stock bonus plans, stock option plans and other incentive plans for any or all of its directors, officers and employees.

(p) To be a promoter, partner, member, associate, or manager of any partnership, joint venture, trust or other enterprise.

(q) To have and exercise all powers necessary or convenient to effect its purposes.

§ 5. Indemnification of Officers, Directors, Employees and Agents

(a) A corporation shall have power to indemnify any person who was or is a party or is threatened to be made a party to any threatened, pending or completed action, suit or proceeding, whether civil, criminal, administrative or investigative (other than an action by or in the right of the corporation) by reason of the fact that he is or was a director, officer, employee or agent of the corporation, or is or was serving at the request of the corporation as a director, officer, employee or agent of another corporation, partnership, joint venture, trust or other enterprise, against expenses (including attorneys' fees), judgments, fines and amounts paid in settlement actually and reasonably incurred by him in connection with such action, suit or proceeding if he acted in good faith and in a manner he reasonably believed to be in or not opposed to the best interests of the corporation, and, with respect to any criminal action or proceeding, had no reasonable cause to believe his conduct was unlawful. The termination of any action, suit or proceeding by judgment, order, settlement, conviction, or upon a plea of nolo contendere or its equivalent, shall not, of itself, create a presumption that the person did not act in good faith and in a manner which he reasonably believed to be in or not opposed to the best interest of the corporation, and, with respect to any criminal action or proceeding, had reasonable cause to believe that his conduct was unlawful.

(b) A corporation shall have power to indemnify any person who was or is a party or is threatened to be made a party to any threatened, pending or completed action or suit by or in the right of the corporation to procure a judgment in its favor by reason of the fact that he is or was a director, officer, employee or agent of the corporation, or is or was serving at the request of the corporation as a director, officer, employee or agent of another corporation, partnership, joint venture, trust or other enterprise against expenses (including attorneys' fees) actually and reasonably incurred by him in connection with the defense or settlement of such action or suit if he acted in good faith and in a manner he reasonably believed to be in or not opposed to the best interests of the corporation and except that no indemnification shall be made in respect of any claim, issue or matter as to which such person shall have been adjudged to be liable for negligence or misconduct in the performance of his duty to the corporation unless and only to the extent that the court in which such action or suit was brought shall determine upon application that, despite the adjudication of liability but in view of all circumstances of the case, such person is fairly and reasonably entitled to indemnity for such expenses which such court shall deem proper.

(c) To the extent that a director, officer, employee or agent of a corporation has been successful on the merits or otherwise in defense of any action, suit or proceeding referred to in subsections (a) or (b), or in defense of any claim, issue or matter therein, he shall be indemnified against expenses (including attorneys' fees) actually and reasonably incurred by him in connection therewith.

(d) Any indemnification under subsections (a) or (b) (unless ordered by a court) shall be made by the corporation only as authorized in the specific case upon a determination that indemnification of the director, officer, employee or agent is proper in the circumstances because he has met the applicable standard of conduct set forth in subsections (a) or (b). Such determination shall be made (1) by the board of directors by a majority vote of a quorum consisting of directors who were not parties to such action, suit or proceeding, or (2) if such a quorum is not obtainable, or, even if obtainable a quorum of disinterested directors so directs, by independent legal counsel in a written opinion, or (3) by the shareholders.

(e) Expenses (including attorneys' fees) incurred in defending a civil or criminal action, suit or proceeding may be paid by the corporation in advance of the final disposition of such action, suit or proceeding as authorized in the manner provided in subsection (d) upon receipt of an undertaking by or on behalf of the director, officer, employee or agent to repay such amount unless it shall ultimately be determined that he is entitled to be indemnified by the corporation as authorized in this section.

(f) The indemnification provided by this section shall not be deemed exclusive of any other rights to which those indemnified may be entitled under any by-law, agreement, vote of shareholders or disinterested directors or otherwise, both as to action in his official capacity and as to action in another capacity while holding such office, and shall continue as to a person who has ceased to be a director, officer, employee or agent and shall inure to the benefit of the heirs, executors and administrators of such a person.

(g) A corporation shall have power to purchase and maintain insurance on behalf of any person who is or was a director, officer, employee or agent of the corporation, or is or was serving at the request of the corporation as a director, officer, employee or agent of another corporation, partnership, joint venture, trust or other enterprise against any liability asserted against him and incurred by him in any such capacity or arising out of his status as such, whether or not the corporation would have the power to indemnify him against such liability under the provisions of this section.

§ 6. Power of Corporation to Acquire Its Own Shares

A corporation shall have the power to acquire its own shares. All of its own shares acquired by a corporation shall, upon acquisition, constitute authorized but unissued shares, unless the articles of incorporation provide that they shall not be reissued, in which case the authorized shares shall be reduced by the number of shares acquired.

If the number of authorized shares is reduced by an acquisition, the corporation shall, not later than the time it files its next annual report under this Act with the Secretary of State, file a statement of cancellation showing the reduction in the authorized shares. The statement of cancellation shall be executed in duplicate by the corporation by its president or a vice president and by its secretary or an assistant secretary, and verified by one of the officers signing such statement, and shall set forth:

(a) The name of the corporation.

(b) The number of acquired shares cancelled, itemized by classes and series.

(c) The aggregate number of authorized shares, itemized by classes and series, after giving effect to such cancellation.

Duplicate originals of such statement shall be delivered to the Secretary of State. If the Secretary of State finds that such statement conforms to law, he shall, when all fees and franchise taxes have been paid as in this Act prescribed:

(1) Endorse on each of such duplicate originals the word "Filed", and the month, day and year of the filing thereof.

(2) File one of such duplicate originals in his office.

(3) Return the other duplicate original to the corporation or its representative.

§ 7. Defense of Ultra Vires

No act of a corporation and no conveyance or transfer of real or personal property to or by a corporation shall be invalid by reason of the fact that the corporation was without capacity or power to do such act or to make or receive such conveyance or transfer, but such lack of capacity or power may be asserted:

(a) In a proceeding by a shareholder against the corporation to enjoin the doing of any act or the transfer of real or personal property by or to the corporation. If the unauthorized act or transfer sought to be enjoined is being, or is to be, performed or made pursuant to a contract to which the corporation is a party, the court may, if all of the parties to the contract are parties to the proceeding and if it deems the same to be equitable, set aside and enjoin the performance of such contract, and in so doing may allow to the corporation or to the other parties to the contract, as the case may be, compensation for the loss or damage sustained by either of them which may result from the action of the court in setting aside and enjoining the performance of such contract, but anticipated profits to be derived from the performance of the contract shall not be awarded by the court as a loss or damage sustained.

(b) In a proceeding by the corporation, whether acting directly or through a receiver, trustee, or other legal representative, or through shareholders in a representative suit, against the incumbent or former officers or directors of the corporation.

(c) In a proceeding by the Attorney General, as provided in this Act, to dissolve the corporation, or in a proceeding by the Attorney General to enjoin the corporation from the transaction of unauthorized business.

§ 8. Corporate Name

The corporate name:

(a) Shall contain the word "corporation," "company," "incorporated" or "limited," or shall contain an abbreviation of one of such words.

(b) Shall not contain any word or phrase which indicates or implies that it is organized for any purpose other than one or more of the purposes contained in its articles of incorporation.

(c) Shall not be the same as, or deceptively similar to, the name of any domestic corporation existing under the laws of this State or any foreign corporation authorized to transact business in this State, or a name the exclusive right to which is, at the time, reserved in the manner provided in this Act, or the name of a corporation which has in effect a registration of its corporate name as provided in this Act, except that this provision shall not apply if the applicant files with the Secretary of State either of the following: (1) the written consent of such other corporation or holder of a reserved or registered name to use the same or deceptively similar name and one or more words are added to make such name distinguishable from such other name, or (2) a certified copy of a final decree of a court of competent jurisdiction establishing the prior right of the applicant to the use of such name in this State.

A corporation with which another corporation, domestic or foreign, is merged, or which is formed by the reorganization or consolidation of one or more domestic or foreign corporations or upon a sale, lease or other disposition to or exchange with, a domestic corporation of all or substantially all the assets of another corporation, domestic or foreign, including its name, may have the same name as that used in this State by any of such corporations if such other corporation was organized under the laws of, or is authorized to transact business in, this State.

§ 9. Reserved Name

The exclusive right to the use of a corporate name may be reserved by:

(a) Any person intending to organize a corporation under this Act.

(b) Any domestic corporation intending to change its name.

(c) Any foreign corporation intending to make application for a certificate of authority to transact business in this State.

(d) Any foreign corporation authorized to transact business in this State and intending to change its name.

(e) Any person intending to organize a foreign corporation and intending to have such corporation make application for a certificate of authority to transact business in this State.

The reservation shall be made by filing with the Secretary of State an application to reserve a specified corporate name, executed by the applicant. If the Secretary of State finds that the name is available for corporate use, he shall reserve the same for the exclusive use of the applicant for a period of one hundred and twenty days.

The right to the exclusive use of a specified corporate name so reserved may be transferred to any person or corporation by filing in the office of the Secretary of State a notice of such transfer, executed by the applicant for whom the name was reserved, and specifying the name and address of the transferee.

§ 10. Registered Name

Any corporation organized and existing under the laws of any state or territory of the United States may register its corporate name under this Act, provided its corporate name is not the same as, or deceptively similar to, the name of any domestic corporation existing under the laws of this State, or the name of any foreign corporation authorized to transact business in this State, or any corporate name reserved or registered under this Act.

Such registration shall be made by:

(a) Filing with the Secretary of State (1) an application for registration executed by the corporation by an officer thereof, setting forth the name of the corporation, the state or territory under the laws of which it is incorporated, the date of its incorporation, a statement that it is carrying on or doing business, and a brief statement of the business in which it is engaged, and (2) a certificate setting forth that such corporation is in good standing under the laws of the state or territory wherein it is organized, executed by the Secretary of State of such state or territory or by such other official as may have custody of the records pertaining to corporations, and

(b) Paying to the Secretary of State a registration fee in the amount of . . . . for each month, or fraction thereof, between the date of filing such application and December 31st of the calendar year in which such application is filed.

Such registration shall be effective until the close of

the calendar year in which the application for registration is filed.

§ 11. Renewal of Registered Name

A corporation which has in effect a registration of its corporate name, may renew such registration from year to year by annually filing an application for renewal setting forth the facts required to be set forth in an original application for registration and a certificate of good standing as required for the original registration and by paying a fee of . . . . A renewal application may be filed between the first day of October and the thirty-first day of December in each year, and shall extend the registration for the following calendar year.

§ 12. Registered Office and Registered Agent

Each corporation shall have and continuously maintain in this State:

(a) A registered office which may be, but need not be, the same as its place of business.

(b) A registered agent, which agent may be either an individual resident in this State whose business office is identical with such registered office, or a domestic corporation, or a foreign corporation authorized to transact business in this State, having a business office identical with such registered office.

§ 13. Change of Registered Office or Registered Agent

A corporation may change its registered office or change its registered agent, or both, upon filing in the office of the Secretary of State a statement setting forth:

(a) The name of the corporation.

(b) The address of its then registered office.

(c) If the address of its registered office is to be changed, the address to which the registered office is to be changed.

(d) The name of its then registered agent.

(e) If its registered agent is to be changed, the name of its successor registered agent.

(f) That the address of its registered office and the address of the business office of its registered agent, as changed, will be identical.

(g) That such change was authorized by resolution duly adopted by its board of directors.

Such statement shall be executed by the corporation by its president, or a vice president, and verified by him, and delivered to the Secretary of State. If the Secretary of State finds that such statement conforms to the provisions of this Act, he shall file such statement in his office, and upon such filing the change of address of the registered office, or the appointment of a new registered agent, or both, as the case may be, shall become effective.

Any registered agent of a corporation may resign as such agent upon filing a written notice thereof, executed in duplicate, with the Secretary of State, who shall forthwith mail a copy thereof to the corporation at its registered office. The appointment of such agent shall terminate upon the expiration of thirty days after receipt of such notice by the Secretary of State.

If a registered agent changes his or its business address to another place within the same . . . .,* he or it may change such address and the address of the registered office of any corporation of which he or it is registered agent by filing a statement as required above except that it need be signed only by the registered agent and need not be responsive to (e) or (g) and must recite that a copy of the statement has been mailed to the corporation.

*Supply designation of jurisdiction, such as county, etc., in accordance with local practice.

§ 14. Service of Process on Corporation

The registered agent so appointed by a corporation shall be an agent of such corporation upon whom any process, notice or demand required or permitted by law to be served upon the corporation may be served.

Whenever a corporation shall fail to appoint or maintain a registered agent in this State, or whenever its registered agent cannot with reasonable diligence be found at the registered office, then the Secretary of State shall be an agent of such corporation upon whom any such process, notice, or demand may be served. Service on the Secretary of State of any such process, notice, or demand shall be made by delivering to and leaving with him, or with any clerk having charge of the corporation department of his office, duplicate copies of such process, notice or demand. In the event any such process, notice or demand is served on the Secretary of State, he shall immediately cause one of the copies thereof to be forwarded by registered mail, addressed to the corporation at its registered office. Any service so had on the Secretary of State shall be returnable in not less than thirty days.

The Secretary of State shall keep a record of all processes, notices and demands served upon him under this section, and shall record therein the time of such service and his action with reference thereto.

Nothing herein contained shall limit or affect the right to serve any process, notice or demand required or permitted by law to be served upon a corporation in any other manner now or hereafter permitted by law.

§ 15. Authorized Shares

Each corporation shall have power to create and issue the number of shares stated in its articles of incorporation. Such shares may be divided into one or more classes with such designations, preferences, limitations, and relative rights as shall be stated in the articles of incorporation. The articles of incorporation may limit or deny the voting rights of or provide special voting rights for the shares of any class to the extent not inconsistent with the provisions of this Act.

Without limiting the authority herein contained, a corporation, when so provided in its articles of incorporation, may issue shares of preferred or special classes:

(a) Subject to the right of the corporation to redeem any of such shares at the price fixed by the articles of incorporation for the redemption thereof.

(b) Entitling the holders thereof to cumulative, noncumulative or partially cumulative dividends.

(c) Having preference over any other class or classes of shares as to the payment of dividends.

(d) Having preference in the assets of the corporation over any other class or classes of shares upon the voluntary or involuntary liquidation of the corporation.

(e) Convertible into shares of any other class or into shares of any series of the same or any other class, except a class having prior or superior rights and preferences as to dividends or distribution of assets upon liquidation.

§ 16. Issuance of Shares of Preferred or Special Classes in Series

If the articles of incorporation so provide, the shares of any preferred or special class may be divided into and issued in series. If the shares of any such class are to be issued in series, then each series shall be so designated as to distinguish the shares thereof from the shares of all other series and classes. Any or all of the series of any such class and the variations in the relative rights and preferences as between different series may be fixed and determined by the articles of incorporation, but all shares of the same class shall be identical except as to the following relative rights and preferences, as to which there may be variations between different series:

(A) The rate of dividend.

(B) Whether shares may be redeemed and, if so, the redemption price and the terms and conditions of redemption.

(C) The amount payable upon shares in the event of voluntary and involuntary liquidation.

(D) Sinking fund provisions, if any, for the redemption or purchase of shares.

(E) The terms and conditions, if any, on which shares may be converted.

(F) Voting rights, if any.

If the articles of incorporation shall expressly vest authority in the board of directors, then, to the extent that the articles of incorporation shall not have established series and fixed and determined the variations in the relative rights and preferences as between series, the board of directors shall have authority to divide any or all of such classes into series and, within the limitations set forth in this section and in the articles of incorporation, fix and determine the relative rights and preferences of the shares of any series so established.

In order for the board of directors to establish a series, where authority so to do is contained in the articles of incorporation, the board of directors shall adopt a resolution setting forth the designation of the series and fixing and determining the relative rights and preferences thereof, or so much thereof as shall not be fixed and determined by the articles of incorporation.

Prior to the issue of any shares of a series established by resolution adopted by the board of directors, the corporation shall file in the office of the Secretary of State a statement setting forth:

(a) The name of the corporation.

(b) A copy of the resolution establishing and designating the series, and fixing and determining the relative rights and preferences thereof.

(c) The date of adoption of such resolution.

(d) That such resolution was duly adopted by the board of directors.

Such statement shall be executed in duplicate by the corporation by its president or a vice president and by its secretary or an assistant secretary, and verified by one of the officers signing such statement, and shall be delivered to the Secretary of State. If the Secretary of State finds that such statement conforms to law, he shall, when all franchise taxes and fees have been paid as in this Act prescribed:

(1) Endorse on each of such duplicate originals the word "Filed," and the month, day, and year of the filing thereof.

(2) File one of such duplicate originals in his office.

(3) Return the other duplicate original to the corporation or its representative.

Upon the filing of such statement by the Secretary of State, the resolution establishing and designating the series and fixing and determining the relative rights and preferences thereof shall become effective and shall constitute an amendment of the articles of incorporation.

§ 17. Subscriptions for Shares

A subscription for shares of a corporation to be organized shall be irrevocable for a period of six months, unless otherwise provided by the terms of the subscription agreement or unless all of the subscribers consent to the revocation of such subscription.

Unless otherwise provided in the subscription agreement, subscriptions for shares, whether made before or after the organization of a corporation, shall be paid in full at such time, or in such installments and at such times, as shall be determined by the board of directors. Any call made by the board of directors for payment on subscriptions shall be uniform as to all shares of the same class or as to all shares of the same series, as the case may be. In case of default in the payment of any installment or call when such payment is due, the corporation may proceed to collect the amount due in the same manner as any debt due the corporation. The by-laws may prescribe other penalties for failure to pay installments or calls that may become due, but no penalty working a forfeiture of a subscription, or of the amounts paid thereon, shall be declared as against any subscriber unless the amount due thereon shall remain unpaid for a period of twenty days after written demand has been made therefor. If mailed, such written demand shall be deemed to be made when deposited in the United States mail in a sealed envelope addressed to the subscriber at his last post-office address known to the corporation, with postage thereon prepaid. In the event of the sale of any shares by reason of any forfeiture, the excess of proceeds realized over the amount due and unpaid on such shares shall be paid to the delinquent subscriber or to his legal representative.

§ 18. Issuance for Shares

Subject to any restrictions in the articles of incorporation:

(a) Shares may be issued for such consideration as shall be authorized by the board of directors establishing a price (in money or other consideration) or a minimum price or general formula or method by which the price will be determined; and

(b) Upon authorization by the board of directors, the corporation may issue its own shares in exchange for or in conversion of its outstanding shares, or distribute its own shares, pro rata to its shareholders or the shareholders of one or more classes or series, to effectuate stock dividends or splits, and any such transaction shall not require consideration; provided, that no such issuance of shares of any class or series shall be made to the holders of shares of any other class or series unless it is either expressly provided for in the articles of incorporation, or is authorized by an affirmative vote or the written consent of the holders of at least a majority of the outstanding shares of the class or series in which the distribution is to be made.

§ 19. Payment for Shares

The consideration for the issuance of shares may be paid, in whole or in part, in cash, in other property, tangible or intangible, or in labor or services actually performed for the corporation. When payment of the consideration for which shares are to be issued shall have been received by the corporation, such shares shall be nonassessable.

Neither promissory notes nor future services shall constitute payment or part payment for the issuance of shares of a corporation.

In the absence of fraud in the transaction, the judgment of the board of directors or the shareholders, as the case may be, as to the value of the consideration received for shares shall be conclusive.

§ 20. Stock Rights and Options

Subject to any provisions in respect thereof set forth in its articles of incorporation, a corporation may create and issue, whether or not in connection with the issuance and sale of any of its shares or other securities, rights or options entitling the holders thereof to purchase from the corporation shares of any class or classes. Such rights or options shall be evidenced in such manner as the board of directors shall approve and, subject to the provisions of the articles of incorporation, shall set forth the terms upon which, the time or times within which and the price or prices at which such shares may be purchased from the corporation upon the exercise of any such right or option. If such rights or options are to be issued to directors, officers or employees as such of the corporation or of any subsidiary thereof, and not to the shareholders generally, their issuance shall be approved by the affirmative vote of the holders of a majority of the shares entitled to vote thereon or shall be authorized by and consistent with a plan approved or ratified by such a vote of shareholders. In the absence of fraud in the transaction, the judgment of the board of directors as to the adequacy of the consideration received for such rights or options shall be conclusive.

§ 21. Determination of Amount of Stated Capital [Repealed]

§ 22. Expenses of Organization, Reorganization and Financing

The reasonable charges and expenses of organization or reorganization of a corporation, and the reasonable expenses of and compensation for the sale or underwriting of its shares, may be paid or allowed by such corporation out of the consideration received by it in payment for its shares without thereby rendering such shares not fully paid or assessable.

§ 23. Shares Represented by Certificates and Uncertified Shares

The shares of a corporation shall be represented by certificates or shall be uncertificated shares. Certificates shall be signed by the chairman or vice-chairman of the board of directors or the president or a vice president and by the treasurer or an assistant treasurer or the secretary or an assistant secretary of the corporation, and may be sealed with the seal of the corporation or a facsimile thereof. Any of or all the signatures [of the president or vice president and the secretary of assistant secretary] upon a certificate may be a facsimile. [s if the certificate is manually signed on behalf of a transfer agent or a registrar, other than the corporation itself or an employee of the corporation.] In case any officer, transfer agent or registrar who has signed or whose facsimile signature has been placed upon such certificate shall have ceased to be such officer, transfer agent or registrar before such certificate is issued, it may be issued by the corporation with the same effect as if he were such officer, transfer agent or registrar at the date of its issue.

Every certificate representing shares issued by a corporation which is authorized to issue shares of more than one class shall set forth upon the face or back of the certificate, or shall state that the corporation will furnish to any shareholder upon request and without charge, a full statement of the designations, preferences, limitations, and relative rights of the shares of each class authorized to be issued, and if the corporation is authorized to issue any preferred or special class in series, the variations in the relative rights and preferences between the shares of each such series so far as the same have been fixed and determined and the authority of the board of directors to fix and determine the relative rights and preferences of subsequent series.

Each certificate representing shares shall state upon the face thereof:

(a) That the corporation is organized under the laws of this State.

(b) The name of the person to whom issued.

(c) The number and class of shares, and the designation of the series, if any, which such certificate represents.

(d) The par value of each share represented by such certificate, or a statement that the shares are without par value.

No certificate shall be issued for any share until such share is fully paid.

Unless otherwise provided by the articles of incorporation or by-laws, the board of directors of a corporation may provide by resolution that some or all of any or all classes and series of its shares shall be uncertificated shares, provided that such resolution shall not apply to shares represented by a certificate until such certificate is surrendered to the corporation. Within a reasonable time after the issuance or transfer of uncertificated shares, the corporation shall send to the registered owner thereof a written notice containing the information required to be set forth or stated on certificates pursuant to the second and third paragraphs of this section. Except as otherwise expressly provided by law, the rights and obligations of the holders of uncertificated shares and the rights and obligations of the holders of certificates representing shares of the same class and series shall be identical.

§ 24. Fractional Shares

A corporation may (1) issue fractions of a share, either represented by a certificate or uncertificated, (2) arrange for the disposition of fractional interests by those entitled thereto, (3) pay in money the fair value of fractions of a share as of a time when those entitled to receive such fractions are determined, or (4) issue scrip in registered or bearer form which shall entitle the holder to receive a certificate for a full share or an uncertificated full share upon the surrender of such scrip aggregating a full share. A certificate for a fractional share or an uncertificated fractional share shall, but scrip shall not unless otherwise provided therein, entitle the holder to exercise voting rights, to receive dividends thereon, and to participate in any of the assets of the corporation in the event of liquidation. The board of directors may cause scrip to be issued subject to the condition that it shall become void if not exchanged for certificates representing full shares or uncertificated full shares before a specified date, or subject to the condition that the shares for which scrip is exchangeable may be sold by the corporation and the proceeds thereof distributed to the holders of scrip, or subject to any other conditions which the board of directors may deem advisable.

§ 25. Liability of Subscribers and Shareholders

A holder of or subscriber to shares of a corporation shall be under no obligation to the corporation or its creditors with respect to such shares other than the obligation to pay to the corporation the full consideration for which such shares were issued or to be issued.

Any person becoming an assignee or transferee of shares or of a subscription for shares in good faith and without knowledge or notice that the full consideration therefor has not been paid shall not be personally liable to the corporation or its creditors for any unpaid portion of such consideration.

An executor, administrator, conservator, guardian, trustee, assignee for the benefit of creditors, or receiver shall not be personally liable to the corporation as a holder of or subscriber to shares of a corporation but the estate and funds in his hands shall be so liable.

No pledgee or other holder of shares as collateral security shall be personally liable as a shareholder.

§ 26. Shareholders' Preemptive Rights

The shareholders of a corporation shall have no preemptive right to acquire unissued shares of the corporation, or securities of the corporation convertible into or carrying a right to subscribe to or acquire shares, except to the extent, if any, that such right is provided in the articles of incorporation.

§ 26A. Shareholders' Preemptive Rights [Alternative]

Except to the extent limited or denied by this section or by the articles of incorporation, shareholders shall have a preemptive right to acquire unissued shares or securities convertible into such shares or carrying a right to subscribe to or acquire shares.

Unless otherwise provided in the articles of incorporation,

(a) No preemptive right shall exist

(1) to acquire any shares issued to directors, officers or employees pursuant to approval by the affirmative vote of the holders of a majority of the shares entitled to vote thereon or when authorized by and consistent with a plan theretofore approved by such a vote of shareholders; or

(2) to acquire any shares sold otherwise than for money.

(b) Holders of shares of any class that is preferred or limited as to dividends or assets shall not be entitled to any preemptive right.

(c) Holders of shares of common stock shall not be entitled to any preemptive right to shares of any class that is preferred or limited as to dividends or assets or to any obligations, unless convertible into shares of common stock or carrying a right to subscribe to or acquire shares of common stock.

(d) Holders of common stock without voting power shall have no preemptive right to shares of common stock with voting power.

(e) The preemptive right shall be only an opportunity to acquire shares or other securities under such terms and conditions as the board of directors may fix for the purpose of providing a fair and reasonable opportunity for the exercise of such right.

§ 27. By-Laws

The initial by-laws of a corporation shall be adopted by its board of directors. The power to alter, amend or repeal the by-laws or adopt new by-laws, subject to repeal or change by action of the shareholders, shall be vested in the board of directors unless reserved to the shareholders by the articles of incorporation. The by-laws may contain any provisions for the regulation and management of the affairs of the corporation not inconsistent with law or the articles of incorporation.

§ 27A. By-Laws and Other Powers in Emergency [Optional]

The board of directors of any corporation may adopt emergency by-laws, subject to repeal or change by action of the shareholders, which shall, notwithstanding any different provision elsewhere in this Act or in the articles of incorporation or by-laws, be operative during any emergency in the conduct of the business of the corporation resulting from an attack on the United States or any nuclear or atomic disaster. The emergency by-laws may make any provision that may be practical and necessary for the circumstances of the emergency, including provisions that:

(a) A meeting of the board of directors may be called by any officer or director in such manner and under such conditions as shall be prescribed in the emergency by-laws;

(b) The director or directors in attendance at the meeting, or any greater number fixed by the emergency by-laws, shall constitute a quorum; and

(c) The officers or other persons designated on a list approved by the board of directors before the emergency, all in such order of priority and subject to such conditions, and for such period of time (not longer than reasonably necessary after the termination of the emergency) as may be provided in the emergency by-laws or in the resolution approving the list shall, to the extent required to provide a quorum at any meeting of the board of directors, be deemed directors for such meeting.

The board of directors, either before or during any such emergency, may provide, and from time to time modify, lines of succession in the event that during such an emergency any or all officers or agents of the corporation shall for any reason be rendered incapable of discharging their duties.

The board of directors, either before or during any such emergency, may, effective in the emergency, change the head office or designate several alternative head offices or regional offices, or authorize the officers so to do.

To the extent not inconsistent with any emergency by-laws so adopted, the by-laws of the corporation shall remain in effect during any such emergency and upon its termination the emergency by-laws shall cease to be operative.

Unless otherwise provided in emergency by-laws, notice of any meeting of the board of directors during any such emergency may be given only to such of the directors as it may be feasible to reach at the time and by such means as may be feasible at the time, including publication or radio.

To the extent required to constitute a quorum at any meeting of the board of directors during any such emergency, the officers of the corporation who are present shall, unless otherwise provided in emergency by-laws, be deemed, in order of rank and within the same rank in order of seniority, directors for such meeting.

No officer, director or employee acting in accordance with any emergency by-laws shall be liable except for willful misconduct. No officer, director or employee shall be liable for any action taken by him in good faith in such an emergency in furtherance of the ordinary business affairs of the corporation even though not authorized by the by-laws then in effect.

§ 28. Meetings of Shareholders

Meetings of shareholders may be held at such place within or without this State as may be stated in or fixed in accordance with the by-laws. If no other place is stated or so fixed, meetings shall be held at the registered office of the corporation.

An annual meeting of the shareholders shall be held at such time as may be stated in or fixed in accordance with the by-laws. If the annual meeting is not held within any thirteen-month period the Court

of . . . . may, on the application of any shareholder, summarily order a meeting to be held.

A special meeting of the shareholders may be called by the board of directors, the holders of not less than one-tenth of all the shares entitled to vote at the meeting, or such other persons as may be authorized in the articles of incorporation or the by-laws.

§ 29. Notice of Shareholders' Meetings

Written notice stating the place, day and hour of the meeting and, in case of a special meeting, the purpose or purposes for which the meeting is called, shall be delivered not less than ten nor more than fifty days before the date of the meeting, either personally or by mail, by or at the direction of the president, the secretary, or the officer or persons calling the meeting, to each shareholder of record entitled to vote at such meeting. If mailed, such notice shall be deemed to be delivered when deposited in the United States mail addressed to the shareholder at his address as it appears on the stock transfer books of the corporation, with postage thereon prepaid.

§ 30. Closing of Transfer Books and Fixing Record Date

For the purpose of determining shareholders entitled to notice of or to vote at any meeting of shareholders or any adjournment thereof, or entitled to receive payment of any dividend, or in order to make a determination of shareholders for any other proper purpose, the board of directors of a corporation may provide that the stock transfer books shall be closed for a stated period but not to exceed, in any case, fifty days. If the stock transfer books shall be closed for the purpose of determining shareholders entitled to notice of or to vote at a meeting of shareholders, such books shall be closed for at least ten days immediately preceding such meeting. In lieu of closing the stock transfer books, the by-laws, or in the absence of an applicable by-law the board of directors, may fix in advance a date as the record date for any such determination of shareholders, such date in any case to be not more than fifty days and, in case of a meeting of shareholders, not less than ten days prior to the date on which the particular action, requiring such determination of shareholders, is to be taken. If the stock transfer books are not closed and no record date is fixed for the determination of shareholders entitled to notice of or to vote at a meeting of shareholders, or shareholders entitled to receive payment of a dividend, the date on which notice of the meeting is mailed or the date on which the resolution of the board of directors declaring such dividend is adopted, as the case may be, shall be the record date for such determination of shareholders. When a determination of shareholders entitled to vote at any meeting of shareholders has been made as provided in this section, such determination shall apply to any adjournment thereof.

§ 31. Voting Record

The officer or agent having charge of the stock transfer books for shares of a corporation shall make a complete record of the shareholders entitled to vote at such meeting or any adjournment thereof, arranged in alphabetical order, with the address of and the number of shares held by each. Such record shall be produced and kept open at the time and place of the meeting and shall be subject to the inspection of any shareholder during the whole time of the meeting for the purposes thereof.

Failure to comply with the requirements of this section shall not affect the validity of any action taken at such meeting.

An officer or agent having charge of the stock transfer books who shall fail to prepare the record of shareholders, or produce and keep it open for inspection at the meeting, as provided in this section, shall be liable to any shareholder suffering damage on account of such failure, to the extent of such damage.

§ 32. Quorum of Shareholders

Unless otherwise provided in the articles of incorporation, a majority of the shares entitled to vote, represented in person or by proxy, shall constitute a quorum at a meeting of shareholders, but in no event shall a quorum consist of less than one-third of the shares entitled to vote at the meeting. If a quorum is present, the affirmative vote of the majority of the shares represented at the meeting and entitled to vote on the subject matter shall be the act of the shareholders, unless the vote of a greater number or voting by classes is required by this Act or the articles of incorporation or by-laws.

§ 33. Voting of Shares

Each outstanding share, regardless of class, shall be entitled to one vote on each matter submitted to a vote at a meeting of shareholders, except as may be otherwise provided in the articles of incorporation. If the articles of incorporation provide for more or less than one vote for any share, on any matter, every reference in this Act to a majority or other proportion of shares shall refer to such a majority or other proportion of votes entitled to be cast.

Shares held by another corporation if a majority of the shares entitled to vote for the election of directors of such other corporation is held by the corporation, shall not be voted at any meeting or counted in determining the total number of outstanding shares at any given time.

A shareholder may vote either in person or by proxy executed in writing by the shareholder or by his duly authorized attorney-in-fact. No proxy shall be valid after eleven months from the date of its execution, unless otherwise provided in the proxy.

[Either of the following prefatory phrases may be inserted here: "The articles of incorporation may provide that" or "Unless the articles of incorporation otherwise provide"] . . . at each election for directors every shareholder entitled to vote at such election shall have the right to vote, in person or by proxy, the number of shares owned by him for as many persons as there are directors to be elected and for whose election he has a right to vote, or to cumulate his votes by giving one candidate as many votes as the number of such directors multiplied by the number of his shares shall equal, or by distributing such votes on the same principle among any number of such candidates.

Shares standing in the name of another corporation, domestic or foreign, may be voted by such officer, agent or proxy as the by-laws of such other corporation may prescribe, or, in the absence of such provision, as the board of directors of such other corporation may determine.

Shares held by an administrator, executor, guardian or conservator may be voted by him, either in person or by proxy, without a transfer of such shares into his name. Shares standing in the name of a trustee may be voted by him, either in person or by proxy, but no trustee shall be entitled to vote shares held by him without a transfer of such shares into his name.

Shares standing in the name of a receiver may be voted by such receiver, and shares held by or under the control of a receiver may be voted by such receiver without the transfer thereof into his name if authority so to do be contained in an appropriate order of the court by which such receiver was appointed.

A shareholder whose shares are pledged shall be entitled to vote such shares until the shares have been transferred into the name of the pledgee, and thereafter the pledgee shall be entitled to vote the shares so transferred.

On and after the date on which written notice of redemption of redeemable shares has been mailed to the holders thereof and a sum sufficient to redeem such shares has been deposited with a bank or trust company with irrevocable instruction and authority to pay the redemption price to the holders thereof upon surrender of certificates therefor, such shares shall not be entitled to vote on any matter and shall not be deemed to be outstanding shares.

§ 34. Voting Trusts and Agreements Among Shareholders

Any number of shareholders of a corporation may create a voting trust for the purpose of conferring upon a trustee or trustees the right to vote or otherwise represent their shares, for a period of not to exceed ten years, by entering into a written voting trust agreement specifying the terms and conditions of the voting trust, by depositing a counterpart of the agreement with the corporation at its registered office, and by transferring their shares to such trustee or trustees for the purposes of the agreement. Such trustee or trustees shall keep a record of the holders of voting trust certificates evidencing a beneficial interest in the voting trust, giving the names and addresses of all such holders and the number and class of the shares in respect of which the voting trust certificates held by each are issued, and shall deposit a copy of such record with the corporation at its registered office. The counterpart of the voting trust agreement and the copy of such record so deposited with the corporation shall be subject to the same right of examination by a shareholder of the corporation, in person or by agent or attorney, as are the books and records of the corporation, and such counterpart and such copy of such record shall be subject to examination by any holder of record of voting trust certificates, either in person or by agent or attorney, at any reasonable time for any proper purpose.

Agreements among shareholders regarding the voting of their shares shall be valid and enforceable in accordance with their terms. Such agreements shall not be subject to the provisions of this section regarding voting trusts.

§ 35. Board of Directors

All corporate powers shall be exercised by or under authority of, and the business and affairs of a corporation shall be managed under the direction of, a board of directors except as may be otherwise provided in this Act or the articles of incorporation. If any such provision is made in the articles of incorporation, the powers and duties conferred or imposed upon the board of directors by this Act shall be exercised or performed to such extent and by such person or persons as shall be provided in the articles of incorporation. Directors need not be residents of this State or shareholders of the corporation unless the articles of incorporation or by-laws so require. The articles of incorporation or by-laws may prescribe other qualifications for directors. The board of directors shall have authority to fix the compensation of directors unless otherwise provided in the articles of incorporation.

A director shall perform his duties as a director, including his duties as a member of any committee of the board upon which he may serve, in good faith, in a manner he reasonably believes to be in the best interests of the corporation, and with such care as an ordinarily prudent person in a like position would use under similar circumstances. In performing his duties, a director shall be entitled to rely on information, opinions, reports or statements, including financial statements and other financial data, in each case prepared or presented by:

(a) one or more officers or employees of the corporation whom the director reasonably believes to be reliable and competent in the matters presented,

(b) counsel, public accountants or other persons as to matters which the director reasonably believes to be within such person's professional or expert competence, or

(c) a committee of the board upon which he does not serve, duly designated in accordance with a provision of the articles of incorporation or the by-laws, as to matters within its designated authority, which committee the director reasonably believes to merit confidence,

but he shall not be considered to be acting in good faith if he has knowledge concerning the matter in question that would cause such reliance to be unwarranted. A person who so performs his duties shall have no liability by reason of being or having been a director of the corporation.

A director of a corporation who is present at a meeting of its board of directors at which action on any corporate matter is taken shall be presumed to have assented to the action taken unless his dissent shall be entered in the minutes of the meeting or unless he shall file his written dissent to such action with the secretary of the meeting before the adjournment thereof or shall forward such dissent by registered mail to the secretary of the corporation immediately after the adjournment of the meeting. Such right to dissent shall not apply to a director who voted in favor of such action.

§ 36. Number and Election of Directors

The board of directors of a corporation shall consist of one or more members. The number of directors shall be fixed by, or in the manner provided in, the articles of incorporation or the by-laws, except as to the number constituting the initial board of directors, which number shall be fixed by the articles of incorporation. The number of directors may be increased or decreased from time to time by amendment to, or in the manner provided in, the articles of incorporation or the by-laws, but no decrease shall have the effect of shortening the term of any incumbent director. In the absence of a by-law providing for the number of directors, the number shall be the same as that provided for in the articles of incorporation. The names and addresses of the members of the first board of directors shall be stated in the articles of incorporation. Such persons shall hold office until the first annual meeting of shareholders, and until their successors shall have been elected and qualified. At the first annual meeting of shareholders and at each annual meeting thereafter the shareholders shall elect directors to hold office until the next succeeding annual meeting, except in case of the classification of directors as permitted by this Act. Each director shall hold office for the term for which he is elected and until his successor shall have been elected and qualified.

§ 37. Classification of Directors

When the board of directors shall consist of nine or more members, in lieu of electing the whole number of directors annually, the articles of incorporation may provide that the directors be divided into either two or three classes, each class to be as nearly equal in number as possible, the term of office of directors of the first class to expire at the first annual meeting of shareholders after their election, that of the second class to expire at the second annual meeting after their election, and that of the third class, if any, to expire at the third annual meeting after their election. At each annual meeting after such classification the number of directors equal to the number of the class whose term expires at the time of such meeting shall be elected to hold office until the second succeeding annual meeting, if there be two classes, or until the third succeeding annual meeting, if there be three classes. No classification of directors shall be effective prior to the first annual meeting of shareholders.

§ 38. Vacancies

Any vacancy occurring in the board of directors may be filled by the affirmative vote of a majority of the remaining directors though less than a quorum of the board of directors. A director elected to fill a vacancy shall be elected for the unexpired term of his predecessor in office. Any directorship to be filled by reason of an increase in the number of directors may be filled by the board of directors for a term of office continuing only until the next election of directors by the shareholders.

§ 39. Removal of Directors

At a meeting of shareholders called expressly for that purpose, directors may be removed in the manner provided in this section. Any director or the entire board of directors may be removed, with or without cause, by a vote of the holders of a majority of the shares then entitled to vote at an election of directors.

In the case of a corporation having cumulative voting, if less than the entire board is to be removed, no one of the directors may be removed if the votes cast against his removal would be sufficient to elect him if then cumulatively voted at an election of the entire board of directors, or, if there be classes of directors, at an election of the class of directors of which he is a part.

Whenever the holders of the shares of any class are entitled to elect one or more directors by the provisions of the articles of incorporation, the provisions of this section shall apply, in respect to the removal of a director or directors so elected, to the vote of the holders of the outstanding shares of that class and not to the vote of the outstanding shares as a whole.

§ 40. Quorum of Directors

A majority of the number of directors fixed by or in the manner provided in the by-laws or in the absence of a by-law fixing or providing for the number of directors, then of the number stated in the articles of incorporation, shall constitute a quorum for the transaction of business unless a greater number is required by the articles of incorporation or the by-laws. The act of the majority of the directors present at a meeting at which a quorum is present shall be the act of the board of directors, unless the act of a greater number is required by the articles of incorporation or the by-laws.

§ 41. Director Conflicts of Interest

No contract or other transaction between a corporation and one or more of its directors or any other corporation, firm, association or entity in which one or more of its directors are directors or officers or are financially interested, shall be either void or voidable because of such relationship or interest or because such director or directors are present at the meeting of the board of directors or a committee thereof which authorizes, approves or ratifies such contract or transaction or because his or their votes are counted for such purpose, if:

(a) the fact of such relationship or interest is disclosed or known to the board of directors or committee which authorizes, approves or ratifies the contract or transaction by a vote or consent sufficient for the purpose without counting the votes or consents of such interested directors; or

(b) the fact of such relationship or interest is disclosed or known to the shareholders entitled to vote and they authorize, approve or ratify such contract or transaction by vote or written consent; or

(c) the contract or transaction is fair and reasonable to the corporation.

Common or interested directors may be counted in determining the presence of a quorum at a meeting of the board of directors or a committee thereof which authorizes, approves or ratifies such contract or transaction.

§ 42. Executive and Other Committees

If the articles of incorporation or the by-laws so provide, the board of directors, by resolution adopted by a majority of the full board of directors, may designate from among its members an executive committee and one or more other committees each of which, to the extent provided in such resolution or in the articles of incorporation or the by-laws of the corporation, shall have and may exercise all the authority of the board of directors, except that no such committee shall have authority to (i) authorize distributions, (ii) approve or recommend to shareholders actions or proposals required by this Act to be approved by shareholders, (iii) designate candidates for the office of director, for purposes of proxy solicitation or otherwise, or fill vacancies on the board of directors or any committee thereof, (iv) amend the by-laws, (v) approve a plan of merger not requiring shareholder approval, (vi) authorize or approve the reacquisition of shares unless pursuant to a general formula or method specified by the board of directors, or authorize or approve the issuance or sale of, or any contract to issue or sell, shares or designate the terms of a series of a class of shares, provided that the board of directors, having acted regarding general authorization for the issuance or sale of shares, or any contract, therefor, and, in the case of a series, the designation thereof, may, pursuant to a general formula or method specified by the board by resolution or by adoption of a stock option or other plan, authorize a committee to fix the terms of any contract for the sale of the shares and to fix the terms upon which such shares may be issued or sold, including, without limitation, the price, the dividend rate, provisions for redemption, sinking fund, conversion, voting or preferential rights, and provisions for other features of a class of shares, or a series of a class of shares, with full power in such committee to adopt any final resolution setting forth all the terms thereof and to authorize the statement of the terms of a series for filing with the Secretary of State under this Act.

Neither the designation of any such committee, the delegation thereto of authority, nor action by such committee pursuant to such authority shall alone constitute compliance by any member of the board of directors, not a member of the committee in question, with his responsibility to act in good faith, in a manner he reasonably believes to be in the best interests of the corporation, and with such care as an ordinarily prudent person in a like position would use under similar circumstances.

§ 43. Place and Notice of Directors' Meetings; Committee Meetings

Meetings of the board of directors, regular or special, may be held either within or without this State.

Regular meetings of the board of directors or any committee designated thereby may be held with or without notice as prescribed in the by-laws. Special meetings of the board of directors or any committee designated thereby shall be held upon such notice as is prescribed in the by-laws. Attendance of a director at a meeting shall constitute a waiver of notice of such meeting, except where a director attends a meeting for the express purpose of objecting to the transaction of any business because the meeting is not lawfully called or convened. Neither the business to be transacted at, nor the purpose of, any regular or special meeting of the board of directors or any committee designated thereby need be specified in the notice or waiver of notice of such meeting unless required by the by-laws.

Except as may be otherwise restricted by the articles of incorporation or by-laws, members of the board of directors or any committee designated thereby may participate in a meeting of such board or committee by means of a conference telephone or similar communications equipment by means of which all persons participating in the meeting can hear each other at the same time and participation by such means shall constitute presence in person at a meeting.

§ 44. Action by Directors Without a Meeting

Unless otherwise provided by the articles of incorporation or by-laws, any action required by this Act to be taken at a meeting of the directors of a corporation, or any action which may be taken at a meeting of the directors or of a committee, may be taken without a meeting if a consent in writing, setting forth the action so taken, shall be signed by all of the directors, or all of the members of the committee, as the case may be. Such consent shall have the same effect as a unanimous vote.

§ 45. Distributions to Shareholders

Subject to any restrictions in the articles of incorporation, the board of directors may authorize and the corporation may make distributions, except that no distribution may be made if, after giving effect thereto, either:

(a) the corporation would be unable to pay its debts as they become due in the usual course of its business; or

(b) the corporation's total assets would be less than the sum of its total liabilities and (unless the articles of incorporation otherwise permit) the maximum amount that then would be payable, in any liquidation, in respect of all outstanding shares having preferential rights in liqidation.

Determinations under subparagraph (b) may be based upon (i) financial statements prepared on the basis of accounting practices and principles that are reasonable in the circumstances, or (ii) a fair valuation or other method that is reasonable in the circumstances.

In the case of a purchase, redemption or other acquisition of a corporation's shares, the effect of a distribution shall be measured as of the date money or other property is transferred or debt is incurred by the corporation, or as of the date the shareholder ceases to be a shareholder of the corporation with respect to such shares, whichever is earlier. In all other cases, the effect of a distribution shall be measured as of the date of its authorization if payment occurs 120 days or less following the date of authorization, or as of the date of payment if payment occurs more than 120 days following the date of authorization.

Indebtedness of a corporation incurred or issued to a shareholder in a distribution in accordance with this Section shall be on a parity with the indebtedness of the corporation to its general unsecured creditors except to the extent subordinated by agreement.

§ 46. Distributions from Capital Surplus [Repealed]

§ 47. Loans to Employees and Directors

A corporation shall not lend money to or use its credit to assist its directors without authorization in the particular case by its shareholders, but may lend money to and use its credit to assist any employee of the corporation or of a subsidiary, including any such employee who is a director of the corporation, if the board of directors decides that such loan or assistance may benefit the corporation.

§ 48. Liability of Directors in Certain Cases

In addition to any other liabilities, a director who votes for or assents to any distribution contrary to the provisions of this Act or contrary to any restrictions contained in the articles of incorporation, shall, unless he complies with the standard provided in this Act for the performance of the duties of directors, be liable to the corporation, jointly and severally with all other directors so voting or assenting, for the amount of such dividend which is paid or the value of such distribution in excess of the amount of such distribution which could have been made without a violation of the provisions of this Act or the restrictions in the articles of incorporation.

Any director against whom a claim shall be asserted under or pursuant to this section for the making of a distribution and who shall be held liable thereon, shall be entitled to contribution from the shareholders who accepted or received any such distribution, knowing such distribution to have been made in violation of this Act, in proportion to the amounts received by them.

Any director against whom a claim shall be asserted under or pursuant to this section shall be entitled to contribution from any other director who voted for or assented to the action upon which the claim is asserted and who did not comply with the standard provided in this Act for the performance of the duties of directors.

§ 49. Provisions Relating to Actions by Shareholders

No action shall be brought in this State by a shareholder in the right of a domestic or foreign corporation unless the plaintiff was a holder of record of shares or of voting trust certificates therefor at the time of the transaction of which he complains, or his shares or voting trust certificates thereafter devolved upon him by operation of law from a person who was a holder of record at such time.

In any action hereafter instituted in the right of any domestic or foreign corporation by the holder or holders of record of shares of such corporation or of voting trust certificates therefor, the court having jurisdiction, upon final judgment and a finding that the action was brought without reasonable cause, may require the plaintiff or plaintiffs to pay to the parties named as defendant the reasonable expenses, including fees of attorneys, incurred by them in the defense of such action.

In any action now pending or hereafter instituted or maintained in the right of any domestic or foreign corporation by the holder or holders of record of less than five per cent of the outstanding shares of any class of such corporation or of voting trust certificates therefor, unless the shares or voting trust certificates so held have a market value in excess of twenty-five thousand dollars, the corporation in whose right such action is brought shall be entitled at any time before final judgment to require the plaintiff or plaintiffs to give security for the reasonable expenses, including fees of attorneys, that may be incurred by it in connection with such action or may be incurred by other parties named as defendant for which it may become legally liable. Market value shall be determined as of the date that the plaintiff institutes the action or, in the case of an intervenor, as of the date that he becomes a party to the action. The amount of such security may from time to time be increased or decreased, in the discretion of the court, upon showing that the security provided has or may become inadequate or is excessive. The corporation shall have recourse to such security in such amount as the court having jurisdiction shall determine upon the termination of such action, whether or not the court finds the action was brought without reasonable cause.

§ 50. Officers

The officers of a corporation shall consist of a president, one or more vice presidents as may be prescribed by the by-laws, a secretary, and a treasurer, each of whom shall be elected by the board of directors at such time and in such manner as may be prescribed by the by-laws. Such other officers and assistant officers and agents as may be deemed necessary may be elected or appointed by the board of directors or chosen in such other manner as may be prescribed by the by-laws. Any two or more offices may be held by the same person, except the offices of president and secretary.

All officers and agents of the corporation, as between themselves and the corporation, shall have such authority and perform such duties in the management of the corporation as may be provided in the by-laws, or as may be determined by resolution of the board of directors not inconsistent with the by-laws.

§ 51. Removal of Officers

Any officer or agent may be removed by the board of directors whenever in its judgment the best interests of the corporation will be served thereby, but such removal shall be without prejudice to the contract rights, if any, of the person so removed. Election or appointment of an officer or agent shall not of itself create contract rights.

§ 52. Books and Records: Financial Reports to Shareholders; Examination of Records

Each corporation shall keep correct and complete books and records of account and shall keep minutes of the proceedings of its shareholders and board of directors and shall keep at its registered office or principal place of business, or at the office of its transfer agent or registrar, a record of its shareholders, giving the names and addresses of all shareholders and the number and class of the shares held by each. Any books, records and minutes may be in written form or in any form capable of being converted into written form within a reasonable time.

Any person who shall have been a holder of record of shares or of voting trust certificates therefor at least six months immediately preceding his demand or shall be the holder of record of, or the holder of record of voting trust certificates for, at least five percent of all the outstanding shares of the corporation, upon written demand stating the purpose thereof, shall have the right to examine, in person, or by agent or attorney, at any reasonable time or times, for any proper purpose its relevant books and records of accounts, minutes, and record of shareholders and to make extracts therefrom.

Any officer or agent who, or a corporation which, shall refuse to allow any such shareholder or holder of voting trust certificates, or his agent or attorney, so to examine and make extracts from its books and records of account, minutes, and record of shareholders, for any proper purpose, shall be liable to such shareholder or holder of voting trust certificates in a penalty of ten per cent of the value of the shares owned by such shareholder, or in respect of which such voting trust certificates are issued, in addition to any other damages or remedy afforded him by law. It shall be a defense to any action for penalties under this section that the person suing therefor has within two years sold or offered for sale any list of shareholders or of holders of voting trust certificates for shares of such corporation or any other corporation or has aided or abetted any person in procuring any list of shareholders or of holders of voting trust certificates for any such purpose, or has improperly used any information secured through any prior examination of the books and records of account, or minutes, or record of shareholders or of holders of voting trust certificates for shares of such corporation or any other corporation, or was not acting in good faith or for a proper purpose in making his demand.

Nothing herein contained shall impair the power of any court of competent jurisdiction, upon proof by a shareholder or holder of voting trust certificates of proper purpose, irrespective of the period of time during which such shareholder or holder of voting trust certificates shall have been a shareholder of record or a holder of record of voting trust certificates, and irrespective of the number of shares held by him or represented by voting trust certificates held by him, to compel the production for examination by such shareholder or holder of voting trust certificates of the books and records of account, minutes and record of shareholders of a corporation.

Each corporation shall furnish to its shareholders annual financial statements, including at least a balance sheet as of the end of each fiscal year and a statement of income for such fiscal year, which shall be prepared on the basis of generally accepted accounting principles, if the corporation prepares financial statements for such fiscal year on that basis for any purpose, and may be consolidated statements of the corporation and one or more of its subsidiaries. The financial statements shall be mailed by the corporation to each of its shareholders within 120 days after the close of each fiscal year and, after such mailing and upon written request, shall be mailed by the corporation to any shareholder (or holder of a voting trust certificate for its shares) to whom a copy of the most recent annual financial statements has not previously been mailed. In the case of statements audited by a public accountant, each copy shall be accompanied by a report setting forth his opinion thereon; in other cases, each copy shall be accompanied by a statement of the president or the person in charge of the corporation's financial accounting records (1) stating his reasonable belief as to whether or not the financial statements were prepared in accordance with generally accepted accounting principles and, if not, describing the basis of presentation, and (2) describing any respects in which the financial statements were not prepared on a basis consistent with those prepared for the previous year.

§ 53. Incorporators

One or more persons, or a domestic or foreign corporation, may act as incorporator or incorporators of a corporation by signing and delivering in duplicate to the Secretary of State articles of incorporation for such corporation.

§ 54. Articles of Incorporation

The articles of incorporation shall set forth:

(a) The name of the corporation.

(b) The period of duration, which may be perpetual.

(c) The purpose or purposes for which the corporation is organized which may be stated to be, or to include, the transaction of any or all lawful business for which corporations may be incorporated under this Act.

(d) The aggregate number of shares which the corporation shall have authority to issue and, if such shares are to be divided into classes, the number of shares of each class.

(e) If the shares are to be divided into classes, the designation of each class and a statement of the preferences, limitations and relative rights in respect of the shares of each class.

(f) If the corporation is to issue the shares of any preferred or special class in series, then the designation of each series and a statement of the variations in the relative rights and preferences as between series insofar as the same are to be fixed in the articles of incorporation, and a statement of any authority to be vested in the board of directors to establish series and fix and determine the variations in the relative rights and preferences as between series.

(g) If any preemptive right is to be granted to shareholders, the provisions therefor.

(h) The address of its initial registered office, and the name of its initial registered agent at such address.

(i) The number of directors constituting the initial board of directors and the names and addresses of the persons who are to serve as directors until the first annual meeting of shareholders or until their successors be elected and qualify.

(j) The name and address of each incorporator.

In addition to provisions required therein, the articles of incorporation may also contain provisions not inconsistent with law regarding:

(1) the direction of the management of the business and the regulation of the affairs of the corporation;

(2) the definition, limitation and regulation of the powers of the corporation, the directors, and the shareholders, or any class of the shareholders,

including restrictions on the transfer of shares;

   (3) the par value of any authorized shares or class of shares;

   (4) any provision which under this Act is required or permitted to be set forth in the by-laws.

It shall not be necessary to set forth in the articles of incorporation any of the corporate powers enumerated in this Act.

§ 55. Filing of Articles of Incorporation

Duplicate originals of the articles of incorporation shall be delivered to the Secretary of State. If the Secretary of State finds that the articles of incorporation conform to law, he shall, when all fees have been paid as in this Act prescribed:

(a) Endorse on each of such duplicate originals the word "Filed," and the month, day and year of the filing thereof.

(b) File one of such duplicate originals in his office.

(c) Issue a certificate of incorporation to which he shall affix the other duplicate original.

The certificate of incorporation, together with the duplicate original of the articles of incorporation affixed thereto by the Secretary of State, shall be returned to the incorporators or their representative.

§ 56. Effect of Issuance of Certificate of Incorporation

Upon the issuance of the certificate of incorporation, the corporate existence shall begin, and such certificate of incorporation shall be conclusive evidence that all conditions precedent required to be performed by the incorporators have been complied with and that the corporation has been incorporated under this Act, except as against this State in a proceeding to cancel or revoke the certificate of incorporation or for involuntary dissolution of the corporation.

§ 57. Organization Meeting of Directors

After the issuance of the certificate of incorporation an organization meeting of the board of directors named in the articles of incorporation shall be held, either within or without this State, at the call of a majority of the directors named in the articles of incorporation, for the purpose of adopting by-laws, electing officers and transacting such other business as may come before the meeting. The directors calling the meeting shall give at least three days' notice thereof by mail to each director so named, stating the time and place of the meeting.

§ 58. Right to Amend Articles of Incorporation

A corporation may amend its articles of incorporation, from time to time, in any and as many respects as may be desired, so long as its articles of incorporation as amended contain only such provisions as might be lawfully contained in original articles of incorporation at the time of making such amendment, and, if a change in shares or the rights of shareholders, or an exchange, reclassification or cancellation of shares or rights of shareholders is to be made, such provisions as may be necessary to effect such change, exchange, reclassification or cancellation.

In particular, and without limitation upon such general power of amendment, a corporation may amend its articles of incorporation, from time to time, so as:

(a) To change its corporate name.

(b) To change its period of duration.

(c) To change, enlarge or diminish its corporate purposes.

(d) To increase or decrease the aggregate number of shares, or shares of any class, which the corporation has authority to issue.

(e) To provide, change or eliminate any provision with respect to the par value of any shares or class of shares.

(f) To exchange, classify, reclassify or cancel all or any part of its shares, whether issued or unissued.

(g) To change the designation of all or any part of its shares, whether issued or unissued, and to change the preferences, limitations, and the relative rights in respect of all or any part of its shares, whether issued or unissued.

(h) To change the shares of any class, whether issued or unissued, into a different number of shares of the same class or into the same or a different number of shares of other classes.

(i) To create new classes of shares having rights and preferences either prior and superior or subordinate and inferior to the shares of any class then authorized, whether issued or unissued.

(j) To cancel or otherwise affect the right of the holders of the shares of any class to receive dividends which have accrued but have not been declared.

(k) To divide any preferred or special class of shares, whether issued or unissued, into series and fix and determine the designations of such series and the variations in the relative rights and preferences as between the shares of such series.

(l) To authorize the board of directors to establish,

out of authorized but unissued shares, series of any preferred or special class of shares and fix and determine the relative rights and preferences of the shares of any series so established.

(m) To authorize the board of directors to fix and determine the relative rights and preferences of the authorized but unissued shares of series theretofore established in respect of which either the relative rights and preferences have not been fixed and determined or the relative rights and preferences theretofore fixed and determined are to be changed.

(n) To revoke, diminish, or enlarge the authority of the board of directors to establish series out of authorized but unissued shares of any preferred or special class and fix and determine the relative rights and preferences of the shares of any series so established.

(o) To limit, deny or grant to shareholders of any class the preemptive right to acquire additional shares of the corporation, whether then or thereafter authorized.

§ 59. Procedure to Amend Articles of Incorporation

Amendments to the articles of incorporation shall be made in the following manner:

(a) The board of directors shall adopt a resolution setting forth the proposed amendment and, if shares have been issued, directing that it be submitted to a vote at a meeting of shareholders, which may be either the annual or a special meeting. If no shares have been issued, the amendment shall be adopted by resolution of the board of directors and the provisions for adoption by shareholders shall not apply. If the corporation has only one class of shares outstanding, an amendment solely to change the number of authorized shares to effectuate a split of, or stock dividend in, the corporation's own shares, or solely to do so and to change the number of authorized shares in proportion thereto, may be adopted by the board of directors; and the provisions for adoption by shareholders shall not apply, unless otherwise provided by the articles of incorporation. The resolution may incorporate the proposed amendment in restated articles of incorporation which contain a statement that except for the designated amendment the restated articles of incorporation correctly set forth without change the corresponding provisions of the articles of incorporation as theretofore amended, and that the restated articles of incorporation together with the designated amendment supersede the original articles of incorporation and all amendments thereto.

(b) Written notice setting forth the proposed amendment or a summary of the changes to be effected thereby shall be given to each shareholder of record entitled to vote thereon within the time and in the manner provided in this Act for the giving of notice of meetings of shareholders. If the meeting be an annual meeting, the proposed amendment of such summary may be included in the notice of such annual meeting.

(c) At such meeting a vote of the shareholders entitled to vote thereon shall be taken on the proposed amendment. The proposed amendment shall be adopted upon receiving the affirmative vote of the holders of a majority of the shares entitled to vote thereon, unless any class of shares is entitled to vote thereon as a class, in which event the proposed amendment shall be adopted upon receiving the affirmative vote of the holders of a majority of the shares of each class of shares entitled to vote thereon as a class and of the total shares entitled to vote thereon.

Any number of amendments may be submitted to the shareholders, and voted upon by them, at one meeting.

§ 60. Class Voting on Amendments

The holders of the outstanding shares of a class shall be entitled to vote as a class upon a proposed amendment, whether or not entitled to vote thereon by the provisions of the articles of incorporation, if the amendment would:

(a) Increase or decrease the aggregate number of authorized shares of such class.

(b) Effect an exchange, reclassification or cancellation of all or part of the shares of such class.

(c) Effect an exchange, or create a right of exchange, of all or any part of the shares of another class into the shares of such class.

(d) Change the designations, preferences, limitations or relative rights of the shares of such class.

(e) Change the shares of such class, into the same or a different number of shares of the same class or another class or classes.

(f) Create a new class of shares having rights and preferences prior and superior to the shares of such class, or increase the rights and preferences or the number of authorized shares, of any class having rights and preferences prior or superior to the shares of such class.

(g) In the case of a preferred or special class of shares, divide the shares of such class into series and fix and determine the designation of such series and the variations in the relative rights and preferences between the shares of such series, or authorize the board of directors to do so.

(h) Limit or deny any existing preemptive rights of the shares of such class.

(i) Cancel or otherwise affect dividends on the shares of such class which have accrued but have not been declared.

§ 61. Articles of Amendment

The articles of amendment shall be executed in duplicate by the corporation by its president or a vice president and by its secretary or an assistant secretary, and verified by one of the officers signing such articles, and shall set forth:

(a) The name of the corporation.

(b) The amendments so adopted.

(c) The date of the adoption of the amendment by the shareholders, or by the board of directors where no shares have been issued.

(d) The number of shares outstanding, and the number of shares entitled to vote thereon, and if the shares of any class are entitled to vote thereon as a class, the designation and number of outstanding shares entitled to vote thereon of each such class.

(e) The number of shares voted for and against such amendment, respectively, and, if the shares of any class are entitled to vote thereon as a class, the number of shares of each such class voted for and against such amendment, respectively, or if no shares have been issued, a statement to that effect.

(f) If such amendment provides for an exchange, reclassification or cancellation of issued shares, and if the manner in which the same shall be effected is not set forth in the amendment, then a statement of the manner in which the same shall be effected.

§ 62. Filing of Articles of Amendment

Duplicate originals of the articles of amendment shall be delivered to the Secretary of State. If the Secretary of State finds that the articles of amendment conform to law, he shall, when all fees and franchise taxes have been paid as in this Act prescribed:

(a) Endorse on each of such duplicate originals the word "Filed," and the month, day and year of the filing thereof.

(b) File one of such duplicate originals in his office.

(c) Issue a certificate of amendment to which he shall affix the other duplicate original.

The certificate of amendment, together with the duplicate original of the articles of amendment affixed thereto by the Secretary of State, shall be returned to the corporation or its representative.

§ 63. Effect of Certificate of Amendment

Upon the issuance of the certificate of amendment by the Secretary of State, the amendment shall become effective and the articles of incorporation shall be deemed to be amended accordingly.

No amendment shall affect any existing cause of action in favor of or against such corporation, or any pending suit to which such corporation shall be a party, or the existing rights of persons other than shareholders; and, in the event the corporate name shall be changed by amendment, no suit brought by or against such corporation under its former name shall abate for that reason.

§ 64. Restated Articles of Incorporation

A domestic corporation may at any time restate its articles of incorporation as theretofore amended, by a resolution adopted by the board of directors.

Upon the adoption of such resolution, restated articles of incorporation shall be executed in duplicate by the corporation by its president or a vice president and by its secretary or assistant secretary and verified by one of the officers signing such articles and shall set forth all of the operative provisions of the articles of incorporation as theretofore amended together with a statement that the restated articles of incorporation correctly set forth without change the corresponding provisions of the articles of incorporation as theretofore amended and that the restated articles of incorporation supersede the original articles of incorporation and all amendments thereto.

Duplicate originals of the restated articles of incorporation shall be delivered to the Secretary of State. If the Secretary of State finds that such restated articles of incorporation conform to law, he shall, when all fees and franchise taxes have been paid as in this Act prescribed:

(1) Endorse on each of such duplicate originals the word "Filed," and the month, day and year of the filing thereof.

(2) File one of such duplicate originals in his office.

(3) Issue a restated certificate of incorporation, to which he shall affix the other duplicate original.

The restated certificate of incorporation, together with the duplicate original of the restated articles of incorporation affixed thereto by the Secretary of State, shall be returned to the corporation or its representative.

Upon the issuance of the restated certificate of incorporation by the Secretary of State, the restated articles of incorporation shall become effective and shall supersede the original articles of incorporation and all amendments thereto.

§ 65. Amendment of Articles of Incorporation in Reorganization Proceedings

Whenever a plan of reorganization of a corporation has been confirmed by decree or order of a court of competent jurisdiction in proceedings for the reorganization of such corporation, pursuant to the provisions of any applicable statute of the United States relating to reorganizations of corporations, the articles of incorporation of the corporation may be amended, in the manner provided in this section, in as many respects as may be necessary to carry out the plan and put it into effect, so long as the articles of incorporation as amended contain only such provisions as might be lawfully contained in original articles of incorporation at the time of making such amendment.

In particular and without limitation upon such general power of amendment, the articles of incorporation may be amended for such purpose so as to:

(A) Change the corporate name, period of duration or corporate purposes of the corporation;

(B) Repeal, alter or amend the by-laws of the corporation;

(C) Change the aggregate number of shares or shares of any class, which the corporation has authority to issue;

(D) Change the preferences, limitations and relative rights in respect of all or any part of the shares of the corporation, and classify, reclassify or cancel all or any part thereof, whether issued or unissued;

(E) Authorize the issuance of bonds, debentures or other obligations of the corporation, whether or not convertible into shares of any class or bearing warrants or other evidences of optional rights to purchase or subscribe for shares of any class, and fix the terms and conditions thereof; and

(F) Constitute or reconstitute and classify or reclassify the board of directors of the corporation, and appoint directors and officers in place of or in addition to all or any of the directors or officers then in office.

Amendments to the articles of incorporation pursuant to this section shall be made in the following manner:

(a) Articles of amendment approved by decree or order of such court shall be executed and verified in duplicate by such person or persons as the court shall designate or appoint for the purpose, and shall set forth the name of the corporation, the amendments of the articles of incorporation approved by the court, the date of the decree or order approving the articles of amendment, the title of the proceedings in which the decree or order was entered, and a statement that such decree or order was entered by a court having jurisdiction of the proceedings for the reorganization of the corporation pursuant to the provisions of an applicable statute of the United States.

(b) Duplicate originals of the articles of amendment shall be delivered to the Secretary of State. If the Secretary of State finds that the articles of amendment conform to law, he shall, when all fees and franchise taxes have been paid as in this Act prescribed:

(1) Endorse on each of such duplicate originals the word "Filed," and the month, day and year of the filing thereof.

(2) File one of such duplicate originals in his office.

(3) Issue a certificate of amendment to which he shall affix the other duplicate original.

The certificate of amendment, together with the duplicate original of the articles of amendment affixed thereto by the Secretary of State, shall be returned to the corporation or its representative.

Upon the issuance of the certificate of amendment by the Secretary of State, the amendment shall become effective and the articles of incorporation shall be deemed to be amended accordingly, without any action thereon by the directors or shareholders of the corporation and with the same effect as if the amendments had been adopted by unanimous action of the directors and shareholders of the corporation.

§ 66. Restriction on Redemption or Purchase of Redeemable Shares [Repealed]

§ 67. Cancellation of Redeemable Shares by Redemption or Purchase [Repealed]

§ 68. Cancellation of Other Reacquired Shares [Repealed]

§ 69. Reduction of Stated Capital in Certain Cases [Repealed]

§ 70. Special Provisions Relating to Surplus and Reserves [Repealed]

§ 71. Procedure for Merger

Any two or more domestic corporations may merge into one of such corporations pursuant to a plan of merger approved in the manner provided in this Act.

The board of directors of each corporation shall, by resolution adopted by each such board, approve a plan of merger setting forth:

(a) The names of the corporations proposing to merge, and the name of the corporation into which they propose to merge, which is hereinafter designated as the surviving corporation.

(b) The terms and conditions of the proposed merger.

(c) The manner and basis of converting the shares of each corporation into shares, obligations or other securities of the surviving corporation or of any other corporation or, in whole or in part, into cash or other property.

(d) A statement of any changes in the articles of incorporation of the surviving corporation to be effected by such merger.

(e) Such other provisions with respect to the proposed merger as are deemed necessary or desirable.

§ 72. Procedure for Consolidation

Any two or more domestic corporations may consolidate into a new corporation pursuant to a plan of consolidation approved in the manner provided in this Act.

The board of directors of each corporation shall, by a resolution adopted by each such board, approve a plan of consolidation setting forth:

(a) The names of the corporations proposing to consolidate, and the name of the new corporation into which they propose to consolidate, which is hereinafter designated as the new corporation.

(b) The terms and conditions of the proposed consolidation.

(c) The manner and basis of converting the shares of each corporation into shares, obligations or other securities of the new corporation or of any other corporation or, in whole or in part, into cash or other property.

(d) With respect to the new corporation, all of the statements required to be set forth in articles of incorporation for corporations organized under this Act.

(e) Such other provisions with respect to the proposed consolidation as are deemed necessary or desirable.

§ 72A. Procedure for Share Exchange

All the issued or all the outstanding shares of one or more classes of any domestic corporation may be acquired through the exchange of all such shares of such class or classes by another domestic or foreign corporation pursuant to a plan of exchange approved in the manner provided in this Act.

The board of directors of each corporation shall, by resolution adopted by each such board, approve a plan of exchange setting forth:

(a) The name of the corporation the shares of which are proposed to be acquired by exchange and the name of the corporation to acquire the shares of such corporation in the exchange, which is hereinafter designated as the acquiring corporation.

(b) The terms and conditions of the proposed exchange.

(c) The manner and basis of exchanging the shares to be acquired for shares, obligations or other securities of the acquiring corporation or any other corporation, or, in whole or in part, for cash or other property.

(d) Such other provisions with respect to the proposed exchange as are deemed necessary or desirable.

The procedure authorized by this Section shall not be deemed to limit the power of a corporation to acquire all or part of the shares of any class or classes of a corporation through a voluntary exchange or otherwise by agreement with the shareholders.

§ 73. Approval by Shareholders

(a) The board of directors of each corporation in the case of a merger or consolidation, and the board of directors of the corporation the shares of which are to be acquired in the case of an exchange, upon approving such plan of merger, consolidation or exchange, shall, by resolution, direct that the plan be submitted to a vote at a meeting of its shareholders, which may be either an annual or a special meeting. Written notice shall be given to each shareholder of record, whether or not entitled to vote at such meeting, not less than twenty days before such meeting, in the manner provided in this Act for the giving of notice of meetings of shareholders, and, whether the meeting be an annual or a special meeting, shall state that the purpose or one of the purposes is to condiser the proposed plan of merger, consolidation or exchange. A copy or a summary of the plan of merger, consolidation or exchange, as the case may be, shall be included in or enclosed with such notice.

(b) At each such meeting, a vote of the shareholders shall be taken on the proposed plan. The plan shall be approved upon receiving the affirmative vote of the holders of a majority of the shares entitled to vote thereon of each such corporation, unless any class of shares of any such corporation is entitled to vote thereon as a class, in which event, as to such corporation, the plan shall be approved upon receiving the affirmative vote of the holders of a majority of the shares of each class of shares entitled to vote thereon.

Any class of shares of any such corporation shall be entitled to vote as a class if any such plan contains any provision which, if contained in a proposed amendment to articles of incorporation, would entitle such class of shares to vote as a class and, in the case of an exchange, if the class is included in the exchange.

(c) After such approval by a vote of the shareholders of each such corporation, and at any time prior to the filing of the articles of merger, consolidation or exchange, the merger, consolidation or exchange may be abandoned pursuant to provisions therefor, if any, set forth in the plan.

(d) (1) Notwithstanding the provisions of subsections (a) and (b), submission of a plan of merger to a vote at a meeting of shareholders of a surviving corporation shall not be required if—

(i) the articles of incorporation of the surviving corporation do not differ except in name from those of the corporation before the merger,

(ii) each holder of shares of the surviving corporation which were outstanding immediately before the effective date of the merger is to hold the same number of shares with identical rights immediately after,

(iii) the number of voting shares outstanding immediately after the merger, plus the number of voting shares issuable on conversion of other securities issued by virtue of the terms of the merger and on exercise of rights and warrants so issued, will not exceed by more than 20 percent the number of voting shares outstanding immediately before the merger, and

(iv) the number of participating shares outstanding immediately after the merger, plus the number of participating shares issuable on conversion of other securities issued by virtue of the terms of the merger and on exercise of rights and warrants so issued, will not exceed by more than 20 percent the number of participating shares outstanding immediately before the merger.

(2) As used in this subsection—

(i) "voting shares" means shares which entitle their holders to vote unconditionally in elections of directors;

(ii) "participating shares" means shares which entitle their holders to participate without limitation in distribution of earnings or surplus.

§ 74. Articles of Merger, Consolidation or Exchange

(a) Upon receiving the approvals required by Sections 71, 72 and 73, articles of merger or articles of consolidation shall be executed in duplicate by each corporation by its president or a vice president and by its secretary or an assistant secretary, and verified by one of the officers of each corporation signing such articles, and shall set forth:

(1) The plan of merger or the plan of consolidation;

(2) As to each corporation, either (i) the number of shares outstanding, and, if the shares of any class are entitled to vote as a class, the designation and number of outstanding shares of each such class; or (ii) a statement that the vote of shareholders is not required by virtue of subsection 73(d);

(3) As to each corporation the approval of whose shareholders is required, the number of shares voted for and against such plan, respectively, and, if the shares of any class are entitled to vote as a class, the number of shares of each such class voted for and against such plan, respectively.

(b) Duplicate originals of the articles of merger, consolidation or exchange shall be delivered to the Secretary of State. If the Secretary of State finds that such articles conform to law, he shall, when all fees and franchise taxes have been paid as in this Act prescribed:

(1) Endorse on each of such duplicate originals the word "Filed," and the month, day and year of the filing thereof.

(2) File one of such duplicate originals in his office.

(3) Issue a certificate of merger, consolidation or exchange to which he shall affix the other duplicate original.

(c) The certificate of merger, consolidation or exchange together with the duplicate original of the articles affixed thereto by the Secretary of State, shall be returned to the surviving, new or acquiring corporation, as the case may be, or its representative.

§ 75. Merger of Subsidiary Corporation

Any corporation owning at least ninety per cent of the outstanding shares of each class of another corporation may merge such other corporation into itself without approval by a vote of the shareholders of either corporation. Its board of directors shall, by resolution, approve a plan of merger setting forth:

(A) The name of the subsidiary corporation and the name of the corporation owning at least ninety per cent of its shares, which is hereinafter designated as the surviving corporation.

(B) The manner and basis of converting the shares of the subsidiary corporation into shares, obligations or other securities of the surviving corporation or of any other corporation or, in whole or in part, into cash or other property.

A copy of such plan of merger shall be mailed to each shareholder of record of the subsidiary corporation.

Articles of merger shall be executed in duplicate by the surviving corporation by its president or a vice president and by its secretary or an assistant secretary, and verified by one of its officers signing such articles, and shall set forth:

(a) The plan of merger;

(b) The number of outstanding shares of each class of the subsidiary corporation and the number of such shares of each class owned by the surviving corporation; and

(c) The date of the mailing to shareholders of the subsidiary corporation of a copy of the plan of merger.

On and after the thirtieth day after the mailing of a copy of the plan of merger to shareholders of the subsidiary corporation or upon the waiver thereof by the holders of all outstanding shares duplicate originals of the articles of merger shall be delivered to the Secretary of State. If the Secretary of State finds that such articles conform to law, he shall, when all fees and franchise taxes have been paid as in this Act prescribed:

(1) Endorse on each of such duplicate originals the word "Filed," and the month, day and year of the filing thereof,

(2) File one of such duplicate originals in his office, and

(3) Issue a certificate of merger to which he shall affix the other duplicate original.

The certificate of merger, together with the duplicate original of the articles of merger affixed thereto by the Secretary of State, shall be returned to the surviving corporation or its representative.

§ 76. Effect of Merger, Consolidation or Exchange

Upon the issuance of the certificate of merger or the certificate of consolidation by the Secretary of State, the merger or consolidation shall be effected.

When such merger or consolidation has been effected:

(a) The several corporations parties to the plan of merger or consolidation shall be a single corporation, which, in the case of a merger, shall be that corporation designated in the plan of merger as the surviving corporation, and, in the case of a consolidation, shall be the new corporation provided for in the plan of consolidation.

(b) The separate existence of all corporations parties to the plan of merger or consolidation, except the surviving or new corporation, shall cease.

(c) Such surviving or new corporation shall have all the rights, privileges, immunities and powers and shall be subject to all the duties and liabilities of a corporation organized under this Act.

(d) Such surviving or new corporation shall thereupon and thereafter possess all the rights, privileges, immunities, and franchises, of a public as well as of a private nature, of each of the merging or consolidating corporations; and all property, real, personal and mixed, and all debts due on whatever account, including subscriptions to shares, and all other choses in action, and all and every other interest of or belonging to or due to each of the corporations so merged or consolidated, shall be taken and deemed to be transferred to and vested in such single corporation without further act or deed; and the title to any real estate, or any interest therein, vested in any of such corporations shall not revert or be in any way impaired by reason of such merger or consolidation.

(e) Such surviving or new corporation shall thenceforth be responsible and liable for all the liabilities and obligations of each of the corporations so merged or consolidated; and any claim existing or action or proceeding pending by or against any of such corporations may be prosecuted as if such merger or consolidation had not taken place, or such surviving or new corporation may be substituted in its place. Neither the rights of creditors nor any liens upon the property of any such corporation shall be impaired by such merger or consolidation.

(f) In the case of a merger, the articles of incorporation of the surviving corporation shall be deemed to be amended to the extent, if any, that changes in its articles of incorporation are stated in the plan of merger; and, in the case of a consolidation, the statements set forth in the articles of consolidation and which are required or permitted to be set forth in the articles of incorporation of corporations organized under this Act shall be deemed to be the original articles of incorporation of the new corporation.

§ 77. Merger, Consolidation or Exchange of Shares Between Domestic and Foreign Corporations

One or more foreign corporations and one or more domestic corporations may be merged or consolidated in the following manner, if such merger, consolidation or exchange is permitted by the laws of the state under which each such foreign corporation is organized:

(a) Each domestic corporation shall comply with the provisions of this Act with respect to the merger, consolidation or exchange, as the case may be, of domestic corporations and each foreign corporation shall comply with the applicable provisions of the laws of the state under which it is organized.

(b) If the surviving or new corporation in a merger or consolidation is to be governed by the laws of any state other than this State, it shall comply with the provisions of this Act with respect to foreign corporations if it is to transact business in this State, and in every case it shall file with the Secretary of State of this State:

(1) An agreement that it may be served with process in this State in any proceeding for the enforcement of any obligation of any domestic corporation which is a party to such merger or consolidation and in any proceeding for the enforcement of the rights of a dissenting shareholder of any such domestic corporation against the surviving or new corporation;

(2) An irrevocable appointment of the Secretary of State of this State as its agent to accept service of process in any such proceeding; and

(3) An agreement that it will promptly pay to the dissenting shareholders of any such domestic corporation, the amount, if any, to which they shall be entitled under provisions of this Act with respect to the rights of dissenting shareholders.

The effect of such merger or consolidation shall be the same as in the case of the merger or consolidation of domestic corporations, if the surviving or new corporation is to be governed by the laws of this State. If the surviving or new corporation is to be governed by the laws of any state other than this State, the effect of such merger or consolidation shall be the same as in the case of the merger or consolidation of domestic corporations except insofar as the laws of such other state provide otherwise.

At any time prior to the filing of the articles of merger or consolidation, the merger or consolidation may be abandoned pursuant to provisions therefor, if any, set forth in the plan of merger or consolidation.

§ 78. Sale of Assets in Regular Course of Business and Mortgage or Pledge of Assets

The sale, lease, exchange, or other disposition of all, or substantially all, the property and assets of a corporation in the usual and regular course of its business and the mortgage or pledge of any or all property and assets of a corporation whether or not in the usual and regular course of business may be made upon such terms and conditions and for such consideration, which may consist in whole or in part of cash or other property, including shares, obligations or other securities of any other corporation, domestic or foreign, as shall be authorized by its board of directors; and in any such case no authorization or consent of the shareholders shall be required.

§ 79. Sale of Assets Other Than in Regular Course of Business

A sale, lease, exchange, or other disposition of all, or substantially all, the property and assets, with or without the good will, of a corporation, if not in the usual and regular course of its business, may be made upon such terms and conditions and for such consideration, which may consist in whole or in part of cash or other property, including shares, obligations or other securities of any other corporation, domestic or foreign, as may be authorized in the following manner:

(a) The board of directors shall adopt a resolution recommending such sale, lease, exchange, or other disposition and directing the submission thereof to a vote at a meeting of shareholders, which may be either an annual or a special meeting.

(b) Written notice shall be given to each shareholder of record, whether or not entitled to vote at such meeting, not less than twenty days before such meeting, in the manner provided in this Act for the giving of notice of meetings of shareholders, and, whether the meeting be an annual or a special meeting, shall state that the purpose, or one of the purposes is to consider the proposed sale, lease, exchange, or other disposition.

(c) At such meeting the shareholders may authorize such sale, lease, exchange, or other disposition and may fix, or may authorize the board of directors to fix, any or all of the terms and conditions thereof and the consideration to be received by the corporation therefor. Such authorization shall require the affirmative vote of the holders of a majority of the shares of the corporation entitled to vote thereon, unless any class of shares is entitled to vote thereon as a class, in which event such authorization shall require the affirmative vote of the holders of a majority of the shares of each class of shares entitled to vote as a class thereon and of the total shares entitled to vote thereon.

(d) After such authorization by a vote of shareholders, the board of directors nevertheless, in its discretion, may abandon such sale, lease, exchange, or other disposition of assets, subject to the rights of third parties under any contracts relating thereto, without further action or approval by shareholders.

§ 80. Right of Shareholders to Dissent and Obtain Payment for Shares

(a) Any shareholder of a corporation shall have the right to dissent from, and to obtain payment for his shares in the event of, any of the following corporate actions:

(1) Any plan of merger or consolidation to which the corporation is a party, except as provided in subsection (c);

(2) Any sale or exchange of all or substantially all of the property and assets of the corporation not made in the usual or regular course of its business, including a sale in dissolution, but not including a sale pursuant to an order of a court having jurisdiction in the premises or a sale for cash on terms requiring that all or substantially all of the net proceeds of sale be distributed to the shareholders in accordance with their respective interests within one year after the date of sale;

(3) Any plan of exchange to which the corporation is a party as the corporation the shares of which are to be acquired;

(4) Any amendment of the articles of incorporation which materially and adversely affects the rights appurtenant to the shares of the dissenting shareholder in that it—

(i) alters or abolishes a preferential right of such shares;

(ii) creates, alters or abolishes a right in respect of the redemption of such shares, including a provision respecting a sinking fund for the redemption or repurchase of such shares;

(iii) alters or abolishes a preemptive right of the holder of such shares to acquire shares or other securities;

(iv) excludes or limits the right of the holder of such shares to vote on any matter, or to cumulate his votes, except as such right may be limited by dilution through the issuance of shares or other securities with similar voting rights; or

(5) Any other corporate action taken pursuant to a shareholder vote with respect to which the articles of incorporation, the bylaws, or a resolution of the board of directors directs that dissenting shareholders shall have a right to obtain payment for their shares.

(b) (1) A record holder of shares may assert dissenters' rights as to less than all of the shares registered in his name only if he dissents with respect to all the shares beneficially owned by any one person, and discloses the name and address of the person or persons on whose behalf he dissents. In that event, his rights shall be determined as if the shares as to which he has dissented and his other shares were registered in the names of different shareholders.

(2) A beneficial owner of shares who is not the record holder may assert dissenters' rights with respect to shares held on his behalf, and shall be treated as a dissenting shareholder under the terms of this section and Section 81 if he submits to the corporation at the time of or before the assertion of these rights a written consent of the record holder.

(c) The right to obtain payment under this section shall not apply to the shareholders of the surviving corporation in a merger if a vote of the shareholders of such corporation is not necessary to authorize such merger.

(d) A shareholder of a corporation who has a right under this section to obtain payment for his shares shall have no right at law or in equity to attack the validity of the corporate action that gives rise to his right to obtain payment, nor to have the action set aside or rescinded, except when the corporate action is unlawful or fraudulent with regard to the complaining shareholder or to the corporation.

§ 81. Procedures for Protection of Dissenters' Rights

(a) As used in this section:

(1) "Dissenter" means a shareholder or beneficial owner who is entitled to and does assert dissenters' rights under Section 80, and who has performed every act required up to the time involved for the assertion of such rights.

(2) "Corporation" means the issuer of the shares held by the dissenter before the corporate action, or the successor by merger or consolidation of that issuer.

(3) "Fair value" of shares means their value immediately before the effectuation of the corporate action to which the dissenter objects, excluding any appreciation or depreciation in anticipation of such corporate action unless such exclusion would be inequitable.

(4) "Interest" means interest from the effective date of the corporate action until the date of payment, at the average rate currently paid by the corporation on its principal bank loans, or, if none, at such rate as is fair and equitable under all the circumstances.

(b) If a proposed corporate action which would give

rise to dissenters' rights under Section 80(a) is submitted to a vote at a meeting of shareholders, the notice of meeting shall notify all shareholders that they have or may have a right to dissent and obtain payment for their shares by complying with the terms of this section, and shall be accompanied by a copy of sections 80 and 81 of this Act.

(c) If the proposed corporate action is submitted to a vote at a meeting of shareholders, any shareholder who wishes to dissent and obtain payment for his shares must file with the corporation, prior to the vote, a written notice of intention to demand that he be paid fair compensation for his shares if the proposed action is effectuated, and shall refrain from voting his shares in approval of such action. A shareholder who fails in either respect shall acquire no right to payment for his shares under this section or section 80.

(d) If the proposed corporate action is approved by the required vote at a meeting of shareholders, the corporation shall mail a further notice to all share-holders who gave due notice of intention to demand payment and who refrained from voting in favor of the proposed action. If the proposed corporate action is to be taken without a vote of shareholders, the corpora-tion shall send to all shareholders who are entitled to dissent and demand payment for their shares a notice of the adoption of the plan of corporate action. The notice shall (1) state where and when a demand for payment must be sent and certificates of certificated shares must be deposited in order to obtain payment, (2) inform holders of uncertificated shares to what extent transfer of shares will be restricted from the time that demand for payment is received, (3) supply a form for demanding payment which includes a request for certification of the date on which the shareholder, or the person on whose behalf the shareholder dissents, acquired beneficial ownership of the shares, and (4) be accompanied by a copy of sections 80 and 81 of this Act. The time set for the demand and deposit shall be not less than 30 days from the mailing of the notice.

(e) A shareholder who fails to demand payment, or fails (in the case of certificated shares) to deposit certificates, as required by a notice pursuant to subsection (d) shall have no right under this section or section 80 to receive payment for his shares. If the shares are not represented by certificates, the corporation may restrict their transfer from the time of receipt of demand for payment until effectuation of the proposed corporate action, or the release of restrictions under the terms of subsection (f). The dissenter shall retain all other rights of a shareholder until these rights are modified by effectuation of the proposed corporate action.

(f) (1) Within 60 days after the date set for demand-ing payment and depositing certificates, if the corporation has not effectuated the proposed corpor-ate action and remitted payment for shares pursuant to paragraph (3), it shall return any certificates that have been deposited, and release uncertificated shares from any transfer restrictions imposed by reason of the demand for payment.

(2) When uncertificated shares have been released from transfer restrictions, and deposited certificates have been returned, the corporation may at any later time send a new notice conforming to the require-ments of subsection (d), with like effect.

(3) Immediately upon effectuation of the proposed corporate action, or upon receipt of demand for payment if the corporate action has already been effectuated, the corporation shall remit to dissenters who have made demand and (if their shares are certificated) have deposited their certificates the amount which the corporation estimates to be the fair value of the shares, with interest if any has accrued. The remittance shall be accompanied by:

(i) the corporation's closing balance sheet and statement of income for a fiscal year ending not more than 16 months before the date of remit-tance, together with the latest available interim financial statements;

(ii) a statement of the corporation's estimate of fair value of the shares; and

(iii) a notice of the dissenter's right to demand supplemental payment, accompanied by a copy of sections 80 and 81 of this Act.

(g) (1) If the corporation fails to remit as required by subsection (f), or if the dissenter believes that the amount remitted is less than the fair value of his shares, or that the interest is not correctly deter-mined, he may send the corporation his own estimate of the value of the shares or of the interest, and demand payment of the deficiency.

(2) If the dissenter does not file such an estimate within 30 days after the corporation's mailing of its remittance, he shall be entitled to no more than the amount remitted.

(h) (1) Within 60 days after receiving a demand for payment pursuant to subsection (g), if any such demands for payment remain unsettled, the corpora-tion shall file in an appropriate court a petition requesting that the fair value of the shares and interest thereon be determined by the court.

(2) An appropriate court shall be a court of compe-tent jurisdiction in the county of this state where the registered office of the corporation is located. If, in the

case of a merger or consolidation or exchange of shares, the corporation is a foreign corporation without a registered office in this state, the petition shall be filed in the county where the registered office of the domestic corporation was last located.

(3) All dissenters, wherever residing, whose demands have not been settled shall be made parties to the proceeding as in an action against their shares. A copy of the petition shall be served on each such dissenter; if a dissenter is a nonresident, the copy may be served on him by registered or certified mail or by publication as provided by law.

(4) The jurisdiction of the court shall be plenary and exclusive. The court may appoint one or more persons as appraisers to receive evidence and recommend a decision on the question of fair value. The appraisers shall have such power and authority as shall be specified in the order of their appointment or in any amendment thereof. The dissenters shall be entitled to discovery in the same manner as parties in other civil suits.

(5) All dissenters who are made parties shall be entitled to judgment for the amount by which the fair value of their shares is found to exceed the amount previously remitted, with interest.

(6) If the corporation fails to file a petition as provided in paragraph (1) of this subsection, each dissenter who made a demand and who has not already settled his claim against the corporation shall be paid by the corporation the amount demanded by him, with interest, and may sue therefor in an appropriate court.

(i) (1) The costs and expenses of any proceeding under subsection (h), including the reasonable compensation and expenses of appraisers appointed by the court, shall be determined by the court and assessed against the corporation, except that any part of the costs and expenses may be apportioned and assessed as the court may deem equitable against all or some of the dissenters who are parties and whose action in demanding supplemental payment the court finds to be arbitrary, vexatious, or not in good faith.

(2) Fees and expenses of counsel and of experts for the respective parties may be assessed as the court may deem equitable against the corporation and in favor of any or all dissenters if the corporation failed to comply substantially with the requirements of this section, and may be assessed against either the corporation or a dissenter, in favor of any other party, if the court finds that the party against whom the fees and expenses are assessed acted arbitrarily, vexatiously, or not in good faith in respect to the rights provided by this section and section 80.

(3) If the court finds that the services of counsel for any dissenter were of substantial benefit to other dissenters similarly situated, and should not be assessed against the corporation, it may award to these counsel reasonable fees to be paid out of the amounts awarded to the dissenters who were benefitted.

(j) (1) Notwithstanding the foregoing provisions of this section, the corporation may elect to withhold the remittance required by subsection (f) from any dissenter with respect to shares of which the dissenter (or the person on whose behalf the dissenter acts) was not the beneficial owner on the date of the first announcement to news media or to shareholders of the terms of the proposed corporate action. With respect to such shares, the corporation shall, upon effectuating the corporate action, state to each dissenter its estimate of the fair value of the shares, state the rate of interest to be used (explaining the basis thereof), and offer to pay the resulting amounts on receiving the dissenter's agreement to accept them in full satisfaction.

(2) If the dissenter believes that the amount offered is less than the fair value of the shares and interest determined according to this section, he may within 30 days after the date of mailing of the corporation's offer, mail the corporation his own estimate of fair value and interest, and demand their payment. If the dissenter fails to do so, he shall be entitled to no more than the corporation's offer.

(3) If the dissenter makes a demand as provided in paragraph (2), the provisions of subsections (h) and (i) shall apply to further proceedings on the dissenter's demand.

§ 82. Voluntary Dissolution by Incorporators

A corporation which has not commenced business and which has not issued any shares, may be voluntarily dissolved by its incorporators at any time in the following manner:

(a) Articles of dissolution shall be executed in duplicate by a majority of the incorporators, and verified by them, and shall set forth:

(1) The name of the corporation.

(2) The date of issuance of its certificate of incorporation.

(3) That none of its shares has been issued.

(4) That the corporation has not commenced business.

(5) That the amount, if any, actually paid in on subscriptions for its shares, less any part thereof disbursed for necessary expenses, has been returned to those entitled thereto.

(6) That no debts of the corporation remain unpaid.

(7) That a majority of the incorporators elect that the corporation be dissolved.

(b) Duplicate originals of the articles of dissolution shall be delivered to the Secretary of State. If the Secretary of State finds that the articles of dissolution conform to law, he shall, when all fees and franchise taxes have been paid as in this Act prescribed:

(1) Endorse on each of such duplicate originals the word "Filed," and the month, day and year of the filing thereof.

(2) File one of such duplicate originals in his office.

(3) Issue a certificate of dissolution to which he shall affix the other duplicate original.

The certificate of dissolution, together with the duplicate original of the articles of dissolution affixed thereto by the Secretary of State, shall be returned to the incorporators or their representative. Upon the issuance of such certificate of dissolution by the Secretary of State, the existence of the corporation shall cease.

§ 83. Voluntary Dissolution by Consent of Shareholders

A corporation may be voluntarily dissolved by the written consent of all of its shareholders.

Upon the execution of such written consent, a statement of intent to dissolve shall be executed in duplicate by the corporation by its president or a vice president and by its secretary or an assistant secretary, and verified by one of the officers signing such statement, which statement shall set forth:

(a) The name of the corporation.

(b) The names and respective addresses of its officers.

(c) The names and respective addresses of its directors.

(d) A copy of the written consent signed by all shareholders of the corporation.

(e) A statement that such written consent has been signed by all shareholders of the corporation or signed in their names by their attorneys thereunto duly authorized.

§ 84. Voluntary Dissolution by Act of Corporation

A corporation may be dissolved by the act of the corporation, when authorized in the following manner:

(a) The board of directors shall adopt a resolution recommending that the corporation be dissolved, and directing that the question of such dissolution be submitted to a vote at a meeting of shareholders, which may be either an annual or a special meeting.

(b) Written notice shall be given to each shareholder of record entitled to vote at such meeting within the time and in the manner provided in this Act for the giving of notice of meetings of shareholders, and, whether the meeting be an annual or special meeting, shall state that the purpose, or one of the purposes, of such meeting is to consider the advisability of dissolving the corporation.

(c) At such meeting a vote of shareholders entitled to vote thereat shall be taken on a resolution to dissolve the corporation. Such resolution shall be adopted upon receiving the affirmative vote of the holders of a majority of the shares of the corporation entitled to vote thereon, unless any class of shares is entitled to vote thereon as a class, in which event the resolution shall be adopted upon receiving the affirmative vote of the holders of a majority of the shares of each class of shares entitled to vote thereon as a class and of the total shares entitled to vote thereon.

(d) Upon the adoption of such resolution, a statement of intent to dissolve shall be executed in duplicate by the corporation by its president or a vice president and by its secretary or an assistant secretary, and verified by one of the officers signing such statement, which statement shall set forth:

(1) The name of the corporation.

(2) The names and respective addresses of its officers.

(3) The names and respective addresses of its directors.

(4) A copy of the resolution adopted by the shareholders authorizing the dissolution of the corporation.

(5) The number of shares outstanding, and, if the shares of any class are entitled to vote as a class, the designation and number of outstanding shares of each such class.

(6) The number of shares voted for and against the resolution, respectively, and, if the shares of any class are entitled to vote as a class, the number of shares of each such class voted for and against the resolution, respectively.

§ 85. Filing of Statement of Intent to Dissolve

Duplicate originals of the statement of intent to dissolve, whether by consent of shareholders or by act of the corporation, shall be delivered to the Secretary of State. If the Secretary of State finds that such statement conforms to law, he shall, when all fees and franchise taxes have been paid as in this Act prescribed:

(a) Endorse on each of such duplicate originals the word "Filed," and the month, day and year of the filing thereof.

(b) File one of such duplicate originals in his office.

(c) Return the other duplicate original to the corporation or its representative.

§ 86. Effect of Statement of Intent to Dissolve

Upon the filing by the Secretary of State of a statement of intent to dissolve, whether by consent of shareholders or by act of the corporation, the corporation shall cease to carry on its business, except insofar as may be necessary for the winding up thereof, but its corporate existence shall continue until a certificate of dissolution has been issued by the Secretary of State or until a decree dissolving the corporation has been entered by a court of competent jurisdiction as in this Act provided.

§ 87. Procedure after Filing of Statement of Intent to Dissolve

After the filing by the Secretary of State of a statement of intent to dissolve:

(a) The corporation shall immediately cause notice thereof to be mailed to each known creditor of the corporation.

(b) The corporation shall proceed to collect its assets, convey and dispose of such of its properties as are not to be distributed in kind to its shareholders, pay, satisfy and discharge its liabilities and obligations and do all other acts required to liquidate its business and affairs, and, after paying or adequately providing for the payment of all its obligations, distribute the remainder of its assets, either in cash or in kind, among its shareholders according to their respective rights and interests.

(c) The corporation, at any time during the liquidation of its business and affairs, may make application to a court of competent jurisdiction within the state and judicial subdivision in which the registered office or principal place of business of the corporation is situated, to have the liquidation continued under the supervision of the court as provided in this Act.

§ 88. Revocation of Voluntary Dissolution Proceedings by Consent of Shareholders

By the written consent of all of its shareholders, a corporation may, at any time prior to the issuance of a certificate of dissolution by the Secretary of State, revoke voluntary dissolution proceedings theretofore taken, in the following manner:

Upon the execution of such written consent, a statement of revocation of voluntary dissolution proceedings shall be executed in duplicate by the corporation by its president or a vice president and by its secretary or an assistant secretary, and verified by one of the officers signing such statement, which statement shall set forth:

(a) The name of the corporation.

(b) The names and respective addresses of its officers.

(c) The names and respective addresses of its directors.

(d) A copy of the written consent signed by all shareholders of the corporation revoking such voluntary dissolution proceedings.

(e) That such written consent has been signed by all shareholders of the corporation or signed in their names by their attorneys thereunto duly authorized.

§ 89. Revocation of Voluntary Dissolution Proceedings by Act of Corporation

By the act of the corporation, a corporation may, at any time prior to the issuance of a certificate of dissolution by the Secretary of State, revoke voluntary dissolution proceedings theretofore taken, in the following manner:

(a) The board of directors shall adopt a resolution recommending that the voluntary dissolution proceedings be revoked, and directing that the question of such revocation be submitted to a vote at a special meeting of shareholders.

(b) Written notice, stating that the purpose or one of the purposes of such meeting is to consider the advisability of revoking the voluntary dissolution proceedings, shall be given to each shareholder of record entitled to vote at such meeting within the time and in the manner provided in this Act for the giving of notice of special meetings of shareholders.

(c) At such meeting a vote of the shareholders entitled to vote thereat shall be taken on a resolution to revoke the voluntary dissolution proceedings, which shall require for its adoption the affirmative vote of the holders of a majority of the shares entitled to vote thereon.

(d) Upon the adoption of such resolution, a statement of revocation of voluntary dissolution proceedings shall be executed in duplicate by the corporation by its president or a vice president and by its secretary or an assistant secretary, and verified by one of the officers signing such statement, which statement shall set forth:

(1) The name of the corporation.

(2) The names and respective addresses of its officers.

(3) The names and respective addresses of its directors.

(4) A copy of the resolution adopted by the shareholders revoking the voluntary dissolution proceedings.

(5) The number of shares outstanding.

(6) The number of shares voted for and against the resolution, respectively.

§ 90. Filing of Statement of Revocation of Voluntary Dissolution Proceedings

Duplicate originals of the statement of revocation of voluntary dissolution proceedings, whether by consent of shareholders or by act of the corporation, shall be delivered to the Secretary of State. If the Secretary of State finds that such statement conforms to law, he shall, when all fees and franchise taxes have been paid as in this Act prescribed:

(a) Endorse on each of such duplicate originals the word "Filed," and the month, day and year of the filing thereof.

(b) File one of such duplicate originals in his office.

(c) Return the other duplicate original to the corporation or its representative.

§ 91. Effect of Statement of Revocation of Voluntary Dissolution Proceedings

Upon the filing by the Secretary of State of a statement of revocation of voluntary dissolution proceedings, whether by consent of shareholders or by act of the corporation, the revocation of the voluntary dissolution proceedings shall become effective and the corporation may again carry on its business.

§ 92. Articles of Dissolution

If voluntary dissolution proceedings have not been revoked, then when all debts, liabilities and obligations of the corporation have been paid and discharged, or adequate provision has been made therefor, and all of the remaining property and assets of the corporation have been distributed to its shareholders, articles of dissolution shall be executed in duplicate by the corporation by its president or a vice president and by its secretary or an assistant secretary, and verified by one of the officers signing such statement, which statement shall set forth:

(a) The name of the corporation.

(b) That the Secretary of State has theretofore filed a statement of intent to dissolve the corporation, and the date on which such statement was filed.

(c) That all debts, obligations and liabilities of the corporation have been paid and discharged or that adequate provision has been made therefor.

(d) That all the remaining property and assets of the corporation have been distributed among its shareholders in accordance with their respective rights and interests.

(e) That there are no suits pending against the corporation in any court, or that adequate provision has been made for the satisfaction of any judgment, order or decree which may be entered against it in any pending suit.

§ 93. Filing of Articles of Dissolution

Duplicate originals of such articles of dissolution shall be delivered to the Secretary of State. If the Secretary of State finds that such articles of dissolution conform to law, he shall, when all fees and franchise taxes have been paid as in this Act prescribed:

(a) Endorse on each of such duplicate originals the word "Filed," and the month, day and year of the filing thereof.

(b) File one of such duplicate originals in his office.

(c) Issue a certificate of dissolution to which he shall affix the other duplicate original.

The certificate of dissolution, together with the duplicate original of the articles of dissolution affixed thereto by the Secretary of State, shall be returned to the representative of the dissolved corporation. Upon the issuance of such certificate of dissolution the existence of the corporation shall cease, except for the purpose of suits, other proceedings and appropriate corporate action by shareholders, directors and officers as provided in this Act.

§ 94. Involuntary Dissolution

A corporation may be dissolved involuntarily by a decree of the . . . . court in an action filed by the Attorney General when it is established that:

(a) The corporation has failed to file its annual report within the time required by this Act, or has failed to pay its franchise tax on or before the first day of August of the year in which such franchise tax becomes due and payable; or

(b) The corporation procured its articles of incorporation through fraud; or

(c) The corporation has continued to exceed or abuse the authority conferred upon it by law; or

(d) The corporation has failed for thirty days to appoint and maintain a registered agent in this State; or

(e) The corporation has failed for thirty days after change of its registered office or registered agent to file in the office of the Secretary of State a statement of such change.

§ 95. Notification to Attorney General

The Secretary of State, on or before the last day of December of each year, shall certify to the Attorney General the names of all corporations which have failed to file their annual reports or to pay franchise taxes in accordance with the provisions of this Act, together with the facts pertinent thereto. He shall also certify, from time to time, the names of all corporations which have given other cause for dissolution as provided in this Act, together with the facts pertinent thereto. Whenever the Secretary of State shall certify the name of a corporation to the Attorney General as having given any cause for dissolution, the Secretary of State shall concurrently mail to the corporation at its registered office a notice that such certification has been made. Upon the receipt of such certification, the Attorney General shall file an action in the name of the State against such corporation for its dissolution. Every such certificate from the Secretary of State to the Attorney General pertaining to the failure of a corporation to file an annual report or pay a franchise tax shall be taken and received in all courts as prima facie evidence of the facts therein stated. If, before action is filed, the corporation shall file its annual report or pay its franchise tax, together with all penalties thereon, or shall appoint or maintain a registered agent as provided in this Act, or shall file with the Secretary of State the required statement of change of registered office or registered agent, such fact shall be forthwith certified by the Secretary of State to the Attorney General and he shall not file an action against such corporation for such cause. If, after action is filed, the corporation shall file its annual report or pay its franchise tax, together with all penalties thereon, or shall appoint or maintain a registered agent as provided in this Act, or shall file with the Secretary of State the required statement of change of registered office or registered agent, and shall pay the costs of such action, the action for such cause shall abate.

§ 96. Venue and Process

Every action for the involuntary dissolution of a corporation shall be commenced by the Attorney General either in the . . . . court of the county in which the registered office of the corporation is situated, or in the . . . . court of . . . . county. Summons shall issue and be served as in other civil actions. If process is returned not found, the Attorney General shall cause publication to be made as in other civil cases in some newspaper published in the county where the registered office of the corporation is situated, containing a notice of the pendency of such action, the title of the court, the title of the action, and the date on or after which default may be entered. The Attorney General may include in one notice the names of any number of corporations against which actions are then pending in the same court. The Attorney General shall cause a copy of such notice to be mailed to the corporation at its registered office within ten days after the first publication thereof. The certificate of the Attorney General of the mailing of such notice shall be prima facie evidence thereof. Such notice shall be published at least once each week for two successive weeks, and the first publication thereof may begin at any time after the summons has been returned. Unless a corporation shall have been served with summons, no default shall be taken against it earlier than thirty days after the first publication of such notice.

§ 97. Jurisdiction of Court to Liquidate Assets and Business of Corporation

The . . . . courts shall have full power to liquidate the assets and business of a corporation:

(a) In an action by a shareholder when it is established:

(1) That the directors are deadlocked in the management of the corporate affairs and the shareholders are unable to break the deadlock, and that irreparable injury to the corporation is being suffered or is threatened by reason thereof; or

(2) That the acts of the directors or those in control of the corporation are illegal, oppressive or fraudulent; or

(3) That the shareholders are deadlocked in voting power, and have failed, for a period which includes at least two consecutive annual meeting dates, to elect successors to directors whose terms have expired or would have expired upon the election of their successors; or

(4) That the corporate assets are being misapplied or wasted.

(b) In an action by a creditor:

(1) When the claim of the creditor has been reduced to judgment and an execution thereon returned unsatisfied and it is established that the corporation is insolvent; or

(2) When the corporation has admitted in writing that the claim of the creditor is due and owing and it is established that the corporation is insolvent.

(c) Upon application by a corporation which has filed a statement of intent to dissolve, as provided in this Act, to have its liquidation continued under the supervision of the court.

(d) When an action has been filed by the Attorney General to dissolve a corporation and it is established that liquidation of its business and affairs should precede the entry of a decree of dissolution.

Proceedings under clause (a), (b) or (c) of this section shall be brought in the county in which the registered office or the principal office of the corporation is situated.

It shall not be necessary to make shareholders parties to any such action or proceeding unless relief is sought against them personally.

§ 98. Procedure in Liquidation of Corporation by Court

In proceedings to liquidate the assets and business of a corporation the court shall have power to issue injunctions, to appoint a receiver or receivers pendente lite, with such powers and duties as the court, from time to time, may direct, and to take such other proceedings as may be requisite to preserve the corporate assets wherever situated, and carry on the business of the corporation until a full hearing can be had.

After a hearing had upon such notice as the court may direct to be given to all parties to the proceedings and to any other parties in interest designated by the court, the court may appoint a liquidating receiver or receivers with authority to collect the assets of the corporation, including all amounts owing to the corporation by subscribers on account of any unpaid portion of the consideration for the issuance of shares. Such liquidating receiver or receivers shall have authority, subject to the order of the court, to sell, convey and dispose of all or any part of the assets of the corporation wherever situated, either at public or private sale. The assets of the corporation or the proceeds resulting from a sale, conveyance or other disposition thereof shall be applied to the expenses of such liquidation and to the payment of the liabilities and obligations of the corporation, and any remaining assets or proceeds shall be distributed among its shareholders according to their respective rights and interests. The order appointing such liquidating receiver or receivers shall state their powers and duties. Such powers and duties may be increased or diminished at any time during the proceedings.

The court shall have power to allow from time to time as expenses of the liquidation compensation to the receiver or receivers and to attorneys in the proceeding, and to direct the payment thereof out of the assets of the corporation or the proceeds of any sale or disposition of such assets.

A receiver of a corporation appointed under the provisions of this section shall have authority to sue and defend in all courts in his own name as receiver of such corporation. The court appointing such receiver shall have exclusive jurisdiction of the corporation and its property, wherever situated.

§ 99. Qualifications of Receivers

A receiver shall in all cases be a natural person or a corporation authorized to act as receiver, which corporation may be a domestic corporation or a foreign corporation authorized to transact business in this State, and shall in all cases give such bond as the court may direct with such sureties as the court may require.

§ 100. Filing of Claims in Liquidation Proceedings

In proceedings to liquidate the assets and business of a corporation the court may require all creditors of the corporation to file with the clerk of the court or with the receiver, in such form as the court may prescribe, proofs under oath of their respective claims. If the court requires the filing of claims it shall fix a date, which shall be not less than four months from the date of the order, as the last day for the filing of claims, and shall prescribe the notice that shall be given to creditors and claimants of the date so fixed. Prior to the date so fixed, the court may extend the time for the filing of claims. Creditors and claimants failing to file proofs of claim on or before the date so fixed may be barred, by order of court, from participating in the distribution of the assets of the corporation.

§ 101. Discontinuance of Liquidation Proceedings

The liquidation of the assets and business of a corporation may be discontinued at any time during the liquidation proceedings when it is established that cause for liquidation no longer exists. In such event the court shall dismiss the proceedings and direct the receiver to redeliver to the corporation all its remaining property and assets.

§ 102. Decree of Involuntary Dissolution

In proceedings to liquidate the assets and business of a corporation, when the costs and expenses of such proceedings and all debts, obligations and liabilities of the corporation shall have been paid and discharged and all of its remaining property and assets distributed to its shareholders, or in case its property and assets are not sufficient to satisfy and discharge such costs, expenses, debts and obligations, all the property and assets have been applied so far as they will go to their payment, the court shall enter a decree dissolving the corporation, whereupon the existence of the corporation shall cease.

§ 103. **Filing of Decree of Dissolution**

In case the court shall enter a decree dissolving a corporation, it shall be the duty of the clerk of such court to cause a certified copy of the decree to be filed with the Secretary of State. No fee shall be charged by the Secretary of State for the filing thereof.

§ 104. **Deposit with State Treasurer of Amount Due Certain Shareholders**

Upon the voluntary or involuntary dissolution of a corporation, the portion of the assets distributable to a creditor or shareholder who is unknown or cannot be found, or who is under disability and there is no person legally competent to receive such distributive portion, shall be reduced to cash and deposited with the State Treasurer and shall be paid over to such creditor or shareholder or to his legal representative upon proof satisfactory to the State Treasurer of his right thereto.

§ 105. **Survival of Remedy after Dissolution**

The dissolution of a corporation either (1) by the issuance of a certificate of dissolution by the Secretary of State, or (2) by a decree of court when the court has not liquidated the assets and business of the corporation as provided in this Act, or (3) by expiration of its period of duration, shall not take away or impair any remedy available to or against such corporation, its directors, officers, or shareholders, for any right or claim existing, or any liability incurred, prior to such dissolution if action or other proceeding thereon is commenced within two years after the date of such dissolution. Any such action or proceeding by or against the corporation may be prosecuted or defended by the corporation in its corporate name. The shareholders, directors and officers shall have power to take such corporate or other action as shall be appropriate to protect such remedy, right or claim. If such corporation was dissolved by the expiration of its period of duration, such corporation may amend its articles of incorporation at any time during such period of two years so as to extend its period of duration.

§ 106. **Admission of Foreign Corporation**

No foreign corporation shall have the right to transact business in this State until it shall have procured a certificate of authority so to do from the Secretary of State. No foreign corporation shall be entitled to procure a certificate of authority under this Act to transact in this State any business which a corporation organized under this Act is not permitted to transact. A foreign corporation shall not be denied a certificate of authority by reason of the fact that the laws of the state or country under which such corporation is organized governing its organization and internal affairs differ from the laws of this State, and nothing in this Act contained shall be construed to authorize this State to regulate the organization or the internal affairs of such corporation.

Without excluding other activities which may not constitute transacting business in this State, a foreign corporation shall not be considered to be transacting business in this State, for the purposes of this Act, by reason of carrying on in this State any one or more of the following activities:

(a) Maintaining or defending any action or suit or any administrative or arbitration proceeding, or effecting the settlement thereof or the settlement of claims or disputes.

(b) Holding meetings of its directors or shareholders or carrying on other activities concerning its internal affairs.

(c) Maintaining bank accounts.

(d) Maintaining offices or agencies for the transfer, exchange and registration of its securities, or appointing and maintaining trustees or depositaries with relation to its securities.

(e) Effecting sales through independent contractors.

(f) Soliciting or procuring orders, whether by mail or through employees or agents or otherwise, where such orders require acceptance without this State before becoming binding contracts.

(g) Creating as borrower or lender, or acquiring, indebtedness or mortgages or other security interests in real or personal property.

(h) Securing or collecting debts or enforcing any rights in property securing the same.

(i) Transacting any business in interstate commerce.

(j) Conducting an isolated transaction completed within a period of thirty days and not in the course of a number of repeated transactions of like nature.

§ 107. **Powers of Foreign Corporation**

A foreign corporation which shall have received a certificate of authority under this Act shall, until a certificate of revocation or of withdrawal shall have been issued as provided in this Act, enjoy the same, but no greater, rights and privileges as a domestic corporation organized for the purposes set forth in the application pursuant to which such certificate of authority is issued; and, except as in this Act otherwise provided, shall be subject to the same duties, restrictions, penalties and liabilities now or hereafter imposed upon a domestic corporation of like character.

§ 108. Corporate Name of Foreign Corporation

No certificate of authority shall be issued to a foreign corporation unless the corporate name of such corporation:

(a) Shall contain the word "corporation," "company," "incorporated," or "limited," or shall contain an abbreviation of one of such words, or such corporation shall, for use in this State, add at the end of its name one of such words or an abbreviation thereof.

(b) Shall not contain any word or phrase which indicates or implies that it is organized for any purpose other than one or more of the purposes contained in its articles of incorporation or that it is authorized or empowered to conduct the business of banking or insurance.

(c) Shall not be the same as, or deceptively similar to, the name of any domestic corporation existing under the laws of this State or any foreign corporation authorized to transact business in this State, or a name the exclusive right to which is, at the time, reserved in the manner provided in this Act, or the name of a corporation which has in effect a registration of its name as provided in this Act, except that this provision shall not apply if the foreign corporation applying for a certificate of authority files with the Secretary of State any one of the following:

(1) a resolution of its board of directors adopting a fictitious name for use in transacting business in this State which fictitious name is not deceptively similar to the name of any domestic corporation or of any foreign corporation authorized to transact business in this State or to any name reserved or registered as provided in this Act, or

(2) the written consent of such other corporation or holder of a reserved or registered name to use the same or deceptively similar name and one or more words are added to make such name distinguishable from such other name, or

(3) a certified copy of a final decree of a court of competent jurisdiction establishing the prior right of such foreign corporation to the use of such name in this State.

§ 109. Change of Name by Foreign Corporation

Whenever a foreign corporation which is authorized to transact business in this State shall change its name to one under which a certificate of authority would not be granted to it on application therefor, the certificate of authority of such corporation shall be suspended and it shall not thereafter transact any business in this State until it has changed its name to a name which is available to it under the laws of this State or has otherwise complied with the provisions of this Act.

§ 110. Application for Certificate of Authority

A foreign corporation, in order to procure a certificate of authority to transact business in this State, shall make application therefor to the Secretary of State, which application shall set forth:

(a) The name of the corporation and the state or county under the laws of which it is incorporated.

(b) If the name of the corporation does not contain the word "corporation," "company," "incorporated," or "limited," or does not contain an abbreviation of one of such words, then the name of the corporation with the word or abbreviation which it elects to add thereto for use in this State.

(c) The date of incorporation and the period of duration of the corporation.

(d) The address of the principal office of the corporation in the state or country under the laws of which it is incorporated.

(e) The address of the proposed registered office of the corporation in this State, and the name of its proposed registered agent in this State at such address.

(f) The purpose or purposes of the corporation which it proposes to pursue in the transaction of business in this State.

(g) The names and respective addresses of the directors and officers of the corporation.

(h) A statement of the aggregate number of shares which the corporation has authority to issue, itemized by classes and series, if any, within a class.

(i) A statement of the aggregate number of issued shares itemized by class and by series, if any, within each class.

(j) An estimate, expressed in dollars, of the value of all property to be owned by the corporation for the following year, wherever located, and an estimate of the value of the property of the corporation to be located within this State during such year, and an estimate, expressed in dollars, of the gross amount of business which will be transacted by the corporation during such year, and an estimate of the gross amount thereof which will be transacted by the corporation at or from places of business in this State during such year.

(k) Such additional information as may be necessary or appropriate in order to enable the Secretary of State to determine whether such corporation is entitled to a certificate of authority to transact business in this State and to determine and assess the fees and franchise taxes payable as in this Act prescribed.

Such application shall be made on forms prescribed and furnished by the Secretary of State and shall be executed in duplicate by the corporation by its president or a vice president and by its secretary or an assistant secretary, and verified by one of the officers signing such application.

§ 111. Filing of Application for Certificate of Authority

Duplicate originals of the application of the corporation for a certificate of authority shall be delivered to the Secretary of State, together with a copy of its articles of incorporation and all amendments thereto, duly authenticated by the proper officer of the state or country under the laws of which it is incorporated.

If the Secretary of State finds that such application conforms to law, he shall, when all fees and franchise taxes have been paid as in this Act prescribed:

(a) Endorse on each of such documents the word "Filed," and the month, day and year of the filing thereof.

(b) File in his office one of such duplicate originals of the application and the copy of the articles of incorporation and amendments thereto.

(c) Issue a certificate of authority to transact business in this State to which he shall affix the other duplicate original application.

The certificate of authority, together with the duplicate original of the application affixed thereto by the Secretary of State, shall be returned to the corporation or its representative.

§ 112. Effect of Certificate of Authority

Upon the issuance of a certificate of authority by the Secretary of State, the corporation shall be authorized to transact business in this State for those purposes set forth in its application, subject, however, to the right of this State to suspend or to revoke such authority as provided in this Act.

§ 113. Registered Office and Registered Agent of Foreign Corporation

Each foreign corporation authorized to transact business in this State shall have and continuously maintain in this State:

(a) A registered office which may be, but need not be, the same as its place of business in this State.

(b) A registered agent, which agent may be either an individual resident in this State whose business office is identical with such registered office, or a domestic corporation, or a foreign corporation authorized to transact business in this State, having a business office identical with such registered office.

§ 114. Change of Registered Office or Registered Agent of Foreign Corporation

A foreign corporation authorized to transact business in this State may change its registered office or change its registered agent, or both, upon filing in the office of the Secretary of State a statement setting forth:

(a) The name of the corporation.

(b) The address of its then registered office.

(c) If the address of its registered office be changed, the address to which the registered office is to be changed.

(d) The name of its then registered agent.

(e) If its registered agent be changed, the name of its successor registered agent.

(f) That the address of its registered office and the address of the business office of its registered agent, as changed, will be identical.

(g) That such change was authorized by resolution duly adopted by its board of directors.

Such statement shall be executed by the corporation by its president or a vice president, and verified by him, and delivered to the Secretary of State. If the Secretary of State finds that such statement conforms to the provisions of this Act, he shall file such statement in his office, and upon such filing the change of address of the registered office, or the appointment of a new registered agent, or both, as the case may be, shall become effective.

Any registered agent of a foreign corporation may resign as such agent upon filing a written notice thereof, executed in duplicate, with the Secretary of State, who shall forthwith mail a copy thereof to the corporation at its principal office in the state or country under the laws of which it is incorporated. The appointment of such agent shall terminate upon the expiration of thirty days after receipt of such notice by the Secretary of State.

If a registered agent changes his or its business address to another place within the same .... *, he or it may change such address and the address of the registered office of any corporation of which he or it is registered agent by filing a statement as required above except that it need be signed only by the registered agent and need not be responsive to (e) or (g) and must recite that a copy of the statement has been mailed to the corporation.

*Supply designation of jurisdiction, such as county, etc. in accordance with local practice.

§ 115. Service of Process on Foreign Corporation

The registered agent so appointed by a foreign corporation authorized to transact business in this State shall be an agent of such corporation upon whom any process, notice or demand required or permitted by law to be served upon the corporation may be served.

Whenever a foreign corporation authorized to transact business in this State shall fail to appoint or maintain a registered agent in this State, or whenever any such registered agent cannot with reasonable diligence be found at the registered office, or whenever the certificate of authority of a foreign corporation shall be suspended or revoked, then the Secretary of State shall be an agent of such corporation upon whom any such process, notice, or demand may be served. Service on the Secretary of State of any such process, notice or demand shall be made by delivering to and leaving with him, or with any clerk having charge of the corporation department of his office, duplicate copies of such process, notice or demand. In the event any such process, notice or demand is served on the Secretary of State, he shall immediately cause one of such copies thereof to be forwarded by registered mail, addressed to the corporation at its principal office in the state or country under the laws of which it is incorporated. Any service so had on the Secretary of State shall be returnable in not less than thirty days.

The Secretary of State shall keep a record of all processes, notices and demands served upon him under this section, and shall record therein the time of such service and his action with reference thereto.

Nothing herein contained shall limit or affect the right to serve any process, notice or demand, required or permitted by law to be served upon a foreign corporation in any other manner now or hereafter permitted by law.

§ 116. Amendment to Articles of Incorporation of Foreign Corporation

Whenever the articles of incorporation of a foreign corporation authorized to transact business in this State are amended, such foreign corporation shall, within thirty days after such amendment becomes effective, file in the office of the Secretary of State a copy of such amendment duly authenticated by the proper officer of the state or country under the laws of which it is incorporated; but the filing thereof shall not of itself enlarge or alter the purpose or purposes which such corporation is authorized to pursue in the transaction of business in this State, nor authorize such corporation to transact business in this State under any other name than the name set forth in its certificate of authority.

§ 117. Merger of Foreign Corporation Authorized to Transact Business in This State

Whenever a foreign corporation authorized to transact business in this State shall be a party to a statutory merger permitted by the laws of the state or country under the laws of which it is incorporated, and such corporation shall be the surviving corporation, it shall, within thirty days after such merger becomes effective, file with the Secretary of State a copy of the articles of merger duly authenticated by the proper officer of the state or country under the laws of which such statutory merger was effected; and it shall not be necessary for such corporation to procure either a new or amended certificate of authority to transact business in this State unless the name of such corporation be changed thereby or unless the corporation desires to pursue in this State other or additional purposes than those which it is then authorized to transact in this State.

§ 118. Amended Certificate of Authority

A foreign corporation authorized to transact business in this State shall procure an amended certificate of authority in the event it changes its corporate name, or desires to pursue in this State other or additional purposes than those set forth in its prior application for a certificate of authority, by making application therefor to the Secretary of State.

The requirements in respect to the form and contents of such application, the manner of its execution, the filing of duplicate originals thereof with the Secretary of State, the issuance of an amended certificate of authority and the effect thereof, shall be the same as in the case of an original application for a certificate of authority.

§ 119. **Withdrawal of Foreign Corporation**

A foreign corporation authorized to transact business in this State may withdraw from this State upon procuring from the Secretary of State a certificate of withdrawal. In order to procure such certificate of withdrawal, such foreign corporation shall deliver to the Secretary of State an application for withdrawal, which shall set forth:

(a) The name of the corporation and the state or country under the laws of which it is incorporated.

(b) That the corporation is not transacting business in this State.

(c) That the corporation surrenders its authority to transact business in this State.

(d) That the corporation revokes the authority of its registered agent in this State to accept service of process and consents that service of process in any action, suit or proceeding based upon any cause of action arising in this State during the time the corporation was authorized to transact business in this State may thereafter be made on such corporation by service thereof on the Secretary of State.

(e) A post-office address to which the Secretary of State may mail a copy of any process against the corporation that may be served on him.

(f) A statement of the aggregate number of shares which the corporation has authority to issue, itemized by class and series, if any, within each class, as of the date of such application.

(g) A statement of the aggregate number of issued shares, itemized by class and series, if any, within each class, as of the date of such application.

(h) Such additional information as may be necessary or appropriate in order to enable the Secretary of State to determine and assess any unpaid fees or franchise taxes payable by such foreign corporation as in this Act prescribed.

The application for withdrawal shall be made on forms prescribed and furnished by the Secretary of State and shall be executed by the corporation by its president or a vice president and by its secretary or an assistant secretary, and verified by one of the officers signing the application, or, if the corporation is in the hands of a receiver or trustee, shall be executed on behalf of the corporation by such receiver or trustee and verified by him.

§ 120. **Filing of Application for Withdrawal**

Duplicate originals of such application for withdrawal shall be delivered to the Secretary of State. If the Secretary of State finds that such application conforms to the provisions of this Act, he shall, when all fees and franchise taxes have been paid as in this Act prescribed:

(a) Endorse on each of such duplicate originals the word "Filed," and the month, day and year of the filing thereof.

(b) File one of such duplicate originals in his office.

(c) Issue a certificate of withdrawal to which he shall affix the other duplicate original.

The certificate of withdrawal, together with the duplicate original of the application for withdrawal affixed thereto by the Secretary of State, shall be returned to the corporation or its representative. Upon the issuance of such certificate of withdrawal, the authority of the corporation to transact business in this State shall cease.

§ 121. **Revocation of Certificate of Authority**

The certificate of authority of a foreign corporation to transact business in this State may be revoked by the Secretary of State upon the conditions prescribed in this section when:

(a) The corporation has failed to file its annual report within the time required by this Act, or has failed to pay any fees, franchise taxes or penalties prescribed by this Act when they have become due and payable; or

(b) The corporation has failed to appoint and maintain a registered agent in this State as required by this Act; or

(c) The corporation has failed, after change of its registered office or registered agent, to file in the office of the Secretary of State a statement of such change as required by this Act; or

(d) The corporation has failed to file in the office of the Secretary of State any amendment to its articles of incorporation or any articles of merger within the time prescribed by this Act; or

(e) A misrepresentation has been made of any material matter in any application, report, affidavit, or other document submitted by such corporation pursuant to this Act.

No certificate of authority of a foreign corporation shall be revoked by the Secretary of State unless (1) he shall have given the corporation not less than sixty days' notice thereof by mail addressed to its registered office in this State, and (2) the corporation shall fail prior to revocation to file such annual report, or pay such fees, franchise taxes or penalties, or file the required statement of change of registered agent or registered office, or file such articles of amendment or articles of merger, or correct such misrepresentation.

§ 122. **Issuance of Certificate of Revocation**

Upon revoking any such certificate of authority, the Secretary of State shall:

(a) Issue a certificate of revocation in duplicate.

(b) File one of such certificates in his office.

(c) Mail to such corporation at its registered office in this State a notice of such revocation accompanied by one of such certificates.

Upon the issuance of such certificate of revocation, the authority of the corporation to transact business in this State shall cease.

§ 123. **Application to Corporations Heretofore Authorized to Transact Business in this State**

Foreign corporations which are duly authorized to transact business in this State at the time this Act takes effect, for a purpose or purposes for which a corporation might secure such authority under this Act, shall, subject to the limitations set forth in their respective certificates of authority, be entitled to all the rights and privileges applicable to foreign corporations procuring certificates of authority to transact business in this State under this Act, and from the time this Act takes effect such corporations shall be subject to all the limitations, restrictions, liabilities, and duties prescribed herein for foreign corporations procuring certificates of authority to transact business in this State under this Act.

§ 124. **Transacting Business Without Certificate of Authority**

No foreign corporation transacting business in this State without a certificate of authority shall be permitted to maintain any action, suit or proceeding in any court of this State, until such corporation shall have obtained a certificate of authority. Nor shall any action, suit or proceeding be maintained in any court of this State by any successor or assignee of such corporation on any right, claim or demand arising out of the transaction of business by such corporation in this State, until a certificate of authority shall have been obtained by such corporation or by a corporation which has acquired all or substantially all of its assets.

The failure of a foreign corporation to obtain a certificate of authority to transact business in this State shall not impair the validity of any contract or act of such corporation, and shall not prevent such corporation from defending any action, suit or proceeding in any court of this State.

A foreign corporation which transacts business in this State without a certificate of authority shall be liable to this State, for the years or parts thereof during which it transacted business in this State without a certificate of authority, in an amount equal to all fees and franchise taxes which would have been imposed by this Act upon such corporation had it duly applied for and received a certificate of authority to transact business in this State as required by this Act and thereafter filed all reports required by this Act, plus all penalties imposed by this Act for failure to pay such fees and franchise taxes. The Attorney General shall bring proceedings to recover all amounts due this State under the provisions of this Section.

§ 125. **Annual Report of Domestic and Foreign Corporations**

Each domestic corporation, and each foreign corporation authorized to transact business in this State, shall file, within the time prescribed by this Act, an annual report setting forth:

(a) The name of the corporation and the state or country under the laws of which it is incorporated.

(b) The address of the registered office of the corporation in this State, and the name of its registered agent in this State at such address, and, in case of a foreign corporation, the address of its principal office in the state or country under the laws of which it is incorporated.

(c) A brief statement of the character of the business in which the corporation is actually engaged in this State.

(d) The names and respective addresses of the directors and officers of the corporation.

(e) A statement of the aggregate number of shares which the corporation has authority to issue, itemized by class and series, if any, within each class.

(f) A statement of the aggregate number of issued shares, itemized by class and series, if any, within each class.

(g) A statement, expressed in dollars, of the value of all the property owned by the corporation, wherever located, and the value of the property of the corporation located within this State, and a statement, expressed in dollars, of the gross amount of business transacted by the corporation for the twelve months ended on the thirty-first day of December preceding the date herein provided for the filing of such report and the gross amount thereof transacted by the corporation at or from places of business in this State. If, on the thirty-first day of December preceding the time herein provided for the filing of such report, the corporation had not been in existence for a period of twelve months, or in the case of a foreign corporation had not been authorized to transact business in this State for a period of twelve months, the statement with respect to business transacted shall be furnished for the period between the date of incorporation or the date of its authorization to transact business in this State, as the case may be, and such thirty-first day of December. If all the property of the corporation is located in this State and all of its business is transacted at or from places of business in this State, then the information required by this subparagraph need not be set forth in such report.

(h) Such additional information as may be necessary or appropriate in order to enable the Secretary of State to determine and assess the proper amount of franchise taxes payable by such corporation.

Such annual report shall be made on forms prescribed and furnished by the Secretary of State, and the information therein contained shall be given as of the date of the execution of the report, except as to the information required by subparagraphs (g) and (h) which shall be given as of the close of business on the thirty-first day of December next preceding the date herein provided for the filing of such report. It shall be executed by the corporation by its president, a vice president, secretary, an assistant secretary, or treasurer, and verified by the officer executing the report, or, if the corporation is in the hands of a receiver or trustee, it shall be executed on behalf of the corporation and verified by such receiver or trustee.

§ 126. Filing of Annual Report of Domestic and Foreign Corporations

Such annual report of a domestic or foreign corporation shall be delivered to the Secretary of State between the first day of January and the first day of March of each year, except that the first annual report of a domestic or foreign corporation shall be filed between the first day of January and the first day of March of the year next succeeding the calendar year in which its certificate of incorporation or its certificate of authority, as the case may be, was issued by the Secretary of State. Proof to the satisfaction of the Secretary of State that prior to the first day of March such report was deposited in the United States mail in a sealed envelope, properly addressed, with postage prepaid, shall be deemed a compliance with this requirement. If the Secretary of State finds that such report conforms to the requirements of this Act, he shall file the same. If he finds that it does not so conform, he shall promptly return the same to the corporation for any necessary corrections, in which event the penalties hereinafter prescribed for failure to file such report within the time hereinabove provided shall not apply, if such report is corrected to conform to the requirements of this Act and returned to the Secretary of State within thirty days from the date on which it was mailed to the corporation by the Secretary of State.

§ 127. Fees, Franchise Taxes and Charges to be Collected by Secretary of State

The Secretary of State shall charge and collect in accordance with the provisions of this Act:

(a) Fees for filing documents and issuing certificates.

(b) Miscellaneous charges.

(c) License fees.

(d) Franchise taxes.

§ 128. Fees for Filing Documents and Issuing Certificates

The Secretary of State shall charge and collect for:

(a) Filing articles of incorporation and issuing a certificate of incorporation, ... dollars.

(b) Filing articles of amendment and issuing a certificate of amendment, ... dollars.

(c) Filing restated articles of incorporation, ... dollars.

(d) Filing articles of merger or consolidation and issuing a certificate of merger or consolidation, ... dollars.

(e) Filing an application to reserve a corporate name, ... dollars.

(f) Filing a notice of transfer of a reserved corporate name, ... dollars.

(g) Filing a statement of change of address of registered office or change of registered agent, or both, ... dollars.

(h) Filing a statement of the establishment of a series of shares, ... dollars.

(i) Filing a statement of intent to dissolve, ... dollars.

(j) Filing a statement of revocation of voluntary dissolution proceedings, ... dollars.

(k) Filing articles of dissolution, ... dollars.

(l) Filing an application of a foreign corporation for a certificate of authority to transact business in this State and issuing a certificate of authority, ... dollars.

(m) Filing an application of a foreign corporation for an amended certificate of authority to transact business in this State and issuing an amended certificate of authority, ... dollars.

(n) Filing a copy of an amendment to the articles of incorporation of a foreign corporation holding a certificate of authority to transact business in this State, ... dollars.

(o) Filing a copy of articles of merger of a foreign corporation holding a certificate of authority to transact business in this State, ... dollars.

(p) Filing an application for withdrawal of a foreign corporation and issuing a certificate of withdrawal, ... dollars.

(q) Filing any other statement or report, except an annual report, of a domestic or foreign corporation, ... dollars.

§ 129. **Miscellaneous Charges**

The Secretary of State shall charge and collect:

(a) For furnishing a certified copy of any document, instrument, or paper relating to a corporation, ... cents per page and .... dollars for the certificate and affixing the seal thereto.

(b) At the time of any service of process on him as agent of a corporation, ... dollars, which amount may be recovered as taxable costs by the party to the suit or action causing such service to be made if such party prevails in the suit or action.

§ 130. **License Fees Payable by Domestic Corporations**

The Secretary of State shall charge and collect from each domestic corporation license fees, based upon the number of shares which it will have authority to issue or the increase in the number of shares which it will have authority to issue, at the time of:

(a) Filing articles of incorporation;

(b) Filing articles of amendment increasing the number of authorized shares; and

(c) Filing articles of merger or consolidation increasing the number of authorized shares which the surviving or new corporation, if a domestic corporation, will have the authority to issue above the aggregate number of shares which the constituent domestic corporations and constituent foreign corporations authorized to transact business in this State had authority to issue.

The license fees shall be at the rate of .... cents per share up to and including the first 10,000 authorized shares, ... cents per share for each authorized share in excess of 10,000 shares up to and including 100,000 shares, and .... cents per share for each authorized share in excess of 100,000 shares, whether the shares are of par value or without par value.

The license fees payable on an increase in the number of authorized shares shall be imposed only on the increased number of shares, and the number of previously authorized shares shall be taken into account in determining the rate applicable to the increased number of authorized shares.

§ 131. **License Fees Payable by Foreign Corporations**

The Secretary of State shall charge and collect from each foreign corporation license fees, based upon the proportion represented in this State of the number of shares which it has authority to issue or the increase in the number of shares which it has authority to issue, at the time of:

(a) Filing an application for a certificate of authority to transact business in this State;

(b) Filing articles of amendment which increased the number of authorized shares; and

(c) Filing articles of merger or consolidation which increased the number of authorized shares which the surviving or new corporation, if a foreign corporation, has authority to issue above the aggregate number of shares which the constituent domestic corporations and constituent foreign corporations authorized to transact business in this State had authority to issue.

The license fees shall be at the rate of .... cents per share up to and including the first 10,000 authorized shares represented in this State, ... cents per share for each authorized share in excess of 10,000 shares up to and including 100,000 shares represented in this State, and .... cents per share for each authorized share in excess of 100,000 shares represented in this State.

The license fees payable on an increase in the number of authorized shares shall be imposed only on the increased number of such shares represented in this State, and the number of previously authorized shares represented in this State shall be taken into account in determining the rate applicable to the increased number of authorized shares.

The number of authorized shares represented in this State shall be that proportion of its total authorized shares which the sum of the value of its property located in this State and the gross amount of business transacted by it at or from places of business in this State bears to the sum of the value of all of its property, wherever located, and the gross amount of its business, wherever transacted. Such proportion shall be determined from information contained in the application for a certificate of authority to transact business in this State until the filing of an annual report and thereafter from information contained in the latest annual report filed by the corporation.

§ 132. **Franchise Taxes Payable by Domestic Corporations**

The Secretary of State shall charge and collect from each domestic corporation an initial franchise tax at the time of filing its articles of incorporation at the rate of one-twelfth of one-half of the license fee payable by such corporation under the provisions of this Act at the time of filing its articles of incorporation, for each calendar month, or fraction thereof, between the date of the issuance of the certificate of incorporation by the Secretary of State and the first day of July of the next succeeding calendar year.

The Secretary of State shall charge and collect from each domestic corporation an annual franchise tax, payable in advance for the period from July 1 in each year to July 1 in the succeeding year, beginning July 1 in the calendar year in which such corporation is required to file its first annual report under this Act, (Alternative 1: at the rate of ...... of ...... per cent of the amount represented in this State of the stated capital of the corporation, as determined in accordance with accounting practices and principles that are reasonable in the circumstances, as disclosed by the latest report filed by the corporation with the Secretary of State) (Alternative 2: at the rate of ...... cents per share up to and including the first 10,000 issued and outstanding shares, and ...... cents per share for each issued and outstanding share in excess of 10,000 shares up to and including 100,000 shares, and ...... cents per share for each issued and outstanding share in excess of 100,000 shares).

[If Alternative 2 is enacted, the following paragraph should be deleted.]

The amount represented in this State of the stated capital of the corporation shall be that proportion of its stated capital which the sum of the value of its property located in this State and the gross amount of business transacted by it at or from places of business in this State bears to the sum of the value of all of its property, wherever located, and the gross amount of its business, wherever transacted.

§ 133. **Franchise Taxes Payable by Foreign Corporations**

The Secretary of State shall charge and collect from each foreign corporation authorized to transact business in this State an initial franchise tax at the time of filing its application for a certificate of authority at the rate of one-twelfth of one-half of the license fee payable by such corporation under the provisions of this Act at the time of filing such application, for each month, or fraction thereof, between the date of the issuance of the certificate of

authority by the Secretary of State and the first day of July of the next succeeding calendar year.

The Secretary of State shall charge and collect from each foreign corporation authorized to transact business in this State an annual franchise tax, payable in advance for the period from July 1 in each year to July 1 in the succeeding year, beginning July 1 in the calendar year in which such corporation is required to file its first annual report under this Act, (Alternative 1: at the rate of ...... per cent of the amount represented in this State of the stated capital of the corporation, as determined in accordance with accounting practices and principles that are reasonable in the circumstances, as disclosed by the latest annual report filed by the corporation with the Secretary of State) (Alternative 2: at a rate of ...... cents per share up to and including the first 10,000 issued and outstanding shares represented in this State, and ...... cents per share for each issued and outstanding share in excess of 10,000 shares up to and including 100,000 shares represented in this State, and ...... cents per share for each issued and outstanding share in excess of 100,000 shares represented in this State).

[If Alternative 2 is enacted, the following paragraph should be deleted.]

The amount represented in this State of the stated capital of the corporation shall be that proportion of its stated capital which the sum of the value of its property located in this State and the gross amount of business transacted by it at or from places of business in this State bears to the sum of the value of all of its property, wherever located, and the gross amount of its business, wherever transacted.

§ 134. **Assessment and Collection of Annual Franchise Taxes**

It shall be the duty of the Secretary of State to collect all annual franchise taxes and penalties imposed by, or assessed in accordance with, this Act.

Between the first day of March and the first day of June of each year, the Secretary of State shall assess against each corporation, domestic and foreign, required to file an annual report in such year, the franchise tax payable by it for the period from July 1 of such year to July 1 of the succeeding year in accordance with the provisions of this Act, and, if it has failed to file its annual report within the time prescribed by this Act, the penalty imposed by this Act upon such corporation for its failure so to do; and shall mail a written notice to each corporation against which such tax is assessed, addressed to such corporation at its registered office in this State, notifying the corporation (1) of the amount of franchise tax assessed against it for the ensuing year and the amount of penalty, if any, assessed against it for failure to file its annual report; (2) that objections, if any, to such assessment will be heard by the officer making the assessment on or before the fifteenth day of June of such year, upon receipt of a request from the corporation; and (3) that such tax and penalty shall be payable to the Secretary of State on the first day of July next succeeding the date of the notice. Failure to receive such notice shall not relieve the corporation of its obligation to pay the tax and any penalty assessed, or invalidate the assessment thereof.

The Secretary of State shall have power to hear and determine objections to any assessment of franchise tax at any time after such assessment and, after hearing, to change or modify any such assessment. In the event of any adjustment of franchise tax with respect to which a penalty has been assessed for failure to file an annual report, the penalty shall be adjusted in accordance with the provisions of this Act imposing such penalty.

All annual franchise taxes and all penalties for failure to file annual reports shall be due and payable on the first day of July of each year. If the annual franchise tax assessed against any corporation subject to the provisions of this Act, together with all penalties assessed thereon, shall not be paid to the Secretary of State on or before the thirty-first day of July of the year in which such tax is due and payable, the Secretary of State shall certify such fact to the Attorney General on or before the fifteenth day of November of such year, whereupon the Attorney General may institute an action against such corporation in the name of this State, in any court of competent jurisdiction, for the recovery of the amount of such franchise tax and penalties, together with the cost of suit, and prosecute the same to final judgment.

For the purpose of enforcing collection, all annual franchise taxes assessed in accordance with this Act, and all penalties assessed thereon and all interest and costs that shall accrue in connection with the collection thereof, shall be a prior and first lien on the real and personal property of the corporation from and including the first day of July of the year when such franchise taxes become due and payable until such taxes, penalties, interest, and costs shall have been paid.

§ 135. Penalties Imposed upon Corporations

Each corporation, domestic or foreign, that fails or refuses to file its annual report for any year within the time prescribed by this Act shall be subject to a penalty of ten per cent of the amount of the franchise tax assessed against it for the period beginning July 1

of the year in which such report should have been filed. Such penalty shall be assessed by the Secretary of State at the time of the assessment of the franchise tax. If the amount of the franchise tax as originally assessed against such corporation be thereafter adjusted in accordance with the provisions of this Act, the amount of the penalty shall be likewise adjusted to ten per cent of the amount of the adjusted franchise tax. The amount of the franchise tax and the amount of the penalty shall be separately stated in any notice to the corporation with respect thereto.

If the franchise tax assessed in accordance with the provisions of this Act shall not be paid on or before the thirty-first day of July, it shall be deemed to be delinquent, and there shall be added a penalty of one per cent for each month or part of month that the same is delinquent, commencing with the month of August.

Each corporation, domestic or foreign, that fails or refuses to answer truthfully and fully within the time prescribed by this Act interrogatories propounded by the Secretary of State in accordance with the provisions of this Act, shall be deemed to be guilty of a misdemeanor and upon conviction thereof may be fined in any amount not exceeding five hundred dollars.

§ 136. Penalties Imposed upon Officers and Directors

Each officer and director of a corporation, domestic or foreign, who fails or refuses within the time prescribed by this Act to answer truthfully and fully interrogatories propounded to him by the Secretary of State in accordance with the provisions of this Act, or who signs any articles, statement, report, application or other document filed with the Secretary of State which is known to such officer or director to be false in any material respect, shall be deemed to be guilty of a misdemeanor, and upon conviction thereof may be fined in any amount not exceeding .... dollars.

§ 137. Interrogatories by Secretary of State

The Secretary of State may propound to any corporation, domestic or foreign, subject to the provisions of this Act, and to any officer or director thereof, such interrogatories as may be reasonably necessary and proper to enable him to ascertain whether such corporation has complied with all the provisions of this Act applicable to such corporation. Such interrogatories shall be answered within thirty days after the mailing thereof, or within such additional time as shall be fixed by the Secretary of State, and the answers thereto shall be full and complete and shall be made in writing and under oath. If such interrogatories be directed to an individual they shall be answered by him, and if directed to a corporation they shall be answered by the president, vice president, secretary or assistant secretary thereof. The Secretary of State need not file any document to which such interrogatories relate until such interrogatories be answered as herein provided, and not then if the answers thereto disclose that such document is not in conformity with the provisions of this Act. The Secretary of State shall certify to the Attorney General, for such action as the Attorney General may deem appropriate, all interrogatories and answers thereto which disclose a violation of any of the provisions of this Act.

§ 138. Information Disclosed by Interrogatories

Interrogatories propounded by the Secretary of State and the answers thereto shall not be open to public inspection nor shall the Secretary of State disclose any facts or information obtained therefrom except insofar as his official duty may require the same to be made public or in the event such interrogatories or the answers thereto are required for evidence in any criminal proceedings or in any other action by this State.

§ 139. Powers of Secretary of State

The Secretary of State shall have the power and authority reasonably necessary to enable him to administer this Act efficiently and to perform the duties therein imposed upon him.

§ 140. Appeal from Secretary of State

If the Secretary of State shall fail to approve any articles of incorporation, amendment, merger, consolidation or dissolution, or any other document required by this Act to be approved by the Secretary of State before the same shall be filed in his office, he shall, within ten days after the delivery thereof to him, give written notice of his disapproval to the person or corporation, domestic or foreign, delivering the same, specifying the reasons therefor. From such disapproval such person or corporation may appeal to the .... court of the county in which the registered office of such corporation is, or is proposed to be, situated by filing with the clerk of such court a petition setting forth a copy of the articles or other document sought to be filed and a copy of the written disapproval thereof by the Secretary of State; whereupon the matter shall be tried de novo by the court, and the court shall either sustain the action of the Secretary of State or direct him to take such action as the court may deem proper.

If the Secretary of State shall revoke the certificate of authority to transact business in this State of any foreign corporation, pursuant to the provisions of this Act, such foreign corporation may likewise appeal to the .... court of the county where the registered office of such corporation in this State is situated, by filing with the clerk of such court a petition setting forth a copy of its certificate of authority to transact business in this State and a copy of the notice of revocation given by the Secretary of State; whereupon the matter shall be tried de novo by the court, and the court shall either sustain the action of the Secretary of State or direct him to take such action as the court may deem proper.

Appeals from all final orders and judgments entered by the .... court under this section in review of any ruling or decision of the Secretary of State may be taken as in other civil actions.

§ 141. Certificates and Certified Copies to be Received in Evidence

All certificates issued by the Secretary of State in accordance with the provisions of this Act, and all copies of documents filed in his office in accordance with the provisions of this Act when certified by him, shall be taken and received in all courts, public offices, and official bodies as prima facie evidence of the facts therein stated. A certificate by the Secretary of State under the great seal of this State, as to the existence or non-existence of the facts relating to corporations shall be taken and received in all courts, public offices, and official bodies as prima facie evidence of the existence or non-existence of the facts therein stated.

§ 142. Forms to be Furnished by Secretary of State

All reports required by this Act to be filed in the office of the Secretary of State shall be made on forms which shall be prescribed and furnished by the Secretary of State. Forms for all other documents to be filed in the office of the Secretary of State shall be furnished by the Secretary of State on request therefor, but the use thereof, unless otherwise specifically prescribed in this Act, shall not be mandatory.

§ 143. Greater Voting Requirements

Whenever, with respect to any action to be taken by the shareholders of a corporation, the articles of incorporation require the vote or concurrence of the holders of a greater proportion of the shares, or of any class or series thereof, than required by this Act with respect to such action, the provisions of the articles of incorporation shall control.

§ 144. Waiver of Notice

Whenever any notice is required to be given to any shareholder or director of a corporation under the provisions of this Act or under the provisions of the articles of incorporation or by-laws of the corporation, a waiver thereof in writing signed by the person or persons entitled to such notice, whether before or after the time stated therein, shall be equivalent to the giving of such notice.

§ 145. Action by Shareholders Without a Meeting

Any action required by this Act to be taken at a meeting of the shareholders of a corporation, or any action which may be taken at a meeting of the shareholders, may be taken without a meeting if a consent in writing, setting forth the action so taken, shall be signed by all of the shareholders entitled to vote with respect to the subject matter thereof.

Such consent shall have the same effect as a unanimous vote of shareholders, and may be stated as such in any articles or document filed with the Secretary of State under this Act.

§ 146. Unauthorized Assumption of Corporate Powers

All persons who assume to act as a corporation without authority so to do shall be jointly and severally liable for all debts and liabilities incurred or arising as a result thereof.

§ 147. Application to Existing Corporations

The provisions of this Act shall apply to all existing corporations organized under any general act of this State providing for the organization of corporations for a purpose or purposes for which a corporation might be organized under this Act, where the power has been reserved to amend, repeal or modify the act under which such corporation was organized and where such act is repealed by this Act.

§ 148. Application to Foreign and Interstate Commerce

The provisions of this Act shall apply to commerce with foreign nations and among the several states only insofar as the same may be permitted under the provisions of the Constitution of the United States.

§ 149. Reservation of Power

The ....* shall at all times have power to prescribe such regulations, provisions and limitations as it may deem advisable, which regulations, provisions and limitations shall be binding upon any and all corporations subject to the provisions of this Act, and the ....* shall have power to amend, repeal or modify this Act at pleasure.

*Insert name of legislative body.

§ 150. Effect of Repeal of Prior Acts

The repeal of a prior act by this Act shall not affect any right accrued or established, or any liability or penalty incurred, under the provisions of such act, prior to the repeal thereof.

§ 151. Effect of Invalidity of Part of this Act

If a court of competent jurisdiction shall adjudge to be invalid or unconstitutional any clause, sentence, paragraph, section or part of this Act, such judgment or decree shall not affect, impair, invalidate or nullify the remainder of this Act, but the effect thereof shall be confined to the clause, sentence, paragraph, section or part of this Act so adjudged to be invalid or unconstitutional.

§ 152. Exclusivity of Certain Provisions [Optional]

In circumstances to which section 45 and related sections of this Act are applicable, such provisions supersede the applicability of any other statutes of this state with respect to the legality of distributions.

§ 153. Repeal of Prior Acts

(insert appropriate provisions).........

Appendix

F

DICTIONARY OF LEGAL TERMS
(Abridged and Adapted from Black's Law Dictionary, 5th Edition.)

A

abatement of nuisance See **nuisance**

abstract of title A condensed history of the title to land, consisting of a summary of the material or operative portion of all the conveyances which in any manner affect the land, or any estate or interest therein, together with a statement of all liens, charges, or liabilities to which the same may be subject, and of which it is in any way material for purchasers to be apprised.

acceptance *Commercial paper* Acceptance is the drawee's signed engagement to honor the draft as presented. It becomes operative when completed by delivery or notification. U.C.C. § 3–410.

Contracts Compliance by offeree with terms and conditions of offer.

Sale of goods U.C.C. § 2–606 provides three ways a buyer can accept goods: (1) by signifying to the seller that the goods are conforming or that he will accept them in spite of their nonconformity, (2) by failing to make an effective rejection, and (3) by doing an act inconsistent with the seller's ownership.

accession An addition to one's property by increase of the original property or by production from such property. E.g., A innocently converts the wheat of B into bread. U.C.C. § 9–315 changes the common law where a perfected security interest is involved.

accommodation An arrangement made as a favor to another, usually involving a loan of money or commercial paper. While a party's intent may be to aid a maker of note by lending his credit, if he seeks to accomplish thereby legitimate objects of his own, and not simply to aid the maker, the act is not for accommodation.

accommodation party A person who signs commercial paper in any capacity for the purpose of lending his name to another party to an instrument. U.C.C. § 3–415.

accord and satisfaction A method of discharging a claim whereby the parties agree to accept something in settlement, the "accord" being the agreement and the "satisfaction" its execution or performance. It is a new contract that is substituted for an old contract, which is thereby discharged, or for an obligation or cause of action and that must have all of the elements of a valid contract.

account Any account with a bank, including a checking, time, interest or savings account. U.C.C. § 4–194. Also, any right to payment, for goods or services, that is not evidenced by an instrument or chattel paper. E.g., account receivable.

adhesion contract Standard "form" contract, usually between a large retailer and a consumer, in which the weaker party has no realistic choice or opportunity to bargain.

adjudication The giving or pronouncing of a judgment in a case; also the judgment given.

administrator A person appointed by the court to manage the assets and liabilities of an intestate (person dying without a will). A person who is named in the will by testator (person dying with a will) is called the executor. Female designations are administratrix and executrix.

adverse possession A method of acquisition of title to real property by possession for a statutory period under certain conditions. There may be different periods of time, depending on whether the adverse possessor has color of title. See also **constructive adverse possession; prescription; tacking.**

affidavit A written statement of facts, made voluntarily, confirmed by oath or affirmation of party making it, and taken before an authorized officer.

affirmative defense A response that attacks the plaintiff's legal right to bring an action as opposed to attacking the truth of the claim. E.g., accord and satisfaction; assumption of risk; contributory negligence; duress; estoppel.

agency Relation in which one person acts for or represents another by the latter's authority.
Actual agency Exists where the agent is really employed by the principal.
Agency by estoppel One created by operation of law and established by proof of such acts of the principal as reasonably lead to the conclusion of its existence.
Implied agency One created by acts of parties and deduced from proof of other facts.

alienation Every mode of passing realty by the act of the party, as distinguished from passing it by the operation of law. See also **restraint on alienation.**

allegation A statement of a party setting out what he expects to prove.

annul To annul a judgment or judicial proceeding is to deprive it of all force and operation.

answer Any pleading setting up matters of facts by way of defense. The answer is the formal written statement made by a defendant setting forth the ground of his defense.

anticipatory breach of contract (or **anticipatory repudiation**). The unjustified assertion by a party that he will not perform an obligation that he is contractually obligated to perform at a future time. See U.C.C. §§ 610 & 611.

apparent authority Such principal power that a reasonable person would assume an agent has in light of the principal's conduct. It includes the power to do whatever is usually done in order to carry into effect the principal power conferred.

appeal Resort to a superior (appellate) court to review the decision of an inferior (trial) court or administrative agency.

appearance A technical coming into court as a party to an action, as plaintiff or as defendant. The party may actually appear in court, or he may, by his attorney, enter his appearance by filing written pleadings in the case, or by filing a formal written entry of appearance.

appellant A party who takes an appeal from one court to another. He may be either the plaintiff or defendant in the original court proceeding.

appellee The party in a cause against whom an appeal is taken; that is, the party who has an interest adverse to setting aside or reversing the judgment. Sometimes also called the "respondent."

appurtenances Things appurtenant pass as incident to the principal thing. Sometimes an easement consisting of a right of way over one piece of land will pass with another piece of land as being appurtenant to it.

arbitration The reference of a dispute to an impartial (third) person chosen by the parties who agree in advance to abide by the arbitrator's award issued after a hearing at which both parties have an opportunity to be heard.

arrest of judgment The act of staying a judgment, or refusing to render judgment in an action at law, after verdict, for some matter intrinsic appearing on the face of the record, which would render the judgment, if given, erroneous or reversible.

articles of incorporation (or **certificate of incorporation**) The instrument under which a corporation is formed. The contents are prescribed in the particular state's general incorporation statute.

articles of partnership A written agreement by which parties enter into a partnership, to be governed by the terms set forth therein.

assignment A transfer of the rights to real or personal property, usually intangible property such as rights in a lease, mortgage, sale agreement or partnership.

attachment The process of seizing property, by virtue of a writ, summons, or other judicial order, and bringing the same into the custody of the court for the purpose of securing satisfaction of the judgment ultimately to be entered in the action. While formerly the main objective was to coerce the defendant debtor to appear in court, today the writ of attachment is used primarily to seize the debtor's property in the event a judgment is rendered.

Distinguished from execution See **execution.**

Also, the process by which a security interest becomes enforceable. Attachment may occur upon the taking of possession or upon the signing of a security agreement by the person who is pledging the property as collateral.

attestation The act of witnessing an instrument in writing, at the request of the party making the same, and subscribing it as a witness. Execution and attestation are clearly distinct formalities; the former being the act of the party, and the latter of the witnesses only.

B

bailee The party to whom personal property is delivered under a contract of bailment.

bailment A delivery of personal property in trust for the execution of a special object in relation to such goods, beneficial either to the bailor or bailee or both, and upon a contract to either redeliver the goods to the bailor or otherwise dispose of the same in conformity with the purpose of the trust.

bailor The party who delivers goods to another in the contract of bailment.

bankrupt The state or condition of one who is unable to pay his debts as they are, or become, due.

bankruptcy act The Act was substantially revised in 1978, effective October 1, 1979. Straight bankruptcy is in the nature of a liquidation proceeding and involves the collection and distribution to creditors of all the bankrupt's non-exempt property by the trustee in the manner provided by the Act. The debtor rehabilitation provisions of the Act (Chapters 11 and 13) differ however from straight bankruptcy in that the debtor looks to rehabilitation and reorganization, rather than liq-

uidation, and the creditor looks to future earnings of the bankrupt, rather than property held by the bankrupt to satisfy their claims.

beneficiary One who benefits from act of another. See also **third party beneficiary.**

Incidental A person who may derive benefit from performance on contract, though he is neither the promisee nor the one to whom performance is to be rendered. Since the incidental beneficiary is not a donee or creditor beneficiary (see **third party beneficiary**), he has no right to enforce the contract.

Trust As it relates to trust beneficiaries, includes a person who has any present or future interest, vested or contingent, and also includes the owner of an interest by assignment or other transfer and, as it relates to a charitable trust, includes any person entitled to enforce the trust.

bequest A gift by will of personal property; a legacy. Disposition of realty in will is termed "devise." See also **devise; legacy.**

Residuary bequest A gift of all the remainder of the testator's personal estate, after payment of debts and legacies, etc.

Specific bequest One whereby the testator gives to the legatee all his property of a certain class or kind; as all his pure personalty.

bill of lading Document evidencing receipt of goods for shipment issued by person engaged in business of transporting or forwarding goods and it includes airbill. U.C.C. § 1–201(6).

bill of sale A written agreement, formerly limited to one under seal, by which one person assigns or transfers his right to or interest in goods and personnal chattels to another.

binder A written memorandum of the important terms of contract of insurance which gives temporary protection to insured pending investigation of risk by insurance company or until a formal policy is issued.

blue sky laws A popular name for state statutes providing for the regulation and supervision of securities offerings and sales, for the protection of citizen-investors from investing in fraudulent companies.

bona fide Latin. In good faith.

bond A certificate or evidence of a debt on which the issuing company or governmental body promises to pay the bondholders a specified amount of interest for a specified length of time, and to repay the loan on the expiration date. In every case a bond represents debt—its holder is a creditor of the corporation and not a part owner as is the shareholder.

by-laws Regulations, ordinances, rules of laws adopted by an association or corporation for its government.

C

capital Accumulated goods, possessions, and assets, used for the production of profits and wealth. Owners' equity in a business. Often used equally correctly to mean the total assets of a business. Sometimes used to mean capital assets.

capitalization To record an expenditure that may benefit in the future as an asset, rather than to treat the expenditure as an expense of the period of its occurrence. Different tax consequences flow from whether an expenditure is "capitalized" or "expensed".

cause of action The ground on which an action may be sustained.

caveat emptor Latin. Let the buyer beware. This maxim is more applicable to judicial sales, auctions, and the like, than to sales of consumer goods where strict liability, warranty, and other laws protect.

certificate of deposit A written acknowledgment by a bank or banker of a deposit with promise to pay to depositor, to his order, or to some other person or to his order. U.C.C. § 3–104(2)(c).

certification of incorporation See **articles of incorporation**.

certiorari Latin. To be informed of. A writ of common law origin issued by a superior to an inferior court requiring the latter to produce a certified record of a particular case tried therein. It is most commonly used to refer to the Supreme Court of the United States, which uses the writ of certiorari as a discretionary device to choose the cases it wishes to hear. The trend in state practice has been to abolish such writ.

chancery Equity; equitable jurisdiction; a court of equity; the system of jurisprudence administered in courts of equity.

charter An instrument emanating from the sovereign power, in the nature of a grant. A charter differs from a constitution in that the former is granted by the sovereign, while the latter is established by the people themselves.

Corporate law An act of a legislature creating a corporation, or creating and defining the franchise of a corporation. Also a corporation's constitution or organic law; that is to say, the articles of incorporation taken in connection with the law under which the corporation was organized.

chattel An article of personal property, as opposed to real property. It may refer to animate as well as inanimate property.

chattel mortgage A pre-Uniform Commercial Code security device whereby a security interest was taken by the mortgagee in personal property of the mortgagor. Such security device has generally been superseded by other types of security agreements under U.C.C. Article 9 (Secured Transactions).

check A draft drawn upon a bank and payable on demand, signed by the maker or drawer, containing an unconditional promise to pay a sum certain in money to the order of the payee. U.C.C. § 3–104(2)(b).

Cashier's check A bank's own check drawn on itself and signed by the cashier or other authorized official. It is a direct obligation of the bank.

civil law Laws concerned with civil or private rights and remedies, as contrasted with criminal laws.

The system of jurisprudence administered in the Roman empire, particularly as set forth in the compilation of Justinian and his successors, as distinguished from the common law of England and the canon law. The civil law (Civil Code) is followed by Louisiana.

close corporation See **corporation**.

code A compilation of all permanent laws in force, consolidated and classified according to subject matter. Many states have published official codes of all laws in force, including the common law and statutes as judicially interpreted, which have been compiled by code commissions and enacted by the legislatures.

codicil A supplement or an addition to a will; it may explain, modify, add to, subtract from, qualify, alter, restrain or revoke provisions in existing will. It must be executed with the same formalities as a will.

cognovit judgment Written authority by debtor for entry of judgment against him in the event he defaults in payment. Such provision in a debt instrument on default confers judgment against the debtor.

collateral security A security given in addition to the direct security, and subordinate to it, intended to guaranty its validity or convertibility or insure its performance.

Banking Some form of security in addition to the personal obligation of the borrower.

collecting bank Any bank handling the item for collection except the payor bank. U.C.C. § 4–105(d).

commercial law A phrase used to designate the whole body of substantive jurisprudence (*e.g.* Uniform Commercial Code; Truth in Lending Act) applicable to the rights, intercourse, and relations of persons engaged in commerce, trade, or mercantile pursuits. See **uniform commercial code.**

commercial paper Bills of exchange (*i.e.* drafts), promissory notes, bank-checks, and other negotiable instruments for the payment of money, which, by their form and on their face, purport to be such instruments. U.C.C. Article 3 is the general law governing commercial paper.

common law As distinguished from statutory law created by the enactment of legislatures, the common law comprises the judgments and decrees of the courts recognizing, affirming, and enforcing usages and customs of immemorial antiquity. As distinguished from ecclesiastical law, it is the system of jurisprudence administered by the purely secular tribunals.

comparative negligence Under comparative negligence statutes or doctrines, negligence is measured in terms of percentage, and any damages allowed shall be diminished in proportion to amount of negligence attributable to the person for whose injury, damage or death recovery is sought.

complainant One who applies to the courts for legal redress by filing complaint (*i.e.* plaintiff).

complaint The pleading which sets forth a claim for relief. Such complaint (whether it be the original claim, counterclaim, cross-claim, or third-party claim) shall contain: (1) a short and plain statement of the grounds upon which the court's jurisdiction depends, unless the court already has jurisdiction and the claim needs no new grounds of jurisdiction to support it, (2) a short and plain statement of the claim showing that the pleader is entitled to relief, and (3) a demand for judgment for the relief to which he deems himself entitled. Fed.R. Civil P. 8(a). The complaint, together with

the summons, is required to be served on the defendant. Rule 4.

confession of judgment See **cognovit judgment.**

conflict of laws That branch of jurisprudence, arising from the diversity of the laws of different nations, states or jurisdictions, that reconciles the inconsistency, or decides which law is to govern in the particular case.

confusion Results when goods belonging to two or more owners become intermixed to the point where the property of any of them no longer can be identified except as part of a mass of like goods.

consanguinity Kinship; blood relationship; the connection or relation of persons descended from the same stock or common ancestor.

conservator Appointed by court to manage affairs of incompetent or to liquidate business.

consideration The cause, motive, price, or impelling influence which induces a contracting party to enter into a contract. Some right, interest, profit or benefit accruing to one party, or some forbearance, detriment, loss, or responsibility, given, suffered, or undertaken by the other.

consignee One to whom a consignment is made. Person named in bill of lading to whom or to whose order the bill promises delivery. U.C.C. § 7–102(b).

consignment Ordinarily implies an agency and denotes that property is committed to the consignee for care or sale.

consignor One who sends or makes a consignment; a shipper of goods. The person named in a bill of lading as the person from whom the goods have been received for shipment. U.C.C. § 7–102(c).

consolidation In *corporate law*, the combination of two or more corporations into a newly created corporation. Thus, A Corporation and B Corporation combine to form C Corporation.

constructive That which is established by the mind of the law in its act of *construing* facts, conduct, circumstances, or instruments. That which has not the character assigned to it in its own essential nature, but acquires such character in consequence of the way in which it is regarded by a rule or policy of law; hence, inferred, implied, or made out by legal interpretation; the word "legal" being sometimes used here in lieu of "constructive."

constructive adverse possession Type of adverse possession that is characterized by performance of certain acts under color of title by an adverse claimant who is not in actual possession of the entire amount of land being claimed. See **adverse possession.**

constructive assent An assent or consent imputed to a party from a construction or interpretation of his conduct; as distinguished from one which he actually expresses.

constructive conditions Conditions in contracts which are neither expressed nor implied but are rather imposed by law to meet the ends of justice.

constructive delivery Term comprehending all those acts which, although not truly conferring a real possession of the vendee, have been held by construction of law to be the equivalent to acts of real delivery.

constructive trust See **trustee.**

contract An agreement between two or more persons which creates an obligation to do or not to do a particular thing. Its essentials are competent parties, subject matter, a legal consideration, mutuality of agreement, and mutuality of obligation.

Output contract A contract in which one party agrees to sell his entire output and the other agrees to buy it; it is not illusory, though it may be indefinite.

Requirements contract A contract in which one party agrees to purchase his total requirements from the other party and hence it is binding and not illusory.

Unconscionable contract One which no sensible man not under delusion, duress, or in distress would make, and such as no honest and fair man would accept. A contract the terms of which are excessively unreasonable, overreaching and one-sided.

Unilateral and bilateral A unilateral contract is one in which one party makes an express engagement or undertakes a performance, without receiving in return any express engagement or promise of performance from the other. Bilateral (or reciprocal) contracts are those by which the parties expressly enter into mutual engagements.

contributory negligence The act or omission amounting to want of ordinary care on part of complaining party, which, concurring with defendant's negligence, is proximate cause of injury.

The defense of contributory negligence is an absolute bar to any recovery in some states; be-

cause of this, it has been replaced by the doctrine of comparative negligence in many other states.

conversion Unauthorized and wrongful exercise of dominion and control over another's personal property, to exclusion of or inconsistent with rights of the owner. See also **trover.**

corporation A legal entity ordinarily consisting of an association of numerous individuals. Such entity is regarded as having a personality and existence distinct from that of its several members and is vested with the capacity of continuous succession, irrespective of changes in its membership, either in perpetuity or for a limited term of years.

Domestic and foreign With reference to the laws and the courts of any given state, a "domestic" corporation is one created by, or organized under, the laws of that state; a "foreign" corporation is one created by or under the laws of another state, government, or country.

Subsidiary and parent Subsidiary corporation is one in which another corporation (called parent corporation) owns at least a majority of the shares, and thus has control.

Close corporation A corporation whose shares, or at least voting shares, are held by a single shareholder or closely-knit group of shareholders.

Corporation de facto One existing under color of law and in pursuance of an effort made in good faith to organize a corporation under the statute. Such a corporation is not subject to collateral attack.

Corporation de jure That which exists by reason of full compliance with requirements of an existing law permitting organization of such corporation.

Subchapter S corporation A small business corporation which, under certain conditions, may elect to have its undistributed taxable income taxed to its shareholders. I.R.C. § 1371 *et seq.* Of major significance is the fact that Subchapter S status usually avoids the corporate income tax, and corporate losses can be claimed by the shareholders.

costs A pecuniary allowance, made to the successful party (and recoverable from the losing party), for his expenses in prosecuting or defending an action or a distinct proceeding within an action. Fed.R.Civil P. 54(d); Fed.R.App.P. 39. Generally, "costs" do not include attorney fees unless such fees are by a statute denominated costs or are by statute allowed to be recovered as costs in the case.

count In pleading, the plaintiff's statement of his cause of action. No longer used under Federal Rules of Civil Procedure.

counter offer A statement by the offeree which has the legal effect of rejecting the offer and of proposing a new offer to the offeror. However, the provisions of U.C.C. § 2–207(2) modifies this principle by providing that the "additional terms are to be construed as proposals for addition to the contract."

counterclaim A claim presented by a defendant in opposition to or deduction from the claim of the plaintiff. Fed.R. Civil P. 13. If established, such will defeat or diminish the plaintiff's claim. The two types are compulsory and permissive.

course of dealing A sequence of previous acts and conduct between the parties to a particular transaction which is fairly to be regarded as establishing a common basis of understanding for interpreting their expressions and other conduct. U.C.C. § 1–205(1).

court above—court below In appellate practice, the "court above" is the one to which a cause is removed for review, whether by appeal, writ of error, or certiorari; while the "court below" is the one from which the case is being removed.

covenant Used primarily with respect to promises in conveyances or other instruments dealing with real estate.

Covenant of warranty An assurance by the grantor of an estate that the grantee shall enjoy the same without interruption by virtue of paramount title.

Covenant running with land A covenant which goes with the land, as being annexed to the estate, and which cannot be separated from the land, and transferred without it. A covenant is said to run with the land when not only the original parties or their representatives, but each successive owner of the land, will be entitled to its benefit, or be liable (as the case may be) to its obligation. Such a covenant is said to be one which "touches and concerns" the land itself, so that its benefit or obligation passes with the ownership. Essentials are that the grantor and grantee must have intended that the covenant run with the land, the covenant must affect or concern the land with which it runs, and there must be privity of estate between party claiming the benefit and the party who rests under the burden.

Covenants against incumbrances A stipulation against all rights to or interests in the land which may subsist in third persons to the diminution of the value of the estate granted.

Covenant appurtenant A covenant which is connected with land of the grantor, and not in gross. A covenant running with the land and binding heirs, executors and assigns of the immediate parties.

Covenant for further assurance An undertaking, in the form of a covenant, on the part of the vendor of real estate to do such further acts for the purpose of perfecting the purchaser's title as the latter may reasonably require.

Covenant for possession A covenant by which the grantee or lessee is granted possession.

Covenant for quiet enjoyment An assurance against the consequences of a defective title, and of any disturbances thereupon.

Covenants for title Covenants usually inserted in a conveyance of land, on the part of the grantor, and binding him for the completeness, security, and continuance of the title transferred to the grantee. They comprise covenants for seisin, for right to convey, against incumbrances, or quiet enjoyment, sometimes for further assurance, and almost always of warranty.

Covenant in gross Such as do not run with the land.

Covenant of right to convey An assurance by the convenantor that the grantor has sufficient capacity and title to convey the *estate* which he by his deed undertakes to convey.

Covenant of seisin An assurance to the purchaser that the grantor has the very estate in quantity and quality which he purports to convey.

credit beneficiary See **third party beneficiary.**

cure The right of a seller under U.C.C. to correct a non-conforming delivery of goods to buyer within the contract period. § 2–508.

cy-pres As near as (possible). Rule for the construction of instruments in equity, by which the intention of the party is carried out *as near as may be,* when it would be impossible or illegal to give it literal effect.

D

damage Loss, injury, or deterioration, caused by the negligence, design, or accident of one person to another, in respect of the latter's person or property. The word is to be distinguished from its plural, "damages", which means a compensation in money for a loss or damage.

damages Money sought as a remedy for breach of contract or for tortious acts.

Actual damages Real, substantial and just damages, or the amount awarded to a complainant in compensation for his actual and real loss or injury, as opposed on the one hand to "nominal" damages, and on the other to "exemplary" or "punitive" damages. Synonymous with "compensatory damages" and with "general damages."

Compensatory damages Compensatory damages are such as will compensate the injured party for the injury sustained, and nothing more; such as will simply make good or replace the loss caused by the wrong or injury.

Consequential damages Such damage, loss or injury as does not flow directly and immediately from the act of the party, but only from some of the consequences or results of such act. Consequential damages resulting from a seller's breach of contract include any loss resulting from general or particular requirements and needs of which the seller at the time of contracting had reason to know and which could not reasonably be prevented by cover or otherwise, and injury to person or property proximately resulting from any breach of warranty. U.C.C. § 2–715(2).

Exemplary or punitive damages Damages other than compensatory damages which may be awarded against person to punish him for outrageous conduct.

Expectancy damages Calculable by subtracting the injured party's actual dollar position as a result of the breach from that party's projected dollar position had performance occurred.

Incidental damages Under U.C.C. § 2–710, such damages include any commercially reasonable charges, expenses or commissions incurred in stopping delivery, in the transportation, care and custody of goods after the buyer's breach, in connection with the return or resale of the goods or otherwise resulting from the breach. Also, such damages, resulting from a seller's breach of contract, include expenses reasonably incurred in inspection, receipt, transportation and care and custody of goods rightfully rejected, any commercially reasonable charges, expenses or commissions in connection with effecting cover and any other reasonable expense incident to the delay or other breach. U.C.C. § 2–715(1).

Irreparable damages In the law pertaining to injunctions, damages for which no certain pecuniary standard exists for measurement.

Liquidated damages and penalties Damages for breach by either party may be liquidated in the agreement but only at an amount which is reasonable in the light of the anticipated or actual harm caused by the breach, the difficulties of proof of loss, and the inconvenience or nonfeasibility of otherwise obtaining an adequate remedy. A term fixing unreasonably large liquidated damages is void as a penalty. U.C.C. § 2–718(1).

Mitigation of damages A plaintiff may not recover damages for the effects of an injury which reasonably could have been avoided or substantially ameliorated. This limitation on recovery is generally denominated as "mitigation of damages" or "avoidance of consequences."

de facto In fact, in deed, actually. This phrase is used to characterize an officer, a government, a past action, or a state of affairs which must be accepted for all practical purposes, but is illegal or illegitimate. See also **corporation**, *corporation de facto.*

de jure Descriptive of a condition in which there has been total compliance with all requirements of law. In this sense it is the contrary of *de facto.* See also **corporation**, *corporation de jure.*

de novo Anew; afresh; a second time.

debt security Any form of corporate security reflected as debt on the books of the corporation in contrast to equity securities such as stock; *e.g.* bonds, notes and debentures are debt securities.

deceit A fraudulent and cheating misrepresentation, artifice, or device, used to deceive and trick one who is ignorant of the true facts, to the prejudice and damage of the party imposed upon. See also **fraud; misrepresentation.**

declaration In common-law pleading, the first of the pleadings on the part of the plaintiff in an action at law, being a formal and methodical specification of the facts and circumstances constituting his cause or action. The term "complaint" is now used in the federal courts and in all states that have adopted the Rules of Civil Procedure.

deed A conveyance of realty; a writing signed by grantor, whereby title to realty is transferred from one to another.

defendant The party against whom relief or recovery is sought in an action or suit.

delegation of duties Transferring all or part of one's duties arising under a contract to another.

delivery The physical or constructive transfer of an instrument or of goods from the hands of one person to those of another. See also **constructive delivery.**

demurrer An allegation of a defendant that, even if the facts as stated in the pleading to which objection is taken be true, yet their legal consequences are not such as to put the demurring party to the necessity of answering them or proceeding further with the cause.

The Federal Rules of Civil Procedure do not provide for the use of a demurrer, but provide an equivalent to a general demurrer in the motion to dismiss for failure to state a claim on which relief may be granted. Fed.R. Civil P. 12(b).

deposition The testimony of a witness taken upon interrogatories, not in court, but intended to be used in court. See also **discovery.**

depository bank The first bank to which an item is transferred for collection even though it may also be the payor bank. U.C.C. § 4–105(a).

descent Succession to the ownership of an estate by inheritance, or by any act of law, as distinguished from "purchase."

Descents are of two sorts, *lineal* and *collateral*. Lineal descent is descent in a direct or right line, as from father or grandfather to son or grandson. Collateral descent is descent in a collateral or oblique line, that is, up to the common ancestor and then down from him, as from brother to brother, or between cousins.

devise A testamentary disposition of land or realty; a gift of real property by the last will and testament of the donor. When used as a noun, means a testamentary disposition of real or personal property and when used as a verb, means to dispose of real or personal property by will.

dictum Generally used as an abbreviated form of *obiter dictum,* "a remark by the way;" that is, an observation or remark made by a judge which does not embody the resolution or determination of the court and which is made without argument or full consideration of the point.

directed verdict In a case in which the party with the burden of proof has failed to present a prima facie case for jury consideration, the trial judge may order the entry of a verdict without allowing the jury to consider it, because, as a matter of law, there can be only one such verdict. Fed.R. Civil P. 50(a).

discount A discount by a bank means a drawback or deduction made upon its advances or loans of money, upon negotiable paper or other evidences of debt payable at a future day, which are transferred to the bank.

discovery The pre-trial devices that can be used by one party to obtain facts and information about the case from the other party in order to assist the party's preparation for trial. Under Federal Rules of Civil Procedure tools of discovery include: depositions upon oral and written questions, written interrogatories, production of documents or things, permission to enter upon land or other property, physical and mental examinations and requests for admission. Rules 26–37.

dishonor To refuse to accept or pay a draft or to pay a promissory note when duly presented. U.C.C. § 3–507(1); § 4–210. See also **protest.**

dissolution The dissolution of a partnership is the relation of the partners caused by any partner ceasing to be associated in the carrying on as distinguished from the winding up of the business. See also **winding up.**

dividend The payment designated by the board of directors of a corporation to be distributed pro rata among the shares outstanding.

domicile That place where a man has his true, fixed, and permanent home and principal establishment, and to which whenever he is absent he has the intention of returning.

donee beneficiary See **third party beneficiary.**

dower A species of life-estate which a woman is, by law, entitled to claim on the death of her husband, in the lands and tenements of which he was seised in fee during the marriage, and which her issue, if any, might by possibility have inherited.

Dower has been abolished in the majority of the states and materially altered in most of the others.

draft A written order by the first party, called the drawer, instructing a second party, called the drawee (such as a bank) to pay a third party, called the payee. An order to pay a sum certain in money, signed by a drawer, payable on demand or at a definite time, and to order or bearer. U.C.C. § 3–104.

drawee A person to whom a bill of exchange or draft is directed, and who is requested to pay the amount of money therein mentioned. The drawee of a check is the bank on which it is drawn.

When drawee accepts, he engages that he will pay the instrument according to its tenor at the time of his engagement or as completed. U.C.C. § 3–413(1).

drawer The person who draws a bill or draft. The drawer of a check is the person who signs it.

The drawer engages that upon dishonor of the draft and any necessary notice of dishonor or protest, he will pay the amount of the draft to the holder or to any indorser who takes it up. The drawer may disclaim this liability by drawing without recourse, U.C.C. § 3–413(2).

duress Unlawful constraint exercised upon a person, whereby he is forced to do some act against his will.

E

earnest The payment of a part of the price of goods sold, or the delivery of part of such goods, for the purpose of binding the contract.

easement A right in the owner of one parcel of land, by reason of such ownership, to use the land of another for a special purpose not inconsistent with a general property in the owner. This right is distinguishable from a "license" which merely confers personal privilege to do some act on the land.

Affirmative easement One where the servient estate must permit something to be done thereon, as to pass over it, or to discharge water on it.

Appurtenant easement An incorporeal right which is attached to a superior right and inheres in land to which it is attached and is in the nature of a covenant running with the land.

Easement by estoppel Easement which is created when landlord voluntarily imposes apparent servitude on his property and another person, acting reasonably, believes that servitude is permanent and in reliance upon that belief does something that he would not have done otherwise or refrains from doing something that he would have done otherwise.

Easement by necessity Such arises by operation of law when land conveyed is completely shut off from access to any road by land retained by grantor or by land of grantor and that of a stranger.

Easement by prescription A mode of acquiring title to property by immemorial or long-continued enjoyment, and refers to personal usage restricted to claimant and his ancestors or grantors.

Easement in gross An easement in gross is not appurtenant to any estate in land or does not belong to any person by virtue of ownership of estate in other land but is mere personal interest in or right to use land of another; it is purely personal

and usually ends with death of grantee.

Easement of access Right of ingress and egress to and from the premises of a lot owner to a street appurtenant to the land of the lot owner.

ejectment An action of which the purpose is to determine whether the title to certain land is in the plaintiff or is in the defendant.

emancipation The act by which an infant is set at liberty from the control of parent or guardian and made his own master.

emblements Crops annually produced by labor of tenant. The doctrine of emblements denotes the right of a tenant to take and carry away such crops after his tenancy has ended.

eminent domain Right of the people or government to take private property for public use upon giving of a fair consideration.

entirety Used to designate that which the law considers as one whole, and not capable of being divided into parts.

equitable Just, fair, and right. Existing in equity; available or sustainable only in equity, or only upon the rules and principles of equity.

equitable servitude A restriction on the use of land that is enforceable in an equity proceeding.

equity Justice administered according to fairness as contrasted with the strictly formulated rules of common law. It is based on a system of rules and principles which originated in England as an alternative to the harsh rules of common law and which were based on what was fair in a particular situation.

equity of redemption The right of the mortgagor of an estate to redeem the same after it has been forfeited, at law, by a breach of the condition of the mortgage, upon paying the amount of debt, interest and costs.

equity securities Stock or similar security, in contrast to debt securities such as bonds, notes and debentures.

error A mistake of law, or false or irregular application of it, such as vitiates the proceedings and warrants the reversal of the judgment.

Error is also used as an elliptical expression for "writ of error"; as in saying that *error* lies; that a judgment may be reversed *on error*.

Harmless error In appellate practice, an error committed in the progress of the trial below which was not prejudicial to the rights of the party assigning it and for which, therefore, the court will not reverse the judgment.

Reversible error In appellate practice, such an error as warrants the appellate court in reversing the judgment before it.

escrow A system of document transfer in which a deed, bond, or funds is delivered to a third person to hold until all conditions in a contract are fulfilled; *e.g.* delivery of deed to escrow agent under installment land sale contract until full payment for land is made.

estate The degree, quantity, nature, and extent of interest which a person has in real and personal property. An estate in lands, tenements, and hereditaments signifies such interest as the tenant has therein.

Also, the total property of whatever kind that is owned by a decedent prior to the distribution of that property in accordance with the terms of a will, or, when there is no will, by the laws of inheritance in the state of domicile of the decedent.

Future estate An estate limited to commence in possession at a future day, either without the intervention of a precedent estate, or on the determination by lapse of time, or otherwise, of a precedent estate created at the same time. Examples include reversions and remainders.

estoppel A bar or impediment raised by the law, which precludes a man from alleging or from denying a certain fact or state of facts, in consequence of his previous allegation or denial or conduct or admission, or in consequence of a final adjudication of the matter in a court of law. See also **waiver.**

eviction Dispossession by process of law; the act of depriving a person of the possession of lands which he has held, in pursuance of the judgment of a court.

evidence Any species of proof, or probative matter, legally presented at the trial of an issue, by the act of the parties and through the medium of witnesses, records, documents, concrete objects, etc., for the purpose of inducing belief in the minds of the court or jury as to their contention.

ex parte A judicial proceeding, order, injunction, etc., is said to be *ex parte* when it is taken or granted at the instance and for the benefit of one party only, and without notice to, or contestation by, any person adversely interested.

exception A formal objection to the action of the court, during the trial of a cause, in refusing a request or overruling an objection; implying that the party excepting does not acquiesce in the decision of the court, but will seek to procure its reversal, and that he means to save the benefit of his request or objection in some future proceeding. Under rules practice in the federal and most state courts, the need for claiming an exception to evidence or to a ruling to preserve appellate rights has been eliminated in favor of an objection. Fed.R. Civil P. 46.

executed Completed; already done or performed. The opposite of executory.

execution *Execution of contract* includes performance of all acts necessary to render it complete as an instrument and imports idea that nothing remains to be done to make complete and effective contract.

Execution upon a money judgment is the legal process of enforcing the judgment, usually by seizing and selling property of the debtor.

executor A person appointed by a testator to carry out the directions and requests in his will, and to dispose of the property according to his testamentary provisions after his decease. The female designation is executrix. A person appointed by the court in intestacy situation is called the administrator(rix).

executory That which is yet to be executed or performed; that which remains to be carried into operation or effect; incomplete; depending upon a future performance or event. The opposite of executed.

executory contract See **contracts.**

executory interests A general term, comprising all future estates and interests in land or personalty, other than reversions and remainders.

exemplary damages See **damages.**

express Manifested by direct and appropriate language, as distinguished from that which is inferred from conduct. The word is usually contrasted with "implied."

ex-ship Seller may choose shipper. Risk of loss passes to buyer upon the goods leaving the ship. Buyer is responsible for any landing charges. See U.C.C. § 2–322. See also **F.A.S.**

F

F.A.S. Free alongside. Term used in sales price quotations, indicating that the price includes all costs of transportation and delivery of the goods alongside the ship. See U.C.C. § 2–319(2). See also **ex-ship**

fee simple

Absolute A fee simple absolute is an estate that is unlimited as to duration, disposition, and descendibility. It is the largest estate and most extensive interest that can be enjoyed in land.

Conditional Type of transfer in which grantor conveys fee simple on condition that something be done or not done.

Defeasible Type of fee grant which may be defeated on the happening of an event. An estate which may last forever, but which may end upon the happening of a specified event, is a "fee simple defeasible".

Determinable Created by conveyance which contains words effective to create a fee simple and, in addition, a provision for automatic expiration of estate on occurrence of stated event.

fee tail An estate of inheritance, descending only to a certain class or classes or heirs; e.g., an estate is conveyed or devised "to A. and the heirs of his body," or "to A. and the heirs male of his body," or "to A., and the heirs female of his body." State statutes have dealt variously with estates tail, some converting them into estates in fee simple.

fiduciary A person or institution who manages money or property for another and who must exercise a standard of care in such management activity imposed by law or contract; *e.g.* executor of estate; receiver in bankruptcy; trustee.

financing statement Under the Uniform Commercial Code, a financing statement is used under Article 9 to reflect a public record that there is a security interest or claim to the goods in question to secure a debt. The financing statement is filed by the security holder with the Secretary of State, or similar public body, and as such becomes public record. See also **secured transaction.**

firm offer An offer by a merchant to buy or sell goods in a signed writing which by its terms give assurance that it will be held open is not revocable, for lack of consideration, during the time stated or if no time is stated for a reasonable time, but in no event may such period of irrevocability exceed three months. U.C.C. § 2–205.

fixture An article in the nature of personal property which has been so annexed to realty that it is regarded as a part of the land. Examples include a furnace affixed to a house or other building, counters permanently affixed to the floor of a store, a sprinkler system installed in a building. U.C.C. § 9–313(1)(a).

Trade fixtures Such chattels as merchants usually possess and annex to the premises occupied by them to enable them to store, handle, and display their goods, which are generally removable without material injury to the premises.

FOB Free on board some location (for example, FOB shipping point; FOB destination); the invoice price includes delivery at seller's expense to that location. Title to goods usually passes from seller to buyer at the FOB location. U.C.C. § 2–319(1).

foreclosure Procedure by which mortgaged property is sold on default of mortgagor in satisfaction of mortgage debt.

franchise A privilege granted or sold, such as to use a name or to sell products or services. The right given by a manufacturer or supplier to a retailer to use his products and name on terms and conditions mutually agreed upon.

fraud Elements include: false representation; of a present or past fact; made by defendant; action in reliance thereon by plaintiff; damage resulting to plaintiff from such misrepresentation.

freehold An estate for life or in fee. It must possess two qualities: (1) immobility, that is, the property must be either land or some interest issuing out of or annexed to land; and (2) indeterminate duration.

frustration of purpose doctrine Excuses a promisor in certain situations when the objectives of contract have been utterly defeated by circumstances arising after formation of agreement, and performance is excused under this rule even though there is no impediment to actual performance.

fungibles With respect to goods or securities, those of which any unit is, by nature or usage of trade, the equivalent of any other like unit. U.C.C. § 1–201(17); *e.g.*, a bushel of wheat or other grain.

future estate See **estate**

G

garnishment A statutory proceeding whereby a person's property, money, or credits in the possession or control of another are applied to payment of the former's debt to a third person.

gift A voluntary transfer of property to another made gratuitously and without consideration. Essential requisites of "gift" are capacity of donor, intention of donor to make gift, completed delivery to or for donee, and acceptance of gift by donee.

gift causa mortis A gift in view of death is one which is made in contemplation, fear, or peril of death, and with intent that it shall take effect only in case of the death of the giver.

goods A term of variable content and meaning. It may include every species of personal property or it may be given a very restricted meaning. Sometimes the meaning of "goods" is extended to include all tangible items, as in the phrase "goods and services."

All things (including specially manufactured goods) which are movable at the time of identification to the contract for sale other than the money in which the price is to be paid, investment securities and things in action. U.C.C. § 2–105(1).

grantor A transferor of property. The creator of a trust is usually designated as the grantor of the trust.

guaranty A promise to answer for the payment of some debt, or the performance of some duty, in case of the failure of another person, who, in the first instance, is liable to such payment or performance.

The terms *guaranty* and *suretyship* are sometimes used interchangeably; but they should not be confounded. The distinction between contract of suretyship and contract of guaranty is whether or not the undertaking is a joint undertaking with the principal or a separate and distinct contract; if it is the former it is one of "suretyship", and if the latter, it is one of "guaranty". See also **surety.**

H

hearsay Hearsay evidence is testimony in court of a statement made out of the court, the statement being offered as an assertion to show the truth of matters asserted therein, and thus resting for its value upon the credibility of the out-of-court asserter.

heir A person who succeeds, by the rules of law, to an estate in lands, tenements, or hereditaments, upon the death of his ancestor, by descent and right of relationship.

holder Person who is in possession of a document of title or an instrument or an investment security drawn, issued or endorsed to him or to his order, or to bearer or in blank. U.C.C. § 1–201(20).

holder in due course A holder who takes an instrument for value, in good faith, and without notice that it is overdue or has been dishonored or of any defense against or claim to it on the part of any person.

holograph A will or deed written entirely by the testator or grantor with his own hand and not witnessed (attested). State laws vary with respect to the validity of the holographic will.

I

in personam Against the person. Action seeking judgment against a person involving his personal rights and based on jurisdiction of his person, as distinguished from a judgment against property (*i.e.* in rem). Type of jurisdiction or power which a court may acquire over the defendant himself in contrast to jurisdiction over his property.

in re In the affair; in the matter of; concerning; regarding. This is the usual method of entitling a judicial proceeding in which there are not adversary parties, but merely some *res* concerning which judicial action is to be taken, such as a bankrupt's estate, an estate in the probate court, a proposed public highway, etc.

in rem A technical term used to designate proceedings or actions instituted *against the thing*, in contradistinction to personal actions, which are said to be *in personam.*

Quasi in rem A term applied to proceedings which are not strictly and purely *in rem*, but are brought against the defendant personally, though the real object is to deal with particular property or subject property to the discharge of claims asserted; for example, foreign attachment, or proceedings to foreclose a mortgage, remove a cloud from title, or effect a partition.

inchoate Imperfect; unfinished; begun, but not completed; as a contract not executed by all the parties.

indemnify To reimburse one for a loss already incurred.

indenture A written agreement under which bonds and debentures are issued, setting forth maturity date, interest rate, and other terms.

indicia Signs; indications. Circumstances which point to the existence of a given fact as probable, but not certain.

indorsee The person to whom a negotiable instrument, promissory note, bill of lading, etc., is assigned by indorsement.

indorsement The act of a payee, drawee, accommodation indorser, or holder of a bill, note, check, or other negotiable instrument, in writing his name upon the back of the same, with or without further or qualifying words, whereby the property in the same is assigned and transferred to another. U.C.C. § 3–202 *et seq.*

injunction An equitable remedy forbidding the party defendant from doing some act which he is threatening or attempting to commit, or restraining him in the continuance thereof, such act being unjust and inequitable, injurious to the plaintiff, and not such as can be adequately redressed by an action at law.

Interlocutory injunction Interlocutory injunctions are those issued at any time during the pendency of the litigation for the short-term purpose of preventing irreparable injury to the petitioner prior to the time that the court will be in a position to either grant or deny permanent relief on the merits. A preliminary injunction includes any interlocutory injunction granted after the respondent has been given notice and the opportunity to participate in a hearing on whether or not that injunction should issue. A temporary restraining order differs from a preliminary injunction in that it is issued ex parte, with no notice or opportunity to be heard granted to the respondent.

insolvency In general, state insolvency laws have been superseded by the Federal Bankruptcy Act.

Under U.C.C., a person is insolvent who either has ceased to pay his debts in the ordinary course of business or cannot pay his debts as they fall due or is insolvent within the meaning of the Federal Bankruptcy Law. U.C.C. § 1–201(23).

insurable interest Exists where insured derives pecuniary benefit or advantage by preservation and continued existence of property or would sustain pecuniary loss from its destruction.

insurance A contract whereby, for a stipulated consideration, one party undertakes to compensate the other for loss on a specified subject by specified perils. The party agreeing to make the compensation is usually called the "insurer" or "underwriter"; the other, the "insured" or "assured"; the written contract, a "policy"; the events insured against, "risks" or "perils"; and the subject, right, or interest to be protected, the "insurable interest." Insurance is a contract whereby one undertakes to indemnify another against loss, damage, or liability arising from an unknown or contingent event.

inter alia Among other things.

inter se or **inter sese** Latin. Among or between themselves; used to distinguish rights or duties between two or more parties from their rights or duties to others.

intermediary bank Any bank to which an item is transferred in the course of collection except the depositary or payor bank. U.C.C. § 4–105(c).

intestate A person is said to die intestate when he dies without making a will. The word is also often used to signify the person himself. *Compare* **testator.**

invitee A person is an "invitee" on land of another if (1) he enters by invitation, express or implied, (2) his entry is connected with the owner's business or with an activity the owner conducts or permits to be conducted on his land and (3) there is mutuality of benefit or benefit to the owner.

J

joint tenancy See **tenancy.**

judgment The official and authentic decision of a court of justice upon the respective rights and claims of the parties to an action or suit therein litigated and submitted to its determination.

judgment in personam A judgment against a particular person, as distinguished from a judgment against a thing or a right or *status.*

judgment in rem An adjudication pronounced upon the status of some particular thing or subject matter, by a tribunal having competent authority.

judgment n. o. v. Judgment non obstante veridicto in its broadest sense is a judgment rendered in favor of one party notwithstanding the finding of a verdict in favor of the other party.

jurisdiction The right and power of a court to adjudicate concerning the subject matter in a given case.

jury (From the Latin jurare, to swear). A body of persons selected and summoned by law and sworn to try the facts of a case and to find according to the law and the evidence. In general, the province of the jury is to find the facts in a case, while the judge passes upon pure questions of law. As a matter of fact, however, the jury must often pass upon mixed questions of law and fact in determining the case, and in all such cases the instructions of the judge as to the law become very important.

L

laches Based upon maxim that equity aids the vigilant and not those who slumber on their rights. It is defined as neglect to assert right or claim which, taken together with lapse of time and other circumstances causing prejudice to adverse party, operates as bar in court of equity.

landlord He who, being the owner of an estate in land, or a rental property, has leased it to another person, called the "tenant." Also called "lessor."

lapse The termination or failure of a right or privilege through neglect to exercise it within some limit of time, or through failure of some contingency.

lease Any agreement which gives rise to relationship of landlord and tenant (real property) or lessor and lessee (real or personal property).

The person who conveys is termed the "lessor," and the person to whom conveyed, the "lessee;" and when the lessor conveys land or tenements to a lessee, he is said to lease, demise, or let them.

Sublease, or underlease One executed by the lessee of an estate to a third person, conveying the same estate for a shorter term than that for which the lessee holds it.

leasehold An estate in realty held under a lease. The four principal types of leasehold estates are the estate for years, periodic tenancy, tenancy at will, and tenancy at sufferance.

legacy "Legacy" is a gift or bequest by will of personal property, whereas a "devise" is a testamentary disposition of real estate.

Demonstrative legacy A bequest of a certain sum of money, with a direction that it shall be paid out of a particular fund. It differs from a specific legacy in this respect: that, if the fund out of which it is payable fails for any cause, it is nevertheless entitled to come on the estate as a general legacy. And it differs from a general legacy in this: that it does not abate in that class, but in the class of specific legacies.

General legacy A pecuniary legacy, payable out of the general assets of a testator.

Residuary legacy A bequest of all the testator's personal estate not otherwise effectually disposed of by his will.

Specific legacy One which operates on property particularly designated. A legacy or gift by will of a particular specified thing, as of a horse, a piece of furniture, a term of years, and the like.

letter of credit An engagement by a bank or other person made at the request of a customer that the issuer will honor drafts or other demands for payment upon compliance with the conditions specified in the credit.

letters of administration Formal document issued by probate court appointing one an administrator of an estate.

letters testamentary The formal instrument of authority and appointment given to an executor by the proper court, empowering him to enter upon the discharge of his office as executor. It corresponds to letters of administration granted to an administrator.

levy To assess; raise; execute; exact; tax; collect; gather; take up; seize. Thus, to levy (assess, exact, raise, or collect) a tax; to levy an execution, *i.e.*, to levy or collect a sum of money on an execution.

license License with respect to real property is a privilege to go on premises for a certain purpose, but does not operate to confer on, or vest in, licensee any title, interest, or estate in such property.

lien A qualified right of property which a creditor has in or over specific property of his debtor, as security for the debt or charge or for performance of some act.

life estate An estate whose duration is limited to the life of the party holding it, or some other person. Upon the death of the life tenant, the property will go to the holder of the remainder interest or to the grantor by reversion.

limited partnership See **partnership.**

liquidated Ascertained; determined; fixed; settled; made clear or manifest. Cleared away; paid; discharged.

liquidated damages See **damages.**

liquidation The settling of financial affairs of a business or individual, usually by liquidating (turning to cash) all assets for distribution to creditors, heirs, etc. It is to be distinguished from dissolution which is the end of the legal existence of a corporation. Liquidation may precede or follow dissolution, depending upon statutes.

lost property Property which the owner has involuntarily parted with and does not know where to find or recover it, not including property which he has intentionally concealed or deposited in a secret place for safe-keeping. Distinguishable from mislaid property which has been deliberately placed somewhere and forgotten.

M

maker One who makes or executes; as the maker of a promissory note. One who signs a check; in this context, synonymous with drawer. See **draft**.

mandamus Latin, we command. A legal writ compelling the defendant to do an official duty.

Pleading Like most of the extraordinary writs, the *writ* of mandamus has been abolished under rules practice in favor of a complaint in the nature of mandamus which accomplishes the same object.

mandate A judicial command or precept proceeding from a court or judicial officer, directing the proper officer to enforce a judgment, sentence, or decree.

master See **principal**.

maturity The date at which an obligation, such as the principal of a bond or a note, becomes due.

mechanic's lien A claim created by state statutes for the purpose of securing priority of payment of the price or value of work performed and materials furnished in erecting or repairing a building or other structure, and as such attaches to the land as well as buildings and improvements erected thereon.

mercantile law An expression substantially equivalent to commercial law. It designates the system of rules, customs, and usages generally recognized and adopted by merchants and traders, and which, either in its simplicity or as modified by common law or statutes, constitutes the law for the regulation of their transactions and the solution of their controversies. The Uniform Commercial Code is the general body of law governing commercial or mercantile transactions.

merchant A person who deals in goods of the kind or otherwise by his occupation holds himself out as having knowledge or skill peculiar to the practices or goods involved in the transaction or to whom such knowledge or skill may be attributed by his employment of an agent or broker or other intermediary who by his occupation holds himself out as having such knowledge or skill. U.C.C. § 2–104(1).

merger The fusion or absorption of one thing or right into another; generally spoken of a case where one of the subjects is of less dignity or im-

portance than the other. Here the less important ceases to have an independent existence.

Corporations The absorption of one company by another, latter retaining its own name and identity and acquiring assets, liabilities, franchises, and powers of former, and absorbed company ceasing to exist as separate business entity. It differs from a consolidation wherein all the corporations terminate their existence and become parties to a new one.

Horizontal merger Merger between business competitors, such as manufacturers of the same type products or distributors selling competing products in the same market area.

Vertical merger Union with corporate customer or supplier.

mislaid property Property which an owner has put deliberately in a certain place but owner is unable to remember where he put it, as distinguished from lost property which the owner leaves unwittingly in a place, forgetting its location. See also **lost property**.

misrepresentation Any manifestation by words or other conduct by one person to another that, under the circumstances, amounts to an assertion not in accordance with the facts. A "misrepresentation" that justifies the rescission of a contract is a false statement of a substantive fact, or any conduct which leads to a belief of a substantive fact material to proper understanding of the matter in hand, made with intent to deceive or mislead. See also **deceit; fraud**.

mitigation of damages See **damages**.

mortgage A mortgage is an interest in land created by a written instrument providing security for the performance of a duty or the payment of a debt.

N

negligence The omission to do something which a reasonable man, guided by those ordinary considerations which ordinarily regulate human affairs, would do, or the doing of something which a reasonable and prudent man would not do.

negotiable Legally capable of being transferred by endorsement or delivery. Usually said of checks and notes and sometimes of stocks and bearer bonds.

non sequitur Latin. It does not follow. An inference which does not follow from the premise.

nonsuit Action in form of a judgment taken against a plaintiff who has failed to appear to prosecute his action or failed to prove his case. Under rules practice, the applicable term is "dismissal", not nonsuit. Fed.R. Civil P. 41.

note   See **promissory note.**

novation   A novation substitutes a new party and discharges one of the original parties to a contract by agreement of all three parties. A new contract is created with the same terms as the original one but only the parties are changed.

nuisance   Nuisance is that activity which arises from unreasonable, unwarranted or unlawful use by a person of his own property, working obstruction or injury to right of another, or to the public, and producing such material annoyance, inconvenience and discomfort that law will presume resulting damage.

Abatement of a nuisance   The removal, stoppage, prostration, or destruction of that which causes a nuisance, whether by breaking or pulling it down, or otherwise removing, destroying, or effacing it.

O

obiter dictum   See **dictum**

offer   A manifestation of willingness to enter into a bargain, so made as to justify another person in understanding that his assent to that bargain is invited and will conclude it. Restatement, Second, Contracts, § 24.

output contract   See **contracts.**

P

par   In commercial law, equal; equality. An equality subsisting between the nominal or face value of a bill of exchange, share of stock, etc., and its actual selling value. When the values are thus equal, the instrument or share is said to be "at par;" if it can be sold for more than its nominal worth, it is "above par;" if for less, it is "below par."

parol evidence rule   Under this rule, when parties put their agreement in writing, all previous oral agreements merge in the writing and a contract as written cannot be modified or changed by parol evidence, in the absence of a plea of mistake or fraud in the preparation of the writing. But rule does not forbid a resort to parol evidence not inconsistent with the matters stated in the writing. Also, as regards sales of goods, such written agreement may be explained or supplemented by course of dealing or usage of trade or by course of conduct, and by evidence of consistent additional terms unless the court finds the writing to have been intended also as a complete and exclusive statement of the terms of the agreement. U.C.C. § 2–202.

part performance   In order to establish part performance taking an oral contract for the sale of realty out of the statute of frauds, the acts relied upon as part performance must be of such a character that they can reasonably be naturally accounted for in no other way than that they were performed in pursuance of the contract, and they must be in conformity with its provisions. See U.C.C. § 2–201(3).

partition   The dividing of lands held by joint tenants, coparceners, or tenants in common, into distinct portions, so that they may hold them in severalty. And, in a less technical sense, any division of real or personal property between co-owners, resulting in individual ownership of the interests of each. Division between several persons of property which belongs to them as co-owners; it may be compulsory (judicial) or voluntary. Commonly, the court will order the property sold and the proceeds divided instead of ordering a physical partition of the property.

partnership   An association of two or more persons to carry on, as co-owners, a business for profit.

Partnerships are treated as a conduit and are, therefore, not subject to taxation. The various items of partnership income, gains, and losses, etc. flow through to the individual partners and are reported on their personal income tax returns.

Limited partnership   Type of partnership comprised of one or more general partners who manage business and who are personally liable for partnership debts, and one or more limited partners who contribute capital and share in profits but who take no part in running business and incur no liability with respect to partnership obligations beyond contribution.

payee   The person in whose favor a bill of exchange, promissory note, or check is made or drawn.

payer, or **payor**   One who pays, or who is to make a payment; particularly the person who is to make payment of a check, bill or note. Correlative to "payee."

payor bank   A bank by which an item is payable as drawn or accepted. U.C.C. § 4–105(b).

per capita   This term, derived from the civil law,

is much used in the law of descent and distribution, and denotes that method of dividing an intestate estate by which an equal share is given to each of a number of persons, all of whom stand in equal degree to the decedent, without reference to their stocks or the right of representation. It is the antithesis of *per stirpes*

per stirpes This term, derived from the civil law, is much used in the law of descents and distribution, and denotes that method of dividing an intestate estate where a class or group of distributees take the share which their deceased would have been entitled to, taking thus by their right of representing such ancestor, and not as so many individuals. It is the antithesis of *per capita*

perfection of security interest Acts required of a secured party in the way of giving at least constructive notice so as to make his security interest effective at least against lien creditors of the debtor. See U.C.C. §§ 9–302 through 9–306. In most cases, the secured party may obtain perfection either by filing with Secretary of State or by taking possession of the collateral.

performance See **part performance; specific performance.**

personal property Generally, all property other than real estate.

plaintiff The party who complains or sues in a civil action and is so named on the record.

plea In common law pleading (now obsolete with adoption of Rules of Civil Procedure), any one in the series of pleadings. More particularly, the first pleading on the part of the defendant. In the strictest sense, the answer which the defendant in an action at law made to the plaintiff's declaration, and in which he set up matter of *fact* as defense, thus distinguished from a demurrer, which interposed objections on grounds of *law*.

In equity pleading (now obsolete with adoption of Rules of Civil Procedure), a special answer showing or relying upon one or more things as a cause why the suit should be either dismissed or delayed or barred.

pleadings The formal allegations by the parties of their respective claims and defenses.

Rules or Codes of Civil Procedure Unlike the rigid technical system of common law pleading, pleadings under federal and state rules or codes of civil procedure have a far more limited function, with determination and narrowing of facts and issues being left to discovery devices and pre-trial conferences. In addition, the rules and codes permit liberal amendment and supplementation of pleadings.

Under rules of civil procedure the pleadings consist of a complaint, an answer, a reply to a counterclaim, an answer to a cross-claim, a third party complaint, and a third party answer. Fed.R.Civil P. 7(a).

pledge A bailment of goods to a creditor as security for some debt or engagegment.

Much of the law of pledges has been replaced by the provisions for secured transactions in Article 9 of the U.C.C.

possibility of reverter The interest which remains in a grantor or testator after the conveyance or devise of a fee simple determinable and which permits the grantor to be revested automatically of his estate on breach of the condition.

power of appointment A power of authority conferred by one person by deed or will upon another (called the "donee") to appoint, that is, to select and nominate, the person or persons who are to receive and enjoy an estate or an income therefrom or from a fund, after the testator's death, or the donee's death, or after the termination of an existing right or interest.

power of attorney An instrument authorizing a person to act as the agent or attorney of the person granting it.

power of termination The interest left in the grantor or testator after the conveyance or devise of a fee simple on condition subsequent or conditional fee.

precedent An adjudged case or decision of a court, considered as furnishing an example or authority for an identical or similar case afterwards arising or a similar question of law. See also **stare decisis.**

pre-emptive right The privilege of a stockholder to maintain a proportionate share of ownership by purchasing a proportionate share of any new stock issues.

preference The act of an insolvent debtor who, in distributing his property or in assigning it for the benefit of his creditors, pays or secures to one or more creditors the full amount of their claims or a larger amount than they would be entitled to receive on a *pro rata* distribution. The treatment of such preferential payments in bankruptcy is governed by Bankruptcy Act, § 547.

premium A bounty or bonus; a consideration given to invite a loan or a bargain, as the consideration paid to the assignor by the assignee of a lease, or to the transferor by the transferee of shares of stock, etc. So stock is said to be "at a premium" when its market price exceeds its nominal or face value.

Also, the price for insurance protection for a specified period of exposure.

prescription Prescription is a peremptory and perpetual bar to every species of action, real or personal, when creditor has been silent for a certain time without urging his claim.

Also, acquisition of a personal right to use a way, water, light and air by reason of continuous usage. See also **easement**.

presentment The production of a negotiable instrument to the drawee for his acceptance, or to the drawer or acceptor for payment; or of a promissory note to the party liable, for payment of the same. U.C.C. § 3–504(1).

presumption A presumption is a rule of law, statutory or judicial, by which finding of a basic fact gives rise to existence of presumed fact, until presumption is rebutted. A presumption imposes on the party against whom it is directed the burden of going forward with evidence to rebut or meet the presumption, but does not shift to such party the burden of proof in the sense of the risk of nonpersuasion, which remains throughout the trial upon the party on whom it was originally cast.

prima facie Latin. At first sight; on the first appearance; on the face of it; so far as can be judged from the first disclosure; presumably; a fact presumed to be true unless disproved by some evidence to the contrary.

principal *Law of agency* The term "principal" describes one who has permitted or directed another (*i.e.* agent or servant) to act for his benefit and subject to his direction and control. Principal includes in its meaning the term "master", a species of principal who, in addition to other control, has a right to control the physical conduct of the species of agents known as servants, as to whom special rules are applicable with reference to harm caused by their physical acts.

privity of contract That connection or relationship which exists between two or more contracting parties. The absence of privity as a defense in actions for damages in contract and tort actions is generally no longer viable with the enactment of

warranty statutes (*e.g.* U.C.C. § 2–318), acceptance by states of doctrine of strict liability and court decisions which have extended the right to sue to third party beneficiaries and even innocent bystanders.

probate Court procedure by which a will is proved to be valid or invalid; though in current usage this term has been expanded to generally include all matters and proceedings pertaining to administration of estates, guardianships, etc.

process *Judicial process* In a wide sense, this term may include all the acts of a court from the beginning to the end of its proceedings in a given cause; but more specifically it means the writ, summons, mandate, or other process which is used to inform the defendant of the institution of proceedings against him and to compel his appearance, in either civil or criminal cases.

Legal process This term is sometimes used as equivalent to "lawful process." Thus, it is said that legal process means process not merely fair on its face, but in fact valid. But properly it means a summons, writ, warrant, mandate, or other process issuing from a court.

profit *Mesne profits* Value of use or occupation of land during time it was held by one in wrongful possession and is commonly measured in terms of rents and profits.

Profit à prendre Right to make some use of the soil of another, such as a right to mine metals, and it carries with it the right of entry and the right to remove.

promissory estoppel Arises where there is a promise which promisor should reasonably expect to induce action or forbearance on part of promisee and which does induce such action or forbearance, and where injustice can be avoided only by enforcement of the promise.

promissory note An unconditional written promise to pay a specified sum of money on demand or at a specified date. Such a note is negotiable if signed by the maker and containing an unconditional promise to pay a sum certain in money either on demand or at a definite time and payable to order or bearer. U.C.C. § 3–104.

promoters In the law relating to corporations, those persons are called the "promoters" of a company who first associate themselves together for the purpose of organizing the company, issuing its prospectus, procuring subscriptions to the stock, securing a charter, etc.

protest A formal declaration made by a person interested or concerned in some act about to be done, or already performed, whereby he expresses his dissent or disapproval, or affirms the act against his will. The object of such a declaration is generally to save some right which would be lost to him if his implied assent could be made out, or to exonerate himself from some responsibility which would attach to him unless he expressly negatived his assent.

Notice of protest A notice given by the holder of a bill or note to the drawer or indorser that the bill has been protested for refusal of payment or acceptance. U.C.C. § 3–509.

proximate cause Where the act or omission played a substantial part in bringing about or actually causing the injury or damage and where the injury or damage was either a direct result or a reasonably probable consequence of the act or omission.

proxy (Contracted from procuracy.) Written authorization given by one person to another so that the second person can act for the first, such as that given by a shareholder to someone else to represent him and vote his shares at a shareholders' meeting.

Q

quantum meruit Expression "quantum meruit" means "as much as he deserves" and it is an expression that describes the extent of liability on a contract implied by law. Essential elements of recovery under quantum meruit are: (1) valuable services were rendered or materials furnished, (2) for person sought to be charged, (3) which services and materials were accepted by person sought to be charged, used and enjoyed by him, and (4) under such circumstances as reasonably notified person sought to be charged that plaintiff, in performing such services, was expected to be paid by person sought to be charged.

quasi Latin. As if; almost as it were; analogous to. It negatives idea of identity, but points out that the conceptions are sufficiently similar for one to be classed as the equal of the other.

quasi contract Legal fiction invented by common law courts to permit recovery by contractual remedy in cases where, in fact, there is no contract, but where circumstances are such that justice warrants a recovery as though there had been a promise.

quasi in rem See **in rem.**

quiet To pacify; to render secure or unassailable by the removal of disquieting causes or disputes. This is the meaning of the word in the phrase "action to quiet title," which is a proceeding to establish the plaintiff's title to land by bringing into court an adverse claimant and there compelling him either to establish his claim or be forever after estopped from asserting it.

quitclaim deed A deed of conveyance operating by way of release; that is, intended to pass any title, interest, or claim which the grantor may have in the premises, but not professing that such title is valid, nor containing any warranty or covenants for title.

quorum When a committee, board of directors, meeting of shareholders, legislature or other body of persons cannot act unless a certain number at least of them are present.

R

ratification In a broad sense, the confirmation of a previous act done either by the party himself or by another; as, confirmation of a voidable act.

In the law of principal and agent, the adoption and confirmation by one person with knowledge of all material facts, of an act or contract performed or entered into in his behalf by another who at the time assumed without authority to act as his agent.

real property Land, and generally whatever is erected or growing upon or affixed to land. Also rights issuing out of, annexed to, and exercisable within or about land. See also **fixture.**

receiver A fiduciary of the court, appointed as an incident to other proceedings wherein certain ultimate relief is prayed. He is a trustee or ministerial officer representing court, and all parties in interest in litigation, and property or fund intrusted to him.

recoupment To recover a loss by a subsequent gain. In pleading, to set forth a claim against the plaintiff when an action is brought against one as a defendant.

Under rules practice, recoupment has been replaced by the modern counterclaim.

Set-off distinguished A "set-off" is a demand which the defendant has against the plaintiff, arising out of a transaction extrinsic to the plaintiff's cause of action, whereas a "recoupment" is a reduction or rebate by the defendant of part of the plaintiff's claim because of a right in the defendant arising out of the same transaction.

redemption The realization of a right to have the title of property restored free and clear of the mortgage; performance of the mortgage obligation being essential for that purpose.

Repurchase by corporation of its shares at a price equal to the net asset value of the shares on date a redemption request is received by the corporation.

reformation Equitable remedy used to reframe written contracts to reflect accurately real agreement between contracting parties when, either through mutual mistake or unilateral mistake coupled with actual or equitable fraud by other party, the writing does not embody contract as actually made.

release The relinquishment, concession, or giving up of a right, claim, or privilege, by the person in whom it exists or to whom it accrues, to the person against whom it might have been demanded or enforced.

remainder An estate limited to take effect and be enjoyed after another estate is determined. As, if a man seised in fee-simple grants lands to A for twenty years, and, after the determination of the said term, then to B and his heirs forever, here A is tenant for years, remainder to B in fee.

remand To send back. The sending by the appellate court of the cause back to the same court out of which it came, for purpose of having some further action taken on it there.

remedy The means by which the violation of a right is prevented, redressed, or compensated. Though a remedy may be by the act of the party injured, by operation of law, or by agreement between the injurer and the injured, we are chiefly concerned with one kind of remedy, the judicial remedy, which is by action or suit.

rent Consideration paid for use or occupation of property. In a broader sense, it is the compensation or fee paid, usually periodically, for the use of any property, land, buildings, equipment, etc.

At common law, term referred to compensation or return of value given at stated times for the possession of lands and tenements corporeal.

replevin An action whereby the owner or person entitled to repossession of goods or chattels may recover those goods or chattels from one who has wrongfully distrained or taken or who wrongfully detains such goods or chattels.

repudiation Repudiation of a contract means refusal to perform duty or obligation owed to other party.

requirements contract See **contracts.**

res judicata Rule that a final judgment is conclusive as to the rights of the parties and their privies, and, as to them, constitutes an absolute bar to a subsequent action involving the same claim, demand or cause of action.

rescission An equitable action in which a party seeks to be relieved of his obligations under a contract on the grounds of mutual mistake, fraud, impossibility, etc.

residuary Pertaining to the residue; constituting the residue; giving or bequeathing the residue; receiving or entitled to the residue. See also **legacy,** *residuary legacy.*

respondeat superior Latin. Let the master answer. This maxim means that a master is liable in certain cases for the wrongful acts of his servant, and a principal for those of his agent.

respondent In equity practice, the party who makes an answer to a bill or other proceeding in equity. In appellate practice, the party who contends against an appeal; *i.e.* the appellee. The party who appeals is called the "appellant."

restitution An equitable remedy under which a person who has rendered services to another seeks to be reimbursed for the costs of his acts (but not his profits) even though there was never a contract between the parties.

restraint on alienation A provision in an instrument of conveyance which prohibits the grantee from selling or transferring the property which is the subject of the conveyance. Many such restraints are unenforceable as against public policy and the law's policy of free alienability of land.

reverse An appellate court uses the term "reversed" to indicate that it annuls or avoids the judgment, or vacates the decree, of the trial court.

reversion The term reversion has two meanings, first, as designating the estate left in the grantor during the continuance of a particular estate and also the residue left in grantor or his heirs after termination of particular estate. It differs from a remainder in that it arises by act of the law, whereas a remainder is by act of the parties. A reversion, moreover, is the remnant left in the grantor, while a remainder is the remnant of the whole estate disposed of, after a preceding part of the same has been given away.

revocation The recall of some power, authority, or thing granted, or a destroying or making void of some deed that had existence until the act of revocation made it void. It may be either general, of all acts and things done before; or special, to revoke a particular thing.

right of entry The right of taking or resuming possession of land by entering on it in a peaceable manner.

right of redemption The right (granted by statute only) to free property from the encumbrance of a foreclosure or other judicial sale, or to recover the title passing thereby, by paying what is due, with interest, costs, etc. Not to be confounded with the "equity of redemption," which exists independently of statute but must be exercised before sale. See also **equity of redemption**.

rule against perpetuities Principle that no interest in property is good unless it must vest, if at all, not later than 21 years, plus period of gestation, after some life or lives in being at time of creation of interest.

S

satisfaction The discharge of an obligation by paying a party what is due to him (as on a mortgage, lien, or contract) or what is awarded to him, by the judgment of a court or otherwise. Thus, a judgment is satisfied by the payment of the amount due to the party who has recovered such judgment, or by his levying the amount. See also **accord and satisfaction**.

scienter Latin. Knowingly.

scintilla Latin. A spark; a remaining particle; the least particle.

secured transaction A transaction which is founded on a security agreement. Such agreement creates or provides for a security interest. U.C.C. § 9–105(h).

securities Stocks, bonds, notes, convertible debentures, warrants, or other documents that represent a share in a company or a debt owed by a company.

seisin Possession with an intent on the part of him who holds it to claim a freehold interest.

set-off A counter-claim demand which defendant holds against plaintiff, arising out of a transaction extrinsic of plaintiff's cause of action.

In equity practice it is commenced by a declaration in set-off, though under rules practice (which merged law and equity) it has been displaced by the counterclaim. Fed.R.Civil P. 13.

For the distinction between set-off and recoupment, see **recoupment**.

severance Act of severing, or state of being severed; partition; separation; *e.g.* a claim against a party may be severed and proceeded with separately. Fed.R.Civil P. 21.

Also, the destruction of any one of the unities of a joint tenancy. It is so called because the estate is no longer a joint tenancy, but is severed.

Term may also refer to cutting of the crops, such as corn, wheat, etc., or the separating of anything from the realty.

Shelley's case, rule in Where a person takes an estate of freehold, legally, or equitably, under a deed, will, or other writing, and in the same instrument there is a limitation by way of remainder of any interest of the same legal or equitable quality to his heirs, or heirs of his body, as a class of persons to take in succession from generation to generation, the limitation to the heirs entitles the ancestor to the whole estate.

The rule was adopted as a part of the common law of this country, though it has long since been abolished by most states.

shipment contract Seller is authorized or required only to bear the expense of placing goods with the common carrier and bears the risk of loss only up to such point.

short swing profits Profits made by insider through sale or other disposition of the corporate stock within six months after purchase.

sight draft An instrument payable on presentment.

sole proprietorship A form of business in which one person owns all the assets of the business in contrast to a partnership and corporation.

specific performance The doctrine of specific performance is that, where damages would be an inadequate compensation for the breach of an agreement, the contractor or vendor will be compelled to perform specifically what he has agreed to do; *e.g.* ordered to execute a specific conveyance of land. See Fed.R. Civil P. 70.

With respect to sale of goods, specific performance may be decreed where the goods are unique or in other proper circumstances. The decree for specific performance may include such terms and conditions as to payment of the price, damages, or other relief as the court may deem just.   U.C.C. §§ 2–711(2)(b), 2–716.

stare decisis   Doctrine that, when court has once laid down a principle of law as applicable to a certain state of facts, it will adhere to that principle, and apply it to all future cases, where facts are substantially the same; regardless of whether the parties and property are the same.

statute of frauds   A celebrated English statute, passed in 1677, and which has been adopted, in a more or less modified form, in nearly all of the United States.   Its chief characteristic is the provision that no action shall be brought on certain contracts unless there be a note or memorandum thereof in writing, signed by the party to be charged or by his authorized agent.

statute of limitation   A statute prescribing limitations to the right of action on certain described causes of action; that is, declaring that no suit shall be maintained on such causes of action unless brought within a specified period after the right accrued.

stock   "Stock" is distinguished from "bonds" and, ordinarily, from "debentures," in that it gives right of ownership in part of assets of corporation and right to interest in any surplus after payment of debt.   "Stock" in a corporation is an equity, and it represents an ownership interest, and it is to be distinguished from obligations such as notes or bonds which are not equities and represent no ownership interest.

Capital stock   See **capital.**

Common stock   Securities which represent an ownership interest in a corporation.   If the company has also issued preferred stock, both common and preferred have ownership rights.   Claims of both common and preferred stockholders are junior to claims of bondholders or other creditors of the company.   Common stockholders assume the greater risk, but generally exercise the greater control and may gain the greater reward in the form of dividends and capital appreciation.

Convertible stock   Stock which may be changed or converted into common stock.

Cumulative preferred   A stock having a provision that if one or more dividends are omitted, the omitted dividends must be paid before dividends may be paid on the company's common stock.

Preferred stock   is a separate portion or class of the stock of a corporation, which is accorded, by the charter or by-laws, a preference or priority in

respect to dividends, over the remainder of the stock of the corporation, which in that case is called *common stock.*

Stock warrant   A certificate entitling the owner to buy a specified amount of stock at a specified time(s) for a specified price.   Differs from a stock option only in that options are granted to employees and warrants are sold to the public.

strict liability   A concept applied by the courts in product liability cases in which a seller is liable for any and all defective or hazardous products which unduly threaten a consumer's personal safety.   This concept applies to all members involved in the manufacturing and selling of any facet of the product.

subpoena   A subpoena is a command to appear at a certain time and place to give testimony upon a certain matter.   A subpoena duces tecum requires production of books, papers and other things.

subrogation   The substitution of one thing for another, or of one person into the place of another with respect to rights, claims, or securities.

Subrogation denotes the putting a third person who has paid a debt in the place of the creditor to whom he has paid it, so that he may exercise against the debtor all the rights which the creditor, if unpaid, might have done.

subscribe   Literally to write underneath, as one's name.   To sign at the end of a document.   Also, to agree in writing to furnish money or its equivalent, or to agree to purchase some initial stock in a corporation.

substantial performance   Equitable doctrine protects against forfeiture for technical inadvertence or trivial variations or omissions in performance.

substantive law   The basic law of rights and duties (contract law, criminal law, tort law, law of wills, etc.) as opposed to procedural law (law of pleading, law of evidence, law of jurisdiction, etc.).

suit   "Suit" is a generic term, of comprehensive signification, and applies to any proceeding in a court of justice in which the plaintiff pursues, in such court, the remedy which the law affords him for the redress of an injury or the recovery of a right.

summary judgment   Rule of Civil Procedure 56 permits any party to a civil action to move for a summary judgment on a claim, counterclaim, or cross-claim when he believes that there is no genuine issue of material fact and that he is entitled to prevail as a matter of law.

summons Writ or process directed to the sheriff or other proper officer, requiring him to notify the person named that an action has been commenced against him in the court from where the process issues, and that he is required to appear, on a day named, and answer the complaint in such action.

surety One who undertakes to pay money or to do any other act in event that his principal fails therein.

Guarantor and surety compared A surety and guarantor are both bound for another person. However, a surety is usually bound with his principal by the same instrument, executed at the same time and on the same consideration. On the other hand, the contract of guarantor is his own separate undertaking, in which the principal does not join. A surety is an insurer of the debt or obligation; a guarantor is an insurer of the solvency of the principal debtor or of his ability to pay. Under U.C.C., term "surety" includes a guarantor. § 1–201(40). See also **guaranty.**

T

tacking The term is applied especially to the process of making out title to land by adverse possession, when the present occupant and claimant has not been in possession for the full statutory period, but adds or "tacks" to his own possession that of previous occupants under whom he claims.

tenancy Possession or occupancy of land or premises under lease.

Joint tenancy Joint tenants have one and the same interest, accruing by one and the same conveyance, commencing at one and the same time, and held by one and the same undivided possession. The primary incident of joint tenancy is survivorship, by which the entire tenancy on the decease of any joint tenant remains to the survivors, and at length to the last survivor.

Tenancy at sufferance Only naked possession which continues after tenant's right of possession has terminated.

Tenancy at will Possession of premises by permission of owner or landlord, but without a fixed term.

Tenancy by the entirety A tenancy which is created between a husband and wife and by which together they hold title to the whole with right of survivorship so that, upon death of either, other takes whole to exclusion of deceased heirs. It is essentially a "joint tenancy," modified by the common-law theory that husband and wife are one person.

Tenancy for a period A tenancy for years or for some fixed period.

Tenancy in common A form of ownership whereby each tenant (*i.e.*, owner) holds an undivided interest in property. Unlike a joint tenancy or a tenancy by the entirety, the interest of a tenant in common does not terminate upon his or her prior death (*i.e.*, there is no right of survivorship).

tender An offer of money; the act by which one produces and offers to a person holding a claim or demand against him the amount of money which he considers and admits to be due, in satisfaction of such claim or demand, without any stipulation or condition.

Also, there may be a tender of performance of a duty other than the payment of money.

testator One who makes or has made a testament or will; one who dies leaving a will.

third party beneficiary One for whose benefit a promise is made in a contract but who is not a party to the contract

Creditor beneficiary Where performance of a promise in a contract will benefit a person other than the promisee, that person is a creditor beneficiary if no purpose to make a gift appears from the terms of the promise in view of the accompanying circumstances and performance of the promise will satisfy an actual or supposed or asserted duty of the promisee to the beneficiary.

Donee beneficiary The person who takes the benefit of the contract even though there is no privity between him and the contracting parties. A third party beneficiary who is not a creditor beneficiary. See also **beneficiary.**

title The means whereby the owner of lands or of personalty has the just possession of his property.

tort A private or civil wrong or injury, other than breach of contract, for which the court will provide a remedy in the form of an action for damages.

Three elements of every tort action are: Existence of legal duty from defendant to plaintiff, breach of duty, and damage as proximate result.

tort-feasor One who commits or is guilty of a tort.

trade acceptance A draft drawn by a seller which is presented for signature (acceptance) to the buyer at the time goods are purchased and which then becomes the equivalent of a note receivable of the seller and the note payable of the buyer.

trespass At common law, trespass was a form of action brought to recover damages for any injury to one's person or property or relationship with another.

Trespass to chattels An unlawful and serious interference with the possessory rights of another to personal property.

Trespass to land At common law, every unauthorized and direct breach of the boundaries of another's land was an actionable trespass. The present prevailing position of the courts finds liability for trespass only in the case of intentional intrusion, or negligence, or some "abnormally dangerous activity" on the part of the defendant. Compare **nuisance**.

trover A possessory action wherein plaintiff must show that he has either a general or special property in thing converted and the right to its possession at the time of the alleged conversion. Such remedy lies only for wrongful appropriation of goods, chattels, or personal property which is specific enough to be identified. See also **conversion**.

trust Any arrangement whereby property is transferred with intention that it be administered by trustee for another's benefit.

A trust, as the term is used in the Restatement, when not qualified by the word "charitable," "resulting" or "constructive," is a fiduciary relationship with respect to property, subjecting the person by whom the title to the property is held to equitable duties to deal with the property for the benefit of another person, which arises as a result of a manifestation of an intention to create it. Restatement, Second, Trusts § 2.

Constructive trust Wherever the circumstances of a transaction are such that the person who takes the legal estate in property cannot also enjoy the beneficial interest without necessarily violating some established principle of equity, the court will immediately raise a *constructive trust*, and fasten it upon the conscience of the legal owner, so as to convert him into a trustee for the parties who in equity are entitled to the beneficial enjoyment. Constructive trusts have been said to arise through the application of the doctrine of equitable estoppel, or under the broad doctrine that equity regards and treats as done what in good conscience ought to be done.

Resulting trust One that arises by implication of law, where the legal estate in property is disposed of, conveyed, or transferred, but the intent appears or is inferred from the terms of the disposition, or from the accompanying facts and circumstances, that the beneficial interest is not to go or be enjoyed with the legal title.

Voting trust A trust which holds the voting rights to stock in a corporation. It is a useful device when a majority of the shareholders in a corporation cannot agree on corporate policy.

trustee In a strict sense, a "trustee" is one who holds the legal title to property for the benefit of another, while, in a broad sense, the term is sometimes applied to anyone standing in a fiduciary or confidential relation to another, such as agent, attorney, bailee, etc.

U

ultra vires Acts beyond the scope of the powers of a corporation, as defined by its charter or laws of state of incorporation. By doctrine of ultra vires a contract made by a corporation beyond the scope of its corporate powers is unlawful.

unconscionable contract See **contracts**

underwriter Any person, banker, or syndicate that guarantees to furnish a definite sum of money by a definite date to a business or government in return for an issue of bonds or stock. In insurance, the one assuming a risk in return for the payment of a premium.

undue influence Term refers to conduct by which a person, through his power over mind of testator, makes the latter's desires conform to his own, thereby overmastering the violition of the testator.

uniform commercial code One of the Uniform Laws drafted by the National Conference of Commissioners on Uniform State Laws governing commercial transactions (sales of goods, commercial paper, bank deposits and collections, letters of credit, bulk transfers, warehouse receipts, bills of lading, investment securities, and secured transactions). The U.C.C. has been adopted by all states, except Louisiana.

usage of trade A usage of trade is any practice or method of dealing having such regularity of observance in a place, vocation or trade as to justify an expectation that it will be observed with respect to the transaction in question.

usury Collectively, the laws of a jurisdiction regulating the charging of interest rates. A usurious loan is one whose interest rates are determined to be in excess of those permitted by the usury laws.

V

vendee A purchaser or buyer; one to whom anything is sold. Generally used of the purchaser of real property, one who acquires chattels by sale being called a "buyer." See also **vendor.**

vendor The person who transfers property by sale, particularly real estate; "seller" being more commonly used for one who sells personalty. The latter may, however, with entire propriety, be termed a vendor. A merchant; a retail dealer; a supplier; one who buys to sell. See also **vendee.**

venue "Jurisdiction" of the court means the inherent power to decide a case, whereas "venue" designates the particular county or city in which a court with jurisdiction may hear and determine the case.

verdict The formal and unanimous decision or finding of a jury, impaneled and sworn for the trial of a cause, upon the matters or questions duly submitted to them upon the trial.

vested Fixed; accured; settled; absolute. To be "vested," a right must be more than a mere expectation based on an anticipation of the continuance of an existing law; it must have become a title, legal or equitable, to the present or future enforcement of a demand, or a legal exemption from the demand of another.

vicarious liability Indirect legal responsibility; for example, the liability of an employer for the acts of an employee, or, a principal for torts and contracts of an agent.

void Null; ineffectual; nugatory; having no legal force or binding effect; unable, in law, to support the purpose for which it was intended.

There is this difference between the two words "void" and "voidable": *void* in the strict sense means that an instrument or transaction is nugatory and ineffectual so that nothing can cure it; *voidable* exists when an imperfection or defect can be cured by the act or confirmation of him who could take advantage of it.

Frequently the word "void" is used and construed as having the more liberal meaning of "voidable."

voidable See **void.**

voluntary Resulting from free choice. The word,

especially in statutes, often implies knowledge of essential facts.

W

waiver Terms "estoppel" and "waiver" are not synonymous; "waiver" means the voluntary, intentional relinquishment of a known right, and "estoppel" rests upon principle that, where anyone has done an act, or made a statement, which would be a fraud on his part to controvert or impair, because other party has acted upon it in belief that what was done or said was true, conscience and honest dealing require that he not be permitted to repudiate his act or gainsay his statement. See also **estoppel.**

ward An infant or insane person placed by authority of law under the care of a guardian.

warrant, v. In contracts, to engage or promise that a certain fact or state of facts, in relation to the subject-matter, is, or shall be, as it is represented to be.

In conveyancing, to assure the title to property sold, by an express covenant to that effect in the deed of conveyance.

warrant, n. An order by which the drawer authorizes one person to pay a particular sum of money.

An authority issued to a collector of taxes, empowering him to collect the taxes extended on the assessment roll, and to make distress and sale of goods or land in default of payment.

Stock warrant See **stock.**

warranty A warranty is a statement or representation made by seller of goods, contemporaneously with and as a part of contract of sale, though collateral to express object of sale, having reference to character, quality, or title of goods, and by which seller promises or undertakes to insure that certain facts are or shall be as he then represents them.

The general statutory law governing warranties on sales of goods is provided in U.C.C. § 2–312 *et seq.* The three main types of warranties are: (1) express warranty; (2) implied warranty of fitness; (3) implied warranty of merchantability.

warranty deed Deed in which grantor warrants good clear title. The usual covenants of title are warranties of seisin, quiet enjoyment, right to convey, freedom from encumbrances and defense of title as to all claims.

will A written instrument executed with the formalities required by statutes, whereby a person makes a disposition of his property to take effect after his death.

winding up To settle the accounts and liquidate the assets of a partnership or corporation, for the purpose of making distribution and dissolving the concern.

writ of certiorari See **certiorari.**

writ of error A writ issued from a court of appellate jurisdiction, directed to the judge or judges of a court of record, requiring them to remit to the appellate court the record of an action before them, in which a final judgment has been entered, in order that examination may be made of certain errors alleged to have been committed, and that the judgment may be reversed, corrected, or affirmed, as the case may require.

Index

References are to Pages

†